RIFLES
OF THE WORLD

2nd Edition

John Walter

Published by

krause publications

700 E. State Street • Iola, WI 54990-0001
Telephone: 715/445-2214

www.krause.com

Please call or write for our free catalog of publications. Our toll-free number to place an order or obtain a free catalog is 800-258-0929 or please use our regular business telephone 715-445-2214 for editorial comment and further information.

ISBN: 0-87349-202-1

Library of Congress Catalog No. 93-70481

Printed in the United States of America

To Alison and Adam, who give love and patience in equal measure.

Contents

Foreword **8**

ARGENTINA **9**
- Buenos Aires 9
- Enfield 9
- FMAP 9
- FN (FMAP) 9
- Garand 10
- Mauser 10
- Remington 10

ARMENIAN REPUBLIC **10**
- Kalashnikov 10

AUSTRALIA **10**
- FN (Lithgow) 11
- Lee-Enfield 11
- Martini 11
- Sportco 12
- Steyr (Lithgow) 12

AUSTRIA **12**
- Dschulnigg 12
- FN (Steyr) 13
- Mannlicher 113
- Mauser 14
- Sodia 14
- Voere, autoloading type 17
- Voere, bolt-action type 17
- Winkler 20

AUSTRIA-HUNGARY **20**
- Andrs 20
- Barth & Hohenbrück 20
- Früwirth 20
- Jurnitschek 20
- Krnka, block-action type 20
- Krnka, bolt-action type 21
- Kropatschek 21
- Mannlicher, autoloading type 21
- Mannlicher, bolt-action type 22
- Mosin-Nagant 25
- Odkolek 25
- Schönauer 25
- Schulhof 25
- Spitalsky 26
- Wangler 26
- Wänzl 26
- Werndl 26

BADEN **28**

BAVARIA **28**
- Chassepot 28
- Podewils 28
- Spörer & Harl 29
- Werder 29

BELGIUM **29**
- Albini-Braendlin 30
- Charrin 30
- Clément 30
- Comblain 30
- Dumoulin 31
- Engh 31
- Fabrique Nationale, auto-loading type 31
- Fabrique Nationale, bolt-action type 33
- Fabrique Nationale, break-open type 34
- Fabrique Nationale, slide-action type 34
- Falisse & Trapmann 34
- FN-Saive 34
- FN-Sauer 35
- Francotte 36
- Ghaye 36
- Larsen 36
- Laurent 36
- Lebeau-Courally 36
- Lecocq & Hoffmann 37
- Lenders-Lambin 37
- Marga(-Francotte) 37
- Martini-Francotte 37
- Masquelier 37
- Mauser (state type) 37
- Mauser (FN type) 40
- Mauser, other types 41
- Montigny 42
- Nagant 42
- Pieper (Henri), bolt-action type 42
- Pieper (Henri), lever-action type 42
- Pieper (Henri), revolving-cylinder type 42
- Pieper (Nicolas), auto-loading type 42
- Raick 42
- Terssen 43

BOLIVIA **43**

BRAZIL **43**
- Chuchu 43
- Comblain 43
- FN-Saive (Imbel) 44
- Garand 44
- Mannlicher 44
- Mauser 44
- Pieper 45
- Rossi, lever-action type 45
- Rossi, slide-action type 46
- Vergueiro 46

BRITAIN **46**
- Accuracy International 46
- Adams 48
- Anson & Deeley 48
- Arisaka 48
- Armalon 48
- Aston 49
- Atkin, Grant & Lang 49
- Bacon 49
- Banks 50
- BMS 50
- Braendlin 50
- Brand 50
- BSA, auto-loading type 50
- BSA, bolt-action type 51
- BSA, slide-action type 53
- BSA-Adams 53
- BSA-Enfield 53
- BSA-Lee 54
- BSA-Martini 54
- BSA-Mauser 55
- BSA-Norman, block-action type 55
- BSA-Norman, bolt-action type 55
- BSA-Thompson 56
- Burton, block-action type 56
- Burton, bolt-action type 56
- Byrnes & Benjamin 56
- Carter & Edwards 56
- Churchill 57
- Cogswell & Harrison, block-action type 57
- Cogswell & Harrison, bolt-action type 57
- Cogswell & Harrison, break-open type 58
- Cogswell & Harrison (Mauser) 58
- Cooper, block-action type 58
- Cooper, toggle-action type 58
- Daw 59
- Deeley & Edge 59
- De Lisle 59
- Dickson 59
- Dougall 59
- Enfield, auto-loading type 59
- Enfield, bolt-action type 60
- Enfield-Martini 62
- Esser-Barratt 62
- Farquhar & Hill 62
- Farquharson 63
- Field 63
- Firearms Company 63
- FN-Saive (Enfield) 63
- Fraser 64
- Gamwell 64
- Gibbs 64
- Godsal 64
- Green 65
- Greene 65
- Greener, bolt-action type 65
- Greener, break-open type 66
- Greener-Martini 66
- Griffiths & Woodgate 66
- Hall 66
- Halle 67
- Heckler & Koch (Enfield) 67
- Henry 67
- Holland & Holland 68
- Januszewski (Janson) 68
- Jeffrey 68
- Jeffries 68
- Jenks 68
- Jones, block-action type 69
- Jones, break-open type 69
- Kerr 69
- Lancaster 69
- Lang 69
- Lee-Burton 69
- Lee-Enfield 70
- Lee-Metford 75
- Leetch 76
- Manceaux 77
- Mannlicher 77
- Martini-Enfield 77
- Martini-Henry 78
- Martini-Metford 80
- Martini sporting guns 81
- Mauser 82
- Midland 82
- Morris 82
- Needham 82
- Parker (Lee-Enfield) 82
- Parker-Hale (Lee-Enfield) 82
- Prince 85
- Purdey 85
- Reilly-Comblain 85
- Remington-Lee 85
- Restell 86
- Rexer 86
- Richards, bolt type 86
- Richards, lifting-block type 86
- Richards, dropping-block type 87
- Rigby 87
- Ross 88
- Sharps 88
- Shephard 88
- Snider 88
- Soper 91
- Storm 91
- Swinburn 91
- Terry 92
- Thorneycroft 93
- Thorpe 93
- Turner 93
- Vickers 93
- War Office 94
- Wilson 94
- Wood 95
- Woodgate 95
- Wyley 95

BULGARIA **95**
- Berdan 95
- Kalashnikov 95
- Mannlicher 95

BURMA (MYANMAR) **95**
- Heckler & Koch 95

CANADA **96**
- ArmaLite (Diemaco) 96
- FN-Saive (Long Branch) 96
- Lakefield, autoloading type 96
- Lakefield, bolt-action type 96
- Lee-Enfield 97
- Ross 97
- Savage 100
- Remington 100
- SIG 100
- Winchester 100

CHILE **100**
- Mannlicher 100
- Mauser 100
- Remington 101
- SIG 101
- Winchester 101

CHINA (EMPIRE) **101**
- Haenel 101
- Mauser 101
- Reichsgewehr 101
- Remington-Lee 102

CHINA (REPUBLIC) **102**
- Arisaka 102
- Lee-Enfield 102
- Mannlicher 102
- Mauser 102

CHINA (PRC) **102**
- ArmaLite (Norinco) 102
- Kalashnikov 102
- Mosin-Nagant 103
- Simonov 103
- State designs 104

COLOMBIA **104**
MAUSER.......... 104
CONFEDERATE STATES OF AMERICA **104**
BILHARZ & HALL CARBINES.......... 104
LE MAT REVOLVER CARBINES.......... 104
MORSE CARBINES.......... 105
READ CARBINES.......... 105
ROBINSON CARBINES.......... 105
TARPLEY CARBINES.......... 105
CONGO FREE STATE **105**
MAUSER.......... 105
COSTA RICA **105**
Mauser.......... 105
CUBA **105**
KRAG-JØRGENSEN.......... 105
REMINGTON-LEE.......... 105
WINCHESTER.......... 106
CZECHOSLOVAKIA **106**
Ceská Zbrojovka, auto-loading type.......... 106
Ceská Zbrojovka, bolt-action type.......... 107
Galas.......... 109
Holek, auto-loading type.......... 109
Holek, bolt-action type.......... 110
Janecek.......... 110
Koucky, auto-loading type.......... 110
Koucky, bolt-action type.......... 111
Kratochvil.......... 113
Kyncl.......... 113
Mauser (CSZ, ZB).......... 113
Mosin-Nagant.......... 115
DENMARK **115**
Bang.......... 115
Heckler & Koch.......... 116
Krag-Jørgensen.......... 116
Krag-Petersson.......... 117
Madsen, bolt-action type.......... 118
Remington.......... 118
Snider.......... 120
DOMINICAN REPUBLIC **120**
Cristobal.......... 120
Mauser.......... 121
ECUADOR **121**
Mauser.......... 121
EGYPT **121**
FN-Saive.......... 121
Kalashnikov.......... 121
Ljungmann.......... 121
Remington.......... 121
EL SALVADOR **122**
ESTONIA **122**
ETHIOPIA **122**
FINLAND **122**
Kalashnikov.......... 122
Mannlicher.......... 124
Mauser.......... 124
Mosin-Nagant.......... 124
Pelo.......... 126
Sako, bolt-action type.......... 126
Sako, lever-action type.......... 131
Tampeeren Asepaja.......... 131
Tikka, bolt-action type.......... 131
Tikka, break-open type.......... 133
Valmet, bolt-action type.......... 133
Valmet, break-open type.......... 134
FRANCE **134**
Albini-Braendlin.......... 134
APX.......... 134
Bérenger.......... 134
Berdan.......... 134
Berthier, autoloading type.......... 135
Berthier, bolt-action type.......... 135
Carcano.......... 137
Chabot.......... 137
Chapuis Armes.......... 137
Pierre Chapuis.......... 139
Chassepot.......... 139
Clair.......... 141
CTV.......... 141
Daudetau.......... 141
Descoutoures.......... 141
ENT.......... 142
Gallager.......... 142
Gastinne-Renette.......... 142
Gaucher.......... 142
Gévelot, autoloading type.......... 142
Gévelot, lever-action type.......... 143
Gras.......... 143
Heckler & Koch (MAS).......... 144
Joslyn.......... 144
Kropatschek.......... 144
Lardinois.......... 145
Lebel.......... 145
Lefaucheux Casimir.......... 147
Manceaux & Viellard.......... 147
Manufrance, autoloading type.......... 147
Manufrance, bolt-action type.......... 147
Manufrance, break-open type.......... 149
MAS, autoloading type.......... 149
MAS, bolt type.......... 151
Mauser.......... 152
Meunier.......... 152
Peabody.......... 152
PGM.......... 152
Plastow.......... 153
Remington.......... 153
Robert.......... 153
Roberts.......... 153
RSC.......... 154
Sharps.......... 154
SIG (Manurhin).......... 154
SMFM.......... 154
Snider.......... 155
Springfield(-Allin).......... 155
STA.......... 155
Tabatière.......... 155
Treuille de Beaulieu.......... 155
Unique, autoloading type.......... 155
Unique, bolt-action type.......... 156
Warner.......... 158
Wilson.......... 158
GERMANY **158**
Anschütz, autoloading type.......... 159
Anschütz, bolt-action type.......... 159
GERMANY **166**
Anschütz-Förtner.......... 167
Aydt.......... 168
Blaser, block-action type.......... 168
Blaser, bolt-action type.......... 169
Blaser, break-open type.......... 170
Bock.......... 171
Bornmüller, Simson & Luck.......... 171
Brennecke.......... 171
BRENNEKE-MAUSER SPORTING RIFLES.......... 171
Büchel.......... 171
Burgsmüller.......... 171
Chassepot.......... 171
Dornheim.......... 171
Dreyse.......... 171
DWM.......... 172
Erma, autoloading type.......... 172
Erma, bolt-action type.......... 173
Erma, lever-action type.......... 173
Erma, slide-action type.......... 173
Feinwerkbau.......... 174
FN-Saive.......... 175
Frankonia.......... 175
Gehmann.......... 175
Genschow.......... 175
Gercke.......... 175
Gustloff.......... 175
Haenel, autoloading type.......... 176
Haenel, bolt-action type.......... 177
Halbe & Gerlich.......... 177
Heckler & Koch.......... 177
Heinemann.......... 182
Heym, block-action type.......... 183
Heym, bolt-action type.......... 183
Heym, break-open type.......... 184
Heym-Ruger.......... 186
Hoster.......... 186
Jäger.......... 186
Kalashnikov.......... 186
Keppeler & Fritz.......... 187
Kind.......... 187
Krico, autoloading type.......... 188
Krico, bolt-action type.......... 188
Krieghoff, autoloading type.......... 192
Krieghoff, break-open type.......... 192
Langenhan.......... 194
Lettow.......... 194
Lindner.......... 194
Luger.......... 194
Mannlicher.......... 194
Mauser, autoloading type.......... 195
Mauser, bolt-action type.......... 196
Mayer & Grammelspacher.......... 208
Merkel.......... 208
Mosin-Nagant.......... 209
Müller & Greiss.......... 209
Oesterreich.......... 209
Reichsgewehr (Mannlicher).......... 209
Rheinmetall (Dreyse), autoloading type.......... 210
Rheinmetall (Dreyse), bolt-action type.......... 211
Rheinmetall-Stange.......... 211
Rhöner, bolt-action type.......... 212
Rhöner, break-open type.......... 212
RWS.......... 213
Sauer.......... 213
Sauer-Weatherby.......... 215
Schilling.......... 215
Schmidt & Habermann, block-action type.......... 215
Schmidt & Habermann, bolt-action type.......... 215
Schüler.......... 215
Sempert & Krieghoff.......... 215
Simonov.......... 215
Simson.......... 216
Stahl.......... 216
Thälmann.......... 216
Tirmax.......... 216
Voere, autoloading type.......... 216
Voere, bolt-action type.......... 217
Vom Hofe.......... 219
Walther, autoloading type.......... 219
Walther, block-action type.......... 221
Walther, bolt-action type.......... 221
Weihrauch, block-action type.......... 224
Weihrauch, bolt-action type.......... 225
GREECE **226**
Gras.......... 226
Heckler & Koch (EBO).......... 226
Mannlicher.......... 226
Mauser.......... 226
Mylona.......... 226
GUATEMALA **226**
HAITI **227**
Remington-Lee.......... 227
HESSEN **227**
Chassepot.......... 227
HONDURAS **227**
Mauser.......... 227
Remington (Enfield).......... 227
HUNGARY **227**
Kalashnikov.......... 227
Mannlicher.......... 227
Mosin-Nagant.......... 228
INDIA **229**
FN-Saive (Ishapur).......... 229
Kalashnikov (Ishapur).......... 229
Lee-Enfield.......... 229
INDONESIA **229**
Arisaka.......... 229
Garand.......... 229
IRAN **229**
Heckler & Koch.......... 229
IRAQ **230**
Lee-Enfield.......... 230
IRELAND (EIRE) **230**
Lee-Enfield.......... 230
ISRAEL **230**
FN-Saive (IMI).......... 230
Galil (Kalashnikov).......... 230
Mauser.......... 231
ITALY **231**
Armaguerra (Revelli).......... 231
Armi-Jager, autoloading type.......... 231
Armi-Jager, bolt-action type.......... 232
Beretta, autoloading type.......... 232
Beretta, bolt-action type.......... 235
Beretta, break-open type.......... 236
Bernardelli.......... 236
Breda.......... 237
Carcano.......... 237
Cei-Rigotti.......... 238
Daffini.......... 238
Doersch & von Baumgarten.......... 238
FAVS.......... 238
Franchi.......... 238
Garand.......... 238
Mannlicher-Carcano.......... 238
Mauser.......... 240
Pedersoli.......... 240
Perugini-Visini.......... 242
Pieri.......... 242
Pietta.......... 242

Rizzini (FAIR Techni-Mec)	242
SAB, bolt action type	242
SAB, break-open type	243
Sabatti	243
Scotti	243
Uberti	243
Vetterli	244
Zanardini	246
Zoli (Angelo)	246
Zoli (Antonio), bolt-action type	246
Zoli (Antonio), break-open type	246

JAPAN 247
Arisaka	247
Chassepot	250
Garand	250
Howa, autoloading type	250
Howa, bolt-action type	250
Mannlicher-Carcano	251
Mauser	251
Murata	251
Simple Rifles	252

KOREA (PRK) 252
Kalashnikov	252
Mosin-Nagant	252
Simonov	252

KOREA (REPUBLIC) 253
Arisaka	253
ArmaLite	253
Dae Woo	253

LATVIA 253
| Mauser | 253 |

LIBERIA 253
| Mauser | 253 |

LITHUANIA 253
| Mauser | 253 |

LUXEMBOURG 253
| Mauser | 253 |

MANCHURIA 53
| Mauser | 253 |

MEXICO 254
Arisaka	254
FN-Saive	254
Mauser	254
Mondragon, autoloading type	255
Mondragon, bolt-action type	256
Remington	256
Whitney	256

MOROCCO 257
| Beretta | 257 |
| Garand | 257 |

NETHERLANDS 257
Beaumont	257
Kalashnikov (NWM)	257
Mannlicher	257
Mauser	258

NEW ZEALAND 259
Lee-Enfield	259
Parker-Hale	259
Remington-Lee	259

NICARAGUA 259
| Mauser | 259 |

NIGERIA 259
| FN-Saive | 259 |
| Garand | 259 |

NORWAY 259
Heckler & Koch	259
Jarmann	259
Kammerladningsgevær	260
Kongsberg	261
Krag-Jørgensen	261
Krag-Petersson	263
Landmark	263
Lund	263
Mauser	264
Remington	265

ORANGE FREE STATE 265
| Mauser | 265 |

PAKISTAN 265
| Heckler & Koch | 265 |

PARAGUAY 266
| Mauser | 266 |

PERSIA 266
| Mauser | 266 |

PERU 266
| Mauser | 267 |
| Remington-Lee | 267 |

PHILIPPINES 267
ArmaLite	267
Arms Corporation, autoloading type	267
Arms Corporation, bolt-action type	267

POLAND 268
Kalashnikov	268
Mauser	268
Mosin-Nagant	268

PORTUGAL 268
Guedes	268
Heckler & Koch (FBP)	269
Kropatschek	269
Mannlicher	270
Mauser	270
Richards	270
Snider	270
Vergueiro	270

PRUSSIA 270
Bock	271
Bornmüller	271
Chassepot	271
Doersch & von Baumgarten	272
Dreyse	272
Luck	276
Poppenburg	276
Spangenberg & Sauer	276

ROMANIA 276
Kalashnikov	276
Mannlicher	276
Mauser	277
Peabody	277
Peabody-Martini	277

RUSSIA, MODERN 277
Kalashnikov	277
Nikonov	278
Tula	278

RUSSIA, TSARIST 278
Arisaka	278
Baranov	278
Berdan, block-action type	278
Berdan, bolt-action type	279
Fedorov	280
Gillet-Trummer	280
Greene	280
Karle	280
Krnka	281
Mosin-Nagant	281
Nagant	282
Norman (Terry)	282
Winchester	282

SAUDI ARABIA 283
| Heckler & Koch | 283 |
| Mauser | 283 |

SAXONY 283
| Chassepot | 283 |
| Drechsler | 283 |

SERBIA 283
Green	283
Martini	284
Mauser	284

SIAM 285
Arisaka	285
Mannlicher	285
Mauser	285

SINGAPORE 285
| ArmaLite | 285 |
| Chartered Industries | 285 |

SOUTH AFRICA 286
FN-Saive (Lyttelton)	286
Galil (Lyttelton)	286
Lee-Enfield	287
Musgrave	287
Vergueiro	287

SPAIN 287
Amiel	287
Berdan	287
CETME	288
García Saez	289
La Rosa	289
Mata	290
Mauser: bolt-action	290
Núñez de Castro	292
Peabody	292
Remington	292

Snider	294
Soriano	294
Winchester	294

SWEDEN 294
FN (FFV)	294
Friberg-Kjellman	295
Galil (FFV)	295
Hagström	295
Heckler & Koch (FFV)	295
Husqvarna (FFV)	295
Ljungmann (Husqvarna)	297
Mauser (Carl Gustaf)	297
Remington	298
Sjögren	298
Stiga (Mauser)	298

SWITZERLAND 299
Abegg	299
End	299
Flisch	299
Flury	299
Frey	299
Gamma & Infanger	299
Grünig & Elmiger	299
Hämmerli	300
Heeren	300
Kaestli	301
Mannlicher	301
Martini	301
Milbank-Amsler	302
Neuhausen	302
Pauly	302
Peabody	302
Schmidt (-Rubin)	303
SIG	305
SIG-Sauer	308
Stamm	308
Tanner	309
Vetterli	310

TAIWAN 312
| Armalite | 312 |
| Garand | 312 |

THAILAND 312
| Arisaka | 312 |

TRANSVAAL (ZAR) 312
| Mauser | 312 |
| Richards | 312 |

TURKEY 312
Berthier	312
Heckler & Koch	312
Mauser	312
Peabody	313
Peabody-Martini	314
Reichsgewehr (Mannlicher)	314

URUGUAY 314
Daudetau-Mauser	314
Mauser	314
Remington	314

U.S.A. 314
Allen (Ethan), block-action type	314
Allen (Ethan), plug-action type	314
Allen (Hiram)	314
Alpha Arms	315
AMAC	315
American Industries (Calico)	315
AMT, autoloading type	315
AMT, bolt-action type	315
ArmaLite	316
Armstrong & Taylor	321
A-Square	321
Auto-Ordnance	321
Ball	321
Ballard	322
Bannerman	323
Beal	323
Beals	323
Berdan, block-action type	323
Berdan, bolt-action type	324
Bighorn	324
Blake	324
Boswell	324
Broadwell	324
Broughton	324
Brown	324
Browning, autoloading type	324
Browning, block-action type	324
Browning, bolt-action type	325
Browning, lever-action type	326
Brown Standard	328
Bruce	328

Bullard, block-action type............ 328
Bullard, lever-action type 328
Burgess............................ 328
Burke.............................. 328
Burnside........................... 329
Burton............................. 330
Bushmaster 330
Century 330
Chaffee-Reece...................... 330
Champlin 331
Charter Arms 331
Chipmunk 331
Clerke 331
Cochran........................... 331
Coleman 331
Colt, autoloading type.............. 331
Colt, bolt-action type............... 331
Coltsman Standard Sporting Rifle 332
Coltsman Standard Sporting Rifle 332
Colt, lever-action type.............. 332
Colt, slide-action type.............. 332
Conover (Empire)................... 333
Conroy 333
Cooper............................ 333
Crescent 334
Cullen 334
Daisy.............................. 334
Dakota............................ 334
Davenport 334
Dodge 335
DuBiel 335
Durst.............................. 335
Elliott 335
Enfield 335
Evans 336
Fajen 336
Field 336
Firearms International.............. 336
Fitzgerald 336
FN-Saive........................... 336
Fogerty, bolt-action type............ 336
Fogerty, lever-action type........... 337
Franklin........................... 337
Freeman 337
Gallager 337
Garand 338
Gibbs, bolt-action type 341
Gibbs, break-open type 341
Golden Eagle 341
Golden State 341
Goulding 341
Gray.............................. 341
Greene............................ 341
Grendel 342
Grillett 342
Gross............................. 342
Gwyn & Campbell 342
Hall............................... 342
Hammond 344
Hampden.......................... 344
Harrington & Richardson, autoloading type 344
Harrington & Richardson, bolt-action type. 344
Harrington & Richardson, break-open type 345
Harrington & Richardson,
   block-action type,............... 345
Harrington & Richardson, slide-action type 346
Hartung (Klein).................... 346
Harvey 346
Hayden 346
Henry 346
High-Standard...................... 347
Hoffmann 347
Holden 347
Hopkins & Allen.................... 347
Hotchkiss 348
Howard 348
Howe.............................. 348
HS Precision 348
Hubbell 348
Hyper............................. 348
Ithaca 348
Iver Johnson 349
Jaeger 349
Jenks (Barton)..................... 349
Jenks (William)..................... 349
Jennings 350
Johnson, autoloading type........... 351
Johnson, swinging-barrel type........ 351
Johnson Associates.................. 351
Joslyn 351
Joslyn-Tomes....................... 352
Kimber 352
Knight............................. 354

Kodiak 354
Krag-Jørgensen 355
Laidley............................ 356
Lamson 357
Lee, block-action type.............. 357
Lee, bolt-action type............... 357
Lee, pivoting-barrel type............ 358
Lee-Cook.......................... 358
Lindner 358
Ljutic............................. 359
McMillan 359
Marathon 360
Marlin, autoloading type............ 360
Marlin, bolt-action type............. 362
Marlin, lever-action type............ 364
Marlin, slide-action type............ 370
Marston 371
Mauser............................ 371
Maynard 371
Meigs............................. 373
Merrill 373
Merrill, Latrobe & Thomas 373
Milbank 373
Miller............................. 374
Mix & Horton...................... 374
Montana Armory 374
Morgenstern........................ 374
Morse............................. 374
Mosin-Nagant 374
Mossberg, autoloading type.......... 375
Mossberg, block-action type.......... 375
Mossberg, bolt-action type........... 375
Mossberg, lever-action type.......... 379
Mossberg, slide-action type.......... 380
Mullins 380
National 380
National Ordnance.................. 380
Navy Arms 381
Needham 381
New England Firearms 381
Newton 381
Opus 382
Page-Lewis 382
Palmer 382
Parkhurst-Lee 382
Peabody........................... 382
Peabody-Martini 383
Pedersen 383
Percy 383
Perry 384
Pitcher 384
Plainfield 384
Poultney........................... 384
Rahn 384
Ranger............................ 384
Red Willow 385
Remington, autoloading type......... 385
Remington, block-action type......... 387
Remington, bolt-action type.......... 390
Remington, lever-action type......... 397
Remington, slide-action type......... 398
Remington-Hepburn 399
Remington-Keene 400
Remington-Lee 400
Richardson......................... 401
Roberts 402
Robertson & Simpson 402
Robinson 402
Roper............................. 402
Rowe 402
Ruger, autoloading type............. 403
Ruger, block-action type 404
Ruger, bolt-action type 406
Ruger, lever-action type 408
Russell (-Livermore) 408
Savage, autoloading type............ 408
Savage, block-action type........... 408
Savage, bolt-action type............. 409
Savage, break-open type............. 416
Savage, lever-action type............ 416
Savage, slide-action type............ 417
Schenkl 418
Schroeder, Salewski & Schmidt 418
Sears, Roebuck 418
Sharps (i) 418
Sharps (ii) 422
Sharps-Borchardt................... 422
Sharps & Hankins 423
Shilen............................. 423
Shiloh 424
Smith (Dexter)..................... 424
Smith (Gilbert)..................... 424
Smith (Isaac)...................... 425

Smith & Wesson.................... 425
Smoot............................. 425
Sneider 425
Snell 426
Snider............................. 426
Spencer........................... 426
Spencer-Roper 427
Springfield, bolt-action type......... 427
Springfield (-Allin)................. 430
Springfield Armory, Inc. 433
Standard (Smith) 434
Starr 434
Stevens (J.), autoloading type........ 434
Stevens (J.), block-action type....... 435
Stevens (J.), bolt-action type 436
Stevens (J.), break-open type........ 437
Stevens (J.), slide-action type........ 438
Stevens (J.), swinging-barrel type..... 438
Stevens (W.X.)..................... 439
Stoner............................ 439
Storm 439
Straw 439
Symmes 439
Thomas........................... 440
Thompson.......................... 440
Thompson/Center 440
Tiesing 441
Trabue 441
Triplett & Scott 441
Ultra Light 441
Underwood......................... 442
Universal 442
Updegraff.......................... 443
Van Choate........................ 443
Varner............................. 443
Voere (KDF) 443
Volcanic 443
Ward-Burton 443
Warner............................ 444
Weatherby, autoloading type 444
Weatherby, bolt-action type 444
Wesson 446
White 446
Whitney 446
Whitney-Remington Patterns 446
Whittemore........................ 447
Wichita............................ 447
Wickliffe 447
Wilson & Flather 447
Winchester, autoloading type 447
Winchester, block-action type 451
Winchester, bolt-action type......... 452
Winchester, lever-action type........ 461
Winchester, slide-action type........ 468
Winchester-Hotchkiss 468
Winchester-Lee 469
Winslow 470
Wolcott............................ 470
Wright & Brown.................... 470

USSR **470**
Degtyarev, autoloading type.......... 470
Dragunov 471
Fedorov 472
Izhevsk............................ 472
Kalashnikov 474
Konstantinov 476
Margolin........................... 476
Mosin-Nagant 477
Roshchepey 479
Ross.............................. 479
Rukavishnikov 479
Serdyukov & Kraskov SNIPER RIFLE Vintovka
   Serdyukova-Kraskova, 'VSS' 479
Simonov 479
Sudaev 481
Tokarev 481
TOZ, autoloading type.............. 484
TOZ, bolt-action type............... 485

VENEZUELA **485**
FN-Saive 485
Mauser 485

YEMEN **485**

YUGOSLAVIA **485**
Kalashnikov 485
Mauser 487
Simonov 487

Bibliography **488**

Glossary **493**

Foreword

A glance at this new edition of *Rifles of the World*, originally published in 1993, will show that a great change has taken place. The book is much larger and, we hope, very much better than its predecessor.

Rifles of the World was originally produced in Britain and handled in the USA by DBI, now a division of Krause Publications. However, restrictions on the size of the first edition, made by the demands of the British market, forced a series of choices to be made: small-caliber rimfires were excluded, and so was anything firing a combustible cartridge. These artificial restrictions undoubtedly reduced the value of the first *Rifles of the World* to the US collector. In addition, the sub-division of the book by manufacturer was never universally popular, and so a return to the tried and tested country-by-country basis has now been made.

Most of the restrictions on coverage have now been abandoned, though coverage is still devoted to breechloaders. A start has been made on the 22 rimfires; cap-locks and needle guns have been included, and some break-open representatives will also be found. However, the enormity of the subject means that only the surface has been scratched—deeply, I hope—and help is still welcomed.

One of the most pleasing aspects of the publication of the first edition was the feedback from specialist collectors, who corrected mistakes and enlarged entries which had previously been sketchy. I cannot thank everyone personally and hope that a corporate 'thanks' will suffice. But I feel I must single out Ian Hogg, a friend of long standing, for assistance above and beyond the call of duty.

I also owe a great debt to Anthony Carter of Tharston Press, author of the standard works on German bayonets; to Richard Brown of Ken Trotman Ltd, Britain's premier gun-book dealer; to John Knibbs of Birmingham, for access to his unrivalled knowledge of the rifles produced by BSA; to Herb Woodend, Curator of the MoD Pattern Room Collection in the Royal Ordnance Factory, Nottingham; to David Penn, Keeper of the Department of Firearms in the Imperial War Museum, London; to Jan Lenselink of the Royal Dutch Arms and Army Museum in Delft; to Joseph J. Schroeder of Handgun Press, Glenview, Illinois; to Claus Espeholt of Grenaa; and to Karl Schäfer of Pirmasens and Hans-Bert Lockhoven of Köln.

Many illustrations have been provided by the manufacturers, but a large number were supplied by Karl Schäfer and others come from my own archives. Those marked 'HBL' appear by courtesy of Hans-Bert Lockhoven; pictures marked 'W&D' and 'W&W' came from the archives of the British auctioneers Weller & Dufty (Birmingham) and Wallis & Wallis (Lewes) respectively.

'Calvó' identifies a drawing taken from Juan L. Calvó's *Armamento Reglamentario y Auxiliar del Ejercito Español*; 'FMW' from James E. Hicks' *French Military Weapons* (1964 edition); 'FP&P', from Jaroslav Lugs' book *Firearms Past & Present* (1976); 'GdW', from Schott's *Grundriss der Waffenlehre* (1878); 'Greener', from W.W. Greener's *The Gun and Its Development* (1910 edition) or *Modern Breech Loaders* (1871); 'Kromar', from *Repetier- und Automatische Handfeuerwaffen der Systeme Ferdinand Ritter von Mannlicher* (1900); and 'USMF', from James E. Hicks' *US Military Firearms* (1962).

No-one with a broad interest in firearms can hope to know as much about each facet of the subject as a specialist who may have been collecting a particular gun-type for fifty years. I'm no exception to this rule, but I hope that one of the strengths of this new *Rifles of the World*—and it is extensively changed—lies in even-handed treatment of American and European guns. Several 'listings' books already cover the same subject, but most treat US guns much more comprehensively than European products.

One of the most pleasing aspects of compilation work is the great enthusiasm of many manufacturers, though some major players failed to react to requests for assistance and a few sections reflect a lack of cooperation. It would be churlish to single out any particular agency for criticism, but I would like to thank the most helpful respondents individually—J.G. Anschütz GmbH of Ulm/Donau; Blaser-Jagdwaffen GmbH of Isny/Allgau; FAIR Techni-Mech of Gardone Val Trompia; Heym GmbH & Co. of Gleichamberg; Pietro Beretta SpA of Gardone Val Trompia; Bill Hulse of Edgar Brothers Ltd, Macclesfield; Rolf Westinger of Feinwerkbau-Westinger & Altenburger GmbH, Oberndorf a.N.; Bernhard Knöbel, Vice-President (Marketing) of H. Krieghoff GmbH, Ulm/Donau; Anne-Marie Ramakers of Aug. Lebeau-Courally, Liege; Davide Pedersoli & Co. s.n.c. of Gardone Val Trompia; Alfonso Puzzo of Fratelli Pietta, Gussago, Brescia; Ralph Krawczyc of Rhöner; Ronald Bartos and Lynn Johnson of Savage Arms, Inc., Westfield, Massachusetts; SIG of Neuhausen; Springfield Armory, Inc., of Geneseo, Illinois; Eric Brooker of Thompson-Center Arms Co., Inc., Rochester, New Hampshire; Edward Horton and Simon Brown of Viking Arms Ltd, Harrogate; and Antonio Zoli of Gardone Val Trompia.

Lastly, I must thank Charles Hartigan, for his faith in commissioning this second edition; Harold Murtz for casting his expert editorial eye over a script which had run roughshod over the agreed length-limit; and Ken Ramage of Krause Publications, for taking the project through its most difficult stages to print.

John Walter
Hove, England, 1998

ARGENTINA

Argentine firearms are often marked with the national Arms, which, in the case of Mauser rifles, is usually stamped into the receiver-top above the chamber. This takes the form of two hands clasping a Liberty Cap on a pole within a wreath of laurel. Rifles may also be found with the marks of the naval and military academies ('ESCUELA NAVAL' and 'ESCUELA MILITAR' respectively).

• Buenos Aires

This name was given to Chassepot-type rifles, musketoons and carbines made in Belgium by Francotte of Liége. The guns served Argentine forces as the 'Mo. 1869,' but were subsequently replaced with Remingtons. It is suspected that at least a few of the Chassepot copies were converted to fire metal-case ammunition, but details are lacking. For information about history, construction and dimensions, see 'France: Chassepot'.

• Enfield

The Remington Arms Company is said to have supplied Model 40 rifles to the Argentine army in the mid 1930s, at about the time large numbers were sent to Honduras (q.v.). The guns are said to have chambered the 7.65x53 rimless cartridge and to have borne the national arms above the chamber. However, this 'Argentine contract' has never been substantiated.

• FMAP

The state-owned ordnance factory developed a small caliber rifle in the late 1970s, intending to replace the 7.62mm FSL in front-line service. The FARA 83 bore much the same relationship to the FSL as Fabrique Nationale's CAL had with the original FAL (see 'Belgium'), but had been abandoned by the mid 1980s – said to have been due to budgetary restrictions, but more probably due to unexpected teething troubles.

MODEL 83 AUTOMATIC RIFLE
Fusil Automatico del Republica de Argentina Modelo 83, 'FARA 83'

Made by Fábrica Militar de Armas Portatiles 'Domingo Matheu,' Rosario, Santa Fé, about 1984-9.

Total production: 2500-3000? **Chambering:** 5.56x45, rimless. **Action:** locked by rotating lugs on the bolt into the receiver walls; gas operated, selective fire.

39.35in overall (29.5in with stock folded), 8.27lb without magazine. 17.8in barrel, 6-groove rifling; RH, concentric. Detachable box magazine, 30 rounds. Three-position rear sight graduated to 400m (435yd). 3165fps with SS109 ammunition; 775±50rpm. Knife bayonet.

Developed to supersede the 7.62mm FSL, this conventional-looking rifle embodied a rotating-bolt lock instead of a tilting block and made extensive use of stampings to save weight. The butt of glass-reinforced synthetic fiber could be swung to the right alongside the receiver, and grooves in the short plastic forend accepted the legs of an optional bipod. The FARA rear sight had open notches for 200m (220yd) and 400m (435yd), accompanied by a special 100m (110yd) Tritium-insert setting for use in poor light in conjunction with an auxiliary front sight.

• FN (FMAP)

A few thousand 30-06 Mle 49 (SAFN) rifles were acquired in 1950, apparently for the navy. They were followed a decade later by the first FAL rifles; many surviving SAFNs were subsequently

The FARA 83 on field exercises.

altered to accept the 20-round FAL magazine in the interests of standardisation, but were then withdrawn into store.

Substantial numbers of Types 50-00 FAL II, 50-61 Para and 50-63 Para rifles were provided from Belgium before the first licence-built guns emanated from Fábrica Militar de Armas Portatiles 'Domingo Matheu' of Rosario, Santa Fé.

FAL-TYPE AUTOMATIC RIFLES
Fusil Semiautomatico Livano, 'FSL'

A typical army rifle was marked 'FABRICA MILITAR DE ARMAS PORTATILES–ROSARIO' over 'INDUSTRIA ARGENTINA,' behind the maker's encircled 'FM' on the right side of the receiver; 'F.S.L.-Cal.-7,62-002' lay on the left rear side. Argentine-made guns have been supplied to other countries in South and Central America. By 1981, about 129,680 standard and 8,460 heavy-barrel guns had been made when work in the Rosario factory ceased. Argentinian FAL-type guns have also been supplied from Rosario to Colombia, Honduras, Peru (FSL, FSL Para), and Uruguay (FSL, FSL Para).

SIMILAR GUNS

5.56mm version. The 7.62 FSL rifles were destined to be replaced in front-line service by the 5.56mm FARA 83 (see 'FMAP', above), but progress was soon halted. To save money, therefore, the Rosario factory developed a small caliber version of the FSL, sharing many of the parts of the original 7.62mm gun – excepting the barrel, the bolt, the magazine and the feed components. Subtle changes to the gas system have been made to handle the different pressure/time curve of the 5.56x45 round, though external appearance remains virtually unchanged.

The 5.56mm FSL is currently being made in a full-length infantry pattern ('Tipo Infanteria') and a short-barreled paratroop gun ('Tipo Paracudista') with a folding butt. The standard gun is 42.9in long, has a 21in barrel and weighs 9.6lb without its magazine; the paratroop model is 40.15in long (30.3in with the butt folded), with

The Argentine version of the FAL, in its short-barreled form.

a 18.05in barrel and an empty weight of 9.25lb. Thirty-round magazines and two-position 'L'-type rear sights for 150m (165yd) and 250m (275yd) are common to both types.

• Garand

The US government supplied nearly thirty thousand M1 Garand rifles prior to 1964, many being issued to the navy along with Beretta BM-59 rifles supplied directly from Italy. Some Garands were converted by Fabrica Militar de Armas Portatiles 'Domingo Matheu' in the 1960s to accept the standard Beretta-type twenty-round box magazine.

• Mauser

The government purchased Mausers to replace Remington single-shot rifles and, apparently, Lee bolt-action rifles chambered for the 11mm Spanish cartridge. The guns usually bear 'MAUSER ARGENTINO' on the left side of the receiver and the national Arms above the chamber, though, owing to a law promulgated during the 1930s, the chamber-marks may have been ground away.

MODEL 1891 RIFLE
Fusil Mauser Argentino Mo.1891

Made by Ludwig Loewe & Co., Berlin, 1891-6; and Deutsche Waffen- und Munitionsfabriken, Berlin, 1897-1900.

Total production: not known. **Chambering:** 7.65x53, rimless. **Action:** locked by two lugs on the bolt head engaging recesses in the receiver ring behind the chamber as the bolt handle is turned down.

48.65in overall, 8.8lb empty. 29.15in barrel, 4-groove rifling; RH, concentric. Fixed charger-loaded box magazine, 5 rounds. Ramp-and-leaf sight graduated to 2000m (2185yd). 2130fps with Mo. 1891 ball cartridges. Mo. 1891 sword bayonet.

This was adopted after extensive trials, an order for 180,000 rifles being passed to Loewe. The rifle was an improved Turkish M1890 (q.v.), though the changes were comparatively few: a rotating lock-bolt was added to retain the magazine, guide ribs were added to the bolt sleeve, and the handguard extended forward as far as the barrel band. The rear sight had a small leaf for 350m (385yd) in addition to the large leaf graduated to 2000m. Most 1891-type rifles were altered after 1909 for the spitzer-bulleted 'Bala S' cartridge.

SIMILAR GUNS

Model 1891 carbine. The 'Carabina Mauser Argentina Mo. 1891' – 37in long, with a 17.65in barrel – was introduced in 1893 for the cavalry and artillery. It was stocked to the muzzle, had a plain nose cap and barrel band, and the bolt handle was turned down against the stock. A sling bar and ring assembly was fitted beneath the wrist. The rear sight was graduated to 1200m (1310yd), but a handguard still ran from the front of its base to the band. Empty weight was about 7.25lb. Thirty thousand guns were ordered from Loewe in 1891, but the deliveries were not made for some time: rifles were presumably accorded priority. Some surviving guns were adapted to receive a sword bayonet, apparently in the mid 1920s.

MODEL 1909 RIFLE
Fusil Mauser Argentino Mo. 1909

Made by Deutsche Waffen- und Munitionsfabriken, Berlin, 1909-14; and Fábrica Militar de Armas Portatiles, Rosario, about 1942-59.

Total production: an unknown quantity in Germany, plus possibly 85,000 in Argentina. **Chambering:** 7.65x53, rimless. **Action:** locked by two lugs on the bolt head engaging recesses in the receiver ring behind the chamber as the bolt handle was turned down, and by a safety lug opposing the bolt handle.

49.15in overall, 8.97lb empty. 29.15in barrel, 4-groove rifling; RH, concentric. Internal charger-loaded box magazine, 5 rounds. Tangent-leaf sight graduated to 2000m (2185yd). 2705fps with Mo. 1909 'S' ball cartridges. Mo. 1909 sword bayonet.

Ordered in Germany in 1909, this was a standard 1898-type Mauser with a tangent-leaf sight and a hinged magazine floor-plate, released by a small catch set into the trigger guard. The left charger guide, however, was provided by an upward extension of the spring-loaded bolt stop. The handguard ran from the receiver ring to the narrow spring-retained barrel band, and the nose cap was a German 'H' type.

Though the first deliveries of rifles were apparently accompanied by German 1898-type épée bayonets, these broke too easily and

had a short service career; most rifles, therefore, were subsequently fitted with adaptors for the sturdier Mo. 1891 sword bayonet.

The advent of the Second World War in Europe stemmed the flow of small arms from Belgium and Czechoslovakia. Consequently, the Argentine government decided in 1940 to begin work in the Rosario factory, the first Mauser rifles being delivered in 1942.

SIMILAR GUNS

Model 1909 cavalry carbine. Made by DWM or FMAP, this had a full-length stock with a straight-wristed butt and a hand-guard running from the receiver ring to the barrel band. It was 42.5in long, had a 21.65in barrel and weighed about 8.5lb. The rear sight was a 1400m (1530yd) tangent-leaf pattern and a lug for the Mo. 91 bayonet projected beneath the forend.

Model 1909 mountain carbine. Also identified as an engineers' weapon (were there two differing patterns?), this has an 'H'-type nose cap for the Mo. 1909 bayonet and a 1400m rear sight. The carbines, which were about 41.3in overall, may have been cut down from full-length rifles. Production continued in Rosario for many years, amounting to 20,220 in 1942-59.

Model 1909 sniper rifle. A few specially-selected guns were fitted with 4x German-made telescope sights. Their bolt handles were turned down against the stock to prevent them fouling the sight body during the reloading cycle.

OTHER GUNS

Large quantities of Mle 24 and Mle 30 short rifles were purchased from Fabrique Nationale of Herstal in the period between the two world wars. Additional FN Mausers were purchased in the late 1940s, though the numbers involved were small.

• Remington

Large numbers of 11mm Spanish-pattern guns were purchased from E. Remington & Sons in 1875-86. Issued as Mo. 1875 (rifle) and Mo. 1879 (carbine), they were accompanied by Ames-made bayonets. Smaller quantities of improved 'Mo. 1902' rifles, chambering 7.65x53 smokeless ammunition, were purchased from the Remington Arms Company in the first years of the twentieth century.

ARMENIAN REPUBLIC

• Kalashnikov

Among the surprises at the Defendory International Show in Athens in October 1996 was the appearance of an indigenous assault rifle.

ASSAULT RIFLE MODEL 3 AK-3
Manufacturer unknown.

Currently in production? **Chambering:** 5.45x39, rimless.

Detachable box magazine, 30 rounds. Tangent-leaf sight graduated to 500m (545yd). 2330fps with ball ammunition; about 600rpm. No bayonet.

The AK-3 is an uncomplicated adaptation of the AK-74, with the box magazine behind the pistol grip and a shoulder plate attached to the back of the black-phosphated receiver. The only major alteration in the operating system, the pinning of the bolt carrier to the piston rod, is purely a manufacturing expedient and does not affect the basic cycle.

The bullpup layout allows overall length to be substantially reduced, but requires the sights to be carried high above the receiver on riser blocks; optional optical or electro-optical sights can be mounted in a bracket attached to the left side of the receiver. The pistol grip and the short vertically ribbed forend are made of a dark-green plastic material.

AUSTRALIA

The tardy confederation of Australia, which did not occur until 1900, meant that individual states purchased weapons of their own. Consequently, New South Wales bought 450 Henry dropping-block breechloaders in the 1870s (long and short rifles, artillery carbines and cavalry carbines), followed by 577 Snider artillery carbines in 1885-6; Queensland bought Calisher & Terry caplock breechloaders with German-made saber bayonets, then some special 303 Martini-Enfield rifles with attachment bars for bushed P/1887 sword bayonets; South Australia is known to have used 577 P/53 Enfield rifle-muskets converted in Birmingham to the Braendlin(-Albini) breech system; Victoria acquired 577 Snider conversions in the 1880s; and Western Australia bought a thousand commercial 303 Lee-Speed rifles from BSA&M Co. in 1892.

Australian guns may be distinguished by their markings, which included the Lithgow factory mark in various guises; 'MA' originally represented 'Made in Australia,' but came to signify Lithgow when a chain of sub-contractors was established during the Second World War. These included government-owned factories in Bathurst ('BA'), Forbes ('FA'), Orange ('OA') and Wellington ('WA'). Most of the stocks and handguards came from the Slazenger factory in Sydney and displayed 'SLAZ.' Property marks have included 'DD' and 'D,' or state markings such as 'TAS.' and 'W.A.' for Tasmania and Western Australia.

- ## FN (Lithgow)

L1A1 RIFLE
Made by the Lithgow Small Arms Factory, New South Wales, about 1958-78.

Total production: not known. **Chambering:** 7.62x51 NATO, rimless. **Action:** as Belgian FAL (q.v.). 44.7in overall, 12lb loaded. 20.95in barrel, 6-groove rifling; RH, concentric.

Detachable box magazine, 20 rounds. Sliding aperture sight, graduated to 600yd. 2750fps with L2A2 ball cartridges. L1A2 knife bayonet.

The Australian Army adopted the British L1A1 rifle on 1st March 1957, preparing a production line in the government-owned factory immediately. The first Lithgow-made guns were delivered into store in March 1959. Excepting markings, they were identical with British-issue weapons – with wood furniture and anti-fouling grooves cut in the side of the bolt carrier. The carrying handles were generally synthetic, and had shallow finger grooves. Australian L1A1-type guns have been supplied from Lithgow to Barbados, Fiji, Jamaica, Malaysia, New Zealand and Singapore. The Steyr AUG, adopted in the mid 1980s, has superseded the L1A1 in Australian service, though large numbers of the older guns are still being held in reserve.

SIMILAR GUNS
L1A1-F1 rifle. A shortened version of the basic L1A1, this was introduced about 1973. It was 41.95in overall, had an 18.2in barrel and weighed 10.82lb loaded.

L2A1 rifle. This was a heavy-barreled version of the basic infantry rifle, 44.75in overall with a 20.95in barrel and a loaded weight of 15.2lb. The magazines held 20 or 30 rounds, and the tangent-bar sight was graduated to 1000yd. Unlike the L1A1, the L2A1 would not accept a bayonet. Though made in substantial numbers prior to the early 1970s, operating problems caused it to be withdrawn from front-line units in favor of the heavier but much more efficient Bren Gun (L4). Surviving L2A1 rifles were re-issued to second-line and ancillary units.

- ## Lee-Enfield

Prior to 1939, the Australian forces were armed with standard British SMLE Mks III and III* (No. 1 Mk III and No. 1 Mk III*) rifles made in a government factory that had been established in Lithgow, New South Wales, in 1912. The guns dated from 1913-29, 1938-45 and 1953-6.

The Australian Lee-Enfields were virtually identical with British prototypes; however, apart from a few made immediately prior to the First World War with walnut stock blanks supplied from Britain, they were stocked in a selection of native woods. As these were softer than walnut, minor changes were made to the bedding. Minor changes in the machining of components were also to be found, and rectangular apertures were cut through the front-sight protectors of many rifles during the Second World War to facilitate removal of the sight blade without detaching the nose-cap assembly.

The Australians also made a heavy-barreled model for military target shooting. Distinguished by a large 'H' on the knox-form and on the right side of the butt, many were impressed into military service in 1940-5.

NUMBER 1 MARK 3* H (T) (AUST.) RIFLE
Sniper rifle
Made by the Royal Australian Small Arms Factory, Lithgow, New South Wales, 1944-6.

Total production: see notes. **Chambering:** 303, rimmed. **Action:** locked by a single lug on the bolt body engaging the receiver, and by the rear of the bolt guide rib abutting the receiver bridge as the bolt handle was turned down.

44.55in overall, 10.3lb with sight. 25.2in barrel, 5-groove rifling; LH, concentric. Detachable box magazine, 10 rounds. Tangent-leaf sight graduated to 2000yd. 2440fps with Mk VII ball cartridges. No. 1 Mk 1 sword bayonet.

About 2500 of these heavy-barrel SMLEs were ordered to supplement the No. 3 Mk I* (T) sniper rifles on 10th November 1944. They had Aldis telescope sights, offset to the left; cheekpieces were occasionally fitted, as were additional sling swivels on the front trigger guard screw.

Only 1612 rifles had been completed when the project was terminated in 1946. They were made from old actions, and may be misleadingly dated as early as 1915. All but four hundred had P/1918 (Aust.) sights in special high mounts, the exceptions having Pattern 1918 (Aust.)/1 sights in low mounts. Very few of these weapons were ever used, though a few were issued in the 1970s pending the introduction of a new gun.

NUMBER 1 MARK 3 RIFLE, SHORT PATTERN
Made by the Royal Australian Small Arms Factory, Lithgow, New South Wales, 1944.

Total production: at least 105, including prototypes. **Chambering:** 303, rimmed. **Action:** as No. 1 Mk 3* H (T), above.
DATA FOR LONG-BARREL VERSION
39.55in overall, 7.8lb empty. 20.2in barrel, 5-groove rifling; LH, concentric. Detachable charger-loaded box magazine, ten rounds. Pivoting 'L' rear sight for 200yd and 500yd. About 2180fps with Mk VII ball cartridges. Knife bayonet.

This experimental short rifle was made in the Lithgow factory in 1944. Prototypes were given 18in (short) and 20in (intermediate) barrels in search of a handier weapon for jungle fighting. The intermediate barrel was preferred, and a hundred additional guns were made for trials in March. However, the prototype No. 6 (q.v.) held greater potential and the No. 1 was abandoned. Its bayonet was subsequently adapted for the Owen sub-machine gun.

NUMBER 6 RIFLE
Made by the Royal Australian Small Arms Factory, Lithgow, New South Wales, 1945.

Total production: at least 200. **Chambering:** 303, rimmed. **Action:** generally as No. 1 Mk 3* H (T), above.
DATA FOR LONG-BARREL VERSION
39.5in overall, 7.5lb empty. 19in barrel, 5-groove rifling; LH, concentric. Detachable charger-loaded box magazine, ten rounds. Tangent-leaf rear sight graduated to 2000yd. About 2130fps with Mk VII ball cartridges. Knife bayonet.

Four batches of about fifty near-identical guns were made in 1945, differing only in the buttplates (brass or rubber) and sights. Half the guns had No. 1 tangent-leaf rear sights ('No. 6 Mk 1') while the remainder had pivoting aperture sights on the rear of the receiver ('No. 6 Mk 1/1').

The rifles were similar to the British No. 5 jungle carbine, but were built on the older No. 1 action. They had half-stocks and handguards, retained by a single band, and multiple grasping grooves were cut in the forend.

The pattern was approved in the autumn of 1945, but the Australian No. 6 was declared obsolete before production began. A few survivors were altered in 1954 for the 7.62x51 NATO cartridge and given detachable twenty-round box magazines to satisfy a Royal Australian Air Force specification. Margins of safety in the action proved insufficient, however, and the project was abandoned.

- ## Martini

CADET RIFLES
Made by Auguste Francotte & Co., Liége, about 1900-3 (25,000?); the Birmingham Small Arms Co. Ltd, Small Heath, about 1907-14 (75,000?); and W.W. Greener Ltd, Birmingham, about 1907-14 (50,000?).

Chambering options: 297/230 or 310. **Action:** locked by the tip of the operating lever propping the breechblock behind the chamber.
DATA FOR A TYPICAL EXAMPLE
Chambering: 310, rimmed 44.75in overall, 8.95lb empty. 29in barrel, 4-groove rifling; RH, concentric? Ramp-and-leaf sight (see notes). About 1200fps with 120-grain bullet. Special reduced-scale P/53 socket bayonet.

Substantial quantities of these small-action trainers were acquired by the governments of Victoria and Western Australia from 1900 onward. The first batches were apparently ordered from

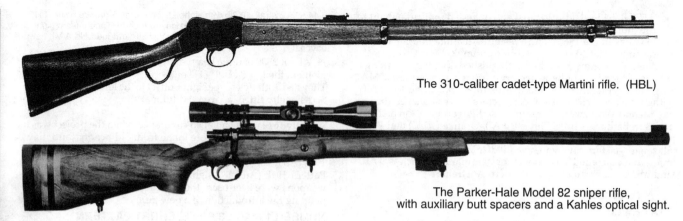

The 310-caliber cadet-type Martini rifle. (HBL)

The Parker-Hale Model 82 sniper rifle,
with auxiliary butt spacers and a Kahles optical sight.

Francotte, as the British manufacturers were struggling to satisfy demands of the Second South African (Boer) War. Purchases continued after 1900 on behalf of the newly formed Commonwealth of Australia.

The original guns had military-style stocks with a single barrel band near the muzzle, a cocking indicator on the right side of the receiver, and ramp-and-leaf rear sights similar to the Martini-Enfields. However, additional guns were ordered from BSA and Greener in Britain c. 1907. They were similar to the original Belgian pattern, but the rear sights had SMLE-type protecting wings.

Writing in 1910, William Greener suggested that 310 'Sharpshooter Cadet Rifles' and 297/230 'Miniature Patterns' were bought for adults and juniors respectively. They may be distinguished from commercial guns by 'VIC.,' 'W.A.' or 'COMMONWEALTH OF AUSTRALIA' marks.

• Parker-Hale

The Australian authorities adopted a variant of the British Parker-Hale M82 sniper rifle in the mid 1980s. Issued as the 'Rifle, 7.62mm, Sniper System,' it was fitted with a 1200-TX barrel, a Kahles Helia Zf.60 6x42 telescope sight, and precision open sights. For additional details, see **'Britain.'**

• Sportco

Sporting Arms Ltd. of Adelaide, better known by the brandname 'Sportco,' made a range of rim- and centerfire sporting rifles from the 1960s until purchased by Omark Indusries in c. 1980. Clearly inspired by American rivals, the Sportco guns are rarely seen outside Australia and have proved difficult to catalog. The information given below undoubtedly only includes part of the product range.

SPORTCO MODEL 71S RIFLE

Made by Sporting Arms Ltd., Adelaide, South Australia.
Total production: not known. **Chambering**: 22 Long Rifle rimfire. **Action:** no mechanical breech lock; blowback operation, semi-automatic only.

42in overall, 6lb empty. 24in barrel, 4-groove rifling; RH, concentric. Detachable box magazine, 10 rounds. Spring-leaf and elevator rear sight. 1050fps with standard ball ammunition.

This autoloader – introduced about 1966 and still being made ten years later – had a tubular receiver containing the bolt, with a charging handle protruding from the right side of the feed way. The butt of the half-stock had a straight comb and a plain pistol grip; the tip of the forend was distinctively squared. A safety catch appeared on the rear right side of the receiver, the trigger guard was a stamped strip, and grooves in the receiver-top could accept telescope-sight mounting bases.

Small numbers of the Australian Sportco Model 71 autoloading rifle were issued in the British services under the designations L29A1 and L29A2, for automatic weapons training, but were rapidly superseded by the 5.56mm L98 Cadet Rifle.

SIMILAR GUNS

Sportco Model 87A rifle ('Sportomatic M87A'). This is believed to have been contemporary with the M71S, with a tube magazine beneath the barrel and a half-stock with a rounded pistol grip. It may be abandoned by 1967, but details are lacking.

SPORTCO HORNET RIFLE
Made by Sporting Arms Ltd, Adelaide, South Australia.

Total production: not known. **Chambering**: 22 Hornet, rimmed. **Action:** apparently locked by rotating two lugs on the bolt body into recesses in the receiver bridge as the bolt handle turned down.

42in overall, 6.6lb empty. 23.5in barrel, 4-groove rifling; RH, concentric. Detachable box magazine, 5 rounds. Tangent-leaf rear sight. 2425fps with 46-grain bullet.

A conventional bolt-action design, this rifle had a squared receiver – suitably grooved to accept optical sights – and a half-stock with a low Monte Carlo comb on the butt. The pistol grip and the forend were checkered; and thin white spacers separated the woodwork from the pistol grip cap and the buttplate. The trigger guard was a stamped strip, and a large spring-leaf release catch lay immediately behind the magazine well. Swivels were placed beneath the butt and forend. The Sportco Hornet may not have been particularly successful, as importation into Britain had been discontinued by 1970.

SPORTCO MODEL 44 RIFLE
Made by Sporting Arms Ltd, Adelaide, South Australia, about 1971-80.
Total production: not known. **Chambering**: 7.62x51 (308 Winchester), rimless. **Action:** locked by rotating three lugs on the bolt body into the barrel extension as the bolt handle turned down.

45.25in overall (with butt spacers), 10.25lb empty. 26.5in barrel, 4-groove rifling; RH, concentric. Single shot only. Parker Hale PH5C aperture rear sight. 2850fps with standard ball ammunition.

This target rifle was a departure from the tried and tested Lee and Mauser-action guns popular in Australia, relying on a three-lug lock connecting with the barrel instead of the receiver. The trigger was adjustable to 4-4.5lb, the safety catch lay on the right side of the upper tang behind the cocking piece, and the barrel was allowed to float freely in the half-length forend/handguard assembly. Parker-Hale PH5C vernier-adjustable aperture (back) and FS22A replaceable-insert tunnel (front) sights were customary, but other options were supplied to suit national competition requirements.

The Sportco 44 was used in small numbers by the Australian police and armed forces as a sniper rifle, but was superseded in the mid 1980s by the Parker-Hale Model 82.

• Steyr (Lithgow)

The AUG, efficient and sturdy, performed well enough in comparative trials for the '5.56mm Rifle F8' to be adopted in 1985. Initial orders for 85,000 rifles were given to the Lithgow small arms factory, eighteen thousand being destined for New Zealand. The first issues were made to the Australian Army in 1988. Lithgow-made rifles have also been offered commercially throughout Australasia; F88 was the standard rifle, F88C was a carbine with a 407mm barrel, the receiver of F88S was adapted for night-vision sights, and the heavy-barreled F88-203 had a 40mm M203 grenade launcher.

AUSTRIA

Details of pre-1918 Mannlicher, Wänzl, Werndl and other rifles will be found in the the chapter devoted to Austria-Hungary.

• Dschulnigg

Karl Dschulnigg of Salzburg, basically a custom gunsmith, made sporting rifles on Mauser, Mannlicher and Sako actions in virtually any chambering the customer requested.

SPORTING RIFLE

The basic Mauser action in a good-quality stock. The cut-out in the left receiver wall was generally filled and refinished. The butt had a straight comb, a small round cheekpiece, and a slender pistol grip with hand-cut checkering. The checkered forend had a shallow schnabel tip. Single or double triggers were fitted to order, within a typically European trigger guard bow. A deluxe 'Grade I' rifle offered a walnut stock, with a sharply curved pistol grip and a contrasting rosewood forend tip.

SIMILAR GUNS

Excepting the Tiger pattern, most Dschulnigg rifles were supplied with double triggers unless the purchaser specified otherwise. Open sights, when fitted, comprised a hooded ramped blade (or bead) and a folding leaf.

Chamois Model rifle. This was similar to the Ibex type, though its butt had a Monte Carlo comb and a conventional pistol grip cap; the slender forend had an oblique-cut tip. Checkering was often replaced by carved oakleaves.

Ibex Model rifle. Distinguished by a modernistic stock with a straight-cut forend tip, an exaggerated pistol grip cap, and a broad beaver-tail forend, these guns also had silver-inlaid engraving on the receiver and magazine floorplate, though gold inlay could be substituted on request.

Ram Model rifle. This had a schnabel-tip ebonite forend, a roll-over comb, and oakleaf carving instead of checkering. The bolt handle was spatulate.

Roebuck Model rifle. Essentially similar to the Ram type, this could be distinguished by a different engraving pattern.

Tiger Model rifle. Similar to the Chamois pattern, excepting for a hog's back comb and a squared Bavarian-style cheekpiece, this gun also customarily had a squared ebonite forend.

Top Hit rifle. This was similar to the standard pattern, but had a beech stock with a Monte Carlo comb and skip-line checkering. A radial magazine floor-plate latch was popular, with sights comprising a hooded ramped blade and an adjustable folding leaf. Most guns were supplied with extended safety catches and mounts for optical sights.

• FN (Steyr)

MODEL 58 ASSAULT RIFLE
Sturmgewehr 58, StG. 58

Made by Steyr-Daimler-Puch AG, Steyr, 1959-75.
Total production: not known. **Chambering:** 7.62x51 NATO, rimless.
Action: as Belgian FAL (q.v.).

44.7in overall, 9.37kg empty. 21.1in barrel, 6-groove rifling; RH, concentric. Detachable box magazine, 20 rounds. Sliding aperture sight graduated to 600m (655yd). 2750fps with standard NATO ball rounds. No bayonet.

The first Austrian service rifles were supplied from Fabrique Nationale in 1958, during the period in which tooling was being undertaken in Steyr. The perfected StG. 58 was distinguished by a fluted sheet-metal forend. According to FN records, the guns originally had the muzzles threaded for a combination grenade launcher and muzzle brake/compensator, a two-piece extractor; a butt with a nose cap, and a trap in the buttplate for cleaning material. They lacked bipods and could not be loaded from chargers. Carrying handles were ribbed synthetic cylinders.

Production runs had been completed by 1975. The StG. 58 was superseded in 1981 by the StG. 77 (Steyr AUG), and the FAL-type weapons were gradually passed to the reserve.

• Mannlicher

The earliest Mannlicher conversions for the 8mm German service cartridge seem to date from 1918; most M1895/24 guns, however, served Bulgaria and Yugoslavia. Details of pre-1918 designs will be found in the 'Austria-Hungary' chapter.

MILITARY WEAPONS

MODEL 1895/24 SHORT RIFLE

Possibly converted in the Steyr factory, this was an adaptation of the 1895-pattern Mannlicher for the ubiquitous German 7.9x57 cartridge. The barrels were shortened to 23.6in, giving an overall length of 43.3in and a weight of about 7.7lb, and charger guides were added to the front of the receiver bridge. The modified magazines, with integrally welded clips to hold the cartridges, could be loaded from the standard German-style stripper clips; the clip-

ejection port in the base of the magazine body had a sheet-metal cover. The rear sights were usually graduated to 2000m (2185yd), muzzle velocity being about 2700fps with German S-Patrone.

M1930 SHORT RIFLE

Converted in the Steyr factory, this chambered a new 8x56 rimmed cartridge standardized in collusion with Hungary to replace the venerable 8x50 pattern. Converted guns were difficult to distinguish externally from 1895-type short rifles, excepting for rear sight graduations extending to 2000m (2185yd). They were 39.4in overall, had 19.7in barrels and weighed 6.88lb. Muzzle velocity was 2395fps and the Austro-Hungarian M1895 knife bayonet with an auxiliary front sight was used.

SPORTING GUNS

Production began again in the early 1920s, guns being identical to pre-1918 patterns. Details of the post-war Models 69, 72 and SBS will be found under 'Steyr, bolt type,' below.

REPETIER-PIRSCHBÜCHSE

Made in Steyr by Österreichische Waffenfabriks-Gesellschaft (c. 1921-34) and Steyr-Daimler-Puch AG (1934-40, 1950-71).
Total production: not known. **Chambering options:** see notes. **Action:** as Austro-Hungarian guns (q.v.).

DATA FOR A TYPICAL 1932-VINTAGE RIFLE

Chambering: 6.5x54, rimless. 45.05in overall, 7.45lb empty. 23.6in barrel, 4-groove rifling; RH, concentric. Internal rotary magazine, 5 rounds. Block-and-leaf sight. 2250fps with 126-grain bullet.

Production resumed with permission from the Allied authorities in 1921, the earliest guns being assembled from pre-war parts. The first entirely new examples dated from 1923-4, though the manufacturing pattern remained unchanged. The first guns chambering the 7.62x63 cartridge (30-06) originated in this era for sale in North America.

The rifles retained the block-and-leaf rear sight or *Klappvisier*, though the popularity of optical patterns soon increased. Short-barreled Repetier-Pirschbüchsen were chambered for 6.5mm, 8mm, 9mm or 9.5mm cartridges; long-barreled half-stocked guns ('Hochrasanz-Modelle') were usually supplied for 7x64, 7.62x63 or 8x60. Other chamberings could be supplied to order, e.g., a 9.3x53 pattern was particularly popular in Switzerland. Longer barrels than normal, multi-leaf Express sights, optical- or aperture-sight mounts, sling eyes on barrel collars, engraving and stock carving were also available.

Production ceased c. 1940 in favor of war-work, the Steyr factory being re-tooled for the Kar. 98k under German supervision. Assembly of sporting rifles is believed to have continued on a small scale until 1942.

The first post-war (or 1950-pattern) sporters were based on the pre-war design, though the bolt handle was refined and the safety catch was moved from the cocking piece to the rear right side of the bridge. This had the important effect of reducing the comparatively slow lock time of the original rifles. Initially chambered only for the 6.5x54 and 270 Winchester cartridges, guns were offered from 1951 in 257 Roberts and 30-06 in the hope of attracting orders from North America; 7x57 and 9.3x62 followed for the European market in 1952. Typically, they had 24in barrels, walnut half-stocks with straight-comb butts, capped pistol grips, and rounded rosewood forend tips.

Many of the guns sold in the USA had single triggers, though the double set pattern retained much of its popularity in Europe. In 1952, in an attempt to modernize the design, the bolt handle was swept backward and the stock detailing improved. Chamberings remained unchanged from 1950.

A revised stock was introduced in 1956, with a Monte Carlo comb and spacers accompanying the forend-tip, pistol grip cap and buttplate. Additional 243 Winchester, 7x57 and 308 Winchester chamberings appeared in this period. A universal stock with a Monte Carlo comb (but lacking a cheekpiece) was introduced in 1961, but production ceased in the early 1970s in favor of the improved Model 72 (q.v.).

SIMILAR GUNS

Short rifle. This was made with a full-length 'Mannlicher' stock, and had a 20in barrel.

Carbine. Distinguished by a barrel measuring merely 18.3in, this 6.5x54 pattern was also made in small numbers.

• Mauser

Austrian gunsmiths, especially those in the gunmaking center of Ferlach in the Kärnten district. The earliest guns were usually built on refurbished wartime military actions, though newer examples, however, use actions bought-in from companies such as Fabrique Nationale. Among the principal manufacturers have been Dschulnigg of Salzburg, and Sodia and Winkler of Ferlach.

• Sodia

Franz Sodia of Ferlach was best known in the 1950s for good-quality sporting rifles built on the Mannlicher-Schönauer but then turned to the Mauser.

MODEL 1963 RIFLE

Apparently built on refurbished actions, engraved to order—was offered in a sporting stock with a Bavarian-style cheekpiece and an oddly humped comb. The drop at the comb was small and the pistol grip radius was much tighter than that found on many British- or US-style rifles. The forend had a short tip with an unusually sharp schnabel profile, the front swivel eye was fixed to the barrel, and a plain folding-leaf sight was used. A 23.6in barrel was standard, gun weight averaging 7.2lb. Chamberings included 220 Swift, 243 Winchester, 6.5x57, 270 Winchester, 7x57, 7x64mm, 30-06, 308 Winchester, 8x57, 338 Winchester, 9.3x62 or 9.3x64.

SIMILAR GUNS

Model 1964 Super Express rifle. This was similar to the standard 1963 pattern listed previously, but accepted 5.6x61, 7x66 Vom Hofe, 6.5x68 or 8x68 RWS cartridges.

Steyr, autoloading type

The Mannlicher-pattern bolt action rifles are covered in their own section. Since the end of the Second World War, Steyr-Daimler-Puch has made a range of automatic weapons including the futuristic Armee-Universal-Gewehr (AUG). The company has also developed the Steyr ACR, chambered for a special flechette cartridge; this gun is described and illustrated in *Military Small Arms of the 20th Century*, p.135.

Austrian-made AUG rifles have been tried in small numbers by many military and paramilitary organizations. Tunisia was an early convert to the Steyr design, purchasing sizeable numbers from 1978 onward; Saudi Arabia may have bought as many as 100,000 in 1980-92; and Oman purchased about 30,000 in 1982-3. See also '**Australia**'.

The AUG was adopted in Ecuador in 1987, deliveries apparently being complete by 1990. It is also the service rifle of the Irish Free State (Eire), adopted early in 1988 after trials against the Belgian FNC, British L85A1, French FAMAS, German G41, Israeli Galil, Italian AR 70/90, Swiss SG-550 and US M16A2.

ARMEE-UNIVERSAL-GEWEHR (AUG)
Sturmgewehr 77, or StG. 77
Made by Steyr-Daimler-Puch AG, Steyr.
Currently in production. **Chambering:** 5.56x45, rimless. **Action:** locked by rotating lugs on the bolt into the barrel extension; gas operated, selective fire.
DATA FOR A TYPICAL RIFLE

31.2in overall, 9lb with loaded magazine. 20in barrel, 6-groove rifling; RH, concentric. Detachable box magazine, 30 or 42 rounds. Integral 1.5x optical sight. 3180fps with M193 ball ammunition; 650 rpm. No bayonet.

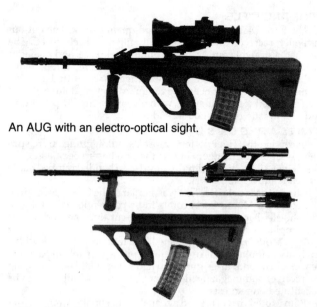

An AUG with an electro-optical sight.

The AUG dismantles easily into its major components.

This bullpup was developed specifically for the Austrian army in the late 1970s. Gas is tapped from the barrel to strike one of the bolt-carrier guide rods, which rotates the bolt.

The AUG divides into six major component groups: barrel, receiver (cast integrally with the optical sight bracket), trigger, bolt, magazine and butt. Changing the barrel transforms the rifle into a light support weapon, a carbine or submachine gun. The direction of ejection can be altered merely by changing the bolt and replacing the ejection-port cover.

The synthetic frame, in black or olive green, is common to all sub-variants. Barrels include 13.8in, 16in and 20in patterns (without sights); 20in with a front sight; 20in with an integral M203 grenade launcher; and a heavy 24.45in unit carrying a bipod. The standard receiver has an integral optical sight mount, but alternatives offered an open rear sight or ('N' pattern only) conventional optical sight mounts. Three differing trigger systems and three bolts allow the purchaser to choose from a semi-automatic version, or selective-fire guns firing automatically from the open- or closed-bolt position. The contents of the transparent plastic magazines can be seen at a glance.

The futuristic lines of the AUG are difficult to mistake, with prong-type flash suppressors and a pivoting hand grip ahead of the trigger guard. Light pressure on the trigger fires single shots; strong pressure, where appropriate, allows the mechanism to cycle automatically. A safety bolt runs laterally through the frame. The first series-made rifles were delivered in 1978.

SIMILAR GUNS

AUG-A1. This is a post-1980 designation for the standard selective-fire rifle.

The Steyr-Mannlicher SSG-69 has proved a popular sniping rifle.

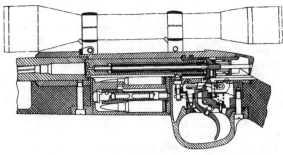

A sectional drawing of the action of the SSG-69.

AUG-P ('Polizei' or 'Police'). A short-barreled selective-fire or semi-automatic version of the basic AUG, this fires from a closed bolt.

Steyr, bolt-action type

This section contains details of the modified rear-locking Steyr design, customarily regarded (wrongly) as a 'Mannlicher.' The genuine Steyr-made front-locking Mannlicher-Schönauer rifles and carbines are included in the appropriate section above.

MILITARY WEAPONS

MODEL 69 SNIPER RIFLE

Scharfschützengewehr 69, SSG 69

Made by Steyr-Daimler-Puch AG, Steyr.

Currently in production. **Chambering options:** 243 Winchester or 308 Winchester only. **Action:** locked by three lugs on the bolt engaging recesses in the receiver behind the magazine as the bolt handle turns down.

DATA FOR A TYPICAL SSG P-I

Chambering: 7.62x51 NATO (308 Winchester), rimless. 44.5in overall, 8.7lb without sights. 25.6in barrel, 4-groove rifling; RH, concentric. Detachable spool magazine, 5 rounds. Optical sight. 2690fps with SS77 ball ammunition.

Adopted by the Austrian army in 1969, and then by military and police forces throughout the world, this was built on a heavy version of the standard short action in which the receiver extended forward to enclose the chamber. A spool magazine was standard, though a ten-round detachable box was also available.

The original SSG-69, sold commercially in North America as the 'SSG Marksman,' had a walnut or Cycolac stock of brown or olive green; spacers adjusted the butt length when necessary. Most military-issue rifles had optical sights, though 'Match Target' guns sold commercially had a micro-adjustable aperture rear sight and a replaceable-element tunnel at the muzzle. Major metal parts were usually phosphated to eliminate reflections.

The standard rifle was re-designated 'P-I' on the introduction of the P-II pattern in 1988, when a 243 Winchester chambering option was also introduced.

SIMILAR GUNS

SSG P-II. Introduced in 1988, this has a heavy barrel and a large bolt-handle knob instead of the slender spatulate type, the original 1969-type rifle being retrospectively designated 'P-I.'

SSG P-III. Dating from 1992, this is simply a P-I with aperture-sight bases, a heavy 23.6in barrel, and an American-made synthetic H-S Precision stock.

SSG P-IV. Offered only in 308 Winchester, this had an unusually short 16.7in barrel with a flash-hider and a stock of black or green Cycolac.

SPORTING GUNS

RIMFIRE PATTERNS

Steyr-Daimler-Puch also made substantial quantities of a 22LR rimfire sporting rifle in 1953-69. Known as the 'Standard,' this had a detachable five-round magazine, a 19.7in barrel, and a walnut half-stock with a plain pistol grip and a simple round-tipped forend. The sights consisted of a blade at the muzzle and a small fixed notch-plate on the barrel immediately ahead of the chamber. Bolt handles were generally swept slightly backward, but the trigger guard was a simple stamped strip.

The deluxe pattern or *Luxusmodell* (1955-67?) was recognizable by its full-length stock, which had checkering on the capped pistol grip and the forend. The rear sight was moved forward, the front sight was ramped, and a swivel was fixed through the forend. The trigger guard was usually the spurred bow favored on the center-fire Mannlicher-Schönauer rifles.

MODEL 1969 RIFLE

Alternatively known as 'Model 67'

Made by Steyr-Daimler-Puch AG, Steyr.

Total production: not known. **Chambering options:** see notes. **Action:** as M69 sniper rifle, above.

DATA FOR A TYPICAL FULL-STOCK MODEL

Chambering: 243 Winchester, rimless. 39.15in overall, 6.88lb empty. 20in barrel, 4-groove rifling; RH, concentric. Detachable box magazine, 3 rounds. Folding-leaf sight. 3070fps with 100-grain bullet.

Developed in 1967 to replace the supposedly obsolescent Mannlicher-Schönauer, these guns had six lugs (in two rings of three) on the bolt to lock into the receiver behind the magazine well. A substantial part of the bolt is placed under compressive stress during firing (cf., Lee-Enfield), but the system has proved sturdy enough in practice. One substantial gain from construction of this type is that cartridges feed directly into the chamber instead of crossing the space left for locking lugs. As the perfected detachable spool magazine positions cartridges more consistently than a thin-lipped box, feed is practically flawless.

Introduced commercially in 1968, the first sporting rifles had a neat spatulate bolt handle and a safety catch on the right side of the solid-bridge receiver immediately behind the bolt handle. The "monk's cowl" bolt shroud was unmistakable.

Most magazines had a skeletal spool inside a transparent case, though box magazines could be fitted to order.

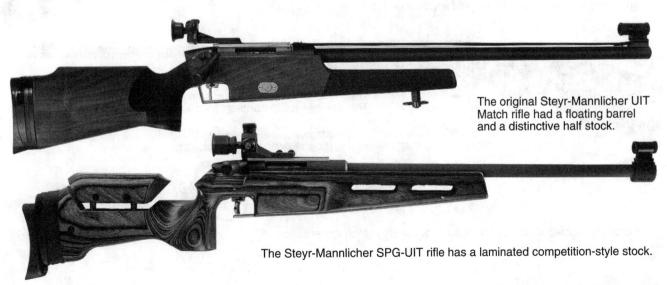

The original Steyr-Mannlicher UIT Match rifle had a floating barrel and a distinctive half stock.

The Steyr-Mannlicher SPG-UIT rifle has a laminated competition-style stock.

THE GUNS

In addition to the standard guns, deluxe patterns or *Luxusmodelle* have been made on the basis of practically any of the individual guns described below. The spool magazines were generally replaced by three-round boxes and steel floorplates, while the safety catch was moved to the upper tang. A single trigger, set by pushing the trigger-lever forward, was regarded as standard instead of optional. The stock lacked the hunched appearance of the standard patterns, the pistol grip being lengthened. Bavarian-style cheekpieces and hog's back combs were customary. Excepting the Model S, half-stocked guns had a rosewood schnabel tip and the front sling swivel lay on a barrel collar. Metalwork and stock wood were decorated to order.

Match-UIT rifle. Made in single shot or magazine-feed versions from 1984 onward, in 243 or 308 Winchester only, these rifles had the forend of the stock cut away to allow the barrel to float freely. The straight bolt handle had a large synthetic knob, and the trigger could be adjusted longitudinally. Aperture sights were standard and a woven 'mirage band' ran from the receiver ring to the front-sight block. A typical rifle was about 44.5in overall, had a 25.6in barrel, and weighed about 10.9lb with its sights.

Model L rifle ('Light'). These, also built on the short action, chambered the 5.6x57, 243 Winchester and 308 Winchester rounds. They were made in the same three basic variants as the SL. A heavy-barrel Varmint derivative was introduced in 1969, with stippling on the pistol grip of the half-stock, and a 222 option was announced in 1971.

Model M rifle ('Medium'). This 1973-vintage variant was built on a similar action to the Model L, enlarged to accept cartridges such as 6.5x57, 270 Winchester, 7x57, 7x64, 30-06, 8x57 and 9.3x62. Additional 6.5x55 and 7.5x55 options were introduced for the Model M in 1977. The rubber recoil pad was ventilated and a contrasting rosewood forend tip was fitted.

Model M Professional rifle. This was a minor variant of the standard Model M (above) with a warp-proof Cycolac synthetic stock.

Model S rifle ('Standard'). Offered from 1970 in 6.5x68, 7mm Remington Magnum, 300 Winchester Magnum, 375 H&H Magnum or 8x68S, 'Model S' rifles were built on the largest of the new actions. The receiver was strengthened to withstand pressures generated by high-power cartridges. Conventional pistol grip stocks with low Monte Carlo combs and ventilated rubber buttplates were retained; rosewood forend tips and pistol grip caps had thin white spacers.

Model SL rifle ('Super Light'). Made with the shortest of the three basic actions, this has been offered in 222 Remington, 222 Remington Magnum, 223 Remington and 5.2x50 Magnum. The double set trigger was standard, though a single-trigger system could be substituted to order. A folding-leaf rear sight was used in conjunction with a ramp-mounted blade. SL rifles had half- or full-length stocks with skip-line checkering on forends and pistol grips, low Monte Carlo combs, plastic pistol grip caps and rubber shoulder plates.

SL Varmint patterns were introduced in 1969, with heavy barrels, and a half-stock with a stippled pistol grip. Seven short slots were cut through the forend. Heavy-barrel 222 options appeared for the standard Model SL rifles in 1971.

Model S/T rifle ('Standard / Tropical'). Announced in 1974, this shared the 'S'-pattern action. Supplied only for the 9.3x64, 375 H&H Magnum or 458 Winchester Magnum cartridges, the guns had 25.6in barrels (23.6in option in 458 only), weighed up to 9.25lb and were fitted with four-round magazines. Their Express-type or multi-leaf rear sights were mounted on very distinctive squared blocks.

The Model M Professional Steyr-Mannlicher has a synthetic half-stock.

This Model S Luxus (deluxe) Steyr-Mannlicher has a Bavarian-style stock with a squared cheekpiece and a schnabel-tip forend.

The Model S/T rifle is the largest in the Steyr-Mannlicher range. This gun has a compartment for a spare magazine in the butt side.

An optically-sighted Model SL, the lightest of the Steyr-Mannlicher range.

MODEL 72 SPORTING RIFLE

Made by Steyr-Daimler-Puch AG, Steyr, c. 1972-7.

Total production: not known. **Chambering options:** see notes. **Action:** locked by rotating lugs on the bolt engaging recesses in the receiver as the bolt handle was turned down.

DATA FOR A TYPICAL MODEL S

Chambering: 8x68S, rimless. 45.85in overall, 8.75lb empty. 24in barrel, 4-groove rifling; RH, concentric. Detachable spool magazine, 4 rounds. Block-and-leaf sight. 3250fps with 180-grain bullet.

Made only for a few years, this rifle was apparently introduced to guard against the failure of the rear-locking action to handle high pressures effectually. The Model 72 lugs lay on the bolt head, though construction was otherwise similar to the Model 69.

THE GUNS

Model 72L rifle. The 'L' ('Light') variant was based on the short action, chambered for the 22-250 Remington, 5.6x57, 6mm Remington, 243 Winchester, 6.5x57, 270 Winchester, 7x57, 7x64, 308 Winchester or 30-06 cartridges. Barrels were 22in long; stocks and fittings were similar to the Model 69.

Model 72M rifle. The medium-size guns were larger and heavier than the 'L' versions, but embodied the short action and chambered the same cartridges.

Model 72S rifle. A long 'S' ('Standard') action was chambered for 6.5x68, 7mm Remington Magnum, 8x68S, 9.3x64 or 375 H&H Magnum ammunition. A 24in medium-weight barrel was standard, rifles averaging 8.4lb.

Model 72S/T rifle. Introduced in 1974 in 300 Winchester Magnum, 9.3x64, 375 H&H Magnum or 458 Winchester Magnum, this was identical with the Model S excepting for its heavy 24in barrel and a weight in excess of 8.8lb.

MODEL 96 SBS SPORTING RIFLE
'Safe Bolt System'

Made by Steyr-Mannlicher AG, Steyr, 1996 to date.

Currently in production. **Chambering options:** 6.5x57, 270 Winchester, 7x64, 7mm Remington Magnum, 30-06, 300 Winchester Magnum, 8x68S and 9.3x62. **Action:** locked by two groups of two lugs on the bolt head engaging recesses in the barrel extension as the bolt handle is turned down.

DATA FOR A TYPICAL 7x64 EXAMPLE

44.7in overall, 7.5lb empty. 23.6in barrel, 4-groove rifling; RH, concentric. Detachable box magazine, 4 rounds. Folding open rear sight. 2620fps with 173-grain bullet.

Announced in 1996, this represents a new approach to Steyr rifle design, abandoning the tried and tested rear-lug system of the Model 69 in favor of a new twin double-lug frontal lock with a rotary motion of about 70 degrees. This enables high-pressure cartridges to be fired without putting a substantial portion of the bolt body under compressive stress and has a beneficial effect on accuracy. The SBS 96 also pays particular attention to safety. A slider on the upper tang behind the cocking piece can be set to the firing, loading or trigger-locked positions; the bolt can only be removed when the trigger is immobilized. An active firing-pin safety allows the gun to be carried securely when the bolt handle is turned down against the stock, automatically releasing the set-trigger until the safety has been taken off, and the magazine can be locked in an intermediate position to prevent cartridges being fed into the chamber.

The SBS has the distinctive appearance of a classic modern Steyr-Mannlicher product, with an elegant action broken only by the ejection port and a characteristically streamlined cocking-piece shroud with an indicator pin. The standard select walnut half-stock has a hog's back comb, a Bavarian-style cheekpiece and a rosewood schnabel tip. One swivel lies beneath the butt, and the other under the barrel ahead of the forend. The standard trigger is a combination design incorporating a setting mechanism, but a direct-acting pattern can be obtained to order.

SIMILAR GUNS

SBS 96 Stutzen or 'Ganzschaftmodell.' Offered in all of the standard chamberings listed above, this is a short-barreled variant with a full-length 'Mannlicher' stock. It is 40.15in long, has a 20in barrel and weighs about 7.1lb.

Scout or 'Steyr Scout.' Announced in 1997 after long-term collaboration with the American Jeff Cooper, this 308 Winchester sniper rifle offers several unusual features. The free-floating 19.1in barrel lies within a large-diameter sleeve and a folding bipod is formed integrally with the forend. A spare staggered-row box magazine can be carried in the under-edge of the Zytel butt, which also has an adjustable shoulder plate. A special 2.5x28 Leupold Model 8 optical sight, with unusually long eye relief, can be mounted on a Picatinny Rail on the barrel sleeve ahead of the feed way to eliminate ejection problems. The rifle is 39.55in long with two spacer-plates for the butt; it weighs only 6.95lb, including the telescope sight and two empty five-round magazines.

• Voere, autoloading type

The move from Germany to Austria in 1978, though accompanied by a considerable stockpile, led to the abandonment of many of the older Voere guns. Even though many of the 22 patterns remained available into the 1980s, only the Models 0014, 2114S and 2115 were actively promoted under the Voere–Austria mark. Details of these and many other pre-1978 guns will be found in the German section.

MODEL 2185 MATCH RIFLE
Präzisions-Selbstlade-Sportbüchse M2185

Introduced in 1991, this was a modification of the original gas-operated M2185 (see 'Germany'), possibly built on actions left over from pre-1978 production. The most obvious features were the laminated competition-style stock with an anatomical pistol grip and a deep square forend, an extension of trigger guard to house the magazine-release catch, and a special sight-mounting rail above the receiver. Some guns were also fitted with muzzle brake/compensators.

SIMILAR GUNS

M2185SM or 'Super Match.' This variant of the basic autoloading design had an elevating comb and a buttplate which could slide vertically in its channel-block.

• Voere, bolt-action type

Only the Models 1007 Biathlon, 1013, 1014, 2155, 2165, 2175, 2202 and 2204 were actively promoted under the Voere–Austria mark after the move from Germany to Austria in 1978. Details of these and many other pre-1978 guns will be found in the German section.

The first Titan II and Titan Menor rifles were made in Germany, but production had been comparatively meager. Consequently, as they provided the basis for the first Voere–Austria patterns, they are considered here.

From 1st March 1988, after another reorganisation, the Voere business was merged with Kufsteiner Gerätebau und Handelsgesellschaft mbH to form 'Voere–Kufsteiner Gerätebau- und Handelsgesellschaft mbH.' Voere continued to make bolt-action rifles, but rights to the Titans were sold to Mauser-Werke Oberndorf GmbH to fund development of the VEC-91 rifle and its caseless cartridge.

TITAN II
Also known as 'Model 225' or 'Mauser Model 99'

Made by Voetter & Co., Vöhrenbach, Schwarzwald (c.1976-8); by Tiroler Jagd- und Sportwaffenfabrik GmbH & Co., Kufstein (1978-87); and by Mauser-Werke Oberndorf GmbH (1987-94?).

Total production: not known. **Chambering options:** 5.6x57, 243 Winchester, 25-06 Remington, 6.5x55, 6.5x57, 6.5x68, 270 Winchester, 7x57, 7x64, 7mm Remington Magnum, 7mm vom Hofe, 7.5x55, 300 H&H Magnum, 300 Winchester Magnum, 30-06, 308 Norma Magnum, 308 Winchester, 8x57, 8x68S, 9.3x62, 9.3x64, 375 H&H Magnum or, at extra cost, 458 Winchester. **Action:** as Model 2130, above.

DATA FOR A TYPICAL LUXUSMODELL

Chambering: 7mm vom Hofe Super Express, rimless. 46.45in overall, 7.45lb empty. 25.6in barrel, 4-groove rifling; RH, concentric. Detachable box magazine, 5 rounds. Folding-leaf leaf sight. 3280fps with 170-grain bullet.

Changes made to the basic Titan design in the mid 1970s created the Titan II, later known as the Model 225. The receiver was streamlined, a new safety (part of the trigger system) appeared above the right side of the stock behind the bolt handle, and the contours were refined.

The Titan II could be fitted with the conventional single trigger, a double set trigger, or a single 'Rückstecher' set by pushing the solitary trigger lever forward. Butts generally had hog's back combs, and round tipped cheekpieces.

As the Titan II had proved to be robust, three Weatherby Magnum chamberings (.257, 270 and 300) were added in the early 1980s to satisfy the North American market. In 1987, however, responsibility for the Model 225 Titan II passed to Mauser-Werke and some guns were sold in North America as the 'Mauser Model 99.' Chamberings were initially restricted to the 257 Weatherby Magnum, 270 Weatherby Magnum, 7mm Remington Magnum, 300 H&H Magnum, 300 Weatherby Magnum, 300 Winchester Magnum, 30-06 Springfield, 308 Norma Magnum, 8x68S, 338 Winchester Magnum, 9.3x64 or 375 H&H Magnum rounds, but others have subsequently been supplied to order.

SIMILAR GUNS

Titan II Luxusmodell (Model 225 Luxus). The deluxe version featured selected woodwork, and a separate rosewood forend tip in addition to the otherwise standard rosewood pistol-grip cap. The forend tip, pistol grip cap and ventilated rubber butt pad were all accompanied by white spacers.

Model 2145 Match (Model 225 Match) Introduced *c.* 1977, this was a moving-target ('LS,' Laufende Scheibe) rifle built on the standard action. It had a heavier barrel than normal, a special stock with an upright pistol grip, and six ventilation slots through the forend. The pistol-grip and forend were stippled, open sights were omitted, and the shotgun type trigger was standard. The gun was about 1180mm long and weighed 4.2kg; the standard chambering was 308 Winchester, but other versions were made to order. After

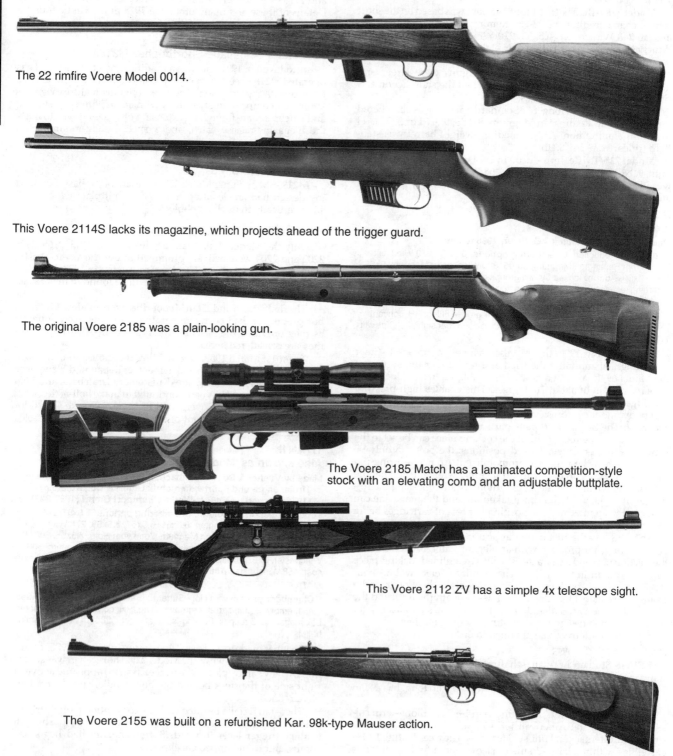

The 22 rimfire Voere Model 0014.

This Voere 2114S lacks its magazine, which projects ahead of the trigger guard.

The original Voere 2185 was a plain-looking gun.

The Voere 2185 Match has a laminated competition-style stock with an elevating comb and an adjustable buttplate.

This Voere 2112 ZV has a simple 4x telescope sight.

The Voere 2155 was built on a refurbished Kar. 98k-type Mauser action.

The Voere Model 2165, built on refurbished Mauser actions, offers a streamlined cocking-piece shroud and a refined stock.

The Voere Titan Menor rifle may also be encountered as the Mauser 'Model 99.'

The VEC-91 is Voere's mould-breaking caseless-cartridge rifle.

the Titan II became known as the Model 225, the 2145 Match was apparently renamed '225 Match' without any change in the basic pattern.

TITAN MENOR
Made by Voetter & Co.,Vöhrenbach, Schwarzwald (c. 1976-8); and by Tiroler Jagd- und Sportwaffenfabrik GmbH & Co., Kufstein (1978-87).
Total production: not known. **Chambering options:** 222 Remington, 222 Remington Magnum, 223 Remington or 5.6x50. **Action:** locked by rotating two lugs on the bolt head into the receiver wall as the bolt was turned down, and by the bolt-handle base turning down into its seat.
DATA FOR A TYPICAL EXAMPLE
   Chambering: 222 Remington, rimless. 42.15in overall, 6.28lb empty. 23.6in barrel, 6-groove rifling; RH, concentric. Detachable box magazine, 3 rounds. Folding-leaf rear sight. 3200 fps with 50-grain bullet.

A version of the Titan II was introduced *c.* 1976 for 22/5.6mm centerfire cartridges, but few had been made before the move to Austria occurred. The Titan Menor had an ejection port rather than the entire upper surface of the receiver cut away. It accepted any of the standard triggers. Stock options paralleled those of the Titan II (above), though an additional high-comb version was made for moving-target shooting.

SIMILAR GUNS
   Model 3145 Match (or 'LS'). This moving-target rifle was built on the standard action. It had a heavy barrel and lacked open sights. Direct-action trigger systems (Flintenabzüge) were standard. The stock had a high comb, an upright pistol-grip and a forend with six ventilating slots. Offered only in 222 or 223 Remington, the rifles were 45.25in long and weighed 8.6lb without sights.
   Model 3145 DJV. This single-shot rifle was intended for shooting under German national regulations. It could be distinguished externally from the 3145 Match pattern by the absence of a detachable magazine and by the deep forend. It weighed about 9.25lb.

TITAN III
Also known as 'Model 226'
Made by Tiroler Jagd- und Sportwaffenfabrik GmbH & Co., Kufstein (1985-7); and by Mauser-Werke Oberndorf GmbH (1987-95?).
Total production: not known. **Chambering options:** 22-250 Remington, 243 Winchester, 6.5x55, 6.5x57, 25-06 Remington, 270 Winchester, 7x64, 7.5x55, 30-06 or 308 Winchester. **Action:** generally as Titan II, above.

DATA FOR A TYPICAL MODEL 226 TITAN III
   Chambering: 22-250 Remington, rimless. 42.15in overall, 6.28lb empty. 23.6in barrel, 6-groove rifling; RH, concentric. Detachable box magazine, 5 rounds. Fixed-leaf rear sight. 3725 fps with 55-grain bullet.

Model 226 or Titan III rifles, available commercially in standard and deluxe variants from 1986 onward, utilized a small 225-type action. The rear of the receiver was noticeably more angular than the smooth diagonal of the Titan II and the bolt shroud was shorter. In addition, the trigger-guard was a light recurved-strip pattern and the recoil bolt associated with the Titan II stock was omitted. The standard and deluxe Monte Carlo-pattern stocks duplicated the Titan II (q.v.) types.

White spacers were omitted from the stocks of Mauser-marked guns, while a classical pattern with a straight comb and a schnabel forend tip became available as an option.

VEC-91 SPORTING RIFLE
Also known as 'Lightning' in the USA
Made by Tiroler Jagd- und Sportwaffenfabrik GmbH & Co., Kufstein (1991 to date).
Currently in production. **Chambering options**: 5.7mm or 6mm UCC, caseless. **Action:** locked by two lugs on the bolt head engaging recesses in the receiver behind the chamber as the bolt handle turns down.
DATA FOR A TYPICAL EXAMPLE
   Chambering: 5.7x26, caseless. 39.1in overall, 6.2lb empty. 20.45in barrel, 4-groove rifling; RH, concentric? Detachable box magazine, 5 rounds. Folding-leaf rear sight graduated to 200m (220yd) About 3300fps with 55-grain bullet.

This is one of the most remarkable innovations in sporting-rifle design in recent years, though whether the investment in caseless-ammunition technology—a great financial risk—will ever be repaid is still the subject of debate. The trigger can be adjusted to give a release pressure from about 5oz to 6.5lb. Excepting the closed-receiver design and electronic ignition, powered by batteries in the pistol grip, the VEC-91 is a surprisingly conventional design. The walnut half stock has a Bavarian-style hog's back comb, a squared cheekpiece, and a schnabel-tip forend. Checkering appears on the pistol grip and forend, and swivels lie beneath the barrel and the butt.

VEC-91BR, 1994 to date. This is a single shot derivative of the basic pattern, with a heavy 20.45in barrel and a synthetic bench-rest style stock with a broad flat-bottom forend.

VEC-91HB or 'Varmint,' 1994 to date. Distinguished by a 22in medium-heavy barrel, this magazine-feed rifle will be found in a black synthetic or bi-color laminated wood stock. No open sights are provided.

VEC-91SS, 1994 to date. Mechanically identical with the standard gun, this has a black synthetic straight-comb half stock and matte-finish metalwork. Open sights are not provided.

• Winkler

Benedikt Winkler of Ferlach made sporting rifles on the basis of refurbished military Mauser actions. The Model 80N, made to order in virtually any caliber the purchaser cared to specify, had a 26in barrel and weighed about 7.5lb. It was usually supplied with a straight-comb pistol grip half stock with a small oval cheekpiece, and had a plain forend with a rounded tip.

The Model 80L ('Luxusmodell') was similar, but had an engraved action and, occasionally, carving on the stock instead of checkering. Most rifles were fitted with double set trigger systems and a magazine floor-plate latch.

AUSTRIA-HUNGARY

Guns manufactured after the disbandment of the Habsburg or Austro-Hungarian Empire in 1918, even if based on pre-1918 designs, will be found in the sections devoted to Austria and Hungary.

• Andrs

Surviving examples of this experimental breechloading rifle usually prove to have been built on the Werndl (q.v.), or at least incorporate a substantial number of its parts. Developed for trials in Austria-Hungary, the Andrs system relied on a primitive bolt-action. The hammer of the back-action lock was retracted to half cock; the bolt handle was then pushed forward to release it from a retaining shoulder on the receiver, and raised to allow the bolt to be pulled back. It is suspected that the Andrs rifle extracted and ejected more efficiently than the drum-breech Werndl, but was not deemed good enough to displace the latter in Austro-Hungarian service.

• Barth & Hohenbrück

Also known as 'Barth-Hohenbrück.' Credited to two Bohemian gunmakers – Anton Barth of Reichenau became better known in the 1870s – this breechloading system was a barely disguised copy of the Krnka lifting-block (q.v.) altered to contain a spring-loaded striker suited to self-contained metal-case ammunition. Most of the conversions were built on rifle-muskets – e.g., British-type P/53 Enfields or Swiss 1863-type short rifles (*Stutzer*) – but a few may have been made from scratch. The principal difference between the Barth & Hohenbrück and the original Krnka system lay in the use of the hammer tip to lock the block in place as the gun fired.

• Früwirth

This early repeating mechanism is credited to a Viennese gunsmith. The basic Werndl-Holub drum-breech was soon seen as cumbersome and incapable of transformation into a magazine-loader.

Though experiments with quickloaders were undertaken throughout the 1870s, none was deemed acceptable; nor did the younger Krnka's experiments with an assortment of quick-loading (*Schnell-lader*) rifles in the 1870s provide lasting results.

Shortly after the first Werndls had been introduced, the Früwirth rifle appeared with a tubular magazine beneath the barrel. Though clearly based on the then-new Swiss Vetterli rifle, the Früwirth carbine had sufficient merit to be issued to gendarmerie units.

MODEL 1872 GENDARMERIE CARBINE

Made by Österreichische Waffenfabriks-Gesellschaft, Steyr, 1870-5.
Total production: about 12,000. **Chambering:** 11x36R. **Action:** locked by the bolt handle rib abutting the receiver ahead of the bridge as the bolt handle turns down.

40.9in overall, 8.13lb empty. 22.45in barrel, 6-groove rifling; RH, concentric. Tube magazine under barrel, 6 rounds. Ramp-and-leaf sight graduated to 600 paces (505yd). 975fps with M1867 carbine round. M1854 socket bayonet.

The first carbines were issued for trials in 1869, possibly chambered for an 11x36 rimmed cartridge. On 23rd May 1872, the Früwirth was formally adopted for the Cisleithanischen Gendarmerie. The bolt handle rib sufficed as a lock; no ejector was fitted; and the cocking piece had a prominent spur or 'Jäger grip.' The straight-wrist stock had a trigger guard with a spurred rearward extension, similar to that of the Werndl carbine of the day. There was a small nose cap, a swivel on the under-edge of the butt, and a sling loop anchored laterally through the forend.

In 1873, the army briefly considered the gun as an Extra-Corps-Gewehr. Unfortunately, it proved to be too fragile to withstand even the 1867-pattern carbine cartridge. Issue of the Früwirth was extended in 1874 to the Tiroler Landesschützen, but surviving guns had all been withdrawn into store by 1890.

• Jurnitschek

Alfred Jurnitschek von Wehrstedt, of Puchberg bei Wels, patented a distinctive bolt-action rifle in 1887. The box magazine – holding a staggered row of five cartridges – was in the form of an elongated wedge-shape housing or follower pivoted under the forend.

• Krnka, block-action type

Sylvestr Krnka was a dedicated but unlucky and largely unsuccessful inventor. His first breechloading design, perfected in 1849, was apparently built on the basis of an Austrian rifled musket. This was altered by cutting away part of the breech and adding a transverse bar-like locking block – precursor of the American Joslyn (q.v.) – in a large bronze receiver. A small handle on the right side lifted the locking bar up and to the left to give access to the chamber.

BAR-LOCK GUNS

The 1849 pattern was followed by a series of guns of the same general type, but extremely difficult to classify. The earliest were primitive, without positive breech-locking features, but later examples became increasingly sophisticated. The design of individual components was greatly refined, and interlocks were added between the hammer and locking-bar to prevent the breech opening prematurely.

Krnka rifles of this type were apparently used in Montenegro in the mid-1860s. They had side-action caplocks, plain straight-wrist stocks, and leaf-and-slider rear sights. Rifles similar in principle, though differing greatly in detail, were adopted in 1869 by the Russian army (q.v.).

RAPID-LOADING RIFLES

Krnka's work with single shot rifles culminated in the *Schnelladegewehr* ('rapid-loading rifles'), with the operating lever and hammer combined in a single component. The flip-open breech was operated by a cocking lever and a spring. Pressing the tip of the lever forward retracted the striker, which locked the breech shut, and simultaneously raised the breechblock until it sprang open automatically. Completing the movement of the lever cocked the striker, a new cartridge was placed in the chamber, and the breech-locking bar was pressed shut against its spring. The gun could then be fired, and the cycle began again.

Some rapid-loading rifles were converted from existing weapons – e.g., Russian rifle-muskets or Austrian Werndls – and others were specially built for trials. Some had levers on the right side of the breech in front of the trigger guard; others had knobs on side-hammers, relying on extensions of the hammer body to trip the breech.

The perfected version developed in 1874-7, perhaps inspired by the British Soper (q.v.), relied on a combination of the operating lever and the breech-bar. The handle on the right side of the breech – resembling a conventional bolt handle – was pulled back to disengage from a retaining notch, then allowed to rise with the locking bar against the pressure of the breech-spring. A spent case was expelled during the opening stroke, a new cartridge was inserted in the chamber, and the handle and breech-bar were pushed back to the locked position.

The Schnelladegewehr failed to excite military interest in Austria-Hungary, where commitment to the drum-breech Werndl was already being challenged by the first magazine rifles. Even Krnka realized that the days of single shot weapons were drawing to a close, and abandoned the lifting-block gun in the late 1870s to concentrate on repeaters.

Krnka, bolt-action type

Sylvestr and Karel Krnka perfected a bolt-action gun in 1887-9 with a detachable box magazine and the operating handle on a sleeve at the back of the action. This was subsequently developed into a more refined version. Unfortunately Österreichische Waffenfabriks-Gesellschaft and Ferdinand von Mannlicher had such an iron grip on Austro-Hungarian ordnance affairs that the Krnka rifle – despite its merits – had little chance of adoption in its native country.

The original guns incorporated a patented 'safety extractor' in the form of a 'V'-spring which could remove a spent case if the regular extractor failed. They also had detachable box magazines containing five, 10, 15 or even 20 rounds.

1889-TYPE RIFLES

The formation of the Krnka Repeating Rifle Co. Ltd in London in 1888, to promote the rifles in trials being undertaken in Russia and Romania, was accompanied by the development of improved patterns: No. 1 was a two-lug straight-pull action with a five-round staggered row magazine; No. 2 was a similar gun with three locking lugs; No. 3 was a turn-bolt design; and No. 4 was apparently a variant of No. 2. The guns were loaded from a stripper clip, which was thrown clear when the bolt was closed to chamber the first round. The follower doubled as a hold open, and a small lever could be released to drop the magazine. This served as a cut-off, allowing the rifle to be single-loaded.

Unfortunately, the London venture failed in 1891. The final Krnka bolt-action design of the mid-1890s was a complex design with a large locking lug on a separate bolt head and a rib bearing on the bridge of the split receiver. The bolt handle was still mounted on a sleeve, the striker was unusually long and probably contributed to a very slow lock time. The detachable box magazine could be loaded from special stripper clips, and the cut-off or magazine release catch was mounted in a separate small-diameter guard ahead of the trigger. The design was too complex to challenge simpler and sturdier designs which had appeared in the early 1890s, and vanished into history.

Kropatschek

The failure of the Früwirth carbine to interest the Austro-Hungarian army cleared the way for a rifle designed by Alfred von Kropatschek. The first guns were submitted to the Minister of War on 24th September 1874. They had a conventional action inspired by the German Mauser, using the bolt rib to lock against the receiver, and had a Vetterli-type tube magazine in the forend.

By 1876, the Kropatschek was being declared as 'suitable for adoption' – which simply allowed a lengthy program of minor improvements to drag on into the 1880s. Leopold Gasser of Vienna patented a spring-loaded loading gate in 1879, adapting existing Winchester patterns, which was used on 'Gasser-Kropatschek' rifles tested in Austria-Hungary in the early 1880s. However, the rise of the box magazine restricted distribution – except in France, where the popularity of the Kropatschek in Indo-China and Equatorial Africa eventually created the Lebel (q.v.).

MODEL 1881 GENDARMERIE CARBINE
Sometimes known as 'M1874/81'

Made by Österreichische Waffenfabriks-Gesellschaft, Steyr, 1882-5.
Total production: 9200? **Chambering:** 11x36R. **Action:** locked by the bolt rib abutting the receiver ahead of the bridge as the bolt handle turns down.

41.1in overall, 8.37lb empty. 22.45in barrel, 6-groove rifling; RH, concentric. Tube magazine in forend, 6 rounds. Ramp-and-leaf sight graduated to 600 paces (505yd)? 1005fps with M1877 (carbine) cartridges. Socket bayonet?

A smaller version of the army trials rifles, with a single barrel band and the bolt handle turned downward, the 'Repetier-Karabiner für königlich Ungarnische Landesvertheidigung' was adopted on 19th June 1881. The gun was somewhat similar to the earlier Früwirth (q.v.), but the striker had an integral cocking piece instead of an external hammer.

Issue of the M1881 was extended in the late summer of 1881 to the Bosnian gendarmerie, and then to the Austrian Landesgendarmerie from 17th March 1882. However, surviving guns had been replaced by 1900 with the 1890-pattern Mannlichers discarded by the army.

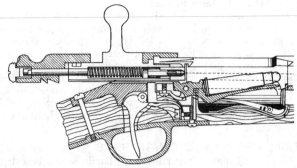

The action of the 1878-type Kropatschek rifle, which inspired the French Lebel. (FP&P)

1881-TYPE TRIALS RIFLES

Made by Österreichische Waffenfabriks-Gesellschaft, Steyr, 1881-4.
Total production: not known. **Chambering:** 11x58R. **Action:** as M1881 gendarmerie carbine, above.

50.85in overall, 10.03lb empty. 31.25in barrel, 6-groove rifling; RH, concentric. Tube magazine in forend, 8 rounds. Ramp-and-leaf sight graduated to 1600 paces (1345yd). 425fps with M1877 cartridges. Sword bayonet.

Sizable quantities of these were issued for field trials with the Austro-Hungarian army, possibly in several differing versions. The guns had a one-piece straight-wristed stock with two barrel bands and a nose cap. The straight bolt handle projected ahead of the split-bridge receiver and the rear sight was mounted on the barrel-top ahead of the chamber. Swivels lay on the under-edge of the butt and on the underside of the middle barrel band, and the trigger guard had a rearward 'Jäger' spur. The cleaning rod appears to have been set into the left side of the forend and the bayonet lug lay on the right side of the nose cap. A magazine cut-off button lay beneath the bolt, projecting into either of two large-diameter holes bored into the underside of the bolt handle guide rib.

SIMILAR GUNS

Navy rifle. The pattern identified here with the military trials has also been listed as the 'Navy Rifle M1884' – a problem which is compounded by the issue of the 'Torpedo-Boots Gewehr' from 28th October 1893 to the crews of torpedo-boats. The imperial navy was comparatively small in 1890, and the Kropatschek trials rifles may have been sufficient to satisfy the needs of the navy immediately after the Mannlicher had been adopted in 1886. The Torpedo-Boots Gewehr may simply have been shortened to save space aboard the tiny warships, as an alternative explanation that they had been altered for the 8x50R cartridge depends on the Kropatschek action being strong enough to withstand pressures generated by smokeless cartridges.

Mannlicher, autoloading type

Ferdinand von Mannlicher, trained as a railway engineer, turned to small-arms design in the late 1870s. His earliest manually-operated designs were often complicated and inefficient, and the same was true of the earliest self-loaders. Though more acceptable guns had been tested in the 1890s, von Mannlicher's death in 1904 removed the guiding hand. Perhaps the best of the designs were tested posthumously, but virtually all work had ceased by 1908 in favor of other ideas. The detailed story of Mannlicher's attempts to interest the army in his guns has still to be told.

HANDMITRAILLEUSE

Tested in 1885, this was an early attempt to provide an automatic rifle. The recoil-operated gun fed from a 10-round gravity magazine above the left side of the breech. When the gun fired, the barrel recoiled until a strut or 'tongs' (zange) dropped into a well in the frame and allowed the breechblock to run back against a powerful spring. The block then returned, stripping a new round from a carrier pivoted in the left wall of the receiver into the chamber, and raised the tongs into their upper position. The barrel and bolt then ran back into battery and reconnected the trigger system ready for the next shot. The Handmitrailleuse was a clumsy weapon, with a wood half-stock, finger grooves in the short forend, and a ladder-type rear sight folding down above the breech. It was not successful; perhaps only a couple were ever made.

1891-TYPE AUTOMATIC RIFLE

An improved version of the Handmitrailleuse, this was locked by a transverse lug on the top rear of the tongs engaging a recess on the underside of the bolt. The lock was broken when a shoulder in the frame, ahead of the fixed clip-loaded magazine, cammed the tongs downward as the recoil stroke commenced. The rifle had a short two-piece stock joined in front of the rear sight. The sliding barrel was contained in a sheet-metal jacket, and the nose cap had a bayonet lug on the right side. The sear, disconnector and hold-open system was too complicated to be durable, and, like its immediate predecessor, the 1891-pattern rifle was a failure.

MODEL 1893 SEMI-AUTOMATIC RIFLE

The first of the delayed-blowback Mannlichers to be extensively tested by the Austro-Hungarian army as an infantry weapon, this was made in two very different patterns.

One type relied on steeply-pitched lugs on the bolt head rotating against the resistance provided by the seats in the receiver – similar, perhaps, to the better known Thompson patterns of the 1920s (see 'USA'). The one-piece stock had a straight-wrist butt, a single band, and a nose cap with a stacking rod. A lug for a sword bayonet lay on the right side. A clip-loaded single column magazine projected beneath the stock, well ahead of the trigger guard.

The other series of rifles was built on straight-pull bolt systems, with the bolt head connected with body by cam-lugs moving in helical grooves. The principal visible difference was the position of the bolt handle, which reciprocated in a straight path on the right side of the breech and did not intrude into the sight-line during the operating cycle as it did in the turning-bolt design.

Neither rifle was successful, trials indicating that they extracted too violently to function efficiently unless special ammunition and adequate lubrication were used.

MODEL 1895 SEMI-AUTOMATIC RIFLE

This was a quirky gas-operated design, externally resembling a lever-action Winchester, with a two-piece stock and a full-length handguard above the barrel. A five-round magazine was contained in the receiver. A cocking handle on the right side of the receiver could be used to load the chamber for the first shot and cock the hammer. When the gun fired, however, gas tapped from the bore forced the cocking slide back – cocking the hammer, pivoting the breechblock sideways to remove the lateral locking lug from its recess in the receiver behind the chamber, and operating the 'L'-shape extractor on the right side of the breech. Though the action was extremely compact, it was unacceptable militarily.

MODEL 1900 SEMI-AUTOMATIC RIFLE

This improved gas-operated design provided the basis for the most efficient of the Mannlichers, perfected posthumously in 1905-8. Gas tapped from the bore ahead of the chamber forced an operating rod backward so that its tip, protruding through a slot in the left side of the receiver, could rotate the bolt about 45 degrees anti-clockwise to disengage the bolt handle base from its seat in the receiver. The guns were hammer fired, with detachable five-round spool magazines in a detachable housing beneath the feed way. Guides for stripper-clips were machined into the receiver. Pistol grip butts were accompanied by separate forends, with full-length handguards and a single band. A combined stacking rod and bayonet lug lay on the underside of the Swiss-style nose cap.

Guns of this pattern initially suffered from a weak breech-lock, rapid erosion of the gas port, and the intrusion of the charging handle into the sight line during the firing cycle. However, greatly improved forms were still being tested in Germany and Austria-Hungary as late as 1908.

The action of an 1893-type Mannlicher automatic rifle. (Kromar)

• Mannlicher, bolt-action type

The earliest designs, characterized by their impracticality, were unsuccessful – four patterns failed the British trials in the early 1880s – but some of the later guns were much more efficient.

1895-type Mannlichers found limited success in the export markets, selling to Bulgaria and Siam in quantity, but were soon overshadowed by guns derived from the Gew. 88 (see 'Germany – Reichsgewehr: bolt-action') and later Mannlicher-Schönauers (see 'Greece').

The Reichsgewehr amalgamated a modified Mannlicher-type clip-loaded magazine with a bolt adapted from the M1871/84 Mauser. A patent infringement suit ensued over the use of a clip system in the German magazine and Österreichische Waffenfabriks-Gesellschaft was subsequently allowed to incorporate the Gew. 88-type bolt in export rifles. The Haenel (q.v.) rifle was little more than a Gew. 88 with an improved magazine.

The cataloging of Mannlicher rifles was greatly assisted by the publication of Konrad von Kromar's *Repetier- und Automatische Handfeuerwaffen der Systeme Ferdinand Ritter von Mannlicher* (1900, reprinted 1976), which provided the basis – perhaps not acknowledged as fully as it should have been – for W.H.B. Smith's *Mannlicher Firearms*.

MILITARY WEAPONS

1880-TYPE RIFLE
Repetir-Gewehr mit Rohrbündel-Magazin in Kolben

This gun had an extraordinary triple tube magazine in the butt, a rotating feed block, and a bolt reminiscent of the French Gras. It had a two-piece stock with a massive central receiver, a single barrel band, and a nose cap with the bayonet lug on the right side. Cumbersome and pig-headedly complicated, it predictably failed its trials.

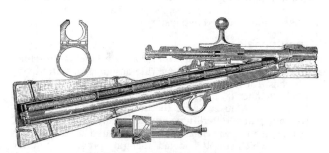

The 1880-pattern Mannlicher rifle had an extraordinary triple magazine in the butt.

The first of the box-magazine Mannlichers dated from 1881. (Kromar)

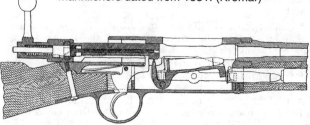

The 1882-type Mannlicher rifle was a turn-bolt design with a tube magazine. (Kromar)

1881-TYPE RIFLE
Repetir-Gewehr mit anhangbarem Magazin M1881

Distinguished by a box magazine with a straight-line follower-lifter powered by a coil spring, this rifle was locked by a pair of lugs on the two-part bolt engaging the receiver bridge. A socket bayonet could be locked around the front sight.

SIMILAR GUNS

1882-type rifle, 'Repetir-Gewehr mit Vorderschaft-Magazin M1882.' This shared the basic action of the 1881-type rifle, but had an eight-round tube magazine under the barrel (though a ninth cartridge could be placed on the elevator and a tenth in the chamber). The one-piece stock contained a loading gate similar to the Gasser-Kropatschek pattern, one barrel band was used, and a sword bayonet could be attached to a lug on the right side of the nose cap.

1882-type rifle, 'Repetir-Gewehr mit Aufsteckbarem Magazin M1882.' Otherwise similar to the tube-magazine design, this had two barrel bands, a simple nose cap, and accepted a socket bayonet. The gravity-feed seven-round magazine on the right side of the receiver had an unbalancing effect when attached.

1884-TYPE RIFLE

This was the first of the straight-pull bolt systems ('Geradzug-Verschluss'), with two lugs on a locking piece connecting the bolt head or *Kammer* with the body or *Griffstück*. Fed from a five-round gravity magazine offset on the left side of the receiver, the 11mm rifle had a one-piece straight-wrist stock with a single band and a nose cap accepting a sword bayonet. Swivels lay beneath the butt and band.

1885-TYPE TRIALS RIFLE
Repetier-Gewehr 'Österreichische Vorlage'
Made by Österreichische Waffenfabriks-Gesellschaft, Steyr, 1885.
Total production: about 1520. **Chambering:** 11x58R. **Action:** locked by pivoting a bar under the back of the bolt into the bolt-way floor as the bolt handle was pushed forward.

52.3in overall, about 10.45lb empty. 31.8in barrel, 6-groove rifling; RH, concentric. Integral clip-loaded box magazine, 5 rounds. Ramp-and-leaf sight graduated to 1600 paces (1310yd). 1445fps with M1877 ball cartridges. Special épée bayonet.

The shortcomings of the Werndl were so evident by the end of the 1870s that a commission was charged with the development of a magazine rifle. After unsuccessfully testing an assortment of weapons – including Spitalsky, Winchester, Mannlicher, Kropatschek-Gasser, Kropatschek-Kromar, Schulhof, Odkolek, Schönauer and Lee patterns – interest centered on an improved form of the 1884-pattern Mannlicher.

The complexity of the earlier helical-channel bolt head was replaced by a simple bar cammed into engagement with the receiver immediately behind the bolt well. The 1885-patent design also accepted a clip through the top of the open action, cartridges being forced up by a driver arm until the last one had been chambered, fired and extracted.

The one-piece stock had a pointed pistol grip, the two bands and the nose cap being pinned in place. A bayonet lug lay on the right side of the nose cap. The cleaning rod lay beneath the muzzle, a Werndl-type rear sight was fitted and, as well, a large radial catch on the right side of the magazine casing to eject spent clips.

MODEL 1886 RIFLE
Infanterie-Repetier-Gewehr M1886
Made by Österreichische Waffenfabriks-Gesellschaft, Steyr, 1886-8.
Total production: about 90,000. **Chambering:** 11x58R. **Action:** as 1885-type trials rifle, above.

52.2in overall, 9.95lb empty. 31.8in barrel, 6-groove rifling; RH, concentric. Integral clip-loaded box magazine, 5 rounds. Quadrant sight graduated to 1500 paces (1230yd). 1445fps with M1877 ball cartridges. M1886 knife bayonet.

Large-scale field trials of the 1885-pattern Mannlicher, undertaken in the Spring of 1886, showed the need for improvements. The clip-catch was greatly simplified and moved to the lower back of the magazine casing; the leaf-type rear sight was replaced by a tangent pattern; the stock was refined and lightened; the cleaning rod under the muzzle was deleted; and the nose cap was redesigned to accept a stacking rod.

The 11mm Repetier-Gewehr M1886 was officially approved on 20th June 1886, and production began even though concurrent trials had shown an 8mm cartridge to have greater potential. It had a straight-pull bolt and a prominent flat-sided magazine case protruding ahead of the trigger guard bow. The slider of the rear sight could be extended leftward to be used in conjunction with a pin on the left side of the front band for distances up to 2300 paces (1885yd).

There were two screw-retained barrel bands, and a nose cap with a stacking rod beneath the muzzle and a lug on the left side for bayonet. Sling swivels lay beneath the middle band and on the under-edge of the butt.

SIMILAR GUNS

Model 1886-90. This designation was applied to surviving 1886-type rifles which had been converted to 8mm in 1892.

1887-TYPE RIFLE
Repetir-Gewehr mit Trommel Magazin M1887

This marked a return to the bridge-locking two piece turn-bolt-action, which was fitted with an eight-round spring-driven drum magazine beneath the feed way. A two-piece stock was used, with one band and a nose cap. A socket bayonet could be locked around the base of the front sight and the trigger guard had a 'Jäger' spur. Rifles of this type were submitted to the Austro-Hungarian army trials of 1887-8, but were soon replaced by the 1887/88 pattern (below).

1887/88-TYPE RIFLE

This was the first of the Mannlicher rifles to embody a spool magazine patented by Otto Schönauer, which was amalgamated with a straight-pull bolt system with the locking lugs on the connector-piece between the bolt head and the body. The eight-round magazine, which had a single-finger follower, could be loaded from a special stripper clip (*Patronen-Packet*). The one-piece stock had a pistol grip butt, two screwed bands, and a nose cap with a stacking rod and a bayonet lug on the right side. Swivels appeared beneath the butt and the middle band, and a quadrant rear sight lay on the barrel. Trials showed the rifle to be too complicated for arduous service, and so it was rejected in favor of the M1888 Mannlicher.

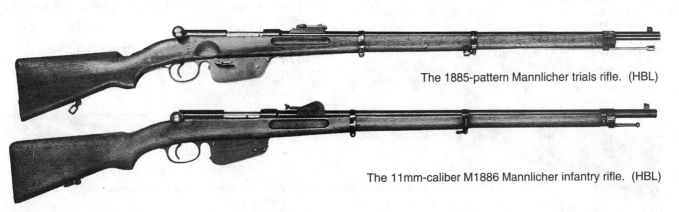

The 1885-pattern Mannlicher trials rifle. (HBL)

The 11mm-caliber M1886 Mannlicher infantry rifle. (HBL)

MODEL 1888 RIFLE
Infanterie-Repetier-Gewehr M1888

Made by Österreichische Waffenfabriks-Gesellschaft, Steyr, 1888-96. Total production: 350,000? **Chambering:** 8x50R. **Action:** as M1886 rifle, above.

50.45in overall, 8.9lb empty. 30.1in barrel, 4-groove rifling; RH, concentric. Integral clip-loaded box magazine, 5 rounds. Quadrant sight graduated to 1700 paces (1395yd). 2015fps with M1888 ball cartridges. M1888 knife bayonet.

No sooner had mass-production of the M1886 begun than the results of the small caliber trials drew attention to the grave mistake in accepting the obsolescent 11mm pattern. Archduke Rudolf, the Inspector of Infantry, was made scapegoat for the embarrassment.

Work on the M1886 ceased in 1887, and trials began again. Major contenders were a Belgian-made Schulhof, an 1887-pattern Mannlicher with a drum magazine (soon withdrawn), the M1887/88 Mannlicher-Schönauer, and a new small caliber version of the 1886-type Mannlicher service rifle. The trials board predictably recommended the simplest solution – the 8mm variant of the M1886 rifle.

The 1888-model rifle was identical with its predecessor, apart from chambering a smaller cartridge and having a differently graduated rear sight. The auxiliary long-range sighting system sufficed for 1800-2500 paces (1475-2050yd). Owing to the reduced diameter of the cartridge base, the magazine case of the M1888 is noticeably shallower than the M1886.

The adoption of smokeless powder in 1890 forced changes to be made in the sights. Most existing guns were modified by attaching plates marked for the M90 cartridge over the old 1888-type black-powder graduations on the side of the quadrant-base.

SIMILAR GUNS

Model 1888-90. Rifles made after 1890-1, generally known under this designation, had newly made sights graduated to 1800 paces (1475yd). Long-range sights on the left side of the gun – an extension to the rear sight slider and a protruding pin on the front band – were used for distances up to 3000 paces (2460yd).

MODEL 1890 CAVALRY CARBINE
Kavallerie-Repetier-Karabiner

Made by Österreichische Waffenfabriks-Gesellschaft, Steyr, 1891-6. Total production: not known. **Chambering:** 8x52R. **Action:** locked by two lugs on a detachable bolt head engaging the receiver when the bolt handle was pushed forward.

39.55in overall, 7.28lb empty. 19.6in barrel, 4-groove rifling; RH, concentric. Integral clip-loaded box magazine, 5 rounds. Quadrant sight graduated to 2400 paces (1970yd). About 1790fps with M1888 ball cartridges. No bayonet.

Perfection of the M1888 rifle turned thoughts toward a carbine. The experimental guns of 1889 were simply cut-down rifles, but their weak dropping-bar lock ensured that only a few were made. A new action, introduced in 1890, reverted to the helical-grooved bolt head system of Mannlicher's first straight-pull action; tests in 1887-8 had shown that this was much stronger than the bar-lock.

The M1890 cavalry carbine embodied a much shorter action than its predecessors, allowing the trigger guard to flow straight into the magazine casing, and the knurled-head cocking piece lay almost directly above the trigger. The gun had a one-piece walnut stock with a simple nose cap without a stacking rod; sling swivels lay on the left side of the forend and stock-wrist.

SIMILAR GUNS

M1890 gendarmerie carbine. Adopted in 1892, this variant of the cavalry gun accepted the standard knife bayonet and had a stacking rod on the nose cap.

1894-TYPE RIFLE
Repetier-Gewehr mit Packetladung M1894

This was basically a small caliber amalgamation of the Gew. 88-type bolt and a detachable staggered-row box magazine loaded from a five-round stripper clip. Made in calibers as small as 5.5mm (.217) and 6mm (.236), the rifle had a one-piece straight-wrist stock, with one band and a simple nose cap with a bayonet lug on the right side. A handguard ran from the chamber to the barrel band, and a 2000m (2185yd) leaf-type rear sight was fitted.

MODEL 1895 RIFLE
Repetier-Gewehr M1895

Made by Österreichische Waffenfabriks-Gesellschaft, Steyr, 1895-1918; and Fémáru Fegyver és Gépgyér, Budapest, 1897-1918. Total production: 3.5 million? **Chambering:** 8x50R. **Action:** as M1890, above.

50.1in overall, 8.35lb empty. 30.1in barrel, 4-groove rifling; RH, concentric. Integral clip-loaded box magazine, 5 rounds. Leaf sight graduated to 2600 paces (2130yd). 2035fps with M1893 ball cartridges. M1895 knife bayonet.

Trials held in 1892 failed to convince the authorities that calibers as small as 5.5mm were worthy enough to challenge 8mm. However, it was equally clear that even the new 1888-pattern rifles were poor compared with the latest European advances, and that their weak bar-locks could not withstand the pressures generated by high velocity cartridges.

An improved infantry rifle was adopted in 1895, incorporating a straight-pull action adapted directly from the cavalry carbine of 1890. The M1895 had a full-length handguard and a leaf-pattern rear sight. Sling swivels lay beneath the butt and barrel band, while the bayonet lug lay beneath the nose cap with a stacking rod on the left side. The magazine clip could be ejected by opening the bolt and releasing the catch in the front edge of the trigger guard.

Though the straight-pull action was acceptable enough in peacetime, and even under the temporary stress of battle, it was prone to jamming in mud and snow. The slender barrel also proved to be prone to warping in the heat of rapid fire. The Austro-Hungarian authorities would have issued a Mannlicher-Schönauer had not World War I begun.

SIMILAR GUNS

Model 1895 cavalry carbine. Two patterns of this gun appeared in 1896, with full-length stocks and handguards. A hooked spur on the cocking piece distinguished them from the 1890 pattern. Bayonets could not be attached, but swivels lay on the left side of the barrel band and butt-wrist. Carbines were 39.5in overall, weighed 6.8lb empty, had a 19.7in barrel, and were sighted to 2400 paces (1970yd).

Model 1895 short rifle, 'Repetier-Stutzen M1895.' The Stutzen or Extra-Corps-Gewehr – otherwise similar to the cavalry carbine – had swivels on the under side of the butt and barrel band. It accepted a special 1895-type knife bayonet with an auxiliary front sight on top of the muzzle ring to compensate for changes in point-of-impact if the gun was fired with the bayonet attached. Some guns were given additional swivels in 1907, allowing them to be used by mounted or dismounted units alike.

1896-TYPE RIFLE
Repetier-Gewehr mit Packetladung M1896

A turning-bolt design with two rows of four small lugs on the solid bolt head, this also had a spurred cocking piece attached to the striker assembly. The single-row magazine was forged integrally with the trigger guard bow, and had panels milled in its outer sides to save weight.

Made in calibers as small as 6mm (.236), the gun had a slender one-piece stock with a straight-wrist butt and a full-length handguard retained by a single band and a simple Swiss-style nose cap with a combination stacking rod and a lug for a lightweight sword bayonet.

MODEL 1904 RIFLE

Made by Österreichische Waffenfabriks-Gesellschaft, Steyr. Total production: not known. **Chamberings:** 8x57 and others. **Action;** locked by rotating lugs on the detachable bolt head into the receiver as the bolt handle turns down.

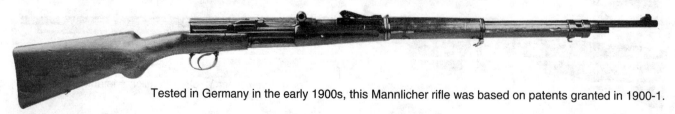

Tested in Germany in the early 1900s, this Mannlicher rifle was based on patents granted in 1900-1.

DATA FOR A TYPICAL EXAMPLE

Chambering: 8x57, rimless. 48.25in overall, 8.85lb empty. 28.55in barrel, 4-groove rifling; RH, concentric. Clip-loaded integral magazine, 5 rounds. Leaf sight graduated to 2000m. 2250fps with ball ammunition. Optional knife or sword bayonet.

This was a large caliber version of the series that had included the Romanian and Dutch Mannlichers. It had a straight-grip stock, and a handguard running from the receiver ring to the barrel band. The magazine case resembled that of the Gew. 88, but the barrel jacket of the German gun was absent; a bayonet lug lay on the right side of the nose cap.

Sales of 1904-pattern Mannlichers were few, largely owing to the phenomenal success of the Mauser. Österreichische Waffenfabrik had even tooled to make the latter as part of a cartel encompassing itself, DWM, Fabrique Nationale and Mauser.

However, substantial quantities of 1904-pattern Mannlichers went to China (perhaps being the basis for the Hanyang pattern), and nearly eleven thousand were purchased by the Ulster Volunteer Force in about 1913-14 together with a little over 9,000 Gewehre 88. It is suspected that these all came from A.L. Frank of Hamburg.

UVF guns often bore 'FOR GOD AND ULSTER' in a cartouche around the Red Hand of the O'Neills, the provincial badge. Many were seized by the British before entering Ireland, and were used for home defense during World War I.

OTHER GUNS

A few Austro-Hungarian units – particularly the Landwehr – used Gewehr 88 as the 'Repetier-Gewehre M 13.' These chambered the standard 8x57mm cartridge. It is assumed that they were supplied in the early days of World War I, when Austria-Hungary lacked serviceable weapons; it is not known whether they came from Germany or had been stored by the Steyr factory since the termination of German orders in the mid-1890s.

SPORTING GUNS

Prior to the perfection of the Schönauer rotary magazine, the Mannlicher rifle had had little commercial success; few sportsmen liked the clip loaded magazine, except possibly in Germany. The advent of a magazine which could be loaded with loose cartridges changed the situation appreciably, as the Mannlicher was sturdy; furthermore, owing to the split-bridge receiver design, its bolt was easy to use.

The first sporters were identical mechanically with the Greek M1903 service rifle, though greater care was taken over surface finish and better stocks were fitted. They were very popular in Britain (q.v.), where many were sold by gunmakers such as George Gibbs of Bristol and John Blanch of London.

REPETIER-PIRSCHBÜCHSE

Made by Österreichische Waffenfabriks-Gesellschaft, Steyr, about 1903-16.

Total production: not known. **Chambering options:** see notes. **Action:** locked by rotating lugs on the detachable bolt head into the receiver as the bolt handle turns down.

DATA FOR A TYPICAL SHORT RIFLE

Chambering: 6.5x54, rimless. 39.1in overall, 6.65lb empty. 17.7in barrel, 4-groove rifling; RH, concentric. Internal rotary magazine, 5 rounds. Block-and-leaf sight. 2245fps with 8.2-gram bullet.

Introduced commercially in 1904, the 1903-pattern sporting rifle was offered only in 6.5x54. Most were made as short rifles (Repetier-Pirschstutzen), with full-length stocks, but long-barreled half-stock examples were also available. The military-style action could be loaded from a charger, a safety catch lay on top of the cocking piece, and the bolt handle was a flattened spatulate form inspired by the German Kar. 88.

Butts had a straight comb, a small oval cheekpiece and a rounded pistol grip. The grip and forend were checkered, a steel nose cap was fitted, and a sling ring was held by a bolt through the stock and a small collar on the barrel. A trap in the buttplate housed a four-piece cleaning rod, and sometimes also two additional cartridges.

The rear sight (Klappvisier) had a standing block for 100m, with folding leaves for 200m or – alternatively – 200m and 300m. A double set trigger mechanism was customary, but single-trigger guns were also made.

A variant chambered for the 9x56 cartridge appeared in 1905, identical with the 6.5mm gun except for a 500mm barrel. It was

followed in 1908 by 8x56 (Austrian) and, apparently, 8x57 (German) chamberings.

A 9.5x56 version was introduced early in 1910, and a special 10.75x63 option was announced shortly before World War I began – perhaps in 1912 or 1913, though few had been made when fighting began. Note: cartridges were widely designated by bullet diameter in pre-1918 Austria-Hungary, causing confusion as the standard 6.5mm varieties were classed as '6.7mm.'

• Mosin-Nagant

The Austro-Hungarian forces on the Eastern Front captured sizable quantities of Russian rifles in 1914-15, and had also received large numbers taken by the Germans. From 1916 onward, therefore, guns were issued in Austro-Hungarian service with Russian ammunition. When supplies of cartridges began to run short, some rifles were converted in the Wiener-Neustadt Armory for the standard 8x50R round. The original Russian-style socket bayonets were retained wherever possible, but some crude Austro-Hungarian substitutes have been reported.

• Odkolek

Adolf Freiherr von Odkolek von Augezd (Ujezd) deserves recognition as the inventor of the Hotchkiss gas operated machine gun, though the honor is customarily denied him. Odkolek was also responsible for a quirky repeating rifle patented in Germany in February 1889.

1889-TYPE RIFLE

The bolt was moved by a rack-and-pinion mechanism after the spurred trigger guard had been unlatched and pushed forward, cocking the hammer automatically as the bolt started back. A vertically-moving locking block was dropped to release the bolt by a rocking lever and a cam-lug on the rack. The patent drawings suggest that an 8x50R prototype was built on the stock of the 1888-pattern Mannlicher rifle. A strange six-round box magazine was hung on the right side of the breech, with a slot in the body to show the state of loading; a cut-off on the magazine allowed the rifle to be used as a single-loader when required. The Odkolek rifle could have been operated very rapidly in perfect circumstances, but primary extraction is likely to have been bad; series production would have been nightmarish.

1903-TYPE RIFLE

Adolf von Odkolek was granted an Austrian patent in May 1903 to protect the locking system operated by a lug on a massive striker sliding inside the breechblock to engage bars or transverse bolts in the receiver. These ideas were incorporated in experimental machine guns, and a few automatic rifles were also apparently made.

• Schönauer

See 'Greece – Mannlicher-Schönauer: bolt-action.'

• Schulhof

Josef Schulhof's first guns were masterpieces of impossible machining and unnecessary fragility. They were made in such a variety of styles and shapes that output was restricted. There is no evidence that series production was ever undertaken, with the possible exception of the so-called '1887 model.'

THE GUNS

1882-type rifle. The first of these 'Model I' rifles were apparently built on the basis of adapted Vetterli actions, even though the basic design could be adapted to virtually any bolt-action rifles – e.g., Mauser, Gras or Berdan. At least one survivor has an Italian Pieri-type thumb trigger on the right side of the breech. A partitioned 'tandem magazine,' beneath a hinged cover on the left side, held 6+5+4 rounds in the butt with four in the feed tube and another in the chamber.

A detail view of a typical Schulhof rotary-magazine rifle, probably made for trials in France in the 1880s. (W&D)

The magazine could be loaded in a single motion with a special cardboard charger-box, but worked efficiently only if four rounds had previously been worked into the feed tube. Trials predictably showed the Model I Schulhof to be unreliable and much too cumbersome. It was replaced by the Model II of 1883.

1883-type rifle. An improved form of the butt-magazine rifle, retaining the basic principles of its predecessor, this had a simpler single-chamber five-round butt magazine and a five-round feed tube. It was tested in Austria-Hungary and Portugal, without success. Though the magazine system had the advantage of being replenished even when the rifle was ready to fire, the complexity was too great. The Model II also failed its trials, and had been replaced by the mid-1880s by a greatly improved rifle with a rotary magazine.

1886-type rifle. This had a sturdy receiver separating the straight-wrist butt from the forend, and a hinged cover (with viewing slots) on the right side of the magazine casing.

1887-type rifle. Essentially similar to the preceding gun, this had a magazine which had been refined in many details. The turning-bolt-action had two locking lugs, a two-piece stock was used, and a prominent magazine housing lay ahead of the trigger guard. Substantial quantities of rotary-magazine rifles were made in Liége, perhaps by Francotte, and performed creditably in military trials. Chambered for the then-experimental 8mm Austro-Hungarian cartridge, a typical survivor is about 50in overall and weighs 8.8lb. The rear sight is a quadrant pattern, and a lug on the muzzle accepts a sword bayonet. Unfortunately for Schulhof, none of his rifles performed well enough to be adopted; his death in 1890 brought work to an end.

• Spitalsky

Antonin Spitalsky, an employee of Österreichische Waffenfabriks-Gesellschaft, patented his first bolt-action repeating rifle in 1879. Made experimentally on the basis of the 1871-type Mauser, initially with seven- and then six-shot magazines, the Spitalsky guns were initially chambered for the 11mm German and 11mm Austro-Hungarian service cartridges. Later purpose-built guns incorporated Gras and Mauser features.

Konrad von Kromar improved the basic 1879-pattern rifle in 1882 by fitting an eight-round magazine with a cut-off, allowing it to be used as a single-loader, but Spitalsky himself produced the perfected design in 1884. This rifle, which also had an eight-round magazine, was tested extensively (but ultimately unsuccessfully) in France and Austria-Hungary. The rifles were probably made in the Steyr factory.

• Wangler

Developed by a Bohemian gunmaker, Ignaz Wangler of Kutna Hora (best known for Lefaucheux-type sporting guns), this was a variation of the sliding-barrel construction favored by patentees such as the Belgian gunmaker Ghaye (q.v.). Pulling down the tip of the underlever first withdrew the support of a pivoting frame-mounted locking bar from the barrel-block, then moved the barrel forward by a rack-and-pinion mechanism. Many guns had a self-cocking back-action lock with an external hammer; the survivors are usually double-barrel smooth-bores, but rifled single-barrel sporting rifles were also made in small numbers.

• Wänzl

The disastrous Seven Weeks War of 1866, when the Austrian army had been crushed by the Prussians, highlighted the conservatism of the Austrian ordnance and the quest for a suitable breech-loader began. Submissions included caplocks and metallic-cartridge rifles, but, after extensive trials, a swinging block-action breech-loading transformation – developed by a Viennese gunsmith – was adopted on 28th January 1867.

MODEL 1866 RIFLE
Infanterie-Gewehr M1863/66
Converted by Österreichische Waffenfabriks-Gesellschaft, Steyr, 1867-9?
Production total: 120,000. **Chambering:** 13.9x33, rimfire. **Action:** locked by lowering the breechblock behind the chamber.

52.3in overall, 9.42lb empty. 34.85in barrel, 4-groove rifling; RH, concentric. Ramp-and-leaf sight graduated to 1100 paces (925yd). 1280fps with M1867 rifle cartridges. M1854 socket bayonet.

These guns were converted from caplock 'Lorenz' rifle-muskets. Wrought-iron or steel barrels were used, depending on the

manufacturing pattern (1854 or 1863 respectively); 1863-type guns also had smaller lock plates.

The weapons had straight-wristed one-piece stocks, with two spring-retained bands and a heavy nose cap. A cleaning rod was carried beneath the barrel, while swivels lay on the middle band (unusually close to the nose cap) and under the butt. The bayonet had a locking ring and a distinctive diagonal attachment slot. (Note: original rifle-muskets are often known by an '1862' pattern-date.)

SIMILAR GUNS
Model 1866 short rifle. These conversions of old Jäger-Stutzen had heavy octagonal barrels with the muzzle crowns turned down to accept a sword-bladed bayonet with a locking ring around the socket-base.

The Ordinäre Stutzer of 1853 was originally rifled with four grooves and sighted to 1000 paces, while the pillar-breech Dornstutzer of 1854 once had a heavy ramrod and sights graduated to 1200 paces. The guns all had key-retained barrels, with swivels through the forend (above the cleaning-rod pipe) and on the under-edge of the butt. Trigger guards ended in a finger-spur, while the rear sights were curved-leaf 'grasshopper' patterns.

Survivors had been converted to fire expanding-ball ammunition after 1863, when they had been assimilated in a single group. Virtually all of those remaining in service in 1866 were converted to the Wänzl system. A typical Stutzer M1853/63/66 was 43.5in overall, weighed 10.4lb, and had a 26in barrel. The 1853-pattern socket bayonet was used.

Model 1866 gendarmerie carbine. The Extra-Corps-Gewehre M1853/66 and M1863/66 were converted from the caplocks of 1853 (iron barrel, large lock plate) and 1863 (steel barrel, small lock plate). Used by gendarmerie, sappers, pioneers and ancillary troops, they had a band in addition to a nose cap, accepted the M1854 socket bayonet, and had standard-weight 24in barrels. Overall length was generally about 41.6in, weight averaged 9.1lb, and the ramp-and-leaf sights were graduated to 500 paces.

• Werndl

Experiments to find a new rifle, undertaken concurrently with the conversion trials (see 'Wänzl'), created great interest. The Breech-loading Commission demanded that muzzle velocity should exceed 1115fps, but more than a hundred designs were considered before the commission selected the Austrian Würzinger and the American Remington as the most desirable.

A Remington rolling block was recommended for adoption on 29th November 1866 and guns were readied for trials. However, rumors put about by the Austro-Hungarian authorities that the Remington breech was unsafe allowed a rifle designed by Josef Werndl and Karl Holub to enter.

Werndl rifles were confined to Austria-Hungary, except for small-scale deliveries to Persia and Montenegro (23,000 and 20,000 respectively). After the introduction of Mannlichers in the 1880s, guns were passed down through second-line and lines-of-communication troops to the Landwehr and then into store. Survivors were reissued during World War I.

MODEL 1867 RIFLE
Infanterie- und Jägergewehr M1867
Made by Österreichische Waffenfabriks-Gesellschaft, Steyr, 1867-74.
Total production: 600,000. **Chambering:** 11x42R. **Action:** locked by rotating the breech-drum to seal the chamber.

50.3in overall, 9.75lb empty. 33.65in barrel, 6-groove rifling; RH, concentric. Ramp-and-leaf sight graduated to 1400 paces (1180yd). 1425fps with M1867 rifle cartridges. M1867 saber bayonet.

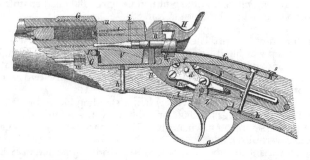

A sectional drawing of the 1867-pattern Werndl rifle.

The Werndl-Holub breech system was officially adopted on 28th July 1867, the decision being widely acclaimed in Austria. The subsequent manufacture of guns in the new Steyr factory contributed greatly to its prosperity.

The principal feature of the M1867 was the drum-breech, which, while sturdy and secure, compromised extraction. The rifle had a one-piece stock with a straight wrist, and a back-action lock with an external hammer. There were two screwed barrel bands and a nose cap; swivels lay under the middle band and butt. A cleaning rod was carried beneath the muzzle.

The rear sight leaf was graduated to 1200 paces with a 'V'-notch in the top edge for 1400 paces. A bayonet lug appeared on the right side of the muzzle. Standard infantry-pattern trigger guards were plain ovals, but a finger spur was substituted for Jäger units.

SIMILAR GUNS
Model 1867/77 rifle. With effect from 25th December 1878, most surviving rifles were adapted to chamber a new long-body 11x58R cartridge. They were officially known as 'M1867/77.'

MODEL 1867 CARBINE
Karabiner M1867
Made by Österreichische Waffenfabriks-Gesellschaft, Steyr, 1867-74.
Total production: 11,000. Chambering: 11x36R. Action: as M1867 infantry rifle, above.

39in overall, 7lb empty. 22.45in barrel, 6-groove rifling; RH, concentric. Ramp-and-leaf sight graduated to 600 paces (505yd). 980fps with M1867 carbine cartridges. M1867 saber bayonet.

Adopted at the same time as the infantry rifle, in 1867, this had a nose cap but lacked barrel bands. A knob appeared on the hammer instead of a spur. Werndl carbines originally chambered a short-case necked 11mm cartridge developing appreciably less power than the rifle pattern.

SIMILAR GUNS
Model 1867/77 carbine. The adoption of a more powerful cartridge, in December 1878, led to a change in the chambering. The modified carbines were usually known under this particular designation.

MODEL 1873 RIFLE
Infanterie- und Jägergewehr M1873
Made by Österreichische Waffenfabriks-Gesellschaft, Steyr, 1873-8.
Total production: 500,000? Chambering: 11x42R. Action: as M1867 infantry rifle, above.

49.8in overall, 9.27lb empty. 33.1in barrel, 6-groove rifling; RH, concentric. Ramp-and-leaf sight graduated to 1400 paces (1180yd). About 1460fps with M1867/73 ball cartridges. M1873 saber bayonet.

The drum-breech proved to be very susceptible to fouling, becoming increasingly difficult to rotate until it jammed altogether; constructional weaknesses were discovered in the receiver; and rear sight leaves regularly snapped. The action was extensively revised in 1872-3 by Antonin Spitalsky, who had succeeded Josef Werndl as head of the technical section of the Steyr factory. The sight-base and the sight leaf were strengthened; the receiver sides were flattened; the lock-plate was redesigned with a central hammer; the bayonet attachment was improved by using an internal coil-spring and stud; and the standard cartridge was revised.

On 10th February 1873, the new rifle was formally approved. It was similar to its predecessor, though the central hammer and modified receiver casing were obvious differences.

Troubles encountered with the original Wildburger-pattern rifle cartridge, in addition to jams and extraction failures, were solved only when a strengthened Roth-type case appeared in 1874.

SIMILAR GUNS
Model 1873/77 rifle. This was no more than an 1873-type rifle adapted to chamber a modified long-case cartridge approved in December 1878. Outwardly all but identical with the unaltered guns, a revised example could be distinguished by its rear sight.

MODEL 1873 CARBINE
Karabiner M1873
Made by Österreichische Waffenfabriks-Gesellschaft, Steyr, 1874-8.
Total production: 100,000 (all types). Chambering: 11x36R. Action: as M1867 infantry rifle, above.

39.5in overall, 7.17lb empty. 22.85in barrel, 6-groove rifling; RH, concentric. Ramp-and-leaf sight graduated to 600 paces (505yd). Performance: as M1867 carbine, above. M1873 saber bayonet.

Accepted on 6th November 1874, the revised or 1873-pattern carbine had a low-profile hammer and a nose cap, but lacked barrel bands. One swivel was anchored through the forend and the other lay on the trigger guard.

SIMILAR GUNS
Extra-Corps-Gewehr M1873. Adopted at the same time as the carbine, the gendarmerie rifle had a single barrel band and accepted the 1854-type socket bayonet. It weighed about 8.2lb.

Model 1873/77 carbine. Modifications were subsequently made to surviving 1873-type carbines to chamber the improved cartridge adopted in December 1878.

MODEL 1877 RIFLE
Infanterie- und Jägergewehr M1877
Made by Österreichische Waffenfabriks-Gesellschaft, Steyr, 1878-85.
Chambering: 11x58R. Otherwise generally as M1873, except rear sight (graduated to 2100 paces [1770yd]) and a muzzle velocity of 1490fps with M1877 rifle cartridges.

Trials of improved cartridges in 1875-7 led to a better rifle adopted at the end of 1877. The principal differences between the old M1873 and new M1877 rifles – and the assorted conversions – lay in the sights; rifles chambering the new long-case M1877 cartridge would not fire the short-case 1867 pattern, though unconverted guns were deliberately left in the Landwehr and Honved to expend existing supplies.

The improved cartridge was issued from 25th December 1878. It seems that no 1877-type rifles had been issued by this time, and thus that there was no need to re-graduate sights. The adoption of improved propellant in 1881 raised velocity slightly (apparently to about 1525fps) and allowed the rear sight graduations to be increased to 2200 paces or 1855yd.

MODEL 1877 CARBINE
Karabiner M1877
Made by Österreichische Waffenfabriks-Gesellschaft, Steyr, 1878-85.
Chambering: 11x36R.

Otherwise generally as M1873 carbine, except the rear sight (graduated to 1600 paces [1345yd]) and a muzzle velocity of 1005fps with M1877 carbine cartridges.

This was approved in 1878 to replace the 1867 and 1873-pattern guns. The new cartridge was interchangeable with its predecessors, but much more powerful. Consequently, the 1877-pattern

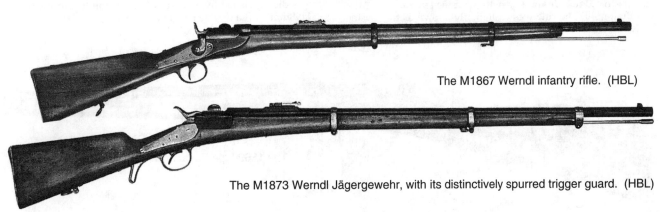

The M1867 Werndl infantry rifle. (HBL)

The M1873 Werndl Jägergewehr, with its distinctively spurred trigger guard. (HBL)

Kropatschek-designed sight was graduated to 1600 paces compared with only 600 paces for the original carbine round.

OTHER GUNS

Werndl carbines were to be found with bronze barrels (so-called 'Alpine Models' but possibly naval) or cut to pistol proportions, generally chambering the 11mm 'Zimmergewehr-Ladekonus' of 1871 and 1877 and intended for short-range practice. Some Zimmer-Karabiner may have been used by paramilitary units, but most were intended for civilian use. Though the Werndl was never very popular commercially, a few sporters were made in the early 1870s. They were often distinguished by excellent quality and copious engraving on the action, but others – generally very plain – were adapted from military weapons in 1890-1910.

BADEN

• Terry

The state army made limited use of a short bolt-action breech-loading gun of this type, issued to the riflemen (*Jäger*) as the 'Jägerbüchse M1863.' This was a simplified form of the British Terry (q.v.), with a sturdy collar-mounted bolt handle at the rear of the cylindrical breech instead of a folding handle doubling as a loading-port cover. The guns had a back-action caplock, a quadrant-type rear sight and a spurred trigger guard. The butt had a straight wrist, with a single band around the forend accompanying the nose cap. The unprotected loading port on top of the breech was vulnerable to the entry of rain and moisture.

BAVARIA

Bavaria, after allying with Austria against Prussia in the Seven Weeks War of 1866, remained independent until incorporated into the German Empire in 1871. Though the Bavarian ordnance department was gradually subjugated to Prussia, sufficient importance was retained for some years; the 1871-pattern Mauser rifle, for example, was not accepted in Bavaria until 1877, and the indigenous Werder rifle remained in front-line service into the 1880s.

• Chassepot

The Bavarians seem to have made the first attempts to alter the Chassepot, experimenting with an 11mm M/69 (Werder) cartridge in the early part of 1871. They also tried to negotiate a contract for ten thousand conversions with Österreichische Waffenfabriks-Gesellschaft, but reluctantly sold the greater part of their captured French rifles – apparently unaltered – in 1876.

• Podewils

In 1865, the Bavarian authorities formed the Handfeuerwaffen-Versuchscommission – a committee to develop a conversion system for the army's rifle muskets as well as a new breechloading rifle. The initial favorites were the French Manceaux transformation (q.v.) and a needle gun developed by von Borse, which was known colloquially as the 'Bückeburger Jägergewehr.' Other triallists included guns submitted by Högel, Mattenheimer, Oberleutnant Braumüller of the Bavarian army, and Edward Lindner.

The eventual result was the adoption of a system developed on the basis of the Lindner breech by the commandant of the Amberg manufactory, Freiherr von Podewils, with the assistance of Adolf von Braumühl. The rifle was customarily known as the 'System Podewils-Lindner-Braumühl,' though only the rudiments of the

This drawing of the Franco-Prussian War era shows Bavarian soldiers foraging in the Loire Valley during the Franco-Prussian War of 1870-1. They are using Lindner-type rifles.

Lindner system were retained. It was issued as a temporary measure pending the introduction of a purpose-built Werder (q.v.).

MODEL 1858/67 RIFLE

Assembled in the Royal Bavarian rifle manufactory, Amberg, from parts made by sub-contractors (see text).

Total production: about 113,300. **Chambering:** 13.9mm, rimmed. **Action:** locked by an interrupted-screw engaging threads in the rear of the receiver as the bolt handle was turned.

DATA FOR A TYPICAL EXAMPLE

51.25in overall, 10.23lb empty. 35.95in barrel, 4-groove rifling; RH, concentric. Single shot only. Leaf rear sight graduated to 600 paces. 1280fps with 425-grain bullet. M1858 socket bayonet.

These conversions of the 1858-pattern rifle muskets were easily distinguished by the tubular extension of the receiver behind the lock plate to accept the massive bolt. Fifteen manufacturers were involved in the work; the first 86,000 actions, for example, were made by Maschinenfabrik Augsburg (10,000), Maschinenbau-Gesellschaft Nürnberg (70,000) and Werkstätte L.A. Riedinger (6000). More than eighty thousand rifles had been assembled in the Amberg factory by the autumn of 1867; by the end of February 1869, 113,277 of an estimated stock of 116,000 M1858 rifle muskets had been altered.

The Lindner conversion was very sturdy, and surprisingly efficient for a gun of its type. The M1858/67 rifles saw action during the Franco-Prussian War in the hands of some of the Bavarian infantry regiments, but were relegated to the Landwehr when sufficient supplies of Werder rifles became available. When these were in their turn displaced by the Mausers, the old Lindners were either recalled into store or sold to military-surplus dealers such as Benny Spiro or A.L. Frank.

The basic Lindner rifle could be recognized by the bolt protruding behind the external hammer of the side-lock, and was stocked with two bands and a nose cap. The basic rear sight was apparently graduated only to 600 paces (*Schritt*).

SIMILAR GUNS

Schützen-Gewehr (Marksman's rifle). This was a minor variation of the infantry rifle with a special 1200-pace rear sight.

Jägerbüchse. Issued to men of the Bavarian rifle battalions, this was distinguished by a short barrel (overall length was merely 1198mm) and a double trigger system which embodied a setting lever.

The 1869-type Bavarian Werder carbine. (HBL)

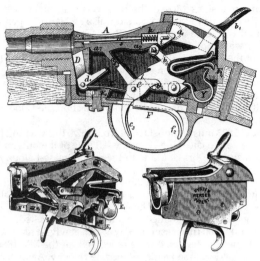

A drawing of the action of the Bavarian Werder rifle.

• Spörer & Harl

These employees of the government arms factory in Amberg patented a bolt-action rifle in Germany in 1882. The basic mechanism was adapted from the 1871-type Mauser, but a gravity-feed case magazine in the butt fed the breech by a Hotchkiss-like feed way and elevator system.

• Werder

Credited to Johann-Ludwig Werder, director of the Cramer-Klett'schen Établissements in Nuremburg, this block-action mechanism was patented in Bavaria in June 1868.

As the Lindner conversion was only a temporary solution, trials to find a new breech-loader began in Bavaria in the summer of 1868. The series resolved into a four-cornered contest between the Austrian Werndl, a Colt-made Berdan, a Mauser-Norris and the Bavarian Werder.

The indigenous Werder showed promise, though bad ammunition jammed continually. Once a new cartridge had been perfected in the Amberg manufactory, Werder and Werndl rifles were acquired for field trials. The Werndl was rejected after continual breech-jamming, and a straight fight developed between the Werder and the Colt-Berdan. Additional experiments failed to separate the contestants, so an example of each was shown to the king, Ludwig II; predictably, the Werder was adopted.

To load the Werder, the front trigger was pressed forward to release the block-prop, dropping the breech block automatically and kicking the spent case out of the breech. After a new cartridge had been inserted, pulling back on the spur of the operating lever (protruding upward from the rear right side of the action) raised and locked the block. The action could be worked extremely rapidly, earning the M/69 the sobriquet *Blitzgewehr* ('Lightning Rifle') during the Franco-Prussian War – though only about half the Jäger-Bataillone and parts of three infantry regiments had been suitably equipped.

MODEL 1869 RIFLE
Rückladungsgewehr M/1869, System Werder

Made by the rifle factory in Amberg (125,000?), relying heavily on sub-contractors; and Handfeuerwaffen-Productionsgenossenschaft, Suhl (20,000).
Total production: in the region of 150,000. **Chambering:** 11x50, rimmed. **Action:** locked by propping the breechblock behind the chamber.

51.2in overall, 9.68lb unladen. 35in barrel, 4-groove rifling; RH, concentric. Ramp-and-leaf sight graduated to 1000 schritt? 1465fps with M/1869 ball cartridges. M/1869 saber bayonet.

About a thousand Liége-made rifles were delivered for trials against Steyr-made Werndls in 1868. The experimental 1868-type rifle differed from the perfected M/1869 largely in the manner of stocking – it had one band instead of two – and accepted the French Mle. 66 saber bayonet. Most surviving trials guns were converted into M/69 carbines in 1870.

The M/69 rifle was approved on 18th April 1869. It was difficult to mistake for any other design, owing to the twin levers in the trigger guard and the position of the breech-lever spur. However, the ultimate fate of the Werder was sealed when the Bavarians were pressured into accepting the Prussian Mauser infantry rifle – though little was done until 1877.

SIMILAR GUNS

Model 1869, altered ('Aptierte M/1869'). Trials were undertaken in 1874 with M/69 rifles chambering the 11mm Mauser cartridge, two hundred converted rifles being issued in December. Early in 1875, despite evidence of continual breakages, the authorities recommended adopting the Reichspatrone conversion. The plans received royal assent on 5th June 1875; by 1st November 1876, Amberg had produced 124,540 'aptierte M/69' rifles by rechambering the old barrels and fitting new 1871-pattern rear sights.

MODEL 1869 CARBINE

Made by Maschinenfabrik 'Landes,' Munich (4000); and Auguste Francotte & Cie, Liége (4000).
Total production: 8600, including conversions. **Chambering:** 11mm, rimmed. **Action:** as M/1869 infantry rifle, above.

37.8in overall, 7.72lb unladen. 21.65in barrel, 4-groove rifling; RH, concentric. Ramp-and-leaf sight graduated to 500 schritt? About 1150fps with M/1869 ball cartridges. No bayonet.

Adopted on 1st July 1869, this was made only in small quantities. The first six hundred were converted from surviving 1868-type trials rifles, but new guns were subsequently made in Munich and Liége. Francotte also apparently made a Werder gendarmerie rifle, a variant of the standard carbine accepting a socket bayonet.

NEW MODEL 1869 RIFLE
Rückladungsgewehr M/1869, neues Muster

Continual problems during trials showed that converted M1869 rifles were unlikely to be durable, and so the M/1869 n.M. – chambered for the standard 11x60 'Reichspatrone' – was substituted on 21st July 1875. The extractor and receiver had been strengthened; the chamber, barrel, sights and nose cap being 1871-pattern Mauser designs to ensure at least partial conformity with the new imperial standards.

About 25,000 new actions were made by Maschinenfabrik Augsburg and assembled in Amberg with barrels and stocks made locally or purchased from Österreichische Waffenfabriks-Gesellschaft of Steyr.

The Bavarian army finally approved the Mauser in August 1877, allowing the surviving Werder rifles to be relegated to foot artillerymen and then eventually to store. Re-issue had been completed by July 1882.

BELGIUM

Belgian service weapons can often be identified by the royal cyphers. These generally take the form of a crowned script or Roman letter – 'A' for Albert, 'L' for Leopold, 'B' for Baudoin. The guns also bear an encircled 'GB' (*Gouvernement Belge*) and inspectors' marks in the form of capital letters surmounted by crowns or stars.

A typical M1853/67 Albini-Braendlin infantry rifle conversion.

• Albini-Braendlin

This system was designed by Augusto Albini, an Italian army officer, but perfected with the assistance of Francis Braendlin – associated with Albini in British patents of 1866-7. The gun was tested throughout Europe, but adopted only in Belgium.

The essence of the breech was a locking bolt attached to the hammer-body. Rotating the hammer to half cock withdrew the bolt and allowed the breechblock handle to be lifted, extracting a spent case to be tipped from the feed way. Once the gun had been reloaded, the breech block was closed and the hammer thumbed back to full cock. Pressing the trigger allowed the hammer to fly forward, whereupon the locking bolt entered the back of the breech block and struck the firing pin.

After testing differing rifles, including the Remington, the Belgians selected the Albini-Braendlin breech owing to the ease with which existing rifle-muskets could be converted.

MODEL 1867 RIFLE
Fusil d'Infanterie Mle 1867
Apparently made in Liége by Dresse-Laloux & Cie.
Total production: not known. **Chambering:** 11.4x50mm, rimmed. **Action:** locked by a sliding bolt entering the back of the breechblock as the hammer fell.

DATA FOR AN M1853/67 CONVERSION
53.05in overall, 10.07lb unladen. 34.75in barrel, 4-groove rifling; RH, concentric. Ramp-and-leaf sight graduated to 1100m (1205yd). 1365fps with Mle 1867 ball cartridges. Mle 1867 socket bayonet.

Most of these infantry rifles were converted from an assortment of obsolete guns. The new barrel was copied from the Chassepot, with French-style rifling. The guns all had one-piece stocks, with two sprung barrel bands and a large nose cap; swivels lay under the middle band and ahead of the trigger guard. Mle 1777/1867 rifles were issued only to fortress artillerymen and reservists, allowing the other conversions to serve line infantry and riflemen pending the introduction of newly-made weapons. Issue of the Albini-Braendlin was extended in 1869 to the Garde Civique, but no guns had been delivered when the Comblain (q.v.) was substituted in 1871.

SIMILAR GUNS
Model 1777/1867 rifle. This designation was sometimes applied to Mle 1867 rifles converted from 1777-pattern flintlock muskets, acquired from France in the 1840s, which had already been converted to caplock and had a typically Belgian back-action lock plate.

Model 1841/67 rifle. A conversion of the 1841-pattern cap lock rifle-musket.

Model 1853/67 rifle. This version of the Mle 67 rifle was a transformation of the 1853-pattern rifle-musket, a small caliber gun issued with Minié expanding ball ammunition.

Model 1867/1901 rifle. Many surviving rifles were adapted for rural gendarmerie after 1901, and the distinctions between the several classes of conversion (which had not always been used) were finally abandoned. Barrels and stocks were shortened, the nose cap was discarded, and barrel was smooth-bored to about 13.9mm for shot cartridges. A notch on the breechblock hinge sufficed as the rear sight, with a blade on the barrel above the forend tip. Most of these adaptations had been withdrawn by 1910.

Model 1873 rifle. This was simply a newly-made version of the Mle 1867 (q.v.), with an improved extractor adapted from the Terssen conversions. Most of the guns were made in Liége by Fabrique d'Armes de l'État, and possibly also by Henri Pieper & Cie.

Model 1777/1873 musketoon. This *Mousqueton*, or gendarmerie rifle, was another Dresse-Laloux conversion. It shared the action of the Mle 1867 rifle, but chambered an 11.4x42 cartridge and was merely 45.25in long. Converted from an old French flintlock musket, it weighed 8.27lb and had a 26.75in barrel. The butt was plain and the mounts were brass. Gendarmerie bayonets were basically diminutives of the Mle 1867, with shortened elbows and flattened blades.

Model 1873 musketoon. Dating from 1874, this was an 11.4x42 short rifle with a cheek-piece on the left side of the butt and iron fittings instead of brass. Made in Liége by Dresse-Laloux & Cie (and perhaps also by Henri Pieper & Cie), it was 45in long, had a 26.75in barrel and weighed 8.02lb. A ramp-and-leaf rear sight was graduated to 600m (655yd) and muzzle velocity with ball cartridges was about 1155fps. The Mle 1873 also apparently had a sling ring on the wrist, which the Mle 1777/1873 lacked.

Model 1873/80 rifle. From 1880 onward, newly-made Mle 1873 rifles (but not conversions) were re-sighted for the Mle 1880 cartridge, which developed a higher muzzle velocity. A notch on the extended slider of the new 1400m (1530yd) back-sight leaf could be used for ranges up to 2100m (2295yd) in conjunction with a stud on the middle band.

Model 1873/1901 rifle. Some surviving 1873-type rifles were eventually converted for rural gendarmerie in 1901 (see 'M1867/1901', above), but had been discarded by 1914.

• Clément

Also known as 'Clément-Neumann'. Introduced prior to 1910, this carbine was based on patents granted in 1903-8 to Charles Ph. Clément of Liége.

CLÉMENT AUTOMATIC CARBINE
Carabine Automatique 'Clément'
Made by Fabrique d'Armes Charles Ph. Clément, Liége, about 1909-14.
Total production: not known. **Chambering:** 401 Winchester, rimless. **Action:** no mechanical breech lock; blowback operation, semi-automatic only.

42.5in overall, 7.85lb empty. 23.6in barrel, 4-groove rifling; RH, concentric. Detachable box magazine, 5 rounds. Block and folding leaf rear sight graduated to 200m (219yd). 2140fps with 200-grain bullet.

The gun was based on the Clément pistols of the day, but the breechblock – cocked by prominent grips on the top rear of the action – reciprocated inside the receiver. The walnut butt had checkering on the rounded pistol grip, and the checkered forend had a horn or ebonite tip. The barrel was usually octagonal, and the large slab-sided receiver had a magazine in the trigger guard housing. Clément's business was acquired in 1913 by the Neumann brothers (Neumann Frères et Cie), and guns sold commercially after this date were marked 'Clément-Neumann'. They were not particularly successful, however, and production stopped, never to resume, when the Germans invaded Belgium in 1914.

• Comblain

This was created by Hubert-Joseph Comblain of Liége. The standard Belgian-type Comblain was exported to Greece in 1873 (eight thousand rifles and five hundred musketoons) and then to Chile and Peru. A special pattern was made for Brazil.

The M1873 Albini-Braendlin rifle.

The M1871 Comblain musketoon.

Compact for its day and surprisingly durable, the basic action comprised a sturdy receiver with the breech lever (doubling as the trigger guard) pivoted at the lower front edge. Pulling the lever lowered the breech block – which contained the hammer, trigger and main spring – to disengage the locking shoulders and then moved it radially. The hammer cocked during the opening motion, at the end of which the extractor withdrew the spent case from the chamber.

MILITARY WEAPONS

MODEL 1870 CIVIL GUARD CARBINE
Carabine de la Garde Civique Mle 1870

Made by the 'Petit Syndicat,' Liége (Ancion & Co., Dresse-Laloux & Co., Auguste Francotte, and Pirlot-Frésart & Co.).

Total production: not known. **Chambering:** 11.4x50mm, rimmed. **Action:** locked by an operating lever combined with the trigger guard propping the breechblock behind the chamber.

47.25in overall, 9.83lb empty. 31.8in barrel, 4-groove rifling; RH, concentric. Ramp-and-leaf sight graduated to 1000m (1095yd)? 1410fps with Mle 1870 ball cartridges. Mle 1868 saber bayonet.

Adopted on 26th March 1870 to supersede the Albini-Braendlin, supplies of which had not reached the Garde Civique, this 'carbine' – virtually a full-length rifle – was easily identified by its massive receiver and the housing immediately behind the trigger. It had a two-piece stock, the single band and simple nose cap being retained by springs. A cleaning rod was contained in the forend, projecting beneath the barrel, while swivels lay beneath the band and on the under-edge of the butt. Set in a distinctive washer, a retaining bolt ran laterally through the forend immediately below the rear sight, the leaf of which hinged at the front of the bed. A bayonet lug and tenon lay on the right side of the muzzle.

SIMILAR GUNS

Model 1882 (Fusil d'Infanterie de la Garde Civique Mle 1882). A modified gun, slightly longer than the Mle 1870 Garde Civique carbine but otherwise essentially similar, was adopted to cure faults in the original design. The breech lever was simplified; the hammer was altered so that the mechanism could be cocked or uncocked at will; and a half-cock safety notch appeared.

MODEL 1871 SHORT RIFLE
Mousqueton Mle 1871

Made by the 'Petit Syndicat' (see above).

Total production: 7500? **Chambering:** 11.4x42mm, rimmed. **Action:** as Mle 1870, above.

31.5in overall, 6.68lb unladen. 17.9in barrel, 4-groove rifling; RH, concentric. Ramp-and-leaf sight graduated to 500m (550yd). 970fps with ball cartridges. No bayonet.

Adopted on 15th July 1871 for the regular cavalry, this was little more than a shortened Mle 1870 Garde Civique carbine. The short forend was retained by a nose cap and a transverse bolt. Swivels lay beneath the nose cap and butt.

SIMILAR GUNS

Model 1871/83 short rifle. Many Mle 1871 guns were altered for the engineers and supply corps from 1883 onward, to approximate to the Mle 1882 Garde Civique rifle (q.v.). As the musketoons were stocked to the muzzle, a new screw-retained barrel band and a new nose cap were required. A sling bar was fitted to the under-edge of the stock immediately behind the breech lever, and a cleaning rod lay beneath the muzzle. The new rear sight was graduated to 1070m (1170yd).

A few guns were altered in the early 1890s to accept the Mle 1867 bayonet. These had a new barrel band (fitted with a swivel) and a simple nose cap, sufficient of the muzzle being exposed to accept the bayonet socket. The second swivel lay on the under-edge of the stock.

SPORTING GUNS

Sporters made in Liége in 1870-80 were soon overhauled by better designs; though the Comblain was strong enough to handle most of the medium-power sporting cartridges of its period, its unhandsome looks were a drawback. A few guns were stocked and completed in Britain, probably from components supplied by Francotte; usually displaying a 'small action' instead of the full-size military type, these often bear the marks of E.M. Reilly & Co. of Oxford Street, London. Edward Reilly had collaborated with the Belgian inventor in the Reilly-Comblain rifle of the mid 1860s.

• Dumoulin

Dumoulin & Fils of Milmort, near Liége, made Mauser-type sporters, originally on the basis of refurbished war-surplus Kar. 98k-type actions, but then on the basis of new components purchased from Fabrique Nationale.

MR-2 SPORTING RIFLE

The standard rifle had a refurbished action, a straight-comb butt and a rounded forend tip of ebony, rosewood or horn. The pistol grip and the forend were checkered; swivels lay under the butt and on the barrel; and the leaf sight was graduated for 100-300m (110-330yd).

SIMILAR GUNS

MR-5. A deluxe version of the MR-2, this had a block-and-leaves sight set into the front of a short rib stretching forward from the chamber. The receiver was invariably engraved with scrolls or foliation.

Type A. These rifles were built on new actions purchased from Fabrique Nationale. Chambered for 375 H&H Magnum cartridges, they had Monte Carlo combs and tapering forends with short rounded ebony or rosewood tips. Two- or three-leaf Express sights were let into quarter-ribs, hinged magazine floorplates were fitted, and the front swivel was attached to the barrel ahead of the forend.

Type DM. Chambered for 7x57, 7.65x53 or 8x57 ammunition, these were also built on new FN actions. Their stocks usually exhibited an exaggerated pistol grip cap, a notch-back Monte Carlo comb, and a squared reverse-cut ebonite forend tip; checkering was skip-line or basket-weave. Williams sights were fitted.

RIMFIRE GUNS

In addition to centerfire sporting rifles, Dumoulin Frères have made rimfire patterns. These have included the Model 569, a single shot 22LR rifle with fixed sights and a 23.6in barrel – most unusually fitted with a top-rib. The Model 570 was similar, but had a 27.95in barrel; the Model 570TR apparently had a 30in barrel and a specially selected deluxe walnut stock.

• Engh

Promoted by SA Manufacture Liégeoise d'Armes à Feu, guns of this pattern were entered in the Belgian army trials of 1888-9. Production of military-test and sporting rifles is believed to have exceeded fifty. The essence of the straight-pull action was a massive handle, protruding upward from the receiver, which could be pulled backward to rotate locking shoulders on the handle-base out of the receiver. The handle and the breech block could then be pulled straight back.

The magazine spool of the original pattern could be removed once its housing had been pivoted downward at the breech. The radial release catch lay immediately ahead of the trigger guard. A two-piece stock was used, with a cleaning rod set into the left side of the forend. This gun was superseded by a lighter version with a protruding single-column magazine case, a one-piece straight-wrist stock, and a half-length handguard running forward from the receiver ring to the barrel band.

A longitudinal section of the interesting Engh rifle.

• Fabrique Nationale, auto-loading type

See also 'Browning Arms Company' in the chapter devoted to the USA.

BROWNING AUTOMATIC CARBINE
Carabine Automatique Browning or 'Auto-22'

Made by Fabrique Nationale d'Armes de Guerre, Herstal-lèz-Liège, 1914, 1920-40 and 1947-76; and by the Miroku Firearms Company, Kochi, 1976 to date.

Currently in production. **Chambering options:** 22 Short or Long Rifle rimfire. **Action:** no mechanical breech lock; blowback, semi-automatic only.

DATA FOR A TYPICAL EXAMPLE

Chambering: 22 Long Rifle. 37in overall, 4.74lb empty. 19.25in barrel, 4-groove rifling; RH, concentric. Tube magazine in butt, 11 rounds. Spring-leaf and elevator sight. About 1050fps with 40-grain bullet.

This gun was made in accordance with patents obtained by John Browning in 1908, though production did not begin in Belgium until January 1913. Browning was so convinced that the design would be successful that he ordered fifty thousand guns for the North American market on his own account.

The simple tube-magazine autoloader had an enclosed hammer, a half-length forend, and a separate butt with a port cut in the butt to allow the magazine to be half-filled without opening the breech. The 22 LR rifle was more popular; the original 22 Short version, with a 22.75in barrel and a sixteen-cartridge magazine, was only made in small numbers.

No sooner had production begun, than the Germans invaded Belgium and work ceased until 1920. Interrupted once again by war and its aftermath (1940-7), production then proceeded unhindered until passed to Miroku. Guns were still being made in 1997, despite the introduction of newer and supposedly better designs.

THE GUNS

Model A. Made until the mid-1960s, but still available from dealers' stocks until 1968, this was the most basic version. Offered in 22LR with an eight-round magazine or 22 Short (eleven rounds), it had a plain semi-pistol grip butt and a slender forend. Originally offered with a fixed open rear sight, the guns made in the 1960s had a spring leaf-and-elevator rear sight and weighed about 4lb empty. The barrel and forend can be detached by releasing a catch and rotating the ribbed barrel collar through 90 degrees.

Model B. This was an improved version of the Model A, with a checkered pistol grip butt and a broad semi-beavertail forend. Deluxe examples have been made with engraving on the receiver and woodwork specially selected for its attractive grain.

BAR Deluxe (Grades III-VI). Three of these highly decorative deluxe guns – Grades III-V – were introduced in 1971, differing in finish; concurrently, the standard rifle was re-designated 'Grade I' and the original deluxe version became 'Grade II'. The new Grade III had a grayed steel receiver with trophy heads (deer and antelope on standard guns, elk and moose on magnums) set in fine English style scrollwork. Grade IV was similar, but had full-figure representations of the animals between reduced end-panels of heavier baroque scrollwork; Grade V had complete game scenes with gold animal inlays. Triggers were gold plated and the woodwork was selected walnut, hand-checkered and carved.

Owing to limited demand, Grades II, III and V were abandoned in 1974. Grade IV remained as a stock item until the mid-1980s, but was then superseded by guns made individually to order until Grade VI appeared in 1988. Offered in a blue or grayed finish, Grade VI guns had woodwork specially selected for its figuring and gold-finished game scenes in low relief on the receiver – a fox and squirrel on the right, and a beagle and rabbit on the left.

HIGH-POWER SEMI-AUTOMATIC RIFLE

Made by Fabrique Nationale d'Armes de Guerre, Herstal-lèz-Liège, 1910-14, 1921-31.

Total production: about 4910. **Chambering:** 35 Remington. **Action:** no mechanical breech lock; blowback, semi-automatic only.

40.5in overall, about 7.8lb empty. 22in barrel, 4-groove rifling; RH, concentric. Detachable box magazine, 5 rounds. Folding-leaf rear sight. 2180fps with 200-grain bullet.

This gun was made in accordance with a patent granted to John Browning in October 1900, which was also licensed to Remington. Consequently, the FN rifle was essentially similar to the Remington Model 8 (q.v.). The principal external differences lay in the solid matted rib above the barrel, and in the two-leaf rear sight.

LIGHT AUTOMATIC CARBINE
Carabine Automatique Légère, 'CAL'

Made by Fabrique Nationale d'Armes de Guerre, Herstal-lèz-Liège, 1966-74?

Total production: 30,000? **Chambering:** 5.56x45, rimless. **Action:** locked by rotating lugs on the bolt into engagment with the receiver; gas operated, selective fire.

DATA FOR A TYPICAL FIXED-BUTT EXAMPLE

38.6in overall, 8.48lb with loaded 20-round magazine. 18.4in barrel, 6-groove rifling; RH, concentric. Detachable box magazine, 20 or (later) 30 rounds. Pivoting-'L' sight for 150/250 or 250/400 metres. 3250fps with M193 bullet; 850±50 rpm. 'Flash-hider' tube bayonet.

The 5.56mm CAL was not particularly successful, and was replaced by the FNC.

The first attempts were made to adapt the FAL to 5.56mm (.223) in 1963, but the tilting-block locking system lacked the camming action to ease spent cases out of the chamber. Extraction was not reliable enough to satisfy potential users.

Prototypes of the Carabine Automatique Légère were demonstrated in 1967. The gun retained the proven gas system and trigger of the FAL, but a rotating bolt was substituted for the tilting block. Series production began in 1969.

Despite the different mechanism, the CAL was externally much like its 7.62mm predecessor, with a synthetic butt and pistol grip. A version with a folding tubular butt could also be supplied. Forends were unnecessarily complex ventilated sheet-steel stampings; selectors lay on the left side of the receiver above the trigger, being marked 'S,' '1,' '3' and 'A' – for safety, single shots, bursts, and fully automatic operation respectively.

By 1975, however, the CAL had been abandoned. Prone to extraction failures, it was too expensive and had appeared at a time when many armies had either just re-equipped with 7.62mm NATO standard weapons or were still to be convinced of the efficacy of the 5.56mm bullet.

Guns had been tested extensively in Belgium and elsewhere, but had never challenged the 5.56mm AR-15/M16A1 and HK33. Gabon and Lebanon purchased a few in the early 1970s, but the CAL was then replaced by the sturdier FNC.

BROWNING AUTOMATIC SPORTING RIFLE
Also known as 'BAR'

Made by FN Herstal SA, Herstal-lèz-Liège, 1967 to date.

Currently in production. **Chambering options:** 243 Winchester, 270 Winchester, 280 Remington, 7mm Remington Magnum, 30-06, 300 Winchester Magnum, 308 Winchester or 338 Winchester Magnum. **Action:** locked by rotating seven lugs on the bolt head into the receiver; gas operated, semi-automatic only.

DATA FOR A TYPICAL AFFÛT

Chambering: 270 Winchester, rimless. 43.2in overall, 7.65lb empty. 20.05in barrel, 4-groove rifling; RH, concentric. Detachable box magazine, 5 rounds. Spring-leaf and elevator sight. About 3115fps with 130-grain bullet.

Locked by rotating the bolt, this gas-operated rifle – unrelated to the pre-1918 BAR – is popular and efficient. Its design is usually credited to Val Browning, son of John.

The modern Browning Automatic Rifle is an elegant centerfire design. The patented hinged floor-plate/detachable box magazine unit allows the box to be replenished without removing it. The standard rifle has an open rear sight, and extensive checkering on the walnut pistol grip butt and forend. The earliest deluxe examples had scroll engraving on the grayed receiver sides, gold-plated triggers and woodwork chosen for its figuring.

SIMILAR GUNS

BAR Affût. This was the post-1985 name for the original rifle, described above. A 280 Remington chambering was introduced in 1988.

BAR Battue. Introduced in the mid-1980s, this had a small folding-leaf rear sight let into a quarter-rib. The standard rifle was renamed 'Affût' (q.v.) to distinguish it from the Battue pattern.

BAR Big Game Special Edition. Six hundred of these were made in small numbers in 1987-8, in 30-06 only. They had gold-plated triggers and silver-gray receivers engraved with mule deer on the left and white-tails on the right; each scene was accompanied by a single trophy head inlaid in gold.

BAR Deluxe. This was the original version, with engraving on the receiver and specially-selected woodwork.

BAR Magnum. The first 300 Winchester Magnums were introduced in 1969. They measured 45.1in overall, with a four-round magazine, and had six-groove rifling. The 338 Winchester option was added in 1988.

FN AUTOMATIC CARBINE
Fabrique Nationale Carabine, 'FNC'
Made by FN Herstal SA, Herstal-lèz-Liège, 1982 to date.
Currently in production. **Chambering:** 5.56x45, rimless. **Action:** generally as CAL, above.
DATA FOR A TYPICAL TYPE 2000

39.25in overall with butt extended, 9.6lb with loaded magazine. 17.7in barrel, 6-groove rifling; RH, concentric. Detachable box magazine, 30 rounds. Pivoting-'L' sight for 250/400 metres (275/435yd). 3000fps with SS109 bullet; 650±50 rpm. Optional knife bayonet.

The successor to the ill-starred CAL (q.v.), the FNC was developed hurriedly in 1975-7 to participate in NATO standardisation trials. However, development work had not been completed and the rifle was soon withdrawn from competition; it had been entered at too early a stage, and did not perform as well as FN had hoped.

By 1980, protracted testing had revealed that problems centered mainly on the much simplified construction – stampings and welded seams being much in evidence – but also that the basic gas and rotating-bolt locking systems were efficient enough. Rifles were successfully entered in trials in Sweden in 1981-2, and performed well enough to convince the Belgian army of their merits. About ten thousand guns were sold to the Indonesian air force in 1982. Finally, in 1989, after issuing the FNC to airborne forces for some years, the Belgian government finally indicated that the 5.56mm gun would gradually replace the 7.62mm FAL in universal service.

An FNC fitted with an optical sight.

SIMILAR GUNS
FNC Model 90.00. The guns were supplied with a folding skeleton butt of tubular steel, but a fixed polyamide butt was available on request; the bayonet, where used, was a variant of the US M7. Barrels and chambers were chromed to minimise the effects of propellant fouling, and a three round burst-fire mechanism could be supplied whenever required. No distinction was originally drawn between the two differing rifling patterns, making a turn in 12in and 7in to suit the Belgian 5.56mm SS109 and US 223 M193 bullets.

FNC Model 92.00. This was the original designation for the standard short-barreled carbines, with 1-in-12 or 1-in-7 rifling; they were 35.85in long, had 14.15in barrels, and weighed 8.15lb.

FNC Type 0000. Also originally known as 'Model 90.00,' this is the current designation for the standard long-barreled FNC with 1-in-12 rifling suited to the Belgian SS109 bullet.

FNC Type 2000. This is simply a variant of the Type 0000 adapted for the US 223 M193 bullet, with rifling which makes a turn in 7in.

FNC Type 6000. This was a short-barreled carbine with 1-in-12 rifling for the Belgian SS109 bullet.

FNC Type 6040. This was a 'Law Enforcement' pattern, restricted to semi-automatic operation. The rifling had a pitch of 1-in-12.

FNC Type 7000. Mechanically identical with the Type 6000, this had 1-in-7 rifling suited to the US M193 bullet.

FNC Type 7030. This was a minor variant of the 6040 Law Enforcement carbine, with 1-in-7 rifling.

OTHERS
In addition to service in Belgium and Sweden, the FNC is currently being made under license in Indonesia. The Indonesian air force purchased 10,000 guns from FN in 1982 whereafter, in April 1984, the government signed a licensing agreement permitting manufacture in the state arsenal. Assembly is believed to have begun in 1987. The weapons bear a Garuda mark on the receiver or magazine housing.

No other large-scale purchases of FNC have yet been identified, though guns have been supplied for trials in many countries; small batches may also have found their way into Africa, the Middle East, South and Central America through dealers and intermediaries.

• Fabrique Nationale, bolt-action type
See also **'Browning Arms Company'** in the chapter devoted to the USA. The decision to make rimfire sporting guns was taken as early as November 1896, when the Board of Directors voted to make fifty thousand simple 22 bolt-action sporting rifles.

FN-CARABINE
Made by Fabrique Nationale d'Armes de Guerre, Herstal-lèz-Liège, 1898-1914 and about 1920-35. Chambering options: 22 Short, 6mm Flobert and 9mm Flobert (see text). **Action:** locked by turning the bolt-handle base down ahead of the receiver bridge.
DATA FOR A TYPICAL 22 EXAMPLE

31.5in overall, 3.55lb empty. 17.7in barrel, 4-groove rifling; RH, concentric. Single shot only. Fixed open-notch rear sight. About 755fps with 29-grain bullet.

Available as a rifled 22 or smooth-bored for 22 rimfire or 6mm Flobert cartridges, this was FN's most basic sporting rifle – built on the simplest of 'Mauser' action, which meant simply that it was a bolt action pattern! The plain half-stock had a short round-tipped forend, but lacked a buttplate. The barrel and action were held in the stock by a threaded bolt beneath the chamber.

SIMILAR GUNS
22 deluxe pattern. Though retaining the action of the most basic 22, this had a walnut stock with checkering on the pistol grip and forend. The trigger guard was a machined forging instead of a stamped strip, and swivels lay beneath the butt and barrel. The guns were 41.3in long, with 23.6in barels, and weighed 4.3-4.6lb.

22 military trainer. Embodying the standard action, this had a full-length forend with a single barrel band and a simple nose cap which could take a knife bayonet. The butt had a straight wrist, the trigger guard was usually a machined forging, and the rear sight was a leaf-and-slider type.

9mm pattern. This shared the action of the 22 Short gun, but had a 23.6in barrel, weighed about 5lb, and was customarily fitted with a special pivoting-lever extractor on the right side of the breech.

22 T-BOLT RIFLE
Made by FN Herstal SA, Herstal-lèz-Liège, 1965-74.
Total production: not known. **Chambering:** 22 Long Rifle rimfire (see text). **Action:** locked by a pivoting bar in the bolt mechanism.

41.35in overall, 5.5lb empty. 24in barrel, 4-groove rifling; RH, concentric. Box magazine in stock, 5 rounds. Williams ramp-type rear sight. About 1050fps with 40-grain bullet.

The FN-Browning B124 Express over/under double rifle, with its exchangeable shotgun barrels.

The standard or 'T-1' version of this straight-pull rimfire rifle had a half stock with a straight comb, a pistol gripped butt and a rounded forend. The bolt handle lay at the rear right side of the receiver, and the manual safety catch on the tang locked the trigger and bolt. The receiver top was grooved for optical-sight mounts.

The rifles could feed 22LR rimfire ammunition from the magazine, but could fire 22 Short or Long if cartridges were loaded individually into the chamber; a special magazine-block could ease the feeding of single rounds. The T-Bolt rifle – never especially successful – was replaced in the mid 1970s by a rimfire version of the A-Bolt. The deluxe or 'T-2' version had a better stock, with checkering on the pistol grip and forend, and a Williams aperture sight on the receiver bridge.

• Fabrique Nationale, break-open type
EXPRESS DOUBLE RIFLE
Made by Fabrique Nationale d'Armes de Guerre and FN Herstal SA, Herstal-lèz-Liège.

Currently in production. **Chambering options:** 7x65R or 9.3x74R. **Action:** locked by a sliding bolt beneath the breech engaging the under-lug as the top-lever closes.

DATA FOR A TYPICAL 7x65MM PATTERN

About 42in overall, 7.6lb empty. 25.6in barrel, 4-groove rifling; RH, concentric. Double barreled; two shots only. Folding rear sight. 2885fps with 135-grain bullet.

This is basically an improved version of the Browning-designed 'Superposed' over-and-under shotgun, patented in 1925 and introduced commercially in 1931. Among the revisions have been the addition of automatic compensation for wear in the breech and the top-lever system. The base-plate and walls of the frame have been strengthened to withstand the pressures generated by rifle ammunition.

The standard gun is offered with checkering on the pistol grip and schnabel-tip forend, engraving on the action – English bouquet, scrollwork, or game scenes – and a single-trigger mechanism. The rear sight is set into a quarter-rib, but optical sights can be used if appropriate mount bases have been fitted.

The deluxe pattern is identical mechanically, but has a straight wristed 'swan-neck' butt, with a curved belly, and a three-piece forend. The wood is chosen for its delicate figure, and the engraving is low-relief Renaissance tracery on a matted ground.

• Fabrique Nationale, slide-action type
See also **'Browning Arms Company'** in the chapter devoted to the USA.

BROWNING REPEATING CARBINE
Carabine à Répétition Browning, 'Trombon'
Made by Fabrique Nationale d'Armes de Guerre, Herstal-lèz-Liège, 1921-74.

Total production: about 152,000. **Chambering:** 22 Long Rifle rimfire. **Action:** locked by propping the bolt in place behind the chamber as the slide handle moved forward?

39in overall, 4.8lb empty. 22in barrel, 4-groove rifling; RH, concentric. Tube magazine beneath the barrel, 15 rounds. Spring-and-elevator rear sight. 1050fps with 40-grain bullet.

This was a typical slide-action repeater, derived from the Browning-designed external-hammer Winchester of 1890 (q.v.). It was essentially similar to the 22 autoloader, but had the magazine beneath the barrel instead of contained in the butt. The guns customarily had butts with shallow pistol grips, and circumferentially ribbed slide handles enveloping the magazine tube.

• Falisse & Trapmann
These gunmakers devised a bolt-action rifle about 1862. The mechanism relied on a bolt handle which, in addition to providing a locking effect of its own against the split receiver bridge, engaged a locking lug in a slot in the receiver-top and another in the bolt-way floor. The large knurled-edge disc screwed to the back of the bolt was a distinctive feature. Few surviving Falisse & Trapmann guns have been reported, but an illustration in Rudolf Schmidt's *Die Handfeuerwaffen* (Bern, 1875) suggests that at least one was built on the lines of the British P/53 (Enfield) rifle musket; these guns had been made in quantity in Liége in the 1850s, and parts were undoubtedly available at very little cost.

• FN-Saive
The origins of these gas-operated auto-loading rifles, originally developed in the late 1930s, are obscure. Owing to the similarity of the breech-locks, it is suspected that Dieudonné Saive was familiar with the Tokarev – but it is not known whether this was due to supply of information from the Soviet Union, or if weapons captured by the Finns in the opening stages of the Winter War had been examined in Herstal. It has also been suggested that the inspiration was provided by experimental auto-loading rifles prepared in France prior to the First World War.

Whatever the source may have been, the SAFN and FAL rifles proved to be successful militarily – in the latter's case, almost unbelievably so.

EARLY PROTOTYPES
The Germans invaded Belgium before Saive and his team had completed preliminary work on the rifle. Many technicians subsequently escaped from Herstal (taking some blueprints with them) and eventually set to work in Britain, where the prototype SLEM – 'Self-Loading, Experimental Model' – was made in about 1943.

The experimental rifles developed into the Mle 49 or SAFN rifle after the end of the Second World War; this in turn led to the Fusil Automatique Léger (or LAR, 'Light Automatic Rifle') in the early 1950s.

MODEL 1949 RIFLE
Fusil Semi-automatique Mle 1949 ('SAFN')
Made by Fabrique Nationale d'Armes de Guerre, Herstal-lèz-Liège, about 1949-52.

Total production: 160,000? **Chambering options:** 7x57, 7.65x53, 7.9x57 or 30-06. **Action:** locked by tilting the bolt into engagment with the receiver; gas operated, selective fire.

DATA FOR A BELGIAN MILITARY EXAMPLE

Chambering: 30-06, rimless. 43.7in overall, 9.48lb empty. 23.2in barrel, 4-groove rifling; RH, concentric. Integral box magazine loaded from a

The SAFN or M1949 rifle, predecessor of the FAL.

The standard 7.62x51 FAL.

stripper clip, 10 rounds. Tangent-leaf and aperture sight graduated to 1500m (1640yd). 2720fps with 150-grain bullet. Mle 49 knife bayonet.

Development work on the experimental British SLEM rifle (q.v.) was completed in Herstal in 1947-8, and a production line had been readied. The rifle was adopted by the Belgian army as the '.30 Fusil Semi-automatique Mle 1949,' though it has also been known as the SAFN ('Semi-Automatic, Fabrique Nationale'). The term 'ABL', often misleadingly applied as a designation, arose from the property mark – 'Armée Belge Leger' – which was a combination of French ('Armée Belge') and Flemish ('Leger Belge').

The Mle 49 had a tall squared receiver, carrying the rear sight and its prominent guards, and the conventional pistol grip stock was held by a single swivel-carrying band. The rear swivel lay on the under-edge of the butt. A handguard ran from the chamber to the rear sight/gas-port block, and a bayonet bar lay beneath the exposed muzzle. The magazine was loaded from chargers, suitable guides being milled in the receiver-top ahead of the rear sight base. Muzzle brake/compensators were optional, and guns could be supplied to order in semi-automatic and selective-fire versions.

A sniper version with a telescope sight made by Société Belge d'Optique et d'Instruments de Précision was issued in small numbers, but was replaced first by optically-sighted FALs and then by FN-Mauser bolt-action rifles.

Though large-scale export orders had been fulfilled by 1952, the Mle 49 rifle proved to be unsuitable for prolonged arduous use. It was unbalanced by the height of the receiver, handled clumsily, and breakages in the trigger system sometimes led to unexpected automatic fire. Thus the Mle 49 was replaced by the FAL.

SAFN-type guns were supplied from Herstal to the Belgian Congo (Zaire), by way of the Belgian army; and to Colombia, Egypt, Indonesia and Luxembourg.

LIGHT AUTOMATIC RIFLE
Fusil Automatique Leger, 'FAL'
Made by Fabrique Nationale d'Armes de Guerre, Herstal-lèz-Liège, 1953 onward.

Total production: several million. **Still available. Chambering options:** 7x49mm or 7.62x51mm. **Action:** generally as Model 49, above.

DATA FOR A TYPICAL TYPE 50-64 PARA

Chambering: 7.62x51 NATO, rimless. 42.9in overall (33.25in with stock folded), 8.6lb empty. 21in barrel, 6-groove rifling; RH, concentric. Detachable box magazine, 20 rounds. Pivoting 'L'-sight for 150m (165yd) and 250m (275yd). 2750fps with standard NATO ball cartridges. Bayonet: optional.

A prototype FN assault rifle, chambered for the German 7.9mm intermediate (Kurz) cartridge, was demonstrated in 1948 at the company's Zutendael proving range. Development continued until, in 1950, trials were undertaken with standard (No. 1) and 'bullpup' (No. 2) rifles. Neither was made in quantity; No. 2 was abandoned owing to its poor handling characteristics, bad balance, and concern that the firer's cheek was too near the chamber should the case-head fail.

In 1951, however, the No. 1 rifle was enlarged to chamber the semi-experimental British 280 (7x49) cartridge. The resulting weapons had wood furniture with a ribbed forend, and a plain muzzle with no additional fittings. They were capable of fully-automatic fire, cyclic rate being 675±25rpm. Rejection of the 280 round in 1952, principally by the US Army, persuaded FN to rechamber the assault rifle for the 30 T65 pattern proffered by the Americans. The work was undertaken in Liége by Dieudonné Saive and Ernest Vervier.

Similar internally to the 280 rifles, the 7.62mm (.30) pattern had a folding carrying handle and a swell-pattern wooden forend with a short ribbed section. The standard barrel had a six-slot compensator, and the magazine well was still cut higher on the left side than the right. Detachable bipods, flash-hiders and grenade launchers were optional; and a knife bayonet with a conventional hilt could be attached.

Small-scale series production began in 1953 to provide guns for field trials in the principal NATO armies, and the first of a great many export orders – for Venezuela – was fulfilled. The earliest Venezuelan weapons chambered the British 280 cartridge.

The perfected rifle was adopted by the Belgian army in 1956. It had charger guides on the receiver; a smooth muzzle with neither grenade launcher nor flash suppressor; a nose-cap butt and a plain buttplate without a trap. A tubular bayonet doubled as a flash

suppressor/compensator if necessary, and the handguard was usually an injection-moulded plastic pattern. Synthetic furniture replaced the wood pattern as standard in 1963. The forend generally had a groove along the lower edge to accept the legs of the bipod, even though this was rarely fitted to infantry-weight rifles. Three cooling slots were standard.

SIMILAR GUNS

FAL Compétition, or 'LAR Competition'. Intended for 'Military Match' target-shooting competitions, this 308 Winchester (7.62x51) semi-automatic version of the FAL was made in small batches from about 1962 onward. About 44.5in long, with a 24.2in barrel (including the flash hider), it weighed 10lb with an empty magazine; the furniture was customarily graphite-color plastic.

FAL Type 50-00. This designation was applied from the 1970s onward to distinguish the standard or infantry-pattern FAL – 42.9in overall, 9.37lb empty, with nylon furniture, a fixed butt and a tubular flash suppressor. It was capable of firing fully automatically. Finish was usually durable gray phosphating.

FAL Type 50-64 Para. This had a folding cocking handle, and a change in the position of the breechblock return spring owing to the folding tubular-frame butt. It was similar mechanically to the standard infantry rifle.

FAL Type 50-63 Para. Measuring only 40.15in overall, or about 30.3in with the butt folded, this shortened gun had a folding cocking handle and a 300m (330yd) battle sight. It weighed about 8.25lb and had a 17.15in barrel. The hold-open and carrying handle of the 50-64 Para were omitted.

FAL Type 50-41 ('Fusil Automatique Lourd', 'LAR HB'). Introduced in 1958, this was special heavy-barrel FAL with a sturdier handguard, wood or synthetic furniture, and a combination flash suppressor/muzzle brake. A folding bipod was provided to suit a light support role, but the FALO was never successful – partly owing to its fixed barrel, which overheated if fire was sustained, but largely owing to an inexplicable tendency to fire twice and then jam on the third round of automatic fire. Consequently, some users of FAL-type rifles (e.g., Britain) never purchased heavy barrel versions, and others such as Australia soon withdrew them from front-line service. Many have since seen use as sniper weapons, as their weight was advantageous and fully automatic operation was unnecessary. The guns were typically 45.25in overall, weighed 13.25lb without the thirty-round magazine, and had sliding aperture sights graduated to 600m (655yd). Bayonets could not be mounted.

OTHER USERS

Belgian FAL-type guns have been supplied to many military forces, including –

Bahrain, in 1968.	Lebanon, in 1956.
The Belgian Congo (Zaire), in 1961.	Liberia, in 1962.
Burma, by way of Germany.	Libya, in 1955.
Burundi.	Luxembourg.
Cambodia (Kampuchea) in 1960.	Malawi, in 1974.
Chad.	Mauritania, apparently supplied by way of Cuba.
Chile in 1960.	
Colombia.	Morocco, in 1963.
The Congo People's Republic.	The Netherlands (FAL and FALO), in 1961.
Cuba.	
The Dominican Republic.	Oman.
Dubai (United Arab Emirates).	Paraguay, in 1956.
Eire.	Peru, FAL and FAL Para.
Ecuador.	Portugal, in 1959.
Ethiopia, possibly supplied by way of Chile or Colombia.	Qatar.
	Rwanda.
Ghana.	Saudi Arabia.
Greece (FAL and FAL Para).	Syria, in 1956.
Haiti.	Tanzania.
Honduras.	Thailand, in 1961.
Indonesia, in 1958.	Tunisia.
Kuwait (FAL and FAL Para), in 1957.	Turkey, by way of Germany.
	Uganda (possibly).

• FN-Sauer

FN Herstal SA made a small quantity of FN-Sauer rifles in 1977-82. Based on the Sauer Model 80, the Belgian rifle was distinguished by a massive forged-steel receiver separating the forend from the hog's back butt. The pistol grip and forend were checkered, and a ventilated rubber buttplate was standard. The chamberings included 270 Winchester, 7x64, 7mm Remington Magnum, 30-06, 300 Winchester Magnum and 8x68S.

• Francotte

One of Belgium's leading gunmakers since the early nineteenth century, though never renowned as particularly innovative, Francotte made bolt-action and break-open sporting guns prior to 1939, often for sale in North America through agencies such as Von Lengerke & Detmold or Abercrombie & Fitch.

Mauser-type rifles are currently being offered in three action lengths – short, standard and magnum – for chamberings as diverse as 218 Bee and 505 Gibbs Magnum. They generally have exquisitely checkered stocks and extensive engraving on the action. Box- and side-lock Double Rifles are also being promoted in a wide range of chamberings, alongside a single-barreled box-lock gun in 6.5x50R, 7x57R and 7x65R. See also '**Marga(-Francotte)**' and '**Martini-Francotte**'.

• Ghaye

Developed in the 1850s by a Liége-based gunsmith, this sliding-barrel system was operated by an underlever ahead of the trigger. The original pattern was hinged at the tip of the forend, pulling the barrel forward by means of an intermediate link when the lever-grip was pulled down.

Ghaye rifles were made for military trials and sporting use, in a wide variety of sizes and styles. Back-action locks were customary, with a shallow wooden insert in the barrel-supporting frame and an additional wooden forend beneath the barrel unit. Military prototypes have a barrel band and a nose cap; sporters and shotguns are usually half-stocked, or may lack the forend entirely. Engraving was popular and the tip of the underlever was often decoratively scrolled.

Owing to simplicity, and despite its inability to withstand high chamber pressures, the Ghaye system was popular in Belgium. Many minor modifications were made, the most popular being a reversal of the layout so that the operating-lever pivot lay immediately ahead of the trigger and the handgrip lay at the tip of the forend. Easier to handle than the standard design, this ensured that the breech-link pushed the barrels away from the standing breech instead of pulling them.

Made by Jamat-Smits of Liége, this Ghaye-type rifle displays its sliding barrel. (W&D)

• Larsen

August Larsen of Liége patented a butt-magazine system in 1883. Similar to the Schulhof type, the gravity-feed mechanism was incorporated experimentally in guns such as the 1871-pattern German Mauser and the Dutch Beaumont. Some guns had a multi-chamber butt compartment, with a capacity of 7+5+3 rounds (and one in the feeder), or, alternatively, a simple single-chamber design with a capacity of five rounds plus three in the feed-tube. A reciprocating lugged elevator bar transferred cartridges from the magazine to the chamber as the bolt was operated.

• Laurent

Dating from the 1860s, this breech-loading system was invented by a Liége-based gunmaker. A variation of designs such as Ghaye's, the barrel and forend were slid forward after a lever on the right side of the breech ahead of the back-action lock had been raised through 90 degrees to release the locking collar from the interrupted-thread cut into the barrel. The barrel could then be tipped downward to give access to the chamber. Also made in the guise of a shotgun or experimental military rifle, a typical 451 (56 Bore) Laurent sporter had a three-quarter stock with a straight checkered wrist, a round barrel, engraved metalwork and a spurred trigger guard. The rear sight was a minuscule quadrant type.

• Lebeau-Courally

Founded in 1865 and trading under the current title since 1896, Société Anonyme Continentale pour la Fabrication des Armes à Feu Lebeau-Courally has been one of Belgium's leading makers of high quality sporting guns for many years. However, though twentieth-century output has included Mauser sporting rifles, the range currently concentrates on break-open patterns; the standard chambering options are meagre compared with manufacturers such as Krieghoff or Blaser, but what the guns lack in versatility they more than compensate in the quality of construction and beauty of decoration.

OVER/UNDER DOUBLE RIFLES

Ambassadeur. Offered in 9.3x74R, with additional 20-Bore shotgun barrels, this has a distinctive three-piece forend with the fillets alongside the barrels. The sidelocks, breech, trigger guard and top lever are engraved with gold-inlaid oak leaves and high-relief game scenes on a blackened steel ground. Double triggers are standard fittings, and the butt generally has a straight wrist.

Battue. Intended for use against driven game, in 9.3x74R only, this short-barreled gun has a pistol grip butt and a standing-block rear sight let into the top of the quarter-rib. The Renaissance-style floral relief engraving, on the customary dark ground, is enhanced with gold inlaid vine-leaf and stem work. Finely detailed hunting scenes – e.g., deer, wild boar – appear on the sideplates and the underside of the frame. Double trigger are standard.

SIDE-BY-SIDE DOUBLE RIFLES

Ardennes. This is an Anson & Deeley-type boxlock in 9.3x74R, with a scalloped rear edge to the frame. Fine English scroll engraving appears on the action and fences, while the action flats end in tear-drop finials. The gun has a double-trigger mechanism, a checkered pistol grip butt, and a folding rear sight set into the tip of the double rib.

Big Five. Originally created for the film *In the Blood*, and chambered for the 458 Winchester Magnum, this gun is a classic sidelock with a straight-wrist butt. Big Fives are also supplied with an exchangeable set of 375 H&H Magnum barrels with telescope-sight mount blocks on the quarter-rib. The decoration consists largely of acanthus-leaf work and gold-line inlays, accompanying African game scenes – an elephant beneath the frame, rhinos on the sideplates, a leopard on the top lever.

Safari. Made only in 470 Nitro Express, this Big Game rifle has double sidelocks and a reinforced frame. High-relief matted-ground Renaissance tracery is cut into the action, barrels, rib and pistol grip cap, with finely detailed trophy heads (e.g., Cape Buffalo) in panels. Mounted on the quarter-rib, the Express-type rear

The Lebeau-Courally Safari 470 Nitro Express side-by-side double rifle.

The Lebeau-Courally Tyrol, a single-barrel design in 7x65.

sight has a fixed block for 50m and folding leaves for 100m and 150m; double triggers are standard.

SINGLE RIFLE

Tyrol. Offered in 7x65R only, this break-open design had a single side-lock on the left side with a matching sideplate on the right. The barrel is octagonal, locked in the frame by a double-bite slide and a double Greener ('Kersten') crossbolt. An ejector and a set-trigger can be supplied on request. The decoration is customarily fine English scroll and bouquet engraving, with oak leaves on the fences and trophy heads – chamois, moufflon, ibex – in the panels. Bases for telescope mounts are integral with the quarter-rib.

• Lecocq & Hoffmann

Lecocq & Hoffmann of Brussels offered Mauser-type sporting rifles prior to 1940 and again in the 1955-70 period. Built on refurbished military-surplus actions, the post-war standard model had a half-stock with a straight comb. The shallowly curved pistol grip and tapering round-tipped forend were extensively checkered; a multi-leaf Express rear sight appeared on a short rib and a detachable magazine floorplate was used. Chamberings included 8x60, 9x57, 9.3x62, 9.5x57 and 10.75x68.

A big-game rifle was made for the 375 H&H Magnum round. It had a tangent-leaf or Express rear sight, a four-round magazine and a double set trigger system. Pre-war guns had flat panels alongside the action, rounded pistol grips and schnabel-tip forends; post-war examples usually had ventilated rubber butt-plates, capped pistol grips and rounded forends.

• Lenders-Lambin

This bolt-action needle rifle, developed in Liége in the 1860s, was intended as an inexpensive method of converting caplock rifle muskets; examples of the British P/53 (Enfield) and the French Mle 57 are known to have been among them. A cylindrical extension attached to the breech contained a bolt with a small handle on the right side. The handle was turned up to the left to allow the bolt to slide backward in its channel, exposing the chamber to receive a new cartridge.

The guns retained conventional side- or back-action locks and external hammers, but some were altered to fire a proprietary cartridge with an internal priming pellet in the base. A pin on the nose of a spring-steel striker bar, attached to the top of the barrel behind the rear sight, passed through a hole drilled vertically in the breech. The hammer struck the pin downward into the priming pellet as the gun fired, but the spring-steel bar then pulled the pin back out of the chamber as the hammer was drawn back to half-cock to allow the breech to be opened. This type of ignition was rapidly overtaken by rim- and centerfire metal-case ammunition, and the Lenders-Lambin rifle had disappeared by 1870.

• Marga(-Francotte)

Uldarique Marga, an officer in the Belgian infantry, began his designing activities in the 1880s and was still actively engaged in development of autoloaders in 1909.

The earliest bolt-action rifles were made in accordance with a series of patents granted in 1889-92. The so-called 'Model 1888' had a very simple striker system with a 'V'-spring contained in the bulbous bolt handle – a feature clearly inspired by the Dutch Beaumont (q.v.) – and a sliding safety catch lay on the back of the bolt where the cocking piece would normally appear. Patents of

addition granted in 1891 and 1892 added a clip-fed magazine and an improved extractor respectively.

All Marga rifles had an interrupted-thread lock on the rear of the bolt body. They seem to have pressed the 1889-pattern Mauser close in the Belgian army trials of 1888-9, but ultimately encountered no tangible success.

1888-TYPE TRIALS RIFLE

Made by August Francotte & Co., Liége, 1888.
Total production: 500? **Chambering:** 7.65x53, rimless. **Action:** locked by an interrupted thread in the form of multiple lugs rotating into the bridge of the receiver as the bolt handle was turned down.

51.1in overall, 9.2lb empty. 30.8in barrel, 4-groove rifling; RH, concentric? Integral box magazine, 5 rounds. Leaf sight graduated to 1900m. 2050fps with Mle 89 standard ball ammunition. Knife bayonet.

These rifles were easily recognized by the protruding magazine, formed as part of the trigger guard, and by the unusually large bolt handle. They had one-piece stocks with a straight-wrist butt, two screwed bands, and a bayonet lug beneath the plain nose cap. Swivels lay under the butt and center band; a cleaning rod lay under the forend, and there was a notable reduction in the depth of the forend ahead of the back band.

Rifles of this type do not appear to bear manufacturer's markings, so the attribution to Francotte should be treated with caution unless an inspection mark in the form of a small crowned 'A.F.' can be found.

SIMILAR GUNS

1894-type rifle. About 2500 of these were made by Francotte about 1894-1902, mostly (but possibly not exclusively) in 7.65x53. The guns shared the basic bolt and extractor design of their predecessors, but an internal staggered-row 5-round box magazine was substituted for the protruding single-row type. The one-piece stock had a straight wrist and a single screwed barrel band, with a hand guard running from the receiver ring to the band. The tangent-leaf sight was graduated to 2000m (2185yd) and the plain nose cap had a lug on its underside, apparently for the standard 1889-pattern Belgian knife bayonet.

These Marga rifles (possibly designed for trials in Brazil) were still being actively promoted by Francotte as late as 1900, when they were exhibited at the Paris Exposition Universelle. A typical example is marked 'A. FRANCOTTE' and 'A LIÉGE' on the left side of the receiver. Most survivors chamber the 7.65x53 cartridge, though 7x57 and 303 examples are said to exist. It also seems likely that sporting guns may have been made alongside rifles destined for military trials.

• Martini-Francotte

The British-pattern Martini was extensively copied in sporting guns made in Liége in 1880-1910, principally by Auguste Francotte. Many guns incorporated Francotte's patented cocking indicator, whose blade protruded above the right receiver wall, and also had safety catches.

Belgian-made guns can usually be identified by their proof marks, even though marked as a product of another company; the Braendlin Armoury Co. Ltd of Birmingham, active until 1888, purchased many of its rifles in Liége and Francotte maintained an agency in London for about twenty years from 1873 onward.

• Masquelier

Manufacture d'Armes de Chasse Masquelier of Liége offered AMD-1, AMD-2 (both in 8x68S) and AMD-3 (7x64) rifles on the basis of FN-Mauser actions. The AMD-2 was simply an AMD-1 with engraving on the receiver and better-quality woodwork. The rifles had slender pistol grip stocks with Monte Carlo combs and rounded forends with a contrasting rosewood or ebony tip. Thin white spacers generally accompanied the shoulder pad, pistol grip cap and forend tip. (Note: Masquelier may have purchased the guns from Raick Frères..

• Mauser (state type)

This section contains details of the Belgian government-issue guns, which were made by several different contractors. See also **'Mauser (FN): bolt action'**.

In 1886, the Belgian militry authorities began testing rifles submitted by Francotte, Jarmann, Kropatschek, Lee, Mauser, Nagant and Schulhof. None of these was successful, and new tests began

The 7.65x53 M1889 infantry rifle, the first successful small-bore Mauser.

in 1888 with small caliber rifles. These included the Mauser C/88 and C/89; a Liége-made Schulhof; 'Engh' rifles made by SA Manufacture Liégeoise d'Armes à Feu; a Pieper; and several Lee designs. On 12th July 1889, Alard Bormans and Henri Pieper signed a contract on behalf of Fabrique Nationale d'Armes de Guerre to produce 150,000 of whatever pattern of repeating rifle the Belgian government ultimately accepted; on 22nd October, the Minister of War obtained a licence to allow Mauser rifles to be made in accredited private factories. In June 1891, however, Ludwig Loewe proposed to license FN's Mauser production directly, the offer was quickly accepted, and a revised contract was signed in Berlin on 26th November.

MODEL 1889 RIFLE
Fusil d'Infanterie Mle 1889

Made by Fabrique Nationale d'Armes de Guerre, Herstal-lèz-Liége (275,000?); by Fabrique d'Armes de l'État, Liége, about 1895-1914; by Anciens Éstblissements Pieper, Herstal-lèz-Liége; and by Hopkins & Allen, Norwich, Connecticut, 1914-16 (about 8000); a few were also made in Britain during the First World War.

Total production: not known. **Chambering:** 7.65x53, rimless. **Action:** locked by two lugs on the bolt head engaging recesses in the receiver ring behind the chamber as the bolt handle turns down.

50.2in overall, 8.88lb empty. 30.7in barrel, 4-groove rifling; RH, concentric. Fixed box magazine loaded from a stripper clip, 5 rounds. Ramp-and-leaf sight graduated to 1900m (2080yd). 2050fps with Mle 89 ball cartridges. Mle 89 knife bayonet.

After extensive testing, the authorities decided to adopt a much-improved Mauser rifle. Tooling had begun by the end of January 1891 and, on 31st December, Fabrique Nationale delivered the first four rifles to the Ministry of War. The 'Fusil à Répétition, système Mauser, Modèle de 1889' was formally adopted on 6th February 1892. It was the first true small caliber Mauser. The one-piece bolt was derived from that of the Gew. 88, with two symmetrical locking lugs, but the handle turned down behind the solid bridge of the receiver and a cocking-piece housing or bolt-shroud was screwed into the rear of the perfected bolt (C/89 prototypes had used a lug attachment system).

The charger-loaded magazine was an improvement on Mannlicher clip patterns, as the charger was not essential to the action. Consequently, the magazine was simpler, less prone to mis-feed, and could be replenished with single rounds. A suitable guide was milled into the leading edge of the receiver bridge, its companion being formed by an extension of the spring-loaded bolt stop to hold the charger in place. Spent chargers were thrown clear as the bolt closed.

The rifle had a straight wristed one-piece stock; a housing for the follower-arm pivot projected from the lower front edge of the magazine case. A single spring-retained barrel band and a nose cap with a bayonet lug on its underside were used, but the barrel had a full-length annular jacket inspired by the Gew. 88. Sling swivels lay beneath the barrel band and on the under-edge of the butt.

By 30th June 1893, more than forty thousand Mle 89 rifles had been delivered to the army; daily production had stabilized at 250 rifles, 25,000 bullets and 25,000 cartridge cases. The last of the 150,000 rifles was delivered on 31st December 1894. Another Belgian government contract for 1889-type rifles was given to Fabrique Nationale in June 1903, followed by another in November 1906.

Large numbers of Mle 89 rifles were seized by the Germans when the First World War began. Many were issued without alteration, but some were apparently converted to fire the standard German 8x57mm cartridge. The remnants of the Belgian army fighting alongside the French placed production contracts with Hopkins & Allen after the fall of Belgium. In addition, a syndicate of exiles acquired facilities to make Mle 89 rifles in England. These are marked simply 'ÉTAT BELGE' and 'BIRMINGHAM' above the chamber.

The knife bayonet was replaced by the Mle 24 épée pattern in the mid 1920s, and conversion to Mle 89/36 (q.v.) standards began in 1935.

SIMILAR GUNS

Model 1889 Civil Guard rifle (Mle 89 de la Garde Civique). On 11th February 1896, issue of the infantry rifle was extended to the Corps Spéciaux de la Garde Civique, accompanied by a bayonet with a blade of 11.8in instead of the standard 9.8in.

Model 1889 sniper rifle (Mle 89 pour Tireur d'Élite). Introduced in 1916 in small numbers, this was little more than a standard infantry rifle with an offset mount for a suitable telescope sight on the left side of the receiver. The action could still be charger-loaded. Winchester sights were most common, but other patterns were used in small numbers.

MODEL 1889 CAVALRY CARBINE
Carabine de Cavallerie, Mle 1889

Made by Fabrique d'Armes de l'État, Liége, about 1892-1914.

Total production: not known. **Chambering:** 7.65x53, rimless. **Action:** as Mle 1889 rifle, above.

34.85in overall, 6.65lb empty. 15.75in barrel, 4-groove rifling; RH, concentric. Fixed box magazine loaded from a stripper clip, 5 rounds. Ramp-and-leaf sight graduated to 1900m (2080yd). About 1835fps with Mle 89 ball cartridges. No bayonet.

Adopted in 1892, this was simply a much shortened form of the infantry rifle. The bolt handle was turned downward, the rear sight was mounted on the chamber reinforce, and the forend extended only to the barrel band. This exposed a considerable length of the barrel jacket and cleaning rod.

A slotted plate was screwed to the left side of the butt to accept a stud on the carrying harness. Early carbines had a distinctive

Belgian infantry machine-gunners with a Maxim. Note the M1889 rifle and bayonet carried by the man on the right.

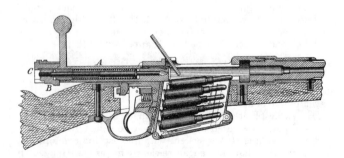

A longitudinal section of the M1889 Mauser action.

The Belgian M1889 cavalry carbine.

The Belgian M1889 (Mauser) fortress artillery musketoon.

pivoting cover to protect the stud-slot, but this was eventually abandoned.

MODEL 1889 CADET CARBINE
Carabine des Enfants de Troupe, Mle 1889
Made by Fabrique d'Armes de l'État, Liége, about 1899-1914.
Total production: not known. **Chambering:** 7.65x53, rimless. **Action:** as Mle 1889 rifle, above.

41.15in overall, 7.78lb empty. 21.65in barrel, 4-groove rifling; RH, concentric. Fixed box magazine loaded with a stripper clip, 5 rounds. Ramp-and-leaf sight graduated to 1900m (2080yd). About 1920fps with Mle 89 ball cartridges. Mle 89 knife bayonet.

This gun – apparently dating from 1899 – was similar to the carbine issued to dismounted gendarmerie and fortress artillery, but had a straight bolt handle and the barrel band lay midway between the rear sight base and the nose cap. Few were made.

MODEL 1889 GENDARMERIE AND ARTILLERY CARBINE
Carabine pour le Gendarmerie à Pied et de l'Artillerie de Fortresse, Mle 1889 ('carbine for dismounted gendarmerie and fortress artillery')
Made by Fabrique d'Armes de l'Èta about 1899-1914.
Total production: not known. **Chambering:** 7.65x53, rimless. **Action** and other details as Mle 1889 cadet carbine, above.

Issued from 9th May 1904, this shared the action, stock, and barrel band/nose cap of the infantry rifle. The barrel band lay closer to the nose cap than rear sight base, distinguishing it from the otherwise similar cadet carbine. The bolt handle was generally turned downward. Described as 'avec yatagan,' the gun took a long-bladed bayonet. In 1916, however, surviving bayonets in the hands of the gendarmerie were replaced by the Mle 16 épée type.

MODEL 1889 GENDARMERIE CARBINE
Carabine pour Gendarmerie à Cheval, Mle 1889 ('carbine for mounted gendarmerie')
Made by Fabrique d'Armes de l'Èta about 1904-14.
Total production: not known. **Chambering:** 7.65x53, rimless. **Action:** as Mle 1889 rifle, above. Dimensions generally as Mle 89 cavalry carbine.

A minor 1904-vintage variant of the cavalry carbine, this had a conventional-length stock – though the barrel band was almost directly behind the nose cap. A sling swivel on the band was used in conjunction with a bracket screwed to the right side of the butt. A long-blade ('yatagan') version of the Mle 89 knife bayonet was issued until the First World War, when it was replaced by the Mle 16 épée pattern with a shortened Mle 82 (Comblain) blade.

MODEL 1889 CYCLISTS' CARBINE
Carabine pour les Cyclistes de la Garde Civique, Mle 1889 ('carbine for the cyclists of the civil guard')
Made by Fabrique d'Armes de l'État from 1907 until about 1912, this 7.65mm carbine apparently had a modified safety that could not be applied when the gun was cocked. The rear sight was graduated to 1200m (1310yd), a sling bar lay on the left side of the band, and a swivel was attached to the left side of the butt.

MODEL 1916 CARBINE
Carabine pour Mitrailleurs, Batteries d'Infanterie et Agents de Transmission, Mle 1916 ('carbine for machine gunners, infantry-gun crews and despatch riders')
This was adopted for a selection of special and ancillary troops during the First World War. It was similar to the 1889-type carbine issued to dismounted gendarmerie and fortress artillery, but had a 23.6in barrel and a sling bar in the left side of the butt.

MODEL 1935 SHORT RIFLE
Fusil Mle 1935
Made by Fabrique Nationale d'Armes de Guerre, Herstal-lèz-Liége, 1935-40 (see text).
Total production: not known. **Chambering:** 7.65x53, rimless. **Action:** locked by two lugs on the bolt head turning into recesses in the receiver ring behind the chamber as the bolt handle turns downward, and by a safety lug opposing the bolt-handle base.

43.6in overall, 9lb empty 23.45in barrel, 4-groove rifling; RH, concentric. Internal box magazine loaded from a stripper clip, 5 rounds. Tangent-leaf sight graduated to 2000m (2185yd). 2350fps with Mle 35 ball cartridges. Mle 24 épée bayonet.

This 1935-vintage rifle was a standard 1898-pattern Mauser, with a non-rotating extractor, a safety lug on the bolt and most of the refinements found on the Gew. 98. The barrel jacket was abandoned and the magazine lay within the stock. The barrel band and the nose cap both hinged open for removal, an open stacking swivel was fitted, and the bayonet lug projected beneath the nose cap.

The earliest examples were converted in the state arms factory – Fabrique d'Armes de l'État — from Gew. 98 received as reparations from Germany after the end of the First World War. Production of new guns had hardly begun in the FN rifle factory when the Germans invaded Belgium once again in 1940. Work stopped immediately. A few sniper rifles were distinguished by ring mounts above the chamber and on the receiver bridge, and by a special rubber cheekpiece fitted in a metal cradle on the comb of the butt.

MODEL 1889/36 SHORT RIFLE
Fusil Mle 1889/36
Apparently converted by Fabrique d'Armes de l'État, Liége; and by Anciene Établissements Pieper, Herstal-lèz-Liége, 1936-40.
Total production: 7500-10,000? **Chambering:** 7.65x53, rimless. **Action:** as Mle 1889 rifle, above.

43.05in overall, 8.32lb empty. 23.6in barrel; 4-groove rifling; RH, concentric. Fixed box magazine loaded from a stripper clip, 5 rounds. Tangent-leaf sight graduated to 2000m (2185yd). 2350fps with Mle 35 ball cartridges. Mle 24 épée bayonet.

The conversion of Mle 89 rifles to Mle 35 standards began in the Pieper factory in 1936. The resulting weapon combined the action and shortened stock of the Mle 89 with the barrel, sight, forend and hinged nose cap of the Mle 35. A recoil bolt was added through the stock beneath the chamber. The German invasion of Belgium brought operations to a halt in 1940 after only a few thousand rifles had been transformed. Work does not seem to have been resumed after 1945.

• Mauser (FN type)

By the middle of 1894, Fabrique Nationale had supplied Mauser rifles and cartridges to the Netherlands, Spain, Serbia, Brazil, Chile, Brazil, China, Norway and Costa Rica. In December, Chile approached the company to place an order for sixty thousand Mauser-system rifles, but Mauser objected to the fulfilment of non-Belgian orders and the irritated Chileans placed the order with Loewe. In December 1894, Mauser asked Fabrique Nationale to cease using the patents covering the 1893 or Spanish-pattern Mauser on the grounds that these were not part of the original 1891-vintage agreement.

Backed by a campaign in the Belgian Press and parliament, Fabrique Nationale tried to fight the injunction throughout 1895, but it was eventually decided at a high level in the government that there were no real grounds for objection. FN conceded the case. In February 1896, therefore, FN and Loewe amicably negotiated a new contract with Mauser.

Finally, in January 1897, a production agreement was signed by the principal manufacturers of Mauser rifles – FN, Mauser, DWM and OEWG – under which each was allocated a specific quota. Contract work continued until August 1914, ceased for the duration of the First World War and then resumed in 1919.

By 1940, FN Mauser rifle production since 1899, excluding Belgian orders, amounted to at least 517,000. In addition to the guns considered here individually, the company had made at least 143,000 'unattributed' examples for France, Greece, Lithuania, Paraguay, Peru, Venezuela and Yemen.

MODEL 1922 RIFLE
Fusil d'Infanterie Mle 1922
Made by Fabrique Nationale d'Armes de Guerre, Herstal-lèz-Liége, 1922-5.

Total production: 50,000? **Chambering options:** 7x57, 7.65x53 or 7.9x57. **Action:** locked by two lugs on the bolt head turning into the receiver ring behind the chamber as the bolt was turned down, and by a safety lug opposing the bolt-handle base.
DATA FOR A TYPICAL EXAMPLE
Chambering: 7x57, rimless. About 48.7in overall, 8.85lb empty. 29.15in barrel, 4-groove rifling; RH, concentric. Internal box magazine loaded from a stripper clip, 5 rounds. Tangent-leaf sight graduated to 2000m (2185yd). 2575fps with FN ball cartridges. FN export-pattern bayonet.

Introduced in 1922, these were the first post-war Mausers to be made in the reconditioned and re-equipped Herstal factory. The Mle 22 was mechanically similar to the Gew. 98, but had the standard export fittings – a tangent-leaf rear sight, a handguard running forward from the receiver ring, and a conventional bayonet attachment incorporating a muzzle ring. The barrel band was particularly narrow and the nose cap was as simple as it could be.

Though Mle 22 FN Mausers went to Brazil, the market for full-length rifles was declining fast. The Mle 24 short rifle described below soon proved to be much more popular.

SIMILAR GUNS
Model 1922 carbine (or 'mousqueton'). This was made in comparatively small numbers, as the market for military weapons had declined greatly at the end of the First World War. It was easily recognized by the fittings, particularly the nose cap.

MODEL 1924 SHORT RIFLE
Fusil Court Mle 1924
Made by Fabrique Nationale d'Armes de Guerre, Herstal-lèz-Liége, 1924-40 and 1946-54.

Total production: 650,000? **Chambering options:** 7x57, 7.65x53 or 7.9x57. **Action:** as M1922 rifle, above.
DATA FOR A TYPICAL EXAMPLE
Chambering: 7.65x53mm, rimless. 42.9in overall, 8.4lb empty. 23.25in barrel, 4-groove rifling; RH, concentric. Internal charger-loaded box magazine, 5 rounds. Tangent-leaf sight graduated to 2000m (2185yd). 2380fps with FN ball cartridges. FN export-pattern bayonet.

A short rifle appeared in 1924 to supplement, then replace the Mle 1922. It had a conventional 1898-pattern Mauser action and a non-rotating extractor. Though a straight-wrist stock was offered for a short period, virtually all known guns have a pistol grip pattern with a single band and either a simple nose cap or a German 'H' pattern. The mounts were retained by springs let into the right side of the forend. A handguard generally ran either from the receiver ring to the forend, or only as far as the barrel band. Swivels generally lay under the band and on the under-edge of the butt, but variations were sometimes made by individual purchasers. Production ceased when the Germans invaded Belgium in May 1940, though the Fabrique Nationale factory subsequently made parts for the Kar. 98k. Work began again after the end of the Second World War.

SIMILAR GUNS
Model 1924 rifle. This was made in very small numbers. It was identical mechanically with the short rifle, but had a longer barrel and forend. The nose cap was usually a German-inspired 'H' type.

Model 1924 carbine. This was also made in small numbers, being shorter and lighter than the short rifle. The bolt handle was generally turned down towards the stock.

Model 1924/30 short rifle. Whether these are Mle 24 brought up to Mle 30 standards or simply an alternative designation for the true Mle 30 has not been resolved.

Model 1930 short rifle. Modifications were made to the basic Mauser action in the late 1920s, advancing the designation appropriately. It is believed that they were largely changes of dimension, and that, externally at least, the weapons remained similar to their predecessors. Attempts have been made to link the changes to matters of nose cap, handguard and stock design, but these were largely controlled by the purchaser and may not have been the arbiters. Production of Mle 30-type rifles began again in 1946, though demand was never great. Too many war-surplus weapons were available for the pre-war markets to be re-established.

Training rifle. FN also made a special 22 version of the Model 24/30 short rifle after the Second World War had ended. Externally similar to the full-bore guns, the rimfire pattern was easily identified by its small caliber, the simplified bolt, and a blacked or phosphated finish.

MODEL 1935/46 SHORT RIFLE
Fusil Mle 1935/46
Made by Fabrique Nationale, Herstal, 1946-53.

Total production: possibly 5000 conversions and about 10,000 new guns. **Chambering:** 30-06, rimless. **Action:** as Mle 1935 rifle, above.
43.5in overall, 8.95lb empty. 23.2in barrel, 4-groove rifling; RH, concentric. Internal box magazine loaded from a stripper clip, 5 rounds. Tangent-leaf sight graduated to 2000m (2185yd). About 2740fps with US M2 ball cartridges. Mle 24 épée bayonet.

Conversion of surviving Mle 35 rifles (see 'Mauser, State types') for the US service cartridge began in 1946, owing to the tremendous quantities of war-surplus guns and ammunition provided to re-equip the Belgian armed forces. Alterations included a groove cut across the face of the chamber to accommodate the longer American cartridge, and the guides on the receiver re-cut to accept US stripper clips.

SIMILAR GUNS
Model 1950. Production of new 30-06 Mle 30-type guns began in FN's Herstal factory. The magazine well was lengthened, though the grooved chamber face was retained. The guides accepted the standard American stripper clip. Internally, the raceway for the left locking lug was milled through the shoulder in the receiver ring in typical post-1946 FN fashion. A typical rifle

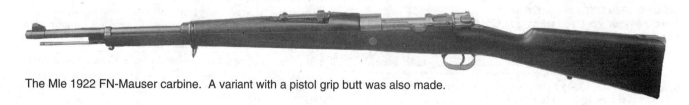

The Mle 1922 FN-Mauser carbine. A variant with a pistol grip butt was also made.

was marked with a crowned 'B' above the chamber, the cypher of King Baudoin, above the property mark and date – 'ABL', '1953'.

MODEL 30-11 SNIPER RIFLE

Made by Fabrique Nationale Herstal SA, Herstal, about 1975-87.
Total production: 500? Chambering options: 7.62x51 NATO or 7.9x57.
Action: as Mle 1935 rifle, above.
DATA FOR A TYPICAL EXAMPLE
   Chambering: 7.62x51 NATO. 43.9in overall, 10.7lb without sights. 19.7in barrel (excluding flash hider), 4-groove rifling; RH, concentric. Internal box magazine, 5 rounds. Optical sight. 2785fps with standard ball ammunition.

This was a refined version of the standard Mle 30 short rifle, adapted for precision shooting. A special heavy barrel was fitted, the trigger was capable of limited adjustment, and the entire rear end of the extraordinary butt could slide vertically. The length of the butt could be altered by adding wooden spacers.

Though most rifles were fitted with mounts for optical or electro-optical sights, a few were supplied with Anschütz aperture sights. A rail set into the underside of the forend accepted a hand-stop or sling mount, and even a MAG-type bipod. Some guns were made with flash eliminators, and a few had a detachable 10-round box magazine.

SPORTING GUNS

Fabrique Nationale made sporting rifles in small numbers prior to the First World War – apparently to use old 1893-pattern actions that had remained in stock since the 1890s. Chambered for 7x57 or 7.65x53 cartridges, they cocked on the closing stroke of the bolt and were stocked in minimal English fashion, with straight combs and slender round-tipped forends.

POST-1924 SPORTING RIFLES

Guns made between the wars were based on the 1924-pattern military action. The most popular version had a straight-comb half-stock, though fully stocked examples are known. However, production does not seem to have been excessive.

Work on 1924-type sporting rifles began again in 1947, the earliest being assembled from a selection of pre-war and wartime parts. Bolt handles were swept downward, though the first guns retained a simple military-style single-stage trigger. The chamberings were initially 7x57, 8x57 and 30-06 only, 270 Winchester being added in 1948.

Changes were soon made: the underside of the bolt-handle knob was checkered, the military-style trigger was altered to give a single pressure, the magazine floorplate release was improved, and the left wall of the receiver retained its height where the thumb cut-away would normally lie. In the autumn of 1948, the safety was altered to limit its rotation (but remained on top of the bolt shroud) and the stripper-clip guides were deleted. Alternative 220 Swift, 257 Roberts, 250-3000 Savage and 300 Savage chamberings were available by the beginning of 1950; 243 Winchester, 244 Remington, 308 Winchester, 8x60S, 9.3x62, 9.5x57 and 10.75x68 were subsequently added.

Most of the rifles had straight combs and generously proportioned forends with rounded tips. Their barrels were usually 24in long, weights were 7.5-8.2lb, and the magazines held five rounds. Guns intended for sale in North America had Monte Carlo-type stocks and Tri-Range rear sights; most European examples had straight combs and folding two-leaf sights.

SIMILAR GUNS

Presentation-grade guns were introduced in the mid 1950s, with selected stocks and engraved metalwork, but were discontinued in 1963.

200-SERIES GUNS

Known as the Deluxe or 'Serie 200' after the introduction of the 300-pattern guns in 1957, the standard FN-Mauser action was discontinued in the early 1960s – though new guns were available from dealers' stock for several years.

SIMILAR GUNS

Magnum version. This appeared in 1953, based on the standard action with the magazine box and the bolt head altered to accommodate the 300 or 375 H&H Magnum cartridges. It was abandoned about 1963, having been offered for the 264 Winchester, 7mm Remington, 300 Winchester or 458 Winchester magnum rounds in addition to the original Holland & Holland types. Magazine capacity was restricted to three cartridges instead of the customary five.

Bench Rest. The first of these single shot actions appeared in 1955, with a solid-base receiver. Three differing bolts accepted 222 Remington, 30-06, or the belted magnums.

300-SERIES GUNS

In the mid 1950s, Fabrique Nationale developed the 'Serie 300' action, announced in Europe in 1956 and later known as the 'Supreme'. Characterized by a radial safety on the right side of the action behind the bolt handle, it had a smooth-topped receiver bridge and a modified trigger mechanism. A hinged magazine floorplate was standard, the release catch being set into the front of the trigger guard bow. The trigger itself was a minor adaption of the Sako No. 4.

The actions were successful commercially, being used by Colt, Harrington & Richardson, High Standard and Marlin. They were being made in several patterns by 1970, ranging from the No. 1, for standard-length cartridges (e.g., 270 Winchester and 30-06), to the No. 7 for magnums such as 264 or 338 Winchester; the receiver design remained unchanged, alterations being made only to the magazine and the bolt where necessary. The No. 6 Bench Rest pattern could be supplied with three differing bolts, depending on cartridge case-head diameter.

• Mauser, other types

In addition to the military Mausers, and the guns made by Fabrique Nationale, many Belgian gunsmiths have made sporters. Most of these have been built either on refurbished ex-military actions (though very rarely the Mle 1889) or on commercial-finish actions purchased from Fabrique Nationale. Separate entries will be found for Dumoulin & Fils, Aug. Francotte, Lecocq & Hoffmann, Manufacture d'Armes de Chasse Masquelier and Raick Frères.

The standard FN-Mauser sniper rifle, showing its unusual butt.

• Montigny

The Brussels gunsmith Joseph Montigny is best known for his participation in the design and production of the *Mitrailleuse*, a primitive European machine gun. He also made a quantity of sporting rifles and shotguns embodying a variation of the breech mechanism pioneered by the Swiss-born gunmaker Samuel Pauly (q.v.). The breech cap, pivoted laterally on the chamber, could be lifted upward when a catch inside the operating-lever ring had been released from the upper tang. As the cap was lifted upward, it released a flap-like toggle lock, rotated the striker or hammer to half cock (depending on individual construction), and withdrew the breech-bolt so that the chamber could receive a new cartridge. Closing the breech forced the toggle joint below the axis of the breech and re-locked the action. Cocking was completed by pressing the lever projecting vertically ahead of the trigger guard.

• Nagant

Perhaps best known as a maker of revolvers, Manufacture d'Armes E. & L. Nagant Frères ('Nagant Brothers arms manufactory') of Liége was the principal European licensee of the Remington rolling-block breech system; countless thousands of rifles, short rifles and carbines were made prior to the 1890s to satisfy military contracts and commercial demand. The Nagant Remingtons also included double-barreled constabulary pistols and quirky side-by-side shotguns embodying a modified Belgian-patent breech mechanism. A smooth-bore Cape Rifle of this type—sold by Christie's in 1997—was 43.25in overall, had 27.5in stub-twist barrels and weighed about 8.19lb. The Nagants also made a few hundred bolt-action rifles for trials held in Russia (q.v.) in 1889-90; the precursors of the Mosin-Nagant, these are described in greater detail in the appropriate section.

• Pieper (Bayard), autoloading type

These guns were made by Anciens Établissements Pieper of Herstal, successors to Henri Pieper & Co. in 1905. The products were customarily sold under the 'Bayard' brandname.

BAYARD SEMI-AUTOMATIC CARBINE

Made by Anciens Établissements Pieper, Herstal-lèz-Liége, about 1908-13.

Total production: not known. **Chambering options:** 22 Short or 22 Long rimfire. **Action:** no mechanical breech lock; blowback, semi-automatic only.
DATA FOR DELUXE 'HALF-AUTOMATIC' 22 LONG PATTERN
42.9in overall, 4.45lb empty. 23.6in barrel, 4-groove rifling; RH, concentric. Single shot only. Block and two-leaf rear sight graduated to 150m (165yd). 1055fps with 29-grain bullet.

These were 22 rimfire guns with walnut half-stocks. Most of them had checkering on the shallow pistol grips, and were often 'take-down' designs relying on a knurled-head bolt beneath the forend to hold the action in the stock. The trigger guard was usually as stamped metal strip.

The guns were made in several patterns, but have proved difficult to classify. They had cylindrical receivers, charging handles on the right side of the bolt and a prominent spring-leaf ejector on the left side of the breech. However, though some had tube magazines in the butt, most appear to have been 'half-automatic' – single shot guns which ejected automatically, but had to be reloaded manually.

THE GUNS
Standard pattern. This had a short stock with a tapered forend; a 19.7in barrel gave it an overall length of 38.6in, weight being only 3.5lb. Swivels were fitted under the butt and on the tip of the forend, and a fixed standing-block rear sight appeared on the barrel above the breech.

Deluxe pattern. This was larger than the ordinary version, and had a walnut stock with checkering on the pistol grip and forend. The rear sight was usually a small standing 50m block with leaves for 100m and 150m.

• Pieper (Henri), bolt-action type

An improved form of the Pieper rifle, with a bolt based on the Mauser and the handle locking down into a slot in the receiver bridge, was allegedly made for Brazil (q.v.) in 1894.

1888-TYPE TRIALS RIFLE

Made by Henri Pieper & Cie, Liége, 1888-90.

Total production: a few hundred? **Chambering options:** 7.65x53 and possibly others. **Action:** locked by an interrupted-thread in the form of multiple lugs rotating into the receiver bridge as the bolt handle was turned down.
DATA FOR A TYPICAL 7.65MM EXAMPLE
52in overall, about 10lb empty. 32in barrel, 4-groove rifling; RH, concentric. Internal rotary magazine, 6 rounds. Tangent-leaf sight graduated to 1900m. About 2000fps with 187-grain bullet. Sword bayonet.

This interesting rifle was patented by Henri Pieper in February 1888. Large and cumbersome, it had a multi-lug bolt, a rotary magazine, a pivoting cut-off lever on top of the receiver bridge, and a hammer-fired trigger system cocked as the bolt rode backward. The rifle had a straight-wrist butt with a separate forend and a full-length handguard; the single band was reinforced with a cap-type nose band formed as part of a barrel sleeve and bayonet lug assembly. The front sight was mounted on the sleeve, but several inches of the muzzle protruded.

• Pieper (Henri), lever-action type

A distinctive 'gas-seal' design was patented in Belgium in 1885. An underlever – combined with the trigger guard – pulled the barrel forward to break the seal formed with the mouth of the cartridge case, indexed the cylinder, cocked the hammer, and then moved the barrel back to its closed position. Unfortunately, the design was too complex to justify the meager gains in performance; as it was also incapable of handling the powerful cartridges demanded for military service, Henri Pieper abandoned the gas-seal carbine in favor of the 1888-patent bolt-action rifle decribed previously.

• Pieper (Henri), revolving-cylinder type

The Pieper company made a series of gas-seal revolvers in addition to rifles and shotguns, though they were overshadowed by the better-known Nagants. However, revolving carbines were also made in substantial numbers in the early 1890s; most seem to have been supplied to Mexico, where they were used by the rural gendarmerie. Details will be found under 'Mexico: Nagant'.

• Pieper (Nicolas), autoloading type

PIEPER SEMI-AUTOMATIC CARBINE

Made by Nicolas Pieper & Cie, Liége, about 1908-13.

Total production: not known. **Chambering options:** 22 Short, 22 Long or 22 Long Rifle rimfire (see text). **Action:** no mechanical breech lock; blowback, semi-automatic only.
DATA FOR DELUXE 'HALF-AUTOMATIC' 22 SHORT PATTERN
42.9in overall, 4.45lb empty. 23.6in barrel, smooth-bored. Single shot only. Block and two-leaf rear sight graduated to 150m (165yd). 775fps with 29-grain bullet.

These guns, unrelated to the Bayard series made by Anciens Établissements Pieper (q.v.), were also generally single shot auto-ejecting 'half-automatics' operated by blowback. Though magazine-fed versions may have been made, none has yet been reported. The Piepers had simple cylindrical receivers, with charging handles on the right side of their reciprocating bolts.

THE GUNS
Junior pattern. Made only in 22 Short, this was a 'take-down' gun, with a bolt beneath the forend. It had a simple half-stock with a straight wrist and a small rearward bar on the trigger guard, and weighed only about 2.9lb. The rear sight was a simple fixed block.

Standard pattern. Slightly larger than the junior gun, weighing 3-3.2lb, this could handle the three rimfire chamberings interchangeably. It had a better stock with checkering on the pistol grip and (sometimes) on the slender forend; swivels lay beneath the butt and on the forend-tip.

Military trainer. Usually chambered for the 22 Short cartridges, these had straight-wrist butts with forends stretching virtually to the muzzle. A single barrel band and a plain nose cap were fitted, while a primitive socket bayonet could be attached around the front-sight base. The rifles weighed 3.4-3.5lb without the bayonet.

• Raick

Raick Frères of Liége made substantial quantities of Mauser-type sporting rifles, initially built around refurbished wartime actions and then on new examples purchased from Fabrique Nationale.

MODEL 155 SPORTING RIFLE

This was the basic pattern available in 1965, built on an FN action and a conventional half-stock. Barrels measured 21.65-24in; standard chamberings were 243 Winchester, 6.5x55, 270 Winchester, 280 Remington, 7x57, 30-06, 308 Winchester, 8x60, 358 Winchester and 9.3x62. Magazines held five rounds.

SIMILAR GUNS

Model 156 Magnum. This was a four-shot version of the standard 155 pattern, chambered for the 7mm Remington Magnum, 300 Winchester Magnum and 375 H&H Magnum rounds.

Model 160 Carbine. Mechanically identical with the Model 155, this had a 20.45in barrel and a full-length 'Mannlicher' stock.

Model 161 Magnum Carbine. This was a variant of the Model 160, offered in the same chamberings as the Model 156 but distinguished by a short barrel and a full-length stock.

Model 165 Big Game Rifle. Built on the FN-Mauser action, this had barrels of 21.65-25.6in and a ventilated rubber butt pad. The guns had folding-leaf Express sights on a quarter rib, and the front swivel eye lay on the barrel instead of forend.

• Terssen

Credited to the commandant of the Manufacture d'Armes de l'État in Liége, this was unique to Belgium. Problems with the first Albini-Braendlin breech were apparently bad enough to prevent the Belgians re-equipping sufficiently quickly. The Terssen system was adopted as a temporary measure, but was not perpetuated once Albini-Braendlin and Comblain weapons were available in quantity.

It relied on a longitudinal locking bolt in the breech block entering a recess in the rear face of the receiver. Rotating the operating handle withdrew the bolt into the block, after which the breech could be pivoted upward. A conventional Snider-type striker ran diagonally down through the block. Terssen conversions had a more effective extractor than the pivoted Albini-Braendlin type, though this was rectified on the later (1873 model) Albini. It is suspected that the Terssen breech was more prone to jamming.

MODEL 1777-1868 RIFLE
Fusil d'Infanterie Mle 1777-1868

Converted in Liége; agency or agencies unknown (by "Le Petit Syndicat des Fabricants d'Armes"?).

Total production: not known. **Chambering:** 11x50R, rimmed.

53in overall, 10.6lb empty. 34.75in barrel, 4-groove rifling; RH, concentric. Single shot only. Ramp-and-leaf rear sight graduated to 1100m (1205yd). 1370fps with Mle 1867 ball cartridges. Mle 1867 socket bayonet (see text).

This was an adaption of French Mle 1777 flintlock muskets, which had already received a Belgian back-action lock. There were two barrel bands and a simple nose cap, with swivels beneath the middle band and under-edge of the butt. Line infantry were issued with the standard socket bayonet, but the saw-backed Mle 1868 or Mle 1880 sword patterns used by the engineers required a lug and tenon on the right side of the rifle muzzle. Survivors were relegated to second-line units as soon as the new Mle 1873 Albini-Braendlin became available in quantity.

MODEL 1848-68 MUSKETOON

These rifles were altered from the cap lock pillar-breech rifle adopted in 1848. They had new French-style barrels retained by a single band and a simple nose cap. A typical example was 51.1in overall, had a 31.5in barrel and weighed 10.3lb. The lug and tenon for the Mle 1868 saber bayonet lay on the right side of the muzzle and the original rear sight was graduated to 1100m (1205yd). Muzzle velocity was 1330fps.

SIMILAR GUNS

Model 1848-68-80 musketoon. Some 1848-68 guns were altered to fire the Mle 1880 ball cartridge, being distinguished by new Halkin-type ramp-and-leaf sights graduated to 1400m (1530yd). A second sighting notch, cut in the left side of the extended slider-block, was used in conjunction with a sighting stud on the left side of a new band (between the original band and nose cap) for ranges up to 2100m or 2295yd.

BOLIVIA

The standard receiver-top crest was a pastoral scene – including a llama and a wheatsheaf – within a circlet containing 'BOLIVIA' and nine stars. It was surmounted by a condor and backed by a trophy of arms and flags. Later guns were often simply marked 'EJÉRCITO DE BOLIVIA'.

MAUSER RIFLES.

The earliest small caliber acquisition was the Modelo 1895, identical with the Mo. 1891 Argentine rifle, except for markings. It was made by Ludwig Loewe & Co. in Berlin. The Mo. 1907 rifle and short rifle were standard German 1904- or export-pattern guns, believed to have been supplied by Deutsche Waffen- und Munitionsfabriken.

Mo. 1950 short rifles were made by Ceskoslovenská Zbrojovka of Brno in 1950-2, as the 7.65x53 'Fusil Mauser Boliviano Serie B-50'. They were essentially vz. 24 short rifles, though the stock and stamped-sheet bands were based on those of the wartime Kar. 98k. A single spring let into the right side of the forend sufficed to hold the band and the nose cap. The buttplate was a stamped 'bucket' pattern and the trigger guard and magazine floor-plate assembly were stamped from a single strip. Swivels lay under the band and butt. The B-50 was 43.3in overall, weighed 8.58lb and had a 23.6in barrel. Its tangent-leaf sight was graduated to 2000m (2185yd) and a Czechoslovakian export-pattern bayonet was used.

Bolivia also used 7.65mm vz. 24/26 short rifles, purchased in the late 1920s from Ceskoslovenská Zbrojovká, and a few 7.65mm Standard-Modell guns supplied from Mauser-Werke in the 1930s.

REMINGTON-LEE RIFLES

Bolivia purchased about 1950 1885-type rifles from Hartley & Graham of New York in April 1891. They are believed to have been chambered for the 11mm Spanish (.433) cartridge, but it is not known if special markings were ever applied.

SIG RIFLES

The army purchased about five thousand SG 510-4 rifles in the 1960s, followed in 1980-5 by a substantial quantity of 5.56mm SG 540-type guns made in France by Manurhin.

BRAZIL

Brazilian firearms often display a mark based on the national Arms. Customarily accompanied by 'ESTADOS UNIDOS DO BRASIL' (or simply 'E.U. do Brasil') on the guns, the crest consists of a large five-point prismatic star impaled on a sword, point uppermost. A constellation of five stars – the Southern Cross – lies within a circlet of twenty small stars on the center of the prismatic star. The device is generally contained within a wreath of laurel and coffee, and may be placed on a stylized sunburst.

• Chuchu

This interesting mechanism, designed by Athanase Chuchu and unique to Brazil, was incorporated in gendarmerie musketoons (*Mosquete do Policia*) made in Liége in the late 1870s for issue in Bahia. An operating lever on the right side of the breech was pulled back to cock the hammer, then outward to swing the entire breech block laterally to the right. The spent case was extracted as the movement was completed. Chuchu remained active for many years, receiving three US firearms patents in 1885-1904, but none of his other designs is known to have reached production status.

• Comblain

Details of the construction and background history of this gun will be found under 'Belgium: Comblain'.

MODEL 1874 RIFLE

Manufacturer unknown – possibly Auguste Francotte & Co., Liége.
Total production: not known. **Chambering:** 11.4x53, rimmed. **Action:** as Belgian guns (q.v.).

47.2in overall, 10.25lb empty. 31.6in barrel, 4-groove rifling; RH, concentric. Ramp-and-leaf sight graduated to 1200m (1310yd)? Performance: not known. Socket bayonet?

This was a variant of the orginal gun, but lacked a cocking spur on the breech block as the hammer was carried inside a shroud.

The standard IMBEL-made version of the 7.62x51 Belgian FAL.

The 5.56mm IMBEL-made MD-1 rifle.

The rear swivel was carried on a special plate screwed to the front of the receiver, and the lower tang – projecting backward from the receiver – was made separately rather than being forged integrally as in the Belgian prototype.

• FN-Saive (Imbel)

Fabrique Nationale supplied small numbers of 30-06 SAFN in the early 1950s, apparently for the marines and navy. Small quantities of Belgian-made FAL rifles followed in the early 1960s, and a licence was granted to permit production in the government factory (Fábrica de Armas) in Itajubá under the supervision of Industria de Material Belico de Brasil ('Imbel').

FN-made rifles bore the company name on the right side of the frame above the pistol grip; 'EXERCITO BRASILEIRO' appeared in the panel milled out of the frame (on the right side above the magazine) together with the national Arms.

Standard FAL-type rifles were then made in Brazil as the M964 (fixed butt) and M969A1 (folding butt), the latter being issued largely to airborne forces and marines. Their markings were essentially similar to the Belgian-made originals, excepting that the maker's name on the receiver usually read 'FABRICA DE ITA-JUBA–BRASIL' and 'FZ. 7.62 M 964' lay on the left above the selector lever. Brazilian guns had plain-sided receivers instead of the milled-panel FN type.

• Garand

Like Argentina, Brazil received large numbers of M1 Garands in the early 1950s. Some were subsequently converted in the Itajuba factory for the 7.62x51 cartridge and accepted the standard twenty-round FAL magazine.

• Mannlicher

About 3400 7x57 rifles were apparently purchased from Österreichische Waffenfabriks-Gesellschaft of Steyr early in the 20th century, perhaps to offset a temporary shortage of Mausers. These guns are said to have been 'Gew. 88', but it seems more likely that they were made to the improved 'Model 1904' pattern (see 'Austria-Hungary – Mannlicher: bolt action'). Distinctive markings, if any, have not been identified.

• Mauser

Like many South American countries, Brazil has bought vast numbers of Mauser-action rifles since the 1890s. Unlike most neighboring states, excepting Argentina and Chile, Brazil has also made its own Mauser rifles in the Itajuba ordnance factory.

MODEL 1894 RIFLE

Adopted after extensive tests, the 7x57 Fuzil Mo. 1894 was virtually identical with the Spanish Mo. 1893 (q.v.) excepting for a cylindrical bolt head. The magazine-follower tail was rounded so that the bolt shut on an empty chamber after the last round had been ejected.

The guns were made by Ludwig Loewe & Co. of Berlin (1894-6), Deutsche Waffen- und Munitionsfabriken, Berlin, (1897-9?), and Fabrique Nationale d'Armes de Guerre, Herstal (1894-9). They were 48.6in overall and weighed 8.85lb empty. The 29.05in barrels had concentric four-groove twisting to the right. The charger-loaded magazine held five rounds, the leaf sight was graduated to 2000m (2185yd), and the Mo. 1894 knife bayonet could be mounted.

SIMILAR GUNS

Model 1894 carbine. This was a shortened version of the rifle, measuring about 37.4in overall with a 17.7in barrel. The rear sight was graduated to 1400m (1530yd), the bolt handle was straight, and the rifle-type nose cap assembly lacked the bayonet bar. A sling bar and ring lay beneath the straight-wrist butt.

MODEL 1904 RIFLE
Also known as the 'Mo. 1907'
Made by Deutsche Waffen- und Munitionsfabriken, Berlin, 1904-14.

Total production: 20,000? **Chambering:** 7x57, rimless. **Action:** locked by two lugs on the bolt engaging recesses in the receiver behind the chamber as the bolt handle was turned down, and by an additional lug on the bolt-handle base engaging its recess.

48.5in overall, 8.82lb empty. 28.95in barrel, 4-groove rifling; RH, concentric. Ramp-and-leaf sight graduated to 1200m (1310yd)? 2700fps with standard ball ammunition. Mo. 1894 sword bayonet.

This embodied an 1898-type Mauser action and had a pistol grip stock, but shared the nose cap of the Mo. 1894 so that the same bayonet could be used. Swivels lay under the barrel band and butt. Sights were originally identical with the Mo. 1894 type.

SIMILAR GUNS

Model 1907 carbine. The 7x57 'Carabina Mo. 1907', issued to cavalry and artillerymen, was supplied from Deutsche Waffen-und Munitionsfabriken in 1907-12. It had a 1898-pattern action and has often been mistakenly identified as the 'Mo. 1908'. The short pistol grip stock had a handguard running from the chamber ring to the single screw-clamping barrel band, and the nose cap had a bayonet lug. One swivel lay on the left side of the band, with the other on a short bar attached to the under-edge of the butt behind the pistol grip. A tangent-leaf sight graduated to 2000m (2185yd) was used.

Model 1908 rifle. Made by Deutsche Waffen- und Munitions-fabriken of Berlin in 1908-14, and by Fabryka Bronie w Radomu in 1935-8, this was about 49.15in overall, weighed 8.88lb and had a 29.15in barrel. It had a pistol grip stock with a handguard running from the chamber ring to the solitary barrel band; the German 'H' type nose cap accepted a bayonet with a muzzle ring; and the tangent-leaf sight was graduated to 2000m (2185yd). Swivels lay under the band and butt, and a washer was held in the right side of the butt by a slotted-head screw. Some guns have been seen with the DWM name and the Oberndorf address, which may suggest that work was sub-contracted to Mauser.

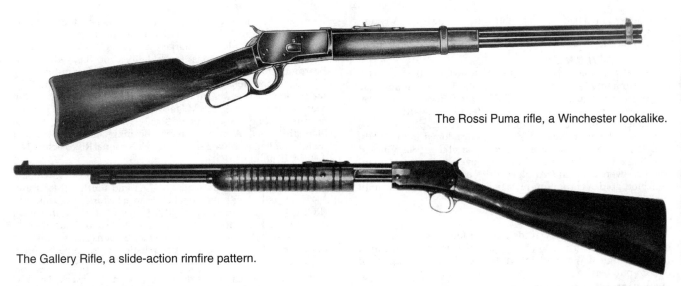

The Rossi Puma rifle, a Winchester lookalike.

The Gallery Rifle, a slide-action rimfire pattern.

Model 1908 short rifle. Virtually identical with the full-length gun, apart from dimensions (41.9in long with a 22.05in barrel), this was generally found with the bolt handle turned down toward the stock. The 2000m rear sight was retained.

Model 1922 short rifle. These 7mm guns – 39.2in long, weighing about 6.8lb – were purchased from Fabrique Nationale in the early 1920s. They had 1898-type actions in a stock with a straight-wrist butt and 1400m (1530yd) rear sights. A short bayonet lug lay beneath the muzzle, and swivels lay beneath the band and butt.

Model 1924 short rifles. These 7x57 guns were purchased from Czechoslovakia in 1931, by Brazilian insurgents. They bore nothing but commercial Ceskoslovenská Zbrojovka markings, but had the bolt handles turned down against a recess in the stock. Many were captured by government forces and added to the army inventory.

Model 1935 rifle and short rifle. These were 'Standard Modell' Mausers, purchased in Germany in 1935-7. The long rifle was essentially similar to the Gew. 98 (then known as the 'Karabiner 98b'), with a tangent rear sight, but the bolt handle was straight and the front swivel lay under the barrel band. It was about 49.25in long and weighed about 9.8lb. The short rifle was similar, but merely 42in long; its bolt handle was bent down toward a recess in the stock.

Other types. An order for 100,500 7x57 vz. 08/33 and vz. 12/33 guns is said to have been placed in Czechoslovakia by Brazil in 1938, but had hardly been begun when the Germans entered Czechoslovakia in 1939. Production then commenced in Brazil.

MODEL 1908/34 RIFLE
Made by Fabrica de Armas de Itajuba, about 1940-55.
Total production: not known. **Chambering:** 30-06, rimless. **Action:** as M1904, above.

43.75in overall, 9.2lb empty. 23.6in barrel, 4-groove rifling; RH, concentric. Tangent-leaf sight graduated to 2000m (2185yd). 2750fps with ball ammunition. Sword bayonet.

This was a Brazilian-made version of the 1908-pattern short rifle described previously, the major change being the adoption of the standard US 30 cartridge. Some of the guns were made from reclaimed actions, but others were newly made; the stocks are customarily of a South American hardwood, with a grain unlike the walnut patterns supplied from Europe prior to 1939. The rifles are marked 'Mo. 08/34 30' on the left side of the chamber. Bolt handles turn down against a recess in the stock.

SIMILAR GUNS
Model 1954. This was a variant of the Model 08/34 with a stamped-sheet 'boot' buttplate and the muzzle threaded to mount a grenade launcher. Rifles of this type are marked 'Mo. 30 M954' on the left side of the chamber.

• Pieper
The parentage of these rifles remains a mystery; Brazil had ordered Mauser-type rifles from Fabrique Nationale in June 1894 and it seems unlikely that trials were still underway when these 'Piepers' (which have a vague affinity with Nagant trials rifles sent to Russia in 1890) were being made. However, by the end of 1894, Mauser was trying to prevent FN making guns incorporating the 1893-type action and magazine. An explanation that the 'Pieper' rifle was an *alternative* to the Mauser – built on spare 1894-type Brazilian Mauser receivers – seems worthy of consideration.

MODEL 1894 RIFLE
Fabrique Nationale d'Armes de Guerre, Herstal-lèz-Liége, 1894.
Total production: see text. **Chambering:** 7x57, rimless. **Action:** locked by two lugs on the bolt head engaging recesses in the receiver as the bolt handle turns down, and by the base of the bolt handle turning into its seat.

About 48in overall, 9lb empty. 29.0in barrel, 4-groove rifling; RH, concentric. Internal box magazine, 6 rounds. Leaf-and-slider sight graduated to 2000m (2185yd). 2700fps with standard ball ammunition. Sword bayonet.

Rifles of this type, customarily associated with Henri Pieper (see **'Belgium'**), are said to have been supplied to enable field trials to be undertaken in competition with the Mauser. Survivors display the Brazilian Arms over the chamber, and are marked 'ESTADOS UNIDOS DO BRAZIL' above 'FAB. NAT. ARMES. HERSTAL 1894' on the left side of the receiver. They have a one-piece stock with a straight wrist, lack a handguard, and a plain nose cap carries the front sight on top and the bayonet lug on the right side. Swivels lie on the butt and band.

The bolt has two lugs on its head, and the handle locks into a right-angle channel in the bridge. The spur of the hammer, protruding behind the bolt, is pushed back automatically as the bolt opened.

• Rossi, lever-action type
Amadeo Rossi SA Metalúrgica e Munições of São Leopoldo, best known as a maker of revolvers and shotguns, has also made a limited range of cartridge rifles. In addition to the lever- and slide-action guns listed below, Rossi made a simple 'Model 6' 22LR bolt-action saloon rifle in 1951-61.

Many Rossi-made guns have been sold in the USA, principally by Interarms of Virginia. Cataloging individual variants has been handicapped by a tendency to sell them as the 'Model 92' – to capitalize on identification with the original Winchesters – instead of the native Argentine pattern-numbers.

MODEL 67 PUMA RIFLE
Made by Amadeo Rossi SA, São Leopoldo.
Currently in production. **Chambering:** 357 Magnum, centerfire. **Action:** locked by sliding bars engaging the bolt as the operating lever is raised.

37in overall, 6.17lb empty 20in barrel, 6-groove rifling; RH, concentric. Tube magazine beneath barrel, 10 rounds. Spring-leaf and elevator rear sight. 1590fps with 157-grain bullet.

This was a slight modification of the Model 92 Winchester (q.v.), designed by John Browning. Capable of firing 357 Magnum and 38 Special cartridges interchangeably, introduced in July 1976 and given a 'K'-prefix number from December. The Model 67 had a straight-wrist butt, a spring-loaded loading gate on the right side of the receiver, and a half-length forend with a single band. An additional retaining band encircled the barrel and the tube magazine at the muzzle. The exposed hammer had a half-cock safety notch.

SIMILAR GUNS

Model 77 Puma. This was a 38 Special version of the Model 67, dating from July 1977. Mechanically identical with its immediate predecessor, but unable to chamber 357 ammunition, it was given a 'B'-prefix serial number from November 1977 onward.

Model 65 Puma (designation unconfirmed). Experimental 44 variants of the basic Puma design were developed in the 1970s, but did not enter commercial production until the 1980s. Offered in 44 Magnum or 44-40 WCF, they were never made in great quantity; however, the standard blued rifles and engraved versions with blue, gold or chromium-plate finish remained available until 1987-9.

• Rossi, slide-action type

Guns sold in the USA, principally by Interarms of Virginia, have often been sold as 'Model 65' – to capitalize on identification with the original Winchesters – instead of the native Argentine pattern-numbers.

MODEL 37 GALLERY RIFLE

Made by Amadeo Rossi SA, São Leopoldo.

Currently in production. **Chambering options:** 22 Short, 22 Long or 22 Long Rifle, rimfire. **Action:** locked by a sliding block engaging the bolt as the slide handle is pushed forward.

38.65in overall, 5.33lb empty. 23in barrel, 6-groove rifling; RH, concentric. Tube magazine beneath barrel, 13 22LR rounds. Spring-leaf and elevator rear sight. 1050fps with standard ball ammunition.

Based on the Winchester Model 62, this rifle can handle all three types of rimfire cartridge interchangeably, the magazine capacity with Short and Long rounds being sixteen and twenty respectively. The straight-wrist hardwood butt and slab-side receiver are accompanied by a cylindrical slide handle that has circumferential grooves; the exposed hammer has a half-cock safety notch, and a mechanical interlock prevents the gun firing until the action is securely locked. Rifles made after March 1969 had 'G'-prefix numbers. A stainless-steel variant appeared in the mid 1980s, but it is not known if this was accompanied by a change in designation.

SIMILAR GUNS

Model 57 Gallery Junior. Introduced in March 1970, this was made for Harrington & Richardson as the 'Model 749.' Distribution elsewhere was limited, and production ceased in 1972. The most distinctive feature was the short barrel (16.5in), which ended level with the tip of the tube magazine.

Model 59 Gallery Magnum. Introduced in February 1981, this is a variant of the M37 chambered for the 22 Winchester Magnum rimfire cartridge. Magazine capacity is merely ten rounds. The M59 is 39.4in long and weighs about 5.2lb.

Model 73 Gallery Junior II. An improved version of the short-lived M57, this appeared in September 1975 and is still being made. It is 30.5in long, has a 16.5in barrel, and weighs 4.6lb; magazine capacity ranges from twelve 22LR to eighteen 22 Short rounds.

• Vergueiro

DWM sold about five thousand Vergueiro-type rifles to the federal police, probably in 1910-12 to use parts left over from the Portuguese contract. The guns were practically identical with the standard Portuguese Mo. 904, but were adapted for the 7x57 cartridge; their chamber tops displayed the Brazilian enwreathed-star Arms above 'F.P.D.F.' (Força Policia Distrito Federal).

BRITAIN

British rifles often display 'W↑D', signifying the War Department. This superseded the Board of Ordnance ('B↑O') in the mid-19th Century. A 'V.R.' ('Victoria Regina') may appear on guns made between 1888 and 1901; alternatives include 'E.R.' ('Edwardius Rex'), 1901-10 or 1936; 'G.R.' ('Georgius Rex'), 1910-36 or 1936-52; and 'E.R.' ('Elizabeth Regina') from 1952 to date.

Guns made by the Royal Small Arms Factory at Enfield Lock were usually marked 'ENFIELD' or 'EFD'. Guns made in BSA's Small Heath factory bore 'B.S.A. & M. CO.' (Birmingham Small

Arms & Munitions Company) until 1897, when the company reverted to original 'B.S.A.' marks. Those made by the London Small Arms Co. Ltd. were marked 'L.S.A. CO.' or, alternatively, 'L.S.A. CO. LD.' Rarer marks include 'B.E.' or 'B.E. CO.' for the Beardmore Engineering Co. Ltd. (found only on Martini-Enfields), 'H.R.B.' for the Henry Rifled Barrel Company, 'N.A. & A. Co.' for the National Arms & Ammunition Co. Ltd. of Birmingham (on Martini-Henry guns), 'V.S.M.' for Vickers, Sons & Maxim Ltd. (on charger-loading Lee conversions only, 1911-12), 'S.S.A.' for the Standard Small Arms Company, Birmingham (1916-18), and 'N.R.F.' for its short-lived successor, the National Rifle Factory No. 1 (1918-19 only).

During World War II, No. 4 rifles were made by Enfield, the BSA factories in Small Heath (M47A) and Shirley (M85B and M47C), together with the Royal Ordnance factories in Fazakerley (ROF [F], FY, or F) and Maltby (ROF [M] or RM). No. 4 rifles were also supplied to Britain from Small Arms Ltd. of Long Branch, Toronto (an 'LB' monogram), and by the Stevens Arms Company of Chicopee Falls, Massachusetts (a distinctive squared 'S', often in a box-border).

Designation marks take the form 'I' or 'II*' for Marks I and II* respectively, the 'star' being the standard method of indicating an improved pattern. 'M.E.', 'M.H.' and 'M.M.' represent Martini-Enfield, Martini-Henry and Martini-Metford respectively. Prefixes 'A.C.' and 'C.C.' denote artillery and cavalry carbines, though the marks can be difficult to decipher – 'II C. I', for example, is a Mark II Carbine (type unspecified), 'First Class'.

When the Lee-Enfield appeared, it was so similar to the Lee-Metford that the prefix 'L.E.' was used to distinguish it. Thereafter, a series of descriptive prefixes had to be used: 'C.L.L.E.' for 'Charger-Loading Lee-Enfield'; 'COND.L.E.' for 'Converted Lee-Enfield' (not 'condemned'); or 'SHT.L.E.' for 'Short Lee Enfield'. After World War I, with the adoption of a new system of designations, the butt-shoe marks read 'NO. 1 MK. VI' or 'NO. 4 MK. 1'. By 1940, marks had been transferred from the butt-shoe of the Lee-Enfield to the left side of the receiver, a typical example reading 'No4 Mk1 ROF (F)' over '2/45' for February 1945. The 7.62mm Lee-Enfield conversions bore marks such as 'RIFLE 7.62MM L8A3' over '(CR 62 GA)'.

Among countless lesser marks have been 'A.T.' for guns fitted with an Aiming Tube, or sub-caliber trainer; 'D.P.' for those relegated to Drill Purposes; 'EY.' for 'Emergency' patterns; 'FTR' or 'F.T.R.' for 'Factory Thorough Repair' (i.e., a complete overhaul); 'N.I.' for 'Non-Interchangeable'; 'P.W.' for guns which were issued in a 'part-worn' condition; 'S-X' for 'Strengthened Extractor' (Mk III Martini-Henry rifles only); and 'U P' for 'unproved'.

The British Army used unit markings extensively prior to World War I. However, though they were customarily listed in the official *Instructions to Armorers*, very little information is currently available. The best source is an Appendix in Bernd Rolff's *Im Dienste Ihrer Majestät* (Schwäbisch Hall, Germany, 1994).

• Accuracy International

This small-volume manufacturer promotes a purpose-built sniper rifle, adopted by the British Army (at the expense of the Parker-Hale Model 85) after trials lasting several years.

Developed from 1982 onward by a team led by Malcolm Cooper, and introduced in 1985, the PM featured a bolt with a fully enclosed head and a 60-degree throw. The construction of the breech was also unusual, as the barrel screwed into an extension of the receiver and was held in place with a barrel collar. The lugs on the bolt head passed through appropriate slots in the collar and were then turned so that they locked into place. This system allowed the barrel collar to be replaced when wear increased headspace unacceptably, and also simplified construction.

The PM had some initial teething troubles, arising from manufacturing problems, but the initial difficulties were soon overcome. Though the original PM rifle has recently been discontinued in favor of the improved AW pattern, sales have been made to more than twenty countries. Accuracy International rifles have also successfully overcome rival submissions to win sniper rifle competitions in Belgium, Germany, the Netherlands and Sweden.

The Accuracy International PM sniping rifle.

L96A1 SNIPER RIFLE
Also known as Model 'PM'

Made by Accuracy International Ltd., Portsmouth, Hampshire, 1986-95.
Chambering: 7.62x51 NATO, rimless. **Action:** locked by three lugs on the bolt engaging a locking collar on the barrel as the bolt handle (which doubled as a fourth lug) was turned down.

DATA FOR A TYPICAL EXAMPLE

44.25in overall, 14.33lb with sights and bipod. 25.75in barrel, 4-groove rifling; RH, concentric. Detachable box magazine, 10 rounds. Optical sight. 2825fps with ball ammunition.

Among the most interesting features of the PM was the modular construction, which has since become fashionable among the makers of specialized target and precision sniping rifles. Two 'stock sides', made of tough plastic with olive drab finish, were bolted onto the aluminum chassis supporting the action to overcome the warping which can occur when one-piece wood stocks are used in unfavorable conditions.

The action cocked partly on opening and partly on the closing stroke of the bolt, the trigger was adjustable, and the safety catch blocked the trigger, the bolt and the firing pin simultaneously. Lock time was particularly fast.

The basic PM rifle is easily recognized by the shape of its angular thumb-hole half stock, and by the prominent stock-side retaining bolts. It was often seen with a bipod and a small monopod or 'Quick Action Spike'. Excepting the Long Range pattern, which was a single shot, all PM rifles fed from a detachable box magazine.

SIMILAR GUNS

PM Counter-Terrorist rifle. This was offered in 7.62mm NATO, with Schmidt & Bender 6x42 or 2.5-10x56 sights.

PM Covert rifle. Derived from the PM Moderated rifle described below, this was designed to dismantle into a wheeled suitcase. The most obvious features of the assembled rifle were the pistol grip immediately behind the trigger and a butt which could be swung to the left to lie alongside the receiver.

PM Infantry rifle. This 7.62x51 rifle had a 6x42 sight, but a folding rear sight graduated to 700yd was usually fitted on the receiver above the bolt handle to work in conjunction with a protected blade at the muzzle.

PM Long Range rifle. Distinguished by its single shot action, offering increased rigidity compared with the box-magazine type, this was usually fitted with Schmidt & Bender 12x42 or Leupold 10x/16x M1 sights, and chambered for the 7mm Remington Magnum or 300 Winchester Magnum rounds in search of better accuracy at greater distances than the standard 7.62x51 NATO round could achieve.

PM Moderated rifle. Fitted with a 6x42 optical sight, this had a full-length sound moderator suited to special subsonic 7.62x51mm ammunition.

PM Super Magnum rifle. Developed for the 338 Lapua Magnum cartridge (8.6x70), this PM variant was developed partly to increase the distance at which reliable hits could be obtained and partly to improve anti-materiel performance. It was only made in small numbers before being replaced by the AW-type Super Magnum described below.

'AW' SNIPER RIFLE
Also known as the 'Arctic Warfare' pattern

Made by Accuracy International Ltd., Portsmouth, Hampshire, 1992 to date.
Chambering: 7.62x51 NATO, rimless. **Action:** as PM rifle, above.

46.5in overall, 14lb with sights and bipod. 26in barrel, 4-groove rifling; RH, concentric. Detachable box magazine, 10 rounds. Optical sight. 2825fps with ball ammunition.

An improved version of the Accuracy International PM sniper rifle, this was developed in 1986-7 for trials in Sweden, where it was eventually adopted as the PSG-90. The bolt action has been improved by changes in the design of individual components, and an anti-icing system allows the rifle to operate reliably in temperatures as low as -40°C. A three-position safety lever on the right side of the receiver behind the bolt handle can be used to withdraw the firing pin, but the bolt may be locked ('full lock') or left free to open ('half lock'). The stainless steel barrel has an optional muzzle brake to reduce the recoil sensation, a multi-adjustable bipod can be fitted at the tip of the forend or to an optional hand-stop on the accessory rail. Open sights can be provided to support the standard Schmidt & Bender 6x42 or Hensoldt 10x42 telescope patterns. The rear section of the thumbhole butt can be slid vertically.

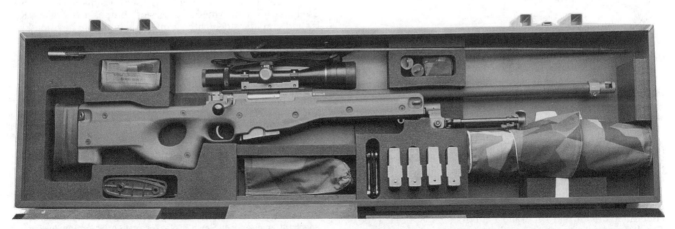

The Accuracy International AW rifle with a Hensoldt 10x42 telescope sight and accessories in its aluminum case.

SIMILAR GUNS

AWP or 'Police' rifle. Introduced in 1997 in 243 Winchester or 7.62x51 (.308 Winchester), this derivative of the AW fitted with a medium-weight 24in stainless-steel barrel and a 3-12x50 Schmidt & Bender sight.

AWS rifle (also known as 'AW Suppressed' or 'AW Silenced'). Otherwise similar to the standard AW rifle, this has a full-length sound suppresser and performs best with special subsonic ammunition.

Super Magnum rifle or 'SM-94'. This resembles the standard AW externally, but has a strengthened six-lug bolt. A section of the butt can be slid vertically. The standard 338 Lapua Magnum (8.6x70) rifle is about 49.9in long, has a 27in barrel, and weighs about 15.5lb with sights and bipod. The magazine contains five rounds. A 26in barrel has been supplied for the 7mm Remington Magnum and 300 Winchester Magnum versions.

• Adams

Developed in the 1860s, this usually took the form of a transformation of a P/53 ('Enfield') rifle-musket, one 577 example being rejected unfired by the British Army in 1868. The Adams action relied on a breechblock which, after the hammer of the conventional external-hammer sidelock had been retracted, lifted up around a longitudinal pin on the right side of the breech. This allowed a combustible cartridge to be pushed into the chamber manually.

• Anson & Deeley

This name is given to the first commercially successful hammerless box-lock shotgun, patented in 1875 (British Patent 1756/75) jointly by William Anson and John Deeley. This particular specification was filed while Anson was still working as foreman of the Westley Richards 'gun action room', which he left in 1877 to trade on his own account. A subsequent patent of addition – 1833/83 of 1883 with Deeley – protected modifications to the Anson & Deeley design. The breech system had the lock mechanism mounted directly on the action instead of separate sideplates.

Anson & Deeley's design was originally known as the 'Body Action', but subsequently became better known as a 'boxlock'. A safety lever mounted on the side of the action of the earliest guns was soon replaced by a sliding catch on the tang behind the top lever.

The first guns were made by Westley Richards of Birmingham, but the patent was subsequently licensed to several leading gunmakers and eventually – after protection had lapsed – was simply copied far and wide. In addition to shotguns, which are by far the most numerous embodiment of the system, large numbers of double-barreled rifles have been made. Many of those made while the patents were still in force were marked 'A. & D. PATENT' somewhere on the action, but most of the newer examples do not acknowledge their origins.

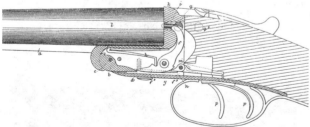

The basic Anson & Deeley box-lock action, from the original British patent.

• Arisaka

The British authorities ordered at least 150,000 of these Japanese guns shortly after World War I began in August 1914, a mixed batch of 30th and 38th Year Type rifles – plus some carbines – being delivered in 1914-15. Most were old examples with Japanese markings, but a few seem to have been newly made.

Suitably refurbished, the weapons were issued to the British Army from 24th February 1915 as the 'Rifle, Magazine, 256-inch, Pattern 1900' (30th Year Type) and 'Pattern 1907' (38th Year Type). The designations were based on the date of issue in the Japanese

army instead of approval. Most of the rifles were used by training battalions, but a passage from *Seven Pillars of Wisdom* by T.E. Lawrence (Lawrence of Arabia) suggests that at least a few reached Arabia. It is assumed that they had been landed by warships, and thus that they were part of twenty thousand Arisaka rifles issued to the Royal Navy from 15th June 1915 to free Lee-Enfields for land service. Japanese rifles also served the Royal Flying Corps and its 1918-vintage successor, the Royal Air Force.

The Arisakas were soon recalled, the navy guns being replaced by Canadian Ross rifles in April-June 1917. About 128,000 assorted Japanese guns were subsequently sent from Britain to Russia, and the patterns were declared obsolete in British service in 1921.

• Armalon

This gunmaking business developed the BGR to compete in the British Army sniping-equipment trials held in the 1980s. It was built from commercially available components at the last moment, to accompany Armalon's variant of the Schmidt & Bender 6x42 optical sight. Adjudged too late for testing, the BGR was abandoned after a few prototypes had been made; ironically, the 6x42 sight was adopted in conjunction with the Accuracy International PM rifle.

ARMALON BGR
'British-German Rifle'

Armalon Ltd., London, about 1985

Total made: a few prototypes only. **Chambering:** 7.62x51, rimless. **Action:** locked by three lugs on the bolt head engaging recesses in the barrel when the bolt handle was turned down.

47.2in overall, 14.5lb with bipod and sight. 27.6in barrel, 4-groove rifling; RH, concentric. Detachable box magazine, 5, 10 or 20 rounds. Optical sight. 2790ft/sec with standard ball ammunition.

These rifles were assembled from a selection of components. The bolt system is a modified German Krico (q.v.) benchrest pattern, with a special short-fall firing pin to reduce lock time to an absolute minimum, and an adjustable two-stage trigger was fitted. The heavy barrel was prominently fluted to improve cooling, and had an integral five-port compensator. The conventional one-piece thumbhole half stock – with an adjustable comb and buttplate – was intended to be wood, carbon fiber composite, or a blend of carbon fiber, Kevlar and glass-reinforced plastic.

ARMALON PR
'Practical Rifle'

Made by Armalon Ltd., London, on the basis of a Remington action.

Currently in production. **Chambering options:** 222 Remington, 22-250, 243 Winchester, 243 Winchester or 308 Winchester/7.62x51. **Action:** locked by two lugs on the bolt head engaging recesses in the receiver wall as the bolt handle turns downward.

DATA FOR A TYPICAL 223 EXAMPLE

43.7in overall, 12lb with sights and bipod. 24in barrel, 6-groove rifling; RH, concentric. Detachable box magazine, 20 or 30 rounds. Optical sight. 3170ft/sec with standard ball ammunition.

Introduced in 1990, these rifles are based on the Remington Model 700; once intended principally for Practical Rifle competitions, they are now seen as specialist sniping/SWAT equipment. Based principally on the Remington Model 700 Police or 40-XB target rifle (though Varmint and other variants have also been used), the PR retains the H-S Precision composite fiberglass, Kevlar and graphite stock with an integral aluminum bedding-block and accessory rail.

The 308 guns have been altered to use M14-type magazines, which tests had shown to be particularly efficient feeders; the 223 version customarily uses twenty-round Colt AR-15 magazines, avoiding the feed problems which occasionally arise with thirty-round patterns. The Armalon features a new one-piece trigger guard/magazine housing, with an extended magazine release catch. A Jewell or Timney trigger may be fitted, the bolt handle is often enlarged, and the longitudinal fluting reduces barrel weight without sacrificing rigidity.

ARMALON PC
'Pistol Carbine'

Made by Armalon Ltd., London, on the basis of a No. 4 Lee-Enfield action.

Currently in production. **Chambering options:** 9mm Parabellum, 38 Special, 10mm Auto, 40 Smith & Wesson or 45 ACP. **Action:** locked by a lug on the rear of the bolt engaging a recess in the receiver wall, and by

The Armalon version of the wartime De Lisle carbine, built on Lee-Enfield components: 45-caliber (top) or 9mm Parabellum (bottom).

the bolt guide rib abutting the receiver bridge as the bolt handle is turned down.

DATA FOR A TYPICAL 9MM EXAMPLE

35.5in overall, 8.3lb empty. 16in barrel, 6-groove rifling; RH, concentric. Detachable box magazine, 16 rounds. Folding-leaf rear sight on receiver. About 1250ft/sec with standard ball ammunition.

Offered from 1997 on the basis of extensively altered Lee-Enfield actions, these carbines fire a variety of pistol ammunition. The bolt head has been altered to feed the new cartridges, the bolt stroke has been greatly reduced, a new ejector is installed in the feed way, and a reversed cock-on-opening striker mechanism has been developed. The PC is instantly recognizable by its compact dimensions, the shortened forend/handguard asssembly, and the protruding muzzle carrying the original front sight. An Italian-made magazine protrudes from a new magazine housing let into the underside of the stock.

• Aston

Gunsmith James Aston, Armorer to the School of Musketry in Hythe, Kent, was also the designer of a dropping-block action. Patented in several countries in 1873 (e.g., U.S. Patent 138,837), the guns were operated by pressing down on a straight-shank radial lever on the right side of the receiver. This not only dropped the breech, extracting and ejecting the spent case, but also cocked the internal hammer.

If the four-digit numbers on survivors can be trusted, substantial quantities of Aston rifles were made – mostly by Hollis & Sheath of Birmingham. A typical 450 example had a butt with checkering on the straight wrist, and an extensively checkered

forend with a crudely defined Henry Tip. The 27in round barrel, pinned into the forend, was marked **'James Aston Patent. School of Musketry. Hythe.'** This does not, however, indicate that it was ever the property of this particular British Army establishment but only that Hythe was the basis of Aston's gunsmithing operations.

• Atkin, Grant & Lang

Atkin, Grant & Lang of St James, London, was a 1960s amalgamation of the businesses of Henry Atkin, Stephen Grant & Sons, and Joseph Lang & Son. All three of these original London gunmakers made sporting rifles under their own names, apparently including a few Mausers created around actions purchased in Germany. Similar guns have been made in more recent times.

In 1965, Atkin, Grant & Lang was offering the budget-price 'Charles Lancaster' rifle on the basis of a standard military-surplus 1898-pattern Mauser action. Chambered for 243 Winchester, 270 Winchester, 30-06 or 308 Winchester rounds, it had a 24in barrel, weighed about 7lb, and had a walnut stock with a Monte Carlo comb. A ventilated rubber recoil pad was used, and the pistol grip had a separate cap (synthetic or ebonite). Checkering appeared on the pistol grip and forend, the rounded tip of the latter being rosewood or ebony on better-quality guns. Sights comprised a ramped blade and a 100-yard block with folding leaves for 200 or 300 yards.

• Bacon

The first bolt-action rifles of this type were submitted to the British trials begun at the end of 1866. One was summarily rejected on the grounds that it was incomplete, and the other, despite proving to be very accurate, failed owing to its complexity.

FIRST-PATTERN GUNS

A patent was granted in 1868 to Lieutenant Francis Bacon of the Royal Marine Artillery, protecting a double-barrel sporter and a single-barrel rifle suitable for military use. The action was locked by turning the bolt handle down until a rib on the bolt body abutted a shoulder in the receiver. A sliding breech cover moved with the bolt, and ejection was upward. The first Bacons were extremely complicated, particularly the bolt and bolt head, and would have been difficult to make.

A solitary rifle took part in the 1868 breech mechanism trials, but was wrecked by a premature explosion while the breech was being closed. This ended the military career of the Bacon rifle before it had begun, though it was to enjoy greater success as a double-barreled shotgun.

IMPROVED-PATTERN GUNS

Patented in December 1870, this was a refinement of the 1868 design with a simpler bolt and sear which slid diagonally in the bolt plugs. Primary extraction was improved, ejection was by gravity through a port cut through the underside of the stock, and the tip of the strikers doubled as cocking indicators.

Mindful of the premature explosion which had occurred in the military trials, Bacon not only ensured that the striker could not be released until the breech was locked shut but also included a manually-operated radial safety lever on the left side of the stock behind the bolt.

A 12-bore example sold at auction in 1996 was marked **"Bacon's Patent No. 343"**, referring not to the patent but instead to the quantity of guns made under a royalty agreement. This suggests that production was substantial by the standards of the day, though the proportion of rifled guns to smoothbores is not known. The manufacturer is believed to have been Henry Walker & Company of 14 St Mary's Row, Birmingham, who was claiming in the mid-1870s to have been the "sole maker of Bacon's Patent Gun" for several years.

• Banks

Often associated with the gunmaking business of John Rigby & Co., of London and Dublin, this falling block action was operated by a curved radial lever – pivoted at the front right side of the receiver – which was depressed with the thumb to lower the block. A typical 450 rifle had a straight-wrist butt, a plain forend held to the barrel with a lateral key, and a 29in round barrel. The rear sight, graduated to 300yd, consisted of a standing block with two small folding leaves.

• BMS

These rifles, developed in the late 1980s, all incorporate bolts locked by wedges which are cammed outward as the handle is turned (cf., Sauer 80/90 series). The movement of the bolt handle is merely 22 degrees.

MILCAM RIFLE

BMS Trading Ltd., London.

Currently in production. **Chambering:** 5.56x45 (.223). **Action:** locked by pivoting wedges on the bolt head engaging recesses in the receiver when the bolt handle is turned down.

40in overall, 7.25lb empty. 20in barrel, 6-groove rifling; RH, concentric. Detachable box magazine, 10 or 30 rounds. Rotating aperture sight graduated to 500m? 3110ft/sec with M193 ball ammunition. U.S. ArmaLite-pattern knife bayonet.

This was designed to answer a need for a 5.56mm bolt-action rifle, appealing to purchasers with limited resources or a preference for manually-operated weapons. The principal novelty – apart from caliber – lies in the cam-operated bolt locking system. The Milcam can be supplied to fire the U.S. M193 or NATO SS109 bullets, which require differing rifling patterns, and will accept any NATO-standard magazine or optical sight mounts. The rifles are otherwise conventional, with wooden stocks and barrel-top handguards running forward from the chamber. The standard barrels measure 20in, but longer patterns can be obtained to order. They have three-slot compensators and will generally accept an American-pattern knife bayonet.

SIMILAR GUNS

Milcam HB rifle. A minor variation of the standard Milcam, this heavy-barrel pattern has been offered as a low-cost sniper rifle. Empty weight is about 8lb without sights.

Snicam rifle. Featuring a free-floating heavy barrel and a refined stock with an adjustable buttplate and cheekpiece, this version of the Milcam series is also usually fitted with a bipod. The pitch of the rifling may make a turn in 7in, 9in or 12in, suiting the U.S. M196 tracer, NATO SS109 and US M193 ball cartridges respectively. Snicam rifles have 24in barrels and weigh about 11lb without bipod and sights.

Polcam rifle. Intended for police and security agencies, this is a simplified form of the Snicam with the barrel, bolt and receiver of blackened stainless steel. The pitch of the rifling is one turn in 8.5in, to handle virtually any type of 5.56mm bullet interchangeably with comparatively little accuracy loss.

• Braendlin

Francis Augustus Braendlin, who may have had Belgian origins, made lifting-block guns in accordance with patents granted in 1863-5 for improvements to the Mont Storm (see **'Storm'**) system. He then became involved with Augusto Albini (see **'Belgium: Albini-Braendlin'**). Rifles were made on both patterns, and it is assumed that the five hundred 577 converted P/53 'Braendlin' (Albini-Braendlin) rifles acquired from Holland & Holland by the purchasing agents for South Australia emanated from Birmingham. They were accompanied by modified P/53 socket bayonets adapted by the Birmingham gunmaker William Tranter. A few sporting rifles were also made in Britain on the Braendlin-Albini action.

• Brand

This was made by Calisher & Terry of Birmingham, in accordance with a patent granted to Richard Brand in 1853 and a patent of addition granted to William Terry in 1855 to provide better ignition and an improved cartridge. Brand's Carbine typically had a swinging ring-type handle on the rear of the bolt-like breech, a sidelock, a half-stock and a trigger guard with a rearward spur. A small block and folding-leaf rear sight was fitted above the breech. An advertisement for Calisher & Terry published in *Pigot & Co.'s Birmingham Directory* of 1858 shows a Brand carbine, but it seems that it was dropped in favor of the Terry pattern shortly afterward.

• BSA, auto-loading type

BSA was Britain's largest privately-owned gunmaking business, and, therefore, became involved with a variety of firearms. Some were made in the Tool Room, commissioned by individual inventors; others were made in small batches on a commercial basis, such as the Carter & Edwards or Soper actions.

Information concerning BSA's commercial output has been very difficult to obtain. Fortunately, John Knibbs of P & J Springs of Birmingham, England, very kindly offered details from his forthcoming book dealing with BSA's entire commercial output,

The BSA Model 28-P auto-loading rifle.

and the summary presented here is undoubtedly the most accurate currently available.

Among the automatic firearms made in the Small Heath works prior to World War I was a recoil-operated rifle chambering 7mm Eley Special (7x63 or 276) cartridges. This was tested by the British Army in April 1913, but proved to be unreliable. Its action was locked by rotating the entire barrel through 45 degrees to release the bolt. The five-round magazine was loaded from a stripper clip, overall length was about 49.3in, the barrel measured 25.25in, and empty weight was about 10.4lb. An improved rifle tested in July 1913 was rejected partly because it was still unreliable, and partly because manual operation was unsatisfactory.

MODEL 28-P RIFLE

Made by BSA Guns Ltd., Birmingham, 1949.

Total production: 12-15. **Chambering:** 280, rimless. **Action:** locked by displacing the breechblock laterally into a recess in the left receiver wall; gas operated, selective fire.

DATA FOR A TYPICAL EXAMPLE

42in overall, 9.4lb with an empty magazine. 20in barrel, 5-groove rifling; RH, concentric. Detachable box magazine, rounds. Optical sight. About 2275ft/sec with standard ball ammunition; 300rpm. Knife bayonet.

The Model 28-P semi-automatic was developed by Claude Perry and Roger Wackrow to compete with the EM-2 and other rifles in the British Army trials of 1949-50. The rifle had a distinctively squared receiver with an integral optical sight and a pistol gripped half stock. The trigger system incorporated a rack-and-pinion and weight mechanism to slow the rate of automatic fire, with the radial-lever selector—marked 'A', 'R' and 'S' for automatic operation, single shots and safety respectively—protruding from the left side of the stock alongside the receiver. The flash hider doubled as a grenade launcher, and could accept a bayonet which is assumed to have been adapted from the No. 5 pattern.

A 28-P rifle was tested at Enfield in the summer of 1950, but was not particularly accurate; a premature explosion revealed a potentially serious weakness in the breech and, though a revised version subsequently performed adequately, the project was abandoned.

RALOCK SPORTING RIFLE

Made by BSA Guns Ltd., Birmingham, 1949-51.

Total production: a few thousand. **Chambering:** 22 Short or 22 Long Rifle, rimfire. **Action:** locked by a radial block sealing the chamber; blowback, semi-automatic only.

DATA FOR A 22LR TYPICAL EXAMPLE

38.75in overall, 6lb empty. 22in barrel, 6-groove rifling; RH, concentric. Tube magazine in the butt, 8 rounds. Spring-and-elevator rear sight. 1050ft/sec with standard ball ammunition.

The Ralock, made in takedown form, had an interesting patented radially-moving breech, and was cocked by pushing forward on the trigger guard. The 22 Short version had a magazine capacity of twelve rounds.

ARMATIC SPORTING RIFLE

Made by BSA Guns Ltd., Birmingham, 1963-9.

Total production: less than 5000. **Chambering:** 22 long rifle rimfire. **Action:** locked by a reciprocating bolt sealing the chamber; blowback, semi-automatic only.

40.5in overall, 5.5lb empty. 20.25in barrel, 6-groove rifling; RH, concentric. Detachable box magazine, 10 rounds. Spring-and-elevator rear sight. 1100ft/sec with 40-grain bullet.

The Armatic was a replacement for the Ralock, with a much more conventional bolt mechanism and a double-row box magazine ahead of the trigger guard. The gun fired from a closed breech, which improved accuracy. The tubular receiver (grooved for optical-sight mounts) had four distinctive circumferential angled slots above the magazine housing, and the pistol grip beechwood half-stock had a straight comb.

• BSA, bolt-action type

The first BSA sporting rifles were built on Lee-Metford and Lee-Enfield actions (q.v.), but work on these stopped when World War I began. Postwar efforts were concentrated on high-power rifles chambered – mistakenly, perhaps – for a new range of proprietary cartridges. The guns were built on the British modified Mauser action featured by the Pattern 1914 rifles (see **'Enfield'**) and then, when supplies of P/14 actions ran short, on war-surplus 1898-type Mausers.

In addition to the pre-1914 Lee-pattern sporting rifles and the patterns based on the Mauser or P14 actions, BSA also made a range of simple guns derived from the War Office Miniature Rifle (q.v.). Most were chambered for 22 rimfire ammunition, though there were a few 297/230 and even apparently some 310 examples among them.

Developed in the period immediately after the end of World War II, the perfected BSA bolt-action rifles relied on a standard Mauser two-lug locking system – though the third or safety lug was abandoned in favor of the bolt handle locking down into a seat in the receiver.

A non-rotating collar-type extractor was retained until the late 1950s. An entirely new firing mechanism then appeared, with a rotary safety catch on the right side of the bolt shroud, while an adjustable trigger was combined with the bolt stop and ejector.

Standard BSA rifles were sold in the U.S. by Galef, Herter's and others, before a sole distributorship was granted to the Ithaca Gun Company (q.v.) in the mid-1970s. Herter's also sold barreled Monarch actions as ' U9'.

NUMBER 1 RIMFIRE RIFLE

Made by the Birmingham Small Arms Co. Ltd. and BSA Guns Ltd., Birmingham, 1908-39.

Total production: many thousands. **Chambering:** 22 Long Rifle rimfire. **Action:** locked by turning the bolt handle base down into its seat in the receiver.

37in overall, about 4.1lb empty. 19.5in barrel, 4-groove rifling; RH, concentric? Single shot only. Fixed open-notch rear sight. 1050ft/sec with 40-grain bullet.

These guns were based on the War Office Miniature Rifle (q.v.), developed as a military trainer and exhibited in quantity for the first time at Bisley in 1906. BSA was one of the principal contractors, making large numbers in accordance with a government order, but then continued to develop the basic pattern for commercial sale. Several patents were granted to BSA, Augustus Driver and George Norman prior to 1914, beginning with no. 1000/07 of 1907. Some of the patent specifications showed an improved design with two opposed locking lugs, a shrouded bolt head and twin extractors.

The original No. 1 was shorter and lighter than its War Office prototype. It had a straight-comb half-stock with a short rounded forend. Some guns were made with a folding butt, operated by releasing a catch on the tang behind the cocking piece. Most BSA-made guns of this type had twin extractors, and the rear sight was often the adjustable rising-blade pattern associated with the air rifles of the day.

SIMILAR GUNS

No. 1A rifle (later known as 'No. 2'). This was similar to the No. 1, but had a micrometer-adjustable rear sight. It was also supplied with a plate above the stock-wrist to take the BSA No. 8 or No. 8A folding aperture sight.

SPORTSMAN RIFLE

Made by BSA Guns Ltd., Birmingham, 1947-55.

Total production: many thousands. **Chambering:** 22 Long Rifle rimfire. **Action:** locked by turning the bolt handle base down into its seat in the receiver.

DATA FOR A TYPICAL EXAMPLE

44in overall, about 5.7lb empty. 25.25in barrel, 6-groove rifling; RH, concentric. Single shot only. Open spring-and-elevator rear sight. 1100ft/sec with 40-grain bullet.

When production of commercial firearms resumed after World War II, BSA's designers seized the opportunity to refine the pre-1939 small caliber sporters, which dated back to the venerable War Office Miniature Rifle of 1906. The result was the Sportsman series. A basic single shot pattern – apparently distinguished by 'J', 'JA', 'JB' or 'JC' prefix serial numbers – was accompanied by a series of magazine-feed variants.

SIMILAR GUNS

Sportsman Five rifle. This was the basic magazine rifle, with a detachable five-round box ahead of the trigger guard. The plain half-stock had a shallow pistol grip and a straight comb. Serial numbers were prefixed 'K', 'KA', 'KB', 'KC' or 'KD', indicating that a number of minor changes had been made during the production life.

Sportsman Ten rifle. Mechanically identical with the 'Five', this had a ten-round tube magazine beneath the barrel and an 'L'-prefixed number.

Sportsman Fifteen rifle. Most popular of the Sportsman patterns, this had a fifteen-round tube magazine.

ROYAL SPORTING RIFLE
Also known as 'Hunter'
Made by BSA Guns Ltd., Birmingham, 1954-9.
Chambering options: (short action) 22 Hornet or 222 Remington; (medium action) 243 Winchester, 257 Roberts, 7x57mm, 300 Savage or 308 Winchester; (long action) 270 Winchester, 30-06 or 458 Winchester.
Action: locked by two lugs on the bolt head engaging recesses in the receiver behind the chamber as the bolt was turned downward, and by the bolt handle base entering its seat.
DATA FOR A TYPICAL EXAMPLE

Chambering: 222 Remington, rimless. 43.88in overall, 7.55lb empty. 24in barrel, 6-groove rifling; RH, concentric. Internal box magazine, 4 rounds. Folding-leaf rear sight. 3200ft/sec with 50-grain bullet.

The first of BSA's centerfire sporting rifles appeared in 1954. The magazine floorplate was released by a pivoting catch in the front of the trigger guard, and dovetails for optical-sight mounts were milled into the top of the receiver. The stock had a low Monte Carlo comb, a cheekpiece, and a checkered pistol grip; the checkered forend had a plain rounded tip.

A medium-length action was announced in 1956. A guide rib was added to the bolt, gas-escape ports were provided, and short blind holes were drilled down into the receiver-top dovetails to anchor optical sight mounts. The profile of the forend was changed to incorporate a schnabel tip but, except dimensions, the medium-action gun was practically identical with its shorter predecessor.

The long-action rifle of 1957 was essentially the same as the medium-action version, but had a modified chambering system. Instead of a Mauser 1898-type receiver ring, the BSA barrel was counter-bored to take the entire bolt head. The Royal was superseded by the Majestic (q.v.) in 1959, though assembly continued until the end of 1960.

SIMILAR GUNS

Featherweight rifle. Introduced in 1958, this rifle amalgamated a 22in barrel with a lightened version of the medium (.222 or 243) or long action (.270 or 30-06). The thickness of the left receiver wall was greatly reduced to save weight, and the optional 'Besa' muzzle brake was often fitted. This consisted simply of counter-boring the barrel and cutting gas-escape ports through to the bore.

.458 pattern. This variant of the basic Royal design was strengthened to handle the recoil of the 458 Winchester Magnum cartridge, and had a recoil bolt in the stock. It was particularly popular in central Africa.

SUPERSPORT FIVE SPORTING RIFLE
Made by BSA Guns Ltd., Birmingham, 1955-67.
Total production: many thousands. **Chambering:** 22 Long Rifle rimfire.
Action: an improved form of the Sportsman rifle, above.
DATA FOR A TYPICAL EXAMPLE

40.5in overall, 6lb empty. 21.0in barrel, 6-groove rifling; RH, concentric. Detachable box magazine, 5 rounds. Tangent-leaf rear sight. 1100ft/sec with 40-grain bullet.

This improved Sportsman had a new enclosed bolt, a radial safety lever on the right rear side of the breech behind the bolt handle recess, an improved extractor, and a greatly refined stock. Some guns had the alternative spring-leaf and elevator rear sight; serial number sequence ran from 'S' through 'SA' and 'SB' to 'SC'.

SIMILAR GUNS

Century 22 Match Rifle. This was built on the basis of the Supersport action, but had a 26in heavy barrel and a target-type half-stock with a contoured pistol grip and a broad forend. A swivel eye was screwed into the tip of the forend. Single shot guns had a spring-retained filler block in the receiver instead of a magazine, but the standard five-shot magazines could be substituted if required. Serial numbers customarily had a 'V' prefix.

MAJESTIC-SERIES SPORTING RIFLES
Made by BSA Guns Ltd., Birmingham, 1959-65.
Chambering options: see text. **Action:** as Royal series, above.
DATA FOR A TYPICAL MEDIUM-ACTION EXAMPLE

Chambering: 243 Winchester, rimless. 41.75in overall, 7.55lb empty. 22in barrel, 6-groove rifling; LH, concentric. Internal box magazine, 4 rounds. Folding-leaf sight graduated to 300yd. 3070ft/sec with 100-grain bullet.

Introduced in 1959, this was an improved BSA Royal (q.v.). A small extractor and a plunger-type ejector were mounted on the bolt head, the enclosed cocking piece had a small red plastic indicator pin, and a few minor changes were made in the trigger mechanism. The safety catch remained on the cocking piece. A folding-leaf rear sight and a hooded-ramp front sight were standard. The stock retained the low comb and cheekpiece of its predecessors, with checkering on the pistol grip and the schnabel-tip forend.

The artificial distinction between the short and medium actions was finally abandoned in 1961, but the Majestic series was replaced by the Monarch (q.v.) in 1965.

THE GUNS

Imperial rifle. Obtainable in 270 Winchester, 30-06 or 458 Winchester, this was the long-action version of the basic pattern.

Featherweight rifle. Available in 222 (short action), 243 and 308 (medium action), or 270 and 30-06 (long action), this had a row of gas vents along the muzzle beneath the front sight ramp.

Regent rifle. This was the short-action version, which was really little more than the medium-length Viscount with a smaller magazine. It was offered in 22 Hornet and 222 Remington only.

Viscount rifle. The standard or medium-action pattern, this was chambered for the 243 or 308 Winchester cartridges. It is described above.

MONARCH SPORTING RIFLE
Made by BSA Guns Ltd., Birmingham, 1965-74.
Chambering options: (medium action) 222 Remington, 243 Winchester or 308 Winchester; (long action) 257 Roberts, 270 Winchester, 7mm Remington Magnum, 300 Winchester Magnum or 30-06. **Action:** as Royal series, above.
DATA FOR A TYPICAL EXAMPLE

Chambering: 243 Winchester, rimless. 43.75in overall, 7.15lb empty. 22in barrel, 6-groove rifling; LH, concentric. Internal box magazine, 4 rounds. Folding-leaf sight graduated to 300 yards. 3070ft/sec with 100-grain bullet.

Introduced in 1965 to replace the Majestic, this had a rocking safety on the right side of the receiver behind the bolt handle. The trigger system was simplified and a few minor changes were made in the magazine, though the rifle otherwise resembled its predecessors. Monarch actions were made in two patterns – long and medium – and the Featherweight was abandoned. The flat dovetailed rails were replaced in 1968 by a round-top receiver drilled and tapped for conventional mounting bases, but the Monarchs were superseded by the improved CF-2 (q.v.) in 1974.

SIMILAR GUN

Varmint rifle, 1967-74. Chambered only for 222 Remington or 243 Winchester cartridges, this gun had a 24in heavy barrel, lacked open sights and weighed about 9lb.

CF-2 SPORTING RIFLES
Made by BSA Guns Ltd., Birmingham, 1974-86.
Chambering options: 222 Remington, 22-250, 223 Remington, 243 Winchester, 6.5x55, 7x57, 7x64, 7mm Remington Magnum, 270 Winchester, 300 Winchester Magnum, 30-06 or 308 Winchester. **Action:** an improved version of the Royal series, above.
DATA FOR A TYPICAL EXAMPLE

Chambering: 7x64, rimless. 44.4in overall, 8.05lb empty. 23.6in barrel, 5-groove rifling; LH, concentric. Internal box magazine, 4 rounds. Williams ramp-pattern rear sight. 2950ft/sec with 160-grain bullet.

Though announced in 1974 as a replacement for the Monarch, the first supplies of this rifle did not become available until the summer of 1975. The basic CF-2 was a refinement of its predecessors, with a one-piece forged bolt and a shrouded bolt face.

A plunger-type ejector and a broad extractor claw were set into the bolt head so that full-size locking lugs could be retained. An indicator pin protruded from the top of the bolt plug and a rocking safety catch, part of the separate trigger unit, protruded from the stock behind the bolt handle.

The guns originally had a roll-over Monte Carlo comb, with skip-line checkering on the pistol grip and forend; accompanied by a white spacer, the separate forend tip had an unusual 'wedge' joint with the stock. This stock pattern was abandoned on standard CF-2 rifles in the early 1980s, being restricted thereafter to the heavy-barrel rifle.

The BSA CF-2 Stutzen.

The magazine floorplate was released by a catch on the front upper face of the trigger guard. Williams sights were standard, and among the options was a set trigger with an additional reverse-curved lever in the front of the trigger guard.

A 6.5x55 chambering option was introduced for the standard CF-2 in 1982 to boost sales in Scandinavia, but work ceased when BSA Guns Ltd. collapsed in 1986. The machinery and most of the parts were apparently sold to Pakistan, but production has never recommenced (though parts can still be obtained in Britain for all BSA CF-series rifles).

SIMILAR GUNS

CF-2 carbine, 1984-6. This amalgamated the barrel of the Stutzen with the stock of the standard rifle. Offered for all the chamberings except the two magnum types, it was not especially popular and was made only in small numbers.

CF-2 Classic rifle, 1985-6. Built on the standard CF-2 action, this had a distinctively angular bolt plug and an oil-rubbed stock with a straight-comb butt. The forend tip was rounded.

CF-2 Heavy Barrel rifle (or 'Varmint'), about 1977-85. A heavy 24in barrel could be supplied in any of the standard chamberings, the resulting guns weighing up to 9.5lb.

CF-2 Regal Custom rifle, 1985-6. These rifles had a stock with a Monte Carlo comb and ebonite caps on the pistol grip and forend; bolt handles were flattened. Actions were engraved to order, but production seems to have been very limited.

CF-2 Stutzen, 1982-6. Introduced in all the standard chamberings except 7mm Remington Magnum and 300 Winchester Magnum, this was mechanically identical with the rifle. It was 41.4in long, had a 20.6in barrel and weighed about 7.8lb; the principal distinguishing feature was a full-length stock with a separate schnabel forend tip. The Stutzen stock lacked the roll-over comb, white spacers and high gloss finish of its predecessors.

CF-2 Varminter rifle, 1985-6. Little more than a heavy-barrel version of the Classic (q.v.), this lacked open sights.

CFT TARGET RIFLE

Made by BSA Guns Ltd., Birmingham, 1982-6.
Chambering: 7.62x51 NATO/308 Winchester only. **Action:** as Royal series, above.

47.6in overall, 10.85lb with sights. 26.5in barrel, 4-groove rifling; RH, concentric. Single shot only. Parker-Hale aperture sight. 2860ft/sec with 150-grain bullet.

Introduced in 1982, this single shot rifle was built on a modified CF-2 action. It had a solid-top receiver, a solid bottom plate where the magazine throat would normally lie, and a pistol grip butt that could accept spacer plates. A rail for a hand-stop was let into the underside of the broad plain-tipped forend. Micro-adjustable competition sights were usually fitted, though the mounting rail above the receiver could also accept optical or electro-optical sights.

SIMILAR GUN

A CFT with a four-round box magazine, developed as a sniper rifle, was entered by the Sterling Engineering Co. Ltd. of Dagenham in the British Army trials of the early 1980s. Unfortunately, BSA collapsed before guns could be offered commercially.

• BSA, slide-action type

The 22 long rifle rimfire Repeating Rifle was a modified takedown copy of Fabrique Nationale's hammerless Browning-pattern slide-action repeater. Introduced in 1923 with a six-round box magazine, the original version was joined in 1925 by a variant with a 15-round under-barrel tube magazine. Barrels measured 21.5in. Several thousand guns – less than 10,000 – were made in 1923-39.

• BSA-Adams

This rifle, designed by a British Army officer and promoted by the Fairfax Arms Syndicate Ltd. of London, was briefly exhibited to the British Army in December 1921 as the 'Browne-Adams'. Initially rejected untried as unsatisfactory, it reappeared as the 'Fairfax-Adams' in June 1922 and then as a 'new model' – made by BSA – in September 1924. It was eventually rejected in the Spring of 1928, on the grounds that it was potentially dangerous.

TRIALS PATTERN

Made by BSA Guns Ltd., Birmingham, 1924-5.
Chambering: 303, rimless. **Action:** locked by lugs on a rotating bolt entering recesses in the receiver wall; gas operated, semi-automatic only.

47.7in overall, 10.3lb empty. 26.4in barrel, 5-groove rifling; LH, concentric. Detachable box magazine, 5 rounds. Leaf sight on receiver, graduations unknown. About 2400ft/sec with Mk VII ball ammunition. P/1914 sword bayonet?

A BSA-Adams numbered '1' was held in the BSA collection until the early 1970s, and other guns survive in military collections. They had one-piece pistol grip stocks and wooden handguards above the barrel. The forend, bands and nose cap were the same as the P/1914 bolt-action rifle ('Enfield'). The magazine could be loaded through the action with stripper clips, and the rear sight was carried on a bracket, attached to the left side of the stock, which curved up and over the receiver. Gas was tapped from a port on the right side of the breech, alongside the chamber, and pushed back on a small piston on the front right side of the bolt. However, hot gases eroded the port and piston chamber much too quickly. The operating cycle was too violent, giving perpetual extraction

The breech of a BSA-Adams rifle.

failures, and the damage caused to the cartridge cases was deemed to be unacceptable.

• BSA-Enfield

These guns were built of the basis of refurbished P/14 actions (see **'Enfield'**), though it has been suggested that they were unfinished components left over from pre-war production of experimental 276 P/1913 rifles.

HIGH-POWER MODEL
Also known as 'Model 1923'

Made by BSA Guns Ltd., Birmingham, 1921-5.
Chambering options: 26 BSA, 33 BSA and 40 BSA. **Action:** locked by two lugs on the bolt head engaging recesses in the receiver as the bolt handle was turned down, and by the bolt handle base entering its seat.
DATA FOR A TYPICAL EXAMPLE
Chambering: 26 BSA, belted rimless. 48in overall, 8lb empty. 26in barrel, 5-groove rifling; LH, concentric? Internal charger-loaded box magazine, 5 rounds. Rear sight: see notes. 3100ft/sec with 110-grain bullet.

The Explosives Trades Ltd. cartel – created from Kynoch, Eley and Nobel – formed a 'Rifle Committee' in 1919 to perfect a range of sporting rifle cartridges based on a pre-war Eley design. The project was unsuccessfully offered to Holland & Holland in 1920, and then, with greater success, to BSA.

These sporters, based on the P/1914 action, appeared in 1926. They offered an angular half-stock, and had a short cylindrical bolt handle. The rear sight protectors on the receiver bridge were milled down around a compact twin-aperture sight and an additional folding-leaf sight (for 150yd and 300yd) was placed on the barrel.

Most of the cannibalized 1914-type actions had been used by 1927; consequently, BSA developed a new sporting rifle based on the P/14 ('Enfield') action. However, only about five of these improved prototypes were made and the project was never launched commercially.

LATER GUNS

BSA also converted several thousand British P/14 and U.S. M1917 rifles to sporting pattern in 1949-53. These had pistol grip half-stocks, but could be distinguished from the 1923 pattern by the cranked bolt handle. Offered in five grades from extremely plain to highly decorative, the conversions were available in 303 (P14 actions), 270 Winchester and 30-06 (M1917), and had 'H', 'HA' or 'M' prefixes to their serial numbers.

• BSA-Lee

The Birmingham Small Arms & Munitions Co. Ltd. ('BSA&M Co.') offered its first Lee-type rifles commercially in 1892, utilizing actions taken from regular production runs. A change to Enfield rifling was made about 1896, though the guns were outwardly similar to their Metford-barreled predecessors. Details paralleled those of the contemporary army rifles (q.v.), except that commercial proof marks were used and 'LEE-SPEED PATENTS' replaced British government marks.

Among the most desirable of these military-style rifles were those that had been made for volunteer units prior to the British Army reforms of 1908, and several thousands sold to the British South Africa Company prior to the abortive Jameson Raid into the Transvaal in 1896. Others went to India and Afghanistan.

Details of the military 303 Lee-action rifles built by BSA – and some of the 22 rimfire trainers – will be found in the Lee-Metford and Lee-Enfield sections.

HIGH-VELOCITY SPORTING PATTERN RIFLES
Made by the Birmingham Small Arms Co. Ltd., Small Heath, about 1902-14.
Chambering options: 7x57, 303, 8x51R, 32-40 Winchester or 375 Flanged Nitro Express (9.5x57). Action: locked by a single lug on the bolt body engaging a recess in the receiver and by the rear of the bolt guide rib abutting the receiver bridge as the bolt handle was turned down.
DATA FOR A TYPICAL NO. 2
Chambering: 303, rimmed. 43.5in overall, 7.55lb empty. 24in barrel, 5-groove rifling; RH, concentric. Detachable box magazine, 5 rounds. Block-and-leaves sight. About 2140ft/sec with 190-grain bullet.

Inspired by a rise of interest in the magazine sporting rifle, and particularly by some of the guns produced by enterprising gunsmiths on the basis of the Trade Pattern action, BSA introduced its own sporters about 1902.

Built on the action of the Lee-Enfield Mk I, with a plain Lee-Metford type cocking piece, the Pattern No. 1 BSA had its bolt handle turned down and slightly forward in the manner of the standard military carbines. The two-piece stock offered a pistol grip butt, and a half-length forend with a rounded rosewood, horn or ebonite tip. The barrel had a full-length top rib mounting a Cape-pattern rear sight graduated to a thousand yards; the front sight was usually a bead with protecting wings.

Production was apparently stopped in 1914. Though a few sporting rifles and carbines may have been sold in the early 1920s from store, none has yet been seen with the post-1919 trading style 'BSA Guns Ltd.'

SIMILAR GUNS

Heavy Pattern No. 1. A special variant of the No. 1 sporter was made for the 375 'Flanged' (rimmed) Nitro Express cartridge; it was identical with the standard No. 1, but had a heavyweight barrel, a four-round magazine and an express rear sight consisting of a standing block and two small folding leaves. The front sight was usually a blade or barleycorn with a sheet-steel hood.

Pattern No. 2. This was a cheaper version of No. 1, with a plain barrel.

Pattern No. 3. Distinguished by a plainer stock and a safety catch mounted on the cocking piece, the No. 3 customarily had a Cape-pattern rear sight and protected front-sight bead – though BSA No. 9 aperture sights could be fitted if required.

MAGAZINE SPORTING PATTERN CARBINES
Made by the Birmingham Small Arms Co. Ltd., Small Heath, about 1902-14
Chambering options: 7x57, 303, 8x51R or 375 Flanged Nitro Express.
Action: as BSA sporting rifle, above.
DATA FOR A TYPICAL NO. 3
Chambering: 303, rimmed. 40.5in overall, 7.35lb empty. 21in barrel, 5-groove rifling; LH, concentric. Detachable box magazine, 5 rounds. Leaf sight graduated to 2000yd. About 1900ft/sec with 215-grain bullet.

Introduced concurrently with the BSA Lee-Enfield sporting rifle described previously, these were also offered in four differing patterns.

THE GUNS
Pattern No. 1, "for officers' use". Chambered only for 303 ammunition, this had a military-style butt with the unique semi-pistol grip. Checkering on the butt and forend distinguished the No. 1, which accepted the P/1888 bayonet, from many otherwise similar service-issue carbines.

Pattern No. 2. This was basically a No. 1 stocked virtually to the muzzle, with a horn or ebonite forend tip.

Pattern No. 3, 'Trade Pattern'. Little more than a plain version of No. 1, this lacked checkering on the stock. It also had a military-type rear sight and a safety catch on the cocking piece.

Pattern No. 4. This seems to have been a hybrid with a 22in barrel, a cocking-piece safety, the military-style butt and a half-length forend. Cape-type rear sights were popular. Unlike the other carbines in this series, the No. 4 could chamber 7x57 Mauser rimless or 8x51 French rimmed cartridges.

• BSA-Martini

One of the leading contractors supplying Martini-Henry rifles to the British authorities, BSA was well placed to make sporting rifles embodying the same action. However, though a decision was taken in December 1884 to make Trade Pattern 'Rook Rifle' (small) and 'Sporting Rifle' (large) actions for individual gunmakers to complete, there is no evidence that BSA marketed Martini-type sporters of its own prior to the early 1900s. Though guns have been identified with BSA from the pre-1900 period, most of them prove to have been completed on BSA-made actions, identified by a small Piled Arms trademark, or to have been altered at a later date from BSA-made military rifles.

About 1906, however, a large order for Martini-action 310 training rifles was received from Australia (q.v.), supplementing guns which had previously been acquired from Francotte. Another large Australian order was placed with W.W. Greener (q.v.), but it is suspected that, owing to the colossal quantities involved, BSA may have made the Greener-Martini actions as well as its 'own-brand' type.

Small caliber sporting/target BSA-Martini rifles could be obtained even before 1914, though it was not until the formation of BSA Guns Ltd. in 1919 that promotion of guns of this pattern was undertaken in earnest. When production of the BSA-Martini began again after the end of World War II, however, the range was reduced to a single good-quality target rifle.

The BSA-Martini Internationals were very successful, being made in surprisingly large quantities for many years; indeed, the Mk V ISU, the last of the line, was still being made when BSA finally stopped making cartridge rifles in 1986.

SMALL-BORE RIFLES
Made by the Birmingham Small Arms Co. Ltd. and BSA Guns Ltd., Birmingham, about 1907-39.
Total production: many thousands. Chambering options: see text.
Action: locked by the tip of the underlever propping the breechblock behind the chamber.
DATA FOR A TYPICAL NO. 15 EXAMPLE
46in overall, 9.45lb empty. 29in barrel, 6-groove rifling; RH, concentric? Single shot only. Aperture sight on tang. 1100ft/sec with 40-grain bullet.

The guns made between the world wars have proved difficult to catalog; as work is still underway, therefore, only some of the individual patterns are listed here. The BSA-Martini detachable action was based on the Francotte type, with a distinctive high rounded back and a blade-type cocking indicator protruding (on the early models) from the upper right side of the breechblock. Sporting guns usually had straight-wrist butts and short round-tipped forends, though many of the better target rifles had pistol grip butts with the flat-tip operating lever shaped accordingly.

SIMILAR GUNS

No. 4. This was the first of the series, chambered for the 310 Cadet and other small centerfire cartridges.

No. 6. This was being offered in the 1930s in 25-20 WCF and 32-20 WCF. The barrel measured 25in.

No. 12. This was a 22 LR rimfire target rifle, with a 29in barrel and a weight of about 8.7lb. It had a straight-wrist butt, a conventional hooked operating lever, and a short forend with a panel of checkering on each side. One swivel lay on the underside of the barrel, with another beneath the forend directly ahead of the receiver.

No. 12/15. Produced in small numbers shortly after the end of World War II, this was basically the No. 12 action amalgamated with the improved pistol grip butt and broadened forend of the Model 15 (q.v.). The serial number had a 'P' prefix.

No. 13. A smaller version of No. 12, with a 25in barrel and a weight of only 6.5lb. A target version was made with a Parker (later Parker-Hale) No. 7 rear sight on the upper tang behind the breech, whereas a sporting variant had a simpler Parker 'Sportarget' sight.

No. 15. Another of the 22 LR target guns, this had a more robust action than the No. 12/15, a heavy 29in barrel, a broad beavertail forend, and a pistol grip butt with a squared cheekpiece. It weighed about 9.6lb, though an extra-heavy version reached 11lb. The rear sight was customarily a micro-adjustable BSA No. 30, the front sight being a BSA No. 20 tunnel pattern.

Centurion. This was a modified version of the No. 15, with a special 29in match-quality barrel guaranteed to make 1.5in groups at 100yd. The flat barrel rib was file-cut to minimize reflections.

INTERNATIONAL TARGET RIFLES

Made by BSA Guns Ltd., Birmingham, 1950-86.
Total production: many thousands. **Chambering:** 22 Long Rifle rimfire. **Action:** as BSA-Martini, above.
DATA FOR A TYPICAL 'ISU' EXAMPLE
43-44in overall (depending on butt spacers), 10.75lb empty. 28in barrel, 6-groove rifling; RH, concentric. Single shot only. Aperture sight on receiver. 1110ft/sec with 40-grain bullet.

The original BSA Martini-International Match rifle, subsequently designated 'Mark I', was introduced in 1950. Fitted with Parker-Hale sights, it had a pistol grip butt with a cheekpiece and an angular forend with a hand-stop on the underside. A single swivel was mounted on the hand-stop body for a single-point sling. Guns could be obtained with a 26in medium- or 29in heavyweight barrel, weight being 11-14lb. Their serial numbers were prefixed with 'U', 'UA' or 'UB'.

SIMILAR GUNS

Mk II, 1953-60. Sold in light and heavy patterns, this had an improved trigger system, better ejection, and refined woodwork. The forend was held by hooking it into the front of the receiver and by a single bolt running up into the underside of the barrel. A rail beneath the forend had five positions for the hand stop, and blocks for telescope-sight mounts were attached to the top of the barrel. Serial numbers were usually prefixed 'UB', 'UC', 'UD', 'F', 'FB' or 'FC'.

Mk III, 1959-70? Distinguished by numbers with a 'UF' prefix, this was a greatly improved form of the Mk II, with a free-floating barrel held in the greatly extended receiver by two large cap-head bolts on the left side. An 'I'-section rail ran forward from the receiver to support the forend, allowing the hand stop infinite adjustment. The Mk III was particularly successful and was made in large quantities.

ISU, 1968-86. This was a minor variant of the Mk III, adapted to comply with the International Shooting Union (ISU/UIT) 'Standard Rifle' rules. The trigger was improved, a vertically-adjustable buttplate was fitted, the cheekpiece was flattened, and the heavy barrel lacked the optical-sight mounting bases. The loading trough was angled, and the forend attachment was changed from the standard 'I'-strut to an improved 'V' pattern. The sights were customarily Parker-Hale PH1 Special (front) and PH25E (back) target patterns. Right- and left-hand actions could be obtained.

Mk V Match Rifle, about 1974-86. This was an improved form of the ISU pattern, but had an extra-heavy tapered barrel (1.1in diameter at the breech) and the optical-sight mounting bases were restored. The guns weighed 12.75lb and could be obtained with right- or left-hand actions.

• BSA-Mauser

BSA made a few sporters and some experimental military rifles in the mid 1920s, on the basis of refurbished war-surplus actions. The BSA reference collection still contained several BSA-Mauser rifles when it was dispersed in 1971. A typical example – chambered for a 303 Magnum cartridge – had a 26in barrel in a full-length pistol grip stock, with a handguard above the barrel and a bayonet lug beneath the nose cap. The buttplate was a brass SMLE type with a hinged trap.

The action had a detachable magazine floorplate, and a special vertical-leaf rear sight was mounted on the receiver bridge behind the stripper clip guides. A similar gun tested by the British authorities as the 'Model 1925 No. 1' was stocked in the manner of the SMLE Mk VI rifle, with a diced forend. It accepted a spike bayonet and had a special aperture sight on the receiver bridge, graduated to 1100yd.

• BSA-Norman, block-action type

Smooth-bore rifles for the Indian police were ordered in substantial numbers in the late 1920s to replace worn-out Martini-Henry conversions. BSA initially supplied 577/490 guns built on Martini actions, often with a patented trigger-blade safety system dating from 1929, but these were accompanied by an unknown quantity of guns built on a proprietary action.

INDIA POLICE CARBINE
Made by BSA Guns Ltd., Birmingham, about 1929-32.
Total production: not known. **Chambering:** 577/490 Spherical Ball, rimmed. **Action:** locked by the tip of the underlever propping a vertically-moving block behind the chamber.
42.5in overall, about 9lb empty. 25.63in barrel, smooth-bored. Single shot only. Standing-block rear sight. Performance not known. P/1888 sword bayonet.

These guns were stocked similarly to the SMLE, with a British-style butt and a full-length wooden barrel guard, but had a Martini-type nose cap. The steel buttplate contained a hinged-lid trap for the pull-through, and an automatic safety rose from the tang behind the receiver as the action was cocked.

• BSA-Norman, bolt-action type

Among the oddest bolt systems ever to be touted for military use, this had its origins in 'travelling block' rifles exemplified by the British Godsal (q.v.). BSA has been credited with the manufacture of the last experimental Godsal rifles – most had previously been the work of Webley & Scott – and a connection between the two guns can be made.

Patented by George Norman in December 1911, the BSA-Norman rifle had a two-lug Mauser-type bolt inclined at 9 degrees to the axis of the bore. When the breech was opened, the bolt and (at least on the military version) the stock-slide cover ran back down the comb. The face of a separate non-rotating bolt head was maintained at right angles to the bore during the operating stroke. The goal had been to allow the firer to operate the gun without disturbing his sight-line, but the rifles had such strange handling characteristics that this goal was never reached and the trials held in March 1913 were a disaster. The project was immediately abandoned.

The breech of the BSA-Norman inclined bolt rifle. (W&D)

EXPERIMENTAL MILITARY RIFLE

Made by BSA Guns Ltd., Birmingham, about 1911-12.

Total production: six? **Chambering:** 7mm Eley Special (7x63), rimless. **Action:** locked by two lugs on the bolt head engaging recesses in the receiver wall behind the chamber as the bolt handle turned down, and by the bolt handle base entering its seat.

43.5in overall, about 9.2lb empty. 24in barrel, 5-groove rifling; LH, concentric. Internal box magazine, 5 rounds. Folding-leaf rear sight graduated to 2000yd? About 2750ft/sec with ball ammunition. Sword bayonet.

The rifles cannot be mistaken, owing to the angled bolt with its handle alongside the trigger aperture. The shape of the butt, which lacked a comb, was also most distinctive. The rear sight was carried on a high bridge on the rear of the receiver, and the military-pattern prototypes had an intermediate position on the bolt release catch which served as a magazine cut-off.

British records suggest that two differing guns were submitted in 1912, followed by four – one made 'to a new pattern' – in time for trials held in 1913. One survives in sporting form with a checkered walnut half-stock, and another (the 'new pattern'?) has long-range sights and a radial safety lever on the right side of the receiver behind the bolt.

• BSA-Thompson

BSA, licensee of the patents protecting the Thompson automatic rifle (see **'USA'**), made a handful of the 1923-type Thompsons in the 1920s. Some of these were completed as 'heavy rifles' – really a form of light machine gun – with folding bipods and finned barrels. Surviving examples suggest that there were two series, light and heavy, and that at least six were made in each group.

The first submission was made in April 1924, followed by a test of an improved rifle at the beginning of 1926. The improved BSA-Thompson had a shortened action with a straight-pull cocking handle mounted at the rear of an independent bolt sleeve. Like its American-designed predecessors, however, it was still locked by a steeply pitched screw thread on the bolt engaging a bronze 'nut' or locking collar in the breech. At least one 7.9mm-caliber gun of this pattern survives; it has a British-style butt and a rear sight mounted on the extreme rear of the receiver.

A competition was arranged in the autumn of 1927 between a BSA-made Thompson, a Colt-made Thompson supplied by BSA, an improved BSA-Thompson, a gas-operated BSA, the BSA-Adams and a Farquhar-Hill. The report, submitted on 30th May 1928, indicated that the BSA-made Thompson narrowly beat the 'improved' BSA-Thompson with the Farquhar-Hill third. However, as none of the submissions was acceptable, BSA's interest in the Thompson-type rifles soon waned.

The BSA-Thompson heavy automatic rifle. (W&D)

• Burton, block-action type

James Burton, an American, is perhaps best known for his efforts to create a Confederate arms industry during the Civil War. However, he also served as chief engineer of the Royal Small Arms Factory, Enfield, in 1855-60 and lived in London from 1863 until his final return to the U.S. in 1868. Burton designed several firearms, but no relevant patents have been found and their chronology is difficult to determine.

1858-TYPE CARBINE

Made by the Royal Small Arms Factory, Enfield, 1858.

Total production: very few. **Chambering:** 500, combustible cartridge, fired by a caplock. **Action:** Locked by sliding the breechblock vertically in the frame.

34in overall, 6.08lb empty. 18in barrel, 5-groove rifling; RH, concentric. Single shot only. Multi-leaf rear sight for distances up to 500yd. No bayonet.

This experimental cavalry weapon resembled the Sharps, which may have provided the inspiration and may also explain the absence of traceable patents. The Burton design had a back-action lock, a distinctive rear sight, and an unusually long forend with a swivel-carrying band near the tip. The most obvious feature was the locking catch on the tip of the combination operating lever/trigger guard, which may also have prevented the trigger releasing the hammer unless the lever was properly closed.

TRIALS-PATTERN RIFLE

Known officially as the 'Burton No. 1', this was submitted to the British Army trials of 1867. Its breechblock was pivoted beneath the barrel and lowered by a handle in front of the trigger guard. The striker retracted automatically as the breech opened. Spent cases supposedly fell downward and out of an ejection port cut in the stock, but this feature did not prove acceptable in rapid fire. Six 577-caliber guns were made for the British trials; they had 32.5in barrels with six-groove rifling making a turn in 48in. Stocks were in one piece, with a back-action lock and three bands. The rifles had London proof marks.

• Burton, bolt-action type

TRIALS-PATTERN RIFLE

The 'Burton No. 2' rifle tested by the British authorities in 1867, in contrast with the block-action No. 1 (q.v.), was a bolt-action design. Six 577-caliber guns – probably London-made – were submitted to the British trials; they had 33in barrels with six-groove rifling making a turn in 48in. Their stocks were in one piece, there were three bands, and a P/1853 socket bayonet could be fitted when required.

The gun was regarded highly, placing second to the Henry in the trials compared with fifth for the Burton No. 1. It has been suggested that the basis of the design was provided by patents granted to another American engineer, Bethel Burton (q.v.), but no relationship between James and Bethel Burton has yet been proved.

• Carter & Edwards

The subject of patents granted to Henry Carter and George Edwards in 1866-9, these rifles were perhaps the best of the British bolt-action designs of their day.

The first guns were submitted to the British trials of 1866-7. Rifle No. 1 was overweight and could not be fired owing to an error in its construction; No. 2 was summarily rejected owing to misfiring and uncertain extraction; but an 'Improved Model' was retained for consideration.

1866-PATENT GUNS

Several constructional alternatives were shown in the 1866 patent, including one unhandy striker-fired gun with a tubular receiver extending back over the wrist. An alternative with an internal or shrouded bolt and a hammer firing system was also offered. The handle lay at the front of the bolt, the action being locked by the handle entering a recess in the receiver and by a small stud in the bolt way entering a seat in the bolt. A hinged breech cover could be housed against the left side of the stock when not required.

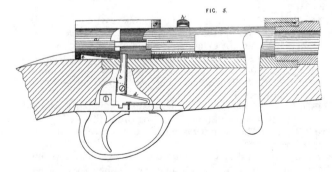

The improved Carter & Edwards 'Chassepot conversion' action, from the British patent.

1867-PATENT GUNS

The 'Improved Model' tried in 1867 had an internal hammer and an inertia striker, the design of the components ensuring that no cartridge could be fired until the bolt had been locked shut. The auxiliary locking stud in the bolt way was abandoned, and the ejector was improved.

The Carter & Edwards rifles were much simpler than the competing Bacon (q.v.), but were clearly capable of improvement and a greatly refined 1867-patent design was entered in the breech-mechanism trials of 1868.

Much easier to make than its predecessors, the 1867-type rifle was offered in two patterns – with a light iron breech shroud or an open-top action. It had a very neat butter knife bolt handle placed well forward, and a cross-bolt safety catch on the trigger plate. The trigger was combined with the sear for simplicity, and the hammer could not reach the striker until the bolt was locked.

A hundred actions were ordered in 1868 from the Birmingham Small Arms Co. Ltd. by the 'Carter-Edwards Breech Loading Rifle Co. Ltd.' of London. It is suspected that these were subsequently barreled, stocked and finished by William Scott & Sons of 47 Princip Street, Birmingham. At least one gun was used in the military breech-mechanism trials of 1868, but fell victim to the ban placed on all bolt-action designs after the accidental destruction of a Bacon and a Wilson rifle. This was particularly hard on Carter and Edwards, as their gun had been the only one to negotiate the additional safety trials without a blemish. The remaining actions were completed as sporting guns.

1869-PATENT GUNS

In the summer of 1869, Carter & Edwards patented a simple metallic cartridge adaptation of the Chassepot needle rifle and an improvement of their own rifle. The 1869-type gun had an improved self-cocking action with the bolt handle turned downward. The sear, which doubled as the bolt stop, slid vertically; articulated with the trigger, it was driven by a single spring. Interfaces between the bolt body and cocking piece ensured that the gun could not be fired until the breech was locked, and a safety in the form of a rotating collar on the left side of the breech prevented the cocking piece moving forward far enough for the striker to reach the cartridge.

Six complete guns of this type were made in the BSA toolroom in the Spring of 1871, possibly for military trials, but Scott & Sons failed in 1875 and work on Carter & Edwards rifles ceased. Henry Carter had meanwhile sued the Mauser brothers and Hiram Berdan for patent infringement but was unable to prove his claims.

• Churchill

Churchill (Gunmakers) Ltd. of London, created from Robert Churchill & Company since the end of World War II, has made rifles embodying Mauser actions supplied by ZCZ in Yugoslavia.

'ONE OF ONE THOUSAND' RIFLE

This was made for Interarms, Churchill's parent, to celebrate the American company's twentieth anniversary in 1973. Offered in 270 Winchester, 7mm Remington Magnum, 300 Winchester Magnum, 30-06, 308 Winchester, 375 H&H Magnum or 458 Winchester Magnum, the rifle had a 24in barrel and weighed 8.0-8.5lb; the magazine held five standard or three magnum cartridges. The half-stock had a straight comb, checkering on the pistol grip and forend, and a rounded ebonite tip. Express-type sights and quick-detachable swivels were standard. (Note: the Churchill brand name has also been associated with bolt action rifles made in Italy by FIAS and sold in North America by Kassnar.)

• Cogswell & Harrison, block-action type

Though renowned more for bolt action and break-open rifles, Cogswell & Harrison have also made single shot patterns using a variety of actions. The most popular seems to have been the Farquharson (q.v.), which was still being promoted in the 1920s. A typical 303 example had a case-hardened receiver with 'Best Bouquet' engraving, a pistol grip butt with a straight comb, and a short forend with a plain tip. A three-leaf express sight was mounted on a quarter-rib, sling eyes lay beneath the barrel and the butt, and a sliding safety could be found on the tang.

• Cogswell & Harrison, bolt-action type

This well-established gunmaker exploited a unique turning-bolt action patented in March 1900 by Edgar Harrison. The patent specifications illustrate a large rifle with a magazine of suitable dimensions for centerfire cartridges such as the 303 or 7.65mm Mauser.

Named after the company's telegraphic code-name, the Certus mechanism was built around a stubby rotating bolt head set into a reciprocating block. When the handle was lifted, disengaging the locking lugs from the receiver, bolt and block could be slid backward along rails set into the stock. The extractor and ejector are built into the bolt head and block respectively. The safety catch was a radial lever on the right rear side of the block, and most guns had readily detachable barrels.

The Certus action has some affinities with the British Godsal (q.v.). Though it was conceived as an express rifle, its initial applications seem to have been to rimfire and small caliber patterns. A few shotguns were also made. Production seems to have ceased in 1914; post-1918 Cogswell & Harrison sporters were built on standard Mauser actions.

CERTUS EXPERT MARKSMAN'S RIFLE

Made by Cogswell & Harrison, London, about 1900-12.
Total production: not known. **Chambering:** 220 (.22 WCF?), centerfire.
Action: locked by three lugs on the bolt head engaging recesses in the receiver when the bolt handle was turned down.

About 40in overall, 4.5lb empty. 22in barrel, 6-groove rifling; RH, concentric? Single shot only. Fixed open rear sight. 1500ft/sec with 45-grain bullet?

This small rifle was offered in the Cogswell & Harrison catalog of 1900 in plain or engraved versions. It had a walnut half-stock, checkered on the wrist and forend. The rear sight was an exchangeable 'V' or peep-plate sliding in a channel on the back of the traveling block. Like all Certus patterns, the barrel was readily detachable.

By 1906, an improved version had been introduced 'with Military Sights for Miniature Rifle Clubs, Target & Gallery Shooting'. This was usually distinguished by an exposed knurled head on the cocking piece and the rear sight of the War Office Miniature Rifle (q.v.), though other versions have been reported. The standard 220 chambering was supplemented by 297/230; rimfire guns were also made in small numbers.

SIMILAR GUNS

Rook & Rabbit Rifle. Offered in plain, engraved or 'Best' quality, this was an enlarged version of the Expert Marksman's Rifle chambered for 250 or 295 centerfire cartridges. By 1906, an improved gun had been introduced 'for Rooks, Rabbits, Small Game & Practice', with a heavier stock and a flat base to the pistol grip. A simple rear sight on the traveling block could be supplemented by a multi-leaf sight on the barrel ahead of the chamber. The standard chamberings were 220, 250 and 295 centerfire.

CERTUS EXPRESS SPORTING RIFLE

Made by Cogswell & Harrison, London, about 1902-10.
Total production: a few hundred? **Chambering options:** 256 Mannlicher, 303, 375/303 Axite, 318 Accelerated Express, 360 Nitro Express No.2, and many other British sporting rounds. **Action:** as Expert Marksman's Rifle, above.

The Certus sporting rifle.

DATA FOR TYPICAL EXAMPLE

Chambering: 303, rimmed. 48.25in overall, 7.67lb empty. 27in barrel, 5-groove rifling; LH, concentric. Detachable box magazine, 4 rounds. Express sight. 2050ft/sec with 210-grain bullet.

The first rifles of this type followed the 1900 patent specification drawings closely, with one-piece stocks and detachable box magazines. A radial safety lever lay on the right side of the breechblock, and the tail of the striker acted as an indicator when the mechanism was cocked.

The barrel, held in the receiver by interrupted-thread screw, could be removed by turning it through 90 degrees after a bolt running upward into the forend ahead of the magazine had been loosened.

Most guns of this pattern had impeccably checkered pistol grip half-stocks with an unusually short forend, sometimes retained by a transverse key set in oval escutcheons. The sights reflected the customer's specifications; though express or Cape patterns predominated, they may range from simple open notches to military-style tangent-leaves.

SIMILAR GUNS

Guns were made to what is assumed to have been an improved design – though this has been associated with Westley Richards & Co. Ltd., to whom Cogswell & Harrison may have granted a license. Some rifles had magazines, but most were single shot.

The principal improvement concerned the detachable barrel, locked into the receiver by a lateral quick-release bolt. The breech mechanism was simplified – the bolt handle was sometimes no more than an open ring – and the striker-locking safety was usually replaced by a trigger-lock type. Owing to the slab-type barrel-lock housing, a two-piece stock was necessary. Butts had straight wrists or pistol grips; forends were plain or horn tipped.

• Cogswell & Harrison, break-open type

Renowned for shotguns built on box- or sidelock actions, Cogswell & Harrison has also regularly made double rifles on the same basic patterns. These are notoriously difficult to classify, as they have often been built to order. Details of a typical pattern are listed below.

HIGH VELOCITY DOUBLE RIFLE

Made by Cogswell & Harrison, London, 1920-39.

Total production: not known. **Chambering:** 470, rimmed. **Action:** locked by a double-bite and cross bolt controlled by a top lever.

DATA FOR TYPICAL EXAMPLE

About 40.5in overall, 11.25lb empty. 26in barrel, 4-groove rifling; RH, concentric. Double barrels, two shots only. Express sight. 2200ft/sec with 500-grain bullet.

This was listed in the 1920 catalog as a hammerless ejector of the 'Finest Quality', with extensive bouquet or scroll engraving on the breech, detachable sidelocks, and an elongated action-strap with a "Stalker's Stop" on the sliding safety button. It was also offered in lesser grades, as a side- or box-lock ejector, and will be encountered with a variety of butts ranging from plain straight-wrist to pistol grip examples with cheekpieces and hog's back combs. Most guns had multi-leaf express sights mounted on a matted top rib between the barrels.

• Cogswell & Harrison (Mauser)

Production of the proprietary Certus action seems to have been stopped by World War I, as the Cogswell & Harrison catalog of 1920 shows only Mauser-type guns.

SUPER HIGH VELOCITY SPORTING RIFLE

Made by Cogswell & Harrison, London, 1920-39.

Chambering: 370 rimless. **Action:** Locked by turning the two lugs on the bolt head into their recesses behind the chamber, and the lug opposing the bolt head into its seat in the receiver.

DATA FOR TYPICAL EXAMPLE

.370, rimless. 44.2in overall, 8.25lb empty. 24in barrel, 4-groove rifling; RH, concentric. Internal box magazine, 3 rounds. Express sight. 2850ft/sec with 270-grain bullet.

These were built in plain or 'Best' forms on refurbished military actions, betrayed by the hole bored through the front trigger guard web. Initially chambered only for the 250 rimless belted and 370 rimless cartridges (subsequently renamed '.375 Super'), they were offered in takedown form with a jointing plate set vertically in the stock ahead of the chamber. The half-stock had an oval cheekpiece, with checkering on the pistol grip and the forend; engraving appeared on the action, and the bolt handle was bent downward against the woodwork. Guns were offered with a 'deadened' (i.e., 'matted') sighting rib, with extra sights and a sight cover in the pistol grip. A folding peep sight could even be attached to the cocking piece.

By 1929, the standard chamberings had become 250/300 Savage, 275 Super, 300 US Cartridge (30-06), 318 High Velocity and 375 Super; in 1965, Cogswell & Harrison was offering a series of Mauser-action rifles, built on old German or new FN actions.

INDIVIDUAL GUNS

Longford. Available in 30-06 or 308 Winchester only, this was the basic pattern; built on a war-surplus action, it had a 22in barrel and a plain pistol grip stock with a straight comb. Swivels lay under the butt and round tipped forend. The rear sight was usually a tangent-leaf.

Special Model. Offered in 7x57mm Mauser, 30-06, 300 H&H Magnum, 308 Winchester, 9.3x62mm Mauser, 9.5mm Nitro Express, 375 H&H Magnum, 404 Nitro Express or 458 Winchester, this gun had a better-quality stock than the Longford and greater attention was paid to finish. Barrels measured 22-26in. The front swivel lay on the barrel, and a folding-leaf rear sight was usually fitted. Rosewood or ebonite forend tips were customary.

Take Down. Similar to the Special, this had an interrupted-screw joint between the action/butt group and the barrel/forend.

De Luxe. Essentially the same as the Special Model, De Luxe guns had a select walnut stock (with a straight or Monte Carlo comb). The action was usually engraved with scrollwork. A Cape or express sight lay above the barrel on a quarter-rib, though a curious folding peep sight was also often attached to the bolt plug. De Luxe rifles were chambered to order.

• Cooper, block-action type

Joseph Cooper of Birmingham was a prolific patentee, receiving fourteen patents for breech-loading rifles in 1853-69. Typical of the earliest designs was a chamber which was drawn back and then tipped laterally when a cam-lever on the right side of the breech was lifted through 90 degrees. A typical 30-bore sporting rifle of this type had a 31in octagonal barrel with twelve-groove rifling and a walnut half stock with a checkered wrist and forend. The barrel was held in the forend, which had a separate horn tip, by a transverse key set in oval escutcheons. The engraved sidelock had a flat-body hammer, and a small standing block rear sight with a single folding leaf was dovetailed into the top surface of the barrel.

• Cooper, toggle-action type

Among Joseph Cooper's later inventions was a toggle-lock breech patented in 1864 (no. 1816), which was incorporated in good-quality caplock rifles made by Cooper & Goodman. The toggle was released by a thumb catch on the right side of the breech, sometimes accompanied by an additional locking latch which had to be released simultaneously by the finger and thumb of the trigger hand. Customarily completed in military style, though often intended for target shooting, the Copper & Goodman guns often had a curved brace running from the back of the action to the back of the butt-wrist; this supported a special rear sight when shooting prone from the back position. Color case-hardened sidelocks, checkered walnut stocks, and English-style scroll or best-bouquet engraving are also often present.

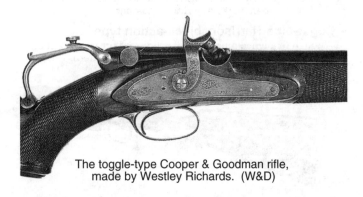

The toggle-type Cooper & Goodman rifle, made by Westley Richards. (W&D)

• Daw

London gunsmith George Daw patented a 'drop-down' or break-open action in 1861, exhibiting guns of this particular type at the International Exhibition of 1862. A lever under the trigger guard was pushed down to withdraw the sliding locking bolt in the frame beneath the barrel block. The Daw system was applied to pin- and centerfire rifles, but was most commonly encountered on shotguns. Like most of the simple-but-weak locking systems of the early 1860s, it was soon replaced by more efficient designs.

• Deeley & Edge

The Deeley & Edge rifle – developed for military use, but successful only for sporting purposes or match-shooting – was originally an underlever pattern, patented by John Deeley and James Edge of Birmingham in 1873 and improved in 1878. A hollow breechblock contained the hammer, trigger lever and all the associated springs. Pulling down on the spur of the trigger guard (suitably offset to the right) lowered the breechblock and cocked the hammer.

The rifle was efficient enough, but the integration of the lever and the trigger guard was less acceptable militarily than the separate lever and trigger guard of the Martini-Henry. The modified (or 'Improved') pattern was somewhat like the earlier Field (q.v.), but had a compact solid block, containing only a small inertia-pattern striker.

The block was lowered by a projection on the thumb-lever boss directly engaging a finger on the underside of the breechblock. The internal hammer cocked as the thumb-lever rotated. Though lacking the extracting qualities of long-lever actions, the 1881-type Deeley & Edge rifle was a simple and efficient design.

Virtually all of these guns were made by Westley Richards & Co. Ltd., John Deeley having succeeded Westley Richards in 1872. The rifles were made alongside proprietary Westley Richards pivoting-block rifles (q.v.) and a selection of Improved Martini patterns. Both types of Deeley & Edge rifle were made concurrently.

BREECH-LOADING MILITARY RIFLE
1877 pattern
Made by Westley Richards & Co. Ltd., Birmingham.

Total production: not known. **Chambering options:** 450 and other centerfire chamberings. **Action:** locked by the operating lever propping the breechblock behind the chamber.
DATA FOR A TYPICAL EXAMPLE
 Chambering: 500/450 No. 2, rimmed. 49.8in overall, 9.04lb empty. 33in barrel, 7-groove rifling; LH, composite. Ramp-and-leaf sight graduated to 1400yd. 1355ft/sec with 480-grain bullet. Sword or saber bayonet, supplied to order.

This gun was immediately recognizable by its breechblock, the top edge being dished to form a loading tray, and by the spur on the operating lever/trigger guard bent outward to the right. A straight-wrist butt and full-length forend were standard, the latter being hooked into the receiver and retained by a single band at the muzzle. The band carried the bayonet lug and a swivel, the other swivel appearing on the underside of the butt. A radial safety lever on the operating lever locked the trigger when the action was closed.

IMPROVED SPORTING RIFLE
1881 pattern
Made by Westley Richards & Co. Ltd., Birmingham.

Total production: not known. **Chambering options:** many large-caliber pre-1900 British sporting cartridges. **Action:** similar to 1877 pattern above, but operated by a side-lever.
DATA FOR A TYPICAL EXAMPLE
 Chambering: 500/450 No. 1 Express, rimmed. 43.15in overall, 8.10lb empty. 26in barrel, 5-groove rifling; RH, concentric. Multiple-leaf sight. 1900ft/sec with 270-grain bullet.

This rifle had a strong external affinity with the Farquharson (q.v.), except that the breech lever lay on the receiver-side instead of around the trigger guard. Internally, the Deeley & Edge pattern was much simpler. A typical sporting rifle offered a pistol grip butt and a half-length forend, woodwork being extensively checkered. Swivels appeared on the underside of the barrel ahead of the forend tip and under the butt. A three-leaf express rear sight graduated for 100yd, 200yd and 500yd was fitted to the matted rib above the round barrel. The front sight was a small silvered bead.

• De Lisle

Offered to the British authorities by William De Lisle in 1943, this was basically a Lee-Enfield action adapted to fire 45 ACP cartridges through a large-diameter silencer made integrally with the gun. The goal was a short-range silent weapon for Special Operations. A few prototypes were made in the Dagenham factory of the Ford Motor Company by adapting old SMLE actions. These performed well enough for a 500-gun contract to be given to the Sterling Engineering Co. Ltd.

DE LISLE CARBINE
Made by the Sterling Engineering Co. Ltd., Dagenham, Essex, 1944-5.
Total production: less than 200 (see text below). **Chambering:** 45 ACP, rimless. **Action:** generally as Lee-Enfield rifles (q.v.).
DATA FOR A STANDARD EXAMPLE
 35.75in overall, 8.25lb empty. 7.25in barrel, 6-groove rifling; RH, concentric. Detachable box magazine, 7 rounds. Tangent-leaf sight graduated to 200yd. About 1050ft/sec with ball ammunition. No bayonet.

Built on a No. 1 Mk III* rifle action, the standard carbine was readily identified by the narrow magazine protruding ahead of the trigger and the large-diameter silencer housing above the slender forend. The rear sight lay on top of the casing at the breech. The first order called for 450 standard and fifty paratroop guns, but, though the quantities were subsequently increased, work stopped after only 106 had been accepted. However, a few carbines were subsequently salvaged from government rejects or assembled from parts; the total, therefore, is believed to have approached 200.

SIMILAR GUNS
Airborne pattern (or Paratroop). This was a variant of the standard carbine with a folding butt and an auxiliary pistol grip. Fifty were to be included in the first 500-gun delivery, but there is no evidence that anything other than prototypes were ever made.

• Dickson

John Dickson & Sons of Edinburgh, best known for the Round Action double-barrel shotguns (and a few sporting rifles of the same pattern), also offered Mauser-type sporting rifles on old German or new FN actions. A typical 1960s-vintage Caledonian Model – chambered for 243, 270 or 308 Winchester cartridges – had a 22in barrel and a quintessentially British express rear sight on a short rib. Walnut stocks with Monte Carlo combs and rounded forends were standard.

• Dougall

James Dougall of Edinburgh (and later London) patented his Lock Fast action in the early 1860s. This relied on a sidelever, working on an eccentric made integrally with a transverse pin, to draw the barrels forward far enough from conical discs in the standing breech to allow them to drop down. Made in rifled pinfire and centerfire versions, as well as smooth-bore shotguns, the Lock Fast system was particularly popular in the 1870s before being superseded by better designs.

• Enfield, auto-loading type

This title signifies participation in design by the Royal Small Arms Factory – founded in Enfield Lock, Middlesex, but closed in the late 1980s when operations moved to Nottingham. The only truly Enfield-designed rifles to attain service status are the British Army's current autoloader and the sturdy Mauser-type bolt-action Pattern 1914. Coverage here is restricted to these rifles and (in the case of the P/1914) their direct descendants. Details of the Lee-Enfield will be found in the 'Lee' section, while the British L1A1 is considered below under 'FN-Saive (Enfield)'.

SLEM RIFLE

Based on pre-war Belgian prototypes, a few 'Rifles, 7.92mm, Self-Loading, Experimental Model No. 1 (SLEM No. 1) were made at Enfield in 1944 to a design prepared by Dieudonne Saive and émigré FN technicians attached to the Small Arms Group, Cheshunt. Two thousand SLEM-type 'Rifles, Automatic, 7.92mm' were ordered in 1946 for field trials, though the command was soon rescinded and very few were ever made. They were very similar to the Mle. 49 SAFN (see 'Belgium'), but the handguard ran only to the barrel band, the pistol grip was much slimmer, and the rear sight lacked protecting wings.

The SLEM rifle, an experimental predecessor of the FAL.

The 5.56mm L85A1 rifle replaced the
4.85mm IW. This is an XL70E3 prototype

INDIVIDUAL WEAPON
Also known as the IW, SA-80 or L85
**Made by the Royal Small Arms Factory and Royal Ordnance pic,
Enfield Lock (to 1988) and Nottingham (1988 to date).**

Currently in production. **Chambering:** 5.56x45, rimless. **Action:** locked by rotating lugs on the bolt into engagement with recesses in the receiver; gas operated, selective fire.

DATA FOR A TYPICAL L85A1

30.9in overall, 10.95lb with loaded magazine. 20.4in barrel, 6-groove rifling; concentric, RH. Detachable box magazine, 30 rounds. Optical sight. 3085ft/sec with SS109 bullet.

Trials to find a new small caliber service rifle for the British Army began about 1967, a 6.25x43 cartridge being tested in 1969-71. The 6.25mm round – a 92-95-grain bullet in a necked 280 case – was a potentially effective compromise between the 5.56x45 and 7.62x51 rounds; it promised to be accurate, and had better hitting power (and a longer effective range) than the US 5.56mm M193 bullet. However, it was heavier than the 5.56mm pattern and thoughts turned instead to lightening the rifleman's burden.

A 5x44 cartridge appeared in 1970 and a finalized 5mm pattern of 1972 was renamed '4.85x44'. It was given a 49mm case in 1973, and more than a million rounds were expended during development trials. Once the cartridge design had been stabilized, work began on a suitable rifle. The project team was initially led by the late John Weeks, then a lieutenant colonel in the British Army. The design of the rifle owed much to Sydney Hance, who had been involved with the abortive 280 EM-2 (q.v.).

The new 4.85mm Infantry Weapon (IW) differed greatly from the EM-2 internally, though both guns favored the bullpup layout. Its multi-lug bolt was adapted from the Stoner (Armalite) patterns, trial models being bullpup adaptations of AR-18 and Stoner 63

The current British service rifle, the 5.56mm L85A1.

rifles. On 14th July 1976, the new guns were publicly unveiled. Four basic guns were demonstrated, two rifles and two Light Support Weapons (LSW).

SIMILAR GUNS
L85A1. The XL70E3 was adopted in 1985 as the '5.56mm Rifle L85A1'. Compact dimensions and the universal issue of an optical sight have been welcomed, but the basic 5.56mm IW has been unsuccessful in competitive military trials – e.g., in Australia and Eire – and has encountered many unforeseen teething troubles. Field service in the Gulf War revealed serious problems attributed more to manufacturing deficiencies and poor-quality ammunition than design faults, but reports of widespread dissatisfaction throughout the British Army began to gain credence. The inability of the firer to choose the direction of ejection (cf., French FAMAS) was the target of much criticism, particularly as it also compromised the utility of the rifle in an urban environment. Though the worst of the teething troubles have now been overcome, it is still hard to see the British Army keeping long-term faith with the L85.

L98A1 cadet rifle. Developed in 1984 and designated 'L98A1' in 1985, this shared the outline of the autoloader but was charged manually by retracting the handle on the right side of the breech. The optical sight was replaced by a pivoting-'L' sight let into the fixed carrying handle. A ten-round magazine was developed specifically for this weapon, though the standard twenty- and thirty-round IW types would interchange if required. So, too, would the NATO-standard US M16A1 pattern. Cadet Rifles were about 29.75in long, had a 19.5in barrel and weighed about 9lb.

SA-80. The commercial designation of the L85A1.

XL64E5. This was the standard 4.85mm pattern, with the mechanism designed to eject spent cases to the right. The XL64 was entered in NATO trials in 1977, which eventually standardized the thirty-round US M16A1 magazine, the French grenade launcher, and the Belgian FN SS109 5.56mm bullet. However, agreement reached among the other participants left the British 4.85mm guns isolated.

XL68E2. A variant of the XL64E5 set to eject to the left. Comparatively few of these were made, as the decision was soon taken to issue rifles of only one basic pattern.

XL70E3. This was a 5.56mm version of the 4.85mm XL64, developed in 1981. It could be identified by the simplified receiver, which had a straight under-edge. The first series-production guns were made in the Enfield factory in 1983 for field trials and issued in the summer of 1984. The XL70 followed the fashionable straight-line bullpup layout, with the magazine protruding behind the pistol grip, and mounted the 4x 'Sight, Unit, Small Arms, Trilux, L9A1' (SUSAT). The shoulder pad, handguard and pistol grip were nylon and the construction relied heavily on stampings, pressings and spot-welding.

• Enfield, bolt-action type
This Mauser-based system was developed in Britain, but mass-produced in the U.S. The original rifles were accurate and sturdy – apart from the flimsy ejector. Sights were excellent and a long sight radius promoted good shooting.

In 1910, increasingly worried that the German Gewehr 98 and the US M1903 Springfield developed considerably greater muzzle velocity than the short Lee-Enfield, the British Small Arms Committee was asked to list features to be incorporated in an entirely new rifle. As much of the SMLE was to be retained as possible, but a Mauser-pattern action was to be used and an aperture rear sight substituted for the open notch. The first experiments were undertaken with a converted M1903 'Enfield-Springfield', but a much-modified rifle and an experimental 276 cartridge were being recommended for field trials early in 1912.

MILITARY WEAPONS

PATTERN 1913 RIFLE

Made by the Royal Small Arms Factory, Enfield, Middlesex, 1913-14.
Total production: at least 1250. **Chambering:** 276, rimless. **Action:** locked by two lugs on the bolt head rotating into their seats in the receiver as the bolt handle turned down, and by the bolt handle base entering its seat.

46.2in overall, 8.56lb empty. 26in barrel, 5-groove rifling; LH, concentric. Internal charger-loaded box magazine, 5 rounds. Leaf sight graduated to 1900yd. 2785ft/sec with 276 Ball Mk I. P/1913 sword bayonet.

A thousand 'Rifles, Magazine, 276-inch, Pattern 1913' were issued for trial in 1913. They had an aperture sight between prominent protectors above the rear of the receiver, ahead of the bolt handle. The leaf was graduated 400-1900yd, with a fixed aperture or battle sight for 600yd and an auxiliary long-range sight on the left side of the distinctively British-style one-piece stock. The magazine platform held the action open when the last round had been fired and ejected. Four diagonal grasping grooves appeared on each side of the forend immediately ahead of the breech, but were unpopular with firers.

The rifles undertook trials successfully, though there had been a tendency to misfire and trouble had been experienced with the charger guides. However, only poor magazine feed caused any real worry. Optimistically, in 1914, the British authorities recommended the 276 rifle as a replacement for the 303 Lee-Enfield.

PATTERN 1914 RIFLE

Made by the Winchester Repeating Arms Company, New Haven, Connecticut, 1915-16 (235,530); Remington Arms-Union Metallic Cartridge Company, Ilion, New York, 1915-16 (about 432,300); and the Remington Arms of Delaware Company, Eddystone, Pennsylvania, 1915-16 (about 450,000).
Total production: 1,117,850. **Chambering:** 303, rimmed. **Action:** as P/1913, above.

46.15in overall, 9.12lb empty. 26in barrel, 5-groove rifling; LH, concentric. Internal charger-loaded box magazine, 5 rounds. Leaf sight graduated to 1650yd. 2525ft/sec with 303 Ball Mk VII. P/1913 sword bayonet.

When World War I began in the summer of 1914, no production line for the 276 P/1913 (see above) existed and the entire project was abandoned. To alleviate shortages caused by mobilization, however, a contract for 200,000 'Rifles, Magazine, 303-inch, Pattern 1914' was agreed with Winchester on 24th November 1914. Similar contracts had previously been signed with Remington Arms–UMC. The perfected Winchester-adapted rifle was accepted on 22nd March 1915 and ordered into immediate mass production. Test-firing of the first Ilion-made Remington rifles took place in October.

The P/1914 was similar to the experimental 276 P/1913, but had a conventional grasping groove in the forend and the magazine was adapted for rimmed 303 cartridges. Rear sight graduations ranged from 200yd to 1650yd, the battle-sight aperture being set for 400yd and the long-range sights on the left side of the forend sufficing for distances up to 2600yd.

Final assembly in the Winchester factory in New Haven began in January 1916, and three differing sub-variants were introduced to British service on 21st June. Suffixes were used to distinguish them; though individual parts were generally interchangeable between guns of the same make, the products of each of the major factories differed sufficiently to prevent full compatibility.

The Mark I* was approved in December 1916. The most important changes were the lengthening of the left locking lug on the bolt and alterations to its seat in the receiver ring. These guns had additional five-point stars on the bolt handle, chamber, and right side of the butt. Mk I* rifles with finely-adjustable rear sights had a pattern mark with an additional 'F' suffix.

In the autumn of 1916, the British greatly reduced their orders. Winchester ceased work in December, though assembly in the Ilion (Remington) factory continued into 1917.

When the ever-increasing certainty of war became evident in 1939, surviving No. 3 rifles were hastily refurbished for reissue from 24th June onward. The long-range sight aperture bar and dial pointer were removed. At least 677,000 guns were altered, mostly at Enfield or by Holland & Holland of London. They were initially used for training, and then issued to the Local Defence Volunteers (later known as the 'Home Guard') where they served loyally until sufficient supplies of No. 4 Lee-Enfields had been ensured. They were eventually declared obsolete in July 1947.

SIMILAR GUNS

Mark I (E). This designation was applied to rifles made in the Eddystone factory in 1915-16. The parts were often marked 'ERA'.

Mark I (R). This distinguished guns made by Remington–UMC in 1915-16. Their parts were customarily marked 'RA'.

Mark I (W). Winchester-made rifles (1915-16) were given this designation. Many of the parts were simply marked 'W'.

Mark I* (E). This designation was applied to rifles made in the Eddystone factory in 1916. The parts were often marked 'ERA'. Pattern marks may be encountered with an additional 'F' suffix, which indicates a rear sight capable of finer than normal adjustments.

Mark I* (R). These guns were made by Remington–UMC in 1917; parts may display 'RA'. Guns with finely-adjustable rear sights will have an additional 'F' suffix in the pattern mark.

Mark I* (W). Dating from 1916, these Winchester-made rifles often had parts marked 'W'. Some may also have an additional 'F' fine-sight suffix (see above).

Mark I* (W) T. From 11th April 1918, the P/14 Mk I* (W) was adopted as the official British Army sniper rifle. Mounts for the P/1918 Aldis telescope sight (carried centrally above the bolt) were added on the left side of the breech and rear sight protector, long-range sights being removed. About two thousand rifle/sight combinations had been assembled prior to the Armistice.

No. 3 Mk I. In 1926, surviving P/1914 rifles were recalled to store and re-classified. The distinction between the three manufacturing patterns was dropped at this time.

No. 3 Mk I*. This was simply the post-1926 designation of the P/1914 Mk I*. Guns with finely adjustable rear sights had an additional 'F' suffix. ('No. 3 Mk I* [F]').

No. 3 Mk I* (T). Applied to P/1914 sniper rifles, usually of Winchester origin, this mark was applied only after 1926.

No. 3 Mk 1* (T) A. A few of these sniper rifles were made by BSA in Birmingham (at least seventy-nine of them) and by Alex Martin & Company of Glasgow (at least 421). Dating from 1940, they had a wooden cheekpiece and an Aldis sight in a low mount offset to the left of the bore.

SPORTING GUNS

Though its strength was unquestioned, the P/1914 action was rarely used by gunmakers. Most preferred the 1898-pattern Mauser, which could be transformed into an elegant sporting gun with little trouble; the Enfield-designed rifle, conversely, had prominent rear sight protectors on the receiver bridge and a particularly ugly bolt handle. In the 1920s, however, BSA (q.v.) introduced a range of rifles built on the Enfield system; the company is suspected to have manufactured many (if not all) of the actions incorporated in the P/1913 trials rifles, even though they were supposedly made at Enfield, and would have been a prime contractor had not World War I intervened. It is highly likely that BSA had incomplete actions in store.

The Pattern 1914 'Enfield' rifle.

SNIPER RIFLE, EXPERIMENTAL MODEL

The SREM, a bullpup bolt-action pattern developed in 1944, was the final expression of the short-rifle theories promoted by inventors such as Thorneycroft (q.v.). It was operated by pressing a catch set into the left side of the stock above the pistol grip, to release two diametrically-opposed bolt lugs, then retracting the grip to eject the spent case. The bolt moved down into the butt during its backward stroke. The grip was then returned to strip a new round from the magazine into the chamber and the action re-locked automatically for the next shot.

The 7.92x57 SREM had a very unconventional appearance. Several different versions were considered, but the perfected prototype was about 38in long, had a 23.75in barrel. It weighed about 9lb. A folding-leaf rear sight lay above the chamber, with fixed ring mounts for an optical sight offset to the left side of the breech. The five-round magazine was contained in the stock directly above the pistol grip. The forend and front sight were similar to those of the No. 5 rifle ('Lee-Enfield Jungle Carbine') – then in the development stage – and the distinctive combless butt had a ventilated rubber shoulder pad. A rudimentary cheekpiece was formed in the left side of the butt.

The SREM was an advanced design for its day, but faced too many teething troubles and was abandoned in the knowledge that progress was being made with autoloaders. Only a few prototypes were ever made in the Enfield tool room.

• Enfield-Martini

This was an abortive stage between the 450 Martini-Henry service rifles and the first 303 magazine rifles. Only comparatively small numbers of 402 guns were made, and most were subsequently converted to 450 and thence to 303. The earlier history will be found in the sections devoted to the Martini-Henry, Martini-Metford and Martini-Enfield, and subsequent progress in the Lee-Metford chapter.

MARK I RIFLE

Made by the Royal Small Arms Factory, Enfield, 1887-8.
Total production: 21,730 Pattern No. 1 and 43,000 Pattern No. 2.
Chambering: 402, rimmed. **Action:** locked by an underlever propping the pivoting breechblock behind the chamber.
DATA FOR PATTERN NO. 1
49.5in overall, 9.13lb empty. 33in barrel, 7-groove rifling; LH, ratchet. Ramp-and-leaf sight graduated to 2000yd. 1570ft/sec with ball cartridges. Enfield-Martini sword bayonet.

Derived from the experimental 40-caliber P/82 and P/83 rifles, the 'Rifle, Enfield-Martini, 402-inch (Mark I), with cleaning rod' was sealed on 17th April 1886 to guide manufacture of a thousand guns for troop trials. It was similar to the P/83, but the long-range sights were replaced by an elevating leaf. The safety bolt, narrowed butt and curious forend were all retained.

Production was approved in 1887 before the final trial reports had been submitted. Complaints were soon being voiced; no-one liked the quick-loader, and there had been extraction troubles.

Though production of Pattern No. 1 rifles had started, Pattern No. 2 was substituted on 13th May 1887. This reverted to the standard Martini-Henry forend and bayonet bar, the unpopular safety bolt had been superseded by a small cocking indicator, and the

British soldiers of the 1880s are pictured with Enfield-Martini rifles, which can be identified by the length of the operating lever and the shape of the receiver-back.

quick-loader attachment plate was abandoned. The operating lever was lengthened to give more power to the extractor.

Work of these rifles continued until 1888, but most were subsequently converted from 402 to 450.

• Esser-Barratt

This slide-action rifle – at least in its prototype stages – was based on converted Austro-Hungarian 1895-pattern straight-pull Mannlichers. The bolt handle was replaced by a 'U'-shape plate 'covered with a suitable material', sliding in a channel in the forend, which was connected with the bolt by an extension rod on each side of the breech.

MILITARY-PATTERN TRIALS RIFLE

Converted by the Esser-Barratt Repeating Arms Co. Ltd., Birmingham, about 1906-7.
Total production: at least one. **Chambering:** 303. **Action:** locked by two lugs on the bolt head engaging recesses in the receiver as the bolt closed.
DATA FOR A TYPICAL EXAMPLE, 1906
50in overall, 'less than 8lb with bayonet and strap'. 30in barrel, 4-groove rifling; RH, concentric. Fixed box magazine, five rounds. Tangent-leaf sight graduated to 2000yd? 2230ft/sec with Mk VI ball rounds. Austrian-pattern knife bayonet.

The Esser-Barratt rifle was unmistakable, owing to its resemblance to the 1895-type Mannlicher and the slide-grip on the forend. A safety catch lay on the cocking piece, with a lever on the right side of the magazine case to depress the clip until the bolt could no longer strip the top round into the chamber. One 303 rifle was tested at Bisley in the summer of 1906, firing five shots in two seconds and forty shots in less than a minute. This may still survive incomplete in a British collection, and an article in *Engineering* in November 1906 suggested that a 22 caliber trainer and a shotgun were also being made.

• Farquhar & Hill

These recoil-operated rifles were patented in Britain in 1906 by Moubray Gore Farquhar – a 'Gentleman' of Aboyne, Aberdeenshire – and Birmingham gunmaker Arthur Hill. Farquhar and Hill subsequently protected a series of improvements to the basic design in 1907-22, culminating in the Beardmore-Farquhar light machine gun of the 1920s.

THE EARLY GUNS

A 10lb 8x57 prototype was submitted in May 1908, but limited testing suggested a weakness in the forend; a modified gun tried in September extracted too poorly to impress the Chief Superintendent of the Ordnance Factories, who did not regard the design as promising. Farquhar & Hill persisted, however, and another gun was tested at the School of Musketry in November with better results.

A new 7.65x53 gun was demonstrated at Bisley in the summer of 1909, with a shortened bolt. The bolt-catch mechanism had been removed, the springs had been improved, and weight had reduced to only 8lb 3oz 'without boring lightening holes in the butt'. The rifle was still loaded through a hinged trap under the stock ahead of the trigger guard, as the ten-round magazine requested by the Small Arms Committee had not been perfected. The trials were ruined by the poor quality of the British-made 7.65mm cartridges and development continued.

IMPROVED DESIGNS

By 1915, Farquhar and Hill had developed a more robust version of the original rifle, with a two-piece stock jointed ahead of the detachable box magazine, a handguard running the length of the barrel, and a pivoting rear sight on the extreme rear of the receiver. A sword bayonet could be attached to a boss and a lug on the nose cap. By 1917, the rifle had gained an auxiliary pistol grip beneath the forend and a ten-round drum magazine permanently attached to the rifle.

Three dummy cartridges were welded permanently into the magazine, one to the front and rear sprockets and the others linked to the lower sprocket alone. The uppermost dummy doubled as a cartridge platform and hold-open. The rifle performed creditably in its trials and is said to have been provisionally adopted for the British Army. However, the end of World War I brought a new (and possibly reasonable) assessment that even the perfected Farquhar-Hill was too complicated and too lightly built to survive arduous service.

A typical Farquhar-Hill rifle.

An experimental rifle submitted by Webley & Scott was placed only third behind the Thompson and BSA-Thompson automatic rifles in the trials of 1925, and the entire project was abandoned shortly afterward.

• Farquharson

Designed by John Farquharson and patented in Britain in May 1872, this is regarded as the classic English dropping-block action. Beloved by purists owing to its strength and elegance, the block is lowered by pulling the breech lever downward to expose the chamber through the intermediacy of a link. As the action opens, it cocks the hammer and pivots the extractor to clear the chamber of a spent case. An improved version designed by William Ruger in the USA (q.v.) in the 1960s has been very successful commercially.

The original Farquharsons were made by George Gibbs of Bristol, who supplied actions to other gunmakers in the period before the patents expired. Subsequently, guns were offered by gunmakers such as W.J. Jeffrey & Company. The ability to handle powerful cartridges in safety and a lengthy period in vogue – from the 1870s until after World War I – ensured that the Farquharson has been made in a profusion of sizes and styles.

MILITARY RIFLE
Gibbs-Farquharson-Metford Pattern
Made by George Gibbs & Company, Bristol.

Total production: not known. **Chambering:** 450 Government pattern, rimmed **Action:** locked by an underlever propping the breechblock behind the chamber.

DATA FOR A TYPICAL EXAMPLE

49.9in overall, about 9lb empty. 32.65in barrel, 7-groove rifling; RH, polygonal. Ramp-and-leaf sight graduated to 1400yd. 1315ft/sec with rolled-case ball cartridges. Sword bayonet.

The first of the Gibbs Farquharson rifles, distinguished by their Metford-pattern rifling, were introduced to the sporting rifle market in 1877 – to great acclaim. Work continued into the 20th Century, products ranging from plain military-style guns to the finest target rifles with heavy barrels and vernier sights.

Most of the military-style guns pre-date the introduction of the Lee-Metford in 1888; they had straight-wrist butts and full-length forends retained by two screwed bands, the upper band usually carrying a standard bayonet lug on the right side. Swivels lay beneath the muzzle band and the butt.

SPORTING RIFLE
Jeffrey-Farquharson Improved or 1904 Pattern
Made by W.J. Jeffrey & Company, London.

Total production: not known. **Chambering options:** many differing large-caliber British sporting cartridges. **Action:** as Military Rifle, above.

DATA FOR A TYPICAL EXAMPLE

Chambering: 450/400 Nitro Express, rimmed. 43.75in overall, 8.45lb empty. 26in barrel, 4-groove rifling; LH, concentric. Express sight. 2100ft/sec with 400-grain bullet.

The first Jeffrey-made guns appeared toward the end of the 19th Century, an assortment of differing patterns being introduced prior to 1914. A typical gun of the 'improved' or 1904 pattern, with a radial safety on the right side of the receiver, offered a checkered pistol grip butt and a slender forend with a plain round tip. Sling eyes lay under the butt and on the barrel ahead of the forend; a five-leaf express sight (100-500yd) lay on a quarter-rib and a vernier sight could be mounted on the tang behind the receiver.

• Field

This sporting rifle – another of the classic English dropping-block systems – was designed by William Field of Birmingham and patented in Britain in May 1877.

Thumbing the operating lever forward moved the depressor-link past its locked position; projections on the tip of the depressor then ran along tracks cut diagonally into each side of the breech-block, lowering the block into the receiver. The initial movement of the operating lever cocked the hammer; at the end of the stroke, the block struck the extractor and cleared the chamber. Pulling the lever back closed the breech, rotating the upper tip of the depressor behind the center of the axis pin to lock the breechblock closed.

The Field action was compact, strong and simple, but extraction was inferior to rivals with extended operating levers (e.g., Farquharson). The original rifles were marketed by the Field Rifle Company, formed in 1885 and active until 1898, but were probably made in Birmingham by gunmakers such as Greener or Westley Richards. Most guns had external hammers and inertia strikers in the breechblock, but a few hammerless versions were made.

MATCH RIFLE
Greener-Field Pattern
Made by W.W. Greener, Birmingham.

Total production: not known. **Chambering options:** a selection of large-caliber British sporting cartridges. **Action:** locked by a side-lever propping the breechblock behind the chamber.

DATA FOR A TYPICAL EXAMPLE

Chambering: 303, rimmed. 45in overall, 9.92lb empty. 28.25in barrel, 7-groove rifling; LH, polygonal. Ramp-and-leaf sight graduated to 1400yd. 2050ft/sec with 215-grain bullet.

The Field, like many comparable English designs, was made in styles ranging from ultra plain (for volunteers and military-style target shooting) to the finest match rifles. A typical example of the best pattern offered a heavy round barrel with a full-length matted rib, an exchangeable-element front sight with a spirit level, and a vernier aperture rear sight on the tang. The butt had a checkered pistol grip with a horn cap, and the forend displayed checkering and a Henry-pattern tip.

• Firearms Company

The Firearms Co. Ltd. of Bridgwater, England, has been making the 'Alpine' Mauser-action sporting rifle for many years. The actions, once refurbished war surplus, have apparently been purchased from Belgium (FN) and Spain (Santa Barbara).

ALPINE MODEL RIFLE

This 1965-vintage pattern was made with a plastic-finished wood stock in 243 Winchester, 270 Winchester, 30-06 or 308 Winchester. It had a 24in barrel, weighed about 7.5lb and had a five-round magazine. The sights comprised a hooded ramped blade and an adjustable Williams ramp.

SIMILAR GUNS

Custom Grade. By 1991, guns were being made in Custom and Supreme grades, chambered for 22-250, 7mm Remington Magnum and 8mm Remington Magnum in addition to those previously listed. Standard guns had 23in barrels and five-round magazines; magnums had 24in barrels and three-round magazines. The walnut stock generally displayed skip-line checkering.

Supreme Grade. This was a deluxe form of the Custom pattern, with specially-selected woodwork, engraving on the action, and greater attention to details such as pistol grip caps and forend tips.

• FN-Saive (Enfield)

The first comparative trials undertaken in 1951 against the EM-2 ('Rifle No. 9 Mk 1' – see 'Januszewski/Janson') favored the 280 FN rifle. Though field trials undertaken in the summer were inconclusive, progress being made in Herstal was sufficient for the adoption of the No. 9 rifle to be rescinded in October. The failure of the 7.62mm EM-2 to challenge the Belgian rifle was resolved in December 1953, when five thousand FALs were ordered from Fabrique Nationale.

Known as the L1A1, the British version of the FN FAL saw front-line service for many years. This gun is fitted with a Pilkington PE Pocketscope electro-optical sight.

L1A1 RIFLE

Made by the Royal Small Arms Factory, Enfield Lock, Middlesex, 1958-75 (a million?); and BSA Guns Ltd., Shirley, Warwickshire, 1958-64 (150,000).

Total production: more than 1.15 million. **Chambering:** 7.62x51 NATO, rimless. **Action:** as Belgian FAL (q.v.).

45in overall (standard butt), 11.19lb with full magazine. 21in barrel, 6-groove rifling; RH, concentric. Detachable box magazine, 20 rounds. Sliding aperture sight graduated to 600yd. 2750ft/sec with L2A2 ball rounds. L1A3 knife bayonet.

The first thousand rifles were delivered in two differing models in 1954. After protracted trials and political wrangling lasting several years, the rifle was ultimately adopted in 1957 as the L1A1. Apart from differences in detail, and the absence of a selective-fire capability, its construction duplicates that of the FN FAL (see **'Belgium'**).

British L1A1-type guns have been supplied from Enfield to a selection of Commonwealth and British-aligned countries, including Bangladesh, Belize, Botswana, The Gambia, Ghana, Guyana, Kenya, Mauritius, Sierra Leone, Swaziland, Trinidad & Tobago, and Zambia.

SIMILAR GUNS

L1A1. The X14E1 was formally adopted as the 'Rifle, 7.62mm, FN, L1A1' on 1st March 1957. Capable only of single shot fire, the standard infantry rifle had wooden furniture and a folding cocking handle on the left side of the receiver. Charger guides were abandoned and a longitudinally slotted muzzle-brake/compensator was fitted. Four lengths of butt were made (short, standard, long and extra long) to suit individual soldiers. The thirty-round L4 (Bren gun) magazine could be used with the L1A1 rifle if necessary.

X8E1. Dating from 1954, these experimental 'Rifles, 7.62mm, FN, BR X8E1' had open sights, but lacked flash suppressors.

X8E2. This was simply a variant of the E1 pattern with an EM-2 type optical sight mounted on the receiver.

X8E3. This was an improved version of the X8E1, with an American-type flash suppressor.

X8E5. A refined form of the X8E3 fitted with a folding cocking handle.

X14E1. Channels were cut in the bolt carrier in 1956 to reduce the likelihood of accumulated fouling jamming the action, and testing of improved prototypes continued. By the end of the year, Fabrique Nationale had supplied 14,530 trial guns to Britain since 1954.

• Fraser

The name of Daniel Fraser of Edinburgh will be encountered on a variety of bolt-action rifles, including Mannlicher, Lee-Speed/Lee-Enfield and Ross patterns. However, a proprietary dropping-block action (patented in Britain in 1877) was also used commercially.

The mechanism had several interesting features, including a locking button beneath the head of the operating lever – though this was absent from some early guns, those with small actions

(e.g., for so-called 'Rook Rifle' cartridges) or simply sometimes omitted on request. A toggle-type depressor-lever assembly opened the breech, and a mainspring ran forward on a separate bracket beneath the barrel. The hammer pivoted on the same axis as the main depressor lever to strike a cut-away firing pin in the upper part of the breechblock.

IMPROVED BREECH-LOADING RIFLE

Made by Daniel Fraser & Co., Edinburgh, about 1878-1914.

Total production: several hundred? **Chambering options:** a variety of British sporting cartridges.

Action: operated by a lever propping the breechblock behind the chamber.

DATA FOR A TYPICAL EXAMPLE

Chambering: 450/400 Black Powder Express (2.38in case), rimmed. 44.3in overall, 8.38lb with sight. 27in barrel, 5-groove rifling; LH, concentric. Optical sight. 1750ft/sec with 230-grain bullet.

This typical Fraser-breech rifle, bearing the action number 215 (i.e., the 215th gun made by Fraser to the relevant patent), was sold at auction in 1997. The elegant butt, with a cheekpiece and a checkered pistol grip, was retained by a massive bolt running up through the pistol grip into the back of the color case-hardened body. 'Best Bouquet' engraving appeared on the metalwork, and the short forend had the hooked beak – known generically as a 'Henry Tip' – that characterized early British attempts to copy the original German schnabel pattern.

A sliding trigger-blocking safety catch lay inside the guard, but alternative shotgun-pattern tang buttons and a superfluous lever to hold the hammer at half cock could also be obtained. Fraser-Patent telescope sights could supplement or replace multi-leaf express rear sights, but precise cataloging is difficult; the rifles were made to order, varying greatly in size, finish, stock and decoration.

• Gamwell

This experimental rifle was designed in the early 1900s by Harry Gamwell, a gunsmith employed by Hooton & Jones of Liverpool. Patented by Harry & Charles Gamwell in April 1904, it was built on a standard Lee-Metford action. The bolt mechanism ran back along the butt comb and the trigger was moved forward ahead of the chamber. A double magazine – two standard ten-round patterns brazed together – was inserted in the underside of the butt.

The Gamwell rifle was an extraordinary design with few real merits. It was clumsy and badly balanced when loaded with twenty rounds, the bolt handle was awkwardly placed, and the proximity of the chamber to the marksman's cheek probably gave uncomfortable vibrations each time the gun was fired.

• Gibbs

George Gibbs of Bristol is best known for the Gibbs-Farquharson-Metford match rifles, built in surprising quantities on the single shot Farquharson (q.v.) dropping-block action. A typical 461 example, no. 14433 of about 1887-8, bore the action number '568'; it had a 28in barrel, a bolted side-safety, and weighed 7.65lb.

Gibbs also imported substantial numbers of Mannlicher (q.v.) actions into Britain prior to World War I, using them as the basis for fine-quality sporting guns. Mauser-type rifles were chambered for the 256 Gibbs Magnum cartridge, introduced in 1913, and for the 505 Rimless Magnum of 1910-11. These actions were purchased directly from Oberndorf prior to 1914, though post-1920 guns showed greater variety.

• Godsal

This intriguing rifle, which originated in the early 1890s, was intended to show the shortcomings of the Lee-Metford. However – despite vocal backing – its inventor was never able to persuade the British Army that his guns had real merit.

Major P.T. Godsal had been commissioned into the 52nd Regiment in 1860, but retired his commission in 1880 to become adjutant of the Eton College Volunteers and devote more than twenty years to firearms design. His rifle embodied a 'traveling block', really no more than a short bolt, running in tracks on the upper edge of the combless butt. The earliest guns were built privately, but later patterns (though embodying long Lee-Enfield barrels and fittings) were the work of Webley.

The Godsal 'travelling-block' rifle.

EXPERIMENTAL RIFLE

Made by P. Webley & Sons or Webley & Scott Ltd., Birmingham, Warwickshire.

Total Production: a handful, about 1895-1910. **Chambering:** 303, rimmed. **Action:** locked by two lugs on the bolt head engaging seats in the receiver as the bolt handle was turned down.

DATA FOR A TYPICAL EXAMPLE

44.1in overall, 7.15lb empty. 30in barrel, 5-groove rifling; LH, concentric. Internal box magazine, 5 rounds. Leaf rear sight with a stepped bed, graduated to 1000yd. P/1888 sword bayonet.

The Godsals are easily distinguished by the short bolt or 'traveler', which slides down rails on top of the stock wrist (cf., Cogswell & Harrsion Certus). The bolt body, which is only about .75in long, occupies the space between the bolt head and the striker housing. The sear bar lay on the right side of the breech behind the bolt handle recess. The magazine is contained in the stock directly behind the trigger, shrouded by the oddly shaped woodwork. The butt narrowed behind the magazine to assist a bayonet thrust.

The perfected Godsal had some good features, particularly as the twin lugs locked immediately behind the chamber, and the compact construction of the bolt/block system has recently found favor on some of the Blaser designs (q.v.). However, the quirky stock and the handling characteristics were not acceptable militarily. The success of the shortened Lee-Enfields made efforts to fit full-length barrels within compact dimensions irrelevant prior to 1914.

• Green

First noted by the British Army in May 1863, this was a bolt-action conversion of the P/53 (Enfield) rifle musket credited to Charles, Edwin & John Green of Birmingham. A receiver was substituted for the breech plug so that a sliding bolt could be added. A small bolt handle was free to rotate within a flat-top shroud or cover. One lug on the bolt body turned into a recess in the left side of the receiver or 'shoe'; another lug, on the underside of the bolt handle sleeve, locked transversely into a slot in the receiver floor. A gutta-percha washer on the bolt head served as an obturator, though the Green was never regarded as truly gas tight. The bolt could be removed from the action simply by pressing forward on the back of the trigger lever, which retracted a retaining rod into the receiver.

The Green rifle was never successful in Britain, though made in small numbers in sporting guise. However, a modified form was briefly adopted in Serbia (q.v.) to convert caplock rifle muskets.

TRIALS RIFLE

Made by or possibly for C., E. & J Green, Birmingham, Warwickshire.
Total production: at least six, 1864. **Chambering:** 577 combustible cartridge; fired by a cap lock. **Action:** locked by turning lugs on the bolt into recesses in the receiver (see text, above).

54in overall, 9.5lb empty. 39in barrel, 3-groove rifling; RH, concentric. Single shot only. Leaf rear sight with a stepped bed, graduated to 1000yd. About 1000ft/sec with standard expanding-ball ammunition. P/1853 socket bayonet.

An experimental rifle was followed by six of the forty-eight P/1853 rifle muskets supplied to seven different manufacturers for conversion in 1864; the Greens were numbered 43-48. Recognizable by the bolt handle on the rear of the action (turning down to the left) and by the light sheet-iron bolt cover, the guns had a standard Enfield sidelock, a one-piece stock and three Baddeley bands. They were not particularly successful, however, and did not participate in later trials.

SPORTING RIFLES

A few Green-type sporters are known, mostly marked by E.M. Reilly & Co. of London. A typical example – 'GREEN BROS.

PATENT NO. 43' – was half-stocked in walnut, with checkering on the wrist and forend. A cleaning rod was held beneath the barrel in two brass pipes; the rear sight was a leaf pattern graduated to 900yd; and the furniture was steel. A rearward extension of the trigger guard bow provided a finger rest. The bolt was held in the closed position by a spring catch on the handle, which had to be released before the breech could be opened.

• Greene

This was patented in the U.S. in June 1854 by John Durrell Greene, and is considered in greater detail in the relevant section. The American Civil War carbines had 22in barrels, four inches longer than their British equivalents.

A gun fitted with a Maynard Tape Primer was successfully tested at Hythe in the summer of 1855. Accuracy up to 400yd proved to be as good as any carbine that had been submitted, no leakage of gas was detected, and, even after firing nearly three hundred rounds without cleaning, a fire rate of nine rounds per minute was still possible.

To load the gun, it was only necessary to put the hammer to half cock, press the front trigger, rotate the barrel slightly to the right, and pull it forward to disengage the locking lugs. The barrel was then swung over to the right for loading.

TRIALS CARBINE

Made by the Massachusetts Arms Company, Chicopee Falls, Massachusetts.

Total production: 2000, 1857-8. **Chambering:** 55, combustible cartridge; fired by a cap lock. **Action:** locked by a fence on the frame preventing the barrel moving laterally.

34.5in overall, about 7lb empty. 18in barrel, 3-groove rifling; RH, concentric. Single shot only. Leaf-type rear sight graduated to 600yd. No bayonet.

This was a distinctive design, with a Maynard tape primer system and the barrel above a tubular longitudinal pivot. There were two 'triggers' (one was actually the barrel-release catch) within a single guard. A back-action cap lock was fitted, a sling ring lay beneath the butt, and a patch box with a hinged iron lid was set into the right side of the butt.

The guns ordered in 1856 had all been delivered into store by March 1858. A hollow spike projecting from the standing breech was intended to pierce the cartridge when the action closed, but protracted trials at Enfield and Woolwich failed to produce a suitable cartridge. The Greene Carbines, which were otherwise eminently serviceable, were held in store for many years. A myth has arisen that they were sold back to the Federal government – or, perhaps, some independent state authority – during the American Civil War. However, 1,947 were still in store in the Tower of London in 1866.

• Greener, bolt-action type

Best known for single shot sporting guns, W.W. Greener & Company of Birmingham marketed a distinctive bolt-action repeating rifle with a rotary magazine – perhaps an American-made Blake (q.v.) type – and a pivoting ejection port cover doubling as the rear sight base. Chambered for 45-caliber cartridges of unknown type, one rifle measured 45.4in overall, had a 24in barrel and weighed in the region of 9lb empty. The distinctive two-piece stock had a checkered wrist and half-length forend, sporting-type swivel eyes appearing on the barrel and butt. Nothing is known about the origin of the rifle, which is presumed to date from the late 1880s.

Greener also offered Lee-Enfield sporting and military rifles prior to 1914. These were rarely anything other than standard BSA-made guns with Greener marks, the No. 1 Sporting Rifle being most popular; according to *The Gun and Its Development* (1910), 303 or 375 Magazine Action Rifles were being offered with 'sporting finish, and well engraved'; with a plain finish; or with a short barrel. Long Lee-Enfield rifles, 'specially sighted and tested for Match shooting' were also to be found. Other guns incorporated BSA actions with Greener's own stocks and fittings.

• Greener, break-open type

William Wellington Greener offered a wide variety of single- and double-barreled sporting guns prior to 1914. They included 'Double Barrel High Velocity Rifles' ranging from straightforward Anson & Deeley boxlocks (the cheapest option) through under-lever and 1873-patented Triple Wedge-Fast actions to the proprietary Facile Princeps pattern. Hammer and hammerless guns were made in black-powder and smokeless chamberings from a 310 'Miniature' to the awesome 500 Express. The more expensive guns were customarily made to order, with extensive engravings and a selection of optional extras.

• Greener-Martini

William Wellington Greener was among the first of the British gunsmiths to offer guns for club shooting. Most of these rifles were based on the Martini breech, and on the many thousands of Cadet rifles made for the Australian government prior to World War I.

Though large-caliber sporting rifles were offered on the service-type Martini action, they were regarded as the most basic guns in the range. Farquharson (q.v.) or Webley actions were preferred, the former being stocked and barreled in the greater quantity. Chamberings ranged from 303 to 450 Nitro Express.

The Greener-Martini rifle, 1910. (Greener)

ROOK RIFLE
Also known as the 'Rook & Rabbit Rifle'
Made by W.W. Greener, Birmingham.

Total production: many thousands. **Chambering:** 310, rimmed. **Action:** locked by propping the breechblock behind the chamber with the tip of the operating lever.

DATA FOR A TYPICAL EXAMPLE

About 41.5in overall, 6.5lb empty. 26in barrel, 4-groove rifling; RH concentric? Single shot only. Block and leaf sight graduated to 150yd. 1200ft/sec with 120-grain bullet.

These rifles were often fitted with Greener's Improved Martini action, a take-down pattern operated by a radial lever on the front left side of the body. A cocking indicator and a safety lever lay on the right side of the breech. Butts were pistol grip or straight-wrist patterns, invariably checkered, and the checkered forend had a separate horn tip. The operating lever of guns with a pistol grip butt terminated in a small ring finial, though the straight-wrist type conformed with the classic serpentine military form. The rear sight was usually a simple block-and-leaf design; tough multi-leaf express sights, often set into a matted top rib, were popular alternatives.

SIMILAR GUNS

Miniature Club Rifle. Offered in 22 rimfire, or 297/230 and 297/250 centerfire, this was a takedown design with the customary locking lever on the lower left side of the body. A short round-tip forend and a plain straight-wristed butt were standard fittings. The sights were 'sporting' or 'military', the former consisting of a bead and a block-and-leaf whereas the latter was a combination of a barleycorn and a 300yd leaf-and-slider unit. An 'Orthoptic Wind-Gauge Peep Sight' or special competition sights with verniers and spirit levels could be fitted to order. A high-polish 'Sporting Finish' cost an additional guinea (21/-, £1.05), which was half the price of the most basic gun!

Sharpshooter's Club Rifle. This was essentially similar to the Miniature Club pattern, but chambered the 310 centerfire cartridge and was sighted to 300yd. The 'Mk I' had a fixed barrel, 'Mk II' embodied Greener's Improved Martini (take-down) action, and the Cadet Model, 'as supplied to Commonwealth of Australia',

could be supplied from stock for the 297/230 round. Unlike the other guns in the series, the Cadet examples had a forend which extended virtually to the muzzle.

TRADE AND OTHER PATTERNS

In addition to the small caliber or Miniature rifles listed above, Greener also made hammerless top-lever and hammer sidelever Rook Rifles, alongside a 'Martini Service Pattern' chambered for 22 rimfire or – occasionally – the 297/230 centerfire cartridges. This duplicated the full-size Martini-Enfield rifles, with a 30in barrel and an empty weight of about 8.5lb.

Guns and actions made by Greener were supplied to sporting-goods agencies, as well as many other well-known gunmakers. Typical of these were E.M. Reilly & Company and the Army & Navy Co-operative Stores Ltd. of London, but many other names will be found. The origins of the guns may be difficult to determine, though some are said to bear 'W.W.G.' or a discreet encircled-elephant trademark.

• Griffiths & Woodgate

Patented in 1892 by engineer William Griffiths and army officer Herbert Woodgate, this was not only one of the earliest auto-loading rifles to be offered to the British Army, but also deserved more than summary rejection.

When the gun fired, the barrel and bolt moved back together until the barrel was halted by spring collar striking the receiver. The bolt was turned by a handle operating in a cam slot in the receiver, continuing back alone to eject the spent case and forcing the hammer down until it was held on the sear. A spring returned the bolt to strip a new round into the chamber and revolve the locking lugs back into engagement.

A patent granted in 1892 improved the lockwork, adding a disconnector and safety features to allow controlled single shot fire. The patent showed a two-piece stock and a modified magazine case with a greater gap between the back of the magazine and the trigger guard.

The performance of the Griffiths & Woodgate rifle remains conjectural, though a more refined weapon than some of its exact contemporaries, and Woodgate (q.v.) subsequently made improvements of his own.

The Griffiths & Woodgate rifle. (Greener)

EXPERIMENTAL RIFLE
1892 patent type
Maker unknown.

Total production: at least one. **Chambering:** 303, rimmed. **Action:** locked by rotating four lugs on the bolt into the barrel extension; recoil operated, semi-automatic only.

51in overall, 10.06lb empty. 30in barrel, 5-groove rifling; LH, concentric. Detachable box magazine, 8 rounds. Leaf sight graduated to 1700yd. 1800ft/sec with standard ball ammunition?

Submitted by the Automatic Rifle Syndicate, the rifle had a one-piece stock with two bands and a handguard running from the breech to the rear band. The special front band was combined with the front sight. The barrel return spring lay on the left side of the barrel, a depressor catch was fitted to the right side of the magazine case, and the rear sight lay above the ejection port. See also 'Woodgate'.

• Hall

This idiosyncratic autoloader was designed in 1944 by Major John Hall, an Australian infantry officer. A British Patent was granted in February 1945 – no. 589,394 – but there is no evidence that anything other than a wooden model had been made. The Hall was a bullpup design with the ten-round staggered-coloumn magazine in the butt and a charging handle beneath the receiver behind the pistol grip. The breech was locked by a vertically-sliding block, which was much more compact than a bolt. The Hall was only about 26.5in long, but had a 19in barrel. The project is said to have been abandoned early in 1947, but the rifle was officially designated 'EM-3' in January 1948 and it is possible (if unlikely) that additional progress had been made.

• Hallé

A most interesting, but unsuccessful design, this rifle was promoted in the early 1900s by the Hallé Automatic Firearms Syndicate of London. The patentees were Clifford Hallé and Marguerite Ribbentrop, described respectively as 'Lecturer' and 'Spinster'. The first patent of 1901 protected a recoil-operated rifle with a 'regulating lever' in the barrel extension, which pivoted in the base of the fixed magazine housing to control the backward movement of the bolt after the resistance of sprung 'abutment pieces' in the frame had been overcome. The perfected design, patented in 1902, substituted a multi-lever pantograph or 'lazy tongs' above the breech for the regulating lever, allowing the magazine to be improved. The patent drawings show the tongs fixed above the chamber, compressed when at rest, but the guns tested in 1904-6 had the action reversed so that the tongs (anchored at the rear) were compressed on firing.

When the 1902-pattern gun fired, the barrel and breech moved back together until the abutment pieces were moved out of engagement. The barrel was stopped, allowing the bolt to move backward under control of the lazy tongs to the end of its stroke. Springs returned the mechanism to battery, stripping a new round into the chamber and allowing the abutment pieces to swing back into the bolt way.

MILITARY-PATTERN TRIALS RIFLE

Probably made by William Moore & Grey, London, about 1903-6.
Total production: at least three. **Chambering options:** 7x57 Mauser and 303. **Action:** locked by two spring-loaded flaps in the receiver wall closing behind the bolt; combination recoil/delayed blowback operation, semi-automatic only.
DATA FOR A TYPICAL 7MM EXAMPLE, 1906
About 52in overall, 9.75lb empty. 28.8in barrel, 4-groove rifling; RH, concentric. Fixed box magazine, five rounds. Tangent-leaf sight graduated to 1600m (1750yd)? 2196ft/sec with 173-grain bullet. Sword bayonet.

The Military Model Hallé rifle, tried at Bisley in the summer of 1904 and – in an improved form – at Enfield in May 1906 had a one-piece stock with a straight-wrist butt, a handguard from the chamber to the barrel band, and a simple nose cap with a bayonet lug. It could be charged simply by pulling down on an underlever doubling as the trigger guard, retracting the bolt and cocking the internal hammer. The magazine was charged simply by inverting the gun, opening the base plate, and inserting the cartridges. The standard magazine held five, but a 14-round extended pattern was also tried.

The Hallé performed very well at Bisley, where it proved to be accurate and pleasant to fire. Many observers preferred it to the competing Rexer; the Enfield testers were less impressed, as the sand test proved to be difficult to negotiate and the difficulties of dismantling the gun without armorers' tools was in conflict with established military requirements.

• Heckler & Koch (Enfield)

G3-type rifles have been made by the Royal Small Arms Factory in Enfield, apparently to utilize manufacturing capability that would otherwise have stood idle while the 5.56mm SA-80 rifle was being developed to replace the L1A1 (FAL). Guns have been exported in great quantity – mainly, but not exclusively, to British-orientated countries. However, the British Army has never adopted G3 or HK33 rifles as standard issue, though favor has been found with police marksmen and anti-terrorist groups. British-made guns generally exhibited the designation, 'G3A3', plus 'EN' (for Enfield) on the left side of the magazine housing; the first two digits of the serial number sometimes gave a clue to the date of assembly.

• Henry

A sturdy and efficient dropping-block action, this was made in small numbers for sporting use. Henry patented the first of a series of improved rifles with internal hammers in 1870, but they were too delicate to have widespread appeal.

An Alexander Henry external-hammer sporting rifle. (W&D)

A prototype was presented to the British breech-loading rifle trials of 1865. Its dropping block was controlled by a lever under the breech, and a conventional external hammer was fitted. A second series of trials, undertaken in 1867, revealed the Henry to be good enough to be entered into the Prize Competition. Six more guns had been made by mid-October. They had 34in 455-caliber barrels, rifled with seven grooves.

In February 1868, Henry was awarded 600 pounds for the best breech mechanism entered in the government trials. The Peabody and Martini had been ranked sixth and seventh respectively, but a third series of trials ended with Martini, Henry and Westley Richards rifles being recommended.

By 1869, after Westley Richards had withdrawn his rifle, the contest between the Enfield-modified Martini and an improved Henry resolved in favor of the former. Concurrently, ammunition trials approved of a 450 Henry-rifled barrel – though its cartridge was considered to be too long – and the Martini-Henry (q.v.) was created.

MILITARY PATTERN

Made by Alexander Henry & Company, Edinburgh, 1870-5; and the National Arms & Ammunition Co. Ltd., Sparkbrook, Birmingham, 1872-5.
Total production: not known. **Chambering:** 450, rimmed. **Action:** locked by an underlever propping the breechblock behind the chamber.
DATA FOR A TYPICAL EXAMPLE
49.2in overall, 8.84lb empty. 33in barrel, 7-groove rifling; LH, composite. Ramp-and-leaf sight graduated to 1400yd. 1315ft/sec with rolled-case ball cartridges. Socket or saber bayonet.

Small-scale production began about 1870 for the volunteer units and officers who required rifles chambering service cartridges. A typical military-style Henry rifle had a two-piece stock and a short receiver. The hammer often lay on the left side of the receiver, to facilitate loading from the right, and an operating lever – pivoted at the lower front of the receiver – fitted around the stylish trigger guard. The lever was locked by a small sliding-plunger catch. The straight-wrist butt and the forend were essentially similar to those of the P/53 Enfield rifle-musket, with three (later two) screw-clamping bands.

Lacking suitable facilities of his own, Alexander Henry granted a license to the National Arms & Ammunition Co. Ltd., which made a few rifles in an attempt to gain military orders. These were never forthcoming and the military rifles were abandoned about 1875.

SPORTING PATTERN

Made by Alexander Henry & Co., Edinburgh.
Total production: several thousand. **Chambering options:** a selection of large-caliber British sporting-rifle cartridges. **Action:** as Military Pattern, above.
DATA FOR A TYPICAL EXAMPLE
Chambering: 450, rimmed. 45.6in overall, 7.94lb empty. 28in barrel, 7-groove rifling; LH, composite. Single shot only. Block-and-leaf rear sight. 1600ft/sec with 325-grain bullet.

The Henry rifle was usually chambered for the standard British service cartridges – 577 and then 450 – but lasted into the small-bore era. Rifle no. 2831, dating from about 1872, bears an action number '773' which shows that production had already been substantial. Excepting a very few 'improved' guns with internal hammers, the back-action lock and external hammer were retained on the right side of the breech. Sporters usually had half stocks with rounded-tip forends, though sights ranged from military ramp-and-leaf patterns to plain blocks. The most obvious feature was the plunger-type catch on the operating lever, which locked into the trigger guard. Quality was very good, the fit of wood to metal being exemplary. Delicate scroll engraving often appeared on the hammer, lock and action.

Unfortunately, as the guns were made largely to order, accurate cataloging is very difficult – they varied greatly in size, finish, stock, and decoration. In addition, Henry actions were regularly stocked and barreled by other gunmakers. A gun by John Dickson & Son of Edinburgh, serial no. 3530, was sold at auction in 1997; Dickson had made more than eighty Henry rifles by the time this particular example was completed.

• Holland & Holland

Holland & Holland of London, trading as a limited-liability company from 1899 onward, is renowned for high-quality shotguns and double rifles. The company has also offered Mauser rifles chambering 240 Belted Rimless Nitro Express cartridges (introduced about 1923); 244 Belted Rimless Magnum (about 1955); 275 Belted Rimless Magnum Nitro Express (date unknown); 300 Holland's Super Thirty, subsequently known as the 300 H&H Magnum (1925); 375 Belted Rimless Magnum Nitro Express, subsequently known as 375 H&H Magnum (1912); and the 400/375 Belted Nitro Express (1905).

Holland & Holland has made small quantities of Best Quality Magazine Rifles and Deluxe Magazine Rifles in recent years, usually on the basis of FN Mauser actions. Available in 240 Apex, 300 H&H Magnum ('Super Thirty Model') and 375 H&H Magnum only, with four-round magazines and 24in barrels, they usually displayed stocks of the finest quality. Straight combs were considered to be standard, with simple oval cheekpieces and round-tip forends. The folding-leaf sights were often set on a short barrel rib, and a recoil bolt ran through the stock beneath the chamber.

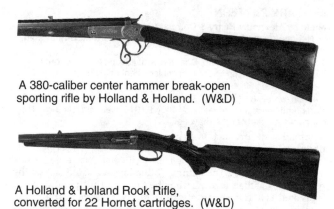

A 380-caliber center hammer break-open sporting rifle by Holland & Holland. (W&D)

A Holland & Holland Rook Rifle, converted for 22 Hornet cartridges. (W&D)

• Januszewski (Janson)

This rifle was developed from the unsuccessful EM-1 (Korsac) light machine gun by an Anglo-Polish team led by Stefan Januszewski and Sydney Hance, beginning life in the autumn of 1947 with the first of the hand-made prototypes. Patented in August 1951 (no. 723,090), the gun was locked by a variation of the pivoting-flap system devised in the 1870s by Friberg, a Swedish army officer, and subsequently used most successfully in the Soviet Degtyarev light machine gun and the German Gew. 43.

EM-2 RIFLE
Rifle, Automatic, 280in, EM-2 (CEAD), codenamed 'Yellow Acorn' or 'Mamba'

Made by the Chambons Tool Co., Hammersmith, London (six); by the Royal Small Arms Factory, Enfield Lock (30-35); BSA Guns Ltd., Shirley, Warwickshire (at least eight); and Canadian Arsenals Ltd., Long Branch, Ontario (10).

Total production: 55-60, including prototypes. **Action:** locked by pivoting flaps on the breechblock into the receiver walls; gas operated, selective fire. **Chambering:** 280, rimless.

35in overall, 9.25lb with a loaded magazine. 24.5in barrel, 4-groove rifling; RH, concentric? Detachable box magazine, 20 rounds. Integral optical sight. 2415ft/sec with 140-grain bullet; 625±25rpm. Knife bayonet.

The EM-2 was a bullpup design, with the magazine behind the pistol grip and the shoulder plate attached to the end of the receiver. It had an external affinity with the competing EM-1 (see **'Thorpe'**) pattern, but was made by traditional methods from machined forgings. The fixed rear sight was permanently attached to the carrying handle, though an adjustable 'Long Arm' sight was also developed. Five experimental guns were made at Cheshunt and Enfield, and then twenty 'semi-production' guns (two from

The 280-caliber EM-2 rifle.

Chambons and eighteen from Enfield) appeared in time for NATO trials at Aberdeen Proving Ground in February-April 1950. These showed that the EM-2 had some advantages – it was compact, handled well and dismantled easily – but also drew attention to serious flaws. The breech and trigger system was too complicated, leading to excessive parts breakages, and accuracy was very poor.

Though the British government approved the EM-2 for service as the 'Rifle 7mm No. 9 Mk 1' in 1951, the U.S. Army, backed by the French, refused to accept the 280 cartridge as a suitable NATO standard. Eventually, in October 1951, the new Conservative government rescinded approval; in December 1953, the British Army ordered five thousand FAL rifles for troop trials and the EM-2 was abandoned.

SIMILAR GUNS

No. 9 X1E1. BSA made six guns for trials with the US 30 T65 cartridge, and Enfield then made fifteen similar 'No. 9 X1E1' rifles numbered EN100-EN114.

EM-2 HV. Four 'High Velocity' rifles were made by Chambons in 1950, chambered for the 7x49, 7x51 or 30-06 cartridges, and ten additional guns (numbered 1-10 in their own series) were subsequently made by Canadian Arsenals Ltd. in 7x51mm.

No. 9 X1E2. Fifteen of these prototypes were ordered from BSA in 1952, but only a few were made. They lacked the selective-fire capability of the X1E1, as the problems of firing even 280 cartridges from the lightweight EM-2 had proved insuperable.

Small caliber guns. Several surviving EM-2 rifles were converted for the experimental 6.25x45 cartridge in the 1970, acting as test-beds for the development of a new intermediate round which was eventually rejected in favor first of a 4.85mm design and secondly the ubiquitous 5.56x45 now chambered by the L85 service rifle.

• Jeffrey

An advertisement placed in *Arms & Explosives* in 1892 by W.J. Jeffrey & Company of London – formed from Jeffrey & Davies in 1891 – reveals that a range of hammerless shotguns (including double rifles) was accompanied by a variety of Martini-action rifles. In addition to service-pattern 'Military Rifles and Carbines', three sporting variants could be obtained. The No. 1 Jeffreys-Martini had a checkered pistol grip butt, often with a rudimentary cheekpiece, and a spatulate operating lever with a back-curled tip. The action was readily detachable, a pivoting safety or cocking indicator could be fitted to the right side of the body, and the short checkered forend had a horn tip. The barrel, which could be round or octagonal, was retained by a transverse wedge set in oval escutcheons; rear sights were customarily Cape patterns. The No. 2 Martini was a sporting carbine, whereas No. 3 was a variant of No. 1 with a full-length ramrod carried beneath the barrel in brass pipes.

Jeffrey was an early devotee of the Mannlicher (q.v.) action, including a few 1895-type Dutch actions imported prior to 1905. However, the Mauser action was preferred for the proprietary 280 Rimless cartridge (developed about 1913), the 303 Magnum (1919), 333 Rimless Nitro Express (1911), 404 Rimless Nitro Express (about 1909); and the devastating 500 Rimless Nitro Express (about 1913).

• Jeffries

George Jeffries, a gunmaker working in Norwich, patented a distinctive breech system in 1862. This relied on an underlever to move the breech radially along a radial slot in the floorplate until it cleared the standing breech. The Jeffries system was sturdy, if cumbersome, compared with the break-open designs. Guns were made in substantial numbers in the 1865-75 period, not only by Jeffries but also by 'Best' makers such as Joseph Wilson of London. Shotguns predominated, but a few rifles – pinfire and centerfire – were included among them.

• Jenks

A few of these American-designed carbines were made in Liége in 1840 – perhaps by Malherbé. Tried with the British cavalry in

1841, they were disliked so greatly that the survivors were immediately returned to store. Three were still in the Tower of London armories in 1916.

The mechanism was operated by placing the hammer at half-cock and then lifting the grips of the top lever, which lay above the breech. The lever (pivoted in the wrist of the butt) then broke the lock and retracted the bolt to expose the chamber for loading.

The carbines were typical of the sturdy British designs of the 1830s, with Lovell's back-action cap lock and the barrel held in the stock by a transverse bolt. A small standing-block rear sight lay ahead of the chamber, and the rear tang of the brass trigger guard was formed into a small scroll or finger rest.

• Jones, block-action type

Developed in the early 1880s by a Philadelphian, Owen Jones, best known for his work on the quirky British 476 Enfield revolver, this was the only successful magazine conversion of the block-action Martini-Henry rifle. The prototype had a box magazine in its butt, and was operated by a reciprocating handle on the right side of the receiver. A thumb-trigger firing mechanism protruded from the juncture of the receiver and stock immediately behind the handgrip.

Trials showed that the basic principles worked, and so an improved gun was built in the Enfield small arms factory in 1883. A sliding four-spur handgrip was placed beneath the butt, and a cut-off lever was added to the top side of the receiver ahead of the thumb trigger.

The slab-sided receiver had obvious Martini affinities. Sliding the handgrip down its track under the butt tilted the locking block out of engagement with a shoulder inside the receiver and then pulled it back down inside the wrist of the butt. Simultaneously, the carrier pivoted to raise a new cartridge from the magazine to a point where, on the return stroke, the breechblock rammed the new round into the chamber before swinging the back of the block back of the block into engagement with the locking shoulder.

Trials revealed that the Owen Jones had a slight superiority over the Lee patterns in rapid fire, and so work continued. The last prototypes had a Burton-type hopper magazine instead of a tube, and a conventional trigger replaced the thumb pattern. The slide was changed to a two-spur 'hand width' design and a radial-lever cut-off catch was set into the lower right side of the butt. The rifles had a two-piece stock with a combless butt and a ventilated Arbuthnot-pattern forend. They were replaced by the simpler Improved Pattern, with 113 parts instead of 121.

IMPROVED MODEL RIFLE

Made by the Royal Small Arms Factory, Enfield, 1886.
Total production: 150? **Chambering:** 402, rimmed. **Action:** locked by pivoting the rear of the locking block up into the rear of the receiver.

51.5in overall, 10.4lb empty. 33.2in barrel, 7-groove rifling; RH, concentric. Hopper magazine on the left side of the receiver, 5 rounds. Leaf rear sight with a stepped bed, graduated to 2000yd. 1570ft/sec with 384-grain bullet. P/1876 socket bayonet?

The Owen Jones rifle cannot be mistaken for other patterns, owing to the slider beneath the butt, the Martini-like receiver and the hopper magazine. The handguard ran from the chamber to the band, enveloping the rear sight, and the swivels lay beneath the band and the toe of the butt. The elevator and cut-off switch of the

The breech of the hopelessly
complicated 402-caliber Owen Jones rifle.

preceding guns were eliminated, and the safety catch became a radial lever ahead of the trigger on the left side of the breech.

Enfield was asked to make a hundred rifles early in 1886, for troop trials, but the order was immediately increased to five thousand to equip the Royal Navy. This hasty request was then reduced to 2000, before the first series-made Owen Jones was dispatched to the Admiralty from Enfield on 1st October 1886. Trials against the Improved Lee and Lee-Burton confirmed the suspicions of those who regarded the Owen Jones as ridiculously complicated and jam-prone. The entire program was abandoned at the end of 1886. Guns have been seen with numbers as high as 115, but the production total is still unknown.

• Jones, break-open type

Henry Jones of Birmingham obtained four British Patents for 'drop-down barrel actions' in 1859-70, among them being an efficient modification of the Lefaucheux (q.v.) underlever locking system. Jones's improvement relied on a helical lug on the underlever stem to engage with notches in both sides of the barrel lump simultaneously, drawing it securely downward as the operating lever was closed. The Jones system was simple, sturdy, and adopted by many of the leading gunmakers of the day for hammer-type double rifles. Chambered for a variety of pinfire and centerfire cartridges, these guns enjoyed a heyday in the 1865-75 period before being overtaken by more efficient bolting systems.

• Kerr

This bolt-action rifle – "similar to Wilson's" (q.v.) – was submitted to the British Army trials of 1865, but rejected unfired. Built on the basis of a P/53 Enfield rifle-musket and often recorded officially as the 'Carr' it retained an external caplock and fired a special combustible cartridge. An improved pattern chambered for centerfire Boxer ammunition was tested in 1868, when it was admitted to the competition until, unluckily, all the bolt-action systems were rejected as potentially dangerous. The later Kerr still featured an external hammer, but had a rebounding striker and a slight camming action on the closing stroke to seat cartridges more efficiently.

• Lancaster

Charles William Lancaster of London made another of the early underlever breech-loading guns, smooth-bore and rifled alike. The system was similar to the much more successful Jones-patent design (q.v.), but closing the lever pulled an extension on the underlug back until it engaged in a recess beneath the standing breech.

• Lang

Joseph Lang of London was granted British patent 1785/67 of 1867 to protect a pinfire breechloader locked by an underlever, one of the first of its type to be offered commercially. However, Lang died in 1869 and exploitation of his design was greatly inhibited. Though most of the surviving examples are shotguns, a few rifled guns were made.

• Lee-Burton

Developed in the mid-1880s, the Patent Double Magazine Rifle developed by the American Bethel Burton (q.v.) attracted sufficient attention to be included in the British *Treatise on Military Small Arms and Ammunition* in 1888.

Based on a series of patents granted in the U.S. in 1859-80, the rifle had an interrupted-screw bolt, a tube magazine in the forend and a hopper on the left side of the receiver. Cut-off devices on both sides of the receiver enabled cartridges to be selected from the tube or the hopper at will, or even for both magazines to be held in reserve while single rounds were loaded directly into the chamber. The standard ten-round hopper could be replaced by a special skeletal pattern accepting four-round expendable clips. The twenty-shot dual-magazine proved to be too heavy and too complicated.

The first Burton rifles tested by the British Army seem to have been submitted to military trials in 1882, when the 1880-patent interrupted-screw pattern test gun – chambered for the 45 Gatling cartridge and stocked in British style – was rejected on the grounds that extraction and ejection were poor.

The authorities were sufficiently impressed by the side-mounted hopper magazine to make three 45-caliber Burton rifles in the Enfield factory in 1883. However, the interrupted-screw

The Lee-Burton rifle (Enfield pattern).

breech system was deemed to be inferior to the simpler Lee two-lug type, and so a combination of Lee bolt and Burton magazine was developed instead. Chambered for the 402 (Enfield-Martini) cartridge, this proved to be efficient enough to be entered in long-term trials against the Lee and the Owen Jones.

Only about thirty guns of the initial 150-gun order were made before the order was suspended in favor of an improved rifle. They had Arbuthnot-pattern ventilated forends held by a single band at the muzzle.

IMPROVED LEE RIFLE WITH BURTON MAGAZINE

Made by the Royal Small Arms Factory, Enfield.

Total production: 327, 1887-8. **Chambering:** 402, rimmed. **Action:** locked by rotating two lugs on the rear of the bolt into their recesses in the receiver.

50.2in overall, 10.25lb empty. 30.2in barrel, 7-groove rifling; RH, ratchet. Gravity-feed hopper magazine on the left side of the receiver, 5 rounds. Leaf rear sight with a stepped bed, graduated to 2000yd. 1550ft/sec with 384-grain bullet. P/1886 sword bayonet?

These guns had two-piece stocks, with Martini-Henry pattern forends held by two bands. The bayonet stud lay on the right side of the front band. The hopper on the right side of the receiver could be pushed downward to its lower stop to cut off the magazine supply and allow the gun to be used as a single-loader.

Trials undertaken in 1887-8 showed the futility of continuing with the Owen Jones (q.v.), and also that the box magazine of the Improved Lee rifle was preferable – even though the hopper could be refilled when the rifle was locked and ready to fire. The Lee-Burton was abandoned, about thirty guns being converted to accept a box magazine. It was superseded by the Enfield-Lee with Speed's cut-off and ultimately by the Lee-Metford.

• Lee-Enfield

No sooner had the perfected Lee-Metford (q.v.) rifle entered service in quantity than the Mk I Cordite 303 cartridge (approved in November 1890 but not made for some time) proved to wear out Metford-rifled barrels very quickly. Trials undertaken by the authorities led to the approval of new concentric 'Enfield' rifling with five square-shouldered grooves.

MILITARY WEAPONS

MARK I RIFLE

Made by the Royal Small Arms Factory, Enfield Lock, Middlesex (171,100); the Royal Small Arms Factory, Sparkbrook, Birmingham (46,200); the Birmingham Small Arms & Metal Co. Ltd., Small Heath (64,300); and the London Small Arms Co. Ltd., Bow (about 35,600).

Total production: about 317,200. **Chambering:** 303, rimmed. **Action:** locked by a lug on the bolt body engaging a recess in the receiver as the bolt is turned down, and by the rear of the bolt guide rib abutting the receiver bridge.

49.5in overall, 9.50lb empty. 30.2in barrel, 5-groove rifling; LH, concentric. Detachable box magazine, 10 rounds. Ramp-and-leaf sight graduated to 1600yd. 2060ft/sec with Mk II ball cartridges. Pattern 1888 sword bayonet.

Sealed on 11th November 1895, the 'Rifle, Magazine, Lee-Enfield, 303-inch (Mark I)' had the new rifling and the front sight moved to the left. The marking on the butt socket read 'L.E.' ('Lee-

Enfield') instead of 'L.M.' for 'Lee-Metford'. Mechanically, however, the Lee-Enfield was all but identical with its Lee-Metford predecessor.

SIMILAR GUNS

Charger Loading Mark I (N) rifle. Approved in 1914, the 'Rifle, Magazine, Charger-Loading, Lee-Enfield, Naval Service, 303-inch (Mark I)' resembled the Charger Loading Mk I* (q.v.) and had an identical charger bridge. The original long rifle sights were altered for Mk VII ammunition, the leaf being graduated to 1900yd and marked 'C.L.' in the bottom left corner.

Charger Loading Mark I* (N) rifle. This was simply a Mk I* Lee-Enfield adapted to Mk I (N) standards; it was approved on 2nd October 1914.

Charger Loading Mark II rifle. Approval of the bridge-type stripper-clip guides allowed this rifle to be sealed on 1st July 1907. More than 300,000 Mk I and I* rifles had been adapted by Enfield, Vickers, BSA and LSA by 1913.

Converted Mark I rifle. Sealed on 2nd November 1903, this was such a complex adaptation of the Lee-Metford Mk I* that few guns were altered before the design was declared obsolete in 1906.

Mark I* rifle. Sealed on 7th August 1899, the Mk I* Lee-Enfield lacked a clearing rod and the associated rod groove in the underside of the forend; Mk I rifles modified to Mk I* standards have a fillet of wood in the groove. About 590,000 new Mk I* rifles were made by the government small arms factories in Enfield (241,550) and Sparkbrook (83,300), by the Birmingham Small Arms & Metal Co. Ltd. (192,000), and by the London Small Arms Co. Ltd. (about 74,000). With effect from February 1906, the trigger let-off was lightened to 5-7lb to match the SMLE, but the conversion of many Lee-Enfields to the 22 rimfire Aiming Tube (q.v.) system began in 1907. These were marked 'A.T.', though a few survivors were changed back to 303 in 1939-40.

MARK I CARBINE

Made by the Royal Small Arms Factory, Enfield Lock.

Total production: about 14,000. **Chambering:** 303, rimmed. **Action:** as Lee-Enfield Mk I, above.

39.3in overall, 7.44lb empty. 20.75in barrel, 5-groove rifling; LH, concentric. Detachable box magazine, 6 rounds. Ramp-and-leaf sight graduated to 2000yd. 1940ft/sec with Mk II ball cartridges. No bayonet.

Approved on 17th August 1896, the 'Carbine, Magazine, Lee-Enfield, 303-inch (Mark I)' resembled the Lee-Metford equivalent, but lacked the sling bar. An 'L.E.C.' mark ('Lee-Enfield Carbine') appeared on the butt socket.

SIMILAR GUN

Mark I* carbine. Sealed on 7th August 1899, this was identical with the preceding Mk I carbine except for the omission of the clearing rod. Production amounted to about 26,650, exclusively in the Enfield factory.

NO. 1 IMPROVED PATTERN RIFLE

Made by the Royal Small Arms Factory, Enfield Lock, Middlesex, 1901.

Total production: at least 100. **Chambering:** 303, rimmed. **Action:** as Lee-Enfield Mk I, above.

A 303Charger-Loading Lee-Enfield Mk II rifle, with bridge-type stripper-clip guides.

DATA FOR A TYPICAL EXAMPLE

44.55in overall, 8.38lb empty. 25.2in barrel, 5-groove rifling; LH, concentric. Detachable box magazine, ten rounds. Tangent-leaf rear sight graduated to 2000yd. About 2030ft/sec with Mk II ball cartridges. Pattern 1888 sword bayonet.

This was produced by the Royal Small Arms Factory in 1901, in response to complaints made during the Second South African War – for example, that the Lee-Enfield was too complicated and contained too many springs.

The No. 1 Improved pattern had a lightened barrel and butt, a full-length handguard, and an improved nose cap to remove the strain of a fixed bayonet from the barrel. The sights were changed and the safety catch was revised. The most important advance, however, was the advent of a Watkin & Speed charger-loading system.

MODIFIED (SHORTENED) PATTERN RIFLE

Made by the Royal Small Arms Factory and issued for trials in the autumn of 1901, this was basically a No. 1 Improved rifle with additional refinements and a special sword bayonet. About 1060 were made.

The Pattern A (Watkin & Speed) rear sight had a front-hinged leaf graduated from 200yd to 2000yd; the competing Pattern B was hinged at the rear. The safety was changed and an internal barrel band was used. Short, normal and long butts were tested, as well as differing bayonets.

The shortened trials rifles were popular, despite minor problems, and comparative trials with a selection of standard full-length rifles revealed little change in accuracy. Almost all survivors were altered to SMLE standards in about 1903-4 – and then converted for Aiming Tube use in 1906-7 before being discarded. Consequently, very few will now be found in their original state.

MARK I SHORT RIFLE

Made by the Royal Small Arms Factory, Enfield Lock, Middlesex (133,450); the Royal Small Arms Factory, Sparkbrook, Birmingham (14,650); the Birmingham Small Arms Co. Ltd., Small Heath (150,000); and the London Small Arms Co. Ltd., Bow (about 65,000).
Total production: 363,100. **Chambering:** 303, rimmed. **Action:** as Lee-Enfield Mk I, above.

44.55in overall, 8.15lb empty. 25.2in barrel, 5-groove rifling; LH, concentric. Detachable box magazine, 10 rounds. Tangent-leaf sight graduated to 2000yd. 2230ft/sec with Mk VI ball cartridges. Pattern 1903 sword bayonet.

By the end of 1902, a perfected trials rifle had been forthcoming. Changes included provision of an 'eared' front sight, and a modified handguard.

It subsequently became the 'Rifle, Short, Magazine, Lee-Enfield, 303-inch (Mark I)' on 23rd December 1902. Production began immediately, but many minor alterations were soon required and the pattern was re-sealed several times. Guns made for naval service were fitted with cut-offs from August 1903 onward, and the manufacturing pattern was re-sealed on 14th September.

The basic Mark I pattern was sealed again in September 1906. The use of the cut-off was extended to land service from October, and a shortened lead from the chamber to the bore was also approved during the year. An improved U-notch replaced the 'V' on the back-sight leaf in 1907.

SIMILAR GUNS

Converted Mark I short rifle.** Accepted for naval service in January 1908, this SMLE was transformed by Royal Navy ordnance depots in Chatham, Plymouth and Portsmouth. Despite being fitted with Mk III sights, the guns all retained the original two-piece stripper-clip guides on the bridge and bolt head. A large 'N' appeared on the left side of the receiver shoe. Surviving guns were re-sighted for Mk VII ball ammunition and given bridge-type stripper-clip guides in 1912. Complementary changes were made in the stock and the incurving front sight protectors were straightened.

Converted Mark I* short rifle.** This rifle was sealed on 22nd August 1914 to guide adaptation of the earlier Mk I* (q.v.) for Mk VII cartridges.

Converted Mark II short rifle. Sealed on 16th January 1903, though final approval was withheld until November, the Converted Mk II was adapted from Mk I or Mk I* Lee-Enfields and a few old Mk II or II* Lee-Metfords. New short barrels were fitted; stripper-clip guides appeared on the receiver and bolt head; there were new sights; and the original stock was greatly modified. Owing to improvements made in the Converted Mk II*, the pattern for the preceding Converted Mk II was re-sealed in September 1906.

Converted Mark II* short rifle.** Approved on 15th March 1906 and adapted from old Lee-Metfords (Mks II, II*) or Lee-Enfields (Mks I, I*), this was comparable with the standard SMLE Mk I* (q.v.).

Converted Mark II** short rifle.** Modified by the navy ordnance depots in Chatham, Plymouth and Portsmouth, these short rifles were accepted for naval service in July 1908. They were similar to the Converted Mk I** (q.v.), originally retaining two-piece stripper-clip guides. Surviving guns were re-sighted for Mk VII ball ammunition in 1912 and fitted with bridge-type stripper-clip guides. Changes to the stock and sight protectors were made at the same time.

Converted Mark II** short rifle.** Introduced in 1909, this was practically identical with the Converted Mk II**. Two-piece stripper-clip guides were used. Most of the remaining rifles were re-sighted for Mk VII ball ammunition in 1912, receiving bridge-type stripper-clip guides, minor changes to the stock, and straightened front-sight protectors.

Mark I* short rifle.** Approved on 27th March 1906, the Mk I* SMLE had a trap in the buttplate for the oiler and pull-through, a swivel on the butt, and a modified magazine. More than sixty thousand guns of this type were made in the Enfield factory, and another three thousand 'India Pattern' examples in Ishapore.

Mark I A.T. short rifle This centerfire training rifle embodied the 23-caliber Mk I 'Aiming Tube' (a sub-caliber barrel insert). It was approved in November 1903, but so many problems were discovered that a satisfactory pattern was not sealed until 1906. The guns were generally rebuilt from SMLE trials rifles and classified as 'Non-Interchangeable'. They displayed 'A.T.' and 'N.I.' on the body, bolt, barrel and butt. On 13th December 1907, however, the 22 rimfire SMLE Mk I trainer was substituted.

MARK III SHORT RIFLE

Made by the Royal Small Arms Factory, Enfield Lock, Middlesex (2.235 million including 'peddled' guns, 1907-22); the Birmingham Small Arms Co. Ltd., Small Heath (about two million, 1907-43); by the London Small Arms Co. Ltd., Bow (430,000, 1907-19); by the Standard Small Arms Company, Birmingham (1916-18); by the National Rifle Factory No. 1 (1918-19); and many other contractors (see notes).
Total production: about 4.67 million Mk III and Mk III* rifles in Britain, plus 1.4 million in Lithgow (Australia) and 640,600 in Ishapore (India).
Chambering: 303, rimmed. **Action:** as Lee-Enfield Mk I, above.

44.55in overall, 8.66lb empty. 25.2in barrel, 5-groove rifling; LH, concentric. Detachable box magazine, 10 rounds. Tangent-leaf sight graduated to 2000yd. 2440ft/sec with Mk VII ball cartridges. Pattern 1907 sword bayonet.

Service soon showed that the bolt-head stripper-clip guide loosened much too quickly to be useful. The first monoblock bridge-type guides were developed experimentally in 1906. Trials occupied several months, until Enfield-pattern stripper-clip guides and an improved Watkin & Speed sight were adopted for a new Mk III SMLE on 26th January 1907. The nose cap was lightened and the rear sight protectors were altered.

The adoption of the Mk VII cartridge in 1910, raising velocity from 2230ft/sec, required the sights to be adapted for the differing trajectory of the new lightweight projectile; changes to the original dial sight were made either by altering the existing graduations or replacing the dial plate entirely. In the summer of 1911, the magazine and the receiver body were modified to ensure that the pointed Mk VII bullet fed properly.

SIMILAR GUNS

Converted Mark IV short rifle. Sealed on 17th June 1907, this was little more than the Converted Mk II (q.v.) improved to SMLE Mk III standards. It weighed about 8.9lb.

Mark III* short rifle.** Approved on 2nd January 1916, this SMLE embodied changes to raise production to levels demanded by the advent of war. The most obvious external change was the omission of long-range sights. BSA had also discarded the cut-off plate from a few Mk III rifles made in the autumn of 1915, but the component was soon officially reinstated; however, the authorities subsequently relented, making the cut-off mechanism optional until the end of World War I in November 1918. A simplified cocking piece with grooved flat sides was introduced in August 1916.

Mark III EY and Mark III* EY short rifles. Announced 'for the record' in December 1918, though in use since mid 1916, 303 Emergency Pattern Lee-Enfields were old, worn or damaged weapons with their forends lashed with cable or copper wire to minimize splintering should the barrel burst.

Mark III (T) and Mark III* (T) short rifles. Shortly after World War I began, the earliest SMLE sniper rifles were fitted with fragile Galilean sights consisting simply of two widely separated lenses. By mid-1915, however, conventional telescope sights were becoming popular. A typical Periscopic Prism Company sight was 12in long, with a 9-degree field of view and range drums graduated for 100-600yd. Male dovetails on the sight rings fitted into a bar brazed to the left side of the SMLE action.

By 1918, the sturdy 2.5x sights made by Aldis Brothers of Birmingham were preferred. A typical example had a 19mm objective lens and a range drum calibrated '1' to '6' (100-600yd). Figures published in the 1920s revealed that 9790 Mk III and Mk III* SMLE sniper rifles had been made during World War I.

No. 1 Mk III short rifle. Guns remaining in service after May 1926 were re-designated 'No. 1 Mk III', production of rifles of this type finally ending in the BSA Small Heath, Redditch and Shirley factories (M47A, M47B and M47C respectively) in 1943. Extensive use had been made of sub-contractors but, apart from insignificant changes to parts such as the cocking piece, few alterations had been made since the end of World War I.

No. 1 Mk III* short rifle. The post-1926 designation of the Mark III* SMLE authorised during World War I.

.22 MARK I SHORT RIFLE

Converted from Mk I* Lee-Metfords, this was approved on 13th December 1907. The magazine and the cut off were discarded, a new barrel was fitted, and the forend was shortened. The original nose cap was retained, but the bayonet bar was removed. A Mk III rear sight and a new rear handguard was fitted. The bolt was altered to accept an auxiliary bolt head and a one-piece striker, though the '.22 No. 2 Bolt Head', with a two-piece inertia striker assembly, was adopted in December 1910. At least six thousand of these trainers were converted in the Enfield factory. They were 44.3in long, had a 25.2in barrel, and weighed 8.4lb; the eight-groove rifling turned to the right.

SIMILAR GUNS

.22 Mark I* short rifle. Dating from October 1911, the Mk I* was a Mk I with a modified Pattern No. 2 bolt head and revised sights approximating to a SMLE firing Mk VII ammunition.

.22 Mark II (N) short rifle. This Naval Service trainer was converted from Lee-Metford Mk II rifles with effect from January 1912. It could be distinguished from the Mk I and Mk I* by the forend, which lacked the finger groove of the older patterns. Only about a thousand guns were converted in Enfield.

.22 Mark III short rifle. This rimfire short rifle – approved in August 1912 – was a transformation of the SMLE Converted Mks II and II*. It had a new 22-caliber barrel, the No. 2 bolt head (with a two-piece striker) and a Mk III rear sight. The Parker-Hiscock magazine was approved for the 22 Mk III in December 1915. This

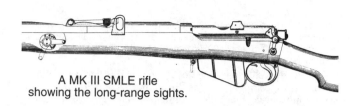

A MK III SMLE rifle showing the long-range sights.

consisted of a five-round insert and feed spring contained within a 303 magazine body, with a prominent depressor lever on the rear right side of the magazine body. The magazine was not successful; after 1925, therefore, a standard magazine devoid of spring and follower was used to catch spent cases. About eleven thousand rifles were converted by BSA, LSA and Enfield.

.22 Mark IV* short rifle. Introduced in November 1921, this trainer was converted from SMLE Mk III and III* rifles. It had a solid barrel and a new bolt head, the cut off and magazine being discarded. Surviving P/1914 rimfires (q.v.) were altered to Mk IV and Mk IV* standards when they returned for repair.

No. 2 Mk IV* short rifle. This was a post-1926 designation for the 22 Mk IV*. As many as thirty thousand of these 22 training rifles were made; most were conversions, but a few new guns were made in Enfield in the 1920s and work was still underway in Lithgow ('No. 2 Mk 4/1') and Ishapur in the 1950s.

.22 MARK I RIFLE
Alternatively known as '.22 Mark I Long Rifle'

This was approved for the Royal Navy in February 1912, the guns being conversions of Mk II Lee-Metfords retaining the full-length stocks and a nose cap with a bayonet bar. The barrels were new, and the bolt head was altered to receive the two-part No. 2 striker assembly. Rifles were about 49.5in long, had 30.2in barrels with eight-groove rifling, and weighed 8.75lb.

SIMILAR GUNS

.22 Mark I* rifle. This had originally been a Mk II* Lee-Metford or a Mk I/Mk I* Lee-Enfield, with a radial safety lever on the right side of the cocking piece. About four thousand guns were converted in Enfield.

.22 Mark II rifle. Approved for Land Service in November 1911, the 22 Mk II was originally a Mk II* Lee-Metford or a Mk I/Mk I* Lee-Enfield. It was intended to duplicate the sighting arrangements of the Charger-Loading Lee Enfield, but lacked the bridge for the stripper-clip.

PATTERN 1914 22 RIFLE

The 'Rifle, Short, 22 Rim Fire, Pattern 1914', approved on 24th May 1915, had a tubed barrel, a bolt head with an inertia striker, and an improved extractor. The sights were appropriately marked for 25yd. It was made exclusively by A.G. Parker & Co. Ltd. and Westley Richards & Co. of Birmingham, from SMLE Converted Mk II and Converted Mk II* rifles, and renamed 'P/14 No. 1' after the adoption of the No. 2 pattern described below.

Originally a single-loader, it could be fitted with a Parker-Hiscock magazine from the end of 1915 onward. Unfortunately, the magazines proved to be very unreliable and their value in rapid-

The SMLE Mk I rifle.

The Lee-Enfield Mk I cavalry carbine, with a safety lever on the cocking piece. (W&W)

fire training was questionable. They were replaced after 1925 by standard 303 magazine cases without springs and followers, which caught spent cases after extraction.

An aperture rear sight fitting onto the long-range sight arm was issued from April 1917 to prepare firers for the 303 P/14.

SIMILAR GUNS

Pattern 1914 No. 2 rifle. Adopted in April 1916, this was a conversion of the SMLE Mk III and Converted Mk IV. Confined to Enfield, production may not have exceeded two thousand.

Pattern 1914 long rifle. Also approved in April 1916, this was a conversion – perhaps experimental – of the Charger Loading Lee Enfield Mk I*, using the tubed barrel and modified bolt head. It is suspected that only a few of these conversions were made.

PATTERN 1918 22 RIFLE

This 22 rifle was approved in July 1918, an adaptation of SMLE Mk III and Converted Mk IV rifles to accept 'conveyors' – 303-shape adapters into which a 22 rimfire cartridge was inserted. Apart from requiring a tubed barrel, modifications to the bolt head, and a special ejector, the P/18 was identical with 303 service rifles. It proved unexpectedly temperamental, and was declared obsolete soon after the end of the war. Only about 950-1000 guns are believed to have been made in the Enfield small arms factory.

MARK V SHORT RIFLE

Made by the Royal Small Arms Factory, Enfield Lock, Middlesex, 1922-4.
Total production: 20,000. **Chambering:** 303, rimmed. **Action:** as Lee-Enfield Mk I, above.

DATA FOR SMLE MK V

44.55in overall, 8.65lb empty. 25.15in barrel, 5-groove rifling; LH, concentric. Magazine: detachable charger-loaded box, 10 rounds. Aperture sight graduated to 1400yd. 2440ft/sec with Mk VII ball cartridges. Pattern 1907 sword bayonet.

The 'Rifle, Short, Magazine, Lee-Enfield, 303-inch Mark V' was approved in 1922, with aperture sights on the body behind the stripper-clip guides, and an additional 'battle sight' to be used when the sight was folded down. A reinforcing band appeared behind the nose cap, while the handguard reached back to the chamber ring.

SIMILAR GUNS

No. 1 Mk VI rifle. Extensive trials revealed that the Mk V was far from ideal, and introduction was canceled in 1924 in favor of experiments with the Mk VI. The new gun, which appeared during the summer, had a heavy barrel, a modified body and an improved rear sight with distinctive protecting wings. Only a few inches of the muzzle protruded from the forend.

No. 1 Mk VI Model B rifle. Developed in 1930, this lacked buttplate checkering. At least 1025 were made in 1930-1. In 1933, two thousand additional 'Model B' trials rifles were made with raised left body walls and plain forends. Most surviving Model B rifles

A British infantryman from the end of the 'Redcoat' era holds a Long Lee-Enfield rifle.

British infantrymen armed with SMLE rifles pose 'somewhere in France' in 1916.

were converted to No. 4 standards and issued to the British Army in 1940, shortly after the withdrawal from Dunkirk. Diced forends and fluted handguards distinguished them.

No. 1 Mk VI Model C rifle. Tests were undertaken during the mid-1930s with more than fifty examples of this rifle.

No.1 Mk VI Model D rifle. This, the final experimental pattern prior to the approval of the Rifle No. 4 (q.v.), was abandoned after only a handful had been made.

NUMBER 4 MARK I RIFLE

Made by BSA Guns Ltd., Redditch and Shirley, 1940-5 (665,000); by the Royal Ordnance Factories, Fazakerley (619,900) and Maltby (737,500), 1942-5.
Total production: about 2.022 million in Britain. **Chambering:** 303, rimmed. **Action:** as Lee-Enfield Mk I, above.

44.45in overall, 9.06lb empty. 25.2in barrel, 2- or 5-groove rifling; LH, concentric. Detachable charger-loaded box magazine, 10 rounds. Leaf sight graduated to 2000yd. 2440ft/sec with Mk VII ball. No. 4 spike bayonet.

Approved on 15th November 1939 on the basis of the No. 1 Mk VI Model B trials rifle (above), the No. 4 Mk I was not issued until the Spring of 1942. Rough machining and the six-inch spike bayonet soon received adverse comments, as the advantages of the new weapon initially passed unnoticed.

Many changes were made to fittings during World War II to simplify mass production. There were, for example, several No. 4 rear sights ranging from the Mk 1, graduated from 200yd to 1300yd in fifty-yard increments, to the Mk 2 rocking 'L' for 300yd and 600yd.

Two-groove rifling was approved in 1941, and used until declared obsolete in July 1945. The early flared-rim cocking piece was replaced first with a flat three-groove pattern and then an entirely plain type. Buttplates on wartime guns were often mazak alloy instead of gunmetal, while stock wood was often inferior and sling swivels were reduced to bent wire.

SIMILAR GUNS

No. 4 Mk I* rifle. Approved in June 1941, this was made only in Canada and the U.S. The action body was modified and the 'catch-head, breech bolt' was omitted. Production of these guns was considerable: Small Arms Ltd. of Long Branch, Toronto, made 910,700 Mk I and Mk I* rifles (including 330,000 for Britain), and the Savage Arms Company of Chicopee Falls, Massachusetts, made about 1.236 million guns. Though these totals included a few No. 4 Mk I rifles, the vast majority were made to the Mk I* pattern.

The Lee-Enfield Mk III rifle.

A drawing of the commercial Lee-Speed action. (Greener)

No. 4 Mk 1/2 rifle. This was a revision of original British-made No. 4 Mk 1 rifles to Mk 2 standards, undertaken from 1949 onward.

No. 4 Mk 1/3 rifle. Similar to the Mk 1/2, this was a post-1949 conversion of North American-made No. 4 Mk I* rifles to Mk 2 standards. Production of Mk 1/2 and Mk 1/3 rifles is believed to have reached 360,000, with all but a few thousand Enfield conversions being undertaken in Fazakerley.

No. 4 Mk I (T) rifle. Shortages of suitable sniping equipment in the early stages of World War II were solved by fitting Aldis sights to P/14 rifles, and by converting about 1400 No. 1 Mk VI trials rifles to No. 4 standards. Auxiliary cheekpieces were authorized in September 1940.

The perfected No. 4 Mk I (T) rifles, approved on 12th February 1942, were issued with No. 32 telescope sights. The No. 32 Mk I sight weighed 2lb 3oz, had a 19mm objective lens, a 9-degree field of view, and a range drum graduated 100-1000yd. Much conversion work was sub-contracted to Holland & Holland (code 'S51'), who completed 26,442 of about 28,500 sniper rifles. BSA-made guns were preferred, though a few Stevens-Savage examples were used in 1942.

No. 4 Mk 2 rifle. Approved on 4th December 1947 to replace the unsuccessful No. 5, this was not introduced until 1949. The trigger was mounted on the underside of the body instead of on the trigger guard, so the revised Mk 2 forend could not be exchanged with the earlier type. No. 4 Mk 1 rear sights were used. Made exclusively in the Enfield factory, production is believed to have exceeded 450,000.

NUMBER 5 MARK 1 RIFLE
'Lee-Enfield Jungle Carbine'

Made by BSA Guns Ltd., Shirley (81,330); and the Royal Ordnance Factory, Fazakerley (169,810).

Total production: about 251,000. **Chambering:** 303, rimmed. **Action:** as No. 4 Mk 1, above.

Armed with SMLE rifles and fixed bayonets, British infantrymen march through occupied Cologne in 1919.

39.5in overall, 7.16lb empty. 18.7in barrel (excluding flash hider), 5-groove rifling; LH, concentric. Detachable charger-loaded box magazine, 10 rounds. Leaf sight graduated to 800yd. About 2100ft/sec with Mk VII ball cartridges. No. 5 knife bayonet.

The Lee-Enfield 'Jungle Carbine' arose from a 1943-vintage request for a lighter weapon for use in the Far East. Trials undertaken in 1944 with shortened rifles proved that accuracy was acceptable, but that recoil increased. Formally approved on 23rd May 1945, the No. 5 Mk 1 was made with the three standard butts, a half-length forend and a modified No. 4 Mk 1-type rear sight. Guns were ordered from the BSA and Fazakerley factories, where work on the No. 4 stopped. However, the popularity of the Jungle Carbine was temporary: accuracy was poor. As experiments failed to pinpoint the cause, the No. 5 was declared obsolete in 1947.

NUMBER 7 MARK 1 RIFLE

Experiments were made in the 1930s, but no new training rifles appeared until prototypes based on the No. 4 and No. 5 303 rifles were made by BSA in 1944-5. The No. 4 look-alike was approved in the late 1940s by the Air Ministry, as the 'Rifle, .22in, No.7 Mk 1'.

The supersession of the Lee-Enfield by the L1A1 was accompanied by the demise of the training rifles, many of which were sold to rifle clubs. Others, however, were stripped of their woodwork and re-issued as sub-caliber artillery trainers under the designation 'L2A1'.

The No. 1 Mk V rifle was an early post-war attempt to improve the SMLE.

The No. 4 Mk II rifle, the 'SMLE' of the Second World War.

The No. 5 Mk I Lee-Enfield Jungle Carbine was not successful.

The L39A1 was a target-shooting version of the Lee-Enfield.

SIMILAR GUNS

No. 8 Mk 1 rifle. Instead of standardizing on the air force's No. 7 (q.v.), the army approved the Rifle No. 8 Mk 1 in September 1948. It had a half-stock, a refined pistol grip butt and, eventually, greatly refined sights graduated to 100yd. Made by the Royal Ordnance Factory in Fazakerley and apparently also in the BSA Shirley factory, it measured 41.8in overall, had a 23.9in barrel rifled with six-groove clockwise twist, and weighed 8lb 8oz.

No. 9 Mk 1 rifle. The 'Rifle, .22in, No. 9 Mk 1' was a variant of the No. 7 made for the Royal Navy in 1957-9 by Parker-Hale Ltd. Unlike the newly-made RAF rifles, the No. 9 was converted by tubing the barrels of existing No. 4 weapons.

L8A1 RIFLE

Made by the Royal Small Arms Factory, Enfield Lock, Middlesex
Total production: not known. **Chambering:** 7.62x51, rimless. **Action:** as Lee-Enfield Mk I, above.
DATA FOR L39A1
46.5in overall, 9.72lb empty. 27.55in barrel, 4-groove rifling; RH, concentric. Detachable charger-loaded box magazine, 10 rounds. Micro-adjustable aperture sight. 2770ft/sec with standard ball cartridges.

7.62mm conversions of the 303 No. 4 Lee-Enfield formed the L8 series of the 1960s. The basic pattern, the L8A1, was based on the No. 4 Mk 2. Conversion kits comprising a new barrel, a modified extractor, a new magazine and a charger-guide insert were made in the Royal Small Arms Factory, Enfield (marked 'UE') and by the Sterling Engineering Co. Ltd. of Dagenham ('US').

SIMILAR GUNS

L8A2 rifle. This was based on the No. 4 Mk 1/2, which was itself a conversion to Mk 2 standards of British-made rifles No. 4 Mk I.

L8A3 rifle. Based on the No. 4 Mk 1/3, this used a North American-made No. 4 action which had already been modified to Mk 2 standards.

L8A4 rifle. This was a conversion of original unaltered British-made No. 4 Mk 1 rifles. It does not seem to have been produced in large numbers.

L8A5 rifle. Based on the No. 4 Mk 1*, this used unaltered North American-made actions.

L39A1 rifle. Touted commercially as the 'Enfield Envoy', this rifle had a sporting-style half stock and aperture sights. Used by the British armed forces for competitive shooting, it was invariably built on a Mk 2 action with the trigger pivoted on the underside of the body.

L42A1 sniping rifle. Adopted on 24th August 1970 for issue to British snipers, prior to the introduction of the L96A1 in the mid 1980s, the L42A1 was converted from existing No. 4 Mk 1 (T) rifles and had the trigger lever pivoted on the trigger guard. It has been issued with the 'Telescope, Straight, Sighting, L1A1' (the old No. 32 Mk 3).

Three British soldiers pose with No. 1 Mk III SMLE rifles, 1942.

SPORTING GUNS

The Lee action, owing to its alleged weaknesses, has never been popular among sportsmen except in areas of British dominance. But even British gunsmiths promoted it apathetically; supplying good-quality sporting rifles built on Mauser actions, which commanded far higher prices, was far more to their taste.

The Lee system has had two principal periods in vogue. It was reasonably popular prior to 1914, and again after World War II when colossal numbers of military surplus No. 1 and No. 4 rifles became available.

The principal manufacturers were BSA, W.W. Greener, A.G. Parker, Parker-Hale and Westley Richards. Their products are all listed separately. Many individual British gunmakers handled Lee-type sporters, usually bought wholesale from BSA. These will usually bear a discreet 'Piled Arms' proofmark on the action.

• Lee-Metford

Developed in the U.S., then perfected in the U.S. and Britain, Lee guns were service issue in Britain and the British Empire – and in many former colonies after independence had been gained (e.g., India and Pakistan). Lee-Enfields were also used in Iraq and the Irish Free State (Eire) prior to 1939; many others were sold to Belgium, Denmark, Egypt, Greece, the Netherlands, Norway, Thailand, and Turkey in the post-1945 era.

The first turning-bolt Lee design, with a single locking lug, sold in small numbers to warring factions in South and Central America while encountering continual apathy in the US Army. An improved two-lug mechanism was then perfected in Britain, where the 303 Magazine Rifle Mk I (Lee-Metford) was adopted for military service in 1888.

Though the perfected British-type Lee served with honor through world wars and many lesser conflicts, criticism has always been made of its design. Placing the locking lugs behind the magazine put much of the bolt body under stress during firing.

However, few problems arose when 303 cartridges were used, and though occasional bolt failures were reported when conversions to 7.62x51mm were made in the 1960s, the deficiencies were exaggerated. Judged from a purely military standpoint, the Lee has been a great success.

THE FIRST STEPS

The Lee appeared in Britain at the end of March 1880, when three 1879-pattern rifles and two carbines chambering the 45-caliber drawn-case Gatling cartridge were among a selection of guns tried by the Small Arms Committee.

A final report made on 21st March 1881 noted that, despite niggling extraction problems, the 45 Lee had performed best of the submissions.

Keen to adopt a magazine rifle, the British Admiralty recommenced trials in the summer of 1882. Participants included Lee (M1882) and Spencer-Lee rifles. By April 1883, a new Lee rifle chambering the 45-70 US Army cartridge was being tested at Enfield, impressing the authorities sufficiently for a 402 'Improved Lee' to be built in the Enfield factory; it had a one-piece Arbuthnot-type stock.

In 1887, a 43 (11mm Spanish) 1885-type Remington-Lee (q.v.) rifle passed an outstanding test. Three hundred guns were ordered for trials against the Lee-Burton, receiving the British War Department property mark on the right side of the butt. The trials resolved in favor of the box magazines of these U.S.-made guns at the expense of the Burton hopper. However, development of an 8mm smokeless cartridge in France persuaded the British to abandon the ineffectual 402, experimental work revealing that a 298 Rubin bullet offered flatter trajectory, better accuracy and greater penetration.

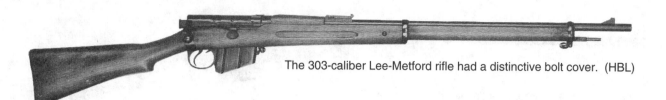

The 303-caliber Lee-Metford rifle had a distinctive bolt cover. (HBL)

MILITARY WEAPONS

TRIALS PATTERNS

Made by the Royal Small Arms Factory, Enfield Lock, Middlesex, 1888.
Total production: at least 437 rifles and 51 carbines. **Chambering:** 303, rimmed. **Action:** locked by a single lug on the bolt body engaging a recess in the receiver as the bolt handle was turned down, and by the rear of the bolt guide-rib abutting the receiver bridge.

DATA FOR A TYPICAL RIFLE
49.9in overall, 9.09lb empty. 29.5in barrel, 7-groove rifling; LH, concentric. Detachable box magazine, seven rounds. Ramp-and-leaf rear sight graduated to 1600yd. About 1800ft/sec with ball cartridges. Sword bayonet.

A 303 rifle chambering a straight-case cartridge was approved early in 1888. It had a distinctive butt with a continuous comb and a straight wrist. A bolt-head release catch lay on the right side of the receiver and a long ejector was let into the left side of the bolt-way. The design of the box magazine, the cut-off and the long-range dial sight was credited to Joseph Speed of the Enfield factory. A Martini-style upper band accepted a special sword bayonet.

Experiments were continued throughout the autumn of 1888 with a selection of rimmed, rimless and semi-rim necked cartridge cases. Many minor changes were also made to the rifle, which gained Rigby's patented nose-cap, Lewes-pattern sights and an eight-round single-row magazine. The ejector was simplified, a new safety catch appeared on the left side of the receiver, and a handguard was added behind the rear sight. The result was the Lee-Metford.

MARK I RIFLE

Made by the Royal Small Arms Factory, Enfield Lock, Middlesex (189,000); by the Royal Small Arms Factory, Sparkbrook, Birmingham (63,000); by the Birmingham Small Arms & Metal Co. Ltd., Small Heath (67,500); and by the London Small Arms Co. Ltd., Bow (about 40,000).
Total production: about 360,000 Mk I and Mk I*. **Chambering:** 303, rimmed. **Action:** as Lee-Metford trials rifle, above.
49.5in overall, 9.5lb empty. 30.2in barrel, 7-groove rifling; LH, polygonal. Detachable box magazine, 8 rounds. Ramp-and-leaf sight graduated to 1800yd. 1830ft/sec with Mk I (black powder) ball rounds. Pattern 1888 sword bayonet.

Sealed on 12th December 1888, the perfected 'Rifle, Magazine, 303-inch (Mark I)' had a modified rear sight and a long-range dial plate (for 1800-3500yd) on the left side of the forend. The first issues were made in December 1889, but problems soon arose with the Lewes sights.

The forend groove was abandoned in 1890; changes were made to prevent handguards breaking; and a disc for regimental markings was added to the butt after 30th September 1890.

A combined front sight protector and muzzle-stop was adopted in January 1891, and the rifles were re-designated 'Lee-Metford Mk I' on 8th April. A reversion to 'V'-and-barleycorn sights was made in 1892. Sights had been graduated on the basis that smokeless propellant would be available immediately, but the appearance of a satisfactory cordite load had been delayed by unforeseen manufacturing problems.

SIMILAR GUNS

Mark I* rifle. Omitting the safety catch from 31st December 1890 advanced the designation of the Magazine Rifle Mk I. The 'Lee-Metford Mk I*' terminology was adopted on 8th April 1891.

MARK II RIFLE

Made by the Royal Small Arms Factory, Enfield Lock, Middlesex (84,350); by the Royal Small Arms Factory, Sparkbrook, Birmingham (47,900); by the Birmingham Small Arms & Metal Co. Ltd., Small Heath (73,100); and by the London Small Arms Co. Ltd., Bow (46,700).
Total production: about 252,000. **Chambering:** 303, rimmed. **Action:** as Lee-Metford trials rifle, above.

49.50in overall, 9.50lb empty. 30.22in barrel, 7-groove rifling; LH, polygonal. Detachable box magazine, 10 rounds. Ramp-and-leaf sight graduated to 1600yd. 1830ft/sec with Mk I (black powder) cartridges. Pattern 1888 sword bayonet.

A prototype rifle with a lightened barrel and a staggered-row box magazine appeared in September 1890. The barrel band and safety catch had been omitted; changes were made in the bolt head, the bolt cover and the cut-off mechanism. The dial sight ranged to 2800yd.

A hundred trials rifles appeared in October, ten with sights calibrated for cordite and the remainder for black powder. Testing was completed in April 1891, but changes were soon made. They included the approval of a new bolt head, designed by Deeley & Penn, and the reappearance of the lower band.

On 12th April 1893, the 'Rifle, Magazine, Lee-Metford, 303-inch (Mark II)' was finally sealed, though production had begun in October 1892.

SIMILAR GUNS

Charger Loading Mark II rifle. Though the pattern was sealed in 1907, replacement Metford-rifled barrels were in such short supply that work stopped in 1909. The few transformations were mostly fitted with Enfield-type barrels before receiving stripper-clip guides and SMLE-type sights in 1913-14.

MARK I CARBINE

Made by the Royal Small Arms Factory, Enfield Lock, Middlesex, 1894-6.
Total production: 18,700. **Chambering:** 303, rimmed **Action:** as Lee-Metford trials rifle, above.
39.9in overall, 7.43lb empty. 20.8in barrel, 7-groove rifling; LH, polygonal. Detachable box magazine, 6 rounds. Ramp-and-leaf sight graduated to 2000yd. About 1680ft/sec with Mk I (black powder) rounds. No bayonet.

At least 150 trials carbines were made between 1st April 1892 and 31st March 1894. The finalized design was sealed for cavalry use in June 1894 and again in September. The Mk I carbine was little more than a short infantry rifle with a safety catch on the right side of the cocking piece. The bolt handle knob was flattened and bent forward to facilitate inserting the carbine into a saddle bucket, and the magazine faired neatly into the underside of the forend. The guns had a sling bar and a marking disc on the right side of the butt, and a 'D'-ring on the left side of the butt socket.

The 'D'-ring was abandoned with effect from 6th March 1896, and a leather back-sight cover, held to the forend by two protruding-head screws, was approved in the autumn of the same year.

AIMING-TUBE GUNS

The earliest trainers were simply old 303 rifles with worn-out barrels, converted for Aiming Tubes. Also known as 'Morris Tubes' after their inventor, they were simply sub-caliber liners retained by knurled muzzle collars. Most fired a low-power 23 centerfire '.297/.230' cartridge.

The first Lee-Metford pattern was approved in December 1891, to be joined by a shortened version for carbines in May 1895. Lee-Metford Aiming Tubes would also fit long Lee-Enfields. Most guns were marked 'M.T.' or 'A.T.' and had a special bolt head. The last 23-caliber Aiming Tube was approved for Naval Service in February 1910 to expend existing ammunition.

SPORTING GUNS

Though neither BSA nor LSA offered purpose-built Lee-Metford sporting rifles, 'Trade Pattern' actions were supplied to individual gunmakers for completion. Consequently, a variety of half-stocked guns will be found with express sights and other special fittings.

• Leetch

Originally known as a gun-wadding maker, Leetch had become a gunmaker in London's Cavendish Square by 1858 and was granted four British patents for breechloaders prior to 1866.

Most surviving Leetch firearms display a laterally-moving sidelever action made in accordance with British patent 2235/58 of 1858, though a few have a lever which lifts upward. One gun was exhibited before the Board of Ordnance as early as November 1853, and a test of a short rifle, with a 33in barrel, followed in 1854.

MILITARY WEAPONS

BREECH-LOADING CARBINE

Military pattern

Maker unknown, but presumed to have been one of the better-known London gunmakers of the day.
Total production: a few, about 1854. **Chambering:** 577, combustible cartridge; fired by a cap lock. **Action:** locked by wedging the chamber in the frame with a side lever.

DATA FOR A TYPICAL EXAMPLE
36.35in overall, 6.75lb empty. 17.25in barrel, 3-groove rifling; RH, concentric. Single shot only. Leaf-type rear sight with a stepped bed, graduated to 500yd. No bayonet.

The Leetch carbine was operated by putting the hammer to half-cock, then pulling the side lever out and downward. The first movement withdrew the nose of the chamber from a narrow seat in the barrel before tipping the chamber down and clear of the breech. A combustible cartridge could be loaded from the front.

The motions were then reversed to replace the chamber in the breech, the final movement of the side lever camming the chamber forward to make a seal. A locking bolt was driven forward as the hammer fell, to prevent the breech opening as the gun fired.

A short-barreled Leetch was tried against a Sharps in 1855, firing 130 rounds without a misfire, and the adoption of the Leetch carbine for cavalry was formally approved on 19th July 1855. An order for fifteen thousand was passed to the Royal Manufactory at Enfield, but attention was soon drawn to the fact that spilled powder grains could prevent the breech closing or that a bullet jarred forward across the joint of the breechblock and barrel effectively locked the action shut.

The official order was reduced to two thousand guns in January 1856, but none had been delivered by early 1859; no government-order gun may ever have been completed.

SPORTING GUNS

Though the Leetch carbine was a failure in its role as a cavalry weapon, the breech was efficient enough by mid-19th Century standards to encourage the construction of other guns. Small numbers of sporting guns will be found, often differing in the details of the locking mechanism or the design of the stock. They customarily offer checkering, engraving, and better standards of finish than the plain military products.

• Manceaux

Designed in France by Manceaux & Vieillard (q.v.), these guns featured a breechbolt or 'plunger' operated by raising the breech cover, turning it slightly clockwise and then drawing the mechanism to the rear to expose the chamber. Obturation was achieved – apparently most successfully – by a coned bolt head meshing with a tapered hollow collar.

TRIALS CARBINE

Made by the Royal Small Arms Factory, Enfield.
Total production: 3-6, 1858. **Chambering:** 472, combustible cartridge; fired by a cap lock. **Action:** locked by rotating a rib on the breechbolt into engagement with shoulders in the receiver.

DATA FOR A TYPICAL EXAMPLE
40in overall, 7.30lb empty. 24.75in barrel, 6-groove rifling; RH, concentric. Single shot only. Block and multi-leaf rear sight for distances up to 500yd. No bayonet.

The experimental Manceaux carbine outshot even the Westley Richards carbine – regarded as the most accurate of the British caplock breechloaders – but the delicacy of its cartridge and the complexity of the obturator caused its rejection. The guns were similar externally to the Terry (q.v.) patterns, with a government-style sidelock and a hammer with an unusually long shank, but the breech cover lay on top of the action instead of the right side.

Enfield-made Manceaux carbines came in several types, including at least one gun with an 18in barrel and a patch box set into the right side of the butt.

• Mannlicher

These guns were popular in Britain early in the 20th Century, where sporting rifles were built on military 1893, 1895, or 1903-pattern actions imported by many well-known gunsmiths. Guns will be found with marks applied by (among others) Thomas Bland, John Dickson & Son, W.W. Greener, Holland & Holland, W.J. Jeffrey, MacNaughton and Joseph Woodward. Work continued for many years, one 6.5mm Dickson-made gun being reliably dated from 1931-2. The original 6.5x53 Dutch or 6.5x54 Mannlicher-Schönauer chamberings are most common; however, pre-1939 examples may handle cartridges as large as the 375 Rimless Nitro Express.

Stocks customarily followed the typically British minimalist form, with straight combs, small oval cheekpieces and delicately contoured pistol grips. Many rifles were made in takedown form, locked by interrupted threads or screws through the breech, while others – intended for long-range target shooting – had vernier sights on the heel of the butt. Cocking-piece aperture sights, patented triggers and adapted magazines were often proffered, together with Henry-type forend tips and express or Cape rear sights.

• Martini-Enfield

These 303 conversions represented the final stage in the development process begun by the 450 Martini-Henry (q.v.) and a minor progression from the 303 Martini-Metford (q.v.). Guns of this type had a long and useful life, being passed successively from the regular army to territorial units and then even to Boy Scouts and Boys' Brigade units. Many were stored to emerge in World War II to arm Local Defence Volunteers and the Home Guard.

MARK I RIFLE

Made by the Royal Small Arms Factory, Enfield, 1896-7.
Total production: 48,610. **Chambering:** 303, rimmed. **Action:** locked by the tip of the operating lever propping the breechblock behind the chamber.

46.5in overall, 8.31lb empty. 30.2in barrel, 5-groove rifling; LH, concentric. Ramp-and-leaf sight graduated to 1800yd. About 1970 ft/sec with Mk I (Cordite) ball cartridges. P/1895 socket bayonet.

Formally approved on 4th October 1895, the 'Rifle, Martini-Enfield, 303-inch (Mark I)' was converted from the Mk III Martini-Henry. Its new barrel had Enfield rifling, accepted a socket bayonet and had a rear sight graduated for cordite ammunition. The handguard ran to the back-sight base, swivels lay on the butt and lower band, and an open piling swivel graced the upper band.

Contact between the barrel and the forend or nose-cap of Martini-Enfield guns of all types was relieved from October 1901 onward in search of improved accuracy.

SIMILAR GUNS

Mark I* rifle. Approved in February 1903 after complaints emanating from South Africa, this was simply a standard Mk I Martini-Enfield with the new laterally-adjustable front sight (high, normal and low).

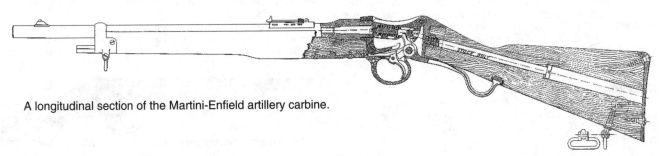

A longitudinal section of the Martini-Enfield artillery carbine.

The Martini-Enfield carbines were popular with juvenile training units after the First World War, shown by this British Boys Brigade company photographed in 1920.

Mark II rifle. Approved on 11th February 1896, this Martini-Enfield was a conversion of Mark II 45 Martini-Henry rifles. It had a larger cocking indicator than the Mk I, but was otherwise similar. Production of Mk II rifles slightly exceeded forty thousand: 33,020 were made in the Royal Small Arms Factory in 1896-1903, and another seven thousand were contributed by the Beardmore Engineering Co. during the Second South African (Boer) War of 1900-1. Beardmore guns were marked 'B.E.CO.'.

Mark II* rifle. This was a post-1903 conversion of the Mk II Martini-Enfield, with new front sights.

MARK I CAVALRY CARBINE
Made by the Royal Small Arms Factory, Enfield, 1898-1904.
Total production: 6870. **Chambering:** 303, rimmed. **Action:** as Martini-Enfield rifle, above.

37.3in overall, 6.56lb empty. 21.4in barrel, 5-groove rifling; LH, concentric. Ramp-and-leaf sight graduated to 2000yd. About 1690ft/sec with Mk I (Cordite) ball cartridges. No bayonet.

Approved on 20th August 1896, these differed from the comparable Martini-Metford patterns only in rifling and sights. About 5900 were converted from Mk II Martini-Henry rifles. Guns converted after the abolition of the clearing rod on 11th May 1899 had solid forends.

MARK I ARTILLERY CARBINE
Made by the Henry Rifled Barrel Co. Ltd., Hoxton (1896-7), and the Royal Small Arms Factory, Enfield, 1897-9.
Total production: 44,720. **Chambering:** 303, rimmed. **Action:** as Martini-Enfield rifle, above.

37.3in overall, 7.28lb empty. 21in barrel, 5-groove rifling; LH, concentric. Ramp-and-leaf sight graduated to 2000yd. About 1690ft/sec with Mk I (Cordite) ball cartridges. P/1888 sword bayonet.

The 'Carbine, Martini-Enfield, Artillery, 303-inch (Mark I)' – converted from a Mark III Martini-Henry rifle – was approved for issue on 6th November 1895.

SIMILAR GUNS
Mark II artillery carbine. Sealed on 6th December 1897, this was converted from Mk I and Mk III Martini-Henry artillery patterns. The forend was retained by a pin instead of a hook. Production was confined to the Henry Rifled Barrel Co. and the Royal Small Arms Factory in Enfield (1898-1900), totalling about 26,000 guns.

Mark III artillery carbine. Converted from the Mark II Martini-Henry rifle, the Mk III Martini-Enfield artillery carbine was sealed in July 1899. However, the original pattern was speedily re-sealed with an offset front sight in wing-type protectors. The Mk III was similar to the Mark II Martini-Metford artillery carbine, but had an Enfield barrel and modified sights. It also had a solid forend. About 32,540 Mk III carbines were converted, mainly by the Royal Small Arms Factory (1900-4) though a few thousand came from the Beardmore Engineering Co. in 1900-1.

COLONIAL PATTERNS
The first of 965 303 Martini-Enfield Mk II cavalry carbines was made for New South Wales in 1903, work being completed within a year. They were converted from Mk I Martini-Henry artillery carbines.

• Martini-Henry
See also Enfield-Martini, Martini-Enfield, Martini-Metford, and Westley Richards Martini. Perfected in Switzerland in the 1860s, these rifles saw service in Britain (Martini-Henry, Martini-Metford and Martini-Enfield types), Portugal (Martini-Henry), the South African Republic (Westley Richards Martini), Romania (Peabody-Martini) and Turkey (Peabody-Martini). They were briefly adopted in Serbia (Martini-Henry), and ex-British rifles were used in Japan.

BACKGROUND
Swiss-born Friedrich Martini offered a prototype to rifle trials held in Aarau in 1866. The mechanism was patented in Britain in July 1868, where, after extensive improvements by technicians in the government small-arms factory in Enfield, it was approved for service.

The Martini is widely believed to have been an adaptation of patents filed in the U.S. by Henry Peabody (q.v.); Martini himself acknowledged his rifle to be 'an improvement on the Peabody'. However, as dropping-block rifles were scarcely new, Peabody and Martini agreed to mutually beneficial terms prior to 1873: Peabody-Martini rifles emanated from the U.S. even as the Martini-Henry was being made in Britain.

The true Martini breech contained a sturdy block with a transverse pivot through the rear upper tip, inserted in a hollow box-type receiver. Pushing the breech lever downward dropped the front of the breechblock to reveal the chamber, extracting the cartridge as it did so. If the movement was swift enough, the spent case flew clear of the gun and a new round could be pushed into the chamber manually. Returning the breech lever raised the front of the block and cocked the internal striker.

The action was very strong but, like all guns in its class, did not extract particularly well in adverse conditions. Some versions also had an inferior trigger pull, though this was rarely true of the effectual target rifles made in Europe.

The inherently poor extracting qualities of the Martini breech were particularly evident when firing coiled-case 450 cartridges in hot and dusty conditions, or when the chamber was foul.

The original British version of the self-cocking striker also promoted a very poor trigger pull, which modifications did little to cure. This allowed enterprising gunmakers such as Swinburn or Westley Richards to amalgamate the basic breech mechanism with a simple hammer-type trigger. Yet Martini-Enfields remained in yeomanry and then Territorial Army hands until World War I; some still served colonial police in 1939.

THE FIRST STEPS
Competitions were held in the Spring of 1867 to find suitable single shot and magazine rifles. Though the Henry (q.v.) dropping-block rifle almost managed to satisfy the War Office criteria, its cartridge was too poor; similarly, the Burton No. 2, which had much to commend it, failed at long range. However, trials with a variety of breech systems began again almost immediately. Only three rifles remained after an endurance trial – Martini, Henry and Westley Richards.

A modified Martini was made at Enfield in 1868 under supervision of the inventor. Final trials showed little superiority over the Henry, though the Martini was simpler and more compact. The Royal Small Arms Factory made four prototype Martini-Henry rifles in 1869, differing from each other only in detail. Apart from a weakness in the cartridge indicator, the rifles worked well.

TRIALS RIFLE
Sealed on 1st October 1869, this had swivels on the forend, trigger guard and butt. A cocking indicator pivoted on the right side of the action and the safety catch protruded from the trigger guard ahead of the trigger lever.

The most obvious features were the short-wrist butt and an unusually long action body. About two hundred rifles were made in the Enfield factory in 1869. Chambered for a rimmed 450 car-

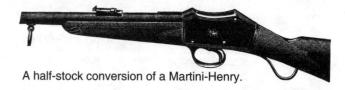

A half-stock conversion of a Martini-Henry.

tridge, they were 51in overall, weighed 9.34lb and had a 35in barrel with seven-groove composite rifling.

Even as the long-chamber rifles were being issued for trials, William Eley successfully necked a cartridge case to give the powder capacity of the original straight Martini-Henry round in appreciably less overall length. Ten rifles were prepared to test it, eight sharing the long action of the original two hundred trials guns and the remaining two being specially shortened. Two new short-action guns were made to solve production problems; twenty-four more were then made for ammunition trials.

By February 1871, the rifle committee reported that the short-chamber gun should be adopted for service immediately, an opinion endorsed by the Council of Ordnance on 30th March.

MARK I RIFLE

Made by the Royal Small Arms Factory, Enfield, 1871-6.

Total production: not known. **Chambering:** 450, rimmed. **Action:** locked by the tip of the operating lever propping the breechblock behind the chamber.

DATA FOR PATTERN NO. 3 RIFLE

49in overall (with short butt), 8.75lb empty. 33.2in barrel, 7-groove rifling; LH, composite. Ramp-and-leaf sight graduated to 1400yd. 1315ft/sec with rolled-case ball cartridges. Elcho-type sword bayonet (originally).

The long-butt 'Rifle, Breech-Loading, Martini-Henry (Mk I)' was sealed on 3rd June 1871, with a sword bayonet and a selection of accessories. An improved trigger was approved on 21st November, though the appropriate pattern was sealed only in September 1872. The 'Bayonet, Sword, Martini-Henry Mk I' (Elcho pattern) was superseded in November 1872 by a bushed P/53 socket pattern.

The Pattern No. 3 or 'Approved Mk I' rifle was accepted on 17th July 1874. It had a split-steel block axis pin, a modified cleaning rod, a longer butt than its predecessors, and a plain buttplate. The edges of the trigger guard had been rounded and the safety catch was discarded. Issues of the new rifle were made toward the end of the year.

The swivel on the butt was eliminated on 20th January 1875, though rifles issued to the Rifle Brigade and the 60th Rifles were exempted.

MARK II RIFLE

Made by the Royal Small Arms Factory, Enfield, 1877-81; by the Birmingham Small Arms & Metal Co. Ltd., Small Heath, 1880-90; and by the London Small Arms Co. Ltd., Bow, 1880-7.

Total production: not known. **Chambering:** 450, rimmed. **Action:** as Mk I rifle, above.

49.5in overall (with long butt), 8.66lb empty. 33.2in barrel, 7-groove rifling; LH, composite. Ramp-and-leaf sight graduated to 1400yd. 1350ft/sec with solid-case ball cartridges. P/76 socket bayonet.

Trouble with the Mk I trigger led to cancellation of the original Sealed Pattern while trials of modified weapons were undertaken. Formally approved on 25th April 1877, the 'Arm, Interchangeable, Rifle, Breech-loading, Martini-Henry, with cleaning rod (Mark II)' lacked the tumbler rest and tumbler-rest axis screw.

The upper surface of the breechblock was browned, the rear sight 'V'-notches were deepened, and changes to the trigger ensured that the trigger guard plate shrouded the trigger lever well enough to reduce jamming caused by debris. The trigger screw and trigger spring were modified, and the pull-off was improved. Changes in the trigger and the lengthened butts – 14in and 14.5in – reduced complaints of excessive recoil.

Guns were only made by the Royal Small Arms Factory, Enfield, until the approval of the Mark III in August 1879. However, the Trade then began to make Mark II Martini-Henrys: the last Mk II ordered from BSA was not forthcoming until June 1890.

Martini-Henry rifles had a nose cap with a bayonet lug on the right side. The original converted P/53 or later P/76 socket bayonets were issued to rank and file, a bushed P/58 or P/60 saber pattern being issued to engineers, marine artillery and Serjeants of the Line.

MARK I CAVALRY CARBINE

Made by the Royal Small Arms Factory, Enfield, 1877-82.

Total production: not known. **Chambering:** 450, rimmed. **Action:** as Mk I rifle, above.

37.7in overall, 7.5lb empty. 21.4in barrel, 7-groove rifling; LH, composite. Ramp-and-leaf sight graduated to 1000yd. About 1100ft/sec with ball cartridges. No bayonet.

The first experiments were made at Enfield in June 1871. A Martini-type carbine tested in May 1873 had a strong recoil and a badly shaped stock. Cartridge loading and bullet weight were subsequently reduced, but recoil and accuracy declined correspondingly.

Fifty guns were issued to the hussars in 1875, and, finally, the Pattern No. 6 carbine was approved on 15th June 1876. The weapon was fully stocked, with two bands, a special nose cap, and a distinctive half-cock thumb-piece on the right side of the body above the scaled-down cocking indicator.

The half-cock was abandoned before the 'Carbine, Breech-loading, Martini-Henry (Mark I)' was sealed on 24th September 1877. The forend was retained by a hook, rather than the stud-and-pin of the Mk II rifle; the size of the cocking indicator was greatly reduced; two reinforcements appeared on the breech instead of one; and breakages were minimized by altering the striker and breechblock assembly.

A back-sight cover was adopted in April 1879, anchored over two screws in the forend. The forend retaining hook was re-shaped in August 1880, requiring changes in the Pattern Arm. Swivels were then reinstated in August 1882.

GARRISON ARTILLERY CARBINE

Less than a hundred of these 450-caliber guns were made in the Royal Small Arms Factory, Enfield, once the pattern had been approved for issue on 9th April 1878. The Garrison Artillery carbine was similar to the cavalry carbine, but took a sword bayonet.

MARK I ARTILLERY CARBINE

Made by the Royal Small Arms Factory, Enfield, 1888-9.

Total production: approximately 57,210. **Chambering:** 450, rimmed. **Action:** as Mk I rifle, above.

37.7in overall, 7.66lb empty. 21.4in barrel, 7-groove rifling; LH, composite. Ramp-and-leaf sight graduated to 1000yd. About 1100ft/sec with ball cartridges. P/58 saber bayonet.

The 'Carbine, Breech-loading, Rifled, with Cleaning Rod, Martini-Henry, Interchangeable, Artillery (Mark I)' was sealed on 21st July 1878 to replace the abortive Garrison Artillery Carbine (q.v.). The swivels were carried under the butt and upper band.

MARK III RIFLE

Made by the Royal Small Arms Factory, Enfield, 1881-8.

Total production: not known. **Chambering:** 450, rimmed. **Action:** as Mk I rifle, above.

DATA FOR LONG-BUTT PATTERN

49.5in overall (long butt), 9.06lb empty. 33.2in barrel, 7-groove rifling; LH, composite. Ramp-and-leaf sight graduated to 1400yd. 1350ft/sec with solid-case ball cartridges. P/76 socket bayonet.

Sealed on 22nd August 1879, this refinement of the Mark II had a forend that hooked into the front of the receiver (then officially termed the 'body'). Changes were made to the breechblock and sights, in addition to the striker and the striker hole in the front face of the breechblock.

The Martini-Henry Mk II rifle, 1874.

The Mk III rifle was almost identical externally with its predecessor, with a two-piece stock and two screw-clamped barrel bands. The most obvious feature was the greatly reduced size of the cocking indicator.

The first rifles were delivered into store in 1881, though the advent of the Mk III was not announced in the official *List of Changes* until 1st March 1882.

PATTERN 1882 RIFLE

About fifty-three of these emanated from the Royal Small Arms Factory, Enfield, in 1882-4. Conventional Martini-action rifles firing a rimmed 40 cartridge developing a muzzle velocity of about 1570ft/sec, they were 49in overall, weighed 9.17lb empty, and had 33.19in barrels with nine-groove ratchet rifling. The goal was to flatten trajectory by reducing the size of the bore.

They had combless butts, and the body was cut away behind the block axis pin to facilitate grip. A long-range leaf appeared on the left side of the rear sight base, to be used in conjunction with a detachable bar-type front sight on the left side of the upper band. The forend was cut down so that the barrel merely rested on top of it and a quirky safety disc pivoted in the trigger guard.

SIMILAR GUNS

Pattern 1883 rifle. This was an improved P/82, all but two of the earlier rifles being upgraded. Nine- and seven-groove rifling were tried, and the handguard was revised. The lower band was solid, the sights were refined, and a safety bolt was added. Enfield-pattern quick-loaders could be attached to a bracket on the right side of the body. Guns weighed 9.11lb without the detachable long-range sight.

MARK IV RIFLE
First pattern

In 1881, to simplify logistics, the army authorities decided to adapt the Martini-Henry for the 45 Gatling machine gun cartridge, which was preferable to adapting the Martini-Henry pattern for machine guns. At least forty rifles were altered by inserting an annular bushing in a reamed-out chamber.

Trials at the School of Musketry showed that the accuracy of the original and converted guns had been comparable. Gatling cartridges raised muzzle velocity by 60-70ft/sec, but recoil had also risen perceptibly. The performance of the improved ammunition being used in the then-experimental Gardner Guns was so satisfactory that the Mk IV rifle was sealed on 1st October 1881. However, issuing similar but non-interchangeable cartridges made no sense: in mid-January 1882, therefore, the Mk IV was abandoned.

About a hundred guns had been made in the Enfield factory. They were 49.5in overall and weighed 9.06lb. Their 33.2in barrels had composite seven-groove rifling, the ramp-and-leaf sight was graduated to 1400yd, and muzzle velocity was about 1400ft/sec.

MARK IV RIFLE
Later pattern

Made by the Royal Small Arms Factory, Enfield, 1888-9.

Total production: about 21,750 Pattern A, 42,900 Pattern B and 34,330 Pattern C. **Chambering:** 450, rimmed. **Action:** as Mk I rifle, above.

DATA FOR PATTERN B

49.3in overall (long butt), 9.13lb empty. 33in barrel, 7-groove rifling; LH, composite. Ramp-and-leaf sight graduated to 1400yd. 1350ft/sec with solid-case ball cartridges. P/76 socket bayonet.

The advent of the 303 cartridge left 65,000 402 Enfield-Martini (q.v.) rifles in varying stages of completion. Re-boring to 45 – without altering the external barrel profile – was sanctioned on 15th September 1887.

THE GUNS

Mark IV Pattern A rifle. This was a major reconstruction, salvaging only the butt, furniture, handguard, barrel and block of the original 402 rifle. The body was a new second-pattern from store.

Mark IV Pattern B rifle. Converted from 402 Pattern No. 2, these rifles shared a similar body, but their front sights lay on a short ramp.

Mark IV Pattern C rifle. The rifles were made from stored parts and had a longer knoxform. Barrels measured 33.2in, increasing overall length to 49.5in with the long butt.

MARK II ARTILLERY CARBINE
Made by the Royal Small Arms Factory, Enfield, 1893-6.
Total production: 38,410. **Chambering:** 450, rimmed. **Action:** as Mk I rifle, above.

37.7in overall, 7.56lb empty. 21.4in barrel, 7-groove rifling; LH, composite. Ramp-and-leaf sight. About 1100ft/sec with ball cartridges. Converted P/58 saber bayonet.

The Mk II artillery carbine, sealed on 16th June 1892, was converted from the Mk II rifle. The barrel was shortened, the muzzle being turned down to receive the guard ring of the bayonet. The forend finished about 1in from the muzzle (distinguishing Mks II and III); a new upper band carried the bayonet lug. Rear sight, swivels, butt disc and cleaning rod were new. Surviving Mk II carbines were reduced to Drill Purpose status in 1902.

SIMILAR GUN

Mark III artillery carbine. Supposedly converted from Mk III rifles, this was approved in 1894 but never sealed. It had a special cleaning rod, retained the original rifle front sight, and had a forend terminating about 2in from the muzzle.

• Martini-Metford

This was an intermediate stage between the 450 Martini-Henry (q.v.) and the 303 Martini-Enfield (q.v.), most guns being discarded, relegated to store or converted to Enfield-rifled standards early in the 20th Century when supplies of Metford-pattern barrels began to run low.

MARK I RIFLE

Approved by the Secretary of State for War on 30th July 1889, the 'Rifle, Martini-Henry, 303-inch (Mark V)' was converted from the 45 Mark III rifle. The barrel, breechblock, striker, extractor, sights and many minor components were exchanged; Lewes sights were standard, the rear sight being graduated for black powder ammunition.

Only prototypes seem to have been made, doubtless owing to the comparative complexity of the conversion. They were 49.75in overall, weighed 8.78lb, and had 33.25in barrels with polygonal seven-groove rifling. The ramp-and-leaf sight was graduated to 1900yd, muzzle velocity with 303 Mk I ball cartridges was about 1850ft/sec, and the P/1888 bayonet could be mounted.

MARK II RIFLE
Made by the Birmingham Small Arms & Metal Co. Ltd., Small Heath, 1890-1.
Total production: 9600. **Chambering:** 303, rimmed. **Action:** as Mk I Martini-Metford rifle, above.

49.75in overall, 9.69lb empty. 33.25in barrel, 7-groove rifling; LH, polygonal. Ramp-and-leaf sight graduated to 1900yd. About 1850ft/sec with Mk I ball cartridges. P/1887 sword bayonet.

This conversion of Mk II Martini-Henry rifles was approved on 10th January 1890. The pattern was formally sealed on 18th June 1891 and renamed 'Rifle, Martini-Metford, 303-inch (Mark II)' in August.

The 303 barrel shared the external contours of the 45 version it replaced, allowing the existing bands, furniture and bayonet to be retained. The Lewes sights were replaced by 'V'-and-barleycorn patterns in 1892. The replacement rear sights were originally graduated to 1600yd for black powder loads, but were subsequently altered to 1800yd for cordite.

MARK I CAVALRY CARBINE
Made by the Henry Rifled Barrel Co. Ltd., Hoxton, and the Royal Small Arms Factory, Enfield (1892-4).
Production total: see text. **Chambering:** 303, rimmed. **Action:** as Mk I Martini-Metford rifle, above.

37.65in overall, 8.09lb empty. 21in barrel, 7-groove rifling; LH, polygonal. Ramp-and-leaf sight graduated to 1000yd. About 1650ft/sec with Mk I ball cartridges. No bayonet.

Formally approved in May 1892, the 'Carbine, Martini-Metford, Cavalry, 303-inch (Mark I)' was converted from the Martini-Henry Cavalry Carbine Mk I. Its new barrel shared the profile of the original, but the nose-cap was shortened and the cleaning rod was replaced.

THE GUNS

In 1894, most guns were given new rear sights suited to ammunition loaded with cordite and graduated to 1400yd (Mk I, I*, II, II*) or an improbable 2000yd (Mk III). Guns with replacement

Enfield-rifled barrels (fitted in 1896 or later) subsequently became 'Martini-Enfield Mark I' regardless of original pattern.

Mark I cavalry carbine. The original design, described above. Made by the Henry Rifled Barrel Co. and in the Enfield factory. Production totaled 11,150 (including Mk I*).

By 1893, Lewes sights were being replaced with standard 'V'-and-barleycorn patterns, rear sight graduations initially remaining unchanged but eventually altered to 1400yd for cordite ammunition. Many guns converted after mid October received front sight protectors, allowing their designations to advance to 'Mark I*'. Earlier examples were often upgraded when returning for repair.

Mark II cavalry carbine. This was converted from Mk I Martini-Henry artillery examples, apparently for issue to horse and field artillery. About 850 were altered in the Enfield factory in 1892-3. The original bayonet bar disappeared, and the rear swivel was removed from the under-edge of the butt. Sight-cover retaining screws appeared on the forend beneath the rear sight. Mk II guns weighed 8.25lb.

Mark II* cavalry carbine. A post-1893 version of the Mk II with standard 'V'-and-barleycorn sights.

Mark III cavalry carbine. Converted from Mk II Martini-Henry rifles, this was approved in July 1892 and re-sealed in December with front sight protectors. It had a new breechblock, had an overall length of 37.3in and weighed 7.69lb. The front edge of the body was ground down to enable the rifle-type sights to be seen at low elevations, and a brass marking disc appeared on the butt. There were 4,300 examples made for the British Army in the Royal Small Arms Factory in 1892-6.

Mark III cavalry carbine, 'Colonial Pattern'. A few Mk III carbines, fitted with abbreviated wooden handguards, were shipped to Natal in 1895. The deliveries of about five hundred guns were completed the following year.

MARK I ARTILLERY CARBINE
Made by the Royal Small Arms Factory, Enfield, 1893-4.
Production total: unknown. **Chambering:** 303, rimmed. **Action:** as Mk I Martini-Metford rifle, above.

37.65in overall, 7.77lb empty. 21.4in barrel, 7-groove rifling; LH, polygonal. Ramp-and-leaf sight graduated to 1000yd. About 1650ft/sec with Mk I ball cartridges. P/1888 sword bayonet.

Approved in May 1892, but re-sealed in June 1893 once front sight protectors had been added, Martini-Metford Mk I artillery carbines were transformations of Mk I Martini-Henry artillery patterns. New barrels, new bands, and a nose-cap taking a bayonet were fitted. The original Lewes sights were replaced after 1893 by 'V'-and-barleycorn fittings, though graduations remained unchanged. However, rear sights graduated to 1400yd for cordite were fitted from 1894 onward.

In 1896, Mk I Martini-Metford artillery carbines with replacement Enfield-pattern barrels were renamed 'Martini-Enfield Mk III' (q.v.).

SIMILAR GUNS
Mark II artillery carbine. Approved on 11th October 1893, this was similar to the Mk III Martini-Metford cavalry carbine, but accepted a sword bayonet. The gun was 37.31in long, and weighed about 7.06lb empty. Enfield made about 2750 of them in 1894-6, but survivors were fitted with new 303 barrels and became 'Mk II' Martini-Enfields thereafter.

Mark II* artillery carbine. The Mk II* was little more than a Mk II with a newly-made breechblock. Experiments showed that the original 45 pattern could be retained, whereupon the Mk II* was abandoned.

Mark III artillery carbine. This Martini-Metford was approved on 8th March 1894, but re-sealed in December after changes had been made. A conversion of a Mk III Martini-Henry rifle, its forend was retained by a hook rather than a pin. It had 2000yd sights and a 21.00in barrel, measured 37.3in overall, and weighed 7.19lb. The carbines were newly made by the Birmingham Small Arms & Metal Co. Ltd. of Small Heath (1895-8) and the London Small Arms Co. Ltd. of Bow (1896-8), production totaling about 47,000.

COLONIAL PATTERNS
The first of five hundred 303 Martini-Metford rifles with iron butt traps ordered by South Australia was dispatched in 1891, the last gun following in 1893. Sights were adjusted for black powder cartridges.

Seven hundred similar rifles were sent to Western Australia in 1894, sighted for black powder ammunition and fitted with brass traps. A thousand near-identical rifles went to Canada in the same era.

760-800 rifles sighted for the 303 Mk I (Cordite) cartridge were prepared for the government of Natal in 1895, despatch being completed in 1896. These had a short handguard running to the rear sight base.

• Martini sporting guns
An attractive combination of strength and simplicity has suited the Martini breech to many differing applications. The adoption of the Martini-Henry for service in the early 1870s, and ready availability of government-pattern 'large' actions, persuaded many gunsmiths to create military-pattern rifles for volunteers and target shooting. These were distinguished from the official patterns only by superior finish, better woodwork, checkering on the wrist and forend, adjustable sights, and flat-faced or carefully counterbored muzzles.

Sporters came in far greater variety. The most popular chambering was initially the government 450 cartridge though, after the Martini-Henry service rifle had been superseded in the late 1880s by the Lee-Metford, emphasis shifted to cartridges such as 500/450 No. 1 Express, 461 Gibbs and 500 No. 2 Express.

The marks of many leading British gunmakers will be encountered on Martini sporting rifles – e.g., John Rigby, Cogswell & Harrison, Daniel Fraser and John Blanch – together with lesser lights such as C.G. Bonehill, Alfred Field or Silver & Son. However, actions often prove to have been 'Trade Patterns' made by the major military contractors, BSA and the London Armory Company. Others were acquired from Westley Richards, who made a series of government-type actions and a modified pattern embodying a Francotte-patent cocking indicator protruding above the right receiver wall.

Many 'small action' guns were also made, often on the basis of the so-called Cadet Martini action introduced early in the 20th Century. Though these guns were usually chambered for 310 cartridges, a whole series of options from 297/230 Short and 297/250 to 360 No. 5 could be encountered; these guns were often known as 'Rook Rifles' owing to their role in controlling vermin.

Countless thousands of 22 rimfire Martini rifles have been made in Britain, including conversions of substantial quantities of military-surplus actions by Greener, Bonehill and others for the Society of Miniature Rifle Clubs and, subsequently, the National Rifle Association. BSA was still making excellent 22 Martini-International target rifles in the mid 1980s. The products of BSA, W.W. Greener and Vickers Ltd. are covered separately.

FIELD-MARTINI SPORTING RIFLE
Made by or for Alfred Field & Co., London.
Total production: unknown. **Chambering:** 500/450 No. 1 Express, rimmed. **Action:** locked by the tip of the operating lever propping the breechblock behind the chamber.

45in overall, 7.85lb empty. 28.5in barrel, 7-groove rifling; LH, composite. Cape-pattern multi-leaf rear sight. 1900ft/sec with 270-grain bullet.

This interesting rifle, dating from the early 1890s, offered several departures from the classical British Martini-Henry. It had a high-back or 'Mark IV' action (possibly purchased from Westley Richards) with an additional radial safety lever on the right side, and a pistol grip butt. The grip and forend were extensively checkered, and a barrel key set in German silver escutcheons. The operating lever had a pierced-ring terminal.

A sturdy brass-tipped wooden clearing rod was carried in pipes attached to a rib beneath the octagonal barrel, sling eyes

The British Martini-Henry was often converted sporting use, particularly in India or the Middle East. Guns are commonly found with engraving and damascening.

appearing on the rearmost pipe and the under-edge of the butt. The Cape-type rear sight had four small folding leaves (100yd, 200yd, 300yd and 400yd) plus a large leaf for 500-1000yd.

• Mauser

The home market was too small to justify production of indigenous Mausers, though BSA touted a modified **P/14** (see **'Enfield'**) and Vickers briefly promoted rifles with actions made by DWM prior to 1918.

Prior to 1914, the magazine rifle struggled to gain a foothold in a market dominated by single shot block-action rifles and the shotgun-like double rifles beloved by big-game hunters in Africa and India. The inability of the Lee action to handle cartridges powerful enough to down rhino and elephant created a niche for the Mauser. Most British gunmakers bought actions in Germany or simply imported complete rifles; many marked by W.J. Jeffrey & Co. of London prior to 1914, for example, seem to have been made in Suhl by Sauer & Sohn.

TYPICAL RIFLES

Anglo-German sporters, though engraved and often stocked in somewhat minimal British style, rarely deviated from the tested 1898-pattern action. Minor components such as safety catches and magazine floorplates occasionally showed proprietary features, but the bolt mechanism was rarely altered. The most obvious differences concerned the sights, but even these blurred as the years passed.

German ammunition makers developed many cartridges powerful enough to satisfy British sportsmen, but poor bullet design – real or imagined – hindered the export success. Until 1939, therefore, most of the 'British Mausers' chambered special proprietary cartridges.

Some of the special cartridges chambered in British-made Mauser sporters were extremely hard-hitting, Jeffrey's 500 Rimless Nitro Express being the most powerful available prior to 1939. They were also often very large, necessitating deepened magazine cases to contain three, four or five rounds. However, except these modifications, the rifles were generally much the same as their German rivals. Folding-leaf express sights were preferred to tangent-leaf types, and the use of folding aperture sights (usually attached to the cocking piece) was encouraged.

Entries will be found for many individual gunmakers: Atkin, Grant & Lang; Churchill (Gunmakers) Ltd.; Cogswell & Harrison; John Dickson & Sons; Firearms Co. Ltd.; George Gibbs; Holland & Holland; W.J. Jeffrey & Company; Midland Gun Company; James Purdey & Sons Ltd.; Parker-Hale Ltd.; Westley Richards & Co. Ltd.; and John Rigby & Company.

• Midland

The 'Midland Gun Company' was a trading name used by Parker-Hale (q.v.) to promote the 'Midland Model 2100' rifle, built on an 1893-type Spanish Mauser action. The style has been perpetuated by Parker-Hale's successor, the Gibbs Rifle Company (USA, q.v.).

• Morris

Richard Morris was responsible for the first successful sub-caliber barrel-insert system to be marketed in Britain, though his earliest patents protected conventional box magazines. A patent granted in 1886 protected a 'conveyor' or carrier mechanism, and 5786/87 of 20th April 1887 allowed a claim for a box magazine with an external depressor. Morris continued to improve his designs, including a 'magazines for rifles' protected by British Patents 2306/90 and 4522/90 of 1890. Morris's Aiming & Sighting Apparatus Company was formed in 1883 to exploit these patents, but was reorganized in 1888 as Morris Tube Ammunition & Safety Range Co. Ltd.

The 'Morris Tube' was approved for the Lee-Metford rifle in 1891 in conjunction with a 297/230 centerfire cartridge. Morris Tubes had the advantage of allowing the rifle to revert to 303 ammunition if necessary, but were not particularly accurate and were replaced after 1908 by permanently-placed 22 rimfire Aiming Tubes.

• Needham

Henry Needham was one of the most progressive gunmakers operating in England in the middle of the 19th Century, and one of the few to champion the needle gun. Needham's design relied on a cylindrical chamber, with a spatulate handle, which could be pivoted out of the receiver to receive a primitive needle-fire cartridge with the priming pellet in the center of a zinc base. The striker mechanism (patented in January 1849) cocked automatically as the handle rose, and a radial safety lever usually lay behind the operating handle.

Guns of this pattern were customarily made as double-barrel shotguns, but a few single-barrel rifles were made for trials. They were not successful militarily – the cartridge was unacceptable and the breech leaked too much gas – but the commercial market was much more accommodating; Needham even gained a gold medal at the Great Exhibition held in London in 1851.

An improved form of the swinging breech was developed by Joseph & George Needham, sons of Henry, in the mid 1860s. Offered commercially for a few years, and tested experimentally as a rifle-musket conversion in Britain and the U.S. (where it was patented in May 1867), the design was not handy enough to succeed. The breechblock swung out of the right side of the receiver when the hammer had been retracted to half-cock, automatically extracting a spent case. The breech was locked shut at the instant of firing by the nose of the external hammer, a feature which some testers regarded as inadequate even though the British were satisfied with it.

• Parker (Lee-Enfield)

Alfred G. Parker & Co. Ltd. of Birmingham, a part of Parker-Hale (q.v.) after 1936, offered Lee-Enfield sporters built on the SMLE Mk III or No. 1 action. Most of these prove to have been refurbished military weapons, though a few may have been purchased, new, from BSA.

• Parker-Hale (Lee-Enfield)

Parker-Hale continued to make Lee-Enfield sporting rifles after succeeding A.G. Parker & Co. in 1936. Work began again after World War II, continuing into the 1970s even though the bulk of the company's efforts was aimed at perfecting the Mauser-action rifles (q.v.).

SPORTING MODEL RIFLE

Made by Parker-Hale Ltd., Birmingham, about 1953-75.

Chambering: 303, rimmed. **Action:** as BSA sporting rifle, q.v.

DATA FOR A TYPICAL SUPREME NO. 1

41.50in overall, 8.00lb empty. 22.00in barrel, 5-groove rifling; RH, concentric rifling. Detachable box magazine, 5 rounds. Tangent-leaf sight graduated to 2000yd. About 2080ft/sec with 190-grain bullet.

The first of these rifles, later known as the Standard and De Luxe No. 1, were converted from military surplus Mk III SMLE in the early 1950s. They retained their charger guides, but had a half-length forend and the original rear sight protectors were removed. The standard pattern had a 10-round magazine and an open front sight; the De Luxe version had its front sight on a special ramp and a five-round magazine.

SIMILAR GUNS

Supreme No. 1. This was introduced in 1958 to satisfy increasingly discerning clientele. Though retaining the original military-pattern action, complete with charger guides, it had a new pistol grip butt with a sculpted Monte Carlo comb, and a checkered round-tipped forend.

Custom No. 1. Dating from 1965, this embodied a refurbished SMLE action with the unsightly charger guides removed and the left wall of the receiver adapted so that an adjustable side mount for an optical sight could be fitted. The butt had a ventilated recoil pad, and was separated by white spacers from the pistol grip cap and obliquely-cut forend tip. A simple spring and elevator rear sight was standard on these guns.

Custom No. 4. This Lee-Enfield was practically identical to the Custom No. 1, but built on the newer action; however, though this was stronger than the No. 1, there is no evidence that Parker-Hale ever offered chamberings other than 303.

• Parker-Hale (Mauser)

Parker-Hale made its first Mauser rifles in the 1960s on the basis of actions purchased in Spain. Work continued until 1990, when interest in the guns passed to the Gibbs Rifle Company (q.v.). Excepting the Model 2100 Midland pattern, discussed separately,

Parker-Hale Mausers featured a classic 1898 Mauser action with two locking lugs on the bolt head and a safety lug on the bolt body.

MODEL 1000 SAFARI RIFLE

Introduced about 1965, this had a Santa Barbara action (Spain, q.v.) complete with a cut-away receiver and a conventional safety mechanism on top of the bolt shroud. A five-round magazine with a hinged floorplate (Model 1000) or a detachable box magazine (1000C) could be obtained. Standard chamberings were 243, 270 or 308 Winchester, plus 30-06. The walnut half-stock had a Monte Carlo comb, a capped pistol grip, and a forend with a plain rounded tip. The checkering was conventional; swivels were fitted under the butt and forend. Sights comprised a simple folding leaf dovetailed into the barrel and a ramp-mounted bead with a tubular hood. A typical 270-caliber 1000C was 43in overall, weighed 7.05lb empty, and had a 22in barrel rifled with four grooves turning to the right. The detachable box magazine held four rounds.

SIMILAR GUNS

Model 1000 Standard. Apparently dating from the mid 1980s this model had a plain walnut stock with a low Monte Carlo comb, impressed checkering on pistol grip and forend, and a diced nylon buttplate. Obtainable in nine regular chamberings, the guns were 43in overall and weighed 7.25lb.

Model 1000 Safari Magnum. Only made in 375 H&H Magnum, this had the rear sight mounted on a short block and an additional recoil bolt through the stock beneath the chamber. A ventilated rubber buttplate was fitted, and the forend had a schnabel tip. The rifles were 44.5in overall, had 24in barrels and weighed 8.5lb.

MODEL 1100 RIFLE

The Model 1100 (dating from 1968) had a safety catch on the right side of the receiver and the bolt handle swept downward. The magazine floorplate was released by a catch in the front of the guard. Chamberings were restricted to 243 Winchester, 270 Winchester, 7mm Remington Magnum, 30-06 or 308 Norma Magnum.

SIMILAR GUN

Model 1100 De Luxe Safari. This amalgamated the stock pattern of the 1100 Safari Magnum (above) with the new action.

MODEL 1200 SUPER SAFARI RIFLE

This was originally made in two versions – Model 1200, with a traditional five-round magazine with a hinged floorplate, and the 1200C with a detachable four-round box magazine ('clip' in Parker-Hale terminology). Standard chamberings were 243 Winchester, 270 Winchester and 30-06. A typical 243 rifle was 43in overall, weighed 6.8lb and had a 22in barrel with four-groove concentric rifling. The internal box magazine held five rounds and a folding-leaf sight was fitted. All Super Safari rifles had half-stocks with roll-over Monte Carlo combs; ventilated rubber buttplates; contrasting rosewood forend tips; white spacer-plates separating the stock from the buttplate, pistol grip and forend tip; and skip-line checkering.

SIMILAR GUNS

Model 1200 Magnum. Characterized by a 24in barrel, 1200M rifles were made only in conventional style for 7mm Remington or 308 Norma magnum ammunition. Three-round magazines were standard.

Model 1200 TX. This target rifle was fitted with a PH5 aperture sight. It had a straight comb, a plain pistol grip and a half-length forend. Made only for the 308 Winchester (7.62x51 NATO) cartridge, it was 46.5in long, had a 26in barrel and weighed about 11lb with sights.

OTHER GUNS

From 1969 onward, presentation-grade (1200P) and Varmint (1200V) models were made, the former having quick-detachable swivels and a scroll-engraved action while the latter – chambered for 22-250, 6mm Remington, 243 Winchester or 25-06 – offered a 24in heavy barrel without sights. The 1200P was abandoned in 1975.

MODEL 1261 RIFLE

The Model 1261 (1968-9) was chambered only for the 222 Remington cartridge and offered with a detachable box magazine. It had the Safari De Luxe stock and weighed 7.3lb, but was replaced by the 1200V.

MODEL 81 CLASSIC RIFLE

Announced in 1983, the M81 Classic had a straight-comb walnut stock with hand-cut checkering on the pistol grip and forend. The rubber shoulder pad was accompanied by a black spacer, while quick-detachable swivels lay under the butt and forend. A Williams ramp-pattern rear sight could be fitted, though optical sights were popular; set triggers were among the options. Chambered for 22-250, 243 Winchester, 6mm Remington, 270 Winchester, 6.5x55, 7x57, 7x64, 7mm Remington Magnum, 30-06, 300 Winchester Magnum or 308 Winchester rounds, the M81 Classic was about 44.5in overall and weighed 7.7lb.

SIMILAR GUNS

Model 81 African. These rifles featured engraving on the actions, folding-leaf express rear sights on a quarter-rib, and an additional recoil lug. The front swivel lay on the barrel instead of the stock. Chamberings were restricted to 300 H&H Magnum, 308 Normag, 375 H&H Magnum or 9.3x62. Overall length was about 45in, weight averaging 9lb without sights.

MODEL 1200 SUPER RIFLE

This, sharing the action of the M81 series, had a gold-plated trigger. Its half-stock had a roll-over Monte Carlo comb, white spacers, and a ventilated rubber recoil pad. A contrasting rose-

The Parker-Hale Africa Magnum rifle.

The Parker-Hale 1200 Super rifle.

The Parker-Hale 1200 Standard rifle.

wood forend tip was customary. The 1200 Super was 44.5in long, weighed 7.5lb, and was chambered similarly to the M81 Classic.

SIMILAR GUNS

Model 1200M Super Magnum. These rifles duplicated the 1200 Super type described previously, but were chambered for the 7mm Remington, 300 Winchester and 308 Norma magnum cartridges.

Model 1200C and **1200CM Super-Clip.** Both of these patterns had detachable box magazines restricted to three rounds only.

MODEL 1100 RIFLE

Dating from 1984, the Lightweight pattern chambered the same cartridges as the 1200 Super (above), but its 22in barrel gave an overall length of 43in. An empty weight of just 6.5lb was obtained by hollowing the bolt handle, fitting an alloy trigger guard/floorplate assembly, and slimming the schnabel-tip stock.

Chambered only for 375 H&H Magnum, 404 Jeffrey and 458 Winchester Magnum ammunition, Model 1100M African Magnums (46in long, 9.5lb) had a heavy barrel and a strengthened stock containing an additional recoil bolt. The Monte Carlo comb was shallower than normal, the forend had a rudimentary schnabel tip, and a ventilated shoulder pad was standard.

MODEL 82 SNIPER RIFLE

Made by Parker-Hale Ltd., Birmingham, 1983-90.

Total production: several thousand? **Chambering:** 7.62x51 NATO, rimless. **Action:** generally as Parker-Hale sporting rifles, above.

45.75in overall, 10.6lb without sights. 26in barrel, 4-groove rifling; RH, concentric. Internal box magazine, 4 rounds. Aperture or optical sights: see text. 2825ft/sec with standard ball ammunition.

This, the earliest of Parker-Hale's specialized sniper rifles, derived from the company's lengthy target-shooting traditions. The rifle was adopted by Australia and New Zealand (as the 'Rifle, 7.62mm, Sniper System'), and in Canada as the Rifles C3 and C3A1.

The M82 amalgamates a conventional 1898-type Mauser action with a heavy barrel and an adjustable trigger system contained in a detachable self-contained unit. The safety locks the trigger, bolt and sear simultaneously. The walnut half-stock could be supplied with a one-piece butt (for use with standard sights) or a special butt with a rear section which could be slid vertically; this allowed the first generation of electro-optical sights to be used in comfort, as their horizontal axis was considerably above that of a standard telescope sight. The butt could be lengthened with spacers, and a

rail for accessories such as bipods or hand-stops was let into the underside of the forend. Most of the Australian and New Zealand rifles were fitted with adjustable rear sights in addition to the Kahles Helia Zf60 6x42 telescope; the Canadian guns, however, used Kahles Helia or 10x Unertl optical and Parker-Hale PH5E/TX aperture sights interchangeably.

SIMILAR GUNS

L81A1 Cadet Rifle. The success of the M82 encouraged Parker-Hale to enter a single shot cadet rifle in British Ministry of Defense trials. A sturdy gun with a short butt and half-length forend, this was officially approved for issue as the L81A1. The action was specially bedded in epoxy resin, accuracy being claimed as a half-minute of angle at 100yd. A folding leaf sight lay on top of the strengthened receiver, and a replaceable-element tubular front sight was fitted at the muzzle. The L81A1 was 46.75in long, had a 26in barrel, and weighed 10.9lb.

M83 NATO Target Rifle. This was simply a commercial name for the L81A1 described previously.

M84 Mk II Canberra. This target rifle had an ambidextrous walnut stock with stippling on the pistol grip and forend. It was 48-49.5in overall, depending on butt spacers, and weighed 11.5lb with sights and hand-stop. A full-length accessory rail lay under the forend; PH5E aperture sights were used.

M84 Mk II Bisley. Similar mechanically to the Canberra, the Bisley Model was made with plain right- or left-hand stocks.

MODEL 85 SNIPER RIFLE

Made by Parker-Hale Ltd., Birmingham, 1986-90, and by the Gibbs Rifle Co., Martinsburg, West Virginia, 1991 to date.

Total production: several thousand? **Chambering:** 7.62x51 NATO, rimless. **Action:** generally as Parker-Hale sporting rifles, above.

45.25in overall, about 13.75lb with sight and bipod. 27.5in barrel, 4-groove rifling; RH, concentric. Detachable box magazine, 10 rounds. Aperture or optical sights: see text. 2825ft/sec with standard ball ammunition.

This sniper rifle was developed to compete in British Army trials held in the mid 1980s. The detachable box magazine was a notable improvement on the internal magazine of the preceding Model 82, and the elongated bolt handle (inspired by the Canadian C3A1) made operation easier if a bulky electro-optical sight was fitted.

The walnut half-stock – which could be brown, black or camouflage pattern – had extensive stippling on the pistol grip and

The Parker-Hale M84 Bisley target rifle.

The Parker-Hale M84 Canberra target rifle.

The Parker-Hale L81A1 target rifle.

The Parker-Hale M87 Heavy Varmint rifle.

The Parker-Hale
M85 sniping rifle.

forend to improve grip in adverse conditions. The length of the butt could be adjusted with spacers, and an optional vertically-sliding butt section could be obtained to order. A rail let into the underside of the forend accepted bipods, hand stops, sling anchors and similar accessories. Open sights in the form of a folding rotary aperture above the receiver bridge and a protected open blade at the muzzle could also be fitted if required.

The British Army assessed the M85 as 'fit for service', but the Accuracy International PM rifle (q.v.) was preferred; however, Parker-Hale subsequently managed to sell the Model 85 to police and paramilitary organisations worldwide before rights to the Parker-Hale rifles were sold to the Navy Arms Company. Production began in the Gibbs Rifle Company factory in 1991.

SIMILAR GUNS

Model 86. Derived from the M85, this 7.62mm target rifle had a detachable five-round box magazine and could accept an optical sight. Stocks resembled the Canberra pattern.

Model 87. Adapted from the M86 for moving-target shooting, this had a distinctive heavyweight 26in barrel and a squared forend with restricted amounts of stippling. An optical sight was standard. A typical example was 45in long and weighed 10lb; chamberings included 243 Winchester, 6.5x55, 30-06, 300 Winchester Magnum or 7.62x51 NATO.

• Prince

The origins of this particular weapon, seen as a suitable replacement for the unsuccessful Leetch (q.v.) pattern, remain obscure. The designer is believed to have been the William Prince listed in London in the census of 1841 as a 'Journeyman Gunmaker', though confirmation is lacking. British official correspondence of the 1860s records the address of 'Mr. Prince' as 88 Piccadilly.

The locking mechanism relied on a short tapered chamber with two sturdy lugs, attached to the standing breech. The barrel was detached simply by turning the handle – protruding vertically downward ahead of the trigger – through 15 degrees, to disengage seats in the barrel with the lugs on the chamber. The barrel was then simply pushed forward. A combustible paper cartridge could be inserted in the chamber, the barrel was replaced, the hammer was retracted, a cap was placed on the nipple, and the gun could then be fired.

The Prince system was a failure militarily, though sporting guns were also made on the principle. The barrel was not supported well enough to withstand arduous service, and the breech undoubtedly leaked gas. British attention shifted to the Sharps, and then to the Greene carbine.

A single Prince rifle was submitted to the British trials of 1866, but was rejected unfired on the grounds that it was too long, extremely inaccurate, and 'not sufficiently strong for military purposes'.

TRIALS CARBINE

Maker unknown.

Total production: a hundred? **Chambering:** 577, combustible cartridge; fired by a caplock. **Action:** locked by engaging lugs on the breech in seats in the detachable barrel.

DATA FOR A TYPICAL EXAMPLE

About 36in overall, 6.25lb empty. 20in barrel, 3-groove rifling; RH, concentric. Single shot only. Leaf-type rear sight with a stepped bed, graduated to 1100yd. No bayonet.

The Prince carbine is difficult to mistake, owing to the breech-lever projecting downward in front of the square-fronted trigger guard. Military-pattern guns had a one-piece stock with a short forend, a back-action cap lock was fitted, and the rear sight lay above the chamber. A small spring-loaded bolt in the underside of the trigger guard bow projected into a recess in the operating handle to prevent the breech springing open unexpectedly.

SPORTING GUNS

Several guns of this type have been recorded, including a 22-bore example with a 30in barrel, two bands, a back-action lock, bronze furniture, and a circular iron-lidded patch box set into the side of the butt. This particular rifle bore, in addition to an acknowledgment of Prince's patent, the marks of Robert S. Garden of Piccadilly, London. Active from 1852 until 1888, Garden is regarded as a 'gun supplier' and is unlikely to have been the manufacturer.

• Purdey

Best known for shotguns and double rifles, James Purdey & Sons Ltd. of London have made some of the most desirable of all Mauser-type sporters. Guns dating prior to 1939 customarily incorporate Oberndorf-made actions, whereas the origin of post-war specimens generally proves to be Fabrique Nationale. Some of the rifles made in the 1950-65 period, however, were built around refurbished Kar. 98k or similar actions; typically, they were chambered for 7x57 Mauser, 300 Nitro Express, 375 Nitro Express (.375 H&H Magnum) or 404 Nitro Express (.404 Jeffrey, 10.75x73). Barrels were usually about 22in long, while stocks took the classical English form with a straight comb and a plain rounded forend tip. Express sights were commonly fitted.

• Reilly-Comblain

Patented in 1868, this was a pivoting-block design operated by a cranked lever on the right side of the breech. Customarily built on the basis of a British P/53 ('Enfield') rifle-musket, the Reilly-Comblain had a distinctive slender hammer with a vertical shank. Tested in Britain in 1867-68, it was rejected as inferior to rival designs. However, a few guns were subsequently made for sporting use and survivors are still occasionally encountered.

• Remington-Lee

Three hundred 1885-pattern guns were acquired for trials against the Lee-Burton (q.v.) in 1887. Numbered in the 46000 group, they bore the 'W↑D' mark of the War Department on the stock. Magazine cut-off units were fitted on the right side of the receiver by the Royal Small Arms Factory, Enfield, before field trials began. Additional details will be found under **'U.S.: Remington-Lee'.**

The breech of a typical Prince carbine,
made by William Garden. (W&D)

A 433-caliber Remington-Lee rifle tested by the British in 1887.

• Restell

Patented in 1857 by Thomas Restell of Birmingham, these guns were made in military or sporting forms. The essence of the system was a lever on the left side of the breech which, when lifted, automatically retracted the hammer to half-cock and slid the breech-block backward to expose the chamber. Unfortunately, the Restell carbine – at least in its original pattern – lacked any type of locking device to prevent gas leaks blowing the breech open and was not particularly successful.

TRIALS CARBINE

Maker unknown, but presumed to have been in Birmingham.
Total production: a handful, 1858-9. **Chambering:** 500, combustible cartridge; fired by a cap lock. **Action:** locked by the breechblock abutting a shoulder in the back of the receiver.

36in overall, 6.20lb empty. 20in barrel, 6-groove rifling; RH, concentric. Single shot only. Leaf-type rear sight with a stepped bed, graduated to 1000yd. No bayonet.

This experimental cavalry carbine, furnished in the manner of the regulation muzzle-loaders, was tested by the British Army in the late 1850s. The gun has a full-length stock, two screwed bands, a conventional sidelock, and swivels beneath the butt and front band. One survivor has a swivel rammer, but another has a plain nose cap. Guns are often misleadingly marked 'LONDON', as Restell was trading in Birmingham in 1857-73.

• Rexer

Promoted by the Rexer Arms Co. Ltd. of London, together with a light machine gun, this rifle was operated by allowing the barrel and bolt to recoil, locked together, almost to the end of the operating stroke. Shortly before the end of travel was reached, cam tracks inside the charging-handle collar disengaged lugs on the bolt head from recesses in the barrel behind the chamber. The bolt was then held back while a spring returned the barrel to battery. Once the shooter had released pressure on the trigger, the bolt-catch was tripped and the bolt ran forward to chamber a new round. The lugs were revolved back into their locked position at the end of the closing stroke, and the gun was ready to fire again.

Though the guns worked surprisingly well, the excessive length of the recoil stroke and the unusual disconnector mechanism were potential weaknesses. Unfortunately, a disagreement over patents ended in a court decision in favor of Dansk Rekylriffel Syndikat AS (promoters of the Madsen guns) and the Rexer company was ultimately liquidated.

MILITARY-PATTERN TRIALS RIFLE

Made by (or more probably for) the Rexer Arms Co. Ltd., London, about 1904-7.
Total production: a handful. **Chambering options:** 6.5x55 Swedish Mauser, possibly also 7x57 and 303. **Action:** locked by two lugs on the bolt head engaging recesses in the barrel as the bolt closed; long recoil operation, semi-automatic only.
DATA FOR A TYPICAL 6.5MM EXAMPLE
50in overall, 9.33lb empty. 26.5in barrel, 4-groove rifling; RH, concentric. Detachable box magazine, five rounds. Tangent-leaf sight graduated to 1600m (1750yd)? 2200ft/sec with 157-grain bullet. Sword bayonet.

Two Rexer rifles were demonstrated at Bisley in the summer of 1904, in competition with the Hallé pattern. One gun was tested in the Enfield small arms factory in the same period. Chambered for the 6.5mm Swedish Mauser cartridge, the Rexer performed creditably even though regarded as too fragile for service. It had a one-piece stock with a straight-wrist butt, a half-length cleaning rod set into the right side of the stock, and two barrel bands. The front band carried a mounting lug, but, owing to the projection of several inches of muzzle from the barrel sleeve, any bayonet would have required a long blade and it is suspected that none was ever fitted.

• Richards, bolt type

Westley Richards & Co. Ltd. of Birmingham, one of the few provincial gunmakers to challenge 'Best London' work for quality, was another of many to offer BSA-made rifles.

A few Lee-Speed and Lee-Enfield sporting rifles were chambered for the proprietary 303/375 Axite cartridge introduced about 1906. The 215-grain bullet developed a muzzle velocity of 2500 ft/sec, making it more powerful than the regular service-type 303. The Axite cartridge may have tested the original Lee-Enfield action to its limits, as survivors are rare. Consequently, Richards relied on Mausers – made from about 1909 onward – to chamber cartridges such as the company's proprietary 318 Nitro Express and 425 Rimless Magnum.

• Richards, lifting-block type

Initially patented in Britain in March 1858, the Westley Richards carbine was gradually refined until it was generally regarded as the best of the British caplock breech-loading systems.

An open-topped box-like barrel extension received a breech-bolt attached to the actuating lever. The shape of the lever earned the sobriquet 'Monkey Tail'.

The earliest guns could be fired while the lever was still slightly open, but a safety interlock was soon added. The first guns also had a hook on the obturating pad to pull the base wad of the cartridge out of the breech when the action was opened. Later guns had a plain coned bolthead, obturation becoming a secondary function of the cartridge base wad. Each wad was simply pushed out of the muzzle by the next shot.

Monkey Tail carbines worked satisfactorily, except that breeches leaked gas when in bad repair and the action could be stiff in very cold conditions.

PATTERN NO. 1 CARBINE

Made by Westley Richards & Company, Birmingham, Warwickshire.
Total production: about 400. **Action:** locked by a projection on the breechblock, attached to the underside of the top lever, bearing against a shoulder in the bottom of the receiver.

Chambering: 450, combustible cartridge, fired by an external cap lock. 36in overall, 6.55lb empty. 20in barrel, octagonal rifling; RH, concentric. Single shot only. Leaf-type rear sight with a stepped bed, graduated to 800yd. No bayonet.

Design of the carbine had stabilized by 1860. Pattern No. 1 was sealed on 29th April 1861, two thousand guns being ordered from Westley Richards soon afterward. Unfortunately, after the first batches had been delivered, it was discovered that the chambers were too long; production stopped while the ordnance authorities, whose mistake it had been, considered alternatives. Production had proceeded too far to stop work on 404 guns, which were completed to the original design.

SIMILAR GUNS

Pattern No. 2 carbine. This was simply No. 1 with a correct short chamber; 544 guns of this type were made.

An improved metallic-cartridge Westley Richards rifle, c. 1867. (W&D)

A typical Pattern No. 5 Westley Richards 'Monkey Tail' carbine.

Pattern No. 3 carbine. This was a No. 2 with minor improvements. Production amounted to 387 guns.

Pattern No. 4 carbine. Sealed on 3rd January 1862, the 665 guns of this type exhibited detail changes. The nipple was moved forward. A fence was added to the nipple lump, round studs were used on the trigger plate, the front sight bed became oval, and the nose cap was refined.

Pattern No. 5 carbine. Twenty thousand of these were ordered from Enfield in the autumn of 1864, though the Pattern Arm was not sealed until March 1866. The guns were machine-made and classed as 'Interchangeable'; 19,000 had been received into store by 31st March 1867. They were 35.9in long and weighed 6.5lb. The barrel was retained by a single Baddeley band, furniture was iron, and the butt was drilled longitudinally for the breech scraper and rammer-tip.

MILITARY RIFLES

The first Westley Richards rifles were ordered in the Spring of 1860, 112 being issued for trials by May 1861 though all but fourteen were subsequently altered to a modified pattern. They had 39in barrels. One of the oddest features of the rifles, shared with the carbines, was that they shot much better foul than clean. A few 450 short rifles were made for trials with the Royal Navy in 1862, with no lasting results, and some large-bore (.577) rifles were made for the government trials of 1864.

The most numerous of 'Monkey Tail' rifles, however, are survivors of two thousand offered to the British authorities in 1863. Unauthorized changes made by the inventor soon attracted official disapproval – e.g., a non-standard rear sight had been used, and a lateral bolt through the forend displaced one of the bands – and only 230 had been delivered by May 1865. They had 36in barrels, long operating levers extending back down the stock wrist, and weighed about 9.4lb.

A manufacturing pattern was finally sealed in September 1865, but the reluctance of Westley Richards to develop a metallic-cartridge conversion seems to have brought the entire project to a standstill. The impending trials of better weapons then rendered the caplocks obsolete.

OTHER GUNS

. Large numbers of military weapons, apparently including rifles and carbines, were delivered to Portugal (q.v.) in the late 1860s.

Sporting guns were also made in a variety of designs. Some have pistol grip stocks, with checkering on the grip and forend; others may have engraving on the action and lock plate, or have been converted to fire metal-case ammunition. Richards himself patented a series of improvements to the basic lifting-block action, including a rimfire conversion (1864) and a centerfire pattern (1866).

Westley Richards also patented an improved form of the Monkey Tail, cocked automatically as the breech lever was raised. Patented in 1866, this relied on a linkage connecting the hammer and the breech mechanism. A 450-caliber gun of this type was submitted to trials in Britain in 1867, but was rejected on the grounds that its dimensions did not meet the specification. It was replaced by the first of the inventor's dropping-block rifles described below.

• Richards, dropping-block type

These pivoting-block action rifles were designed and developed in Britain. The first of Westley Richards' rifles was patented in Britain in 1868, but was withdrawn from army trials when likely to place third behind Martini and Henry rivals. Continual improvements culminated in British patents granted in 1870.

Essentially simple, though not as compact as the Martini, the action relied on a pivoting Peabody-type breechblock tipped by the head of an operating lever pivoted transversely at the lower front of the receiver. A simple trigger and sear system released an internal hammer, which cocked automatically as the breechblock descended. The hammer shared the operating-lever axis pin, while the main spring ran forward beneath the barrel. The worst feature was the sear spring, bent downward at an odd angle.

Westley Richards retired in 1872, selling his operations to John Deeley (see **'Deeley-Edge'**). Production seems to have been transferred to the National Arms & Ammunition Company, to which relevant patents had been licensed, but reverted to Westley Richards & Co. in the 1880s. However, in later years, the company made extensive use of conventional Martini-type actions with special detachable triggers. Quality was good, as Richards had a reputation as the only Birmingham gunmaker of his era able to compete with the established 'Best London' makers as an equal.

BREECH-LOADING RIFLE
Also known as the 'Patent Central-Fire Breech-Loading Military & Sporting Rifle'
Made by Westley Richards & Company (1870-2) and Westley Richards & Co. Ltd., Birmingham, about 1873-92.

Chambered: many large-caliber British black-powder sporting cartridges. **Action**: pivoting-block, with an operating lever ahead of the trigger guard.
DATA FOR A TYPICAL EXAMPLE
Chambering: 500 No. 2 Express, rimmed. 44.88in overall, 7.50lb empty. 28.00in barrel, 5-groove rifling; LH, concentric? Standing-block sight for 200yd. 1870ft/sec with 300-grain bullet.

Invariably distinguished by an operating lever with a ring tip beneath the trigger guard, these sporting rifles were introduced in the early 1870s and generally built to individual requirements; each differed in detail, though the action remained the same.

Most had a two-piece stock with a straight-wrist butt curved to fit against the back of the receiver, owing to the use of butt-tangs instead of a Martini-type socket, but a few were made with one-piece stocks enveloping the action. A radial trigger-blocking safety lever appeared on the right side of the receiver and a detachable lock was usually fitted.

The finely checkered wrists and half-length forends, the latter occasionally retained by a transverse key, often had plain rounded horn tips. Some rifles had sling eyes on the barrel and butt, while simple, Cape or express sights could be fitted to order. Guns were made to individual specifications and vary greatly in detail.

• Rigby

John Rigby & Company of London was renowned for single shot rifles built on Farquharson, Banks and similar actions. The company also offered Mauser-action rifles chambered for 275 Rimless cartridges (1907); 350 Rimless Magnum (1908); 400/350 Nitro Express (1899); and 416 Rigby (1911). Most of the actions were bought in Oberndorf prior to World War I, but later examples showed greater diversity.

RIGBY 243 RIFLE

This was being built in 1965 on a refurbished action. Chambering 243 Winchester, with a barrel of 21in or 25in, it had a pistol grip half-stock with a Monte Carlo comb.

SIMILAR GUNS

Rigby 275. Chambered for the 7x57mm Mauser cartridge, this had a traditional straight-comb butt and a rounded half pistol grip. The front swivel eye lay on the barrel and the rear sight was a leaf pattern.

Big-Bore Magazine Rifle. Available in 375 H&H Magnum, 404 Jeffrey or 416 Rigby, this customarily had a sturdy stock with a Monte Carlo comb and a rounded forend tip. A recoil bolt ran laterally through the forend beneath the chamber. The pistol grip had a shallow English-style curve, plus a cap of horn, ebony, rosewood or steel. One swivel eye was carried on a collar around the barrel, ahead of the forend. Magazines were deepened to accept four of the large-diameter cartridges. Sights comprised folding leaves (often set into a quarter-rib) and a replaceable-element tunnel.

• Ross

In September 1914, shortly after World War I began, the British government ordered 100,000 Mk III Ross rifles from Canada. Deliveries were erratic and the contract was finally cancelled in March 1917, after 66,590 guns had been accepted, owing to the appropriation of the Ross Rifle Company's Quebec factory by the Canadian government. Most of the rifles were used for training purposes, but 45,000 were issued to the Royal Navy in the Spring of 1917 to replace unwanted Japanese Arisakas.

The Ross rifle was declared obsolete in British service in November 1921, but surviving guns were reissued in 1940 to the Royal Canadian Navy and auxiliary units. A few thousand were sent to Britain for the Home Guard. Soon displaced by more efficient No. 3 (P/14) and US M1917 Enfield rifles, most of the Ross guns ended their days aboard merchant ships.

In addition to military-issue rifles, substantial quantities of Ross sporters were stocked, barreled and sold in Britain – principally by Charles Lancaster of London. Most of these used Canadian-made actions (see **'Canada: Ross'**).

• Sharps

These American-made guns are described in greater detail in the relevant section. Only one pattern was issued for British Army trials in the 1850s, but was acquired in surprisingly large numbers.

A Sharps carbine had been tested by the British authorities in April 1854, and another, with a Maynard primer, followed in February 1855. Twelve 577 guns were then made in the Enfield manufactory tool room; issued for trials in July 1855, they were so successful that the British ordered six thousand carbines from the U.S. in January 1856. All had been delivered by 31st March and were sent to India for trials with cavalry units. Ultimately, however, the Westley Richards (q.v.) 'Monkey Tail' design was preferred and the Sharps carbines were ultimately returned to store in Britain.

PATTERN 1855 CARBINE

Made for the Sharps Rifle Mfg Co. by Robbins & Lawrence, Windsor, Vermont, 1856-8.

Quantity: 6000. **Action:** dropping-block action, operated by a lever under the breech.

DATA FOR A SECOND-PATTERN EXAMPLE

Chambering: 56, combustible cartridge, fired by a caplock. 35.5in overall, 7.38lb empty. 18in barrel, 5-groove rifling; RH, concentric. Single shot only. Block and four-leaf rear sight graduated to 600yd. About 950ft/sec with a 475-grain bullet. No bayonet.

Guns of this type all had Maynard primers, a sling bar and ring on the left side of the breech, a single brass barrel band, and a patch box set into the right side of the butt. The first version had standard 577 Enfield pattern three-groove rifling making a turn in 78in; overall length was about 37in, the barrel measured 20in and the guns weighed 7lb 9oz. Later examples were made to a modified pattern with an 18in 551-caliber barrel, rifled with three grooves making a turn in 48in. Carbines of this type were 35in long and weighed 7lb 6oz.

• Shephard

Experimental rifles of five differing patterns were submitted to the British trials of 1864 by E. Clarence Shephard of Shephard & Newton, along with claims that 20,000 carbines were being altered in the U.S. to 'Plan No. 1'. Twelve of the forty-eight P/1853 rifle-muskets converted to seven differing breech systems in 1864-5 were 'Shephards', six chambering rimfire cartridges and six adapted for service-pattern combustible ammunition. They were excluded from the trials on the basis that their ammunition was too fragile and too dangerous to fire. With weights averaging 10.1lb – one weighed 10lb 12-1/4oz – the Shephards were also much too heavy. The trial reports describe them as having a center hammer and a two-piece stock, and leave no doubt from the description of the breech that they were early forms of the rolling block Remingtons (q.v.).

• Snider

This American design, best known for service in Britain, was also used in Denmark and Spain – and, in a modified form, by France as the 'Tabatière' (q.v.).

The essence of the Snider breech was a hinged block developed by Jacob Snider the Younger in association with François Eugène Schneider of Paris. Patents granted in Britain in 1864 protected an improved sideways-tipping block which could be retracted on its axis pin to extract the spent case.

The Snider was reliable once problems of premature opening had been overcome, solved in Britain with the Improved or 'Bolted' breech of the Pattern III infantry rifle (q.v.). The short 577 coiled-case cartridge proved to be more reliable in hot and arid conditions than the later 450 design, and most British cavalrymen were sorry to receive Martini-Henry carbines instead of their Sniders.

Eventually, many British guns found their way abroad, particularly to Portugal and Japan. Several alleged 'proprietary' breech systems were very similar in principle to the Snider. They included the French Tabatière, submitted in questionable circumstances after a proper Snider conversion had been tentatively approved.

THE FIRST STEPS

Made by Potts & Hunt and chambered for French Pottet cartridges, the Snider trials rifle of 1865 was susceptible to jamming. However, it was regarded as very strong; very little of the original stock needed to be cut away, unlike many of its rivals. The absence of the American Joslyn trials rifle promoted the Snider's cause appreciably, though the British Secretary of State preferred the Storm conversion. This accepted standard combustible cartridges and could be loaded from the muzzle in an emergency.

Many inventors subsequently questioned the originality of the Snider breech, but only Thomas Wilson of Birmingham benefited by a grant of one-tenth of the royalty payments.

MILITARY WEAPONS

CONVERTED PATTERN 1853 RIFLE, PATTERN NO. 1

Made by the Royal Small Arms Factory, Enfield (conversions and new guns, 1866-73); the Birmingham Small Arms Co. Ltd., Small Heath (conversions and new guns, 1867-73); and by the London Small Arms Co. Ltd., Bow (conversions and new guns, 1868-72).

Total production: about 815,000 (all types). **Chambering:** 577, rimmed. **Action:** locked by swinging the breechblock behind the chamber, where it was locked by the fall of the hammer and (Pattern III breech only) a separate bolt.

*DATA FOR PATTERN II** RIFLE*

54.25in overall, 9.13lb empty. 36.5in barrel, 3-groove rifling; RH, concentric. Ramp-and-leaf sight graduated to 950yd. 1240ft/sec with Mark IX ammunition. P/53 socket bayonet.

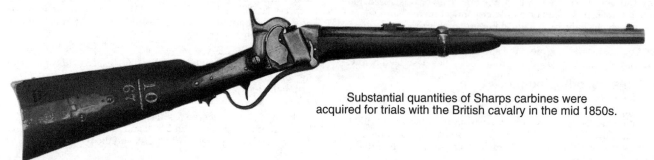

Substantial quantities of Sharps carbines were acquired for trials with the British cavalry in the mid 1850s.

An alteration of P/53 rifle-muskets with a Snider breech was sealed on 25th November 1865 as the "Musket, Rifled, Enfield P/53, converted on Snider's Principles". The first guns were delivered late in March 1866. They proved more accurate than the P/53 caplock and fired three times faster with practically no misfires or jamming. Results were so pleasing that the wholesale conversion of rifle-muskets began at Enfield immediately.

A perfected 'Pattern I' was approved on 18th September 1866, conversion contracts being placed with the Birmingham Small Arms Co. Ltd. and the London Small Arms Co. Ltd. to supplement the output of Enfield. Based on the P/53 rifle-musket, the Snider had a new receiver and breechblock unit ('shoe' in contemporary terminology). It was readily identified by its great length and three screwed bands.

SIMILAR GUNS

Pattern I* rifle. This was a conversion of Pattern I guns to Pattern II standards, with a partially squared countersink. The designation applied only to altered P/53 rifle muskets.

Pattern II* rifle. Approved in November 1866, the new long-base Mark II cartridge – with a squared case rim – necessitated a change in the breeches of Sniders converted from the P/53 rifle-musket and the Lancaster engineers' carbine. These were altered to 'Pattern II*' standards by squaring the counter-sink for the case groove.

Pattern II** rifle. Introduced in 1867, this was simply a Pattern II* with additional modifications to the extractor, and the underside of the breechblock extended to cover the entire case-head; the receiver was revised and the nipple was shortened.

Pattern III rifle. It soon became clear that Snider actions showed a tendency to open prematurely as they began to wear. However, even though development of a 450 Martini-Henry (q.v.) was proceeding steadily, large numbers of new Sniders were still needed to re-equip the standing army.

Trials with differing locking catches led to the approval of 'Pattern G', designed by Edward Bond of the London Small Arms Company and approved on 13th January 1869. Pattern III guns embodying this 'Improved' or 'Bolted' action also had a steel barrel, a strengthened receiver and a squared-off hammer face. The knurled-head latch set into the left side of the breechblock was most distinctive.

The first Pattern III rifles were issued in the summer of 1870. Military weapons displayed royal cyphers and government property/inspectors' marks, while commercial examples bore a large 'S' transfixed by an arrow.

By 1874, however, the first Martini-Henry rifles were being issued to infantry regiments on Home Service. Work was completed at home and abroad by the end of 1875, and the Snider was clearly becoming obsolescent. Large numbers were withdrawn into store, though about five thousand Snider rifles were assembled in 1879 in the Royal Small Arms Factory, Sparkbrook, Birmingham, from a mixture of old P/53 parts and new Pattern III actions.

Most of the Sniders serving the volunteers and militia had been replaced with the Martini-Henry by 1885. An inventory taken on 1st April revealed that 166,340 Sniders were in store.

CONVERTED P/1855 ENGINEER CARBINE

The 577 'Lancaster Engineer Carbine, P/55, converted on Snider's Principles' was sealed on 30th October 1866. About five thousand were transformed in Pimlico in 1866-7. Guns may be found with Pattern I, I* or II* breeches, but the II** type is most common. A minor change had been made to the snap-cap, which was attached to the front of the trigger guard by a new retaining chain.

The P/55 (which was really a short rifle) had two brass bands and a lug-and-tenon for the P/55 saber bayonet on the right side of the muzzle. Its back-sight leaf hinged at the front of the base and the lower swivel lay under the butt. Guns were replaced from 1879 by the Martini-Henry. They were 47.9in overall, weighed

8.17lb empty and had a 29.15in barrel with Lancaster's oval-bore rifling. The ramp-and-leaf sight was graduated to 1150yd.

CONVERTED P/1858 NAVAL SHORT RIFLE

About 53,000 transformations – and 570 new guns – emanated from the Royal Small Arms Factory, Enfield, in 1866-72. Similar to the Serjeants' P/60 (q.v.), but with two brass bands and brass mounts, the modified naval P/58 was approved on 7th August 1867. The bayonet bar lay on the right side of the muzzle, the ramrod was lightened to act as a cleaning rod, and the stock was second-grade wood.

Except a handful made in 1869 with improved bolted actions, the guns all exhibit Pattern II** breeches. P/58 rifles were 48.75in overall, weighed 8.95lb, and had 30.5in barrels rifled with three grooves. Their ramp-and-leaf sights were graduated to 1000yd. Most Royal Navy guns were replaced after 1876 by Martini-Henry rifles.

SIMILAR GUN

Yeomanry Pattern short rifle. In 1871, the first of at least twelve thousand guns was altered for the yeomanry, work continuing until the 1880s. The rear swivel was moved to the underside of the butt and the P/59 cutlass bayonet was replaced with an altered P/60 saber.

CONVERTED PATTERN 1856 CAVALRY CARBINE

Made by the Royal Small Arms Factory, Enfield Lock, Middlesex (14,560 new guns and 14,390 conversions, 1866-72); the Royal Small Arms Factory, Sparkbrook, Birmingham (2460 new guns from old parts, 1882-4); the Birmingham Small Arms & Metal Co. Ltd., Small Heath (1200, 1874); C.G. Bonehill, Birmingham (2000, 1879).

Total production: 34,610 (all guns except Trade, India and colonial patterns). **Chambering:** 577, rimmed. **Action:** as converted P/53 infantry rifle, above.

DATA FOR PATTERN II** CARBINE

37.4in overall, 7.10lb empty. 19.25in barrel, 5-groove rifling; RH, concentric. Ramp-and-leaf sight graduated to 600yd. 995ft/sec with Mark IX ammunition. No bayonet.

Approved on 2nd May 1867, this conversion used the Pattern II** breech. It was applied to the original Pattern No. 1 (P/56) and Pattern No. 2 (P/61) carbines indiscriminately, the original 'P/56' designation being used for all the Sniders, as the modified half-stock gave the cavalry carbine the appearance of a new design. The Baddeley-type (screwed) band was retained by a pin driven through the stock, a two-piece cleaning rod was carried in a butt-trap, and a snap-cap was secured by a chain attached to the trigger guard bow. A ring slid on a bar anchored in the stock on the left side of the breech.

SIMILAR GUNS

Pattern III (or 'No. 3') carbine. Approval of the Pattern III (Bolted) breech in 1869 allowed the production of cavalry carbines to begin again. They had new stocks, and could be distinguished by the latch on the left side of the breech; in addition, 'III' appeared on the receiver and 'STEEL' lay on the left side of the barrel. Replacement of the Sniders by the Martini-Henry began in 1878, and had been completed within two years.

Guard carbine. The first batches of at least 400 guns were smooth-bored for military guard purposes in 1897, being issued with buckshot cartridges. Work continued until 1900 or later.

CONVERTED PATTERN 1860 SERJEANT'S RIFLES

Made by the Royal Small Arms Factory, Enfield, Middlesex (31,710 conversions and 17,750 new guns, 1866-72); the Royal Small Arms Factory, Sparkbrook, Birmingham (5000 new guns in 1873-4); the Birmingham Small Arms & Metal Co. Ltd., Small Heath (at least 4420 for the British Army, 1876); the London Small Arms Co. Ltd., Bow; and the National Arms & Ammunition Co. Ltd., Birmingham.

A Snider rifle, converted from a P/53 ('Enfield') rifle-musket.

The breech of a 'commercial' Snider rifle sold by the Army & Navy Stores. (W&D)

Total production: about 80,000, including Trade, India and colonial patterns. **Chambering:** 577, rimmed. **Action:** as converted P/53 infantry rifle, above.

DATA FOR PATTERN II** RIFLE

48.7in overall, 8.75lb empty. 30.5in barrel, 5-groove rifling; RH, concentric. Ramp-and-leaf sight graduated to 1000yd. 1200ft/sec with Mark IX ammunition. P/60 saber bayonet.

The transformation of the caplock P/60 short rifle (and a few examples of the 1861 pattern) to the Snider system was approved on 6th March 1867. It had a Pattern II** breech. There were two barrel bands, and a bayonet lug on the right side of the muzzle; swivels appeared beneath the band and butt. Easily confused at a glance with the engineer carbine (q.v.), the back-sight leaf of the P/60 hinged at the back of the block instead of the front.

SIMILAR GUNS

Pattern III (or 'No. 3') serjeant's rifle. The first new guns were made at Enfield in 1869, with iron barrels and the Pattern III or Bolted Action. Obvious features were the locking latch on the left side of the breech, the new flat-face hammer and 'III' on the receiver. They served until replacement by the Martini-Henry began in 1874.

CONVERTED PATTERN 1861 ARTILLERY CARBINE

Made by the Royal Small Arms Factory, Enfield, Middlesex (37,560 conversions and 7500 new guns, 1867-72); the Royal Small Arms Factory, Sparkbrook, Birmingham (17,000 conversions in 1871-3 and 460 new guns from old parts in 1882-4); the Birmingham Small Arms & Metal Co. Ltd. and the Birmingham Small Arms & Munitions Co. Ltd., Small Heath (at least 11,200 new guns in 1871-6); the London Small Arms Co. Ltd., Bow (6000 new guns in 1871-4); and C.G. Bonehill, Birmingham (2100 new guns in 1880).

Total production: at least 81,820, excluding Trade, India and colonial patterns. **Chambering:** 577, rimmed. **Action:** as converted P/53 infantry rifle, above.

DATA FOR PATTERN II** CARBINE

40.25in overall, 7.48lb empty. 21.5in barrel, 5-groove rifling; RH, concentric. Ramp-and-leaf sight graduated to 600yd. 1005ft/sec with Mark IX ammunition. P/61 saber bayonet.

Approved on 2nd May 1867 and converted from the Pattern No. 3 (P/61) caplock, this also received the Pattern II** breech. Unlike the P/56 cavalry carbine, it had a full-length forend, a conventional cleaning rod, and brass furniture. The bayonet bar lay on the barrel.

SIMILAR GUN

Pattern III (or 'No. 3') artillery carbine, newly made. The adoption of the improved bolted action (Pattern III) on 13th January 1869 allowed the Snider artillery carbine to be revised, substantial quantities of new guns being made – though doubtless using many parts that had been in store. Furniture remained brass, but the barrels usually prove to be steel rather than iron. Replacement by Martini-Henry carbines began in 1880. In April, however, 2100 new Snider artillery carbines were ordered from Bonehill of Birmingham. Though otherwise identical with the standard Pattern III, they lacked bayonets and could be fitted with leather cavalry-type rear sight protectors.

Pattern IV (or 'No. 4') artillery carbine. A new Snider artillery carbine was sealed on 4th September 1885 for cadets. It was stocked to the muzzle, with a bar on the front band, and accepted a saber bayonet. Barrels were rifled with three grooves instead of five, and the rear sight was a standard rifle pattern with altered graduations; swivels lay under the front band and butt, while a snap-cap chain was attached to the front of the trigger guard bow. Cadet-pattern artillery carbines were officially re-designated 'Mark IV' in 1891.

ROYAL IRISH CONSTABULARY PATTERN

Converted in the government factory in Pimlico, London (1869-71 and possibly later), and by the Royal Small Arms Factory, Sparkbrook, Birmingham (1869 and 1881-3).

Total production: at least 16,910. **Chambering:** 577, rimmed. **Action:** as converted P/53 infantry rifle, above.

DATA FOR PATTERN II** CARBINE

41.1in overall, about 7.3lb empty. 22.5in barrel, 3-groove rifling; RH, concentric. Ramp-and-leaf sight graduated to 900yd. 1020ft/sec with Mark IX ammunition. Bayonet: see notes.

Accompanied by a saw-backed sword bayonet designed by Colonel William Dixon, this was approved on 16th July 1867. Converted from old two-band P/56 Short Rifles, it had iron furniture and was stocked virtually to the muzzle. The bayonet lug lay on the right side of the front band. Swivels lay under the front band and butt. rear sights were altered short-rifle patterns. Most Pimlico guns had Pattern II** actions, but some guns were made in Birmingham in 1869 with Pattern III (Bolted) breeches – though they were still converted from P/56 short rifles and had three-groove rifling. Work even began again in Birmingham in 1881, to provide replacements for guns lost by attrition.

YEOMANRY CARBINE

Made by the Royal Small Arms Factory, Sparkbrook, Birmingham, 1881-4.

Total production: at least 4,500. **Chambering:** 577, rimmed. **Action:** as converted P/53 infantry rifle, above.

DATA FOR PATTERN II** CARBINE

37.9in overall, 7lb empty. 19.15in barrel, 3-groove rifling; RH, concentric. Ramp-and-leaf sight graduated to 600yd. 995ft/sec with Mark IX ammunition. No bayonet.

Formally sealed on 19th July 1880, the 'Carbine, breech-loading, rifled, with cleaning rod, Snider, Yeomanry, Interchangeable, with cover, leather, rear sight, Mk I' was the last service-pattern Snider to be adopted in Britain. A conversion of P/53 Snider long rifles, it was longer in the butt than other carbines and lacked side-nail cups for the sling bar. Most guns had Pattern II** breeches and three-groove rifling.

GAOL, OR CONVICT CIVIL GUARD CARBINE

Approved on 25th September 1867, these 577 guns were converted in the Pimlico factory; 330 had been adapted by March 1868 from P/53 rifle-muskets. They were 41in overall, weighed about 7.5lb, and had 21.5in barrels. Pattern II** breeches and three-groove rifling were standard; however, rear sights and swivels were omitted. Forends were rounded off ahead of the band, and the special socket bayonet had a triangular-section blade.

INDIA AND COLONIAL PATTERNS

The principal private contractors – particularly the Birmingham Small Arms & Metal Co. Ltd. and the London Small Arms Co. Ltd. – continued to make Sniders long after work had stopped at Enfield. Among the many orders was one for 2,000 short rifles with saw-back bayonets, ordered for New Zealand in 1871 and fulfilled by BSA. The Agent-General for New Zealand also ordered 1,000 short rifles and 400 artillery carbines in May 1878; 2,000 short rifles in August 1879; and 500 cavalry carbines in December 1879. These were all fulfilled by BSA&M Co., except 460 short rifles supplied as part of the August 1879 contract by the National Arms & Ammunition Co. Ltd.

India acquired 1800 special short rifles in 1875, accompanied by socket bayonets; they had two bands and barrels measuring 30.5in. They were followed by 9170 short rifles with P/60 saber bayonets (ordered in December 1876) and 2130 cavalry carbines (1877-9). Indian guns were almost always made by the Birmingham Small Arms & Metal Co. Ltd., though the National Arms & Ammunition Co. Ltd. made three thousand of the 1876 contract.

SPORTING GUNS

Though many French Tabatiéré-type guns were converted into rudimentary hunting rifles in 1880-1900, the Snider was not popular among discerning sportsmen. Its period in vogue in Britain was comparatively short, owing to the emergence of better breech-loading rifles almost contemporaneously with the advent of the perfected Bolted Action. However, fine-quality rifles were proffered by the principal military contractors – the Birmingham and London Small Arms companies – and small quantities of good-quality guns were made for the volunteers by gunmakers such as Thomas Turner of London and Birmingham; Parker, Field & Company of London; Alexander Henry of Edinburgh; or James Kerr & Company of London. The actions were usually acquired from BSA, whose marks will often be found on them. An acknowledgement of Snider's patents (a large 'S' transfixed by an arrow) may also appear.

The Bolted Action was preferred. Woodwork was often excellent, with checkering on the wrist and forend; improvements were evident in the locks, while the metalwork could be lightly engraved. Furniture was generally iron instead of brass and the service-pattern sights were greatly refined. Most of the 'Volunteer Sniders' were full-length rifles, though some short patterns are also known.

• Soper

This swinging-block rifle, designed by William Soper of Reading, was patented in Britain in 1865 (an underlever action) and 1867 (for the side-mounted operating lever). It was renowned as the gun that arrived too late for inclusion in the British Army trials, but the truth was more prosaic; the Soper did arrive, but the committee decided in 1867 that though the performance 'both for accuracy and rapidity, was very satisfactory, the breech mechanism [was thought] to be too complicated'. Pressing the operating lever downward cocked the hammer, retracting the striker as it did so, and allowed the breech to spring open to the right. Spent cases were extracted and ejected automatically.

The mechanism was simple and efficient, and proved capable of incredibly rapid fire; on one occasion, certified by many onlookers, sixty shots were fired in a minute. Why it failed to attract greater attention remains a mystery, as suggestions that extraction was uncertain are rebutted by the contemporaneous rapid-fire trials. Perhaps the gun was simply unlucky enough to be promoted by a provincial gunmaker with meager manufacturing facilities. The earliest guns were made in Soper's own workshop, though post-1870 actions – if not the guns themselves – were apparently made by BSA.

IMPROVED BREECH-LOADING RIFLE

Made by William Soper, Reading, Berkshire (1868-70); and possibly also by the Birmingham Small Arms Co. Ltd., Small Heath (actions only, 1870-8?).

Total production: several hundred? **Chambering options:** many large-caliber pre-1885 British sporting cartridges. **Action:** locked by placing the breechblock across the frame behind the chamber.

DATA FOR A TYPICAL SPORTING PATTERN

Chambering: 450, rimmed. 44.15in overall, 8.03lb empty. 28in barrel, 7-groove rifling; LH, composite. Standing block sight. 1440ft/sec with 370-grain bullet.

By the early 1870s, Soper was promoting guns which ranged from fine-grade sporters to extremely plain examples destined for military-style target shooting or members of the volunteer movement. The guns had one-piece stocks – rare among contemporary block-action guns – with the operating lever at the end of a serpentine plate let into the right side of the stock beneath the breech.

A typical sporter offered a pistol grip butt and a short forend with a Henry-pattern tip. The round barrel had a full length top rib, suitably matted, and the rudimentary rear sight was accompanied by a small silver-tipped blade at the muzzle. Swivels lay under the butt and barrel, while a small safety catch appeared behind the trigger lever.

• Storm

The origins of this gun have been disputed, as the inventor has been claimed as American, Belgian or British. The earliest traceable patent was granted in the U.S. in July 1856, protecting the basic tipping-chamber construction and a locking bolt actuated by the fall of the hammer. Storm – who has been listed as 'William Mount Storm', 'William Mont Storm' or even 'William Montgomery Storm' – was clearly an American, beginning his designing career in New York sometime prior to 1853.

Though one of the Storm patents protected a breechblock which slid vertically, the rifles tested in Britain all embodied the lifting-chamber design. The 'Mont Storm Gun Works' traded briefly in Birmingham, under the management of Francis Braendlin (q.v.), when the chances of success in Britain seemed high.

TRIALS RIFLE

Made by, or more probably for the Mont Storm Gun Works, Birmingham, Warwickshire.

Total production: about 400. **Chambering:** 577, combustible cartridge; fired by a caplock. **Action:** locked by a hammer-propelled bolt entering the back of the pivoting chamber as the gun fired.

54in overall, 8.9lb empty. 39in barrel, 3-groove rifling; RH, concentric. Single shot only. Leaf rear sight with a stepped bed, graduated to 1000yd. About 1000ft/sec with standard expanding-ball ammunition. P/1853 socket bayonet.

Submitted to the British authorities by Charles Phelps, the 'Mont Storm' breech mechanism was seen as an ideal conversion system for the Enfield rifle muskets, as it did not weaken the stock too greatly and could fire combustible cartridges.

Six experimental alterations of the P/53 Enfield were delivered in December 1864; numbered 37-42, they were part of a total of 48 Enfields issued for conversion to seven manufacturers. They performed well enough to allow a decision to alter three thousand muzzle-loading guns for field trials to be taken in 1865.

Unfortunately, though the Pattern Arm was sealed on 7th October and again on 25th November 1865, only 66 Mont Storms had been delivered when problems with the special patented skin cartridge caused a suspension of work in February 1866. Work eventually ceased after the initial 400-gun batch had been completed. The Mont Storm conversion had been overtaken by the Snider and the introduction of metal-case ammunition.

SIMILAR GUNS

Mont Storm rifles were made in small numbers for Volunteer use, and possibly also in sporting guise. Pseudo-military patterns usually duplicated 577 Short Rifles (the Naval P/58 being favored), with 33in barrels, two barrel bands, and a bayonet bar on the right side of the muzzle. Several have been reported with the marks of Walter Adams the Younger of Birmingham, who may have made the guns for the Mont Storm Gun Works.

• Swinburn

Designed and developed by John Swinburn, this pivoting-block mechanism was the subject of several British patents granted in 1872-7 even though it was little more than a variant of the popular Martini.

The Model 1875 had a lever on the right side of the receiver to re-cock the striker should the gun misfire. The striker was hit by a hammer powered by a 'V'-type main spring. The straight-wrist butt was attached by tangs, creating space for the trigger mechanism behind the receiver; consequently, though it had a more effectual trigger, the Swinburn was neither as compact nor as durable as the Martini-Henry when fired with comparable ammunition.

Guns with British Government-pattern 450 Henry barrels were bought to arm militia and irregulars during the Zulu War of 1879 and the First South African War of 1881. They remained in service until the advent of Martini-Metfords.

MODEL 1875 RIFLE

Marked as a product of Swinburn & Son, Birmingham, but probably made by Westley Richards & Co. Ltd.

Total production: at least 1200. **Chambering:** 450, rimmed. **Action:** locked by the tip of the operating lever propping the breechblock behind the chamber.

49.5in overall, 9.31lb empty. 33in barrel, 7-groove rifling; LH, composite. Ramp-and-leaf sight graduated to 1400yd. 1350ft/sec with solid-case ball cartridges. Special sword bayonet.

An order for three hundred rifles was placed on 15th July 1875 by way of V. & R. Blakemore of London, Crown Agents for Natal. The Swinburns resembled the Mk II Martini-Henry (q.v.) externally, but the shaping of the rear of the body differed and the shank of the operating lever was practically straight.

A hundred additional rifles were ordered through the Crown Agents on 24th April 1876. Like the earlier batches, they were viewed at the government small arms repair factory in Birmingham. Volunteers in Natal then ordered 1500 rifles and carbines in 1878, apparently in equal proportions, directly from the manufacturer. A hundred additional guns were sent to Natal in 1886. They are believed to have been assembled from old parts – possibly by Westley Richards, as Swinburn had ceased trading three years earlier.

Swinburn-Henry rifles and carbines were finally withdrawn from service in favor of Martini-Metfords in 1895, though survivors remained in store for at least another decade.

Men of the Natal field forces,
pictured in 1879 with Swinburn-Henry carbines.

SIMILAR GUN

Carbine. The short-barrel Swinburn was similar to the rifle, except for reduced dimensions (39.3in long, 7.5lb empty). It had a plain forend with neither bands nor nose cap. All guns could take bayonets – a few special bowie-blade examples were made for the carbines – though issue of leather rear sight covers was apparently restricted to carbines. About 2100 carbines were made: sixty were ordered on 15th July 1875, followed by about 1250 on 24th June 1876, perhaps 750 more in 1878, and a few in 1886.

IMPROVED SPORTING RIFLE

Made by (or perhaps for) Swinburn & Son, Birmingham, about 1876-83.
Total production: a few hundred? **Chambering options:** a variety of large-caliber British black powder sporting cartridges. **Action:** as Model 1875, above.
DATA FOR A TYPICAL EXAMPLE
Chambering: 360 Express (black powder load), rimmed. 43.4in overall, 7.27lb empty. 26in barrel, 3-groove rifling; LH, concentric. Folding-leaf sight for 100yd, 200yd and 300yd. 1500ft/sec with 200-grain bullet.

The first sporters appeared in 1876. They are now rarely seen, as trading soon ceased. Surviving examples display typical English characteristics: slender pistol gripped butts with straight combs, plain round-tipped forends, express-pattern rear sights, simple trigger mechanisms, and – in some cases – restrained scroll engraving. Swinburn ceased trading in 1883, halting work on the dropping-block action. A few rifles may then have been completed by Westley Richards.

• Terry

Made in accordance with a British Patent granted to William Terry in 1856, but probably inspired by the Brand pattern (q.v.), this was made in a variety of calibers, sizes and styles. Popular among the sporting fraternity, the Terry carbine was also recommended for service with the British Army on 23rd August 1858 – though not without severe misgivings.

Substantial, but unknown numbers of Terry carbines were used by both sides during the American Civil War. Henry Calisher sold two hundred in New York in 1861, probably privately, but the most famous owner was the Confederate General James 'Jeb' Stuart.

Terry's patent protected a crude bolt-action mechanism with a breech cover, pivoted to the bolt, which was pulled outward and then rotated to disengage the retaining lugs. Retracting the bolt then exposed the chamber for loading. Unfortunately, poor manufacturing tolerances and rapid deterioration of the obturating pad in the bolt head allowed gas leaks which were bad enough to blow the breech cover open.

MILITARY WEAPONS

PATTERN NO. 1 CARBINE

Made by Calisher & Terry, Birmingham, with locks supplied from the Tower of London.
Total production: several hundred. **Chambering:** 568, combustible cartridges; fired by a cap lock. **Action:** locked by rotating two lugs on the rear of the bolt body into seats in the receiver.
DATA FOR A TYPICAL EXAMPLE
36.75in overall, 6.55lb empty. 19.65in barrel, 3-groove rifling; RH, concentric. Single shot only. Leaf and stepped-block rear sight graduated to 500yd. No bayonet

Sealed on 21st December 1858, this had three-groove rifling making a turn in 78in. The gun could be identified by the tubular extension of the breech, running back behind the long-shank hammer to house the bolt. A conventional sidelock was used. The Terry could be distinguished from the Manceaux (q.v.) design by the position of the hinged bolt cover, which lay on the right side of the breech instead of on top.

The barrel was held in the stock with two bands, a sling bar was anchored to the left side of the stock with two side-nails, and the furniture was iron. Guns of this type were issued to the 18th Hussars in sufficient numbers to be considered a regulation pattern.

SIMILAR GUNS

Pattern No. 2 carbine. Sealed in November 1860, this had a 539-caliber 21in barrel, and five-groove rifling making a turn in 36in. Measuring 38in overall, the gun weighed 6.2lb. It had a single barrel band and a rear sight similar to that of the contemporary P/61 cavalry carbine.

Pattern No. 3 carbine. Sealed on 9th March 1861, this was identical with No. 2, but had a Baddeley-pattern barrel band and lacked the band swivel.

IMPROVED PATTERN

Made to a modified design patented by Henry Calisher in July 1866, a combustible-cartridge gun of this type was submitted to trials undertaken in Britain in 1867. The rifle was rejected as it had to be held horizontally to prevent the bolt closing (or the cartridge falling out of the breech), and because the gas seal depended on the 'accurate fitting of two surfaces which are liable to become worn'.

SPORTING GUNS

Substantial quantities of Terry rifles, carbines and even shotguns were made for sale commercially. However, it is very difficult to classify them as so many were made to individual order – with features such as long barrels, pistol grip butts, checkering, engraving or multi-leaf rear sights.

SPORTING RIFLE

Made by John Blanch & Son, London, about 1862.
Total production: not known. **Chambering:** 52-bore (.451) combustible cartridges; fired by a cap lock. **Action:** as military carbine, above.
DATA FOR A TYPICAL EXAMPLE
50.75in overall, 8.25lb empty. 36in barrel, 3-groove rifling; RH, concentric. Single shot only. Leaf-type rear sight graduated to 1100yd.

This particular rifle had a round barrel, but octagonal patterns are known from other sources. Delicate scroll engraving appeared on the bolt handle, the case-hardened lock plate, the hammer and the trigger guard. The full-length walnut stock was accompanied

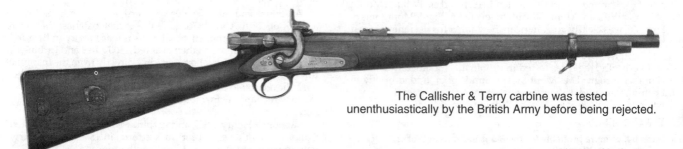

The Callisher & Terry carbine was tested
unenthusiastically by the British Army before being rejected.

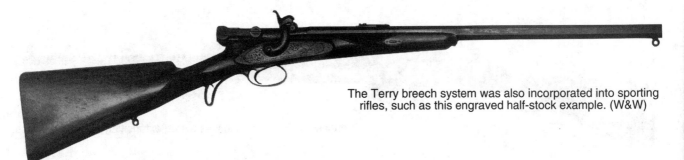

The Terry breech system was also incorporated into sporting rifles, such as this engraved half-stock example. (W&W)

by an engraved iron buttplate and two engraved barrel bands. The lock plate bore the marks of Blanch & Son of Gracechurch Street, London, and the breech bore an acknowledgment of Terry's patent.

Though this particular gun was the product of a well-known gunmaker, Calisher & Terry maintained an office of their own in London in the 1860s. This justified the application of 'London' marks (even though the guns were made in Birmingham) to capitalize on the excellent reputation of London gunmakers compared with the English provincial trade.

• Thorneycroft

The origins of this rifle present a mystery. It has been linked with the commander of Thorneycroft's Mounted Rifles – volunteers serving in the Second South African (Boer) War of 1899-1902 – who was a particularly vocal advocate of short rifles. However, British Patent 14,622 of 1901 records the inventor as James Baird Thorneycroft, an 'Ironmaster' of Mauchline, Ayrshire.

His rifle was somewhat similar to the Godsal (q.v.). Its bolt/block unit had a carefully shaped wooden shroud; and the rear sight was usually comparable with that of the SMLE. As the bayonet fits onto a boss at the muzzle, the surviving gun probably dates from 1903 or later. It was specifically developed for cavalry, hence the care with which everything was clothed in wood.

Like the Godsal, the Thorneycroft had a magazine in the wrist of the butt immediately behind the trigger. However, though this permitted a long barrel, it restricted the capacity of the magazine to five rounds. In addition, the gun was awkward to use; not only was aim disturbed to reload after each shot, owing to the position of the bolt, but the grip for the trigger-finger hand was very uncomfortable.

• Thorpe

This rifle was developed experimentally by a team led by Stanley Thorpe, to compete with the Januszewski (q.v.) EM-2. Based on German prototypes – notably the StG. 45M of World War II – the first attempt was a conventional-looking gun chambered for the 7.9x33 Kurzpatrone. This was soon revised into bullpup form, with the magazine behind the pistol grip and the shoulder pad attached directly to the receiver; it was also a brave attempt to introduce some of the manufacturing techniques pioneered in Germany, relying on pressing, stamping and welding at the expense of traditional machining. However, British industry proved to be incapable of mastering this new technology in the post-1945 depression, and the chance to develop a precursor of the CETME – inspired by the same prototypes – was lost.

EM-1 RIFLE
Rifle, Experimental, 280in EM-1 (CEAD), code name 'Cobra'
Made by the Royal Small Arms Factory, Enfield, 1949-50.
Total production: 6-10. **Chambering:** 280, rimless. **Action:** locked by rollers in the breechblock engaging the receiver walls; gas operated, selective fire.

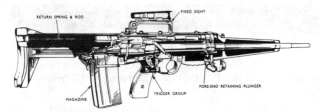

A general-arrangement drawing of the Thorpe (EM-1) rifle.

36in overall, 10.88lb with loaded magazine. 24.5in barrel, 4-groove rifling; RH, concentric? Detachable box magazine, 20 rounds. Integral optical sight. 2415ft/sec with 140-grain bullet; 450±25rpm. Knife bayonet.

The EM-1 was a distinctive design; similar externally to the EM-2, it could be recognized by the shape of the two-piece wooden forend and the design of the flat-sided receiver – a flimsy pressing by Turner Bros. of Birmingham. The firing mechanism embodied an efficient extractor and a linear hammer, offset to the right of the barrel extension, which gave a particularly good trigger-pull. However, though the breechblock was much simpler than its EM-2 equivalent, the EM-1 was extremely difficult to field-strip and had an unnecessarily fragile hold-open; the cocking plate in the firing train would also have been prone to failure.

The first EM-1 was proved at Enfield in December 1949. Three guns had been readied for comparative trials in the U.S. in 1950, but the project was then canceled in favor of the EM-2. The Thorpe rifle failed largely because it could not be manufactured with the technology of the day. But it seems probable that it would have made a better weapon in the long term than the lighter but more complicated EM-2.

• Turner

Thomas Turner of Birmingham was granted a British Patent in 1864 to protect a caplock rifle with a lifting breech. A pivoting block could be raised to give access to the chamber once a cross-bolt catch at the rear of the receiver had been released. Several 450-caliber rifles of this pattern survive, perhaps intended for British military trials held prior to 1865. A typical example has a 36.5in barrel, a military-pattern walnut stock with a straight wrist, two barrel bands, a nose cap, and a case-hardened external-hammer sidelock.

The breech of a Turner-type P/53 Enfield conversion. (W&D)

• Vickers

Vickers Ltd. is best known for machine guns, but would have been the primary private manufacturer of the P/14 (Enfield) rifle had not war begun in 1914.

The company subsequently made a short-lived attempt to diversify into sporting guns after the end of World War I to maintain employment in the Crayford and Erith factories. Simplified Martini-action target rifles were made in the 1920s, distinguished by round-topped bodies and one-piece stocks. In addition, probably owing to pre-war links with Deutsche Waffen- u. Munitionsfabriken (one of the principal makers of Mauser rifles), Vickers offered a few high-power sporting rifles in the same era. It is assumed that they were made on actions supplied from Germany, but the quantity is assumed to have been small and none could be traced for examination.

The Vickers-Pedersen rifle was tested extensively, without success.

Vickers was also a licensee of the patents granted to John Pedersen to protect his toggle-action rifle (see 'USA'). Pedersen even traveled to Britain to develop tooling for his rifle, which – or so Vickers believed – had been 'adopted' by the US Army in 1928. The first two Vickers-made guns were submitted to the Small Arms Committee in 1929, passing their trials successfully enough for additional experiments to be undertaken in 1931-3; eventually, however, the Vickers-Pedersen was rejected after placing second to the Holek ZH 29 in the final eliminator. It has been claimed, however, that at least two hundred rifles and a handful of carbines were made.

• War Office

Practically every British service weapon could be included under this particular heading; though the Snider, Martini and Lee actions were all proprietary designs, the service patterns incorporated a considerable amount of modifications made by technicians in the government-owned Enfield small-arms factory. Guns of these patterns, however, will be found listed in the British chapter under the original inventors' names. The exception to this general rule, however, is the rimfire training rifle developed in the early 1900s.

Lessons learned from the war against the Boers (1899-1902) gave target-shooting a great boost in Britain, leading, among other things, to the formation in 1902 of the National Small-Bore Rifle Association (NSRA) and the encouragement of 'Miniature Rifle Shooting'. This was initially fulfilled by small caliber Martini-breech rifles, imported American 22 rimfires of various types, and by service rifles fitted with adapters such as the Morris or Aiming Tubes.

In 1905, the War Office invited submissions of small-bore training rifles from leading British gunmakers. Most of the rifles submitted were based on the Martini breech, though Cogswell & Harrison submitted a Certus and there were a number of adaptations of the 303 service rifles. Mindful of the fact that the SMLE was a bolt-action design, and possibly also of the fact that the French trainers included a reduced scale version of the Lebel, the War Office rejected the submissions and produced an 'in house' design of its own. Manufacture was contracted out to BSA and LSA, but other gunmakers subsequently made close copies prior to 1914.

The War Office Miniature Rifle, developed to appeal to the rifle clubs, was unsuccessful. The Martini-action guns proved to be far more accurate, even though their value as military trainers was questionable. Consequently, the War Office pattern was not made in vast numbers, though it did provide the basis for improved sporting guns marketed by BSA from 1910 onward.

WAR OFFICE MINIATURE RIFLE

Made by the Birmingham Small Arms Co. Ltd., Small Heath, Birmingham; by the London Armory Co. Ltd., Bow, London; and probably by other gunmakers such as W.W. Greener, about 1907-14.

Total production: at least 160,000. **Chambering options:** 22 Long rimfire, 22 Long Rifle rimfire, 297/230 centerfire. **Action:** locked by turning the bolt handle base down into its seat in the receiver.
DATA FOR A TYPICAL 22 LR EXAMPLE
41.5in overall, 5.5lb empty. 23.5in barrel, 4-groove rifling; RH, concentric. Single shot only. Tangent-leaf sight graduated to 200yd. 1050ft/sec with 40-grain bullet.

This was a simple bolt-action rifle intended to duplicate the handling characteristics of the SMLE, though it was much too light, usually had a differently placed bolt handle, and the butt had a true pistol grip instead of the uniquely British semi-pistol grip design. War Office contracts were placed with BSA (100,000 guns) and LSA (60,000?) in 1906, for the use of "all branches of the Armed Forces, Cadet Corps, Boys' Clubs, Working Men's Clubs [and] Public School Cadet Forces". By the summer of 1907, BSA-made guns were being advertised commercially at an attractively low price.

The guns were made in several styles, including a full-stock pattern with two barrel bands, and a more popular half- or three-quarter-stocked design with a single band. Some of the earliest government-purchased rifles are dated – LSA no. 4323 and BSA no. 25175, for example, were made in 1907 and 1908 respectively.

BSA-made guns were typically three-quarter stocked and had an internal band in the forend, with swivels beneath the butt and band. A safety catch often lay above the cocking-piece, and a few examples had detachable five-round box magazines ahead of the stamped-strip trigger guard. The wind-gauge rear sights, with SMLE-type protectors, were usually graduated from 25yd to 200yd.

• Wilson

Thomas Wilson of Birmingham, a most prolific patentee, was eventually granted a share of the Snider royalties. This alternative bolt-action design was among the earliest bolt-type conversions mooted for the P/1853 (Enfield) rifle muskets, as details were being submitted to the British authorities as early as April 1860.

Altered in accordance with a patent dating from 1859, the breech plug of the old caplock was substituted by a new open-topped receiver. A bolt or 'plunger' slid in the receiver, being held in place by a wedge sliding laterally behind the hammer. This was released by pulling back on the articulated finger-piece on the rear of the bolt. An India-rubber obturator on the bolt-head minimized gas leaks.

1859-PATENT TRIALS RIFLE

Made by, or more probably for Thomas Wilson of Birmingham, Warwickshire.

Total production: at least six, 1864. **Chambering:** 577 combustible cartridge; fired by a cap lock. **Action:** locked by pushing a wedge laterally through the receiver and bolt.

The Wilson breech relied on a sliding bolt locked by a transverse key. This is a P/53 'Enfield' rifle-musket conversion. (W&W)

54in overall, 9.75lb empty. 39in barrel, 3-groove rifling; RH, concentric. Single shot only. Leaf rear sight with a stepped bed, graduated to 1000yd. About 1000ft/sec with standard expanding-ball ammunition. P/1853 socket bayonet.

Six rifles – numbered 7-12 – were among nearly fifty P/53 rifle muskets converted to seven differing breech systems in 1864-5. They had a one-piece straight-wrist stock, a government-pattern sidelock, and three Baddeley bands. The knurled finger-piece on the back of the bolt and the rounded head of the locking wedge immediately behind the hammer were most distinctive. Though the Wilson rifles performed well, the Snider was preferred. They were replaced by the improved or 1867 pattern in subsequent trials.

1867-PATENT TRIALS RIFLE

Made for Thomas Wilson of Birmingham, Warwickshire, 1867-70. Total production: a few hundred? **Chambering:** 50, centerfire. **Action:** locked by rotating two lugs on the bolt sleeve into their recesses in the receiver.

53.5in overall, 9.3lb empty. 39in barrel, 5-groove rifling; RH, concentric. Single shot only. Leaf and stepped-bed rear sight graduated to 1000yd. Bushed P/1853 socket bayonet.

Improved Wilson rifles appeared in the British trials of 1866-8. The gun tested in 1867 was a needle-fire pattern chambering a combustible cartridge with an India-rubber base wad. The needle was driven by a rib and spring. The rifle was successful enough to be 'retained for further consideration', but was replaced by a centerfire pattern with striker driven by a coil spring.

The bolt of the perfected gun was pushed home with the ball of the palm, until a locking collar at the rear could be rotated to the left to engage the lugs with their seats in the receiver. The rifles were easily identified by the absence of an external hammer and by the tubular receiver, with a stubby rear-mounted bolt handle mounted on a collar. They were eventually rejected when a premature breech explosion destroyed one gun, though similar weapons were submitted to trials held throughout Europe. Small numbers were even sold to France during the Franco-Prussian War of 1870-1.

• Wood

Charles F. Wood of Enfield patented an extraordinary rifle in 1888, deriving partly from advances in rifle design but also from the design of mechanical machine guns – the top-mounted strip-feed magazine (10-12 rounds) clearly owed much to the Nordenfelt and Gardner guns. The Wood rifle was operated by a sliding straight-pull handle on the right side of the breech, but was much too complicated and cumbersome to succeed, and was all too soon eclipsed by better designs.

• Woodgate

Herbert Woodgate, co-designer of the Griffiths & Woodgate rifle (q.v.), patented an improved recoil-operated rifle in October 1894. The return spring was moved beneath the barrel, the bolt head locked directly into the receiver behind the chamber, and the cam-track was moved to the inside of the left receiver wall. The trigger was also simplified. The rifle fired when the bolt was released to follow the barrel, a projection on the receiver striking the firing-pin head protruding from the bolt handle shank. This happened just as the bolt lugs were revolved into engagement – a very unusual variation of the slam-fire principle which probably resulted in poor accuracy. There is no evidence that guns were made in quantity in accordance with Woodgate's patent, as the firing mechanism would have been difficult to make; however, it is assumed that at least one prototype existed.

• Wyley

Gunsmith James Wyley (or Wylie) obtained a patent in 1864 to protect caplock breechloaders with sliding, hinged or laterally-

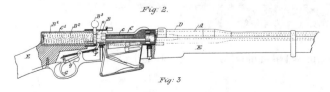

The Woodgate rifle, from the British patent.

moving chambers. A typical 450-caliber (52 Bore) example of the Wyley rifle had a barrel which could be turned through 90 degrees to release an interrupted-thread connection, then pulled forward and pivoted to the left to give access to the chamber. The rifle had a back-action lock, an elegant butt with checkering on the straight wrist, and a scrolled trigger guard. The checkered forend was held to the barrel by a transverse key set in oval escutcheons. The block and leaf rear sight was graduated to merely 150yd – this particular gun was a short-range 'Park Rifle' – and the 33in round barrel gave an overall length of about 48.5in. A modified Wyley rifle was submitted to the British authorities in 1867, but was rejected on the basis that the 'breech bolt is liable to be detached from the rifle in opening the breech' and that better bolt action designs were already under consideration.

BULGARIA

• Berdan

The Russian-pattern bolt action Berdan infantry rifle and cavalry carbine were apparently adopted by the newly autonomous Bulgarian army as the 'M1880', serving until the adoption of the Austro-Hungarian Mannlicher. They were identical with Russian issue, but bore the 'crown A' cypher of Alexander I.

• Kalashnikov

The People's Army was initially armed with rifles made in Poland (q.v.). A typical example – made by Factory 11 in 1963 – had a machined-steel receiver, a wooden forend, a plain wood pistol grip, and a cleaning rod beneath the barrel. The solid 'C'-section folding butt, actuated by a press-stud on the left side, had an open 'U'-shape shoulder piece and no visible rivets. The selector bore 'C' above 'P'. Production of AK rifles began in State Factory No. 10 about 1965. Plastic furniture was fitted, the pistol grip being crudely checkered, and selectors were marked 'Ад' and 'Е--'. A cleaning rod was carried under the barrel, but the gun did not accept a bayonet. Production switched to the AKM in the early 1970s, and then to a facsimile of the AK-74 in the mid-1980s.

A Bulgarian-made 7.62x39 Kalashnikov AKS, with a folding butt.

• Mannlicher

The Bulgarian army used M1888 and M1895 rifles, supplied by Österreichische Waffenfabriks-Gesellschaft in 1890-2 and 1897-1901 respectively. They were identical with Austro-Hungarian weapons, excepting that they bore Bulgarian arms over the chamber, rampant lion inspectors' marks, and the 'crowned F' cypher of Prince Ferdinand. Several thousand 8mm M1895 rifles were converted in the early 1920s to 'M95/24' short rifles, chambering the German 7.9x57 cartridge. Most of the work appears to have been undertaken at Steyr.

BURMA (MYANMAR)

• Heckler & Koch

The first G3 were acquired from Heckler & Koch in 1963. By 1975, indigenous production of the G3A2 was under way. A modified heavy-barrel variation has also been made, apparently only after 1980. It has a special Burmese-designed bipod, but is otherwise similar to the standard G3-type service rifle.

CANADA

• ArmaLite (Diemaco)

The Canadian army has replaced the 7.62mm C1 rifle (FN FAL, q.v.) with the 5.56mm C7 rifle and C8 carbine, known to Colt as the models 715 and 725 respectively. Developed from a government contract given to Diemaco in the Spring of 1983, the C7 and C8 are essentially variations of the M16A2 with a simpler pivoting-leaf rear sight, a thirty-round nylon magazine and a Colt-pattern butt trap. The C8 has a short barrel and a telescoping XM177E2-type butt. The three-round burst-fire mechanism was discarded in favor of the standard fully-automatic setting.

Orders for nearly eighty thousand C7 rifles and 1570 C8 carbines were approved in 1984. Batches of C7 rifles were delivered in the summer of 1985, the first of the all-Canadian made guns appearing at the end of 1987.

Though some of the earliest guns were marked differently, C7 rifles display 'CANADA/FORCES/CANADIENNES' under a stylized maple leaf on the left side of the magazine housing, above the designation, caliber and serial number. The left side of the receiver ahead of the selector displays 'MADE IN CANADA' and 'FABRIQUE AU CANADA' above Diemaco's trademark.

The Royal Canadian Mounted Police have used commercial-pattern Colt AR-15 sporting rifles and carbines in small numbers.

A Canadian soldier is pictured during the competitive trials which led to the adoption of the ArmaLite AR-15A2 as the 'C7' rifle.

• FN-Saive (Long Branch)

These guns were Canadian-made variants of the FN FAL, described in greater detail in the Belgian section.

C1 AUTOMATIC RIFLE

Made by Canadian Arsenals Ltd, Long Branch, Ontario, 1957-68.
Total production: not known. **Chambering:** 7.62x51 NATO, rimless.
Action: as Belgian FAL (q.v.).
DATA FOR A TYPICAL C1A1

44.72in overall, 9.37lb without magazine. 21.00in barrel, 6-groove rifling; RH, concentric. Detachable box magazine, 20 rounds. Folding rotating aperture sight graduated to 600yd. 2750ft/sec with standard NATO ball rounds. C1 knife bayonet.

The first trials undertaken in 1954 with the experimental EX-1 and EX-2 rifles – essentially similar to the British X8E1 and X8E2, with fixed and optical sights respectively – convinced the Cana-

dian authorities of their merits. About two thousand were acquired from Fabrique Nationale in 1954-5.

The C1 rifle was adopted in June 1955. It differed from the British X8E5 and X14E1 rifles (which became the L1A1) in the addition of charger guides to the receiver. It also had a unique rotating-disc rear sight. The furniture was wood and a cylindrical flash suppressor was fitted.

The first issues were made in 1956. A typical receiver mark – on the left side above the pistol grip – read RIFLE, 7.62MM FN (C1).

SIMILAR GUNS

C1D rifle. A selective-fire C1, differing from the army rifle only in the selector and trigger mechanism, was adopted by the Royal Canadian Navy in 1958 as the 'Rifle, 7.62mm, FN, C1D'.

C1A1 and C1A1D rifles. The rigours of service showed that the original firing pin could fail to retract into the breech block automatically if the tip was deformed, igniting the cartridge before the breech was properly locked. The adoption in 1959 of a two-piece firing pin and a new plastic carrying handle advanced the designation to C1A1 (army) or C1A1D (navy, selective fire). The 7.62mm C1A1 was superseded in 1984 by the 5.56mm C7 rifle (a modified M16A1), but many of the large-caliber weapons are still being held in reserve in Canada.

C2 rifle. This heavyweight C1, introduced in 1958, shared the same basic characteristics but had a combination forend/bipod with wood strips attached to the metal legs. The gas tube was exposed above the heavy barrel and a three-position selector lever appeared on the left side of the receiver above the pistol grip. The guns were 44.72in long, weighed 15.28lb with loaded magazine, had sliding-aperture rear sights graduated to 1000yd, and could not accept bayonets. Their cyclic rate was about 710rpm. The upper left side of the pistol grip was rebated to allow the selector to rotate, and a mark such as 'RIFLE AUTO 7.62MM FN C2' was found on the left side of the receiver.

C2A1 rifle. The supersession of the original one-piece firing pin by a two-piece design, introduced with the C1A1 infantry rifle, was extended to the C2 in 1960. The designation advanced to C2A1, though only the markings and the plastic carrying handle distinguished the two patterns externally.

• Lakefield, autoloading type

The Lakefield Arms Company made a limited range of good-quality 22 rimfire sporting and target rifles from about 1990 until 1996, when the business was acquired by Savage (see 'USA').

MODEL 64B SPORTING RIFLE

Made by Lakefield Arms Company, Quebec, 1990-96.
Total production: not known. **Chambering:** 22 LR, rimfire. **Action:** no mechanical lock; blowback, semi-automatic only.

40.1in overall, 5.63lb empty. 20.25in barrel, 4-groove rifling; RH, concentric. Detachable box magazine, 10 rounds. Spring-leaf and elevator rear sight. 1050ft/sec with 40-grain bullet.

Similar to many rifles in its class, the 64B (still being marketed by Savage) had a walnut-finished hardwood half-stock with a low Monte Carlo comb, a plastic shoulder plate, and checkering on the pistol grip and forend. The receiver – suitably grooved for optical-sight mount bases – had a rounded back, continuing the contours of the butt, and a safety catch set into the rear right side; the charging handle lay in the ejection port cut in the right side of the receiver above the detachable box magazine. A separate hold-open held the bolt back after the last case had been ejected.

• Lakefield, bolt-action type

These guns were all based on an identical action. However, though comparatively simple, they were good enough to attract the attention of Savage – the name under which several of them are still being marketed.

A typical Lakefield rifle, now distributed as the Savage 64-F.

A typical Lakefield rifle, now distributed as the Savage Mk II-LV.

MARK I SPORTING RIFLE
Made by Lakefield Arms Company, Quebec, 1990-95.
Total production: not known. **Chambering:** 22 LR, rimfire. **Action:** locked by the base of the bolt handle turning down into its seat on the receiver.

39.5in overall, 5.75lb empty. 20.5in barrel, 4-groove rifling; RH, concentric. Single shot only. Spring-leaf and elevator rear sight. 1050ft/sec with 40-grain bullet.

The basic rifle of the Lakefield range, this had a walnut-finish half stock with a low Monte Carlo comb and checkering on the pistol grip and forend. A radial safety lever protruded from the right side of the stock behind the bolt handle. Also offered as a smooth-bore, the Mark I was usually blued and had grooves on the receiver to accept optical-sight mount bases.

SIMILAR GUNS
Mark IY, 1990-6. Still being offered by Savage, this reduced-scale 'youth' pattern was destined for firers of small stature. Overall length was reduced to 37in, the barrel measured 19in, and empty weight was about 5.2lb.

Mark II, 1990-6. Essentially similar to the Mark I, this rifle had a detachable ten-round magazine with a noticeable curve. Still available from Savage.

Mark IIY. A variant of the Mark II with a short barrel and butt, intended for the 'youth' market.

Model 90B, 1991-6. This was a Biathlon target-rifle derivative of the basic Lakefield action, accompanied by five 5-round magazines, a spare magazine holder, and folding protectors on the competition sights. Now made under the Savage brandname, the 90B was about 39.65in long, had a 21.5in barrel and weighed 8.25lb without magazines.

Model 91S, 1992-6. Derived from the 91T described below, this target rifle was intended for metallic silhouette competitions. It could be recognized by its high-comb butt and optical sights, the receiver-top being drilled and tapped to accept the appropriate mounting bases.

Model 91T, 1991-6. Now known as the Savage 900TR, the basic Lakefield single shot 22LR target rifle had a heavy 25in barrel, giving an overall length of about 43.65in and a weight of 8lb without its micro-adjustable aperture sights. The hardwood stock had a deep forend with an accessory rail and hand-stop; the comb was straight, the pistol grip was stippled, and the forend had an obliquely-cut tip.

Model 91TR, 1991-6. Otherwise identical with the 91T, this had a detachable five-round box magazine.

Model 93 Magnum, 1994-6. Essentially similar to the Mark II, this chambered the 22 Winchester Magnum rimfire cartridge. A five-round detachable box magazine was retained.

• Lee-Enfield
After using the standard British-pattern Snider, Martini-Henry and Lee-Metford rifles, the Canadians elected to follow independent lines by adopting the Ross (q.v.) in 1903. The spectacular failure of the Ross in the First World War led to the belated standardisation of the SMLE in 1916, though no manufacture occurred until the Long Branch factory, operated by the government-owned Small Arms Ltd, tooled for No. 4 rifles in 1940.

NUMBER 4 MARK I* RIFLE
The Canadian-made Lee-Enfield rifles, many of which were used by the British Army, followed this improved pattern. Unique to North American production, the Mk I* had a distinctively shaped safety catch. Some guns had C Mk 2 and C Mk 3 rear sights; fabricated from stampings, these were broadly similar to the British Mks 3 and 4 respectively.

Canadian guns were regarded as very well made, had serial numbers such as '12L1926' and bore an 'LB' monogram maker's mark. By 31st December 1945, Long Branch had made about 905,730 No. 4 Mk I and I* rifles for the British and Canadian forces. Canadian rifles normally displayed 'DC' ('Dominion of Canada') or simply 'C', often accompanied by a Broad Arrow.

NUMBER 4 MARK I* (T) RIFLE
Substantial quantities of sniper rifles had also been assembled, the total by the end of 1945 standing in the region of 1140 – some for Britain and the remainder for Canada. The actions were selected for accuracy and carefully stocked in the manner of the standard British No. 4 Mk I (T) (q.v.), though a few, intended for trials, have been found with pistol grip butts and a roll-over Monte Carlo comb.

A selection of optical sights was used, including the standard C No. 32, the No. 32 Trade Pattern (a commercial Lyman Alaskan sight in a Griffin & Howe mount), and the C No. 32 Mk 4. Made by Research Enterprises Ltd of Montreal, the Mk 4 sight was subsequently redesignated 'C No. 67'.

NUMBER 4 LIGHTWEIGHT RIFLE
The only other Canadian development of note was this weapon, with a one-piece stock and every conceivable attempt to save weight. The gun measured 42.10in overall had a 22.75in barrel and weighed less than 6lb. About fifty were made in 1944.

• Parker-Hale
The Canadian forces adopted the British Parker-Hale M82 sniper rifle as the 'Rifle, 7.62mm C3'. This Mauser-action weapon was fitted with a Kahles 6x42 telescope sight, but could also accept aperture-type competition sights. Spacers were issued to allow marksmen to adjust the length of the butt to their personal requirements. The C3A1 was an improved form of the C3, with a detachable six-round box magazine instead of the five-round internal type. The receiver was strengthened, a bipod was fitted to facilitate observation duties, and the bolt-handle knob was lengthened to clear the 10x Unertl sight. The acquisition of rights to the Parker-Hale rifles by the Midland Arms Company (see 'USA') has compromised the long-term utility of the C3 and C3A1, and it is believed that the Canadians are currently seeking a suitable replacement.

• Ross
Perhaps the most vilified of all twentieth-century military rifles, though often a first-class sporter, the Ross owed its brief glory to the refusal of the British to supply Canadian troops with Lee-Enfields during the Second South African War of 1899-1902. The design is customarily credited to Sir Charles Ross, a talented but opinionated engineer who received his first British patent in 1893. Ross had simply adapted the 1890-pattern Austrian Mannlicher to suit his own purposes, even though it had performed badly in many official trials. In this lay the seeds of disaster.

The perfected Ross action relied on threaded helical ribs on the bolt engaging threads inside the bolt sleeve. When the bolt was pulled back, the ribs rotated the locking lugs out of the receiver wall. However, though the Ross worked reasonably well when clean – and firing good-quality ammunition – war in the trenches emphasised the ease with which the action could be jammed by mud or heat generated during rapid fire.

There was little doubt that the Ross action was very fast in perfect conditions; in addition, when properly locked, it was unusually strong. However, quality control was poor and problems soon became apparent. After part of a bolt blew back into the face of a Royal North West Mounted Policeman during shooting practice in 1906, costing the firer an eye, RNWMP Ross rifles were recalled into store. Survivors were exchanged for improved Mk II rifles in 1909.

Accidents involving 1905-type actions may have been due to faulty engagement of the locking lugs, or the trigger releasing the striker before the breech was properly locked. In most of the later 1910-pattern guns, however, the bolt could be rotated under the extractor after the bolt-sleeve had been removed from the bolt-way. Though the bolt sleeve would re-enter the receiver, the bolt could not lock on the closing stroke and slammed back on firing. If the bolt-stop then failed, the bolt flew back out of the gun with potentially disastrous consequences.

Though the British ordered substantial quantities of Mk III Ross rifles in 1914, reports of bolts flying out of the Ross as it fired were already multiplying. Adjustments were made in 1916 to the extractor groove, and the addition by armorers in France of a rivet or screw in the bolt sleeve prevented bolts being wrongly assembled. However, the improvements came too late to prevent the unpopular Ross being replaced by the short Lee-Enfield in the autumn of 1915. Tests showed that jamming often arose simply from the bolt-stop damaging the rearmost locking thread, but the Canadians had lost all confidence in their rifle and the authorities were in no position to correct the faults.

The Ross Rifle Company ceased trading in March 1917, when its facilities were seized by the Canadian government, but $2 million compensation was paid to Sir Charles Ross in 1920.

MILITARY RIFLES

Ross submitted a military version of his 1900-pattern sporting rifle to the Canadian militia in 1901. The prototype shot accurately and performed adequately in rapid fire, but comprehensively failed an endurance test negotiated by the competing Lee-Enfield. A Ross rifle was taken to Britain shortly afterwards, but was rejected by the Small Arms Committee in favor of the shortened Lee-Enfield.

The Canadians were forced into adopting the Ross largely because Britain was unwilling to supply sufficient Lee-Enfield rifles at a time when the Second South African (Boer) War still raged. The pattern for the 'Rifle, Ross, 303-inch, Mark 1' was sealed in April 1902, and a contract for 12,000 rifles was signed in March 1903. The Ross Rifle Company was formed in the autumn of 1903, and construction of a purpose-built factory began in Quebec.

The first army-contract rifles were completed early in 1905, initially using many parts bought in from Billings & Spencer and Mossberg, but deliveries of rifles to the militia and carbines to the Royal North-West Mounted Police had already begun.

MARK I RIFLE
Also known as 'Military Model 1905'
Made by the Ross Rifle Company, Quebec.
Total production: about 5000. **Chambering:** 303, rimmed. **Action:** locked by two lugs on the bolt head engaging the receiver wall when the bolt handle was pushed forward.

47.65in overall, 8.03lb empty. 28in barrel, 4-groove rifling; RH, concentric. Internal box magazine, 5 rounds. Tangent sight graduated to 2500yd, then 2200yd. 2000ft/sec with Mk II ball ammunition. No bayonet.

The first 'Rifles, Ross, 303-inch, Mark I' were delivered to the Department of Militia and Defence in August 1905. The Mk I had a pistol grip stock and a barrel band. A nose cap carried the bayonet lug and a piling swivel; sling swivels lay on the band and under the butt. The Mk I rear sight had a long leaf graduated to 2500yd, which predictably proved to be too fragile and was replaced by a shorter 2200yd pattern.

The magazine featured the so-called 'Harris Controlled Platform', with a depressor behind the rear sight on the right side of the forend. This could be actuated by the thumb to allow cartridges to be dropped into the magazine. The cut-off lay on the side of the stock above the trigger guard.

SIMILAR GUNS

Mk II rifle (i). Announced in 1905 and delivered in February 1907, this retained the 28in barrel and the Harris magazine. It had

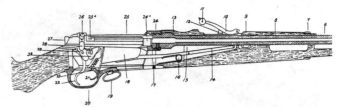

A longitudinal section of the 303-caliber Mk II Ross rifle.

a longer handguard than the Mk I, and the barrel band was moved noticeably forward. A high-sided receiver was adopted, the design of the bolt sleeve was improved, a hooked cut-off lay inside the trigger guard, and the rear swivel lay ahead of the guard. A strengthened Mk III rear sight was introduced in 1907, distinguished by its flat-top elevator bar.

Mark II rifle (ii). In 1912, to hide the growing list of modifications, the Canadians re-designated the 30.5in-barreled Mk II** as the 'Rifle, Ross Mk II'.

Mark II* rifle. This was a modified form of the original Mk II, with changes to the magazine lever and a new German-style tangent-pattern Mk II rear sight with a rotating-collar micrometer system that permitted the sight to be elevated in ten-yard increments. Guns of this type were offered in 'Military Standard', 'Military Target' or 'Military Presentation' grades.

Mark II** rifle. After a tremendous number of minor changes had been made, this rifle appeared with a 30.5in barrel, an improved 'flag' safety catch instead of a press-catch, a longer nose cap (not unlike that of the US Krag-Jørgensen), and a broader barrel band. The cut-off mechanism was omitted. Most rifles had simpler handguards and leaf-type rear sights made by the Sutherland Sight Company (which had been renamed 'Canada Tool & Specialty Company' by 1911). These sights lay mid-way between the receiver ring and the barrel band. Some Mk II** rifles were specially built in 1909 for military target shooting, with heavy barrels, modified forends, and a Ross battle sight mounted on the receiver bridge.

Mark II*** rifle. Introduced in 1909, this had a 28in barrel and a Sutherland sight ahead of a prominent steel housing abutting the receiver ring. The cut-off was reinstated and the safety reverted to the press-catch design.

Mark II***** rifle. Dating from 1910, this was another of the 28in-barreled guns, distinguished from the Mk II*** by a simpler housing immediately behind the Sutherland sight.

Mark I short rifle. This was a post-1912 designation for all short-barrel Ross rifles other than the Mks II*** and II*****.

Mark II short rifle. In 1912, wishing to hide the ever-growing list of modifications, the Canadian authorities reclassified the 28in-barreled Mks II*** and Mk II***** as 'Rifles, Short, Ross Mk II'.

Sniper Model. This was a short-lived variant of the Mark II*, with an optical sight carried in a special mount bolted to the stock. It could also be fitted with a BSA-pattern vernier aperture sight.

MARK III RIFLE
Also known as 'Military Model 1910' or (misleadingly) as the 'Model 1912'
Made by the Ross Rifle Company, Quebec.
Total production: about 400,000 (including British guns). **Chambering:** 303, rimmed. **Action:** locked by multiple lugs on the bolt head engaging the receiver wall as the bolt was pushed forward.
DATA FOR A TYPICAL MK III

50.36in overall, 9.85lb empty. 30.25in barrel, 4-groove rifling; LH, concentric. Integral box magazine, 5 rounds. Folding leaf sight graduated to 1550yd. 2520ft/sec with Mk VII ball ammunition. Sword bayonet.

A Mark II rifle, with a Harris-pattern magazine.

The Mk III Ross rifle.

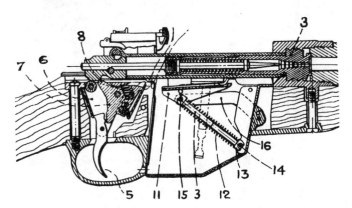

The action of the Mk III Ross rifle.

Approved in the summer of 1911, this was the principal weapon of the Canadian Expeditionary Force in 1914, though guns had only just reached the troops before hostilities began. The Mk III featured a 'triple-thread interrupted screw double-bearing cam bolt head', owing more to Ross's desire to create a suitable action for powerful sporting-rifle cartridges than military desirability.

The new bolt locked vertically instead of horizontally in an attempt to improve the feed stroke, and the substitution of a five-round in-line box magazine for the original Harris platform type was an improvement – particularly as the Mk III could be loaded from a stripper clip. The magazine cut-off and bolt stop were combined in a single small lever on the left side of the receiver bridge.

The unwieldy Mark III Ross was characterized by the protruding magazine housing, shallow pistol grip, and – orignally – by a folding bridge-mounted aperture rear sight.

SIMILAR GUNS

.280 Military Match rifle. Introduced in 1912 for military-style target shooting, this was essentially similar to the Mark III excepting for an internal box magazine and a 26in barrel. Guns of this pattern were unbelievably successful at Camp Perry and Bisley in 1913, US NRA rules being rapidly re-written to exclude them.

Mark IIIB (or '3B') rifle. A modified version of the original Mk III, which was then retrospectively known as the 'IIIA', this was approved in October 1915. It had a simplified rear sight and, apparently, an SMLE-type cut off.

Mk III sniper rifle. Some Ross rifles were retained for sniping, fitted with American 1908 or 1913-model Warner & Swazey sights offset to the left to clear the charger guides. Ironically, these were perhaps the most accurate of all pre-1918 sniper rifles.

SPORTING GUNS

Ross designed his first sporting rifle in 1895-6, the relevant patent being granted in Britain in 1897. The earliest Magazine Sporting Rifles were not particularly successful, though made in Britain and the USA.

1897-TYPE SPORTING RIFLE

This was a straight-pull design with the operating handle at the extreme rear of the receiver, though the principal distinguishing feature – all but invisible externally – was a combination of the sear and the hammer in a hinged sub-assembly. Cam-lugs and helical cam-tracks between the sleeve and the bolt were used to revolve the locking lugs into engagement with the receiver, rotation of the sleeve being prevented by ribs sliding in guideways in the receiver. The rifles had a single-column magazine accepting a clip of four 303 cartridges.

A few guns were made in Hartford, Connecticut, under the supervision of Joseph Bennett (manufacturing was undertaken by Billings & Spencer and Mossberg), while others were made in London by Charles Lancaster. A typical example had a 26in barrel and a straight-wrist butt, though pistol grip patterns were obtainable to order.

1900-TYPE SPORTING RIFLE

Similar in dimensions and performance to the 1897 pattern, this had an improved bolt mechanism with a conventional spring-loaded striker instead of the hinged hammer / sear unit. The action cocked on closing. Externally similar to its predecessor, the 1900 rifle had a 26in barrel and a pistol grip half stock with checkering on the grip and forend. However, perhaps only about 25 guns were made in Hartford before the perfected or 1903 pattern appeared.

1903-TYPE SPORTING RIFLE

Though the earliest guns of this type emanated from Hartford, most were assembled in the new Ross Rifle Company factory in Quebec from parts made largely by sub-contractors in the USA.

Rifles customarily had pistol grip half stocks. The Harris-patent double row magazine was contained within the stock, though the tip of the depressor lever protruded from the top right side of the forend behind the two-leaf rear sight. A magazine cut-off lay on the right side of the stock above the front web of the trigger guard.

Bennett-made Hartford guns were exclusively in 370 caliber, but actions were sent from Canada to be barreled, stocked and finished by Charles Lancaster & Co. of London in chamberings ranging from 256 (6.5mm) Mannlicher to 370 Express. The guns completed in Britain were made largely to individual order, and can vary greatly in configuration.

MILITARY-TYPE SPORTING RIFLES

A few sporting rifles were built in 1906 on military Mk II actions. Their walnut half stocks had short forends with a single encircling barrel band. Many similar guns, of course, were subsequently converted from surplus military rifles – in many cases, long after the First World War had ended. These were often altered on an individual basis, and impossible to catalog on anything other than a generalized basis.

MODEL R SPORTING RIFLE

This appeared in 1907, built on the 1905-pattern action with modified threaded locking lugs. Chambered for 303 cartridges, with a 28in barrel, Model R rifles were little more than military actions in half stocks. An improved five-round internal magazine

A typical 280-caliber M-1910 Ross sporting rifle.

retained a Harris controlled-platform magazine, though the rear sight became an open spring-leaf and elevator pattern.

SIMILAR GUNS

Match Target Rifle. A 280 Ross rifle fired by F.W. Jones created a sensation by winning major prizes at the 1908 Bisley meeting, including the Match Rifle Aggregate. The gun was found to have an overweight barrel, whereupon Jones disqualified himself, but the Ross name had been established. The Match Target was a single shot rifle embodying a modified 1905-type action (with threaded locking lugs), a pistol grip half stock and a floating 30.5in barrel; it was typically 51 long and weighed about 9lb empty. Sights often comprised a vernier-adjustable folding leaf on a mount embedded in the heel of the butt, with a large cross-hair lens unit with a spirit level at the muzzle.

Model E rifle. Also dating from 1907, available in 35 WCF as well as 303, these rifles had a neatly proportioned half-stock with checkering on the pistol grip and forend.

Scotch Deer Stalking Rifle. Alternatively known as the 'High Velocity Sporting Rifle', this was simply a 280 version of the Model E.

RIMFIRE SPORTING RIFLE

Made by the Ross Rifle company, Quebec, 1912-14.

Total production: not known (25,000?). **Chambering:** 22 Long Rifle. **Action:** locked by a pivoting bar beneath the bolt.

40.2in overall, about 5lb empty. 21.5in barrel, 4-groove rifling; RH, concentric. Single shot only. Aperture rear sight. 1050ft/sec with 40-grain bullet.

Made only until the First World War began, this popular little rifle embodied a straight-pull action locked by a bar controlled by an independent release lever. It had a walnut half-stock with a plain pistol grip and a round-tipped forend. The adjustable aperture sight was placed at the extreme rear of the tubular receiver and a safety catch ran through the stock immediately above the trigger.

SIMILAR GUNS

Cadet Rifle. Built on the same action as the 22 sporter, this had a full-length forend and a sleeve-like nosecap carrying a bayonet lug. The front sight had protecting 'wings'.

MODEL R-1910 SPORTING RIFLE

Made by the Ross Rifle Company, Quebec.

Total production: not known. **Chambering options:** 280 Ross, 303 or 35 WCF (see notes). **Action:** locked by multiple lugs on the bolt head engaging the receiver wall as the bolt was pushed forward.

DATA FOR A TYPICAL E-10

Chambering: 280 Ross, rimless. 48.5in overall, 7.35lb empty. 28in barrel, 4-groove rifling; LH, concentric. Integral box magazine, 4 rounds. Folding-leaf sight. 3050ft/sec with 140-grain bullet.

The first R-1910 rifles appeared commercially in 1913. The basic gun (in 303 only) was built on a conventional action, with a protruding magazine case and a 26in barrel. It had a plain pistol grip walnut half-stock and an adjustable spring-leaf and elevator rear sight.

Production of sporting rifles ceased on the outbreak of the First World War in 1914, though assembly apparently continued into 1915. The perfected patterns had enjoyed a brief period in vogue, selling extremely well before the stopping power of their high-velocity lightweight bullets was questioned.

SIMILAR GUNS

E-1910 rifle, 1913-14. Offered only in 303 or 35 WCF, this was an adaptation of the 'R' type, but the pistol grip and forend were checkered. The rear sight was a folding two-leaf Express type.

M-1910 rifle, 1914 only. The 280 M-10 had a 28in barrel and an elegant checkered half-stock with a schnabel-tipped forend. An internal magazine was fitted, resulting in a much smoother outline than its immediate predecessors. The sight was generally a folding leaf on the barrel, though an optional folding aperture pattern could be dovetailed into the receiver bridge. Most Ross sporters carried a sling eye on a barrel collar, protruding behind the forend tip.

• Savage

Details of the history, development and construction of this lever-action rifle will be found in the USA section.

MODEL 1899 RIFLE

Made by the Savage Arms Company, Utica, New York, 1914-15.

Total production: 500? **Chambering:** 303 Savage, rimmed. **Action:** locked by displacing the tail of the breech block upward into the receiver as the operating lever was closed.

49.95in overall, 8.75lb empty. 28in barrel, 6-groove rifling; RH, concentric. Integral rotary box magazine, 5 rounds. Ramp-and-leaf sight graduated to 2000yd. 2180ft/sec with 180-grain bullet. Special knife bayonet.

The commencement of war in August 1914 found Canada with insufficient rifles to mobilize efficiently. Among the many weapons acquired to free service-pattern Ross rifles for the Canadian Expeditionary Force were these lever-action Savages, purchased by leading businessmen in Montreal to arm local militia. The rifle had a full-length forend, military-style sights, a barrel band, and a nose cap with a lug for a knife bayonet with a unique pivoting locking latch beneath the pommel. A cleaning rod protruded beneath the muzzle. It is assumed that the guns served until the end of hostilities, and were then discarded. Very few survivors are known.

CHILE

Chilean firearms can often be identified by a mark adapted from the National Arms. This consists of a star on a horizontally divided shield supported by a *huemal* (Andes deer) and a condor.

• Mannlicher

Substantial quantities of 1888-type 8x50R Austro-Hungarian rifles were purchased from Österreichische Waffenfabriks-Gesellschaft for use against the insurgents in the civil war of 1891-2, but the guns do not seem to have been specially marked.

• Mauser

Adopted to replace a selection of obsolescent Comblain, Winchester and Mannlicher rifles, these Mausers may be identified by chamber crests. A similar mark was often impressed on the side of the butts, and many guns bore 'MAUSER CHILENO' on the left side of the receiver.

MODEL 1895 RIFLE

The first examples of the 7x57 'Fusil Mauser Chileno Mo. 1895' were supplied by Ludwig Loewe, though others came from Deutsche Waffen- und Munitionsfabriken in 1897-1900. They were 48.5in overall, weighed 8.64lb, and had 29.05in barrels rifled with four grooves twisting to the right. Muzzle velocity was 2700ft/sec with standard ball cartridges.

The internal charger-loaded box magazine held five rounds and the tangent-leaf sight was graduated to 2000m (2185yd). The rifles were identical with the Mo. 1893 Spanish Mauser rifle excepting for conventional cylindrical-head bolts, and the tail of the magazine follower was rounded so that the action closed automatically on an empty chamber. An auxiliary shoulder on the receiver behind the bolt handle was intended to act as a last-ditch safety should the action fail on firing.

The stock had a straight wrist, a handguard ran forward from the receiver ring to the barrel band, and the nose cap bore a lug for the Mo. 1895 bayonet. Swivels lay on the band and butt.

SIMILAR GUNS

Model 1895 carbine. The 'Carabina Mauser Chilena Mo. 1895' was only 37.3in long, with a 18.3in barrel, and weighed about 7.5lb. It had a 1400m (1530yd) rear sight, a standard nose cap, and could accept a bayonet. The swivels lay on the left side of the band and on the left side of the butt behind the wrist.

Model 1895 short rifle. The 'Mosqueton Mauser Chileno Mo. 1895' was identical with the rifle, but was merely 41.2in long and had a 1400m rear sight. The bolt handle turned down toward the stock, and slings swivels lay on the left side of the butt and band.

MODEL 1904 RIFLE

The 7x57 Fusil Mauser Chileno Mo. 1904 was supplied only in small numbers by Deutsche Waffen- und Munitionsfabriken in 1904-6. It is believed to have been a standard 1898-pattern export Mauser with a pistol grip stock and a nose cap adapted to take the standard Chilean knife bayonet. Markings would distinguish it from a Brazilian rifle.

MODEL 1912 RIFLE

Made by Österreichische Waffenfabriks-Gesellschaft, Steyr, Austria, 1912-14.

Total production: 20,000? **Chambering:** 7x57, rimless. **Action:** locked by two lugs on the bolt engaging recesses in the receiver behind the chamber as the bolt handle was turned down, and by a supplementary lug on the bolt-handle base engaging its recess.

48.9in overall, 9.06lb empty. 28.95in barrel, 4-groove rifling; RH, concentric. Tangent-leaf sight graduated to 2000m (2185yd). 2700ft/sec with standard ball ammunition. Mo. 1894 sword bayonet.

Supplied in small numbers prior to the First World War, this was a standard 1898-type rifle with a pistol grip butt and an 'H'-type nose cap. A marking disc lay on the side of the butt and 'MOD-ELO 1912' was struck into the metalwork beneath the chamber crest.

SIMILAR GUNS

Model 1912 short rifle. Identified principally by its size – 41.8in long, with a 21.65in barrel – and a rear sight graduated only to 1400m (1530yd), this had the bolt handle turned down toward the stock.

Model 1935 carbine. About five thousand of these 21.45in-barreled guns were purchased from Mauser-Werke AG in 1935. Destined for the Cuerpo dos Carabineros, they had a pistol grip stock with an unusually broad barrel band and an 'H'-type nose cap. The sling fittings lay on the left side of the butt-wrist and barrel band. The bolt handle turned down over a recess on the stock. The guns were about 42in long and weighed 8.6lb. They had 'C.Ch.' serial-number prefixes, and a chamber mark consisting of crossed rifles, 'CHILE', 'ORDEN Y PATRIA' and the designation.

• Remington

About ten thousand Spanish-type Remington rifles were apparently purchased for the Chilean army in the late 1870s. It is assumed that they bore distinctive identifying marks.

• SIG

About fifteen thousand SG 510-4 rifles were purchased in the 1960s from SIG, by way of Beretta. A licence was also acquired to permit FAMAE of Santiago to begin production. Work had scarcely begun, however, when the SG 540 was substituted in 1986. Production is still underway for the Chilean armed forces. Military rifles apparently bear the national Arms on the right side of the receiver – described in detail in the Mauser section – and 'EJER-CITO DE CHILE'.

• Winchester

Substantial quantities of 1886-type 44-40 rifles were purchased by the insurgents in the civil war of 1891-2. Surviving weapons may have been added to the government inventory at the end of hostilities, but none of the guns seem to have been specially marked.

CHINA (EMPIRE)

Chinese ordnance affairs are among the most confusing of all. Not only was China customarily used as a dump for virtually any obsolescent weapon, particularly during the period in which European powers were jostling to influence Imperial affairs, but the ability of the Chinese to copy virtually anything has made cataloging a nightmare. British Enfield rifle-muskets and Snider conversions, French Chassepot and Gras rifles, and even surplus weaponry from the American Civil War have been reported with Chinese marks.

This period was followed by reliance on repeaters such as the US Remington-Lee, Austro-Hungarian Mannlichers and the Gewehr 88, before the Chinese held a competition to find a new infantry rifle in the early 1900s. Competitors included a Mauser, a Mannlicher-Schönauer and a Haenel, all chambered for a 6.8mm round and marked accordingly. The Mauser was victorious, but the revolution of 1911 intervened before much could be done.

• Haenel

An unsuccessful competitor in the trials of 1906-7, this was an improved form of the Gewehr 88. Details of its construction and history are listed under 'Germany'.

1907-TYPE TRIALS RIFLE

Made by C.G. Haenel, Waffenfabrik, Suhl, 1907.

Total production: 250-500? **Chambering:** 6.8x57, rimless. **Action:** locked by two lugs on the bolt head engaging their seats in the receiver as the bolt handle was turned down.

47.95in overall, 8.53lb empty. 27.95in barrel, 4-groove rifling; RH, concentric. Internal charger-loaded box magazine, 5 rounds. Tangent-leaf sight graduated to 2000m (2185yd). Special Haenel sword bayonet.

These guns bore few marks other than 'Mod. 07. Cal. 6,8mm.' on the left side of the action ahead of the clearance cutaway. The Haenel, though serviceable enough, was less efficient than its Mauser rival and is presumed to have been rejected after field trials.

• Mauser

The Chinese sought substantial quantities of weapons in Europe in 1875, eventually ordering 26,000 1871-type rifles from Waffenfabrik Mauser. It is suspected that the German government underwrote the order to ensure a German manufacturer benefited in a time of economic hardship, though, as Mauser's facilities were being used to their limit, the original guns may have been supplied by Österreichische Waffenfabriks-Gesellschaft of Steyr – supplier of more than seventy thousand 1871-pattern Mauser rifles to China, Japan, Honduras, 'Republica Oriental' (Uruguay) and the Transvaal prior to 1885.

THE EARLY GUNS

The 1871-pattern rifles delivered in 1876 bore nothing but the manufacturer's markings and, perhaps, Chinese ideographs. They were identical mechanically with the standard German version (q.v.). Rifles with German military proof and inspectors' marks also served in China, but most of these were purchased early in the twentieth century from military surplus. A few new 1871-type carbines were acquired in the 1870s, followed in 1906 by a thousand German army-surplus examples.

An unknown quantity of 7x57 guns is said to have been ordered by the government from Waffenfabrik Mauser AG about 1896, though the period of delivery is no longer known. The guns seem to have duplicated the 1895-pattern Chilean rifle (q.v.), but may have borne ideographs on the receiver. They were 48.5in overall, weighed 8.64kg empty, and had 29.05in barrels. Their tangent-leaf sights were graduated to 2000m (2185yd) and a variant of the Spanish Mo. 1893-type sword bayonet is said to have been used.

1906-TYPE TRIALS RIFLE

A few 7mm-caliber rifles were purchased from Germany for field trials. They were standard 1898-pattern guns (49.2in overall, 8.55lb empty) with the 1904-type heavyweight cocking piece, a tangent-leaf rear sight, and a handguard stretching forward from the receiver ring to the barrel band. Sling swivels lay beneath the band and on the under-edge of the butt behind the pistol grip. The simple nose cap anchored a short attachment bar, requiring a bayonet with a conventional muzzle ring.

SIMILAR GUNS

Model 1907 rifle. The Chinese acquired a selection of rifles – including a Mauser, a Haenel and a Mannlicher-Schönauer – chambered for a unique 6.8x57 cartridge, similar to the 7mm pattern but with a shallower neck taper. The guns were all clearly marked '6,8MM MOD. 07'. The Mauser won the trials, and Waffenfabrik Mauser and possibly also Deutsche Waffen- und Munitionsfabriken then delivered a few thousand rifles of this type to China. The 1911 revolution intervened before substantial deliveries could be made; enough guns remained in Germany to equip two German infantry regiments during the First World War. However, the Chinese then simply copied the Mauser in the early 1920s.

Model 1907 carbine. This gun had the bolt handle turned downward. Stocked to the muzzle and unable to accept a bayonet, it was about 41in long, had a 21.65in barrel, weighed a little over 8lb, and was sighted to 1400m (1530yd).

• Reichsgewehr

The Chinese were enthusiastic purchasers of the Gewehr 88, sufficient guns being acquired from Loewe and Österreichische Waffenfabriks-Gesellschaft to equip front-line troops in the Sino-Japanese War of 1894. Additional examples were purchased in 1907, once Gewehre 98 had been issued to the German armies, and the post-1916 Hanyang (see 'China [Republic]', below) was little more than a minor variant of the German prototype.

• Remington-Lee

The Chinese acquired substantial quantities of Remington-Lee rifles and carbines in the 1880s, the total being estimated as 8000-10,000. It is probable that the orders were never fulfilled, possibly because of default, as Remington still had 1016 guns 'with Chinese marks' on hand in 1889.

MODEL 1882 RIFLE

Chambered for the 45-70-500 or 43 (11mm Spanish) cartridges, the guns had Diss-pattern magazines. Two notches on the back rib of the magazine allowed the rifle to be used as a single loader, holding the magazine in reserve until given a sharp tap to raise it into the feed position.

The rifles were supplied with 28in or 32in barrels adapted to take a German-made sword or standard Remington socket bayonet interchangeably; this was accomplished simply by cutting the bayonet lug back until it cleared the base of the socket. Chinese ideographs customarily appeared on the receiver ring.

SIMILAR GUNS

Model 1882 carbine. This shared the rifle action, but the barrel measured a mere 20.5in and weight averaged 7.5lb, compared with 8.7-8.9lb for the full-length weapons.

CHINA (REPUBLIC)

The imperial regime was overthrown in 1911, being replaced with a supposedly democractic republic which lasted until itself overthrown by the Communists in 1949. However, there was considerable internal discontent throughout this period – not to mention the bloody war with Japan – and the history of Chinese ordnance remains unclear.

• Arisaka

Large quantities of ex-Japanese Type 99 rifles were altered after 1946 for the 7.9x57 cartridge, which was similar in size and shape to the rimless 7.7x58 Type 99. Work was allegedly undertaken for the 'Nationalist North China Army'. The original barrel was shortened and re-chambered, then replaced in the receiver; the magazine was altered slightly, but little else was done apart from grinding the chamber markings away and refinishing most of the parts.

• Lee-Enfield

At least forty thousand Stevens-Savage No. 4 Mk I* Lee-Enfield rifles were supplied under aid programmes agreed between China and the USA early in the Second World War. It is assumed that they bore appropriate markings.

• Mannlicher

These guns were modified versions of the German Reichsgewehr, substantial quantities being made in the Chinese arsenals prior to the mid 1920s. They lacked the barrel jacket of their German prototype, and generally had a slender stock with a shallow pistol grip.

HANYANG RIFLE

Made by Hanyang arsenal, perhaps with the assistance of other contractors.
Total production: unknown. **Chambering:** 8x57, rimless. **Action:** locked by two lugs on a detachable bolt head engaging recesses in the receiver as the bolt handle was turned down.

49.25in overall, 8.5kg empty 29.25in barrel, 4-groove rifling; RH, concentric. Integral clip-loaded box magazine, 5 rounds. Tangent-leaf sight graduated to 2000m (2185yd). About 2070ft/sec with ball cartridges. Sword bayonet.

The history of these guns, sometimes erroneously known as the Type 88, is far from clear. It is assumed that production began after the 1911 revolution, or, more probably, after the beginning of the First World War cut supplies from Germany. The Hanyang used a copy of the Gewehr 88 action, with a clip-loaded magazine, but lacked the barrel jacket. The forend and handguard had more in common with pre-1914 export Mannlichers, and the bayonet lug lay beneath the nose cap. A swivel usually lay on the sprung rear band. Hanyangs may also be found with a semi-pistol grip stock with little drop at the toe. Like the original straight-wrist patterns, these guns have 8.08mm (.318) bores and chamber M1888 cartridges. Some guns were adapted to use stripper clips, apparently in the 1930s.

• Mauser

MODEL 1907 RIFLE

The first guns of this type were supplied from Mauser and DWM prior to the 1911 revolution (see 'China [Empire]', above). Post-revolutionary copies were made in a factory identified by a mark of two interlocking diamonds, possibly in the early 1920s. The Chinese-made guns lack the finish of the pre-1914 German examples, and are probably made of poorer material.

SIMILAR GUNS

Model 1912 rifle. A few 8x57 guns of this pattern, identical with the Chilean (q.v.) version apart from markings, were supplied by Österreichische Waffenfabriks-Gesellschaft shortly before the First World War began in Europe.

MODEL 21 SHORT RIFLE

This 7.9x57 Mauser is enigmatic, said to have been made by Kwantung arsenal in 1932-7 for the Kuomintang (North China Army). Copied from the FN Mle. 30, it was identifiable by poor quality workmanship and Chinese markings on the receiver. The handguard from the receiver ring to the nose cap distinguished it from the Chiang Kai-Shek rifle. A typical example was 43.6in long, had a 23.6in barrel, and weighed 8.65lb. Its rear sight elevated to 2000m (2185yd).

CHIANG KAI-SHEK SHORT RIFLE

Several million of these copies of the 'Standard Modell' Mauser were made by state arsenals prior to 1949. Work is believed to have begun shortly before the Sino-Japanese war, as some guns have been seen dated '25-11' – November 1935, counting from the revolutionary year of 1911 as '1'. Though displaying a German-style rear sight and handguard, quality was far poorer than a genuine Mauser; stocks were roughly shaped, and a crude groove was cut into the forend. A typical 7.9x57 example – made by the 'double diamond' factory – was about 43.5in long, with a 23.6in barrel, and weighed nearly 9lb; its tangent-leaf sight was graduated to 2000m (2185yd).

SIMILAR GUNS

A few guns of this type, as well as a few based on the Czechoslovakian vz. 24, have been reported with folding bayonets adapted from the Japanese 44th year Arisaka (q.v.) cavalry carbine. It is assumed that these were made in the late 1940s, possibly from parts found in Mukden arsenal, but details are lacking.

OTHER PATTERNS

FN supplied 24,220 Mle. 24 and Mle. 30 7.9mm short rifles in 1930-4, followed by 164,500 more Mle. 30 examples in 1937-9. The Chinese also acquired about seventy thousand Czech-made vz. 98/22 rifles in the 1920s, and then about 100,000 7.92mm vz. 24 (mostly) short rifles in the mid 1930s.

A few Mauser 'Standard Modell' guns followed in 1935-7, with banner marks over the chamber and 'B'-prefix numbers. Some of these have stocks with grasping grooves in the forend, with conventionally mounted swivels beneath the butt and band; others – perhaps later – have plain forends and standard German-style slot and bar sling fittings. Short rifles predominated, but a few carbines were also supplied.

CHINA (PRC)

• ArmaLite (Norinco)

The China North Industries Corporation (Norinco) has made a few M16A1 copies as the 'Type CQ' or Model 311, the latter being a semi-automatic sporter. The guns are immediately recognizable by their curved pistol grip, with moulded-in decoration, and the humped under-edge of the gray butt.

• Kalashnikov

TYPE 56 ASSAULT RIFLE

Made by State Factory 66, 1956-73; and an unknown factory under Norinco control.

The Type 56 (Kalashnikov) carbine.
This particular gun lacks its bayonet.

Total production: 15-20 million, 1973 to date? **Chambering:** 7.62x39, rimless. **Action:** locked by rotating lugs on the bolt head into engagement with the receiver; gas operated, selective fire.

DATA FOR A TYPICAL TYPE 56

34.25in overall, 9.81lb with empty magazine. 16.35in barrel, 4-groove rifling; RH, concentric. Detachable box magazine, 30 rounds. Tangent-leaf sight graduated to 800m (875yd). 2330ft/sec with M43 ball cartridges; 775±50rpm. Type 56 folding bayonet.

The People's Republic was an early convert to the Kalashnikov, beginning production in the late 1950s. The standard Type 56 originally had wooden furniture and a machined steel receiver, with a knife-blade bayonet attached to a block beneath the muzzle.

A triangular-blade bayonet replaced the shorter knife pattern about 1959, though the method of attachment remained the same. In the mid 1960s, however, production was switched to a stamped-sheet AKM-type receiver without altering the basic designation. Bolt covers were usually plain-surface AK-pattern instead of the ribbed version associated with the Soviet-made AKM. Chinese rifles still bore standard ideographs on the selector, though export patterns were usually marked 'L' and 'D'. Furniture remained wooden, pistol grips being plain, and the triangular bayonet was retained. Machining marks were usually very evident, minor parts were often very crudely made, fitting was sloppy, and a curious semi-matte finish was adopted.

Production apparently switched about 1973 from Factory 66 to a plant run under the supervision of the North Chinese Industries Corporation; these guns are often marked 'M22' and have 'N'-prefix serial numbers. Quality of Norinco Kalashnikovs is noticeably better than Factory 66's military output.

SIMILAR GUNS

NM-47. Distinguishing a heavy-barrel version of the basic Norinco-made Type 56-1, this has been used in North America though its status remains uncertain

Type 56-1. This had a squared 'U'-section butt, with an open 'U'-shape shoulder piece and two rivets each side. The Chinese-ideograph selector markings were most distinctive, as was the '66-in-triangle' factory mark on the left side of the receiver ahead of the designation (e.g., 56-1 --) and the serial number. The folding butt of the post-1965 Type 56-1 displayed two spot welds on each side, behind the pivot, and a swivel was often found on the top edge of the butt instead of the left side.

Type 56-2. Introduced in the mid 1970s, this variant had a metal skeleton stock folding to the right against the receiver-side. A reddish-brown plastic cheekpiece was the principal distinguishing characteristic. Some guns of this type have been seen with a tubular butt, apparently inspired by the FNC; it is assumed that these date from the 1980s, but information is lacking.

Type 56-5. This designation has been applied to Norinco-made guns restricted to semi-automatic fire.

Type 81. Dating from 1981, this adaptation of the AK-74 chambered the 5.45x39 cartridge. Made with fixed or folding butts, the guns were otherwise very similar to the then-current Types 56 and 56-1. (Note: a derivative of the Type 63 rifle, described below, seems to have been offered as the 'Type 81 semi-automatic carbine'. The Kalashnikov is regarded as the 'Type 81 submachine gun', a distinction carried over from the Type 56 patterns.)

Type 84. Introduced commercially in 1985 for the 5.56x45 cartridge, this has a barrel rifled with six grooves but is otherwise similar to the Type 81. Fixed and folding-butt guns have been reported, apparently designated Type 84 and Type 84-1 respectively.

Type 86. A bullpup adaptation of the Type 81/Type 84 series was announced under this designation in the late 1980s, but it is doubtful if series production has ever been undertaken: few have been seen in the West.

• Mosin-Nagant

The People's Republic made Mosin-Nagant Type 53 carbines. They are virtually identical with the Soviet obr. 1944g, but were marked '53 --' on the receiver and often bore the encircled-triangle mark of Factory 66. Production ceased in favor of SKS and AK copies in the late 1950s.

• Simonov

TYPE 56 RIFLE

Made by Factory 26 and Factory 138.

Total production: in excess of five million? **Chambering:** 7.62x39, rimless. **Action:** locked by tilting the tail of the bolt downward into the receiver; gas operated, semi-automatic only.

44.15in overall, 8.5lb empty. 20.45in barrel, 4-groove rifling; RH, concentric. Integral charger-loaded box magazine, 10 rounds. Tangent-leaf sight graduated to 1000m (1095yd). 2410ft/sec with Soviet Type PS ball cartridges. Integral folding bayonet.

Though differing in detail, the Chinese SKS shared the general characteristics of its Soviet prototype (q.v.). The earliest guns were generally made of blued steel and had knife-bladed bayonets. Their safety heads were fluted or sometimes checkered.

Later examples had triangular-blade bayonets, apparently to rationalize production with the Type 56-1 (Kalashnikov); guns made by Factory 26 were generally quite good quality, but the products of Factory 138 often had investment-cast receivers and presented a decidedly inferior appearance.

Virtually all displayed the factory mark and designation on the left side of the receiver, accompanied by a serial number, seemingly sequential, that sometimes ran to seven digits. Production in Factories 26 and 138 alone, on the basis of serial numbers, could have exceeded 22 million; given the enormous size of the Chinese militia, this is not beyond the realms of probability. However, it is suspected that other guns – e.g., the Type 56-1 Kalashnikov – may have been included in the same series.

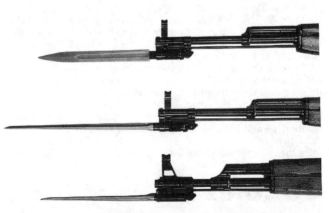

A comparison of the folding bayonets of the Soviet SKS (top), the Chinese Type 56 Simonov rifle (center), and the Chinese Type 56-1 Kalashnikov carbine (bottom).

The Type 56 (Simonov) rifle. Note the folding bayonet.

The Type 68 rifle.

SIMILAR GUNS

Type 84. An improved 7.62mm 'Type 84' SKS with a twenty-round Kalashnikov-type magazine was advertised in the mid 1980s, accompanied by a 5.56x45 export version designated 'Type EM3611'.

• State designs

Little is known about the genesis of these unusual rifles which, though sharing the lines of the SKS (Simonov) carbine, embody a rotating bolt and a gas system adapted from the Kalashnikov. At least part of the design work has been credited to Tang Wen-Li, but several differing patterns have been reported and the information given below should still be treated with caution.

TYPE 63 RIFLE

Made by State Factory No. 90?

Total production: unknown. **Chambering:** 7.62x39, rimless. **Action:** locked by rotating lugs on the bolt into the barrel extension; gas operated, semi-automatic only.

40.75in overall, 7.65lb without magazine. 20.45in barrel, 4-groove rifling; RH, concentric. Detachable box magazine, 15 rounds. Tangent-leaf sight graduated to 1000m (1095yd). 2410ft/sec with Soviet M43 cartridges; 750±25 rpm. Integral knife bayonet.

Adopted in 1963, this rifle had a conventional appearance, with a crudely shaped hardwood stock and a bayonet which pivoted back on a block on the muzzle (behind the sight) to lie under the forend. Oddly, the magazine could be loaded through the top of the open action, suitable stripper-clip guides being milled into the rear edge of the ejection port.

Series production of the original Type 63 rifle began in 1965, several million being made. They were distinguished by machined-steel receivers. It is suspected, owing to the curious magazine arrangements and the absence of a grenade launching capability, that the Type 63 was intended for the people's militia rather than the regular forces for whom the 7.62mm Type 56 and 5.45mm Type 84 (Kalashnikov) assault rifles remained standard.

SIMILAR GUNS

Type 68. Introduced in 1969, this had a stamped receiver, minor changes in the action, and a synthetic handguard.

Type 73. This differed from its predecessors primarily in the addition of a fully automatic capability and the substitution of the standard AK-type thirty-round magazine for the smaller pattern of the earlier Types 63 and 68.

Type 81. Dating from 1983, this variant of the Type 73 – apparently for commercial sale – had a three-round burst firing capability instead of the fully automatic setting.

Type 81-1. Identical mechanically with the standard Type 81, this was distinguished by its folding butt. (Note: the 'Type 81' designation has also been applied to a modernized variant of the standard Type 56 carbine [SKS]. The confusion has probably arisen from the external affinity of the Type 63 and its successors with the original Type 56.)

COLOMBIA

Colombian-issue guns bore either 'Ejercito de Colombia' or the national crest on the chamber top. Surmounted by a condor and set on two pairs of national flags, the shield contained a pome-granate and two cornucopiae above a Liberty Cap, two sailing ships and a depiction of the isthmus of Panama.

• Mauser

Small numbers of Loewe-made 7.65x53 Mo. 1891 (Argentine pattern) and 7x57 DWM-made 'Mo. 1904' rifles were acquired, the latter being identical with the Brazilian guns of the same year. Ordered from Österreichische Waffenfabriks-Gesellschaft shortly before the outbreak of the First World War, the 7x57 Mo. 1912 was identical with the Mexican pattern (q.v.). Hostilities began before work was completed, the guns being diverted to the Austro-Hungarian army.

About five thousand Czech 'vz. 12 mex.' 7mm short rifles with 21.9in barrels were acquired in 1929, followed by a few 7x57 Mo. 1929 short rifles from Steyr-Solothurn AG. Sizable quantities of Mle. 24/30 short rifles came from Fabrique Nationale in the early 1930s, plus some similar vz. 24 guns from Ceskoslovenská Zbrojovka.

Many of the Herstal- and Brno-made weapons were converted to 30-06 in the early 1950s, when FN supplied an unknown number of new 'Mo. 1950' rifles chambered for the American cartridge. A typical 30-06 rifle – 43in overall, with a 22.75in barrel – displayed a large '.30' on top of the receiver bridge, with 'R. FAMAGUE' and the date (e.g., '1953') on the left side of the receiver. The marks showed that it was converted ('Reformado') by Fabrica de Material de Guerra in Bogota. The chamber mark is usually accompanied by 'COLOMBIA' and 'FUERZA MILITARES'.

CONFEDERATE STATES OF AMERICA

The life of the Confederacy was brief, confined, indeed, to the period of the American Civil War (1861-5). The Confederate ordnance lacked the resources of its Federal counterpart, which could call on virtually all of the gunmaking districts of the USA. Consequently, the quantities of breechloaders made in the Southern states breechloaders were pitifully small.

Most of the guns purchased in Europe were muzzle-loaders, but there were also substantial numbers of British-made Terry (q.v.) carbines and a few French Perrin revolver-rifles.

• Bilharz & Hall Carbines

Made by Bilharz, Hall & Co. – sometimes listed as 'Bilharz, Hull & Co.' – of Pittsylvania, Virginia. Production amounted to only about a hundred rising-block 54 caplock breechloaders with 21in browned barrels. Generally marked 'P' over 'CS' on the frame and the breechblock, they were operated by swinging the combined underlever/trigger guard downward. Several types of lever-locking catch are known. A sling ring and bar were fitted to the left side of the frame beneath the breech. The butt and forend were made of walnut, the single barrel band was usually brass (though iron examples are known), and the back-action lock had a hammer with a short straight shank.

• Le Mat Revolver Carbines

Made in small numbers, apparently in Belgium. A nine-shot capped cylinder fed the 42-caliber part-octagonal/part round upper barrel, but a selector on the hammer nose allowed a single charge of shot to be fired through the 63-caliber smooth-bore barrel doubling as the cylinder axis pin. These weapons were patented in 1856-9 by a French-American physician, Jean François Alexandre Le Mat, a colonel in the Louisiana militia. Prototypes were made by Krider of Philadelphia. However, excepting a few hundred guns made in New Orleans prior to the Civil War and a few guns made in Britain in 1861, the bulk of production was undertaken elsewhere – apparently in Liége by A. Francotte & Cie. A typical carbine was 38.3in long and weighed about 7.7lb.

• Morse Carbines
Based on the experimental breechloading conversions of the 1850s (see 'USA'), though made for the Confederate ordnance in a very different form. They could be identified by the extensive use of brass, which included the massive frame, the finger-rest trigger guard, the buttplate and the nose cap. The top lever was hinged at the rear of the frame, which had a detachable plate on the right side. The cocking spur was mounted centrally, and the rear sight was a simple standing block. The guns often have decorative 'tiger stripe' butts and forends. About a thousand 50-caliber examples with 20in barrels were made under the inventor's personal supervision in the State Military Works in Greenville, South Carolina, but only the last few bore the Morse name. Though the guns were reasonably easy to make, the special metal-case ammunition taxed production facilities to the full.

• Read Carbines
The work of Keen, Walker & Co. of Danville, Virginia. About 275 of these 54-caliber breechloaders of this type were made in accordance with a patent granted in March 1863 to Nathan Read. The tipping breech was operated by an underlever combined with the trigger guard. The guns had a 22.5in barrel, a brass frame, and a combless walnut butt similar in appearance to the Maynard type (see 'USA'). The hammer was pivoted inside the frame, but was offset to the right to allow the fixed sights to be used. A sling bar and ring lay on the left side of the breech, and the buttplate was made of iron.

• Robinson Carbines
Copies of the dropping-block Sharps. Several thousand were made in 1864 by the S.C. Robinson Arms Manufactory of Richmond, Virginia; the factory was then evacuated to Tallahassee in the face of the Union advance, but production of the carbines may never have recommenced. The 52in-caliber Robinson carbines were usually dated as well as numbered. They had 21in barrels, weighed about 7.5lb, and were close copies of the Sharps carbines externally – though individual components differed greatly in detail. The buttplate and bands were brass, and a bar-and-ring assembly was fixed to the left side of the breech.

• Tarpley Carbines
Made by Tarpley, Garrett & Co. of Greensboro, North Carolina, in accordance with a Confederate patent granted in February 1863 to Jere H. Tarpley. Another of the tipping-breech designs, the 52-caliber guns had 23in round barrels, iron mounts, and weighed about 6.9lb empty. Producton was apparently confined to 1863-4.

CONGO FREE STATE

• Mauser
According to Korn's book *Mauser-Gewehre und Mauser-Patente* (1908), Mauser supplied 7.65x53 1894-type rifles to arm the European elements of the army of this Belgian-sponsored state. It is not yet known which of the rifle-makers was responsible, nor if distinctive markings were applied.

COSTA RICA

The Costa Rican Arms consisted of a shield depicting nine stars, above an isthmus of three volcanoes separating two sailing ships. This does not seem to have been applied to the Mausers, however, and so it is assumed that the orders were too small or too sporadic to be considered as 'contract patterns'.

• Mauser
MODEL 1895 RIFLE
This virtual duplicate of the 1895-type Chilean rifle was purchased from Ludwig Loewe & Co. (1895-6) and then Deutsche Waffen- und Munitionsfabriken (about 1897-1900). The quantities involved were small – perhaps no more than ten thousand – and survivors are rarely encountered.

MODEL 1910 RIFLE
Made by Waffenfabrik Mauser AG of Oberndorf am Neckar in 1911-14 and chambered for the 7x57 rimless cartridge, it was 48.8in overall, had a 29.15in barrel and weighed about 8.75lb. Virtually identical with the Gew. 98, the guns had 2000m (2185yd) tangent-leaf sights and standard 'export' stock arrangements with a hand-guard running forward from the receiver ring to the band. The simple nose cap had a bayonet lug on its underside.

The most obvious feature, however, was the shrouded bolt-face enveloping the case rim, patented in Germany in February 1898 but rarely used on service weapons. The face of the chamber had a recess for the extractor, necessitating precise machining and reassembly after repair. Altering the bolt forced Mauser to omit the small lug on the bolt-edge that supported the cartridge case during the feed stroke and extraction.

OTHER PATTERNS
FN supplied some 7x57 Mle. 24 short rifles in the 1930s. They had standard pistol grip stocks, and a 'H'-type nose cap with a short bayonet lug. Bolt handles were generally straight. The guns were about 43.3in long, had 22.5in barrels and weighed about 8lb; they were sighted to 2000m (2185yd).

CUBA

A variety of firearms was acquired after independence from Spain had been declared as a result of the Spanish-American War. These were used to arm the Guardia Rurales, an armed gendarmerie which operated until the Cuban army was formed in 1909.

• Krag-Jørgensen
The Cuban army received a selection of about nine thousand US Army-surplus 30-40 Krag carbines in 1912. These replaced the assorted Winchester and Lee patterns which had been serving the Guardia Rurales.

• Remington-LEE
About three thousand 1899-pattern rifles and carbines were purchased in 1905-7 to arm the Guardia Rurales. Chambering the 30-40 Krag cartridge, the rifles had 29.5in barrels, accepted detachable magazines, and could be fitted with a standard Remington knife or sword bayonet. They were about 49.5in overall and weighed about 8.5lb. Some guns have been reported with a shield bearing the national arms above the chamber, but this does not seem to have been common to all of them. The Remington-Lee carbines, which outnumbered the rifles by about two to one, had half-stocks and did not accept bayonets. They had 20in barrels, were about 39.5in long, and weighed 7.5lb.

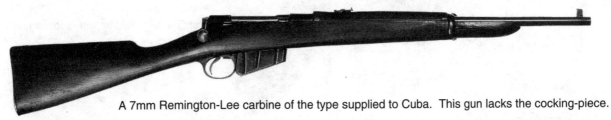

A 7mm Remington-Lee carbine of the type supplied to Cuba. This gun lacks the cocking-piece.

• Winchester

It has been claimed that about ten thousand 1895-type 30-40 lever action rifles were purchased for the Guardia Rurales in 1906. Rapidly displaced by Krag-Jørgensens, they were sold out of service in 1914. They had apparently been acquired by the US Army for service in the Philippines soon after the Spanish-American War, but had never been issued.

CZECHOSLOVAKIA

Guns used by the Czechoslovakian forces were distinguished by a distinctive crowned twin-tailed Lion of Bohemia with a shield on its breast. They may also show 'CSK' or 'CSZ' for Ceskoslovenská ('Czechoslovakia') and Ceskoslovenská Státni Zbrojovky ('Czechoslovakian state factory'). The export weapons usually bore the marks of Ceskoslovenská Zbrojovka of Brno.

Czechoslovakia seized independence from Austria-Hungary at the end of the First World War, gaining the nucleus of an efficient arms industry – in the form of the Skoda company – and many Austro-Hungarian, German and Russian rifles. A factory was subsequently created in Brno to make Mausers, equipped with Austro-Hungarian or German machinery supplied as war reparations.

The Mauser-type bolt-action rifles – made in vast numbers between the wars – are covered in the 'Mauser (CSZ, ZB)' section below. The earliest autoloaders included the Netzsch and the Praga, which owed more to light machine gun design and are not included here. However, lighter guns were developed by Karel Krnka from designs which had originated in the early twentieth century; his 'K' rifle of the mid 1920s became the CZ HB, after work credited to Benes, then the 'Model S' rifle and finally the vz. 39, which was extensively tested against the Holek (q.v.) designs before eventually becoming the vz. 39; it was provisionally adopted in 1939, but German occupation – first the Sudetenland, and then the entire country prior to the Second World War – brought progress to a standstill.

The arms industry was rebuilt after 1945 on the basis of the work of some talented designers. Uniquely, among the constituents of the Warsaw Pact, Czechoslovakia managed to retain independence of thought, issuing the vz. 58 assault rifle when all the other armies were carrying Kalashnikovs. Recent political changes have led to the concentration of the former Czechoslovakian state-owned gunmaking facilities in the Czech Republic, and it is suspected that this change will be accompanied by greater commercial activity.

• Ceská Zbrojovka, auto-loading type

A selection of guns of this type has been developed since the 1920s, beginning with the Krnka-designed 'K' rifle and progressing to the latest LADA series. A few guns of uncertain attribution are listed below, but others are considered under the names of the principal designers: e.g., 'Kratochvil'.

'HB' AUTOMATIC RIFLE

Credited to Eduard Benes, this was designed to compete with the 'K'-type (Krnka) rifle promoted by the Brno organisation. The first trials were undertaken in 1927.

MODEL 'S' AUTOMATIC RIFLE

Developed from the 'HB' pattern in 1929, at least ten of these were made in 7.92x57. They were gas-operated and were appar-

A Czech soldier with the Model 58 assault rifle fitted with an infra-red sight.

ently locked by tilting the breechblock downward into the receiver floor. The gas tube and piston assembly lay beneath the barrel; the tangent-leaf sight lay on the top of the one-piece forend/hand-guard unit; stripper-clip guides were machined in the edge of the receiver immediately behind the feed way; and a large detachable box magazine was fitted.

The charging handle lay on the right side of the receiver above the magazine. The short sheet-metal fore-guard had three ventilation slots. Swivels lay beneath the butt and band. The barrel, forend and upper receiver, pivoted to the butt and standing frame, could be tipped downward once a plug at the rear of the frame had been turned to release them. A combined safety lever and selector was set into the right side of the butt behind the magazine.

SIMILAR GUNS

CZ 35. This was a refinement of the 'S' pattern, with a better stock and an additional retaining band around the forend. The receiver was noticeably rounded, and the catch on the rear of the receiver was altered. Thirty or more were made in 7.92x57.

MODEL 38 AUTOMATIC RIFLE
Samocinná puska CZ 38

Credited to Vaclav Polanka and Jan Kratochvil, this was based on the CZ 35. The half-stock had a separate wooden forend with a ventilated barrel guard and a sheet-metal extension reaching to the gas-port assembly. The detachable box magazine held ten rounds, and the safety catch was moved to the rear of the receiver. A distinctive strap-and-clamp attachment was fitted to the right side of the butt; swivels were to be found on the left side of the butt-wrist and the forend cap band; and the rear sight lay immediately behind the stripper-clip guides on the top of the receiver.

The CZ 38 was provisionally adopted as the vz. 39, presumably to enable large-scale field trials to be undertaken, but the German occupation of Czechoslovakia brought work to an end. Surviving rifles were pressed into emergency Wehrmacht service at the end of the Second World War.

The Model 58V assault rifle, with a folding butt.

The CZ 511 rimfire auto-loading rifle, with the original straight-comb butt.

The CZ 611 rimfire sporter.

MODEL 2000 ASSAULT RIFLE
Formerly known as LADA
Made by Ceská Zbrojovka, Uhersky Brod.

Currently in production. **Chambering:** 5.56x45, rimless. **Action:** locked by rotating lugs on the bolt into the receiver; gas operated, selective fire.

33.45in overall (24.2in with butt folded), 7lb with empty magazine. 15.05in barrel, 6-groove rifling; RH, concentric. Detachable box magazine, 30 rounds. Tangent-leaf rear sight graduated to 800m (875yd). 2985ft/sec with standard 62-grain bullet; 800±50rpm.

Optional knife bayonet.

Development of this weapon began in the Prototypa design bureau in 1983, under the supervision of Jiri Klecec. The original pattern is said to have incorporated a tilting-block locking system adapted from the vz. 24 machine gun, but the experimental guns field-tested in 1989-90, derived from the AK-74, had a rotating bolt. Work on the SRAZ project – soon renamed LADA – was completed in the mid 1990s in the Ceská Zbrojovka factory, when a decision was taken to concentrate on 5.56x45 and the 5.45x39 version was abandoned. The guns were renamed 'CZ 2000' in 1997, but their future is currently uncertain.

The assault rifle can also be configured as a carbine or a light machine gun. The butt folds by pressing a catch on the left side and swinging it forward along the right side of the receiver. The action is derived from the Kalashnikov, and has a modified AKM-type breech cover locked in place by a cross-pin. A four-position selector on the left side of the receiver is marked '30' for automatic fire, '3' for a burst, '0' for safe and '1' for single shots; the bursts are controlled by a pawl and ratchet unit. The pistol grip, forend and barrel guard are all made of fiberglass-reinforced styrene foam, and the rear sight has two sturdy steel-wire protectors.

SIMILAR GUNS
LADA carbine. This is a shortened version of the assault rifle, with a conical flash-hider / muzzle brake instead of the longer slotted type associated with the rifle and light machine gun. The carbine is 26.6in long (17.1in with the butt folded), has a 7.3in barrel, and weighs 6.1lb with an empty magazine.

• Ceská Zbrojovka, bolt-action type

Once best known as the principal Czechoslovakian manufacturer of handguns, CZ has also made sporting guns in the Uhersky Brod factory. This resulted from a reorganisation of the state-run firearms industry in the 1960s, freeing the Brno facilities to concentrate on other things. Consequently, many guns once identified under the 'Brno' name are currently being marketed under the CZ banner. See also 'Koucky' for details of pre-1960 designs which are still being made by CZ, and 'Mauser' for details of the earliest military rifles.

CZ 452-2E SPORTING RIFLE
Made by Ceská Zbrojovka, Uhersky Brod.

Currently in production. **Chambering options:** 22 Long Rifle and 22 Winchester Magnum rimfire. **Action:** locked by the bolt-handle base entering its seat as the bolt handle is turned down.

DATA FOR A TYPICAL CZ 452-2E

42.65in overall, 6.61lb empty. 24.8in barrel, 4-groove rifling; RH, concentric. Detachable box magazine, 5 or 10 rounds. Tangent-leaf rear sight graduated to 200m (220yd). 1050ft/sec with standard ball ammunition.

This is a modernized version of the ZKM 452 (see 'Koucky', below), though the differences are comparatively minor. The standard gun has a lacquered beechwood half-stock with a hog's back comb, lacking checkering, and the slender forend has a schnabel tip. Swivels lie beneath the butt and forend. Metalwork is customarily blued. The safety catch lies on top of the cocking piece, the trigger guard remains a stamped strip, a single shot adaptor can replace the magazine when necessary, and muzzle can be threaded to accept sound moderators.

SIMILAR GUNS
CZ 452-2E Lux. Mechanically identical with the standard version, this has polished blue metalwork and a walnut stock with checkering on the pistol grip.

CZ 452-2E Style. This is distinguished by a black synthetic half-stock with an overall roughened texture instead of checkering. The barrel, receiver, trigger guard and magazine are plated with nickel.

CZ 452-2E Special. A minor variant of the Lux, this has a beech stock with a checkered pistol grip.

CZ 452-2E Junior. Easily identified by its greatly shortened butt and barrel, this was specially developed for children. Offered in either of the regular chamberings, it is merely 32.15in long, has a 16.2in barrel and weighs about 4lb. The rear sight is usually a simple spring-leaf and elevator pattern.

CZ 453 Standard. This is a short-barreled version of the basic 452-2E rifle – only offered in 22 LR rimfire – with a rocking 'L' sight, a straight-comb butt suited to optical sights, and a greatly simplified trigger mechanism. The muzzle may be threaded to

The CZ 550 Standard rifle.

accept a sound moderator. The plain half-stock is beech. Overall length is 40.75in, the barrel measures 22.45in, and weight averages 6.2lb.

CZ 453 Lux. Distinguished by a walnut stock with checkering on the pistol grip, this is otherwise identical with the standard 453-type rifle.

CZ 513 Farmer. This is a short-barreled version of the CZ 453, sharing the simple trigger system. It has a plain beech half-stock with a rounded forend tip, and a spring-leaf and elevator rear sight. The plain hog's back comb lacks checkering. Made only for the 22 LR rimfire cartridge, often with the muzzle threaded for a sound moderator, the Farmer is 38.95in long and weighs about 6.1lb; the barrel contributes 20.85in of the overall length.

CZ 527 SPORTING RIFLE
Also known as the 'Fox'
Made by Ceská Zbrojovka, Uhersky Brod.
Currently in production. **Chambering options:** 22 Hornet, 222 Remington or 223 Remington. **Action:** locked by a two lugs on the bolt head engaging recesses in the receiver as the bolt handle was turned down, and by the bolt-handle base entering its seat.
DATA FOR A TYPICAL 222 EXAMPLE
42.4in overall, 6.17lb empty. 23.6in barrel, 4-groove rifling; RH, concentric. Detachable box magazine, 5 rounds. Standing block rear sight. 3180ft/sec with 50-grain bullet.

Introduced about 1990, this is an improved form of the ZKM 465 with a 'Mauser-type' forward-locking bolt and a claw extractor. A double trigger mechanism embodying a setting element was fitted, the rear sight was adjustable, and a radial safety lever appeared on the right side of the receiver behind the bolt handle. The standard gun had a beechwood half-stock, with swivels beneath the butt and forend. The box magazine was set in a housing formed by a continuation of the trigger guard and the receiver-top was formed to accept optical-sight mounts.

SIMILAR GUNS

CZ 527 Lux. This differed from the standard rifle only in the design of the stock, which was made from walnut and had a hog's back comb and a cheekpiece. The pistol grip and forend were checkered.

CZ 527 FS. A full-stocked version of the basic pattern, this had a 20.45in barrel. Overall length was merely 38.45in, weight averaging 5.95lb.

CZ 537 SPORTING RIFLE
Made by Ceská Zbrojovka, Uhersky Brod.
Production total: not known, but belived to have been small. **Chambering options:** 270 Winchester, 30-06 or 308 Winchester. **Action:** locked by two lugs on the bolt head engaging recesses in the receiver as the bolt handle was turned down.
DATA FOR A TYPICAL 270 EXAMPLE
44.75in overall, 7.63lb empty. 23.6in barrel, 4-groove rifling; RH, concentric? Detachable box magazine, 5 rounds. Adjustable rear sight. 3165ft/sec with 130-grain bullet.

This was a large-caliber version of the CZ 527, introduced in 1991, with a forged one-piece bolt and a single trigger incorporating a set element. A cocking indicator was also fitted. The walnut half stock had a checkered pistol grip and forend, and a sturdy recoil pad was fitted. Sling swivels lay beneath the butt and barrel. The CZ 537 was rapidly replaced by the CZ 550 (q.v.), and is rarely seen.

SIMILAR GUNS

CZ 537 Sniper. This was a variant of the standard rifle with a plain wooden half stock and a heavy large-diameter barrel. An optical sight and a bipod were normally fitted.

CZ 550 SPORTING RIFLE
Made by Ceská Zbrojovka, Uhersky Brod.
Currently in production. **Chambering options:** see text, below. **Action:** locked by two lugs on the bolt head engaging recesses in the receiver as the bolt handle was turned down.
DATA FOR A TYPICAL CZ 550 STANDARD EXAMPLE
Chambering: 9.3x62, rimless. 44.7in overall, 7.28lb empty. 23.6in barrel, 4-groove rifling; RH, concentric? Integral box magazine, 5 rounds. Fixed open-notch rear sight. 2280ft/sec with 285-grain bullet.

Readily identified by its long cocking-piece shroud, with a notable taper, this rifle is basically a much-modified Mauser with a traditional sprung-claw extractor. A two-position safety lever appears behind the bolt handle, though a three-position alternative (which allows the bolt to be opened with the safety applied) can be supplied to order. The three-position safety has an additional white dot on the cocking-piece shroud. The single trigger can be set simply by pushing it forward. The tip of the firing pin doubles as a cocking indicator, and a radial catch on the left rear of the receiver – the cocking-piece being cut away appropriately – releases the bolt from the bolt way. A press-button on the left side of the cocking-piece shroud can be used in conjunction with the trigger or the bolt handle to release the sear and lock the striker, which simplifies dismantling.

The 'Standard' rifle has a straight-comb walnut half stock with checkering on the pistol grip and the round-tipped forend. Swivels lie beneath the forend and the butt, fixed or detachable magazines can be obtained, and the rear sight (when fitted) is a simple open block. Mounting bases for optical sights can be fitted on rails above the chamber and the receiver bridge, though a cylindrical receiver or a proprietary Magnum Research flat-top pattern can be obtained on request. The optional receivers are drilled and tapped for sight-mount bases. Standard chamberings are currently 6.5x55, 270 Winchester, 7x57, 7x64, 30-06 or 9.3x62 (internal magazine), and 243 Winchester or 308 Winchester (detachable magazine).

SIMILAR GUNS

CZ 550 Battue. Intended for shooting at driven game, this is basically a 550 Lux (q.v.) with a 20.45in barrel and the rear sight set into a quarter-length ramp. Guns can be supplied in all the regular chamberings, with internal or detachable magazines.

CZ 550 Battue FS. This is simply a 550 Battue with a full-length stock.

CZ 550 FS. Sharing the Bavarian-style butt with the Lux version, this has a full-length stock and a 20.45in barrel; overall length is about 41.55in, though weight remains unchanged. Chamberings are identical with the CZ 550 Standard.

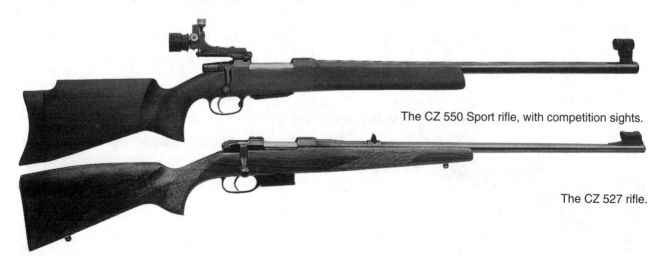

The CZ 550 Sport rifle, with competition sights.

The CZ 527 rifle.

CZ 550 Lux. The deluxe version of the standard rifle, offered in the same chamberings, this has a Bavarian-style walnut half stock with a low hog's back comb and a squared cheekpiece. The forend tip is rounded rather than a schnabel form. A ventilated rubber buttplate is customary.

CZ 550 Magnum. Similar to the Standard pattern, but with a long action, this may be chambered for 7mm Remington Magnum, 300 Winchester Magnum, 375 H&H Magnum, 416 Remington Magnum, 458 Winchester Magnum cartridges. The rifles are typically 46.45in long, have 25in barrels, and weigh 9.25lb; their rear sights – graduated to 300m (330yd) – have a standing block and two folding leaves.

CZ 550 Magnum Lux. Identical mechanically with the Magnum, this has the deluxe Bavarian-style stock.

CZ 550 MC. This is a minor variant of the 550 Standard with a Monte Carlo comb, a rounded cheekpiece and a ventilated rubber buttplate.

CZ 550 Minnesota. Intended specifically for the North American market, supplied in all the CZ 550 Standard chamberings, this has a checkered walnut half-stock with a ventilated rubber buttplate and less drop at the heel than the other guns in the 550 series. This suits it specifically to optical sights, and no open sights are fitted.

CZ 550 Sport. Readily distinguishable by its stippled target-style stock, with a high comb, an adjustable buttplate, an extended pistol grip and a deep forend, the 550 Sport also has a heavy barrel. Sights comprise an Anschütz micro-adjustable aperture pattern on an adaptor attached to the receiver bridge and a replaceable-element tunnel at the muzzle. Available only in 308 Winchester, the CZ 550 Sport is about 45.3in long, has a 25.6in barrel, and weighs 10.35lb with its sights. Box-magazine feed is standard, though a single shot adaptor can be obtained. An adjustable comb and an accessory rail can be fitted on request.

CZ 700 SNIPER RIFLE
Odstrelovacská puska CZ 700 Sniper
Made by Ceská Zbrojovka, Uhersky Brod.
Currently in production. **Chambering:** 308 Winchester. **Action:** locked by two rows of three lugs on the bolt engaging recesses in the receiver bridge as the bolt handle was turned down.

48.45in overall (with flash suppressor), 13.67lb with sight and bipod. 25.6in barrel, 4-groove rifling; RH, concentric? Detachable box magazine, 10 rounds. Optical sight. 2970ft/sec with 150-grain bullet.

This purpose-built sniping weapon, a replacement for the short-lived CZ 537 (q.v.), abandons the Mauser bolt for an unusual rear-locking multi-lug pattern suited to the exchangeable-barrel concept. The butt of the laminated half stock has an elevating comb and an adjustable buttplate, the anatomical pistol grip is set vertically, and the trigger can be adjusted for let-off pressure as well as position within the rudimentary trigger guard. The fluted barrel is allowed to float freely, the bolt handle has an enlarged wooden knob, and a bipod can be fitted to the rail beneath the forend.

SIMILAR GUNS
Silenced pattern. The CZ 700 can be fitted with a special 17.7in barrel within a large-diameter suppressor casing. This is designed to handle special subsonic ammunition loaded with 200-grain bullets. The rifle is about 47.85in overall and weighs 14.75lb without sights or bipod.

• Galas
The first post-war sporters were conventional Mausers (q.v.), but they were soon supplemented by the ZG 47, built on a Mauser action modified by Otakar Galas. Most other Czechoslovakian bolt-action rifles have been Koucky designs.

ZG 47 SPORTING RIFLE
Made by Ceskoslovenská Zbrojovka, Brno, 1949-63.
Total production: about 20,000. **Chambering options:** see text. **Action:** locked by rotating two lugs on the bolt head into recesses in the receiver walls as the bolt handle was turned down, and by a safety lug opposing the bolt-handle base entering its seat.
DATA FOR A TYPICAL ZG 47 A
Chambering: 9.3x62, rimless. 45.3in overall, 6.95lb empty. 23.6in barrel, 4-groove rifling; RH, concentric. Internal box magazine, 4 rounds. Block-and-leaves sight. 2360ft/sec with 285-grain bullet

Introduced in 1947, this retained a Mauser bolt with a collar-pattern extractor, but the firing pin was locked by a radial safety catch on the right side of the bolt shroud. The bolt handle was lowered, an adjustable single-stage trigger was fitted, the magazine had a hinged floorplate, and the sight rails were machined into the top of the receiver. Rifles were chambered for a variety of sporting cartridges, including 6.5x57, 270 Winchester, 7x57, 7x64, 30-06, 8x57, 8x60, 8x64, 9.3x62 and 10.75x68. They could also be adapted to order for special loads – e.g., 5.6x61 Vom Hofe – provided that overall cartridge length was less than 3.35in. The ZG 47, often considered to be the finest of all Czechoslovakian-made sporting rifles, was superseded in the early 1960s by the ZKK 600 (see 'Koucky', below).

SIMILAR GUNS
ZG 49-Sn. A specialized sniping rifle chambered for a special 7.92x64 cartridge, this was made in small numbers in 1949. A typical example is marked '0018' – assumed to be the serial number – and 'grv 49', presumed to be a factory code and date.

ZG 51-Sn. An improved form of the ZG 49-Sn, abandoned in favor of a Mosin-Nagant adaptation under Russian pressure.

ZK 474. This single shot 7.92x57 target rifle was never made in quantity, though the existence of gun '070', dated 1950, indicates that at least one batch was made.

• Holek, auto-loading type
Emanuel Holek first attained prominence in the late 1920s, when a 276 version of his ZH 29 rifle was submitted for trials in the USA. This was the first of a lengthy series of gas-operated autoloaders.

MODEL 29 AUTOMATIC RIFLE
Made by Ceskoslovenská Zbrojovka, Brno.
Chambering options: 276, 7x57, 30-06, 7.92x57 and others. **Action:** locked by displacing the bolt into the receiver wall; gas operated, semi-automatic only or selective fire.
DATA FOR A TYPICAL 7.92MM EXAMPLE
45.3in overall, 9.88lb empty. 21.45in barrel, 4-groove rifling; RH, concentric. Detachable box magazine, 5, 10 or 25 rounds. Tangent-leaf sight graduated to 1400m (1530yd). 2690ft/sec with ball ammunition. Knife or sword bayonet.

The ZH 29 is said to have been developed in response to a request made by China in the late 1920s for an auto-loading rifle. A 276 gun was submitted to US Army trials, but did not perform well enough to challenge the Pedersen and Garand patterns.

The earliest ZH 29 rifles had their conventional wooden forends and handguards retained by a single band. Some were semi-automatic, but others could also fire automatically. Later rifles had distinctive ribbed aluminum forends to dissipate the additional heat generated on firing.

The ZH 29 was always beautifully made, but badly suited to mass production; the locking mechanism, particularly, was difficult to machine accurately and prone to jamming in adverse conditions. Most rifles also had a unique hold-open system; when the magazine had been replenished, pressing the trigger allowed the breech to

The ZH 39 rifle.

close and chamber a fresh round. A second pull on the trigger then fired the gun. However, this attracted unfavorable comment.

The ZH 29 was tested enthusiastically in South America, Europe and the Far East in 1930-2, but only the Chinese acquired large numbers (beginning with 150 7.92mm rifles purchased in 1929). Limited sales were also made to Ethiopia and, allegedly, Siam.

SIMILAR GUNS

ZH 32 rifle. A modified rifle was tested unsuccessfully in 1932 by Romania and Turkey under this designation. Published photographs reveal no obvious differences externally, and so it is assumed that the improvements were internal.

ZH 39 rifle. By 1938, the Holek tilting-bolt mechanism had been adapted so that the gas tube and piston system lay above the barrel. The resulting ZH 39 had a more modern appearance than its predecessors, with a short forend and a ventilated sheet-steel handguard. The clearing rod was carried above the barrel. However, though the rifle was submitted for trials in Britain and elsewhere, the German invasion of Czechoslovakia in 1939 brought development to an end.

MODEL 58 ASSAULT RIFLE
Samopal vz. 58

Apparently made by Ceskoslovenská Zbrojovka, Povaske Strjirny (code 'she'), about 1960-73.

Total production: not known. **Chambering:** 7.62x39, rimless. **Action:** generally as Kratochvil vz. 52, below.

DATA FOR A TYPICAL VZ. 58 P

33in overall, about 8.75lb with a loaded magazine. 15.75in barrel, 4-groove rifling; RH, concentric. Detachable box magazine, 30 rounds. Tangent-leaf sight graduated to 800m (875yd). 2295ft/sec with Soviet M43 cartridges; 800±50 rpm. Knife bayonet.

This weapon arose from a competition held in 1953 to find a Kalashnikov-type assault rifle, field trials being undertaken with the ZK 503, CZ 522 and ZB 530. The trials resolved in favor of the Holek design, but production of an improved version was deferred while the mechanism was adapted for the 7.62mm Soviet M43 cartridge. The relevant alterations have been credited to Josef Cermák.

Full-scale production of the Samopal vz. 58 P (*Pechotni*, 'infantry') began in 1958. Though superficially resembling the Kalashnikov, the vz. 58 had a tilting-block locking system and an axial striker instead of a swinging hammer. The selector lay on the right side of the receiver above the pistol grip.

Many of the earliest guns had wooden butts, pistol grips and forends, but reddish-brown plastic/wood-fiber patterns had appeared by about 1960. Some of the newest guns had nylon polymer fittings. Most guns were phosphated externally, but some have been reported with a baked-on gray-green finish. They are currently still in service, but will probably be replaced by the 5.56mm CZ 2000 assault rifle.

SIMILAR GUNS

Model 58 V. Intended for armored and airborne units, this had a single-strut metal butt folding to the right alongside the receiver.

Model 70 (utocna puska 70). This was a 5.45x39 version of the vz. 58, developed experimentally in 1976-8; small batches of guns were made for field trials, but the project was eventually abandoned – perhaps owing to Soviet pressure, or simply to budgetary restrictions.

• Holek, bolt-action type

Emanuel Holek also developed simplified bolt-action rifles in the late 1940s for trial against a Kyncl-modified Mauser. The series culminated in the 7.5mm P-5 of 1949, tentatively approved in 1950 as the 7.62x45 P-6. Owing to rapid progress with automatic weapons, however, the bolt-action project was abandoned in 1951.

A Janecek-type Mauser rifle, made alongside the autoloaders in the mid 1930s.

• Janecek

The gunmaker Frantisek Janecek produced auto-loading rifles in a factory in the Michl district of Prague. Developed in 1936-7, the guns were delayed blowbacks operated by an interesting combination of fluted chambers and cartridge cases, floated on a cushion of propellant gas, which slid backward to operate the bolt. The guns – at least ten were made – had one-piece pistol grip stocks, cylindrical receivers and detachable box magazines. The finalized version had a guard above the barrel which ran forward from the chamber to the spring-retained 'H' nose cap and bayonet bar assembly. A single retaining band was fitted. The charging handle lay on the right side of the receiver above the magazine, and a tangent-leaf rear sight was set into the barrel guard. However, the breech mechanism could not be developed to compete satisfactorily with more conventional CZ and ZB designs, and the Janecek project was abandoned in the 1938. Guns of this type are said to have been recovered from German combat units in 1944-5, but the rifles usually prove to be CZ 'S' and vz. 39 patterns.

• Koucky, auto-loading type

The products of Josef and Frantisek Koucky have included a wide range of auto-loading and bolt-action guns. The centerfire sporters have been particularly successful, being widely distributed in the West since the late 1950s, but a range of autoloaders was also made.

ZK 371 AUTOMATIC RIFLE
Samocinná puska ZK 371

This was the first of Josef Koucky's auto-loading rifles to reach trial status. An embrionic design locked by a tilting block, it had a stock based on the contemporaneous Czechoslovakian Mausers – even to the 'H'-type nose cap and bayonet bar assembly. The gas port and tube assembly lay above the barrel, midway between the chamber and the muzzle, necessitating an elevated aperture rear sight on the extreme rear of the receiver. A finger groove was cut into the forend, the stock being extended downward to contain the five-round magazine. Guides for stripper clips were milled into the front edge of the receiver behind the feed way. Only a few ZK 371 rifles were made, as they served only as prototypes for the ZK 381 (q.v.).

ZK 381 AUTOMATIC RIFLE
Samocinná puska ZK 381

This gas-operated tilting-block design was a refinement of the ZK 371; at least thirty were made, mostly chambered for the 7.92x57 cartridge. The most obvious characteristic was the massive slab-sided receiver, which divided the pistol grip butt from the forend. The 2000m (2185yd) tangent-leaf sight lay on top of the receiver behind the feed way, and a detachable box magazine replaced the internal pattern associated with the ZK 371. The slender barrel protruded from the short forend and barrel guard, ahead of the gas-port housing. The front sight was placed on top of an elevated block, above the bayonet lug, and a six-port muzzle-brake/compensator was fitted to the barrel. Swivels lay under the butt and beneath the back of the gas-port assembly.

The 7.92mm ZK 420 rifle.

The 7.5mm-caliber ZK 472 rifle.

SIMILAR GUNS

ZK 381 Au II. This was a minor variant of the standard gun, made for trials in the USSR in August 1938. Chambered for the 7.62x54R cartridge, it had a straight-wrist butt and a noticeably curved magazine. The trial was extremely successful – ten thousand shots were put within a metre-square target at 1000m (1095yd) – but nothing came of this particular exhibition.

ZK 391 AUTOMATIC RIFLE
Samocinná puska ZK 391

This 7.92mm-caliber autoloader was an improved form of the ZK 381, with a one-piece stock adapted from the vz. 24 (Mauser) short-rifle pattern. The gas port was moved forward behind the bayonet bar, to reduce the violence of the operating stroke, and a standard 2000m (2185yd) tangent-leaf rear sight was let into the barrel guard. Stripper-clip guides were milled in the receiver-top behind the feed way and a detachable ten-round magazine was fitted.

The ZK 391 was efficient enough to attract German interest and, in 1944, an attempt was made to begin production in the Armaguerra factory in Cremona. However, the Second World War ended before much progress had been made. The ZK 391 'Italsky model' was similar to the standard Czechoslovakian rifle, but had a large single-port muzzle brake, a squared-base pistol grip, and a hinged magazine case reminiscent of pre-war Beretta designs.

ZK 420 AUTOMATIC RIFLE
Samocinná puska ZK 420
Made by Ceskoslovenská Zbrojovka, Brno.
Chambering options: see text. **Action:** locked by lugs on a rotating bolt engaging the receiver; gas operated, semi-automatic only.
DATA FOR A TYPICAL EXAMPLE
Chambering: 7.92x57, rimless. 41.65in overall, 10.54lb loaded. 21.65in barrel, 4-groove rifling; RH, concentric. Detachable box magazine, 10 rounds. Tangent-leaf sight graduated to 1000m (1095yd). 2690ft/sec with ball ammunition. No bayonet.

Though the design has its origins during the war, the perfected ZK 420 prototype did not appear until the summer of 1945. Numbered '002', it had a conventional forend and nose cap assembly, a rifle-type tangent-leaf rear sight set into the handguard, and a curious integral magazine which could be loaded with stripper clips through the top of the action.

SIMILAR GUNS

ZK 420S rifle. A few semi-production guns were made for trials in 1946 under this designation, with a detachable box magazine, a half-stock, and a sight with protective wings on top of the receiver. At least 150 rifles were made in 7mm, 30-06 or 7.92mm, for tests in countries as disparate as Britain, Ethiopia, Israel and Switzerland. However, though the ZK 420 worked well enough, it was expensive to mass-produce and offered no real advantages over existing guns. Owing to progress with smaller intermediate-cartridge patterns, the project was abandoned in 1949.

ZK 425 AUTOMATIC RIFLE

This was a simplified version of the ZK 420, incorporating stampings and pressings. The receiver was squared, the trigger guard was a stamped steel strip, and the gas tube ran back above the barrel from a transfer-port housing combined with the front sight. The pistol grip stock had a single band and a cup-shape nose cap retained by a spring.

ZK 472 AUTOMATIC RIFLE
Made by Ceskoslovenská Zbrojovka, Brno.
Total production: at least fifty. **Chambering:** 7.5mm, rimless. **Action:** locked by lugs on a rotating bolt engaging the receiver; gas operated, semi-automatic only.
39.4in overall, 6.5lb empty. 19.7in barrel, 4-groove rifling; RH, concentric. Detachable box magazine, 10 or 15 rounds. Tangent-leaf sight graduated to 1000m (1095yd). Performance not known. No bayonet.

The first two examples of this variant of the ZK 420, developed for Czech military trials, were delivered in the Spring of 1949. Tests against against the Kyncl-designed ZJ 481 and the Kratochvil CZ 493 suggested that the Koucky design was the best, and 35 were acquired in the summer of 1949 for field trials. The ZK 472 remained the favorite until an improved CZ 493 appeared in March 1950; this became the CZ 502 and, ultimately, the vz. 52 service rifle.

The Koucky design was abandoned in August 1950 – not because it was poor, but simply that the CZ pattern was perceived to be better. Most half-stocked ZK 472 rifles were chambered for the Czechoslovakian 7.5mm intermediate cartridge, but a few may have been adapted experimentally for the 7.62x39 Russian pattern. The detachable box magazine could be loaded from a stripper-clip through the open action.

ZKW 561 SPORTING RIFLE
Made by Ceska Zbrojovka, Uhersky Brod.
Total production: many thousands. **Chambering:** 22 Long Rifle, rimfire.
Action: no mechanical lock; blowback operation, semi-automatic only.
38.75in overall, about 6lb. 22.25in barrel, 4-groove rifling; RH, concentric? Detachable box magazine, 8 or 16 rounds. Adjustable aperture sight graduated to 75m (82yd). 1080ft/sec with standard ball ammunition.

These guns were designed by the Koucky brothers, and were originally associated with the 'Brno' brand name. They have, however, always been made in Uhersky Brod and are now being marketed under the Ceska Zbrojovka name.

The ZKW 561 was a small autoloader with a pistol grip half stock. The receiver was pierced only by an ejection port on the right side and by the magazine feed way beneath. Dismantling could be undertaken without tools. Though a small aperture sight was fitted, the ZKW 561 was intended to be fitted with an optical sight, suitable rails being provided above the receiver for the mounting bases.

SIMILAR GUNS

CZ 511. A modernized form of the ZKW 561, incorporating minor internal improvements, this has been made in large numbers. The standard rifle – 38.6in long, 5.4lb – has a beechwood half-stock without checkering, and a two-position 'L' or 'flip' rear sight graduated for 50m and 100m. The magazine holds eight rounds. The muzzle may be threaded on request to take a sound moderator, for use in conjunction with special subsonic 22 ammunition.

CZ 511 Lux. Mechanically identical with the standard pattern, this may be distinguished by a walnut stock with checkering on the pistol grip.

CZ 511 Special. Essentially similar to the Lux pattern, this has a beechwood stock with a checkered pistol grip.

• Koucky, bolt-action type

Most of these rifles have been credited to Josef and Frantisek Koucky. They have been one of the great strengths of the post-1948 firearms industry, as they offered some of the best manufacturing standards to be found in the Soviet bloc. Though developed in the Koucky design office in Brno, they have always been made by Ceská Zbrojovka.

ZKM 451 SPORTING RIFLE
Also known as the 'Brno Model 1'
Made by Ceská Zbrojovka, Uhersky Brod.
Total production: many thousands. **Chambering:** 22 Long Rifle, rimfire.
Action: locked by the bolt-handle base entering its seat as the bolt handle is turned down.
40.95in overall, 4.55lb empty. 22.85in barrel, 4-groove rifling; RH, concentric? Detachable box magazine, 5 rounds. Standing-block rear sight with two folding leaves. 1080ft/sec with standard ball ammunition.

Introduced in 1946, this rifle was an instantaneous success. Bearing some resemblance to the pre-war Winchester Model 52,

The ZKK 601 sporting rifle.

it was an elegant but sturdy design with a simple half stock and a pistol grip butt. The trigger guard was a stamped strip, a prominent gas-escape hole was bored through the right side of the chamber, and a rail on top of the receiver could accept optical-sight mounting bases. The rear sight was mounted on a barrel-collar, and a laterally pivoting safety catch was attached above the cocking piece. Later guns made under the Ceska Zbrojovka brand are listed as the 'CZ 452 series', above.

SIMILAR GUNS

ZKM 451-Ex sporting rifle, or Brno Model 1-Ex. Mechanically identical with the Model 1, this version had a tangent-leaf rear sight adjustable to 200m (220yd).

ZKM 452 sporting rifle, or Brno Model 2. This was a refinement of the Model 1 with a select walnut stock; the forend had a graceful schnabel tip. Barrels customarily measured 23.6in, but a 25in version was made in small numbers.

ZKM 454 training rifle. This derivative of the Model 1, designed as a rimfire replica of the 7.92mm vz. 24, had a full-length stock with a finger groove in the forend. A handguard lay above the forend, a single band was fitted, and the nose cap was a simpler form of the standard military 'H' pattern. A tangent-leaf rear sight with unusually shallow range-curves was set into the handguard ahead of the chamber.

ZKM 455 target rifle, or Brno Model 3, 1949-56. This was an adaptation of the Model 1 with a heavy barrel, a deep forend, and an enlarged anatomical pistol grip. Checkering appeared on the pistol grip and forend of the earliest guns, but was soon abandoned. A vernier-adjustable aperture rear sight was attached to a bar mount on top of the receiver bridge.

ZKM 456 target rifle, or Brno Model 4, 1957-62. A replacement for the Model 3, this offered a better trigger mechanism and an improved safety catch.

ZKM 573 sporting rifle, or Brno Model 5, 1957-73. This was an improved form of the Model 1, with changes in the trigger and safety systems.

ZKW 465 SPORTING RIFLE
Also known as 'CZ 365'
Made by Ceska Zbrojovka, Uhersky Brod.
Total production: 40,000, 1949-73. **Chambering options:** 218 Bee, 22 Hornet or 222 Remington. **Action:** locked by two lugs on the bolt body engaging recesses in the receiver as the bolt handle turns down, and by the bolt-handle base entering its seat.

DATA FOR 22 HORNET VESRION
41.5in overall, 6.25lb empty. 22.75in barrel, 4-groove rifling; RH, concentric? Detachable box magazine, 5 rounds. Standing-block rear sight with two folding leaves. 2430ft/sec with 46-grain bullet.

Design of this Koucky 'miniature Mauser' was completed in 1946, though it is believed to have had wartime origins. Basically an enlargement of the ZKM 451, the principal changes concerned the re-location of the safety catch on the right side of the receiver behind the bolt handle, where it could be set by moving it upward with the thumb. The trigger guard was enlarged and amalgamated with the slanted magazine housing; the magazine-release catch

lay inside the front of the guard. The perfected rifle had a straight-comb half-stock, originally with a slender schnabel-tip forend. The pistol grip and forend were checkered. Rifles chambered for anything other than the 22 Hornet cartridge are very rare, as production was small.

ZKK 600 SPORTING RIFLE
Made by Ceska Zbrojovka, Uhersky Brod, about 1962-95.
Total production: not known.
Chambering options: see notes.
Action: locked by two lugs on the bolt head entering recesses in the receiver wall as the bolt handle turned down, and by a safety lug opposing the bolt handle entering its seat.
DATA FOR A TYPICAL EXAMPLE
Chambering: 8x60S, rimless. 43.7in overall, 6.9lb empty. 23.6in barrel, 4-groove rifling; RH, concentric. Internal box magazine, 5 rounds. Folding-leaf sight. 2770ft/sec with 187-grain bullet.

Unquestionably the most successful sporting rifle made in eastern Europe since 1945, this interesting 1960-vintage Koucky design was basically a Mauser – with a safety lug opposing the bolt handle base and a full-length collar pattern extractor. It also retained the undercut bolt face, preventing double loading. The standard trigger mechanism was an excellent single pattern, though a special set design could be obtained for the ZKK 600 and ZKK 601.

This could be recognized by an auxiliary blade set into the main trigger lever. It was set simply by pushing the lever forward, allowing a light pressure on the auxiliary blade to fire the gun. A small open rear sight was set into the receiver bridge, where it could be raised when required, though a folding-leaf sight was often also mounted on the barrel. A rotary safety lay on the right side of the bolt shroud. The ZKK series was replaced by the CZ 550 patterns (q.v.) in the mid 1990s.

THE GUNS

ZKK 600 rifle. Designed for cartridges with an overall length of 3.15in (80mm) and a maximum case diameter of 472 (12mm), this has been chambered for 270 Winchester, 7x57, 7x64, 30-06 Springfield, 8x57, 8x60, 8x64 (all with five-round magazines) and 10.75x68 (four rounds). The 7x57 and 7x64 options were both discontinued in 1989.

The standard half-stock originally offered a niggardly proportioned forend; most butts have had straight combs, but Monte Carlo patterns have occasionally been offered for use with high-mounted optical sights. The pistol grip and the rounded-tip forend were checkered, the receiver was usually phosphated, and most of the other metal parts were blued. Most rifles displayed the CZ trademark, 'MADE IN CZECHOSLOVAKIA', the designation, and dated proof marks (e.g., '68' for 1968).

ZKK 601 rifle. Designed for cartridges with a 2.76in (70mm) overall length, this has chambered the 222 Remington, 222 Remington Magnum, 223 Remington, 243 Winchester or 308 Winchester rounds. The 223 option was abandoned in 1991. Magazines held five rounds, or six in 222 only. A typical gun was 43.1in overall, had a 23.6in barrel and weighed 7.2lb.

The original ZKM 452 rifle.

The vz. 52 auto-loading rifle.

ZKK 602 rifle. Developed for cartridges with a maximum overall length of 3.74in (95mm) and a body diameter no greater than 551 (14mm), the ZKK 602 has chambered the 300 Winchester Magnum, 8x68S (discontinued in 1990), 358 Norma Magnum, 375 H&H Magnum, 404 Jeffrey, 416 Rigby (1990 only) or 458 Winchester Magnum rounds. A typical rifle had a 25in barrel, measured 45.25in overall and weighed about 9.25lb. The depth of the forend was increased to accommodate a five-round magazine and recoil bolts were fitted through the stock.

ZKB 680 FOX II SPORTING RIFLE
Made by Ceská Zbrojovka, Uhersky Brod, 1968-90.
Total production: not known. **Chambering:** 222 Remington only. **Action:** similar to ZKK 600, above.
42.4in overall, 5.78lb without magazine. 23.6in barrel, 6-groove rifling; RH, concentric. Detachable box magazine, 5 rounds. Ramp-pattern sight. 3115ft/sec with 50-grain bullet.

This rifle was little more than a ZKW 465 (q.v.) with a short Mauser action instead of the simplified 'miniature' pattern. A wing-type safety lay on the bolt shroud and a box magazine was used. The half-stock generally offered a low Monte Carlo comb, with checkering on the pistol grip and forend, and a contrasting forend tip. A double set-trigger was also often fitted.

• Kratochvil

The period of German occupation, which ended in 1945, left the Czechoslovakian authorities with an unusually detailed knowledge of German weaponry. Substantial quantities of the Gew. 43 (Walther) autoloader were impressed into temporary service, but the army wanted a new weapon based on an intermediate cartridge. A directive published in August 1946, asking for a rifle chambering a full-power 7.62mm cartridge was rapidly revised around an intermediate pattern developed from short-case rounds originating in Brno prior to 1945.

A 7.5x45 round was successfully tested in 1947, and a selection of prototype rifles was acquired. Ceská Zbrojovka of Strakonice submitted two guns – one operated by gas, the other a blowback – to compete against two gas-operated weapons promoted by Ceskoslovenská Zbrojovka of Brno. Trials showed that the CZ 147, designed by Josef Kratochvil, was the most promising; the Czechsolovakian army was willing to adopt the finalized 7.5mm CZ 475 (with a sliding rod bayonet beneath the muzzle), but pressure brought to bear by the USSR to standardize calibers led to the 7.62mm CZ 493. Two CZ 493 rifles were submitted in 1949 for trials against the ZK 472 (Koucky) and ZJ 481 (Kyncl), but the testers decided that the ZK 472 promised the most. However, ten more CZ 493 rifles were acquired in the summer of 1949, and an improved CZ 493 submitted in March 1950 was ultimately preferred – perhaps mistakenly – to the ZK 472.

Distinguished by a laterally-swinging knife bayonet on the right side of the forend, the improved CZ 493 became the CZ 502 of 1951 once improvements had been made to the extractor. Field trials held in 1951 showed that the CZ 502 was acceptably accurate and sufficiently durable for service.

MODEL 52 AUTOMATIC RIFLE
7.62mm Samonabijecki puska vz. 52
Made by Ceskoslovenská Zbrojovka, Uhersky Brod (code 'tgf').
Chambering: 7.62x45, rimless. **Action:** locked by displacing the bolt into the receiver; gas operated, semi-automatic only.
39.55in overall (bayonet folded), 9.15lb empty. 20.45in barrel, 4-groove rifling; RH, concentric. Detachable box magazine, 10 rounds. Tangent-leaf sight graduated to 1000m (1095yd). 2445ft/sec with Z 50 cartridges. Folding bayonet.

This rifle, formally adopted on 20th March 1952, was a lightened version of the CZ 502 lacking the gas-regulator system. However, problems with pre-production guns were not solved until a modified prototype (the CZ 521) appeared. Series production began in 1953, the first guns entering service the following summer. They embodied a tilting-bolt locking system, powered by an annular short-stroke piston; oddly, the locking lugs lay at the front of the bolt.

Though the box magazine was detachable, the rifle could also be reloaded through the open action, suitable stripper-clip guides being milled in the receiver-top behind the ejection cutaway. The one-piece pistol grip stock, made of walnut or beech stained a yellowish-brown, had a trap in the butt for a cleaning rod, oil can and accessories.

SIMILAR GUNS
Model 52/57 rifle. The desire to unify the weapons of the Soviet-block states was discussed in 1954, prior to the signing of the Warsaw Pact. As a result of pressure applied by the USSR, the Czechoslovakian authorities revised the vz. 52 to accept the 7.62x39 M43 Soviet intermediate cartridge, which had a shorter case than the Z 50 pattern. The modified gun was known as 'vz. 52-57'; it was sighted to 900m (985yd) for the slower Russian-style bullet, weighed 9.48lb empty, and had a distinctively sloped magazine base plate. Some guns were newly made, but it seems that others were converted from the vz. 52. The advent of the more efficient vz. 58 (q.v.) caused work to be abandoned.

Unfortunately, despite compact dimensions, the vz. 52 and vz. 52/57 were never popular; the cumbersome integral bayonet had an unbalancing effect, and the locking mechanism proved unsatisfactory in service. The guns were withdrawn from the armed forces once supplies of the vz. 58 had been assured, and exported to countries which were then sympathetic to Communism – e.g., Egypt, Syria, Cuba and Nicaragua. Rifles of this type are still to be found throughout Africa.

• Kyncl

Josef Kyncl, employed by the Janecek company, submitted the experimental ZJ 481 rifle to the military trials held in the summer of 1949; two patterns were tested, one with a gas-piston system and the other with a direct-impingement system. Known as the 'AK' ('Automat Kyncl'), both were forms of delayed blowback. Ten pistonless guns were then suppiled in mid 1949 for extended trials, but not enough improvement had been made and the design was rejected in March 1950 in favor of the competing CZ and Koucky (Brno) rifles.

• Mauser (CSZ, ZB)
MAUSER-JELEN TRIALS RIFLE
Short rifle: Puska Mauser-Jelená
Chambered for the 7x57 cartridge, the first rifles made in 1919 were standard 1898-type Mausers with non-rotating extractors and special sword bayonets. Most guns had a distinctive pistol grip stock and a handguard running from the receiver ring to the muzzle. The magazine floorplate was often fitted with a quick-release lever similar to those found on Mauser sporters.

The most distinctive feature was the nose cap assembly inspired by the British SMLE, which ran back under the forend to an intermediate screw-clamped band. The ring on the bayonet cross-guard fitted around a boss on the nose cap beneath the muzzle. Sling swivels appeared on the underside of the true barrel band – which lay some way behind the auxiliary nose-cap fitting – and on the under-edge of the butt.

Several hundred rifles were manufactured in 1921 by Ceskoslovenská Statni Zavody na Vyrobu Zbrani, including at least 150 in 7x57 and a roughly comparable quantity in 7.92x57. Most were

The vz. 98/29 Mauser rifle.

The vz. 24 short rifle.

issued to the Czechoslovakian army, but some went to Yugoslavia. In 1922, however, the Jelen-type Mauser was abandoned in favor of a copy of the pre-war Steyr-made Mo. 1912 Mexican rifle.

MILITARY WEAPONS
MODEL 1898/22 RIFLE
Puska vz. 98/22
Made by Ceskoslovenská Statni Zavody na Vyrobu Zbrani, Brno, 1923-4; and Ceskoslovenská Zbrojovka AS, Brno, 1924-30.
Total production: not known. **Chambering:** 7.92x57, rimless. **Action:** as Jelen-pattern rifle, above.
DATA FOR TYPICAL RIFLE
48.8in overall, 9.3lb empty. 29.15in barrel, 4-groove rifling; RH, concentric. Internal box magazine loaded from a stripper clip, 5 rounds. Tangent-leaf sight graduated to 2000m (2185yd). 2855 fps with standard ball cartridges. Standard vz.23 knife or sword bayonets.

Adopted for service with the Czech army in 1922, this was little more than a slightly improved Mo. 1912 Steyr-made Mexican Mauser, with a pistol grip stock and a handguard running from the receiver ring to the barrel band. A German 'H'-pattern nose cap was used, a front sight hood was fitted, and the swivels lay in conventional positions beneath the band and butt.

In 1924, the state-owned factory was reorganized as a private company to encourage exports. The 98/22-pattern long rifles were initially popular with purchasers, but vz. 24 short rifles soon attained greater renown.

SIMILAR GUNS
Model 1898/22 short rifle, káatká puska vz. 98/22. This was simply a short version of the standard 98/22 rifle, with a barrel of about 23.6in. It does not seem to have been made in large numbers.

Models 23 and 23A short rifles. The first of these short rifles was based on the German Kar. 98 AZ, but stocked more in the manner of the Gew. 98. The action was essentially that of the vz. 98/22 rifle, but minor improvements were made internally, the barrel was shortened, and the handguard extended to the nose cap. Swivels lay on the under-edge of the butt and on the underside of the barrel band. Most vz. 23 short rifles incorporated old or cannibalized parts, whereas vz. 23A examples were entirely newly made. The barrel band was noticeably closer to the German 'H'-type nose cap than the receiver ring.

MODEL 1924 SHORT RIFLE
Krátká puska vz. 24
Made by Ceskoslovenská Statni Zavody na Vyrobu Zbrani, Brno, 1923-4 (prototypes only); and by Ceskoslovenská Zbrojovka AS, Brno, 1924-40.
Total production: hundreds of thousands. **Chambering options:** 7x57, 7.65x53 or 7.92x57. **Action:** as Jelen-pattern rifle, above.
DATA FOR A TYPICAL EXAMPLE
Chambering: 7.92x57, rimless. 43.25in overall, 9.13lb empty. 23.25in barrel, 4-groove rifling; RH, concentric. Internal box magazine loaded from a stripper clip, 5 rounds. Tangent-leaf sight graduated to 2000m (2185yd). 2755 fps with standard cartridges. Standard vz. 23 or vz. 24 sword bayonets.

The perfected short rifle appeared at a time when the government rifle factory was being reorganized. It was very similar to the vz. 23, but the design of the forend had been improved and the band – retained by a lateral bolt in Austrian fashion – was moved back until it was approximately mid-way between the nose cap and the receiver ring.

An additional bolt was placed laterally through the pistol grip and a finger groove invariably appeared on the forend beneath the rear sight. Some (but by no means all) guns had their bolt handles turned down against a recess in the side of the stock.

The first large export orders were placed in 1925, and sufficient guns had been delivered to the Czechoslovakian army by 1929 – about 80,000 vz. 23/vz. 23A, plus 40,000 vz. 24 – for issue to infantry, cavalry and armored divisions.

Work continued until the Brno factory was seized by the Germans in 1939. Most existing vz. 24 short rifles were sequestered, serving the Wehrmacht as the 'Gew. 24 (t)', and production continued. Rifles made under HWaA supervision had German-style butts with sling slots and hollow washers to assist dismantling the firing pin. The first of the stamped 'bucket'-type buttplates appeared in the summer of 1942.

Production of the Kar. 98k began in 1942, distinguished from the German prototype largely by its markings ('dot' code). Work ceased in the face of the Russian advance at the end of 1944, after about 1.25 million guns had been made.

MODEL 1933 GENDARMERIE CARBINE
Krátká puska vz.33 pro cetnictvo a financi stráz
Made by Ceskoslovenská Zbrojovka AS, Brno, 1933-9.
Chambering: 7.92x57, rimless. **Action:** as Jelen-pattern rifle, above.
39.2in overall, 7.67lb empty. 19.3in barrel, 4-groove rifling; RH, concentric. Internal charger-loaded box magazine, 5 rounds. Tangent-leaf sight graduated to 1000m (1095yd). 2560 fps with standard ball cartridges. Standard vz. 24 sword bayonet.

The military version of the vz. 16/33 export carbine was bought by the Czechoslovakian authorities in small quantities. It was essentially a diminutive vz. 24, but had a small-diameter receiver ring and flutes were milled out of the receiver sides below the line of the stock to save weight. The bolt-handle knob was hollowed and a fixed sling bar was held to the left side of the barrel band. Swivels lay beneath the band and butt. About 12,740 guns were acquired for the gendarmerie and 5300 for the treasury guards in 1934, followed in 1938 by 2730 additional gendarmerie and 2270 treasury-guard guns. Work continued under German auspices in the early stages of World War II, until the modified Gew. 33/40 (q.v.) was adopted by the Wehrmacht in 1940. Assembly of the vz. 33 continued until late in 1941.

CZ CONTRACT PATTERNS
Huge quantities of Mauser-type weapons were exported prior to 1939. They included the vz.98/22 rifle, vz.23 and 23a short rifles, and vz.24 short rifle (above), as well as the 'JC' short rifle, 'L' short rifle and carbine described below.

MODEL 1898/29 RIFLE
Puska vz. 98/29
Made by Ceskoslovenská Zbrojovká AS, Brno, 1933-9.
Chambering options: 7x57 or 7.92x57. **Action:** as Jelen-pattern rifle, above.
DATA FOR TYPICAL VZ. 98/29 SHORT RIFLE
Chambering: 7.92x57, rimless. 38in overall, 8.31lb empty. 17.9in barrel, 4-groove rifling; RH, concentric. Internal box magazine loaded from a stripper clip, 5 rounds. Tangent-leaf sight graduated to 2000m (2185yd). 2510 fps with standard ball cartridges. Standard vz. 23 sword bayonet.

Offered for sale from 1930 onward, the 98/29 was a minor adaptation of the vz. 98/22 rifle. The rifle generally had a much broader barrel band than the vz. 98/22 pattern (which was unusually narrow), the front sight block was extended upward to protect the sight blade, and an open piling swivel was added on the under

The Model 54 sniper rifle.

side of the nose cap. A third swivel was generally fitted through the front of the trigger guard web, in addition to those under the band and on the under-edge of the butt. The additional bolt through the pistol grip, characteristic of the vz. 24, was lacking from the vz. 98/29.

SIMILAR GUNS

Model 08/33 short rifle. Made for Brazil in 7x57, this may also have accepted the Brazilian Mo. 1908 bayonet.

Model 12/33 carbine. This ultra-short weapon generally chambered the 7.92mm cartridge and could mount a vz. 23 bayonet. The gun was a lightened vz. 24 intended for use in hot climates; consequently, it was particularly popular in Central and South America. It was derived from the 'vz. 12 mex.' pattern supplied to Mexico in the late 1920s.

Model 16/33 carbine. The shortest of the group, this provided the basis for the Czech vz. 33 service weapon described above.

Models 32 and 35 short rifles. Guns of this type usually prove to have been minor variations of the vz. 24 – e.g., the Peruvian Mo. 32 short rifle had a small-diameter receiver ring and a reversed safety lever.

Model 98/29 short rifle. Derived from the vz. 24, this was a shortened 98/29 rifle with the same band, nose cap and front-sight guard, but the bolt handle was turned down against a recess in the side of the stock and a fixed sling bar was added to the left side of the band to supplement the conventional swivel.

Model JC short rifle. A lightened version of the standard vz. 24.

Model L short rifle. Also made in carbine form, this is believed to have been developed at the request of the Lithuanians; it chambered the British 303 rimmed cartridge, and accepted a surplus Austro-Hungarian 1895-pattern knife bayonet. The gun may be recognized by the magazine, which protruded slightly from the underside of the stock ahead of the trigger guard, and by the bayonet lug on the underside of the nose cap.

SPORTING GUNS

Ceskoslovenská Zbrojovka of Brno made its first sporting rifles in the early 1930s, apparently to compete against the products of Oberndorf. They had military-style actions, with cut-outs milled in the left side of the receiver, and classical wing-type safety catches. The Model A was a half-stock rifle; Model B was a fully stocked carbine. The bolt handles were generally turned downward and – on most carbines at least – spatulate. A double set trigger mechanism was standard, together with a delicate pierced-web trigger guard. Chambering options included 7x57, 8x57 and 8x60S.

MODEL 21 SPORTING RIFLE
Also known as 'Model 21H'

Made by Ceskoslovenská Zbrojovka AS, Brno, about 1937-40, 1946-50. Total production: said to have been 46,000. **Chambering options:** 6.5x57, 7x57, 7x64, 8x57, 8x60S and 9x57. **Action:** as Jelen-pattern rifle, above.

DATA FOR TYPICAL EXAMPLE

Chambering: 9x57, rimless. 42.1in overall, 7.16lb empty. 22.05in barrel, 4-groove rifling; RH, concentric. Internal box magazine loaded from a stripper clip, 5 rounds. Folding rear sight. 2090 fps with 275-grain bullet.

The original Mauser-type sporting rifles were supplemented shortly before the German invasion of Czechoslovakia by the

Model 21, built on a 'small ring' receiver. The bolt handle was spatulate, turned downward and shaped to clear an optical sight. The safety catch was moved to the left side of the bolt shroud, where it locked the firing pin, and the left receiver wall retained its full height. Magazines held five rounds, and folding rear sights were standard. The half-stocks generally had checkering on the pistol grip and forend.

Production began again after the end of World War II. The receivers of post-1946 guns usually had squared sight-mount bases, and the double set trigger mechanism was a popular accessory. The Thalson Import Company of San Francisco sold some 7x57 guns in the U.S. after World War II as the Models 721 and 722, but the pre-war Mauser-pattern rifles were replaced after the 1948 revolution by the ZG 47 – a modified Mauser credited to Otakar Galas (q.v.).

SIMILAR GUNS

Model 22 or 'Model 22F'. This was a full-stocked 'Mannlicher' variant of the half-stocked Model 21, usually offered with a 20.45in barrel.

• Mosin-Nagant

After the revolution of 1948, Czechoslovakia continued to produce Mauser-type rifles. A modified sniper rifle (ZG 49 Sn), submitted to trial by Otakar Galas in the late 1940s, was developed into the ZG 51 Sn, but a change of heart – perhaps influenced by the Soviet Union – led to the development of the similar ZG 51/91/30 on the Mosin-Nagant action.

MODEL 1954 SNIPER RIFLE
Odstrelovacská Puska vz. 54.

Made by state factories, 1954-7. **Chambering:** 7.62x54R, rimmed. **Action:** locked by two lugs on a detachable bolt head engaging recesses in the receiver behind the chamber as the bolt handle was turned down. 48.45in overall, 11.46lb without sights. 28.75in barrel, 4-groove rifling; RH, concentric. Integral box magazine loaded from a stripper clip, 5 rounds. Tangent-leaf sight graduated to 2000m (2185yd). 2640 fps with Type D ball cartridges.

Built on specially finished, but otherwise standard obr. 1891/30 actions, this sniper rifle was developed to share a special 7.62mm ball cartridge being made for the Goryunov machine gun. It had a pistol grip half-stock and a handguard running forward from the receiver ring. There was a single band at the tip of the forend and a grasping groove beneath the rear sight. Owing to the free-floating barrel, the vz. 54 was accurate and dependable. However, it was never made in large numbers.

DENMARK

• Bang

Credited to Søren H. Bang, this Danish rifle was patented in Britain in 1904 and tested by many armies in the early years of the twentieth century. A typical unsuccessful submission to the U.S. Army occurred in 1911. On 23rd December 1919, the Ordnance Board was asked to adapt the Bang rifle for cavalry use; and finally, in August 1928, the army tested an improved 256 gun against a 30

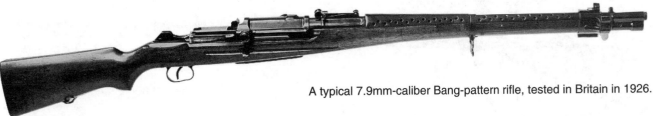
A typical 7.9mm-caliber Bang-pattern rifle, tested in Britain in 1926.

primer-actuated M1924 Garand, the 30 Thompson Auto Rifle, and two versions of the 276 T1 Pedersen. Though touted for some time, the muzzle-cup system of the Bang rifle was ultimately found wanting on trial – even though the German Gew. 41 (Mauser and Walther) were merely adaptations of the basic design.

• Heckler & Koch

The army received its first Rheinmetall or H&K-made Gevær M/66 (G3) in 1966-7, on lease from the Federal German government. The selector mechanism, normally set for single shots, could be altered with a special key to allow fully-automatic fire. In 1977, the G3A5-type Gevær M/75 superseded the earlier M/66 pattern. The guns were still in universal service in the mid-1990s, though trials were being undertaken with 5.56mm designs.

• Krag-Jørgensen

Aware by 1887 that their standard Remington rolling-block infantry rifles were obsolescent, the Danes sought an alternative. Five hundred Lee-type Førsøgsrepetergevær m/1 ('Model 1 repeating trials rifle') were issued in April but, though reports indicated great superiority over the Remingtons, the rifle commission was not convinced of their merits.

After tests had been undertaken with the latest weapons, including the French Lebel and some Austro-Hungarian Mannlichers, the Krag-Jørgensen was adopted in 1889.

MODEL 1889 RIFLE
Gevær m/89

Made by Geværfabriken Kjobenhavn and Kobenhavns Tøjhus, Copenhagen, 1890-1915; and by Hærens Tøjhus, Copenhagen, 1915-21.

Total production: about 118,000. **Chambering:** 8x58R, rimmed. **Action:** locked by a single lug on the bolt head engaging a recess in the receiver when the bolt handle was turned down, and by the bolt-guide rib abutting the receiver bridge.

52.3in overall, 10.1lb empty. 37.4in barrel, 6-groove rifling; RH, polygonal. Integral pan magazine, 5 rounds. Leaf sight graduated to 2000m (2185yd) – see notes. 1970 fps with m/89 ball cartridges. m/89 knife or m/15 sword bayonets.

Accepted in June 1889, the original rifle was sighted for the 8mm m/89 cartridge, with a 250-metre standing block and a leaf graduated to 1800m (1970yd). A notch in the leaf-top sufficed for 2000m (2185yd). The gun lacked any safety features other than the potentially dangerous half-cock notch. It had a barrel jacket inspired by the Gew. 88, a straight-gripped stock, two barrel bands, and a hooked cocking piece spur. The first series-made guns were accepted on 19th January 1890, bulk deliveries commencing in the summer.

SIMILAR GUNS

Model 1889-08 rifle. On 19th September 1908, the Danes adopted the pointed-bullet m/08 cartridge (muzzle velocity: 2460 fps) and the sights were modified to give a maximum range of 2100m or 2295yd. The auxiliary sights for the m/89 cartridge on the left side of the barrel band and the back-sight notch plate were discarded.

Model 1889-10 rifle. From 23rd June 1910, a cocking-piece safety catch credited to C.C.G. Barry – an armorer attached to the Royal Danish Life Guards – was added to the right side of the receiver behind the bolt handle; most pre-1910 survivors were adapted when returning for repair.

Rifles made or thoroughly overhauled after February 1915 were given new barrels, with a modified chamber, and the m/15 sword bayonet superseded the m/89 knife type on 22nd August 1916. A few m/16 periscope sights were also issued in this period. Barrels made after 1925 had four-groove concentric rifling, which replaced the original six-groove Rasmussen pattern.

Shortly before the Germans invaded Denmark at the beginning of World War II, a few m/89-10 rifles were issued to the Royal Danish Navy to replace venerable m/67-96 and m/67-97 Remingtons. However, the Germans had sequestered at least 60,000 assorted Krag rifles and carbines by 1942, then took an additional fifty thousand after finally disarming the Danish forces on 29th August 1943.

MODEL 1889 CAVALRY CARBINE
Ryttergevær or Rytterkarabin m/89.
Made by Kobenhavns Tøjhus, Copenhagen, 1912-13.
Total production: about 2600. **Chambering:** 8x58R, rimmed. **Action:** as m/89 rifle, above.

43.3in overall, 8.9lb empty. 23.6in barrel, 6-groove rifling; RH, polygonal. Internal pan magazine, 5 rounds. Tangent-leaf sight graduated to 2000m (2185yd). About 2035 fps with m/08 ball cartridges. No bayonet.

The standard cavalry carbine or Ryttergevær m/89 (renamed 'Rytterkarabin' in 1924), little more than a shortened version of the infantry rifle, was adopted in 1912 after protracted trials. The barrel jacket of the rifle was replaced by a conventional wooden handguard, the buttplate was omitted, and a new rear sight was developed. A large grooved stud was screwed laterally into the left side of the stock-wrist, level with the back of the trigger guard, to accept the m/05 leather suspender carried over the cavalryman's back. The guns all had 'R'-prefix numbers.

MODEL 1889 ENGINEER CARBINE
Ingeniørkarabin m/89.
Made by Hærens Tøjhus, Copenhagen, 1917-18.
Total production: approximately 4000. **Chambering:** 8x58R, rimmed.
Details otherwise generally similar to m/1889 cavalry carbine, except that the m/15 sword bayonet was used.

Approved as a rifle in 1917, this gun resembled the cavalry carbine (q.v.). However, it had barrel bands closer to the muzzle and accepted a bayonet. There was only a single production run, gun-numbers being prefixed by 'I'. The earliest issues were made in May 1918. In 1924, the rifle was officially reclassified as a carbine.

MODEL 1889-23 CAVALRY CARBINE
Rytterkarabin m/89-23.
Made by Hærens Rustkammer, Copenhagen, 1923-6.
Total production: about 4600. **Chambering:** 8x58R, rimmed.
Details generally similar to m/1889 cavalry carbine, except that the m/15 sword bayonet was used.

Experimental short Krag-Jørgensens were made for the border guards and customs service in 1922. Additional trials then led to the approval of the m/89-23 on 28th June 1923. Most of the carbines were converted from old m/89-10 rifles, and it is suspected that only a few hundred were newly made. They all exhibit Rasmussen polygonal rifling, which was abandoned in 1925.

MODEL 1889-24 INFANTRY CARBINE
Fodfolkskarabin m/89-24.
Made by Hærens Rustkammer, Copenhagen, 1923-32; and by Hærens Vaabenarsenal, Copenhagen, 1932-40.
Total production: see notes. **Chambering:** 8x58R, rimmed. **Action:** as m/89 rifle, above.

43.5in overall, 8.73lb empty. 24in barrel, 6-groove rifling; RH, polygonal. Internal pan magazine, 5 rounds. Tangent-leaf sight graduated to 2000m (2185yd). About 2040 fps with m/08 ball cartridges. m/15 sword bayonet.

The first examples of this short rifle were converted from old infantry patterns in 1923. rear sights were replaced, but the barrel jacket and the original band arrangements were retained. Converted weapons were given an 'F' prefix to their serial numbers and can be distinguished by old marks on the receiver: e.g., 'GEVÆRFABRIKEN KJOBENHAVN 1893 M.89'.

Rasmussen polygonal rifling was abandoned in 1925 in favor of a more conventional four-groove concentric pattern, and the chambering was revised in January 1928. Issue was extended to the infantry machine gun companies during the same year.

The M1889-10 Krag-Jorgensen rifle.

A longitudinal section of the Danish
1889-type Krag-Jørgensen rifle.

Production of a few new guns began in the Copenhagen factory in 1929. Their receivers bear the correct designation – e.g., 'HÆRENS RUSTKAMMER 1931 M.89-24' – to distinguish them from the 'M.89'-marked conversions. Serial numbers nonetheless have an 'F' prefix.

Important modifications in the trigger mechanism were introduced in September 1930. Issue of the m/89-24 was extended to mortar units in 1931, and then to the crews of anti-tank guns in 1937. Shortages of serviceable weapons during the German occupation of Denmark caused production to resume, but the poor condition of the machinery and constant sabotage restricted output to less than 3500 guns (April 1944-May 1945). Most were m/89-24 infantry carbines.

MODEL 1889-24 ARTILLERY CARBINE
Artillerikarabin m/89-24.
Made by Hærens Rustkammer, Copenhagen, 1925-30.
Total production: approximately 5,000, including the conversions.
Chambering: 8x58R, rimmed.
Otherwise similar to the m/89-23 cavalry carbine; no bayonet.

The first batches of these guns were converted from m/89 infantry rifles in 1925. Otherwise essentially similar to the 1924-pattern infantry carbine, they retained the original leaf sight. A large triangular sling swivel lay on the second barrel band – the infantry type had been rectangular – and a large stud protruded from the left side of the straight stock-wrist behind the trigger guard. The bolt handle turned down toward the stock, a finger groove was cut into the forend, and a brass marking disc appeared on the right side of the butt.

MODEL 1928 RIFLE
A few hundred of these marksmen's rifles, or *Finskydningsgevær*, adopted in February 1928, were made by Hærens Rustkammer of Copenhagen prior to 1931. The rifle was little more than an infantry weapon with a large-diameter free-floating barrel. Though a handguard stretched to the tip of the forend of the walnut half-stock, the woodwork was kept from direct contact with the barrel surface. A hooded-blade or globe front sight replaced the open barleycorn found on other Danish Krags, while a micro-adjustable aperture rear sight on the left side of the receiver replaced the standard tangent pattern. Virtually all m/28 rifles chambered the 8mm m/08 cartridge; a typical gun was 46.1in long, had a 23in barrel, and weighed 11.75lb. They were numbered in the same series as m/89-24 infantry carbines, but their actions displayed 'fsk' and 'm/1928'.

A new lightweight spurless cocking piece was introduced in 1929 to reduce lock time. Older guns were modified while under repair. Bolt handles were turned downward on newly made rifles from 1930 onward.

SIMILAR GUNS
Model 1928-31 rifle. A few of these marksmen's rifles were made in 1932 for the rimless 6.5x55 Norwegian rifle cartridge. Apparently intended for military-style 300m target-shooting, they are rarely encountered outside Scandinavian collections.

SPORTING GUNS
Substantial numbers of Krag-type Salongevær and Salonkarabin m/89 were made for reduced-caliber training. They fired Flobert primer-propelled ammunition held in a special chamber insert.

Single shot target rifles were also made in a number of calibers, and actions were supplied to individual gunsmiths. These sporting rifles are uncommon, however, owing to the superiority of guns based on the Mannlicher and Mauser actions.

• Krag-Petersson
MODEL 1877 NAVY CARBINES
Flådens magasin-karabin m/1877
Made by Geværfabrik Kjobenhavn, 1877-80.
Total production: 1500? **Chambering:** 11.35mm, rimfire. **Action:** as Norwegian M/1876, q.v.

37.5in overall, 8.93lb empty. 20.1in barrel, 5-groove rifling; RH, concentric. Tube magazine under barrel, 7 rounds. Ramp-and-leaf sight graduated to 1500 alen (1030yd)? About 1085 fps with standard ball rounds. No bayonet.

Adopted in 1877, the royal navy's magazine carbine was very similar to the Norwegian rifle, except in size and magazine capacity. It lasted in front-line Danish service until the issue of Krag-Jørgensen rifles in the early 1890s. The m/1877 had a two-piece stock and a barrel band with a swivel. The second swivel lay under the butt. The forend ran to the muzzle, where the nose cap was retained by a sturdy cross-pin.

• Løbnitz
Credited to a Copenhagen gunmaker, Nicolai Johan Løbnitz, this was the prototype of the chamber-loading guns which enjoyed a brief period in vogue in the middle of the 19th Century. Løbnitz-pattern carbines also also served the Danish cavalrymen in small numbers.

The mouth of the chamber was lifted by turning a radial lever on the right side of the breech. Most guns had a separate butt and forend (some short-barrel carbines had no forend at all), and were fired by an under-hammer cap lock; the trigger – which latched into a notch on the hammer until pressed – was often simply a spring-steel leaf anchored in the inside face of the massive brass trigger guard. Løbnitz chamber-rifles were tested extensively by many European armies, but only the Danes used them in their original form; the Norwegian Kammerladningsgevær (q.v.), credited to Scheel, had a more conventional trigger system even though under-hammer ignition was retained.

• Madsen, autoloading type
Formed in 1896, Dansk Rekylriffel Syndikat ('DRRS' or 'DRS') sought to exploit a recoil-operated rifle patented by Julius Rasmussen. This had been developed from an unsuccessful prototype created in the 1880s by Lieutenant Madsen, later Minister of War. It was only moderately efficient, but a light machine gun derivation proved to be extremely successful.

The Madsen machine gun had been overtaken by more modern designs by 1945, and its manufacturer then attempted to diversify – with only minimal success.

MADSEN-LJUNGMANN AUTOMATIC RIFLE
Made by Dansk Industri Syndikat A/S 'Madsen', Herlev.
Chambering options: 7.9x57 and others. **Action:** locked by tilting the back of the bolt down into the floor of the receiver; gas operated, semi-automatic only.

Otherwise generally as Swedish and Egyptian rifles (q.v.), except that a Danish-type knife bayonet was used.

Impressed by the success of the Swedish Ag-42, the Madsen company negotiated a license with the inventor in the hope of persuading the Danish army to adopt the rifle to replace the Krag-Jørgensen once the German occupation had ceased.

The first 1945-vintage prototypes were chambered for – among others – the 7x57 and 7.9x57 cartridges, which were larger and more powerful than the 6.5mm Swedish pattern. Consequently, the Danish rifle had a more robust mechanism than the Ag-42.

As the earliest Madsen-Ljungmann prototypes had been prone to extraction failures and case-head separations, the gas tube was coiled around the barrel to lengthen the distance from the barrel-port to the bolt carrier face. This extended the delay before the breech opened, but made the rifles much more difficult to clean than their Swedish antecedents.

Work on the Madsen-Ljungmann dragged on into the early 1950s, with few tangible results. The rifles could be recognized by their nose caps, with an attachment bar for a conventional bayonet, and by the ventilated sheet-steel handguard above the forend.

The Krag-Petersson navy rifle.

DENMARK

LIGHT AUTOMATIC RIFLE
Also known as 'LAR' or 'Madsen A-Carbine'
Made by Dansk Industri Syndikat AS 'Madsen', Copenhagen.
Total production: not known, but comparatively small. **Chambering:**
7.62x51, rimless. **Action:** locked by rotating lugs on the bolt head into the
barrel extension; gas operated, selective fire.
DATA FOR A SLIDING-BUTT EXAMPLE
43.3in overall (butt extended), 10.23lb with empty magazine. 20.6in barrel
(rifled portion only), 4-groove rifling; RH, concentric. Detachable box
magazine, 20 rounds. Aperture sight graduated to 600m (655yd). 2705 fps
with ball ammunition; 575±25 rpm. Optional knife bayonet.

DISA designer Gunnegaard Poulsen began development of
this rifle in 1957, a handful of 7.62x39 examples being made for
trials in Finland in 1958. A spherical piston-rod head entered a
recess in the tubular bolt carrier; after the gun had been fired, the
piston struck the carrier backward, rotating the bolt through 37
degrees to disengage the locking lugs.

The prototype rifles, which had one-piece wood stocks and
short tubular compensators, were tested in 1960 but were not successful enough to persuade the Finns to abandon a Kalashnikov
copy. The improved 7.62mm LAR appeared in 1962. Many of the
major parts were made of high-tensile aluminum alloy, including
the receiver, while the bore and parts of the gas system were chromium plated to minimize fouling. The perfected rifles could be
recognized by the floating barrel, protruding from the ventilated
sheet-steel guard between the gas-piston tube and a support rail.
A short wooden forend was fitted, though the butt could be fixed
wooden, sliding-bar or fixed-tube patterns. Most guns were
accompanied by a detachable bipod, which clipped to the bayonet
scabbard when not required.

Though the LAR would undoubtedly have made an efficient
weapon had development continued, it could not challenge established market leaders such as the FN FAL and Heckler & Koch G3.
As the project looked unlikely to repay the effort that had been
invested in it, the Madsen rifle was abandoned in 1965.

• Madsen, bolt-action type
MODEL 47 RIFLE
'Madsen Light Military Rifle'
Made by Dansk Industri Syndikat AS 'Madsen', Copenhagen.

Total production: not known. **Chambering options**: see notes. **Action:**
locked by lugs on the bolt head engaging recesses in the receiver as the
bolt handle was turned down.
DATA FOR A TYPICAL COLOMBIAN EXAMPLE
Chambering: 7.62x63 (U.S. 30-06), rimless. 43.3in overall, 8.5lb empty.
23.45in barrel, 4-groove rifling; concentric. Internal box magazine, 5 rounds.
Tangent-leaf sight graduated to 900m (985yd). 2705 fps with ball
ammunition. Knife bayonet.

Specifically intended for sale in areas where soldiers were of
small stature, this most distinctive 1948-vintage rifle had a split-
bridge receiver with the bolt handle acting as a safety lug. The
pistol grip stock had a short handguard running from the chamber
to the barrel band. Guns were also fitted with rudimentary muzzle
brakes and rubber buttplates.

Touted in chamberings ranging from 6.5mm to 8mm (including
7x57, 7.65x53, 7.9x57 and 30-06), the Madsen was not especially
successful. Too many military surplus weapons were available at
modest prices, and the only order known to have been fulfilled
was for about 5,000 guns placed by the government of Colombia
about 1957. Chambered for the U.S. 30 rimless cartridge, these
rifles bore the national crest on a circular medallion let into the left
side of the stock. They were apparently used by the navy as the
'Modelo 58'.

• Remington
MODEL 1867 RIFLE
Bagladeriffel m/1867
**Made by E. Remington & Sons, Ilion, New York, 1867-70 (40,540); and
by Geværfabrik Kjobenhaven, 1870-88.**
Total production: about 80,000, excluding conversions? **Chambering:**
11.7x51R, rimfire (see notes). **Action:** locked by shoulders on the hammer
body engaging the underside of the radial breech block.
50.4in overall, 9.25lb empty. 35.7in barrel, 5-groove rifling; RH,
concentric. Ramp-and-leaf sight graduated to 2000 alen (1370yd). About
1230 fps with m/1867 ball cartridges. m/1867 saber bayonet.

Chambered for a rimfire cartridge, this rifle had a straight-wrist
butt and a forend with three spring-retained bands. The bayonet
lug and tenon lay on the right side of the muzzle, and there were
swivels under the middle band and butt. The rear sight lay close
to the receiver, the leaf being hinged at the front.

The conversion of some surviving guns to m/67/93 standards
began in 1893 (see below), but the advent of the m/89 Krag-Jørgensen rifle led to the withdrawal of the 11.7mm Remington rifles

The Madsen-Ljungmann rifle,
developed experimentally
from a Swedish design.

The Madsen Light
Automatic Rifle (LAR).

from the infantry in 1896. They were converted for a centerfire cartridge and re-issued to coast and fortress artillerymen as 'm/67/96'. The obvious feature was a greatly lengthened back-sight leaf graduated to 2100m (2295yd).

MODEL 1867 CARBINE
Karabinen for rytter, artilleri og ingeniør, m/1867
Made by E. Remington & Sons, Ilion, New York, 1867-70 (1800); and by Geværfabrik Kjobenhaven (5200), 1870-1908.
Total production: 7000, excluding conversions. **Chambering:** 11.7x51R, rimfire (see notes). **Action:** as m/1867 rifle, above.

DATA FOR ENGINEER CARBINE
36in overall, 6.95lb empty. 21.05in barrel, 5-groove rifling; RH, concentric. Ramp-and-leaf sight graduated to 1500 alen (1030yd). 870 fps with m/1867 ball cartridges. No bayonet.

Introduced in 1867, the first of these guns was little more than a shortened m/67 infantry rifle. The solitary barrel band was held by a spring under the half-length forend.

THE GUNS
Model 1867 artillery carbine. This short rifle could be identified by the position of the sling swivels beneath the butt and barrel band, and by the lug-and-tenon for a sword bayonet on the right side of the muzzle.

Model 1867 cavalry carbine. The original type carried its sight on a muzzle band, and is believed to have had a sling stud or ring on the left side of the breech. Bayonets could not be mounted, and the back-sight leaves were hinged at the back of the block.

Model 1867 engineer carbine. This was similar to the artillery pattern, with swivels on the band and butt, but could not mount a bayonet.

MODEL 1867/93 NAVY RIFLE
Flådens Bagladeriffel m/1867/93
Converted by Geværfabriken Kjobenhaven, 1893-5.
Production total: not known. **Chambering:** 8x58R, rimmed. **Action:** as m/1867 rifle, above.

40.25in overall, 8.4lb empty. 29.15in barrel, 6-groove rifling; RH, polygonal. Ramp-and-leaf sight graduated to 2000m (2185yd). About 1920 fps with m/1889 ball cartridges. m/1893 sword bayonet.

These were made from m/1867 rifles. They had a new barrel and forend, and a full-length handguard. Two bands and a special nose cap were fitted, the bayonet lug-and-tenon appearing on the right side of the muzzle. The rear sight lay immediately ahead of the receiver.

MODEL 1867/96 CAVALRY CARBINE
Rytterkarabin m/1867/96
Converted by Geværfabriken Kjobenhavn, 1897-1908.
Production total: about 3000. **Chambering:** 11.7x51R, rimmed. **Action:** as m/1867 rifle, above.

Otherwise similar to unaltered m/1867 carbines except rear sight (ramp-and-leaf pattern graduated to 1200 metres [1310yd]) and muzzle velocity (935 fps).

Introduced in 1897, this was a conversion of the m/1867 carbine for cavalry service pending development of a Krag-type carbine. Chambering centerfire ammunition, it originally had swivels on the underside of the butt and band. The back-sight leaf was apparently re-graduated, but was otherwise the same as the original 1500-alen (1030yd) pattern and hinged at the back of the base. Surviving carbines were recalled in 1905 for modification, receiving a new butt with the swivel on the left side. The second swivel was fitted to a collar on the barrel. Distinguished by its hinged aluminum lid, the distinctive butt-comb magazine could hold 10 rounds vertically. Cartridges could be transferred if required to a quick-loader fixed to the right side of the forend ahead of the breech. The modified Remington carbine lasted until replaced by the Krag m/89 Rytterkarabin about 1914.

• Schultz & Larsen
Best known for its custom gunsmithing work prior to 1939, Schultz & Larsen made a small number of carbines for the Danish police during World War II, progressing in the early 1950s to a modest range of improved rim- and centerfire guns. In addition, large numbers of German Karabiner 98k were converted for the Danish rifle association in the 1950s. Details of these half-stocked target rifles will be found in the Mauser section.

MODEL 1942 POLICE RIFLE
Rigspolitikarabin m/42 (Rplt.42)
Made by Schultz & Larsen Geværfabrik, Otterup, 1942-3.
Total production: about 600, 1942-3. **Chambering:** 8x58R, rimmed. **Action:** locked by four lugs on the bolt head turning into the receiver behind the magazine as the bolt handle turned down, and by the bolt-handle base entering its seat.

43.6in overall, 8.65lb empty. 22.65in barrel, 4-groove rifling; RH, concentric. Integral box magazine, 4 rounds. Fixed sight regulated for 200m (220yd). 2130 fps with ball ammunition. No bayonet.

The first guns of this type were delivered in 1942. Chambered for the standard 8mm rimmed Danish service cartridges, they had one piece pistol grip stocks extending to the muzzle. A handguard ran forward from the chamber under the single band. A simple nose cap was fitted, swivels appearing under the band and butt. The receiver was tubular, with a large oval ejection port, and the single-column magazine (integral with the trigger guard) protruded beneath the stock. Unlatching the floorplate allowed cartridges to be loaded singly into the magazine. Persistently disrupted by sabotage, work finally finished after only a few hundred guns had been completed.

MODEL 54 SPORTING RIFLE
Made by Schultz & Larsen Geværfabrik, Otterup, about 1954-73.
Total production: not known. **Chambering options:** see notes. **Action:** as M1942 police carbine, above.

DATA FOR A TYPICAL 68DL SPORTER
Chambering: 308 Winchester, rimless. 44.5in overall, 7.5lb empty. 24in barrel, 4-groove rifling; RH, concentric. Internal box magazine, 4 rounds. Optical sight. 2850 fps with 150-grain bullet.

The first sporting rifles were made in 1953 by adapting the 1942-pattern police carbine to accept an internal magazine, the ejection port being broadened to allow cartridges to be loaded through the open action.

SIMILAR GUNS
Model 54J. These magazine-fed sporting rifles were offered commercially in 270 Winchester, 7x61 Sharpe & Hart or 30-06 Springfield. Barrels measured 24in (270 or 30-06) and 26in (7x61). The half-stocks had a Monte Carlo butt and cheekpiece, with checkering on the pistol grip and forend.

Model 54M ('Match'). This 300m Free Rifle was built on a special single shot action. Most guns chambered the Norwegian 6.5x55 rimless service round, though some were made for 30-06, 308 Winchester and other American cartridges. Set triggers and 27.55in heavy barrels were standard, weight totaling a little over 15.4lb with the hooked buttplate and a hand-rest beneath the forend. Thumb-hole stocks were customary.

Model 61M. Introduced in 1961, this 22LR rimfire Free Rifle was distinguished by a refined thumbhole half-stock with squared contours. Weight rose to about 16.5lb, sights were improved, and the pistol grip invariably had adjustable heel-rests. Hand stops, articulated hand rests, and sling anchors were among the optional extras which could be fitted to the accessory rail beneath the squared forend.

Model 62M. This 1962-vintage adaptation of the rimfire Model 61M was chambered for the 308 Winchester (7.62x51 NATO) cartridge. Externally, however, the two guns were much the same except for the size and shape of the ejection port.

Model 65. Dating from 1965, this was an improved sporting rifle chambered for 270 Winchester, 7x61 Sharpe & Hart, 30-06, 308 Winchester, 308 Norma Magnum or 358 Norma Magnum ammunition. The gun had an elegant Monte Carlo stock with white spacers accompanying the pistol grip cap and the ventilated rubber shoulder pad; the forend tip was rounded. The bolt handle was swept backward in a curve until the grasping ball lay above the trigger.

Model 65DL. No more than a deluxe variant of the Model 65, this had a half-stock with a rosewood forend tip and pistol grip cap.

Model 68. This sporter was similar to the 1965 patterns, but the curve of the bolt handle was reduced, an improved radial safety catch appeared on the right side of the bolt shroud, and a recessed bolt head was used. Rifles were made in about twenty chamberings, including several magnums, but work seems to have been abandoned about 1973.

Model 68DL. This deluxe version of the Model 68 had a specially selected walnut half-stock with a rosewood forend tip and pistol grip cap.

MODEL 52 TARGET RIFLE

Made by Schultz & Larsen Geværfabrik, Otterup, about 1953-60.

Total production: at least 15,000.

Chambering options: 6.5x55 and 30-06. **Action:** locked by two lugs on the bolt engaging recesses in the receiver behind the chamber as the bolt handle was turned down, and by the third lug opposing the bolt-handle base entering its seat.

DATA FOR A TYPICAL 6.5MM EXAMPLE

47.65in overall, 9.5lb empty. 27.55in barrel, 4-groove rifling; RH, concentric. Internal box magazine, 5 rounds. Aperture rear sight graduated to 500m (545yd). 2720 fps with 139-grain bullet.

These guns were produced to satisfy the needs of the Danish shooting association, which sought replacements for the Krag-Jorgensen. The basis for the conversion were Gew. 24 (t) and Kar. 98k seized from the Germans at the end of World War II; the Czechoslovakian guns were preferred, as their quality reflected pre-war origins. Schultz & Larsen fitted a target-grade barrel, adapted the magazines for the longer 30-06 cartridge, honed the trigger mechanism, and cut the military stock to half-stock proportions. A new swivel was added to the forend tip. The sights were intended to supplicate the Garand patterns, as surplus 30 M1 rifles had become the service rifle of the Danish army. The rear sight was a click-adjustable aperture pattern graduated from 200m (220yd) to 500m (545yd); attached to the receiver bridge, it projected forward far enough to prevent the use of stripper clips.

SIMILAR GUNS

Model 58. This was a modified form of the M52 with a micro-adjustable Schultz & Larsen M24 aperture sight on the receiver and a replaceable-element tunnel sight at the muzzle. It chambered the 308 Winchester round (7.62x51 NATO), but retained the adapted military stock.

Model 58E. Sharing the refurbished Mauser action, this was specifically built for the British market. A heavier barrel was set in a new target-style half-stock with a high comb, a cheekpiece and a rubber shoulder plate. Two swivels lay beneath the forend. The sights were customarily Parker M68 or comparable aperture patterns with the eyepiece farther back than the Danish designs. A typical rifle was 47.8in long and weighed 11.1lb.

• Snider

The Danish army adopted the Remington rolling block in 1867; however, not enough money could be spared to re-equip immediately and a Snider conversion was also approved.

M1848-65 SHORT RIFLE
Bagladeriffel m/1848-65

Converted in the Geværfabrik Kjobenhavn, 1866-8.

Total production: not known. **Chambering:** 16.9mm, rimfire. **Action:** locked by swinging a longitudinally-pivoting block behind the chamber.

52.15in overall, 9.7lb empty. 34.05in barrel, 6-groove rifling; RH, concentric. Single shot only. Tangent sight graduated to 900 alen (615yd). 1065 fps with standard ball cartridges. m/1848 socket bayonet.

These guns were adapted from an old 1848-type pillar-breech rifle, the work being undertaken in the state firearms factory in 1866-8. The original barrels were fitted with a breech block swinging to the left, and the Dahlhoff sight was graduated for 300-900 Danish ells. Some rifles also retained the patch box in the right side of the butt, but many were re-stocked (using the original bands and nose-cap). Trigger guards and sideplates were brass, remaining mounts being iron. One swivel lay under the butt, the other being held by a screw through the middle band.

M1853-66 NAVY RIFLE
Flådens Bagladeriffel m/53-66

Converted in the Geværfabrik Kjobenhavn, 1866.

Total production: about 2250. **Chambering:** 16.9mm, rimfire. **Action:** as m/48-65, above.

47.25in overall, 8.93lb empty. 28.5in barrel, 6-groove rifling; RH, concentric. Single shot only. Tangent sight graduated to 600 alen (410yd). About 990 fps with standard ball cartridges. m/1848 socket bayonet.

This was originally a pillar-breech weapon, 5,000 of which had been bought in Liége – apparently from Malherbé – by the Schleswig-Holstein rebels. After the failure of the 1848 insurrection, 2540 guns were adapted in Kronborg in 1853-5 and issued to the Danish navy.

The barrel was retained by keys, a bayonet bar lay on the right side of the muzzle, and the back sling swivel lay on the spurred brass trigger guard. The rear sight was a Dahlhoff 'grasshopper' pattern, and the brass-hilted sword bayonet had a double-edged blade. The Snider-type breeches apparently opened to the right.

DOMINICAN REPUBLIC

• Cristobal

Unusually, for such a small country, the Dominican Republic created an effectual arms factory in San Cristobal in the late 1940s – largely to use the talents of fugitive firearms designers from Hungary and Italy. The first weapon to be produced was a submachine gun, copied from the Beretta Mo. 1938, but work then concentrated on a light automatic rifle chambering the U.S. 30 M1 Carbine cartridge.

Cristobal carbines were popular in Central America, selling in quantity to Cuba in addition to service with the Dominican Republic armed forces. Production has been estimated in excess of 200,000, but details are lacking.

CRISTOBAL CARBINE MODEL 2

Made by Armeria San Cristobal.

Total production: not known. **Chambering:** 30 M1 Carbine, rimless. **Action:** delayed blowback; semi-automatic only.

37.2in overall, 7.85lb without magazine. 16.2in barrel, 4-groove rifling; RH, concentric. Detachable box magazine, 30 rounds. Spring-leaf and elevator sight. 1870 fps with standard ball cartridges; 575±25 rpm. No bayonet.

Designed by the Hungarian Pal Kiraly and introduced in about 1955, the Cristobal M2 had a Beretta-like appearance externally, relying on the mechanism of that submachine gun to give single shots from the front trigger or fully automatic fire by pressing the rear trigger. Internally, however, a lever connected the lightweight bolt head and the heavy body. When the gun fired, the resistance of the lever had to be overcome before the bolt body began to move backward, delaying the opening of the breech until the chamber pressure had dropped to a safe level; this was much the same system that had been used in Kiraly's Hungarian submachine guns a decade earlier.

SIMILAR GUNS

Model 3. Field service showed that the M2 overheated in automatic fire. The improved M3 (or 'Mk 3') of 1961 discarded the original wooden handguard for a perforated sheet-steel forend and could accept an FN export-pattern knife bayonet. A few guns were made with a tubular folding butt, but were only issued in limited quantities.

MODEL 62 RIFLE

Made by Armeria San Cristobal.

Total production: not known. **Chambering:** 7.62x51, rimless. **Action:** locked by displacing the rear of the breech block into the receiver floor; gas operated, semi-automatic.

42.5in overall, 10.47lb with loaded magazine. 21.25in barrel, 4-groove rifling; RH, concentric. Detachable box magazine, 20 rounds. Ramp sight graduated to 600m (655yd)? 2705 fps with standard ball cartridges. No bayonet.

Introduced about 1962, this unexceptional infantry rifle was created by combining the proven gas system of the U.S. Garand/M14 rifle with the efficient locking system of the FN FAL. It had a conventional pistol grip stock, ending well short of the muzzle, and a short sheet-steel handguard above the forend.

By the time the rifle was ready for production (about 1966), the advent of better weapons and the movement of the U.S. toward a smaller caliber halted work after only a couple hundred M62 rifles had been made.

A drawing of the Cristobal Carbine.

• Mauser

Some ex-Brazilian Mo.1908 rifles and short rifles were acquired by the Dominicans in the early 1950s. They were refinished in the government arms factory in San Cristobal, but were soon displaced by surplus U.S. weapons and sold on the commercial market. Brazilian markings were ground away and a new identifier added to the left side of the receiver – 'ARMERIA F.A. REP. DOM.' with a date and a new serial number.

ECUADOR

• Mauser

These guns were marked 'EJERCITO DEL EQUATOR' or 'EJERCITO EQUATORIANO' on the receiver. The chamber-top crest comprised an oval landscape featuring the Chimborazo volcano rising, below a shining sun, out of a sea on which a steamer rode. The device was surmounted by the obligatory condor, had a fasces at its base, and was backed by two pairs of national flags plus a wreath.

PRE-1914 PATTERNS

The earliest Mausers were Argentine-type 7.65x53 Mo. 1891 (q.v.), followed by 7.65mm 'Mo. 1907' (1904 Brazilian-type) rifles and a handful of carbines of unknown designation.

LATER PATTERNS

Substantial quantities of Czechoslovakian 7.65mm vz. 24 short rifles and vz. 12/33 carbines were purchased during the 1930s, while Fabrique Nationale supplied additional short rifles in the 1940s.

EGYPT

• FN-Saive

Fabrique Nationale supplied the Egyptian army with substantial quantities of 7.9x57 SAFN rifles in the days of King Farouk. They were later superseded by the Hakim, based on the Swedish Ljungmann rifle (q.v.). The Egyptian rifles may be recognized partly by the chambering, and also by Arabic numerals on the rear sight.

• Kalashnikov

The armed forces have used Soviet-made AK and AKM rifles in addition to several million AKM-type rifles made by 'Factory 54' of Maadi Military & Civil Industries Company. The factory was equipped with Soviet assistance in the late 1950s. The gun has a laminated wood butt and forend, and a checkered plastic pistol grip.

• Ljungmann
HAKIM RIFLE
Made by the State Factory 54, Port Said (later Maadi Military & Civil Industries Company).
Total production: not known. **Chambering:** 7.9x57, rimless. **Action:** as Danish Madsen-Ljungmann rifle (q.v.).

47.6in overall, 10.63lb empty. 23.25in barrel, 4-groove rifling; concentric, RH. Detachable box magazine, 10 rounds. Tangent-leaf sight graduated to 1000m (1095yd). 2855 fps with standard ammunition. Sword bayonet.

A combination of the overthrow of King Farouk and the comparative failure of the SAFN rifle in service created the need to establish an indigenous small arms industry. This was undertaken in 1954 with machine tools purchased from Husqvarna in Sweden.

Production of the Hakim rifle began in 1955. It was essentially similar to the Swedish Ag-42.B, sharing the straight-tube gas system and aberrant cocking system, but was appreciably heavier and its gas port could be adjusted to allow for variations in ammunition pressure. It was stocked to the muzzle, with a single retaining band, and had a wooden handguard from the chamber to the nose cap. A perforated muzzle brake/compensator appeared ahead of the front sight block. In addition to Arabic markings on the backsight leaf, the rifle was usually dated on the front left side of the receiver above its serial number.

The Hakim was acceptably accurate, but heavy, unwieldy, and made to such fine tolerances that it was prone to jam in sandy conditions. The Egyptians eventually substituted the lighter and more reliable Kalashnikov.

RASHID RIFLE
Made by the State Factory 54, Port Said (later Maadi Military & Civil Industries Company).
Total production: not known. **Chambering:** 7.62x39, rimless. **Action:** as Hakim rifle, above.

42.4in overall, about 8.25lb empty. 22.45in barrel, 4-groove rifling; concentric, RH. Detachable box magazine, 10 rounds. Tangent-leaf sight graduated to 1000m (1095yd). 2395 fps with standard ammunition. Integral folding bayonet.

Apparently dating from the period (1959-60?) in which tooling for the Kalashnikov was being undertaken, perhaps to provide the Egyptian reserve with weapons chambered for the new intermediate cartridge, this was an improved Hakim. It retained the direct-impingement gas system, but the charging handle was attached directly to the bolt carrier and an SKS-type bayonet pivoted on an attachment block behind the front sight.

• Remington
MODEL 1868 RIFLE
Made by E. Remington & Sons, Ilion, 1869-76.

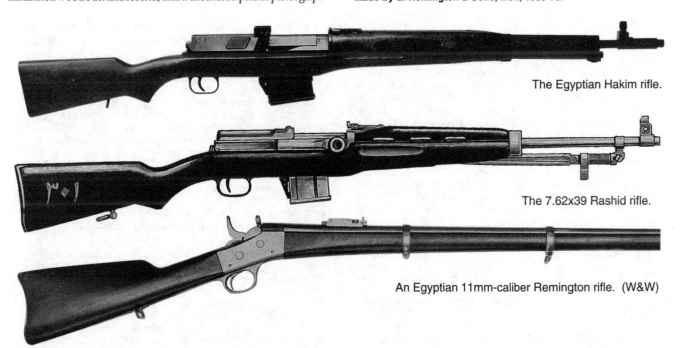

The Egyptian Hakim rifle.

The 7.62x39 Rashid rifle.

An Egyptian 11mm-caliber Remington rifle. (W&W)

Total production: at least 60,000 – see text. **Chambering:** 11.43x50R, rimmed. **Action:** locked by shoulders on the hammer body propping the radial breech block behind the chamber.

50.3in overall, 9.15lb unladen. 35in barrel, 5-groove rifling; RH, concentric. Ramp-and-leaf sight graduated to 1000m (1095yd). 1280 fps with ball cartridges. Saber bayonet.

The Egyptian government gave Remington an order for a substantial quantity of rifles in 1868. An additional order was forthcoming in 1869, but the original 'Egyptian' guns were sold to France during the Franco-Prussian War. The contractual obligations were finally fulfilled when the last of 60,000 rifles was delivered from Ilion in 1876. However, some Egyptian-type rifles and carbines have been seen with the marks of E. & L. Nagant of Liége, to whom Remington had granted a license in the mid-1870s. M1868 rifles had standard American-type rolling blocks, and three spring-retained bands. Swivels appeared beneath the butt and the middle band, while the lug on the right side of the barrel accepted a brass-hilted bayonet made by Ames.

SIMILAR GUNS

M1868 carbine. Small numbers of these guns were also acquired. They had short half-length forends retained by a single band, and were not issued with bayonets.

EL SALVADOR

Mauser

These guns bore a chamber crest of a triangular seascape with five volcanoes, beneath a staff supporting a Liberty Cap on a sunburst. The device was backed by five national flags and usually lay on a wreath. The legend 'RÉPUBLICA DE EL SALVADOR' was also to be found. The earliest Mausers were Chilean-style Mo. 1895 rifles in 7x57, apparently purchased from DWM in about 1900. Later guns included some 7mm vz. 12/33 short rifles acquired from Ceskoslovenská Zbrojovká in the early 1930s.

ESTONIA

Mauser

Czechoslovakian 'L'-model short rifles were purchased in 1931, the guns apparently being supplied with Austrian-style M1895 knife bayonets. Their chambering may have been for the British 303 rimmed round, substantial quantities of which had been sold to Estonia in the early 1920s.

ETHIOPIA

Mauser

Most of these Mausers will be found with the crowned cypher of Haile Selassie I in Amharic letters on the chamber-top, surrounded by a wreath of a grape-vine and an ear of wheat. They may also display a Lion of Judah property mark.

FN supplied 25,000 Mle 24 Mauser short rifles and carbines in 1933-5, and similar quantities of 'Standard-Modell' Mausers – all used as the 'M1933' – were purchased in the same era.

Three contracts were placed with Mauser-Werke in 1933-5. The earliest, perhaps for a few hundred rifles only, was identified by 'A'-prefix serial numbers and the elaborate chamber crest.

The second order was larger, but the pattern of the serial numbers is not known; the third order, however, was taken from the 'B'-prefix commercial series, displayed five-digit numbers, and bore the Mauser banner trademark on the receiver ring. The Lion of Judah lay on the barrel between the back-sight base and the receiver.

FINLAND

The Finns seized the chance to free themselves from Russian shackles soon after the October Revolution and declared independence on 20th July 1919. By 1920, the Finnish army and Protective Corps (*Suojeluskuntain Ylieskunnan*, or Sk.Y) mustered 100,000 men under arms. The initial small-arms influences were largely German (many Finns had fought for the Germans during World War

I), but the capture of Helsinki arsenal led to a reliance on Russian-style Mosin-Nagant rifles, Maxim machine-guns and Nagant revolvers. This influence is still evident, with the adoption of a modified form of the Kalashnikov assault rifle.

• Kalashnikov

The first prototypes of the improved Kalashnikov were made in the mid-1950s, and the 'm/58' Valmet pattern laid the basis for the perfected designs. In addition to Sako- and Valmet-made guns, however, Finland has used the standard Soviet AK as the Rynnakokivääri m/54. The folding-stock version was used by paratroops and police, but all Soviet-made weapons were withdrawn into store in the mid 1980s.

MODEL 1960 ASSAULT RIFLE
Rynnakkokivääri m/60
Made by Valmet Oy, Jyväskylä, 1960-1.
Total production: 600? **Chambering:** 7.62x39, rimless. **Action:** locked by rotating lugs on the bolt head into the receiver; gas operated, selective fire.

36in overall, 9.02lb with empty magazine. 16.55in barrel, 4-groove rifling; RH, concentric. Detachable box magazine, 30 rounds. Tangent-leaf rear sight graduated to 1000m (1095yd). 2330 fps with M43 ball cartridges; 750±25rpm. m/60 knife bayonet.

Derived from the Valmet m/58 prototype, these rifles were very different externally from the Kalashnikov. The plastic forend, tubular steel butt, and rear sight on the receiver cover were distinctive. Two basic patterns were made for field trials.

THE GUNS

Type A rifle. These guns—200 provided by Sako—lacked a trigger guard, relying on a vertical post between the trigger lever and the magazine, and had a fluted forend pierced with ventilation holes. The receiver was a carefully machined forging, selectors were marked 'S' and 'Y', and a bar in the butt was a sling anchor point.

Type B rifle. These were similar to Type A, but had trigger guards released by a spring-catch on the back of the pistol grip; 200 were made by Valmet for field trials. A selection of bayonets was developed, often with Beretta-inspired folding blades, and the butt tubes were usually covered with rubberized insulation. The Valmet mark appeared on the left side of the receiver.

fm/60 rifle. Type B guns were preferred, and so another 200 slightly modified 'fm/60' were delivered for field trials in the winter of 1960. Finally, after additional changes had been made, the Finnish Defence Force approved the modified m/62 (below).

MODEL 1962 ASSAULT RIFLE
Rynnakkokivääri m/62
Made by Valmet Oy, Jyväskylä, 1963-75; and by Oy Sako Ab, Riihimäki, 1963-6.
Total production: not known. **Chambering:** 7.62x39, rimless.
Otherwise generally similar to m/60, above, except bayonet (m/62 knife pattern).

This was adopted to replace the semi-experimental m/60, embodying many detail refinements. The receiver was simplified, and the ribbed plastic handguard and pistol grip took different forms. The furniture was a dark greenish hue on the original Sako-made examples, but black on the later Valmet examples. The gas tube of the original guns generally lay in a stamped liner, with the top exposed, while later ones were often enclosed.

The rear sight attachment was improved in the late 1960s, and a solid-top hood replaced the previous open pattern which had allowed easy access to the adjustable-height front sight element. Selectors were marked • and •••, for single shots and automatic fire respectively; the dots were impressed on early guns but raised on later examples. The serial numbers of Valmet-made guns began at 100001, whereas Sako products commenced at 200001.

SIMILAR GUNS

m/62 rifle, new pattern. From 1972 onward, tritium night sights were fitted to new guns and the rounded rear sight protectors were replaced by taller square versions. Rifles with the original sights were reclassified as 'm/62 PT'. After purchasing small numbers of the m/62/76 (see below), the Finns returned to the folding-butt m/62 in 1985 on the grounds that the machined-steel receiver was more durable than the stamped version. Orders for about 40,000 new guns had been placed with the Sako-Valmet combine by the end of 1988. However, apart from dated markings and minor improvements in the action and sights, they are identical with the original m/62 patterns.

m/62 PT rifle. A post-1972 designation, this was applied retrospectively to m/62 rifles with the original sights. See 'm/62, new pattern', above.

m/62 S rifle. A few semi-automatic m/62-type rifles were sold commercially under this designation; they had fixed or folding tubular butts, though guns touted in the U.S. often had conventional fixed wooden butts and a wooden pistol grip.

MODEL 1971 ASSAULT RIFLE
Rynnakkokivääri m/71
Made by Valmet Oy, Jyväskylä, 1971-3.
Chambering options: 5.56x45 or 7.62x39, rimless. **Action:** as m/60, above.
DATA FOR A TYPICAL 5.56MM EXAMPLE
36.55in overall, 7.92lb with empty magazine. 16.55in barrel, 4-groove rifling; RH, concentric. Detachable box magazine, 30 rounds. Tangent-leaf rear sight graduated to 1000m (1095yd). 3150 fps with M193 ball cartridges; 650±25rpm. m/60 knife bayonet (optional).

Introduced in the early 1970s, this was a short-lived variant of the m/62 with a stamped receiver and a front sight assembly much more like the Soviet AKM than the Finnish m/62 service rifle. The synthetic butt, not unlike that of the Fabrique Nationale CAL (q.v.), was accompanied by a parallel-side forend enveloping the gas cylinder. Most guns had mechanical hold-opens and the rear sight ahead of the ejection port.

5.56mm guns were offered commercially—some semi-automatic examples being sold as 'm/71 S'—while most of the 7.62mm guns were supplied to the Finnish army. The m/71 was soon withdrawn in favor of the improved m/62/76; survivors are apparently still held in store.

MODEL 1976 ASSAULT RIFLE
Rynnakkokivääri m/62/76
Made by Valmet Oy, Jyväskylä, 1976-87, and Sako-Valmet, 1987-90.
Chambering options: 5.56x45 or 7.62x39, rimless. **Action:** as m/60.
DATA FOR A TYPICAL M76W
Chambering: 5.56x45, rimless. 35.95in overall, 8.09lb with empty magazine. 16.55in barrel, 4-groove rifling; RH, concentric. Detachable box magazine, 15, 20 or 30 rounds. Tangent-leaf rear sight graduated to 1000m (1095yd). 3150 fps with M193 ball cartridges; 650±25rpm. m/62 knife bayonet (optional).

After producing a series of prototypes, Valmet introduced the m/76 rifle with a sheet-steel receiver in 1977. This was purchased by the Finnish armed forces in small numbers, but did not prove durable enough to displace the m/62. The rifle has been produced in several variants; in addition to limited sales to the Finnish army, some have been sold to Qatar and Indonesia.

SIMILAR GUNS
m/62/76 rifle. This was the Finnish army designation for the standard 1976-type rifle, with a conventional selector (with safe, single-shot and fully automatic positions) on the right side of the receiver. On 1st January 1987, Sako and Valmet amalgamated as 'Sako-Valmet Oy'. After several changes in the controlling interests, the Sako name was bestowed on a privately capitalized company making rifles and ammunition. Work continued in the Riihimäki and Jyväskylä factories respectively. This led to the development of the so-called 'm/90' and 'm/92' rifles, and then to the RK m/95 TP listed below.

m/62/76 TP rifle. Also applied by the Finnish army, this signified a folding butt (or *Taittoperä*).

Model 76F rifle. This designation was applied to the standard commercial version of the rifle with selective-fire capability and a folding tubular butt.

The Valmet M/62 Kalashnikov rifle and bayonet.

The Valmet M71S Kalashnikov rifle.

The Valmet M62/76 Kalashnikov rifle.

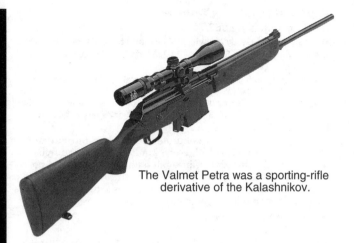

The Valmet Petra was a sporting-rifle derivative of the Kalashnikov.

Model 76P rifle. The standard selective-fire pattern, this had a fixed plastic butt.

Model 76T rifle. Distinguished by a fixed tubular butt, this version of the selective-fire Finnish Kalashnikov was mechanically similar to the other guns in the series.

Model 76W rifle. The suffix indicates that this gun had a fixed wood butt.

Law Enforcement Series. These were minor variants of the standard commercial guns—'F', 'P', 'T' and 'W' versions—with the trigger mechanism adapted to prevent fully-automatic operation.

Model 76B rifle (also known as 'Model 82'). Introduced by Valmet in 1981, this was a bullpup version of the Model 76. The standard action was inserted in a one-piece synthetic stock, reducing overall length to about 27.9in and weight to about 7.3lb. The trigger and pistol grip were moved forward ahead of the magazine, and a special raised rear sight lay ahead of the ejection port. Like most guns of its type, the Model 76B handled oddly. It was never made in quantity.

MODEL 95 ASSAULT RIFLE
Rynnakkokivääri m/95 PT
Made by Sako Oy, Riihimäki, 1995-7.
Total production: not known. **Chambering:** 7.62x39, rimless. **Action:** as m/60, above.

36.8in overall, 9.9lb with loaded magazine. 16.55in barrel, 4-groove rifling; RH, concentric. Detachable box magazine, 30 rounds. Rocking 'L' rear sight for 150m (165yd) and 300m (330yd). 2330 fps with ball cartridges; about 660rpm. m/62 knife bayonet (optional).

Development of this rifle began in 1986, though the first prototypes (known tentatively as the 'm/90') dated from 1989-90. Considerable changes were made to the selector, which was moved to the left side of the receiver where—ironically—it had been placed on the original Kalashnikov prototypes of 1946. A spring-loaded cover plate was added to prevent snow and dust entering the charging-handle slot, and many other improvements were made internally. Unfortunately, the Finnish Defence Force deemed that the alterations were too radical, compromising interchangeability with the existing m/62 and m/62/76 rifles, and so a simpler m/92/62 pattern was substituted.

Adopted as the m/95 TP (*Taittoperä*, 'folding stock'), the rifles have a tubular butt which can be swung forward to lie alongside the receiver. The design of the magazine housing has been changed to give extra support to the magazine, and a rail for optical and electro-optical sights appears on the left side of the receiver. The charging handle has been tipped upward so that, if preferred, it can be retracted with the left hand. The sights have additional open Tritium 'dusk sights' and an improved brake/compensator on the muzzle.

SIMILAR GUNS
m/95 S rifle. This is a semi-automatic sporting version of the basic assault rifle, with a fixed wooden butt instead of the folding metal pattern. The recent end of assault-rifle production in Finland has ensured that it will never be made in quantity.

PETRA SPORTING RIFLE
Made by Valmet Oy, Jyväskylä, 1982-6.
Total production: not known. **Chambering options:** 243 Winchester or 308 Winchester. **Action:** as m/60, above.
DATA FOR A TYPICAL 308 EXAMPLE
39.15in overall, 8.5lb with empty magazine 17.7in barrel, 4-groove rifling; RH, concentric. Detachable box magazine, 10 rounds. Tangent-leaf rear sight graduated to 1000m (1095yd). 2625 fps with FN Match ammunition.

Announced commercially in 1982, this was one of the few attempts to adapt the Kalashnikov for the sporting fraternity. An enlarged Model 76, restricted to semi-automatic fire, it was fitted with a good quality wood butt featuring a straight comb, checkering on the pistol grip and a ventilated rubber recoil pad. The checkered open-top forend was also wood. Swivels lay on the barrel and under the butt, and a mount for an optical sight appeared to the receiver. Finish was excellent.

• Mannlicher
Many Italian-type Mo.1891-38 Mannlicher-Carcano rifles and carbines were supplied to Finland during the Winter and Continuation Wars of 1939-40 and 1941-4. These can usually be identified by the army property mark, 'SA' in a square.

• Mauser
Prior to the development of the long L-61 proprietary action described elsewhere, Sako offered rifles on the FN-Mauser action (1950-7 only). Chambered for the 270 Winchester or 30-06 cartridges, the guns had 24in barrels and weighed about 7.5lb. They had Monte Carlo-pattern half-stocks with plain rounded forend tips, and open folding-leaf rear sights. A Magnum version, with a rubber recoil pad, accepted 300 or 375 H&H Magnum ammunition.

• Mosin-Nagant
Owing to the capture of many Russian rifles in Helsinki armory, the Mosin-Nagant was selected as the standard infantry weapon—though 8,000 ex-German Kar. 98 AZ, obtained from the French, served the cavalry until 1923. The Finns soon began to make changes of their own, but the rifles were always built around original pre-1917 Mosin-Nagant actions repaired and refinished locally.

MODEL 1891 RIFLE
Kivääri m/91
For data, see 'Model 1891 rifle' in the 'Russia (Tsarist): Mosin-Nagant' section.

Many ex-Russian rifles were used with little modification. However, some others—infantry and dragoon patterns alike—will now often be found with modified handguards, and sling rings through slots in the stock which have replaced the original Russian swivels. Rifles which survived into the 1920s received back-sight leaves graduated in metres instead of *arshin*. Some guns will be found with the barrel and forend cut to approximate to the later short rifles; most of these date from the Winter War, but it is not known if the changes were sanctioned officially.

MODEL 1924 RIFLE
Kivääri m/24
Converted by the Sk.Y workshops in Helsinki, 1924-7.

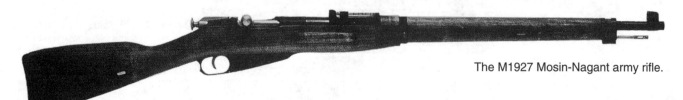

The M1927 Mosin-Nagant army rifle.

The M1939 Mosin-Nagant rifle.

Total production: about 38,000. **Chambering:** 7.62x54R, rimmed.
Action: locked by two lugs on a detachable bolt head engaging recesses in the receiver behind the chamber as the bolt handle was turned down.

51.2in overall, 9.25lb empty. 32.2in barrel, 4-groove rifling; RH, concentric. Integral box magazine loaded from a stripper clip, 5 rounds. Ramp-and-leaf rear sight (see notes). 2885 fps with obr. 1908g ball cartridges. Obr. 1891g socket bayonet.

The Finns ordered 3,000 new 7.62mm barrels from Schweizerische Industrie-Gesellschaft in 1923. These displayed the maker's name on the right side ahead of the breech. In 1924, therefore, the Swiss barrels (which had a step rather than a continuous taper) were fitted to reconditioned actions retrieved from scrapped weapons, creating the m/24 or m/91-24 rifle. The stock-bedding was altered, requiring a new barrel channel, and the front band was pinned to the stock so that the barrel could float.

The conversions were so successful that the Finns made a few small dimensional changes and ordered 10,000 more barrels. Work continued until the Sk.Y workshop moved to Riihimäki in 1927. Most of these rifles retained the original Russian rear sight, though the graduations on the back-sight base—to 1,200 arshin—were replaced by metric near-equivalents running to 850m (930yd). Sight leaves were rarely altered.

Several hundred m/24 were shortened in 1932 by the government rifle factory (VKT) in Jyväskylä, possibly for artillerymen. Work was apparently spread over two years.

MODEL 1927 SHORT RIFLE, ARMY TYPE
Kivääri m/27
Made by Valtions Kivääritedhas, Jyväskylä, 1927-39.
Total production: not known. **Chambering:** 7.62x54R, rimmed. **Action:** as m/1924 rifle, above.
DATA FOR INFANTRY PATTERN
46.65in overall, 9.06lb empty. 26.95in barrel, 4-groove rifling; RH, concentric. Integral box magazine loaded from a stripper clip, 5 rounds. Ramp-and-leaf rear sight (see notes). 2430 fps with heavy ball cartridges. m/27 or m/35 sword bayonet.

Introduced in 1927, these were shortened versions of the m/24 (though otherwise comparable with the earlier design). The nose cap, hinged in the manner of the German Kar. 98 AZ, carried a bayonet lug. The rear sight had an aperture instead of the original open notch and its base was re-graduated to 800m (875yd). The bolt handle was turned down, part of the stock-side being removed to receive it.

Problems with the nose cap, which tended to rotate laterally, were solved in the early 1930s by adding extension plates. Anchored in a recess milled in the side of the nose cap, these ran back along the forend and were retained by transverse bolts.

SIMILAR GUNS
m/27 cavalry rifle. This was identical with the infantry type, but measured only 43.7in overall and weighed 8.77lb.

MODEL 1928 SHORT RIFLE, PROTECTIVE CORPS
Sk.Y kivääri m/28
Made by Suojeluskuntain Ase- ja Konepaja Osakeyhtö ('Sako'), Riihimäki, 1927-30.
Total production: 30,000? **Chambering:** 7.62x54R, rimmed.
Otherwise generally as m/1927 army rifle, above, except weight (9.22lb empty) and bayonet (m/28 Sk.Y or m/35 sword patterns).

Adopted in August 1927, this refinement of the m/24 has been credited to Niilo Talvenheimo, the principal arms inspector of the Protective Corps. The barrel was shortened, the depth and pitch of the rifling were revised, the trigger was improved, and the stock was changed.

The first rifles were assembled in the Sako factory in November using new SIG-made barrels and selected Russian actions. They had a single barrel band and a simple nose cap. The base of the rear sight was re-graduated to 850m (930yd). The first issues were made in 1928.

MODEL 1928-30 SHORT RIFLE, PROTECTIVE CORPS
Sk.Y. kivääri m/28-30
Made by Suojeluskuntain Ase- ja Konepaja Osakeyhti^ ('Sako'), Riihimäki, 1931-40.
Total production: 55,000-60,000? **Chambering:** 7.62x54R, rimmed.
Action: as m/1924 rifle, above.
46.65in overall, 9.61lb empty. 26.95in barrel, 4-groove rifling; RH, concentric. Integral box magazine loaded from a stripper clip, 5 rounds. Tangent-leaf rear sight graduated to 2000m (2185yd). 2430 fps with heavy ball cartridges. m/28 Sk.Y or m/35 sword bayonet.

This improved m/28 rifle had a revised magazine and a greatly improved rear sight, but was otherwise mechanically similar to its predecessors. The barrels were made in the Sako factory, quality proving at least the equal of SIG products.

MODEL 1939 SHORT RIFLE
Kivääri m/39
Made by Suojeluskuntain Ase- ja Konepaja Osakeyhti^ ('Sako'), Riihimäki, 1939-44.
Total production: 70,800? **Chambering:** 7.62x54R, rimmed. **Action:** as m/1924 rifle, above.
46.65in overall, 10.03lb unladen. 26.95in barrel, 4-groove rifling; RH, concentric. Integral box magazine loaded from a stripper clip, 5 rounds. Tangent-leaf rear sight graduated to 2000m (2185yd). 2295 fps with D166 ball cartridges. m/35 sword or m/39 knife bayonet.

Developed in 1938 by a committee drawn from the Department of Defence, the army and the Sk.Y, the m/39 rifle retained the Mausner-pattern rear sight of the m/28-30 Sk.Y rifle. Detail changes included an increase in bore diameter to handle a new ball cartridge, the development of a two-piece stock made in interlocking parts, and the adoption of a two-piece interrupter copied from the Soviet 1891/30 type. Army-type rifling was retained, along with a lightweight barrel to conserve weight.

The rifle was formally approved in the summer of 1939, and production began. On 3rd November 1944, however, owing to the end of the Continuation War with the USSR, the Sk.Y disbanded and Sako was sold to the Finnish Red Cross. Ten thousand incomplete m/39 rifles were sold for conversion into sporting rifles.

OTHER GUNS
Non-standard weapons assembled during the Winter and Continuation Wars (1939-44) were cannibalized from Finnish, Russian and Soviet parts. They are often difficult to categorize.

SNIPER RIFLES
In the late 1980s, after protracted trials with Valmet, Sako and other rifles, the Finnish army adopted a new sniper rifle built on the original Imperial Russian actions. The guns have special heavy

A typical experimental Pelo auto-loading rifle.

barrels, pistol-grip stocks with adjustable combs, and are fitted with modern optical sights. At the time of writing the specifications are still unclear, though the process not only undoubtedly saved costs but also testified to the outstanding durability of the basic Mosin-Nagant. The rifles have now apparently been superseded by bolt-action Sako patterns.

• Pelo

This recoil-operated auto-loading rifle was developed in the 1930s by Carl Pelo, a Finnish army officer. Though tested extensively in several countries—including Sweden and Britain—it was not successful. Production has been estimated at 50-100.

• Sako, bolt-action type

Sako was originally a government-owned repair shop, created in an old brewery in Helsinki but soon progressing to a purpose-built factory and the manufacture of new rifles. Owing to harsh conditions attached by the Soviet Union to the treaty ending the Continuation War, however, Sako was sold to the Finnish Red Cross in 1944. As production of war materiel was no longer possible, sporting rifles were substituted.

The company made modified Kalashnikov (q.v.) assault rifles for the Finnish army in the 1960s, but was amalgamated with the state-owned Valmet organization in 1987. Sako-Valmet has promoted a bolt-action TRG-21 sniper rifle, but the Finnish army apparently preferred modified Mosin-Nagants for some years—a cheaper solution.

The much-modified Mausers are classified by action length: L-461 (short), L-579 (medium) and L-61 (large). Development began in Riihimäki in 1942, work being credited to Niilo Talvenheimo. War with the USSR curtailed progress, though prototype L-42 sporters were made in 1942-4. The perfected L-46 appeared after World War II had ended.

The earliest Sako rifles had a spring-steel extractor dovetailed into the right side of the bolt body—originally patented by Mauser in 1890—and the bolt shroud was attached by a lug (once confined to the L-57 only).

L-46 SPORTING RIFLE

Made in Riihimäki by Oy Sako AB (1946-87) and Sako-Valmet Oy (1987 to date).
Total production: not known. **Chambering options:** see notes. **Action:** locked by two lugs on the bolt head engaging recesses in the receiver wall as the bolt handle was turned downward.

DATA FOR A TYPICAL L-461 VARMINT PATTERN
Chambering: 222 Remington, rimless. 42.9in overall, 8.15lb empty. 23.75in barrel; 6-groove rifling; RH, concentric. Internal box magazine, 6 rounds. Optical sight. 3200 fps with 50-grain bullet.

The first guns were made for the European market in 1946, in 22 Hornet and 7x33. The L-46 had a detachable single-column box magazine, a lugged firing pin and a trigger copied from the Winchester Model 70. Birch half-stocks had low Monte Carlo combs. The bolt handle was straight, a safety catch lay on the left side of the bolt shroud, and the trigger guard/floorplate was a simple stamped strip.

Guns were made for the North American market from 1949 onward, initially in 218 Bee and 22 Hornet. A 222 Remington option was added in 1951 and, in 1952, a distinctive pivoting safety catch on the right side of the bolt shroud was substituted for the unpopular left-side pattern.

THE GUNS

L-46 rifle. This was the basic version, described above. A machined steel trigger guard/magazine floor-plate replaced the stamped-strip version in 1958, and a 222 Remington Magnum

chambering was offered for the first time in 1959. However, the basic short L-46 action was soon refined to become the short-lived L-469 (q.v.).

L-46 Bench-rest rifle. A single-shot variant with a solid-bottom receiver, this was introduced in 1956.

L-469 rifle. Introduced in 1959, this refinement of the L-46 action was not particularly successful; it was abandoned in 1962.

P-46 SPORTING RIFLE

This was the first of the *Pienoiskiväärit*, or small-bore rifles. Development began in 1944, though the perfected prototypes were not made until after the end of World War II and series production did not start until 1947. The P-46 was a simple 22LR rimfire design, relying on the sturdy bolt-handle base to lock the action. The last guns were not sold until 1965, though it is probable that very few had been made since the late 1950s, owing to the introduction of the improved P-54.

SIMILAR GUNS

P-54 rifle, 1954-77. An improved version of the P-46, this was developed in 1952-4. Chambered for the 22LR rimfire cartridge, it had a five-round detachable box magazine, a 22.85in barrel and weighed about 5.65lb. The walnut half-stock had a pistol grip, and the rear sight was a tangent-leaf pattern graduated to 200m (220yd).

P-54T rifle. This was a target-shooting adaptation of the basic P-54, with a heavy barrel and a straight-comb half-stock with a checkered pistol grip and a broadened 'beavertail' forend. The sights consisted of a replaceable-element tunnel and a micro-adjustable aperture, and an adjustable handball could be attached beneath the forend. The buttplate often had a backward projection on the toe; swivels lay beneath the butt and forend. Triggers were adjustable. The 24.5in barrel gave an empty weight of about 8.8lb.

L-461 SPORTING RIFLE

Sako's short-cartridge action was perfected in 1961, work being credited to Eino Mäckinen. First produced in quantity in 1962 as the 'Vixen', the new rifle embodied many of the changes pioneered by the L-57 and L-579 described below. An internal staggered-column box magazine was fitted, the modified trigger had a vertically-moving sear, and a rocking safety lay on the right side of the receiver behind the bolt handle. The firing pin was threaded into the cocking piece, simplifying production.

SIMILAR GUNS

L-461 Model 72 rifle ('Vixen'). The original Vixen was replaced in 1971 by this pattern. A minor change had been made to prevent the bolt guide rib rotating past the fully-open position behind the left locking lug, and then releasing the bolt-stop as the bolt was retracted. However, the manufacturing pattern was short-lived.

L-461 Model 74 rifle ('Vixen'). This was a revised version of the preceding Model 72, dating from 1974, introduced in 222 and 223 Remington as a result of attempts to rationalize the three types of action. The primary goal was to simplify manufacture. Post-1974 L-461 rifles had the same spring-loaded extractor as the L-579 and L-61. The L-461 M74 Vixen had a 22.65in barrel and weighed about 6.5lb. Monte Carlo-type butts were standard, with checkering on the pistol grip and the forend; the forend tip was a plain rounded pattern.

L-461 Model 74 Super Sporter. These guns had deluxe stocks with skip-line checkering; contrasting rosewood pistol-grip caps and forend tips were accompanied by thin white spacers.

L-461 Model 74 Varmint rifle. Easily identified by a heavy barrel and a broad semi-beavertail forend, this rifle weighed about 3.85kg.

The Sako L-461 Hunter rifle, with the standard short action.

L-461 Carbine, 1983-7. A few fully stocked carbines (of a type associated more with the L-579 and L-61 actions), were offered for a few years only in 222 Remington.

L-461 Classic Sporter, 1985-7. This short-lived variant was offered in 17, 222 or 223 Remington chamberings, but had disappeared within two years of its introduction.

L-461 Deluxe rifle. This was similar to the standard pattern, but had a selected stock with skip-line checkering and a contrasting rosewood forend tip. Super Deluxe guns had a hand-carved and checkered stock.

L-461 Heavy Barrel (or 'Varmint Model'). Identifiable by the heavyweight barrel, a broad beavertail forend and an absence of open sights, this was initially made only for the 222 Remington or 223 Remington rounds. The 17 Remington, 22 PPC and 6mm PPC options—previously made to special order—became standard in 1988, but only the three Remington chamberings (.17, 222 and 223) were being offered by 1996.

L-461 Hunter. Little more than a 1987-vintage renaming of the original L-461 A I Sporting Rifle, this was available only in three proprietary Remington chamberings—17, 222 and 223—in 1996.

L-461 Hunter LS ('Laminated Stock'), 1987-9. This appeared in 222 and 223 Remington chamberings only. Made from 36-ply stock-blanks, each stock had a color and pattern of its own. A stainless-steel barrel option was added about the same time.

L-461 Lightweight (or 'Hunter Lightweight'). This was a version of the Hunter with a light barrel and a pared-down stock, saving a substantial amount of weight.

L-461 Lightweight Deluxe. Derived from the Lightweight pattern, this had a select French walnut stock with rosewood pistol grip and forend caps. The top surfaces of the receiver and cocking-piece shroud were checkered to reduce glare, the remaining metalwork was mirror-polished, and skip-line checkering was used.

L-461 PPC rifle. This special single shot variant—usually made with a 23.6in barrel—chambers the 22 PPC and 6mm PPC benchrest cartridges developed by Louis Palmisano and Ferris Pindell in the late 1970s. Initially built only for the promoters of the cartridges, the rifles have since become commercially available. See also 'Heavy Barrel', above, for the magazine-feed version.

L-461 Standard rifle, 1977-87. Built on the 'A I' action, this was introduced in 17, 222 and 223 Remington chamberings, the Vixen name finally disappearing. The most obvious change was the adoption of a plunger-type ejector set into the bolt face. A standard L-461 A I rifle was about 41.9in long, had a 22.55in barrel and weighed 6.2-6.4lb; it had a walnut half-stock with a Monte Carlo comb and a solid rubber shoulder plate. The pistol-grip and forend were hand-checkered. It was renamed 'Hunter' (q.v.) in the mid 1980s.

L-461 Target rifle. Initially offered only in 222 Remington, this had a heavy free-floating barrel in a deep competition-style stock. The cheekpiece was detachable, and four slots were cut laterally through the forend to improve air circulation around the barrel. Unlike the outwardly similar L-579 type, L-461 Target rifles had internal six-round box magazines. They were 42.3in long, had 23.75in barrels and weighed 9.25lb. In 1988, however, the 17 Remington, 22 PPC and 6mm PPC options—previously made to special order—became standard on the Target model. By 1990, the L-461 Target was being chambered exclusively for PPC rounds only and was generally a special single-shot derivative intended for bench-rest shooting with a stiffened solid-bottom receiver.

L-461 Varmint rifle—an alternative name for the 'Heavy Barrel' pattern described above.

L-57 SPORTING RIFLE

Made in Riihimäki by Oy Sako AB (1957-87) and Sako-Valmet Oy (1987 to date).

Total production: not known. **Chambering options:** see notes. **Action:** as L-46, above.

DATA FOR A TYPICAL L-579 HUNTER RIFLE

7x64, rimless. 42.65in overall, 6.83lb empty. 22.55in barrel, 4-groove rifling; RH, concentric. Internal box magazine, 5 rounds. Folding-leaf sight. 2950 fps with 139-grain bullet.

The medium-length L-57 action, introduced in 1957, was developed specifically to handle 243 and 308 Winchester cartridges. Small quantities were made commercially in 1957-9 before teething troubles were encountered.

The L-57 was basically an L-46 lengthened to accommodate cartridges up to 2.75in (70mm) long. A fixed staggered-column box magazine was fitted, feed lips being machined in the underside of the receiver. The magazine floor-plate was hinged, the release catch appearing in the front of the machined-steel trigger guard bow. The catch initially protruded inside the guard, but was subsequently changed so that it could only be operated externally. A trigger with a vertically sliding sear was fitted, adapted from those used on contemporary Sako-Mausers (q.v.).

The first guns were made in standard, deluxe, fully-stocked Mannlicher and heavy barrel patterns. Most heavy-barrel examples had broad semi-beavertail forends.

L-579 SPORTING RIFLE

The perfected L-579 action, developed two years previously, replaced the L-57 in 1961. The initial chamberings were 243 Winchester, 244 Remington, 7.62x39 or 308 Winchester. The most obvious change was the addition of the Sako No. 4 trigger mechanism, with an integral radial safety protruding from the receiver behind the bolt handle.

A new smooth-surface shroud was held to the bolt by a small lug. The bolt-stop housing was retained by two short screws instead of sliding into a dovetailed mortise, and a sliding spring-loaded extractor replaced the earlier fixed claw pattern.

SIMILAR GUNS

L-579 Forester Carbine, also known as 'BL-579', 1964-73. This had a full length forend and a 20.1in barrel. A 22-250 Remington chambering was introduced in 1965, when the 244 option was abandoned.

L-579 Model 72 rifle (Forester). The original Foresters were replaced in the early 1970s, changes being made to prevent the bolt-guide rib over-rotating. The resulting rifle did not last long.

L-579 Model 74 rifle (Forester). Changes were made to the design of the 579-type action so that all three Sako actions were essentially similar. The M74 Forester chambered 22-250, 243 Winchester or 308 Winchester cartridges, had a 22.85in barrel and weighed about 6.8lb.

L-579 Model 74 Super Sporter. This was made with a deluxe stock (see L-461 Model 74 Super Sporter, above).

L-579 Model 74 Varmint rifle. Distinguished by a heavy barrel and supplied in the three standard chamberings, this weighed about 8.8lb.

L-579 Battue rifle, 1992 to date. Intended for use against driven game, this is really little more than a Handy (q.v.) with the rear sight set into the front edge of a raised quarter-rib stretching forward above the barrel from the chamber.

L-579 Carbine, 1977 to date. Measuring just 39.25in overall, this had a 19.4in barrel and weighed about 6.8lb. A joint in the full-length Mannlicher forend was concealed by the barrel band. It was initially made only in 243 Winchester, but a 308 version was introduced in 1985. Some guns will be encountered with the optional detachable five-round box magazine, and current production has an 18.5in barrel.

L-579 Classic Sporter, or 'Classic Rifle', 1980-7 and 1993 to date. Mechanically identical with the standard sporting rifle, this is distinguished by a straight-comb 'classic' stock with an oil finish. It has been made in 243 Winchester only.

L-579 Deluxe rifle. This version of the L-579 Standard had a selected stock with skip-line checkering and a contrasting rosewood forend tip; Super Deluxe guns had a hand-carved stock.

L-579 Fiberclass rifle, 1988-95. Made with a distinctive black fiberglass stock, this was chambered for 22-250, 243 Winchester, 7mm-08 or 308 Winchester ammunition.

L-579 Handy or 'Hunter Carbine', 1986-91. These short-barreled half-stock guns were introduced in 22-250 (discontinued in 1990), 7mm-08 or 308 Winchester. A 243 Winchester option was available in 1991 only. The original carbines were 39.25in overall, had 19.4in barrels and weighed 6.8-6.9lb; later examples had 18.5in barrels. A five-round detachable box magazine could be supplied to special order.

L-579 Handy Fiber, 1989-91. This was simply a variant of the Handy carbine (above) with a black fiberglass stock.

L-579 Heavy Barrel (or Varmint Rifle). Made with a special large-diameter barrel and a broad beavertail forend, initially only in 220 Swift, 22-250, 243 Winchester or 308 Winchester, though a 7mm-08 Remington alternative was offered from 1987 onward and

The Sako L-579 Super Target rifle.

the last 220 Swift examples were sold in 1988. The standard barrel measured 23.75in, giving an overall length of 42.9in and a weight averaging 8.2lb; some guns will have the optional detachable five-round box magazine. Chamberings available in 1996 were confined to 22-250, 243 Winchester, 7mm-08 Remington and 308 Winchester.

L-579 Hunter rifle. This was simply the standard L-579 rifle under another name, introduced in 1987 in 22-250, 243 Winchester, 7mm-08 Remington and 30-06. The last guns chambered for the 220 Swift cartridge were sold in 1988, when an optional detachable five-round box magazine was introduced. A left-hand action was also introduced in 1987.

L-579 Hunter LS ('Laminated Stock'), 1988-95. This had a stock made from 36-ply blanks, and was often fitted with a stainless-steel barrel. Standard chamberings were 22-250, 243 Winchester, 7mm-08 Remington and 308 Winchester.

L-579 Lightweight rifle (or 'Hunter Lightweight'). Chambered for the 22-250, 243 Winchester, 270 Winchester or 7mm-08 Remington rounds, this is distinguished by a slender barrel and stock. It was mechanically identical with the standard Hunter pattern.

L-579 Lightweight Deluxe rifle. This was a variant of the standard Lightweight pattern with a select French walnut stock, rosewood pistol grip and forend caps, mirror-polished bluing and skip-line checkering.

L-579 Standard rifle, 1977-87. This embodied the modernized L-579 A II action, with a streamlined bolt shroud and a plunger-type ejector in the bolt face. The Forester name disappeared. The 'A IIa' rifles chambered 220 Swift or 22-250 Remington rounds; 'A IIb' handled 243 Winchester and 308 Winchester patterns. Renamed 'Hunter' in 1987, the standard rifle had a hand-checkered Circassian walnut stock with a Monte Carlo comb, a pistol-grip and a solid rubber buttplate.

L-579 Super Match rifle. Made in 308 Winchester only, this had a heavy competition-style half-stock with a detachable cheekpiece and four slots cut laterally through the forend. Its barrel floated freely. The special L-579 SM action had a strengthened receiver pierced only by the magazine feed-way and ejection port. A 10-round detachable box magazine was standard.

L-579 Target rifle, 1983-? Offered only in 308 Winchester, these guns had a massive half-stock with a plain forend and a floating barrel. They were 44.75in overall, had 26in barrels, and weighed about 9.9lb. Detachable five-round magazines were standard.

L-579 Varmint rifle. An alternative name for the Heavy Barrel pattern (q.v.), this has gained popularity in recent years.

L-61 SPORTING RIFLES

Made in Riihimäki by Oy Sako AB (1961-87) and Sako-Valmet Oy (1987 to date).

Total production: not known. **Chambering options:** see notes. **Action:** as L-46 with an additional lug on the bolt.

DATA FOR A TYPICAL L-61R HANDY FIBER RIFLE

Chambering: 30-06, rimless. 40.35in overall, 7.16lb empty. 19.3in barrel, 4-groove rifling; RH, concentric. Internal box magazine, 5 rounds. Folding-leaf sight on ramp. 2970 fps with 150-grain bullet.

Development of the L-61 or 'Finnbear' began in 1960 after demands for greater power emanated from North America. A third locking lug was added on the bolt body, ahead of the handle. Announced for 30-06 and 300 H&H Magnum only, it replaced the earlier 'Sako Mauser' or 'U.S. Mauser' rifles. The L-61 was made in standard, deluxe and Mannlicher patterns. Additional 264 Winchester Magnum and 338 Winchester Magnum options were introduced in 1963, followed by 7mm Remington Magnum in 1964 and 300 Winchester Magnum in 1965.

SIMILAR GUNS

Finnsport 2700, 1982-5. This seems to have been introduced in the early 1980s to rid Sako of pre-1977 actions. Chambered for the 270 Winchester, 7mm Remington Magnum, 300 Winchester Magnum or 30-06 cartridges, the 2700 had a plain stock and a 24in barrel. Weight averaged 8lb.

L-61 carbine. A few of these were built on the L-61 action about 1970, with full-length Mannlicher stocks and 20.05in barrels.

L-61 Model 72 rifle (Finnbear), 1972-4. A new version of the basic rifle was created to prevent the bolt guide rib over-rotating as the bolt was operated. Open rear sights were fitted to all but heavy-barrel guns.

L-61 Model 74 rifle (Finnbear), 1974-9. A rationalized manufacturing pattern was approved to simplify production. The changes were comparatively minor. M74 L-61 rifles had 24in barrels accepting 25-06, 270 Winchester, 7mm Remington Magnum, 300 Winchester Magnum, 30-06, 338 Winchester Magnum or 375 H&H Magnum ammunition. The standard stocks had Monte Carlo combs, checkering on the pistol grip and forend, and a plain rounded forend tip.

L-61 Model 74 Super Sporter. The stocks of these rifles had Monte Carlo combs, skip-line checkering, and white spacers accompanying the pistol-grip cap and oblique-cut rosewood forend tip.

L-61 Model 74 Varmint rifle. A few heavy-barrel Varmint rifles, with broad forends, were made in 25-06.

L-61 Battue rifle. Introduced in 1992, this is a variant of the Handy (q.v.) pattern with the rear sight set into the front of a ventilated quarter-rib above the barrel.

L-61 Carbine, 1977 to date. Built on the right-hand action only (L-61R), this is stocked to the muzzle and has a barrel band covering the joint in the forend. Chamberings are restricted to 270 Winchester and 30-06. The first guns were 40.35in long, had a 19.3in barrel and weighed 7.25lb; current examples, however, have 18.5in barrels which reduce length to 39.8in.

L-61 Carbine Magnum, 1985 to date. Now offered only in 338 Winchester and 375 H&H magnum chamberings, these guns have a half-length stock with a rounded forend tip. The 25-06 Remington, 7mm Remington Magnum and 300 Winchester Magnum options were withdrawn in 1991, though new guns continued to be sold from stock for several years.

L-61 Classic rifle (or 'Classic Sporter'), 1980-7 and 1993 to date. Introduced in 270 Winchester, 7mm Remington Magnum and 30-06, this is distinguished by an oil-finish half-stock with a straight-comb butt. It has a 21.75in barrel and weighs about 6.5lb.

L-61 Deluxe rifle. Based on the L-61 Standard sporter, this had a selected stock with skip-line checkering and a contrasting rosewood forend tip; Super Deluxe stocks usually exhibited hand-carved oak leaves.

L-61 Fiberclass Sporter, 1984 to date. Supplied in ordinary or magnum actions, this had a dark charcoal-gray or black synthetic stock with a textured finish and a straight comb. It was initially offered in 25-06, 270 Winchester, 7mm Remington Magnum, 300 Winchester Magnum, 30-06, 338 Winchester Magnum or 375 H&H Magnum. A 280 Remington version appeared in 1989, and a 416 Remington Magnum version in 1991. A left-hand action was made in 1987-9 only.

L-61 Golden Anniversary Model. One thousand special 7mm Remington Magnum 'Golden Anniversary Model' rifles were created to celebrate Sako's 50th birthday.

L-61 Handy ('Handy Carbine' or 'Hunter Carbine'), 1986-91. This half-stocked carbine appeared on the L-61R action, chambered for the 25-06 Remington (discontinued in 1990), 6.5x55, 270 Winchester, 7x64, 7mm Remington Magnum (discontinued in 1990), 30-06. 338 Winchester Magnum or 9.3x62 rounds. A few 375 H&H Magnum examples were made in 1991.

L-61 Handy Fiber rifle, 1989-91. This was a variant of the L-61 Handy carbine with a straight-comb synthetic stock instead of a wooden pattern with a Monte Carlo comb. Standard chamberings included 25-06 Remington, 270 Winchester, 7mm Remington Magnum, 30-06, 300 Winchester Magnum and 338 Winchester Magnum; only the 338 option continued after 1990, though a few 375 H&H Magnum guns were made in 1991.

L-61 Heavy Barrel rifle (or 'Varmint Rifle'). A few of these were chambered for 25-06 or 7mm Remington Magnum, but had been discontinued by 1983.

L-61 Hunter rifle, 1987 to date. This was simply the L-61 Standard sporter under a new name. A stainless-steel barrel option was introduced about 1988, together with new 6.5x55 or 7x64 chamberings. 1996 chamberings were confined to 25-06 Remington, 270 Winchester and 30-06.

L-61 Hunter Lightweight rifle. These rifles were allegedly introduced in the mid-1980s, but, in the absence of confirmation from Sako literature, they are assumed to have been nothing other than the refinements of the standard guns.

L-61 Hunter LS rifle ('Laminated Stock'), 1987-95. Built on the L-61R or L-61R Magnum actions, this had a multi-layer stock blank. A stainless-steel barrel option was introduced about 1988. Chamberings duplicated the standard Hunter pattern.

L-61 Lightweight rifle (or 'Hunter Lightweight'), 1984 to date. This has a slender tapering barrel and an unusually delicate stock, reinforced by a recoil bolt beneath the chamber. Mechanically identical with the L-61 Hunter, it has been chambered for the 25-06 Remington, 270 Winchester, 280 Remington and 30-06 rounds.

L-61 Lightweight Deluxe rifle, 1985 to date. Essentially similar to the standard Lightweight pattern, this had a select walnut halfstock with rosewood pistol grip and forend caps. The top surfaces of the receiver and the cocking-piece shroud were finely checkered, the remaining metalwork was highly polished, and the checkering on the pistol grip and forend was skip-line.

L-61 Lightweight Magnum rifle, 1984 to date. This was distinguished from the standard L-61 Lightweight only by the chamberings, and the designation is often regarded as artificial. Guns have been made for a selection of magnum cartridges, including 7mm Remington, 300 Weatherby, 300 Winchester, 338 Winchester, 375 H&H and 416 Remington patterns.

L-61 Long Range Hunter rifle. Introduced in 1996 in 25-06 Remington, 7mm Remington Magnum and 300 Winchester Magnum, this has a 26in fluted barrel and a gloss-finish Monte Carlo-type half-stock. Optical sights are standard.

L-61 Magnum rifle (or 'Hunter Magnum'), 1987 to date. Built on the 'L-61 A V Mag' action, these rifles accepted 7mm Remington, 300 Winchester, 338 Winchester or 375 H&H magnum rounds. The guns had 24.4in barrels, measured 45.3in overall, and weighed 7.3-8.2lb depending on barrel length and stock-wood density. The half-stock had a Monte Carlo comb and a rubber buttplate, with hand-cut checkering on the pistol grip and forend. A recoil bolt ran through the stock beneath the chamber. A 300 Weatherby Magnum option was added to the Hunter series in 1989, followed by 416 Remington Magnum in 1991. Magnum chamberings available in 1996 were 270 Weatherby, 7mm Remington, 7mm Weatherby, 300 Weatherby, 300 Winchester, 338 Winchester, 340 Weatherby, 375 H&H and 416 Remington. A left-hand action has also been offered, and Deluxe and Super Deluxe-pattern Magnums have been made in small numbers.

L-61 Safari rifle, 1981 to date. Made on the L-61R Magnum action, this was chambered for several popular cartridges: 7mm Remington, 300 Winchester, 338 Winchester or 375 H&H Magnums. The butt had a straight comb, two transverse recoil bolts (one on some more recent guns) ran through the stock, and an Express rear sight lay above the barrel on a traditional quarter-rib. A typical rifle was 43.3in overall, had a 20.45in barrel and an empty weight of about 9.25lb. The 300 Winchester Magnum option was dropped in 1989, followed in 1991 by 7mm Remington Magnum, but 416 Remington Magnum was added in 1992.

L-61 Standard rifle, or 'L-61 Sporter', 1978-87. A new-pattern rifle appeared in the late 1970s, with a streamlined bolt shroud and a bolt-mounted ejector. The Finnbear name was dropped. The new rifle was known to the factory as 'L-61 A V'—i.e., the fifth action—and existed in three patterns: right-hand (L-61R), left-hand (L-61L, introduced in 1987) and magnum (L-61R Mag). The earliest 'A V' rifles were chambered for 25-06 Remington, 270 Winchester, 30-06 or 9.3x62. Barrels were customarily 22.85in, giving an overall length of about 43.3in; weight was about 7.5lb. This pattern was renamed 'Hunter' in the late 1980s.

P-72 SPORTING RIFLE
Also known as 'Finnscout'
Made by Oy Sako Ab, Riihimäki, 1972-83?

Total production: not known. **Chambering:** 22 LR rimfire. **Action:** locked by the bolt-handle base entering its seat in the receiver as the bolt handle was turned down

41in overall, 6.75lb empty. 22.5in barrel, 6-groove rifling; RH, concentric. Detachable box magazine, 5 rounds. Williams-type adjustable open ramp-type rear sight. 1080 fps with 40-grain bullet.

This replaced the obsolescent P-54 in the early 1970s. A conventional rimfire action with a 45-degree bolt lift was set in a plain walnut-finish half-stock with a straight comb and a rounded forend. The synthetic buttplate was accompanied by a thin white spacer.

SIMILAR GUNS
P-72 Finnscout Junior rifle, 1972-5. Mechanically identical with the standard P-72 Sporter, this had a noticeably shorter butt.

P-72 Finnscout HB rifle ('Heavy Barrel'), 1972-83? Mechanically identical with the standard rifle, this had a 23.6in barrel which raised average weight to about 7lb. The half-stock had a straight comb and a semi-beavertail forend, but lacked checkering.

P-72 Finnscout Hornet rifle, 1975-82. Chambered for the centerfire 22 Hornet cartridge, this is believed to have a supplementary locking lug and a longer magazine. It does not seem to have been made in large numbers.

P-72 Finnscout Super Sporter, 1972-85? This had a walnut half-stock, with a cheekpiece and a Monte Carlo comb. The pistol grip and the forend were extensively checkered.

P-78 Biathlon rifle ('P-78AH'), 1982-5. Characterized by a special synthetic half-stock with stippling on the pistol grip and the deep forend, this was intended for biathlon competition shooting—*Ampumahiihtopienoiskivääri*, 'biathlon small-bore rifle'. It was 43.9in long, had a 26in barrel, and weighed 10.35lb. Four spare magazines were carried under the concave butt, the shoulder plate was fixed, and a special match-type trigger was provided. A carrying harness and competition sights were standard fittings, the muzzle and tunnel-pattern front sight being protected by a hinged

The Sako L-61 with a full-length Mannlicher stock.

The Sako L-61 Safari rifle.

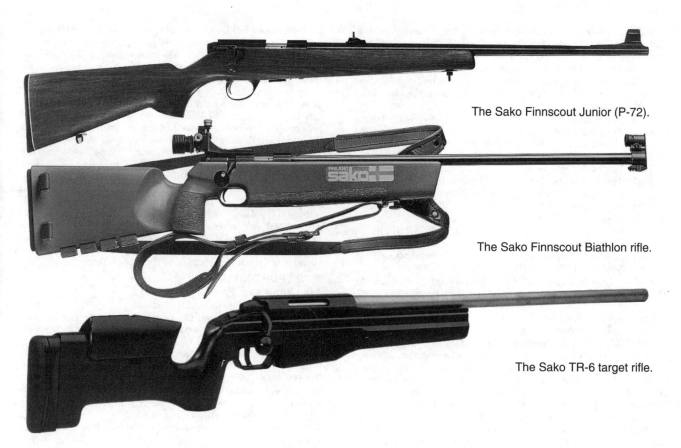

The Sako Finnscout Junior (P-72).

The Sako Finnscout Biathlon rifle.

The Sako TR-6 target rifle.

cover. The first stock pattern had a straight forend; the later type, however, had a deep section ahead of the trigger guard and a short broad beavertail nearer the forend tip. Most guns had adjustable weights in the forend tip and pistol grip.

TRG SPORTING RIFLE

Made by Oy Sako Ab, Riihimäki.

Currently in production. **Chambering options:** 243 Winchester, 6.5x55, 7mm-08 Remington, 270 Winchester or 30-06. **Action:** locked by three lugs on the bolt head engaging recesses in the receiver behind the chamber as the bolt handle is turned down.

DATA FOR A TYPICAL EXAMPLE

Chambering: 7mm-08 Remington, rimless. 43.5in overall, 7.35lb empty. 22in barrel, 4-groove rifling; RH, concentric. Detachable box magazine, 5 rounds. Fixed open rear sight. 2715 fps with 154-grain bullet.

Introduced in 1995, the TRG action moves away from the modified Mauser action in favor of a symmetrical three-lug bolt with a 60-degree rotation. The safety catch—which locks the trigger, bolt and firing pin—lies inside the trigger guard. The standard rifle ('TRG-S' or 'TRG-Sporter') has a reinforced polyurethane Monte Carlo-type half-stock, a free-floating barrel, and an adjustable trigger. The metal surfaces have a matte 'satin' blue finish.

SIMILAR GUNS

TRG-M rifle. The Magnum version of the standard gun—built on a long action—is currently being offered for the 270 Weatherby, 7mm Remington, 300 Winchester, 338 Winchester, 340 Weatherby, 375 H&H and 416 Remington magnum cartridges. Except the four-round 375 pattern, the magazine holds five rounds; barrel length is customarily 24in.

TRG-21 sniper rifle. Built on a standard TRG action, in 7.62x51, this has a free-floating barrel and a synthetic half-stock attached to an aluminum-alloy frame. The butt can be lengthened with spacers, and the height or rake of the comb can be adjusted by altering the cheekpiece. The receiver rail will accept mounts for optical and electro-optical sights, though folding open sights are provided for emergency use. The trigger can be adjusted for release pressure (2.2-5.5lb). Most guns had bipods fixed to the front of the stock frame, and the combination muzzle brake/flash hider was threaded to accept a sound-suppressor. The rifle is 46.3in long, has a 26in barrel, and weighs 10.47lb without sights. Its detachable box magazine holds 10 rounds.

TRG-41. A variant of the TRG-21, difficult to distinguish externally, this chambers the 338 Lapua Magnum cartridge and has a four-round magazine.

SSR MARK 1 SILENCED RIFLE

Made by Oy Sako Ab, Riihimäki.

Total production: not known. **Chambering:** 7.62x51 NATO, rimless. **Action:** as L-46, above.

46.25in overall, 9.04lb without sights. 18.3in barrel, 4-groove rifling; RH, concentric. Detachable box magazine, 5 rounds. Optical sight. 985 fps with special subsonic ball ammunition.

Derived from the standard Sako target rifle, built on the medium-length L-579 A II action, the SSR had a one-piece wooden half-stock with a target-style pistol grip. A bipod was attached beneath the forend, but the most distinctive feature was the full-length silencer developed by Sako in collaboration with Oy Vaimeninmetalli ('Vaime'). There is a rail for NATO-standard optical or electro-optical sight mounts, but no open sights are provided. Maximum effective range with the special subsonic ammunition is about 300m (330yd).

SIMILAR GUNS

SSR Mark 3 rifle. Chambered for the 22 Long Rifle rimfire cartridge, this is said to have been developed at the request of police and anti-terrorist agencies for use in situations—e.g., in urban environments—where the greater penetration of the 7.62mm bullet was a hazard.

FINNFIRE SPORTING RIFLE

Made by Oy Sako Ab, Riihimäki.

Currently in production. **Chambering:** 22 LR rimfire. **Action:** locked by two lugs on the bolt engaging seats in the receiver behind the chamber as the bolt handle turns down.

40.5in overall, 5.35lb empty. 22in barrel, 4-groove rifling; RH, concentric. Detachable box magazine, 5 rounds. Fixed open rear sight. 1080 fps with 40-grain bullet.

Introduced in 1994, this has a short action with a 50-degree rotation. The walnut half-stock has a Monte Carlo comb and cheekpiece, and a short rounded forend. Checkering appears on the pistol grip and forend. The single-stage trigger is adjustable for release pressure and let-off point. An optional 23.6in heavy barrel can be obtained to order.

• Sako, lever-action type

These were introduced to compete with the American rifles that had a stranglehold on the European market. They were never as successful as the Sako bolt-action guns, owing partly to robust competition and partly to high price.

VL-63 SPORTING RIFLE
Finnwolf

Made by Oy Sako AB, Riihimäki (1962-75).

Total production: not known. **Chambering options:** 243 Winchester or 308 Winchester. **Action:** locked by lugs on the bolt rotating into recesses in the receiver walls as the lever formed integrally with the trigger guard is closed.

DATA FOR A TYPICAL 243 RIFLE

42.5in overall, 6.75lb empty. 22.95in barrel, 4-groove rifling; RH, concentric. Detachable box magazine, 4 rounds. Optical sight. 3070 fps with 100-grain bullet.

Developed in 1959-62, this lever-action rifle fed from a box to allow pointed-nose or 'spitzer' bullets to be used. A rack-and-pinion mechanism revolved the bolt, and a lateral safety bolt ran through the breech-lever web behind the trigger.

Also known as the VL-63, after the year in which it was introduced, the Finnwolf had a one-piece half-stock with a Monte Carlo comb and a right- or left-hand cheekpiece. Hand-cut checkering graced the pistol grip and forend. The single-column magazine protruded slightly beneath the stock.

SIMILAR GUNS

VL-73 rifle, 1973-5. This was a modified version of the VL-63 gun with a four-round staggered-column magazine fitting flush with the stock, but comparatively few were ever made.

• Tampeeren Asepaja

This small gunmaking business is renowned for a straight-pull bolt-action rifle locked by a toggle-lever. This was extensively promoted in the early 1980s for competition shooting—specifically the biathlon—where rapidity of fire and minimum disturbance of aim were great assets. A few thousand rifles were made to this innovative design, but did not find the success their promoters were seeking and proved unable to challenge the pre-eminence of conventional bolt-action patterns.

FINNBIATHLON-22 TARGET RIFLE

Made by Tampeeren Asepaja Oy, Tampere, about 1978-83.

Total production: not known. **Chambering:** 22LR, rimfire. **Action:** locked by a toggle lever attached to the bolt.

42.5in overall (with one butt spacer), 9.9lb without sights. 23.6in barrel, 4-groove rifling; RH, concentric. Detachable box magazine, 5 rounds. Micro-adjustable aperture rear sight. 1080 fps with 40-grain bullet.

Made in right- or left-hand versions, the Finnbiathlon-22 was easily distinguished by its toggle-lever action, a system which has since found favor elsewhere (cf., German Anschütz-Förtner type). Its concave butt-face was pierced with holes for the biathlon harness; a pivoting flap or 'snow guard' protected the tunnel-type front sight and the muzzle; and a special frame set into the forend side held four spare magazines. The trigger was adjustable. The length of the butt could be altered with specially curved spacers,

and up to 3.9oz (110gm) of additional weights could be inserted in the forend.

• Tikka, bolt-action type

Tikka sporters were originally derived from the 1898-pattern Mauser, omitting the safety lug in favor of the bolt handle turning down into its seat in the receiver. They were unremarkable mechanically, but proved to be sturdy and very dependable. In 1987, however, a wholesale reorganization of the Finnish arms industry led to the incorporation of Oy Tikkakoski in Sako-Valmet Oy in 1989. The Valmet 412 shotgun series (which included a double rifle) was thereafter marketed under the Tikka name, though the production machinery had been sold to Italy. The Tikka 55 and 65 rifles were replaced by what ultimately became the 590/690 series.

MODEL 55 SPORTING RIFLE

Made by Oy Tikkakoski Ab, Tikkakoski.

Total production: not known. **Chambering options:** 17 Remington, 222 Remington, 22-250, 6mm Remington, 243 Winchester or 308 Winchester. **Action:** locked by two lugs on the bolt head rotating into recesses in the receiver wall when the bolt handle was turned down, and by the bolt-handle base turning down into its seat.

DATA FOR A TYPICAL EXAMPLE

Chambering: 243 Winchester, rimless. 42.15in overall, 7.15lb empty. 580mm barrel, 4-groove rifling; RH, concentric. Detachable box magazine, 3 rounds. Folding leaf sight. 3070 fps with 100-grain bullet.

Apparently introduced in the mid 1960s, the Tikka 55 Standard had a radial safety catch on the right side of the breech behind the bolt handle, and a magazine-release catch in the guard ahead of the trigger lever. The plain oil-finished hardwood stock had a pistol grip, a low Monte Carlo comb and a ventilated rubber shoulder pad. Checkering appeared on the pistol-grip and forend; swivels lay beneath the butt and the forend. The bolt handle was swept slightly backward. An optional large-diameter bolt-knob was popular—particularly in areas where gloves were used. The rounded forend tips of standard and deluxe rifles were replaced in 1980 by oblique-cut squared designs. The Model 55 was superseded in 1989 by the improved Tikka 558 described below.

SIMILAR GUNS

Tikka 55 DL rifle ('Deluxe'), 1965-89. This had a walnut stock with a roll-over comb. The pistol-grip cap was rosewood, accompanied by a white-line spacer. The forend tip—square-cut after 1980—was also rosewood, cut obliquely and separated from the stock wood by another spacer. Checkering was conventional or a skip-line pattern.

Tikka 55 Sporter, 1977-89. This was chambered for the 222 Remington, 22-250 Remington, 243 Winchester or 308 Winchester cartridges. Also known as the 'Heavy Barrel' or 'Varmint' pattern, it had a 24.4in barrel and a heavy stock. Overall length was about 43.3in, and weight averaged 9lb. The robust pistol grip was almost vertical, and the forend was deeper than normal. Owing to the depth of the stock ahead of the trigger, a special extension was fitted to otherwise standard three-round magazines. Stippling ran from the forend to the pistol grip. One swivel lay on the right side of the straight-comb butt; its partner slid on a rail beneath the forend. Open sights were customarily omitted.

The basic Tikka Model 55, with a plain stock.

The Tikka Model 55 Sport rifle, with a detachable box magazine.

FINLAND

Tikka 55 SSP rifle. This was essentially similar to the M55 Sporter, but had micro-adjustable competition sights.

Tikka 55 Super Sporter (also known as 'Sniper' or 'Master'), 1983-9. Easily identified by its Cycolac stock, with a vertically sliding exchangeable cheekpiece, this gun had a fluted barrel—giving rigidity without increasing weight unnecessarily—and a weight attached to the muzzle by two cap-head bolts. Optical sights were retained by quick-release clamping mounts, while a bipod could be attached to the rail beneath the forend.

MODEL 65 SPORTING RIFLE

Made by Oy Tikkakoski Ab, Tikkakoski.

Total production: not known. **Chambering options:** see notes. **Action:** as Model 55, above.

DATA FOR A TYPICAL STANDARD EXAMPLE

Chambering: 6.5x55, rimless. 42.5in overall, 7.5lb empty. 22.05in barrel, 4-groove rifling; RH, concentric. Detachable box magazine, 5 rounds. Optical sight. 2560 fps with 144-grain bullet.

Dating from the early 1970s, this was little more than a Model 55 enlarged to chamber magnum cartridges. The cocking-piece shroud was extended, owing to longer striker travel, and the bolt handle base was smoothed. Free-floating barrels promoted excellent accuracy. The stocks of the standard Tikka 65 rifle duplicated the corresponding '55' model. Five-round magazines were standard. Production ceased in 1989 in favor of the improved Model 658.

SIMILAR GUNS

Tikka 65 DL rifle ('Deluxe'). This shared the stock of the 55DL pattern described above.

Tikka 65 Wildboar Model (sometimes known as the 'Trapper' in North America). Introduced in 1977 in 30-06 or 308 Winchester, this had a 20.5in barrel and a quarter-rib rear sight. The pistol grip cap and forend tip were rosewood, but spacers were not used.

Tikka 65 Sporter (also known as 'Heavy Barrel' or 'Varmint'). Initially offered in 6.5x55 Mauser, 270 Winchester, 30-06 or 308 Winchester, this was introduced in 1978. Many were fitted with the wooden buttplates required in moving-target competitions. Sporters were 43.7in overall, had 23.6in barrels and weighed 9.9lb. Their magazines held seven rounds. Additional 7x64, 7mm Remington Magnum and 300 Winchester Magnum chamberings were added in 1979.

Tikka 65 Super Sporter. Dating from 1983, this was identical with the Model 55 Super Sporter (q.v.) apart from a longer receiver required to handle magnum-length ammunition.

Tikka 65A rifle (or '65A-308'). This extraordinary rifle, apparently introduced in 1985, offered a special deep beavertail forend with a bipod attachment. The 10-round magazine was contained in an auxiliary wood housing and the anatomical plastic pistol grip anchored a tubular metal butt ending in an adjustable shoulder pad. A wooden comb-block could be slid along the butt-tube when required.

TIKKA 590 POPULAR SPORTING RIFLE

Made by Oy Tikkakoski Ab, Tikkakoski.

Currently in production. **Chambering options:** 17 Remington, 222 Remington, 22-250, 223 Remington, 243 Winchester or 308 Winchester. **Action:** locked by two lugs on the bolt head engaging recesses in the receiver behind the chamber as the bolt handle is turned down.

DATA FOR A TYPICAL EXAMPLE

Chambering: 22-250, rimless. 42.15in overall, 7.05lb empty. 22.45in barrel, 4-groove rifling; RH, concentric. Detachable box magazine, 3 rounds. Folding leaf sight. 3730 fps with 55-grain bullet.

This rifle originated in the 1980s as a replacement for the earlier patterns. It was originally introduced as the 'Tikka 558' and 'Tikka 658', indicating that it had been developed in 1988 to replace the

Models 55 and 65, but only prototypes had been made before improvements were made and the designations changed to '590' and '690'. Series production then began. Made by the Sako factory in Jyväskylä, the action has noticeably squarer contours than its predecessors and a high wall on the left side of the receiver. The barrel was allowed to float freely in the stock, the two-lug bolt enclosed the base of the cartridge case, and a special short extractor was fitted. The trigger was adjustable, the bolt shroud was streamlined, a radial safety catch lay on the right side of the action behind the bolt handle, and the receiver-top was grooved for optical sight mounts. The magazine-release catch was recessed in the underside of the stock. The 590 Popular version—the basic version—had an oil-finished walnut half-stock with a Monte Carlo comb and cheekpiece; the buttplate was a fixed synthetic pattern. Checkering appeared on the pistol grip and the rounded forend. A left-hand action has also been made in limited numbers.

SIMILAR GUNS

These guns are all chambered for the same six cartridges listed above. A set trigger is among the optional extras.

Tikka 590 Popular Battue rifle, 1991 to date. Also known as the 'Whitetail', particularly in North America, this has a 20.65in barrel and a straight-comb butt. The most obvious feature, however, is the rear sight—let into the front of a short ventilated rib running forward from the chamber. Battue rifles are about 40.35in long and weigh 6.83lb empty.

Tikka 590 Popular Continental rifle, 1991 to date. Distinguished by a broadened semi-beavertail forend and a heavy barrel, often made of stainless steel, this customarily lacks open sights. The five-round magazine, optional with the other rifles in the series, is regarded as standard. Rifles are typically 43.7in long, have 23.6in barrels, and weigh about 8.15lb. They are sometimes advertised as the 'Tikka Varmint' in North America.

Tikka 590 Popular Deluxe rifle, 1990 to date. This differs from the standard pattern principally in the design of the stock, which has a rollover comb and cheekpiece. The buttplate is rubber; the pistol grip cap and forend tip are rosewood.

TIKKA 690 POPULAR SPORTING RIFLE

This is a long-action version of the 590, the differences increasing overall length by 10mm (.4in) though the barrels remain unchanged. Weight is about 3-4oz greater than the corresponding short-action guns. Standard chamberings are 25-06 Remington, 6.5x55, 270 Winchester, 7x64, 30-06 and 9.3x62.

SIMILAR GUNS

Tikka 690 Popular Battue rifle. This gun retains the 20.65in barrel of the 590 Battue, but weighs a little over 7lb; it is distinguished principally by the length of the action.

Tikka 690 Popular Continental rifle. Identical with the corresponding 590 pattern except for action length, this is 44.1in long, has a 23.6in barrel and weighs about 8.35lb.

Tikka 690 Popular Deluxe rifle. A minor variant of the standard rifle, this amalgamates the long action and a select walnut half-stock with a rollover comb. The pistol grip cap and forend tip are rosewood.

TIKKA 690 MAGNUM SPORTING RIFLES

Chambered for the 7mm Remington, 300 Winchester or 338 Winchester magnum cartridges, these guns share the standard long action. Most dimensions parallel their 690 equivalents, though the standard 690 Popular Magnum has a 24.4in barrel and measures 44.5in overall; weight averages 7.5lb. Battue, Continental and Deluxe versions are made. Magazines hold three rounds, except for the four-round type fitted as standard to the Continental but optional on the others.

The Tikka Model 65 Master rifle, with optical sight, fluted barrel and muzzle weight.

The Tikka Master Battue rifle.

TIKKA 595 MASTER SPORTING RIFLE

Generally similar to the short-action 590 series, this is distinguished by a special buttplate relying on a system of sliding rods and spacers to adjust the length and rake to suit individual shooters. Offered in the same chamberings as the 590 rifles, the 595 series contains—in addition to the standard Master—the Master Continental, the Master Deluxe and the Master Trapper. The Continental and Deluxe patterns are duplicates of their 590-type equivalents, but the Trapper (which is basically a Battue without the quarter-rib) has a plain 20.65in barrel; iron sights are not provided.

SIMILAR GUNS

Tikka 695 Master rifles. Made in the same four patterns as the 595 series (standard, Continental, Deluxe and Trapper), these can be identified by the combination of long action and adjustable buttplate system. Chamberings are the same as the 690 series.

Tikka 695 Magnum rifles. Offered in standard, Continental, Deluxe and Trapper versions, these are duplicates of the 690 Magnums with adjustable buttplates.

• Tikka, break-open type

The Tikkakoski company, enveloped in the Sako-Valmet group, gained responsibility for the Valmet (q.v.) shotguns, combination guns and double rifles; these replaced the Tikka 77 series. Surviving 412-S rifles were sold in the 9.3x74R chambering into the early 1990s, but were then replaced by the Italian-made 512-S.

TIKKA 512-S EXPRESS DOUBLE RIFLE

Made for Oy Tikkakoski, Tikkakoski, by Fratelli di Stefano Marocchi SRL, Zanano di Sarezzo, Italy, 1992 to date.

Currently in production. **Chambering options:** see text. Data and performance generally as Valmet 412-S, below.

Advertised as the 'European Gun', this is little more than a Valmet 412-S with detail improvements in the action, made under license on machinery sold to Marocchi by Sako-Valmet. Accompanied by interchangeable-barrel shotguns and combination guns, the 512-S Express has a silver-gray finish on the action (most Valmet guns were case hardened) and 24in barrels. The standard chamberings are currently 7x65R, 7.62x53R, 30-06, 308 Winchester, 8x57IRS and 9.3x74R; the 30-06 and 308 versions are normally supplied without ejectors.

• Valmet, bolt-action type

In addition to Kalashnikov-type (q.v.) assault rifles and center-fire sporters, Valmet Oy was renowned for good-quality rimfire rifles—in particular, for the 'Finnish Lion' patterns. A bolt-action sniper rifle was developed in the mid 1980s, but, owing to a wholesale reorganization of the Finnish arms industry, Valmet amalgamated with Sako (q.v.) in 1987.

ORAVA SPORTING RIFLE

This was a 22-caliber junior rifle with a plain pistol-grip butt and a short forend with a finger groove. The barreled action could be detached simply by releasing the large nut protruding beneath the forend ahead of the stamped-strip trigger guard. The Orava had a 19.7in barrel, measured 36.4in overall, and weighed about 3.9lb. Swivels lay under the barrel and the butt.

ERÄ SPORTING RIFLE

This was a substantial 22LR rimfire sporting rifle with a detachable five-round magazine. A typical example weighed 6.15lb and was 41.75in long with a 23.6in barrel. The locking system apparently consisted of the bolt handle base entering its seat and a small auxiliary lug entering the receiver wall. Sights consisted of a ramped blade and a tangent-leaf graduated to 200m (220yd). The walnut half-stock, with a long round-tipped forend, had swivels beneath the forend and butt. Checkering was usually absent.

FINNISH LION ISU STANDARD TARGET RIFLE

Made by Valmet Oy, Tourula, Jyväskylä, 1966-87?

Total production: not known. **Chambering:** 22LR, rimfire. **Action:** locked by turning the bolt-handle base into its seat in the receiver.

44.9in overall, 10.65lb empty. 27.55in barrel, 6-groove rifling; RH, concentric. Single-shot only. Micro-adjustable aperture rear sight. 1080 fps with standard ball ammunition.

Once one of the most popular target rifles—designed in 1965 by a team led by Lt. Col. Eiino Vuorimies—this offered an ideal combination of good manufacturing quality, excellent performance, and low price. The standard rifle could be identified by the design of its stock, which had a distinctive shroud over the upper part of the pistol grip and a squared checkered panel on the deep forend. A hand stop and sling anchor could be attached to an accessory rail beneath the forend, and the adjustable shoulder plate was controlled by a large knurled-head nut on the right side of the butt. The rear sight was mounted on an adjustable bar on the left side of the receiver, which required the front sight to be canted to the left to maintain the sight line.

SIMILAR GUNS

Note: the identification of a pre-war 'Finnish Lion' rifle, allegedly dating from 1937, seems to have arisen from confusion with a little-known 22LR 'Lion' pattern made in Tallinn in Estonia.

The Valmet Model 86 sniping rifle.

Finnish Lion Champion rifle, 1966-72. Intended for Free Rifle competitions, this had a thumbhole stock with an adjustable hooked buttplate, a double trigger system capable of being set to a release pressure of just 100gm, and an anatomically-shaped adjustable wooden hand rest beneath the forend. An adjuster was originally mounted on top of the shoulder plate, but was eventually moved to the right side. The heavy 28.35in barrel gave a total weight of about 14.33lb without the competition sights.

Finnish Lion International rifle, 1978-87. This was a variant of the ISU Standard, sold without sights to enable the purchaser to comply with the regulations of individual authorities; standard or thumbhole stocks could be supplied to order.

Finnish Lion Junior rifle. This was a simpler version of the full-size rifle, sharing the same action, with a plain pistol-grip half-stock. A finger groove ran the length of the forend.

Finnish Lion Match rifle, 1966-87. The perfected guns of this type had a stock with a notable 'flat' projecting back from the chamber above the pistol grip. The butt had an extending hooked-toe shoulder plate, a hand-stop was fitted beneath the forend, and a forked wooden hand rest could be attached if required. Match rifles usually had medium-weight barrels and single triggers.

MODEL 86 SNIPER RIFLE

Made by Valmet Oy, Tourula, Jyväskylä, 1986-7.

Total production: very few. **Chambering:** 7.62x51, rimless. **Action:** locked by three lugs on the bolt head engaging the receiver behind the chamber as the bolt handle was turned down.

47.65in overall, 12.57lb without bipod and sights. 27.55in barrel, 4-groove rifling; RH, concentric. Detachable box magazine, 5-9 rounds. Optical sight. 2495 fps with 185-grain D-46 bullet.

Apparently designed to meet the requirements of the Finnish army, seeking to replace its Mosin-Nagant sniping equipment, the M-86 was a large but conventional design capable of hitting a 5.9in (15cm) target consistently at 500m (545yd). The butt of the wood or reinforced-fiberglass half-stock had an elevating comb and an adjustable shoulder plate. A short rail let into the under side of the squared forend accepted a sling anchor, and a bipod could be fitted to the forend tip. The pressure required to release the match-pattern trigger could be adjusted from 25oz to 4.5lb, and a radial safety lever was pivoted on the right side of the trigger housing to protrude from the stock behind the bolt handle. Sights could include competition, telescope or electro-optical patterns, and the barrel was usually fitted with a muzzle brake/flash suppressor.

• Valmet, break-open type

MODEL 412-S DOUBLE RIFLE

Made by Valmet Oy, Tourula, Jyväskylä, 1982-9.

Total production: several thousand. **Chambering options:** 243 Winchester, 30-06, 308 Winchester, 375 H&H Magnum or 9.3x74R. **Action:** locked by a sliding bar beneath the action engaging lugs on the underside of the barrel-lump as the top lever was closed.

DATA FOR A TYPICAL EXAMPLE

Chambering: 9.3x74R, rimless. About 40.5in overall, 7.5lb empty. 24in barrel, 4-groove rifling; RH, concentric. Double barrels, two shots only. Fixed open rear sight. 2280 fps with 285-grain bullet.

Part of a 'shooting system' which included a range of shotguns and combination guns, the 412-S was a sturdy and efficient box-lock design with superposed or 'over-and-under' barrels. Distin-

The Valmet Model 412S Double Rifle,
with exchangeable barrel units.

guished by a rib between the barrels, it had a sliding safety on the tang and a selector bolt in the trigger lever. The standard ambidextrous walnut butt had a Monte Carlo comb, but lacked a cheekpiece. The pistol grip and the forend were both extensively checkered. Swivels were fitted beneath the butt and lower barrel, and the rear sight was set into the front part of the stepped barrel rib. The last guns were sold under the Tikka brand (q.v.). The guns were customarily supplied with ejectors, except for the non-ejecting 30-06 pattern; the 243, 308 and 375 options were all abandoned in 1987.

SIMILAR GUNS

Model 412-K rifle, 1982-9. Offered in 30-06 and 308, this non-ejecting gun could be identified by the absence of the rib between the barrels.

FRANCE

French rifles bear very distinctive marks. Inscriptions such as 'MANUFACTURE IMPÉRIALE' (prior to 1870) or "MANUFAC-TURE D'ARMES" (post 1872) often appear on the left side of the receiver above the name of the arsenal—e.g., cursive St. Étienne—ahead of a designation such as 'MLE. 1866', 'MLE. 1874' or 'MLE. 1886-93'.

An 'MI' mark ('MA' after late 1870) appears on the right side of the barrel alongside the breech, together with the initial of the factory and the date ('S 1868': Saint-Étienne, 1868). The left side of the barrel displays a serial number such as 'G49693' underneath and to the rear of the rear sight base; while the initials of the steel supplier, the Directeur de la Manufacture and the Contrôleur Principale—'AF', 'B' and 'D' on a typical Chassepot—lie on the upper left-side flat of the barrel octagon behind the sight.

The proof mark, the month-number and an inspector's mark usually appeared under the barrel. The serial number is repeated in whole or in part on most of the pieces, together with inspectors' marks taking the form of small raised letters in squares, circles or diamonds.

French rifles customarily had a circular stamp on the right side of the butt, displaying the month of manufacture, the initial of Contrôleur Principal and the factory director, and then the factory abbreviation (e.g., 'S' for Saint-Étienne) and the year of manufacture.

In addition to the regulation patterns, the French government bought substantial quantities of non-standard weapons in times of national emergency. This was particularly true of the Franco-Prussian War of 1870-1, when an amazing variety of guns was acquired by the 'Gouvernement de la Défense Nationale'; virtually anything which could shoot was pressed into service with the Gardes Mobiles.

• Albini-Braendlin

A few of these Anglo-Belgian rifles, possibly made commercially by the Braendlin Armory in Birmingham, were acquired during the Franco-Prussian War. The quantities involved were presumably small—certainly no more than a few thousand. For additional details, see **'Belgium'**.

• APX

This designation was applied to a series of automatic rifles developed prior to World War I by the Établissement Technique de l'Artillerie de Puteaux. They competed against the CTV (q.v.) patterns, but were not successful.

• Bérenger

Jean Bérenger, a renowned Parisian gunsmith active in the middle of the 19th Century, made a substantial quantity of sporting guns with a breech-chamber which pivoted sideways when a radial lever beneath the forend was turned. The system was not sophisticated enough to enjoy anything other than a short period in vogue. The guns themselves customarily had two-piece stocks, and often displayed copious engraving on the slab-sided frame which housed the breech mechanism.

• Berdan

Two differing patterns were acquired during the Franco-Prussian War—2431 'M1866 Berdan-Springfield' rifles chambered for a '.58 Remington' cartridge, and 11,188 converted Spanish rifle-muskets chambered for the 11mm Spanish Remington cartridge. For additional details, see **'U.S.A.'** and **'Spain'** respectively.

• Berthier, autoloading type

In addition to his better-known bolt-action rifles, Adolphe Berthier was also responsible for some automatic weapons. Though often considered as light machine-guns, some of these were closer in design and dimensions to automatic rifles. A gas-operated pattern was submitted to the French in 1908, but nothing came of an encouraging trial. Similarly, a gun tested by the U.S. Army in May 1920 also failed. In mid-November 1921, an improved Berthier rifle was tested in the U.S. against Thompson Auto Rifles PC and Mark V, but did not prove acceptable. Berthier's greatest legacy was the British Vickers-Berthier light machine gun and its successor, the Vickers 'K'.

• Berthier, bolt-action type

Guns of this system, unique to France at first, were also supplied to Russia and Greece during World War I. Berthier rifles were used by the Kingdom of Serbs, Croats and Slovenes (later Yugoslavia) in the early 1920s; and also, more recently, throughout what was once the French colonial empire.

The Berthier action was a modified Lebel (q.v.), with the locking axis changed from horizontal to vertical and the substitution of a clip-loaded magazine for the forend tube.

Though elegant and quite popular in France, the Berthier action was also awkward, and a gap between the bolt and the right side of the magazine above the receiver allowed dirt to enter. Rigorous service during World War I soon revealed the weakness of the slender rifle stock, and also that accuracy was generally inferior to that of the Lebel. Consequently, small numbers of the sturdier and more durable Mle 86/93 rifles were retained after 1918 for grenade-launching and sniping.

THE FIRST STEPS

In 1887, attempts were being made to provide a suitable carbine for the French cavalrymen when news reached the authorities of Adolphe Berthier's adaption of the Mle 86 (Lebel) action to accept an Austrian Mannlicher-style magazine. Official approval to build a prototype Berthier rifle was withheld until May 1888, while the military experimented with Lebel-type guns. When these failed, the first Berthier infantry rifles appeared. Trials held at Mont-Valérien soon showed the superiority of the Berthier over the Lebel in rapid fire.

1888-type rifle. The ten experimental 8mm Berthier infantry rifles made at the Ateliers de Puteaux in 1888 embodied many Mle 86 parts. However, panels were milled out of the receiver to save weight and the archaic tube magazine beneath the barrel had been replaced by a four-round clip-loaded box. The magazine floorplate was released by a latch in the front of the trigger guard, and a radial lever on the right side of the receiver expelled a loaded clip. Swivels lay on the butt and the barrel band.

1889-type musketoon. The experimental infantry rifles were followed by the first "Mousqueton d'Artillerie" (a short rifle accepting a bayonet), similar to the rifle except that the clip-expelling mechanism was abandoned and the bolt handle was turned down against the stock. Swivels were fitted under the butt and the barrel band.

1889-type carbine. A prototype Berthier-system cavalry carbine offered a streamlined magazine case protruding beneath the receiver, and the bolt handle was moved forward about 0.8in to make the gun easier to handle. A small button inside the front of the trigger guard retained the clip in the magazine.

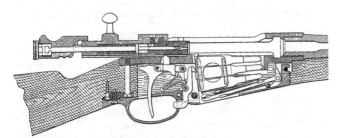

A longitudinal section of the Berthier action.

A Hotchkiss machine-gun crew with Franco-British troops. Note the 1892-type Berthier musketoon shouldered by the man in the foreground.

1890-type rifle. The original infantry rifles, with bolt lugs which locked horizontally, were followed by ten Puteaux-made vertical-locking Berthiers. Trials of these rifles began on 28th February 1890 against ten lightened Lebel short rifles promoted by the École Normale de Tir, which were little more than abbreviated Mle 86 Lebels with the magazine capacity reduced to six rounds.

MODEL 1890 CAVALRY CARBINE
Carabine de Cavallerie Mle 1890
Made by the state manufactory, Saint-Étienne, 1890-4.
Chambering: 8x51R, rimmed. **Action:** locked by two lugs on the detachable bolt head engaging recesses in the receiver wall behind the chamber when the bolt handle was turned down.

37.2in overall, 6.66lb empty. 17.85in barrel, 4-groove rifling; LH, concentric. Clip-loaded internal box magazine, 3 rounds. Ramp-and-leaf sight graduated to 2000m (2185yd). 2090 fps with Balle 1886 D. No bayonet (see notes).

Adopted in March 1890 and eventually issued to dragoons, hussars and mounted riflemen (Chasseurs)—together with colonial cavalrymen (Spahis)—this was a minor revision of the experimental 'Numéro 2.bis' trials gun. The original carbines had a conventional stock, a loose sling ring on the left side of the barrel band, and a swivel on the under edge of the butt. They were sighted for the Balle 1886 M, leaves being graduated to 1800m (1970yd) with a 2000m (2185yd) notch on the top edge.

The sights were revised for the Balle 1886 D in 1901, the 2000m setting being moved to the body of the leaf. A sling bar appeared on the left side of the butt from 1904 onward, with a fixed ring on the barrel band.

SIMILAR GUNS

Mle 90 T. 15. Introduced in 1915, this was adapted to accept a standard Mle 92 sword bayonet, the modified nose cap being moved back far enough to admit the bayonet hilt beneath the muzzle. Sights were graduated for the Balle 1886 D.

Mle 90 T. 27. Dating from 1927, this version had a modified nose cap with a rudimentary piling hook. The cleaning-rod channel on the left side of the forend was filled with a fillet of wood.

MODEL 1890 CUIRASSIER CARBINE
Carabine de Cuirassiers Mle 1890
Made by the state manufactory, Saint-Étienne, 1890-4.
Chambering: 8x51R, rimmed. Otherwise as Mle 1890 cavalry carbine except weight (about 6.55lb empty).

Sharing the standard Mle 90 action, this carbine was introduced in 1890 to arm the heavy cavalry. Its extraordinary stock had a quirky combless butt suited to firers wearing a steel breast-plate. A leather buttplate replaced the cast-iron pattern, and sights were graduated for the original Balle 1886 M. From 1901, however, the rear sights were adapted for the Balle 1886 D (though still graduated to 2000m).

A M1892 Berthier musketoon, with bayonet.

SIMILAR GUNS

Mle 90 T. 15. Some guns were adapted in 1915 for the standard Mle 92 sword bayonet, a new nose cap being moved back to receive the hilt.

MODEL 1890 GENDARMERIE CARBINE
Carabine de Gendarmerie Mle 1890.
Made by the state manufactory, Saint-Étienne, 1890-4.
Chambering: 8x51R, rimmed. Otherwise as Mle 1890 cavalry carbine, except weight (6.83lb empty) and bayonet (Mle 90 épée pattern).

Introduced in 1890, this was similar to the cavalry carbine (q.v.) but had a nose cap with a protruding stud to enter the pommel of the bayonet. Guns were originally sighted to 2000m (2185yd) for the Balle 1886 M, but the sights were revised after 1901 for the Balle 1886 D.

MODEL 1892 ARTILLERY MUSKETOON
Mousqueton d'Artillerie Mle 1890
Made by the state manufactory, Saint-Étienne, 1892-1916.
Chambering: 8x51R, rimmed. Otherwise generally as Mle 1890, except bayonet (Mle 92 sword pattern).

Adopted in 1892 for issue to artillerymen and, eventually, to the customs service, the Mle 92 musketoon was a derivative of the 1890-pattern cavalry carbine with the nose cap and barrel adapted for a different bayonet. A cleaning rod was carried in a channel hollowed out of the left side of the forend. A sling ring was fixed to the left side of the barrel band, and a barred sling recess appeared in the left side of the butt.

SIMILAR GUNS

Mle 92 T. 27. Approved in 1927, this lacked the cleaning rod, its channel being filled with a glued-in wooden fillet, sanded smooth and refinished. Despite the care with which the alterations were made, however, the line of the original channel was usually clearly discernible.

MODEL 1902 COLONIAL RIFLE
Fusil Mle 1902
Made by the state manufactory, Saint-Étienne, 1902-14.
Chambering: 8x51R, rimmed. **Action:** as Mle 1890 cavalry carbine, above.
44.35in overall, 7.98lb empty. 24.9in barrel, 4-groove rifling; LH, concentric. Clip-loaded internal box magazine, 3 rounds. Ramp-and-leaf sight graduated to 2000m (2185yd). 2275 fps with Balle 1886 D. Mle 02 épée bayonet.

This rifle was introduced in 1902 to arm colonial troops in Annam, Cambodia and Tonkin in French Indo-China—and, therefore, is often known as 'de Tirailleurs Indo-Chinois'. Lighter, handier and more efficient than the standard Mle 86 Lebel, it was the first Berthier rifle to be issued in quantity in the French armed forces.

The action was essentially that of the Mle 90 cavalry carbine, but the production life of the rifle was shortened by the introduction of the Mle 07/15 (below). Original guns were sighted for the Balle 1886 M, to expend existing supplies of ammunition. The rear sight had a standing block for 250m (275yd), ramps for 400-800m (435-875yd), and a folding leaf for 900-1900m (985-2075yd). The 2000m (2185yd) setting was a small 'V'-notch in the top edge of the leaf body. Bolt handles were bent downward.

The sights were altered after 1909 for the Balle 1886 D. The original sight was retained, but the leaf was graduated to 2400m (2625yd) and the sighting notch was deepened appreciably. Some sights were newly made—their bases are generally marked 'N'—but many others were simply altered from the original pattern.

A few surviving rifles were converted in the Saint-Étienne factory in 1937 for 7.5mm rimless ammunition (see '**Model 1902/37**').

MODEL 1907 COLONIAL RIFLE
Fusil Mle 1907
Made by the state manufactory, Saint-Étienne, 1907-14.
Chambering: 8x51R, rimmed. **Action:** as Mle 1890 cavalry carbine, above.

51.4in overall, 8.42lb empty. 31.6in barrel, 4-groove rifling; LH, concentric. Clip-loaded internal box magazine, 3 rounds. Ramp-and-leaf sight graduated to 2000m (2185yd). 2300 fps with Balle 1886 D. Mle 07 épée bayonet.

The success of the Mle 02 rifle, which was ideally suited to the small stature of the French colonial units raised in the Far East, persuaded the authorities to adopt a modified full-size gun for the Senegalese sharpshooters (*Tirailleurs Sénégalais*) in 1907.

The Mle 07 lacked a cleaning rod, as the relevant equipment was carried separately. Sights were initially graduated for the Balle 1886 M, and the bolt handle was bent downward. From 1910 onward, the rear sights of surviving guns were altered to 2400m (2625yd) for the Balle 1886 D.

MODEL 1907/15 RIFLE
Fusil d'Infanterie Mle 1907/15
Made by the state manufactories in Châtellerault, Saint-Étienne and Tulle, 1915-17; by Manufacture d'Armes de Paris, 1915-18 (components only); by Établissements Contin-Souza, Paris, 1915-18; by Société Française Delaunay-Belleville, 1915-18; and by the Remington Arms-Union Metallic Cartridge Company, Ilion, New York, 1915-16 (9440 only).
Chambering: 8x51R, rimmed. **Action:** as Mle 1890 cavalry carbine, above.
51.4in overall, 8.4lb empty. 31.6in barrel, 4-groove rifling; LH, concentric. Clip-loaded internal box magazine, 3 rounds. Ramp-and-leaf graduated to 2400m (2625yd). 2300 fps with Balle 1886 D. Mle 15 épée bayonet.

The opening stages of World War I soon showed the weaknesses of the Mle 86 Lebel rifle; the French were aware of them, but parsimony had prevented the introduction of a superior Berthier prior to 1914. Lengthening the Mle 92 artillery musketoon to infantry rifle proportions, even though the three-round clip was retained, bought time while a modified rifle was developed.

Adopted in 1915, the Mle 07/15 rifle was essentially similar to the 1907 colonial pattern (above), except for its straight bolt handle and a cleaning rod let into the left side of the forend.

Fitted with the standard internal three-round clip-loaded magazine, Mle 07/15 guns fed from the Chargeur Mle 90 and were sighted for the Balle 1886 D. They were issued to some of the infantry units raised in 1916-18.

SIMILAR GUNS

Mle 07/15 T. 16. Small numbers of these rifles were modified in 1917 to accept the five-round Mle 16 clip. Though possessing the same sheet-metal magazine cases protruding beneath the stock, they lacked the handguard of the true Mle 16 and bore markings such as 'ST.-ETIENNE Mle 1907-15' on the left side of the receiver.

Mle 07/15 M. 34. This was a conversion for the 7.5mm Balle 1929 C; see below.

MODEL 1916 RIFLE
Fusil d'Infanterie Mle 1916
Manufacturers: generally as Mle 1907/15 (q.v.), except for some of the lesser contractors and Remington-UMC.
Total production: 1.5 million? **Chambering:** 8x51R, rimmed. **Action:** as Mle 1890 cavalry carbine, above.
51.4in overall, 9.24lb empty. 31.6in barrel, 4-groove rifling; LH, concentric. Clip-loaded box magazine, 5 rounds. Ramp-and-leaf sight graduated to 2400m (2625yd). 2300 fps with Balle 1886 D. Mle 15 épée bayonet.

Issued from 1916 onward, to many of the regiments raised in 1917-18, this was little more than an adaptation of the Mle 07/15 to accept a five-round clip. The opportunity was also taken to provide a hinged cover for the spent-clip aperture, though the firer had to pull the cover downward when the gun was being used unless he wanted the spent clip to remain in the magazine. Guns were sighted for the Balle 1886 D and had a handguard running from the receiver ring under the barrel band.

The sight line was raised above the handguard in 1920, requiring a new sight base, and a slider with a square notch replaced the original 'V'-type. New sights display 'A' on their components.

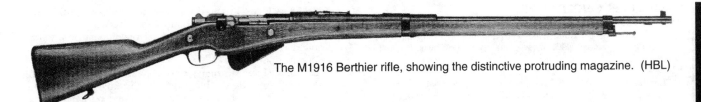

The M1916 Berthier rifle, showing the distinctive protruding magazine. (HBL)

Adaptation of guns for the Balle 1932 N was approved in 1932, necessitating changes in sights and chambering (though much of the work appears to have been delayed until after 1945). By 1939, the Mle 16 served much of the French army. It was also to be found on colonial service.

MODEL 1892-16 ARTILLERY MUSKETOON
Mousqueton d'Artillerie Mle 1892 M. 16
Manufacturers: generally as Mle 1916 rifle (q.v.).
Chambering: 8x51R, rimmed. **Action:** as Mle 1890 cavalry carbine, above.

37.2in overall, 7.16lb empty. 17.85in barrel, 4-groove rifling; LH, concentric. Clip-loaded box magazine, 5 rounds. Ramp-and-leaf sight graduated to 2000m (2185yd). 2090 fps with Balle 1886 D. Mle 92 sword bayonet.

Introduced in 1916 to equip artillerymen and mounted troops, the "Mousqueton d'Artillerie Mle 92 Modifié 1916" served motorized and armored units, infantry machinegunners and some colonial units by 1939. It was retained by the gendarmerie, customs service and prison guards into the 1960s.

Basically a newly made variation of the Mle 92, with the magazine deepened to accept the Mle 16 clip, the gun had the sling ring fixed to the left side of the barrel band and a barred sling recess cut into the left side of the butt.

The earliest examples were made without the handguard that was soon added above the barrel, and a cleaning-rod channel was cut into the left side of the forend. Sights were graduated for the 8mm Balle 1886 D, but the sight line was raised in 1920 and the sight-block was given a deep squared notch instead of the original 'V'. New parts were marked 'A'.

SIMILAR GUNS
Mle 92/16 T. 27. Introduced in 1927, this gained a stacking rod on the nose cap, and the cleaning-rod channel was filled with a wooden fillet. The first batches of musketoons were re-sighted and re-chambered for the Balle 1932 N in the early 1930s, though most of the work may have been undertaken after 1945.

MODEL 1907-15-34 SHORT RIFLE
Fusil d'Infanterie Mle 07/15 M. 34
Made by the state manufactory in Saint-Étienne, 1934-9.
Chambering: 7.5x54, rimless. **Action:** locked by two lugs on the detachable bolt head engaging recesses in the receiver wall as the bolt handle was turned down.

42.5in overall, 8.11lb empty. 22.85in barrel, 4-groove rifling; RH, concentric. Charger-loaded internal box magazine, 5 rounds. Tangent-leaf sight graduated to 900m (985yd). 2675 fps with Balle 1929 C. Mle 15 épée or Mle 15 sword bayonets.

Something better than the Berthier was clearly needed in the 1920s—experiments eventually led to the MAS 36 (q.v.)—but, in the interim, the sharply tapering 8mm Lebel cartridge was replaced by the rimless 7.5mm Balle 1924 C. Some Lebel-type rifles were experimentally modified for this round (Mle 1886 M. 27, q.v.), but had no long-term influence.

The improved 7.5mm Balle 1929 C replaced the 1924 pattern in 1929, whereupon the first experiments to adapt the Berthier rifles

to rimless cartridges were made. Many existing Mle 07/15 rifles were modernized after 1934 while development of the MAS 36 was completed.

SIMILAR GUNS
Infantry pattern. This had a straight bolt handle, a swivel on the under edge of the butt, a handguard above the barrel, and accepted the Mle 86/15 épée bayonet. Most metal parts were phosphated.

Cavalry pattern. Similar to the infantry rifle, this had a sling bar on the left side of the butt, a bent-down bolt handle, and accepted the Mle 92/15 sword bayonet. Issue was restricted to a few regiments in 1939.

MODEL 1902-37 SHORT RIFLE
Fusil Mle 1902/37
Converted by the state manufactory in Saint-Étienne, 1938-9.
Total production: a few hundred. **Chambering:** 7.5x54, rimmed. **Action:** as Mle 07/15 M. 34, above.

42.3in overall, 8.05lb empty. 22.45in barrel, 4-groove rifling; RH, concentric. Charger-loaded internal box magazine, 5 rounds. Tangent-leaf sight graduated to 900m (985yd). 2675 fps with Balle 1929 C. Mle 02 épée bayonet.

Adopted in 1937, this was a transformation of the old Mle 1902 colonial rifle (q.v.) to approximate the new Mle 07/15 M. 34. It retained the original turned-down bolt handle, but displayed a mark such as 'TYPE SE-MAS 1902 M 37' on the left side of the receiver.

• Carcano
These needle-rifles were used by the Gardes Mobiles during the Franco-Prussian War of 1870-1. It is suspected that they were acquired from the Italian government, which was intending to re-equip with the bolt-action Vetterli. For additional details, see 'Italy'.

• Chabot
Patented in several countries by Cyprien Chabot in the mid 1860s (e.g., U.S. Patents 47163 of April 1865 and 49718 of September 1865), this breechloading system had much earlier antecedents. A short cylindrical breech-bolt attached to a frame or 'cap' pivoted transversely on the side of the chamber. A hook on the top rear of the cap was used to lift the bolt clear of the breech, automatically activating a sliding extractor in the right wall of the chamber as it rose. Chabot guns seem to have been built for trials on the basis of several different military cap locks, including French Mle 57 rifle-muskets, Swiss 10.4mm 1863-pattern short rifles (Stutzer), and U.S. 1861-pattern Springfields.

• Chapuis Armes
This gunmaking business is among Europe's best-known manufacturers of break-open rifles—single barrel, side-by-side double barrel and over/under designs. What the range lacks in diversity, it more than repays in decoration.

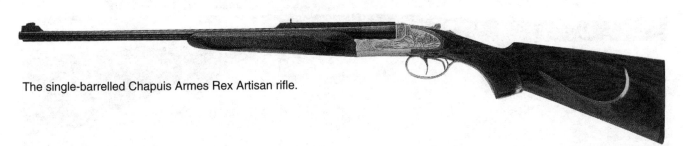

The single-barrelled Chapuis Armes Rex Artisan rifle.

OURAL EXEL SINGLE RIFLE

Made by Chapuis Armes, Saint-Bonnet-le-Château.

Currently in production. **Action:** locked by a double under-lug engaging the locking bar as the top lever closes. **Chambering options:** see text, below.

DATA FOR A TYPICAL EXAMPLE

Chambering: 6.5x68R, rimmed. 40.8in overall, 6.06lb empty. 23.6in barrel, 4-groove rifling; RH, concentric. Single shot only. Fixed open rear sight. 3770 fps with 93-grain bullet.

This is a boxlock of exceptional quality, with a double-hook 'Blitz'-pattern action. The standard gun— known as the 'Exel'—has a walnut pistol grip butt with a straight comb and a rounded Monte Carlo-type cheekpiece; checkering appears on the pistol grip and on the slender schnabel-tip forend. The pistol grip cap is customarily ebonite. The trigger is usually a single pattern, but a double 'set' unit is available on request; a sliding safety catch is fitted on the tang. The front sight is a ramped blade, and the rear sight is set into the front tip of the quarter-rib. 6.5x57R and 7x65R are regarded as the standard chamberings, but options include 243 Winchester, 6x62R Frères, 6.5x65R RWS, 6.5x68R, 7mm Remington Magnum, 270 Winchester and 300 Winchester Magnum. A 1.5-6x42 Zeiss optical sight and fine English scroll engraving are also standard.

SIMILAR GUNS

Oural Luxe. This deluxe pattern displays special individually signed scroll engraving extending onto the fences, with a game scene beneath the action body ahead of the trigger guard. The trigger guard has a long tang extending back down the pistol grip to the chiseled steel grip cap.

Oural Elite. Distinguished by additional sideplates, though still built on the basic boxlock action, this allows more game scenes to be shown. Only the finest-quality walnut blanks are used to make the butt and the forend.

PROGRESS UGEX DOUBLE RIFLE

Made by Chapuis Armes, Saint-Bonnet-le-Château.

Currently in production. **Chambering options:** see text, below. **Action:** locked by a double under-lug engaging the locking bar as the top lever closes.

DATA FOR A TYPICAL EXAMPLE

Chambering: 7x65R, rimmed. 40.75in overall, 7.15kg empty. 23.6in barrel, 4-groove rifling; RH, concentric. Double barrel, two shots. Fixed open rear sight. 2820 fps with 162-grain bullet.

Basically a double-barreled version of the Oural (q.v.), this offers the same exemplary quality. Chamberings currently include 7x65R, 8x57IRS and 9.3x74R, with 30 Blaser and 8x75RS as optional extras. The standard version—known as the 'Ugex'—has a pistol grip butt with a straight comb, but lacks a cheekpiece; the forend is a round-tipped form. A quarter-rib appears on the barrel above the breech; the boxlock is decorated with fine 'Best Bouquet' or English scrollwork; and a double-trigger system is standard. Individual guns can be supplied as ejectors or non-ejectors according to purchasers' whims. Sling swivels can be added beneath the barrel and butt, and an optical sight can be mounted. A 21.65in barrel option is also popular.

SIMILAR GUNS

Progress Brousse. A big-game rifle chambered for cartridges such as the 375 Holland & Holland (standard), 416 Rigby or 470 Nitro Express (options), this has an ejecting boxlock action with reinforced sides and a butt with a Monte Carlo-type cheekpiece. The engraving usually consists of English scrollwork. A sturdy rubber shoulder pad is fitted, and an express sight is let into the front of the quarter-rib. The 375 rifle has a 25.6in barrel and weighs about 9.25lb; the large-caliber versions, with 23.6in barrels, average 10.4lb.

Progress Hgex Imperial. Similar mechanically to the Hgex Supreme, this version has exhibition-quality woodwork. Game scenes and Renaissance-style foliate scrolls appear on a matted deep-cut ground. A small rounded cheekpiece is customary, gun weight averaging 7lb.

Progress Hgex Supreme. Another variation of the Chapuis boxlock side-by-side double, this 'Grande Luxe' gun is distinguished by its decoration—game scenes and bordered Engish scrollwork—and by the small rounded German-style cheekpiece on the pistol grip butt. The standard chamberings are 7x65R, 30 Blaser, 8x57IRS, 8x75RS and 9.3x74R.

Progress Jungle. Similar to the Brousse, and offered in the same chamberings, this can be identified by the sideplates extending backward from the boxlock. The game-scene engraving is also more extensive.

Progress Rex. A variant of the basic boxlock design, made in ejecting and non-ejecting forms, this has additional sideplates engraved with game scenes.

Progress Rex Artisan. This is simply a custom-made version of the Rex, with extensive English-scroll and game-scene engraving. The woodwork of the butt and forend is six-star walnut.

Progress Rgex. This is a deluxe form of the Progress Ugex, with a select walnut stock and an additional game scene beneath the action body. The butt usually has a Monte Carlo-type cheekpiece and a chiselled steel pistol grip cap. An additional 300 Winchester Magnum chambering is currently being offered with this rifle.

Progress Rgex Artisan. A custom-made version of the standard Rgex, this has walnut of the finest quality; game-scene and scroll engraving appears on the action, the fences, the extended trigger guard and the pistol grip cap. The cheekpiece is generally a Monte Carlo pattern.

Progress Savane. This is a variant of the Brousse and Jungle models with 'Holland & Holland' fences and a sinuous 'moustache' reinforce on the sides of the action body. The engraving pattern is a combination of Renaissance matted-ground foliate tracery and African game scenes.

SUPER ORION C-5 DOUBLE RIFLE

Made by Chapuis Armes, Saint-Bonnet-le-Château.

Currently in production. **Chambering options:** see text, below. **Action:** locked by a double under-lug engaging the locking bar as the top lever closes.

DATA FOR A TYPICAL EXAMPLE

Chambering: 9.3x74R, rimmed. 38.9in overall, 3.15kg empty. 21.65in barrel, 4-groove rifling; RH, concentric. Double barrel, two shots. Fixed open rear sight. 2280 fps with 285-grain bullet.

The Super Orion is basically an over-and-under version of the Progress side-by-side double rifle, fitted with an exchangeable recoil absorber and a short barrel (though a 23.6in option is also available). The standard rifle—a non-ejector known as the 'C-5'—can be supplied from stock in 7x65R, 8x57IRS and 9.3x74R, with 30 Blaser and 8x75RS as surcharged alternatives. The guns have a plain walnut butt, with checkering on the pistol grip, and a deep forend with a schnabel tip. A double-trigger system is standard, the rear sight is set into the tip of the quarter-rib, and swivels lie beneath the butt and forend. The engraving pattern is usually fine English scrollwork.

SIMILAR GUNS

Note: a Bergstutzen version of the Super Orion was introduced in 1997, distinguished by barrels of differing caliber. Applicable to any of the individual versions—from the C-10 to the Imperial—the upper barrel can be chambered for 7x65R, 8x57IRS or 9.3x74R, with a lower barrel for 6.5x57R or 7x65R.

The Chapuis Armes Super Orion Artisan over/under Double Rifle.

Super Orion C-10. This is an ejecting version of the C-5, otherwise identical mechanically and supplied in the same chamberings.

Super Orion C-15. Supplied as an auto-ejector, though a non-ejecting version is optional, this is basically a C-10 with better-quality woodwork and a Monte Carlo cheekpiece on the butt. The pistol grip has a steel cap.

Super Orion C-25. Identical with the C-15, this has additional sideplates and, therefore, more extensive engraving. The scroll-work was accompanied by game scenes on the sideplates and the underside of the action body. Ejecting and non-ejecting versions can be obtained.

Super Orion C-115 Artisan. The first of the custom-made patterns, this has six-star walnut woodwork with a Monte Carlo cheekpiece on the straight-comb butt. The tang of the trigger guard extends down the pistol grip to meet the metal pistol grip cap. The engraving pattern combines matted-ground foliate scrollwork with game scenes.

Super Orion C-125 Artisan. Essentially similar to the C-115, this has a boxlock with additional sideplates; these are engraved with fine English scrollwork and game scenes.

Super Orion Excellence. Supplied in ejecting form (though a non-ejector can be obtained to order), the finest of the Chapuis Armes over/under double rifles has a six-star walnut butt with a small rounded cheekpiece. The trigger mechanism is usually a single non-selective design. Renaissance-style foliate tracery and game-scene engraving offers the highest quality.

Super Orion Prestige. Distinguished by the sideplates extending back from the boxlock, this is similar to the Excellence—apart from the opportunity for more extensive engraving.

• Pierre Chapuis

Trading independently of Chapuis Armes, though with strong family links, Pierre Chapuis of Saint-Bonnet-le-Château concentrates more on excellence of decoration than a variety of guns.

THE GUNS

The Pierre Chapuis range consists of side-by-side and over/under double rifles, built on a modified Anson & Deeley action with reinforced-side action bodies and a patented replaceable recoil seat. Ejectors and single-trigger systems are among the optional features. The side-by-side rifles have pistol grip butts with rounded cheekpieces and round-tipped forends. The over/under patterns, however, have Bavarian-style woodwork with low hog's back combs, squared cheekpieces, and forends with schnabel tips. Chamberings are normally restricted to 8x57IRS and 9.3x74R.

THE STYLES

These guns are set apart by their decoration, which can include pierced pistol grip caps and buttplates, engraved forend caps, and stocks ranging from a straightforward straight-comb design with a small oval cheekpiece to a 'Sologne' pattern with a bellied stock and matching cheekpiece. Pierre Chapuis will even supply a butt 'à la Française', carved into the head of a red deer behind the straight wrist.

Artisan. Applied to the guns with extended sideplates, this is equivalent to the 'Classique' boxlock design, with color case-hardening on the action body and English scroll engraving. However, the walnut is generally a better grade, and the pistol grip cap and shoulder plate are pierced steel.

A cased Pierre Chapuis double-barrelled over/under rifle.

Beaugency. The finest of the boxlock styles, this combines the coin finish with Louis XVI scroll engraving and game scenes on the sides and underside of the action body. The woodwork is generally five-star walnut.

Chambord. The sideplate equivalent of Fontainebleau, this has the hardened coin finish and scroll-engraved bordering to the game scenes.

Classique. The most basic form of the boxlock guns (side-by-side and over/under alike), this has a color case-hardened action body with light English scroll engraving.

Fontainebleau. Distinguished by a hardened mirror-polish 'coin' finish, this combines red deer and wild boar scenes with scroll-engraved borders. The forend cap and trigger guard are a matched set.

Versailles. The best of Pierre Chapuis' work, this sideplate pattern matches Louis XVI scrollwork with game scenes engraved in a combination of depths. The game-scene backgrounds may range in color from sky blue to rich purple.

• Chassepot

A Prussian Dreyse breech-loading rifle—surrendered in 1850 to the French authorities—was tested at the École Militaire de Vincennes, but the breech was not considered to be gas-tight and its performance was inferior to the standard French rifle-muskets.

By the mid-1860s, however, spurred on by Manceaux and other inventors, the French had realized that their Minié-pattern muzzle-loaders were obsolescent.

The eventual beneficiary of this process was Antoine Alphonse Chassepot, whose first rifle had been patented in November 1857. Although a Manceaux-Vieillard rifle (q.v.) was tried successfully in 1862, the experimental bolt-action Chassepot was being preferred by 1864. This led to the experimental 'Fusil Chassepot des essais du camp de Châlons' and, after alterations had been made to the bolt, the trigger and the stock, to the "Fusil d'Infanterie Modéle 1866."

Chassepots first saw service in campaigns in northern Italy in 1867-68. Their excellent performance did not escape the attention of Prussian military observers who reported that not only had development of the Dreyse needle guns stagnated, but also that French technology had overtaken them.

TRIALS GUNS
Fusils et carabines Chassepot des essais
Probably made by the imperial manufactory in Châtellerault, 1858-64.
Total production: several hundred. **Action:** locked by lugs on the bolt body engaging recesses cut in the receiver walls as the bolt handle was turned down.

DATA FOR A TYPICAL RIFLE

Chambering: 13.5mm combustible cartridge, fired by a cap lock. 51.4in overall, 8.2lb empty. 31.9in barrel, probably 4-groove rifling; RH, concentric. Single-shot only. Leaf-and-slider rear sight. About 1310 fps with ball ammunition. Saber-Lance de Cent Gardes.

The first Chassepot, patented in 1857, retained a back-action cap lock. The breech mechanism comprised a bolt which could be opened by releasing the spring catch, raising the handle and pulling the bolt backward to expose the chamber.

The essence of the Chassepot system was the special india-rubber washer that lay between the bolt body and the bolt head. When the rifle was fired, the bolt head was forced backward, squeezing the india-rubber *obturateur* outward against the chamber wall. Unfortunately, although this provided a surprisingly good gas-seal for a few shots, excessive heat generated in rapid-fire could reduce the resilience of the india-rubber washer until it disintegrated.

12mm Chassepot carbines were tested by three cavalry regiments in 1860, competing against the Manceaux & Vieillard system. They were successful enough to encourage the manufacture of experimental 13.5mm-caliber infantry rifles and Carabines de Chasseurs; by 1864, the Chassepot, though acknowledged to be imperfect, was preferred to its rivals. However, the pervading influence of the Prussian Dreyse needle rifles persuaded the French to adapt the Chassepot system to a similar style. The result was the so-called 'Camp de Châlons' rifle of 1865, described below.

1865-TYPE TRIALS RIFLE
Fusil Chassepot des essais du camp de Châlons
Probably made by the imperial manufactory in Saint-Étienne, 1865.

Total production: about 400. **Action:** locked by turning the bolt-handle rib down so that it abuts the receiver. **Chambering:** 11mm, combustible cartridge.

51.2in overall, 9.05lb empty. 32.3in barrel, 4-groove rifling; LH, concentric. Single-shot only. Leaf-and-slider rear sight. Performance not known. Mle 1861 saber bayonet.

This, the experimental forerunner of the perfected Mle 1866 infantry rifle, was made for extended trials. It was fired by a long spring-loaded needle in the bolt, the detachable bolt head being held by a screw through the extension of the bolt-handle base. An india-rubber washer lay between the bolt body and the head to seal the breech as the gun fired.

The needle fitted onto a supporting pillar attached to the cocking piece, and a guide roller was fitted on the cocking-piece to reduce friction. A small chamber was formed behind the cartridge base to aid combustion of the black-powder propellant.

The cocking piece had to be pulled back manually before the bolt could be opened. Half-raising the bolt handle while simultaneously retracting the cocking piece allowed a small blade-like *pièce d'arrét* in the forward extension of the cocking piece to engage a small guide-way in the rear of the bolt body. This safety feature prevented the needle reaching the cartridge base and prevented further rotation of the bolt. The cocking piece had then to be fully retracted before the bolt could be opened.

The gun had a straight-wrist stock, the barrel being held by a brass band and a brass nose cap. Swivels lay beneath the band and the butt. The cocking piece and the trigger lever both had a notable backward slant, and the back-sight leaf was hinged at the rear of the mounting block. The saber bayonet had a short recurved quillon and wooden grips held to the tang with two bolts.

MODEL 1866 RIFLE
Fusil d'Infanterie Mle 1866
Made by the state manufactories in Châtellerault, Saint-Étienne and Tulle; and in Birmingham, Brescia, Liége, London, Planencia and Vienna.

Total production: 1.5 million? **Action:** locked by turning the bolt-handle rib down so that it abuts the receiver.

Chambering: 11mm, combustible cartridge. 51.35in overall, 9.13lb empty. 32.3in barrel, 4-groove rifling; LH (changed to RH from 1868?), concentric. Single-shot only. Stepped base leaf-and-slider rear sight graduated to 1200m (1310yd). 1330 fps at 25m from the muzzle. Mle 1866 saber bayonet.

Adopted on 30th August 1866, the first guns were ordered from the Saint-Étienne factory. The state-owned facilities were unable to meet Napoleon III's demands for 400,000 guns in the first year, so large numbers of Mle 1866 rifles—perhaps 100,000—were ordered from Cahen-Lyon & Cie. This company had acquired commercial rights to the Chassepot bolt head, but was forced to sub-contract production to gunmakers throughout Europe. Though these guns were inspected and re-proved by the French state arsenals, few were fully interchangeable and they were discarded as soon as possible after the Franco-Prussian War. It has been estimated that only about 50,000 Cahen-Lyon rifles were delivered in 1868-70.

Serial-number letter suffixes identify the individual manufacturer, which is especially valuable if the receiver marks have been erased. The code for the Mle 1866 was 'A', 'B' and 'C' for Châtellerault; 'D' and 'E' for Mutzig; 'F'-'H', 'J'-'N', 'P' and 'Q' for Saint-Étienne; 'R', 'S' and 'T' for Tulle; 'X' for the "Commission d'Armement de 1870/71"; and 'Z' for isolated purchases of saber bayonets. Letters 'U' and 'V' were reserved for Cahen-Lyon.

The Mle 1866 was very similar to the experimental Camp de Châlons trials gun of 1865. However, the cocking piece was altered, the trigger lever was noticeably more vertical, a dismantling screw was added on the right side of the receiver behind the bolt handle,

and the back-sight leaf pivoted at the front of its bed instead of the rear.

The barrel of the Mle 1866 rifles was held in the stock by a single band and a nose-cap. Mounts were iron. One swivel was attached to the band and the other lay on the underside of the butt. A cleaning rod was carried under the forend, and a bayonet could be mounted on lug-and-tenon at the muzzle.

Changes were made to the cocking piece in 1867, when the dished back surface gave way to a simple convex curve. Checkering on the back of the bolt handle was abandoned at the same time, and the rifling was changed from left- to right-hand twist.

The first issues were made in September 1866 to the Bataillon des Chasseurs à Pied de la Garde, and the front-line infantry regiments had all had been re-equipped by April 1868. By July 1870, 1,037,555 Chassepots were on the inventory. About 30,000 of these had been issued to the navy.

The state arsenals were delivering about 30,000 guns monthly when the Franco-Prussian War began, and made about 122,000 between 17th September 1870 and 22nd February 1871. However, the losses during the war are said to have included 665,327 French needle guns. Most of these were captured by the Germans (see 'Prussia' and 'Saxony').

The government factories were making 45,000 Mle 1866 rifles annually by 1872, when about a million remained serviceable. Few changes were made in the post-war era, as it was obvious that the days of the needle-gun were numbered. However, rear sights were fitted with an extending leaf after about 1873, graduated to 1600m (1750yd), and a few guns were fitted experimentally with the Haberlin 'tige baionnette' (a rod pattern) in 1873-4.

Production ceased in favor of the Gras (q.v.) in 1875. Many of the needle guns were converted to accept the new 11mm metal-case cartridges, but unaltered guns served the French navy until replaced by the Kropatschek in 1879-80. Some others were sold abroad, notably to Japan and China.

MODEL 1866 COLONIAL RIFLE
Fusil pour la cavalerie d'Afrique

Twelve thousand of these guns were made in Saint-Étienne in 1869, numbered 1-12000 in their own series. Intended to be carried on a bandolier, they were identical with the infantry rifle except for an additional central barrel band carrying the front swivel. The rear swivel was held ahead of the trigger by a screw running laterally through washers set in the stock. The mounts were iron.

MODEL 1866 CAVALRY CARBINE
Carabine de Cavallerie Mle 1866
Made by the state manufactories in Châtellerault, Saint-Étienne and Tulle.

Total production: not known. **Action:** generally as Mle 1866 rifle, above. **Chambering:** 11mm, combustible cartridge.

46.25in overall, 7.83lb empty. 27.65in barrel, 4-groove rifling; RH, concentric. Single-shot only. Stepped base leaf-and-slider rear sight graduated to 1000m (1095yd). 1295 fps at 25m from the muzzle. No bayonet.

Introduced until shortly after hostilities had commenced in 1870, the first issues of this shortened version of the Mle 1866 infantry rifle were made to the mounted units of the Garde Impériale. The finalized guns were brass mounted, the barrel was held in the stock by two bands and a nose cap, and the spatulate bolt handle was turned down against the stock. Butts were about 0.4in shorter than the infantry-rifle pattern, making the carbines easier to use on horseback.

The swivels were attached to the middle band and the extended front web of the trigger guard, though experimental weapons were made with combinations of sling rings and bars.

The M1866 Chassepot infantry rifle.

Model 1866 GENDARMERIE CARBINES
Carabine de Gendarmerie à Cheval Mle 1866 and Carabine de Gendarmerie à Pied Mle 1866
Made by the state manufactories in Châtellerault, Saint-Étienne and Tulle.
Total production: not known. **Action:** generally as Mle 1866 rifle, above.
DATA FOR A FOOT GENDARMERIE EXAMPLE
Chambering: 11mm, combustible cartridge. 46.25in overall, 7.78lb empty. 27.65in barrel, 4-groove rifling; LH (later RH), concentric. Single-shot only. Stepped base leaf-and-slider graduated to 1000m (1095yd). 1295 fps at 25m from the muzzle. Mle 1866 saber bayonet.

These guns were similar to the cavalry carbine, with turned-down bolt handles. The mounted gendarmerie carbine had the customary three bands (one doubling as the nose cap), but accepted a quadrangular-bladed socket bayonet which locked around the base of the front sight. The foot gendarmerie carbine lacked the middle band, had the back swivel on the underside of the butt, and accepted the standard saber bayonet. A few short-barrel guns were made experimentally in 1873, but never in great quantity.

MODEL 1866 ARTILLERY MUSKETOON
Mousqueton d'Artillerie Mle 1866
Made by the state arsenals in Châtellerault, Saint-Étienne and Tulle.
Total production: not known. **Action:** generally as Mle 1866 rifle, above.
Chambering: 11mm, combustible cartridge.
39in overall, 7.1lb empty. 20.05in barrel, 4-groove rifling; RH, concentric. Single-shot only. Stepped-base leaf-and-slider rear sight graduated to 1000m (1095yd). 1195 fps at 25m from the muzzle. Mle 1866 saber bayonet.

Introduced in 1873, this was the shortest member of the Chassepot series even though it had the full-length butt. Artillery musketoons had two brass bands (one forming the nose cap), swivels on butt and band, and accepted the standard saber bayonet. The spatulate bolt handle was turned down against the stock.

OTHER GUNS
A few Chassepot-type wall guns (*Fusils de Rempart*) were also made for trials. They had 18mm-caliber 35.4in barrels, were about 60.25in long and weighed 20.95lb. They had two steel bands and a steel nose cap. The Hurtu & Hautin rifle, made in Paris during the war of 1870-1, was also externally similar to the Chassepot.

• Clair
The three Clair brothers—Benoît, Jean-Baptiste and Victor—were gunsmiths working in Saint-Étienne. They are renowned for making the first practicable gas-operated shotgun, but also made a handful of automatic rifles operating on the same basic principles. Patents were sought in the late 1880s, German Patent 49,100 being among the earliest to be granted in 1889. Propellant gas was tapped from the bore and led back to strike a piston, which in turn unlocked the breech.

Much controversy has surrounded the Clairs' activities; owing to the unreliability of the first generation of smokeless propellant, their sporting guns never achieved widespread recognition and it has become fashionable to undervalue their work.

• CTV
These prototype automatic rifles were developed by the Commission Technique de Versailles (CTV) and the Établissement Technique de l'Artillerie de Puteaux (APX). They dated from 1903-10.

The first four guns, two each from Versailles (CTV No. 1, CTV No. 2) and Puteaux (APX No. 3 and APX No. 4), had long-recoil actions. They were also known as C1-C4 respectively, but were too complicated and prone to excessive breakages.

They were replaced about 1908 by the 8mm Fusil C8, derived from the C5-C7 series begun by Chauchat and Sutter in 1906. The C8 was made in small quantities for field trials. It was operated by long recoil and had a rotating bolt with an interrupted-screw lock. The magazine relied on a standard three-round Mannlicher-type clip (Chargeur Mle 90), overall dimensions being similar to those of the Mle 1902 Berthier.

• Daudetau
A turning-bolt rifle designed by Commandant Louis Daudetau in the late 1880s, this was patented in Britain in December 1890. The rifles were chambered for cartridges ranging from 6x51 to 8x60. No great success was encountered in France, though 6.5x53.5 guns went to Portugal in 1899-1900; they were apparently used for field trials prior to the emergence of the Mannlicher-Schönauer and then the Vergueiro-Mauser. Daudetau rifles and carbines were sold to El Salvador and Paraguay in the late 1890s, while Uruguay selected the 6.5x53.5 No. 12 Daudetau cartridge for weapons converted from 1871-type Mausers in Saint-Denis. These are described in greater detail in the 'Uruguay' chapter. Production ended in the early 1900s, after about 5,000 had been made, but Daudetau-type sporting rifles were still being made in the 1920s (see 'MAS, bolt-action type').

MODEL 1896 NAVY RIFLE
Experimental pattern
Made by Compagnie des Forges et Aciéries de la Marine, Saint-Chamond, but marked as a product of Société Française des Armes Portatives, Saint-Denis, Paris (see notes).
Chambering: 6.5x53.5, semi-rim. **Action:** locked by two lugs on the detachable bolt head engaging recesses in the receiver behind the chamber when the bolt handle was turned down.
50.65in overall, 8.71lb empty. 32.5in barrel, 4-groove rifling; LH, concentric. Integral charger-loaded box magazine, 5 rounds. Leaf sight graduated to 2000m (2185yd). 2525 fps with Daudetau No. 12 ball cartridges. Special épée bayonet.

The first Daudetau rifles were tested by the French navy in the mid 1890s, at a time when cartridges smaller than the regulation 8x51 (Lebel) pattern were being tested throughout Europe. The direct inspiration was probably the 1895-type Lee 236 (6mm) straight-pull rifle adopted by the U.S. Navy in 1895.

The Daudetau guns had split-bridge receivers and a two-lug bolt inspired by the Lebel. The charger was needlessly complex, and the box-magazine case was formed integrally with the small trigger guard; the trigger aperture was almost circular, giving the rifles an unmistakable appearance.

Several hundred 1896-pattern rifles were issued in 1896-7. It is suspected that the actions were made in Saint-Étienne by Manufacture Française des Armes et Cycles, despite the contradictory markings on the rifles themselves. They had a one-piece walnut stock with a handguard running forward from the chamber under the broad retaining band, the band and nose cap being retained by springs. A stacking rod lay on the right side of the nose cap and a cleaning rod was set into a channel in the left side of the forend. Swivels lay beneath the band and the butt. The bayonet was essentially similar to the Mle 86 (Lebel) type, with a similar spring-loaded locking collar, but the left side of the hilt was grooved to clear the head of the cleaning rod.

Germany was showing no inclination to accept a small-caliber cartridge by 1899, so the French army elected to issue the improved 8mm Balle D instead of the 6.5mm Daudetau and the navy soon followed suit. Experiments with a selection of improved bolt-action rifles developed by Daudetau and the École Nationale de Tir (ENT) had ceased by 1902.

• Descoutoures
Another of the many experimental breechloading systems produced in the middle of the 19th Century, this was the invention of gunmaker Michel Descoutoures. The prototypes are said to have

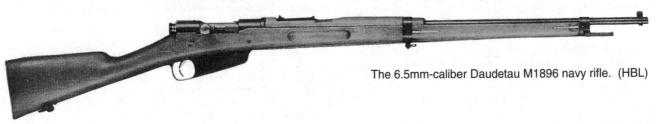

The 6.5mm-caliber Daudetau M1896 navy rifle. (HBL)

been made in a Paris workshop in 1850-1 on the basis of Mle 1842 rifled muskets. These had back-action cap locks, two sprung brass bands, and a large brass two-strap nose cap.

A large rotating disc was placed vertically, with a radial operating lever on the right side of the breech. This was lifted through 90 degrees to allow a combustible cartridge to be inserted into the mouth of a loading chamber in the disc, which was then rotated back to the closed or firing position. Probably drawing much of its inspiration from the 'turret guns' developed in the U.S. (cf., Cochran), the rotating-disc action was unnecessarily cumbersome and particularly prone to gas-leakage.

Descoutoures patented a swinging-barrel design in 1865, but there is no evidence that this was ever made in quantity.

• ENT

These rifles, including a series of small-caliber bolt-action guns, were developed in the École Normale de Tir. Two types of turning-bolt 6mm rifle were tested in 1896, with two-piece stocks but an otherwise Berthieresque profile; a 7mm gun was tried in 1898, with a pump-type 'U'-section actuator under the action beneath the chamber; and a 6mm straight-pull gun of 1901 had a lateral bar-lock with a pivoting bolt-lever running back along the right side of the pistol grip. These guns were never made in quantity, though they were subjected to extensive trials. Work ended about 1902.

The École Normale also promoted a series of automatic rifles prior to World War I. There were at least four gas-operated Rossignol designs with retractable locking lugs (ENT No. 1 or B1, B2, B4, B5); two short-recoil Belgrand rifles (ENT No. 2 or B3 and B6); a Chezaud rifle (B7) and a Vallarnaud (B8), also operated by short recoil. None of these guns was especially successful, as CTV and STA designs (q.v.) were preferred.

• Gallager

The French purchased about 2,500 of these carbines during the Franco-Prussian war of 1870-1, chambered for the 56-56 Spencer rimfire cartridge. For additional details see '**U.S.A.**'.

• Gastinne-Renette

This Parisian gunmaking business made breech-loading sporting guns with a barrel which, when a catch had been released, tipped sideways to the left on a longitudinal pivot. A rifle of this pattern was submitted for trials with the Cent Gardes in 1854 (see 'Treuille de Beaulieu'). The Gastinne-Rennette gun had a back-action lock, an external hammer, and a straight-wrist half stock. A single band encircled the barrel and the forend, and a simple nose cap was fitted. The rifle was about 45.3in long, weighed 6.25lb and accepted the 'saber-lance' bayonet. The 13mm self-contained cartridge had a metal base and a cardboard body, but the joint proved to be too weak and the components separated too often in the breech to be acceptable.

• Gaucher

This gunmaking business, trading in Saint-Étienne, made simple bolt-action rifles. These were marketed under a range of brand names and, at the time of writing, the distinctions are still unclear.

MODEL B-3 COLIBRI SPORTING RIFLE
Made by Gaucher Armes, Saint-Étienne, 1960-75?
Total production: not known. **Chambering options:** a variety of rimfire and Flobert cartridges—see text below. **Action:** locked by turning the bolt-handle rib down against the front of the receiver bridge.
DATA FOR A TYPICAL EXAMPLE
Chambering: 22LR rimfire. 43.7in overall, 4.75lb empty. 25.6in barrel, 4-groove rifling; RH, concentric? Single-shot only. Tangent-leaf sight graduated to 200m (220yd). 1080 fps with standard ball ammunition.

This was a simple bolt-action rifle with the handle turning down ahead of the bridge. The B3 pattern had a half stock, with checkering on the pistol grip and a finger groove in the slender schnabel-tipped forend. The front sight was a hooded ramped blade; the rear sight was a conventional tangent-leaf design.

SIMILAR GUNS

In addition to the rifled guns, a range of smoothbores handled cartridges as large as 14mm. These are considered as bolt-action shotguns, and are not included below.

Model B-Star. A 6mm Flobert version of the Model C-Star (q.v.).

Model B1-Colibri. Believed to have been the basic 22 model, this had a straight wristed hardwood half-stock and a fixed rear sight.

Model B2-Colibri. This was a simpler version of the 22 B3, weighing only 4.3lb. The major difference is believed to have been the stock, which was a pistol-grip hardwood type.

Model B5-Colibri. Possibly a version of the 22 B3 with a longer barrel (25.6in?) and a heavier stock, the meager published details of this gun indicate a weight of 5lb.

Model BL-Colibri. This was chambered for the 6mm Flobert cartridge instead of a 22 rimfire.

Model C-Star. Chambered specifically for 9mm black-powder cartridges, this rifle, built on the standard Gaucher bolt-action, was 43.7in long and had a 25.2in barrel; empty weight was about 4.2lb. The half-stock had a pistol grip, the front sight was a ramped blade, and the rear sight was a tangent-leaf type with a slider.

Model D-Colibri. This shared the basic bolt-action, but chambered 9mm Flobert ammunition and had a slender pistol-grip stock of selected walnut. It weighed merely 3.85lb.

Model G-Star. A variant of the Model C-Star, this chambered 22 rimfire ammunition: Short, Long and Long Rifle, interchangeably.

Model L. Mechanically identical with the Model T, this accepted 6mm Flobert ammunition.

Model T. This was a version of the Model V chambering the 22 Short, Long or Long Rifle cartridges, probably interchangeably.

Model V, or Fauvette. A 9mm junior gun intended for black-powder cartridges, this was 39in long, had a 21.65in barrel, and weighed only about 2.87lb. It had fixed sights and a hardwood half-stock with a very shallow pistol grip.

• Gévelot, autoloading type

Gévelot was also responsible for a range of autoloading sporting guns marketed under the 'Gévarm' brand. Most of the guns lacked extractors, relying on residual propellant gases to expel spent cases, and had the firing pins fixed in the bolt so that the action fired as the breech closed.

MODEL A SPORTING RIFLE
Made by Gévelot SA, Saint-Germain-Laval, 1960-75?
Total production: not known. **Chambering:** 22LR, rimfire. **Action:** no mechanical lock; blowback, semi-automatic only.
DATA FOR A TYPICAL MODEL A-3.
41.25in overall, 6.25lb empty. 21.65in barrel, 4-groove rifling; RH, concentric? Detachable box magazine, 8 rounds. Tangent-leaf sight graduated to 100m (110yd). 1080 fps with standard ball ammunition.

This rifle had a cylindrical receiver with a fluted end cap, distinguishing the 'A' series from the round-backed 'E'. The charging handle lay on the right side, immediately behind the ejection port, and the magazine protruded beneath the gun. The French walnut half-stock had checkering on the pistol grip and schnabel-tipped forend. Sights consisted of a tangent-leaf with graduations for 25-100m (27-110yd) on the barrel, and a tunnel with five interchangeable elements at the muzzle, but the top of the receiver was grooved for telescope sight bases.

SIMILAR GUNS

Model A-6. This was a variant of the A-3 with a plain stock, lacking the checkering. Its sights consisted simply of a small fixed blade at the muzzle and a spring-leaf and elevator on the barrel.

Model A-7. Equipped similarly to the A-3, with a tangent-leaf rear sight and a tunnel-pattern front sight at the muzzle, this had the plain pistol-grip half-stock. Unlike the other guns in the series, the A-7 fired from a closed breech and was thus more accurate.

Model A Rafale. This was a selective-fire variant of the standard gun, made for export. A radial lever under the stock on the left side of the trigger could be turned clockwise—to 'R'—to give automatic fire.

MODEL E SPORTING RIFLE

This 22LR blowback sporter was easily distinguished from the Gévarm 'A' series by the slab-sided round-back receiver and two-piece stock. The butt had a straight comb, with thin white-line spacers between the woodwork and the synthetic pistol-grip cap and shoulder plate. The Model E had a 19.3in barrel and a spring-leaf and elevator rear sight.

• Gévelot, lever-action type

Best known as a developer of ammunition, Gévelot was also responsible for a distinctive needle rifle. Dating from the 1860s, the action embodied an underlever formed as part of the trigger guard. A spring-catch pivoting in the finger spur held the lever closed. The hammer had to be retracted to half-cock before the bolt could be opened, but the interaction of a notch on the back of the trigger with a recess in the lever-locking catch ensured that the gun could not fire until the bolt was properly locked.

Gevelot rifles are usually stocked in military style, with two sprung bands, a nose cap, and a leaf-and-slider rear sight. They were not successful enough to have been made in quantity.

An improved form of the needle gun, chambering centerfire cartriges, was the subject of U.S. patent 68,786 of 10th September 1867 granted to Marshall Pidault & Georges Elièze 'dit Lagièze'. Rights to the invention were assigned to Gévelot. The sliding bolt was operated by a radial lever and sector-plate on the right side of the breech.

These guns were made in small numbers, surviving examples being numbered as high as 150. A typical 11mm two-band military rifle was 49.8in long with a 29.5in barrel, and weighed about 10.2lb. A lug and bar for a saber bayonet lay on the right side of the muzzle, and a small tangent-leaf sight was attached to the barrel behind the rear band.

• Gras

This rifle, perfected in the early 1870s, proved to be long-lived. It was also adopted in Greece in 1876.

By 1871, rapid progress being made in Germany had frightened the French into reconsidering their Mle 1866 ('Chassepot') needle rifle. Though the French weapon was ballistically more efficient than the Dreyse needle guns, the annular India-rubber obturating washer on the Chassepot bolt head lost elasticity during prolonged fire.

Trials began in March 1872 with a Dutch Beaumont rifle, which performed well. On 8th May 1873, however, army captain Basile Gras presented a Chassepot needle rifle converted to chamber a metal-case cartridge. The Gras bolt was comparatively simple, with a separate head carrying the extractor and a satisfactory lock being provided by the abutment of the bolt handle rib against the receiver bridge. No ejector was fitted, spent cases being tipped from the bolt way by the head of a screw doubling as the bolt stop.

Prototypes had a Chassepot-type safety system, in which the cocking piece could be retracted and rotated to rest on the back of the receiver. This prevented the firing pin reaching the chambered round, but also prevented the bolt handle being locked down and was abandoned on service rifles.

A final elimination trial with Gras and Beaumont rifles began at the end of April 1874, resolving in favor of the French design.

MODEL 1874 RIFLE
Fusil d'Infanterie Mle 1874

Made by the government small arms factories in Châtellerault, Saint-Étienne and Tulle, 1874-87; and by Österreichische Waffenfabriks-Gesellschaft, Steyr, 1876-7 (bolts only).

Total production: not known, but more than a million. **Chambering:** 11x59R, rimmed. **Action:** locked by bolt handle rib abutting the receiver ahead of the bridge as the handle was turned down.

51.4in overall, 9.24lb empty. 32.3in barrel, 4-groove rifling; LH, concentric. Ramp-and-leaf sight graduated to 1800m (1970yd). 1445 fps with Mle 1874 ball ammunition. Mle 1874 épée bayonet.

Adopted on 7th July 1874, the Gras rifle was externally similar to the preceding Mle 1866 Chassepot needle rifle. However, the detachable bolt head provided a visible distinction. The one-piece stock was accompanied by a single band and a simple nose cap, both mounts being retained by springs. Swivels lay on the under-side of the band and on the under-edge of the butt, and a lug-and-tenon for the bayonet lay on the right side of the muzzle. The back-sight leaf, graduated to 1400m (1530yd), had an extending portion serving ranges up to 1800m (1970yd).

The first bulk deliveries were made from the state arsenals in 1875. Concurrently, conversion of old Chassepots began.

SIMILAR GUNS

Model 1866/74. Chassepots were changed simply by boring-out the breech to receive a short liner chambering the Gras cartridge. The receivers were modified, and a new Mle 1874 bolt was substituted. 'Mle 1866/74' conversions had smaller back-sight leaves graduated to 1300m (1420yd), with the sliding extension to 1700m (1860yd). However, some of these conversions received new barrels during their lives (distinguished by 'N' on the upper surface near the breech).

The converted rifles initially retained their Mle 1866 saber bayonets. Though they were gradually adapted to take the Mle 1874 épée, the program, still incomplete, was abandoned in September 1880 and the Mle 1866 sabers were retained with unmodified guns.

Model 1874/80 (Mle 1874 M.80). The addition from 1880 of an annular channel and a longitudinal groove cut into the left side of the bolt way helped gas to escape should the primer rupture or the case head fail – a worrying occurrence with pre-1879 ammunition, though strengthening the cartridge case head reduced the problem to manageable proportions. Altered guns were designated 'Mle 1874 Modifié 1880', the distinction between Mle 1866/74 and Mle 1874 being abandoned at this time.

Magazine conversions. Many guns were converted experimentally in 1883-5 – e.g., Gras-Vernet, Gras-Spitalsky and Gras-Lee. Few of these were made in quantity, though batches were altered in 1885 to approximate to the new Kropatschek infantry rifle (q.v.).

Small caliber conversions. The first large-scale withdrawals from line infantrymen were made in 1887 with the advent of sufficient Mle 1886 Lebel rifles. Surviving Gras rifles were issued for service in World War I, many being modified for the 8mm cartridge in 1914-15.

Grenade launchers and flare guns. Substantial numbers were adapted in 1914-18 to provide the 'Bombarde DR' (a grenade thrower) and the 'Fusil-Signaleur'. The latter was patented by Louis Chobert of Paris, and is usually so marked.

MODEL 1874 CAVALRY CARBINE
Carabine de Cavallerie Mle 1874

Made by the government small-arms factories in Châtellerault, Saint-Étienne and Tulle, 1874-87.

Total production: not known. **Chambering:** 11x59R, rimmed. **Action:** as Mle 1874 rifle, above.

46.25in overall, 7.85lb empty. 27.65in barrel, 4-groove rifling; LH, concentric. Ramp-and-leaf sight graduated to 1100m (1205yd). 1405 fps with Mle 1874 ball ammunition. No bayonet.

Adopted in 1874, concurrently with the infantry rifle, this was simply a shortened gun with an additional spring-retained barrel band and the bolt handle turned down toward the stock. Swivels lay under the middle band and and in front of the trigger guard. Unlike similar mounted gendarmerie carbines (below), cavalry patterns were stocked almost to the muzzle and did not accept a bayonet. Some were converted Chassepots (Mle 1866/74), others were newly made (Mle 1874). Most service weapons were modified after 1880 to facilitate the escape of gas in the event of a case head failure (Mle 1874 M.80). Replacement by the Berthier-pattern magazine carbines began in the early 1890s, and most Gras carbines had been sold out of service by 1914.

MODEL 1874 MOUNTED GENDARMERIE CARBINE
Carabine de Gendarmerie à Cheval Mle 1874

Made by the government small-arms factories in Châtellerault, Saint-Étienne and Tulle, 1874-87.

The M1874 Gras rifle. (HBL)

A Gras M1874 M80 cavalry or gendarmerie rifle.

Chambering: 11x59R, rimmed.

Otherwise generally as cavalry carbine, except for bayonet (Mle 1874 socket pattern).

Identical with the cavalry patterns, with an additional barrel band and a turned-down bolt handle, these accepted special bayonets. Some were old Chassepot conversions (Mle 1866/74), others were newly made (Mle 1874), and most post-1880 survivors were adapted to ease escape of gas from a failed case head or a ruptured primer (Mle 1874 M.80).

MODEL 1874 DISMOUNTED GENDARMERIE CARBINE
Carabine de Gendarmerie à Pied Mle 1874.
Made by the government small-arms factories in Châtellerault, Saint-Étienne and Tulle, 1874-87.
Chambering: 11x59R, rimmed.

Otherwise as cavalry carbine, above, except bayonet (Mle 1866 saber pattern).

This was little more than an infantry rifle shortened to carbine length. It had one band bearing the swivel, and a plain nose cap. A lug and tenon for the bayonet lay on the right side of the muzzle. The cavalry carbine rear sight was used, and the bolt handle was turned down against the stock.

Some guns were conversions (Mle 1866/74); others were newly made (Mle 1874). Post-1880 survivors were altered by cutting a channel and groove inside the bolt way to protect the firer from gas escaping from a failed case head; these were designated 'Mle 1874 M.80', distinctions between converted and newly-made guns being abandoned.

MODEL 1874 ARTILLERY MUSKETOON
Mousqueton d'Artillerie Mle 1874
Made by the government small-arms factories in Châtellerault, Saint-Étienne and Tulle, 1874-87.
Total production: not known. **Chambering:** 11x59R, rimmed. **Action:** as Mle 1874 rifle, above.

39in overall, 7.19lb empty. 20.05in barrel, 4-groove rifling: LH, concentric. Ramp-and-leaf sight graduated to 1250m (1365yd). 1330 fps with Mle 1874 ball ammunition. Mle 1866 saber bayonet.

Adopted to replace the earlier Mle 1866 (Chassepot) pattern, this was a much-shortened infantry rifle. It had the same band and nose cap, but the rear sight differed and the bolt handle was turned down against the stock. The saber bayonet was retained, a suitable lug and tenon appearing on the right side of the muzzle. Some guns were Mle 1866/74 conversions; others were newly-made Mle 1874. Most

North African tribesmen with an M1874 Gras artillery musketoon.

surviving musketoons were adapted after 1880 to protect the firer should gas escape from a failed cartridge ('Mle 74 M.80').

MODEL 1874/80/14 RIFLE
Fusil Mle 1874 M.80 M.14
Converted by government- and privately-owned factories, 1914-15.
Chambering: 8x51R, rimmed. **Action:** as Mle 1874 rifle, above.

51.4in overall, 9lb empty. 32.3in barrel, 4-groove rifling; LH, concentric. Ramp-and-leaf sight graduated to 2000m (2185yd). 2295 fps with Balle 1898 D. Mle 1874 épée bayonet.

This emergency conversion of many surviving Gras rifles – Mle 1874 and Mle 1866/74 – to fire the 8mm Lebel cartridge was accepted in the early weeks of World War I. No changes were made in the basic action, as trials showed that the Gras was sturdy enough to handle the comparatively small increases in chamber pressure.

However, a minor change was made to the face of the detachable bolt head, to accept the different case head shape, and the barrel and back-sight assembly were replaced. A short wooden handguard ran from the receiver ring under the barrel band, but the original mounts were retained.

Many 8mm conversions were shipped to the colonies after 1920, where they remained until the end of World War II. Others were still being used in 1939 by airfield guards of the Armée de l'Air.

GRAS-CHASSEPOT TRAINING RIFLES

Among the many minor and experimental adaptations of the Gras rifle were substantial quantities of converted Mle 1866 Chassepot rifles chambered for reduced-charge ammunition. Introduced in 1881 for short-range training purposes, these had Gras-type bolts, a short chamber, and a special rear sight graduated to only 40m (45yd).

SPORTING GUNS

Like most single shot rifles of its type, the Gras was not particularly popular commercially until thousands of military surplus weapons, displaced by magazine-loaders, began to reach the market at the end of the 19th Century. Many of them were subsequently converted to shotguns – the action had ample reserves of strength – and exported to the French colonial empire in Africa and the Far East.

NOUVELLE TARGET RIFLE

A few of these guns were built on modified Gras actions by a Parisian gunsmith, Arthur Nouvelle. Authorized for army shooting matches in the early 1880s, they had a micro-adjustable quadrant rear sight, a special cheek-piece butt with a hooked wooden buttplate, and blued metalwork. Marks such as 'NOUVELLE' and 'BTE S.G.D.G.' usually lay on the left side of the receiver.

• Heckler & Koch (MAS)

H&K-type rifles have been made by Manufacture Nationale d'Armes in Saint-Étienne (MAS, subsequently part of GIAT) and exported in quantity to countries within the French sphere of dominance – even though the army, satisfied with the 5.56mm FAMAS, never showed great interest in the G3 or HK33. A typical rifle made for the Lebanese army bore 'G3 CO' and a serial number on the left side of the magazine housing, together with a 'MAS' mark.

• Joslyn

About 6600 of these distinctive lifting-breech carbines were acquired, in 56-56, 56-52 and 56-50 Spencer rimfire chamberings. For additional details, see 'U.S.A.'.

• Kropatschek

The Kropatschek was more popular in France than in its native Austria-Hungary, 50,000 being purchased from Steyr or made in

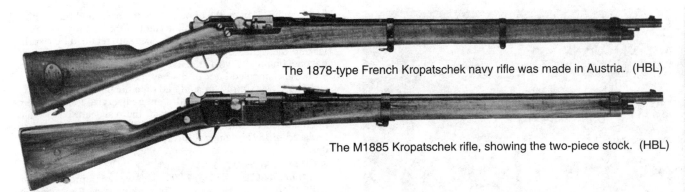

The 1878-type French Kropatschek navy rifle was made in Austria. (HBL)

The M1885 Kropatschek rifle, showing the two-piece stock. (HBL)

the French ordnance factories. However, their service life was greatly curtailed by development of 8mm smokeless-propellant cartridges. Chamber pressures rose too far for the Gras-type Kropatschek bolt to handle safely, owing to the simple bolt handle rib lock, and a symmetrical two-lug pattern was developed in 1885-6. This soon became known as the Lebel (q.v.).

MODEL 1878 NAVY RIFLE
Fusil de Marine Mle 1878
Made by Österreichische Waffenfabriks-Gesellschaft, Steyr, 1878-9.
Total production: 25,000. **Chambering:** 11x59R, rimmed. **Action:** locked by the bolt-guide rib abutting the receiver ahead of the bridge as the bolt handle was turned downward.

48.95in overall, 9.92lb empty. 26.2in barrel, 4-groove rifling; RH, concentric. Tube magazine in forend, 7 rounds. Ramp-and-leaf sight graduated to 1800m (1970yd). 1495 fps with Mle 74 ball cartridges. Mle 78 épée bayonet.

Tests undertaken by the French Navy in midsummer 1877 – with Hotchkiss, Krag-Petersson and Kropatschek rifles – resolved in September in favor of the Kropatschek. After approval of a cartridge-stop or cut-off mechanism, the trials rifle was adopted on 28th June 1878 to replace the aging Mle 1866 (Chassepot) needle guns which were then still in naval service.

The first Kropatschek rifle to encounter real success, it amalgamated the action of the single shot French Mle 1874 (Gras) with a tube magazine in the forend inspired by the Swiss Vetterli. The rifle had two screw-clamped barrel bands and a full-width nose cap with a bayonet lug on the right side. This accepted a special bayonet with a flat-backed hilt. Swivels lay under the rear band and butt.

MODEL 1884 RIFLE
Fusil d'Infanterie Mle 1884.
Made by the government small-arms factories in Châtellerault and Saint-Étienne, 1884-5.
Chambering: 11x59R, rimmed. **Action:** as M1878, above.

48.95in overall, 9.39lb empty. 29.25in barrel, 4-groove rifling; RH, concentric. Tube magazine in forend, 8 rounds. Ramp-and-leaf sight graduated to 1900m (2080yd). 1495 fps with Mle 74 ball cartridges. Mle 74 épée bayonet.

Developed in 1883 by two employees of the Châtellerault arms factory, arms inspector Close and Commandant Lespinasse, this was little more than a French-made Mle 1878.

The first guns were converted in 1884 from Mle 74 M.80 rifles, being distinguished by a new one-piece stock with a prominent grasping groove in the forend. Known as 'Mle 74/84' or 'Mle 74/

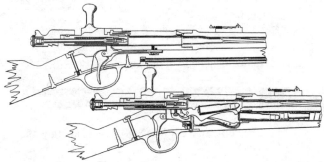

A comparison of the Gras and Kropatschek actions. (FMW)

80 M. 84', they had a single barrel band and a nose cap, retained by springs, but the bayonet bar lay on the right side of the muzzle. The cut-off lever rotated in a depression in the stock behind the bolt handle.

Newly-made Mle 1884 rifles had a cleaning rod let into the left side of the stock; and the nose cap was clinched inward beneath the muzzle so that the lug would accept the raised pommel of the standard Mle 1874 bayonet. In addition, the magazine tube protruded a short distance forward beneath the muzzle. Most metal parts were browned, whereas naval Mle 1878 rifles had been polished to resist corrosion.

MODEL 1885 RIFLE
Fusil d'Infanterie Mle 1885.
Made by the Manufacture d'Armes de Saint-Étienne, 1885-7.
Chambering: 11x59R, rimmed. **Action:** as M1878 rifle, above.

48.95in overall, 9.26lb empty. 29.55in barrel, 4-groove rifling; RH, concentric. Tube magazine in forend, 8 rounds. Ramp-and-leaf sight graduated to 1900m (2080yd). 1495 fps with Mle 74 ball cartridges. Mle 74 épée bayonet.

The perfected version of the French Kropatschek was easily distinguished by the separation of butt and forend by a deep metal receiver. The rifle was otherwise very similar to the Mle 1884, with the same clinched nose cap, but had only one band. Swivels lay under the band and on the under-edge of the butt. The bolt handle rib was plain: Mle 78 and Mle 84 rifles had two blind holes in the right side of the rib beneath the bolt handle to receive the cut-off button. The Mle 1885 cut-off protruded from the bottom of a prominent housing on the right side of the receiver ahead of the trigger. Though the Kropatschek rifle was soon replaced by the Lebel, it remained in service long enough to serve French forces in Indo-China.

SIMILAR GUNS
Model 1874/85. These were converted from Mle 74 M.80 Gras rifles, but the changes were so extensive that the identity of the original guns was all but lost. However, they bore their original markings on the barrel and other major components.

Improved patterns. A few guns made toward the end of production in 1887 had the Lebel-type cut-off set into the receiver, which allowed the entire side panel to be milled flush.

• Lardinois
Also known as 'Lardenois'. Very little is known about this particular breech-loading system, which is assumed to have originated in France or possibly Belgium about 1850. A variation of the tipping-chamber system, it was operated by a radial lever pivoting on the right side of the breech directly ahead of the back-action lock and external hammer. Surviving guns are stocked in military style, with stepped-base leaf-and-slider rear sights; some bear a distinctly Russian appearance, which may suggest that they were made for the trials held there in the 1860s, but it is also likely that sporting patterns once existed.

• Lebel
This rifle was designed and perfected in France in the mid 1880s on the basis of the Mle 1885 Kropatschek (q.v.). The Mle 1886/93 was used by several European countries during World War I – it armed some of the Belgian troops fighting alongside the French on the Western Front, for example – and about 86,000 were shipped to Russia in 1915-16. Others served Greece and Czechoslovakia into the early 1920s.

French soldiers parade with Lebel rifles
in Paris on Bastille Day, 14th July 1916.

THE FIRST STEPS

Worried by the experiments then being undertaken in Germany with semi-experimental 1882-type Mauser rifles, which had a tube magazine, the French sought an efficient rival by modifying the Mle 1878 Kropatschek (q.v.) in 1883. This was not successful enough to merit adoption, but, in 1885, the Commission d'Étude des Armes á Répétition produced an improved Kropatschek with a modified bolt.

Work had hardly begun on the new rifle when Paul Vieille produced an effectual smokeless powder. This allowed the caliber of the service rifle to be reduced to 8mm, but increased chamber pressures appreciably. As the margins of safety in the single-lug Gras-Kropatschek bolt action were not great enough for the Mle 1885 rifle to be adapted directly, modified rifles were completed with a symmetrical two-lug bolt head proposed by Colonel Bonnet.

The poorest feature of the new rifle was the retention of a tube magazine, credited to Colonel Gras but probably owing more to government insistence that a new rifle should hold at least as many cartridges as the German M71/84 Mauser. The perfected French gun was adopted in 1887. It had a Kropatschek-type tube magazine in the forend and a modified cartridge elevator. The bolt was basically that of the Mle 1874 (Gras), but the separate bolt head had two lugs that locked horizontally behind the chamber. The sturdy receiver and two-piece stock of the Mle 1885 were retained. The new gun soon became known as the 'Lebel' after the commandant of the École Normale de Tir, who had personally directed most of the trials undertaken in the Camp de Châlons. Colonel Lebel protested, but the name soon gained common currency.

MODEL 1886 RIFLE
Fusil d'Infanterie Mle 1886

Made by government small-arms factories in Châtellerault, Saint-Étienne and Tulle, 1886-1919 (Mle 1886 and Mle 1886 M.93 rifles); and by the Manufacture d'Armes de Paris, Saint-Denis, 1915-18 (Mle 1886 M.93 rifles only).

Total production: 3.5-4 million (all types). **Chambering:** 8x51R, rimmed.
Action: locked by two lugs on a detachable bolt head engaging recesses in the receiver behind the chamber as the bolt handle was turned downward.

51.45in overall, 9.22lb empty. 32.1in barrel, 4-groove rifling; LH, concentric. Tube magazine under barrel, 8 rounds. Ramp-and-leaf sight graduated to 2000m (2185yd). 2075 fps with Balle 1886 M. Mle 1886 épée bayonet.

The Mle 1886 rifle was adopted on 22nd April 1887. It had a distinctive two-piece stock, separated by a massive machined-steel receiver; typically French, this can only be confused with the semi-experimental Mle 1885 (see 'Kropatschek'). The butt was bolted to the tangs and the forend was retained by a single spring-retained

band. Swivels lay on the underside of the band and butt, while a radial cut-off lever was set in the right side of the receiver above the front of the trigger guard. The nose cap, retained by a spring let into the right side of the forend, had a boss that entered the bayonet pommel. Two distinctive tenons under the muzzle mated with the channeled back of the bayonet hilt. The original back-sight base was simply tin-soldered onto the barrel.

No sooner had the new rifles entered service than problems were reported. The worst concerned the rear sight base, which often loosened during rapid fire, so the original pattern was replaced in 1892 by one with claws extending down around the barrel.

SIMILAR GUNS

Model 1886/93 (Mle 1886 M.93). This was an improved pattern with a lighter striker retainer in the cocking piece and a stacking rod on the right side of the nose cap. A special non-rotating obturator (*tampon-masque*) on the bolt head behind the locking lugs deflected gas escaping from a case head failure. The claw-type back-sight base was altered at about this time, but does not seem to have been a cornerstone of the improvements.

Work began in 1900 to adapt rear sights for the Balle 1898 D, which had a muzzle velocity of 2300 fps. This required a new back-sight leaf graduated to 2400m (2625yd). The first modified guns were issued in 1901. The useless 'safety notch' on the cocking piece was abandoned in 1902, which left the Lebel rifle with no form of applied safety whatsoever. When World War I began in Europe in 1914, the Mle 86 M.93 rifle equipped virtually all front-line infantrymen – though colonial troops carried Mle 1902 or Mle 1907 Berthiers (q.v.). Only during 1917 did the Lebel begin to give way to the Mle 1907/15 and Mle 1916 (Berthier) rifles, and even then the older guns were retained by marksmen.

Model 1886/93 sniper rifle. Selected rifles were fitted with a 3x Mle 1916 telescope sight on the left side of the receiver. By 1920, four Mle 1886 M.93 rifles were still being issued to each infantry regiment section. Three were used to fire Vivens-Bessières rifle grenades, as the Lebel was stronger than any of the Berthiers; the fourth, retained as a sniper's weapon, mounted a 3x Mle 1916 or Mle 1921 telescope sight.

Model 1886/93/27 (Mle 1886 M.93 M.27). The advent of a new rimless cartridge encouraged the authorities to consider the design of their infantry rifles, and a few Mle 1886 M.93 Lebel rifles were converted in 1927. The principal improvements were a five-round Mauser type staggered-row magazine, which replaced the elevator mechanism in the receiver beneath the bolt, and a new barrel/rear sight assembly. A handguard ran forward from the receiver ring past the barrel band, though the original nose cap was retained.

Charger guides were added, the ejector was improved, and changes were made to the bolt head for the rimless cartridge. Guns were issued for field trials in 1928, but were not deemed successful. Converted in the Tulle factory, they were 43.55in long, had 23.6in barrels, and weighed 7.85lb. The tangent-leaf sight was graduated

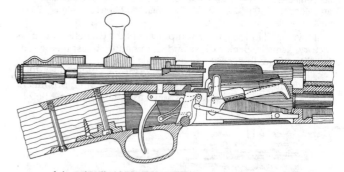

A longitudinal section of the Lebel rifle. (FP&P)

The 8mm-caliber M1886/93 Lebel infantry rifle.

FRANCE

to 900m (985yd), any 1886-type épée bayonet would fit, and muzzle velocity was 2830 fps.

Unfortunately, the original 7.5x58 rimless Balle 1924 C had been abandoned by the time the guns had been completed. Though an improved short-case Balle 1929 C appeared, progress with new rifles (see 'MAS') soon rendered the converted Lebel obsolete.

MODEL 1886/35 SHORT RIFLE

Fusil Mle 1886 R.35

Apparently converted in Châtellerault, 1936-9.
Total production: not known.
Chambering: 8x51R, rimmed.
Action: as M1886 rifle, above.

37.7in overall, 8.3lb empty. 17.7in barrel, 4-groove rifling; LH, concentric. Tube magazine under barrel, 3 rounds. Ramp-and-leaf sight graduated to 2000m (2185yd). 1985 fps with 1886 Balle D. Mle 1935 épée bayonet.

A decision was taken in 1935 to shorten many of the Mle 1886 M.93 rifles held in reserve, providing a handy weapon for cavalrymen and motorized units while tooling for the MAS 36 was undertaken. The barrel, forend and magazine tube were greatly shortened, though little else was necessary. The new barrel band had a fixed sling ring on the left side, a bar being added to the left side of the butt; the rear swivel on the butt-edge was retained. In common with most other tube-magazine designs, the cartridge capacity could be improved when necessary by placing a fourth round on the elevator and a fifth in the chamber.

However, the alterations had not been completed when World War II began in 1939. A few Mle 1886 R.35 rifles were issued to men on home service when fighting started, but most had already been sent to Africa.

A decision was taken in 1945 to modify Mle 1886 M.93 R.35 rifles (and a few surviving Mle 1886/93 guns) for the Balle 1932 N before passing them to the reserve. This involved re-cutting the chamber to accept a longer bullet, and the opportunity was taken to strengthen the striker spring. Modified guns were marked 'N' on the barrel near the breech and stored for the reserve.

• Lefaucheux

Casimir Lefaucheux was granted his first patent in 1827, and by 1832 had perfected a drop-barrel sporting gun locked by a lever beneath the forend. This accepted paper-case cartridges with a reinforced cardboard base, fired by a conventional caplock.

Guns of this type were tested by the French artillery committee in 1833, but were rejected partly because they leaked gas too badly but also because the ammunition was unfit for military service. The advent of metal-base pinfire cartridges in the mid 1830s, however, improved performance greatly.

Turning the tip of the operating lever to the right released lugs on a vertical bolt from recesses cut in two blocks ('breech lumps' or simply 'lumps') on the underside of the barrel-block. The barrels could then be tipped down at the muzzle, elevating the chambers for reloading. Most guns had back-action caplocks with external hammers, but the basic construction proved to be so popular that it was copied, adapted and improved by many other European gunmakers. However, the breech remained comparatively weak and could not be adapted to handle high pressures without bolting the top of the barrel block into the standing breech.

• Manceaux & Vieillard

These Parisian gunmakers were responsible for experimental military rifles embodying a bolt action and an expanding conical metal obturator on the bolt head. The bolt was opened by raising

A patriotic postcard produced in Britain during the First World War shows a French soldier with a Lebel rifle.

the breech cover, rotating it to disengage the locking lug, then retracting the bolt to give access to the chamber. A special combustible cartridge was used, and a safety system prevented the breech being opened if the hammer had been cocked – or, alternatively, the hammer being cocked until the breech had been locked shut.

The Manceaux & Vieillard system was a qualified success, as substantial quantities of guns were made for field trials held in France in 1862-4. It also performed creditably in Britain (q.v.).

1862-TYPE TRIALS RIFLE

Possibly made in the manufactory in Châtellerault.
Total production: not known. **Chambering:** 12mm combustible cartridge, fired by a caplock. **Action:** locked by a lug on the bolt engaging a shoulder on the receiver?

56.1in overall, 9.88lb empty. 36.2in barrel, 6-groove rifling; RH, concentric. Single shot only. Fixed open-notch rear sight. Performance unknown. Socket bayonet.

The experimental Manceaux & Vieillard infantry rifle was distinguished by two sprung brass bands, a brass nose cap, and a fixed rear sight. The rifles were extensively tested by the army, but were disliked. They were awkward to load, and, as the fragility of the cartridges promoted misfiring, so they were abandoned in favor of the promising bolt-action Chassepot (q.v.).

SIMILAR GUNS

Carbine. Intended for the Chasseurs, this was a surprisingly large gun: 52.15in long and weighing 9.65lb. Retaining the bands and nose cap of the infantry rifle, it is believed to have been designed for a sword bayonet. It also had a leaf-and-slider rear sight graduated to 1200m (1310yd).

Musketoon. Destined for the cavalry, this carbine-type short rifle was stocked virtually to the muzzle and did not take a bayonet. It had a single barrel band in addition to the standard nose cap, and the rear sight was graduated only to 1000m (1095yd). Overall length was about 47.2in; empty weight averaged 8.5lb.

Gardes Mobiles pattern. Manceaux continued to make his proprietary rifles for some years after they had been rejected by the French authorities, marking them 'J. ↑ M.'. Some were issued to irregular units during the Franco-Prussian War of 1870-1. A typical example measured 49.8in overall, weighed 9.25lb, and accepted a standard French-type socket bayonet.

• Manufrance, autoloading type

Manufacture Française d'Armes et Cycles, known after World War II as 'Manufrance SA', marketed small quantities of a semi-automatic 22 carbine, patented by an engineer named Sidna. Little is currently known about the production history of this particular gun.

CARABINE REINA

Made by Manufrance SA, Saint-Étienne, about 1954-75.
Total production: not known. **Chambering:** 22 Long Rifle, rimfire. **Action:** no mechanical breech lock; blowback, semi-automatic only.
DATA FOR MODEL 446

41.75in overall, 4.85lb empty. 22.05in barrel, 6-groove rifling; RH, concentric. Detachable box magazine, 8 or 15 rounds. Fixed rear sight regulated for 50m (55yd). 1080 fps with 40-grain bullet.

Introduced commercially in the early 1950s, this gun had a one-piece half-stock. The pistol grip butt had a Monte Carlo comb, a grasping groove in the forend lay beneath the rear sight, and the pistol grip cap and buttplate were accompanied by decorative white spacers. The cocking lever and ejection port lay on the right side of the cylindrical receiver. Reina carbines were issued to personnel of the French prison service from the mid 1950s until replaced in 1971 by the MAS 49/56.

THE GUNS

Model 446. This was the basic pattern described above, with a plain half-stock with a straight comb.

Model 450. Also chambering the 22LR cartridge, this had a 22.85in barrel and a 150m (165yd) tangent-leaf rear sight. Its deluxe stock had a cheekpiece, a Monte Carlo comb, and checkering on the pistol grip and forend. Empty weight was averaged 5.5lb.

• Manufrance, bolt-action type

This well-known French gunmaking business was responsible for a wide variety of shotguns, sporting rifles and handguns, together with an impressive array of accessories. The rifles were made on two basic actions – the unique Manufrance-designed 'Buffalo' series and the 'Rival', which served as a high-power sporter. Mauser-action rifles have also been seen.

BLACHON ACTION

Better known as the 'Buffalo', this was the work of a director of Manufrance, Pierre Blachon. Originally patented in France in 1897, the mechanism was a clever combination of a bolt action and the travelling-block system popular in the late 19th Century. Its essence lay in a sturdy receiver, a reciprocating breech-piece or *Culasse mobile*, and an operating handle attached to a short cylindrical collar containing the locking recesses. The barrel was screwed into the receiver from the rear, and had locking lugs formed in its periphery. Starting with the action locked and fired, the handle was raised to disengage the recesses in the collar from the lugs on the barrel. This allowed the collar and the breech-piece to be drawn back until, near the end of the stroke, an extension of the breech-piece running forward beneath the barrel activated the sturdy extractor. The trigger and an associated breech-release lever lay in the stock, but the reciprocating sear was pinned in the breech-piece. The action was not only extremely sturdy, but also very simple; it was ideally suited to single shot weapons owing to the position of the extractor-operating extension, and was never adapted to magazine feed. Shotguns were also made, usually in 12mm or 14mm, and Buffalo-type rifles were still being made in the 1970s.

BUFFALO CARBINE

Made by Manufacture Française d'Armes et Cycles and Manufrance SA, Saint-Étienne, about 1900-77.

Total production: hundreds of thousands (all types). **Chambering:** 9mm Flobert. **Action:** locked by turning recesses in the bolt collar over lugs on the external surface of the barrel.

DATA FOR A TYPICAL PRE-1939 EXAMPLE

39.5in overall, 4.85lb empty. 22.45in barrel, 6-groove rifling; RH, concentric. Single shot only. Fixed open-notch rear sight. Performance not known.

The most basic of the Buffalo rifles, often encountered with a smooth-bore suited equally to ball or shot cartridges, this gun had a two-piece stock. It had a straight-wrist butt and lacked a buttplate. Sling swivels lay under the butt and on the front of the forend tip. In addition to the standard rifle, however, a series of better-quality patterns was offered; these ranged from improved finish and checkering on the pistol grip, to elaborately decorated rifles with scalloped-edge woodwork and fluted or octagon barrels.

SIMILAR GUNS

Except the Sport, Junior and target-shooting variants, Buffalo rifles were all made in variants ranging from the most basic to highly decorative.

Buffalo. The basic 9mm Flobert rifle was being sold as the Model 602 by the 1960s, accompanied by the Models 608 and 614. The 608 had a lightly engraved receiver and checkering on the stock and forend, but the 614 was a deluxe version with selected woodwork and surprisingly extensive decoration.

Buffalo-Canardière. An alternative name for the 'Buffalo-Mitraille' (q.v.).

Buffalo-Champion. The best of the Manufrance rifles of this pattern, apart from the Super-Champion (q.v.), this was 47.25in long and weighed 12.13lb. It had an adjustable trigger, a micro-adjustable tangent sight which could be slid along a rail on the barrel, a replaceable-element front sight, and a special heavy pistol gripped butt. The spurred buttplate was accompanied by spacers, allowing the distance from the shoulder to the trigger to be adjusted. A spherical palm-rest was fitted beneath the receiver ahead of the trigger. Champion rifles could be obtained in 22 Extra Short, 22 Short, 22 Long and 22 Long Rifle.

Buffalo-Concours. Destined for target shooting, this rifle could be identified by its heavy barrel and decorative finish. The pistol grip butt had a cheekpiece; the buttplate was spurred; and the tangent-leaf rear sight could be slid along a rail to adjust eye relief. The front sight was customarily an adjustable hooded blade carried on a muzzle collar.

Buffalo-Eureka. This interesting rifle had two bores in its oval barrel, a smooth 9mm being placed above a rifled 6mm to give the shooter the choice of accuracy, a larger projectile or even a charge of shot. Rimfire and Flobert ammunition was used. The guns were

39.5in long, and weighed 5.3lb empty. They had a fixed open-notch rear sight.

Buffalo Fédérale. Alternatively known as the Model 724, this 22LR rimfire target rifle had a 25.6in barrel and weighed about 7.7lb. It was fitted with a special half-stock, with a deep rounded forend, and had competition sights. Among the optional extras were Perfex barrels with solid or ventilated ribs.

Buffalo Junior. Destined for youthful cadets, this rifle – in 22 Long Rifle or 6mm rimfire – amalgamated the basic construction of the Buffalo series with a forend extending almost to the muzzle. Two bands were used, one doubling as a nose cap, and a grasping groove lay beneath the rear sight. The sight was usually a tangent-leaf pattern elevated by rotating a knob on the right side of the base; lateral adjustments were controlled by a drum on the right side of the notch-plate block. A pivoting hood protected the ramped-blade front sight.

Buffalo Match. The Model 730 was a good-quality target rifle with a pistol grip half-stock with a deepened forend. Fitted with a 25.6in barrel, the Match pattern weighed about 8.4lb without its micro-adjustable aperture (back) and replaceable-element tunnel (front) sights.

Buffalo-Mitraille. This was a unique variant of the basic Blachon bolt mechanism, with three bores in a single large-diameter barrel and a unique triple-position extractor sliding in the floorplate. The rifle was intended as a fowling piece, firing three 22LR rimfire cartridges simultaneously. It had a three-leaf rear sight graduated to 150m (165yd), measured 41.75in overall, and weighed about 5.85lb empty. A post-1946 version – sold as the Model 674 – was 42.5in long, weighed 7lb, and had a simpler 100m sight.

Buffalo-Slave. This was a typical Buffalo-type rifle, offered as the 'Modèle A' (8mm rimmed) or 'Modèle B' (32-20). The 8mm version shared the ammunition of the French 1892-pattern ordnance revolver. The rifles had a separate butt with a shallow pistol grip, held to the receiver by a sturdy longitudinal bolt. The half-length forend had a grasping groove beneath the a four-leaf rear sight graduated to 200m (220yd). The guns measured 41.75in overall and weighed 5.7-5.8lb.

Buffalo-Sport. Distinguished by a plain straight-wrist butt and half-stock, this gun chambered 22 cartridges ranging from Extra Short to Long Rifle interchangeably. The rear sight was usually a spring-leaf elevated by a slider. The Sport pattern was being sold in the 1960s as the Model 710 (.22LR only), with a straight-wrist butt and a spring-leaf rear sight adjusted by a small screw; it was about 39.4in long and weighed 5.1lb. The essentially similar Model 716, in 22LR or 6mm rimfire, had a longer barrel and a tangent-leaf sight graduated to 200m (220yd). It measured 43.7in overall and weighed about 5.4lb.

Buffalo-Stand. Intended for target shooting, this rifle had checkering on the forend and pistol grip, and a crescent-shape buttplate. The adjustable tangent-leaf rear sight was shared with the Buffalo-Junior (q.v.), and the fixed-blade front sight was usually attached to a screwed collar. Four different 22 rimfire chamberings were offered: Extra Short, Short, Long and Long Rifle.

Buffalo-Super-Champion. The best of the entire range, this target rifle was essentially similar to the Buffalo-Champion described above. However, it had a double trigger mechanism with a setting system; an articulated palm rest was fitted beneath the receiver; and an additional Lyman aperture sight often lay on the left side of the receiver. A wide range of accessories could be obtained, including a detachable auxiliary forend grip. The Super Champion chambered a variety of 22 rimfire cartridges, including the No. 7 or Extra Long pattern which was particularly favored in Switzerland.

DAUDETAU ACTION

RIVAL SPORTING CARBINE
Carabine à Répétition 'Rival'

Made by Manufacture Française d'Armes et Cycles de Saint-Étienne.

Total production: not known, but probably less than 1500. **Chambering:** 8x51R, rimmed. **Action:** locked by turning lugs on the bolt head into corresponding recesses in the receiver immediately behind the chamber.

46.45in overall, 8.15lb empty. 25.6in barrel, 4-groove rifling; RH, concentric. Fixed box magazine, four rounds. Multi-leaf rear sight (see text). 2065 fps with 230-grain bullet.

Drawings published in the Manufrance catalogs of the 1920s show quite clearly that this was built on a Daudetau (q.v.) action, raising the possibility that the rifles allegedly constructed by Société Française d'Armes Portatives were actually made in Saint-Étienne. However, though testimonials from places as far apart as the Ivory Coast and Rio de Janeiro testified to the efficacy of the Rival, no example could be traced for inspection and it is suspected that production was comparatively meager.

Catalog illustrations show that the gun retained the military-style action, with the bolt handle turned downward ahead of the receiver bridge, and had a projecting flat-sided magazine case formed integrally with the trigger guard bow.

The one-piece stock had checkering on the shallow pistol grip and the elongated two-piece forend. One swivel lay beneath the butt, but the other, though protruding through the forend, was attached to a collar on the barrel. Sights varied from a folding three-leaf design, with the leaves sharing a common pivot, to an express pattern with a pivot for each leaf. The front sight was generally a ramped blade, and (in 1926 at least) a $2^1/2$x optical sight could be supplied; this fitted to distinctive high-set mounts, the rear mount being attached to the left side of the receiver to allow the bolt handle to move backward.

MAUSER ACTION

Few French gunsmiths made good use of the Mauser action until modern times, the traditional enmity between France and Germany ensuring that pre-1939 French sporting rifles were generally built on actions of other types. However, Manufrance SA (formerly Manufacture Française d'Armes et Cycles) offered Mauser-action sporting rifles into the late 1960s.

RIVAL SPORTING RIFLE

Built around refurbished wartime actions, with the cutaway on the left side of the receiver filled and the charger guides removed, these included the Model 462 Rival (10.75x68) and Model 463 Rival (375 H&H Magnum). The guns had four-round magazines, were 43.9in long, had 23.6in barrels, and weighed 7.95lb. Their straight-comb stocks had rounded forends, and three-leaf express sights were common.

POPULAIRE ACTION

These rifles were simple single shot patterns locked by the base of the bolt handle rib, though offering good manufacturing quality and a spring-loaded extractor which slid in the base of the feed way.

POPULAIRE CARBINE

Made by Manufacture Française d'Armes et Cycles de Saint-Étienne.
Total production: hundreds of thousands. **Chambering options:** see text below. **Action:** locked by turning the base of the bolt handle rib down against a shoulder on the receiver bridge.
DATA FOR A TYPICAL EXAMPLE
Chambering: 9mm Flobert. 37.4in overall, 3.3lb empty. 21.65in barrel, smooth-bore. Single shot only. Fixed open-notch rear sight. Performance not known.

The most basic of these guns had a straight-wrist hardwood half-stock, though checkering was offered on an optional walnut stock, and engraved deluxe patterns could be obtained to order. The bolt handle turned down ahead of the split-bridge receiver. The action could be uncocked by raising the bolt handle horizontally and pressing the trigger, though this is not recommended.

By the mid 1960s, the standard 9mm carbines were being sold as the Model 502, rifled or smooth-bore. The Model 508 was similar, but had checkering on the stock and engraving on the action; the Model 514 was a deluxe version with a better stock and engraving on most of the metal surfaces.

SIMILAR GUNS

Populaire Junior. Also known as the Model 526, this was a post-1945 version of the Scolaire pattern. Chambered for the 6mm rimfire cartridge, it had a full-length 'military style' straight-wrist stock and a spring-leaf rear sight elevated by a small screw. Overall length was about 41.35in; weight averaged 4.5lb.

Populaire Scolaire. Intended for the use of youthful cadets and the members of the Sociétés de Tir, this was a version of the basic rifle with a straight-wristed stock extending almost to the muzzle. There were two bands, the front one doubling as a nose cap, and a grasping groove beneath a spring-leaf rear sight adjustable by a screw running vertically into the barrel. The bolt handle was turned down, and swivels usually lay beneath the butt and rear band. The chambering was 22 Extra Short ('5.5mm Extra-courte') or 6mm rimfire.

Populaire-Sport. Chambered for the 22 Extra Short rimfire cartridge, this was only available in a plain-finish pattern with a straight-wrist half-stock. The rear sight was usually a spring-leaf type. Known by the 1960s as the 'Model 520', the Populaire-Sport was then being chambered only for 6mm rimfire ammunition. It was about 39.5in long and weighed 4lb.

• Manufrance, break-open type

Manufacture Française d'Armes et Cycles made a variety of double rifles on the basis of proven shotgun actions. Most had conventional side- or boxlocks, but a few were made on the idiosyncratic Ideal system.

EXPRESS

Made by Manufacture Française d'Armes et Cycles de Saint-Étienne.
Total production: not known. **Chambering options:** 8x51R, 405 WCF or 450 No. 2 Nitro express. **Action:** locked by a sliding plate engaging two 'bites' (notches) in the under-lump, and by a top lever engaging a doll's head extension entering the standing breech ('Triple Lock').
DATA FOR A TYPICAL EXAMPLE
Chambering: 450 No. 2 Nitro express, rimmed. 43in overall, about 14.8lb empty. 28in barrel, 6-groove rifling; RH, concentric. Double barrels, two shots. Four-leaf express rear sight graduated to 300m (330yd). 2175 fps with 450-grain bullet.

This massive rifle was originally made with external-hammer back locks and inertia firing pins, though some guns made in the 1930s had Anson & Deeley boxlocks. Pistol grip butts and multi-leaf express sights were standard, with checkering on the pistol grip and forend, and extensive Best Bouquet or scroll engraving on the case-hardened action. Twin triggers and ejectors were standard.

EXPRESS IDEAL

Made by Manufacture Française d'Armes et Cycles de Saint-Étienne.
Total production: not known. **Chambering:** 8x51R, 405 WCF or 450 No. 2 Nitro express. **Action:** locked by a sliding plate engaging three 'bites' (notches) in the under-lump, and by a side-lever engaging a doll's head extension entering the standing breech ('Quadruple Lock').
DATA FOR A TYPICAL EXAMPLE
Chambering: 405 WCF, rimmed. 41.2in overall, 14.33lb empty. 26in barrel, 6-groove rifling; RH, concentric. Double barrels, two shots. Four-leaf express rear sight graduated to 300m (330yd). 2200 fps with 300-grain bullet.

Instantly recognizable by the position of the barrel-locking lever, which was set into the right side of the breech, this double rifle also embodied a quadruple locking system. Straps set in either side of the butt strengthened the pistol grip. Ejectors and twin triggers were customary, though variations were doubtless made to order; considerable variety certainly exists among decoration. A multi-leaf express sight was mounted on a short rib above the breech.

• MAS, autoloading type

These rifles were confined largely to the French army and the forces of former French colonies. The introduction of a rimless 7.5mm cartridge in 1924, followed by the appearance of a new pattern in 1929, encouraged experimentation with semi-automatic rifles. The government factory in Saint-Étienne produced a series of prototypes between the wars, the earliest being based on the Mle 1918 RSC (q.v.) and the last sharing the basic action of the Russian Tokarev. MAS rifles proved to be sturdy and reliable, though they handled clumsily. The action relied on gas tapped from the top of the barrel, from where it bled back to impinge directly on the bolt carrier; as the carrier began to move back, it lifted the rear of the breech block above the locking shoulder in the receiver and the whole mechanism reciprocated to reload the chamber on the return stroke.

MAS 44 RIFLE
Fusil automatique MAS 44

Made by the Manufacture d'Armes de Saint-Étienne, 1946-70.
Total production: not known. **Chambering:** 7.5x54, rimless. **Action:** locked by a tilting block engaging the receiver; gas operated, semi-automatic only.
42.35in overall, 8.97lb empty. 22.85in barrel, 4-groove rifling; LH, concentric. Detachable box magazine, 10 rounds. Tangent-leaf sight graduated to 1200m (1310yd). 2790 fps with Balle 1929 C. MAS 36 rod bayonet.

The FA MAS used in conjunction
with TN 2-1 observation binoculars.

Work began in the autumn of 1944 to perfect the pre-war MAS 39 semi-automatic rifle for series production. The first batches of about 1,000 MAS 44 rifles were delivered in 1946, for field trials with marine commandos serving in Indo-China.

The rifle shared the two-piece stock, fittings, bayonet and magazine of the bolt-action MAS 36, but had a deep receiver containing the breechblock and carrier assembly. The charging handle protruded from the front right side of the feed way, and the rear sight lay immediately in front of the shooter's eye.

SIMILAR GUNS

MAS 44-A. Introduced in 1948, this modified MAS 44 was developed to fire grenades, a suitable muzzle and sight being fitted. Bayonets were abandoned on these guns.

MAS 49. Experiments began in 1949 with modified rifles, some chambered for the US 30-06 service cartridge and others fitted with an assortment of grenade launchers or folding stocks. Production of the finalized MAS 49 began in Saint-Étienne in 1951. It was practically identical with the MAS 44, but lacked the bayonet and had a differing stripper-clip. The gas tube, shorter than the MAS 44 version, was bent to follow the contours of the barrel. This allowed the forend and handguard to be modified, reducing empty weight to about 8.66lb.

The first guns were issued to selected marksmen in the early 1950s, virtually all being fitted with the Mle 1953 telescope sight and a hard rubber cheekpiece on the butt. Production of the MAS 49 ceased in favor of the improved MAS 49/56 (below) in 1957, though the two guns co-existed in the army before being relegated to the reserve in the 1970s.

MAS 49/56 RIFLE
Fusil automatique MAS 49/56
Made by the Manufacture d'Armes de Saint-Étienne, 1957-70.
Total production: not known. **Chambering:** 7.5x54, rimless. **Action:** as MAS 44, above.

40.25in overall, 8.55lb empty. 22.85in barrel, 4-groove rifling; LH, concentric. Detachable box magazine, 10 rounds. Tangent-leaf sight graduated to 1200m (1310yd). 2750 fps with Balle 1929 C. MAS 56 knife bayonet.

This was developed in the mid 1950s to replace the MAS 49, production beginning in 1957. The rifle was equipped to fire NATO-standard rifle grenades; a special sight was pivoted to the back of the front-sight mounting block, and the launcher collar/muzzle brake had a diameter of 866 (22mm). The special bayonet, which locked behind the muzzle brake, had two attachment rings. The butt duplicated the MAS 49 pattern, but the half-length forend and handguard – retained by a single band – created space for the grenade-launcher sight. Accessories included the Mle 1953 telescope sight, a rubber cheekpiece, and two types of sponge-rubber buttplate.

SIMILAR GUNS

MAS 49/56 SN. About 250 rifles destined for security police (*Sûreté Nationale*) were converted in the mid 1960s to fire 7.62x51 NATO ammunition, the grenade launcher being modified to fire tear gas and other specialized ammunition.

MAS 49/56 M-SE. This was a special competition-shooting version of the 49/56 ('modifié Saint-Étienne'), formally approved on 10th July 1971. Converted from new or reconditioned guns by ERM, Poitiers, it had an improved trigger with a shorter hammer fall, and a pistol grip stock based on that of the bolt-action FR F-1.

MAS 56 RIFLE

Prototype locked-breech assault rifles replaced unsuccessful delayed-blowback MAS 54 and MAS 55 patterns in 1956. The new gun had a distinctive wooden butt and a circular-section pistol grip. Its gas system and Tokarev-type tilting-block lock were adapted from the MAS 49/56, though direct impingement of gas on the face of the bolt carrier was replaced by a short-stroke piston. The half length wooden forend led to a ventilated sheet-steel guard, and the muzzle had a 49/56-type grenade launcher.

SIMILAR GUNS

MAS 58. This 1958 revision of the 1956 design had a modified receiver, a new rear sight, a carrying handle, and plastic furniture.

MAS 59. The 'Fusil Automatique MAS Type AP 59', derived from the MAS 58, had a supplementary pistol grip ahead of the magazine. The rear sight lay directly above the front grip.

MAS 62 RIFLE
Fusil d'Assaut MAS 56
Made by the Manufacture d'Armes de Saint-Étienne, 1963-5.
Total production: about 1000. **Chambering:** 7.62x51 NATO, rimless. **Action:** as MAS 44, above.

40.75in overall, 9.3lb without magazine. 19.7in barrel, 4-groove rifling; LH, concentric. Detachable box magazine, 20 rounds. Drum sight graduated to 600m (655yd). 2760 fps with ball ammunition. MAS 56 knife bayonet.

The perfected MAS 62 was little more than a MAS 58 simplified for series production. It had a more conventional pistol grip than its predecessors, and the shaping of the plastic butt and forend was refined. The metal parts were phosphated, the rear sight was moved rearward, and a selector appeared above the pistol grip on the left side of the receiver. It was marked 'M', 'C' and 'S' for fully-automatic fire, single shots, and safety respectively.

The 7.5mm MAS 49 auto-loading rifle.

The gun was issued with a special detachable bipod, which could be carried on the bayonet scabbard. The bipod fitted at the muzzle or under the forend.

In 1967, the French tentatively adopted the MAS 62 after protracted trials. However, the trend toward small calibers led to a reassessment of requirements and the gun was abandoned in favor of the 5.56mm FA MAS (q.v.) – the prototype of which was displayed in the summer of 1973.

MAS ASSAULT RIFLE
Fusil d'Assaut MAS, 'FA MAS' or 'FAMAS'
Made by Manufacture d'Armes de Saint-Étienne (subsequently part of Groupement Industriel des Armements Térrestres [GIAT], Saint-Cloud).

Currently in production. **Chambering:** 5.56x45, rimless. **Action:** delayed blowback, selective fire.

29.8in overall, 8.66lb with bipod and empty magazine. 19.2in barrel, 3-groove rifling; RH, concentric. Detachable box magazine, 25 rounds. Aperture sight regulated for 300m (330yd). 3150 fps with M193 ball ammunition; 950 rpm. Knife bayonet.

The first prototypes of this idiosyncratic bullpup rifle were exhibited at Satory in June 1973, though design work had hardly been completed. The perfected A3 prototypes were issued for field trials in 1976 and series production began in 1979. The first issues to the French army occurred early in 1980.

Known to the soldiery as *Le Clairon* ('The Bugle'), the FA MAS cannot be mistaken for any other gun owing to ultra-compact dimensions and the lengthy carrying handle. The rear sight was let into the rear of the handle. The bipod folded back along the sides of the receiver, above the pistol grip, and the direction of ejection could be changed simply by altering the position of the extractor on the bolt and reversing the cheekpiece.

The action was charged by a handle on top of the receiver, beneath the carrying handle. No positive lock was fitted, as a transverse lever connecting the bolt and bolt carrier delayed the opening of the breech until chamber pressure dropped to a safe level.

Packaged in a replaceable synthetic box, the trigger system relied on a ratchet escapement to fire three-shot bursts. The selector in the trigger guard could be moved from 'S' ('sûr', safe) to '1' or 'R' – for single- or multiple shots respectively. With the main selector set to 'R' and the burst-fire selector under the trigger on '0', the FA MAS would fire fully automatically; if the settings were 'R' and '3', however, a three-round burst ensued.

The rifle has been successful enough to satisfy the authorities, though the delayed blowback system is only marginally strong enough to handle high-pressure 5.56mm cartridge; extraction failures occur even though the chamber is fluted. However, the FA MAS remains the principal French service weapon.

SIMILAR GUNS

Modèle de Police. Small numbers of these have been made, with a 14.15in barrel and an overall length of just 23.2in. Destined to replace the MAT 49 submachine gun, the police rifle lacked the bipod and had a simplified forend with a short carrying handle.

• MAS, bolt type

Developed in France in the 1930s, these rifles have been confined largely to the French army and the forces of former French colonies in Africa and the Far East.

The MAS 36 and its derivatives were sturdy and durable, though safety features were poor and the bolt was more awkward

The MAS 36 CR 39 rifle, folded into its butt.

to manipulate than some more conventional rivals. However, they gave excellent service for many years.

THE EARLIEST GUNS

The introduction in 1924 of a rimless 7.5mm cartridge, which was far better ballistically than the venerable 8mm rimmed pattern, forced the French to re-examine their infantry weapons. The rifles had originally been developed in the 1880s and were in need of improvement.

Prototype rifles were offered from Tulle and Saint-Étienne in the late 1920s. Virtually all had magazines loaded from stripper clips, and had socket or spike bayonets which could be reversed into the forend when not required. The MAT 1932 rifle had a two-piece stock and a simple bolt. The operating handle was bent forward so that its ball lay immediately above the trigger guard. Development of the MAT 1932 then produced the MAS 34, the 'B1' version being accepted for service in 1935 as the 'MAS 36'.

MAS 36 SHORT RIFLE
Fusil MAS 36
Made by Manufacture d'Armes de Saint-Étienne, 1937-40 and 1945-53.
Total production: not known. **Chambering:** 7.5x54, rimless. **Action:** locked by two lugs on the bolt body engaging recesses in the receiver behind the magazine well as the bolt was turned down.

40.25in overall, 8.27lb empty. 22.65in barrel, 4-groove rifling; LH, concentric. Internal charger-loaded box magazine, 5 rounds. Tangent-leaf sight graduated to 1200m (1310yd). 2790 fps with Balle 1929 C. MAS 36 rod bayonet.

Approval of the MAS 34 B1 rifle allowed a production line to be readied for the MAS 36 rifle in 1935. The pistol grip butt was separated from the forend and handguard by a massive forged receiver containing the one-piece bolt. No safety catch was provided, and the bolt handle was bent forward so that it came easily into the hand. The rear sight lay on the rear of the receiver, immediately ahead of the firer's eye.

The single barrel band, which carried a swivel, was accompanied by a machined nose cap carrying the front sight. The spike-type bayonet lay in a channel in the forend and a stacking rod protruded from the right side of the nose cap.

Though the first deliveries had been made in 1937, comparatively few MAS 36 rifles had reached French infantrymen when the Germans invaded France in 1940. The major metal parts of pre-war guns were generally phosphated, though some were painted black—perhaps those made hurriedly in 1939-40—and others were browned for the navy and marines.

Production of MAS 36 rifles began again in 1945, post-war guns embodying a tunnel-pattern front-sight protector and sheet-metal mounts. The rear sight was modified so that the adjustment rack lay on the sight base instead of the leaf. A sling bar lay on the left side of the butt and a fixed ring appeared on the left side of the barrel band.

The 7.5mm MAS FR-F1 sniping rifle.

SIMILAR GUNS

MAS 36 CR 39. Adopted for airborne infantry and alpine ski-troops in 1939, this was simply a short MAS 36 with a slotted aluminum butt which could be folded forward around the trigger and lower part of the receiver. It was 34.85in long, had a 17.7in barrel, and weighed 8.49lb. Muzzle velocity fell to 2560 fps.

MAS 36 training rifles. Production of modified 5.6mm rifles began under German supervision in 1941. These had barrel liners, but retained the original chamber so that adaptors in the shape of the 7.5mm round could be used. The adaptors contained a firing pin allowing the centerfire striker to ignite rimfire ammunition.

MAS 36 Competition. The first of about fifty long-barreled single-shot competition rifles chambering the 8mm Balle 1932 N appeared in 1947. It was 47.25in overall, weighed a little under 11lb, and had an aperture sight on the receiver. A ramp-mounted front sight appeared on the barrel, the band was omitted, and the nose cap was greatly simplified. Swivels lay under the forend and butt.

MAS 36 LG 48. Some guns were modified in the late 1940s to accept the 1948-type grenade launcher. These 'LG 48' had a folding sight-arm on the left side of the new machined-steel nose cap, which also had an eared front sight protector. Grenade range was varied by rotating a collar around the muzzle.

MAS 36 LG 51. A NATO-standard grenade launcher was approved in 1951. Rifles modified in 1952-5 ('LG 51') had an elongated ribbed muzzle and the pivoting grenade-sight arm was set into the top upper part of the handguard. A few guns were chambered for 30-06 and 7.62mm NATO cartridges, but 7.5x54 remained standard.

FR F-1 TYPE A

Fusil à Répétition, Modèle F-1 Type A

Made by Manufacture d'Armes, Saint-Étienne (subsequently part of Groupement Industriel des Armements Térrestres [GIAT], Saint Cloud).

Chambering options: 7.5x54 or 7.62x51. **Action:** as MAS 36, above.

DATA FOR A TYPICAL EXAMPLE

Chambering: 7.62x51, rimless. 44.75in overall, 12lb with bipod and magazine. 21.75in barrel (excluding muzzle brake), 4-groove rifling; RH, concentric. Detachable box magazine, 10 rounds. Folding leaf sight. 2790 fps with SS77 ball ammunition. No bayonet.

This sniper rifle, introduced in 1964, was developed from the MAS pattern described above. The work was credited to the factory design bureau and a leading French rifleman, Jean Fournier.

The military FR F-1 'Type A' or "Tireur d'Élite" had a distinctive wood butt with a shallow pistol grip, a separate hand grip immediately behind the trigger, and a slender floating barrel protruding from the enveloping forend. A bipod and a muzzle brake were usually fitted. Wooden spacers could be used to lengthen the butt, and two differing detachable synthetic cheekpieces could be obtained.

A lever-pattern magazine catch lay on the right side of the receiver. The magazine was generally fitted with a detachable rubber cover; when the magazine was inserted into the feed way, the cover was simply pushed over the magazine base. Service rifles were usually fitted with the 3.8x Mle 1953 L.806 optical sight, though guns used by the police and anti-terrorist agencies exhibit 1.5-6x Zeiss Diavari patterns.

SIMILAR GUNS

FR F-1 'Type B', or 'Tir Sportif'. This target rifle lacked the bipod of the military Type A, and had a micro-adjustable aperture sight attached to a bar-mount above the receiver. It weighed about 9.9lb without its magazine.

FR F-1 Grande Chasse. A sporting-rifle derivative of the basic design, this has been made in small numbers with an APX L.804 sight and a simplified trigger.

FR F-2. Introduced in 1984, this improved pattern was offered only in 7.62x51. The strengthened bipod was mounted on a yoke around the barrel, immediately ahead of the receiver, and the wooden forend was replaced by a plastic-coated metal frame. The barrel was enclosed in a plastic sleeve in an attempt to reduce the effect of radiated heat on the sight picture, and possibly also to reduce the risk of infra-red detection.

FR-G1. This was an 'export version' of the FR-F2, lacking the thermal sleeve. A conventional wooden forend was fitted, and the bipod had fixed-length legs.

FR-G2. Otherwise identical with the G1 version, this could be identified by its adjustable bipod legs.

• Mauser

A few Mle 30 short rifles were purchased from Fabrique Nationale in the mid 1930s, apparently to undertake trials against the experimental MAS 36 (q.v.).

M1898 SHORT RIFLE

Production of a slightly modified Kar. 98k (see 'Germany: Mauser, bolt-action type') continued in the Mauser factory after the end of World War II. The guns were destined for French police units, though they were eventually returned to arm West German border guards. They were similar to the so-called *Kriegsmodell*, with bucket-shape buttplates and crude sheet-steel bands/nose caps held to the forend with wood screws. The most recognizable feature was the stacking rod beneath the muzzle, where the cleaning rod would normally lie; the unique hexagonal extension of the rod was threaded to screw into the forend face. In 1946, the French bowed to international pressure and ceased production in Oberndorf at the beginning of May. However, many ex-German Kar. 98k served in Indo-China into the early 1950s.

• Meunier

Also known as 'STA', this semi-automatic rifle was designed by Colonel Meunier of the Section Technique de l'Artillerie on the basis of experiments undertaken in 1897-1910 with a variety of gas- and recoil-operated CTV, ENT and STA rifles (qq.v.). The Meunier rifle apparently worked reliably enough in the hands of well-trained specialists during World War I, but was complicated and difficult to make; its brief success was due to a temporary absence of simpler RSC (q.v.) guns.

FUSIL A6

Assembled in the Manufacture d'Armes de Tulle, with parts from Châtellerault and Saint-Étienne, 1916-17.

Total production: about 1010. **Chambering:** 7x59, rimless. **Action:** locked by lugs on the bolt head rotating into recesses in the receiver; recoil operated, semi-automatic only.

50.9in overall, 8.91lb empty. 28.35in barrel, 4-groove rifling; LH, concentric. Integral charger-loaded box magazine, 6 rounds. Leaf sight graduated to 2300m (2515yd). 2610 fps with ball cartridges. Special sword bayonet.

The A6 rifle was provisionally adopted in 1910 after successfully undergoing field trials. Construction of a production line began in Tulle in 1913, but increasing likelihood of war delayed progress and only pre-production samples had been made by August 1914. Limited series production eventually began in 1916, owing to unexpected problems with the prototypes of the Mle 1917 RSC rifle.

The one-piece stock of the A6 had a small sharply-pointed pistol grip, with ventilation slots in the forend between the barrel band and the special nose cap. A short handguard ran under the band. Sling swivels lay on the underside of the band and butt, and a lug under the nose cap accepted a modified Mle 1892-type sword bayonet.

The A6 rifle had a hollow-headed straight bolt handle and was loaded from a Mauser-type stripper clip, suitable guides being milled in the receiver; a radial safety lever lay on the right side of the trigger guard. About 750 Meunier rifles were issued to selected marksmen in 1917, but, owing to shortages of special ammunition, survivors had been replaced by March 1918 with the Mle 1917.

• Peabody

The French purchased 34,530 Peabody rifles and carbines of the 1862 or external-hammer pattern during the Franco-Prussian War. The long arms were chambered for the 11mm Spanish cartridge, whereas the carbines handled the 56-52 Spencer cartridge.

There were also 16,056 British Enfield-Peabody transformations, made in Birmingham. These had a top-lever protruding behind the hammer and chambered a 58-caliber cartridge. For additional details, see 'USA: Peabody'.

• PGM

PGM Précision is best known for a series of high-quality target rifles, introduced in the 1980s, but has now entered the sniper rifle field with the 'Ultima Ratio' ('UR') series.

ULTIMA RATIO SNIPER RIFLE

Made by PGM Précision, Les Chavannes, 1989 to date.

Currently in production. **Chambering options:** 7.62x51 is standard, but others can be obtained to order. **Action:** locked by three lugs on the bolt head engaging seats in the receiver behind the chamber when the bolt handle is turned down.

DATA FOR A TYPICAL 'INTERVENTION' EXAMPLE

Chambering: 7.62x51 NATO. 40.55in overall, 12.13lb without sights. 18.5in barrel, 4-groove rifling; RH, concentric. Detachable box magazine, 5 rounds. Optical sight. 2740 fps with standard ball ammunition.

Named after the manufacturer's trademark, the UR rifles combine a sturdy bolt-action system with exchangeable modules allowing the system to be adapted to specific requirements. The trigger is an adjustable match-quality unit, a safety catch lies on the left side of the receiver, and a rail will accept a range of optical sight mounts.

Individual components are mounted on a rigid aluminum alloy frame. An adjustable bipod is attached to the tip of the frame ahead of a short wooden forend, while the rear of the unit carries the ambidextrous pistol grip, the sliding comb, the butt and the adjustable shoulder plate.

THE GUNS

UR Intervention. The standard rifles have barrels measuring 18.5in or 23.6in, recognizable by prominent circumferential fins. They are locked in place by an Allen bolt, and can be readily exchanged. A full-length sound-suppressed barrel unit can also be used when necessary.

UR Commando I. This is little more than a short version of the UR Intervention, usually fitted with a 18.5in barrel which is deeply fluted instead of finned.

UR Commando II. The principal feature of this PGM variant is the folding butt, which lacks the prominent wooden under-block of the Intervention and the Commando I. Releasing a catch allows the butt to be swung forward along the left side of the receiver.

UR Europa. This UR Intervention is offered commercially in a variety of chamberings. It shares the basic features of the military patterns, but customarily lacks the bipod.

UR Magnum. This is simply a long-action version of the Europa, generally adapted for the 300 Winchester Magnum cartridge though other chamberings can be obtained to order.

ULTIMA RATIO HECATE II RIFLE

Made by PGM Précision, Les Chavannes, 1989 to date.

Currently in production. **Chambering:** 12.7x99, rimless. **Action:** generally as Ultima Ratio sniper rifle, above.

54.35in overall, 30.42lb without sights. 27.55in barrel, 4-groove rifling; RH, concentric. Detachable box magazine, 7 rounds. Optical sight. 2815 fps with US M2 ball ammunition.

This is a long-range sniping or anti-matériel version of the standard PGM Ultima Ratio design, differing from the 7.62mm patterns largely in dimensions. Bolt action and modular construction are retained, but the stock can be detached and the heavy barrel—fluted in its perfected form—has a large muzzle brake. A folding carrying handle is provided; and the safety catch has been moved to the right side of the receiver.

The earliest examples of the Hecate II had a plain barrel with a three-port muzzle brake and used the folding bipod associated with the US M60 machine guns. Newer guns have a purpose-built bipod with adjustable-length legs. An optional monopod can be attached beneath the butt to give additional support.

• Plastow

Made in the Châtellerault manufactory about 1850, on the basis of Mle 42 rifled muskets, this system relied on a block which fell vertically through a mortise in the breech housing when the support of a screwed stud (running up through the reinforced bolster of the trigger guard) was removed by turning its head a half-turn clockwise. The block dropped far enough to allow a combustible cartridge to be pushed manually into the chamber, where it was fired by a conventional percussion cap. However, the Plastow system did not perform well enough to impress the French army and was abandoned after only a handful of conversions had been made.

• Remington

The initial purchases occurred in 1870, during the Franco-Prussian War, when many Remingtons were acquired by the Gouvernement de la Défense Nationale.

They included 63,030 58 rimfire Springfield rifle-muskets with rolling-block breeches; about 21,120 56-50 rimfire Remington-Geiger carbines; 16,940 50-70 US Navy-type M1870 Remington rifles; 100,000 Egyptian-contract 11.43mm rifles; 49,960 additional Egyptian-pattern rifles, in accordance with French requests; 3,700 11mm Spanish-model rifles; and 9,200 'Greek' Remingtons of unknown pattern.

MODEL 1915 RIFLE

In 1915, the authorities ordered 100,000 'Mle 1897/02' guns from the Remington Arms Company. The contract was largely complete by November 1918. The rifles and carbines were substantially the same as the Mo. 1897 Mexican patterns (q.v.), but had an improved ejector patented in October 1901. They chambered the standard 8x51 round and were sighted to 2400m (2625yd), though a few in 7x57—with 2000m sights—were supplied from stock while adjustments were made for the French cartridge.

The rifles were issued for the duration of World War I as 'Fusils Remington Mle 1915', to non-combatants, lines-of-communication units and the heavy artillery. Survivors were sent to Indo-China in the 1920s.

• Robert

This gunmaker promoted a Pauly-like gun in the early 1830s, chambering a cartridge with a tubular primer projecting back from the cartridge base. A large hollow breech-piece or 'cap' was pivoted on the sides of the breech. A lever attached to the cap ran back down the wrist of the butt to end in a flattened ring, which was held against the comb by a spring-finger extending upward through the butt from the lower tang. The breech was opened simply by pulling upward on the ring, allowing the remnants of the old cartridge to be removed and a fresh cartridge to be placed in the receiver. A roller-tipped arm cocked the internal hammer automatically as the breech opened, allowing the tip of the hammer to protrude ahead of the trigger guard to double as a cocking indicator.

Guns of this pattern were tested unenthusiastically by the French army alongside the double-barreled Lefaucheux (q.v.), but were deemed to be unacceptable. The cartridge, with an unprotected tube primer projecting axially from its base, was clearly unsuited to military service. But others disagreed with the military view; the judges at the Paris Exposition in 1834, for example, recognized the merits of the Robert system—a technologically advanced design by 1830s standards—with the award of a gold medal.

1833-TYPE TRIALS RIFLE

Possibly made in the manufactory in Châtellerault.

Total production: not known. **Chambering:** 16mm, tube-fire. **Action:** locked by the rear of the breech-cap closing the chamber, and by lugs in the cap engaging recesses in the receiver floor.

55.9in overall, 8.71lb empty. 33in barrel, 3-groove rifling; RH, concentric? Single-shot only. Fixed open-notch rear sight. Performance unknown. Mle 1822 socket bayonet.

Based on the Mle 1822 flintlock musket, this had a full-length stock with a straight wrist butt. There were two brass bands—one held with a spring, the other by the swivel—and a sturdy two-strap nose cap; a bayonet could be mounted when required, locking around the base of the front sight. An internal spring-hammer, cocked automatically as the breech opened, fired the gun when the trigger was pressed.

• Roberts

Several thousands of the 'Roberts-Springfield transformation, M1866' were acquired by the French authorities during the Franco-Prussian War of 1870-1. The total is not known with certainty, but they chambered a 58 cartridge—apparently identical with the so-called Enfield-Peabody pattern (British Snider type?)—and had a conventional external cap-lock. For additional details, see **'USA: Roberts'**.

• RSC

Also known as 'Saint-Étienne', this rifle was designed in 1915-16 by Ribeyrolles, Sutter and Chauchat. The RSC rifle was created once it had been realized that the Fusil A6 (Meunier) was too complicated to mass-produce satisfactorily.

Gas was tapped from the underside of the RSC barrel to impinge on a piston and drive back the operating rod—exposed on the right side of the breech—to rotate and disengage the multiple interrupted-screw type lugs on the separate bolt head. Rigorous service showed the Mle 1917 rifle to be surprisingly efficient, though continual refinements ultimately led to the Mle 1918. Series production of the latter did not commence until after the Armistice.

The RSC was undoubtedly among the best semi-automatic rifles produced during World War I, but was handicapped by the clumsy French cartridge.

MODEL 1917 RIFLE
Fusil Mle 1917

Assembled by Manufacture d'Armes, Saint-Étienne, with parts supplied from the government factories in Tulle and Châtellerault plus the privately-owned Hotchkiss factory in Saint-Denis, 1917-18.
Total production: 86,330. **Chambering:** 8x51R, rimmed. **Action:** locked by rotating multiple lugs on the bolt into the receiver; gas operated, semi-automatic only.

52.3in overall, 11.45lb empty. 31.5in barrel, 4-groove rifling; LH, concentric. Integral charger-loaded box magazine, 5 rounds. Leaf sight graduated to 2000m (2185yd). 2295 fps with Balle 1898 D. Mle 86/15 épée bayonet.

Experiments began in 1915 with prototypes adapted from Mle 86/93 Lebel rifles. These showed sufficient promise for work to continue throughout the year, and the RSC rifle was provisionally adopted in May 1916. An assembly line was readied in Saint-Étienne, but problems slowed progress so greatly that limited quantities of the Fusil A6 (Meunier, q.v.) were made as an expedient.

The first batches of Mle 1917 rifles were assembled early in 1917, issues being ordered (in March) on a scale of sixteen to each company of the line infantry regiments. The guns had distinctive two-piece stocks and a rounded magazine case projecting beneath the receiver. The band and nose cap were essentially similar to those of the Mle 1916 Berthier bolt-action rifle, and the standard bayonet was retained. The handguard ran from the front of the rear sight base, over the top of the band to approximately half-way to the nose cap.

A prominent operating slide reciprocated on the right side of the receiver, a stubby retracting handle appearing on the bolt. A safety button protruded on the right side of the receiver between the trigger guard and the magazine, a manual hold-open lever being added shortly after series production commenced.

By the end of the year, sufficient quantities were available for general issue to begin; RSC rifles were usually given to the squad leaders and the best marksmen.

SIMILAR GUNS

Mle 1917 Mousqueton. Active service showed the Mle 1917 to be reliable, but too clumsy for trench warfare. Small numbers of a shortened 'Mousqueton' were made, with a different nose cap moved back around the gas-port assembly. Minor improvements were also made in the action.

Mle 1917/35. Most survivors were converted to manual straight-pull operation in the late 1930s, simply by blocking the gas port. These guns seem to have been held in reserve in 1939, though a few may have served the Gardes Mobiles in the opening stages of World War II.

MODEL 1918 SHORT RIFLE
Fusil Mle 1918

Assembled by Manufacture d'Armes, Saint-Étienne, with parts supplied from the government factories in Tulle and Châtellerault, 1918-19.

Total production: 9500? **Chambering:** 8x51R, rimmed. **Action:** as Mle1917, above.

43.25in overall, 10.47lb empty. 22.85in barrel, 4-groove rifling; LH, concentric. Integral charger-loaded box magazine, 5 rounds. Leaf sight graduated to 2000m (2185yd). 2150 fps with Balle 1898 D. Mle 86/15 épée bayonet.

This was an improved form of the Mle 1917, shorter and lighter but otherwise essentially similar. The handguard ran from the front of the receiver to the nose cap; a lever on the right side of the receiver held the action open after the last case had been ejected; and a tubular sleeve prevented débris entering the charging-handle slot.

Production began in the late summer, but no guns had been issued by the Armistice and only a few thousand of them were made in 1919 before the project was abandoned. Some were issued for service in Morocco in the early 1920s, but the introduction of a 7.5mm rimless cartridge rendered them obsolescent.

SIMILAR GUNS

Mle 1918/35. Surviving Mle 1918 rifles were converted in the late 1930s to the manually-operated 'Mle 1918/35' simply by blocking the gas port. The charging stroke was appreciably stiffer than a conventional bolt-action rifle, making the conversions unpopular. They were brought out of store briefly in 1939, to arm the Gardes Mobiles, and a few were changed back to semi-automatic operation merely by unblocking the gas port.

• Sharps

French records suggest that acquisitions during the Franco-Prussian War of 1870-1 included 7334 1863-type rifles and carbines chambered for the 52 combustible cartridges, and 1270 50-70 'Model 1866' metallic-cartridge carbine conversions. For additional details, see **'USA: Sharps'**.

• SIG (Manurhin)

The 540-series guns were licensed to Manurhin of Mulhouse in about 1975—not only so that they could enter trials with the advantageous backing of a French manufacturer, but also to permit export without contravening Swiss law. French-made 540-series rifles have been distributed much more widely than their SIG equivalents, especially among former French colonies in Africa. Large numbers have also been sold in Bolivia, Chile, Ecuador, Nicaragua and Paraguay. Some were supplied to Indonesia and others have gone to the Lebanon.

Substantial quantities of Manurhin SG 540 rifles—perhaps 20,000—were acquired by the French army in the late 1970s pending issue of the 5.56mm FAMAS. Though now displaced from front-line service, they were retained by the Foreign Legion and overseas units as late as 1990. The first issues were made to French contingents serving with United Nations forces in Lebanon in 1978-9.

• SMFM

Société Moderne de Fabrications Mécaniques ('SMFM') of Saint-Étienne made a range of simple bolt-action rifles distinguished by the position and design of the operating handle, which was bent forward and down in the manner of the French MAS 36 service rifle.

MODEL 702 SPORTING RIFLE
'Modèle 702 Olympique'

Made by Société Moderne de Fabrications Mécaniques, Saint-Étienne, 1960-75?

Total production: not known. **Chambering options:** a variety of 22 and 6mm rimfire cartridges—see text below. **Action:** locked by turning a lug on the bolt-body down against the front of the receiver bridge.
DATA FOR A TYPICAL EXAMPLE
Chambering: 22LR rimfire. 41.75in overall, 4.45lb empty. 23.6in barrel, 4-groove rifling; RH, concentric? Single-shot only. Tangent-leaf sight graduated to 200m (220yd)? 1080 fps with standard ball ammunition.

The 1917-type RSC semi-automatic rifle, the only truly successful design of its type to be used during the First World War. (HBL)

These guns were easily identified by the design of the bolt handle and the exposure of the locking lug in the feedway ahead of the receiver bridge. The front sight was a hooded ramped blade, the rear sight being a conventional tangent-leaf design. The pistol grip half-stock was customarily plain, with a rounded tip to the short forend. Checkering was absent.

SIMILAR GUNS

In addition to the rifled guns, SMFM also made a limited range of 9mm smooth-bored 'Ranch' guns. These are considered as bolt-action shotguns, however, and are not included below.

Model 701. This was a variant of the Model 702, chambered for the 6mm rimfire cartridge; it retained the noticeably short forend.

Model 703. A derivative of the 6mm-caliber Model 701, this had the long forend extending about half-way along the barrel

Model 704 Olympic. Essentially similar to the Model 702, this 22-caliber gun shared the long forend.

Model 709. This was an improved form of the Model 704, with the long forend and a rounded cheekpiece on the butt. It chambered the 6mm cartridges.

Model 710. Otherwise identical with the Model 709, this chambered 22 rimfire ammunition.

• Snider

Desperate for serviceable weapons of any type, the French government contracted for a quantity of British-type 'Snider-Enfield' rifles in 1870. Twenty thousand breechloaders—mainly Sniders—were bought in Birmingham, together with the 21,400 BSA-made Pattern III (Bolted) Snider actions required to convert obsolescent muzzle-loading P/53 Enfield rifle-muskets and P/58 short rifles purchased at the same time. There is no evidence that this contract was completed, but some work was undoubtedly undertaken before the end of hostilities. For additional details, see **'Britain: Snider'.**

• Springfield(-Allin)

The US authorities seized the chance to sell 25,281 obsolescent 'Springfield-Allin transformation, M1866' rifles for use in the Franco-Prussian War (1870-1). They chambered the 50-70 center-fire cartridge. For additional details, see **'USA: Springfield-Allin'.**

• STA

This designation covered a variety of autoloaders developed in 1894-1916. STA No. 4 (later reclassified 'Fusil A1') was a gas-operated Pralon-Meunier design dating from 1897. It was locked by rotating interrupted-thread type lugs into seats in the receiver. The No. 4 was followed by a series of improved rifles, STA No. 5-STA No. 7 (also known as Fusils A2, A3 and A5). The carbine-length A4 rifle was extensively tested in 1900-1 by the cavalry, but the original rifles were superseded by STA No. 6 (7mm Fusil A6). This was adopted officially and is described under 'Meunier'.

• Tabatière

Though Mle 66 Chassepot (q.v.) needle rifles served regular troops, the French still needed to convert obsolescent cap-locks for second-line and militia units. Trials led to the adoption in 1867 of a Snider-type breech. Jacob Snider's executors protested, but the French cited the existence of earlier patents—notably Clairville's of 1853—to avoid licensing fees. By 1870, 342,120 converted guns were available to serve Gardes Mobiles, local militia and franc-tireurs. The French system was known colloquially as 'à Tabatière'—'like a snuff-box'—and opened to the right. Unlike the British Snider, which rotated to the left, it was cut down behind the breech to form a loading tray.

M1867 RIFLE
Fusil d'Infanterie Mle 1867

These guns were adapted by gunmakers in Paris, Versailles, Alsace and Liége from cap-lock Mle 57 rifle-muskets. They had two brass bands and an elaborate brass nose cap. A new iron receiver (often bronze on improved-pattern guns) was added to the existing barrel, suitably shortened to accommodate it. The hammer had a typically French straight spur. The guns chambered a rimmed 17.8x35 centerfire cartridge, were 56in long and weighed 9.8lb; their 37.7in barrels had four-groove concentric rifling. A pivoting-leaf rear sight was graduated to 600m (655yd), muzzle velocity was 1050 fps, and the Mle 1847 socket bayonet could be mounted.

The breechblock of the original guns, lacking a method of locking it shut, was prone to open on firing if the parts had worn; consequently, a retaining catch (*Bouton-Arrêt*) was added in 1868. Improved-pattern guns had a broader shoulder behind the breech block than their predecessors.

M1867 RIFLE
Fusil de Dragon Mle 1867

Similar to the infantry pattern described previously, with two brass bands and the elaborate nose cap, this was only 52.05in overall and weighed 9.37lb. The barrel was 33.5in long, muzzle velocity was 1025 fps and the Mle 1847 socket bayonet was retained. Only improved 'locking' actions seem to have been used.

M1867 CARBINE
Carabine de Chasseurs Mle 1867

This rifle-length 'cavalry carbine' was adapted from the Mle 1859 cap-lock. It could be distinguished from the other Tabatières by its dimensions, though the band and nose cap were sprung instead of screwed. The carbine was 49.5in overall, had an 31.8in barrel and weighed 10.25lb. The leaf sight was graduated to 1000m (1095yd); and a lug-and-tenon for the Mle 1842 M.59 saber bayonet lay on the right side of the muzzle.

OTHER CONVERSIONS

Many cap-lock muskets were altered for the Tabatière breech during the war of 1870-1. Most common was the Mle 1822 T.bis, but adaptations of Napoleonic 'An IX' flintlocks are known. Surviving Tabatière rifles were reduced to reserve status by the mid 1870s and almost all had been discarded by 1885, many undergoing conversion to hunting rifles or shotguns.

• Treuille de Beaulieu

Invented by an artillery officer, this quirky design was operated by pulling down the breechblock—a finger spur protruded beneath the stock—until the block was held in its lower or open position by a spring-guard around the trigger. When the trigger was pressed, the block was thrown upward to close the breech and 'slam fire' a special cartridge. The cartridge case had a locating or extraction pin on top, and a primer pellet on the underside.

MODEL 1854 ROYAL BODYGUARD MUSKETOON
Mousqueton de Corps de Cent Gardes
Made by the Imperial Manufactory, Châtellerault, 1854-8?

Total production: not known. **Chambering:** 9x46, rimmed. **Action:** locked by a vertically sliding breechblock, supported by a spring.

46in overall, 6.77lb empty. 29.35in barrel, 4-groove rifling; RH, concentric? Single-shot only. Folding-leaf rear sight. Performance: said to have been 1800 fps with ball ammunition. Saber-lance bayonet.

The Cent Gardes musketoon was a distinctive design, with the spring-steel trigger guard doubling as the breechblock catch. It had a one-piece straight-wrist stock with a single brass band and a substantial two-strap brass nose cap. A lengthy portion of the muzzle was exposed to enable the extraordinary 'Sabre-Lance de Cent Gardes' to be attached; this had a basket guard and a long double-fullered blade. A fixed bayonet almost doubled the length of the rifle, the combination measuring 84.3in.

SIMILAR GUNS

Modified pattern. Experience showed that the Cent Gardes musketoon was far from perfect. Modifications made in the 1860s included the replacement of the spring-guard with a conventional brass trigger guard, and the removal of the cocking spur to the top rear of the breechblock. The rear sight was also moved forward from above the chamber, increasing eye relief; and the heavy saber-lance bayonet was lightened by shortening the blade and removing the basket guard.

Mousqueton Treuille de Beaulieu. A shortened version of the Cent Gardes rifle was developed experimentally as a cavalry weapon. The barrel was shortened, the band was combined with the nose cap, and the stock was lightened. No bayonet could be fitted. The guns were about 41in long, had 27.95in barrels and weighed about 6.2lb.

• Unique, autoloading type

Manufacture d'Armes des Pyrénées Françaises (MAPF), formed after World War I in Hendaye, in the Basque region of south-western France, is best known as a maker of automatic pistols. However, production of rifles began in the early 1950s and—with the aid of a gold medal gained at the 1996 Olympic Games—now threatens to dominate production.

MODEL X51 SPORTING RIFLE

Made by Manufacture d'Armes des Pyrénées Françaises, Hendaye, about 1951-70.

Total production: not known. **Chambering:** 22 Long Rifle, rimfire. **Action:** no mechanical breech-lock; blowback, semi-automatic only.

DATA FOR A TYPICAL EXAMPLE

36.6in overall, 5.3lb empty. 19.7in barrel, 4-groove rifling; RH, concentric. Detachable box magazine, 5 rounds. Spring-leaf and elevator rear sight. 1080 fps with 40-grain bullet.

This was a straightforward design with a slab-sided receiver separating the pistol grip butt from the short round-tipped forend. A charging plunger protruded from the forend beneath the barrel, and the five-round magazine (the standard fitting) was contained in a housing made integrally with the trigger guard. An automatic magazine safety was accompanied by a manual bolt, originally an optional extra, which ran laterally through the trigger guard housing. A 23.6in barrel could also be obtained to order.

SIMILAR GUNS

Model F11. This is a licensed FA MAS look-alike (see 'MAS: autoloading type'), with the charging lever on top of the receiver beneath the extended carrying handle. Chambered for the 22LR rimfire cartridge, it has a 10- or 20-round magazine, measures about 33in long, has a 22.05in barrel, and weighs 8.28lb. A manual crossbolt safety catch is a standard fitting, and automatic systems prevent the gun being fired with the magazine or stock removed.

Model G21. Discontinued about 1990, this was similar to the X51.bis. However, it was charged by a conventional handle on the right side of the receiver ahead of the ejection port. It had a one-piece half stock with a short over-barrel guard, and military-style blade and aperture sights; the detachable four-position rear sight (25-150m) lay at the extreme rear of the receiver. The trigger guard and the magazine housing were made in a single piece. The G21 was 33.45in long, had a 17.9in barrel, and weighed 5.85lb. Magazines held two, five or 10 rounds.

Model X51.bis. Originally introduced in the 1950s as a deluxe version of the X51, this has now superseded the original pattern. A tangent-leaf rear sight replaced the simpler spring-leaf design, and a ramped-blade front sight was used. The stock design was

refined, and optional two- and 10-round magazines were introduced to cater for restricted export markets. The X51.bis is typically 40.55in long, with a 23.6in barrel, and weighs 5.95lb empty.

• Unique, bolt-action type

Manufacture d'Armes des Pyrénées Françaises makes a wide variety of rifles. The rimfire bolt-action patterns share a common mechanism, locked by a combination of the bolt-handle base in its seat and an opposed lug in the receiver wall, but have recently been joined by an efficient centerfire pattern.

MODEL T66 MATCH RIFLE

Made by Manufacture d'Armes des Pyrénées Françaises, Hendaye, 1966-92?

Total production: not known. **Chambering options:** 22 Long Rifle, rimfire. **Action:** locked by a lug on the rear of the bolt entering its recess in the receiver wall, and by the bolt-handle base turning down into its seat.

DATA FOR A TYPICAL EXAMPLE

44.1in overall, 10.8lb empty. 25.6in barrel, 4-groove rifling; RH, concentric. Single shot only. Micro-adjustable aperture rear sight. 1080 fps with 40-grain bullet.

Available in right- and left-hand forms, this was the best of the rimfire target rifles made in France prior to the emergence of the Unique T2000. Intended for 25m prone shooting, it had a squared half stock with a vertical pistol grip and (on later guns) a low elevating comb. The buttplate could be slid vertically in its mounting plate, extensive stippling appeared on the pistol grip and forend, and competition sights consisted of an aperture unit above the bolt and a replaceable-element tunnel at the muzzle. Later guns had the sides of the forend cutaway to allow the barrel to float freely in the stock, and a sling-anchor or hand stop could be slid along the accessory rail beneath the forend.

SIMILAR GUNS

Model T Audax. Offered in 22 Short or 22LR rimfire, this was a sporting rifle with a plain hardwood half-stock. It was 39.2in overall, had a 21.65in barrel, and weighed 6.4lb. The detachable box magazine usually held five rounds, though a 10-round pattern was optional. The safety bolt worked laterally.

Model T Dioptra. Still available in 1997 in 22LR rimfire, this is an Audax with a walnut stock and a 'flag' safety which locks the firing pin. The cheekpiece and comb are Monte Carlo patterns; thin white spacers lie between the woodwork and the pistol grip cap and shoulder plate; and the tip of the forend—once fashionably

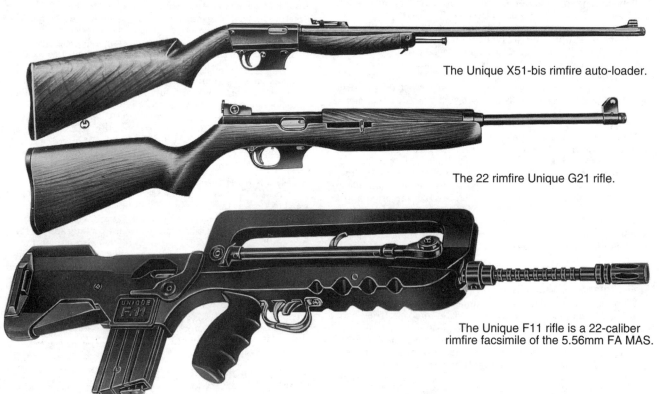

The Unique X51-bis rimfire auto-loader.

The 22 rimfire Unique G21 rifle.

The Unique F11 rifle is a 22-caliber rimfire facsimile of the 5.56mm FA MAS.

squared—is now more rounded. A tangent-leaf rear sight graduated to 200m (220yd) was fitted to the barrel. The guns are typically 41.15in long, have 23.6in barrels, and weigh about 6.8lb; magazines hold five or 10 rounds. A left-hand action has also been made in small numbers.

Model T Dioptra Magnum. This is a variant of the Dioptra chambering the 22 Winchester Magnum rimfire cartridge. Magazines hold five rounds.

Model T/SM. Based on the Model T Audax, this has a five-round box magazine and a short heavy barrel suited to metallic-silhouette shooting. The trigger is adjustable and a safety catch locks the firing pin. The half stock usually has a fixed butt, with stippling on the pistol grip and the forend, but the T/SM may be encountered in a match-pattern stock (right- or left-hand) with an elevating comb. Aperture or optical sights can be fitted to grooves machined in the receiver-top, and the barrel can float freely in the forend in a quest for better accuracy. Available chambered for the 22LR rimfire with magazines of five or 10 rounds, or in 22WMR with a five-round magazine only, the T/SM is about 38.4in long, has a 19.7in barrel and weighs 6.75lb without sights.

Model T/SM Biathlon Junior. Mechanically similar to the standard T/SM, this accepted the harness used in biathlon shooting and will sometimes be found with a hinged protective flap on the muzzle.

Model T/SM Magnum. Otherwise identical with the T/SM, this accepted the 22 Winchester Magnum rimfire cartridge instead of 22 LR. The designation was dropped in the early 1990s, when both chamberings were included under the 'T/SM' banner.

Model T/SM Match Junior. Essentially similar to the T/SM, this 22LR rifle had a short butt—with an adjustable shoulder plate—and an accessory rail set into the underside of the forend.

Model T791. Derived from the T66, this short-lived variant was intended for biathlon competitions. It measured 40.15in overall and weighed about 10.15lb with its sights. The deep forend contained a five-round magazine, with the release catch set into the right side of the stock beneath the ejection port; four spare magazines were set in the under-edge of the butt, the shoulder plate was fixed, the special biathlon harness could be attached, and the muzzle had a hinged protective cover.

MODEL T2000 STANDARD RIFLE
Made by Manufacture d'Armes des Pyrénées Françaises, Hendaye.
Currently available. **Chambering:** 22 Long Rifle, rimfire. **Action:** as T66, above.

DATA FOR A TYPICAL EXAMPLE

About 46in overall, 11.35lb empty. 27.95in barrel, 4-groove rifling; RH, concentric. Single shot only. Micro-adjustable aperture rear sight. 1080 fps with 40-grain bullet.

This is a modernized version of the T-66, with a flat-bottomed receiver and a fully adjustable trigger. The barrel is customarily a fluted medium-weight stainless-steel design. The walnut half-stock has an elevating comb, and a buttplate which can be slid in its channel-plate. Stippling appears on the anatomical pistol grip and the deep forend; an accessory rail is let into the underside of the forend. The rudimentary trigger guard is formed by a short steel strip attached to the forend. Sights consist of an aperture unit and a replaceable-element tunnel. A left-hand action has also been made in small numbers.

SIMILAR GUNS

T2000 Free Rifle. Fitted with a 71cm fluted medium-heavy or cylindrical heavyweight stainless-steel barrel, this has a walnut or laminated two-color beech stock. The elevating comb is accompanied by an extending buttplate with an articulated hook. An accessory rail is let into the underside of the forend. Weight with the medium-heavy barrel is about 14.66lb. Among the extras are a left-hand action.

T2000 Free Rifle, lightweight. Introduced in 1997, this features a 71cm fluted medium-weight barrel. A colored stock and a left-hand action are among the many options.

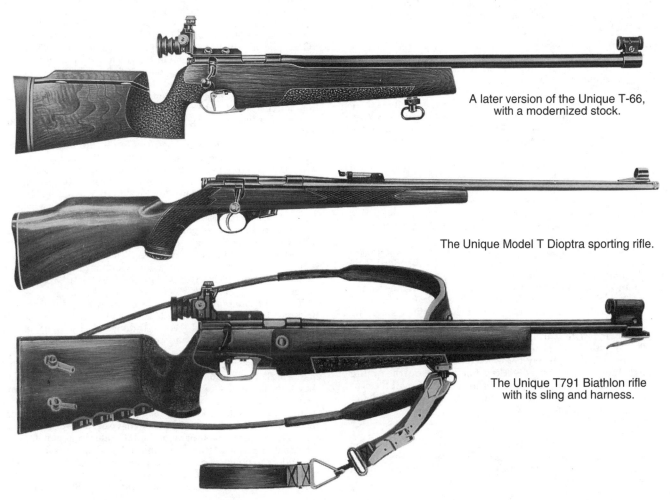

A later version of the Unique T-66, with a modernized stock.

The Unique Model T Dioptra sporting rifle.

The Unique T791 Biathlon rifle with its sling and harness.

The Unique T3000 UIT Standard Rifle.

TGC SPORTING RIFLE
Fusil de Chasse

Made by Manufacture d'Armes des Pyrénées Françaises, Hendaye.
Currently available. **Chambering options:** 243 Winchester, 6.5x55, 270 Winchester, 7mm-08, 7x64, 7mm Remington Magnum, 300 Winchester Magnum, 30-06, 308 Winchester or 9.3x62. **Action:** locked by three lugs on the bolt head engaging recesses in the barrel directly behind the chamber, and by the bolt-handle base turning down into its seat.

DATA FOR A TYPICAL EXAMPLE

Chambering: 7x64, rimless. About 44in overall, 8lb empty. 25.6in barrel, 4-groove rifling; RH, concentric. Detachable box magazine, 5 rounds. Fixed open rear sight. 2885 fps with 154-grain bullet.

Featuring an interchangeable-barrel system, the TGC has a squared solid-top receiver with an ejection port on the right side. The three-lug bolt has a large synthetic tear-drop knob on the operating handle, and a safety button behind the bolt handle can be used to lock the striker. The standard two-color half stock has a Monte Carlo comb, and extensive stippling on the pistol grip and schnabel-tipped forend. Alternatives include walnut stocks, and checkering instead of stippling. The angular trigger guard has a noticeably triangular rear web. A rail above the receiver accepts aperture or optical sights, though the TGC sporter is customarily fitted with a fixed open rear sight and a ramped front sight beneath a hood. A magazine release catch will be found on the right side of the floor-plate beneath the stock.

SIMILAR GUNS

TGC Battue. Made with a short detachable forend and exchangeable barrel, allowing the gun to be taken apart for transport, this is intended for use against driven game. The comb is usually shorter than the sporting version, however, and a ventilated quarter-rib carries the rear sight; magazine capacity is three magnum or five standard rounds, chamberings being 243 Winchester, 6.5x55, 270 Winchester, 7mm-08, 7x64, 7mm Remington Magnum, 300 Winchester Magnum, 30-06, 308 Winchester or 9.3x62. A typical rifle weighs 8.15lb.

TGC Varmint. This variant can be obtained in 6mm BR, 243 Winchester, 7mm-08, 300 Winchester Magnum. 300 Savage, 30-06, or 308 Winchester. It has a fixed-comb half stock with an interchangeable-barrel system; optional extras include a match-pattern stock with a low elevating comb, and a hand-stop and a detachable bipod to slide on the accessory rail beneath the forend. Stainless-steel or fluted barrels can also be obtained.

T3000 Standard Rifle. This single shot target rifle, adaptable to accept a 10-round magazine, may be used for Standard Rifle and Military Rapid Fire competitions. A magazine-release button is usually set into the right side of the stock beneath the ejection port. The stock is identical with that of the T2000 rimfire rifle, apart from minor changes required to accept the centerfire action. The T3000 Standard weighs 12lb when fitted with a 25.6in barrel.

T3000 Free Rifle. This is a single shot version of the standard T3000, with a solid-floor receiver and a 27.95in fluted medium-weight or cylindrical heavy barrel; weight averages 15.3lb with the lighter of the two barrels. Stocks duplicate those of the rimfire T2000 Free Rifle, with a few insignificant changes to suit the centerfire action. The T3000 Free Rifle can be obtained with a left-hand action, or with a colored stock.

• Warner

The French purchased 2500 of these carbines during the Franco-Prussian War of 1870-1, some chambered for the proprietary 52 Warner cartridge and others for the 56-50 Spencer rimfire. For additional information, see **'USA: Warner'**.

• Wilson

A few examples of this rare British-made breechloading carbine were bought during the Franco-Prussian War for the Gardes Mobiles, but the quantities involved were undoubtedly very small. For additional details, see **'Britain: Wilson'**.

GERMANY

Unit markings. The most common of these identify line infantry regiments of the Prussians and their allies ('R') or the Bavarian line infantry regiments ('B...R.'); in 1908, there were 182 and 23 of these units respectively. Reserve infantry regiments used a cursive 'R', while the stampings applied by regimental machine gun companies ('...R.M.G....') may also be encountered. Marks struck during World War I may not always take the prescribed form, owing to the inexperience of conscripted armorers; 'I.R.', 'J.R.' ('J' being an alternative form of 'I'), 'Inf.R.' and other variations of the standard infantry-regiment mark will all be found.

There were 14 Prussian rifle battalions ('J') in 1908, plus two Bavarian equivalents ('B...J.'). Marks signifying the five regiments of foot guards ('G.R.'), five guard-grenadier regiments ('G.G.R.'), the solitary Garde-Füsilier-Regiment ('G.F.R.'), the Lehr-Infanterie-Bataillon ('L.I.B.'), the single Bavarian Leib-Regiment ('B.L.R.'), the Garde-Jäger-Bataillon ('G.J.') or the Garde-Schützen-Bataillon ('G.S.') may also be found, though each is comparatively scarce.

The Prussian establishment in 1908 included 24 dragoon ('D.') regiments, 17 hussar ('H.') regiments, eight regiments of heavy cavalry (Kürassiere, 'K'), and 16 regiments of lancers ('U', Uhlanen). There were also two guard-dragoon ('G.D.'), one guard-hussar ('G.H.') and three guard-lancer regiments ('G.U.').

Particularly interesting is evidence of service in the Prussian royal bodyguard (Regiment der Gardes du Corps, 'G.d.C.'), or with the mounted riflemen (Jäger zu Pferde, 'J.P.'). The Bavarian light horse (Cheveaulegers) applied marks including 'B.' and 'Ch.', while the Bavarian heavy cavalry regiments used 'B.' and 's.R.'. Marks such as 'F.A. ...' and 'F.E.A....' indicate service with the airmen (Flieger-Abteilungen). An 'R.G.' mark was applied by the Reichsgendarmerie, operating prior to 1918 in the province of Alsace-Lorraine (Elsass-Lothringen).

Colonial-service weapons were marked prior to 1912 with 'K.S.' ('Kaiserliche Schutztruppe'), and thereafter with the stampings of each individual force – e.g., 'Sch.D.O.A.234.' on a rifle issued to the protective forces in German East Africa; or 'Sch.Tr.D.S.W.A.' (Schuztrupp Deutsch-Südwestafrika) on a bandolier.

The most common of the marks applied by the pre-1918 navy, the Kaiserliche Marine, included 'M.D.' and 'W.D.' for the sailors (Matrosen) and dockyard (Werften) divisions. The mark of the Torpedo-Division ('T.D.') and the coastal artillery batteries or Marine-Artillerie-Abteilungen ('M.A.A.') are more rare. The marines, or Seebataillone, applied marks such as 'II.S.B.2.35.'; the marks of III. See-Bataillon ('III.S.B....') are especially desirable, as they indicate service in the German Chinese colony of Tsingtau prior to 1914.

Individual unit markings of the type introduced in 1923 took the form of '2./J.R.15.5.', which would have been the fifth weapon issued to the second company of the 15th infantry regiment. The combinations 'A.R.', 'N.A.', 'Pi.' and 'R.R.' signified respectively an artillery regiment, a communications unit (Nachrichten-Abteilung), a pioneer battalion, and a cavalry (Reiter) regiment; 'Kdtr.' was Kommandantur, a district command, and 'Ü.Pl.' signified the

The Model 520/61.

administrative staff of a training ground or Truppenübungsplatz. Navy marks of the Reichsmarine period generally took the ultra-simple form of a number prefixed 'N.' or 'O.', for the Nordsee (North Sea) and Ostsee (Baltic) districts.

The police markings introduced by the Prussian regulations of 1922 employed the prefixes 'S', 'P' and 'L' for Schutzpolizei, police schools, and air-surveillance detachments respectively; 'S.Ar.II 2.15.', therefore, was the 15th weapon issued to 2nd precinct of the second sub-district of the Arnsberg area command. 'S.D.' and 'S.S.' were the marks of the Schutzpolizei in Düsseldorf and Schneidemühl – not the the Sicherheitsdienst and the Schutzstaffel. The Bavarian Landespolizei applied marks such as 'M.5.25.' (the 25th gun issued to the fifth precinct of the München district). By 1932, however, the Prussian system had become 'K' for Kriminalpolizei, 'S' for Schutzpolizei and 'L' for Landjägerei: 'S.Br.II.15.' was the 15th gun issued to the second ('II') district of the Schutzpolizei in Breslau.

A major hindrance to identifying these marks has always been the unreliability of existing sources; German commentators have identified more than 400 mistakes in one booklet which many U.S. collectors regard as invaluable, and it is fair to claim that no English-language source is entirely error-free. However, the recent publication of the painstaking work of Don Bryans and Joachim Görtz – based entirely on German sources – goes much of the way to resolving the problems. Though it deals specifically with the Parabellum or 'Luger', many of the markings are as applicable to rifles as they are to the handguns.

• Anschütz, autoloading type

MODEL 520 SPORTING RIFLE

Made by J.G. Anschütz GmbH, Ulm/Donau.

Chambering: 22 LR rimfire only. **Action:** no positive breech-lock; blowback operation, semi-automatic only.

40.95in overall, 6.28lb unladen. 21.65in barrel, 4-groove rifling; RH, concentric. Detachable box magazine, 10 rounds. Folding-leaf sight. 1050 fps with 40-grain bullet.

This was a 22LR rimfire autoloader with the butt and forend separated by the receiver. The mechanism fed from a detachable box magazine ahead of the trigger. The sights usually consisted of a simple folding leaf and a ramp-mounted blade, but an optional tangent-leaf rear sight could be obtained. The simple trigger was adjustable; swivels lay under the butt and forend; and a radial safety lever lay on the right side of the trigger guard web.

SIMILAR GUNS

Model 520. This was the standard gun, described above. It was restricted to 'export only' after about 1973, though the 520/61 pattern continued to be available in Germany.

Model 520/61. This was a longer version of the standard 520, with a 24in barrel. It was 43.3in overall and weighed 6.4lb.

Model 522 or '522 Luxus'. The deluxe version of the standard gun had a walnut cheek-piece butt with hand-cut checkering on the pistol grip. The forend was a broad or semi-beavertail pattern. Receivers generally had a distinctive crackle finish, though the gun was mechanically identical with the 520. The deluxe pattern had been abandoned by 1973.

Model 522/61 or '522/61 Luxus'. Discontinued in 1983, this was simply a long-barreled deluxe pattern, amalgamating the 24in barrel with the walnut stock.

Model 525 or '525H', 1983-7. This was a minor variant of the Model 522, with a wooden barrel guard and a Williams peep-and-ramp rear sight on the back of the receiver. A 20.05in barrel gave the gun an overall length of 38.6in and a weight of about 6.17lb.

Model 525/61, 1983-95. This differed from the standard 525 only in the length of the barrel – 24in instead of 20.05in. Overall length was about 42.5in.

• Anschütz, bolt-action type

Like many of the large German gunmakers who survived into the post-1945 era, Anschütz made bolt-action rimfire rifles prior to World War II. Catalogues dating from the early 1930s suggest that they were originally simple *Tesching,* light rifles ranging from 4mm 'parlour rifles' (Zimmerstützen) through 22 Long Rifle sporting guns to 9mm Flobert smoothbores. Cataloguing is still hindered by a lack of reliable information, but many of the guns were simply marked 'JGA' (Julius Gottfried Anschütz). The cursive form popular in the mid 1930s is now often mistakenly read as 'IGA'.

Work began again in the early 1950s, when it is assumed that some of the pre-war Zella-Mehlis designs were simply put back into production. *Preisliste für Waffenersatzteile und Büchsenmacherwerkzeuge,* a "price list of gun parts and gunsmiths' tools" published about 1957 by Gustav Genschow, illustrates a drawing of a pre-1939 'JGA-Tesching' and lists (without giving any details) the Models 1380-5, 1389, and 1396-7; the chamberings are given only as 4mm, 6mm and 9mm – a Zimmerstutzen primer-propelled cartridge and two Floberts.

Anschütz rifles still regularly win medals at the highest levels. The company's trigger systems have always been among the very best, giving very rapid lock times; manufacturing quality is impeccable; and the Anschütz competition sights are widely used on other guns – a fitting tribute to the skill with which they are made.

The Savage Arms Company handled Anschütz products in the U.S. (about 1964-81) before passing the agency to Precision Sales International, Inc. Most guns were sold in North America under their original designations, but there have been exceptions: standard 22 Hornet Model 1432 and 222 Remington Model 1532 sporting rifles, for example, were once promoted as the Savage-Anschütz 'Model 54 Sporter' and 'Model 153 Sporter' respectively. The standard European Models 1432 and 1532 were being sold in the U.S. in the early 1990s as '1432 (or 1532) Custom'.

A few bolt-action 22 rimfire Savage rifles were sold in Europe in the mid 1960s under the designations AS 1415, AS 1416, AS 1515 and AS 1516. It is suspected (but not yet confirmed) that this was an expedient pending the introduction of Anschütz's own rimfire sporters.

FLOBERT I ACTION

The simplest and most primitive of the four Anschütz bolt actions offered little other than good manufacturing quantity. It was confined to a handful of rimfire and Flobert-ammunition guns, but was abandoned in the 1980s.

1360-SERIES SPORTING RIFLES

Made by J.G. Anschütz GmbH, Ulm/Donau.

Total production: not known. **Chambering:** 22 LR rimfire only. **Action:** locked by rotating the bolt handle down into its seat in the receiver.

DATA FOR A TYPICAL MODEL 1363

38.6in overall, 4.95lb empty. 21.65in barrel, 4-groove rifling; RH, concentric. Single shot only. Spring-leaf rear sight. 1050 fps with 40-grain bullet.

This rifle would fire virtually any 22 cartridge from a BB Cap to Long Rifle (5.6mm LfB). It had a simple walnut-finish hardwood stock, with a low Monte Carlo comb, a plain pistol grip and a simple forend. The trigger guard was a stamped-steel strip and the trigger was capable of a limited degree of adjustment.

THE GUNS

Model 1363. Described above, this was made until about 1973.

Model 1363 E. An improved version of the original 1363, with a rounded pistol grip, an adjustable trigger, and a few insignificant improvements in the action, this was introduced in 1973.

Model 1365. Chambered for 9mm Flobert ammunition, this was a larger version of the 1363 pattern: 42.5in long, with a 25.6in barrel and weighing about 5.07lb. It was superseded by the 'E' pattern in 1973. A new-pattern Model 1365 appeared in 1976 and was made until 1994.

Model 1365 E. Dating from 1973, this adjustable-trigger gun replaced the original 1365; apart from the rounding of the pistol grip, however, there were few visible differences.

FLOBERT II ACTION

This simple bolt system – a more robust version of the now-obsolete Flobert I – is confined to the lowest grades of Anschütz rifles. It still relies on the bolt handle seat to lock the bolt, but is usually accompanied by a surprisingly good trigger. All the rifles featuring the Flobert II action, apart from the Achiever (q.v.), display a radial safety on the left side of the receiver.

1380-SERIES SPORTING RIFLES

Made by J.G. Anschütz GmbH, Ulm/Donau.

Total production: not known. **Chambering options:** 4mm Übungsmunition or 22 rimfire. **Action:** locked by rotating the bolt handle down into its seat in the receiver.

DATA FOR A TYPICAL MODEL 1386 Z

Chambering: 4mm Übungsmunition. 38.95in overall, 5,07lb empty. 21.65in barrel, 4-groove rifling; RH, concentric. Single shot only. Tangent-leaf rear sight. 300 fps with 7-grain bullet?

The basic 1380-series gun, the Model 1386, was chambered for 22 cartridges ranging from 22 BB and CB caps to 22 Short and 22 Long Rifle rimfire (all of which could be fired interchangeably). The gun was essentially similar to the 1363 pattern described previously, but had a stronger breech mechanism and a better rear sight. It was abandoned in 1973.

THE GUNS

Model 1386. This was the 22 version, described above. It was also offered as a 'Model 1386 FA' or 'Model 1386 FB', the suffixes indicating sale with 4x15 optical sights differing in the design of the graticles.

Model 1386 Z. Chambering 4mm primer-propelled ammunition, this was a parlour rifle (or *Zimmerstutzen*) intended solely for ultra-short range practice. It was also discontinued in 1973.

Model 1388. This single shot gun chambered 22 ammunition (BB Caps to Long Rifle rimfire). Intended as a basic trainer, it had a walnut-finished hardwood half-stock, with a low Monte Carlo comb and a plain pistol grip. A simple spring-leaf rear sight may be encountered, but a sturdier tangent-leaf pattern was more common. Checker panels were pressed into the pistol grip from 1977 onward, and rifles of this type were still available in 1984. A typical example was 37.8in long, had a 19.7in barrel, and weighed about 4.85lb.

Model 1389. Dating from 1973, this was a deluxe version of the 1388 pattern, with a cheekpiece on the butt and checkering on the pistol grip.

1400-SERIES FLOBERT II SPORTING RIFLES

Models 1400 and 1400 D. Introduced some time prior to 1971, but discontinued in 1972, the Model 1400 was a 22LR sporting rifle with a hardwood stock with a plain pistol grip, an adjustable trigger, a tangent-leaf rear sight, and a detachable magazine for five or 10 rounds. It was 38.95in long and weighed 5.18lb. Guns were also offered with 4x15mm optical sights, gaining 'FA' or 'FB' suffixes depending on the graticle design. The 1400 D was a minor variant of the standard 1400 pattern with a non-adjustable direct-acting trigger.

Models 1440 and 1440 D. The deluxe versions of the basic 1400 pattern, discontinued in 1972, had walnut Monte Carlo-type cheek-piece stocks. Checkering appeared on the pistol grip and on the forend, which had a schnabel tip. Swivels lay under the butt and forend. Mechanically identical to the 1440 version, the 1440 D had a simple non-adjustable trigger system.

Models 1441 D and 1441 E. Introduced in 1972, the short-lived 22LR Model 1440 D shared the tangent-leaf rear sight of the contemporary 300-series air rifles. A plain walnut-finish hardwood stock featured a low Monte Carlo comb and checkering on the pistol grip. The gun, which had a 22in barrel and a detachable box magazine (5 or 10 rounds), was replaced about 1975 by sporting guns built on the Model 64 action. Model 1441 E differed solely in the design of the trigger, which was capable of a limited amount of adjustment.

Models 1442 D and 1442 E. Similar mechanically to the 1441 pattern, these had a walnut stock with a low Monte Carlo comb, a cheekpiece, and checkering on the pistol grip and forend. Swivels lay beneath the butt and forend. The trigger of the 'D' pattern was a simple direct-acting pattern, whereas the 'E' pattern could be adjusted.

Models 1443 D and 1443 E. Essentially similar to the Model 1442, these guns had walnut-finish hardwood stocks. The basic pattern had a non-adjustable trigger mechanism ('D') in an attempt to restrict the price; the 1443 E trigger, however, was capable of limited adjustment.

Models 1449 and 1449 D, 1982-92? Otherwise identical with the Model 1388, these chamber 22LR rimfire ammunition and feed from a detachable box magazine holding five (standard) or 10 (optional) rounds. The 1449 is a junior model, with a 16.15in barrel, an abbreviated stock, no checkering and no buttplate; overall length was merely 32.3in, weight being about 3.5lb. The 'D' version had a direct-acting non-adjusting trigger unit.

Model 1450, 1976 to date. This 22LR rifle, feeding from a detachable box magazine, combines the action of the Model 1449 (q.v.) with the more impressive stock of the Model 1388. This has had panels of checkering impressed on the sides of the pistol grip since the late 1970s.

1400-SERIES FLOBERT II TARGET RIFLES

Model 1450 Biathlon, 1994 to date. This basic 22LR rifle was intended as a trainer for junior biathlon competitors. It had a three-slot forend, a detachable five-round box magazine, and an extended non-slip buttplate with a rod-like hook. A slide rail and

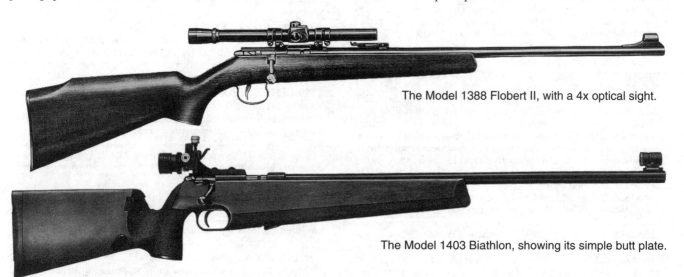

The Model 1388 Flobert II, with a 4x optical sight.

The Model 1403 Biathlon, showing its simple butt plate.

hand stop lay beneath the forend, and provision was made on the butt and forend to anchor a simple biathlon sling.

Model 1451 AST ('Achiever Super Target'), 1994 to date. This beginner's target rifle has a stock with an adjustable buttplate, stippling on the pistol grip and forend, and three blind slots on the forend sides. It is usually fitted with the No. 6805 rear sight.

Mark 2000. Dating from 1982, this 22LR rimfire was Anschütz's basic target rifle prior to the introduction of the Achiever (q.v.). It accepted the No. 6732 aperture sight and had a large-diameter heavy barrel. Its plain hardwood stock had a low straight comb and a durable plastic buttplate. The Mark 2000 was intended specifically for novice and junior shooters, being the lightest of all conventional Anschütz target patterns.

Achiever. Designed primarily to meet the regulations of the National Rifle Association of America (NRA), this amalgamated the standard Flobert II action with a distinctive stock with a stippled pistol grip and three lateral slots in the forend. The buttplate could be adjusted vertically, and spacer-plates allowed the butt to be lengthened as a junior shooter grew. Unlike other guns in the Flobert II series, the Achiever had a safety catch on the right side of the action immediately behind the bolt handle. Its No. 5066 two-stage trigger can be adjusted by a gunsmith, but is usually regulated to 44oz (1250gm). A simplified set of sights, known as the 'No. 1', was specifically developed for the Achiever.

MODEL 64/MATCH 64 ACTION

Though some of the smaller sporting rifles made good use of the sophisticated Match-Verschluss 54, they were so expensive that a cheaper action was developed in the early 1960s. Known as the Match 64 (or 'Model 64'), this was developed to replace the Flobert II and soon became popular on the lowest-grade sporting and target rifles.

MODEL 64 MS

Introduced in 1982, this was intended for metal silhouette shooting – and, primarily, the North American market. It shared the stock of the 1808 MS and 5418 MS patterns (q.v.), but had a simpler bolt mechanism.

1400-SERIES MATCH 64 TARGET RIFLES

Made by J.G. Anschütz GmbH, Ulm/Donau.

Chambering: 22 LR rimfire. **Total production:** not known. **Action:** locked by rotating the bolt handle down into its seat in the receiver.

DATA FOR A TYPICAL MODEL 1403

44.1in overall, 7.72lb empty. 26in barrel, 4-groove rifling; RH, concentric. Single shot only. Aperture rear sight on the receiver. 1050 fps with 40-grain bullet.

These guns all embody the Match 64 action, which filled a gap between the unsophisticated Flobert II and the efficient-but-expensive Match 54 pattern.

THE GUNS

Most of the sporting guns may be obtained with a choice of a direct-acting single trigger ('D' patterns) or a sophisticated double-trigger unit with a 'set' ('St' patterns).

Model 1403, about 1965–88. Seen as an inexpensive alternative to the Model 1411 (q.v.), this intermediate target rifle embodies the mechanical refinement of the Model 64 action and a match-

grade trigger system. The stock is the 'prone' pattern, with a shallow forend, an adjustable buttplate and a fixed comb; stippling will be found on the pistol grip. The trigger is adjustable down to 35oz (1000gm), and the No. 6705 aperture rear sight is standard. The forend was deepened from 1978, when the design of the trigger guard was also improved. The bolt handle shank was bent backward from 1984 onward.

Model 1403 Biathlon, about 1977–87. This junior Biathlon rifle had a plain slab-sided butt, a wooden buttplate, and sling anchors at the back of the pistol grip. A special aperture rear sight, No. 6707, had a hinged protective flap to keep snow out of the peep hole.

Model 1403 D. This variant of the basic 1403 has a simplified direct-acting non-adjustable trigger mechanism with a release pressure of about 49oz (1400gm).

Model 1403 Rep., 1985–8. A variant of the single shot 1403, this was distinguished by its detachable 10-round box magazine.

1400-SERIES MATCH 64 SPORTING RIFLES

Models 1415 and 1415 D. Introduced prior to 1971, the 1415 pattern had a walnut-finish beechwood half-stock with a rounded forend, a straight comb, and an adjustable trigger. The gun was 40.95in long, with a 22.85in barrel, and weighed about 6.17lb; a detachable box magazine held five or 10 rounds, and a tangent-leaf rear sight was standard. The stock was improved in 1984, when a straight comb replaced a shallow Monte Carlo design. The 'D' version offered a fixed non-adjustable trigger system.

Model 1416 Classic. These rifles were offered with three differing trigger systems: the standard pattern, adjustable for let-off; a fixed direct-acting type ('D'); or a double-trigger Jagdstecher ('St') incorporating a setting element. Classics had 22.85in barrels, were about 40.95in long and weighed 6–6.25lb.

Models 1416 D and 1416 St. Differing solely in the design of the trigger system, these 22LR rifles were similar to the 1415, but had walnut stocks with schnabel forend tips, low Monte Carlo combs, cheekpieces, and skip-line checkering on the forend and pistol grip. A folding-leaf or tangent-leaf rear sight was customarily fitted.

Model 1416 DL Classic. This was the only rifle in the series to be offered with a left-hand action, but was mechanically identical with the 1416 D pattern.

Model 1418 or '1418St'. Distinguished by a full-length Mannlicher stock with a hog's back comb, a Bavarian-style cheekpiece, and swivels beneath the butt and forend, this rifle had a 19.7in barrel. The detachable magazine held five or 10 cartridges. Though usually fitted with the two-trigger Jagdstecher ('St') mechanism, guns are known with the single-stage direct-acting 'D' pattern.

1500-SERIES MATCH 64 SPORTING RIFLES

Made by J.G. Anschütz GmbH, Ulm/Donau.

Chambering: 22 Winchester Magnum rimfire. **Action:** as 1400 series, above.

DATA FOR A TYPICAL MODEL 1516 CLASSIC

40.95in overall, 6.17lb empty. 22.85in barrel, 4-groove rifling; RH, concentric. Detachable box magazine, 5 rounds. Aperture rear sight on the receiver. 2015 fps with 40-grain bullet.

The Model 2000 (or 'Mark 2000') target rifle was built on the Flobert II action.

The 22 rimfire Model 1416 Classic sporting rifle.

The Model 1418 St Classic had a full-length Mannlicher stock and a double trigger.

These guns were a more powerful version of the otherwise comparable 22 LR 1400-series types described previously. The enlarged magazine provided the most obvious recognition feature.

THE GUNS

Models 1515 and 1515 D. Introduced prior to 1971, these were identical with the 1415 pattern except for chambering. The stock was walnut-finish hardwood, and the trigger was adjustable or, in the 1515 D, a fixed direct-acting pattern. The stock was improved in 1984, when the original shallow Monte Carlo comb was replaced by a straight design.

Models 1516, 1516 D and 1516 St. The 1516 was similar to the Model 1515 (q.v.), with an adjustable trigger, but had a walnut stock with a low Monte Carlo comb, a cheekpiece, and skip-line checkering on the forend and pistol grip. The forend had a schnabel tip. The introduction of an improved manufacturing pattern in the late 1970s led to the creating of additional 'D' and 'St' versions, with single direct-acting ('D') and double set ('St') triggers respectively.

Model 1516 Classic. Introduced in 1982, this could be acquired in the same three versions as the equivalent 22 LR Model 1416 described above.

Model 1518 or '1518 St'. A 22WMR equivalent of the 22LR Model 1418, this had a full-length Mannlicher stock with a hog's back comb, a squared Bavarian-style cheekpiece, and skip-line checkering. The double-trigger mechanism was standard. Rifles of this type were 37.8in long, had 19.7in barrels, and weighed about 5.5lb. They also had tangent-leaf rear sights and detachable four-round box magazines.

MODEL 54/MATCH 54 ACTION

The elegant 'Model 54' action has been the cornerstone of Anschütz's success, used – in varying forms – on all 22 rimfire Anschütz rifles until the advent of the Model 64/Match 64 series, and also on 22 Hornet and 222 Remington guns. The '54'-type action operated similarly to the Flobert II version, but the lock provided by the bolt handle base was reinforced by a lug on the opposite side of the body. The extractors were twinned; manufacturing quality was improved. The Match 54 action was updated in 1978 by the adoption of a short tapered cocking piece with a signal pin, which protruded when the striker was cocked. The bolt handle ball was enlarged, and the shank was swept backward.

1400-SERIES MATCH 54 TARGET RIFLES

Made by J.G. Anschütz GmbH, Ulm/Donau.

Total production: not known. **Chambering:** 22 LR rimfire. **Action:** locked by the bolt handle base engaging the receiver as the handle was turned down, and by an opposed lug on the base entering its recess.

DATA FOR A TYPICAL MODEL 1407

44.5in overall, 10.8lb empty. 26in barrel, 4-groove rifling; RH, concentric. Single shot only. Aperture rear sight on the receiver. 1050 fps with 40-grain bullet.

This group contains the finest of the earliest Anschütz target rifles, which provided the basis for the 1900 and 2000 series of the 1990s. The most obvious recognition features lie in the design of

the stocks; mechanically, except for the trigger mechanism, the rifles are all practically identical. The Model 1403, which is often included in this group, was built on the simpler Match 64 action.

THE GUNS

Models 1407 UIT Standard and 1407 D. The 1407 was the basic target rifle, combining the Match 54 action with a walnut target-style stock with a fixed comb and a deep forend. The pistol grip and parts of the stock were stippled to improve grip, and an accessory rail was let into the underside of the forend. The buttplate was adjustable. Sights comprised the No. 6522 replaceable-element tunnel at the front and a No. 6702 or No. 6705 micro-adjustable aperture rear sight; trigger pressures were adjustable down to about 6.2oz (175gm). The Model 1407 was replaced by the 1807 type (q.v.) in the early 1980s. The 1407 D version had a single-stage non-adjustable trigger, giving a pressure of 15.9oz (450gm) or 49oz (1400gm).

Model 1407 Z. Comparatively rarely encountered, this was a Zimmerstutzen ('parlour rifle') firing 4mm primer-propelled ammunition suited to indoor practice. The trigger was adjustable, but the gun was too expensive to justify its function and sold only in very small numbers.

Model 1408 ED 'UIT Laufende Scheibe'. Introduced prior to 1971 for moving-target competitions, this 22LR rifle had a distinctive walnut stock with a fixed comb and an adjustable wooden buttplate. The bolt handle was enlarged, the trigger was a non-adjustable match pattern giving a pressure of 17.6oz (500gm) or 53oz (1.5kg) – achieved by changing the spring – and an optical sight was fitted. Overall length was 45.25in, weight being about 9.25lb without sights.

Model 1408 ED Super. Introduced in 1973, this was an improved 1408 ED with a thumb-hole stock and an elevating comb. A left-hand version was also made in small numbers. A projecting spur was added to the butt-plate heel in 1977, when a special multi-part muzzle weight was introduced. However, the Model 1408 was replaced after 1981 by the Model 1808 (q.v.).

Model 1409. Intended for three-position shooting, this 22LR rimfire rifle was little more than a 1407 with a thumb-hole stock. The trigger could be adjusted down to 6.2oz (175gm), and the standard aperture rear sights (No. 6702 or No. 6705) were fitted. The Model 1409 was 44.5in long, had a 27.15in barrel, and weighed about 12.13lb.

Model 1409 Z. This was a Zimmerstutzen version of the standard 22 Model 1409, chambered for 4mm primer-propelled ammunition. It was never made in large numbers.

Models 1410 and 1410 D. Dating from 1977, these were simpler versions of the Model 1413. They lacked the adjustable heel-rest on the pistol grip, and had a deep forend to compensate for the absence of the auxiliary hand rest. The 1410 was superseded in the early 1980s by the 1910 pattern. The 'D' version was distinguished solely by its single-stage fixed-pressure trigger.

Models 1411 and 1411 D. Introduced prior to 1971, the 1411 was basically a variant of the 1407 pattern intended for prone

The Model 1411 target rifle, with an elevating comb.

shooting. It had a plain walnut stock with a fixed comb and cheek-piece, a stippled pistol grip, and a shallow forend; an elevating comb system was adopted in 1973. The trigger could be adjusted down to 4.2oz (120gm) and the standard aperture rear sights could be used. The rifle was 45.65in long, had a 27.15in barrel, and weighed about 11.9lb. Model 1411 D had a direct-acting non-adjustable trigger offering release pressures of 17.6oz (500gm) or 49oz (1400gm), but was otherwise identical with the standard pattern.

Models 1413, 1413 D and 1413 St. These Match Rifles had a special walnut thumb-hole stock with an omni-adjustable butt-plate and an adjustable heel-rest on the pistol grip. A special palm rest – originally a stirrup pattern but a block on post-1978 guns – lay beneath the forend, and the trigger-release pressure (Model 1413 only) could be adjusted down to about 4.2oz (120gm). The guns were 44.5-46.1in long, depending on the butt-plate spacers, and had 27.15in barrels. Weight was usually 15.2-15.5lb. The standard No. 6702 or No. 6705 aperture sights were used. Model 1413 D was a version of the Match Rifle with a single-stage trigger regulated to either 15.9oz (450gm) or 49oz (1400gm); 1413 St had a two-trigger system which could give a release-pressure of 7.1oz (200gm) or, if the 'set' element was used, merely 0.9oz (25gm).

Model 1427 Biathlon, 1973-82. A minor variant of the Model 1407 (q.v.) with a five-round magazine and a special carrying strap, this was very unsophisticated compared with later equipment. In 1977, however, an entirely new stock was adopted with a plain slab-side butt, a wooden buttplate with an alloy hook, and new front and rear sights with folding protectors. The 1427 pattern, which was also made with a left-hand action, was eventually superseded by the Model 1827.

1400-SERIES MATCH 54 SPORTING RIFLES

These rifles were discontinued in 1987-8, though new guns from dealers' stocks continued to be sold into the 1990s.

Models 1422 D and 1422 St. Abandoned in 1988, these 22LR rimfire sporters had a walnut half-stock, with a contrasting pistol grip cap and a schnabel-tipped forend. The butt had a roll-over Monte Carlo comb, and there was skip-line checkering on the pistol grip and forend. Sling swivels lay on the underside of the forend and butt. The Model 1422 was 42.1in long, had a 22.85in barrel, and weighed about 6.6lb. The action, with a safety on the left side of the receiver, fed from a detachable five-round box magazine, and there was a folding open rear sight. A single-stage direct-acting trigger was standard. The 'St' variant, however, was fitted with a double set trigger system.

Model 1422 Classic. Available with either trigger system ('D' and 'St' suffixes), this sporting rifle was similar to the 1422 D except for a straight-comb butt and a plain rounded forend tip.

Model 1424. Introduced in 1973, this was a 22LR sporter with a half-stock and a Bavarian-style cheekpiece.

1430-SERIES SPORTING RIFLES
Made by J.G. Anschütz GmbH, Ulm/Donau.
Total production: not known. **Chambering:** 22 Hornet only. **Action:** as 1400 Match 54 target rifles, above.
DATA FOR A TYPICAL MODEL 1432 D
43.3in overall, 6.72lb empty. 24in barrel, 4-groove rifling; RH, concentric. Detachable box magazine, 5 rounds. Folding-leaf sight. 2690 fps with 45-grain bullet.

The Models 1430, 1431 and 1432 were all introduced in 1965. The original guns had 23.2in barrels and weighed about 6.6lb. Model 1430 A was the most basic, with a plain hardwood stock with a Monte Carlo comb and a slab-sided forend with an oblique-cut tip.

THE GUNS
Model 1430 A, 1965-72. This was the original pattern, described above.

Models 1430 D and 1430 St, 1972-88. These revised guns shared the action of the Model 1432, but had plainer stocks. Checkering and cheekpieces were omitted, and the roll-over comb was replaced by a low Monte Carlo pattern. The forend tips were cut obliquely, and the machined trigger guard was replaced with a simple stamped strip. Folding-leaf rear sights became customary. The 'St' pattern had a double-trigger unit (*Jagdstecher*) instead of the direct-acting 'D' type.

Model 1431 A, 1965-73. This was similar to the 1430 A, but apparently had a better quality walnut stock with a cheekpiece and a roll-over comb. Double-bordered checker panels appeared on the pistol grip and the forend.

Model 1432 A, 1965-73. Distinguished by a walnut half-stock with a hog's back comb (a roll-over pattern was substituted about 1967), this also had a schnabel-tip forend. The pistol grip was accompanied by a white spacer, skip-line checkering being used on the pistol grip and forend. Swivels lay on the underside of the forend and butt.

Model 1432 Classic, 1982-8. This gun had a straight comb and a deep round-tip forend, hand-cut checkering appearing on the pistol grip and forend. In common with many of the better models in the Anschütz range, the trigger guard was a machined forging (a casting on later guns) and could protect single or double triggers – 'D' or 'St' subvarieties.

Models 1432 D and 1432 St, 1972-88. These replaced the 1432 A, the major difference concerning the stock. The butt had a roll-over comb, skip-line checkering appeared on the pistol grip, and there were swivels under the butt and schnabel-tip forend. Direct-acting ('D') or adjustable set trigger ('St') systems were used, together with folding-leaf or tangent-leaf rear sights. The guns were 43.3in long, had 24in barrels, and weighed about 6.85lb. Their detachable box magazines held four cartridges.

Model 1432 E. Offered commercially from 1975 onward, this was a competition rifle satisfying the Deutsche Jägerschafts-Ver-

The Model 1413 Super Match Free Rifle, with a palm rest and a hooked buttplate.

The Model 1432 EK St was intended for moving-target shooting.

band (hunting association). It shared the basic action of the 22LR version introduced several years previously, but had a plain half-stock with a deep forend, a vertical pistol grip, a high straight comb, and a wooden buttplate with rubber spacers. The forend and the pistol grip were stippled to improve grip. The two-stage No. 1432 E-U3 trigger was adjustable to give a pull of 10.5-17.6oz (300-500gm). Open sights were absent, as telescope types were used in competition.

Model 1432 E D. Externally similar to the 1432 E, this had a special direct-acting single stage 1432 E-U1 trigger mechanism, which gave a fixed pull of 17.6oz (500gm).

Model 1432 E KSt. Intended for DJV-style competition shooting, this had a distinctive butt and extensive stippling on the under-surface of the deep forend. A ventilated rubber buttplate was standard and the unique match-quality two-stage No. 5039E trigger system (*Kombiniertem-Stecher-Abzug*, 'KSt'), incorporated a reverse-curve set-lever. The pressure was 7.1oz (200gm), or merely 0.9oz (25gm) if the setting mechanism had been used.

Model 1432 E St. Destined for competitions run under DJV rules, this gun was introduced in 22LR in 1971. It had a walnut stock with a fixed comb and a synthetic buttplate. The pistol grip took sporting (instead of target) form, and stippling appeared on the grip and forend. No open sights were fitted, as an optical sight was obligatory. The rifle had a hunting-style double-trigger system abjustable down to a release pressure of 10.6oz (300gm); it was about 45.3in long and weighed 7.94lb without sights. The rimfire chambering was found to be too weak, and was superseded by 22 Hornet centerfire in 1973. A change was made to the stock about 1977, when a ventilated rubber buttplate appeared and the pistol grip cap was abandoned. The stippling was extended along the entire underside of the forend. The E St guns had a special No. 1432 E St-U4 trigger – Jagdstecher ('St') – giving a pull as low as 10.6oz (300gm).

Model 1433 St Luxus. Introduced in 1976, this rifle had a standard double set trigger, a 19.7in barrel and a full-length 'Mannlicher' stock. The butt had a low European-style comb and a small rounded cheekpiece. Skip-line checkering appeared on the forend and pistol grip, and the schnabel tip was usually rosewood.

Models 1434 D and 1434 St, 1973-88. Similar to the Models 1432 D and St (above), these had a butt with a more typically European cheekpiece and a lower comb than the Monte Carlo roll-over pattern. The pistol grip was shortened and had a differing style of cap, while swivels appeared beneath the butt and the schnabel-tip forend.

1520-SERIES SPORTING RIFLES
Made by J.G. Anschütz GmbH, Ulm/Donau.

Total production: not known. **Chambering:** 22 Winchester Magnum rimfire. **Action:** as 1400 Match 54 target rifles, above.
DATA FOR A TYPICAL MODEL 1522 CLASSIC
43.3in overall, 6.62lb empty. 24in barrel, 4-groove rifling; RH, concentric. Detachable box magazine, 4 rounds. Folding-leaf sight. 2015 fps with 40-grain bullet.

These rifles are all but identical with the 1422 series described above, though they chamber 22 WRM instead of 22LR rimfire.

SIMILAR GUNS
Model 1522 Classic, about 1983-8. This had a straight comb and a deep round-tip forend, with hand-cut checkering on the pistol grip and forend. It could be obtained with single or double triggers – 'D' or 'St' subvarieties.

Models 1522 D and 1522 St, about 1974-88. Distinguished from each other by the design of the trigger mechanism, these had a plainer stock than the 1522 Classic.

Model 1524. Introduced in 1973, this was basically a 22 WMR version of the 22LR Model 1424 (q.v.). The stock had a hog's back comb and a Bavarian-style cheekpiece. Skip-line checkering appeared on the pistol grip and the forend had a schnabel tip.

Models 1549 and 1549 D, 1983-91? Included here for convenience, despite the numerical designation, these were simple 22 Winchester Magnum rimfire junior rifles with a 17.3in barrel and an overall length of just 34.25in. They had four-round magazines and a choice of adjustable two-stage (standard) or single-stage direct-acting ('D') triggers.

1530-SERIES SPORTING RIFLES
Made by J.G. Anschütz GmbH, Ulm/Donau.

Total production: not known. **Chambering:** 222 Remington only. **Action:** as Model 1430, above.
DATA FOR MODEL 1533 ST LUXUS
39.4in overall, 6.5lb empty. 19.7in barrel, 4-groove rifling; RH, concentric. Detachable box magazine, 3 rounds. Folding-leaf sight. 3200 fps with 49-grain bullet.

The earliest of the 222 rifles, the Model 1530 A, was introduced in 1965. It was otherwise identical with the 1430-series 22 Hornet patterns described above. Most of the guns were replaced by the equivalent 1700-series designs in the early 1990s.

SIMILAR GUNS
Model 1530 Classic, 1982-7. This was made in 'D' and 'St' subvarieties, depending on the trigger mechanism.

Models 1530 D and 1530 St, 1973-88. Distinguished by a plain stock and a single direct-acting ('D') or double set ('St') trigger, this was simply a 222 version of the M1430 (q.v.).

Model 1531 A, 1965-73. Generally comparable with the rimfire Model 1431 A (q.v.), this was one of the original manufacturing patterns.

Model 1532 Classic, 1982-8. Made in 'D' or 'St' subvarieties, this rifle had a straight-comb butt and a rounded forend tip.

Models 1532 D and 1532 St, 1973-88. These single-trigger ('D') or double-trigger ('St') guns had a roll-over Monte Carlo butt and a large pistol grip. Forends were schnabel tipped.

Models 1532 E D and 1532 E St, 1973-88. These rifles were made with DJV-style competition stocks and either a single direct-acting ('D') or a double ('St') trigger mechanism.

Model 1533 St Luxus, 1976-88. This was characterized by a full-length stock and a double set-trigger. Like most of the other guns in this series, it was discontinued when the first 1700-series guns appeared.

Models 1534 D and 1534 St, 1973-88. Identified by a butt with a hog's back comb, a rounded cheekpiece and a small pistol grip, as well as by a single direct-acting ('D') or double set ('St') trigger system, this was introduced in the early 1970s. Skip-line checkering was used, and swivels lay beneath the butt and the schnabel-tipped forend.

MODEL 1568 SPORTING RIFLE (i)
Made by J.G. Anschütz GmbH, Ulm/Donau.

Total production: not known. **Chambering options:** 270 Winchester, 7x57 or 7x64. **Action:** locked by two lugs rotating into their seats immediately behind the chamber as the bolt handle was turned down, and by the bolt handle base turning down into its recess.
DATA FOR A TYPICAL EXAMPLE
Chambering: 7x57, rimless. 44.5in overall, 7.5lb empty. 24in barrel, 4-groove rifling; RH, concentric. Detachable box magazine, 4 rounds. Folding-leaf rear sight. 2560 fps with 139-grain bullet.

A few sporting guns of this type, built on 700-type actions supplied by Krico (q.v.), were made in 1971-3. They had walnut stocks

The Model 1434 St, with a Bavarian-style half stock and a double trigger.

with roll-over combs, a Wundhammer-swell pistol grip, and skip-line checkering on the pistol grip and schnabel-tip forend. The box magazine was released by a catch in the front of the trigger guard.

THE GUNS

Models 1568 D and 1568 St. The standard version could be obtained with a direct-acting single-stage trigger ('D') or a double-trigger system embodying a setting element ('St'). Folding- or tangent-leaf rear sights will also be encountered.

Models 1574 D and 1574 St. Built on a 600-series Krico short action, these were chambered for the 222 Remington, 222 Remington Magnum or 243 Winchester rounds. The design of the trigger system distinguished the 'D' and 'St' versions.

MODEL 1568 SPORTING RIFLE (ii)

Production of centerfire sporting rifles built on Krico actions ceased in 1973, when they were replaced by a modified pattern reflecting the agreements between Anschütz and Savage. The second-type Model 1568, therefore, was a Savage 110C action matched with a European-style stock similar to that of the preceding Krico-action 1568. Chambered for 270 Winchester or 7x64 ammunition, the Savage-Anschütz sporters had the magazine release catch set into the right side of the stock. The double-trigger system was standard.

1700-SERIES SPORTING RIFLES

Made by J.G. Anschütz GmbH, Ulm/Donau.

Currently in production. **Chambering options:** 22 LR rimfire, 22 WM rimfire, 22 Hornet or 222 Remington. **Action:** as 1400 Match 54 target rifles, above.

DATA FOR A TYPICAL MODEL

1742 Chambering: 222 Remington, rimless. 43.5in overall, 7.61lb empty. 24in barrel, 4-groove rifling; RH, concentric. Detachable box magazine, 3 rounds. Folding-leaf sight. 3200 fps with 49-grain bullet.

Introduced in 1988, the Model 1700 was little more than an improved 1532 with a heavyweight barrel and an improved action. The standard 222 rifle had a plain walnut-finish beech stock with a straight-comb butt and a simple round-tip forend. Checkering was pressed into the pistol grip only. A single trigger was standard, but a double 'set' pattern could be substituted on request.

THE GUNS

All guns of the 1700 series could be obtained with single triggers ('E' suffix patterns) or double-trigger No. 5004 Jagdstecher units with 'set' elements ('St' variant). The series was greatly refined in 1989-90, when separately-numbered caliber groups appeared. The '4'-suffix guns, owing to the design of the Bavarian-style stock (*Bayernschaft*), have been marketed in North America as the 'Bavaria' series. The guns all have swivels beneath the butt and the forend.

Models 1700 D and 1700 St, 1988-90. These were the original 222 rifles, made with 61cm barrels and three-round magazines. They were about 43.3in long and weighed 6.6-6.9lb depending on the density of the stock wood. See text, above.

Model 1700 Classic, 1988-91. Similar to the standard M1700, but with a 23.6in barrel and a weight of about 7.5lb, this had a walnut stock with hand-cut checkering on the forend and pistol grip. A separate pistol grip cap was fitted, and the trigger was gold plated.

Model 1700 Deluxe or 'Luxusmodell', 1988-90. This had a walnut stock with a roll-over Monte Carlo comb, a contrasting rosewood pistol grip cap, a schnabel-tip forend, and skip-line checkering.

Model 1710, 1990 to date. The 22 LR 1710 has the plain walnut-finish beech stock with a straight comb and rounded forend. Checkering was rolled into the pistol grip only (cf., Classic pattern, below).

Model 1712, 1990 to date. Deluxe variants of Model 1710, these rifles had stocks with roll-over Monte Carlo combs, contrasting pistol grip caps, and schnabel tips. Skip-line checkering appeared on the pistol grip and forend.

Model 1714, 1990 to date. This was a variant of the 1710 with a Bavarian stock or *Bayernschaft,* with a squared cheekpiece and a hog's back comb. Skip-line checkering and a schnabel forend tip were customary.

Model 1716, 1989 to date. This 22 LR rifle was finished in the 'Classic' pattern, with a straight-comb walnut stock, a synthetic pistol grip cap, and conventional checkering on the pistol grip and

round-tipped forend. Folding- (standard) or tangent-leaf (optional) rear sights could be fitted.

Model 1720, 1990 to date. This was the first of the 22 Winchester Magnum rimfire variants in the 1700 series, with the standard plain walnut-finish beech stock.

Model 1722, 1990 to date. A Luxusmodelle derived from the 22 WMRF Model 1720, this rifle had a half-stock with a roll-over Monte Carlo comb and a schnabel tip on the forend (see Model 1712, above).

Model 1724, 1990 to date. This was distinguished by its Bavarian-style half-stock, with a squared cheekpiece and a hog's back comb.

Model 1726, 1989 to date. Featuring the 'Classic' stock, these guns could be obtained with folding- (standard) or tangent-leaf (optional) sights.

Model 1730, 1989 to date. This was similar to the 1710 and 1720 patterns, with the plain walnut-finish beech stock, but chambered the 22 Hornet cartridge.

Model 1732, 1989 to date. A Luxusmodelle 1730, this had a half-stock with a roll-over Monte Carlo comb on the butt and schnabel tip to the forend.

Model 1734, 1989 to date. Distinguished by a squared cheekpiece and hog's back comb, this was the 'Bavarian' version of the 1730 series.

Model 1736, 1989 to date. Featuring the so-called 'Classic' stock – see Model 1716, above – this could be fitted with folding- (standard) or tangent-leaf (optional) rear sights.

Model 1740, 1989 to date. Chambered for the 222 Remington cartridge and built on a strengthened version of the basic Match 54 action, this had the plain walnut-finish beech stock. It replaced the Model 1700.

Model 1742, 1989 to date. A deluxe version of 222 Model 1740, this had a stock with a roll-over Monte Carlo combs and a schnabel-tipped forend.

Model 1744, 1989 to date. Often known as the 'Bavaria' on account of the squared cheekpiece and hog's back comb, this was mechanically identical with the standard Model 1740.

Model 1746, 1989 to date. Featuring an adaptation of the Anschütz 'Classic' stock (see 'Model 1716'), this could be obtained with a choice of rear sights: standard folding or optional tangent-leaf patterns.

1800-SERIES TARGET RIFLES

Made by J.G. Anschütz GmbH, Ulm/Donau.

Total production: not known. **Chambering:** 22 LR rimfire. **Action:** as 1400 Match 54 target rifles, above.

DATA FOR A TYPICAL MODEL 1813

44.5-46.1in overall (depending on butt spacers), 15.43lb empty. 27.15in barrel, 4-groove rifling; RH, concentric. Single shot only. Micro-adjustable aperture rear sight. 1050 fps with 40-grain bullet.

The sophisticated M1813 Super Match was introduced in 1981, replacing the 1413 pattern. The telescope-sight mount bases were omitted from the barrel, but the most important change was the advent of a better trigger unit (No. 5018) and a lengthened trigger guard with a front web containing a bolt which played an integral part in the action-retaining system. An improved articulated butt-plate and hook were adopted in 1985. The 1813 may also be encountered with a block attached to the accessory rail beneath the forend instead of the swivelling hand-rest which was commonly fitted.

THE GUNS

Model 1803, 1987 to date. This replaced the 1403 pattern (q.v.). It had a beech stock with three slots in the forend, a synthetic comb, and stippling on the pistol grip and forend.

Models 1807 and 1807 D, 1981-7. This gun was intended for UIT standard rifle (25m) competitions. The original pattern had a walnut stock with three lateral slots in the forend, with extensive stippling running the length of the underside of the forend back as far as the trigger plate. The pistol grip was also extensively roughened, the synthetic cheekpiece was adjustable, and the butt-plate could be slid vertically in its channel-piece. The standard Model 1807 had an adjustable two-stage trigger. The 1807 D was a minor variant with a single-stage trigger.

Model 1807 Rep., 1985-7. This was simply a 22LR Model 1807 with a detachable 10-round magazine.

The Model 1807 UIT-Standard, with beech stock and cheekpiece.

Model 1807 Z. This 'Z' (Zimmerstützen, 'parlour rifle') is still available. Firing 4mm M20 primer-propellant ammunition, it is intended for ultra-short range indoor practice and is generally accompanied by a stock duplicating that of the Model 1803. However, some 1807 Zimmerstützen actions will be encountered in the newer 1907 stock.

Model 1808 D-RT Super, 1995 to date. A replacement for the 1808 ED Super described below, this 22 LR moving-target gun had a skeletal butt with a separate adjustable comb and a wooden buttplate. The forend had stippled sides raised to the top of the barrel, and the barrel was customarily fitted with a muzzle weight.

Model 1808 ED Super, 1981-95. This moving-target rifle combined a Model 54 action with a thumb-hole stock. The stock had a broad stippled forend, an elevating comb/cheek-piece unit, and a wooden buttplate which slid in a vertical channel. Optical sights were standard; in addition, after 1985, the ED Super was given a long shroud extending forward of the muzzle to carry three adjustable weight collars. This restricted barrel length while simultaneously facilitating a smooth swing on the target. A 17.6oz (500gm) single-stage trigger was standard.

Model 1808 MS. Intended for silhouette shooting, this 1985-vintage rifle is mechanically identical with the 1808 ED Super; however, its stock is much more conventional. There is extensive stippling under the forend, as well as on the pistol grip, but the butt has a fixed cheekpiece and a simple solid rubber buttplate.

Model 1809. Introduced in 1981, this was a variant of the Model 1810 – described below – chambering 4mm primer-propellant ammunition to allow Free Rifle training indoors.

Models 1810 and 1810 D. Introduced in 1981, these match rifles were much like the Model 1807 – with adjustable two-stage (standard guns) or less sophisticated single-stage ('D') triggers – but had an adjustable buttplate with a prominent hook. A new articulated hook mechanism was adopted in 1985.

Models 1811 and 1811 D. The Model 1811 was a variant of the 1810 destined for shooting from the prone position, with a much lower comb and a shallow forend. The 'D' version had the alternative single-stage direct-acting trigger mechanism instead of the standard two-stage type.

Models 1813 Super Match, 1813 D and 1813/1807. The standard Super Match is described in the text, above. Model 1813 D had a simpler direct-acting trigger, and the 1982-vintage 1813/1807 – 'M1813 in M1807 stock' – fitted the action and trigger of the 1813-pattern Super Match into a simpler stock.

Model 1827 B. Intended for Biathlon matches, this replaced the Model 1427 (q.v.) in 1982. The sights had hinged snow caps, the front cap doubling as a muzzle protector; it blocked the sight line to force the firer to expose the muzzle before shooting began. Four auxiliary magazines are set in the under edge of the butt to facilitate reloading, the buttplate is wood with a short straight hook, and a special double-shoulder harness is required to carry the gun centrally on the skier's back. The 1827 uses the standard Model 54 action, with a large grasping knob suited to gloves, and has a walnut stock. The design of the stock was revised in 1985, when an auxiliary muzzle weight was introduced.

1900-SERIES TARGET RIFLES
Made by J.G. Anschütz GmbH, Ulm/Donau.
Currently in production. **Chambering:** 22 LR rimfire. **Action:** as 1400 Match 54 target rifles, above.
DATA FOR A TYPICAL MODEL 1907
44.5in overall, 10.8lb empty. 26in barrel, 4-groove rifling; RH, concentric. Single shot only. Micro-adjustable aperture rear sight. 1050 fps with 40-grain bullet.

The Anschütz Model 1907 (.22LR) is the current designation for what was known prior to 1987 as the '1807'. The current pattern features the superb two-stage No. 5018 trigger, mated with the Match 54 action. The earliest guns were assembled in the 1807 stock, which had three slots in the forend and a synthetic comb, but this was rapidly superseded by the perfected 1900-series design. Made in beech, this has an adjustable comb/cheekpiece and an extensible butt-plate mount retained by prominent synthetic snap-locks let into the woodwork. The stock also has distinctive decorative fluting running the length of the forend sides. A walnut stock option was introduced in 1989, followed by a multi-color laminate pattern in 1995; a short-butt option and an improved No. 7002 rear sight appeared in 1996.

SIMILAR GUNS
Model 1903, 1995 to date. This is a modernized form of the obsolescent Model 1403, with an adjustable comb and a tapered three-slot forend. The stock is generally walnut or a colored wood laminate.

Models 1907 and 1907 D. The standard 1907 is described in the text above; the 'D' variant had a single-stage trigger mechanism.

Model 1907 Z. The 'Z' suffix indicates that this Zimmerstutzen variant fired 4mm primer-propelled cartridges to permit safe indoor or ultra short-range practice.

Model 1909 Z. Another of the 4mm-caliber practice rifles – similar to, but simpler than the Model 1910 – this was distinguished by a thumb-hole butt, an articulated buttplate and a deep forend with three slots.

Models 1910 and 1910 D, 1987 to date. This was originally no more than the 1810 renamed, but a modernized stock had appeared by 1988. The Model 1910 is intended for 50m rifle shooting, sharing the heavy barrel and match trigger of the Model 1913

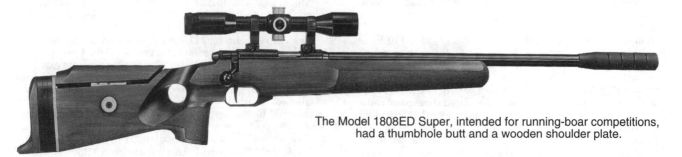

The Model 1808ED Super, intended for running-boar competitions, had a thumbhole butt and a wooden shoulder plate.

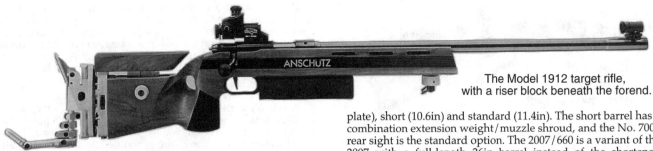

The Model 1912 target rifle, with a riser block beneath the forend.

Free Rifle (q.v.). The plainer stock lacks the adjustable palm-rest shelf of the 1913, and the forend has been deepened to allow a standing marksman to shoot without needing an auxiliary hand rest. The multi-adjustable hooked buttplate and elevating comb/cheek-piece system of the 1913 are both retained. The No. 7002 aperture rear sight was offered as an option from 1995 onward. The 1910 D was mechanically identical, but has a single-stage trigger mechanism.

Models 1911 and 1911 D, 1987 to date. These embody the 1913-type action and a heavy barrel in a stock designed specifically for prone shooting. This has a comparatively shallow forend and butt, and a low comb/cheek-piece unit. The No. 7002 rear sight was usually fitted after 1995. The differences between the variants concern the trigger, which in the 1911 D is a single-stage pattern.

Model 1912 Sport Rifle. Announced at the beginning of 1997 for a new shooting discipline, this is a version of the 1913 accompanied by the No. 6805 or No. 7002 rear sight. A stippled rectangular riser-block runs forward from the trigger guard beneath the forend. Fitted with a 26in barrel, the rifle is about 45.65in long (depending on butt length) and weighs 11.53lb without its sights. The walnut stock has a thumb-hole grip, a cheekpiece which can be adjusted for cant and rake, and a sophisticated articulated buttplate. A true left-hand version, with the bolt reversed, can be obtained to order.

Model 1913, 1987 to date. Top of the company's range of target rifles at the time of its introduction, this superseded the 1813 pattern. Destined for 50m Free Rifle competitions, the Model 1913 has distinctive features such as a hooked buttplate; an elevating comb/cheek-piece unit; and an adjustable palm-rest on the pistol grip. The standard Match 54 action (right or left-handed) is mated with a heavy barrel. A rail beneath the comparatively shallow forend accepts a hand rest, a riser block or a hand-stop. New post-1995 stocks – made of walnut or colored laminate – have a cheekpiece/comb unit adjustable for cant and rake, a stock with three blind slots, and the sides of the forend raised to be level with the barrel top. The No. 7002 rear sight is regarded as standard.

Model 1913/1807 (or 'M1913 National in M1807 stock'). For those who wish to use the same basic gun in a number of competitions, the basic 1913 action can be fitted into an 1807-pattern stock suitable for 25m shooting.

Model 1913 D. This is simply a version of the Model 1913 fitted with a single-stage 'D' trigger, instead of the otherwise standard adjustable No. 5018 type.

2000-SERIES TARGET RIFLES

Made by J.G. Anschütz GmbH, Ulm/Donau.

Currently in production. **Chambering:** 22 LR rimfire. **Action:** as 1400 Match 54 target rifles, above.

DATA FOR A TYPICAL MODEL 2013

43.7-46.1in overall (depending on butt and spacers), 15.43lb empty. 19.7in barrel within a 27.15in shroud/barrel unit, 4-groove rifling; RH, concentric. Single shot only. Micro-adjustable aperture rear sight. 1050 fps with 40-grain bullet.

These guns are most readily recognized by the new integrated action/barrel construction, derived from the Match 54 pattern, which has squarer contours compared with the older guns in the Anschütz range.

THE GUNS

Models 2007 and 2007/660, 1995 to date. This amalgamates the integrated action with a conventional beech or walnut stock with three blind slots, horizontal grooves and the 'snap fastener' comb/cheekpiece unit. The fixed part of the butt has been offered since 1996 in three basic lengths: extra short (9.8in excluding the butt-plate), short (10.6in) and standard (11.4in). The short barrel has a combination extension weight/muzzle shroud, and the No. 7002 rear sight is the standard option. The 2007/660 is a variant of the 2007 with a full-length 26in barrel instead of the shortened shrouded pattern.

Model 2012 Sport Rifle. Announced at the beginning of 1997, accompanying the Model 1912 (q.v.), this is basically a 2013 with a stippled rectangular riser-block running forward from the trigger guard, and supplementary weights on tracks below and alongside the barrel ahead of the forend tip. Fitted with a 26in barrel, the rifle is about 45.65in long – depending on butt length – and weighs 12.95lb without sights; the walnut stock has a thumb-hole grip and an articulated buttplate. A true left-hand version, with the bolt reversed, can also be obtained.

Models 2013 Super Match and 2013/690, 1995 to date. Developed to replace the Model 1913, this combines the integrated action with weight tracks above and below the barrel ahead of the forend tip. The short barrel is usually fitted with a combination muzzle weight/extension shroud, and an improved comb is adjustable for cant and rake. The walnut stock has three blind slots and decorative horizontal grooving on the forend, the butt hook is articulated, and a palm-heel rest can be attached to the accessory rail. The No. 7002 rear sight is standard. The 2013/690 pattern has a full-length 27.15in barrel instead of the shrouded type.

MODEL 5418 TARGET RIFLE

Also known as '5418 MS', this was introduced in 1982 and offered in a left-hand version from 1983 onward. Developed largely for the North American market, it is intended for metal silhouette shooting. Differing from the 1808 MS (q.v.) largely in the use of a short large-diameter barrels, it lacks the extension shroud and adjustable collar weights.

BR-50 TARGET RIFLE

This single shot 22LR pattern was introduced in 1996 for bench-rest shooting. It amalgamates the 2000-series integrated action and a heavy 19.7in barrel inside a 22.8in barrel/muzzle weight assembly. The black synthetic stock has a 1911-type butt and an elevating comb, while the broad forend has a flat underside to improve grip. Weight averages 11.5lb.

BAVARIAN SERIES

Introduced in 1988, the Bavarian (22LR, 22 Magnum, 22 Hornet or 222 Remington) is basically an amalgamation of the standard Match 54 action with a special Bayernschaft or Bavarian-style stock. This has a tighter pistol grip than guns such as the 1422 or 1522, but its most obvious feature is the squared cheekpiece typical of guns from this particular geographical area.

• Anschütz-Förtner

MODEL 1827 BT TARGET RIFLE

Unique among Anschütz's products, the 1827 BT ('Biathlon Target') rifle of 1985 embodies a straight-pull bolt. Though otherwise identical with the standard Model 1827 B, the BT pattern has a distinctive cylindrical receiver with a knurled steel lever fixed vertically to the tip of the bolt-operating handle. When the lever is pulled with the index finger, the locking lugs are retracted and the bolt will come straight back; pressing the bolt closed with the thumb – an action that can be done virtually without disturbing aim – reloads the chamber and locks the bolt.

The stock was extensively revised in 1995, when the magazine holder was transferred to the forend. The butt was cut away to save weight, and an adjustable comb was fitted. A special non-slip butt-plate consisted of a simple plate with a small rod-like hook projecting at the base. The special sights had hinged protective flaps.

• Aydt

Aydt-Haenel, Aydt-Ideal or *Aydt-Reform.* This swinging-block action, unique to Germany and central Europe, was patented by

A detail view of an Aydt rifle.

Carl Wilhelm Aydt in 1884. It was very successful commercially, though not strong enough for high-pressure cartridges.

The essence of an Aydt mechanism was a block, hollowed to contain the hammer, which pivoted under the barrel and was locked in place by a shoulder on the operating lever. When the lever was depressed, the mechanism unlocked and the block rotated downward until its upper edge lay level with the base of the chamber. As the block reached the end of its travel, the extractor pulled the spent case from the chamber. Haenel-made guns usually had an external extractor lever on the left side of the receiver, but internal patterns will be found on other makes. The hammer was held on the sear and cocked as the action closed.

Aydt-type guns will be encountered in great diversity, owing to the stocking and finishing of actions by individual gunsmiths throughout Germany for more than 50 years. Set triggers and good-quality aperture sights were standard fittings, operating levers were plain or eleborately shaped, and the butts came in a wide range of shapes and styles. The most popular were the Schützen patterns, with high combs and adjustable hook-style buttplates.

HAENEL-AYDT TARGET RIFLE
Made by C.G. Haenel, Suhl, about 1890-1925.
Total production: many thousands. **Chambering options:** many European cartridges, with 8.15x46.5R predominating. **Action:** locked by a shoulder on the operating lever propping the swinging block behind the chamber.
DATA FOR A TYPICAL EXAMPLE
   Chambering: 8.15x46.5R. 47.05in overall, 11.07lb empty. 31.1in barrel, 4-groove rifling; RH, concentric. Aperture sight on rear tang. 1805 fps with 151-grain bullet.

The Haenel-made 'Original-Aydt' had an external extractor and, in most cases, a lever that locked the barrel in place; the entire action could be dismantled without tools. An elaborately looped operating lever/trigger guard simply sprung into place over a stud integral with the lower tang. The tang was retained by a small spring catch behind the lever-retaining stud. Double set triggers were regarded as essential fittings, instead of an optional extra. Barrels were usually octagonal, though round and specially fluted examples are known; the half-length forend, often with a schnabel tip, was keyed to the barrel. The butt often displayed a dished Tyrolean cheekpiece, though Bavarian, Swiss and other regional variations were made to order. Elaborate engraving was popular, while an aperture sight on the tang often replaced the quadrant rear sight on the barrel.

AYDT-REFORM TARGET RIFLE
Made by August Schüler, Suhl, about 1910-35.
Total production: many thousands. **Chambering options:** a variety of European cartridges. **Action:** as Haenel-Aydt, above.
DATA FOR A TYPICAL EXAMPLE
   Chambering: 6.5x27R. 44.95in overall, 10.76lb empty. 29.15in barrel, 4-groove rifling; RH, concentric. Aperture sight on rear tang. 1560 fps with 82-grain bullet.

Dating from about 1910, this was an improved version of the Aydt with an internal extractor and a radial-lever locking catch on the lower tang behind the triggers. Apart from these changes, however, the modified Aydt was essentially similar to the 1884 pattern; most rifles were made for Schützen purposes, with elaborate operating levers, high-comb butts and ultra-sophisticated sights, but plainer sporting guns were also made.

OTHER GUNS
A simpler version of the Aydt-Reform, known as the 'Aydt-Ideal' or simply 'Ideal', may also have been made by Schüler. The Original Zentrum – often credited to a gunmaker named Neumann and claimed to have been a modified Aydt – was actually built on a Martini-type action.

• Blaser, block-action type
This metalworking company (which the first edition of *Rifles of the World* unwittingly placed in Switzerland) turned to guns only in the late 1970s. Thanks to the enthusiasm of owner Gerhard Blenk and his staff, Blaser products are among the most innovative of today's sporting guns.

BL-820 SPORTING RIFLE
Made by Blaser-Jagdwaffen GmbH, Isny/Allgäu.
Total production: not known. **Chambering options:** 5.6x50R Magnum, 6.5x57R, 6.5x68R, 7x57R, 7x65R, 222 Remington, 243 Winchester, 300 Winchester Magnum, 30-06 or 308 Winchester. **Action:** locked by a lever combined with the trigger guard propping a dropping block in position behind the chamber.
DATA FOR A TYPICAL EXAMPLE
   Chambering: 6.5x68R. 39.75in overall, 6.65lb empty. 23.6in barrel, 4-groove rifling; RH, concentric? Single shot only. Folding-leaf sight. 3610 fps with 93-grain bullet.

Introduced commercially in 1982, but only made until about 1991, this elegant rifle offered a compact action contained almost entirely within the receiver. Pushing the trigger guard spur down opened the action around a pivot at the front of the action-plate, and dropped the locking block to expose the chamber. Once the breech had been closed, the hammer had to be cocked manually.

• Blaser, bolt-action type
Developed in the early 1980s and introduced in 1984, rifles of the original R-84 series had a bolt in a non-rotating housing which slid back along rails on top of the receiver (cf., Certus – see 'Britain'). Lugs on the bolt head locked directly into the barrel, allowing the

The open action of the Blaser BL 820, showing its compact design.

The Blaser BL 820 single-shot rifle.

receiver to be made of lightweight alloy. The R-93, however, features a unique patented locking mechanism with a segmented collar or multi-lug unit on the bolt head. This is operated simply by pulling the bolt handle backward, which withdraws the collar segments flush with the bolt body during the first phase of the opening stroke, when the bolt lever rocks back before the bolt comes free. The design offers full circumferential support to the bolt, unlike conventional lug systems, and has a self-centering effect.

The Blaser R-84, showing the unorthodox design of the bolt and carrier.

R-84 SPORTING RIFLE
Made by Blaser-Jagdwaffen GmbH, Isny/Allgäu, 1985-9.
Total production: not known. **Chamberings**: see text. **Action**: locked by three locking lugs rotating into the barrel behind the chamber as the bolt handle was turned down.

DATA FOR A TYPICAL EXAMPLE

Chambering: 280 Remington, rimless. 40.95in overall, 7.05lb empty. 23.05in barrel, 4-groove rifling; RH, concentric? Blind magazine, three rounds. Optical sight. 2820 fps with 165-grain bullet.

Built on the original three-lug action, the R-84 had a safety – pivoted on the rear of the mobile bolt-housing – which could lock the bolt and the firing pin. Readily detachable free-floating barrels carried the optical-sight mount. The straight-comb butts and round-tip forends (designed by Magnum Arms of Canada, Inc.) were made of Circassian walnut.

The standard R-84 was offered in 22-250, 243 Winchester, 6mm Remington, 25-06, 270 Winchester, 280 Remington or 30-06. A left-hand action was made in small numbers from 1988 onward.

SIMILAR GUNS
R-84 Magnum, 1985-9. About 41.95in overall, with a 24in barrel and a weight of 7.28lb, these guns have chambered 257 Weatherby, 264 Winchester, 7mm Remington, 300 Weatherby, 300 Winchester, 338 Winchester and 375 H&H magnum cartridges.

SR-850, 1989-93. An improved form of the R-84, this had a similar action and exchangeable barrel, but was styled more conventionally and had an exposed hammer.

R-93 STANDARD SPORTING RIFLE
Made by Blaser-Jagdwaffen GmbH, Isny/Allgäu.
Currently in production. **Chambering options**: originally 22-250, 243 Winchester, 6.5x55 Mauser, 270 Winchester, 7x57 Mauser, or 308 Winchester. See also text below. **Action**: locked by a multi-segment collar engaging a shoulder in the barrel behind the chamber as the bolt handle is closed.

DATA FOR A TYPICAL EXAMPLE

Chambering: 6.5x55mm, rimless. 40.15in overall, 6.94lb empty. 22.7in barrel, 4-groove rifling; RH, concentric. Blind box magazine, 3 rounds. Optical sight. 2720 fps with 139-grain bullet.

Introduced commercially in 1994, on the basis of the circum-ferential-segment action, the R-93 also has a special 'searless' trigger mechanism operating on a toggle principle. Cocking is undertaken manually by pressing in the safety slide on the rear of the bolt unit (which locks the bolt and the striker) before each shot. An intermediate position allows the gun to be unloaded, but remain uncocked.

An alloy receiver containing the bolt and trigger mechanism separates the walnut butt from the forend. The butt orginally had a straight comb and a forend with a shallow schnabel tip, but the post-1995 pattern has slight hog's back comb and a plain round-tip forend. Sling eyes lie beneath the butt and on the front tip of the forend. The magazine projecting forward from the receiver is contained entirely within the forend, the cartridge tips being protected by rubber pads.

Barrels and rear sights are combined in separate readily exchangeable units, though the bolt head must be replaced if a change of caliber-group is required (e.g., from Mini to Standard Caliber, or from Standard to Magnum). New *Standardkalibergruppe* chambering options introduced in 1995-6 have included 6.5x55 RWS, 6x57, 7x64, 8x57IS and 9.3x62.

SIMILAR GUNS
R-93 Attaché Introduced in 1996 specifically to fit into an attaché case, this shortened R-93 has an instantly detachable optical sight and a special fluted 20.45in barrel, conserving weight without compromising strength. Intended for hunters operating in uplands, mountains and comparable terrain, it is available in all regular chamberings. Attaché rifles are typically about 39in long, the weight of the standard version averaging 5.5lb.

R-93 Deluxe, or 'Luxusmodell'. The R-93 – like other Blaser products – can be obtained in deluxe versions offering exemplary quality. The decoration can range from arabesques and 'Best English' scrollwork to depictions of elk, bear and buffalo on the central receiver panels.

R-93 Grand Luxe. These patterns have extensive engraving on the straps and panels of the receiver – usually oakleaf, bouquet or English scrollwork – and woodwork of the best quality. The bolt handle may also be decoratively turned wood. The 'Royal' version is the top of the entire range, with – for example – high-relief engraving, gold inlay on the game scenes, woodwork carved with fish-scale checkering and floral bouquets.

R-93 ISU Standard (or 'UIT Standard'). Introduced in 1996 for target shooting, this version has a free-floating barrel with an extension shroud carrying the front sight and a non-reflective mirage band. The shroud effectively extends the 23.6in barrel to about 29.9in. The black or multi-colored synthetic stock has an adjustable wooden cheekpiece/comb unit and a sliding buttplate. Anschütz or Grünel aperture rear sights are fitted on a rail attached to the left side of the stock. Made in single- or 10-shot versions, the R-93 ISU Standard can be chambered for the 222 Remington, 223 Remington, 243 Winchester, 6mm PPC, 6mm Norma BR, 6.5x55 Mauser, 7.5x55 or 308 Winchester rounds.

R-93 Magnum Caliber. Distinguished from the standard R-93 largely by the barrel – 24.7in long instead of 22.7in – this is offered for cartridges such as 257 Weatherby Magnum (abandoned in 1995), 7mm Remington Magnum, 300 Winchester Magnum, 300 Weatherby Magnum, 338 Winchester Magnum or 375 H&H Magnum. Overall length is about 42.15in, weight averages 7.1lb and the magazine holds three rounds.

R-93 Medium Caliber. This group of R-93 chamberings was announced in 1996, initially comprising 6.5x68, 7.5x55, 8x68S and 9.3x64. Mechanical details remain unchanged from the Standard Caliber group, but the bolt head differs in detail.

R-93 Mini-Caliber. Chambered only for the 222 or 223 Remington cartridges, but mechanically identical with the standard pattern, this is the smallest gun in the series; retaining a 22.05in barrel, it weighs about 6.6lb. Magazines hold four rounds.

R-93 Prestige. Applied to any version of the R-93, this is the most basic of the decorated versions. The guns usually have a small oval arabesque panel on the receiver-side, but lack the engraving coverage of the true Luxusmodell.

R-93 Safari. Intended for use against large game, chambered only for the 375 H&H Magnum or 416 Remington Magnum rounds, this has a 24.7in heavyweight barrel and the open sights are supplied as standard fittings. Safari rifles are about 46.05in long and weigh 9.7lb without the optical sight and mounts.

The action of the Blaser R93, showing the wood insert in the receiver.

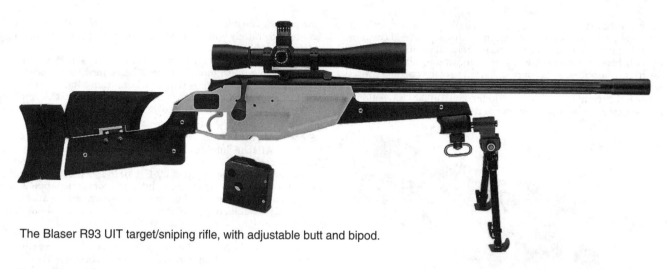

The Blaser R93 UIT target/sniping rifle, with adjustable butt and bipod.

• Blaser, break-open type

Blaser has recently introduced a range of multi-barrel guns, including a two-barrel rifle described below. The unusual *Bock-drilling* has two different rifled barrels and a single smooth-bore.

K-77A STANDARD SPORTING RIFLE

Made by Blaser-Jagdwaffen GmbH, Isny/Allgäu, 1978-94?

Total production: not known. **Chambering options:** originally 22-250, 243 Winchester, 6.5x55 Mauser, 270 Winchester, 280 Remington, 7x57, 7x65R or 30-06. See also text below. **Action:** locked by a shoulder on top of a separate block entering a recess in the barrel when the top lever was actuated.

DATA FOR A TYPICAL EXAMPLE

Chambering: 7x65R, rimmed. 39.55in overall, 5.62lb empty. 23.05in barrel, 4-groove rifling; RH, concentric. Single shot only. Optical sight. 3050 fps with 123-grain bullet.

This single shot rifle incorporated a special locking block, which not only relieved the receiver of strain but also made cross-bolts, doll's head extensions and other additional locking devices superfluous. The original rifle had an alloy receiver – often highly decorated – separating the straight-comb Circassian walnut butt from the rounded forend, the surfaces of the pistol grip and forend being extensively checkered. Swivels lay on the barrel and the butt, and a slide on the tang behind the top-lever could be used to cock or de-cock the trigger mechanism.

SIMILAR GUNS

K-77A Deluxe or 'Luxusmodell'. The deluxe version, obtainable in regular or magnum chamberings, had engraving on the receiver and carving on the stock. The pistol grip cap was often sterling silver, decorated with a game scene or the owner's initials.

K-77A Magnum. This was a minor variant of the standard gun – 40.55in long, with a 24in barrel. It could be obtained in 7mm Remington Magnum, 300 Winchester Magnum and 300 Weatherby Magnum.

K-95 STANDARD SPORTING RIFLE

Made by Blaser-Jagdwaffen GmbH, Isny/Allgäu, 1995 to date.

Currently in production. **Chambering options:** 22 Hornet, 222 Remington, 5.6x50 Magnum, 5.6x52R, 243 Winchester, 6.5x55 Mauser, 6.5x55R RWS, 6.5x57R, 6.5x65R RWS, 6.5x68R, 270 Winchester, 7x57R, 7mm Remington Magnum, 7.5x55, 30-06, 308 Winchester, 30R Blaser, 300 Weatherby Magnum, 300 Winchester Magnum, 8x57R, 8x75RS, 8x68S or 9.3x74R. **Action:** as K-77A, above.

DATA FOR A TYPICAL EXAMPLE

Chambering: 6.5x57R, rimmed. 40.15in overall, 5.4lb empty. 23.6in barrel, 4-groove rifling; RH, concentric. Single shot only. Standing-block rear sight for 150m (165yd). 3230 fps with 93-grain bullet.

An improved form of the K-77A, with a new trigger, an improved cocking slide, refinements in detail and a modified optical-sight mounting system, the K-95 has been offered in a variety of options. Most of the standard guns offer a walnut butt with a low hog's back comb, a generously proportioned pistol grip, and a squared Bavarian-style cheekpiece with a fluted under edge. Skip-line checkering appears on the pistol grip and the slender schnabel-tipped forend.

The distinction between the standard and magnum versions – sometimes perpetuated in the K-77A – is now rarely used: only a single type of K-95 is advertised, even though Magnum chamberings are customarily accompanied by a 25.6in barrel.

SIMILAR GUNS

K-95 Classic. Made since in 1996, this is a minor variant of the standard rifle with a folding rear sight set into a quarter-rib on top of the barrel. It can be obtained in any of the standard chamberings.

K-95 Deluxe or 'Luxusmodell'. These deluxe patterns offer decoration on the receiver-sides ranging from English scrollwork to wild boar or red deer.

K-95 Grand Luxe. Applied to any K-95, this is the best of the deluxe guns. It is distinguished by the outstanding quality of the woodwork and the extent and quality of the engraving. This usually takes the form of 'Fine English' scrollwork.

K-95 Prestige. The most basic of the decorated versions of the K-95 may be identified by the bouquet-and-stipple decoration on the sides of the receiver.

B-750/88 SPORTING RIFLE
Bergstutzen 750/88

Made by Blaser-Jagdwaffen GmbH, Isny/Allgäu, 1995 to date.

Currently in production. **Chambering options:** (top barrel) 22 Hornet, 222 Remington, 5.6x50R Magnum or 5.6x52R; (bottom barrel) 5.6x50R Magnum, 5.6x52R, 243 Winchester, 25-06, 6.5x57R, 6.5x65R RWS, 270 Winchester, 7x57R, 7x65R, 308 Winchester, 30R Blaser, 8x57R IS, 8x75RS or 9.3x74R. **Action:** locked by a sliding block in the base of the breech intercepting a lug on the barrel lump.

DATA FOR A TYPICAL EXAMPLE

Chambering: 22 Hornet/.270 Winchester. 40.15in overall, 6.83lb empty. 23.6in barrel, 4-groove rifling; RH, concentric. Double barreled, two shots only. Standing-block rear sight. 2430 fps with 46-grain bullet (22 Hornet) and 3170 fps with 130-grain bullet (270 Winchester).

This rifle is typical of the *Bergstutzen*, a two-caliber design popular in the upland districts of central Europe. Based on a boxlock action shared with the company's shotguns and combination guns, the Blaser version lacks the top-bolt found on many rival

The Blaser K-77 Deluxe single-barrel rifle.

designs. However, it has proved to be amply strong enough for the pressures involved with the cartridge options.

SIMILAR GUNS

Deluxe patterns. The standard gun has a plain-sided receiver, but a selection of Prestige, Luxus and Grande Luxe designs can be obtained. These are similar to the K-95 patterns described above. The butts customarily have a low hog's back comb and a squared Bavarian-style cheekpiece; the forends have a slight schnabel tip; and skip-line checkering is preferred.

• Bock

Otto Bock of Berlin made sporting rifles embodying Oberndorf-made Mauser actions. Many were chambered for the then-proprietary 9.3x62 cartridge, developed by Bock in about 1905.

• Bornmüller, Simson & Luck

These Suhl-based gunsmiths patented a modification of the 1871-pattern Mauser in 1882. A case magazine, loaded through a hinged flap on the right side of the butt, relied on a spring-lever feed to elevate the cartridges into the chamber. Cartridge capacity seems to have been 11 rounds – five in the magazine, five in the feed tube and one in the chamber. An improved 1884 pattern was essentially similar, but had a 'lazy tongs' multi-lever pantograph-type feeder bar in the butt.

• Brennecke

Wilhelm Brenneke of Leipzig and Berlin was basically a developer of ammunition, his Mauser-type rifles embodying Oberndorf actions. The first guns, made about 1912, chambered a special 8x64 round. A 7x64 Brenneke cartridge was introduced during World War I, followed by a 9.3x64 pattern in 1924. This was chambered in conventional Mauser-type sporters. However, many guns were modified in Brenneke's workshops before being stocked. Typical of the improvements were a raised left receiver wall, an improved floorplate release, and a ball-catch on the receiver to keep the bolt handle shut. The 8x64 cartridge was reintroduced in the late 1950s by W. Brenneke GmbH of Berlin-Schöneberg, descended directly from the pre-1945 company.

• BRENNEKE-MAUSER SPORTING RIFLES

By 1965, Brenneke was offering an assortment of Mauser-action rifles, older versions embodying war-surplus Kar. 98k actions while newer ones used newly-made FN-Mauser patterns. Most of the older guns had the thumb-cut on the left side of the receiver filled and the receiver-side refinished to hide their origins.

THE GUNS

Model 1. Available in 7x64, 8x64S or 30-06, this offered a 26in barrel and weighed about 7.3lb empty. It had a slender stock with a slight hog's back comb, a small round cheekpiece, and a ventilated butt pad. A pistol grip cap and a contrasting forend tip were used. Checkering was hand cut. The sights were usually a hooded ramped blade and a folding leaf, but optical-sight mounts could be encountered on the bridge and on the barrel. Models 1A and 1B had double and single triggers respectively.

Model 2. This was a 'carbine' version of the Model 1, made in 'A' (double trigger) and 'B' (single trigger) subvariants with a 23.6in barrel.

Model 3. Intended as a big-game rifle, this had a 26in or 26.8in barrel and weighed 9.1lb. It chambered 9.3x64 rounds and had a single trigger.

• Büchel

This system, patented by Cuno Büchel in 1887, was unique. The breechblock originally contained the entire lock mechanism, including the hammer and double set triggers. When the operating lever was depressed, the entire block moved radially down around a pivot at the lower front edge of the receiver. The lever was held

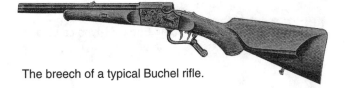

The breech of a typical Buchel rifle.

in its closed position by a distinctive notched-nose catch set into its rearward spur.

By the turn of the century, however, the system had become more compact. Post-1900 rifles, therefore, embodied a shorter action with only the hammer contained within the block. Pivoted to the operating lever, the block moved vertically in the receiver; the trigger system was fitted into the stock behind the receiver and did not move when the lever was depressed.

Büchel rifles were often disguised by brand names 'Tell' or 'Luna'. Most had locking latches on the rearward spur of the operating lever, but looped levers may be found on the largest examples. Rifles may also bear other gunmakers' names, obscuring their origins.

TELL SPORTING RIFLE

Made by Ernst Friedrich Büchel, Suhl, about 1890-1939.
Total production: many thousands. **Chambering options:** a selection of European and American cartridges, with 8.15x46.5R predominating.
Action: locked by an operating lever doubling as the trigger guard propping the breechblock behind the chamber.

DATA FOR A TYPICAL EXAMPLE, ABOUT 1910

Chambering: 5.6x35R, rimmed. 42.3in overall, 8.51lb empty. 26.8in barrel, 4-groove rifling; RH, concentric. Block-and-leaf sight. 2015 fps with 46-grain bullet.

The later rifle of 1910, with a vertically-moving block action, could be mistaken at a glance for an Aydt (q.v.). However, it had a characteristic locking latch on the operating lever spur and a raised wall on the left side of the receiver. The right wall was cut level with the base of the chamber to facilitate loading. A sliding safety catch lay on the tang, behind the cocking-indicator pin. A double set trigger mechanism was standard on these guns, particularly those destined for Schützen competitions. Barrels were invariably octagonal, though half-octagon, round and fluted patterns were also made.

• Burgsmüller

H. Burgsmüller & Söhne of Kreiensen am Harz manufactured sporting rifles and combination guns prior to 1914. Usually built on Oberndorf-made 1898 type actions, the rifles were comparatively conventional; the combination guns, however, were curious-looking weapons with a separate shotgun barrel beneath the rifled pattern. The breech of the shotgun, locked by a lever running forward beneath the forend, swung outward to the left for loading. A separate hammer protruded from the stock alongside the left side of the bolt shroud and was generally fired by the front trigger.

• Chassepot

Though converted some years after the Franco-Prussian War had ended, the unification of the German armies had only just begun. Guns are listed under 'Bavaria', 'Hessen', 'Prussia' and 'Saxony'.

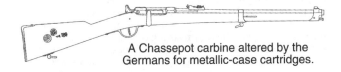

A Chassepot carbine altered by the Germans for metallic-case cartridges.

• Dornheim

G.C. Dornheim of Suhl – one of Germany's principal wholesalers of guns and hunting goods – marketed 'Gecado'-brand Mauser sporters between the wars, but they were invariably made elsewhere. The business was purchased by Albrecht Kind in 1940.

• Dreyse

These sporting rifles owed their existence to the needle guns (Zündnadelgewehre) developed by Johann-Nikolaus Dreyse in the 1830s. The needle guns had been very successful, but their day had passed by 1870.

Franz von Dreyse, the son of Johann-Nikolaus, patented a convertible centerfire version of his father's original bolt-action needle gun (see 'Prussia: Dreyse') in February 1874. Guns of this type are often found in conjunction with a special rifled-chamber liner or *Rotationskammer*, patented in August 1875, which allowed smooth-bore guns to fire cartridges such as the German 11mm Reichspatrone with greater accuracy.

A typical 1874-type Dreyse carbine, probably made for military trials.

Sporting guns were made in the Sömmerda factory from the mid 1870s until the Dreyse assets were purchased by Rheinische Metallwaaren- und Maschinenfabrik (see 'Rheinmetall') in 1901.

SPORTING RIFLE

Made in Sömmerda by Waffenfabrik von Dreyse (about 1875-1900).
Chambering: see text. **Action:** Locked by turning the bolt handle downward until its base abuts the receiver ahead of the bridge.
DATA FOR A TYPICAL EXAMPLE

10.4x42mm, rimmed. 1085mm overall, 3.92kg unladen. 700mm barrel, 5-groove rifling; RH, concentric. Aperture sight on tang, and quadrant sight on barrel. 430m/sec with 17-gram bullet.

The earliest guns shared the general split-bridge 'Z slot' receiver of the perfected needle guns, but had a separate bolt head carrying an extractor claw and a conventional spring-loaded firing pin lay inside the bolt body. Except the earliest transitional models, which had to be cocked separately in the manner of their needle-gun predecessors, Dreyse cartridge rifles cocked automatically as the bolt closed. The handle was usually bent downward into a spatulate form.

A typical sporter had an octagonal barrel held in a straight-wrist half-stock by a transverse key set in small silver-plated escutcheons. The action was lightly engraved and, typical of southern German guns, the trigger guard had a separate horn finger rest instead of a pistol grip. A small quadrant sight appeared on the barrel.

The perfected Dreyse rifles of 1885 had a simplified action, often advertised by less discerning dealers as 'Mauser' or – marginally more realistically – 'Mauser Type'. The resemblance was nothing more than superficial, and then only to the single shot 1871 pattern.

REPEATING RIFLES

Franz von Dreyse patented an unsuccessful bolt-action repeater in 1884. A tube magazine lay beneath the barrel, and the cartridge elevator moved vertically on the tips of sprung pivoting levers forming an 'A' shape.

• DWM

Deutsche Waffen- und Munitionsfabriken AG ('DWM') of Berlin is best known as the maker of Mauser rifles, Maxim machine guns and Parabellum (Luger) pistols. In addition, one toggle-locked automatic rifle survives incomplete in France and German archives are said to contain references to others.

The surviving rifle bears an external resemblance to a gun patented in the U.S. in 1914 by Hugo Borchardt, with the link mechanism connected to the return spring by a short chain, but DWM may also have made another toggle-lock rifle patented in Britain in 1907 by Karl Ebert. Investigative work is still necessary.

• Erma, autoloading type

The rifles of this type are based on the U.S. 30 M1 Carbine; they were apparently developed in the late 1960s to satisfy requests from the U.S., but have since been marketed enthusiastically in Europe. Though they bear a close resemblance to their prototypes externally, the Erma rifles – especially the blowbacks – are quite

different internally. The guns will often be found with the marks of Wischo (Wischo–Wilsker & Co. GmbH of Erlangen), a major German-based distributor.

MODEL 1 CARBINE
EM-1, also known as 'Model 69'?
Made by Erma-Werke GmbH, München-Dachau.
Currently in production. **Chambering:** 22LR rimfire. **Action:** no mechanical breech lock; blowback, semi-automatic only.

35.45in overall, 6.62lb without magazine. 17.7in barrel, 4-groove rifling; RH, concentric. Detachable box magazine, 10 rounds. Ramp-type rear sight graduated to 100m (110yd). 1050 fps with 40-grain bullet.

The EM-1 has a military-style beechwood half-stock with a shallow pistol grip and a forend running forward from the chamber to the single retaining band. The butt is slotted for the sling. An adjustable peep-type sight – graduated for 25m-100m – lies on top of the receiver behind the feed way, and a radial safety lever appears on the right side of the front trigger guard web. Grooves for telescope-sight mount bases are also present on the receiver top.

SIMILAR GUNS

EGM Sport. Distinguished by a black synthetic stock with a thumbhole grip and a textured finish, this was introduced in 1995. It is sometimes identified as the 'EGM-1 Sport' – a designation rightly applied only to the laminated wood-stock version listed below.

EGM-1, sometimes known as 'Model 70'. Mechanically identical with the 22LR EM-1, this lacks the slot cut vertically through the butt. The front sight was an open ramped blade, and swivels lay beneath the butt and forend. Magazines containing 2, 5, 10 and 15 rounds are available to suit individual purchasers or local legislation.

EGM-1 Sport. Introduced in 1995, this is readily distinguished by its laminated wooden stock with a thumbhole grip.

MODEL SG-22 CARBINE
ESG-22
Made by Erma-Werke GmbH, München-Dachau.
Currently in production. **Chambering:** 22 Winchester Magnum rimfire. **Action:** locked by displacing the heel of the breech-bolt downward; gas operated, semi-automatic only.

38in overall, 6.72lb without magazine. 19.3in barrel, 4-groove rifling; RH, concentric. Detachable box magazine, 5 or 12 rounds. Ramp-type rear sight graduated to 100m (110yd). 2015 fps with 40-grain bullet.

This is a modified locked-breech version of the basic blowback action, set in a sporting-style walnut stock. The butt has a low Monte Carlo comb, the forend tip is cut obliquely, the rear sight has been moved forward to the edge of the feed way, and the front sight is a generously ramped blade. Magazines holding five or 12 rounds are regarded as standard.

SIMILAR GUNS

ESGM-1. This is identical with the EM-1, but chambers the 22 Winchester Magnum rimfire cartridge.

ESGM-22. A variant of the EGM-1 in 22 Winchester Magnum rimfire. The stock is usually beech.

An Erma M1-type carbine.

• Erma, bolt-action type

The small caliber rifles made by Erma-Werke of Erfurt were all based on a simple turning-bolt action, locked by seating the base of the bolt handle in its recess. The receiver was cylindrical, with an ejection port placed slightly to the right of the center line of the feed way and the bolt handle track in a similar location. The most distinctive feature was the radial safety catch, which lay on the web at the front of the trigger guard.

MODEL 1 SPORTING RIFLE
Erma-Kleinkaliberbüchse Sportmodell Nr. 1
Made by Erma-Werke, B. Geipel GmbH, Erfurt (about 1930-40).
Total production: not known. **Chambering**: 22 Long Rifle (5.6mm Nr. 6), rimfire. **Action**: locked by turning the base of the bolt handle down into its seat in the receiver.

43.3in overall, 7.06lb empty. 26in barrel, 4 grooves; RH twist, concentric. Single shot only. Tangent-leaf rear sight graduated to 200m (220yd). 1050 fps with 40-grain bullet.

The basic pattern had a walnut half-stock with checkering on the pistol grip and a grasping groove in the side of the forend beneath the rear sight. The sight was graduated for 30-200m (33-220yd). The standard front sight was a barleycorn pattern mounted on a ramp, but other options were available to order. The swivel eyes lay under the forend and butt.

SIMILAR GUNS
Sportmodell Nr. 2. This was a minor variant of Nr. 1, chambering the 22 Extra Long (5.6mm Nr. 7) rimfire cartridge.

Sportmodell Nr. 3. This was apparently a variant of Nr. 2 with an adjustable screw-elevated tangent rear sight (Schraubvisier).

Dioptermodell Nr. 3a. This target shooting adaptation of Nr. 3, apparently also chambered for the 22 Extra Long cartridge, could be fitted with a micro-adjustable diopter sight on the rear of the receiver above the bolt way. It was also often fitted with the standard tangent-type rear sight on the barrel.

Meisterschaftsbüchse Nr. 4. A heavyweight version of Nr. 3, this had checkering on the square-bottom pistol grip and on the sides and underside of the forend. A selection of open sights could be obtained.

Diopter-Meisterschaftsbüchse Nr. 4a. The finest rimfire rifle in the pre-war Erma range, this was a Nr. 4 fitted with a micro-adjustable diopter sight above the bolt way.

MODEL 61 RIFLE
Erma-Gewehr 61, or 'E-61'
Made by Erma-Werke GmbH, München-Dachau, about 1969-85.
Total production: not known. **Chambering**: 22LR rimfire. **Action**: locked by the base of the bolt handle entering its seat in the receiver.

38.2in overall, 4.85lb empty. 19.5in barrel, 4-groove rifling; RH, concentric. Single shot only. Tangent-leaf rear sight graduated to 100m (110yd). 1050 fps with 40-grain bullet.

This was a very basic design, abandoned in the 1980s. The action was set in a hardwood half-stock with a low Monte Carlo comb and a short forend with an obliquely-cut tip. The trigger guard was a simple stamped strip, but grooves for telescope-sight mounting bases were cut in the top of the tubular receiver.

SIMILAR GUNS
Model 62 rifle, about 1969-85. Also known as the 'E-62', this was a minor variant of the E-61 with a detachable five-round box magazine and a weight of about 5.07lb.

MODEL 100 SNIPER RIFLE
SR-100
Made by Erma-Werke GmbH, München-Dachau.
Currently in production. **Chambering options**: 300 Winchester Magnum, 308 Winchester or 338 Lapua Magnum. **Action**: locked by three lugs on the bolt engaging recesses in the bolt handle extension behind the chamber as the bolt handle is turned down, and by the bolt handle base entering its seat.
DATA FOR 338 VERSION

51.4in overall, 15.22lb empty. 29.55in barrel, 6-groove rifling; RH, concentric. Detachable box magazine, 5 rounds. Optical sight. 2965 fps with 250-grain bullet.

The SR-100 is a distinctive design with a 60-degree throw and a readily exchangeable barrel/bolt/magazine unit. The barrel is seated firmly in the receiver by a camming clamp, and the receiver is bedded securely in an aluminum block set into the stock. A multi-adjustable match-quality trigger can be varied from 400gm (14.1oz) to 2kg (4.4lb). The safety lever lies on top of the cocking piece, and a muzzle brake is supplied to reduce the recoil sensation. The thumbhole-grip stock, a wood-laminate type, has an accessory rail beneath a forend pierced with three lateral slots. The cheek-piece and the buttplate are both adjustable, and a retractable monopod is housed in the underside of the butt.

• Erma, lever-action type

The company has been making a limited range of rimfire Winchester facsimiles for many years, but has also been responsible for a copy of the Gallager carbine of the American Civil War period. Work on the replica seems to have been confined to the 1980s and the quantities involved were comparatively small.

MODEL 712 SPORTING RIFLE
Erma-Gewehr 712, 'EG-712'
Made by Erma-Werke GmbH, München-Dachau.
Currently in production. **Chambering**: 22 Short, Long or LR rimfire, interchangeably. **Action**: locked by a strut propped into the underside of the breech-bolt by the tip of the operating lever.
DATA FOR 22 LONG LOADING

35.85in overall, 5.29lb empty. 18.5in barrel, 4-groove rifling; RH, concentric. Tube magazine beneath barrel, 17 rounds. Spring-leaf and elevator rear sight. 1035 fps with 29-grain bullet.

Introduced as the 'Erma Saddle Gun' in 22LR only, this is a simplified rimfire facsimile of the Winchester Model 94 with an exposed hammer and rails machined in the receiver to accept telescope-sight mounting blocks. The straight-wrist butt is made of walnut or beech, and the short forend is held by a single band encircling the barrel. Later versions of the EG-712 can chamber any of the three major rimfire cartridges, magazine capacity being 15 22LR or 21 22 Short rounds.

SIMILAR GUNS
EG-73. A minor variant of the EG-712, this chambers the 22 Winchester Magnum rimfire round. It is 37.4in long, has a 19.3in barrel and weighs 5.5lb empty; magazine capacity is restricted to 10 rounds.

EG-712 deluxe (Luxusmodell). This is the same as the standard gun, apart from an octagonal barrel and fine English-style scroll engraving on the silver-plated receiver.

• Erma, slide-action type
MODEL 722 SPORTING RIFLE
Erma-Gewehr 722, 'EG-722'
Made by Erma-Werke GmbH, München-Dachau, about 1973-88.
Total production: not known. **Chambering**: 22 Short, Long or LR rimfire, interchangeably. **Action**: locked by a strut propped into the underside of the breech-bolt by the tip of the operating lever.
DATA FOR 22 SHORT LOADING

35.85in overall, 5.29lb empty. 17.7in barrel, 4-groove rifling; RH, concentric. Tube magazine beneath barrel, 21 rounds. Spring-leaf and elevator rear sight. 855 fps with 29-grain bullet.

An Erma lever-action rifle.

This was a modified version of the EG-712, with a ribbed slide handle instead of the underlever mechanism; the hardwood butt customarily had a straight wrist. Alternative magazine capacities were 15 22LR or seventeen 22 Long rounds. Sometimes known as the 'EP-722', this slide-action rifle was not as successful as its lever-action equivalent, and seems to have been abandoned in the late 1980s.

• Feinwerkbau

Feinwerkbau–Westinger & Altenburger GmbH & Co. KG of Oberndorf/Neckar are best known for airguns, but successfully diversified into small-bore rifles in the late 1970s. The goal was to provide airguns and cartridge rifles with the same stock design to satisfy multi-discipline marksmen.

MODEL 2000 ISU STANDARD RIFLE
Alternatively known as 'UIT Standard'

Made by Feinwerkbau–Westinger & Altenburger GmbH, Oberndorf/Neckar.

Total production: not known. **Chambering:** 22LR rimfire. **Action:** locked by the bolt handle base turning down in its seat, and by a lug on the bolt handle collar engaging its recess in the receiver.

44.1in overall, 10.8lb with sights. 26.35in barrel, 4-groove rifling; RH, concentric. Single shot only. Adjustable aperture rear sight. 1050 fps with 40-grain bullet.

This was the original small-bore Feinwerkbau, made in a variety of styles. The original stock design, based on the LG300S Match L air rifle, had an angular fixed-comb butt, a vertical pistol grip, a prominent black plastic pistol grip cap (subsequently abandoned) and extensive stippling on the tapering slab-sided forend. The trigger was adjustable, and the buttplate could be slid vertically in its channel. Micro-adjustable competition sights were standard.

SIMILAR GUNS

Model 2000 Junior. This short-barreled lightweight version of the ISU Standard pattern originally had a stepped underside to the forend, though post-1985 guns reverted to a short straight design. M2000 Junior rifles were about 39.5in long, had 22.05in barrels and weighed about 9.25lb with sights.

Model 2000 ISU Universal (or 'UIT Universal'). This was identical with the ISU Standard, but had an adjustable elevating comb instead of the fixed-height type.

Model 2000 ISU Moving Target ('UIT Laufende Scheibe'). Comparatively short lived, this variant could be identified by the very short half-stock with a thumbhole grip, an elevating comb and a wooden shoulder plate. The long barrel had an under-rail for the stipple-finish fore grip and the adjustable sliding weights. Optical sights were obligatory.

Model 2000 Super Match. This was a Free Rifle derivative of the ISU Standard, with a laminated thumbhole stock with an adjustable heel-rest at the base of the grip. The elevating comb was minutely adjustable, and the buttplate was articulated. The slender forend had an accessory rail for the hand stop, a hand rest, and the anchor-block for a stabilizer rod (with sliding weights) which

extended beneath the barrel. Additional movable weights slide along the barrel top above the forend, the back weight being encased in wood. The hand rest could be replaced with a tilting riser block if required. A mechanical trigger mechanism was standard, but could be replaced with a patented electronic pattern. Guns could also be obtained with a true left-hand stock and action.

MODEL 2600 ISU UNIVERSAL RIFLE

This was introduced in 1984 to succeed the 2000 series (q.v.), embodying a simplified action – the safety catch was omitted – and a new laminated wooden stock based on the pioneering Model 600 air rifle. Often made of alternating natural/colored sheets, the stock has a prominent flute running forward from the trigger aperture. The comb could be elevated, the shoulder plate could slide vertically in its channel, and the trigger was a multi-adjustable match pattern.

SIMILAR GUNS

Model 2600 Super Match, 1987-95. A Free Rifle derivative of the standard Model 2600, this could be identified by the elevating comb – which had a squared rear face – and by the articulated-hook shoulder plate. The shallow forend had an accessory rail for a riser block, a universal hand rest, a hand-stop or the stabilizer anchor. The stabilizer bar and its sliding weights extended forward beneath the barrel.

MODEL 2602 ISU UNIVERSAL RIFLE

This is currently the standard Feinwerkbau target rifle, distinguished by a laminated stock (often partly colored) and a prominent flute running forward from the trigger aperture. An elevating comb, an adjustable buttplate and an accessory rail let into the underside of the forend are standard fittings. The trigger is a match pattern, adjustable from 50gm to 180gm, with a shoe which can be altered for length and rake. The streamlined micro-adjustable aperture rear sight is accompanied by a replaceable-element tunnel front sight.

The M2602 is 43.3-44.5in long, depending on butt spacers, weighs about 11lb empty, and has a 26.35in heavy free-floating barrel with an external diameter of .866 (22mm). A heavier .945 (24mm) barrel can be obtained to order, raising weight to 11.7lb. An optional short-barrel system, paired with a weighted barrel sleeve and a new large-diameter front sight, was introduced in 1996.

SIMILAR GUNS

Model 2602 Super Match. Intended for Free Rifle competitions, this shares the Universal action but has an articulated butt-plate hook, a precision-adjustable elevating comb unit, and an adjustable hand rest attached to the accessory rail. It is 47.2-48.5in long – depending on butt spacers – and has an extra-heavy 26.35in barrel; weight averages 13lb without sights. The trigger can be adjusted from 50gm to 180gm (1.8-6.3oz). A short barrel/weight-sleeve combination was offered from 1996 onward.

Model 2602 Sport. Introduced in 1996, this is basically a lightweight Super Match with a short muzzle weight and a slender tapering forend. A hand rest or a riser-block can be fitted to the

The Feinwerkbau Model 2600 Super Match target rifle.

The Model 2602 Universal rifle, with sleeve-type barrel weight and elevating comb.

The Favorit Safari rifle, shown here cocked, is built on a refurbished Mauser action.

accessory rail, and a simplified form of the articulated-hook butt-plate is usually present. The rifles are 48-50in long, and weigh about 12.75lb with a heavy 26.35in barrel; the extra-heavy barrel increases weight to 13.45lb. The stock is usually a natural/red-stained laminate.

• FN-Saive
In the late 1950s, the Federal German authorities acquired about 100,000 FN-made guns for the Bundesgrenzschutz in the days before the army (Bundesheer) was properly re-created. Known as the 'Gewehr 1', these served only until supplies of the Gewehr 3 (made by Rheinmetall and Heckler & Koch) became available in 1959. After a period in store, most of the German FAL-type rifles were sold to Turkey.

• Frankonia
Waffen-Frankonia of Würzburg has handled large numbers of Mauser-pattern sporting rifles, usually built on refurbished 1898-type military actions. The origins of these rifles remain unclear; they were still being offered in the mid 1990s.

FAVORIT SPORTING RIFLE
This gun was being advertised in 1965 in a pistol grip half-stock with a slight hog's back comb and a small round cheekpiece. Available in 243 Winchester, 6.5x57, 7x57, 7x64, 270 Winchester, 30-06, 308 Winchester, 8x57, 8x68S, 9.3x62 or 9.3x64, it had a double-trigger system (within the cramped military-style trigger guard) and a folding-leaf rear sight.

SIMILAR GUNS
Favorit De Luxe. Offered as a 6.2lb 'Leichtmodell' (in 243, 6.5x57, 7x57, 7x64 or 8x57 only) or as a 7.3lb Standardmodell in all the regular chamberings. The lightweight gun had a slender stock with a Monte Carlo comb, a ventilated rubber butt pad, a contrasting square-cut forend tip, and skip-line checkering. The standard rifle had a shallow hog's back comb, a small rounded cheekpiece, a rounded forend and conventional checkering.

Favorit Druckjagd. Distinguished by a rear sight mounted on the tip of a ventilated quarter-rib, this version had a short Stutzen-length barrel in a half-stock.

Favorit Safari. This was similar to the standard gun, except for its single trigger, ventilated rubber shoulder pad and recoil bolt; it was chambered for 8x68S, 375 H&H Magnum, 9.3x62, 9.3x64 or 458 Winchester.

Favorit Stutzen. As the name suggests, this was a short-barreled gun with a full-length 'Mannlicher' stock.

• Gehmann
Walter Gehmann of Karlsruhe (see 'Vom Hofe', below), has made Mauser-type 'Original Vom Hofe' rifles on the basis of actions purchased from Husqvarna. Offered with double triggers, twin lateral recoil bolts and sharply curved pistols grips, the rifles generally had 24.4in or 26.8in barrels and three-cartridge magazines. Chamberings were restricted in 1965 to 5.6x61 Vom Hofe, 7x66 Vom Hofe and 6.5x68 RWS. Gehmann also designed the unique short-action rifle made by Mauser (q.v.).

• Genschow
Gustav Genschow & Co. AG of Berlin, Durlach bei Karlsruhe and Alstadt-Hachenburg sold many Mauser-type sporters in 1920-39. Almost all were made elsewhere, even though Genschow maintained substantial gunsmithing facilities in its principal warehouses. Genschow Mausers often bore nothing but the well-known 'Geco' trademark. The business was eventually acquired by Dynamit Nobel in 1959.

• Gercke
Patented in Germany in 1884 by Karl Gercke of Berlin, and improved in 1886, this was the variant of the Martini tipping breech with a hammer type firing mechanism. The breech was opened by turning a radial lever on the right side of the receiver; mounted on an eccentric plate, the lever dropped the front of the breechblock to cock the hammer and expel a spent case. A new round could be inserted in the chamber manually, and the operating lever was then returned to lift the block behind the chamber.

• Gustloff
This delayed blowback system was credited to engineer Karl Barnitske, head of the Gustloff-Werke small-arms development bureau. It dated from the end of World War II. The action of the VG 1-5 was a sophisticated concept, though its value was reduced by poor construction. Gas was bled from multiple barrel ports into the bolt sleeve, to fill the annular gap between the surface of the barrel and the inside of the barrel casing. The gas then pressed against the bolt-sleeve to oppose the opening stroke of the breech until pressure in the chamber had dropped to a safe level.

MODEL 1-5 PEOPLE'S RIFLE
Volksgerät or Volksgewehr 1-5, 'VG. 1-5'
Made by Gustloff-Werke, Weimar (code 'dfb')?

Total production: a few thousands? **Chambering:** 7.9x33, rimless.
Action: the opening of the breech was opposed by a gas-delay system – see text, above.

34.85in overall, 9.72lb without magazine. 14.85in barrel, 4-groove rifling; RH, concentric. Detachable box magazine, 30 rounds. Folded-strip sight for 100m (110yd). About 2120 fps with standard ball cartridges. No bayonet.

Very little is known about the background of this interesting gun, except that development began in the late summer of 1944 when the Russians began menacing eastern Germany.

The short rifle was very crudely made, with a sheet-steel barrel casing, and the badly shaped butt and forend were riveted to the

The crude VG 1-5 was made towards the end of the Second World War, when time and materials were in short supply.

frame. However, the mechanism worked well enough to handle the 7.9mm Kurz cartridge in reasonable safety – though prone to jamming from heat expansion or excessive fouling.

Small-scale production began in late January 1945, apparently on the initiative of the Gauleiter of Thüringen. Survivors often have marks such as 'Th.1017' stamped or branded into the butt – but none displays the Waffenamt marks that would prove official recognition. Production lasted for no more than a few months.

• Haenel, autoloading type

By 1916, the Germans had realized that neither the standard 8mm rifle cartridge nor the 9mm Parabellum pistol pattern was suited to an 'all-purpose' role.

Experimentation was stopped by Treaty of Versailles, but, by the late 1920s, details of experimental 7.65x27 and 7.65x35 Swiss cartridges, developed in 1919-21, had reached German hands by way of Waffenfabrik Solothurn. In 1933, Rheinisch-Westfälische Sprengstoff AG and Gustav Genschow & Co. AG both produced intermediate cartridges on the basis of the rimmed 8.15x46.5R sporting round. The case length was soon reduced from 1.77-1.81in to 1.57in, and a jacketed spitzer bullet weighing about 75 grains appeared. Genschow was granted an army development contract in 1935.

Experimentation continued until, by 1937, Genschow was using cases measuring 1.46-1.81in and bullets weighing 75-82 grains. Rheinmetall-Borsig's cartridge had a .284 diameter bullet in a 1.44in bottleneck case, and a BKIW/DWM pattern initially had a 1.54in case. However, not one of the prototypes were entirely successful and so the army authorities recruited Polte-Werke of Magdeburg to the development programme in 1939. Progress was soon being made and the 7.9mm 'Kurz-Patrone' (7.9x33) was perfected.

MODEL 42 (H) ASSAULT RIFLE
Maschinenkarabiner 42 (H), 'MKb. 42 (H)'

Made by C.G. Haenel AG, Suhl, 1942-3, with the assistance of sub-contractors.

Total production: a few hundred. **Chambering:** 7.9x33, rimless. **Action:** locked by shoulders on a tilting block engaging the receiver; gas operated, selective fire.

37in overall, 10.74lb empty. 14.35in barrel, 4-groove rifling; RH, concentric. Detachable box magazine, 30 rounds. Tangent-leaf sight graduated to 800m (875yd). 2100 fps with standard ball cartridges; 575±50 rpm. No bayonet (prototypes), or S. 84/98 (finalized design).

By April 1938, Wa-Prüf 2 (the research and development bureau of the Heereswaffenamt) had given Haenel a contract for a selective-fire Maschinenkarabiner chambering Polte's newest cartridge. The gun was designed largely by Hugo Schmeisser, basic work being complete by 1940.

Transforming the Haenel prototype for mass production was entrusted in 1941 to Merz-Werke GmbH of Frankfurt am Main, whose experience with metal stamping, precision casting and spot-welding was unrivalled in Germany. The gas tube lay above the barrel, extending forward almost to the muzzle; and a curved 30-round box magazine lay ahead of the trigger aperture. The rifles fired from an open breech.

In 1942, however, the Heereswaffenamt disrupted progress by altering the basic specifications to include a bayonet lug and provision for a grenade launcher; only 25 guns were delivered in November, and 91 in December. Strenuous efforts were made to solve problems as soon as they arose, and the 500 guns delivered in January 1943 represented a shortfall of only 200. The first full combat trials were apparently undertaken in the Spring by SS Division 'Wiking'. After seeking the troops' opinions personally, Hitler revised his low opinion of the assault rifle concept and ordered the Mkb.42 (H) into production at the expense of the FG. 42 and Gew. 43.

MODEL 43 ASSAULT RIFLE
Maschinenpistole 43, 'MP 43'

Made by C.G. Haenel Waffen- und Fahrradfabrik (code 'fxo'), Suhl, 1943-5; and by Erfurter Maschinenfabrik B. Geipel GmbH 'Erma-Werk' ('ayf'), Erfurt, 1943-5. Mauser-Werke AG ('byf') of Oberndorf and an unidentified company using the code 'sup' made receivers. Lesser contractors included Merz-Werke Gebr. Merz ('cos'), Frankfurt am Main; Württembergische Metallwarenfabrik ('awt') of Geislingen-Steige; J.G. Anschütz Germania Waffenfabrik, Zella-Mehlis; Progress-Werk Wörnlein & Zellhofer ('kqf'), Nürnberg; J.P. Sauer & Sohn ('ce'), Suhl; Erste Nordböhmische Waffenfabrik Adolf Rossler ('fnh'), Niederinseidel; and Lothar Walther Zeug- und Metallwarenfabrik of Zella-Mehlis.

Total production: 325,000 (all types)? **Chambering:** 7.9x33, rimless. **Action:** as MKb. 42 (H), above.

37in overall, 10.85lb empty. 14.35in barrel, 4-groove rifling; RH, concentric. Detachable box magazine, 30 rounds. Tangent-leaf sight graduated to 800m (875yd). 2100 fps with standard ball cartridges; 550±50 rpm. No bayonet.

Though the rival Walther prototype (MKb. 42 [W], q.v.) was lighter, better balanced and more accurate, the simpler Haenel was easier to make in quantity. It was adopted in 1943 once an adaptation of the Walther hammer-fired trigger mechanism had replaced the original striker. The finalized rifle also fired from a closed breech.

The MP. 43 of 1943 was the first weapon of its type to be mass-produced. Relying on an untried sub-contract system, production did not always proceed smoothly; many of the components made by outworkers had to be hand-finished to fit and deliveries were erratic. Its influence on post-war thinking was appreciably greater than the contribution to the campaign history of World War II.

THE GUNS

MP. 43. This had a ball-tipped rod projecting from the gas-port assembly instead of the original extended gas tube.

MP. 43/1. The muzzle of these guns was modified to accept a special grenade launcher (MP. GwGrGt. 43); most other versions had a short muzzle for the Kar. 98k-type launcher. Most MP. 43/1 and some MP. 44 rifles had side-rails accepting the Zf. 4 optical sight or the Zielgerät 1229 'Vampir' night sight.

MP. 44. The basic gun was renamed in 1944 to emphasize the beginning of mass production, though no modifications had been made.

StG. 44. The MP. 44 was eventually renamed 'Sturmgewehr 44' (StG. 44) in recognition of its capabilities. A few guns were even fitted with curved-barrel units (*Krummläufe*), originally designed

The MKb. 42 (H) was the prototype Haenel assault rifle.

for armored-vehicle crews but ultimately developed to fire around street corners. They included the 30-degree 'Vorsatz J', the 40-degree 'Vorsatz J' and the 90-degree 'Vorsatz P'.

StG. 45 (H). Trials of Mauser, Rheinmetall-Borsig and Grossfuss assault rifles, deferred from the previous November, began in January 1945. Haenel submitted the StG. 45 (H) – a greatly simplified MP. 43 – but only one gun survived the war.

• Haenel, bolt-action type

These were modifications of the so-called Commission Rifle action (see 'Reichsgewehr'), which had been made by Haenel in some numbers. The original clip-loading feature was superseded by a patented detachable floorplate magazine which could be loaded with loose rounds.

Haenel is also said to have completed a few Mauser-action sporting rifles immediately after the end of World War I. However, though Haenel had been making Gew. 98 since 1915, no guns could be traced for examination. Haenel sporters usually prove to be pre-1920 variations on the Gew. 88 or the similar 'Improved Model' rifle.

MODEL 1907 RIFLE
Aptierte Haenel-Gewehr M1907

Made by C.G. Haenel, Waffenfabrik, Suhl, 1907-10.

Total production: not known. **Chambering:** 8x57, rimless. **Action:** as Gew. 88 (see 'Reichsgewehr', below).

47.95in overall, 8.53lb empty. 27.95in barrel, 4-groove rifling; RH, concentric. Internal charger-loaded box magazine, 5 rounds. Tangent-leaf sight graduated to 2000m (2185yd). About 2805 fps with S-Patrone. No bayonet in German service?

Apparently developed in 1906-7 for sale to China (q.v.), this rifle had a 1888-type bolt, modified by the addition of a bolt-guide rib and a gas-escape port bored into the bolt body. The lugs locked vertically into the receiver behind the chamber. Stripper-clip guides were machined into the receiver, a clearance cut away was milled out of the left receiver wall, and the bolt handle was turned down against the stock. The Mannlicher-style clip-loaded magazine was replaced by an internal box with Haenel's 1906-patent pivoting floorplate. The bayonet fitting was a 'T'-lug, on an extension of the nose cap, and a boss surrounding the clearing rod.

A few rifles remained in store in Germany when World War I began in 1914. Some were issued for service in their original 6.8mm chambering, but others were modified for the standard 8mm service cartridge. They were probably issued to Landsturm troops or recruiting depots to free Gew. 88 for front-line service; though the Haenel was a better weapon than the Gew. 88, too few guns were available to become regulation issue.

MODEL 1909 SPORTING RIFLE
Haenel-Jagdbüchse M1909

Made by C.G. Haenel, Waffen- und Fahrradfabrik, Suhl, 1909-14.

Total production: 10,000? **Chambering options:** 7x57, 8x57 or 9x57. **Action:** as Gew. 88 (see 'Reichsgewehr', below).

DATA FOR A TYPICAL EXAMPLE

Chambering: 9x57, rimless. 44.1in overall, 6.95lb empty. 22.85in barrel, 4-groove rifling; RH, concentric. Internal box magazine, 5 rounds. Block-and-leaves sight. 1855 fps with 281-grain bullet.

This was simply the 1907-type military rifle in sporting guise, amalgamating a modified 1888-type action with an internal box magazine distinguished by a patented detachable floorplate. However, though Haenel-Mannlichers were perhaps the most efficient of true Gew. 88 derivatives, they were not made in sufficient numbers to challenge the supremacy of Mauser.

THE GUNS

Grade I sporting rifle. It had a walnut pistol grip half-stock, a barleycorn front sight on a matted saddle, and a simple rear sight with a standing block plus a small folding leaf. The metal parts were blacked. The basic rifle cost about 20 per cent less than a comparable Mauser prior to World War I.

The 1909-type Haenel-Mannlicher sporting rifle.

The MP. 43, seen here being examined by a senior British officer, was little more than a perfected form of the MKb. 42. (H)

Grade II sporting rifle. This offered better finish than Grade I, with flat sideplates on the stock alongside the action, a cheek-piece on the butt and an additional set-trigger.

Grade III sporting rifle. These guns were an improvement on Grade II. They had a silver-bead front sight on a long matted-top saddle, and a tangent-leaf sight graduated to 1000m (1095yd).

• Halbe & Gerlich

Halbe & Gerlich (Halger-Waffenfabrik) of Kiel and later Hamburg, made their first Mauser-type rifles about 1923. These chambered the 244 Halger Magnum round, though the range was later enlarged to include 280 Halger Magnum, 30-06, 335 Halger Belted Magnum, 375 H&H Magnum and 404 Rimless Nitro Express. The rifles were essentially similar to the standard Oberndorf Mauser sporters of the period between the wars, though they were often made with half-octagonal barrels and had a mount for an optical sight set forward on the barrel ahead of the receiver ring. Their claim to fame lay in chamberings.

• Heckler & Koch

Heckler & Koch was acquired in the 1990s, first by the British Royal Ordnance plc and then by British Aerospace after the German government had withdrawn support from the caseless-cartridge G11 project. At the time of writing, production of the 5.56mm HK series had been moved to the Royal Ordnance factory in Nottingham, where it is continuing alongside the British SA-80/L85 rifle (see **'Britain: Enfield, autoloading type'**), but the future is still not clear.

The Heckler & Koch-made versions of the CETME – the 7.62mm G3 and the 5.56mm HK33/G41 series – have been outstandingly successful. Though they lack the cam-assisted extraction of a well-designed rotating-bolt lock, a fluted chamber reduces the problem to manageable proportions. As the roller-lock is symmetrical, and stresses in the action are balanced, the G3 is regarded as very accurate.

In addition to the many guns listed below, the Bundeswehr (and some police units) have used modified 7.62mm HK11 and HK11E 'rifles' under the designations G8 and G8A1. Though sometimes used in a sniping role, owing to their heavy barrels, they are regarded here as light machine guns – the G8, indeed, can be belt fed.

BACKGROUND

A promising trial of the Spanish CETME (q.v.) rifle was undertaken in Germany in 1955. After an abortive variant had been produced for a short 7.62mm round, the rifle was revised for the U.S. 30 T65 cartridge (later 7.62x51 NATO) and the German defense ministry ordered about 400 for trials in 1956 – apparently through Heckler & Koch, though the guns were made in Spain. Tests were satisfactory, but many changes were requested and the finalized German gun (differing considerably from its Spanish prototype) fired from a closed bolt at all times.

An early 7.62mm G3A3 rifle with a first-generation Zeiss intensifier sight.

In 1958, the license granted by CETME to the Dutch NWM organization was transferred to Heckler & Koch; after gaining extensive experience of the rifle by supplying machine tools to facilitate its production, H&K had become keen to enter the arms-making industry.

MODEL 3 AUTOMATIC RIFLE
Gewehr 3

Made by Heckler & Koch GmbH & Co., Oberndorf/Neckar, and by contractors in many other countries.

Total production: not known, but undoubtedly several millions. **Chambering:** 7.62x51 NATO. **Action:** the opening of the breech is delayed by rollers engaging the barrel-collar walls; gas operated, selective fire.
DATA FOR A TYPICAL G3A3

40.15in overall, 9.68lb with magazine. 17.7in barrel, 4- or 6-groove rifling; RH, polygonal. Detachable box magazine, 20 rounds. Rear sight: see notes. 2590 fps with NATO ball cartridges; 550±50 rpm. G3 knife bayonet (optional).

Sufficient 'B'-type CETME rifles were purchased in Spain to permit Bundeswehr field trials to begin on 1959. The first-pattern German derivative of the Spanish design was approved for service in 1960, replacing the Gewehr 1 (FAL). It had a rocking-'L' rear sight (*Klappvisier*), a bipod and a folding carrying handle.

A modified G3 was adopted in 1963, with a drum sight (*Drehvisier*) which rotated around its axis – markedly forward of vertical – to present a 100m (110yd) notch or apertures for 200m-400m (220-435yd) ahead of the firer's eye. The bipod and carrying handle were abandoned.

The G3 was made largely of pressings and stampings, but was undoubtedly sturdy and durable. It had a conventional fixed butt and a sheet metal forend with ventilating slots. The folding cocking handle lay above the forend on the left side of the bolt-extension tube. A magazine protruded beneath the receiver, the release catch appearing between the back of the magazine and the front of the trigger guard bow, and a radial selector lever lay above the pistol grip. Most pre-1975 guns were marked 'S' (top), '1' (middle) and 'F' (bottom) for safety, single shots, and fully automatic fire respectively, the markings being repeated on the right side of the receiver where an engraved line on the selector spindle indicated the fire-state.

The designation and the maker's mark lay on the left side of the magazine housing, ahead of the serial number – e.g., 'G3 HK 20472' – and above the date of acceptance ('5/62' for May 1962). The right side of the housing dis-

A Bundeswehr soldier on maneuvers carries a G3A4 rifle.

played the dates on which the gun was rebuilt, generally at intervals of about five years. Most markings reveal the work to have been undertaken by Heckler & Koch, though some was done by army ordnance depots. Guns made for the West Berlin police were marked 'MAS' to avoid infringing agreements preventing distribution of German-made guns in Berlin.

SIMILAR GUNS

G3A1. Delayed by prolonged trials, this was not formally approved until October 1963. The retractable butt slid in grooves pressed into the sides of the receiver and was locked by a catch under the special receiver cap. The rifle measured about 31.5in with the stock retracted, and weighed 10.23lb with an empty magazine.

G3A2. This variant was approved in June 1962. The principal change seems to have been the advent of a free-floating barrel, improving accuracy. Many older guns were rebuilt to G3A2 standards during overhaul and had an additional 'FS' mark on the left side of the magazine housing beneath the original date of manufacture.

G3A3. Adopted in December 1964, this had a solid synthetic butt (cf., G3A4 below). Changes had been made in the design of the front sight, and a modified flash-suppressor/muzzle brake was approved to fire NATO standard grenades.

A three-round burst mechanism was developed in 1968, though generally omitted from the German service rifles. The burst-fire capability was usually added to the selector levers, giving a fourth position, but was sometimes substituted for the autofire option. Changes were made in 1974 to simplify the pistol grip, the forend and the selector lever. Additional changes were made in 1986, when synthetic butt/pistol grip sub-frames and ambidextrous safety catches were adopted. The safety mark became a white diagonal cross superimposed on a white bullet in a rectangular border; single shot fire was indicated by a red bullet, three-shot bursts by three red bullets, and fully automatic operation by seven red bullets.

G3 Zf. Some otherwise standard rifles, selected for accuracy, have been sold as sniper's weapons under this designation (Zf., *Zielfernrohr* or 'telescope sight'). They are uncommon.

G3A4. This, adopted simultaneously with the G3A3, had a retractable butt.

G3A5, G3A6 and G3A7. These were special versions developed for Denmark, Iran and Turkey respectively. Details will be found in the appropriate sections.

G3 SG/1. This sniper rifle supplemented the otherwise-standard G3 Zf. (q.v.) in 1973. SG/1 rifles were built on actions which had shown exemplary accuracy during test-firing, and had a special set-trigger system. This could only be used with the selector lever set to 'E', whereupon the small blade protruding ahead of the pistol grip was pressed to 'set' the front trigger. The adjustable pull could be set as low as 2.75lb, compared with 5.7lb if the setting mechanism was not used; the rifle could be fired simply by pressing the conventional trigger lever. If the selector lever was moved after the mechanism had been set, but before a shot was fired, the system reverted to normal operation. Most G3 SG/1 rifles had a bipod, an auxiliary cheekpiece, and a Zeiss 1.5-6x optical sight.

G3 TGS. Dating from 1985, the G3 Tactical Group System ('TGS') featured an HK79 grenade launcher instead of the standard forend/handguard assembly. Unladen gun weight rose to about 11.9lb. The auxiliary trigger lay on the left side of the HK79 frame above the barrel, and a ladder-pattern grenade-launching sight was fitted on the receiver top – subsequently replaced by a radial drum on the forend. The breech of the single shot launcher dropped open after it had been unlatched, though the striker had to be cocked manually.

G3 INKAS. Announced in 1987, this was offered with fixed or retractable butts. The rifles had an integral infra-red laser sighting system used in conjunction with Philips Elektro-Spezial BM-8028 image intensifying goggles. Built into the cocking handle tube, the laser projector was controlled by a switch behind the front sight.

MODEL 32 AUTOMATIC RIFLE
Gewehr HK32

Made by Heckler & Koch GmbH & Co., Oberndorf/Neckar.

Total production: not known. **Chambering:** 7.62x39 M43, rimless. **Action:** as G3, above.

DATA FOR A TYPICAL HK32A2

36.2in overall, 8.05lb with magazine. 15.35in barrel, 6-groove rifling; RH, polygonal. Detachable box magazine, 20, 30 or 40 rounds. Drum sight graduated to 400m (435yd). 2360 fps with Soviet PS ball cartridges; 600±25 rpm. H&K knife bayonet (optional).

Though a few CETME rifles had been made for the Soviet 7.62mm intermediate cartridge in the late 1950s, apparently for trials undertaken by NATO in Europe, some years passed before Heckler & Koch offered similar weapons. Introduced in 1965, the HK32 was a diminutive G3 with a checkered plastic forend/handguard.

SIMILAR GUNS

HK32A2, 1965-82? This was a fixed-butt pattern.

HK32A3, 1965-82? A retractable-stock version of the basic rifle, this was about 37in overall, or 28.75in with the stock retracted. It weighed 8.8lb.

HK32KA1, 1967-82? Based on the HK32A3, this variant had the barrel shortened to 12.65in. Fixed or retractable-butt guns were available to order. The latter measured 34.05in overall – 26.4in with the butt retracted – and weighed 8.69lb with an empty twenty-round magazine. It would not accept a bayonet, owing to minimal protrusion of the barrel from the forend, and muzzle velocity declined to about 2175 fps.

MODEL 33 AUTOMATIC RIFLE
Gewehr HK33

Made by Heckler & Koch GmbH & Co., Oberndorf/Neckar.

Total production: not known. **Chambering:** 5.56x45. **Action:** as G3, above.

DATA FOR A TYPICAL HK33A3

37in overall (28.75in with stock retracted), 8.73lb with empty 20-round magazine. 15.35in barrel, 6-groove rifling; RH, polygonal. Detachable box magazine, 20, 30 or 40 rounds. Drum sight graduated to 400m (435yd). 3150 fps with M193 ball cartridges; 600±25 rpm. H&K knife bayonet (optional).

Inspired by the appearance of the AR-15 (M16) rifle, Heckler & Koch modified the G3 action in 1963 to produce a small caliber prototype; the first series-made HK33 rifles were released in 1965. They were externally similar to the HK32 (above), but chambered the standard U.S. 5.56mm cartridge.

SIMILAR GUNS

HK33A2. The standard fixed-butt rifle was 36.2in overall and weighed 7.95lb with an empty magazine.

HK33A3. This was simply a retractable-butt variant of the HK33A2, mechanically identical with its prototype.

HK 33 Zf. Based on the HK33A2, this was a selected (but otherwise standard) rifle with an optical sight. It has been touted with only limited success.

HK33KA1. This short-barreled gun appeared in 1967, generally accompanied by a retractable butt. A fixed butt was optional, but compromised the compactness gained by shortening the barrel. The HK33KA1 shared the dimensions of the HK32KA1 (q.v.), but weighed 8.5lb with an empty magazine.

HK33E. The original HK33, successful enough to attract limited military interest, developed into the improved 33E pattern in 1983. By 1985, the HK33E had gained a synthetic pistol grip sub-frame. The improved ambidextrous safety catch/selector system incorporated a three-shot burst-fire mechanism.

HK33EC A2. This was a fixed-butt gun with a special forest green camouflage finish, introduced to minimize heat-absorption at high temperatures.

HK33ES A2. A version of the EC A2 pattern with a two-tone desert sand camouflage finish.

HK33EC A3. Mechanically identical with the EC A2 gun, this was distinguished by its retractable butt.

HK33ES A3. An ES A2 with a retractable butt.

HK33KC and HK33KS. These were short-barreled retractable-stock guns with forest green and desert sand camouflage respectively.

The 5.56mm HK33A2 rifle, the first-generation of Heckler & Koch's small-caliber/high velocity rifles.

The retractable-butt HK33A3.

MODEL 36 AUTOMATIC RIFLE
Gewehr HK36

Made by Heckler & Koch GmbH & Co., Oberndorf/Neckar.
Total production: very few. **Chambering:** 4.56x36, rimless. **Action:** as G3, above.

35in overall, 6.33lb without magazine. 14.95in barrel, 4-groove rifling; RH, polygonal? Detachable box magazine, 30 rounds. Collimator sight for 300m (330yd). 2560 fps with ball cartridges; 1100±50 rpm. No bayonet.

Revealed in 1971, this experimental lightweight rifle fired a cartridge which had been developed jointly by CETME and Heckler & Koch in 1967-8. An asymmetrical tungsten-carbide bullet core was intended to compensate for the reduction in hitting power. The rifle embodied the standard roller-locked delayed blowback action, but was much lighter than the HK33. The slender barrel protruded from the forend, all furniture being synthetic. A fixed-power collimator sight was contained within the carrying handle, a Betalight source providing illumination in poor light.

Many of the earliest guns had detachable box magazines, but later examples had fixed boxes with hinged covers. Fixed or telescoping butts were provided, most weapons having burst-firing capabilities (two to five rounds, depending on pattern) in addition to normal selective fire. The small caliber trials were abandoned in the mid 1970s, after encouraging progress had been made with the G11 and its consumable cartridge.

MODEL 41 AUTOMATIC RIFLE
Gewehr 41

Made by Heckler & Koch GmbH & Co., Oberndorf/Neckar.
Total production: not known. **Chambering:** 5.56x45mm, rimless. **Action:** as G3, above.

DATA FOR A TYPICAL G41

39.25in overall, 9.04lb with magazine. 17.7in barrel, 6-groove rifling; RH, polygonal. Detachable box magazine, 30 rounds. Drum sight graduated to 400m (435yd). 3150 fps with M193 ball cartridges; 825±50 rpm. H&K knife bayonet (optional).

Introduced in 1983 to replace the HK33, this incorporated a mechanical hold-open and a bolt-closing device on the right side of the action inspired by the M16A1. The ejection port was fitted with a hinged cover, the magazine attachment and optical-sight mounts were altered to conform with NATO standards, and Tritium sight inserts were fitted. The guns were designed for a minimum life of 20,000 rounds. Retractable-butt rifles were 38.75in overall and weighed 9.48lb.

The major component-groups of the G41.

New synthetic butt/pistol grip sub-frames were adopted in 1986, together with an ambidextrous safety catch. The safety mark became a white diagonal cross superimposed on a white bullet; single shot fire was indicated by a red bullet, three-shot bursts by three red bullets, and fully automatic operation by seven red bullets.

SIMILAR GUNS

G41K. This was a short-barrel derivative, overall length being about 5.1in less than the standard weapons.

G41 TGS. Announced in 1985, this was fitted with a 40mm HK79 grenade launcher beneath the forend. The oldest guns had a ladder-pattern auxiliary sight on top of the receiver, in front of the standard drum, but this was soon replaced by a radial sight on the right side of the forend.

G41K TGS. This was simply a short-barreled rifle fitted with the TGS system described previously.

G41 INKAS. Similar to the similarly named G3 variant (q.v.), this rifle had an integral infra-red laser projector in the cocking-handle tube. The projector was used in conjunction with Philips Elektro-Spezial BM 8028 goggles. Guns will be found with fixed or retractable butts.

G41K INKAS. This was simply a combination of the standard short-barrel rifle and the electro-optical sighting system.

MODEL 1 PRECISION SNIPER RIFLE
Präzisions-Scharfschützengewehr 1, 'PSG-1'

Made by Heckler & Koch GmbH & Co., Oberndorf/Neckar.
Total production: not known. **Chambering:** 7.62x51 NATO, rimless. **Action:** as G3, above.

The 5.56mm G41 replaced the HK33 in Heckler & Koch's product range.

The G41TGS had an integral grenade launcher and a ladder-type auxiliary rear sight.

The PSG-1 is among the leading semi-automatic sniping rifles.

47.55in overall, 17.85lb without magazine. 25.6in barrel, 4-groove rifling; RH, concentric. Detachable box magazine, 5, 10 or 20 rounds. Optical sight. 2675 fps with SS77 ball cartridges. No bayonet.

Introduced in 1985, this G3 derivative had a butt with a detachable saddle-type cheekpiece (similar to those found on H&K light machine guns) and a shoulder-plate adjustable for length and rake. The separate anatomical walnut pistol grip had an adjustable palm rest. A special heavy-weight barrel was used, though the standard G3 action was limited to semi-automatic fire. Special attention to the trigger gave a smooth 3.3lb pull. Mounted and adjusted as an integral part of the weapon, the 6x42 optical sight had an illuminated range-finding reticle graduated for 100-600m (110-655yd).

MODEL 3 MILITARY SNIPER RIFLE
Militär-Scharfschützengewehr 3, 'MSG-3'
Made by Heckler & Koch GmbH & Co., Oberndorf/Neckar.
Total production: not known. **Chambering:** 7.62x51mm NATO, rimless.
Action: as G3, above.
DATA FOR A TYPICAL EXAMPLE

43.3in overall, 11.68lb without magazine. 19.7in barrel, 4-groove rifling; RH, concentric. Detachable box magazine, 5 or 20 rounds. Drum sight graduated to 400m (435yd). 2625 fps with NATO cartridges. No bayonet.

Built from 1988 onward on the basis of specially selected G3 actions restricted to semi-automatic fire, these had specially honed (but otherwise standard) triggers. Bolt-closing devices were fitted to reduce cocking noise. Developed specifically for the Bundeswehr and German police, the MSG-3 had a standard barrel, an adjustable comb and buttplate, a fixed-leg bipod, and conventional open sights.

SIMILAR GUNS
MSG-90. This was a variant of the MSG-3 with a heavyweight barrel and a bipod with adjustable legs. About 45.85in overall, it weighed 14.1lb. The drum sight was customarily omitted.

MODEL R3 AUTOMATIC RIFLE
Gewehr R3
Made by Heckler & Koch GmbH & Co., Oberndorf/Neckar.
Chambering: 5.56x45mm, rimless. **Action:** as G3, above.
DATA FOR A TYPICAL GR3C A2

36.2in overall, 8.65lb with empty magazine. 15.35in barrel, 6-groove rifling; RH, polygonal. Detachable box magazine, 20, 30 or 40 rounds. Optical sight. 3150 fps with M193 ball cartridges; 600±25 rpm. H&K knife bayonet (optional).

Adapted from the HK33/G41 series in the mid 1980s, and introduced in 1988, these guns had simple 1.5x optical sights – adjustable for elevation and windage – on a permanent receiver top mount. Most of the dimensions paralleled the HK33 equivalents, though GR3 patterns were all about 10oz heavier.

THE GUNS
GR3C A2. This was the basic fixed-butt rifle, with forest-green camouflage on the receiver and forend.
GR3S A2. Mechanically identical with the GR3C version, this had a desert sand camouflage finish.

GR3C A3. Similar to the A2 pattern, this had a retractable butt and forest-green finish.
GR3S A3. A variant combining a retractable butt and desert sand camouflage.
GR3KC. This was a straightforward amalgamation of a short barrel, a retractable stock, and forest green camouflage.
GR3KS. Identical with the GR3KC pattern in all respects except coloring, this was given desert sand camouflage.

MILITARY USERS
Heckler & Koch rifles – particularly those made in Germany, Britain and France – have achieved a truly worldwide distribution. In addition to the countries considered individually (Burma, Britain, Denmark, France, Iran, Norway, Pakistan, Sweden) the following have been identified:

Bahrain: G3A3 (H&K).
Bangladesh: G3A2 (Pakistani surplus) and G3A3 (H&K).
Bolivia: G3A3 (H&K).
Brunei: G3A3 (H&K).
Chad: G3A3 (H&K).
Chile: 500 HK33 from Heckler & Koch in 1975.
Colombia: 30,000 G3 delivered from Heckler & Koch in the early 1970s.
Dominican Republic: G3A3 (H&K).
Eire: HK33 (H&K).
El Salvador: about 2500 HK33 from Heckler & Koch in the early 1970s.
Gabon: G3A3 (MAS).
Ghana: about 12,000 G3 and G3A1 rifles supplied by Heckler & Koch prior to 1965, and an unknown quantity of HK33 rifles (supplied from Enfield?).
Guyana: G3 (H&K).
Haiti: G3A4 (H&K).
Indonesia: G3 (H&K, Rheinmetall) and G3A1 (Heckler & Koch) prior to 1965, plus G3 SG/1 (H&K).
Italy: G3 SG/1 (H&K) for police, carabinieri and special forces only.
Ivory Coast: G3A3 (MAS).
Kenya: 20,000 G3A3 supplied from Enfield in the 1970s.
Lebanon: G3A3 (MAS). HK33 from MAS and Enfield in the early 1970s, for police and the presidential guard.
Liberia: a few G3 and G3A1 supplied by Heckler & Koch prior to 1965.
Malawi: G3A3 (H&K).
Malaysia: G3 SG/1 (H&K). About 50,000 HK33 from Heckler & Koch in the early 1970s.
Mauritania: G3A3 (MAS).
Morocco: G3A3 (MAS).
Niger: G3A3 (MAS).
Nigeria: G3A3 and G3A4 (Enfield).
North Yemen: G3A3 (Saudi Arabian).
Paraguay: G3 and G3A3 (H&K).
Portugal: HK33 (assembled by FBP from H&K parts?).
Qatar: G3A3 (Enfield).
Senegal: G3A3 and HK33A1 (MAS).
Sudan: G3, G3A3 and G3A4 (H&K).

The HK270 rifle.

The HK940 rifle.

Tanzania: G3A3 and HK33 (Enfield?).
Thailand: about 30,000 HK33, assembled from German-made parts in the 1970s.
Uganda: G3 and G3A3 (provenance unknown).
United Arab Emirates: G3A3 (Enfield or Saudi Arabian) used in Sharjah, Dubai and Abu Dhabi.
Upper Volta: G3A3 (MAS).
Zaire: G3A3 (probably Enfield).
Zambia: G3A3 (Enfield).

SPORTING GUNS

The HK-91, derived from the HK33, was limited to semi-automatic fire and had a recoil pad on the butt. Optional small-capacity magazines were offered to non-military purchasers.

SL-6 SPORTING RIFLE

Made by Heckler & Koch GmbH & Co., Oberndorf/Neckar.
Total production: 10,000-15,000? **Chambering:** 5.56x45. **Action:** as G3 rifle, above.

39.95in overall, about 7.72lb empty. 17.7in barrel, 6-groove rifling; RH, polygonal. Detachable box magazine (see notes). Drum sight graduated to 400m (435yd). 3200 fps with M193 ball cartridges.

The first of these guns were made in the mid 1970s, apparently to fulfill a 25,000-gun order from police in Colombia (subsequently aborted). They had a three-quarter stock with a handguard above the barrel. A barred plate was let into the left side of the butt to retain a sling; and a radial safety lever appeared in the left side of the stock above the trigger guard. Magazines holding two rounds were intended for the West German sporting market, though 10-round patterns were available for export.

SIMILAR GUNS

SL-7. This was a variant of the SL-6 chambered for the 7.62x51 NATO round. The two patterns were almost identical externally, and are very difficult to tell apart.

HK770 SPORTING RIFLE

Made by Heckler & Koch GmbH & Co., Oberndorf/Neckar.
Total production: not known. **Chambering options:** 270 Winchester or 308 Winchester. **Action:** as G3 rifle, above.
DATA FOR A 308 EXAMPLE

44.5in overall, 8.05lb empty. 17.7in barrel, 6-groove rifling; RH, polygonal. Detachable box magazine (see notes). Folding-leaf sight. 2675 fps with ball cartridges.

Introduced commercially in 1978, these similar-looking guns share squared trigger guard/magazine floorplates, multi-slot muzzle brakes, and a folding cocking handle on the right side of

the investment-cast receiver. Radial safety levers were set into the left side of the stock, the magazine catch appearing in the front of the trigger guard.

The fine-quality walnut stocks had pistol grips, hog's back combs and squared cheekpieces. Cut checkering usually graced the pistol grip and forend, but some guns have been highly decorated. Swivels lay under the butt. Standard German-market magazines contain only two rounds, though three- and nine-round patterns have been made for export purposes.

THE GUNS

HK270. The smallest of these H&K sporting rifles, this simple blowback is chambered for the 22 LR rimfire cartridge. The magazine customarily holds two rounds, though 5- and 20-round options are available.

HK300. Essentially similar to the HK270—except for the better stock and cheekpiece-style butt—this is chambered for 22 Winchester Magnum rimfire ammunition.

HK630. Chambered for 223 Remington cartridges, this was 42.15in overall and weighed 7.05lb. The magazine usually holds two rounds, though four- and 10-round options have been offered.

HK770. This rifle has been offered only in 270 Winchester and 308 Winchester chamberings. Data are given in the table above.

HK940. Available only in 30-06, this weighed 8.6lb and measured 47.25in overall, though short-barrel variants have also been offered in small numbers.

• Heinemann

The Selbstladegewehre ('self-loading rifles') Rh. 28 and Rh. 29 were designed by Karl Heinemann for Rheinmetall. They had distinctive lateral toggle-locks on the right rear of the receiver, box magazines protruding from the left side of the receiver, and Bang-type muzzle cups to trap and divert propelling gases onto the actuating rod. At least 50 were made in a variety of shapes and sizes, some in military guise and others masquerading as sporters – probably for presentation purposes. At least one rifle was recovered from German 'last-ditch' forces at the end of World War II. The toggle-lock was far too complicated and too expensive to make for military service, particularly at a time when the first gas-operated rifles were being perfected.

The SL-6 rifle.

• Heym, block-action type

MODEL 550 COMBI DOUBLE RIFLE

Made by Friedrich Wilh. Heym GmbH & Co., Gleichamberg.

Chambering: not announced at the time of writing. **Action:** locked by tenons on the separate breechblock sliding in grooves on the barrel block.

DATA FOR A TYPICAL EXAMPLE

9.3x74R, rimmed. About 40.5in overall, about 7.7lb empty. 23.6in barrel, 4-groove rifling; RH, concentric? Double barrel, two shots. Open rear sight. 2460 fps with 247-grain bullet.

Announced in 1996, for delivery in 1997, this gun is a fascinating combination of the traditional break-open breech and a dropping-block action. Pulling down on the lever that doubles as a trigger guard pivots the locking block away from the standing breech until it releases the barrel-block to drop downward.

The Combi has a pivoting 'clasp'-type safety lever set into the underside of the pistol grip, in addition to a sliding button on the tang. The butt has a slight hog's back comb, accompanied by a squared Bavarian-style cheekpiece, and hand-cut checkering appears on the pistol grip and forend.

The basic Combi can be obtained with a shotgun or rifled barrel uppermost. The bottom barrel, which is readily exchangeable, is invariably a rifle – a separate fixed 'double smooth-bore' unit is available to convert the Combi to a conventional shotgun. This form of modular construction allows the owner to create a double-barrel rifle either with two barrels of the same caliber (550B) or two which differ (to form a Bergstutzen or '550BS').

SIMILAR GUN

Model 550BS Combi ('Bergstutzen'). This is little more than a two-caliber version of the Model 550. The larger-caliber rifle barrel is always uppermost – e.g., 9.3x74R, above 5.6x52R or 22 Hornet.

• Heym, bolt-action type

Established in Suhl in 1865, Heym made sporting guns until the end of World War II, the company's reputation being firmly established when the first hammerless three-barrel rifle-shotgun (*Drilling*) was patented in Germany in 1891. Production of sporting guns resumed after World War I had ended, continuing with scarcely an interruption until 1945. Operations were subsequently re-established in the small Bavarian town of Münnerstadt, where the first post-war firearms were made in 1952, but a move back to Gleichamberg in Thüringen occurred in 1996.

Heym made classical Mauser-type sporters for many years. The oldest were based on refurbished wartime actions, though later examples used FN-Mauser actions. Heym then made modified rifles for Mauser (q.v.) before progressing to the SR-20 series. Recent large-caliber rifles have reverted to traditional Mauser actions.

MODEL 20 SPORTING RIFLE
Usually known as 'SR 20'

Made by Friedr. Wilh. Heym GmbH & Co., Münnerstadt.

Currently in production. **Chambering options:** see text, below. **Action:** locked by two lugs on the bolt head engaging the receiver wall as the bolt handle turns down.

DATA FOR A TYPICAL SR 20N

Chambering: 7x57, rimless. 44.5in overall, 7.05lb empty. 24in barrel, 4-groove rifling; RH, concentric. Internal box magazine, 5 rounds. Folding-leaf sight. 2625 fps with 162-grain bullet.

The termination of the agreement with Mauser-Jagdwaffen (q.v.) left Heym with a substantial quantity of parts for the Mauser Model 3000, 3000 Magnum and 4000 rifles. Heym's management decided to continue work, creating the 'SR 20' series after a few changes had been made. The safety catch was moved from the bolt shroud to the receiver immediately behind the bolt handle, where it could be thumbed back to safe and pushed forward to fire; a third (central) position locked the bolt shut.

THE GUNS

SR 20 Alpine, 1989-95. Replacing the SR 20L, this was minor adaption of the Trophy pattern, with a 20.05in barrel and a full-length Mannlicher-style stock with a steel forend cap.

SR 20 Classic, 1984-95. Introduced in the same chambering options as the 20N and 20G, and renamed 'Classic Sportsman' in 1989, the Classic had a straight-comb butt, a rounded forend tip and a shallower pistol grip. Engraving was applied to order.

SR 20 Classic Safari, 1990-5. Built on the longest Heym action, this has been chambered for 404 Jeffrey, 425 Express or 458 Winchester Magnum. It had a 24in barrel and a three-leaf Express rear sight; recoil bolts appeared beneath the chamber and through the pistol grip. The forend tip was joined to the stock vertically, but lacked the accompanying spacer; the butt was a classically styled straight-comb pattern with little drop at the heel.

SR 20D, 1988-93? Intended for snap-shooting, the Drückjagd-büchse had a short barrel and a ventilated quarter-rib.

SR 20F ('Fiberglas'), 1988-95. This had a classically-styled brown or black synthetic stock, but was identical mechanically with the standard SR 20N described below.

SR 20G, 1975 to date. These guns were originally chambered only for 6.5x68S, 7mm Remington Magnum, 8x68S, 300 Winchester Magnum and 375 H&H Magnum ammunition. Their barrels measured 25.6in, making them longer and slightly heavier than the SR 20N.

The SR 20G was still in production in 1997, when the list of chamberings had grown greatly – 22-250 Remington, 6x62 Frères, 243 Winchester, 25-06, 6.5x55, 6.5x57, 6.5x64 Brenneke, 6.5x65 RWS, 6.5x68, 270 Winchester, 7x57, 7x64, 7mm Remington Magnum, 30-06, 300 Winchester Magnum, 308 Winchester, 8x57, 8x64S, 8x68S, 8.5x63 Rebated, 338 Winchester Magnum, 9.3x62, 9.3x64, 9.5x66SE, 375 H&H Magnum and 10.3x60R.

SR 20L, about 1977-89. This had a 20.05in barrel and a full-length Mannlicher-style stock. It was available in all regular calibers except 9.3x62.

SR 20M, 1988-95. This single shot Match rifle – destined for competition shooting – was offered only in 6.5x55 or 308 Winchester. The SR 20M had a near-vertical pistol grip and a beavertail forend; it weighed about 9.5lb without sights, and was about 44.5in long.

SR 20N, 1975 to date. This was the original standard sporting rifle, built on right- or left-hand actions. It had a Monte Carlo half-stock with a rosewood pistol grip cap and a schnabel pattern forend tip. Chamberings were originally restricted to 5.6x57, 243 Winchester, 6.5x55, 6.5x57, 270 Winchester, 7x57, 7x64, 30-06 Springfield, 308 Winchester and 9.3x62. By 1997, however, it was being offered in a much wider range of options (see SR 20G, above).

SR 20 Trophy, 1989-95. This had a distinctive quarter-rib on an octagonal barrel measuring 22.05in for standard chamberings or

The SR20M rifle.

The SR20N rifle.

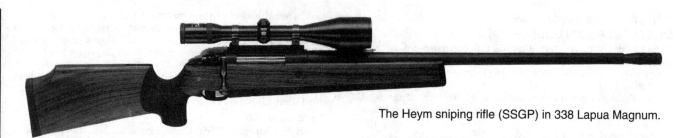

The Heym sniping rifle (SSGP) in 338 Lapua Magnum.

24in for the magnums. The front swivel was attached to the barrel ahead of the forend tip.

SR 40. Chambered only for 222 Remington, 223 Remington or 5.6x50 Magnum, this was a short-action version of the SR 20. Made with a 24in barrel, it was about 43.9in long and weighed 6.5-6.7lb. It was abandoned in 1995.

MODEL 30 SPORTING RIFLE
Usually known as 'SR 30'
Made by Friedr. Wilh. Heym GmbH & Co., Gleichamberg.
Currently in production. **Chambering options:** 243 Winchester, 270 Winchester, 30-06, 308 Winchester, 6x62 Frères, 6.5x55, 6.5x57, 6.5x65 RWS, 7x57, 7x64, 8x57, 8x64 or 9.3x62. **Action:** locked by six bearing balls in the bolt head engaging the receiver wall as the bolt is pushed forward.
DATA FOR A TYPICAL EXAMPLE
   Chambering: 9.3x62, rimless. 44.5in overall, 7.05lb empty. 23.6in barrel, 4-groove rifling; RH, concentric. Detachable box magazine, 5 rounds. Folding-leaf sight. 2280 fps with 285-grain bullet.

This gun, introduced in 1996, presents a departure from the tried and tested Mauser-type bolt system embodied in the SR20 series. The SR 30 has a unique bolt with retractable locking lugs, in addition to excellent safety features. It is easily recognizable by the tubular receiver – with an elongated ejection port on the right side, and a wooden bolt handle knob. The magazine-release catch is set into the lower edge of the stock ahead of the trigger guard.

Special attention has been paid in the design to safety features, including a 'combination trigger' which automatically uncocks the mechanism if the bolt is opened without firing. The standard walnut half-stock, with hand-cut checkering, has a contrasting rosewood forend tip and pistol grip cap. The buttplate is solid rubber. A squared Bavarian-style cheekpiece and a slight hog's back comb are standard, but Monte Carlo combs and other features can be obtained to order.

MAGNUM EXPRESS SPORTING RIFLE
Made by Friedr. Wilh. Heym GmbH & Co., Münnerstadt (prior to 1995) and Gleichamberg (1996 to date).
Currently in production. **Chambering options:** 300 Weatherby Magnum, 338 Lapua Magnum, 375 H&H Magnum, 378 Weatherby Magnum, 404 Jeffrey Rimmed, 416 Rigby, 425 Express, 450 Ackley, 458 Winchester Magnum, 460 Weatherby Magnum, 500 A-Square, or 600 Nitro Express. **Action:** locked by two lugs on the bolt head engaging recesses in the receiver wall as the bolt handle turns down, and by a third lug on the bolt body entering its recess.
DATA FOR A TYPICAL EXAMPLE
   600 Nitro Express, rimless. 45.3in overall, 9.83lb empty. 24in barrel, 4-groove rifling; RH, concentric? Internal box magazine, 3 rounds. Express sight. 1970 fps with 895-grain bullet.

This Heym-made rifle, introduced in 1989, could have been included in the Mauser section owing to the presence of a third or safety lug on the bolt and a full-length collar-pattern extractor. A Timney trigger was fitted and the safety catch was moved back to the bolt shroud. Twin vertical recoil lugs were used, though the stock was externally similar to the SR 20 Classic Safari described above. Rifles of this type were still being made in 1997 as the 'Express' model.

• Heym, break-open type
In addtiion to the multi-barrel rifles listed below, Heym also makes a range of shotguns and combination guns (including *Drill-inge*) on the same basic actions.

MODEL 25BS DOUBLE RIFLE
Made by Friedr. Wilh. Heym GmbH & Co., Gleichamberg.

Currently in production. **Chambering options:** 22 Hornet, 222 Remington, 222 Remington Magnum, 22-250 Remington, 223 Remington, 5.6x50 Magnum, 5.6x52R, 6x62 Frères, 243 Winchester, 6.5x55, 6.5x57, 6.5x65R, 7x57, 7x65R, 30R Blaser, 30-06, 308 Winchester or 8x57. **Action:** locked by double under lugs, controlled by a radial lever on top of the action body.
DATA FOR A TYPICAL EXAMPLE
   Chambering: 6.5x57, rimless. 39.75in overall, 6.07lb empty. 23.6in barrels, 4-groove rifling; RH, concentric? Double barrels, two shots. Open rear sight. 3310 fps with 93-grain bullet.

Introduced in 1996, this is a lightweight over-and-under double rifle with an aluminum alloy receiver and the patented de-cocking/safety system designed to prevent the gun firing if it is dropped. There are two triggers, the usual sliding safety (with an integral cocking-indicator pin) on the tang behind the top lever, and a shallow quarter-rib.

The walnut butt has a checkered pistol grip with a synthetic cap, a low hog's back comb, and a squared Bavarian-style cheekpiece. The plain round-tip forend is also extensively hand-checkered. Swivels will be found beneath the butt and on the lower barrel immediately ahead of the forend.

The Model 25 is usually considered as a combination gun with one smooth-bore and one rifled barrel ('BF' – *Bockbuchsflinte*), but a version with two rifled barrels ('BS' – *Bergstutzen*) is also made. The second rifled barrel is simply inserted in the upper smooth-bore tube.

Guns can be obtained in five grades, ranging from the plain 'Standard', with engraved borders on the action, to the 'Exclusiv' with extensive floral-scroll and game-scene engraving.

MODEL 37BK TRIPLE RIFLE
Made by Friedr. Wilh. Heym GmbH & Co., Münnerstadt (prior to 1995) and Gleichamberg (since 1996).
Currently in production. **Chambering options:** see text. **Action:** locked by double under-lugs and double Greener cross-bolts, controlled by a radial lever on top of the action body,.
DATA FOR A TYPICAL EXAMPLE
   Chambering: 22 Hornet (upper barrels) and 7x65R (lower barrel). 41.75in overall, 7.83lb empty. 25in barrels, 4-groove rifling; RH, concentric? Three shots. Open rear sight. 2430 fps with 46-grain bullet (upper barrels); 2530 fps with 173-grain bullet (lower barrel).

Introduced in 1995, this is a variation of the standard side-lock Model 37 Drilling. The gun has separate cocking levers for each striker, unbreakable spiral springs, and a combination safety catch and cocking-indicator pin on the tang. The lower barrel is cocked separately, and the front lever of the two-trigger system incorporates a 'set' element to promote precision marksmanship.

Bases for optical-sight mounts are set into the top surface of the rib between the upper barrels. The woodwork is walnut, with hand-cut checkering on the pistol grip and forend. The pistol grip has a separate cap – synthetic, or rosewood in deluxe patterns – and the low hog's back comb is accompanied by a squared Bavarian-style cheekpiece.

Chamberings available at the end of 1996 included 22 Hornet, 222 Remington, 222 Remington Magnum, 5.6x50 Magnum, 5.6x52R, 6.5x57, 243 Winchester, 6.5x55, 6.5x57, 6.5x65 RWS, 270 Winchester, 7x57, 7x65R, 30R Blaser, 30-06, 308 Winchester, 8x57, 8x75RS, and 9.3x74R.

MODEL 44B SPORTING RIFLE
Made by Friedr. Wilh. Heym GmbH & Co., Gleichamberg, 1996 to date.
Currently in production. **Chambering options:** see text. **Action:** as Model 37BK, above.
DATA FOR A TYPICAL EXAMPLE
   5.6x50 Magnum, rimless. 40.55in overall, 6.06lb empty. 23.6in barrel, 4-groove rifling; RH, concentric? Single shot. Open rear sight. 3590 fps with 50-grain bullet.

Introduced in 1996, after the return to Thüringen, this elegant octagonal-barreled single shot rifle is a typical high-quality Heym product. The boxlock action (with false side-plates extensions) is a modified Anson & Deeley pattern, and the sliding safety catch on the tang has a locking button. Opening a cocked gun automatically releases the trigger, preventing the gun firing accidentally.

The standard Model 44 has a pistol grip butt with a low hog's back comb and a squared Bavarian-style cheekpiece; the forend has a rosewood schnabel tip, the pistol grip has a rosewood cap, the buttplate is plain rubber, and swivels lie beneath the butt and forend. The rear sight is let into a quarter-rib, which also has integral bases for optical-sight mounts.

The Model 44 is normally supplied with 'Best Bouquet' and game scene engraving on the sideplates, but can be obtained to special order with more extensive decoration – including high-relief work on the action and basketweave checkering on the pistol grip and forend.

A wide range of chamberings was being offered in 1997: 22 Hornet, 222 Remington, 222 Remington Magnum, 5.6x50 Magnum, 5.6x52R, 5.6x57, 223 Remington, 6x62 Frères, 243 Winchester, 6.5x55, 6.5x57, 6.5x65 RWS, 270 Winchester, 7x57, 7x65R, 30R Blaser, 30-06, 308 Winchester, 8x57, 8x75RS, 9.3x74R, and 10.3x60R.

MODEL 55B DOUBLE RIFLE

Made by Friedr. Wilh. Heym GmbH & Co., Münnerstadt (prior to 1995) and Gleichamberg (1996 to date).

Currently in production. **Chambering options:** see text. **Action:** as Model 37BK, above.

DATA FOR A TYPICAL EXAMPLE

Chambering: 7x65R, rimmed. 41.75in overall, 7.94lb empty. 25in superimposed barrels, 4-groove rifling; RH, concentric? Two shots. Open rear sight. 3050 fps with 123-grain bullet.

Displaying an Anson & Deeley-type boxlock, this double rifle is a variant of the Model 55F shotgun and 55BF or 55BSS combination guns.

The walnut butts have Bavarian-style cheekpieces and slight hog's back combs. The rear sight is let into the traditional quarter-rib, and the action is customarily engraved with scroll-and-game motifs (though the extent and design varies to order). The Model 55B was available in 1985 in chamberings including 7x65R, 30-06, 308 Winchester, 8x57, 9.3x74R and 375 H&H Magnum. By 1997, the options had grown to 270 Winchester, 7x65R, 300 Winchester Magnum, 30-06, 308 Winchester, 8x57, 8x75RS, 9.3x75RS, 375 H&H Magnum, 10.3x60R, 416 Rigby, 458 Winchester Magnum and 470 Nitro Express.

SIMILAR GUNS

Model 55BS. The Bergstutzen or 'mountain rifle' is supplied with rifled barrels chambering different cartridges, and with twin set-triggers. The smaller-diameter upper barrel fires 5.6x50R Magnum or 222 Remington, while the lower one can be chambered for any of the standard Heym cartridges.

MODEL 80B DOUBLE RIFLE

Made by Friedr. Wilh. Heym GmbH & Co., Gleichamberg.

Currently in production. **Chambering options:** 7x65R, 30R Blaser, 30-06, 8x57, 8x75R S, 9.3x74R or 10.3x60R; 375 H&H Magnum and others have been supplied to order. **Action:** locked by double under-lugs, controlled by a radial lever on top of the action body.

DATA FOR A TYPICAL EXAMPLE

Chambering: 30-06, rimless. 40.75in overall, 7.05lb empty. 23.6in side-by-side barrels, 4-groove rifling; RH, concentric? Double barrel, two shots. Open rear sight. 2990 fps with 150-grain bullet.

Introduced in 1996, this elegant double-barreled hunting rifle features a narrow action built on a modified Anson & Deeley boxlock (Model 80B) or a Purdey/Greener sidelock (80BS/SS) with a

The open action of Heym's box-lock Model 55B rifle, showing one of the underlugs and the double lugs for the toplever-activated cross-bolt.

radial top lever and a sliding safety on the tang. Double triggers are standard, though a single-trigger option and a special *Handspanner* version – cocked manually by a slider on the tang – can be obtained on request.

The Model 80 is normally supplied with Arabesque or oak leaf engraving on the action body and around the barrels at the breech. A straight-comb butt with an English-style oval cheekpiece is regarded as standard, with other types (e.g., Bavarian cheekpiece or a Monte Carlo comb) available to order. The checkered panels on the pistol grip and forend are also edged with scroll and oak leaf motifs. High-relief game scenes and additional engraving can be applied on request.

SIMILAR GUNS

Model 80BS. This is a Bergstutzen with barrels of differing calibers, the right-hand barrel being the larger of the two. Chambering options available by the beginning of 1997 included 7x57, 7x65R, 30R Blaser, 30-06. 8x57, 8x75RS or 9.3x74R in one barrel, and 22 Hornet, 222 Remington, 222 Remington Magnum, 5.6x50 Magnum or 5.6x52R in the other.

Model 80BS/SS. Available in the same chamberings as the 80BS pattern, this differs solely in the substitution of side-locks for the boxlock.

MODEL 88B DOUBLE RIFLE

Made by Friedr. Wilh. Heym GmbH & Co., Münnerstadt (prior to 1995) and Gleichamberg (1996 to date).

Currently in production. **Chambering options:** 7x65R, 30R Blaser, 30-06, 8x57, 8x75RS, 9.3x74R or 375 H&H Magnum. **Action:** generally as Model 37BK, above.

DATA FOR A TYPICAL EXAMPLE

Chambering: 9.3x74R, rimmed. 41.9in overall, 8.27lb empty. 25in barrels, 4-groove rifling; RH, concentric? Double barrel, two shots. Express sight. 2280 fps with 285-grain bullet.

This is a classical side-by-side double rifle, embodying an Anson & Deeley boxlock (Model 88B) or a Purdey-style intercepting-sear sidelock (88B/SS), and all the many refinements to be expected of Heym. Sliding safety catches are mounted on the upper tang, and loaded-chamber indicators are inlet in the top of the action body alongside the top lever. Heym side-by-side double rifles can be supplied with extractors, ejectors or the company's special selective ejector.

Many standard guns made prior to 1995 displayed American-style butts with Monte Carlo combs, while the deluxe patterns invariably had straight or hog's back combs; the guns made in Gleichamberg, however, have straight-comb butts with rounded cheekpieces. English-style scroll engraving may be encountered on the action, with gold-line inlay on the breech.

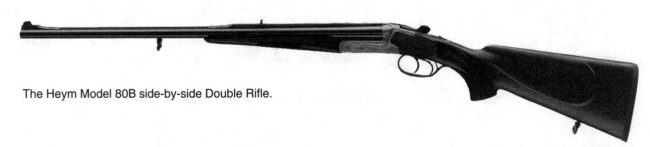

The Heym Model 80B side-by-side Double Rifle.

The open breech of the Heym Model 80B Safari rifle, showing the cross-bolt protruding from the left of the breech.

SIMILAR GUNS

Model 88BS. This was a Bergstutzen derivative of the basic Model 80B, with barrels of differing caliber. The chambering options available in 1997 were 6.5x57, 6.5x65 RWS, 7x57, 7x65R, 30R Blaser, 30-06 and 8x57 for the larger barrel; and 22 Hornet, 222 Remington, 222 Remington Magnum, 5.6x50 Magnum or 5.6x52R for the smaller one.

Model 88BS/SS. This is simply a version of the 88BS with side-locks instead of a boxlock. It is particularly favored for the deluxe guns, owing to the greater surface area of metal presented for engraving.

Model 88 Safari. Introduced in 1990 and often encountered with superb decoration, this is simply a large-caliber version of the standard side-lock type Model 88. The additional Greener cross-bolts suit the 88-type action better than the simpler '80' pattern to the pressures involved in firing cartridges powerful enough to down African game. Made only in 375 H&H Magnum, 458 Winchester Magnum and three Nitro Express rounds – 470, 500 and 600 – it can weigh as much as 10lb.

• Heym-Ruger

Ruger No. 1 actions have been used as the basis for guns engraved and stocked in European style, and are described in greater detail in the relevant part of the USA section. Heym abandoned work on them in the early 1990s.

HR 30 SPORTING RIFLE

Made by Sturm, Ruger & Co., Inc., Southport, Connecticut, but completed by Friedrich Wilh. Heym GmbH & Co., Münnerstadt.
Total production: believed to have been less than 1000. **Chambering options:** see notes. **Action:** locked by shoulders on the operating lever propping the breechblock behind the chamber.
DATA FOR A TYPICAL EXAMPLE
  Chambering: 7x65mm, rimmed. 40.15in overall, 6.72lb empty. 23.6in barre l, 6-groove rifling; RH, concentric. Single shot only. Folding-leaf sight. 2525 fps with 173-grain bullet.

The first guns were built around U.S.-made actions in the late 1970s. The basic pattern had a round barrel, a single set Canjar trigger and open sights, though claw-pattern optical-sight mounts have been a popular alternative. HR 30 rifles have been chambered for 243 Winchester, 6.5x57R, 6.5x68R, 270 Winchester, 7x64, 7x65R, 300 Winchester Magnum, 30-06, 308 Winchester, 8x68S, 9.3x72R or 10.3x60R.

SIMILAR GUNS

HR 38. This was identical with the HR 30, except that it had an octagonal barrel. Most rifles were stocked in walnut. Chamberings were 6.5x57R, 6.5x68R, 8x68S or 10.3x60R. Standard actions offered game-and-oakleaf engraving, but 'Modell HR 38 Exclusiv' had side-plate extensions on the receiver.

HR 30L Carbine. This had a full-length Mannlicher pattern stock. Bavarian cheekpieces invariably had scalloped lower edges. Owing to its comparatively short barrel, the Carbine was not available in magnum chamberings.

• Hoster

Albert Hoster patented a repeating rifle in 1887. A turning-bolt design, it had a rotary-feed magazine driven by a spring. Guns were made experimentally for the 11mm Mauser cartridge, magazine capacity being eight rounds. They had dial-type cartridge remaining indicators on the left side of the receiver and two-piece stocks with straight-wrist butts. A pivoting safety lever lay ahead of the trigger inside the guard.

• Jäger

These simple bolt-action rifles were sold in the U.S. by A.F. Stoeger & Co. and Charles Daly prior to 1939, but production was never large. Little is known about their history.

HEROLD SPORTING RIFLE
Herold-Repetierbüchse

Made by Franz Jäger & Co., Suhl.
Total production: not known; probably quite small. **Chambering options:** 5.6x35R or 22 Hornet. **Action:** locked by rotating a lug on the bolt body into the receiver, and by the bolt handle turning down into its seat.
DATA FOR A TYPICAL EXAMPLE
  Chambering: 22 Hornet, rimmed. 43.7in overall, 7.76lb empty. 24in barrel, 4-groove rifling; RH, concentric. Internal box magazine, 5 rounds. Folding-leaf sight. 2690 fps with 45-grain bullet.

Introduced in the mid 1930s, this rifle was built on an action which was euphemistically advertised as a 'miniature Mauser'. It existed in grades ranging from plain-stock sporters to deluxe guns with selected woodwork and engraved actions. The cylindrical receiver had a large ejection port, the bolt handle was turned downward, and a double set trigger mechanism was common. The most distinctive feature was the magazine, which consisted of a light sheet steel box attached to the floorplate.

• Kalashnikov

The German Democratic Republic used Soviet-made AK rifles from 1957 until indigenous production commenced in Suhl two years later. These particular guns may have Russian and East German marks, but the quantities involved seem to have been small and survivors are rarely seen.

KALASHNIKOV MACHINE PISTOL
Maschinenpistole Kalashnikow, MPi-K

Production of a minor variant of the Soviet rifle began in 1959 in the former Sauer factory ('VEB Ernst Thälmann Werke'). About 1.3-1.5 million were made about 1959-66. The guns had wood butts, forends and handguards, but lacked the cleaning rod and butt-trap of their Soviet prototypes and did not accept bayonets. Selectors were marked 'D' and 'E'. A curious night sight, comprising a luminous slider on rails, could be clipped onto the aperture in the front-sight mounting block. East German guns may be identified by marks such as '64 R 4925' on the left side of the receiver. The first two digits represent the date of manufacture – e.g., '64' is 1964. The guns also display a principal inspector's mark in the form of a letter inside a circle of dots.

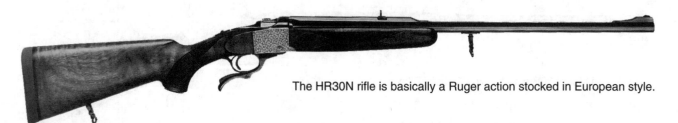

The HR30N rifle is basically a Ruger action stocked in European style.

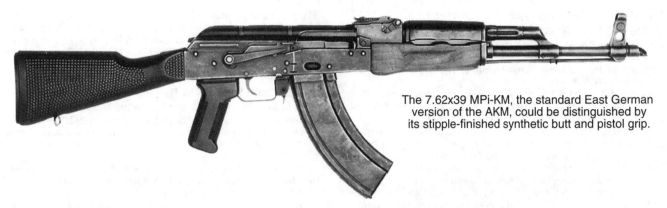

The 7.62x39 MPi-KM, the standard East German version of the AKM, could be distinguished by its stipple-finished synthetic butt and pistol grip.

SIMILAR GUNS

MPi-KS. This had a plain-sided folding butt, but was otherwise similar to the basic MPi-K.

MPi-KM. Based on the AKM, these rifles appeared in 1965. They had wood butts, though later examples were fitted with plastic handguards, wooden forends, and blue-gray plastic butts with a distinctive stippled finish. Most guns had a cleaning rod. About two million were made prior to the mid 1980s.

MPi-KMS. This was a minor variant of the MPi-KM with a distinctive butt, which swung to the right; the locking latch protruded from the receiver beneath the butt-rod. The pressed-steel shoulder piece was retained by two rivets. Selectors bore 'D' above 'E', and date/serial marks such as '71 H 7472'.

MPi-K 74. A copy of the AK-74 was introduced about 1983, but production was stopped by the reunification of Germany and does not seem to have been large.

• Keppeler & Fritz

These rifles are based on a single type of bolt action, with a sturdy receiver pierced only by the ejection port and the bolt handle guide way. Locking depends on no fewer than seven lugs on the bolt. Keppeler & Fritz also offer adaptors allowing Anschütz rimfire rifle actions – specifically the Models 1407, 1413, 1807, 1810 and 1913 – to be fitted into the distinctive rail-pattern stock. This produces a series of small caliber rifles (*Kleinkalibergewehre*) promoted as the Standard, Sport and International patterns.

STANDARD RIFLE
Grosskaliber-Standardgewehr
Made by Keppeler & Fritz GmbH, Fichtenberg.

Currently in production. **Chambering options:** 222 Remington, 223 Remington, 243 Winchester, 7mm-08 Remington, 7.5x55, 308 Winchester, or 8x57IS.

DATA FOR A 7.5X55 EXAMPLE

1130mm overall, 5.3kg empty. 650mm barrel, 4-groove rifling; RH, concentric? Single shot only. Adjustable aperture rear sight. 2650 fps with 180-grain bullet.

Destined for 300m (330yd) shooting competitions, this gun can be identified by its distinctive walnut stock. The action is bedded in the stock in thermoplastic material. The comb is fixed, the butt-plate can be slid vertically, and a prominent 'knuckle' protrudes backward above the pistol grip. Three ventilating slots are cut laterally through the forend, and an accessory rail will accept hand-stops, hand rests or sling anchors.

Alternatively, the stock of the Anschütz Model 1907 match rifle can be used (though restricted to 222 and 223). This has an elevating comb and an extending buttplate controlled by plastic snap-locks let into the butt-side. Anschütz aperture sights and mirage bands are also standard. The direct-acting trigger is adjusted to give a release pressure of 3.3lb (1.5kg), but can be replaced if required with a match pattern adjustable down to 3.5oz (100gm). Left-hand actions are also made.

SIMILAR GUNS

Long Range Rifle. Made only in 308 Winchester, this is similar to the Standard pattern except that the barrel is 30in long. The Keppeler-style stock is used.

Sport rifle (Sportgewehr). A short variant of the Long Range Rifle, also available only in 308, this has a 25.6in barrel.

Free Rifle (Grosskaliber-Freigewehr). Based on the standard Keppeler action, this has a stock with a thumbhole grip, an articulated butt-plate hook, and an elevating comb. Thermoplastic bedding is used to ensure a consistent contact between metal and woodwork. A match-quality trigger can be adjusted down to about 3.5oz (100gm). The 25.6in heavy barrel gives a total weight of about 14.1lb. A left-hand action has also been made in small numbers.

Alternatively, a Keppeler action, chambered for the 222 and 223 Remington rounds only, can be fitted in the stock of the rimfire Anschütz 1913 Free Rifle (q.v.).

Special Free Rifle. The principal distinguishing feature of this rifle is its alloy rail-type stock, terminating in a mounting block with an adjustable hook-type shoulder plate sliding on rods. A small wooden cheekpiece – often a multi-color wood laminate – is attached to the top of the rail behind the receiver, and a separate wood-laminate anatomical pistol grip appears beneath the bolt mechanism. A shallow two-strip forend is bolted to the rail beneath the free-floating 25.6in barrel. The rifle is about 45.8in long, depending on the position of the butt, and weighs 13.2lb without its sights. It has been made for 222 Remington, 223 Remington, 6mm BR, 6mm PPC, 7mm-08 Remington and 308 Winchester cartridges, but other chamberings can be provided on request.

Sniper Rifle. This was an experimental 7.62x51 (308 Winchester) adaptation of the Keppeler action, unsuccessfully submitted to the German military sniper-rifle trials of the early 1990s.

• Kind

Albrecht Kind AG ('Akah') of Nürnberg and Berlin was another of the wholesalers that sprang to prominence in the period between the wars. Mauser-action sporting guns have been reported with the company's trademarks – 'Akah', 'Eichel', 'Schutzmann' and 'Tanne' – but were undoubtedly made elsewhere, and evidence of the actual manufacturer should be sought from a close inspection of the guns. Business was re-established in the 1950s from a new headquarters in Hunstig bei Dieringshausen.

MERKUR SPORTING RIFLE

This was among many sporting rifles offered under the Akah brand, and was often identified by the code-number '6939'. Built on refurbished Kar. 98k-type actions, possibly by Kriegeskorte (q.v.), Merkur rifles had beech or walnut sporting half-stocks with hog's back combs and small oval cheekpieces. Checkering appeared on the capped pistol grip and the shallow schnabel-tipped forend. Folding-leaf rear sights were fitted and the front swivel eye lay on the barrel ahead of the stock. Chamberings included 243 Winchester, 6.5x57, 270 Winchester, 7x57, 7x64, 30-06, 308 Winchester or 8x57mm. The guns were typically 44.5in long, had 23.6in barrels and weighed 7.1lb; five-cartridge magazines were standard.

SIMILAR GUNS

Saturn. The Merkur originally had a double set trigger system, whereas the Saturn – though otherwise identical – had a conventional single trigger. About 1968, however, the categories were merged under the Merkur name.

Merkur-Super. Dating from about 1968, this had a butt with a Monte Carlo comb and a ventilated rubber shoulder pad. A contrasting forend tip was fitted. The standard barrel length remained 23.6in, though a 6.5x58 chambering option was added. A new 25.6in barrel was introduced in 1971, chambered only for 7x64, 8x68S, 9.3x63 or 9.3x64.

• Krico, autoloading type
MODEL 260 SPORTING RIFLE
Made by Krico GmbH, Jagd- und Sportwaffenfabrik, Stuttgart, about 1962-80.

Total production: not known. **Chambering:** 22 LR, rimfire. **Action:** no mechanical lock; blowback, semi-automatic only.

About 40.5in overall, 5.73lb empty. 22.45in barrel, 4-groove rifling; RH, concentric. Detachable box magazine, 5 rounds. Three-leaf rear sight graduated to 100m (110yd). 1080 fps with 40-grain bullet.

An inexpensive 22LR rimfire blowback autoloader, distinguished by excellent quality and reliable performance, this had a Bavarian-type half-stock with a squared cheekpiece, a low hog's back comb and a schnabel forend tip. Accompanied by detachable box magazines containing two, five or 10 rounds, the 260 could be used as a single-loader if required. A radial safety catch lay on the right rear side of the receiver, and grooves for optical-sight mounting bases were machined in the receiver top.

SIMILAR GUNS
Model 250A, 1962-80? This was a variant of the 260 with a tube magazine beneath the barrel, raising capacity to eighteen 22LR rounds. A plain pistol grip half-stock and the three-leaf rear sight were standard fittings.

Model 260EA, 1962 to date. Distinguished by a walnut-finish hardwood half-stock with a low Monte Carlo comb, this was a simpler and cheaper version of the Model 260. It had a rubber buttplate; checkering on the pistol grip and forend; and sling swivels beneath the butt and forend.

• Krico, bolt-action type
Kriegeskorte & Co., now better known as Krico GmbH, converted standard Mauser military-action rifles to effective sporters in the early 1950s. The company then proceeded to a short-action 'Miniature Mauser' – dating from 1956-62 – before the first of the proprietary guns appeared in 1962, distinguished by its streamlined bolt shroud and a radial safety catch above the stock behind the bolt handle. The company moved from Stuttgart to Vohburg-Irsching in 1994, when the opportunity was taken to refine the range of guns; the current products are listed at the end of the section below.

Krico rifles have been offered in the U.S. under many names (e.g., 'Tradewinds Husky 5000'). The original importer was Tradewinds, Inc., of Tacoma, Washington (1968-82). After a short interregnum, the agency passed to Beeman Precision Arms of Santa Rosa, California (1983-90), and then to Mandall Shooting Supplies, Inc., of Scottsdale, Arizona.

The Wolverine, sold by O&L Guns, Inc., of Seminole, Texas, was little more than a barreled 700 Magnum action in a U.S.-made stock; it was distinguished by a quarter-rib on the barrel.

THE STUTTGART GUNS
MODEL 120 SPORTING RIFLE
Abandoned about 1988, this was the most basic of the Krico rifles. Locked by allowing the base of the bolt handle to enter its seat in the receiver, the Model 120 was chambered for the 22LR rimfire cartridge. The detachable box magazine held five rounds.

The plain beech half-stock, which lacked checkering, had a low Monte Carlo comb and a synthetic buttplate. The trigger guard was a simple stamped strip, and the simple 'L' type simple spring-leaf and slider rear sight was fitted. The Model 120E was a single shot variant, and the Model 120S had a straight-pull 'Krico-Kitzmann' bolt system.

MODEL 300E SPORTING RIFLE
Made by Krico GmbH, Jagd- und Sportwaffenfabrik, Stuttgart.

Total production: not known. **Chambering options:** 22 LR or 22 Winchester Magnum rimfire. **Action:** locked by the bolt handle base turning down into its seat in the receiver.

DATA FOR 22LR VERSION

38.3in overall, 5.5lb empty. 19.7in barrel, 4-groove rifling; RH, concentric. Detachable box magazine, 5 rounds. Tangent-leaf rear sight graduated to 200m? 1100 fps with 40-grain bullet.

Though locked only by the base of the bolt handle, unlike the essentially similar Krico 22 Hornet equivalents (q.v.), these guns are more than strong enough to handle the pressures of the rimfire cartridges. The 300E has a plain half-stock with a Monte Carlo comb, and checkering on the pistol grip and forend. The forend tip is generally cut obliquely. A radial safety lever will be found on the right side of the action behind the bolt handle, and the tail of the striker protrudes from the cocking piece to double as an indicator pin. The single-trigger mechanism (regarded as the standard fitting) is shared with the Model 260 autoloader described above.

SIMILAR GUNS: FIRST SERIES
These rifles were often distinguished with an 'ST' or 'St' suffix if they were fitted with the standard double-trigger unit, though the distinction was dropped when the 'second series' began.

Model 302. This 22LR rimfire rifle was the basic variant of the series, with a beech pistol-gip half-stock and a three-leaf rear sight graduated to 100m (110yd). Barrels measured 24.8in, and weight averaged 6.2lb.

Model 302D. A deluxe version of the standard 302, in 22LR rimfire, this had a double trigger and a Bavarian-style walnut half-stock with a schnabel-tipped forend.

Model 302E. Chambered for the 22LR rimfire cartridge, this had a stock with a Monte Carlo comb, a single trigger and a tangent-type 'LA' rear sight.

Model 302L. A minor variant of the Model 302, this had a 200m (220yd) tangent-leaf sight instead of the three-leaf pattern.

Model 302SA. A most distinctive version of the standard 22LR rimfire rifles, this had a full-length silencer doubling as the barrel casing.

Model 304. Distinguished by a full-length stock and a 22.45in barrel, this had the Bavarian-style stock and chambered the 22LR cartridge. A three-leaf rear sight and a double-trigger unit, incorporating a set element, were regarded as standard.

Model 304L. This was simply a Model 304 with a 200m (220yd) tangent-leaf rear sight replacing the three-leaf pattern.

Model 310. Offering a 22.45in barrel and plain half-stock with a rounded forend tip, this was an economy version of the 304. Checkering was absent.

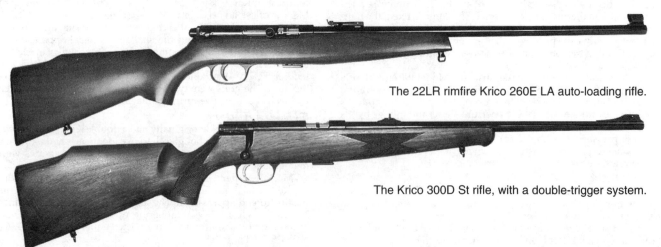

The 22LR rimfire Krico 260E LA auto-loading rifle.

The Krico 300D St rifle, with a double-trigger system.

The Krico 320L, with a 'Mannlicher' stock and a double trigger.

Model 311. This was a deluxe version of the Model 310, with checkering on the pistol grip and forend of a select walnut half-stock.

Model 352. Apart from chambering – 22 Winchester Magnum rimfire – this was identical with the Model 302 (q.v.).

Model 352D. Mechanically identical with the deluxe Model 352D, described above, this chambered the 22WMRF cartridge.

Model 352E. This was a variant of the Model 302E (above) chambered for the 22 Winchester Magnum rimfire cartridge.

Model 354. Chambering the 22 WMRF cartridge, this was simply a more powerful version of the Model 304 described above.

SIMILAR GUNS: SECOND SERIES

Model 300D. This amalgamates the basic action with a double set trigger unit. It also has a Monte Carlo-style walnut half-stock with a shallow schnabel tip on the forend.

Model 300E. A single-trigger gun with a tangent-leaf rear sight and a beech stock with a Monte Carlo comb, this is described in the text above.

Model 300 Luxus (or 'Deluxe'). This features a double-trigger mechanism and a Bavarian-style walnut stock with a hog's back comb and a squared cheekpiece.

Model 300SA. Fitted with a large-diameter sound moderator, acting as a barrel casing, this is a most distinctive gun. Double triggers are standard.

Model 320L. Mechanically identical with the 300D, this has a full-length Mannlicher stock with a hog's back comb, a squared Bavarian-style cheekpiece and a decorative pistol grip cap.

Model 330S. Discontinued in 1992, this was a single shot UIT 25m target rifle with a conventional competition stock and aperture sights. It had an adjustable buttplate, extensive stippling on the pistol grip, and an accessory rail inlet under the forend; unfortunately, it did not prove capable of challenging the domination of Anschütz and Walther in this particular discipline.

Model 340. This 22LR target rifle, intended for DJV moving target competitions, has a deep butt with a squared cheekpiece, a fixed wooden (or rubber) buttplate, and a broad 'beavertail' forend. Stippling is applied extensively to the pistol grip and under the forend. The 340, which can only be used with optical sights, has a heavy barrel and the standard double set trigger.

Model 340S. Destined for moving-target competitions, this 22LR pattern has a 23.6in barrel, a double trigger mechanism, and a distinctive stock with seven slots in the forend. Unlike the standard 340, it also has sling swivels.

Model 340S Silhouette, or '340 Sil'. Developed from the standard Model 340 especially for North American competitions, made in 22LR only, this has a single match-quality trigger unit and a short barrel. The half-stock lacks the deep broad forend of its near-relation, but has a ventilated rubber shoulder plate.

Model 360S Biathlon. Built on the Krico-Kitzmann straight-pull bolt system, this had a competition stock with a vertical pistol grip. Stippling appeared on the pistol grip and the forend, and four spare magazines were set in the underside of the butt.

Model 360S2 Biathlon. Made only in small numbers, this shared the action of the 360S Biathlon. However, the extraordinary stock had a separate pistol grip, an under-arm rod on the toe of the shoulder plate, and an unusually deep forend extending backward to form a rudimentary trigger guard. Rocking the pistol grip backwards opened the bolt mechanism. Four magazines could be carried in the underside of the butt.

MODEL 400D SPORTING RIFLE

Made by Krico GmbH, Jagd- und Sportwaffenfabrik, Stuttgart.
Total production: not known. **Chambering:** 22 Hornet. **Action:** locked by two lugs on the bolt engaging recesses in the receiver behind the bolt handle, and by the bolt handle base entering its seat.

42.9in long, 7.12lb empty. 23.6in barrel, 4-groove rifling; RH, concentric. Detachable box magazine, 5 rounds. Standing-block rear sight. 2690 fps with 45-grain bullet.

Introduced in 1983, these guns were based on the company's proven 300-series rimfires, with additional locking lugs behind the bolt handle base. The radial safety lever was retained in its familiar position behind the bolt handle on the right side of the receiver. The 400D had a hog's back comb, a low squared cheekpiece, and an imperceptibly schnabel-tipped forend; a thick rubber shoulder pad was used and the pistol grip had a separate cap. The double trigger unit was standard.

SIMILAR GUNS

Model 400E. The basic rifle had a plain half-stock with a low Monte Carlo comb and a thin plastic or rubber shoulder plate. Simple checkering panels appeared on the pistol grip and forend, while swivels lay under the forend and butt. A single double-pressure trigger was usually fitted.

Model 420L. This had the double trigger and a full-length Mannlicher-type stock; the barrel measured 19.7in barrel instead of 21.65in.

Model 430S. Identified by a deep beavertail forend and a notably squared cheekpiece, this single shot 22LR rimfire target rifle also had a double set trigger. A conventional match-pattern trigger was obtainable on request.

Model 440S. Otherwise similar to the 430S, this magazine-feed gun had a double trigger (a match pattern was optional) and a slender forend with seven longitudinal slots.

MODEL 530S TARGET RIFLE

This short-lived 22LR pattern was intended for moving-target competitions. It had a movable trigger shoe, an enlarged bolt-ball, and stippling on the pistol grip and the flat-bottom forend. The most obvious feature, however, was the control switch and indi-

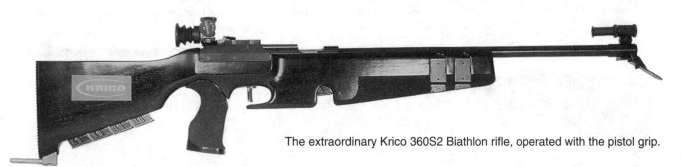

The extraordinary Krico 360S2 Biathlon rifle, operated with the pistol grip.

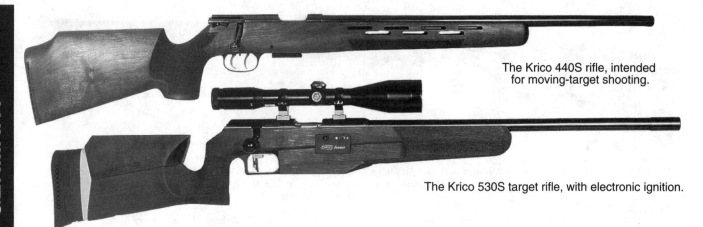

The Krico 440S rifle, intended for moving-target shooting.

The Krico 530S target rifle, with electronic ignition.

cator light for the electronic trigger on the right side of the forend beneath the chamber. Optical sights were standard.

SIMILAR GUNS

Model 540S Silhouette. Built on the same action as the 530S, this shared the electronic trigger (though the switch plate lay on the right side of the butt). The butt comb and shoulder plate were fixed, the pistol grip was stippled, and stippling also ran the entire length of the underside of the forend.

MODEL 600 SPORTING RIFLE

Made by Krico GmbH, Jagd- und Sportwaffenfabrik, Stuttgart.

Total production: not known. **Chambering options:** see notes. **Action:** locked by two lugs on the bolt head engaging recesses in the receiver as the bolt handle is turned down, and by the bolt handle base entering its seat.

DATA FOR A TYPICAL MODEL 620L

Chambering: 5.6x50 Magnum, rimless. 43.65in overall, 7.54lb empty. 21.65in barrel, 4-groove rifling; RH, concentric. Detachable box magazine, 3 rounds. Ramp sight. 3590 fps with 50-grain bullet.

The first of these guns was introduced in 1962 to replace the previous Mauser-pattern rifle. The 600 series was built on a modified Mauser action, with dual opposed lugs on the bolt head and a simplified bolt shroud – black plastic on most guns. A small extractor claw was let into the side of the bolt head and a plunger-type ejector lay in the shrouded bolt face. The chronology of the early rifles is difficult to unravel. By 1964, however, a wide selection was being offered.

SIMILAR GUNS; FIRST SERIES

Designations have been seen with 'St' (Stecher) or 'E' (Einzelabzug) suffixes indicating the trigger design.

Models 601-606. The original 600 series were similar short-action guns. They were about 43.7in long, had 23.6in barrels and weighed an average of 6.9lb. The back-sight block was usually regulated for 100m (110yd), with folding leaves for 200m (220yd) and 300m (330yd). The half-stocks had hog's back or 'Bavarian' combs, low squared cheekpieces, and schnabel-tip forends. Checkered panels graced the pistol grip and forend. Dark plastic buttplates and pistol grip caps were accompanied by white spacer plates, while swivels lay beneath the forend and butt. Detachable box magazines were standard, capacity being dependent on chambering.

The basic Krico guns were all offered in the same five chamberings, the last digit of the designation acting as an indicator – '1' for 222 Remington; '2' for 222 Remington Magnum; '3' for 243 Winchester; '5' for 308 Winchester; and '6' for 5.6x57. The Model 602, therefore, accepted 222 Remington Magnum cartridges; Model 606 was chambered 5.6x57 ammunition. Most rifles sold in Europe

were fitted with double set triggers, though many exported to North America had the simpler single-stage mechanism.

Models 601K-606K. Guns in the 'K' series were identical with the basic 600 pattern, but had Monte Carlo butts and angular squared-tip forends. Barrels measured 23.6in, except in 222 (21.65in) and 5.6x57mm (24in).

Models 607 and 607K. Dating from 1966, these chambered the 22-250 Remington round. The basic pattern does not seem to have been popular and had been discontinued by 1969, though the 'K' version survived into the 1980s.

Models 621-626. The 620 series was similar to the 600 group, but had 21.65in barrels and were about 41.7in overall. They had the full-length Mannlicher-style forends with sling loops and steel nose caps.

Model 641. Intended for use under Deutsche Jägerschafts-Verband or Deutsche Schützenbund rules, this competition rifle (in 222 Remington) had a high-comb Monte Carlo butt suited to optical sights. Its rounded forend had an oblique-cut rosewood tip. Double set triggers were standard, though single-trigger units could be supplied to order.

Model 643. Identical with the 641 except for chambering (243 Winchester), a typical example was 43.7in overall, had a 23.6in barrel and weighed 7.7lb.

SIMILAR GUNS: SECOND SERIES

The range was extensively redesigned in 1983, when the identifying suffixes were abandoned. The new basic models were the Krico 600 and 620, available in a selection of chamberings. The guns all had walnut stocks, with a distinctive hog's back comb and the Bavarian-type cheekpiece, though there were appreciable differences in the forends. The suffix letter 'D' signifies guns with double trigger systems. Standard 600-series chamberings – for all except Model 600A – were 222 Remington, 5.6x50 Magnum, 243 Winchester or 308 Winchester; in addition, 17 Remington, 222 Remington Magnum, 22-250, 223 Remington and 5.6x57 have been supplied to order.

Model 600A. The half-stock of this plainly finished double-trigger rifle ended in a shallow schnabel-tipped forend. A thin rubber shoulder plate was standard. Swivel eyes were fitted, but not open sights. The 23.6in barrels were chambered only for 222 Remington, 243 Winchester or 308 Winchester.

Model 600E. Subsequently known as '600D', these rifles had 23.6in barrels, double triggers (other patterns were optional), and better-quality stocks than the otherwise comparable 600A. Ventilated rubber shoulder plates were used, together with neater schnabel tips and attractively machine-jewelled bolts. Standard

The Krico 600D sporting rifle.

chamberings were 222 Remington, 5.6x50 Magnum, 243 Winchester and 308 Winchester; optional chamberings were initially 17 Remington, 222 Remington Magnum, 223, 22-250 and 5.6x57 RWS.

Model 600EAC. A few rifles were offered under this designation in the early 1980s, with straight-comb butts, rounded forends and single-stage triggers. Production was small.

Model 600 Luxus (or 'Deluxe'). These guns had specially selected stocks with separate rosewood schnabel tips, and a spatulate handle graced the machine-jewelled bolt. Sights comprised an open notch and a gold-plated blade. Single triggers embodying a setting element were standard, though alternatives could be requested. A left-hand action was introduced in 1985.

Model 620L. This gun had a 21.65in barrel and a full-length Mannlicher stock. Double set triggers were standard.

Model 620 Luxus. This was a variant of the standard 620L with the single set trigger mechanism instead of the two-trigger type. A left-hand version appeared in 1985.

Model 630S. This single shot rifle (.222 Remington, 243 and 308 Winchester, plus 223 Remington to order) was intended for the DJV 'hunting' competitions. Consequently, it had a half-stock with a deep forend, a massive butt with a low Monte Carlo comb, and a fixed ventilated rubber buttplate. The forend and pistol grip were extensively stippled.

Model 640L. This dual purpose target/sporting rifle, available in the same chamberings as the 650S (q.v.), with a 23.6in barel, amalgamated the heavy-barreled 640S action and a sporting style half-stock with a rounded rosewood forend tip. Checkering lay on the pistol grip and forend, and the buttplate was solid rubber.

Model 640S. This rifle exhibited a detachable box magazine, the double trigger system, and a match stock with seven longitudinal slots through the forend. Chambered for the 222 Remington, 223 Remington, 22-250, 243 Winchester or 308 Winchester rounds, the Krico 640S had a fixed cheekpiece and a solid rubber shoulder plate.

Model 640S Sniper, now known simply as '640 Sniper'. Essentially similar to the 640S, this gun (in 222 and 223 Remington, 243 and 308 Winchester only) had a buttplate adjustable for height and rake, plus a comb that could be elevated with a special key. A muzzle brake appeared on the phosphated barrel, a single-stage trigger was standard, and the bolt-ball was enlarged to facilitate grip. The 640S Sniper provided the basis for the British Armalon (q.v.) BGR in the mid 1980s.

Model 650S Benchrest, or simply '650S'. Available additionally in 22-250, this single shot rifle was similar to the 630S apart from a heavier barrel and a more conventional stock. The single match-quality trigger was regarded standard, but alternatives could be fitted on request.

MODEL 701 SPORTING RIFLE

Made by Krico GmbH, Jagd- und Sportwaffenfabrik, Stuttgart.
Total production: not known. **Chambering options:** see notes. **Action:** as 600 series, above.

DATA FOR A TYPICAL EXAMPLE

Chambering: 7x64, rimless. 44.15in overall, 7.45lb empty. 23.6in barrel, 4-groove rifling; RH, concentric. Detachable box magazine, 3 rounds. Ramp sight. 2625 fps with 173-grain bullet.

Introduced in 1962, this was a long-action 601 chambered for 270 Winchester, 7x57, 7x64 or 30-06 cartridges. Fitted with a 23.6in barrel, it was about 44.1in long, or .4in (10mm) greater than the short-action guns. The basic manufacturing patterns were refined in 1983, though the action was unchanged. The new guns were identical with corresponding variants in the 600 group, apart from the longer bolt and receiver.

SIMILAR GUNS

Model 700A. This was a plain gun with a double trigger and a 23.6in barrel chambering the 7x64 or 30-06 rounds only. It lacked fixed sights, but was drilled and tapped to accept mounting bases for a telescope.

Model 700D. Dating from 1982 and distinguished by a double trigger unit incorporating a 'set' element, this was available in 6.5x57, 7x64 or 30-06 as standard, options including 6.5x55, 7x57, 270 Winchester and 9.3x62.

Model 700 Luxus Magnum (or 'Deluxe Magnum'). This amalgamated the 25.6in barrel with a special single trigger incorporating a setting element. A left-hand version was made from 1985 onward.

Model 700D Magnum. This shared the standard long action, but had a 25.6in barrel instead of the standard 23.6in type. Usually chambering 300 Winchester Magnum or 8x68S, the rifle has also been supplied to order in 6.5x68, 7mm Remington Magnum, 7.5x55 or 9.3x64. The double trigger was standard.

Model 700E. This was simply a larger version of the Model 600E described previously, retaining a double trigger system.

Model 700EAC. A few guns of this pattern were made in the early 1980s. They had straight-comb butts, rounded forends and single-stage triggers, but production was minuscule.

Model 700 Luxus (or 'Deluxe'). Distinguished by a better stock, this had a single trigger incorporating a setting element and a gold bead front sight. It was otherwise identical with the 700D, though a left-hand action appeared in 1985.

Model 720D Magnum. This was simply a minor variant of the Model 700D with a full-length Mannlicher-style stock.

Model 720L. A full-stocked 'Mannlicher' version of the standard 700L, this double-trigger gun was offered in the same chamberings as the Model 700D.

Model 720 Luxus ('or 'Deluxe'). Mechanically identical with the other 700-series guns, this had a single trigger with a setting element and a gold-bead front sight. A left-hand version was introduced in 1985.

Model 740S. Offered only in 6.5x55, with a 23.6in heavy barrel and a double trigger, this was identical with the Model 640S target rifle (q.v.) except for the chambering and the length of the action.

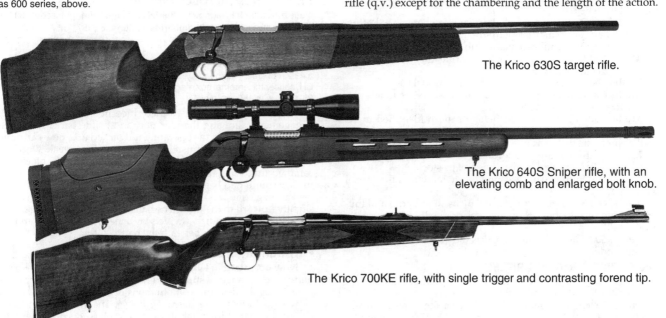

The Krico 630S target rifle.

The Krico 640S Sniper rifle, with an elevating comb and enlarged bolt knob.

The Krico 700KE rifle, with single trigger and contrasting forend tip.

The Krico 720L St, with a full-length stock and a short barrel.

Model 740S Magnum. This was simply a variant of the 740S (above) in 7.5x55. The barrel measured 25.6in.

THE VOHBURG-IRSCHING RANGE

The move from Stuttgart led to a reduction in the number of patterns available from Krico, the current range being summarized below.

300-SERIES SPORTING RIFLES

Model 300 or '300 Standard'. This was previously known as the 'Model 300E', the most basic pattern of the type.

Model 300L or 'Luxus'. The deluxe model, previously known as '300D', with a better stock and a rosewood schnabel forend tip.

Model 300SA or 'Schallabsorber'. Originally known as the Model 300D SA, this is a double-trigger gun fitted with a sound moderator.

Model 300 Silhouette. Formerly known as the 'Model 300LS'.

Model 300 Stutzen. This short-barreled variant, distinguished by a full-length Mannlicher stock, was previously known as the 'Model 320L'.

400 SERIES SPORTING RIFLES

This range contained most of the original 22 Hornet guns, assimilated with several of the 300-type 22LR and 22WMR target rifles.

Model 400 or '400 Standard'. Originally known as the Model 400E, this was the most basic gun in the range.

Model 400E or 'Einzellader'. This was a single shot version of the basic magazine-feed rifle, formerly known as the Model 330S, with a solid receiver floor conferring greater rigidity.

Model 400L or 'Luxus'. The deluxe pattern, formerly known as '400D', had a better stock than the standard pattern.

Model 400 Match. Formerly known as the Models 340S or 440S, the current version of this rifle has a short barrel with a muzzle weight. The buttplate is fixed, and the trigger has a movable synthetic shoe.

Model 400 Silhouette. Destined for metallic-target shooting, this was previously sold as the 'Model 340S Silhouette'.

600-SERIES SPORTING RIFLES

The basic 'Model 600' seems to have been what was originally known as the Model 600D.

Model 600B or 'Benchrest'. This was originally known as the 'Modell 650S Benchrest' in Stuttgart days.

Model 600DJ or 'Druckjagd'. Known elsewhere as a 'Battue' (driven game) gun, this 1996 introduction is distinguished by a short barrel and a ventilated quarter-rib carrying the rear sight.

Model 600 Einzellader. A single shot rifle, this was originally known as the Model 630S.

Model 600 Jagd. Formerly known as the Model 640L.

Model 600KE or 'Economy'. This was a basic 1996-vintage pattern with a beechwood stock.

Model 600L or 'Luxus'. The deluxe pattern identified by its double-trigger mechanism, barrel-mounted front swivel, and well-appointed stock was previously known as the Model 600L.

Model 600 Match. Simply the Model 640S under another name, this was easily identified by the design of its stock.

Model 600 Sniper. This was previously known as the Model 640 Sniper.

Model 600 Stutzen. Distinguished by its short barrel and full-length Mannlicher-style stock, this was originally known as the Model 620L.

Model 600V or 'Varmint'. This was the post-1995 designation for the Model 600A.

700-SERIES SPORTING RIFLES

Model 700V or 'Varmint'. This is the current designation for the Model 700A, described above.

Model 700KE or 'Economy'. Introduced in 1996, this is a plain-stock version of the 700D. The wood is beech instead of walnut.

Model 700DJ or 'Druckjagd'. Distinguished by a rear sight set into a ventilated quarter-rib, this is the short-barreled 'Battue' or driven-game version of the basic rifle.

Model 700 Luxus. The deluxe pattern, formerly known as the Model 700L, has a fine-quality Bavarian stock with a separate rosewood forend tip.

Model 700 Luxus S. Introduced in 1996, this is a variant of the standard deluxe rifle (700 Luxus) with a cocking slide on the upper tang behind the bolt mechanism.

Model 700 Stutzen. Formerly known as the Model 720L, this has a short barrel and a full-length Mannlicher-style stock.

MODEL 902 SPORTING RIFLE

This 'Safety Repeating Rifle' – the latest in the Krico range – features fashionably modular construction (cf., Sauer, Steyr-Mannlicher). Externally similar to the 700 Luxus S, it is easily recognized by the alloy frame anchoring the butt and the forend. The frame is usually supplied with inset panels of wood, though engraved nickel plates are optional.

Based on a three-lug bolt locking directly into the barrel extension, the action is made in three lengths (short, standard and large). The bolt handle is spatulate and the exchangeable barrels each have a loaded-chamber indicator. Barrel lengths are 19.7in (Stutzen), 22.5in (standard) and 24.4in (magnums). The double trigger mechanism incorporates a 'set' element, which is re-set automatically if the bolt is opened. Detachable box magazines hold three or five rounds, the latter being optional. Gun weight averages 6.8lb empty.

The Bavarian-style butt has a low hog's back comb and a squared cheekpiece. The slender forend has a separate schnabel tip of rosewood. Checkering appears on the pistol grip and forend; swivels lie beneath the barrel and the butt.

• Krieghoff, autoloading type

This interesting gas-operated design was developed in the mid 1930s, but only a few had been made when World War II brought production to a halt. The gun was light, handy and had an unusually compact action, though the distance between the pistol grip and the trigger lever was too great for small hands.

HIGH-POWER AUTOLOADING RIFLE

Made by Heinrich Krieghoff Waffenfabrik, Suhl, Thuringia, about 1937-9. Total production: 250? Chambering options: 6.5x57, 7x57, 8x57IS, 8x60. Action: locked by a block moving vertically behind the chamber; gas operated, semi-automatic only.

DATA FOR 8X60 VERSION

41.2in overall, 7.25lb empty. Barrel length not known, 4-groove rifling; RH, concentric. Internal box magazine, 4 rounds. Block-and-leaf back sght. 2820 fps with 159-grain bullet.

The front part of the two-piece breechblock dropped out of engagement, allowing the rear portion to slide back. The spent case was ejected, and the operating rod picked up a new cartridge on the return stroke to push it forward into the breech. Once the cartridge had entered the chamber, the front part of the block was cammed up to seal the breech. The action remained open when the last round had been ejected.

The magazine was offset to the left of the breech, ejection being slightly upward to the right. The half-stock had checkering on the pistol grip and forend; the swivels lay beneath the butt and around the operating-rod tube beneath the barrel.

• Krieghoff, break-open type

Now operating in Ulm, but based in Suhl prior to 1945, Krieghoff makes a range of superb side-by-side and over/under shotguns, double rifles, and combinations of smooth-bore and rifled barrels (including three-barrel *Drillinge*). The quality of the metalwork and wood-to-metal fitting is exemplary; decoration can be

The Krieghoff Ultra 20 Double Rifle.

applied from comparatively plain engraving to the finest high-relief inlay work.

Most of the current guns incorporate standard features, such as the Krieghoff Universal Trigger System and the Combi cocking device. The trigger has been designed specifically to preserve crisp operating characteristics, but preventing the accidental 'doubling' (firing a second shot unbidden) which has often plagued double rifles chambering powerful ammunition. The Combi mechanism allows the rifles to be carried with the hammers down – the safest position – but they can be cocked simply by pushing forward on the slide on the tang. If the slide is locked forward, the action re-cocks automatically each time it is opened; alternatively, the hammers can be lowered safely (even if the chambers are loaded) simply by pushing the slide forward as far as it can go, then gently allowing it to move back to the rear or uncocked position.

Only the purpose-built rifles are listed below; Krieghoff also offers combination rifle/shotguns, as well as EL-65 sub-caliber inserts to convert shotgun barrels to rifles.

CLASSIC STANDARD DOUBLE RIFLE
Made by H. Krieghoff GmbH, Ulm/Donau, Germany.
Currently in production. **Chambering options:** 7x65R, 30R Blaser, 30-06, 308 Winchester, 8x57IRS, 8x75RS or 9.3x74R. **Action:** locked by a slide in the frame engaging two lumps on the underside of the barrel-block, and by an extension of the block entering the face of the standing breech.
DATA FOR A TYPICAL EXAMPLE
   Chambering: 9.3x74R, rimmed. 40.75in overall, 7.6lb empty. 23.5in barrel, 4-groove rifling; RH, concentric? Double barreled: two shots only. Fixed-leaf rear sight. 2280 fps with 285-grain bullet.

The Classic is a streamlined boxlock rifle. The side-by-side barrel units (which include shotgun types) can be readily exchanged when required. The gun has a sliding self-adjusting locking wedge and an automatic safety to ensure that the hammers cannot be released until the action is closed. A detachable wedge between the muzzles allows a gunsmith to re-regulate the points of impact if necessary. Optional fittings include a single trigger, 21.5in barrels, and folding or Express sights set into the standard quarter-rib. Some guns have small Arabesque engraving on the action, which, though optional in Europe, is regarded as standard in North America. The straight-comb butt may have a conventionally rounded or a squared Bavarian-style cheekpiece; checkering graces the pistol grip and the slender schnabel-tip forend; and swivels will be found beneath butt and barrel.

SIMILAR GUNS
Classic Big Five. Intended to down the largest African game, this is chambered for a selection of high-power cartridges: 375 H&H Magnum, 375 H&H Magnum Flanged Nitro-Express, 416 Rigby, 458 Winchester Magnum, 470 Nitro Express, 500/416 Nitro Express 3in (introduced in 1997) and 500 Nitro Express 3in. The guns have 23.5in barrels and weigh about 9.5lb, depending on the grain of the woodwork. They are customarily fitted with 'BreaK-O' recoil-reducers in the butt – particularly in the larger chamberings – and have a hinged front trigger to protect a finger on the rear trigger from the effects of recoil. The sights may be a squared back notch and a squared front blade, or a 'V'-notch with a pearl bead.

Classic-S. This variant is recognizable by the sideplates, though the action is still a boxlock. It provides the basis for decoration, ranging from simple scrollwork to high-relief game scenes inlaid with precious metal.

HUBERTUS STANDARD SPORTING RIFLE
Made by H. Krieghoff GmbH, Ulm/Donau, Germany.
Currently in production. **Chambering options:** 222 Remington, 22-250 Remington, 5.6x50R Magnum, 5.6x52R, 243 Winchester, 6x62R Frères, 6.5x55, 6.5x57, 6.5x57R, 6.5x65R, 270 Winchester, 7x57, 7x57R, 7x64, 7x65R, 30R Blaser, 30-06, 308 Winchester, 8x57IRS or 8x75RS. **Action:**

locked by a slide in the frame engaging two lumps on the underside of the barrel-block.
DATA FOR A TYPICAL STEEL-FRAME EXAMPLE
   Chambering: 6.5x57R, rimmed. About 41in overall, 6.1lb empty. 23.62in barrel, 4-groove rifling; RH, concentric? Single shot only. Fixed-leaf rear sight. 3230 fps with 93-grain bullet.

Introduced in 1996, this is a single-barrel version of the Classic, sharing the Universal Trigger System and the Combi cocking mechanism. The guns are usually fitted with straight-comb butts with squared Bavarian-style cheekpieces, and have slender forends with elegant schnabel tips. Swivels lie beneath the butt and barrel, and a fixed rear sight is set into the front of the sculpted quarter-rib. Guns with aluminum alloy frames are about 12oz lighter than the steel version, and a 21.65in barrel is among the many options.

SIMILAR GUNS
Hubertus Magnum. Built on the standard steel frame, this is chambered for 270 Weatherby Magnum, 7mm Remington Magnum or 300 Winchester Magnum cartridges. It may also be fitted with the 'BreaK-O' recoil-reducer, which increases an empty weight of about 7lb by 14oz.

Hubertus-S. Mechanically identical with the standard pattern, this has a steel boxlock with sideplates. The 'S' version forms the basis for the ornate deluxe options.

TECK DOUBLE RIFLE
Made by H. Krieghoff GmbH, Ulm/Donau, Germany.
Currently in production. **Chambering options:** (standard guns) 7x65R, 30R Blaser, 30-06, 308 Winchester, 8x57IRS, 8x75RS or 9.3x74R. **Action:** locked by a slide in the frame engaging two lumps on the underside of the barrel-block, and by a cross-bolt intercepting extensions on the barrel-block face.
DATA FOR A TYPICAL BOCKDOPPELBÜCHSE
   Chambering: 7x65R, rimmed. 42in overall, 7.35lb empty. 25in barrel, 4-groove rifling; RH, concentric? Double-barreled: two shots only. Fixed-leaf rear sight. 2820 fps with 162-grain bullet.

Also offered as a shotgun and a combination gun, the Teck over/under double rifle is built on a classic boxlock action. Ejectors can be fitted if required and the frame may be aluminum alloy instead of steel, saving about 12.5oz. The earliest Teck was a self-cocker with a safety catch on the tang, but guns can now be obtained with a special double set trigger, a single selective trigger, the patented Krieghoff Universal Trigger System, or the Combi cocking mechanism. Barrels measuring 21.65in can be supplied on request. The butts have a slight drop-comb, an oval cheekpiece, and checkering on the pistol grip; forends are customarily round-tipped, with extensive checkering on the sides. A small fixed rear sight is fitted to the tip of the quarter-rib, and a ventilator is often fitted between the muzzles.

SIMILAR GUNS
Teck Bergstutzen. Built on the standard Teck action, this offers 21.65in barrels of differing calibers. The chamberings are usually 22 Hornet, 222 Remington Magnum, 5.6x50R Magnum or 5.6x52R in the lower barrel, with 243 Winchester, 6x62R Frères, 6.5x57, 6.5x57R, 6.5x65R, 270 Winches-

The breech of the 'Big Five' Double Rifle.

ter, 7x57, 7x57R, 7x64, 7x65R, 30-06, 308 Winchester, 8x57IRS, 8x75RS or 9.3x74R in the upper barrel.

ULM DOUBLE RIFLE

Made by H. Krieghoff GmbH, Ulm/Donau, Germany.

Currently in production. **Chambering options:** (standard guns) 7x65R, 30R Blaser, 30-06, 308 Winchester, 8x57IRS, 8x75RS or 9.3x74R. **Action:** generally as Teck, above.

DATA FOR A TYPICAL BOCKDOPPELBÜCHSE

Chambering: 30-06, rimless. 42in overall, 7.28lb empty. 25in barrel, 4-groove rifling; RH, concentric? Double-barreled: two shots only. Fixed-leaf rear sight. 2990 fps with 150-grain bullet.

Krieghoff's finest over/under guns, these have beautifully-engineered detachable sidelocks and a safety slide on the upper tang. Double triggers are standard fixtures, the rear sights are mounted on quarter-ribs, and the woodwork is similar to that of the Teck.

SIMILAR GUNS

Ulm Bergstutzen. Chambered for the same cartridges as the Teck version, this has 21.65in barrels of differing caliber.

Ulm Primus. These are simply extra-quality versions of the standard guns, with superb engraving and specially selected woodwork.

ULTRA-20 DOUBLE RIFLE

Made by H. Krieghoff GmbH, Ulm/Donau, Germany.

Currently in production. **Chambering options:** (standard guns) 7x65R, 30R Blaser, 30-06, 308 Winchester, 8x57IRS, 8x75RS or 9.3x74R. **Action:** locked by a slide in the frame engaging two lumps on the underside of the barrel-block.

DATA FOR A TYPICAL STEEL-FRAME BOCKDOPPELBÜCHSE

Chambering: 308 Winchester, rimless. 40.8in overall, 7.35lb empty. 23.62in barrel, 4-groove rifling; RH, concentric? Double-barreled: two shots only. Fixed-leaf rear sight. 2625 fps with 168-grain bullet.

Also made as a 20-bore shotgun or a three-barrel *Drilling*, this over/under rifle has a steel or lightweight aluminum alloy frame (saving about 13oz). Two hammers are mounted inside the box-lock frame, and a manual cocking slide lies on the upper tang behind the top lever. A single-trigger option is often fitted to the guns that are destined to serve solely as double rifles, though the standard two-trigger unit is preferred if the optional shotgun barrels are to be used. Woodwork consists of a Bavarian-style walnut butt – with a drop-comb and a squared cheekpiece – and a schnabel-tipped forend. Extensive checkering appears on the pistol grip and forend sides.

SIMILAR GUNS

Ultra-20 Bergstutzen. Distinguished by its 21.65in barrels, this mountain rifle has a large-caliber barrel above a smaller one. The chambering options are basically the same as the Teck Bergstutzen described above.

Ultra-20 S, Bergstutzen and Bockdoppelbüchse. Identical with the standard guns in all other respects, these have plates extending backward on the sides of the action; they provide the basis for the most decorative of the deluxe patterns.

Ultra-20 Bockdoppelbüchse TS. Introduced in 1996, this variant incorporates a free-floating (*Thermostabil*, 'TS') barrel assembly – unaffected by heat – with a proprietary three-point radial adjustment system to regulate the point of impact.

• Langenhan

Best known after 1925 as a maker of airguns, but once renowned for the 'FL' autoloading pistols, Friedrich Langenhan of Zella-Mehlis also built rimfire sporting rifles on a particular form of dropping-block action.

'F.L.' TARGET RIFLE
'F.L.'-Kleinkaliberbüchse

Made by Friedrich Langenhan, Zella-Mehlis (1922-38?).

Total production: several thousand. **Chambering:** 22 Long Rifle (5.6mm Nr. 6), rimfire. **Action:** locked by the underlever propping the sliding breechblock behind the chamber.

44.1in overall, 7.61lb empty. 28.25in barrel, 4 grooves; RH twist, concentric. Single shot only. Micro-adjustable tangent rear sight. About 1085 fps with 40-grain bullet.

Langenhan's target rifle embodied a breechblock which slid vertically in the slab-sided receiver, operated by a lever combined

The Langenhan 'FL' single-shot dropping-block rifle.

with the trigger guard. The basis of the design seems to have been the Aydt (q.v.), though the two differed greatly in detail internally.

A typical rifle had an octagonal barrel, though round and part-octagonal/part-round alternatives could be obtained. The butt was customarily a pistol grip pattern with a high hog's back comb. The forend usually took a broad form with noticeable flats next to the breech. Swivel eyes were fitted to the barrel and butt.

The standard barrel-mounted rear sight could be supplemented by a micro-adjustable diopter mounted on a pillar attached the upper tang of the receiver; the front sight was a ramped blade, barleycorn, bead or replaceable-element tunnel.

Special guns of this type were made for export, particularly to Switzerland, with hooked buttplates, special cheekpieces, set triggers, hinged palm-rests beneath the forend, and sights of the finest patterns.

Work on these rifles – sometimes identified only by 'FL' or 'FLZ' marks – seems to have ceased shortly before World War II began, though Langenhan was still trading in 1945. Essentially similar rifles were still being made by Weihrauch (q.v.) in the early 1990s.

• Lettow

Otto von Lettow of Danzig patented an improved dropping-block breech mechanism in 1887. Its features included a hammer and an associated coil spring carried within the breechblock, and a separate operating lever curved around the trigger guard. The guard, decoratively spurred in typically mid-European style, contained a two-trigger mechanism incorporating a set element. Though no Lettow-marked guns have been reported, many sporting rifles embodying similar constructional features were made in Suhl and the surrounding districts prior to 1914.

• Lindner

Adolf Lindner of Berlin patented a distinctive lever-action rifle in 1887. A radial breechblock pivoted around a transverse pin in the lower part of the receiver ahead of the trigger guard. The hammer had a special short-fall design, minimizing lock time, and a sliding extractor was activated automatically as the breechblock rotated backward. The patent drawings suggest a design which was mature enough to have been manufactured, but no guns of this type have yet been traced.

• Luger

This rifle was the subject of patents granted in 1893-4 to protect extractors, ejectors, special ammunition clips, and a safety system which prevented the gun firing if the detachable bolt head had been lost. Possibly developed by Ludwig Loewe & Co., seeking to avoid paying royalties to Mauser, the Luger rifle was derived from the Gewehr 88 (see 'Reichsgewehr'). Greatly resembling its predecessor, the Luger design lacked the barrel jacket and had a quadrant-arm rear sight; guides for a stripper clip were added above the feedway – the magazine would also accept Mannlicher or Luger clips – and the abbreviated handguard stopped short of the barrel band. The cocking piece was noticeably more rounded than the Gew. 88 pattern, while a radial clip-expelling lever lay on the lower right side of the magazine case.

A Luger rifle chambering an experimental 6mm rimless cartridge was successfully tested by the U.S. Navy in November 1894, but the advent of the Lee Straight Pull rifle (see **'USA: Winchester-Lee'**) ruined its chances of adoption. Tests were also undertaken in the Netherlands in 1895, and the existence of a sporting-rifle action marked by Deutsche Waffen- und Munitionsfabriken suggests that work continued into 1897. As many as 500 Luger rifles may have been made, though confirmation is lacking.

• Mannlicher

A few Austro-Hungarian Mannlicher bayonets have been found with standard German property and inspectors' marks. They include M1888 examples usually dated 1910-2 and a few of 1895 type dating from 1917. Their history is still obscure. It has been suggested that Mannlicher rifles were acquired to offset a temporary shortage of Mausers prior to 1914 or, alternatively, during the war to offset a temporary shortage of weapons. Neither case is proven, though Bavaria *did* purchase Steyr handguns in 1916-18. See also 'Reichsgewehr (Mannlicher)'.

MODEL 1898/40 SHORT RIFLE Gewehr 98/40
Made by Fémáru Fegyver és Gépgyér, Budapest, 1941-4.
Chambering: 7.9x57mm, rimless. **Action:** locked by two lugs on the bolt head rotating into their seats in the receiver as the bolt handle was turned down.

43.2in overall, 9lb empty. 23.6in barrel, 4-groove rifling; RH, concentric. Internal charger-loaded box magazine, 5 rounds. Tangent-leaf sight graduated to 2000m (2185yd). 2475 fps with sS-Patrone. S. 84/98 bayonet.

The first of these guns, adapted from the Hungarian 35.M pattern, was delivered from 'Metallwaren-, Waffen- und Maschinenfabrik' – the Hungarian state firearms factory in Budapest, code 'jhv' – in the Spring of 1941. Unlike its Hungarian predecessors, the Gew. 98/40 had a German-style charger-loaded magazine, a 1.6in bayonet bar, sights for the sS-Patrone, a bolt handle turned downward, and a sling-slot in the butt. Its British-type butt was held in the action-body socket by a sturdy bolt running up through the butt-body and pistol grip. Production ended in the autumn of 1944, when the advance of the Red Army made work impossible. The Gew. 98/40 was sturdy and reliable, though the butts occasionally worked loose. It provided the basis for the Hungarian 43.M service rifle (q.v.).

• Mauser, autoloading type

Most of the guns were characterized by the needless complexity so characteristic of the pre-1914 period; though some were made in substantial numbers, they invariably failed field trials.

Ironically, the only lasting contribution made by the Mauser organization to autoloading rifle design was the gas-operated roller-locked breech system. Originated by Wilhelm Stähle, then perfected by a research team led by Ernst Altenburger and Ludwig Vorgrimmler, this provided the basis for the CETME and Heckler & Koch rifles (q.v.).

C/98 AUTOMATIC RIFLE
Patented in Germany in February 1898-May 1899, this relied on two pivoting bars in a prominent housing at the front of the receiver. When the gun was fired, the barrel ran back inside its casing; after traveling about .4in (10mm), the bars were cammed out of engagement, the barrel stopped, and the breechblock ran back alone to cock the internal hammer. A spring in the left side of the receiver returned the block to battery, stripping a new round into the chamber. The block rejoined the barrel, the barrel/receiver assembly moved forward, and the locking bars were cammed back into engagement.

The rifle shown in the patent specifications – at least one survives – had a magazine case integral with the extended trigger guard. A bolt-type charging slide lay on the right side of the receiver and a prominent radial 'wing' safety catch appeared on the back of the breech cover.

A rifle pictured in *Mauser-Gewehre und Mauser-Patente* (1908), possibly a later example, has an internal magazine and a small oval trigger guard. A company of an infantry regiment was issued with C/98 rifles in 1901, but the trials were not successful.

C/02 AUTOMATIC RIFLE
Protected by a series of patents, the most important being granted in November 1902, this clumsy weapon replaced the C/98. After the gun had fired, the barrel and bolt recoiled across the magazine well. At the end of the rearward stroke, a rapid-pitch thread in the multi-piece bolt rotated the locking lugs out of engagement; the bolt was then held back as springs returned the barrel to its original position. The final movement of the barrel

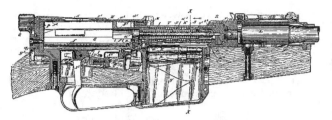

A longitudinal section of an early Mauser autoloading design, from a patent granted in 1902.

operated the ejector and tripped the retaining latch, whereupon the bolt ran back to battery, stripping a fresh round into the chamber and re-locking the lugs.

Though the C/02 apparently extracted spent cases better than its predecessor, the bolt was needlessly complicated and the excessive mass of the moving parts made accurate shooting difficult. Revisions were being patented as late as 1905, but the project was abandoned shortly afterwards; production may have been substantial, as one rifle is reportedly numbered '137'. The original patent shows an integral magazine case/trigger guard assembly, but most survivors have internal magazines and oval trigger guards. A folding charging handle on the right side could be used to operate the breech manually, though the pull would have been very stiff.

C/06-08 AUTOMATIC RIFLE
This marked a return to short-recoil principles. A lesser design embodied a pivoting saddle – much more compact, but also more complicated. The guns pictured by Korn are numbered '2' (flap lock) and '15' (saddle lock), but flap-lock guns have been reported with numbers as high as 50. C/06-08 rifles were eventually replaced by the delayed-blowback M1915.

MODEL 1915 AUTOMATIC RIFLE
Mauser Flieger-Gewehr und Flieger-Karabiner
Made by Waffenfabrik Mauser AG, Oberndorf.
Total production: 200-250? **Chambering:** 8x57, rimless. **Action:** delayed blowback – see text below.
DATA FOR A TYPICAL RIFLE
49.15in overall, 10.45lb empty. 26.55in barrel, 4-groove rifling; RH, concentric. Detachable box magazine, 10 or 20 rounds. Tangent sight graduated to 2000m (2185yd). 2510 fps with S-Patrone. S. 98, S. 98/05 or S. 84/98 bayonet.

Based on a patent granted in October 1906, the C/06-08 rifle was made in small numbers in 1907 for field trials. Some rifles had leaf sights instead of the Lange tangent pattern, and a selection of magazines was tried. Most guns were stocked similarly to the Gew. 98 and accepted bayonets without muzzle rings.

When the gun fired, the barrel and receiver slid backward for about 15mm. During this time, locking bars were cammed into the sides of the receiver to release the breechblock to reciprocate. The action was cumbersome and unreliable; the slender locking bars were particularly prone to breakage.

Mauser designers were doggedly persisting with the flap-lock when World War I began. Consequently, a few half- and full-stocked guns (similar in concept to the C/12-14 pistol) were issued in 1915, each costing six times as much as gas-operated Mondragons which had been purchased in Switzerland.

The fully-stocked rifles had standard Gew. 98 pattern nose caps, accepted bayonets, and were tested in the trenches of the Western Front. Most of the half-stock patterns were initially used

The Mauser-Fliegerkarabiner was an awkward and cumbersome gun.

for air service. Experience showed the Mondragon (q.v.) to be preferable and the Mausers were rapidly withdrawn. Surviving guns seem to have been reissued to the navy.

MODEL 35 AUTOMATIC RIFLE

Dating from the mid 1930s, this had a two-part rotating bolt unlocked by a short recoil system. Extensively tested by the German army, it was not efficient enough to be adopted.

The breech of the 1935-pattern Mauser rifle.

MODEL 41 RIFLE
Gewehr 41 (M)

Made by Mauser-Werke AG, Oberndorf (code 'byf').
Total production: 6700, 1941. **Chambering:** 7.9x57, rimless. **Action:** locked by rotating lugs on the bolt into the receiver; gas operated, semi-automatic only.

46.15in overall, 10.15lb empty. 21.65in barrel, 4-groove rifling; RH, concentric. Integral box magazine, 10 rounds. Tangent-leaf sight graduated to 1200m (1310yd). 2425 fps with sS-Patrone. S. 84/98 bayonet.

The Heereswaffenamt, or army weapons office, issued specifications for a semi-automatic rifle to Mauser, Walther and others in 1941. Mauser's submission, the 'Gewehr 41 (M)', used the muzzle-cup operating system developed in the early 1900s by the Danish inventor Søren Bang (q.v.). Propellant gas drove an actuating rod back beneath the barrel to unlock a two-piece 'straight-pull' bolt, patented by Mauser engineers in 1935-6.

The Gew. 41 (M) was stocked similarly to the Kar. 98k, accepted the standard bayonet, and could be loaded from stripper clips or with loose rounds; the main identifying feature was the bolt-type charging handle protruding from the lower right rear of the receiver. However, protracted field trials showed that the rival Walther-developed Gew. 41 (W) was preferable; production of the Mauser rifle, therefore, was meager.

GERÄT 06 ASSAULT RIFLE

Inspired by the success of the MP. 43, Mauser created this 'machine carbine' around a gas-operated roller-locked breech system originated by Wilhelm Stähle (see **'Spain: CETME'**). Developed for German army trials early in 1943, Gerät 06 was a gas-operated locked-breech weapon chambering the 7.9mm intermediate (Kurz) cartridge. It had a straight-line layout and the rear sight was carried on a high block. The detachable box magazine was close to the trigger/pistol grip group and a cranked cocking aperture lay on the left side of the breech. A sheet-metal barrel casing was accompanied by a distinctive muzzle-brake/compensator.

SIMILAR GUNS

Gerät 06 No. 2. Dating from 1944, this resembled its predecessor but lacked the muzzle brake.

Gerät 06 (H). Readied for trials in the summer of 1944, this had a modified breech with rollers which simply delayed the opening stroke. This allowed the gas system to be discarded. The German authorities were too suspicious of delayed blowbacks to approve the modified rifle, though Mauser favored it for its simplicity.

OTHER RIFLES

In addition to the intermediate-cartridge guns, Mauser also developed autoloaders chambering the 7.9x57 round in 1944-5. A few were readied for trials, though the quantities involved are no longer known.

• Mauser, bolt-action type

This section contains details of the principal Mauser-made service rifles used in Germany, and also of the sporting rifles built in Oberndorf. Many of the 'contract' guns and some of those embodying modified Mauser actions (e.g., Arisaka, Enfield, Springfield) are covered separately. Mausers were widely used throughout the world, estimates of production running as high as 100 million. Good sources of additional information are Ludwig Olson's authorititative *Mauser Bolt Rifles* (F. Brownell & Son, 1976) and the more recent *Mauser Military Rifles of the World* by Robert Ball (Krause Publications, 1996).

THE EARLIEST GUNS

The first steps had been taken in 1867, when Mauser developed a self-cocking bolt-action rifle on the basis of the Dreyse needle gun. The prototypes were built on old Württemberg rifle-muskets.

The 'C/67' is now sometimes known as the 'Mauser-Norris' rifle, owing to participation of Remington salesman Samuel Norris in its development. It had been rejected by the Württemberg state army at the beginning of the year, and then also by Austria-Hungary. In 1870, however, Paul and Wilhelm Mauser submitted an improved 'C/70' rifle to the Prussian army. Trials in the Spandau musketry school continued throughout the period of the Franco-Prussian War, until only the Mauser and the Bavarian Werder (q.v.) remained. On 9th December 1871, therefore, the Mauser was provisionally adopted pending the development of a satisfactory safety mechanism.

MILITARY RIFLES

The steady improvement in design began with the single shot M1871, progressing through the Serbian M78/80 and the German M71/84 to the Turkish rifle of 1887 and then the Belgian Mle. 89 – the first box-magazine gun. Major advances were made with the Spanish Mauser of 1893, the first to have its magazine contained in the stock, and then with the German rifle of 1898 and its third 'safety' locking lug.

Prior to 1914, most rifles were supplied by Gebrüder Mauser and Waffenfabrik Mauser AG, Ludwig Loewe & Co. (only until the end of 1896), Deutsche Waffen- und Munitionsfabriken (from 1st January 1897), Österreichische Waffenfabriks-Gesellschaft and Fabrique Nationale d'Armes de Guerre. Indeed, in 1897, a cartel had been formed to divide production among the major participants: the agreement lasted until 1914.

The collapse of Germany in 1918 broke the domination of the pre-war supply ring. Alone among the pre-1914 participants, Fabrique Nationale managed to re-establish a flourishing export market under the growing challenge of Ceskoslovenská Zbrojovka. However, as purchases were generally smaller than they had been in the heady days prior to World War I, weapons were often simply supplied from stock.

MODEL 1871 RIFLE
Infanterie-Gewehr M1871

Made by the Königlich Gewehrfabrik, Spandau, 1872-84; by Österreichische Waffenfabriks-Gesellschaft, Steyr, 1873-8; by Gebr. Mauser & Co., Oberndorf, 1873-84; by

The Gewehr 41 (M) was an unsuccessful embodiment of a Bang-type muzzle cup.

The 1871-pattern Mauser infantry rifle.

Productionsgenossenschaft, Suhl, 1876-82; and by the National Arms & Ammunition Co. Ltd, Birmingham, 1876-8.

Chambering: 11x60R, rimmed. **Action:** locked by the bolt-guide rib abutting the receiver ahead of the bridge.

52.95in overall, 10.1lb empty. 33.65in barrel, 4-groove rifling; RH, concentric. Leaf sight graduated to 1600m (1750yd). 1410 fps with Reichspatrone M1871. M1871 sword bayonet.

Adopted on 22nd March 1872, this had a straight-wrist stock, two spring-retained barrel bands, and a nose cap with a bayonet lug on the right side. Swivels lay on the trigger guard and under the middle band. The rear sight had a small leaf for 400m (435yd), and a large one, with a sliding extension, for 500-1600m (545-1750yd).

The Bavarian government ordered 100,000 rifles from the Amberg factory in May 1872, but the facilities were occupied converting Werders (q.v.); Württemberg ordered a similar quantity from the Mauser brothers in December 1873.

The first series-made Spandau rifle was presented to the Kaiser on 22nd March 1875 and, in February 1876, the Prussian authorities ordered 180,000 additional guns from the 'Productionsgenossenschaft Suhl'; 100,000 were sought from Österreichische Waffenfabriks-Gesellschaft in July, and 75,000 from the National Arms & Ammunition Co. Ltd in Birmingham at about the same time. British-made guns were marked 'N.A. & A. CO.' in a triangle, but the order was never completed; deliveries may only have totaled 6,000.

By 31st December 1877, Österreichische Waffenfabriks-Gesellschaft had delivered more than 474,000 rifles to the armies of Prussia and Saxony alone. About 26,000 guns were sold to China in the late 1870s, and other small export orders were fulfilled; most of the purchases, however, were made after the 1871-pattern Mauser had been declared obsolete.

Comparatively few mechanical changes were made to the rifle, though a hardened insert was pinned into the rear of the bolt guide rib after 1882 – to reduce wear – and the bolt-stop screw gained a retaining pin. An ejector was also added in this period.

On 28th January 1884, however, the Kaiser signed an order suspending production of 1871-type rifles, and the single shot weapons were gradually withdrawn from regular units as supplies of the Gew. 71/84 (q.v.) became available from 1886 onward. The old guns were passed down through the active reserve, the Landwehr and Landsturm until – by about 1900 – they had either been sold or placed in store. A.L. Frank of Hamburg ('Alfa') was still advertising large numbers of them commercially in 1911.

SIMILAR GUNS

Balloon guns. Surviving Gew. 71 were re-issued in 1914 to free better weapons for active service, and some are said to have been re-bored to fire incendiary ammunition. Doubt has recently been cast on this claim, with the suggestion that the Germans would have used the 1898-type Mauser action for any anti-balloon weapon. However, the British used substantial quantities of 12-bore shotguns against German observation balloons in the first few months of the war; their cartridges could hold large enough charges of phosphorus to remedy the lack of a suitable small caliber incendiary bullet.

Obsolescent single shot Mauser actions could undoubtedly have accepted a large-bore barrel much easier than their small caliber successors. The caliber of the 'anti-balloon guns' is usually listed as 13mm (.512), but they may have chambered 28-bore (.550) shotgun ammunition. Unfortunately, no gun of this type has yet been traced.

Improved patterns. Tests were undertaken early in 1877 with 500 guns modified in the Spandau factory to receive an improved striker, retaining nut and cocking-piece assembly. The new component was not adopted; though it improved the certainty of ignition, lock-time was also increased greatly.

The 1871-pattern infantry rifle was also taken by many inventors as the basis of magazine conversions. Most of these were simply 'add-on' patterns, feeding by gravity or springs. Some fed automatically, but others required the cartridges to be transferred to the chamber manually.

Typical of these designs were the 1878 Holub design, with a tube magazine above and to the left of the barrel; Schano's of 1879, which had a cylinder on the left side of the breech; and Louis Schmeisser's 1882 design, with a drum on the right side of the gun ahead of the feedway. Franz von Dreyse patented a tube magazine attached to the left side of the action in 1879 and a centrally-mounted detachable box in 1882; Mauser added a box magazine

The Mauser factory in Oberndorf, photographed in 1909.

offset to the right of the breech; and Ludwig Loewe & Co. promoted a 'U'-shape magazine running from the right side of the gun underneath the stock to feed from the left. Adolf Lindner of Berlin championed a gravity-feed box magazine in 1883, offset to the left side of the receiver. Individual cartridges were retracted automatically on the opening stroke of the bolt, then pushed forward into the chamber as the action closed.

MODEL 1871 SHORT RIFLE
Jägerbüchse M1871

Made by the Königlich Gewehrfabrik, Danzig, 1876-84; by Österreichische Waffenfabriks-Gesellschaft, Steyr, 1876-7; and by Gebr. Mauser & Co., Oberndorf, 1876-81.

Total production: not known. **Chambering:** 11x60R, rimmed. **Action:** as M1871 rifle, above.

48.8in overall, 9.85lb empty. 29.5in barrel, 4-groove rifling; RH, concentric. Leaf sight graduated to 1600m (1750yd). 1370 fps with Reichspatrone M1871. M1871 Hirschfänger (sword) bayonet.

Adopted on 18th January 1876, this was similar to the infantry rifle. However, the Jägerbüchse had only one barrel band, the trigger guard terminated in a spurred finger rest, and the rear sling swivel lay beneath the butt instead of through the trigger guard.

Changes were made to the rear sight, the bolt-guide rib and the bolt-stop screw in 1882 (see 'Model 1871', above), but the rifles were rapidly displaced by Gew. 71/84. Many seem to have been given to the navy or, alternatively, despatched to Germany's overseas colonies in Africa or the Far East. Marks applied by the Schutztrupp Deutsche Ost-Afrika ('Sch.D.O.A.') are particularly common. Surviving guns were brought out of store in 1914, though most were discarded during World War I.

MODEL 1871 CARBINE
Karabiner M1871

Made by Österreichische Waffenfabriks-Gesellschaft, Steyr, 1876-7; by Arbeitsgemeinschaft Haenel, Suhl, 1877-85 ; by V.C. Schilling, Suhl, 1877-85; and by Gebr. Mauser & Co., Oberndorf, 1876-81.

Total production: 150,000? **Chambering:** 11x60R, rimmed. **Action:** as M1871 rifle, above. 39.15in overall, 7.54lb empty.

19.9in barrel, 4-groove rifling; RH, concentric. Leaf sight graduated to 1200m (1310yd). 1280 fps with Karabiner-Patrone M1871. No bayonet.

Development of an experimental carbine commenced in January 1875, a prototype being tested at Spandau in May. On 31st August 1876, therefore, the Karabiner M1871 was adopted for dragoons, hussars and lancers, replacing Chassepot carbines altered to fire metal-case ammunition.

The Mauser carbine had a single spring-retained barrel band; a full-length stock; a nose cap from which the muzzle scarcely protruded; a turned-down bolt handle; a small rear sight; and a sling-swivel under the foot of the butt. Prussian carbines were made in Steyr and Suhl; Württemberg issue came directly from Mauser.

By 31st December 1877, Steyr had delivered 60,000 carbines to Prussia and Saxony alone. Issue of carbines was extended to the cuirassiers from 12th April 1884, but replacement of Karabiner M1871 by the 1888-pattern magazine carbines began in 1890. One thousand surplus carbines were sold out of store to China in 1906.

SIMILAR GUNS

Gendarmerie-Gewehr M1871, or 'Landjäger-Gewehr'. This was introduced in Württemberg in 1876 to arm the Königliches Land-

The Mauser Karabiner 1871, with a full stock and the bolt handle turned down.

jäger-Korps, or rural gendamerie. Essentially similar to the Karabiner M1871, the guns can be identified by a lug for a sabre bayonet on the right side of the nose cap and by marks prefaced 'K.L.K.'.

Grenz-Aufseher-Gewehr M1879. Adopted on 29th November 1879, these special carbine-length rifles were made by Schilling of Suhl for the *Grenz- und Steueraufseher zu Fuss,* the Prussian corps of border guards and customs officials. The guns had simple two-position rocking rear sights, Dreyse-style stock fittings, and could accept sword bayonets. About 2500-3000 were made in 1880-1.

MODEL 1882 RIFLE

The experimental Infanterie-Repetier-Gewehr C/1882, developed from the Serbian M78/80 rifle, was patented in Germany in March 1882. It was 52.95in overall, weighed 10.1lb empty, and had a 33.65in barrel rifled with four grooves. A tube magazine lay under the barrel, the leaf sight was graduated to 1600m (1750yd), and an 1871-type bayonet could be mounted on the muzzle and nose cap.

Mauser delivered 2,000 rifles in the summer of 1882 for trials with garrison battalions in Darmstadt, Königsberg and Spandau. The guns incorporated many 1871-pattern components, but had new receivers. Testing revealed that they were not durable enough for service, highlighting premature magazine ignition which was speedily cured by a new flat-nose bullet and deep-seating the primers. The result was the Gew. 71/84 (q.v.).

MODEL 1871/84 RIFLE
Infanterie-Gewehr M1871/84

Made by the arms factories in Danzig, Erfurt and Spandau, 1885-9; by the Königlich bayerisches Gewehrfabrik, Amberg, 1886-90; and by Waffenfabrik Mauser AG, Oberndorf, 1885-7.

Total production: 950,000? **Chambering:** 11x60R, rimmed. **Action:** locked by the bolt-guide rib abutting the receiver ahead of the bridge.

51.05in overall, 10.16lb empty. 31.5in barrel, 4-groove rifling; RH, concentric. Tube magazine in forend, 8 rounds. Leaf sight graduated to 1600m (1750yd). 1410 fps with Reichspatrone 71/84. S. 71/84 knife bayonet.

An improved version of the C/82 rifle, this was adopted everywhere except in Bavaria on 31st January 1884. Bavarian adoption occurred in May.

The Gew. 71/84 was similar externally to the single shot M1871, but an elevator was added beneath the bolt way, and a tube magazine, loaded through the top of the open action, ran forward beneath the barrel. The short-blade bayonet had a muzzle ring.

Prussian guns were made in the principal government arsenals; Bavarian guns came from Amberg; and Württemberg's were supplied by Waffenfabrik Mauser. The first rifles were delivered from

Large amounts of captured equipment were pressed into service during the First World War. These Landsturm men, guarding British prisoners of war, are carrying 1871-pattern Mauser rifles fitted with Belgian Mle 1889 bayonets.

Spandau, Erfurt and Danzig in 1885. The first Amberg-made guns were sent into store in January 1886.

The depth of the rifling grooves was halved (to .059) with effect from 14th November 1885, though the change was not made in Bavaria until the end of 1886.

Though the advent of the French Lebel (q.v.) was soon to make the Gew. 71/84 obsolescent overnight, issues were made to the army corps in Elsass-Lothringen (Alsace-Lorraine) in July 1886. One thousand sectioned actions had previously been distributed to facilitate training.

The Germans nearly adopted an experimental 8mm Gew. 71/84 with an extra locking lug, mooted in 1887. Sense prevailed, however, and the Gew. 88 (see 'Reichsgewehr') was taken instead. Issue of Gewehre 88 in 1890 allowed the first 71/84-type rifles to be withdrawn to serve the active reserve, the Landwehr, and then the Landsturm before being stored or sold. Many ultimately found their way into the navy, where the obsolescence was less obvious. Surviving guns, and those retrieved from wholesalers such as A.L. Frank, were issued in 1914 to free better weapons for active service.

SIMILAR GUNS

Model 71/84-type carbines exist, in addition to Jägerbüchsen with a single barrel band and a swivel on the butt midway between the toe and the trigger guard. Their history has yet to be explained in detail.

MODEL 1896 RIFLE
Kleinkalibriges-Gewehr M1896

Made by Waffenfabrik Mauser AG, Oberndorf, 1896-7.

Total production: at least 2185. **Chambering options:** 6x58, 7.65x64, 8x57 and probably others. **Action:** locked by two lugs on the bolt head engaging recesses in the receiver behind the chamber as the bolt handle was turned down.

DATA FOR A 6MM EXAMPLE

Chambering: 6x58, rimless. 49.2in overall, 8lb empty. 29.15in barrel, 6-groove rifling; RH, concentric. Internal box magazine loaded from a stripper clip, 5 rounds. Tangent-leaf sight graduated to 2000m (2185yd). 2800 fps with 130-grain bullet? Special sword bayonet.

This experimental Mauser was apparently ordered to enable trials to be undertaken with small caliber ammunition, as its action bore a greater resemblance to the 1894-pattern Swedish Mauser rifle than it did to the Gew. 88/97.

The guns had a non-rotating extractor, a shrouded bolt head, an auxiliary locking lug on the underside of the bolt body, and an under-cut extractor to prevent double loading. The straight-wrist stocks were retained by a single sprung band, and a small nose cap had a bayonet lug on its right side. A half-length cleaning rod was normally carried in the forend; swivels lay under the band and on the under edge of the butt; and a handguard ran from the receiver ring to the band. The rear sight was carried above the handguard on a short sleeve around the barrel.

The earliest guns cocked as the bolt was closed, but later examples cocked on opening. The effort was eased by increasing the diameter of the bolt behind the handle to lengthen the cocking-cam track.

Trials eventually resolved in favor of the existing 8mm cartridge. As Mauser had improved the basic rifle, and as the German army wanted refinements of its own, the 1896-type gun was abandoned. It is highly likely that some were rebarreled and re-stocked, as specimens have been reported in 7.65mm and 8mm.

MODEL 1888/97 RIFLE
Infanterie-Gewehr M1888/97 ('Gew. 88/97')

Made by Waffenfabrik Mauser AG, Oberndorf, 1895.

Total production: about 2000. **Chambering:** 8x57, rimless. **Action:** locked by two lugs on the bolt head engaging recesses in the receiver behind the chamber as the bolt handle was turned down, and by a safety lug opposing the bolt handle base entering its seat.

49.15in overall, 8.77lb empty. 29.15in barrel, 4-groove rifling; RH, concentric. Internal box magazine loaded from a stripper clip, 5 rounds. Tangent sight graduated to 2000m (2185yd). 2065 fps with Patrone 88. Special sword and épée bayonets.

Delivered in the summer of 1895, this was an adaptation of the contemporary Mauser rifles – made in Oberndorf but incorporating features requested by the army. It had the 1895-patent third or 'safety' locking lug, a cocking-piece housing with an integral gas-deflector flange, and gas-escape holes in the bolt body. The action cocked on opening.

Formally accepted in Prussia, Saxony and Württemberg on 11th March 1897 (21st April in Bavaria), after trials against 6mm-caliber Mausers, the Gew. 88/97 had a uniquely squared Lange tangent-pattern rear sight and a full-length barrel jacket. The straight-wrist stock had a single barrel band, carrying the front swivel, and there were two closely spaced nose bands. The tubular-steel hilts of the bayonets slid over (and locked onto) the cleaning-rod housing beneath the barrel jacket, the basic idea of isolating the bayonet from the barrel having been patented by Mauser in October 1895. Before the Erfurt factory could begin production, the Gewehr 88/97 was abandoned in favor of the improved 1898-pattern rifle.

MODEL 1898 RIFLE
Infanterie-Gewehr M1898 or 'Gewehr 98'
Made by the government small-arms factories in Danzig, Erfurt and Spandau, 1900-18; and by the Königlich bayerisches Gewehrfabrik, Amberg, 1903-7. Rifles were also made by Waffenfabrik Mauser AG, Oberndorf am Neckar, Württemberg, 1904-18; by Deutsche Waffen- und Munitionsfabriken, Berlin, 1904-18; by Simson & Co., Suhl, 1915-18; by C.G. Haenel, Suhl, 1915-18; by V.C. Schilling & Co., Suhl, 1915-18; and by Waffenwerk Oberspree, Kornbusch & Co., Niederschönweide bei Berlin, 1915-18 (acquired by DWM in 1916).
Total production: in excess of five million. **Chambering:** 8x57, rimless. **Action:** as Gew. 88/97, above.

49.2in overall, 9.02lb empty. 29.15in barrel, 4-groove rifling; RH, concentric. Internal box magazine loaded from a stripper clip, 5 rounds. Tangent sight graduated to 2000m (2185yd). 2855 fps with S-Patrone. S. 98 sword bayonet.

Adopted in the armies of Prussia, Saxony and Württemberg on 5th April 1898, to replace the Gew. 88/97, this was a standard Mauser with a third (safety) lug, a guide rib, an under-cut extractor and a shrouded bolt face. The bolt-sleeve lock was introduced, the travel of the firing pin was reduced to accelerate lock time, and a large-diameter receiver ring enhanced strength. The mechanism cocked as the bolt was opened and the internal box magazine could be loaded from a stripper clip or with loose rounds.

Gew. 98 were originally accompanied by the Seitengewehr 98, with a rib along the back of the blade and a very distinctive hilt. The sturdy twin-band nose cap had an unusually long bayonet-attachment bar, giving a rigid mount without the assistance of a muzzle ring.

By 1899, sufficient rifles had been made to allow large-scale troop trials to commence. As few important faults were revealed, tooling for mass production began immediately. The first issues were made in 1901 to the navy, the East Asian Expeditionary Force, and the three premier Prussian army corps. The rifle was then adopted in Bavaria on 2nd May. Rearmament of virtually all reg-

A sniper of Reserve Infanterie-Regiment Nr. 91 (armed with an optically-sighted Gewehr 98) takes aim, observed by colleagues with binoculars and a trench periscope.

ular units was completed by 1907, and most of the Reserve and active Landwehr had been re-equipped with Gewehre 98 by 1912.

Lugs were added to the firing pin in 1902, in accordance with a patent granted to Mauser in May 1901. They aligned with shoulders in the unlocked bolt to prevent accidental firing.

The first private contracts were placed in 1904 with Waffenfabrik Mauser AG and Deutsche Waffen- und Munitionsfabriken, for 290,000 and 210,000 rifles respectively. A perfected self-sprung brass-body charger was introduced in October, remaining standard issue until the end of World War I.

The change from the Patrone 88 to the improved high-velocity S-Patrone, mooted in 1903, was made with effect from 1st October 1905. The modified Lange sight was much taller than its predecessor, and its slider was greatly revised. Converted rifles received a 2.5mm 'S' above the chamber and on the barrel behind the rear sight base.

An auxiliary front sight (*Hilfskorn*) was developed in World War I to allow accurate shooting at 100m, as the graduations on the post-1905 Lange sight began at 400m (435yd). From 19th November 1915, the marking disc on the butt of all rifles – infantry, sniper or otherwise – was replaced by two washers with a central hole connected by a short metal tube. The tip of the firing pin was inserted in the hole while the bolt was being dismantled, preventing damage which could promote a misfire.

An emergency program began in 1916 to accelerate production. Parts made by the many sub-contractors were assembled in the government factories by experienced armorers. Unfortunately, these guns required too much hand fitting for the system to be useful. Rifles which were successfully test fired bore a large star above the chamber, and were known as *Stern-Gewehre* ('Star Rifles'). Their parts were rarely completely interchangeable.

Minor changes were made in 1917 to simplify Gew. 98 components, and the standards of finish began to deteriorate perceptibly. Bolts were browned instead of blued, and differing stock woods were used.

SIMILAR GUNS
Gewehr 98/17. This refined (but semi-experimental) rifle appeared in 1917, with a tangent-leaf rear sight, a cylindrical barrel, a stamped-steel bolt-cover and a hold-open. Five thousand

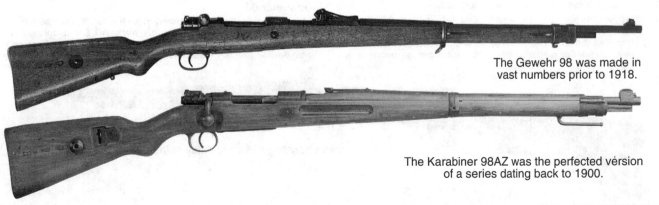

The Gewehr 98 was made in vast numbers prior to 1918.

The Karabiner 98AZ was the perfected version of a series dating back to 1900.

were ordered from Simson of Suhl for trials, but the first batch was not forthcoming until March 1918.

Gewehr 98/18 (or 'Gewehr 18'). Developed privately by Waffenfabrik Mauser, this had a detachable box magazine, a bolt stop included in the trigger system, an improved stock and a new mechanical hold-open. It was too late to see war service. A few hundred were made for field trials, but never issued; they were apparently destroyed after the Armistice.

Model 1907. Originally destined for China, but retained in store in Oberndorf either because of the intervention of revolution or non-payment for previous consignments, these guns armed two German line infantry regiments (nos. 261 and 262) when World War I began. They were practically identical with the Gew. 98, but had the modified 1904-type action, a tangent-leaf sight, a simple nose cap, and accepted a bayonet with a muzzle ring. It is generally accepted that about 15,000 were available.

Karabiner 98b. Rifles retained by the Reichswehr after 1920 were given simple tangent-leaf rear sights. The swivel-bearing barrel band was replaced; the *Klammerfuss* under the butt was superseded by a lateral sling slot; and the bolt handles were turned down into a stock recess. Known as 'Karabiner 98b' to distinguish them from the former Kar. 98 AZ, which had been renamed 'Karabiner 98a', these guns usually display a '1920' property mark in addition to (or instead of) their original date-marks.

Radfahrer-Gewehr 98. Introduced for cyclists about 1902, this was no more than a Gew. 98 with the bolt handle turned down into a depression in the stock.

Scharfschützen-Gewehr 98. Adopted in 1915 to make uniform the equipment of the snipers, who had previously been armed with an assortment of sporting rifles, this was mechanically identical with the standard Gew. 98. The bolt handle was bent down against a special stock recess, and two ring mounts held a 4x Goerz or Zeiss telescope sight. The sight was offset to the left so that the magazine could still be loaded from a stripper-clip. The sight drums were graduated to 1000m (1095yd) in 100-metre increments, except in Bavaria where they were graduated for 200m, 400m and 600m (220yd, 435yd and 655yd) only.

MODEL 1898 CARBINE
Karabiner 98

Made by the Königlich Gewehrfabrik, Erfurt, 1900-1.

Total production: perhaps 3000. **Chambering:** 8x57, rimless. **Action:** as Gew. 88/97, above.

37.2in overall, 7.35lb empty. 17.1in barrel, 4-groove rifling; RH, concentric. Internal box magazine loaded from a stripper clip, 5 rounds. Tangent sight graduated to 1200m (1310yd). 1855 fps with Patrone 88. No bayonet.

Apparently adopted in June 1900, this was a diminutive of the standard infantry rifle with a small Lange-pattern rear sight, a spatulate bolt handle turned down against the stock, and a plain nose cap from which only the muzzle crown protruded. A handguard ran from the rear sight to the muzzle.

Owing to the lack of a bayonet lug, inhibiting use by the artillery and Train, the first Karabiner 98 was abandoned in 1902. Most of the surviving guns were converted in 1902-3 to form *Zielkarabiner*, short-range practice rifles chambering special 5mm primer-propelled ammunition.

MODEL 1898A CARBINE
Karabiner 98A

Made by the Königlich Gewehrfabrik, Erfurt, 1902-5.

Total production: perhaps 7500. **Chambering:** 8x57, rimless. **Action:** as Gew. 88/97, above.

37.2in overall, 7.54lb empty. 17.1in barrel, 4-groove rifling; RH, concentric. Internal box magazine loaded from a stripper clip, 5 rounds.

Tangent sight graduated to 1200m (1310yd). 2610 fps with S-Patrone. S. 98 sword bayonet.

Adopted to replace the Karabiner 98 on 26th February 1902, this had a Gew. 98-type nose cap assembly placed – curiously – well back from the muzzle. Consequently, the Kar. 98A had a short wooden forend ahead of the nose cap. The nose cap was retained by a transverse slotted-head bolt instead of the customary spring, and carried the standard 1.6in bayonet bar.

Experiments began in 1904 to adapt the Kar. 98A for the S-Patrone, but the flash and excessive muzzle blast of the new cartridge was excessive in such a short-barreled gun, and the Kar. 98AZ (below) was substituted in 1905.

MODEL 1898 AZ CARBINE
Karabiner 98 AZ

Made by the government small arms factories in Danzig (1912-4) and Erfurt (1908-18); and by the Königlich bayerisches Gewehrfabrik, Amberg, 1909-12.

Total production: perhaps 1.5 million. **Chambering:** 8x57, rimless. **Action:** as Gew. 88/97, above.

42.9in overall, 8.18lb empty. 23.2in barrel, 4-groove rifling; RH, concentric. Internal box magazine loaded from a stripper clip, 5 rounds. Tangent-leaf sight graduated to 2000m (2185yd). 2755 fps with S-Patrone. S. 98/05 sword bayonet.

Trials began in June 1906 with about 800 long-barrel carbines, all but 100 being fitted with stacking rods. By mid-summer 1907, work had shown that recoil and muzzle blast were more acceptable in the long-barrel guns than the short Kar. 98A. However, a bayonet lug was demanded and changes were required in the stock.

Official adoption of the *Karabiner 98 mit Aufplanz- und Zusammensetzvorrichtung* (Kar. 98 AZ) occurred on 16th January 1908. The external diameter of the receiver ring was noticeably smaller than the Gew. 98 type. A full-length handguard lay above the barrel, a simple tangent-leaf rear sight was used, and a unique hinged nose cap appeared behind an ultra-short muzzle. The front sight had prominent protectors; a stacking rod protruded beneath the nose cap; and a hemispherical bolt handle, with a checkered back face, turned down into the stock. The curve of the pistol grip was tightened to combat additional recoil. The standard bayonet had a 15.7in fullered blade tapering gradually outward toward the tip. Saw-backed versions were issued to NCOs, in traditional German fashion.

The first issues of the Kar. 98 AZ were made to Prussian cavalry in 1909, and extended to the foot artillerymen in 1910. When war began in 1914, the guns were being carried by cavalry; by foot artillerymen; by cyclists attached to infantry regiments, riflemen, sharpshooters and pioneers; by the independent machine gunners; by the telegraphists and the field-telephonists; by airship and motor-transport units; and in parts of the Train.

The flash from the S-Patrone was soon found to char the back of the bayonet grips if the Kar. 98 AZ was fired with the bayonet fixed. To prevent unnecessary damage, therefore, a sheet-steel flash guard was added along the back of the bayonet hilt from the summer of 1915 onward.

SIMILAR GUNS

Karabiner 98a. No changes were made to the guns retained by the Reichswehr after 1920, though they were renamed 'Karabiner 98a' to distinguish them from the Kar. 98b – a minor adaption of the full-length Gewehr 98.

MODEL 1898K SHORT RIFLE
Karabiner 98k

Made by Mauser-Werke AG, Oberndorf am Neckar, Württemberg (code 'S/42', '42', 'byf' or 'svw'); by Mauser-Werke AG, Berlin-Borsigwalde ('S/243', '243' or 'ar'); by Sauer & Sohn, Suhl ('S/147', '147' or 'ce'); by Berlin-Lübecker Maschinenfabrik, Lübeck ('S/237' or '237'); by

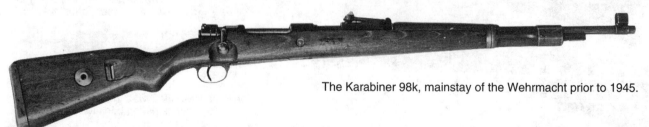

The Karabiner 98k, mainstay of the Wehrmacht prior to 1945.

This Karabiner 98k has a 1.5x Zf. 41 long-relief optical sight.

The action of a wartime Karabiner 98k, made by 'bcd' in 1943.

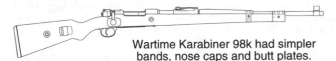

Wartime Karabiner 98k had simpler bands, nose caps and butt plates.

Waffenwerk Brünn AG, Brno ('dot'); by Fabrique Nationale d'Armes de Guerre, Herstal-lèz-Liége ('ch'); by Feinmechanische Werke GmbH, Erfurt ('S/27', '27' and 'ax'); by Gustloff-Werke, Weimar ('bcd'); and by Steyr-Daimler-Puch AG, Steyr/Oberdonau ('660', 'bnz').

Total production: 9-11.5 million (see text). **Chambering:** 7.9x57, rimless. **Action:** as Gew. 88/97, above.

43.7in overall, 8.64lb empty. 23.6in barrel, 4-groove rifling; RH, concentric. Internal box magazine loaded from a stripper clip, 5 rounds. Tangent-leaf sight graduated to 2000m (2185yd). 2475 fps with S-Patrone. S. 84/98 knife bayonet.

Superficially resembling the full-length Kar. 98b, the Karabiner 98k of 1935 was recognizable by its reduced dimensions. The action and tangent-leaf rear sight were unchanged, and the stock was similar in virtually all respects except length. There was a single barrel band, and the 'H'-type nose cap was accompanied by a 1.6in bayonet bar beneath the muzzle. The sling attachment consisted of a slot in the butt and a short fixed bar on the left side of the barrel band.

Production totals are uncertain, owing to a lack of reliable information concerning pre-1939 production. However, it is known that about 7.41 million guns were made during World War II (excluding sniper rifles) and that output peaked in 1944, when 1.92 million guns were made by a variety of contractors.

SIMILAR GUNS

Fallschirmjäger-Karabiner 98k. The paratroop rifles were developed in 1941 for trials, work spilling over into 1942. One pattern had a hinged butt; another used a detachable barrel with an interrupted-screw joint ahead of the receiver. After the costly invasion of Crete, however, the faith of the military hierarchy in mass airborne assaults abated.

Gebirgsjäger-Karabiner 98k. Identifiable by the steel plate on the left side of the butt, small numbers of these guns were made in the early 1940s.

Kriegsmodell 98k. Manufacturing standards fell as the fighting progressed, creating the so-called 'War Model' of 1942. Distinguishing characteristics included stamped nose caps, barrel bands and butt-plates, crudely finished trigger guards, and thinly varnished stocks. Most guns – but by no means all – had laminated stocks, the result of trials that had stretched through the 1930s. Plywood laminates resisted warping better than the conventional one-piece patterns, did not require lengthy maturing, and were less wasteful of raw material.

Zielfernrohr-Karabiner 98 (or Zf.-Kar. 98). Introduced in 1941, these Kar. 98k were selected for their accuracy. Early combinations used 4x Zf. 39 sights made by Zeiss, Leitz, Goerz, Hensoldt and others; during the war, however, smaller 1.5x Zf. 40, Zf. 41, Zf. 41/1 and Zf. 41/2 patterns became common.

Zf. 39 had separate 'turret' mounts, on top of the receiver bridge and the chamber, or – more rarely – a one-piece twin ring mount clamped onto a rail on the left side of the receiver; 1.5x sights slid into a rail on the rear sight, where they were held by a spring-loaded catch. A few guns were fitted in 1944-5 with the Zf. 4 sight, developed for the Gew. 43 (q.v.), in a rearward-slanting twin-ring monoblock. The Zf. 4 was shorter and stubbier than the Zf.39. Production of Zielfernrohr-Karabiner 98k amounted to about 126,000 in 1941-5, output peaking at 57,255 guns in 1943.

MODEL 24 (T) SHORT RIFLE
Gewehr 24 (t)

The subjugation of Czechoslovakia in 1939 provided the Germans with large numbers of Kar. 98k-type vz. 24 and vz. 24/30 short rifles made in Brno by Ceskoslovenská Zbrojovka. There were also a few vz. 98/22 and vz. 98/29 long rifles, approximating to the Karabiner 98b.

However, in addition to existing guns impressed into German service (which generally retain their original Czechoslovakian army markings), production continued until a decision was taken in 1942 to concentrate on the Kar. 98k. About 330,000 Gew. 24 (t) were made under German control; they bear nothing but standard military proof marks and WaA inspectors' marks.

MODEL 29 (P) SHORT RIFLE
Gewehr 29 (p)

This German designation was applied to the 1898-pattern Mauser short rifles being made in the government factories in Radom and Warsaw when the Germans overran Poland (q.v.) in 1939. It has often been claimed that production ceased in 1940 – so that the factories could concentrate on the Kar. 98k – but official records indicate that nearly 370,000 Polish-type weapons were made under German supervision prior to 1942.

MODEL 29/40 SHORT RIFLE
Gewehr 29/40

Made by Steyr-Daimler-Puch AG, Steyr/Oberdonau (code '660' or 'bnz'). Otherwise similar to Kar. 98k – q.v.

This was a variation of the Steyr-made 'export Mauser', apparently issued largely to the Luftwaffe. About 300 rifles were assembled in 1940 from a combination of old parts destined for the Steyr (or 'Steyr-Solothurn') 1929 and 1931-pattern export rifles, and others taken from cannibalized Polish Karabinek wz. 29.

Only a handful of the so-called 'Gewehr 29/40' were made. Note the design of the nose cap and the pointed Austrian-style pistol cap.

A variant of the G33/40 with a slide-swinging butt
or Klappschaft, probably for paratroop use.

The Gew. 29/40 was identical with the Kar. 98k apart from its distinctive nose cap, a handguard stretching from the receiver ring to the nose cap, and a pointed Austrian-style pistol grip. Unlike the Austrian guns made prior to 1939, the 29/40 accepted the German knife bayonet.

MODEL 33/40 SHORT RIFLE
Gewehr 33/40
Made by Waffenwerk Brünn AG, Brno (code 'dot'), 1941-3.
Total production: 131,500, 1940-2. Chambering: 7.9x57, rimless.
Action: generally as Gew. 88/97, above.
38.95in overall, 8.33lb empty. 19.3in barrel, 4-groove rifling; RH, concentric. Internal box magazine loaded from a stripper clip, 5 rounds. Tangent-leaf sight graduated to 1000m (1095yd). 2250 fps with S-Patrone. S. 84/98 knife bayonet.

Officially adopted by the Wehrmacht on 16th October 1940, the Gewehr 33/40 had originally been introduced as the 'Krátá cetniká puska vz.33' for the Czechoslovakian police and the gendarmerie responsible for protecting the country's financial institutions.

Production of the minuscule carbine continued under German supervision until emphasis switched to the Kar. 98k; most Gew. 33/40 were issued to the mountain troops (Gebirgsjäger) and had special reinforcing plates on the left side of the butt. They had a German-style nose cap, but a full-length handguard ran forward from the front of the rear sight. Unlike the original vz. 33, the 33/40 accepted the S. 84/98. Work ceased in 1942 in favor of the Kar. 98k.

MODEL 1898 PEOPLE'S RIFLE
Volkskarabiner 98, 'VK. 98'
The ultimate deterioration of the bolt-action rifles was the crude *Volksgewehr* or "People's Rifle". The earliest apparently dates from the autumn of 1944, though specifications had been circulated some months previously. The goal was a simplified weapon which could be made with a minimum of machine time or raw material; the results included simplified Kar. 98k developed by Mauser-Werke; Volkskarabiner 98 (VK. 98) made by Steyr-Daimler-Puch (code 'bnz'), Walther ('qve') and others; and the Volksgewehre contributed by many anonymous machine shops. VK. 98 chambered the standard sS-Patrone and, except the final patterns, had conventional Mauser bolt actions.

Most VK. 98 had half-stocks, fixed-notch rear sights and roughly stepped or cylindrical barrels. However, though their finish was rough, they were not as poorly made as the Volksgewehre. Chambering full-power 7.9mm S-Patrone or the intermediate Pist. Patr. 43, Volksgewehre have been credited to 'Erma-Werke', Erfurter Maschinenfabrik B. Geipel GmbH (code 'ayf'), but it is suspected that many other contractors were to have been involved had World War II continued into the summer of 1945.

Most had stamped and welded receivers, and simple bolts with one or two locking lugs. They had plain cylindrical bolt handles made from bar-stock, roughly planed woodwork (often with separate butts and forends), and could accept neither bayonets nor grenade launchers. Though Gew. 43-pattern magazines were usually fitted, some of the last and crudest Volksgewehre were single shot only.

No official orders governing the introduction of these Volkswaffen have ever been found, and, though production in the first three months of 1945 is believed to have totalled about 53,000 guns, no breakdown by individual pattern appears to survive. The HWaA was ordered to develop an efficient weapon (which is assumed to have been the Volkskarabiner 98), but it seems much more likely that the most crudely made guns were procured on a purely local basis.

MILITARY-CONTRACT PATTERNS
Waffenfabrik Mauser made large quantities of rifles for export prior to 1914, but most of these are considered in the country-by-country registers; their history was intertwined with the guns made by the other participants in the original 1897-vintage cartel.

During the 1920s, however, aware of the export successes of Fabrique Nationale and Ceskoslovenská Zbrojovka, Mauser-Werke AG began development of a comparable short rifle. The work was completed in the late 1920s and assembly of components made secretly in Oberndorf began in a factory in Kreuzlingen, Switzerland, in 1929-30. Overt production did not begin until the last restrictions of the Treaty of Versailles had been shrugged aside in 1933. By this time, Mauser's rivals had established an unassailable dominance on the export markets.

The earliest orders seem to have been placed by China, though Paraguay and Ethiopia were also keen. The most important variation was the 'Postal Rifle' (*Reichspost-Gewehr*), purchased by the German mail service. This was practically a Kar. 98k, but had a narrow barrel band and a nose cap which was pinned to the forend instead of held by a spring. Genuine Reichspost guns were marked appropriately on the side of the butt, but the term was also used to camouflage sales of rifles to paramilitary formations of the SA and SS.

A few small-scale orders were forthcoming throughout the 1930s from Ethiopia, China and Portugal, but, after 1934, the bulk of Mauser rifles went to the Wehrmacht. So important were the early military deliveries that supplies to the paramilitary ceased, forcing the SA, so it is said, to acquire rifles from Fabrique Nationale.

MODEL 1933 SHORT RIFLE
Mauser Standard-Model
Made by Mauser-Werke AG, Oberndorf am Neckar, 1932-44.
Total production: 235,000? Chambering: 7.9x57, rimless. Action: locked by two lugs on the bolt head engaging recesses in the receiver behind the chamber as the bolt was turned down, and by a safety lug opposing the bolt handle base entering its seat.
DATA FOR A REPRESENTATIVE CARBINE
41.55in overall, 8.5lb empty. 21.65in barrel, 4-groove rifling; RH, concentric. Internal box magazine loaded from a stripper clip, 5 rounds. Tangent-leaf sight graduated to 2000m (2185yd). 2800 fps with standard ball ammunition. Sword bayonet.

The export-pattern Mausers were essentially similar to the 1924-model short rifles offered by Fabrique Nationale and Ceskoslovenská Zbrojovka. However, unless otherwise specified by the customer, they had a German-type exchangeable-bed rear sight and a handguard running from the front of the rear sight base only as far as the barrel band. An 'H'-type nose cap was fitted. Most short rifles had finger grooves in the forend, but these were customarily omitted from carbines. The bolt handles of the latter were generally turned downward: most rifle examples were straight.

Manufacture stopped in 1940 for the duration of the war though, curiously, guns were still assembled for commercial sale. The post-war Allied CIOS report indicates that 8,800 'sporting rifles' were produced in 1940-4.

MODERN PATTERNS
MODEL 93 SNIPER RIFLE
Also known as 'SR 93'
Made by Mauser-Werke Oberndorf GmbH, Oberndorf/Neckar, 1994 to date.
Total production: a few hundred? Chambering options: 7.62x51, 300 Winchester Magnum, 338 Lapua Magnum and others to order. Action: locked by two lugs on the bolt head engaging recesses in the receiver behind the chamber when the bolt handle is turned down.
DATA FOR A TYPICAL EXAMPLE
Chambering: 300 Winchester Magnum. 48.45in overall, 12.9lb without sights. 25.6in barrel, 4-groove rifling; RH, concentric. Detachable box magazine, 6 rounds. Optical sight. 2985 fps with ball ammunition.

The SR 93 Sniper was developed to meet the needs of the German army, though it was ultimately rejected in favor of the British Accuracy International Super Magnum (q.v.). The Mauser design is based on the fashionable modular frame construction, allowing a free-floating barrel to be used in a search for greater accuracy. The barrel has a slotted muzzle brake and is deeply fluted to facilitate cooling.

Enveloped in a rounded synthetic forend, the under edge of the frame provides a rail for accessories such as bipods or hand-stops. The components of the butt – including a synthetic pistol grip, a cheekpiece and an adjustable buttplate – are all mounted on the frame. A telescoping monopod in the butt can be used to support the gun when appropriate.

The safety lever and magazine catch are duplicated, allowing ambidextrous operation, and, most unusually, the bolt handle can be moved from the right side to the left at will.

CENTERFIRE SPORTING GUNS

The rise of big-game hunting, particularly in Africa and India, created a rapidly growing need for sporting rifles. This was initially satisfied by single shot and shotgun-style double rifles, until the widespread issue of military magazine rifles caused hunters to question whether they should carry guns which gave a speedy third, fourth or fifth shot.

The leading military rifles – Lee-Enfield, Mannlicher and Mauser – understandably attracted the greatest attention prior to 1914. However, owing to the rearward position of its locking lugs, the Lee was comparatively weak; and the magazine of most pre-1900 Mannlichers required a special clip, acceptable militarily but much less appropriate for sportsmen. Only the Mauser had impeccable credentials.

Though Mauser actions were supplied to individual gunsmiths prior to 1900 – the Briton George Gibbs, for example, obtained Husqvarna-made examples from Sweden as early as 1899 – commitment to huge military orders prevented Waffenfabrik Mauser participating with any real enthusiasm.

About 1899, however, the Mauser Repetier-Pirschbüchse was introduced. This used the standard 1898-pattern action, usually fitted with the heavyweight cocking piece associated with the export-pattern rifle of 1904. The Mausers could withstand surprisingly high chamber pressures, encouraging ammunition makers in Germany and Britain to develop new cartridges.

Mauser supplied enormous numbers of actions to custom gunmakers prior to 1914, most being identified only by trademarks on the underside of the receiver. Details of the most important agencies are listed separately. After about 1930, Mauser also finished many 7.9mm Standard-Modell (Kar. 98k) rifles for commercial sale. These were offered to those who needed a military-style weapon.

MAUSER-ACTION PATTERNS

MODEL 1898 SPORTING RIFLE
Pirschbüchse C/98
Made by Waffenfabrik Mauser AG, Oberndorf am Neckar, 1899-1910.
Total production: 50,000? **Chambering options:** 6x57, 6.5x54, 6.5x57, 7x57, 8x51, 8x57, 9x57, 9.3x57 or 10.75x57. **Action:** locked by two lugs on the bolt head engaging receses in the receiver behind the chamber as the bolt turned down, and by a safety lug opposing the bolt handle entering its recess.
DATA FOR A TYPICAL EXAMPLE
  Chambering: 9x57, rimless. 44.95in overall, 7.15lb empty. 23.55in barrel, 4-groove rifling; RH, concentric. Internal box magazine loaded from a stripper clip, 5 rounds. Block-and-leaves sight graduated to 300m (330yd). 2100 fps with 247-grain bullet.

This was introduced in 1899 in a limited range of chamberings based on the standard military cartridge case – 7x57, 8x57 and 9x57. Rifles were offered in a selection of half- and full-stock patterns with 23.6in barrels and a 1000m (1095yd) tangent-sight or a simple block- and-leaf *Jagdvisier*. Mausers all had rounded pistol grips with extensive checkering, and notably slender stocks. Ribbed rubber buttplates offered prior to 1910 often bore 'WM' monograms ('Waffenfabrik Mauser'); later ones used the better-known banner trademark. A standard military-pattern magazine floorplate was used. Bolt handles were invariably turned down and front sights appeared on ramps forged integrally with the barrel. Swivels lay on the butt and barrel collar or band. Set-trigger systems were optional.

MILITIA MODEL
Wehrmannbüchse und Einheitsgewehr
Made by Waffenfabrik Mauser AG, Oberndorf am Neckar, about 1900-15.
Total production: not known. **Chambering:** 8.15x46.5R, rimmed. **Action:** as Model 1898 sporter, above.
DATA FOR A TYPICAL SPECIMEN
  49.2in overall, 9.2lb empty. 29.15in barrel, 6-groove rifling; RH, concentric. Sights: see notes. 1800 fps with 150-grain bullet.

Dating from the beginning of the 20th Century, this was little more than a single shot version of the Gew. 98. A few rifles have been reported with magazines, but a wood block generally confined them to single loading; these are believed to be ex-military conversions. Virtually all the rifles chambered a low-power cartridge, credited to a Suhl gunmaker called Fröhn, which had been standardized by the German hunting associations prior to 1914.

The bolt-way had a solid base on purpose-built guns, shaped into a loading tray, and the bolt head lacked the cut away rim of the service weapon. The *Einheitsgewehr* ('universal rifle') could be supplied with exchangeable military or sporting-style triggers. An adjustable aperture sight could be fitted to the left rear of the receiver to facilitate target shooting.

Production continued into the post-war era, when a short-lived version with a sleeve-type receiver and an ejection port was offered.

MODEL 1908 SPORTING RIFLE
Mauser-Pirschbüsche C/98-08
Made by Waffenfabrik Mauser AG, Oberndorf am Neckar, 1908-15.
Total production: not known. **Chambering options:** 6x58, 6.5x54, 7x57, 8x57, 9x57, 9.3x62 or 10.75x68. **Action:** as M1898 sporter, above.
DATA FOR A TYPICAL SPECIMEN
  Chambering: 6x58, rimless. 44.9in overall, 6.67lb empty. 23.6in barrel, 4-groove rifling; RH, concentric. Internal box magazine loaded from a stripper clip, 5 rounds. Tangent-leaf sight graduated to 1000m (1095yd). 2790 fps with 127-grain bullet.

Very similar externally to the C/98, this was offered from 1908-9 onward in half- and full-stock versions with 23.6in barrels and a selection of sights. Most popular was the block-and-leaves *Jagdvisier*, but a 1000m (1095yd) tangent-leaf pattern was also favored. A 500m (550yd) tangent sight with lateral or 'drift' adjustment was less common.

MODEL 1908 SPORTING CARBINE
Mauser-Pirschbüsche C/98-08
Made by Waffenfabrik Mauser AG, Oberndorf am Neckar, 1908-15.
Total production: not known. **Chambering options:** 6.5x54, 6.5x58, 7x57, 8x57 or 9x57. **Action:** as M1898 sporter, above.
DATA FOR A TYPICAL SPECIMEN
  Chambering: 6.5x54, rimless. 40.9in overall, 6.35lb empty. 19.7in barrel, 4-groove rifling; RH, concentric. Internal box magazine loaded from a stripper clip, 5 rounds. Block-and-leaves sight graduated to 300m (330yd). 2360 fps with 120-grain bullet.

This carbine had a full stock with a slight swell or hand-stop under the forend behind the front sling swivel. The barrel band and the nose cap were carried internally, the *Jagdvisier* and radial lever floorplate release were standard, and the trigger guard had a recurved front web.

MODEL 1908 ARMY RIFLE
Mauser-Armee-Pirschbüsche C/98-08
Made by Waffenfabrik Mauser AG, Oberndorf am Neckar, 1908-15.
Total production: not known, but comparatively small. **Chambering options:** 7x57, 8x57 or 9x57. **Action:** as M1898 sporter, above.
DATA FOR A TYPICAL SPECIMEN
  Chambering: 8x57, rimless. 44.9in overall, 6.55lb empty. 23.6in barrel, 4-groove rifling; RH, concentric. Internal box magazine loaded from a stripper clip, 5 rounds. Block-and-leaves sight graduated to 300m (330yd). 2315 fps with 200-grain bullet.

Introduced by 1910, this gun had a half-stock, a marking disc on the butt and a standing-block sight. Army-type rifles had stepped-cylinder barrels instead of the continuously tapering sporting patterns, and military-style magazine floorplates replaced the lever-locked unit associated with other Mausers.

MODEL 1908 BIG-GAME RIFLE
Mauser-Afrika-Pirschbüsche C/98-08
Made by Waffenfabrik Mauser AG, Oberndorf am Neckar, 1909-14.

Total production: not known. **Chambering options:** 8x57, 9.3x62 or 10.75x68. **Action:** as M1898 sporter, above.

DATA FOR A TYPICAL SPECIMEN

Chambering: 9.3x62, rimless. 52.8in overall, 8.33lb empty. 31.5in barrel, 4-groove rifling; RH, concentric. Internal box magazine loaded from a stripper clip, 5 rounds. Sights: see notes. 2265 fps with 285-grain bullet.

Apparently derived from a long-barreled 1908-type sporter, originally made with a three-quarter stock and a short handguard running from the chamber to the barrel band, this was specifically intended for sale in India and southern Africa. It was designed to compete with rifles offered by British gunmakers such as George Gibbs, Holland & Holland and others – many of which, ironically, had been built on actions supplied from Oberndorf.

German-made guns were usually appreciably cheaper than the custom-built English guns, and could be supplied from stock. They were fitted with long barrels 'of best Krupp Steel', and had a ramped silver-bead front sight. The Cape-type rear sight, on a prominent base, had two small folding leaves and a large leaf-and-slider. The checkered pistol grip of the half-stock had a horn cap; the forend had a rounded horn tip. The bolt handle was turned down, eyes for detachable swivels lay under barrel and butt, and a double set trigger was available to order.

MODEL A SPORTING RIFLE

Made by Mauser-Werke AG, Oberndorf am Neckar, 1922-41.

Total production: not known. **Chambering options:** (small action) 250-3000 Savage, 6.5x54 or 8x51; (medium action) 7x57, 30-06, 8x60, 9x57 or 9.3x62; (large action) 280 Ross, 318 Rimless Nitro Express, 10.75x68 or 404 Rimless Nitro Express. **Action:** as M1898 sporter, above.

DATA FOR A TYPICAL PATTERN NO. 2 GUN

Chambering: 8x60, rimless. 44.9in overall, 7.4lb empty. 23.6in barrel, 4-groove rifling; RH, concentric. Internal box magazine loaded from a stripper clip, 5 rounds. Tangent-leaf sight graduated to 1000m (1095yd). 2540 fps with 195-grain bullet.

Introduced about 1922, for the British market, these rifles were offered in three mechanically-identical actions, differing only in the length of the receiver and the depth of the magazine; the medium and large actions had large-ring receivers, whereas the smallest had the so-called 'small ring' type. The rear sight was carried on a distinctive base ahead of the chamber, the front sight being mounted on a ramp.

Pattern No. 1 rifles had an express rear sight, with a block for 100m (110yd) and four small folding leaves for 200-500m (220-545yd); Pattern No. 2 had the 1000m tangent-leaf sight.

The magazine floorplates were released by a pivoting catch inside the trigger guard. The stock had a checkered pistol grip, usually with a metal cap, and a hard rubber buttplate. A forend tip of rosewood or buffalo horn was usually fitted to German-made guns. Swivel eyes lay under the butt and on a collar around the barrel.

Though guns varied in detail, military-style two-stage triggers and express rear sights were standard. Optional extras included partly or fully octagonal barrels, set triggers, or an additional sliding safety catch on the receiver-side or tang. Manufacture ceased in 1941, though small-scale assembly continued until 1944.

SIMILAR GUNS

Model B. Available in the same chamberings as the Model A, this standard post-war sporting rifle was essentially similar to the pre-1914 C/98-08. The radial-lever magazine floorplate release was retained, while the half-stock had a cheekpiece, a checkered pistol grip – generally with a metal cap – and a schnabel tip. The standard rear sight was a multi-leaf pattern appropriate for ranges up to 300m (330yd).

A small panel of checkering with distinctive concave borders lay beneath the rear sight. A tapered-cylinder barrel was standard, but half- or full-octagon versions were available. Two-stage military, direct-action or double set triggers could be supplied to order.

Model K. Chambered only for the 250-3000 Savage, 6.5x54 or 8x51 cartridges, this gun was 42.4in overall, had a 21.65in barrel, and weighed 6.06lb unladen. It was the small (*Kleine*) version of the sporting rifle, essentially similar to Model B, but with a short action, a small-diameter receiver ring, and a tapered-cylinder barrel.

Model M. This full-stocked version of the Model B was available in 6.5x54, 7x57, 30-06, 8x51, 8x60 or 9x57. A typical example was 41in overall and weighed 6.95lb empty; its barrel measured 19.7in. The guns had a spatulate bolt handle and a magazine floor-

plate released by a catch in the trigger guard. The nose cap was external, and a ribbed steel buttplate contained a trap for cleaning equipment.

The usual options were available, though the three-leaf sight and the double set triggers seem to have been considered as standard fittings.

Model S. This lightweight version of the Model M (q.v.) was chambered only for the 6.5x54, 7x57, 8x51, 8x60 or 9x57 cartridges. It was 40.85in overall, weighed 6.53lb empty, and had a 19.55in barrel. A normal ball-type bolt handle was used instead of the spatulate form, and the magazine floorplate release was a radial lever. The stock extended to the tip of the muzzle, the nose cap being fitted internally, and there was usually a slight hand-stop swell at the mid-point of the forend. A solid rubber buttplate was fitted.

MODEL 2000 SPORTING RIFLE

Made by Friedr. Wilh. Heym GmbH & Co., Münnerstadt.

Chambering options: see text. **Total production:** not known. **Action:** locked by two lugs on the bolt head engaging recesses in the receiver wall as the bolt handle turns down.

DATA FOR A TYPICAL EXAMPLE

Chambering: 270 Winchester, rimless. 44.5in overall, 7lb empty. 24in barrel, 4-groove rifling; RH, concentric. Internal box magazine, 5 rounds. Folding-leaf sight. 3170 fps with 130-grain bullet.

Apparently introduced in 1968 for sale by Mauser Jagdwaffen GmbH of Oberndorf, as the 'Mauser 2000', this Heym-made rifle had a bolt-mounted ejector and a short extractor claw let into the bolt body. The safety catch lay on the right side of the bolt shroud: thumbed upward, it locked the firing pin, though the bolt could still be opened. The basic gun could be fitted with single-stage, adjustable or double set triggers. Standard stocks had a Monte Carlo comb and cheekpiece, and a rubber shoulder plate. The rounded tip was separated from the obliquely cut forend by a white spacer. Checkering appeared on the pistol grip and forend.

Standard chamberings apparently included 5.6x57, 243 Winchester, 6.5x57, 270 Winchester, 7x57, 7x64, 7mm Remington Magnum, 30-06, 308 Winchester, 8x57, 8x60S, 9.3x64 and 375 H&H Magnum.

SIMILAR GUNS

Mauser Model 3000, 1971-4. The original rifle was replaced by a gun with a full-length bolt-guide rib, to prevent binding. The stocks gained skip-line checkering and squared forend tips. The Model 3000 was sold in similar chamberings to its predecessor, had a 22in or 24in barrel and weighed 6.75-7.25lb. Owing partly to the success of the Model 66 and also to the impending introduction of the Model 77 (q.v.), Mauser-Jagdwaffen ceased purchasing the Heym-made rifles in the early 1970s. Heym then continued production and distribution under its own name, as the 'SR 20'.

Mauser Model 3000S, 1971-4. This was a variant of the Model 3000 with skip-line checkering on the stock and forend, and a ventilated shoulder pad.

Mauser Model 3000M ('Magnum'), 1971-4. A variant of the Model 3000 accepting 7mm Remington Magnum, 300 Winchester Magnum or 375 H&H Magnum cartridges, this had a 26in barrel and weighed about 8lb unladen. A three-round magazine replaced the standard five-round type.

Mauser Model 4000, 1971-4. This was a short-action 'varmint' rifle, based on the Model 2000 but offered in 222 or 223 Remington only. It had a solid rubber shoulder pad and a folding-block rear sight.

MODEL 77S SPORTING RIFLE
Jagdrepetier Modell 77S

Made by Mauser-Jagdwaffen GmbH, Oberndorf/Neckar, 1977 to date.

Total production: not known. **Chambering options:** see notes. **Action:** locked by three lugs on the bolt engaging in the receiver bridge as the bolt handle turns down.

DATA FOR A TYPICAL EXAMPLE

Chambering: 7x64mm, rimless. 43.3in overall, 7.75lb empty. 23.6in barrel, 4-groove rifling; RH, concentric. Detachable box magazine, 5 rounds. Block and folding-leaf sight. 2950 fps with 139-grain bullet.

Introduced in quantity in 1978, this rifle had a detachable magazine with the release catch in the forend of the half-stock. Hog's back combs and schnabel forend tips were standard. The safety catch lay on the right side of the bolt plug, and a button controlling

The Mauser Model 77, with an optical sight mounted on the short barrel rib.

the action of the set trigger protruded from the stock behind the bolt handle. Opening the action automatically returned the trigger to normal operating mode.

The standard chamberings included 243 Winchester, 270 Winchester, 6.5x57, 7x64, 30-06 and 308 Winchester.

SIMILAR GUNS

Model 77SM. Offered with a special 25.6in barrel, this accepted high power rounds such as 6.5x68, 7mm Remington and 300 Winchester Magnums, 8x68S, 9.3x62, 9.3x64 or 10.3x60.

Model 77 Afrikamodell. A special heavyweight derivative of the 77SM, this was chambered solely for the 375 H&H Magnum round.

Model 77 Sportsman. Made with a 23.6in heavy barrel, but lacking open sights, this was offered in 243 and 308 Winchester only. It weighed 10.7lb with a Zeiss Diavari 2.5-10x52 optical sight. It had a Monte Carlo-type butt and an accessory rail was let into the underside of the forend.

Model 83 UIT Standardgewehr. Available from 1983 in single shot or magazine-fed versions, and offered only in 308 Winchester, this was specifically developed for 300m (330yd) target-shooting. Built on an improved 77-type action, it had a match-quality trigger and a competition stock with an adjustable shoulder plate and butt-comb.

Model 83 UIT Freigewehr. Similar to the 83 UIT Standardgewehr, this rifle had a hooked buttplate, a thumb-hole butt, and an adjustable palm rest beneath the forend. It was destined for 300m Free Rifle competitions.

MODEL 86 SNIPER RIFLE
Scharfschützengewehr 86, 'SG 86' or 'SR 86'
Made by Mauser-Jagdwaffen GmbH, Oberndorf/Neckar, 1987 to date.
Total production: not known, but not large. **Chambering:** 308 Winchester only. **Action:** locked by turning two lugs on the bolt head into their recesses in the receiver, directly behind the chamber.

50.15in overall, 11.55lb without sights. 28.9in barrel (including flash-hider), 4-groove rifling; RH, concentric. Detachable box magazine, 9 rounds. Optical sight. 2855 fps with 150-grain bullet.

Chambered exclusively for the 308 Winchester round (7.62x51 NATO), this retained the basic shape of the Model 83; however, the bolt had lugs locking into the receiver ring instead of the bridge in a search for better accuracy. The sight rail above the breech was lowered and a laminated stock was used. Fluted to save weight while retaining rigidity, the barrel had an efficient flash suppressor/muzzle brake. A synthetic/thumbhole-type stock option was announced in 1989.

SHORT-ACTION (GEHMANN) GUNS
MODEL 66S SPORTING RIFLE
Made by Mauser-Jagdwaffen GmbH, Oberndorf/Neckar, 1965 to date.
Chambering options—Group I: 243 Winchester, 6.5x57, 270 Winchester, 7x64, 30-06 or 308 Winchester. Group II: 9.3x64 only. Group III: 6.5x68, 7x66 vom Hofe or 8x68S. Group IV: 7mm Remington Magnum, 300 Winchester Magnum, 375 H&H Magnum or 458 Winchester. **Action:** locked by turning lugs on the bolt head into recesses in the barrel extension, and by the bolt handle turning down into its seat.
DATA FOR A TYPICAL EXAMPLE

Chambering: 7x66 vom Hofe, rimless. 39.05in overall, 8.05lb empty. 23.6in barrel, 4-groove rifling; RH, concentric. Internal box magazine, 3 rounds. Block and folding-leaf rear sight. 3295 fps with 170-grain bullet.

Designed by Walter Gehmann of Karlsruhe in the early 1960s, this unique short action presents a complete departure from traditional Mausers. The reduction in length is due largely to the location of the magazine between the trigger and the bolt, and by telescoping the bolt and bolt carrier.

As the bolt is retracted to open the breech, the handle strikes the bolt-carrier bridge; bolt and carrier then run back together over the wrist of the stock. The ejector and extractor are both carried in the bolt head; a safety catch lies on the right side of the cocking-piece shroud; and the bolt stop protrudes from the right side of the stock above the trigger.

The prototype was exhibited at the international arms fair (IWA) in Nürnberg in 1965, and series-made guns were introduced commercially in 1966. Cap-head bolts retaining the receiver ring and the rear sight block can be loosened, allowing the barrel/receiver ring assembly to be replaced after the bolt had been opened. Shutting the action automatically indexes the barrel, the retaining bolts are replaced, and the gun is ready for use.

The Gehmann-system Mauser Model 66 has an unusually short action: note the position of the bolt handle.

The Mauser Model 66 sniper rifle.

The Model 66S has a walnut half-stock with a hog's back comb, a ventilated rubber buttplate, a rosewood or ebonite pistol grip cap, and a rounded rosewood forend tip. Checkering lies on the pistol grip and forend, with swivels appearing under butt and barrel. A double set trigger is regarded as standard, though a single trigger (with a setting button on the upper tang) and a two-stage match trigger are among the optional alternatives.

SIMILAR GUNS

Model 66ST ('Stutzen'). This shares the basic action and half-stock of the 66S, but had a 20.85in barrel. It has been marketed as the '660 Ultra' in the U.S..

Model 66SM. This gun amalgamates the standard action and barrel with a Monte Carlo comb, modified pistol grip contours and a schnabel forend tip.

Model 66SM Carbine. A short form of the 66SM, this offers a 20.85in barrel, a full-length stock, a straight comb, and a Bavarian cheek piece.

Model 66S Magnum and 66SM Magnum. These are identical with the standard rifles, but have 25.6in barrels, larger-diameter bolt faces and deeper magazines.

Model 66D or Diplomat. Made in several patterns—e.g., 66S, 66SM and 66 Magnum—these guns have selected stocks and display engraved game motifs on the receiver: red and roe deer, or red deer and wild boar.

Model 66SD or 'Super Deluxe'. These richly decorated guns, made only to order, feature complex checkering, scroll engraving and baroque stock carving.

Model 66SP. Introduced in 1976, this sniper rifle has been chambered only for the 308 Winchester/7.62x51 NATO cartridge. Specially selected for accuracy, the action is fitted to a heavy barrel with an efficient flash-hider/muzzle brake. The massive wood stock has a thumbhole grip, an adjustable cheek piece, and a butt which can be lengthened with spacers. Zeiss Diavari 1.5-6x42 optical sights are usually fitted. A typical gun is 44.1in overall, has a 26.75in barrel, and weighs 13.78lb with its sight. The internal box magazine holds three rounds.

The 66SP offers advantages over most conventional bolt-action patterns, including ultra-fast lock time and—owing to the position of the handle—the chance to operate the bolt with minimal disturbance of aim. Mauser-Gehmann sniper rifles have been used in small numbers by military, paramilitary and police throughout the world, but the restricted magazine capacity is generally regarded as disadvantageous.

RIMFIRE SPORTING GUNS

Mauser-Werke made a series of good-quality 5.6mm rimfire patterns from the 1920s onward. These were built on three basic actions: the original lightweight pattern, which lacked a safety catch; a strengthened pattern with a rotary safety catch on the bolt body; and a version of the Deutsches Sportmodell with a flag-type safety on top of the cocking piece.

Cataloguing the rimfires is complicated by a coding system used by Mauser to identify individual patterns. Interpreting these prefixes and suffixes is still subject to dispute; however, though few were used on the guns themselves, they clearly had a logical basis.

MODEL 300 SPORTING RIFLE
M.W.-Karabiner Eb 300
Made by Mauser-Werke AG, Oberndorf am Neckar, Württemberg.
Total production: not known. **Chambering:** 5.6mm Nr. 6 (22 Long Rifle), rimfire. **Action:** locked by turning the base of the bolt handle down into its seat in the receiver.

36.8in overall, 3.95lb empty. 19.7in barrel, 4 grooves; RH twist, concentric. Single-shot only. Fixed standing-block rear sight. 1080 fps with 40-grain bullet.

This was the smallest of the Mauser-Werke ('M.W.') sporting rifles, intended for juniors. It had a pistol grip half-stock with a short butt, and a plain round barrel. Built on the most basic of the actions, it lacked a safety catch. The gun was often catalogued as 'Eb 300', the prefix denoting an *Einzellader*—'single-loader' (i.e., single-shot)—in a stock of *buchholz* (beech).

SIMILAR GUNS

En 310. This variant of the Eb 300 shared an identical action and the 19.7in barrel. The 'n' in the designation signified a better-quality stock made of *nussbaum* (walnut).

El 320. A larger version of the En 310, with a 23.6in barrel and a weight of about 4.3lb, this had a walnut stock with a checkered pistol grip. A simple adjustable rear sight took the form of a standing block with a thumbscrew elevator, and the swivels could be found beneath the barrel and butt. The significance of 'l' in the designation is unclear, but may have identified the light-pattern 23.6cm barrel (*leichtlauf*).

MODEL 340
M.W.-Sportbüchse Es 340
Made by Mauser-Werke AG, Oberndorf am Neckar, Württemberg.
Total production: not known. **Chambering:** 5.6mm Nr. 6 (22 Long Rifle), rimfire. **Action:** generally as Model 300, above.

42.9in overall, 7.05lb empty. 25.6in barrel, 4 grooves; RH twist, concentric. Single shot only. Tangent-leaf sight graduated to 200m (220yd). 1080 fps with 40-grain bullet.

This was a larger version of the 320, with a heavy barrel, an elongated forend mounting a sling swivel, and a choice of sights. The most popular seems to have been a military-style tangent-leaf design with a slider, curiously graduated for distances of 30m, 50m, 80m, 100m, 125m, 150m, 180m and 200m (33-220yd). This was sometimes fitted with a laterally-adjustable notch plate, or could be replaced by a *Schraubvisier*—a sight which, though taking the general pattern of the tangent-leaf design, was adjusted vertically by a large screw running down into the bed plate.

It has been suggested that a missing '330' pattern may have been similar to the Es 340. Some 1930s catalogues specifically describe the 340 as a 'heavyweight pattern', suggesting that a short-lived lighter version had once been made. Details are currently lacking.

MODEL 350
M.W.-Meisterschafts Kleinkaliber Büchse Es 350
Made by Mauser-Werke AG, Oberndorf am Neckar, Württemberg.
Total production: not known. **Chambering:** 5.6mm Nr. 6 (22 Long Rifle), rimfire. **Action:** generally as Model 300, above.

44.9in overall, 7.72lb empty. 25.6in barrel, 4 grooves; RH twist, concentric. Single-shot only. Micro-adjustable tangent-leaf rear sight. 1080 fps with 40-grain bullet.

The Es 350 was a heavyweight target-shooting version of the rimfire Mausers, originally made with the first-pattern action lacking a safety catch. This had been changed by 1932 for the modified design with a safety catch on the bolt body and an improved adjustable trigger mechanism. Customarily known as the Es 350N, the 's' apparently indicating a heavy barrel (*schwerlauf*) and 'N' the new model (*Neuer Art*), guns of this type had a walnut half-stock with checkering on the pistol grip and forend. The swivels lay under the forend and butt. Aperture rear sights could be mounted on the receiver, and a variety of open and hooded front sights was available. The Glaser catalogue of 1933 lists the barrel length as 27.55in (70cm), though all the rifles which could be traced for examination had the standard 25.6in (65cm) pattern.

MODEL 410
M.W.-Mehrlader-Karabiner Mm 410
Made by Mauser-Werke AG, Oberndorf am Neckar, Württemberg.
Total production: not known. **Chambering:** 5.6mm Nr. 6 (22 Long Rifle), rimfire. **Action:** generally as Model 300, above.

40.75in overall, 5.07lb empty. 23.6in barrel, 4 grooves; RH twist, concentric. Detachable box magazine, 5 rounds. Tangent-leaf sight graduated to 200m (220yd). 1080 fps with 40-grain bullet.

This was also known as the Mm 410—*Mehrlader*, 'repeater', and *mittelgewicht* for a medium-weight 23.6in barrel. Seen as a multi-shot version of the En 310 (q.v.), it was apparently introduced in the late 1920s with the improved or 'safety catch' action and a pistol grip half-stock with a finger groove in the forend. The swivels lay beneath the butt and barrel.

By 1932, however, an improved deluxe version (*Luxusausführung*) had appeared. Its half-stock had checkering on the grip, and the forend had a shallow schnabel tip. The rear sight, which was originally a simple block-and-thumbwheel pattern, became a tangent-leaf *Kurvenvisier* adjustable from 33yd (30m) to 220yd (200m).

SIMILAR GUNS

Ms 420. A repeating Sportbüchse, this was essentially similar to the Mm 410. However, it had the standard 25.6in heavy barrel and a pistol grip half-stock with an extended forend. Overall length was about 43.3in, weight being in the region of 6.75lb. The front swivel—fitted to the barrel of the Mm 410—lay beneath the forend of the

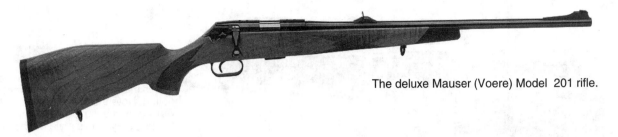
The deluxe Mauser (Voere) Model 201 rifle.

Ms 420. It is assumed that deluxe versions were also made, lacking the forend groove. The standard tangent-leaf sight was often replaced with a screw-elevated Schraubvisier or the micro-adjustable tangent-leaf sight associated with the Es 350 target rifle.

GERMAN SPORTS MODEL
Deutsches Sportmodell ('DSM')

Made by Mauser-Werke AG, Oberndorf am Neckar, and many other contractors (see text).

Total production: hundreds of thousands. **Chambering:** 5.6mm Nr. 6 (22 Long Rifle), rimfire. **Action:** locked by turning the bolt handle down into its recess in the receiver, and by a lug opposite the handle entering a recess in the receiver.

43.7in overall, 8.37lb empty. 27.55in barrel, 4 grooves; RH twist, concentric. Single-shot only. Tangent-leaf sight graduated to 200m (220yd). 1080 fps with 40-grain bullet.

The origin of this rifle is still an open question. Though customarily credited to Mauser-Werke, on purely circumstantial evidence, the Deutsches Sportmodell was probably developed semi-officially—perhaps by the national shooting organization, which supervised marksmanship training with a decidedly military slant. The name 'Deutsches Sportmodell' was deliberately misleading. The first guns varied in appearance; some were half-stocked, but many forends were extended much closer to the muzzle. However, very few (if any) DSM had fittings such as bayonet bars. Their actions varied considerably in detail, and it is suspected that the original DSM criteria—whatever they were—were not particularly restricting.

Though chambering rimfire ammunition, most of the guns have the barrels offset from the bolt so that a simple centerfire-type striker could be used. They all have 'wing'-pattern safety catches on top of the rear of the bolt, and are generally locked simply by turning the bolt handle down into its seat in the receiver. Compared with the magazines of most rimfire sporting rifles made in Germany prior to 1935, which often abutted the trigger guard, the DSM magazine was placed well forward. The rear sight was invariably a tangent-leaf pattern, graduated from 25m or 30m to 150 or 200m (27-220yd).

Among the manufacturers of DSM were J.G. Anschütz ('J.G.A.') of Zella-Mehlis; Berlin-Suhler Waffen- & Fahrzeugwerk ('BSW') of Suhl; Bolte & Anschütz ('B.u.A.') of Zella-Mehlis; G.C. Dornheim AG of Suhl ('Gecado'); Erma-Waffenfabrik B. Geipel of Erfurt; Gustav Genschow & Co. AG of Berlin-Treptow ('Geco'); C.G. Haenel of Suhl; Gustloff-Werke of Suhl; Mauser-Werke AG of Oberndorf; Bernh. Paatz of Suhl ('BP'); Simson & Co. of Suhl; Carl Walther of Zella-Mehlis; Hermann Weihrauch of Zella-Mehlis ('H.W.Z.'); and Venuswaffenwerk Oskar Will of Zella-Mehlis ('VWW' monogram).

Not all of these businesses necessarily traded simultaneously; Simson, for example, was succeeded first by BSW and secondly by Gustloff, and Dornheim is believed to have ceased working independently in 1940. In addition, barreled actions were stocked and finished by many lesser gunsmiths for sporting use, and a tremendous variety of guns will be found—ranging from short-barreled full-stock carbines or 'Stutzen' to sophisticated target rifles.

SIMILAR RIFLES

As far as the Mauser products are concerned, the Sportmodell action provided a basis for a range of single-shot and magazine-feed rifles. These superseded the previous 'B' series described above, though the original designations were retained. The guns had their barrels and receivers grooved to accept optical-sight mounts.

Series production is believed to have stopped about 1940, but small-scale assembly may have continued virtually until the end of the war for training and vermin control.

Es 340B. A single-shot pattern, made in plain and deluxe versions, this had a 25.6in barrel and a pistol grip half-stock. The tangent-leaf rear sight was standard.

Es 350B. Intended for target shooting, this heavy-barrel rifle was usually fitted with a micro-adjustable tangent-leaf rear sight. However, a special diopter sight could be attached to the receiver bridge if required.

Ms 350B. This was simply a magazine-feed version of the Es 350B target rifle. A wooden block could be obtained to allow the rifle to be used in competitions where magazines were banned.

Mm 410B. This was the smaller of the two magazine-feed sporting guns, with a 23.6in medium-weight barrel. The front sling swivel lay on the barrel instead of under the forend, which had a shallow schnabel tip.

Ms 420B. The larger of the sporting-rifle derivatives of the basic DSM design had a 25.6in barrel, but was otherwise similar to the Mm 410B (q.v.).

Kleinkaliber-Wehrsportgewehr (KKW). Once the last restrictions of the Treaty of Versailles had been cast away, training rifle facsimiles of the Kar. 98k were built on the DSM action from about 1936 onward. These small-caliber military sport rifles had military-style stocks and fittings which included a sling bar on the left side of the barrel band, a sling slot cut through the butt, and even a bayonet bar beneath the muzzle.

Made by many of the contractors listed previously, KKW are all very similar. Some variations will be found—e.g., Gustloff guns customarily had a distinctive ejector plate in the bottom of the feed way—but the rifles were operated in much the same way as the Kar. 98k.

OTHER SPORTERS

Very few Mauser-system sporters were made in Germany prior to 1918, other than those emanating from Waffenfabrik Mauser AG or created around Oberndorf-made actions. Watertight patent legislation prevented any large-scale exploitation of the Mauser action virtually until the beginning of World War I; Schilling and Haenel, for example, continued to offer guns based on the obsolescent Gew. 88 (see 'Reichsgewehr').

After 1920, however, the scene changed dramatically; tens of thousands of war-surplus guns were available for customization, and the major manufacturers still had huge stockpiles of unused parts. A few thousand actions could keep a moderate-size gunmaker busy for years.

Proven strength and ready availability of the Mauser action encouraged independent gunsmiths—particularly in and around Suhl—to stock and finish sporting rifles in their own name. The list that follows, therefore, can be little more than a guide to the most important participants.

Among the many German gunmakers offering Mauser-action sporting rifles, often built around proprietary cartridges, have been Otto Bock of Berlin; Wilhelm Brenneke of Leipzig and Berlin; H. Burgsmüller & Söhne of Kreiensen am Harz; G.C. Dornheim of Suhl; Waffen-Frankonia of Würzburg; Walter Gehmann of Karlsruhe; Gustav Genschow & Co. AG of Berlin, Durlach bei Karlsruhe; C.G. Haenel of Suhl and Alstadt-Hachenburg; Halbe & Gerlich (Halger-Waffenfabrik) of Kiel and later Hamburg; Friedr. Wilh. Heym GmbH & Co. of Münnerstadt, Bavaria; Albrecht Kind AG ('Akah') of Nuremburg and Berlin; Kriegeskorte & Co. of Stuttgart; Gebr. Merkel of Suhl; Müller & Greiss of Munich; J.P. Sauer & Sohn of Suhl; V. Chr. Schilling of Suhl; E. Schmidt & Habermann of Suhl; Waffenfabrik August Schüler of Suhl; Sempert & Krieghoff of Suhl; Simson & Company of Suhl; Voetter & Co., originally of Vöhrenbach in Schwarzwald; Vom Hofe & Scheinemann of Berlin; and Carl Walther Sportwaffenfabrik of Ulm/Donau. All these manufacturers are listed separately.

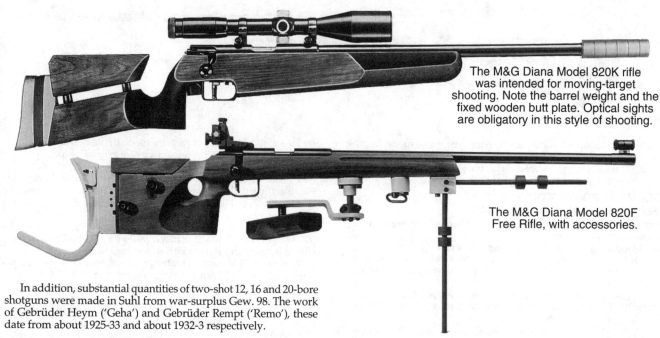

The M&G Diana Model 820K rifle was intended for moving-target shooting. Note the barrel weight and the fixed wooden butt plate. Optical sights are obligatory in this style of shooting.

The M&G Diana Model 820F Free Rifle, with accessories.

In addition, substantial quantities of two-shot 12, 16 and 20-bore shotguns were made in Suhl from war-surplus Gew. 98. The work of Gebrüder Heym ('Geha') and Gebrüder Rempt ('Remo'), these date from about 1925-33 and about 1932-3 respectively.

• Mayer & Grammelspacher

Best known for its 'Diana'-brand airguns, Mayer & Grammelspacher made single shot cartridge rifles from about 1979 to 1994. All were based on a sturdy action with a radial safety lever on the stock behind the bolt. The goal was to persuade marksmen to use the company's products in several disciplines by matching stock profiles and handling characteristics with the air rifles.

Owing to a successful marketing relationship with Dynamit Nobel, Diana 820 rifles will often be encountered under the RWS brand.

MODEL 820S TARGET RIFLE

Made by Dianawerk Mayer & Grammelspacher GmbH & Co. KG, Rastatt/Baden.

Total production: not known. **Chambering:** 22 Long Rifle, rimfire. **Action:** locked by a lug on the bolt body and the base of the bolt handle engaging their seats in the receiver.

44.5in overall, 10.35lb without sights. 26in barrel, 4-groove rifling; RH, concentric. Single shot only. Micro-adjustable aperture rear sight. 1080 fps with 40-grain bullet.

Intended for 25m competition-shooting, this gun was available in right- or left-hand forms. The trigger was adjustable from 1.8oz (50gm) to 8.8oz (250gm), and had a movable tongue. The rear sight was either the Diana M75T01 (subsequently known as the M76) or the improved Model 82 pattern. The stock was walnut, with a comb elevating on cylindrical spacers and a shoulder plate which could slide in its channel-plate. The pistol grip and the rounded forend were extensively stippled. A flat-base riser block was fixed to the underside of the stock ahead of the trigger guard aperture.

SIMILAR GUNS

Model 820F, 1988-94. An improved form of the 820S, this was destined for 50m Free Rifle competitions. Apart from a change in the rear of the action, which was cut obliquely and had a more prominent safety-lever head, the most obvious difference lay in the stock. This had a massive slab-sided thumbhole butt, with an elevating comb and an adjustable hooked shoulder plate. The forend had an imperceptible taper and a short decorative flute. An accessory rail set in the underside of the forend accepted a hand

rest, a hand stop or an anchor-block for the stabilizer rod and its sliding weights. The rod could be set horizontally, beneath the barrel, or vertically downward. Excluding the butt hook, the 820F was 45.8in long, had a 27.15in barrel, and weighed about 15.3lb; the trigger could be set for release pressures between 1.4oz (40gm) and 8.8oz (250gm).

Model 820K, 1981-94. Introduced for Running Boar competitions, this was easily identified by its wooden buttplate and a short barrel with adjustable weights at the muzzle. An optical sight was standard. The 820K measured 44.5in overall (50.4in with an optional barrel extension), had a 26in barrel, and weighed 9.48lb without sights. The trigger, adjustable from 10.6oz (300gm) to 24.7oz (700gm), could be converted at will from double-pressure to a direct-acting type.

Model 820L, 1988-94. This UIT Standard three-position rifle shared the stock of the Model 100 air gun. A prominent 'rib' or shelf ran from the pistol grip to the chamber, on each side of the forend, and the trigger guard was a quirky zig-zag plate wedged between the front of the pistol grip and the deepened forend. The elevating comb on the butt-top and the bellied butt were distinctive. The 820L could be fitted with a butt-plate hook when necessary; it was about 44.5in long, had a 26in barrel, and weighed about 10.6lb without sights.

Model 820SF, 1981-7? A special long-barreled gun, this was often fitted with riser blocks beneath the sights and had a high comb for 'head up' shooting styles. It was about 45.7in long, had a 27.15in barrel, and weighed 11lb without sights.

• Merkel

Gebr. Merkel of Suhl stocked and completed Mauser sporters prior to World War II—though best known for shotguns, double rifles and combination guns of impeccable quality. Merkel used genuine newly-made actions, purchased from Obendorf and acknowledged in the company's advertising literature.

A typical post-war Merkel side-by-side Double Rifle, in this case a Model 140.

Rifles could be supplied in any of the standard Mauser chamberings. Typically, they had long barrels (usually about 28in) and were stocked almost to the muzzle. The pistol grip was checkered, while the forend was usually made in two pieces with a diagonal joint behind the front sling loop. The barrels were half-octagonal with a matted top rib, and had a combined block-and-leaf rear sight (*Jagdvisier*). Set triggers were common, and the receiver was often engraved; the individual details, however, were left to the whims of the purchaser. By 1939, the company was owned by Adolf Schäde and trading as 'Suhler Waffenwerk Gebr. Merkel'.

• Mosin-Nagant

Many Russian rifles were captured on the Eastern Front during the opening stages of World War I. Some were retained by the German army, to serve recruiting depots and lines-of-communications troops until the end of hostilities. Others went to the navy to destroy floating mines. A few were converted to handle the standard 8x57 service cartridge, but so much ammunition had been captured that most guns were simply issued unaltered. However, changes were often made so that German-style bayonets could be fitted. The revisions usually comprised a muzzle tube with a bayonet lug, requiring the original forend to be cut back.

• Müller & Greiss

Müller & Greiss of Munich made a few Mauser-action rifles chambering a special 9.5x73 Magnum cartridge shortly before World War I. The cartridge was apparently created by necking the British 404 Rimless Nitro Express.

• Oesterreich

In 1886, Rudolf Oesterreich of Berlin patented a repeating rifle of the so-called 'Bohemian School', with a combination breechblock/carrier hinged at the top rear of the receiver. The gun was operated by pushing forward on the ring-tipped lever protruding beneath the receiver, which lowered the block to receive a cartridge from the under-barrel tube magazine. Retracting the lever then lifted the cartridge into the firing position, the chamber being formed partly by the shaped inner surface of the receiver-top and partly by the top surface of the carrier; the gun could be fired by pulling the ring-lever farther back. Alternatively, the striker could be cocked manually and then released by the ring lever.

Wear rapidly upset the precision of this type of chambering and, as the Oesterreich system was too complex, success was elusive. A few sporting rifles of this type may have been made. Inferior extraction was a perpetual problem with guns of the mechanical-repeater class.

• Reichsgewehr (Mannlicher)

In 1887, the German authorities decided to improve the Gewehr 71/84 by adding a second locking lug. Suitable machinery was ordered in December. In 1888, however, mindful of the introduction of the Mle 86 (Lebel) rifle in France, the Germans realized that a better weapon than a converted Gew. 71/84 was needed. The resulting *Reichsgewehr* or 'commission rifle' had a bolt developed by Louis Schlegelmilch and a clip-loaded magazine, inspired by Mannlicher but modified by the Gewehr-Prüfungs-Kommission so that the clip would load either way up. The barrel jacket was designed by Armand Mieg and, to save time, the rifling was simply copied from the French pattern.

Experiments with pre-production guns made in Spandau in April-May 1888 resolved the question of caliber in favor of 8mm; production began in October to permit field trials to be undertaken.

MODEL 1888 RIFLE
Gewehr 88

Made by the government small-arms factories in Danzig, Erfurt and Spandau (750,000?); by the Königlich bayerische Gewehrfabrik, Amberg (100,000?); by Ludwig Loewe & Co., Berlin-Charlottenburg (425,000); by Österreichische Waffenfabriks-Gesellschaft, Steyr (300,000); and by private contractors in Suhl (100,000?).
Total production: in excess of 1.68 million in 1888-97. **Chambering:** 8x57, rimless. **Action:** locked by turning two lugs on a detachable bolt head into recesses in the receiver behind the chamber.

49in overall, 8.6lb empty. 29.15in barrel, 4-groove rifling; RH, concentric. Integral clip-loaded box magazine, 5 rounds. Leaf sight graduated to 2050m (2240yd). 2065 fps with Patrone 88. S. 71 sword bayonet (S. 71/84 in Bavaria).

The Gew. 88 was adopted in Prussia, Saxony and Württemberg on 12th November 1888. Issue began in the autumn of 1889 to XV. and XVI. Armeekorps, stationed in Alsace-Lorraine; and sufficient guns had been delivered to allow most line infantry regiments to re-equip by 1st August 1890.

The barrel was strengthened in January 1891, a large dot thereafter being struck into the receiver and barrel side. Excessive gas leakage from the ruptured primers of defective cartridges was minimized from 1894 onward by fitting striker heads with gas deflection flanges, and new rifling was introduced on 7th July 1896. Guns fitted with altered or newly made barrels—some had been re-rifled satisfactorily—usually displayed a 3mm letter 'Z' on top of the chamber and a 7mm 'Z' on the butt.

The Gewehre 88 were gradually replaced by the Gew. 98 after 1900, and relegated to the Reserve, Landwehr and Landsturm. Many of them were sold to China in 1907, and others apparently went to South America. When World War I began in 1914, the 88/S and 88/05 rifles were retrieved from the Landwehr and issued to front-line units to overcome a shortage of serviceable Mauser-type weapons. They were withdrawn again at the end of the year, but about 120,000 88/05 and 88/14 rifles remained nominally on the army inventory in 1918. Many of these were serving in Turkey (q.v.), where they remained after hostilities had ceased.

SIMILAR GUNS

Gewehr 88S. The approval of the S-Patrone on 3rd April 1903 caused a change in bore-diameter and chambering, though it was 1905 before any wholesale changes were made. Only guns with new 'Z'-pattern barrels were altered, receiver-tops gaining an additional 3mm 'S'. A 7mm-high 'S' was often repeated on the side of the butt. A new sight leaf was graduated to 2000m (2185yd), the supplementary leaf on the original sight being abandoned.

Gewehr 88/05. Adopted on 3rd January 1907, these rifles were converted from standard Gew. 88 and may be found with 'Z' and 'S' marks above the chambers. They were loaded from a

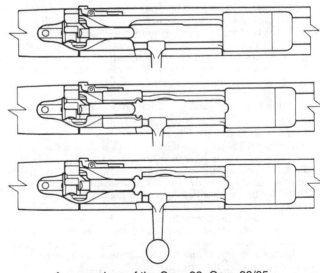

A comparison of the Gew. 88, Gew. 88/05 and Gew. 88/14, viewed from the top.

A typical Gewehr 88/05. Note the stripper-clip guide block on the receiver bridge.

The Gewehr 91. (HBL)

pressed-tin stripper-clip, blocks containing suitable guides being screwed to the top of the receiver bridge.

The left side of the receiver wall was ground out to enable the thumb to press the cartridges fully down into the magazine well, and a channel was milled across the breech face so that the pointed-nose S-Patrone could be used. As the comparatively bulky clip was no longer used, the magazine was narrowed and shortened internally; a spring-loaded cartridge retainer was added, and the opening in the bottom of the magazine was closed by a pressed-steel cover. It has been estimated that 370,000 Gew. 88 were converted to 88/05 standard in the Spandau factory in 1906-7.

Gewehr 88/14. These wartime expedients, approximating to the 88/05 pattern, were hastily altered from Gew. 88/S from December 1914 on into the summer of 1915. Stripper-clip guides were formed by protrusions welded onto the front of the receiver bridge. The left wall of the receiver was cut away, and a groove was milled across the face of the chamber. The opening in the bottom of the magazine was blocked by a sheet-steel cover, the magazine well being shortened and narrowed for the S-Patrone. Work was rushed, finish being inferior to the peacetime 88/05 conversions, and it is reckoned that about 75,000 guns were converted.

MODEL 1888 CARBINE
Karabiner 88
Made by C.G. Haenel, Suhl, 1889-95; by V.C. Schilling, Suhl, 1890-5; and by the Königlich Gewehrfabrik, Erfurt, 1891-6.
Chambering: 8x57mm, rimless. **Action:** as Gew. 88, above.
37.5in overall, 6.88lb empty. 17.15in barrel, 4-groove rifling; RH, concentric. Integral clip-loaded box magazine, 5 rounds. Leaf sight graduated to 1200m (1310yd). 1885 fps with Patrone 88. No bayonet.

Adopted for the armies of Prussia, Saxony and Württemberg on 19th January 1890, after protracted trials, this was a short version of the Gewehr 88. It had a turned-down bolt handle, a full-length stock, and a plain nose-cap with 'ears' around the front sight. A single spring-retained barrel band was used, with a fixed sling bar on the left side, and a sling-anchor point was cut through the butt. By March 1890, sufficient carbines had been delivered to begin issue to each Prussian cavalry squadron.

The incidence of ruptured barrels was reduced from 1891 onward by modifying barrel contours. Chamber tops thereafter bore a large dot. New striker heads with gas deflection flanges were fitted from 1894, and the rifling grooves were deepened in barrels made after July 1896 (chambers were marked 'Z').

SIMILAR GUNS
Gewehr 91. Though classified by the German army as a rifle, this was a carbine-length weapon issued to artillerymen. Made by Haenel, Schilling and the Erfurt factory in 1891-6, the Gew. 91 was much the same size as the Kar. 88 and weighed 7.12lb. It was adopted for the foot artillerymen of Prussia, Saxony and Württemberg on 25th March 1891.

The principal distinctive feature was an additional stacking rod, integral with a steel plate let into the underside of the forend immediately behind the nose-cap. Striker heads with gas deflection flanges were fitted from 1894 to minimize gas leakage, in the event of a primer rupture or case-head failure, and the chambers of post-July 1896 barrels (with modified rifling) were marked 'Z'.

Gewehr 91S. Conversion of surviving guns for the new S-Munition began in 1905, altered guns gaining a large 'S' on top of the chamber. Survivors were re-issued when World War I began; consequently, many will be found with markings applied by munitions columns and similar minor formations.

Karabiner 88 mS (mit Seitengewehr, 'with bayonet'). A few Kar. 88 were modified during World War I by adding bayonet-attachment bars on the right side of the muzzle. Nothing else is known about them.

Karabiner 88S. The first carbines to be converted for S-Munition were issued in 1905, bearing an additional chamber-top 'S'. Owing to the short barrel, they had a particularly unpleasant muzzle blast. The Kar. 88 was superseded by the Karabiner 98 AZ (q.v.) in January 1908 and the last survivors were withdrawn from regular units in 1910. Some were placed in store, but many were sold commercially. Survivors were re-issued in the autumn of 1914 to ancillary units.

SPORTING GUNS
Rifles based on the 'Mannlicher' action embodied in the Gew. 88 enjoyed a period in vogue prior to 1914. Though many were stocked and finished by independent gunsmiths on the basis of military-surplus actions, new patterns almost always prove to have been made in Suhl by Haenel or Schilling. Both manufacturers continued production long after the Gew. 88 had been displaced in the German army by the perfected Mauser.

Classifying these guns is often very difficult, as they may bear nothing but a retailer's name; stocks, barrels and fittings offered such great diversity that dating is also problematical.

MODEL 1888 SPORTING RIFLE
Made in Suhl by C.G. Haenel & Co. or V.C. Schilling & Co.
Total production: not known. **Chambering options:** see notes. **Action:** Locked by turning two lugs on the detachable bolt head into recesses in the receiver immediately behind the chamber.
DATA FOR A TYPICAL EXAMPLE
Chambering: 9x63, rimless 41.8in overall, 7.39lb empty. 21.65in barrel, 4-groove rifling; RH, concentric. Integral clip-loaded box magazine, 5 rounds. Block-and-leaves rear sight. 2445 fps with 185-grain bullet.

The first sporting rifles, introduced in the early 1890s, were essentially similar to the military Gewehr 88 (q.v.). They lacked the superfluous barrel jacket, had better stocks, and were often fitted with set triggers.

As time passed, better guns appeared. Most accepted 8x57 German service ammunition, though some examples were chambered for the 9x57 or 9.3x57 rounds. By 1911, 6.6x57 and 9x63 versions were also being offered. Military-style *Wehrmannbuchsen* fired the 8.15x46.5R cartridge.

A typical gun made by Haenel at the turn of the century had a good quality pistol grip half-stock, with extensive checkering on the grip and the horn tipped forend. A sling eye was brazed to the underside of the barrel, a block-and-leaf rear sight was fitted, and the front sight was a silvered bead. A double set trigger was customary.

A differing Schilling gun had an octagonal barrel and a full-length forend held to the barrel by two transverse keys set in escutcheons. It had a spring-loaded ejection port cover under the magazine case and a hinged aperture sight on the wrist. The action was lightly engraved overall.

In 1915, however, the German authorities ordered Haenel and Schilling to tool for the Gew. 98; production of the older actions ceased. Though most 1888-type sporters were made before World War I, therefore, a few were undoubtedly assembled in the early 1920s from surplus rifles and old parts.

• Rheinmetall (Dreyse), autoloading type
DREYSE SEMI-AUTOMATIC CARBINE
Dreyse-Selbstladekarabiner
Made by Rheinische Metallwaaren- & Maschinenfabrik, Sömmerda, 1907-14.
Total production: not known. **Chambering:** 7.65mm Auto only. **Action:** no mechanical breech lock; blowback, semi-automatic only.
37.4in overall, 4.95lb empty. 18in barrel, 4-groove rifling; RH, concentric. Detachable box magazine, 6 rounds. Standing-block rear sight. About 1350 fps with 73-grain bullet.

Designed by Louis Schmeisser, this was an adaptation of the better-known Dreyse pistols. The separate butt had a shallow rounded pistol grip, with checkering, and the short plain forend had a small schnabel tip. Swivels lay beneath the butt and barrel.

The magazine was detachable. A large grooved reciprocating charging block slid on top of the receiver, and a radial safety lever lay on the right side above the trigger guard. Dreyse carbines were made in considerable numbers, proving popular with police units—particularly, it seems, the Royal Gendarmerie of Saxony, whose 'K.S. Gend.' marks will sometimes be found.

• Rheinmetall (Dreyse), bolt-action type

These sporting rifles owed their existence to the needle guns (Zündnadelgewehre) developed by the Prussian Johann-Nikolaus Dreyse in the 1830s. Franz von Dreyse, the son of Johann-Nikolaus Dreyse, patented a convertible needle-fire/centerfire bolt mechanism in 1874. However, even the improved Dreyse cartridge rifles were markedly inferior to the Mauser; as the latter grew in importance, so the Dreyse fortunes declined. The company's assets were purchased by Rheinische Metallwaaren- und Maschinenfabrik in 1901, allowing curiously archaic pistols, light automatic carbines and sporting rifles to be produced under the 'Dreyse' brand until the end of World War I. An autoloading rifle designed by Karl Heinemann was promoted unsuccessfully in the 1920s by what had become known as 'Rheinmetall'.

DREYSE SPORTING RIFLES

A typical RM&M-made 'Dreyse' of 1910 differed little from its pre-1900 equivalents. Barrels were usually octagonal, retained by transverse keys, and the bolt handle was bent downward ahead of the simplified split receiver bridge. The half-stock had a checkered wrist, prominent flats lay alongside the action, and the forend had a schnabel tip. Some guns had pistol grips, but the horn finger rest remained popular.

Double set triggers and light engraving were customary on better-grade examples, together with a small pillar-type aperture sight that folded into the elongated upper tang.

Owing to the comparatively weak locking system, the guns were restricted to blackpowder ammunition or low pressure smokeless loads. Among the popular rimmed cartridges were 6.5x27, 8.15x46.5, 9.3x57, 9.3x72, 11x65 or 11.15x52.

DREYSE TARGET RIFLES

These had heavier barrels and better sights than the sporters. Trigger guards were elaborately spurred or scrolled; set triggers were standard. German-style rifles had straight-wrist butts and plain shoulder plates, whereas Swiss-style guns had squared cheek pieces and heavy hooked shoulder plates. Most rifles were chambered for the rimmed 8.15x46 or 9.5x47 rounds, though Swiss 10.4x38 rimfire or 10.4x42 (Vetterli) centerfire cartridges enjoyed local success.

• Rheinmetall-Stange

Developed for Rheinmetall by Louis Stange, this rifle relied on a long-stroke piston/bolt carrier rotating lugs on the bolt head into engagement with the receiver walls. When the mechanism was set to fire semi-automatically, the firing pin (mounted on the bolt carrier and released from the front sear notch) could reach the cartridge only after the trigger had been pressed; when firing fully automatically, the bolt and bolt carrier were released together from the rear position.

Once an empty magazine had been removed, the bolt remained open only if the selector was set for automatic fire; pulling the trigger then allowed the bolt to close, stripping a new round into the chamber. The bolt carrier immediately followed and the gun fired. If semi-automatic fire had been selected, the bolt closed on an empty chamber as the magazine was withdrawn and had to be retracted manually. Not without faults—it was too light to control when firing automatically and had an oddly placed magazine—the FG. 42 was a brave attempt to provide a full-power assault weapon.

BACKGROUND

In 1940, the Luftwaffe requested a special rifle for the paratroops (Fallschirmjäger). The gun was to be less than 39.4in (1000mm) long and no heavier than the Kar. 98k, yet remain capable of firing standard full-power 7.9mm cartridges automatically. The army rejected the goals as unattainable, so the Luftwaffe hierarchy simply contacted established arms-makers independently.

MODEL 42 PARATROOP RIFLE
First pattern: Fallschirmjägergewehr 42 or FG. 42 I
Made by Heinrich Krieghoff Waffenfabrik, Suhl ('fzs').

Total production: not known, see text below. **Chambering:** 7.9x57, rimless. **Action:** locked by two lugs on the bolt rotating into the receiver walls; gas operated, selective fire.

38.9in overall, 9.66lb without magazine. 20in barrel, 4-groove rifling; RH, concentric. Detachable box magazine, 10 or 20 rounds. Folding aperture sight graduated to 1200m (1310yd). 2395 fps with sS ball cartridges; 800±50 rpm. Rod-type bayonet.

The Stange design was preferred to a rising-block Krieghoff prototype. Series production of the FG. 42 began in Suhl in 1944 after development had been completed in the Rheinmetall-Borsig factory in Sömmerda. The paratroop rifle had a distinctive straight-line layout with folding sights, a pressed-steel butt, a sharply-angled pistol grip to improve control, a short wooden forend/handguard, and a permanently attached bipod under the front of the receiver. The box magazine fed laterally from the left side and the reversible bayonet was carried beneath the barrel. Production in 1944 amounted to only 527 guns, which suggests that very few first-pattern FG. 42 were ever made.

MODEL 42 PARATROOP RIFLE
Second pattern: Fallschirmjägergewehr 42 or FG. 42 II
Made by Heinrich Krieghoff Waffenfabrik, Suhl ('fzs'); and Rheinmetall-Borsig AG, Sömmerda ('bmv', parts only?).

Total production: 3000-3500? **Chambering:** 7.9x57, rimless. **Action:** as FG. 42 I, above.

41.7in overall, 11.13lb empty. 20.65in barrel, 4-groove rifling; RH, concentric. Detachable box magazine, 20 rounds. Folding aperture sight graduated to 1200m (1310yd). 2395 fps with sS ball cartridges; 750±30 rpm. Simplified rod bayonet.

Combat experience and a critical shortage of valuable manganese steel caused the FG. 42 to be completely redesigned. The muzzle brake was improved; the bipod could be moved forward beneath the muzzle, improving stability in automatic fire; and a variable-orifice gas regulator was provided to handle fluctuating ammunition pressure or the effects of fouling. The trigger mechanism became detachable, and the position of the safety catch was changed. A hinged cover kept debris out of the bolt way when the magazine was removed, while a deflector ensured that spent cases were ejected harmlessly.

The first-pattern FG. 42, customarily credited to Krieghoff.

The revised FG. 42, made by Rheinmetall in 1945.

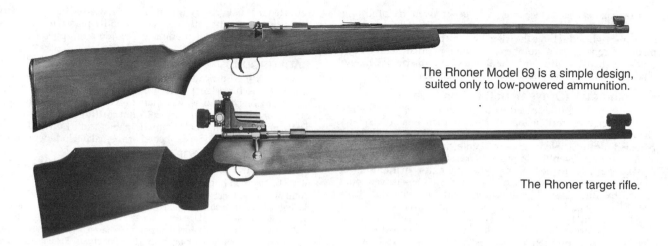

The Rhoner Model 69 is a simple design, suited only to low-powered ammunition.

The Rhoner target rifle.

The new rifle had a wooden butt and a conventional plastic pistol grip, raked much less sharply than its predecessor. The flash-hider was a bulky ribbed pattern instead of the earlier pierced cylinder. The bolt stroke was lengthened to reduce parts-breakage attributed to the violent action of the FG. 42 I. Consequently, the second-pattern rifle was longer and heavier than its predecessor and had a lower cyclic rate. Production was apparently confined to the earliest days of 1945, and is said to have totaled 3873.

• Rhöner, bolt-action type

Rhöner Sportwaffenfabrik, founded in Weissbach in 1959, began to make sporting rifles in 1966, when the 'SM' ('Sport und Munition') trademark was adopted. The company is better known for its break-open rifles, described below, but also makes a small range of bolt-type guns.

MODEL 69A SPORTING RIFLE

Made by Rhöner Sportwaffenfabrik GmbH, Oberelsbach-Weisbach.
Currently in production. **Chambering:** 22 Long Rifle, rimfire. **Action:** locked by turning the base of the bolt handle down into its seat in the receiver.

39.4in overall, 5.07lb empty. 23.6in barrel, 4-groove rifling; RH, concentric. Single shot only. Fixed open rear sight. 1080 fps with 40-grain bullet.

The Model 69a is an inexpensive beginner's gun, with the simplest of bolt actions in a plain beech half-stock with a low Monte Carlo comb and an obliquely cut forend tip. The trigger has a double-pressure release, and a sliding safety catch lies on the left side of the receiver. A telescope sight can be fitted to the receiver rails if required.

SIMILAR GUNS
Rhöner also makes a 9mm Flobert version of the 69a, known as the Model 69; however, this is a smooth-bore firing shot cartridges.

Model 69 Match. Based on the same basic design as the 69a, but with a straight bolt handle and sturdier construction, this light-weight target rifle has a half-stock with a high comb, a deep slab-sided forend, and stippling on the pistol grip. A micro-adjustable aperture sight can be fitted to the receiver rails, with a replaceable-element tunnel at the muzzle. The Model 69 Match has a heavy 23.6in barrel, giving it an overall length of 40.35in and a weight of about 7.1lb without sights.

• Rhöner, break-open type

This small range of single shot rifles (and a few double-barreled combination guns) is built on a self-adjusting wedge-locked action operated by an underlever. Introduced in the 1970s, the Rhöner rifles have proved to be popular and durable.

MODEL 75 SPORTING RIFLE

Made by Rhöner Sportwaffenfabrik GmbH, Oberelsbach-Weisbach.
Currently in production. **Chambering options:** 22 Winchester Magnum rimfire or 22 Hornet. **Action:** locked by a wedge intercepting a shoulder on the barrel block when the underlever closes.
DATA FOR 22 HORNET VERSION

39.4in overall, 6.5lb empty. 23.6in barrel, 4-groove rifling; RH, concentric. Single shot only. Fixed open rear sight. 2430 fps with 46-grain bullet.

These guns have a distinctively rounded receiver with foliate scroll decoration, a protruding hammer spur, and an operating lever curling around the trigger guard.

The trigger may be a direct-acting type or incorporate a setting element. Model 75 rifles are stocked in two pieces; the butt has a

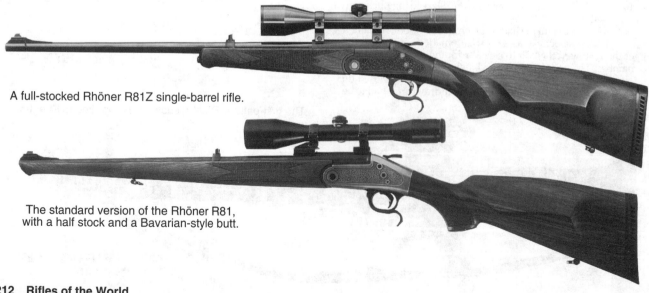

A full-stocked Rhöner R81Z single-barrel rifle.

The standard version of the Rhöner R81, with a half stock and a Bavarian-style butt.

hog's back comb and checkering on the pistol grip, whereas the forend has a checkered panel and a schnabel tip. The receiver is blued and is grooved for optical-sight mounting bases. Swivels lie beneath the butt and forend.

SIMILAR GUNS

Note: Rhöner also makes combination guns embodying the same basic action. These can be recognized by the over/under two-barrel construction.

Model 75L. This is a deluxe version or *Luxusmodell*, with an antique gray finish to the receiver and a squared Bavarian-style cheek piece on the butt. An optional five-cartridge magazine, with a hinged lid, can be set into the underside of the butt; finish and decoration match the receiver.

Model R81. Chambered for 22 Hornet, 222 Remington or 5.6x50R Magnum ammunition, this is a strengthened version of the basic design. The receiver may be blued or antique gray, the set trigger is standard, and the stock magazine may be fitted. A Bavarian-style butt displays the customary hog's back comb and a squared cheek piece. The guns are 39in long, have 23.6in barrels, and weigh about 6.6lb. Swivels lie beneath the butt and barrel.

Model R81S. Top of the Rhöner break-action range, this is distinguished by a Bavarian-style stock with a full-length forend; a ventilated rubber buttplate is a popular optional extra.

Model R81Z. Mechanically identical with the R81, this is a 'take-down' design.

• RWS

RWS-brand guns, perpetuating the pre-war trademark of Rheinisch-Westfälische Sprengstoff AG, have been marketed in recent years by Dynamit Nobel of Troisdorf/Oberlar. The most common centerfire bolt-action cartridge rifles are made by Kriegeskorte ('Krico', q.v.), but some Mausers—apparently emanating from Spain—have also been offered.

• Sauer

J.P. Sauer & Sohn of Suhl was an early convert to the bolt system, making a few high-class sporting rifles from about 1901 until the beginning of World War I on the basis of Mannlicher and Mauser actions. The business was also responsible for single shot dropping-block and break-open guns, but little is currently known of these; some even seem to have been sold under the 'Tell' brand-name customarily associated with Ernst Friedrich Büchel (q.v.).

The Mauser rifles were generally engraved, and often had ultra-slim forends held to the barrel by a transverse key set in oval escutcheons. Horn trigger guards and notable flats in the woodwork beneath the receiver were popular on Sauer products, though they should not be taken to indicate a Sauer sporter in the absence of the company's name or wild-man trademark.

The post-war version of Sauer & Sohn, after undertaking sub-contract work for Weatherby (q.v.) in the Eckenförde factory, developed a unique bolt with three locking flaps retracting into the cylindrical body as the bolt handle rose. As the handle turned down into its seat on the return stroke, the flaps were cammed outward into the receiver wall. This allowed the surface of the bolt to be entirely smooth, greatly simplifying the machining of the receiver.

Owing to the position of the locking flaps behind the magazine well, placing much of the bolt under compressive stress at the moment of firing, headspace problems were predicted when the first guns appeared. The fears soon proved to be groundless.

MODEL 80 SPORTING RIFLE
Made by J.P. Sauer & Sohn, Eckenförde/Holstein.
Currently in production. **Chambering options:** see notes. **Action:** locked by camming three retractable lugs into seats in the receiver behind the magazine well as the bolt handle is turned down.
DATA FOR A TYPICAL EXAMPLE
  Chambering: 25-06, rimless. 43.7in overall, 7.94lb unladen. 24in barrel, 4-groove twist; RH, concentric. Detachable box magazine, 3 rounds. Folding-leaf rear sight. 3440 fps with 90-grain bullet.

Introduced in 1973, these rifles had the distinctive bolt patented in 1970-2. A cocking indicator appeared in the bottom of the bolt-way, a loaded-chamber indicating pin lay on the left side of the breech, and a shotgun-pattern safety slid on the upper tang behind the bolt shroud. The standard medium-action Model 80 was made for 25-06, 270 Winchester or 30-06. A short-action rifle was introduced in 1974 for 22-250, 243 Winchester or 308 Winchester.

SIMILAR GUNS

Model 80 Magnum. This chambered 7mm Remington or 300 Winchester rounds.

Model 80 Super Magnum. This was the largest and most powerful chambering available with the standard medium-length action, handling the 458 Winchester Magnum cartridge. A typical rifle was 43.7in long, had a 24in barrel, and weighed about 7.95lb.

Model 90 Medium. A new standard pattern, introduced in 1982, this had a 22.45in barrel chambering 270 Winchester, 7x64 or 30-06 cartridges. The guns were about 43.3in long and weighed 7.5lb. Their selected walnut stocks had rosewood pistol grip caps and forend tips. Comb and cheek piece followed classical Bavarian hog's back form, and a ventilated rubber shoulder plate was popular. Swivels lay on the barrel ahead of the forend tip and under the butt. 6.5x57 and 9.3x62 options were added for all standard medium-action guns in 1983, though 22-250 was abandoned about 1986.

Model 90 Stutzen. These were medium-action rifles with full-length Mannlicher stocks. They were 40.95in long, had 20.05in barrels and weighed 7.7lb.

Model 90 Junior. Available only in 22-250 Remington, 243 and 308 Winchester, this was about 0.8in shorter in the butt than the standard medium-length pattern. It was 42.5in long and weighed 7.3lb. A 222 Remington option was introduced in 1983, but abandoned about three years later.

Model 90 Stutzen Junior. This was a short-butt version of the Model 90 Stutzen, sharing the same chamberings; it had a 20.05in barrel and an overall length of 40.15in.

Model 90 Magnum. These rifles were chambered for 6.5x68, 7mm Remington Magnum, 300 Weatherby Magnum, 300 Win-

The Sauer Model 90 Magnum sporting rifle.

The Sauer (or 'SIG-Sauer') SSG2000 sniper rifle, right side.

The barrel of the Sauer 2000 is held in the receiver by the three cap-head bolts seen below the chamber. Note also the multiple locking lugs on the bolt head.

chester Magnum, 8x68S, 375 H&H Magnum or 9.3x64 Brenneke cartridges. Barrels measured 26in, except for the 23.6in 375 pattern.

Model 90 Safari. Available only in 458 Winchester Magnum, this had a strengthened stock with two transverse recoil bolts. A typical rifle was 44.9in long, had a 23.6in barrel and weighed 10.6lb.

SSG 2000 SNIPER RIFLE
Scharfschützengewehr 2000
Made by J.P. Sauer & Sohn, Eckenförde/Holstein.

Total production: not known. **Chambering options:** 223 Remington, 7.5x55, 300 Weatherby Magnum or 308 Winchester. **Action:** as Model 80, above.

DATA FOR A TYPICAL EXAMPLE

Chambering: 7.5x55, rimless. 47.65in overall, 14.6lb with sight. 24in barrel, 4-groove twist; RH, concentric. Detachable box magazine, 4 rounds. Optical sight. 2640 fps with 180-grain bullet.

This was introduced in 1983 to provide SIG (Switzerland, q.v.) with a sniper rifle. Built on a Model 90 action, the SSG 2000 had a heavy barrel ending in a slotted compensator. The competition-type thumbhole half-stock had an adjustable shoulder plate and a separate comb controlled by an elevating wheel. An accessory rail was let into the underside of the angular forend; the pistol grip and the sides of the forend were stippled to improve grip.

Guns were supplied with Zeiss Diatal ZA 8x56 or Schmidt & Bender 1.5-6x42 telescope sights. Among the accessories were butt-spacers, tripods and mirage bands.

MODEL 200 SPORTING RIFLE
Made by J.P. Sauer & Sohn, Eckenförde/Holstein.
Currently in production. **Chambering options:** see notes. **Action:** locked by rotating multiple lugs into the barrel extension as the bolt handle turns down.

DATA FOR A TYPICAL STEEL-RECEIVER MAGNUM

Chambering: 6.5x68, rimless. 46.45in overall, 8.33lb unladen. 25.6in barrel, 4-groove twist; RH, concentric. Detachable box magazine, 4 rounds. Folding-leaf rear sight. 3770 fps with 93-grain bullet.

The cylindrical bolt of this interesting rifle, introduced in 1986, carried two banks of three lugs on a reduced-diameter head. These locked directly into the barrel extension, isolating the receiver from stress and allowing an alloy receiver to be offered as an option. Three large cap-head bolts clamped the barrel into the receiver ring, facilitating a change of caliber.

The magazine-release catch was recessed into the floorplate, the safety catch lay in the front web of the trigger guard, and an indicator protruded from the back of the bolt shroud when the striker was cocked. The trigger could be replaced by an optional 'set' system with a button substituting for a setting lever.

Butt and forend were separated by a sliver of receiver metal beneath the bolt handle, tenons on the wood engaging under-cut edges in the receiver shoulder. The butt was retained by a bolt which ran up through the pistol grip and into the receiver. The spatulate bolt handle could be replaced with an optional rounded alternative, and the front sling swivel bush was screwed horizontally into the forend tip.

Assuming the relevant barrel, magazine and bolt were available, chamberings were easily exchanged. Group I rifles handled 243 Winchester, 25-06 Remington, 6.5x55, 6.5x57, 270 Winchester, 7x64, 30-06, 308 Winchester or 9.3x62 cartridges. Bolts were common to all options except 243; magazines, to all but 243 and 308 (which share case-head dimensions) plus 9.3x62.

The Group II magazine was common to all chamberings. However, bolt IIa handled 6.5x68 and 8x68S, while bolt IIb was confined to the 7mm Remington, 300 Winchester or 300 Weatherby Magnum.

Standard rifles had a straight-comb walnut butt and a simple forend with a plain rounded tip, though synthetic carbon fiber patterns have also been made. The pistol grip and forend were checkered; the shoulder plate was solid rubber.

SIMILAR GUNS

Model 200 Lux. The 200 Lux and Lux E patterns were identical with the standard guns, except for their selected woodwork. Lux rifles also had gold-plated triggers and jeweled bolts. The 'Lux E' was a richly decorated version of the basic 200 Lux, engraved in any of seven basic styles.

Model 200 Europa (sometimes listed as 'Europe'). This gun had a stock with a low hog's back comb and a Bavarian-style cheek piece.

Model 200 Europa Lux and Lux E. These were the deluxe-pattern guns, with rosewood schnabel forend tips. The metalwork of the 'E' pattern was extensively engraved in a variety of styles.

Model 200 USA. This rifle was basically a Europa with a Monte Carlo comb and cheek piece. Its forend had a plain rounded tip.

Model 202. Introduced in 1994, this was an improved form of the Model 200 with a modified safety system. A safety button has been added to the tang, behind the cocking piece, and a safety-release catch lies in the trigger guard directly ahead of the trigger. The release has to be moved to the firing position before the trigger can be set, and re-sets automatically if the bolt is opened. The half-stock has a Monte Carlo comb and cheek piece, with checkering

The Sauer Model 200 rifle.

The new Sauer 200 UIT target rifle.

on the pistol grip and the forend. The pistol grip cap and the schnabel forend tip are both rosewood. Chamberings are currently 243 Winchester, 25-06, 6.5x55, 6.5x57, 270 Winchester, 7x64, 30-06, 308 Winchester and 9.3x62. The standard Model 202—with three- or five-round magazines—can be distinguished from the Europa model by the deeper forend.

Model 202 Alaska. Currently offered only in three magnum chamberings—300 Weatherby, 300 Winchester and 375 H&H—this 8.8lb gun is easily identifiable by a sturdy laminated beechwood half-stock. The steel components are phosphated, alloy parts being anodized. Magazine capacity may be three or four rounds.

Model 202 Europa (known as 'Europe' in most English-speaking markets). This differs from the standard rifle principally in the design of the stock, which has a much more slender forend with a pronounced schnabel tip, and in the addition of jewelling on the bolt.

Model 202 Europa Lux and Lux E. These are deluxe forms of the standard rifle, with select walnut half-stocks. Slender forends with schnabel tips, contrasting rosewood caps, bolt jewelling, and a range of engraving styles may be obtained.

Model 202 Hunting Match. Distinguished by a heavy 26.35in barrel and a straight-comb half-stock with an accessory rail let into the underside of the forend, this is available in 6.5x55 and 308 Winchester only. Typically, it weighs 10.15lb without the bipod. An alternative butt with a Monte Carlo comb (but lacking a cheek piece) is available to order.

Model 202 Magnum. Identical mechanically with the standard rifle, this chambers the 6.5x68, 7mm Remington Magnum, 300 Winchester Magnum, 300 Weatherby Magnum, 8x68S and 375 H&H Magnum cartridges. A 25.6in barrel is provided for all options except 375 H&H (23.6in only). Magnum rifles are 46.05in long and weigh about 8.35lb; magazine capacities are two or four rounds.

Model 202 Mannlicher. Offered in all the standard '202' chamberings, this has a full-length Bavarian-style stock with a squared cheek piece and a hog's back comb. It is 40.95in long, has a 20.05in barrel, and weighs about 6.65lb with the optional alloy receiver. A muzzle brake may be fitted to reduce recoil.

• Sauer-Weatherby

SAUER-WEATHERBY SPORTING RIFLE
Made by J.P. Sauer & Sohn, Eckenförde, 1965-72.

Total production: not known. **Chambering options:** see notes. **Action:** as Weatherby Mark V rifle (see 'USA: Weatherby, bolt-action type').

DATA FOR A TYPICAL EUROPA

Chambering: 8x68S, rimless. 47.25in overall, 9.05lb empty. 26in barrel, 4-groove rifling; RH, concentric. Internal box magazine, 3 rounds. Folding-leaf rear sight. 3050 fps with 195-grain bullet.

Introduced in 1965 to capitalize on the great potential of the nine-lug action being made for Weatherby, the Europa rifle was stocked in European fashion. The Monte Carlo comb was shallower and the contours were much more rounded than the standard American stock. A double set trigger was regarded as standard, though conventional single-trigger options were also available.

The 24in-barreled rifle was available in three Weatherby Magnum chamberings—270, 7mm and 300—or 30-06. The guns measured 45.25in overall and weighed about 7.95lb. A 26in-barreled version could be supplied in 6.5x68, 7x64, 8x68S, or occasionally even 460 Weatherby Magnum.

SIMILAR GUNS

Junior pattern. Confined to 224 Weatherby Magnum, with a short six-lug action, this rifle had a four-round magazine and a plastic shoulder plate. It was 45.25in long and weighed 6.65lb.

• Schilling
V. Chr. Schilling of Suhl completed Gew. 98 actions left over from wartime production. They were offered in a variety of chamberings—e.g., 6x58 Förster, 6.5x61 or 8x75—but were often anonymous. Others bore a tiny 'V.C.S.' somewhere on the action. Operated by Ludwig Bornhöft from about 1919, business failed about 1934.

• Schmidt & Habermann, block-action type
The attribution of this system to one of the larger gunmaking establishments in the Suhl district rests entirely on the appearance

of 'S. & H.' marks on rifles bearing the names of two other makers. Guns have been reported by Franz Kettner of Suhl (to whom the design has also been attributed) or Theodor Kommer of Zella-Mehlis. All embody identical actions, which were made in several sizes.

Walter Glaser of Zürich offered a series of excellent-quality sporters embodying this action in the period between the wars. Owing to the strength of the mechanism, they could chamber 'any sporting cartridges of between 6.5 and 11mm caliber'. The sturdy breechblock, which contained the hammer and an inertia firing pin, moved vertically when the operating lever ahead of the trigger guard was pushed down and forward to break the lock.

Rifles from the 1920s were usually much less individualistic than pre-1914 equivalents, as the excesses of Schützen-style butts were replaced by straight-wrist or pistol grip sporting patterns. Combs were invariably of hog's back type, cheek pieces being either rounded or the squared-edge patterns favored in Germany and Switzerland. Barrels were usually partly or fully octagonal, though round examples are known.

STANDARD PATTERN
Made by E. Schmidt & Habermann, Suhl, about 1920-39.

Total production: not known, but many thousands. **Chambering options:** many European and American cartridges, with 8.15x46.5R predominating. **Action:** locked by an intermediate block and the operating lever propping the breechblock behind the chamber.

DATA FOR A TYPICAL EXAMPLE

Chambering: 8.15x46.5R, rimmed. 44.9in overall, 7.41lb empty. 28.15in barrel, 4-groove rifling; RH, concentric. Quadrant sight graduated to 800m (875yd). 1805 fps with 150-grain bullet.

A typical rifle had a color case-hardened action with a lightly engraved breechblock. A set-trigger lever accompanied the conventional lever within the trigger guard, and the operating lever was curved around the guard in the fashion of many German-made break-action shotguns. The pistol grip butt displayed a hog's back comb and a small rounded cheek piece; the forend, held to the barrel by a key set in oval silver escutcheons, had a shallow schnabel tip. The half-octagonal barrel carried a Swiss-style quadrant rear sight at the breech, and a replaceable blade lay on a ramp at the muzzle.

• Schmidt & Habermann, bolt-action type
E. Schmidt & Habermann of Suhl made a 'Model 21' short-action Mauser rifle in 6.5x54, 8x51 and 250-3000 Savage. This was basically a modified Gew. 98 with a special knurled cocking-piece knob—not unlike that of the U.S. M1903 Springfield—and a simplified safety system. Schmidt & Habermann also handled conventional Mauser-pattern sporting rifles, often identified only by a small 'S & H' mark (cf., Sempert & Krieghoff).

• Schüler
Richard Schüler, junior partner with his brother Oskar in the well-established Waffenfabrik August Schüler of Suhl, developed a 11.2x60 cartridge from the old Reichspatrone 71 about 1913. This was chambered in a selection of sporting rifles, some single-shot and others embodying Mauser actions. Its distinctive 'rebated' case rim, smaller than the case head, was necessary to fit the recessed Mauser bolt face. The 11.2x72 Magnum cartridge appeared in the early 1920s, suitable rifles being made for Schüler by Sempert & Krieghoff.

In 1923, however, Schüler produced an awesome 12.7x70 cartridge, similar to the 500 Jeffrey Rimless, for use on the biggest game southern Africa had to offer. The rifle was very large and heavy, with a large-diameter barrel befitting its caliber. The pistol grip stock was similarly massive, but the magazine box still protruded beneath the forend ahead of the trigger. The magazine floor-plate catch was usually a radial-lever pattern. The last proprietary Schüler round, 6.5x68, appeared in the early 1930s.

• Sempert & Krieghoff
Sempert & Krieghoff of Suhl were merged into Heinrich Krieghoff in 1924, though retaining a separate identity until the 1930s. Mauser-action sporting rifles were stocked for general sale, and also for supply to August Schüler of Suhl in the immediate post-1920 period. An 'S. & K.' mark was used (cf., Schmidt & Habermann).

GERMANY

• Simonov
KARABINER-S
Made in the former Sauer & Sohn factory, Suhl.
Total production: perhaps 1.5 million. **Chambering:** 7.62x39, rimless. Otherwise generally as Soviet SKS except rear sight (graduated to 800m [875yd]) and a knife-type folding bayonet.

Production of the Karabiner-S appears to have begun in Suhl in the mid 1950s. The guns were closely patterned on the Soviet version, but had a sling slot through the butt and lacked the cleaning rod. A knife-type bayonet was fitted, the stock was generally a laminated pattern stained a yellowish shade, and the safety-catch head was ribbed. The left side of the receiver bore marks such as '60 K 1234'—the year of production ('60'=1960) and the serial number.

• Simson
Simson & Company of Suhl, appointed prime contractor to the German army in the immediate post-1919 period, is said to have completed some Gew. 98 actions in sporting-rifle form. The company became 'Berlin-Suhler Waffen- und Fahrzeugwerke GmbH' in 1932, but was nationalized in the mid 1930s; by 1940, it had become a division of 'Gustloff-Werke'.

There were also many 22 (5.6mm) rimfire patterns. An absence of information makes these difficult to catalogue, but they are known to have ranged from a junior carbine up to sophisticated Sportbüchsen.

PRECISION CARBINE
Simson-Präzisions-Karabiner
Made by Simson & Co., Suhl (1927-32), and by Berlin-Suhler Waffen- & Fahrzeugwerke, Suhl (1932-40).
Total production: unknown. **Chambering options:** 22 Short rimfire or 22 Extra Long rimfire (see text). **Action:** locked by turning the bolt handle down into its recess in the receiver.
DATA FOR A 22 SHORT EXAMPLE
41.35in, 3.5lb empty. 23.6in barrel, 4-groove rifling; RH, concentric. Single-shot only. Standing-block rear sight. 855 fps with 29-grain bullet.

This gun was made in several patterns, sharing an identical split-receiver bolt system and a spatulate handle turning down ahead of the trigger. The chamberings included 5.6mm Nr. 2 and 5.6mm Nr. 7, better known as the 22 Short and 22 Extra Long rimfire cartridges respectively. Otherwise similar Flobert guns (6mm and 9mm) were customarily smooth-bores, whereas rimfire patterns were rifled.

An extractor-plate slid back in a channel in the bottom of the feed way as the bolt was opened, expelling a spent case if appropriate. The guns had plain beech half-stocks, usually with swivels under the barrel and forend.

A 21.65in barrel was often fitted to 9mm-caliber guns instead of the 23.6in type, while a deluxe rifle had checkering on the pistol grip of a walnut half-stock and an adjustable block-and-thumbwheel rear sight.

SIMILAR GUNS
Neues Modell ('new model'). Introduced in 1932, this was distinguished by the design of the receiver. Instead of a broad cutaway ahead of the bolt handle to expose the feed way, a small oval ejection port was cut in the top surface to improve rigidity. Made only with the standard 23.6in barrel, the rifles were available for 5.6mm Nr. 7 or 6mm rimfire cartridges. An optional double-trigger mechanism could be obtained to order.

Kleinkaliberbüchse Modell 1933. This was a minor variation of the new-model guns, with a 25.6in barrel, an adjustable trigger, a 200m (220yd) tangent-leaf sight, and a 'striker safety' to prevent firing until the breech was locked. The ball-type bolt handle was bent slightly downward. Chambered only for the 5.6mm Nr. 7 rimfire cartridge, the rifle could be obtained to order with a double-trigger system. Empty weight was 5.95lb.

SPORTING GUN
Simson-Sportbüchse
Made by Simson & Co., Suhl (1927-32), and by Berlin-Suhler Waffen- & Fahrzeugwerke, Suhl (1932-40).
Total production: unknown. **Chambering:** 22 Extra Long rimfire. **Action:** generally as Precision Carbine, above.
43.13in overall, 6.65lb empty. 25.6in barrel, 4-groove rifling; RH, concentric. Single-shot only. Tangent-leaf rear sight graduated to 200m (220yd). 1080 fps with 40-grain bullet.

Built on the improved action—which ejected upward to the right through an oval port—this gun had a radial safety lever on the left side of the breech, and a sturdy pistol grip half-stock with a finger groove beneath the rear sight. The trigger was adjustable, swivels lay under the butt and forend, and a screw-adjusted rear sight (*Schraubvisier*) could be substituted for the militaristic tangent-leaf pattern.

• Stahl
Two types of rifle designed by Richard Stahl of Suhl may be encountered. The rarer, dating from 1869, embodied a self-cocking pivoting-block action operated by a bulky two-part lever in the enlarged trigger guard ahead of the trigger. The more successful 1873-pattern—similar externally to the Martini—was operated by a breechblock extension lever running down the right side of the stock wrist. By 1880, Stahl had turned to true Martini-action rifles at the expense of his own designs. He was succeeded by his son, Bernhard, but business had ceased by 1914.

• Thälmann
VEB Fahrzeug- und Jagdwaffenfabrik 'Ernst Thälmann' was the trading name of the nationalized firearms industry of the German Democratic Republic, based on elements of the pre-1945 gunmaking industry working in and around Suhl. Most of the rimfire 'Thälmann' rifles seem to have been made in the former Simson (BSW/Gustloff-Werke) factory and show characteristics of pre-1939 designs—see 'Simson'.

MODEL 91 SPORTING RIFLE
Little is known about the breadth of the pre-1970 range, except that it included this 22LR rimfire bolt-action sporting rifle. This gun was about 39.5in long, had a 20.5in barrel, weighed about 6.4lb and had a detachable five-round magazine. The beech half-stock had a straight comb and a pistol grip, but apparently lacked a cheekpiece and checkering.

SIMILAR GUNS
Model 91L rifle. This was a variant of the standard Model 91 with a full-length Mannlicher-style stock.

Model 92 rifle. Based on the Model 91, this chambered the 5.6x35R Vierling cartridge, which was popular in central Europe prior to the emergence of the 22 Hornet in the late 1950s. It is assumed that a supplementary locking lug was added to the bolt; though the Vierling cartridge was not particularly hard-hitting, it was appreciably more powerful than the 22 rimfires.

Model 92L rifle. Mechanically identical with the 5.6x35R pattern described previously, this could be identified by its distinctive full-length stock.

'World Master' small-bore rifle (KK-Weltmeisterbüchse). This had a 29.9in barrel, measured 46.8in overall, and weighed 15.4lb; a shorter 26.7in barrel was apparently optional. The pistol grip half-stock had a deep rounded forend, a sliding shoulder plate. The trigger could be adjusted for release pressure and pull-length. Sights comprised a micro-adjustable aperture pattern on the receiver and an exchangeable-element tunnel at the muzzle.

• Tirmax
TIRMAX AUTOMATIC CARBINE
Maker unknown, about 1909-14.
Total production: not known, but probably very few. **Chambering options:** 7.65mm Browning and 9mm Browning Long. **Action:** no mechanical lock; blowback operated, semi-automatic only.
DATA FOR A TYPICAL 7.65MM EXAMPLE
40.95in overall, 6.07lb empty. 22in barrel, 4-groove rifling; RH, concentric. Detachable box magazine, 6 rounds. Combination block and folding-leaf rear sight. 1350 fps with 73-grain bullet.

This is generally regarded as German, though Belgian provenance can also be argued. Operated by simple blowback principles and capable of being dismantled without tools, it had a sturdy round-topped receiver. A straight-comb butt with a checkered semi-pistol grip and a small round cheek piece was separated from the forend by a receiver. Swivels lay beneath the butt and the barrel. The cocking slide lay on the left side, immediately behind the forend, and the magazine projected ahead of the trigger. A safety bolt ran laterally through the trigger guard housing, and the magazine release projected inside the front of the guard. The hammer-fired action had a cocking indicator on the left side of the receiver.

The Voere Model 2115.

• Voere, autoloading type

Voere has had an interesting history. The business was founded in the 1950s in the small Bavarian town of Vöhrenbach in the Schwarzwald ('Black Forest'), close to the border between Austria and Germany, and traded there until 1978. It was then renamed 'Tiroler Jagd- und Sportwaffenfabrik Voere GmbH & Co. KG' and moved to the Kufstein in the Austrian Tyrol.

In addition to many bolt-action patterns, Voere has made a surprisingly broad range of blowback rimfire and gas-operated centerfire autoloaders. The first guns were apparently introduced in the early 1960s.

MODEL 2114S SPORTING RIFLE

Made by Voetter & Co., Vöhrenbach, Schwarzwald, about 1963-78.
Total production: not known. **Chambering:** 22LR rimfire. **Action:** no mechanical lock; blowback, semi-automatic only.

37.8in overall, 5.73lb empty. 18.1in barrel, 4-groove rifling; RH, concentric. Detachable box magazine, 10 rounds. Fixed open rear sight. 1080 fps with 40-grain bullet.

This 22LR rimfire semi-automatic, distinguished by a prominent trigger guard extension block filling the gap behind the detachable box magazine. It has an adjustable single-stage trigger, and can be converted to fire single shots by locking the cocking handle. Fixed open sights are standard, though an adjustable tangent-leaf rear sight can be supplied; the front sight is a hooded blade on a short ramp. A rotary safety collar at the back of the receiver locks the firing pin. The walnut-finish Monte Carlo-type hardwood stock has a shallow cheekpiece and a rounded forend. Sling swivels are fitted beneath the barrel and butt.

SIMILAR GUNS

Model 1014 rifle. This embodies a similar autoloading action to the 2114, but has a distinctive military-style stock with a handguard, a straight-comb butt and the front swivel mounted on a barrel band. Like most of the guns in this series, it can fire single shots merely by locking the cocking handle after reloading. The Modell 1014 has an adjustable aperture rear sight on top of the receiver above the trigger, and a wing-pattern safety protrudes from the receiver end-cap. Magazines hold eight or 15 rounds, and the guns weigh about 6lb empty.

Model 2100 rifle. Little is known about this gun, advertised by Wischo of Erlangen (a distributor) in the mid 1960s. It is believed to have been the prototype of the Model 2114, with a beech stock. Published dimensions indicate a length of 40.6in with a 19.7in barrel, and a weight of 6.28lb with an eight-round magazine.

Model 2101 rifle. This was a variant of the Model 2100 with a deluxe walnut stock.

Model 2115 rifle. This is essentially similar to the 2114 pattern, but has hardwood stock with a small rounded German-style cheekpiece, checkering on the pistol grip and forend, and a slight hog's back comb; white spacers accompany the pistol grip cap and buttplate. Sling swivels are standard.

MODEL 0014 SPORTING RIFLE

Made by Voetter & Co., Vöhrenbach, Schwarzwald, about 1965-78.
Total production: not known. **Chambering:** 22LR rimfire. **Action:** no mechanical lock; blowback, semi-automatic only.

37.6in overall, 5.07lb empty. 17.9in barrel, 4-groove rifling; RH, concentric. Detachable box magazine, 10 rounds. Fixed open rear sight. 1080 fps with 40-grain bullet.

This small sporting rifle has a walnut-finish hardwood stock, a plain pistol grip, a low Monte Carlo comb, and a squared forend with an obliquely cut tip. The bolt can be locked in a safety notch when required. A detachable box magazine protrudes ahead of the trigger group—a fifteen-round option is available—and fixed open sights, though an adjustable tangent-leaf rear sight can be fitted on request.

SIMILAR GUNS

Model 0015 rifle (designation unconfirmed). A long-barreled deluxe pattern, with a 21in barrel and an overall length of 41in, this was being advertised in Britain in 1968. The walnut half-stock had a Monte Carlo comb, a cheekpiece on the left side of the butt, a rosewood pistol grip cap, and an obliquely cut rosewood forend tip.

MODEL 2185 SPORTING RIFLE

Made by Voetter & Co., Vöhrenbach, Schwarzwald (about 1975-8).
Total production: not known. **Chambering options:** 5.6x50, 5.6x57, 222 Remington, 222 Remington Magnum, 223 Remington, 6.5x57, 243 Winchester, 270 Winchester, 7x64, 30-06, 308 Winchester or 9.3x62. **Action:** locked by rotating lugs on the bolt into the receiver wall; gas operated, semi-automatic only.

DATA FOR A TYPICAL EXAMPLE

Chambering: 5.6x57, rimless. 45.85in overall, 7.6lb empty. 20.45in barrel, 4-groove rifling; RH, concentric. Detachable box magazine, 2 rounds. Fixed open rear sight. 3410 fps with 74-grain bullet.

This large autoloader was introduced for sporting use in the mid 1970s, though sales have been relatively small. Its three-quarter pistol grip stock had a hog's back comb and a schnabel forend tip. A ventilated shoulder pad and ports on the side of the muzzle beneath the front-sight block reduced the recoil sensation. The detachable box magazine was placed well forward of the trigger guard, which was a simple stamped strip. A few guns were sold under the 'Voere-Austria' banner (see **'Austria'**) from 1978 onward.

• Voere, bolt-action type

The original German-based business passed in 1978 to Tiroler Jagd- und Sportwaffenfabrik GmbH & Co. of Kufstein, and continued under a 'Voere–Austria' banner (see **'Austria: Voere, bolt-action type'**).

Cataloguing the German-made Voere rimfire rifles is still handicapped by a lack of information from the earliest days, and by camouflaging of the Voere model numbers by over-zealous distributors in Britain and North America.

GARDEN GUN

This was a simple design with a split-bridge receiver, possibly originating in the 1950s and discontinued about 1968. Offered in 22LR, 6mm rimfire and 9mm Flobert (ball and shot), rifled or smooth-bored, the gun was about 39.5in long, had a 23.6in barrel, and weighed merely 4.4lb. Most guns had straight-comb halfstocks with a pistol grip and a short forend with a finger groove. However, some 9mm examples have been reported with low Monte Carlo combs and a 25.6in barrel.

MODEL 2055 SPORTING RIFLE

Precursor of the 2100 series, this 22LR rifle (possibly dating from 1958-65) had an improved action with the bolt at the rear. It was about 39.4in long, had a 23.6in barrel—differing sources give differing dimensions—and weighed 4.4-4.5lb. The straight-comb beech stock lacked checkering, a 200m (220yd) tangent-leaf rear sight was fitted, and there was a finger groove in the short forend.

SIMILAR GUNS

Model 2056 rifle. This was simply a variant of the 2055 chambering 9mm Flobert ammunition, and was invariably a smoothbore.

MODEL 2155 SPORTING RIFLE
Repetierbüchse M2155

Made by Voetter & Co., Vöhrenbach, Schwarzwald (about 1967-78)
Subsequently made in Austria (q.v.).
Total production: not known. **Chambering options:** 5.6x57, 22-250, 243 Winchester, 25-06 Remington, 6.5x55, 6.5x57, 270 Winchester, 7x57, 7x64, 7.5x55, 30-06, 308 Winchester, 8x57IS or 9.3x62. **Action:** locked by rotating two lugs on the bolt head into the receiver wall behind the chamber as the bolt was turned down, and by the safety lug entering its seat.

DATA FOR A TYPICAL 2155/1

Chambering: 6.5x55, rimless. 46in overall, 7lb empty. 24in barrel, 4-groove rifling; RH, concentric. Internal box magazine, 5 rounds. Folding-leaf rear sight graduated to 200m (220yd). 2720 fps with 139-grain bullet.

The Voere Model 2155 was based on a refurbished Mauser actions.

The first Mauser-type firearms were made from military-surplus actions in the 1950s. The most basic rifle available in the mid 1970s—known as the 2155/1—was built on a Kar. 98k-type action with a spatulate bolt handle. The walnut stock had a Bavarian-style cheekpiece and a hog's back comb; skip-line checkering lay on the pistol grip and forend. Single or double trigger units could be fitted to order.

SIMILAR GUNS

Model 2155/2 rifle. Mechanically identical with the 2155/1, this had a walnut-finish stock with a Monte Carlo comb and cheekpiece. Double set triggers were usually fitted.

Model 2155/3 rifle. This amalgamated a refurbished Kar. 98k action with a refined stock, with a larger panel of checkering on the rounded forend. The pistol grip lacked the synthetic cap of the '/1' and '/2' variants, and the contours of the Monte Carlo-style butt were refined.

Model 2155/4 rifle. This is believed to have been applied to a short-barreled fully stocked gun, made only in small numbers.

Model 2155/5 rifle. Lacking confirmation, this designation is said to have identified a variant of the 2155 with a straight-comb 'classic' butt.

Model 2155 Lux rifle. This deluxe pattern, with a greatly refined stock of select French walnut, was apparently built on new FN-made actions instead of refurbished wartime patterns. The magazine floor-plate release catch was set in the front web of the trigger guard bow.

Model 2165 rifle. The Repetierbüchse 2165 was an improved 2155 with a double set trigger, an elegant bolt shroud and a streamlined bolt handle. The safety catch lay on the upper tang. Detachable box or internal hinged floor-plate magazines were available; the walnut stock had a hog's back comb and a squared Bavarian cheekpiece. Skip-line checkering appeared on the pistol grip and forend, and a rosewood schnabel tip was standard. Chamberings duplicated the 2155 model.

Model 2165 Special rifle, or 'Magnum'. These were mechanically identical with the standard pattern listed previously, but had 25.6in barrels and measured 46.25in overall; weight averaged 7.3lb. Chamberings were customarily 6.5x68, 7mm Remington Magnum, 300 Winchester Magnum, 8x68S and 9.3x64.

Model 2175M rifle (or 'Medium'). The Voere 2175 had a Bavarian-style walnut half-stock, but the bolt shroud was a short cylinder and a pivoting safety protruded from the stock behind the bolt handle. A selection of single and double triggers was offered.

Model 2175L rifle (or 'Light'). The short or 'L' action chambered 222 and 223 Remington, 223 Remington Magnum or 5.6x50 Magnum.

Model 2175S rifle ('Special' or 'Magnum'). This version handled the same powerful long-case cartridges as the 2165 Special described above.

MODEL 2202 SPORTING RIFLE

Made by Voetter & Co., Schwarzwald (about 1975-8); subsequently made in Austria (q.v.).

Total production: not known. **Chambering:** 22LR. **Action:** locked by turning the bolt handle down into its seat in the receiver.

38.95in overall, 5lb empty. 21.25in barrel, 4-groove rifling; RH, concentric. Single shot only. Tangent-leaf rear sight graduated to 150m (165yd)? 1080 fps with 40-grain bullet.

A single-shot gun, this is chambered specifically for 22LR rimfire ammunition. It has a simple hardwood half-stock with a pistol grip and a low Monte Carlo comb, fixed open sights, a simple trigger, and a safety catch that locks the firing pin. Some older examples will be found with a fixed open rear sight.

SIMILAR GUNS

Note: The earliest guns were made with fixed open rear sights, but later examples usually display the tangent-leaf pattern—once optional. Swivels (also optional) may be found beneath the butt and forend of any individual 2200-series gun.

Model 2200 rifle. The most basic gun in the series, this was a smooth-bore chambered for 6mm rimfire cartridges.

Model 2201 rifle. Mechanically identical with the 2200, this had a rifled barrel.

Model 2201N rifle. A deluxe version of the standard guns, this was distinguished by a walnut stock or *Nussbaumschaft*, with a cheekpiece on the left side of the butt and checkering on the pistol grip and forend.

Model 2202 rifle. Described above, this was also offered with a 4x optical sight as the '2202 VZ' (*Visierung-Zielfernrohr*, 'telescope sighted')

Model 2203 rifle. Mechanically identical with the 2202, this was distinguished by the addition of a shallow cheekpiece on its Monte Carlo-type butt. It was also offered in a 'VZ' configuration.

Model 2204 rifle. Essentially similar to the 2202 pattern, this chambers 9mm Flobert cartridges, measures 44.5in overall, has a 26.6in smooth-bore barrel, and weighs only 4.5lb empty. The sights were basic, comprising a fixed open notch and a bead at the muzzle. Ball or shot cartridges could be used interchangeably.

Model 2204N rifle. This was a deluxe version of the standard 2204, with a walnut half-stock with a shallow cheekpiece on the left side of the butt. The pistol grip and the forend were checkered.

MODEL 2107 SPORTING RIFLE

Made by Voetter & Co., Vohrenbach, Schwarzwald (about 1971-8).

Total production: not known. **Chambering:** 22LR. **Action:** locked by turning the bolt handle down into its seat in the receiver.

38.95in overall, 5lb empty. 21.25in barrel, 4-groove rifling; RH, concentric. Detachable box magazine, 5 or 8 rounds. Tangent-leaf rear sight graduated to 200m (220yd). 1080 fps with 40-grain bullet.

The Model 2107, the most basic of the magazine-feed Voere rimfire rifles, is distinguished by a walnut-varnished beech half-stock with a Monte Carlo comb, a plastic buttplate and a squared forend. The safety catch is a small button protruding above the stock behind the bolt handle; it locks the trigger when applied. Swivels lie beneath the butt and forend. Guns remaining after 1978 were subsequently sold as the 'Model 107' by Tiroler Jagd- und Sportwaffenfabrik of Kufstein (see **'Austria: Voere, bolt-action type'**).

SIMILAR GUNS

Note: A compact standing-block rear sight with a folding leaf was an optional extra on deluxe guns.

Model 1007 Biathlon rifle. This is a five-, eight- or 15-shot bolt-action rifle with distinctive sliding safety catch at the rear of the receiver and a tangent-leaf sight immediately ahead of the bolt handle. It has a pseudo-military stock similar to that of the Modell 1014 and a single-stage trigger.

Model 1013 rifle. This is essentially similar to the M1007, but chambers 22WRM and comes with a five- or 10-round magazine. It is also available with a double set trigger.

Model 2108 rifle. A deluxe version of the 2107, this has a walnut stock with a cheekpiece, a rosewood pistol grip cap, and skip-line checkering on the pistol grip and forend. It was also available with an optical sight, as the '2108 VZ'.

Model 2109 rifle. This was a single shot version of the M2107, lacking the magazine but otherwise identical. The 2109 VZ was an optically-sighted derivative.

Model 2110 rifle. A deluxe version of the 2109, this single shot 22LR gun could be identified by its walnut stock, by the white spacer accompanying the plastic buttplate, and by skip-line checkering on the pistol grip and forend. A 'VZ' variant was also made.

Model 2112 rifle. Also made in 'VZ' (optical sighted) guide, this was the best of the Voere 22LR repeaters. The select French walnut half-stock had hand-cut checkering and a rosewood forend tip accompanied by a white spacer.

Model 2113 rifle. Chambered for the 22 Winchester Magnum rimfire round, with five- or 10-round magazines, this had a sturdier action with an additional locking lug. It was often fitted with a double set trigger and given an 'St.' suffix.

Model 2116 rifle. Dating from about 1966-72, this was apparently a replacement for the 'Garden Gun' mentioned previously, measuring 39.4in overall and weighing only 4lb. The solid-bridge receiver may have been an alloy casting, and the bolt handle lay above the rear of the trigger guard; the trigger lever was placed unusually far forward. The plain walnut-finish hardwood half-stock had a Monte Carlo comb, but lacked a cheekpiece.

Model 2117 rifle. Introduced prior to 1965, this was an early form of the Model 2107, with a five-round magazine and the 200m tangent-leaf rear sight. It had a plain hardwood half-stock, lacking checkering and a cheekpiece. The front swivel lay on the tip of the forend beneath the barrel.

Model 2118 rifle. This was a deluxe version of the 2117, with a checkered walnut stock.

TITAN 2130 E
Also known as the 'Shihar'
Made by Voetter & Co., Schwarzwald (c. 1967-76).

Total production: not known. **Chambering options:** 243 Winchester, 6.5x57, 270 Winchester, 7x57, 7x64, 30-06, 308 Winchester, 8x57 or 9.3x62. See also notes. **Action:** locked by rotating three lugs on the bolt head into the receiver wall as the bolt was turned down, and by the bolt handle base entering its seat.

DATA FOR A TYPICAL EXAMPLE

Chambering: 30-06, rimless. 44.1in overall, 7.05lb empty. 23.6in barrel, 4-groove rifling; RH, concentric. Detachable box magazine, 5 rounds. Folding-leaf rear sight graduated to 200m (220yd). 2800 fps with 165-grain bullet.

Easily recognizable by its lofty angular receiver, this 1967 introduction had a fluted bolt with three symmetrically-placed lugs. The cartridge-case head was entirely enclosed in the bolt face. Bolt throw was about 60 degrees, and a safety catch protruded from the back of the angular bolt shroud. Lock time was claimed to be the fastest of all production rifles.

Most of the rifles had Monte Carlo half-stocks, with skip-line checkering on the forend and pistol grip. A ventilated rubber shoulder pad was fitted. The pistol grip caps and reverse-cut forend tips were rosewood, accompanied by thin white spacer plates. Most stocks had an oiled finish, though lacquered versions could be supplied on request.

THE GUNS
Model 2130 E rifle. A special single set trigger system ('E', *Einzelzüngelstecher*) could be substituted for the double pattern to order, though the guns were otherwise mechanically identical.

Model 2130 F rifle. This variant had a direct-acting shotgun-pattern trigger ('F', *Flintenabzug*).

Model 2130 St rifle. Fitted with a double set trigger (*Doppelzüngelstecher*, 'St'), this was regarded as the standard Titan rifle. By 1973, the chambering options had been enlarged to include 25-06, 7mm Remington Magnum, 300 Winchester Magnum, 308 Norma Magnum and 375 H&H Magnum. Standard rifles had 23.6in barrels; Magnum patterns measured 25.6in. Magazine capacity was 3-5 rounds, depending on chambering. In 1976, however, the Model 2130 was replaced by the improved Titan II.

• Vom Hofe
Vom Hofe & Scheinemann of Berlin made their first sporting rifles on the basis of 1898-pattern Mauser action about 1927. From 1931, Ernst-August vom Hofe continued business after the withdrawal of his partner, developing the 6.2x73mm Super Express (Belted) cartridge soon afterward. A 7x73mm cartridge replaced the

6.2mm pattern in 1933 and business moved to Karlsruhe in 1936. Almost immediately, the 5.6x61mm Super Express cartridge was introduced commercially. The first Vom Hofe Super Express rifles date from this period, built on Oberndorf-made actions with barrels supplied by Christoph Funk and Triebel-Gewehrfabrik of Suhl.

In 1955, Walter Gehmann (q.v.) of Karlsruhe succeeded to the business of vom Hofe (who had died some years earlier) and the 7x66mm Super Express was announced little more than a year later.

• Walther, autoloading type
Surprisingly little is known about the chronology of these rifles, though experiments undertaken by Fritz and Erich Walther dated back to the 1930s.

The unsuccessful flap-lock Gew. 41 (W) was superseded by the perfected Gew. 43, which shared the locking mechanism but had a greatly improved gas system. When the Gew. 43 fired, gas was tapped from the bore into a hollow piston chamber and the actuating rod was forced back against the breech cover. The cover pulled the firing pin away from the breech as it retreated, camming the locking arms into the breech block, and then reciprocated to eject, cock the hammer, strip a fresh round into the chamber and re-lock the breech.

The perfected Walther rifle proved to be very efficient, though the workmanship and quality of material left much to be desired.

MODEL 1 SPORTING RIFLE
Walther-Selbstlade-Kleinkaliberbüchse Modell 1
Made by Carl Walther Waffenfabrik, Zella-Mehlis, about 1931-40?

Quantity: at least 15,000 (all types). **Chambering:** 22 Long Rifle, rimfire. **Action:** blowback, no positive lock.

40in overall, 4.4lb empty. 20in barrel, 4 grooves; RH twist, concentric. Detachable box magazine, 5 rounds. Standing block and multi-leaf rear sight. About 1080 fps with standard ammunition.

Walther's first rimfire autoloading rifle was a sophisticated product compared with many of its rivals, offering a detachable box magazine and a sliding safety catch on the tang behind the receiver. The operating handle, mounted on the bolt-retracting collar, was placed well forward in the feed way.

Advertised as a *Schonzeitbüchse* ('close-season gun'), it had a walnut half-stock with checkering on the pistol grip. Swivels lay beneath the barrel and butt. Five-round magazines were standard, but a nine-round unit could be obtained to order; with one round in the chamber, this raised capacity to a maximum of 10 shots. Alternatively, a magazine block could be acquired to convert the rifle into a single-shot auto ejector.

SIMILAR GUNS
Model 2 rifle. This 'Sportbüchse' was a heavier version of the Model 1, with a 24.8in barrel and a bulkier half-stock with a grasping groove in the sides of the forend. The rear sight was usually a tangent-leaf pattern graduated from 30m to 200m. The rifle was about 44in long, weighed 7.04lb, and could accommodate a micro-adjustable diopter sight on the rear of the receiver.

MODEL 41 RIFLE
Gewehr 41 (W)
Made by Carl Walther Waffenfabrik, Zella-Mehlis, Thüringen (code 'ac'); and Berlin-Lübecker Maschinenfabrik 'duv').

Quantity: 122,800. **Chambering:** 7.9x57mm, rimless. **Action:** Locked by camming flaps in the bolt outward into recesses in the receiver walls; gas operated, autoloading.

45.5in overall, 10.1lb empty. 22in barrel, 4-groove rifling; RH, concentric. Charger-loaded integral box magazine, 10 rounds. Tangent-leaf sight graduated to 1200m. 2460 fps with sS ball cartridges. S. 84/98 sword bayonet.

Cocked by retracting the breech cover, this rifle shared the Bang-type muzzle cup system with the competing Mauser pattern

The Gewehr 41 (W) was a comparatively unsuccessful design.

The Gewehr 43, derived from the Gew. 41 (W), was a much better gun.

(q.v.)—presumably in accordance with army instructions. However, the Gew. 41 (W) had its operating rod above the barrel instead of below, and the breech-locking system differed greatly from that of the Gew. 41 (M).

The Walther rifle, preferred to its Mauser rival, was officially adopted in December 1942 and an initial order for 70,000 guns was approved. The mechanical hold-open of the trials rifles was eliminated and the safety system was improved.

Though nearly 92,000 rifles were made in 1943, combat experience in Russia soon showed the undesirability of the muzzle-cup system in adverse conditions. Consequently, the Gew. 41 was abandoned in favor of the Gew. 43 (below) though series production continued into the first months of 1944.

MODEL 42 (W) ASSAULT RIFLE
Maschinenkarabiner 42 (W), MKb. 42 (W)
Made by Carl Walther Waffenfabrik, Zella-Mehlis, Thüringen (code 'ac').

Quantity: 2,800? **Chambering:** 7.9x33mm, rimless. **Action:** Gas-operated autoloading action, locked by rotating lugs on the bolt into the receiver.
DATA FOR A 'PRODUCTION' GUN

37.3in overall, 9.7lb with empty magazine. 16.2in barrel, 4-groove rifling; RH, concentric. Detachable box magazine, 30 rounds. Tangent-leaf sight graduated to 800m. 2128 fps with ball cartridges; 575±50 rpm. S. 84/98 sword bayonet.

Walther produced a weapon to compete with the Haenel prototype (q.v.). The gun was successfully demonstrated to the authorities at the end of 1941. In January 1942, therefore, a contract for 200 pre-production guns was approved—but only two guns had been made by July. Trials at the Kummersdorf firing-range revealed that the Haenel and Walther carbines worked well enough to be issued for field trials. Both were ordered into limited production: Walther was to make 500 guns in October, and attain 15,000 per month by March 1943.

Changes in the basic WaA specification then disrupted progress, but eventually, in February 1943, the combined efforts of Walther and Haenel exceeded the 1,000-gun production target by 217.

Made largely from pressings and stampings, the MKb. 42 (W) was superficially similar to the Mkb. 42 (H), but fired from a closed breech at all times, had a more obvious 'straight-line' layout, and carried the rear sight on a tall block. A cylindrical forend casing contained an annular gas piston/barrel construction.

Service trials showed that the Haenel gas system was easier to maintain and more reliable in adverse conditions—some testing had been undertaken in what had once been Soviet territory. The Walther was promptly abandoned.

MODEL 43 RIFLE
Gewehr 43
Made by Carl Walther Waffenfabrik, Zella-Mehlis, Thüringen (code 'ac'); Berlin-Lübecker Maschinenfabrik ('duv', 'qve'); and Gustloff-Werke, Weimar ('bcd').

Quantity: at least 402,700 (see text). **Chambering:** 7.9x57mm, rimless. **Action:** as Gew. 41 (W), above.

44.8in overall, 8.5lb without magazine. 22in barrel, 4-groove rifling; RH, concentric. Detachable box magazine, 10 rounds. Tangent-leaf sight graduated to 1200m. 2460 fps with sS ball cartridges. No bayonet.

Adopted on 30th April 1943 to replace the unsatisfactory Gew. 41, but retaining the breech-locking system of its predecessor, this rifle had a conventional port-and-piston gas system adapted from the Soviet Tokarev (q.v.). A detachable box magazine protruded beneath the stock ahead of the trigger guard bow.

The Gew. 43 was an excellent design, but had been ordered into full-scale production at a time when the German arms industry was in decline and was prone to parts-breakage. External finish was notably poor, as work was concentrated on key internal components.

It had a laminated pistol grip half-stock with a full-length handguard in wood or plastic. The gas-tube, piston and actuating rod lay above the barrel. A sling-slot was cut through the butt, a fixed bar appearing on the left side of the forend band, and a rail for the Zf. 4 telescope sight lay on the right side of the receiver.

Production began slowly—only a little over 3,000 guns were completed in 1943—but accelerated rapidly: 299,800 Gew. 43 were delivered in 1944. Unfortunately, sub-contracting reduced the value of what was potentially among the best semi-automatic rifles of World War II, and so many were lost in Russia that they are now comparatively scarce. Among the parts supplied from subsidiary contractors were many of the barrels, which may be found with the 'dnv' code associated with Fahr AG of Stochach.

The total production prior to 31st March 1945 is said to have totaled 402,713, 53,435 of these being Gew. 43 Zf. However, Berlin-Lübecker Maschinenfabrik reportedly made another 15,000 guns in the first week of April 1945, and, with Walther's contribution, it is probable that total production reached 430,000 or more.

SIMILAR GUNS
Gewehr 43 Zf (*Zielfernrohr*, 'telescope sight'). This was a specially selected sniper version of the basic Gew. 43. However, though 22,000 were made in 1944 and 31,500 in the first three months of 1945, the Walther proved to be much less accurate than the bolt-action sniper rifles derived from the Kar. 98k. This was partly due to poor-quality ammunition, partly to declining manufacturing standards—particularly in the last few weeks of the war—and partly to the unavoidable movement in the action as the gun fired.

Karabiner 43. Many attempts have been made to define the differences between the Gew. 43 and the Kar. 43, but the latter was simply the former renamed in April 1944. A few changes were subsequently made to accelerate production: machining was simplified, the cleaning rod was eliminated, some guns lacked the mechanical hold-open and others had an additional bolt-guide rib.

WA2000 SNIPING RIFLE
Made by Carl Walther Sportwaffenfabrik, Ulm/Donau, about 1982-8.
Total production: very few. **Chambering options:** 7.5x55, 7.62x51 or 300 Winchester Magnum. **Action:** locked by rotating seven lugs on the bolt into recesses in the receiver walls; gas operated, semi-automatic only.

The Mkb. 42 (W) was an unsuccessful entrant in the first assault-rifle trials.

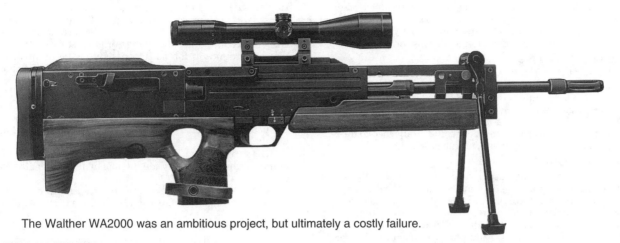

The Walther WA2000 was an ambitious project, but ultimately a costly failure.

DATA FOR A 300 EXAMPLE

35.65in overall, 17.53lb with sight and magazine. 25.6in barrel, 6-groove rifling; RH, concentric. Detachable box magazine, 6 rounds. Optical sight. 3215 fps with 168-grain bullet.

This was developed specifically for the 300 Winchester Magnum cartridge, seeking better long-range performance than the standard 7.62x51 NATO pattern could give. The bullpup-type WA2000 was built around a cradle-mounted barrel, with the receiver doubling as the butt and cheek-piece support. An ambidextrous thumbhole-type pistol grip lay at the front of the receiver below the breech; the hammer-type trigger, disconnector and magazine unit were built into a detachable sub-frame beneath the receiver; and a bipod was pivoted on the upper barrel-cradle bar. A Schmidt & Bender 2.5-10x56 optical sight was standard.

Though great things were expected of the WA2000, reports of its performance differed: some ascribed its failure simply to excessive cost, but others suggest that serious teething troubles could not be overcome without investment which was unlikely to be recouped.

• Walther, block-action type

Introduced in 1985, these rifles feature a block action locked by a lever on the receiver-side. The goal was a simpler mechanism that could be made more easily than the traditional, but complicated Walther bolt unit.

UIT-BV-UNIVERSAL TARGET RIFLE

Built around a *Blockverschluss* ('block action'), this shared the adjustable-comb stock of the bolt-action UIT-Universal pattern (q.v.), but had a squared receiver with the operating lever on the right side. When the gun had been fired, pulling the lever out of the receiver unlocked the breech and drew the breech-block back until the spent case was ejected. A new round was placed in the chamber and the operating lever could be returned to its original position in the receiver wall, shutting the breech. The system was reliable enough, but failed to challenge bolt-action designs and was abandoned in 1990.

SIMILAR GUNS

UIT-E-Universal rifle (sometimes known as the 'UIT-BV-E-Universal'), 1986-90. This was a variation of the standard BV pattern with an electronic trigger, substituted for the standard mechanical one in an attempt to reduce lock time.

• Walther, bolt-action type

Like many of the German gunmaking businesses struggling to survive in the 1920s, Walther turned to the production of small-caliber sporting rifles. However, instead of relying on the unsophisticated split-bridge bolt actions preferred by many rivals (e.g., Simson), Fritz Walther developed a distinctive design of his own. This was easily identified by the position of the bolt handle, which was forged integrally with a large-diameter locking collar on the rear of the bolt body. This allowed a cylindrical receiver to be used in a quest for greater rigidity. An attempt was also made to reduce the movement of the striker—and hence lock time—to a practicable minimum, travel being merely 2in. The Walthers also cocked on the opening movement of the bolt instead of during the closing stroke.

MODEL V SPORTING RIFLE
Walther-Kleinkaliberbüchse Modell V
Made by Carl Walther Waffenfabrik, Zella-Mehlis, about 1928-40?
Quantity: at least 25,000 (all types). **Chamberings:** 22 Long Rifle, rimfire.
Action: locked by rotating lugs on the bolt handle collar into recesses in the back of the receiver.

DATA FOR A TYPICAL EXAMPLE

.22 Long Rifle, rimfire. 44.8in overall, 7lb empty. 26in barrel, 4 grooves; RH twist, concentric. Single-shot only. Spring-leaf and slider rear sight, graduated to 200m. About 1080 fps with standard ammunition.

This sporting rifle had a plain pistol grip half-stock, with a grasping groove in the forend beneath the rear sight. Swivels lay beneath

The Walther factory in Ulm/Donau.

The UIT-E-Universal target rifle.

the barrel and the butt. These Walthers shot very accurately; targets reproduced in the Glaser catalogue of 1933 show two impressive 10-shot groups obtained at 50 metres with Model V rifles no. 17423 and 18932, also indicating that production was considerable.

SIMILAR GUNS

Meisterbüchse. This was a target-shooting version of the Modell V, sharing the same general lines but usually chambered for the 5.6mm Nr. 7 rimfire cartridge (22 Extra Long). The pistol grip was checkered, the front swivel-eye lay under the forend instead of beneath the barrel, and a micro-adjustable tangent rear sight was supplied. A special diopter sight could be attached to the rear left side of the receiver with a clamping screw.

POST-WAR GUNS

Walther's basic rimfire action dated from the early 1950s, but is none the worse for its age: countless international championships were still being won with it when Walther decided to concentrate on pistols and air guns in 1990. The basic action locked by using the base of the bolt handle and an opposed lug engaging the receiver wall—copied by many other manufacturers, but rarely with Walther's attention to detail. Special attention was paid to the mechanical triggers, resulting in fast lock times and a smoothness shared only by Anschütz and Feinwerkbau rifles.

KKJ SPORTING RIFLE

Made by Carl Walther Sportwaffenfabrik, Ulm/Donau, about 1957-81.
Chamberings: 22LR rimfire, 5.6x35R Vierling, 22 Hornet or 222 Remington. See notes. **Action:** locked by two lugs on the rear of the bolt rotating into the receiver as the bolt handle is turned down.
DATA FOR A TYPICAL KKJ-HV
Chambering: 5.6x35R Vierling, rimmed. 40.35in overall, 5.85lb empty. 22.05in barrel, 4-groove rifling; RH, concentric. Detachable box magazine, 5 rounds. Tangent-leaf sight graduated to 200m (220yd). 2015 fps with 46-grain bullet.

The first small-caliber rimfire sporting rifles (*Kleinkaliber-Jagdbüchsen*) were introduced in 1957, followed in 1959 by the first centerfire guns. The bolt had two lugs, one of which was combined with the bolt handle base; a lateral safety catch, which could be applied only when the gun was cocked, ran through the stock above the rear web of the trigger guard. Conventional single two-stage or double set trigger units could be supplied to order.

The half-stocks were originally pistol grip patterns, with a straight comb and a small oval cheekpiece, but a few two-piece Mannlicher-style (full length) versions were made. Steel buttplates or rubber shoulder pads were optional, and a 23.6in barrel could be substituted for the standard pattern on request. An elevating comb/cheek-piece unit was introduced in 1962 to satisfy users of optical sights, but was never popular and had been abandoned by 1966.

By the end of the 1960s, rationalization of the Walther small-bore rifles led to the KKJ being fitted with the action of the target rifles. This had a safety sleeve attached to the bolt, and required part of the left side of the stock to be cut down behind the receiver. Until 1972, however, the sporting guns also retained the original safety bolt through the stock. A shallow hog's back comb replaced the straight pattern in this period. The new stock was about a half-inch longer than its predecessors, overall length being 40.8in, and weight rose to 6.1lb.

The 222 Remington chambering proved to generate too much pressure for the rear-locking Walther action, and had been discontinued by 1973; very few guns had been made. Eventually, in 1981, the entire series (except the KJS) was abandoned.

THE GUNS

KJS target rifle ('SSV'), 1970-82. The first single-shot *Jagdliche Sportschiessen* ('Game Shooting') rifles were chambered for 22LR

rimfire, 22 Hornet or 222 Remington cartridges. The double set trigger was customary, though a special match pattern could be supplied to order. The half-stock had a high comb and a squared cheekpiece. Stippling covered the upright pistol grip and much of the deep round-tip forend. Open sights were omitted. Widely known in English-speaking markets as the SSV ('Single-shot, Varmint'), the guns weighed 7.7lb.

KJS-II target rifle, 1982-90. This differed from the KJS largely in the form of the stock—which was more rounded—and the stippling on the forend, which stopped short of the tip. A rubber shoulder pad was customary and the 60cm barrel had a small muzzle weight.

KKJ carbine (or 'KKJ-Karabiner'), 1960-5? Made only in small numbers, this was readily identifiable by its full-length 'Mannlicher-style' stock.

KKJ rifle, 1957-81. The original rimfire pattern could be identified by the tangent-leaf rear sight, which was graduated to 125m (137yd).

KKJ-E carbine, 1960-3. This was a short-lived single shot version of the fully stocked gun, lacking the customary magazine fittings.

KKJ-E rifle, 1957-63? Lacking the standard box magazine, this was a single shot version of the KKJ. It was never popular; production is suspected to have been small.

KKJ-H rifle, or 'KKJ-Ho', 1959-81. Chambered for the 22 Hornet centerfire cartridge, this retained the five-round box magazine. A deep magazine—to the base of the trigger guard—and a 200m (220yd) tangent-leaf rear sight distinguished it from the 22LR rimfire pattern, which had 125m sights. Barrels were 22.05 or 23.6in. Fitted with the longer barrel option, the rifles were 41.6in long and weighed about 7lb.

KKJ-HE rifle, 1959-63? Mechanically identical with the KKJ-H (q.v.), this was restricted to single shots.

KKJ-Ma rifle, 1963-81. This was a minor variant of the standard KKJ, chambered for the 22 Winchester Magnum rimfire cartridge instead of 22LR. Distinctions between the standard and magnum rimfire chamberings were gradually dropped in the 1970s, and the guns were considered simply as 'KKJ'. The sights and magazine resembled the KKJ-H types instead of the standard 22LR versions.

KKJ-V rifle, 1959-63. Mechanically identical with the standard KKJ, this magazine-feed gun was chambered for the 5.6x35RVierling cartridge, a European near-equivalent of the 22 Hornet (see KKJ-H).

KKJ-VE rifle. Otherwise similar to the KKJ-V (q.v.), this was restricted to single shots. Vierling patterns soon lost their popularity, the last being sold in 1964, and the single-shot guns were never as popular as the repeating types.

KKM target rifle, or 'KK-Master', 1959-68. Intended for three-position shooting, this was basically a modified KKJ action—with a wing-type safety catch on the cocking piece—in a half-stock with a deep rounded forend and an anatomical pistol grip. The cheekpiece was squared and the buttplate could slide vertically in its channel. Competition micrometric aperture/replaceable-element tunnel sights were standard fittings, the match-stype trigger was adjustable, and a sling-anchor was fixed beneath the forend. Weight was about 9.9lb. Left-hand stocks could be obtained on request, but an extended 'crossover' bolt handle extension sometimes had to be used in conjunction with the right-handed action.

KKM-II target rifle, 1959-65? This was a minor variant of the standard KKM with a hook-pattern buttplate and a rail beneath the forend to accept the base of the palm-rest. The pistol grip and forend were checkered. Weight averaged 12.1lb.

KKM-Match target rifle, 1960-8. Intended for Free Rifle competitions, this had a massive half-stock with a thumbhole butt. The

The Walther KKS sporting rifle, made in rim- and centerfire chamberings.

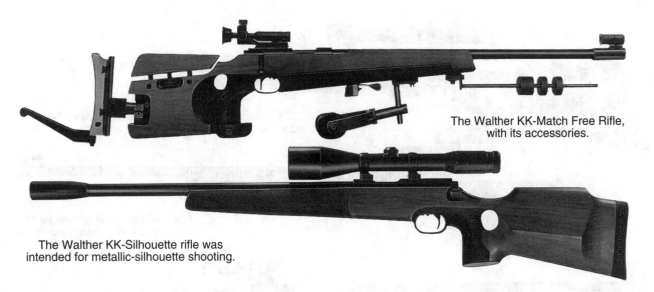

The Walther KK-Match Free Rifle,
with its accessories.

The Walther KK-Silhouette rifle was
intended for metallic-silhouette shooting.

anatomical pistol grip had an adjustable heel-rest, and the special front sight had a large diameter disc. KKM-Match rifles weighed about 15.7lb with the standard tapered barrel, or 17.4lb with the optional cylindrical type. An optional set-trigger system consisted of a slender setting lever, curved to follow the contours of the front of the trigger guard bow, and a knurled cylindrical release.

KKM-UIT target rifle. Introduced in 1962, this was the prototype of the series of target rifles intended for national and international list. They are covered separately, below.

KKS-D target rifle, 1960-5. Comparatively short-lived, this was a simple 22LR rimfire target-shooting adaptation of the KKJ with a non-adjustable match trigger, a fixed rubber buttplate, a low Monte Carlo comb, and a micrometric aperture rear sight. The butt lacked a cheekpiece, but had checkering on the pistol grip. The guns weighed 8.38lb.

KKS-V target rifle. This was a basic form of the KKS-D: mechanically identical, stocked similarly, but with a tangent-leaf rear sight instead of the micro-adjustable aperture pattern. Very few of these guns were made.

MODEL A SPORTING RIFLE

Made by Carl Walther Sportwaffenfabrik, Ulm/Donau, 1955-74.
Total production: several thousand? **Chambering options:** 6.5x57, 270 Winchester, 7x57, 7x64, 30-06, 8x57IS, 9.3x62 or 375 H&H Magnum. **Action:** locked by two lugs on the bolt head engaging recesses in the receiver as the bolt handle was turned down, and by a safety lug entering its seat in the receiver

DATA FOR A TYPICAL EXAMPLE

Chambering: 7x64, rimless. 42.3in overall, 7.4lb empty. 23.6in barrel, 4-groove rifling; RH, concentric. Internal box magazine, 5 rounds. Open folding-leaf rear sight graduated to 200m (220yd). 2885 fps with 154-grain bullet.

The first of these Mauser-type rifles were built on refurbished actions in the mid 1950s, but were eventually replaced by the JR pattern. They had conventional half-stocks, originally with low straight combs, small rounded cheekpieces and a shallow schnabel tip to the forend. Swivels lay beneath the barrel and butt. By 1963, however, the stock had acquired a Monte Carlo comb and cheekpiece, and a round-tipped forend. Hand-cut checkering appeared on the pistol grip and forend. A unique safety bolt ran laterally through the stock above the trigger.

SIMILAR GUNS

Model A rifle. This had a double set trigger mechanism. Sights consisted of a pearl bead on a ramp at the muzzle and a folding two-leaf rear sight. Chamberings are listed in the data table; 243 Winchester and 8x60mm options were added in the early 1960s.

Model A carbine. Small numbers of these double-trigger guns were made with full-length Mannlicher-style stocks. They were normally chambered only for 6.5x57mm and 7x57mm rounds (22in barrels), though 7x64mm and 8x57mm (24in barrels) could be obtained on request.

Model B rifle. This was a minor variant of the Model A, with a simple single-trigger mechanism.

Model B carbine. This was simply a fully-stocked version of the Model B, with a single trigger.

UIT-SPECIAL TARGET RIFLE

Made by Carl Walther Sportwaffenfabrik, Ulm/Donau, 1961-91 (all types)
Total production: not known. **Chambering:** 22LR, rimfire. **Action:** as KKJ rifle, above.

43.9in overall (with one butt spacer), 10.8lb with sights. 25.6in barrel, 4-groove rifling; RH, concentric. Single shot only. Micro-adjustable aperture rear sight. 1080 fps with 40-grain bullet.

The original UIT Standard rifle was a version of the KKJ, introduced in 1962. It was superseded by the 'Special' pattern, which had a stock with a deep squared forend and an angular butt with a straight under-edge and a sliding shoulder plate. The vertical pistol grip was stippled instead of checkered. The trigger had a straight lever and release pressure could be adjusted from 3.5oz to 21.2oz (100-600gm). A bolt lock was added to the safety system, a graduated accessory rail was let into the underside of the forend, and competition-grade sights were fitted.

Several changes were made to the UIT-Special during its life. A significant revision in 1982 led to the reappearance of the deep squared forend—which had lost favor on other guns—and an elongated trigger aperture.

SIMILAR GUNS

KK-Match rifle, 1969-90. The acme of the Walther bolt-action rifles, this had a selected walnut stock with every conceivable accessory—an elevating comb; a buttplate adjustable for length, cant and height; a heel rest on the pistol grip; a palm rest sliding along the accessory rail under the forend; and a balance-weight rod running forward from the forend tip. The original comb/cheekpiece was raised on spacers and slid diagonally upward to adjust its position; this system was replaced in 1973 by the 'Model 72' screw elevator, which was itself substituted by an improved design in 1975. The auxiliary balance-weight rods on post-1975 guns protrude from a block attached to the accessory rail. The rifles were typically 47.6in long and weighed 16.3lb without the forend rest or balance weights.

KK-Silhouette rifle, 1982-90. Rifles of this type (42.4in, 8.36lb) were similar to the UIT-LS pattern, but had a fixed-comb stock and a ventilated rubber buttplate. Enlarged bolt handle knobs and optical sights were standard. A typical example was 41.75in long, with a 23.6in barrel, and weighed 8.38lb without its sights.

UIT-Lochschaft rifle, 1972-4. Distinguished by its thumbhole-style butt, this was mechanically identical with the UIT Special. It was made in very small quantities, owing to a rule change which banned stocks of this type from three-position competitions.

UIT-LS rifle (*Laufende Scheibe*, 'moving target'), 1970-90. Intended for increasingly popular metallic-target shooting, these guns had thumbhole stocks. They were 42.7in long, had 23.6in barrels, and weighed about 8.6lb without their optical sights. The stock had a short rounded forend, extensively stippled, and an adjustable comb. The earliest comb relied on a slender wooden

The Walther UIT-Laufende Scheibe (Running Boar) target rifle had a fixed wooden butt plate and an elevated comb.

The Walther UIT-Match target rifle, with high comb and stippled forend.

The Walther UIT-Match Universal rifle, with an adjustable comb.

fillet entering a vertical slot in the butt, but this was replaced in 1972 by an improved design relying on elevating rods and a screw-clamp. The LS guns also had a 7.8oz muzzle weight and an adjustable wooden buttplate. The trigger was pre-set to 17.7oz (500gm), and the bolt knob was enlarged.

UIT-Match rifle, 1979-87? The walnut stocks of these guns have distinctive tapering forends, extensively stippled.

UIT-Match-Universal rifle, 1981-90. Universals have an adjustable four-position comb adjusted by removing the retaining bolt, inserting the elevator pillars in the desired holes (each pillar has two positions) and then replacing the retaining bolt. The system is quirky, but the selected position cannot be knocked out of position as easily as some screw-elevated combs; 44.8in, 11lb.

UIT-Prone rifle (or 'UIT-Liegend'), 1971-85? Specially adapted for shooting in the prone position, this had a shallow forend with an adjustable weight protruding from the forend tip beneath the barrel. An elevating comb with a saddle-like cheekpiece was used.

UIT-Special-R rifle (*Repetier*, 'repeating'), 1982-5. This was a version of the UIT-Special with a detachable five-round box magazine, intended for rapid-fire training.

UIT-Super rifle, about 1976-81. Intended for universal use, this could be identified by the slender forend with a short deepened section immediately ahead of the trigger guard. Made only in small numbers, it was rapidly replaced by the UIT-Match and UIT-Match Universal patterns.

MODEL JR SPORTING RIFLE
Jagd-Repetier-Gewehr
Made by Carl Walther Sportwaffenfabrik, Ulm/Donau, 1974-8.
Total production: 5000? **Chambering options:** 7x64, 7.5x55, 308 Winchester, 8x68S or 9.3x64. See notes. **Action:** locked by three lugs on the bolt head engaging recesses in the receiver as the bolt handle turned down.

DATA FOR A TYPICAL JRM
Chambering: 8x68S, rimless. 44.3in overall, 8.31lb empty. 25.6in barrel, 4-groove rifling; RH, concentric. Internal box magazine, 3 rounds. Open folding-leaf sight graduated to 200m (220yd). 3050 fps with 196-grain bullets.

A replacement for the adaptations of the 1898-type Mauser, this had a three-lug bolt with a 60-degree throw and a conical plastic grasping knob. Unusual features included a pivoting firing-pin safety mechanism, a bolt lock, and a special 'silent' lateral magazine-release button—through the stock beneath the bolt way—which could be activated only when the safety catch was applied.

Standard rifles, available only in 7x64 and 308 Winchester, had 24.4in barrels. The Monte Carlo-type half-stock had a plain round tipped forend, though a semi-beavertail forend could be supplied if required. Machine-cut checkering was applied to the pistol grip and the forend sides, and the ventilated rubber shoulder pads were accompanied by plain dark spacers. Swivels lay under the butt and forend.

SIMILAR GUNS
JR Jagdschiessen rifle (or simply 'JR Jagd'). These rifles were specially designed for moving-target shooting. Chambered only for the 7.5x55 or 308 Winchester rounds, they were instantly recognizable: the stock had an upright pistol grip, the buttplate was adjustable, and the separate comb could be elevated by a knurled finger wheel. A large spherical bolt handle knob replaced the conical type and the quirky magazine-release system was discarded. The grip and forend were extensively stippled.

JR Magnum rifle. Distinguished by a 25.6in barrel, these were chambered only for the 8x68S or 9.3x64 rounds.

• Weihrauch, block-action type
This gunsmithing business was founded in Zella St Blasii in 1899, making large quantities of sporting guns—including Martini

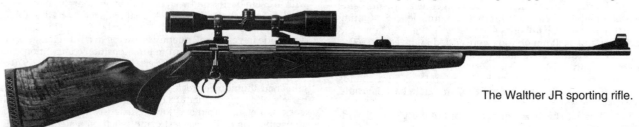

The Walther JR sporting rifle.

The Weihrauch HW52J, a modern version
of the pre-war Langenhan target rifle.

rifles—until 1939. Re-established in Bavaria after World War II, the company is now best known for Arminius-brand revolvers and high-quality sporting air guns.

HW 52 SPORTING RIFLE

Made by Hermann Weihrauch KG, Mellrichstadt, about 1952-88.
Total production: not known. **Chambering options:** 22 LR rimfire, 22 Hornet, 222 Remington or 5.6x50R. **Action:** locked by raising the breechblock behind the chamber with the tip of the operating lever.

DATA FOR A TYPICAL HW 52J

Chambering: 5.6x50R, rimmed. 41.35in overall, 7.28lb empty. 25.6in barrel, 4-groove rifling; RH, concentric. Open folding-leaf leaf sight graduated to 200m (220yd). 3280 fps with 56-grain bullet.

Introduced in 1952, this single-shot rifle was based on a pre-war Langenhan pattern. It had a lateral safety bolt and a finely adjustable trigger; set triggers were available to order. The earliest butt seems to have been a simple design with a shallow hog's back or straight comb and a small oval cheekpiece. However, a Monte Carlo type was standardized in the early 1970s.

SIMILAR GUNS

Luxusmodell. Deluxe patterns have been offered with skip-line checkering on the pistol grip; a ventilated rubber buttplate; and a rosewood forend tip. Thin white spacers separated the tip from the forend, the nylon pistol grip cap from the butt, and the buttplate from the stock wood. The actions often displayed scroll engraving.

HW 52MM rifle ('Match Model'). A special target rifle, this had a 27.55in heavy barrel. The action was enclosed in a one-piece stock, with a squared Bavarian-style cheekpiece and a hog's back comb. The buttplate was a rubber crescent design. A micro-adjustable aperture sight could be mounted on a block attached to the upper tang behind the breech; the front sight was a replaceable-element tunnel. Most MM rifles chambered rimfire ammunition, but a few were made for the 22 Hornet cartridge.

• Weihrauch, bolt-action type

HW 60J SPORTING RIFLE

Made by Hermann Weihrauch KG, Mellrichstadt.
Currently in production. **Chambering options:** 22 LR rimfire, 22 WMR, 22 Hornet or 222 Remington. See notes. **Action:** locked by two lugs engaging recesses in the receiver as the bolt was turned down.

DATA FOR A TYPICAL EXAMPLE

Chambering: 22 Hornet, rimmed. 41.7in overall, 6.5lb empty. 22.85in barrel, 4-groove rifling; RH, concentric. Detachable box magazine, 4 rounds. Open fixed-block rear sight. 2690 fps with 45-grain bullet.

The first of these rifles, dating from the early 1960s, embodied a good-quality bolt action with a locking lug supplementing the bolt handle base. A sliding safety appeared on the left side of the receiver. The half-stock of the HW 60J—the standard sporting version or *Jagdbüchse*—had a hog's back comb and an oval cheekpiece. Checkering appeared on the pistol grip and schnabel-tipped forend; a ventilated rubber butt pad was fitted; and swivels lay under the butt and forend. The receiver was grooved for optical sight mounts. Changes were made to the shape of the magazine base about 1982, when projecting grooves were added to facilitate removal, and a double set trigger option was offered. Magazines hold five 22LR rounds, four 22 Magnum or 22 Hornet rounds, but only three 222 Remingtons.

SIMILAR GUNS

HW60 Match. Chambered for 22LR rimfire ammunition only, this is intended for standard 25-metre UIT competition shooting. Built on the standard 60-series action, it has a heavyweight 26in barrel and aperture sights. The stock features a deep forend, extensively stippled, and a near-vertical pistol grip improves control. The cheekpiece is a conventional slab-sided pattern and the adjustable buttplate slides vertically in its channel. An accessory rail is

The Weihrauch HW60J sporting rifle,
chambered for rimfire ammunition.

The Weihrauch HW66 is
intended for moving-target shooting.

A Weihrauch HW660 Match rifle with a laminated stock.

let into the underside of the forend. Like virtually all Weihrauch guns, the HW60 Match (45.3in long, 10.7lb) has a finely adjustable trigger.

HW 66. Introduced in 1985 in 22 Hornet or 222 Remington, this was built on a single-shot version of the HW 60 action and could be fitted with conventional double-stage, single set or double set triggers. The heavy 22.05in stainless-steel barrel reduced overall length to about 41.15in, though weight increased to 8.5lb without sights. Its competition-style stock had a squared cheekpiece, a straight comb, and a broadened forend. Stippling covered the pistol grip and most of the underside of the forend.

HW66 DJV. Intended for moving-target competition shooting, these rifles have a short barrel, a half-stock with extensive stippling on the underside of the shallow forend, and a fixed rubber buttplate.

HW660 Match. This is a variant of the HW60 Match, differing primarily in the design of the stock. Its features include an adjustable-height comb and two slots cut laterally through the forend. A multi-color laminated stock was introduced in 1995.

GREECE

• Gras

Adopted in 1876 to replace the unsuccessful indigenous Mylona rifle, the Gras was made in Steyr by Österreichische Waffenfabriks-Gesellschaft: 57,000 rifles and 6,000 carbines had been delivered by the end of 1877. Many found their way in the early 20th Century to minor Balkan states (e.g., Montenegro), displaced by magazine rifles. Others were taken out of store to serve second-line troops during the Balkan Wars.

• Heckler & Koch (EBO)

About 1974, the Greek army purchased G3A3 and G3A4 rifles for field trials. They were successful enough for a manufacturing license to be acquired. The first of 200,000 guns ordered from Elleniki Biomichanica Oplon of Anjion was accepted in 1979. Greek-made weapons have a distinctive diamond-shape 'EBO' trademark on the left side of the receiver, and selectors marked 'AB' (top), 'BB' (middle) and 'BP' (bottom). The rifles were still in front-line service in 1997.

• Mannlicher

The Greeks were originally armed with 1888- and 1895-pattern Mannlichers, supplied in small numbers by Österreichische Waffenfabriks-Gesellschaft prior to 1900. A desire for a gun of their own led the authorities to consider the Mannlicher-Schönauer rifle then being tested in Portugal. Its spool magazine appeared to feed more precisely than box patterns. Chamber-tops of Greek rifles normally displayed a crowned shield bearing a cross above the designation 'Y.1903' or 'Y.1903/14', with the maker's mark (e.g., STEYR 1909) on the left side of the receiver.

MODEL 1903 RIFLE

Made by Österreichische Waffenfabriks-Gesellschaft, Steyr, 1902-14. **Total production:** not known. **Chambering:** 6.5x54, rimless. **Action:** locked by two lugs on a detachable bolt head engaging recesses in the receiver as the bolt handle turns downward.

48.25in overall, 8.31lb empty. 28.55in barrel, 4-groove rifling; RH, concentric. Internal charger-loaded spool magazine, 5 rounds. Tangent-leaf graduated to 2000m (2185yd). 2230 fps with M1903 ball cartridges. M1903 knife bayonet.

After extensive testing, the Mannlicher-Schönauer was officially adopted in 1903. The rifle was essentially similar to the experimental 1900 Portuguese pattern (q.v.), its action being all but identical. The one-piece stock, with a semi-pistol grip, had a half-

length handguard and two bands. Grasping grooves in the sides of the forend turned upward at the breech to facilitate removing the handguard. The band nearest the muzzle – with a bayonet lug on its underside – acted as a nose cap, while a half-length cleaning rod was carried in the forend.

The magazine floorplate could be removed by depressing its retaining spring and turning through 90 degrees; alternatively, the magazine could be emptied by opening the bolt and pressing a catch on the right side of the receiver alongside the feed way.

These weapons rapidly gained a reputation for smooth operation, generally reckoned as better than any military magazine rifle with the possible exception of the U.S. and Norwegian Krag-Jørgensens.

SIMILAR GUNS

Model 1903 carbine. The cavalry and artillery carbine, which accepted the standard bayonet, was simply a shortened rifle with a sling ring on the left side of the barrel band and a swivel on the side of the butt. It was about 40.35in long, had a 18.5in barrel and weighed 7.78lb empty. The rear sight was graduated to about 1600m (1750yd) and muzzle velocity fell to 2055 fps.

MODEL 1903/14 RIFLE

Made by Österreichische Waffenfabriks-Gesellschaft, Steyr, 1914; and Società Italiana Ernesto Breda, Brescia, 1926-9. **Total production:** not known. **Chambering:** 6.5x54, rimless. Otherwise generally as M1903 rifle, above, except weight (about 8.44lb empty).

The basic Mannlicher-Schönauer action was retained for this rifle, but the handguard ran the full length of the barrel, the grasping grooves no longer had the distinctive rearward upturn, and a stacking rod was added to the left side of the nose cap. Few guns emanated from Steyr before the beginning of hostilities stopped work.

With stocks of M1903 and M1903/14 rifles declining, the government placed an order for 100,000 rifles and about 10,000 carbines in Italy in the mid-1920s. Apart from marks (e.g., 'BREDA 1927'), however, they were identical with pre-1914 Steyr-made weapons.

SIMILAR GUNS

Model 1903/14 carbine. Except for the shortened barrel and forend, and the appearance of the swivels on the left side of the barrel band and butt, this was identical with the corresponding rifle. Bolt handles are occasionally found bent downward, but this was not universal.

• Mauser

These guns generally have a chamber mark in the form of a crowned shield bearing a short-armed cross. This appears above the designation, e.g., 'Y-1930'. Though normally reliant on Mannlicher-Schönauers, the Greek army bought a few 7.9mm Mle 30 short rifles from Fabrique Nationale in the 1930s.

• Mylona

This was an unsuccessful dropping-block gun, unique to Greece. Adopted in the early 1870s and made in small numbers, it was soon replaced by the sturdier and more efficient Gras.

GUATEMALA

Mauser

Guatemalan rifles usually display a chamber-top mark consisting of a quetzal bird perched on a scroll reading 'Libertad de 15 de Set. de 1821' (liberation day), with crossed swords and rifles within a laurel wreath. They include Czechoslovakian 7mm vz. 12/33 short rifles purchased in the mid- 1930s.

The M1903 Greek Mannlicher-Schönauer rifle. (HBL)

The M1934 rifle was based on the M17 Enfield, but lacked the rear sight and its protectors above the receiver bridge.

HAITI

• Remington-Lee

The government of this small island bought about 2,000 1882-type rifles from Hartley & Graham of New York in July 1889. It is assumed that they were chambered for the 11mm (.43) Spanish Remington cartridge.

HESSEN

• Chassepot

Ludwig Baer pictures an ex-French Mle 1866 rifle with a shortened muzzle and a special nose cap. The bolt handle has been turned down, the overall length reduced to about 46.5in, and the weight to about 8.8lb. This gun is said to have been the work of Garde-Dragoner-Regiment Nr. 23, raised and garrisoned in the Grand-duchy of Hessen.

HONDURAS

• Mauser

These guns are rarely encountered in collections, though 7x57 Mo. 1895 Chilean-type rifles are said to have been purchased prior to 1914, and some Standard-Modell Mausers followed in the 1930s. The national crest comprised a triangular volcano, flanked by two towers, set in front of a pyramid on a grassed field. The device was set inside an oval border bearing the date of independence, 15th September 1821.

• Remington (Enfield)

The Remington Arms Company supplied about 3,000 modified M1917 Enfield rifles to Honduras in the mid-1930s. Apparently issued as the 'Mo. 1934', but known commercially as the 'Model 40', these chambered the 7x57 cartridge and had new stepless-base tangent rear sights protruding from the handguard above the grasping groove. A new open barleycorn front sight was used. The original folding sight on the bridge of the receiver was removed and the protecting wings had been milled away, but the guns were otherwise similar to the U.S. 30 M1917 Enfields (q.v.).

HUNGARY

• Kalashnikov

MODEL 55 ASSAULT RIFLE

The original Geppistoly AK-55, made by Fegyver é Gáz-készülékgyár (FÉG) of Budapest about 1955-65, had a cleaning rod but lacked a bayonet lug. Manufacturing quality was surprisingly good, with the stock, checkered pistol grip and forend all being solid wood. Selectors were marked '1' for semi-auto and '∞' for full-auto firing. The serial number was usually stamped into a panel milled out of the left side of the receiver, but manufacturer's marks were rarely present.

SIMILAR GUNS

AKM-63. Introduced in 1963 and made until the late 1980s, this FÉG product, initially made with a wood butt, had a unique metal forend formed integrally with the receiver. A supplementary pistol grip lay ahead of the magazine. The butt and pistol grip became gray-blue or dark-green polypropylene. Selectors still bore '1' and '∞'.

AMD-65. Dating from 1966, this was a shortened derivative of the AKM with a simple tubular butt and a rubber buttplate. The butt could be folded by pressing a slotted-head catch under the receiver behind the rear pistol grip. The short barrel had a distinctive two-port muzzle brake/compensator. Both pistol grips were grayish-green plastic, serial numbers appeared on the left side of the receiver, and selectors were marked in their customary Hungarian manner. Some guns were subsequently converted for grenade firing, acquiring a launcher on the muzzle, a special optical sight above the receiver on a mounting plate, and a shock-absorbing tubular butt.

NGM-81. Production of an indigenous variant of the 5.45mm AK-74 began about 1981 under this designation, though only a few guns were made. Effort was instead concentrated on a good-quality 5.56x45 variant intended for export. Made only with a fixed butt and a wooden forend, the NGM had a chromium-lined bore.

• Mannlicher

In 1931, the authorities adopted a rimmed 8mm cartridge to replace the old Austro-Hungarian 8x50 design. The new round, known as the 31.M in Hungary, was initially used in modified 1895-type straight-pull Mannlichers – rifles, short rifles and carbines alike. These were essentially similar to the Austro-Hungarian patterns (q.v.), but had new rear sights and new front-sight protectors. A large 'H' was stamped into the chamber. Service life was brief, as the adoption of the 35.M rifle caused the conversions (which suffered perpetual extraction difficulties) to be withdrawn into store. Survivors were reissued for service in 1940.

MODEL 1935 SHORT RIFLE
Huzagol 35.M
Made by Fémáru Fegyver és Gépgyár, Budapest, 1936-42.
Total production: not known. Chambering: 8x56R, rimmed. Action: as M1931, above.

43.7in overall, 8.88lb empty. 23.6in barrel, 4-groove rifling; RH, concentric. Integral clip-loaded box magazine, 5 rounds. Tangent-leaf sight graduated to 2000m (2185yd)? 2395 fps with 31.M ball cartridge. 35.M sword bayonet.

Work began in 1933 on a new infantry rifle with a turning-bolt action, retaining the best features of the 1895-pattern Mannlicher but designed specifically around the 31.M cartridge and thus more durable than its predecessors.

Adopted in 1935, the 35.M rifle had a split-bridge receiver and a British-style two-piece stock, the butt being held in the receiver by a sturdy bolt. A turning-bolt action was preferred, though the spur-type cocking piece of the 1895-model rifle was retained. The rifle was clip-loaded and had a projecting magazine case. Swivels lay beneath the butt and the barrel band, and the front face of the nose cap carried a small projecting stud to enter the bayonet pommel.

MODEL 1943 SHORT RIFLE
Huzagol 43.M
Made by Femaru Fegyver és Gépgyár, Budapest, 1944-50.
Chambering: 8x56R.

Otherwise as 35.M rifle, above, except dimensions (43in overall, 8.64lb empty), magazine (internal 5-round box loaded from a stripper-clip) and bayonet (43.M sword pattern).

The unexpected success of the German Gew. 98/40 – a modification of the 35.M being made in Budapest under contract – persuaded the Hungarians to adopt a new rifle in 1943. The 43.M, which had a Mauser-type magazine, was little more than a Gew. 98/40 with Hungarian-style barrel band, nose cap and sling swivels.

Production was interrupted by the end of World War II after only a few thousand had been made. Work began again about 1947, but apparently ceased in the early 1950s.

HUNGARY

• Mosin-Nagant

Substantial quantities of Mosin-Nagant guns were made by FÉG of Budapest in the early 1950s. Production seems to have been confined to good-quality copies of the obr. 1944g carbine and obr. 1891/30g sniper rifle, known as 44.M and 48.M respectively.

The standard Hungarian-made 7.62x39 Kalashnikov.

The AMD-65, a Kalashnikov derivative with its stock extended.

The AMD-65 with its folding stock detached.

The action of the Gew. 98/40 (later adapted as the Hungarian 43.M rifle). Note the British-style butt retaining bolt and the unusually long cocking-piece assembly. Photo enlarged to show detail.

228 Rifles of the World

INDIA

• FN-Saive (Ishapur)

About 1963, India began to make a version of the FN FAL in the state-owned Ishapur rifle factory. Known as the 'Rifle IASL' or 'Indian Army Self-Loading', it was distinguished by the *Asoka* – the national crest of four lions on a pillar-cap – on the right side of the receiver. See also remarks under 'Kalashnikov', below.

• Kalashnikov (Ishapur)

Production problems have always been encountered with the IASL 7.62mm rifle, partly because the Indians had copied the FAL without the benefit of a licence and were making parts which interchanged with neither the British-style imperial-measure guns nor metric-standard European patterns.

By the mid- 1980s, a decision had been taken to re-equip with a 5.56mm-caliber rifle and trials with guns derived from the Kalashnikov by Armament Research & Development Establishment in Poona were completed with the adoption in 1990 of the 5.56mm Indian Small Arms System (INSAS). This consists of an automatic carbine, an assault rifle and a light support weapon.

To replace surviving bolt-action 7.62mm Lee-Enfields as quickly as possible, particularly for service in the Punjab, the Indian government acquired 100,000 assorted 7.62x39 AKM-type weapons from Russia, Hungary, Romania and possibly even Israel in 1990-2.

INSAS ASSAULT RIFLE

Made by the Ishapur ordnance factory.

Currently in production. **Chambering:** 5.56x45, rimless. **Action:** locked by rotating lugs on the bolt into the receiver walls; gas operated, selective fire.

37.2in overall, 9.04lb with loaded magazine. 18.25in barrel, 6-groove rifling; RH, concentric. Detachable box magazine, 22 rounds. 'L'-type rear sight graduated to 400m (435yd). 3000 fps with ball ammunition; 650±50rpm. Optional tool bayonet.

The INSAS rifle is a typical Kalashnikov derivative, with a chrome-plated bore, but has a selector lever on the left side of the receiver above the pistol grip and can fire a three-shot burst as well as fully automatically. The transparent plastic magazine was adapted from the Steyr AUG type, but has a smaller capacity than is now customary. The rear sight lies on the rear of the breech cover, and the plastic butt and forend assemblies – differing considerably from their Russian prototypes – were apparently based on the fittings of the Israeli Galil rifle.

SIMILAR GUNS

The INSAS rifle is also offered with a folding butt, which can be swung forward along the right side of the receiver. These guns are about 37.8in long with the butt extended, folding to 29.5in when required. A short-barrel carbine has also been developed, but has yet to enter series production.

• Lee-Enfield

The Indian Army, part of British Establishment until independence was gained in 1947, was initially armed from Britain. Early in the 20th Century, however, powder mills in the town of Ishapore (now Ishapur) were converted to an arms factory, the first guns being made in 1905.

Gradually, a series of 'India Pattern' weapons was approved. Though they followed British prototypes, changes were authorized to suit local conditions. Differing buttplates were fitted, often to allow pull-throughs and cleaning material to be carried in the butts of rifles that were not similarly fitted in Britain; changes to stocks accounted for climate or unskilled labour.

INDIA PATTERN LEE-ENFIELDS

Indian-made rifles were distinguished by butt-socket marks such as 'ISHAPORE' or 'R.F.I.' ('Rifle Factory, Ishapur', post-1950) and 'I.P.' for 'India Pattern'. SMLE rifles made after 1950 substituted an *Asoka* for a crowned 'E.R.I.' cypher (1905-10, 1936) or 'G.R.I.' (1910-47). The Asoka comprised four lions on top of a column – not tigers, as had been claimed – though only three animals are visible. Property marks included 'I' beneath a Broad Arrow, while stock roundels displayed names such as Ferozepore or Allahabad.

THE GUNS

Carbine, India Pattern. Approved on 8th January 1904, this was issued to the Sappers & Miners with the P/1888 sword bayonet. A standard rifle-type nose cap was fitted with a Martini-pattern swivel, a second swivel being added on the under-edge of the butt. Survivors were re-chambered in 1924 for 303 Mk VII cartridges and the back-sight graduations were altered. The maximum sighting distance was 1,000 yards.

Rifle, India Pattern, Mk I*. This was simply a Mk I* Long Lee-Enfield with a short rifle butt, which had a trap for cleaning materials and the pull-through.

Rifle, India Pattern, Charger Loading Mk I. A variation of the Mk I long Lee-Enfield, this had one charger guide attached to the receiver bridge and the other brazed to the bolt head. Transformation was underway well before similar work began in Britain. Many guns were converted for bridge-type charger guides after 1912, and re-classified 'Mk II I.P.'.

Rifle, India Pattern, Charger Loading Mk I*. This was created by fitting charger guides to Mk I* long Lee-Enfield rifles. Rifles converted for bridge-type charger guides after 1912 were re-classified as 'Mk II I.P.'.

Rifle, India Pattern, Charger Loading Mk II. This conversion of British-made Mks I and I* long rifles was approved on 8th September 1909, the original weapons gaining SMLE Mk III bridge-type charger guides instead of the less efficient bolt-and-bridge design.

Rifle, India Pattern, Charger Loading, Mk II*. Approved in 1910, this was the Mk II rifle (described above) fitted with a Mk I* SMLE-type butt, shoulder plate and inletted butt swivel.

Rifle, India Pattern, single shot. Approved by the Secretary of State for India in December 1909, 2,000 full-length guns were made at Enfield in 1911-12 for Frontier Levies. The magazine-well was filled with a sturdy wood block, and a special trigger guard/magazine plate was used. Beginning in 1913, most guns were altered to accept a Martini-type swivel through the front of the trigger guard, the butt swivel being removed.

Short Rifle, India Pattern, Mk I*. Sealed on 30th August 1910, this was simply the standard British Mk I SMLE fitted with a Mk I* butt, butt-plate, and inletted swivel.

Short Rifle, India Pattern, single shot. This was approved on 21st August 1923. The magazine aperture was filled with a wood block and a special trigger guard/magazine plate was manufactured. Single shot rifles were made at Ishapore into the 1930s, for issue to troops whose loyalty was not above suspicion.

Rifle 7.62mm No. 1 Mk 3*. These were made in the late 1950s for the 7.62x51mm cartridge – an interim measure while tooling for the IA SL rifle (an FAL variant) was being undertaken. Distinguished by their squared box magazines, the Lee-Enfields were made of better-grade steel than their 303 predecessors to withstand the high-pressure 7.62mm ammunition.

INDONESIA

• Arisaka

Large numbers of 38th Year Type and Type 99 rifles, taken from the Japanese occupation forces, were used by insurgents fighting against Dutch rule – and then by the newly-formed army once Indonesia had gained independence in 1949. Most rifles remained in their original state, though some will be found with crude replacement stocks and others with a bluish enamel finish. The army property mark was a small five-point star.

• Garand

In addition to production of BM-59 rifles in the state factory in Bandung, Indonesia received 55,000-78,000 M1 Garands (estimates vary) and a handful of M1C rifles from the USA prior to 1971. Substantial quantities of Italian-made M1 and BM-59 rifles were also supplied. A *Garuda* – a mythical half-human bird – lay across the receiver-back above the serial number.

IRAN

• Heckler & Koch

In the early 1970s, Iran placed an order with Heckler & Koch for sizable quantities of German-type G3A3 and G3A4 rifles. Production of the modified G3A6 subsequently began in the state small arms factory at Mosalsalasi. Prior to the Islamic Revolution of 1979, this factory was said to be making 145,000 G3-type rifles annually, but output declined until only about 50,000 guns were being made by the mid-1980s.

IRAQ

• Lee-Enfield

The government purchased new No. 1 Mk III Lee-Enfield short rifles from Britain in the mid-1930s, an order for 16,000 being passed to BSA Guns Ltd in 1935. As these guns were newly made instead of being cannibalized from old parts, they lacked British markings; instead, they bore a reversed angular 'S' in a triangle.

IRELAND (EIRE)

Ireland was integral with the United Kingdom prior to 1922, when the Irish Free State (Eire) gained independence from the six counties ('Northern Ireland') remaining loyal to the British.

• Lee-Enfield

Work began in Enfield in 1905 to create 10,000 Constabulary Carbines from obsolescent rifles. They had a very distinctive nose cap, and feathers of wood were generally let into the forend channel. Butt discs were marked 'R.I.C.' ('Royal Irish Constabulary'); the last of them was dispatched to Ireland in 1906.

ISRAEL

• FN-Saive (IMI)

The army acquired the first of many FAL rifles in the early 1960s, the guns remaining regulation issue until the advent of the 5.56mm M16A1 and Galil rifles. The earliest weapons were purchased directly from Fabrique Nationale, but later examples were assembled by Israeli Military Industries. These had FN-made receivers, but the remaining components were made locally.

Guns emanating from IMI exhibited changes suggested by combat in desert conditions: the butt had a lower comb; the forend was pressed-metal, with a short finely-fluted wooden grip; the cocking handle was modified to double as a bolt-closing device; the front sight/gas plug assembly was improved; and the dismantling catch was recessed to reduce the chances of accidentally opening the receiver.

Distinguishing marks included the Defense Force badge of a sword and an olive branch on a six-point Star of David above a scroll. Inspectors' and property marks also appeared, the serial number commencing with the date of manufacture – e.g., '6312539' on a gun made in 1963.

• Galil (Kalashnikov)

The Israeli authorities, keen to establish an arms industry but dissatisfied with the FAL, elected to produce a modified Kalashnikov in the late 1960s. Known as the Galil, in honor of the engineer responsible for the transformation, the Israeli rifle approximates to the Finnish m/62 – indeed, the earliest guns are said to have incorporated unmarked Valmet-made receivers.

GALIL AUTOMATIC RIFLE

Made by Israeli Military Industries, Ramat ha-Sharon.
Currently in production. **Chambering options:** 5.56x45 or 7.62x51, rimless.
Action: locked by rotating lugs on the bolt head into the receiver; gas operated, selective fire.

DATA FOR 5.56MM GALIL ARM

Chambering: 5.56x45, rimless. 38.55in overall (29.2in with stock folded), 9.26lb with bipod. 18.1in barrel, 6-groove rifling; RH, concentric. Detachable box magazine, 12, 25 or 50 rounds. Pivoting aperture sight for 300m (330yd) and 500m (545yd). 3200 fps with M193 ball cartridges; 650±50 rpm. Knife bayonet (optional).

The performance of AKM rifles in the Six-Day War of 1967 impressed the Israelis greatly. Work began immediately to amalgamate the basic Kalashnikov action, improved in detail, with a simpler gas system lacking a regulator. The basic ARM rifle of 1971 had a tubular plastic pistol grip and a tubular skeletal butt folding to the right to lie alongside the receiver. A radial selector lay on the right side, closing the ejection port when set to its uppermost (safe) position. The charging handle was bent upward so that the rifle could be cocked with either hand, and a folding carrying handle lay above the chamber. The earliest rifles had fluted wooden forends, but later examples usually had synthetic components.

The standard 5.56mm (223) ARM had a bipod, hinged to the gas block to double as a wire cutter. A short flash-suppresser/compensator was fitted to the muzzle and a short U.S.-type bayonet could be attached. Among the most obvious features of the Galil was the rear sight at the rear of the breech cover, accompanied by projecting ears and a folding 100m night sight with luminescent tritium dots.

A typical example was marked 'A.R. GALIL' above '5.56 x 45', 'IMI' and 'ISRAEL' on the left side of the receiver. Safety catches under the thumb on the left side of the pistol grip were marked 'S', 'A' and 'R'. Export patterns were generally marked in English; Israeli Defense Force rifles, stamped in Hebrew, also displayed a sword and olive branch inside a six-point star on the left side of the receiver above the pistol grip.

Many guns made after about 1980 may bear the Israeli Military Industries trademark of a sword and an olive branch superimposed on a cogwheel; serial numbers usually run vertically upward on the front left side of the receiver immediately behind the forend.

SIMILAR GUNS

5.56mm Galil AR. This was a long-barreled ARM without the bipod and cranked charging handle, and had a simplified synthetic forend.

5.56mm Galil SAR. A short-barrel pattern, this was 33.5in long, folded to 24.2in, had a 13in barrel and weighed about 8lb.

7.62m Galil ARM. The 7.62mm patterns were noticeably larger and heavier than the 5.56mm guns and had bulkier magazines with virtually no curve. The ARM was 41.35in long, had a 21in barrel, and weighed 9.48lb. The rifles fired SS77 ball ammunition at about 2790 fps.

The 7.62mm Galil ARM.

The 5.56mm Galil SAR.

7.62mm Galil AR. A version of the ARM weighing 8.7lb.

7.62mm Galil SAR. This short version of the basic design folded to 24.2in, had a 15.75in barrel, and weighed 8.25lb.

Galil Sniper. Developed for Israeli army snipers in the early 1980s, this special semi-automatic 7.62mm AR-type Galil had a heavyweight barrel and a large tubular muzzle brake/compensator. A two-stage trigger was fitted, while the bipod was moved back to pivot on the receiver instead of the gas block, relieving the barrel of unnecessary stress that could reduce accuracy. The folding wooden butt had a cheek piece and a ventilated rubber recoil pad. The guns were about 43.9in overall (33.05in with stock folded), had 19.7in barrels and weighed 14.1lb with the bipod. A standard two-position aperture rear sight was fitted to the receiver, but a bracket attached to the left side of the receiver accepted a 6x40 Nimrod sight or any NATO-standard infra-red and image-intensifying night-vision patterns.

Hadar II. Intended for police use, and also occasionally sold as a sporting rifle, the Hadar II of 1987 had a standard 7.62mm AR action set into a three-quarter length wooden stock with an unmistakable thumb-hole butt and a radial safety lever set into the left side of the pistol grip. The rifles were about 38.6in overall and weighed 9.6lb empty.

• Mauser

Immediately after the Israeli state was formed in 1947, many thousands of ex-German Kar. 98k rifles were refurbished and reissued. These guns almost always display their old marks in addition to new Israeli ones. In 1949, the authorities decided to purchase an entire Kar. 98k production line from Switzerland – at enormous cost – and installed it in a new factory in Ramat ha-Sharon (now Israeli Military Industries, IMI). However, the advent of efficient semi-automatic rifles caused the Mauser to be abandoned in favor of the FN FAL after only a few new guns had been made. Manufacture then concentrated on old German actions, and others purchased from Fabrique Nationale in the 1950s. Survivors have been re-barreled for the 7.62x51 NATO round since the 1960s.

ITALY

Cataloguing Italian-made rifles is complicated by the vast numbers of shotgun-like doubles made in the traditional gunmaking area centered on Brescia. Though the products of major manufacturers such as Beretta have always been subjected to critical scrutiny, much less is known about the output of the smaller workshops and work has still to be done before a reliable overview can be offered.

• Armaguerra (Revelli)

This rifle was designed by Gino Revelli, son of Abiel Bethel Revelli—best known for the Fiat-Revelli machine guns and the Glisenti pistol. Several guns were successfully tested by the Italian army in the summer of 1939, allowing an order for 10,000 to be given to Società Anonima Revelli Manifattura Armiguerra (better known by the telegraphic codename 'Armaguerra'). A factory was erected in Cremona to make the guns, but a change in caliber from 7.35mm to 6.5mm hindered progress. It is believed that, had hostilities continued into 1945, the Cremona factory would have made the Czechoslovakian ZK 391 'Italsky model' at the expense of the Revelli design.

MODEL 39 AUTOMATIC RIFLE
'Fucile Armaguerra Mo. 39'
Made by Società Anonima Revelli Manifattura Armiguerra, Genoa and Cremona, about 1940-3.

Total production: 500? **Chambering options:** 6.5x52 and 7.35x52mm, rimless. **Action:** locked by pivoting a block under the bolt into engagement with the receiver; short-recoil operation, semi-automatic only.

DATA FOR A TYPICAL 6.5MM EXAMPLE

46.05in overall, 8.16lb empty. 23.6in barrel, 4-groove rifling; RH, concentric. Integral clip-loaded magazine, 6 rounds. Quadrant-leaf rear sight graduated to 300m (330yd)? 2290 fps with Mo. 91-95 ball ammunition. Mo. 1891 sword bayonet (optional)

The Armaguerra rifle had a barrel which slid back through about 10mm (.4in) to release the locking block and allow the bolt to reciprocate. The one-piece stock had a shallow pistol grip and a ventilated barrel guard. Prominent retaining bolts ran laterally through the stock into the receiver behind the trigger and beneath the rear sight, and the nose cap—with characteristically Italian rearward extensions—was relieved to accommodate the sliding barrel. The rounded magazine case projected beneath the stock. The oddest feature of the Mo. 39, however, was the charging lever; combined with the forward sling-swivel anchor, it had to be drawn back by pulling the sling.

• Armi-Jager, autoloading type

Jager-Armi di Armando Piscetta & C. SRL of Milan, now better known as 'Armi-Jager', has made autoloading rifles ranging from a few traditionally styled sporters—introduced in the 1960s—to present-day rimfire facsimiles of the M16.

MODEL AP-61 SPORTING RIFLE

This 22LR autoloader had a cylindrical receiver containing the bolt and return spring assembly. The barrel measured 21.65in, overall length was 42.4in, and empty weight averaged 5.51lb. The detachable box magazines held five or 10rounds, though a curved 20-round pattern was an optional extra. The AP-61 was very similar to the Daffini Model 11 (q.v.). The sights consisted of a ramped blade and a spring-leaf and elevator, though mounting bases for an optical sight could be attached to the grooved receiver-top. The half-stock had an elongated forend, a plain pistol grip and a low Monte Carlo comb, but lacked a cheekpiece.

SIMILAR GUNS
Model AP-61L rifle. This was simply a deluxe variant of the standard rifle, offering a better stock with skip-line checkering on the pistol grip and forend.

MODEL AP-66 SPORTING RIFLE

Sharing blowback principles with the AP-61, this had a short slab-side action with the charging handle on the left side instead of the right. The magazines (6- or 18-rounds) ran up through a prominent web made integrally with the trigger-guard bow, and the rear sight was contained in prominent protectors on top of the receiver behind the ejection port. The AP-66 was stocked in a single piece of walnut. The butt had a Monte Carlo comb, but lacked a cheekpiece; checkering was also absent.

The Armi-Jager CAR-15 lookalike,
with a long barrel to comply with legal restrictions.

SIMILAR GUNS

Model AP-66L rifle. The deluxe version had checkering on the pistol grip and the square-tipped forend. A Monte Carlo comb and a deep rounded cheekpiece were standard.

MODEL AP-74 SPORTING RIFLE

Made by Armi-Jager, Milan.
Currently in production. **Chambering options:** 22LR rimfire or 7.65mm Auto. **Action:** no mechanical breech lock; blowback, semi-automatic only.
DATA FOR A TYPICAL 22 EXAMPLE
39in overall, 6.5lb empty. 19.75in barrel, 4-groove rifling; RH, concentric. Detachable box magazine, 10 or 14 rounds. Adjustable rear sight set in carrying handle. 1080 fps with 40-grain bullet. AR-15 knife bayonet.

This was a simplified version of the 5.56mm AR-15 (see 'U.S.A: ArmaLite'), with a particularly accurate outline—including the carrying handle and prong-type flash suppressor. Standard rifles had synthetic furniture, but a deluxe version has been made with a wooden butt, pistol grip and forend.

SIMILAR GUNS

AR-74 carbine. This variant of the ArmaLite lookalike has a sliding tubular butt and a short forend. It also has the full-length barrel, to avoid transgressing restrictive laws, and looks a little odd!

AP-74 Commando carbine. Sharing the basic AR-74 action, this 1976 introduction has a distinctive butt (said to have been inspired by the Uzi submachine gun) set beneath the return-spring tube. The underside of the wood forend is grooved to improve grip, and the carrying handle on top of the receiver has been replaced by a low ramp.

• Armi-Jager, bolt-action type

Armi-Jager made a few sporting rifles in the 1960s on the basis of refurbished military 1898-type Mauser actions.

CENTERFIRE GUNS

Offered in 220 Swift, 243 Winchester, 6.5x57, 270 Winchester, 7x57, 7x64, 30-06, 308 Winchester or 8x57, these had half-stocks with Monte Carlo combs and checkering on the pistol grip and round-tipped forend; thin white spacers accompanied black plastic shoulder plates and pistol grip caps. A folding-leaf rear sight was often supplemented by a micro-adjustable peep-sight fitted to the receiver bridge.

MODEL AP-62 TARGET RIFLE

This was locked simply by the base of the bolt handle entering its seat. However, a heavy 26in barrel was fitted, and the beech half-stock was a competition pattern. Checkering appeared on the pistol grip and the deep rounded forend; a shallow cheekpiece lay on the right side of the butt; and the shoulder plate was hard rubber. Weight was about 9.9lb. The sights consisted of a replaceable-element tunnel at the muzzle and a Weihrauch-type micro-adjustable aperture unit above the back of the receiver. The trigger had a double pressure, and a sling-anchor or hand stop could be fitted beneath the forend.

MODEL AP-65 UNIVERSAL SPORTING RIFLE

This interesting small-caliber bolt-action rifle had an exchangeable barrel, the standard chamberings including (in 1965) 22LR rimfire, 6mm rimfire, 22 Winchester Magnum rimfire and 9mm Flobert. The Flobert barrels were generally smooth-bores, whereas the 22 patterns were invariably rifled. A pistol grip half-stock was customary.

• Beretta, autoloading type

A series of semi-automatic rifles was made during the 1930s, under the supervision of Tullio Marengoni. By 1939, however, the Beretta had been rejected in favor of the Armaguerra design (q.v.).

The company's guns have all been gas-operated, and all but the Model 57 have relied on rotating-bolt locks. In spite of the efforts of Marengoni, little success was encountered prior to 1945; since World War II, however, far greater success has been achieved with adaptations of the popular U.S. 30 M1 Garand and many export orders were fulfilled in the 1960s. The Garand-based rifles were supplemented by the 5.56mm AR-70 and then, after protracted trials, replaced by the perfected AR-70/90 assault rifle in the mid 1980s.

5.56mm Beretta AR-70 and AR-70/90 rifles, in varying guises, have been supplied in quantity to—among others—the forces of Jordan and Malaysia. They have also been manufactured under licence in Morocco (q.v.).

MODEL 1931 RIFLE
Fucile automatico Beretta Mo. 931

Made by Pietro Beretta SpA, Gardone Val Trompia (Brescia), 1932-5.
Total production: not known. **Chambering:** 6.5x52, rimless. **Action:** locked by rotating lugs on the bolt into the receiver; gas operated, semi-automatic.
45.45in overall, 8.97lb empty. 23.6in barrel, 4-groove rifling; RH, concentric. Integral box magazine, 6 rounds. Quadrant sight graduated to 1500m (1640yd). 2295 fps with ball cartridges. Mo. 1891 sword bayonet

Subjected to Italian army trials in the early 1930s, this was an orthodox gas-operated weapon with a recoil-spring housing protruding back above the straight-wrist butt. The lower part of the integral clip-loaded magazine case pivoted forward when the catch on the side of the butt was released. Ventilating holes were cut through the forend and half-length handguard.

SIMILAR GUNS

Model 1937 rifle. This was an improved 7.35mm version of the Mo. 1931. It was 41.75in long, had a 19.1in barrel and weighed 8.69lb. A notched block sufficed as a 300m (330yd) sight and the Mo. 91-38 knife bayonet could be attached when required. The

The 6.5mm Beretta M1931 auto-loading rifle.

The 7.35mm Beretta Model 1937 rifle.

Mo. 1937 shared the rotating-bolt locking system of its predecessor, but chambered a more potent cartridge.

The magazine was altered to eliminate the pivoting section, and stripper-clip guides were added to the front of the recoil-spring housing. The butt was given a shallow pistol grip; ventilating holes were cut through the half-length handguard; and the forend between the barrel band and the nose cap was replaced by a fluted metal casing.

MODEL 1957 CARBINE
Also known as 'P-30'
Made by Pietro Beretta SpA, Gardone Val Trompia (Brescia), 1957-62.
Total production: not known. Chambering: 30 M1 Carbine, rimless.
Action: locked by tilting the bolt downward into the receiver; gas operated, semi-automatic only.

37.1in overall, 6.5lb without magazine. 17.9in barrel, 4-groove rifling; RH, concentric. Detachable box magazine, 30 rounds. Pivoting 'L' sight for 150m (165yd) and 300m (330yd). 1970 fps with ball cartridges; 500±30 rpm.

U.S. M4 knife bayonet
Designed by Tullio Marengoni in the early 1950s, this was inspired by the M1, M1A1 and M2 Carbines supplied to Italy by the U.S. Government. Its action relied on a tilting-block lock adapted from the Soviet Tokarev; except the charging handle and bolt carrier, no visible parts moved during the firing cycle.

The carbine was usually supplied with a pistol grip stock, with flutes in the forend and ventilating holes in the handguard. However, folding-butt examples with a separate pistol grip were available to order, and a sheet-metal handguard was often fitted. The most distinctive feature was the double-trigger system, the rear lever permitting fully automatic fire by disengaging the auxiliary sear.

BM-59 RIFLE
Fucile automatico Beretta, Mo. 1959
Made by Armi Pietro Beretta SpA, Rome.
Total production: not known. Chambering: 7.62x51, rimless. Action: locked by rotating lugs on the bolt head into the receiver; gas operated, semi-automatic or selective fire.
DATA FOR BM-59 ITAL TIPO ALPINI

43.7in overall (with butt extended), 10.75lb with empty magazine. 19.35in barrel, 4-groove rifling; RH, concentric. Detachable box magazine, 20 rounds. Tangent sight graduated to 2000m (2185yd). 2665 fps with NATO SS77 ball cartridges; 800rpm. M7-type knife bayonet.

The first BM-59 guns, dating from 1958, were simply shortened selective-fire 7.62x51 M1 Garands (q.v.) with detachable box magazines.

SIMILAR GUNS
BM-59D rifle. Introduced in 1959, this was a variant of the standard BM-59 with an auxiliary pistol grip behind the trigger.

BM-59R rifle. This 1959-vintage rifle was a BM-59 with a rate-reducing device built into the trigger mechanism.

BM-59GL rifle. Dating from 1959-60, this was a minor variant of the BM-59 with a grenade launcher on the muzzle.

BM-59 Mk I rifle. This had an improved trigger system and a 'tri-compensator'—a muzzle fitting serving as a muzzle brake, flash suppresser and compensator, but also capable of accepting a U.S.-style M1 bayonet or Mecar rifle grenades.

BM-59 Mk II rifle. Essentially similar to the BM-59 Mk I, this had a pistol grip behind the trigger guard to aid control when firing automatically, a winter trigger, a bipod attached to the gas tube, and a hinged shoulder strap on the buttplate.

BM-59 Mk III rifle. This lacked the otherwise standard bipod, but had an additional pistol grip ahead of the magazine and a folding steel stock strong enough to withstand grenade launching.

BM-59 Mk IV rifle. Intended as a light support weapon, this had a heavy barrel and a stock not unlike that of the later U.S. M14A1 (q.v.).

BM-60 CB rifle. Introduced in 1960, this could fire three-round bursts instead of the usual full-automatic fire.

BM-59 Mk Ital rifle. After extensive trials, the Italian army adopted this BM-59 variant in 1962. The service rifle had a conventional pistol gripped wood stock, a bipod around the gas tube, and a grenade-launcher sight folding down behind the front-sight block. Marks on a typical army rifle included 'BM-59' over 'CAL. 7,62 NATO' above 'BERETTA–ARMI' and 'ROMA', in four lines across the receiver behind the rear sight. Commercial and contract weapons generally bore 'P. BERETTA–BRESCIA–ITALIA' and the date of manufacture above 'B M 59–CAL. 7,62 NATO' and the serial number. These marks lay on the rear left side of the receiver below the rear sight.

BM-59 Ital rifle, 'Tipo Alpini'. Intended to arm Alpine troops, this had a folding butt and a pistol grip behind the trigger.

BM-59 Ital rifle, 'Tipo Paracudisti'. The paratroop rifle had a short barrel and a detachable compensator.

BM-59 Ital A rifle. This was simply a standard Ital with a folding butt.

BM-59 SL rifle. Restricted to semi-automatic fire, this was an adapted M1 Garand with a detachable box magazine.

AUTOMATIC CARBINE
Carabine automatiche Beretta, 'CAB'
Made by Pietro Beretta SpA, Gardone Val Trompia, about 1962-88.
Total production: not known. Chambering: 22LR, rimfire. Action: no mechanical breech lock; blowback, semi-automatic only.
DATA FOR THE STANDARD 'SPORT' PATTERN

About 40in overall, 6.06lb without magazine. 20.45in barrel, 6-groove rifling; RH, concentric. Detachable box magazine, 5, 10 or 20 rounds (later 4, 8 or 20 rounds). Open-block and two-leaf rear sight graduated to 200m (220yd). 1080 fps with 40-grain bullet.

The original 22 'Sport' rifle had a walnut half-stock with a straight comb. The butt lacked a cheekpiece, though the forend had a schnabel tip. Locking the cocking handle down in its recess

The Beretta BM59 Mark Ital rifle, derived from the Garand.

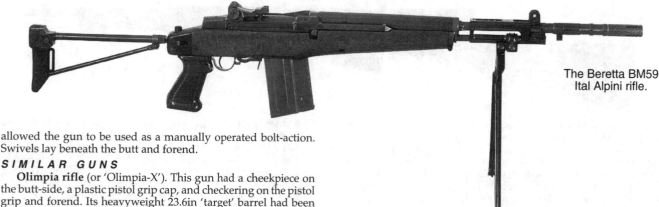

The Beretta BM59 Ital Alpini rifle.

allowed the gun to be used as a manually operated bolt-action. Swivels lay beneath the butt and forend.

SIMILAR GUNS

Olimpia rifle (or 'Olimpia-X'). This gun had a cheekpiece on the butt-side, a plastic pistol grip cap, and checkering on the pistol grip and forend. Its heavyweight 23.6in 'target' barrel had been given a phosphated anti-glare finish by the 1980s, and the rear sight was adjustable for drift as well as elevation. An aperture rear sight could be attached to the upper tang behind the receiver when required. Weight averaged 8lb without competition sights.

Super Sport rifle. Similar to the Tipo Olimpia, this rifle orig-nally had a select walnut stock with a Monte Carlo comb and small oval cheekpiece. However, the guns being made in the early 1980s had a plainer stock lacking the cheekpiece. The original checkering had also given way to a skip-line pattern. An optical sight could be fitted above the receiver if required.

MODEL 70 ASSAULT RIFLE
Fucile d'Assalto AR-70

Made by Pietro Beretta SpA, Gardone Val Trompia (Brescia), 1970-83.
Total production: not known. **Chambering:** 5.56x45, rimless. **Action:** locked by rotating two lugs on the bolt into the receiver; gas operated, selective fire.

DATA FOR A PRE-1975 EXAMPLE

38.95in overall, 7.56lb without magazine. 17.7in barrel, 4-groove rifling; RH, concentric. Detachable box magazine, 30 rounds. Tangent-leaf sight graduated to 500m (545yd). 3050 fps with ball cartridges; 625±25 rpm. Optional knife bayonet.

Announced in 1970 after development lasting five years, this presented a conventional appearance even though its receiver was made largely of pressings. The earliest AR-70 had a ribbed syn-thetic forend. The pistol grip was originally checkered wood, but was soon changed to a synthetic pattern matching the forend.

A rotary selector lay above the pistol grip on the left side of the receiver (up for automatic fire, back for single shots, down to lock the trigger); the charging handle was on the right side; and con-ventional sights were accompanied by folding grenade-launching patterns. Sling loops lay on the left side of the gas-port block and on the left side of the butt.

AR-70 rifles accepted optical or electro-optical sights. A bipod and carrying handle transformed them into light support weapons,

and an American-style knife bayonet could be fitted when required. By 1983, substantial quantities of Beretta rifles had been purchased by the Italian air force and special counter-terrorist units.

The perfected versions of the AR-70 and its derivatives offered many detail changes compared with the earliest guns. The folding stock was strengthened, and the original ribbed handguard was replaced by a fluted pattern with ventilation slots. However, field trials and paramilitary service showed that improvements could still be made.

SIMILAR GUNS

SC-70 rifle. This was a folding-butt derivative of the AR-70, comparable in size and capable of accepting the same range of auxiliary sights.

SC-70 rifle, 'versione corta'. This ultra-short version of the SC-70 appeared in 1974. It was 32.3in overall with the stock extended (23.5in when folded), had a 12.6in barrel, and weighed 7.08lb without the magazine. The grenade-launching sights and the muzzle sleeve were omitted.

MODEL 70-90 ASSAULT RIFLE
Fucile d'Assalto AR-70/90

Made by P. Beretta SpA, Gardone Val Trompia (Brescia), 1985 to date.
Currently in production. **Chambering:** 5.56x45, rimless. **Action:** as Mo. 70, above.

DATA FOR A 1988-VINTAGE EXAMPLE

39.2in overall, 8.69lb without magazine. 17.7in barrel, 6-groove rifling; RH, concentric. Detachable box magazine, 30 rounds. Tangent-leaf sight graduated to 500m (545yd). 3050 fps with ball cartridges; 625±25 rpm. Optional knife bayonet.

Rigorous service trials revealed minor flaws in the AR-70 and a light machine-gun derivative designated 'Mo. 70/78'. Work began in 1984 to revise the design so that guns could participate in Italian army trials, and the first AR-70/90 rifles appeared in

The Beretta Olimpia X rimfire auto-loader.

The first version of the 5.56mm Beretta AR70 rifle.

The 1983-type 5.56mm Beretta AR70 rifle.

The 5.56mm Beretta AR70/90 rifle, 1992.

1985. The Beretta was finally selected to replace the aging 7.62mm BM-59 in Italian service in 1990, and the first large-scale deliveries were made in 1992.

The major change was internal. The bolt of the AR-70 had reciprocated on rails pressed into the receiver, but this method was not strong enough to satisfy the army and so hardened steel rails were inserted in the AR-70/90 frame.

The new straight-line layout was achieved by raising the heel of the butt, and a detachable carrying handle was added on top of the receiver. An ambidextrous selector/safety catch unit was fitted, while changes were made to the receiver and pistol grip. Bipods could be removed at will.

SIMILAR GUNS

SC-70/90 rifle. This was the standard folding-butt version of the AR-70/90, though the two patterns were otherwise identical.

SCS-70/90 carbine. A short-barreled version of the SC-70/90, this lacked the grenade-launching tube on the muzzle.

SCP-70/90 carbine. Intended for paratroop use ('Tipo Paracudisti'), this short-barreled gun had a folding stock, a grenade launcher on the muzzle, and an auxiliary folding sight on the gas-port block.

• Beretta, bolt-action type

SUPER OLIMPIA TARGET RIFLE

Made by Pietro Beretta SpA, Gardone Val Trompia, 1962-70?
Total production: not known. **Chambering:** 22LR, rimfire. **Action:** locked by the base of the bolt handle entering its seat in the receiver as the bolt is turned down.

42.5in overall, 10.6lb with sights. 25.6in barrel, 6-groove rifling; RH, concentric. Single shot only. Micro-adjustable aperture rear sight. 1080 fps with 40-grain bullet.

A good quality competition rifle, with a squared butt and a deep oblique-tipped forend, this had an adjustable two-stage trigger regulated to a 17.6oz (500gm) release. The pistol grip and forend were checkered. Sights comprised the customary aperture pattern, mounted on the receiver above the bolt handle, and a replaceable-element tunnel at the muzzle.

MODEL 500 SPORTING RIFLE

Made by Pietro Beretta SpA, Gardone Val Trompia, 1984-90.
Total production: not known. **Chambering options:** see notes. **Action:** locked by two lugs on the bolt engaging recesses in the receiver wall behind the chamber as the bolt handle was turned down, and by the bolt-handle base entering its seat.

DATA FOR A TYPICAL 500S EXAMPLE
Chambering: 223 Remington, rimless. 42.7in overall, 7.15lb empty. 23.6in barrel, 6-groove rifling; RH, concentric. Internal box magazine, 5 rounds. Open ramp sight. 3245 fps with 55-grain bullet.

Beretta's bolt-action rifle was basically a Mauser. The extractor was a small claw let into the side of the bolt head; the plunger-type ejector was mounted in the recessed bolt face. The Mo. 500 (short action) rifles—chambered only for 222 or 223 Remington cartridges—had a half-stock with a Monte Carlo comb, a North American-style cheekpiece, and a plain rounded forend tip. An optical sight was standard, no open sights being provided.

SIMILAR GUNS

Model 500DL rifle. The deluxe or 'Custom Grade' guns had a high-quality walnut half-stock with a low hog's back comb, a small oval cheekpiece, a ventilated rubber buttplate, and checkering on the pistol grip and forend. A schnabel tip was standard.

Model 500S rifle. This was a variant of the standard gun supplied with a Williams-type adjustable open sight on the barrel and a ramped blade at the muzzle.

Model 500 Sniper rifle, 1985-9. Initially offered only in 7.62x51 NATO (308 Winchester), this had a heavy barrel with a conical muzzle brake/flash suppresser. An adjustable bipod was attached

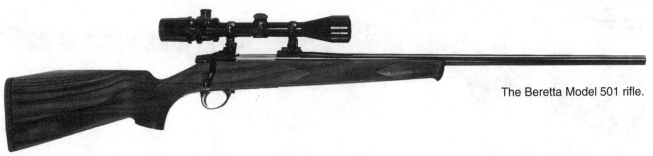

The Beretta Model 501 rifle.

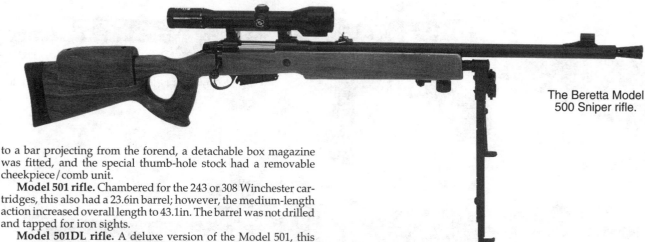

The Beretta Model 500 Sniper rifle.

to a bar projecting from the forend, a detachable box magazine was fitted, and the special thumb-hole stock had a removable cheekpiece/comb unit.

Model 501 rifle. Chambered for the 243 or 308 Winchester cartridges, this also had a 23.6in barrel; however, the medium-length action increased overall length to 43.1in. The barrel was not drilled and tapped for iron sights.

Model 501DL rifle. A deluxe version of the Model 501, this was distinguished by a better Bavarian-style stock (see Model 500DL, above).

Model 501S rifle. This was simply an open sighted version of the medium-action Model 501.

Model 502 rifle. Available in 270 Winchester, 7mm Remington Magnum, 30-06 or 375 H&H Magnum, these long-action guns customarily had 24.4in barrels, increasing overall length to 44.3in and average weight nearer 8lb.

Model 502DL rifle. The deluxe version of the long-action Beretta had a superior Bavarian-style walnut half-stock with a hog's back comb.

Model 502S rifle. Mechanically identical with the Mo. 502, this was identified by its iron sights. An optical sight could still be fitted when required.

• Beretta, break-open type

Renowned for a wide range of high-quality shotguns in addition to handguns, submachine guns and automatic rifles, Beretta has also made a limited quantity of Double Rifles.

THE BASIC PATTERNS

Model S689 rifle. Introduced in the early 1980s, this over/under box-lock pattern was discontinued in 1991. Chambered only for the 30-06 or 9.3x74R rounds, it had automatic ejectors and a double trigger system. The guns typically had 23in barrels and weighed about 7.7lb. The action body was nickel-plated prior to 1985, but color case-hardened thereafter.

Model SSO Express rifle. Made from 1987 to date, this over/under game rifle—often weighing 10.5-11lb—has been offered in 375 H&H Magnum, 9.3x74R or 458 Winchester Magnum. An auto-ejecting sidelock design, with double triggers and case-hardened lock plates, the SSO often provides the basis for superb engraving. The barrels usually measure 23.6in or 25.6in, and the butts may be pistol grip or straight-wrist types.

Model 455 rifle, 1990 to date. Distinguished by its side-by-side barrels, this has detachable sidelocks. Built virtually to individual specifications, the 455 has been chambered for a variety of big-game cartridges: e.g., 375 H&H Magnum, 416 Rigby, 458 Winchester Magnum, 470 Nitro Express, and 500 3in Nitro Express. Barrels are usually 23.6in or 25.6in long, and weight can exceed 12lb. The Model 455 EELL (the extra-deluxe version) has game scenes and English-style Best Bouquet engraving on the action body, allied with specially selected exhibition-grade walnut woodwork. The butts generally have pistol grip wrists.

• Bernardelli

SEMI-AUTOMATIC CARBINE
Carabine Semi-Automatiche ('CSA')

Made by Vincenzo Bernardelli SpA, Gardone Val Trompia, about 1962-85.

Total production: not known. **Chambering options:** 22LR rimfire or 9mm Flobert. **Action:** no mechanical breech lock; blowback, semi-automatic only.

DATA FOR 22 EXAMPLE

40.15in overall, 5.18lb empty. 20.85in barrel, 4-groove rifling; RH, concentric. Detachable box magazine, 10 rounds. Open-block rear sight with a folding leaf. 1080 fps with 40-grain bullet.

Made with an eye to low-cost production, this gun has a die-cast receiver. A simple blowback feeding from a detachable box magazine ahead of the trigger, the CSA usually has a butt with a Monte Carlo comb; the pistol grip and the round-tipped forend are usually checkered.

SIMILAR GUNS

Flobert version. This measured 43.7in overall and had a 24.4in barrel; weight averaged 5.75lb. Guns of this type usually had plain forends and a plain pistol gripped hardwood stock with a Monte Carlo comb. Magazine capacity was merely three rounds, and the sights were rudimentary.

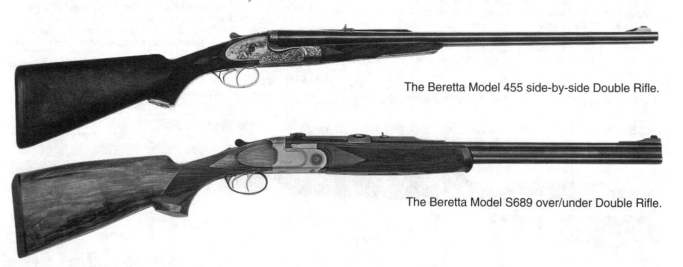

The Beretta Model 455 side-by-side Double Rifle.

The Beretta Model S689 over/under Double Rifle.

• Breda

Also known as 'Breda-Fiorini', this early assault rifle was developed in Italy in the 1930s by Sestilio Fiorini—head of the Breda technical department. The PG rifle was originally chambered for the 6.5mm rifle cartridge in the forlorn hope that it would interest the Italian army, but was never entirely successful.

The rifle was very heavy, in spite of its compact dimensions. Gas was tapped from a port at the muzzle to strike an annular piston; this released the locking block and allowed the breechblock and carrier to reciprocate. The gun fired single shots from a closed bolt, but relied on a complicated ratchet-type escapement to fire four-round bursts from an open-bolt position.

Military sales were few and far between, the only known large-scale delivery going to Costa Rica shortly before World War II began.

MODEL PG SHORT RIFLE
Moschetto Automatico Breda Mo. PG
Made by Società Italiana Costruzioni Meccaniche Ernesto Breda, Brescia, 1935-6.
Total production: 850? Chambering: 7x57, rimless. Action: locked by a pivoting block; gas operated, semi-automatic only.

43.9in overall, 11.57lb empty. 17.9in barrel, 4-groove rifling; LH, concentric. Detachable box magazine, 20 rounds. Quadrant sight graduated to 2000m (2185yd). Bayonet: see notes.

Introduced in 1935, the PG was a stubby gun with a protruding magazine case not unlike that of the Italian Mannlicher-Carcano service rifle. Feed lips were machined on the inside of the receiver instead of relying on a shaped magazine throat. The one-piece stock had a sling aperture and bar in the butt. A handguard ran forward from the back-sight base. The double-band nose cap assembly, which surrounded the piston, had a swivel on the left side of the rear band and a bayonet lug on its underside; the bayonet was shared with Costa Rican Mauser rifles.

Receivers were invariably marked 'GOBIERNO DE COSTA RICA' above the chamber, together with the gun designation, the serial number and a date (e.g., '1935-XIII', 'XIII' representing the thirteenth year of the Italian Fascist era commencing in 1923).

• Carcano

The incorporation of independent states in the Italian confederation was accompanied by an urgent need to rationalize and modernize the infantry weapons. A commission was formed in 1866 to investigate breech-loading rifles, testing a wide variety of weapons. However, the authorities rejected those firing metal-case ammunition or requiring separate primers. This left only the needle guns of Chassepot, Dreyse and Doersch & von Baumgarten.

Ease of conversion was the principal reason for selecting the Doersch & von Baumgarten system (q.v.), which required less radical changes to the breech than its rivals. However, problems with experimental Dreyse-type ammunition led to the abandonment of the German-designed breech in favor of a combination of Doersch and Dreyse features credited to Salvatore Carcano.

Patented in Italy in July 1867, the Carcano breech consisted of an 'L'-shape channel formed in the existing barrel to receive a rudimentary bolt. A bracket was inserted in the stock behind the breech to support the bolt during its travel, and the stock was adapted to house a new hammer and trigger mechanism; the apertures for the lock plates of the original guns were sealed with fillets of wood.

Carcano rifles were operated by pulling a cocking knob on the back of the action, retracting the needle and allowing the bolt handle to be lifted. The bolt was then pulled back. A cartridge was

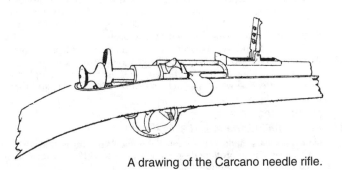

A drawing of the Carcano needle rifle.

placed in the chamber, and the bolt was pushed foward until the handle could be turned down to re-lock the mechanism. The thumb piece on the needle-tube was then pushed forward to set the trigger mechanism, and the gun could be fired.

MODEL 1860/67 RIFLE
Fucile di Fanteria Mo. 1860/67
Converted by the Regia Fabbrica d'Armi, Turin, about 1868-70.
Total production: 50,000? Chambering: 17.5mm combustible cartridge.
Action: locked by turning the base of the bolt handle down into contact with a shoulder on the receiver.

55.5in overall, 9.59lb empty. 36in barrel, 4-groove rifling; RH, concentric. Single-shot only. Leaf-pattern rear sight. 1035 fps with 556-grain bullet. Socket bayonet.

The standard rifle was a clumsy-looking weapon; owing to the chosen method of conversion, the trigger mechanism was moved about 2cm (.8in) forward to a position where it was difficult to grasp. The bolt handle was also placed well forward, directly above the swivel on the front web of the trigger guard. One of the two sprung brass bands carried a swivel, and a heavy brass nose cap was used. The standard rear sight had a single folding leaf with three sighting apertures and a 'V' in its top edge.

Most of the original stocks were retained—suitably patched—though a few guns (sometimes known as 'M1868') received newly-made one-piece replacements without the characteristic flats alongside the breech. The cleaning rods were retained initially, but then discarded; the channels were filled with cork. The head of a spring-loaded safety catch protruded in the guard ahead of the trigger. Most guns are marked 'PRIVATIVA' ('Patented') and 'S. Carcano' on the breech.

MODEL 1856/67 CARBINE
Carabina di Bersaglieri Mo. 1856/67
Converted by the Regia Fabbrica d'Armi, Turin, about 1868-70.
Total production: a few thousand. Chambering: 17.5mm combustible cartridge. **Action:** generally as M1860/68 rifle, above.

49.9in overall, 9.93lb empty. 31.3in barrel, 4-groove rifling; RH, concentric. Single-shot only. Leaf-pattern rear sight. 985 fps with 556-grain bullet. Sword bayonet.

This was essentially similar to the M1860/67 rifle, but the middle band and the nose cap were placed unusually close together and the rear sight leaf had an adjustable slider. The hilt of the bayonet, inspired by Swiss practice, slid in a tube fitted to the right side of the muzzle and was retained by a spring catch.

MODEL 1844/67 ARTILLERY MUSKETOON
Moschetto di Artigliera Mo. 1844/67
Converted by the Regia Fabbrica d'Armi, Turin, about 1868-70.
Total production: a few thousand. Chambering: 17.5mm combustible cartridge. **Action:** generally as M1860/68 rifle, above.

43.1in overall, 7.72lb empty. 24.4in barrel, 4-groove rifling; RH, concentric. Single-shot only. Tangent-type rear sight. 905 fps with 556-grain bullet. Sword bayonet.

These guns shared the action of the infantry rifle, but were much smaller. They had a single band and a nose cap, both made of brass, and a small (but very distinctive) tangent sight lay above the breech. Swivels lay beneath the butt and the barrel band. The bayonet, which had a double-edged blade, was attached in the same manner as the Bersaglieri type described above.

SIMILAR GUNS

M1844/67 Engineers' musketoon. This was identical with the artillery pattern, but accepted a socket bayonet instead of a sword pattern. It was also used by the Italian navy (Regia Marina).

MODEL 1860/67 GENDARMERIE MUSKETOON
Moschetto di Carabinieri Mo. 1860/67
Converted by the Regia Fabbrica d'Armi, Turin, about 1868-70.
Total production: a few hundred only? **Chambering:** 17.5mm combustible cartridge. **Action:** generally as M1860/68 rifle, above.

45.25in overall, 7.94lb empty. 26.75in barrel, 4-groove rifling; RH, concentric. Single-shot only. Leaf-type rear sight? 930 fps with 556-grain bullet. Socket bayonet.

Very little is known about this weapon, which seems to have had only a single barrel band accompanying the brass nose cap. The rear sight is believed to have been similar to that of the infantry rifle, with sighting slots, though some reports suggest that a simple fixed block was used. The bayonet was also shared with the M1860/67 rifle.

• Cei-Rigotti

Patented in Italy in 1895 by Major Amerigo Cei-Rigotti, this autoloading rifle was demonstrated in the British Royal Small Arms Factory, Enfield, in March 1901. Three series of 10 rounds were fired at a 24ft-wide target at a distance of 200yd; the inventor fired 10 rounds in 19 seconds, including the time taken to clear a jam, but the accuracy was poor. The test was repeated by the Enfield Proof Master, who fired one round for practice and then nine for accuracy in 17 seconds. Results were judged good for such rapid fire. The rifle was then set to fire automatically, firing 10 rounds in less than two seconds. Owing to the high incidence of jams, the Cei-Rigotti was rejected, though development work is believed to have continued until at least 1905. The rifles typically resembled the Mannlicher-Carcano short rifles, being stocked virtually to the muzzle, and would accept the 1891-type sword bayonet. However, a prominent bolt-support track extended back over the wrist of the butt, and the reach from the wrist to the trigger was excessive.

The 6.5mm Cei-Rigotti automatic rifle, tested in Britain in 1900.

• Daffini

Libero Daffini of Brescia offered sporting rifles built on surplus Kar. 98k actions in 1955-70. Often marketed under the brand name 'Lida', they were chambered for 30-06 or 8x57 cartridges; typical examples had 21.65in barrels and pistol grip stocks with Monte Carlo combs.

Daffini also made a 22LR rimfire autoloading sporting rifle (very similar to the Armi-Jager AP-61) under the designation 'Model 11'. This was a conventional blowback pattern with a detachable four- or eight-round magazine. The 20.05in barrel gave an overall length of 39.2in and an empty weight of about 5.5lb. Made in a single piece, the half-stock had a pistol grip and a low Monte Carlo comb, but usually lacked checkering. The sights consisted of a ramped blade and a spring-leaf and elevator.

• Doersch & von Baumgarten

This needle-fire mechanism, developed in Prussia (q.v.), was initially selected as an ideal method of modernizing the Italian muzzle-loading rifle muskets. The royal arms manufactory in Turin made substantial quantities of breech-loading guns for trials with the Italian army, on the basis of the M1856 carbine and M1860 rifle musket.

The first trials showed that the breech was acceptably gas tight, but also that the Dreyse-type cartridges supplied by the Laboratorio Pirotecnico were virtually useless. When the ammunition was changed to a version of the 1860-pattern combustible cartridge with an additional cardboard base, gas leaks increased greatly; the problem was partly solved by adding a rubber washer to the base of the cartridge, which increased the risk of jamming. As the drawbacks of the ammunition clearly outweighed the constructional advantages of the breech, the Doersch & von Baumgarten system was abandoned in favor of the Carcano design (q.v.).

• FAVS

Fabbrica Armi Valle Susa di Guglielminotti (FAVS) of Villarfochardio/Torino offered refurbished military surplus actions in the mid 1960s. These were set in slender three-quarter length stocks. Monte Carlo combs, schnabel-tip forends, and skip-line checkering were standard. Barrels measured 23.6in or 25.6in and were chambered to order; double triggers were also supplied on request. Most guns had engraving on the receiver and magazine floorplate.

In addition to the centerfire patterns, FAVS made rimfire sporters. These included the Cocher-22, a single-shot 22LR pattern with a cylindrical receiver and an automatic safety; the rear sight was a sturdy block, and the front sight was a blade on a low ramp. The guns weighed about 4.9lb with a 23.6in barrel.

The Beter-6 and Beter-9 shared the same action as the Cocher pattern, but chambered Flobert ammunition and had sights which comprised nothing more than a pin and a notch.

• Franchi

Luigi Franchi SpA of Fornaci, near Brescia, made small numbers of the 7.62mm LF-59 in the early 1960s. These gas-operated rifles bore a superficial resemblance to the FN FAL, and were also locked by tilting the tail of the breechblock down against a transverse shoulder in the receiver. The piston was forged integrally with the bolt carrier, and the return spring was housed in a telescoping tube in the back of the receiver. Fixed and folding-butt versions were made, but the Italian army preferred the Beretta BM-59 and the LF-59 faded quietly into obscurity. A typical example was 40.6in long, had a 20.85in barrel, and weighed about 9.5lb. A 20-round detachable box magazine was used, cyclic rate being about 625rpm.

• Garand

Italy received 232,000 M1 Garand rifles from the USA in 1950-70, in addition to guns made by Beretta (see 'BM-59 rifle'). War-surplus examples can be recognized by their original makers' marks and serial numbers in the U.S. Army ranges.

With the approval of the U.S. authorities, Beretta began to tool in 1950 to make the standard M1 Garand. The first series-made gun was delivered to the Italian army in 1952. Small export orders were subsequently gained from Denmark and Indonesia.

By 1958, after nearly 100,000 guns had been made, Beretta realized that advances being made elsewhere—in particular, the adoption of the M14 by the U.S. Army—were making the basic M1 obsolescent. A team led initially by Domenico Salza and then by Vittorio Valle shortened the original M1 and fitted a detachable magazine. The pre-production or prototype series included the M1 LS, a short rifle retaining the original clip-loaded magazine, and the BM-58 with a detachable box pattern.

• Mannlicher-Carcano

By 1887, the Italians had realized that the Vetterli rifles (q.v.) were obsolescent. The introduction of the Lebel in France and—most importantly—the adoption of the 8mm M1888 Mannlicher by arch-rival Austria-Hungary forced the authorities to form an infantry weapon commission. This commenced work in the school of musketry, Parma, at the end of 1888. The president was General Gustavo Parravicino.

In December 1889, the committee reported on trials with more than 50 rifles submitted by (among others) Vitali, Bertoldo, Mauser and Lee. None had proved ideal. A decision was taken in March 1890 to adopt a 6.5mm cartridge, and 10 differing breech systems were tested for suitability. Eventually, manufacturing problems were referred to the government arsenals; progressive rifling was adopted, and the cartridge was perfected in the Bologna munitions factory.

A report recommending the Mannlicher magazine in preference to Lee, Mauser and other patterns was made on 23rd April 1891. The major contestants in subsequent trials were the 'Mauser-Mannlicher Terni Tipo 2'—essentially similar to the Gew. 88, with Italian-pattern sights but no barrel jacket—and 'Fucile italiano No. 1', a modified Mannlicher developed in Regia Fabbrica d'Armi de Torino by a team led by Salvatore Carcano.

Captured and war surplus ex-Italian guns equipped some Albanian, Ethiopian, Greek and Yugoslavian troops during and immediately after World War II. Most of these were soon replaced by more effective weapons such as British Lee-Enfields and German Kar. 98k Mausers.

MODEL 1891 RIFLE
Fucile di Fanteria Mo. 1891

Most guns were made by the Regia Fabbrica d'Armi Terni, 1892-1937; some were also produced—generally prior to 1912—in Brescia, Torino and Torre Annunziata.

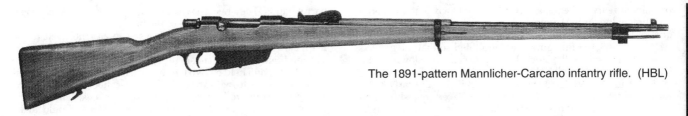

The 1891-pattern Mannlicher-Carcano infantry rifle. (HBL)

Total production: 4-4.5 million? **Chambering:** 6.5x52, rimless. **Action:** locked by two lugs on a detachable bolt head engaging recesses in the receiver as the bolt handle was turned down.

50.47in overall, 8.33lb empty. 30.7in barrel, 4-groove rifling; RH, concentric. Integral clip-loaded box magazine, 6 rounds. Quadrant sight graduated to 2000m (2185yd). 2295 fps with Mo. 91-95 ball cartridges. Mo. 1891 sword bayonet.

On 5th March 1892, the army infantry-weapons commission recommended adoption of 'Fucile No. 1 ter', a modified form of Torino's Fucile italiano No. 1. The war ministry concurred on 29th March, when the M1891 or Mannlicher-Carcano rifle was formally approved.

It had a one-piece straight-wrist stock and a protruding magazine case. Unlike Austro-Hungarian service rifles, the Italian gun accepted reversible clips; adopting a small-caliber cartridge also allowed one extra round to be carried. The M1891 had a split-bridge receiver, but its bolt was simpler than the Mannlichers based on the Gew. 88 and the safety was nothing more than a projecting plate between the rear of the bolt body and the cocking piece. The bolt could be removed simply by holding the trigger back. A typically Italian quadrant sight lay on the barrel ahead of the chamber; swivels appeared under the butt and rear band; and a conventional bayonet lug lay beneath the nose cap. Maker's marks—e.g., a crown above 'R.E. TERNI'—lay on the barrel ahead of the receiver and on the right side of the butt.

The first rifles were issued in the Spring of 1894, but the bolt-head was almost immediately strengthened pending the introduction of the smokeless Mo. 91-95 cartridge (approved in February 1896). Trials undertaken from August 1904 with a thousand modified rifles brought a change in the handguard in 1905; a modified extractor was adopted in 1907.

By April 1913, monthly production of rifles in the Terni factory had risen to about 2500. At this time, production of carbines was centered on Brescia, the factories in Torino and Torre Annuziata being partially closed down.

When World War I commenced in the summer of 1914, the Italian army inventory stood at 700,000 Mo. 1891 rifles. When the Armistice was concluded on 11th November 1918, the Terni factory alone had made 2,063,750 rifles since the outbreak of hostilities.

MODEL 1891 CAVALRY CARBINE
Moschetto Mo. 1891
Mostly made by the Fabbrica Nazionale d'Armi, Brescia; some were also made in Terni.

Total production: 750,000-1,000,000 moschetti of all types. **Chambering:** 6.5x52, rimless. **Action:** as Mo. 1891 rifle, above.

37.5in overall, 6.97lb empty (walnut stock). 17.75in barrel, 4-groove rifling; RH, concentric. Integral clip-loaded box magazine, 6 rounds. Quadrant sight graduated to 1500m (1640yd). 2085 fps with Mo. 91-95 ball cartridges. Integral folding bayonet.

This was adopted on 9th June 1893 for cavalry, carabineri (mounted gendarmerie) and cyclists. The original carbine had a straight-wrist half-stock, a recoil bolt running laterally through the stock beneath the receiver ring, a turned-down bolt handle, and a folding bayonet attached to a special muzzle block. The bayonet was locked by a sliding catch on the blade, changed about 1897 to become a radial lever on the right side of the muzzle block.

The recoil bolt was abandoned in 1900, and a handguard ran from the rear sight to the combined barrel band/nose cap. At about this time, the bayonet attachment became a push-button on the muzzle block. A few cavalry carbines were made in 1940 with barrels strengthened in the chamber area, the rear sight being moved farther forward.

SIMILAR GUNS
Model 1891 royal bodyguard carbine. A variant of the cavalry carbine was adopted for the 'Squadrone Reali Carabinieri Guardie del Re' and, subsequently, for the guard of the president of the Italian republic. It had a handguard, a turned-down bolt handle, and a special nose cap into which the socket bayonet could be reversed. The bolt, nose cap, magazine body and parts of the rear sight were gilded, other metal parts being blued.

MODEL 1891 TS CARBINE
Moschetto Mo. 1891 per Truppe Speciali
Most were made by the Fabbrica Nazionale d'Armi, Brescia, though some emanated from Terni.

Total production: 750,000-1,000,000 moschetti of all types. **Chambering:** 6.5x52, rimless.

Otherwise as Mo. 1891 cavalry carbine except for weight (7.1lb empty) and bayonet (Mo. 1891 TS pattern—see text).

This carbine was adopted for the Truppe Speciali in 1897. The original nose cap was similar to that of the rifle, with a bayonet lug, but carried a swivel on its rear edge. The second swivel lay on the underside of the butt. A recoil bolt ran through the stock beneath the receiver ring and the bolt handle was straight.

The recoil bolt was abandoned in 1900, the bolt handle was turned down, and a modified nose cap was approved. This had a

An M1891 Mannlicher-Carcano cavalry carbine. (HBL)

The Model 1891TS Mannlicher-Carcano with the 1928-pattern grenade launcher.

prominent rearward extension for the front swivel and a lateral attachment lug for the bayonet. The press-stud on the special bayonet protruded from the end of the pommel.

About 1908, the first guns were modified so that the swivels lay on the left side of the stock. Work proceeded so slowly that it was not completed until 1913.

Surviving Mo. 91 TS carbines were recalled in the early 1920s for modification. The old nose cap was replaced by a shortened version (accepting the standard sword bayonet) and a new swivel-bearing sprung band was added. A few TS carbines were subsequently fitted with a grenade launcher (*Annesso trombonico Mo. 28*) on the right side of the forend. Grenades were fired by removing the bolt from the carbine and inserting it in the bolt-way of the launcher.

MODEL 1891-24 CARBINE
Moschetto Mo. 1891-24

Converted by the Fabbrica Nazionale d'Armi, Terni. **Chambering:** 6.5x52, rimless. Otherwise generally as Mo. 1891 carbine, except bayonet (Mo. 91 sword pattern).

This was created in 1924 simply by shortening full-length infantry rifles, particularly those returning for major repairs to the barrel or forend. The Mo. 91-24 had the modified nose cap and barrel-band assembly of the modified Mo. 91 TS carbine, but retained the full-size rear sight of the rifle—though the graduations were suitably altered to compensate for reduced muzzle velocity.

MODEL 1891-38 SHORT RIFLE
Fucile Mo. 1891-38

Made by the Fabbrica Nazionale d'Armi, Terni.

Total production: not known. **Chambering:** 6.5x52, rimless. **Action:** as Mo. 1891 rifle, above.

42.3in overall, 7.63lb empty. 22.15in barrel, 4-groove rifling, RH, concentric. Integral clip-loaded box magazine, 6 rounds. Fixed-notch sight for 300m (330yd). 2150 fps with Mo. 91-95 ball cartridges. Mo. 1938 knife bayonet.

This modified Mo. 1891 was introduced in 1938 to expend 6.5mm ammunition before all service rifles were converted to 7.35mm. The Mo. 91-38 rifle was identical with the 7.35mm Mo. 38 (q.v.), but retained the original barrel and bolt. A barrel band with a swivel on the left side was approved in 1940, when the nose cap received distinctive extensions.

MODEL 1891-38 CARBINE
Moschetto Mo. 1891-38

Converted by the Fabbrica Nazionale d'Armi, Terni.

Chambering: 6.5x52, rimless.

Otherwise as Mo. 1891 carbine, above, apart from rear sight (fixed notch for 200m [220yd]) and bayonet (see notes).

These conversions of the 6.5mm cavalry and Truppe Speciali carbines, authorized in 1938, retained their original barrels and bolts. The rear sight was modified, but transformations were uncommon. Cavalry carbines had a folding bayonet; the TS patterns accepted a Mo. 91 sword bayonet.

MODEL 1938 SHORT RIFLE
Fucile Mo. 1938

Converted by the Fabbrica Nazionale d'Armi, Terni, 1939-40.

Total production: not known. **Chambering:** 7.35x52, rimless. **Action:** as Mo. 1891 rifle, above.

40.15in overall, 8.11lb empty. 22.15in barrel, 4-groove rifling; RH, concentric. Integral clip-loaded box magazine, 6 rounds. Fixed-notch sight for 300m (330yd). 2475 fps with Mo. 38 ball cartridges. Mo. 1938 knife bayonet.

Experience with the 6.5mm round in World War I suggested that it lacked power, and troubles in the Italian colonies in North Africa highlighted its shortcomings. In the mid-1930s, therefore, experiments began in Terni under the supervision of Colonel Giuseppe Mainardi. With the co-operation of Bombrini Parodi Delfino and Società Metallurgica Italiana, a satisfactory 7.35mm bullet was created. This could be loaded in the 6.5mm cartridge case with minimal alterations.

The 1938-pattern rifle was initially made by converting surviving Mo. 1891 guns. A selection of new parts was needed—from the barrel and bolt to the bands and stock—and a new folding-blade knife bayonet appeared. The guns could be recognized by a simple rear sight and, initially, by an absence of intermediate

barrel bands. They had a swivel on the left side of the nose cap and a fixed bar on the left side of the butt.

Weaknesses in the forend and nose-cap assembly led to the reappearance in 1939 of a barrel band with a swivel on the left side. The modified nose cap had small rearward extensions, let into the forend sides and held by two lateral pins. In 1940, however, a decision was taken to withdraw all 7.35mm-caliber guns from the armed forces and re-issue 6.5mm versions. This was taken on the grounds that the commencement of World War II would make wholesale rearmament too great a risk. The large-caliber rifles were apparently given to the militia.

MODEL 1938 CARBINE
Moschetto Mo. 1938

Converted by the Fabbrica Nazionale d'Armi, Terni.

Chambering: 7.35x52, rimless.

Otherwise as Mo. 1891 carbine, except for rear sight (fixed notch for 200m [220yd]), performance (2380 fps with Mo. 1938 ball cartridges) and bayonet.

Mostly converted from the Mo. 91 cavalry carbines, retaining the folding bayonet, the Mo. 38 had a new 7.35mm barrel and bolt. The otherwise similar Mo. 38 TS carbine had a barrel band and a nose cap accepting the Mo. 91 sword bayonet. Adjustable rear sights were replaced by fixed notches. Surviving guns were passed to the militia after 1940.

MODEL 1940 RIFLE

Adopted officially but never made in quantity, the Fucile Mo. 1940 was an improved Mo. 1891 with a distinctive rotary-elevator rear sight. A few hundred guns were made by the Terni manufactory, but World War II prevented full-scale production. Chambered for the 6.5x52 cartridge, the rifle was 46.25in overall and weighed 8.18lb. Its 27.15in barrel had concentric four-groove rifling and the magazine accepted the standard six-round clip. Muzzle velocity was 2245 fps with Mo. 91-95 ball cartridges and the Mo. 1891 sword bayonet could be attached to the muzzle.

MODEL 1941 RIFLE

The Mo. 1941, credited to Major Roberto Boragine, was recognizable by its shortened barrel and reduced-scale 1000m (1095yd) quadrant sight. Constant-twist rifling replaced the original progressive variety, but few guns were made before the major part of the Italian armed forces surrendered to the Allies in 1943. Perhaps only 1,000 were made in the Terni factory. Chambered for the 6.5x52 cartridge, they were 46.15in long, had 27.15in barrels and weighed 8.2lb empty.

MODEL 1938-43 SHORT RIFLE
Moschetto Mo. 1938-43

Chambering: 7.9x57, rimless.

Otherwise generally as Mo. 1891 carbine, above, except magazine (integral 5-round box), rear sight (fixed notch for 300m [330yd]) and performance (about 2050 fps with sS-Patrone). The Mo. 1891 sword bayonet was used.

Small quantities of these weapons were made in 1944—apparently in the Armaguerra factory in Cremona—for the co-belligerent forces fighting alongside the Germans. The barrel was bored for the standard 7.9mm German service cartridge, suitable adjustments being made to the bolt-head face, and a semi-circular channel was milled vertically across the chamber to allow the rounds to be pushed down into the magazine. A modified clip was welded into the magazine to retain the cartridges, which had to be loaded as singles owing to the absence of stripper-clip guides. A large 'S' was struck into the chamber-top, with '7.9' ahead of the rear sight.

The quality of the alterations was very poor; and the action was only marginally strong enough for such a powerful cartridge.

• Mauser

Several Italian gunmakers have offered sporting rifles built on Mauser actions, originally cannibalized from wartime service rifles but later built on commercial actions purchased from suppliers such as Fabrique Nationale. See separate entries for Libero Daffini, FAVS, Armi-Jager, Società Armi Bresciane and Sabatti SpA. Modified Mauser-type guns have also been made by—amongst others—Beretta and Antonio Zoli.

• Pedersoli

Davide Pedersoli & C. SNC of Gardone Val Trompia is best known for replica firearms, ranging from Japanese matchlocks, English dueling pistols and Kentucky rifles to a selection of Rem-

The Pedersoli Kodiak Mk IV
black-powder Double Rifle.

ington, Sharps and 'Trapdoor Springfield' (Springfield-Allin) breech-loaders. An exposed-hammer double rifle is also being made.

KODIAK MARK IV DOUBLE RIFLE

Made by Davide Pedersoli & C. SNC, Gardone Val Trompia, 1987 to date.
Currently in production. **Chambering options:** 8x57IRS, 9.3x74R or 45-70 (see text). **Action:** locked by a bar in the action engaging the underlugs of the barrel-block when the top lever closes.

DATA FOR A TYPICAL EXAMPLE
Chambering: 45-70, rimmed. 40.55in overall, 9.7lb empty. 24in barrel, 6-groove rifling; RH, concentric. Double barreled, two shots only. Multi-leaf rear sight. 1320 fps with 405-grain bullet.

These guns were based on a handful of double rifles built by Colt in the 1880s on the basis of the 1878-model shotgun action. The 45-70 Mark IV, currently being sold as the 'Model 890-S', has a straight-comb walnut butt with checkering on the shallow pistol grip and the short rounded forend. The color case-hardened side-action locks have rebounding hammers, the buttplate is normally rubber, and the swivels lie beneath the butt and barrel. The rear sight is an express pattern with an open notch and three folding leaves.

SIMILAR GUNS

Short-barrel guns. The original 45-70 rifle was supplemented by a shorter gun chambered for the 8x57IRS or 9.3x74R cartridges. Also known as the 'Model 892-S', the smaller version is 38.6in long, has a 22.05in barrel, and weighs about 8.15lb; four-groove rifling is standard.

Deluxe patterns. Both versions of the Kodiak can be supplied in a *Versione Lusso* (890-L and 892-L), with a grayed satin finish on the frame, locks and major metal fittings. The barrels are browned and the woodwork is selected for its figuring.

REMINGTON ROLLING BLOCK RIFLE

The history of these radial-block designs will be found under 'U.S.A.: Remington, block-action type'. Pedersoli examples may be found with engraving, particularly on the receiver.

THE GUNS

Cavalry rifle. Essentially similar to the Infantry pattern (below), offered in 357 and 45-70, this has a part-octagonal/part-round 30in barrel. The rear sight is fixed. Overall length is 45.75in, weight being about 12.1lb. Post-1997 rifles may have steel or brass barrel bands.

Infantry rifle. This has a color case-hardened receiver and a single brass band around the barrel and short forend; the butt is a plain straight-wrist type. Fixed sights are standard. Offered in 357 Magnum and 45-70, the rifles have 26in or 30in blued octagonal barrels giving an overall length of 42.7in or 46.75in; weights average 11.7lb for the short rifle and 12.8lb for the longer version. Optional steel barrel bands were introduced in 1997.

Long Range 'Creedmoor' rifle. Made in 357 Magnum and 45-70, with a 30in octagonal barrel, this has a checkered pistol grip butt and a checkered forend with a shallow lip. Though a spring-leaf and elevator sight is fitted to the barrel, the gun also has a tunnel-type sight at the muzzle and a folding 'Creedmoor' aperture sight on the upper tang behind the breech. The rifles are typically 45.75in long and weigh 10.5lb.

Target rifle. Offered with a lightweight blued octagonal barrel and a brightly polished receiver, this is supplied with a spring-leaf and elevator rear sight. However, competition sights can be fitted to the muzzle and tang if required. Chambered for the 357 Magnum or 45-70 cartridges, the Target Model is 45.75in long and weighs 9.8lb.

SHARPS DROPPING-BLOCK RIFLE

These guns are described in greater detail under 'U.S.A.: Sharps, dropping-block type'. The Pedersoli versions are often encountered with select walnut woodwork and engraving on components such as the receiver, hammer, lock plate, and patchbox.

CAP-LOCK GUNS

1859 Berdan Model rifle. This is identical with the Infantry pattern described below, except that it is fitted with a double set trigger mechanism.

1859 Cavalry Model carbine. Essentially similar mechanically with the Infantry pattern (q.v.), this 54-caliber Sharps has a patch box on the right side of the butt, a short forend retained by a single band, and a sling ring/bar assembly on the left side of the receiver. The guns are 39.15in long, have 22.05in barrels, and weigh 7.5lb.

1859 Sporting Model rifle. Guns of this type have 32in 54-caliber octagonal barrels, a checkered straight-wrist butt with a patch box, and a lipped half-length forend. The front sight is adjustable, and a double set trigger is standard. Overall length is 48.8in, weight being about 8.6lb.

1859 Infantry Model rifle. The basic model of the Pedersoli Sharps series has a plain straight-wrist butt with a patch box on the right side, and a full-length forend with three steel bands. Swivels lie beneath the butt and the middle band. A locking catch holds the underlever/trigger guard closed. The 54-caliber rifles are 46.85in long, have 29.9in blued barrels, and weigh 8.38lb.

1863 Cavalry Model carbine. This is simply an 1859-type carbine made without the patch box.

1863 Sporting Model rifle. Mechanically identical with the 1859 type, this also retains the straight checkered-wrist butt and the double trigger. However, it lacks the patch box.

CARTRIDGE GUNS

1874 Cavalry Model carbine. This is a 45-70 version of the 1863-pattern caplock carbine, with a plain sided butt. The barrel measures 22in.

1874 Civilian Model carbine. Identified by a 24in round barrel, giving an overall length of 41.15in and a weight of 8.15lb, this has a straight-wrist butt and a plain lipped forend. The barrel band which characterizes the military-style carbines is absent.

1874 Infantry model rifle. Identical with the 1859-pattern cap lock, but chambered for the 45-70 cartridge, this retains the long three-band forend and even the patch box on the butt side.

1874 Silhouette model rifle. Introduced in 1997 in 45-65 or 45-70, this has a 31.9in octagon barrel and a double trigger. The woodwork consists of a checkered pistol grip butt and a half-length lipped forend. Weight averages 8.6lb.

1874 Sporting Model rifle. A 45-65 version of the 1863-pattern Sporting Model cap lock, this is rifled with a special twist. It has a set trigger, a 32in round barrel, and a half-length lipped forend. The guns are about 48.8in long and weigh 8.6lb. A *Versione Lusso* offers grayed satin finish on the receiver, though the barrel is blued.

SPRINGFIELD-ALLIN RIFLE

Details of the background of these rifles will be found under 'U.S.A.: Springfield (-Allin)'. Pedersoli versions (introduced in 1997) are faithful recreations of the originals, but may be found with additional engraving.

THE GUNS

1873-model U.S. Army rifle. This is distinguished by a full-length straight-wrist stock with two sprung bands and a small steel nose cap. Swivels lie beneath the butt and the front band, and a cleaning rod is carried beneath the muzzle. Chambered for the

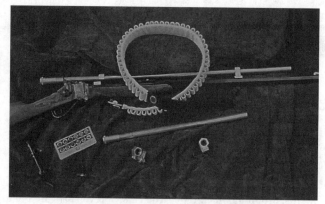

An 1874 Sporting Model Pedersoli Sharps
rifle with accessories and an optical sight.

45-70 cartridge, the rifle is 51.9in long, has a 32.6in barrel with three-groove rifling, and weighs 8.38lb. The rear sight is graduated to 500yd.

1873-model U.S. Cavalry carbine. A short version of the rifle, this has a half-length forend held by a single sprung band. It is 41.3in long, has a 21.95in barrel, weighs about 7lb, and has a 400yd rear sight.

1875-model Officer's Rifle. Easily distinguished by the checkered-wrist half-stock, with a single sprung band and a steel forend tip, this has a set trigger and a folding Creedmoor-type tang sight. The lock plate and hammer are color case-hardened. A full-length cleaning rod is carried in pipes beneath the 26in barrel. Overall length is 45.3in; weight is about 7.95lb.

• Perugini-Visini

This gunmaking business—trading in Gardone Val Trompia—made a selection of Mauser-pattern sporting rifles prior to 1985, basing most of them on refurbished military actions. There were also a number of Anson & Deeley-type box-lock single- or double-barreled rifles, sold under brand names such as Eagle, Express, Selous, Super Express and Victoria. The Express and Super Express were over/under designs, the others having their barrels side by side. As most of the Perugini-Visini rifles were built to order, they will be encountered in a wide range of chamberings and styles. They are, therefore, extremely difficult to catalogue.

• Pieri

Giacomo Pieri is best known for his thumb-trigger system, developed in the 1860s and protected in many countries in the mid 1870s; U.S. Patent 166,138 of 27th July 1875 is typical. Interestingly, this patent records Pieri as 'Jacques' and his residence as 'Ghisoni, Corsica'—which may suggest that he may have been born a French subject instead of an Italian. The patent was also rather strangely assigned to William Smith of London, though the prototype rifles were probably made in the Glisenti factory in Brescia. At least one Swiss Vetterli rifle was made with a thumb-trigger of this type, on the upper tang behind the bolt, and many other experiments were undertaken: a British Martini-Henry showing similar characteristics also survives. Pieri was granted a later U.S. Patent in April 1886 to protect a breech-loading rifle with a magazine, but no guns of this type are known.

• Pietta

Best known for a wide range of caplock revolvers, Fratelli Pietta also make a reproduction of the Smith carbine (q.v.), originally patented shortly before the American Civil War began.

SMITH BREECH-LOADING CARBINE
Made by Fratelli Pietta di Giuseppe & C. SNC, Gussago/Brescia.
Currently in production. **Chambering:** 50 combustible cartridge, fired by a cap lock. **Action:** locked by a spring-lever on top of the barrel engaging a stud in the frame.

39in overall, 7.72lb empty. 29.15in barrel, 4-groove rifling; RH, concentric? Single shot only. Leaf-and-slider rear sight graduated to 500yd. Performance not known. No bayonet.

This is a surprisingly faithful reproduction of the original break-open design (see 'U.S.A.: Smith, break-open action'). Pressing upward on a catch in the front of the trigger guard lifts the spring-lever to allow the barrel to drop down around a pivot in the lower front of the receiver or frame. The blued barrel is octagonal to the single band, then round to the muzzle. The 'Artillery Model' has swivels on the band and butt, whereas the 'Cavalry Model' has a ring-and-bar assembly on the left side of the color case-hardened receiver. The straight-wrist butt and half length forend are walnut.

• Rizzini (FAIR Techni-Mec)

This gunmaking business specializes in fine-quality over/under shotguns and combination guns, built on a dependable boxlock action. Double-barreled rifles are also being made.

SAFARI DOUBLE RIFLE
Made by FAIR Techni-Mec SNC di Isidoro Rizzini & C., Marcheno (Brescia).
Currently in production. **Chambering options:** 7x57R, 7x65R, 30-06, 8x57IRS, 9.3x74R or 444 Marlin. **Action:** locked by a bar in the action engaging two underlugs on the barrel block as the top lever closes.
DATA FOR A TYPICAL 'SAFARI STANDARD'
Chambering: 444 Marlin, rimmed. 46in overall, 6.65lb empty. 26.75in, 4-groove rifling; RH, concentric. Double-barreled, two shots only. Fixed open rear sight. 2400 fps with 240-grain bullet.

Built on the action of the FAIR 20-bore shotgun, the standard Safari rifle has a blued box-lock and a prominent rib between the barrels. A safety slider on the upper tang, automatic ejectors and a single trigger are customary. The rear sight is set into the front edge of a low quarter-rib. Checkering appears on the pistol grip of the straight-comb butt, and on the lipped forend; swivels lie under the butt and lower barrel.

SIMILAR GUNS

Safari Deluxe rifle. This can be distinguished by the quality of the woodwork, and by the Bavarian-style butt with a hog's back comb and a squared cheekpiece. A rubber buttplate replaces the standard synthetic type. Actions are usually finished black, often with engraved-line bordering.

Safari Prestige rifle. Essentially similar to the deluxe version, this has select walnut woodwork and side-plates on the action. The guns are extensively engraved with game scenes and scrollwork.

• SAB, bolt action type

Società Armi Bresciane Srl ('SAB') has marketed 'Linea Renato Gamba' firearms, including handguns, shotguns, combination guns, and bolt-action rifles.

RGZ 1000 GAME RIFLE
Made by Società Armi Bresciane SRL, Gardone Val Trompia.
Total production: not known. **Chambering options:** 270 Winchester, 7x64, 7mm Remington Magnum and 300 Winchester Magnum. **Action:** locked by two lugs on the bolt head engaging recesses behind the chamber as the bolt handle was turned down, and by the safety lug entering its seat.
DATA FOR A TYPICAL EXAMPLE
Chambering: 7x64, rimless. 42.4in overall, 7.7lb empty. 23.6in barrel, 4-groove rifling; RH, concentric. Internal box magazine, 5 rounds. Williams ramp-pattern rear sight. 2885 fps with 154-grain bullet.

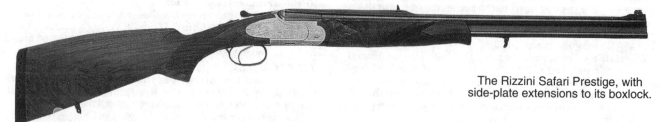

The Rizzini Safari Prestige, with
side-plate extensions to its boxlock.

The SAB/Gamba Prinz 498 rifle.

This sporter had a Mauser-pattern bolt with the bolt handle turned down against the stock and swept backward. A radial safety catch protruded from the stock behind the bolt handle. The Game rifle had an adjustable rear sight and a double set trigger; the walnut Monte Carlo-style half-stock—with checkering panels on the pistol grip and forend—had a contrasting rosewood schnabel tip and pistol grip cap. Swivels lay beneath the butt and forend, and the buttplate was usually a ventilated rubber design.

SIMILAR GUNS

RGZ 1000 Battue rifle. This had a 20.45in barrel, a fixed rear sight formed in the front edge of a quarter-rib, and a single direct-acting trigger.

• SAB, break-open type

MUSTANG SPORTING RIFLE

Made by Società Armi Bresciane SRL, Gardone Val Trompia.
Currently in production. **Chambering options:** 5.6x50R, 222 Remington Magnum, 6.5x57R, 270 Winchester, 7x65R or 30-06. **Action:** locked by a bar in the action engaging underlugs on the barrel block, and by a Greener-type crossbolt intercepting two lugs projecting from the breech face as the top lever closes.

DATA FOR A TYPICAL EXAMPLE

Chambering: 6.5x57R, rimmed. 42.5in overall, 6.15lb empty. 25.6in barrel, 4-groove rifling; RH, concentric. Single shot only. Fixed open rear sight. 2855 fps with 108-grain bullet.

The Mustang usually has a Holland & Holland-type sidelock, a double set trigger mechanism, and a distinctive barrel rib with bases for hook-in telescope sight mounts. The walnut butt has a straight comb, a Monte Carlo-type cheekpiece, a checkered pistol grip, and a ventilated rubber shoulder pad. The forend, which is also checkered, has a parrot-beak tip. Decoration comprises Renaissance-style vine-leaf engraving, in relief on a dark matted ground, though game scenes can be added on request. Special custom-made guns may have English 'Best Bouquet' engraving, scrollwork, or bordered game scenes.

SAFARI EXPRESS DOUBLE RIFLE

Made by Società Armi Bresciane SRL, Gardone Val Trompia.
Currently in production. **Chambering options:** 7x65R, 9.3x74R or 375 H&H Magnum. **Action:** generally as Mustang, above.
DATA FOR A TYPICAL EXAMPLE

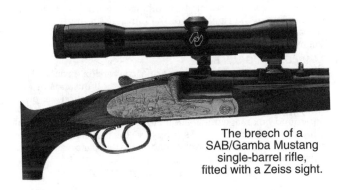

The breech of a SAB/Gamba Mustang single-barrel rifle, fitted with a Zeiss sight.

Chambering: 375 H&H Magnum. 41.8in overall, 9.9lb empty. 25in barrel, 4-groove rifling; RH, concentric. Double-barreled; two shots only. Fixed open rear sight. 2590 fps with 300-grain bullet.

This gun, usually built on an over/under boxlock action (though some sidelocks have apparently been made under the same designation), has a Bavarian-style pistol grip butt with a hog's back comb and a small rounded cheekpiece. The forend has a rounded tip.

Cocking-indicator blades lie alongside the top lever, a sliding safety appears on the upper tang, a double trigger is fitted, and the swivels are attached beneath the butt and the lower barrel. The 375 guns usually lack the otherwise-standard automatic ejectors. Coin-finish action bodies are usually engraved with foliate engraving and game scenes in relief, but other styles can be applied to order.

OTHER GUNS

Express Maxim rifle. Built on a sidelock action, this shares the stock design and engraving style of the over/under Express. Chamberings include 375 H&H Magnum, 416 Remington Magnum, 458 Winchester Magnum and 470 Nitro Express.

• Sabatti

Fabbrica Italiana Armi Sabatti SpA ('FIAS') of Gardone Val Trompia built the Carabina Rover 87 around a conventional modified Mauser action, a neat spatulate bolt handle, and an internal magazine with a detachable floorplate. The standard rifle offered a classic straight-comb stock, whereas the deluxe Rover 87DL had a Monte Carlo comb. Chamberings in the 22in barrel included 243 Winchester, 25-06, 7mm Remington Magnum, 270 Winchester, 300 Winchester Magnum, 30-06 or 308 Winchester.

Sabatti has also made—in addition to a wide range of box-lock shotguns—a selection of over/under double rifles under the designation 'Model 340 Express'. The standard pattern had a pistol grip butt with a hog's back comb, a small oval cheekpiece, a double trigger, and a rear sight set into a quarter-rib. The Model 340 Express EDL was very similar, but had a squared Bavarian-style cheekpiece and better engraving. Chamberings are believed to have included 270 Winchester, 30-06 and 9.3x74R, but information is still lacking.

• Scotti

Alfredo Scotti-Douglas built a number of experimental rifles in a small factory in Brescia, including a range of autoloaders. The Modelo X was the most successful. Produced in the 10th year of the Fascist era (1932), it was stocked in the fashion of the Mo. 1891 Mannlicher-Carcano infantry rifle and utilized the standard six-round clip.

The Scotti carbine, however, usually had a separate pistol grip behind the trigger, and the so-called 'naval anti-aircraft rifle' had a detachable box magazine. It also had a hand grip on the forend and a shotgun-style sighting rib to facilitate snap shooting. Quadrant rear sights were fitted to most Scotti long arms.

Scotti rifles relied on a blow from a short-stroke piston to rotate the bolt out of engagement, whereupon residual pressure in the chamber forced the spent cartridge case back with sufficient force to open the breech. The inventor also converted a few British P/14 rifles to operation of this type in 1938-9, but World War II intervened before progress could be made.

• Uberti

Best known as a maker of reproduction caplock and cartridge revolvers, Aldo Uberti & C. SAS is also the leading manufacturer of replica lever-action Henry and pre-1873 Winchester rifles. Additional details of the guns will be found under 'U.S.A.: Henry' and 'U.S.A.: Winchester, lever-action type'.

1860-PATTERN HENRY RIFLE

Recognizable by its brass frame and lack of a forend, this 44-40 has an octagonal barrel made integrally with the full-length magazine. The straight-wrist butt has a sturdy crescent-shape brass buttplate. Rifles of this type are typically 43.75in long, have 24.25in barrels and weigh about 9.25lb. A pivoting leaf-pattern rear sight is fitted on the barrel directly in front of the receiver. Guns have also been offered with modern gun blue, traditional charcoal blue, 'white' or chrome-plated finishes. Engraved versions have also been offered, including a '1 of 1000' design.

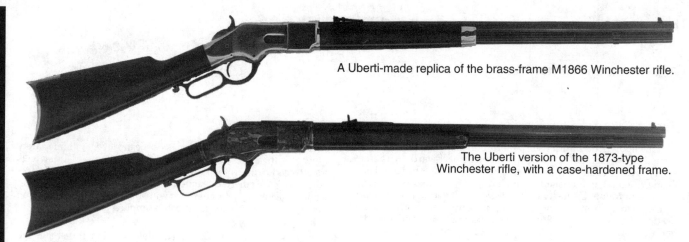

A Uberti-made replica of the brass-frame M1866 Winchester rifle.

The Uberti version of the 1873-type Winchester rifle, with a case-hardened frame.

SIMILAR GUNS

1860-pattern Henry carbine. A short version of the rifle, with a 22.25in barrel, this measures 41.75in overall and weighs about 9lb.

1860-pattern Henry Trapper carbine. This differed from the standard guns only in barrel length, which was merely 16in.

1866-PATTERN WINCHESTER SPORTING RIFLE
Also known as '1866 Yellow Boy'

Based on the Henry, the earliest lever-action Winchester had a loading gate on the right side of its brass frame and a short wooden forend. The Uberti replica shares these features, together with a brass forend tip. The 24.25in octagonal barrel is accompanied by a separate full-length magazine tube. Offered in 22LR rimfire, 22 Winchester Magnum rimfire, 38 Special or 44-40, the guns are 43.75in long and weigh about 8.15lb empty.

SIMILAR GUNS

1866-pattern Winchester carbine. Similar to the full-length rifle, this has a 19in round barrel and a plain-tipped forend with a single barrel band. The front sight is combined with a small nose band around the barrel and magazine tube. A sling ring is attached to the left side of the receiver beneath the hammer. The guns are 38.3in long and weigh about 7.38lb.

1866-pattern Winchester Indian Carbine. Identical mechanically with the standard carbine, this is distinguished by etched decoration on the receiver sides—incorporating a portrait of Red Cloud—and optional brass tacks on the butt and forend.

1866-pattern Winchester Indian Rifle. This is simply a version of the Sporting Rifle with the etched 'Red Cloud' receiver and optional brass-tack decoration.

1866-pattern Winchester Trapper carbine. Mechanically identical with the standard carbine, this was made with a 16in barrel.

1873-PATTERN WINCHESTER SPORTING RIFLE

Originally derived from the 1866 model, this was notable for its iron frame—color case-hardened steel in most facsimiles. The forend has a blued steel tip, and the leaf-pattern rear sight has been replaced with a spring-leaf and elevator pattern. Chamberings are 22LR rimfire, 22 Winchester Magnum rimfire (both discontinued in 1991), 38 Special, 44-40 and 45 Long Colt (added in 1992); the Uberti M1873 was originally restricted to a 24.25in octagonal barrel, though 20in and 30in 44-40 options were added in 1990. The standard barrel gave an overall length of about 43.3in and a weight averaging 8.2lb. A variety of finishes has been offered, together with a '1 of 1000' pattern.

SIMILAR GUNS

1873-pattern Winchester carbine. Distinguished by a 19in tapered round barrel and a short plain-tipped forend held by a single barrel band, this also has a sling ring on the left side of the receiver. A leaf-type rear sight is fitted, and the front sight lies immediately behind the muzzle band. Overall length is about 38.3in, weight being about 7.4lb.

• Vetterli

The unification of Italy created standardization problems in ordnance circles. Rigorous trials undertaken in 1868-9 subsequently convinced the Italians of the merits of the Swiss Vetterli breech, but not of the tube magazine. Italy had a larger army than Switzerland and the cost of re-arming with magazine rifles was prohibitive. Italian weapons, therefore, were originally single-loaders.

MODEL 1870 RIFLE
Fucile di Fanteria Mo. 1870

Made by the Fabbrica d'Armi Pietro Beretta, Gardone Val Trompia; by the royal manufactories in Torino (Turin) and Torre Annunziata; and by the Officina Costruzione d'Artiglieria, Rome.

Total production: not known. **Chambering:** 10.35x47, rimmed. **Action:** locked by two lugs on the bolt body engaging recesses in the receiver behind the elevator well as the bolt handle was turned down.

52.95in overall, 9.08lb empty. 33.85in barrel, 4-groove rifling; RH, concentric. Single-shot only. Quadrant sight graduated to 1000m (1095yd). 1410 fps with Mo. 1870 ball cartridges. Mo. 1870 sword bayonet.

The standard infantry rifle was easily distinguished from the Swiss M1869 (q.v.) by the lack of a magazine, and by the slender stock ending well short of the muzzle. The Italian gun had a safety catch on the right side of the breech behind the bolt handle, and a rotating ejection port cover with a knurled-head button. It also had a spurred trigger guard, two screw-clamping barrel bands, and a small nose cap. The mounts were all made of iron. A lug for the bayonet lay on the right side of the muzzle. An improved Vecchi-pattern quadrant sight was adopted in 1881, graduated to 1200m.

SIMILAR GUNS

Model 1870-87 rifle. A magazine conversion proposed by Giuseppe Vitali was approved in 1887, many thousands of Mo. 1870 rifles being converted in 1888-95. Though the action was practically unchanged, a new floorplate supported a detachable four-round box magazine loaded either singly or from a special stripper clip. A central spiral spring gave the magazine its unique appearance, and a support rail was added to the rear of the receiver to prevent the bolt rocking when open.

The standard M1870 Vetterli infantry rifle.

The 10.35mm M1870/87 Vetterli-Vitali rifle. Note the magazine and the bolt-support rail.

The M1870/87/16 rifle, a 6.5mm-caliber conversion of the Vetterli-Vitali.

The introduction in 1890 of cartridges loaded with smokeless propellant, generating a muzzle velocity of 2000 fps, permitted the rear sights to be graduated to 1600m (1750yd). Surviving guns were converted to 6.5mm from 1916 onward.

Substantial numbers of obsolescent Mo. 70/87 rifles were sold in 1912 to the Ulster Volunteer Force, an ultra-Conservative paramilitary force raised in Northern Ireland to fight—if necessary—against Home Rule. The guns were apparently military surplus bought in Germany, perhaps from Benny Spiro or A.L. Frank of Hamburg. In addition to original Italian ordnance marks, they often bore 'FOR GOD AND ULSTER', or 'U.V.F.' and the Red Hand of the O'Neill family on a shield (taken from the Provincial Arms).

MODEL 1870 TS SHORT RIFLE
Moschetto per Truppe Speciali Mo. 1870
Manufacturers: as Mo. 1870 rifle (q.v.).
Total production: not known. **Chambering:** 10.47x35, rimmed. **Action:** as Mo. 1870 rifle, above.
43.1in overall, 9.3lb empty. 24in barrel, 4-groove rifling; RH, concentric. Quadrant sight graduated to 500m (545yd). 1345 fps with Mo. 1870 ball cartridges. Mo. 1870 TS épée bayonet.

This 1872-vintage firearm, a shortened version of the infantry rifle, was intended for special-service units (*Truppe Speciali*). It had a short barrel, a single barrel band, and a plain trigger-guard bow. The bayonet had a distinctive two-edged blade with a central rib. Post-1881 guns were fitted with a Vecchi rear sight graduated to 1000m (1095yd); older weapons were adapted when returning for repair.

SIMILAR GUNS
Model 1870/87 TS short rifle. A decision was taken in 1887 to fit surviving guns with four-round Vitali box magazines ('Mo. 1870/87'), work being undertaken over a period of several years, and the introduction in 1890 of cartridges loaded with smokeless propellant allowed sights to be graduated to 1400m (1530yd). Some Mo. 1870/87 TS short rifles were subsequently converted to accept 6.5mm ammunition during World War I.

MODEL 1870 CAVALRY CARBINE
Moschetto Mo. 1870
Manufacturers: as Mo. 1870 rifle (q.v.).
Total production: not known. **Chambering:** 10.47x35, rimmed. **Action:** as Mo. 1870 rifle, above.
36.55in overall, 7.78lb with bayonet. 17.7in barrel, 4-groove rifling; RH, concentric. Quadrant sight graduated to 500m (545yd). 1230 fps with M1870 ball cartridges. Mo. 1870 socket bayonet.

Adopted for the cavalry in 1872, this was little more than a rifle action in a short half-stock. The trigger guard had a plain bow, and the nose cap (which carried the front sling swivel) had a cranked appearance. The long-bladed bayonet, which locked round the front sight, could be reversed when not required; half the blade ran back inside the forend, a half-length cleaning rod being carried in a butt trap. An improved Vecchi-pattern rear sight was approved in 1881, extending the sight-range to 1000m (1095yd).

SIMILAR GUNS
Model 1870 gendarmerie carbine. A longer version of the cavalry weapon, this was adopted for the Carabineri in 1875. It shared the same general characteristics, but was the same length as the Mo. 1870 TS (q.v.) and weighed about 9lb with its socket bayonet.

Model 1870/87 carbine. Surviving 1870-pattern carbines were adapted for the four-round Vitali box magazine from 1890 onward, when the approval of ammunition loaded with smokeless propellant allowed the sights on the Carabineri guns to be altered to 1400m (1530yd). Though contemporary Italian manuals also show the short-barrel cavalry carbine with these extended sights, none could be traced for inspection. Survivors were converted during World War I for the 6.5mm cartridge.

MODEL 1882 NAVY RIFLE
Fucile di Marina Mo. 1882
Made by the Fabbrica d'Armi, Terni?
Total production: a few thousand. **Chambering:** 10.35x47, rimmed.
Action: as Mo. 1870 rifle, above.
47.65in overall, 8.93lb empty. 28.75in barrel, 4-groove rifling; RH, concentric. Tube magazine under barrel, 8 rounds. Quadrant sight graduated to 1400m (1530yd). 1310 fps with Mo. 1870 ball cartridges. Mo. 1870 sword bayonet.

This gun was adopted only by the Italian navy, principally for the use of the marine infantry. It was basically a standard Mo. 70 rifle with a tube magazine beneath the barrel, giving the forend a massive appearance. Unlike the Swiss guns, which had a separate loading port on the right side of the receiver, the Mo. 82 magazine loaded through the top of the open action.

Often known as the 'Vetterli-Bertoldo'—apparently honoring the president of the navy trials board—these guns had a plain stock, two sprung barrel bands and an exposed muzzle carrying a bayonet lug. Swivels lay on the underside of the butt and the rear barrel band, while the cleaning rod was carried in a channel cut into the left side of the forend.

A few surviving Vetterli-Bertoldo rifles were adapted in 1890 for the four-round Ferraciú box magazine, apparently for trials. An elongated triangular casing was fitted beneath the bolt way, relying on a spring-loaded lifter arm to raise the cartridges. Though the balance of the rifle improved perceptibly, improvements were purely temporary; Vetterli rifles were soon replaced in navy service by the Mo. 1891 Mannlicher-Carcano.

MODEL 1870-87-15 RIFLE
Fucile di Fanteria Mo. 1870/87/15
Believed to have been converted in the Terni arsenal, and possibly also by gunsmiths in the Gardone area.
Total production: not known. **Chambering:** 6.5x52, rimless. **Action:** as Mo. 1870 rifle, above.
52.95in overall, 10.19lb empty. 33.85in barrel, 4-groove rifling; RH, concentric. Fixed clip-loaded box magazine, 6 rounds. Quadrant sight graduated to 2000m (2185yd). 2395 fps with Mo. 1891/95 ball cartridges. Mo. 1870/15 sword bayonet.

Conversion of obsolescent Mo. 1870/87 Vetterli-Vitali rifles was authorized in 1916, partly to offset losses of M1891 (Mannlicher-Carcano) guns and partly to arm newly-raised units. The work consisted of boring out the original barrel, inserting a rifled liner, changing the sights, and substituting a Mannlicher magazine for the old Vitali box type.

Owing to the position of the locking lugs, the Vetterli breech was only just strong enough to withstand the pressures generated by the 6.5mm cartridge. Consequently, the rifles were relegated to artillery, lines-of-communication and militia units wherever possible. However, some served colonial infantrymen in North Africa until the last of the Italian forces capitulated in 1941.

SIMILAR GUNS

Carbines and short rifles. Mo. 1870/87 TS musketoons, Mo. 1870/87 cavalry carbines and Mo. 1870/87 Carabinieri carbines (the last named only in minuscule numbers) were all adapted for the 6.5mm cartridge. Their history parallels that of the rifles, but most were discarded after 1918.

• Zanardini

Armi Zanardini of Brescia has made a wide range of shotguns, combination guns and double-barreled rifles. Though chambering details are lacking, these rifles are known to have included a selection of side-by-side patterns—the Express boxlock, and the sidelock Bristol and Oxford—as well as the Koenig over/under boxlock.

• Zoli (Angelo)

Prior to the demise of his business in 1987, this gunmaker made the 'Leopard Express' boxlock double rifle in 7x65R, 30-06, 308 Winchester and 375 H&H Magnum. The guns had double triggers and straight-comb walnut butts with checkered pistol grips.

• Zoli (Antonio), bolt-action type

Founded in 1945, this gunmaking business is renowned for a variety of shotguns and combination rifles. However, though Zoli offers the 'Slug' (a smooth-bore adapted to fire 12-bore slugs) and some Double Rifles, effort is concentrated on a bolt-action rifle embodying a Husqvarna-designed 'modified Mauser' action with twin opposed lugs on the bolt head, a guide rib made integrally with one of the locking lugs, a bolt-mounted plunger-type ejector and a recessed bolt-face.

AZ 1900 SPORTING RIFLE

Made by Antonio Zoli SpA, Gardone Val Trompia.
Currently in production. **Chambering options:** 243 Winchester, 6.5x55mm, 6.5x57mm, 270 Wheaton, 270 Winchester, 7mm Remington Magnum, 30-06, 300 Winchester Magnum, 308 Winchester, 338 Winchester Magnum or 9.3x62. **Action:** locked by two lugs on the bolt head rotating into the receiver wall as the bolt is turned down, and by the bolt handle base entering its seat.

DATA FOR A TYPICAL EXAMPLE

Chambering: 270 Wheaton, rimless. 46.5in overall, 7.75lb empty. 25.6in barrel, 4-groove rifling; RH, concentric. Detachable box magazine, 4 rounds. Folding leaf rear sight. 3000 fps with 150-grain bullet.

Introduced in 1989, the AZ 1900 has a neatly contoured bolt shroud and a radial-lever safety catch on the right side of the action behind the bolt handle. The safety locks the machine-jeweled bolt and firing pin, though a catch protruding from the right side of the stock alongside the receiver bridge can release the bolt to allow the chamber to be cleared. The magazine floor-plate is held by a catch set into the front of the trigger guard. Standard barrel lengths were originally 20.85in and 23.6in, but the shorter is now confined to the Battue versions. The walnut half stock has a Monte Carlo-type comb and cheekpiece, with checkered panels on the pistol grip and the rounded forend. Swivels lie under the forend and the butt. Left-hand actions and set-trigger guns are also made in small numbers.

SIMILAR GUNS

Note: though a distinction has often been drawn between the standard and magnum chamberings, Zoli currently lists all of them under a single heading.

AZ 1900 Anniversary rifle. Made in 1995 to celebrate Zoli's 50th anniversary, this had a select walnut Monte Carlo-style half stock with a rosewood pistol grip cap and forend tip. A silver trademark medallion was set into the pistol grip cap, with a gold version behind the cocking-piece shroud. The left side of the receiver displayed *50th Anniversary 1945-1995 Antonio Zoli* in gold-inlaid script.

AZ 1900 Battue rifle. Available in right- or left-hand versions, distinguished by a ventilated quarter-rib above the barrel (carrying the rear sight), this also has a short barrel.

AZ 1900 carbine (or '1900C'). This designation has been applied to the short-barrel (20.85in) version of the standard rifle, but does not have official sanction.

AZ 1900 Lux rifle (or '1900DL'). This deluxe version offers a select walnut—but otherwise standard—stock and etched decoration on the bright-finished action.

AZ 1900 Lux Battue rifle. Combining the quarter-rib sighting system, the deluxe stock and an etched action, this is intended for snap shooting.

AZ 1900M rifle. Dating from 1991, this featured a Bell & Carlson stock composed of graphite, kevlar and carbon fiber with baked-on woodgrain finish and moulded checkering. Chamberings were restricted to 243 Winchester, 6.5x55, 270 Winchester, 30-06 and 308 Winchester, barrel-length being 20.85in.

AZ 1900M Lux. The deluxe version of the synthetic-stock rifle had etched decoration on the action., but was mechanically identical to the standard guns.

AZ 1900 Stutzen. Identifiable by its full-length 'Mannlicher-style' stock, made of a single piece of walnut, with a Monte Carlo-style butt and a schnabel-tip forend. The barrel is attached to the stock by a special three-point system, which includes an elastic bush doubling as the front swivel mount.

AZ 1900 Stutzen Battue. The ventilated quarter-rib, carrying the rear sight, distinguishes this from the standard full-stock Zoli sporter.

AZ 1900 Stutzen Lux (or '1900SDL'). The deluxe pattern can be distinguished from the standard pattern by the stock, made of a better grade of walnut, and by the engraving on the receiver.

AZ 1900 Super Lux rifle. Readily identifiable by the select walnut stock, which has a rosewood forend tip and a silvered trademark medallion set into the rosewood pistol grip cap, this also has skip-line checkering. The action is customarily engraved with oak leaf or game scene motifs.

• Zoli (Antonio), break-open type

EXPRESS DOUBLE RIFLE

This is a box-lock over/under pattern with a straight-comb butt with a checkered pistol grip and a rounded cheekpiece. The forend, which is also checkered, has a rounded tip. Double triggers are fitted, embodying a setting mechanism for the lower barrel. Chamberings have included 7x57, 7x65R, 30-06, 308 Winchester and 9.3x74R, extraction being manual. Barrel length was usually 25.6in.

SIMILAR GUNS

Express E rifle. This is simply the auto-ejecting version of the standard non-ejecting pattern.

The Zoli AZ1900 rifle.

The Zoli 'Savana E' side-by-side Double Rifle.

Express EM rifle. This has a single trigger system and was customarily fitted with automatic ejectors. It has been made in all the Express chamberings except 7x57.

SAVANA EXPRESS RIFLE

Apparently discontinued in the early 1990s, this box-lock side-by-side non ejector was chambered for the 7x65R, 30-06, 308 and 9.3x74R cartridges. It had a pistol grip butt with a slight hog's back comb, checkering on the pistol grip, and a Monte Carlo-type cheekpiece. The forend—which was also checkered—had a slender rounded tip.

SIMILAR GUNS

Savana E rifle. This was the auto-ejecting form of the standard gun.

Savana L rifle ('Lux'). This was a deluxe version of the basic gun, with better-quality Bavarian-style woodwork with a squared cheekpiece and a low hog's back comb. The action body was decorated with foliate engraving.

Savana Trophy. Intended for game hunting, this was chambered only for the 375 H&H Magnum cartridge. It had a 25.6in barrel and weighed 8.8-9lb.

JAPAN

Prior to 1930, Japanese service weapons were designated according to the reign period (nengo) of each emperor reckoned from the restoration of 1868; thus, 1890 was the '23rd Year' of Emperor Meiji's reign. The system was maintained through the Taisho period (1912-26) and into the Showa era before being replaced by a calendar based on the mythical foundation of Japan in 660 BC. After 1929, therefore, terms such as 'Type 94' were used, 1934 being '2594' reckoned by the absolute calendar.

Receivers of pre-1945 Japanese small-arms displayed an imperial chrysanthemum and a mixture of pictographs derived from Chinese (kanji) and a phonetic alphabet used to assimilate foreign words into Japanese (katakana). Marks on a rifle read '38 Year Type'. Chrysanthemums were often defaced on guns due for surrender, to avoid shaming the emperor and thus reflecting badly on the patriotism of the soldier.

By about 1932, when the serial numbers of Meiji 38th Year rifles had exceeded two million, a cyclical numbering system was adopted. Individual blocks (1-99999) were identified by small encircled katakana prefixes, the sequence being taken from the traditional poem Iroha. Numerical values can be given to these symbols, but they should be regarded as letter-groups.

Arsenal identification marks were arbitrary; Tokyo and Kokura used a pile of cannon balls, while Nagoya had two stylized fighting fish. The principal navy mark was a large anchor.

• Arisaka

This sturdy turning-bolt action was designed and developed in Japan. The British, Chinese, Indonesian, Korean, Russian and Thai guns are described separately; Finnish guns were taken from the Russians, while those used in Burma came from the Japanese.

When the Japanese became embroiled in war with China in 1894, they encountered the German Gew. 88 ('Reichsgewehr', q.v.) in combat. This showed that tube-magazine repeaters such as the Murata were less efficient than those with clip-loaded box magazines. A committee chaired by Colonel Nariake Arisaka was appointed to develop a new rifle, soon concluding that the Mauser action was preferable.

The perfected Meiji 38th Year Type rifle was distinguished by good-quality workmanship and excellent material. Except rifles made toward the end of World War II, which were often very poor, the Arisaka action was exceptionally strong and durable. It relied on a Mauser twin-lug lock, and had a Mauser-type trigger. However, the reciprocating bolt cover and distinctive method of stocking were uniquely Japanese.

MODEL 1896 TRIALS RIFLE
Meiji 29th Year Type
Made by the Imperial artillery arsenal, Koishikawa, Tokyo, 1896-7.
Total production: not known. **Chambering:** 6.5x50, semi-rimmed.
Action: locked by two lugs on the bolt head engaging recesses in the receiver when the bolt handle was turned down, and by the base of the handle engaging its slot.

50.05in overall, 9lb empty. 31in barrel, 4-groove rifling; RH, polygonal. Internal box magazine loaded with a stripper clip, 5 rounds. Leaf sight graduated to 2000m (2185yd). About 2495 fps with ball cartridges. Bayonet: not known.

Made between July 1896 and April 1897, these guns had a modified Mauser action, chambered a 6.5mm semi-rim cartridge, and had a most distinctive safety hook protruding from the cocking piece. Trials rifles lacked a handguard.

MODEL 1897 RIFLE
Meiji 30th Year Type
Made by the Imperial artillery arsenal, Koishikawa, Tokyo, 1899-1907.
Total production: at least 550,000. **Chambering:** 6.5x50, semi-rimmed.
Action: as 29th Year Type rifle, above.
DATA FOR RIFLE

50.15in overall, 8.85lb empty. 31.05in barrel, 4- or 6-groove rifling; RH, polygonal. Internal box magazine loaded with a stripper clip, 5 rounds. Leaf sight graduated to 2000m (2185yd). 2540 fps with Meiji 30th Year Type ball cartridges. Meiji 30th Year Type sword bayonet.

Trials indicated that the experimental 29th Year Type rifle could be improved, the perfected version being adopted in February 1899. The resulting 30th Year Type had a stock with a shallow pistol grip, a single spring-retained barrel band, and a plain nose cap carrying a bayonet lug on its underside.

A grasping groove was cut into the forend and a handguard ran from the front of the rear sight base to the barrel band. The swivels lay beneath the butt and band. The receiver had a distinctive bridge with an angular slot into which the bolt handle locked; a prominent hook on the bolt plug acted as a safety catch.

In 1900, the tangs of the receiver and trigger guard were extended to reinforce the stock wrist. Most early guns were made with one-piece stocks, but an increasing shortage of suitable blanks led to development of a two-piece butt with a separate toe pinned and glued in place.

SIMILAR GUNS

Model 1897 carbine. A cavalry carbine was produced simply by shortening the standard rifle, omitting the handguard and substituting a smaller rear sight graduated to 1500m (1640yd). It was 37.85in overall; had an 18.9in barrel with six-groove polygonal rifling; weighed 7.47lb empty; and was mechanically identical with the standard rifle. It also accepted the same bayonet. At least 40,000 guns of this type were made.

Most of the original back-sight leaves were adapted after 1905 for the 38th Year ball cartridge, which had a heavier bullet than the 30th Year pattern. New leaves could be identified by the 2000m

The Meiji 30th Year Type rifle, 1897. (HBL)

The 6.5mm Meiji 38th Year Type rifle, 1905.

setting, which was a 'V'-notch cut in the upper edge. Carbine sights do not seem to have been altered.

MODEL 1902 RIFLE
Meiji 35th Year Type

Made by the Imperial artillery arsenal, Koishikawa, Tokyo, about 1903-6. Total production: 35,000? **Chambering:** 6.5x50, semi-rimmed. **Action:** as 29th Year Type rifle, above. 50.2in overall, 8.97lb empty.

31.1in barrel, 6-groove rifling; RH, polygonal. Internal box magazine loaded with a stripper clip, 5 rounds. Tangent-leaf sight graduated to 2000m (2185yd). 2540 fps with Meiji 30th Type ball cartridges. Meiji 35th Type sword bayonet.

As the 30th Year system proved a disappointment – even though at least 600,000 guns had been made by 1905 – this improved rifle was accepted in February 1902. It had an enlarged cocking piece; a new gas port on the bolt; an enlarged bolt knob; a better bolt head; an improved feed ramp; a sliding spring-loaded breech cover; a tangent rear sight; and a handguard extending back to the receiver ring.

Now widely regarded as naval issue, the gun may have been intended to substitute for the 1897 pattern until the Russo-Japanese War proved that more radical changes were required. If so, then 1902-pattern rifles would have been issued to the navy only after the army had received the first of the perfected Meiji 38th Year Type rifles. Confirmation from Japanese sources is still lacking, however.

MODEL 1905 RIFLE
Meiji 38th Year Type

Made by the Imperial artillery arsenal, Koishikawa, Tokyo, 1907-32; by the Imperial army arsenal, Kokura, 1932-3; by the Imperial army arsenal, Nagoya, 1933-41; by Heijo ordnance factory (Jinsen arsenal), Korea, about 1938-9; by Mukden arsenal, Manchuria, 1940-4; by Nanking and Tientsin arsenals, North China, about 1944 (mostly from sub-contracted parts).

Total production: at least three million. **Chambering:** 6.5x50, semi-rimmed. **Action:** locked by two lugs on the bolt head engaging recesses in the receiver as the bolt turns down, and by the base of the bolt handle entering its seat in the receiver.

50.2in overall, 9.08lb empty. 31.45in barrel, 4- or 6-groove rifling; RH, polygonal. Internal box magazine loaded with a stripper clip, 5 rounds. Leaf sight graduated to 2400m (2625yd). 2495 fps with Meiji 38th Year Type ball cartridges. Meiji 30th Year Type or Type 97 sword bayonets.

Experience in the Russo-Japanese War (1904-5) revealed shortcomings in the standard Meiji 30th Year Type rifle, including the bolt-mounted extractor/ejector system, the separate bolt head, and jamming by dust and mud.

By mid May 1906, a modified rifle had been developed with a simplified bolt, a non-rotating extractor, a reciprocating bolt cover and a large knurled safety shroud on the cocking piece. It was accepted immediately.

Production in Koishikawa continued until numbers in the original cumulative sequence exceeded 2,031,000. Work then recommenced at *i-1*, equivalent to number 2,000,000, with a simplified notch safety head replacing the previous lug pattern in the *mu* series. Nagoya's first series had *no* prefix characters, production running to the *ku* series, a sheet-metal buttplate being substituted for the earlier forged type.

SIMILAR GUNS

Type 97 sniper rifle. The perfected sniping weapon was adopted in 1937 after trials that had lasted more than a decade. The bolt handle was lengthened and bent downward; a monopod was added beneath the forend; and an optical-sight mount on the left side of the receiver was pegged and screwed in place. About

19,500 guns were assembled in Kokura (5500 in 1938-9) and Nagoya (14,000 in 1938-41). They weighed about 11.25lb.

The 2.5x Type 97 sight was held in a baseplate dovetail by a radial latch. Mounting the sight on the left side of the gun facilitated use of a stripper clip, but made the gun-and-sight combination awkward to use. A rotary sleeve on the telescope body controlled elevation, though the sniper relied on a comparatively complicated graticule to estimate deflection.

Shortened guns. Alteration of full-length 38th Year Type rifles was sanctioned in 1941 to offset shortages of 7.7mm short rifles. The barrel was cut to about 640mm, increasing handiness but sharpening muzzle blast. District inspectors' stamps on the butt identified the converter as Nagoya arsenal.

MODEL 1905 CARBINE
Meiji 38th Year Type

Made by the Imperial artillery arsenal, Koishikawa, Tokyo, 1907-32 (about 235,000); by the Imperial army arsenal, Nagoya, 1933-9 (25,000?); and by Mukden arsenal, Manchuria (a few thousands?).

Total production: 270,000 or more. **Chambering:** 6.5x50, semi-rimmed. **Action:** as M1905 rifle, above.

37.9in overall, 7.38lb empty. 19.15in barrel, 4- or 6-groove rifling; RH, polygonal. Internal box magazine loaded with a stripper clip, 5 rounds. Leaf sight graduated to 2000m (2185yd). 2395 fps with Meiji 38th Year Type ball cartridges. Bayonet: as comparable rifle.

This was adopted in 1907 for issue to cavalry, until the advent in 1911 of the Meiji 44th Year Type (q.v.). Production of the original design then continued for artillerymen and ancillary units.

About 215,000 were made in Tokyo prior to the change to pre-fixed numbers, two blocks following before production transferred to Nagoya and probably ultimately to Mukden. Apart from its reduced dimensions, the 1905 pattern carbine was essentially similar to the infantry rifle, with a handguard running from the front of the rear sight base to the nose cap.

MODEL 1911 CAVALRY CARBINE
Meiji 44th Year Type

Made by the Imperial artillery arsenal, Koishikawa, Tokyo, 1912-37; by the Imperial army arsenal, Nagoya, about 1933-8; and by Mukden arsenal, Manchuria, about 1939-42.

Production total: not known. **Chambering:** 6.5x50mm, semi-rimmed. Otherwise as 1905-type carbine except dimensions (38in long, 8.95lb empty) and bayonet (integral folding pattern).

This cavalry carbine, adopted in 1911, superseded the 1905 pattern (q.v.). It had a unique folding bayonet attached to the nose cap. Originally confined exclusively to Koishikawa, work was eventually transferred to Nagoya.

The earliest bayonet mounting block was very short, with the two lateral retaining bolts close together; the uncommon second pattern, dating from the mid 1920s, was greatly extended rearward and had a quillon on the right side of the muzzle block; the third was similar, but the rear bolt, moved back even farther, lay on a hemispherical extension of the sideplate. There were also two differing patterns of cleaning rod chamber in the butt, the later type containing a sheet-steel liner.

MODEL 1939 RIFLE

Made by the Toriimatsu factory of the Imperial army arsenal, Nagoya, 1940-5; by Dai-Nippon Heiki Kogyo, Notobe, about 1940-2; by Kayaba Kogyo, Tokyo, about 1940-2; by the Imperial army arsenal, Kokura, 1940-5; by Toyo Juki, Hiroshima, 1941-5; by Tokyo Juki, Tokyo, about 1943-4; and by Jinsen arsenal, Korea, about 1942-5 (all types).

Total production: at least 3.5 million. **Chambering:** 7.7x58, rimless. **Action:** as M1905 rifle, above.

The Meiji 44th Year Type cavalry carbine, 1911. Note the folding bayonet.

The 7.7mm Type 99 rifle, 1939.

The Type 99 sniping rifle.

DATA FOR TYPE 99 SHORT RIFLE

45.25in overall, 8.37lb empty. 25.85in barrel, 4-groove rifling; RH, polygonal. Internal box magazine loaded with a stripper clip, 5 rounds. Leaf sight graduated to 1500m (1640yd). 2395 fps with Type 99 ball cartridges. Type 99 sword bayonet.

The 38th Year rifle remained the standard infantry weapon until combat experience in the Sino-Japanese war, against troops armed with 7.9mm-caliber rifles, emphasized the poor long range performance of the Japanese 6.5mm rifle cartridge.

Kokura arsenal subsequently modified 300 guns for an experimental 7.7mm semi-rimmed round. Tests at Futsu proving ground showed the conversion to be effective, allowing specifications for a new rifle to be finalized in April. Two rifles based on the standard 38th Year Type were then tested against modified 38th Year and 44th Year Type carbines.

As the carbines had an unacceptably severe muzzle blast and Kokura's simplified breech action failed its endurance tests, the Nagoya 'Rifle Plan No. 1' was developed into the long Type 99 rifle by May 1939.

SIMILAR GUNS

Type 99 long rifle. A few thousand of these, without prefixed numbers, were made in the Toriimatsu factory. They were judged too clumsy and replaced by the shortened pattern; 50in overall, the long rifles had 31.15in barrels and weighed about 9.15lb. The rear sight was graduated to 1700m (1860yd).

Type 99 short rifle. Rejection of the long rifle in 1940 in favor of a shortened pattern, removing the need for separate carbines, allowed production to be undertaken in several factories simultaneously. As this was long before any major military reverses had been suffered, quality was good. For example, the Type 99 short rifles made in the Toriimatsu factory under Nagoya arsenal supervision showed all the regular production features – including the anti-aircaft lead bars on the rear sight – for at least six number blocks.

Type 99 sniper rifle. Introduced in 1942, this retained the basic features of the preceding Type 97, including the mount, bolt and monopod. The earliest Kokura-assembled guns featured 2.5x sights, but the 10,000 or so Nagoya-made guns used the improved 4x Type 2. Apart from a few Type 4 sights made toward the end of the war, with adjusting bolts in the front mounting ring, Japanese patterns lacked external adjustments.

Type 99 substitute. Attempts to conserve raw material led in 1943 to the Substitute Type 99, also known as 'Type 99 Model 2' or 'Type 3' rifle. This was characterized by use of low grade steel, omission of bolt cover and sling swivels, and the deletion of chrome from the boltface and the bore. Nagoya-made guns, for example, soon exhibited a two-screw nose cap; the bolt knob became cylindrical; the rear sight ultimately became a fixed block; the grasping groove in the forend was eliminated, and the buttplate changed from metal to wood. Solid barrel bands and welded safety shrouds appeared toward the end of 1944. The last guns were truly awful; that they worked at all was a tribute to the exceptional strength of the action.

PARATROOP RIFLES

All data for Type 2

Made by the Imperial army arsenal, Nagoya, 1943-4.
Total production: see text. Chambering: 7.7x58, rimless. Action: as M1905 rifle, above.

45.3in overall, 8.93lb empty. 24.4in barrel, 4-groove rifling; RH, polygonal. Internal box magazine loaded from a stripper clip, 5 rounds. Leaf sight graduated to 2400m (2625yd). 2370 fps with Type 99 ball cartridges. Type 99 sword bayonet.

The Japanese were very slow to develop efficient submachine guns. Consequently, the paratroops had to rely on comparatively clumsy infantry rifles until the 1st Army Technical Research Institute developed the Type 0 (or 'Type 100') rifle in 1940.

SIMILAR GUNS

Type 0. This incorporated an interrupted-thread joint between the barrel and receiver to allow rapid dismantling into two major components. Nagoya arsenal converted 500 standard Type 99 short rifles to permit field trials.

Type 1. Dating from 1941, this was no more than a 38th Year Type carbine with a folding butt. It was developed to safeguard against the failure of the interrupted-screw system. Surviving guns were pressed into service at the end of the war.

Type 2. As the interrupted-thread lock of the Type 0 proved to be inefficient, so a sliding wedge was substituted in October 1942. This gun, the Type 2, was standardized in May 1943; production of 25,000 began immediately. The omission of a monopod and the rough surface finish betrayed late-war origins.

TRAINING RIFLES

Prior to 1942, the Japanese made reduced-scale 38th Year Type rifles to train juvenile cadets. Except smooth-bored 38th Year and Type 99 rifles, the trainers had a simplified receiver with integrally-cast tangs and a detachable smooth-bore barrel. Niggardly proportioned one-piece stocks were ideally suited to rejected

The Type 2 Paratroop rifle, 1942.

wood blanks. However, as pressures generated by regular ball ammunition would have wrecked training rifles, 'for blank ammunition only' was usually marked on receiver or butt in Japanese ideographs.

EMERGENCY RIFLES

Late in 1944, when the quality of rifle production had declined appreciably, emergency weapons were produced. The most effectual combined old 1902-pattern actions with barrels originally destined for training rifles. These '35th Year Type Substitute Rifles' could be recognized by the design of the rear sight (graduated to 1600m [1750yd] with an aperture on the slider), a flat sheet metal buttplate and, unusually, a one-piece stock with an almost straight wrist. A very distinctive screw thread was found on the barrel surface ahead of the receiver ring. Some guns saw front-line service on Okinawa.

SPECIAL NAVY RIFLE

Made by Yokosuka navy arsenal in 1945, this amalgamated a cast-iron training rifle receiver with a barrel modified to receive the locking lugs directly in the enlarged chamber – allowing ball ammunition to be fired without blowing the gun apart. About 12,500 rifles were made, initially with adjustable sights but later with fixed notches. Buttplates and barrel bands were generally crudely cast, and the finish was black stove enamel. The earliest guns were marked 'Special' and often displayed a large anchor mark; later guns were marked 'Special Type 99', but the last bore nothing but an anchor on their receivers.

• Chassepot

The lengthy development of the Murata rifle (q.v.) and the need to develop suitable manufacturing capacity delayed the introduction of a purpose-built Japanese breechloading rifle until 1880.

The urgent need for weapons in the immediate aftermath of the Satsuma Rebellion was solved by purchasing guns in Europe, including a large number of surplus Chassepot needle guns. It is suspected that these included a quantity of guns captured by the Germans during the Franco-Prussian War, but some may have been acquired from manufacturers who still had undelivered guns to hand when the Franco-Pussian War began. Surviving rifles and bayonets usually show signs of earlier French ownership, but some bear no marks other than those applied by the Japanese – which can include large ideographs painstakingly constructed from tiny triangular or arrowhead punch-marks.

Many of the Japanese Chassepots were converted to chamber the 11x60 rimmed Murata cartridge in the 1880s and issued as an expedient until Murata rifles appeared in quantity. Chassepots of this type customarily had new bolts with a leaf-type extractor on the bolt head.

• Garand

Experiments undertaken in the 1920s and 1930s with automatic rifles had no lasting results, so the Sino-Japanese war, which began in 1937, was fought with conventional Arisaka (q.v.) rifles. When the Pacific War began in 1941, Japanese troops soon found themselves at a disadvantage against U.S. troops armed with Garands. The navy appears to have provisionally adopted the Type 4 recoil-operated rifle in 1944, based on contemporary Swiss practice, but the weapon was unsuccessful. The problems were eventually solved simply by adapting the Garand for the 7.7mm Japanese semi-rim rifle cartridge, but no series production had been undertaken by the end of the war.

TYPE 5 AUTOMATIC RIFLE

Made by the Imperial navy arsenal, Yokosuka, 1945.

Total production: about 250 sets of parts. **Chambering:** 7.7x58, rimless. **Action:** locked by rotating lugs on the bolt head into recesses in the receiver; gas operated, semi-automatic only.

43.25in overall, 9.13lb empty. 23.15in barrel, 4-groove rifling; RH, polygonal. Integral box magazine loaded from stripper clips, 10 rounds. Tangent-leaf sight graduated to 1200m (1310yd). 2395 fps with Type 99 ball cartridges. Standard Type 99 sword bayonet?

Unlike the M1 Garand, which required a special magazine clip, the Type 5 could be loaded with single rounds or from standard rifle stripper-clips. Unfortunately, Japanese metallurgy had deteriorated so greatly that the Type 5 was never perfected. With widespread dislocation of Japanese industry by U.S. bombing, only a few sets of components were found in Yokosuka when the war ended. There is no evidence that more than 100-130 guns ever saw action.

• Howa, autoloading type

Best known as a contractor to the Japanese defence forces, Howa made the Weatherby Vanguard actions from the early 1970s onward; once the exclusive licensing agreement had expired, however, these Sako-type bolt-action rifles also appeared in North America under the Howa brand.

TYPE 64 RIFLE

64-Shiki jidoju

Made by Howa Machinery Company, Nagoya, 1965-85.

Total production: about 250,000. **Chambering:** 7.62x51, rimless. **Action:** locked by tilting the breech block into the receiver; gas operated, selective fire.

38.95in overall, 9.72lb empty (with bipod). 17.7in barrel, 4-groove rifling; RH, concentric. Detachable box magazine, 20 rounds. Folding aperture sight graduated to 400m (440yd). 2295 fps with Type 64 ammunition; 500±25 rpm. Type 64 knife bayonet.

A search to find an autoloader for the Japanese forces began in earnest in 1958, when a team of military personnel and Howa civilian technicans under the leadership of General Koni Iwashita began test-firing in April.

Experiments with R-1 and R-2 rifles – with decidedly ArmaLite exteriors, though differing internally – continued until the Howa-pattern R-6 appeared. This progressed through several stages until the 'R-6E (Modified)' was approved for production; most of the minor variants differed in sights, charging facilities, forends and muzzle brakes.

Adopted in April 1964, the Type 64 was an amalgam of several European designs. However, the rifle was characterized by attention to detail to reduce length and weight to suit the stature of the average Japanese soldier. Special reduced-charge 7.62mm cartridges were fired, though conventional full-power rounds could be used if the gas regulator was adjusted accordingly.

The Type 64 had a short-stroke piston system and a distinctive straight-line layout, with a linear hammer running back into the butt housing. The handguard was a ventilated metal pressing, a bipod was fitted, and a shoulder strap folded on the buttplate. Production ceased in 1985, pending the investigation of 5.56mm designs.

• Howa, bolt-action type

MODEL 1500 SPORTING RIFLE

Made by Howa Machinery Company, Nagoya.

Currently in production. **Chambering:** see text. **Action:** locked by lugs on the bolt head rotating into the receiver wall, and by the bolt handle turning down into its seat.

DATA FOR A TYPICAL EXAMPLE

Chambering: 270 Winchester, rimless. 44.5in overall, 7.8lb empty. 24in barrel, 4-groove rifling; RH, concentric? Internal box magazine, 5 rounds. Williams ramp sight. 3140 fps with 130-grain bullet.

Known in Japan as the Howa 1500 and in America until recently as the Weatherby Vanguard Standard (VGS), this 1973-vintage introduction had a distinctive angular web ahead of the trigger guard to house the release catch for the detachable magazine floorplate. Standard guns have been chambered for the 22-250 Remington, 243 Winchester, 25-06, 270 Winchester or 30-06 cartridges.

The Type 5 navy rifle of 1945 was a Japanese version of the M1 Garand, with a box magazine.

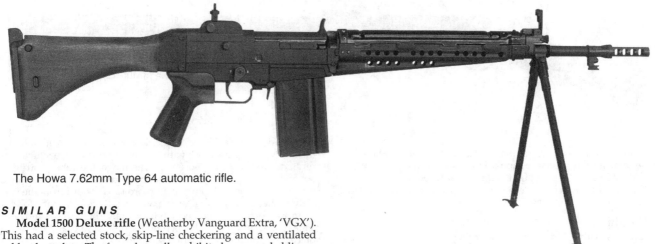

The Howa 7.62mm Type 64 automatic rifle.

SIMILAR GUNS

Model 1500 Deluxe rifle (Weatherby Vanguard Extra, 'VGX'). This had a selected stock, skip-line checkering and a ventilated rubber buttplate. The forend usually exhibited a squared oblique-cut tip, while the tapered barrel was drilled and tapped for optical sight mounts.

Model 1500 Extra Deluxe rifle (Weatherby Vanguard Extra Deluxe, 'VGX Deluxe'). Made with a heavier barrel than the standard guns, and minor improvements in the action, this was introduced for the cartridges chambered by the VGS and VGL – the short action being restricted to 22-250 Remington or 243 Winchester. It could also be supplied for the 300 Weatherby and 338 Winchester Magnums.

Model 1500 Hunter rifle (Weatherby Vanguard Classic II). This had a straight-comb stock lacking a forend tip. U.S.-market rifles had the proprietary Weatherby pistol grip cap; Japanese examples were plain.

Model 1500 Lightning rifle (Weatherby Vanguard Weather-mark, 'VGM'). This appeared in 1989 with a black or green CarboLite stock. Offered in 223 Remington, 243 Winchester, 308 Winchester (short action) and 270 Winchester, 7mm-08, 7mm Remington Magnum or 30-06 (standard action), it was identical mechanically with the regular guns.

Model 1500 Magnum rifle (Weatherby Vanguard Magnum, 'VGM'). This was indentical mechanically with the standard pattern, but was chambered for the 7mm Remington Magnum or 300 Winchester Magnum cartridges and had a three-round magazine.

Model 1500 Short rifle (Weatherby Vanguard Light, 'VGL'). Made from 1984 onward for 22-250, 223 Remington, 243 and 308 Winchester, this had a special short action. Similar 22-250 and 223 'varmint' versions also had heavyweight cylindrical barrels.

Model 1500 Synthetic rifle (Weatherby Vanguard Fiberguard, 'VGF'). Introduced in 1985, this offered a matt-blued action set in a textured Forest Green synthetic stock. The rifle has been built around short (223, 243 or 308) or standard actions (270, 7mm Remington Magnum or 30-06). A 20in barrel was used, overall length being 40-40.5in.

Model 1500 Trophy. Distinguished by a butt with a Monte Carlo comb and cheek piece, this gun also had the pistol grip-cap separated from the butt-wood by a white spacer.

• Mannlicher-Carcano

I-TYPE RIFLE

Assembled by Fabbrica Nazionale d'Armi, Terni, 1938-9; major sub-contractors included the Italian government factories in Gardone (RSFAE) and Brescia (FNAB), plus Pietro Beretta SpA.

Total production: 60,000. **Chambering:** 6.5x50, semi-rimmed. **Action:** locked by two lugs on a detachable bolt head engaging recesses in the receiver as the bolt handle was turned down.

49.7in overall, 8.97lb empty. 30.6in barrel, 4-groove rifling; RH, concentric? Internal box magazine loaded with a stripper clip, 5 rounds. Leaf sight graduated to 2400m (2625yd). 2475 fps with Meiji 38th Year Type ball cartridges. Meiji 38th Year Type sword bayonet.

Embroilment in a war with China caught the Japanese authorities with too few rifles to satisfy mobilization. However, a mutual trade agreement allowed large numbers of hybrid rifles to be ordered in Italy in 1937. These combined Japanese-style barrels, sights, bayonets and stocks with the Mannlicher-type split-bridge actions.

The butts of some rifles were shortened in 1940 by 0.75in (20mm), suiting them to troops of small stature. The I-type rifles were replaced by the Type 99 in 1941, survivors being relegated to training duties.

• Mauser

The Arisaka rifle, widely regarded as a much-modified Mauser, is covered separately. The Japanese made 8mm Mauser rifles for Siam (q.v.) prior to 1914, and also apparently supervised work on 7.9mm rifles in the Mukden factory in the puppet state of Man-

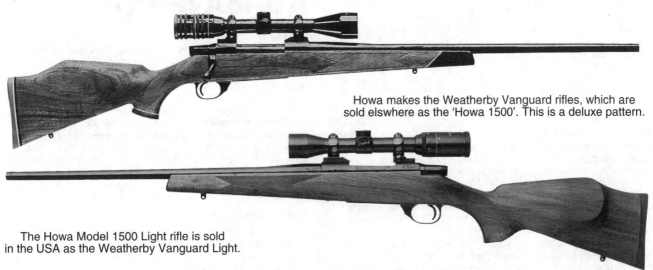

Howa makes the Weatherby Vanguard rifles, which are sold elswhere as the 'Howa 1500'. This is a deluxe pattern.

The Howa Model 1500 Light rifle is sold in the USA as the Weatherby Vanguard Light.

The Meiji 22nd Year Type
(Murata) infantry rifle, 1889.

chukuo (Manchuria, q.v.) in the 1930s. Substantial numbers of these Manchurian guns were apparently used during World War II, alongside many conventional Mausers captured in China from 1937 onward. Some Chinese guns are said to have been rebarreled to fire Japanese 6.5mm or 7.7mm cartridges.

• Murata

Contact with Chinese troops carrying Mauser, Snider and Chassepot rifles highlighted the poverty of the Japanese arms industry in the years before the Satsuma Rebellion of 1877. The government created a technical commission in 1875 to inquire into the guns being made and used in Europe, despatching Major Tsuneyoshi Murata (1838-1921) to France, Germany, Switzerland, the Netherlands and Italy in 1876-7. By combining features suggested by the Mauser, Gras and Beaumont rifles, Murata successfully created the first Japanese-made breechloader. Ordnance factories were established in Tokyo and Osaka, where production of the new gun and its metal-case cartridge began in 1880.

MODEL 1880 RIFLE
Meiji 13th Year Type
Made by the Imperial ordnance factory, Koishikawa, Tokyo, 1880-6.
Total production: at least 100,000. **Chambering:** 11x60, rimmed. **Action:** locked by the bolt guide rib abutting the receiver ahead of the bridge as the bolt handle turns down.

51.55in overall, 9.1lb empty. 33.05in barrel, 5-groove rifling; LH, concentric. Ramp-and-leaf sight graduated to 1600m (1750yd). 1485 fps with 13th Year Type cartridges. 13th Year Type sword bayonet.

Inspired by the French Gras rifle and distinguished by its stubby bolt handle, the first or 13th Year Type Murata of 1880 had a one-piece stock with a straight wrist. The front band doubled as a nose cap – with the bayonet bar on the right side – while the rear band carried a swivel. Another swivel lay on the under edge of the butt.

SIMILAR GUNS
16th Year Type cavalry carbine. Introduced in 1883, this apparently had a 20in barrel and a stock extending to the muzzle. Weight was 7.15lb and the rear sight ranged to 1200m (1310yd).

18th Year Type. An improved bolt mechanism was adopted in 1885. The original 13th Year Type stock was refined, with a lower comb and a shoulder at the rear of the receiver. The trigger guard bow was simplified (the earlier pattern had a bulkier rear tang) and the protrusion of the barrel ahead of the forend tip was reduced. A small auxiliary bayonet mounting tenon appeared on the left side of the muzzle; consequently, the 18th Year Type bayonet was not interchangeable with its 13th Year Type predecessor.

18th Year Type cavalry rifle. Made only in small numbers, this seems to have had 25.2in barrel – much longer than a carbine – and was stocked to the muzzle; bayonets could not be mounted. However, very few guns were produced before the 22nd Year Type magazine rifle appeared.

MODEL 1889 RIFLE
Meiji 22nd Year Type
Made by the Imperial artillery arsenal, Koishikawa, Tokyo, 1888-97.
Total production: more than 100,000. **Chambering:** 8mm, rimmed. **Action:** locked by two lugs on the bolt head engaging recesses in the receiver behind the chamber as the bolt handle was turned down.

47.5in overall, 8.68lb empty. 29.5in barrel, 4-groove rifling; RH, concentric. Tube magazine under barrel, 8 rounds. Ramp-and-leaf sight graduated to 2000m (2185yd). About 1850 fps with 22nd Year Type cartridges. 22nd Year Type sword bayonet.

An experimental Meiji 20th Year Type magazine rifle, inspired by the Austro-Hungarian Kropatchek (q.v.), was issued for field trials in 1887. In 1889, after minor changes and improvements had

been made, the Meiji 22nd Year rifle was duly approved. It had a distinctive one-piece stock with a straight-wrist butt, a single barrel band and a sturdy nose cap. The magazine tube protruded beyond the nose cap to receive the cross-guard ring of the strange little knife bayonet. A short handguard ran forward from the rear sight to the rear band, and dicing was usually found on the forend to improve grip. Swivels lay on the underside of the band and butt; a magazine cut-off lever lay behind the bolt handle; and the three-piece cleaning rod was carried separately by NCOs.

Field service in the Sino-Japanese war of 1894 highlighted the shortcomings of the Murata, and work began to develop the more efficient rifle that became known as the Arisaka (q.v.).

SIMILAR GUNS
Model 1894 carbine (Meiji 27th Year Type). Made by the Imperial artillery arsenal in Koishikawa, this was a shortened version of the 22nd Year rifle – 37.5in long, 6.85lb empty – with a six-round magazine and a 1600m (1750yd) rear sight. Introduced in 1894, it had a spring-retained barrel band and a shortened magazine tube which did not protrude past the nose cap. Swivels appeared on the underside of the forend and butt for the artillery, or on the left side of the barrel band and butt for cavalrymen.

• Simple Rifles

These were made in China, for the Japanese occupation forces, at the end of World War II. The least desirable of all the crude but otherwise conventional Japanese emergency weapons, the first single shot 'Simple Rifle' fired the 7.7mm Type 99 round – yet could be made on an ordinary lathe. The cartridge predictably proved much too powerful in the absence of suitable high-tensile steel, and so the design was speedily revised for the 8mm pistol cartridge.

Simple Rifles had slab-pattern butts and split-bridge receivers. Locking relied on the base of the bolt handle, while the trigger system often consisted simply of a spring and lever engaging directly in the cocking piece. The intention to make millions of Simple Rifles was thwarted by the end of the war. One example measured 30.9in overall, had an 11.8in smooth-bore barrel and weighed 6lb. The only contractors thus far identified are Toa Iron-works, Shanghai; Nanking arsenal; the Sixth Army repair depot, Tung-Shan; and the Chi-Fo, Wang-Shih and Shu-Chow work-shops in Tung-Shan.

KOREA (PRK)

• Kalashnikov

Production of the Type 58 began in the People's Republic of Korea in 1959. A straightforward copy of the Soviet AK, the guns had cleaning rods but lacked bayonet lugs. They were made with solid wooden butts and smooth-tapering forends instead of the original beaver-tail type. Pistol grips may be solid or (apparently later) laminated wood. Selector markings were most distinctive, and the serial number on the left side of the receiver was generally prefixed by a large encircled star. The Type 68 of 1970 was basically an AKM with an AK-type trigger mechanism. The standards of manufacture were poor. However, sufficient production (at an annual rate of 150,000 in the early 1980s) has been undertaken in Factories 61 and 65 to allow substantial numbers of AK and AKM-type rifles to be exported.

• Mosin-Nagant

A poor-quality copy of the Soviet obr. 1891/30g rifle was made in the 1950s, apparently as the 'Type 30'. It was distinguished by a large encircled five-point star, preceding the serial number on the left side of the receiver.

The 5.56mm Dae Woo K2 assault rifle.

• Simonov

At least a million Type 63 carbines were made by the state factories in 7.62x39. They were essentially similar to the Chinese Type 56, but the rear sight was graduated to 800m (875yd) and a knife-type folding bayonet was used. The standards of workmanship and finish were poor, the bolt carrier usually being phosphated. A cleaning rod was retained; the stock and hanguard were generally wood laminates; a swivel often lay on the under edge of the butt. The safety-catch head and bolt handle were ribbed; most other SKS derivatives have knurled bolt handles.

KOREA (REPUBLIC)

• Arisaka

The conversion of selected weapons for the 30-06 cartridge began under American supervision in Tokyo artillery arsenal in 1951. By the middle of 1952, about 126,500 short and 6650 long Type 99 rifles had been altered. They were apparently intended for South Korean gendarmerie – though possibly only a handful had been issued by the end of the Korean War in 1953. In addition to the new chambering, the magazine box was lengthened for the new cartridge and a prominent groove was cut across the face of the breech to facilitate charger loading. Japanese chamber marks were removed and the receivers were given a gray phosphated finish.

• ArmaLite

A licensed copy of the M16A1 (Colt Model 603-K) has been built in what was once the government-owned Pusan arsenal, after the U.S. Military Aid Program had provided nearly 27,000 M16A1 rifles from U.S. Army stores. The indigenous rifles bore 'MADE IN KOREA' above an acknowledgment of the license on the right side of the magazine, the designation and 'K'-prefix serial number appearing on the left. Production is said to have approached 600,000 before work finished about 1985. The selector was marked in Korean. In 1983, the Pusan facilities were sold to Dae Woo Precision Industries (q.v.).

• Dae Woo

Development of a series of weapons to replace the M16A1 in Korean service began when the government-owned arms factory in Pusan was transferred to private control in 1983, with the intention of freeing the country's small arms from U.S. dominance. The prototype rifles appeared in 1984, series production beginning a year later.

K1 AUTOMATIC CARBINE

Made by Dae Woo Precision Industries, Pusan.

Currently in production. **Chambering:** 5.56x45, rimless. **Action:** locked by rotating lugs on the bolt into recesses in the walls of the receiver; gas operated, selective fire.

30.9in overall (stock extended), 6.28lb empty. 10.35in barrel, 4-groove rifling; concentric, RH. Detachable box magazine, 30 rounds. Adjustable aperture sight. 3130 fps with standard M193 bullet.

The K1 carbine of 1985, equivalent to the U.S. Army XM177E2 (see 'U.S.A.: Armalite'), combined the direct-impingement gas system of the M16 with the bolt carrier and twin recoil-guide rod assembly of the AR-18. The lower part of the hinged receiver resembled the M16A1 type, though the upper section differed greatly; the integral carrying handle was replaced by a prominent

sight protector and the butt had more of a drop at the wrist. One swivel lay on the barrel ahead of the handguard, with the other on the back left side of the receiver. The K1 could fire single shots, three-round bursts or fully automatically; selectors displayed markings in Korean or English.

SIMILAR GUNS

K1A1 carbine. This had a longer barrel than the K1, to minimize muzzle flash, but shared the construction of its predecessors and has also been offered in semi-automatic 'Law Enforcement' form.

K2 rifle. This shared the basic construction of the K1 carbine, but had a full-length barrel and a solid polyamide butt swinging to the right instead of a retractable pattern. The gas system was changed to a long-stroke piston adapted from the Soviet Kalashnikov, and the muzzle-brake/compensator could accept standard rifle grenades. Like the K1, the K2 had a short fluted handguard and checkering on the pistol grip. It was 38.9in overall, weighed 7.38lb empty and had an 18.3in barrel.

Others. Guns were sold in the U.S. in the late 1980s by Stoeger Industries of Hackensack, New Jersey, as the Max-1 and Max-2 Auto Carbines – the K1A1 and K2 respectively.

LATVIA

• Mauser

About 15,000 vz. 24 short rifles were purchased from Ceskoslovenská Zbrojovka in 1935. It is not known whether they bore any distinctive markings.

LIBERIA

• Mauser

Mle. 24 short rifles were bought from Fabrique Nationale in the 1930s, but details are lacking. The arms consisted of a shield bearing a star above 11 vertical bars.

LITHUANIA

• Mauser

In 1931, the army apparently bought small quantities of Czechoslovakian-made 'L'-model short rifles chambering the British rimmed 303 cartridge. Whether these were issued to the army or to a gendarmerie has not been determined, as 7.92mm vz. 24 short rifles had been purchased from Ceskoslovenská Zbrojovka in 1926-7 and some 7.9mm Fabrique Nationale Mle. 30 short rifles followed in 1935-8. These were all used as 'Model 24.L'. The chamber mark was a highly stylized crown beneath 'GINKLU FONDAS' ('arms fund') and the date of manufacture.

LUXEMBOURG

• Mauser

A few rifles were supplied prior to 1900 to equip the tiny state army. The guns are believed to have been similar to the 1895 Chilean pattern (q.v.), but special markings – if any – have not been identified.

MANCHURIA

• Mauser

Mukden arsenal made curious Mauser rifles, apparently in the period of the Japanese inspired Manchukuo state (1932-45). The 7.9x57 'Mukden Mausers', apparently dating from about 1933-9, appear to have been created with Japanese technical assistance. They had an 1898-type Mauser action, with the third (safety) lug and a non-rotating extractor, but changes were made to the firing pin assembly and the bolt plug had an elongated housing for the main spring. There were two gas-escape holes in the receiver ring, the bolt handle was a typically Japanese oviform type, and a reciprocating sheet-steel cover could be attached over the receiver. A typical rifle was 48.8in overall, with a 29.15in barrel. Its internal charger-loaded box magazine held five rounds and the tangent-leaf sight was graduated to 2,000m.

In about 1938, Mukden arsenal re-tooled to make the 7.7mm Type 99 Japanese Arisaka short rifle. However – toward the end of World War II – some Mausers were modified for the Japanese 6.5mm semi-rim round, gaining an auxiliary block in the back of the magazine well to compensate for the appreciable reduction in the length of the cartridge.

MEXICO

• Arisaka

Faced with revolution, in 1910, the government ordered about 40,000 38th Year Type Arisakas to supplement the existing Mausers. The rifles – and a few carbines – were made in Koishikawa. They were practically identical with the standard Japanese service patterns, but chambered 7x57 cartridges (necessitating a different rear sight leaf) and the nose caps were altered to accept the standard Mexican bayonets. Eagle-and-cactus chamber motifs accompanied 'REPUBLICA MEXICANA', a liberty cap and 'R M' being struck into the barrel near the breech. However, the overthrow of president Porfirio Diaz in 1911 canceled orders after less than 5,000 guns had been delivered. The remainder were stored in Japan until 1914.

• FN-Saive

The Belgian-pattern FAL was adopted as the standard service weapon in 1963, serving until superseded in the late 1970s by the Heckler & Koch G3. The earliest guns were acquired from Belgium; later ones were assembled by the government factory (Fábrica de Armas) in Mexico City. They may be identified by the Mexican eagle-on-cactus badge on the side of the magazine housing, or by 'REPUBLICA MEXICANA' marks.

• Mauser

These rifles invariably bear the national arms above the chamber. Inspired by Aztec legend, these show an eagle – perched on a cactus – with a snake in its beak. The marks were usually accompanied by 'REPUBLICA MEXICANA' or 'R M'.

MODEL 1893

The Spanish national manufactory in Oviedo has sometimes been identified with the production of 1895-type Mexican Mausers (see below). However, the guns in question seem to have been standard Mo. 1893 Spanish rifles – which had a different bolt head – supplied to the Mexican government or possibly acquired by insurgents in the early years of the 20th Century. They bear the Spanish arms over the chamber and the maker's name on the left side of the receiver.

MODEL 1895 RIFLE
Fusil Mauser Mexicano Mo. 1895

Made by Ludwig Loewe & Co., Berlin (1895-6); and Deutsche Waffen- und Munitionsfabriken, Berlin (1897-1901).

Total production: 50,000? **Chambering:** 7x57, rimless. **Action:** locked by two lugs on the bolt head engaging recesses in the receiver walls when the bolt handle was turned down.

48.6in overall, 8.75lb empty. 29.1in barrel, 4-groove rifling; RH, concentric. Internal charger-loaded box magazine, 5 rounds. Leaf sight graduated to 2000m (2185yd). 2395 fps with standard ball cartridges. Mo. 1895 sword bayonet.

This rifle was adopted after extensive tests, proving to be simpler and more durable than the 1893-model Mondragon. The contract was placed with Ludwig Loewe & Co., but only a few guns were made before work was passed to DWM at the beginning of 1897. The rifle was virtually identical with the Spanish Mo. 1893 (q.v.), but had a normal cylindrical bolt head.

SIMILAR GUNS

Model 1895 carbine (Carabina Mauser Mexicana Mo. 1895). Adopted at the same time as the 1895-pattern rifle – for cavalry and artillerymen – this was simply a shortened gun with a small rear sight graduated to 1400m (1530yd), the bolt handle turned down against the stock, and the sling mounts lay on the left side of the butt and barrel band. It was 37.5in long, had a 18.3in barrel, and weighed 7.5lb empty. About 10,000 carbines seem to have been made.

MODEL 1902 RIFLE
Fusil Mauser Mexicano Mo. 1902

Made by Deutsche Waffen- und Munitionsfabriken, Berlin, 1902-4 (38,000); and Österreichische Waffenfabriks-Gesellschaft, Steyr, 1906-7 (40,000).

Total production: 78,000? **Chambering:** 7x57, rimless. **Action:** locked by two lugs engaging recesses in the receiver behind the chamber as the bolt handle turned down, and by a safety lug opposing the bolt bolt handle base entering its seat.

48.6in overall, 8.85lb empty. 29.1in barrel, 4-groove rifling; RH, concentric. Internal charger-loaded box magazine, 5 rounds. Leaf sight graduated to 2000m (2185yd). 2395 fps with standard ball cartridges. Mo. 1895 sword bayonet.

Adopted in 1902 to supersede the Mo. 1895, this embodied an 1898-type action with a non-rotating extractor and a gas-shield on the bolt plug. The rifle was otherwise similar to its predecessors, with a straight-wrist stock and a simple nose cap with a lug for the standard Mo. 1895 bayonet.

MODEL 1907 RIFLE
Fusil Mauser Mexicano Mo. 1907

Made by Österreichische Waffenfabriks-Gesellschaft, Steyr, 1907-10.
Total production: not known. **Chambering:** 7x57, rimless.

Otherwise generally as Mo. 1902 (above) except: 48.8in overall, 8.93lb empty. Mo. 1907 sword bayonet.

Ordered in Austria-Hungary, this was mechanically similar to the earlier Mo. 1902. However, it had a pistol grip stock and a simple band-type nose cap with a short bayonet bar. The position of this attachment bar beneath the barrel forced a change to be made in the bayonet. From about 1925 onward, the original rear sight leaf was replaced by a 1800m (1970yd) pattern after the introduction of heavy-ball ammunition suited to rifles and machine guns alike.

MODEL 1910 RIFLE
Fusil Mauser Mexicano Mo. 1910.

Made by Fábrica Nacional de Armas, Mexico City, about 1913-35.
Total production: about 40,000.

Otherwise generally as Mo. 1902 (above).

A Czechoslovakian-made 'Carbine vz. 12 Mex.' of the 1930s.

Plans were readied in 1909-10 to make the first indigenous Mauser-type rifle, though they were interrupted by revolution in 1911 and it is believed that the first series-production guns were not forthcoming until about 1913. The rifles duplicated the preceding Mo. 1902, with 1898-type actions, straight-wrist stocks, and nose caps adapted for the original knife bayonet. They bore the factory name – 'FABRICA NACIONAL DE ARMAS' – around an elaborate version of the national arms over the chamber, adding a half-wreath of laurel to the eagle-on-cactus motif; 'MEXICO D.F.' and the date of manufacture lay below the wreath.

The introduction of heavy-ball ammunition for rifles and machine guns caused back-sights to be revised to 1800m (1970yd) after about 1925.

SIMILAR GUNS

Model 1910 carbine and Model 1912 carbine. These were also made in small quantities – perhaps totaling no greater than 4,000. They had a straight-grip butt, with sling mounts on the left side of the band and wrist. Overall length was about 37.6in, the barrel measured 17.5in, and empty weight was 7.83lb without the sling. The rear sight was a tangent-leaf design graduated to 1400m (1530yd).

MODEL 1912 RIFLE
Fusil Mauser Mexicano Mo. 1912
Made by Österreichische Waffenfabriks-Gesellschaft, Steyr, 1913-14.
Total production: not known. **Chambering:** 7x57, rimless.

Otherwise generally as Mo. 1902 (above) except 48.9in overall, 9.06lb empty. Tangent-leaf sight graduated to 2000m (2185yd). Mo. 1907 sword bayonet.

Tortuous progress with the FNA-made Mo. 1910 forced the Mexican government to order another batch of rifles from Austria in 1912. The Mo. 1912 had a large-ring receiver, a pistol grip stock, a tangent-leaf rear sight, and an 'H'-type nose cap taking a bayonet with the muzzle ring close to the hilt-back.

Deliveries had hardly started when the First World War cut supplies. Many Mexican rifles were issued to Austro-Hungarian units, survivors being altered to 7.9mm in 1919-20 for the Kingdom of Serbs, Croats and Slovenes (where they were used as 'M24B').

SIMILAR GUNS

Model 1912 short rifle. Made only in small numbers, this was a short-barrel version of the standard rifle, with the bolt handle turned down against the stock and a tangent-leaf rear sight graduated to only 1400m (1530yd). The guns were about 41.7in long and weighed 8.8lb.

MODEL 1924 SHORT RIFLE
Fusil Mauser Mexicano Mo. 1924
Made by Fabrique Nationale d'Armes de Guerre, Herstal-lèz-Liége, 1926-7 (25,000); and Ceskoslovenská Zbrojovká, Brno, 1932-3 (5000?).
Total production: 30,000? **Chambering:** 7x57, rimless. **Action:** generally as Mo. 1902 (q.v.).
DATA FOR A BELGIAN-MADE GUN

43in overall, 8.5lb empty. 23.45in barrel, 4-groove rifling; RH, concentric. Internal box magazine loaded with a stripper clip, 5 rounds. Tangent-leaf sight graduated to 2000m (2185yd). Mo. 1924 sword bayonet.

These guns included Mle. 24 short rifles purchased from Fabrique Nationale and vz. 12/33 short rifles acquired from Czechoslovakia in the 1930s. Brno-made examples were slightly shorter than the FN pattern, measuring 41.9in overall with 21.85in barrels. They also had the bolt handles turned down and 'H'-type nose caps instead of the simpler FN design.

The guns all had pistol grip stocks with full-length handguards, and were customarily marked with an eagle-and-cactus motif and 'REPUBLICA MEXICANA 1924' above the chamber. Brno prod-

ucts were marked 'FABRICA CHECOSLOVACA DE ARMAS' over 'S.A. BRNO' on the left side of the receiver.

SIMILAR GUNS

Model 1924 carbine. A few of these were also supplied from FN. They had the bolt handle turned down toward the stock, a simple nose cap, and a handguard extending to the barrel band. Swivels lay under the butt and band; bayonets could not be mounted. The guns were about 35.6in long, had 15.15in barrels, and weighed 7.5lb. Their tangent-leaf sights were graduated to 1400m (1530yd).

MODEL 1936 SHORT RIFLE
Fusil Mauser Mexicano Mo. 1936
Made by Fábrica Nacional de Armas, Mexico City, 1936-51.
Total production: not known. **Chambering:** 7x57, rimless. **Action:** generally as Mo. 1902, (q.v.).

42.9in overall, 8.33lb empty. 23.25in barrel, 4-groove rifling; RH, concentric. Internal box magazine loaded with a stripper clip, 5 rounds. Tangent-leaf sight graduated to 1500m (1640yd). About 715m/sec with standard ball cartridges. Mo. 1895 knife or Mo. 1936 sword bayonet.

Adopted in 1936 to replace the Mo. 1910, this combined an 1898-type Mauser action with the bands, nose cap and cocking-piece of the U.S. M1903 Springfield rifle. It had a pistol grip stock with the forend swelling slightly ahead of the magazine floorplate, and the bolt handle was turned downward. American-style swivels lay on the butt and barrel band, with an open stacking swivel on the nose cap. The top of the chamber displayed an elaborate Mexican Crest.

MODEL 1954 SHORT RIFLE
Fusil Mauser Mexicano Mo. 1954
Made by Fábrica Nacional de Armas, Mexico City, 1954-5.
Total production: at least 7500. **Chambering:** 30-06, rimless. **Action:** as Mo. 1936, above.

About 44.1in overall, 9.65lb empty. 24in barrel, 4-groove rifling; RH, concentric. Internal charger-loaded box magazine, 5 rounds. Rocking-leaf aperture sight on receiver bridge (see text). About 2770 fps with U.S. M2 Ball cartridges. Mo. 1936 sword bayonet.

A sudden influx of war-surplus U.S. weapons, particularly M1 Garands, persuaded the Mexicans to adapt the basic Mo. 1936 to fire 30-06 cartridges. The conversion was formally approved in 1954.

Alterations to the face of the chamber allowed the longer cartridges to pass into the modified magazines. The resulting rifles, often using receivers salvaged from earlier guns (dated prior to 1950), had laminated stocks and the trigger guards and magazine floorplates were made from a single continuous stamping. The rear sight was an aperture pattern on the receiver bridge, inspired by the U.S. M1903A3, though some guns were fitted with the 1500m (1640yd) tangent-leaf pattern associated with the Mo. 1936.

The left side of the receiver behind the chamber was marked marked 'CAL. 7.62mm' over 'MOD. 54', showing that the gun fired the U.S. 30-06 round – 7.62x63 in metric dimensions.

Faced with the increasing availability of semi-automatics, the Mexicans abandoned the 30-06 Mauser in 1955-6, after only a few had been assembled.

• Mondragon, autoloading type

The first autoloading rifle to encounter real success was the work of a talented Mexican army officer, Manuel Mondragon. After developing a unique straight-pull bolt-action rifle described below, Mondragon began work on a gas-operated autoloader in the mid 1890s. However, many years passed before a patent was sought in the U.S. in August 1904.

Gas was tapped from the bore into an expansion chamber under the barrel, forcing a piston back against the bolt actuator. As the actuator moved back, it rotated the locking lugs out of engagement with the receiver walls. Slight camming action helped

The M1908 Mondragon rifle.

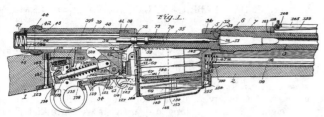
A section of the Mondragon rifle, from its US Patent.

to extract the spent cartridge case, then the mechanism ran back to eject before returning to chamber a new round.

A pivoting claw on the bolt handle could disconnect the bolt assembly from the recoil spring during the cocking stroke, turning the rifle into a manually operated straight-pull pattern if the gas port had been closed – though the action was difficult to retract.

The finalized Mondragon was prone to jamming and breakages. Though it was greatly superior to most pre-1914 designs, and has the distinction of being the first autoloader to become official issue, service with the German army in the First World War rapidly revealed major shortcomings.

MODEL 1908 RIFLE
Fusil Automatico de 7mm 'Porfirio Diaz', Modelo de 1908.
Made by Schweizerische Industrie-Gesellschaft, Neuhausen, 1909-11.
Chambering: 7x57, rimless. Otherwise as German FSK. 15 (q.v.), except magazine (clip-loaded eight-round box) and a special bayonet.

Two 7mm prototypes were unsuccessfully tested in Britain in the summer of 1903, failing the sand test though efficient enough when clean. The rifle was officially adopted in Mexico in 1908, and a contract for 4,000 guns was placed in Switzerland. The barrels were apparently to measure about 29.5in, though this was soon reduced to 24.4in on production guns.

They were conventional-looking autoloaders, with a one-piece straight-wrist stock (most of the prototypes had two-piece stocks) and a handguard stretching forward from the chamber to a nose cap from which the gas regulator protruded. A lug for the unique trowel bayonet lay under the muzzle, one swivel lay on the barrel band and another lay beneath the butt.

Mexican-service rifles had an enwreathed eagle perched on a cactus, with a snake in its beak, above the chamber; 'RM' ('Republica de Mexico') marks also appeared, while the 'Mo. 1908' designation and maker's mark – 'FABRICA DE ARMAS NEUHAUSEN SUIZA' – lay on the top rear of the receiver.

The first batch of 400 guns reached Mexico early in 1911, but revolution in May then toppled Diaz. The new government seems to have seized on unreliability and excessive parts-breakage to cancel the order, leaving SIG with substantial quantities of unwanted guns. Some modified 7.5x55 examples were tested by the Swiss army – with detachable ten- or 20-round box magazines – but had no lasting effects. The remaining rifles were sold to Germany in 1915.

• Mondragon, bolt-action type
Work began on these interesting guns in 1891, seeking to provide the Mexican army with a new rapid-firing repeater. The first prototypes were made in 1892, and 50 Swiss-made guns were successfully field-tested in Mexico in September 1894. The report was enthusiastic, apart from regarding the auto-firing feature as superfluous, but the cost of re-equipping the army was prohibitive; Mausers were purchased instead.

1893-TYPE RIFLE
Made by Schweizerische Industrie Gesellschaft, Neuhausen, Switzerland.
Total production: 130-150 (all types)? **Chambering:** 6.5mm, rimless.
Action: locked by rotating multiple lugs on the bolt into engagement with the receiver as the bolt handle is pushed forward.

48in overall, 7.5lb empty. 29in barrel, rifling profile unknown. Integral clip-loaded box magazine, 8 rounds. Quadrant-leaf rear sight graduated to 2600m (2845yd). About 2150 fps with ball ammunition. Sword bayonet.

The Mondragon rifle was an interesting straight-pull design, with a sliding handle on the right side of the receiver operating a separate bolt by way of a lug riding in a helical cam-way. One series of locking lugs engaged directly behind the chamber, and

another group locked into the receiver-bridge behind the magazine well. A massive slab-sided receiver separated the straight-wrist butt from the hollow one-piece forend. The simple nose cap carried the lug for a Swiss-style saw-backed bayonet, but the most interesting feature of the design, however, was a radial selector operating on a semi-circular plate set into the right side of the stock above the trigger. This could be set to a safe position (locking the trigger) or to give single shots; a third position isolated the trigger mechanism, allowing the gun to fire automatically as the breech was closed. This was intended to give a high volume of fire as soldiers advanced at walking pace.

SIMILAR GUNS
1894-type rifle. Though the 1893 pattern was ultimately rejected by the Mexican authorities, Mondragon continued development in Switzerland. The perfected gun chambered a unique 5.2x68 cartridge firing its 90-grain 'piston bullet' at 2850 fps. Ammunition was made in Germany by Polte of Magdeburg. The excessive chamber pressures required two sets of five locking lugs, with another group of five at the rear of the bolt to act as a gas shield. The rifles came in a variety of sizes, being largely experimental; a typical example was 53in long, had a 34.5in barrel and weighed 7.69lb empty. It was loaded with an eight-round 'en bloc' clip, had a 2600m quadrant-leaf sight, and retained the auto-firing feature. The selector plate was marked 'A', 'L' and 'R', for automatic fire, safety and single shots respectively.

• Pieper
Henri Pieper supplied the Mexicans with substantial quantities of revolving-cylinder carbines, embodying a patented gas-seal system. The cylinder was cammed forward over a short conical seat on the rear of the barrel, preventing the escape of gas from the cylinder/barrel joint.

MODEL 1893 CARBINE
Made by Henri Pieper & Cie, Liége, Belgium, about 1895-7.
Total production: 500? **Chambering:** 8mm Nagant. **Action:** a cylinder was revolved by the trigger mechanism for each shot.

36in overall, 6.5lb empty. 19.75in barrel, 4-groove rifling; RH concentric? Cylinder, 9 rounds. Stepped base leaf-and-slider rear sight, graduated to 900m (985yd). Performance unknown.

These carbines – issued to rural gendarmerie – had a distinctive hollowed one-piece wooden forend, with a single band and a swivel. The second swivel lay on the left side of the straight butt wrist. The lock was double-action, the hammer was exposed to allow manual cocking, and the yoke-mounted cylinder could be swung out of the frame to the right for loading. There is some evidence that prototypes were chambered for a 7.65mm cartridge (DWM case 485 was for a 'Mex.-Revol.-Karabiner'), but the perfected version used an 8mm type loaded with a 125-grain bullet. Mexican issue numbers run into the 200s, though the manufacturer's numbers run up to at least 350.

• Remington
The government bought 10,000 11mm Spanish type rifles from Remington in the early 1870s, and then ordered 3,000 additional rifles in 1877. A thousand 'convertible carbines' could fire 50-70 centerfire or 56-50 Spencer rimfire cartridges as required. They were 36in long, had 20.45in barrels and weighed 6.75lb.

Mexican rifles were marked 'R. DE MEXICO' or 'RM' on the barrel, although those marked after 23rd July 1894 displayed an additional Liberty Cap on a sunburst. The 1897-pattern guns bore the eagle-on-cactus above the receiver.

MODEL 1897 RIFLE
Made by the Remington Arms Company, Ilion, New York, 1897-1902.
Total production: not known. **Chambering:** 7x57, rimless. **Action:** locked by shoulders on the hammer body propping the radial breechblock behind the chamber.

45.5in overall, 8.5lb empty. 30in barrel, 5-groove rifling; RH, concentric. Ramp-and-leaf sight graduated to 1900m (2080yd). 2100 fps with Mo. 1895 ball cartridges. Remington 'export' knife or sword bayonets.

Several thousand of these guns were purchased in 1897 from Marcellus Hartley & Company, Remington's agents. They had straight-wrist butts, handguards running from the receiver to the spring-retained barrel band, and a band-like nose cap with a bayonet lug and a swivel. The other swivel lay under the butt. Rear sights had protecting wings and the barrels were marked '7 M.M.-S.M.' ('7mm caliber, Spanish model').

SIMILAR GUNS

Model 1897 carbine. This was a short version of the rifle – 36in overall – with a half-stock and a rounded forend tip. It did not accept a bayonet. A sling ring lay on the left side of the receiver, while swivels were to be found on the right side of the butt and band. The rear sight was graduated to 1300m (1420yd).

• Whitney

WHITNEY MILITARY MODEL

Made by the Whitney Arms Company, Whitneyville, Connecticut, 1872-80.

Total production: not known. **Chambering:** 11x58, rimmed. **Action:** Locked by shoulders on the hammer body and an auxiliary cam propping the radial breechblock behind the chamber.

50.5in overall, 9.5lb empty. 35in barrel, 4-groove rifling; RH, concentric? Ramp-and-leaf sight graduated to 1200yd. 1440 fps with 375-grain bullet. Socket bayonet.

The standard Laidley & Emery-type Whitney military rifle of 1872 – available in 433 Spanish, 45-70 or 50-70 – had a full-length forend retained by three bands; swivels lay on the band nearest the muzzle and through the front web of the trigger guard bow. About 2,000 rifles were purchased directly from Whitney in 1877, on behalf of the Mexican government. They are usually distinguished by a liberty-cap-on-sunburst above 'R M' for 'Republica Mexicana'. The rifles accepted socket bayonets with conventional locking rings. These could fit the carbines in an emergency, but were never issued to mounted troops. Whitney could supply sabre patterns to order when required to do so, but there is no evidence that they were ever used in Mexico.

SIMILAR GUNS

Carbine. A half-stocked carbine was offered with a sling ring and bar anchored in the left side of the receiver; it was about 36in long, had a 20.5in barrel and weighed about 7.2lb. The ramp-and-leaf rear sight was usually graduated to 600 yards. About 500 carbines accompanied the rifles purchased from Whitney in 1877.

MOROCCO

• Beretta

The Beretta Model 57 carbine was initially purchased from Beretta, with a license to make guns in the government factory in Fez (Manufacture d'Armes de l'État de Fès). Moroccan-made guns seem to date from 1960-5, but the quantities were small.

• Garand

Beretta granted a license to enable the BM-59 to be made in the government ordnance factory in Fez, but work was confined to the assembly of components imported from Italy; special markings, if any, have yet to be identified.

NETHERLANDS

• Beaumont

A turning-bolt mechanism developed by a well-established gunmaker, E. de Beaumont of Maastricht, this was inspired by the Chassepot needle rifle. Principal among its unique features was the position of the striker spring, a 'V'-type leaf being inserted in the hollow two-piece bolt handle instead of a conventional coil pattern in the annular space between the striker body and the inner surface of the bolt. The action was simple, with a separate bolt head retained by a screw through the rib. The extractor lay beneath the bolt head when the action was open, but no ejector was fitted.

A longitudinal section of the Beaumont action.

The Beaumont was developed to replace Dutch Snider conversions in 1870. The strange striker spring assembly was an Achilles heel; not only was it more prone to breaking than the coil patterns, but it also prevented development of Beaumont-type carbines with turned-down bolt handles. Articulated springs were not durable enough, so Remingtons were purchased instead.

Rigorous use showed the Beaumont rifle to be more fragile than many of its rivals, though an experimental conversion of a Chassepot pressed Gras prototypes hard in the French trials of 1873-4.

MILITARY WEAPONS

MODEL 1871 RIFLE

Infanterie-Geweer M1871

Made by E. de Beaumont, Maastricht; by P. Stevens, Maastricht; and by J.J. Bär, Delft.

Total production: not known. **Chambering:** 11.3x50, rimmed. **Action:** locked by rotating the bolt-guide rib downward until it abuts the front face of the receiver bridge.

51.95in overall, 9.66lb empty. 32.7in barrel, 4-groove rifling; RH, concentric. Quadrant sight graduated to 1100 paces (about 825yd). 1330 fps with M1871 ball cartridges. M1871 socket bayonet.

This rifle, adopted in 1870, was externally reminiscent of the Chassepot or Gras. However, it had a distinctive rear sight, a safety button on the right side of the receiver bridge, and a concave rear face to the trigger guard (French designs were oval). Mounts comprised a single barrel band and a nose cap, swivels being fitted beneath the band and butt.

The safety system, which had originally locked the bolt in the half-rotated position, was abandoned in 1876. New rear sights, designed by Captain In de Betou of the Royal Netherlands army, were fitted from 1879 onward. These had a new leaf graduated to 1300m (1420yd) for the 1878- or Harsveldt-pattern cartridge, with a muzzle velocity of about 435m/sec (1425 fps). The cartridge case was lengthened by .08in (2mm), necessitating changes to the chamber, and the diameter of the bullet was reduced slightly to promote better performance in the existing barrels. Guns of this type are often designated 'M1879' or 'M1871/79', but it is not known whether these had official status. The last unaltered M71 rifles lasted in store and colonial service until the First World War.

SIMILAR GUNS

M1871/88. The adaptation of surviving rifles for the Italian-designed Vitali box magazine began in 1888. The work involved adding a bolt-mounted ejector and cutting away the lower part of the feed way to accept a case containing four rounds. The magazine follower was propelled by a coil spring around a guide-rod, the protruding housing for which gave the Vitali magazine its distinctive shape. A magazine cut-off was also added at this time. Surviving front-line M1871-88 rifles were replaced by Mannlichers in the late 1890s, though large numbers were still being held in reserve in 1914.

The 1879-type Beaumont infantry rifle and its socket bayonet.

SPORTING GUNS

Few sporters embody the Beaumont action, though some were doubtless made in the Netherlands toward the end of the nineteenth century. However, many obsolete rifles were converted into 20-bore shotguns prior to 1914 and exported to the Dutch colonies in the East Indies and Central America.

• Kalashnikov (NWM)

In the late 1970s, Nederlandse Wapen- en Munitiefabriek (NWM) negotiated a licence to make a modified form of the Israeli Galil known as the MN-1. This was touted as a replacement for the 7.62mm FAL, though this Belgian gun remained in front-line service while extensive trials were undertaken with 5.56mm patterns. Though the FNC was regarded as the long-term favorite to replace the FAL, the decision was taken in 1995 to adopt the Canadian-made Diemaco C7 (M16A1) rifle.

• Mannlicher

The adoption of small caliber magazine rifles throughout Europe placed the army of the Netherlands at a disadvantage. The Dutch maintained a small colonial empire and did not wish to be outgunned by potential aggressors, so a Mannlicher was adopted to replace the M1871/88 (Beaumont-Vitali).

TRIALS RIFLES

Made by Österreichische Waffenfabriks-Gesellschaft, Steyr, 1892-5.

Total production: 1000? **Chambering:** 6.5x53, rimmed. **Action:** locked by two lugs on a detachable bolt head engaging seats in the receiver immediately behind the chamber as the bolt handle was turned down.

50.8in overall, 9.13lb empty. 31.1in barrel, 4-groove rifling; RH, concentric. Integral clip-loaded box magazine, 5 rounds. Quadrant sight graduated to 2100m (2295yd). 2410 fps with ball cartridges. Experimental épée bayonet?

The army acquired substantial numbers of rifles for field trials in the 1890s. They were virtually identical with the M1892 Romanian Mannlicher (q.v.) except for detail differences – a special rear sight, an enlarged bolt handle, and an additional guide rib on the bolt body. The bayonet lug lay under the nose cap. Unlike the Romanian gun, which would accept a bolt in the unlikely event of the head being omitted during reassembly, the Dutch rifle could not receive a wrongly assembled bolt unless the bolt stop was depressed manually.

MODEL 1895 RIFLE
Infanterie-Geweer M1895

Made by Österreichische Waffenfabriks-Gesellschaft, Steyr, 1895-1902; and by the Artillerie-Inrichtingen, Hembrug, 1901-20.

Total production: not known. **Chambering:** 6.5x53, rimmed. **Action:** as Mannlicher trials rifles, above.

51in overall, 9.48lb empty. 31.1in barrel, 4-groove rifling; RH, concentric. Integral clip-loaded box magazine, 5 rounds. Quadrant sight graduated to 2000m (2185yd). 2425 fps with M1895 ball cartridges. M1895 épée bayonet.

This was an adaptation of the preceding 1892-pattern trials rifle, sharing a split-bridge receiver. The magazine projected beneath the stock. The butt had a straight wrist, a handguard ran forward from the receiver ring to the spring-retained barrel band, and the nose cap carried a projecting bayonet bar similar to that found on the British Lee-Metford.

A few guns were converted to 8mm in 1917, and others were cut down in the early 1930s to produce No. 5 carbines for the Dutch air force. In addition, many Mannlichers were converted in the Netherlands Indies during the Japanese occupation (1942-5), accepting Japanese regulation Type 99 7.7mm semi-rim ammunition, and others were converted in Indonesia after 1949 for the British rimmed 303 cartridge.

SIMILAR GUNS

7.9mm conversions. Substantial quantities of 1895-type rifles were altered in Hembrug in 1910 to chamber the German 7.9x57 rimless cartridge shared with the Dutch Lewis and Schwarzlose machine guns. Muzzle velocity rose to about 2880 fps, but the project was not successful. The 7.9mm guns are customarily listed as 'M1917' in English-language sources (including the first edition of *Rifles of the World*) and have been associated with machine gunners; this is an old established error which should now be corrected.

Practice rifle. The *Geweer tot kamerschietoefeningen* – of uncertain vintage – was chambered for low-powered 5.5mm (.22) centerfire cartridges which could be loaded in a special five-round clip; the rifle was basically an M1895 infantry pattern, but weighed 10.35lb. It was prominently marked 'K.S.O.' on the right side of the butt.

MODEL 1895 CARBINE NO. 1
Karabijn M1895 A.1

Made by Österreichische Waffenfabriks-Gesellschaft, Steyr, 1897-1904; and by the Artillerie Inrichtingen, Hembrug, 1902-20.

Total production: not known. **Chambering:** 6.5x53, rimmed. **Action:** as M1895 rifle, above.

37.5in overall, 6.85lb empty. 17.7in barrel, 4-groove rifling; RH, concentric. Integral clip-loaded box magazine, 5 rounds. Quadrant sight graduated to 2000m (2185yd). 2050 fps with M1895 ball cartridges. M1871 socket bayonet.

A half-stocked carbine was issued to the cavalry and horse artillery from about 1897. A handguard was omitted, and the forend narrowed perceptibly ahead of the single barrel band. Fixed sling bars lay on the left side of the barrel band and on the left side of the butt close to the buttplate.

Most carbines were improved after 1915 to the 'New Model' (*Nieuw Model*) standards, which included pinning and gluing a wooden fairing to the left side of the magazine to stop the uniform being abraded when the gun was slung over the shoulder. Surviving guns of original pattern were reclassified as 'Old Model' (*Oude Model*) to distinguish them. The cavalry carbine stock was adapted in the 1920s to receive a conventional nose cap, and a short M1895 cavalry-pattern bayonet was adopted at much the same time.

SIMILAR GUNS

Model 1895 Carbine No. 2. Adopted about 1899 for the Korps Marechaussee (military gendarmerie), this was a variant of the No. 1 or cavalry pattern with a conventional full-length stock. There were two bands, the front one doubling as a nose cap, and a special bayonet – locked by a spring – could be rotated into place on the right side of the muzzle. When reversed, the tip of bayonet blade abutted a shoulder on the right side of the rear band. Swivels lay beneath the barrel band and butt. Details were generally similar to No. 1, except for an empty weight of 7.1lb and the attachment of a folding bayonet. Old and new-model variants are known.

Model 1895 Carbine No. 3. Believed to have been adopted about 1904 for the fortress artillery, engineers and sappers, the No. 3 carbine had a distinctive handguard running forward past the nose cap and over the top of the muzzle. It was issued with a long-bladed bayonet to compensate for the lack of reach. The swivels lay on the underside of the barrel band and the under-edge of the butt. The gun weighed 6.9lb and accepted the long M1895 épée bayonet. Old and new-model variants are known.

Model 1895 Carbine No. 4. The No. 4 carbine of 1908 was a minor variant of the No. 3, for cyclists and machine gunners, with a conventional handguard assembly ending at the nose cap. The swivels lay on the left side of the forend – owing to the lack of a barrel band – and on the side of the butt. Old and new-model variants are known. New swivels were added beneath the band and nose cap in 1939.

The M1895 Mannlicher rifle, with its distinctive sword bayonet.

The No. 4 carbine, with post-1939 sling swivels.

Model 1895 Carbine No. 5. Adopted in 1938 for issue to personnel of the anti-aircraft and motorized artillery units, this was made by cutting down full-length rifles. It lacked the wood fillet on the magazine side, had a rifle-type nose cap, and could be identified by original manufacturing marks. The No. 5 carbine was 37.8in long, weighed 7.85lb empty, and had a 17.9in barrel; the rear sight was graduated to 2000m (2185yd).

Model 1911 KNIL carbine. This colonial pattern was made in small numbers for the Royal Netherlands Indies Army (KNIL); its bolt handle was turned down, and it accepted a strange knife-bladed bayonet with a bar hilt.

• Mauser

MODEL 1948 GENDARMERIE CARBINE
Made by Fabrique Nationale d'Armes de Guerre, Herstal-lèz-Liége, Belgium.
Total production: not known. **Chambering:** 7.9x57, rimless. **Action:** locked by two lugs on the bolt head engaging seats in the receiver behind the chamber, as the bolt handle was turned down, and by a third lug opposing the bolt handle base entering a recess in the receiver.

37.2in overall, 7.5lb empty. 17.3in barrel, 4-groove rifling; RH, concentric. Internal box magazine, 5 rounds. Tangent-leaf rear sight graduated to 1400m (1530yd). About 2650 fps with standard ball cartridges. FN 'export' type knife bayonet.

These short-barreled guns were purchased after the Second World War for the gendarmerie and police. A few were acquired in 1961 for the short-lived defense forces in Papua, which was incorporated into Indonesia within a year of issue.

The bolt handle was turned down against the stock, the 'H'-type nose cap had a short bayonet bar, and there were swivels under the band and butt. The handguard ran forward from the chamber to the band.

Carbines of this type were handy weapons, but suffered from an awesome muzzle blast. They displayed the crowned cyphers of the Dutch queens – 'W' for Wilhelmina (1948) and 'J' for Juliana (1948 onward) – above the chamber on the butt.

NEW ZEALAND

• Lee-Enfield
Lacking production facilities, New Zealand traditionally relied on British and Australian weapons. In response to requests, Enfield made about 1,500 'Carbines, Magazine, Lee-Enfield, fitted to receive P/88 Sword-bayonet' in 1901-3. The diameter of the muzzle was increased, while the sights duplicated those of the Martini-Enfield Artillery Carbine Mk III. The guns were 40.31in overall, had 21in barrels and weighed about 7.5lb; 'NZ' usually appeared on the butt, together with a Broad Arrow.

• Parker-Hale
The New Zealand forces currently use the Australian version (q.v.) of the 7.62x51 Parker-Hale M82 sniping rifle.

• Remington-Lee
Five hundred 43 (11mm Spanish) M1885 Lee-action rifles were purchased in 1887, during one of the periodic 'Russian Invasion' scares. The guns were numbered at random in the 41500-44000 group, and had 'N Z' over '87' on the receiver ring. They were extremely unsuccessful in service, though the faults were subsequently attributed to the poor quality of locally-made ammunition. Some of the rifles were converted to rudimentary sporters, but few survive.

NICARAGUA

• Mauser
Some 7x57 vz. 23 rifles and vz. 12/33 carbines were ordered from Ceskoslovenská Zbrojovka in the 1930s. Though some were apparently marked in Czechoslovakian, most bore their maker's name in Spanish and a version of the National Arms above the chamber. This comprised five volcanoes and a Liberty Cap on a staff, rising out of a seascape beneath a sunrise and a rainbow.

NIGERIA

• FN-Saive
The basic FAL was adopted in 1967. Most were made in Belgium, though some Enfield-made L1A1 rifles were supplied from Britain. A license to make make FALs in the Kaduna ordnance factory was purchased in the mid 1970s, superseding the Beretta BM-59 (q.v.), but no production was ever undertaken.

• Garand
The Nigerian government purchased a license to make the BM-59 in Kaduna. However, the civil war interrupted plans and there is no evidence that guns were made. Nigerian Garands invariably prove to have been made in Italy.

NORWAY

• Heckler & Koch
In 1964, the German-style Automatisk Gevær 3 (G3A3 type) was adopted for service with the army, tooling beginning immediately in Kongsberg Våpenfabrikk. The first Norwegian-made AG3 was assembled in 1966-7. However, production has always been slow and periodic shortages have been resolved by buying rifles from Germany. The army has also acquired substantial numbers of 5.56x45 Heckler & Koch rifles for trials, but future requirements are currently unclear.

• Jarmann
The mechanism of this magazine rifle relied on a turning bolt, adapted from the French Gras (q.v.), and a Kropatschek-inspired tube magazine in the forend beneath the barrel which could be loaded through the top of the open action. Like virtually all similar rifles, the Jarmann could carry a ninth cartridge on the elevator and a 10th in the chamber.

Experimental Jarmanns were tested extensively by a joint Norwegian-Swedish army board in 1878-9, but the Swedes decided to

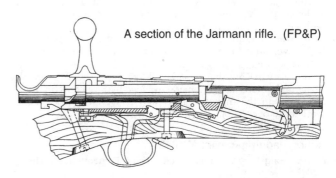

A section of the Jarmann rifle. (FP&P)

retain the single shot Remington. However, about 500 Jarmann rifles were made in Eskilstuna in 1880-2 by the Swedish state gun factory – Carl Gustafs Stads Gevärsfactori – for trials in Norway. These had a selection of magazines (including gravity-feed box patterns), and a variety of knife, sword, folding and rod bayonets.

A typical rifle, with a five-round gravity feed magazine offset to the right side of the receiver, had three bands and a block-and-leaf rear sight. Chambered for a 10.15x61 rimmed cartridge, it was about 52.95in long and had a 32.3in barrel. The bolt cocked on opening.

The success of the Jarmann persuaded the Norwegians to continue, having settled on a tube magazine. About 1,000 trials guns were then made in Sweden in 1882-3.

MODEL 1884
Infantry rifle: Jarmann Repetergevær M /1884
Made by Kongsberg Våpenfabrikk, 1884-9.

Total production: about 28,000 (all types), 1884-97. **Chambering:** 10.15x61, rimmed. **Action:** locked by a single lug on the bolt engaging a recess in the receiver as the bolt handle was turned down.

52.95in overall, 9.75lb empty. 32.6in barrel, 4-groove rifling; LH, concentric. Tube magazine under barrel, 8 rounds. Tangent-leaf sight (see notes). 1360 fps with M/86 ball cartridges. M/84 épée (army) or knife (navy) bayonets.

This indigenous design was adopted for the Norwegian army and navy in 1884. The bolt handle was set well forward above the trigger guard even though the receiver had a solid bridge. The one-piece walnut or birch stock had a single spring-retained band and a pinned nose cap, with a bayonet lug on its right side.

The original rear sight was graduated to 1500m (1640yd) with an auxiliary 'long range' sight on the left side of the forend for distances up to 2400m (2625yd). After a minor change had been made in the ammunition in 1886, the rear sight was re-graduated to 1600m (1750yd) and the long range sight on the forend was adjusted accordingly.

Limited quantities of Jarmann rifles were sold commercially, presumably to members of the Norwegian shooting association (Skytterlag). However, the Jarmann was rapidly overhauled by better small caliber designs and replaced after 1895 by the Krag-Jørgensen.

SIMILAR GUNS
M/1884/87. Though several minor alterations were made to the M/1884, this was the only major variant of the original gun. It was distinguished by a magazine cut-off added on the left side of the receiver.

Carbines. Several types of short-barreled gun were made experimentally, often in reasonable numbers. They included a single shot pattern stocked virtually to the muzzle, and a shortened version of the infantry rifle with a six-round magazine and a spatulate bolt handle turned down against the stock.

• Kammerladningsgevær

The inspiration for these strange, but surprisingly long-lived guns was the Danish Løbnitz chamber-loader (q.v.), though changes were made to the firing system for Norwegian service. The work is often credited to gunsmith F.W. Scheel.

Guns of this type are easily identified, though changes made during their service lives – particularly to the sights – can hinder the identification of individual models. The original sights were all graduated in alen, each equivalent to about 24.7in.

The large box-like receiver contained a chamber which could be elevated at the mouth by turning the lever on the right side of the breech. An underhammer caplock within a large bow-like spring was standard; unlike the original Danish guns, however, the Norwegian patterns all had conventional trigger guards.

Most Kammerladningsgeværer were made in the government manufactory in Kongsberg (marked 'K' beneath a crown), though substantial quantities were made in Liége by Francotte (marked 'I.P.', or with the maker's name) and in Herzberg by Crause (marked 'R' over 'C.H.').

MODEL 1842 RIFLE
Kammerladningsgevær M/1842
Made by Kongsberg Våpenfabrikk (400) and A. Francotte, Liége (100), 1842-6.

Total production: 500. **Chambering:** 18-bore (16.8mm) combustible cartridge, fired by a cap lock. **Action:** locked by rotating the breech-chamber into line with the barrel.

55.7in overall, 12.13lb empty. 36.7in barrel, 6-groove rifling; RH, concentric. Single shot only. Standing-block sight for 200 alen (135yd). About 1165 fps with ball ammunition. Socket bayonet.

Issued largely for extended trials, these guns had a chamber diameter of 13-bore – .710in (18.03mm). The stock, made of walnut (or occasionally birch on Kongsberg-made guns), had a straight grip. The barrel was held in the forend by two barrel bands and a nose cap, the mounts being held by springs. Swivels lay under the middle band ahead of the hammer-spring. All the mounts, including the trigger guard and the buttplate, were brass.

Most 1842-pattern rifles were subsequently converted by the substitution of the M/49 and M/55 rear sights, and by the substitution of the 1846-type bayonet (with an angular slot and a locking ring) for the original straight-slot design, which was retained by a spring.

MODEL 1846 RIFLE
Kammerladningsgevær M/1846
Made by Kongsberg Våpenfabrikk (3000?), A. Francotte, Liége (1500), and Crause of Herzberg (1500), 1846-50.

Total production: about 6000. **Chambering:** 18-bore (16.8mm) combustible cartridge, fired by a cap lock.

Otherwise generally as M/1842, above, except for the use of the 1846-pattern socket bayonet.

This was the perfected series-made version of the 1842-type chamber-loading rifle, with a better bayonet – retained by a locking ring – and a few internal improvements. They are now usually found with the improved M/1855 rear sight instead of the original fittings.

MODEL 1848 CADET RIFLE
'Officers Academy rifle': Krigsskolens kammerladnings-gevær M/1848 med sabelbajonett

Made exclusively by Kongsberg Våpenfabrikk, several patterns of this short rifle were issued to cadets. They were considerably shorter than usual – 2in, 7.5in or 12in – to account for the changing stature of the cadets as they grew. Apart from the reduction of the barrel fittings to a single band and a nose cap, the most distinctive feature was the bar on the muzzle to accept the 1848-pattern sabre bayonet.

MODEL 1849 RIFLE
Kammerladningsgevær M/1849
Made by Kongsberg Våpenfabrikk (6500?), A. Francotte, Liége (2000), and Crause of Herzberg (2000), 1849-54.

Total production: about 10,500. **Chambering:** 18-bore (16.8mm) combustible cartridge, fired by a cap lock.

Otherwise generally as M/1842, above, except for the sights and bayonet.

This was little more than an improved M/1846. The rear sight, placed behind the chamber, consisted of a standing block for 200 alen (135yd) and leaves for 300 and 400 alen (205yd and 275yd). However, sharpshooters' rifles had an additional leaf-type sight on the barrel suitable for ranges up to 800 alen (550yd) and most of the original sights were subsequently replaced by the M/1855 pattern. Small improvements were made in the action, the most visible being the broadened hammer ears. The 1846-type socket bayonet was usually issued with the M/1849 rifle.

MODEL 1855 RIFLE
Kammerladningsgevær M/1855
Made by Kongsberg Våpenfabrikk, 1855-60.

Total production: about 4000. **Chambering:** 18-bore (16.8mm) combustible cartridge, fired by a cap lock.

Otherwise generally as M/1842, above, except for the sights and bayonet.

This was the first real improvement in the chamber-loading rifle since the original batches had been made in 1842. The principal change lay in the adoption of the M/1855 expanding bullet, replacing the M/1842 ball, which increased both range and accuracy.

Carried on a broad band around the barrel, the new two-leaf rear sight had a standing notch for 300 alen (205yd) on the short leaf and settings for 400-700 alen (275-480yd) on the longer one; a notch in the top of the longer leaf sufficed for 800 alen (550yd). Two barrel bands and a nose cap were retained, though the under-edge of the butt had a much more 'bellied' appearance than its much straighter predecessors.

The serial numbers of the M/1855 ran on from those of the 1849 pattern, but many older guns were converted to 1855 standards in the late 1850s and early 1860s. These can be identified by the presence of makers' and other marks dating back to an earlier period.

SIMILAR GUNS

M/1855 med sabelbajonett. This special infantry rifle, made in small numbers, was little more than an M/1849 adapted to accept the 1848-type sabre bayonet. It was issued to infantry NCOs and the NCOs and men of the rifle battalions and light infantry units. The combination of a long barrel and a heavy bayonet was much too clumsy, so the bayonet was rapidly reduced to sidearm status.

MODEL 1857 CAVALRY CARBINE
Kammerladnings-kavalenkarabin M/1857
Made by Kongsberg Våpenfabrikk, 1857-9.

Total production: not known. **Chambering:** 12.55mm combustible cartridge, fired by a cap lock. **Action:** generally as M/1842 (q.v.).

37.5in overall, 5.73lb. 17.9in barrel, 6-groove rifling; RH, concentric. Single shot only. Leaf-type rear sight graduated to 400 alen (275yd). About 970 fps with ball ammunition. No bayonet.

The most distinctive features of this carbine, apart from its compact dimensions, were the partial enclosure of the receiver-box in the birch stock and the extension of the forend almost to the muzzle. The band, nose cap, trigger guard and buttplate were all brass, and a large swivel ring was attached to the left side of the stock alongside the receiver.

MODEL 1859 SHORT RIFLE
Kort kammerladningsgevær M/1859
Made by Kongsberg Våpenfabrikk, 1859-62.

Total production: 1500? **Chambering:** 18-bore (16.8mm) combustible cartridge, fired by a cap lock. **Action:** as M/1842 (q.v.).

49.5in overall, 10.5lb. 30.3in barrel, 6-groove rifling; RH, concentric. Single shot only. M/1855-pattern two-leaf rear sight. About 1075 fps with ball ammunition. Sabre bayonet.

This was the first short-barrel gun to achieve general issue. It had a single barrel band and a nose cap, and a bar on the right side of the muzzle to accept the sabre bayonet of the M/1825 pillar-breech rifle. Issued to sharpshooters, riflemen and infantry NCOs, it was numbered in the same sequence as the M/1849 and M/1855.

SIMILAR GUNS

Conversions of the M/1842, M/1846 and M/1849 rifles to M/1859 standards are known. Most have their barrels and forends cut by 6-6.5in, and the middle band moved forward to become a nose cap. Conversions can usually be identified by old marks and signs of alteration, and by the use of a socket bayonet instead of the sabre type.

MODEL 1860 RIFLE
Kammerladningsgevær M/1860
Made by Kongsberg Våpenfabrikk, 1861-7.

Total production: 8500? **Chambering:** 11.77mm combustible cartridge, fired by a cap lock. **Action:** generally as M/1842 (q.v.).

55.1in overall, 9.65lb empty. 36.5in barrel, hexagonal Whitworth-type rifling; RH, concentric. Single shot only. Two-leaf rear sight graduated to 750 alen (515yd). Performance: not known. Socket bayonet.

This improved small-bore rifle had a chamber diameter of .485 (12.33mm). It was little more than a lightened version of the M/1855, with a straight-wrist stock, two barrel bands and a nose cap. Furniture was brass, including the trigger guard and the buttplate. The socket bayonet was similar to the 1846 type, but had a smaller internal diameter. The most obvious feature of the new rifle-musket, however, was the hexagonal bore.

Sharpshooters were issued with rifles which had rear sights with an additional leaf-and-slider graduated to 1500 alen (1030yd). A few extra guns, mounted in iron with a horn forend tip, were made for sale to members of the national shooting association (Skytterlag). Many of these display a retainer-spring for a socket bayonet of 1842 type, though there is no evidence that bayonets were ever issued. Shooting association guns were often subjected to the Landmark metallic-cartridge conversion (q.v.) instead of the Lund pattern favored by the army.

MODEL 1860 SHORT RIFLE
Kort kammerladningsgevær M/1860 med sabelbajonett
Made by Kongsberg Våpenfabrikk, 1862-7.

Total production: about 3500. **Chambering:** 11.77mm combustible cartridge, fired by a cap lock.

Otherwise generally as M/1860, above, except for the bayonet.

This was a shorter version of the infantry rifle, inspired by the 18mm M/1859, with only a single band in addition to the nose cap. A lug on the right side of the muzzle accepted a version of the M/1825/60 sabre bayonet with a smaller muzzle ring. A few similar guns were made for the national shooting association, with iron mounts (instead of brass) and a special horn-tip forend.

MODEL 1862/66 FOOT ARTILLERY CARBINE
Kammerladningskarabin for fotartilleriet M/1862/66
Made by Kongsberg Våpenfabrikk, 1866-8.

Total production: not known (1000?). **Chambering:** 11.77mm combustible cartridge, fired by a cap lock.

Otherwise generally as M/1857, above, except for the bayonet and sights.

Twenty experimental carbines were made in the Kongsberg factory in 1859 for trials with the artillery. They had short round barrels with a single barrel band, a nose cap, and a bayonet lug on the right side of the muzzle. Trials were concluded successfully in 1862, but lack of funds caused the project to be deferred for several years. The perfected carbines had rear sights with a standing block for 200 alen (135yd), and two small leaves for 400 alen (275yd) and 600 alen (410yd). The sabre bayonet was similar to the 1860 pattern, but had a shorter hilt.

MODEL 1865 CAVALRY CARBINE
Kammerladnings-kavalenkarabin M/1865
Made by Kongsberg Våpenfabrikk, 1866-8.

Total production: not known (1000?). **Chambering:** 11.77mm combustible cartridge, fired by a cap lock.

Otherwise generally as M/1862/66, above, except for the bayonet.

This was very similar to the foot artillery carbine, with the same forend and barrel-band arrangement, but lacked the bayonet lug and had a sling ring on the left side of the breech.

• Kongsberg

These rifles, introduced in 1993, replaced the conventional Mauser-action patterns being made in the formerly state-owned ordnance factory. The essence of the system was a new three-lug bolt with a 60-degree throw.

CLASSIC SPORTING RIFLE
Made by Kongsberg Våpenfabrikk, Kongsberg.

Currently in production. **Chambering options:** 22-250, 243 Winchester, 6.5x55 Mauser, 270 Winchester, 30-06 or 308 Winchester.
DATA FOR A 6.5MM EXAMPLE

44in overall, 7.5lb empty. 23in barrel, 4-groove rifling; RH concentric. Internal rotary magazine, 4 rounds. Ramped open rear sight. 2720 fps with 139-grain bullet.

This is a conventionally half-stocked rifle with a pistol grip butt, a straight comb, and a rubber shoulder pad. The receiver is drilled to accept telescope-sight mount bases. The adjustable trigger is accompanied by a three-position safety lever on the right side of the action behind the bolt handle, and special attention is paid to the design of the claw-type extractor. A left-hand action has also been offered.

SIMILAR GUNS

Magnum. This is a minor variant of the Classic, with a longer action and a 26in barrel. It is chambered for the 7mm Remington, 300 Winchester or 338 Winchester magnum cartridges, and has a three-round magazine. Weight averages 7.8lb.

Thumbhole (or 'Sniper'). Offered only in 22-250 and 308, with a 23in heavy barrel, this variant has a thumbhole-type walnut stock with a broad forend and an adjustable elevating comb. The forend and the pistol grip are both stippled. The enlarged bolt knob facilitates grip, an optical sight is regarded as standard, and spacers can be used to lengthen the butt.

• Krag-Jørgensen

The Krag bolt-action rifle has a distinctive 'case' magazine in the receiver beneath the bolt, feeding cartridges laterally. The Danish loading gate hinges forward; U.S. and Norwegian patterns hinge down. The comparatively weak one-lug action, which precluded the adoption of high power cartridges, caused the rapid replacement of the U.S. Krag-Jørgensen by the 30 Springfield magazine rifle (q.v.), which was a modified Mauser. Most of the Danish and Norwegian guns, however, lasted into the 1950s.

Ole Krag, director of the government small arms factory in Kongsberg, reported in 1887 that progress in Denmark would soon make the then-new Norwegian Jarmann rifle obsolete. In January 1888, therefore, the Defence Ministry sanctioned trials to find a new small caliber service rifle. By 1892, extensive trials had narrowed the choice to guns submitted by Mauser, Mannlicher and Krag & Jørgensen.

The commission made its final report on 3rd May 1893. A Krag-Jørgensen was unanimously approved, 50 hand-made experimental guns being ordered from Kongsberg to facilitate troop trials in the late summer. Once these had been concluded, the rifle was officially adopted on 21st April 1894.

MODEL 1894 RIFLE
Krag-Jørgensengevær M/1894

Made by Österreichische Waffenfabriks-Gesellschaft, Steyr, 1895-8 (29,000 guns); Fabrique Nationale d'Armes de Guerre, Herstal-lèz-Liége, 1895 (a few); and Kongsberg Våpenfabrikk, 1896-1935 (125,000).

Total production: about 155,000. **Chambering:** 6.5x55, rimless. **Action:** locked by a single lug on the bolt head engaging a recess in the receiver behind the chamber as the bolt handle was turned down, and by the bolt-guide rib abutting the bridge.

49.6in overall, 8.93lb empty. 29.9in barrel, 4-groove rifling; LH, concentric. Internal pan magazine, 5 rounds. Tangent-leaf sight graduated to 2000m (2185yd). 2395 fps with M/97 ball cartridges. M/1894 knife or M/1912 sword bayonets.

The Norwegian Krag was a considerable improvement on the Danish m/1889 (q.v.). Its rimless cartridge minimized feed troubles, while the downward-hinged magazine gate doubled as a loading platform.

Like all Krags, the M/1894 magazine could be replenished even when the action was cocked and locked, though a rotary cut-off isolated the magazine when required. The locking lug turned down into the receiver immediately behind the chamber, additional security being provided by the abutment of the bolt guide rib on the front of the receiver bridge and by the bolt handle seating in the receiver.

The rifles had an elegant pistol grip walnut stock (birch on later guns) with a finger groove beneath the rear sight. A handguard ran from the receiver ring to the rear barrel band. The bands were retained by springs let into the left side of the stock, and did not touch the 'floating' barrel. Swivels usually lay on the upper band and on the underside of the butt, while a stacking swivel was fitted on the fore-band. A half-length cleaning rod was carried under the barrel. Sights were graduated for the M/94 cartridge, and a Mauser-type safety lay on the cocking piece. The later navy guns lacked the butt-trap.

The combination bolt-stop/hold-open was abandoned in 1897. Whether changes were made for the improved cartridge is not known, as the trajectories of the M/94 and M/97 bullets seem to have been similar.

The Royal Norwegian navy received its first rifles in 1901, taken from the commercial series (numbered 2511-3010, and apparently 3011-5906), and work began in Kongsberg in 1905 to adapt 1,000

standard rifles (89601-90600) to accept German Ajack 4x optical sights for issue to marksmen. Conversion was completed in 1907, but the sights proved to be unreliable in sub-zero conditions and so the guns reverted to standard form after the introduction of the m/23.

Experiments with pointed bullets, begun in 1905, culminated in 1923 in the adoption of the M/1923 spitzer. Revisions to the rear sight – which was graduated to 2200m (2405yd) – were not completed until 1938!

SIMILAR GUNS

Model 1923 marksman's rifle (Skarpskyttegevær M/1923). This replaced the standard M/1894 pattern when the Ajack optical sight proved to be unreliable in sub-zero conditions. The M/23 rifle had an open micro-adjustable aperture sight ('Dioptersikte M/23'), graduated to 1000m (1095yd), and a full-length stock with a handguard, two barrel bands, and a M/1912-type nose cap. The radius of the pistol grip was rather sharper than the standard M/1894 pattern and checkering improved grip. The special heavy 'floating' 26.2in barrel had a muzzle diameter of .668 rather than the standard .591. Sling swivels lay on the underside of the second barrel band and on the under-edge of the butt. About 320 M/1923 rifles were made by Kongsberg Våpenfabrikk in 1923-5, but virtually all were subsequently converted to M/1930 standards.

Model 1925 marksman's rifle (Skarpskyttegevær M/1925). Little more than an 1894-type infantry rifle with the aperture sight, this also had a large-diameter heavy barrel and a front sight with eared protectors. The guns were apparently numbered in the standard M/94 series, but their receivers displayed 'M.25' in addition to 'M/1894'. About 110 were made Kongsberg Våpenfabrikk in 1926-7. The M/25 was superseded by the much improved 1930-type sniper rifle described below.

Model 94/43 short rifle. The Krag-Jørgensen served reliably until World War II, when some M/1894 rifles were modified to M/1912 length during the German occupation. Fitted with front sight protectors, the conversions displayed German ordnance marks.

MODEL 1895 CAVALRY CARBINE
Krag-Jørgensenkarabin for Kavaleriet M/1895
Made by Kongsberg Våpenfabrikk, 1896-1912.

Total production: 5000. **Chambering:** 6.5x55, rimless. **Action:** as M/1894 rifle, above.

39.95in overall, 7.5lb empty. 20.45in barrel, 4-groove rifling; LH, concentric. Internal pan magazine, 5 rounds. Tangent-leaf sight graduated to 2000m (2185yd). 2100 fps with M/1923 ball cartridges. No bayonet.

This neat half-stock carbine, introduced in 1895, had a short handguard running from the receiver ring to the rear sight base. Its action was identical with the M/1894 rifle. The forend, narrowing abruptly to save weight, was retained by a single sprung barrel band. Swivels lay on the left side of the band and under the butt behind the pistol grip.

The hold-open/bolt-stop was abandoned in 1897, and the carbines made from 1908 until production ceased had the rear swivel on the left side of the guard.

SIMILAR GUNS

Model 1906 cadet carbine (Krag-Jørgensenkarabin for Skoler). This was identical with the M/95 cavalry carbine except for the omission of the handguard to save weight. Colloquially known as 'gutte karabin' or "boys' carbines", these guns were used for

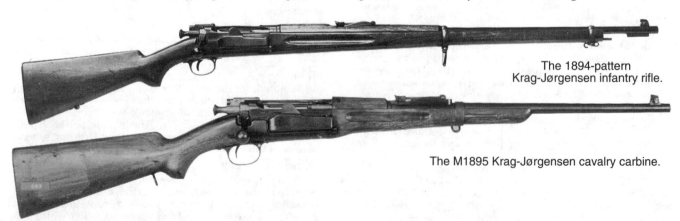

The 1894-pattern Krag-Jørgensen infantry rifle.

The M1895 Krag-Jørgensen cavalry carbine.

marksmanship training in the Norwegian secondary schools, where shooting with reduced-charge ammunition was regularly practiced at 100m (110yd). About 3320 were made by Kongsberg Våpenfabrikk in 1906-12.

MODEL 1897 MOUNTAIN ARTILLERY AND ENGINEER CARBINE
Krag-Jørgensenkarabin for bergartilleriet og ingeniørvåpnet M/1897
Made by Kongsberg Våpenfabrikk, 1897-1911.
Total production: less than 2000. **Chambering:** 6.5x55, rimless.
Otherwise generally as M/1895, above.

Dating from 1897, this was practically identical with the cavalry carbine described previously – except that the rear swivel lay 4in from the toe of the butt instead of behind the pistol grip.

MODEL 1904 ENGINEER CARBINE
Krag-Jørgensenkarabin for ingeniørvåpnet M/1904
Made by Kongsberg Våpenfabrikk, 1904-15.
Total production: a few thousands. **Chambering:** 6.5x55, rimless. **Action:** as M/1894 rifle, above. Otherwise generally as M/1897 carbine, except weight (8.4lb empty) and provision for mounting the M/1894 knife or M/1912 sword bayonets.

Introduced in 1904, this was similar to the M/1897 (q.v.). However, it was stocked to the muzzle and had two spring-retained barrel bands. The full-length handguard and half-length cleaning rod increased the overall weight, while swivels lay under the front barrel band and on the left side of the trigger guard.

SIMILAR GUNS
Model 1907 field-artillery carbine (Krag-Jørgensenkarabin for feltartilleriet). About 2,000 of these were made in Kongsberg in 1907-15. They were intended to replace the M/1895 cavalry carbine in the field artillery units, and were identical with the M/1904 pattern apart from the position of the swivels – one on the left side of the rear barrel band and the other on the under-edge of the butt about 4in from the toe.

MODEL 1912 SHORT RIFLE
Krag-Jørgensenkarabin M/1912
Made by Kongsberg Våpenfabrikk, 1912-35.
Total production: 30,120. **Chambering:** 6.5x55, rimless. **Action:** as M/1894 rifle, above.
43.55in overall, 8.86lb empty. 24in barrel, 4-groove rifling; LH, concentric. Internal pan magazine, 5 rounds. Tangent-leaf sight graduated to 2000m (2185yd). 2330 fps with M/1923 ball cartridges. M/1912 sword bayonet.

Trials began in 1909 with a shortened Krag-Jørgensen intended for universal issue, many of the prototypes having pivoting or rod bayonets. The adoption of the M/1912 was duly approved in 1912.

The walnut pistol gripped stock – birch in later examples – had a full-length handguard with a grasping groove beneath the M/1894 tangent sight, which virtually abutted the receiver ring. The guard extended to a nose cap from which only a small portion of the muzzle protruded. The bayonet lug lay under the nose cap, while the single barrel band carried a sling swivel on the left side. The short cleaning rod could be pushed through an eye on the nose cap during stacking. The second swivel lay on the under-edge of the butt, an auxiliary sling-hole being bored through the trigger guard bow.

Field service revealed a weakness in the stock where it joined the nose cap. A steel collar integral with the nose cap was added to guns made after 1916, older examples receiving an auxiliary bolted-on band when returning for repair. Army guns numbered below 21678 had bent-down bolt handles, but subsequent ones were straight.

The rear sight was revised from 1923 onward for the M/1923 cartridge, graduations changing to 2200m (2405yd). The alterations were made over a period of years. However, the M/1912 was not as successful as had been hoped and never entirely replaced the M/94 in Norwegian service.

MODEL 1930 MARKSMAN'S RIFLE
Skarpskyttegevær M/1930
The perfected 6.5mm Krag-Jorgensen sniper rifle had a half-stock and a free-floating super-heavy 29.9in barrel with a muzzle diameter of .827 (21mm). A single broad band retained the barrel and the handguard. The blade-type front sight had a tubular protector; swivels lay on the under-edge of the butt and under the

forend behind the band; and receivers bore additional 'M/30' marks. About 150 guns were made in the Kongsberg factory in 1931-4, and about 90 M/23 rifles were converted to 1930 standards. These can be recognized by the older marks on the receiver.

SPORTING GUNS
MODEL 1894
About 33,900 army-type M/1894 rifles – numbered from 1 – were made in the Kongsberg factory for private use, plus 4500 (numbered 3001-7500) by Österreichische Waffenfabriks-Gesellschaft. A hundred rifles were even purchased in 1896 by sympathetic anti-British German purchasers for use by the Boers during the Second South African War of 1899-1902. Regrettably, the numbers of these guns have yet to be identified.

Kongsberg also made approximately 1590 M/1912 short rifles for sale commercially, in addition to substantial quantities of sniper rifles – including 310 M/23 (numbered 2001-2310), 1,080 M/25 and a few M/30.

Guns sold privately, or to the Norwegian rifle association, lacked the butt-trap found on army issue. Service-issue guns usually bore the 'OII' or 'H7' monograms of Oscar II and his successor, Haakon VII, but the bolts of commercial guns had an axe-carrying rampant lion.

MODEL 1948
After the end of World War II, 'new' Krag-Jørgensens were assembled from M/1912 carbine actions and surplus Colt machine gun barrels. Their chambers were suitably strengthened for the 7.9mm German service cartridge. Sold commercially for target shooting, the M/48/51 had an aperture sight in front of the chamber whereas the M/48/53 had a folding open sight for 100-300 metres (110-330yd).

• Krag-Petersson
This quirky magazine rifle, credited to Norwegian Ole Krag and Swedish engineer Axel Petersson, was inspired by the block-action Lee rifle of the early 1870s.

The basis of the Krag-Petersson mechanism was a hammer-like actuating lever above the breech. Pulling the lever back dropped the breech block to receive a cartridge from the magazine beneath the barrel, extracting the spent case as it did so. At the end of the stroke, the block halted and a new cartridge was pushed into the breech manually until it entered the chamber, riding over the extractor as it did so. Pushing the operating lever half-forward until it was held on the trigger lever then closed the breech; pressing the trigger fired the gun.

MODEL 1876 NAVY RIFLE
Marinen Repetergevær M/1876
Made by Kongsberg Våpenfabrikk, 1876-7.
Total production: not known. **Chambering:** 12.17mm, rimfire. **Action:** locked by a pivoting block raised behind the chamber by a hammer-lever.
49.2in overall, 9.75lb empty. 31.8in barrel, 6-groove rifling; RH, polygonal. Tube magazine under barrel, 9 rounds. Ramp-and-leaf sight graduated to 2200 alen (1510yd)? About 1200 fps with ball cartridges. Sword bayonet.

Introduced in 1876, this rifle had a two-piece stock with a straight-wrist butt and three screwed barrel bands. One swivel lay under the middle band, with the other on the under-edge of the butt. In 1878, however, aware of the serious shortcomings of the Krag-Petersson, a committee of Swedish and Norwegian officers understandably rejected it in favor of the Jarmann (q.v.). The spurned rifle subsequently competed in Spain in 1881, with an equal lack of success.

• Landmark
This metallic-cartridge conversion system, apparently the work of an enterprising Christiana (Oslo) gunsmith, was applied in the late 1860s to the Kammerladningsgeværer or 'chamber-loading rifles'. The new two-piece breechblock distinguished it from the one-piece Lund pattern favored by the army. Landmark-converted M/1860 rifles, long or short, generally prove to have been either sold commercially or used by members of the national shooting association (Skytterlag).

• Lund
This was a conversion of the old caplock Kammerladningsgevær (chamber-loading rifle) to fire metal-case ammunition. A solid breech block, containing a firing pin and an extractor, replaced the original hollow tube-like chamber. A distinctive semi-

circular leaf spring enclosed the underhammer beneath the forend ahead of the trigger guard. Lifting the breech lever rotated the chamber upward around a pivot at the rear of the receiver. Extraction was poor, however, and the modified weapons were regarded as an expedient pending the acquisition of sufficient Remington rifles. They lasted in second-line service into the 1880s.

MODEL 1860/67 RIFLE
Langt Lunds gevær M/1860/67
Converted by Kongsberg Våpenfabrikk, 1868-9.

Total production: 4500. **Chambering:** 11.77mm, rimfire. **Action:** see Kammerladningsgevær, above.

55.7in overall, about 11lb empty. 36.6in barrel, 6-groove rifling; RH, polygonal. Ramp-and-leaf graduated to 900 alen (615yd). About 1300 fps with M/1867 ball cartridges. M/1846 socket bayonet.

The original M/1860 rifle – derived from the M/1849 musket – featured hexagonal Whitworth-type rifling. The M/1860 long rifle resembled the earlier M/1855, with three spring-retained bands, but was much more slender. The rear sight was originally a two-leaf rocking pattern, but guns issued to marksmen had a tangent-leaf sight graduated to 1500 alen (1030yd). The first issues were made in 1862. A variant with iron furniture instead of brass, and a horn-tipped forend, was made for the Norwegian rifle association.

SIMILAR GUNS
Model 1867 rifle. About 1600 new guns were made in 1869-70. All these weapons were given a new rear sight. Survivors were renamed "12mm Lund's Rifle-musket M/1867" in 1879.

MODEL 1860/67 SHORT RIFLE
Kort Lunds gevær M/1860/67
Converted by Kongsberg Våpenfabrikk, 1868-9.

Total production: 1800. **Chambering:** 11.77mm, rimfire. **Action:** as M/1867 infantry rifle, above.

49.4in overall, 10.25lb empty. 30.3in barrel, 6-groove rifling; RH, polygonal. Ramp-and-leaf sight graduated to 900 alen (615yd). About 1230 fps with M/1867 ball cartridges. M/1860 sword bayonet.

This short rifle had two spring-retained barrel bands instead of three, and a bayonet bar on the right side of the muzzle. It accepted a special sword bayonet with a muzzle-ring diameter of .736 (18.7mm). Most guns were conversions.

SIMILAR GUNS
Model 1867 rifle. About 750 of these were made in the Kongsberg factory in 1869-70. Surviving weapons were renamed "12mm Lund's Rifle M/1867" in 1879. A few supplied to the rifle association had iron furniture and horn-tip forends.

MODEL 1865/69 CAVALRY CARBINE
Lunds karabin for kavaleriet M1865/69
Converted by Kongsberg Våpenfabrikk, 1868-9.

Total production: about 1250. **Chambering:** 11.77mm, rimfire. **Action:** as M/1867 infantry rifle, above.

36.8in overall, 8.6lb empty. 17.7in barrel, 6-groove rifling; RH, polygonal. Ramp-and-leaf sight graduated to 800 alen (550yd). About 1065 fps with M/1867 ball cartridges. No bayonet.

Almost identical to the M/1862 artillery carbine, the chamber-loading cavalry carbine of M/1865/69 originally lacked swivels. A sling ring lay on the left side of the stock alongside the breech. The 1869-vintage Lund system conversions of this carbine were designated 'M/1865/69' and given new sights.

SIMILAR GUNS
Model 1869 cavalry carbine. This was simply a newly-made M/1865/69, identical in almost every respect except markings. Only about 600 were made in 1870, as the chamber-loader was superseded in front-line service by the Remington.

Model 1869/77 cavalry carbine. A minor change was made in 1877 to the cavalry carbines, when the sling ring was replaced by a swivel on the trigger guard. A new double-band nose cap and swivel were adopted at this time.

MODEL 1866/69 ARTILLERY CARBINE
Lunds karabin for artilleriet M/1866/69
Converted by Kongsberg Våpenfabrikk, 1868-9.

Total production: about 1000. **Chambering:** 11.77mm, rimfire. **Action:** as M/1867 infantry rifle, above.

36.6in overall, 8.65lb empty. 17.5in barrel, 6-groove rifling; RH, polygonal. Ramp-and-leaf sight graduated to 800 alen (550yd). About 1065 fps with M/1867 ball cartridges. M/1862 sabre bayonet.

The original chamber-loading artillery carbine of 1862 was little more than a short-barreled M/1860 rifle. It had a birch stock and brass furniture. Swivels lay on the nose cap and under the butt, the barrel accepting a special short-hilted bayonet. Virtually all guns had received new two-leaf sights (400 and 600 alen, 275 and 410yd) in 1866, but the approval for conversion to the Lund system was soon given, the resulting 'M/1866/69' carbines having 800-pace (550yd) sights.

SIMILAR GUNS
Model 1869 artillery carbine. A newly-made gun of this pattern will be dated '1869' or later, but production amounted to merely 500.

OTHER GUNS
About 1,000 Lund conversions of the 18-bore (16.8mm) M/1855 rifle-musket were made in Kongsberg in the late 1860s, receiving new 800-alen (550yd) rear sights. The one-piece stock had flats alongside the action and three barrel bands, the front band doubling as the nose cap. M/1857 socket bayonets were used, but the weapons were soon withdrawn.

SPORTING GUNS
The Lund conversion was rarely used on anything other than military guns, as the Landmark (q.v.) conversion, embodying a hinged two-piece breech block, was preferred commercially. In addition, a few guns have been seen amalgamating a modified Martini pivoting block with the side-mounted eccentric lever. Unique to Norway, these were generally the work of Hagen of Christiana (Oslo).

• Mauser
Many ex-German Kar. 98k were issued to the Norwegian army after the end of World War II, offsetting a shortage of Krags. These short rifles retained their German military proof and inspectors' marks, but may bear additional Norwegian stamps on the receiver or stock.

Some guns were converted in the late 1940s for the U.S. 30-06 (7.62x63) round, apparently for issue to the home guard, and many others were altered in the late 1950s to chamber the 7.62x51 rimless cartridge; rifles of this type are usually marked 'HÆR' ('army') on the left side of the chamber, and 'KAL 7.62 m/m' on the left side of the barrel. A groove was milled vertically across the chamber face of the 30-06 version to accept the longer cartridges and the feed aperture in the base of the receiver was appropriately widened.

MODEL 59 RIFLE
Made by Kongsberg Våpenfabrikks, 1959-70?

Total production: not known. **Chambering options:** 6.5x55, 30-06, 7.62x51 or 7.9x57. **Action:** locked by two lugs on the bolt rotating into their seats immediately behind the chamber as the bolt handle is turned down, and by a lug opposite the bolt-handle base entering a recess in the receiver.

48.45in overall, 9.88lb with sights. 27.55in barrel, 4-groove rifling; RH, concentric. Detachable box magazine, 5 rounds. Adjustable aperture rear sight graduated to 600m (655yd). 2755 fps with 7.62x51 ball cartridges.

Specially selected actions were used as the basis for 30-06 target rifles issued to the army, given to the national shooting association, or sold commercially. The first of these had a floating barrel in a special half-stock, with a new handguard (held by a single band) and a near-vertical pistol grip. A special aperture rear sight, developed by Kongsberg in collusion with the Norma ammunition factory, was fitted on the receiver bridge. The bolt handle was customarily turned downward. The Kongsberg factory maintained a lucrative business in converted Mausers for many years, and a modernized pattern (see below) is still the army sniping rifle.

SIMILAR GUN
Model 59F1. This was a variant of the 30-06 M59, introduced in 1964 after the adoption of the Heckler & Koch G3 automatic rifle. Army sniping rifles were issued with a 4x Hertel & Reuss telescope sight in a bracket-type mount on the left side of the receiver.

Model 59 single shot target-shooting versions were also made. These had the feed aperture in the bottom of the receiver filled to increase rigidity in the action.

NM149MS TARGET RIFLE

Made by Våpensmia A/S, Dokka.

Currently in production. **Chambering:** 7.62x51, rimless. **Action:** as M59, above.

44.1in overall, 12.45lb with sights. 23.6in barrel, 4-groove rifling; RH, concentric. Detachable box magazine, 5 rounds. Sights: see text. 2750 fps with ball cartridges.

Adopted by the army and police in 1988, this sniper rifle is based on a refurbished 1898-type Mauser action. A new heavy-weight cold-forged barrel is fitted, and a stiffening bar, which doubles as a rail for a Schmidt & Bender 6x42 sight, is fitted over the magazine aperture. Alternatively, an aperture sight can be substituted for use in conjunction with a conventional blade-type front sight.

The beech stock is a resin-impregnated laminate, with an optional adjustable comb. The trigger is an adjustable match-quality design, and a detachable box magazine replaces the traditional internal Mauser pattern – the sight-rail, though it does not interfere with ejection, prevents the magazine being loaded through the top of the open action.

• Remington

MODEL 1867 RIFLE
Remingtongevær M/1867

Made by Husqvarna Vapenfabrikk, 1867-8 and 1872-3 (5,000); Kongsberg Våpenfabrikk, 1869-90; and by the Hovedarsenalet, Christiana, about 1875-6 (a few hundred, assembled from Kongsberg parts).

Total production: about 5500. **Chambering:** 12.17mm, rimfire. **Action:** locked by shoulders on the hammer body propping the radial breechblock behind the chamber.

53.45in overall, 9.92lb empty. 37.3in barrel, 6-groove rifling; RH, concentric. Ramp-and-leaf sight (see notes). 1250 fps with M/1867 ball cartridges. M/1860 sabre bayonet.

Adopted in 1867, this rolling-block rifle chambered a copper-case rimfire cartridge. Norwegian-made guns usually had two-piece birch stocks, with iron furniture – including three screw-retained bands – and a brass buttplate, though the first 3,000, made in Sweden, were marked with an 'H' (for 'Husqvarna') and had iron buttplates.

The first Kongsberg-made guns appeared in 1869, marked with a crowned 'K'; Hovedarsenalet weapons bore a crowned 'A'. A Krag sight with distinctive protective wings, graduated to 1500 alen (1030yd), had been substituted for the British Enfield tangent-leaf pattern.

Changes were made in the action in 1871, when a revised gun was approved. As most of the revisions were internal, the M/1867 designation was retained even though the guns had a single lateral screw through the back of the receiver instead of two. The cartridge designation was changed to '12mm' in 1879, without affecting chambering.

MODEL 1888 CAVALRY CARBINE
Remingtonkarabin for kavaleriet M/1888

Converted by Kongsberg Våpenfabrikk, 1888-92.

Total production: not known. **Chambering:** 8x58 (?), rimmed. **Action:** as M/1867 rifle, above.

40.35in overall, 8.37lb empty. 24.2in barrel, rifling pattern unknown. Ramp-and-leaf sight graduated to 1600m (1750yd). About 1790 fps with ball cartridges. No bayonet.

Issue of the Jarmann (q.v.) repeater freed substantial quantities of single shot Remington rifles in the late 1880s. Some were converted to centerfire in 1889, and cut to carbine length for the cavalry. They had new half-stocks and a barrel band with a swivel on the left side. A sling bar was fixed to the left side of the the butt.

SIMILAR GUNS

M/1888 engineers carbine (Remingtonkarabin for ingeniørvåpnet). This was similar to the cavalry weapon, but had swivels on the underside of the band and butt. The engineer pattern often had a single extractor whereas virtually all cavalry guns possessed two.

MODEL 1891 CAVALRY CARBINE
Remingtonkarabin for kavalleriet M/1891

Converted by Kongsberg Våpenfabrikk in 1891-5, these were modifications of the earlier 1888 models with a single extractor

and a safety catch for the firing pin. The axis pins of the hammer and breechblock were held by a pivoting retainer on the right side of the receiver. The half-length forend was held by a single barrel band at its tip, and a short handguard ran from the receiver to the back-sight base. The cavalry carbine had its swivels on the side of the butt and band. Issue of the cavalry carbine was extended in 1892 to the mountain artillery (Bergartilleriet).

SIMILAR GUNS

M/1891 engineers carbine (Remingtonkarabin for ingeniørvåpnet). This was much the same as the cavalry pattern described previously, but had swivels beneath the butt and band.

ORANGE FREE STATE

• Mauser

The ordnance affairs of the Oranje Vrij Staat (OVS), a short-lived independent republic in southern Africa, remain mysterious. However, shortly after the Jameson Raid into neighbouring Transvaal in January 1896, an order was placed in Germany to offset shortages of modern magazine rifles in the hands of the state army.

MODEL 1896 RIFLE

Made by Ludwig Loewe & Co. and Deutsche Waffen- und Munitionsfabriken AG, Berlin, 1896-7.

Total production: see text. **Chambering:** 7x53, rimless. **Action:** locked by two lugs on the bolt head rotating into their seats in the receiver as the bolt handle was turned down.

48.6in overall, 8.73lb empty. 29.05in, 4-groove rifling; RH, concentric. Internal box magazine, 5 rounds. Tangent-leaf rear sight graduated to 2000m (2185yd). Knife bayonet.

True OVS rifles followed the 1893 (Spanish) pattern, but had cylindrical-head bolts and chambered a short-necked 7x53 cartridge. An 'O.V.S.' mark lay above the serial number on the left side of the receiver, usually accompanied by 'MOD. MAUSER' and the date of manufacture. This has led to the mistaken identification of two patterns (i.e., '1896' and '1897'). The serial number was customarily repeated on the left side of the stock below the receiver mark.

The first 800-1000 guns, dated 1896, used Loewe-made receivers with a distinctive 'LC' monogram. However, they may not have been delivered until after the formation of Deutsche Waffen- und Munitionsfabriken on 1st January 1897. The remaining guns all had the well-known DWM monogram trademark over the chambers.

Work was halted in 1899 by the Second South African War after substantial quantities had been delivered. The exact figures remain in dispute: estimates as great as 18,000 have been made, but gun no. 8631 has additional Chilean marks, and it may be that only about 8,000 of a 10,000-gun contract were delivered. The 'missing' 10,000 may have been Spanish 1893-pattern guns, supplied from Germany or Oviedo. Spanish-type knife bayonets were also acquired in small numbers by the Orange Free State, though very rarely used in battle; a version of the 1871-pattern German sword bayonet with a reversed quillon has also been identified with these rifles.

About 1800-2000 half-complete guns were re-chambered for the 7x57 cartridge and sold to Chile (q.v.). They bore Chilean as well as OVS markings.

PAKISTAN

• Heckler & Koch

The army purchased the first of many G3, G3A2 and G3A3 rifles about 1967, together with a license to make the G3A2 sub-variant in the government ordnance factory in Wah. In 1986, the G3A3 was substituted for the G3A2 and production continued. The Pakistani-made version had a broad forend, the furniture being a speckled brown plastic; most metal parts were phosphated and then lacquered. Rifle bipods and the special knife bayonets were made by a local sub-contractor. The rifles were still regulation service issue in 1997, though experiments with 5.56mm patterns are apparently underway.

PARAGUAY

The firearms issued in Paraguay often display a mark consisting of a star on a stylized sunburst within a wreath, usually encircled by 'REPUBLICA DEL PARAGUAY'.

• Mauser

PRE-1900 PATTERNS

Small quantities of Mo. 1895 (Chilean type) rifles were purchased from DWM in the late 1890s. They can usually be distinguished by their markings.

MODEL 1907 RIFLE

The Fusil Mauser Paraguayano was made by Deutsche Waffen- und Munitionsfabriken in 1907-12. Chambered for the 7.65x53 rimless cartridge, the rifle was very similar to the then-current Gew. 98, with safety lugs and non-rotating extractors, and even had a Lange-pattern rear sight. However, the heavy 1904-type cocking piece was used and the 'H'-type nose cap accepted a standard German export-model bayonet with a muzzle ring. Swivels lay on the underside of the butt and barrel band.

A typical example measured 49.1in overall, weighed 9.06lb, and had a 29.15in barrel with concentric four-groove rifling. The tangent sight was graduated to 2000m (2185yd) and the Mo. 1907 knife bayonet could be fitted.

SIMILAR GUNS

M1907 carbine. The Carabina Mauser Paraguayana Mo. 1907 was similar to the infantry rifle, but its stock extended to the muzzle and the plain nose cap protruded upward to protect the front sight. Bayonets could not be mounted. A sling mount lay on the left side of the spring-retained barrel band and a sling slot was cut through the butt. The rear sight was changed to a Mauser-type tangent-leaf pattern and the bolt handle turned down against the stock.

MODEL 1927 RIFLE

The Fusil Mo. 1927 was ordered in Spain, being made by Fábrica Nacional de Armas, Oviedo, c. 1927-32. Though mechanically similar to the guns supplied in 1907, it had a combination bolt stop/ stripper-clip guide. Rifles required a bayonet with the muzzle ring abutting the back of the hilt, but were usually fitted with an auxiliary-lug attachment so that 1895-type bayonets could be used. Full-length rifles were similar to the Gew. 98, with a pistol-grip stock and an 'H' nose cap. Conversion to 7.9x57 began in the early 1950s.

SIMILAR GUNS

M1927 short rifle. The Mosqueton Mo. 1927 shared the action of the full-length rifle, but had a straight-wrist stock. The bolt handle was often (but not invariably) bent downward. The gun was about 43.3in overall, weighed 8.65lb and had a 23.45in barrel rifled with four grooves turning to the right. The tangent-leaf sight was graduated to 2000m (2185yd).

M1927 carbine. Stocked virtually to the muzzle, where a simplified nose cap was fitted, the Carabina Mo. 1927 could not accept a bayonet. The action was identical with the rifle; however, the bolt handle was turned down against the stock and a sling loop lay on the left side of the barrel band.

OTHER PATTERNS

Standard-Model Mausers were bought in the mid-1930s, and FN-made Mle 24 'Mo. 1935' short rifles followed in the late 1930s. More FN rifles were acquired after the end of the Second World War. Many surviving Mle 24-type guns were converted to 7.9x57 in the 1950s.

PERSIA

Persian guns had an elaborate chamber mark comprising a stylized scimitar-wielding lion on a sunburst—beneath the distinctive Pahlavi Crown—surrounded by a wreath of laurel and oak leaves.

• Mauser

The earliest rifles seem to have been of Chilean Mo. 1895 pattern, but pre-1914 Mauser records give no other details.

MODEL 1310 RIFLE

Made by Ceskoslovenská Zbrojovka, Brno, 1931-9

Total production: said to have been 80,000. **Chambering:** 7.9x57, rimless. **Action:** locked by two lugs on the bolt head engaging recesses in the receiver behind the chamber as the bolt handle was turned down, and by a safety lug opposing the bolt handle base entering its seat.

DATA FOR SHORT RIFLE

38in overall, 8.33lb empty. 17.9in barrel, 4-groove rifling; RH, concentric. Internal charger-loaded box magazine, 5 rounds. Tangent-leaf sight graduated to 2000m (2185yd). 2755 fps with standard ball cartridges. Standard vz. 23-type sword bayonet.

A substantial quantity of vz. 98/29 rifles was ordered in Czechoslovakia in 1931. The guns chambered the 7.92mm cartridge and were apparently known as 'M1310', suitable Arabic marks appearing on the receiver.

SIMILAR GUNS

M1310 carbine. About 10,000 of these short rifles were delivered in the early 1930s. Mechanically identical with the M1310 rifle, they could be distinguished by their compact dimensions and a turned-down bolt handle.

M1317. In 1938, an order for about 100,000 vz. 98/29 (or 'M1317') rifles—including some vz. 24 short rifles—was agreed, but had not been completed when the Germans occupied Czechoslovakia.

MODEL 1328 SHORT RIFLE

Made by the state rifle factory, Mosalsalasi.

Total production: not known. **Chambering:** 7.9x57, rimless. **Action:** as M1310, above.

38.2in overall, 8.6lb empty. 18.1in barrel, 4-groove rifling; RH, concentric. Internal charger-loaded box magazine, 5 rounds. Tangent-leaf sight graduated to 1500m (1640yd)? About 2380 fps with standard ball cartridges. Standard vz. 23-type sword bayonet.

Made from 1949 onward in an arms factory erected with Czechoslovakian assistance, this was a modified vz. 98/29 carbine. The barrel-band and nose cap were stamped from steel sheet, and retained by a single spring let into the forend. A sling slot, cut through the butt in German fashion, could be used in conjunction with a fixed bar on the left side of the barrel band. A sling ring was also fitted through the front web of the trigger guard.

OTHER GUNS

Approximately 10,000 vz. 24 short rifles were acquired from Ceskoslovenská Zbrojovka in the early 1930s, together with some Mle 24 short rifles from Fabrique Nationale.

PERU

These guns are invariably distinguishable by the chamber mark. The national arms comprised a shield divided into three, with a llama and a cinchona tree (in the upper compartments) above a cornucopia. The shield was usually superimposed on two pairs of national flags, surmounted by a sunburst and surrounded by a wreath. The legends 'REPUBLICA DEL PERU' or, latterly, 'REPUBLICA PERUANA' may also appear.

The Czechoslovakian-made vz.98/29 carbine was popular in Persia.

• Mauser

MODEL 1891 RIFLE

About 30,000 examples of the Fusil Mauser Peruano Mo. 1891 were made by Ludwig Loewe & Co. in 1892-5. They chambered the 7.65x53 cartridge, but were identical with the then-current Argentine gun (q.v.) except for markings. The rifles were 48.6in overall, weighed 9.04lb, and had 29.05in barrels. The standard leaf sight was graduated to 2000m (2185yd) and an Argentine-type sword bayonet was used.

A program began in 1912 to convert most surviving Mo. 1891 rifles to handle improved pointed-bullet ammunition. These guns can be recognized by the substitution of a Lange-type tangent rear sight for the original leaf design.

MODEL 1909 RIFLE

Made by Waffenfabrik Mauser AG in Oberndorf am Neckar, about 50,000 of the 7.65mm Fusil Mauser Peruano Mo. 1909 were delivered in 1910-14. An 1898-pattern Mauser, with an auxiliary lug on the bolt and a non-rotating extractor, the rifle used the heavy 1904-type cocking piece. An 'H'-type nose cap accepted a standard German S. 98 bayonet. The Peruvian gun—49.15in long, 9.33lb empty—was mechanically similar to the Argentine Mo. 1909, but had a Lange tangent rear sight graduated to 2000m (2185yd) and lacked the special magazine floor-plate release catch in the front of the trigger guard.

OTHER PATTERNS

Peru purchased some 600 7.65x53 vz. 24-pattern short rifles from Ceskoslovenská Zbrojovka in 1930, and then 5,000 'vz. 32' (or 'Mo. 1932') short rifles in 1934. Subsequent guns—Mo. 1935 short rifles and a few carbines—seem to have been acquired from Fabrique Nationale, a few being delivered after 1945. Pre-1939 guns usually had the action of the safety catch reversed compared with their successors. Many surviving guns were converted to chamber the 30-06 cartridge in the early 1950s, owing to the ready availability of U.S. war surplus ammunition.

• Remington-Lee

The Peruvian authorities purchased 1,000 43-caliber M1882 rifles from Hartley & Graham of New York in May 1889. It is not known if distinguishing marks were used. For additional details, see 'U.S.A.: Remington-Lee'.

PHILIPPINES

• ArmaLite

About 50,000 Model 613 (XM16E1) rifles were purchased from Colt in 1965-70, and 27,000 M16A1 rifles were provided under the U.S. Military Aid Program in 1975-6. In 1967, however, a license was granted to Elisco Tool Company of Manila. Elisco has since made Model 613-P rifles, in addition to a Model 653-P carbine with a 14.5in barrel and a telescoping tubular butt. The left side of the magazine housing displays suitable marks ('Made by Elisco Tool for the Republic of the Philippines') above a 'P'-prefix serial number; an acknowledgment of the license appears on the right. Selector marks are in English.

• Arms Corporation, autoloading type

Trading prior to 1980 as Squires, Bingham & Co., using the brand name 'Squibman', this gunmaking business makes a wide range of small caliber rifles. Guns will be encountered with the marks of Armscorp Precision of San Mateo, California, Ruko Products, Inc., of Buffalo, New York, and KBI Inc. of Harrisburg, Pennsylvania—the principal North American importers in 1980-91, 1991-97 and 1997 onward respectively.

MODEL 1600 SPORTING RIFLE
Also known as 'Model 16P'

Made by the Arms Corporation of the Philippines, Makati, Rizal, 1986 to date.

Currently in production. **Chambering:** 22LR, rimfire. **Action:** no mechanical breech lock; blowback, semi-automatic only.

38.5in overall, 6.25lb empty. 18.25in barrel, 4-groove rifling; RH, concentric. Detachable box magazine, 10 or 15 rounds. Aperture-type rear sight. 1080 fps with 40-grain bullet.

This was the basic blowback semi-automatic pattern, based—loosely—on the lines of the ArmaLite AR-15 (M16) rifle. The trigger housing has been extended to form a magazine housing, a pistol grip has been added, and a carrying handle lies on top of the receiver. The butt and forend are customarily made of ebony or mahogany instead of synthetic material.

SIMILAR GUNS

Model 1600R, 1986-94. Mechanically identical with the M1600, this is distinguished by a retractable tubular stainless-steel butt and a forend with ventilation slots.

Model 1600C, 1986-7. This short-lived variant of the basic ArmaLite look-alike had a 19.5in barrel and a glass-fiber reinforced butt. The one-piece forend enveloped the barrel.

Model 1600W, 1986-7. A variant of the M1600C, this could be identified by its wooden butt and forend.

MODEL 2000P SPORTING RIFLE
Originally known as the 'Model 20P'

This shared the action of the M1600, but offered a conventional pistol grip half-stock made of mahogany. The 20.75in barrel gave an overall length of about 40.6in, weight averaging 5.8lb. Ten-round magazines and open sights were standard, though mounts for an optical sight could be fitted to the receiver rails.

SIMILAR GUNS

Model 2000 (or '20D', '2000D'),1986-7. This was a version of the M2000P with a checkered Pulong Dalaga stock and adjustable sights.

Model 2000C (or '20C'), 1990 to date. The stock of this rifle, inspired by the M1 Carbine, had a barrel band and a steel buttplate. Barrel length was merely 16.5in, giving an overall length of 38.1in. The sights comprise spring-leaf and slider, on the barrel, and a ramped blade at the muzzle.

Model 2000S, 1990 to date. Essentially similar to the M2000P, this 'Classic' has a mahogany half-stock with a Monte Carlo comb and cheekpiece; hand-cut checkering appears on the pistol grip and forend.

Model 2000SC, 1990 to date. A deluxe version of the basic design, this 'Super Classic' has a checkered American walnut half-stock with a Monte Carlo comb. The bolt is machine-jeweled, the metalwork is highly polished, and a rubber butt pad is fitted. Swivels lie beneath the butt and forend.

MODEL 50-S SPORTING RIFLE

Marketed prior to 1991 as the 'PPS-50', and inspired by pre-1945 Soviet submachine guns, this was distinguished by a ventilated barrel casing and a 16.5in barrel. The box magazines held 25 or 30 rounds, though a drum was also made in small numbers.

MODEL AK-22S SPORTING RIFLE

Introduced in 1986, this is a rimfire facsimile of the AK-47 (Kalashnikov). Capable only of semi-automatic fire, it has an 18.5in barrel, a fifteen-round box magazine, and mahogany woodwork. The AK-22F—made from 1989 to date—is mechanically identical with the 'S' pattern, but has a folding butt.

• Arms Corporation, bolt-action type

MODEL 1400P SPORTING RIFLE
Also known as 'Model 14P'

Made by the Arms Corporation of the Philippines, 1986 to date.

Currently in production. **Chambering:** 22LR, rimfire. **Action:** locked by the bolt handle base entering its seat in the receiver.

40.5in overall, 6lb empty. 23in barrel, 4-groove rifling; RH, concentric. Detachable box magazine, 5 rounds. Open rear sight. 1080 fps with 40-grain bullet.

This was the basic design, introduced in 1986. It can be distinguished by its simple sights, and by a plain half-stock which lacks checkering.

SIMILAR GUNS

Model 1400D ('14D' or '14 Deluxe'), 1987-8 and 1990 to date. Mechanically identical with the 14P, this has adjustable sights and checkering on the pistol grip of the Pulong Dalaga stock.

Model 1400LW, 1990 to date. A variant of the Model 14P with a 10-round magazine, this 'Light Weight' gun has a mahogany stock with checkering on the pistol grip and the schnabel-tipped forend. The buttplate is customarily hard rubber.

Model 1400SC, 1990 to date. Also known as the 'Super Classic', this is distinguished by an American walnut half-stock with a Monte Carlo comb and a contrasting forend tip. The bolt is usually machine-jeweled.

Model 1500, 1986 to date. Essentially similar to the M1400P, this chambers the 22 Winchester Magnum rimfire cartridge, has a 21.5in barrel, and weighs about 6.5lb. Five-round magazines are standard.

Model 1500LW, 1990 to date. This is simply a variant of the Model 1400LW chambered for magnum rimfire ammunition.

Model 1500SC, 1990 to date. Distinguished by its Monte Carlo stock, made of walnut instead of mahogany, this is a magnum rimfire version of the Model 1400SC.

MODEL 1800 SPORTING RIFLE

A few samples of these 22 Hornet derivatives of the Model 1500 were made in 1986-7. They had 23in barrels, five-round magazines, and weighed about 6.6lb. The mahogany half-stock had a checkered pistol grip and a Monte Carlo-type cheekpiece and comb; the forend was round-tipped. It is suspected that the centerfire cartridge strained the action to its limits, even though a secondary locking lug had been added opposite the bolt handle base.

POLAND

• Kalashnikov

Polish Kalashnikovs will usually display an '11-in-oval' factory mark, the date and a prefixed serial number (e.g., '1964' and 'MK12891').

KALASHNIKOV MACHINE PISTOL

Production of the Pistolet Maszynowy Kalasznikow (PMK), alternatively known as the Karabinek Automatyczny Kalasznikow (Kbk-AK), began in the principal state firearms factory in Radom in the early 1960s. The PMK was essentially similar to the original Soviet gun, but had wooden furniture, a checkered pistol grip and a selector marked 'C' and 'P'. The rifles had cleaning rods but, unlike Soviet issue, were not issued with bayonets.

SIMILAR GUNS

PMK-S. This had a folding butt—a 'C'-section pressing—with a 'U'-type shoulder piece.

PMK-DGN. Alternatively known as the 'Kbk.g wz/60', this grenade-launching variant was apparently made in a former Perkun factory in Warsaw. Adapted to fire F1/N60 anti-personnel and PGN-60 anti-tank grenades from the LON-1 launcher, it had a special leaf sight, a special small-capacity magazine, and a gas-cylinder cut-off valve marked 'O' and 'Z'. Trapezoidal metal plates were added to each side of the butt.

PMK-M. Production of an AKM-type rifle began in Factory No. 11 in 1966-7. It had a laminated forend and handguard, in addition to a checkered plastic pistol grip. Manufacturing quality was quite good, the stamped receiver and bolt cover, together with most of the minor external parts, being well blacked. Selectors bore 'C' and 'P', and a cleaning rod lay beneath the muzzle. The base of the short muzzle attachment was extended to serve as a rudimentary compensator.

PMK-MS. This was identical with the PMK-M, except for a folding stock with three rivets, three spot-welds and two short flutes on each side of the pressed-steel strut. It rotated upward.

Radom Hunter. Intended for commercial sale, this is simply a 7.62x39 AKM action—restricted to semi-automatic fire—in a wooden stock.

MODEL 88 ASSAULT RIFLE
Karabinek automatyczny wz. 88, Kbk. wz. 88

Designed by a team working in Zaklady Metalowe Lucznik, Radom, led by Bogdan Szpaderski, this was a Polish variant of the AK74S with an additional three-round burst-firing capability and an East German-style folding butt. The gas port assembly was altered, the selector lever lay on the left side of the receiver above the trigger, and tritium night-sight elements were added to the sights. Some guns will be encountered with the 40x46 Kbk-g wz. 74 grenade launcher beneath the forend.

SIMILAR GUNS

Kbk. wz. 89. This was a fixed-butt version of the 5.45x39 wz. 88, intended for export. Sales have been few, however, and work is now concentrating on the 5.56mm patterns.

Kbk. wz. 90 'Tantal'. Chambered for the 5.56x45 cartridge, this variant of the wz. 88 has a straighter magazine with strengthening ribs, and a muzzle brake doubling as a grenade launcher. The folding stock is retained.

Kbk. wz. 90 'Onyks'. A short-barrel version of the Tantal, this resembles the Soviet AKMS-U (q.v.), with a short forend and an abbreviated conical flash-hider. The short-range rear sight lies on an extension of the sight block carried backward above the ejection port.

• Mauser

The Poles, who inherited large numbers of ex-German guns, began production of 1898-type long and short rifles in the rifle factory in Warsaw after the end of the First World War. Production had moved to Radom by the late 1920s. Guns usually had a large displayed eagle on the chamber above the maker's marks.

MODEL 1898 RIFLE
Pusek wz. 98

Made by the Polish government rifle factory (Panstwowa Fabryka Karabinow) in Warsaw, c. 1923-9, these were simply copies of the German Gew. 98 (q.v.)—apparently built on ex-German machinery from Danzig arsenal. The full-length rifle, made only in small numbers, was difficult to distinguish from the German pattern. Production seems to have exceeded 125,000.

SIMILAR GUNS

Karabinek wz. 98. The short rifle had a sling bar on the left side of the stock, in addition to swivels under the band and on the under edge of the butt. A distinctive stacking rod with a squared elbow protruded from the nose-cap extension beneath the forend.

MODEL 1929 SHORT RIFLE
Karabinek wz. 1929
Made by Fabryka Broni w Polska, Radom, 1929-40.
Total production: not known. **Chambering:** 7.9x57, rimless. **Action:** locked by two lugs on the bolt head engaging recesses in the receiver behind the chamber as the bolt handle was turned down, and by a safety lug entering its seat.

43.4in overall, 9.02lb empty. 23.6in barrel, 4-groove rifling; RH, concentric. Internal charger-loaded box magazine, 5 rounds. Tangent-leaf sights graduated to 2000m (2185yd). 2475 fps with German S-Patrone. wz. 29 sword bayonet.

Inspired by the FN Mle. 24 and the Czechoslovakian vz. 24 short rifles, this was adopted in 1929 to supersede the wz. 98. Production began in 1930 in the newly equipped Radom arms factory. The gun was very similar to the Brno-made vz. 24, with the barrel band retained by a transverse bolt and a handguard running from the elongated receiver ring to the nose cap.

A cleaning rod lay under muzzle, the front-sight block was continued upward to protect the sight blade, and the bolt handle turned down against a recess cut in the side of the stock. Swivels lay on the underside of the butt and forend. A sling bar was let into the left side of the butt.

The wz. 29 was the standard infantry weapon when the Germans invaded Poland in 1940. Production continued in Radom until 1942, ceasing after about 370,000 guns had been supplied to the Wehrmacht. A few Polish short rifles were subsequently converted in Austria to Gew. 29/40 standards (see 'Germany: Mauser, bolt-action type').

• Mosin-Nagant

The earliest Polish Mosin-Nagant, introduced in the late 1920s, was a converted Russian rifle with a new 7.9mm-caliber barrel and the magazine altered to feed rimless cartridges.

MODEL 91/98/25 RIFLE

This had a German-style nose cap and bayonet bar, a swivel on the side of the barrel band and another on the left side of the butt. The gun was about 43.3in overall, had a 23.6in barrel and weighed 8.15lb.

SIMILAR GUNS

Copies of Soviet obr. 1944g carbines and obr. 1891/30 rifles—the latter usually reserved for snipers—were made in the 1950s. They were identical with the original patterns, but bore Polish factory marks.

PORTUGAL

• Guedes

This rifle was developed for the Portuguese army in 1882-4, largely through the work of army lieutenant Luis Guedes Dias.

About 50 11mm-caliber guns were made in Portugal in 1884, but the advent of smokeless propellant in France—accompanied by a small-caliber cartridge—caused the project to be revised for an 8mm rimmed cartridge before production began. Owing to a lack of suitable facilities in the Lisbon arsenal, the contract was placed in Austria-Hungary.

The breechblock of the rifle, containing the trigger, hammer and multi-purpose spring, was moved down and then slightly back from the face of the breech as the rear of the trigger guard was depressed. A spent case was thrown clear by a sturdy sliding extractor/ejector at the end of the opening stroke.

MODEL 1885 RIFLE
Made by Österreichische Waffenfabriks-Gesellschaft, Steyr, 1885-6.
Total production: see text. **Chambering:** 8x60R, rimmed. **Action:** locked by propping the breechblock behind the chamber with an underlever.

47.9in overall, 9.04lb empty. 33.25in barrel, 4-groove rifling; concentric, RH. Ramp-and-leaf sight graduated to 2000m (2185yd). 1705 fps with 247-grain bullet. Mo. 1885 sword bayonet.

A contract for 40,000 rifles was placed with OEWG in 1885, the company being asked to alter the mechanism from 11mm to 8mm while tooling was underway. The rifle had a straight-wrist butt and a long forend retained by two bands, the bayonet lug appearing on the right side of the band nearest the muzzle. Among the most distinctive features were the breech lever combined with a trigger guard, a safety lever alongside the trigger, and a rear sight leaf—hinged at the front of its base—with a sliding long-range extension.

The Mo. 1885 was abandoned in March 1886 in favor of the Kropatschek (q.v.), though the accompanying bayonets were all accepted. The change is widely assumed to have been due to the preference for a magazine rifle, but the 8mm Guedes was not as successful as the 11mm prototypes. The original 8mm round may have been too weak in the rim to extract reliably in adverse conditions, and excessive pressure directed back through the reduced-diameter chamfered cartridge-case base strained the hollow breechblock.

Ownership of the remaining rifles had passed to OEWG in 1887, when the Portuguese contract had been canceled. About 2700 guns were purchased by the Transvaal in the mid 1890s, followed by 5,000 more in 1897; several thousand also went to the Orange Free State. The Transvaal contracts were arranged through Alfred Field & Co. of Birmingham by way of Stein & Hunter of Cape Town.

• Heckler & Koch (FBP)
In an effort to equip the Bundeswehr as quickly as possible, the German government ordered G3-type rifles from Fabrica Militar de Braco de Prata ('FBP') in 1961. The design was then adopted for Portugal's armed forces—as the 'Espingarda automatica Mo. 961'—to make full use of the production run. The Mo. 961 was identical with the G3, except markings.

A modified Mo. 963 was approved in 1963, made to G3A2 standards with a drum-pattern rear sight instead of the rocking-'L' of the Mo. 961. The Mo. 963 remained the principal Portuguese service rifle into the 1990s, though small quantities of 5.56mm Galil and HK33 rifles were purchased in the mid 1980s for field trials.

• Kropatschek
The Portuguese adopted a Kropatschek to replace the single-shot Guedes (q.v.). Marks on the left side of the receiver included 'OE.W.F.G. STEYR', above the date of manufacture; the cypher of Luis I, a crowned 'L'; and the designation 'M 1886'.

MODEL 1886 RIFLE
Espingarda Mo. 1886
Made by Österreichische Waffenfabriks-Gesellschaft, Steyr, 1885-8.

Total production: 49,000. **Chambering:** 8x60R, rimmed. **Action:** locked by the bolt rib abutting the receiver ahead of the bridge as the bolt handle was turned down.

51.95in overall, 10.07lb empty. 31.55in barrel, 4-groove rifling; RH, concentric. Tube magazine in forend, 8 rounds. Ramp-and-leaf sight graduated to 2000m (2185yd). 1755 fps with Mo. 1886 ball cartridges. Mo. 1886 sword bayonet.

Worried by the obsolescence of the Mo. 1885 Guedes rifle, which had only just been approved, the Portuguese ordered 40,000 Kropatschek rifles in July 1886. The standard infantry rifle was an improved form of the French Mle. 1878, with a bolt adapted from the German Gew. 71/84 pattern and an elevator/cut off mechanism credited to an ordnance officer named Dechambès.

The straight-grip walnut stock had two screw-clamping barrel bands, with swivels on the butt and middle band. The nose cap had a bayonet lug on its right, and the cleaning rod was set into the left side of the forend. The trigger guard had a distinctive finger spur.

A supplementary order for 6,000 rifles was agreed on 30th October 1886, followed by an additional three thousand in 1887. A smokeless cartridge was approved about 1896, increasing muzzle velocity to about 2265 fps; rear sight graduations were altered to 2200m (2405yd), though the designation of the rifles remained unchanged.

SIMILAR GUNS
Model 1886/89. Guns fitted with handguards in the Arsenal do Exército in Lisbon in 1889 were known as 'Mo. 86/89', but not all Portuguese Kropatscheks were so treated; it is suspected that the modified guns were issued to colonial troops, to reduce the adverse effect of radiated barrel-heat on the sight picture. The last colonial guns were not withdrawn until 1961.

MODEL 1886 SHORT RIFLE
Mosqueton Mo. 1886
Made by Österreichische Waffenfabriks-Gesellschaft, Steyr, 1888.
Total production: 4800. **Chambering:** 8x60R, rimmed. **Action:** as Mo. 1886 rifle, above.

45.85in overall, 9.37lb empty. 25.85in barrel, 4-groove rifling; RH, concentric. Tube magazine in forend, 6 rounds. Ramp-and-leaf sight graduated to 2000m (2185yd). 1560 fps with Mo. 1886 ball cartridges. Mo. 1886 sword bayonet.

Ordered in March 1888, specifically for the use of Treasury guards, this was simply a short version of the Mo. 1886 rifle with the same fittings and fixtures. Most short rifles were altered after 1896 for more powerful ammunition, receiving 2200m (2405yd) rear sights. Muzzle velocity rose to 2000 fps.

MODEL 1886 CARBINE
Made by Österreichische Waffenfabriks-Gesellschaft, Steyr, 1885-94.
Total production: 4000. **Chambering:** 8x60R, rimmed. **Action:** as Mo. 1886 rifle, above.

40.35in overall, 8.85lb empty. 20.5in barrel, 4-groove rifling; RH, concentric. Tube magazine in forend, 5 rounds. Ramp-and-leaf sight graduated to 1500m (1640yd). 1280 fps with Mo. 1886 ball cartridges. Mo. 1886 sword bayonet.

Three thousand carbines were ordered from Steyr on 30th October 1886. They were similar to the infantry rifles, but had a short forend and only a single barrel band. The carbines were stocked almost to the muzzle, the bayonet lug being set back on the side of the barrel behind the nose cap to compensate for reduced muzzle protrusion. A thousand additional carbines were purchased in 1894.

The Portuguese adopted a cartridge loaded with smokeless propellant purchased in Austria-Hungary from about 1896 onward. A few Kropatschek carbines are said to have been re-chambered in this period for a semi-experimental 6.5mm round—for issue to mounted units—but the guns may have been purpose-built French Daudetaus (q.v.).

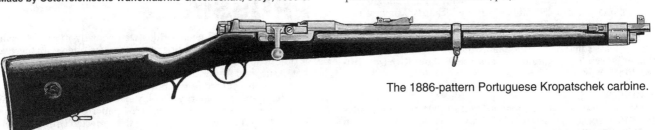

The 1886-pattern Portuguese Kropatschek carbine.

The Portuguese M1904 Vergueiro rifle, made in Germany.

• Mannlicher

The army acquired about 1,000 OEWG-made 6.5mm Mannlicher-Schönauer trials rifles—essentially similar to the Greek M1903 (q.v.)—after two had successfully undertaken trials in 1900.

TRIALS RIFLES

Purchased in 1901, these guns had one-piece stocks with a shallow pistol grip. A handguard ran forward from the receiver ring to the spring-retained barrel band. The bayonet lug lay on the underside of the nose cap and a half-length cleaning rod was carried beneath the muzzle. Sling swivels were to be found on the under edge of the butt and barrel band.

Unlike contemporaneous box-feed Mannlichers, the M1900 had its Schönauer magazine entirely within the stock. The magazine floorplate could be detached by pivoting it laterally through 90 degrees. The rifle had a standard Mannlicher-type bolt, essentially similar to that of the M1895 Dutch rifle, but the center of the guide rib was milled away to save weight; the bolt-knob was also hollowed out.

Trials failed to convince the Portuguese that the many merits of the rotary magazine outweighed its complexity, and, ultimately, the Vergueiro rifle was developed instead.

• Mauser

Portuguese guns used after the revolution of 1909 generally bore the national Arms above the chamber. These consisted of a shield inside a shield, containing five small shields each charged with five discs; seven castles lay around the edge of the outer shield, the whole being placed on an armillary sphere (a navigating instrument) and surrounded by a wreath of laurel leaves. Prior to 1937, however, the Mauser had not been popular in Portugal.

MODEL 1937 SHORT RIFLE
Espingarda Mo. 937
Made by Mauser-Werke AG, Oberndorf/Neckar, Germany, 1937-43.
Total production: not known. **Chambering:** 7.9x57, rimless. **Action:** locked by two lugs on the bolt head turning into recesses in the receiver behind the chamber as the bolt handle was turned down, and by a safety lug entering its seat.
DATA FOR MO. 937-A

43.45in overall, 8.75lb empty. 23.6in barrel, 4-groove rifling; RH, concentric. Internal box magazine loaded with a stripper clip, 5 rounds. Tangent-leaf rear sight graduated to 2000m (2185yd). 2800 fps with standard ball ammunition. Mo. 937 sword bayonet.

The original Mo. 937 was a 'Standard Modell' Mauser, similar to the Kar. 98k with German-style slot-and-bar sling mounts. In 1938, however, a modified 'Mo. 937-A' was substituted, with swivels under the butt and barrel band. The front sight could be adjusted laterally in a diagonal slot, and the mounting-block edges were extended upward to protect the sight blade. The last deliveries were made in 1943, but guns remaining in store in Oberndorf in 1944 were issued to the Wehrmacht once a sling slot had been cut in the butt and the barrel band had been changed.

• Richards

The Portuguese, traditionally allied with Britain, bought substantial quantities of 450-caliber Westley Richards 'Monkey Tail' rifles and carbines in 1867-70. Some of these were subsequently converted to fire metal-case ammunition, though it is suspected that at least some of the alterations included the addition of a Snider breech. For additional details, see '**Britain: Richards, lifting-block type**'.

• Snider

The Portuguese government ordered 10,000 Snider long rifles (with P/53 socket bayonets) and 1200 cavalry carbines from Britain in 1874. The War Office passed the contract to the Birmingham

Small Arms & Metal Co. Ltd in October; guns were delivered by the middle of 1875 to replace altered Westley Richards 'Monkey Tail' weapons in the line infantry and élite cavalry.

• Vergueiro

This rifle was developed after trials held in 1900-2 showed the Mannlicher-Schönauer to be efficient, but too expensive for the Portuguese treasury. The best features of the 1898-pattern Mauser were simply combined with a split-bridge receiver and a simplified bolt based on the Mannlicher-Schönauer (i.e., a modified Reichsgewehr). Ironically, the Vergueiro rifles were all made in Germany.

MODEL 1904 RIFLE
Espingarda 6.5 Mo. 1904
Made by Deutsche Waffen- und Munitionsfabriken, Charlottenburg, Berlin, about 1904-9.
Total production: at least 70,000 – see text. **Chambering:** 6.5x58, rimless. **Action:** locked by two lugs on the bolt head engaging recesses in the receiver wall as the bolt handle was turned down.

48.15in overall, 8.37lb empty. 29.05in barrel, 4-groove rifling; RH, concentric. Internal charger-loaded box magazine, 5 rounds. Tangent-leaf sight graduated to 2000m (2185yd). 2345 fps with Mo.1904 ball ammunition. M1904 sword bayonet.

The Vergueiro-Mauser rifle was easily recognized by the receiver, with the bolt handle turning down ahead of the split bridge to act as a safety lug should the front lugs fail. A separate bolt head and a simplified cocking piece/safety mechanism eased manufacturing problems in an effort to reduce costs. Unlike some other rifles with detachable bolt heads, however, the Vergueiro could not be assembled unless the head had been secured.

Rifles cocked partly during the opening stroke and partly as the action closed. The floorplate of the internal staggered-column magazine could be released by a catch inside the front of the trigger guard. The one-piece walnut stock had a shallow pistol grip, and a handguard ran from the chamber ring to the solitary sprung band. A bayonet bar lay ahead of the narrow nose cap, above the protruding half-length cleaning rod. Swivels lay under the band and butt.

A typical rifle was marked 'ESPINGARDA PORTUGUEZA 6,5 MOD. 1904' on the left side of the receiver above the DWM name. Chambers bore either the crowned 'CI' cypher of Carlos I (reigned 1889-1909) or, apparently, the 'M2' of his short-lived successor Manuel II (1909-10 only). Work may have been completed by the 1910 revolution; few, if any, deliveries were made thereafter. The original contract is believed to have been for about 100,000 guns.

SIMILAR GUNS
Model 1904/39 rifle. Owing to the adoption of the 7.9mm Mo. 937 Mauser (q.v.), many surviving Mo. 1904 rifles were converted in the Lisbon arsenal for the new cartridge. Known as 'Mo.904/39', they had 23.5in barrels and front sights protected by prominent wings. A transverse bolt was added beneath the chamber to handle increased recoil.

PRUSSIA

The Dreyse-made needle rifles were usually marked 'Soemmerda ND' on the left rear side of the receiver, often with the year of production; double dates (e.g., '1842–1849') usually indicated that issue had been delayed. Government-made guns were marked with a spread eagle above 'DANZIG' or 'SPANDAU'.

Later guns customarily displayed their designation on the receiver in Fraktur script—the 1854-pattern Jägerbüchse, for example, was marked 'MOD. 54' and the perfected Dreyse carbine bore 'MOD:57'. The 1860-pattern fusilier rifles were marked

'F.G.MOD.60', whereas the M1862 infantry rifles had 'Z.G.MOD. 62' and the 1865 Jäger rifle displayed 'ZB MOD.65'. The perfected pioneer rifle was marked 'Z.P.G.M69'. Guns fitted with steel barrels were marked 'STAHL'.

A royal cypher often appeared on the right side of the butt, sometimes accompanied by a two-digit date. Later guns sometimes bore the cypher—crown-over-'FW' before 1871 or 'W' thereafter—on the left side of the barrel below the rear sight, together with the date of manufacture. Guns made after 28th August 1852 also often bore a 10mm roman letter on the left side of the butt: 'A' represented *Ausschuss*, or unserviceable; 'D' indicated a *Defensionsgewehr*, relegated to garrison use; 'E' signified an *Exerzierwaffe*, suitable only for training purposes; and 'L.B.'—*Landes-Bewaffnung*—showed that a gun had been relegated to the Landsturm.

Long ('L.A.') or short ('K.A.') butt-length options were introduced in 1862, but were usually applied only to the infantry rifles. Unit markings could indicate a Jäger battalion—e.g., '2.J.3.35.' for Jäger-Bataillon Nr. 2—while naval marks included 'K.M.' and 'I.M.D.', for 'Königliche Marine' (royal navy) and I. Matrösen-Division (first sailors division) respectively. Most marks of this type were stamped letter-by-letter into the buttplate.

• Bock

Rudolf Bock of Potsdam made a few breech-loading caplock rifles in the early 1850s. The action relied on a radial lever on the right side of the receiver camming the barrel forward, away from the standing breech, so that the muzzle could tip down to elevate the chamber for loading. Typical of these guns was a 25-bore carbine, with a 23.2in octagonal barrel and a box-lock hammer offset to the right side of the breech. The two-trigger mechanism incorporated a set element, the trigger guard was spurred, and an adjustable rear sight was fitted on the receiver alongside the hammer.

• Bornmüller

Richard Bornmüller of Suhl made a needle gun in the 1860s. Resembling a simplified Doersch & von Baumgarten (q.v.) design in some respects, it had a self-cocking needle mechanism, an extended receiver bridge and a locking lug in the form of a long guide rib. It is believed to have been offered as a military weapon (without success) and perhaps more appropriately as a sporting gun.

Carle

The needle rifles attributed to J.F.C. Carle (also listed as 'Carlé', 'Karl' or 'Karle') are something of a mystery. One gun was submitted to the British trials of 1865, but the official description suggests that the 'improvements patented by Mr Carle', were applied to a break-open Dreyse. A gun of this type was granted protection in the U.S. in February 1866—see **'Russia, Tsarist: Karl'**.

At the end of 1867, however, Ludwig Loewe & Co. applied to protect the design of an 'improved needle gun' naming the inventor as Carle, a Hamburg ship- and insurance broker; a patent was duly granted in February 1868. However, within a few weeks, a complaint was filed by Simson & Luck on the grounds that the Carle design was a virtual duplicate of the Luck (q.v.) pattern.

The Carle system had, meanwhile, been officially adopted in Russia. It is assumed that some agreement was subsequently reached—conversion of rifle-muskets in Russia continued until 1869.

• Chassepot

By the end of the Franco-Prussian War, the Germans had captured huge quantities of Mle 1866 needle rifles, as well as many Tabatière breech-loaders and other obsolete weapons.

The Bavarian pioneer battalions are said to have been given ex-French rifles with shortened muzzles, but other rifles were modified unofficially by regimental armorers.

After the war had finished, attempts to convert the Chassepots for metallic cartridges began. These were intended for cavalrymen and auxiliary units, as it had been realized that the introduction of a Mauser cavalry carbine would be delayed.

THE GUNS

Owing to a shortage of Dreyse-type cavalry carbines (which were universally disliked), many cavalry units were hastily

A drawing of the Prussian cavalry-carbine conversion of the 1866-type French Chassepot rifles.

re-armed in 1870-1 with captured French rifles. Many of these subsequently had their muzzles shortened and the lug-and-bar bayonet fixings removed. They were then re-issued with captured combustible paper-case ammunition.

Experiments were undertaken in 1872 with Chassepots chambered for the Reichspatrone 1871, an 11mm cartridge which had been adopted for the then-experimental Mauser. Finally, on 6th March 1873, Kaiser Wilhelm I sanctioned conversion of needle-rifles which were being held in store.

MODEL 1871 CARBINE
Aptierter Chassepot-Karabiner M1871
Altered by the Prussian government factory in Herzberg, Österreichische Waffenfabriks-Gesellschaft and others.
Total production: at least 275,000 (see below). **Chambering:** 11x60R, rimmed. **Action:** locked by turning the bolt guide-rib down in front of the receiver bridge.

39.15in overall, 7.88lb empty. 20.45in barrel, 4-groove rifling; LH, concentric. Single-shot only. Tangent-leaf rear sight graduated to 1500m (1640yd). 1310 fps with Reichspatrone 1871. No bayonet.

By the autumn of 1874 the GPK had decided, after lengthy trials, that the Prussian prototype Chassepot carbine was sufficiently battle-worthy. It differed from the Saxon M1873 (q.v.) in minor respects. A new plug-type bolt head was retained by a flush-ground transverse pin, instead of a slotted-head screw, and the front part of the bolt handle base extension was cut away.

An extractor was added in the bottom of the bolt-way; a gas-escape hole was bored through the rear of the receiver ring into the chamber; the old firing needle was replaced with a robust striker; and the guide roller under the original cocking-piece head was replaced by a fixed semi-circular rib.

The Prussians simply bored-out the Mle 1866 breech to receive a tubular liner with a reamed-out chamber for the new metallic-case cartridge—simple, strong and reliable, and with minimal effects on stock, sights and barrel fittings.

The barrel retained its octagonal breech section, carrying the original tangent-leaf rear sight. The stock continued to the muzzle, ending in a distinctive steel nose-cap with front sight guards, and a short cleaning rod was carried in the forend. The barrel was held in the stock by a single spring-retained band. Swivels lay under the barrel band and butt.

French markings on the receiver were often retained—e.g., 'MANUFACTURE IMPERIALE' over 'Mutzig' and 'MLE. 1866'. However, the marks on the barrel octagon were all replaced by inspectors' marks and a large crown over 'W'. Original marks on the butt were defaced, additional German markings customarily including a large cursive crowned-'W' cypher. Many guns also bore a stylized eagle and 'DEUTSCHES REICH'. French serial numbers were often still evident.

The Prussian transformation was approved late in 1874, the French journal *Le Spectateur Militaire* noting that the first mass-produced Chassepot conversion and the first Mauser infantry rifle were both shown to the Kaiser on 22nd March 1875. *Italia Militare* recorded that 208,600 Chassepots were altered in 1875 and that they were then being carried by 'the cavalry, the train, the siege artillery and the pioneers'. By 31st December 1877, Österreichische Waffenfabriks-Gesellschaft had despatched 54,900 carbines to Prussia and Saxony.

Issues were extended on 31st August 1876 to the lancers, with the exception of trumpeters and NCOs, and a further 25 carbines were issued to each cuirassier squadron from 30th November 1880. Chassepot-type carbines were soon replaced with Mausers, though the cuirassiers did not relinquish theirs until 1884. Unaltered French rifles served the Landwehr until the early 1880s, when survivors were sold to dealers owing to shortages of French-pattern combustible ammunition.

A typical Doersch & von Baumgarten rifle, possibly made for trials in Britain in the mid 1860s. Note the position of the bolt handle, which is slightly open.

• Doersch & von Baumgarten

Johannes Doersch and Cramer von Baumgarten of Suhl, attempting to remedy what they saw as the bad features of the Dreyse (q.v.), developed an improved needle rifle in the early 1860s. Shortening the needle mechanism and moving the handle to the rear of the bolt produced a much more compact design, with a single lug which passed through the receiver bridge to be turned clockwise to its locked position.

Doersch & von Baumgarten rifles were tested successfully in Italy (q.v.), but problems with Italian-made ammunition caused them to be rejected in favor of the Carcano. However, at least 1,000 guns were made for the Jäger-Korps of the principality of Schaumburg-Lippe, where they were adopted (as the 'Modell 1861') on 15th April 1862. The rifles were fully stocked, had a patch-box on the left side of the straight-wrist butt, accepted a sword bayonet, and were fitted with a spurred trigger guard. Their service life was short, as the men of the Jäger-Korps were incorporated in the Prussian army in 1867.

Experimental military rifles were tested in Britain and elsewhere, without success, and sporting guns were made on the same action—perhaps by Bornmüller, Simson & Luck of Suhl. The sporters often have double trigger systems, octagonal barrels, and half-stocks. Trigger guards may be made of horn instead of metal.

• Dreyse

The earliest of Johann Nikolaus Dreyse's *Zündnadelgewehre* ('needle guns') appeared in the 1820s, remarkable chiefly for the use of a long needle-like firing pin to detonate mercuric fulminate contained within a combustible paper cartridge.

The muzzle-loading sporting guns originally had a spring-loaded needle assembly in the rear of the breech, cocked by a radial lever on the barrel-side. One gun embodying this mechanism was submitted to the Kriegsministerium in 1827, but was rejected by the ultra-conservative Prussian ordnance authorities.

Royal patronage subsequently enabled Dreyse to persuade the war ministry to undertake new trials in 1832-6. The first breech-loader, submitted in 1833, was operated by a simple sliding bolt with a projecting handle which turned down into a locking recess in the receiver.

Men of the 48th infantry regiment fight in woodland during the Franco-Prussian War of 1870-1. Note the Dreyse needle guns.

Exhaustive field-trials undertaken in 1836 showed that the rifles had great potential, and so 155 were delivered to the Prussian Army in 1839 from Dreyse's workshop in Sömmerda. These fired a self-contained cartridge containing a round lead ball, lubricated with tallow, in a special papier-mâché sabot. The .598-diameter ball was propelled by 66 grains of powder, ignited by a pellet of mercuric fulminate in the base of the sabot.

The needle-gun was adopted on 4th December 1840 and Dreyse was soon given an order for 60,000 rifles. Issue was delayed for some time, owing to production problems, but campaigns undertaken in 1849 showed the Dreyse to be far superior to muzzle-loaders serving the Prussians in Schleswig-Holstein and Baden. However, the gas seal between the barrel extension and the bolt required careful machining.

Gas-blast from worn Dreyse breeches led many military authorities to overlook that the guns could be loaded while prone, on horseback or on the move, and the impressive rate of fire was widely regarded as a waste of ammunition.

The bolt mechanism of the 1841-pattern infantry rifle was locked simply by abutting the bolt handle base on the receiver bridge. Assuming the mechanism to be in its fired state, the thumb-piece attached to the inner portion of the bolt was retracted, withdrawing the needle through its protective housing. A leaf spring locked the breech unless the needle mechanism had been properly retracted.

The bolt handle was rotated toward the left until it cleared the locking shoulder, then drawn back through the receiver bridge to expose the chamber. A cartridge was placed in the feed-way and pushed forward with the finger until it rested against the step between chamber and barrel. The bolt was returned, then rotated to the right through about 25 degrees to lock. The needle sleeve was then returned to its initial position.

As the needle was being held by the sear bar attached to the trigger mechanism, closing the sleeve also compressed the needle-spring. Pressing the trigger against the resistance offered by its spring disengaged the sear. The needle-spring then drove the needle through the base of the special paper-clad cartridge and through the propelling charge to ignite the primer. The primer ignited the main powder charge, driving the bullet down the bore and out of the muzzle. Air drag then pulled the sabot away. An expansion chamber (*Luftkammer*) was cut inside the bolt face to collect fouling débris and improve combustion.

The worst feature of the Dreyse was the design of the cartridge, though the dangers of accidental ignition in transit were substantially reduced by burying the primer in a papier-mâché buffer. However, the needle was susceptible to corrosion and prone to breakage.

Each soldier carried two spare needles and a cleaning kit for the expansion chamber in the front of the bolt, while corporals (*Unteroffiziere*) carried spare main springs.

MODEL 1841 RIFLE
Leichte-Percussions-Gewehr M1841
Made by Waffenfabrik von Dreyse, Sömmerda.

Total production: 650,000? **Chambering:** 15.43mm combustible cartridge. **Action:** locked by the base of the bolt handle abutting the receiver, ahead of the bridge, as the bolt handle was turned down.

56.1in overall, 10.95lb empty. 35.7in barrel, 4-groove rifling, RH, concentric. Single-shot only. Block and two-leaf rear sight graduated to 600 paces (1847 pattern). 965 fps with 1847-pattern ammunition. M1841 socket bayonet.

The first Dreyse could easily be distinguished by the length of its bolt mechanism and by its brass furniture. The cylindrical barrel had a short octagonal section ahead of the breech, carrying the rear sight, and was held in the stock by three spring-retained bands.

The swivels were attached to the middle band and the elongated trigger guard, which ended in a small curled-over spur.

The stock had characteristic flats alongside the action, with a rudimentary cheekpiece on the left side of the butt. Sixty thousand Zündnadelgewehre were ordered from Dreyse in 1841, but the first deliveries were not made until the end of 1842 and large-scale issues were delayed for some years. From about 1843 onward, the original curled-over terminal on the trigger guard was replaced by a straight form.

The original lead-ball cartridge (*Patrone mit Rundkugel*) was replaced by an improved M1847 pattern. The new oviform projectile promised longer range and better accuracy, and so the sights were duly revised. The sights were revised again after the introduction of the M1855 cartridge, when a block and three-leaf pattern appeared. The large leaf was regulated for 600/700 paces (450/525yd). At about the same time, the Dreyse was renamed 'Infanterie-Gewehr Modell 1841' owing to the introduction of the M1839/55 (Minié) rifle-musket.

Production ceased in 1865 in favor of the 1862-pattern infantry rifle, but 448,510 1841-model rifles remained on the Prussian inventory when mobilization for the Franco-Prussian War began in July 1870. Though the 1862-pattern Dreyse rifle had been introduced some years earlier, many infantry regiments carried the older guns. Surviving 1841-type Dreyse rifles were declared obsolescent on 15th August 1872 and relegated to the Landwehr.

MODEL 1849 SHARPSHOOTER'S RIFLE
Jägerbüchse M1849

Made by Waffenfabrik von Dreyse, Sömmerda.

Total production: about 5000. **Chambering:** 15.43mm combustible cartridge. **Action:** generally as M1841, above.

49.2in overall, 10.05lb empty. 31.1in barrel, 4-groove rifling, RH, concentric. Single-shot only. Block and three-leaf rear sight graduated to about 600 paces (475yd). 905 fps with 1847-pattern ammunition. M1849 sword bayonet (Garde-Hirschfänger).

Adopted on 11th December 1851, this rifle was used only by the Garde-Jäger and Garde-Schützen. Unfortunately, identification of the production pattern is still uncertain. Von Menges suggested that the gun had a shortened [*komprimiert*] lock and receiver, measuring 5.9in instead of 9.95in for the M1841. This had been made possible by a change in the obturating system. 'The chamber mouth does not slide over the barrel extension,' noted von Menges, 'but has a plug-type extension … that fits in a recess cut in the chamber. Escaping powder gases could consequently place the shooter in more peril… .'

This breech sealing system proved inferior to the regular Dreyse pattern; though perpetuated on the 1855 and 1857 carbines, where a short action was essential, it was abandoned on subsequent long arms.

The barrel of the M1849 was retained in the stock by a lateral key and screws instead of bands. The nose-cap was brass, and the 'T'-lug for the bayonet was brazed to the muzzle. Swivels were attached through the forend and on the underside of the butt. The trigger-guard bow had a long finger-rest, and prominent flats appeared on the stock alongside the breech. The butt had a cheekpiece on the left side and an iron shoulder plate.

From 1855 onward, a new sight with four leaves was provided, though the guns that remained in service were speedily replaced by the Zündnadelbüchse M1854. By July 1870, only 2973 1849-type

guns were still on the inventory; they were discarded immediately after the Franco-Prussian War.

MODEL 1854 SHARPSHOOTER'S RIFLE
Zündnadelbüchse M1854

Made by the Royal Prussian arsenal, Spandau (1855-60).

Total production: about 30,000. **Chambering:** 15.43mm combustible cartridge. **Action:** generally as M1841, above.

49in overall (bayonet retracted), 10.1lb empty. 30.9in barrel, 4-groove rifling, RH, concentric. Single-shot only. Block and four-leaf rear sight graduated to 800 paces (600yd). 905 fps with 1855-pattern ammunition. M1854 rod bayonet

Intended to equip the élite Jäger-Bataillone, this short rifle was adopted on 22nd March 1855. The action was merely 6.7in long, and had a prominent reinforce where the bolt handle base abutted the receiver. The barrel was cylindrical, apart from a short octagonal portion at the breech carrying the multi-leaf rear sight, and was held in the stock by two bands and a special nose-cap. The nose-cap had a locking catch for the rod bayonet. One swivel was attached to the middle band and the other lay beneath the butt.

The M1854 was superseded by the Zündnadelbüchse M1865 (q.v.) in 1866-8. Many surviving M 1854 rifles were reissued to the navy, while others were converted to u/M pioneer rifles (q.v.). Navy-issue guns had their barrels brightly polished instead of browned and will usually display characteristic unit marks.

By 1870, the 1854-type rifles had all been discarded apart from those serving the navy and those that had been converted. By 1875, even the navy rifles had been replaced by Mausers.

MODEL 1855 CAVALRY CARBINE
Karabiner M1855

Made by Waffenfabrik von Dreyse, Sömmerda (about 1855-65), and by Crause & Co., Herzberg (1871 only).

Total production: 85,000-90,000. **Chambering:** 15.43mm combustible cartridge. **Action:** generally as M1841, above.

31.7in overall, 6.35lb empty. 15.05in barrel, 4-groove rifling, RH, concentric. Single-shot only. Block-and-leaf rear sight graduated to 300 paces (225yd). 740 fps with 1847-pattern ammunition. No bayonet.

By the mid-1850s, with the Dreyse needle-rifles in service in quantity, the military authorities were keen to replace the motley collection of muzzle-loading carbines and pistols being carried by the cavalry.

In May 1855, therefore, 25 men in each dragoon and hussar regiment were given needle carbines with wrought-iron barrels. The guns had an ultra-short action, lacking the reinforced bridge. The coned bolt head entered a milled-out circumferential recess in the chamber mouth, but allowed gas leaks to escape backwards into the shooter's face; normal Dreyse actions tended to deflect it forward and upward.

SIMILAR GUNS

Model 1857. On 3rd February 1859, the perfected needle-fire carbine was finally accepted. It was identical with its 1855-pattern predecessor except that a steel barrel had been substituted for the original wrought-iron pattern. Guns were issued to all ranks of the dragoon and hussar regiments other than NCOs and trumpeters, who retained their cap-lock pistols.

The cylindrical barrel had a short octagonal section at the breech, carrying the rear sight, and was held in the stock by an iron nose-cap. The stock had a brass buttplate and the customary flats alongside the receiver. The trigger guard lacked a finger-rest,

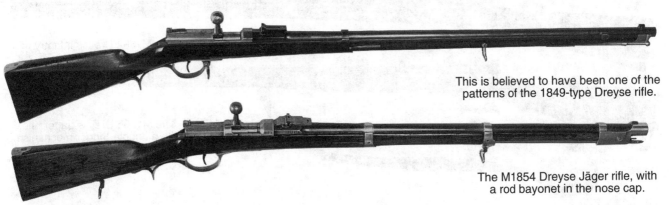

This is believed to have been one of the patterns of the 1849-type Dreyse rifle.

The M1854 Dreyse Jäger rifle, with a rod bayonet in the nose cap.

but anchored a large saddle ring and had a stud for a leather bolt-retaining strap.

There were 54,172 Dreyse carbines in the army inventory in July, and, early in 1871, 500 were supplied to the Bavarian Army. These were issued to Chevaulegers (light cavalry) on the scale of 80-90 to each regiment.

In addition, at least 26,663 replacement carbines were made for the Prussians in Herzberg in 1871. They had conventional sling swivels, but the stocks lacked cheekpieces and receiver-side flats.

The introduction of converted Chassepot and new M1871 (Mauser) cavalry carbines ensured that 1857-pattern guns had been removed from front-line service by 1876. Many were given rifle-type slings and sling swivels, then stored for issue to stretcher bearers.

MODEL 1860 FUSILIER RIFLE
Zündnadel-Füsiliergewehr M1860
Made by Waffenfabrik von Dreyse, Sömmerda (about 1860-8).
Total production: 130,000? **Chambering:** 15.43mm combustible cartridge. **Action:** generally as M1841, above.

51.2in overall, 10.43lb empty. 30.9in barrel, 4-groove rifling, RH, concentric. Single-shot only. Block and two-leaf rear sight graduated to 800 paces (600yd). 905 fps with 1855-pattern ammunition. M1860 sword bayonet (Füsilier-Seitengewehr).

Adopted on 4th August 1860, this rifle was intended for eight élite regiments formed by reserve infantrymen. Mechanical details paralleled the M1841 (q.v.), but the action was made to finer tolerances.

The barrel bands so characteristic of older Dreyse infantry rifles were replaced by a transverse key through the stock above the ramrod tailpipe. The furniture was brass, including the two ramrod pipes, the nose cap, and the trigger-guard bow. A 'T'-lug on the right side of the barrel accepted the pommel slot of the sword bayonet. The swivels lay through the fore-stock and the front of the trigger-guard bow. The stock lacked a cheekpiece, but retained the flats alongside the bolt mechanism. The buttplate was cast iron.

The M1860 Dreyse fusilier rifle.

SIMILAR GUNS
Altered Model 1860 ('aptierte nach Beck'). 101,865 M1860 rifles remained available when mobilization for the Franco-Prussian War began in July 1870, but many underwent the Beck Transformation (q.v.) in 1871-2. These guns have a prominent screw-head on the bolt, ahead of the handle, and an improved rear sight. The last of the modified M1860 rifles passed to the Landwehr in the mid 1870s, after Mauser rifles had been issued.

MODEL 1862 RIFLE
Zündnadelgewehr M1862
Made by Waffenfabrik von Dreyse, Sömmerda, and by the Royal Prussian manufactories in Danzig and Spandau (about 1862-70).
Total production: 600,000? **Chambering:** 15.43mm combustible cartridge. **Action:** generally as M1841, above.

53.55in overall (long butt), 10.45lb empty. 33.1in barrel, 4-groove rifling, RH, concentric. Single-shot only. Block and two-leaf rear sight graduated to 700 paces (525yd). 965 fps with 1855-pattern ammunition. M1862 socket bayonet.

An improved version of the M1841 infantry rifle was adopted on 28th July 1862. It was better made than its predecessor, slightly smaller, had refined sights, and lacked a cheekpiece on the butt.

The cylindrical barrel had a short octagonal section at the breech, mounting the rear sight, and was held in the stock by spring-retained bands. Unlike the 1841 patterns, the springs ran forward. Swivels lay beneath the middle band and through the trigger guard. The stock had the customary flats alongside the bolt and a cast-iron buttplate. A cleaning rod was still carried beneath the barrel.

Production seems to have been slow, as only a handful of infantry regiments had re-equipped by the beginning of the Austro-Prussian War in 1866. The success of the French Chassepot needle rifle in campaigns undertaken in the late 1860s then highlighted the weaknesses of the Dreyse action.

There were about 434,567 M 1862 rifles on the army inventory when the Franco-Prussian War began in 1870, compared with nearly 450,000 of the older 1841 model. Conversion work had already begun on the M1860, M1862, M1865 and M1869 rifles, but only three regiments were equipped with 'Beck' rifles (all 1862-pattern) during the war. Work continued after hostilities had ceased; the journal *Italia Militare* claimed that an improbable 729,703 had been altered by the end of 1873, but many commentators regard this as a misprint. Numerous M1862 rifles were re-issued in 1873-4 to the foot artillery (often distinguished by 'A.F.' in their markings); the remaining infantry rifles had all been withdrawn by the mid-1870s.

SIMILAR GUNS
Altered Model 1862 ('Aptierte nach Beck'). On 10th March 1870, a modified bolt credited to Johannes Beck—but inspired by the Chassepot—was officially adopted. Muzzle velocity rose from 965 fps to 1115 fps, and performance improved accordingly.

A new bolt head, inside the old gas expansion chamber, was secured by a large screw on top of the bolt ahead of the handle. A leather washer was squeezed outward between the bolt head and the bolt body when the gun was fired, providing an effective gas seal until the washer material deteriorated.

Minor alterations were made to the interior of the bolt body, and new rear sights were fitted. These offered a block for 200 paces, a small leaf for 300 paces, and a large one—with a sliding body—graduated to 1200 paces (800yd).

MODEL 1865 SHARPSHOOTER'S RIFLE
Jägerbüchse M1865
Made by Waffenfabrik von Dreyse, Sömmerda, and by the Royal Prussian manufactory in Spandau (about 1865-72).
Total production: 40,000? **Chambering:** 15.43mm combustible cartridge. **Action:** generally as M1841, above.

48.45in overall (long butt), 9.66lb empty. 30.25in barrel, 4-groove rifling, RH, concentric. Single-shot only. Block and four-leaf rear sight graduated to 900 paces (675yd). 925 fps with 1855-pattern ammunition. M1865 sword bayonet (Hirschfänger).

An experimental derivative of the fusilier rifle was issued in 1865 to two Jäger battalions, and the perfected Zündnadelbüchse

The M1862 Dreyse infantry rifle.

The M1865 Dreyse Jäger rifle, with a double-trigger mechanism.

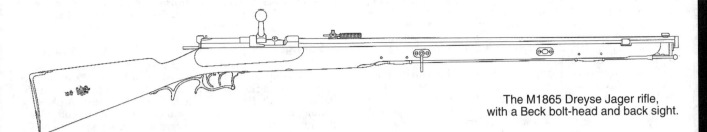

The M1865 Dreyse Jager rifle, with a Beck bolt-head and back sight.

M1865 was adopted on 16th March 1866. The major mechanical difference between the M1862 and M1865 rifles concerned the double set trigger of the latter, which promoted better accuracy.

The M1865 had two trigger levers in the trigger-guard bow. The back lever could be used to fire the gun with a creeping pull characteristic of military weapons; the front or hair-trigger, however, could be adjusted until the pull weight was virtually nil.

The octagonal barrel was held in the stock by a transverse screw and a transverse key, and the nose cap was made largely of brass. The straight-grip stock lacked a cheekpiece, but retained a cast-iron buttplate. Two finger spurs on the trigger guard provided an excellent identification feature.

There were 29,896 M1865 rifles in the Prussian army inventory in July 1870. They were replaced by Mausers in the mid 1870s and handed on to the Landwehr, where some were supposedly altered to use Mle 66 sabre bayonets captured from the French during the Franco-Prussian War.

SIMILAR GUNS

Altered Model 1865 ('Aptierte nach Beck'). At least 10,000 guns were given the Beck breech after the Franco-Prussian War had ended.

PIONEER RIFLE, U/M PATTERN
Zündnadel-Pioniergewehr u/M
Made by the Königlich Gewehrfabrik, Spandau (about 1865-72).

Total production: 12,000-15,000. **Chambering:** 15.43mm combustible cartridge. **Action:** generally as M1841, above.

43.3in overall (long butt), about 8lb empty. 26.55in barrel, 4-groove rifling, RH, concentric. Single-shot only. Block-and-leaf rear sight graduated to 300 paces (225yd). About 875 fps with 1855-pattern ammunition. M1865 sword bayonet (Pionierfaschinenmesser).

Adopted on 16th November 1865, this was converted from the M1854. The discarded Jägerbüchsen were converted by removing the rod bayonet assembly, the barrel bands, 5.5in of the barrel, and the old rear sight.

The u/M pioneer rifle had a plain forend with a transverse screw to hold the barrel and sling swivel. A bayonet lug was brazed to the right side of the muzzle and a new nose cap replaced the rod-bayonet assembly. The bayonet channel beneath the forend was filled with a wooden sliver. The second swivel lay beneath the butt, behind the trigger guard. Unlike the 1869 type (q.v.), the u/M stock retained a cheekpiece on the left side of the butt. Converted rifles were still marked 'MOD. 54' on the receiver.

Zündnadel-Pioniergewehre were officially renamed 'umgeändertes Modell' (converted model) on 25th January 1869, distinguishing them from the new M1869, and the inventory on 15th July 1870 stood at 12,449 pioneer rifles of all types.

MODEL 1869 PIONEER RIFLE
Zündnadel-Pioniergewehr M1869
Made by the Königlich Gewehrfabrik, Spandau (about 1869-72).

Total production: 8,000? **Chambering:** 15.43mm combustible cartridge.

Otherwise generally the same as the u/M pattern, above, except that it weighed about 8.45lb and accepted the M1869 Pionierfaschinenmesser.

Adopted on 25th January 1869, this was little more than a variant of the Zündnadel-Pioniergewehr u/M. The short action was similar to that of the u/M pioneer rifle, apart from noticeable differences in the machining on the top of the receiver. All 1869-type rifles had plain forends, the barrels being retained by transverse screws which also anchored the front swivel.

A bayonet lug lay on the right side of the muzzle behind the nose cap, and a cleaning rod was carried under the forend in two pipes. The second sling swivel lay under the butt behind the trigger guard. The one-piece walnut stock lacked the cheekpiece found

on the left side of the slimmer u/M butts. Consequently, 1869-type guns weighed 7-8oz more than the conversions.

SIMILAR GUNS

Altered Model 1869 ('Aptierte nach Beck'). Only 2202 M1869 pioneer rifles had been inventoried by 15th July 1870, but production continued after the Franco-Prussian War. A few were converted to the Beck system, but even these had soon been replaced by the first Mausers.

OBSOLESCENT PATTERNS

German fear of France, culminating in the Franco-Prussian War of 1870-1, led to the conversion of many guns which—in calmer days—would have been considered unworthy of attention.

At least 80,000 emergency weapons were produced in 1868-71, including breech-loading conversions of obsolete Prussian cap-locks and minor-state muskets. The best source of details is Rolf Wirtgen (editor), *Das Zündnadelgewehr. Eine militärtechnische Revolution im 19. Jahrhundert*, published by E.S. Mittler Söhne in 1990.

Austrian-pattern guns ('Ö/M'). These were converted from Lorenz rifle-muskets captured during the short Austro-Prussian War of 1866. Gustav Lehmann, in *Die Mobilmachung 1870/71*, lists the quantities on hand in July 1870 as 35,599 'Defensions-Zündnadelgewehre Ö/M' and 1958 short 'Defensions-Zündnadelbüchse Ö/M'. These guns all used the short Dreyse carbine action. Altered in Suhl, most were destined to remain in store or on garrison duties during the war.

Baden patterns. The state army of Baden provided 950 'B/M' needle-rifle conversions.

Brunswick patterns. There were 3397 'Br/M' guns, but few of these ever saw active service and virtually all were discarded as soon as hostilities had finished in 1871.

Hessen patterns. 'H/M' guns (*Hessisches Muster*, Hessian pattern) had originally belonged to the army of the grand duchy. Lehmann lists them as 'Füsilier-Gewehre H/M' (2832 on hand in the summer of 1870) and 'Zündnadelgewehre H/M' (5297).

Nassau patterns. According to Lehmann, 4547 of a 'Na/M' needle gun came from this particular state.

Prussian patterns. Defensions-Zündnadelbüchsen u/M were converted from Prussian Jägerbüchsen M35/48, 8862 remaining on hand in July 1870. The guns had begun life in 1810 as flintlock Neuer Corpsbüchsen, but had been altered to cap-lock during the mid-1830s and then for a Thouvenin-type pillar breech in the late 1840s. The Dreyse conversion, undertaken in Sömmerda, was apparently adopted in 1868; it could be recognized by the distinctive bayonet bar on the right side of the muzzle. There were also 17,358 converted (u/M) Prussian cavalry carbines.

Saxon patterns. The cavalrymen carried the Dreyse-type Reiterkarabiner M1863 in 1870.

Württemberg patterns. Two Dreyse-system infantry rifles were issued in this period (M1867, M1868).

SPORTING GUNS

The Dreyse sporting guns were initially built on a very different action from the military patterns. Though the essence of the needle-fire mechanism was retained, the barrels (most were double-barreled) were moved forward and then laterally by an eccentric plate when a lever beneath the forend was turned to the right. The needle assemblies were inserted in solid-face receivers, but usually required the needle-catch head to be retracted before the needle sleeve itself could be pulled back; returning the sleeve left the needle cocked and ready to fire.

Dreyse sporting guns typically had half- or full-octagon barrels, or round barrels with an octagonal chamber. They had short half-stocks with straight-wrist butts. The trigger guards could be iron, brass, wood or sometimes horn, spurs and finger-rests being common. Guns with rifled barrels customarily had standing-block rear sights with folding leaves—usually only two—for longer ranges; smooth-bores had simple fixed-block sights. Shotguns, rifles and even an occasional pistol were made in the Dreyse factory in Sömmerda until the 1870s.

Single-barrel Dreyse sporters were usually built on the military-style bolt action. These guns often displayed spatulate bolt handles, extensive scroll engraving on the receiver, octagonal barrels, set-triggers, special sights, and refined stocks with spurred or finger-rest trigger guards of wood or horn.

Many rifles made after about 1875 could accept needle- or center-fire cartridges interchangeably, in accordance with a patent granted to Franz von Dreyse (see **'Germany: Dreyse'**).

• Luck

Carl August Luck, a gunsmith trading in Suhl, developed a needle rifle in the 1860s. Patented in May 1865, this was essentially a precursor of the better-known Carle type. When Carle received his patent in 1868, Simson & Luck objected on the grounds of infringement. The results of this are not clear, but, in view of a potentially lucrative agreement reached by Ludwig Loewe & Co. (Carle's backers) with Russia, it is suspected that the parties reached an amicable conclusion.

The existence of the Luck rifle was made known to the British authorities in October 1865, but none was available for trial. An illustration in Rudolf Schmidt's *Die Handfeuerwaffen* (1875) suggests that a typical Luck-made rifle had a ring-tipped folding lever above the back of the breech, screwed barrel bands, and two folding leaves attached to the back-sight block. The round barrel had an octagonal breech, the profile being continued in the open-topped receiver.

• Poppenburg

Invented by Carl-Johann von der Poppenburg of Suhl and patented in the U.S. in October 1865 (no. 50,760), this was an interesting variation on the needle-gun theme. The cartridge was loaded into the mouth of a chamber which sprang out of the receiver after a spring-catch on the top of the needle sleeve had been pressed to allow the sleeve to be retracted. Pushing the sleeve back into the receiver cocked the needle and re-locked the breech chamber as it was closed. A Poppenburg rifle submitted by John Benson & Co.

of London was tested by the British authorities in 1865, but was rejected owing to its cumbersome design and the unreliability of the breech-opening spring.

• Spangenberg & Sauer

This gunmaking partnership, predecessors of J.P. Sauer & Sohn (q.v.), developed an improved needle gun about 1869. It had two opposed locking lugs on the head of the bolt, and could apparently be cocked automatically as the breech was closed. A pivoting spring-loaded safety catch lay on the right side of the bolt behind the stubby handle. The Spangenberg & Sauer action was so easily converted to chamber metal-case cartridges that unaltered guns are rarely (if ever) found.

ROMANIA

• Kalashnikov

Made in the arms factory in Cugir from 1960 onward, the AI (AK) rifle was little more than a copy of the Soviet pattern, with a selector marked 'S', 'FA' and 'FF'.

The improved AIM (AKM)—introduced in the mid-1960s—had a plastic pistol grip, a laminated butt, a laminated handguard, and a laminated forend with an integral pistol grip. It also had a stamped bolt cover, a 1000m rear sight, a cleaning rod and a bayonet lug. The rear sling swivel lay on the under-edge of the butt, though many guns have been reported with it removed to the left side of the butt-wrist. Romanian Kalashnikovs generally bore an arrowhead-in-triangle mark on the left side of the receiver, ahead of the date (e.g., '1967') and a serial number.

• Mannlicher

MODEL 1892 RIFLE

Made by Österreichische Waffenfabriks-Gesellschaft, Steyr, 1892.

Total production: not known. **Chambering:** 6.5x53R, rimmed. **Action:** locked by two lugs on a detachable bolt head engaging seats in the receiver as the bolt handle was turned down.

48.3in overall, 8.95lb empty. 28.55in barrel, 4-groove rifling; RH, concentric. Integral clip-loaded box magazine, 5 rounds. Tangent-leaf sight graduated to 2000m (2185yd). 2230 fps with ball cartridges.

The Romanian AKM-type Kalashnikov, known as the 'AIM'.

The Romanian AIM (Kalashnikov), with a forty-round magazine.

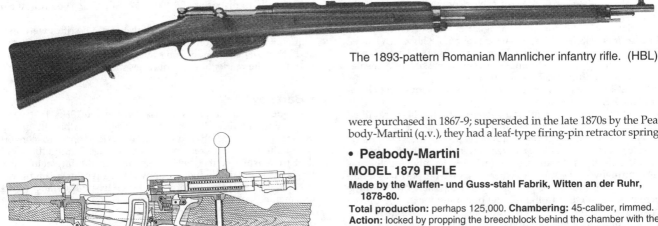

The 1893-pattern Romanian Mannlicher infantry rifle. (HBL)

A sectional drawing of the
Romanian M1893 Mannlicher rifle.

Acquired for field trials in 1892, these were the first Mannlicher-type rifles to embody lessons learned from the Gew. 88. They had straight-grip stocks and two barrel bands; the front band, doubling as a nose cap, carried the bayonet lug on the right side. The handguard ran from the receiver ring to the rear band.

There were swivels under the rear band and the butt-edge, while a half-length cleaning rod lay beneath the muzzle. Chamber-tops were marked 'ARMA MD. 1892' below a crown, with 'STEYR 1892' on the left side of the receiver. The guns were readily distinguishable by their plain-sided magazines.

MODEL 1893 RIFLE
Made by Österreichische Waffenfabriks-Gesellschaft, Steyr, 1893-1914.
Total production: 100,000 by 1907. **Chambering:** 6.5x53R, rimmed. **Action:** as M1892, above.

48.3in overall, 9.06lb empty. 28.55in barrel, 4-groove rifling; RH, concentric. Integral clip-loaded box magazine, 5 rounds. Tangent-leaf sight graduated to 2100m (2295yd). 2400 fps with M1893 ball cartridges. M1893 knife bayonet.

An improved form of the 1892 trials rifle, this had an additional stacking rod on the left side of the nose cap and prominent reinforcing ribs on the lower sides of the magazine housing. Internally, a change was made to the left locking lug and the bolt stop so that the bolt could be re-inserted only if properly assembled; otherwise, the bolt stop had to be lifted manually.

Like the earlier gun, the M1893 had a gas-escape port in the bolt and a secondary cocking-piece notch on the rear of the bolt to assist dismantling. The chamber-top marking read simply 'Md.1893' beneath a crown.

SIMILAR GUNS
Model 1893 carbine. This was adopted about 1903 for cavalry and artillerymen. About 37.5in overall, with a 17.7in barrel and a weight of 7.25lb, it was identical with the rifle apart from size, the turned-down bolt handle, and the absence of a barrel band. A swivel lay on the left side of the butt, with a loop on the left side of the nose cap.

• Mauser
7.92mm vz. 24 short rifles were purchased from Ceskoslovenská Zbrojovka to supplement the service-issue Mannlichers. These had a chamber-mark comprising the cypher of Michael I (four crowned letters 'M' forming a cross) or Carol II (a crowned encircled 'CC' monogram in a laurel wreath). Confusion exists over the dating of these guns, owing to the fact that Carol II—most unusually—interrupted Michael's reign. It is suspected that they date from 1929-33.

• Peabody
Prior to gaining independence in 1878, Romania was an autonomous province of the Turkish empire. About 30,000 Peabody rifles

were purchased in 1867-9; superseded in the late 1870s by the Peabody-Martini (q.v.), they had a leaf-type firing-pin retractor spring.

• Peabody-Martini
MODEL 1879 RIFLE
Made by the Waffen- und Guss-stahl Fabrik, Witten an der Ruhr, 1878-80.
Total production: perhaps 125,000. **Chambering:** 45-caliber, rimmed. **Action:** locked by propping the breechblock behind the chamber with the tip of the underlever.

49in overall, 9.6lb empty. 33.25in barrel, 5-groove rifling; RH, concentric. Ramp-and-leaf rear sight apparently graduated to 1600m (1750yd). About 1490 fps with ball cartridges. Socket bayonet.

This Peabody-Martini—the first rifle to be adopted after independence had been gained—was practically identical with the Turkish M1874 (q.v.). Differences were purely minor. The Romanian rifle was stocked almost to the muzzle, had two barrel bands, and the back-sight leaf was hinged at the rear. Sling swivels appeared on the front band, ahead of the trigger guard, and on the underside of the butt.

SIMILAR GUNS
Model 1879 carbine. A few of these were acquired for issue to cavalrymen. They had a half-length forend retained by a single band and did not accept a bayonet.

RUSSIA, MODERN

The disintegration of the Soviet bloc led to the concentration of the Soviet small-arms factories in renascent Russia (e.g., Izhevsk, Kovrov, Tula), but also to a wholesale reduction in military production. This has been accompanied by reassessments of existing equipment, and a competition has even been undertaken to find an assault rifle to supersede the AK-74M. Elimination trials undertaken with eight differing guns are said to have resolved in 1996 in favor of the Nikonov design, but there is no evidence that series production is to begin in the immediate future; the proven durability of the Kalashnikov may yet defeat its more sophisticated rival.

• Kalashnikov
Though reports have suggested that the Kalashnikov is to be replaced in Russian service with the AN-94 (Nikonov) assault rifle when funds permit, the manufacture of more than fifty million AK, AKM and AK-74 weapons suggests that there is still life in a design of proven durability. A variant of the AK-74M entered in the Russian 'Abakan' trials has provided the basis for the 'Hundred Series' Kalashnikovs announced in 1995. The basic design has also been adapted to provide the Saiga 20-bore and 410 semi-automatic shotguns.

MODEL 101 ASSAULT RIFLE
Avtomat Kalashnikova, obr. 101
Made by the Izhevsk ordnance factory.
Chambering: 5.56x45, rimless. **Action:** locked by rotating lugs on the bolt into the receiver walls; gas operated, selective fire.

37.15in overall, 7.52lb empty. 16.35in barrel, 4-groove rifling; RH, concentric. Detachable box magazine, 30 rounds. Tangent-leaf sight graduated to 1000m (1095yd). 2985 fps with ball ammunition, 600±25rpm Optional tool bayonet.

This is a minor variation of the AK-74M (see 'USSR'), with an additional burst-firing capability, changes to the muzzle-brake/compensator unit, and minor improvements to the plastic furniture. The AK101 weighs about 8.05lb with a loaded magazine.

SIMILAR GUNS
AK102. This short-barreled version of the AK101, comparable with the Soviet AKM-SU, apparently has a short flash-hider and

a simplified 300m (330yd) sight carried on an extension of the back-sight block running back above the ejection port.

AK103. Intended for export to agencies which retain the original 7.62x39 M43 cartridge, this weighs about 7.83lb with a loaded 20-round magazine. Muzzle velocity is only about 2350 fps, cyclic rate remaining about 600rpm. The muzzle-brake / compensator associated with the AK-74 is also retained.

AK104. Otherwise identical with the AK102 (above), this chambers the 7.62x39 cartridge.

AK105. A minor variant of the AK102, this has been modified for the ex-Soviet bloc 5.45x39 cartridge.

AKT. This was an unsuccessful derivative of the Kalashnikov developed in the Tula design bureau for inclusion in the 'Abakan' assault-rifle trials. Modifications included lengthening the gas tube virtually to the muzzle, where the take-off port was amalgamated with the front-sight block, reducing the violence of the action in an attempt to lighten the operating parts. The breech cover was simplified and the butt-sides were recessed to save weight, but only a few prototypes were made.

• Nikonov

MODEL 94 ASSAULT RIFLE
Avtomat Nikonova obr. 94, 'AN-94'
Apparently made by the Izhevsk ordnance factory.
Chambering: 5.45x39 and possibly also 5.56x45, rimless. **Action:** see text, below.

37.15in overall, 8.64lb empty. Barrel length unknown (16.5in?), 4-groove rifling; RH, concentric. Detachable box magazine, 30 rounds. Tangent-leaf sight graduated to 1000m (1095yd). 2950 fps with ball ammunition, 1800/600rpm. Optional tool bayonet.

Developed in the late 1980s, this rifle was first noticed in the West in 1992, when it was mistakenly identified as the 'Abakan' (the code name applied to the Russian military assault-rifle trials). A cloak of secrecy still shrouds the project, but the Nikonov is believed to be a gas-operated delayed blowback. The Russians claim it uses 'indirect [or "shifted pulse"] impulse' to achieve efficiency twice that of the AK-74 and 50 per cent greater than the M16.

The original rifles were tested with 30- or 60-round magazines, but the latter proved to be too clumsy. The butt was an angular pattern and the forend had a projection on the underside to prevent the support hand sliding back in automatic fire. The developed versions have a light 'L' butt (folding to the right) with the under-edge cut away, a ribbed plastic forend with ventilating slots, and a prominent bulbous forend / compensator. The gas tube lies beneath the barrel. The selector lever has been moved to the left side of the receiver above the pistol grip, where it can be activated with the thumb of the trigger hand; in addition to the locked or safe position, it can be set to give single shots, a two-round burst or automatic fire.

One of the oddest features of the Nikonov design is its ability to fire the two shots (three in the prototypes) at a prodigious rate of 1800-2000rpm, though a cable and cog system then drops the cyclic rate to 600rpm. The secret of this performance may lie in a loading tray holding a second round ready to be rammed into the breech after the first or chambered round has been fired without the need to strip it from the magazine.

The AN-94 has an external affinity with the Kalashnikov, though the breech cover is more angular, the pistol grip lies farther back, and the muzzle fittings are unmistakable. The rear sight lies at the rear of the breech cover, and a bracket for optical / electro-optical sights is attached to the left side of the receiver.

RUSSIA, TSARIST

The caliber of most pre-1917 Russian firearms was expressed in *line*, an indigenous measurement equal to a tenth of an inch; sights were customarily graduated in *arshin* (paces), each being equal to about 28in.

• Arisaka

The authorities, desperately short of efficient weapons, managed to obtain 600,000 6.5mm Arisaka rifles in 1914-15. Virtually all of these were old 30th Year Type guns, stored since improved patterns had been issued in 1907-9. The Japanese also seized the

opportunity to dispose of 35,400 7x57 38th Year Type rifles held since the Mexican revolution of 1911.

About 128,000 30th Year and 38th Year Type rifles were subsequently supplied from Britain (q.v.) in 1916. Most had British and Japanese markings; as some subsequently passed to Finland, therefore, the marks of four countries may be found on a single gun.

• Baranov

Made in small numbers for trials in the late 1860s, this was a very minor modification of the lifting-block Albini-Braendlin breech system (see 'Belgium'). It was developed to convert 1856-pattern rifle-muskets to fire metallic-case ammunition, but the Krnka rival described below was cheaper and simpler to make. It is not yet known whether Baranov was a government employee charged with adapting the original design to suit Russian production methods, or whether he was simply a promoter. No surviving examples have been reported, though it seems that several hundred were made.

• Berdan, block-action type

The original Berdan was a block-action breech-loader, supplied to the Russian Army by Colt. This was not particularly successful in service, and, after a succession of accidents, it was replaced by the bolt-action Berdan No. 2 in the 1870s.

MODEL 1868 RIFLE
Pekhnotniya vintovka Berdana obr. 1868g
Made by Colt's Patent Fire Arms Mfg Co., Hartford, Connecticut, U.S., 1869-70.
Total production: 30,000. **Chambering:** 10.67x58R, rimmed. **Action:** a pivoting breechblock was locked behind the chamber by the passage of the striker.

53in overall, 9.37lb empty. 32.5in barrel, 6-groove rifling; RH, concentric. Single-shot only. Leaf-type rear sight graduated to 1400 paces (1090yd). About 1450 fps with ball ammunition. Obr. 1868g socket bayonet.

These guns embodied the improved linear striker patented in the U.S. in March 1869, and had a Cyrillic inscription on top of the barrel top. There were two screw-clamped iron barrel bands, and the trigger guard had a small spur on the rear tang. Swivels lay on the front band and trigger guard bow; a cleaning rod was carried under the barrel.

SIMILAR GUNS
Model 1868 carbine. Dating from about 1873, this was simply a shortened version of the infantry rifle, stocked to the muzzle and unable to accept a bayonet. The carbines are believed to have been converted from rifles, but may only have been used for field trials.

• Berdan, bolt-action type

At the time of its adoption in 1871, the Berdan No. 2 bolt-action rifle was among the most powerful of all those being issued in European armies, the flatness of its trajectory causing particular worries in British and French ordnance circles. However, production was slow; the Russians did not manage to re-equip even front-line infantrymen until the mid-1870s. On 1st July 1914, the Berdan inventory still stood at 362,400 7.62mm and 10.67mm rifles, plus a small number of 7.62mm carbines.

MODEL 1870 RIFLE
Pekhotniya vintovka Berdana obr. 1870g
Made by the Birmingham Small Arms Co. Ltd. Small Heath, 1870-3 (30,000 only); and by the Imperial arsenals in Tula and Izhevsk, about 1874-92.

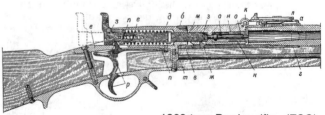

1868-type Berdan rifle. (ESO)

Total production: in excess of one million. **Chambering:** 10.67x58R, rimmed. **Action:** locked by the bolt-guide rib abutting the receiver bridge as the bolt handle was turned down.

53.35in overall, 9.77lb empty. 32.8in barrel, 6-groove rifling; RH, concentric. Ramp-and-leaf sight graduated to 1500 paces (1165yd). 1435 fps with obr. 1870 ball cartridges. Obr. 1870g socket bayonet.

Trials were completed in 1869 with prototypes supplied from the U.S. An order for 300,000 rifles was then placed with BSA on 24th October 1869, delivery of 30,000 being requested by 1st February 1871. One hundred guns were supplied for trials in 1870 and, on 1st February 1871, the Russians finally adopted the perfected experimental rifle. Approval of the bayonet followed on 4th March, and the decision was also taken to begin production in the Tula factory.

Suitable machinery was ordered from Greenwood & Batley of Leeds. A few guns were made in Leeds to test the production line; these guns were then used for trials in Britain, France and elsewhere. Production finally began in the Tula factory in 1874, and in Izhevsk about 1878.

The standard rifle had two screw-clamping bands and a conventional trigger guard. The rear sight had graduations for 200-500 paces on the ramp and 600-1500 paces on the leaf, which hinged at the front of the sight bed. Marks in Cyrillic lay on the barrel-top.

SIMILAR GUNS
Berdan-Krnka. Some guns were fitted with a Krnka 'rapid loader' in 1877, consisting of a 10-round canvas cartridge-box strapped to a plate on the left side of the forend ahead of the chamber. Experiments with quick-loaders and magazine attachments for the Berdan were still underway in 1881.

Berdan-Lutkovskiy. The six-round Lutkovskiy magazine, which hung on the left side of the breech, achieved limited service status—at least for extended troop trials.

Berdan-Schulhof. Several hundred guns may have been converted to the idiosyncratic Schulhof butt-magazine system for trials in the mid-1880s (see 'Austria-Hungary: Schulhof').

MODEL 1870 CARBINE
Karabina Berdana obr. 1870g
Made by the Imperial arsenal, Tula, about 1874-5.
Total production: not known. **Chambering:** 10.67x58R, rimmed. **Action:** as M1870 rifle, above.

38in overall, 6.17lb empty. 18.7in barrel, 6-groove rifling; RH, concentric. Ramp-and-leaf sight graduated to 1000 paces (780yd)? 1190 fps with obr. 1870 ball cartridges. No bayonet.

Little more than a shortened version of the infantry rifle with a single barrel band and a forend running almost to the muzzle, this does not seem to have been made in great numbers and is rarely encountered. It may have been confined to field trials with the cavalry and artillery, and has not been widely recognized as a regulation pattern.

MODEL 1870 DRAGOON RIFLE
Dragunskaya vintovka Berdana obr. 1870g
Made by the Imperial arsenals in Tula and Izhevsk, 1875-92.
Total production: not known. **Chambering:** 10.67x58R, rimmed. **Action:** as M1870 rifle, above.

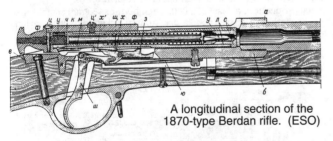

A longitudinal section of the 1870-type Berdan rifle. (ESO)

48.7in overall, 7.9lb empty. 28.35in barrel, 6-groove rifling; RH, concentric. Ramp-and-leaf sight graduated to 1400 paces (1090yd). 1265 fps with obr. 1870 ball cartridges. No bayonet.

Dating from 1875, this modified version of the infantry rifle had a plain stock and sling slots instead of swivels. The two slender bands were retained by springs. An auxiliary dismantling screw on the left side of the receiver mated with a groove cut into the left side of the bolt.

SIMILAR GUNS
Model 1870 cossack rifle (Kazachya vintovka Berdana obr. 1870g). About 48in long and weighing 7.45lb empty, this was introduced at the same time as the dragoon rifle. It was easily distinguished by the replacement of the trigger and trigger guard with an exposed reeded-drum or 'ball' trigger. Three barrel bands were fitted, two being retained by friction and one by a spring. Sling slots were cut through the butt and forend, the cleaning rod was carried almost completely internally, and the barrel-top rear sight was set so far back that it almost touched the receiver.

Several cossack rifles have been reported with barrels and overall lengths approximately an inch greater than given by the Russian official figures. These discrepancies have yet to be resolved.

THREE LINE BERDAN-MODEL RIFLE
Drelineinaya Pekhotniya vintovka Berdana
Conversion was apparently undertaken in Liége.
Total production: not known. **Chambering:** 7.62x54R, rimmed. **Action:** locked by two lugs on the bolt head engaging recesses in the receiver as the bolt handle was turned down, and by the base of the bolt-handle rib abutting the receiver bridge.

52.05in overall, 9.33lb empty. 31.55in barrel, 4-groove rifling; RH, concentric. Ramp-and-leaf sight graduated to 2700 paces (2100yd). 1985 fps with obr. 1891g ball cartridges. Altered obr. 1870 socket bayonet.

Approval for conversion of serviceable 10.67mm Berdan rifles to accept standard 1891-type cartridges was apparently given about 1895. The work was entrusted to contractors in Liége; the rifles generally displayed Belgian proof marks, but rarely gave clues to the contractor. Auguste Francotte & Cie, Em. & L. Nagant and Anciens Établissements Pieper have all been suggested, as more than 200,000 may have been altered.

Apparently confined to the infantry rifle and cavalry carbine, the changes were made by fitting a new barrel, greatly strengthened in the chamber area; by milling a new locking-lug recess and raceway in the bottom of the receiver; and by substituting a new bolt head with twin locking lugs to withstand the additional pressure. An obr. 1891g rear sight was fitted.

SIMILAR GUNS
Cavalry carbine. Though conversion of Berdan-type rifles had been undertaken in the 1890s, some time elapsed before carbines were treated similarly—and then only as an expedient while the Mosin-Nagant magazine pattern was being perfected. The work is believed to have been undertaken in Tula, necessitating a new barrel and alterations to the bolt-head and receiver floor.

• Fedorov

Vladimir Fedorov proposed a recoil-operated modification of the Mosin-Nagant as early as 1905, but it may never have been built. He turned his attention to recoil operation in 1907, producing working prototypes in the Sestroretsk factory in 1908-9.

The basic action relied on two blocks pivoted on the barrel extension. When the mechanism recoiled, a projection on the standing frame pulled the locking blocks downward at the rear to release the bolt to reciprocate alone.

MODEL 1913 TRIALS RIFLE
Avtomaticheskaya vintovka V. Fedorova optniy obr. 1913g
Made by the Imperial ordnance factory, Sestroretsk, 1913-14.

The standard obr. 1870g Berdan infantry rifle.

Total production: at least 150. **Chambering:** 6.5x50, semi-rimmed.
Action: locked by pivoting blocks on the barrel extension into engagement with the bolt; recoil operated, selective fire.

About 49.4in overall, 10.15lb empty. 31.5in barrel, 6-groove rifling; RH, polygonal. Integral box magazine, 5 rounds. Tangent-leaf sight graduated to 2000 paces (1555yd)? 2395 fps with 38th Year Type ball cartridges. Obr. 1891g socket bayonet?

Trials undertaken at the Oranienbaum proving ground in 1910 indicated the superiority of the Fedorov rifle over a rival Tokarev pattern. The 7.62mm Fedorov was eventually approved for field trials in 1912. It was long, very clumsy, and had a butt with a distinctively shaped pistol grip. The box magazine protruded beneath the stock ahead of the trigger; a fire-selector lever lay on the top edge of the stock above the trigger; and a wooden handguard ran from the rear sight to the sheet-metal forend. However, the rimmed 7.62mm cartridge promoted mis-feeds and jams.

In 1913, the inventor obtained permission to use the Japanese semi-rimless 6.5mm cartridge and an improved 'obr. 1913' rifle was produced. It was very similar externally to the 1912 (7.62mm) pattern, though the magazine differed slightly.

Trials undertaken in 1914 against the Tokarev and a selection of foreign-made rivals, including the Sjögren and the Bang, revealed the 1913-type Fedorov to be potentially the best—but still much too unreliable. Work ceased at the beginning of the First World War to concentrate on Mosin-Nagant infantry rifles.

MODEL 1916 RIFLE
Avtomaticheskaya vintovka V. Fedorova obr. 1916g
Made by the Imperial ordnance factory, Sestroretsk, 1916-17.

Total production: about 350. **Chambering:** 6.5x50, semi-rimmed. **Action:** as 1913-pattern rifle, above.

38.4in overall, 9.8lb without magazine. 20.45in barrel, 6-groove rifling; RH, polygonal. Detachable box magazine, 25 rounds. Leaf sight graduated to 2000 paces (1555yd)? 2310 fps with 38th Year Type ball cartridges. Japanese 38th Year Type sword bayonet?

This was basically an improved 1913-type rifle, embodying the same short-recoil action and locking system, but distinguished by its new detachable box magazine.

There was a rudimentary forward hand grip, and the sheet metal forend had been greatly shortened. The earliest guns all had plain-bodied magazines and a rear sight with three sighting notches. They lacked hold opens or stripper-clip guides. By October 1916, enough rifles had been made to equip a company of the 189th infantry regiment. However, production in the Sestroretsk factory proceeded painfully slowly—even though many of the earlier 1913-type rifles were cannibalized to make Avtomats. The October Revolution stopped production altogether.

• Gillet-Trummer

Claimed by V.G. Fedorov to date from 1863, when it was tested in several forms (infantry and dragoon rifles, carbine and pistol), this gun is still the subject of controversy. Donald Webster—in *Military Bolt Action Rifles, 1841-1918*—suggests that the design was undertaken in two stages: an original design by a Belgian gunsmith named Gille or Gillet, and then modified by F.F. Trummer of the Tula manufactory.

The drawings reproduced by Webster show that the Gillet-Trummer system was applied to the 1856-pattern rifle musket, and also to a short two-band gun presumably intended for cavalry or artillerymen. The question remains, however, whether the gun shown is indeed a 'Gillet-Trummer' (which Fedorov unfortunately does not illustrate), or the so-called 'Obturator Rifle M1860'. This may simply be the Russians' first attempt at making the Greene rifle, described in greater detail below, which may suggest that Gillet and Trummer were both Tula employees.

• Greene

Apart from the Egyptians, only the Russians made real use of the fascinating bolt-action rifle developed in the 1850s by the American John Durrell Greene. Greene is known to have traveled to Russia in 1859, where his design was greeted enthusiastically. However, though 3,000 guns are said to have been ordered, these are customarily confused with the perfected 1862-type rifles made during the American Civil War.

Greene's immediate legacy in Russia was possibly to allow guns to be converted in a state manufactory (most probably Tula)

to fire his 1857-patent 'obturating cartridge'. This relied on a perpetual double-bullet system to seal the breech.

There were marked differences in construction between the rifles shown in Greene's patents of 1857 and 1862. In addition, Rudolf Schmidt, in *Die Handfeuerwaffen* (1875), illustrates a 'Russisch Obturatorgewehr M1860' chambering a Greene-type cartridge. Accepting an elastic interpretation of the published drawings, this gun could be connected with the so-called Gillet-Trummer design even though the description of the action of the latter given by Donald Webster does not fit the Schmidt picture.

The M1860 has a bolt handle which cams the bolt forward when properly shut. The handle can be lifted and then turned to the right to allow the bolt to be retracted through the split receiver bridge. This exposes the chamber to receive a loose bullet and then an entire cartridge in a manner described in detail in the U.S.A. section.

Clearly, much investigative work remains to be done. Eventually, however, several thousand Greene rifles seem to have been supplied directly from the U.S. to arm marksmen. Their service life was short, owing to the advent of better guns.

SHARPSHOOTER'S RIFLE
Made by A.H. Waters, Milbury, Massachusetts, 1862.

Total production: 3000, 1862-3. **Chambering:** 55-caliber combustible paper cartridge, fired by a caplock. **Action:** locked by rotating two lugs on the front of the bolt into their seats in the receiver.

52.75in overall, 9.88lb empty. 35.05in barrel, oval-bore rifling; RH. Single-shot only. Leaf-pattern rear sight with a stepped base, probably graduated to 1200 paces (945yd). 1065 fps with a 310-grain bullet? Socket bayonet.

This unique rifle was easily identified by the position of the bolt handle, and by an underhammer cap-lock beneath the forend ahead of the trigger. It had three bands—two retained by springs and the nose cap held by a pin—with swivels beneath the butt and middle band. The rear sight was apparently the standard American pattern with the leaf pivoted at the rear of the bed (if the illustration in Fedorov's book can be trusted), but may have been graduated in paces instead of to the customary 800yd.

• Karle

The identity of the inventor of this needle rifle has been questioned many times, needlessly: Johannes Friedrich Christian Carle of Hamburg was granted protection for a self-cocking adaptation of the Dreyse needle-fire sporting gun—e.g., US Patent 52,938 of 27th February 1866—and a rear-locking gun was patented in Germany in February 1868.

The Russian rifle was operated by lifting the bolt handle (which retracted the needle and its sleeve), then turning the bolt to the left to disengage the locking lugs. The bolt could be retracted to expose the chamber, before being pushed forward, turned to the right and folded downward to its rest position.

Inspired more by the French Chassepot than the Prussian Dreyse, the primer lay in the base of the combustible cartridge instead of directly behind the bullet.

MODEL 1867 RIFLE
Converted by the imperial manufactory, Tula, 1867-70.

Total production: at least 225,000. **Chambering:** 15.2mm combustible paper cartridge, fired by a needle lock. **Action:** locked by rotating two lugs on the mid-section of the bolt into their seats in the receiver.

52.75in overall, 9.95lb empty. 35.1in barrel, 4-groove rifling; RH, concentric. Single-shot only. Tangent rear sight graduated to 600 paces (465yd). 1000 fps with 548-grain bullet. Socket bayonet.

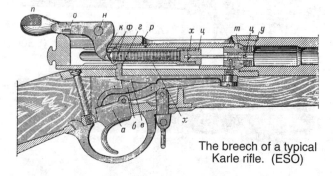

The breech of a typical Karle rifle. (ESO)

These were built on the basis of 1856-pattern rifle muskets, retaining three screwed bands and the original rear sights, but were easily identified by the lever on the top of the bolt and by the lack of an external hammer. Sharpshooters' rifles had 1200-pace (935yd) sights, though infantrymen made do with the 600-pace type. The guns all had small finger rests beneath the butt wrist, with swivels on the trigger guard and middle band. The original lock plate was replaced on most guns by a wooden fillet let into the stock-side, but rifles will also be encountered with one-piece replacement stocks.

• Krnka

The perfected Russian rifle-musket conversion was the work of the Bohemian gunmaker Sylvestr Krnka (see 'Austria-Hungary'). A simple swinging breechblock contained a sturdy inertia-type striker, which was hit by a new hammer mounted on the existing 1856-type back-action lock plate. The Krnka conversion, which fired a centerfire metallic-case cartridge, was the most efficient of the conversion schemes adopted by the Russian army; several hundred thousand guns were converted prior to the introduction of the bolt-action Berdan (q.v.) in the mid-1870s.

MODEL 1869 RIFLE
Converted by the imperial manufactories in Izhevsk, Sestrotesk and Tula, 1870-5.
Total production: at least 350,000. **Chambering:** 15.2mm, rimmed.
Action: locked by a laterally swinging breechblock.
52.75in overall, 9.92lb empty. 35.55in barrel, 4-groove rifling; RH, concentric. Single-shot only. Tangent rear sight graduated to 1200 paces (935yd). 1075 fps with 570-grain bullet. Socket bayonet.

The Krnka rifles all seem to have had the 1200-pace tangent sight previously associated with guns developed for sharpshooters. A massive bronze receiver was attached to existing 1856-type barrels, and the back-action lock was altered to accept the new straight-spur hammer. The stock was modified to accept the new breech mechanism—weakening it ahead of the lock—but retained the standard screwed bands, the trigger guard with its finger spur beneath the stock wrist, and the swivels on the trigger guard and middle band.

SIMILAR GUNS
Model 1869 dragoon rifle. Sharing the action of the infantry rifle, this short-barreled gun was only 48.15in long. According to Fedorov, it weighed 7.61lb.

• Mosin-Nagant

This Russo-Belgian design was also used in Montenegro, in Turkey, and (after 1945) by many Soviet-aligned armies. Large quantities were also made in the People's Republic of China.

The action was based on a French-style bolt, inspired by the Lebel, with a detachable head and a cocking piece which could be retracted and turned to the left as a safety measure. Though clumsy, the mechanism was durable and free of serious weaknesses; the interrupter ensured an unusually good feed with the badly shaped 7.62x54R cartridge. Consequently, the rifle remained in service with some Russian satellite armies well into the 1960s; many guns are still held in reserve.

THE FIRST STEPS

By 1888, the authorities had realized that the Berdan rifle was obsolete. Though experimental rifles submitted by Mauser and Kro-patschek were tested, the indigenous butt-magazine Mosin and the Lutkovskiy, based on the Berdan, were regarded as more promising.

Single- and five-shot Mosin rifles were submitted for trials in 1889, along with some five-shot Belgian Nagants, and testing continued throughout the summer of 1890 with 300 Mosins, 100 Nagants and 100 single-shot Berdans lined down to 7.62mm. The best features of the magazine rifles were then combined to form the Mosin-Nagant, though the participation of Mosin was widely overlooked until Soviet days.

MODEL 1891 RIFLE
Pekhotniya vintovka obr. 1891g
Made by the ordnance factories in Tula, Sestroretsk and Izhevsk, 1892-1922 (about 7.25 million); by the Manufacture d'Armes de Châtellerault, 1893-6 (503,540); by the New England Westinghouse Company, 1915-17 (770,000); and by the Remington Arms-Union Metallic Cartridge Co., Bridgeport, Connecticut, 1915-17 (840,310).
Total production: at least 9.36 million. **Chambering:** 7.62x54R, rimmed.
Action: locked by two lugs on a detachable bolt head engaging recesses in the receiver behind the chamber as the bolt handle turned down.
51.9in overall, 8.95lb empty. 32.3in barrel, 4-groove rifling; RH, concentric. Integral box magazine loaded from a stripper clip, 5 rounds. Ramp-and-leaf sight graduated to 2700 paces (2100yd). 1985 fps with obr. 1891g ball cartridges. Obr. 1891g socket bayonet.

Adopted in April 1891, this was immediately recognizable by its length. The earliest examples had a finger rest extending backward from the trigger guard. The split-bridge receiver was octagonal and the wooden hand-guard ended level with the rearmost screw-clamping barrel band. Swivels lay ahead of the magazine and beneath the front band, though it is alleged that rifles intended for guard units had the back swivel on the underside of the butt. The flat rear sight leaves were originally graduated to 2700 paces (2100yd) for the round-nose obr. 1891g bullet.

By 1892, 3.29 million guns had been ordered from the principal Russian arsenals. Tula delivered the first rifles in the autumn, though only 1440 had been made by the end of December. Mass production began in 1893 and, by the end of 1896, Tula, Izhevsk and Sestroretsk had contributed 1.47 million combat-worthy rifles and 32,440 trainers to the total of a little over two million. As a shortage of machine-tools in Russia restricted production, the French arms factory in Châtellerault also made obr. 1891g rifles in this period. The finger-rest behind the trigger guard was deleted in 1894, and insignificant changes were made in the action.

Combat experience in the Russo-Japanese War of 1904-5 proved that rifles were very badly sighted at short range. As the old round-nose bullet performed poorly at long distances, the pointed obr. 1908g—subsequently designated 'Type L'—was issued in quantity from 1910 onward. Back sights were fitted with new curved leaves graduated to 3200 paces (2490yd), but retained the original sight base. A recoil bolt was added through the forend above the front of the magazine.

On 1st January 1914, the inventory stood at 3.427 million obr. 1891g rifles—but more than five million men were mobilized in the summer and supplies of weapons fell woefully short of needs. In December, therefore, the Chief of Staff ordered the acquisition of weapons regardless of caliber. Contracts for 1.5 million and 1.8 million guns were agreed with Remington-UMC and the New England Westinghouse Corporation in 1915.

By 1st January 1917, deliveries had amounted to only 131,440 Remington-UMC and 225,260 Westinghouse rifles. This shortfall was partly offset by the greatly improved performance of the Russian ordnance factories, which, by 1st October 1917, had completed nearly 3.3 million Mosin-Nagants since 1st July 1914. Work on infantry rifles ceased in 1922 in favor of the dragoon rifle.

MODEL 1891 COSSACK RIFLE
Kazachya vintovka obr. 1891g
Made in the ordnance factories in Tula, Sestroretsk and Izhevsk.
Chambering: 7.62x54R, rimmed. Otherwise generally as obr. 1891g infantry rifle, except dimensions (48.6in overall, 8.66lb empty, 29.9in barrel).

The Cossack rifle was little more than a shortened infantry rifle with a handguard extending as far as the rear sight base. The barrel bands were retained by springs, sling slots were cut laterally through the butt and the forend (protected by oval blued steel washers) and a modified cleaning rod was provided. The serial numbers had a distinctive 'KA3' prefix.

Production of the Cossack rifle was greatly reduced after Russian cavalry had been unable to dominate well-trained

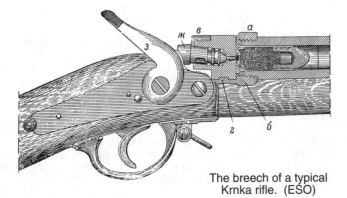

The breech of a typical Krnka rifle. (ESO)

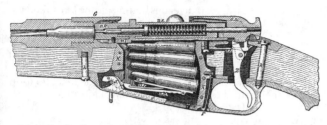

A longitudinal section of the standard
obr. 1891g Mosin-Nagant rifle.

machine-gunners during the Russo-Japanese War—a failure attributed in military circles to cowardice! The Russian army inventory still contained 204,390 Cossack rifles on 1st January 1914, but production stopped in 1915 in favor of dragoon rifles.

SIMILAR GUNS

Model 1891 dragoon rifle (Dragunskaya vintovka). This was a near-duplicate of the Cossack rifle with a different cleaning rod. It was issued without a bayonet, although the standard socket pattern could be mounted if required. Serial numbers had no particular distinction. The introduction of the obr. 1908g ball cartridge led to the 3200-pace sights being fitted, work continuing until 1911 or later. The inventory taken on 1st January 1914 included 540,270 dragoon rifles.

In 1922, the Red Army standardized the dragoon rifle as a substitute for the full-length infantry pattern. Production continued into the early 1930s; consequently, guns will be found with imperial or post-Revolutionary marks.

MODEL 1907 CARBINE
Karabin obr. 1907g

Made by the ordnance factories in Tula, Sestroretsk and Izhevsk.
Total production: not known. **Chambering:** 7.62x54R, rimmed. **Action:** as obr.1891g infantry rifle, above.

40.15in overall, 7.51lb empty. 20.05in barrel, 4-groove rifling; RH, concentric. Integral box magazine loaded from a stripper clip, 5 rounds. Leaf sight graduated to 2000 paces (1555yd). 1805 fps with obr.1891g ball cartridges. No bayonet.

The first Mosin-Nagant carbine pattern (obr. 1907g or '1891/ 07') was issued to the Tsar's artillery and cavalrymen from 1908 onward. It was much shorter than the infantry rifle and the stock extended so close to the muzzle that the standard socket bayonet could not be mounted. The diminutive ramp-and-leaf rear sight was originally graduated to about 1600 paces (1245yd). The adoption of the obr. 1908g cartridge caused a change in sights in 1910, when it is suggested that a few changes were made in the 1907-type carbine—perhaps in the stock—and an improved pattern was substituted. However, it is not known whether the popular 'obr. 1910g' designation has an official standing. The inventory of car-

A comparison of the back sight of the Mosin-Nagant rifles:
the original 1891 pattern (right), the modified curved-leaf
type of 1908 (center), and the tangent-leaf type
associated with the Soviet obr. 1891/30g rifle (left).

bines stood at 118,660 on 1st January 1914, including 25,000 converted Berdans.

• Nagant

At least 100 bolt-action rifles were supplied for field trials with selected Russian army units in 1890, and it is assumed that substantial quantities of prototypes had been made; one surviving gun, for example, is numbered '127'. The Nagant rifle was a conventional gun with the protruding magazine case; its most distinctive feature was the receiver bridge, which had an 'L'-shape slot to receive the bolt handle. The guns proved to be less durable than the competing Mosin pattern, though the interrupter-controlled magazine feed was better; consequently, the Russians combined the best features of the rival designs to produce the Mosin-Nagant (q.v.).

• Norman (Terry)

Made in surprisingly large quantities, this was a modification of the bolt action credited to the English gunsmith William Terry (q.v.). Changes were made by a Tula employee named Ivan Grigorovich Norman—who may well have had British ancestry. Like the Karle and Krnka conversions, the Terry-Norman was built on the basis of the rifle musket of 1856.

A tubular rearward extension, tapering outward, was added to the existing barrel and closed by a large threaded plug. The plug was cut to allow the bolt to pass once it had been turned through a quarter-circle to disengage the locking shoulders. The handle was formed as part of a curved breech cover and lay flat on top of the breech when the mechanism was ready to fire. Though the Russian guns were easier to load than the original Terry pattern, bad gas leaks could flip the breech cover up into the firer's face. Field service soon showed that the Norman-Terry rifle had too many disadvantages, and work stopped in favor of better designs.

MODEL 1866 RIFLE

Converted by the imperial manufactory, Tula, 1866-7.
Total production: 60,000? **Chambering:** 15.2mm combustible paper cartridge, fired by a caplock. **Action:** locked by rotating two shoulders on the bolt body to bear on the closing plug of the breech.

52.75in overall, about 10lb empty. 36.6in barrel, 4-groove rifling; RH, concentric. Single-shot only. Tangent rear sight graduated to 600 paces (465yd). 985 fps with 540-grain bullet. Socket bayonet.

Another of the conversions of the 1856-pattern Russian rifle musket (cf., Karle, Krnka), this retained the original back-action lock and the barrel-band arrangement. It was easily identified by tapered tubular extension on the breech, with flattened sides, which accepted the bolt mechanism. The flattened operating handle—part of the breech cover—was pivoted to the rear of the bolt body.

SIMILAR GUNS

Model 1866 cavalry carbine. Claims have been made that 30,000 Terry-Norman cavalry carbines were also made. None could be traced for examination and the details of construction are still unclear.

• Winchester

MODEL 1915 RIFLE
Vintovka Vinchestya, obr. 1915g

Made by the Winchester Repeating Arms Company, New Haven, Connecticut, 1915-17.
Total production: 295,000? See text. **Chambering:** 7.62x54R, rimmed. **Action:** locked by a vertically-sliding bar intercepting the reciprocating bolt as the operating lever was closed.

45.65in overall, 9.04lb empty. 28.05in barrel, 4-groove rifling; RH, concentric. Integral box magazine loaded from a stripper clip, 5 rounds. Ramp-and-leaf sight graduated to 2700 paces (2100yd). About 2690 fps with Type L ball cartridges. Winchester export-pattern bayonet.

The beginning of the First World War found the Russian ordnance with far too few weapons to arm the many millions of men being mobilized. An approach to Winchester resulted in the production of Mosin-Nagants in North America, and also in an order for 300,000 M1895 lever-action rifles (known as 'obr. 1915g' in Russia).

Production began immediately. The guns followed the standard commercial pattern, but chambered the rimmed Russian rifle cartridges and were sighted accordingly. Stripper-clip guides lay above the receiver and a handguard ran from the receiver ring to the band. The first 5,000 rifles had bayonets with 10in blades, but later examples had a 16in type.

The 7.62mm-caliber Winchester obr. 1915g rifle.

The fall of the Tsar and the ensuing unrest caused deliveries to cease in 1917. Winchester recorded the dispatch of 293,816 rifles while the Russians claimed to have received 299,000, but these figures have been strongly disputed in recent years by Winchester collectors and the actual total remains in doubt.

SAUDI ARABIA

• Heckler & Koch (al-Khardj)

After initial supplies had come from Germany and Britain, the Saudi authorities acquired a license in 1968 permitting guns to be made in the government arms factory at al-Khardj. The rifles generally bore crossed scimitars beneath a palm tree on the left side of the receiver, above 'KINGDOM OF SAUDI ARABIA' in Arabic and English. They bore their designation and serial number (in Arabic) on the left side of the magazine housing. The G3 was superseded by the Steyr AUG in 1980, though large numbers of the older rifles were still in service in 1992.

• Mauser

FN-Mauser short rifles were acquired in the late 1930s (the kingdom in its present form dates from 1932). The guns were apparently chambered for 7.9x57 cartridges, but it is not known how they were marked.

SAXONY

This state became part of the German Empire (*Deutsches Reich*) during the Franco-Prussian War, the Saxon army gradually merging into the Imperial forces. Apart from surviving Chassepot conversions, therefore, Saxon troops carried Mauser rifles from the mid-1870s onward. Post-1875 guns can sometimes be identified by the cyphers of the Saxon kings Albert and Georg, 'AR' and 'GR' respectively.

• Chassepot

MODEL 1873 CARBINE
Aptierter Chassepot-Karabiner M 1873
Altered in the government factory in Dresden.
Total production: at least 10,000. **Chambering:** 11x60, rimmed. **Action:** locked by the bolt guide rib down abutting the receiver bridge when the bolt handle was turned down.

37.6in overall, 6.95lb empty. 18.8in barrel, 4-groove rifling: LH, concentric. Single shot only. Block-and-leaf sight graduated to 1500 metres (1640yd). About 1150 fps with Reichspatrone 1871. No bayonet.

The Bremer-Einhorn Transformation consisted of reaming a new chamber in the abbreviated French barrel, which was then screwed back into a segment of the original barrel remaining within the receiver to act as a bush. As the barrel no longer bedded properly in the stock, however, noticeable gaps could be seen immediately in front of the receiver.

The new flush-headed bolt plug was retained by a transverse screw through the base of the bolt handle rib. A conventional extractor was added, and the needle assembly was replaced by a striker and coil spring. Saxon carbines customarily retained the French-style cocking-piece guide roller, and some had a safety lever on the left rear of the receiver. The original full-length bolt-handle ribs were retained, but stocks were shortened to half length; swivels lay beneath the new nose-cap and under the butt. The leaf of the new rear sight was hinged at the rear of the bed, which lay farther from the breech than the French or Prussian designs.

The original receiver markings were replaced by 'MOD.73' but the others remained intact – excepting those on the discarded breech. New serial numbers were added to the left side of the barrel, the receiver, and the rear portion of the bolt-handle rib. The Bremer-Einhorn conversions were adopted on 27th May 1875 for Train-Bataillon Nr. 12, but the barrels proved to be too weak ahead of the breech and the guns were replaced in the 1880s by the Karabiner M1871.

• Drechsler

Developed about 1863, this was an experimental infantry rifle embodying a bolt system inspired by the British Terry pattern (q.v.). A folding operating lever/cover plate lay on top of the breech, protecting the loading port. The lever could be lifted and turned to the right to allow the locking lug to pass through the reinforced receiver ring as the bolt was retracted. This motion exposed the chamber so that a combustible cartridge could be inserted manually, to be fired by a conventional external-hammer back-action lock after the bolt had been closed.

The status of the Drechsler system remains unclear. Some were clearly made for trials – several examples survive – but the quantity involved is still not known. The army of the kingdom of Saxony was subsequently equipped with Prussian-pattern Dreyse needle rifles, and then, after the formation of the German Empire, with the metallic-cartridge Mausers.

SERBIA

These guns were usually distinguishable from their markings, which, after independence had been gained from Turkey in 1878, included the pavilioned Arms of a double-headed eagle on a shield. This usually lay above the chamber. Inscriptions were customarily in Cyrillic after the 1880s – a script shared only with Russia among the major European powers. The 1878/80-pattern Mausers were customarily marked in German in a single line, but the later magazine rifles showed greater diversity: a typical M99/07S was marked 'AUSTRIYSKA/ORUZHNA FABRIKA/SHTAYER' in three lines of Cyrillic on the left side of the receiver, whereas an M1910 bore 'ORUZHNA FABRIKA MAYSERAA' above 'OBERNDORF A/N.' on the left side of the receiver.

• Green

The ordnance history of Serbia during the period of Turkish suzerainity (1829-78) is still shrouded in mystery. Among the firearms said to have been used was the bolt-action 'Green' rifle, which most Anglo-American authorities have – wrongly – assumed to have been the American Greene pattern, attributing the lack of a terminal 'e' to the difficulties of transliterating Cyrillic. The basis for the conversion was the lesser known *British* Green (q.v.).

MODEL 1867 RIFLE
Gryn-Puska
Converted by the Kraguyevac Armory, 1867-8.
Total production: said to have been about 16,000. **Chambering:** 13.8mm combustible cartridge, fired by an external caplock. **Action:** locked by a lug on the bolt body engaging the receiver wall and another formed in the bolt-handle base locking in the floor of the receiver.

56.7in overall, 9.9lb empty. 37.4in barrel, 4-groove rifling; RH, concentric. Single shot only. Stepped base leaf-and-slider sight, graduations unknown. About 1050 fps with 465-grain bullet. Socket bayonet.

Incorporating improvements suggested by Major Mladen Jankvic, which included combining the rear lug with an eccentric base on the bolt-handle, this bolt-action system remained recognizably the work of the Green brothers of Birmingham. The rifle-muskets retained their locks and hammers, in addition to the one-piece stocks, twin barrel bands and separate nose caps. About 12,000 survived to serve second-line units in campaigns undertaken against the Turks in 1876, but they leaked so badly that the Green breech was replaced with a Peabody-Roberts pattern and metal-case ammunition.

• Martini

The government ordered 100,000 450-caliber Martini-Henry rifles from 'an English company' in 1880. It is suspected that this was the National Arms & Ammunition Co. Ltd. of Birmingham, but that only a few hundred guns were supplied owing to disputes between NA&A Co. and the principal manufacturers of Martini-Henry rifles for the British government. In 1881, owing to lack of progress, the Mauser-Milovanovic (q.v.) was substituted for the Martini-Henry.

• Mauser

Trials began in 1879 to find a rifle for the army. It soon became clear that the 1871-type Mauser was likely to win once changes requested by the trials commission had been made.

Perfected by 1880, the trials rifle operated similarly to the German service rifle, but had a neater trigger guard and a rail extending back from the receiver above the wrist. This prevented the cocking piece from rotating, but also prevented the shooter placing his thumb comfortably over the wrist. A small coil spring was added around the safety-catch spindle, allowing the cocking piece to be dismantled without tools, and an extractor/ejector was fitted to the bolt head.

MODEL 1878/80 RIFLE

Made by Waffenfabrik Mauser, Oberndorf, 1881-7.

Total production: 120,000. **Chambering:** 10.15x63R, rimmed. **Action:** locked by the bolt guide rib abutting the receiver ahead of the bridge.

50.8in overall, 9.85lb empty. 31.5in barrel, 4-groove rifling; RH, concentric. Single shot only. Leaf sight graduated to 2025m (2215yd). 1670 fps with ball cartridges. M1880 sword bayonet.

On 14th February 1881, Mauser won a contract for the M78/80 rifle, colloquially known as the Mauser-Milovanovic. Major Kosta Milovanovic of the arsenal in Kragujevac had been responsible for a number of new features, the most important (but least obvious) being rifling grooves whose width reduced from breech to muzzle. This was apparently intended to improve obturation, but was a needless manufacturing complication.

The M78/80 was long and clumsy, typical of its era, and had a straight-wrist stock. The receiver-base continued backward above the wrist of the stock, undoubtedly adding support to the bolt when open but also making the hand-hold uncomfortable. There were two screw-clamped bands and a nose cap with a bayonet lug on the right side. Swivels lay on the underside of the butt and on the rear band. A cleaning rod lay under the barrel. A few surviving guns were chambered for the standard 7x57 round in the early 1900s (see 'M1880/1907', below).

MODEL 1885 CAVALRY CARBINE
Also known as the 'Mauser-Koká'

Made by Waffenfabrik Mauser, Oberndorf am Neckar, 1885-6.

Total production: 4,000. **Chambering:** 10.15x63mm, rimmed. **Action:** as M1878/80, above.

37.6in overall, 8.27lb empty. 18.3in barrel, 4-groove rifling; RH, concentric. Tube magazine in forend, 5 rounds. Leaf sight graduated to 1200m (1310yd)? 1525 fps with ball cartridges. No bayonet.

The first modern magazine carbines were purchased from Mauser about 1885. Mechanically similar to the contemporaneous M1871/84 German infantry rifle, with a tube magazine inspired by the Kropatschek, they had the extended cocking-piece rail at the back of the receiver even though the Milovanovic decreasing-

width rifling had been abandoned. One-piece stocks, extending to the muzzle, had an unusually long wrist; a single sprung band and a simple nose cap were used. Owing to the absence of a bayonet, it is assumed that the guns were issued to the cavalry.

SIMILAR GUNS

Model 1885 artillery rifle. This seems to have been a longer version of the cavalry carbine, holding an extra cartridge in the magazine and accepting a sword bayonet.

MODEL 1880/06 AND MODEL 1880/07 RIFLES
Also known as 'M80/6' or 'M80/7'

Manufacturer: see text below.

Total production: a few thousand. **Chambering:** 7x57, rimless. **Action:** see notes.

50.7in overall, 9.95lb empty. 30.95in barrel, 4-groove rifling; RH, concentric. Integral charger-loaded box magazine, 5 rounds. Leaf sight graduated to 2000m (2185yd). About 2330 fps with ball cartridges. M1880 sword bayonet.

The first of these rifles was adapted from the single shot M78/80 in 1906, a new barrel and a protruding single-row magazine being provided. However, the earliest 'M1880/06' rifles – locked only by the abutment of the bolt-handle rib on the receiver – proved too weak to withstand the pressures generated by the new cartridges. Later 'M1880/07' batches, therefore, had a special housing on the right side of the receiver for a locking lug cut in the front end of the bolt rib.

The addition of a 'C' suffix to these designations, particularly the 1907 type, still poses questions. The suggestion that the conversion work was undertaken by Österreichische Waffenfabriks-Gesellschaft in Steyr – see M1899/07, below – instead of in the Kraguyevac factory is worthy of consideration.

MODEL 1899 RIFLE

Made by Deutsche Waffen- und Munitionsfabriken, Berlin, 1899-1906; and by Österreichische Waffenfabriks-Gesellschaft, Steyr, 1907-10.

Total production: not known. **Chambering:** 7x57, rimless. **Action:** locked by rotating two lugs on the bolt head into the receiver behind the chamber.
DATA FOR A TYPICAL EXAMPLE

48.45in overall, 8.88lb empty. 29.15in barrel, 4-groove rifling; RH, concentric. Internal charger-loaded box magazine, 5 rounds. Leaf sight graduated to 2000m (2185yd). About 2330 fps with ball cartridges. M1899 knife bayonet.

The first orders for these rifles, similar mechanically to the Chilean Mo. 1895, were placed with DWM and OEWG in 1899. Deliveries continued until about 1903. They had straight-wrist stocks with handguards running from the receiver ring to the barrel band, and simple nose cap with a bayonet lug on its underside. A cleaning rod was carried in the forend. Swivels lay on the under edge of the butt and beneath the band.

Though the guns can be identified by the makers' names, the Austrian-made examples are clearly marked 'M1899C' above the chamber The suffix has perplexed many commentators: some have inexplicably deciphered it as 'C' for 'Cartridge', others have seen it as a Cyrillic 'S' for 'Serbia'. The most plausible explanation is that it is indeed 'S', but represents 'Steyr' – a distinction being drawn between the guns supplied from Germany and those made in Austria, perhaps on the grounds of partial- or even non-interchangeability.

SIMILAR GUNS

Model 99/07S rifle. More rifles were acquired from Österreichische Waffenfabriks-Gesellschaft in 1907. They were stocked in the manner of the original DWM-made pattern, but had improvements in the action. A thumb-cut in the left wall of the receiver facilitated the use of stripper clips and the bolt head enclosed the cartridge case-head.

Model 99/08S rifle. Additional deliveries were made from OEWG in 1908. Guns were marked '99/08C' instead of '99/07C'. The differences are not clearly understood, but are suspected to have been minor – possibly an adaptation of the bolt head, or simply a matter of differing rear sight graduations.

Model 1908 carbine. Purchased in small numbers for cavalry and artillerymen, this was simply a shortened version of the Steyr-made rifle. About 37.5in long, it had a 17in barrel and an empty weight of about 7lb. The stock extended to the muzzle and had a pointed Austrian-style pistol grip. Tangent-leaf rear sights were graduated to 1500m (1650yd), but bayonets could not be mounted.

A manufacturer's drawing of the single shot M78/80 Mauser rifle.

Conversions. The Yugoslavian army altered substantial quantities of 99/07 and 99/08 rifles in the 1920s to chamber the 7.9x57mm round, the work being undertaken in the Kraguyevac factory.

MODEL 1910 RIFLE
Made by Waffenfabrik Mauser AG, Oberndorf, 1910-12.
Total production: not known (40,000?). **Chambering:** 7x57, rimless. **Action:** locked by rotating two lugs on the bolt head into the receiver behind the chamber, and by a safety lug opposing the bolt handle engaging its seat.

48.75in overall, 9.06lb empty. 29.15in barrel, 4-groove rifling; RH, concentric. Internal charger-loaded box magazine, 5 rounds. Tangent-leaf rear sight graduated to 2000m (2185yd). About 2330 fps with ball cartridges. M1899 knife bayonet.

Ordered in 1911, during a period of unrest which culminated in the Second Balkan War, this was a Gew. 98-type gun with a straight bolt handle, an enclosed bolt head (identical with the 1910-type Costa Rica Mauser), and a standard 'export' stock. A handguard ran from the receiver ring to the narrow band, and the simple nose cap carried a bayonet lug.

SIAM

• Arisaka
The Siamese army used a selection of obsolescent Japanese 30th and 35th Year type rifles, converted for the 8x50R and 8x52R service cartridges prior to 1920. Most of the guns were fitted with new one-piece stocks, deepened ahead of the trigger guard to accommodate the large-diameter 8mm cartridges in the magazine, and had tangent-leaf rear sights graduated to 2000m (2185yd). A typical specimen was 48.95in long and had a 30.35in barrel; a *Chakra* (war-quoit) and a date in Sanskrit numerals lay above the chamber.

• Mannlicher
Readily identified by the *Chakra* and Sanskrit numbers, substantial numbers of 1888 and 1888-90 Mannlichers were supplied to the Siamese army in the 1890s. They did not prove successful enough to have long-lasting influences on the country's ordnance affairs, as a Japanese-made Mauser rifle was adopted in 1902.

• Mauser
Substantial quantities of obsolescent 1871-type Mauser rifles were purchased in Europe at the end of the nineteenth century, recognisable by chamber-top *Chakra* and Sanskrit markings in addition to the original German ordnance marks. The earliest small caliber rifles were of 1898 pattern, with the safety lug and a non-rotating extractor. Supplied by Waffenfabrik Mauser in small numbers in 1901-2, chambering the 8x50R cartridge, they were used for field trials.

MODEL 1902 RIFLE
Also known as 'Type 45'
Made by the Imperial artillery arsenal, Koishikawa, Tokyo, about 1903-8.
Total production: not known. **Chambering:** 8x50R, rimmed. **Action:** generally as German Gew. 98 (q.v.).

49.1in overall, 8.55lb empty. 29.15in barrel, 4-groove rifling; RH, concentric. Internal charger-loaded box magazine, 5 rounds. Tangent-leaf sight graduated to 2000m (2185yd). About 2050 fps with Type 45 ball cartridges. Type 45 sword bayonet.

This was adopted in 1902 ('RS 121' on the Siamese calendar) to replace the earlier Mannlichers. The guns had angular stocks with pointed Japanese-style pistol grips and unusually long receiver tangs to strengthen the wrist. A handguard ran forward from the receiver ring to the barrel band, its rear surface being reduced so that the manually operated bolt cover could be slid forward when the gun was to be fired.

Swivels lay under the spring-retained barrel band and on the under-edge of the butt, and a bayonet bar appeared directly beneath the muzzle. Internally, the magazine case was sloped so that the rims of the cartridges would not interlock.

SIMILAR GUNS
Type 42/66 rifle. Surviving rifles were adapted from 1923 onward for the 8x52 Type 66 cartridge, which had a pointed bullet and would not interchange with its predecessor. The principal

external change concerned the back-sight ramps, which were much lower.

30-06 conversions. A few rifles were adapted in the early 1950s for the standard U.S. rifle cartridge, their barrels being shortened appreciably at the same time.

MODEL 1904
Possibly known as the 'Type 47'
Made by Waffenfabrik Mauser AG, Oberndorf am Neckar, Württemberg, Germany.
Total production: not known. **Chambering:** 7x57, rimless. **Action:** as German Gew. 98 (q.v.).

48.8in overall, 8.8lb empty. 29.25in barrel, 4-groove rifling; RH, concentric. Internal box magazine loaded from a stripper clip, 5 rounds. Tangent-leaf rear sight graduated to 2000m (2185yd). 2395 fps with standard ball ammunition. Sword bayonet.

Distinguished by a *Chakra* on the receiver bridge and Sanskrit numerals, these rifles were supplied to the Siamese prior to World War I, perhaps to offset a temporary shortage of weapons (which would explain the non-standard caliber). They had heavy barrels, but were otherwise standard export patterns; the barrel band was narrow, the bayonet lug lay beneath the simple nose cap, and the stock had a shallow pistol grip.

MODEL 1923 SHORT RIFLE
Also known as Type 66
Made by Imperial artillery arsenal, Koishikawa, Tokyo?
Total production: not known. **Chambering:** 8x52R, rimmed. **Action:** as M1902, above.

41.9in overall, 8.05lb empty. 22.05in barrel, 4-groove rifling; RH, concentric. Internal charger-loaded box magazine, 5 rounds. Tangent-leaf sight graduated to 1200m (1310yd). About 2100 fps with Type 66 ball cartridges. Type 66 sword bayonet.

Dating from about 1923, these may have been converted for cavalry or artillery use from Type 45 long rifles. They had a simplified barrel band, sling mounts on the left side, and a Japanese-type nose cap. The muzzle ring of the special bayonet lay well away from the back of the hilt.

SINGAPORE

• ArmaLite
An order was placed with Colt in 1966 for 18,000 standard and 2,300 heavy-barrel CAR-15 rifles. Only a little over 3,000 had been delivered before February 1967, when the authorities negotiated a license to make 150,000 rifles.

Production was entrusted to Chartered Industries Ltd. (CIS), with technical assistance from Colt. The first guns were made in 1970, work continuing for about a decade; about 30,000 of a total approaching 185,000 rifles were shipped to Thailand. The SAR-80 was then derived from the AR-18 by way of the Sterling Automatic Rifle.

Singapore-made rifles bore the 'CiS' trademark on the left side of the magazine housing, above an acknowledgment of the licensing agreement. The left side of the receiver ahead of the selector was marked "COLT'S GOVT. MODEL" over 'M16' over 'CAL. 5.56MM'.

• Chartered Industries
This engineering company first became involved in the arms industry in the late 1960s, when a contract to produce M16-type rifles (see 'ArmaLite') was negotiated on behalf of the newly-independent Singapore state. Making ArmaLites involved the payment of licensing fees; when work on the M16 came to an end, therefore, CIS produced the SA-80 – an adaption of the ArmaLite AR-18 by way of the abortive Sterling Light Automatic Rifle.

The SA-80 and its successor, the SR-88, have been designed with a view to simplifying production. Their construction relies heavily on stampings and sheet-metal fabrication, reducing costs substantially compared with the M16.

SA-80 AUTOMATIC RIFLE
Made by Chartered Industries of Singapore Ltd, later Chartered Firearms Industries Pty Ltd, Singapore.

The Sterling Light Automatic Rifle, prototype of the SA-80 and SR-88.

The 5.56mm SR-88A rifle.

Chambering: 5.56x45mm, rimless. **Action:** Gas-operated autoloading action, locked by rotating lugs on the bolt into the barrel extension.

38.1in overall, 6.9lb without magazine. 18.1in barrel, 6-groove rifling; RH, concentric. Detachable box magazine, 20 or 30 rounds. Rocking-leaf sight. 3180 fps with standard ball cartridges, 700 rpm. Optional knife bayonet.

The first prototypes of this assault rifle were revealed in 1978, most of the design studies being undertaken in England by the Sterling Engineering Co. Ltd. of Dagenham, work being credited to Frank Waters and L. James Sullivan. Series production began in Singapore in 1981.

The rifle was locked by a rotating Stoner-pattern bolt. It could be identified by 'crackle' finish on the receiver, and by a tapering synthetic forend with vertical ribs behind the front sight. Thinner finger grooves lay on the underside ahead of the magazine. An M16 magazine and a standard muzzle brake/grenade launcher were fitted, bipods and a folding butt being optional.

SR-88 ASSAULT RIFLE
Made by Chartered Firearms Industries, Singapore.
Chambering: 5.56x45mm, rimless. **Action:** as SA-80, above.

38.2in overall, 8lb without magazine. 18.1in barrel, 6-groove rifling; RH, concentric. Detachable box magazine, 20 or 30 rounds. Adjustable aperture sight. 3180 fps with standard ball cartridges; 750 rpm. Optional knife bayonet.

This 1988-vintage improved version of the SA-80 had a slotted handguard to improve barrel ventilation, a folding carrying handle, and a new adjustable aperture pattern rear sight. The U.S. M203 grenade launcher could be attached to the underside of the forend when required. The butt, handguard and pistol grip were made of fiberglass-reinforced nylon, and – profiting from U.S. Army experiences in Vietnam – the bore and gas-tube were chromium plated to reduce the effects of fouling. Bipods and a folding skeletal butt could be supplied on request.

SOUTH AFRICA

The Union of South Africa was formed by integrating former British and Dutch colonies after the end of the Second South African War in 1902. British influence remained paramount until independence was declared in 1960.

• FN-Saive (Lyttelton)

The government obtained FAL-type rifles from Fabrique Nationale immediately after gaining independence in 1960. The earliest guns had plain muzzles without flash suppressors, and accepted a tube-hilt bayonet. They had two-piece extractors, butts with nose caps, and lacked the butt trap for cleaning equipment. The handguard was synthetic. South African weapons were usually distinguished by a property mark comprising 'M' within 'U'.

In 1963, under the terms of a licence granted by FN to the South African Armament Corporation, Pty ('Armscor'), the first indigenous rifles were delivered to the Defence Force from Lyttleton Engineering Co., Pty, of Pretoria. These were essentially similar to the Para FAL, with a tube-frame butt folding to the right. The 1974-vintage R2 was simply a shortened form of the original rifle, reducing weight by about 450gm. R1 and R2 rifles were superseded by the Galil-type R4 in the early 1980s.

South African R1-type guns have been supplied to Lesotho; Rhodesia (Zimbabwe); South West Africa (Namibia) and Swaziland.

• Galil (Lyttelton)

After protracted trials, the South African government adopted the '5.56mm Rifle 4' (R4) in 1982, to replace the 7.62mm R1 (FAL) as well as some G3 weapons seized in the Angolan borderland. Made by the Lyttleton Engineering Co., Pty, of Pretoria, the R4 was a minor adaption of the Israeli Galil (q.v.). The forend and pistol grip were made of fiberglass-reinforced plastic; the butt, steel on the original IMI guns, was similarly synthetic to reduce the effects of the hot South African climate. The butt was lengthened, giving an overall dimension of about 39.5in, and changes were made in the bipod, gas system, receiver and rifling to suit SADF requirements. The rifles weighed about 9.4lb without the standard 35-round magazine. Adopted in 1987 to supplement and eventually replace the R4, the 5.56mm R5 was similar to its predecessor excepting for the omission of the bipod and a 5.1in reduction in barrel length. A typical R5 is about 34.4in long and weighs about 8.5lb.

• Lee-Enfield

Formed in 1900 during the Second South African (Boer) War, the Union of South Africa was armed with Lee-Enfield rifles until the approval of the R1 (FN FAL) in the early 1960s. The guns were usually distinguished by a 'U' property mark. No substantial manufacturing has ever been undertaken, apart from replacement barrels marked 'U' over crossed pennants above 'P'.

• Musgrave

Designed by members of a well-known South African gunmaking family, Musgrave rifles were based on the proven Mauser action. Though series production began in the early 1970s, the Mauser-type rifles were replaced in the late 1970s by modified Model 80 and Model 90 patterns.

RSA NR-1 RIFLE
Made by Musgrave Manufacturers & Distributors (Pty) Ltd, Bloemfentein, 1970-6.
Chambering: 308 Winchester only. **Action:** Turning-bolt action, locked by lugs on the bolt-head and the bolt handle turning down into its seat.

About 46.5in overall, 10lb without sights. 26.45in barrel, 4-groove rifling; RH, concentric? Aperture sight. 2625 fps with 180-grain bullet.

This single shot target rifle seems to have been developed for the South African Rifle Association, and possibly also as a military trainer. Built around a much-modified Mauser action, which cocked on closing, the NR-1 was distinguished by a massive tubular receiver, pierced only by an ejection port, and a plain straight-comb half-stock with a handguard running forward from the chamber. A band around the forend bore a swivel, though an accessory rail was often let into the underside of the forend. A rubber buttplate was standard, the barrel was a special heavyweight pattern, and micro-adjustable sights were fitted.

NR-5 SPORTING RIFLE
Made by Musgrave Manufacturers & Distributors (Pty) Ltd., Bloemfontein, 1971-6.
Chambering: 243 Winchester, 270 Winchester, 7mm Remington Magnum, 30-06 or 308 Winchester, and 458 Winchester Magnum to special order only. **Action:** as NR-1, above.
DATA FOR A TYPICAL EXAMPLE
.270 Winchester, rimless. 46.70in overall, 8.25lb empty. 25.75in barrel, 4-groove rifling; RH, concentric? Internal box magazine, 5 rounds. Optical sight. 2900 fps with 150-grain bullet.

Introduced in 1971, the NR-5 or Premier had a good-quality walnut stock with a low Monte Carlo comb and a slender pistol grip. Checkering appeared on the pistol grip and forend, the separate olivewood grip-cap and forend tip contrasting with the dark finish of the stock. A ventilated shoulder pad was fitted to the butt and studs for readily detachable swivels lay beneath the forend and butt toe.

SIMILAR GUNS
NR-6. Also sold as the 'Valiant', this had a 24in barrel and a simpler stock with a straight comb. Skip-line checkering appeared on the pistol grip and forend, the grip cap and forend tip being abandoned. Sights usually comprised a folding leaf and a ramped blade.

• Vergueiro

The South African authorities purchased 25,000 of these 6.5mm rifles from Portugal in 1915, to replace Lee-Enfields which had been issued to South African units serving in Europe. They were identical with the Portuguese (q.v.) service rifle, being distinguished only by the presence of property marks consisting of a Broad Arrow within 'U'.

SPAIN

The principal distinguishing mark has been a simplified form of the national Arms, consisting of a crowned shield with a quartering of a castle, a lion, vertical bars and a chain – taken from the Arms of Castile, Leon, Aragon and Navarre respectively.

• Amiel

This was a Snider-like conversion of an 1859-pattern short rifle (Carabina de Cazadores Mo. 57/59) with the axis pin on the left side of the breechblock. Its principal claim to individuality lay in the cranked lever pinned to the hammer-body which opened the breech and drew the extractor bar backward as the hammer was retracted. The rifle chambered a 15mm centerfire cartridge ignited

by the external hammer striking an 'L'-shape bar let into the top of the breechblock. Guns were tested by the Spanish authorities in the 1860s, but little else is known. They had a one-piece stock with a straight wrist, two screwed bands, a brass nose cap, and a leaf-and-slider rear sight behind the rear band. A socket bayonet could be mounted when required.

• Berdan

Trials began in 1865 with more than a hundred breech systems, the authorities selecting the 'No. 3' Berdan after minor changes had been made. Berdan conversions chambered a rimmed cartridge with a nominal caliber of 15mm. Once the hammer had been thumbed back to halfcock, the breechblock could be lifted up and forward by a small lever. The nose of the original hammer was bent up and back to strike the firing pin running through the breechblock.

MODEL 1867 RIFLE
Fusil para Infanteria Mo. 1867
Converted by several contractors – see text.
Total production: not known. **Chambering:** 15mm, rimmed. **Action:** locked by the hammer wedging the breechblock in its closed position.

54.7in overall, 9.45lb empty. 36.2in barrel, 4-groove rifling; RH, concentric. Single shot only. Ramp-and-leaf sight graduated to 1000m (1095yd). 1195 fps with Mo. 1867 ball cartridges. Mo. 1857 socket bayonet.

Adopted on 14th December 1867, these weapons were converted by Ybarzabal of Eibar, Orbea Hermanos y Cia of Eibar, and Euscalduna of Planencia from Mo. 59 rifle-muskets originally made in the government factory. Locks bore the original marks – a crown over an 'AR' monogram, above 'O' for 'Oviedo' and the date.

The one-piece stock had three screw-clamping bands and a small nose cap. Swivels lay under the butt on the elongated trigger guard tang, and on the middle band; the cramped trigger guard was characteristic of Spanish designs of the 1850s.

M1867 SHORT RIFLE
Fusil para Cazadores Mo. 1867
Converted by several contractors – see text.
Total production: not known. **Chambering:** 15mm, rimmed. **Action:** as Mo. 1867 rifle, above.

48.45in overall, 8.45lb empty. 30.3in barrel, 4-groove rifling; RH, concentric. Single shot only. Ramp-and-leaf sight graduated to 900m (985yd). 1100 fps with Mo. 1867 ball cartridges. Mo. 1857 socket bayonet.

This was similar to the infantry pattern. Converted from Mo. 1857 and Mo. 1857/59 caplocks, the two differing patterns were stocked similarly with two screw-clamping bands and identical ramrods. However, the Mo. 57 had a more generous trigger guard bow and a round-edged buttplate; the Mo. 57/59 had the cramped trigger guard and a much flatter buttplate. Similarly, though both were hinged at the rear, the Mo. 57 sight ramp rose toward the muzzle while the Mo. 57/59 type rose at the breech.

MODEL 1867 CARBINE
Carabina para Artilleria e Ingenieros Mo. 1867
Converted by several contractors – see text.
Total production: not known. **Chambering:** 15mm, rimmed. **Action:** as Mo. 1867 rifle, above.
DATA FOR A TYPICAL 'MO. 58/67'
48.45in overall, 8.31lb empty. 30.3in barrel, 4-groove rifling; RH, concentric. Single shot only. Ramp-and-leaf sight graduated to 900m (985yd). 1100 fps with Mo. 1867 ball cartridges. Mo. 1858 sword bayonet.

This compact weapon shared the action of the infantry rifle. It was approved on the basis of the rifled engineer carbine of 1858, which was a variant of the Carabina Rayada para Cazadores Mo. 57/59 (above) with the bands moved closer together to expose more of the muzzle. Artillerymen carried the Machete Bayoneta Mo. 1858, which had a broad falchion-like blade and a cast-brass grip; unlike any comparable Spanish pattern, it also had a socket and locking ring on the guard.

The Mo. 1861 engineer carbine was altered in small numbers. Its machete bayonet (Mo. 1861) had a conventional guard and a spring-and-stud attachment mechanism in the pommel. The 'Mo. 61/67' carbine had less of the muzzle exposed than the otherwise similar Mo. 58, the bayonet lug and tenon distinguishing it from the 'para Cazadores' Mo. 57/59 adaptation.

MODEL 1867 NAVY RIFLE

A few 'Carbines for marine infantry' (Carabina para Infanteria de Marina, Mo. 1867) were converted from Mo. 1858 caplock naval short rifles which had been made by Juan Aldasoro of Eibar in 1860-1. They were similar to the infantry short rifle (above), with the rear sight and buttplate of the Mo. 57 – the latter in brass – plus the Mo. 59 trigger guard. The bayonet had a cast-brass hilt.

• CETME

The essence of this roller-delayed breech may be traced back to the German MG.42, and to experiments preceding the introduction of the MP.43 – the first modern-style assault rifle.

Mauser began work in 1942 on a roller system credited to Wilhelm Stähle. Locked at the instant of firing, it tapped propellant gas from the bore to propel a piston backward. The piston moved the rear part of the breechblock back until the locking rollers could move inward into the space thus created. A spring in a butt-tube returned the mechanism to re-load the chamber. The front part of the breechblock stopped against the rear face of the barrel at the end of the loading stroke while the rear portion, still moving, forced the rollers out into the locking recesses.

By 1943, however, Mauser's technicians had discovered that the mechanism worked satisfactorily without the piston assembly. The backward thrust generated on firing through the base of the cartridge case was sufficient to unlock the rollers. Unfortunately, the military authorities were deeply suspicious of the delayed-blowback Gerät 06.H, which remained a privately-promoted project, and had only just commissioned 30 locked-breech assault rifles (Gerät 06 or StG.45 [M]) when the war ended.

After the Oberndorf factory had fallen into Allied hands, the French continued work until the spring of 1946. Prototype assault rifles chambering 30 M1 Carbine ammunition were subsequently made in Mulhouse under the supervision of ex-Mauser engineer Ludwig Vorgrimmler.

By 1951, the focus of attention shifted to Spain, where Vorgrimmler had moved. As the Spanish army was in desperate need of modern weapons, the Instituto Nacional de Industrias formed the Centro de Estudios Técnicos de Materiales Especiales (CETME) in Madrid to exploit the German ideas. Prototype assault rifles were completed in 1952.

They embodied the retarded-blowback roller lock and chambered a special 7.9x40 cartridge in an effort to balance an ability to fire fully automatically with the need to keep a gun weighing less than 8.8lb under proper control. The original 105-grain bullet had a copper jacket and a lightweight aluminum core, exposed at the tip; starting out at about 2625 fps, the streamlined bullet was said to be capable of piercing most steel helmets at 1000m (1095yd).

In March 1954, impressed by the CETME rifles, the Spanish government invited Heckler & Koch to resolve mass-production problems and the success of the project was assured.

CETME ASSAULT RIFLE, 7.62MM
Fusil d'Asalto CETME
Made in the Oviedo factory of Empresa Nacional de Militares 'Santa Barbara'.

Total production: not known. **Chambering options:** 7.62x51 CETME or 7.62x51 NATO. **Action:** locked by rollers engaging the barrel-collar walls; delayed blowback, selective fire.

DATA FOR A TYPICAL MODELO C

Wooden handguard pattern. **Chambering:** 7.62x51 NATO, rimless. 39.95in overall, 9.88lb with empty magazine. 17.7in barrel, 4-groove rifling; RH, concentric. Detachable box magazine, 20 rounds. Drum sight graduated to 400m (435yd). 2560 fps with NATO ball cartridges; 600±50 rpm. CETME knife bayonet.

The pre-production guns of 1954 were made for the 7.9mm CETME cartridge. Consisting largely of sheet-steel pressings, they had a straight-line layout with a tube containing the cocking handle above the barrel. The butt and pistol grip were wood, while a folded bipod provided a very uncomfortable forward hand grip. The straight base of the magazine housing was a prolongation of the receiver; the selector lever lay on the left side above the pistol grip; and a tangent-leaf rear sight appeared on top of the action above the trigger aperture. A multi-port muzzle brake was standard, though a detachable grenade launcher could be fitted when required.

Typical markings included 'FUSIL DE ASALTO' above 'C.E.T.M.E.' over the serial number (e.g., 'No. 433') on the left side of the magazine housing.

Promising trials were undertaken in Germany in 1955. After an abortive variant had been produced for a special short-case 7.62mm round, the rifle was revised for the U.S. 30 T65 cartridge which was destined to become NATO standard.

SIMILAR GUNS

CETME Modelo A (also often known as 'Series A'). These 7.62x51mm rifles were made in Spain in the mid 1950s. They were essentially similar to the pre-production examples, but had a straighter magazine, a rotating carrying handle on the bolt-tube, and an oblique-cut magazine housing. A typical marking read 'F.A. CETME' over a number (e.g., 'A-356'). The guns fired automatically from an open-bolt position. The rifle was licensed to NWM in the Netherlands in 1956, to take part in contemporaneous army trials that eventually resolved in favor of the FAL. The Germans had also become very interested in the CETME and development subsequently passed to Heckler & Koch (q.v.).

CETME Modelo B. The Spanish government adopted this version for service in 1958. A grenade launcher and a sheet-metal forend had been added, and the mechanism was simplified by eliminating the open-bolt automatic firing capabilities.

CETME Modelo C. Approved in 1965, this resulted from a decision taken in 1964 to standardize the 7.62mm NATO cartridge (loaded with the FN-designed SS77 bullet) instead of the lower-powered Spanish pattern. The rifle was strengthened to withstand

The 5.56mm CETME Model L rifle, on its bipod.

additional chamber pressure and recoil impulse, and a combination flash-hider/grenade launcher was fitted to the muzzle.

A typical Modelo C rifle was marked with 'F.A.-CETME-C' and the Santa Barbara logo (a sword transfixing a cogwheel) on the left side of the magazine housing ahead of 'cal. 7.62 mm.' and above a serial number such as 'ET*68913*'. Selectors were marked 'T' (top), 'S' (middle) and 'R' (bottom) for single shots, safety, and fully automatic fire respectively. In 1984, the 7.62mm CETME rifles were superseded in Spanish service rifle by the 5.56mm Modelo L rifle (described below), though re-equipment has been so gradual that large numbers of 7.62mm guns remain in the inventory of ancillary forces or are being maintained in store.

Chad, the Congolese Republic, the Dominican Republic, Guatemala and Mauritania have all purchased substantial quantities of CETME-type rifles (principally Model C) for front-line service. Several Scandinavian countries, Pakistan and Portugal have acquired sizable numbers for trials.

CETME Modelo C Sniper. A few heavy-barreled rifles have been made. Fitted with optical sights and restricted to semi-automatic fire, they were not especially successful; imported weapons and the Mauser-type Santa Barbara C-75 rifle have apparently been preferred in Spain – certainly in the hands of counter-terrorist and police units.

CETME Modelo D. Developed in 1978, this was an improved version of the 'C' pattern, but served only as a development prototype for the Modelo E.

CETME Modelo E. Developed in 1981-2 from the 'D' pattern, this was little more than a CETME Modelo C with improvements to the ejector, sights and handguard. Greater use was made of synthetic parts and some guns had burst-firing capabilities, but series production does not seem to have been undertaken owing to the perceived shift towards 5.56mm ammunition at the expense of 7.62mm.

CETME Modelo R. Announced in 1982, this was a short-barreled 'port-firing' weapon intended for armored troops. The muzzle was adapted to fit a ball mount, the butt was replaced by synthetic cap, and the cocking handle was moved backward to clear the short cylindrical forend.

CETME Sport. Derived from the Modelo C, this differed from military-issue guns only in its trigger mechanism – which was limited to semi-automatic fire – and the addition of a recoil pad on the butt. A typical rifle imported into the U.S. in the mid 1960s was marked CETME "SPORT" on the left side of the magazine housing above the 'S'-prefix serial number; 'MADE IN SPAIN' usually appeared on the right above the marks of the importer, Mars Equipment Corporation of Chicago, Illinois. Selectors were marked 'S' (safe) above 'F' (fire). Like all similar rifles, the CETME did not make an effectual sporter and sales were commensurately small.

CETME ASSAULT RIFLE, 5.56MM

Made in the Oviedo factory of Empresa Nacional de Militares 'Santa Barbara'.

Currently in production. **Chambering:** 5.56x45, rimless. **Action:** as 7.62mm version, above.

DATA FOR A TYPICAL MODELO L1

36.5in overall, 7.55lb with empty magazine. 15.75in barrel, 6-groove rifling; RH, concentric. Detachable box magazine, 30 rounds. Pivoting-'L' sight for 200m (220yd) and 400m (435yd). 3180 fps with NATO ball cartridges; 750 rpm. Optional CETME knife bayonet.

Development of a small caliber version of the 7.62mm CETME rifle began in the late 1970s. The perfected Modelo L shared the basic delayed blowback roller-lock system, but was designed with an eye to simplifying production. The pistol grip was molded integrally with the butt and a synthetic handguard was used.

The earliest guns had rotating four-position drum sights (100-400m), and used special 20-round magazines. Their selectors had an additional 'R' position, giving a three-round burst, but this was subsequently reduced to the status of an optional extra.

In 1984, the Modelo L was adopted by the Spanish army to supplement and ultimately replace the 7.62mm rifles. The first rifles were delivered to the army in 1987, by which time orders for about 60,000 had been placed. A typical marking read 'CETME 5.56 (.223)' in three lines on the left side of the magazine housing. An 'L'-prefix serial number usually lay on the left side of the receiver above the trigger.

The CETME Model L rifle in the hands of a member of the Spanish special forces.

SIMILAR GUNS

CETME Modelo L1. This was a minor variant of the 'L' pattern – accepting the NATO standard U.S. M16-type 30-round magazine – but was destined more for export than Spanish service. L1-type rifles have three-position selectors and a simplified two-position rear sight; bipods and optical sights have been used, but are not in general service.

CETME Modelo LC. This compact version of the basic assault rifle offered a 12.6in barrel, with a short expansion chamber behind the flash suppresser, and was fitted with a retractable butt. It was 33.85in long (26.2in with butt retracted) and weighed 7.05lb.

• García Saez

Patented by Cosmé García Saez in the mid 1860s (U.S. Patent 45,801 of 3rd January 1865), this disc-breech system was tested extensively – if unsuccessfully – by the Spanish army. The disc rotated in a two-piece housing, which was clamped together by a helical lug on the spindle of the locking latch to improve the gas seal. Pressing the head of the latch to the right released the clamp and allowed a small projecting slotted-head button on top of the breech housing to rotate the disc back until the mouth of the chamber was visible. The disc was then loaded, rotated forward again, the clamp was tightened, and the gun was ready to fire.

Built on a standard 1859-pattern short rifle (Carabina de Cazadores M. 57/59), the García Saez pattern had a straight-wrist stock, two sprung bands and a simple brass nose-cap. Swivels lay beneath the forend and butt. The back-action caplock had an external hammer, and a stepped-base leaf-and-slider rear sight was fitted to the barrel.

• La Rosa

The work of José Ramón la Rosa, this breechloader had a barrel which could pivot axially when a small catch on the receiver was pressed forward. Sporting guns were made under the name 'Larrosa', but the experimental military paterns were probably made by the Fábrica de Trubia about 1860.

EXPERIMENTAL SHORT RIFLE

Carabina La Rosa

Made by the Fábrica de Trubia, about 1860.

Total production: not known. **Chambering:** 15mm, pinfire. **Action:** the swinging barrel was locked by a spring catch on the receiver.

52in overall, about 9lb empty. 36.8in barrel, 4-groove rifling; RH, concentric. Single shot only. Standing-block rear sight. About 975 fps with ball ammunition. Socket bayonet.

Similar in size to the Carabina de Cazadores, these guns had a back-action lock with an external hammer, a straight-wrist butt, and a forend with two bands and a small brass nose cap. The bands were both sprung and bolted; swivels lay beneath the butt and the rear band.

SIMILAR GUNS

Carbine. A 'Mosqueton la Rosa' was also made, with an overall length of about 39in and a barrel measuring 23.8in. However, whether this was a repair of the broken short rifle or a genuinely experimental pattern – perhaps to be tested by the cavalry – remains open to doubt.

• Mata

The invention of a Spanish army officer, Onofre Mata, this 1883-patent magazine rifle was based on the Remington rolling block. An operating lever on the right side of the breech was used to transfer cartridges from the case magazine in the butt to the chamber by way of an elevator tube. Capacity seems to have been five rounds in the butt and five in the tube.

• Mauser: bolt-action

Trials with a few Turkish 1887-pattern Mausers began in 1887-8, but were not successful. The appearance of smokeless propellant in France then shifted interest to smaller-caliber weapons.

MODEL 1891 TRIALS RIFLE
Fusil Mauser Mo. 1891

Made by Waffenfabrik Mauser AG, Oberndorf am Neckar, 1891.
Total production: 1200. **Chambering:** 7.65x53, rimless. **Action:** locked by two lugs on the bolt head engaging recesses in the receiver behind the chamber as the bolt handle was turned down.

48.75in overall, 9.06lb empty. 29.15in barrel, 4-groove rifling; RH, concentric. Semi-fixed box magazine loaded from a stripper clip, 5 rounds. Leaf sight graduated to 2000m (2185yd). About 2065 fps with ball cartridges.

In accordance with a royal decree of 2nd December 1891, Turkish-type Mausers were acquired for trials with the Regimiento de Infanteria Saboya No. 6 and the Batallón de Cazadores de Puerto Rico No. 19. Bolt heads were modified to eliminate double-loading, the face being partially under-cut, and a spring-loaded plunger was added in the right locking lug. The manufacturer's mark customarily appeared in a single line on the left side of the receiver.

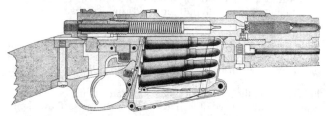

A longitudinal section of the 1891-type Spanish Mauser rifle.

SIMILAR GUNS

Argentine-type guns. Immediately prior to adoption of the Mo. 1893 rifle, the Spanish purchased 10,000 7.65mm Mo. 1891 rifles and 5,000 Mo. 1891 carbines from the Argentine government. These appear to have been delivered directly from the Loewe factory, but already had Argentine marks on the left side of the receiver; however, chamber-tops were plain. The guns were issued to Spanish colonial troops in Africa and the Ejercito de Ultramar in Cuba.

MODEL 1892 RIFLE
Fusil Mauser Español Mo. 1892

Made by Waffenfabrik Mauser, Oberndorf am Neckar, 1893-4.
Total production: 5000-8000? **Chambering:** 7x57, rimless. **Action:** as Mo. 1891, above.

48.6in overall, 9.05lb empty. 29.05in barrel, 4-groove rifling; RH, concentric. Fixed box magazine loaded from a stripper clip, 5 rounds. Leaf sight graduated to 2000m (2185yd). About 2200 fps with ball cartridges. Mo. 1892 sword bayonet.

Adopted on 30th November 1892, this was basically a Turkish rifle in 7mm caliber, but with the improvements made in the 1891 troop trials gun. It had a non-rotating 1892-patent extractor and a detachable floorplate and follower, a catch being set into the

straight front magazine-edge. The trigger system was altered so that the sear could not release the striker unless the bolt was fully locked.

A guide rib was added in the left side of the receiver, the cocking piece was attached to the firing pin with interrupted lugs, and the safety catch had a third (vertical) position to assist dismantling. The handguard ran from the front of the rear sight base to the barrel band.

The acquisition of 20,000 guns was authorized on 21st July 1893, followed by an extra 10,000 on 27th August. However, very few rifles were ever delivered owing to advent of the improved Mo. 1893 (q.v.). Those that lasted until about 1907 were given Mo. 1893-type rear sights and handguards running from the receiver ring to the barrel band. The Spanish Arms appear on the chamber-top above the place and date of manufacture – e.g., 'BERLIN 1894'.

MODEL 1892 CARBINE
Carabina Mauser Española Mo. 1892

Made by Ludwig Loewe & Co., Berlin, 1893-5.
Total production: 10,000. **Chambering:** 7x57, rimless. **Action:** as Mo. 1891, above.

37.15in overall, 7.28lb empty. 17.5in barrel, 4-groove rifling; RH, concentric. Fixed box magazine loaded from a stripper clip, 5 rounds. Leaf sight graduated to 1200m (1310yd). About 1835 fps with ball cartridges. No bayonet.

Stocked to the muzzle, this had a plain nose cap and barrel band, and its bolt handle was turned down against the stock. A sling bar and ring lay under the straight butt-wrist.

The purchase of 5,000 carbines was authorized on 21st July 1893, followed by a similar supplementary order on 27th August.

MODEL 1893 RIFLE
Fusil Mauser Español Mo. 1893

Made by Ludwig Loewe & Co., Berlin (1893-6); by Deutsche Waffen-und Munitionsfabriken, Berlin (1897-9); and by Fábrica Nacional de Armas, Oviedo, 1896-1943.
Total production: 206,830 in Germany (apparently including carbines) and more than two million in Spain. **Chambering:** 7x57, rimless. **Action:** as Mo. 1891, above.

48.6in overall, 8.71lb empty. 29.05in barrel, 4-groove rifling; RH, concentric. Internal box magazine loaded from a stripper clip, 5 rounds. Leaf sight graduated to 2000m (2185yd). About 2230 fps with Mo. 1895 ball cartridges. Mo. 1893 sword bayonet.

Adopted on 7th December 1893, this was the first Mauser to feature a magazine, contained entirely within the stock, which could be loaded from a stripper clip. The initial contract is said to have been for 251,800 rifles and 25,000 carbines, but may include the 40,000 1892-pattern guns described above. The earliest guns bore markings such as 'MAUSER ESPAÑOL MODEL 1895' above 'MANUFACTURA LOEWE BERLIN' on the left side of the receiver.

The Mo. 1893 was mechanically identical with its predecessor, though the safety catch was retained by a lug on the bolt plug engaging the safety-catch head. The safety could only be applied when the action was cocked. The lower portion of the bolt face was squared to improve cartridge feed (abandoned on later Mausers) and the development of an improved stripper clip allowed both guides to be milled into the front of the receiver bridge.

Previous Spanish guns relied on an upward extension of the spring-loaded bolt stop to provide the left guide. Unlike some essentially similar guns (e.g., Brazilian Mo. 1894), the Mo. 1893 would not close on an empty chamber until the magazine follower had been depressed manually.

The perfected Mo. 1895 cartridge was approved on 1st October 1895, issue commencing in earnest after this date. Production began in Oviedo in 1896. All but a few of the guns made in Spain had the left side of the receiver cut to about half-depth to facilitate loading.

The Model 1893 Spanish Mauser rifle. (HBL)

The design of the back-sight slider was improved in May 1906, the striker was strengthened in February 1907, and the approval of an improved cartridge in 1913 – with a muzzle velocity of 2790 fps – led to a modification of sight leaves. Finally, on guns made from 1933 onward, the basic action was improved by Antonio Ramirez de Arellano and José García Menéndez. The cocking piece and safety mechanism were modified, changes were made to the striker and bolt face, and a new ejector was fitted to cure breakages.

SIMILAR GUNS

Model 1893 carbine. Distinguished by a single barrel band and a short round-tipped forend ending some distance from the muzzle, this may have been experimental; the only known specimens were made by Loewe in 1896. No bayonet lug was provided.

MODEL 1895 CARBINE
Carabina Mauser Española para Plazas Montadas Mo. 1895
Made by Ludwig Loewe & Co., Berlin, 1896-7; and by Fábrica Nacional de Armas, Oviedo, 1896-1915.

Total production: about 22,500 in Germany and an unknown number in Spain. **Chambering:** 7x57, rimless. **Action:** as Mo. 1891, above.

37.4in overall, 7lb empty. 17.55in barrel, 4-groove rifling; RH, concentric. Internal box magazine loaded from a stripper clip, 5 rounds. Leaf sight graduated to 1400m (1530yd). About 2180 fps with Mo. 1895 ball cartridges. No bayonet.

Adopted on 7th May 1895, this was simply a short Mo. 1893, stocked to the muzzle, with a small rear sight and the bolt handle turned down. A change was made in 1896 to the barrel band, which gained a sling ring on the left side, and a sling bar was fixed in the left side of the butt in addition to the bar-and-ring assembly beneath the wrist. A half-depth cut in the left side of the receiver was added to facilitate charger-loading. A typical Spanish-made carbine bore the mark of a crown, 'FABRICA DE ARMAS', 'OVIEDO' and '1905' above the chamber.

MODEL 1913 SHORT RIFLE
Mosqueton Mauser Español Mo. 1913
Made by Fábrica Nacional de Armas, Oviedo, 1907.

Total production: not known. **Chambering:** 7x57, rimless. **Action:** as Mo. 1891, above.

37.2in overall, 7.12lb empty. 17.55in barrel, 4-groove rifling; RH, concentric. Internal box magazine loaded from a stripper clip, 5 rounds. Leaf sight graduated to 1400m (1530yd). About 2180 fps with Mo. 1895 ball cartridges. Mo. 1893 sword bayonet.

The guns of this pattern were made in 1907, apparently for trials with the artillery. Mechanically identical with the cavalry carbine, they had swivels under the barrel band and the butt. They were subsequently issued in 1914 for field trials, as the 'Mo. 1913', presaging adoption of the Mo. 1916 short rifle. From 2nd April 1918, surviving musketoons were issued to buglers of the cavalry squadrons.

MODEL 1916 SHORT RIFLE
Mosqueton Mauser Español Mo. 1916
Made by Fábrica Nacional de Armas, Oviedo, 1916-51; and by Industrias de Guerra de Cataluña, Tarrasa, about 1936-9.

Total production: not known. **Chambering:** 7x57, rimless. **Action:** as Mo. 1891, above.

Spanish soldiers on parade with Mauser rifles, 1931.

41.35in overall, 8.27lb empty. 21.7in barrel, 4-groove rifling; RH, concentric. Internal box magazine loaded from a stripper clip, 5 rounds. Tangent sight graduated to 2400m (2625yd). About 2705 fps with Mo. 1913 'S' ball cartridges. Mo. 1913 sword bayonet.

This was adopted on 14th November 1916 to replace the short-barreled Mo. 1895 carbine, which was not suited to the ballistics of the 1913-pattern cartridge. The Mo. 1916 had a full-depth cut-out on the left of the receiver to facilitate reloading from a stripper clip, and additional gas-escape holes in the bolt body and chamber-side. The original rear sight was a Lange-style tangent pattern. The straight-wrist stock had a single barrel band and a standard nose cap, retained by springs let into the underside of the forend; the bolt handle turned down. A pivoting swivel on the left side of the band was used in conjunction with a bar on the left side of the butt. A typical rifle had a chamber-mark comprising a simplified form of the national Arms above 'LA CORUÑA'.

Prominent protectors appeared on the front-sight block after 1918, and the basic design was upgraded in 1933 in much the same way as the Mo. 1893 rifle (q.v.).

SIMILAR GUNS

Carbine. A variant of the short rifle was made with a 17.7in barrel, a rounded forend and a small rear sight. Whether this was intended for gendarmerie, for a paramilitary force, or simply for trials has not been determined.

Civil War pattern. To accelerate production during the hostilities (1936-9), the Lange sight was replaced with a simpler tangent-leaf pattern graduated to 2000m (2185yd). The hinged magazine floorplate and the release catch pivoted in the front of the trigger guard were substituted by a detachable floorplate, and a recoil bolt was added through the forend beneath the chamber. A second bolt was often used to strengthen the wrist of the stock.

The guns made during the Civil War often bear the Falangist emblem of a crossed sword and Fasces above the chamber.

Conversions. Many surviving Mo. 1916 short rifles were altered from 1943-4 onward for the standard German 7.9mm cartridge, owing to the adoption of the Mo. 943 described below. Some guns were given new pistol grip stocks, with a finger groove in the forend and new swivels.

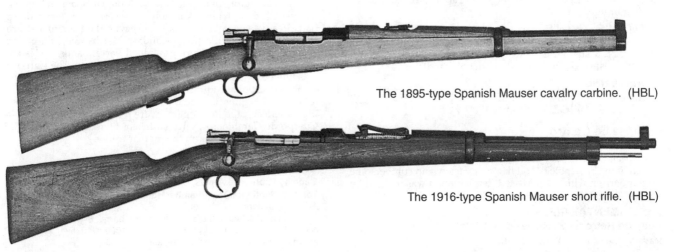

The 1895-type Spanish Mauser cavalry carbine. (HBL)

The 1916-type Spanish Mauser short rifle. (HBL)

MODEL 1898 CONVERSIONS

Substantial quantities of war-surplus Gew. 98 were rebarreled in the 1920s and early 1930s to fire the 7x57 cartridge. New 2000m (2185yd) tangent-leaf sights were fitted, and the original German chamber marks were replaced with Spanish versions: e.g., 'OVIEDO 1928'. They also bear 'ENTUBADOS A 7M/M', indicating the change in caliber.

STANDARD MODEL RIFLE

These 7x57 guns were acquired in small quantities immediately prior to (and possibly also during) the Spanish Civil War of 1936-9. They had straight-wrist butts, straight bolt handles, and 'H'-type nose caps placed unusually close to the solitary barrel band. About 42in long, with 22in barrels, they weighed 8.2lb.

A few 7.9x57 guns were also purchased in this period, with pistol grip butts and finger grooves in the forends. Some also had bolt handles which turned down against a a cutaway in the stock-side.

MODEL 1943 SHORT RIFLE
Fusil Mauser Español Mo. 1943

Made by Fábricas Nacional de Armas, Oviedo and La Coruña, 1943-59.
Total production: not known. **Chambering:** 7.9x57, rimless. **Action:** locked by two lugs on the bolt head engaging recesses in the receiver behind the chamber, and by a safety lug opposing the bolt-handle base entering its seat.

43.5in overall, 8.62lb empty. 23.6in barrel, 4-groove rifling; RH, concentric. Internal box magazine loaded from a stripper clip, 5 rounds. Tangent-leaf sight graduated to 2000m (2185yd). 2460 fps with Mo. 1943 ball cartridges? Mo. 1943 knife bayonet.

This was adopted in 1943 to replace the 7mm Mo. 1916 short rifle, owing to the widespread issue of machine guns chambering the German-pattern service cartridge.

The Mo. 1943 was a conventional 1898-pattern weapon, essentially similar in size and mechanical characteristics to the German Kar. 98k, but had a straight bolt handle and a short grasping groove in the forend. A handguard ran from the receiver ring to the band. Sling swivels lay under the butt, and on the left side and under the barrel band; a sling bar appeared on the left side of the butt. The nose cap was very similar to the 'H' pattern of German guns, but accepted a bayonet with a muzzle ring. An adapter enabled any of the earlier Mo. 1893 and Mo. 1913 bayonets to be used when required.

MODEL 8 RIFLE
Fusil a Repetición Mo. 8, 'FR-8'

Made by Fábricas Nacional de Armas de La Coruña, 1953-5?
Chambering: 7.62x51, rimless. **Action:** as Mo. 1943, above.

38.95in overall, 8.27lb empty. 18.5in barrel, 4-groove rifling; RH, concentric. Detachable box magazine, 5 rounds. Rotating-disc rear sight graduated to 400m (435yd). 2790 fps with standard ball cartridges. Mo. 69 CETME knife bayonet.

This was a conversion of the Mo. 1943 short rifle, chambered for the standard NATO cartridge. The stock was cut back to the barrel band, a grenade launcher was added to the muzzle, and the bayonet was attached to a tubular extension bar beneath the muzzle. A new rear sight revolved in a vertical bracket fixed to the receiver bridge.

SIMILAR GUNS

Model FR-7. This was a conversion of Mo. 1893 and Mo. 1916 rifles to FR-8 standards – identified by their simpler actions, straight-wrist stocks and turned-down bolt handles.

OTHER GUNS

About 4,000 7mm Mexican Mausers with an 1898-type bolt were acquired for trials in the early 1900s.

• Núñez de Castro

This rifle was one of the leading competitors of the Remington in the trials of 1870, but owed a debt to its rival in the interlocking design of the breechblock and hammer. Heavy and cumbersome by comparison with the perfected Remington, it was rejected by the army after protracted testing.

EXPERIMENTAL RIFLE
Fusil de Retrocarga Núñez de Castro

Made by Euscalduna, Placencia, 1870.

Total production: not known. **Chambering:** 11mm, centerfire. **Action:** locked by the interaction of the hammer with the breechblock.

48in overall, about 9.48lb empty. 32.3in barrel, 5-groove rifling; RH, concentric. Single shot only. Leaf-and-slider rear sight graduated to 1300m (1420yd). About 1085 fps with ball ammunition. Socket bayonet.

The Núñez de Castro rifle resembled a crude copy of the Remington externally, and was also operated by initially thumbing back the hammer spur to release the breechblock. However, the block was dropped by pulling the underlever/trigger guard assembly downward and the main spring was anchored beneath the barrel. The rifle had a straight-wrist butt; the forend was held by two sprung bands; there was a vestigial brass nose cap; and a swivel lay beneath the front band. The design of the massive receiver was unmistakable, with a straight hammer spur and an underlever. The rear swivel lay on the front edge of the receiver and the back-sight leaf was hinged at the front of its bed.

• Peabody

COLONIAL MODEL RIFLE
Fusil Peabody do Ejercito de Ultramar

Made by the Providence Tool Company, Providence, Rhode Island, about 1868-9.
Total production: perhaps 25,000. **Chambering:** 56-50 Spencer rimfire. **Action:** locked by propping a radial block behind the chamber with an underlever combined with the trigger guard.

54.05in overall, 9.95lb empty. 35.9in barrel, 3-groove rifling; RH, concentric? Leaf-pattern rear sight graduated to 500m (545yd). 1230 fps with ball cartridges. Socket bayonet (U.S. M1855 pattern?).

These guns were ordered in 1868 for service with the Spanish colonial army (*Ejercito de Ultramar*), based in Cuba. They were conventional Peabody patterns, with back-action locks, and had three spring-retained bands. Swivels lay on the middle band and beneath the receiver ahead of the breech lever. Internally, the firing-pin retractor had a coil spring. Most of the guns originally chambered the Spencer rimfire cartridge, though some supplied in 1870 are said to have handled the standard 11mm (.43) Spanish Remington cartridge.

SIMILAR GUNS

Colonial Model Carbine (Tercerola Peabody do Ejercito de Ultramar). This was a shortened version of the rifle, 38.2in long with a 19.95in barrel and an empty weight of 8.5lb. It had a simpler sight, and the half-length forend was held by a single band. A sling ring was attached to the left side of the stock level with the hammer-pivot screw. About 5,000 are believed to have been acquired.

• Remington

AMERICAN-PATTERN RIFLE
Fusil Remington Norteamericano

Made by E. Remington & Sons, Ilion, New York, 1870.
Total production: 100,000-115,000? **Chambering:** 11x58R, rimmed. **Action:** locked by shoulders on the hammer body rotating under the radial breech-block.

50.3in overall, about 9.26lb empty. 35.1in barrel, 5-groove rifling; RH, concentric. Ramp-and-leaf sight graduated to 1000yd. 1365 fps with U.S.-made ball cartridges. Socket bayonet (two blade lengths).

The Remington rolling block was adopted in Spain on 24th February 1871, though approximately 32,000 (of a 75,000-gun order) had already been delivered for service with the Ejército de Ultramar in Cuba. The rifle was a standard North American-pattern Remington, with three spring-retained barrel bands, a cleaning rod beneath the muzzle, and a concave buttplate. The sight leaf was hinged at the back of its block.

Two additional contracts were placed in the U.S. in 1874 for a total of 60,000 guns, but were probably never completed. Surviving American-type Remingtons were relegated after 1878 to the Cuerpo de Carabineros, once sufficient Oviedo-made Mo. 1871 rifles were available to arm the regular troops.

MODEL 1870 CARBINE
Carabina Remington para Carabineros, Mo. 1870

Made by Fábrica de Armas, Oviedo, 1870-1.
Total production: 6000. **Chambering:** 11x58R, rimmed. **Action:** as American-pattern rifle, above.

42.15in overall, about 8.6lb empty. 27.15in barrel, 6-groove rifling; RH, concentric. Ramp-and-leaf sight graduated to 1000m (1095yd). About 1150 fps with ball cartridges. Socket bayonet.

Adopted by the provisional government during an interregnum, in 1870, this was similar to the American rifle described previously but had only two bands. Swivels lay under the butt and the rear band. The curve of the butt comb was greater than on the later Spanish guns, and the buttplate was flatter.

SHORT RIFLE
Mosqueton Remington, 'fabricación Vascongada'
Made by Orbea Hermanos and others, 1870-1.

Total production: not known. **Chambering:** 11x58R, rimmed. **Action:** as American-pattern rifle, above.

46.85in overall, about 8.85lb empty. 32.3in barrel, 6-groove rifling; RH, concentric. Back sight: as Mo. 59 rifle (see 'Berdan'). 1295 fps with ball cartridges. Socket bayonet.

Made during the Carlist War, probably in 1870 (and apparently in the Basque region of northern Spain), these guns often differ in detail. A typical example had two screw-clamping barrel bands, swivels beneath the butt and rear band, and a transverse barrel-retaining screw set in lugged washers. The rear sight leaf hinged at the rear of its bed.

ROYAL BODYGUARD RIFLE
Fusil Remington para Guardias del Rey
Made by Fábrica de Armas de Oviedo, 1870-1.

Total production: 1000? **Chambering:** 11x58R, rimmed. **Action:** as American-pattern rifle, above.

51.75in overall, 9.37lb empty. 37in barrel, 6-groove rifling; RH, concentric. Ramp-and-leaf sight graduated to 1000m (1095yd). 1310 fps with Mo. 1871 ball cartridges. Special sword bayonet.

Apparently authorized specifically to equip the bodyguard of the king, Amadeo I, this rifle was little more than a longer version of the Mo. 1871 described below. It was introduced in advance of the infantry weapon, presumably owing partly to the demands of protocol but partly to the small numbers required. The guns had three barrel bands, while a bayonet lug lay on the right side of the muzzle. The bayonet had an unusually long double-edged blade – 27.55in – and a backward-pointing finial on top of the guard.

MODEL 1871 RIFLE
Fusil Remington Mo. 1871
Made by Fábrica de Armas de Oviedo, 1871-93; and by Euscalduna, Planencia, about 1872-4.

Total production: not known, but 350,000 were made in Oviedo. **Chambering:** 11x58R, rimmed. **Action:** as American-pattern rifle, above.

51.75in overall, 9lb empty. 37in barrel, 6-groove rifling; RH, concentric. Ramp-and-leaf sight graduated to 1000m (1095yd). 1310 fps with Mo. 1871 ball cartridges. Mo. 1871 socket bayonet.

Adopted on 24th February 1871, this was the standard Spanish infantry rifle for many years. It had three screw-clamping barrel bands, and a small rear sight with the leaf hinged at the rear of the attachment block. There were three screws and the axis-pin retaining plate on the left side of the receiver, and a transverse bolt through the rear of the forend. Swivels lay under the butt and middle band. The cleaning rod protruded beneath the muzzle, and the bayonet locked around the front-sight base.

A minor variation of the basic rifle was made by Euscalduna. Instead of the firing-pin retractor found on the standard Oviedo guns, a spring-loaded inertia-type pin was used.

By decree of 26th January 1875, the rolling block was declared the only breech-pattern approved for the Spanish army. The original iron bands were substituted by new steel patterns from 30th April 1883, their form being revised with effect from 8th November.

SIMILAR GUNS
Modelo 1871/89. From 22nd May 1889 onward, many surviving Mo. 1871 Remington rifles were re-chambered for the new 11mm Mo. 1889 cartridge developed by Lieutenant Colonel Luis

Freire y Góngora and Captain José Brull y Seoane. Muzzle velocity increased to 1475 fps, maximum range-setting being increased by adding an auxiliary front sight on the left side of the front barrel band and an extended back-sight slider with an additional 'V'-notch. Screw-clamping bands were adopted to replace the spring-retained type. Most guns of this type were conversions, but about 1,000 new examples were made in the Oviedo manufactory in 1892-3. The Remington was eventually declared obsolete on 26th March 1909, survivors subsequently passing to the Guardia Civil, the gendarmerie and the militia.

MODEL 1871 SHORT RIFLE
Mosqueton Remington Mo. 1871
Made by Euscalduna, Planencia, date unknown.

Total production: not known. **Chambering:** 11x58R, rimmed. **Action:** as American-pattern rifle, above.

42.5in overall, about 8.85lb empty. 27.95in barrel, 6-groove rifling; RH, concentric. Ramp-and-leaf sight graduated to 1000m (1095yd). 1215 fps with Mo. 1871 ball cartridges. Mo. 1871 socket bayonet.

Dating from about 1873, this short rifle had two barrel bands, conventional swivels and accepted a standard socket bayonet. It may simply have been one of many non-standard weapons made at the time of the Carlist War; alternatively, it may be a short-lived experimental pattern.

MODEL 1871 CARBINE
Tercerola Remington Mo. 1871
Made by Fábrica de Armas de Oviedo, 1871-85.

Total production: 25,880. **Chambering:** 11x58R, rimmed. **Action:** as American-pattern rifle, above.

37.9in overall, 7.23lb empty. 23.15in barrel, 6-groove rifling; RH, concentric. Leaf sight graduated to 600m (655yd). 1170 fps with Mo. 1874 ball cartridges. No bayonet.

Adopted on 24th February 1871 to replace the caplock of 1855, this was apparently considered as semi-experimental. Its half-stock was held by a single screw-clamping barrel band and a small rear sight lay on the barrel. Swivels beneath the band and butt were accompanied by a ring on a bar attached to the left side of the receiver.

MODEL 1874 SHORT RIFLE
Mosqueton Remington Mo. 1874
Made by Fábrica de Armas de Oviedo, 1874-91.

Total production: 15,500. **Chambering:** 11x58R, rimmed. **Action:** as American-pattern rifle, above.

37.9in overall, 7.65lb empty. 23.15in barrel, 6-groove rifling; RH, concentric. Ramp-and-leaf sight graduated to 600m (655yd). 1170 fps with Mo. 1874 ball cartridges. Mo. 1874 socket bayonet.

Adopted on 23rd December 1874 to equip the engineer corps and garrison artillerymen (los Ingenieros y Artilleros de Plaza), this was a variant of the Mo. 1871 rifle with two bands and the small carbine-type rear sight. Issue was extended in 1879 to the military service corps (Brigada de Administración Militar), but surviving guns were withdrawn in 1911.

SIMILAR GUNS
Security Corps Carbine. About 700 Mo. 1874 short rifles were re-chambered for the Freire & Brull cartridge after withdrawal in 1911-12, and then reissued to the security corps. They apparently served on until the Spanish Civil War began in 1936.

MODEL 1889 CARBINE
Carabina Remington para Dragones, Mo. 1889
Made by Fábrica de Armas de Oviedo, 1888-90.

Total production: 650? **Chambering:** 11x58R, rimmed. **Action:** as American-pattern rifle, above.

46.25in overall, 8.71lb empty. 31.55in barrel, 6-groove rifling; RH, concentric. Leaf sight graduated to 1200m (1310yd). 1455 fps with Mo. 1889 ball cartridges. No bayonet.

The 1871-model Spanish Remington infantry rifle.

Two short Spanish Remingtons: the 1874-pattern musketoon (top) and the 1871-type half-stock cavalry carbine (bottom).

This was adopted in May 1889 after 50 experimental guns had been issued in 1888 for trials with the cavalry. It was the first new Remington to be introduced since the mid 1870s, as well as being the first rolling block carbine to be officially adopted for widespread service in the Spanish army. The Mo. 1889 had two screw-clamping bands and a modified rear sight, though its action was essentially that of the 1871-type rifle.

OTHER GUNS

In addition to the regulation patterns and recognizable guns from the Carlist War, Spanish Remingtons may be found with a variety of non-standard characteristics. Often assembled from cannibalized parts and offering inferior quality, these 'Modelos de Recomposición' date from the 1870s. Incorporating old American- or Spanish-made components, they exhibit a wide variety of lengths, weights and fittings.

• Snider

The history of these guns is something of a mystery. They appear to have originated during the Carlist Wars (1873-5), probably made for one of the feuding factions.

SHORT RIFLE

Guns of this type may have been made for use in Cuba (where the fighting was at its worst), but more probably emanate from one of the Spanish provinces favoring the royalist cause. A typical example had a back-action lock and the cramped trigger guard bow characteristic of Spanish guns of the 1860s. The new Snider-type breech swung to the right, while the rear sight was similar to that of the 1871-model Spanish Remington rifle (q.v.). The mark 'LA AZPEITIANA', on top of the breech ahead of the new breech-block, has defied interpretation.

At least two basic versions of these rifles were made, individual examples differing in length and weight. The guns allegedly destined for riflemen (*Versión Cazadores*) accepted a socket bayonet, while the *Versión Zouavos* had a brass-hilted sabre type with an unusually shallowly-curved blade. They all chambered the 11mm Remington cartridge. A typical example was 50.4in overall, weighed about 9.25lb, and had a 35.45in barrel rifled with four grooves. Its ramp-and-leaf sight was graduated to 1000m (1095yd).

• Soriano

Made by a Madrid gunsmith in the mid 1850s, this was a much-modified Dreyse needle gun. A hundred guns were briefly tested by a Spanish cavalry regiment in 1855, without success, and a small quantity was made for sale commercially. The Soriano carbine had the bolt enclosed within the breech, except for the operating handle slot, and seems to have cocked automatically as the bolt was closed. A trigger button was set into the right side of the stock, sometimes in proximity to a breech-locking catch. A surviving gun is 41.35in long, has a 27.55in barrel, and chambers a 15mm combustible cartridge. Cartridges are inserted in a port beneath the forend and fed into the chamber by gravity after inverting the gun. The straight-wrist stock is made from a single piece of walnut and has a small brass forend tip. The swivels lie beneath the butt and forend, and a small standing-block rear sight is fitted above the breech.

• Winchester

The Spanish bought small numbers of 1873 type muskets and carbines from Winchester in 1878, the former having three barrel bands, and the latter a band and a nose cap. Muskets apparently had leaf-pattern rear sights and could accept socket bayonets. The Winchester soon proved efficient enough to be copied.

MODEL 1873 CARBINE
Tercerola Winchester Mo. 1873
Made by Fábrica de Artilleria, Oviedo, 1891-2.

Total production: apparently 2500. **Action:** the reciprocating breech-bolt was locked behind the chamber by a toggle joint. **Chambering:** 10mm, rimmed (44-40 WCF).

38.25in overall, weight unknown. 19.95in barrel, 4-groove rifling; RH, concentric? Tube magazine under barrel, 10 rounds. Leaf sight graduated to 800m (875yd). About 1265 fps with Spanish-made cartridges. No bayonet.

Production of these carbines began in the Oviedo factory in 1891, work being completed in 1892. They were to be issued to the royal bodyguard and the 14th troop of the Guardia Civil. By an order of 2nd December 1893, the guns were officially designated 'Tercerola Mo. 1873'. They were essentially similar to American-made guns purchased in 1878-9, but quality was noticeably poorer. An encircled crown, 'OVIEDO' and the date were stamped into the right side of the butt, together with the serial number (e.g., 'No. 1711').

SWEDEN

• FN (FFV)

MODEL 5 ASSAULT RIFLE
Automatkarbin 5, Ak-5
Made by FN Herstal SA (1984-6), and by Forenade Fabriksverken AS, Eskilstuna (1986 to date).

Chambering: 5.56x45, rimless. Generally as Belgian FNC, (q.v.), except dimensions (39.65in overall with butt extended, 8.6lb empty).

Trials undertaken with a variety of weapons resolved in 1982 in favor of the FNC, which apparently performed acceptably in sub-zero. The Swedish government then purchased a license allowing FFV to develop the design for Nordic service. The Ak-5 was adopted in 1984 to replace the 7.62mm Ak-4 (Heckler & Koch G3, q.v.).

Detail changes compared with the original Belgian FNC included enlargement of the trigger guard and cocking handle – facilitating use with arctic mittens – and a major change in the forend, which gained distinctive cross-hatching. The three-round burst-firing mechanism was sensibly discarded and the metal parts were given a green enamel protective finish.

The earliest Ak-5 were supplied by FN while tooling was undertaken in Eskilstuna; however, the first batches of an initial 80,000-gun order were delivered by FFV early in 1987 and production was still underway in 1997.

The FFV Ak-5, derived from the Belgian FN FNC pattern.

The FFV Model 890C was a modification of the Galil (Kalashnikov).

• Friberg-Kjellman

One of these rifles – incorporating a flap-lock designed in the 1870s by D.H. Friberg and subsequently patented in Sweden by Rudolf Kjellman – was submitted to the British Small Arms Committee in 1905 though no tests of the 6.5x55 gun were undertaken until February 1909; like many of the earliest designs, it performed well enough as a self-loader but was found wanting when operated manually.

• Galil (FFV)

FFV Ordnance acquired a license to make modified Israeli Galil rifles in the late 1970s, small quantities of the resulting Model 890C rifle being supplied for government trials. They could be distinguished by deeply ribbed forends and trigger guards large enough to admit a gloved finger. Trials resolved in favor of the Belgian FNC – adopted in Sweden as the Ak-5 – and the FFV rifle was abandoned.

The FFV890C in use as a grenade launcher.

• Hagström

Patented in 1867 by A. Hagström of Stockholm, this 12.2mm-caliber needle rifle was tested extensively by the Swedish army before being rejected in favor of the Remington. The gun had a two-piece stock and a large angular receiver, resembling an elongated Remington rolling block pattern. This contained the breechblock and the needle mechanism, which was cocked by retracting the thumb piece before opening the breech. A radial operating lever, pivoted on the right side of the breech, was raised from its locating block on the side of the forend and rotated back through about 170 degrees. The initial movement of the lever spindle cammed the breechblock away from the breechface, breaking the gas seal, and the front of the breechblock then dropped to admit a new cartridge into the chamber. Hagström needle guns were made in rifle or carbine form, but were rapidly overtaken by better designs.

• Heckler & Koch (FFV)

The 7.62mm Automatkarabin 4 (Ak-4) was adopted in 1963, licenses being acquired to permit production by Husqvarna Våpenfabrik as well as the government-owned Carl Gustafs Stads Gevarsfactori in Eskilstuna. The first Swedish-made rifles were delivered in 1965.

A reorganization of the state-owned arms factories in 1971 created 'Forenade Fabriksverken' (FFV or FFV Ordnance), and production of Ak-4 rifles was concentrated in the Eskilstuna factory. However, after trials spread over three years, the Ak-4 was superseded in 1984 by the Ak-5 – a minor modification of the FN Herstal 5.56mm FNC. The first deliveries of the new rifle were made in 1986, allowing the oldest of the Heckler & Koch patterns to be withdrawn.

• Husqvarna (FFV)

The earliest sporting rifles made by Husqvarna Våpenfabriks AB embodied the standard 1896-pattern Swedish Mauser action, though a near-facsimile of the pre-war Belgian FN Mle.24 pattern was substituted in 1946. Changes were made in the mid 1950s and early 1960s, but the bolt retained the full-length collar-type extractor and the safety lug until the end of production.

A redesigned action was announced in 1969 but, in 1971, the private Husqvarna and government-owned Carl Gustafs Stads Gevärsfactori were amalgamated under the Forenade Fabriks-verken (FFV) banner.

The FFV Model 2000 'Carl Gustav' sporting rifle.

Operations were concentrated in Eskilstuna, and Husqvarna sporting rifles were marketed thereafter by Viking Sport Arms AB. However, they were often sold under the 'Carl Gustaf' or 'Carl Gustav' (sic) brand names, particularly in North America. The perfected guns were sold by Smith & Wesson from 1970 onward and will be encountered with the distinctive S&W trademark instead of Swedish markings. The agency then passed for a few years to Stoeger Industries. Rifles were offered by Harrington & Richardson during the early 1980s, but these embodied original Mauser-type actions.

1896-TYPE SPORTING RIFLES

Small numbers of sporting rifles were built prior to 1940 on the 1896-pattern Swedish military Mauser action, most chambering 6.5x55 or 9.3x57 rounds. A typical rifle had a straight-comb half-stock, with a shallow pistol grip and the hint of a schnabel tip to the forend.

1898-TYPE SPORTING RIFLES

The first 1898-type Mauser sporting rifles were made in the late 1930s, the earliest being chambered for the 9.3x57 cartridge though 6.5x55, 7x57, 9.3x62 and others had been added by the end of World War II. The actions were mostly German, supplied as part-payment for machine-tools, steel and roller bearings.

SIMILAR GUNS

FN-Husqvarna, 1947 pattern. The earliest post-war Husqvarna sporting rifles were built around actions purchased from Fabrique Nationale (q.v.) and had birch stocks. They chambered 6.5x55, 8x57 or 9x57 ammunition.

FN-Husqvarna, 1950 pattern. This model, intended for sale in North America, was stocked in walnut instead of birch. Most guns had straight-comb stocks, but Monte Carlo patterns became increasingly popular as the years passed. Chamberings usually prove to be 220 Swift, 270 Winchester or the ubiquitous 30-06.

FN-Husqvarna, Model 1951. Essentially similar to the Model 1950, this pattern featured a safety catch altered so that it cleared an optical sight in low mounts.

HUSQVARNA-MAUSER SPORTING RIFLES

The FN-Husqvarna rifles were replaced by the HVA action, introduced about 1968. The new rifle embodied a small-ring action, lacking the reinforcing collar in the receiver, and the left wall retained its height throughout its length. The bolt shroud was streamlined, a radial safety was added to the right side of the receiver behind the bolt handle, and the ejector was moved to eliminate the slot cut through the relevant locking lug. Bolt handles were generally swept down and back.

THE GUNS

Crown Grade rifle, Models 3000 and 3100. These rifles had walnut half-stocks with ebonite pistol grip caps and forend tips; the Model 3000 had a Monte Carlo comb, whereas the otherwise-identical Model 3100 had a straight pattern. Chamberings included 243 Winchester, 270 Winchester, 7x57, 30-06 or 308 Winchester. Most rifles had five-round magazines and 23.6in barrels; weight averaged 7.5lb.

Imperial Custom rifle, Models 6000 and 6100. Made from 1968 until about 1971, these were variations of the Model 3000 or 3100 with a walnut stock selected for its attractive figuring, an improved trigger and a three-leaf rear sight.

Imperial Custom Lightweight rifle, Models 7000 and 7100. Variations of the 4000 series, these featured better stocks, triggers and sights. Production was apparently confined to 1968-70.

Lightweight rifle, Models 4000, 4100, 4500 and 4600. Sharing the action of the Crown Grade version, these guns had 20.45in barrels and weighed about 6.3lb. The slender stock had a Monte Carlo (4000) or straight (4100) comb, and a delicate schnabel tip on the tapering forend. Models 4500 and 4600 – sometimes listed as '456' – had the standard Lightweight action in a full-length Mannlicher stock. The 4500 pattern had a Monte Carlo comb, whereas its near-relation was straight.

Presentation Grade rifle. A few P-3000 guns were made in the late 1960s, with specially selected walnut stocks and contrasting rosewood accessories. The actions were cursorily engraved.

HVA SPORTING RIFLE
Also known as 'Carl Gustaf'

Made by Husqvarna Våpenfabriks AB, Huskvarna, 1968-71; and by Forenade Fabriksverken, Eskilstuna, 1971-83.

Total production: not known. **Chambering options:** see notes. **Action:** locked by rotating two lugs on the bolt head into recesses in the receiver, and by the bolt-handle base turning down into its seat.

DATA FOR A TYPICAL CARL GUSTAF SPORTER

Chambering: 6.5x55mm, rimless. 47.45in overall, 9.45lb without sights. 26.95in barrel, 4-groove rifling; RH, concentric. Internal box magazine, 5 rounds. Optical sight. 2560 fps with 145-grain bullet.

Introduced commercially in 1969, this much-modified Mauser retained the twin bolt-head lugs, but they were changed to fan-tail shape and the right-hand lug was given an additional guide rib to perfect an ultra-smooth operating stroke.

The recessed bolt face contained the plunger-type ejector, and a short extractor claw was let into the bolt body above the right lug. The conventional Mauser third (safety) lug was abandoned, the bolt-handle base sufficing, and the bolt shroud was neatly streamlined. The hinged magazine floorplate was controlled by a catch let into the front web of the trigger guard.

In 1971, the markings on the rifles changed from Husqvarna (often simply a crowned 'H') to Viking Arms or FFV. The major U.S. distributor was Smith & Wesson, but the agreement lapsed in 1972 and Carl Gustaf rifles were then sold by Stoeger Industries until the mid-1970s.

THE GUNS

Model 8000 (or 'Imperial Grade'), 1969-77. This continued a numerical sequence begun by the standard Mausers. Offered in 6.5x55, 270 Winchester, 7mm Remington Magnum, 300 Winchester Magnum, 30-06 or 9.3x62, it had a selected walnut stock with a rosewood forend tip, a machine-jeweled bolt and an engraved magazine floorplate. The receiver was drilled and tapped for optical sight mounts, open sights being customarily omitted. The M8000 was renamed 'Grade III' (Trofé, or Deluxe) in 1971.

Model 9000 (or 'Crown Grade'), 1970-7. This was a simpler form of the 8000 pattern with a standard Monte Carlo-type butt and a folding open rear sight. The M9000 was renamed 'Grade II' (Special) in 1971.

Sporter, 1972-82. Known in the U.S. as the 'Swede', it had a plain European-style stock with either a Monte Carlo butt and rounded forend tip, or a straight-comb butt and schnabel-tip forend. These rifles invariably had 24in barrels and were chambered for 22-250, 243 Winchester, 25-06, 6.5x55, 270 Winchester, 7x64, 30-06, 308 Winchester or 9.3x62; magazines held five rounds, except 9.3mm (four rounds only).

Magnum, 1973-7. This was a version of the Sporter (q.v.) with a ventilated buttplate instead of a solid rubber pattern. Chamberings included 7mm Remington Magnum and 300 Winchester Magnum, magazine capacity being three and four rounds respectively.

Varmint-Target rifle ('V-T'), about 1975-7. This appeared in 222 Remington, 22-250, 243 Winchester or 6.5x55. Magazines held five rounds in all chamberings except 222, which contained six. The plain walnut stock had a Wundhammer pistol grip, and the heavyweight barrel was allowed to float freely. The bolt handle was enlarged and the trigger could be adjusted without removing the stock.

MODEL 2000 SPORTING RIFLE

Made by Forenade Fabriksverken, Eskilstuna, 1991 to date.

Currently in production. **Chambering options:** 243 Winchester, 6.5x55, 270 Winchester, 7mm Remington Magnum, 7x64, 300 Winchester Magnum, 30-06 or 308 Winchester. **Action:** locked by rotating three lugs on the bolt head into recesses in the receiver, and by the bolt-handle base turning down into its seat.

DATA FOR A TYPICAL EXAMPLE

Chambering: 7x64, rimless. 43.9in overall, 7.5lb empty. 24in barrel, 4-groove rifling; RH, concentric. Internal box magazine, 3 rounds. Optical sight. 2885 fps with 170-grain bullet.

Introduced in 1991, the Model 2000 is a departure from the previous FFV-made rifles, as the original two-lug bolt has been replaced with a short-throw three-lug pattern. An adjustable roller-bearing trigger has been fitted, though the three-position safety catch still lies on the right side of the receiver behind the bolt handle. The barrel floats freely, though the rifle is stocked similarly to the preceding Model 8000.

• Ljungmann (Husqvarna)

Also known as *'Eklund-Ljungmann'*. This gas-operated rifle owed its adoption to the enlargement of the Swedish armed forces during World War II, at a time when Mauser rifles were in short supply. As the principal suppliers in Belgium and Czechoslovakia were under German control, and unable to simply accelerate production of m/38 rifles in the state arms factory, the Swedish authorities decided to introduce an untried autoloader made by a private contractor. A prototype Ljungmann rifle – said to have been based on Soviet Tokarevs captured in Finland – was given to an experienced production engineer, Erik Eklund, progressing so speedily that series production commenced within a year. That the rifle worked at all was a considerable feat; field service subsequently revealed flaws, but they concerned constructional details rather than the basic direct-impingement gas system and the locking mechanism.

MODEL 42 AUTOMATIC RIFLE
Automatiskgevär 42 and 42.B

Made by Husqvarna Våpenfabriks AB, Huskvarna.

Total production: not known. **Chambering:** 6.5x55, rimless. **Action:** as Danish Madsen-made pattern (q.v.).

47.45in overall, 10.25lb empty. 24.5in barrel, 4-groove rifling; concentric, RH. Detachable box magazine, 10 rounds. Drum-type sight graduated to 800m (875yd). 2460 fps with standard ammunition. M/96 knife bayonet.

Production began in the privately owned Husqvarna factory in 1942, in an attempt to boost Swedish rifle production without interrupting work on standard M/38 Mauser rifles in the government's Eskilstuna plant.

The bolt of the Ag-42 rested in a carrier, being cammed upward to disengage the receiver floor as propellant gas forced the carrier backward. Though the rifle had a conventional full-length stock, with a handguard from the chamber to a short distance ahead of the barrel band, it also had an unusual charging action: the sliding breech cover – carrying charger guides – was pushed forward to connect with the bolt mechanism, then retracted to open the breech. The cover disengaged at the end of its rearward stroke, allowing the bolt components to close automatically.

Unlike most other pre-1945 rifles, gas was taken from the bore to impinge directly on the bolt-carrier face without intermediate pistons or rods. This had the merit of simplicity, but was prone to fouling; consequently, the rifle never became universal issue in the Swedish army, being issued on the basis of a few guns per squad to provide additional firepower.

A typical example bore the date on the left side of the breech, split into groups of two digits by the crowned-'C' royal cypher (e.g., '19 [cypher] 43'). The serial number lay below the date, and was generally repeated on the left side of the bolt carrier to facilitate assembly.

SIMILAR GUNS

Ag-42 with modified gas system. A few batches of rifles were made in the late 1940s with a large-diameter chamber mid-way along the gas tube, minimizing the effects of fouling and simultaneously reducing the violence of the action to allow for variations in ammunition. However, most Swedish cartridges were loaded consistently enough to operate standard rifles efficiently and the modifications were soon abandoned.

Ag-42.B. An improved rifle was adopted in 1953. The extractor and the trigger mechanism were strengthened, a stainless-steel gas tube reduced fouling, and a rubber roller on the right side of the breech cover prevented cartridge cases being damaged during ejection. Minor changes were also made to the sights and magazine. Work ceased in the mid 1950s, whereupon the machinery was presumably sold to Egypt (see 'Hakim').

• Mauser (Carl Gustaf)

Sweden accepted the Mauser after trials had been undertaken with Mauser, Mannlicher, Lee, Krag-Jørgensen and other patterns.

Most types of Swedish service rifle may be encountered with Finnish property marks (generally 'SA' within a square), showing that they were supplied during the Winter War before neutrality prevailed. A Danish coin replacing the marking disc in the butt denotes guns supplied in 1946-8 to replace Krags sequestered by the Germans.

MODEL 1894 CARBINE
Karabin M/1894

Made by Waffenfabrik Mauser AG, Oberndorf am Neckar, Germany, 1894-6; and by Carl Gustafs Stads Gevärsfactori, Eskilstuna, about 1900-15.

Total production: not known. **Chambering:** 6.5x55, rimless. **Action:** locked by rotating two lugs on the bolt head into recesses in the receiver behind the chamber.

37.4in overall, 7.3lb empty. 17.3in barrel, 4-groove rifling; RH, concentric. Internal box magazine loaded from a stripper clip, 5 rounds. Leaf sight graduated to 1600m (1750yd). About 2130 fps with M/1894 ball cartridges. No bayonet.

An order for 5,000 guns was authorized in August 1894. The carbine was mechanically similar to the Mo. 1893 Spanish rifle (q.v.), but the safety could be engaged with the striker almost fully forward and a distinctive angular extension appeared on the cocking piece. The M/1894 had a straight-wrist full length stock and a handguard running forward from the receiver ring to the band. The edges of the nose cap carried upward to protect the sight blade, while a sling bar on the left side of the band was used in conjunction with a slot cut through the butt.

A total of 7,185 guns was ordered from Mauser in 1895 but, after the adoption of the M/1896 rifle, the carbine was revised in 1899. A cut-out on the left side of the receiver facilitated charger loading, but most other changes were internal. Production began in the state manufactory in Eskilstuna in 1900.

SIMILAR GUNS

M1894/17. From 1917 onward, the nose cap was altered so that a sword bayonet could be attached. The new design – inspired by the British SMLE – comprised a boss beneath the muzzle and a long rearward extension with an attachment lug. Production continued in the Carl Gustafs Stads Gevärsfactori until about 1932.

The introduction of the improved M/1941 cartridge, with a trajectory differing from the M/1894 pattern for which the sights had been calibrated, was solved by adding sight-setting information on the right side of the butt of the guns that survived into the 1940s.

The Swedish M1894 Mauser carbine. (HBL)

The Swedish 1896-pattern infantry rifle.

MODEL 1896 RIFLE
Gevär M/1896

Made by Waffenfabrik Mauser AG, Oberndorf am Neckar, 1899-1904; by Carl Gustafs Stads Gevärsfactori, Eskilstuna, about 1900-32; and by Husqvarna Våpenfabrik, Huskvarna.

Total production: not known. **Chambering:** 6.5x55, rimless. **Action:** as M1894, above.

49.45in overall, 8.97lb empty. 29.1in barrel, 4-groove rifling; RH, concentric. Internal box magazine loaded from a stripper clip, 5 rounds. Leaf sight graduated to 1600m (1750yd). 2380 fps with M/1894 ball cartridges. M/1896 knife bayonet.

Adopted in 1896, this was an improved form of the M/1894 carbine. It was very similar to its predecessor, but part of the left side of the receiver was cut away (to facilitate loading from a stripper clip) and the guide rib was moved from the receiver-wall to the bolt body. A gas-escape hole was added in the receiver ring.

The rifle had a straight-wrist stock, with a handguard from the receiver ring to a simple barrel band. A monopod could be fitted to the nose-cap eye, while the tube-hilted bayonet locked onto the angled lug beneath the cleaning-rod boss. The back-sight leaf pivoted at the front of the bed; swivels lay under the band and butt.

A contract for 45,000 rifles was given to Mauser in 1899, tooling in the Swedish state rifle factory beginning at much the same time.

SIMILAR GUNS

M/1938 short rifle. This was practically identical with the M/1896, but the bolt handle was turned down, the barrel was cut to 23.6in and overall length reduced to 44.1in.

M/1896/41 rifle. The advent of an improved M/1941 cartridge, with a velocity of 2625 fps, required an additional sight-setting plate on the butt. The '41' designation suffix, however, does not seem to have had official status.

M/1941 sniper rifle. This was a selected M/1896 with its bolt handle bent downward and a telescope-sight mount clamped in a dovetail plate on the side of the receiver. German Ajack 4x90 or Swedish 3x65 AGA M/1942 or M/1944 optical sights were used.

MODEL 1939 SHORT RIFLE
Gevär M/1939

The ever-increasing chance of war in Europe persuaded the Swedish authorities to create a special rifle for the machine gun units, chambered for the 8mm M/1932 cartridge to simplify ammunition supply. A few altered Kar. 98k were issued for field trials, as the M/1939, but these predictably revealed that the recoil of the 8mm round – firing a 221-grain bullet at 2525 fps – was unmanageable in a shoulder weapon.

SIMILAR GUNS

M/1940 short rifle. A few thousand of these guns were assembled by Carl Gustafs Stads Gevärsfactori in 1940, using Kar. 98k-type actions supplied by Mauser. They were readily distinguishable by the muzzle brake attached to the barrel. Never successful, M/40 rifles were rapidly replaced by 6.5mm versions when it became clear that Swedish neutrality would be respected.

SPORTING GUNS

Large numbers of Model 63 target rifles were made on the basis of the proven 1896-pattern Swedish military action; lacking the third or safety lug associated with the 1898-type Mausers, this cocked on closing. Changes were made to the action to reduce the lock time. Chambered for the 6.5x55 or 7.62x51 NATO cartridges, the M63 rifle had a distinctive half stock with a deep butt and an upright pistol grip. A handguard ran from the receiver ring to the tip of the forend. A single band was used; swivels lay under the forend and butt; and competition-pattern aperture sights were customary. Bolt handles may be straight, slightly bent, or turned down against the stock.

The Carl Gustaf factory was amalgamated with the Husqvarna operations in 1971, forming Forenade Fabriksverken, but work on the Model 63-type Mausers had already ceased.

• Remington

The first M/1867 Remington rifles (30,000) and carbines (3,000) were purchased in America, though production soon began in Husqvarna Våpenfabrik. The guns were much the same as the Norwegian patterns (q.v.); indeed, the first 3,000 Norwegian infantry rifles were made in Sweden before production began in the Kongsberg factory. It is assumed that the rifles and carbines were subject to alterations during their career, but, at the time of writing, details are still not known. They probably duplicated progress in Norway, where conversion of rifles to 8mm centerfire carbines began in 1888.

• Sjögren

Carl Sjögren of Stockholm received his first Swedish patent in December 1900, improving his design in several stages. The most common form operates on a type of delayed blowback, built around an inertia block inside the reciprocating breech housing. When the gun fired, recoil threw the whole gun backward; however, the inertia block tended to move *forward* relative to the rearward motion of the gun. This compressed the inertia-block spring, which then pushed the inertia block back to disengage the lock. The entire breech unit was driven back by residual gas pressure, extracting the spent case, then returned under spring pressure to reload the chamber and re-lock the action.

Only a few Sjögren rifles were made, but the system did find favor as a shotgun; several thousand were made in Denmark – prior to about 1908-15 – for Svenska Våpen- och Ammunitions-fabriken of Stockholm.

MILITARY-PATTERN TRIALS RIFLE
Made by Haandvaabenværkstederne, Copenhagen, Denmark, about 1907-12.

Total production: at least ten (see text). **Chambering options:** 6.5x55 Mauser, '7.63mm rimless' (30-06?) or 8mm Krag. **Action:** locked by pivoting flaps on the breechblock engaging recesses in the receiver; delayed blowback, semi-automatic only.
DATA FOR A TYPICAL 7.63MM EXAMPLE

45.5in overall, 8.3lb empty. 24.5in barrel, 4-groove rifling; RH, concentric. Internal box magazine, five rounds. Tangent-leaf sight graduated to 1600m (1750yd). Performance not known. M/96 Swedish knife bayonet.

The perfected rifles locked by pivoting two flaps or 'angle bars' laterally into recesses in the receiver, whereas the tube-magazine shotguns relied on a flap moving vertically beneath the breechblock. Six rifles were ordered in 1906, four being delivered in 1907 and two (one in carbine form) in 1908. In addition, three Russian Mosin-Nagants were converted in 1911.

A Sjögren rifle chambered for a '7.63mm rimless cartridge' – promoted by the Normal Powder & Ammunition Co. Ltd of Hendon – was exhibited in Britain in 1908 and tested in the Enfield factory in October with encouraging results. Stocked similarly to the Swedish Mauser rifles, it had a one-piece straight-wrist butt, a single barrel band, a handguard from the chamber to the band, and a nose cap adapted to take a bayonet. A re-cocking lever lay on the back of the breechblock.

• Stiga (Mauser)

Stiga AB of Tranås made sporting rifles based on refurbished M1896 military actions. Guns were being offered in the mid 1960s in 270 Winchester, 30-06 or 8x57. They had 23.6in barrels and weighed about 7.15lb empty. The plain straight-comb half stocks had checkered pistol grips and slender forends terminating in a schnabel tip. Single-trigger systems were standard, though a double set pattern could be fitted to order.

SWITZERLAND

• Abegg

The essence of this Swiss breechloading system, patented in 1851 and often erroneously listed as 'Abezz' or "d'Abezz", was a chamber which could be swung out to the right of the frame as the underlever was moved to the left. The lever was usually bent to follow the contours of the trigger guard.

Guns of this pattern were often converted from Swiss Federal 10.4mm cap-lock short rifles or Stutzer. Sporting versions had special butts, set triggers, and greater attention to detail, but the lack of a positive breech-locking system was sufficient of a handicap to limit the life of the Abegg system to less than a decade.

• End

Patented in July 1914 by Gotthard End, this rifle was submitted to the Swiss army by SIG in 1915 but was confined to military trials. It had front-mounted locking lugs and a separate Schmidt-type bolt actuator. The action was much shorter than the 1911-pattern service rifle, but was unsuccessful. A surviving rifle—lacking a serial number—is 41.35in long, has a 23.2in barrel and weighs 8.75lb empty. The re-cocking ring is positioned horizontally and the detachable box magazine containing six rounds lies directly ahead of the trigger guard, though the gun otherwise resembles the 1911-type Schmidt carbine.

• Flisch

Developed by Franz Flisch from a single shot design patented by Rudolf Schmidt in 1873, this rifle had a tube magazine beneath the barrel. A vertically-oscillating block in the receiver was operated by a stud on an external slide working in a cam-groove. When the operating handle attached to the slide was pulled backward, the hammer was cocked and the breech-block was dropped to receive a cartridge from the magazine; pulling the slide farther backward then lifted the breechblock until the new cartridge was in line with the bore. Pushing the handle forward then rammed the cartridge into the chamber and dropped the block behind it.

At least one Flisch rifle was made in the Eidgenössische Waffen-fabrik in 1873/4. Incorporating many Vetterli rifle parts—including the spurred trigger guard and diced forend—the gun was 49.8in long, had a 26in barrel, and weighed 10.1lb. The magazine held 12 cartridges.

The Flisch rifle could be operated rapidly when clean, but was prone to extraction problems. It had a two-piece stock with a straight wrist. A safety catch on the right side of the receiver locked the operating slide in the forward position.

• Flury

The Swiss authorities became so obsessed with straight-pull bolts that many alternative designs were considered prior to World War I. They included this rifle, which could be loaded with the bolt locked shut. The work of gunmaker Flury of Aesch, it never progressed past the prototype stage. A surviving 7.5mm example made by the Eidgenössische Waffenfabrik in 1901 is 49.8in long, has a 30.7in barrel and weighs 10.4lb with an empty 12-round magazine. It is recognizable by a flat-section actuating bar on the right side of the squared breech housing.

• Frey

This unsuccessful rifle, patented in Switzerland in November 1907 by Adalbert Frey, was promoted by SIG in the 1906 military trials. A surviving example is 51.4in long, has a 30.3in barrel, and weighs about 8.66lb. The staggered-row magazine holds six 7.5mm cartridges and the standard quadrant rear sight was retained. The most obvious recognition feature was the large ring-headed cocking piece, and the bolt track running back above the trigger.

• Gamma & Infanger

Designed and patented by two gunmakers working in Altdorf, this 10.4mm rimfire rifle was an unsuccessful rival of the bolt-action Vetterli. A tube magazine inspired by the Henry rifles tested in Switzerland in 1865-6 was combined with a reciprocating bolt operated by an underlever doubling as a trigger guard. The breech was locked by the upper bar of a hollow block dropping into a transverse groove in the bolt when the operating lever was closed. The receiver, with its distinctive pivoting loading port on the right side, separated the straight-wrist butt from the forend. The Gamma & Infanger rifle was made experimentally for military trials, and possibly also—briefly—as a sporting rifle.

• Grünig & Elmiger

Once renowned for Lienhard-brand sub-caliber trainers, Grünig & Elmiger have also made target rifles based on the Swiss Kar. 31 service rifle. Modern rifles embody a proprietary action, though the stocks and sights were originally purchased from Anschütz.

SPORTING/TARGET RIFLES
Matchkugelbüchsen: Standard and Luxusmodelle
Made by Grünig & Elmiger AG, Jagd- und Sportwaffenfabrik, Malters.
Currently in production. **Chambering options:** 222 Remington, 5.6x50 Magnum, 243 Winchester, 6.5x55, 7x57, 7x64, 7.5x55, 308 Winchester, 8x57, 8x68S and others. **Action:** locked by lugs on the bolt head engaging the receiver when the bolt handle turns down.

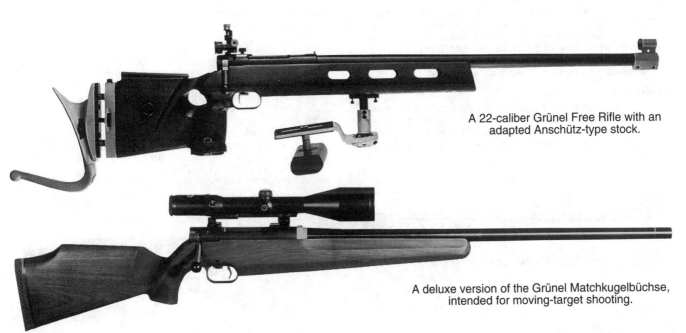

A 22-caliber Grünel Free Rifle with an adapted Anschütz-type stock.

A deluxe version of the Grünel Matchkugelbüchse, intended for moving-target shooting.

The Grünel Super Target 200 CISM rifle.

DATA FOR A TYPICAL EXAMPLE

Chambering: 5.6x50 Magnum, rimless. 44.7in overall, 8.71lb empty. 26in barrel, 6-groove rifling; RH, concentric. Optical sight. 3590 fps with 49-grain bullet.

Introduced in the early 1970s, these rifles, intended for sporting-style target shooting, usually have a special trigger mechanism. The rear lever is set by pushing the reversed lever in the front of the guard forward. Grünel rifles have free-floating barrels and solid beaver-tail forends, and can weigh 8.3-11lb depending on caliber.

UIT STANDARD TARGET RIFLE

Made by Grünig & Elmiger AG, Jagd- und Sportwaffenfabrik, Malters, about 1975-88.

Total production: not known. **Chambering options:** 222 Remington, 243 Winchester, 6.5x55, 7.5x55 or 308 Winchester. **Action:** as Matchkugelbüchse, above.

DATA FOR A TYPICAL MATCHGEWEHR 300

Chambering: 308 Winchester, rimless. 45.3in overall, 15.26lb without hand rest. 26.95in barrel, 4-groove rifling; RH, concentric. Micro-adjustable aperture rear sight. 2690 fps with ball ammunition.

These Grünel target rifles shared the action of the Matchkugelbüchsen (q.v.), but had differing triggers. The Matchgewehr UIT Standard had an Anschütz-pattern competition stock, with lateral slots in the forend of guns made after about 1983, and a direct-action trigger with a pull of 3.3lb. Most rifles also had a matted strap or 'mirage band' above the barrel.

SIMILAR GUNS

Grünel 300 LM (Liegendmodell). This is similar to the UIT Standard, but is designed for prone-position shooting. The forend is shallower and the butt-comb, adjustable on most post-1985 examples, slopes downward to the pistol grip. A direct-acting trigger is standard, though others can be supplied on request.

Grünel Matchgewehr 300. Made until about 1988, this had an adjustable trigger mechanism and a thumbhole stock. The comb, hooked shoulder plate and pistol grip palm rest were also adjustable, and a hand rest could be fitted beneath the slotted forend.

Grünel Super Target 200/40 Free Rifle. Modernized guns appeared in 1987 with new stocks and optional electronic triggers. The Super Target replaced the Matchgewehr 300 (above).

Grünel Target 200 rifle. This is a modernized version of the UIT Standard pattern, introduced in the late 1980s.

• Hämmerli

Now best known for its exemplary target pistols, Hämmerli has also made a substantial quantity of rifles—sporting guns based on the standard Mauser action, and target rifles based on the Martini or Schmidt-Rubin patterns. These are all noted in the relevant sections.

MODEL 700 SPORTING RIFLE

This was a standard Kar. 98k Mauser—complete with cutaway receiver wall and stripper-clip guides—in a walnut half-stock with a straight comb, a small round cheekpiece, a ventilated rubber shoulder pad, and a schnabel tip forend. The pistol grip and forend were checkered. Standard chamberings were 6.5x55, 6.5x57, 270 Winchester, 7x64, 7.5x55, 300 H&H Magnum, 30-06, 308 Winchester, 8x57, 8x60S, 9.3x62 or 10.3x60, but others could be supplied on request. Hämmerli Mausers usually had swivels on the butt and barrel, and adjustable folding-leaf sights.

SIMILAR GUNS

Model 701 rifle. This was identical with the 700 pattern, but had a double set trigger instead of the military pattern.

Model 705 rifle. This was a variant of the single-trigger Model 700, with the same Kar. 98k-type action, but had a finer stock with a Monte Carlo cheekpiece and comb.

Model 706 rifle. Mechanically identical with the Model 705, this featured a double trigger system.

Model 710 rifle. This shared the stock and single-trigger system of the Model 705, but the receiver and magazine floor-plate were engraved.

Model 711 rifle. A double-trigger version of the Model 710, this was made only in small numbers.

Model 715 rifle. Distinguished by extensively engraved metalwork and a carved select-grain stock, this deluxe pattern was only made in small numbers.

OTHER TYPES

The last Schmidt-Rubin rifles (National and Olympia models) were made in 1959, but were not sold until the early 1960s. To fill the gap, therefore, improved turning-bolt Free Rifles made by Hans Tanner (q.v.), were sold under the Hämmerli name from 1965 until the early 1970s.

• Heeren

This dropping-block action—particularly popular in Switzerland—was patented in 1880 by Christian Heeren, who gave his domicile as 'Paris' in patent applications but was an officer in the Baden State army. The original patent was apparently filed in Austria-Hungary.

The Heeren system was unique in that its operating lever, combined with the trigger guard, was pulled downward at the front to lower the breechblock—the opposite of most other systems. The result was a compact and surprisingly simple gun, but one in which the extraction leverage was comparatively poor. The modified Würthrich-Heeren has a special patented extractor to minimize this weakness.

The lever-locking catch was pivoted in the front of the guard. Among other idiosyncratic features was the exposure of what was effectively the spur of the hammer in the guard behind the trigger lever. The hammer was cocked during the opening stroke, but could be uncocked or re-cocked manually at will.

A half-stocked Würthrich-Heeren sporting rifle.

Like many European single-shot actions, the Heeren was barreled and stocked by many independent gunsmiths in Germany, Austria-Hungary, Switzerland, Britain and elsewhere. Examples have been noted with the marks of makers as disparate as Carl Stiegle Hofgewehrfabrik of München, Thomas Bland of London, and Walter Glaser of Zürich. The popularity of the Heeren was due as much to its strength as compact design, as it was more durable than many of its rivals (e.g., Aydt or Büchel) and could chamber comparatively powerful cartridges. A modernized Heeren-type rifle is still available from Würthrich.

HEEREN-GLASER SPORTING RIFLE
Made by W. Glaser, Zürich, about 1925-50.

Total production: not known. **Chambering options:** 7x57, 7x65, 8x57, 8x60R, 9.3x53R, 9.3x72R or 9.3x74R. **Action:** locked by propping the dropping block behind the chamber, with the tip of the operating lever engaging the receiver.
DATA FOR A TYPICAL EXAMPLE
Chambering: 8x60R, rimmed. 37.8in overall, 6.66lb empty. 23.6in barrel, 4-groove rifling; RH, concentric. Block-and-leaf rear sight. 2525 fps with 196-grain bullet.

A typical Glaser-made rifle dating from the early 1930s had a walnut butt with a straight comb, a rounded cheekpiece, and a checkered pistol grip with a horn cap. The full-length forend had checkering and a hand-stop swell at the mid point. Glaser-made actions were often highly decorative, and bases were sometimes provided on the half-octagonal barrel for sight mounts.

WÜRTHRICH-HEEREN SPORTING RIFLE
Made by W. Würthrich Jagd- und Sportwaffen, Lützelflüh, 1977-93?

Total production: not known. **Chambering:** see notes. **Action:** generally as Heeren-Glaser, above.
DATA FOR A TYPICAL EXAMPLE
Chambering: 8x60S, rimless. 39.75in overall, 6.95lb empty. 25.6in barrel, 4-groove rifling; RH, concentric. Optical sight. 2770 fps with 187-grain bullet.

Introduced in 1977, this modernized Heeren was locked by a catch set into the trigger-guard web. The trigger mechanism—patented in Switzerland in 1978—was also derived from the original design. The hammer struck the firing pin through an intermediate 'firing piece' only when the breech was securely closed. A manual safety catch on the side of the receiver locked the firing piece securely in place.

Only about 250-300 guns had been made by by the early 1990s, and their status is uncertain. Round barrels have been regarded as standard, with half- or fully-octagonal versions supplied on special request. The half-length and Mannlicher-style pistol grip stocks have squared cheekpieces with fluted under-edges. Receivers are usually engraved with deer, chamois or ibex, while the stocks may display foliate carving.

A detail view of a highly decorated Würthrich-Heeren rifle.

• Kaestli
Designed about 1867 by a gunmaker, L. Kaestli of Altstätten, this rifle was operated by lowering an underlever/trigger guard unit pivoted on a saddle attached externally to the forend. This pulled the breech-block vertically downward, allowing a cam on the rear of the block to retract the striker until it was held on the sear. The striker housing was offset diagonally on the right side of the breech, giving unobstructed access to the chamber once the action had been cocked. The striker struck the 10.4mm rimfire cartridge on the right edge.

• Mannlicher
MODEL 1893 CARBINE
Repetier-Karabiner M1893
Made by Schweizerische Industrie-Gesellschaft, Neuhausen, 1895-1900; and by the Eidgenössische Waffenfabrik, Bern, 1898-1905.

Total production: 7750. **Chambering:** 7.5x53.5R, rimmed. **Action:** locked by revolving two lugs on a detachable bolt head into seats in the receiver as the bolt closed.

40in overall, 6.8lb empty. 21.65in barrel, 4-groove rifling; RH, concentric. Detachable box magazine, 6 rounds. Quadrant sight graduated to 1200m (1310yd). 1835 fps with M1890 ball cartridges. No bayonet.

The 1889-pattern Schmidt action was too long and too clumsy to be incorporated in a carbine and so, on 29th June 1893, trials began with two Neuhausen turning-bolt designs; turn-bolt and straight-pull Mannlichers; a Mauser turn-bolt with Rubin's modifications; and straight-pull actions designed by Vogelsang and Krauser.

The compactness of the straight-pull Mannlicher action, more than 3in shorter than Schmidt's, allowed the adoption of the M1893 carbine on 1st March 1895. These guns had a straight-wrist stock with a German-style sling-anchor slot in the butt, a full-length handguard, and a single barrel band. They were stocked to the muzzle.

• Martini
The products of south Germany, northern Austria and Switzerland are often difficult to separate, unless their provenance is clearly marked.

The first sporting guns were made by Friedrich von Martini in Frauenfeld, almost always featuring a cocking indicator protruding above the rear right side of the receiver and a pivoting safety lever immediately ahead of the trigger guard. The chambering customarily proves to be 10.4mm rim- or center-fire.

Once the true Martini action had become established, other gunsmiths copied it; however, as many of the actions were hand-made, great variety in construction could be found. For example, guns made by F.W. Kessler & Co. of Suhl invariably had an unusually narrow action set in a one-piece stock. Swiss Martini rifles often had locking catches on the breech-block axis pin, facilitating dismantling, while their detachable floorplates contained the entire trigger mechanism. The lock work usually lay behind the receiver, unlike the British military guns, allowing the trigger guard to be combined with the elaborately looped breech lever. Butts, forends and sights were all subject to variety.

Many rifle actions emanating from central Europe were cut down behind the breech so that the barrel could be cleaned from the rear. Though this did not in itself compromise strength, the strain of firing was taken on the breech-block axis pin, and excessive displacement of this pin in relation to the centerline of the bore increased the chances of failure. Consequently, some guns lack the strength of the true Martini-Henry or Peabody-Martini actions.

This is sometimes reflected in low-power chamberings: 6.5x27, 8.15x46.5 or 9.5x47. Sturdier guns accepted such proven hunting cartridges as 9.3x72 or 11.15x65.

HÄMMERLI-MARTINI TARGET RIFLE
Made by Rudolf Hämmerli & Co., Lenzburg.

Total production: not known. **Chambering:** 7.5x55, rimless. **Action:** locked by pivoting the breechblock behind the chamber with the tip of the operating lever/trigger guard.
DATA FOR A TYPICAL 1930-VINTAGE EXAMPLE
55.7in overall (including butt-plate hook), 11.3lb without the palm-ball. 33.65in barrel, 4-groove rifling; RH, concentric. Quadrant sight graduated to 1200m (1310yd). 2050 fps with 189-grain bullet.

The first rifles made by Johann Ulrich Hämmerli in 1887 rapidly attained a reputation for strength and outstanding accuracy, gaining a gold medal from the inaugural world shooting championships held in Lyon in 1897.

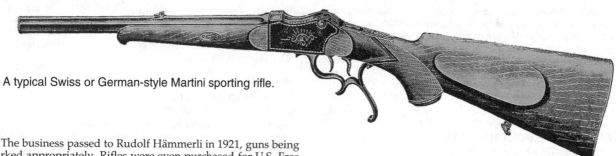

A typical Swiss or German-style Martini sporting rifle.

The business passed to Rudolf Hämmerli in 1921, guns being marked appropriately. Rifles were even purchased for U.S. Free Rifle teams. By 1932, target rifles were being made for sale under the Hämmerli name, alongside actions to be stocked and completed elsewhere. Many leading Swiss gunmakers (e.g., Waffen-Glaser of Zürich) purchased them.

A typical Martini-Match-Stutzer offered a butt with a Tyrolean cheekpiece and a ram's horn terminal. A forked shoulder plate, adjustable for height and cant, also had a hook. The underside of the wrist and the forend were extensively checkered, while the breech lever—combined with the trigger guard—had a looped rear spur and an open forward hand-grip. An adjustable palm-ball was fitted to a threaded socket under the front of the receiver.

Production of Martini rifles ceased in 1940, owing to mobilization in Switzerland and an impending concentration on war work.

• Milbank-Amsler

Patented in the U.S. by Isaac Milbank in 1866, then adapted by Rudolf Amsler of Schaffhausen, this swinging-block mechanism was adopted by the Swiss on 22nd December 1866. The block hinged laterally once the hammer had been retracted to half-cock; a spring-loaded striker ran slightly diagonally through it. About 76,700 guns had been altered by the beginning of 1869 by 20 gunmakers, the most important single contribution being made by Schweizerische Industrie-Gesellschaft.

MODEL 1851-67 SHORT RIFLE
Converted by a variety of gunmakers

Total production: many thousands. **Chambering:** 10.4x38R, rimfire. **Action:** locked by swinging a laterally-opening breechblock behind the chamber.

49.6in overall, 9.92lb empty. 29.5in barrel, 4-groove rifling; RH, concentric. Single shot only. Quadrant rear sight graduated to 1200m (1310yd). 1360 fps with M1867 ball cartridges. Special bayonet (see text).

This was a cap-lock Stutzer, originally adopted in May 1851, adapted to fire a 10.4mm rimfire cartridge with a slight neck. Distinguished by a double set trigger, the gun had a tube-like bayonet housing on the right side of the muzzle. The massive buttplate had an overturned finial on the lower tip; the upper tip contained a pricker for the cap-lock, replaced by a screwed-in finial on the cartridge version.

SIMILAR GUNS

Model 1856-67 rifle. Converted from the old cap-lock Jäger weapon, accepted in September 1856 (but issued in quantity only in 1859), this short rifle had two bands and accepted a socket bayonet. It was 51.95in long, had a 34.05in barrel, and weighed about 9.33lb. The quadrant rear sight was graduated to 1000m (1095yd).

Model 1863-67 rifle. This infantry rifle was converted from a cap-lock. Approved in December 1863, it had two barrel bands and accepted the 1863-pattern socket bayonet. The back swivel lay on the trigger guard instead of beneath the butt. The M63-67 was 54.33in long, 2.4in greater than the otherwise similar M1856-67, and weighed about 10.25lb. The barrel measured 36.45in, and the quadrant rear sight was graduated to 1000 schritt.

Model 1864-67 rifle. Similar to the M1851-67, with a double set trigger, this had a conventional lug for the M1867 sabre bayonet on the right side of the barrel. The guard ring slipped over the cylindrical muzzle of the otherwise octagonal barrel. The basis for the conversion was a Stutzer adopted in December 1864. The guns were 49.5in long, had 29.6in barrels and weighed about 10lb; their quadrant sights were graduated to 1000 schritt.

Converted French weapons. In 1867-70, the Swiss transformed 56,370 French Mle 1840 T. 59 and Mle 1842 T. 59 infantry rifles to fire a stubby 18mm rimfire cartridge. The principal distinction lay in the back-action lock on the earlier gun, the newer type displaying a sidelock. These antiquated guns were discarded as soon as Vetterli rifles had displaced Swiss-pattern Milbank-Amsler conversions from first-line service. Many were subsequently smooth-bored and sold as shotguns.

• Neuhausen

Designed in 1887-8, but not patented in Switzerland until July 1889, this rifle had a bolt with an annular actuator collar rather than the separate side-mounted pattern of the competing Schmidt rifle (q.v.); however, its twin lugs still locked into the receiver behind the magazine well.

The first Neuhausens were converted from Vetterli actions. They were promising enough to persuade the Swiss army to order ninety near-identical 7.5mm guns from Schweizerische Industrie-Gesellschaft to facilitate extended trials.

NEUHAUSEN TRIALS RIFLE
Made by Schweizerische Industrie-Gesellschaft, Neuhausen am Rheinfalls.

Total production: at least 100. **Chambering:** 7.5x53.5, rimless. **Action:** locked by revolving two lugs on the bolt into seats in the receiver behind the magazine as the bolt closed.
DATA FOR GUN NO. 99

51.2in overall, 8.86lb empty. 30.3in barrel, 3-groove rifling; RH, concentric. Detachable box magazine, 12 rounds. Quadrant rear sight graduated to 2000m (2185yd). 1875 fps with experimental ball cartridges. Sword bayonet.

The basic rifle had a solid-bridge receiver with a straight-pull bolt and a stubby bolt handle. Most guns had either a ring (early) or a hook (later) safety protruding from the back of the bolt. The one-piece stock had a straight wrist, and a handguard ran the length of the barrel. A single barrel band was used in conjunction with a nose cap carrying a bayonet lug on its underside.

The magazine was separated from the trigger guard by a catch set into a low housing. Swivels lay under the band and on the under edge of the butt.

• Pauly

Many of the earliest advances had been made in France, where the Swiss gunmaker-inventor Samuel Pauly obtained a patent protecting a breech-loader as early as 1812. One of the most remarkable features of Pauly's gun, which was locked by a pivoting block behind the breech, lay in its self-contained cartridge: a stiff paper sleeve, set in a moulded leather base containing a fulminate pellet. The primer could be struck by a 'piston' running through the breech-block. Some guns were even fired by the heat generated when air was compressed rapidly, but the concept was much too radical to achieve tangible success. The French Robert rifles (q.v.) were derived from Pauly's prototypes.

• Peabody

MODEL 1867 ENGINEER RIFLE
Genie-Gewehr system Peabody M1867

Made by the Providence Tool Company, Providence, Rhode Island, 1867-8.

Total production: 15,000. **Chambering:** 10.4x38R, rimfire. **Action:** as original American-made guns (q.v.).

51.55in overall, 9.7lb empty. 32.8in barrel, 3-groove rifling; RH, concentric. Quadrant sight graduated to 800m (875yd). 1425 fps with M1867 ball cartridges. M1863 socket bayonet.

A large quantity of these rifles, adopted on 14th June 1867, was ordered from America. About 5,000 were issued to riflemen (Scharfschützen) in 1868, pending perfection of the Vetterli magazine rifle; the others were stored.

The remaining guns were given to engineers in 1872. Surviving guns were modified after 1875 by changing the extractor and altering the striker-block to a more conventional form. Altered guns had a narrow extractor blade with a tapering tip, protruding at the base of the chamber.

The guns that survived in 1877 received Swiss-made barrels. These were about 32.3in long, reducing overall length to 51.1in, and had a distinctive 3.1in octagonal section at the breech; the original American-made barrel was a tapering cylinder. Modified guns, often known as 'M1867/77' or 'M1877', served the Landwehr for 10 years. It has been claimed that Swiss Peabody rifles were converted to center-fire in this period, but none has been examined.

• Schmidt (-Rubin)

Eduard Rubin (1846-1920) developed the first successful small-caliber copper-jacketed bullets that could withstand velocities higher than were normal in the 1880s. Rubin cartridges with a caliber of 8.1-9.6mm were tested against an 8.6mm Hebler pattern in Switzerland in 1882. The Hebler cartridge, which had a papier-mâché core, attained a prodigious velocity but the Rubin pattern proved to be far more accurate.

In 1884, Schweizerische Industrie-Gesellschaft converted 130 Vetterli (q.v.) rifles to fire 7.5mm and 8mm Rubin cartridges. Most were adapted from obsolete infantry weapons, but a few had been trial guns of 1873-5: these had a distinctive bolt-support guide extending back above the wrist of the butt.

Also chambered for Rubin ammunition, Rudolf Schmidt's first straight-pull bolt mechanism of 1885 relied on an actuating rod, set in a channel on the right side of the breech, to rotate the bolt through a helical channel cut in the bolt sleeve. Twin lugs were provided midway along the bolt sleeve, locking into the receiver directly above the trigger.

THE EARLIEST TRIALS RIFLES

Though the relevant patent was not granted until September 1889, the first rifles had been submitted for trials in December 1885. They had protruding box magazines, 1881-pattern quadrant sights, finger spurs behind the trigger guard, diced bolt-knobs and diced forends.

By 1888, trials were centering on 11 improved Schmidts and a similar number of 'Neuhausen' (q.v.) guns promoted by Schweizerische Industrie-Gesellschaft. The Schmidts, chambered for an experimental 1888-pattern Rubin cartridge, had a distinctive nose cap/bayonet lug assembly, quadrant sights, a lateral safety bolt on top of the receiver, and a selection of differing magazine release catches.

Ninety more guns of each design were ordered in the autumn of 1888 for field trials. By this time, the Schmidt rifle had acquired a ring on the cocking piece, doubling as a safety catch. Ultimately, the Schmidt system, simpler and easier to use, was preferred to the SIG design.

MODEL 1889 RIFLE
Infanterie-Repetier-Gewehr M1889
Made by Eidgenössische Waffenfabrik, Bern, 1891-7.
Total production: about 212,000—see text. **Chambering:** 7.5x53.5, rimless. **Action:** locked by revolving two lugs on the rear of the bolt sleeve into seats in the receiver ahead of the trigger.

51.25in overall, 10.69lb empty. 30.7in barrel, 3-groove rifling; RH, concentric. Detachable box magazine, 12 rounds. Quadrant sight graduated to 2000m (2185yd). 1935 fps with M1890 ball cartridges. M1889 sword bayonet.

This rifle was officially adopted on 26th June 1889. Tooling had already begun in the state factory, and so the first deliveries were surprisingly speedy. The M1889 was a most unusual design, with a characteristically Swiss nose cap/bayonet lug/stacking rod assembly, and a receiver with a noticeable gap between the trigger

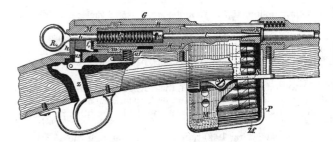

A sectional drawing of the 1889-type Schmidt rifle.

guard and the magazine. The great length of the bolt weakened the Schmidt system greatly. Production ceased in 1897 after 211,890 rifles and 40-50 Exerzierwaffen had been delivered.

MODEL 1889/96 RIFLE
Infanterie-Repetier-Gewehr M1889/96
Made by Eidgenössische Waffenfabrik, Bern, 1897-1912.
Total production: 127,000. **Chambering:** 7.5x53.5, rimless. **Action:** similar to the M1889, above, excepting that the lugs lock into the receiver behind the magazine well.

51.2in overall, 9.94lb empty. 30.7in barrel, 3-groove rifling; RH, concentric. Detachable box magazine, 12 rounds. Quadrant sight graduated to 2000m (2185yd). 1935 fps with M1890 ball cartridges. M1889 sword bayonet.

The inherent weaknesses of the 1889-pattern Schmidt action were recognized after protracted experience with the standard 7.5mm 1890-pattern cartridge had been gained. As soon as attempts were made to increase the muzzle velocity, the problems intensified.

Testing of 50 modified rifles allowed the improved Vogelsang/Rebholz action to be adopted on 27th September 1897. Though the 1889/96 rifle resembled its predecessor externally, the locking lugs had been moved to the front of the bolt-sleeve. This strengthened the action, by placing less of the sleeve under compressive stress, and reduced the gap between the trigger and the magazine by 0.4in.

The rifles were reclassified as the '[Infanterie-]Gewehr 89/96' in 1909; by November 1912, 127,050 service rifles and about 20 Exerzierwaffen had been made.

In 1913, as a result of a decree signed on 13th January 1911, conversion of 1896-type rifles to approximate to the 1911 pattern began in the Eidgenössische Waffenfabrik. By 1st March 1920, 135,770 rifles had been altered. They had four-groove rifling and chambered the Ordonnanz 11 cartridge.

MODEL 1897 CADET RIFLE
Kadettengewehr M1897
Made by Eidgenössische Waffenfabrik, Bern, 1898-1927.
Total production: 7900. **Chambering:** 7.5x53.5mm, rimless. **Action:** as M1889/96 rifle, above.

43.5in overall, 7.78lb empty. 23.3in barrel, 3-groove rifling; RH, concentric. Quadrant sight graduated to 1200m (1310yd). 1855 fps with M1890 ball cartridges. M1892 socket bayonet.

The Kadettengewehr was adopted on 27th July 1898 after trials with guns derived from the Mannlicher cavalry carbine and the Schmidt-system rifles. The single-shot M1897 had a special quadrant sight with differing sets of graduations for the Ordonnanzpatrone (to 1200m on the left side) or the reduced-charge Kadetten-Patrone (to 400m on the right). In addition to standard guns, about 40 sub-caliber trainers were also made.

MODEL 1900 SHORT RIFLE
Kurzgewehr M1900
Made by Eidgenössische Waffenfabrik, Bern, 1901-11.

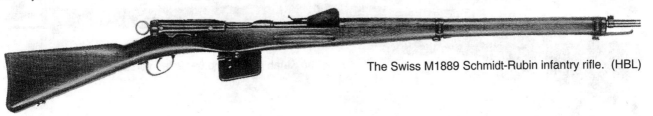

The Swiss M1889 Schmidt-Rubin infantry rifle. (HBL)

Total production: 18,750. **Chambering:** 7.5x53.5, rimless. **Action:** as M1889/96 rifle, above.

43.5in overall, 8.36lb empty. 23.3in barrel, 3-groove rifling; RH, concentric. Detachable box magazine, 6 rounds. Quadrant sight graduated to 1200m (1310yd). 1855 fps with M1890 ball cartridges. M1897 épée or saw-back M1906 sword bayonets.

Adopted on 9th April 1901, the Kurzgewehr was based on the 1896-pattern action; apart from its length, the smaller magazine and reduced-range sight, it was similar to the M89/96 infantry rifle.

Many surviving 1900-type guns were among the 26,340 carbines and short rifles converted to '1911' standards by Eidgenössische Waffenfabrik in 1913-20. Accepting 7.5mm Ordonnanz 11 cartridges, they had four-groove rifling.

MODEL 1905 CAVALRY CARBINE
Kavallerie-Karabiner M1905
Made by Eidgenössische Waffenfabrik, Bern, 1906-11.
Total production: 7900. **Chambering:** 7.5x53.5, rimless. **Action:** as M1889/96 rifle, above.

42.15in overall, 8lb empty. 21.65in barrel, 3-groove rifling; RH, concentric. Detachable box magazine, 6 rounds. Quadrant sight graduated to 1500m (1640yd). 1805 fps with M1890 ball cartridges. No bayonet.

Preceded by a handful of experimental designs—including one with a folding stock and another with a three-piece cleaning rod carried beneath the forend—the Karabiner 05 was adopted in 1905 to replace the 1893-type Mannlicher. Stocked virtually to the muzzle, preventing the attachment of bayonets, it had a full-length handguard and a sling-slot in the butt.

A decree signed on 13th January 1911 ordered the Eidgenössische Waffenfabrik to modify 26,340 surviving M1900 short rifles and M1905 carbines to approximate to the 1911 pattern. The work was undertaken in Bern in 1913-20. The converted guns had four-groove rifling and chambered 7.5x55 1911-type cartridges.

MODEL 1911 RIFLE
Gewehr 11
Made by Eidgenössische Waffenfabrik, Bern, 1913-19.
Total production: 133,000. **Chambering:** 7.5x55, rimless. **Action:** locked by revolving two lugs on the front of the bolt sleeve into the receiver behind the magazine well.

51.5in overall, 10.03lb empty. 30.7in barrel, 4-groove rifling; RH, concentric. Detachable box magazine, 6 rounds. Tangent-leaf sight graduated to 2000m (2185yd). 2640 fps with M1911 ball cartridges. M1892 socket, M1889 sword or saw-backed M1906 bayonets.

A universal increase in muzzle velocity, arising from widespread adoption of pointed-bullet ammunition, caused further problems with the Swiss rifles. Trials were undertaken in 1908-10 with modified bullets and rifles embodying a strengthened Vogelsang/Rebholz action. Apart from the tangent sight, these guns resembled their predecessors externally—though, once dismantled, three large holes were found to be bored through the bolt sleeve to reduce weight.

The perfected [Infanterie-]Gewehr 11 was formally approved on 10th January 1913, together with adaptations of several earlier weapons. The new guns had a strengthened action, a hold-open to signify an empty magazine, a pistol grip stock and an improved rear sight.

MODEL 1911 CARBINE
Karabiner 11
Made by Eidgenössische Waffenfabrik, Bern, 1914-33.
Total production: 184,200. **Chambering:** 7.5x55, rimless. **Action:** as M1911 rifle, above.

43.45in overall, 8.65lb empty. 23.3in barrel, 4-groove rifling; RH, concentric. Detachable box magazine, 6 rounds. Tangent-leaf sight graduated to 1500m (1640yd). 2475 fps with M1911 ball cartridges. Bayonet: as M1911 rifle.

Adopted concurrently with the 1911-pattern infantry rifle in January 1913, to replace the short rifle and cavalry carbine, this was readily distinguished by its short barrel and stock. It was mechanically identical with the rifle.

MODEL 1931 SHORT RIFLE
Karabiner 31
Made by Eidgenössische Waffenfabrik, Bern, 1933-58.
Total production: 582,230. **Chambering:** 7.5x55, rimless. **Action:** locked by revolving two lugs on the front of the bolt sleeve into the receiver behind the chamber.

43.6in overall, 8.85lb empty. 25.65in barrel, 4-groove rifling; RH, concentric. Detachable box magazine, 6 rounds. Tangent-leaf sight graduated to 1500m (1640yd). 2560 fps with M1911 ball cartridges. M1889, M1889/18, M1918, M1889/55 or saw-backed M1914 sword bayonets.

By 1930, it had become clear that important changes were required in the 1911-type Schmidt action to keep abreast of improved technology. On 22nd January 1932, therefore, the Bundesrat approved the manufacture of about 20 experimental short rifles; the Karabiner 31 was formally adopted on 16th June 1933.

Great changes had been made in the action which, though retaining the essence of the original Schmidt principle, locked into the receiver ring rather than behind the magazine well. In addition, the bolt did not project as far beyond the bolt carrier, reducing the length compared with the 1896-type action by 2.4in.

The Karabiner 31 had a longer barrel than the Karabiner 11, which was of similar overall length. An improved sight was fitted, and the semi-pistol grip stock—with a sling bar let into the left side of the butt—was retained by a clamping nose cap accepting any of the standard Swiss sword bayonets.

Military production finished in 1958 after more than half a million Karabiner 31 had been made in the Bern factory. A hundred otherwise standard examples were supplied in the 1930s to equip the élite Swiss Guard (or 'Papstliche Schweizergarde') in the Vatican; these guns were apparently numbered 249047-249146.

SNIPER RIFLE MODEL 1931/42
Zielfernrohr-Karabiner 31/42
Made by Eidgenössische Waffenfabrik, Bern, 1944-5.
Total production: 2240. **Chambering:** 7.5x55, rimless.
Otherwise as Kar. 31, above, excepting weight (9.44lb empty).

Experiments had been undertaken with optically-sighted Karabiner 11 as early as 1919, but the project had been shelved until trials with Karabiner 31 and Zeiss, Wild, Gerber and Kern sights began in 1935 in the Schiess-schule Walenstadt.

Though the low-power Kern sight was accepted in November 1940 and a hundred experimental carbines had been manufactured in 1943, the perfected Zf.-Kar. 31/42 was not approved until

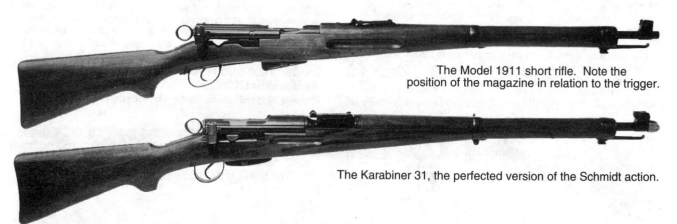

The Model 1911 short rifle. Note the position of the magazine in relation to the trigger.

The Karabiner 31, the perfected version of the Schmidt action.

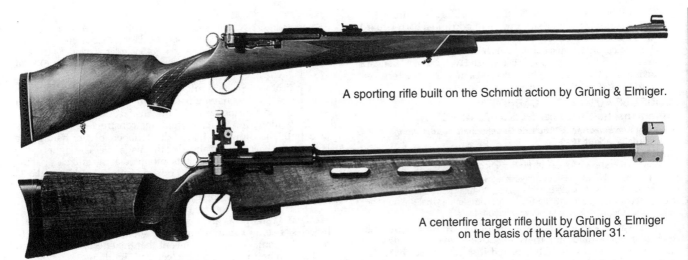

A sporting rifle built on the Schmidt action by Grünig & Elmiger.

A centerfire target rifle built by Grünig & Elmiger on the basis of the Karabiner 31.

1st July 1944. It had a 1.8x sight, offset on the left side of the receiver alongside the bolt. Each sight had a small auxiliary tangent sight and a unique pivoting periscope head.

SIMILAR GUNS

Model 31/43 sniper rifle. Otherwise identical with its 31/42 predecessor, this had an improved 2.8x sight on the left side of the receiver. Production was confined to 1945-6.

SNIPER RIFLE MODEL 1955
Zielfernrohr-Karabiner 55
Made by Eidgenössische Waffenfabrik, Bern, 1957-9.
Total production: 4150. **Chambering:** 7.5x55, rimless.
Otherwise as Kar.31, above, excepting overall length (47.55in) and weight (13.5lb with sight).

Featuring a top-mounted Kern 3.5x sight (graduated to 800m [875yd]), this rifle was adopted in 1956 to replace the M31/42 and M31/43. The 1955-type guns had a special half-stock with a checkered pistol grip, a folding bipod and a special muzzle brake.

SPORTING GUNS

In addition to regulation weapons and 13,260 commercial Karabiner 31 (the last being sold in 1972), the Swiss authorities accepted a short rifle with an aperture sight on 11th January 1963. Intended for use in military-style shooting matches, 'Präzisionskarabiner' Models 70 and 74 were made for UIT full-bore (70-M and 74-M) and biathlon (70-B, 74-B) competitions. The two '74' guns had a distinctive cut-away stock, and the biathlon guns were fitted with special shoulder harnesses.

Schmidt-type actions have been stocked and barreled by Grünig & Elmiger, Hämmerli, Tanner and others in a wide selection of calibers and chamberings—mostly for target shooting. However, the excessive length of pre-1931 actions made them less suitable for sporting purposes than Mauser or Mannlicher designs.

Schmidt & Jung

This gunmaking partnership submitted a rifle to the Swiss army trials of 1865. It had a small breech-bolt which could be raised out of the barrel by pivoting it around an axial pin on the left side of the action. An operating lever on top of the bolt could be turned forward to lock into a small forked block on the right side of the barrel. A spring-loaded striker inside the bolt cocked automatically as the operating lever was swung back.

The trials gun was a 10.4mm cartridge conversion, built on components salvaged from an 1863-pattern short rifle (Stutzer). The Schmidt & Jung design was too primitive to impress the trials board, however, and was passed over in favor of more efficient rivals.

• SIG

Also known as Fabrique d'Armes de Neuhausen, Schweizerische Industrie-Gesellschaft ('SIG'), Société Industrielle Suisse or Waffenfabrik Neuhausen, the premier privately-owned Swiss gunmaking company has a history dating back to the middle of the 19th Century. In addition to work on the Vetterli and Schmidt(-Rubin) service rifles, semi-experimental Neuhausen (q.v.) straight-pull bolt actions were developed unsuccessfully in the late 1880s.

SIG made a wide variety of autoloading rifles between the wars. A gas-operated 7.5mm KEG prototype, adapted from the promising KE-7 light machine-gun, was refined into the N-42 to compete in the mid 1940s with the AK-44 promoted by the Eidgenössische Waffenfabrik. Neither rifle was acceptable, even though a few hundred improved N-42 rifles, designated SK-46 (or 'N-46'), were made for trials.

MODEL 46 AUTOMATIC RIFLE
Selbstlade-Karabiner Modell 46, 'SK-46'
Made by Schweizerische Industrie-Gesellschaft, Neuhausen am Rheinfalls, 1946-50.
Total production: not known. **Chambering options:** 7.5x55 or 7.9x57.
Action: locked by camming the breechblock into the receiver wall; gas operated, semi-automatic only.
DATA FOR A 7.9MM EXAMPLE
44.3in overall, 9.9lb empty. 23.6in barrel, 4-groove rifling; RH, concentric. Detachable box magazine, 5 or 10 rounds. Tangent-leaf rear sight graduated to 1500m (1640yd). 2700 fps with standard ball ammunition. Standard 1889-pattern sword bayonet.

The SK-46 tapped gas from the bore near the chamber, leading it back to strike the head of a piston formed as an extension of the bolt body. The bolt lay in the chamber on the right side of the breech, where it acted on the breechblock by means of a stud riding in a cam groove. As the bolt began to move back, it pulled the tail of the breechblock out of engagement with the receiver; the breechblock then ran back to the limit of its travel, before returning to strip a new round into the chamber. At the end of the closing stroke, the stud cammed the breechblock back into engagement with the receiver and the gun was ready to be fired again.

The SIG Model 46 (SK46) semi-automatic rifle.

The full-length stock was similar to the Kar. 31 pattern (see 'Schmidt [-Rubin]'), with a shallow pistol grip and a barrel guard running from the chamber to the nose cap. However, the piston and bolt assembly lay in a cylindrical chamber on the right side of the breech and the box magazine was placed well forward beneath the action. A 2.2x optical sight could be clamped on the receiver, offset to the left to allow the open sights to be used.

MODEL 53 AUTOMATIC CARBINE
Automatische-Karabiner Modell 53, 'AK-53'
Made by Schweizerische Industrie-Gesellschaft, Neuhausen/ Rheinfalls, about 1949-50.

Total production: not known. **Chambering:** 7.5x55. **Action:** locked by rotating the barrel into contact with the breech; gas operated, automatic only.

39.4in overall, 10.8lb without magazine. 23.6in barrel, 4-groove rifling; RH, concentric. Detachable box magazine, 20 rounds. Tangent-leaf rear sight graduated to 1200m (1310yd). 2460fps with standard ball ammunition; 300rpm. Standard 1889-pattern sword bayonet.

This was an extraordinary design for the 1950s; though small quantities were made for trials, the AK-53 was never likely to appeal to prospective purchasers and it is hard to see how SIG hoped to succeed.

When the gun fired, gas was led back from the barrel port to strike the head of the gas piston. This drove the piston back, compressing its spring, until the piston-body engaged the actuator tube. The piston and actuator tube were then returned by the spring, rotating the barrel to release its lugs and moving it *forward* from the standing breech. The spent case was ejected. A spring in the barrel casing then brought the barrel, actuator-tube and piston assembly back to re-lock the breech.

Though the AK-53 was a locked-breech design, avoiding the vibrations that had plagued earlier 'slam-fire' blow-forward systems, it was clumsy and needlessly complicated. It had a straight-wristed half-stock with a separate wooden pistol grip immediately behind the trigger and a large-diameter barrel casing carrying the front sight and a bayonet lug. Owing to the low rate of fire, single shots could be fired by rapidly pressing and releasing the trigger.

MODEL 55 AUTOMATIC RIFLE
Also known as 'AM-55'

The authorities remained dissatisfied until the AM-55 was developed in Neuhausen in the mid 1950s under the supervision of Rudolf Amsler. Inspiration for this rifle came in the early 1950s from wartime German designs, specifically the StG. 45 (M) (see **'Spain: CETME'**). As the gun fired, generating pressure that tended to thrust the cartridge case backward, two short round-tip flaps anchored in the bolt-head were forced to retract into their housing. Resistance was provided partly by careful attention to the angled entry of the flaps into the receiver wall and partly by the inertia of the heavy bolt body. The whole mechanism then reciprocated to reload; as the bolt closed, the body forced the locking flaps outward into the receiver wall. Extraction was violent enough to demand a fluted chamber, but the weapon soon attained a reputation for reliability in untaxing Swiss service. Whether this could be sustained by less disciplined users, or in desert or arctic warfare, is another matter entirely.

MODEL 510 AUTOMATIC RIFLE
Also known as SG 510 or Stgw. 57
Made by SIG, Neuhausen am Rheinfalls.

Total production: at least a million (all types). **Chambering options:** see notes. **Action:** locked by engaging pivoting bolt-mounted struts in the receiver walls; delayed blowback, selective fire.

DATA FOR A TYPICAL STGW.57

Chambering: 7.5x55, rimless. 43.5in overall, 12.25lb with bipod and empty magazine. 22.95in barrel, 4-groove rifling; RH, concentric. Detachable box magazine, 24 rounds. Folding pillar sight graduated to 800m (875yd). 2495 fps with ball ammunition; 475-500 rpm. Stgw. 57 knife bayonet.

The prototype AM-55 rifle (subsequently renamed Selbstladegewehr [SG] 510-0), having passed army tests, was approved for service as the 'Sturmgewehr 57' or "Fusil d'Assault Mle 57".

Easily identified by its straight-line construction and rubberized butt, the Stgw. 57 had a short ribbed plastic handguard beneath the barrel jacket ahead of the magazine. The sights could be folded, and the bipod could be mounted at the muzzle or at the breech. The standard 24-round box magazine could be replaced when necessary by the 30-round type associated with the lMG. 25, or by a special six-round version for grenade-launching blanks.

The Stgw. 57 was very expensive to make, though quality was excellent. Weight was great enough to mask the effects of a rapid breech stroke, and accuracy was very good. However, firing automatically from a closed bolt meant that the effects of barrel heat had to be monitored to prevent 'cook off' ignitions.

Production of the Stgw. 57 ceased in 1983 after about 585,000 had been made. Most of the work was undertaken by SIG, though some final assembly apparently occurred in the Eidgenössische Waffenfabrik in Bern.

SIMILAR GUNS

Model 510-1 rifle, or SG 510-1. Introduced in 1958 in search of exports, this was little more than an Stgw. 57 chambering the 7.62x51 NATO cartridge.

Model 510-2 rifle, or SG 510-2. This was a lightened variant of the SG 510-1 with a wooden butt and a slimmer barrel jacket.

Model 510-3 rifle, or SG 510-3. Distinguished primarily by dimensions and chambering—the 7.62x39 Russian M43 round—this gun was similar mechanically to the others in the series. However, it had a short barrel and its magazine was sharply curved. The bayonet stud lay on the barrel jacket behind the sight assembly to compensate for the shortened muzzle. Changes to the woodwork and sights (eliminating the original straight-line configuration) were made shortly after the introduction of the SG 510-4 in the 1960s.

Model 510-4 rifle, or SG 510-4. Introduced in 1963-4, this chambered 7.62x51 NATO ammunition. Made with a 19.9in barrel, the gun was 39.95in long; weight averaged 10.5lb with a bipod and an empty 20-round magazine. Cyclic rate was about 600 rpm. A new wooden forend/handguard assembly and curved-comb butt sacrificed some of the advantages of straight-line layout so that sturdier fixed sights could be used. A bipod could be fitted above the barrel jacket behind the front sight, and the muzzle was adapted to double as a grenade launcher.

The SG 510-4 sold comparatively well in South America, especially in Bolivia and Chile, but was too expensive to interest major armies. Swiss laws preventing the export of certain classes of weapon often proved to be too inhibiting.

AMT sporting rifle. In addition to military-surplus Stgw. 57, limited to semi-automatic operation for sale in the U.S. as the 'PE-57', SG 510-3 and 510-4 rifles have also been advertised for sporting purposes. The most notable variant has been the 308 AMT. Restricted to single shots and obtainable with five- or 10-round magazines (plus the standard military 20-round pattern), this 'sporter' offered a folding winter trigger and a bipod. A combination of high price and ultra-military appearance kept sales to a minimum.

The Swiss Stgw. 57, known commercially as the SIG SG510.

The 5.56mm SIG SG530-1 was not particularly successful.

MODEL 530 AUTOMATIC RIFLE
Also known as SG 530

Made by SIG, Neuhausen am Rheinfalls, 1967-71.

Total production: not known. **Chambering:** 5.56x45, rimless. **Action:** generally as SG 510, above, but gas operated.

DATA FOR A TYPICAL SG 530-1

37.6in overall, 7.2lb without box magazine. 15.35in barrel, 4-groove rifling; RH, concentric. Detachable box magazine, 20 or 30 rounds. Rotating aperture sight graduated to 400m (435yd). 2870 fps with SS109 ball ammunition; 600rpm. Optional knife bayonet.

Committed to the Stgw. 57, the Swiss army showed little interest in the improved SG 510-4. SIG then produced its first 5.56mm rifle, retaining the two-part bolt and pivoting locking flaps but adding a gas piston assembly above the barrel to operate what had become a positive lock. Gas was tapped from the barrel as the gun fired, impinging on the piston head to force the rear part of the bolt carrier back far enough for the locking flaps to disengage the receiver wall.

The action ran back until the return spring asserted itself, stripping a fresh round into the chamber and forcing the flaps back into their locked position as the breech closed.

Trials undertaken in 1971 revealed that the breech system was not suited to the high pressure 5.56mm round. As the SG 530 was expensive to make, work concentrated thereafter on the simpler SG 540.

MODEL 540 AUTOMATIC RIFLE
Also known as SG 540

Made by SIG, Neuhausen am Rheinfalls.

Total production: not known. **Chambering options:** 5.56x45 or 7.62x51. **Action:** locked by rotating lugs on the bolt head into the receiver walls; gas operated, selective fire.

DATA FOR A TYPICAL SG 542

Chambering: 7.62x51 NATO, rimless. 39.4in overall, 8.97lb with bipod and empty magazine. 18.3in barrel, 4-groove rifling; RH, concentric. Detachable box magazine, 20 rounds. Drum sight graduated to 600m (655yd). 2690 fps with SS77 ball ammunition; 625±25 rpm. Optional knife bayonet.

Introduced in 1972, this replaced the unsuccessful SG 530. A rotating-bolt lock was used and the guns were simplified externally. Prototypes had wooden furniture, but synthetic components were soon substituted. The gas regulator was adjustable. A selector lever lay on the left side of the receiver above the pistol grip, with the settings displayed through a small circular aperture. Single shots and (optional) three-shot bursts could be fired, or the gun could be set to operate automatically. A Heckler & Koch-type rear sight was used, a bipod folded under the forend, and special attention was paid to dismantling; pressing a catch on the left side of the receiver, above the magazine release, allowed the entire barrel/forend/breech assembly to swing open. A manufacturing license was sold to Manurhin in 1975 (see **'France: SIG [Manurhin]'**), and the first guns were made in Mulhouse in 1977-8.

THE GUNS

Model 540 rifle, or SG 540. The standard rifle could be obtained in fixed or folding-butt patterns. It was 37.4in long, had a 18.1in barrel, and weighed 7.16lb without magazine or bipod; alternatively, it measured 28.35in with the butt folded, and weighed about 7.28lb.

Model 541 rifle, or SG 541. Dating from 1979, this modified SG 540 was developed for trials against a rival Eidgenössische Waffenfabrik prototype. Made in two barrel lengths, the rifle had a synthetic skeleton butt, an integral bipod and a modified selector/safety catch with the markings stamped into the outside of the receiver. The Swiss army provisionally adopted the SG 541 in 1983,

to replace the aging Stgw. 57, but shortage of funds delayed final acceptance. When sufficient money was eventually forthcoming, the design had progressed to the SG 550 (q.v.).

Model 543 carbine, or SG 543. The short-barreled derivative of the SG 540 was 31.7in long, had a 11.8in barrel and weighed 6.5lb without magazine. The bipod was omitted. Folding-butt examples collapsed to only 22.45in overall.

MODEL 550 AUTOMATIC RIFLE
Also known as SG 550

Made by SIG, Neuhausen am Rheinfalls.

Currently in production. **Chambering:** 5.56x45, rimless. **Action:** as SG 540, above.

DATA FOR STGW.90

39.4in overall (butt extended), 9.04lb with bipod and empty magazine. 20.8in barrel, 6-groove rifling; RH, concentric. Detachable box magazine, 20 or 30 rounds. Drum sight graduated to 500m (545yd). 3215 fps with U.S. M193 ball ammunition. Knife bayonet.

Little more than an improved SG 541—practically indistinguishable externally—these guns were adopted by the Swiss Army in 1984 as the 'Sturmgewehr Modell 90' (Stgw.90). They retain the operating system of the SG 540, but the previously optional three-round burst firing mechanism has been standardized. The folding plastic butt has a distinctive central void, and transparent plastic magazines are issued. Bipods are fitted as standard beneath the forend.

The first of about 600,000 series-made Stgw. 90 were issued for service in 1986, the intention being to issue each new recruit a 5.56mm rifle while the aging 7.5mm Stgw. 57 was phased out—a process that took nearly 10 years.

SIMILAR GUNS

Model 550 Sniper rifle, PSG 550, or SG 550 Sniper. Batches of these rifles were made for evaluation in 1991, though limited series production did not begin until 1995. The PSG 550 can be identified by its heavy barrel, by the heel-rest on the pistol grip, by an adjustable comb and by an extending buttplate. An optical sight is attached to a rail above the breech, and a bipod is customarily fitted beneath the forend.

Final assembly of the SG550 in SIG's Neuhausen factory.

The SIG SG551 SWAT, with short barrel, cheekpiece, Hensoldt optical sight, and triple magazine unit.

The ultra-compact SIG 552 Commando.

Model 550 Sporter. This is a minor variant of the SG 550, restricted to semi-automatic fire. About 30,000 had been sold commercially by mid 1995.

Model 551 carbine, or SG 551. This 'headquarters weapon' is basically a simplified version of the SG 550 with a barrel measuring only 14.1in. It cannot accept a bayonet. A 'SWAT' version developed for close-range sniping work has a cheekpiece on the butt and a rail for an optical sight above the breech.

Model 551LB carbine, or SG 551LB. This is simply an SG 551 with a long muzzle and a bayonet lug on the gas-port block.

Model 552 Commando. This is a short-barreled varsion of the basic design, with a folding butt. The ventilating holes in the compact forend are round instead of slotted.

• SIG-Sauer

MODEL 3000 SNIPER RIFLE
Scharfschützengewehr 3000, 'SSG 3000'
Made by Schweizerische Industrie Gesellschaft, Neuhausen am Rheinfalls.
Currently in production. **Chambering:** 7.62x51 NATO. **Action:** locked by two rows of three lugs on the bolt head engaging recesses in the barrel when the bolt handle was turned down.

46.45in overall, 11.8lb without sights. 24in barrel, 4-groove rifling; RH, concentric. Detachable box magazine, 5 rounds. Optical sight. 2790 fps with standard ball ammunition.

This rifle, a successor to the SSG 2000 (see 'Germany'), was built around the Sauer 200 action. This reverted to a front-locking system, which promised better accuracy than the rear-locking 'wedge' lugs of the earlier gun. The action is built on modular principles, with a detachable barrel and a 'packaged' trigger mechanism. A left-hand action can also be obtained.

The wooden stock may be in a single piece or a laminate. The buttplate and cheekpiece are both adjustable. Four slots are cut laterally through the forend. The trigger may be a single- or two-stage type, the sliding safety catch locks the trigger, bolt and firing pin, and an indicator pin protrudes from the breech when a round has been chambered.

The receiver rail is specifically designed to accept a 1.5-6x24 Hensoldt optical sight, but an alternative NATO-standard pattern can be obtained on request. SSG 3000 rifles will also accept a 22-caliber conversion unit, facilitating short-range practice. Other accessories include a mirage band, a bipod, a hand-stop and a sling anchor.

• Stamm

Hans Stamm of Saint Gallen, originally working in collusion with Adolf Sauerer of Arbon, developed a range of firearms prior to World War I. These included the 'Volkerbund' pistols and a series of bolt-action rifles.

Stamm was granted several Swiss patents in 1910-14 to protect straight-pull actions, rear sights, magazines, barrel bands and other fittings. A stud inside the bolt-sleeve rode in a helical groove in the bolt body to rotate two lugs on the bolt head into recesses in the receiver directly behind the chamber—a much stronger arrangement than the service-type Schmidt.

The guns were extensively tested by the Swiss authorities from about 1907 until at least 1912; survivors bear serial numbers as high as 20. However, despite the advantages of the Stamm bolt (which were appreciable), the clumsy Schmidt system was retained. This decision was undoubtedly influenced by the existence in the Eidgenössische Waffenfabrik of a production line for the Vogelsang/Rebholz-modified Schmidts, which could be readily adapted to make new 1911-pattern guns.

A typical experimental Stamm rifle, chambered for an experimental precursor of the 1911-type 7.5x55 cartridge, was 48.6in long, had a 27.65in barrel, and weighed 9.3lb. The detachable box magazine held six rounds in two rows. The gun could be recognized by the compact action, a distinctive 1910-patent rear sight with an elevator arm, and a nose cap with prominent apertures in the sides.

• Tanner

André Tanner began his gunmaking exploits in a converted garage in 1955, where the earliest target rifles were made. By 1960, a small factory had been opened in Neuenburg but a move to Fulenbach occurred in 1964. By this time, the rifles were attracting considerable attention. A distribution agreement with Hämmerli—signed in 1965—allowed the Free Rifles to enter series production. When Hämmerli participation ended in 1970, Tanner's operations were strong enough to survive on their own.

STANDARD UIT-STUTZER

This single-shot rifle features the company's sturdy bolt action, with three locking lugs and a safety catch on the right rear side of the action to lock the bolt. The action can only be loaded when the

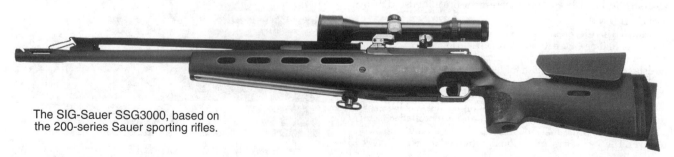

The SIG-Sauer SSG3000, based on the 200-series Sauer sporting rifles.

catch is set to 'Safe'. UIT-Stutzer are fitted with mechanical triggers adjustable from 3.5oz (100gm) to 4.4lb (2000gm), allowing them to be used as Free Rifles as well as in UIT Standard competitions, where trigger-pull weight is limited to 3.3lb (1500gm). The walnut Olympia-Schaft has an interchangeable cheekpiece and an adjustable rubber buttplate. Checkered alloy plates inset in each side of the forend facilitate grip.

SIMILAR GUNS

Repetierstutzer. A repeating version of the UIT-Stutzer features a nine-round box magazine, running up through the stock ahead of the trigger. A 10th round can be placed directly into the chamber. Excepting the magazine, the two Stutzers are externally identical; internally, however, the bolt head of the repeater has two lugs instead of three.

SUPER MATCH 50M CARBINE

This is intended for use as a Free Rifle, as it is fitted with a thumb-hole stock, an adjustable hooked buttplate and a hand-rest beneath the forend. It has a heavy large-diameter barrel, contributing to the all-up weight of about 13.9lb, and offers a 'System Tanner' trigger adjustable between 0.7oz (20gm) and 14.1oz (400gm). The trigger mechanism must be cocked with a lever protruding beneath the guard before the trigger lever can release the sear.

Several patterns of hand-rest may be obtained—ball, cylindrical or universally adjustable—and a balance-weight rod may be attached under the tip of the forend. In common with most of the Tanner series, the sights are offset to the left.

FREE RIFLE
Matchstutzer 300m

Made by André Tanner, Werkstätte für Präzisionswaffe, Fulenbach. Currently in production. **Chambering options:** 7.5x55 or 308 Winchester. **Action:** locked by rotating lugs on the bolt head into the receiver wall and the bolt handle is turned down, and by the bolt-handle base entering its seat.

DATA FOR A TYPICAL 300M PATTERN
Chambering: 7.5x55, rimless. 45.65in overall (with buttplate retracted), 14.88lb without hand rest. 28.9in barrel, 4-groove rifling; RH, concentric. Micro-adjustable aperture rear sight. 2655 fps with 177-grain bullet.

The first rifles were made on the Tanner action in 1962, with three symmetrically-spaced lugs on a separate bolt head. They have a massive receiver pierced only by the ejection port, and a special trigger set by a lever protruding beneath the trigger guard.

The massive half-stock has a thumbhole grip and a hooked butt-plate which can be adjusted for height and length. The straight comb is fixed. An accessory rail is let into the underside of the stock, with alloy finger-plates on either side of the forend. Many accessories are available, including competition sights, hand rests and mirage bands.

A distinctive aluminum bedding block was added between the barrel and receiver from 1966 onward. Tests soon showed that this was effective enough to become a Tanner hallmark.

UIT SHORT RIFLE
UIT-Stutzer

Made by André Tanner, Werkstätte für Präzisionswaffe, Fulenbach. Currently in production. **Chambering options:** 7.5x55 or 308 Winchester. **Action:** as Free Rifle, above.
DATA FOR A TYPICAL MAGAZINE-FEED MODELL 85
Chambering: 308 Winchester, rimless.
44.7in overall (with standard buttplate), 11.9lb with sights. 26in barrel, 4-groove rifling; RH, concentric. Detachable box magazine, 9 rounds. Micro-adjustable aperture rear sight. 2610 fps with 180-grain bullet.

Introduced in 1980, the first of the 300-metre Standard UIT rifles was based on the Tanner Free Rifle. The single-shot version retained the original three-lug bolt, whereas the magazine-fed version had only two lugs. The trigger-pull could be adjusted between about 7.1oz (200gm) and 6.6lb (3kg). Competition-pattern diopter rear sights and replaceable-element 'tunnel' front sights were standard. A safety catch protruded above the stock behind the bolt handle.

Made of good quality walnut, the stock had an adjustable shoulder pad, a stippled pistol grip, a fixed straight comb, and a long slot through the forend. An accessory rail was also fitted.

SIMILAR GUNS

Model 85 rifle. This improved UIT pattern was introduced in 1985 to capitalize on an increase in the maximum permissible weight from 11lb (5kg) to 12.1lb (5.5kg). It can be identified by the stock, which has a revised pistol grip and a replaceable cheekpiece; aluminum grasping plates are still set in the forend sides. The trig-

A typical Tanner centerfire sporting rifle.

The Tanner Matchstutzen 300, intended for Free Rifle competitions.

The Tanner sniper rifle.

ger has been altered to give an adjustment range of 3.5-71oz (100-2000gm) and the safety catch—which locked the bolt instead of the firing pin—has been moved forward to the right side of the receiver bridge ahead of the bolt handle.

Model 85 Sniper rifle. Dating from 1987 (but made only in small numbers), this was offered with a shortened heavy barrel, a plain forend and a bipod. Optical sights were customary.

• Vetterli

Designed by Friedrich Vetterli, this bolt-action rifle was used only in Switzerland and Italy. Vetterli had joined the Schweizerische Industrie-Gesellschaft Waffen-Department in 1864, and had soon developed a metallic-cartridge gun by combining a bolt inspired by the Dreyse with a Henry-type tube magazine. At the time the Vetterli was adopted by the Swiss army, it represented a significant advance: nowhere else in Europe had a magazine-feed rifle been accepted for universal military service. Its large-capacity magazine permitted an aimed fire-rate of 21 or more shots per minute, and, even if the bolt-lugs were not ideally positioned, the gun was sturdy enough for untaxing Swiss service.

Even though the Swiss Vetterli fired rimfire ammunition, it remained in service until replaced by the Schmidt(-Rubin) in the 1890s.

TRIALS RIFLE, 1867

The 'Repetier Gewehr M1867' had a distinctive external ring hammer, hung centrally below the rear of the bolt. A pivoting loading cover lay on the right side of the receiver, and a distinctively spurred trigger guard was fitted. The 1863-pattern quadrant sight was retained; the cleaning rod was channeled in the left side of the stock; and an 1863-pattern socket bayonet could be fitted.

MODEL 1869 RIFLE
Repetier-Gewehr M1869

Made by Schweizerische Industrie-Gesellschaft, Neuhausen, 1869-74 (total quantity: 59,000); by the Eidgenössische Montier-Werkstätte, Bern, 1869-75 (8900); by the Eidgenössische Waffenfabrik, Bern, 1875-8 (14,060); by Cordier & Cie, Bellefontaine, 1869-73 (4000); by W. von Steiger, Thun, 1869-74 (15,200); by Ost-Schweizerische Buchsenmacher, St Gallen, 1869-74 (8700); by Rychner & Keller, Aarau, 1869-73 (9700); by Valentin Sauerbrey, Basel, 1869-73 (7000); and by the Zürich Zeughaus, 1869-73 (1500).
Total production: 128,060. Chambering: 10.4x38R, rimfire. Action: locked by rotating two lugs on the bolt body into seats in the receiver behind the elevator-well as the bolt handle was turned down.

51.95in overall, 10.27lb empty. 33.1in barrel, 4-groove rifling; RH, concentric. Tube magazine under barrel, 12 rounds. Quadrant sight graduated to 1000 schritt. 1425 fps with M1867 ball cartridges. M1863 socket bayonet.

Provisionally approved on 8th January 1869, the first Swiss rifle (often known as the 'M1868/69') could be distinguished principally by its cleaning rod, which was set into the left side of the stock. Experience soon showed that the cleaning rod was easily damaged. Changes were made, the improved 'M1869' being accepted by the federal parliament on 1st August 1869 and declared regulation issue in December.

The modified gun was 51.2in overall, weighed 10.16lb and had an 11-round magazine, though a 12th round could be carried on the elevator and a 13th in the chamber. Its cleaning rod was carried in the forend under the barrel; a knurled ring was added to the cocking-piece head to facilitate re-cocking in the event of a misfire; a gas-escape hole was added above the chamber; and the loading-gate cover was modified so that the small transverse bolt on the front of the action acted as a limit-stop.

Changes were made in 1870, the most obvious being the substitution (from 20th August) of a transverse key through the forend—beneath the rear sight—for a spring which had been set in the right side of the forend at the joint with the receiver. The small threaded bolt that had previously limited the rotation of the loading-gate cover was also omitted.

SIMILAR GUNS

Model 1869/71 rifle. The introduction in 1871 of a new short rifle, described below, was accompanied by a change in the rifle with effect from 31st December. The 'M1869/71' rifle (which accepted the new quadrangular-blade M1871 socket bayonet) was distinguished by an improved elevator system and a simplified receiver, lacking the loading-gate cover and the leaf spring that had previously appeared on the left side. The two bands, nose cap and diced forend were all retained, though the rear sight was graduated to 1000m (1095yd) and weight rose to about 10.4lb.

Shortened guns. Small numbers of M1869 rifles were shortened in 1878 to offset shortages of true 1871-type carbines. A typical example was 37.2in long, with a 19.1in barrel, and weighed 8.6lb. Though the central barrel band and nose cap were retained, shortening the muzzle prevented a bayonet being used.

MODEL 1870 CADET RIFLE
Kadetten-Gewehr M1870

Made by Schweizerische Industrie-Gesellschaft, Neuhausen, 1870-3.
Total production: not known. Chambering: 10.4x38R, rimfire. Action: as M1869 rifle, above.

45.25in overall, 7.16lb empty. 26.75in barrel, 4-groove rifling; RH, concentric. Quadrant sight graduated to 600m (655yd). About 1300 fps with M1867 ball cartridges.

The single-shot cadet rifle was authorized by the Eidgenössische Militärdepartment on 22nd November 1870. Made exclusively by SIG, it had a one-piece stock resembling the Italian Vetterli rifles (q.v.) but did not take a bayonet.

MODEL 1871 CARBINE
Repetier-Karabiner M1871

Made by Eidgenössische Montierwerkstätte, Bern, 1871-2 (500?); and by Rudolf Pfenninger, Stäfa, 1872-4 (about 2500).
Total production: about 3000. Chambering: 10.4x38R, rimfire. Action: as M1869 rifle, above.
DATA FOR A FIRST-PATTERN GUN

36.7in overall, 7.16lb empty. 18.5in barrel, 4-groove rifling; RH, concentric. Tube magazine under barrel, 6 rounds. Block-and-leaf rear sight graduated to 400m (435yd)—see notes. 1230 fps with M1867 ball cartridges. No bayonet.

Adopted on 20th February 1871, this had a rotating ejection-port cover, a straight-edge forend and a spatulate bolt handle. The rear sight was a small standing block for 225m with folding leaves for 300m and 400m. Only about 200-250 carbines of this type were made.

A sliding Thury-pattern tangent rear sight graduated for 225-300m (245-330yd) was approved on 14th May 1872. At about the same time, the guns acquired a bolt handle with a conventional grasping knob, a forend with a notable step, and a modified receiver lacking the leaf spring on the left side.

A Schmidt-pattern sight was accepted on 4th November 1874 and apparently fitted to carbines as they returned for repair—production had been completed in August.

MODEL 1871 SHORT RIFLE
Repetier-Stutzer M1871

Made by Schweizerische Industrie-Gesellschaft, Neuhausen, 1871-4 (1000); by the Eidgenössische Montierwerkstätte and by the Eidgenössische Waffenfabrik, Bern, 1872-9 (about 15,000).
Total production: about 16,000. Chambering: 10.4x38R, rimfire. Action: as M1869 rifle, above.

The Model 1869/71 Vetterli infantry rifle. This example lacks the dicing usually found on the forend.

310 Rifles of the World

A 10.4mm rimfire Model 1878 Vetterli rifle.

49.6in overall, 10.2lb empty. 30.9in barrel, 4-groove rifling; RH, concentric. Tube magazine under barrel, 10 rounds. Quadrant sight graduated to 1000m (1095yd). 1375 fps with M1867 ball cartridges. M1871 socket bayonet.

The standard Vetterli infantry rifle was supplemented from 27th February 1871 by this gun, intended for the riflemen. A Thury double set trigger was adopted in December. Stutzer were shorter than infantry rifles; had only a single barrel band; and were fitted with special heavy buttplates.

MODEL 1878 RIFLE
Repetier-Gewehr M1878
Made by the Eidgenössische Waffenfabrik, Bern, 1878-81.
Total production: about 100,000. **Chambering:** 10.4x38R, rimfire.
Action: as M1869 rifle, above.
52.2in overall, 10.1lb empty. 33.1in barrel, 4-groove rifling; RH, concentric. Tube magazine under barrel, 12 rounds. Quadrant sight graduated to 1200m (1310yd). 1425 fps with M1867 ball cartridges. M1878 sword bayonet.

Experiments undertaken in 1872 to improve the Vetterli rifle created a variation with a bolt guide above the wrist of the stock, and another with a twin magazine containing more than 20 rounds. Trials rifles usually had one-piece stocks; at least one had an 1875-patent Pieri thumb-trigger, on the upper tang behind the bolt, and a finger spur replacing the trigger guard.

An improved Repetier-Gewehr was adopted on 30th April 1878. The action was little more than that of the M1869/71, though detail improvements had been made internally; externally, the gun had only a single barrel band, lacked stock-dicing, and mounted a sword bayonet. The Schmidt quadrant sight had a shorter leaf than its predecessor.

SIMILAR GUNS
Model 1878 short rifle, 'Repetier-Stutzer M1878'. Made by the Eidgenössische Waffenfabrik, Bern, this was simply a minor variant of the M1878 infantry rifle fitted with a Schmidt-type set trigger. Consequently, there are two trigger levers inside the spurred guard. Production amounted to 5410 guns in 1878-81.

MODEL 1878 CARBINE
Repetier-Karabiner M1878
Made by the Eidgenössische Waffenfabrik, Bern, 1879-85.
Total production: 1720. **Chambering:** 10.4x38R, rimfire. **Action:** as M1869 rifle, above.
36.55in overall, 7.28lb empty. 18.5in barrel, 4-groove rifling; RH, concentric. Tube magazine under barrel, 6 rounds. Quadrant sight graduated to 600m (655yd). 1230 fps with M1867 ball cartridges. No bayonet.

Adopted on 30th April 1878 for dragoons, this shared the action of the rifle and Stutzer, but was greatly shortened and had a stepped forend. A pivoting loading-gate cover was retained, but the spur on the trigger guard was omitted and the guns would not accept a bayonet. The carbines often lacked the gas-escape holes found on rifle receivers.

SIMILAR GUNS
Border Guard carbine. About three hundred guns were modified in 1895 for issue to the Grenzwächterkorps, when supplies of the purpose-built M1878 (below) began to run short. The cavalry-carbine conversions had an additional swivel on the nose cap.

MODEL 1878 BORDER-GUARD CARBINE
Repetier-Karabiner für Grenzwächterkorps, M1878
Made by the Eidgenössische Waffenfabrik, Bern, about 1880-1.
Total production: 400. **Chambering:** 10.4x38R, rimfire. **Action:** as M1869 rifle, above.
37.2in overall, 7.36lb empty. 19.1in barrel, 4-groove rifling; RH, concentric. Tube magazine under barrel, 6 rounds. Quadrant sight graduated to 600m (655yd). 1230 fps with M1867 ball cartridges. Sword bayonet.

Approved for issue to the border guards about 1880, this was virtually an M1878 carbine with an additional barrel band (carrying the front swivel) and a rifle-type nose cap with a bayonet lug.

MODEL 1881 SHORT RIFLE
Repetier-Stutzer M1881
Made by the Eidgenössische Waffenfabrik, Bern, 1881-7.
Chambering: 10.4x38R, rimfire. **Action:** as M1869 rifle, above.
52in overall, 10.19lb empty. 33.05in barrel, 4-groove rifling; RH, concentric. Tube magazine under barrel, 12 rounds. Quadrant sight graduated to 1600m (1750yd). 1425 fps with M1867 ball cartridges. M1878 sword bayonet.

Adopted on 22nd March 1881, this gun had the modified Schmidt Quadrantenvisier, with graduations for 225-1200m and an extending sight leaf intended for 1600m; it also had an improved Schmidt set-trigger system, though the changes from the earlier (1878) pattern were not obvious externally.

SIMILAR GUNS
Model 1881 rifle, 'Repetier-Gewehr M1881'. Made by the Eidgenössische Waffenfabrik, Bern, and also known as 'M1878-81', the last Swiss Vetterli rifle was adopted on 1st November 1881. It had an improved Schmidt Quadrantenvisier with an extending leaf, shared with the M1881 Stutzer (above), but was otherwise difficult to distinguish from the 1878 infantry pattern. Production lasted until 1887.

POLICE CARBINES
Some seven shot 'carbines'—they were actually 45in long compared with only 36.6in for the Repetier-Karabiner M1871—were made for cantonal police in the early 1870s. They had single barrel bands and accepted the standard 1863-pattern socket bayonet.

SPORTING GUNS
The Vetterli was never very popular with the sporting fraternity, though many thousands of obsolescent single-shot Italian military rifles were converted either to shotguns or rudimentary sporters in the 1890-1914 era. Most of the rifles simply had the forend remodeled.

Some Swiss magazine rifles were converted for target shooting, though commercial versions are now scarce: the guns were clumsy and comparatively low powered. However, a few good quality sporting guns were made. Some were made from new parts in the 1870s, but most prove to have been later adaptations of obsolescent military actions. The forend and magazine tube were shortened to half-length and set triggers were popular. Engraving sometimes graced the receiver, with carving on the stock.

A typical single shot target rifle had a 33.5in octagonal barrel with a quadrant sight. A double set trigger was fitted, the trigger guard was spurred, and the half-stock had a schnabel tip. The butt had a squared German-style cheekpiece and a hooked shoulder plate.

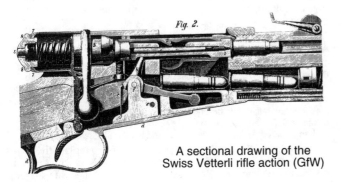
A sectional drawing of the Swiss Vetterli rifle action (GfW)

TAIWAN

• Armalite

The government, which had been making the M14 under license in the Hsing-Ho factory in Kao-Hsiung, proceeded in the mid 1970s to the 5.56mm Rifle Type 65 (i.e., 'M1976'). This mated an M16-type frame with a modified receiver/barrel assembly with a gas-piston system adapted from the AR-18. A pivoting rear sight lay on top of the raised rear of the receiver.

• Garand

The U.S. Military Aid Program supplied 173,730 M14 rifles prior to 1975, and the Springfield Armory production machinery had been sold to the Nationalist Chinese in 1967. Production of the 'Type 57' rifle began in 1968. Prior to gun number 048665, the ideographs across the rear of the receiver read 'Rifle 762' above '57 Type China' and the arsenal mark (a stylized encircled fire-wheel); later guns display ideographs reading 'Rifle 762 57 Type' above 'Made in Republic of China' over the arsenal mark. More than a million guns had been made by the end of the 1980s. They were identical with the last of the American-made rifles, though their stocks were generally cruder and a more noticeable flat appeared directly behind the receiver.

THAILAND

• Arisaka

The Thai army received ex-Japanese rifles of all types after 1945, some Type 99 short rifles being altered for the U.S. 30-06 cartridge. Undertaken in the government ordnance depot in Bangkok in the early 1950s, the conversion was essentially similar to the Korean type (q.v.). Thai guns often bore Sanskrit numbers and a disc-like *Chakra*, but the Japanese marks were left untouched.

TRANSVAAL (ZAR)

• Mauser

The Mausers used by the Zuid Afrikaansche Republiek (ZAR), also known as the Transvaal, were ordered from DWM through the intermediacy of Krupp after the Jameson Raid of January 1896 showed the poverty of the country's arsenal. They supplemented orders for obsolescent Westley Richards Martini-Henry rifles and Steyr-made Portuguese Guedes rifles.

MODEL 1896 RIFLE

Purchase of as many as 50,000 DWM-made rifles was authorized in 1896, though only about 37,000 had been delivered by the start of the Second South African War in 1899. The rifles were virtually identical with the Chilean Mo.1895 (q.v.), though whether they chambered 7x53 or 7x57 cartridges has not been determined. A typical example was 48.6in overall, had a 29.05in barrel and weighed 8.8lb. Its leaf sight was graduated to 2000m (2185yd) and a typical German export-pattern sword pattern could be fitted when required. Oddly, though many OVS guns survive in collections, few ZAR examples exist. The reason for this is not clear.

• Richards

Owing to the supply of 'monkey tail' breechloaders converted for centerfire cartridges in the 1880s, Westley Richards & Co. Ltd had established a relationship with the two independent Dutch orientated states in southern Africa—the Orange Free State (OVS, 'Oranje Vrij Staat') and the South African Republic (ZAR, 'Zuid Afrikaansche Republiek'). The Martini rifles were ordered before relations with Britain deteriorated.

RICHARDS-MARTINI RIFLE

Made by Westley Richards & Co. Ltd, Birmingham, 1896-7.
Total production: see notes. **Chambering:** 450, rimmed. **Action:** locked by pivoting the breechblock behind the chamber with the tip of the operating lever.

49.55in overall, 9lb empty. 33.25in barrel, 7-groove rifling; RH, composite. Ramp-and-leaf rear sight graduated to 1200yd. 1350 fps with solid-case ball cartridges. No bayonet issued?

These rifles had already been ordered when the Jameson Raid (in January 1896) revealed a desperate need for modern firearms. No more than 10,000 Westley Richards Martini guns had been delivered by 1897, against orders said to have totaled 36,000, owing to growing political unrest and impending deliveries of Mausers.

Created from unfinished Mark IV actions made in the early 1880s by the National Arms & Ammunition Company factory in Sparkbrook, Birmingham, the guns had a distinctive Francotte-type cocking indicator protruding above the right receiver wall. A patented knurled-head catch on the lower front right of the receiver allowed the entire breech mechanism to be taken out of the receiver.

The rifles displayed 'MADE SPECIALLY FOR Z.A.R.' on the right side of the receiver, with the manufacturer's mark on the left and a date in a triangle—e.g., '1897'—on top of the barrel.

SIMILAR GUNS

Carbine. A short-barreled version of the rifle was also made in small numbers, generally stocked almost to the muzzle and apparently incapable of accepting a sword or sabre bayonet.

TURKEY

The firearms and accessories used in Turkey are notoriously difficult to classify. Though they customarily follow specific patterns—e.g., Mauser or Peabody-Martini—local alterations often blur their origins. This is particularly true of the wholesale changes made to ex-German Gew. 88 by the Ankara military factory in the period between the world wars, and the multitude of non-standard bayonets originating in the same era.

Turkish rifles made prior to about 1926 can usually be identified by marks in Arabic; in addition, many of the more modern Mausers have a *Toughra* (a calligraphic symbol unique to each ruler) on the chamber top.

• Berthier

The Turkish forestry service is said to have been equipped with altered French Mle 07 Berthier (q.v.) rifles, possibly sold as surplus immediately after World War II. The barrels and stocks were shortened to carbine length, inspiration for the new nose cap—perhaps even the components themselves—being provided by the 1908-type Turkish Mauser carbine. The bolt handle was bent downward, but the three-round clip-loaded magazine and the original rear sight were retained. Most of the guns reported (all dated '1948') also had a protective sheet-steel shroud between the front of the receiver and the rear sight. Guns are typically 41.7in overall, have 21.75in barrels and weigh about 7.6lb empty.

• Heckler & Koch

The army bought the first G3A3 and G3A4 rifles—'G3 Otomatic Piyade Tüfegi'—from Heckler & Koch in the early 1970s, together with a license to make guns in the government-sponsored Makina v Kimya Endustrisi (MKE) factory in the Kurumü suburb of Ankara. Indigenous production does not seem to have begun until 1977, the first guns being assembled in 1978. Turkish-made G3A7 guns have a distinctive retractable butt and display an encircled 'MKE' trademark on the right side of the magazine housing. They are generally phosphated and then lacquered.

• Mauser

The Turks were among the first to order Mauser-type magazine rifles in quantity. A feature of the initial contract was a clause forcing the substitution of a better rifle should one be adopted elsewhere.

MODEL 1887 RIFLE

Made by Waffenfabrik Mauser, Oberndorf am Neckar, 1888-90.
Total production: about 210,000 rifles and 15,000 carbines. See text.
Chambering: 9.5x60R, rimmed. **Action:** locked by turning a lug on the bolt into a recess in the receiver, and by the bolt guide rib abutting the receiver ahead of the bridge.

49.25in overall, 9.23lb empty. 29.9in barrel, 4-groove rifling; RH, concentric. Tube magazine in forend, 8 rounds. Leaf sight graduated to 1600m (1750yd). 1755 fps with ball cartridges. M1887 sword bayonet.

Trials began in 1886 to find a magazine rifle to replace the Peabody-Martini. Once the decision to adopt a new Mauser had been taken, an order for 500,000 rifles and 50,000 carbines was shared

The 1887-pattern Turkish Mauser carbine. (HBL)

by Waffenfabrik Mauser and Ludwig Loewe & Co. Before work began, however, the contractors decided that Mauser should make all the Turkish guns while Loewe accepted contracts for the German Gew. 88.

The new rifle chambered a powerful black-powder cartridge, necessitating an additional locking lug, but was externally similar to the Gew. 71/84. It had a straight-wrist stock, a single spring-retained barrel band, and a nose cap with a bayonet lug on the right side. The swivels lay on the underside of the nose cap and in the front web of the trigger guard, and a German-type rear sight was attached to the barrel ahead of the octagonal chamber reinforce.

Owing to progress with the 1889-type Mauser in Belgium, the Turkish authorities invoked the substitution clause in the original contract in 1890. Production of M1887 rifles stopped in the Oberndorf factory after about 225,000 had been made. A few carbines had been among them.

MODEL 1890 RIFLE
Made by Waffenfabrik Mauser, Oberndorf am Neckar, 1891-3.
Total production: 245,000? **Chambering:** 7.65x53, rimless. **Action:** locked by two lugs on the bolt head engaging recesses in the receiver as the bolt handle was turned down.

48.7in overall, 8.85lb empty. 29.15in barrel, 4-groove rifling; RH, concentric. Semi-fixed box magazine loaded from a stripper clip, 5 rounds. Leaf sight graduated to 2050m (2240yd). 2130 fps with ball cartridges. M1890 sword bayonet.

A variant of the Belgian Mle 1889 rifle, this was adopted in 1890 to replace the obsolescent M1887. It had a plain barrel, stepped to allow for expansion during rapid fire without upsetting the stock bedding. A one-piece sear was fitted and the magazine—though intended to be permanent—could be removed by pressing a catch set into the front face of the trigger-guard. The rear sight was carried on a sleeve around the barrel, while a curiously abbreviated handguard ran forward from the sight base. The guard did not reach the solitary spring-retained band. The nose cap assembly was simpler than that of the M1887, carrying its bayonet lug on the underside. Swivels lay on the band and butt.

SIMILAR GUNS
Model 1890 carbine. The first batches of about 30,000 carbines were supplied in 1892 to arm cavalry and artillerymen. About 39.15in overall, with 19.7in barrels and a weight of 7.7lb, they were similar mechanically to the rifles. However, the stock extended to the muzzle (preventing bayonets being mounted) and bolt handles were turned down. The rear sight was apparently graduated to merely 1200m (1310yd).

Turks in the First World War, with 1898-type German Mausers.

MODEL 1893 RIFLE
Made by Waffenfabrik Mauser, Oberndorf am Neckar, 1894-9.
Total production: 201,100. **Chambering:** 7.65x53, rimless. **Action:** as M1890, above.

48.6in overall, 8.95lb empty. 29.05in barrel, 4-groove rifling; RH, concentric. Fixed box magazine loaded from a stripper clip, 5 rounds. Leaf sight graduated to 2000m (2185yd). 2130 fps with ball cartridges. M1890 sword bayonet.

The approval of the Spanish Mo. 1893 caused the Turks to request an improvement on their 1890-pattern rifle. The new gun was a virtual duplicate of the Spanish weapon, but had a conventional cylindrical bolt and a unique cut-off lever in a housing on the right side of the receiver beneath the bolt way. An extension of the bolt stop doubled as the left charger guide, and Arabic markings lay on the receiver.

MODEL 1903 RIFLE
Made by Waffenfabrik Mauser, Oberndorf am Neckar, 1903-6.
Total production: not known. **Chambering:** 7.65x53, rimless. **Action:** locked by two lugs on the bolt head engaging recesses in the receiver as the bolt handle was turned down, and by a safety lug opposite the bolt-handle base entering its seat.

48.6in overall, 9lb empty. 29.05in barrel, 4-groove rifling ; RH, concentric. Integral box magazine loaded from a stripper clip, 5 rounds. Tangent-leaf sight graduated to 2000m (2185yd). 2130 fps with ball cartridges. M1903 sword bayonet.

True to their policy of keeping abreast of developments in Germany, doubtless influenced by restrictive clauses in the original 1887-vintage contract, the Turks purchased large quantities of this Gew. 98-like rifle prior to 1914.

The M1903 resembled the contemporary German service rifle externally, though it had a standard rear sight, a handguard extending from the receiver ring to the band, and a bayonet lug under the simple nose cap. The cocking-piece was longer and heavier than the German pattern, and the bolt stop was extended upward to form the left stripper-clip guide. The stock had a pistol grip; swivels lay under the band and butt.

SIMILAR GUNS
7.9mm conversions. From the mid 1920s onward, the first batches of M1903 rifles were converted to chamber the 7.9x57 rimless cartridge—large quantities of which had been supplied to assist pro-German Turkey during World War I.

MODEL 1908 CARBINE
Made by Waffenfabrik Mauser, Oberndorf am Neckar, 1903-6.
Total production: not known. **Chambering:** 7.65x53, rimless. **Action:** as M1903, above.

41.15in overall, about 8.25lb empty. 21.65in barrel, 4-groove rifling; RH, concentric. Integral box magazine loaded from a stripper clip, 5 rounds. Leaf sight graduated to 1600m (1750yd)? 2080 fps with ball cartridges. No bayonet.

This gun, virtually a short rifle, was acquired to replace the earlier 1890 pattern in the hands of the cavalry and artillerymen. It had a pistol-grip stock, a spring-retained barrel band, and a simple nose cap carried upward to protect the front-sight blade. The bolt handle was turned down toward the stock, and sling mounts lay on the left side of the band and butt. Many surviving guns were converted for the standard 7.9x57 cartridge from 1925 onward.

OTHER GUNS
Turkey also purchased 7.92mm vz. 98/22 rifles from Czechoslovakia in the early 1920s. Many ex-German Gew. 88 and Gew. 98 were still in service in the mid 1920s, when substantial quantities of replacement bolts were made in Brno.

• Peabody
No mention was made in Peabody literature reliably dated to 1870, suggesting that the Turkish order dates from about 1871. The

guns were standard external-hammer types with back-action locks and leaf type firing-pin retractor springs.

• Peabody-Martini
MODEL 1874 RIFLE
Made by the Providence Tool Company, Providence, Rhode Island, 1874-9.

Total production: about 600,000 rifles and 50,000 carbines. **Chambering:** 45, rimmed. **Action:** locked by pivoting the breechblock behind the chamber with the tip of the operating lever.

49in overall, 9.55lb empty. 33.2in barrel, 5-groove rifling; RH, concentric. Ramp-and-leaf rear sight. About 1490 fps with ball cartridges. Bayonet: see notes.

The Turks were among the first to buy sizable quantities of the Peabody-Martini rifle, ordering 400,000 in 1874. It has been suggested that they unsuccessfully approached the British before turning to the Providence Tool Company, but the case is not proven.

The Turkish Peabody-Martini was almost impossible to distinguish at a glance from a British Martini-Henry, apart from an 1869-type safety lever ahead of the trigger guard. Rifles were fully stocked, with two barrel bands; infantry rifles apparently accepted a standard socket bayonet, but others, possibly for riflemen and Élite units, were issued with a distinctive leather-gripped sword pattern. Sling swivels generally lay under the front barrel band, immediately ahead of the trigger guard, and on the under-edge of the butt. A large radial cocking indicator lay on the right rear side of the receiver.

SIMILAR GUNS
Model 1874 carbine. The Turks also ordered 25,000 guns for their cavalry, placing other (smaller) orders into the late 1870s until total acquisitions approached 50,000. The carbines had half-length forends, retained by a single band, and would not accept bayonets.

• Reichsgewehr (Mannlicher)
Large quantities of Gew. 88, 88/05 and 88/14 were left in Turkey by the Germans at the end of World War I. Many were subsequently reconditioned in the 1920s and 1930s, receiving a new pistol grip stock. The barrel jacket was discarded, the magazines were altered to use standard Gew.98-type stripper-clips, and a new 2000m (2185yd) tangent-leaf rear sight was fitted. Most of these guns will display a large star-and-crescent mark on the receiver ring, accompanied by a conversion date—e.g., '1928', or '32' for 1932. A 'TC' monogram for *Türkiye Cumhuriyeti* ('Republic of Turkey') may also be present, together with the 'AS.FA' mark of the military factory or *Askeri Fabrika* in Ankara.

URUGUAY

These rifles will usually be found with the national Arms over the chamber. These comprised a quartered oval, beneath a rising sun, displaying the scales of justice, the citadel of Montevideo, a horse and a bull. The mark lay within a laurel wreath; 'REPUBLICA ORIENTAL DEL URUGUAY' or 'REPUBLICA ORIENTAL' also appeared.

• Daudetau-Mauser
Though Uruguay is said to have acquired a sizable quantity of 1871-type Mauser rifles in the 1880s, apparently from Österreichische Waffenfabriks-Gesellschaft, these bore nothing but 'Republica Oriental' marks. However, more rifles of this pattern were acquired in the 1890s in questionable circumstances.

Substantial quantities of Mauser rifles and carbines were converted by (or possibly for) Société Française des Armes Portatives of Saint-Denis, Paris, and are appropriately marked with a cursive 'S.F.A.P.' over 'St. Denis' above the chamber. The guns were re-barreled for the 6.5x53.5 Daudetau No. 12 semi-rim cartridge, the bands and nose caps being replaced by typically Daudetau patterns. The rear sight was a 2000m (2185yd) tangent-leaf pattern, and a special French-style épée bayonet was used.

Chronology is disputed. Marks on a typical rifle show that it had been made in 1879 and issued to German units from 1882; proof and inspectors' are all German military patterns. As it bears no Uruguayan identification, suggestions have been made that the Dovitiis-Mauser rifles (named after the supervising Uruguayan

engineer) were acquired not by the government but by one of the many revolutionary factions active prior to 1910. Alternatively, the rifles may have been bought as an expedient pending the delivery of 1895-type Mausers; their front-line life would thus have been very short, lasting from 1895 only until 1898. Information is still being sought in South America.

• Mauser
PRE-1914 PATTERNS
Ten thousand 7x57 Mo. 1895 rifles, 4,000 Mo. 1895 carbines and 4.5 million cartridges were ordered from Fabrique Nationale in March 1896. The contract is believed to have been shared with DWM. An unknown quantity (25,000?) of Mo. 1904 Mauser rifles was subsequently purchased from DWM prior to 1914.

POST-1914 PATTERNS
About 6,000 Czechoslovakian vz. 32 7.65mm short rifles were delivered in 1937, to serve as the 'Mo.1934'; some 7mm Mle. 24-type short rifles were also purchased from Fabrique Nationale in the same era.

• Remington
The army acquired Spanish-type three-band rifles and two-band short rifles in the late 1870s, apparently issuing them as 'Mo. 1879'. The mark 'REPUBLICA ORIENTAL' lay on top of the barrel ahead of the receiver.

U.S.A.

• Allen (Ethan), block-action type
SPORTING RIFLE
Made in Worcester, Massachusetts, by Allen & Wheelock (prior to 1865), E. Allen & Co. (1865-71) and Forehand & Wadsworth (1872-80?).

Total production: 7,500? **Chambering options:** 22, 32, 38 or 44 rimfire, and 44 centerfire. **Action:** a vertically-moving block is propped behind the chamber by the operating lever.
DATA FOR A TYPICAL PRE-1865 EXAMPLE

Chambering: 44 Long, rimfire. 41.9in overall, 8.1lb empty. 25.85in barrel, 5-groove rifling; RH, concentric. Single shot only. Standing-block rear sight with a small folding leaf. 825 fps with 225-grain bullet.

Made in accordance with a patent granted to Ethan Allen in September 1860, guns of this type were operated by releasing the blade-type latch in a pillar forming the rear web of the trigger guard, and then pulling down on the operating lever to lower the block in the deeply recessed frame. An extractor slid in the barrel block immediately below the chamber, and the detachable barrel was held by a 'take-down' screw. The butt was held to the frame by a longitudinal bolt running up through the straight wrist, the shoulder plate was concave, and a short forend was attached to the barrel.

Allen rifles usually had half-octagon barrels, though lengths and styles may vary. They have a detachable plate on the left side of the receiver, and may be found with a distinctive pivoting-pointer rear sight which was also a feature of the 1860 patent. Options including superior woodwork, checkering and long barrels were available to order.

• Allen (Ethan), plug-action type
Among the wide range of patents granted to Ethan Allen during his working life was U.S. no. 13,154, granted in July 1855 to protect a faucet breech. Sporting rifles of this type were made by Allen & Wheelock of Worcester, Massachusetts, until the American Civil War began. A typical 44-caliber example had a 30in part-round, part-octagonal barrel; the case-hardened iron receiver contained a back-action caplock with an external hammer; and the butt had a crescent-shape shoulder plate. A patch-box with a circular iron lid, set in a decorative mounting plate, was let into the right side of the butt. The rear sight was a spring-leaf design with an elevator plate sliding in a groove in the top of the barrel.

• Allen (Hiram)
Two carbines were submitted to the U.S. Army trials of 1865. Tested as Guns No. 1 and No. 2, they were operated by pulling up on a back-hinged lever on top of the butt wrist. This system—

possibly patented in a perfected form by Hiram Allen in 1871—allowed the entire breech-block and hammer mechanism to slide back down a track. The guns had a Ballard-type receiver with long supplementary side-straps running down the wrist. The separate butt had a straight comb and wrist, and the half-length forend was retained by a single band. The rear sight seems to have been a standing block ahead of the chamber.

• Alpha Arms

This company made a limited range of bolt action sporters designed by Homer Koon, based on a three-lug bolt mechanism with a 60-degree throw.

ALPHA MODEL 1 SPORTING RIFLE

Made by Alpha Arms, Inc., Flower Mound, Texas, 1982-5.
Total production: limited quantities only. **Chambering options:** 243 Winchester, 7mm-08 and 308 Winchester. **Action:** locked by three lugs on the bolt head engaging the receiver as the bolt handle was turned down.
DATA FOR A TYPICAL 7MM-08 EXAMPLE
39.5in overall, 6.3lb empty. 20in barrel, 4-groove rifling; RH, concentric? Internal box magazine, 4 rounds. Optical sight. 2715 fps with 154-grain bullet.

The original Alpha Model 1 had a medium-length action and a comparatively short barrel. The satin-finish half-stock had a Monte Carlo comb, but lacked a cheekpiece. An aluminum bedding-block system was used and the trigger guard/magazine floor-plate assembly was coated in Teflon. Improved rifles were introduced in 1985, with short, regular or magnum-length actions. Made to order with barrels of 20-24in, they could be chambered for virtually any cartridge the customer cared to specify from 17 Remington to 458 Winchester Magnum. Alpha rifles were all made in right- or left-hand versions.

SIMILAR GUNS
Alaskan Model, 1985-7. Identifiable by a stainless-steel barreled action, with Nitex-coated lesser metal parts, these guns customarily had wood laminate stocks (though a few synthetic examples were made). Chamberings were apparently confined to 308 Winchester, 350 Remington Magnum, 358 Winchester Magnum and 458 Winchester Magnum.
Custom Model, 1985-7. Offered in 243 Winchester, 25-284, 7mm-08, 284 Winchester or 308 Winchester, this had a superbly grained oil-finished Claro walnut half-stock with a straight comb and a metal Niedner pistol grip cap. The shoulder plate was hard rubber. Forend caps were generally ebony, though rosewood patterns were sometimes substituted. The checkering panels on the grip and forend were invariably divided by sinuous rib bands.
Grand Slam Model, 1985-7. This duplicated the Custom pattern, but had a stock of AlphaWood (a composite of fiberglass and wood pulp).

ALPHA JAGUAR SPORTING RIFLE

Made in several variations in 1987-8, apparently based on a 'modified Mauser' two-lug action, this could be ordered in chamberings ranging from 222 Remington to 338 Winchester Magnum. Grade I had a sliding safety; Grade II had a Douglas barrel; Grade III had a three-position safety lever, inspired by the Winchester Model 70; and Grade IV was a lightweight version of Grade III. Production seems to have been very small.

• AMAC

The American Military Arms Corporation succeeded to the business of Iver Johnson in the early 1980s but continued to use the earlier trade name. In addition to 50-caliber anti-matériel rifles, AMAC also made a copy of the 30 M1 Carbine (see 'Winchester') and has offered a single-shot bolt-action 22 rimfire rifle known as the Model 2000 or "Li'l Champ Bolt 22". Intended for juniors, this gun measures 33in overall, has a 16.3in barrel and weighs about 2.63lb. Erma-made rimfire rifles (q.v.) have also been distributed in the U.S.A. as the 'U.S. Carbine 22', 'Wagonmaster Lever Action' and 'Targetmaster Pump Action'.

• American Industries (Calico)

American Industries once manufactured the fascinating Calico rimfire rifles, and a short-barrel 'pistol' derivative—the M-100P—built on an identical action. The guns are now made by Calico Light Weapons Systems.

M-100 CARBINE

Made by Calico Light Weapons Systems, Bakersfield, California.

Currently in production. **Chambering:** 22LR rimfire. **Action:** no mechanical breech lock; blowback, semi-automatic only.

35.8in overall (stock extended), 5.75lb loaded. 16in barrel, 4-groove rifling; RH concentric. Detachable helical-feed box magazine, 100 rounds. Open rear sight. 1080 fps with 40-grain bullet.

The M-100 has a light alloy frame, a folding stock and a ribbed synthetic handguard. The unique magazine, made from high-strength thermoplastic, has a silent winder with a spring-release clutch to facilitate loading. Two clear ports allow the state of loading to be assessed at a glance. Most unusually, the magazine lies on top of the action; it is claimed to be more efficient and lighter-per-round than conventional box patterns.

SIMILAR GUNS
Liberty series. These two guns (Liberty 50 and Liberty 100) are essentially similar to the 22 rimfires, but chamber the 9x19, or '9mm Luger' cartridge.
M-100S (Sporter) This was an M-100 with a wooden hand-guard and combination pistol grip/butt unit.
M-105 Sporter. Introduced in 1987, this was similar to the M-100, but had a separate wood butt and forend. The pistol grip was synthetic.

• AMT, autoloading type

Arcadia Machine & Tool, Inc., has offered a selection of rifles built on a version of the Automag II gas-assisted blowback action.

LIGHTNING SPORTING RIFE

Introduced in 1986 in 22LR rimfire only, this could be obtained with a 17.5in bull or tapered barrel. The satin-finish stainless steel action is stocked in warp-resistant fiberglass-filled nylon, with a skeletal butt which pivots forward to lie along the right side of the action. A 30-round box magazine is standard.

SIMILAR GUNS
Hunting Rifle, 1992-6. This 22LR autoloader has a black synthetic stock with a Monte Carlo-type comb and cheekpiece. A compartment in the butt, reached by detaching the shoulder pad, contains cleaning equipment, spare ammunition and a survival knife. The magazine is a 10-round rotary design.
Magnum Hunter. Introduced in 1995 in 22 Winchester Magnum rimfire, this has a detachable 10-round box magazine. Overall length with a 20in free-floating barrel is about 40.5in, empty weight averaging 6lb. The black fiberglass/nylon half-stock has a straight comb, and lacks a cheekpiece.
Small Game [Hunting] Rifle. Also known as the 'SGH', this appeared in 1986 in 22LR and 22 Winchester Magnum rimfire (not handled interchangeably). The SGH has a 22in heavyweight barrel, a fixed butt, and is intended to be fitted with an optical sight. A detachable 10-round box magazine is used.

• AMT, bolt-action type

AMT SPORTING RIFLE

Made by AMT, Irwindale, California.

Currently in production. **Chambering options:** see text. **Action:** locked by two lugs on the bolt head engaging recesses in the receiver as the bolt handle turns down, and by the bolt-handle base entering its seat in the receiver.
DATA FOR A TYPICAL EXAMPLE
Chambering: 6mm PPC, rimless. 47.5in overall, 8.25lb empty. 26in barrel, rifling profile not known. Internal box magazine, 3-5 rounds depending on chambering. Optical sight. 3140 fps with 70-grain bullet.

These rifles are supplied in two basic patterns. The single shot version has a conical breech system, allied with a post-1964 Winchester Model 70-type extractor and a pre-1964 three-position safety; the magazine-feed gun, however, has a standard Mauser-type extractor. The guns are supplied in short, medium or long actions for right- or left-handed use. The half-stocks are typically 'classic composite' on the standard guns, and McMillan or HS-Precision patterns on the deluxe versions. Single shot chamberings are currently 22 Hornet, 22 PPC, 22-250, 222 Remington, 223 Remington, 243 Winchester, 243 'A', 6mm PPC, 6.5x08, 7mm-08 and 308 Winchester. Magazine rifles can be obtained in 22-250, 223 Remington, 243 Winchester, 243 'A', 6mm PPC, 25-06, 6.5x08, 270 Winchester, 7x57 Mauser, 7mm-08, 7mm Remington Magnum, 30-06, 300 Winchester Magnum, 7.62x39, 308 Winchester, 338 Winchester Magnum, 375 H&H Magnum, 416 Remington, 416 Rigby and 458 Winchester Magnum.

• ArmaLite

The story of this controversial rifle began with the ArmaLite Division of Fairchild Engine & Airplane Corporation, formed in the autumn of 1954 to promote guns embodying aluminum alloy parts and foam-filled synthetic furniture. The autoloading 7.62x51 AR-3, designed by ArmaLite's chief engineer Eugene Stoner, was locked by a variation of the rotating bolt patented in the 1930s by Melvin Johnson (q.v.).

A small tube ran along the left side of the breech to direct propellant gas through the receiver wall into a chamber formed between the bolt and the bolt carrier. The bolt carrier was forced backward on firing, rotating the bolt to disengage the lock; when the carrier had moved back a short distance, it closed the port on the receiver side and cut off the gas supply.

Though only a few AR-3 rifles were ever made, they led to the AR-10 and, ultimately, to the AR-15. *The Black Rifle. M16 Retrospective* by R. Blake Stevens and Edward C. Ezell (Collector Grade Publications, Inc., Toronto, 1987) remains the best source of information about the AR-15/M16 series.

ARMALITE AR-10 RIFLE

Made by Artillerie-Inrichtingen, Zaandam, under license from ArmaLite, Hollywood, California.

Total production: about 5500. **Chambering:** 7.62x51 NATO, rimless. **Action:** locked by multiple lugs on the bolt head rotating into the barrel extension; gas operated, semi-automatic only.

DATA FOR TYPICAL RIFLE

41.3in overall, 6.85lb without magazine. 20in barrel, 4-groove rifling; RH, concentric. Detachable box magazine, 20 rounds. Pivoting-leaf sight. 2700 fps with M59 ball cartridges: Optional knife bayonet.

The 30-06 prototype showed enough promise for a 308 Winchester version to be made in the summer of 1955. Successfully tested at Fort Benning, a third experimental rifle ('AR-10A') had a plastic butt filled with foam, a large muzzle-brake/compensator and a charging handle on the receiver side.

About 50 semi-production AR-10B rifles were made in 1956, with a new gas tube above the barrel and an improved bolt carrier. A rifled steel liner lay inside an alloy barrel casing, and the charging handle was moved to the top of the receiver beneath the carrying handle.

Trials held in Springfield in the winter revealed that additional development was needed, but experiments with an improved rifle—in January 1957—ended disastrously when a bullet came out of the side of the barrel. Metallurgical analysis revealed flaws in the composite barrel, and a conventional steel pattern was substituted.

ArmaLite had granted manufacturing rights to the state-owned Artillerie-Inrichtingen in the hope that a Dutch government order would follow. ArmaLite retained the North American sales agency; Sidem International SA of Brussels was granted Europe and North Africa; Cooper-Macdonald, Inc., of Baltimore took charge of Australasia and the Far East; and, belatedly, Interarms of Alexandria, Virginia, assumed responsibility for southern Africa, plus Central and South America.

Several AR-10 derivatives appeared in 1958, among them a carbine/submachine gun, a sniper rifle and a light machine gun. The earliest AI-made rifles had perforated full length handguards. The ejection-port cover was held by a plunger instead of a spring-clip, and the original compensator was replaced by an open prong-type suppresser capable of handling rifle grenades. However, this seriously compromised the ability of the AR-10 to fire fully automatically; later guns had a new barrel with a slotted suppresser and circumferential ribs to support a grenade tail. A fluted wooden handguard appeared behind an abbreviated sheet-metal casing,

and the selector was altered so that the safety position was forward instead of upward.

Most rifles had an assortment of marks on the left side of the magazine housing, including the 'ARMALITE AR10' designation and an 'AI-in-a-triangle' trademark above the serial number. AR-10 rifles were optimistically touted worldwide in 1959. The design finished a creditable second to the FAL in South African trials of 1960, but a failed endurance test in Nicaragua lost a 7500-gun order for the National Guard.

When the Dutch also rejected the ArmaLite in favor of the FAL, Artillerie-Inrichtingen lost interest and work in Zaandam stopped. However, Interarms sold about 350 AI-made guns to Guatemala and perhaps 1750 to the Sudan, while Sidem had sold Portugal about a thousand South African-style guns—with a telescoping charging handle and an improved trigger—and Cooper-Macdonald disposed of a few in Burma.

ARMALITE AR-15 RIFLE

Tests undertaken in 1952-3 with an M2 Carbine chambering a shortened 222 Remington cartridge suggested that small-caliber high velocity bullets and light automatic rifles had a future. Though the experiments incurred official disapproval, the U.S. Army authorities prepared a specification in 1957 for a small-caliber selective fire rifle with a magazine capacity of at least 20 rounds but a loaded weight no greater than 6lb. Accuracy and trajectory were to be at least equal to the 30-caliber service rifle cartridge to 300yd, with wounding power equal to or preferably better than the 30 M1 Carbine pattern. The weapon was to chamber any suitable 22 cartridge.

Robert Fremont and James Sullivan altered the AR-10 to fire a modified 222 Remington round, avoiding lengthy ammunition development but accepting a penalty in the form of a small-capacity cartridge case. High velocity could be achieved only through high chamber pressures.

The first rifles weighed 6.12lb with a loaded 25-round magazine and were 37.5in overall. They had steel barrels and hollow fiber-glass-reinforced plastic butts. Muzzles were plain cylindrical, the selector lever rotated up to the safety position and the charging handle still lay beneath the carrying handle. About 20 of these early guns were made. The 'encircled Pegasus' ArmaLite trademark lay on the left side of the magazine housing above 'AR-15' and the Hollywood address.

Differences of opinion among Army experts had, meanwhile, increased the performance requirements from 300yd to 500yd. ArmaLite solved this by substituting the 222 Remington Special (known as 223 Remington from 1959) for the original 222 round, increasing propellant capacity. The AR-15 then gained a serious rival—the Winchester 224 Light-Weight Military Rifle ('WLAR'), created by Ralph Clarkson by amalgamating the best features of the company's previous autoloaders.

Ten AR-15 rifles were delivered in March 1958. Tests undertaken at Fort Benning, Aberdeen Proving Ground and Fort Greely were highly successful. Though doubts about the lethality of small-diameter bullets persisted, the AR-15 and the WLAR performed better than the 30-caliber T44E4. The ArmaLite was most reliable, though adversely affected by the use of 224E2 cartridges; the Winchester rifle could not chamber 222 Remington Special.

Trials suggested that the AR-15 charging handle should be moved to the rear of the receiver, as it could not be grasped through an arctic mitten and became too hot to hold during rapid fire. The safety position on the selector was altered to point forward, barrel weight was increased, and a flash suppresser was added. Magazine capacity was reduced to 20 rounds to compensate for weight added elsewhere.

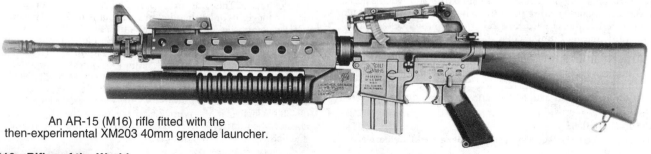

An AR-15 (M16) rifle fitted with the then-experimental XM203 40mm grenade launcher.

Fierce opposition from the Office of the Chief of Ordnance to the small-caliber high velocity concept was soon magnifying problems out of all proportion. An examination of optimal calibers then led to the rejection of 222-caliber in favor of 258.

Rifle trials recommenced on 1st December 1958, but the M14 was reaffirmed as the 'only rifle suitable for military use'; not surprisingly, Fairchild lost interest in the ArmaLite and licensed it to Colt in February 1959. The formation of ArmaLite, Inc., followed in 1961. However, Eugene Stoner and his design team had departed to join the Cadillac Gage Company (see 'Stoner').

The first Colt-made rifles ('AR-15 Model 01') were completed in December 1959, and modest orders were soon being fulfilled for Malaysia and India. The butts and handguards of the earliest guns had a mottled brown finish, later painted green. A rampant Colt trademark lay on the left side of the magazine housing, above 'ARMALITE' (plus 'AR15' on later examples), 'Patents Pending', the designation '01' and the serial number.

By 1960 Colt was advertising that, among other things, the AR-15 could fire more shots without cleaning than any rival. The U.S.A.F., actively seeking to replace obsolescent M2 Carbines, then requested that the AR-15 be reviewed. Trials confirmed accuracy and reliability, the failure rate being less than three rounds per 1,000, and the 223-caliber rifle was grudgingly cleared for Air Force scrutiny.

Trials were so encouraging that the U.S.A.F. asked for 8500 guns. Congress rejected the request, but growing interest in Vietnam could not be ignored. In January 1962, therefore, the 5.56mm Rifle AR-15 (later XM16, then M16) was classified as U.S.A.F. standard.

XM16 AND M16 RIFLES

On 15th May 1962, purchase of 20,000 guns was approved by Congress for the U.S.A.F., Navy SEALs and American advisers in Vietnam. The guns were soon being hailed as a suitable replacement for virtually all the existing service small-arms.

Owing to the lack of progress with the SPIW project, the U.S. Army soon renewed interest in the AR-15, acquiring 338 'XM-16' rifles in the autumn of 1962 for trials against the M14 and the Kalashnikov. After many tribulations, in 1963, the Secretary of the Army recommended the purchase of up to 100,000 AR-15 rifles for Army airborne units and special forces.

But the ArmaLite still had its enemies. Major faults were blamed—justifiably—on poor quality control of guns and ammunition, and minor problems continued to arise with exasperating frequency. Unfortunately, by ordering that only unavoidable changes should be made, the Secretary of Defense had ensured that correctional work was too often left undone.

New 1-in-12 rifling (instead of 1-in-14) was accepted on 26th July 1963 to safeguard bullet performance in sub-zero conditions. The Army then insisted on manual closure of the breech if a cartridge failed to chamber correctly, though neither the U.S.A.F. nor the USMC concurred and XM-16 rifles were made for some time alongside the XM16E1 pattern.

XM16E1 RIFLE

The addition of a 'forward assist', a bolt-closing plunger designed by Foster Sturtevant, allowed the breech to be closed manually. The handle lay on the rear right side of the XM-16 receiver above the pistol grip and advanced the designation to 'XM16E1'. Eventually, on 4th November 1963, Colt received the first large government contract—85,000 XM16E1 rifles for the Army and 19,000 M16s for the Air Force.

The first M16 and XM16E1 rifles were delivered in the Spring of 1964. They were similar to the AR-15, except that the butt and handguard were blacked, the charging handle had become a 'T'-bar, the firing pin was altered to minimize slam-firing tendencies, and the flash suppresser was strengthened. Magazine bodies were changed from steel to alloy. Marks included a rampant Colt on the left side of the magazine housing ahead of 'COLT' over 'AR-15'. Then—in four lines—came the property mark, the caliber, 'MODEL 02' and the serial number.

Reports of severe problems had filtered back from Vietnam by the beginning of 1965. Though many were traced to lack of maintenance, persistent extraction failures and misfires due to the bolt carrier rebounding from the breechface were much more serious.

The original buffer (made of compressible ring springs) was replaced in December 1966 by a multi-weight Sturtevant design, which not only cured the rebound problem but also reduced the cyclic rate and partly corrected the tendency of the bolt to run forward again after the last round had been fired.

Trials undertaken at Frankford Arsenal in December showed that the supposedly perfected service rounds jammed five times more frequently than those used throughout the original trials. Though better propellant was adopted in May 1966, fouling continued to plague the rifles for some months. However, Colt was given a second contract, signed on 16th June 1966 and later extended to 836,810 guns valued at $91.7 million. The future of the AR-15 was assured.

On 29th June 1966, a contract for nearly 20,000 XM148 (Colt CGL-4) 40mm grenade launchers for the XM16E1 was passed to Colt, the first shipment leaving for Vietnam in December. The XM148 proved to be a disaster, and was abandoned in 1967 after only 34,000 had been made. It was replaced by the AAI XM203 launcher, standardized in the summer of 1968 as the M203.

A new slotted compensator was approved in September 1966 and, in December, the Secretary of the Army reported that the XM16E1 was 'generally superior' for Army use. The ArmaLite rifle was recommended for adoption at the expense of the Stoner Model 63.

M16A1 RIFLE

Made by Colt's Patent Fire Arms Mfg. Co., Hartford, Connecticut; Harrington & Richardson, Worcester, Massachusetts; and the Hydra-Matic Division, General Motors Corporation, Ypsilanti, Michigan.

Total production: substantial. **Chambering:** 5.56x45, rimless. **Action:** as AR-10, above.

DATA FOR M16

39in overall, 6.31lb without magazine. 20in barrel (excluding flash suppresser), 6-groove rifling; RH, concentric. Detachable box magazine, 20 or 30 rounds. Pivoting-leaf sight. 3250 fps with M193 ball cartridges; 700-800 rds/min. M7 knife bayonet.

The XM16E1 was reclassified as 'M16A1' on 28th February 1967. On 3rd May, however, the Ichord Congressional Sub-Committee began its first deliberations into the controversy surrounding the rifle, reporting in October—oblivious of important details—that the entire program had been mishandled.

A chrome-plated chamber was approved to minimize extraction failures on 26th May 1967 and, on 30th June, the U.S. government bought manufacturing rights from Colt for $4.5 million plus a royalty on guns made under government license.

Reluctant to rely on Colt as the only supplier of ArmaLite rifles, the Department of Defense sought alternative contractors. On 19th April 1968, provisional contracts (eventually totaling 240,000 guns apiece) were agreed with the Hydra-Matic Division of General Motors and Harrington & Richardson—in circumstances that raised more than a few eyebrows in Congress.

Each new contractor delivered rifles from 1969 onward, easily distinguished by 'HYDRA-MATIC DIV.' over 'G.M. CORP.' on the left side of the magazine housing or 'HARRINGTON & RICHARDSON' on the left side of the receiver ahead of the selector. The Harrington & Richardson guns also displayed a prominent encircled lion trademark over 'H&R' on the magazine housing.

By the end of 1968, Colt reported that sales had amounted to 183,950 M16 (including about 40,000 export and commercial guns) and 830,630 XM16E1/M16A1.

The first 30-round magazines became available in 1969, though the requirement had arisen three years earlier. In November 1969, Colt accepted a 'definitized' contract (an amalgamation of two smaller orders provisionally awarded in 1968) for 740,800 M16A1 and a thousand M16 rifles. Colt and GM Hydra-Matic received new contracts in 1970 for 458,440 and 229,620 M16A1 rifles respectively. The GM-made rifles, despite doubts raised at the outset in Congress, were extremely well made.

XM16E2 AND M16A2 RIFLES

Heedless of U.S. Army apathy, the Marine Corps embarked on a program of improvements in 1980, eventually persuading the Joint Services Small Arms Program managers to acquire 50 Colt-made M16A1E1 rifles in November 1981.

The M16A1E1, having demonstrated its superiority, was officially designated M16A2 in September 1982 even though adoption was delayed until November 1983. The major changes concerned the new rear sight and a heavy barrel with 1-in-7 twist. The suppresser was redesigned to double as a muzzle brake, the pistol grip contours were refined, and the stock was filled with nylon foam. A three-shot burst mechanism replaced the fully-automatic capability of the M16A1.

The U.S. Army was initially scathing about the USMC improvements, especially as the change in rifling pitch prevented M193 ball ammunition being used. The burst-fire system also disliked, as the ability to fire automatically had offset the lack of confidence many individual soldiers still had in the 'knock-down' performance of small-caliber bullets. From 1985, however, the Army began to purchase M16A2 rifles in substantial quantities.

COMMERCIAL AND OTHER AR-15/M16-TYPE GUNS

Note: only guns chambering the 5.56x45 cartridge are included; the few 9x19 (9mm Parabellum) derivatives have been ignored on the grounds that they are submachine guns, and Squad Automatic Weapons are effectively light machine guns.

The changes made since the first edition of *Rifles of the World* have benefited greatly from publication of 'Colt M16 Model Numbers', contributed to the August 1993 issue of *Small Arms World Report* by Edward C. Ezell, C. Reed Knight and Robert E. Roy. However, identifying the guns often presents problems—particularly as the manufacturer's model numbers no longer appear on the receiver side.

In addition to Colt, ArmaLite guns are also being offered under other names—e.g., ArmaLite, Inc., of Geneseo, Illinois; Eagle Arms, Inc. (supplied by ArmaLite); and Olympic Arms. Knight's Armament Company of Vero Beach, Florida, is currently making a range of comparable guns under the 'Stoner' banner.

RIFLES

Model 601 AR-15. The original M16-type guns were offered commercially as the 'Colt Automatic Rifle' ('CAR'), alternatively known as the 'Model 01'.

Model 602 AR-15. These were the first XM16E1 rifles with the bolt-assist system. Government-issue guns are marked 'PROPERTY OF U.S. GOVERNMENT'; commercial and development guns are not.

Model 603 AR-15. This was the Colt designation for the perfected M16A1, with the bolt assist, a 20in barrel, and 1-in-12 rifling. Guns may also be found with Hydra-Matic (General Motors) or Harrington & Richardson marks.

Model 603K AR-15. A special model of the M16A1 made for the Korean armed forces, this is suitably marked in Korean—but has 'K'-prefix serial numbers below the designation 'M16A1'.

Model 604 AR-15. This was the U.S. Air Force designation for the standard M16 rifle, lacking the bolt assist.

Model 613 AR-15. An export version of the Model 603, retaining the bolt-assist system, this lacks U.S. government marks. A 20in barrel and 1-in-12 rifling remain standard. A similar gun made by Elisco in the Philippines is designated 'Model 613P'.

Model 614 AR-15. Lacking the bolt-assist device, this is basically a commercial 'export' version of the M16. A similar gun made in Singapore (q.v.) by Chartered Industries is designated 'Model 614S'.

Model 645 M16A2. This is the current standard U.S. Army rifle, with 1-in-7 twist, three-round burst firing instead of automatic-fire capability, and a fully adjustable rear sight. Guns have been made by Colt and by FN Mfg. Inc. of Columbia, South Carolina. Model 645E was an experimental adaptation with a pivoting front sight; an optical sight could be fitted to the rail vacated by the detachable carrying handle.

A US Army soldier pictured after the successful invasion of Grenada. Note the 'forward assist' or bolt-closing device on the receiver immediately above his right hand.

Model 655 AR-15 Sniper Rifle. Built experimentally on the basis of the Model 614 frame, but with a bolt assist in the receiver, this had adjustable open sights, an optical-sight mount and a sound suppresser. Only a few were made. The Model 656 was similar mechanically, but had a low-profile receiver lacking the standard carrying handle.

Model 701 M16A2. This is the commercial or 'export' version of the standard U.S. Army rifle, with the bolt-assist system and the ability to fire automatically restored in place of the three-round burst; 1-in-7 twist is standard.

Model 703 M16A2. Made for the United Arab Emirates, this gun lacks the three-shot burst capability (replaced by full-automatic operation) and the rear sight requires a special adjuster tool.

Model 705 M16A2 or 'M16A2E3'. Distinguished by a bolt assist and a three-round burst capability, this also has windage-adjustable sights.

Model 707 M16A2. This rifle combines the three-round burst capability and the adjustable rear sight of the M16A2 with a standard medium-weight M16A1 barrel.

Model 711 M16A2. Another of the guns embodying a combination of features, this is basically an M16A2 with the sights, automatic-fire capability and barrel of the M16A1. Sometimes advertised as the 'AR-15A2 Sporter II', it may be encountered with a commercial-pattern magazine restricted to five rounds.

Model 715 M16A2. Made by Diemaco, this is the standard Canadian C7 service rifle (q.v.).

Model 901 M16A3. Essentially similar to the Model 701, this combines fully-automatic capabilities with a flat-top receiver (lacking the carrying handle) and is thus suited to optical sights. The earliest receivers are marked 'M16A2'.

Model 905 M16A3. Basically a modified version of the M705, this shares the flat-top receiver of the M901. A three-round burst-firing mechanism replaces the fully-automatic capability.

HEAVY-BARREL RIFLES

Model 606 AR-15 HB. Originally known as the 'AR-15 Model 06', and also as the 'Heavy Assault Rifle M1', this heavy-barrel assault rifle weighed 7.5lb without its magazine or accessories. The 20in barrel had a 1-in-12 twist; the bolt assist was omitted. A Colt-modified BAR or standard M2 rifle-type bipod could be attached when required. The Model 606A had a bolt-assist mechanism, and the Model 606B had a four-position selector and an additional three-round burst facility. Several hundred were made for U.S. Army SAWS trials.

Model 611 AR-15 H-Bar. A commercial version of the Model 606, this lacked the bolt-assist mechanism. Model 611P was made specially for the Philippines (q.v.), where it has been made by the Elisco Tool Company with 'RP'-prefix serial numbers.

Model 616 AR-15 H-Bar. This is an export version of the Model 606, lacking the bolt-assist fittings.

Model 621 AR-15 H-Bar. A variant of the Model 603 (M16A1) rifle, intended for export sales, this retains the bolt-assist mechanism.

Model 737 M16A2 H-Bar. The commercial semi-automatic AR-15A2 H-Bar, introduced at the end of 1985, was similar to the M16A2—sharing the adjustable rear sight and case deflector, but the barrel diameter is maintained throughout its length (unlike that of the military M16A2). The 1-in-7 rifling twist is standard, together with the M16A1-type fixed rear sight and a fully-automatic capability.

Model 741 M16A2 H-Bar. A minor variant of the Model 737, this features the fully adjustable 'A2'-type rear sight. Introduced in 1987, the short-lived AR-15A2 Delta H-Bar—apparently derived from the M741—had a rubber-armored 3-9x optical sight on a special mount and an ambidextrous cheekpiece, under-cut to allow the charging handle to be retracted. The Delta H-Bar rifle weighed about 10lb with its sight.

Model 941 M16A3 H-Bar. Otherwise similar to the Model 741, retaining features such as the bolt assist and the adjustable rear sight, this has a flat-top receiver without a carrying handle.

CARBINES

Model 605A AR-15 carbine. Several prototypes of these were made, the earliest having a 16in barrel and a special short handguard. It could also fire two-shot bursts, necessitating a four-position selector. A bolt assist was fitted. The finalized commercial semi-automatic had a 16in barrel, a short (but otherwise standard) handguard and a collapsible butt. It was 35in overall (31.75in with the butt retracted) and weighed about 5lb with a loaded magazine. The Model 605B had an additional burst-firing capability, requiring an additional or fourth position on the selector. It also had a full-length handguard, with the muzzle of the 15in barrel protruding.

Model 651 AR-15 carbine. This was an export version of the M16A1-type carbine, with a bolt assist and a 14.5in barrel. The butt was a full-size fixed pattern.

Model 652 AR-15 carbine. Little more than a minor variant of the M651, this lacked the bolt-assist device and was thus basically a variant of the M16.

Model 653 AR-15 carbine. This could be distinguished from the M651, which it otherwise resembled, by the telescoping butt. A version made by Elisco in the Philippines ('Model 653P') has 'RP'-prefix serial numbers.

Model 654 AR-15 carbine. Derived from the Model 652, this displays a telescoping butt instead of the standard fixed pattern.

Model 720 M16A2 carbine. Known during development as the 'XM-4', then standardized as 'M4', this is a short M16A2 with a 14.5in barrel.

Model 723 M16A2 carbine. Intended for sale to the United Arab Emirates, though also used in small numbers by the U.S. Special Forces, this amalgamates an M16A1-type rear sight with a 14.5in barrel.

Model 725 M16A2 carbine. Made in Canada by Diemaco (q.v.), this gun serves the Canadian armed forces as the 'C8'. A version has also been made (as the M725A) with a fixed M16A1-type rear sight and a three-round burst instead of the fully-automatic capability.

Model 727 M16A2 carbine. Supplied to U.S. Special Forces, among other units, this is little more than a Model 725 with the fully-automatic capability restored at the expense of the three-round burst.

Model 925 M16A3 carbine. This amalgamates a flat-top receiver with the remaining features of the Model 725, including the three-round burst system.

Model 927 M16A3 carbine. A flat-top receiver pattern, this substitutes the ability to fire fully automatically for the three-round burst of the M925.

SUBMACHINE GUNS (5.56MM)

Model 231 Port Firing Weapon. Standardized in 1979, this lacks sights and is restricted to automatic fire. It lacks a butt—only the buffer protrudes from the rear of the receiver—and has a

A short-barreled Colt CAR-15 with a British Davin IRS-218 night sight.

rapid-pitch screw thread on the front of the barrel casing. The screw mates with a suitable ball mount in the U.S. Army M2 Bradley Fighting Vehicle. Known during development as the 'XM231', the gun can be dismounted in an emergency and fired by using the carrying handle as a rudimentary sight. The earliest prototypes had sliding butts, but these were soon abandoned.

Model 607 AR-15 submachine gun. The first experimental pattern had a 10in barrel, a sliding butt and a 3.5in flash suppresser. It lacked the bolt-assist system.

Model 608 CAR-15 Survival Rifle. Originally known simply as the Model 08, this shared the 10in barrel of the submachine gun, but had a fixed tubular butt, a truncated pistol grip and a cylindrical handguard. It was 29in overall and weighed 4.8lb without its magazine. Only 10 were made before the project was abandoned.

Model 609 AR-15 submachine gun or 'Commando' (XM177E1). Also known as the 'Army Model No. 1', this was an abbreviated version of the standard M16A1 rifle, with a bolt assist and a 10in barrel. The butt and pistol grip were shortened. Some of the earliest examples were fitted with a telescoping version of the conventional butt, though this was soon replaced by a tubular pattern. The submachine gun attracted the interest of the U.S. Army, which ordered 2815 in June 1966. First deliveries were made

A Colt CAR-15 with an M203 grenade launcher and an MWG drum magazine.

A Colt AR-15 A2 Sporter II (M16A1 type).

The XM-231 Port Firing Weapon was basically a cut-down M16 rifle.

in November. They retained the 10in barrel and had an unsatis-factory 4.5in flash-hider with a small-diameter exit port.

Model 610 AR-15 submachine gun (XM177). Acquired for tri-als with the U.S.A.F. in 1967, this lacked the bolt assist. The stock was a sliding type. Model 610B was similar, but had an additional three-round burst-firing capability and, therefore, a fourth posi-tion on the selector.

Model 619 AR-15 submachine gun. A commercial version of the M609, this retains the bolt-assist components.

Model 620 AR-15 submachine gun. Otherwise identical with the Model 610, this is a commercial variant of the M16 pattern and lacks the bolt assist.

Model 629 AR-15 submachine gun (XM177E2). Incorporating the bolt assist, and thus basically a shortened M16A1, this had an 11.5in barrel and a 4.5in flash suppresser.

Model 630 AR-15 submachine gun. This was the U.S.A.F. equivalent of the Model 629, lacking the bolt assist and thus a short-ened M16.

Model 639 AR-15 submachine gun. An 'export' or commercial-sale version of the Model 629, this lacked U.S. government markings.

Model 640 M16 submachine gun. Distinguished from the Model 639 by the absence of the bolt-assist unit, this was a com-mercial equivalent of the M630.

Model 649 AR-15 submachine gun. This revised form of the Model 609, with a 14in barrel but lacking the bolt assist, was made for the U.S.A.F. The receiver was marked 'GAU-5/A/A'.

Model 733 M16A2 Commando. Incorporating the full-auto-matic capability instead of the three-round burst, this also has a 11.5in barrel, a fixed rear sight, and 1-in-7 twist. The Model 733A is identical, but is restricted to bursts instead of automatic fire.

OTHER AR-15/M16 SERIES USERS

It is often difficult to assess whether rifles have been acquired directly from Colt on a commercial basis, through U.S. military aid programs, or from intermediaries. In the list that follows, 'M16' or 'M16A1' infers U.S. military surplus; guns supplied by Colt are given their commercial designations in accordance with the desig-nations given previously. In addition to countries covered sepa-rately—Canada, China, Korea, the Philippines, Singapore, Taiwan—many others have used ArmaLite-type rifles and carbines:

Australia (2500 assorted Models 613, 614 and 653, 1965-73).
Barbados (U.S. Army surplus).
Belize (ex-British M16 and some Colt Model 613, 1978-86).
Bolivia (M16A1, U.S. Army surplus?).
Brazil (Model 614 for Air Force, M16A1 for police and M16A2 for special anti-terrorist forces).
Britain (several thousand Model 614, plus a few Models 613 and 653, were purchased about 1967-80 for Special Forces and Limited Theatre use).
Brunei (Models 613 and 653).
Burma (M16A1, U.S. Army surplus?).
Cameroons (Model 613).
Chile (approximately 5500 M16A1 and Model 613, 1974-7).
Costa Rica (U.S. Army surplus?).
Denmark (acquired for police in the early 1970s).
Dominican Republic (at least 6,000 M16A1 and Model 613).
Ecuador (10,000-12,000 M16A1, Model 613 and Model 653).
El Salvador (32,600 M16A1, 1981-4).
Fiji (M16A1, M16A2 and Model 701).
Gabon (Model 613).
Ghana (roughly 5000-6500 M16A1 and Model 613).
Greece (about 500 Models 701 and 723 for the special forces).
Grenada (about 250 U.S. Army surplus M16A1).
Guatemala (U.S. Army surplus M16A1).
Haiti (500 Model 613).
Honduras (10,000 M16A1 and Model 613, 1977-83).
Indonesia (at least 78,500 M16A1 and Model 613, 1971-81).
Israel (97,000 M16A1, 65,000 Model 613 and 45,000 Model 653, 1970-85).
Jamaica (about 500 Model 613 and 100 Model 653).
Jordan (68,000 M16A1, 1967-75).
Kampuchea (ex-U.S. M16A1).
Lebanon (50,000 ex-U.S. Army M16A1, and 20,000 new Model 613 rifles distinguished by 'AL'-prefix numbers).
Lesotho (Models 613 and 653).
Liberia (Models 613 and 701).
Malaysia (about 200,000 Model 613 and 5000 Model 653).
Morocco (M16A1, Model 613 and Model 653).
New Zealand (Model 613).
Nicaragua (M16A1 and Model 613).
Nigeria (Korean-made).
Oman (Model 613).
Panama (M16A1 and Model 613).
Papua New Guinea (U.S. Army surplus).
Peru (U.S. Army surplus).
Qatar (about 4000 Model 613 and 2500 Model 653, 1981-3).
Somalia (U.S. Army surplus?).
South Africa (security police).
Sri Lanka (M16A1 and Model 723).
Thailand (89,000 U.S. Army surplus M16A1 in 1972-81, 55,000 Model 613 in 1975-85, and about 30,000 CIS Model 614-S in 1973-4.
Trinidad & Tobago (Model 613?).

A typical AR-18 rifle.

Tunisia.
Turkey (Models 711 and 723 for security forces).
Uganda (Model 616?).
United Arab Emirates (Models 613, 653, 703 and 727, from 1979 to date).
Uruguay (U.S. Army surplus).
Vietnam [South] (6,000 M16 and 938,000 M16A1, 1966-75).
Zaire (military surplus).

ARMALITE AR-18 RIFLE

Made by or for the ArmaLite Corporation, Costa Mesa, California, 1969-82; by Howa Machinery Ltd. Nagoya, Japan, 1972-3; and by the Sterling Engineering Co. Ltd, Dagenham, England, 1976-8.
Total production: not known. **Chambering:** 5.56x45, rimless. **Action:** as AR-10, above.

DATA FOR AR-18 RIFLE
38in overall, 7.18lb with loaded magazine. 18.25in barrel, 6-groove rifling; RH, concentric. Detachable box magazine, 20 or 30 rounds. Pivoting-leaf sight. 3185 fps with M193 ball cartridges; 700-800 rds/min. Optional knife bayonet.

Designed by Eugene Stoner specifically for tank and armored-vehicle crewmen, the 1961-vintage 7.62mm AR-16 rifle was promoted as an inexpensive alternative to the M14. Composed largely of stampings and parts that could be turned on a lathe, the rifle had a wooden butt that hinged to the left. It weighed about 8.75lb and had a 15in barrel, but only three were made.

After the defection of Stoner and his design team to the Cadillac Gage Corporation in 1963, Arthur Miller scaled-down the AR-16 for the 5.56mm cartridge. The resulting AR-18 had a tappet-type piston system in a tube above the barrel. The bolt carrier reciprocated on two guiding rods in the pressed-steel receiver, the integral charging handle doubling as a bolt-closure device. The gas system could not be adjusted, but the selector could be set for safety, semi-automatic or fully automatic fire. Like most of the 5.56mm Stoner-inspired rifles, the AR-18 had seven lugs on the rotating bolt; the position of the eighth was occupied by the extractor claw.

The AR-18 was unsuccessfully tested by the U.S. Army in 1964, still in the prototype stage, but even the refined guns purchased in 1965 generated little interest. Finally, a license was granted to Howa about 1969. Production was small, but included a few 223-caliber AR-180 sporters with distinctive wood stocks. Sterling Engineering briefly participated in the AR-18 program from 1976 onward, before developing an automatic rifle of its own (see **'Singapore: CIS'**).

• Armstrong & Taylor

A gun of this type, made in accordance with U.S. patent 37,025 of November 1862, was submitted to the U.S. Army trials of 1865. However, it was not among those that were selected for photography and may have been rejected in the examination stages. Designed by James Armstrong and John Taylor of Augusta, Kentucky, the barrel rotated on a longitudinal pin to expose the chamber; a cam-track cut in the barrel pin operated the extractor automatically as the breech was opened. Small numbers of Armstrong & Taylor sporting guns were made in the 1860s by the Norwich Arms Company of Norwich, Connecticut.

• A-Square

The products of this company—semi-custom rifles and proprietary ammunition, including some powerful big-game cartridges—gained nationwide acceptance only in the late 1980s.

HANNIBAL MODEL SPORTING RIFLE

Made by A-Square Co., Inc., Madison, Indiana (1983-91), and Bedford, Kentucky (1991 to date).

Currently in production. **Chambering options:** see notes. **Action:** locked by two lugs on the bolt head engaging recesses in the receiver as the bolt handle is turned down.

DATA FOR A TYPICAL RIFLE
Chambering: 9.3x62, rimless. About 45.5in overall, 9.42lb empty. 26in barrel, 4-groove rifling; RH, concentric? Integral box magazine, 5 rounds. Express sight. 2330 fps with 285-grain bullet.

Built on a modified P/17 Enfield (q.v.) action, the Hannibal has an adjustable target-type trigger and a manual safety catch on the bolt shroud. Most guns offer hand checkered oil-finished Claro walnut stocks, with the company's patented Coil-Chek recoil suppresser, a straight comb and a deep pistol grip with a notably tight radius; excellent bedding was achieved with a composite steel and fiberglass insert. Some synthetic stocks (apparently Du Pont Rynite) have also been used.

Two sturdy bolts ran laterally through the stock to dissipate recoil effects. Three-leaf Express sights could be fitted to order, but most purchasers have preferred guns with bases for optical-sight mounts.

A wide variety of chamberings has been offered. Group I rifles have been offered in 270 Winchester (prior to 1990 only), 30-06 or 9.3x62 (from 1988). Group II options have included 7mm Remington Magnum, 300 Winchester Magnum, 308 Norma Magnum (prior to 1987), 338 Winchester Magnum, 416 Taylor (from 1988), 425 Express (from 1989) and 458 Winchester Magnum.

Group III Hannibals have been made for cartridges such as 7mm STW (1990), 300 H&H Magnum, 300 Weatherby Magnum, 8mm Remington Magnum (from 1988), 340 Weatherby Magnum, 9.3x64 (from 1988), 375 H&H Magnum, 375 Weatherby Magnum, 375 JRS (1990 only), 404 Jeffrey (from 1991), 416 Hoffmann, 416 Remington Magnum (introduced in 1989), 450 Ackley Magnum, 458 Lott (from 1989) and 470 Ruark (1990 only).

Group IV rifles have been made for a selection of proprietary A-Square rounds—including 338, 375, 460 Short, 460 Long, 495 and 500—as well as 378 Weatherby Magnum, 404 Jeffrey (1988-91 only), 416 Rigby and 460 Weatherby Magnum. The largest guns weigh up to 11.75lb.

SIMILAR GUNS

Hamilcar Model Rifle, 1994 to date. This is a lightweight version of the Hannibal, chambered for cartridges including 25-06, 6.5x55, 257 Weatherby Magnum, 264 Weatherby Magnum, 270 Weatherby Magnum, 270 Winchester, 7x57, 7mm Remington Magnum, 7mm STW, 7mm Weatherby Magnum, 280 Remington, 30-06, 300 Weatherby Magnum, 300 Winchester Magnum, 338-06 or 9.3x62.

CAESAR MODEL SPORTING RIFLE

Dating from 1984, this is built on a Remington Model 700 action and supplied only in a wood stock. A left-hand version has been made in small numbers. Chamberings of groups I, II and III rifles generally duplicate those of the Hannibal pattern described previously, but Caesar rifles are not offered in A-Square magnum versions and are about 8oz lighter than comparable Hannibals.

• Auto-Ordnance

Best known for the Thompson submachine gun—also offered in long-barreled semi-automatic forms—this gunmaking business was also the promoter of the Thompson autoloading rifles (q.v.). Most of the manufacturing was undertaken by Colt. Another business of the same name, established in West Hurley, New York, currently makes a range of Colt-Browning type pistols in addition to Thompson submachine gun look-alikes.

• Ball

This repeating carbine was made in accordance with a series of patents granted in 1863-4 to a talented engineer, Albert Ball,

The A-Square Hannibal,
built on a modified M17 (Enfield) action.

who perfected the design in the employment of E.G. Lamson & Company.

The cartridge elevator or 'carrier' formed part of the breech-block. This carrier took a cartridge from the tube magazine beneath the barrel, transported it to the chamber, then extracted and ejected the spent case. The chamber was formed partly by the inside contours of the frame and partly by the cartridge elevator, but proved to be a serious weakness in an otherwise efficient design; chambering precision deteriorated as the components began to wear.

REPEATING CARBINE

Made by E.G. Lamson & Co., Windsor, Vermont.

Total production: 1500? **Chambering:** 56-50 Spencer, rimfire. **Action:** locked by pivoting the underlever to prop the cartridge carrier in place behind the chamber.

37.6in overall, 7.38lb empty. 20.7in barrel, 5-groove rifling; RH, concentric. Tube magazine in forend, 9 rounds. Folding-leaf rear sight. About 900 fps with 435-grain bullet. No bayonet.

On 6th June 1864, the federal government placed an order for 1,000 guns. The action had been designed for a special 50-caliber cartridge, but the authorities ordered Lamson to use 56-50 Spencer cartridges to simplify ammunition supply. Consequently, the perfected carbine would hold nine Spencer or 12 Ball cartridges.

Ball carbines had a two-piece stock with a tube magazine in the forend. There were two iron barrel bands, the barrel was blued, and the case-hardened receiver had a side hammer. The guns ordered by the federal authorities were all delivered into store on 14th May 1865, but were too late to see service and were eventually sold at auction.

SIMILAR GUNS

Sporting carbines. A few of these were made after the end of the American Civil War, chambered for the 44 Henry rimfire cartridge. One gun was submitted to the U.S. Army trials of 1865-6, but was not among those that were photographed. This may simply indicate that the design was already too well known or, alternatively, that it was rejected in the examination stages.

• Ballard

Patented by Charles Ballard in November 1861, this dropping-block design was very successful. The breechblock contained the hammer, trigger mechanism and springs. When the operating lever was pushed down, the front of the block—loosely pivoted in the rear of the frame—dropped radially down and away from the chamber, disengaging the back of the breechblock from shoulders in the receiver behind the hammer.

The pre-1873 extractor bar, under the barrel, was actuated by a large stud projecting from the underside of the forend. The stud was slid backward manually.

The rifles were made in Worcester, Massachusetts, first by Ball & Williams (1861-4) and then by R. Ball & Company (1864-6)—though a few had been made in 1862-3 by Dwight Chapin & Company of Bridgeport, Connecticut, under contract to Merwin & Bray. Postwar production passed to Merrimack Arms & Mfg. Co. (1867-9) and thence to the Brown Mfg. Co. (1869-73), both of Newburyport, Massachusetts.

When the Brown Mfg. Co. failed, rights to the Ballard were acquired by Schoverling & Daly of New York in 1873; manufacture was licensed two years later to John Marlin of New Haven, Connecticut. Marlin-made rifles show many detail improvements on pre-1873 examples, though the earliest often incorporated Brown-made parts. The butt was attached by a bolt running up through the wrist into the back of the receiver; an automatic extractor replaced the old manually-operated pattern; and the breechblock was made in two halves.

The layout of the operating springs was changed, but not for the better: the original coil-pattern trigger spring was more reliable than the folded-leaf replacement.

Owing to its strength and availability, the Ballard action was used as the basis for many custom guns—prior to 1890, even Marlin made non-standard examples to order.

1865 TRIALS CARBINE

The gun submitted to the U.S. Army trials of 1865-6 (photographed as 'No. 3') was identical with those being made at the end of the American Civil War. The short forend was held by a single screwed band, and swivels lay beneath the band and butt.

NO. 1 HUNTING RIFLE

Made by J. M. Marlin, New Haven, Connecticut, 1876-80.

Total production: not known. **Chambering options:** 44 rim and centerfire, 44 Ballard Long, 44 Ballard Extra-Long, or 45-70. **Action:** locked by propping the breechblock behind the chamber with the tip of the operating lever.

DATA FOR A TYPICAL EXAMPLE

Chambering: 44 Ballard Extra Long. 45.25in overall, 8.05lb empty. 30in barrel, 6-groove rifling; RH, concentric. Single shot only. Standing-block rear sight. 1320 fps with 265-grain bullet.

Introduced in 1876, the first Marlin-made Ballard rifles were advertised with a round barrel (26-30in), a blued frame, a Marlin-patent automatic extractor, and a special reversible firing pin for rim- or center-fire ammunition. The original rifle was renamed 'No.1' when additional patterns appeared, and a 45-70 chambering was introduced in addition to 44 Ballard Long and Extra-Long.

SIMILAR GUNS

No. 1 1/2 Hunter's Model, 1879-83. Chambered for 40-63 Ballard or 45-70 Government cartridges, the No. 1 1/2 was a No. 1 with an extra-heavy wrought iron frame. A typical rifle was 47.3in overall, with a 32in round barrel, and weighed 10.07lb. A rifle-type buttplate and Rocky Mountain sights were standard.

No. 1-3/4 Far West Model, 1879-82. Introduced in 1879, for 40-65 Ballard Everlasting or 45-70 Government rounds only, this was a minor variant of the No. 1 1/2 distinguished externally only by its double set trigger.

No. 2 Sporting Model, 1876-89. Introduced in for 32-, 38-, 41- or 44-caliber rim- and center-fire cartridges, this had an octagonal barrel, a reversible firing pin, and a blued frame. A variant chambering '.44 Colt and Winchester Center-Fire' (44-40 WCF) was added in 1882, but 41 Extra Long and 44 Extra Long were abandoned. The 32-caliber version was sold with a 28in barrel, and weighed 8.25lb; 38-caliber patterns had 30in barrels and weighed 8.75lb; 44-caliber examples, also generally made with 30in barrels, were about 45.25in overall and weighed 9lb empty. Most had Rocky Mountain sights.

No. 3 Gallery Model, 1876-89. Featuring a 24-30in octagon barrel and open sights, this was chambered only for the 22 Short and Long rimfire rounds. A 'Fine' or deluxe pattern ('No. 3F') was made in 1882-7 with a pistol grip butt and an 'Off Hand' buttplate.

No. 3 1/2 Target Model, 1880-1. Chambered only for the 40-55 Everlasting cartridges, this had a 30in octagon barrel, peep-and-globe sights, and a shotgun-type buttplate.

No. 4 Perfection Model, 1876-89. This was intended for hunting in 38-, 40-, 44-, 45- and 50-caliber centerfire, and usually had open Rocky Mountain sights. So-called 'Everlasting Shells', specifically intended for reloading, were recommended for the No. 4. It had an octagonal barrel (26-32in) and an extra-heavy heavy case-hardened receiver. By 1881-2, guns had been chambered for the proprietary 32-40, 38-50, 38-55, 40-63, 40-65, 40-70 and 44-75 Ballard cartridges, plus 44-77 Sharps and the 45-70 or 50-70 Government patterns. In 1883, however, Marlin had reduced the options

A Civil War-period Ballard carbine. The knob protruding from the forend works the manual extractor. (W&W)

to 32-40, 38-55 or 40-63 only. A typical 40-63 example, with a 30in round barrel, was about 45.35in overall and weighed 9.95lb empty.

No. 4 1/2 Mid-Range Model, 1878-81. The No. 4 1/2 rifle had a pistol grip butt and a half-length forend, woodwork being extensively checkered. The barrels were half- or fully octagonal, and an improved peep-and-globe sight system was fitted. A typical 40-90 example was about 45.5in overall, had a 30in barrel and weighed 10.25lb. Chamberings included 38-50 Ballard, 40-70 Sharps, 40-90 Ballard, 40-90 Sharps, 44-75 Ballard, 44-77 Sharps, 44-90 Sharps (2.63 and 2.88in cases) or 44-100 Ballard, plus 45-70 and 50-70 Government.

No. 4 1/2 A.1 Mid-Range Model, 1879-83. A minor variant of the No. 4 1/2, this had a fine English walnut half-stock, Marlin's improved 800yd Vernier rear sight, and a wind-gauge front sight with bead and aperture discs. The frame was engraved, the optional shotgun- or rifle-type buttplate was rubber, and every part was 'finished in the best manner'. Frames usually displayed 'Mid-Range A.1' in an engraved panel.

No. 5 Pacific Model, 1876-89. This was a modified No. 4 (q.v.), with an extra-heavy iron frame, a heavy octagonal barrel (30-32in), double set triggers, and—unlike other Ballards—a cleaning rod beneath the muzzle. Rocky Mountain sights were standard. New 40-85 and 45-100 options were announced in 1882. Weights ranged from 10lb for the 38-55 version to 12lb for the 45-100 type. A typical 32in-barreled 45-caliber example was 47.3in overall. By the time production ended, rifles had been chambered for 38-50 Ballard, 38-55 Ballard, 40-63 Ballard, 40-65 Ballard, 40-70 Sharps, 40-85 Ballard, 40-90 Ballard, 44-40 Winchester, 44-75 Ballard, 44-77 Sharps, 45-70 Government or 45-100 Ballard cartridges.

No. 5 1/2 Montana Model, 1882-3. Essentially a heavier No. 5, this had a ring-tip breech lever instead of a spur and chambered for the 45-caliber Sharps cartridge (2.88in case). Rifle- or shotgun-style buttplates were supplied to order. A typical gun was 47.15in long, had a 30in barrel and weighed about 13.6lb.

No. 6 Schuetzen Model, 1876-89. Known as the 'Off-Hand Model', this was intended for European-style target shooting popular in the eastern U.S.A. Originally chambered only for 40-65 and 44-75 cartridges, it had a half-octagonal barrel and weighed up to 15lb. A double set-trigger system was standard. Most guns were fitted with Marlin's 800yd short or mid-range Vernier peep rear sights. Hand-made straight-wrist 'German' (Swiss) style butts, with a cheekpiece and a nickel plated hook-pattern shoulder plate, were standard fittings.

By 1883, the chambering options—which had included 32-40 Ballard, 38-50 Ballard, 38-55 Ballard, 40-65 Ballard or 44-75 Ballard—were being restricted to 32-40 or 38-50. A typical 38-50 example, with a 30in barrel, was 48.05in overall (including the butt-plate hook) and weighed 14.11lb.

No. 6 1/2 Off Hand Model, 1876-89. Also known as the 'No. 6 1/2 Rigby', this rifle was little more than a modified No. 6. The 'German'-pattern walnut butt had a checkered pistol grip and a Farrow shoulder plate. The barrels, measuring 28in or 30in, were bought from John Rigby & Company of London. Marlin 800yd mid-range Vernier rear sights and wind-gauge pattern front sights were standard fittings. The receivers of most rifles were engraved with scrollwork, though differences in pattern are known. A typical 28in-barreled rifle measured 44.5in overall and weighed 10.12lb.

No. 7 Long-Range Model, 1877-82. About 50.5in overall with a 34in barrel and a weight of 10.25lb, the No. 7—chambered only for the 45-100 Ballard cartridge—had a half-octagon barrel and an improved 1300yd Vernier rear sight. The wind-gauge front sight was supplied with bead and aperture discs, plus a spirit level. Hand-made pistol grip butts were standard, with scroll engraving on the action, checkering on the pistol grip, and a schnabel-tipped forend.

No. 7 A.1 Long Range Model, 1877-80. These were deluxe variants of the No.7, with Rigby barrels, special 'extra handsome English walnut stocks', rubber shoulder plates, and Vernier sights of the finest pattern.

No. 7 A.1 Extra Model, 1876-8. A few of these were made with high-quality engraving and wood selected for its superb figuring.

No. 7 Creedmoor Model. These were basically leftover No. 7 actions, assembled in 1885-6 from parts on hand and advertised as an illusory 'new pattern'.

No. 8 Long Range Model. The first or old-pattern No. 8 also had a pistol grip butt, though much plainer than the standard No. 7.

No. 9 Long Range Model. This was simply No. 8 with a straight-wrist butt. Production ended about 1882.

Union Hill Models, No. 8 new and No. 9 new patterns, 1884-9. Introduced to compete in the medium-price target rifle market, these had half-octagon barrels (28in or 30in) and pistol grip butts with cheekpieces. A nickeled Farrow 'Off Hand' buttplate was usually supplied. Double set triggers and peep-and-globe sights were standard on the No. 8, the otherwise similar No. 9 being made with a single trigger. Looped finger levers were common on rifles sold after 1887. A typical gun with a 30in barrel, chambering the 32-40 Ballard round, was 46.5in overall and weighed 9.65lb.

No. 10 Schuetzen Junior Model. Offered only for the 32-40 or 38-55 Ballard cartridges, this 1884-vintage target rifle—often fitted with a short butt—was essentially the same as the No. 8 Union Hill pattern described previously. However, it had a heavy octagonal barrel and a 800yd Vernier-type Mid Range rear sight. A typical 32-caliber example was 48.5in overall and weighed 11.85lb. Its barrel measured 32in.

• Bannerman

Francis Bannerman & Sons of New York was best known for their unparalleled success—at least in the Anglo-American world—as military surplus dealers, selling everything from cap badges to armed yachts. The collection of so much raw material enabled Bannerman to assemble rifles which match no known pattern.

MANNLICHER-SPRINGFIELD RIFLE

This was a combination of the Reichsgewehr action (see 'Germany') and a 1903-type Springfield 30-caliber barrel with the chamber altered to accept the 7.65mm Mauser cartridge. The gun also had a Krag-type tangent-leaf rear sight.

MAUSER-SPRINGFIELD RIFLE

In 1914-15, as a patriotic acknowledgement of their Scottish ancestry, the Bannermans supplied a thousand rifles to help the British war effort. They were based on M1903 Springfield receivers, originally condemned because of brittleness, which had subsequently been subjected to remedial heat treatment by R.F. Sedgley of Philadelphia. These were given Krag barrels, re-chambered for the 303 British rimmed cartridge, and fitted into Springfield stocks. Sights and trigger guards were provided by the Krag; handguards and magazine followers were reclaimed from Mausers. The company crest and an arched 'BANNERMAN' appeared above the chamber.

Unfortunately, the guns would not handle British military ammunition satisfactorily, and were accordingly reduced to Drill Purpose status on inspection—an unfortunate end to a generous gesture. They had probably been set-up for Canadian ammunition, which, when serious problems occurred with the Ross rifles, was found to be smaller in the body than its British equivalent.

• Beal

Beal Carbine No. 4, tested by the U.S. Army in 1865, had a two-piece stock and a half-length forend held by a single sprung band. The buttplate was a crescent pattern, but the most obvious feature was the sheath trigger. It is believed that the gun operated by swinging the chamber and barrel unit laterally. No patentee has yet been identified.

• Beals

The better known gun of this name was the work of Fordyce Beals—better known as a handgun designer—who developed a rifle with a barrel which slid forward when the underlever was operated. The subject of three patents granted between June 1864 and January 1866, protecting the action and extraction/ejection systems, a 44-caliber Beals sporting rifle was made in small numbers by E. Remington & Sons. It had a straight-wrist butt with a crescent-shape shoulder plate, a half-octagon barrel and a closed-loop underlever similar to the Henry or Winchester types.

A wooden model of a lever-action gun with a toggle-locked two-wedge breech system, possibly resembling the National carbine (q.v.) in spirit if not detail, was submitted to the U.S. Army in 1872 by A.C. Beals, who may have been Fordyce Beals' son. However, nothing else is known.

• Berdan, block-action type

These guns were designed by General Hiram Berdan, who had achieved lasting fame in the American Civil War as the instigator of the federal sharpshooters regiments.

The breech system—similar to many of the transformations offered in the mid-1860s—was patented in the U.S.A. in February

1866. A gun of this type was submitted to the U.S. Army trials of 1865-6, but was not among those that were photographed at the time. This may simply indicate that the design was regarded as too well known, or that it had been rejected in the examination stages. Two other guns (conversions of a 577-caliber British Enfield and a 58-caliber U.S. Springfield rifle-musket) were tried in 1867, when they performed very well. However, the Springfield-Allin was preferred and the only real success encountered by the Berdan lifting-block system occurred in Spain (q.v.).

Berdan also developed an action relying on a straight-line striker instead of a clumsy external hammer; this was the subject of a U.S. patent granted in March 1869. Drawing back the striker allowed the breechblock to be raised, extracting a spent case and gaining access to the chamber. A cartridge was then inserted, the breech was shut and the gun could be fired; the mechanism was locked at the moment of discharge by the striker-nose running forward into the back of the breechblock. Made by Colt, substantial quantities of 1869-type guns were supplied to Tsarist Russia (q.v.).

• Berdan, bolt-action type

Patented in the U.S.A. in November 1870, this rifle served only in Russia (q.v.) and Bulgaria. It was a straightforward design, derived from the old Dreyse and Chassepot needle rifles, with a sturdy split-bridge receiver and a short bolt body with a massive rib doubling as a locking shoulder.

The cocking piece was prevented from rotating by a 'finger' projecting forward into the receiver. A spring-loaded striker ran through the center of the bolt to ignite the cartridge; an extractor was mounted in the guide rib; and—on the patent drawings at least—the ejector lay in the bottom of the receiver beneath the bolt way. Russian-made rifles lacked ejectors, forcing the firers to tip spent cases out of the receiver.

• Bighorn

The Bighorn Rifle Company of Orem and subsequently American Fork, Utah, made sporting rifles on commercial Mauser actions in 1983-7, apparently FN or Spanish Santa Barbara types. Made to individual specifications in chamberings from 22-250 Remington to standard medium-length magnums, the Bighorn rifle usually had a good quality straight-comb half-stock with hand-cut checkering and a rounded ebony or rosewood forend tip. Two barrels were supplied with each gun.

• Blake

This interesting but obscure rifle was designed by John Blake of New York City. Two 30-caliber prototypes were tested by the U.S. Army in 1891-3, but were unable to challenge the Krag-Jørgensen. Both were stocked in military fashion, had seven-round spool magazines, and weighed 9.63lb.

Blake subsequently sought a patent, granted in July 1898, and rifles were advertised commercially in Grades A (best) to D (plain). The standard 'D'-grade rifle was offered in 236 Lee, 7x57, 30-40 Krag, 30-30 Winchester or proprietary 400 Blake chamberings. The magazine accepted a detachable seven-round spool. Barrels are said to have measured 18-30in, the profile being round, octagon or partly octagonal. Weights were claimed to be 7.5-9lb, depending on barrel length; stocks had straight or pistol grip wrists.

Surviving rifles are extremely scarce, and it seems as though series production was never undertaken; however, one gun reportedly bears a three-digit number and another may have borne the marks of the British gunmaker W.W. Greener (q.v.), suggesting some export sales.

• Boswell

The name of Charles Boswell was originally among the leading London gunmakers, renowned for shotguns and double-barreled rifles of impeccable quality. In 1988, however, the business was purchased by U.S. interests and moved—lock, stock and barrel—to Charlotte, North Carolina. A limited quantity of rifles is made annually, based on Anson & Deeley box-lock or Holland & Holland sidelock designs. Chamberings have ranged from 300 Express to the mighty 600 Nitro Express.

• Broadwell

Lewis Broadwell was granted a U.S. patent in August 1865 to protect a rifle opened by turning the trigger guard to the right, which used a rapid-pitch screw thread to drop the breech plug. A variation on a well-tried theme, with ancestry dating back to the Frenchman de la Chaumette (1714) and the better-known Ferguson of the Revolutionary War period, there is no evidence that the Broadwell rifle was ever made in quantity. The inventor is better known for his machine gun feed, and for collaborating with Murray Durst (q.v.).

• Broughton

John Broughton of New York submitted three differing rifles to the U.S. Army breech-loading rifle trials of 1872. Gun No. 18, a 50-caliber musket, embodied a variation of the radial breechblock patented in April 1868 (no. 76,595). This relied on an underlever to disengage a 'locking brace', pivoting in the frame, from a shoulder in the radial block before the breech could open. The rifle had a distinctive appearance, with the tip of the breechblock protruding above the step in the elongated frame and an exposed hammer spur at the rear.

Gun No. 45, another 50-caliber musket, had a chamber-block which swung out to the right of the gun when the locking bolt had been slid back and the thumb-catch had been pressed. The general design resembled the Needham type (q.v.), and was equally unacceptable. Broughton Gun No. 79, a 42-caliber musket, relied on a vertically swinging block pivoted at the front of the chamber. This was locked by a combination of the hammer nose and the firing-pin sleeve—fitted with a thumb latch—entering the standing breech.

• Brown

The Brown Precision Co. of Los Molinos, California, introduced the 'High Country' sporting rifle in about 1975; it was still being made in 1992. Offered with a fiberglass stock, the rifle had a Model 700 Remington action and an internal five-round magazine (four in 7mm); chambering options included 243 Winchester, 25-06, 270 Winchester, 7mm Remington Magnum or 30-06. German-made Blaser (q.v.) bolt-action rifles were imported prior to 1989.

• Browning, autoloading type

Details of most of these will be found elsewhere—see **'Belgium: FN, autoloading type'**. However, a modified form of the BAR was introduced in 1993 as the 'BAR Mark II Safari'. This has a new hold-open system and a detachable trigger, with changes to the gas system and buffer unit to improve reliability. The BOSS system (see bolt-action guns, below) can be supplied with optically-sighted Mark II guns.

• Browning, block-action type

This dropping-block breech mechanism was patented by John Browning in October 1879 (U.S. 220,271), though commercial success awaited the introduction of a slightly modified pattern by Winchester in 1885. It is one of the sturdiest and most compact of its type ever to have been made, and still attracts many copyists— e.g, Clerke Recreation Products, Falling Block Works, Montana Armory, and Serrifile.

The breechblock slid vertically in the sturdy receiver, the external hammer being pivoted in the block. As the operating lever was depressed, the pressure of the mainspring was taken off the hammer, and the breechblock rose imperceptibly to release the toggle-type lock formed by the link bar. Further movement pulled the breechblock down into the receiver, lowering the hammer past

The Browning BAR Mk II rifle.

the sear until the chamber was exposed for extraction, ejection and reloading.

Returning the lever closed the breech and—by connecting the hammer and sear—cocked the trigger mechanism and rotated the link-bar to its locked position. The gun could then be fired. Alternatively, the hammer could be dropped under thumb control with the trigger pressed; just before the face of the hammer reached the breechblock, the trigger could be released and the hammer retracted until the sear engaged a safety notch in the hammer body. To fire, the hammer had then to be thumbed back to full-cock before pressing the trigger.

1878-PATTERN RIFLE

John Browning began work on his dropping-block action in 1878, seeking to improve on the popular Sharps (q.v.). J.M. Browning & Brother of Ogden, Utah, began to make rifles to special order in 1880, though doubt has been cast on the traditional production estimate of 600 and the supposed transfer of partly completed rifles when John and Matthew Browning sold rights to the Winchester Repeating Arms Company in 1883. Very few original rifles survive and is suspected that only 150-200 were made. They were very similar to the later 'High Wall' Winchesters (q.v.), but their receivers were not as angular and the joint between the butt and receiver was straight instead of curved. Browning rifles also had heavier hammers than their Winchester counterparts and were simpler internally.

MODEL 78 SPORTING RIFLE
Also known as 'B-78'

Made for the Browning Arms Company, Morgan, Utah, by the Miroku Firearms Mfg Co., Kochi, Japan,1973-83.

Total production: not known. **Chambering options:** see text. **Action:** locked by propping the breechblock behind the chamber with the tip of the operating lever.

DATA FOR A TYPICAL EXAMPLE

Chambering: 30-06, rimless. 42in overall, 7.63lb empty. 26in barrel, 6-groove rifling; RH, concentric. Single shot only. Spring-leaf and elevator rear sight. 2910 fps with 150-grain bullet.

This Japanese-made 're-creation' of the original 1878 pattern rifle was chambered for the 22-250, 6mm Remington, 270 Winchester or 30-06 cartridges. It had a straight receiver/butt joint and the receiver tangs were reduced to a minimum. The standard barrels were octagonal, though a round pattern was optional. The checkered schnabel-tipped forend was accompanied by a pistol grip butt with a cheekpiece, a Monte Carlo comb and a solid rubber shoulder plate. Changes made in the B-78 action created the Model 1885 (below).

SIMILAR GUNS

Model 78 Bicentennial rifle. Work on 1,000 special 45-70 rifles celebrating the U.S. Bicentennial began in 1975, a simplifed version subsequently being offered commercially with a 24in octagon barrel, a straight-comb butt, and a die-cast concave shoulder plate.

MODEL 1885 SPORTING RIFLE

Made for the Browning Arms Company, Morgan, Utah, by the Miroku Firearms Mfg Co., Kochi, Japan,1987 to date.

The Browning M85 rifle, a recreation of the legendary Winchester-made gun.

Currently in production. **Chambering options**: see text. **Action:** as Model 78, above.

DATA FOR A TYPICAL EXAMPLE

Chambering: 45-70, rimmed. 43.5in overall, 8.75lb empty. 28in barrel, 4-groove rifling; RH, concentric. Single shot only. Spring-leaf and elevator rear sight. 1320 fps with 405-grain bullet.

Miroku delivered the first examples of this improved B-78 in the Spring of 1988, similar externally to their predecessors but with a cartridge-case deflector (behind the breechblock) which could be adjusted to suit left- or right-handed shooters. The straight-wrist butt had a plain solid-rubber shoulder plate, while the half-length forend had a schnabel tip. Open sights were standard fittings on the 45-70 version, though the others—22-250, 6mm Remington, 25-06, 270 Winchester, 7mm Remington Magnum or 30-06—were tapped and drilled for optical-sight mounts. The original M1885 has been known since 1995 as the 'High Wall' pattern, owing to the introduction of a lighter Low Wall type.

SIMILAR GUNS

Model 1885 Low-Wall rifle, 1995 to date. Made with a light-weight receiver and a tapering 24in octagon barrel, this has a pistol grip butt and a schnabel-tip forend. Chamberings are currently restricted to 22 Hornet, 223 Remington and 243 Winchester; a typical gun is 39.25in long and weighs 6.25lb. The frame is blued.

Model 1885 BPCR rifle, introduced in 1996. Small numbers of these have been made for the 40-65 and 45-70 cartridges, with 30in octagon barrels, and color case-hardening on the frame and lever. The rear sight is a Vernier-adjustable peep pattern mounted on the tang behind the hammer, and the globe-type front sight has an integral spirit level. BPCR rifles are 46.2in long and weigh about 11lb.

• Browning, bolt-action type

This section contains details of the rifles marketed under the Browning Arms Company name. Browning also handles a wide variety of handguns and shotguns. Though some of the pistols are made in the U.S.A., most of the longarms are made in Belgium or Japan.

BROWNING-MAUSER SPORTING RIFLE

The Browning Arms Company—then of St. Louis, Missouri—offered rifles built on FN-Mauser actions from 1959 onward. They had simplified triggers, inspired by the Winchester Model 70, and a modified bolt stop which could be pressed inward to release the bolt. A safety slider lay on the tang behind the bolt shroud. The earliest guns were chambered for 243 Winchester, 264 Winchester Magnum, 270 Winchester, 300 H&H Magnum, 30-06, 308 Winchester, 338 Winchester Magnum, 375 H&H Magnum or 458 Winchester Magnum cartridges. Others (e.g., 7mm Remington Magnum and 308 Norma Magnum) were added at a later date.

The Browning-Mausers were available until 1974; however, the 243 and 308 Winchester options were abandoned when the Sako medium-action sporters were introduced in 1965. Standard rifles had 22in barrels and weighed 7.1-7.2lb. Buttplates were solid rubber. Magnums had 24in barrels, weighed about 8.25lb, and were fitted with ventilated-rubber shoulder pads.

SIMILAR GUNS

Safari Grade. These guns had folding-leaf rear sights, select walnut stocks with Monte Carlo combs, and hand-cut checkering on the pistol grip and forend.

A long-barreled Browning A-Bolt Magnum rifle.

A stainless-steel Browning
A-Bolt rifle, with a left-hand action.

Medallion Grade. Introduced in 1961, this had scroll engraving on the receiver and barrel. A ram's head was engraved on the floorplate; select walnut was used for the stock; and the pistol grip caps and forend tips were rosewood.

Olympian Grade. Guns of this type had an engraved blued barrel, but the receiver and trigger guard/floorplate assembly were engraved satin-chrome. A gold-inlaid motif appeared on the pistol grip cap of the beautifully figured walnut half-stocks.

BROWNING-SAKO SPORTING RIFLE

Browning also sold Sako L-461 and L-579 rifles in 1963-74, chambered for the 222 Remington, 222 Remington Magnum, 22-250, 243 Winchester, 264 Winchester Magnum, 284 Winchester Magnum or 308 Winchester cartridges.

BBR LIGHTNING SPORTING RIFLE

Made for the Browning Arms Company, Morgan, Utah, by the Miroku Firearms Mfg Co., Kochi, Japan, 1979-84.

Chambering options: 25-06, 270 Winchester, 7mm Remington Magnum, 30-06 or 300 Winchester Magnum. **Action:** locked by rotating three lugs on the bolt into seats in the receiver as the bolt handle turned down.

DATA FOR A TYPICAL EXAMPLE

Chambering: 25-06, rimless. 44.7in overall, about 8lb empty. 24in barrel, 4-groove rifling; RH, concentric. Detachable box magazine, 4 rounds. Spring-leaf and elevator rear sight. About 3100 fps with 100-grain bullet.

Introduced in 1979, this embodied a three-lug locking system with a 60-degree throw. The plunger-type ejector was recessed in the shrouded bolt face and a small claw-pattern extractor was fitted. The box magazine/hinged floorplate unit was shared with the BAR autoloader. The standard rifle had a checkered pistol grip butt with a low Monte Carlo comb and a plain synthetic shoulder plate. The checkered forend had a rounded rosewood tip. The BBR, never entirely successful, was superseded by the 'A-Bolt' pattern.

A-BOLT HUNTER

Made for the Browning Arms Company, Morgan, Utah, by the Miroku Firearms Mfg Co., Kochi, Japan, 1986 to date.

Chambering options: see text. **Action:** generally as BBR, above.

DATA FOR A TYPICAL EXAMPLE

Chambering: 280 Remington, rimless. 42.75in overall, 6.65lb empty. 22in barrel, 4-groove rifling; RH, concentric. Detachable box magazine, 4 rounds. Optical sight. About 2900 fps with 150-grain bullet.

Introduced in 1985, this is an improved form of the Miroku-made BBR (q.v.), sharing the short-throw three-lug action. It has a fluted bolt with a short extractor set into one of the locking lugs, and a cocking indicator which protrudes from the back of the bolt sleeve when the striker is cocked. A shotgun-style sliding safety catch lies on the upper tang behind the bolt. The BAR-type magazine system was retained, with an additional patented scissors-type cartridge elevator.

The A-Bolt rifle was introduced in standard and short actions, a strengthened version of the former sufficing for magnum chamberings. Hunter rifles had a pistol grip half-stock with a straight comb, and checkering on the pistol grip and the round-tipped forend. A plain rubber buttplate was fitted.

Short-action guns have been chambered for the 22-250, 243 Winchester, 257 Roberts, 7mm-08 Remington and 308 Winchester rounds; standard-action options have included 25-06, 270 Winchester, 280 Remington or 30-06. Magnums accepted 7mm Remington, 300 Winchester, 338 Winchester or 375 H&H Magnum cartridges. A left-hand action was introduced in 1987 in 270 Winchester, 7mm Remington Magnum, 30-06 and 375 H&H Magnum only.

SIMILAR GUNS

Note: all 'A-Bolt' rifles were upgraded to Mark II standards in 1995 after small changes had been made in the basic action. Externally, however, the 'Mk II' guns are practically indistiguishable from the original type. In addition, all of the rifles excepting the Micro-Medallion can be fitted with the BOSS barrel vibration modulator/muzzle brake attachment.

Camo Stalker rifle, 1988-91? This rifle chambered the 270 Winchester, 30-06 or 7mm Remington Magnum rounds. It was distinguished by a laminated stock made from wood dyed alternately black and green; metal parts had a matt blue finish.

Composite Stalker rifle, 1988-91 and 1994 to date. Derived from the Stainless Stalker (q.v.)—offered additionally in 25-06 and 280 Remington, plus 300 and 338 Winchester Magnum—this has a textured gray-black stock of graphite-reinforced fiberglass.

Eclipse rifle, 1996 to date. Easily identified by its gray-black wood laminate thumbhole stock, this heavy-barrel variant (built on the long or short actions) can be obtained in most of the standard Hunter chamberings.

Gold Medallion rifle, 1988 to date. Made in 270 Winchester, 7mm Remington Magnum or 30-06, this offers a European-style stock with a palm-swell grip and a Monte Carlo comb. The buttplate, pistol grip cap and contrasting forend tip are separated from the woodwork with brass spacers; the receiver flats are engraved with scrollwork and GOLD MEDALLION is inlaid on the right side ahead of the bolt handle.

Medallion rifle, 1987 to date. Introduced to satisfy more discerning clientele, this has high-gloss woodwork, darkened bolt flutes and scrollwork on the receiver flats. An otherwise identical left-hand action is made in 270 Winchester, 7mm Remington Magnum, 30-06 and 300 Winchester Magnum only. A 375 H&H Magnum chambering appeared in 1988, but was discontinued in the early 1990s; the 300 Winchester Magnum option was withdrawn in 1995.

Micro-Medallion rifle, 1988 to date. Available in short-action form only, handling the 22 Hornet, 22-250, 223 Remington, 243 Winchester, 257 Roberts, 7mm-08 Remington or 308 Winchester rounds, this is a diminutive Medallion with a 20in barrel, a short butt and a three-round magazine. About 39.5in long, it weighs 6.1lb.

Stainless Stalker rifle, 1987 to date. Distinguished by a composite stock of graphite and fiberglass, this has a stainless steel barrel/receiver and matte-gray metalwork. Chamberings are restricted to 22-250, 223 Remington, 243 Winchester, 270 Winchester, 7mm Remington Magnum, 7mm-08, 30-06, 308 Winchester and 375 H&H Magnum.

Varmint rifle, 1994 to date. This heavy-barrel gun has a distinctive wood laminate stock with a straight-comb butt and a palm-swell grip. It is available in 22-250, 223 Remington and 308 Winchester only.

• Browning, lever-action type

Additional information concerning pre-1945 guns will be found in the 'Winchester: lever-action type' section.

MODEL 1886 SPORTING RIFLE

Made for the Browning Arms Company, Morgan, Utah, by the Miroku Firearms Mfg Co., Kochi, Japan, 1986.

Total production: 7000. **Chambering:** 45-70, rimmed. **Action:** as 1886-type Winchester (q.v.).

45in overall, 9.4lb empty. 26in barrel, 4-groove rifling; RH, concentric. Tube magazine beneath barrel, 8 rounds. Spring-leaf and elevator rear sight. 1320 fps with 405-grain bullet.

In 1986, the Browning Arms Company announced the manufacture of replica Winchester rifles, work being sub-contracted to Miroku in Japan. The Standard or Grade I rifle, had an octagonal barrel and a full-length tube magazine. The blued receiver was accompanied by a classically styled forend, and a straight-wrist butt with a rifle-type shoulder plate. Another 7,000 guns were made in 1992.

SIMILAR GUNS

Model 71 carbine, or 'B-71', 1986-7. Identical with the rifle, this had a 20in barrel and weighed about 7.8lb; 4000 were made.

Model 71 High Grade carbine, or 'B-71', 1986-7. Three thousand of these deluxe carbines were made, with checkering on the butt and forend and a scroll-engraved grayed receiver.

Model 71 rifle, or 'B-71', 1986-7. Introduced on the Miroku-made M1886 action, this had a half-length magazine for four 348 Winchester cartridges. A 24in round barrel gave an overall length of 43in and a weight averaging 8.15lb. The forend and pistol grip butt were plain walnut, though a few guns were made with straight-wrist butts. Production totaled 3,000.

Model 71 High Grade rifle, or 'B-71', 1986-7. A duplicate of the standard pattern, this had gloss-finish checkered woodwork and a scroll-engraved grayed-steel receiver; three thousand were made.

M1886 Grade I carbine, 1992. About seven thousand 45-70 carbines were made with 22in barrels, an overall length of 40.8in, and a weight of 8.3lb.

M1886 Grade II carbine, 1992. A deluxe version of the standard 1886-pattern carbine, 3,000 of these engraved-receiver guns were made.

M1886 Grade II rifle, 1986. Three thousand of these were made with gloss instead of satin-finished woodwork, and engraved scrollwork, elk and bison on the receiver-side.

M1886 Montana Centennial rifle. A limited edition of 2,000 guns was made to celebrate the 100th anniversary of the admission of Montana to the Union in 1886. They had a reproduction of the state seal on the receiver-side.

MODEL 92 SPORTING RIFLE
Also known as 'B-92'
Made for the Browning Arms Company, Morgan, Utah, by the Miroku Firearms Mfg Co., Kochi, Japan,1979-85.
Total production: 7,000. **Chambering options:** 357 Magnum or 44 Magnum. **Action:** as 1892-type Winchester (q.v.).
DATA FOR 357 VERSION
37.5in overall, 6lb empty. 20in barrel, 4-groove rifling; RH, concentric. Tube magazine beneath barrel, 11 rounds. Spring-leaf and elevator rear sight. 1650 fps with 158-grain bullet.

A modern version of the original carbine was announced in 1979 as the 'Browning B-92'. The classically-styled straight-wrist butt was separated from the half-length forend by the blued receiver. A single band was fitted around the forend. Among the derivatives of the basic B-92 have been the Centennial Model, made in limited numbers in 44 Magnum only, and the BCA Commemorative celebrating the third anniversary of the founding of the Browning Collectors Association.

SIMILAR GUNS
Model 53 rifle, 1990. Five thousand guns of this type were made in 32-20 WCF, with a seven-round tube magazine and a 22in tapered round barrel. The walnut straight-comb butt had checkering on the pistol grip and a plain shotgun-type shoulder plate.

Model 65 Grade I rifle, 1989-90. Production of this variant, chambered for the 218 Bee cartridge, amounted to 3,500. They had 24in barrels, plain pistol grip butts with steel shoulder plates, and broad semi-beavertail forends.

Model 65 High Grade rifle, 1989-90. Only 1,500 deluxe High Grade guns of this type were made, with checkered woodwork and gold-inlaid game scenes on the grayed scroll-engraved receiver.

MODEL 1895 SPORTING RIFLE
Made for the Browning Arms Company, Morgan, Utah, by the Miroku Firearms Mfg Co., Kochi, Japan,1984.
Total production: 10,000 (all types). **Chambering options:** 30-40 or 30-06. **Action:** as 1895-type Winchester (q.v.).
DATA FOR 30-40 VERSION
42in overall, 8lb empty. 24in barrel, 4-groove rifling; RH, concentric. Integral box magazine, 4 rounds. Spring-leaf and elevator rear sight. 2430 fps with 180-grain bullet.

This was essentially similar to the original Winchester-made Browning design, though the lower arm of the operating lever-trigger guard assembly was pivoted to lock the lever into the lower tang behind the trigger when the action was closed. The standard guns had a straight-wrist butt and a half-length schnabel tip forend. Six thousand 30-06 examples had been made before a 30-40 Krag version was announced in 1985, additional production totaling 2,000. Sales were slow, however, and new guns were still being offered in 1990.

SIMILAR GUNS
Model 1895 High Grade rifle, 1984-5. These had scrollwork and an elk-and-bison scene on the grayed receiver, woodwork being selected walnut with hand-cut checkering. Production amounted to 1,000 in each chambering.

BLR SPORTING RIFLE
Made for the Browning Arms Company, Morgan, Utah, by the Miroku Firearms Mfg Co., Kochi, 1972-81.
Total production: not known. **Chambering options:** 243 Winchester or 308 Winchester. **Action:** locked by rotating eight lugs on the bolt into the receiver walls as the operating lever was closed.
DATA FOR A TYPICAL EXAMPLE
Chambering: 243 Winchester, rimless. 39.75in overall, 6.95lb empty. 20in barrel, 4-groove rifling; RH, concentric. Detachable box magazine, 4 rounds. Spring-leaf and elevator sight. About 3000 fps with 100-grain bullet.

Designed by Val Browning in Belgium, prototypes of this rifle were made in Herstal though series production was sub-contracted to Japan. The rotating-bolt action was amply strong enough to handle powerful sporting cartridges, giving the BLR an advantage over many rival lever-action repeaters, and the trigger system was mounted on the operating lever to prevent pinching. The checkered straight-wrist butt had a ventilated rubber recoil pad, and a short checkered forend had a single barrel band. A half-cock position on the hammer and an inertia firing pin provided an element of safety.

SIMILAR GUNS
BLR-81 rifle, standard action, 1981-95. An improved BLR with a six-lug bolt, this was offered in 22-250, 243 Winchester, 308 Winchester and 358 Winchester. The straight butt wrist was lengthened, and a white-line spacer usually accompanied the ventilated rubber buttplate. A gold-plated trigger lever was fitted and the magazine-release catch was improved; the BLR-81 magazine did not project beneath the receiver as markedly as the original BLR type. The hammer spur could be folded down at half-cock to provide an additional safety feature. A 257 Roberts option was announced in 1985, followed in 1987 by three Remington chamberings—222, 223 and 7mm-08. A plain solid rubber plate replaced the ventilated pattern, the accompanying spacer being discarded.

BLR-81 rifle, Magnum or long action, 1991-5. A special variant was introduced to handle 270 Winchester, 7mm Remington Magnum or 30-06 rounds. The barrel measured 22in (24in in 7mm only), giving a length of 42.5in and a weight of 8.5lb.

BLR-81 Lightning, 1996 to date. A modified version of the BLR-81, retaining most of the other original features (e.g., the folding hammer spur and half-cock safety system), this was introduced in two sizes. The standard-action guns are chambered for the 22-250, 223 Remington, 243 Winchester 7mm-08 or 308 Winchester cartridges, and have four-round magazines. The long-action guns are being made for 270 Winchester, 30-06 or 300 Winchester Magnum; guns are typically 42.9in long, with a 22in barrel, and weigh about 7lb. A pistol grip butt and a rounded forend are standard.

• Brown Standard
The Brown Standard Fire Arms Company, based in New York, made self-cocking dropping-block rifles with a partially enclosed

The Browning BLR-81.

spurless hammer. Resembling the British enclosed-hammer Henry rifles of the early 1870s, the gun was patented in 1883 by John H. Brown. It was offered as a half-stocked sporter or a fully stocked military rifle, with a leaf sight on top of the breech ahead of the chamber, but the venture seems to have failed by 1886.

• Bruce

Two magazine rifles were submitted by Lucien Bruce of Springfield, Massachusetts, to the U.S. Army trials of 1891. The subject of patents granted in 1890—in particular, 432,507 of 22nd July—the 30-caliber guns had five-round magazines and weighed 9.63lb empty. Unable to convince the authorities of their merits, the Bruce rifles never reappeared.

• Bullard, block-action type

These individualistic rifles were designed in the early 1880s by James Bullard to compete with the popular Winchesters and Marlins. They were simplifications of the lever-action rifles described below, locked by a very similar pivoting block but lacking the extended receiver.

TARGET RIFLE
Made by the Bullard Repeating Arms Company, Springfield, Massachusetts, about 1885-7.

Total production: not known. **Chambering options:** see notes. **Action:** locked by propping the breechblock behind the chamber with the tip of the operating lever.
DATA FOR A TYPICAL SPECIMEN

Chambering: 38-45, semi-rimmed. About 45.5in overall, 8.85lb empty. 28in barrel, 4-groove rifling; RH, concentric? Vernier peep-type rear sight on rear tang. 1385 fps with 190-grain bullet.

These guns were made in a variety of rim- and centerfire chamberings to satisfy target shooters and huntsmen alike. Production was short-lived, owing to the failure of Bullard to compete with Winchester.

SIMILAR GUNS
Military Model rifle. A few 45-70 guns were stocked as military-style muskets, with a full-length forend, two bands, and swivels under the band and butt. Most of them would accept the regulation 1873-pattern socket bayonet.

Military Model carbine. This was similar to the rifle, but had a half-length forend and a single band. Bayonets could not be mounted.

Schuetzen Model. The finest single-shot Bullard, this had a hooked Swiss-style buttplate and a spurred trigger guard. Made with a 30in barrel, it could weigh 12lb.

Target Model. This and the essentially similar 'Hunting & Target' rifles were made with 28in round, half-octagon or fully octagonal barrels, and could be obtained with straight-wrist or pistol grip butts. Spring-leaf and elevator sights were usually fitted, though the target rifles often had peep-and-globe patterns.

• Bullard, lever-action type

Patented by James Bullard in August 1881 and October 1883, this was locked at the rear by a pivoting block inspired by the Remington rolling block—though the Bullard bolt was moved by levers and rack-and-pinion gear. The operating stroke was extremely smooth, allowing Bullards to regularly win rapidity trials. However, unable to compete effectively against Winchester and Marlin, the company failed in 1890. Liquidation was concluded in 1891.

LEVER-ACTION SPORTING RIFLE
Made by the Bullard Repeating Arms Company, Springfield, Massachusetts, about 1884-7.
Chambering options: 32-40, 38-45, 40-75, 40-90, 45-60, 45-75, 45-85 or 50-115 Bullard, plus 45-70 Government. **Action:** a reciprocating bolt was locked by a pivoting block operated by the underlever.
DATA FOR A TYPICAL RIFLE

Chambering: 50-115 Bullard, semi-rimmed. About 47.75in overall, 9.57lb empty. 28in barrel, 4-groove rifling; RH, concentric? Tube magazine under barrel, 11 rounds. Spring-leaf and elevator rear sight. 1535 fps with 300-grain bullet.

The standard or 'medium frame' rifle was originally offered with 26in or 28in round, half-octagon or fully octagonal barrels chambered for 40-90 rounds; 32-40 and 38-45 options were added in 1885-6. A short seven-round magazine tube was also popular.

Weights ranged from 7.5lb for the small '32-40-105' sporter to 9.75lb for a '50-115-300 Express Rifle' with an optional pistol grip butt. Bullards had a dated appearance, and the absence of a conventional loading gate was also notable. Standard guns had straight-wrist stocks, though checkered butts or forends could be ordered. Receivers were often color case-hardened.

THE GUNS
Express Rifle. Chambered only for 50-115 ammunition, this was the most powerful member of the Bullard series. It had a 28in round barrel and a full-length magazine.

Heavy Frame Sporter. These guns chambered 40-60, 40-75, 45-70 or 45-85 cartridges, had 28in barrels, and were usually fitted with full-length 11-round magazines.

Medium Frame Sporter. This was the standard-weight gun described above.

Military Model muskets. Made only in small numbers, these had a 30in barrel and a full length forend retained by two bands. They accepted a socket bayonet.

Military Model carbine. Essentially a shortened musket, this had a 22in barrel and a short forend retained by a single band.

• Burgess

These guns accorded with patents granted to prolific Andrew Burgess in 1873-82. Rifles made by Whitney and then Colt (q.v.) had a simple action. The operating lever—doubling as the trigger guard—extended up into the breech, where its short rear face rested against the rear of the receiver and an extension arm ran forward along the top inner surface of the receiver. The breechblock was pivoted to the tip of the extension arm. When the operating lever was pulled downward, the locking arm moved down and away from the rear face of the receiver; simultaneously, the extension arm retracted the breechblock. The spent case was ejected as the elevator raised a new cartridge into the path of the returning breechblock.

BURGESS REPEATING RIFLE
Also known as 'Whitney-Burgess' or 'Whitney-Kennedy'
Made by the Whitney Arms Company, Whitneyville, Connecticut, 1877-88.

Total production: not known. **Chambering options:** 32-20, 38-40, 40-60, 44-40 and 45-60 Winchester, or 45-70 Government. **Action:** locked by propping the breech-bolt behind the chamber with the operating lever.
DATA FOR A TYPICAL RIFLE

Chambering: 45-60 Winchester, rimmed. 46.5in overall, 8.72lb empty. 28in barrel, 4-groove rifling; RH, concentric? Tube magazine under barrel, 15 rounds. Spring-leaf and elevator rear sight. 1315 fps with 300-grain bullet.

A rifle exhibited by Andrew Burgess at the Centennial Exposition of 1876 attracted the attention of Eli Whitney, who purchased a manufacturing license in 1877. Two muskets were entered unsuccessfully in U.S. Army trials in 1878, but an improved cartridge elevator patented by Samuel Kennedy in May 1879 was added soon afterward. The rifle subsequently—and misleadingly—became known as the 'Whitney-Kennedy'. It had a large flat-side receiver, a small loading gate with an oval cartridge depression, and a niggardly proportioned open-loop lever. Measuring 24-28in, the barrel could be round, half-octagon or fully octagonal; double set triggers, selected woodwork, engraving, and special sights were among the optional extras. Production ceased when Whitney was acquired by Winchester in 1888.

SIMILAR GUNS
Carbine. Made only in small numbers, this was basically a version of the rifle with a 20in barrel and a shortened magazine.

Light Model rifle. Introduced in 1886, this small-action gun was protected by additional patents issued to Burgess in 1880 and 1883. It was offered only as a 32-20 sporting gun (with a 24in round, half-octagon or fully octagonal barrel) or a 38-40 military-style musket. The sporter was 41.75in overall and weighed 8.75lb empty.

• Burke

John Burke of Sycamore, Illinois, was granted U.S. patent 55,613 of June 1866 to protect a break-open breech mechanism. Sporting rifles were made in small numbers on this system, which had a sliding locking bolt in the frame and an automatic extractor. A rifled carbine was submitted to the U.S. Army trials of 1865-6, but was not among those selected for photography, and the gun may simply have been rejected in the examination stages. Nothing more is known about it.

• Burnside

The prototype of this gun had been made in Springfield Armory as early as the autumn of 1853, but the first patent to be granted to Ambrose Burnside—British 2581/55—was not approved until 15th November 1855; U.S. patent no. 14,491 followed on 23rd March 1856.

The Burnside carbine was operated by pressing a lever beneath the hammer, exposing the mouth of the two-piece breechblock to accept a tapered copper cartridge case. The case was inserted backward into the block through the top of the frame; the protruding bullet seated in the mouth of the chamber as the breech closed. The flash from a conventional percussion cap ignited the powder through a small hole in the base of the cartridge case.

One gun tested at Washington Navy Yard in 1859 fired 500 shots without malfunctioning, though 30 of the aimed shots missed the eight-feet square target at 500 yards.

Burnside and his backers had organized the Bristol Fire Arms Company in May 1855, and a prototype carbine was tested favorably by the U.S. Army in March 1856. Two hundred guns were ordered in April. However, the failure to attract large-scale orders forced Burnside to sell his patents to his creditors in the autumn of 1857. The Bristol Fire Arms Company was eventually reorganized under new management in May 1860. Burnside held shares in this venture, but took no part in the day-to-day running of the business.

The external caplock made Burnside's carbines popular with the military authorities, which were often extremely suspicious of any gun chambering self-contained ammunition. Between 1st January 1861 and 30th June 1866, therefore, the Federal Government bought 55,567 Burnsides, making the design third only to the Spencer and the Sharps in popularity. However, it was obsolescent by the time hostilities ceased, and the Burnside Rifle Company transformed itself into the Rhode Island Locomotive Works in 1867.

BURNSIDE CARBINE, BRISTOL TYPE
'First Pattern', 1856
Made by the Bristol Fire Arms Company, Bristol, Rhode Island, 1856-8.
Total production: 275? **Chambering:** 54 Burnside, externally primed. **Action:** locked by tipping the breechblock with a lever on the right side of the frame.

40in overall, 6.8lb empty. 22in barrel, 5-groove rifling; RH, concentric. Single-shot only. Standing-block sight. Performance not known. No bayonet.

Two hundred Bristol-type Burnsides were purchased by the U.S. Army in April 1856, though teething troubles delayed delivery until January 1858. Late delivery caused a 1,000-gun order placed in November 1857 to be rescinded, and only two other guns are known to have been delivered to the army. A handful of sporting guns was also made. First-pattern Burnsides could be identified by the breech-lock lever, which curved round beneath the external hammer, and by the absence of a forend. Perfected guns also had a tape-primer system behind the hammer.

BURNSIDE CARBINE, FOSTER TYPE
'Second Pattern', 1860
Made by the Bristol Fire Arms Company, Bristol, Rhode Island.
Total production: 900? **Chambering:** 54 Burnside, externally primed. **Action:** locked by a propping the tipping breechblock behind the chamber.

39.5in overall, 6.82lb empty. 21.2in barrel, 5-groove rifling; RH, concentric. Single-shot only. Block- and two-leaf rear sight. Performance not known. No bayonet.

On 21st September 1858, the U.S. Army ordered 709 carbines from the Bristol Fire Arms Company. About 690 of them were accepted between December 1860 and May 1861, 24 guns being rejected from the last consignment. A prototype had been tested by the U.S. Army in February 1860, being regarded as inferior to the Smith and Maynard patterns, but salvation was to be found in the Civil War. Second-pattern Burnsides lacked the tape primer and the original side-mounted locking lever, but did incorporate an improved breechblock patented by George Foster on 10th April 1860 (U.S. no. 27,874). Releasing a catch inside the front of the trigger guard bow allowed the guard-bow/operating lever to be pulled downward to expose the chamber. A bar-and-ring lay on the left side of the breech, with a solitary swivel appeared beneath the butt. The guns bore acknowledgments of Burnside's and Foster's patents—on the frames and operating levers respectively—together with the serial number. The original wrapped-foil straight-taper cartridge case was replaced by a one-piece bellmouth Foster case, with a circumferential groove inside the mouth containing wax to lubricate the bullet.

SIMILAR GUNS
Burnside carbine, Foster type, 'Improved' or 'Third Pattern'. Introduced late in 1861, this had a strengthened hammer (with a shorter nose) and a short wooden forend held to the barrel with a single iron band. Production is believed to have amounted to 1500-1600 guns: 800 were supplied directly to the U.S. Army, and another 719 reached the army by way of Schuyler, Hartley & Graham.

BURNSIDE CARBINE, HARTSHORN TYPE
'Fourth pattern', 'New Model' or 'M1863'
Made by the Burnside Rifle Company, Providence, Rhode Island, 1862.
Total production: 6900-7000?

Otherwise generally as Burnside-Foster pattern, above, except for a block, peep and leaf sight graduated to 500yd.

In July 1861, soon after the Civil War began, large-scale orders were obtained beginning with a request from the State of Louisiana for 1,000 carbines (June 1861). Meanwhile, an improved gun incorporating an articulated or 'double-pivot' breechblock had been developed by Burnside Rifle Company sales agent Isaac Hartshorn (U.S. patent no. 38042 of 31st March 1863), though a pattern arm had been deposited with the Federal authorities in May 1862 and bulk deliveries had commenced in October.

The modifications enabled the mouth of the chamber to be lifted farther back in the frame as the action was opened, easing the task of inserting a fresh cartridge. The guns resembled their immediate predecessors externally, though the 'L'-shape hinge-pin head was a distinctive identifying feature.

SIMILAR GUNS
Burnside carbine, Hartshorn-Bacon type, 'Fifth Pattern'. About 44,000 of these were made by the Burnside Rifle Company in 1862-5. The Hartshorn breechblock was much more efficient than its predecessors, but required two motions to close the breech—first to tip the block and secondly to close the lever. The gun would jam if the motions were performed in the wrong order. The perfected carbine, therefore, incorporated a pin designed by George Bacon (patented in July 1863), which followed a cam-track cut in the side of the breechblock to tip the breechblock automatically as the operating lever was closed. By far the greatest number of Burnside carbines have this feature, which was a great boon to efficiency. Most of them have an acknowledgment of Burnside's patent on the lock plate, with 'MODEL OF 1864' and the serial number on the frame. A government inspector's mark (e.g., cursive 'RKW') was usually stamped into the left side of the butt-wrist.

A typical M1865 Burnside carbine, embodying the Hartshorn double-hinge breech. (W&W)

Conversions. Apart from a few Confederate muzzleloading transformations of Burnside breechloaders, a few 1864-type carbines were modified to fire centerfire ammunition. Probably undertaken in the 1870s, these can be recognized by the quality of work—presumably undertaken by individual gunsmiths—and by the presence of pre-1865 markings. The cartridges chamber directly in the breech, the breechblock being modified to contain the striker mechanism.

MODEL 1865 CARBINE

Apparently made in Ilion, New York State.

Quantity: 100? **Chambering:** 54 Burnside rimfire. **Action:** similar to the caplock pattern (q.v.).

39.5in overall, 7lb empty. 21in barrel, 5-groove rifling; RH, concentric. Single-shot only. Block, peep and leaf sight graduated to 500yd. Performance not known. No bayonet.

This was apparently made in small numbers, perhaps for the U.S. Army trials of 1865-6 (though there is no evidence of participation). Clearly marked 'Model of 1865' on the top of the frame, together with an acknowledgment of Burnside's patent and 'ILION, N.Y', it was derived from the Hartshorn-pattern carbine. Special tapered-case rimfire ammunition was fired by a short striker, driven downward by the elongated hammer nose. The presence of a special extractor beneath the chamber suggests that the gun was made for the Fosters, perhaps by Remington; G.P. & G.F. Foster received two patents in 1865-6 for improved extraction systems. The quirky rimfire Burnside was not successful enough to be made in quantity and the project was abandoned.

• Burton

Apart from the U.S. Army's flirtation with the Ward-Burton (q.v.), the Burton rifles enjoyed their greatest successes in Britain (q.v.). Bethel Burton of Brooklyn, New York, was granted his first U.S. patent for a 'breech-loading firearm' in December 1859 and his last, for an automatic rifle, posthumously in March 1905.

1859-PATENT RIFLE

This had a two-piece bolt with a non-rotating head carrying the nipple and its fence. The rear section was locked by a short multi-rib lug—a small part of an interrupted thread—with a stubby handle at the rear. The hammer of the conventional sidelock could strike the cap only when the bolt was fully forward, and a small chamber behind the chamber, cut entirely through the stock, was intended to allow gas leaks and debris to escape. A coned breech provided a rudimentary gas seal, but few rifles of this type were made.

LATER GUNS

1868 type. Burton did not produce another bolt-action rifle until after the end of the American Civil War, when he received a U.S. patent in August 1868. This gun was locked by a substantial interrupted-thread screw turning into the receiver bridge, a system common to all of the Burton rifles made prior to the 1880s. The striker and its spring lay inside the bolt, the breech slide was connected with what Burton called a 'recoil block', a separate bolt head was used, and articulating the simple vertically sliding sear with the trigger lever allowed a single spring to be used.

1869 type. The first magazine version of the Burton rifle was patented in 1869. The trigger was extended to form a carrier to transfer cartridges to the chamber from the tube magazine beneath the barrel when the action was opened. The breech slide, the striker tube and the inner part of the bolt head were all fluted to minimize the effects of fouling.

1873 type. A Burton-type rifle with alterations made by General W.G. Ward was granted field trials by the U.S. Army in 1871 (see 'Ward-Burton'), but Burton continued to refine his own design. A patent granted to 'B. and W.G. Burton' in October 1873 protected an improved magazine-feed gun with the carrier operated by the bolt, an improved bolt-mounted ejector pin activated by striking the sear bar on the back stroke, and a magazine cut-off to allow single-shot operation.

1880 type. Patented in the U.S.A. and Britain, this was another interrupted-screw system. Changes were made to the firing system, locking the sear until the bolt had been rotated to its closed position, and the extractor was improved. The carrier, pivoted in the frame ahead of the trigger guard, was raised on the back stroke of the bolt. The ejector pin was forced forward by striking the carrier lever. A magazine tube beneath the barrel could be isolated

by rotating the half-round spindle of the cut-off lever to prevent cartridges moving backward onto the carrier. The rifle was loaded from the underside, a spring-loaded gate lever being pivoted to the carrier block.

One of the major claims, however, was the addition (or substitution for the under-barrel tube) of a secondary gravity-feed or 'hopper' magazine on the left wall of the receiver. This was extended sideways to end in a vertical throat closed by a hinged lid which could be held open by a spring catch. Cartridges fed by gravity onto the carrier or bolt-way floor, the normal capacity being four rounds.

A sliding cut-off between the receiver and the secondary magazine could be activated by a radial lever. The magazine could also be fitted with a special sheet-steel extension to raise capacity to 12 rounds. Interestingly, the patent drawings show a rimless cartridge to improve the efficiency of the feed. Magazines of this type found very little favor in the U.S.A., but were enthusiastically tested by the British in the 1880s.

• Bushmaster

Made by the Gwinn Arms Company of Winston Salem, North Carolina (1973-7), and Bushmaster Firearms, Inc., of North Windham, Maine (1977-90), this 5.56x45 gas-operated autoloading rifle amalgamated a tipping-bolt lock with the gas system of the Kalashnikov assault rifle. The bolt locked at the top on the earliest guns, but laterally in later examples. The original alloy frame gave way to a sturdier machined steel forging, and a folding butt was developed to supplement the standard fixed wooden pattern. A typical gun had an 18.5in barrel and weighed 6.25lb with an empty M16-type 30-round magazine. Bushmaster was acquired by Quality Products Company in 1990 and production ceased in 1991; the current 'Bushmaster' guns are modified ArmaLites.

• Century

Century International Arms, Inc., of St. Albans, Vermont, has refurbished a variety of military actions in good-quality beech half-stocks with Monte Carlo butts, checkered capped pistol grips, and round-tipped forends. The guns available in 1997 included the 'Centurion 14', built on modified Enfield (Mauser) actions chambered for 7mm Remington and 300 Winchester Magnum cartridges; the 'Enfield Sporter No. 4', a modified Lee-Enfield in 303 British; the 'Swedish Sporter No. 38' in 6.5x55; the 'Custom Sporter', built on a small-ring Mauser action in 7.62x39 or 308 Winchester; and the 'Deluxe Custom Sporter'—another Mauser—in 243, 270 and 308 Winchester, or 30-06.

• Chaffee-Reece

Patented in February 1879 by Reuben Chaffee and General James Reece of Springfield, Massachusetts, this gun had a bolt-operated oscillating double-rack feed mechanism. Retracting the bolt pushed the mobile rack down the magazine until special retainers slipped behind the cartridge rims; the fixed rack simply held the cartridges in place. Closing the bolt lifted the mobile rack, pulling the cartridges forward, until the bolt face caught the rim of the first cartridge and pushed it into the chamber.

Unlike the competing Hotchkiss rifle (q.v.), which had a conventional tube magazine, the Chaffee-Reece system separated the cartridge noses from the primers of the preceding rounds. A prototype rifle was submitted to the U.S. Army trials of 1882, placing second behind the Lee and ahead of the Hotchkiss. The trial report recommended acquiring substantial numbers of each rifle for field trials, but the backers of the Chaffee-Reece lacked suitable facilities.

After unsuccessfully approaching Colt, General Reece asked the Ordnance Department to make the rifles in Springfield Armory in 1883, costs being minimized by using the old Ward-Burton machinery. The guns were withdrawn into storage after the field trials had been completed; as late as 1907, Francis Bannerman &

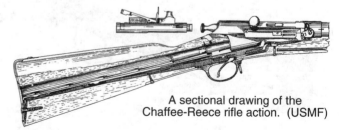

A sectional drawing of the
Chaffee-Reece rifle action. (USMF)

Sons were still offering 100 Chaffee-Reece rifles acquired from U.S. Army stores in the mid-1890s.

MODEL 1882 RIFLE

Made by the National Armory, Springfield, Massachusetts, 1884.

Total production: 750. **Chambering:** 45-70, rimmed. **Action:** locked by the base of the bolt-handle rib abutting the receiver-bridge as the bolt handle was turned down.

49in overall, about 9lb empty. 27.9in barrel, 3-groove rifling; RH, concentric. Tube magazine in butt, 5 rounds. Ramp-and-leaf rear sight graduated to 1,200yd. About 1,300 fps with standard ball cartridges. M1873 socket bayonet.

Readied for trials by midsummer 1884, Chaffee-Reece rifles used a government-pattern stock and resembled the 1879-model Hotchkiss externally. The rack magazine proved to be unreliable and difficult to maintain. As the bolt had to be operated to load each cartridge through the butt-trap, the Chaffee-Reece was ranked below the Hotchkiss in the final assessments made in 1885. Neither rifle challenged the Lee. A 30-caliber derivative appeared unsuccessfully in the U.S. Army magazine-rifle trials of 1891.

• Champlin

Patented by Jerry Haskins, rifles have been made to this interesting design since 1968 on a 'to order' basis; output has never been large. The essence of the action is a three-lug bolt, each lug being backed by a lengthy guide/safety rib. When the action is closed, the lugs rotate into their seats in the receiver and the guide ribs turn ahead of (but do not abut) the receiver bridge.

SPORTING RIFLE

Made by Champlin-Haskins Firearms, Inc. (about 1968-70), and by Champlin Firearms, Inc., Enid, Oklahoma (1971 to date).

Chambering options: virtually anything to order. **Action:** locked by rotating three lugs on the bolt head into seats in the receiver as the bolt handle turns down.

DATA FOR A TYPICAL EXAMPLE

Chambering: 340 Weatherby Magnum, belted. 44.9in overall, 8.15lb empty. 26in barrel, rifling pattern unknown. Integral box magazine, 3 rounds. Express-type rear sight. 2850 fps with 250-grain bullet.

The first Champlins had receivers machined from steel forgings. They could be identified by their distinctive bolt and elegant lines, which included an octagonal receiver and bolt shroud. The recessed bolt face accommodated a plunger-type ejector, the extractor claw being set into one of the locking lugs. Trigger guards were sometimes square backed, and often tapered from front to back. The forged-steel receivers were replaced with machined investment castings in 1971, though the basic features remained unchanged. By 1990, the company was offering rifles of the highest quality, with round, octagonal, tapered octagon or ribbed octagon barrels; stocks were being made to individual specifications, with right or left-hand actions, but were usually Circassian walnut with steel pistol grip caps and butt-plate traps. The tang safety (once optional) had become standard, with a bolt-shroud safety substituted to special order. Canjar triggers have always been fitted.

• Charter Arms

Best known for its revolvers, this company also made the 22 LR rimfire AR-7 Explorer survival rifle. A simple blowback feeding from a detachable eight-round box magazine ahead of the trigger guard, the Explorer dismantles readily into four major components: butt, magazine, action and barrel. No tools are required, as the barrel is retained by a large threaded collar and the action is held in the butt by catches. The parts can then be stowed inside the hollow butt, which is made of buoyant cycolac and ensures that the gun will float.

• Chipmunk

Originally made by Chipmunk Manufacturing, Inc., of Medford, Oregon, under U.S. patents 4,416,077 and 4,457,094, single shot Chipmunk rifles chamber 22 Short, Long or Long Rifle cartridges interchangeably, or the 22 Magnum to special order. Rifles are typically about 30in overall, with a 16.1in barrel, and weigh 2.5lb despite a walnut stock. They have rebounding firing pins, blocked automatically to prevent accidental discharge, and a low-profile bolt handle which will clear the optional optical sights. The Chipmunk has been specifically targeted at 'kids, campers, backpackers, survival and trappers', though the absence of a mag-

azine is disadvantageous. The guns are currently being made by the Oregon Arms Company of Prospect, Oregon, in standard and deluxe patterns.

• Clerke

Made by Clerke Recreation Products of Santa Monica, California, this modernized Winchester (Browning) single shot action was offered in chamberings such as 22-250, 222 Remington, 223 Remington, 243 Winchester, 6mm Remington, 250 Savage, 257 Roberts, 25-06, 264 Winchester, 270 Winchester, 7mm Remington Magnum, 300 Winchester Magnum, 30-06, 30-30 Winchester, 375 H&H Magnum, 45-70 or 458 Winchester. A typical 375 H&H Magnum version was 41.75in long, had a 26in barrel, and weighed about 8lb. Production was apparently confined to 1972-5.

The standard rifle had a round barrel, a walnut pistol grip butt; and a forend with a schnabel tip. The under edge of the deepened forend lay below the base of the receiver. The receiver was generally color case-hardened and the lever—unlike most Winchester patterns—curved to follow the pistol grip. No open sights were fitted. A deluxe version, with an adjustable trigger and half-octagon barrel, had checkered woodwork.

• Cochran

Protected by U.S. patents 47,088 of April 1865 and 52,679 of February 1866, granted to John Webster Cochran—best known for his 'Turret Gun' (an early repeater)—Gun No. 5 tested by the U.S. Army in 1865-6 embodied the tip-up chamber operated by an under-lever. The carbine-style half-stock was a two-piece design, with a single band on the forend. A sling ring lay on the left side of the receiver and a folding-leaf rear sight lay on the barrel ahead of the breech.

• Coleman

A gun of this type was submitted to the U.S. Army trials of 1865-6, but was not among those that were photographed at the time. This may simply indicate that it was rejected in the examination stages. Charles Coleman of Worcester, Massachusetts, was granted two gun-related patents in the 1860s—35,217 of May 1862, for a breech which swung back and down, and 59,500 of November 1866 (posthumously) for a drop-down breech/trigger system released by pulling a ring lever in the rear of the guard. It is not known which of these systems was submitted to the Army trials.

• Colt, autoloading type

Colt is best known as the major initial contractor for the 223-caliber ArmaLite (q.v.) AR-15/M16 series rifles, which are still in production. However, the company has also toyed with a few 22 rimfires.

COLTEER SPORTING RIFLE

This was a simple blowback design with a straight-wrist walnut butt separated by a blacked alloy receiver from the 'Western-style' forend, which had a single barrel band. A magazine for 15 22 LR rimfire rounds lay beneath the 19.4in barrel, with a small clamping band behind the ramped front sight. The rear sight was a traditional spring-leaf and elevator type. About 25,000 guns were made in 1964-75.

SIMILAR GUNS

Courier rifle, 1970-4. This was similar to the Colteer mechanically, but had a pistol grip butt and a beavertail forend.

Stagecoach rifle, 1965-75. Mechanically identical with the Colteer, this had a 16.5in barrel, reducing magazine capacity to 13 rounds; empty weight was 4.65lb. The walnut butt and forend were accompanied by a roll-engraved stagecoach hold-up scene, and a leather thong was fastened to the saddle ring on the left side of the receiver. Total production is said to have approached 25,000.

• Colt, bolt-action type

Colt's Patent Fire Arms Mfg Co. (Colt Industries, Firearms Division) of Hartford, Connecticut, offered a selection of bolt-action sporting rifles from the late 1950s to the 1980s. However, none was an original design: they were simply assembled on the basis of actions purchased in Europe.

COLTEER SPORTING RIFLE

Dating from 1957-66, this simple single shot 22 rimfire rifle could fire Short, Long and Long Rifle ammunition interchange-

The Colt-Sauer rifle was a minor variant of the German-made Sauer 90.

ably. It had a plain walnut half-stock with a pistol grip, and a spring-leaf and elevator rear sight on the barrel. Barrels were 20in or 22in, giving a length of 37.5-39.5in and an empty weight of 5-5.2lb. About 50,000 guns were made.

COLT-ROOT PATTERNS

Two carbines of this type were submitted to the U.S. Army trials of 1865-6 by Colt's Patent Fire Arms Mfg Co., and tested as No. 53 and No. 54. They were based on U.S. patent 65,509, granted posthumously in June 1867 to Elisha Root. The carbines had a one-piece half-stock with a cocking spur on the right side of the breech above the trigger, and a forend held by a single band. Swivels were fitted to the barrel band and (rather oddly) to the back web of the trigger guard. The action was opened by pulling upward on the half-ring behind the breech, which raised the bolt out of a locking recess and allowed it to be retracted until the chamber was exposed. Other guns of this type were made, but it is unlikely that the total exceeded a dozen.

COLTSMAN STANDARD SPORTING RIFLE
Mauser type; originally known as 'Model 57'

These were built on the improved Supreme action in 1957-61, first by the Jefferson Mfg. Co. of North Haven, Connecticut (5,000 only, 1957), and then by the Kodiak Mfg. Co. (1957-61). Most of the guns had a safety catch on the receiver behind the bolt handle, and a conventional internal magazine. They had a 22in barrel and a plain straight-comb butt, lacking a cheekpiece. The guns were all available in 300 H&H Magnum or 30-06 only, had five-round magazines and weighed between 7 and 7.3lb.

SIMILAR GUNS

Coltsman Custom rifle. This had a selected walnut stock with a Monte Carlo comb and cheekpiece.

Coltsman Deluxe rifle. Offered with a 24in barrel and better woodwork than the standard pattern, this had checkering on the pistol grip and forend.

COLTSMAN STANDARD SPORTING RIFLE
Sako type

Built in 1960-3 on L-57 Sako actions, this had a straight-comb butt and a rounded forend. Chamberings were restricted to 243 or 308 Winchester. Later guns (1963-5) were built on the L-461 (short), L-579 (medium) or L-61 (long) actions, depending on the chambering. Guns were available in 222 Remington, 222 Remington Magnum, 223 Remington (L-461); 243 Winchester or 308 Winchester (L-579); and 264 Winchester Magnum, 270 Winchester, 30-06 or 300 H&H Magnum (L-61).

SIMILAR GUNS

Coltsman Custom rifle. This had skip-line checkering and a ventilated shoulder pad; the separate pistol grip cap and obliquely cut forend tip were rosewood

Coltsman Deluxe rifle. This pattern was similar to the standard Coltsman, but the wood offered better quality and a Monte Carlo butt was used.

COLT-SAUER SPORTING RIFLE

Marketed exclusively by Colt in 1973-85, the Colt-Sauer Rifle (25-06 Remington, 270 Winchester, 7mm Remington Magnum, 30-06 or 300 Winchester Magnum) had an American-type walnut stock with a Monte Carlo comb. The rosewood pistol grip cap and forend tip, plus the rubber shoulder pad, were accompanied by white spacers. A 300 Weatherby Magnum option was added about 1979.

SIMILAR GUNS

Grand African Rifle. Offered in 458 Winchester only, this had a stock of dense-grain bubinga wood. Though little larger than the standard guns, it weighed 9.4lb or more.

Grand Alaskan Rifle. Similar to the standard guns, these chambered the 375 H&H Magnum cartridge.

Short Action Rifle. This was similar to the standard Colt-Sauer, but chambered 22-250 Remington, 243 Winchester or 308 Winchester ammunition.

• Colt, lever-action type

The first Colt repeating rifle to chamber metal-case ammunition was the so-called 'Colt-Burgess', produced with an eye on a lucrative market dominated by Winchester. However, Winchester threatened to start making cartridge revolvers to compete against the Single Action Army, so Colt stopped making Burgess-type guns in 1884.

NEW MAGAZINE RIFLE
Also known as 'Colt Burgess'

Made by Colt's Patent Fire Arms Mfg. Co., Hartford, Connecticut, 1883-4.

Total production: 6,400. **Action:** locked by propping the bolt behind the trigger with the tip of the operating lever.

DATA FOR A TYPICAL RIFLE

Chambering: 44-40 Winchester, rimmed. 43.25in overall, 8.72lb empty. 25.5in barrel, 4-groove rifling; RH, concentric? Tube magazine under barrel, 15 rounds. Spring-leaf and elevator rear sight. 1,310 fps with 200-grain bullet.

The first 44-40-200 centerfire sporting rifles and a short-barrel carbine appeared in November 1883. The Colt-made rifles offered round, half-octagon or fully octagonal barrels; carbines had a 20in round barrel, weighed 7.3lb and had 12-round magazines. Decoration and specially selected woodwork were available to order, but guns of this type are very rare. The Colts were similar externally to the Winchesters, but the receiver stopped only a short distance ahead of the loading gate. In 1884, under threat from Winchester, Colt stopped making Burgess-type guns after only 3,810 rifles and 2,590 carbines had been made.

• Colt, slide-action type

Made exclusively by Colt, the repeater patented by William Elliott in 1883 encountered modest commercial success. The mechanism was locked by a Burgess-type pivoting wedge beneath the breech bolt and could be fired merely by operating the slide with the trigger held back. The first guns had troublesome ejectors, but problems were soon overcome and a reputation for reliability was acquired in the mid-1880s. Eventually, however, the Lightning Magazine Rifle succumbed to the simpler Winchesters and the high-pressure smokeless cartridge.

LIGHTNING MAGAZINE RIFLE

Made by Colt's Patent Fire Arms Mfg. Co., Hartford, Connecticut, 1884-1900.

Total production: 89,780. **Chambering options:** 32-20, 39-40 and 44-40 Winchester (no authenticated 25-20 WCF gun has yet been found). **Action:**

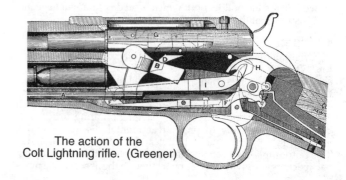

The action of the Colt Lightning rifle. (Greener)

locked by a pivoting wedge under the breech bolt engaging the receiver as the slide handle is returned.

DATA FOR A TYPICAL EXAMPLE

Chambering: 38-40 Winchester, rimmed. 43.6in overall, 8.15lb empty. 26in barrel, 6-groove rifling; LH, concentric? Tube magazine under barrel, 15 rounds. Spring-leaf and elevator rear sight. 1330 fps with 180-grain bullet.

This unique rifle was introduced in the autumn of 1884. Standard medium-frame Lightnings were offered with a round or octagonal barrel. They resembled lever-action Winchesters and Marlins externally, but lacked the finger lever; instead, a short wooden forend slid on tracks on the magazine tube. Straight-wrist butts were normal, but special sights, finishes and woodwork were available. Some guns displayed an auxiliary bolt-locking arm designed by Carl Ehbets and a set trigger mechanism credited to Frederick Knous (patented in April and December 1885 respectively), but these were soon abandoned.

The earliest small-frame rimfire and large-frame Express rifles were introduced in 1887, barrels acknowledging additional patents granted in 1885-7. Apart from differences in size, the most obvious feature was the breech cover, added to the medium-frame guns at this time—pre-1887 examples had an exposed breech bolt.

The Lightning was officially discontinued in 1900, though very little production had been undertaken since the mid- 1890s. Some had been purchased for the San Francisco Police Department, but orders of this magnitude were few and far between.

SIMILAR GUNS

Carbine. Little more than a diminutive of the standard rifle, this had a 20in barrel and a 12-cartridge magazine.

Baby Carbine. Chambered for 44-40, and experimentally for 32-20, this lightweight variant appeared in 1885 with a special 20in barrel, a 12-round magazine and a weight of just 5.3lb.

LIGHTNING EXPRESS RIFLE

Made by Colt's Patent Fire Arms Mfg. Co., Hartford, Connecticut, 1887-94.

Total production: 6500. **Chambering options:** 38-56, 40-60, 45-60 and 45-85 WCF, plus 50-95 Winchester Express. **Action:** as Lightning Magazine Rifle, above.

DATA FOR A TYPICAL EXAMPLE

Chambering: 45-85 Winchester, rimmed. 45.75in overall, 9.92lb empty. 28in barrel, 6-groove rifling; LH, concentric? Tube magazine under barrel, 10 rounds. Spring-leaf and elevator rear sight. 1510 fps with 300-grain bullet.

Designed for powerful black powder cartridges, these were offered with round or octagonal barrels. The largest cartridges tested the action to its limits, until 'racking' eventually afflicted the slide mechanism. All chamberings were abandoned in 1894, though new guns continued to be available from dealers' stocks for some years.

SIMILAR GUNS

Carbine. This was little more than a shortened rifle, with a 22in barrel and a weight of about 9lb.

Baby Express Carbine. Made only in small numbers, this 8lb gun was rapidly abandoned, owing to poor sales and inherent constructional weaknesses.

• Conover (Empire)

Jacob Conover patented a simple rifle design in July 1866, assigning rights to the Empire Breech-Loading Fire Arms Company of New York City. The breechblock pivoted laterally when a projecting lug on the right side was lifted. A rudimentary lock was provided by the nose of the falling hammer entering a recess in the block immediately before striking the firing pin. A gun of this type may have been entered in the U.S. Army trials of 1867 as the 'Empire No. 1', but only the 'Empire No. 2' (submitted by George Walter but of unknown origin) was actually fired. The No. 2 relied on a tipping barrel locked by a spring-loaded latch.

• Conroy

William Conroy submitted a 50-caliber musket to the U.S. Army trials board of 1872. Accepted as 'No. 84', it apparently failed its initial trials and was rejected. Details of the design are unclear; however, Loughlin Conroy of New York was granted two U.S. patents in 1867-9 to protect a radial breechblock and hammer system operated by an underlever doubling as the trigger guard;

sporting guns of this pattern are said to have been made in small numbers, but none could be traced for examination. Loughlin Conroy was also granted U.S. patent 145154 (December 1873), protecting a pivoting-block design operated by an lever beneath the breech; this automatically put the hammer to half-cock and retracted the firing pin before the block opened. It seems probable that a prototype 1873-patent gun was the mysterious 'No. 84'.

• Cooper

These guns rely on a three-lug bolt system introduced in 1991, initially concentrating on short-case cartridges developing moderate pressures. This allowed the lugs to be placed in the middle of the bolt body, though a front-locking derivative of the basic design has been developed for the Model 22.

MODEL 21 VARMINT EXTREME RIFLE
Classic pattern

Made by Cooper Arms, Stevensville, Montana.

Currently in production. **Chambering:** see notes. **Action:** locked by rotating three lugs on bolt into seats in the receiver walls as the bolt handle turns down.

DATA FOR A TYPICAL EXAMPLE

Chambering: 17 Remington, rimless. 43.1in overall, about 7lb empty. 23.75in barrel, 4-groove rifling; RH, concentric. Single shot only. Optical sight. 4020 fps with 25-grain bullet.

Introduced in 1994, this rifle has been offered in 17 Remington, 17 Mach IV, 221 Fireball, 222 Remington, 222 Remington Magnum, 223 Remington and 223 PPC. The stainless-steel barrel is allowed to float in the forend of the walnut straight-comb half-stock, which has a plain broad forend.

SIMILAR GUNS

Model 21 Custom Classic rifle, 1994 to date Distinguished by select Claro walnut, this also has a Monte Carlo-style butt with a high comb and a cheekpiece.

Model 21 Bench Rest rifle, 1996 to date. This is supplied with a Jewell trigger and a flat-bottom forend.

Model 36 BR-50, 1994 to date. Destined for bench-rest shooting, this has a single shot action in a black synthetic MacMillan stock. It has a 22in cylindrical barrel, measures 40.5in overall, and weighs 6.8-7lb.

Model 36 Classic Sporter, 1995 to date. This 22 rimfire pattern shares the standard three-lug action, but has a detachable five-round box magazine. The 22.75in barrel gives an overall length of 42.5in and an empty weight of 7lb.

Model 36 Custom Classic Sporter, 1995 to date. A deluxe version of the standard pattern, this has a select walnut stock with a Monte Carlo-style comb and cheekpiece.

Model 36 Featherweight, 1996 to date. Mechanically identical with the Model 36 Classic Sporter, this has a black synthetic half-stock. Weight averages 6.5lb.

Model 36 Montana Trailblazer, 1996 to date. A lightweight tapering barrel gives this wood-stocked gun a weight of just 6.25lb.

Model 38 Centerfire Sporter, 1991-4. Offered only in 17 CCM and 22 CCM chamberings, this had a 23.75in Shilen barrel and a checkered Claro walnut Monte Carlo-type half-stock with swivels under the butt and forend. A Pachmayr butt pad was standard. The single-stage trigger was adjustable. Guns were typically about 42.5in long and weighed 8lb.

Model 40 Centerfire Classic Sporter, 1996 to date. This is a modified version of the Model 36, sharing the three-lug action, but chambers the 22 Hornet or 22 K-Hornet cartridges. It has a 23in barrel and weighs about 7lb empty.

Model 40 Centerfire Custom Classic Sporter, 1996 to date. Distinguishable by the design of its Claro walnut half-stock, which has a Monte Carlo comb and cheekpiece, this is otherwise similar to the standard Model 40.

Model TRP-1 rifle, 1991-5. This was a single shot 22LR rimfire ISU target gun, with a 22in Shilen barrel and a weight of about 10lb. A competition-style stock had an elevating comb and an adjustable buttplate, and Anschütz sights could be fitted.

MODEL 22 PRO-VARMINT EXTREME RIFLE

Introduced in 1996 in 22-250, 220 Swift, 6mm PPC, 243 Winchester, 25-06 and 308 Winchester, this has a front-locking three-lug bolt. The 26in barrel is allowed to float in the forend of the half-stock.

SIMILAR GUNS

Model 22 Benchrest rifle. This is supplied with a Jewell trigger.

Model 22 Black Jack. Otherwise identical with the standard wood-stocked gun, this has a synthetic McMillan stock.

• Crescent

The Crescent Firearms Company was acquired by H. & D. Folsom in 1893, though the name was retained until the formation of the Crescent-Davis Corporation (1930) and its ultimate disappearance into the Savage-Stevens conglomerate in 1932. Consequently, the Crescent rifle may be encountered with the name of Folsom or any one of a large number of distributors.

SPORTING RIFLE

Made by the Crescent Firearms Company, Norwich, Connecticut, about 1891-1915.

Total production: not known. **Chambering options:** 22 Short, 22 Long Rifle, 25 Stevens or 32 Long rimfire, and 25-20 (25 SS) centerfire. **Action:** locked by propping the breechblock behind the chamber with the hammer body.

DATA FOR A TYPICAL EXAMPLE

Chambering: 25-20, rimmed. 37.85in overall, 4.8lb empty. 24in barrel, 4-groove rifling; RH, concentric. Single shot only. Standing-block rear sight. 1410 fps with 85-grain bullet.

Best known as a shotgun manufacturer, supplying many thousands of guns to a wide variety of wholesalers, Crescent also made a small rolling-block rifle which could be classed as a blatant copy of the Remington No. 4 (q.v.) had it not been for a conical takedown wedge. This ran laterally through the receiver from the left, and could be released by turning a lever-headed bolt on the right. The system was patented on 14th April 1891, perhaps by Frank Foster; the gun-barrels were appropriately marked. Barrels were usually round, butts had straight wrists, and the short forends tapered to a plain tip. Open sights were standard, but it is assumed that more sophisticated fixtures could be obtained to order.

• Cullen

In April 1869, Thomas Cullen of San Francisco received U.S. patent no. 88,853 to protect the design of a complicated risingblock repeating rifle with a revolving cluster of four tube magazines in the butt. Operated by an underlever, a gun of this type was allegedly submitted to U.S. Army trials. It was clumsy, delicate and much too complicated to succeed.

• Daisy

Best known as a maker of air guns, the Daisy Company has occasionally flirted with cartridge guns—including the abortive Daisy-Heddon VL system of the 1960s. This consisted of a 22-caliber caseless cartridge ignited by an air blast (see 'Switzerland: Pauly'), but only about 23,000 guns were made in 1968-9.

MODEL 2201 LEGACY SPORTING RIFLE

Made by the Daisy Mfg. Co., Rogers, Arkansas, 1989-92

Total production: not known. **Chambering:** 22 LR, rimfire. **Action:** locked by the base of the bolt handle abutting the receiver.

36.5in overall, 6.7lb empty. 22in barrel; 12-groove rifling; RH, concentric. Single shot only. Adjustable rear sight. 1080 fps with 40-grain bullet.

The brief to designer Jerry Haskins appears to have been to develop guns that incorporated visual references to American shooting heritage. Consequently (apart from the autoloading M2203), the Legacy rifles all displayed a turning-bolt action and an odd combination of an octagonal barrel and synthetic wood-grain stocks. The detachable trigger unit could be removed for safe keeping. The 2201 had a synthetic half-stock with an adjustable buttplate; the 'take-down' barrel was a steel liner within an alloy sleeve; and the receiver was grooved to accept telescopesight mounts. Swivels lay beneath the butt and forend.

SIMILAR GUNS

Note: the guns could all be converted to shotguns simply by substituting a smooth-bore barrel for the rifled version. Combination sets were also available.

Model 2202 rifle, 1989-92. Based on the M2201, this had a detachable 10-round rotary magazine.

Model 2203 rifle, 1989-92. The autoloading Legacy fed from a seven-round box magazine.

Model 2211 rifle, 1989-92. This was simply the Model 2201 with a walnut-finished hardwood half-stock. The Models 2212 and 2213 were similar derivatives of the 2202 and 2203 respectively.

Model 2221 rifle, 1988 only. This was apparently the original version of the single shot M2201. Made only in small quantities, it was rapidly superseded by the improved version.

Model 2222 rifle, 1988 only. An original form of the magazine-feed Model 2201, only a few guns of this type were made.

• Dakota

Dakota Arms was formed by amalgamating two smaller companies with extensive gunmaking experience. The objective was to produce the Model 76 rifle, an improved Winchester Model 70 (q.v.) built to the high-quality manufacturing standards that had ruled prior to 1964.

DAKOTA 76 CLASSIC RIFLE

Made by Dakota Arms, Inc., Sturgis, South Dakota, 1988 to date

Total production: not known. **Chambering options:** see text. **Action:** locked by rotating lugs on the bolt head into the receiver as the bolt handle is turned down, and by the bolt-handle base entering its seat.

DATA FOR A TYPICAL EXAMPLE

Chambering: 338 Winchester Magnum, rimless. 42.5in overall, 7.50lb empty. 23in barrel, 4-groove rifling; concentric, RH? Internal box magazine, 3 rounds. Williams ramp sight. 3000 fps with 200-grain bullet.

Introduced in 1988, this has a Mauser collar-pattern extractor, an adjustable trigger, a Winchester three-position safety, and a trigger guard/floorplate assembly machined from a single piece of steel. A special combination bolt stop, gas shield and bolt guide was patented by Peter Grisel in 1985. The standard Classic rifle has a straight-comb butt and a rounded forend tip, with hand-cut checkering and a solid rubber shoulder pad. The separate pistol grip cap is usually steel.

Chamberings have included 257 Roberts, 270 Winchester, 280 Remington, 7mm Remington Magnum, 300 Winchester Magnum, 30-06, 338 Winchester Magnum, 375 H&H Magnum or 458 Winchester Magnum, but others have been made to order.

SIMILAR GUNS

Alpine Rifle. Introduced in 1988, this was a lightweight version with a slender stock and a blind magazine.

Rigby Rifle. This 1990-vintage enlargement of the basic action had a deepened stock to accept a four-round magazine, recoil bolts through the wrist and forend, and a 24in heavy barrel. A standing-block rear sight is standard. Chambered for 404 Jeffrey, 416 Rigby, 416 Dakota or 450 Dakota, it could weigh 10lb.

Safari Grade Rifle. Offered in 300 Winchester Magnum, 338 Winchester Magnum, 375 H&H Magnum or 458 Winchester Magnum only, this had a one-piece magazine unit and a gloss-finished walnut stock. The butt originally had a Monte Carlo comb and cheekpiece, but this was changed to a straight-comb type in 1990.

Short Action Rifle. Announced in 1989 in 22-250, 243 Winchester, 6mm Remington, 250-3000, 7mm-08 Remington or 308 Winchester, this offers a scaled-down action and a 21in barrel. It has been made in Classic Grade, and in an 'Alpine Grade' with a slim stock and a blind magazine.

• Davenport

William Davenport was a prolific inventor and the driving force behind the Davenport Fire Arms Company, best known for its shotguns. Like the nearby Crescent (q.v.) business—also a shotgun manufacturer—Davenport made a few rifles, on the basis of a dropping-block action patented in December 1891.

BROWNIE SPORTING RIFLE

Made by the Davenport Fire Arms Company, Norwich, Connecticut, about 1891-1902.

Total production: several thousand? **Chambering options:** 22 Short, 22 Long Rifle, 32 Short or 32 Long rimfire. **Action:** locked by propping the breechblock behind the chamber with the operating lever.

DATA FOR A TYPICAL EXAMPLE

Chambering: 32 Long, rimfire. 38.6in overall, 4.37lb empty. 23.9in barrel, 5-groove rifling; RH, concentric. Single shot only. Standing-block rear sight. 950 fps with 90-grain bullet.

Apparently incorporating parts purchased from Hopkins & Allen, the Davenport rifle had a coil-type mainspring in a tunnel bored beneath the chamber, relying on an extension strut to operate the rebounding hammer. A safety notch on the hammer body was intercepted by the trigger after each shot. The detachable barrel was locked by a lug engaging a transverse bar in the frame, and by a lever-headed bolt running laterally through the frame-front. Round barrels were customary, though part- and full-octagon versions may have been available to order. The earliest guns had a hook-type operating lever, but a later version, bearing an additional October 1897 patent date to protect the 'shell ejecting device', had a looped design. Later guns were also often marked 'THE BROWNIE'; their barrels were contained in a breech-sleeve, and the take-down lever could be folded into the frame.

• Dodge

William Dodge, often working in collusion with his son Phillip, received several U.S. patents in 1866-72. Excepting the 1866-patent rifle, which drew inspiration from the Spencer (q.v.), the designs were usually variations on the radial-block system exemplified by the Remington rolling block. They often relied on a two-part or compound breechblock embodying a 'locking brace', combined with auto-retracting firing pins and mechanical breech locks. However, there is no evidence that Dodge rifles were ever made in quantity.

• DuBiel

Created in 1975 by John Tyson and Joseph DuBiel, this company made rifles with a patented five-lug bolt system. This allowed the extractor to pass between two lugs rather than requiring one to be partially cut away, and gave a compact 36-degree throw. Work ceased in 1990.

DUBIEL SPORTING RIFLE

Made by the DuBiel Arms Company, Sherman, Texas, 1978-90.
Total production: not known. **Chambering options:** virtually any from 22-250 to 458 Winchester Magnum. **Action:** locked by rotating lugs on the bolt head into the receiver as the bolt handle was turned down, and by the bolt-handle base entering its seat.
DATA FOR A TYPICAL EXAMPLE
   Chambering: 300 Winchester Magnum, rimless. 43.5in overall, 7.5lb empty. 24in barrel, rifling pattern not known. Internal box magazine, 3 rounds. Optical sight. 3400 fps with 150-grain bullet.

Though made in surprisingly large numbers, the DuBiel rifle was really a custom pattern and could be chambered for almost any cartridge the purchaser specified. Right- or left-hand actions were available from stock, and often had Canjar triggers and Douglas barrels. The Classic stock had a straight comb; the Modern Classic was similar, but had contrasting ebonite pistol grip cap and forend tip. The Rollover pattern had a distinctive Monte Carlo comb, while the design of the Thumbhole butt was self-explanatory. Thumbhole Mannlicher stocks extended to the muzzle, usually being confined to barrels measuring less than 22in. Most stocks prove to be walnut or maple, though some laminated examples were made. The guns had a neat bolt shroud and a sliding tang safety (omitted from thumbhole-stock guns), while the magazine floorplate locking lever was reminiscent of pre-1939 Mauser sporters.

• Durst

Murray Durst of Wheatland, California, developed repeating rifles in the 1890s. Early collaboration with Lewis Broadwell (q.v.), who is believed to have contributed the magazine, soon gave way to solitary effort. Gun No. 31 in the U.S. Army trials of 1891 was a 30-caliber Durst, with a 10-round magazine and an empty weight of 8.25lb, and a U.S. patent was granted in August 1893 to protect an improved turning-bolt rifle with a rotary magazine. A gun of this pattern was tested by the U.S. Navy in 1894, chambering an experimental 6mm (.236) semi-rimless cartridge. However, the testers preferred first the Luger and then the straight-pull Lee, and the Durst was rejected.

• Elliott

William Elliott of Plattsburg, New York, and then New York City, was a talented inventor and prolific patentee. Though renowned for handguns, often developed in collusion with Remington, Elliott also developed rifles. These included a single shot underlever design with a breech which slid backward, carrying the side hammer (1862); a backward-sliding breech operated by a toplever (1863); and a series of radial-block systems dating from 1865.

Gun No.24 and Carbine No. 80 entered in the 1872 U.S. Army trials were both 50-caliber Elliott designs. Somewhat similar to the single shot Lee rifles of the same era (q.v.), they were operated by retracting the hammer. The backward stroke of the hammer pivoted the front of the breechblock downward, though the hammer automatically returned to half-cock when released. A cartridge was inserted and the hammer was once again pulled back to full-cock to close the breech. The subject of patents granted in December 1870 and May 1871, guns of this type had a long receiver with a prominent hammer spur. However, they were not successful and it is assumed that only a few were made—perhaps in the Remington tool room.

• Enfield

MODEL 1917

Made in 1917-19 by the Winchester Repeating Arms Company, New Haven, Connecticut; by the Remington Arms-Union Metallic Cartridge Company, Ilion, New York; and by the Remington Arms of Delaware Company, Eddystone, Pennsylvania.
Total production: approximately 2.513 million. **Chambering:** 30-06, rimless. **Action:** as British P/1914 (q.v.).
   46.3in overall, 9lb empty. 26in barrel, 5-groove rifling; RH, concentric. Internal box magazine loaded from a stripper-clip, 5 rounds. Leaf-pattern rear sight graduated to 1600yd. 2750 fps with M2 ball cartridges. M1917 sword bayonet.

The entry of the U.S.A. into World War I in 1917 revealed that only 740,000 Springfield and obsolescent Krags were on hand. Production had been so radically curtailed that a decision was taken to re-chamber the British P/1914 for the standard 30-06 rimless cartridge. The 30-06 case was longer than the 303-caliber pattern, though its body diameter was comparable and only minor changes were needed in the magazine. Enfield-type rifling could be retained merely by adjusting the bore diameter.

The 'Rifle, Caliber 30, Model of 1917' was very similar externally to its British predecessor. The rimless cartridge improved feed, and Enfield-type rifling unexpectedly resisted wear better than the Springfield type. By 11th November 1918, the Eddystone factory had made 1,181,910 rifles; Remington had supplied 545,540, and Winchester had contributed 465,980. Springfield Armory and Rock Island Arsenal had made only 313,000 M1903 rifles in the same period.

The U.S. Army considered substituting the M1917 for the M1903 in 1919, but the Enfield was unpopular with the rank-and-file and the production facilities remained in private hands.

Almost a million refurbished rifles were placed in store in 1920, many survivors being sent to Britain in 1941 as part of the Lend-Lease program. Official records reveal only an order for 50,000, but Ian Skennerton, in *The U.S. Enfield*, notes the total to have been 119,000. After a series of accidents, most of the guns used in Britain gained broad red stripes around the forend and butt to remind firers that they chambered the 30-06 cartridge instead of the 303 type.

The first batches of 143,000 new 30-caliber M1917 barrels were made in 1942 by the High Standard Manufacturing Company of New Haven, Connecticut (four-groove, right twist), and Johnson Automatics, Inc. of Providence, Rhode Island (two-groove, right twist).

The M17 Enfield rifle, a 30-caliber
version of a British design.

An Evans magazine carbine.

• Evans

This idiosyncratic gun was patented by Warren Evans of Thomaston, Maine, in 1868-71. Wisely ignored by the U.S. Ordnance Department, it was apparently used by the Russian navy in the late 1870s. The action relied on a Spencer-like radial breech-block, fed from a capacious Archimedean screw magazine containing a four-fluted cylindrical cartridge carrier and a spiral-wire cartridge separator.

The magazine tube doubled as the spine of the butt. The carrier made a quarter-turn each time the trigger guard/operating lever was thrown, ejecting the spent case before presenting a new round to the breech.

PATENT MAGAZINE RIFLE

Made by the Evans Rifle Manufacturing Company, Mechanic Falls, Maine, 1871-7.

Total production: a few thousand. **Chambering:** 44 Evans (short), rimmed. **Action:** locked by propping a radial breechblock behind the chamber with the tip of the operating lever.

DATA FOR MILITARY RIFLE

47.25in overall, 10.11lb empty. 30in barrel, 4-groove rifling; RH, concentric? Tube magazine in butt, 34 rounds. Ramp-and-leaf rear sight graduated to 1000yd. About 850 fps with 215-grain bullet. M1873 socket bayonet?

The rifle was promoted for its 'military potential' by Merwin & Hulbert from 1871, but the mechanism was clumsy and delicate. Evans rifles could not be mistaken; they had massive receivers with an ejection port on the right side and the tube magazine running back through the split butt. A small latch lay beneath the serpentine operating lever and the hammer was concealed in the receiver. The mechanism could be fired as a single-loader merely by depressing the operating lever far enough to eject, but not far enough for the breechblock to receive a new cartridge from the magazine. The action had to be operated to turn the feed-cylinder for each and every cartridge inserted in the magazine. An Evans rifle was submitted to U.S. Army trials in 1872, but predictably failed the dust and rust tests.

THE GUNS

Military Rifle. This had a full-length forend held by two bands, and accepted a socket bayonet.

Carbine. These had a 22in barrel, a half-stock and a single band.

Sporting Rifle. Despite the failure of Merwin & Hulbert to convince prospective purchasers of the merits of the military musket, a sporting rifle appeared in 1874. Sporters had octagonal barrels measuring 26-30in and weighed about 10lb loaded. The forend was generally checkered, and often had a horn or pewter tip.

NEW MODEL PATENT RIFLE

Made by the Evans Rifle Manufacturing Company, Mechanic Falls, Maine, 1877-80.

Chambered: 44 Evans (long), rimmed. **Action:** as Patent Magazine Rifle, above.

The action of the extraordinary Evans carbine.

DATA FOR SPORTING RIFLE

43.25in overall, 9.64lb empty. 26in barrel, 4-groove rifling; RH, concentric? Tube in butt magazine, 26 rounds. Ramp-and-leaf sight graduated to 1000yd. About 1200 fps with 280-grain bullet.

The improved rifle of 1877 was offered in the same varieties as its predecessor, but could be identified by its semi-external hammer and sliding ejection-port cover. A prominent locking catch lay on the underside of the operating lever, which had a recurved tip. Half-stocked carbines had 22in barrels; sporters had round, half-octagon or fully octagonal barrels measuring 26-30in, and weighed up to 10lb.

About a thousand rifles were purchased during the Russo-Turkish War of 1877-8, apparently for the Imperial Russian navy, but Evans went into liquidation in 1880 and work on his idosyncratic design ceased.

• Fajen

Reinhart Fajen Mfg. Co., Inc., of Warsaw, Missouri, stocked and completed large numbers of Acra S-24 rifles on Santa Barbara actions. They were bedded with synthetic Acraglas in pursuit of consistent accuracy.

• Field

Two carbines of this otherwise anonymous design were tested by the U.S. Army in 1865. Listed as No. 6 and No. 7 (as 'Field' or 'Fields'), they embodied a dropping-block action controlled by the ring-tipped underlever. Both guns lacked forends and had small folding-leaf sights on the barrel; they also had distinctive straight-shank hammers. Tentative links have been made with Edwin Field of Springfield, Massachusetts, a firearms patentee in the 1880s, but have yet to be proved.

• Firearms International

Firearms International Corporation of Washington, DC, in addition to importing standard Finnish-made Sako rifles, sold sizable numbers of the Musketeer rifle. Built on an FN-Mauser action and dating from 1963-72, these had comparatively plain pistol grip half-stocks with Monte Carlo combs. Bolt handles were generally turned downward, and open sights were customarily omitted. Standard chamberings included 243 Winchester, 25-06, 270 Winchester, 30-06 or 308 Winchester (five-round magazines), plus 264 Winchester Magnum, 7mm Remington Magnum or 300 Winchester Magnum (three rounds). Barrels usually measured 24in, weights averaging 7.3lb.

• Fitzgerald

Walter Fitzgerald of Boston was granted U.S. patent 45,919 in January 1865, protecting a radial breech-block mechanism operated by an under lever doubling as a trigger guard. A tube magazine in the butt fed a new round into the chamber each time the breech was opened. A Fitzgerald carbine was apparently submitted to the U.S. Army trials of 1865, but was not amongst those that were photographed at the time and may have been rejected in the examination stages.

• FN-Saive

The U.S. Army experimented with the perfected FAL or 'Rifle, 30 T48' in the early 1950s. About 15 guns were made by the High Standard Manufacturing Company of Hamden, Connecticut, in 1954; and a further 500—numbered from 4001 upward—by Harrington & Richardson of Worcester, Massachusetts, in 1955. Including the flash-hider, they measured about 44.5in overall and weighed 9.43lb with an empty magazine. The competing T44 rifle was preferred, eventually becoming the M14 (see 'Garand').

• Fogerty, bolt-action type

These guns were made in acordance with patents granted to Valentine Fogerty in February 1869 and July 1871, though work had probably finished long before the latter (sought in the summer of 1869) had actually been granted. The first examples were made for U.S. Army trials, but were not successful enough to encourage additional development.

The receiver was bored through to receive a multi-piece bolt, which was basically a hollow cylinder with two lugs at the rear. The bolt had a non-rotating collar to prevent it being removed inadvertently from the gun and also to support the motion of the bolt during the operating stroke. A firing pin or 'lock-bolt' lay within the bolt body and had a short straight operating handle.

To operate the gun, the bolt handle was raised vertically through a quarter-turn and drawn back, taking the lock-bolt and the bolt sleeve with it. The pivoted carrier then threw the extracted case out of the loading port and clear of the breech. A new cartridge was placed in the carrier, and the bolt was returned to lock. Camming action ensured that the firing pin did not touch the case base during the loading stroke.

A safety notch on the lock-bolt ensured that the gun would not fire if dropped on the butt. Pulling back on the handle then put the gun into half- or full-cock when needed.

MILITARY-MODEL RIFLE

Made by the American Repeating Rifle Co., Boston, Massachusetts, 1869.
Total production: 10? **Chambering:** 58, rimfire. **Action:** locked by two lugs on the rear of the bolt abutting shoulders in the rear of the receiver.

45.9in overall, about 9.6lb empty. 30in barrel, 3-groove rifling; concentric. Single-shot only. Two-leaf sight for 200 and 500yd? Performance not known. Socket bayonet.

The gun had a standard Springfield-style stock, three sprung bands, with swivels on the trigger guard and middle band. A repeating version was also made experimentally. This had a tube magazine in the butt, operated by a sliding rod set into the right side of the forend.

• Fogerty, lever-action type

The Fogerty rifle is often mistaken at a cursory glance for a Spencer (q.v.), sharing similar external contours, a tube magazine in the butt, and lever operation.

Valentine Fogerty of Boston, Massachusetts, was granted a U.S. patent in February 1865 to protect a tube magazine operated with a sliding grooved rack instead of a spiral spring. A second patent granted in October 1866—part-assigned to Paul Todd—incorporated the rack-feed magazine in a suitable lever-action gun.

The gun was in the same general class as the Spencer; it loaded through a sliding shutter or trap in the buttplate. The front cartridge lay in a recess behind and slightly to the right of the barrel. When the lever was opened, the breechblock swung down and back, allowing the spent case to be withdrawn onto the carrier and flipped clear of the breech. The rifle was then canted to the left to allow a new cartridge to roll onto the carrier.

As the lever was closed, the carrier rose, the breechblock pushed the cartridge into the chamber, and the carrier moved forward into a recess below the breech. The magazine rack moved forward to place another round in the feed recess. The first model, made in small quantities by the Fogerty Rifle Company of Boston, had a hammer and lock plate let into the stock.

Gravity feed was most unsatisfactory, however, and an improved force-feed mechanism was patented in October 1868. An additional cammed finger was used to feed the cartridges positively onto the new two-piece carrier. These second-pattern guns had the detachable lock mechanism set into a rearward extension of the frame.

Fogerty rifles were made in small numbers until the assets of the American Repeating Rifle Co. were acquired by Winchester in August 1869.

MILITARY-MODEL RIFLE, 1868 TYPE

Made by the Fogerty Rifle Co., Boston, Massachusetts, and by the American Repeating Rifle Co., Boston, Massachusetts, 1868-9.
Total production: 100? **Chambering:** 56-50 Spencer, rimfire. **Action:** locked by a vertically-moving block operated by the trigger guard.
DATA FOR RIFLE
48in overall; about 9.5lb empty. 30in barrel, 3-groove rifling; concentric. Tube magazine in the butt, 7 rounds. Leaf-and-slider rear sight graduated to 1200yd? Performance not known. Socket bayonet.

This was offered in long and short form. The barrel of the full-stock rifle was retained by three screwed bands, the middle band carrying a swivel. The 20-inch barrel of the carbine was held in the short forend by a single band, and a sling bar lay on the left side of the breech. The magazines were usually loaded through a port in the butt trap, but a few guns are known—all 45-caliber carbines—with a loading port in the rear left side of the butt.

SPORTING-MODEL RIFLE

Made by the Fogerty Rifle Co., Boston, Massachusetts, and by the American Repeating Rifle Co., Boston, Massachusetts, 1868-9.
Total production: 1500-2000? **Chambering:** 40 rimfire. **Action:** as military rifle, above.
44.1in overall; about 9lb empty. 26.2in barrel, 3-groove rifling; concentric. Tube magazine in the butt, 7 rounds. Standing-block rear sight. Performance not known.

This gun had a half-octagon barrel and a short forend with a brass or pewter tip. A cut-off button (fitted to all but the earliest guns) protruded beneath the butt immediately ahead of the trigger. It could be pushed upward to disconnect the magazine feed mechanism. An optional adjustable rear sight could be fitted on the tang running down the butt wrist behind the hammer.

• Franklin

This was a tube magazine repeater designed by General William Franklin and made by Colt's Patent Fire Arms Mfg. Co. in Hartford, Connecticut. Submitted unsuccessfully to the 1878 U.S. Army trials, development of the Colt-Franklin rifle continued for several years; patents were still being granted on a refinements of the basic pattern as late as 1885.

• Freeman

Austin Freeman of Binghampton, New York, patented a radial-block breech mechanism in January 1872. The principal claims to novelty concerned the interlocking shoulders on the block and hammer body. Three 50-caliber Freeman muskets were tested by the U.S. Army in 1872—as No. 50, No. 59 and No. 76—but none passed the initial examination stages and details of their construction are lacking. It is assumed that they were radial-block patterns, but a patent protecting a flattened block rotating around a vertical pivot in the frame was granted in December 1873; at least one of the submissions may have been of this type.

• Gallager

The first patent granted by the U.S. Patent Office to Mahlon J. Gallager of Savannah, Georgia, was dated 12th July 1859. Developed in collaboration with William Gladding, this gun had a split chamber with a pivoting breech-piece and a tipping barrel. The action was unlocked by rotating the trigger guard laterally. It was also remarkable chiefly for its strange self-primed pinfire cartridge with an oviform case.

The basic design was subsequently improved by Gallager, who received U.S. patent no. 29,157 on 17th July 1860 to protect a more conventional gun with a barrel which simultaneously moved forward and tipped down to give access to the chamber. The breech lever doubled as a trigger guard.

The Gallager carbine, made by Richardson & Overman during the Civil War. (W&W)

Unfortunately, Gallager placed half the chamber in the standing breech and the remainder in the barrel. Even though the carbines were normally issued with Poultney's or Jackson's patent cartridges, they were notorious for jamming.

When the breech was opened after firing, the barrel moved straight forward before tipping upward at the breech. Owing to the absence of an extractor, however, spent cases usually stuck fast in the breech or the barrel. A special combination tool was issued with each gun, but was easily lost and too flimsy to remove the most obstinate cases.

Soldiers regarded the Gallager as greatly inferior to any of the breech-loaders chambering metal-case ammunition. The federal government acquired 22,728 carbines prior to 30th June 1866, but they scarcely represented a bargain.

1861-PATTERN CARBINE

Made by Richardson & Overman, Philadelphia, 1861-4.

Total production: at least 20,000. **Action:** locked by the trigger guard/breech lever. **Chambering:** 52-caliber combustible cartridge, fired by a caplock.

39.2in overall, 7.55lb empty. 22.25in barrel, 3-groove rifling; RH, concentric. Single-shot only. Block and three-leaf rear sight graduated to 500yd. 900-1000 fps, depending on cartridge. No bayonet.

The standard Gallager lacked a forend and relied on a conventional side-hammer caplock for ignition. It had iron mounts and a patch box on the right side of the butt. A ring-and-bar assembly was attached to the left side of the breech. A typical example bore an acknowledgement of Gallager's 1860 patent on the lock plate, together with 'MANUFACTD. BY' above 'RICHARDSON & OVERMAN', 'PHILADA.' and the serial number. Despite severe shortcomings, the federal government purchased 17,728 caplock Gallager carbines between 31st August 1861 and 10th December 1864. Others were acquired by other units raised in individual states and through private purchase.

SIMILAR GUNS

Carbine, cartridge type. Five thousand guns, made to a modified pattern chambering 56-50 Spencer rimfire cartridges, were ordered in May 1864. The last batches were delivered into Federal store in June 1865.

Sporting patterns. Though the Gallager made a poor military weapon, small quantities were converted after the end of the American Civil War to handle a variety of metal-case cartridges. Others were converted to shotguns.

• Garand

John Garand was granted U.S. patent 1,892,541 to protect his perfected rifle on 12th April 1930. Gas tapped from a port under the muzzle forced a spring-loaded operating rod backward, acting on a roller on the right side of the bolt to rotate the lugs out of engagement with the receiver. The bolt and operating rod assembly retreated, ejecting a spent case and re-cocking the hammer, then returned to reload the chamber and re-lock the bolt for another shot.

The worst feature was the idiosyncratic magazine, which required a special clip and would not accept single cartridges. The clip ejected automatically after the last shot had been fired, which was at best a nuisance and at worst potentially fatal in situations where silence was required. In spite of these flaws, however, the M1 rifle gave the U.S. soldier a great advantage over his opponents.

THE FIRST STEPS

The U.S. Army's dormant interest in automatic rifles was rekindled by the submission of Bang and Murphy-Manning patterns in 1911. Though neither performed impressively, they inspired trials with a selection of guns in 1916-18. Garand's first efforts—dating from 1920-4—relied on the backward movement of a deep-seated primer to unlock the breech on firing. The guns worked well enough, but required special ammunition. They were tested against Thompson, Hatcher-Bang and Berthier rifles and then, from 1924 onward, against the highly promising delayed-blowback Pedersen.

Primer-actuated Garands were not made in quantity, though an order for 24 of the 276-caliber 1922-type guns was completed in the summer of 1924. Tests of the promising Pedersen rifle in 1926 were followed by extended trials undertaken with 10 modified Thompson Auto Rifles and 10 improved or 1924-model Garands.

An inconclusive report was submitted on 15th June 1926 and, at the end of July, the Ordnance Board ordered a Garand to be made for standard 30-caliber ball ammunition. The crimped-in primers of the service cartridges forced John Garand to abandon the primer-actuated locking system in favor of gas operation, settling on a muzzle port and a piston-operating rod under the barrel after experimenting with a Bang-type muzzle cup.

In March 1927, the Cavalry Board reported that the field trials of primer-actuated Garand, delayed-blowback Thompson and recoil-operated Springfield rifles had failed to resolve the competition. By the end of the year, therefore, a gas-operated 276-caliber Garand had also been sanctioned. Throughout the Spring of 1928, the Infantry and Cavalry Boards experimented with 276-caliber Tl Pedersen Rifles, submitting highly favorable reports in April. In June, however, the 'Pig Board' was appointed to consider the hitting power of rifle ammunition, followed by the creation of the Semi-Automatic Rifle Board (SRB) to supervise trials on behalf of the U.S. Army, Navy and Marine Corps.

On 13th August 1928, the SRB representatives tested the primer-actuated M1924 Garand, the 30-caliber Thompson Auto Rifle, two versions of the 276-caliber Tl Pedersen and an improved 256-caliber Bang. Another inconclusive report was submitted on 21st September. Experiments with the 30-caliber Garand ceased in February 1929, as the 276-caliber design was preferred.

The second series of SRB rifle trials was programmed for 1st July, but so few guns appeared that the committee postponed the acceptance date to 15th August 1929. The original submissions—Brauning, Colt-Browning, Holek, T1 Pedersen, T3 Garand and Thompson—were joined only by a Rheinmetall rifle and an incomplete White.

Submitted on 24th October, the trial board's report suggested that work on the 30-caliber Garand should recommence, and a prototype T3 pattern was ordered from Springfield Armory on 14th November 1929. The Ordnance Board tested two more rifles submitted by Joseph White of Boston in 1930, but found them to be less rugged than either the Pedersen or the Garand.

In the Spring of 1931, Springfield Armory completed the 20 276-caliber T3E2 Garands and dispatched them for trials against the T1 Pedersens. The third series of SRB trials lasted from 9th October 1931 to 4th January 1932, involving the T1E1 Garand (30-caliber), the T1 Pedersen, the T3E2 Garand and the renascent White Rifle.

THE EARLY DESIGNS

The original 1920-pattern primer-actuated Garand was withdrawn for improvement in May 1920, to be replaced in November 1921 by the improved 'M1921'.

Model 1922 rifle. An order for 24 of these guns, essentially similar to the M1921, was approved in March 1922. Tests against the Thompson Auto Rifle PC (or 'M1922') in the summer of 1925 showed that the Garand had greater promise, but that there was still much work to do. Improvements led to the 1924 pattern.

Model 1924 rifle. This improved M1922 was tested at Fort Benning against 10 Thompson Auto Rifles. The report of 15th June 1926 was inconclusive. Subsequently, however, the construction of the first 30-caliber Garand was authorized.

T1E1 rifle. The first gas-operated 30-caliber Garand appeared by the end of 1927. Trials were undertaken throughout 1928 against M1924 primer-actuation Garands, Thompson Auto Rifles, T1 Pedersen rifles and a 6.5mm Bang. The 30-caliber Garand was abandoned in February 1929. However, after tests undertaken throughout the summer of 1929—with Brauning, Colt-Browning, Holek, T1 Pedersen, T3 Garand, Thompson, Rheinmetall and White rifles—work on large-caliber Garand recommenced. A suitable T1E1 prototype was ordered from Springfield Armory on 14th November, though the gun did not appear until the autumn of 1931—breaking its bolt on trial. The T1E1 was successfully re-tested in March 1932 and 77 guns were ordered to a slightly modified design to facilitate field trials.

T1E2 rifle. These 30-caliber Garands, ordered in March 1932, were essentially similar to the later M1 pattern described below. On 3rd August 1933, the T1E2 designation was formally changed to 'Semi-Automatic Rifle, Caliber 30, M1'. Fifty guns were sent to the Infantry Board and 25 to the cavalrymen in May 1934, but so many complaints had been received that the guns were withdrawn for modification and did not reappear for more than a year. Trials of improved guns were completed by October 1935, allowing the

An M1C Garand sniper rifle
with an M73B1 sight.

M1 to be recommended for service and cleared for procurement by the Assistant Secretary of War on 7th November.

T3E2 rifle. In the Spring of 1931, Springfield Armory completed twenty of these 276-caliber Garands for trials against the T1 Pedersens until a suitable 30-caliber rifle became available. As the Federal government was viewing progress with increasing anxiety, a meeting was held in Washington DC on 4th January 1932. The retention of 276-caliber was confirmed, production of 125 T3E2 Garands in Springfield Armory being authorized. However, as a result of General Douglas MacArthur's intervention, the reduction in caliber (and the order for T3E2 rifles) was rescinded on 25th February 1932 and interest in T1E1 Garand was renewed.

M1 RIFLE

Made by the Springfield Armory, Springfield, Massachusetts (4.617 million, 1937-57); by the Winchester-Western Division of Olin Industries, New Haven, Connecticut (513,580, 1940-5); by Harrington & Richardson, Inc., Worcester, Massachusetts (445,600, 1951-4); and by the International Harvester Corporation, Chicago, Illinois (457,750, 1951-4).

Total production: about 6.034 million. **Chambering:** 30-06, rimless.
Action: locked by rotating lugs on the bolt head into the receiver; gas operated, semi-automatic only.

43.5in overall, 9.5lb empty. 24in barrel, 4-groove rifling; RH, concentric. Internal clip-loaded box magazine, 8 rounds. Tangent rear sight graduated to 2000yd. 2740 fps with M2 ball cartridges. M1 sword bayonet.

The M1 Garand was standardized on 9th January 1936, but manufacturing problems delayed the first deliveries of machine-made guns until September 1937. The rifle had a one-piece pistol grip stock extending almost to the muzzle, allowing only the last few inches of the gas tube and barrel to protrude. A handguard ran forward from the receiver ring, and the solitary band carried a swivel; the other swivel lay beneath the butt. The magazine was contained within the stock, while a distinctive tangent rear sight was fitted to the receiver behind the feed way.

Daily production in the Springfield factory reached 100 by the beginning of September 1939. Unfortunately, the early problems seriously damaged the M1's reputation long before samples were badly received at the 1939 National Matches, and a major redesign of the gas-cylinder assembly and barrel had to be authorized on 26th October. In February 1940, the Ordnance Committee ruled that no further action be taken with the promising Johnson rifle (q.v.) in case it affected remedial work on the Garand.

By 10th January 1941, Springfield Armory was making 600 M1 rifles a day, and the first of Winchester's 65,000-gun 'educational' contract had also appeared. By September 1943, Springfield Armory had reached a production total of 100,000 and was adding 4,000 daily.

Garand production by VJ-Day amounted to about 4.028 million; 600,000 or more were made immediately after the war, and work began again during the Korean conflict. A production license was granted to Beretta (q.v.) in 1952 to make new guns to honor NATO/SEATO contracts. The M5 knife bayonet was approved in 1955. The conventional muzzle ring of the M1 pattern was replaced by a small rearward-facing spigot on the upper part of the guard, which locked into the gas-plug housing beneath the barrel. M1 rifle production finally ended on 17th May 1957.

SIMILAR GUNS

M1C sniper rifle (known during development as 'M1E7'). Standardized in July 1944, this had an M73 (Lyman Alaskan) or M73B1 (Weaver 330) telescope sight in a Griffin & Howe side mount. M1C rifles were often issued with the conical T37 flash-hider, subsequently standardized as the M2. They weighed 11.2-11.5lb with their sights.

M1 Ceremonial Pattern. These were single-shot M1 conversions, made for the American Legion and the Veterans of Foreign Wars for saluting purposes.

M1D sniper rifle (known during development as 'M1E8'). Standardized in September 1944, this was generally issued with the M81 or M82 optical sight, the former offering a cross-hair reticle while the M82 had a post pattern. Like the M1C, the M1D was often found with the T37 (M2) flash hider.

M1E5 rifle. An alternative designation for the original folding-butt version of the compact T26 rifle (q.v.).

M1E7 rifle. A designation applied during the development phase of the M1C sniper rifle (q.v.), adopted in the summer of 1944.

M1E8 rifle. This designation was used during the development of the 1944-vintage M1D sniper rifle, described below.

M1E14. A shortage of M14 and M16 rifles in the early 1960s prompted the U.S. Navy to develop a special chamber insert to enable the 30-06 M1 to fire 7.62x51 NATO cartridges. Patented by naval officer Richard Haley and civilian James O'Conner, then developed by H.P. White Laboratories, Inc., it consisted of a small sleeve in the front of the chamber to compensate for the shorter case-neck and different shoulder of the NATO round. The insert was retained in the gun simply by firing two eight-round clips to expand it against the existing chamber walls. The first 10 M1E14 rifles—subsequently officially redesignated 'Rifle, 7.62mm, Mk 2 Model 0'—were successfully converted by the American Machine & Foundry Company of York, Pennsylvania, in the summer of 1964.

M1 NM rifle ('National Match'). These rifles mated specially-selected actions with barrels of proven accuracy, and had special attention paid to their triggers. The first batches were made in 1953 (800 new guns) and the last in 1963, when 3640 service rifles were rebuilt. Production totaled a little less than 45,000: 21,390 new guns and 23,460 rebuilds.

Mark 2 Model 0 rifle. Production of the perfected version of the M1E14 (above) began in 1965, but insert-ejection problems were encountered as soon as the modified rifles entered service. An improved insert was hastily developed by the Navy Weapons Production Engineering Center in Crane, Indiana, to cure the faults. Production was surprisingly large: AMF made 17,050 Model 0 guns with the first-pattern chamber insert, before a modified 'Model 1' version was adopted. The rifles were all marked '7.62 M.M.' on the rear of the receiver.

Mark 2 Model 1 rifle. These were comparable to the Mk 2 Mod. 0, but the design of the chamber insert was improved. About 5,000 Model 1 Garand conversions were made by the American Machine & Foundry Company, and 12,050 by Harrington & Richardson.

Mark 2 Model 2 rifle. This designation was applied to 7.62x51 Garand conversions with new barrels, 8750 being supplied by Harrington & Richardson.

T20 rifle. The use of fully-automatic assault rifles by the Germans encouraged the Ordnance Department to develop the first selective-fire Garands in 1944. Beginning work in the Spring, the design staff of the Springfield Armory had completed this gun by the end of August to compete against the Remington-sponsored T22. In September 1944, however, the Army Ground Forces headquarters revised the basic specification and the guns were withdrawn for modification.

T20E1 and T20E2 rifles. The first of these improved selective-fire designs was tested at Aberdeen Proving Ground in January/February 1945. The T20E1 was judged to be almost acceptable and 100 improved T20E2 rifles were successfully tested in May; 100,000 were to be ordered in 1945-6, but the war ended before the contract could be placed.

T22 rifle. This was an early selective-fire Garand built by Remington to compete with the Springfield-designed T20. It was replaced by the improved T22E1 in the summer of 1944.

T22E1 rifle. An improved version of the abortive T20. Trials undertaken at Aberdeen Proving Ground in the early months of 1945 revealed that, though some promise was being shown, more work was needed. The project was not abandoned until the Spring of 1948.

T26 rifle. This folding-butt derivative, also known as the 'M1E5', was developed in Springfield in late summer 1944 but proved to be too weak. In July 1945, however, Colonel William Alexander of the Pacific Warfare Board requested 15,000 short M1 rifles for jungle warfare. About 150 prototypes were subsequently converted in the ordnance workshops of the 6th Army in the Philippines, one being sent to Springfield Armory for review. Springfield subsequently developed the T26 Wood Stock Garand from this sample, but the project was canceled when fighting in the Pacific ended.

T27 rifle. Based on the M1, this chambered the 30 T65 cartridge, but the project terminated in March 1948.

T35 rifle. Fifty of these semi-automatics, based on the M1, were built before the project terminated in 1950—to be briefly revived in the mid 1950s without success.

T36 rifle. This was a derivative of the T20E2 with a lightweight barrel designed by Lloyd Corbett at Springfield Armory in November 1949; it chambered the 30-caliber T65 cartridge and was capable of selective fire. Suspended by the outbreak of the Korean War in 1950, the project was soon resurrected and the rifle became the T44.

M14 RIFLE

Made by the Springfield Armory, Springfield, Massachusetts (167,100, 1958-62); by Harrington & Richardson, Inc., Worcester, Massachusetts (537,580, 1959-64); by the Winchester-Western Division of Olin Industries, New Haven, Connecticut (356,500, 1959-64); and by Thompson-Ramo-Woolridge, Inc., Cleveland, Ohio (319,160, 1962-4).

Total production: 1.38 million. **Chambering:** 7.62x51 NATO, rimless.
Action: as M1 Garand, above.
DATA FOR STANDARD M14
44in overall, 8.56lb empty. 22in barrel, 4-groove rifling; RH, concentric. Detachable box magazine, 20 rounds. Tangent sight graduated to 1500yd. 2750 fps with M59 ball cartridges. Cyclic rate 725-775 rds/min. M6 knife bayonet.

Suspended in 1951 by the intervention of the Korean War, work on a modernized Garand created the T44 by amalgamating the action of the T20E2 with the gas cylinder of the T25 and the magazine of the abortive T31. Tested extensively against the T25 and the FN FAL ('T48' to the U.S. Army), the T44, chambered for the 30-caliber T65 cartridge, performed so well that the Ordnance Department pressed strongly for improvement. A heavy-barrel T44E1 appeared in October.

After procuring a few FAL rifles—3200 were purchased in Belgium in 1950-6—testing was undertaken at Fort Benning in August 1952. The FAL was preferred, ahead of the new T44, the T25 and the British EM-2. The T25 and EM-2 were eliminated, but the Ordnance Board was still impressed by the performance of the T44 and instructed Springfield to make 500 for trials against 500 T48 FAL-type rifles ordered from Harrington & Richardson.

On 15th December 1953, the 30-caliber (7.62) T65 cartridge was approved as a NATO standard, the perfected T65E3 being standardized by the Ordnance Committee in August 1954. Arctic trials undertaken in the winter of 1954 showed that the T44 rifle performed much better in sub-zero conditions than the T48—but after remedial work on the latter, additional trials in 1954-5 were tied.

However, the T48 rifle failed the Fort Benning 'Combat Course Test' so comprehensively that it was withdrawn so that British and Belgian representatives could supply their latest weapons for comparison. Surviving T48 rifles were then rebuilt in Springfield Armory to incorporate lessons learned in the Sudan by the British. A final test at Fort Benning in April 1956 showed that the T44 and

T48 were equally suitable for adoption. The Ordnance Board recommended the indigenous T44 on the grounds that it was lighter and better suited to U.S. production techniques.

Five years of trials with the T44 series (T44E2-T44E6) were finally resolved on 1st May 1957, when the T44E4 was adopted as the '7.62mm Rifle M14' and the T44E5 was accepted as the heavy-barreled M15 respectively.

The M14 was essentially similar to the Garand internally, though the detachable box magazine, shortened gas tube, and pistol grip half-stock were most distinctive. The selector on many guns (unofficially known as 'M14 M[odified]') was plugged to restrict them to semi-automatic fire, though a standard three-position selector could be substituted when required.

The earliest M14 rifles were made with wooden stocks and handguards, but the guard soon became ventilated fiberglass-reinforced plastic; finally, a durable synthetic stock and a ribbed non-ventilated handguard were adopted.

Work ceased in 1963, and the production machinery was sold to the government of Taiwan (q.v.) in 1967. In 1968, however, severe shortages of efficient sniper rifles—particularly in Vietnam—led to a demand for 1800 specially selected M14-type rifles fitted with 3-9x Leatherwood Adjustable Ranging Telescopes (ART). Modified M14-based rifles are still being marketed in the U.S.A. by Springfield Armory, Inc. (q.v.).

SIMILAR GUNS

M14A1 rifle. Introduced in 1960, this was a selective-fire M14. Five differing butts were tested before the M14E2 was standardized as the 'Rifle, 7.62mm, M14A1'. Credited to Captain Durward Gosney of the U.S. Army Infantry Board, the M14A1 employed the standard M14 action, but had a stabilizer over the compensator and would not accept a bayonet. A bipod with adjustable telescoping legs was fitted, the straight wooden stock had a vertical pistol grip behind the trigger, a folding forward hand grip was often fitted, and the rubber buttplate had a folding shoulder strap. Handguards were invariably synthetic.

M14E1 and M14E2 rifles. These designations were applied to experimental predecessors of the M14A1 (q.v.).

M14M rifle. This designation was applied unofficially to otherwise-standard M14 rifles which had been restricted to semi-automatic fire by plugging the selector.

M14 NM rifle ('National Match'). The first of these rifles appeared in 1963, with specially selected 'accurized' barrels and fiberglass-bedded barrels. The M14 usually outshot the FAL, which was ascribed by many to the superiority of a rotating bolt (which moves in a straight line) over a displaced block.

M15 rifle. Similar internally to the M14, the M15 had a heavy barrel, a fixed-leg bipod attached to the gas cylinder, a strengthened stock, and a folding shoulder strap on the buttplate. Made only in small numbers, the unsuccessful M15 was declared obsolete on 17th December 1959.

T44 series (T44E1-T44E6). The designation applied to the development model of the M14.

M21 rifle. Known during development as the XM21, this sniper-rifle derivative of the M14 was thoroughly tested against the Marine Corps Remington 700, the MAS FR-F1 and the Steyr SSG-69. The modified Garand proved to be as accurate as any of its rivals at long range, particularly when fired with M118 match ammunition, and so conversion of 1435 National Match (NM) pattern M14 rifles to XM21 standards began in 1970 in Rock Island Arsenal. The XM21 was formally standardized in December 1975 as the M21. It remained the standard U.S. Army sniper rifle until recent approval of the bolt-action 7.62mm Remington Model 24 Sniper System. During the XM21 development period, about 300 M14 National Match rifles were fitted with M84 sights as a temporary measure.

OTHER USERS

In addition to Argentina, Brazil, Indonesia, Italy, Morocco, and Nigeria, where guns were either made or assembled from parts, many other countries have used Garands; the colossal numbers of M1 rifles made in 1936-57 enabled countless thousands to be distributed to friendly forces through the U.S. Military Aid Programs. Virtually all of the rifles retained their American marks and numbers, unlike those newly made in Italy or Taiwan. Among major M1 users have been:

Denmark (69,810 'Gevær m/50' supplied prior to 1964, some subsequently converted to 7.62x51).

Ethiopia (20,700 M1 plus an unknown quantity of Beretta BM-59 rifles).

France (232,500, 1950-64).

Federal Republic of Germany (46,750 prior to 1965).

Greece (186,090 M1 and 1880 M1C/M1D prior to 1975).

Iran (165,490 prior to 1964).

Israel (up to 60,000 prior to 1975).

Jordan (25,000-30,000 prior to 1974).

Laos (36,270, 1950-75).

Norway (72,800 prior to 1964).

Pakistan (possibly 150,000 prior to 1975).

Paraguay (30,750 prior to 1975).

Philippines (34,300 M1 and 2630 M1D in 1950-75).

Saudi Arabia (34,530 prior to 1975).

South Korea (296,450, 1964-74).

South Vietnam (220,300 M1 and 520 M1C/M1D, 1950-75).

Thailand (about 40,000 prior to 1975).

Turkey (312,430, 1953-70).

Venezuela (55,670 M1, prior to 1975).

In addition, the U.S. armed forces abandoned nearly a million 30-caliber M1/M2 Carbines, M1 Garand and M14 rifles in Vietnam in the mid 1970s. M14 rifles have been less widely distributed than the M1, large-scale users including Ethiopia (23,450 in 1971-4) and Israel (at least 22,500 prior to 1975).

• Gibbs, bolt-action type

The Gibbs Rifle Company of Martinsburg, West Virginia, succeeded to the rifle-making operations of Parker-Hale (Britain, q.v.) in 1990. Substantial numbers of complete and partly-complete rifles were accompanied by a large quantity of parts, allowing rifles to be marketed under the Gibbs name until 1995.

The Model 1300C Scout appeared in 1992 to use spare 1200-series components. It had a 20in barrel with a muzzle brake, a laminated birch stock, and a detachable 10-round box magazine. Chambered only for the 243 or 308 Winchester cartridges, it was about 41in overall and weighed 8.5lb.

The Midland Model 2100 rifle, unlike the British-made gun of the same designation, was built on a modified 1898-pattern action. Offered in 22-250, 243 Winchester, 6mm Remington, 6.5x55, 7x57, 7x64, 300 Winchester Magnum, 30-06 or 308 Winchester, it had a walnut stock with a low Monte Carlo comb; 43in long with the standard 22in barrel, it weighed 7lb. The Model 2600 was similar, but had a plain hardwood stock; the Model 2700 Lightweight, announced in 1992, had a slender barrel, an alloy trigger guard/floorplate unit, and a lighter stock; the Model 2800 was a minor variant with a laminated birch Monte Carlo-pattern stock.

• Gibbs, break-open type

Patented by Lucius Gibbs in January 1856, the carbine relied on a trigger guard lever to tip the barrel upward at the breech. Unlike the otherwise similar Gallager (q.v.) carbine, the Gibbs pattern fired a combustible paper cartridge; an annular collar in the breechface expanded momentarily to act as a gas seal. A conventional side-hammer caplock was used, the flash from the cap passing down the nipple channel and out along the hollow axis of the conical cartridge-piercing spigot.

BREECH-LOADING CARBINE

Made for William Brooks of New York City by William Marston, the Phoenix Armory, New York City, 1863.

Total production: no more than 1100. **Chambering:** 52-caliber combustible cartridge, fired by a caplock. **Action:** a tipping barrel is locked in place by the operating lever.

39in overall, 7.37lb empty. 22in barrel, 6-groove rifling; concentric. Single-shot only. Three-leaf rear sight for ranges to 500yd. Performance not known. No bayonet.

On 18th December 1861, the Ordnance Department contracted with Brooks for 10,000 carbines; lacking facilities of his own, Brooks sub-contracted most of the work to Marston. Deliveries commenced in April 1863, but the Phoenix Armory was destroyed on 13th June—during the New York Draft Riots—and work on the carbines ceased after only 1052 had been accepted. They had conventional wooden forends, barrels held by a single band, and a distinctive closed ring on the breech-lever tip.

• Golden Eagle

Golden Eagle Rifles of Houston, Texas, imported Model 7000 bolt-action rifles made in Tochigi, Japan, by Nikko Firearms. Available in wide range of chamberings, including 270 Winchester and 300 Weatherby Magnum, the standard 'Model 7000 Golden Eagle Big Game' had 24in or 26in barrels; Grade I was the standard pattern, with a walnut half-stock, Grade II was the deluxe pattern with better-quality woodwork. A Model 7000 African Rifle was also offered in 375 H&H Magnum and 458 Winchester Magnum only. Work was confined to 1976-81.

• Golden State

Golden State Arms Corporation of Pasadena, California, made the Centurion Model 100 (plain), 200 (deluxe) and other rifles on the basis of the Spanish Santa Barbara action. Dating from the mid 1960s, they ranged from plain guns with blind three-cartridge magazines to conventional patterns with hinged magazine floorplates.

• Goulding

Gun No. 11 in the U.S. Army trials of 1865 was a carbine submitted by John Goulding of Worcester, Massachusetts, in accordance with his U.S. patent 42,573 of May 1864. It was little more than a minor variant of the Warner pattern (q.v.), with a hinged breechblock and an extractor lever protruding beneath the forend. A cam-lock thumb lever lay on the right side, just in front of the hammer, to improve the security of the breech.

• Gray

Joshua Gray of Boston submitted three carbines to the U.S. Army trials of 1865, where they were tested as Guns No. 12-14. Made in accordance with U.S. patent 54,068, granted in April 1866, they were easily distinguished by large slab-sided receivers and a sliding magazine tube—the subject of a patent granted in July 1865—in the forend beneath the barrel. The breech mechanism, operated by an underlever doubling as the trigger guard, was based on a block which was pulled radially back and down to expose the chamber for reloading. A sling ring lay on the left side of the receiver, and there was a leaf-and-slider sight on top of the barrel.

The Gray conversion system tested by the U.S. Army in 1867, however, was made to an older design patented in June 1865. Built as a Springfield rifle-musket, the rifles were locked by a pivoting toplever. This could be pulled upward at the rear to release locking shoulders from their abutment with the receiver and then retract the breechblock. The Gray rifle worked well on trial, though the small size of the breech-handle grip was criticized. However, other submissions were preferred and nothing more was done.

• Greene

James Durrell Greene received his first U.S. patent in June 1854, to protect the pivoting-barrel carbine described in the British section. This was followed by two patents for a self-contained cartridge and an under-hammer bolt-action rifle. A successful test of a bolt-action gun in August 1857 persuaded the U.S. Army to order 100, but Greene preferred to travel to Europe where a 3000-gun order was obtained from Russia (q.v.) in 1859. A small quantity—possibly 350—may also have been sold to Egypt.

An improvement to the bolt-action design was patented in February 1862. When the Civil War began, Greene was commissioned in the Union Army and, after a few hundred of his guns had gone to Massachusetts volunteers, strenuous efforts were made to sell them to the Ordnance Department.

Though tests undertaken in the late Spring of 1862 were unfavorable, Greene and his backers persisted until 900 guns and accessories were ordered in January 1863.

GREENE RIFLE

Made by A.H. Waters & Co., Milbury, Massachusetts.

Total production: at least 4000. **Chambering:** see text. **Action:** locked by rotating two lugs into their seats behind the chamber as the bolt handle was turned down.

52.5in overall, 10lb empty. 36in barrel, oval bore rifling; RH. Single-shot only. Leaf-type rear sight with a stepped base, graduated to 800yd. About 990 fps with a 550-grain bullet. Socket bayonet.

The Greene swivelling-barrel carbine.
This particular gun, a trials piece, bears
British marks on the lock plate and butt. (W&W)

This underhammer rifle had a straight-wristed one-piece stock with three sprung bands, and swivels beneath the butt and middle band. Lancaster-pattern oval bore rifling measured .530 and .546 on its minor and major axes respectively. The self-contained combustible cartridge had a projectile inserted in its base.

The breech was opened by pressing a release catch on the tang, rotating the bolt handle to the right, and retracting the bolt to expose the chamber. A single bullet was placed in the chamber, and the bolt handle was pushed forward to its limit to allow the bolt-sleeve to seat the bullet at the front of the chamber. The bolt was then re-opened, a combustible cartridge was dropped into the breech, and the action was closed and locked.

Consequently, a properly loaded rifle had one projectile ahead of the charge and a second bullet acting as a gas-seal. The rear or 'gas-seal' bullet was pushed forward after firing to allow another cartridge to be inserted.

Though the Greene could be used as a muzzle-loader if the chamber became too foul, the quirky loading procedure and the underhammer caplock were heartily disliked. The 900-gun order was completed in March 1863—promptly, by Civil War standards—but the rifles were still in store when hostilities ceased. They were eventually sold at auction in the 1890s.

• Grendel

S-16 SNIPER RIFLE

Made by Grendel, Inc., Rockledge, Florida, about 1992 to date.
Currently in production. **Chambering:** 7.62x36 Grendel. **Action:** generally as ArmaLite AR-15/M16 series (q.v.).

39.1in overall; 10.5lb with magazine, but without sights. 16in barrel, 6-groove rifling; RH, concentric. Detachable box magazine, 20 rounds. Optical sight. 1075 fps with ball ammunition.

This rifle combines the gas-operated rotating-bolt action of the proven ArmaLite with a full-length silencer. However, instead of relying on a subsonic version of a standard 5.56x45 or 7.62x51 cartridge—which are inevitably compromises—Grendel preferred to develop a unique cartridge to reproduce at 300yd the performance of a 9mm Parabellum bullet as it leaves a pistol muzzle. This was achieved largely by enlarging the mouth of the standard 5.56mm case to accept a much heavier bullet, which ensures that the muzzle velocity remains consistently below the speed of sound. The rifle is similar externally to the M16A1, but has a 'second hand' spur on the underside of the butt and a Picatinny Rail for optical or electro-optical sights instead of a carrying handle. A rail conforming with NATO standards can be substituted.

• Grillett

Guns No. 15-17 tested by the U.S. Army in 1865 were carbines submitted by Alexander Grillett of Philadelphia, who had received an appropriate U.S. patent (no. 45,152) in November 1864. Locked by a radial-block mechanism, they had one-piece half-stocks with a single band encircling the forend. A sling ring was mounted on a short bar on the left side of the breech above the trigger, and a small folding leaf sight lay on the barrel. A short straight cocking spur protruded from the right side of the action.

• Gross

Patented in August 1859 by Henry Gross of Tiffin, Ohio, this odd-looking gun was marketed as the 'Gross'; as the 'Cosmopolitan', named after the manufacturer; as the 'Gwyn & Campbell', after the owners of Cosmopolitan; or as the 'Union', owing to a mark appearing on many guns.

GROSS CARBINE

Made by the Cosmopolitan Arms Co., Hamilton, Ohio.
Total production: 1500? **Chambering:** 52-caliber combustible cartridge, fired by a caplock. **Action:** locked by propping the pivoting chamber-block in place with the trigger guard lever.

39in overall, 6.6lb empty. 19in barrel, 3-groove rifling; RH, concentric. Single-shot only. Leaf-and-slider rear sight graduated to 700yd. Performance not known. No bayonet.

These guns were ordered to arm volunteers mustered in Illinois. They lacked forends, and were operated by pulling the breech lever down to pivot the breechblock face upward; a separate breech cover, with an integral loading groove, dropped to allow a cartridge to be pushed into the chamber.

True Gross/Cosmopolitan guns had a serpentine breech lever, doubling as a trigger guard, with the tip curving to lock into a catch on the frame. They also had a rounded hammer shank. About 1140 of them were purchased by the federal authorities in 1862.

• Gwyn & Campbell

Once the order for Gross carbines (q.v.) had been fulfilled, Edward Gwyn and Abner Campbell simplified the action of the Gross carbine. U.S. patent 36,709 of October 1862 protected a grooved breechblock which simply dropped at the front to expose the chamber.

GWYN & CAMPBELL CARBINE

Made by Gwyn & Campbell, Hamilton, Ohio.
Total production: 10,000? **Chambering:** 52-caliber combustible cartridge, fired by a caplock. **Action:** generally as Gross pattern, above.

39.2in overall, 6.55lb empty. 20.1in barrel, 3-groove rifling; RH, concentric. Single-shot only. Leaf-and-slider rear sight graduated to 700yd. Performance not known. No bayonet.

Similar to the earlier Gross pattern, lacking a forend, this had a ring-and-bar sling mount on the left side of the breech. The breech lever locked into the front of the catch on the underside of the butt. A case-hardened lock plate had a hammer with flattened sides, the barrel was sometimes tinned (for shipboard use?), and the rear sight had been simplified. The federal government purchased 8202 Gwyn & Campbell carbines prior to 30th June 1866, and it is assumed that others were sold commercially.

SIMILAR GUNS

Improved pattern. Two carbines were tested by the U.S. Army in 1865, as Guns No. 18 and No. 19. Improvements had been made in the trial guns, but doubt remains over details. One was externally similar to the Spencer (q.v.), but lacked the butt magazine and had an additional reverse-curve catch inside the front of the trigger guard. The other carbine had a distinctive centrally-hung hammer with a low spur, lacked a forend, and displayed slender reinforcing straps running down the wrist on both sides of the butt. A ring-and-bar appeared on the left reinforcing strap. The rear sight was a small stepped-base folding-leaf unit on the barrel.

• Hall

On 21st May 1811, Captain John Hall and his agent, William Thornton of Washington DC, patented a breech-loading rifle with a detachable breech chamber supporting the lock-work. U.S. Army trials undertaken in 1813 and 1816 were successful enough to encourage the purchase of 100 'Patent Rifles' in January 1817. Experience with these led directly to the adoption of the M1819 rifle, the first breech-loader ever to be issued for military service on a large scale.

The Hall rifle could be fired with surprising rapidity, tests suggesting that the regulation muzzle-loaders could fire only 37-43 shots for each 100 from the breech-loader. However, large powder charges were required to overcome tendencies to leak gas at the breech—even though the Hall was not particularly powerful. Tests

U.S.A.

in the early 1840s revealed that the muzzle velocity of the Hall-North carbine was considerably less that the otherwise comparable Jenks.

Production of Hall-system guns was surprisingly large, allowing 1575 rifles and 3520 carbines to be bought back into federal store from state reserves during the Civil War. An inventory prepared on 31st December 1862 showed that 827 flintlock and 1592 caplock rifles remained in the federal arsenals. Several thousand others, acquired from a variety of sources, were used by the Confederate Army.

Note: the caliber of the Halls was customarily assessed on the basis of 'balls per pound', and the actual bore diameter was considerably smaller—e.g., the true caliber of '.54' guns was 52.

MODEL 1819 RIFLE
Made by the U.S. government manufactory, Harper's Ferry, Virginia (19,680, 1823-40), and by Simeon North, Middletown, Connecticut (5700, 1829-36).
Total production: at least 25,480. **Chambering:** 54-diameter ball, flintlock ignition. **Action:** detachable hinged-breech unit, locked by a catch ahead of the trigger guard.
DATA FOR A GUN DATED 1837
52.75in overall, 10.25lb empty. 32.65in barrel, 16-groove rifling; RH, concentric. Single shot only. Fixed standing-block rear sight. 1475 fps with a 70-grain powder charge. Socket bayonet.

A contract signed on 19th March 1819 allowed the U.S. Government to make 1000 Hall-system rifles, though a lack of machine tools delayed the first deliveries until 1823. The cock and frizzen were offset to the right of the breechblock to allow sight to be taken, and the trigger could be adjusted by turning a screw set into the sear. The barrel was held in the straight-grip stock by two bands and a nose cap, sprung until 1831 and pinned thereafter. A swivel was attached to the middle band, and the trigger guard extended backward to form a finger spur.

Once the initial order had been completed, in 1824, work on another 1000-gun contract began. The barrel was then shortened slightly and a third contract, for 6000, followed on 22nd April 1828. Work continued for another 16 years, though the final batches were made as caplocks (Model 1841, below); the last flintlock was completed in the late summer of 1840.

Harper's Ferry guns were marked 'J.H. HALL' and sometimes also 'H. FERRY' above 'US' and the date of manufacture. On 15th December 1828, however, as Harper's Ferry was unable to satisfy demands being made by individual states, 5000 Hall rifles were ordered from Simeon North. These lacked the finger-spur on the trigger guard, and the breech-latch was attached to the trigger guard plate instead of the breechblock. North received additional orders totaling 5200 in July 1829 and January 1835, but deliveries were never completed.

MODEL 1833 CARBINE
Made by Simeon North, Middletown, Connecticut (1833-4).
Total production: 1026. **Chambering:** 54-diameter ball, fired by a caplock. **Action:** a hinged chamber was locked by a lever on top of the breech.
45in overall, 8.25lb empty. 26.2in barrel, smooth-bore. Single-shot only. Fixed standing-block sight. About 1320 fps with a 70-grain charge. Rod bayonet

Authorized for the First Regiment of Dragoons in 1833, this was the first caplock firearm to be issued in the U.S. Army. The barrel was held in the half-length stock with two bands, with a rod bayonet which could be extended beneath the muzzle and locked by a tongue on the retaining spring entering a groove cut across the bayonet body. A sling ring was anchored in the rearward exten-

sion of the trigger guard, and a chamber under the butt (protected by a hinged lid) contained patches and cleaning material.
SIMILAR GUNS
Model 1836 carbine. At least 2500 of these large-caliber (.69?) guns were made by Simeon North in 1836-9. About 40in overall, with an empty weight of 8.22lb, they had 21in smooth-bore barrels and rod bayonets. Often erroneously listed as the 'Model 1837', these guns were ordered for the Second Regiment of Dragoons on 20th June 1836. Stocks and other components were cannibalized from 1819-pattern flintlock rifles, but the breech mechanism was newly made. However, an eye-bolt was added through the stock wrist to hold the sling ring, and a hole was bored through the hammer neck. North obtained a contract for 10,000 1836-type Hall carbines in 1839, but few had been completed when the improved or 1840 pattern was substituted.

Militia carbines. These rifled Halls, often wrongly listed as the 'Model of 1836', are believed to have been supplied to the Alabama State Militia in 1838-9. They fired a 54-diameter ball through a 52-caliber barrel.

MODEL 1840 CARBINE
Patch and Huger types
Made by Simeon North, Middletown, Connecticut.
Total production: about 6500. **Chambering:** 54-diameter ball, fired by a caplock. **Action:** generally as M1833 carbine, above.
40in overall, 7.9lb empty. 21in barrel, smooth-bored. Single shot only. Fixed standing-block sight. About 1270 fps with a 70-grain charge. No bayonet.

This gun was authorized in September 1839, but production was deferred until North had completed a previous order. Work began in January 1840, but even the Ordnance Office realized that the Hall carbine could be improved; production was thus restricted to five hundred.

The short-barreled guns had a conventional ramrod instead of the fragile rod bayonet. The breech was unlocked by pivoting an 'L'-shape elbow lever forward from its rest position, against the trigger guard, then pressing upward to release the breechblock latch. This system was credited to U.S. Government arms inspector Nahum Patch. By 2nd May 1840, the unpopular elbow lever had been replaced by a fish-tail pattern proposed by Captain James Huger. Approximately 6000 Huger-lever carbines were delivered between August 1840 and July 1843.
SIMILAR GUNS
Model 1842 carbine, 1842-3. About 1000 of these guns were made in the government manufactory in Harper's Ferry, the last regulation-pattern Halls to be made there. They had Huger-pattern breech levers, modified trigger guard bows, brass furniture, and a swell-head ramrod. The drop at the heel of the butt was greatly reduced in an attempt to improve shooting comfort. Breechblocks were marked, typically, 'H.FERRY', 'US' and '1842' in three lines.

Model 1843 carbine, 1843-50. The 52-caliber Hall-North 'Improved Model of 1840' (or M1843) lacked the rod bayonet. A bar-and-ring ran from the second barrel band back along the left side of the receiver. A typical gun was about 40in long, weighed 8.1lb empty and had a 21in smooth-bore barrel. Simeon North supplied 1000 carbines with Huger fish-tail levers in 1843, followed by 500 guns with the side-mounted lever patented in July 1844 by North & Savage (U.S. no. 3686). The North & Savage lever—pulled downward to release the breechblock—was fitted to about 10,000 of the 11,000 1843-type carbines made by North.

Model 1843 carbine, rifled pattern, 1861-2. Five thousand Hall carbines (mostly M1843), were sold from New York Arsenal in the summer of 1861 to Arthur Eastman of Manchester, New Hampshire. They were re-sold to Simon Stevens of New York, rifled, and

The M1819 Hall-pattern
flintlock breech-loader. (W&W)

sold back to the commanding general of the Army Department of the West at such high prices that a full-scale Congressional investigation was authorized.

MODEL 1841 RIFLE

Made by the U.S. Government manufactory, Harper's Ferry, Virginia (1841-4).

Total production: 3190. **Chambering:** 54-diameter ball, fired by a caplock. **Action:** generally as M1840 carbine, above.

52.5in overall, 9.8lb empty. 32.5in barrel, 7-groove rifling; RH, concentric. Single-shot only. Fixed standing-block sight. 1475 fps with a 70-grain charge. Socket bayonet.

Hall died in 1840, but Harper's Ferry continued to make caplock long arms. Though many 1819-type flintlocks were converted, true 1841-type rifles shared the action of the 1840 carbine. Their Huger 'fish tail' unlatching lever was mounted on a latch plate made integrally with the trigger guard, and the rifling extended to the muzzle. The trigger guard lacked the finger rest, and the rear swivel apparently lay under the butt.

• Hammond

Carbines No. 20 and No. 21 tested by the U.S. Army in 1865 were the work of Henry Hammond of Providence, Rhode Island. Made in accordance with U.S. patent no. 44,798, granted in October 1864, they were modifications of the 'Bulldog' single-shot pistol. The barrel tipped sideways to eject or load. The stock was made in two pieces, with a half-length forend held by a single band.

• Hampden

Two experimental bolt-action rifles of this type, submitted by T.B. Wilson of Springfield, Massachusetts, were tested by the U.S. Army in 1891 without success. Both had magazines containing five 30-caliber rimmed cartridges, and weighed about 8lb apiece. Wilson obtained patents protecting his bolt-action designs in 1896-8, assigning the rights to Charles Billings of Hartford, Connecticut, which suggests that Billings & Spencer or their associates may have made the prototypes. Nothing else is known.

• Harrington & Richardson, autoloading type

Once trading from Gardner, Massachusetts, the long-established Harrington & Richardson, Inc., ceased trading in 1986. It was succeeded by H&R 1871, Inc., which offers a limited range of guns under its own name and also that of 'New England Firearms'. Prior to its demise, Harrington & Richardson—best known for inexpensive handguns—offered rifles ranging from autoloaders to shotgun-like break-open patterns.

MODEL 60 SPORTING RIFLE

Designed by Eugene Reising, this 45-caliber blowback was derived from the wartime Reising submachine gun. Production was confined to 1944-6. The gun had an 18.3in barrel and weighed about 7.5lb with an empty twelve-round box magazine (a 20-round pattern was optional). The plain pistol grip half-stock had a straight comb, with swivels beneath the butt and the slab-sided forend. A spring-leaf sight was attached to the extreme rear of the receiver.

SIMILAR GUNS

Model 65 Military rifle (known commercially as the 'General'), 1944-6. Developed as a trainer for the U.S. Marine Corps, this 22LR rimfire version of the Model 60 had a 23in heavy barrel and a half-stock with a butt-profile based on the M1 Garand. The detachable box magazine contained 10 rounds, a Redfield No. 70 peep sight was mounted on the rear of the receiver, and the front sight had eared protectors. Empty weight was about 9lb.

Model 150 Leatherneck rifle, 1949-53. Based on the Model 65, this had a 22in barrel and weighed only 7.25lb. The rear sight was an open spring-leaf pattern and the capacity of the box magazine was restricted to five rounds.

Model 151 Leatherneck rifle, 1949-53. This was a minor variant of the M150 with an adjustable Redfield No. 70 peep sight on the receiver.

Model 165 Leatherneck rifle, 1945-61. Essentially similar to the Model 65, this had a lighter 23in barrel and an open ramped front sight, though the Redfield receiver sight and the 10-round magazine were retained. Weight averaged 7.7lb.

MODEL 360 ULTRA AUTOMATIC RIFLE

Made by the Harrington & Richardson Arms Co., Worcester, Massachusetts, 1965-78.

Total production: not known. **Chambering options:** 243 or 308 Winchester **Action:** locked by rotating lugs on the bolt head into the receiver walls; gas operated, semi-automatic only.

DATA FOR A TYPICAL 243 EXAMPLE

44.5in overall, 7.45lb empty. 22in barrel, 4-groove rifling; RH, concentric. Detachable box magazine, 3 rounds. Williams ramp rear sight. 3500 fps with 80-grain bullet.

Introduced as the 'Model 308', this was renamed when the 243 option was added in 1967. An efficient and popular gun, it had a one-piece half-stock with checkering on the pistol grip and forend. The comb was customarily a roll-over design, the buttplate was rubber, and swivels lay beneath the butt and rosewood-tipped forend.

MODEL 800 LYNX RIFLE

Dating from 1958-60, this was a 22LR autoloader with a detachable five- or 10-round box magazine. It had a 22in barrel and weighed about 6lb. The pistol grip half-stock had a Monte Carlo comb sloping markedly upward towards the heel, and a synthetic trigger guard; a spring-leaf and elevator rear sight lay on the barrel.

MODEL 755 SAHARA RIFLE

Made only from 1963-71, for the 22 Short, Long or Long Rifle cartridges, this was a diminutive single shot auto-ejector operated by simple blowback. It had a pistol grip stock with a full-length forend. Weight was only about 4lb with the standard 18in barrel.

SIMILAR GUNS

Model 760 rifle, 1965-70. This was identical mechanically with the Sahara type, but had a conventional Monte Carlo-style pistol grip half-stock.

MODEL 700 SPORTING RIFLE

Made by Harrington & Richardson, Inc., Gardner, Massachusetts, 1979-85.

Total production: not known. **Chambering:** 22 Winchester Magnum rimfire. **Action:** no mechanical breech lock; blowback, semi-automatic only.

43.5in overall, 6.5lb empty. 22in barrel, 4-groove rifling; RH, concentric. Detachable box magazine, 5 or 10 rounds. Folding open-notch rear sight. 2000 fps with 40-grain bullet.

Made only from 1977-85, this was the only U.S.-made autoloader chambering the 22 WMR cartridge. The walnut half-stock had a pistol grip, a roll-over comb and a squared forend. The Model 700 received considerable critical acclaim when it appeared, but praise could not offset the comparative scarcity and high cost of magnum rimfire ammunition.

SIMILAR GUNS

Model 700DL rifle, 1979-85. This was a deluxe version, with a better stock and checkering on the pistol grip and forend.

• Harrington & Richardson, bolt-action type

MODEL 265 "REG'LAR" RIFLE

Introduced in 1946, this was a simple 22LR rimfire design locked by the base of the bolt handle turning down into its seat. The plain pistol grip half-stock had a short rounded forend. A 10-round detachable magazine and a 22in barrel were fitted; a Lyman No. 55H rear sight was used in conjunction with a ramped blade at the muzzle. Weight averaged 6.5lb. The last guns were made in 1961.

SIMILAR GUNS

Note: most of the earlier Harrington & Richardson rimfire rifles of this type were chambered specifically for 22 Long Rifle ammunition rather than all 22s interchangeably.

Model 250 Sportster rifle, 1948-61. Similar to the 265 pattern, this had a 23in barrel, a five-round magazine, and an open spring-leaf rear sight.

Model 251 rifle, 1948-55. This was a minor variant of the Model 250 with a Lyman No. 55H rear sight.

Model 365 Ace rifle, 1946-7. Lacking a magazine, this single shot pattern had a 22in barrel and a Lyman No. 55H rear sight. The pistol grip stock was a plain design with a short rounded forend.

Model 450 rifle, 1948-61. This was similar to the Model 451, but the choice of sights was left to the purchaser.

Model 451 Medalist, 1948-61. Intended for target shooting, this had a 26in barrel and a special half-stock with an extended slab-side forend; swivels lay beneath the butt and forend, and the detachable magazine held five rounds. The gun weighed about 10.5lb with a Lyman No. 524F rear sight on the breech and a No. 77 exchangeable-element tunnel at the muzzle.

Model 465 Targeteer rifle, 1946-7. Derived from the 265 pattern, this 9lb gun had a 10-round magazine and a 25in barrel. The sights consisted of a Lyman No. 57 peep unit on the breech and a ramped bead at the muzzle.

Model 466 Targeteer Junior rifle, 1948-51 (numerical designation uncertain). Guns of this type had a 20in barrel, a five-round magazine and a special short butt; weight was about 7lb. A Redfield Model 70 peep sight was mounted on the receiver, with a Lyman No. 17A at the muzzle.

Model 750 Pioneer rifle, 1954-84. A single shot gun capable of handling the three standard 22 rimfire cartridges interchangeably, this had a plain half-stock with a pistol grip and a low Monte Carlo comb. The trigger guard was generally a synthetic molding. The original pattern had a slender forend with an oblique tip, but this was changed in 1979 to a more conventional round-tip form; a 'Fluid Feed' loading platform was added, the trigger guard was changed, and the curve of the pistol grip was refined.

Model 751 rifle, 1971. Distinguished by a full-length forend held by a single barrel band, this was not particularly successful; very few were made.

Model 765 Pioneer rifle, 1948-54. Capable of handling 22 Short, Long or Long Rifle rounds interchangeably, this single shot gun weighed about 5lb with a light 24in barrel. The plain pistol grip half-stock had a short forend, and a spring-leaf and elevator rear sight was standard.

Model 852 Fieldsman rifle, 1952-3. This short-lived gun had a tube magazine beneath its 24in barrel, capacity being 14-21 rounds depending on cartridge length: 22 Short, Long and Long Rifle cartridges could be handled interchangeably. A plain pistol grip half-stock and a spring-leaf and elevator sight were fitted. Weight averaged 5.5lb.

Model 865 Plainsman rifle, 1949-86. Chambered specifically for the 22LR rimfire round, this had a detachable five-round box magazine and a 22in or 24in barrel.

Model 866 rifle, 1971. Only a few of these were made, distinguished by the full-length forend with a single barrel band.

MODEL 300 SPORTING RIFLE

Built on a Sako action in 1965-82, this was offered in 22-250 (L-461 action), 243 Winchester (L-579), 270 Winchester (L-61), 30-06 (L-61), 308 Winchester (L-579), 7mm Remington or 300 Winchester Magnums (both L-61). A typical 1974-vintage rifle was 42.5in overall, had a 22in barrel and weighed 7.75lb. The Williams ramp sight had a folding leaf, and the American-style stock had a roll-over comb. Forend tips and pistol grip caps were usually rosewood.

SIMILAR GUNS

Model 301 rifle, 1967-82. Similar to the M300, this had a full-length stock; it was 39in long, had an 18in barrel and weighed 7.25lb. Chamberings were identical except for the omission of the 22-250 option.

Model 317 Ultra Wildcat rifle, 1968-76. Introduced on the L-461 action, this was originally chambered only for the 17 Remington round—though 17/223, 222 and 223 options were added before the model was discontinued. The Monte Carlo-pattern half-stock had checkering on the pistol grip and forend. Pistol grip caps and forend tips were rosewood.

Model 317P rifle. A deluxe version of the M301, this had a better stock with basket-weave checkering.

Model 333 rifle, 1974. Built in small numbers on the Sako L-61 action, for the 7mm Remington Magnum or 30-06 cartridge only, this had a plain ambidextrous beech stock lacking a cheekpiece.

MODEL 300 ULTRA RIFLE

Built on an FN-Mauser action in 1967-82, this could be obtained in 22-250, 243 Winchester, 25-06, 270 Winchester, 7mm Remington Magnum, 300 Winchester Magnum, 30-06 or 308 Winchester chamberings. The half-stock had a roll-over comb, a contrasting forend tip, and checkering on the pistol grip and forend. Williams ramp sights were standard. The standard 22in barrel gave an overall length of 42.5in; weight averaged 7.7lb.

SIMILAR GUNS

Model 301 Ultra Carbine. Distinguished by a full-length stock, with a low Monte Carlo comb, this was available in all regular chamberings except 22-250. Overall length with an 18in barrel was 39in, weight being about 7.25lb. A simple folding-leaf rear sight was used.

Model 330 Hunter's Rifle, 1967-72. Similar mechanically to the Model 300, offered in all chamberings except 22-250, this had a plain ambidextrous Monte Carlo-comb half-stock, lacking a cheekpiece.

Model 370 Ultra Medalist rifle, 1968-73. A dual-purpose varmint/target pattern built on the FN Supreme action, this had a plain walnut stock with a roll-over comb, a sculpted pistol grip, and a broad semi-beavertail forend. Offered only in 22-250, 6mm Remington or 243 Winchester, it had a heavy 24in barrel and weighed about 9.5lb. Open sights were not supplied.

Model 340 rifle, 1982-4. This was built on a Swedish Husqvarna-Mauser action, with a 22in barrel chambered for the 243 Winchester, 270 Winchester, 7x57, 30-06 or 308 Winchester rounds; weight averaged 7.3lb. The half-stock had a straight comb and a rounded forend; the buttplate was a ventilated rubber pattern, and the checkering was hand-cut.

MODEL 5200 SPORTING RIFLE
Made by Harrington & Richardson, Inc., Gardner, Massachusetts, 1982-6.

Total production: not known. **Chambering:** 22 LR rimfire. **Action:** locked by the base of the bolt handle turning down into its seat in the receiver.

24in barrel, 4-groove rifling; RH, concentric. Detachable box magazine, 5 rounds. Aperture rear sight on the receiver. 1080 fps with 40-grain bullet.

This rifle was sturdy and attractive, though the bolt handle and the flimsily stamped trigger blade attracted adverse comment. However, the recessed bolt face and dual extractors were excellent features, and performance was surprisingly good. The straight-comb walnut stock had hand-cut checkering on the pistol grip and the rounded forend, and a peep sight was fitted to the receiver bridge; the front sight was a hooded blade. The magazine catch was recessed into the combination trigger guard/floorplate.

SIMILAR GUNS

Model 5200 Match Rifle, 1982-6. Distinguished by a 28in heavy barrel, giving an overall length of 46in and a weight of 11lb, this had a fully adjustable trigger and the patented 'Fluid Feed' loading platform inherited from the Model 750. An accessory rail let into the underside of the squared forend accepted an adjustable hand stop or sling-anchor.

• Harrington & Richardson, break-open type
MODEL 158 TOPPER JET SPORTING RIFLE
Made by the Harrington & Richardson Arms Co., Worcester, Massachusetts, 1963-7.

Total production: not known. **Chambering:** 22 Remington Jet. **Action:** locked by a bar in the action engaging the barrel-block.

37in overall, 6.5lb empty. 22in barrel, 4-groove rifling; RH, concentric. Single shot only. Folding open-notch rear sight. 2460 fps with 40-grain bullet.

This was a straightforward adaptation of the popular Harrington & Richardson single-barrel shotgun, opened by pressing a catch on the right side of the receiver alongside the exposed central hammer. The Topper Jet had a case-hardened receiver separating the pistol grip butt from the plain rounded forend. A ventilated rubber shoulder pad and a Lyman rear sight were standard. The customary 22-caliber barrels could be exchanged for 410 or 20-bore shotgun patterns.

SIMILAR GUNS

Model 155 rifle, 1972-82. Built on the standard 158-type action, this was offered only in 44 Remington Magnum or 45-70. A brass cleaning rod lay beneath the barrel, and a barrel band encircled the elongated forend. The butt had a straight wrist; barrels were 24in or 28in.

Model 157 rifle, 1976-86. Distinguished by a full-length forend, this was offered only in 22 Winchester Magnum rimfire, 22 Hornet and 30-30.

Model 158C rifle, 1963-86. This was a simplified form of the Topper Jet, with a plain straight-wrist butt, a synthetic shoulder plate, and a blacked receiver. Chamberings included 22 Hornet, 30-30, 357 Magnum, 357 Maximum and 44 Magnum.

• Harrington & Richardson, block-action type
H&R CENTENNIAL RIFLE

Ten thousand of these 45-70 guns were made to celebrate the 100th anniversary of Harrington & Richardson in 1971. Based on the 'Trapdoor Springfield' Officer's Rifle of 1875 (see 'Springfield [-Allin]'), they had a checkered straight-wrist half-stock with a metal forend tip. The action, lock plate, band and buttplate were engraved, and a large oval commemorative plaque lay on the right side of the butt. A full length cleaning rod was carried in a pipe beneath the 26in barrel.

SIMILAR GUNS

Custer Commemorative Carbine, Officer's Pattern, 1973. Only 25 of these were made, with gold-inlay engraving on the metalwork and a Vernier sight on the tang. They were accompanied by a mahogany case.

Custer Commemorative Carbine, Enlisted Man's Pattern, 1973. These cased gold-inlaid guns were similar to the Officer's type, but had the military stepped-base and leaf rear sight on the barrel; 243 were made.

Model 171 carbine, 1972-81. Offered only in 45-70, this replica of the 1873-type Springfield cavalry carbine had a straight-wrist walnut half-stock with a single band encircling the forend and the 22in barrel. Overall length was about 40in, weight averaging 7lb. A simple folding-leaf Lyman rear sight was fitted.

Model 171DL carbine, 1972-86. Otherwise identical with the Model 171, this had checkering on the pistol grip, a stepped-base and leaf rear sight, and engraving on the action.

Model 172 carbine, 1972-81. This was offered with a select walnut stock, checkering, silver plating on many of the metal parts, a Vernier aperture sight on the tang, and a 'grip adapter' (a primitive detachable pistol grip) beneath the wrist.

Model 173 rifle, 1972-81. Essentially similar to the H&R Centennial rifle, this long-barreled gun had a cleaning rod and a checkered half-stock, but lacked the stock plaque.

Model 174 Little Big Horn carbine, 1972-84. This was a minor variant of the Model 171DL, with the Vernier-mounted tang sight and a grip adapter.

Model 178 rifle, 1973-80. A replica of the 45-70 rifle, with a 32in barrel, this had a leaf-type rear sight and an empty weight of about 8.63lb. The barrel was held in the full length forend by two bands.

• Harrington & Richardson, slide-action type
MODEL 422 SPORTING RIFLE

Dating from 1956-8, this short-lived pattern had a tube magazine beneath the barrel; cartridge capacity was 15-21, as the mechanism would accommodate any of the three standard 22 rimfire cartridges. The Model 422 had a grooved slide handle and a plain pistol grip butt. Weight was about 6lb with a 24in barrel.

• Hartung (Klein)

A few bolt action needle-fire sporting guns emanated from the Taunton, Massachusetts, workshop of G.P. Foster. They were constructed in accordance with U.S. patent 6871, granted in November 1849 to Charles (Karl) Hartung of Reichlingen in Prussia. Though rights to the invention had been assigned to John B. Klein of New York City and production was begun enthusiastically, the commercial market was so unimpressed that distribution of 'Klein' needle guns was confined largely to the New England states. Hartung needle rifles were customarily half-stocked, with deeply concave buttplates and octagonal barrels held in the forend by a transverse key.

• Harvey

The 30-caliber T25 lightweight automatic rifle arose from a specification issued by the Office of the Chief of Ordnance in September 1945 to provide a weapon locked by something other than the Garand-type rotating bolt. Developed by Earle M. Harvey at Springfield Armory, the T25 pivoted a strut in the breechblock down against a shoulder in the receiver.

T25 RIFLE

Characterized by a straight-line layout, a separate pistol grip and folding sights, the T25 was about 43.3in overall. It weighed 7.5lb and had a cyclic rate of 750rpm.

SIMILAR GUNS

T25E1 rifle. This was a heavy-barreled version of the standard gun, weighing about 9.5lb. Work stopped on the introduction of the improved T47, and was formally abandoned in November 1951.

T47 rifle. An improved version of the T25, this was tested from October 1951 onward against the T44 before being discarded in the Spring of 1953. It combined the T25 operating system with a conventional stock, and fired from a closed bolt at all times. The standard gun was about 44.8in overall, weighed 8.4lb, and had an excessive cyclic rate of 850rpm.

T47E1 rifle. An improved form of the heavy-barrel T25E1, this was otherwise comparable with the T47.

• Hayden

Hiram Hayden of Waterbury, Connecticut, received U.S. patent no. 45,945 in December 1864 to protect a trunnioned breech-block which was propped in place by a cone-nose block activated by a sliding wedge and an underlever. The block moved back and then rotated upward at the rear to expose the chamber.

A patent granted in August 1866 (no. 56,939) protected a sliding-bolt breech operated by the hammer. Thumbing back the hammer spur unlocked and then slid back the bolt, raising a fresh cartridge from the under-barrel magazine on the elevator. At the limit of the backward travel, a spring was tripped to close the bolt automatically. Locking was effected by the fall of the hammer. A Hayden carbine (type unknown) was submitted to the U.S. Army trials of 1865, but was not among those that were selected for photography.

• Henry

The New Haven Arms Company, maker of the Volcanic (q.v.) guns, was facing collapse by 1861. Salvation came in the form of a lever-action rifle which had been developed from the ineffectual Volcanic by Benjamin Henry. Protected by U.S. patent 30,446 of October 1860, assigned to Oliver Winchester, the gun chambered a 44-caliber rimfire cartridge which was far more powerful than the Volcanic Rocket Ball.

Though the Henry rifle retained the toggle-lock of the preceding Volcanic, it had a new hollow carrier block doubling as an ejector and many minor improvements.

HENRY'S PATENT REPEATING RIFLE
Made by the New Haven Arms Company, New Haven, Connecticut, 1861-6.

Total production: about 13,500. **Chambering:** 44-25-216 (44 Henry) rimfire. **Action:** locked by a toggle-joint beneath the bolt, operated by a swinging lever forming the trigger guard.

DATA FOR A TYPICAL EXAMPLE

43.5in overall, 9.25lb empty. 24in barrel, 6 grooves; RH twist, concentric. Tube magazine beneath the barrel, 12 rounds. Folding leaf-and-slider rear sight on the barrel or receiver. 1050 fps with 216-grain bullet? No bayonet.

The first guns had a true bore diameter of .420in, each of the six grooves being .005in deep; the rifling had a progressively steepening twist from breech to muzzle. Iron frames were used for the first 200 guns, though the perfected manufacturing pattern reverted to bronze and a catch was added beneath the wrist of the butt to hold the finger lever. The rear sights lay on the barrel instead of the receiver, though many transitional examples are known.

The walnut butt had a straight wrist and a concave brass buttplate with a trap for the multi-part cleaning rod. Henry rifles—unlike the later Winchesters—lacked forends. Barrels measured 24-32in, giving gun weights ranging from 9.2lb to 10lb, though the 24in type was regarded as standard.

Series-made Henry rifles, available from the summer of 1862, were purchased in quantity by federal volunteers even though the Ordnance Department was unhelpful. After the Spencer rifle (q.v.)

The 'Color Bearers and Guard' of the 7th Illinois volunteer infantry regiment. Pictured by Matthew Brady, c. 1863, with Henry rifles.

The Henry rifle lacked a forend and originally had an iron frame; this modern replica, though dimensionally identical, has a brass frame.

had been approved in 1863, attitudes softened to the extent that 1731 Henry rifles and 4.5 million cartridges had been acquired by May 1865. Government-purchase guns can be identified by 'C.G.C.' marks applied by the inspector, Charles G. Chandler. About 8000 other Henry rifles were used by state and volunteer units during the Civil War.

The advent of the Blakeslee Quick Loader (patented in 1864) elevated the separate-cocking Spencer Rifle to rank with the Henry, but none of the other breechloaders of 1861-5 could compare so favorably. Though prone to extractor breakages, the Spencer was the more durable; Henry rifles often suffered damage to the fragile magazine tubes and had a delicate firing pin.

The Henry rifle was also low-powered by rifle-musket standards. Its great assets were speed and accuracy; trials undertaken in Switzerland with an 1866-model Winchester, which fired similar 44 rimfire ammunition, showed that even an untrained rifleman could achieve 20 unaimed shots in a minute with a surprisingly good chance of hitting a target.

• High-Standard

Better known for its handguns, the High Standard Mfg. Co. of Hamden, Connecticut, made a few thousand High-Power rifles in 1962-6 on the basis of Mauser actions purchased from Fabrique Nationale. The Field Model sporter—offered only in 270 Winchester or 30-06—had a 22in barrel and a four-cartridge magazine. Its plain hardwood stock had a straight comb and a rounded forend tip. A 'De Luxe' pattern had a checkered walnut stock, with a Monte Carlo comb and quick-detachable swivels. Folding-leaf rear sights were standard, though Redfield or Lyman peep sights were sometimes fitted to the receiver.

A series of 22 rimfire blowback autoloading rifles was also offered under the 'Sport-King' brand name. These tube-magazine guns included a carbine, with a straight-wrist butt and a band around the forend (1964-73); a deluxe pattern with a checkered Monte Carlo-style stock (1966-75); the 'Field' pattern, with a plain pistol grip half-stock (1960-6); and the 'Special' (1960-6), which was a basically a Field pattern Sport-King with a Monte Carlo comb and a beavertail forend.

• Hoffmann

The Hoffmann Arms Company of Cleveland, Ohio, and Ardmore, Oklahoma, marketed substantial numbers of Mauser-action rifles immediately after World War II, often chambering proprietary 276 or 300 Hoffmann cartridges. A few guns were fitted with the Howe-Whelen aperture rear sight, which replaced the bolt shroud; but complexity and high cost made this fitting unpopular.

• Holden

Cyrus B. Holden of Worcester, Massachusetts, was granted two U.S. patents to protect breechloading firearms—34,859 of 1st April 1862 and 42,139 of 29th March 1864. The hammerless 58 rimfire single-shot rifles and carbines made by Armsby & Harrington in accordance with the 1862 patent had an open-sided frame containing a block and a cocking slide (with suitable finger holes) which were retracted manually after the trigger guard had been depressed. They had straight wrist butts and short forends held by a single brass band.

Guns of this type were being advertised as late as 1880, when the blued standard and nickel-plated deluxe 44 Long rimfire versions were being made with 28in octagonal barrels. The 1864-patent gun had a sliding block pulled down with a finger ring, but does not seem to have been exploited in quantity. Cyrus Holden continued to make drop-barrel and falling-block rifles on his own account from about 1873 until shortly before his death in December 1906.

• Hopkins & Allen

Trading in Norwich, Connecticut, this long-established gunmaking business (independent until 1915) made a wide range of revolvers, rifles and shotguns. These included single shot radial- and dropping-block longarms. Hopkins & Allen built guns for many distributors, marking them with many brand names. The most important agencies were Merwin, Hulbert & Co. and Hulbert Brothers & Co. of New York, but among the many lesser known marks was 'Rev-o-Noc' applied at the request of Hibbart, Spencer, Bartlett & Co. of Chicago.

RADIAL-BLOCK DESIGNS
NO. 722 SPORTING RIFLE

Made only in 22 rimfire, with an 18in round barrel and simple open sights, this had a color case-hardened frame and a straight-wrist butt. The forend was exceptionally short. A large ring-head 'take-down' bolt protruded beneath the frame ahead of the trigger guard. The action was a simple 'rolling block' operated by a small stud-like handle on the right side of the breechblock. The No. 722 was neither well-made nor particularly sturdy, yet was made in substantial numbers under a variety of brand names. A military trainer was made on the same action, with a 26in barrel and an extended forend held by a single barrel band.

NO. 822 SPORTING RIFLE

Made by Hopkins & Allen, Norwich, Connecticut, about 1890-1915.
Total production: not known. **Chambering options:** 22 Short or 22 Long Rifle rimfire. **Action:** locked by propping the breechblock behind the chamber with the hammer body.
DATA FOR A TYPICAL EXAMPLE
Chambering: 22 Short, rimfire. 35.9in overall, 3.5lb empty. 21.3in barrel, 4-groove rifling; RH, concentric. Single shot only. Standing-block rear sight. 900 fps with 29-grain bullet.

This was a sturdier form of the basic rolling-block action, operated by a lever doubling as the trigger guard. A spring-catch was built into the back of the lever where, engaging with the lower tang, it helped to hold the action shut. Straight-wrist butts and small tapering forends were standard, and the take-down bolt ran vertically up into the frame ahead of the breech.

SIMILAR GUNS

No. 832 rifle. Identical mechanically with the 822 pattern, this was chambered for the 32 Long rimfire cartridge.

No. 3922 rifle. Built on the same small action, this was a target shooting or 'Schuetzen' version of the No. 822 with a hooked buttplate, improved peep sights, and an optional double trigger. It weighed about 5.5lb.

The open-action of the 1883-pattern Winchester-Hotchkiss rifle, showing the bolt about to feed a cartridge from the magazine.

DROPPING-BLOCK TYPE

NO. 922 SPORTING RIFLE

Originally known as the 'Junior Model'

Made by Hopkins & Allen, Norwich, Connecticut, about 1890-1915.

Total production: not known. **Chambering options:** 22 Short, 22 Long or 22 Long Rifle rimfire. **Action:** locked by propping the vertically-moving breechblock behind the chamber with the operating lever.

DATA FOR A TYPICAL EXAMPLE

Chambering: 22 Long, rimfire. 39.6in overall, 5.13lb empty. 24in barrel, 4-groove rifling; RH, concentric. Spring-leaf and elevator rear sight. Standing-block rear sight. 1050 fps with 29-grain bullet.

Chambered for 22 rimfire ammunition and protected by patents granted in 1885-90, this was a true dropping-block action with a take-down bolt placed vertically ahead of the trigger guard (original guns), or laterally through the frame ('New Model' guns). Rollers were often incorporated in the lever and the hammer to smooth the operating process, but the guns seem to have been made in batches and will often differ in detail. Most have 24in or 26in barrels—round, part- or full-octagon—and straight-wrist butts, though pistol grips are common.

SIMILAR GUNS

No. 925 rifle. Identical mechanically with the 922, built on the same small action, this was chambered for the 25 rimfire cartridge.

No. 932 rifle. Possibly originally known as the 'Senior Model', this gun had a larger action than the 922, with the ring-headed take-down bolt running vertically (original pattern) or laterally ('New Model') through the frame beneath the chamber. Chamberings included 25-20 Single Shot centerfire, 32 Long rimfire, 32 Long centerfire, 32-20 WCF and 32-40 WCF.

No. 938 rifle. Identical with the Model 932, this was chambered for the 38 Long rimfire, 38-40 WCF, 38-55 and 44-40 WCF rounds. A few 38-55 guns were apparently made on the large dropping-block shotgun action, which had a raised panel on each side of the frame and lacked the 'take-down' feature.

No. 3925 rifle. A 25-20 target-shooting 'Schuetzen' version, usually built on the larger of the two standard rifle actions, this had a folding Vernier peep sight on the tang and a globe sight at the muzzle. The butt had a hooked shoulder plate.

• Hotchkiss

The earliest Hotchkiss bolt-action rifles, patented in 1869-75, were metallic-cartridge firing adaptations of the French Chassepot (q.v.) needle guns. These cocked automatically and, in their finalized form, seated the cartridge in the chamber with a camming action as the bolt was closed. Safety interlocks were also developed to prevent the guns firing before the breech was securely shut. In 1876, however, Hotchkiss patented an improved bolt-action gun with a tube magazine in the butt. This formed the basis for the Winchester-Hotchkiss patterns (q.v.).

• Howard

Patented in October 1862 by Sebre Howard, and improved in September-October 1865 by Charles Howard, this breechloader was made for its promoters—Howard Brothers of New Haven, Connecticut—by Whitney.

THUNDERBOLT RIFLE

Made by the Whitney Arms Company, Whitneyville, Connecticut, 1865-9.

Total production: not known. **Chambering options:** a selection of rimfire cartridges. **Action:** locked by a lug on the operating lever rising behind the breech-bolt.

DATA FOR A 1867 TRIALS GUN

Chambering: 56-46 Spencer rimfire. 49.5in overall, about 9lb empty. 33in barrel, rifling profile not known. Single shot only. Ramp and leaf sight graduated to 1000yd? 1210 fps with 330-grain bullet. Socket bayonet.

The Howard rifle was a lever-action pattern with a straight-wrist butt, a distinctive tubular receiver and—in most cases—a slender forend held by two bands. The patent specification shows a special tube bayonet which could be reversed so that the hollowed blade pointed back along the barrel, but the gun submitted to trials in New York State in 1867 probably accepted a conventional 1855-type socket pattern.

SIMILAR GUNS

Thunderbolt carbine. Made in small numbers for military and commercial sale, this lacked a forend and had a simple folding rear sight. Customarily chambered for the 44 Long rimfire cartridge, the carbines were about 37.5in long, had 21in barrels, and weighed only about 6lb. Charles Howard 'of New York' submitted two carbines to the U.S. Army trials of 1865, where they were tested unsuccessfully as No. 23 and No. 23a.

• Howe

Frederick W. Howe of Providence, Rhode Island, was granted U.S. patent 46,671 (March 1865) to protect a distinctive radial-block breech. The lock mechanism was contained in a pivoting frame in the wrist of the stock, released by pressing the rear 'trigger' and pulling the self-contained unit downward around a transverse pivot beneath the chamber. A rifle was tested by the U.S. Army in 1865, as 'No. 22', but failed to leave a lasting impression. It had a two-piece stock with a forend held by three sprung bands. One of the bands, mounting the rear swivel, lay unusually close to the breech; this allowed the second swivel to be carried under the middle band. A folding leaf sight was brazed to the top of the barrel.

• HS Precision

HS Precision, Inc., of Rapid City, South Dakota, makes custom stocks and barrels. The company has also completed commercially-purchased actions—generally the Remington 700—as the Pro-Series, which includes 'Sporter/Varmint' and 'Tactical Marksman' patterns. These are often supplied in take-down form.

• Hubbell

William Hubbell of Philadelphia was responsible for two breechloading systems. Though rifles and carbines were advertised commercially in 1847-50, and though they were undoubtedly made in small quantities, the design was not good enough to withstand competition from Sharps and others. Hubbell worked on to patent a toggle-type breech system in June 1867, but is best known for his work with heavy ordnance.

1844-PATENT GUNS

Patented in January 1844, this breechloading system relied on a separate block or chamber pivoted on an axial rod on the left side of the breech. An identical rod on the right served to index the chamber by stopping the downward travel of the chamber-handle as the breech was closed.

The earliest guns relied on nothing but the inertia of the hammer to keep the breech shut as the gun fired, but later examples often had a pin in the breech face which slid into the rear of the chamber as the hammer fell. Most guns were caplocks; a few cartridge conversions are known, but these seem to have been undertaken long after the original date of manufacture.

Held to the breech merely by the two breech rods and a slender supporting frame, the barrel of the Hubbell was comparatively weak. In addition, lacking any form of camming action to make a proper seal, the breech was prone to leak gas.

1867-PATENT GUNS

Hubbell's rifle-musket conversion—the subject of U.S. patent 65,812—was tested in 1867, based on a standard 58-caliber Springfield. It embodied a form of toggle lock opened by pulling upward on a lever ahead of the chamber. Pivoting at the rear, the lever broke the lock and pulled the breechblock back from the breech face. However, the design needed a three-piece striker and was more complicated than many rival designs. Ammunition problems during the endurance trial caused the gun to be withdrawn, never to return.

• Hyper

The Hyper Gun Company of Jenks, Oklahoma, made a single shot dropping-block rifle for a few years prior to 1984. Opreated by an underlever combined with the trigger guard, it was made in small numbers in a staggering variety of chamberings.

• Ithaca

The Ithaca Gun Company is best known as a principal U.S. distributor for Tikka and BSA rifles, in addition to handling many 22 rimfire Erma-made lever-actions such as the 'Model 72'. The company's principal claim to fame, however, rests on the single shot Model 49—derived from the Martini system.

MODEL 49 SADDLEGUN

Made by the Ithaca Gun Co., Inc., Ithaca, New York State, 1961-78.

Total production: not known. **Chambering options:** 22 Short, 22 Long or 22 Long Rifle rimfire, interchangeably. **Action:** locked by a pivoting breechblock behind the chamber with the tip of the operating lever.

33.5in overall, 5.25lb empty. 18in barrel, 6 grooves; RH twist, concentric. Single shot only. Spring-leaf and elevator rear sight. 1080 fps with 40-grain bullet.

Modeled externally on the lever-action Winchesters, complete with a dummy tube magazine under the barrel, this junior rifle has a Martini breech. The rebounding hammer must be cocked manually for each shot. The butt had a straight wrist, often with impressed checkering, and the 'carbine style' forend had a barrel band.

SIMILAR GUNS

Model 49 Deluxe, 1962-74. Mechanically identical with the standard gun, this had gold plating on the hammer and trigger, better-quality woodwork, and swivels beneath the butt and forend.

Model 49 Magnum, 1962-78. Chambered for the 22 Winchester Magnum cartridge, the action of this variant was suitably strengthened.

Model 49 Presentation, 1964-74. Similar to the deluxe pattern, this had a roll-engraved receiver and a gold nameplate on the butt. It could be obtained in regular or magnum rimfire chambering.

Model 49 Repeater, 1968-71. Similar externally to the single shot guns, this was modified internally to feed from a tube magazine beneath the 20in barrel. The hammer was cocked automatically for each shot. Capacity was 15-21 rounds, depending on cartridge length.

Model 49 St Louis Bicentennial, 1964. Two hundred of these, based on the 49DL (suitably inscribed), were made to celebrate the 200th anniversary of the founding of the Missouri state capital.

Model 49 Youth, 1962-78. This was identical with the standard gun except for the length of the butt.

• Iver Johnson

Iver Johnson's Arms, Inc., of Fitchburg, Massachusetts, entered the M1 Carbine-making business by purchasing the assets of the Plainfield Machine Company (q.v.) and moving to Middlesex, New Jersey, in 1977. The business of Universal Sporting Goods was purchased in 1983, after a move to Jacksonville, Arkansas, but Iver Johnson was itself liquidated in 1986.

The assets of the company were acquired by the American Military Arms Corporation and the 'Iver Johnson' name ceased to be associated with the M1 Carbine in 1987. However, the Iver Johnson name reappeared in 1992 on the 50th birthday M1 Carbines. Appropriately roll-engraved, these have a figured walnut stock and an American flag medallion set into the butt.

PM-30 CARBINE

The Iver Johnson PM-30 was made in several versions; 'HB' was the standard blued gun, with a beech stock; 'WB' was blued, with a walnut stock; and 'WS' was a stainless-steel version. Most chambered the 30 M1 cartridge, but others accepted the more potent 5.7mm MMJ. After the demise of Iver Johnson, AMAC continued to sell the Models 3103, 3203 and 3200 Paratrooper models—the Iver Johnson PM30HB, PM30WB and SC30FB respectively—under its own name.

SIMILAR GUNS

SC-30 ('Survival Carbine'), 1983-6. This was also made in several patterns. The 'SS' was made of stainless steel, with a black DuPont Xytel butt with a separate pistol grip behind the trigger; folding-butt 'FB' and 'FS' guns were essentially similar, finish being blue or stainless steel respectively.

• Jaeger

Paul Jaeger, Inc., of Grand Junction, Tennessee, introduced the Jaeger African, Alaskan and Hunter rifles in 1989. All three were built on commercial (most probably Spanish) Mauser actions.

AFRICAN RIFLE

This was chambered for 375 H&H, 416 Taylor or 458 Winchester Magnum cartridges, had a graphite-reinforced synthetic stock and weighed about 9lb. The hooded front sight, fitted on a muzzle band, was accompanied by a folding night sight; the rear sight was a fixed block adjusted for 50yd.

SIMILAR GUNS

Alaska Rifle. Chambered for the 7mm Remington, 300 Winchester or 338 Winchester magnum rounds, guns of this type had Douglas Premium barrels, Williams rear sights, silver bead front sights, and matte blue-black metalwork. They weighed about 8lb.

Hunter Rifle. This had a Bell & Carlson composite Kevlar-reinforced fiberglass stock with a crackle finish. Offered in 243 Winchester, 257 Roberts, 25-06, 280 Remington, 7x57, 7mm-08, 30-06 or 308 Winchester chamberings, the guns had 22in or 24in Douglas Premium barrels and weighed about 7lb. A laminated wood stock was optional.

• Jenks (Barton)

The three guns submitted to the U.S. Army trials of 1865 by Barton Jenks, son of Alfred, were characterized by a multi-part breech with a radial locking lever which bore against a shoulder in the rear of the receiver. A sliding extractor lay beneath the barrel. This system was patented in an improved form in February 1868. Trials guns Nos. 24-26 were all carbines, with one-piece stocks and half-length forends held by a single sprung band. A ring-and-bar appeared on the left side of the butt behind the trigger guard, and a folding leaf sight lay above the breech.

• Jenks (William)

The breech of the single-shot carbine patented in May 1838 by William Jenks of Columbia, South Carolina, was sealed by a 'plunger' or piston sliding into the back of the chamber from the rear. The toggle-type breech was opened by an elongated cover, pivoted at the back of the action, which broke the lock and withdrew the breechblock to expose the chamber.

Though the Jenks action sometimes leaked gas, the breech lever deflected blast down and away from the shooter's face. The perfected caplock Jenks had a very distinctive side-hammer—known as the 'mule ear'—and cannot be mistaken for any other weapon. Trials in 1841 confirmed its potential, and an endurance test ceased only when the nipple split after 14,813 shots had been fired.

A Board of Officers, meeting at Washington arsenal in 1845, recommended adoption; unfortunately, troop trials proved catastrophic (largely because attempts to use Hall or standard musket cartridges were made) and surviving guns were being held in storage by 1860. Many of them were transformed by James Merrill (q.v.) into conventional side-hammer caplocks during the Civil War. However, a very few unaltered Jenks carbines were taken by Confederate forces from Norfolk Navy Yard, in September 1861, and 2800 others were purchased by A.M. Eastman of Manchester, New Hampshire. The Eastman guns were rifled by W.W. Marston of New York, and the carbines among them were fitted with conventional swivels; their fate is uncertain, though they were presumably sold to federal militiamen.

MODEL 1839 MUSKETOON

Made by the Chicopee Falls Co., Chicopee Falls, Massachusetts.
Total production: 100. **Chambering:** see text. **Action:** locked by a sliding bolt actuated by a hinged lever on top of the breech.

42.25in overall, 7.2lb empty. 25.65in barrel, smooth-bore. Single shot only. Fixed standing-block sight. 1650-1700 fps, depending on charge. No bayonet.

The first Jenks flintlock, successfully tested in Watervliet Arsenal in 1838-9, was followed by 100 64-caliber smooth-bore muske-

A 9mm Parabellum version of the Iver Johnson M1 Carbine.

toons with barrels held by two pinned brass bands. Fifty guns were issued for trials, but the reports were unfavorable and the guns were sent into store in Springfield. About 65 survivors were converted to caplock in 1843.

SIMILAR GUNS

Carbine. A few shortened guns were tested by the cavalry. They were 36in long, had 19.5in barrels and weighed only about 6.3lb.

Navy musket. Concurrently with the army trials, the U.S. Navy bought a few 54-caliber muskets with 36in barrels. These are assumed to have been caplocks.

MODEL 1841 NAVY MUSKET

Made by the Nathan Ames Manufacturing Company, Chicopee Falls, Massachusetts, 1841-5.

Total production: 1000. **Chambering:** 54-diameter ball, fired by a caplock. **Action:** generally as M1839 musketoon, above.

52.5in overall, 6.8lb empty. 35.4in barrel, smooth-bore. Single-shot only. The tail of the breech lever formed the rear sight. 1685 fps with a 70-grain charge. Socket bayonet.

The U.S. Navy ordered 1500 guns from Jenks in August 1841, comprising 1000 rifle-length weapons with 36in barrels and 500 24in-barreled carbines. The rifles had been delivered by December 1844, but only carbine orders followed. These guns were most distinctive, as the laterally-moving hammer gave them a streamlined appearance; they were also very lightly built. Muskets had three brass bands and accepted a conventional socket bayonet. Lock plates were marked 'N.P. AMES', 'SPRINGFIELD' and 'MASS.' in three lines, with 'Wm JENKS' at the rear; the barrel bore a navy inspector's mark and the date.

SIMILAR GUNS

Navy carbines. The first 500 were delivered in the summer of 1843. They had two brass bands and were stocked virtually to the muzzle; bayonets could not be mounted. A large sling ring lay under the butt immediately behind the trigger guard. Total production eventually amounted to 4200.

Army carbines. On 23rd January 1844, 40 of these were delivered—20 smooth-bores and 20 specially rifled 'for the dragoons'. Trials were so discouraging that nothing further was done with the Jenks in U.S. Army service.

MODEL 1845 NAVY CARBINE

Made by E. Remington & Son, Ilion, New York State, 1846-7.

Total production: 1000.

Otherwise generally similar to the 1841-pattern carbine, above.

Ordered by the U.S. Navy on 22nd September 1845, these were the first military firearms to incorporate a Maynard Tape Primer. This was contained in a chamber immediately behind the hammer, protected with a hinged lid. Lock plates were customarily marked "REMINGTON'S', 'HERKIMER' and 'N.Y.' in three lines; barrels displayed 'W.JENKS', 'USN', 'RP', 'P', '1847' and 'CAST STEEL' in five. Straight-shank hammers and double ear actuating levers were fitted, while the loading aperture in the top of the breech was oval instead of the circular design found on Ames-made guns.

A typical Jenks 'Mule Ear' sidehammer carbine. (W&W)

• Jennings

The origins of this rifle, predecessor of the lever-action Winchester M1866, lay in the work of Walter Hunt of New York. Hunt was granted two relevant U.S. patents in 1848-9, one for a 'Rocket Ball' and the other protecting the design of a primitive 'Piston Breech and Firing-cock Repeating Gun'.

Rights to the Hunt patents were originally assigned to George Arrowsmith of New York City, but Arrowsmith had soon sold them to a syndicate led by the railroad tycoon Courtlandt Palmer. The rifle was improved by Lewis Jennings, but inefficient ignition, low-powered ammunition and a lack of mechanical advantage in the operating mechanism presaged commercial failure. Palmer canceled the 5000-gun contract long before it had been completed, and the last few guns may even have been completed as muzzle-loaders.

The Hunt and Jennings patents were then licensed to Horace Smith and Daniel Wesson, and development continued under the 'Volcanic' brand name (q.v.).

HUNT-JENNINGS RIFLE

Made by Robbins & Lawrence, Windsor, Vermont, 1848-52.

Total production: a few hundred? **Chambering:** 54-caliber self-contained ball, fired by a pill-lock. **Action:** locked by a toggle system behind the bolt, operated by a swinging trigger lever.

DATA FOR A TYPICAL EXAMPLE

44in overall, about 9lb empty. 26in barrel, 7 grooves; RH twist, concentric. Tube magazine beneath the barrel, 20 rounds? Standing-block rear sight. About 500 fps with 130-grain bullets.

The Hunt rifle had a ring-tipped lever behind the trigger guard, which was swung forward to break the toggle lock and retract the bolt or 'slider'. A separate ring-headed feed lever ahead of the trigger was pressed to lower the cartridge carrier, then released to raise a Rocket Ball into position. Returning the operating lever rammed the ball into the chamber and the gun was ready to fire.

This was clearly too clumsy to succeed, so the project was entrusted to Lewis Jennings. Jennings eventually received a patent on 25th December 1849, his patent model being a 54-caliber pill-lock with a 34in barrel, an overall length of 53in, and a 20-shot tube magazine beneath the barrel. Among its novelties were a two-part magazine follower, and the combination of the operating levers to undertake all the cocking/loading functions with a single ring-headed trigger.

The existence of an English patent combining the Hunt ammunition and a Jennings-like rifle, granted to Stephen Taylor in December 1847, suggests that development was completed earlier than widely supposed—and also that Jennings had undertaken his work long before the appropriate U.S. patent had been granted.

The first-pattern Jennings rifle of 1848 had the ring trigger/operating lever inside a conventional guard; the magazine tube ended level with the muzzle. A later gun (1849-52) dispensed with the guard and had a magazine ending a few inches behind the muzzle. Most of the rifles had blued receivers and case-hardened hammers, the barrels and magazine tubes being browned. They customarily bore the name of the manufacturer, but were also marked 'C.P. DIXON. AGENT. N.Y.'

Richard Lawrence of Robbins & Lawrence subsequently claimed to have made many of the changes to the Jennings rifles, but the basis for his claims is unclear.

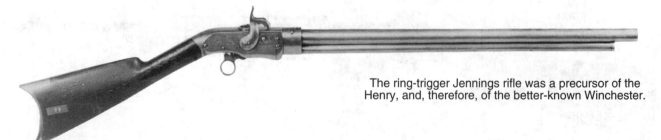

The ring-trigger Jennings rifle was a precursor of the Henry, and, therefore, of the better-known Winchester.

A small number of box-magazine sporting rifles were made before production of the better-known rotary-magazine Johnson military rifle began.

• Johnson, autoloading type

The prototype Johnson Automatic Rifle was tested in 1936, the relevant U.S. patent being granted in September 1937. More than 20 experimental examples were made by Marlin and Taft-Pierce before the design was settled. As the original intention had been to develop a sporting rifle in parallel with the military version, some guns even had checkered walnut half-stocks, box magazines and Lyman aperture rear sights.

The action was a novel combination of short recoil and an eight lug bolt, which subsequently reappeared on the ArmaLite series. Melvin Johnson, an officer in the Marine Corps Reserve, was a highly vocal (and often controversial) champion of his rifle and had powerful friends; only the intervention of the Secretary for War prevented the U.S. Senate debating the adoption of the 'Semi-Automatic Rifle, 30 M2' in the summer of 1940.

MODEL 1941 RIFLE

Made by Johnson Automatics Mfg. Co., Cranston, Rhode Island, 1942-4.
Total production: 70,000? **Chambering options:** 7x57 or 30-06. **Action:** locked by rotating lugs on the bolt head into the receiver; recoil operated, semi-automatic only.

DATA FOR A TYPICAL 30-06 EXAMPLE

45.5in overall, 9.50lb empty. 22in barrel, 4-groove rifling; RH, concentric. Detachable rotary drum magazine, 11 rounds. Spring-leaf and ramp rear sight graduated to 1000yd. About 2700 fps with M2 ball ammunition. Special knife bayonet.

A prototype was tested at Fort Benning in the Spring of 1938, and then at Aberdeen Proving Ground from August onward. Trials of an improved 30-caliber rifle, held in December 1939, persuaded the Ordnance Board to take the Johnson rifle seriously. In February 1940, however, the authorities ordered interest in the Johnson to cease in case remedial work on the Garand (q.v.) was adversely affected.

Tests showed that the Garand was compact and more durable, but the Johnson magazine could be reloaded even with the bolt closed. In addition, the feed lips were machined in the receiver, reducing jamming, and the barrel was readily detachable.

Trials undertaken in November 1940 by the U.S. Marine Corps, in San Diego, favored the M1903 Springfield at the expense of new M1 Garands with the post-1939 gas assembly, two well-worn Taft-Pierce Johnson rifles, and four differing Winchesters. As the Johnsons had each fired more than 10,000 rounds before trials began, and as the Winchesters were hardly out of the development stage, the conclusions were not altogether unexpected.

Spurned by the U.S. government, Johnson sold a substantial number of rifles to the Netherlands government-in-exile in the autumn of 1940. Destined for service with the Royal Netherlands Indies Army (KNIL), the perfected weapon was most distinctive, with a two-piece stock separated by the magazine housing. A pierced sheet-steel jacket surrounded the barrel, which moved back on firing to unlock the bolt. The stock wrist was noticeably shallow, as the return spring lay in a tube in the butt.

The KNIL contract was canceled when the East Indies surrendered to the Japanese in 1942, apparently before any large-scale deliveries had been made. Production was thereafter diverted to the U.S. Marines. Johnson rifles saw active service in the Pacific and European theaters, but the mechanism was more likely to jam under combat conditions than the Garand, and the slender barrel proved susceptible to damage.

A few hundred rifles apparently went to Chile, chambered for the 7x57 rimless cartridge, but it is unclear if delivery was made in 1942 or after 1945.

• Johnson, swinging-barrel type

William Johnson of Cincinnati, Ohio, received two U.S. patents in 1862-4 to protect firearms loaded by pivoting the barrel assembly laterally to the right on a sturdy tapered pin set into the lower part of the breech. However, doubt remains concerning the relationship between Johnson and A.H. Rowe (q.v.), whose patent shows a gun which is so similar to Johnson's that the resemblance cannot be entirely coincidental. Two Johnson carbines of an improved pattern, No. 27 and No. 28, were supplied to the U.S. Army trials of 1865. Made without forends, they had a small block-and-leaf rear sight. The action seems to have been locked by the hammer blade as the latter struck the primer of the chambered round.

• Johnson Associates

Johnson Automatics Associates, Inc., of Hope Valley, Rhode Island, marketed a series of modified M1 Carbines chambered for a potent 5.7mm MMJ cartridge—which may justifiably be regarded as the predecessor of the current 5.56x45 round. Production ceased in the early 1960s.

• Joslyn

Benjamin Joslyn was among the most enthusiastic of the gunmakers active during the American Civil War, but also among the most controversial. He contributed caplock revolvers and two differing carbines to the roster of breechloaders in Federal service, but quality was often very poor and the inventor was still embroiled in disputes with the government long after the war had ended.

MODEL 1855 NAVY RIFLE

Made by A.H. Waters & Co., Milbury, Massachusetts.
Total production: not known. **Chambering:** 58-caliber combustible cartridge, fired by a caplock. **Action:** locked by an elongated block pivoted upward around the chamber.

45.8in overall, 8lb empty. 30in barrel, 3-groove rifling; concentric. Single-shot only. Leaf-and-slider rear sight graduated to 800yd. Performance not known. Sword bayonet.

Made in accordance with a patent granted to Joslyn in August 1855, 500 of these guns were ordered on 9th September 1859 from Joslyn's agent, William Freeman of New York. Owing to problems with Waters & Co., delivery was delayed until the Spring of 1861 and it has been suggested that no more than 200 of the 500-gun order were ever delivered. The guns had conventional side-hammer caplocks, half-stocks, and barrels held with a single band. The furniture was brass, and a sabre bayonet could be mounted if required. The breech lever on top of the stock-wrist could be lifted with a large finger ring, exposing the chamber; steel rings in the breech-face expanded momentarily on discharge to form a gas seal.

SIMILAR GUNS

Model 1855 carbine. Trials undertaken successfully by the U.S. Army in September 1857 led to the purchase of 50 of these 54-caliber carbines in November. They were similar to the Navy rifles, with half-stocks, brass furniture and a single barrel band, but were only 28.3in long and weighed 7.25lb. The 22.5in barrel could accept a bayonet.

MODEL 1861 CARBINE

Made by B.F. Joslyn Fire Arms Co., Stonington, Connecticut.
Total production: not known. **Chambering:** 56-56 Spencer, rimfire. **Action:** locked by a breechblock pivoting laterally behind the chamber.

38.75in overall, 6.63lb empty. 22in barrel, 3-groove rifling; concentric. Single shot only. Three-leaf rear sight for ranges up to 500yd. Performance not known. No bayonet.

This carbine replaced the inefficient and unpopular 1855-type gun. Chambering metal-case cartridges and protected by a patent granted in October 1861, the prototypes appeared in 1861; series production began a year later. A laterally-hinged block, known as a 'cap', partially enveloped the standing breech and opened to the left when the locking catch was released. A patent of addition, granted in June 1862, added cam surfaces to improve cartridge seating and primary extraction. The Federal ordnance purchased

860 Joslyns from Bruff, Bros. & Seaver of New York City in 1861-2, assigning most of them to units raised in Ohio. At the end of 1862, however, Joslyn acquired a much larger contract and began volume deliveries of the improved 1862-pattern gun (below) in mid-August 1863.

SIMILAR GUNS

Model 1862 carbine. Made in Stonington, this was essentially similar to the 1861 type but chambered the 56-52 Spencer rimfire cartridge. It had a 22in barrel and measured 38.9in overall. Furniture was brass. There were long upper tangs, a hook on the breech cap, and a single block hinge. The extractor plate was retained by screws.

Model 1862 carbine, improved pattern. A few transitional guns made in 1864 combined the basic 1862-type action with the improved breech-cap release catch.

Model 1864 carbine. At least 5,000 of these were made. They were similar to the 1861 pattern, but a checkered finger-piece was let into the underside of the breech hook to improve the lock. The firing-pin shroud was cylindrical, a gas vent was added on top of the breech cap, and the upper tang was shortened. Guns numbered above about 11000 had double-hinge breeches. They were generally marked '1864' on the lock plate, and the breech-cap markings lay on the back surface instead of on top. Furniture was iron. The federal government purchased 10,201 metallic-cartridge Joslyn carbines (all types) from 1st May 1863 until 25th February 1865, though only about half the orders had been fulfilled when hostilities ceased. The contract was promptly cancelled on the grounds that the guns failed to meet specifications.

Trials pattern, 1865. Benjamin Joslyn submitted two carbines to the U.S. Army trials of 1865-6. Tested as 'No. 28a' and 'No. 29', they were much the same as the perfected swinging-block Civil War pattern. The trial guns had a one-piece half-stock, with a single band encircling the forend and a sling ring-and-bar—mounted on a slender round-cornered rectangular plate—set into the left side of the stock above the trigger.

MODEL 1865 RIFLE

Made by the Springfield Armory, Springfield, Massachusetts, 1865.
Total production: 3007. **Chambering:** 56-56 Spencer, rimfire. **Action:** as 1861-type carbine, above.

52in overall, 9.15lb empty. 35.5in barrel, 3-groove rifling; concentric. Leaf-and-slider rear sight graduated to 500yd. About 1050 fps with 350gr bullet. M1855 socket bayonet.

In view of the acrimonious exchanges between Joslyn and the federal government, it was ironic that this should have been the first breechloading rifle to be made in quantity in Springfield Armory. Derived from the regulation M1863 rifle-musket, 5000 Joslyns were ordered in the winter of 1864.

Though enough guns had been delivered by April 1865 to equip two infantry regiments, they were too late to see active service and production stopped before deliveries had been completed. About 1600 of them were converted in Springfield in 1871 for the 50-70 centerfire cartridge, but were sold almost immediately to an American dealer and thence to France. After serving the Gardes Mobiles in the closing stages of the Franco-Prussian War, many Joslyn rifles were seized by the Germans. Sold to Belgium, they were ultimately converted to shotguns and shipped to Africa.

• Joslyn-Tomes

One gun of this type—'Gun No. 40'—was tested by the U.S. Army in 1872. Made in accordance with a patent granted to Benjamin Joslyn in November 1870, the basis of the action was a hammer pivoting on the bolt. Pulling back the hammer spur disengaged the lower tip of the hammer from its recess in the floorplate. The hammer and the bolt could then be retracted to expose the chamber, extracting and ejecting a spent case as they ran back. When the bolt had been returned, pressing the trigger released the cocked hammer; before the striker could be driven forward onto the rim of a new cartridge, however, the lower tip of the hammer entered its seat and locked the action shut. The Joslyn-Tomes rifle (probably licensed to Henry Tomes of Tomes, Melvain & Co. of New York) was rejected on the grounds that many of the rival breech-locking systems operated more positively.

• Kimber

Founded as 'Kimber of Oregon, Inc.' in 1979, this gunmaking business became renowned for a range of high-quality rim- and centerfire bolt-action rifles. However, the original business failed in 1991 and—though the Warne family regained the use of the name—work did not recommence until 1994. Slightly modified forms of the Model 82, 84 and 89 rifles are now being offered by 'Kimber of America, Inc.'

MODEL 82 SPORTER

Made by Kimber of Oregon, Inc., Clackamas, Oregon.
Total production: not known. **Chambering options:** 22 Long Rifle rimfire, 22 Winchester Magnum rimfire, 22 Hornet. **Action:** locked by rotating two lugs on the bolt body into the receiver walls as the bolt handle was turned down.
DATA FOR A TYPICAL EXAMPLE

Chambering: 22 Winchester Magnum, rimfire. 40.5in overall, 6.38lb empty. 22in barrel, 6-groove rifling; RH, concentric. Internal box magazine, 4 rounds. Folding-leaf rear sight. 2000 fps with 40-grain bullet.

This rimfire sporter had a rugged two-lug bolt, an adjustable trigger and a flush-fitting magazine. Its walnut half-stock had a polished steel pistol grip cap, and a checkered steel buttplate. Centerfire versions shared the same rear-locking action, and the safety catch was originally a radial pattern behind the bolt handle.

SIMILAR GUNS

Note: '82A'-type guns (1986-8) had an improved bolt mechanism, and were made in right- or left-hand form; '82B' patterns (right-hand only, 1988-91) also had improvements in the striker system, reducing lock time, and a swept-back bolt handle.

Model 82 All-American Match rifle, 1990-1. Similar to the M82 Government Model, this single shot 22 LR gun had a 25in barrel and an adjustable single-stage trigger. The buttplate could slide vertically in its channel-block, and the pull could be lengthened with spacers.

Model 82 Brownell Commemorative rifle, 1986. Five hundred of these were made to mark the death of Leonard Brownell. They had full-length stocks.

Model 82 Cascade rifle, 1983-5. This had a Monte Carlo cheek-piece and comb, but lost popularity once the Model 84 appeared.

Model 82 Centennial rifle (or '22LR Centennial'), 1987. Made to celebrate the 100th anniversary of the introduction of the 22LR

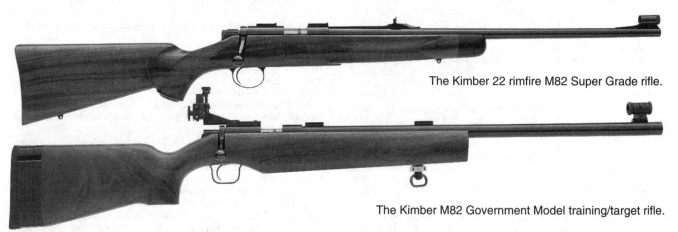

The Kimber 22 rimfire M82 Super Grade rifle.

The Kimber M82 Government Model training/target rifle.

rimfire cartridge by the J. Stevens Tool & Arms Company, these guns had selected walnut half-stocks, engraved actions, and a special target-grade barrel.

Model 82 Classic rifle, 1982-8. Another name for the standard pattern, this had a 22in barrel.

Model 82 Classic Custom rifle, 1982-8. A better grade of walnut distinguished this from the Classic pattern. A few single shot guns in 218 Bee and 25-20 WCF were made in 1985.

Model 82 Continental rifle, 1987-91. Made only in small numbers in 22LR, 22 Winchester Magnum rimfire and 22 Hornet, this had a full-length Mannlicher-style stock.

Model 82 Custom Match rifle, 1984. About 500 of these guns were made with a French walnut half-stock, rust-blue finish, fine checkering, and chamber dimensions regulated to closer tolerances than normal to handle match-quality ammunition.

Model 82 Deluxe Grade, 1989-90. A replacement for the Classic and Classic Custom patterns, this 22LR gun had an 'AA'-grade walnut half-stock but lacked a cheekpiece. An optional 10-round magazine could also be obtained.

Model 82 Government Model, 1987-9. The U.S. Army adopted a modified 82A for training purposes, with a heavy barrel, an extra-deep forend and a butt with adjustable spacers. A 20,000-gun contract had been fulfilled by 1989, but similar guns were offered commercially in 1990-1.

Model 82 Hunter rifle, 1990. This 22LR pattern had a walnut half-stock, generally of Super America (q.v.) pattern, with a matte-blue finish on the barrel and receiver.

Model 82 Kimber Decennial rifle, 1989. A few of these deluxe guns were made to celebrate the first 10 years of trading. They had slender tapering forends and a distinctive shadowed cheekpiece.

Model 82 Mini Classic, 1988. Made only in 22LR, this had an 18in barrel and a steel shoulder plate on the straight-comb butt. Swivels were fitted beneath the butt and forend.

Model 82 Sporter, 1991. These were minor variants of the standard pattern, made at the end of Kimber's life on old 'A'-type 22LR actions; they had 22in tapering barrels, and checkering on the pistol grip and forend of the comparatively poor-grade stocks. The round-top receiver was supplied with bases for optical-sight mounts.

Model 82 Super America rifle, 1983-8 and 1990-1. Made with a fine-quality walnut half-stock, this also had a checkered steel Niedner buttplate and detachable bases for optical-sight mounts. The 22in barrel was standard. Super America rifles were replaced by the 'Super Grade', only to reappear at the end of Kimber's life.

Model 82 Super Continental rifle, 1987-8. A deluxe form of the standard M82 Continental, this had finer checkering and a better grade of walnut in its stock.

Model 82 Super Grade rifle, 1989. A replacement for the Super America pattern, this was never popular; only a few were sold.

Model 82 Varminter rifle, 1990-1. Built on 22LR 'A'-type actions, these had 25in barrels and rubber shoulder pads instead of steel. Empty weight averaged 8.5lb; the detachable magazines held five (standard) or 10 (optional) rounds.

MODEL 82C SPORTING RIFLE

Kimber of America recommenced production of the Model 84 in 1994, advancing the designation to '82C'. Changes were made in the trigger, and an aluminum-pillar bedding system appeared. The standard 82C Classic rifle (made only in 22 LR rimfire) has a straight-comb half-stock of Claro walnut, with checkering on the pistol grip and round-tip forend. Open sights are not provided, as the receiver is tapped and drilled for optical-sight mount bases.

SIMILAR GUNS

Model 82C Custom rifle, 1995 to date. Though otherwise similar to the 82C Classic, this has a rust-blue finish and a French walnut stock with a Niedner shoulder plate.

Model 82C Stainless rifle, 1996 to date. Little more than an 82C Classic with a stainless-steel barrel, this exhibits a matte-blue action.

Model 82C Super America rifle, 1994 to date. A deluxe version of the standard gun, this has a select walnut stock, a beaded-edge cheekpiece, and an ebony forend tip.

Model 82C SVT rifle ('Stainless Varmint/Target'), 1996 to date. Easily identified by a fluted 18in stainless-steel barrel set in a high-comb walnut half-stock, this single shot gun also has a squared trigger guard with a voided web.

Model 82C Varmint Synthetic, 1996 to date. Distinguished by a matte-blue action and a fluted 20in stainless-steel barrel floating in a synthetic straight-comb half-stock, this weighs about 7.5lb.

MODEL 84 SPORTER
Also known as the 'Model 84 Mini-Mauser'
Made by Kimber of Oregon, Inc., Clackamas, Oregon, 1984-91.

Total production: not known. **Chambering options:** 17 Remington, 22 Hornet, 222 Remington or 223 Remington (see text). **Action:** locked by rotating two lugs on the bolt head into the receiver, and by the bolt-handle base entering its seat.

DATA FOR A TYPICAL SUPER VARMINTER

Chambering: 222 Remington, rimless. 42.5in overall, 7.25lb empty. 24in barrel, 6-groove rifling; RH, concentric. Internal box magazine, five rounds. Optical sight. 3200 fps with 50-grain bullet.

Developed specifically for 222 Remington cartridges, this combined features of the pre-1964 Winchester Model 70—e.g., the safety on the bolt shroud and the spring-loaded ejector—with others provided by the proven 1898-type Mauser. A round-top receiver was adopted in 1986, and a three-position safety replaced the earlier two-position type in 1987.

SIMILAR GUNS

Model 84 Big Bore Sporter, 1991. Derived from the standard M84 Sporter, a few of these were made for the 250-3000 Savage or 35 Remington rounds; the most obvious feature was a red-rubber Pachmayr shoulder pad.

Model 84 Big Bore Super America rifle, 1991. This was a 250-3000 Savage or 35 Remington version of the Super America (q.v.), with a Pachmayr butt pad.

Model 84 Classic rifle, 1984-8. This was another name for the standard rifles, which had a 22in barrel and weighed about 6.3lb. The walnut half-stock had a straight comb and a round-tipped forend. Additional 17 Mach IV, 221 Remington Fireball, 5.6x50, 6x45 and 6x47 chamberings had all been discontinued by 1988.

Model 84 Classic Custom rifle, 1984-8 and 1991. This was a 'Deluxe Grade', with a Claro walnut stock and ebony forend tip; the shoulder plate was a diced steel Niedner pattern.

Model 84 Cascade rifle, 1984-5. Made with a Monte Carlo-style half-stock, this was never popular; few were made.

Model 84 Continental rifle, 1987-91. Easily distinguished by its full-length Mannlicher-style stock, this was introduced only in 222 or 223 Remington, though a 221 Fireball option was added in 1989.

Model 84 Custom Match rifle, 1986. Only about 200 of these guns were made in 222 or 223 Remington. They had a selected walnut half-stock, a rust-blue finish, and chambers held to tolerances fine enough to suit match-quality ammunition.

Model 84 Deluxe Grade rifle, 1989-90. This replacement for the Classic Custom pattern could be recognized by the absence of a cheekpiece. Offered only in three Remington chamberings (17, 222 and 223), it was so unpopular that the Classic Custom made a brief reappearance in 1991.

Model 84 Hunter rifle, 1990. Made only in 17, 222 and 223 Remington chamberings, this had a laminated wood half-stock and matte-blue finish on the metalwork.

Model 84 Kimber Decennial rifle, 1989. Celebrating their manufacturer's 10th birthday, these had a slender tapering forend and a shadowed cheekpiece. The round-top receiver had bases for telescope sight mounts and the buttplate was a steel Niedner design. Chambering was restricted to 223 Remington.

Model 84 Sporter, 1991. Offered with a 22in barrel in 17 Remington, 22 Hornet, 22-250 or 223 Remington, this had a 'A'-grade walnut half-stock and a round-top receiver with bases for optical-sight mounts.

Model 84 Super America rifle, 1984-8 and 1990-1. These guns had walnut half-stocks selected for figuring, beaded cheek-piece edges, and fine hand-cut 22-line checkering. Niedner shoulder plates were standard, but skeletal pistol grip caps or buttplates were available to order. Other options included ebony forend tips, a quarter-rib with express sights, and dicing on the bolt-handle knob. Chamberings in the 22in barrel were restricted to 17 Remington, 22 Hornet, 22-250 or 223 Remington.

Model 84 Super Continental rifle, 1987-8. Essentially similar to the Continental (q.v.), with a full-length forend, this had finer checkering and a select walnut stock. It was available only in 222 and 223 Remington.

The Kimber M89 African Rifle.

Model 84 Super Grade rifle, 1989. A replacement for the Super America pattern (q.v.), apparently lacking a cheekpiece on the butt, this was never particularly popular; the earlier gun was subsequently reintroduced. Super Grade rifles were made in the three standard Remington chamberings—17, 222 and 223.

Super Varminter, 1989-90. A deluxe version of the Ultra Varminter, built to 'Super America' standards, this had selected Claro walnut stock with a beaded-edge cheekpiece and inletted swivel eyes.

Ultra Varminter, 1988-91. Distinguished by a 24in stainless-steel barrel and a laminated birch stock with a straight-comb butt, this was introduced in 17 Remington, 221 Fireball, 222 Remington or 223 Remington. The Fireball chambering was replaced in 1990 by a 22 Hornet option.

MODEL 84C CLASSIC SPORTING RIFLE

This 1996 reincarnation of the Mini-Mauser incorporates the aluminum-pillar bedding system. The standard Classic pattern has a straight-comb walnut half-stock with a round-tip forend. Offered only in 222 or 223 Remington, the rifles are typically 40.5in long (with a 22in barrel) and weigh about 6.8lb.

SIMILAR GUNS

Model 84C SSV rifle, 1996 to date. The 'Single Shot Varmint' pattern, made only in 17 and 223 Remington, has a fluted 25in stainless-steel barrel floating in the beavertail forend of a walnut half-stock.

Model 84C Super America rifle, 1996 to date. Announced in 17, 222 and 223 Remington, this deluxe pattern has a select-quality walnut half-stock with a beaded-edge cheekpiece, finely cut checkering, and a Niedner buttplate.

MODEL 89 BIG-GAME RIFLE

Made by Kimber of Oregon, Inc., Clackamas, Oregon, 1989-91.
Total production: not known. **Chambering options:** see notes. **Action:** generally as Model 84, above.
DATA FOR A TYPICAL EXAMPLE
Chambering: 300 H&H Magnum, belted rimless. 44in overall, 8lb empty. 24in barrel, 6-groove rifling; RH, concentric. Internal box magazine, three rounds. Folding-leaf rear sight. 2980 fps with 180-grain bullet.

Preceded by a series of pre-production guns made in 1987, this had a Mauser-type breech with an inner collar in the receiver ring, a collar-type extractor, an internal box magazine, and a pivoting bolt-stop on the left side of the receiver. The trigger, the safety and the ejector (which rode under the left locking lug) were inspired by the Winchester Model 70. The classically-styled walnut half-stock had a straight comb. In 1990, the design of the bolt-guide and the corresponding receiver rail were improved to smooth the bolt stroke.

THE GUNS

Model 89 African Rifle, 1990-1. Announced in a variety of chamberings, this seems to have been made only in 375 H&H, 416 Rigby and 505 Gibbs. The overall length was 47in; weight was 10-10.5lb. African rifles were stocked in Classic or Classic Custom styles (qq.v.) with very little drop at the heel. An express sight was fitted on a quarter-rib, the front sling swivel eye lay on the barrel, and two lateral recoil bolts were fitted through the woodwork.

Model 89 BGR Classic rifle 1988-9. The standard production version had a walnut half-stock with a cheekpiece and a straight comb; forends were round tipped. The standard chamberings were 270 Winchester, 7mm Remington Magnum, 280 Remington, 30-06, 300 Winchester Magnum, 338 Winchester Magnum or 375 H&H Magnum.

Model 89 BGR Classic Custom rifle, 1988-9. Mechanically identical with the BGR Classic, this had a better stock with an ebony forend tip.

Model 89 Deluxe Grade rifle, 1989-90. This was a version of the BGR with a round-top receiver, a separate ebony forend tip,

and a straight-comb butt lacking a cheekpiece. It was offered either with a 'Featherweight[-profile] barrel'—in 257 Roberts, 25-06, 270 Winchester, 280 Remington, 7x57 and 30-06—or with a medium-weight barrel in 7mm Remington Magnum, 300 H&H Magnum, 300 Winchester Magnum, 338 Winchester Magnum, 35 Whelen or 375 H&H Magnum.

Model 89 Hunter rifle, 1990-1. Supplied only in 270 Winchester, 7mm Remington Magnum, 30-06, 300 Winchester Magnum or 338 Winchester Magnum, this had a laminated wood half-stock and matte-blue finish on the barrel and action.

Model 89 Sporter, 1991. A simplification of the Deluxe pattern, offered only at the end of the company's life, this had a squared-bridge receiver and a standard-grade walnut stock.

Model 89 Super America rifle, 1989 and 1991. These guns, which could be supplied in most of the regular chamberings, had half-stocks made from specially-selected walnut blanks, finely cut checkering, and cheekpieces with a beaded edge.

Model 89 Super Grade rifle, 1989-90. Similar to the Super America version, this had a squared-bridge receiver. The butt lacked a cheekpiece.

K770 CUSTOM SPORTING RIFLE

An improved M89, this was introduced in 1996 in 270 Winchester and 30-06 only. The bolt has been altered so that the lugs lock into the barrel behind the chamber, and the throw of the bolt handle has been changed to 60 degrees. The pillar-bedding system has been retained, the barrel is allowed to float freely in the forend of the walnut half-stock, and the four-round magazine has a hinged floorplate. A Super America pattern offers woodwork selected for its figuring, a beaded-edge cheekpiece, and a special Niedner butt-plate.

• Knight

Bearing an external affinity with the ArmaLite series, the SR-25 was the last of Eugene Stoner's firearm designs to reach production before his death in 1997. The SR-25 is basically an AR-15/M16 revised to accept a 7.62mm cartridge—somewhat ironic, as the 5.56mm AR-15 was a diminution of the unsuccessful 7.62mm AR-10 of the mid 1950s! The commonality of the M16 and the SR-25 is intended to tempt users familiar with the 5.56mm guns to acquire a large-caliber derivative for special duties, e.g., in support of sniper or machine gun teams armed with 7.62mm weapons.

MODEL 25 MATCH RIFLE
Also known as 'SR-25 Match'

Made by Knight's Armament Company, Vero Beach, Florida, 1994 to date.
Currently in production. **Chambering:** 308 Winchester. **Action:** generally as ArmaLite R-15/M16 series (q.v.).
46.25in overall; 9.75lb without sights. 20in barrel, 4-groove rifling; RH, concentric. Detachable box magazine, 10 or 20 rounds. Optical sight. 2785 fps with ball ammunition.

The basic SR-25 Match Rifle has a distinctive flat-top receiver with a Picatinny Rail for optical or electro-optical sights, and a cylindrical barrel jacket retained by a large threaded nut.

SIMILAR GUNS

SR-25 Carbine. A compact version of the basic rifle, this has a 16in barrel; overall length, therefore, is reduced to about 42.5in.

SR-25 Silenced. This is distinguished by a full-length silencer, which replaces the cylindrical barrel jacket/forend of the standard version.

SR-25 Sniper. A heavy-barreled version of the basic rifle, this usually displays a telescoping-leg bipod beneath the forend. Empty weight is about 10.8lb.

SR-25 Sporter. Intended for commercial sale, this reverts to the detachable M16-type carrying handle and adjustable open sights.

• Kodiak

Kodiak Mfg. Co. of North Haven, Connecticut, made rifles on the basis of refurbished 1898-pattern Mauser actions in about 1959-73. Rifles were also made under contract to Colt (q.v.).

MODEL 98 SPORTING RIFLE

Chambered for 243 Winchester, 30-06 or 308 Winchester rounds, this was made with a 20in or 24in barrel and a five-round magazine. It had a plain hardwood stock with a low Monte Carlo comb and impressed checkering on the pistol grip and forend sides.

SIMILAR GUNS

Model 100 Deluxe. This was similar to the Model 98, but had a better quality stock, a ventilated shoulder plate, and a pistol grip cap. Made only with a 24in barrel, it chambered, in addition to the three standard 'Model 98' options, an assortment of magnum cartridges—264 Winchester, 7mm Remington, 300 Winchester, 308 Norma, 338 Winchester, 350 Remington or 358 Winchester. A three-round magazine was standard.

Model 101 Ultra. This was a variant of the Model 100 with a better walnut stock. The comb was a roll-over pattern, the forend tip and pistol grip cap were ebonite, and a ventilated rubber shoulder pad was fitted.

Model 102 Varmint Ultra. Essentially similar to the Model 100, this had a heavy barrel and lacked open sights. It weighed 8.5lb.

• Krag-Jørgensen

Worried by advances in Europe, the U.S. Army decided in 1890 to hold a competition to find a suitable small-bore magazine rifle. Trials with more than 50 guns were concluded in August 1892. Among the submissions had been several Krag-Jørgensen rifles. Krag no. 1 was the 8mm Danish m/89; nos. 2 and 3 were similar 30-caliber guns with a Mauser-type safety, a pivoting ejector and a different cocking piece; no. 4 was no. 2 with a dust cover over the bolt and a downward-opening loading gate; no. 5 was the same as no. 4, without the dust cover; and Krag no. 6 was a variant of no. 5 chambered for a special rimless 30-caliber cartridge.

Krag no. 5 was eventually chosen in preference to Lee no. 3 and the Belgian-type Mauser no. 5 simply because fresh cartridges could be inserted in the magazine when the bolt was shut on a loaded chamber.

MODEL 1892 RIFLE
'U.S. Magazine Rifle, Caliber 30, Model of 1892'

Made by the Springfield Armory, Springfield, Massachusetts, 1894-7. Total production: 24,560. **Chambering:** 30-40, rimmed. **Action:** locked by a single lug on the bolt head engaging a recess in the receiver.

49in overall, 9.38lb empty. 30in, 4-groove rifling; RH, concentric. Internal pan magazine, 5 rounds. Tangent-leaf rear sight graduated to 1900yd. 2000 fps with M1895 ball cartridges. M1892 sword bayonet.

The Krag was officially adopted on 15th September 1892, though production was deferred while trials were undertaken fruitlessly with other U.S.-designed rifles. The first guns were assembled in Springfield Armory on 1st January 1894, but issues were delayed until 6th October.

The straight-grip walnut stock had a grasping groove in the forend and a handguard from the breech to the barrel band. An open stacking swivel was attached to the nose cap, and a lug beneath the nose cap accepted a Swiss-style sword bayonet. The rear sight lacked windage adjustments. The original flat buttplate was replaced by a rounded pattern from 23rd December 1895. By the end of 1896, however, 40 changes had been made to the M1892—though very few guns received all the minor modifications, owing to the adoption of the M1896.

SIMILAR GUNS

Carbines. The first of these were made for trials in 1893 by shortening M1892 rifles by about 8in. A cleaning rod was carried in the stock, a saddle ring appeared on the left side of the wrist, and the nose cap lacked a bayonet lug.

Modified rifles. 1892-pattern Krags altered to 1896 standards after March 1897 can be identified by filled cleaning-rod channels in the forend (a three-piece rod was carried in the butt) and by an M1896 rear sight—often later replaced by the M1901. The final arbiter is usually the receiver marks: '1892' appears on the side-plate instead of 'MODEL 1896'.

MODEL 1896 RIFLE

Made by the Springfield Armory, Springfield, Massachusetts, 1896-9. Total production: about 62,000. **Chambering:** 30-40, rimmed. **Action:** as M1892, above.

49.1in overall, 8.94lb empty. 30in, 4-groove rifling; RH, concentric. Internal pan magazine, 5 rounds. Tangent-leaf rear sight graduated to 1800yd. 2000 fps with M1895 ball cartridges. M1892 sword bayonet.

Standardized on 19th February 1896, this was very similar to the last of the much-modified 1892-type guns—though a three-piece cleaning rod was carried in the butt, and the rear sight had a 'stepless' or continuously curved base. Windage adjustments were still absent.

SIMILAR GUNS

Model 1896 cadet rifle. Adopted in December 1895, this was basically an 1896-type infantry rifle with a full-length cleaning rod and a barrel-band spring. Only about 400 were made in Springfield Armory in 1896-7; they weighed 9.08lb and had tangent-leaf rear sights graduated to 1900yd. Cadet rifles originally lacked swivels, but surviving guns were recalled in November 1900 to be altered, and 1901-pattern rear sights were fitted in 1902-3.

MODEL 1896 CARBINE

Made by the Springfield Armory, Springfield, Massachusetts, 1896-9. Total production: about 22,500. **Chambering:** 30-40, rimmed. **Action:** as M1892, above.

41.15in overall, 7.75lb empty. 22in barrel, 4-groove rifling; RH, concentric. Internal pan magazine, 5 rounds. Tangent-leaf rear sight graduated to 2000yd. About 1750 fps with M1895 ball cartridges. No bayonet.

Approved on 17th May 1895, this gun had a thin-wrist stock, and a saddle ring and bar assembly on the left side of the stock above the trigger guard. A two-piece cleaning rod and an oiler were carried in a butt-trap. Carbine sights were practically identical with those of the rifles, but the leaves were marked with a large 'C'. The cut-offs were reversed in 1900, but most 1896-type carbines were withdrawn in 1901 for militia use and fitted with the 1899-type stock before reissue. Survivors were sold to Cuba (q.v.) in 1912.

MODEL 1898 RIFLE

Made by the Springfield Armory, Springfield, Massachusetts, 1898-1904.

Total production: 324,300. **Chambering:** 30-40, rimmed. **Action:** as M1892, above.

49.15in overall, 9lb empty. 30in barrel, 4-groove rifling; RH, concentric. Internal pan magazine, 5 rounds. Tangent-leaf rear sight graduated to 2000yd. 2200 fps with high-velocity ball cartridges. M1892 sword bayonet.

The first major revision of the U.S. Army Krag was approved on 14th March 1898. The machining of the bolt mechanism,

The US 30-caliber M1892 Krag rifle with a Parkhurst & Warren charging system.

The US 30-caliber M1896 Krag carbine.

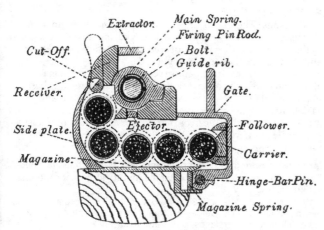

A sectional drawing of the 1898-type Krag rifle.

receiver and the magazine loading gate was greatly simplified, and the bolt-handle seat was milled flush with the receiver. The first M1898 rifles were delivered into store from Springfield in July. They had the M1898 or Dickson-pattern sight with a bullet-drift adjustment and a binding screw on the slider. The guns and their new high-power cartridge reached service in October 1899. Some of them were fitted with a short-lived headless cocking piece, which was abandoned in 1900 after complaints that it prevented the striker being re-cocked after a misfire. The magazine cut-off mechanism had been experimentally reversed in 1897, when a few rifles had been modified for trials, but nothing was done until the change was applied to service weapons made after February 1900.

SIMILAR GUNS

Board of Ordnance and Fortification Rifle, 1902. One hundred of these experimental Springfield-made 30-40 guns were issued for trials in the autumn of 1902. They shared the standard Krag action, but were 45.1in overall, had 26in barrels, and weighed 8.46lb. A special tangent-leaf sight was fitted and the M1892 sword bayonet could be attached at the muzzle. Muzzle velocity was about 1910 fps with M1892 ball cartridges. The short barrel increased muzzle blast and reduced accuracy, though the guns were very popular. However, progress being made with modified Mauser-type rifles was more encouraging and the shortened Krag was abandoned.

Model 1898 carbine, 1898-9. This was essentially similar to the M1896 carbine (q.v.) but had the improved 1898-pattern rifle action. Only about 5000 were made in Springfield, as the high velocity cartridges proved troublesome. Surviving carbines were recalled in the early 1900s to receive 1899-type stocks and new sights. They were about 41.15in long, had 22in barrels and weighed about 7.8lb.

Model 1898 carbine with Parkhurst & Warren Loader, 1900. One hundred guns were converted to this stripper-clip system in mid-summer; tests were favorable, but better progress was being made with a new trials rifle (see 'Springfield, bolt-action type') and the project was abandoned.

Model 1899 carbine, 1899-1904. About 36,000 of these were made in the Springfield factory. Derived from the M1898, they had a plain stock with the forend lengthened by about 3in, and were initially fitted with the 1896-pattern (2000yd) rear sight. A new handguard was approved in 1902, with a special faired projection at the front of the sight base to protect the sight leaf when the carbine was thrust in its saddle scabbard, and the 1901-type Buffington sight replaced the 1896 type in the same era.

Model 1898 rifle with Buffington sight, 1901-2. The disappearance of the high velocity cartridge, which had been with-

drawn once broken locking-lugs had been reported, heralded the 1901-pattern sight with a stepless base and an elongated leaf graduated to 2300yd. The slider could be fitted with a peep, and bullet-drift adjustments were made simply by loosening a clamp-screw and pivoting the entire sight laterally.

Model 1898 rifle with Dickson sight, 1902-4. The 1902-type tangent sight, graduated to 2000yd, was similar to the 1898 pattern. However, it had one sight notch instead of three, and a spring plunger in the slider engaged the leaf-edge serrations.

Model 1898 rifle with Parkhurst & Warren Device, 1900. One hundred rifles were converted at the same time as the carbines described above.

PHILIPPINE CONSTABULARY RIFLE

Converted by the Springfield Armory, Springfield, Massachusetts, 1906-10; by Rock Island Arsenal, Illinois, 1908-10; and by the Manila ordnance depot, 1910-14.

Total production: about 9800. Chambering: 30-40, rimmed. Action: as M1892, above.

41.15in overall, 8.03lb empty. 22in barrel, 4-groove rifling; RH, concentric. Internal pan magazine, 5 rounds. Tangent-leaf rear sight graduated to 2000yd. About 1750 fps with M1892 ball cartridges. M1892 sword bayonet.

Many old Krag-Jørgensen rifles were transformed from 1906 onward into a 'Carbine M1899, altered for Knife Bayonet and Rifle Sling', originally authorized when Springfield modified 350 for Girard College in Philadelphia; 9450 others were converted in 1907-14 to provide native troops in the Philippines with rifles befitting their small stature. Some work was undertaken in the U.S.A., but more was done in Manila.

SPORTING GUNS

The issue of sufficient M1903 Springfield rifles allowed large-scale withdrawal of Krags to begin. In March 1905, therefore, an Act of Congress allowed members of the National Rifle Association to buy Krag rifles. Sales were poor prior to 1917, but war familiarized so many Americans with the bolt action that the situation changed dramatically in the early 1920s. Many Krags were cut to carbine length and given rounded forends (the 'NRA Carbine'), but others were properly re-modeled.

Though the Krag action was not especially strong, its smooth operating stroke and the renowned accuracy of the perfected rifles— appreciably better than the pre-1914 M1903 Springfields at all but long ranges— prompted gunsmiths to alter military-surplus actions. R.F. Sedgley, Inc. of Philadelphia was particularly active, offering large numbers of Krag sporting rifles between the wars. Many were fitted with high-quality Stevens-Pope barrels. Some retained their original 30-40 chambering, but others were converted for 25-35 WCF and a few for 250-3000 Savage.

The Winchester cartridge was popular, but the Savage option proved to be too powerful for the single locking lug. By 1933, *The American Rifleman*, the NRA journal, was already carrying warnings about the undesirablity of re-chambering Krags for the 250-3000 cartridge.

• Laidley

Theodore Laidley, an ordnance officer in the U.S. Army, commanded Frankford Arsenal and Springfield Armory during his career. Service in Springfield inspired him to develop a radial-breech system which avoided problems which had been identified in the earliest Remingtons. A prototype Laidley was made in the Armory in January 1865, followed by several others, and a 50-caliber rimfire 'Carbine No. 33' was tested by the U.S. Army in April. Submitted by 'M.Y. Chick' of New York (camouflaging Laidley's participation), the gun had a two-piece stock with a short forend held by a single band. Its destruction in the overload-charge test was ascribed by Laidley to bad worksmanship, but it reappeared only to be photographed at the conclusion of the trials.

U.S. patent 54,743 was granted to Laidley and Charles Emery in May 1866 to protect a radial-breech system with additional locking bars pivoting on the hammer-axis pin. Several Laidley guns were tested in the Spring of 1866, when the purchase of 50 (together with the Remington, Peabody and Sharps designs) was recommended by the Chief of Ordnance. However, the army commander, General Grant, overturned this suggestion in favor of the Springfield-Allin (q.v.). Colt is said to have made 50 36in-barreled 45- and 50-caliber Laidley rifles in 1867, for trials in Russia, but the project was exploited in the early 1870s by Whitney (q.v.).

A detail view of the Krag rifle with the Parkhurst & Warren Device.

• Lamson

Two guns of this type were tested by the U.S. Army in 1867, one chambering rimfire ammunition and the other adapted for centerfire patterns. The breechblock slid longitudinally in a carrier pivoted to a strap on top of the chamber. The backward movement was very short, just enough to break the contact between the chamber and the breechblock face, but the top-strap was badly damaged during the defective-cartridge tests and the Lamson rifles were withdrawn from competition.

• Lee, block-action type

VERTICALLY-MOVING BLOCK PATTERN
1866-PATTERN RIFLE

In May 1866, a patent was granted to James P. Lee to protect a breechblock which dropped downward through a mortise in the receiver or frame. A 52-caliber gun of this type survives, and it is suspected that at least five were made. The remaining carbine has a bronze frame and a conventional side-hammer lock. The extractor is formed as the front tip of the operating lever/trigger guard, and a spring latch locks around a stud on the tang beneath the stock-wrist. A plate set into the top of the breechblock is supported at the rear as the block drops to deflect ejected cartridge cases.

IMPROVED MARTINI PATTERN
1871-PATTERN RIFLE

This was made in accordance with a patent granted in the U.S.A. in May 1871, assigned to Philo Remington, which combined an underlever and an auto-tripping breechblock. Pressing the lever down to open the breech retracted the firing pin, put the hammer to half-cock, and extracted a spent case as the breechblock reached the bottom of its opening stroke. Inserting a new cartridge tripped the breechblock, which rose far enough to retain the cartridge in the chamber; closing the breech could then be accomplished by the underlever (which left the hammer at half-cock) or simply by thumbing back the hammer to its full-cock position. Though E. Remington & Sons made at least one gun, the unnecessarily complicated 1871-patent Lee was soon superseded by the hammer-action patterns.

HAMMER-OPERATED DESIGNS
1871-PATTERN RIFLE

The failure of the 1871-patent 'Improved Martini Action' encouraged the development of a pivoting-block rifle operated by the hammer, patented by Lee in June 1871. A rifle of this type, made by E. Remington & Sons, was apparently entered in the U.S. Army trials of 1872 as 'Gun No. 54'. It had a solid frame and a two-piece stock. Pulling the hammer to half-cock retracted the firing pin and lowered the breechblock to the loading position, where it struck the tail of the extractor to expel a spent case. Inserting a fresh cartridge tripped the extractor and allowed the breechblock to close automatically; the hammer could then be thumbed back to full-cock to fire the gun.

Gun No. 54 was a simple and compact central-hammer design with a 'U'-shape main spring—possibly its major weakness, as it had been supplemented by the improved 'V'-spring Gun No. 61 even before the U.S. Army trials began.

1872-PATTERN RIFLE

U.S. Army trials Gun No. 61, which retained the earlier 1871-type extractor, was made by Remington in accordance with a patent granted to Lee in January 1872. A 'V'-type main spring lay beneath the breechblock ahead of the two-piece articulated hammer. The thumb piece of the hammer was pushed forward to retract the firing pin, lower the breechblock and extract the spent case. Pulling back on the thumb piece then raised the block and cocked the trigger system. The principal components of the lock were contained in a single sub-assembly and could be detached simply by removing the breechblock pivot pin. Gun No. 61 had a solid receiver and a two-piece stock. It performed well enough to encourage additional development, leading to the 1875-pattern gun described below.

MODEL 1875 RIFLE
Made by the Springfield Armory, Springfield, Massachusetts, 1875.
Total production: 143. Chambering: 45-70, rimmed. Action: locked by propping the breechblock behind the chamber.

49.25in overall, 8.75lb empty. 32.5in barrel, 4-groove rifling; RH, concentric. Single-shot only. Ramp-and-leaf rear sight graduated to 1200yd? About 1250 fps with standard 500-grain bullet. M1873 socket bayonet.

Manufacture of these guns, patented by James Lee in March 1874, began in the Springfield Armory early in 1875. Striking the hammer lever forward with the heel of the palm pivoted the breech down to expose the chamber; a new cartridge was then inserted manually, tripping the breech catch as it entered the chamber. The block then shut automatically. The hammer spur could be retracted to an intermediate position, marked by an audible click, which locked the breechblock and the striker to prevent the trigger releasing the striker until the hammer had been thumbed fully back.

The rifles could be dismantled merely by removing a bolt through the rear tang. They had distinctive Springfield-pattern straight-wrist stocks with two sprung bands. Two swivels were fitted on the band nearest the muzzle and another on the trigger guard bow. A cleaning rod lay beneath the muzzle. The 'U.S.' marks were usually found on the buttplate and on the tang behind the breech.

Issued for trials in the summer of 1875, the Lee rifles could be fired extremely rapidly when clean. But they also had serious flaws. The operating lever had to be kept at half- or full-cock to ensure that the breech remained closed (a feature the military distrusted greatly), and the mechanism was difficult to close without inserting a cartridge to trip the extractor. The guns were recalled to store, to be sold publicly at Rock Island Arsenal, and an interesting experiment came to a premature end.

1877-PATTERN RIFLE

This was an improved form of the 1875 U.S. Army rifle, patented by Lee in August 1877. It had a one-piece rebounding hammer and a refined 'V'-type main spring which controlled all movement. The breech mechanism contained just 15 parts, including seven pins, and was easy to dismantle. Lee entered one rifle in the U.S. Army trials of 1877, from Hartford, Connecticut, but 'Gun No. 25' was unable to challenge the Hotchkiss repeater submitted by Winchester; realizing that the day of the single-shot was passing, Lee turned instead to bolt-action magazine rifles (q.v.).

MAGAZINE RIFLE

At least one of Lee's block-action rifles was altered to use a bandolier magazine patented in April 1875. It was demonstrated in Britain in 1875, without effect, and returned to the U.S.A. with the inventor. The patent drawings suggest that the rifle had a 'U'-shape cartridge box or 'rapid loader' around the action, which could be replenished from the bandolier. Each round was taken from the rapid loader attached to the rifle and inserted into the chamber manually.

• Lee, bolt-action type

See also 'Lee-Cook', 'Remington-Lee' and 'Winchester-Lee'. Details will also be found in the British section. By far the best source of information about the early Lee rifles is *The Remington-Lee Rifle* by Eugene Myszkowski (Excalibur Publications, 1994).

The earliest rifle of this type is believed to have been entered in the U.S. Army trials of 1872, where the unsuccessful 'Gun No. 53'—apparently designed by James Lee and submitted by E. Remington & Sons—was recorded as relying on a camming lever to displace a locking lug on the underside of the sliding breech-bolt down into the receiver floor. No. 53 had a one-piece stock, ejected upward, and may have been the antecedent of the Winchester-Lee ('Lee Straight Pull') rifles of the 1890s.

The key to Lee's success lay in U.S. patent 221,328, granted on 4th November 1879 to protect a bolt-action rifle and its detachable box magazine. The Lee Arms Company was formed in Bridgeport, Connecticut, and about 50 prototypes were made in Sharps' tool

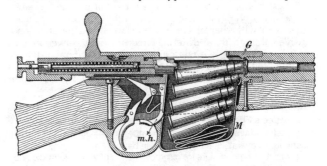

A sectional drawing of the 1879-type Lee rifle.

A typical 1882-pattern Remington-Lee rifle
which replaced the 1879 type. (HBL)

room prior to the collapse of the business in 1881. They varied considerably in detail and few survive.

The perfected version had a handle locking down ahead of the receiver bridge. The greatest problems, however, had concerned the design of the magazine spring and the way in which the cartridges were presented to the chamber. The earliest attempts to develop one-piece zigzag springs failed, and the solution was not found until Hugo Borchardt riveted a series of flat spring steel plates together. The plain-sided Borchardt magazine was eventually patented in March 1882, but was in use by 1881.

The U.S. Navy ordered 300 Lee rifles, but the collapse of Sharps occurred before anything other than the most basic machining could be done on the receivers. The Lee Arms Company then passed the contract to Remington.

MAGAZINE RIFLE, MILITARY PATTERN
Also known as the 'Model 1879'
Made by E. Remington & Sons, Ilion, 1880-4.

Total production: about 8800. **Chambering options:** 43 Spanish or 45-70-500. **Action:** locked by the bolt-guide rib abutting the receiver ahead of the bridge, and by a lug entering the receiver wall as the bolt handle was turned down.

DATA FOR A FIRST-PATTERN U.S. NAVY RIFLE
48.5in overall, 8.5lb empty. 29.5in barrel, 3-groove rifling; RH, concentric. Detachable box magazine, 5 rounds. Ramp-and-leaf rear sight graduated to 1200yd. 1320 fps with ball cartridges. U.S. M1873 socket bayonet.

The U.S. Navy ordered 300 rifles from the Sharps Rifle Company in 1880, to arm newly-commissioning warships and facilitate long-term assessment. The collapse of Sharps forced the contract to be passed to Remington, whose marks appear as well as those of the Lee Arms Company. Almost all 1879-type guns purchased by the Navy bore distinctive inspectors' marks (e.g., 'WWK' applied by Lieutenant Commander William W. Kimball) plus an anchor above 'U.S.'

The bolt handles of the 1879-type rifles locked down ahead of the receiver bridge. The guns had one-piece walnut stocks and two barrel bands, but lacked handguards. Swivels lay on the magazine and on the nose-band. A half-cock notch sufficed as an unreliable safety feature, but the Lee rifles were successful enough to convince the U.S. Navy of their merits and 700 additional guns were purchased. These accepted the standard Remington socket bayonet instead of the 1873-pattern Springfield design, and the magazines were made in accordance with a patent granted to Roswell Cook in September 1884. A sliding spring-detent (on the left side) held the cartridges when the magazine was detached from the gun, but was automatically released when the magazine was pushed into the feed-well.

Most of the earlier 1879-type Navy rifles, which had been issued with the plain-sided Borchardt magazines, were altered to receive the Cook pattern in Navy workshops. Modified guns could accept Borchardt or Cook magazines interchangeably, though second-pattern rifles were restricted to the Cook type.

• Lee, pivoting-barrel type

The earliest of James Lee's forays into firearms design seems to have been his 1862 patent, granted to protect a single shot sheath trigger pistol with a barrel which swung laterally to the left to load. However, though three differing breechloading conversions of 1855-model rifle muskets were submitted to the federal ordnance authorities in 1863—during the American Civil War—nothing was done until 1,000 carbines were ordered from Lee's Fire Arms Company of Milwaukee.

BREECH-LOADING CARBINE
Made by Lee's Fire Arms Company, Milwaukee, Wisconsin, 1865-7.
Total production: several hundred. **Chambering:** 44 rimfire (44 Henry?).
About 38.5in overall, 5.4lb empty. 21.2in barrel, 6-groove rifling; RH, concentric. 'L'-type rear sight for distances up to 500yd. Performance not known. No bayonet.

Prototypes of this carbine were made in Stevens Point, Wisconsin, in 1863. After a test was successfully undertaken in April 1864, the federal government ordered 1000 carbines on 7th May. However, even though rough-bored barrel blanks were purchased from Remington, and sling bars, buttplates and sights came from the Burnside Rifle Company, only 255 carbines had been completed when the Civil War ended. Another 202 had been assembled ready for stocking, but no guns had been delivered owing to disputes about quality and chambering. Lee carbines contained only eight moving parts, had barrels which swung to the right at the breech after the release catch had been pressed, and lacked forends.

A lawsuit was eventually decided in favor of Lee in December 1868, a year after Lee's Fire Arms Company had failed. Many of the carbines were sold commercially, and some of the barreled actions were completed as sporting rifles.

SPORTING RIFLE
Made by Lee's Fire Arms Company, Milwaukee, Wisconsin, 1866-7.
Total production: several hundred. **Chambering options:** 38 Extra Long or 44 Henry rimfire.
DATA FOR A TYPICAL 38-CALIBRE EXAMPLE
44.3in overall, 8.3lb empty. 29.6in barrel, 6-groove rifling; RH, concentric. Fixed-block rear sight. Performance not known.

The end of the Civil War and the failure of the federal government carbine contract left Lee with many unfinished parts. Many of these were subsequently assembled as sporting rifles; serial numbers run as high as 2200, though there is no evidence that more than a few hundred were actually made before production ceased. The sporters were made in a light-barrel pattern weighing about 6.5lb, or a heavy-barrel version weighing up to 8.5lb depending on barrel length and style.

• Lee-Cook

Five of these distinctive-looking rifles were submitted to the U.S. Navy trials of 1894, where they competed against a selection of designs including James Lee's perfected 'straight-pull' gun (see 'Winchester-Lee') and a rifle 'much like the Mauser' submitted independently by the Lee Arms Company.

EXPERIMENTAL RIFLE

Made by the Remington Arms Company in accordance with a patented granted to Roswell Cook in May 1895, this embodied a modification of the Diss-patent bolt used in the 1885-pattern Remington-Lee. The locking lugs lay on the front of the bolt body, but the magazine was a fixed box offset to one side of the receiver.

The Navy trial reports record that guns no. 1, no. 2 and no. 5 had the magazine on the right side of the breech, ejecting to the left; nos. 3 and 4 had the magazine on the left, ejecting to the right. However, the straight-pull Lee was preferred and the interesting Cook-patent rifle was abandoned.

• Lindner

Edward Lindner of New York City, though an American citizen, is believed to have been of German gunmaking stock. He was also a prolific patentee. U.S. patent 14,819, granted in May 1856, protected the first of Lindner's collar-lock designs. This relied on rapid-pitch threads to move the collar forward when the handle was raised, releasing the breechblock to tip upward for loading. This system was subsequently improved by patent 23,378 of 29th March 1859, providing the basis for the guns used in small numbers during the Civil War. A bolt-action conversion credited to Lindner was tested extensively in Austria and eventually adopted in Bavaria (q.v.) in 1867.

CONVERTED MODEL 1841 RIFLE
Made by Allen & Morse, Boston, Massachusetts (100), and by the Amoskeag Mfg. Co., Manchester, New Hampshire (3).
Total production: at least 103. **Chambering:** 54-caliber combustible cartridge, fired by a caplock. **Action:** locked by rotating the breech collar to restrain the breechblock.
48.8in overall, 9.9lb empty. 31in barrel, 6-groove rifling; RH, concentric. Single-shot only. Folding-leaf rear sight graduated to 500yd. Performance not known. No bayonet?

Though Civil War-era Lindners were made in at least three non-standard types—the most basic being imported Austrian muskets, cut to carbine length—a few U.S. regulation rifles were altered in 1861 for Massachusetts cavalrymen. These were the work of Allen & Morse of Boston, who made 100 guns, though at least three prototypes were made by the Amoskeag Mfg. Co.

The breech was opened by turning a short grasping handle to the left, rotating the locking collar until it had moved forward far enough to allow the pivoted breechblock to be lifted to receive a combustible cartridge. Ignition relied on a conventional side-hammer caplock. Alterations included a new upper tang and a strengthened trigger plate, and a new rear sight was fitted. Markings on the breech (apart from original makers' marks) rarely acknowledged anything other than Lindner's 1859 patent.

MODEL 1861 CARBINE

Made by the Amoskeag Mfg. Co., Manchester, New Hampshire.
Total production: at least 1000. **Chambering:** 58-caliber combustible cartridge, fired by a caplock. **Action:** as M1841 rifle, above.

38.5in overall, 6.1lb empty. 20in barrel, 3-groove rifling; RH, concentric. Single shot only. Two-leaf rear sight. Performance not known. No bayonet.

The Lindner carbines had a one-piece walnut half-stock, with the forend and barrel united by a nose cap, but were otherwise very similar to the 1841-pattern conversions described above. Federal ordnance authorities ordered 400 Lindner carbines on 6th November 1861; as these were to be sent to Washington Arsenal within eight days, it is assumed that deliveries were made from stock. Federal purchases eventually totaled only 892 (1861-6), but carbines were also sold to militiamen and volunteers.

• Ljutic

The products of this manufacturing company, in addition to individualistic shotguns, have included one of the most bizarre-looking rifles of recent years. Production apparently ceased at the end of the 1980s, but could easily be resumed if necessary.

SPACE RIFLE

Made by Ljutic Industries, Inc., Yakima, Washington, 1981-8?
Total production: not known. **Chambering options:** 22-250, 30-30 WCF, 30-06 or 308 Winchester. **Action:** see text.
DATA FOR A 22-250 TYPICAL EXAMPLE

44in overall, 8.75lb empty. 24in barrel, rifling pattern not known. Optical sight. 3725 fps with 55-grain bullet.

This extraordinary rifle, resembling a straight tube, cannot be mistaken. Often built to the requirements of individual customers, the Space Rifle loaded by twisting the forend to release the barrel. A striker was cocked by a handle protruding beneath the receiver, the adjustable trigger often being a thumb button. A recoil-absorbing mechanism was built into the butt and the sights were carried in a high mount.

• McMillan

McMillan made small numbers of good quality, but expensive rifles embodying variations on a Mauser-type twin-lug action before a recent reorganization. The guns, which include 50-caliber anti-matériel/long-range sniping rifles, are now being marketed under the Harris Gun Works banner.

SIGNATURE CLASSIC SPORTER

Made by McMillan Gunworks, Inc., Phoenix, Arizona.
Currently in production. **Chambering options:** see notes. **Action:** locked by two lugs on the bolt engaging recesses in the receiver as the bolt is turned down, and by the bolt-handle base entering its seat.
DATA FOR A TYPICAL SIGNATURE ALASKAN

Chambering: 358 Winchester, rimless. 44.4in overall, 8.25lb empty. 24in barrel, 4-groove rifling; RH, concentric. Folding-leaf rear sight. 2250 fps with 250-grain bullet.

Introduced in 1987, these rifles were offered in right or left-hand versions. Short-action Signature Classic Sporters were offered—often with fixed telescope sight rings—in 22-250, 243 Winchester, 6mm Remington, 7mm-08, 284 Winchester, or 308 Winchester; long-action patterns were chambered for 25-06, 270 Winchester, 280 Remington, 7mm Remington Magnum, 300 Weatherby Magnum, 300 Winchester Magnum or 30-06; and the Magnum action was made for 338 Winchester Magnum, 340 Weatherby Magnum or 375 H&H Magnum.

The barrels measured 22-26in, magazines held three magnum or four standard cartridges, and the trigger pressure was set at 3lb. The fiberglass stocks were finished in beige, black, brown or green; synthetic Fibergrain and walnut patterns were optional extras. A version of the Classic Sporter appeared in 1990 with the action and barrel of stainless steel set in a fiberglass stock. The finish was usually natural or black chrome.

SIMILAR GUNS

Signature Alaskan, 1989 to date. Based on the Classic Sporter, this has a folding-leaf rear sight, a barrel band bearing a sling eye, and a walnut Monte Carlo-style stock with a Wundhammer-type pistol grip. Metalwork is generally nickel-plated. Chamberings included 270 Winchester, 280 Remington, 7mm Remington Magnum, 300 Weatherby Magnum, 300 Winchester Magnum, 30-06, 340 Weatherby Magnum, 358 Winchester or 375 H&H Magnum.

Signature Mountain Rifle, 1989 to date. This is a Classic Sporter with a titanium alloy receiver. The stock is usually gray-black fiberglass reinforced with graphite, giving an empty weight of only 5.5lb. Chamberings have included 270 Winchester, 280 Remington, 7mm Remington Magnum, 30-06 or 300 Winchester Magnum.

Signature Super Varminter, 1989 to date. Announced in 220 Swift, 22-250, 223 Remington, 243 Winchester, 6mm Remington, 25-06, 7mm-08 or 308 Winchester, this is distinguished by a heavy barrel, an adjustable trigger and a specially bedded fiberglass or Fibergrain stock.

Talon Safari, 1988 to date. Derived from the Signature series, this embodies a strengthened or 'Safari' action to handle a wide range of magnum cartridges—including 300 H&H, 300 Weatherby, 300 Winchester, 338 Winchester, 340 Weatherby, 375 H&H, 416 Remington, 458 Winchester—plus 404 Jeffrey.

Talon Safari Super Magnum. A heavyweight version of the Talon Safari, this has been chambered for 378, 416 or 460 Weatherby Magnums, plus 416 Rigby. Made with a 24in barrel and a fiberglass stock, the rifles were 43in long and weighed up to 10lb. Express rear sights are usually fitted, with a sling eye on a barrel band. Finish is customarily matt black.

A McMillan Signature Classic sporting rifle with a synthetic stock.

The McMillan M86 sniper rifle.

Talon Sporter, 1991 to date. This has a modified action based on the best features of the Model 70 Winchester and the M1903 Springfield, with a Winchester-type three-position safety. Offered with a choice of walnut or fiberglass stocks, with optional open sights, long-action rifles have been chambered for 25-06, 270 Winchester, 280 Remington or 30-06 cartridges. Strengthened actions have been supplied for 7mm Remington Magnum, 300 H&H, 300 Winchester, 300 Weatherby, 338 Winchester, 340 Weatherby, 375 H&H or 416 Remington Magnum rounds.

MODEL 86 SNIPER RIFLE

Made by McMillan Gun Works, Inc., Phoenix, Arizona, 1986-90.
Total production: not known. **Chambering options:** see notes. **Action:** as sporting guns, above.

DATA FOR A TYPICAL EXAMPLE

Chambering: 300 Winchester Magnum, rimless. 44in overall, 11.25lb empty. 24in barrel, 4-groove rifling; RH, concentric. Optical sight. 3070 fps with 180-grain bullet.

Introduced in 1986, the M86 was chambered for 7mm Remington Magnum, 300 Winchester Magnum or 30-06 ammunition, a special 300 Phoenix chambering being added about 1989. Magazines held three or four rounds, depending on chambering. The rifle offered a match-quality heavy barrel, plus a fiberglass stock with textured surfaces on the pistol grip and forend to improve grip. Most stocks had a camouflage finish. Fixed recoil pads and detachable bipods were standard.

SIMILAR GUNS

Long Range Rifle. This single-shot 14lb pattern—in 7mm Remington Magnum, 300 Phoenix, 300 Winchester Magnum or 338 Lapua—was very similar to the National Match pattern (q.v.), but had a solid-base receiver, a 26in barrel and an adjustable cheekpiece. The buttplate could be moved vertically, canted, or fitted with spacers.

Model 89 Sniper, 1990 to date. An improved form of the M86 with a five-round magazine and a flash suppresser, this has a fiberglass butt which can be lengthened with spacers. The buttplate is adjustable, and a bipod is customarily fitted beneath the forend.

National Match Rifle, 1989 to date. Built on the detachable-box magazine action, this was introduced in 7mm-08 or 308 Winchester and can be identified by a 24in stainless steel barreled action set in a fiberglass ISU-type stock with an adjustable buttplate. An adjustable Canjar trigger is standard, though others have been available to order. A replaceable-element front sight is provided, but the choice of rear sight is generally left to the purchaser. Weight with sights is about 11lb.

• Marathon

Marathon Products, Inc., of Wethersfield, Connecticut, introduced the Sportsman Bush & Field rifle in 1984. Marketed until 1987-8, it was built on a Spanish Santa Barbara action and could be obtained in kit form. Chamberings included 243 Winchester, 270 Winchester, 7x57, 7mm Remington Magnum, 300 Winchester Magnum, 30-06 and 308 Winchester. The standard rifle was about 45in overall, had a 24in barrel and weighed 8lb. It had a walnut stock with a low Monte Carlo comb and a heavy squared-tip forend.

• Marlin, autoloading type

Note: All guns made in 1970—regardless of type—were made with Marlin's 100th anniversary medallion set into the right side of the butt. However, as medallions were sold separately, many owners added them to older guns.

MODEL 50 SPORTING RIFLE

Made by the Marlin Firearms Company, New Haven, Connecticut, 1931-5.
Total production: 5000? **Chambering:** 22 Long Rifle, rimfire. **Action:** no mechanical breech lock; blowback, semi-automatic only.

39.2in overall, 6lb empty. 22in barrel, 6-groove rifling; RH, concentric. Detachable box magazine, 6 rounds. Spring-leaf and elevator rear sight. 1080 fps with 40-grain bullet.

The first of Marlin's autoloaders—made only in small numbers—had a tubular receiver. The half-stock had a shallow pistol grip, and a finger groove lay in the short tapering forend. The knurled head of the take-down bolt protruded beneath the stock between the stamped-steel trigger guard and the detachable box magazine. Unfortunately, the Model 50 fired from an open bolt and had a quirky manually-operated auxiliary extractor; it was never popular, and production was surprisingly small.

SIMILAR GUNS

Model 50E rifle. This was made with a Marlin No. 22 aperture rear sight, used in conjunction with a hooded bead at the muzzle.

MODEL A-1 SPORTING RIFLE

Made by the Marlin Firearms Company, New Haven, Connecticut, 1936-40 (original pattern).
Total production: not known. **Chambering:** 22 Long Rifle, rimfire. **Action:** as Model 50, above.

41in overall, 6lb empty. 24in barrel, 6-groove rifling; RH, concentric. Detachable box magazine, 6 rounds. Spring-leaf and elevator rear sight. 1080 fps with 40-grain bullet.

An improved Model 50, firing from a closed bolt, this originally had a stamped-strip trigger guard and a safety catch protruding beneath the back of the receiver. A modified version, made only in 1941 and 1945-6, had a radial safety on the right rear side of the receiver and a plastic trigger guard. Both types had a walnut half-stock with a pistol grip and a rounded forend.

SIMILAR GUNS

Model A-1C rifle, 1941 and 1945-6. Only offered in the new style, with the modified safety catch and plastic trigger guard, this had a half-stock with a fluted comb and a beavertail forend. Open sights were standard.

Model A-1DL rifle, 1941 and 1945-6. Distinguished from the A-1C by an additional target-type peep rear sight, this also had factory-fitted sling swivels.

Model A-1E rifle, 1936-41 and 1945-6. Otherwise identical with the A-1, made in the two basic patterns, this had an aperture sight on the receiver.

MODEL 88-C SPORTING RIFLE

Made by the Marlin Firearms Company, New Haven, Connecticut, 1948-56.

The Marlin Model 45 carbine.

The Marlin Model 70 rifle.

Total production: not known. **Chambering:** 22 Long Rifle, rimfire. **Action:** no mechanical breech lock; blowback, semi-automatic only.

41in overall, 6.68lb empty. 24in barrel, 6-groove rifling; RH, concentric. Tube magazine in butt, 14 rounds. Spring-leaf and elevator rear sight. 1080 fps with 40-grain bullet.

The first of Marlin's post-war designs was little more than an enlargement of the A-1. The charging handle was attached directly to the front of the bolt, reciprocating in an ejection port instead of a separate slot, and a radial safety appeared at the extreme rear right side of the receiver. The half-stock had a pistol grip and a sturdy rounded forend. A weak point was the tube magazine, set into the butt, which was notoriously difficult to load; an inner tube had to be removed before cartridges could be inserted.

SIMILAR GUNS

Model 88-DL rifle, 1953-6. This deluxe gun had a peep sight on the receiver, checkering on the pistol grip and forend, and factory-fitted sling swivels.

Model 89-C rifle, 1948-61. Easily distinguished from the Model 88, this had a seven-round box magazine protruding beneath the receiver. A 12-round magazine was standardized in 1956, followed a year later by a Monte Carlo-style cheekpiece stock with decorative white spacers accompanying the synthetic buttplate and pistol grip cap.

Model 89-DL rifle, 1953-61. This was simply the 'C' pattern with a peep sight on the receiver and checkering on the pistol grip and forend.

Model 98 rifle, 1957-9. Differing from the 88/89 series in minor respects, this was the only solid-frame gun in the series—the others were take-down types—and had a 15-round magazine in the butt. A loading port was cut in the butt of the pistol grip half-stock, which also had a cheekpiece, a Monte Carlo comb, and a tapering forend; some guns also had aperture sights on the receiver. About 9060 were made.

MODEL 99 SPORTING RIFLE

Made by the Marlin Firearms Company, New Haven, Connecticut, 1959-61.

Total production: 116,240 (including 'branded' guns). **Chambering:** 22 Long Rifle, rimfire. **Action:** as Model 50, above.

39.5in overall, 5.5lb empty. 22in barrel, 6-groove rifling; RH, concentric. Tube magazine beneath barrel, 18 rounds. Spring-leaf and elevator rear sight. 1080 fps with 40-grain bullet.

Designed by Ewald Nichol, the Model 99 and its derivatives have been made in surprisingly large numbers. The short slab-side receiver had a curved back, shaped to follow the curve of the pistol grip, and a large ejection port lay on the front right side. The front of the trigger guard had an elongated web, while a safety bolt ran laterally through the guard behind the trigger lever. The one-piece half-stock had a pistol grip and a straight comb.

SIMILAR GUNS

Model 49 rifle, 1968-78. Though more than 110,000 rifles of this type were made, the first 65,000 were taken by a distributor. Marlin then added the gun to its own range, adding impressed checkering in 1970 and scroll decoration on the receiver in 1971; this created the '49-DL', and the original pattern was abandoned. The rifles were little more than the Model 99 with a distinctive two-piece stock.

Model 60 rifle, 1983 to date. A derivative of the Glenfield Model 60 (q.v.), retaining the plain birch half-stock, this has a 'Wide-Scan' front-sight hood. A hold-open was fitted to guns made after 1985.

Model 60SS rifle, 1993 to date. Easily identified by stainless-steel and nickel plated metalwork, this also has a black/gray birchwood-laminate half-stock and a rubber butt pad.

Model 70 rifle, 1983 to date. An adaptation of the original Glenfield Model 70, this lacked the checkering, barrel band and swivels of its prototype. The front-sight base was attached to the muzzle with screws, and a hold-open was added in 1985. The current version is often listed as 'M70HC', signifying a hardwood stock.

Model 70P carbine ('Papoose'), 1986-95. The shortest of this entire series, this has a 16.25in barrel held in the receiver by a large fluted collar. An interlock ensures that the gun will not fire unless the barrel is secure. The straight comb pistol grip stock extends only to the front edge of the receiver; overall length is 35.3in, weight being pared down to just 3.7lb. The gun is supplied in a red plastic-foam case, which will float if dropped in water.

Model 70PSS carbine, 1996 to date. Basically little more than the Model 70P with a stainless-steel barrel, this also has a black fiberglass-filled stock.

Model 75 rifle, 1983-93? Derived from the Glenfield rifle of the same pattern-number, this had an 18in barrel and a tube magazine restricted to 13 22LR rounds. Empty weight with the standard plain pistol grip half-stock was about 5lb.

Model 99-C rifle, 1961-78. About 105,000 of these were made, with Micro-Groove rifling and gold-plated triggers. A Monte Carlo-style butt and a 'damascened' (machine-jeweled) bolt replaced the original plain versions in 1963, grooves for tip-off telescope-sight mounts were cut in the receiver-top from 1964, and a one-piece front sight/muzzle band appeared in 1969. Impressed checkering—revised at least once—was added to the pistol grip and forend in 1971.

Model 99-DL rifle, 1960-4. Identifiable by a gold-plated trigger and trigger guard, this also had a Monte Carlo-type half-stock with a fluted comb, a rubber buttplate, and thin white decorative spacers. A sling was supplied from 1962 onward. Only about 5280 were made.

Model 99-M1, or '99M1 Carbine', 1966-79. Deliberately constructed to resemble the original M1 Carbine as closely as possible (see 'Winchester, autoloading type'), this had a short nine-round tube magazine in the forend. The Micro-Groove barrel was cut to 18in, a military-type ramp sight was fitted at the muzzle, and a handguard ran from the breech to the barrel band. The guns were about 37in long and weighed 4.75lb. A hold-open was added in 1969, keeping the breech open after the last shot. Total production amounted to about 161,000 guns.

Model 922 rifle, 1993 to date. Chambered for the 22 Winchester Magnum rimfire cartridge, this has a seven-round box magazine and a walnut Monte Carlo-style half-stock. Fitted with a last-shot hold open mechanism, the M922 is 39.75in long and weighs 6.5lb.

Model 989 rifle, 1962-5. Combining a '99'-type action with a detachable seven-round box magazine ahead of the trigger guard, all but the first few guns of this type had a plain Monte Carlo-style half-stock. Production totaled 24,850.

Model 989-M2 carbine, 1965-78. Similar to the 99-M1 pattern, this had an 18in barrel and pseudo-military stock; about 110,000 were made.

Model 990 rifle, 1979-87. Embodying the same basic blowback action as its predecessors, this had a walnut Monte Carlo half-stock with diamond-void checkering on the pistol grip and forend. The tube magazine beneath the 22in barrel, fitted with a patented closure, held 17 22LR cartridges; a hold-open was added in 1985. The guns were typically 40.75in long, weighed 5.5lb, and had a folding notch-plate on the spring-leaf rear sight.

Model 990L rifle, 1992 to date. This has a laminated hardwood half-stock with a black rubber butt pad and swivel eyes beneath the butt and forend. A spring-leaf and elevator rear sight is standard.

The Marlin Model 70P 'Papoose' carbine has a detachable barrel.

Model 995 rifle, 1979-96. Basically a sporting version of the 989-M2 carbine, this had an 18in barrel, a detachable box magazine, and a Monte Carlo half-stock with checkering on the pistol grip and forend. The folding-plate sight was used.

Model 995SS rifle, 1996 to date. This is a minor variant of the M995 with a stainless-steel barrel and bolt.

MODEL 45 CARBINE

Introduced in 1986, chambered for the 45 ACP round, this is a simple blowback autoloader with an angular receiver and a plain half-stock with a rudimentary pistol grip. The release for the seven-round magazine lies inside the front of the trigger guard. Typically 35.5in long, it has a 16.5in barrel and weighs 6.75lb. The receiver is tapped and drilled to accept bases for optical-sight mounts, though a spring-leaf and elevator rear sight is also provided.

SIMILAR GUNS

Model 9 Camp Carbine, 1986 to date. A short-barrel gun with a plain pistol grip half-stock, this is made only in 9mm Parabellum. It has a 16.5in Micro-Groove rifled barrel and a detachable 12-round box magazine.

GLENFIELD SERIES

These were simplified budget-price guns with stocks of birch instead of walnut. In 1983, however, Marlin abandoned the Glenfield brand name and assimilated some of the guns in regular production.

THE GUNS

Glenfield Model 40 rifle, 1979. This was basically a birch-stocked Marlin Model 49-DL, lacking bolt jeweling. The trigger lever was chromed instead of gold-plated.

Glenfield Model 60 rifle, 1966-82. Derived from the Models 99-C or 990, depending on date, this had a birch stock and a simplified spring-leaf rear sight. The impressed decoration usually included a squirrel motif and flutes instead of checkering. The original Model 60G (1960-5) was based on the Marlin Model 99-C.

Glenfield Model 65 rifle, 1968. Made exclusively for the Oklahoma Tire & Supply Company, this was a Glenfield 60 with a lacquered brass magazine tube. Production exceeded 44,000.

Glenfield Model 70 rifle, 1967-83. A simplification of the Marlin 989-M2, with a birch stock and a simpler rear sight, this subsequently became the Marlin Model 70.

Glenfield Model 75 rifle. Derived from the Marlin Model 99-M1, this retained the nine-round tube magazine, the barrel band and the swivels, but lacked the handguard and special aperture sight.

• Marlin, bolt-action type

Note: many minor variations will be found amongst the bolt-action guns—particularly in the design of the front sights, muzzle bands and stock-checkering patterns. Details will be found in Colonel Brophy's book. In addition, all guns made in 1970, regardless of type, had Marlin's 100th anniversary medallion set into the right side of the butt. Medallions were sold separately, however, and many Marlin owners added them to older guns.

MODEL 65 SPORTING RIFLE

Made by the Marlin Firearms Company, New Haven, Connecticut, 1935-7.

Total production: not known. **Chambering options:** 22 Short, 22 Long and 22 Long Rifle rimfire, interchangeably. **Action:** locked by the base of the bolt handle abutting the receiver bridge as the action closed.

40.5in overall, 5.1lb empty. 24in barrel, 6-groove; RH, concentric. Single shot only. Spring-leaf and elevator rear sight. 1080 fps with 40-grain bullet (22LR).

This take-down gun had a solid-bridge receiver and cocked automatically. It had a plain half-stock with a straight-comb butt, a pistol grip, and a finger groove in the schnabel-tipped forend. An open rear sight was used in conjunction with a bead at the muzzle

SIMILAR GUNS

Model 65E rifle. Mechanically identical with the standard gun, this had a No. 22 aperture sight and a hooded bead at the muzzle.

MODEL 100 SPORTING RIFLE

Made by the Marlin Firearms Company, New Haven, Connecticut, 1935-59.

Total production: not known. **Chambering options:** 22 Short, 22 Long and 22 Long Rifle rimfire, interchangeably. **Action:** as Model 65, above.

40.5in overall, 4.5lb empty. 24in barrel, 6-groove; RH, concentric. Single shot only. Spring-leaf and elevator rear sight. 1080 fps with 40-grain bullet (22LR).

A simple take-down design with a split-bridge receiver and a manually cocked action, this originally had a plain straight-comb half-stock. The trigger guard was a recurved stamped strip. After 1940, however, a plastic trigger guard was fitted. A walnut stock was substituted for the plain hardwood pattern in 1957.

SIMILAR GUNS

Model 100-SB rifle, 1941. Made only in small numbers, this smooth-bore was intended to fire shot and ball cartridges with equal facility. It had a standing-block rear sight.

Model 100-S Tom Mix Special, 1937-8. Offered with a peep-type rear sight on the top rear of the receiver, a hooded front sight, and factory-fitted swivels, this was named in honor of a renowned screen cowboy. Exploitation was stopped by Mix's death in an automobile accident in 1940.

Model 101 rifle, 1941 and 1945-77. An improved version of the Model 100, this take-down gun had a better stock with a broad half-beavertail forend, a plastic trigger guard, and a side-mounted safety. It weighed about 5lb. Among the changes made during its production life were the appearance of Micro-Groove rifling and a walnut Monte Carlo-type half-stock, and the addition (in 1959) of a new bolt system with a non-jam throat patented by Thomas Robinson in December 1960. Post-1960 guns had a cocking ring on the rear of the bolt, but this was changed in 1966 to a 'T'-knob.

Model 101-DL rifle, 1941 and 1945. This was a minor variant of the standard 101 with a peep sight on the receiver and a hooded front-sight bead.

Model 101 Crown Prince rifle, 1959. About 7200 of these guns were assembled from parts, which included straight-comb stocks and stamped-strip trigger guards. They were sold as part of a boxed set which included a 4x telescope sight.

MODEL 80 SPORTING RIFLE

Made by the Marlin Firearms Company, New Haven, Connecticut, 1935-9.

Total production: not known. **Chambering options:** 22 Short, 22 Long and 22 Long Rifle rimfire, interchangeably. **Action:** as Model 65, above.

42.5in overall, 5.75lb empty. 24in barrel, 6-groove; RH, concentric. Detachable box magazine, 8 rounds. Spring-leaf and elevator rear sight. 1080 fps with 40-grain bullet (22LR).

This take-down gun was similar to the Model 100, with a split-bridge receiver. The principal recognition feature was the magazine protruding beneath the stock ahead of the trigger guard. The straight-comb butt had a pistol grip, and a finger groove was cut into the side of the forend until 1937. A few guns made in 1939 had Tenite synthetic trigger guards.

SIMILAR GUNS

Model 80-B rifle, 1940. An improved form of the Model 80, this had a better stock, a plastic trigger guard, and a radial safety lever protruding from the stock behind the bolt handle.

Model 80-BE rifle, 1940. This minor variant of the 80-B had an aperture sight on the receiver and a hooded bead at the muzzle.

Model 80-C rifle, 1941 and 1945-71. An improved 80-B, this originally had a broadened semi-beavertail forend. Post-war guns had standard-width forends, but the stock was eventually changed to a walnut Monte Carlo design in 1957; a new streamlined trigger guard was approved in the same era.

Model 80-CSB rifle, 1941. A few of these smooth-bores were made to fire 22 shot or ball cartridges with equal facility.

Model 80-DL rifle, 1941 and 1945-64. Mechanically identical with the open-sighted 80-C, this had an aperture sight on the receiver and a hooded bead at the muzzle.

Model 80-E rifle, 1935-9. Distinguished by a Marlin No. 22 aperture sight on top of the receiver, this was otherwise identical with the original Model 80. A few made in 1939 had the new-style stock and plastic trigger guard.

Model 81 rifle, 1939. Easily identified by the magazine tube beneath the 24in barrel, this had a capacity of 18-24 cartridges depending on length.

Model 81-B rifle, 1940. This could be distinguished from the original Model 81 by the new-style stock and plastic trigger guard, and by the safety catch on the right side of the stock behind the bolt handle.

Model 81-BE rifle, 1940. An aperture sight on the receiver and a hooded bead at the muzzle distinguished this from the otherwise similar 81-B.

Model 81-C rifle, 1941 and 1945-71. This was simply a modernized Model 81-B with a plastic trigger guard and a broad semi-beavertail forend. Post-war guns reverted to a standard forend, though guns made after 1957 had a walnut Monte Carlo half-stock and a new streamlined trigger guard.

Model 81-DL rifle, 1941 and 1945-64. Mechanically identical with the standard 81-C, this had an aperture sight on the receiver and a hooded bead at the muzzle.

Model 81-E rifle, 1939. This was a derivative of the original Model 81, with a Marlin No. 22 aperture sight on the receiver and a hooded bead at the muzzle.

MODEL 322 SPORTING RIFLE

Marlin offered this gun in 1954-7. Built on a standard Sako L-46 action chambered for the 222 Remington cartridge, it had a 24in Marlin barrel with Micro-Groove rifling, measured 42in overall and weighed 7.13lb. Its American-made stock had a straight comb and a rounded forend tip. White spacers accompanied the plastic shoulder plates and pistol grip caps; the checkered panels on the pistol grip and forend had a double-line border. A two-position aperture sight (for 100yd and 200yd) lay on the receiver bridge. Only 5860 guns were made.

SIMILAR GUNS

Model 422 rifle, 1956-8. Rifling in the 322-pattern barrel wore out too quickly to be acceptable, so a Model 422 'Varmint King' appeared, identifiable by its stainless-steel barrel and Monte Carlo butt. Work ceased after merely 350 rifles had been made.

MODEL 122 SPORTING RIFLE

Made by the Marlin Firearms Company, New Haven, Connecticut, 1961-5.
Total production: 5650. **Chambering options:** 22 Short, 22 Long and 22 Long Rifle rimfire, interchangeably. **Action:** locked by the base of the bolt handle abutting the receiver bridge as the action closed.

37.5in overall, 5lb empty. 22in barrel, 6-groove; RH, concentric. Single shot only. Spring-leaf and elevator rear sight. 1080 fps with 40-grain bullet (22LR).

Advertised as a junior target rifle, this introduced the modified bolt system with a no-jam throat and an Auto-Safe trigger patented by Thomas Robinson in March 1961. Applied automatically as the bolt opened, the safety had to be released manually before firing. The line of the solid-bridge receiver was broken only by an oval ejection port, the trigger guard was streamlined, and the comb of the Monte Carlo-style butt sloped markedly down towards the wrist.

MODEL 980 SPORTING RIFLE

Made by the Marlin Firearms Company, New Haven, Connecticut, 1962-71.
Total production: 33,650. **Chambering:** 22 Winchester Magnum rimfire. **Action:** as Model 65, above.

42.9in overall, 6lb empty. 24in barrel, 16-groove; RH, concentric. Detachable box magazine, 8 rounds. Spring-leaf and elevator rear sight. 2000 fps with 40-grain bullet

Comparatively unsuccessful, this was an attempt to provide a more powerful rimfire rifle. It shared the sloped-comb half-stock and streamlined action of the other guns in the series, suitably

strengthened, but the box magazine protruded farther from the underside of the stock. A band-type open front sight was fitted from 1969 onward.

MODEL 780 SPORTING RIFLE

Made by the Marlin Firearms Company, New Haven, Connecticut, 1971-87.
Total production: not known. **Chambering options:** 22 Short, 22 Long and 22 Long Rifle rimfire, interchangeably. **Action:** as Model 65, above.

41in overall, 5.5lb empty. 22in barrel, 6-groove; RH, concentric. Detachable box magazine, 7 rounds. Spring-leaf and elevator rear sight. 1080 fps with 40-grain bullet (22LR).

These guns were a modernization of the '80'-series, embodying an essentially similar action with a radial safety lever protruding from the right side of the stock behind the bolt handle. The top of the receiver was matted to reduce reflections, the Monte Carlo comb took a more conventional form, and the shape of the trigger guard was changed to allow a gloved finger to enter.

SIMILAR GUNS

Model 781 rifle, 1971-87. This was readily identifiable by the tube magazine beneath the barrel, containing 17-25 cartridges (depending on their length).

Model 782 rifle, 1971-87. Chambered for the 22 Winchester Magnum rimfire round, this was an appropriately strengthened 780. The box magazine held seven rounds.

Model 783 rifle, 1971-87. A tube-magazine version of the 22 Magnum rimfire Model 782, this had a capacity of 12 rounds.

Model 880 rifle, 1989 to date. Based on the original 780 pattern, this has the 'Push[-forward]-to-Fire' safety catch and an associated change to the contours of the stock behind the pear-shaped bolt handle. The cocking piece has been revised and the magazines changed so that only 22LR rounds will feed.

Model 880SS rifle, 1994 to date. A stainless-steel version of the standard gun, with some nickel-plated components, this also has a black fiberglass half-stock with molded checkering.

Model 881 rifle, 1989 to date. A revised version of the tube-magazine 781, with the new safety catch and revisions to the cocking piece, this will handle 22 Short, 22 Long and 22 Long Rifle ammunition interchangeably.

Model 882 rifle, 1989 to date. Derived from the Model 782, this displays the changes to the safety system, stock and bolt handle described in the previous entry. The magazine holds seven 22 Winchester Magnum rimfire cartridges.

Model 882L rifle, 1994 to date. A minor variant of the standard gun, this has a black/gray laminated birchwood half-stock.

Model 882SQ rifle, 1996 to date. The 'Squirrel Rifle' has a heavy target-style barrel set in a black synthetic stock with integrally molded checkering. It weighs about 7lb.

Model 882SS rifle, 1995 to date. Mechanically identical with the 882, this has stainless-steel and nickel plated metalwork, set in a black composite fiberglass/polycarbonate stock. Checkering is molded into the pistol grip and forend.

Model 883 rifle, 1989 to date. This is simply a 22 Winchester Magnum pattern with the new, or post-1988 safety system. Its tube magazine holds 12 rounds.

Model 883SS rifle, 1993 to date. Distinguished by stainless-steel and nickel-plated metalwork, this also has a brown bicolor-laminate Monte Carlo half-stock with a rubber shoulder pad.

The Marlin Model 781.

The Marlin Model 782.

A newer Marlin Model 25, with an improved trigger guard and swivel eyes in the stock.

MODEL 15 SPORTING RIFLE

Made by the Marlin Firearms Company, New Haven, Connecticut, 1983.
Total production: comparatively few. **Chambering options:** 22 Short, 22 Long and 22 Long Rifle rimfire, interchangeably. **Action:** as Model 65, above.

38.8in overall, 5.5lb empty. 22in barrel, 6-groove; RH, concentric. Detachable box magazine, 7 rounds. Spring-leaf and elevator rear sight. 1080 fps with 40-grain bullet (22LR).

Little more than a modified Glenfield Model 15 A (q.v.), this lacked the impressed checkering but had standard Marlin sights. The hardwood pistol grip half-stock was fitted with a plastic trigger guard.

SIMILAR GUNS

Model 15Y rifle ('Little Buckaroo'), 1983-7. A junior or 'Youth' version of the standard Model 15, this had a 16.25in barrel and a short-butt half-stock.

Model 15YN rifle, 1988 to date. Identified by the design of the 'New-Style' safety catch, this is the current variant of the Model 15Y.

Model 25 rifle, 1983-7. A box-magazine form of the Model 15, this had a hardwood half-stock, a black-finish trigger, and a plastic trigger guard.

Model 25N rifle, 1989 to date. Introduced to supersede the Model 25, this has the new-pattern safety catch associated with the 880 series.

Model 25M rifle, 1983-8. Chambered for the 22 Winchester Magnum rimfire cartridge, this was basically a Model 782 (q.v.) with a plain birch stock and a simpler front sight.

Model 25MN rifle, 1989 to date. Derived from the 25M, this incorporates the 1988-pattern safety system.

Model 25MB rifle ('Midget Magnum'), 1987-93. Essentially a short version of the Model 25M or 25MN, this had a 16.25in barrel and a special half-stock with a short forend. The gun was easily broken into two parts for transport in its special bag.

MODEL 2000 TARGET RIFLE

Made by the Marlin Firearms Company, New Haven, Connecticut, 1991 to date.

Currently in production. **Chambering:** 22 Long Rifle, rimfire. **Action:** generally as Model 65, above.

41in overall, 8lb empty. 22in barrel, 12-groove; RH, concentric. Single shot only. Micro-adjustable aperture rear sight. 1080 fps with 40-grain bullet (22LR).

Distinguished by a composite fiberglass/Kevlar high-comb half-stock, with an adjustable buttplate and stippling on the pistol grip and forend, this gun also has an accessory rail let into the underside of the forend. An optional five-round box magazine can be fitted if required and the trigger is an adjustable two-stage type. The most obvious feature, however, is the royal blue enamel finish on the stock.

SIMILAR GUNS

Model 2000L rifle. Introduced in 1997, but mechanically identical with the standard gun, this is fitted with a black/gray laminated birchwood stock.

MODEL MR-7 SPORTING RIFLE

Made by the Marlin Firearms Company, New Haven, Connecticut, 1996 to date.

Currently in production. **Chambering options:** 270 Winchester or 30-06. **Action:** locked by lugs on the bolt head engaging recesses in the receiver walls as the bolt is closed.

DATA FOR 270 VERSION

43in overall, 7.5lb empty. 22in barrel, 6-groove; RH, concentric. Detachable box magazine, 4 rounds. Folding-leaf rear sight. 2850 fps with 150-grain bullet

Marlin's first purpose-built centerfire bolt-action sporter, the MR-7 has a comparatively conventional action with a three-position

safety catch and a shrouded cocking piece. It has a straight-comb walnut half-stock, with checkering on the pistol grip and the slender tapering forend. The bolt handle is swept slightly backward.

GLENFIELD SERIES

Marlin made a selection of bolt-action rifles under the Glenfield brand name, with plainer stocks and simpler fittings. In 1983, however, the separate name was abandoned and some—but by no means all—of the guns were integrated with the Marlin product-range. Most Glenfield rifles displayed impressed checkering (often simply ribbing) with a squirrel motif.

THE GUNS

Glenfield Model 10 rifle, 1966-78. This was simply the Model 100G under another name.

Glenfield Model 15, 1979-82. Essentially similar to the Model 10, this had a different cocking knob.

Glenfield Model 20, 1966-81. A new name for the Glenfield 80G; no changes had been made in the gun.

Glenfield Model 25, 1979-82. Essentially similar to the Marlin Model 780, this had a birch stock and an old-style plastic trigger guard.

Glenfield Model 80G rifle, 1965. This was a derivative of the Marlin 80-C, with a birch stock and a simple trigger guard.

Glenfield Model 81G rifle, 1965. Derived from the Marlin 81-C, this had a plain birch stock and a strip-type trigger guard.

Glenfield Model 100G rifle, 1965. Based on the Marlin Model 101, this had a straight-comb birch stock with a recurved stamped-strip trigger guard.

• Marlin, lever-action type

For more detailed information, see William S. Brophy's standard history *Marlin Firearms. A History of the Guns and the Company that made them* (Stackpole Books, 1989). The earliest guns were based on patents granted to Andrew Burgess in 1873-9, allied with an improved cartridge elevator designed by Burgess and John Marlin in December 1881. Later guns were largely the work of Lewis Hepburn, whose first relevant patent dated from 1886.

The original Marlin rifle was very simple. The breech lever extension served as a prop for the longitudinally sliding breech-block. When the gun fired, the strain was taken by the breech-lever pivot pin—theoretically unsound, but more than able to withstand the pressure in practice. Later guns relied on a sliding block or bolt locked by a rising bar. This proved to be most efficient; consequently, the Marlins have been extremely successful, with production of the 1893/1936/336 series reaching three million in 1979.

MODEL 1881 SPORTING RIFLE

Known prior to 1888 simply as the 'Marlin Repeating Rifle'
Made by the Marlin Fire Arms Company, New Haven, Connecticut, 1881-91.

Total production: about 20,540. **Chambering options:** 32-40 Ballard, 38-55 Ballard, 40-60 Marlin, 45-70 Government or 45-85 Marlin. **Action:** locked by propping the bolt in place.

DATA FOR A TYPICAL EXAMPLE

Chambering: 40-60 Marlin, rimmed. 44in overall, 9.88lb empty. 26in barrel, 6-groove rifling; RH, concentric. Tube magazine in forend, 8 rounds. Spring-leaf and elevator rear sight. 1385 fps with 260-grain bullet.

The first top-ejecting prototypes were distributed to Schoverling, Daly & Gales of New York in 1881. They had 28in octagonal barrels chambered for the 40-60 or 45-70 cartridges, and 10-round magazines. The front section of the trigger guard/operating lever had less of a curve than contemporary Winchesters, while the loading gate—with a sliding spring-loaded cover—lay on the lower front right side of the receiver.

Production began in 1882, all but the first 60 guns being made with an improved 1883-patent stirrup-top ejector instead of the original blade. Several barrel options (24-30in) were accompanied by half- or full-length magazines; select woodwork, pistol grip butts, engraving, and special sights were all available to order.

The original heavyweight receiver was soon replaced by a revised pattern lacking the rebated or stepped underside at the joint with the forend. A 45-70 M1881 performed surprisingly well in the US Army repeating rifle trials. Two fingers were added in 1883 to the cartridge elevator or 'carrier' to improve feed, a wedge being used in the small-frame 32- and 38-caliber rifles. Double-set triggers were popular, being fitted to about one in every six guns.

The success of the large-frame guns allowed a medium-frame version to be introduced in 1885, 'specially for export'. Chambered for 40-60 or 45-70 cartridges, it had a 24in or 28in barrel and weighed 8.3-8.8lb. A small-frame adaptation of the M1881 suitable for 32-40 Ballard cartridges was introduced at the end of the year. Offered with standard-weight barrels, it weighed 7.3-7.5lb. A 38-55 Ballard option was added in 1886 and a heavy barrel appeared for the small-frame guns, but production ceased in October 1891. The guns had been made in series with the other Marlins, and so their numbers ran into the 50000s.

MODEL 1888 SPORTING RIFLE

Made by the Marlin Fire Arms Company, New Haven, Connecticut, 1888-9.

Total production: about 4820. **Chambering options:** 32-40 Ballard, 38-40 Winchester or 44-40 Winchester. **Action:** locked by a vertically-sliding bolt actuated by the operating lever.

DATA FOR A TYPICAL EXAMPLE

Chambering: 38-40 Winchester, rimmed. 40.75in overall, 6.72lb empty. 24in barrel, 6-groove rifling; RH, concentric. Tube magazine in forend, 10 rounds. Spring-leaf and elevator rear sight. 1330 fps with 180-grain bullet.

Introduced in 1888, this improved small-action rifle was similar to the M1881 externally as it loaded from the side and ejected upward. Octagon and round barrels were popular, though only 23 guns are known to have been made with the half-octagon option. Frames were normally blued, with the hammer and operating levers color case-hardened. The M1888 embodied changes patented by Lewis Hepburn in December 1886 and October 1887. Its locking mechanism was similar to the Browning-designed Winchesters, which may not have been entirely coincidental.

MODEL 1889 SPORTING RIFLE
Also known as 'Marlin New Safety Repeater'

Made by the Marlin Fire Arms Company, New Haven, Connecticut, 1889-1903

Total production: about 55,120. **Chambering options:** 25-20 Winchester, 32-20 Winchester, 38-40 Winchester or 44-40 Winchester. **Action:** locked by a vertically-sliding bolt actuated by the operating lever.

DATA FOR A TYPICAL EXAMPLE

Chambering: 25-20 Winchester, rimmed. 40.75in overall, 6.8lb empty. 24in barrel, 6-groove rifling; RH, concentric. Tube magazine in forend, 10 rounds. Spring-leaf and elevator rear sight. 1450 fps with 85-grain bullet.

The principal improvement in this rifle, patented by Lewis Hepburn in April 1889, was lateral ejection. Though this required a different bolt and elevator mechanism, the changes allowed a solid-top receiver to be offered. The M1889 was introduced in September in 32-40, 38-40 and 44-40 chamberings, with round or octagonal barrels measuring 24in, 26in or 28in; the 24in octagonal type was most popular. Receivers were blued, with color case-hardened levers and hammers, and a distinctive locking catch lay in the rear of the operating-lever bow; 1889-type rifles could not fire until the lever was fully closed.

Half-length magazines were optional, but uncommon. Plain straight-wrist butts were standard, pistol grips and checkering being supplied on request. Work ceased in 1903, though guns continued to be available for years. Except for the 25-20 WCF version—only 34 guns are known to have been made—the chamberings had proved equally popular.

SIMILAR GUNS

Model 1889 carbine. This was introduced in 1890 with a 20in round barrel, though a few hundred were made with 15in barrels toward the end of the century. Most guns had straight-wrist buts and forends with a barrel band.

Model 1889 musket. About 70 of these fully-stocked guns were made with 30in barrels, military ramp-and-leaf rear sights and provision for a socket or sword bayonet. Swivels lay beneath the nose cap and under the frame ahead of the operating-lever pivot.

MODEL 1891 SPORTING RIFLE
Also known as 'Marlin Safety Rifle, Model 1891'

Made by the Marlin Fire Arms Company, New Haven, Connecticut, 1891-1905.

Production total: see notes. **Chambering options:** 22 Short, 22 Long, 22 Long Rifle rimfire, 32 Short or Long centerfire. **Action:** generally as M1889, above.

DATA FOR A TYPICAL EXAMPLE

Chambering: 32 Long, rimmed. 40.65in overall, 6.5lb empty. 24in barrel, 6-groove rifling; RH, concentric. Tube magazine in forend, 15 rounds. Spring-leaf and elevator rear sight. 850 fps with an 85-grain bullet.

Made in accordance with a patent granted to Lewis Hepburn in August 1890, this was a diminutive rimfire version of the side-loading side-ejecting Marlin. The first guns were made with 24in round or octagon barrels and full-length magazine tubes; only 22 guns were ever made with the optional half-length magazine. The butts were usually straight-wristed, though more than 1000 pistol grip examples were sold.

A revised model with a 26in or 28in barrel appeared in 1892, featuring a tube-loading system patented by John Marlin in March. Guns of this type lacked the gate that had previously appeared on the right side of the receiver; magazines accepted 15 long or 17 short centerfire rounds. The M1891 was eventually discontinued in 1905, though few had been made since 1896. Production totaled 18,650, about 6270 of them being 32-caliber; round barrels had been fitted to about one gun in six.

MODEL 1892 SPORTING RIFLE
Known from 1905 as the 'Model 92'

Made by the Marlin Fire Arms Company, New Haven, Connecticut, 1895-1915.

Total production: 41,000 to 1906. **Chambering options:** 22 Short, 22 Long and 22 Long Rifle rimfire, and 32 Long or 32 Extra Long centerfire. **Action:** generally as M1889, above.

DATA FOR A TYPICAL EXAMPLE

Chambering: 32 Long, rimmed. 42.75in overall, 5.82lb empty. 26in barrel, 6-groove rifling; RH, concentric. Tube magazine in forend, 15 rounds. Spring-leaf and elevator rear sight. 850 fps with 85-grain bullet.

Announced at the beginning of 1896, though production had begun some months previously, this gun succeeded the Model 1891. It ejected laterally from the closed-side receiver and retained the loading-tube system, but lacked the lever-operated trigger safety system; instead, the action was altered so that the firing pin could only reach the chambered round if the lever was completely closed. The M1892 usually chambered rimfire ammunition, but the 32 version could be converted to centerfire simply by changing the firing pin. An octagon or round 24in barrel was standard, though other lengths were available to order. Butts were generally straight-wristed.

A new spring-retained ejector appeared in 1897, and a half-length magazine option was introduced in 1898. The addition of a cut-off mechanism (from 1899 onward) allowed cartridges of differing length to feed satisfactorily, permitting the shooter to mix long and short ammunition indiscriminately.

A 16in carbine barrel was introduced in 1903, followed in 1904 by a cartridge guide in the receiver-top. The guide was short-lived on 32-caliber guns, disappearing again in 1906. The ejector was improved in 1907, the change being signified by two retaining screws on the left side of the receiver, and a serpentine buttplate replaced the original rifle pattern in 1908. The Model 1892 was abandoned in 1915, owing to the advent of war work. Production is believed to have reached about 60,000, about a quarter of this total being 32-caliber.

MODEL 1893 SPORTING RIFLE
Renamed 'Model 93' in 1905

Made by the Marlin Fire Arms Company, New Haven, Connecticut, 1893-1915; the Marlin Firearms Corporation, New Haven, Connecticut, 1922-4; and the Marlin Firearms Company, New Haven, Connecticut, 1926-35.

Total production: 90,000-100,000? **Chambering options:** 25-36 Marlin, 30-30 Winchester, 32 Winchester Special, 32-40 Ballard or 38-55 Ballard. **Action:** generally as M1889, above.

DATA FOR A TYPICAL EXAMPLE

Chambering: 25-36 Marlin, rimmed. 44.25in overall, 7.58lb empty. 26in barrel, 6-groove rifling; RH, concentric. Tube magazine in forend, 10 rounds Spring-leaf and elevator rear sight. 1855 fps with 117-grain bullet.

Patented by Lewis Hepburn in August 1893, to compete with the Winchesters of 1886 and 1892, this incorporated a new locking-bolt system, a two-piece firing pin and an improved elevator. Originally chambered for 32-40-165 and 38-55-255 cartridges, offered in solid frame or take-down versions, the M1893 was an instantaneous success. Round, half- or full-octagon barrels of 20-32in could be obtained, the 26in pattern being regarded as standard when accompanied by a full-length magazine and a straight-wrist butt. Pistol grip butts and engraving could be supplied to order. About 69,000 rifles had been made by 1906, but production stopped in 1915 to concentrate on war work.

SIMILAR GUNS

Model 1893 carbine. Generally chambering 30-30 or 32-40 cartridges in a 20in round barrel, the standard carbine had a full-length magazine, a leaf rear sight, and an empty weight of about 6.75lb. A few were made with 15in barrels in 1898-9. About 4100 carbines of all types had been made by 1906, and it is assumed that, by the end of production in 1915, the total had reached 6000-7500.

Model 1893 carbine, post-1922 version. Offered only in 30-30 or 32-caliber, this had a 20in barrel and a seven-round magazine. Weight averaged 6.8lb. The leaf-and-slider rear sight was graduated to 900yd, and the forend was held by a band.

Model 1893CS 'Sporting Carbine', 1923-36. Essentially similar to its predecessors, this had an abbreviated five-round magazine, a rubber buttplate, and an open spring-leaf rear sight. Advertised 'for big game hunting', it weighed 6.5lb.

Model 1893 Grade B rifle. This rifle was introduced in 1905 for black powder ammunition (.32-40 and 38-55 only), the barrels of regular guns thereafter being marked SPECIAL SMOKELESS STEEL.

Model 1893 Light-Weight Rifle. Made in small numbers in the 1890s, this had a half-length magazine, a slim forend, and a round 18in or 20in barrel.

Model 1893 musket. An 8lb musket derivation, offered with a sword or socket bayonet until about 1905, had a 30in barrel and a full-length forend retained by two bands.

Model 1893 rifle, post-1922 version. When production recommenced after the end of the First World War, the 26in round or octagon barrel was standardized. The gun had 10-round magazines and weighed 7.3lb. The receiver was color case-hardened, the buttplate was blued steel, and Rocky Mountain sights were fitted. Chamberings were restricted to 30-30 Winchester, 32 Winchester Special, 32-40 Ballard and 38-55 Ballard. The two Ballard cartridges and the octagon-barrel option were abandoned in 1935, shortly before work ceased altogether.

MODEL 1894 SPORTING RIFLE
Renamed 'Model 94' in 1906

Made by the Marlin Fire Arms Company, New Haven, Connecticut, 1894-1915; by the Marlin Firearms Corporation, New Haven, Connecticut, 1922-4; and by the Marlin Firearms Company, New Haven, Connecticut, 1926-33.

Total production: very large. **Chambering options:** 25-20 Winchester, 32-20 Winchester, 38-40 Winchester or 44-40 Winchester. **Action:** generally as M1889, above.

DATA FOR A TYPICAL EXAMPLE

Chambering: 44-40 Winchester, rimmed. 41.5in overall, 7.05lb empty. 24in barrel, 6-groove rifling; RH, concentric. Tube magazine in forend, 14 rounds? Spring-leaf and elevator rear sight. 1310 fps with 200-grain bullet.

An improvement of the 1889-pattern Marlin, incorporating features patented by Lewis Hepburn in August 1893, this 1894-vintage side-ejector had the new locking bolt and two-piece firing pin. Customarily fitted with a 24in round or octagon barrel chambering Winchester cartridges, it had a full-length magazine. Barrels of 20-32in were available to order, together with pistol grip butts, short magazines, extra barrels (for the 'Take Down' model), nickel plating and engraving.

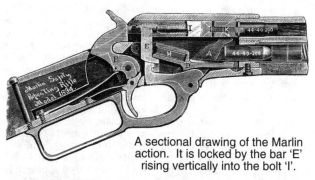

A sectional drawing of the Marlin action. It is locked by the bar 'E' rising vertically into the bolt 'I'.

The 1894-type Marlin 'take-down' rifle broken into its major components.

A half-octagonal barrel appeared in 1901, but was rarely requested and lasted for only six years. After 1903, however, rifle receivers were drilled and tapped for a Hepburn-patent tangent rear sight. Production approached 60,000 guns by 1906, one in five of which had been carbines. Assembly ceased in 1915 to allow the factory to concentrate on war work, but began again in 1922—though the quantities involved were small and it is suspected that work stopped again about 1924. A few small batches of M1894 rifles were assembled from old parts in 1928-9, to be carried in the company's catalogues until 1933.

SIMILAR GUNS

Model 1894 'Baby' carbine. This had a 20in barrel and a short six-round magazine; chambering the 38-40 or 44-40 cartridges, it weighed a mere 5.5lb. A 25-20 option was introduced in 1895.

Model 1894 carbine, 1895-about 1908. The original M1894 carbine had a 20in round barrel or, more rarely, a 15in pattern; the full-length magazines held 12 and nine rounds respectively. The receiver, hammer, buttplate, and forend cap were color case-hardened, though carbine receivers were generally blued.

Model 1894 musket, 1897-1907. Offered with a 30in barrel and a full-length forend retained by bands, this was advertised into the 20th Century. Very few were made, though some had nose caps adapted for surplus British P/1888 sword bayonets.

MODEL 1895 SPORTING RIFLE
Known as 'Model 95' after 1905

Made by the Marlin Fire Arms Company, New Haven, Connecticut, 1895-1915.

Total production: 5300 to 1906. **Chambering options:** 33 Winchester, 38-56 Winchester, 40-60 Marlin, 40-65 Winchester, 40-70 Winchester, 40-82 Winchester, 45-70 Government or 45-90 Winchester. **Action:** generally as M1889, above.

DATA FOR A TYPICAL EXAMPLE

Chambering: 40-82 Winchester, rimmed. 42.5in overall, 8lb empty. 24in barrel, 6-groove rifling; RH, concentric. Tube magazine in forend, 8 rounds. Spring-leaf and elevator rear sight. 1490 fps with 260-grain bullet.

The success of the M1894 Winchester forced Marlin to adapt the 1893-model rifle for the new 30-30 Winchester cartridge, and then to introduce 25-36 Marlin to compete with Winchester's 25-35. The M1895 rifle was specifically created to handle cartridges as

The Model 1894 Marlin rifle. This is the 'take-down' form.

large and powerful as 45-90. Based on Hepburn patents and first listed commercially in 1896, the earliest guns chambered 38-56, 40-65, 40-82, 45-70 or 45-90 cartridges. The standard barrel was a 26in round or octagon pattern, though alternatives—20-32in—could be supplied on request. The maximum length (30in) magazine tube held 10 rounds, though there was a special short three-round magazine, and the conventional half-length design held five (four rounds in 40-82 and 45-90).

Rifle receivers were color case-hardened; carbine examples, however, were invariably blued. Straight-wrist or pistol grip butts were fitted, with tang-mounted sights and several grades of decoration among the many options. A 40-70 chambering was introduced in 1897, followed in 1903 by holes drilled and tapped in the receiver for the Hepburn tangent rear sight. By 1906, production had reached 5300, only 200 of which had been carbines. Only the 33 Winchester and 45-70 chamberings were still being offered in 1915. Assembly then ceased owing to war work, never to resume.

SIMILAR GUNS

Model 1895 carbine. Guns of this type had a 22in round barrel (a 15in option was announced in 1907), a full-length seven-round magazine, and a sling ring on the left side of the receiver. Only 205 had been made by the end of 1906.

Model 1895 Light-Weight Rifle, 1912-15. Introduced to accompany the 33 Winchester cartridge, this had a 24in round barrel, a five-shot half-length magazine and a shotgun-style buttplate. It weighed 7.8lb.

MODEL 1897 SPORTING RIFLE
Renamed 'Model 97' in 1905

Made by the Marlin Firearms Company, New Haven, Connecticut, 1897-1922.

Total production: 75,000? **Chambering options:** 22 Short, 22 Long or 22 Long Rifle rimfire. **Action:** generally as M1889, above.

DATA FOR A TYPICAL EXAMPLE

Chambering: 22 Long, rimfire. 40.8in overall, 5.85lb empty. 24in barrel, 6-groove rifling; RH, concentric. Tube magazine beneath barrel, 18-25 rounds. Spring-leaf and elevator rear sight. 1045 fps with 29-grain bullet.

This take-down gun was made in accordance with a patent granted to Lewis Hepburn in June 1897, protecting a finger-wheel on the right side of the frame which locked the parts together. The gun was otherwise an improved Model 92, chambered exclusively for rimfire ammunition. It had a round barrel of 16-28in, an optional half-length magazine holding 10-16 rounds, and a straight-wrist butt. A pistol grip and folding Vernier tang sights were among the options. Some later guns had flat-top receivers tapped and drilled for a special rear sight patented by Hepburn in June 1903.

SIMILAR GUNS

Model 1897 Bicycle Rifle. Made only in small numbers, this had a 16in round or octagon barrel. The shortened magazine held 10-16 rounds, depending on cartridge length.

MODEL 1936 SPORTING RIFLE
Renamed 'Model 36' in 1937

Made by the Marlin Firearms Company, New Haven, Connecticut, 1936-48.

Total production: not known. **Chambering options:** 30-30 Winchester or 32 Winchester Special. **Action:** generally as M1889, above.

DATA FOR A TYPICAL MODEL 36A

Chambering: 30-30 Winchester, rimmed. 42.4in overall, 6.95lb empty. 24in barrel, 6-groove rifling; RH, concentric. Tube magazine in forend, 5 rounds. Spring-leaf and elevator rear sight. 2220 fps with 170-grain bullet.

Introduced to replace the Model 1893 (q.v.), this exhibited many detail improvements in the action—e.g., a new rounded operating lever and, after the first few guns, a coil-type main spring. The pistol grip butt had a fluted comb, while the broad forend had a slightly convex belly and a steel cap. The standard rifle had a 24in round barrel with a ramped 'Huntsman' front sight, and a short six-round magazine; post-1938 receivers were tapped and drilled for a rear sight. A few guns were assembled in 1945 with receiver-tops sand-blasted to give a matted finish, but the Model 36 was superseded by the Model 336 (q.v.) in 1948.

SIMILAR GUNS

Model 36 ADL rifle, 1940-1 and 1945-6. A deluxe pattern with checkered woodwork, guns of this type had detachable swivels on the magazine tube and butt.

Model 36 carbine, 1937-41. Made with a 20in round barrel and a full-length magazine holding seven rounds, this measured 38in overall and weighed about 6.5lb. Bands appeared around the muzzle and forend.

Model 36SC 'Sporting Carbine'. This combined the general characteristics of the rifle—short magazine, no bands—within the overall dimensions of the carbine.

MODEL 336 SPORTING RIFLE

Made by the Marlin Firearms Company, New Haven, Connecticut (1948-69), and North Haven, Connecticut (1949-69).

Total production: see notes. **Chambering options:** 219 Zipper, 30-30 Winchester, 32 Winchester Special, 35 Remington or 44 Magnum. **Action:** generally as M1889, above.

DATA FOR A TYPICAL POST-1955 336A

Chambering: 32 Winchester Special, rimmed. 43.25in overall, 6.88lb empty. 24in barrel, 16-groove rifling; RH, concentric. Tube magazine in forend, 5 rounds. Spring-leaf and elevator rear sight. 2280 fps with 170-grain bullet.

An improved post-war form of the Model 36, this had a round breech-bolt, a refined extractor, and a conventional ejection port on the right side of the receiver. A folding-leaf rear sight replaced the original Rocky Mountain pattern on all surviving 336 variants in 1971. Gun no. 3000000—suitably engraved—was presented by Marlin to the NRA Museum in 1979.

SIMILAR GUNS

Model 336A rifle, 1949-62 and 1973-80. Chambered only for the 30-30 Winchester and 32 Winchester Special cartridges, the basic 336A rifle had a 24in round barrel rifled with four grooves; a short five-round magazine; a plain pistol grip butt; and a hooded front sight on a ramp. A 35 Remington option was introduced in 1953, chambered in special seven-groove barrels. A pistol grip cap and spacer were added in the early 1950s, but had been abandoned by 1953. Receiver-tops were drilled and tapped for sight mounts from 1956 onward, when 'Micro-Groove' rifling replaced the traditional Ballard patterns. Sixteen grooves were used until 1958, when the 30-30 pattern changed to 22; 12-groove rifling was adopted for the 30-30 Winchester and 35 Remington options in 1968.

The pistol grip cap and spacer were reinstated in 1957, when a new hooded-ramp front sight was adopted, and a gold-plated trigger was standardized in 1959. The receiver top was sand blasted from 1960 to minimize glare, but production ceased shortly afterward. However, the Model 336A reappeared in 1973 with a straight-wrist butt and a new 'Wide-Scan' hooded front sight. When work finally ceased, about 40,000 guns had been made since 1952.

Model 336ADL rifle, 1952-62. Characterized by checkered woodwork and detachable swivels, this deluxe pattern gained a Monte Carlo stock, swivels and a Lyman rear sight in 1957. Only about 5220 guns were made.

Model 336C carbine (known as 'Model 336 Carbine' prior to 1951). Otherwise similar to the rifle, this had a 20in barrel, a full-length six-round magazine, and bands on the muzzle and forend. A 44 Magnum version ('Model 336/44 Magnum') was introduced in 1963 with a 20in barrel and a 10-round magazine, but the 32 Winchester Special and 44 Magnum options were both dropped in 1964. The fluted comb was replaced by a plain design in 1976, and a blued trigger superseded the gold-plated form in 1982.

Model 336CS carbine, 1984 to date. This was simply an improved version of the basic 336C with an additional cross-bolt safety catch.

Model 336ER carbine ('Extra Range'), 1983-4. These guns were made for the 356 Winchester cartridge, but sold so poorly that the project was abandoned after only 2440 had been made. They had 20in round barrels, five-round magazines, and weighed about 6.8lb.

Model 336LTS carbine, 1988-93. This replaced the Texan (336TS) pattern. It had a 16.25in barrel, a straight-wrist butt, a squared operating lever and a five-round full length magazine.

Model 336 Marauder carbine, 1963-4. Offered in 30-30 Winchester and 35 Remington only, this had a 16.25in barrel and weighed 6.3lb. The name proved to be unacceptable commercially, and so the pattern was merged with the Texan in 1964.

Model 336 Octagon rifle, 1973-4. About 2420 of these rifles were made in 30-30. They had 22in octagonal barrels, full-length six-round magazines, and straight-wrist butts with rubber buttplates. The squared operating lever was used and the front sight was a gold bead.

Model 336SC carbine (known as 'Model 336 Sporting Carbine' prior to 1951), 1950-63. This was little more than a 336A with a 20in barrel. Production in the 1952-63 period amounted to 74,220 guns.

Model 336SD carbine, 1954-62. This deluxe 336SC had a Monte Carlo-type Bishop stock and detachable swivels. Production eventually totaled 4390.

Model 336T carbine ('Texan Carbine'). This was announced in 30-30 Winchester and 35 Remington, but was little more than a 336C with a 20in round barrel, a full-length six-round magazine, a straight-wrist butt, and a slim forend. A ramp-mounted front sight replaced the original blade in 1959, and an additional 44 Magnum option was offered in 1962-4. The 35-caliber 336T was abandoned in 1965, when a brass saddle ring was added on the left side of the receiver of the 30-30 version. The operating lever was squared from 1971, when the saddle ring on the receiver-side disappeared. A 'Wide-Scan' hooded ramp-mounted front sight was added in 1972. The fluted comb was replaced by a plain design from 1976 onward, and a blued trigger replaced the gold version in 1982. Barrels were reduced to 18.5in after 1983.

Model 336TDL carbine ('Texan De Luxe'), 1962-3. A deluxe version of the 336T, this had a Texas Longhorn steer superimposed on a map of Texas carved into the right side of the butt. Typical of the gimmickry of its period, the TDL lasted less than a year.

Model 336TS carbine, 1984-8. Essentially a variant of the Texan carbine (336T), this had a new cross-bolt safety catch. It was replaced within a few years by the LTS pattern.

Model 336 Zane Grey Commemorative rifle, 1972. Marlin made nominally 10,000 of these 30-30 WCF guns to celebrate the centenary of the birth of the Western writer Zane Grey.

Model 336 Zipper carbine, 1955-9. Chambering the 219 Zipper cartridge, these guns were similar to the 336SC and weighed about 6.8lb. Barrel-weight was increased by 1lb in 1956 in an abortive attempt to improve accuracy, but the sixteen-groove rifling wore out too quickly; the Zipper variant—never popular—was abandoned after 3230 had been made. Only about a dozen deluxe guns had been included in this total.

MODEL 39 SPORTING RIFLE

Made by the Marlin Firearms Company, New Haven, Connecticut (1922-41 and 1945-69), and North Haven, Connecticut (1969 to date) (all types).

Total production: two million by 1983. **Chambering options:** 22 Short, 22 Long or 22 Long Rifle rimfire, interchangeably. **Action:** generally as M1889, above.

DATA FOR A TYPICAL EXAMPLE

41in overall, 5.75lb empty. 24in barrel, 6-groove rifling; RH, concentric. Tube magazine in forend, 18-25 rounds. Spring-leaf and elevator rear sight. 1080 fps with 40-grain bullet (22LR).

Designed in 1919 under Marlin-Rockwell Corporation supervision, this was introduced commercially in 1922. The action was based on the M1891 rifle, the first lever-action repeater to chamber 22LR rimfire ammunition. A take-down gun with a color case-hardened receiver, it had a full-length tube magazine beneath the octagon barrel (though round barrels and half-length magazines were among the options). A plain pistol grip butt and forend were used, with a concave shoulder plate. An improved ejector was patented by Carl Swebilius in March 1926, but had been used since 1924. The bolt was strengthened in 1932 to eliminate cracks caused by High-Speed ammunition. Production stopped in 1941, but a few guns were made after the Second World War (1945-7).

SIMILAR GUNS

Model 39A rifle, 1939-60. This was essentially similar to the basic Model 39, but had a blued receiver, a round barrel, and a heavier beavertail-type forend. Weight was about 6.5lb. Micro-Groove rifling was adopted in 1954, the lever-loop was rounded instead of squared, and a stock with a fluted comb and white-line spacers was adopted in the early 1960s. The spacers were discarded in 1973.

Model 39A Anniversary rifle, 1960. Made to celebrate Marlin's 90th birthday, this had a chrome-plated barreled action, checkering on the select walnut straight-comb butt and forend, and a squirrel motif carved into the right side of the butt. Only 500 were made.

Model 39A Article II carbine, 1971. Identical mechanically with the Article II rifle, this had a 20in octagon barrel, a straight-wrist butt and a squared operating lever. Production amounted to about 3820 guns.

Model 39A Article II rifle, 1971. Similar to the standard 39A, this was made to celebrate the centenary of the National Rifle Association. It had a 24in octagon barrel, a medallion let into the right side of the receiver, a brass forend cap, and select walnut woodwork. The butt was a pistol grip form with a crescent shoulder plate. About 6265 guns were made.

Model 39A Carbine, 1963-7. About 12,140 of these were made, with straight butts, slender forends, and 20in Micro-Groove barrels. The front sight was a plain open bead, and the magazine held 12-18 rounds depending on cartridge length.

Model 39A Centennial carbine, 1970. One thousand of these guns were sold as matched pairs with Marlin 336 rifles, celebrating the centenary of the Marlin gunmaking business. They had a 20in tapering octagonal barrel, a straight-grip butt, and a medallion set into the right side of the receiver.

Model 39A Century Limited carbine (Model 39ACL or 'CL'), 1970. A cheaper version of the 39A Centennial, this gun had brass furniture and a blued receiver with a brass medallion set into the right side. The 20in barrel was octagonal and the butt had a straight wrist. Production totaled 34,200.

Model 39ADL rifle, 1961-3. A deluxe version of the standard 39A, this was similar to the 90th anniversary pattern (q.v.), but had blued metalwork and a pistol grip butt. Production exceeded 3300 guns.

Model 39A Mountie rifle, 1953-60. This was a variant of the 39A with a straight-wrist butt and a slender forend; it weighed only 6.2lb.

Model 39AS rifle, 1988 to date. Stocked similarly to the 336CS (q.v.), this has a squared breech-bolt reciprocating in the right receiver wall and a patented quick-release locking plug on the magazine tube. Magazine capacity is 19-26 rounds, depending on cartridge length. Guns made since 1992 have had gold-plated triggers and are often known as the 'Model 39AS Golden' pattern.

Model 39A Golden rifle, 1960-92. A minor variant of the standard gun, this offered a gold-plated trigger, sling swivels beneath the butt and forend cap, and a hooded front sight on a prominent muzzle ramp. The 'Golden' qualification was abandoned in 1964 but reintroduced in 1972.

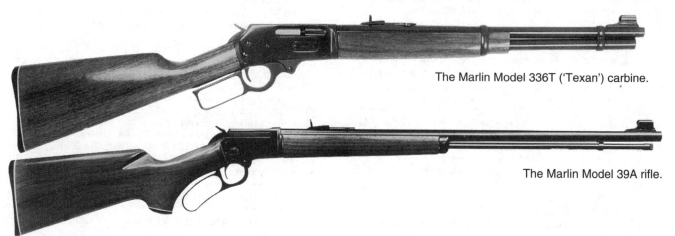

The Marlin Model 336T ('Texan') carbine.

The Marlin Model 39A rifle.

The Marlin Model 444SS rifle.

Model 39A Octagon rifle, 1973. This had a 24in barrel of octagonal form, a bead-type front sight and a slender forend. The pistol grip butt lacked the customary plastic grip cap. Production amounted to about 2550 guns.

Model 39D carbine, 1970-4. This was much the same as the 39M (q.v.), except for a pistol grip butt and a band around the forend.

Model 39M Golden carbine, 1960-92. Distinguished by a 20in round barrel and a straight-wrist butt, this had a gold-plated trigger and a ramped front sight with a protective hood. A spring-leaf and elevator rear sight was fitted, with swivels beneath the butt and forend cap.

Model 39MS carbine, 1988-92. A revised version of the 39M, this had changes in the action and a new quick-release magazine plug.

Model 39M Mountie carbine, 1954-60. Identical with the 39A Mountie rifle, this had a 20in barrel and a magazine capacity of only 15-21 rounds.

Model 39M Octagon carbine, 1973. Limited numbers of these guns were made, with a 20in barrel and a straight-wrist butt. About 2140 were made.

Model 39TDS carbine, 1988-95. Offered with a 16.5in barrel, this had a magazine capacity reduced to 10 22LR or 16 Short cartridges. It also had a straight-wrist stock and a squared operating lever.

MODEL 56 LEVERMATIC SPORTING RIFLE

Made by the Marlin Firearms Company, New Haven, Connecticut, 1955-64.

Total production: about 31,500. **Chambering options:** 22 Short, 22 Long or 22 Long Rifle rimfire. **Action:** locked by a vertically-sliding bolt.

DATA FOR A TYPICAL EXAMPLE

Chambering: 22 Long Rifle, rimfire. 40.6in overall, 5.75lb empty. 22in barrel, 12-groove rifling; RH, concentric. Detachable box magazine, 7 rounds. Spring-leaf and elevator rear sight. 1080 fps with 40-grain bullet.

Designed by Bandell & Neal of Chicago, then perfected by Marlin engineers Ewald Nichol and Thomas Robinson, this action relied on a short-throw lever with a radial movement of just 25 degrees to operate the bolt through a cam-and-roller accelerator. Its one-piece stock—with a Monte Carlo comb and a round-tip forend—presented a departure from traditional Marlin lever-action rifles. The hammer was enclosed in the receiver, which was usually drilled and tapped for optical-sight mounts. The earliest guns had a steel receiver with a squared back, but this was soon replaced with a rounded aluminum-alloy pattern.

SIMILAR GUNS

Model 56DL Clipper King rifle, 1958. Only about 150 of these were offered in a boxed set, accompanied by a 4x optical sight and appropriate mounts. The guns had 12-round magazines and specially marked barrels.

Model 57 Levermatic rifle, 1957-65. This was a tube-magazine version of the Model 56, containing 19-27 rounds depending on cartridge length. It weighed 6.25lb empty. About 35,000 were made, but more than 10,000 were sold through the Western Auto Supply Company and were appropriately marked. Round-backed alloy receivers were replaced after 1959 by squared steel patterns, and a new stock with an oblique-cut forend tip was adopted in 1966.

Model 57M Levermatic rifle, 1959-69. Chambered for 22 Winchester Magnum rimfire ammunition, this had a 24in barrel and a 15-round tube magazine. About 66,900 guns were made.

Model 62 Levermatic rifle, 1963-9. Marlin made about 16,750 of these specially-strengthened guns chambering the 256 Winchester Magnum centerfire cartridge, fired from a barrel rifled with 22 grooves. Readily detachable swivels were added in 1964. In 1966, however, Marlin realized that the 256 cartridge inhibited sales and offered an alternative 30 M1 Carbine chambering. The guns were typically 41.9in long, had 23.25in barrels, and weighed 6.95lb empty.

MODEL 444 SPORTING RIFLE

Made by the Marlin Firearms Company, New Haven, Connecticut (1965-9), and North Haven, Connecticut (1969-71).

Total production: not known. **Chambering:** 444 Marlin only. Lever action, locked by a vertically-sliding bolt.

DATA FOR A TYPICAL PRE-1971 EXAMPLE

42.45in overall, 7.53lb empty. 24in barrel, 12-groove rifling; RH, concentric. Tube magazine in forend, 5 rounds. Spring-leaf and elevator rear sight. 2400 fps with 240-grain bullet.

The advent of the semi-rimmed 444 cartridge—little more than an elongated 44 Magnum—led to the introduction of this gun, adapted from the proven 336 action. It had a straight-wrist butt with a high Monte Carlo comb, a ventilated recoil pad, and a short forend with a swivel-bearing band. A second band appeared behind the muzzle and a Lyman Model 16B rear sight lay on top of the barrel.

SIMILAR GUNS

Model 444S rifle ('Sporter'), 1972-8. A modified version of the original Model 444, this had a handier 22in barrel and a straight-comb pistol grip butt/semi-beavertail forend assembly adapted from the Model 336A. Quick-detachable swivels were fitted. A simplified rear sight replaced the Lyman pattern in 1974, and the muzzle and forend bands were eliminated in 1976.

Model 444SS rifle, 1984 to date. The addition of a cross-bolt safety catch in 1984 advanced the designation to from 'S' to 'SS' and, in 1988, eyes replaced detachable swivels.

GLENFIELD MODEL 36G SPORTING CARBINE

Made by the Marlin Firearms Company, New Haven, Connecticut (1964-6).

Total production: 5930. **Chambering:** 30-30 Winchester only. **Action:** generally as M1889, above.

DATA FOR A TYPICAL GUN

38.25in overall, 7lb empty. 20in barrel, 12-groove rifling; RH, concentric. Tube magazine in forend, 6 rounds. Spring-leaf and elevator rear sight. 2390 fps with 150-grain bullet.

This was little more than a simplified Model 336 (q.v.) marketed under the Glenfield brand name. Most of the guns had round barrels, birch pistol grip butts and birch forends.

SIMILAR GUNS

Model 30 carbine, 1966-72. Replacing the Model 36G, this was identical except for designation. Decorative checkering panels—including a stag's head and oak leaves in the design—were pressed into the pistol grip and forend from 1969. By the end of 1972, about 80,000 Model 30 rifles had been made.

Model 30A carbine, 1973-83. This replaced the Model 30, differing principally in the adoption of a full-length six-round magazine. Impressed checkering was abandoned in 1982, but production ceased a year later after something in excess of 300,000 rifles had been made.

Model 30GT carbine, 1979-80. A variant of the Model 30A with a straight-wrist butt, this had an 18.5in barrel, a full-length magazine and a squared operating lever. About 7740 were made.

Model 30AS carbine, 1983 to date. This replacement for the Model 30A, identical but for markings and the addition of a cross-bolt safety, is now marketed under the Marlin name.

NEW MODEL 1894 SPORTING RIFLE

Made by the Marlin Firearms Company, North Haven, Connecticut, 1969 to date.

Currently in production. **Chambering options:** 218 Bee, 25-20 Winchester, 32-20 Winchester, 357 Magnum, 38 Special, 41 Magnum, 44 Remington Magnum, 44 Smith & Wesson Special or 45 Colt. **Action:** generally as M1889, above.

DATA FOR A STANDARD 1894CL

Chambering: 218 Bee, rimmed. 38.75in overall, 6.25lb empty. 22in barrel, 6-groove rifling; RH, concentric. Tube magazine in forend, 6 rounds. Spring-leaf and elevator rear sight. 2760 fps with 46-grain bullet.

This was introduced after the failure of the 336/44 Magnum, the shorter action being better suited to a handgun cartridge. The

The Marlin New Model 1894CL rifle.

The Marlin New Model 1894CS carbine.

M1894 had a straight-grip butt, a barrel with Micro-Groove rifling, and a band around the forend. The blued receiver, drilled and tapped for sight mounts, had a saddle ring on the left side and a sand blasted top to minimize glare. The saddle ring was abandoned in 1971. A 'Wide-Scan' front sight was adopted in 1974, and the band around the forend and barrel was deleted in 1975. A blued-steel trigger lever replaced the gold-plated pattern from 1980, but the basic Model 1894 was superseded by the 'S' pattern (described below) in 1984.

SIMILAR GUNS

Model 1894C ('Carbine'),1979-84. Introduced in 357 Magnum/38 Special, this was generally similar to the M1894. However, it had an 18.5in barrel, a nine-round magazine, a straight-wrist butt, and bands around the forend and muzzle. The carbine proved extremely popular, more than 90,000 being made before the 1894CS was substituted.

Model 1894CL rifle, 1988 to date. Offered in 25-20 or 32-20, this has a straight-wrist butt, a 22in barrel and a half-length six-round magazine. A 218 Bee chambering was added to the options in 1990.

Model 1894CS carbine, 1983 to date. Introduced in 357 Magnum, this was simply a modification of the basic pattern accepting a cross-bolt safety catch.

Model 1894CM ('Carbine Magnum'), 1969-84. A variant of the standard rifle chambering the 44 Remington Magnum pistol cartridge, this was made only in small quantities.

Model 1894 Cowboy, 1996 to date. Chambered for the 357 Magnum, 44 Magnum 44-40 and 45 Long Colt cartridges, this has a 24in tapered octagon barrel and a 10-round magazine. The butt has a straight wrist and the forend has a blued steel cap; the pistol grip and the forend sides are checkered.

Model 1894M carbine, 1983-6. This comparatively short-lived version of the 1894 design was chambered for the 22 Winchester Magnum rimfire cartridge; about 12,000 guns were made.

Model 1894 Octagon carbine. The design of the elevator was modified in 1973 to feed long-case handgun cartridges. Consequently, about 2960 guns were made in 44 Remington Magnum, with 20in octagonal barrels, straight-grip walnut butts and rubber buttplates.

Model 1894S carbine, 1984 to date. An improved version of the original M1894, this has a 20in barrel and an additional cross-bolt safety catch. Some guns were chambered in 1985 for 41 Magnum, a second group made in 1989 bringing the total to 3540, and a 45 Long Colt option was introduced in 1988.

Model 1894 Sporter. About 1400 of these 44 Magnum guns were made in 1973 with six-round half-length magazines and metal buttplates.

NEW MODEL 1895 SPORTING RIFLE

Made by the Marlin Firearms Company, North Haven, Connecticut, 1972 to date.

Currently in production. **Chambering:** 45-70 Government. **Action:** generally as M1889, above.
DATA FOR A TYPICAL 1895SS

40.5in overall, 7.5lb empty. 22in barrel, 12-groove rifling; RH, concentric. Tube magazine in forend, 4 rounds. Spring-leaf and elevator rear sight. 1810 fps with 300-grain bullet.

Built on the 336-pattern receiver, this was introduced to handle the venerable 45-70 cartridge. It had a straight-wrist butt with a curved rubber buttplate, a squared operating lever and a half-length magazine. The receiver was drilled and tapped for optical-sight mounts, the top being sand-blasted to provide a non-reflecting surface. Early guns had eight-groove rifling.

SIMILAR GUNS

Model 1895S rifle, 1980-4. A pistol grip butt appeared in 1980, with white spacers for the pistol grip cap and buttplate, and a hooded 'Wide-Scan' front sight was fitted.

Model 1895SS rifle, 1984 to date. This had a new cross-bolt safety catch. Swivels were replaced by eyes in 1988.

MODEL 375 SPORTING RIFLE

Made by the Marlin Firearms Company, North Haven, Connecticut, 1980-2.

Total production: about 16,320. **Chambering:** 375 Winchester only. Data otherwise generally as Model 336C, except a muzzle velocity of 2200 fps with 200-grain bullet.

A minor variant of the 336C chambered for a specific cartridge, this was abandoned in 1982 owing to poor sales. New guns were available for some years thereafter.

OTHER PATTERNS

In addition to the rifles marketed under its own and Glenfield names, Marlin has supplied substantial quantities of lever-action rifles to distributors. These have included Coast to Coast Stores of Minneapolis, Minnesota; Cotter & Company of Chicago, Illinois ('West Point' brand); the Firestone Tire & Rubber Company; Montgomery Ward, Inc. ('Western Field'); the Oklahoma Tire & Supply Company ('Otasco'); the J.C. Penney Company of New York ('Formost'); Sears, Roebuck & Company ('Ranger' prior to the Second World War, 'J.C. Higgins' thereafter); United Merchandising, Inc. ('Big 5'); and the Western Auto Supply Company ('Revelation').

Virtually all the centerfire guns have been based on the Marlin Models 30 or 336, though often sold under the distributors' own designations. For example, Montgomery Ward promoted an otherwise standard Marlin 336C with a special recoil pad as the 'EMN-70A'. Otasco's Model 3081—dating from 1981—was a Glenfield 30A with an Alamo medallion let into the butt-side, while the Model 3084 (1984) was a Marlin 30AS with a Mountain Man medallion.

• Marlin, slide-action type

Inspired by the activities of Winchester, Marlin offered a series of rimfire slide-action rifles in the early years of the present century. However, they did not share the success of the company's lever-action patterns and comparatively few were made.

MODEL 18 SPORTING RIFLE
'Marlin Baby Featherweight Repeater No. 18'

Made by the Marlin Firearms Company, New Haven, Connecticut, 1906-8.

Total production: not known. **Chambering options:** 22 Short or 22 Long Rifle rimfire. **Action:** locked by pivoting the locking bolt down against the receiver.
DATA FOR A TYPICAL EXAMPLE

Chambering: 22 Short, rimfire. 35.5in overall, 3.75lb empty. 20in barrel, 6-groove rifling; RH, concentric. Tube magazine beneath barrel, 25 rounds. Spring-leaf and elevator rear sight. 950 fps with 29-grain bullet.

Patented by Lewis Hepburn in 1904, the first of the slide-action Marlins was offered only in a solid-frame pattern with an exposed hammer and a round, part-octagon or octagonal barrel. A half-length tube magazine beneath the barrel held 14 22 Short rimfire cartridges, though a 22 Long Rifle option could be supplied. The straight-wrist butt had a concave shoulder plate and the slide handle was plain. The rear sight was a spring-leaf and elevator type, used in conjunction with an open bead at the muzzle. Later guns offered a take-down feature, but this was simply a readily detachable butt!

SIMILAR GUNS

Model 20 rifle, 1907-11. Offered in 22 Short, 22 Long and 22 Long Rifle, which it would fire interchangeably, the Model 20 was a larger version of the Model 18 with a screw-type take-down system patented by Lewis Hepburn in March 1908. The half-length magazine held 10-15 rounds, though a full-length version was also made (18-25 rounds). The barrel was generally a 24in octagon pattern, giving an empty weight of about 5lb. Slide handles were grooved, though the butts retained the straight wrist.

Model 20S rifle, 1911-13. Soon replaced by the Model 20A, this had a short locking bar. The locking shoulder in the receiver, therefore, no longer lay at the extreme rear.

Model 20A rifle (sometimes known as '20AS'), 1913-22. The perfected form of the Model 20, this had a short locking bar and a modified firing pin. A 22.5in octagon barrel was customary, magazine capacity being 11-15 rounds. A full-length magazine was optional.

Model 25 rifle, 1909-10. A short-lived Gallery Gun, this was chambered only for the 22 Short cartridges or 22 CB Caps. An exposed-hammer take-down design (with a detachable butt like the later version of the Model 18), it had a half-length magazine containing 15 22 Short rounds or 18 CB caps beneath a 23in round barrel. The slide handle was plain and a spring-leaf and elevator rear sight was fitted.

Model 25S rifle, 1911-14. Mechanically identical with the original Model 25, this had a short locking bar.

Model 47 rifle, 1930-1. This exposed hammer take-down gun was little more than a '20A' with a 23in round barrel and an improved magazine. The receiver was color case-hardened, and checkering was cut into the straight-wrist butt and forend. Only about 6,000 guns of this type were made.

MODEL 27 SPORTING RIFLE

Made by the Marlin Fire Arms Company, New Haven, Connecticut, 1909-11.

Total production: not known. **Chambering:** 25 Long rimfire, 25-20 Winchester or 32-20 Winchester centerfire. **Action:** locked by displacing a locking bar in the bolt into the receiver.

DATE FOR A TYPICAL EXAMPLE

Chambering: 32-20 Winchester, rimmed. 42.2in overall, 5.86lb empty. 24in barrel, 6-groove rifling; RH, concentric. Tube magazine in forend, 7 rounds. Spring-leaf and elevator rear sight. 2100 fps with 80-grain bullet.

Built around patents granted to James Wheeler, George Beck and Melvin Hepburn in July 1911, on the basis of guns designed by John Marlin and Lewis Hepburn, this derived from the rimfire Model 20. Introduced in 25-20 or 32-20, in take-down form, it had a pivoting catch on the front right side of the receiver which could be used in conjunction with a thumbscrew on the left (later right) side to detach the barrel/magazine unit. The exposed hammer was retained. The barrel was octagonal; a short magazine tube was fitted; the straight-wrist butt had a crescent buttplate; and a short sliding forend (generally with nine grooves) doubled as the operating handle.

SIMILAR GUN

Model 27S, 1911-32. This was soon substituted for the original pattern, the principal improvement being a button on the right side of the receiver which allowed the action to be opened without dropping the hammer onto the firing pin. A round-barrel option was introduced in 1913, together with a 25-35 Stevens rimfire chambering, but production was stopped by war work in 1916 and did not begin again until 1922. Post-war production concentrated on the round-barrel pattern.

Model 29 rifle, 1913-17. Essentially similar to the Model 20, this had a 23in round barrel, a half-length magazine and a smooth slide handle.

Model 37 rifle, 1923-31. Little more than the Model 29 with a post-war name, this was introduced by the Marlin Firearms Corporation as a 'new' product. The changes from the pre-1917 guns were confined largely to markings.

MODEL 32 SPORTING RIFLE

Introduced in 1915, chambered for 22 Short, 22 Long and 22 Long Rifle cartridges interchangeably, this was an improved takedown slide-action design patented by Carl Swebilius and Theodore Hanitz. It had an internal hammer and a three-quarter magazine holding 10-15 rounds (depending on cartridge length) or 18-25 if the full-length version was preferred. The barrel was usually a 24in octagon pattern, the pistol grip butt had a straight comb, and the forend was ribbed. A spring-leaf and elevator rear sight was used in conjunction with a plain bead at the muzzle. However, the advent of war work stopped production almost as soon as it began, and Model 32 rifles are very rarely seen.

SIMILAR GUNS

Model 38 rifle, 1921-30. This was a post-war version of the Model 32 embodying changes to the lock, ejector and magazine tube patented by Carl Swebilius in 1922-9; the button-type magazine release, added in 1926, is a particularly good aid to dating.

• Marston

William Marston of New York City received a U.S. patent in June 1850 (no. 7443) to protect a distinctive breechloading rifle with a reciprocating bolt contained in an all-metal frame. The bolt was propped in its locked position by a bar extending from the combination trigger guard/underlever, the two components being pinned together with a short 'L'-shape link.

BREECHLOADING SPORTING RIFLE

Marston & Knox of New York City claimed to be making '40 guns a month' in 1853; pistols and rifles, and perhaps a few shotguns, were made in the era before the Civil War began. The rifles had all-metal frames with a loading port cut away on the right side of the breech. A two-trigger mechanism was popular, the butt had a checkered wrist, and the shoulder plate was usually a crescent pattern. A cleaning rod was carried beneath the barrel in two short pipes and a long anchor-tube, and an unusually long hammer-nose was needed to reach the cap nipple. Proprietary Marston cartridges had a lightweight card or thick paper body and a leather-cup base to minimize gas leaks.

• Mauser

In addition to the Mauser-type guns built on American-made actions, some U.S. gunsmiths have refurbished wartime examples and others have purchased components from suppliers such as Fabrique Nationale. Participants have included the Bighorn Rifle Company; the Browning Arms Company; Century International Arms, Inc.; Colt's Patent Fire Arms Mfg Co.; Reinhart Fajen Mfg Co., Inc.; Firearms International Corporation; the Gibbs Rifle Company; the Golden State Arms Corporation; Griffin & Howe, Inc.; Harrington & Richardson; High Standard Mfg. Co.; the Hoffmann Arms Company; Paul Jaeger, Inc.; Kassnar Imports, Inc.; the Kodiak Mfg Company; Marathon Products, Inc.; the Navy Arms Company; Rahn Gun Works; Smith & Wesson; the Stoeger Arms Corporation; Weatherby, Inc.; and the Winslow Arms Company. Details of many of these are listed separately.

• Maynard

Designed by Edward Maynard, a Washington dentist, this carbine was patented in 1856-9. The earliest experiments were undertaken with metal-tube cartridges closed by a waxed paper disc, but Maynard eventually settled on an iron (later brass) tube brazed onto a sturdy perforated base, combining excellent sealing properties with good extraction.

The earliest Maynard carbine was unsuccessful, but its simpler replacement, patented on 6th December 1859, received excellent testimonials. One gun was tried at Washington Navy Yard in October 1859 in the presence of the inventor and Commander John Dahlgren. At a range of 200yd, 237 hits were obtained from 237 shots on a target 3ft broad by 6ft high; at 1300yd, it buried a bullet to its length in oak planks. Maynard carbines were immediately adopted by the U.S. Treasury for service on revenue cutters.

Though large numbers were made during and immediately after the Civil War, interest in the odd-looking Maynard rifle declined greatly in the 1880s in the face of strong competition. The remnants of the business were sold in 1890 to the J. Stevens Arms & Tool Company.

A Maynard carbine of the Civil War era.

A Maynard No. 16 target rifle.

CAPLOCK CARBINE

Made by the Massachusetts Arms Company, Chicopee Falls, Masschusetts, 1860-5.

Total production: 30,000? **Chambering options:** see notes. **Action:** a tipping barrel was locked by the underlever.

DATA FOR A TYPICAL EXAMPLE

Chambering: 50-caliber reloadable cartridge. 36.9in overall, 6.2lb empty. 20in barrel, 3-groove rifling; RH, concentric. Single shot only. Three-leaf rear sight graduated to 500yd. About 1000 fps with 343-grain bullet. No bayonet.

Though the straight-comb wristless butt looked ungainly, Maynards were light and handy. They were loaded by pushing down on a breech lever formed as the trigger guard, tipping the part-octagon barrel so that a new cartridge could be inserted directly into the chamber. The frames and hammers were color case-hardened, a sling ring lay on the left side of the frame, but no forends were used. The earliest guns (35- or 50-caliber) were made with tape primers and a folding rear sight on the tang behind the central hammer. No sling bar was fitted, though a ring sometimes lay on the lower tang behind the breech lever.

Later government guns, made exclusively in 50-caliber, lacked the tape primer and patch box, and had a conventional rear sight on the barrel above the frame hinge. Federal purchases between 1st January 1861 and 30th June 1866 amounted to 20,002 carbines, but many others were probably sold to state militia units.

A Maynard carbine tested by the U.S. Army in the trials of 1865, as 'Gun No. 37', was a standard metallic-cartridge gun of the type used extensively during the American Civil War.

MODEL 1873 SPORTING RIFLE

Made by the Massachusetts Arms Company, Chicopee Falls, Massachusetts, about 1873-5; and by the Maynard Gun Company, Chicopee Falls, Massachusetts, 1876-82 (probably sub-contracted).

Chambering options: see text. **Action:** as caplock gun, above.

DATA FOR A TYPICAL EXAMPLE

Chambering: 35-30 Maynard, rimmed. About 41.5in overall, 7.75lb empty. 26in barrel, 6-groove rifling; RH, concentric. Folding-leaf rear sight on upper tang. 1280 fps with 250-grain bullet.

The manufacture of centerfire rifles began in 1873, but sales were never great. Reliance on idiosyncratic 'thick-rim' cartridges inhibited sales, as the ammunition was difficult to obtain; indeed, most 1873-type rifles were fitted with a rimfire adapter (patented by George Hadley) which could be detached to allow centerfire ammunition to be used. Maynards were usually distinguished by the absence of a forend from all but a few guns, among them being some stocked in Britain. They were often fitted with ring-tip operating levers, though target rifles (particularly the Creedmoor versions) sometimes had wooden pseudo-pistol grips attached to the lever.

THE GUNS

Note: Owing to the ease with which barrels could be changed, a wide range of accessories and to the professed ability of the manufacturers to supply guns to individual requirements, Maynard rifles can be difficult to catalogue. Additional information can be gleaned from *A Guide to the Maynard Breech-Loader* by George J. Layman (Nashoba Publications, 1993).

No. 1 Gallery Rifle, 1873-90. This was a 22 rimfire gun with a 20in or 24in barrel, a straight-wrist walnut butt, and fixed open sights.

No. 2 Gallery & Small Game Hunting Rifle, 1873-90. Similar to No. 1, this had a Beach combination front sight and a folding peep sight on the tang.

No. 3 Hunting & Target Rifle, 1873-90. Made with plain walnut butts and open sights, this was chambered for the 32 Long Rifle rimfire or 32 Short, Long or Extra Long centerfire cartridges. A 32-20 WCF option was added in 1884. The standard barrels measured 24in or 26in.

No. 4 Hunting & Target Rifle, 1873-90. Essentially similar to the No. 3, offered in the same chamberings, this could be identified by its heavier barrel.

No. 5 Hunter's Rifle, 1873-90. Offered only in 38 Extra Long rimfire or 38-55 Maynard centerfire, this was otherwise the same as the No. 4. Barrels measured 26-30in.

No. 6 Sporting Rifle, 1873-90. This was little more than a No. 5 with a folding peep sight on the tang. The standing-notch rear sight on the barrel was retained.

No. 7 Hunter's Rifle, 1873-90. This plain 20in-barreled gun, offered only in 35-30 Maynard, had fixed open sights.

No. 8 Hunter's Rifle, 1873-90. Mechanically identical with the No. 7, offered in the same 35-30 chambering, this had a folding peep sight on the tang behind the hammer.

No. 9 Hunting & Target rifle, 1875-90. Made only with a 26in barrel, this 35-30 or 40-40 centerfire gun had a folding tang-sight in addition to its open barrel sights. It weighed about 7.5lb.

No. 10 Mid Range Target & Hunting Rifle, 1875-90. Available in 35-30, 40-40, 40-60 and 40-70 Maynard, this had a part-octagon barrel, a peep sight on the tang and a Beach combination sight at the muzzle. The open-notch rear sight was retained. Straight-wrist butts were standard, and the guns weighed 8-9lb.

No. 11 Hunter's Rifle, 1875-90. Chambered for a selection of cartridges—.44-60, 44-70, 44-100, 50-50, 50-100 and 55-100 Maynard, plus 45-70 and 50-70 Government—this had a folding peep sight on the tang and the customary open sights on the barrel. Standard barrel lengths were 26-32in.

No. 12 Mid Range Target Rifle, 1876-90. This had a folding peep sight on the tang, a spring-leaf rear sight on the barrel, and a Beach combination sight at the muzzle. Offered only in 40-60 and 40-70 Maynard, it had a 28-32in part-octagon barrel and weighed about 9lb.

No 13 Mid Range Target Rifle, 1876-90. Similar to the No. 12, accepting the same cartridges, this had a Vernier-type peep sight on the tang and a 'Wind Gauge with Spirit Level' front sight.

No. 14 Long Range Creedmoor Rifle, 1876-90. This had a 32in round barrel chambered for the 44-100 cartridge, and a special butt with checkering on the pistol grip. A Vernier tang sight was fitted, with a wind gauge and spirit level. The No. 14 lacked a forend, but often had a rudimentary pistol grip formed by adding a wooden extension to the breech lever.

No. 15 Target Rifle, 1880-90? Distinguished by a hooked Swiss or Schuetzen-style buttplate, this had a checkered straight wrist and a short wooden forend (omitted from guns intended for off hand shooting). It was fitted with a Vernier sight on the tang and a wind-gauge pattern at the muzzle. Supplied with 26-32in part-octagon barrels, the No. 15 could be chambered for the 38-50, 40-60 and 40-70 centerfire cartridges.

A Merrill carbine.

MODEL 1882 SPORTING RIFLE

Made by the Maynard Gun Company, Chicopee Falls, Massachusetts, 1882-9 (probably sub-contracted).

Otherwise generally as 1873 pattern, above.

The perfected Maynard-type sporters of 1882 fired conventional centerfire ammunition, but were not strong enough to withstand the most powerful sporting-rifle cartridges of their day. The 1882 pattern was often classed as an 'Improved Model' to distinguish it from the otherwise similar 1873 design, but the mark did not appear on the gun.

THE GUNS

With the exception of the No. 16 rifle, all the original 1873 patterns were duplicated in 1882 form.

No. 16 Improved Target Rifle, 1882-90. The finest gun in the Maynard range, this had a pistol grip butt with a hooked buttplate. The forend had a shallow schnabel tip, and the heavy barrel took part-octagon form. Chamberings duplicated No. 15 (above).

• Meigs

Josiah Meigs of Lowell, Massachusetts, was granted U.S. patent 36,721 in October 1862 to protect a sliding breech-block locked by a pivoting strut. Few of these guns were made. In May 1866, however, Miegs received U.S. patent no. 54,934 for a vertically-sliding block operated by the reciprocating motion of the trigger guard as it slid on a track in the underside of the stock. This mechanism was subsequently improved in August 1868, when a patent of addition was granted, and a few guns were made on the basis of 1855-pattern Springfield rifle muskets by the Lowell Arms Company of Lowell, Massachusetts. One gun was submitted to the U.S. Army trials of 1865, but was not amongst those selected for photography and was presumably rejected unfired.

• Merrill

The first Merrill design to be accepted officially was a modification of the old Jenks (q.v.) 'Mule Ear' carbines, but this was superseded by a refined version of the sliding-bolt locking system.

The major internal difference between the Jenks and Merrill actions lay in the addition of an annular copper disc on the piston head. The disc was momentarily crushed by the pressure of firing, expanding outward to provide an effective gas-seal. A small lug on the actuating lever automatically cleared the spent cap from the nipple and, by blocking the passage of the hammer to the cap, ensured that the gun could not fire before the action was locked.

The first sale of Merrill-action guns to the federal government was made in June 1861, when 20 carbines, three rifles, a 'Minie Musket' and nine converted Harper's Ferry Rifles (Model 1841) were acquired for trials.

MERRILL-JENKS CARBINE

Issued in the U.S. Navy, this was an Ames-made Jenks (q.v.) adapted to handle combustible paper cartridges. The prototype conversion had been rejected after tests in Washington Navy Yard in February 1858, but an improved version with a conventional side-hammer lock was substituted in June 1858. This was acceptable enough for Merrill to convert 300 Jenks carbines and make 5000 cartridges for extended trials. These duly satisfied the Navy, the conversion being approved on 26th January 1861.

IMPROVED JENKS-PATTERN RIFLE, MODEL 1858

Probably made for Merrill, Thomas & Co. of Baltimore, Maryland, by E. Remington & Sons, Ilion, New York.

Total production: several thousand. **Chambering:** 54-caliber combustible cartridge, fired by a cap-lock. **Action:** locked by a sliding breech-bolt retracted by the operating lever.

48.5in overall, 9.2lb empty. 33in barrel, 3-groove rifling; concentric. Single-shot only. Two-leaf rear sight graduated to 500yd. Performance not known. Sword bayonet.

Nearly 600 Merrill rifles were ordered for the 21st Indiana Volunteer Infantry Regiment in March 1862, an outstanding order for 5000 carbines being reduced accordingly. The guns had barrels held by two brass bands. The original flat knurled breech latches were superseded by a rounded pattern embodying a sprung plunger. Merrill rifles had a reputation for long-range accuracy, and were often prized by marksmen. Though federal government purchases amounted to less than 800 in 1861-3, many others were bought privately.

IMPROVED JENKS-PATTERN CARBINE, MODEL 1858

Probably made by E. Remington & Sons, Ilion, New York, for the promoters.

Total production: 20,000? **Chambering:** 54-caliber combustible cartridge, fired by a cap-lock. **Action:** as 1858-type rifle, above.

37.4in overall, 6.6lb empty. 22.25in barrel, 3-groove rifling; concentric. Single shot only. Three-leaf rear sight for distances up to 500yd. Performance not known. No bayonet.

The first sale of carbines to the federal government occurred in June 1861, when 20 were acquired for trials together with some rifles. The first major purchase occurred when 5000 carbines were ordered on Christmas Eve, 1861; by 30th June 1866, 14,695 had been purchased. The earliest guns had an actuating lever with a flat knurled locking catch and tapering forends; furniture, including the patch box, was brass. Later guns had the modified locking catch on the breech lever, the forend tip was much sturdier, and the patch box was eliminated.

SIMILAR GUNS

Trials-pattern carbine. Gun No. 38 tested by the U.S. Army in 1865 was a metallic-cartridge carbine operated by a top lever pivoted in the butt wrist. It had a one-piece half-stock with a single band. A sling ring and bar lay on the left side of the stock above the trigger guard, and a hinged-leaf sight lay on top of the chamber. Ignition was achieved by striking a firing pin with the hammer of a conventional sidelock.

• Merrill, Latrobe & Thomas

Patented by Merrill in January 1856 and promoted in partnership with Latrobe & Thomas in 1856, this embodied a faucet breech closed by rotating a lateral plug behind the chamber. It was loaded through a hole bored in the plug when the lever was open. The gun was much too complicated; like its original promoters, it soon failed.

1856-PATENT CARBINE

Made by E. Remington & Sons, Ilion, New York, for the promoters, 1855.

Total production: at least 200. **Chambering:** 58-caliber combustible cartridge, fired by a caplock. **Action:** locked by a rotary plug in the breech.

38.1in overall, 7.15lb empty. 22.5in barrel, 3-groove rifling; concentric. Single-shot only. Leaf-and-slider rear sight. Performance not known. No bayonet.

The U.S. Army ordered 170 of these distinctive guns in July 1855. Unlike the prototypes, they had Maynard tape primers set into the lock plate ahead of the hammer. Half-length forends were held by a single brass band, and a patch box with a hinged lid was set into the right side of the butt. A sling ring was attached to the left side of the breech. Supplied before the relevant protection had been granted, the guns were marked 'PATENT APPLIED FOR'.

• Milbank

Isaac Milbank of Greenfield Hill, Connecticut, was granted several firearms patents in 1862-74, but few of his designs encountered tangible success. The only gun known to have been tested by the U.S. Army was made in accordance with U.S. patent 61,751 of 5th February 1867, protecting a breechblock which swung sideways.

Comparable with the Needham system of the same period, the Milbank breech was tested by the U.S. Army in 1867 on a converted 58-caliber Springfield rifle-musket. Milbank subsequently received a patent in December 1868 to protect an improved side-swinging breech, with an internal striker instead of an external side-hammer, but nothing came of either it or a series of bolt-type rifles dating from 1872-4. However, though Milbank was never able to convince the U.S. authorities of the merits of his rifles, a modified form was officially adopted in Switzerland (q.v.) once improvements had been made by Rudolf Amsler.

• Miller

A short-barreled carbine, 'Gun No. 39', tested by the U.S. Army in 1865, was the work of William & George Miller of West Meriden, Connecticut—joint recipients in May 1865 of U.S. patent 47,902. The essence of the design lay in a hinged breechblock which could move up and forward to expose the chamber. A transverse bar on the underside of the breechblock mated with a slot across the top of the receiver when the action was closed.

The Miller carbine had a conventional sidelock, and a one-piece half-stock with a single band. A sling ring and bar lay on the left side of the stock above the trigger guard, and a hinged-leaf rear sight appeared on the barrel directly above the chamber. Another version of the basic design was tested by the U.S. Army in 1867, on the basis of a converted 58-caliber Springfield rifle musket, but was withdrawn after failing the defective cartridge trial.

A few Miller-action guns, often converted from Springfield rifle muskets, were made by the Meriden Mfg. Company in the mid-1860s. However, these often prove to be smooth-bored shotguns.

• Mix & Horton

A gun of this type was submitted to the U.S. Army trials of 1865, but was not among those that were photographed at the time. This may simply indicate that it failed to pass the examination stages. Eugene Mix and Henry Horton of Ithaca, New York State, were granted U.S. patent 41,343 of 19th January 1864 to protect a vertically-sliding block operated by the trigger lever. The hammer was pivoted in the breechblock, which also contained its 'S'-spring, and the extractor was activated automatically at the end of the opening stoke.

• Montana Armory

A re-creation of the M1885 High Wall rifle was available in 1991-5 from the Montana Armory, Inc., of Big Timber. Chambered for 30-40 Krag, 32-40 Winchester, 38-55 Winchester, 40-65 Winchester or 45-70 cartridges, it had a coil-spring action and a 28in octagonal barrel (26in, 30-40 Krag only). The frame, breechblock, operating lever and hammer were color case-hardened. Rocky Mountain sights were fitted.

• Morgenstern

William Morgenstern of Philadelphia was a prolific, if unsuccessful patentee. Beginning with 40,572 of November 1863, granted jointly with E. Morwitz to protect a needle rifle, Morgenstern submitted a variety of sliding-bolt and lifting-block designs. U.S. patent no. 48,133, dating from June 1865, protected a sliding bolt which was retracted by the hammer after being lifted out of engagement with the locking shoulder in the rear of the receiver. A tripping lever allowed the breech to be closed without lowering the hammer. A gun of this type may have been submitted to the U.S. Army trials of 1865, but was not among those that were selected for photography. Most of Morgenstern's subsequent efforts—from U.S. patent 72526 (November 1867) to 93,330 of August 1869—were aimed at perfected a lifting block, which was released by pulling back on a small locking-bolt handle and then pivoted upward around a transverse pivot at the front of the receiver. One exception was the mechanism protected by U.S. patent 74,712 of February 1868, which protected a breechblock which swung on a longitudinal pin once the internal hammer had been set with an external cocking lever.

• Morse

George Morse deserves to be remembered not only as the designer of the first breech-loading rifle to be made in Springfield Armory, but also for the development of an efficient centerfire metal-case cartridge.

His first patent, 15,995 of 28th October 1856, protected a complicated breech system with a sliding bolt-head locked by a strut

attached to a top lever pivoted at the rear of the receiver. A low-slung hammer pivoting on the front of the trigger guard was cocked automatically as the breech opened.

This first design was successfully tested by the U.S. Navy in November 1857 and an order for 125 guns was placed in March 1858. No guns were delivered, as Morse had developed an improved gun—patented in June 1858—with a breechblock pivoting at the back of the top-plate. The patent illustrations show the top-plate moving forward under the hammer blow, to lock under a retaining lip on the frame, but this feature was not incorporated in the guns. The Morse conversion was favorably tested in the summer of 1858, and a decision was taken to alter 2000 guns in the Springfield factory. Work ceased in November 1859, and all relevant patterns, tools and gauges were shipped to Harper's Ferry in the summer of 1860. Few guns had been made when the Confederate forces seized and burned the Harper's Ferry facilities in April 1861.

Morse, a Louisianan, had sufficient Southern sympathies to devote the remainder the American Civil War to producing guns for the Confederacy (q.v.).

MORSE RIFLE

Converted by the Springfield Armory, Springfield, Massachusetts.
Total production: see text. **Chambering:** 58 Morse, centerfire. **Action:** locked by a hammer-propelled bolt entering the breechblock.
DATA FOR AN M1841 RIFLE CONVERSION
48.75in overall, 9.75lb empty. 33in barrel, 6-groove rifling; RH, concentric. Single-shot only. Folding-leaf rear sight. Performance not known. Saber bayonet.

Only 54 guns had been completed by November 1859, and there is little evidence to suggest that any of the 540 which were 'in course of construction' were ever finished. All but a few of the conversions were based on the M1841 rifle, though some 69-caliber M1816 flintlock muskets were altered for trials. Whether any guns were completed in Harper's Ferry is debatable, though some sources put the total of Morse conversions as high as 655. Ten thousand transformations of Model 1842 muskets were ordered in 1860 from the Muzzy Rifle & Gun Manufacturing Company of Worcester, Massachusetts, but only a few prototypes were ever completed.

The 1841-pattern rifle was most distinctive. Its one-piece stock had a straight wrist, and a brass-lid patch box was let into the right side of the butt. A brass barrel band was retained by a spring, and a two-strap brass nose cap carried a swivel. The second swivel lay on the trigger guard. The original rifles were made by a variety of contractors and often exhibit minor differences in detail. Most survivors were bored out to 58-caliber, re-rifled, re-sighted, and altered to accept a sabre bayonet after the introduction of the M1855 rifle musket and its expanding-ball ammunition.

Thumbing back a spur-lever formed from the original cock drew back the internal hammer until it was held on the sear. The breech was then opened by grasping the ears of the firing-pin extension and pulling them backward to withdraw the firing pin from the nose-piece. The front of the top-plate could then be lifted to swing the breechblock and firing pin out of the breech. As this happened, a pivoting strut attached to the back of the breechblock pulled the nose-piece back to expose the chamber and simultaneously extracted a spent case.

A new round could be pushed into the chamber manually, the breech was shut and the trigger could be pressed to release the hammer. This drove a cylindrical bolt forward to lock the breech and strike the firing pin.

• Mosin-Nagant

In 1918, the U.S. government purchased more than a million obr. 1891 rifles from Remington-UMC and the New England Westinghouse Company after the Russian revolution had left the two American manufacturers not only with huge numbers of unwanted guns but also serious financial difficulties. Only 280,050 guns were retained for U.S. Army service, most being used for basic training.

Substantial numbers of 7.62mm Russian-pattern rifles equipped the U.S. divisions sent to Archangel with the Allied intervention forces in 1919, apparently to ease logistics by allowing captured ammunition to be used. The guns, which were accompanied by the Russian-style socket bayonets, were heartily disliked by men accustomed to the M1903 Springfield. Most of them were abandoned in Russia when the Allies finally withdrew in 1920.

The Mossberg Model 353 rimfire
auto-loader, with a forend
doubling as a folding fore-grip.

• Mossberg, autoloading type
MODEL 50 SPORTING RIFLE
Made by O.F. Mossberg & Sons, of New Haven, Connecticut, 1939-41.
Total production: not known. **Chambering:** 22 LR rimfire. **Action:** no
mechanical breech lock; blowback, semi-automatic only.

43.7in overall, 6.8lb empty. 24in barrel, 5-groove rifling: RH, concentric.
Tube magazine in butt, 15 rounds. Spring-leaf and finger-wheel rear sight.
1080 fps with 40-grain bullet.

This gun was characterized more by robust construction than
sophistication. The magazine was contained in the butt, with a
loading port cut on the right side; open sights were fitted on the
barrel, and the half-stock had a plain pistol grip.

SIMILAR GUNS
Model 51 rifle, 1939. This had a heavier cheekpiece stock than
the M50, and a supplementary micrometer sight was attached to
the back of the receiver.

Model 51M rifle, 1939-41 and 1945-6. Identical mechanically
with the Model 51, this had a 20in barrel and a full-length Mannlicher-style stock with a joint in the forend hidden by a sheet-steel
cover. The cheekpiece on guns sold after the end of World War II
was more oval than the pre-1941 wedge shape.

MODEL 151M SPORTING RIFLE
The first post-war gun was derived from the full-stock 51M
pattern described above. Made in 1946-7 and then until 1958 in
subvarieties labelled '(a)', '(b)' and '(c)', the 151M had a new rubber
shoulder pad. Most of the subsequent alterations concerned the
sights and the buttplate.

SIMILAR GUNS
Model 151K rifle, 1950-1. A half-stocked version of the 151M,
this had a Monte Carlo comb and cheekpiece, a rounded pistol
grip, and a bulbous schnabel tip on the forend. The 24in barrel
gave an empty weight of 6lb; aperture sights were absent.

Model 152 carbine, 1948-52. Fitted with an 18in barrel and a
Monte Carlo-type half-stock, this gun had a forend tip which could
be pivoted downward. A seven-round box magazine was fitted,
and the rear sight was a simplified peep on the rear of the receiver.

Model 152K carbine, 1950-7. This was a minor variant of the
152 with an open rear sight on the barrel.

MODEL 350K SPORTING RIFLE
Made by O.F. Mossberg & Sons, of New Haven, Connecticut, 1958-68.
Total production: not known. **Chambering:** 22 Short High-Speed, Long
and LR rimfire. **Action:** generally as Model 50, above.

6.12lb empty. 23.5in barrel, 4-groove rifling: RH, concentric. Detachable
box magazine, 7 rounds. Spring-leaf and finger-wheel rear sight. 1080 fps
with 40-grain bullet.

Embodying a round-topped squared receiver enclosing a hammer mechanism, designed to share components with the 340-series
bolt-action guns (q.v.), this Mossberg rifle had a pistol gripped
half-stock with a Monte Carlo comb. A cheekpiece lay on the left
side of the butt; the forend was rounded; and swivels were placed
beneath the stock. The 350K-A pattern (1960-8) had a fixed rear
sight dovetailed into the barrel.

SIMILAR GUNS
Model 351C carbine, 1965-71. Distinguished by an 18.5in barrel, with a band encircling the barrel and forend, this was a Western-style version of the 350K.

Model 351K rifle, 1958-60. Fitted with a butt magazine holding
15 22LR rimfire rounds, this had a 24in barrel, a Monte Carlo-style
half-stock, and an open spring-leaf rear sight. The 351K-A pattern
(1960-8) had a fixed rear sight.

Model 352 carbine, 1957-9. A short version of the box-magazine rifle, this had an 18.5in barrel, an open rear sight, and a Monte

Carlo butt lacking a cheekpiece. A Tenite forend extension could
swing downward to act as a handgrip. The 350K, 350K-A and
350K-B guns (1960-71) varied in the design of their sights.

Model 353 carbine, 1972-85. A deluxe 352K, with checker-panels pressed into the pistol grip and forend, this had a ramped-blade
sight instead of a bead.

Model 377 Plinkster rifle, 1977-9. Based on the 351K, this had
a 20in barrel and a 15-round tube magazine in the butt of the walnut-finish polystyrene half-stock. The butt had a rollover comb
and a thumbhole-type pistol grip. A 4x optical sight was provided
instead of open sights.

Model 380 rifle, 1980-5. Created to provide a simpler rifle than
the standard Mossbergs, this had a plain walnut-finish half-stock
and simple sights. Available in 22LR rimfire only, it had a butt
magazine and weighed about 5.5lb. The '380S' apparently had a
better stock, but details are lacking.

Model 480 rifle. An alternative name for the 380 pattern, used
briefly in 1985.

MODEL 430 SPORTING RIFLE
Made in 1970-1 only, this had a round-backed slab sided
receiver separating the Monte Carlo-style butt from the short
forend; checkering appeared on the woodwork. A 24in barrel and
an under-barrel tube magazine were standard, capacity being 18
22LR cartridges. The guns were 43.5in long and weighed 6.3lb.

SIMILAR GUNS
Model 432 carbine, 1970-3. A short version of the 430, with a
20in barrel, this had a plain straight-wrist butt and a band around
the forend and barrel.

Model 433 carbine, 1970-3. This was a deluxe pattern with checkering on the Monte Carlo-type butt and the slab-sided forend.

• Mossberg, block-action type
MODEL L SPORTING RIFLE
Made by O.F. Mossberg & Sons, of New Haven, Connecticut, 1929-32.
Total production: not known. **Chambering:** 22 Short, Long and LR rimfire.
Action: locked by propping the breechblock behind the chamber with the
tip of the operating lever. About 38in overall, 5lb empty.

24in barrel, 4-groove rifling: RH, concentric. Single shot only. Spring-leaf
and elevator rear sight. 1080 fps with 40-grain bullet.

This take-down rifle embodied a Martini-type breechblock,
pivoting in the receiver ahead of the exposed hammer spur. The
breech was opened by pulling down on the closed-loop underlever
doubling as the trigger guard; the sides of the receiver were cut
down to facilitate reloading. The rifle had open sights, a plain pistol
grip butt, and a short rounded forend.

SIMILAR GUNS
Model L-1 rifle, 1931. Made only in small numbers, this had a
Lyman No. 2A aperture sight on the tang behind the hammer.

• Mossberg, bolt-action type
O. F. Mossberg & Sons is now renowned as a leading shotgun
manufacturer. Though large numbers of rimfire rifles had been
made prior to World War II, Mossberg was a late convert to the
high-power center-fire sporting rifle. The bolt-action types remained
in production for nearly 20 years, but were never particularly successful in a market dominated by Remington, Ruger, Savage and
Winchester. Mossberg countered criticism with the Pedersen range,
but the venture was short lived and the rifles had all been abandoned
by 1985 in favor of Sako-action guns purchased from Smith & Wesson. Coverage does not include the smooth-bore 'Targos', which,
for the purposes of this edition, are classed as shotguns.

MODEL B SPORTING RIFLE
Introduced in 1930, chambered for the 22 Short, Long and Long
Rifle rimfire cartridges (interchangeably), this had a 22in barrel
and a plain hardwood half-stock with a pistol grip and a rounded
forend. Sights consisted of a spring-leaf on the barrel and a bead
at the muzzle.

Model C rifle, *c.* 1931. Made with a 24in barrel, this single shot pattern had an ivory bead front sight.

Model C-1 rifle, 1932? This target rifle had a walnut stock and Lyman aperture sights, but very few were made.

Model R rifle, 1930-2. Similar to the Model B, this repeater had a 24in barrel and a tube magazine beneath the barrel.

MODEL 10 SPORTING RIFLE

Made by O.F. Mossberg & Sons, of New Haven, Connecticut, 1932-5. Total production: not known. **Chambering:** 22 Short, 22 Long and 22LR rimfire. **Action:** locked by the bolt-handle base turning down into its seat in the receiver.

38.5in overall, 4.15lb empty. 22in barrel, 4-groove rifling: RH, concentric. Single shot only. Fixed open rear sight. 1080 fps with 40-grain bullet.

Made in take-down form, this had a plain straight-comb half-stock with a pistol grip. The front sight was a plain bead; swivels lay beneath the butt and the short rounded forend.

SIMILAR GUNS

Model 20 rifle, 1933-5. A better version of the Model 10, this had a 24in barrel and weighed about 4.5lb. The stock had an additional finger groove in the forend, but the open sights were retained.

Model 30 rifle, 1933-5. This had a 24in barrel, and an empty weight of just 4.5lb. The plain half-stock had a straight-comb butt with a pistol grip and a finger groove in the forend. A peep-type rear sight was used in conjunction with a simple bead at the muzzle.

Model 40 rifle, 1933-5. Otherwise essentially similar to the Model 30, this had a tube magazine beneath the barrel and weighed about 5lb. Cartridge capacity was 16 22LR rounds.

MODEL 14 SPORTING RIFLE

Dating from 1934-5, with 24in barrels, these 22-caliber single shot take-down rifles weighed about 5.25lb. The rear sight was a peep, and the front sight was a hooded ramped blade. The half-stock had a plain straight-comb butt and a broad beavertail forend.

SIMILAR GUNS

Model 34 rifle, 1934-5. Sharing the 24in barrel of the Model 14, this weighed 5.5lb. The half-stock had a straight-comb butt, a plain pistol grip, and a finger groove in the forend. Sights comprised a peep and a hooded ramped blade.

Model 44 rifle, 1934-5. This was a 16-shot 22LR tube-magazine repeater with a plain pistol grip half-stock and a broad forend. A peep-type rear sight was fitted, and the 24in barrel gave a weight of 6lb.

MODEL 25 SPORTING RIFLE

Made by O.F. Mossberg & Sons, of New Haven, Connecticut, 1935-6. Total production: not known. **Chambering:** 22 Short, 22 Long and 22LR rimfire. **Action:** as Model 10, above.

40.6in overall, 5.07lb empty. 24in barrel, 4-groove rifling: RH, concentric. Single shot only. Aperture-type rear sight. 1080 fps with 40-grain bullet.

The sights of this simple junior gun comprised a peep and a hooded ramped blade. The plain pistol grip half-stock had a broad forend with a rounded tip; swivels lay beneath the butt and forend.

SIMILAR GUNS

Model 35 Target Grade rifle, 1935-7. Chambered only for the 22LR rimfire round, this had a heavy 26in barrel and a more robust stock than its predecessors—with a cheekpiece on the straight-comb butt, and a deep forend with angular shoulders ahead of the trigger guard and directly behind the barrel band. Weight was about 8.3lb. The Mossberg No. 4 micrometer sight on the rear of the receiver could be supplemented with a telescope sight in a clamp-type side mount, raising weight to 9.5lb.

Model 42 rifle, 1935-7. Another of the take-down designs, this had a seven-round box magazine ahead of the trigger guard. It was 42in long, had a 24in barrel and weighed about 5.1lb. Peep-type rear sights and ramped-blade front sights were standard. A left-hand action was sold as the 'Model L-42'.

Model 43 rifle, 1937. Identified by a combination of the stamped-strip trigger guard and the deep forend, with an angular step immediately behind the front swivel, this retained the seven-round box magazine. The trigger could be adjusted externally, a four-position front swivel was provided, and the Lyman No. 57MS micrometer rear sight was used in conjunction with a No. 17A tunnel sight at the muzzle.

Model 45 rifle, 1935-7. Essentially similar to the Model 42, this take-down gun had a tube magazine beneath the barrel—increasing capacity to 15 22LR rounds. The plain half-stock had a pistol grip and a slender rounded forend. A Mossberg aperture sight lay on the back of the receiver, with a hooded ramped blade at the muzzle, but a spring-leaf unit was also supplied. The guns were 42.5in long, had 24in barrels and weighed 6.7lb.

Model 46 rifle, 1935-7. This had a heavy target-style stock with a cheekpiece on the butt and an angular shoulder in the forend ahead of the take-down screw; a Mossberg No. 4 micrometer sight was also fitted to the back of the receiver. Guns of this type were 44.5in long, had 26in barrels and weighed 7.5lb.

Model 46T rifle. A minor variant of the Model 46 with a heavier stock, this weighed about 8.3lb.

MODEL 25A SPORTING RIFLE

This introduced the shortened 'Master Action', with a bolt handle which lay at the mid-point of the trigger guard. A lighter cocking piece was fitted (the 'Speed Lock') and a safety catch was added on the upper tang.

SIMILAR GUNS

Model 35A rifle, 1937-8. A modified form of the Model 35, this was often fitted (35A-LS) with Lyman No. 57MS back and No. 17A front sights instead of Mossberg patterns.

Model 42A rifle, 1937-8. This was an improved Model 42, also available in a left-hand (L-42A) version.

Model 45A rifle, 1937-8. Derived from the M45, with the new short action, this was also offered with an 'L-45A' left-hand action.

Model 46A rifle, 1937-9. This was an improved form of the Model 46, usually with an additional open rear sight on the barrel; the cheekpiece was saddle-shape instead of oval, and the front swivel was attached beneath the forend instead of on the tip. A left-hand version was known as 'L-46A', while the Model 46A-LS had Lyman No. 57MS (back) and No. 17A (front) sights.

MODEL 26B SPORTING RIFLE

Made by O.F. Mossberg & Sons, of New Haven, Connecticut, 1938-41. Total production: not known. **Action:** as Model 10, above. **Chambering:** 22 Short, 22 Long and 22LR rimfire.

42.3in overall, 5.45lb empty. 26in barrel, 4-groove rifling: RH, concentric. Single shot only. Micrometer aperture rear sight. 1080 fps with 40-grain bullet.

This take-down pattern introduced a new streamlined form of the Master Action, with a small oval ejection port immediately ahead of the curved-shank bolt handle. The stock and fittings were was also modernized, gaining a triangular fillet at the front of the trigger guard and finger-grooves formed in the pistol grip tang of the guard. Swivels lay beneath the butt and forend. A Mossberg No. 4 aperture sight on the receiver supplemented an open spring-leaf on the barrel, with a hooded ramped blade at the muzzle.

SIMILAR GUNS

Model 26C rifle, 1938-41. Mechanically identical with the Model 26B, this lacked the micrometer receiver sight.

Model 35B rifle, 1938-40. This was a single shot version of the Model 44B, built on the streamlined action but otherwise approximating to the earlier '35' series.

Model 42B rifle, 1938-41. Sharing the general characteristics of the Model 42A (q.v.), this had the improved stock with the grooved pistol grip. The box magazine held five rounds, the barrel measured 24in, and empty weight was about 6lb; a micrometer rear sight was standard.

Model 42C rifle, 1938-41. This was simply a Model 42B with open sights.

Model 42M rifle, 1940-1 and 1944. Derived from Model 42B, with a seven-round box magazine and a 23in barrel, this was easily distinguished by its full-length Mannlicher-style stock, with a cheekpiece on the straight-comb butt and a forend made in two parts. The micrometer rear sight was standard. Guns were typically 40.5in long and weighed 6.8lb; a trap in the buttplate could hold a spare magazine.

Model 42MB rifle, 1942-3. This was supplied to the U.S. and British governments for training purposes; identifiable by the design of the stock, it will also often have official property marks. About 50,000 were made.

Model 43B rifle, 1938-9. A variant of the Model 43A, this had the streamlined action, the web-type trigger guard and a grooved pistol grip.

The Mossberg Model 144 target rifle.
Note the aperture sights, the hand stop,
and the finger grooves formed as
part of the rear trigger guard tang.

Model 44B rifle, 1938-41. The best of the pre-war target rifles, this had a heavy half-stock with a cheekpiece and a grooved pistol grip. The 26in barrel gave an overall length of 43in, and a weight of about 8lb without the detachable seven-round box magazine. The rear sight was a Mossberg No. 4 micrometer type, fitted to the back of the receiver, but the front sight was a hooded ramped blade. A four-position swivel appeared beneath the forend.

Model 44US rifle, 1943-9. Used in substantial numbers (53,000?) by the U.S. armed forces during World War II, this was a minor variant of the 44B with a plainer flush-sided stock and an additional swivel beneath the forend. The back-sight bracket was extended, and the top left side of the receiver was tapped and drilled to receive a telescope-sight mount. Post-war guns were made in several versions—'44US(a)' to '44US(d)'— with changes in the extractor, sights and rifling.

Model 45B rifle, 1938-40. Made with a tube magazine beneath the barrel, capable of holding 15-22 rounds (depending on length), this was supplied with an open spring-leaf and finger-screw rear sight.

Model 46B rifle, 1938-40 and 1945-6. This gun had a 26in barrel and a magazine beneath the barrel, capacity duplicating the Model 46 (though postwar guns had a full-length tube capable of holding 20 22LR rounds). The plain half-stock had a cheekpiece on the butt-side, and the Mossberg-type micrometer rear sight was supplemented by an open sight on the barrel. A ramped blade front sight was used.

Model 46BT rifle, 1938-9. A target-shooting version of the 46B, this had a heavy barrel, a deep forend, and weighed 7.8lb.

Model 46M rifle, 1940-1 and 1946-52. Mechanically identical with the Model 46B, this had a full-length stock with a two-part forend; a broad sheet-steel plate, carrying the front swivel, hid the joint. The barrel- and receiver-mounted rear sights were both present. Several changes were made to the extractors and sights after production resumed in 1946.

MODEL 142A SPORTING CARBINE

Made by O.F. Mossberg & Sons, of New Haven, Connecticut, 1949-57.
Total production: not known. **Chambering:** 22 Short, 22 Long and 22LR rimfire. **Action:** generally as Model 10, above.

34.5in overall, 6.03lb empty. 18in barrel, 4-groove rifling: RH, concentric. Detachable box magazine, 7 rounds. 'Peep'-type rear sight. 1080 fps with 40-grain bullet.

This embodied a refinement of the first pre-war 'Master Action', which was better suited to the box magazine than the later compact streamlined design. The base of the pistol grip was rounded and a low Monte Carlo comb was added to the butt; the most unusual feature, however, was a hinged forend which could be pulled down to improve handgrip. The rear sight was a simple aperture design attached to the receiver above the bolt. Guns made prior to 1954 had a 'T'-shape bolt handle, but post-1954 examples reverted to a ball.

SIMILAR GUNS

Model 140B rifle, 1957-8. Distinguished by a 24.5in barrel, a peep-sight on the receiver and a ramped hooded blade at the muzzle, this was otherwise much the same as the 140K.

Model 140K rifle, 1955-8. Guns of this type had a 24.5in barrel, which gave an overall length of about 41in and weight averaging 5.8lb. The spring-leaf rear sight was accompanied by a post at the muzzle, and the Monte Carlo half-stock had a bulbous schnabel tip.

Model 142K carbine, 1953-7. This was a minor variant of the 142A with an open spring-leaf rear sight on the barrel.

Model 144 rifle, 1949-54. A target-shooting derivative of the basic design, this had a 'T'-type bolt handle, a 26in barrel and weighed about 8lb. The half-stock had a straight-comb butt and a handstop beneath the deep forend. A Mossberg No. 4 micrometer aperture sight was used in conjunction with a hooded ramped blade at the muzzle. The standard four-position front swivel was also used.

Model 144LS rifle, 1954-9. Made with a ball-type bolt handle, this had a Lyman No. 57MS rear sight and a Lyman No. 17A tunnel-pattern front sight. It was replaced by the 144LS-A (1960-79), with a Mossberg S130 rear sight, and finally by the 144LS-B (1979-85) with a 27in barrel and a Mossberg S331 sight.

MODEL 146B SPORTING RIFLE

Made from 1949 until 1954, this was a take-down repeater built on a modification of the pre-war short streamlined action. The bolt-handle shank was straight, and the Monte Carlo-type half-stock had a bulbous schnabel tip. The tube magazine, beneath the barrel, could hold 20 22LR or 30 22 Short rimfire cartridges. The gun had a 26in barrel and weighed about 7lb empty. The 146B-A (1954-8) had a dovetail-mounted rear sight.

MODEL 340B SPORTING RIFLE

Made by O.F. Mossberg & Sons, of New Haven, Connecticut, 1958-81 (B and B-A patterns).
Total production: not known. **Chambering:** 22 Short, 22 Long and 22LR rimfire. **Action:** generally as Model 10, above.

34.5in overall, 6.03lb empty. 18in barrel, 4-groove rifling: RH, concentric. Detachable box magazine, 7 rounds. 'Peep'-type rear sight. 1080 fps with 40-grain bullet.

These guns—replacements for the 140 series—had a new action designed to complement the autoloading patterns, though the bolt handle was placed unusually far forward to maintain the position of the magazine. A concealed-hammer firing mechanism was used instead of the previous striker, which gave a much better trigger action than many inexpensive rimfire designs. The half-stock had a Monte Carlo comb and cheekpiece, and a synthetic buttplate was accompanied by a thin white spacer. The Model 340B (1958-60) was replaced by the 340B-A (1960-81), which had a simpler rear sight dovetailed into the barrel-top.

SIMILAR GUNS

Model 320B Boy Scout target rifle, 1960-71. This was a single shot variant of the 340K, with a 24in barrel and an automatic safety system.

Model 320K rifle, 1958-60. A version of the tube-magazine 346K with a removable loading platform suiting it to single shot use, this weighed 5.8lb and had an automatic safety. The Model 320K-A (1960-80) had a simpler rear sight dovetailed into the barrel surface.

The Mossberg Model 340B rifle,
with a peep sight on the receiver top.

Model 321B rifle, 1972-5. Based on the 321K, this had a peep sight on top of the receiver.

Model 321K rifle, 1972-80. This was a single shot version of the Model 341, with a similar good-quality stock.

Model 340K rifle, 1958-60. Essentially similar to the Model 340B described in the text, this had simple open sights. The 340K-A (1960-81) had the rear sight dovetailed into the barrel.

Model 340M rifle, 1970-1 only. This had an 18.5in barrel and a full-length stock.

Model 341 rifle. Made from 1972 onward, this deluxe pattern had a seven-round box magazine, a 24in barrel and a weight of 6.5lb; the rear sight was an open spring-leaf type. The Monte Carlo-style walnut half-stock had impressed checkering on the pistol grip and forend. Swivels lay beneath the stock.

Model 342K carbine, 1958-60. A short version of the 340K, with open sights and an 18in barrel, this lacked a cheekpiece even though the butt retained a low Monte Carlo comb. The front section of the forend could be pivoted downward to improve grip, and the swivels were placed on the left side of the stock. The Model 340K-A (1960-71) had its rear sight dovetailed into the barrel.

Model 344 rifle, 1985. This was the last version of the box-magazine series, made only in small numbers.

Model 344K carbine, 1985. A short version of the 344, this had an 18.5in barrel and a conventional half-stock.

Model 346B rifle, 1958-60. Mechanically similar to the 340, but with a tube magazine beneath the 24in barrel, this could fire 18 22LR rounds or 25 in 22 Short. The Monte Carlo half-stock had a cheekpiece, and a peep sight was attached to the top rear of the receiver. A few 346B-A rifles were made in 1960-7 with a supplementary open rear sight dovetailed into the barrel.

Model 346K rifle, 1958-60. This was simply a version of the 346B with an open spring-leaf rear sight on the barrel. The Model 346K-A (1960-7) had a simple dovetailed rear sight.

MODEL 640K SPORTING RIFLE
Also known as 'Chuckster'

Made by O.F. Mossberg & Sons, of New Haven, Connecticut, 1959-84 (all types).

Total production: not known. **Chambering:** 22 Winchester Magnum rimfire. **Action:** generally as Model 10, above. 6.05lb empty.

24in barrel, 4-groove rifling: RH, concentric. Detachable box magazine, 5 rounds. Spring-leaf and finger-wheel rear sight. 2000 fps with 40-grain bullet.

Based on the 340-series action—suitably strengthened for powerful ammunition—this rifle had a Monte Carlo-type half-stock with a pistol grip and a cheekpiece, but lacked checkering. The front sight was a simple bead. The original 640 was replaced in 1960 by the K-A version, with a simple open rear sight held to the barrel with a dovetail groove.

SIMILAR GUNS

Model 620K rifle, 1959-60. A single shot Chuckster, this was made only in small numbers. The K-A variant (1960-8) had a simple rear sight dovetailed into the barrel-top.

Model 640KS rifle, 1960-4. Distinguished by a select walnut stock and hand-cut checkering on the pistol grip and forend, this deluxe pattern also had gold plating on the trigger and sights.

Model 640M rifle, 1971 only. The full-length Monte Carlo-style Mannlicher-style stock of this gun was made in a single piece of walnut and had a steel forend cap. The pistol grip and forend were checkered.

Model 642K carbine, 1960-8. Made with an 18.5in barrel, this had a distinctive pivoting forend extension made of black Tenite.

MODEL 800 SPORTING RIFLE

Made by O.F. Mossberg & Sons, Inc., North Haven, Connecticut, 1966-7 (original type).

The Mossberg Model 321K rimfire sporting rifle.

Total production: not known. **Chambering options:** 222 Remington, 22-250 Remington, 6.5mm Remington Magnum, 243 Winchester, 308 Winchester or 350 Remington Magnum. **Action:** locked by six lugs on the bolt head rotating into the receiver behind the chamber, and by the bolt handle turning down into its seat.

DATA FOR A TYPICAL EXAMPLE

Chambering: 243 Winchester, rimless. 42in overall, 6.5lb empty. 22in barrel, 6-groove rifling; RH, concentric. Internal box magazine, 4 rounds. Folding-leaf rear sight. 3500 fps with 80-grain bullet.

Louis Seecamp and Carl Benson began work in 1963 on a new sporting rifle intended, so it is said, to provide Montgomery, Ward & Co., Inc., with a suitable centerfire pattern to sell alongside Mossberg-made Western Field-brand rimfires. Design work was completed in 1965. Production of the Model 800 began in 1966 in 243 and 308 Winchester only.

The rifle had an oddly shaped bolt handle—bent forward above the trigger—and two rows of three lugs on a sub-diameter bolt head; a safety slider lay on the streamlined bolt shroud. The short extractor blade was controlled by a sprung plunger in the bolt head, and the magazine floorplate release lay ahead of the trigger guard.

The earliest guns had walnut pistol grip half-stocks with Monte Carlo combs, the synthetic grip cap and buttplate being accompanied by white-line spacers. The impressed skip-line checkering incorporated a deer-head on the pistol grip and a running buck on the forend.

Model 800A rifle, 1967-78. This was simply a post-1967 designation of the 308-caliber Model 800. Rifles sold with optical sights had an additional 'SM' suffix. The connection between the firing-pin components changed in 1969-70 from lugs to a splined lug and cross-pin.

Model 800AM rifle, 1969-72. Simply a 308 Model 800A, this introduced a 20in barrel, a straight spatulate bolt handle, and a full-length stock. Comparatively few were made.

Model 800AVT rifle, 1971-8. Intended for varmint or target shooting, this was a variant of the Model 800A with a 24in barrel and additional sight bases.

Model 800B rifle, 1967-78. Used from the late 1960s onward, this designation hid a 243-caliber Model 800, with an additional 'SM' suffix if the rifle had an optical sight.

Model 800BM rifle, 1969-72. Made only in small numbers, identified by a straight spatulate bolt handle and a full-length stock, this was a short-barreled Model 800B.

Model 800BVT rifle, 1971-8. This dual-purpose varmint/target shooting rifle was simply a 243-caliber Model 800B with a 24in barrel and additional sight bases.

Model 800C rifle, 1967-78. The introduction of a 22-250 Remington chambering in 1967 forced a change in the designations of the basic Model 800 (see 'A' and 'B' patterns). Rifles sold with optical sights usually had an additional 'SM' suffix.

Model 800CM rifle, 1969-72. A short-lived 22-250 pattern, this introduced a 20in barrel, a straight spatulate bolt handle, and a full-length stock.

Model 800CVT rifle, 1971-8. A dual-purpose derivative of the 22-250 Model 800C, this varmint/target rifle with a 24in barrel and additional optical sight bases.

Model 800D rifle (i), 1968-9. A few rifles were made in 350 Remington, but the chambering was soon abandoned.

Model 800D rifle (ii) or 'Super Grade', 1971-3. This deluxe rifle had a select walnut stock, with a rollover comb, a rosewood pistol grip cap and a rosewood forend tip. It was soon replaced by the Pedersen series (below).

Model 800E rifle, 1968-9. This designation was apparently applied to a few guns made for the 6.5mm Remington Magnum cartridge.

Model 800F rifle, 1970. The advent of a 222 chambering created this variant of the 800 series, but production was very limited.

Model 800V rifle ('Varmint'), 1968-78. This had a heavy 24in barrel and additional optical sight bases. The designation was sub-

The Mossberg Model 800 rifle.

The Mossberg RM-7 rifle.

sequently changed to 'VT' ('Varmint/Target'), which, confusingly, could be added to existing designations—e.g., Model 800BVT was a varmint rifle in 243 Winchester.

MODEL 810 SPORTING RIFLE
Made by O.F. Mossberg & Sons, Inc., North Haven, Connecticut, 1972-8.

Total production: not known. **Chambering options:** 270 Winchester, 7mm Remington Magnum, 30-06 or 338 Winchester Magnum. **Action:** locked by rotating four lugs on the bolt head into the receiver walls behind the chamber.

DATA FOR A TYPICAL 810A

Chambering: 30-06, rimless. 42in overall, 7.75lb empty. 22in barrel, 8-groove rifling; RH, concentric. Detachable box magazine, 4 rounds. Folding-leaf rear sight. 2800 fps with 165-grain bullet.

Dating from 1972, the Model 810 shared the elegant lines of the Model 800, but its bolt had twin lugs in tandem and a conventional firing pin assembly. The adjustable trigger was made in a self-contained unit, and the trigger guard bow/magazine floorplate assembly was steel instead of nylon. The elegant half-stock had a low Monte Carlo comb and a rounded forend, with checkering on the pistol grip and forend. The buttplate and pistol grip cap were accompanied by white spacers.

The introduction of a top-loading magazine in 1975 led to a noticeable reduction in the popularity of the box-magazine guns.

THE GUNS

Note: Rifles sold with factory-fitted optical sights were all given additional 'SM' suffixes—e.g., 'Model 810BHSM' (or, alternatively 'BSMH') was a 7mm Remington Magnum example with optical sights and an internal magazine.

Model 810A rifle, 1972-7. This was the standard 30-06 chambering, with a four-round box magazine.

Model 810AH rifle, 1973-8. Derived from the 810A, this had an internal magazine and a hinged floorplate.

Model 810B rifle, 1972-7. Otherwise identical with the Model 810A, but in 7mm Remington Magnum chambering, this had a three-round magazine.

Model 810BH rifle, 1973-8. This was a minor variant of the 810B (q.v.) with an internal magazine and a hinged floorplate.

Model 810C rifle, 1973-7. Chambered for the 270 Winchester cartridge, this gun had a four-round box magazine.

Model 810CH rifle, 1973-8. Distinguished by an internal magazine and a hinged floorplate, this was otherwise similar to the Model 810C.

Model 810D rifle, 1973-7. Similar to the basic Model 810, apart from a 24in barrel, this chambered the 338 Winchester Magnum cartridge and had a three-round box magazine.

Model 810DH rifle, 1973-8. This was no more than an 810D with an internal top-loading magazine and a hinged floorplate.

RM-7 SPORTING RIFLE
Made by O.F. Mossberg & Sons, Inc., North Haven, Connecticut, 1978-84.

Total production: not known. **Chambering:** 30-06, rimless. **Action:** generally as 810 series, above. 44in overall, 7.45lb empty.

22in barrel, 8-groove rifling; RH, concentric. Internal spool magazine, 5 rounds. Folding-leaf rear sight. 3020 fps with 175-grain bullet.

Introduced to replace the earlier 800/810 rifles, this retained the multi-lug lock. However, the shape of the bolt handle was revised and the bolt shroud was squared. A three-position safety was fitted. The 30-06 RM-7A had a 22in barrel and a five-round magazine, whereas the 7mm Remington Magnum RM-7B had a 24in barrel and a magazine capacity of only four. The walnut stock had a straight comb, checkering on the pistol grip and forend, a black plastic pistol grip cap, and a rubber buttplate. Swivels lay beneath the butt and forend. The RM-7 was abandoned in 1984, owing to lack of success and Mossberg's decision to purchase Sako-action rifles from Smith & Wesson.

PEDERSEN SERIES

The Pedersen Custom Guns Division of Mossberg promoted deluxe versions of the Model 810 (1973-5) as the 'Model 3000'. Grade I had selected woodwork, engraving, silver inlays and a choice of buttplates; Grade II was similar, but lacked the inlays; and Grade III, the most basic, also lacked engraving.

WESTERN FIELD SERIES

Sold by Montgomery, Ward & Co., Inc., of Chicago, these own brand guns included a range of bolt- and lever-action rifles.

THE GUNS

Western Field Model 765. This was a 30-06 Mossberg 810 with a walnut-stained beech stock. Checkering was omitted, the Monte Carlo comb was very shallow, and the buttplate was ribbed plastic.

Western Field Model 775. An original 800-type bolt-action Mossberg, this chambered the 243 Winchester cartridge.

Western Field Model 776. Apart from the chambering—308 Winchester—this was identical with the Model 775.

Western Field Model 782. Sometimes mistakenly listed as 'Model 732', this was a Model 810 in 30-06 or 7mm Remington Magnum, often with distinctive 'Mountain Top' skip-line checkering on the pistol grip and forend.

Western Field Model 786. This was simply a minor variant of the 30-06 Mossberg RM-7A. The magazine held five cartridges.

Western Field Model 787. Little more than an RM-7B, this chambered the 7mm Remington Magnum cartridge and had the customary four-round magazine.

SAKO PATTERNS

Mossberg purchased the remaining Smith & Wesson (q.v.) Model 1500 rifles in 1985, selling them for several years. The Model 1500 Mountaineer and Varmint Deluxe, plus the Model 1700LS, are described in the Smith & Wesson section.

SIMILAR GUNS

Model 1550 rifle. Introduced in 1986, with a detachable box magazine, this chambered 243 Winchester, 270 Winchester or 30-06 cartridges.

Model 1500 Mountaineer rifle. 'Grade I' appeared in 1987 with a straight-comb hardwood stock, guns with walnut Monte Carlo stocks being classed as 'Grade II'. Open sights became optional on both grades.

• Mossberg, lever-action type

MODEL 400 SPORTING RIFLE
Also known as 'Palomino'

Made by O.F. Mossberg & Sons, of New Haven, Connecticut, 1959-64.
Total production: not known. **Chambering:** 22 Short, 22 Long and 22LR rimfire, interchangeably. **Action:** locked by the wedging the bolt behind the breech with the tip of the operating lever.

41in overall, 5.5lb empty. 24in barrel, 4-groove rifling: RH, concentric. Tube magazine beneath barrel, 15-20 rounds depending on cartridge. Spring-leaf and elevator rear sight. 1080 fps with 40-grain bullet.

This rifle had a short slab-sided receiver separating the Monte Carlo-pattern butt from the short squared forend. Checkering

The Mossberg Model 479 carbine, with a pistol grip butt.

appeared on the pistol grip, while thin white spacers accompanied the synthetic pistol grip cap and shoulder plate. The finger-loop underlever was curved to the contours of the pistol grip. Model 400-A rifles had a a fixed rear sight dovetailed to the barrel.

SIMILAR GUN

Model 402 carbine, 1961-71. Much more popular than the rifle, this had an 18.5in barrel (20in after 1964) and a swivel-carrying band around the forend. It weighed merely 4.8lb with an empty magazine.

MODEL 472 SPORTING RIFLE

Made by O.F. Mossberg & Sons, Inc., North Haven, Connecticut, 1974-9.

Total production: not known. **Chambering options:** 30-30 Winchester or 35 Remington. **Action:** locked by a vertically sliding bar intercepting the bolt as the action closed.

DATA FOR A TYPICAL EXAMPLE

Chambering: 30-30 Winchester, rimmed. 38.25in overall, 6.85lb empty (straight-wrist butt). 20in barrel, 8-groove rifling; RH, concentric. Tube magazine beneath barrel, 6 rounds. Spring-leaf and elevator rear sight. 2410 fps with 150-grain bullet.

Introduced in 1972, largely the work of Carl Benson, this incorporated a locking bolt inspired by the Browning-designed Winchesters (q.v.). Unlike the Winchesters, however, the trigger mechanism is attached to the operating lever and a hammer-block safety lever was fitted to the rear left side of the receiver. The side-ejecting Model 472 superficially resembled the Marlin 336, with a loading gate on the side of the receiver and a prominent operating-lever pivot.

THE GUNS

Model 472PC carbine, 1972-8. Identified by a pistol grip butt, this had a 20in barrel and a full-length six-round magazine.

Model 472PR rifle, 1972-8. The basic gun in the series had a pistol grip butt, a 24in barrel and a short five-round magazine.

Model 472SB carbine ('Brush Gun'), 1973-80. Identified by a straight-wrist butt, this had an 18in barrel and a full-length five round magazine. An 'A' suffix indicated a 30-30 gun, 'B' examples chambering 35 Remington.

Model 472SC carbine, 1972-6. This was simply a carbine with a straight-wrist butt.

Model 472SR rifle, 1972-6. A variant of the standard rifle, this had a straight-wristed butt.

Model 479PCA carbine, 1983-5. This 30-30 carbine had a 20in barrel and a six-round magazine.

Model 479PR rifle, 1980-2. Little more than an improved Model 472, this had a hammer-blocking safety bolt. It could be obtained in the same chamberings as the 472, with a similar pistol grip butt.

Model 479SR rifle, 1980-2. Except for the straight wrist butt, this was identical with the 479PR version.

PEDERSEN SERIES

The Pedersen Custom Guns Division of Mossberg marketed a deluxe version of the Model 472 (1975 only) as the 'Model 4700', distinguished by selected woodwork and a broad or semi-beavertail forend.

WESTERN FIELD SERIES

Sold by Montgomery, Ward & Co., Inc., of Chicago, these own brand guns included the Western Field 771, 772 and 778—respectively, a Mossberg Model 472 with straight-wrist butt, a 472 with pistol grip butt, and a standard 479.

• Mossberg, slide-action type

MODEL K SPORTING RIFLE

Made by O.F. Mossberg & Sons, of New Haven, Connecticut, 1922-31.

Total production: not known. **Chambering:** 22 Short, 22 Long and 22LR rimfire. **Action:** locked by rotating lugs on the bolt into the receiver walls on the closing stroke of the operating handle.

About 39in overall, 5.05lb empty. 22in barrel, 4-groove rifling: RH, concentric. Tube magazine beneath barrel, 14-20 rounds depending on cartridge. Spring-leaf and elevator rear sight. 1080 fps with 40-grain bullet.

This had a ribbed slide-handle beneath the barrel, operating through the action bar exposed on the right side of the breech. The straight-wrist butt customarily had a crescent-shape shoulder plate.

SIMILAR GUNS

Model M rifle, 1928-31. Mechanically identical with the Model R, this had a 24in octagon barrel and a pistol grip butt. It weighed about 5.6lb.

Model S rifle, 1927-31. This was a version of the Model K with a 19.75in barrel and a short tube magazine. It is very rarely seen.

• Mullins

John Mullins of Fariston, Kentucky, received four U.S. Patents in 1886-96 to protect 'magazine firearms'. These included a 30-caliber bolt-action rifle tested by the U.S. Army in 1891, which had a three-round magazine and weighed 8.31lb empty. It was not successful enough to survive the initial trials, and very little is known about its construction.

• National

These guns were made in accordance with a patent granted in December 1861 to Daniel Moore of Brooklyn (no. 33,847), which protected the design of a two-piece breechblock. When the underlever was pulled down, the back part of the block dropped down to allow the front part to move back above it to expose the chamber. Though a few guns of this type were presumably made during the American Civil War, the perfected pattern was based on patents granted in 1864-5 to Alfred Bergen and David Williamson. Gun No. 40 tested by the U.S. Army in 1865 was a 50-caliber carbine of Williamson type, but it is believed that sporting rifles were also made.

NATIONAL CARBINE

Made by the National Arms Co., Brooklyn, New York, about 1865-8.

Quantity: a few hundred? **Chambering:** 50-70, rim- and centerfire. **Action:** Locked by wedging the two-part breechblock in place behind the chamber.

39.7in overall, 6.8lb empty. 22.1in barrel, 3 grooves; RH twist, concentric. Single-shot only. Leaf-type rear sight graduated to 800yd. Performance not known. No bayonet.

The National carbine resembled the Peabody (q.v.) externally, with a two-piece stock and a half-length forend held by a single band. However, it was leaner, had a very slender hammer shank curving markedly forward, and was fitted with a box-lock integral with the receiver instead of a separate back-action pattern. The case-hardened receiver contained a breechblock pivoted to the underlever doubling as the trigger guard. When the underlever was pulled down, a slot in the lever body, working in conjunction with a transverse pin in the locking piece, lowered the latter far enough to allow the breechblock to move straight back to expose the chamber. The action was patented by Alfred Bergen & David Williamson in November 1864 (U.S. patent 45,202), and then improved by Williamson alone in March 1865 (46,977).

• National Ordnance

Based in Southern El Monte, California, this company advertised standard and folding-stock M1 Carbines (in 30 or 223 Remington) in the early 1970s. The major parts are believed to have been made in Japan, receivers being investment castings instead

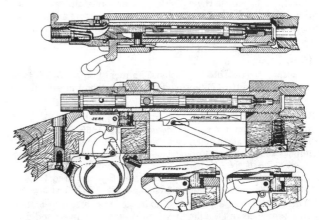

A typical Newton rifle.

of the forged-steel versions favored by Universal. Many of the other parts seem to have been refurbished war surplus. However, the quantities involved do not seem to have been large.

• Navy Arms

The Navy Arms Company of Ridgefield, New Jersey, is best known for its reproduction firearms, particularly the superb replicas of Sharps, Henry, Winchester and other longarms made in Italy. The company also promoted 45-70 conversions of the military Thai ('Siamese') Mauser rifles in the mid-1970s. These had 24in or 26in barrels, weighed 8.2-8.5lb, and had three-round magazines. Bolt handles were generally straight; the plain pistol grip stock had a Monte Carlo comb; and a Williams ramp rear sight was standard. A carbine based on the same action had an 18in barrel, a straight-comb pistol grip half-stock, and a bolt handle which turned downward. It weighed 7.5lb.

A 22LR rifle made in Turkey, based on the pre-1945 German KKW (see **'Germany: Mauser, bolt-action'**), was introduced in 1991. Known as the 'TU-KKW', it had a five-round magazine, a 26in barrel, and an overall length of about 44in. Weight averaged 8lb. A similar TU-33/40 gun (1992-5) was made with a 20.8in barrel, approximating to the original Gew. 33/40 'mountain carbine' of World War II.

• Needham

Patented in the U.S.A. in May 1867 by Englishmen Joseph & George Needham, this rifle relied on a block which swung forward out of the right side of the breech on a vertical pivot. A gun of this type was tested by the U.S. Army in 1867, but rejected on the grounds that locking the block simply with the wedge-shaped hammer nose was not enough. However, shortly after the end of the Civil War, substantial quantities of Springfield rifle-muskets were converted to the Needham system by Alfred Jenks & Son of Bridesburg, Pennsylvania. These guns are said to have seen militia use, but attained greater notoriety as the 'Bridesburg Rifles' acquired by the pro-Irish Fenian Brotherhood for the first attempt to invade Canada in 1866.

• New England Firearms

This trading name is used by H&R 1871, Inc., formed to succeed to some of the assets of the defunct Harrington & Richardson company.

HANDI-RIFLE

Derived from the well-established break-open Harrington & Richardson 150 series, operated by a press-catch on the right side of the frame alongside the exposed central hammer, this 1989 introduction is currently available in 22 Hornet, 223 Remington, 243 Winchester (announced in 1992), 270 Winchester (1994), 280 Remington (1994), 30-30 Winchester, 30-06, 44 Magnum (1995) and 45-70. The guns have 22in barrels, apart from the 26in pattern associated with the 280 Remington chambering.

S I M I L A R   G U N S

Survivor rifle. Introduced in 1996 in 223 Remington and 357 Magnum only, this has a distinctive black plastic thumbhole-style butt and a choice of blue or nickel finish. Storage compartments in the butt and forend can hold ammunition, cleaning equipment and survival gear. Survivors are about 36in long, have a 22in barrel and weigh 6lb.

• Newton

Charles Newton is best known for his cartridges, but deserves recognition as the father of the modern high-velocity sporting rifle. The earliest guns offered by the Newton Rifle Company were built around Mauser actions imported from Germany, but the inventor's thoughts soon turned to an improved design of his own.

The first Newton action had a turning bolt with multiple locking lugs on the head and two auxiliary or safety lugs on the body ahead of the bolt handle. Careful design ensured that the lugs aligned when the breech was open, allowing an unusually slender receiver bridge to be used. The failure of the Newton sporting rifle was due largely to the advent of World War I, though Newton soon proved to be a poor businessman. His second venture fared little better, and, by 1929, he had eschewed the turning-bolt action in favor of a straight-pull pattern. The LeverBolt Rifle Company had been formed in New Haven to exploit the new rifle, but Newton's death in 1932 brought work to an end.

SPORTING RIFLE

Made by the Newton Arms Company, Buffalo, New York, 1916-18.
Total production: 2500-2750? Chambering options: 256, 30, 33 or 35 Newton. **Action:** locked by seven lugs on the bolt head and two on the body engaging recesses in the receiver.
DATA FOR A TYPICAL 30-CALIBRE EXAMPLE
44.1in overall, 6.85lb empty. 24in barrel, 5-groove rifling; RH, polygonal. Internal box magazine loaded from a stripper-clip, 5 rounds. Standing-block rear sight with folding leaves. About 2950 fps with 172-grain bullet.

The 256-, 30- and 35-caliber Newton rifles were announced in April 1916. They had slender stocks with checkering on the pistol grip of the straight-comb butt, and a schnabel tip to the slender forend. A three-position radial safety lay on the right side of the bolt plug, and the detachable magazine floorplate helped to retain the barreled action. The first Newtons had an adjustable set trigger with an auxiliary lever in the back of the trigger guard, and were often fitted with an adjustable column-type sight on the cocking piece. Bolt handles were low enough to clear a telescope.

When the Newton company was liquidated in April 1918, only about half of the 4000 parts-sets had been completed. About 350 rifles were completed and sold in 1919 by the Newton Arms Company liquidators; the inventor, meanwhile, had formed the Charles Newton Rifle Corporation.

A few hundred rifles were subsequently made from old parts, which had been sold to a machine-tool refurbisher by the liquidators. These guns were advertised in 1920 as products of a spurious 'Newton Arms Corporation' until an injunction was granted in July. Quality ranged from barely acceptable to utterly abysmal.

SPORTING RIFLE
Second or 'Buffalo Newton' pattern

Made by the Charles Newton Rifle Corporation, Buffalo, New York, 1921-2; and by the Buffalo Newton Rifle Company, Buffalo, New York (about 1923-4), and New Haven, Connecticut (1925-9).
Total production: 2500 in Buffalo and 400-500 in New Haven.
Chambering options: 256 Newton, 30 Newton, 35 Newton or 30-06.
Action: locked by multiple lugs on the bolt head and one lug on the body turning into seats in the receiver.

A longitudinal section of the Buffalo Newton action.

44.05in overall, 7.42lb empty. 24in barrel, 4-groove rifling; RH, concentric. Internal box magazine, 5 rounds. Standing-block rear sight with folding leaves. About 3100 fps with 123-grain bullet.

This was a modified version of the 1916-type sporter, with an interrupted-thread on the bolt head—easier to machine than the previous lugs—and a greatly simplified cocking piece. The sear doubled as a bolt stop, a prominent recoil bolt ran through the stock below the receiver bridge, and the bolt handle was cranked backward. A reversed set-trigger lever was also distinctive. The Buffalo Newton company was formed in 1922 to promote the new rifle. However, the guns were rarely as well made as the previous pattern and sales suffered accordingly. Trading ceased in 1930.

LEVERBOLT RIFLE

Newton's last design, this was only made in prototype form—though the LeverBolt Rifle Company of New Haven, Connecticut, advertised it in several proprietary Newton chamberings (256, 280, 30 and 35) as well as the obligatory 30-06. The rifle combined a conventional two-lug bolt with a rocking lever, which was substituted for a bolt handle. The project was abandoned when Newton died.

• Opus

Opus Sporting Arms of Long Beach, California, built sporting rifles on the Winchester Model 70 action in 1987-8. Available in standard or deluxe grades, Opus One (6.75lb) had a 24in barrel chambered for the 243, 270 and 308 Winchester cartridges; Opus Two (26in barrel, 7.25-7.5lb) handled the 7mm Remington and 300 Winchester Magnum rounds; and Opus Three, which weighed 10.25lb, could be supplied with a 22in barrel in 375 H&H Magnum or 458 Winchester Magnum.

• Page-Lewis

The Page-Lewis Arms Company began trading immediately after the end of World War I, but was purchased by the Stevens Arms Co. in 1926. For a few years, however, it made substantial quantities of a radial-block rifle patented in April 1923 by George Lewis, a gunsmith who had worked for Stevens prior to 1914. Production began before the patent was granted; the earliest examples were apparently marked 'PAT APP. FOR'.

MODEL A TARGET RIFLE

Made by the Page-Lewis Arms Company, Chicopee Falls, Massachusetts, about 1921-6.

Total production: 15,000 (all types)? **Chambering:** 22 Long Rifle, rimfire. **Action:** locked by propping the swinging breechblock behind the chamber with the operating lever.

33.7in overall, 3.6lb empty. 20in barrel, 4-groove rifling; RH, concentric. Single shot only. Standing-block rear sight. 1075 fps with 40-grain bullet.

This was built on an action fabricated from steel plate, with the lockwork contained within the breechblock. A single coil spring was used to drive the hammer and the trigger, the butt was held by a large longitudinal bolt, and a take-down bolt lay beneath the frame ahead of the trigger guard. The guns had a round barrel, a straight-wrist walnut butt, and a short rounded forend.

SIMILAR GUNS

Model B Sharpshooter rifle. Distinguished by a 24in barrel and a weight of about 4.5lb, this had open sights and a short forend.

Model C Olympic rifle. Sharing the action of the other guns in the series, this had a 24in barrel, a folding aperture sight on the tang and a Beach combination bead-and-globe/blade unit at the muzzle. The forend was extended.

• Palmer

The carbines patented by William Palmer of New York City in December 1863 (41,017) were the first bolt-action patterns firing metal-case ammunition to be adopted in the U.S.A.

PALMER CARBINE

Made by E.G. Lamson & Co., Windsor, Vermont, 1865.

Total production: about 1000. **Chambering:** 56-50 Spencer, rimfire. **Action:** locked by rotating an interrupted screw on the rear of the bolt into recesses in the receiver.

37.31in overall, about 7lb empty. 20.15in barrel, 5-groove rifling; RH, concentric. Single-shot only. Open leaf rear sight. About 950 fps? No bayonet.

The Palmer had a collar-type extractor and a spring-loaded ejector, which elevated it far above many other carbines used during the Civil War. Ignition was supplied by a conventional external

side-hammer. The one-piece half-stock had a straight wrist and a single band. One thousand guns were ordered on 20th June 1864, but, as none had been delivered before mid-June 1865, they were too late to see action in the American Civil War and were sold at auction shortly afterward. 'Gun No. 43' in the U.S. Army trials of 1865 was an unaltered Civil War pattern.

• Parkhurst-Lee

A few fully-stocked rifles and even fewer half-stocked carbines were made by the Remington Arms Company in 1899-1900. Protected by a patent granted to Edward Parkhurst in May 1898 as an improvement on the M1895 Lee straight-pull Navy rifle, the guns had two opposed lugs on the front of the bolt and—originally—a Mauser-type extractor collar. The new combination bolt-stop/ejector, patented by William Larraway in 1897, was accompanied by improvements to the safety.

• Peabody

This pivoting-block action was developed in the U.S.A., but proved to be more popular abroad. The original rifle was patented in July 1862 by Henry Peabody of Boston. A slot under the breechblock opened the action in conjunction with pins on the breech lever. The mechanism was very strong, as it took much of the strain of firing on the rear inner face of the receiver and the position of the breechblock pivot pin prevented the action opening prematurely.

The patent was reissued in 1866, with a rider that pin-and-slot depressors were only one operating method. Peabody then added a lever-and-slot alternative and a pivoting extractor.

Peabody rifles had received great praise from the U.S. Army in 1865. However, though they were much more efficient than the Allin-type Springfield, they could not be created from existing rifle muskets. The deep receiver, two-piece stock and back-action lock required complete re-tooling.

TRIALS-PATTERN MILITARY CARBINE

Made by the Providence Tool Co., Providence, Rhode Island, about 1865-7.

Total production: very few. **Chambering:** 56-50 Spencer, rimfire. **Action:** locked by wedging the pivoting breechblock in place behind the chamber.

39.5in overall, 6.6lb empty. 20.2in barrel, 3 grooves; RH twist, concentric. Single-shot only. Leaf-type rear sight graduated to 800yd. 1150 fps with 350-grain bullet? No bayonet.

Entered in the U.S. Army trials of 1865 on behalf of Henry Peabody of Boston, carbine-length Guns No. 41 and No. 42 both embodied the dropping-block breech system patented in 1862. They had two-piece stocks, with half-length forends held by a single sprung band, and a sturdy box-like color case-hardened receiver containing the breechblock. Ignition was provided by the hammer of a back-action lock hitting a striker plate in the breechblock, and a folding-leaf rear sight lay on the barrel between the band and the breech. No. 42 carried a sling ring and bar assembly on a round-cornered rectangular plate, set into the left side of the wrist above the trigger.

EARLY GUNS

In an 1870-vintage broadsheet, the Providence Tool Company claimed to be making a standard 45-caliber side-hammer or 'Roumanian Model'; the similar 43-caliber 'Spanish Model' with a spiral firing-pin retractor spring; a 'Self-Cocking Gun' with a top-lever depressor and a coil-pattern firing-pin spring; and the 42-caliber (Russian) Peabody-Wessely, a self-cocking design with an internal hammer.

MILITARY MODEL RIFLE

Made by the Providence Tool Company, Providence, Rhode Island, 1867-73.

Total production: not known. **Chambering options:** see notes. **Action:** as trials carbine, above.

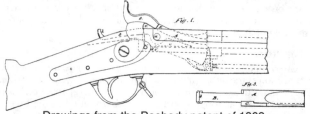

Drawings from the Peabody patent of 1862.

A typical sidehammer Peabody sporting rifle.

DATA FOR A TYPICAL MUSKET
Chambering: 45-70, rimmed. 51.5in overall, 8.95lb empty. 33in barrel, 3-groove rifling; RH, concentric. Leaf-and-slider rear sight graduated to 1200yd. 1275 fps with 405-grain bullet. M1855 socket bayonet.

Catalogues printed in 1871 indicated that military-style muskets, stocked to the muzzle, were available in 43 (11mm Spanish), 45-70 and 50-70 centerfire, plus 50-60 rimfire; military carbines were made in 45- and 50-caliber. The guns were never popular in the U.S.A., though some were purchased on behalf of state militia in Connecticut and Massachusetts. They had straight-wrist butts and full-length forends with two bands. Swivels lay on the nose band, on the front of the trigger guard and under the butt. Some guns had lugs for sword bayonets on the right side of the muzzle, but the lighter socket bayonets were much more popular.

SPORTING GUN

The original 'Peabody Sporting Gun' of 1865 had a half-octagon barrel and a side-barred patch box in the butt. It was superseded in 1866 by a plainer gun chambering a variety of rimfire cartridges, a centerfire version being available by the summer of 1867. A catalogue produced in 1871 indicated that the sporter was available only in 45-70, with a round barrel measuring 20-28in; the standard rear sight was a leaf pattern, though a folding tang sight was optional.

Deluxe guns—with half-octagon or fully octagonal barrels—offered checkering on the stock-wrist and forend, and silver or nickelled escutcheons for the barrel-key. However, the Peabody sporters were too expensive to sell in large numbers and were speedily replaced by the more efficient Peabody-Martini (q.v.); surviving examples are uncommon.

• Peabody-Martini

Friedrich Martini and Henry Peabody reached an agreement over patent licenses in the early 1870s, whereupon Peabody-Martini sporting rifles were substituted for the original Peabody (q.v.) external-hammer pattern. The Providence Tool Company made Peabody-Martini guns for some years. However, the sporters were too expensive to sell in quantity and production seems to have ended in the early 1880s.

IMPROVED SPORTING RIFLE

Made by the Providence Tool Company, Providence, Rhode Island.
Total production: not known. **Chambering options:** see notes. **Action:** a pivoting breechblock was propped behind the chamber by the operating lever.
DATA FOR A TYPICAL NO.2 CREEDMOOR EXAMPLE
Chambering: 44-95, rimmed. About 49in overall, 9.25lb empty. 32in barrel, 4-groove rifling; RH, concentric. Vernier peep sight on tang. 1310 fps with 550-grain bullet.

Among the earliest rifles was a sporter chambered for a necked 45-50 cartridge. The straight-wrist butt was separated from the short tapering forend by the massive receiver, which gave the gun an ungainly appearance. Rear sights were usually spring-leaf and elevator patterns, though other patterns were available on request. Pewter forend tips, select walnut woodwork, fine-quality checkering and engraving could all be supplied on request.

SIMILAR GUNS
Kill Deer Model. This had a plain butt and a round 26in barrel chambered for the 45-70 cartridge. Open Rocky Mountain sights were fitted.

No. 1 Mid-Range Target Model. This appeared in 1876, with a 32in or 30in barrel chambered for 40-70 or 40-90 cartridges. The rear sight was generally an 800yd Vernier-adjustable aperture pattern, used in conjunction with a bead front sight and spirit level.

No. 2 Long-Range Creedmoor Rifle. Made with a 32in half-octagon barrel, this customarily had a long-range (generally 1200yd) aperture sight that could be fitted interchangeably to mounts on the tang or butt heel. The breech lever was extended to curve around a shallow pistol grip on the underside of the butt wrist. It chambered a 44-60 or 44-100 cartridge.

No. 3 What Cheer Model. Named after a well-known rifle range near Providence, this 40-70 or 40-90 pattern of 1877 was essentially similar to the Creedmoor but had a straight-wrist butt and a smaller-caliber 30in barrel.

• Pedersen

John Pedersen, a talented firearms designer and a brilliant production engineer, is now remembered for the Pedersen Device produced during World War I (see 'Springfield, bolt-action type'). However, he was also responsible for many of Remington's slide-action guns, and his brilliantly conceived delayed-blowback toggle-lock rifle so nearly became the U.S. Army service rifle.

The first specifications of the delayed-blowback Pedersen rifle were submitted in February 1924, followed shortly afterwards by the first gun. It greatly impressed the Infantry Board during preliminary demonstrations in January 1926, and was tested by the Ordnance Board on 10th May. Within 10 days, an order for 20 Pedersens had been approved.

T1 RIFLE

Throughout the Spring of 1928, the Infantry and Cavalry Boards experimented with 20 long-barreled and five short-barreled Pedersens, the highly favorable reports being submitted in April 1928. In August 1928, the two versions of the 276-caliber T1 Pedersen were tried successfully against a 30-caliber primer-actuated M1924 Garand, a Thompson Automatic Rifle and an improved 256 Bang.

However, the trials held in 1931 favored the more conventional Garands. The Pedersen toggle-lock was difficult to machine accurately and the waxed cartridge case—necessary to ensure efficient extraction—was unacceptable. The action was more prone to jamming than its rival, and the rising toggle was apt to strike the shooter's helmet. Consequently, the Pedersen system was abandoned even though Vickers Ltd. promoted it enthusiastically in Britain.

• Percy

Three carbines were submitted by John Percy of Albany, New York, to the U.S. Army trials of 1865, where they were tested as Guns No. 44, No. 44a and No. 45. All three embodied an improved form of Percy's U.S. patent no. 39,494, granted in August 1863 to protect 'watertight' internal-hammer construction. The guns were identifiable by their unusually long receivers. They were operated by pressing the lever in the auxiliary guard in front of the trigger, which allowed the barrel to be broken open to expose the chamber. An extractor lever lay on the right side of the breech. The firing mechanism relied on the back lever to cock the action and the front

The 276-caliber Pedersen T2E1 rifle, with the action closed.

lever (the trigger) to release the striker. Percy carbines had iron-frame butts with two separate wood sides held by screws; the half-length forends had a single encircling band.

• Perry

Alonzo Perry of Newark, New Jersey, was granted a U.S. patent in December 1849 to protect a gun with a faucet breech and a magazine in the butt. Though this was never exploited commercially, a radial-breech design patented in November 1854 and improved in January 1855 (U.S. patent 12,244) did encounter limited success.

PERRY CARBINE

Made by (or probably for) Perry's Patent Arms Co., Newark, New Jersey.

Total production: not known, but probably 1000-1500. **Chambering:** 54-caliber combustible cartridge, fired by a caplock. **Action**: locked by a radial breechblock sealing the chamber.

39in overall, 7lb empty. 20.75in barrel, 7-groove rifling; RH, concentric. Single shot only. Standing-block rear sight graduated to 500yd. Performance not known. No bayonet.

The Perry carbine was a half-stock pattern with a prominent closed-ring underlever forming the trigger guard. The frame and external hammer were color case-hardened, and an 'auto-tearing' finger on the breechblock removed—or at least ruptured—the base of the cartridge as it entered the chamber. A 50-cap tube running up through the butt to the breech automatically capped the nipple for each shot. The U.S. Army purchased 200 carbines in April 1855, and others are believed to have gone to the Navy; sporting guns have been reported with four-figure numbers, and it is suspected that production was substantial.

• Pitcher

Henry Pitcher of Neillsville, Wisconsin, obtained four U.S. Patents in 1889-93 to protect a bolt-action magazine rifle, which was promoted by the short-lived Pitcher Automatic Repeating Firearms Company. A five-shot 30-caliber gun weighing 8.63lb was tested by the U.S. Army in 1891, but was rejected in the initial stages of the trials.

• Plainfield

The Plainfield Machine Company of Dunellen and then Middlesex, New Jersey, made a classical M1 Carbine replica (in 22/30, 5.7mm MMJ or 30 M1 Carbine) from the early 1960s onward; most of examples made in the 1970s had ventilated sheet-steel handguards and lacked the bayonet-lug assembly beneath the barrel. The Commando or Paratrooper Model had a forward pistol grip and a sliding skeletal butt; the M1 Sporter had a military-style butt without the sling bar; and the M1 Deluxe Sporter (later known as the 'Plainfielder') had a special half-stock with a Monte Carlo comb and a checkered pistol grip.

The company was acquired by Iver Johnson (see above) in 1975, Iver Johnson moving its own headquarters from Fitchburg to Middlesex in 1977. Production continued thereafter under the Iver Johnson name, the entire enterprise moving to Arkansas in 1982.

• Poultney

A gun of this type was submitted to the U.S. Army trials of 1865, but was not among those that were photographed at the time. This may simply indicate that the weapon was rejected in the examination stages. Thomas Poultney was a partner in Poultney & Trimble of Baltimore. In May 1867, jointly with Silas Crispin, he received U.S. patent 64,701 to protect a breechblock which swung up and forward. A reinforced lip on the right side of the breech acted as a cartridge holder.

• Rahn

Rahn Gun Works of Grand Rapids and then Hastings, Michigan, built sporting rifles around a conventional 1898-pattern Mauser action. Rahn ceased trading in about 1993.

THE GUNS

Deer Series examples had 24in barrels chambered for 25-06, 270 Winchester or 308 Winchester cartridges. A deer's head motif, bordered by oak leaves, was engraved on the floorplate.

Elk Series guns had 26in barrels, and were offered in 6x57, 7mm Remington Magnum or 30-06. An oak leaf-bordered elk's head appeared on the magazine floorplate.

Himalayan Series guns had 24in barrels chambered for 5.6x57 or 6.5x68S cartridges. The floorplate bore a yak-head motif within scroll engraving, and a fiberglass stock was optional.

Safari Series rifles, with 26in barrels, offered the choice of an elephant, a rhinoceros or a Cape Buffalo head on the floorplate. Chamberings ranged from 308 Norma Magnum to 9.3x64. The walnut pistol grip half-stock had a Monte Carlo cheekpiece and a rubber recoil pad; the forend had a shallow schnabel tip.

• Ranger

Designed by Homer Koon, this distinctive action was sold in considerable numbers—left- and right-hand—often to be completed elsewhere. Except rifles made under the Bortmess brand, a vast range of stocks and fittings will be encountered. Few prove to be factory-original.

RANGER SPORTING RIFLE

Made by Ranger Arms Co., Inc., Gainesville, Texas.

Chambering options: see text. **Action:** locked by rotating lugs on the bolt head into the receiver wall as the bolt handle turns down.

DATA FOR A TYPICAL TEXAS MAGNUM

Chambering: 308 Winchester, rimless. 45in overall, 7.28lb empty. 24in barrel, 4-groove rifling; RH, concentric. Internal box magazine, 5 rounds. Optical sight. 2610 fps with 180-grain bullet.

The Ranger rifle of 1967 had three sturdy locking lugs on the bolt head, giving a 60-degree throw. The plunger-type ejector and the short-claw extractor were also carried on the bolt head, which had a recessed face.

The bolt handle unit was screwed into the back of the bolt body, and the streamlined bolt shroud was screwed in turn onto the back of the bolt handle. The trigger mechanism was attached to the trigger guard bow, owing to the inclusion of a lateral safety bolt.

Rifles typically had walnut stock with a roll-over Monte Carlo comb, a contrasting forend tip and pistol grip cap accompanied by thin white spacers, and a ventilated rubber buttplate. However, thumb-hole butts, full-length forends, and a selection of stock woods were also offered.

SIMILAR GUNS

Bortmess Patterns. By 1972, Ranger-made actions were being sold under the banner of the Bortmess Gun Co., Inc., of Scenery Hill, Pennsylvania, fitted with Douglas Premium barrels and differing stock styles. The Classic rifle had a conventional stock, whereas the Big Horn Rifle pattern—for example—had an exaggerated 'half-curl' pistol grip and the height of the cheekpiece was exaggerated by a deeply scalloped heel. The stock was walnut with rosewood accessories. Work ceased in about 1978; by 1980, the Bortmess organization was using Voere actions.

The PMC (Plainfield) Paratrooper, derived from the M1 Carbine.

Ranger Texas Magnum. These have been built on actions accepting magnum-power cartridges comparable in size to the 30-06.

Ranger Maverick. A short-action rifle, single-shot or magazine-fed, this handled cartridges up to the size of 308 Winchester.

• Red Willow

These re-creations of the Marlin-made Ballards (q.v.) were announced by the Red Willow Tool & Armory, Inc., of Stevensville, Montana, in 1992. They chambered 32-40 Winchester, 38-55 Winchester, 40-65 Winchester, 40-70 Ballard, 40-85 Ballard or 45-70 cartridges, though others could be made to order. Options have included tang sights, set triggers, and selected woodwork. The company ceased operations in 1993.

THE GUNS

Red Willow No. 1-1/2 rifle. This was a classic Ballard-type rifle with a 30in barrel, an 'S'-type operating lever and a single trigger.

Red Willow No. 5 Pacific rifle. Distinguished by a 30in octagonal barrel and a ring-pattern operating lever, this also had a double trigger. A typical rifle could weigh as much as 11.5lb.

Red Willow No. 8 rifle. Featuring a 30in half-octagon barrel and a double-set trigger mechanism, this gun had a walnut butt had a cheekpiece, a pistol grip and a nickel-plated 'Off Hand' shoulder plate. It weighed 10lb.

• Remington, autoloading type

Note: Remingtons (whatever their operating system) usually bear 'R.E.P.' or 'REP' in an oval, generally on the barrel near the breech. This is simply the company proof mark.

MODEL 8 SPORTING RIFLE
Subsequently known as the 'Model 8A'
Made by the Remington Arms Company, Ilion, New York, 1906-36.
Total production: not known. **Chambering options:** see text. **Action:** locked by two lugs on the bolt engaging the barrel extension; recoil operated, semi-automatic only.
DATA FOR A TYPICAL EXAMPLE
   Chambering: 32 Remington, rimless. 41in overall, 7.63lb empty. 22in barrel, 6-groove rifling; RH, concentric. Detachable box magazine, 5 rounds. Spring-leaf and elevator rear sight. 2220 fps with 170-grain bullet.

The first centerfire autoloader to be made in North America, this was the work of John Browning. The use of barrel sliding back within a sleeve to unlock the breech had been patented in October 1900 and June 1902, though post-1918 guns listed additional patents granted in May 1907 and February 1911. Chambered for proprietary 25-, 30-, 32- and 35-caliber cartridges, sold only with a round barrel and a box magazine, standard take-down guns had a straight-wrist butt and a separate schnabel-tipped forend, though half pistol grips could be obtained on request. A radial safety lever lay on the right side of the receiver. The Model 8 was offered in six grades—'A' to 'F'—but was superseded in 1936 by the Model 81 (q.v.).

SIMILAR GUNS

Model 81A Woodsmaster rifle, 1936-50. A modernized Model 8, this was chambered for 300 Savage cartridges in addition to Remington's own 30-, 32- and 35-caliber rounds. Woodsmasters were made grades 'A' 'B', 'D' and 'F'. The action was largely unchanged, but the butt had a shallow pistol grip, and the beavertail forend had a plain round tip; weight rose to 8.15lb. The Model 81 was eventually superseded by the Model 740.

MODEL 16 SPORTING RIFLE
Subsequently known as 'Model 16A'
Made by the Remington Arms Co., Ilion, New York, 1914-28.

Total production: 50,000? **Chambering options:** 22 Short, 22 Long Rifle, 22 Winchester or 22 Remington Automatic, rimfire. **Action:** no mechanical breech lock; blowback, semi-automatic only.
DATA FOR 22 REMINGTON AUTOMATIC VERSION
   39.75in overall, 5.75lb empty. 22in barrel, 4-groove rifling; RH, concentric. Tube magazine in butt, 15 rounds. Spring-leaf and elevator rear sight. 950 fps with 45-grain bullet.

Designed by Charles Barnes to compete with the Johnson-pattern Winchesters, this small autoloader was not particularly successful; only the special 22 Remington chambering was still being made by 1918. The Model 16—a take-down design—had a slab-sided receiver with a squared back, a concealed hammer, and a two-part stock. The butt was usually straight-wristed, and the slender forend had a schnabel tip; however, alternative 'C', 'D' and 'F' grades often had extensive decoration.

MODEL 24 SPORTING RIFLE
Subsequently known as 'Model 24A'
Made by the Remington Arms Co., Ilion, New York, 1922-35.
Total production: 75,000-85,000? **Chambering options:** 22 Short or 22 Long Rifle, rimfire. **Action:** as Model 16, above.
DATA FOR 22LR VERSION
   40in overall, 5lb empty. 21in barrel, 4-groove rifling; RH, concentric. Tube magazine in butt, 10 rounds. Spring-leaf and slider rear sight. 1080 fps with 40-grain bullet.

Made in accordance with Belgian patents granted to John Browning in 1913-14 (the first relevant U.S. specification was granted in October 1915), this was essentially similar to the FN-Browning rifle. Introduced before the First World War began. It had a schnabel-tip forend and a long slender receiver. The loading port was cut into the right side of the pistol grip butt; spent cases were ejected downward ahead of the trigger guard. Guns chambered for the 22 Short cartridge usually had 19in barrels.

SIMILAR GUNS

Model 241A Speedmaster rifle, 1935-41 and 1945-51. A modernized 24A, designed to handle regular and high-speed ammunition, this take-down pattern had a butt magazine and a 24in barrel. Checkered panels appeared on the pistol grip and forend. Deluxe guns were offered in 'B' (Special), 'D' (Peerless), 'E' (Expert) and 'F' (Premium) grades; production amounted to 56,000.

MODEL 550A SPORTING RIFLE

Made by the Remington Arms Co., Ilion, New York, 1941 and 1945-71.
Total production: 220,000 (all types). **Chambering options:** 22 Short, 22 Long and 22 Long Rifle rimfire, interchangeably. **Action:** as Model 16, above.
   43.5in overall, 6.25lb empty. 24in barrel, 4-groove rifling; RH, concentric. Tube magazine beneath barrel, 15-22 rounds depending on cartridge length. Spring-leaf and elevator rear sight. 1080 fps with 40-grain bullet.

The most interesting feature of this gun lay in the use of a floating chamber or 'Power Piston' to adapt the action to fire three differing rimfire cartridges. The 550A had a plain hardwood pistol grip half stock, with the head of a radial safety catch protruding above the right side.

SIMILAR GUNS

Model 550P rifle. This had a peep sight on the receiver instead of an open spring-leaf pattern on the barrel.

Model 550G rifle. Sometimes identified as '550-2G' or '550-GS', this was used in shooting galleries. It had a 22in barrel, a screw-eye for a retaining chain, and a spent-case deflector on the right side of the receiver ahead of the charging handle.

MODEL 740A WOODSMASTER RIFLE

Made by the Remington Arms Company, Ilion, New York, 1952 (1955?) to date.

The Remington Model 552 rifle.
Note the case deflector behind the ejection port.

Total production: not known. **Chambering options:** see notes. **Action:** locked by rotating lugs on the bolt into the barrel extension; gas operated, semit-automatic only.

DATA FOR A TYPICAL 742A

Chambering: 280 Remington, rimless. 42in overall, 7.22lb empty. 22in barrel, 6-groove rifling; RH, concentric. Detachable box magazine, 4 rounds. Spring-leaf and elevator rear sight. 2820 fps with 165-grain bullet.

Developed to replace the Model 81, this had a pistol grip butt separated from the forend by a machined steel receiver containing the multi-lug bolt. Chambered initially only for 30-06 or 308 Winchester cartridges, it could be distinguished from the externally similar slide-action Gamemaster—Model 760, q.v.—as the forend ran back as far as the receiver without exposing the operating rods.

The standard rifle had a plain straight-comb butt with a pistol grip, and the beavertail forend was fluted. The open rear sight was usually accompanied by a ramped blade at the muzzle. A 280 Remington option was added in 1957, but the last 740-pattern guns were sold in 1963.

SIMILAR GUNS

Model 740ADL rifle, 1955-63. A deluxe version of the standard rifle, this had checkering on the pistol grip and forend. Its butt could also have a Monte Carlo comb.

Model 740BDL rifle. This was simply an ADL with select-grade woodwork, the high comb being standard.

Model 742A Woodsmaster rifle, 1960-80. Though internal changes were made in this improved 740 (offered in 243 Winchester, 280 Remington, 30-06 and 308 Winchester), the principal changes were cosmetic—the checkering on the straight-comb butt had a fleur-de-lis border, while the beavertail forend had skip-line checkering with foliate edging. A 244 Remington chambering was announced in 1961.

Model 742ADL rifle. Based on the Model 742A, this was distinguished by hand-cut checkering and better-quality woodwork.

Model 742BDL rifle, 1966-80. Another variant of the 742, this gun had a Monte Carlo comb with basket-weave checkering and an angular forend with a reverse-cut tip. The squared receiver-back was unique to the 740 BDL and 760 BDL patterns.

Model 742 carbine, 1962-80. A short variant of the rifle with an 18.5in barrel, made only in 30-06 or 308, this was merely 38.5in overall and weighed about 7lb.

Model 742D Peerless rifle, 1961-80. This deluxe pattern had scroll engraving on the receiver and hand-cut checkering on the half stock.

Model 742F Premier rifle, 1961-80. Premier rifles had scrollwork on the receiver enclosing game scenes inlaid in gold. The wood of the butt and forend was specially selected for its figuring.

MODEL 552A SPEEDMASTER RIFLE

Data generally as Model 550A, above.

Introduced in 1957, this was a modernized 550A without the floating-chamber system. A slab-sided receiver with a round back separated the plain pistol gripped butt from the rounded forend, and a safety bolt ran laterally through the rear web of the trigger guard. A 23in or 25in barrel was fitted, the tube magazine held 15-20 rounds, and the spring-leaf rear sight had an elevator plate.

SIMILAR GUNS

Model 552BDL rifle, 1966 to date. A deluxe version of the 552A, this had checkering on the pistol grip and forend. Ramped sights were fitted to later examples, which often had distinctive fleur-de-lis strapwork checkering.

Model 552C carbine, 1961-77. This had an 21in barrel, but was otherwise the same as the 552A.

Model 552GS rifle, 1957-77. Popular in shooting galleries, this gun was chambered specifically for the low-power 22 Short rimfire cartridge. It will sometimes be found with a screw-eye for a retaining chain, and a synthetic spent-case deflector around the ejection port on the right side of the receiver.

Model 552 Sesquicentennial rifle, 1966. Made in small numbers to celebrate Remington's 150th anniversary, this had an appropriate logo on the left side of the receiver.

NYLON 66 SPORTING RIFLE

Made by the Remington Arms Co., Ilion, New York, 1959-87.
Total production: not known. **Chambering:** 22 Long Rifle, rimfire. **Action:** no mechanical breech lock; blowback, semi-automatic only.

38.5in overall, 5.75lb empty. 19.65in barrel, 4-groove rifling; RH, concentric. Tube magazine in butt, 14 rounds. Spring-leaf and finger-wheel rear sight. 1080 fps with 40-grain bullet.

By far the most successful of the 'Nylon' series, distinguished by injection-moulded futuristic stocks of DuPont Zytel, this was made in Ilion until the rights were sold to CBC in Brazil in the late 1980s. The rifles had slab-sided receivers with a safety slider on the upper tang. The pistol gripped butt—originally only supplied in 'Mohawk Brown'—had a straight comb, and the beavertail-type forend had an integral schnabel tip. Molded checkering was used.

SIMILAR GUNS

Model 10C rifle, 1971-8. This was simply the Nylon 77 masquerading under a new name.

Nylon 66 Apache Black rifle, 1962-84. This was distinguished by black furniture and chromed metalwork, but was otherwise the same as the 'Mohawk Brown' pattern.

Nylon 66 Bicentennial rifle, 1976-7. Mechanically identical with the standard Nylon 66, this had a logo etched into the left side of the receiver to celebrate the 200th anniversary of the Declaration of Independence.

Nylon 66 Seneca Green rifle. A few of these were made in the early 1960s, distinguished by their garish stocks.

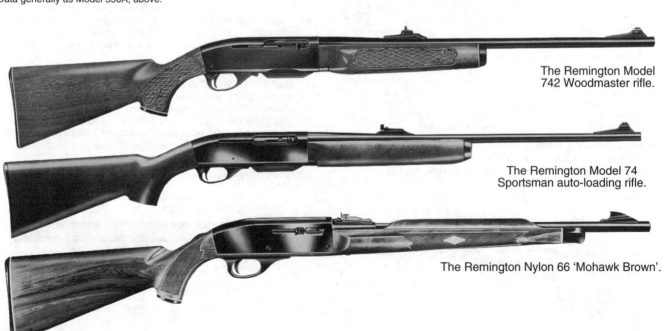

The Remington Model 742 Woodmaster rifle.

The Remington Model 74 Sportsman auto-loading rifle.

The Remington Nylon 66 'Mohawk Brown'.

Nylon 66 Sesquicentennial rifle, 1966. This was made in small numbers to celebrate the 150th anniversary of Remington. A suitable inscription appeared on the left side of the receiver.

Nylon 77 rifle, 1970-1. This was a variant of the Model 66, sold only in small numbers, with a detachable five-round box magazine instead of the butt tube.

Nylon 77 Apache rifle, 1987. A few of these guns were made for the K-Mart chain, from parts on hand. They could be distinguished by bright green stocks.

MODEL FOUR SPORTING RIFLE

Introduced in 1981 to replace the 742 series, the Model Four was initially chambered for 6mm Remington, 243 Winchester, 270 Winchester, 7mm Remington Express (280 Remington), 30-06 or 308 Winchester cartridges. The Model Four had a high gloss polyurethane finish on the woodwork and a Monte Carlo comb on the butt. Checkering appeared on the pistol grip and forend.

SIMILAR GUNS

Model Four Peerless rifle ('4D'), 1981-9. This was a variant of the standard rifle with selected woodwork and an engraved receiver.

Model Four Premier rifle ('4F'), 1981-9. Selected woodwork and engraved receivers, with game scenes inlaid in gold, distinguished these deluxe guns.

Model 7400 rifle. This rifle, with a 22in barrel, was essentially similar to the Model Four but (at least until the mid 1980s) had a much plainer finish.

Model 7400 carbine. These have been made with 18.5in barrels in 30-06 only.

MODEL 522 VIPER SPORTING RIFLE

Made by the Remington Arms Co., Ilion, New York, 1993 to date.
Currently in production. **Chambering:** 22 Long Rifle, rimfire. **Action:** no mechanical breech lock; blowback, semi-automatic only.

40in overall, 4.63lb empty. 20in barrel, 4-groove rifling; RH, concentric. Detachable box magazine, 10 rounds. Williams ramp-type rear sight. 1080 fps with 40-grain bullet.

This distinctive rifle has a synthetic receiver set in a synthetic half stock, both components being finished in matt black. The Viper has a magazine safety in addition to a manual catch, and a manual hold-open as well as an automatic 'last-shot' type. Identification is helped by the design of the stock, which deepens noticeably ahead of the trigger, and by the markedly forward curve of the magazine.

• Remington, block-action type

Copied by Whitney and others, the renowned 'Rolling Block' was developed from the split-breech pattern credited to Leonard Geiger and patents granted to Joseph Rider in the late 1860s.

Rolling blocks were opened by thumbing back the hammer to full-cock and pulling back on the finger spur of the breech piece to give access to the chamber, partially extracting a spent case. After the gun had been reloaded and the breech piece rotated forward to its closed position, a pull on the trigger dropped the hammer. As the hammer fell, shoulders ran forward under the breech piece to direct the thrust generated back through the case-base (as the gun fired) so that the mechanism was locked in its closed position.

The rolling-block was simple and strong. Remington made great capital of its durability, camouflaging comparatively poor extraction, and many hundreds of thousands of guns were sold throughout the world prior to 1914. Many modern versions of the basic design have been made, notably in Italy (by Pedersoli and Uberti) and Spain (by Bonifacio Echeverria). Some of these are considered separately in the appropriate sections.

GEIGER-TYPE GUNS

The carbines purchased by the Federal authorities during the Civil War incorporated the 'split breech' action, designed by Leonard Geiger and perfected by Joseph Rider. Patented in the names of Rider and Remington in 1865, it relied on a high-wall receiver and a radial breechblock containing the hammer. The nose of the hammer struck the rimfire cartridges through a slot in the top surface of the block.

MODEL 1864 REMINGTON-GEIGER CARBINE

Made by E. Remington & Sons, Ilion, New York, 1864-5.
Total production: 20,000. **Chambering options:** 46 rimfire and 56-50 Spencer rimfire. **Action:** locked by shoulders on the hammer body propping the radial breechblock behind the chamber.

DATA FOR A 56-50 GUN

34.25in overall, about 7lb empty. 19.85in barrel, 3-groove rifling; RH, concentric. Single-shot only. Three-leaf rear sight. About 950 fps with Spencer ammunition? No bayonet.

Acknowledging patents granted in 1863-4, the Remington-Geiger action—safe enough with low-pressure loads—was much weaker than the succeeding Rolling Block. However, 15,000 50-caliber carbines were ordered on 24th October 1864. Remington-Geiger carbines had a straight- wrist walnut butt and a separate half-length forend held by a single band. A sling ring lay on the left side of the case-hardended receiver. Remington retrieved most of the 56-50 carbines after the Civil War and re-sold them at a handsome profit to France in 1870-1.

Chambering a notably weaker cartridge—which put less strain on the action—the 46-caliber guns were ordered in January 1865, but few had been delivered before the Civil War ended. Their frames were notably smaller than the 56-50 version, and swivels often lay under the butt and the barrel band.

LATER PATTERNS

Leonard Geiger of Hudson, New York, submitted three differing rifles to the U.S. Army trials of 1865-6. Protected by U.S. Patent 37,501 of January 1863 and tested as Guns No. 8-10, they all relied on variations of the 'Split Breech' system. They had rounded receivers, separate forends held by three sprung bands, one swivel on the middle band, and another swivel in the trigger guard. A stepped-bed leaf sight was used.

Three of the carbines promoted by E. Remington & Sons—Guns No. 46-8—also embodied the Geiger breech, even though combat experience had already shown it to be weak. The Geiger-Remingtons had two-piece stocks, and a sling ring and bar on the left side of the receiver. They did not survive the trials, as the Rider-patent Remington Carbine No. 57 was clearly preferable.

RIDER-TYPE GUNS

An experimental version of this radial-block breech system, promoted by E. Remington & Sons, was tested by the U.S. Army in the trials of 1865-6 as 'Gun No. 57'. Patented by Joseph Rider of Newark, Ohio, in January 1865 (no. 45,797), the 'rolling block' design was far superior to the split-breech Geiger patterns.

Gun No. 57 had a radially-moving breech-block supported by the tumbler on the external hammer, but Gun No. 67 had the hammer mounted centrally. The two-piece half stock had a single band around the barrel and forend.

Though the U.S. Army viewed the Rolling Block without enthusiasm, other agencies were much more interested. Denmark ordered substantial numbers of rifles and carbines in 1867, when the Rider breech also received a silver medal from the Paris Exposition. By 1873, Remington was claiming to have sold 16,500 rifles, carbines and pistols to the U.S. Army; 23,000 to the U.S. Navy; 15,000 Model 1871 Locking Rifles to New York; and 5000 rifle-musket conversions to South Carolina.

A typical Rolling Block sporting rifle, with a heavy octagonal barrel. (W&W)

Among the export orders had been 75,000 rifles and carbines supplied to Spain for use in Cuba, beginning in 1867, and 30,000 guns sent to Sweden from 1868 onward.

Sales of a million military-style rifles were claimed by 1876. These had included the 50-caliber U.S. Model Musket (1871); two converted 58 Springfield rifle-muskets, long and short, which mated the original barrel, stock and furniture with a new action; the 43-caliber (11mm) Spanish Model, with its socket bayonet; the 43-caliber Civil Guard Model, chambered for the 'Spanish or Russian Cartridge' and offered with a saber bayonet; the 43-caliber French Model and saber bayonet, chambered for the 'Egyptian Cartridge'; and a 43- or 50-caliber carbine.

The Remington lasted longer in the U.S. Navy than the U.S. Army; government-issue copper case cartridges extracted so poorly in the 1872-3 trials that the Board of Ordnance favored the Trapdoor Springfield. Though drawn brass cases were soon substituted, the U.S. government was by then committed to the 45-70 M1873 rifle.

MODEL 1870 NAVY RIFLE

Made by the National Armory, Springfield, Massachusetts, 1870-1.
Total production: 22,000 (see text, below). **Chambering:** 50-70, rimmed.
Action: locked by shoulders on the hammer body propping the radial breechblock behind the chamber.

48.65in overall, about 9lb empty. 32.65in barrel, 3-groove rifling; RH, concentric. Ramp-and-leaf sight graduated to 1000yd. 1275 fps with standard ball cartridges. M1870 sword bayonet.

Navy trials began in March 1869, but experimental rolling-block carbines had been purchased in 1867 and there was little surprise when a 50-70 rifle was approved. The regulation Springfield barrel was used, chambered for a Martin cartridge, and the Bureau of Ordnance escutcheon was cast into fish-scale hilt of the Ames-made bayonet.

Ten thousand guns were ordered from Springfield Armory on 3rd February 1870. When the rifles were delivered into navy stores in the summer, the rear sight were seen to be wrongly positioned. The guns were hastily sold to Poultney & Trimble, then re-sold to France during the Franco-Prussian War at a considerable profit. On 27th January 1871, the Chief of the Bureau of Navy Ordnance requested immediate supply of 12,000 properly-sighted rifles.

MODEL 1871 RIFLE

Made by the National Armory, Springfield, Massachusetts, 1870-1.
Total production: at least 32,000. See below. **Chambering:** 50-70, rimmed. **Action:** as M1870 navy rifle, above.

51.75in overall, about 9.25lb empty. 36in barrel, 3-groove rifling; RH, concentric. Ramp-and-leaf sight graduated to 1000yd. 1315 fps with ball cartridges. Socket bayonet.

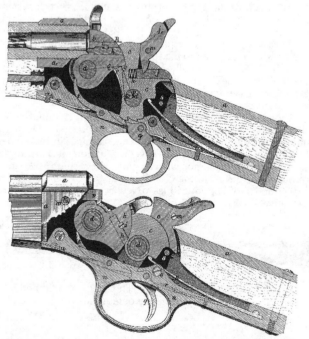

A sectional drawing of the 'Remington Locking Rifle'.

A trial board met in St Louis in March 1870 to investigate the latest rifle designs, eventually reporting that only six among many seemed acceptable—in declining order of preference, Remington, Springfield-Allin, Sharps, Morgenstern, Martini-Henry and Ward-Burton. As 504 rolling-block rifles had been made at Springfield in 1868, their characteristics were well known.

By March 1871, Springfield had made 1008 infantry-pattern Remingtons, with 32.5in barrels, to compete against 1870-pattern Springfield and Sharps conversions. Trials began in midsummer 1871; the Remingtons performed best, though ejection was poor and misgivings were expressed about dust jamming the mechanism.

Ten thousand Model 1871 rifles made at Springfield Armory in 1872 were similar to the 1870-pattern U.S. navy rifles, but had an additional 'Locking Bolt' to prevent accidents occurring when the rolling-block rifles were being loaded at full-cock. The hammer of these guns automatically dropped to half-cock when the breech piece was closed, and had to be retracted manually before firing.

Though the 'Locking Bolt' Remingtons were rejected by army trial boards in 1872-3, 21,000 were purchased by the New York state militia.

SIMILAR GUNS

Model 1871 carbine. Concurrently with 1871 field trials of the army rifle, the U.S. cavalry experimented with 313 50-70 Remington carbines made in Springfield in 1870-1. These had 23.35in barrels and 600yd rear sights, and weighed about 7.8lb. They were tested against 308 Sharps carbines and 341 Model 1870 Springfield carbines. The St. Louis board had recommended that no Remington carbines should be issued until a half-cock loading feature had been added, but this proviso went unheeded. However, by the end of the 1871 trials, rolling-block carbines were rejected in favor of the Springfield-Allin pattern.

SPORTING GUNS

The simplicity, legendary strength and ready availability of the rolling-block action allowed individual gunsmiths—and Remington, indeed—to build guns to individual order. Great variety will be found in chambering, stocks and sights. In 1886, however, the manufacturer's marks changed from the old 'E. REMINGTON & SONS, ILION, N.Y.' to the new 'REMINGTON ARMS CO.' after the failure of the original family business.

NO. 1 SPORTING RIFLE

Made by E. Remington & Sons, Ilion, New York (1867-86); and by the Remington Arms Company, Ilion, New York (1886-90).
Total production: not known. **Chambering options:** 32-20 Winchester, 32-40 Ballard, 38-40 Remington, 40-50 Sharps, 40-70 Remington or Sharps, 43 Spanish, 44 Smith & Wesson, 44-40 Winchester, 44-77 Sharps, 44-90 Creedmoor, 45-70 or 50-70 Government. **Action:** as M1871 rifle, above.
DATA FOR A TYPICAL 44-77 EXAMPLE
45.5in overall, 9.15lb empty. 30in barrel, 5-groove rifling; RH, concentric. Single shot only. Spring-leaf and elevator rear sight. 1460 fps with 365-grain bullet.

The first commercial Rider-pattern Rolling Block eventually acknowledging patents granted in 1864-73. Standard barrels included a 20in round pattern; 26in round, half- or fully-octagonal; and 30in octagonal. However, octagonal barrels from 24in to 34in could be obtained to order. According to an 1876 Remington catalogue, weight ranged from 8.5 to 15lb, depending on barrel-length and design. Optional extras ranged from pisto -grip butts to vernier-adjustable peep-and-globe sights.

SIMILAR GUNS

No. 1 Hunter, Business and Black Hills rifles, 1875-about 1882. These were minor variants of the No. 1 with 28in round barrels, weighing about 7.5lb and invariably chambered for 45-70 cartridges.

No. 1 1/2 Sporting Rifle, 1888-97. A lightened No. 1, this usually had an octagonal barrel, though round and half-octagon patterns were made to order. It chambered rim- and centerfire cartridges ranging from 22- to 38-caliber. A typical 32-20 WCF example was 41.5in long, weighed 7.5lb, and had a 26in barrel. Spring-leaf and elevator sights were standard.

No. 2 Sporting Rifle, 1872-1910. Also known as the 'Gem' or 'New Model Light Rifle', this had an ultra-lightweight action. Made for many centerfire cartridges—and doubtless a few rimfires—it had an octagonal barrel, a straight-wrist butt, and a crescent buttplate. Barrels measured 24-30in, with weight varying between 5.5lb and 8lb. Chamberings included 25-20 Single Shot, 25-20 Winchester, 32-20 Winchester, 32-40 Remington, 38-40 Remington, 38-40 Winchester and 44-40 Winchester. Typically, a 38-40 rifle was 41.15in overall, weighed 6.75lb, and had a 26in barrel.

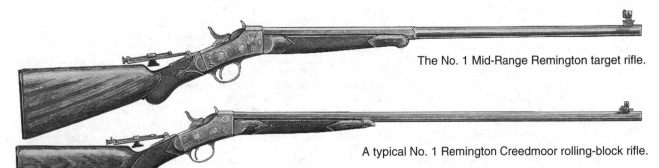

The No. 1 Mid-Range Remington target rifle.

A typical No. 1 Remington Creedmoor rolling-block rifle.

Buffalo Rifle, 1874-about 1890. This had an octagonal or round barrel chambered for cartridges ranging from 40-50 Sharps to 50-70. A typical 44-90 gun was 45.5in long, weighed 10.13lb and had a 30in barrel. Open 'Rocky Mountain' sights were popular, but some guns had sophisticated vernier sights on their tangs.

Mid-Range Target Rifle, 1875-90. Built on the No. 1 action, this had a 28in or 30in half-octagon barrel and chambered cartridges ranging from the 40-50 Sharps to 50-70. A pistol grip butt was usually fitted, together with a globe-pattern front sight and a folding vernier-type aperture rear sight on the tang behind the breech. A representative gun was 45.5in long, had a 30in barrel and weighed 9.8lb.

Short-Range Target Rifle, about 1876-90. Similar to the Mid-Range gun, this had a short half-octagon barrel and chambered rim- and centerfire cartridges ranging from 38 Extra Long to 46 Rimfire. A typical rifle measured 41.5in overall, weighed 9.18lb, and had a 26in barrel. An aperture sight lay on top of the barrel near the breech.

Creedmoor Target Rifle, 1874-91. Built on a specially finished No. 1 action and among the finest rifles of its day, this was named after a range at Creed's Farm on Long Island. It had a 32in octagon barrel chambered for 44-90, 44-100 or 44-105 Remington cartridges, was 48.4in long and weighed about 10.5lb. Stocks were select walnut, with checkered pistol grips, and matching forends terminated in pewter or German silver finials. Vernier peep-and-globe sights and spirit levels could be fitted on the tang behind the hammer. The oldest guns had a special brass-faced 'horse-shoe' shoulder plate on the pistol-grip butt, but later examples used rubber shotgun-type plates.

LIGHT MODEL SPORTING CARBINE

The Remington Arms Company inherited thousands of incomplete rolling-block actions from the moribund Remington & Sons in 1886. Many of these were completed as light or 'Baby' carbines in 1888-1908, reducing stocks of an obsolescent mechanism. Carbines had round barrels, were finished in blue or nickel, and had traditional military-style sights, butt and forend. A sling ring often lay on a 'D'-bar on the left side of the receiver. A typical gun was 35.2in long, had a 20in barrel, and weighed 5.5lb. The leaf sight was graduated to 500yd.

NO. 5 MILITARY/SPORTING RIFLE

Made by the Remington Arms Company, Ilion, New York, 1897-1917.
Total production: many thousands. **Chambering options:** see text, below. **Action:** generally as M1871 rifle, above.
DATA FOR A MEXICAN 7MM EXAMPLE
Chambering: 7x57, rimless. 45.5in overall, 8.65lb empty. 30in barrel, 4-groove rifling; RH, comcentric. Single shot only. Stepped-base and leaf rear sight graduated to 1900yd. 2325 fps with 175-grain bullet.

Introduced in 1897, apparently for sale to the Mexican army, this rolling-block rifle was strengthened for smokeless ammunition. It had a 30in barrel, a forend extending to the muzzle, and a hand guard from the breech to the rear sight base. Many 7x57 guns were supplied to France in 1914 while work commenced on a large order for an 8x51 version. A few 7.62x54mm guns were also supplied to Tsarist Russia in 1915-17.

SIMILAR GUNS

Military carbines. These usually had 22in barrels, straight-wrist butts and short forends held by a single band. Sights were usually leaf patterns graduated to about 1000yd.

Sporting Pattern rifle, 1898-1905. Offered from 1898 with 24-28in barrels, this weighed 7-7.5lb. Chamberings included 7x57, 30 M1903, 30-30 Winchester, 30-40 Krag, 303 British, 32-40 Remington High Powered, 32 Winchester Special and 38-55 Remington High Powered. Butts had a straight wrist, and the rounded forends had a schnabel tip. Eclipsed by its competitors and never popular in North America, the No. 5 sporter was soon abandoned, though new guns continued to be available through the retail trade until the beginning of the First World War.

NO. 4 SPORTING RIFLE

Made by the Remington Arms Company, Ilion, New York, 1890-1933.
Total production: not known. **Chambering options:** 22 Short, 22 Long, 22 Long Rifle, 25 Stevens, 32 Short or 32 Long rimfire. **Action:** generally as M1871 rifle, above.
37.5in overall, 4.5lb empty. 22.5in barrel, 4-groove rifling; RH, concentric. Single shot only. Spring-leaf and slider rear sight. 1080 fps with 40-grain bullet.

Offered in solid-frame or take-down versions, the latter with a radial locking lever on the right side of the frame (patented in July 1902), this embodied a conventional Rolling Block. It could be distinguished from the essentially similar No. 2—built on a pistol action—by the position of the trigger beneath the hammer instead of the block-spur. The standard butt had a straight wrist (a pistol grip type could be obtained to order) and the forend had a rounded tip. The 32-caliber version could be obtained with a 24in octagonal barrel.

SIMILAR GUNS

Model 4S Military Model, 1913-33. Sometimes advertised as the "Boy Scout's Rifle", confined to 22 Short or 22 Long Rifle, this had a full-length stock, a hand guard running from the receiver to the barrel band, sling swivels, and military-style sights. A rudimentary all-metal knife bayonet could be attached beneath the barrel if required.

NO. 6 SPORTING RIFLE

Made by the Remington Arms Company, Ilion, New York, 1901-33.
Total production: not known. Chambering options: 22 Short, 22 Long, 22 Long Rifle, 32 Short or 32 Long rimfire. Action: locked by propping the breechblock behind the chamber as the hammer fell.
34.75in overall, about 4lb empty. 20in barrel, 4-groove rifling; RH, concentric. Single shot only. Fixed open rear sight. 1080 fps with 40-grain bullet.

Though often advertised as a Rolling Block, this small takedown rifle embodied a greatly simplified action which lacked the durability of the No. 2 and No. 4. Fitted with a plain straight-wrist butt and a minuscule rounded forend, the No. 6 could be recognised by its elongated receiver. The head of the dismantling bolt projected beneath the breech, and an optional aperture sight could be fitted to the upper tang.

NO. 7 SPORTING RIFLE

Made by the Remington Arms Company, Ilion, New York, 1903-11.
Total production: not known. **Chambering options:** 22 Short, 22 Long Rifle or 25 Stevens rimfire. **Action:** generally as M1871 rifle, above.
38.1in overall, 6lb empty. 24in barrel, 4-groove rifling; RH, concentric. Single shot only. Folding aperture rear sight. 1080 fps with 40-grain bullet.

Built on the standard pistol action, this had a straight-comb butt with a full pistol grip; the slender forend had a schnabel tip. A hooked Schuetzen-style shoulder plate was sometimes fitted. Barrels were half-octagon patterns, 24-28in long, and the Lyman rear sight was carried on a spur on the frame tip behind the hammer. The front sight was customarily a Beach pattern.

• Remington, bolt-action type

Remington had made such vast numbers of P/1914 and M1917 Enfield (q.v.) rifles during the First World War that an entire warehouse full of parts remained when military production finally ceased. The Model 30 rifle was conceived to make use of them.

The company entered the post-1945 sporting rifle market with a new bolt action developed by a team led by Michael Walker. Markings on Models 721, 722 and 725 usually acknowledge patents granted to John Howell for the extractor (1949) and Michael Walker & Phillip Haskell (1950) for the safety and trigger mechanism. However, though efficient mechanically, the Remingtons lacked the mystique of the Winchester Model 70; sales declined after a promising start, until the advent of the Model 700 in 1962 reversed the trend.

The standard Remington-Mauser action—now regarded as a classic of its type—has twin opposed locking lugs, additional security being provided by the bolt handle turning down into its seat. The extractor and ejector are mounted in the bolt head, which is recessed in a counter-bore in the barrel to minimize problems should the case-head fail during firing.

MODEL 30 SPORTING RIFLE

Made by the Remington Arms Company, Ilion, New York, 1920-40.
Total production: 22,730 (including Model 30S). **Chambering options:** see notes. **Action:** locked by two lugs on the bolt head engaging recesses in the receiver as the bolt handle was turned down, and by the bolt-handle base entering its seat.

DATA FOR A TYPICAL 1938-VINTAGE EXAMPLE
Chambering: 35 Remington, rimless. 42.75in overall, 7.25lb empty. 22in barrel, 5-groove rifling; RH, concentric. Internal box magazine, 5 rounds. Spring-leaf and elevator rear sight. 2210 fps with 200-grain bullet.

This 30-06 sporting rifle—credited to Crawford Loomis and Charles Barnes—shared the M1917 Enfield action, but the barrel was shortened and had a commerically acceptable finish. Guns were offered in 1920 with a pistol grip half stock, a schnabel-tip forend, and an adjustable tangent-slide rear sight graduated to 550yd on the receiver bridge. Proprietary Remington chamberings (25-, 30-, 32- and 35-caliber) appeared about 1923. The rear sight was replaced by a spring-leaf and elevator pattern, the spring being dovetailed into the barrel band.

SIMILAR GUNS

Model 30A rifle, 1932-40. This was a modification of the standard rifle with a free-floating barrel, contact with the barrel-band and forend being eliminated. New 7x57, 7.65x53 and 8x57 chamberings were announced in 1933, replacing the proprietary Remington options. All but 30-06 had gone by 1937. Receivers were drilled and tapped for the first time in 1938 for an optional rear sight, though the spring-and-elevator pattern on the barrel remained standard. The forend was broadened and had a rounded tip.

Model 30 carbine, about 1924-32. This was a short version of the standard sporting rifle with a 20in barrel.

Model 30 Express rifle, 1926-31? The action of this gun was modified to cock on opening, by reducing striker travel. The bolt shroud was shortened and a coil-type ejector spring replaced the original 'sliver' type. The butt comb was raised, the finger groove was eliminated, and checkering was added to the pistol grip and forend. A recoil bolt appeared through the stock beneath the chamber at about the same time, and a guide-rib was added to the bolt body in 1930 to smooth the operating stroke. The firing pin was lightened in an attempt to improve lock time. The bolt shroud was then shortened again, and an additional gas-escape hole was bored into the bolt body near the extractor spring.

Model 30R carbine, 1932-40. A modification of the basic pattern, this had the improved free-floating barrel.

MODEL 30S SPORTING RIFLE

Made by the Remington Arms Company, Ilion, New York, 1930-40.
Total production: not known. **Chambering options:** see notes. **Action:** as Model 30, above.

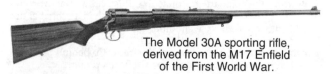
The Model 30A sporting rifle, derived from the M17 Enfield of the First World War.

DATA FOR A TYPICAL EXAMPLE
Chambering: 257 Roberts, rimless. 44.9in overall, 7.95lb empty. 24in barrel, 5-groove rifling; RH, concentric. Internal box magazine, 5 rounds. Aperture rear sight on receiver. 2650 fps with 117-grain bullet.

This had an improved straight-comb stock with a pistol grip cap and a shotgun-style buttplate. A Lyman No. 48R sight was attached to the right side of the receiver and the gold-bead front sight lay on a ramp.

SIMILAR GUNS

Model 30S Special rifle, 1932-40. Changes in the stock and barrel bedding advanced the designation, though the gun was otherwise similar to its predecessor. The 25 Remington and 7x57 options were introduced in 1933; the former was available only with a 22in barrel, and the latter had been abandoned by 1938. A 257 Roberts version was announced in 1934, while a few rifles were apparently made in the late 1930s for the 7.65x53 cartridge—popular in South America.

Model 30SL rifle, 1938-40. This was a minor variant of the original sporting rifle with a Lyman rear sight.

Model 30SR rifle, 1938-40. Otherwise identical with the 30SL pattern, this was distinguished by a Redfield rear sight.

Model 30SX rifle, 1938-40. Intended for use with telescope patterns, this rifle was sold without fixed sights.

MODEL 33 SPORTING RIFLE

Made by the Remington Arms Company, Ilion, New York, 1932-5.
Total production: 263,560 (including NRA rifles). **Chambering options:** 22 Short, 22 Long or Long Rifle rimfire. **Action:** locked by turning the bolt-handle base down ahead of the receiver bridge.

43.25in overall, 4.5lb empty. 24in barrel, 4-groove rifling; RH, concentric. Single shot only. Spring-leaf and elevator rear sight. 1080 fps with 40-grain bullet.

Designed by Crawford Loomis, this was a long, slender and unsophisticated take-down gun with a plain pistol grip stock. The earliest examples had a finger groove in the forend, but this was subsequently abandoned.

SIMILAR GUNS

Model 33 NRA Rifle, 1932-5. Intended for use as a basic junior target rifle, this had Lyman (back) and Patridge (front) sights, swivels beneath the butt and forend, and weighed 5-5.2lb.

Model 34 rifle, 1932-6. An improved repeating version of the Model 33, with changes in the action, this also had a tube magazine beneath the barrel; capacity was 15-22 rounds, depending on the cartridge length. The earliest stocks had finger grooves in the forend. Production totalled 162,940 guns, including the NRA pattern described below.

Model 34 NRA rifle, 1933-6. Mechanically identical with the Model 34, this had the same sights as the Model 33 NRA pattern. It weighed about 5.8lb, but was never made in large numbers.

MODEL 37 RANGEMASTER RIFLE

Made by the Remington Arms Company, Ilion, New York, 1937-54.
Total production: 12,200 (all types). **Chambering:** 22 Long Rifle, rimfire.
Action: generally as Model 33, above.

48.2in overall, 11.75lb empty. 28in barrel, 4-groove rifling; RH, concentric. Detachable box magazine, 5 rounds. Micrometer aperture rear sight. 1080 fps with 40-grain bullet.

Made in accordance with Loomis & Lowe patents, the prototype of all Remington bolt-action target rifles, this allied an improved 1934-type action with a heavy barrel and a high straight-comb half stock with a beavertail forend. The original guns had a military-style band around the forend tip, but this was soon abandoned. A single shot adapter was provided, competition sights were fitted, and bases were provided on the barrel for optical-sight mounts. The trigger guard was a machined steel forging instead of a stamped strip.

SIMILAR GUNS

Model 37 Rangemaster rifle (ii), 1940-1, 1945-54. Changes made in the stock and the action created an improved pattern in 1940, distinguished by the 'Miracle' trigger system and a high-comb Randle stock with a tightened pistol grip but virtually no wrist.

MODEL 41A TARGETMASTER RIFLE

Made by the Remington Arms Company, Ilion, New York, 1936-9.
Total production: 306,880 (all 'Model 41' types). **Chambering options:** 22 Short, 22 Long or 22 Long Rifle, rimfire. **Action:** generally as Model 33, above.

45.6in overall, 5.5lb empty. 27in barrel, 4-groove rifling; RH, concentric. Single shot only. Spring-leaf and elevator rear sight. 1080 fps with 40-grain bullet.

A junior target rifle, this had a sporting-style half stock with a straight-comb pistol grip butt and a rounded forend. The bolt handle was bent downward, and a standard rear sight was attached to the barrel.

SIMILAR GUNS

Model 41AS rifle, 1936-40. Excepting for chambering—.22 Remington Special rimfire—this was identical with the standard gun.

Model 41P rifle, 1936-40. Distinguished by a micrometer aperture sight attached to the left rear of the receiver, this gun also had bases for optical-sight mounts on the barrel.

Model 41SB rifle, 1937-8. This was a smooth-bore version, intended to fire shot or ball cartridges interchangeably. Very few were made.

Model 341A Sportsmaster rifle, 1936-9. Essentially similar to the 41A, this had a bigger stock and a tube magazine beneath the 27in barrel. Cartridge capacity ranged from fifteen 22-caliber LR rounds to 22 of the Shorts. Production of the Model 341 (all types) totalled about 131,600.

Model 341P rifle, 1936-9. A target-shooting version of the basic gun, this had a micrometer-adjustable aperture sight on the rear of the receiver and a hooded front sight. Bases for optical-sight mounts lay on the barrel-top.

Model 341SB rifle, 1937-8. This was a smooth-bore derivative capable of handling shot cartridges.

Model 411 rifle, 1937-9. A special version of the Model 41 made for shooting-gallery use, this chambered 22 CB Cap or 22 Short rimfire ammunition. The safety catch was omitted and a screw-eye was added for a retaining chain. Production amounted to only 1320 guns.

Model 510A Targetmaster rifle, 1939-41 and 1945-62. A single shot design, superseding the Model 41, this had a special loading platform, a streamlined 'self-cocking' bolt, and a radial safety lever behind the bolt handle. The standard 25in barrel gave a weight of about 5.5lb.

Model 510P rifle, 1939-41. Distinguished from the standard M510 by the aperture rear sight on the receiver, and by a Patridge sight at the muzzle, this also generally had blocks for optical-sight mounts on the barrel.

Model 510SB rifle, 1939 only. A few of these smooth-bores were made to fire 22 shot or ball cartridges interchangeably, but they were never popular.

Model 510X rifle, 1964-6. A few of these guns were assembled from parts remaining in stock after production of the 510 series had finished. They could be distinguished by the rear sight, which was a sturdy spring-leaf pattern with a slider instead of an elevator.

Model 511A Scoremaster rifle, 1940-1 and 1945-62. Little more than a repeating version of the Model 510, this had a detachable five-round box magazine in the forend. A spring-leaf and elevator rear sight was standard.

Model 511P rifle, 1940-1. Identifiable by an aperture rear sight on the rear of the receiver, this also had blocks for telescope-sight mounts on the barrel.

Model 511X rifle, 1964-6. These could be identified by the improved rear sight: see Model 510X, above.

Model 512A Sportsmaster rifle, 1940-1 and 1945-62. A version of the Model 341 pattern with the radial-lever safety catch behind the bolt, this retained the tube magazine beneath the barrel but had an improved cartridge feed. A plain pistol grip half stock and a spring-leaf and elevator rear sight were standard fittings.

Model 512P rifle, 1940-1 and 1945-59? Mechanically identical with the 512A, this had a peep sight on the rear of the receiver and a hooded ramped blade at the muzzle; blocks for optical-sight mounts sometimes appeared on the 25in barrel.

Model 512X rifle, 1964-6. This had the improved 'X'-series spring-leaf and slider rear sight, but was otherwise the same as the Model 512A.

Model 513S rifle, 1941 and 1945-56. Only a few of these guns were made before the USA declared war on Japan, series production commencing only in 1945. Based on the 511 design, the 513S had a tapered 27in barrel, a detachable seven-round box magazine (five in post-war examples), and a walnut half stock with checkering on the pistol grip and forend. Swivels lay under the butt and forend.

Model 513TR Matchmaster rifle, 1941 and 1945-69. Offered only in 22LR rimfire, this target rifle had a 27in heavy semi-floating barrel and weighed about 9lb without its seven-round box magazine (six rounds in post-war examples). The patented trigger mechanism had an adjustable stop. Rear sights were usually Redfield patterns, with a replaceable-element tunnel at the muzzle. The sturdy half stock had a beavertail forend and a straight comb which rose at the heel. Sling swivels lay beneath the butt and forend.

Model 514 rifle, 1948-70. This was a simplified form of the basic action, lacking the safety catch. It had a 24in barrel and weighed only 4.7lb.

Model 514BC Boy's Carbine, 1961-71. Made with a 21in barrel, this junior version of the 514 also had a short butt.

Model 514P rifle, 1948-71? This could be distinguished from the standard pattern by the peep sight on the receiver and a ramped hooded blade at the muzzle.

Model 521TL rifle, 1947-69. Little more than a junior version of the Model 513TR (q.v.), this had a 25in barrel and weighed about 7lb in plain its target-style half stock. The aperture rear sight was usually a Lyman No. 57RS micrometer pattern. A short-butt version may have been made in small quantities as the '521TL-JR'.

MODEL 720 SPORTING RIFLE

Made by the Remington Arms Company, Ilion, New York, 1941.
Total production: 2430. **Chambering options:** 257 Roberts, 270 Winchester or 30-06. **Action:** as Model 30, above.
DATA FOR A TYPICAL 720A
Chambering: 30-06, rimless. 44.75in overall, 8lb empty. 24in barrel, 5-groove rifling; RH, concentric. Internal box magazine, 5 rounds. Lyman No. 48R aperture rear sight. 2750 fps with 180-grain bullet.

Developed by the Loomis brothers and Aubrey Lowe in 1941, this offered a refined stock with a fluted comb-tip, a better pistol grip and a broadened forend. A detachable magazine floorplate was fitted, the striker mechanism was altered to reduce lock-time, and the bolt handle was streamlined to improve appearance. Numbered from 40000 upward, the last guns were shipped from the Remington factory in 1944. The ill-starred Model 720 was still being listed in Remington catalogs in 1947, though none had been made for five years.

THE GUNS

Model 720A rifle, 1941-7. Made with a 22in barrel, this could also be fitted with Lyman ('720AL'), Marble-Goss ('720AM') or Redfield ('720AR') receiver sights.

Model 720R rifle, 1941-7. A version of the basic rifle with a 20in barrel, this was available in the same three basic sighting options as the 720A.

Model 720S rifle, 1941-7. Fitted with a 24in barrel, this could have any of the three sighting options.

MODEL 721A SPORTING RIFLE

Made by the Remington Arms Company, Ilion, New York, 1948-62.
Total production: 125,000 (all types)? **Chambering options:** see text.
Action: locked by two lugs on the bolt head engaging the receiver as the bolt handle was turned down.
DATA FOR TYPICAL EXAMPLE
Chambering: 30-06, rimless. 44.25in overall, 7.31lb empty. 24in barrel, 6-groove rifling; RH, concentric. Internal box magazine, 4 rounds. Spring-leaf and elevator rear sight. 2700 fps with 180-grain bullet.

Introduced in January 1949, this rifle chambered 270 Winchester or 30-06 cartridges, a 280 Remington option being added in 1959. The standard gun had a round barrel and a straight bolt handle; its plain straight-comb half stock had a pistol grip and a round tipped forend. The trigger guard was a stamped strip doubling as a floorplate, as a 'blind' magazine was fitted. A small safety catch protruded on the right side of the action behind the bolt handle, and the bolt-stop catch projected into the trigger guard immediately ahead of the finger lever.

SIMILAR GUNS

Model 721A Magnum rifle, 1951-62. This 8.25lb pattern was made for 300 H&H Magnum ammunition only, with a three-round magazine, a 26in barrel, and a recoil pad on the butt. A very few guns were chambered for 264 Winchester Magnum cartridge in 1960.

Model 721AC rifle, 1953-5. This is believed to have had checkering on the pistol grip and forend, but to have been otherwise standard.

Model 721B rifle, 1953-5. A short-lived variant, this had a detachable magazine floorplate.

Model 721BDL rifle, 1955-62. Featuring an improved deluxe stock with a low Monte Carlo comb and a contrasting forend tip, this rifle also had sling swivels. Most examples had Williams ramp-pattern rear sights.

MODEL 722A SPORTING RIFLE

Made by the Remington Arms Company, Ilion, New York, 1949-62.
Total production: not known. **Chambering options:** see text. **Action:** as Model 721, above.

DATA FOR A TYPICAL EXAMPLE

Chambering: 257 Roberts, rimless. 43.25in overall, 6.98lb empty. 24in barrel, 6-groove rifling; RH, concentric. Internal box magazine, 4 rounds. Spring-leaf and elevator rear sight. 2650 fps with 117-grain bullet.

A short-action version of the Model 721, this was offed in customary variety—though not in magnum chamberings. A 222 Remington option became available in 1950, with a 26in round barrel and a five-cartridge magazine. This particular rifle weighed 7.85lb. Subsequent chamberings included 244 Remington (1955, later known as '6mm Remington'); 257 Roberts, 300 Savage and 308 Winchester (1957); 222 Remington Magnum (1958); and 243 Winchester (1961).

SIMILAR GUNS

Model 722AC rifle, 1953-5. This was a short-lived variant with checkering on the pistol grip and forend.

Model 722B rifle, 1953-5. Guns of this type apparently had detachable magazine floorplates.

Model 722BDL rifle, 1955-62. Offering a stock with a Monte Carlo comb and a contrasting forend tip, this also had sling swivels.

MODEL 725ADL SPORTING RIFLE

Made by the Remington Arms Company, Ilion, New York, 1958-61.
Total production: 9850. **Chambering options:** 222 Remington, 243 Winchester, 244 Remington, 270 Winchester, 280 Remington, 30-06, 375 H&H Magnum or 458 Winchester Magnum (see notes). **Action:** as Model 721, above.

DATA FOR A TYPICAL EXAMPLE

Chambering: 244 Remington, rimless. 42.3in overall, 7.04lb empty. 22in barrel, 6-groove rifling; RH, concentric. Internal box magazine, 4 rounds. Spring-leaf and elevator rear sight. 3200 fps with 90-grain bullet.

A short-lived improvement of the Model 721, introduced only in 'ADL' form, this similar to its predecessors but had a detachable magazine floorplate. The safety system was modified to duplicate the original Model 30 ('Enfield') Remington pattern; a third position allowed the bolt to be withdrawn from the receiver. The bolt handle was swept backward, and the shaping of the trigger lever was improved.

SIMILAR GUNS

Kodiak Model rifle, 1961-2. As the decision to replace the 725-type rifle had already been taken, many actions were completed in 375 H&H Magnum or 458 Winchester Magnum. Kodiak guns had 26in barrels with muzzle brakes, recoil bolts through the stock beneath the chamber, and special ventilated rubber recoil pads. They were otherwise standard DL grade, with Monte Carlo combs, hand-cut checkering on the pistol grip and forend, contrasting forend caps, white spacer plates, and swivels under the stock.

MODEL 40 TARGET RIFLE

Made by the Remington Arms Company, Ilion, New York, 1961 to date.
Currently in production. **Chambering options:** see notes. **Action:** as Model 721, above.

DATA FOR TYPICAL MODEL 40XB

Chambering: 222 Remington Magnum, rimless. 46.75in overall, 10.62lb with standard barrel and competition sights. 28in barrel, 6-groove rifling; RH, concentric. Micro-adjustable aperture rear sight. 3300 fps with 55-grain bullet.

The Model 40, originally utilizing a modified Model 722 action, was introduced to handle 22 rimfire ammunition; later guns were

built on an adaptation of the standard Model 700 action, however, and often had a solid-floor receiver to enhance rigidity.

THE GUNS

International Free Rifle, 1964-74. A replacement for the International Match Free Rifle, this embodied the perfected 700-type action and could be identified by the rearward sweep of the bolt handle. Only 107 were made.

International Match Free Rifle, 1961-4. Offered in 22LR rimfire in addition to 222 Remington, 222 Remington Magnum, 30-06 or 308 Winchester centerfire, this was based on the 40X. It had a match-quality trigger and a thumbhole stock. Accessories included adjustable hooked or rubber buttplates, a palm rest, and a hand stop/swivel anchor. Receivers were tapped and drilled for optical-sight mounting bases, and a corresponding mounting block was fitted to the barrel. The guns weighed about 15.5lb with a 28in extra-heavy barrel.

Model 40X rifle, 1961-4. Built on a single-shot 721- or 722-type action, with a solid-floor receiver, this was customarily offered in 222 Remington, 222 Remington Magnum, 30-06 and 308 Winchester (other chamberings were made to order). It had a half-stock with a straight comb and a plain pistol grip. Standard guns lacked checkering, but were supplied with sturdy rubber buttplates. Mounting blocks for optical sights and rails for aperture sights were standard, and an adjustable hand-stop track was let into the underside of the forend.

Model 40XBBR rifle ('Bench Rest'), 1969-90? This gun was available in 22 Remington BR, 222 Remington, 222 Remington Magnum, 223 Remington, 6x47, 6mm BR Remington or 308 Winchester chamberings. It had a plain half-stock with a straight comb and a rounded forend, and weighed 12lb with a heavy 26in stainless-steel barrel.

Model 40XBBR KS ('Bench Rest, Kevlar stock') rifle, 1987 to date. Based on the XBBR of 1969, this had a synthetic stock. Chamberings are currently 22 BR Remington, 222 Remington, 222 Remington Magnum, 223 Remington, 6x47, 6mm BR Remington and 308 Winchester.

Model 40XB KS ('Kevlar stock') rifle, 1987 to date. This variant was introduced only in 220 Swift. It had a 27.25in barrel, weighed about 9.3lb, and was supplied without sights.

Model 40XB Rangemaster rifle, centerfire, 1964 to date. A replacement for the 40X, this single shot gun had a 700-type action and a butt with a straight comb which rose at the heel. The 40XB weighed 9.25lb with the original standard barrel (lacking sights), or about 11.25lb with the heavy pattern. Most post-1980 barrels have been stainless steel. Factory chamberings have included 220 Swift, 222 Remington, 222 Remington Magnum, 22-250, 223 Remington, 6x47, 6mm Remington, 243 Winchester, 25-06, 7mm BR Remington, 7mm Remington Magnum, 30-06, 308 Winchester, 30-338 and 300 Winchester Magnum. The basic heavy-barrel pattern was also made with a five-round magazine, in all options except 25-06, 30-06, 30-338 and 300 Winchester Magnum.

Model 40XB Rangemaster rifle, rimfire, 1964-74. Chambered only for the 22 LR cartridge, this single shot target gun was otherwise similar to the centerfire equivalent. The 28in barrel was set in a target-pattern half-stock with a fixed rubber buttplate and an accessory rail let into the underside of the forend.

Model 40XB Repeater rifle, rimfire, 1964-74. This could be identified by its five-round magazine.

Model 40XC National Match Rifle, 1974-89. Chambered for the 308 Winchester cartridge, this had stripper-clip guides on the front of the receiver bridge for military-match competitions. It weighed about 11lb and had a distinctive walnut half-stock with a vertical thumb-groove pistol grip and a deep forend level with the underside of the trigger guard. An adjustable buttplate and hand stop were supplied, and an optical sight could be attached to the receiver and barrel if required.

Model 40XC National Match KS ('Kevlar Stock') rifle, 1988 to date. This was simply a variant of the National Match pattern with a synthetic stock, standardized in 1990.

The Remington Model 40XB target rifle.

Model 40XR rifle. This single shot heavy-barrel gun had an adjustable buttplate, an elevating comb, and a palm-stop. Blocks for optical-sight mounts appeared on the barrel. Wood stocks were offered until 1989.

Model 40XR Custom Sporter, 1986 to date. This 22LR rimfire pattern has been made in four grades of decoration (I-IV) by the Remington Custom Gun Shop, often to individual requirements.

Model 40XR KS ('Kevlar Stock') rifle, 1988 to date. A modernized version of the original wood-stocked 40XR, this retained the elevating comb and adjustable buttplate of its predecessor.

Model 40XR KS National Match rifle. Offered only in 308 Winchester, with a five-round magazine loaded with a stripper-clip, this had a 24in stainless-steel barreled action and a Kevlar stock with a palm swell and a hand stop. It was 43.5in long and weighed about 11lb.

Model 40X SB rifle, 1957-74. A lightweight version of the 40X Target , this had a 26in barrel and weighed about 10.7lb.

Model 40X Sporter, 1969-77 and 1980. Combining a heavy barrel with an adaptation of the 700ADL half-stock, this was made only in small numbers; most estimates place total production at only 650-675 guns.

Model 40X Target, 1955-74. This single shot 22LR rimfire rifle had a 28in heavy barrel, Redfield Olympic sights, and blocks for telescope-sight mounts on the barrel in addition to a tapped-and-drilled receiver. Weight was about 12.5lb.

NYLON 11 SPORTING RIFLE

Made by the Remington Arms Company, Ilion, New York, 1962-6.
Total production: not known. **Chambering options:** 22 Short, 22 Long or 22 Long Rifle, rimfire. **Action:** generally as Model 33, above. 4.6lb empty.
19.65in barrel, 4-groove rifling; RH, concentric. Detachable box magazine, 6 or 10 rounds. Spring-leaf and finger-wheel rear sight. 1080 fps with 40-grain bullet.

These extraordinary guns had a split-bridge action with a radial safety catch on the right rear side of the receiver behind the spatulate bolt handle. An extraordinary modernistic nylon one-piece stock, with integrally molded checkering, provided an unmistakable recognition feature. A box magazine protruded from the elongated front web/floorplate of the trigger guard.

SIMILAR GUNS

Nylon 10 rifle, 1962-6. Similar to the box-magazine guns, this was restricted to single shots.

Nylon 10SB rifle, 1963-4. These smooth-bores were made to fire shot or ball cartridges interchangeably, but they were never popular and production was correspondingly restricted.

Nylon 12 rifle, 1962-6. This had a tube magazine protruding from the forend beneath the muzzle; 15-22 cartridges could be inserted, depending on their length.

MODEL 700 SPORTING RIFLE

Made by the Remington Arms Company, Ilion, New York, 1962 to date.
Total production: several million? **Chambering options:** see notes.
Action: as Model 721, above.
DATA FOR TYPICAL EXAMPLE
Chambering: 25-06, rimless. 42.35in overall, 7.08lb empty. 22in barrel, 6-groove rifling; RH, concentric. Internal box magazine, 5 rounds. Ramp-pattern rear sight. 3120 fps with 120-grain bullet.

This remodeling of the 720 series has been made in many differing patterns. A one-piece sear replaced the previous two-piece fabrication in 1968, when jeweling was added to the bolt, and the bolt plug was lengthened to enclose the cocking-piece head. A bolt guide-rib system was added in 1974; the rearward sweep of the bolt handle was reduced to prevent the shank from bruising the fingers during recoil; and a special cast stainless-steel magazine follower replaced the folded stamping.

The breech of a Remington Model 700 rifle, fitted with a Leupold Vari-X III 3.5x10-50 adjustable-objective optical sight.

OTHER VARIANTS

Note: Many published designations include the word 'Custom', though even Remington itself has had an ambivalent attitude to its use. The term has been restricted here to genuinely custom products at the expense of standardized deluxe guns.

Model 700ADL rifle, 1962 to date. This had a half-stock with a low Monte Carlo comb. A blind magazine and a short nylon or alloy trigger guard were used on early guns. The butt had a cheek-piece and a Monte Carlo comb, the buttplate was plain rubber, the pistol grip lacked a cap, and the forend tip was rounded. The pistol grip and forend were checkered, and sling-swivel eyes appeared beneath the butt and forend. Williams rear sights were used.

Chamberings have included 222 Remington Magnum (discontinued in 1990), 22-250 and 6mm Remington (both discontinued in 1991), 243 Winchester, 25-06 (until 1991), 270 Winchester, 7mm Remington Magnum, 30-06 and 308 Winchester; all rifles had five-round magazines except the 222 and 7mm Remington Magnum versions, which held six and four rounds respectively. Barrels measured 22in, or 24in in 222, 22-250, 25-06 and 7mm Remington Magnum.

Model 700ADL LS ('Laminated Stock') rifle, 1988 to date. Readily distinguished by the pattern and color of its wood-laminate half-stock, this has been made in 243 Winchester, 270 Winchester or 30-06 only.

Model 700ADL S ('Synthetic') rifle, 1996 to date. Offered in 243 Winchester, 270 Winchester, 7mm Remington Magnum, 30-06 and 308 Winchester, this has a straight-comb fiberglass-reinforced synthetic stock with molded checkering and a black rubber buttplate.

Model 700 APR ('African Plains Rifle'), 1995 to date. Chambered for five popular magnum rounds (7mm Remington, 300 Weatherby, 300 Winchester, 338 Winchester and 375 H&H), this has a 26in barrel set in a wood-laminate stock with hand-cut checkering on the pistol grip and forend. A black shoulder pad is standard.

Model 700 AWR ('Alaskan Wilderness Rifle'), 1994 to date. Recognizable by its matte-gray composite straight-comb stock, made of fiberglass, graphite and Kevlar, this also has a stainless-steel 24in barrel and a satin-blued action. Chamberings are exclusively magnum—7mm Remington, 300 Weatherby, 300 Winchester, 338 Winchester and 375 H&H.

Model 700 AS ('Arylon Stock') rifle, 1989-91. Offered in 22-250, 243 Winchester, 270 Winchester, 280 Remington, 7mm Remington Magnum, 30-06, 300 Weatherby Magnum or 308 Winchester chamberings, this had a matte-black Arylon stock and non-reflective metalwork.

Model 700BDL rifle, 1962 to date. This is now available with short or long action, and in a wide range of chamberings. These have included 17 Remington, 22-250, 222 Remington, 222 Remington Magnum, 223 Remington, 6.5mm Remington Magnum, 243 Winchester, 25-06, 264 Winchester, 270 Winchester, 7mm Reming-

The Remington Model 700ADL rifle.

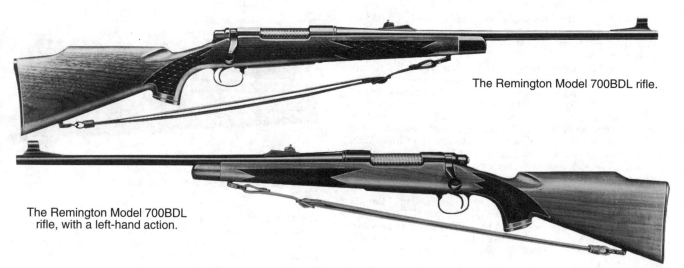

The Remington Model 700BDL rifle.

The Remington Model 700BDL rifle, with a left-hand action.

ton Magnum, 7mm-08, 30-06, 300 Winchester Magnum, 308 Winchester, 8mm Remington Magnum. Production of the 6.5mm and 350 Remington Magnum patterns was confined to 1969, the 264 Winchester chambering disappeared about 1971, and the 8mm Remington Magnum rifle was abandoned in 1991. Additions have included 338 Winchester Magnum and 35 Whelen in 1988, followed in 1992 by 280 Remington and 300 Savage, and 6mm Remington in 1993.

The BDL is essentially an ADL with a better stock with hand-cut skip-line checkering; a detachable magazine floorplate is also fitted. The buttplate, pistol grip cap and contrasting rounded forend tip were all separated from the woodwork by thin white synthetic spacers. A stainless-steel barrel was offered until the early 1970s in the 264 Winchester, 7mm Remington, and 300 Winchester Magnum chamberings only.

A left-hand version of the Model 700BDL was introduced in 1973 in 270 Winchester, 7mm Remington Magnum or 30-06 only. Guns were subsequently made in 22-250 Winchester, 243 Winchester, 7mm Remington Magnum and 338 Winchester Magnum.

Model 700BDL DM ('Detachable Magazine') rifle, 1995 to date. This offers a four-round box magazine in 243 Winchester, 25-06, 270 Winchester, 280 Remington, 7mm-08, 30-06 and 308 Winchester. Magnum options—7mm Remington, 300 Weatherby, 300 Winchester, 338 Winchester—hold three cartridges. The walnut Monte Carlo-style half-stock has a gloss finish.

Model 700BDL European rifle, 1993-5. This is identical with the standard BDL, but has an oil-finish stock instead of the gloss varnish type favored in North America. Chamberings are confined to 243 Winchester, 270 Winchester, 7mm-08, 7mm Remington Magnum and 30-06.

Model 700BDL Limited Classic rifle, 1981-91. Beginning with 7x57, Remington has also offered this gun in a single chambering which changed annually. The pattern was merged with the 700 Classic (below) from 1992.

Model 700BDL SS ('Stainless Steel') rifle, 1993 to date. Available in 270 Winchester, 7mm Remington Magnum, 30-06 and 300

Winchester Magnum, this is built on the basic BDL action, made of matte-finish stainless steel, and has a 24in barrel. The synthetic stock has a cheekpiece and a straight comb.

Model 700BDL SS-DM ('Stainless Steel, Detachable Magazine') rifle, 1995 to date. This is simply the BDL SS with a different magazine. The 'Model 700BDL SS-DM-B' variant, introduced in 1996 in the four magnum chamberings, has an additional muzzle brake.

Model 700C ('Custom Grade') rifle, 1965-89. This was originally a 'semi-production' BDL with a selected stock, skip-line checkering and special high-quality bluing, offered in four grades (I-IV). The designation now reserved for the products of the Remington Gun Shop.

Model 700 CS ('Camo Synthetic') rifle, 1992 to date. Also listed as 'BDL CS', these appeared in 22-250, 243 Winchester, 270 Winchester, 280 Remington, 7mm-08, 30-06 or 308 Winchester (standard guns), in addition to the 7mm Remington and 300 Weatherby Magnum rounds. Except the bolt, metalwork had a non-reflective finish, and the synthetic stock bore Mossy Oak Bottomland camouflage patterns.

Model 700 Classic rifle, 1981-93. This ADL-type gun offered a high-quality walnut stock with a satin finish and a straight comb. Hand-cut checkering graced the pistol grip and forend. Most forends have had rounded tips, though a few schnabel patterns have been made. Post-1990 guns have been offered on a very limited one-chambering-per-year basis—e.g., 220 Swift in 1992 and 375 H&H Magnum in 1996.

Model 700 Classic Magnum rifle, 1981-91. Essentially similar to the Classic pattern, this was chambered for the 7mm Remington Magnum cartridge and had a sturdier rubber buttplate.

Model 700D Peerless rifle, 1965-89. This deluxe variant was distinguished by good-quality woodwork and scroll engraving on the action.

Model 700F Premier rifle, 1965-89. Similar to the 700D or 'Peerless', this had additional game scenes inlaid in gold and the woodwork offered excellent figuring.

The Remington Model 700BDL Varmint Special rifle.

The Remington Model 700 Custom rifle, with a Kevlar stock.

Model 700 FS ('Fiberglass Stock') rifle, 1987-8. This variant offered a straight-comb composite black or black-camouflage half-stock of Kevlar and fiberglass. Right- and left-hand versions were offered. It was chambered for the 243 Winchester, 270 Winchester, 7mm Remington Magnum, 30-06 or 308 Winchester rounds, had a solid rubber recoil pad, and weighed about 6.3lb.

Model 700 Kit Gun, 1987-9. This was simply a standard barreled action accompanied by an inletted but otherwise unfinished ADL-pattern hardwood stock. It could be obtained in 243 Winchester, 270 Winchester, 7mm Remington Magnum, 30-06 or 308 Winchester.

Model 700 LSS ('Laminated, Stainless Steel') rifle, 1996 to date. Derived from the 700BDL, this has a stainless-steel barreled action in a gray-colored wood-laminate half-stock with a Monte Carlo-style cheekpiece and comb. Chamberings are restricted to 7mm Remington Magnum and 300 Winchester Magnum.

Model 700 MTR ('Mountain Rifle'), 1986-95. Also known as the 'BLR Mountain Rifle', this had a 22in tapered lightweight barrel and a straight-comb stock with refined pistol grip contours and an ebony forend tip. Offered initially only in 270 Winchester or 30-06. Additional 243 Winchester, 7mm-08 and 308 Winchester options were announced in 1988, followed by 7x57 in 1990, 257 Roberts in 1991 and 25-06 in 1992. It was about 42.5in long and weighed 6.7lb.

Model 700 MTR Custom KS ('Mountain Rifle, Custom Kevlar Stock'), 1986 to date. Introduced to accompany the standard Mountain Rifle (q.v.), this has a custom-finished Kevlar-reinforced stock with plain or (from 1992) wood-grain finish. Right- or left-hand actions could be supplied to order. Chamberings were initially 270 Winchester, 280 Remington, 7mm Remington Magnum, 300 Winchester Magnum, 30-06 and 375 H&H Magnum, but 8mm Remington Magnum and 338 Winchester Magnum options were added in 1988, followed by 300 Weatherby Magnum and 35 Whelen in 1989. A typical gun weighed about 6.4lb with a 24in barrel.

Model 700 MTN DM ('Mountain, Detachable Magazine') rifle, 1995 to date. A variant of the wood-stocked pattern, with a straight comb and refinements to the pistol grip contours, this has a 22in barrel and a hinged magazine floorplate. Chamberings are currently 243 Winchester, 25-06, 270 Winchester, 7mm-08, 280 Remington and 30-06; magazines hold four rounds. The stock has an oil-rubbed finish.

Model 700 MTR SS ('Mountain Rifle Stainless'), 1993 to date. This combines a 22in tapered barrel with a textured synthetic Mountain rifle half-stock. Chamberings are currently confined to 25-06, 270 Winchester, 280 Remington and 30-06.

Model 700 RS ('Rynite Stock') rifle, 1987-8. Stocked in synthetic Du Pont Rynite, with a gray or gray-camouflage finish, this chambered 270 Winchester, 280 Remington or 30-06 ammunition. Made only in right-hand form with a 22in barrel, it weighed about 7.2lb.

Model 700 Safari [Grade] rifle (or 'BDL Safari'), 1962 to date. This has been offered in 358 Winchester Magnum, 375 H&H Magnum or 458 Winchester Magnum. An 8mm Remington Magnum option was introduced in 1986, followed in 1989 by 416 Remington, but 358 had been abandoned by 1988. They had heavier barrels, reinforced stocks with two recoil bolts, and weighed 8.85lb. The earliest guns had Monte Carlo combs, but many made after the introduction of the Model 700 Classic in 1981 have had straight-comb butts.

Model 700 Safari KS ('Kevlar Stock) rifle, 1989 to date. This was simply a variant of the standard rifle with a 24in barrel and a plain black Kevlar half-stock. Chamberings were restricted to four magnum rounds—8mm Remington, 375 H&H, 416 Remington and 458 Winchester. An optional wood-grain stock finish was introduced in 1992.

Model 700 Sendero rifle, 1994 to date. This is basically a Varmint Synthetic built on a long action, chambered for the 25-06, 270 Winchester, 7mm Remington Magnum and 300 Winchester Magnum. It has a 26in heavy barrel and a straight-comb gray-black mottled composite stock.

Model 700 Sendero SF ('Satin Finish') rifle, 1996 to date. The 26in fluted barrel and the stainless-steel action have a non-reflecting finish.

Model 700 SS ('Stainless Synthetic') rifle, 1992 to date. These guns amalgamated a matte-finish stainless-steel barrel and action with a black textured composite stock. Standard 700BDL SS rifles

were chambered for 25-06, 270 Winchester, 280 Remington or 30-06 Springfield; magnums accepted the 7mm Remington or Weatherby magnum cartridges. Two Winchester magnum options—300 and 338—were added in 1993.

Model 700 VLS ('Varmint, Laminated Stock') rifle, 1995 to date. Made only in 22-250, 222 Remington, 223 Remington, 243 Winchester and 308 Winchester, this has a 26in barrel and a wood-laminate stock with a rubber shoulder pad.

Model 700 VS ('Varmint Special') rifle, or 'BDL VS', 1967 to date. Chambered for 22-250, 222 Remington, 223 Remington, 6mm Remington, 243 Winchester, 25-06 (discontinued in 1989), 7mm-08, or 308 Winchester rounds, this was a short-action BDL with a 24in heavy barrel and no open sights; it weighed 9lb.

Model 700 Varmint Synthetic rifle, 1992 to date. Introduced in 22-250, 223 Remington or 308 Winchester, a 220 Swift option being added in 1993. It was distinguished by an aluminum bedding block running the length of the receiver, a floating barrel, and a straight-comb textured stock of Kevlar, fiberglass and graphite. The stock was a dark gray/black mottle and the metal was blacked.

Model 700 VSS SF ('Varmint Special, Synthetic Satin Finish') rifle, 1994 to date. Little more than a standard VS rifle with a non-reflective finish on the action and the 26in fluted barrel, this is available in 220 Swift, 22-250, 223 Remington and 308 Winchester.

MODEL 600 SPORTING RIFLE

Made by the Remington Arms Company, Ilion, New York, 1964-71.
Chambering options: 222 Remington, 6mm Remington, 243 Winchester, 308 Winchester or 35 Remington. **Action:** as Model 721, above.

DATA FOR A TYPICAL MODEL 600
Chambering: 6mm Remington, rimless. 37.25in overall, 5.95lb empty. 18.45in barrel, 6-groove rifling; RH, concentric. Internal box magazine, 5 rounds. Spring-leaf and elevator rear sight. 3190 fps with 90-grain bullet.

These rifles were introduced in 1964 to compete in the market for cheap and compact brush guns. They had an adapted 700-type short action with the bolt handle cranked forward above the wedge-shape synthetic trigger guard. Box magazines contained five rounds, except the six-round 222 type. The earliest guns had conventional pistol grip half-stocks and tapering forends; they could be easily distinguished by the prominent ventilated barrel rib.

SIMILAR GUNS

Model 600 Magnum rifle. A strengthened version was introduced in 1965 for the 6.5mm Remington Magnum or 350 Remington Magnum cartridges, but had been abandoned by 1967. It was essentially similar to the standard 600, but had a 20in barrel, a four-round magazine, and an integral recoil stop for the sight mounts. The stock was a walnut/beech laminate with swivel eyes beneath the butt and forend.

Model 660 rifle, 1968-71. The basic rifles were superseded by the improved Model 660, having undergone similar changes to the Model 700. The unsightly barrel rib was eliminated, but a contrasting forend tip and spacer were added. Guns were still being sold through wholesalers (as the 'Mohawk 600') several years after production ceased.

Model 660 Magnum rifle, 1968-72. Introduced to replace the Model 600 Magnum, this was chambered for the 6.5mm Remington Magnum or 350 Remington Magnum cartridges. The stocks retained their distinctive laminate pattern.

Mohawk 600 rifle. This brand name was associated with many 660-type rifles sold in the 1970s.

MODEL 788 SPORTING RIFLE

Made by the Remington Arms Company, Ilion, New York, 1967-84.
Chambering options: see notes. **Action:** locked by lugs on the rear of the bolt body engaging seats in the receiver behind the magazine.
DATA FOR A TYPICAL EXAMPLE
Chambering: 223 Remington, rimless. 41.35in overall, 7.19lb empty. 22in barrel, 6-groove rifling; RH, concentric. Detachable box magazine, 4 rounds. Screw-and-leaf rear sight. 3300 fps with 55-grain bullet.

Credited to Charles Morse and Wayne Leek, this budget-priced rifle—a complete departure from the Model 700—was chambered for 222 Remington, 22-250, 30-30 and 44 Magnum. Only one action length was made, though the dimensions of the magazine well and the length of the bolt travel were specifically matched to the chambering. The most obvious feature was the tubular receiver and a bolt with nine small lugs in three rows of three locking into

The Remington Model 788 rifle.

the receiver immediately behind the magazine well. This allowed the receiver to be made from high-grade tubing, the multiplicity of lugs keeping lug-height to a minimum. However, though undeniably rigid, the Model 788 action was not attractive enough to displace the Model 700.

Barrels were usually 22in long, though the 222 and 22-250 guns had 24in patterns; the magazines offered three-round capacity except 222 and 223 (which took four apiece). The plain pistol grip half-stocks had low Monte Carlo combs, though cheekpieces and checkering were omitted to simplify production.

The 6mm Remington and 308 Winchester options were added in 1968, and a left-hand '788L' action (in 6mm and 308 only) appeared in 1969. The Model 788L was finally discontinued in 1981.

MODEL 540X TARGET RIFLE

Made by the Remington Arms Co., Ilion, New York, 1968-74.
Total production: not known. **Chambering:** 22 Long Rifle, rimfire. **Action:** generally as Model 33, above.
45in overall, 8lb empty. 26in barrel, 4-groove rifling; RH, concentric. Single shot only. Micro-adjustable aperture rear sight. 1080 fps with 40-grain bullet.

Introduced on the basis of a new action, lacking the split-bridge receiver of the previous bolt-action rimfires, this gun had a heavy-weight barrel set in a massive half-stock with an anatomical pistol grip. The buttplate could be slid vertically in its channel-block, and a rail for the hand-stop and swivel was let into the underside of the squared forend. The choice of sights was usually left to the purchaser.

SIMILAR GUNS

Model 540XR rifle, 1974-83. Substituted for the otherwise identical 540X, this was intended for three-position shooting. The forend extended down to the underside of the trigger guard, facilitating finger-tip or finger-back support in the standing position.

Model 540XRJR rifle, 1974-83. Essentially the same as the 540XR pattern, this had a short or 'junior' ('JR') butt.

Model 541S Custom Sporter, 1972-84. A sporting gun built on a scroll-engraved 540-series action, this fed from a detachable five-round magazine handling 22 Short, Long and Long Rifle cartridges interchangeably. The barrel was a 24in type, giving a weight of about 6lb with the elegant straight-comb select walnut half-stock.

Checkering appeared on the pistol grip and the forend; the forend tip and pistol grip cap were rosewood.

Model 541T rifle, 1986-92? This was similar to the 541S type, but had plain metalwork and a stock with an ebonite tip. The barrel was drilled and tapped to accept bases for optical-sight mounts.

MODEL 580 SPORTING RIFLE

Made by the Remington Arms Co., Ilion, New York, 1968-78.
Total production: not known. **Chambering options:** 22 Short, 22 Long or 22 Long Rifle, rimfire. **Action:** generally as Model 33, above.
42.5in overall, 4.75lb empty. 24in barrel, 4-groove rifling; RH, concentric. Single shot only. Spring-leaf and elevator rear sight. 1080 fps with 40-grain bullet.

The first of a series of similar-looking rifles derived from the Model 540, these had rails for optical-sight mounts on top of the tubular solid-bridge receiver. The plain ambidextrous half-stock had a low Monte Carlo comb, but lacked a cheekpiece; the generous proportions of the pistol grip and the rounded forend improved handling characteristics, and the stamped-strip trigger guard was large enough to admit a gloved finger.

SIMILAR GUNS

Model 580BR Boy's Rifle, 1971-8. This was simply a minor variant of the standard gun with a short butt.

Model 580SB rifle, 1967-78. Smooth-bored to fire shot or ball cartridges with equal success, this was made only in small numbers.

Model 581 rifle, 1967-83. Distinguished by a detachable six-round box magazine, this resembled the 580 and could be converted to fire single shots with a suitable adapter. A left-hand action was also made in small numbers.

Model 581S rifle, 1987-92? Difficult to distinguish from the original Model 581, this had a five-round magazine and a walnut-finish hardwood stock with a tapering forend.

Model 582 rifle, 1967-83. The tube-magazine version of the 580 could hold 14 22LR or 20 22 Short cartridges. Empty weight was about 5.1lb.

Model 591 rifle, 1970-4. A short-lived adaptation of the basic design, this box-magazine gun was chambered for the 5mm Remington Magnum rimfire cartridge. The pistol grip had a separate synthetic cap and the straight comb had a noticeable notch behind the wrist. About 25,000 guns were made.

Model 592 rifle, 1970-4. Made in similar numbers to the Model 591, this had a 10-round tube magazine beneath the barrel and weighed about 5.6lb empty.

The Remington Model 540XR rimfire rifle.

The Remington Model 541S rifle.

The Remington Model 581 box-magazine rifle.

The Remington Model 582 tube-magazine rifle.

The Remington Model Seven rifle.

MODEL SEVEN

Made by the Remington Arms Company, Ilion, New York, 1983 to date.
Chambering options: see notes. **Action:** as Model 721 above.
DATA FOR A TYPICAL MODEL SEVEN
   Chambering: 7mm-08, rimless. 37.55in overall, 6.38lb empty. 18.5in barrel, 6-groove rifling; RH, concentric. Internal box magazine, 4 rounds. Ramp-pattern rear sight. 2860 fps with 140-grain bullet.

This was designed as an inexpensive short-barreled brush gun. Introduced in 222 Remington (5-round magazine), 6mm Remington, 243 Winchester, 7mm-08 or 308 Winchester (all four rounds), it was little more than a 700-pattern short action in a straight-comb stock with a prominent schnabel tip. A silent side-mounted safety was fitted and the barrel floated freely except for a single bearing point in the tip of the forend. A 223 Remington option was added in 1984, but the 222 version was abandoned soon afterward.

SIMILAR GUNS

Model Seven Custom KS ('Kevlar stock') rifle, 1987 to date. A variant of the Model 7 with a Kevlar-reinforced stock, made to special order, this could be obtained in 223 Remington, 7mm-08, 308 Winchester, 35 Remington or 350 Remington Magnum. It had a 20in barrel, increasing overall length to about 39in, and weighed 5.8lb.

Model Seven Custom MS (Mannlicher-style Stock) rifle, 1993 to date. Distinguished by a wood-laminate stock with a straight comb, a full-length forend and a blackened steel forend cap, this has a 20in barrel; weight averaged 6.75lb. Standard chambering options are 222 Remington, 22-250, 223 Remington, 6mm Remington, 7mm-08, 308 Winchester and 350 Remington Magnum, but 250-3000 Savage, 257 Roberts and 35 Remington versions can be supplied to special order.

Model Seven FS ('Fiberglass Stock') rifle, 1987-90. Made with Kevlar inserts at the stress points in the stock, this has been offered in 243 Winchester, 7mm-08 or 308 Winchester only. It weighs about 5.3lb.

Model Seven SS ('Stainless Steel') rifle, 1994 to date. Offered with a stainless steel action, a 20in barrel and a black synthetic half-stock, this is available in 243 Winchester, 7mm-08 and 308 Winchester.

Model Seven Youth rifle, 1993 to date. This differs from the standard pattern solely in its short-butt hardwood stock. Chamberings are restricted to 243 Winchester and 7mm-08.

MODEL 78 SPORTING RIFLE

Made by the Remington Arms Company, Ilion, New York, 1988-91.
Chambering options: 223 Remington, 243 Winchester, 6mm Remington, 7mm-08, or 308 Winchester. **Action:** as Model 700 above.

   Chambering: 7mm-08, rimless. 37.55in overall, 6.38lb empty. 18.5in barrel, 6-groove rifling; RH, concentric. Internal box magazine, 4 rounds. Ramp-pattern rear sight. 2860 fps with 140-grain bullet.

This short-lived rifle, also known as the 'Model 78 Sportsman', combined a 700-type action with a plain hardwood stock and a plastic buttplate. It was intended to compete in the budget-price market, but was made only in small numbers.

MODEL 24 SNIPER RIFLE
Part of the 'M24 Sniping System'

Made by the Remington Arms Company, Ilion, New York, 1988 to date.
Currently in production. **Chambering:** 7.62x51 NATO. **Action:** generally as Model 700 (q.v.).
   43in overall without butt spacers, 12.25lb without sights. 24in barrel, 5-groove rifling; RH, concentric. Detachable box magazine, 6 rounds. Optical sight. 2615 fps with M118 Special Ball ammunition.

This gun was developed to compete in U.S. Army trials held in 1986, the initial contract being awarded to Remington in the summer of 1987. The M24 was little more than an improved M40A1, or, therefore, a militarized form of the Model 700 (q.v.). The M40X trigger, adapted from the M40 Match Rifle, was capable of a wide range of adjustments. The heavy barrel was specially rifled to suit the 173-grain M118 bullet, though the contract stipulated that the rifles should be capable of conversion if long-term trials showed that the 300 Winchester Magnum was more accurate than the special 7.62mm cartridge.

The pistol grip half-stock is a composite of Kevlar and graphite, with an aluminum bedding-block and a rail beneath the forend to accept a bipod or a hand-stop. The buttplate is adjustable, but the comb is fixed. Optical sights are standard—the purpose-built M24 Sniper Sight was still under development in 1997—but open sights were supplied as part of the basic system for use in emergencies.

Remington supplied 25 rifle/accessory kits for exhaustive preliminary trials ('First Article Testing'), and the first of 2510 series-production rifles was delivered to the U.S. Army in October 1988 for Rangers and Special Forces use.

• Remington, lever-action type
NYLON 76 TRAIL RIDER RIFLE

Made by the Remington Arms Co., Ilion, New York, 1962-4.
Total production: not known. **Chambering options:** 22 Long Rifle, rimfire. **Action:** locked by wedging the bolt behind the chamber with the operating lever.
   37.5in overall, 4.15lb empty. 19.65in barrel, 4-groove rifling; RH, concentric. Tube magazine beneath barrel, 14 rounds. Spring-leaf and finger-wheel rear sight. 1080 fps with 40-grain bullet.

This was a modification of the Nylon 66 autoloader (q.v.), with a short-throw closed loop lever following the curve of the pistol grip behind the trigger. DuPont Zytel stocks were brown or, more rarely, black. Teething troubles were never satisfactorily overcome, and the Nylon 76 was abandoned after only a few thousand had been made.

The Remington Model 78 Sportsman rifle.

• Remington, slide-action type
MODEL 12 SPORTING RIFLE
Subsequently known as 'Model 12A'
Made by the Remington Arms Co., Ilion, New York, 1909-36.
Total production: not known. **Chambering options:** 22 Short, 22 Long or 22 Long Rifle rimfire. **Action:** locked by displacing the bolt lug into the top of the receiver as the slide ran forward.

About 41in overall, 4.5lb empty. 22in barrel, 4-groove rifling; RH, concentric. Tube magazine beneath the barrel, 10-15 rounds depending on cartridge length. Fixed open rear sight. 1080 fps with 40-grain bullet.

The first of the slide-action Remingtons, made in accordance with patents granted in 1909-12 to John Pedersen, this was a hammerless take-down pattern with a straight-wrist butt and a circumferentially grooved slide handle. Made in a wide variety of Grades—from 'A' to 'F'—it had a short slab-side receiver with a rounded back and an ejection port on the right side. The magazine tube was a three-quarter-length design ending well short of the muzzle. Early guns had Remington–UMC marks; later examples had Remington marks only.

SIMILAR GUNS
Model 12B Gallery rifle. This had a 22in octagonal barrel chambered specifically for the 22 Short rimfire cartridge.

Model 12C NRA Target Grade rifle. Readily identifiable by a 24in octagonal barrel and select walnut woodwork, this had a semi pistol grip butt and better sights.

Model 12CS rifle. Made only in small numbers in 'CS', 'DS' and 'FS' Grades, this was chambered for the 22 Remington Special cartridge and had a 12-round magazine.

MODEL 14 SPORTING RIFLE
Made by the Remington Arms Company, Ilion, New York, 1912-36.
Chambering options: see notes. **Action:** as Model 12, above.
DATA FOR A TYPICAL MODEL 141A
Chambering: 30 Remington, rimless. 42.8in overall, 7.15lb empty. 24in barrel, 6-groove rifling; RH, concentric. Tube magazine under barrel, 5 rounds. Spring-leaf and elevator rear sight. 2220 fps with 160-grain bullet.

This was an enlargement of the sturdy Pedersen-designed Model 12 tipping-bolt action to handle centerfire ammunition. A special spiral magazine was used to prevent cartridge noses igniting the primer ahead of them. Standard guns had a straight-wrist butt, a ribbed slide handle, and round barrels. Capable of handling regular and high-speed ammunition, the Model 14 was the first truly successful slide-action centerfire sporting rifle. Optional extras included half pistol grip butts and differing finishes.

SIMILAR GUNS
Model 14 carbine, 1912-34. A variant of the standard rifle-length gun, this had an 18.5in barrel and a straight-wrist stock.

Model 14-1/2 rifle, 1915-25. This derivative was chambered for 38-40 or 44-40 Winchester cartridges. Its action was substantially shorter than that of the guns chambering regular rifle rounds, but the Model 14-1/2 was unpopular and was never made in large numbers.

Model 14-1/2R. A carbine-length version of the standard 14-1/2 rifle, this was similarly unsuccessful.

MODEL 121A FIELDMASTER RIFLE
Made by the Remington Arms Co., Ilion, New York, 1936-41 and 1945-54.
Total production: many thousands. **Chambering options:** 22 Short, 22 Long and 22 Long Rifle, rimfire. **Action:** generally as Model 12, above.

42.5in overall, 6lb empty. 24in barrel, 4-groove rifling; RH, concentric. Tube magazine under barrel, 14-20 rounds depending on cartridge length. Spring-leaf and elevator rear sight. 1080 fps with 40-grain bullet.

The first of a series of highly successful guns made in accordance with Pedersen, Garrison and Loomis patents, the Fieldmaster was a slender design with a plain pistol grip butt and a finely grooved slide handle. The three-quarter-length magazine was retained, stopping well short of the muzzle. Capacity ranged from 14 22LR to 20 22 Short rounds. Many different grades of woodwork, finish and decoration were offered.

SIMILAR GUNS
Model 121S rifle, 1936-40. A minor variant of the standard gun, this was chambered for the 22 Remington Special rimfire cartridge.

Model 121SB rifle, 1936-40. Made in small numbers, this smooth-bore pattern was intended to fire ball and shot cartridges with equal facility.

MODEL 141A SPORTING RIFLE
Made by the Remington Arms Company, Ilion, New York, 1936-50.
Chambering options: see notes. **Action:** as Model 14, above.
Chambering: 30 Remington, rimless. 42.8in overall, 7.15lb empty. 24in barrel, 6-groove rifling; RH, concentric. Tube magazine under barrel, 5 rounds. Spring-leaf and elevator rear sight. 2220 fps with 160-grain bullet.

Made only in 30, 32 or 35 Remington chamberings, available only in standard grade with a 24in round barrel, the Model 141A Gamemaster had a pistol grip butt and a finely ribbed forend. It was discontinued in 1950, though new guns were available from dealers' stocks for some years thereafter.

MODEL 760 GAMEMASTER SPORTING RIFLE
Made by the Remington Arms Company, Ilion, New York, 1952-82 (all patterns).
Chambering options: see notes. **Action:** locked by rotating lugs on the bolt into the barrel extension as the slide ran forward.
DATA FOR TYPICAL MODEL 760A
Chambering: 270 Winchester, rimless. 42in overall, 7.45lb empty. 22in barrel, 6-groove rifling; RH, concentric. Detachable box magazine, 4 rounds. Spring-leaf and elevator rear sight. 2900 fps with 150-grain bullet.

Introduced to replace the Model 141A, the Gamemaster had a pistol grip butt separated from the forend by a machined steel receiver. Renamed '760A' in 1953, after the introduction of the ADL version, the Model 760 was distinguishable from the similar-looking 740 auto-loader by the forend, which exposed several inches of the barrel and operating rods instead of running back to the receiver. Skip-line checkering was pressed into the pistol grip and forend. Chamberings included 223 Remington, 6mm Remington, 243 Winchester, 257 Roberts, 270 Winchester, 280 Remington, 300 Savage, 30-06, 308 Winchester and 35 Remington.

SIMILAR GUNS
Model 760ADL rifle, 1953-63. This had better-quality woodwork than the standard Model 760A, with hand-cut checkering, and was generally offered with a straight comb (though Monte Carlo versions were known). Chamberings included 223 Remington, 6mm Remington, 243 Winchester, 257 Roberts, 270 Winchester, 280 Remington, 300 Savage, 30-06, 308 Winchester and 35 Remington.

Model 760BDL rifle, 1953-82. Introduced in 270 Winchester, 30-06 or 308 Winchester only, this gun displayed high-gloss polyurethane finish on the woodwork and had basket-weave checkering.

Model 760 Bicentennial rifle. Made in 1976 to celebrate the 200th anniversary of the signing of the Declaration of Independence, these guns had suitably engraved receivers.

Model 760 carbine, 1962-80. Made in 270 Winchester, 280 Remington, 30-06 or 308 Winchester chamberings, in standard and deluxe grades, this had an 18.5in barrel and weighed about 7.3lb. A Williams ramp-type rear sight was usually fitted.

The Remington Model 760 carbine.

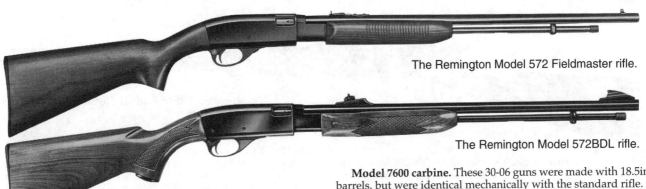

The Remington Model 572 Fieldmaster rifle.

The Remington Model 572BDL rifle.

Model 760D Peerless rifle, 1961-81. Deluxe-grade guns of this pattern had scroll engraving on the receiver and woodwork selected for its decorative grain.

Model 760F Premier rifle, 1961-81. This had scroll engraving and gold-inlaid game scenes on the receiver; woodwork also offered the highest quality.

Model 760 Remington Sesquicentennial rifle. A few of these were made in 1966, in 30-06 only, to celebrate their manufacturer's 150th anniversary. The receivers were appropriately engraved.

MODEL 572A FIELDMASTER RIFLE

Introduced in 1959, this was a much-modernized form of the Model 121 (q.v.). It had a new slab-side receiver—shorter and deeper than its predecessor—with a small ejection port on the front right side. A safety bolt ran laterally through the rear web of the trigger guard, the plain straight-comb butt had a generous pistol grip, and the slide handle was finely grooved. The standard guns had 23in barrels and weighed 5.5lb.

SIMILAR GUNS

Model 572BDL Fieldmaster rifle, 1966-92? This could be distinguished from the 572A by the checkering on the pistol grip and slide handle, though the sights were also ramped.

Model 572BT Lightweight rifle, 1958-62. Similar externally to the standard Fieldmaster, this had an anodized alloy frame and barrel sleeve in 'Buckskin Tan' color. The magazine tube, trigger lever and trigger guard were chromed, and the woodwork (with impressed checkering) was light-stained walnut. Alloy components kept weight down to only a little over 4lb, but durability proved to be suspect and production was soon abandoned.

Model 572CWB Lightweight rifle, 1958-62. This was a variant of the alloy-frame guns in 'Crown Wing Black'.

Model 572 Sesquicentennial rifle, 1966. Made in small numbers to celebrate Remington's 150th anniversary, this had a suitable inscription on the left side of the receiver.

Model 572SB rifle, 1967-78. Made only in small quantities, this was a smooth-bore suited equally to shot or ball ammunition.

Model 572TWB Lightweight rifle, 1958-62. Identical with the 572BT pattern, this had the receiver and barrel-sleeve in 'Teal Wing Blue'.

MODEL SIX SPORTING RIFLE

This was introduced in 1981 to replace the 760 series, though essentially very similar. The walnut woodwork had hand-cut checkering, though Model Six rifles were also made in Peerless and Premier grades. The distinctions between the Models Six and 7600 were lost when the two patterns were merged in the early 1980s under the Model 7600 designation.

SIMILAR GUNS

Model 7600 rifle, 1981 to date. This was originally a plain-finished Model Six. By the mid 1980s, however, the 'Model Six' designation had been abandoned and even the standard Model 7600 rifles featured walnut woodwork with hand-cut checkering. The 22in-barreled Model 7600 rifles were chambered for 6mm Remington, 243 Winchester, 270 Winchester, 280 Remington, 7mm Remington Express, 308 Winchester, 30-06 or 35 Whelen rounds; they had cross-bolt safety catches, Williams ramp sights, and receivers drilled and tapped for optical-sight mounts. Weight averaged 7.5lb.

Model 7600 carbine. These 30-06 guns were made with 18.5in barrels, but were identical mechanically with the standard rifle.

• Remington-Hepburn

Note: Guns made prior to 1886 (and most of those sold for much of 1887-8) were marked as the product of E. Remington & Sons; those dating later than 1888 were made and marked by the Remington Arms Company.

NO. 3 SPORTING RIFLE

Made by the E. Remington & Sons and the Remington Arms Company, Ilion, New York, 1880-92.

Chambering options: see notes. **Action:** locked by propping a radial breechblock behind the chamber with the tip of the operating lever.

Chambering: 38-50 Remington-Hepburn, rimmed. 43.8in overall, 8.5lb empty. 28in barrel, 5-groove rifling; RH, concentric. Single shot only. Spring-leaf and adjusting-screw rear sight. 1320 fps with 255-grain bullet.

Offered in a wide variety of chamberings from 22 rimfire to 45 centerfire, this was very similar to the standard rolling blocks. However, the contours of the receiver were noticeably squarer and a prominent serpentine operating lever—the work of Lewis Hepburn—lay on the right side of the breech. The No. 3 sporter had a rebounding hammer, a 26-30in half- or full-octagon barrel, and a pistol grip butt; the short tapering forend usually had a small pewter tip.

SIMILAR GUNS

No. 3 Improved Creedmoor Rifle, about 1881-91. The advent of the No. 3 sporter created this target rifle, offered in chamberings ranging from 38-40 to 45-90. The guns had round or octagonal barrels, weighed 9-9.5lb and were invariably fitted with a set trigger. Vernier and wind-gauge sights were standard, often incorporating a spirit level. Pistol grip butts and schnabel-tip forends were finely checkered, though cheek-piece butts and special nickel plated Schützen-style buttplates could be supplied to order. A typical 40-70 rifle, with a 34in barrel, measured 49.75in overall and weighed 9.35lb.

No. 3 Long Range Military Creedmoor Rifle, 1882-about 1892. Confined to shooting matches in which military-style stocks were obligatory, this had a steel ramrod, a 34in round barrel and a full-length checkered forend retained by two bands. A typical 44-75-520 example (the only known chambering) was 49.75in long and weighed 10lb; a Vernier sight was fitted to the tang behind the hammer, with a globe pattern at the muzzle.

No. 3 Match Rifle, 1883-1907. Usually sold with a 28in or 30in half-octagon barrel—in chamberings ranging from 25-20 Single Shot to 40-65—this gun had a plain buttplate, a checkered walnut pistol grip butt, and a checkered forend with a tip of pewter or German silver. Sculptured cheekpieces and Schützen-style buttplates could be supplied to order. Typically, a 28in-barreled 40-65 WCF example was 45.75in overall and weighed 8.77lb. A Vernier sight was fitted to the tang behind the hammer.

No. 3 Hunter's Rifle, 1885-about 1907. Usually built on the Hepburn-Walker action, substituting a combination underlever/trigger guard for the Hepburn sidelever, this chambered rim- and centerfire cartridges ranging from 25-20 to 50-70. Sights were generally plain Rocky Mountain patterns, the barrel was a half-octagon type (26-30in), and a checkered pistol grip butt with a curved buttplate was fitted. Tough and comparatively unsophisticated, these guns were regarded as the workhorse of the series; a 38-40 Remington example had a 28in barrel, measured 43.75in overall and weighed 8.03lb.

New Model No. 3, 1893-1912? This was specially strengthened to handle smokeless-powder ammunition, and, as a result, cham-

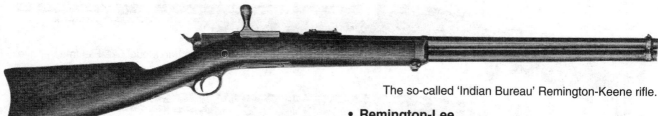

The so-called 'Indian Bureau' Remington-Keene rifle.

bered cartridges such as the 30-30 Winchester, 30-40 Krag, 32 Winchester Special, 32-40 Ballard, 38-55 Ballard or 38-72 Winchester. The octagonal barrel measured 26-30in, and the optional double set trigger unit was often fitted. A representative 38-72 Winchester specimen, weighing 8.04lb with its 26in barrel, was 41.7in long.

No. 3 Schuetzen Match Rifle, 1904-7. Built on the Hepburn or Hepburn-Walker action, this had an impressively scrolled trigger guard. A special Vernier wind-gauge peep sight lay on the tang—with a hooded or tunnel-type front sight—and a shallow cheekpiece appeared on the straight-wrist butt. Hooked Swiss-style butt-plates and folding palm rests were standard. Chambered for 32-40 Ballard, 38-40 Remington, 38-50 Remington or 40-65 Remington ammunition, the half-octagon barrel measured 28in-32in. This gave the rifles a length of 49.5-53.5in (including the buttplate hook) and a weight of 11.5-13lb, but less than 200 were made.

• Remington-Keene

Patented by James Keene of Newark, New Jersey in 1874-7, this bolt-action rifle was tested by the U.S. Army but never adopted in quantity by any military agency.

The bolt relied on a prominent rib turning down into the receiver to provide a satisfactory lock. The loading port lay on the underside of the stock ahead of the trigger, though the magazine could also be loaded from the top through the open action. As the cartridges were securely retained in the elevator during the loading stroke, the Remington-Keene—unlike many tube-magazine rivals—could be loaded and fired upside-down.

REMINGTON-KEENE MILITARY MUSKET
Also known as 'Model 1880'

Made by E. Remington & Sons, Ilion, New York, 1877-80.
Total production: about 5,000. **Chambering**: 45-70, rimmed. **Action**: locked by the bolt-guide rib abutting the front of the receiver bridge as the bolt handle was turned down.

48.5in overall, 9lb empty. 30in barrel, 5-groove rifling; RH, concentric. Tube magazine beneath barrel, 9 rounds. Ramp-and-leaf rear sight graduated to 1200yd. About 1275 fps with standard ball cartridges. M1873 socket bayonet.

Introduced commercially in 1878, the Remington-Keene had a straight-wrist half-stock with a notably 'bellied' under-surface, and a prominent spur on the cocking piece which had to be cocked manually before firing—a safety feature deemed necessary on horseback. The U.S. Navy acquired 250 rifles for shipboard trials in 1880, probably with 30in barrels. The U.S. Army then acquired a similar quantity of guns in 1881, for trials against the Hotchkiss and Remington-Lee. These are said to have had 32.5in barrels.

The Army guns had a full-length stock, two bands, and a cleaning rod set in a channel on the left side of the forend. A cut-off on the left side of the breech allowed them to function as single-loaders. No additional purchases were made.

Carbine. A few 45-70 half-stocked guns were made with 20.5in barrels, giving an overall length of 39.5in and a weight of about 8lb; magazine capacity was reduced to seven cartridges. It is assumed that they were used for military trials, but details are lacking.

Indian Bureau Rifle. About 200 to 250 half-stock 45-70 short rifles with 24in barrels and full-length magazines were purchased on behalf of the U.S. Indian Bureau in 1884. Issued to reservation police, they bore 'U.S.I.D.' and an identification number.

Sporting rifle. A few thousand of these were made in 40-70 Remington, 43 Spanish and 45-70. Most apparently had 24in round or half-octagon barrels and eight-round magazines. Sales were slow, however, and Remington disposed of the remaining stocks of unsold rifles in 1887 at cut-rate prices.

• Remington-Lee

The failure of the Sharps Rifle Company, which was liquidated in 1881, had a beneficial effect on the business of E. Remington & Sons. Remington acquired the uncompleted U.S. Navy contract for Lee magazine rifles, and sensed a great commercial opportunity. Production of the 1879-pattern rifle continued, but work undertaken by Remington designers—particularly Roswell Cook and Louis Diss—soon led to improvements.

MILITARY GUNS
MAGAZINE RIFLE
Also known as the 'Model 1882'

Made by E. Remington & Sons, Ilion, New York, 1882-4.
Total production: about 32,000. **Chambering options**: 43 Spanish or 45-70. **Action**: locked by the bolt-guide rib abutting the receiver bridge and a lug opposing the bolt handle entering the receiver as the bolt handle was turned down.
DATA FOR U.S. ARMY TRIALS RIFLE

Chambering: 45-70-500, rimmed. 52in overall, 8.5lb empty. 32.5in barrel, 3-groove rifling; RH, concentric. Detachable box magazine, 5 rounds. Ramp-and-leaf rear sight graduated to 1200yd. 1320 fps with ball cartridges. M1873 socket bayonet.

Among the rifles tested by the U.S. Army in the summer of 1882 were three Lee patterns—No. 10 and No. 11 were standard 1879-patent rifles, but gun No. 36 had an improved bolt with the handle locking down behind the receiver bridge. On 4th September 1882, the board reported that Lee No. 36 was preferred to 'Chaffee-Reece No. 33' and 'Hotchkiss No. 34' owing to the detachable box magazine and an additional locking lug. A contract for 750 guns was finally signed on 31st May 1884. Remington delivered the 1882-pattern Lee rifles in the late autumn of 1884, enabling field trials against the Springfield-made Chaffee-Reece and Hotchkiss guns supplied by Winchester.

These Lee rifles had one-piece stocks, two bands, and standard Army-type sights. Numbered in the 8800-9800 group, they were marked 'U.S.' and also bore inspectors' marks. Their improved magazines were protected by patents granted to Louis Diss in the summer of 1884, which had two prominent cartridge-guide grooves in the sheet-metal bodies.

The Chief of Ordnance informed the Secretary of War in late 1885 that the Lee had performed better than its rivals. However, most officers still preferred the single-shot 45-70 Springfield and the repeaters were withdrawn.

1882-pattern Lee rifles (and some carbines) were also sold to China, Peru and Haiti. In the autumn of 1891, 208 Army-type M1882 rifles were purchased by the U.S. Navy from William Read, a Boston dealer, and issued to the Massachusetts Naval Brigade. Surviving guns of this type may have rack numbers and 'N B' on the right side of the butt.

IMPROVED MAGAZINE RIFLE
Also known as 'Model 1885'

Made by E. Remington & Sons, Ilion, New York (1886-7); and by the Remington Arms Company, Ilion, New York (1888-95).
Total production: 9000-10,000. **Chambering options**: 43 Spanish or 45-70. **Action**: generally as M1882, above.
DATA FOR A TYPICAL EXAMPLE

Chambering: 45-70, rimmed. 52in overall, 8.9lb empty. 32.5in barrel, 3-groove rifling; RH, concentric. Detachable box magazine, 5 rounds. Ramp-and-leaf sight graduated to 1200yd. 1320 fps with ball cartridges. Remington-type socket bayonet.

This rifle owed its existence to patents granted in March 1885 to Remington employee Louis Diss, protecting the separate bolt head which addressed a problem with the 1882-pattern firing pin. Inserted from the back of the bolt, the older pattern occasionally came out of the back of the gun when the retainer failed. A non-rotating extractor and an enlarged cocking-piece were also fitted, though the stock and sights duplicated those of the M1882.

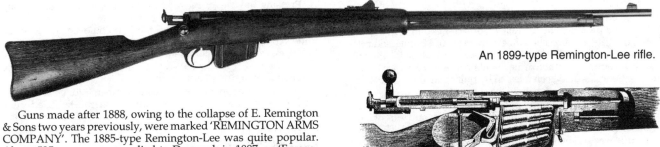

An 1899-type Remington-Lee rifle.

A longitudinal section of the 1899-type rifle.

Guns made after 1888, owing to the collapse of E. Remington & Sons two years previously, were marked 'REMINGTON ARMS COMPANY'. The 1885-type Remington-Lee was quite popular. About 525 guns were supplied to Denmark in 1887, as 'Førsøgsrepetergeværer m/1' (experimental repeating rifles); 350 43-caliber guns went to Britain, and 500 were sold to New Zealand in the same era.

The U.S. Navy accepted nearly 4,000 guns for Navy personnel and naval militia units. The first order for 1610 guns was placed with the Lee Arms Company in August 1888 and then sub-contracted to Remington. The rifles had standard Springfield fittings and sights, and accepted the 1873-pattern socket bayonet.

They were customarily marked with 'USN', an anchor, a Navy serial number (in addition to Remington's), and inspectors' initials. Their service life was short, however, as they were replaced in 1897 by the 236-caliber Winchester-Lee.

SIMILAR GUN

M1885 small caliber rifle. Breech-loading rifle trials undertaken by the U.S. Army in 1890-2 included 10-shot 30-caliber guns submitted on behalf of the Lee Arms Company of South Windham, Connecticut. However, the Lee rifles did not prove acceptable, even though Gun No. 5 reached the final elimination stage; the Krag-Jørgensen was preferred largely owing to the design of its magazine.

M1885 carbine. Only a few 'Remington-Lee Carbines, Improved Model' were made, Remington shipping 25 in 1889 and a single example in 1893. Most of the known survivors from these consignments have 24in barrels, short forends retained by a single band, and a bayonet lug on the right side of the muzzle.

SMALL-BORE MAGAZINE RIFLE
Also known as 'M1899'

Made by the Remington Arms Company, Ilion, New York, 1899-1906.
Total production: 5250-5500.
Chambering options: 6mm Lee, 7x57, 7.65x53, 303 British, 30-30 Winchester or 30-40 Krag. **Action:** locked by two lugs on the bolt head engaging recesses in the receiver as the bolt handle was turned down.
DATA FOR A MICHIGAN NATIONAL GUARD RIFLE
Chambering: 30-40, rimmed. 49.5in overall, 8.50lb empty. 29.5in barrel, 4-groove rifling; RH, concentric. Detachable box magazine, 5 rounds. Ramp-and-leaf rear sight graduated to 2000yd. About 2000 fps with ball cartridges. M1899 knife or sword bayonet.

Introduced in 1898, these guns displayed major mechanical changes in the action. Most of these were due to Louis Diss, who moved the lugs onto a separate bolt head—an adaptation of the bolt developed by Roswell Cook for the abortive side-magazine 'Lee-Cook' rifle (q.v.) of 1893. The standard magazine was a Diss pattern with three cartridge-guide grooves stamped into the sheet-metal body. The most obvious external characteristic, apart from the small-diameter barrel, was the wooden handguard which ran from immediately ahead of the chamber to the barrel band.

The perfected Lee-type turning-bolt rifles did not sell particularly well; though 2001 went to the Michigan National Guard in 1898-9, during a period of 'war fever', they were regarded as most unsatisfactory from the outset (the reasons are still unclear) and had been discarded by the early 1900s. They had Remington Rolling Block-style fittings, including barrel bands, rear sights graduated to 1900yd, and short-blade knife bayonets.

Several thousand guns went to Cuba (q.v.) in 1905, and others are said to have been sold to armies in South and Central America. However, the American design soon lost ground to Mauser south of the Rio Grande.

SIMILAR GUNS

Small-bore magazine carbine. Remington's records indicate that about 3000 carbines were shipped prior to 1907, mostly to Cuba in 1905. A typical carbine had a 20in barrel, a half-length round tipped forend, and a short handguard retained by a single barrel band.

SPORTING GUNS
BLACK POWDER SPORTING RIFLE

Though a few sporting rifles were apparently made as early as 1880, and a few modified 1882-pattern actions were converted to sporting standards about 1886, no purpose-built rifles of this type seem to have been made until 1904. Built on 'Navy actions' (1885 type) which had remained in store, they had 26in round barrels, stocks with shallow pistol grips, and spring-and-slider rear sights. The guns were sold as 'Big-Game Rifles' in 43 Spanish, 44-77, 45-70 or 45-90; they weighed about 8.5lb.

SMALL-BORE SPORTING RIFLE

Made by the Remington Arms Company, Ilion, New York, 1899-1909.
Total production: about 1450. **Chambering options:** 6mm Lee, 7x57, 7.65x53, 303 British, 30-30 Winchester, 30-40 Krag, 32 Winchester Special, 32-40 Winchester, 35 Winchester, 38-55 Winchester, 38-72 Winchester or 405 Winchester. **Action:** as military pattern, above.
DATA FOR A TYPICAL EXAMPLE
Chambering: 38-72 Winchester, rimmed. 46.25in overall, 8.53lb empty. 28in barrel, 4-groove rifling; RH, concentric. Detachable box magazine, 5 rounds. Spring-and-leaf rear sight. About 1475 fps with 275-grain bullet.

Introduced commercially in 6mm, 7mm, 7.65mm, 30-30 and 30-40, this sporter was never successful—simply because the bolt action was unpopular with the American hunting fraternity. Remington-Lee rifles had 24-28in barrels, and weighed 7-9lb depending on whether standard or heavyweight barrels were fitted. Three-groove Diss-pattern magazines were used. The select walnut stocks had checkering on the shallow pistol grips, improving handling characteristics, but the checkered forends tapered rapidly to a very slender tip.

Additional 303, 32-40 and 32 Winchester Special chamberings were announced in 1902, followed in 1903 by 35, 38-55 and 38-72 Winchester options; a 405 Winchester chambering was announced in 1904. Magazine capacity was restricted to four rounds in 32-40 and 38-55 only, the others all handling five.

SIMILAR GUNS

Special Grade rifle. This had a generously proportioned stock of specially selected walnut, a full pistol grip with a pistol grip cap, and a half-octagon barrel.

Target rifle. A few full-stock military and half-stock sporting rifles of this pattern were made in 1899-1900, apparently for international shooting matches. They had special 28in heavyweight barrels; special target rear sights; and Lyman wind-gauge front sights with spirit levels. Perhaps only five to 10 full-stock and 20 to 25 half-stock guns were ever made.

• Richardson

George Richardson, a partner in Richardson & Overman of Philadelphia (maker of Gallager carbines during the American Civil War), was responsible for two firearms tested by the U.S. Army in 1865—Guns No. 49 (rifle) and No. 50 (carbine), which were based on the 1855-pattern Springfield rifle musket and the Gallager carbine respectively. Made in accordance with U.S. patent 43,929 of August 1864, No. 49 had a pivoting breechblock which moved up and forward; No. 50 was a break-open pattern adapted to fire metallic-case ammunition. The principal claim to novelty was the use of a slot-and-double pin system to lock the breech.

• Roberts

Patented in February 1866 by Brevet Brigadier-General Benjamin Roberts and promoted by the Roberts Breech-Loading Arms Co. of New York City, this breechloading conversion of a Springfield rifle-musket was tested by the U.S. Army in 1867. The breechblock swung upward around a pivot above the chamber once a latch which locked into the floorplate had been released by pulling up on a small eared catch on top of the breech behind the external hammer.

The rifle was rejected first by the U.S. Army board and then by the Navy; however, Roberts had powerful friends and fought hard against the Chief of Ordnance to have his gun adopted. Though a 50-70 rifle was still being tried by the U.S. Army in 1872 and small numbers had been adopted by the New York militia, only Serbia used the Roberts conversion in quantity. Most of the guns were made by the Providence Tool Company, better known for the Peabody and Peabody-Martini (q.v.).

• Robertson & Simpson

Patented in the U.S.A. in March 1866 (no. 53,187) by William Robertson of New London, Connecticut, and George Simpson of Hartford, Connecticut, this carbine had an external affinity with the Sharps patterns. It was apparently made in Springfield Armory, and incorporated several original Sharps components. Internally, however, it was locked by a radial block mechanism controlled with an underlever. The half length forend was held by a single band, and a sling ring and bar assembly was fixed to the left side of the butt above the trigger and underlever catch. At least one gun was made for the U.S. Army trials of 1865, where it was tried as Gun No. 52, and a few others were apparently used elsewhere.

• Robinson

These rifles were made in accordance with patents granted to Orvil Robinson of Upper Jay, New York, in 1870-2. Work continued until Adirondack and rights to the Robinson patents were purchased by Winchester.

MAGAZINE SPORTING RIFLE

Made by A.S. Babbitt, Plattsburgh, New York, 1870-4.
Total production: a few hundred? **Chambering:** 44 Long rimfire. **Action:** locked by a pivoting strut beneath the breech-bolt engaging the receiver.

41.9in overall, about 9lb empty. 24.5in barrel, rifling details not known. Tube magazine beneath the barrel, 12 rounds? Spring-leaf rear sight. 825 fps with 220-grain bullet.

This breech of the first-pattern rifle, protected by U.S. patent 103,504 of May 1870, was opened by pressing inward on the prominent ears above the hammer and pulling them backward. This pivoted the rear face of the locking strut out of the receiver floor and retracted the breech-bolt to eject a spent case. A new cartridge then rose on the carrier-block, to be pushed forward into the chamber as the breech was closed.

The rifles had a brass frame with an octagonal barrel above a half-length magazine tube; a decoratively spurred trigger guard appeared beneath the straight-wrist butt. The action was very rapid, though a lack of primary extraction may have proved troublesome with poor ammunition. Robinson patented an improved rifle in 1872, relying on a toggle-like construction with a 'breech-bolt brace' and a linking strut to open the breech-bolt. Prototypes were made in 1872—one was featured in the *Scientific American* in August—but series production by the Adirondack Fire Arms Company of Plattsburgh had only just begun when rights were sold to Winchester in 1874.

• Roper

Sylvester Roper was just one of the many talented engineers raised in New England. Among his many patents—which included sewing machines and hot-air engines—was a quirky repeating rifle. Patented in the U.S.A. in April 1866, this was a 'slam loader' which, by moving each cartridge from the revolving magazine into the barrel, sought to make an ideal gas seal.

When the combination hammer/operating lever was thumbed back, the breech bolt was withdrawn from the cylinder chamber, extracting the spent case and replacing it in the magazine. As the backward bolt stroke was nearing the end, the cylinder, revolving within its shroud, brought the next chamber into line with the breech. The bolt was then held back at full-cock.

Pressing the trigger released the bolt to fly forward, pushing the cartridge out of the cylinder into the barrel, then firing it in a single movement. Alternatively, the bolt could be run forward under control and then retracted to either a safety notch or a half-cock from which sufficient power could be generated to fire the gun. Firing from the half-cock position minimized the shock of the full 'slam fire' stroke.

Prototype Ropers may have been chambered for conventional rimfire cartridges—possibly 38-caliber—but the finalized guns used capped self-contained tubes, the absence of a rim improving the feed stroke.

EARLY PROGRESS

The Roper Repeating Rifle Company of Amherst, Massachusetts, was formed in 1867 under the presidency of Henry Hills, whose Hills Palm Leaf Works undoubtedly made many of the components. The agent of the new company was none other than Christopher Spencer, a close friend of Sylvester Roper.

Production initially concentrated on shotguns; though it is suspected that a few rifles were made in this period, exploitation was delayed until the Roper Sporting Arms Company was formed in March 1869. The new business continued to make four-shot 12-bore shotguns, but added what an 1872-vintage broadsheet called 'The Roper Six-Shooting Rifle'.

ROPER SPORTING RIFLE

Made by the Roper Sporting Arms Company, Hartford, Connecticut, 1872-6.
Total production: estimated as 475-500. **Chambering:** 40-caliber proprietary ammunition. **Action:** locked by the hammer-lever acting as a strut.

41in overall, 9lb empty. 26in barrel, rifling details not known. Rotary magazine, six (common) or five (very rare) rounds. Spring-leaf rear sight. About 1100 fps with ball ammunition.

These guns chambered special self-primed cartridges with the bullets seated entirely in the case. They had distinctive cylindrical magazine shrouds, a small round trigger guard with a rearward spur, and octagonal, half-octagon or round barrels. The short wooden forends, with brass or pewter tips, were held by a bolt; and the straight-wrist butt (which was often finely checkered) had a deeply concave shoulder plate. As the forend and barrel assembly were easily detached from the butt and standing breech, some guns were sold in rifle/shotgun combinations.

CLOVERLEAF RIFLES

Rifles marked by the Roper Repeating Rifle Company of Amherst had four-shot 'cloverleaf' cylinders, but are very difficult to date satisfactorily. The original company was dissolved in 1868, but Roper may have resurrected it. The guns are much more streamlined than their slam-fire predecessors and embody so many improvements that they can only come from a later era—perhaps the mid 1870s, judging by the exceptionally clean lines.

Instead of propelling the entire cartridge forward into the barrel, the action relies on the front trigger withdrawing the bolt and indexing the cylinder. Only .25in of the case-mouth moves forward into the breech to make a seal when the rear trigger fires the gun.

Some of these Roper rifles have center-spindle magazines, others have magazines which can be withdrawn from the frame laterally, and one gun even has a tipping barrel to allow loading from the front. Series production was never undertaken, however, though elements of the two-trigger idea reappeared in the so-called Spencer-Roper series of slide-action guns (q.v.).

• Rowe

Guns No. 55 and No. 56 tested by the U.S. Army in 1865 were made in accordance with U.S. patent 42,227, granted in April 1864 to A.H. Rowe of Hartford, Connecticut. The patent illustrations bore too great a resemblance to the 1862 design of William Johnston (q.v.) to be coincidental, and the relationship between the two men is still debated; writing in *Small Arms Makers*, Robert Gardner suggested that Rowe was forced to hand over his guns to Robbins & Lawrence in 1864—for infringing Lawrence's U.S. patent 8637 of January 1852—but says nothing at all about the links between Johnson & Rowe, and there is evidently more to learn. The trials guns were operated by twisting the barrel unit to the right after a catch on the top of the receiver had been depressed. The guns had two-piece half-stocks with the forend held by a single band, and had folding-leaf sights on top of the barrel ahead of the chamber.

• Ruger, autoloading type

The success of Sturm, Ruger & Company was based on a 22 rimfire pistol, designed by Alexander Sturm and William Ruger, which was introduced commercially in 1949. The company entered the rifle business in the late 1950s with the first of a series of highly successful autoloaders, then progressed to some excellent block- and bolt-action designs.

MODEL 10/22 CARBINE
Also known as '10/22-R' and '10/22-RB'
Made by Sturm, Ruger & Co., Inc., Southport, Connecticut, 1964-9, and Manchester, New Hampshire, 1969 to date.
Currently in production. **Chambering:** 22 LR rimfire. **Action:** no mechanical breech-lock; blowback, semi-automatic only.

37.25in overall, 5lb empty. 18.5in barrel, 6-groove rifling; RH, concentric. Detachable rotary spool magazine, 10 rounds. Folding-leaf rear sight. 1080fps with 40-grain bullet.

Introducing a patented bolt-energy dissipation system and a detachable rotary magazine, this also had a hammer-type ignition system and a cross-bolt safety through the front web of the trigger guard. The original aluminum buttplate was replaced by a synthetic pattern in 1978; the replacement of the original walnut stock by birch (in 1980) advanced the designation from '10/22-R' to '10/22-RB'. The standard guns have a plain birch half stock with a pistol grip and a single band around the forend and barrel. However, a few have been made with wood-laminate stocks, including multi-color or green (1986), brown (1988) and smoke-pattern or tree-bark camouflage (1989). A stainless steel version, known as the 'K10/22-RB', appeared in 1992.

SIMILAR GUNS
Note: Ruger designations will often be found with a 'K' prefix, which signifies a stainless steel barrel and/or action. A few special- or limited-issue versions have also been made in small numbers.

Model 10/22 Canadian Centennial Carbine, 1967. Made to celebrate the hundredth anniversary of the founding of the Canadian federation, this was distinguished by the medallion set into the right side of the butt. There were 4500 guns (10/22-SPCC) with plain stocks and 500 (10/22-SPCCC) with checkering; 1000 of the plain guns were offered as part of a 'cased pair' with Remington Model 742 rifles.

Model 10/22 Deluxe Sporter (10/22-DSP). This had a checkered American walnut half stock. Fixed open sights were standard, though the receiver was drilled and tapped for a tip-off mount adapter.

Model 10/22 International (10/22-X), 1965-9 and 1994 to date. Distinguished by a full-length stock, this was made in comparatively small numbers. About 750 of a checkered-stock version (10/22-XC) were made in 1967-9. The current version has checkering on the pistol grip and forend of its hardwood stock, a rubber buttplate, and a blued steel forend cap.

Model 10/22 Sporter (10/22-SP), 1966-82. A minor variant of the standard 10/22 carbine, this had a finger-groove forend and factory-fitted swivels. About 50,000 guns were made prior to 1971. The 10/22 Sporter Checkered (10/22-SC) was identical apart from the stock; production was confined to 2500 in 1967-8. In 1971, however, checkering was added to the standard stock and work continued on the '10/22-SP New Model' until, in 1981, additional changes created the deluxe version. The standard gun was then discontinued.

Model 10/22 Target (10/22-T), 1996 to date. A target-shooting version of the standard rifle, this has a 20in spirally-fluted heavy barrel and a heavy laminated birchwood half stock. The receiver has bases for 'tip off' scope mounts.

MODEL 44 CARBINE
Also known as 'Model 44-R'
Made by Sturm, Ruger & Co., Inc., Southport, Connecticut, 1959-69, and Manchester, New Hampshire, 1969-85.
Total production: not known. **Chambering:** 44 Remington Magnum only. **Action:** locked by rotating lugs on the bolt into the receiver walls; gas operated, semi-automatic only.
DATA FOR A TYPICAL STANDARD EXAMPLE

36.75in overall, 5.75lb empty. 18.5in barrel, 12-groove rifling; RH, concentric. Tube magazine beneath barrel, 4 rounds. Folding-leaf rear sight. 1830fps with 180-grain bullet.

Externally similar to the rimfire 10/22, this incorporated a locked-breech action. The pistol grip half stock had a plain comb and a concave buttplate. A barrel band lay toward the round forend tip. Open sights were standard, though the receiver was drilled and tapped for optical-sight mounts. A few thousand guns were made in 1962 with a 'Deerstalker' brand name, but this was abandoned after objections had been raised by the Ithaca Gun Company. Very few limited editions of the Model 44 have been made, though Ruger did offer a 25th anniversary model in 1985 with an appropriately engraved receiver.

THE GUNS
Model 44 Deluxe Sporter (44-DSP), 1963-71. This had a walnut stock with a low Monte Carlo comb and a fluted forend. A folding-leaf rear sight was fitted to the barrel, and swivels lay beneath the stock.

Model 44 International (44-X or 44-RSI), 1964-71. Easily identified by its full-length Mannlicher-style stock, this was made only in small numbers.

Model 44 Sporter (44-RS), 1961-78. Differing from the standard pattern largely in the addition of an aperture rear sight, this also had swivels under the butt.

MINI-14 RIFLE
Made by Sturm, Ruger & Co., Inc., Manchester, New Hampshire, 1975 to date.
Currently in production. **Chambering:** 223 Remington only. **Action:** locked by rotating lugs on the bolt into the receiver wall; gas operated, semi-automatic only.
DATA FOR A TYPICAL MINI-14/5

37.15in overall, 6.75lb empty. 18.5in barrel, 6-groove rifling; RH, concentric. Detachable box magazine, 5 rounds. Adjustable aperture rear sight. 3300fps with 55-grain bullet.

Announced at the end of 1973, but not made in quantity until 1975, the Mini-14 relies on a Garand-type rotating bolt powered by a piston attached to the actuator. When the gun fires, propellant gas bleeds from the barrel into the cupped head of the piston surrounding the gas port. The piston receives a sharp backward thrust before clearing the port-cylinder, venting the gas to the atmosphere. Momentum then carries the moving parts back to the limit

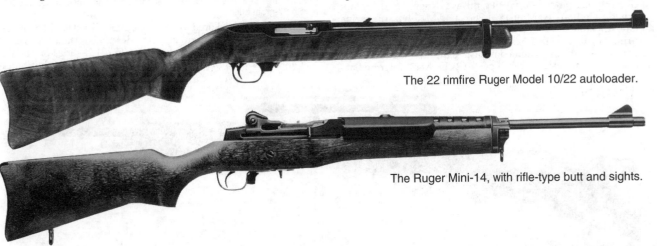

The 22 rimfire Ruger Model 10/22 autoloader.

The Ruger Mini-14, with rifle-type butt and sights.

The Ruger K-Mini-14/5RF
with its folding butt extended.

The Ruger Mini-14/5RF with a
folding butt and military-style back sight.

The Ruger Mini-14, dismantled
into its principal component groups.

of their travel, cocking the hammer, until they can be propelled forward by the return spring.

A ventilated fiberglass handguard covers the actuator slide on the right side of the forend, and the pistol grip half stock contains protective steel liners. The safety catch lies in the front face of the trigger guard. Twenty- and 30-round magazines can be supplied to order.

SIMILAR GUNS

Note: Guns made of stainless steel are designated with a 'K' prefix.

AC556 rifle, 1975-85. A selective-fire derivative of the commercial Mini-14/20GB, this had a modified trigger system and a three-position lever on the right rear of the receiver to select single shots, three-round bursts or fully automatic fire. The cyclic rate was 700-800 rds/min. Owing to light weight and durability, Rugers have proved popular with police and anti-terrorist units throughout the world.

AC556 rifle, folding stock (AC556-F). This was distinguished by its tubular butt, which could be swung forward along the right side of the receiver.

Mini-14/5 folding-stock rifle (14/5-F). Distinguished by a separate plastic pistol grip, this also had a tubular metal butt which folded to the right to give an overall length of only 27.5in.

Mini-14/5 Ranch Rifle (14/5-R), 1982 to date. The original Mini-14 had a conventional wooden handguard with the actuator sliding in an exposed channel on the right side of the forend. This was potentially dangerous, forcing Ruger to develop a fiberglass handguard/actuator cover, introduced with the Ranch Rifle. The gun also has a modified receiver with a folding-leaf rear sight, patented integral optical-sight mount dovetails, and an improved buffer between the actuator slide and the receiver. The bolt stop now doubles as an ejector, and the straight shotgun-style buttplate has subsequently been replaced with the standard Mini-14 pattern.

Mini-14/5 Ranch Rifle, folding stock (14/5-RF), 1985-91? A minor variant of the standard gun, this has a separate pistol grip and tubular butt.

Mini-14/20 rifle, with grenade launcher and bayonet lug (14/20-GB). Dating from the early 1970s, this was Ruger's first attempt to provide a militarized Mini-14. A 20-round M16-type magazine and the M7 knife bayonet were standard fittings.

Mini-Thirty, 1987 to date. This variant of the standard Mini-14 Ranch Rifle—with the patented optical-sight mount and folding rear sight—chambers Soviet-type 7.62x39 M43 intermediate ammunition, which is only marginally inferior to 30-30 Winchester at 150yd.

XGI RIFLE

Developed in 1984-5 for the 243 and 308 Winchester cartridges, this enlarged Mini-14 retained many of the features of the Garand and the gas system, in particular, resembled the M14 design. The XGI had a pistol grip hardwood stock with reinforced steel liners and a ventilated fiberglass guard over the actuating slide. A five-round staggered-row box magazine was contained entirely within the stock, though the 20-round M14 pattern could be substituted. The XGI worked reliably, but was dogged with such severe accuracy problems that Ruger abandoned the project in 1986. Only a few samples were made.

• Ruger, block-action type

The Ruger No. 1 rifle is based on the best of 19th Century British single-shot designs—particularly the Fraser (q.v.), though it has a greater external affinity with the Farquharson. The Ruger breechblock drops at an angle of 3 degrees out of vertical and contains a straight-line striker, struck by the hammer by way of a transfer block; the butt-tang system was replaced by a socket receiving a large bolt running up through the butt.

NUMBER 1 STANDARD RIFLE
Also known as the '1-B' pattern

Made by Sturm, Ruger & Co., Inc., Southport, Connecticut, 1966-9, and Manchester, New Hampshire, 1969 to date.

Chambering options: see notes. **Action:** locked by shoulders on the operating lever propping the breechblock behind the chamber.

DATA FOR TYPICAL EXAMPLE

Chambering: 25-06 Remington, rimless. 42.5in overall, 7.95lb empty. 26in barrel, 6-groove rifling; RH, concentric. Folding-leaf rear sight. 3500fps with 87-grain bullet.

This has a checkered pistol grip butt with a straight comb and a broad forend. A solid rubber shoulder plate is standard, swivels lie under butt and forend, and a safety catch slides on the tang behind the breechblock. A quarter-rib above the breech is tapped

The abortive Ruger XGI rifle.

U.S.A.

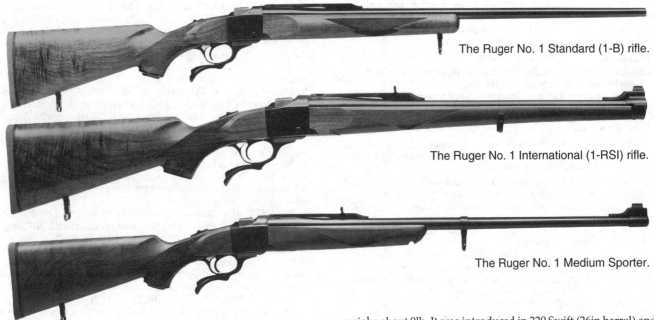

The Ruger No. 1 Standard (1-B) rifle.

The Ruger No. 1 International (1-RSI) rifle.

The Ruger No. 1 Medium Sporter.

and drilled for optical-sight mounts. Chamberings originally included 220 Swift, 22-250 Remington, 6mm Remington, 243 Winchester, 25-06, 270 Winchester, 7mm Remington Magnum, 300 Winchester Magnum and 30-06. A 338 Winchester Magnum option was added in 1973, followed by 280 Remington in 1979 and 300 Weatherby Magnum in 1987. More recent introductions have included 218 Bee, 257 Roberts and 270 Weatherby Magnum. A few guns have also been made for 22 Hornet and 223 Remington.

SIMILAR GUNS

Note: These rifles were originally known by terms such as 'S24H', which identified the barrel length in inches and the barrel-weight—'H' for heavy, 'L' for light and 'M' for medium (standard). Comparatively few special-edition patterns have been made, though 104 rifles were made in 1977, in 7mm Remington Magnum, for the American Hunters 'Hunt of a Lifetime' sweepstakes.

No. 1 Government Model. Offered only in 45-70, this had a 22in barrel, a Henry forend, and a front swivel on the barrel. It weighed about 7.3lb. It was abandoned on the introduction of the No. 3 rifle described below.

No. 1 International Rifle (1-RSI), 1983 to date. Characterized by a full-length stock and a lightweight 20in barrel, this has been offered in 243 Winchester, 270 Winchester, 7x57mm Mauser or 30-06.

No. 1 Light Sporter (1-A). Generally made with a quarter-rib, this 7.25lb rifle had a slender 22in barrel chambering 243 Winchester, 270 Winchester or 30-06. A few guns were also made in 7x57mm. The distinctive Henry forend and a barrel-mounted front swivel were standard fittings.

No. 1 Medium Sporter (1-S). Identifiable by a beaked Henry-type forend tip, an open rear sight set into a quarter-rib and a swivel on the barrel instead of the forend, these guns had 26in barrels chambering the 7mm Remington Magnum or 300 Winchester Magnum cartridges. A 338 Winchester Magnum option was added in 1973, and a 218 Bee version appeared in 1992. A few 45-70 guns have also been made with 22in barrels.

No. 1 Special Varminter rifle (1-V). Fitted with a heavy barrel, drilled and tapped for telescope-sight mounting blocks, this gun

weighs about 9lb. It was introduced in 220 Swift (26in barrel) and a clutch of proprietary Remington chamberings—22-250, 222, 223, 6mm or 25-06 (24in barrels)—but 222 Remington was abandoned in 1974, and 6mm Remington temporarily disappeared in 1990-4; 22PPC and 6mm PPC were added to the list of chamberings in 1993, and a few guns have also been made in 243 Winchester and 280 Remington.

No. 1 Standard/Light Sporter (1-AB), 1980-3. Chambered for the 223 Remington, 270 Winchester, 7x57 or 30-06 rounds, this had a plain forend and a mount for an optical sight on the quarter-rib.

No. 1 Tropical Rifle (1-H). Originally chambered only for 375 H&H Magnum and 458 Winchester Magnum, this gun had a 24in heavy barrel and weighed 8.25-9lb. The Henry forend was standard, and the front swivel was generally carried on a band around the barrel. An open rear sight was set into the quarter-rib. A 416 Rigby option was added in 1990, followed by 404 Jeffrey in 1992 and 416 Remington Magnum in 1993.

NUMBER 3 RIFLE

Made by Sturm, Ruger & Co., Inc., Manchester, New Hampshire, 1972-87.

Total production: not known. **Chambering options:** see notes. **Action:** as No.1 rifle, above.

DATA FOR A TYPICAL EXAMPLE

Chambering: 45-70, rimmed. 38.5in overall, 6lb empty. 22in barrel, 8-groove rifling; RH, concentric. Folding-leaf rear sight. About 1250 fps with modern ball cartridges.

Introduced in 22 Hornet and 30-40 Krag, this modified No.1 had a traditional American-style breech lever with a plain tip. The straight-wrist butt had a curved rifle-type shoulder plate, and the short rounded forend was retained by a single barrel band. A 45-70 version appeared in 1974, but the 30-40 guns were abandoned in 1979. The 223 Remington and 375 Winchester options were added about 1980, though the latter was never popular and had been discarded by 1984. A 44 Remington Magnum option appeared in 1985, but the No. 3 rifle had soon been discontinued.

• Ruger, bolt-action type

The basic action was adapted from the original 1898-pattern Mauser, retaining the non-rotating collar-type extractor. One of

The Ruger 45-70 No. 3 rifle.

the best features—among many—was the front action-retaining bolt, which screwed diagonally upward into the underside of the receiver to give excellent bedding qualities.

MODEL 77 SPORTING RIFLE
Also known as '77-R' and '77-RS'

Made by Sturm, Ruger & Co., Inc., Southport, Connecticut, and Manchester, New Hampshire, 1968-90.

Total production: not known. **Chambering options:** see notes. **Action:** locked by turning two lugs on the bolt head into the receiver wall, and by the bolt-handle base turning down into its seat.

DATA FOR A TYPICAL 77-R

Chambering: 270 Winchester, rimless. 44in overall, 7.53lb empty. 24in barrel, 6-groove rifling; RH, concentric. Internal box magazine, 5 rounds. Optical sight. 3140fps with 130-grain bullet.

The Standard Rifle (77-R) had a half stock with a straight-comb butt, a rubber shoulder plate, and checkering on the pistol grip and forend. A sliding safety catch was set into the upper tang. The receiver had integrally-machined bases for Ruger's own optical-sight mounts. A release catch for the magazine floorplate was let into the trigger guard bow.

The original short-action guns were chambered for the 22-250 Remington, 220 Swift, 6mm Remington, 243 Winchester or 250-3000 Savage cartridges. The shape of the bolt handle was greatly refined in 1971, when long-action rifles were introduced in 25-06, 270 Winchester, 7x57 or 30-06 (five-round magazines), and 7mm Remington Magnum, 300 Winchester Magnum or 338 Winchester Magnum (three-round magazines).

A 280 Remington chambering was offered from 1978 onward on the basis of the 77-R long action, but the 250-3000 option was withdrawn in 1979. However, as compensation, new 308 and 358 Winchester options were made available. The 358 Winchester and 458 Winchester Model 77-R options were abandoned in 1985, followed by the dropping of the 6mm Remington in 1989—when 257 Roberts and 7mm-08 were introduced. The 308 Winchester was abandoned in 1990. Work on the original M77 stopped in favor of the Mk II in 1989, but old-style guns were still being dispatched as late as 1992. A desert camo stock was introduced in 1988, initially in 270 Winchester or 30-06 only.

The Mk II pattern of 1989 (77-R II) was introduced in 6mm Remington, 243 Winchester, 7mm Remington Magnum, 300 Winchester Magnum, 308 Winchester and 338 Winchester Magnum. A 223 Remington option appeared in 1992, followed in 1993-4 by 25-06, 257 Roberts, 6.5x55, 270 Winchester, 280 Remington and 30-06. A Mk II left-hand action (77-LR II) was introduced in 1991, chambered for the 270 Winchester, 7mm Remington Magnum, 300 Winchester Magnum and 30-06 cartridges only.

SIMILAR GUNS

Note: The Mark II rifle of 1989 had an improved trigger and a modified three-position safety system. A Mauser-type collar extractor was fitted, the ejector became a fixed blade, and a patented magazine floorplate latch was set into the front face of the trigger guard.

Model 77 African rifle (77-RSA). This was a minor variant of the 77-R, offered only in 458 Winchester Magnum, with open sights and a sturdier stock. An otherwise standard gun with a Claro or fiddleback walnut stock is said to have been made as the 77-RSC.

Model 77 All Weather Stainless Mk II rifle (77-RP II), 1990 to date. Introduced in 223 Remington, 243 Winchester, 270 Winchester, 308 Winchester or 30-06—plus 7mm Remington Magnum, 300 Winchester Magnum or 338 Winchester Magnum—this gun had stainless steel metalwork, sling loops, and a straight-comb half stock made of fiberglass-reinforced DuPont Zytel with Xenoy inserts in the pistol grip and forend.

Model 77 Deluxe Mk II rifle (77-RSD),1991-3? This had a specially selected straight-comb half stock, with an ebony forend tip, and a quarter-rib on the 22in (standard) or 24in (magnum) barrel. Chamberings were originally 270 Winchester, 7mm Remington Magnum, 300 Winchester Magnum or 30-06; magazine capacity was four rounds.

Model 77 Express Mk II rifle (77-EXP II), 1991 to date. Offered in 270 Winchester, 7mm Remington Magnum, 300 Winchester Magnum and 30-06, with a four-round magazine, this is essentially similar to the Magnum Mk II.

Model 77 International rifle (77-RSI), 1969-91 and 1994 to date. A short-action rifle, with an integral-base receiver and a full-length stock, this had an 18.5in barrel chambered for 22-250, 243 Winchester, 250-3000 Savage or 308 Winchester rounds. The 22-250 and 308 Winchester options were withdrawn in 1991. Long-action 270 Winchester and 30-06 chamberings appeared in 1987, but only a few were made before the Mk II action was substituted.

Model 77 Magnum Mk II rifle (77-RSM II), 1989 to date. Built on the basis of the extra-long Tropical Rifle (q.v.) action, this was strengthened to handle 375 H&H, 404 Jeffrey, 416 Rigby or 458 Winchester cartridges. By 1997, chamberings had been reduced to 375 H&H and 416 Rigby only. The guns, which could weigh as much as 10lb, had quarter-ribs on the barrel and straight-comb half stocks with ebony-tipped forends.

Model 77 Police Rifle Mk II, 1994 to date. Offered in 223 Remington and 308 Winchester (5.56x45 and 7.62x51 NATO), this is about 46.5in overall, weighs 9.75lb without sights, and has a 26in barrel. The internal box magazine holds four rounds.

Based on the 77-V, the Police Rifle was developed for sniping. Its heavyweight stainless steel barrel floats freely in a slender target-style half stock, usually made of walnut or a walnut/beech laminate. Dovetails are machined into the receiver bridge and the chamber-top to accept suitable optical sight mounts. A Harris-type bipod, a sling anchor or a hand stop can be fitted beneath the forend when required.

Model 77 Standard rifle, sighted (77-RS). This designation was applied to a version of the standard rifle fitted with open sights. A Desert Camo stock was introduced in 1988, initially in 270 Winchester or 30-06 only. Mk II guns (77-RS II) were initially restricted to 243 Winchester or 308 Winchester, but short-lived 25-06 and 6mm Remington chamberings appeared in 1990 together with 35 Whelen. By 1994, guns had also been supplied in three magnum chamberings—7mm Remington, 300 and 338 Winchester.

Model 77 Special Top rifle (77-ST). The receiver of these guns, originally offered only in 243 and 308 Winchester, accepted non-Ruger sight mounts. Open sights were standard. Long-action rifles of this type were apparently restricted to 25-06, 270 Winchester or 30-06 (22in barrels) and 7mm Remington Magnum, 300 Winchester Magnum or 338 Winchester Magnum (24in barrels). The

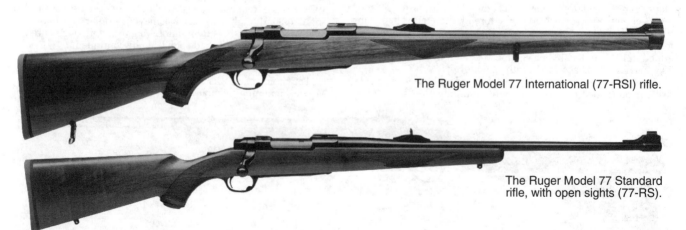

The Ruger Model 77 International (77-RSI) rifle.

The Ruger Model 77 Standard rifle, with open sights (77-RS).

The Ruger Model 77 Tropical Rifle.

The Ruger Model 77 Ultra-Light rifle (77-RL).

300 Winchester Magnum and 338 Winchester Magnum 77-ST chamberings were abandoned in 1979.

Model 77 Tropical rifle (77-RT), 1985-90. This was chambered exclusively for the 458 Winchester Magnum. It had a steel trigger guard/floorplate assembly, a strengthened stock with transverse recoil bolts, and weighed about 8.75lb.

Model 77 Ultra-Light carbine (77-RLS), 1987-90. Introduced in 243 Winchester or 308 Winchester (short-action, discontinued in 1989), and 270 Winchester or 30-06 (long action), this had an 18.5in barrel and weighed 6lb. Folding-leaf sights were standard. A desert camo stock was introduced in 1988, initially in 270 Winchester or 30-06 only. A few Mk II guns were made in 1990, confined to 243 or 308 Winchester.

Model 77 Ultra Light rifle (77-RL), 1983 to date. This short-action gun chambered 243 or 308 Winchester ammunition. It had 20in barrel and weighed a little over 6lb. New 22-250 Remington and 250-3000 Savage options were introduced for the short-action Ultra Light rifle in the mid-1980s, together with long-action 257 Roberts and 270 Winchester patterns, and a 30-06 Ultra Light appeared in 1987. Post-1989 Mk II guns have been offered with 20in barrels, in 223 Remington, 243 Winchester or 308 Winchester.

Model 77 Varmint rifle (77-V), 1968-89. This short-action pattern was introduced in 220 Swift (26in barrel) 22-250, 6mm Remington, 243 Winchester or 25-06 (24in barrels). It lacked open sights and weighed about 9lb. The last 280 Remington guns were sold in 1985, followed by the final 6mm Remingtons in 1987. The Mk II was announced in 1992 in 220 Swift, 22-250, 243 Winchester or 308 Winchester. It had a distinctive laminated stock, with a sharply curved pistol grip and a flat-bellied forend. Weight with a 26in matte-finish stainless steel barrel averaged 9.25lb.

Model 77 Varmint/Target (77-KII VT). This is the current designation for the Mk II Varmint pattern (q.v.), with the Ruger diagonal bedding system and a laminated half stock with a flat-bottom forend. It is now chambered for the 22PPC, 6mm PPC and 25-06 cartridges, in addition to the options listed previously.

MODEL 77/22 SPORTING RIFLE
Also known as the Model 77/22-R
Made by Sturm, Ruger & Co., Inc., Manchester, New Hampshire, 1984 to date.

Currently in production. **Chambering options:** see notes. **Action:** locked by turning two lugs on the bolt into the receiver-bridge wall as the bolt is closed.

DATA FOR A TYPICAL 77/22R

Chambering: 22 LR, rimfire. 39.25in overall, 6.13lb empty. 20in barrel, 6-groove rifling; RH, concentric. Detachable rotary magazine, 10 rounds. Open folding-leaf rear sight. 1080fps with 40-grain bullet.

Ruger's rimfire sporter is beautifully made of fine materials and, apart from a few minor details, is stocked similarly to the Model 77. A three-position 77/22 safety protrudes from the right rear side of the action; when retracted to its farthest point, it locks the action closed. Though the crisp single-stage trigger cannot be adjusted, it remains among the best of its type and the lock-time of 2.7 milliseconds compares favorably with the best target rifles. The Model 77/22 accepts the proven detachable 10-round spool magazine introduced with the autoloading 10/22 (q.v.). Consequently, it has a reputation for flawless feeding.

SIMILAR GUNS

Model 77/22 All Weather Stainless rifle (77/22-RP), 1989 to date. Distinguished by a black fiberglass-reinforced DuPont Zytel half stock, with Xenoy inserts in the pistol grip and forend, this can also be obtained with a stainless steel action (K77/22-RSP).

Model 77/22 All Weather Magnum Stainless rifle (K77/22-RMP), 1990 to date. This simply combines the composite fiberglass, Zytel and Xenoy stock with the magnum rimfire chambering. A variant with open sights is designated 'K77/22-RSMP'.

Model 77/22 Standard rifle, open sights (77/22-RS). Mechanically identical with the standard rifle, this is supplied with open sights.

Model 77/22 Hornet rifle (77/22-RH), 1994 to date. This is a minor variant of the basic rimfire gun strengthened to handle the centerfire 22 Hornet cartridge and fitted with a six-round magazine. An open-sighted version is known as the '77/22-RSH'.

Model 77/22 Magnum (77/22-RM), 1990 to date. Chambered for the 22 Winchester Magnum rimfire cartridge, this has blued

The Ruger Model 77/22RS rifle.

The Ruger 77/44 rifle.

metalwork and a checkered stock. A version with open sights is known as '77/22-RSM'.

Model 77/22 Varmint Stainless rifle (K77/22-VBZ). Chambered for the 22 LR rimfire round, this has matte-finish metalwork, a 24in barrel, and a plain laminated hardwood stock. Magazine capacity is nine rounds. The gun is 43.25in long and weighs 7.25lb. Similar guns chambered for the 22 Winchester Magnum rimfire and 22 Hornet centerfire cartridges are offered as the K77/22-VBM and K77/22-VHZ, with magazine capacities of nine and six rounds respectively.

Model 77/44 rifle (77/44-R). Announced in 1997 in 44 Remington Magnum, this is identical with the standard 77/22 but for chambering and a magazine capacity restricted to four rounds.

• Ruger, lever-action type
MODEL 96/44 SPORTING RIFLE
Made by Sturm, Ruger & Co., Inc., Manchester, New Hampshire, 1996 to date.

Currently in production. **Chambering:** 44 Remington Magnum. **Action:** locked by turning lugs on the bolt into the receiver wall as the bolt is closed.

37.75in overall, 5.88lb empty. 18.5in barrel, 6-groove rifling; RH, concentric. Detachable rotary magazine, 4 rounds. Open folding-leaf rear sight. 1080fps with 40-grain bullet.

Introduced in response to concerns voiced in the US against autoloading rifles, this is basically a manually operated version of the Model 44 with a concealed-hammer firing system. The 96/44 has a hardwood half stock with a pistol grip and a 'carbine band' around the forend. A dovetailed rail machined on top of the receiver accepts telescope-sight mounts, and a safety catch runs laterally through the front web of the trigger guard/operating lever.

SIMILAR GUNS
Model 96/22. This is a 22 LR rimfire version of the basic gun, with an alloy receiver (instead of steel) and a 10-round magazine. The Model 96/22-M is a 22 Winchester Magnum rimfire version, with a nine-round magazine.

• Russell (-Livermore)
Patented in 1882 by Lieutenant A.H. Russell of the US Army, this interesting straight-pull bolt-action rifle was ahead of its time. It had a two-piece stock, and an operating handle mounted on a locking plate which pivoted out of the side of the receiver wall. The receiver, trigger guard and magazine housing were machined in a single piece, with open sides in the magazine case to show the state of feed. The magazine could be replenished at any time simply by inserting a stripper clip of five or six rounds (made of tin-sheet or cardboard) in the mouth of an aperture on the right side of the receiver beneath the bolt way and pressing the cartridges down into the magazine. However, though extensively tested, the Russell rifle had no lasting effect on military equipment. Reports suggest that its locking system was too weak to withstand high-pressure ammunition.

• Savage, autoloading type
Savage Arms, Inc., acquired the Canadian Lakefield (q.v.) gunmaking business in 1994, and has since made most of the guns in the range under its own name. These have included the 22LR rimfire Model 64G autoloader. A synthetic-stock 64F version was introduced in 1997.

MODEL 1912 SPORTING RIFLE
Made by the Savage Arms Company, Utica, New York, 1912-16.
Total production: not known. **Chambering:** 22 Long Rifle, rimfire. **Action:** no mechanical breech lock; blowback, semi-automatic only.

About 37in overall, 4.5lb empty. 20in barrel, 6-groove rifling; RH, concentric. Detachable box magazine, 7 rounds. Spring-leaf and elevator rear sight. 1080fps with 40-grain bullet.

Made only in comparatively small numbers, this was derived from the Savage slide-action guns (q.v.) and shared many of their characteristics. The relationship between the Savage and the similar (but older) Febiger/Batavia rifles, however, has yet to be satisfactorily explained. The M1912 had a round-back receiver, a straight-wrist butt and a short rounded forend.

MODEL 6 SPORTING RIFLE
Made by the Savage Arms Co., Utica, New York (1938-42, 1945-6); Chicopee Falls, Massachusetts (1946-59); and Westfield, Massachusetts (1959-68).
Total production: not known. **Chambering:** 22 Long Rifle, rimfire. **Action:** no mechanical breech lock; blowback, semi-automatic only.

41in overall, 6lb empty. 24in barrel, 6-groove rifling; RH, concentric. Tube magazine beneath barrel, 15 rounds. Spring-leaf and slider rear sight. 1080fps with 40-grain bullet.

Characterized by a round-back receiver flowing smoothly into the pistol grip, this had a simple take-down action set in a walnut half stock. Checkering appeared on the pistol grip, the comb was straight, and the broad round-tipped forend had an angular shoulder alongside the chamber. A safety lever lay on the rear right side of the receiver, and the action could be operated manually by activating a special locking device. Post-war guns had a plain stock with a raised Monte Carlo comb; changes were also made to the sights.

SIMILAR GUNS
Model 6S rifle, 1938-42. This was simply a standard rifle fitted with an aperture rear sight and a hooded front sight. Swivels often lay beneath the butt and forend.
Model 7 rifle, 1939-42 and 1945-51. Essentially similar to the Model 6, this had a detachable five-round box magazine instead of a tube.
Model 7S, 1939-42. An otherwise standard rifle, this was fitted with an aperture rear sight and a hooded front sight.
Model 60 rifle, 1969-72. An improved form of the Model 6 confined to 22LR rimfire, with changes in the action to suit modernized production techniques, this retained the tube magazine under its 20in barrel. The Monte Carlo-type walnut half stock had impressed checkering on the pistol grip and the squared forend.
Model 80 rifle, 1976-89. Mechanically similar to the Model 60, this was distinguished by skip-line checkering, by the protrusion of the safety-lever head above the right side of the stock, and by a fixed open rear sight.
Model 88 rifle, 1969-72. A variant of the Model 60, this had a plain hardwood stock and a bead-type front sight.
Model 90 carbine, 1969-72. A short version of the Model 60, this had a 16.5in barrel, a 10-round tube magazine stopping short of the muzzle, and a plain pistol grip half stock with a Monte Carlo comb. A military-style band around the forend carried the front sling swivel; the rear swivel lay beneath the butt. The rear sight was a folding-leaf type.
Model 987-T rifle (sometimes listed as '981-T'),1981-9. Little more than a modernized Model 60, with a rounded forend and conventional checkering, this had a synthetic trigger guard with a forward-pointing fairing.

• Savage, block-action type
MODEL 71 FAVORITE RIFLE
Made by the Savage Arms Company, Westfield, Massachusetts, 1971.
Total production: 10,000. **Chambering:** 22 Long Rifle rimfire. **Action:** locked by raising the breechblock behind the chamber with the operating lever.

37.5in overall, 4.5lb empty. 22in barrel, 6-groove rifling; RH, concentric. Single shot only. Spring-leaf and elevator rear sight. 1080fps with 40-grain bullet.

This was a facsimile of the 19th-Century Stevens (q.v.) Favorite rifle, with an octagonal barrel and brass plating on the hammer,

The Savage Model 80 rimfire autoloader.

The Savage (Stevens) Model 72 rifle.

The Savage (Stevens) Model 89 rifle.

the front sight and the underlever. A portrait medallion commemorating Joshua Stevens was set into the straight-wrist butt, a decorative 'Stevens Favorite' logo was etched into the receiver-side, and a short curved-belly forend was fitted beneath the barrel.

SIMILAR GUNS

Model 72 Crackshot rifle, 1972-89. A plain version of the Model 7, this had a plain straight-wrist butt, a plain curved-belly forend, and a case-hardened receiver.

Model 74 Little Favorite rifle, 1972-4. Recognizable by its 22in round barrel and black frame, this was otherwise similar to the other guns in the series.

MODEL 89 SPORTING CARBINE

Made by the Savage Arms Company and Savage Arms, Inc., Westfield, Massachusetts (1976-89).

Total production: not known. **Chambering:** 22 Short, 22 Long and 22 Long Rifle rimfire, interchangeably. **Action:** locked by raising the breechblock behind the chamber with the tip of the operating lever.

34.5in overall, 5.6lb empty. 18.5in barrel, 6-groove rifling; RH, concentric. Single shot only. Spring-leaf and elevator rear sight. 1080fps with 40-grain bullet.

Deliberately modeled on the lever-action Winchesters, even to the extent of a simulated under-barrel tube magazine, this is basically a Martini-type single loader. The butt had a straight wrist, the squared forend was held by a band, and an external hammer was fitted.

• Savage, bolt-action type

Already known for a selection of successful rimfire rifles, Savage introduced its first centerfire rifle soon after the First World War had ended. An unsuccessful adaptation of the Mauser action, this was rapidly replaced by the Model 40, with the locking lugs on a sleeve around the rear of the bolt body—simplifying manufacture, though theoretically objectionable.

Centerfire chamberings were also offered with the Models 19 and 23, which incorporated a sleeve with the lugs (and the bolt handle) at the mid-point of the bolt body. This action was only suitable for short cartridges.

The first post-1945 rifles formed the Stevens 322/325/330 series, designed for inexpensive production. They incorporated a variation of the Krag-Jørgensen bolt with one lug on the head and a secondary lock at the rear of the body.

Savage's perfected high-power rifle, designed by Nicholas Brewer, appeared in 1958. Though its twin-lug bolt was an adapted Mauser, the Model 110 had special features of its own. Easily made (if a little complicated), the action operated smoothly and was inherently safe. The ready availability of barreled actions also contributed greatly to success.

Savage Arms, Inc., acquired the Canadian Lakefield (q.v.) gunmaking business in 1994, and has since made most of the Lakefield rimfire guns under its own name. These have included the Marks I and II, the Model 93G Magnum and the 900-series target rifles. Introductions have included the Mk IIFSS and Model 93FSS, with stainless steel actions (1997); and the heavy-barreled Mk IILV (1997).

MODEL 1904 SPORTING RIFLE

Made by the Savage Arms Company, Utica, New York, 1904-17.

Total production: not known. **Chambering:** 22 Short, 22 Long and 22 Long Rifle rimfire, interchangeably. **Action:** locked by turning the base of the bolt handle down ahead of the receiver bridge.

34in overall, 3lb empty. 18in barrel, 6-groove rifling; RH, concentric. Single shot only. Fixed open rear sight. 1080fps with 40-grain bullet.

This was a simple take-down junior rifle, with a plain straight-wrist half stock with a short tapering forend.

SIMILAR GUNS

Model 1905 rifle, 1905-19. Little more than a heavier version of the 1904 pattern, this had a 22in barrel and weighed about 5lb.

MODEL 3 SPORTING RIFLE

Made by the Savage Arms Company, Utica, New York (1933-42, 1945-6), and Chicopee Falls, Massachusetts (1946-52).

Total production: not known. **Chambering:** 22 Short, 22 Long and 22 Long Rifle rimfire, interchangeably. **Action:** as Model 1904, above.

41in overall, 5lb empty. 24in barrel, 6-groove rifling; RH, concentric. Single shot only. Spring-leaf and finger-wheel rear sight. 1080fps with 40-grain bullet.

The most basic of the Savage rifles, this take-down pattern had a simple bolt sliding in a tubular receiver, the operating handle being bent slightly downward. The plain half stock had a butt with a straight comb, a pistol grip, and a rounded forend. A plain bead-type front sight was fitted at the muzzle. Post-war guns generally had 26in barrels, raising the weight to 5.2lb.

SIMILAR GUNS

Model 3S rifle, 1933-42. This was distinguished by an aperture rear sight and a hooded front sight with exchangeable inserts.

Model 3T rifle, 1933-42. A minor variant of the standard Model 3, this had sling swivels beneath the butt and forend.

MODEL 4 SPORTING RIFLE

Made by the Savage Arms Company, Utica, New York (1933-42, 1945-6); Chicopee Falls, Massachusetts (1946-59); and Westfield, Massachusetts (1959-65).

Total production: not known. **Chambering:** 22 Short, 22 Long and 22 Long Rifle rimfire, interchangeably. **Action:** locked by turning the bolt-handle base down into its seat in the receiver.

43.5in overall, 5.6lb empty. 24in barrel, 6-groove rifling; RH, concentric. Detachable box magazine, 5 rounds. Spring-leaf rear sight. 1080fps with 40-grain bullet.

Similar to the Model 3, this take-down rifle was built on a sturdier action with a short solid bridge behind the feedway and a radial-lever safety catch behind the bolt handle. The guns made prior to 1941 had straight-comb half stocks with checkering on the pistol grip and a finger groove (soon abandoned) on the forend. Post-1945 stocks had Monte Carlo combs, but lacked checkering. Several differing rear sights were used.

SIMILAR GUNS

Model 4M rifle, 1962-5. This chambered the 22 Winchester Magnum rimfire cartridge, but was otherwise a standard Model 4 with the plain post-war Monte Carlo stock.

Model 4S rifle, 1933-42. A minor variant of the Model 4, this had an aperture rear sight and a hooded front sight with exchangeable elements.

Model 5 rifle, 1936-42 and 1945-61. Easily distinguished by the tube magazine beneath the barrel—holding 15-21 cartridges, depending on length—this could be found with the pre-war straight comb or post-war Monte Carlo-type half stock.

The Savage (Anschutz) Model 164 rifle.

Model 5S rifle, 1936-42. This was simply a standard rifle fitted with better sights: see Model 4S, above.

MODEL 19 NRA TARGET RIFLE

Made by the Savage Arms Company, Utica, New York, 1919-33.
Total production: about 50,000. **Chambering:** 22 Long Rifle, rimfire.
Action: locked by two lugs on the bolt sleeve engaging recesses at the mid-point of the receiver.

45.5in overall, 8.15lb empty. 25in barrel, 6-groove rifling; RH, concentric. Detachable box magazine, 5 rounds. Micro-adjustable aperture rear sight. 1080fps with 40-grain bullet.

Though the locking system was comparatively weak, it was more than adequate for 22 rimfire ammunition. A port cut into the upper surface of the tubular receiver allowed ejection to be upward and to the right. The NRA rifle had a military-style half stock with a straight comb, an enlarged pistol grip and a plain beavertail forend held by a single swivel-fitted barrel band. An aperture rear sight was used in conjunction with an open blade at the muzzle.

SIMILAR GUNS

Note: Production stopped at the end of 1941, owing to the declaration of war on Japan. Small-scale assembly began again in 1945, the last guns (Model 23D) being shipped in 1947; however, it is unlikely that many major components had been made since the beginning of 1942.

Model 19H rifle, about 1934-41. Built on the 1923-pattern action, this was chambered for the 22 Hornet cartridge and had an aperture rear sight.

Model 19L rifle, 1933-42. Incorporating the speed-lock firing mechanism, this was an otherwise standard Model 19 with a Lyman No. 48Y rear sight on the receiver and a No. 17A replaceable-element tunnel sight at the muzzle.

Model 19M rifle, 1933-42. A target rifle with a heavy 28in barrel and bases for optical sight mounts, this weighed about 9.3lb.

Model 19T rifle ('Target'), 1933-42 and 1945-6. Derived from the Model 19 NRA rifle, this had a sporting-type stock with a plain round-tipped beavertail forend. An improved speed lock firing system was fitted. The first examples apparently had a simple peep-type rear sight; later guns had a micrometer sight on an extension bar attached to the left side of the receiver bridge. The front sight was customarily hooded.

MODEL 20 SPORTING RIFLE

Made by the Savage Arms Company, Utica, New York, 1920-9.

Total production: not known. **Chambering option:** 250 Savage or 300 Savage. **Action:** locked by rotating two lugs on the bolt head into their seats in the receiver behind the chamber.
DATA FOR A TYPICAL PRE-1926 EXAMPLE
Chambering: 300 Savage, rimless. 45.5in overall, 6.03lb empty. 24in barrel, 6-groove rifling; RH, concentric. Internal box magazine, 5 rounds. Spring-leaf and elevator rear sight. 2670fps with 150-grain bullet.

Production of this Mauser-type sporter began in 1920. Offered only with a 22in or 24in round barrel, it had a one-piece half stock with a pistol grip butt and a straight comb. The slender forend tapered to a schnabel tip. The bolt handle was angled slightly back to improve handling characteristics, but the rifle was never popular. The shorter barrel option was abandoned in 1926, when the stock was improved by adding checkering on the pistol grip and forend. Post-1926 rifles often had sling eyes under the stock and a Lyman sight on the bolt shroud. Production ceased in 1928, though assembly continued for a few months.

MODEL 23A SPORTING RIFLE

An improved sporting version of the Model 19, this 22LR rimfire was introduced in 1923. It had a 23in barrel, an oval ejection port, and a detachable five-round box magazine. Weight was about 6lb. The walnut half stock had a straight comb, a pistol grip, and a slender forend with a schnabel tip. Rear sights were customarily spring-leaf and elevator patterns.

SIMILAR GUNS

Model 23AA rifle, 1933-42. A replacement for the Model 23A, with a 25in barrel, this had the 1933-pattern speed-lock firing mechanism. Checkering appeared on the pistol grip and in a small diamond-shape panel beneath the forend. Swivels lay beneath the butt and forend.

Model 23B rifle, 1933-42. Essentially similar to the 23AA version, but chambered for the 25-20 WCF centerfire round, this had a bulkier forend with a rounded tip.

Model 23C rifle, 1925-41 and 1945-6. Derived from the 23A, this handled the 32-20 Winchester cartridge. Production after the end of the Second World War was minimal.

Model 23D rifle, 1934-41 and 1945-7. Introduced simultaneously with the Model 19H (q.v.), chambering the 22 Hornet cartridge, this could be distinguished by an open sporting-pattern rear sight.

MODEL 40 SPORTING RIFLE

Made by the Savage Arms Company, Utica, New York, 1928-40.
Chambering options: 250 Savage, 300 Savage, 30-30 WCF or 30-06.
Action: locked by turning two lugs on a sleeve into seats in the receiver behind the magazine well.

Savage also handled an extensive range of Anschütz rifles, including target rifles such as the Model 64 (top) and Mk 12 (above). Details of these guns will be found in the German section.

U.S.A.

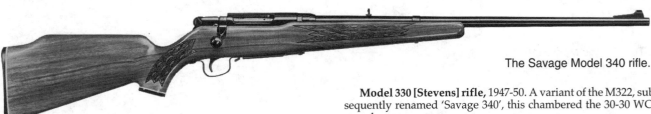

DATA FOR A TYPICAL EXAMPLE

Chambering: 30-30 Winchester, rimmed. 43.25in overall, 7.4lb empty. 22in barrel, 6-groove rifling; RH, concentric. Detachable box magazine, 5 rounds. Spring-leaf and elevator rear sight. 2410fps with 150-grain bullet.

Little more than an enlargement of the sleeve-lock Model 23, with the lugs toward the back of the bolt body, this could still handle some of the most powerful medium-caliber sporting cartridges of its day. The receiver was tubular, the bolt-handle knob lay directly above the trigger, and a small safety catch projected behind the bolt handle. A magazine button lay in the stock beneath the ejection port. The plain wooden half stock had a straight comb, a pistol grip, and a tapering schnabel-tip forend. A 22in round barrel was standard in 250 Savage and 30-30, or 24in in the 300 Savage and 30-06 Springfield options.

Unfortunately for Savage, the unprepossessing 'Super Sporters' lacked the appeal of rivals such as the Winchester Model 54 or Model 70, and were rapidly abandoned.

SIMILAR GUNS

Model 45 Super Sporter. This was a deluxe pattern with checkering on the pistol grip and forend. A Lyman No. 40 aperture sight on the receiver usually supplemented the open sights.

MODEL 340 SPORTING RIFLE

Made by the Savage Arms Company and Savage Arms, Inc., Chicopee Falls, Massachusetts (1957-9), and Westfield, Massachusetts (1959-85).

Total production: 100,000? **Chambering options:** 22 Hornet, 222 Remington, 223 Remington, 225 Winchester or 30-30 Winchester. **Action:** locked by a lug on the bolt head seating in the receiver behind the chamber, and by an auxiliary lug on the back of the bolt body.

DATA FOR A TYPICAL EXAMPLE

Chambering: 222 Remington, rimless. 45.5in overall, 7.35lb empty. 24in barrel, 6-groove rifling; RH, concentric. Detachable box magazine, 4 rounds. Spring-leaf and elevator rear sight. 3200fps with 50-grain bullet.

Introduced in 1947 as the Stevens 320 series (322, 325 and 330), this inexpensive rifle had a tubular receiver and a stamped-strip trigger guard/magazine floorplate assembly. Apart from the 30-30 version, which was three-shot, magazines held four rounds. Among the most obvious identification features were a safety catch on the right rear of the action and a reinforcing rib on the left side of the receiver. The barrel was retained by a threaded collar.

Early guns had round 22in barrels—30-30 examples generally measured 20in—and plain pistol grip stocks with straight combs and round-tip forends.

SIMILAR GUNS

Model 322 [Stevens] rifle, 1947-50. The basic 320-series rifle chambered the 22 Hornet cartridge. It became the Savage Model 342.

Model 325 [Stevens] rifle, 1947-9. A derivative of the basic 320-series design adapted to handle the 250 Savage, this was speedily abandoned when chamber pressures proved to be too high to handle safely.

Model 330 [Stevens] rifle, 1947-50. A variant of the M322, subsequently renamed 'Savage 340', this chambered the 30-30 WCF round.

Model 340 rifle, 1950-85. This was simply the 30-30 Stevens Model 330 under a new Savage-brand name. The distinctions between Models 340 and 342 were abandoned in 1955 when a 222 Remington option became available, all guns being regarded thereafter as '340' (standard pattern) or '340S' (deluxe). A 22in round barrel was standard on the 30-30 version, but a 24in type was supplied with the other chamberings. The advent in 1965 of a low Monte Carlo comb and skip-line checkering improved the stock design; plastic buttplates and grip-caps were fitted, separated from the stock by thin white spacers, and a folding-leaf rear sight replaced the traditional elevator type. The 223 Remington and 225 Winchester chamberings date from this period. Shortly before the Model 340 was finally abandoned—probably about 1983—most guns had a simplified stock lacking checkering.

Model 340C carbine, 1962-4. Offered in all the original options excepting 30-30, this had an 18in barrel. The guns were received unenthusiastically, and production life was short.

Model 340S rifle, 1951-60. A deluxe version of the basic rifle, this had checkering on the pistol grip and forend, an aperture sight on the receiver, and sling eyes beneath the stock.

Model 342 rifle, 1950-5. This was simply the Stevens Model 322 under a new Savage designation, merged into the Model 340 (q.v.) in the mid-1950s.

Model 342S rifle, 1951-5. A deluxe version of the Model 342, this had a better checkered-grip stock, an aperture sight and sling eyes. The distinction between the Models 340S and the 342S lasted only until the mid-1950s, when '340S' was applied to both guns.

MODEL 110 SPORTING RIFLE

Made by the Savage Arms Company and Savage Arms, Inc., Chicopee Falls, Massachusetts (1958-9), and Westfield, Massachusetts (1959 to date).

Currently in production. **Chambering options:** see notes. **Action:** locked by turning two lugs on the bolt head into recesses in the receiver behind the chamber, and by the bolt-handle base entering its seat.

DATA FOR A TYPICAL MODEL 110C

Chambering: 30-06, rimless. 43.5in overall, 6.85lb empty. 22in barrel, 6-groove rifling; RH, concentric. Detachable box magazine, 4 rounds. Spring-leaf and elevator rear sight. 2950fps with 150-grain bullet.

Introduced in 243, 270 and 308 Winchester, plus the ubiquitous 30-06, the Model 110 Sporter had many interesting features. Its barrel was retained by a locking collar; the tip of the sear/bolt stop unit protruded from the stock on the right side of the bridge when the trigger was cocked; and an unusually short cocking-piece head lay behind the bolt handle. A sliding safety catch lay on the upper tang. The butt had a straight comb, the pistol grip and forend were checkered, and the front sight was mounted on a ramp. The receiver-top was drilled and tapped for optical sight mounts.

The action was made in two styles (left and right hand) and two lengths—medium and long. A magnum was introduced in the 1960s, differing from the long pattern only in the diameter of the recess in the bolt face, and actions were offered for sale separately from 1962. The first detachable box magazines appeared in 1966, when a folding-leaf rear sight and skip-line checkering were also introduced. Williams-pattern rear sights have been fitted to all open-sighted rifles made after 1989.

The Savage Model 110B sporting rifle.

The Savage Model 110CL rifle, with a left-hand action.

THE GUNS

Model 110B rifle (i), 1976-89. Introduced in 243 Winchester, 270 Winchester, 7mm Remington Magnum, 30-06 or 338 Winchester Magnum, this was essentially a standard 110E with a select-walnut Monte Carlo stock.

Model 110B rifle (ii), 1989-91. Offered in 22-250 Remington, 223 Remington, 243 Winchester, 270 Winchester, 7mm Remington Magnum, 300 Winchester Magnum, 30-06 and 308 Winchester, the 'new' Model 110B was a minor variant of the 110G with a brown-stained laminated stock and a brown rubber shoulder plate. Made only in small quantities, it was abandoned shortly after a 338 Winchester Magnum option had been introduced.

Model 110BL rifle, 1976-91. This was a left-hand version of the standard 110B, with a reversed bolt.

Model 110C rifle, 1966-86. Offered initially in 22-250, 243 Winchester, 25-06, 270 Winchester, 7mm Winchester Magnum, 300 Winchester Magnum, 30-06 or 308 Winchester, this Savage had a detachable magazine containing three magnum or four ordinary cartridges. The magazine release catch lay on the right side of the stock beneath the receiver, and a new extractor let into the lower locking lug replaced the old 'C'-spring type. A pair of Remington-cartridge options—22-250 and 25-06—were introduced in 1979, with 24in barrels instead of the standard 22in pattern. Neither was popular; the 22-250 lasted until 1984-5, but the last 25-06 examples had gone by 1982. The last 110C rifles were chambered for the 243 Winchester, 270 Winchester, 7mm Remington Magnum or 30-06 rounds.

Model 110CL rifle, 1966-85. Essentially similar to the 110C described previously, this had a left-hand action chambered only for 243 Winchester, 270 Winchester, 7mm Remington Magnum or 30-06—though the last few guns made in 1983-5 may have been confined exclusively to 308 Winchester.

Model 110CY rifle ('Youth'), 1992 to date. These 243 Winchester or 250 Savage rifles were distinguished by a short butt with a 12.5in pull, but were otherwise similar to the 110G. A 223 Remington chambering was added in 1993, followed by 270 Winchester and 308 Winchester in 1994. The 250 Savage option was deleted in 1995.

Model 110D rifle, 1972-88. Similar to the standard rifle, this had a detachable magazine floorplate with a pivoting locking latch. It chambered the three standard Winchester cartridges, plus 7mm Remington Magnum and 300 Winchester Magnum. When assembly of the 110D finally ceased, rifles were being offered in 223 Remington, 243 Winchester, 270 Winchester, 7mm Remington Magnum, 30-06 and 338 Winchester Magnum.

Model 110DL rifle, 1972-88. A left-hand version of the detachable-floorplate 110D, made only in small quantities, the 110DL was being offered in 223 Remington, 243 Winchester, 270 Winchester, 7mm Remington Magnum and 30-06 when it was abandoned.

Model 110E rifle, 1963-88. This replaced the original Model 110 Sporter. It has been chambered for 22-250, 223 Remington and 7mm Remington Magnum in addition to the three standard Winchester cartridges and 30-06. The earliest guns had plain pistol grip stocks with Monte Carlo combs. By the late 1980s, 110E rifles were being offered in 22-250, 223 Remington, 243 Winchester, 270 Winchester, 7mm Remington Magnum, 30-06 or 308 Winchester chamberings.

Model 110EL rifle, 1969-73. A left-hand version of the 110E, confined to 7mm Remington Magnum and 30-06 options, this was made only in small numbers.

Model 110ES rifle ('Super Value'), 1981-5. This was simply the Savage 110E sold under the Stevens name with a 4x optical sight and mounts. Offered in 243 or 308 Winchester only, it had a hardwood stock with plain checkering and a 22in tapered barrel with a simple folding leaf sight.

Model 110F rifle, 1987-94. This was announced in 22-250, 223 Remington, 243 Winchester, 270 Winchester, 7mm Remington Magnum, 300 Winchester Magnum and 30-06 Springfield; 308 Winchester and 338 Winchester Magnum options were added in

1989. A straight-comb black DuPont Rynite stock was most distinctive.

Model 110FL rifle, 1988-94. A left-hand version of the 110F, this was offered in a restricted range of chamberings.

Model 110FLP rifle, 1995 to date. This is a left-hand version of the 110FP, available in the same chamberings.

Model 110FM rifle ('Sierra') 1996 to date. A lightweight rifle with a straight-comb composite graphite/fiberglass half stock and a solid rubber buttplate, the Sierra has a tapered 20in barrel; empty weight is just 6.3lb. Chamberings are restricted to three proprietary Winchester cartridges—243, 270 and 308—together with 30-06.

Model 110FNS rifle ('No Sights'), 1991-4. This was little more than a 110F adapted for use exclusively with optical sights.

Model 110FP rifle ('Police'), 1990 to date. Introducing a heavy 24in barrel and non-reflective finish on the metalwork, this was initially chambered only for the 223 Remington or 308 Winchester rounds. The 110FP was 45.5in overall and weighed about 9lb. It was superseded in 1995 by an improved Tactical version with the composite graphite/fiberglass half stock incorporating the proprietary pillar bedding system and two sling eyes beneath the forend. Chambering options now include 223 Remington, 25-06 Remington, 7mm Remington Magnum, 300 Winchester Magnum, 30-06, and 308 Winchester.

Model 110FX rifle, 1988-9. Made only in small numbers, this had Weaver-type mount bases machined integrally with the receiver. Chamberings duplicated 110F types.

Model 110G rifle, 1989-94. The standard rifle had a 22in barrel (24in for magnums) and a beech half stock with a Monte Carlo-pattern butt and a rubber shoulder plate. Chamberings were originally 22-250, 223 Remington, 243 Winchester, 270 Winchester, 7mm Remington Magnum, 300 Winchester Magnum, 30-06 and 308 Winchester. Standard rifles had five-round magazines, magnum patterns held four. Additional options include 338 Winchester Magnum, introduced in 1991; 250 Savage, 25-06 Remington and 7mm-08 (all dating from 1992); and 300 Savage, which was announced in 1993. The 300 Savage round strained the wood stock too greatly, and, since 1995, has been restricted to the synthetic-stocked 'FL' pattern.

Model 110GC rifle, 1992-4. Readily identifiable by a detachable box magazine, this appeared in 270 Winchester, 7mm Remington Magnum, 300 Winchester Magnum and 30-06.

Model 110GL rifle, 1989-94. A left-handed version of the standard rifle, with a reversed action, this has always been offered in restricted chamberings.

Model 110GLNS rifle, 1991-4. This left-handed 'no sights' rifle was introduced in 270 Winchester, 7mm Remington Magnum and 30-06.

Model 110GNS rifle ('No Sights'), 1991-4. Characterized by reliance on optical sights, this was made in the same chamberings as the standard 110G.

Model 110GV rifle, 1989-4. This varmint rifle, with a heavier barrel than normal, was initially available only in 22-250 or 223 Remington.

Model 110GX rifle, 1989-90. Weaver-pattern mount bases machined into the receiver distinguished this variant. It was not especially popular, however, and was abandoned after only a few guns had been made. The chamberings duplicated those of the standard 110G.

Model 110K rifle, 1986-94. Introduced in 243 Winchester, 270 Winchester, 7mm Remington Magnum, 30-06 and 338 Winchester Magnum, based on the 110D, this had a special laminated camouflage-finish stock.

Model 110M rifle ('Magnum'), 1963-73. Announced at the same time as the Model 110E, this handled a selection of magnum cartridges—264 Winchester, 7mm Remington, 300 Winchester and

The Savage Model 110S rifle, intended for silhouette shooting, had a heavy barrel. Note the extraordinary pattern of stippling.

The Savage Model 110V had a straight-comb butt and stippling running from the pistol grip to the forend.

358 Winchester. It had a long action with an enlarged bolt-face recess, a 24in barrel, and a recoil pad on the butt.

Model 110ML rifle, 1965-73. Made in comparatively small numbers, this was left-hand version of the 110M.

Model 110P rifle ('Premier Grade'), 1964-70. This rifle was introduced in 243 Winchester, 7mm Remington Magnum and 30-06. Barrel lengths were 22in—24in for the 7mm version—and magazines held three 7mm or four other rounds. A French walnut half stock had a cheekpiece and a roll over Monte Carlo comb; a rosewood forend cap was separated from the wood by a thin spacer, and the checkering took skip-line form.

Model 110PE rifle, 1968-70. Presentation Grade Savages were similar to the 110P pattern, but had superbly figured stocks and engraving on the receiver, trigger guard and magazine floorplate. Open sights were rarely fitted.

Model 110PEL rifle, 1968-70. The left-hand Presentation Grade gun was less common than even its rarely encountered right-hand 110PE counterpart.

Model 110PL rifle, 1964-70. This was simply a left-hand version of the Model 110P (q.v.).

Model 110S rifle ('Silhouette'), 1978-94. Chambered only for the 308 Winchester cartridge, this had a heavy tapering 22in barrel set in a distinctive half stock with a short rounded forend and a high comb. The enlarged pistol grip was stippled instead of checkered.

Model 110V rifle ('Varmint'), 1983-94. Sharing the action of the 110D, this had a heavy 26in barrel but lacked sights. Stippling appeared on the pistol grip. The 22-250 round was the standard chambering, though a short-lived 223 Remington option appeared in 1986.

Model 110WLE rifle, 1992-5. Savage's 7x57 'One of One Thousand' rifle was externally similar to the Model 110G, but had a select walnut stock and a laser-etched company logo on the bolt. Additional 250 Savage and 300 Savage options were announced in 1995.

Model 110XP3 rifles. Introduced since 1991, these were 'shooting outfit guns', based on standard 110NS ('No-Sights') patterns. They are supplied with 3-9x Simmons or comparable optical sights and appropriate Kwik-Site ring mounts. Individual variants include the 110F (1992), 110FL (1993), 110G (1991), 110GC/GCL (1994) and 110GL (1993). Chamberings have been restricted to 22-250, 223 Remington, 243 Winchester, 270 Winchester, 7mm Remington Magnum, 300 Winchester Magnum, 30-06 or 308 Winchester.

MODEL 34 SPORTING RIFLE
Sold under the 'Savage-Stevens' or 'Stevens' brands
Made by the Savage Arms Company, Westfield, Massachusetts (1969-81).

Total production: not known. **Chambering:** 22 Short, 22 Long and 22 Long Rifle rimfire, interchangeably. **Action:** generally as Model 1904, above.

39.5in overall, 5.5lb empty. 20in barrel, 6-groove rifling; RH, concentric. Detachable box magazine, 5 rounds. Spring-leaf and elevator rear sight. 1080fps with 40-grain bullet.

A modernized form of the traditional Savage rimfire designs, this had a round-back receiver and a noticeably wedge-shape trigger guard. The bolt handle was placed surprisingly far forward—ahead of the trigger guard—and the Monte Carlo-style half stock had checkering on the pistol grip and the squared forend. The impressed design included diamonds within the checker-panels.

SIMILAR GUNS

Model 34M rifle, 1969-73. This was a strengthened version chambered for the 22 Winchester Magnum rimfire cartridge.

Model 35 rifle, 1982-5. A replacement for the standard M34, this had a six-round magazine. The stock had a rounded forend and a less obvious break between the pistol grip and the butt-comb.

Model 35M rifle, 1982-5. Chambered for the 22 Winchester Magnum rimfire round, this was mechanically similar to the standard Model 35.

Model 46 rifle, 1969-73. Offered only with a plain straight-comb half stock, this repeater had a tube magazine beneath the barrel. It could fire the three basic 22 rimfire rounds interchangeably, capacity being 15 of 22LR type.

Model 63K rifle ('Key-Lock'), 1970-2. This was introduced to improve the safety of junior guns. It had an 18in barrel and a safety catch protruding above the right side of the stock behind the bolt handle. A plain full-length stock had swivels beneath the butt and forend. The most distinctive feature, however, lay in the use of a key to lock the trigger mechanism.

Model 63KM rifle, 1970-2. Otherwise identical with the standard Model 63K, this chambered the 22 Winchester Magnum rimfire cartridge.

Model 65 rifle, 1969-73. A light version of the Model 34, weighing 5lb, this had a ramped front sight instead of a simple blade.

Model 65M rifle, 1969-81. This was simply a Model 65 suitably strengthened for the 22 Winchester Magnum rimfire round.

Model 73 rifle, 1965-80. Made with a 20in barrel and a plain hardwood pistol grip half stock, this lacked a magazine.

The Savage Model 65M rifle.

Model 73Y rifle, 1965-80. A junior version of the Model 73, this had a 18in barrel and a shorter-than-normal butt. It weighed merely 4.5lb.

MODEL 111 CHIEFTAIN SPORTING RIFLE

Made by the Savage Arms Company, Westfield, Massachusetts, 1974-9.

Chambering options: 243 Winchester, 270 Winchester, 7x57, 7mm Remington Magnum or 30-06. **Action:** as Model 110, above.
DATA FOR A TYPICAL EXAMPLE

Chambering: 7mm Remington Magnum, rimless. 44in overall, 8.22lb empty. 24in barrel, 6-groove rifling; RH, concentric. Detachable box magazine, 3 rounds. Open ramp-pattern rear sight. 3020fps with 175-grain bullet.

Little more than a box-magazine variant of the Model 110C, holding four rounds in ordinary or non-magnum chamberings, this was distinguished by a half stock with a plain cheekpiece and a Monte Carlo comb. Heavyweight 22in barrels were standard on all but the magnum option. A Williams rear sight was fitted.

MODEL 111 CLASSIC HUNTER SPORTING RIFLE

Made by the Savage Arms, Inc., Westfield, Massachusetts, 1994 to date.

Chambering options: see text. **Action:** generally as Model 110, above.
DATA FOR A TYPICAL MODEL 111F

Chambering: 25-06 Remington, rimless. 45.5in overall, 7.1lb empty. 24in barrel, 6-groove rifling; RH, concentric. Internal box magazine, 4 rounds. Optical sight. 2990fps with 117-grain bullet.

These guns—the 'Classic Hunter' series—replaced the surviving 110 patterns in 1994, remaining stocks of the earlier guns (excepting the 'CY' and 'FP' types) being used as part of the XP3 shooting kits. The major difference in the 111 series concerns the stock designs.

THE GUNS

Model 111F rifle, 1994 to date. This gun has a synthetic graphite/fiberglass stock with a straight comb and checkering on the pistol grip and forend. The action and barrel are both blued. Standard chamberings include 22-250, 223 Remington, 243 Winchester, 25-06 Remington, 270 Winchester, 7mm Remington Magnum, 300 Winchester Magnum, 30-06, 308 Winchester and 338 Winchester Magnum.

Model 111FAK rifle ('Express') 1995 to date. This rifle combines the standard synthetic straight-comb stock and the blued barreled action with the recoil-reducing AMB ('Adjustable Muzzle Brake') system. Guns are typically 43.5in long, with 22in barrels, and weigh 6.8lb; chambering options have included 270 Winchester, 7mm Remington Magnum, 300 Winchester Magnum, 30-06 and 338 Winchester Magnum.

Model 111FC rifle, 1994 to date. This is simply a 111F with a detachable box magazine (Clip). It has been made only in 270 Winchester, 7mm Remington Magnum, 300 Winchester Magnum and 30-06.

Model 111FL rifle, 1994 to date. A left-hand version of the 111F, this has a reversed action with the bolt handle on the left side of the breech.

Model 111FLC rifle, 1994 to date. A left-handed version of the 111FC, this is available in the same four chamberings.

Model 111FNS rifle, 1994 to date. This is little more than a standard 111F without iron sights.

Model 111G rifle, 1994 to date. The 'G' sub-varieties of the Model 111 have walnut-finish straight-comb hardwood stocks with checkering on the pistol grips and forends. Ventilated rubber buttplates are standard. The 111G can be obtained in all standard 111F chamberings excepting 338 Winchester Magnum.

Model 111GC rifle, 1994 to date. Basically a wood-stocked 111FC, this rifle could be obtained in the same four basic options.

Model 111GL rifle, 1994 to date. A 'reversed' version of the 111G, handling the same cartridges, this had the bolt handle on the left side of the action.

Model 111GLC rifle, 1994 to date. The left-hand version of the wood-stocked 111G, with a detachable box or 'Clip' magazine, this can handle 270 Winchester, 7mm Remington Magnum, 300 Winchester Magnum or 30-06 cartridges.

Model 111GNS rifle, 1994 to date. A 'no sights' version of the standard wood-stocked pattern, this is intended for use with a telescope unit.

Model 111XP3 rifles. Shooting kits have been based around all the individual guns, excepting the 111FAK, 111FM, 111FNS and 111GNS patterns.

MODEL 112V SPORTING RIFLE

Made by the Savage Arms Company, Westfield, Massachusetts (1975-9); and by Savage Arms, Inc., Westfield, Massachusetts (1991 to date).

Chambering: see notes. **Action:** as Model 110, above.
DATA FOR A TYPICAL EXAMPLE

Chambering: 22-250, rimless. 47in overall, 9.22lb empty. 26in barrel, 6-groove rifling; RH, concentric. Optical sight. 3730fps with 55-grain bullet.

The original single-shot 112V varmint rifle was offered in 220 Swift, 222 Remington, 22-250, 223 Remington, 243 Winchester or 25-06. The stock had a straight comb, a deep pistol grip and a heavier forend than normal.

SIMILAR GUNS

Model 112BT rifle, 1994 to date. This magazine-feed gun has a distinctive laminated target-style wood stock, with an elevating comb and three slots cut through the forend. The matte-black receiver contrasts with the stainless steel barrel, the bolt ball has been enlarged, and there are bases for target sights. An accessory rail is let into the underside of the forend. Available initially only in 223 Remington and 308 Winchester, the rifles weigh 10.85lb.

Model 112BT-S rifle, 1995 to date. This is simply a single-shot version of the magazine-feed 112BT, made in 300 Winchester Magnum only.

Model 112BV rifle, 1993-4? A target-shooting version of the basic Model 112, this gun had a laminated wood stock with a high comb and an ambidextrous butt. The otherwise plain pistol grip had a Wundhammer swell. The heavy barrel lacked open sights.

Model 112BVSS rifle ('Long Range') 1994 to date. Little more than the preceding 112BV with a stainless steel barrel, this can also be obtained in 220 Swift—added in 1995.

The Savage Model 111 was a deluxe version of the Model 110.

The Savage Model 111F XP3 rifle is sold as part of a kit which includes a 4x telescope sight and suitable mounts.

The Savage Model 112BT rifle has an elevating comb and a distinctive slotted forend.

The Savage Model 112FV rifle.

Model 112BVSS-S rifle, 1995 to date. This is a single-shot version of the 112BVSS described previously.

Model 112FLVSS rifle, 1993 to date. Easily distinguished by its left-hand action, this was otherwise identical with the 112FVSS pattern.

Model 112FV rifle, 1991 to date. This varmint rifle has a five-round box magazine, a 26in heavy barrel, a black straight-comb DuPont Rynite stock, and a blued barreled action. Made in 22-250 or 223 Remington, it weighs 9lb without sights. A 220 Swift chambering was introduced in 1994, in addition to a pair of swivel eyes in the forend.

Model 112FVS rifle, 1992-4. A single-shot version of the 112FV, this gun offered a solid-floor receiver and greater rigidity in the action. A 220 Swift option was added in 1993, with a 26in barrel and an overall length of 47.5in.

Model 112FVSS rifle, ('Long Range') 1993 to date. Distinguished by a stainless steel action and a synthetic stock, this was introduced in 22-250 and 223 Remington. A modified stock with twin swivel eyes beneath the forend was substituted in 1994.

Model 112FVSS-S rifle, 1994 to date. This is a single-shot version of the 112FVSS, with a rigid solid-floor action.

Model 112R rifle, 1979-83. Made with a five-round internal magazine, this replaced the 112V pattern. Stippling was used instead of checkering on the pistol grips of guns made before the 112R was itself replaced by the Model 110V (q.v.).

MODEL 114CU SPORTING RIFLE

Made by Savage Arms, Inc., Westfield, Massachusetts, 1991-4.
Chambering options: 270 Winchester, 7mm Remington Magnum, 300 Winchester Magnum or 30-06.

Otherwise generally as Model 110, above, but with a detachable magazine.

Also known as the 'Classic Ultra', this was introduced in 1991 but did not become available in quantity until January 1992. It amalgamates the basic 110 action with an American walnut half stock. The butt has a straight comb, a pistol grip cap, and a solid rubber shoulder plate. Checkering is cut rather than impressed, and a Williams ramp rear sight is customary. Standard magazines hold four rounds; magnum magazines contain three.

SIMILAR GUNS

Model 114C rifle ('Classic'), 1996 to date. This gun has a blued action and barrel. Its oil-finished walnut stock has a straight comb, hand-cut plain checkering, and an American-style forend with a rounded tip. Open sights are omitted. Standard chamberings are currently 270 Winchester, 7mm Remington Magnum, 30-06 and 300 Winchester Magnum.

Model 114CE rifle ('Classic European'), 1996 to date. Available in the same chamberings as the 114C, this has skip-line checkering and a slim European-style forend with a schnabel tip. A Williams-type rear sight is standard.

MODEL 116FSS SPORTING RIFLE

Made by Savage Arms, Inc., Westfield, Massachusetts, 1991-4.
Chambering options: 223 Remington, 243 Winchester, 270 Winchester, 7mm Remington Magnum, 300 Winchester Magnum, 30-06 or 338 Winchester Magnum.

Otherwise generally as Model 110, above, with an internal magazine.

The original Savage 116FSS was little more than a synthetic-stock Model 110F with a stainless steel barrel. All 116-type guns were fitted with stainless steel trigger guards from 1st June 1992. The guns are all currently known as 'Weather Warriors'.

SIMILAR GUNS

Model 116FCS rifle, 1992 to date. This was similar to the FSS pattern, but had a detachable box magazine accepting 270 Winchester, 7mm Remington Magnum, 300 Winchester Magnum or 30-06 cartridges.

Model 116FCSAK rifle, 1994 to date. The complicated designation indicates that this particular gun has a detachable box magazine, operated by a button recessed in the stock, together with the adjustable muzzle brake and fluted barrel of the FSAK sub-variety described below.

Model 116FLSS rifle, 1994 to date. A left-hand version of the standard FSS pattern, this is being made in comparatively small quantities.

Model 116FSAK rifle, 1994 to date. This synthetic-stock gun combines an adjustable muzzle brake ('AMB') with a fluted barrel, which promotes rigidity while simultaneously conserving weight.

Model 116FSK rifle ('Kodiak'), 1993 to date. Not available in quantity until the beginning of 1994, this gun has a 22in barrel with a shock suppresser designed to reduce the linear recoil sensation

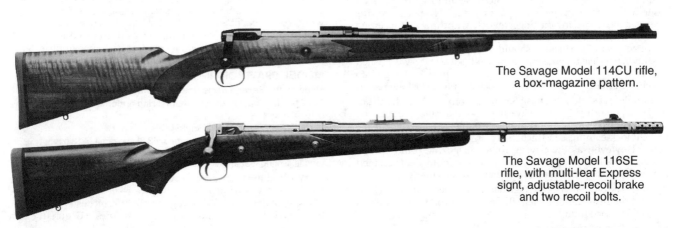

The Savage Model 114CU rifle, a box-magazine pattern.

The Savage Model 116SE rifle, with multi-leaf Express sight, adjustable-recoil brake and two recoil bolts.

by as much as a third. Made only in 338 Winchester Magnum, the gun weighs only 7lb.

Model 116SE rifle ('Safari Express'), 1994 to date. The big game version of the basic Savage action, this has a distinctive select walnut stock with a straight comb and an ebony forend tip. All the metalwork is stainless steel, including a second recoil bolt fitted through the stock. The front swivel lies on a band around the barrel and an Express rear sight has folding leaves for 100, 200 and 300yd. Available in three Winchester Magnum chamberings—300, 338 and 458—the 116SE has a 24in barrel and weighs 8.5lb. This is very light for cartridges generating as much power as 458 Winchester, but the sensation of recoil can be reduced by opening the Adjustable Muzzle Brake ('AMB') unit.

Model 116US rifle ('Ultra Stainless'), 1995 to date. As the designation suggests, this amalgamates stainless steel metalwork with a select walnut straight-comb half stock. The forend has a rounded ebony tip, open sights are omitted, and the barrel is tapped for an optical-sight mount. Standard barrel options have been 22in for 270 Winchester and 30-06, and 24in for 7mm Remington Magnum or Winchester Magnum.

• Savage, break-open type
MODEL 219 SPORTING RIFLE
Made by the Savage Arms Co., Utica, New York (1938-42, 1945-6), Chicopee Falls, Massachussets (1964-59), and Westfield, Massachusetts (1959-65).

Total production: not known. **Chambering options:** 22 Hornet, 25-20, 30-30 and 32-20. **Action:** locked by a bar in the action engaging lugs on the barrel block as the toplever closed.
DATA FOR A TYPICAL EXAMPLE
Chambering: 32-20 WCF, rimmed. 41.5in overall, 6lb empty. 26in barrel, 6-groove rifling; RH, concentric. Single shot only. Spring-leaf and elevator rear sight. 1750fps with 100-grain bullet.

The hammerless 219 was based on Savage's shotguns. It had a box-type receiver separating the plain pistol grip butt from the plain rounded forend, and simple open sights.

SIMILAR GUNS
Model 219L rifle, 1965-7. Made in comparatively small numbers, this had a radial locking lever on the right side of the breech instead of the original toplever.

Model 221 rifle. Offered only with a 26in 30-30 barrel, this was an integral part of the Utility Gun series (Models 221-229). However, these differed only in the gauge and design of the accompanying shotgun barrels.

• Savage, lever-action type
Arthur Savage's first patent was granted in July 1887 to protect a Peabody-Martini rifle with a tube magazine in the butt. Prototypes were made in 45-70 and 44-40, but hinged-block actions were unsuited to magazine feed. By 1889, however, Savage had developed an improved lever-action mechanism and two rifles were submitted to the U.S. Army trials of 1892. They had 34in barrels, and nine-round rotary magazines with radial-arm followers, but were not good enough to beat the Krag-Jørgensen.

In February 1893, Savage received a patent protecting a magazine with each cartridge in a separate cradle. His perfected rifle operated by depressing the finger lever to withdraw a long curved extension from under the rear of the breechblock. The block dropped clear of the locking shoulder in the top of the receiver, to be drawn back clear of the magazine well as the lever was pushed farther down. The return stroke propelled a fresh cartridge into the chamber, then tilted the breechblock up into its locking recess.

Simple and sturdy, the basic Savage action could handle all but the most powerful high-velocity cartridges available prior to 1917. The 22 High Velocity round proved troublesome, as the Savage breechblock compressed fractionally on firing and stretched the cases. However, as the Savage rotary magazine could handle pointed-nose bullets in perfect safety, most handloaders accepted the need to re-size 22HV cases after they had been fired a few times.

Note: The 303 Savage cartridge has always been known in Britain and the British Empire as '301 Savage', to prevent confusion with 303 service rounds.

MILITARY PATTERNS
MODEL 1895 RIFLE AND CARBINE
The original military musket of 1895 chambered 30-40 Krag cartridges, had an eight-round magazine and weighed 8.69lb. The carbine was similar, except for its 22in barrel, half-stock and saddle ring. Very few 1895 Savages were made, as they were soon replaced by an improved design.

SIMILAR GUNS
Model 1899 rifle, 1899-1908. These were offered in 303 Savage and, briefly, in 30-30 Winchester. The rifles were advertised with sword or socket bayonets , the former being the U.S. M1892 (Krag) pattern and the latter apparently a bushed U.S. M1873. A special version of the M1899 was used in Canada (q.v.) during World War I.

Model 1899 carbine, 1899-1908. Distinguished by a 20in barrel, this had a leaf-type rear sight, a sling ring on the right side of the receiver, and a half-length forend retained by a single band. It weighed 7.25lb.

SPORTING GUNS
MODEL 1895 SPORTING RIFLE
Made for the Savage Arms Company, Utica, New York, by the Marlin Fire Arms Company, New Haven, Connecticut, 1895-9.

Total production: about 5000. **Chambering options:** 30-40 Krag or 303 Savage. **Action:** locked by displacing the tail of the breechblock upward into the receiver.
DATA FOR A TYPICAL RIFLE
Chambering: 303 Savage, rimmed. 45.8in overall, 8.05lb empty. 24in, 6-groove rifling; RH, concentric. Integral rotary box magazine, 8 rounds. Spring-leaf and elevator rear sight. 2140 fps with 180-grain bullet.

Made by Marlin in several styles, this was initially chambered for a unique smokeless 303 Savage 'High Velocity' cartridge. Offered with round, half-octagon or fully octagonal barrels, the gun soon presented Winchester and Marlin with an efficient rival.

SIMILAR GUNS
Model 1895 carbine, 1895-9. A few of these were made, with 20in barrels and half-length forends.

Model 1895 commemorative, 1970. A special 'M1895' was made to mark the Savage rifle's 75th anniversary. Mechanically, however, it was a modern Model 99 (q.v.).

MODEL 1899 SPORTING RIFLE
Made by the Savage Arms Company, Utica, New York, 1899-1917.
Total production: 250,000? **Chambering options:** 22 High Velocity, 250 Savage, 25-35 Winchester, 30-30 Winchester, 303 Savage, 32-40 Ballard (Winchester) or 38-55 Winchester. **Action:** as M1895, above.
DATA FOR A TYPICAL EXAMPLE
Chambering: 32-40 Ballard, rimmed. 45.9in overall, 7.65lb empty. 24in barrel, 6-groove rifling; RH, concentric. Integral rotary box magazine, 5 rounds. Spring-leaf and elevator rear sight. 1440 fps with 165-grain bullet.

Though substantial numbers of M1895 sporters had been sold, improvements were soon made in the basic design and production began in 1899 in Savage's new factory. Magazine capacity was reduced (a sixth round could be carried in the breech if required), a cocking indicator was set into the top surface of the bolt, and a firing-pin retractor was added.

The pre-1917 sporter could be obtained with round, half-octagon or fully octagonal 22-26in barrels. Butts originally had straight wrists, though pistol grips, once considered as optional, gradually became standard. Special sights, engraving and selected woodwork could be obtained to order. A 22 high-velocity round designed by Charles Newton (q.v.) was introduced in 1912, followed in 1913 by 250-3000 Savage—another Newton design—offering a muzzle velocity of 3000 fps.

MODEL 99A SPORTING RIFLE
Made by the Savage Arms Company, Utica, New York, 1920-42.
Total production: not known. **Chambering options:** see text. **Action:** as M1895, above.
DATA FOR A TYPICAL MODEL 99E
Chambering: 250 Savage, rimmed. 43.85in overall, 7.13lb empty. 22in barrel, 6-groove rifling; RH, concentric. Integral rotary box magazine, 5 rounds. Spring-leaf and elevator rear sight. 2950 fps with 87-grain bullet.

Work on the lever-action Savage began again after World War I had ended, when the pre-war rifle was re-designated 'Model 99'. Made in 300 Savage, 303 Savage or 30-30 Winchester until 1926, the Model 99A was a minor variant of the pre-1917 gun. It had a

The Savage Model 99C, the last survivor of this long-lived design.

straight-wrist butt, a slender schnabel-tip forend, and a bead-type front sight mounted on a short muzzle ramp.

SIMILAR GUNS

Note: Production ceased at the end of 1941, owing to war with Japan. Stockpiled parts allowed some 99G, 99K, 99R, 99RS and 99T rifles to be assembled in 1942, but work then ceased for the duration of World War II. Details of the guns that reappeared in 1945 will be found under 'Model 99, post-war patterns', below.

Model 99B rifle, 1920-36. This was a take-down version, weighing about 7.5lb instead of 7.3lb; like the other detachable-barrel guns, it had a distinctive metal collar set into the front of the receiver.

Model 99E rifle, 1920-36. A shortened 'carbine' form of the 99A rifle, with a 20in barrel, this could be chambered for 250 Savage, 300 Savage, 303 Savage or 30-30 Winchester cartridges.

Model 99EG rifle, 1936-42. A replacement for the Models 99A, 99B, 99C and 99E, this solid-frame rifle could be obtained available in all standard chamberings. The 99EG had a plain pistol-grip stock and a round-tip forend.

Model 99F rifle ('Featherweight'), 1920-42. A lightened gun with a straight buttplate, made only in take-down guise, this weighed merely 6.5lb with a 22in round barrel. It was chambered for the same cartridges as the 99E.

Model 99G rifle, 1920-42. Mechanically identical with the other Savages, this had checkered panels on the pistol grip and forend.

Model 99H rifle, 1931-42. A carbine-length gun with a solid frame, a straight-wrist butt and a deep round-tip forend, retained by a single band, this chambered 250 Savage, 303 Savage or 30-30 cartridges. Weight was about 6.5lb with a 20in round barrel.

Model 99K rifle, 1931-42. A deluxe rifle with foliate engraving on the receiver, this also had a checkered pistol-grip butt and a checkered schnabel-tip forend. The woodwork was specially chosen for its attractive figuring. A Lyman aperture sight was fitted to the upper tang, and small folding leaf lay on the barrel.

Model 99R rifle, 1936-42. Introduced in 250 Savage (22in barrel) or 300 Savage (24in barrel) and weighing about 7.2lb, this could be distinguished by its pistol-grip butt and a short deep round-tip forend. The pistol-grip and the sides of the forend were checkered. A spring-leaf and elevator rear sight was fitted.

Model 99RS rifle, 1936-42. Mechanically identical with the 99R pattern, this had a Lyman peep sight on the upper tang and a small folding leaf on the barrel.

Model 99T rifle, 1936-42. This lightweight solid-frame gun was offered in 22 High Power, 303 Savage and 30-30 Winchester (22in barrel) or 300 Savage (24in). It had a checkered pistol-grip butt, a round-tip forend, and weighed 7lb.

MODEL 99 SPORTING RIFLE
Post-war patterns

Made by the Savage Arms Company, Chicopee Falls, Massachusetts (1946-59); and Westfield, Massachusetts (1959 to date).

Chambering options: see notes. **Action:** as M1895, above.

DATA FOR A TYPICAL MODEL 99C

Chambering: 284 Winchester, rimless. 45.75in overall, 7.5lb empty. 24in barrel, 6-groove rifling; RH, concentric? Detachable box magazine, 3 rounds. Spring-leaf and elevator rear sight. 2900 fps with 150-grain bullet.

Production recommenced after the end of World War II, beginning with the 99EG, 99R and 99RS patterns. A few minor changes were made, including the addition of checkering on the pistol grip and forend and the introduction of sling-swivel eyes beneath the forend and butt.

The one millionth Model 99 was presented to the National Rifle Association on 22nd March 1960, and ten thousand 308 Winchester 'M1895' rifles were produced in 1970 (on the 99-pattern action) to mark the 75th anniversary of the Savage lever-action rifle. The last rotary-magazine rifles were made in 1982 and, when the Model 99E was abandoned in 1985, only the box-magazine 99C remained in production.

THE GUNS

Model 99A rifle, 1971-82. A modernized version of the pre-war gun of the same designation, this had a sliding safety catch on the tang, a folding-leaf rear sight, and a straight buttplate. It offered a 22in round barrel in 243 Winchester, 250 Savage, 300 Savage and 308 Winchester chamberings.

Model 99C rifle, 1965 to date. Fitted with a detachable box magazine containing three (284 Winchester) or four rounds (243 and 308 Winchester), instead of the traditional rotary pattern, this had a magazine-release button recessed in the right side of the receiver.

Model 99CD rifle, 1965-81. The butt of this deluxe version had a Monte Carlo comb, a shallow cheekpiece, and a pistol grip with skip-line checkering; the forend was a broad semi-beavertail type with a flute running back from the rounded tip. Chamberings seem to have been restricted to 243 Winchester, 250 Savage or 308 Winchester, with four-round magazines.

Model 99DE rifle ('Citation Grade'), 1968-70. A lesser version of the Model 99PE, this was also rapidly abandoned owing to poor sales.

Model 99DL rifle, 1960-73. Little more than a 99F (q.v.) with a Monte Carlo comb and a pistol-grip butt, this deluxe pattern does not seem to have been made in quantity.

Model 99E rifle, 1960-85. This was a short or 'carbine' form of the 99A with a 20in or 22in round barrel chambering 243 Winchester, 250 Savage, 300 Savage or 308 Winchester ammunition. Its pistol grip and notably bulky round-tip forend were skip-line checkered.

Model 99EG rifle, 1946-60. The post-war version of this 1936-vintage introduction was essentially similar to the original pattern, though checkering was added on the pistol grip and forend; 243 Winchester, 308 Winchester and 358 Winchester options were added in 1955 to the original Savage chamberings.

Model 99F rifle ('Featherweight'), 1955-73. A lightened gun, originally made prior to World War II in take-down guise, this was reintroduced in 243 Winchester, 250 Savage or 308 Winchester. Post-1955 guns had checkered pistol grips and forends, were fitted with 22in round barrels, and weighed 6.5lb.

Model 99PE rifle ('Presentation Grade'), 1968-70. This was simply an otherwise standard Model 99 with an elaborately engraved receiver and superbly grained woodwork. Sales were so poor, however, that it was abandoned after only a few hundred had been made.

Model 99R rifle, 1946-60. Originally introduced prior to World War I, this reappeared with a 24in barrel and sling-swivel eyes on the underside of the forend and butt. However, the checkering on the pistol grip was simplified and the checker panel on the forend—basically triangular—no longer continued beneath the gun. The locking catch on the right side of the operating lever was soon abandoned. 1946-type rifles were initially chambered for 250 Savage or 300 Savage cartridges only, though 243, 308 and 358 Winchester options were added in 1955.

Model 99RS rifle, 1946-57. Otherwise identical with the preceding variant, this had a Redfield peep sight on the tang in addition to a small folding leaf on the barrel. Chambering options duplicated those of the 99R (q.v.).

Model 99-358 rifle, 1977-81. This short-lived gun chambered the 358 Winchester round. Apart from its straight-comb butt and ventilated shoulder pad, it was similar to the Model 99CD.

• Savage, slide-action type

Only a single centerfire gun of this type has ever been made, though Savage's 22 rimfires have a lengthy pedigree.

The Savage Model 170 rifle.

MODEL 1903 SPORTING RIFLE
Made by the Savage Arms Company, Utica, New York State, 1903-21.
Total production: not known. **Chambering:** 22 Short, 22 Long and 22 Long Rifle rimfire, interchangeably. **Action:** locked by displacing the locking block into the receiver-top?

40in overall, 5.25lb empty. 24in barrel, 6-groove rifling; RH, concentric. Detachable box magazine, 7 rounds. Spring-leaf and elevator back sight. 1080fps with 40-grain bullet.

The first of Savage's slide-action guns—a 'take-down' design—had a round-back receiver and a sliding safety on the upper tang. The standard butt had a ribbed slide handle, a shallow pistol grip (checkered to order), and a crescent-shape shoulder plate. Its most distinctive feature, however, was the detachable box magazine ahead of the trigger guard. Swivels could be fitted beneath the butt and on a special strap which encircled the barrel. Options included barrels as much as 30in long, and gold or silver- plated metalwork. Decorative versions could be obtained, including the 'Gold Medal Model'.

SIMILAR GUNS
Model 1909 rifle, 1909-15. Similar to the Model 1903, this had a angular receiver, a 20in round barrel and weighed about 4.8lb; the butt and the cylindrical slide handle lacked decoration.

MODEL 1914 SPORTING RIFLE
Also known as the 'Model 14'
Made by the Savage Arms Co., Utica, New York State, 1914-24.
Total production: not known. **Chambering:** 22 Short, 22 Long and 22 Long Rifle rimfire, interchangeably. **Action:** As M1903, above.

40.5in overall, 5.75lb empty. 24in barrel, 6-groove rifling; RH, concentric. Tube magazine beneath barrel, 15-20 rounds depending on cartridge. Spring-leaf and elevator back sight. 1080fps with 40-grain bullet.

Made only in comparatively small numbers, this 'take-down' pattern was a classical tube-magazine repeater derived from the box-feed Model 1903. It had a round-backed receiver, with an ejection port on the right side, and a ribbed slide-handle; the pistol-grip butt lacked checkering. Barrels were octagonal.

SIMILAR GUNS
Model 25 rifle, 1925-9. This was an improved Model 14, with changes in the action.

Model 29 rifle, 1929-42 and 1945-67. An refined Model 25, with additional changes in the action, this 'take-down' gun had checkering on the pistol grip and the slide-handle. Pre-war guns had octagonal barrels; post-war patterns had round barrels and ribbed slide handles. A safety catch worked laterally in the rear web of the trigger guard.

MODEL 170 SPORTING RIFLE
Made by the Savage Arms Company, Westfield, Massachusetts, 1970-81.
Total production: not known. **Chambering options:** 30-30 Winchester or 35 Remington. **Action:** locked by rotating lugs on the bolt into the receiver walls.
DATA FOR A TYPICAL EXAMPLE
Chambering: 35 Remington, rimless. About 43.5in overall, 6.8lb empty. 22in barrel, 6-groove rifling; RH, concentric. Tube magazine under barrel, 3 rounds. Folding-leaf back sight. 2210fps with 200-grain bullet.

A typical shotgun-type rifle, with a short barrel and conventional open sights, the Model 170 had a Monte Carlo butt with a panel of checkering pressed into the pistol grip. The broad fore-end had a short finger groove running back from the tip. A safety catch lay on the upper tang behind the receiver, while swivel eyes appeared beneath the butt and on the front of the magazine-support band under the muzzle.

SIMILAR GUNS
Model 170C carbine, 1974-81. Introduced in 30-30 Winchester only, this had an 18.5in round barrel and a straight-comb butt.

• Schenkl
Patented in June 1857 by John Schenkl of Boston, Massachusetts, this 53-caliber needle rifle was apparently offered commercially in small numbers shortly before the Civil War. One gun was tested by the U.S. Army in the 1857 trials, but was rejected in the preliminary rounds. It had a 23in half-octagon barrel, a straight-comb butt, and a case-hardened receiver. Turning the trigger guard to the right moved the barrel away from the standing breech, to tip forward and expose the chamber. The rear sight was a small quadrant pattern, and a cocking indicator lay on the right side of the breech above the trigger guard.

• Schroeder, Salewski & Schmidt
This interesting needle gun was patented in December 1856 by Herman Schroeder, Louis Salewski and William Schmidt of Bloomington, Illinois. Turning a large knobbed lever on the right side of the forend down and back moved the barrel away from the breech with a rack-and-pinion mechanism; simultaneously, the needle (pivoted to the hammer nose) was forced back to the cocked position. One gun was tested at Washington Arsenal in July 1856, working very well, and 10 were ordered for trials. These performed so poorly that the project was abandoned. Schroeder patented an improved version in June 1861, but this was never exploited.

NEEDLE CARBINE
Made by William Schmidt, New York, 1857.
Total production: at least 11, possibly as many as 100. **Chambering:** 53-caliber self-contained combustible cartridge. **Action:** locked by a rack-and-pinion mechanism.

42.5in overall, about 7lb? 26.75in barrel, 4-groove rifling; RH, concentric. Single shot only. Open block and two-leaf rear sight. Performance not known.

The Schroeder, Salewski & Schmidt gun had a straight-wrist half stock, with a cleaning rod in pipes beneath the barrel and a spurred brass trigger guard. A sliding safety catch beneath the breech ahead of the trigger guard could lock the firing mechanism when necessary. The 10 Army trials guns had a cartouche containing the 'R.H.T.W.' initials of inspector Robert Whitely on the right side of the forend, but it is believed that some guns were sold as sporters prior to 1860 and that some variety may be encountered in fittings.

• Sears, Roebuck
Sears, Roebuck & Co., Inc. of Chicago, Illinois, one of America's leading mail-order houses, sold a few 'Model 52' Sako rifles in 222 Remington in the mid 1950s. They were made by Marlin on the Sako L-46 action. Apart from markings, they were essentially similar to the Marlin Model 322. Many lesser guns have also been sold under the 'Ted Williams' brandname.

• Sharps (i)
The Sharps was the most popular single shot breech-loader purchased by the federal government during the American Civil War. Patented by Christian Sharps on 12th September 1848, the dropping-block mechanism relied on a breechblock which slid downward within a sturdy frame. The combustible cartridge was fired by a conventional side-hammer caplock.

The first guns were made in 1849 by Daniel Nippes of Mill Creek, Pennsylvania. They had obliquely-moving breechblocks instead of the vertical pattern shown in the drawings accompanying the 1848 patent. Carbines were tested by the U.S. Army and U.S. Navy in the autumn of 1850, initially with great success, but prolonged trials showed that the breech could leak gas alarmingly. Among the earliest attempts to provide a satisfactory solution was made by Sharps himself, by inserting a platinum ring in the breechblock face.

The seal was immeasurably improved by letting an expandable gas-check ring into the breechblock face. The first design was patented on 1st April 1856 by Hezekiah Conant of Hartford, Connecticut, but was apparently in use as early as 1855. The Sharps Rifle Company allegedly paid Conant $80,000 for rights to his invention.

The Conant seal was not as effective as its promoters had hoped, however, and the problems were not resolved until Richard Lawrence patented an improved seal in December 1859. Though the U.S. Marine Corps was able to report in 1860 that 'all the earlier troubles encountered with Sharps Carbine' had been corrected, the problem was really eliminated only when the caplocks were converted to fire metal-case cartridges.

Sharps firearms were extremely popular. Though only 5540 New Model examples had been acquired prior to 1861, the Federal government alone purchased 80,512 carbines and 9,141 rifles in 1861-6. Many guns were sold out of service at the end of the Civil War, though the Navy still had 2351 guns in January 1866 and the Army inventory was nearly 50,000. Many of these were subsequently converted for metal-case ammunition, though the U.S. government was still selling caplocks at auction as late as 1890.

MILITARY GUNS
1851-PATTERN CARBINE
Made for the Sharps Rifle Mfg. Co. by Robbins & Lawrence, Windsor, Vermont, 1852-5.
Total production: about 1800. **Chambering:** 52-caliber, combustible cartridge, fired by a caplock. **Action:** the breechblock was raised behind the chamber by a lever under the breech.
DATA FOR A U.S. ARMY TRIALS CARBINE
37.75in overall, 7.8lb empty. 21.6in barrel, 6-groove rifling; RH, concentric. Single-shot only. Open-block rear sight with a folding leaf. About 950 fps with a 450-grain bullet. No bayonet.

The success of the first Sharps firearms led to the formation of the Sharps Rifle Mfg. Co. in the autumn of 1851, production being entrusted to Robbins & Lawrence. The Maynard tape primer was retained, but the trigger guard was forged integrally with the breech lever and the hammer was mounted inside the lock plate. Two hundred carbines were delivered to the U.S. Army in 1853, but production of 1851-pattern carbines and half-stock sporting rifles (q.v.) continued until the mid 1850s.

SIMILAR GUNS
1852-pattern carbine, 1853-4. This embodied a disc priming system patented by Christian Sharps in October 1852. A tube bored vertically in the lock plate, ahead of the hammer, received a thin copper tube full of priming discs raised by a spring-loaded follower. A sliding feed arm propelled a single disc forward over the nipple each time the hammer fell. The guns retained the platinum ring gas-check and the adjustable chamber bushing of their 1851-type predecessors, but had an angular receiver and a conventional outside hammer. The mounts were usually brass.

1853-pattern carbine, 1853-8. A modified form of the 1852 design—made by Robbins & Lawrence prior to 1855 and then by the Sharps Rifle Company—this had a special spring-loaded breech lever pivot-pin retainer instead of a simple leaf spring, and a distinctive serpentine lever on the lower front right side of the receiver. Four hundred carbines were purchased by the U.S. Army in 1853-6, and 200 were purchased in 1857 by the anti-slavery Massachusetts-Kansas Aid Committee. These were subsequently acquired by John Brown to arm anti-slavery factions; 104 were retrieved after Brown's abortive attack on Harper's Ferry Armory in 1859, only to be seized by the Confederate Army in 1861 and refurbished for reissue.

1853-pattern Navy rifle. The 204 rifles purchased by the U.S. Navy and the Marine Corps were half-stocked, with brass furniture and a single barrel band. A small tenon beneath the muzzle accepted the sabre bayonet. The rifles were 44.3in overall, had 28.25in barrels, and weighed 9lb empty; the back-sight leaf was graduated to 800yd.

1855-PATTERN CARBINE
Made by the Sharps Rifle Mfg. Co., Hartford, Connecticut, about 1855-7.
Total production: 6750 carbines (including British contract). **Action:** as 1851 type, above.
DATA FOR U.S. TRIALS CARBINE
Chambering: 52-caliber, combustible cartridge. 37.8in overall, 7.65lb empty. 21.6in barrel, 6-groove rifling; RH, concentric. Single-shot only. Open-block sight with a folding leaf. About 950 fps with 450-grain bullet. No bayonet.

This design arose from a request from Britain (q.v.), where one gun had been tested in 1854 and another, fitted with a Maynard primer, in February 1855. An order for 6000 special 56-caliber guns was placed in January 1856.

Meanwhile, however, 400 52-caliber carbines had been ordered by the U.S. Army in April 1855. Total acquisitions are said to have been 600 1855-type carbines in 1855-7. They were easily distinguished by the tape-priming mechanism on the right side of the receiver, and by the straight neck of the hammer instead of the customary 'S'-shape. A short forend was held by a single band; mounts were almost always brass, though some iron-shod specimens have been reported.

Sharps Rifle Mfg. Co. marks appeared on the carbine barrels, with 'EDWARD MAYNARD' above 'PATENTEE 1855' on the tape primer gate. Official property marks and inspector's initials (e.g., 'U.S.' over 'J.H.' above 'P.') may be encountered on the rear of the barrel.

SIMILAR GUNS
1855-pattern Army rifle, 1855-6. Official acquisitions are said to have totaled merely 25 of these. They had full-length stocks and three bands. A socket bayonet could be mounted at the muzzle.

1855-pattern Navy rifle, 1856-7. The U.S. Navy purchased 200 half-stocked rifles with 28in barrels and 800yd ramp-and-leaf sights. They were 44.25in long, had 28.25in barrels, and weighed about 9lb. Fifty were made with a self-cocking system designed by Rollin White, which linked the hammer with the breech lever, but only 12 were accepted into Navy service.

MODEL 1859 RIFLE
Also known as 'New Model'
Made by the Sharps Rifle Mfg. Co., Hartford, Connecticut.
Total production: see text. **Chambering**: 52-caliber combustible cartridge, fired by a caplock. **Action:** as 1851 type, above.
47.15in overall, 8.75lb empty. 30in barrel, 6-groove rifling; RH, concentric. Single-shot only. Leaf-and-slider rear sight graduated to 700yd. About 1065 fps with 450-grain bullet. Socket bayonet.

The 'New Model' Sharps rifles, modified by Richard Lawrence, had a new stirrup and swivel between the main spring and the tumbler, and the breechblock was altered to move vertically. An improved gas-check ring—patented by Lawrence in December 1859—had been used for at least a year before the New Model was introduced, but the rear sight was new and the addition of a cut-off in the peller-primer mechanism allowed standard caps to be used if required.

THE GUNS
1859-pattern Navy rifle, 1859-62. The U.S. Navy ordered 900 56-caliber rifles on 9th September 1859, with barrels held in the full-length stock by two bands; 1500 additional 52-caliber guns were ordered from John Mitchell of Washington DC in June 1861. Navy rifles had two brass barrel bands, and a short bar and tenon at the muzzle to accept a sword bayonet.

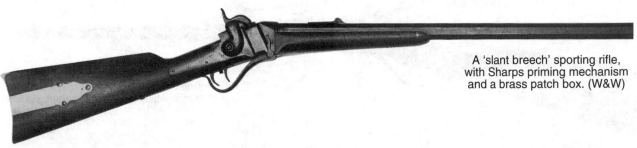

A 'slant breech' sporting rifle, with Sharps priming mechanism and a brass patch box. (W&W)

1859-pattern Army rifle. The first U.S. Army orders for New Model rifles were placed in June 1861, when 109 52-caliber 'Sharps Long Range Rifles with bayonets' were ordered from C.C. Bean of New York. By 30th June 1865, 9350 rifles had been delivered into federal stores. Army rifles were similar to the Navy's—except 600 made with 36in barrels—and had 30in barrels held by three bands. They had case-hardened locks, a patch box set into the right side of the butt, and iron furniture. One swivel was fitted to the middle band and the other lay beneath the butt. Most accepted socket bayonets, locking around the base of the front sight, though some guns with sword-bayonet bars may have been purchased by individual state units.

1859-pattern Sharpshooters rifle. Sharps rifles attained undying fame in the hands of the two regiments of United States Sharpshooters formed in the autumn of 1861 under the supervision of Colonel Hiram Berdan. A thousand rifles with double triggers and 30in barrels were ordered on 27th January 1862, and another 1000 on 6th February. Numbered in batches in the 54500-57800 block, they all bore the cursive 'JT'-in-cartouche mark of government arms inspector John Taylor.

1859-pattern carbine. At least 30,000 of these were made by the Sharps Rifle Mfg. Co. during the American Civil War. A typical 52-caliber U.S. Army example was 38.8in overall, weighed 7.5lb empty, and had a 21.7in barrel. It had a short tapering forend, held to the barrel by a single band, and did not accept a bayonet. Most guns made prior to 1862 had brass furniture, but this was replaced by iron early in the Civil War.

MODEL 1863 RIFLE AND CARBINE

Made by the Sharps Rifle Mfg. Co., Hartford, Connecticut.
Total production: about 65,000 carbines and 5000 rifles.
Otherwise generally as 1859-pattern guns, above.

These revised New Model guns were clearly marked 'MODEL 1863' on the barrel. The changes were comparatively minor: e.g., the dismantling screw in the breechblock was improved and the rear sight was strengthened. The 1863-type sights can be identified by their robust bed, which replaced the standing block and flimsy 'spring bed' of the earlier patterns. Furniture was invariably iron, but the patch box was abandoned some time in the Spring of 1864.

THE FIRST CARTRIDGE GUNS

The U.S. Army trials of 1865 included two dropping-block Sharps carbines, which were tested as No. 58 and No. 59. Though essentially similar to the Civil War patterns, they were chambered for metallic-case ammunition and had an auxiliary reciprocating extractor bolt protected by a patent granted in February 1867. A patch box with a hinged lid was let into the right side of the butt, and a folding-leaf rear sight lay on the barrel.

On 2nd November 1867, the U.S. authorities signed a contract with Sharps to convert caplock guns to take the standard 50-70 centerfire cartridge. Some guns had already been converted to accept a 50-67-487 rimfire cartridge, similar to the 56-50 Spencer pattern, but fitting a suitable striker and extractor had presented difficulties. Eventually, Richard Lawrence perfected an 'S'-shape striker which could be fitted within the existing breechblock design and work began; 31,100 carbines were altered in February-October 1868, followed by 1086 rifles in July-October 1869. The changes to the action were made by Sharps, but the barrels were bored-out, lined and re-rifled in Springfield Armory. The guns served until displaced by the 1873-model Springfields in the mid 1870s.

THE NEW CARTRIDGE GUNS

Unlike many rival designs promoted prior to 1870, the Sharps action was reliable and could handle the most powerful sporting cartridges. Though the cumbersome external hammer and back-action lock were retained, Sharps rifles performed better with metal-case cartridges than combustible ammunition. However, introduction of more efficient guns gradually eroded this superiority and even the improved Borchardt design could not save the company.

MODEL 1870 RIFLE

Made by the Springfield Armory, Springfield, Massachusetts, 1870-1.
Total production: see notes. **Chambering:** 50-70, rimmed. **Action:** generally as 1851 type, above.
49.65in overall, 9lb empty. 32.5in barrel, 3-groove rifling; RH, concentric. Ramp-and-leaf rear sight graduated to 1000yd? 1275 fps with 425-grain bullet. M1855 socket bayonet.

These were issued for U.S. Army field trials. Springfield completed 501 rifles in March 1871 and an additional 500 in July; however, some reports suggest that 2470 rifles and carbines were issued. The difference may have been due to the use of converted guns from store. M1870 rifles amalgamated the fittings and barrels of M1863 caplock rifle-muskets, lined down from 58-caliber, with 1863-type actions taken from Civil War carbines. The guns had full-length forends retained by two bands, though a few three-band examples were also made.

SIMILAR GUNS

M1870 carbine. These had 22in barrels and half-length forends retained by a single band. Their sights were graduated only to about 800yd. The carbines chambered 56-50 Spencer rimfire ammunition, but jammed and misfired too frequently to be acceptable and were discarded after the trials had been completed.

MILITARY MODEL

Made by the Sharps Rifle Mfg. Co., Hartford, Connecticut, 1870-4; and by the Sharps Rifle Company, Hartford, Connecticut, 1874-6, and Bridgeport, Connecticut, 1876-8.
Total production: not known. **Chambering options:** 45-70 Government or 50-70 Government. **Action:** as 1851-pattern carbine, above.
DATA FOR A TYPICAL POST-1873 45-70 EXAMPLE
47.15in overall, 8.85lb empty. 30in barrel, 3-groove rifling; RH, concentric. Ramp-and-leaf rear sight graduated to 1000yd. 1320 fps with 405-grain bullet. Sabre or socket bayonet.

Military-style rifles, based on the original (1869) or perfected (1871) sporting rifles described below, were offered from 1870 until the advent of the Sharps-Borchardt rifle in 1878. They had full-length forends retained by two bands. A few were sold to militia units, but enthusiasm elsewhere was muted.

SIMILAR GUNS

Military Model carbine. This shared the rifle action, but had a 22in barrel, a half-length forend retained by a single band, and a sling ring on the left side of the receiver.

SPORTING GUNS

1848-PATTERN RIFLE

Made by Daniel Nippes, Mill Creek, Pennsylvania, 1849-51.
Total production: about 200. **Chambering:** various, fired by a caplock. **Action:** as 1851-pattern military carbine, above.
DATA FOR A 42-CALIBRE TYPICAL EXAMPLE
48in overall, 9.5lb empty. 30.5in barrel, 5-groove rifling; RH, concentric. Single-shot only. Standing-block rear sight with a folding leaf. 1200 fps with 225-grain bullet?

The earliest Sharps designs made to the 1848 patent, though ordered in May 1849, were distinguished by the patented primer system housed in the frame ahead of the breechblock. This contained a primer-wheel, which could be detached once the swinging cover had been opened.

An 1863-pattern Sharps military carbine, distinguished from the 1859 pattern by the absence of a patch box. (W&W)

Nippes-made rifles had simple back-action locks and the breech-lever was a separate forging which fitted snugly around the trigger guard. A typical sporting rifle of this period had an octagonal barrel, held in the forend by a single lateral key, and a patch box in the butt to hold spare capping discs. Adjustable sights were often fitted—including ladder sights on the butt-wrist—and the mounts were generally brass.

SIMILAR GUNS

1849-pattern rifle. A second contract was placed in November 1849 for a modified rifle with a Maynard tape primer, though production did not begin until the summer of 1850. Most of the guns had iron mounts and a special platinum-alloy sealing ring in the breechblock face which, acting with an adjustable chamber bushing, was intended to prevent gas leaks. Unfortunately, the system was not particularly efficient.

1851-pattern rifle. An improved version of the basic design, this had the breech lever combined with the trigger guard and the hammer carried inside the back-action lock plate. The Maynard tape primer was retained, but the receiver was much more rounded than the angular later guns. About 200 1851-type sporting rifles were made, together with a handful of similar shotguns. Barrels were octagonal or cylindrical, 18-34in long and held in the forend with a single lateral key; caliber could be 36, 44 or 52.

1852-pattern rifle. This was essentially similar to the military rifles and carbines of the same date, embodying the 1852-patent Sharps disc primer system and the outside-hammer lock. Only about 600 guns were made, plus a handful of essentially similar shotguns.

1853-pattern rifle. Production was comparatively meagre—perhaps 2900 sporters and 300 shotguns—but the military-style carbines were also popular commercially. The barrels of the sporting rifles varied from 14in to 39in, but the shortest and longest options were very rare; 24-30in lengths were most popular. A typical 1853-type sporting rifle had a 25.5in 36-caliber octagon barrel.

New Model guns. The Civil War put such great demands upon production that Sharps was unable to make many sporting rifles of the 1859 or 1863 patterns. However, countless thousands of ex-military weapons saw civilian use after hostilities had ceased. A few full-length rifles were converted to fire metal-case ammunition—including the 52-70 Sharps cartridge—and others were remodelled to half-stock design. Shortly after the end of the war, however, Sharps introduced a purpose-built cartridge gun.

IMPROVED BREECH-LOADING SPORTING RIFLE

About 750-1,000 of these were made by the Sharps Rifle Mfg. Co. of Hartford, Connecticut, in 1866-71.

Sharps' first metallic-cartridge rifle was a minor modification of the 1863-type caplock. Based on existing components, it was made in such small numbers that it is now rarely encountered. An improved gun appeared in 1869, with a half-stock and a 26in octagon barrel. Its breechblock contained a cranked firing pin, enabling the side-mounted hammer to ignite a centerfire cartridge, and a new extractor shared the axis pin of the operating lever. The earliest guns chambered 52-70 rim- or centerfire cartridges, soon joined by 44 Berdan Short and 44 Berdan Long cartridges (subsequently known as 44-60 and 44-77 Sharps respectively).

The adoption by the U.S. Army of a 50-70 cartridge in 1870 persuaded Sharps to abandon the proprietary 52-70, as it was preferable to re-tube old barrels to fire military-pattern ammunition. A typical post-1869 rifle, chambering the 44 Berdan Long cartridge (44-77), was 43.15in overall, weighed 8.04lb and had a 26in round barrel.

NEW MODEL SPORTING RIFLE

About 25,000 of these guns were made in Hartford, Connecticut, by the Sharps Rifle Mfg. Co. (1871-4) and the Sharps Rifle Company (1874-6), then in Bridgeport, Connecticut, until 1881. Announced at the beginning of 1871, the new-pattern sporter could handle the most powerful sporting cartridges. The receiver was lengthened to form a loading tray, and the firing pin assembly was modified to improve ignition. The hammer nose was straightened to strike a firing-pin head, set into the rear right side of the breechblock, and the breech lever spring-assembly was revised.

Chamberings were initially restricted to 40 Berdan Short (40-50), 40 Berdan Long (40-70), 44 Berdan Short, 44 Berdan Long (44-77), and 50-70. From 1872 onward, complaints about the effectiveness of the 44 Berdan long bullet on bison were answered with the

50-90 'Big Fifty', in a 2.5in case. By 1873-4, Sharps cartridges were becoming known by their proprietary names. Designations based on case lengths also grew in popularity, as they prevented confusion arising from differing powder charges loaded in otherwise identical cases. For example, the 40-50 cartridge had a 1.563in case, while the 44-90 pattern measured 2.625in.

The first guns appeared in 1873-4 chambered for 45-70 government cartridges, which had replaced the 50-70 type; two versions of the 44-90, for hunting or target use, were also announced in this era.

SIMILAR GUNS

Model 1874 rifle. 1871-type guns were made until the Sharps Rifle Manufacturing Company was succeeded by the Sharps Rifle Company. The 'Model 1874' rifle was identical with its predecessor, but bore the new company name. Catalogues produced in the mid-1870s listed round, half-octagon or fully octagonal barrels (26-30in), and options such as double set triggers or peep-and-globe sights. A gun with an extra-heavy barrel could weigh as much as 15lb, though most examples weighed 8-10lb. Pewter forend tips were characteristic features.

The original necked cartridge-cases were supplemented from 1875 onward by straight patterns, cheaper to make and easier to reload. The first to appear was the 45-75 (2.1in case). Business then moved to Bridgeport, Connecticut.

Rifles leaving the Bridgeport factory after April 1876 bore an additional 'OLD RELIABLE' mark on their barrels. The straight 40-70 (2.5in case) had appeared in March, followed by the first 45-100 (2.875in case) in June. A modified 45-100, in a shorter 2.6in case, was introduced in November.

A 45-90 cartridge appeared in 1877, with a straight 2.4in case, but the Sharps Rifle Company was liquidated in September 1881. Stock-in-hand was still being sold in the mid-1880s, but the famous rifle then disappeared.

Business Rifle, 1874 pattern. This plain-looking gun appeared in the summer of 1876. Offered only with a blued octagonal barrel, it had a double set trigger and open sights. The oil-finished straight wrist butt had a rifle-pattern (concave) buttplate. Chamberings were restricted to 45-70 or a proprietary long-case 45-100 sometimes listed as '45-120'.

Hunter Rifle, 1874 pattern. Available from the Spring of 1875 onward, this is believed to have been a plain-finish sporting gun with a round barrel, a single trigger, and a straight wrist butt with a rifle-type buttplate.

LONG RANGE OR CREEDMOOR RIFLE

The 1873-vintage guns were announced simply as "Sharps' Long Range Rifles", as the Creedmoor name had still to become fashionable. Chambered only for the 44-90 cartridge, with a 2.6in case, they had octagon barrels of 32in or 34in and checkered pistol-grip butts. Vernier sights lay on the upper tang behind the breech; globe-pattern front sights, with wind gauge and spirit level, were fitted at the muzzle. Creedmoor rifles chambered 44-77 cartridges (2.25in or 2.438in cases) in addition to the popular 44-90. The Creedmoor patterns were supplemented in 1876—perhaps superseded—by the Mid- and Long-Range Rifles.

THE GUNS

No. 1 pattern rifle. The first of the three genuine Creedmoor rifles was introduced in 1875. An adaptation of the Long Range Rifle, it had a 32in half- or full-octagon barrel, a checkered pistol-grip butt, and a checkered forend. Straight shotgun-style shoulder plates were standard. A Vernier sight lay on the tang, and a globe-pattern front sight (with wind gauge and spirit level) appeared at the muzzle.

No. 2 pattern rifle. This was similar to No. 1, but had a plain straight-wrist butt and lacked checkering on the forend.

No. 3 pattern rifle. Distinguished by a 30in barrel and a straight-wrist butt, this had a plain aperture sight on the tang instead of the more sophisticated Vernier type.

No. 4 pattern rifle. A short-lived variant, this was plainest of the series. It resembled No. 3, but was stocked in poorer wood.

MID-RANGE RIFLE, NO. 1 PATTERN

Introduced in the Spring of 1876, three differing Mid-Range Rifles were made. The No. 1 (.40-70) had a 30in half- or full-octagon barrel, and a checkered pistol-grip butt with a nickeled rifle-type buttplate. It had a Vernier rear sight on the tang in addition to the conventional open rear sight on the barrel, and the standard globe-pattern front sight—with wind gauge and spirit level—lay on the muzzle.

SIMILAR GUNS

No. 2 pattern rifle. Similar to No. 1, this had a straight-wrist butt and a plainer finish.

No. 3 pattern rifle. Practically identical with No. 2, this chambered the smaller 40-50 (1.875in case) cartridge.

LONG-RANGE RIFLE NO. 1

Announced in the Autumn of 1876, this was really little more than a Mid-Range rifle (q.v.) with a half- or full-octagon barrel of 32in or 34in. Chamberings were 44-90, 45-90 or 45-100, cases measuring 2.625in, 2.4in and 2.6in respectively. Long Range rifles lacked the barrel-mounted rear sight, relying solely on Vernier and globe fittings; the Vernier sight could be mounted on the tang immediately behind the receiver or on the comb of the butt near the heel. The checkered woodwork of the No. 1 pattern was selected for its decorative figuring, and a sterling silver escutcheon was let into the forend.

SIMILAR GUNS

No. 2 pattern rifle. This had a plain forend without the escutcheon and lacked the spirit level on the front sight.

No. 3 pattern rifle. Otherwise identical with No. 2, this had a checkered straight-wrist butt.

NEW OR ENGLISH MODEL, 1875 PATTERN

Encouraged by sales in Europe, Sharps introduced a lightweight barreled action accompanied by a slender butt and forend. The hammer was much more delicate than the sturdy patterns favored in North America. The intention was apparently to provide as heavy a barrel as possible within the 10lb limit imposed in off-hand shooting competitions. Advertised from 1880 in three grades (cf., Mid-Range Rifle), the English Model proved to be very unpopular. Less than 1,000 actions were made, many being completed as standard sporters for sale in John Lower's Sportsman's Depot in Denver, Colorado.

OTHER PATTERNS

Frank Freund of Cheyenne, Wyoming, patented a improved Sharps-type action in August 1876. The round-topped breechblock was allowed to move backward as it dropped. When the breech lever was closed, the block moved up and forward to cam the cartridge-case forward into the breech. Sharps rifles modified by Freund—trading first as 'Freund & Brother' and then as 'The Wyoming Armory'—often had patented 'More Light' sights, with a contrasting line on the back edge of the front-sight blade and an additional aperture in the back-sight leaf beneath the notch. Guns may also be encountered with a patented detachable pistol grip.

A few Wyoming Saddle Guns were made in the early 1880s, embodying hand-made Freund-Sharps actions with notably elongated flat-side receivers, but were too expensive to sell in quantity and no more than 15 were ever completed.

MODERN RE-CREATIONS

The strength and long-established reputation of the Sharps rifles led to a revival in popularity in the 1970s. The first guns were made in Italy, apparently by Pedersoli and others, but were followed in the 1980s by good-quality versions made in the U.S.A. by manufacturers such as C. Sharps and Shiloh Products.

• Sharps (ii)

The C. Sharps Rifle Company of Big Timber, Montana (see also 'Shiloh', below) offered a range of Sharps-type rifles from 1987 onward. Since 1992, they have been distributed under the Montana Armory name.

MODEL 1874 GUNS

Offered in 40-, 44- or 45-caliber, for virtually any suitable chambering, these have been made as Military Rifles, Military Carbines, Business Rifles, Sporting Rifles No. 1 and No. 1 1/2, or Long Range Express Sporting Rifles. A typical sporter had a 30in octagonal barrel and weighed about 9.5lb.

MODEL 1875 GUNS

This was patterned on the improved Sharps rifle, with a greatly simplified slab-sided receiver and a shorter operating lever; however, few of the original guns had been made before the Sharps Rifle Company was liquidated in 1881. Announced in 1986, the re-creation chambered a variety of cartridges from 22 Stevens to 45-90. It had a case-hardened receiver, a round or octagonal barrel, and a straight-wrist butt with a shotgun-style shoulder plate. Individual patterns have included a Sporting Rifle with a 30in octagon barrel; a Saddle Gun with a 26in octagon barrel; a Carbine with a 24in round barrel and a half-length forend retained by a single barrel band; a Business Rifle with a 28in round barrel; and a 1991-vintage Target & Long Range Model with a long-range Vernier sight on the tang, an oval cheekpiece, and a checkered steel shoulder plate.

• Sharps-Borchardt

This hammerless dropping-block breech-loader was based on a patent granted to Hugo Borchardt in December 1876. A modernized version of the familiar Sharps dropping block system of 1848, it was designed to cock the striker as the breechblock descended. The safety lever behind the trigger was applied automatically; when the action had been reloaded and closed, the firer could override the safety by pressing the projecting catch.

Lock-time was very short and the action was extremely strong; so strong, indeed, that modern recreations can handle virtually any sporting cartridge. However, unless carefully honed and adjusted, original Sharps-made rifles had comparatively poor trigger pulls. Despite their short period in vogue, Sharps made about 10,000 military-style Borchardt rifles and 12,500 sporters. The barrels invariably had six-groove concentric rifling twisting to the right. Unfortunately, Sharps was liquidated in September 1881 and development ceased.

NEW MODEL MILITARY RIFLE

Made by the Sharps Rifle Co., Bridgeport, Connecticut, 1878-81.

Total production: about 10,000. **Chambering options:** 45-70 Government or 45-75 Sharps. **Action:** locked by wedging the breechblock behind the chamber with the tip of the operating lever.

DATA FOR A 45-70 EXAMPLE

48.5in overall, 8.98lb empty. 31.15in barrel, 6-groove rifling; RH, concentric. Single-shot only. Ramp-and-leaf rear sight graduated to 1100yd. 1320 fps with 405-grain bullet. M1873 socket bayonet.

The first military-style rifles were introduced in 1878. Their barrels were held in the full-length forends by two bands. Straight-wrist butts were standard. Swivels lay beneath the receiver ahead of the trigger guard and on the underside of the muzzle band. According to catalogue testimonials, Borchardt rifles were bought by the National Guard in Michigan and North Carolina, while the Massachusetts militia acquired a few hundred to train marksmen.

SIMILAR GUNS

Carbines. These were 40.6in overall, had 24in barrels and weighed about 7.65lb; their rear sights were graduated to 900yd. Half-length forends were retained by a single band, and a sling ring lay on the left side of the receiver.

Officer's Model Rifle. This was stocked as a military pattern, but in wood selected for its figuring. It had checkering on the butt-wrist and diced rubber inserts in the receiver-side.

NEW MODEL SPORTING RIFLE

Introduced with a 30in round or octagon barrel, chambered for the 45-70 Government or 45-120 Sharps (2.88in case) cartridges, the 1878-pattern or 'Hammerless' sporter had a half-stock with a straight-wrist butt and a plain rounded forend. Shotgun-style butts were standard. Double triggers and a selection of special finishes were optional. A typical example measured 46.4in overall and weighed 9lb. Its leaf sight was graduated to 1000yd.

SIMILAR GUNS

New Model Business Rifle, 1879-81. Chambered only for the 40-70 Sharps or 40-90 Sharps rounds, this was 44.4in overall (28in barrel) and weighed 8.79lb. It had a blued octagonal barrel and a leaf sight graduated to 1000yd. The oil-finished straight-wrist butt was accompanied by an equally spartan forend.

New Model Express Rifle, 1880-1. Chambered for the 45-100 or 45-120 Sharps cartridges, this was made in small numbers for the African market. The octagonal barrel had a matted top, carrying a British-style multi-leaf express rear sight with platinum centerlines and a front-sight bead. The pistol-grip butt and straight forend were both checkered, sling bars being driven through the woodwork, and the buttplate was a straight rubber shotgun pattern.

New Model Hunters' Rifle, 1879-81. This had a round barrel, a plain forend and a straight-wrist butt with a concave rifle-type buttplate. Chambered only for 40-50 (1.88in case) or 40-70 (2.5in case) Sharps cartridges, it had an open leaf sight graduated to 1000yd. Typically, the rifle was 42.38in overall, had a 26in barrel, and weighed about 8.55lb.

New Model Long Range Rifle or 'Hammerless Long-Range Rifle'. Chambered for the 45-90 Sharps round (2.4in case), this was 51.25in overall with a 34in round barrel and weighed 9.8lb without its sights. The select checkered walnut pistol-grip butt had a rubber shotgun-type shoulder plate. The forend was also checkered, and a wood or rubber plate filled recesses milled out of the receiver sides. The rifles had a Sharps' Long-Range Vernier sight on the tang, graduated to 1800yd, and the globe-type front sight was accompanied by a wind gauge and a spirit level. The standard barrel-mounted rear sight was usually omitted.

New Model Short & Mid-Range Rifle. Chambering 40-70 cartridges with a 2.5in case, this was similar to the Short Range Target Rifle, but had a 30in barrel and, apparently, a Vernier sight suitable for ranges up to 1000yd. Conventional leaf sights were also fitted when requested.

New Model Short Range Target Rifle, 1878-81. This 40-50 gun, chambering a cartridge with a 1.5in case-length, was offered with a Vernier sight intended for distances up to 800yd. A globe-pattern front sight with a wind gauge was standard, together with a checkered pistol-grip butt and forend. A rubber shotgun-style buttplate was fitted. A typical rifle fitted with a 28in round barrel was 44.38in overall and weighed about 9lb.

MODERN RE-CREATIONS

The advent in 1967 of the Sharps Arms Company, promoting a much-modernized Borchardt action, was widely acclaimed—particularly when operations were acquired by Colt. Unfortunately, accuracy problems were so great that the project was abandoned in the mid-1970s. Only about 450 actions had been made by the Bellmore-Johnson Tool Company in Hamden, Connecticut. Not all were assembled, though some were used in highly decorative presentation-grade guns in chamberings ranging from 17 Remington to 458 Winchester. A few modified Borchardt actions were also made in 1972-5 by Artistic Arms of Hoagland, Indiana, but this enterprise also failed after a promising start.

• Sharps & Hankins

The success of the Sharps dropping-block breech system was never mirrored in the uneasy partnership of Christian Sharps and Richard Lawrence, and the inventor eventually lost interest in the Sharps Rifle Manufacturing Company.

Sharps subsequently received U.S. patent 32,790 in July 1861, protecting a firearm loaded by sliding the barrel forward when the trigger guard lever was pressed, and entered into a partnership with William Hankins. Series production of the sliding-barrel guns began in 1862.

OLD MODEL NAVY RIFLE

Made by Sharps & Hankins, Philadelphia, Pennsylvania, 1862.

Total production: 500. **Chambering:** 52 Sharps & Hankins No. 56, rimfire. **Action:** locked by an underlever holding the barrel closed.

47.6in overall, 8.5lb empty. 32.7in barrel, 6-groove rifling; RH, concentric. Single-shot only. Tangent rear sight graduated to 800yd. 975 fps with standard ball ammunition? Socket or sword bayonet.

Five hundred of these rifles were ordered for the U.S. Navy in April-September 1862, all but one hundred being supplied with a sword bayonet. They were fully stocked, with three iron bands, and had swivels beneath the butt and the center band. Markings usually included the makers' names and an acknowledgment of the Sharps patent of 1859.

OLD MODEL CARBINE

Made by Sharps & Hankins, Philadelphia, Pennsylvania, 1862-5.

Total production: about 10,000. **Chambering:** 52 Sharps & Hankins No. 56, rimfire. **Action:** as Old Model Navy Rifle, above.

38.5in overall, 7.4lb empty. 23.5in barrel, 6-groove rifling; RH, concentric. Single-shot only. Tangent rear sight graduated to 800yd. 900 fps with standard ball ammunition? No bayonet.

The Army was more interested in the Sharps & Hankins carbine than in the rifle preferred by the Navy. Short-barreled guns had been bought privately to arm the 9th and 11th New York Volunteer Cavalry in 1862, performing so successfully that the attention of the federal government was gained. The first governmental orders were placed in 1863, the Army eventually receiving 1468 and the Navy taking 6336.

Early or 'Old Model' guns, made in 1862, had a fixed firing pin in the hammer face. They had walnut butts, a brass buttplate, and a swivel beneath the wrist. The barrel was blued or tinned, and the front sight was mounted on a muzzle band.

SIMILAR GUN

New Model or **M1863.** Post-1863 carbines had a floating firing pin in the standing breech, and a safety slider was added on the rear of the frame to block the fall of the hammer. The finalized guns fired metal-case rimfire cartridges known as 'Sharps & Hankins No. 56'. Navy-issue carbines generally displayed inspector's marks (e.g., 'P' over 'H.K.H.') and had a sturdy leather sleeve over the barrel to prevent corrosion.

• Shilen

Founded by Ed Shilen in 1961, to make the high-quality barrels for which it is world famous, this company made its first complete guns in the 1970s. Five models share a turning bolt with dual-opposed locking lugs and a pin-type ejector. Excepting DGA/BP and DGA/BP-S patterns, the contours of the receivers are squared.

DGA SPORTING RIFLE

Made by Shilen Rifles, Inc., Ennis, Texas.

Currently in production. **Chambering options:** see text. **Action:** locked by rotating lugs on the bolt head into the receiver wall.

DATA FOR A TYPICAL DGA SPORTER

Chambering: 284 Winchester, rimless. 44.5in overall, 7.55lb empty. 24in barrel, 4-groove rifling; RH, concentric? Internal box magazine, 3 rounds. Optical sight. 2900 fps with 150-grain bullet.

The standard DGA Sporter and DGA Magnum Sporter were introduced in about 1975 for cartridges with maximum overall lengths of 2.85in and 3.69in respectively. Stocks were American walnut, or fiberglass finished in textured brown, silver, black, red, royal blue or green acrylic enamel.

Cylindrical or tapered barrels were standard, though octagonal patterns have often been made to order to complement the squared lines of the larger actions. The metalwork was either matte ('satin') blue or dulled nickel.

Triggers were sturdy adjustable multi-lever patterns with a pull of about 3lb, though Shilen Competition Triggers (with a pull of 2-6oz) and even an electronic version were supplied on request. Pivoting safety levers were usually fitted to the magazine rifles.

The rigid DGA Single-Shot action has proved popular for long-range silhouette shooting and 'Heavy Varmint' bench-rest competitions. The safety was customarily omitted from single-shot guns, which were often stocked in stable warp-resistant fiberglass. DGA/BP (lightweight) and DGA/BP-S (ultra light) actions were intended for single-shot rifles and silhouette pistols.

THE GUNS

DGA Sporter. These patterns had classic straight-comb butts and round-tip forends. By 1980, Shilen was listing all-caliber chamberings for the Sporter, which was fitted with the 24in No. 2 barrel, though the standard options were regarded as 17 Remington, 220 Swift, 222 Remington, 22-250, 223 Remington, 6mm Remington, 243 Winchester, 250 Savage, 257 Roberts, 284 Winchester, 308 Winchester or 358 Winchester. More than 70 cartridge options ranging from 17 Remington to 458 Winchester Magnum were being listed in 1988.

DGA Bench-Rest. Guns of this type offered unusually broad forends. They customarily accepted 220 Swift, 22-250, 6mm Remington or 308 Winchester, though many others were supplied to order. The 1980 catalogue noted that choice of 'caliber, twist, chambering, [barrel] contour or [barrel] length' was left to the purchaser.

DGA Silhouette. These versions had sharply-pitched high combs suited to optical sights mounted high above the bore. The Silhouette rifles were being offered in 1980 in 7mm-08 or 308 Winchester, in single-shot and magazine-fed forms, but other chamberings could be obtained on request;

DGA Varminter. Characterized by broad forends, these rifles also had sharply-curved pistol grips and low roll-over combs. In 1980, the Varminter was being offered in the same all-caliber option as the Sporter, but had the 25in No. 5 Shilen barrel.

• Shiloh

Shiloh Products, a division of Drovel Tool Company, began trading in Farmingdale, New York, in 1976. After expanding to become the Shiloh Rifle Manufacturing Company, Inc., business moved to Big Timber, Montana, in 1983.

SHILOH SHARPS RIFLES

These have been offered in cap-lock or metal cartridge versions, patterned after the original models of 1863 and 1874 respectively. Shiloh 'Model 1874' cartridge guns, offered in a wide range of chamberings, show great diversity. Virtually all sporting patterns, however, have double set triggers.

THE GUNS

Business Rifle. Otherwise similar to the No. 3 Sporter (q.v.), this had a 28in tapered barrel.

Custom guns. Shiloh has made many guns to special order. Extras have included Schuetzen-style hooked buttplates, pewter forend tips, checkering, oil-finished woodwork and engraving.

Gemmer Model. A recreation of rifles made for John P. Gemmer of St. Louis, a famous Western gunsmith, this had a half-length forend retained by keys and escutcheons. Uniquely, a cleaning rod was carried under the barrel.

Hartford Model. Introduced in 1989, this had a straight-wrist butt with a straight shotgun-style shoulder plate. Distinguishing features included a 'Hartford Collar' (a short cylindrical section on the barrel ahead of the breech) and a pewter or German silver forend tip.

Jaeger Rifle. This was a special lightweight gun with a half-octagonal 26in barrel and a pistol-grip butt.

Long Range Express Sporting Rifle. Distinguished by its 34in tapering-octagon barrel and figured American black walnut woodwork, this had Vernier tang and globe front sights. The pistol-grip butt had a cheekpiece on the left side, the shoulder plate was a rubber shotgun type, while the forend had a schnabel tip.

Military Model. The Shiloh Sharps has also been offered in single-trigger military configurations. The rifle had a three-band stock and a patch box, whereas the carbine had a plain schnabel tip forend. Barrels measured 30in (rifle) or 24in (carbine).

Montana Rifle. Introduced in 1989 to commemorate the State Centennial, this 45-70 rifle was made in three versions: Custom Creedmoor, Hartford, and Bridgeport. The Creedmoor variant, with its Vernier-and-globe sights and beautifully figured woodwork, was especially notable.

Montana Roughrider Rifle. Available with a pistol-grip butt, this had a half- or fully-octagonal barrel measuring 24-34in.

Saddle Rifle. Made with a 26in octagonal barrel and a straight-wrist butt. The butt generally had an oval cheekpiece on the left side.

Sporting Rifle (Deluxe) No. 1. Offered with a 30in tapering octagonal barrel, this had a pistol-grip butt and a schnabel-tip forend.

Sporting Rifle No. 3. Essentially similar to the No. 1 pattern described above, this was sold with a straight-wrist military-pattern butt.

• Smith (Dexter)

Dexter Smith of Springfield, Massachusetts, made firearms in accordance with a series of patents granted in 1867-71 to Martin J. & H.M. Chamberlain (together or alone) to protect a complicated rolling-block breech with a locking or 'safety' cam attached to the trigger. Smith and Martin Chamberlain received a patent in March 1871 to protect an auxiliary locking cam—supplementing the trigger-mounted fitting—and production of shotguns and rifles began in Springfield in 1872.

A 50-caliber musket was tested during the U.S. Army trials of 1872 as 'Gun No. 38'. Often simply listed as the 'Dexter'. It had an exposed central hammer which could be retracted to half- or full-cock before an operating lever on the right side of the breech could be pressed to release the 'locking brace', allowing the radial breech-block to rotate back from the breech face.

The gun was not successful militarily, but about 2500 were made before work stopped in 1874; most were 12- or 16-gauge smooth-bore shotguns. The Smith & Chamberlain guns had a distinctively rounded frame with flats on the sides and a detachable plate on the left, but were much too complicated to compete with rivals such as Sharps or Remington.

• Smith (Gilbert)

On 5th August 1856, Gilbert Smith of Buttermilk Falls, New York, was granted U.S. patent no. 15,496 to protect a method of sealing a gun-breech with an 'elastic lip' on the rear of an enlarged chamber. When the gun was fired, pressure forced the lip momentarily outward against the standing breech to provide a gas-seal. Smith subsequently received Patent no. 17,644 (June 1857) to protect a sliding-barrel gun carrying the cartridge half in the breech and half in the barrel, accurately located by a shoulder in the chamber. The original cartridges had a paper case, but this was subsequently changed to gutta-percha.

The action was locked by a sturdy spring-steel bar projecting back from the top of the barrel over a stud on the standing breech; though popularly associated with Smith's patents, this was not part of his claims to originality. A small catch ahead of the trigger

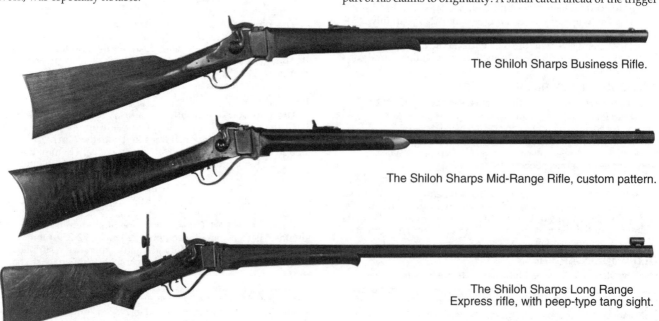

The Shiloh Sharps Business Rifle.

The Shiloh Sharps Mid-Range Rifle, custom pattern.

The Shiloh Sharps Long Range Express rifle, with peep-type tang sight.

The Smith carbine of the
Civil War era. (W&W)

lever was pressed upward to release the bar, allowing the barrel to open.

The Smith carbine tested at Washington Arsenal in the Spring of 1860 was praised for simplicity and an unusually gas-tight breech. However, this opinion was not universal: Major Colston reported to the Commissioners of Virginia Armory later in 1860 that the original paper-cartridge Smith loaded easily when clean, but became so foul after 60 shots that it could not be loaded at all.

SMITH CARBINE

Made by Poultney & Trimble, Baltimore, Maryland; by the
   Massachusetts Arms Company, Chicopee Falls, Massachusetts;
   and by the American Machine Works, Springfield, Massachusetts
   (see text).
Total production: 32,000? **Chambering:** 50 Smith, combustible cartridge, fired by a caplock. **Action:** the tipping barrel was locked by a spring-latch on top of the breech.
DATA FOR A CIVIL WAR GUN.
   39.5in overall, 7.5lb empty. 21.6in barrel, 3-groove rifling; RH, concentric. Single-shot only. Block and single-leaf rear sight. About 950 fps with standard bullet. No bayonet.

The original Smith carbines, made in 1858-60, had a simple standing-block rear sight and a distinctively spurred trigger guard. The half-octagon barrel was held in the forend with a transverse key, and a crescent-shaped buttplate was standard. Swivels were absent. About 300 Smiths were purchased from Poultney & Trimble for U.S. Army field trials shortly before the Civil War began. The 1861 or Civil War-type carbines were simpler, usually with a single barrel band and a ring-and-bar on the left side of the breech.

Poultney & Trimble soon obtained a large order from the federal government. In August 1863, however, the Massachusetts Arms Company passed much of the work on Smith carbines to the American Machine Works to free facilities for the Maynard pattern (q.v.). Intensely irritated, Poultney & Trimble transferred the entire contract for Smith carbines to the American Machine Works in September 1863 and formed a new promoter, the 'American Arms Company', in Chicopee Falls. Smith carbines may be marked by any of the participants, together with an acknowledgment of the June 1857 patent. Federal government inspectors' marks will also appear on service-issue examples. The federal authorities purchased 30,062 Smiths in 1861-6, making them the fourth-ranked carbine after the Spencer, Sharps and Burnside patterns.

The wartime guns originally fired special rubber-case ammunition with a thin paper cover over the flash-hole in the base, but Poultney was assigned a patent granted to Thomas Rodman and Silas Crispin in December 1863 for an improved 'wrapped-metal cartridge with a strengthening disc or cup'. Poultney's patent Metallic Cartridge certainly improved efficiency, though power was limited by the weak breech.

• Smith (Isaac)

Isaac Smith of New York obtained U.S. patent 42,542 in April 1864, protecting a 'safety system for firearms'. Two carbines of this type were tested by the U.S. Army in 1865, as Guns No. 60 and No. 61, with two-piece half-stocks and forends held by a single band. The breech-block lifted laterally—similarly to the Joslyn pattern (q.v.)—and was locked in place by the fall of the central hammer. A small block-type rear sight with a folding leaf lay on top of the barrel in front of the breech.

• Smith & Wesson

Smith & Wesson of Springfield, Massachusetts, best known for handguns, have maintained an occasional interest in rifles. Most of the post-1945 guns were based on Mauser or Sako actions.

MODEL A SPORTING RIFLE

Smith & Wesson distributed Husqvarna-made Mauser-type rifles in 1969-72. The Model A was the Husqvarna 3000 pattern (see 'Sweden: Husqvarna'). Model B was a Husqvarna P-3000. Model C was little more than a minor variant of the Husqvarna Model 4000 Lightweight. Model D was a short 'carbine pattern' with a full-length Mannlicher-style stock and a straight-comb butt. Model E was a variant of the Model D, with a Monte Carlo comb on the butt instead of a straight pattern.

MODEL 1500

Substantial quantities of 1974-type Sako actions were acquired from 1979 onward, probably to allow Sako to introduce new patterns unencumbered by stocks of obsolescent parts. Built on the L-579 or L-61 action, the guns were stocked and finished in North America to be sold as the 'Model 1500' in 243 Winchester (L-579), 270 Winchester, 7mm Remington Magnum or 30-06 (all L-61). The standard rifles had straight-comb half-stocks with a plain rounded forend. Conventional checkering lay on the pistol grip and the square-tipped forend. A 22in barrel was standard in all versions excepting 7mm Remington Magnum (24in), giving a length of 42-42.5in and a weight of 7.5-7.8lb. A Williams ramp rear sight was customary.

The range was enlarged in the early 1980s, by which time the standard Model 1500 was being chambered for 222 or 223 Remington (L-461 action); 243 Winchester or 308 Winchester (L-579); and 25-06 Remington, 270 Winchester, 7mm Remington Magnum, 300 Winchester Magnum or 30-06 (L-61). A walnut Monte Carlo stock was used. In the mid-1980s, however, S&W decided to concentrate on handguns and sold the remaining rifles to Mossberg (q.v.).

THE GUNS

Model 1500 Deluxe, 1979-85. This rifle had a jeweled bolt, a scroll on the magazine floorplate, an S&W pistol-grip cap inlay, and skip-line checkering. No sights were furnished.

Model 1500 Mountaineer, 1983-5. Little more than a standard rifle with a satin finished stock with a straight-comb butt, this was offered in 223 Remington (L-461 action), 243 Winchester (L-579), 270 Winchester, 7mm Remington Magnum or 30-06 (all L-61).

Model 1500 Varmint Deluxe, 1982-5. Introduced on the basis of the Sako L-461 action, this chambered 222, 22-250 or 223 Remington ammunition. It shared the deluxe-pattern Monte Carlo stock and weighed about 9.3lb.

Model 1700LS Classic Hunter, 1983-5. Another of the guns derived from the standard M1500, this had a straight comb and a schnabel-tipped forend. The hand-cut checkering was divided into panels by sinuous ribands. A detachable five-round box magazine was fitted. Chamberings were restricted to 243 Winchester (L-579 action), or 270 Winchester and 30-06 (L-61).

• Smoot

William Smoot of Ilion, New York, submitted a 50-caliber musket to the U.S. Army trials of 1872, where it was listed as 'Gun No. 32'. Possibly made in the Remington Arms Company tool room, it had a slab-sided box receiver containing a radial breechblock. Retracting the thumbpiece of the cam lever projecting above the right receiver wall, after the hammer had been put to half-cock, opened the breech. Smoot obtained a variety of patents for radial-block designs in 1867-72, but none of them seems to have protected the construction of No. 32.

• Sneider

Charles Sneider seems to have been employed by Poultney & Trimble of Baltimore, makers of the carbine patented by Gilbert Smith (q.v.). Sneider's first patent, 27,600 of March 1860, protected a modification of the Smith system with a breech-locking spring which automatically compensated for wear and a release catch or 'lifter' inside the trigger guard. After patenting a range of break-open breech systems, opened by underlevers, Sneider returned to the Smith carbine. U.S. patent 47,755 of May 1865 was granted for a metallic-cartridge conversion with a backward projecting chamber which entered a recess in the standing breech. The hammer was set automatically to half-cock as the breech opened, and a spring-releasing catch was set into the top of the receiver behind the hammer. Interestingly, Silas Crispin of Poultney & Trimble patented a similar improvement to the Smith system in January 1867 (U.S. patent 60,696).

• Snell

Oscar Snell of Williamsburgh, Ohio, submitted three 50-caliber muskets to the U.S. Army trials of 1872; they were tested as Guns Nos. 33, 62 and 101. Very little is known about No. 33, but the others—one rimfire, one centerfire—embodied a slam-firing mechanism eventually patented in July 1874. As the hammer fell to lock the breech, the right side of a cranked arm pivoted on the hammer nose struck the side of the breech. The impact threw the striker, formed by the left side of the arm, against the primer of the chambered round just as the breech closed. As the timing of the action was critical, the Snell system was never successful.

• Snider

Two carbines of this type were submitted to the U.S. Army trials of 1865, where they were tested as Guns Nos. 62 and 63. Made in accordance with U.S. patent 69,941, granted to Jacob Snider Jr of New York in October 1867, they had British-style stocks with three-quarter-length forends ending in a metal cap. Two screwed barrel bands were used, and a cleaning rod was carried beneath the barrel. A lug on the right side of the muzzle presumably accepted a British-style sabre bayonet. The breech-block, hinged longitudinally, tipped to expose the chamber—apparently leftward in the case of Gun No. 62 and to the right on no. 63. Ignition was provided by the hammer of an external sidelock hitting a striker in the breech-block.

• Spencer

Patented in March 1860 (U.S. No. 27,393), this rifle was the work of Christopher M. Spencer, who, with the assistance of Luke Wheelock, produced about 30 prototypes while working for Cheney Brothers Silk Mills Company of Manchester, Connecticut. The patronage of the Cheneys, who were friendly with the Secretary of the Navy, allowed an encouraging trial to be undertaken in Washington Navy Yard on 8th June 1861. An inherent weakness was eventually found in the extractor, but an improved design was patented in July 1862.

The Spencer was a seven-shot repeater with a radial breech-block actuated by a trigger guard lever. Opening the lever dropped the block, allowed the extractor to pull the spent case out of the chamber, and forced the ejector to throw it out of the gun. As the lever closed, the tip of the breechblock picked up the rim of the first cartridge in the butt-tube magazine and fed it into the chamber.

Though the external side-hammer still had to be cocked manually, the Spencer could be fired very rapidly—particularly after a cartridge box patented by Colonel Erastus Blakeslee in Novem-

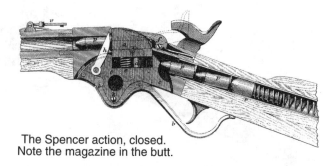

The Spencer action, closed. Note the magazine in the butt.

ber 1864 had been introduced. This held between six and 13 seven-round loading tubes in a wooden block. Reloading was then simply a matter of opening the butt-trap, withdrawing the magazine spring and cartridge elevator, and then simply dropping the cartridges straight out of the Blakeslee loader before replacing the magazine spring.

Note: Great confusion exists over the designations of Spencer cartridges. The original guns had 52-caliber barrels, but fired a straight-case cartridge known as 'No. 56' or 56-56; the Model 1865 Spencer was a 50-caliber gun chambered for government-developed tapered straight-case '56-50' ammunition, which was shared with several other carbines. The 56-52 Spencer round appeared after the Civil War, but would interchange with its 56-50 predecessor.

MODEL 1860 NAVY RIFLE

Made by the Spencer Repeating Rifle Company, Boston, Massachusetts, 1862-3.

Total production: more than 700. **Chambering:** 56-56 Spencer, rimfire. **Action:** locked by propping a radial block behind the chamber.

47in overall, 10lb empty. 30in barrel, 6-groove rifling; RH, concentric. Tube magazine in the butt, 7 rounds. Leaf-and-slider rear sight graduated to 800yd. 975 fps with 435-grain bullet. Sword bayonet

On 22nd June 1861, the U.S. Navy ordered 700 rifles and 70,000 rimfire cartridges for large-scale trials. Navy rifles had case-hardened receivers, three iron bands and accepted brass-hilted sword bayonets made by Collins & Company; 600 were inspected in December 1862 and 703 were received by the Navy Ordnance Department on 3rd February 1863. The Navy bought 300 additional guns in 1863, but these were Army-type guns with socket bayonets; however, six sword-bayonet 'Navy Spencers' were made in 1867 for presentation to the prime minister of Siam.

SIMILAR GUNS

Model 1860 Army rifle, 1862-5. Some of the original Navy trials were attended by Captain Alexander Dyer of the U.S. Army, who reported favorably to his superiors. The Spencer rifle was tested at Washington Arsenal in November 1861—again with favorable results—but Brigadier General Ripley, the Chief of Ordnance, was unimpressed. Exasperated, Charles Cheney turned once more to Secretary of the Navy Gideon Welles, who took the unprecedented step of ordering 10,000 Spencer rifles for the Army. Army rifles were fully stocked, had three bands, and accepted a socket bayonet.

In December 1861, the newly formed Spencer Rifle Manufacturing Company leased half the Chickering piano factory in Boston to cope with demand. However, no guns had been delivered by 29th January 1862, and, after a review of all existing government contracts, the original order was subsequently reduced to 7500. The first 500 guns were delivered into federal store on 31st Decem-

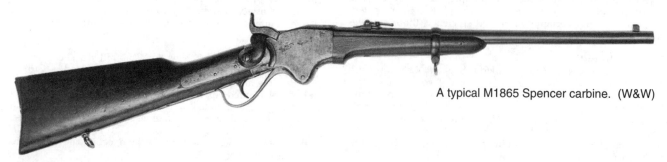

A typical M1865 Spencer carbine. (W&W)

ber 1862; by the end of the Civil War in 1865, 11,472 rifles had been acquired.

Model 1865 rifle, 1865-7. This was a post-war version of the M1860, made only in small numbers. It was customarily offered with a 32in barrel held in the forend with two iron bands and chambered the 56-52 cartridge.

MODEL 1860 CARBINE

Made by and for the Spencer Repeating Arms Company, Boston, Massachusetts, 1862-6 (see text).

Total production: more than 100,000. **Chambering:** 56-56 Spencer, rimfire. **Action:** as Navy rifle, above.

DATA FOR A TYPICAL EXAMPLE

39in overall, 8.23lb empty. 22in barrel, 6-groove rifling; RH, concentric. Tube magazine in butt, 7 rounds. Leaf-and-slider rear sight. 925 fps with 435-grain bullet. No bayonet.

In August 1863, Christopher Spencer met Abraham Lincoln to demonstrate his carbine. The president was greatly impressed, and the future of the weapon was finally assured. The Spencer was robust and fired a heavier bullet than the Henry (q.v.), generating 40 per cent greater muzzle energy than its rival.

The first government-order guns began to reach the troops in the winter of 1862, though many had already been sold to state and volunteer units. They had straight-comb butts and short forends with a single iron band around the barrel. A saddle ring lay on the left side of the breech. Spencer carbines soon proved themselves on the battlefield, where their performance was a revelation. During the Battle of Hoover's Gap, for example, Colonel John Wilder's men were able to maul a far larger band of Confederates thanks to an inventory which consisted largely of Spencers.

SIMILAR GUNS

Model 1865 carbine. These were fitted with a cut-off patented by Edward Stabler of Sandy Springs, Maryland, which held the magazine in reserve by limiting rotation of the breechblock. Guns made to this pattern had 20in three-groove barrels chambering the government-developed 56-50 cartridge. They were made by the Spencer Repeating Arms Company and also by the Burnside Rifle Company, which had delivered 30,496 of a 35,000-gun order by the end of 1865. By 30th June 1866, 94,196 M1860 and M1865 carbines had been delivered into federal stores, though only 50,000 had been issued.

SPORTING RIFLES

The Spencer Repeating Rifle Company made sporting guns in the post-Civil War era. The quantities involved are difficult to judge, however, owing to the delivery of nearly 20,000 1865-type carbines to the U.S. Army after the Civil War had ended, and to the sales of military weapons elsewhere. About 25,000 guns were made in 1865-8 in addition to the carbines, and it is suspected that a substantial portion of these were completed in sporting form.

Most Spencer sporting rifles shared the construction of the perfected carbines, but reverted to six-groove rifling. They were also more delicate, often displaying ring-tip operating levers and pewter or German silver forend tips. Held by transverse keys instead of bands, the barrels could be round or half-octagon patterns chambering the bottlenecked 56-46 rimfire cartridge instead of the 56-52 version. Production was never large, as the assets of the Spencer Repeating Arms Company were sold to the Fogerty Rifle Company in October 1868.

• Spencer-Roper

The basic design was developed by Sylvester Roper (q.v.) in the late 1870s and patented on 4th April 1882 (U.S. no. 255,894), protecting a slide-action breech with a vertically oscillating breech-block. The original prototype apparently had the magazine above the barrel, relying on gravity to expel spent cartridges downward, but the system had soon been refined in collaboration with Christopher Spencer.

SPENCER-ROPER RIFLE

Made by the Spencer Repeating Arms Company, 1882-4.

Total production: at least ten. **Chambering options:** 45-70, 11mm Mauser, 11mm Gras and possibly others. **Action:** locked by pivoting the breech-block into line behind the chamber.

DATA FOR A GERMAN TRIALS MODEL

Chambering: 11x60R, rimmed. 49.4in overall, 10.45lb empty. 32in barrel, 4-groove rifling; RH, concentric. Detachable box magazine, four rounds?

Leaf-and-slider rear sight graduated to 1600m (1750yd). 1410 fps with Reichspatrone 1871. M1871 sword bayonet.

There were apparently two basic types of Spencer-Roper, one ejecting vertically and the other ejecting laterally to the right. A single vertical-ejection gun was made for the U.S. Army magazine-rifle trials of 1882, where it was entered as 'Gun No. 35' but failed to progress to the final series. It had a modified Lee-type box magazine.

When the slide handle was drawn back, it first dropped the block to allow a spent case to be extracted and a cartridge to be taken from the magazine. The block then sprang upward to expel the old case, the new cartridge was pushed into the chamber, and the block returned at the end of the forward handle-stroke to seal the breech.

There were two 'triggers' inside the guard, the cocking/de-cocking lever at the front allowing the striker to be released safely if the rear trigger was pressed at the same time. The mechanism could be re-cocked simply by pressing the front lever forward again.

Spencer-Roper rifles were also tested extensively in Europe in this period. However, the guns sent for trial in France and Germany, built on the general lines of the Gras and the Mauser respectively, had a shorter side-ejecting action with a radial cut-off lever on the right side of the breech below the ejection port. An 11mm survivor of the 1884 French Army trials is 51.25in long and weighs 10.4lb empty.

Though the military rifles failed their trials, more than twenty thousand tube-magazine shotguns sharing the basic action were made by the Spencer Repeating Arms Company and (after 1890) by Francis Bannerman & Sons of New York. A few shotguns were apparently offered as 'rifles', possibly with 12-bore barrels rifled on the Greener 'Paradox' principle.

• Springfield, bolt-action type

This bolt mechanism, based on the Mauser, was unique to the USA—though many war-surplus rifles were used elsewhere after 1945 and others were supplied through Military Aid Programs into the 1960s.

Experience in the Spanish-American War showed that Spanish Mausers were superior to the Krag-Jørgensen. On 2nd October 1900, therefore, a Board of Officers convened at Springfield Armory to test an experimental 'Model 1900' combining the best features of both types of rifle. Its bolt had two locking lugs on the head plus a safety lug provided by the bolt-handle base. A cut-off pivoted above the housing for the Mannlicher pattern clip-loaded magazine.

MODEL 1901 RIFLE

Made by the Springfield Armory, Springfield, Massachusetts, 1901.

Total production: at least 100. **Chambering:** 30-caliber experimental rimless cartridge. **Action:** locked by two lugs on the bolt head engaging recesses in the receiver behind the chamber, and by a 'safety lug' locking down ahead of the receiver bridge.

49.25in overall, 9.47lb empty (with bayonet). 30in barrel, 4-groove rifling; RH, concentric. Integral box magazine loaded from a stripper-clip, 5 rounds. Tangent-leaf rear sight graduated to 2000yd. 2300 fps with 220-grain bullet. M1901 rod bayonet.

This improvement on the experimental rifle of 1900 embodied changes suggested by the trials board. Tested in 1901, it had a straight-wrist butt, a new rear sight, and a rod bayonet. Its magazine could only be loaded through the top of the open action—losing the one real advantage of the Krag, which could be replenished with the bolt closed. Though much the same length as the M1898 Krag, the experimental rifle was appreciably lighter.

Approval was given in 1902 for the manufacture of 5000 M1901 rifles in Springfield, by adapting existing machinery, until the folly of making M1901 and Krag rifles concurrently was realized. Consequently, only 100 M1901 rifles were made (largely by hand) to prevent disrupting production of the Krag-Jørgensen.

MODEL 1903 SHORT RIFLE

Made by the Springfield Armory, Springfield, Massachusetts, 1903-27 (about 1.275 million military M1903); by Rock Island Arsenal, Illinois, 1904-19 (346,780 M1903); and by the Remington Arms Co., Inc., Ilion, New York, 1941-3 (348,090 M1903 and M1903 [Modified]).

Total production: about 1.97 million (all types). **Chambering options:** 30 M1903 or 30-06, rimless. **Action:** generally as M1901, above.

The action of a Springfield-made M1903 rifle.

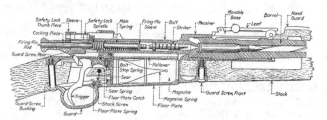

A longitudinal section of the M1903 action.

DATA FOR ORIGINAL PATTERN

Chambering: 30 M1903, rimless. 43.4in overall, 8.5lb empty. 24.2in barrel, 4-groove rifling; RH, concentric. Internal box magazine loaded from a stripper-clip, 5 rounds. Tangent-leaf rear sight graduated to 2000yd. 2300 fps with M1903 ball cartridges. M1903 rod bayonet.

Series production of M1901 rifles had not begun when the advent of the British Lee-Enfield short rifle in 1902 caused the U.S. Army to reconsider. Trials undertaken at Springfield showed that the 1901-type barrel could be reduced to 24in without affecting performance adversely, so the rear sight, handguard, lower band and rod bayonet were suitably modified. The 'United States Magazine Rifle, Caliber 30, Model of 1903' was approved on 19th June 1903. A handguard ran back to the receiver ring.

Production at Rock Island Arsenal began in May 1904 and, by 30th June, Springfield had made 30,000 rifles. Manufacture was suspended on 11th January 1905 while criticisms of the bayonet and barrel length were studied. On 1st April, the Chief of Staff reported that the barrel length was acceptable, but that the rod bayonet should be replaced by a conventional sword pattern. Existing rifles were recalled immediately. They were given new stocks and a nose cap with a bayonet lug.

On 24th May 1905, an improved rear sight was accepted. Graduated to 2400yd, it was based on that fitted to the experimental rifle of 1900. The handguard, front sight and sight-cover were all modified in this period. The leaf of the M1905 sight was hinged at the rear of its base, which was carried on a sleeve.

Inspired by the development of the S-Patrone in Germany, the 'Cartridge, Ball, Caliber 30, Model of 1906' (otherwise known as 30-06) was approved on 15th October 1906. Muzzle velocity rose to 2700 fps, and sight leaves were altered to a maximum range of 2850yd. Re-chambering existing barrels was comparatively easy, though they were shortened by 0.2in; at the same time, a solid tubular back-sight mount replaced the skeletal pattern.

A flute was cut in the top surface of the handguard in 1910 to improve the sight line. The diameter of the drift adjuster on the rear sight was increased perceptibly; a recoil bolt was added through the stock above the front of the trigger guard; the buttplate was checkered; and retaining clips were added in the handguard.

Sufficient rifles had been made by the beginning of November 1913 to allow work to cease in Rock Island Arsenal until February 1917. A Parkerized finish replaced traditional browning in 1917 to simplify production. A second recoil bolt appeared in 1918 through the stock, beneath the chamber, and the bolt handle was bent slightly backward.

Frequent receiver failures, which had been traced to poor heat treatment, were cured by improved manufacturing techniques. Springfield began the new 'double heat treatment' some time prior to receiver no. 800,000 (20th February 1918) while Rock Island Arsenal commenced with 285,507 (11th May 1918).

In early August 1918, in the region of gun no. 320,000, Rock Island Arsenal began making receivers of nickel steel alongside the carbon steel pattern. The situation continued until 1919. Nickel-steel receivers were marked 'NS', but the mark was rarely visible once the rifles had been assembled. Some guns were made in this era with blanks supplied by the Avis Rifle Barrel Company (marked 'AV').

The last rifle to be assembled in Rock Island Arsenal left the factory in June 1918, though at least another 100,000 receivers were made in 1919-20 and production of barrels continued until about 1922. Military production at Springfield Armory had virtually ceased by 1927, though 30-caliber rifles were assembled for National Match target-shooting and the NRA. In late autumn 1928, Springfield began to use nickel-steel receivers—apparently from gun no. 1,301,000 upward.

SIMILAR GUNS

Model 1903 Marksman's rifle. Tests were undertaken in 1907 with optical sights developed by the Warner & Swasey Company of Cleveland, Ohio, in collusion with Frankford Arsenal staff. The experimental 1907-pattern sight was subsequently simplified, and 1,000 'Telescopic Musket Sights, Model of 1908' were ordered from Warner & Swasey. Issue of a few selected rifles to expert marksmen in 1909 failed to reveal serious problems, though the sight was moved forward on the receiver and the rubber eye cup was softened.

A general issue of rifles and 6x M1908 sights was made to marksmen in 1910. The prismatic sights were initially greeted with enthusiasm, but they were very clumsy and uncomfortable. Short eye relief, for example, thrust the rubber eye cup back into the marksman's eye socket on firing. In addition, optical performance was poor.

An improved 5.2x M1913 prismatic optical sight could be identified by the elevation-dial lock nut, which had a cruciform head, and by an eye-piece lock screw ahead of the rubber eye cup. The flat cover plate on the top of the sight body was retained by a dozen screws, whereas the rounded 1908 pattern had been set into its base.

The U.S. authorities finally realized that the prismatic M1913 telescope sight was inferior to straight-tube patterns. A Frankford Arsenal sight, adapted from the Winchester and Goerz designs of the day, was adopted as the M1918 for issue with a modified M1918 (Enfield) sniper rifle. The war ended before Winchester could deliver any sights, and the project was abandoned. The unsatisfactory M1908 and M1913 Warner & Swasey sights were issued to the AEF in 1917, but saw little use.

Model 1903 (Modified) rifle. This was approved on 10th March 1942 to accelerate production. It was basically an M1903 incorporating production expedients, made by Remington in 1941-2 on old machinery leased from Rock Island Arsenal. Among the major changes authorized between March and May 1942 were the deletion of the bolt stop and the advent of stamped bands and nose caps, introduction of simplified band-springs, and adoption of a fabricated trigger guard/magazine floor-plate assembly. The last M1903 (Modified) guns were assembled in March 1943, as the basic pattern had been superseded by the M1903A3 (q.v.).

Model 1903 NRA rifle. From 30th March 1915, a 'flaming bomb' above 'N.R.A.' was applied to rifles sold to National Rifle Association members by the National Board for the Promotion of Rifle Practice.

The M1903 'Style NRA' sporter.

Model 1903 Mark 1 rifle. Developed in 1916 by John Pedersen with the assistance of Remington's Oliver Loomis, this was designed in accordance with the doctrine of 'assault at the walk' to deliver withering fire while advancing across no man's land. Working prototypes for the French Lebel, Russian Mosin and U.S. Springfield rifles were produced in 1917. Few changes were required in the M1903, apart from a minor alteration in the cut-off to lock the Pedersen Device in place. An auxiliary sear was added to the trigger mechanism, and an ejection port was cut through the left side of the receiver.

The shooter only needed to replace the standard bolt with the Pedersen Device and insert the magazine to transform the M1903 Mk 1 (as the altered rifles were known) into a low powered semi-automatic. The Device was little more than a blowback pistol, with a 'slide' behind the receiver bridge and a short barrel extending forward into the chamber. Fitted with the Pedersen Device and a magazine for forty '30 M1918' cartridges, the rifle weighed 10.31lb.

Tests undertaken in 1918 in the presence of General Pershing convinced the U.S. Army that the Pedersen Device—its identity camouflaged as the '30 Automatic Pistol, Model of 1918'—promised greatness. An order for 100,000 was given to Remington, to be made in the Bridgeport factory, and was almost immediately extended to 500,000. However, the war ended before any could be delivered.

About 65,000 Pedersen Devices had been completed before work ceased in 1919, and 101,780 rifles were converted in Springfield Armory in 1919-20. Reappraisal in the calmer post-war conditions centered on the weaknesses of the plan instead of its strengths. The Devices were scrapped in the early 1930s, though the 'Mark 1' rifles served alongside the M1903 until they wore out. They could be identified by the ejection port in the receiver.

Model 1903A1 rifle. This had a modified pistol-grip stock (Style C), which replaced the straight-wrist Style S with effect from 15th March 1929. The change in designation was authorized on 5th December, but few M1903A1 guns were assembled; straight-wrist stocks were still being used in 1939. In 1942, a 'scant pistol grip' was approved to enable under-size or flawed stock blanks to be used. However, this is rarely encountered on surviving guns.

MODEL 1903A3 SHORT RIFLE

Made by the Remington Arms Co., Inc., Ilion, New York (about 707,630); by L.C. Smith-Corona Typewriters, Inc., Pittsburgh, Pennsylvania (about 234,580); and by the Springfield Armory, Springfield, Massachusetts (about 850 in 1956).

Total production: about 943,000. Chambering: 30-06, rimless. Action: as M1901 rifle, above.

43.25in overall, 8.83lb empty. 24in barrel, 2-, 4- or 6-groove rifling; RH, concentric. Internal box magazine loaded from a stripper-clip, 5 rounds. Tangent rear sight graduated to 800yd. 2700 fps with M1906 ball cartridges. M1 sword bayonet.

This simplified M1903, with a profusion of stamped and fabricated parts, was approved on 21st May 1942. The most obvious characteristic was a return to a straight-wrist stock—easier to make, and less wasteful of raw material than a pistol-grip pattern.

The finger groove was omitted and the recoil bolts were replaced with pins. These pins were unsatisfactory, however, and M1903 (Modified) recoil bolts were soon substituted. An open aperture sight lay in an adjustable drift-cradle on top of the receiver bridge behind the stripper-clip guides, and the handguard extended rearward to the receiver ring.

The first M1903A3 rifles were assembled in the Smith & Corona factory in October 1942 and by Remington in December 1942. The stamped trigger guard was deepened ahead of the trigger lever in 1943 to allow a gloved finger better access. Some rifles had two-groove barrels made by Johnson Automatics, Inc., of Providence, Rhode Island (marked 'JA'), or four-groove examples supplied by R.F. Sedgley, Inc., of Philadelphia (marked with an encircled 'S'). A few early M1903A3 used six-groove barrels provided by Savage. The production contracts were canceled in February 1944, though assembly continued until the summer.

SIMILAR RIFLES

M1903A3 National Match Rifle. About 850 of these were produced in Springfield Armory in 1956, using pre-war bolts and milled trigger guards. They had Redfield receiver sights, but were otherwise similar to pre-1945 service guns.

Model 1903A4 rifle. Standardized on 14th January 1943, this variant of the M1903A3 modified for sniping use was made exclusively by the Remington Arms Company factory in Ilion; production amounted to 26,650. Sniper rifles were invariably fitted with Keystone ('K') or Springfield ('S') pistol-grip stocks. The earliest examples had two-groove cut rifling, but later barrels used a four-groove draw-formed pattern. The bolt handle was bent down to clear the 2.5x Telescope M73B1, a militarized Model 330C made in El Paso by the W.R. Weaver Company. It was carried in a Redfield Junior mount.

Finally, on 18th January 1943, 20,000 receivers—numbered 3407088-3427087—were diverted from M1903A3 production for completion to M1903A4 standards. An additional order for 8365 was placed in June. The final batches of M1903A4 rifles were delivered in June 1944, owing to the approval of the M1C Garand with a Lyman Alaskan sight in a Griffin & Howe mount. The June 1943 contract was still apparently incomplete.

SPORTING GUNS

Excluding the output of custom gunsmiths and a few special-purpose rifles made in the Springfield Armory—e.g., the guns made for Theodore Roosevelt in 1903—the Springfield had much less effect on the American sporting rifle scene than its cartridge. The only company to capitalize on its efficiency was R.F. Sedgley, Inc., of Philadelphia, which converted military surplus rifles.

INTERNATIONAL MATCH RIFLE

Springfield made 30-caliber International Match rifles with half-stocks, special set- or multi-lever triggers, palm rests, extended buttplates and a host of other special features. Less than 50 of each pattern were made in 1922-7. Despite refinements such as the Garand Super Speed Firing Mechanism, the modified Springfields were replaced by Martini-action guns. International Match rifles were offered for sale privately, or rebuilt to service pattern and reclassified as 'M1903 Special Target' (M1903A1 after 1928).

MODEL 1903 NATIONAL MATCH RIFLE

Made by the Springfield Armory, Springfield, Massachusetts, 1922-39.
Total production: about 26,950. Chambering: 30-06, rimless.
Otherwise generally as M1903 rifle, above.

Introduced in 1922 specifically for military-style target shooting, which was being promoted enthusiastically by the Director of Civilian Marksmanship (DCM), these were little more than M1903 rifles with barrels selected for accuracy and actions honed for smoothness.

SIMILAR GUNS

Model 1903 rifle, 'Style NM Special', 1922-8. These guns had a standard service-pattern stock, band and nose cap. However, the finger groove in the forend was omitted and a pointed NRA-type pistol grip was used.

Model 1903 rifle, 'Style NB', 1928-9. This was fitted with the clumsy 30-caliber M1922M1 stock, which had been unsuccessfully tested for field service in 1927.

A Remington-made M1903 'Springfield' rifle.

Model 1903 rifle, 'Style SB', 1928-30. Applied to standard service-grade rifles, this indicated use of the 22-caliber M1922M1 stock.

Model 1903 rifle, 'Style NM 1929', 1929-33 and 1936-9. Distinguished by a modified Type C stock, with a refined pointed-tip pistol grip, this remained in vogue for some years even though the headless cocking piece was abandoned in 1930. Assembly began again in 1936, continuing until parts were exhausted.

MODEL 1903 'MATCH SPRINGFIELD' RIFLE

Made by the Springfield Armory, Springfield, Massachusetts, 1922-7.
Total production: about 2000. **Chambering:** 30-06, rimless.

Otherwise as M1903 rifle, above, excepting weight (about 8.25lb without sights) and rear sight.

Dating from 1922, this amalgamated a National Match (q.v.) action, with a headless cocking piece, and a special heavyweight barrel. Blocks for optical-sight mounts appeared on the barrel and a Lyman No. 48B aperture sight was fitted on the right side of the receiver bridge. The 1922-pattern half-stock had a finger groove in the forend, and the solitary barrel band carried a swivel. The second swivel lay under the butt.

MODEL 1922 RIFLE

Made by the Springfield Armory, Springfield, Massachusetts,1922-4
Total production: about 2020. **Chambering:** 22 Long Rifle, rimfire.
Action: locked by a single lug on the bolt body engaging the receiver bridge as the bolt handle was turned down.

43.65in overall, 8.5lb empty. 24in barrel, 4-groove rifling; RH, concentric. Detachable box magazine, 5 rounds. Vernier aperture rear sight. 1080 fps with 40-grain bullet.

The first attempts to make a rimfire rifle retained the bolt-head-mounted locking lugs, but feeding single rounds was difficult. Subsequent attempts relied on the safety lug, which turned down ahead of the receiver bridge; by eliminating the bolt-head lugs and locking recesses, the chamber was brought nearer the bolt way.

Though the M1922 action was externally similar to the 30-caliber M1903, the gun was easily recognized by its pistol grip half-stock. The forend had a single band, a small box magazine projected beneath the stock, and a Lyman No. 48B peep sight was attached to the receiver bridge. Later guns were fitted with a headless cocking piece, but many original guns were upgraded to 1922M1 standards when they returned to Springfield Armory for repairs. These can be identified by the addition of 'M1' to the designation on the receiver.

SIMILAR GUNS

Model 1922M1 rifle, 1925-33. Subsequently known as the 'U.S. Rifle, Cal. 22, M1', this had a new bolt head, an improved firing mechanism with a short striker, a flush-fitting magazine, modifications to the chambering, and a Lyman No. 48C rear sight. The stock was changed to a incorporate a flat-base pistol grip, a service-pattern shoulder plate, and a finger groove in the forend. Metalwork was Parkerized, except for the bright-finish bolt.

Model 1922M1 NRA rifle, 1927-33. Made for civilian use, this was little more than the improved 'M1' action in the original M1922-type half-stock. About 20,000 standard and NRA-pattern M1922M1 guns were made.

M2 rifle, 1933-41. Based on prototypes developed by John Garand, this had a simplified bolt with a one-piece 'short fall' striker and a modified extractor. The stock retained a finger groove in the forend, but had a shallower pistol grip with a deeper thumb well. Guns made after 1934 had a headspace adjuster-screw in the locking lug; this was originally retained by a small transverse set-screw, but later by a copper pin. The last M2 guns had a distinctive Allen-head adjuster. Production amounted to about 7540 guns to the end of the 1940 fiscal year, though work continued into 1942.

Earlier guns upgraded to 'M2' standards were stamped 'M1922M2' or 'M1922M11', depending on whether they had originally been M1922 or M1922M1 examples, and their serial numbers were given 'A' and 'B' prefixes respectively.

Model 1924 International Match Rifle. Twelve of these single shot guns were made in Springfield Armory in 1924. Duplicating the handling characteristics of the 30-caliber match rifles of the day, they had modified 1922-type actions with short-fall strikers. The base of the palm rest occupied the magazine well in the forend. The round-tip half-stock had a hooked buttplate and checkering on the pistol grip. A six-groove 30in barrel was fitted; weight averaged 14lb.

MODEL 1903 NRA SPORTER

Made by the Springfield Armory, Springfield, Massachusetts, 1924-38.
Total production: about 7140. **Chambering:** 30-06, rimless.

Otherwise generally as M1903 rifle, above, excepting weight (about 8.25lb without sights) and rear sight (Lyman No. 48S aperture pattern).

Announced in December 1924 by the Director of Civilian Marksmanship, this owed its existence to a lack of adequate 30-06 sporters. Made to National Match standards, 'Style NRA' guns had barrels duplicating the shape of the standard 22-caliber pattern so that they could fit a standard half-stock. The stocks were distinguished by an additional cut-off cutaway and provision for two transverse recoil bolts. Production of NRA sporters ceased in 1933, though small-scale assembly continued for some time.

SIMILAR GUNS

Model 1903 rifle, 'Style NBA', 1926-8. This used the clumsy M1922M1 stock, with a large flat-based pistol grip and a finger groove in the forend. Only 590 guns were assembled before production reverted to the NRA pattern.

MODEL 1903 'STYLE T' RIFLE

Made by the Springfield Armory, Springfield, Massachusetts, 1929-30.
Total production: about 100. **Chambering:** 30-06, rimless. **Action:** as M1901 rifle, above.

47.2in overall, 10.55lb without sights. 28in barrel, 4-groove rifling; RH, concentric. Internal box magazine loaded from a stripper clip, 5 rounds. Lyman Model 48C aperture rear sight. 2830 fps with M1906 ball cartridges.

This target rifle had a heavy barrel in a modified NRA-type half-stock. Made to National Match standards, it had blocks on the barrel for optical-sight mounts and an aperture sight on the receiver bridge. A Winchester globe-pattern front sight was used, but 'Style T' was not popular enough to justify more than a single short production run.

SEDGLEY SPRINGFIELD SPORTER

Converted by R.F. Sedgley, Inc., Philadelphia, Pennsylvania, about 1925-41, from war-suplus rifles.
Total production: several thousands. **Chambering options:** 218 Bee, 2-R Lovell, 22 Hornet, 220 Swift, 22-3000, 22-4000, 25-35, 250-3000 Savage, 257 Roberts, 270 Winchester, 7x57 or 30-06. **Action:** as M1901 rifle, above.
DATA FOR A TYPICAL EXAMPLE
Chambering: 220 Swift, semi-rimmed. 43.35in overall, 7.27lb empty. 24in barrel, 4-groove rifling; RH, concentric. Internal box magazine, 5 rounds. Lyman Model 48 aperture rear sight. 4100 fps with 48-grain bullet.

The first batches of these guns were built in the mid-1920s on old Springfield Armory or Rock Island Arsenal actions. Among the most interesting are adaptations with the bolt handle on the left side. The walnut half-stocks usually had a straight-comb butt with checkering on the capped pistol grip; forends were also checkered, and often displayed a schnabel tip. Swivels lay beneath the butt and under the internal barrel band. An aperture sight was attached to the receiver bridge, and a hooded bead-type front sight lay on a ramp at the muzzle.

SIMILAR GUNS

Sedgley-Springfield carbine. A few of these 20in-barrel guns were made with a full-length Mannlicher-style stock, but were never popular.

OTHER GUNS

Some 1903-type receivers were made in Japan for the Santa Fé Arms Company of Pasadena, California (possibly 2500 in the mid-1960s), and National Ordnance, Inc., of South El Monte, California (about 23,500 in 1965-70). Apparently produced by investment casting and then assembled in the USA with a variety of military surplus parts, these components had narrow receiver bridges without stripper-clip guides, but offered neither the quality nor the durability of the original machined forgings.

• Springfield (-Allin)

Also known as 'Trapdoor Springfield' or 'Springfield-Allin'.

Advertisements were circulated in 1864 in an attempt to find an effectual means of converting existing rifle-muskets. The Chief of Ordnance, General Dyer, asked Erskine Allin—then Master Armorer at the Springfield Armory—to develop a gun on behalf of the federal government.

Trials completed by April 1865 recommended the Spencer repeater and the single-shot Peabody, but the end of the Civil War removed the need to act quickly. However, the prototype Allin rifle performed well enough in the summer of 1865 to be ordered in quantity for field trials. About 5000 58-caliber rimfire rifles were made in the Springfield factory in 1865-6 from 1863-pattern caplock rifle-muskets and new breechblocks. The block could be swung up to reveal the chamber, but the alteration was much too complicated. The ratchet-pattern extractor was weak and the cartridge performed poorly.

The experimental 1865-pattern Allin was soon replaced by a gun with its barrel lined-down from 58- to 50-caliber. The extractor was greatly simplified, and many detail changes were made. Trials still favored the Berdan as the best conversion system (the Peabody remained the best new rifle), but the 50-caliber Allin was controversially selected for production.

Allin-pattern guns remained regulation U.S. Army firearms until the introduction of the Krag-Jørgensen (q.v.) in the early 1890s. They were then gradually withdrawn, serving the National Guard until about 1905. Those that remained on the official inventory after World War I were stored for the use of state militiamen until the early 1920s.

MODEL 1866 RIFLE

This was a simplification of the original rimfire M1865, with a 'U'-spring extractor instead of the original ratchet mechanism. The 58-caliber barrels were successfully reamed out to .64in to take a liner chambered for the 50-70 centerfire cartridge. Springfield was ordered to convert 25,000 guns on 26th July 1866. They were about 56in overall, had 36.6in barrels, and weighed 9.88lb. Aperture-leaf sights were graduated to 700yd and the M1855 socket bayonet could be mounted.

SIMILAR GUNS

Model 1866 cadet rifle. About 320 of these were made at Springfield, apparently for the U.S. Military Academy at West Point. They incorporated more than a dozen new parts, were 54.8in long, had 34.65in barrels and weighed 8.5lb.

MODEL 1868 RIFLE

Made by the Springfield Armory, Springfield, Massachusetts, 1868-9. Total production: not known. **Chambering:** 50-70, rimmed. **Action:** the breechblock is locked in place behind the chamber with a catch in its rear face.

52in overall, 9.25lb empty. 32.65in, 3-groove rifling; RH, concentric. Leaf-type rear sight graduated to 1000yd. 1210 fps with 50-70-450 ball cartridges. M1855 socket bayonet.

Changes made in this 50-caliber gun included the approval of a new barrel, and the ramrod was held by a stop inserted in the stock. The barrel screwed into a separate receiver, a much stronger arrangement than previous adaptations of existing barrels. Two bands were used instead of three, and a special long-range rear sight was fitted.

SIMILAR GUNS

Model 1869 cadet rifle, 1869-70. Made in small quantities in Springfield, this had a 29.5in barrel and only two bands. Minor variations will be encountered, the final pattern having a flat-face hammer. The earliest batches (sometimes identified as 'M1868') had block-and-leaves rear sights, but later guns had a ramp-and-leaf pattern graduated to 1000yd. They were 51.9in overall and weighed 8.3lb.

MODEL 1870 RIFLE

Made at Springfield in 1870-2, this was virtually identical with its immediate predecessor—the M1868— but the receiver was shortened and the breechblock was relieved behind the hinge to open farther. This prevented the mechanism closing unexpectedly as a new cartridge was being loaded. The ramrod had a double shoulder, and sights were refined. Often regarded as semi-experimental, the M1870 was 51.75in overall and weighed 9.22lb. The barrel measured 32.5in and the leaf sight was graduated to 1000yd.

SIMILAR GUNS

M1870 carbine. Introduced in 1871, this was merely 41.4in overall and weighed 7.92lb. Its barrel was 21.75in long.

MODEL 1873 RIFLE

Made by the Springfield Armory, Springfield, Massachusetts, 1873-80. Total production: about 90,170. **Chambering:** 45-70, rimmed. **Action:** generally as M1868, above.

51.9in overall, 9.21lb empty. 32.4in, 3-groove rifling; RH, concentric. Leaf-type rear sight graduated to 2000yd. 1320 fps with 45-70-405 ball cartridges. M1873 socket bayonet.

Though experiments to reduce the caliber of the standard 50-70 service cartridge and find a better breech-loader continued throughout 1871, the Springfield-Allin was retained at the expense of Remington, Sharps, Ward-Burton and other designs.

In the autumn of 1872, however, a Board of Officers began trials with rifles chambering a new 45-70-405 centerfire cartridge. By January 1873, more than 100 submissions had been reduced to 21, though the Martini-Henry and the Werndl were retained simply as a guide to the performance expected of foreign service weapons. The trials resolved into a contest between Elliot No. 80, Freeman No. 76, Peabody No. 63, Remington No. 86, Springfield No. 69, Ward-Burton No. 97 and the U.S. government-sponsored Springfield No. 99.

Springfield No. 69 was similar to the standard Allin-type M1870 (tested as No. 48), but had a lightened lock plate, a screw instead of the original main-spring bolster, a modified hammer and a simpler stock. However, none of the trial guns could challenge the government entrant and so the 45-caliber Springfield No. 99 was adopted for service. The purchase of a few Ward-Burton magazine rifles was recommended for the cavalry, but subsequently rejected by the Chief of Ordnance.

Formally approved on 5th May 1873, the M1873 rifle was an improved form of the experimental Springfield No. 99. As the Allin breech had cost the U.S. Treasury more than $124,000 to settle patent-infringement claims, the government was reluctant to make wholesale changes. The new rifle was basically an M1870, therefore, but its lock plate was lightened—the edges being squared rather than beveled—and the steel barrel had a smaller external diameter. The hammer body and most of the screws were rounded, while a screw replaced the trigger guard swivel rivet. The top edges of the stock were rounded from the lock plate to the lower band, and the ramrod was changed.

A stacking swivel was adopted in the Spring of 1874, and the first rifles were issued to premier line infantry regiments in the late autumn. A 'Model 1877' rear sight was adopted in January 1877, with differing graduations and an improved sighting notch, only to be altered again in May 1878 (without changing the designation) when a base with curved wing plates replaced the original stepped design.

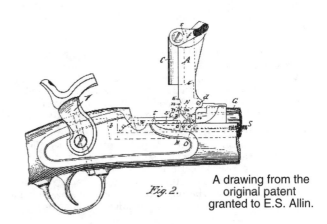

A drawing from the original patent granted to E.S. Allin.

The Model 1873 'Trapdoor Springfield' rifle.

The arch in the underside of the breechblock was flattened from March, creating 'Low Arch' guns in a search for greater rigidity. At about the same time, the firing-pin spring and the corresponding shoulder on the firing pin were abandoned. The widths of the breechblock and receiver were increased in October 1878, when the gas-escape holes in the sides of the receiver were extended rearward.

SIMILAR GUNS

Model 1873 carbine, 1873-8. Identified by a half-stock and a 21.9in barrel, this was 41.3in long and weighed 7.9lb; muzzle velocity with standard 1873 pattern ball cartridges was about 1150 fps. The carbine lacked a butt-trap for the cleaning rods, but a stacking swivel was attached to the solitary barrel band. Bayonets could not be fitted. Cavalrymen in Texas and 'Indian country' finally received their M1873 carbines in 1876. Consequently, men of the Seventh Cavalry fought the Battle of the Little Big Horn in June with brand-new firearms. Total production of 1873-type carbines amounted to about 24,500.

M1873 cadet rifle, 1874-80. Essentially similar to the infantry rifle, this lacked sling swivels and had a different stacking swivel on the upper band. It was 48.9in overall and had a 29.5in barrel. About 5075 guns were made.

M1873 rifle with Metcalfe's Loader, 1876. 1008 of these rifles were made in Springfield Armory. Eight cartridges were carried head upward in a detachable wooden block on the right side of the stock. (Note: as two prototypes had been made for Army trials in 1874, it has been suggested that the guns made in 1876 were destined for militia instead of federal troops.) Confirmation is lacking, however.

Model 1873 rifle, improved pattern, 1880-5. Continual improvements in the 1873 pattern action led in January 1879 to this gun, sometimes known as the 'M1873 Improved', 'M1873 with 1879 Improvements' or (erroneously) as the 'Model 1879'.

A standing plate with two projections (known as a 'buck-horn') improved the rear sight picture. From April 1879, a hole was bored up into the ramrod channel ahead of the trigger guard to reduce fouling. The shape of the buck-horn plate was changed in October 1879, when the distance between the graduations became .04in instead of .02in. The upper surface of the leaf-hinge was flattened in November 1879.

A lip was added to the face of the hammer in January 1880, the notches in the buck-horn rear sight were revised in July 1880, and a heavy-pattern buttplate was formally approved in August 1881.

Several changes were made to the rifle during 1883—the underside of the thumb piece was revised in January, to prevent it striking the lock plate; a straight trigger-lever appeared in March; and a detachable front-sight protector was approved in October. Production figures for the improved rifles are difficult to disentangle from the original 1873 pattern, but are believed to have amounted to about 126,700.

Model 1873 carbine, improved pattern, 1880-1. Approved in the middle of the 1879, this was similar to the original 1873 type. A rifle-type lower band replaced the special stacking-swivel band after December 1879; unlike the rifle, however, the carbine had a butt trap for the cleaning rod. About 15,400 were made.

Model 1873 cadet rifle, improved pattern, 1882-7. These were little more than standard infantry rifles without sling swivels. They were only 48.75in long and had barrels measuring 29.5in. Production is believed to have amounted to about 4520.

MODEL 1875 OFFICER'S RIFLE

Adapted from the contemporary 1873-pattern cadet rifle, this was sold to officers who wanted personal weapons of regulation pattern. The half-stock had checkering on the butt-wrist and a forend with a German silver tip. Scroll engraving appeared on the lock, hammer, receiver, barrel band and buttplate. The globe-pattern front sight folded so that its pin suited the open back-sight notch.

Most rifles had a folding Sharps Vernier peep sight on the butt wrist. The trigger had a normal service-pattern pull, but could be set by pushing it forward. The wooden ramrod had nickel-plated brass ferrules. The guns were 47.4in long, had 26in barrels and weighed 9lb; about 290 were made in 1875-7.

SIMILAR GUNS

Second pattern rifle, 1877-85. The guns made after April 1877 had a detachable pistol grip and an improved Springfield-pattern

tang sight which folded closer to the wrist than the Sharps version. About 135 were made

Third pattern rifle, 1885. A few guns—perhaps 40—were made with proper pistol grip stocks with an elongated schnabel tipped forend, improved sights, and a three-piece cleaning rod in a butt-trap.

LONG RANGE RIFLE

About 150 guns of this type were made at Springfield Armory in 1881, with 32.4in barrels and two spring-retained barrel bands. A typical 45-70 example was 52in overall, weighed 9.9lb. The original rifles—subsequently known as 'Pattern No. 1'—had a Hotchkiss-type buttplate, a full-length stock, a checkered forend, and a checkered wrist with a detachable pistol grip. A Sharps Vernier rear sight lay on the tang above the wrist, and the tunnel pattern front sight had an integral spirit level.

SIMILAR GUNS

Pattern No. 2. This shared the stock design of No. 1, but its improved tang sight was the work of Freeman Bull of Springfield Armory. An adjustable globe-pattern front sight was standard.

Pattern No. 3. Distinguished by a Hotchkiss buttplate and a full-length stock, this had a Bull rear sight on the barrel and a standard front sight.

MARKSMAN'S RIFLE

Springfield made two of these 45-80 guns in 1881 and nine in 1882. They had pistol gripped half-stocks, and special Vernier rear sights on the tang behind the lock plate in addition to the standard 1879-type buck-horn sight on the barrel. The tunnel-type front sights had spirit levels. A 26in cylindrical barrel had six-groove concentric rifling; a three-piece cleaning rod and the dismantling tool were carried in the butt trap. The set-trigger mechanism and the engraved decoration were similar to those of the Officer's Model (q.v.).

MODEL 1880 RIFLE

Approved on 3rd June 1880, after extensive trials had been undertaken with an 1879-vintage prototype, this was the first Allin-type rifle to feature a triangular-section rod bayonet under the barrel. The adoption of the rod bayonet—allegedly approved to lessen the infantryman's burden—simply avoided producing new socket bayonets; those serving in 1880 had all been made before 1865, then altered for the 1873-type rifles by cold-forging the sockets to reduce their diameter. About 1014 M1880 rifles were made in Springfield in 1881. They were essentially similar to the 1873 pattern, but had a special nose cap and two barrel bands.

MODEL 1882 SHORT RIFLE

In February 1882, the Board on Magazine Guns recommended development of a modified 45-caliber rifle with a short barrel, a full-length stock, and an improved lock with a shorter hammer fall. The goal was a rifle that could be issued to infantry and cavalrymen alike. The earliest M1882 short rifles (only 52 were made) had swivels curved to fit the contours of the stock, facilitating the use of saddle scabbards, but these were soon replaced with conventional fittings. Guns were typically 47.5in long, with 27.75in barrels, and weighed about 8.9lb. A few short rifles were subsequently fitted with triangular-section rod bayonets; and a trap in the butt was added to house the shell ejector and dismantling tool.

MODEL 1882 CARBINE

Trials undertaken at Fort Leavenworth failed to persuade cavalrymen of the value of the M1882 short or 'universal' rifle, and so 1003 carbines were made at Springfield in 1886-8 by amalgamating the short-rifle action with a 23.75in barrel. The earliest guns were stocked almost to the muzzle.

The muzzle band was retained by a screw instead of a spring, and a prominent web filled the space under the muzzle. Later guns had heavy barrels, retained by a band behind the rounded stock tip which carried a curved swivel. A standard flat swivel was attached beneath the butt, while a sling ring slid along a bar anchored in the left side of the stock below the breech; tools and a cleaning rod was carried in a butt trap. Buffington wind-gauge rear sights were fitted.

MODEL 1884 RIFLE

Made by the **Springfield Armory, Springfield, Massachusetts**, 1885-90.
Total production: about 200,900. **Chambering:** 45-70, rimmed. **Action:** generally as M1868 rifle, above.

The Model 1884 rifle, showing the distinctive long-range back sight. (W&W)

51.75in overall, about 9lb empty. 32.4in barrel, 3-groove rifling; RH, concentric. Leaf-type rear sight graduated to 2000yd, with a sliding long-range extension. 1320 fps with 45-70-405 ball cartridges. M1873 socket bayonet.

Trials undertaken in 1883 failed to convince the U.S. Army that magazine breech-loading rifles were acceptable, and so this Trap-door Springfield was approved as an expedient. Its Buffington-pattern wind-gauge rear sight had a drift adjustment, the first to be approved for general service in the U.S. Army, and the lower band was altered to accommodate the sight leaf.

Alterations to the sear and tumbler were made in January 1885. New front sights for rifles (.653 high) and carbines (.738) were approved in the same period to prevent guns shooting high at short ranges. The issue of front-sight covers was approved in March 1886. Improvements in the Buffington sight were made in August 1886, when the heads of the wind gauge finger-screws were enlarged to improve grip and to prevent the folded leaf moving laterally by projecting down over the edge of the sight-base. The binding screw was also revised.

A lightweight aluminum-bronze firing pin replaced the original steel pattern in December 1886 to reduce breakages which had plagued the 1873 series since its introduction. The rear edge of the rifle front-sight block was rounded from August 1887 onward; February 1888 brought an improved front-sight protector.

SIMILAR GUNS
M1884 cadet rifle, 1889-93. These were 48.75in long, had 29.5in barrels, and characteristic Buffington sights. Production is believed to have totaled 12,500 guns.

M1884 carbine, 1886-9. Distinguished by their dimensions—41.3in overall, 21.9in barrel—these were also made in small numbers. The Buffington sights distinguished them from the preceding 1879 models. A protector-band for the rear sight was fitted to the carbine from October 1890 onward, and the height of the carbine front-sight was changed from .738in to .728in towards the end of the year. These carbines are often known as 'M1890', but were marked MODEL 1884 on the action. About 20,000 were made.

Model 1884 rifle with positive-cam extractor, 1888. One hundred of these were made in the Springfield Armory. Owing to the imminent introduction of the 1888-pattern rifle (q.v.), the changes were not accepted.

M1884 rifle with rod bayonet, 1885. About 1000 1884-type rifles with cylindrical rod bayonets and refined sights, authorized on 17th December 1884, were issued in the Spring of 1886 for unsuccessful trials with three artillery and 10 infantry regiments.

MODEL 1888 RIFLE
Made by the Springfield Armory, Springfield, Massachusetts, 1890-3.
Total production: about 64,850. **Chambering:** 45-70, rimmed.
Otherwise generally as M1884 rifle, except for the M1888 rod bayonet.

This was the last single-shot rifle to be approved for general issue in the U.S. Army, though the authorities were well aware that production would last only until a suitable magazine rifle had been perfected. Three experimental prototypes were made in 1888, adoption following on 16th August 1889—11 days after the cylindrical rod bayonet had been approved.

• Springfield Armory, Inc.
Trading in Geneseo in Illinois, this business makes M14 derivatives alongside of semi-automatic rifles imported from Brazil (the FN-Saive SAR-4800 in 223 and 308) and Portugal (the Heckler & Koch-type SAR-8 in sporting or counter-sniper form).

M1A RIFLE
This recreation of the M14 (see **'Garand'**) has been made in many patterns, with stocks of walnut, brown or black wood laminate, and black or camouflage-finish fiberglass. Most guns are now sold with a five- or 10-round box magazine, though the original 20-round pattern remains optional. Rifles destined for military

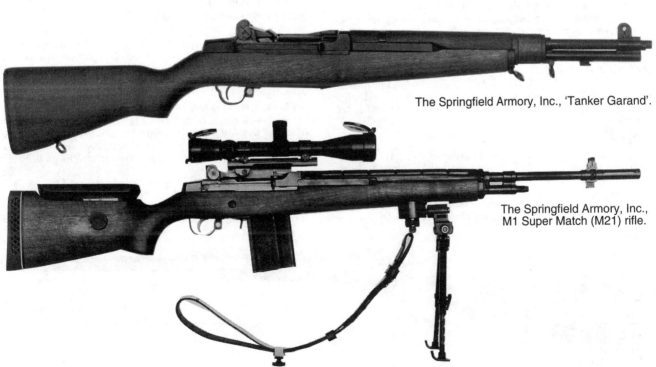

The Springfield Armory, Inc., 'Tanker Garand'.

The Springfield Armory, Inc., M1 Super Match (M21) rifle.

or security-service use are customarily supplied with a bayonet lug. Stabilizers and Harris bipods are among the optional extras.

SIMILAR GUNS

M1A National Match Rifle. Fitted with a half-MOA aperture sight, this has a specially honed trigger and a medium-weight six-groove 'National Match' barrel giving an empty weight of about 10.6lb.

M1A Super Match Rifle. Distinguished by a 22in Douglas Premium barrel, giving a weight of about 11.3lb, this is offered only in a standard walnut stock. The aperture rear sight is adjustable in half-MOA clicks instead of 1MOA.

M1A Tactical Rifle. Resembling the government-issue M21 sniper rifle, this has a special receiver and a 22in Douglas Premium barrel (though Hart stainless steel or Krieger barrels are optional). The target-style stock has a deep butt with an elevating comb, and a mounting plate for optical or electro-optical sights can be fitted to the left side of the receiver. The guns are typically 44.25in long and weigh 11.6lb.

M1A1 Bush Rifle. A short version of the M1, with an 18in barrel, this is 40.5in long and weighs 8.9-9lb depending on the stock material.

M1A1 Scout Rifle. Sharing the dimensions of the short-barreled Bush Rifle, this has a compensator ('stabilizer') on the muzzle and a rail on the barrel for an optical sight with a long eye relief; the barrel guard is a special abbreviated form.

• Standard (Smith)

This short-lived autoloader was patented by Morris Smith in 1906, a substantial part of the interest being assigned to W.D. Condit. Though offered commercially for a few years, the Model G was never successful. Like all gas-operated designs produced before World War I, it was susceptible to variations in ammunition pressure and jammed more readily than recoil-operated Remington or Winchester rivals.

STANDARD RIFLE MODEL G

Made by the Standard Arms Company, Wilmington, Delaware, 1910-12.
Total production: a few thousand? **Chambering options:** 25 Remington, 25-35 Winchester, 30 Remington, 30-30 Winchester or 35 Remington. **Action:** locked by rotating lugs on the bolt into the receiver wall; gas operated, semi-automatic only.
DATA FOR A TYPICAL EXAMPLE
Chambering: 30 Remington, rimless. About 43in overall, 7.7lb empty. 22.35in barrel, rifling pattern unknown. Detachable box magazine, 5 rounds. Spring-leaf and elevator rear sight. 2220 fps with 160-grain bullet.

The first gas-operated autoloading rifle to be manufactured commercially in the U.S.A., this had few other claims to fame. The butt had a straight wrist, the square-top receiver contained an internal hammer, and a box-magazine housing lay ahead of the trigger. A hand-grip around the piston tube, cast from bronze, was decorated with a hunting scene; a catch on the grip disconnected the gas system to allow the action to be operated manually.

SIMILAR GUNS

Model M rifle, 1911-14. Similar to the autoloader, this lacked the piston mechanism and was operated by a sliding hand-grip. It may have been made to rid its manufacturer of unwanted Model G parts.

• Starr

Patented in the U.S.A. on 14th September 1858 by Ebenezer Starr of Yonkers, New York, this single-shot breechloader was tested favorably at Washington Arsenal in January 1858. The testers commented that it would be a better weapon than the rival Sharps carbine if the gas seal could be improved; there had been no misfires, and accuracy had been above average. Unlike the

Sharps design, Starr's breechblock did not shear off the base of the combustible cartridge when the breech closed.

MODEL 1858 CARBINE

Made by the Starr Arms Company, Yonkers, New York, about 1857-64.
Total production: at least 22,000. **Chambering:** 54-caliber, combustible cartridge, cap-lock ignition. **Action:** locked by propping a two-part dropping block behind the chamber.

37.65in overall, 7.4lb empty. 21in barrel, 5-groove rifling; RH, concentric. Single-shot only. Three-position block and leaf rear sight. About 950 fps with 445-grain bullet. No bayonet.

The Starr carbine was similar to the Sharps pattern externally, but had a longer receiver and a distinctive web between the tail of the breech lever and the underside of the butt. A sling ring was fixed to the left side of the frame, the buttplate was brass, and the barrel was held in the forend by a single brass band.

The two-piece radial breechblock was wedged shut at the end of the closing stroke, allowing a deep annular recess in the face of the block to shroud the chamber. A side hammer gave satisfactory ignition as long as the lengthy flash channel was kept clean.

Markings included the Starr Arms Company name on the barrel and lock plate, with an acknowledgment of the master patent on the tang behind the breech. Federal government purchases amounted to 20,601 carbines of this type from 1st January 1861 onward.

MODEL 1865 CARBINE

Made by the Starr Arms Company, Yonkers, New York, 1865-6.
Total production: more than 5000. **Chambering:** 56-50 Spencer, rimfire. **Action and dimensions:** generally as 1858 pattern, above.

On 21st February 1865, 3000 Starr carbines chambered for the Spencer rimfire cartridge were ordered. Otherwise similar to their cap-lock predecessors, they had a new breechblock—containing an ejector—and a modified hammer with a short straight shank. They were so successful that an additional 2000 were soon ordered.

Apart from some conversions and the earliest new-production batches, rimfire Starrs had iron furniture instead of brass. Their markings were unchanged. Though established as an efficient weapon during the Civil War, the 56-50 carbine was tested by the U.S. Army trials board of 1865 without success, as 'Gun No. 65' and 'Gun No. 66'.

• Stevens (J.), autoloading type

Originally dating from the 1930s, these guns were made after Stevens had been acquired by Savage and may bear 'SAV' in a circle. They may occasionally be encountered under the 'Stevens-Savage' brand name, but were more commonly known prior to 1948 as 'Stevens-Springfield'.

MODEL 57 SPORTING RIFLE

Dating from 1939-41 and 1945-7, this simple blowback design had a detachable five-round box magazine. The charging handle occupied a separate slot behind the ejection port, and a black-tipped Buckhorn-series half-stock was used. The '057' pattern had a peep sight on the rear of the receiver in addition to the standard open sights.

SIMILAR GUNS

Model 76 rifle, 1938-41 and 1945-8. Distinguished from the Model 57 by the tube magazine under the barrel, this retained the black-tipped stock. Bead front and spring-leaf and elevator rear sights were fitted, though the '076' version also had a peep sight on the receiver.

Model 85 rifle, 1935-89? A modified version of the Model 76, this had a detachable five-round box magazine. A safety catch lay alongside the receiver above the trigger, and a black-capped forend was used. Guns made after 1948 had a synthetic trigger

The Starr carbine bore an external resemblance to the more familiar Sharps. (W&W)

guard. The Model 085, subsequently known as '85-S', had an additional peep sight above the receiver.

Model 87 rifle, 1935-89? This was simply a tube-magazine version of the Model 85, with a capacity of 15 22LR rimfire rounds. A variant with a peep sight above the receiver, in addition to the open rear sight, was designated '087' or '87-S' after the Stevens-Springfield brand name was abandoned in 1948.

• Stevens (J.), block-action type

Joshua Stevens' earliest rifles, introduced in 1871, were based on a simple tipping-barrel pistol patented in September 1864. The Stevens Arms & Tool Company subsequently made a wide range of sporting guns until the factory was transferred to Remington-UMC in 1916 to concentrate on war work. In 1920, however, the equity was acquired by the Savage Arms Company; Stevens finally merged with its parent in 1936. Guns made before 1886 are usually marked 'J. Stevens & Co.', and those made in 1886-1915 are marked 'J. Stevens Arms & Tool Co.' (or 'A. & T.' instead of 'Arms & Tool'). Many of those made after 1920 will also display 'SAV' in a circle.

'SIDEPLATE' SPORTING RIFLE

Made in Chicopee Falls, Massachusetts, by J. Stevens & Company (1885-6) and the J. Stevens Arms & Tool Company (1886-92).
Total production: no more than 2000. **Chambering options:** see notes.
Action: the radial block is propped behind the chamber by a toggle-link.
DATA FOR A TYPICAL SPORTING RIFLE
Chambering: 25-20 Single Shot, rimmed. 45in overall, 8.25lb empty. 30in barrel, 6-groove rifling; RH, concentric. Fixed-notch rear sight. 1410 fps with 85-grain bullet.

Patented in 1884-5, this was the first Stevens rifle to embody a radial breechblock. An arm on the block, secured by a threaded bolt, ran forward under the chamber. Able to pivot loosely, it was connected with the sturdy breech lever—which doubled as the trigger guard—through a short intermediate toggle-link which held the breech closed during firing. A rocking-blade extractor was activated as the breechblock descended.

Side-plate rifles were too complex to be made cheaply, and removal of the right side to give access to the action reduced the durability of the frame.

SIMILAR GUNS

Sideplate target rifle. These were made in small numbers, typically with a straight-wrist butt, an off hand shoulder plate, a heavy half-octagon barrel, and Vernier-and-globe sights.

'LITTLE SCOUT' SPORTING RIFLE
Also known as No. 14

Operated by pulling back on a small stud attached to the right side of the radial breechblock—once the hammer had been retracted to full cock—this simple take-down gun had a one-piece straight-wrist half-stock (with a short tapering forend) and a pinched stamped-strip trigger guard. Sights consisted of a small bead at the muzzle and a simple fixed notch at the breech. Made only in 1906-8 in 22 Long Rifle chambering, with an 18in barrel, the Little Scout weighed only 2.8lb.

SIMILAR GUNS

No. 11 Junior rifle, 1924-33. Mechanically similar to the No. 14-1/2, with the improved spring-strut, this had a one-piece stock similar to the original No. 14—though the trigger guard was larger and a take-down screw lay beneath the forend.

No. 14-1/2 Little Scout, 1909-33. An improved form of the original No. 14, this had a two-piece stock, take-down construction, and a July 1907 patent-date in the barrel markings. The operating-spring strut was pinned directly to the hammer and breechblock.

'FAVORITE MODEL' SPORTING RIFLE

Among the most popular of the Stevens target rifles, this simple take-down dropping-block design was aimed at junior or cost-conscious marksmen. The first guns—bearing an October 1889 patent date—seem to have been made in the early 1890s, with a ring through the take-down bolt and a bowed mainspring held in the lower tang by a lug. This was replaced by an improved version (displaying an additional 1894 patent date) with a flat mainspring held by a stud. This in turn lasted until a heavier version appeared in 1915, with a knurled-head take-down bolt, a flat-top breech-block, and a coil spring instead of the riband form. The original extractor was moved from the left side of the action to the center about 1901, but was replaced by an improved automatic type on post-1904 22 rimfire guns (but not the larger rim- and centerfires).

THE GUNS

Note: A smooth-bore 'No. 20' version was made for 22 or 32 shot cartridges.

No. 17 rifle, 1894-1935. Offered only for the 22 Long Rifle, 25 Stevens, 32 Long and 32 Extra Long rimfire cartridges, this had a 24in octagonal barrel and weighed about 4.5lb. The butt had a straight wrist, the short tapering forend had a slight 'belly', and the spring-leaf and elevator rear sight was accompanied by an open bead or blade at the muzzle. Post-1915 'heavy action' guns had round barrels.

No. 18 rifle, about 1894-1915. This was a variant of the No. 17 with a Vernier sight on the tang, a leaf-type sight on the barrel, and a Beach combination sight at the muzzle.

No. 19 rifle, about 1894-1915. Distinguished by Lyman sights at the muzzle and on the tang, this also had an open leaf-type rear sight on the barrel.

No. 21 Bicycle Rifle, about 1896-1905. A short version of the No. 17, this had an 18in barrel (others were available to order) and could be packed in a special canvas carrying case. It was not made in quantity, and may have been replaced by a short-barreled No. 21 Lady Model target rifle.

No. 27 rifle, about 1915-35. This was simply a No. 17 gun with an octagonal barrel.

No. 28 rifle, about 1915-22. A minor variant of No. 18, this had an octagonal barrel and composite sights.

No. 29 rifle, about 1915-27. Mechanically identical with No. 17, this had an octagonal barrel and Lyman sights on the tang and muzzle.

'IDEAL MODEL' SPORTING RIFLE

Made in Chicopee Falls, Massachusetts, by J. Stevens Arms & Tool Company (1886-1916) and the J. Stevens Arms Company (1918-35).
Total production: many thousands. **Chambering options:** see notes.
Action: generally as Side-plate pattern, above.
DATA FOR A TYPICAL NO. 44 IDEAL
Chambering: 32-20 Winchester, rimmed. 42.5in overall, 7.75lb empty. 26in barrel, 6-groove rifling; RH, concentric. Spring-leaf and elevator rear sight. 1290 fps with 100-grain bullet.

Improvements to the sideplate action created the 1889-pattern 'Favorite Model' (q.v.). In 1893, the mechanism was enlarged and strengthened to handle centerfire rounds such as 32-40 and 38-55 Ballard and the No. 44 rifle appeared. The earliest rifles bear an October 1889 patent date instead of the April 1894 improvement.

Cheap, yet capable of outstanding accuracy and renowned for the quality of its barrel, the rifle was the mainstay of the Stevens line for many years. The most common variant had a 26in half-octagon barrel, a straight-wrist butt, and a short wooden forend with a schnabel tip. Nickel plating, engraving and specially finished woodwork were among the many options.

The Stevens (Savage) Model 89 rifle.

Barrels were generally half-octagon, though round and full-octagon types are known; the products of the renowned barrel-smith Harry Pope were particularly desirable. Frames were originally color case-hardened, and many of the better guns had set triggers.

Ideal rifles were popular, sturdy, accurate., and chambered for a variety of rim- and centerfire cartridges—e.g., 22 Long rimfire, 25 Rimfire, 25-20 Single Shot, 32 Long and Extra Long rimfire, 32 Long and Extra Long centerfire, 32-20 Winchester, 32-35 Stevens, 32-40 Winchester, 38 Long Center Fire, 38-40 Winchester, 38-55 Ballard or 44-40 Winchester.

A straight-case 25-25 cartridge, designed by Captain William Carpenter of the U.S. Army, was introduced for the No. 44 rifle in 1895, followed in 1897 by a 25-21 version. By the end of the nineteenth century, however, it was realized that cartridges as powerful as 38-55 Ballard strained the Ideal action excessively and chamberings were reduced to nothing more potent than 32-20 Winchester.

A 28-30-120 cartridge credited to Charles Herrick was introduced in 1900, and the extractor was moved centrally from the left side of the action; the pivot screws were replaced with heavier bolts to increase durability. A tension screw in the breechblock, which helped to keep the breech lever closed, was abandoned in this era.

The 32-25-150 or '32 Stevens Ideal' option was added about 1903, and a spring-and-plunger lever retainer was used on Ideal rifles made after introduction of the improved No. 44-1/2 in 1906. Stevens Ideal rifles were made until the advent of war work in 1916. When production began again after World War I, however, only the No. 44 reappeared.

A variant of the basic No. 44 with a specially narrowed lightweight receiver is said to have been promoted as the 'Lady' or 'English' pattern, but confirmation is lacking.

SIMILAR GUNS

No. 45 rifle, 1894-1916. This was very similar to No. 44, but had a hooked 'Off Hand' buttplate.

No. 48 rifle. These guns usually had a spur-type breech lever, a shallow pistol grip, a cheekpiece on the butt, and an off hand shoulder plate.

No. 49 rifle. Virtually identical to No. 48, this had a full pistol grip butt. It was widely sold as the 'Walnut Hill' model (named after a local rifle range) when fitted with 800yd mid-range Vernier sights.

No. 52 rifle, 'Schuetzen Junior'. This was a light target rifle with a 28in barrel, mid-range sights, a pistol grip butt, a sharply pitched comb, a cheekpiece, and a hooked Swiss-style shoulder plate; the breech lever was usually spurred, but could be looped.

No. 53 rifle. This was simply a version of No. 52 with a 30in barrel and a rear sight graduated to 1200yd.

No. 54 rifle. Basically a No. 52 with a 32in barrel and 1200yd sights, this also had a hinged hand-rest beneath the forend and a 'Schuetzen' breech lever with a small spur ahead of a distinctive wood-block inset in a loop.

No. 414 Armory Model rifle, 1912-32. This military-style gun, characterized by a long semi-beavertail forend retained by a single band, had a 26in round barrel. A Lyman Vernier sight was mounted on the receiver, the butt was a straight-wrist type, and swivel eyes lay under the butt and band. Made only for the 22 Long Rifle rimfire cartridge, the No. 414 weighed about 8lb.

'CRACK-SHOT' SPORTING RIFLE

Dating from 1900, this had a simplified radial-block action which, once the hammer had been retracted to full-cock, could be opened simply by pressing a lever on the right side of the frame. The lever was pulled up to close the breech after a new cartridge had been pushed into the chamber, and the hammer locked the components in place as it fell. However, the Crack-Shot was neither particularly well made nor especially strong; chambered only for the 22 Long Rifle or 32 Long rimfire cartridges, the guns had 20in round barrels, stepped ahead of the forend, and weighed about 3.75lb. The earliest examples had an automatic safety-slide behind the hammer, which had to be held back manually as the trigger was pressed, but this was rapidly abandoned. Many owners subsequently removed the safety-slide spring, altering operation from automatic to manual. Production of Crack-Shots had ceased by 1913.

'IMPROVED IDEAL MODEL' SPORTING RIFLE
Also known as No. 44-1/2

Made in Chicopee Falls, Massachusetts, by the J. Stevens Arms & Tool Company (1904-16).

Chambering options: see notes. **Action:** the dropping block is propped behind the chamber by the operating lever.
DATA FOR A TYPICAL SPORTING RIFLE
Chambering: 38-40 Winchester, rimmed. 43.5in overall, 7.95lb empty. 28in barrel, 6-groove rifling; RH, concentric. Vernier rear sight on tang. 1330 fps with 180-grain bullet.

The finest of all the Stevens target rifles, this shared the lines of the Ideal series but had a true dropping-block action. The breechblock, canted back by the finger lever, dropped at a slight angle to the vertical until it was held against the rear of the receiver by a spring plunger beneath the barrel. As the breech was closed, the breechblock was cammed forward sufficiently to seat all but the tightest cartridges in the chamber.

The use of a sturdy steel forging instead of a weaker malleable casting ensured that the No. 44-1/2 receiver could handle high-pressure ammunition. However, the inclusion of a hammer-fly—to protect the tip of the trigger if the hammer slipped during cocking—was a source of potential danger. A firing pin retractor was added in 1908, but, owing partly to declining demand and partly to war-work, the No. 44-1/2 was discontinued during World War I.

'CRACK SHOT' SPORTING RIFLE
Also known as No. 26

Offered only in 22 Long Rifle or 32 Long Rimfire, this 1913-patent take-down design was a lever-operated variant of the Little Scout. Recognizable by the construction of the breech, with the barrel on top of the receiver, it had a straight-wrist butt and a short tapering forend. Sights consisted of a simple standing block and a small bead. The No. 26-1/2 was a smooth-bore chambered for shot cartridges. Though work stopped in 1939, a few guns were made during World War II—possibly in 1943-4—with pistol grip butts, round-belly forends and spring-leaf and elevator rear sights. Their receivers were held together with pins instead of screws.

'NEW MODEL WALNUT HILL' TARGET RIFLE
Also known as 'No. 417'

Introduced in 1932, replacing the obsolescent No. 47 Walnut Hill, this was customarily chambered for the 22 Long Rifle rimfire cartridges, though a few No. 417 and 417-1/2 guns were made for the centerfire 22 Hornet round. Additional chamber pressure strained the action beyond its limits, and the Hornet option was rapidly withdrawn. The No. 417 usually had a 28in round barrel, and weighed about 10.5lb owing to the heavy target-pattern woodwork. The ball-tipped breech lever was curved to follow the underside of the pistol grip.

SIMILAR GUNS

No. 417-1/2 rifle, 1932-40. This was simply a No. 417 with a lighter sporting-style stock, weighing only 8.6lb.

No. 417-0 rifle, 1934-47. Distinguished by a Lyman No. 52L rear sight on the receiver, the last rifles of this type were sold after the end of World War II—but were probably assembled from old parts.

No. 417-1 rifle, 1934-40. Similar to the 417-0 pattern, this had a Lyman No. 48L sight on the receiver.

No. 417-2 rifle, 1934-40. A minor variant of the No. 417 Walnut Hill rifle, this was identified by a Lyman No. 144 Vernier sight on the tang.

No. 417-3 rifle, 1934-40. These were supplied without sights, allowing owners to complete them to their own specifications.

No. 418 rifle, 1932-40. Made only in 22 Long Rifle rimfire, this had a 26in barrel and a standard short operating lever even though a pistol grip butt was standard. A Lyman No. 144 Vernier sight was mounted on the tang, with a blade at the muzzle. The forend was a rounded semi-beavertail pattern, but weight averaged only 6.5lb.

No. 418-1/2 rifle, 1934-40. A minor variant of No. 418, also made in 22 WRF and 25 Stevens rimfire, this had a Lyman No. 2A Vernier sight on the tang and a gold bead at the muzzle instead of a blade.

• Stevens (J.), bolt-action type

Most of these guns were made after Stevens had been acquired by Savage, and may occasionally be found under the 'Stevens-

Savage' brand name. However, they were more commonly known as 'Stevens-Springfield' prior to 1948.

'LITTLE KRAG' SPORTING RIFLE

Very little is known about this tiny take-down gun, chambered for 22 Short, 22 Long or 22 Long Rifle cartridges, except that it was introduced about 1899 and was still available in 1910. Offered only with a 20in round barrel, it had a one-piece half-stock with a tiny tapering forend. The trigger guard was scrolled.

NO. 15 SPORTING RIFLE

Originally known as the 'Stevens-Springfield Model 15', this was a simple single shot design locked by turning the bolt-handle base down ahead of the receiver. The action was much shorter than the other Stevens designs, allowing the bolt handle to lie almost directly above the trigger. Typically, a gun had a 22in round barrel and weighed about 3.75lb.

SIMILAR GUNS

Model 15 rifle, new pattern, 1948-65. This was a post-war modification of the original gun, sold under the Stevens name. It had a 24in barrel, weighed 5lb, and featured an improved half-stock.

Model 15Y rifle, 1958-65. A junior version of the basic Model 15, this had a 21in barrel and a short butt.

NO. 53 SPORTING RIFLE

Introduced in 1931, this single shot design relied on the bolt-handle base locking down ahead of the split receiver bridge. Capable of chambering 22 Short, 22 Long, 22 Long Rifle and possibly also the 22 WRF rimfire rounds interchangeably, the No. 53 was also made for the 25 Stevens rimfire cartridge. The 24in round barrel gave a weight of about 5.5lb. The original pistol grip half-stock had a plain forend with a finger groove. In 1935, however, the gun seems to have been re-launched as the 'Model 53 Buckhorn'; the finger groove was eliminated and a black ebonite forend tip was added. Production stopped at the end of 1941 for the duration of World War II, beginning again in 1945; the last guns were apparently assembled in 1948.

SIMILAR GUNS

Note: Several of the guns were offered in an '0'-prefix series (e.g., Model 053), signifying the addition of a peep sight on the rear of the receiver above the cocking piece.

Model 56 rifle, 1933-41 and 1945-8. Essentially similar to the Model 53, this was a short-bridge design with a detachable five-round box magazine. It was modified to Buckhorn-series standards after 1935.

Model 66 rifle, 1931-5. Sometimes known as 'No. 66', this was a tube-magazine repeater with a capacity of 13-19 rounds depending on type: 22 Short, 22 Long and 22 Long Rifle rimfire rounds could be used interchangeably. A manual safety catch protruded from the rear right side of the long-bridge receiver, and the plain pistol grip half-stock had a finger groove in the forend. The rear sight was an open spring-leaf and elevator; the front sight was an open bead.

Model 419 rifle, 1932-6. This was a junior target-shooting version of the Model 53, with the same split-bridge action. It had a plain half-stock, a 26in round barrel, and weighed about 5.6lb. A Lyman No. 55 aperture rear sight was used in conjunction with a hooded blade at the muzzle.

MODEL 66 SPORTING RIFLE

Introduced in 1936 to replace the earlier 'No. 66', this had a modified receiver with the bolt-handle base locking down behind a solid bridge. The 'Buckhorn' black-tipped stock was mated with a 24in barrel and a tube magazine holding 15-21 rounds. The Model 066 had an additional peep sight on the receiver.

SIMILAR GUNS

Model 419 rifle, 1937-48. This target gun was built on a solid-bridge receiver, cut-down behind the bolt handle. The head of a radial safety lever protruded from the top of the heavy competition-style stock above the trigger, and the stamped-strip trigger guard was extended to become a floorplate for the detachable five-round box magazine. The guns weighed about 9.5lb with 26in round barrels. An aperture sight was fitted to the rear of the receiver, a replaceable-element globe appeared at the muzzle, and swivel eyes lay beneath the butt and forend. Many guns of this pattern were acquired for training purposes during World War II, and may be found with 'U.S. PROPERTY' on the receiver.

MODEL 82 SPORTING RIFLE

This Stevens-Springfield was a simple single shot take-down pattern with a plain hardwood pistol grip half-stock with a long finger groove in the forend. Made in 1935-9 for the 22 Short, 22 Long and 22 Long Rifle rimfire cartridges, which it would fire interchangeably, the Model 82 had a 22in barrel and weighed about 4lb. A spring-leaf and elevator rear sight was used in conjunction with a gold bead at the muzzle. Though a split bridge was used, the tubular construction was carried to the rear of the receiver; the Buckhorn-series receivers were cut down behind the bolt handle.

SIMILAR GUNS

Model 83 rifle, 1935-9. This was a heavier version of the Model 82, built on an identical action. Chambered for 22 Short, 22 Long, 22 Long Rifle and 22 WRF cartridges (apparently interchangeably), or 25 Stevens rimfire ammunition, it had a 24in barrel and a walnut stock.

Model 86 rifle, 1935-41 and 1945-65. Sharing the action of the Model 82, this had a half-length tube magazine beneath the barrel (containing 15-21 rounds depending on cartridge length). Post-1948 versions had the Buckhorn-series half-stock (with a black forend cap) and a synthetic trigger guard. The '086' pattern, later known as '86-S', had an additional peep sight on the receiver.

MODEL 84 SPORTING RIFLE

Though essentially similar to the Model 82, this had a detachable box magazine and was built on a solid-bridge action. Made in small numbers before World War II began, it was reintroduced in 1945 and lasted until 1965. Guns made after the abandonment of the Stevens-Springfield name in 1948 had Buckhorn-series stocks with black forend caps; the bolt handle was revised, and a synthetic trigger guard replaced the stamped-strip type. The Model 084—known as '84-S' after 1948—had a peep sight on the receiver.

• Stevens (J.), break-open type

These guns bore a variety of markings, beginning with 'J. Stevens & Co.', which seems to have lasted until 'J. Stevens Arms & Tool Co.' (often with 'A. & T.' substituted for 'Arms & Tool') was adopted in 1886. This mark lasted until 'J. Stevens Arms Company' was substituted in 1915.

'TIP-UP' SPORTING RIFLE

The first of Joshua Stevens' rifles were made on the basis of a patent granted in September 1864. Introduced in 1872 in 22, 32, 38 and 44 rimfire chamberings, the early guns had a conventional trigger guard (instead of a sheath) and the firing pin lay in the breech instead of the hammer face. The oddly shaped frame was a casting—originally nickel-plated brass, then malleable iron and finally steel—and the barrel was held in the frame by a spring-loaded transverse 'L'-shape latch. Pressing the button on the left

Some of the rifles encountered under the Stevens name are included in the Savage section (q.v.). This is a Model 34.

side of the frame disengaged the lock and allowed the muzzle to tip down, expelling a spent case and exposing the chamber.

The original guns had 24in half-octagon (light) or octagon (heavy) barrels, though barrel lengths up to 36in could be supplied to order. Gun weights were 6.5-8lb, depending on barrel. The straight-wrist butt had a concave shoulder plate and a trigger guard with a small semi-circular spur near the tip of the rear tang. The rear sight was usually a simple folding leaf-and-slider on the rear of the barrel, but Vernier tang sights could be fitted to order. Nickel plating was customary, and 'extra fancy stocks' could be obtained.

A shotgun was introduced on the same basic action, followed in 1875 by the first centerfire guns. Originally chambered only for the 38-35 Stevens, 38-45 Stevens or 44 Long cartridges, these usually had 24in or 26in barrels.

SIMILAR GUNS

No. 1 Open Sight Model, 1886-96. Chambered for the 32 Long, 38 Long and 44 Long rimfire cartridges, this had a 24in octagonal barrel and weighed about 8lb. Open sights, a serpentine trigger guard, and nickel plating on the frame and concave shoulder plate were standard. The straight-wrist butt had an oil finish. Options included extra-long barrels and specially-selected woodwork.

No. 2 Open Sight Model, 1887-1902. Offered only in 22 Long Rifle rimfire, this had a 24in octagonal barrel and weighed 6.5lb or 7.5lb, depending on the barrel type.

No. 3 Peep Sight Model, 1887-95. Essentially similar to the No. 1 pattern, offered in the same chamberings, this had a 24in half- or full-octagon barrel. A Beach-pattern front sight pivoted to give a bead-and-globe or a blade, and a Vernier aperture sight was fitted on the tang. Most guns also had an open rear sight on the barrel.

No. 4 Peep Sight Model, 1887-96. A variant of the No. 3 chambering 22 Short rimfire ammunition only, this was eventually superseded by guns chambering the more effective Long Rifle pattern.

No. 5 Expert Model Model, 1887-1902. Essentially similar to the No. 2, this had a Beach-type front sight, an open rear sight on the 24in half-octagon barrel, and a folding Vernier sight on the tang. The butt was varnished, and the frame and shoulder plate were nickel plated. The guns weighed 6.75lb or 7.75lb, depending on barrel. Chamberings included 22 Short, 22 Long Rifle, 25 Stevens and 32 Long rimfire, in addition to 32-20, 38-40 and 44-40 WCF; by 1897, however, the options had been reduced to 22 Long Rifle rimfire.

No. 6 Expert Model, 1887-97. This was little more than the No. 5 with selected woodwork and better finish.

No. 7 Premier Model, 1887-1902. Distinguished by a Swiss-style 'Schuetzen' buttplate and a short wooden forend, this had varnished woodwork and nickel plating on the frame. A Vernier sight on the tang could be used in addition to the open rear sight on the barrel; the front sight was a Beach-type bead. Weight was 7lb or 7.75lb, depending on barrel. Chamberings were initially 22 Short, 22 Long, 22 Long Rifle, 25 Stevens and 32 Long rimfire, and 32-20, 38-40 and 44-40 WCF. By 1897, however, only the 22 Long Rifle version was still available.

No. 8 Premier Model, 1887-95. A deluxe form of the No. 7, this was characterized by superior woodwork and better finish.

No. 9 Range Rifle, 1888-96. This was made in a selection of chamberings, including 32 Long, 38 Long and 44 Long rimfire, and centerfire rounds such as 22-10-45 Stevens, 32-20 WCF, 32-35 Stevens, 38-35 Stevens, 38-40 WCF and 44-40 WCF. It had a 24in half- or full-octagon barrel, though longer patterns could be fitted to order; the straight-wrist butt had a Schuetzen-style shoulder plate, though the forend was plain. Weights could be as much as 9.25lb.

No. 10 Range Rifle, 1888-96. A deluxe variant of the No. 9, this could be identified by its superior checkered-wrist butt and forend.

No. 11 Lady Model, 1889-96. Mechanically similar to the No. 7, this lightweight (5lb) small-frame gun had a half-octagon 24in barrel, a schnabel-tip forend and a concave buttplate. Chamberings were restricted to 22 Short, 22 Long and 25 Stevens rimfire ammunition.

No. 12 Lady Model, 1889-96. A deluxe form of the No. 11, this had checkering on its oil finished straight-wrist butt and forend.

No. 13 Lady Model, 1889-1902. Chambered for the 22 Short, 22 Long Rifle or 25 Stevens rimfire cartridges, this was a variant of No. 11 with a Beach-type front sight and a folding Vernier peep sight on the tang. The options were reduced in 1897 to the 22 Long Rifle pattern only.

No. 14 Lady Model, 1889-96. This was simply a deluxe version of No. 13, with better woodwork and checkering on the butt and forend.

No. 15 Crack-Shot Rifle, about 1898-1901. Similar to the No. 7 pattern, this had a Lyman Vernier peep sight on the tang and an ivory bead sight at the muzzle. Chamberings are said to have included 22 Short, 22 Long Rifle, 25 Stevens, 32 Long, 38 Long and 44 Long rimfire, plus a selection of Winchester and Stevens centerfire options, but very few guns had been made when the improved radial-block Crack-Shot rifle appeared in 1901.

'MAYNARD JUNIOR' SPORTING RIFLE
Also known as 'No. 15'

Derived from the original Maynard rifle (q.v.), this was operated by pushing the trigger guard downward to lift the chamber up and away from the standing breech. Offered in 1903-14 in 22 Long Rifle rimfire only, it had an 18in half-octagon barrel and simple open sights. The shaping of the walnut butt and forend was crude, and the receiver was built up around a malleable iron casting. Weight was only 2.9-3lb.

SIMILAR GUNS

Note: No. 12-1/2 and No. 15-1/2 were smooth-bore guns chambered for rimfire shot cartridges, and the 44-caliber Model 101 was a shotgun built on the No. 12 action.

No. 12 Marksman rifle, 1912-33. This was a sturdy tip-breech pattern derived from the Maynard Jr, but much more durable. Made only in take-down form, with a knurled-head release bolt beneath the forend immediately ahead of the barrel pivot, the Marksman had a straight-wrist butt. A fixed open rear sight was customary, though some guns were fitted with a spring-leaf and elevator type. Chamberings were restricted to the 22 Long Rifle, 25 Long and 32 Long rimfire cartridges.

• Stevens (J.), slide-action type
'VISIBLE LOADING' SPORTING RIFLE
Also known as 'No. 70'

Dating from 1907-34, this was Stevens' only foray into a market dominated by Winchester and Remington. It was an archaic-looking design with an exposed hammer and breechblock, and a half-length tube magazine beneath the 22in barrel. Magazine capacity was 11-15 rounds, as the 22 Short, 22 Long or 22 Long Rifle rimfire cartridges could be used interchangeably. The plain butt had a pistol grip, and the slide handle was ribbed. Conventional bead and spring-leaf and elevator sights were fitted. The gun was made in a number of patterns (Nos. 70-72, including '1/2' versions), but the differences between them are not clearly understood. Sights, finish and barrel construction were clearly the most important arbiters.

• Stevens (J.), swinging-barrel type
'SURE-SHOT' SPORTING RIFLE

Dating from the 1890s, this was the only gun of its type in the Stevens range. The barrel could turn laterally to the right once a locking catch on the left side of the frame had been depressed. The Sure-Shot had a pivoting take-down lever beneath the frame ahead of the trigger, a firing pin was anchored in the standing breech behind the chamber, and a straight-wrist butt was fitted. Production is believed to have been confined to 1891-7, and was presumably never large. The Sure-Shot was replaced by the more sophisticated Crack-Shot rolling block guns.

THE GUNS

No. 23 rifle. This was the basic version, described above, with a fixed standing-notch rear sight.

No. 24 rifle. Distinguished by peep-and-globe sights shared with the Stevens Pocket Rifles (which were little more than long-barreled pistols), this was otherwise the same as the No. 23.

No. 25 rifle. A Beach-pattern combination globe/blade front sight and a folding Vernier peep sight on the tang identified this version of the Sure-Shot, which retained the open rear sight on the barrel.

No. 26 rifle. Mechanically identical with the No. 23, this gun was fitted with Lyman Vernier peep and globe sights.

• Stevens (W.X.)

Patented in January 1864 by W.X. Stevens of Worcester, Massachusetts (U.S. no. 41,242), three carbines of this pattern were tested by the U.S. Army in 1865 as Guns No. 69-71. A short spur behind the trigger was pulled back to release the breech/trigger guard unit, which dropped downward at the rear to expose the chamber. The guns had two-piece half-stocks with forends held by a single band, and a sling bar and ring on the left side of the receiver. A small folding-leaf rear sight was fitted to the barrel.

• Stoner

These guns were widely touted as the successors to the ArmaLite series (q.v.), appeared after Eugene Stoner and his development team had been lured away from the original promoters. The Stoner series held great promise, but teething troubles and manufacturing problems ultimately prevented success.

MODEL 62 RIFLE

Made by the Cadillac Gage Corporation, 1963-9.

Total production: 150? **Chambering:** 7.62x51, rimless. **Action:** generally as ArmaLite AR-10 (q.v.).

42in overall, 8.9lb without magazine. 20in barrel (excluding flash suppresser), 6-groove rifling; RH, concentric. Detachable box magazine, 30 rounds. Pivoting-leaf rear sight. 2750 fps with M59 ball cartridges. Optional knife bayonet.

This rotating-bolt autoloader embodied a gas piston instead of the ArmaLite direct-impingement system, owing to the assignment of Stoner's original patents to Colt. The piston lay in a tube above the barrel, the charging slide and handle rode on rails on the left side of the receiver, and the furniture was wooden. Most prototypes were semi-automatic, though some were adapted experimentally to fire automatically at 600 rds/min. Though optimistically advertised as part of a multi-weapon system, the Model 62 offered too few advantages over guns such as the FAL.

MODEL 63 RIFLE

Made by the Cadillac Gage Corporation, 1963-9.

Total production: 3500 guns of all types. **Chambering:** 5.56x45, rimless. **Action:** generally as ArmaLite AR-10 (q.v.).

40.25in overall, 9.65lb with loaded magazine. 20in barrel (excluding flash suppresser), 6-groove rifling; RH, concentric. Detachable box magazine, 30 rounds. Pivoting-leaf rear sight. 3250 fps with M193 ball cartridges; 620-680 rds/min. Optional knife bayonet.

The strength of interest in high-velocity small caliber ammunition persuaded Cadillac Gage to revise the Model 62 for the 223 Remington (5.56x45) round in 1963, entrusting work to James Sullivan and Robert Fremont.

Conceived as an integral part of a weapons system, the rifle was heavier than the AR-15, but the long-stroke gas-piston system not only avoided the fouling problems that plagued the ArmaLite but also generated enough power to lift an ammunition belt. The M62 presented a neat, if very conventional appearance. The charging handle was mounted on a non-reciprocating slide, and most guns had synthetic furniture instead of wood.

In 1964, the Stoner multi-weapon project was licensed to Mauser-IWK AG, but transferred to Nederlandsche Wapen- en Munitiefabriek 'de Kruithoorn' NV (a Mauser subsidiary) in 1965. However, U.S. Army trials held in 1967 revealed sufficient flaws for the 5.56mm Stoner guns to be upgraded to '63A' standards.

SIMILAR GUNS

Model 63A rifle, 1968-71. An improvement of the original Model 63, this had a new ejection-port cover, an extended magazine housing, and changes in the gas system. A reciprocating charging handle on the receiver-top doubled as a bolt-closing device. The selector had only two positions, owing to the addition of a separate safety catch.

Model 63A carbine. Little more than a short-barrel rifle, the perfected version of this gun had a folding skeletal-tube butt instead of the original 'synthetic slab'.

XM22 carbine. This designation was applied by the U.S. Army to Model 63A carbines acquired for evaluation.

XM22E1 rifle. The perfected Model 63A Stoner rifle was tested extensively by the U.S. authorities, but failed to displace the established ArmaLite series—though the XM207E1 light machine-gun was classified as limited standard and issued to U.S. Navy SEAL teams as the 'Mk 23 Mod. 0'.

• Storm

This breechloader was patented in July 1856 by William Mont Storm of New York City. The breechblock could be raised by a small handle or stud to expose the chamber. Storm also claimed that the tapered mouth aligned the block and bore, and that a special sliding sleeve or 'bolt valve' improved obturation.

Two converted muskets were submitted to trials at West Point in August 1857. Though these failed, and though a decision was taken in 1858 to concentrate on the Morse conversion, the Ordnance Department still saw promise in the Storm system. Progress was also made in Britain (q.v.).

STORM RIFLE

Four hundred 1841-type rifles—some original 54-caliber examples and others in 58-caliber—were altered in Harper's Ferry in 1859, but field trials showed that they leaked gas too badly. The Storm conversions were stored until the Harper's Ferry facilities were destroyed by Confederate forces in 1861. However, an order for 2000 similar carbines, destined for Indiana militiamen, was given to Schuyler, Hartley & Graham in March 1862. About 500 had been completed by C.R. Alsop of Middletown, Connecticut, by the end of 1862, but they were all rejected by Federal inspectors. Schuyler, Hartley & Graham subsequently sold them on the open market. The emergence of better designs rapidly consigned Storm's efforts to history even though metallic-cartridge versions were tried by the U.S. Army in 1867 and again in 1872.

• Straw

These curious carbines—tested by the U.S. Army in 1865 as Guns Nos. 64, 67 and 68—were operated by sliding the barrel forward and then flipping the breechblock laterally to the left. The receiver formed the greater part of the forend (except for a separate tip), the hammer was mounted centrally, and a folding peep sight was fitted on the upper tang. A small ring-lever, used to slide the barrel forward, lay ahead of the conventional trigger. No. 64 had the butt in two parts, attached to an iron frame by four screws on each side; Nos. 67 and 68, however, were stocked much more conventionally.

• Symmes

Patented in November 1858 by John E. Symmes, a U.S. Army officer serving in Watertown Arsenal, New York, this carbine was made in small numbers for trials. The principal novelty was an 'elastic lip' on the breechblock face to gain satisfactory obturation.

The Stoner Model 63A1 rifle.

BREECH-LOADING CARBINE

Manufacturer unknown (Springfield Armory?).

Total production: at least 20. **Chambering**: 54-caliber, combustible cartridge, fired by a caplock. **Action**: the breechblock was propped behind the chamber by the tip of the operating lever.

38.4in overall, about 7.75lb empty. 21.9in barrel, 5-groove rifling; RH, pentagonal. Single shot only Standing-block rear sight with a folding leaf. Performance not known. No bayonet.

The guns were stocked in two parts, with the forend running almost to the muzzle; there were two barrel bands, and a hinged-lid brass patch box was let into the left side of the straight-wrist butt. A prominent housing for the capping mechanism lay on the right side of the breech, forcing the short straight-shank hammer to be set unusually high on the back-action lock plate. Combined with the trigger guard, the operating lever had a prominent 'locking joint' behind the trigger. The breechblock, which was pivoted transversely below the chamber, moved down and back. Two hundred guns were ordered in 1856, but only 20 are known to have been completed; surviving examples are unmarked, apart from 'LT. SYMMES PATENT'.

• Thomas

Patented in April-May 1872 by John F. Thomas of Ilion, New York, 50-caliber musket 'No. 44' tested by the U.S. Army in 1872 had a radial-block breech deriving from the Remington Rolling Block. It was not successful.

• Thompson

The delayed-blowback Thompson rifle, promoted by the Auto-Ordnance Corporation in the U.S.A. and by BSA Guns Ltd in Britain, was based on a patent granted in March 1915 to James L. Blish. Blish claimed that the friction created between two differing metals sliding together under pressure was sufficient to hold the breech closed until pressure had dropped. The Thompson rifles relied on a screw-lock system, though the better-known (and much more successful) Thompson submachine gun had a sliding wedge-piece.

THE GUNS

The earliest guns, made under contract to Auto-Ordnance by Colt's Patent Fire Arms Mfg. Co., were tested by U.S. Army in May 1920 with promising results. Their most obvious characteristic was the great length of the action in relation to the barrel, and the magazine placed well forward of the trigger guard. The M1921(or 'PC') rifle had a pistol grip half-stock with a ventilated barrel guard, and the bayonet lug and front swivel were attached to the barrel behind the front sight. Steeply-pitched threads on the bolt engaged in seats in the receiver, and a sturdy charging handle was attached to the bolt head. When the gun was fired, the screw-thread was not supposed to rotate until the pressure holding it against its seat dropped to a safe level. In practice, the breech opened with great rapidity. The lock was marginal; the breech leaked gas; the reciprocating movement of the charging handle was dangerous; and ejection was sometimes violent enough to stick mouths of cartridge cases into wood planks placed too close to the gun.

Tests of Thompson Auto Rifles PC and Mark V and an improved Berthier, undertaken in November 1921, showed that none was acceptable. Unfavorable reports of trials with an improved Thompson were filed in June 1925, and 10 modified 'Model D' Thompson Auto Rifles tried against M1924 Garands at Fort Benning also failed to impress. A 30-caliber Thompson was tried against the 30-caliber primer-actuated M1924 Garand, 276-caliber Tl Pedersen and 256-caliber Bang in the summer of 1928,

when it was finally eliminated. Work had ceased entirely by the early 1930s.

• Thompson/Center

This company, in addition to break-open guns, makes carbine derivatives of the Contender and Encore dropping-block pistols. Break-open guns were made in the 1980s, but work is now concentrating on black-powder muzzleloaders.

CONTENDER CARBINE

Made by Thompson/Center Arms, Rochester, New Hampshire, 1985 to date.

Currently in production. **Chambering options**: 22 Long Rifle rimfire, 22 Hornet, 223 Remington, 7mm TCU, 7x30 Waters, 30-30 Winchester, 35 Remington, 357 Magnum, 357 Remington Maximum or 44 Reminton Magnum. **Action**: a dropping-block is propped behind the chamber by the operating lever.

DATA FOR A TYPICAL EXAMPLE

Chambering: 7x30 Waters, rimless. 34.85in overall, 5.1lb empty. 21in barrel, 4-groove rifling; RH, concentric. Single shot only. Adjustable tangent-leaf rear sight. 2700 fps with 120-grain bullet.

This was made simply by attaching a long barrel, a round-tip forend and a pistol-grip walnut butt to the frame of the standard pistol. Barrels can be exchanged simply by removing the forend, tapping the hinge-pin clear of the frame, then detaching the barrel-block. Most guns are blued, with cougar motifs on the receiver-sides; butts and forends are usually walnut. The Contender has a simple tip-barrel action, but embodies an automatic hammer-blocking safety system and a selective rimfire/centerfire firing pin. The 1997 options are restricted to 17 Remington, 22LR rimfire, 22 Hornet, 223 Remington, 7x30 Waters, 30-30 Winchester and 375 Winchester chamberings.

SIMILAR GUNS

Contender Stainless carbine, 1993 to date. Chambered for the 22LR rimfire, 22 Hornet, 223 Remington, 7x30 Waters, 30-30 Winchester or 375 Winchester, this has a stainless steel barreled action and is customarily supplied with black DuPont Rynite butts and forends.

Contender Youth carbine. Available only in blue—in 22 Long Rifle rimfire and 223 Remington centerfire—this has a 16.25in barrel and a short butt, giving an overall length of about 29in and a weight averaging 4.55lb.

TCR MODEL 83 HUNTER SPORTING RIFLE

Made by Thompson/Center Arms, Rochester, New Hampshire, 1983-7.

Total production: not known. **Chambering options**: 22-250, 223 Remington, 243 Winchester, 7mm Remington Magnum or 30-06. **Action**: the tipping barrel was locked by a bar engaging an underlug.

DATA FOR A TYPICAL EXAMPLE

Chambering: 243 Winchester, rimless. 39.35in overall, 6.8lb empty. 23in barrel, 4-groove rifling; RH, concentric. Single shot only. Folding-leaf rear sight. 2920 fps with 105-grain bullet.

Operated by a top lever, this sporting rifle offered an interchangeable-barrel system. The plain straight-comb butt and forend were made of walnut, and a set trigger mechanism could be fitted.

SIMILAR GUNS

Model 83 Aristocrat rifle, 1983-6. This was made with select walnut woodwork, a cheekpiece on the butt, and checkering on the forend. A double set trigger mechanism was standard.

Model 87 Hunter rifle, 1987-95. An improved TCR83 pattern, this was chambered for the 22 Hornet, 222 Remington, 22-250, 223 Remington, 243 Winchester, 270 Winchester, 7mm-08, 30-06 or 308

The Thompson/Center Contender carbine, with a stainless-steel barrelled action.

The Thompson/Center Encore rifle.

Winchester cartridges; 375 H&H and 416 Remington magnum options were briefly added in 1992, followed by 32-40 Winchester in 1993. The barrels were either 23in medium or 25.9in heavy patterns, gun weights ranging from 6.85lb to 7.6lb. Heavy barrels usually lacked open sights, as optical sights were used. Sling swivels lay beneath the pistol grip butt and the finger-grooved forend.

Model 87 Hunter Deluxe rifle, 1987-95. Mechanically identical with the standard gun, this had select walnut woodwork and a double trigger system.

ENCORE CARBINE

Made by Thompson/Center Arms, Rochester, New Hampshire, 1997 to date.

Currently in production. **Chambering options:** see text. **Action:** similar to the Contender, above.

DATA FOR A TYPICAL EXAMPLE

Chambering: 7mm-08, rimless. 38.5in overall, 6.75lb empty. 24in barrel, 4-groove rifling; RH, concentric. Single shot only. Folding-leaf rear sight. 2860 fps with 140-grain bullet.

Essentially similar to the Contender, though the barrel units do not interchange, the Encore is easily identified by a reinforced frame suited to high-power centerfire ammunition. Its features include an automatic hammer safety, a broad hammer spur, and exchangeable barrels which are are drilled and tapped for optical-sight mounting bases. The standard folding-leaf rear sight can be replaced with a tangent-leaf type when necessary. The ambidextrous butt and schnabel-tip forend are made of walnut. The standard 24in-barrelled guns are available in 22-250, 223 Remington, 243 Winchester, 270 Winchester, 7mm-08, 30-06 and 308 Winchester; the 26in heavy-barreled version—supplied with a deep round-tip forend—can be obtained only for the 7mm Remington and 300 Winchester Magnum cartridges.

• Tiesing

Frank Tiesing of North Haven, Connecticut, designed a repeating rifle submitted by the Whitney Arms Company to the U.S. Army trials of 1878. It is believed to have been a 45-caliber lever-action design with a tube magazine beneath the barrel, but details are lacking.

• Trabue

William Trabue of Louisville, Kentucky, patented a bolt-action repeater with a cylindrical receiver which was closed apart from the lateral ejection port. Spring feed from the under-barrel tube magazine forced a cartridge back up a curved exit path until the tip of the cartridge rim was stopped by a recess in the top inner surface of the receiver. As the bolt was pushed forward, a finger projecting forward from the bolt head tipped the cartridge horizontally—allowing it to be pushed into the chamber as the bolt closed—and confined the next round to the magazine. Promoted by the Trabue Arms Company, a gun of this type was unsuccessfully submitted to the U.S. Army magazine-rifle trials of 1881. It is possible that a few sporters were also made to the same basic design.

• Triplett & Scott

Among the most interesting of the repeating firearms introduced during the American Civil War were the guns developed by Triplett & Scott of Columbia, Kentucky, in accordance with a patent granted to Louis Triplett in December 1864. One gun of this type was submitted to the U.S. Army trials of 1865, but was not among those that were selected for photography. Another was submitted by William Scott to the 1872 trials, where it was listed as 'Carbine No. 3'. The Triplett & Scott was acceptably efficient, judged by the standards of the Civil War repeaters, but was too fragile to compete effectively with the Winchester and other post-war designs.

MAGAZINE CARBINE

Made by the Meriden Mfg. Co., Meriden, Kentucky, 1864-70?
Total production: not known. **Chambering:** 44 Henry or 56-50 Spencer rimfire. **Action:** locked by retaining the barrel on a latch.

DATA FOR A 56-50 EXAMPLE

38in overall, 7.25lb empty. 22in barrel, 3-groove rifling; RH, concentric. Tube magazine in butt, 7 rounds. Open-block rear sight. 925 fps with standard ball cartridges. No bayonet.

Said to have been used by Kentucky militiamen at the end of the Civil War, this gun was operated by unlatching the barrel, rotating it through 180 degrees to receive a cartridge from the port on the frame-tip, then turning the barrel back to the firing position. The butt unit was set noticeably lower than the barrel, which gave Triplett & Scott guns an unmistakable appearance. Carbines had half-length forends held with a single band; sporting guns often had long barrels, superior woodwork and different sights.

• Ultra Light

These rifles incorporate a conventional bolt with dual-opposed locking lugs, made in right- ('R' suffix) or left-hand ('L') versions. A silhouette pistol has also been made on the Model 20 receiver.

MODEL 20 SPORTING RIFLE

Made by Ultra-Light Arms, Inc., Granville, West Virginia, 1987 to date.
Currently in production. **Chambering:** see notes. **Action:** locked by rotating two lugs on the bolt head into the receiver wall, and by the bolt handle entering its seat.

DATA FOR A TYPICAL EXAMPLE

Chambering: 7mm-08 Remington, rimless. 41.5in overall, 4.75lb empty. 22in barrel, 4-groove rifling; RH, concentric. Detachable box magazine, 3 rounds. Folding-leaf rear sight. 2850 fps with 140-grain bullet.

Built on several differing action lengths, Ultra Light rifles have Timney triggers and patented sear-locking safety levers protruding from the stock behind the bolt handle. Graphite-reinforced Kevlar stocks have a straight comb and a rubber recoil pad; their matte ('suede') or glossy DuPont Imron epoxy finishes include black, brown or green, plus Woodlands, Desert or Treebark Camo.

THE GUNS

Model 20 rifle. Short-action rifles have been offered in 22-250 Remington, 6mm Remington, 243 Winchester, 250-3000 Savage, 257 Roberts, 7mm-08 Remington, 7x57, 7x57 Ackley, 284 Winchester or 300 Savage chamberings.

Model 20S rifle. This was the smallest of the several otherwise identical actions. Fitted with a Douglas Premium No. 1 barrel, it has been chambered for the 17 Remington, 22 Hornet, 222 Remington or 223 Remington rounds.

Model 24 rifle. Built on an intermediate-length action, this is intended for 25-06 Remington, 270 Winchester, 280 Remington or 30-06 ammunition.

Model 28 rifle. Long-action guns of this type, offered with a 24in Douglas Premium No. 2 barrel and a recoil arrestor (KDF or Ultra Light patterns), can be chambered for 264 Winchester, 7mm Remington Magnum, 300 Winchester Magnum or 338 Winchester

Magnum cartridges. Model 28 rifles are about 45in overall and weigh merely 5.75lb.

• Underwood

A gun of this type was submitted to the U.S. Army trials of 1865, but was not among those that were photographed and may have been rejected in the examination stages. Henry Underwood of Tolland, Connecticut, received U.S. patent 38,772 in June 1863 to protect a tap or 'faucet' breech. This was rotated to the open position by retracting the hammer to half-cock; pulling it back to full cock then closed the breech again.

• Universal

Universal Sporting Goods, Inc., of Hialeah and Miami, Florida, made a variety of M1 Carbine derivatives from the early 1960s until the company was purchased by Iver Johnson (q.v.) in January 1983. The facilities were moved to Arkansas in the summer of 1984, consolidating Iver Johnson's M1 Carbine monopoly. Iver Johnson continued to sell Universal-branded Carbines as late as 1988, the Models 1003 and 5000PT lasting until the very end.

UNIVERSAL M1 CARBINES

The original Universal M1 Carbine was a straightforward copy of the military-pattern gun, though most reviewers agreed that it was not only better made but also shot much more reliably than the wartime products. By 1965, the range comprised M1A, M1B, M1BB, M1BN, M1BG, M1OS and the M1 Ferret.

THE GUNS

M1A Carbine, or 'Military Model', 1962-72. The basic Universal carbine had an 18in barrel, fixed sights, polished blue finish and a straight-comb butt. It was known after 1972 as the 'Model 1000'.

M1B Carbine, 1962-72. This was an otherwise-standard M1A with a sandblasted finish instead of blueing, and was known after 1972 as the Model 1005.

M1BB Carbine, 1962-72. A version of the standard M1B, retaining the matte finish, this was distinguished by a bayonet-mounting lug beneath the barrel.

M1BN Carbine, 1962-72. A deluxe version of the standard Model 1B, this displayed extensive nickel plating.

M1BG Carbine, 1962-72. Distinguished by 18-carat gold electroplating on some of the components, this was otherwise similar to the Model M1B.

M1OS Carbine, 1962-72. This had a characteristic Monte Carlo-pattern stock, but was otherwise standard.

M1 Ferret, 1964-72. Though easily identified by its chambering—256 Winchester instead of 30 M1 Carbine—this was still basically an M1 Carbine replica.

Model 1000 Carbine, or 'Military Model'. This was the post-1972 designation for the standard M1A. It had a blued finish, fixed sights and a birch stock.

Model 1002 Carbine. This was apparently a version of the Model 1A with a sheet-steel handguard.

Model 1003 Carbine, 1972-88. This was a post-1972 designation for the M1A with a 16, 18 or 20in barrel, blue finish, adjustable sights and a birch stock. It was known from about 1981 as the 'Model 1941'.

Model 1004 Carbine. A post-1972 designation, this identified a minor variant of the M1A with an optical sight.

Model 1005 Carbine, or '1005SB'. This was applied after 1972 to the M1B, with an oil-finished Monte Carlo-pattern walnut stock and a high-gloss blue 'Super Mirrored' finish.

Model 1006SS Carbine, or '1006 Stainless'. A stainless steel version of the M1, this was introduced in 1982. It had an 18in barrel and a birch stock.

Model 1010 Carbine, 1010N or '1010 Nickel'. The nickel-plated version of the basic M1B was introduced in 1972, but was rapidly discontinued. However, it had been reintroduced by 1981 as the '1010N'. A ventilated sheet-steel handguard was standard.

Model 1015 Carbine, 1015G or '1015 Gold', 1972-88. This was a 1972-vintage designation for the M1BG, featuring gold plating; '1010G' was in use by 1981.

Model 1020TB Carbine or '1020 Teflon'. Distinguished by DuPont 'Raven Black' Teflon-S finish on the metal parts, this gun also had a Monte Carlo-style stock.

Model 1025TCO Carbine. Made only in small quantities, this gun had an olive drab/camouflage Teflon finish.

Model 1030 Carbine. This variant was made with a distinctive gray Teflon-S finish.

Model 1941 Carbine. Little more than the Model 1000 or 1003 under a different name, this was also offered as the special 'M1941 Commemorative Carbine' (or 'GI Commemorative')—made in 1981 to celebrate the 40th anniversary of the adoption of the M1 Carbine. It had a bayonet lug and a special medallion in the side of the black walnut butt.

Model 1256 Carbine. This designation was applied to the standard 256 Ferret after the introduction of the '2566' version in 1982.

Model 2200 Leatherneck. A 22 rimfire version of the basic design, this had a birch stock, blue finish, and an 18in barrel. It was apparently a blowback design.

Model 2566 Carbine. This stainless steel version of the 256 Ferret dated from 1982.

Model 5000 Carbine, 5000PT or 'Paratrooper', 1980-8? A folding metal stock inspired by the German MP. 38 (Schmeisser) pattern distinguished the Model 5000, which was mechanically identical with the other guns in the series.

Model 5006 Carbine, 5006PS or '5006 Paratrooper Stainless'. This was simply an M5000 made of stainless steel.

Model 5016 Carbine. Announced in 1983, this variant of the M5000PT had a 16in barrel instead of the standard 18in pattern.

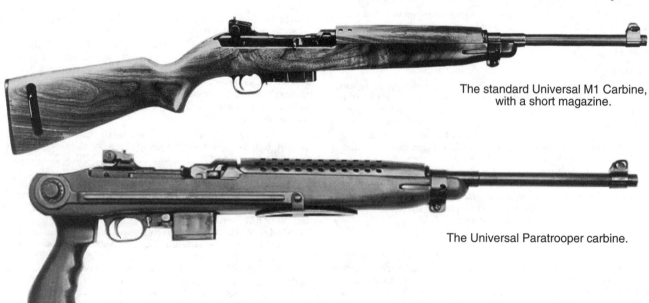

The standard Universal M1 Carbine, with a short magazine.

The Universal Paratrooper carbine.

• Updegraff

Horace Updegraff submitted a 50-caliber musket—'Gun No. 42'—to compete unsuccessfully in the U.S. Army trials of 1872. It had a radial breechblock protected by patents granted in September 1871 (from Fort Laramie, Wyoming) and August 1872 (from Smithfield, Ohio), but was clearly inspired by the Remington rolling block.

• Van Choate

Silvanus Van Choate of Boston, Masschusetts, received a series of patents protecting bolt-action guns in 1869-72. Tested as 'Gun No. 34', a rifle submitted to the U.S. Army trials of 1872 had a split-receiver with a bolt handle turning down into a deep seat cut in the right receiver wall; the hammer was mounted centrally in the stock behind the bolt. It was chambered for a special 45-70-420 centerfire cartridge. Van Choate rifles are said to have been made by the Brown Mfg. Co. (See 'Ballard'), which suggests that sporting guns may have been offered in small numbers.

• Varner

Varner Sporting Arms, Inc., of Marietta, Georgia, made a replica of the original Stevens Favorite 22 rimfire lever-action falling block rifle in three styles—field, sporter and presentation. The guns had 21.5in half-octagonal barrels, attractively color case-hardened receivers, and a large ring-head take-down bolt beneath the receiver ahead of the action-lever pivot.

• Voere (KDF)

Large numbers of Voere rifles were sold in North America by Kleinguenther's, Inc., of Seguin, Texas—originally without modification (as 'K-14 Insta-Fire' [Model 2130] and 'K-15 Insta-Fire' [Titan II]). However, the subsequent creation of KDF, Inc., allowed rifles to be stocked and completed in the U.S.A. Special attention paid to a patented pillar bedding system allowed KDF to guarantee that rifles would better half-MOA at 100yd.

K-15 AMERICAN SPORTING RIFLE

Introduced in 1991 on the basis of the Voere Titan II, this contains sufficient U.S.-made parts to be classed as an indigenous product. It has been offered in 25-06 Remington, 257 Weatherby Magnum, 270 Winchester, 270 Weatherby Magnum, 300 Weatherby Magnum, 300 Winchester Magnum, 30-06, 338 Winchester Magnum, 340 Weatherby Magnum, 375 H&H Magnum, 411 KDF Magnum, 416 Remington Magnum or 458 Winchester Magnum chamberings. Standard guns have four-round magazines; magnum patterns hold one cartridge less. Classic straight comb, Monte Carlo or thumbhole stocks may be select walnut, walnut/maple laminate or composite Kevlar/carbon fiber patterns.

• Volcanic

In the summer of 1854, Horace Smith & Daniel Wesson opened a workshop in Norwich, Connecticut, to exploit patents granted to Walter Hunt and Lewis Jennings (q.v.) in 1848-9. Smith had obtained protection for an improved version of the Jennings rifle, operated by an underlever combined with the trigger guard, and this was followed in 1854 by an adaptation which cocked the hammer automatically as the bolt ran back.

Production of new guns began immediately, but Smith & Wesson soon sold rights to the 'Rocket Ball Rifle' to concentrate on revolvers, and the tools, fixtures, gauges and components were moved from Norwich to New Haven. About 1200 guns had been made by Smith & Wesson, but all but a handful had been pistols.

The Volcanic Repeating Fire Arms Company continued to make guns until the summer of 1857, but sales were never brisk. The small projectiles generated very little power and the mercuric fulminate propellant—which was exceptionally corrosive—ruined the bore unless it was cleaned regularly.

The New Haven Arms Company was formed on 1st May 1857 to purchase the Volcanic patents. Benjamin Henry became works superintendent and production of the 'Volcanic Repeating Fire Arms' continued.

VOLCANIC CARBINE

Made by the Volcanic Repeating Firearms Company, New Haven, Connecticut (1855-7); and by the New Haven Arms Company, New Haven, Connecticut (1857-61).
Total production: 5000 (all types)? **Chambering options:** see text.
Action: locked by a toggle-joint beneath the bolt, operated by a swinging lever forming the trigger guard.

DATA FOR A TYPICAL NEW HAVEN ARMS COMPANY EXAMPLE
Chambering: 41-caliber self-priming ball ammunition. 39in overall, 7.5lb empty. 21in barrel, 7 grooves; RH twist, concentric. Tube magazine beneath the barrel, 25 rounds. Adjustable sight on the back of the receiver. About 550 fps with 110-grain bullet.

The guns were lever-action repeaters, loaded through a port cut in the underside of the magazine tube near the muzzle. Blunt tipped Hunt-type Rocket Ball were used. True Volcanics included 36 and 44-caliber carbines with barrels of 16, 21.5 and 25in, and magazines containing 20, 25 and 25 balls respectively. The frames were bronze, with blued barrels and magazine tubes; the operating lever/trigger guard was case-hardened; and the straight-wrist butt had a concave brass shoulder plate. Lacking a forend, Volcanic carbines resembled the later 44 rimfire Henry rifle (q.v.), but—apart from a handful of Smith & Wesson-made iron-frame guns—the receivers were noticeably shorter.

An 1859-vintage New Haven Arms Company broadsheet was still advertising carbines in 'No. 2' bore (41-caliber), with barrels of 16.5in, 21in and 25in, but production had practically ceased when the Civil War began.

• Ward-Burton

This rifle combined a turning-bolt action derived from patents granted to Bethel Burton (q.v.) in 1859-68 with an 1871-patent extractor/ejector system credited to William Ward. One of its best features was the retraction of the firing pin into the bolt as the breech opened.

Some units issued with trials rifles were enthusiastic, owing to efficient extraction and ejection, but the novelty soon palled and the Allin-type Springfield was preferred.

MODEL 1871 TRIALS RIFLE

Made by the Springfield Armory, Springfield, Massachusetts, 1871-2.
Total production: at least 1015. **Chambering:** 50-70, rimmed. **Action:** locked by engaging interrupted threads on the rear of the bolt body with the receiver.

51.9in overall, about 9lb empty. 32.65in barrel, 3-groove rifling; RH, concentric. Ramp-and-leaf sight graduated to 1200yd? 1250 fps with standard ball cartridges. M1855 socket bayonet.

The Ward-Burton impressed the St. Louis U.S. Army trials board of 1870 sufficiently to be recommended for field trials. The extractor and ejector were mounted on the detachable bolt head; a bolt-lock catch lay on the right side of the receiver; and a spring-loaded firing pin ran through the bolt. On 31st May 1871, General Alexander Dyer, the Chief of Ordnance, informed the Secretary of War that a thousand rifles had been ordered. By March 1872, when field trials began, more than a thousand had been made. One was entered in the breechloading rifle trials as the 'Ward-Burton Musket, No. 26', but failed to challenge the supremacy of the Springfield-Allin. Survivors are now very rarely encountered.

SIMILAR GUNS

Model 1871 single shot carbine. A short-barreled version of the trials rifle, this had a half-length forend held by a single band; 317 were made in Springfield in 1871-2.

Model 1871 magazine carbine. 'Ward-Burton Magazine Carbine, no. 97' was also tested by the St. Louis board. The tube magazine under the barrel, the cartridge elevator and the sliding cut-off had all been developed by Burton and Ward in 1869-71. No. 97 was successful enough to be recommended for a trial with the cavalry, but the Chief of Ordnance strongly disagreed and nothing more was ever done.

A drawing of the Ward-Burton rifle action. (USMF)

The 44 rimfire Warner carbine of the Civil War period. The extractor lever may be seen beneath the breech ahead of the frame. (W&W)

• Warner

Made in accordance with patents granted to James Warner in 1864, this had a breech-block which swung laterally up and to the right to expose the chamber. An extractor lever under the forend, ahead of the receiver, could then unseat the spent case.

MODEL 1864 CARBINE

Made by the Greene Rifle Works, Worcester, Massachusetts, 1864-5. Total production: at least 4000. **Chambering options:** 50 Warner rimfire or 56-50 Spencer rimfire. **Action:** locked by latching the breechblock behind the chamber.

DATA FOR A TYPICAL EXAMPLE

37.2in overall, 6.8lb empty. 19.9in barrel, 3-groove rifling; RH, concentric. Single-shot only. Open leaf rear sight. About 950 fps with Spencer ammunition. No bayonet.

The federal government acquired 4001 of these brass-frame carbines, 1501 chambering a special 50-caliber cartridge (ordered January-November 1864) and 2500 for the government-standard 56-50 rimfire round (26th December 1864). The last guns were delivered into ordnance stores in the Spring of 1865.

A thumb-piece adjacent to the hammer of first-type Warners had to be pressed before the breech-block could be moved laterally by a lug projecting on its left side. The sling ring was held in an eye-bolt which ran through the frame. Later guns had a sliding breech-block catch and a sling bar on the left side of the frame. The straight-wrist butt proved to be too weak to withstand rigorous service, and the manual extractor was ineffectual.

Submitted to the U.S. Army trials of 1865 as Guns No. 72 and 73, the Warner carbines duplicated the Civil War pattern. The breech-blocks hinged to the right (No. 72) or the left (No. 73), but too few improvements had been made to the basic design to impress the testers.

• Weatherby, autoloading type

MARK XXII SPORTING RIFLE

Made for Weatherby by Pietro Beretta SpA, Gardone Val Trompia, Italy (1964-9); by Howa Industries, Nagoya, Japan (1969-81); and in the U.S.A. (1982-9).

Total production: not known. **Chambering:** 22 Long Rifle, rimfire. **Action:** no mechanical breech lock; blowback, semi-automatic only.

DATA FOR A TYPICAL XXII CLIP

42.1in overall, 6.2lb empty. 24in barrel, 4-groove rifling; RH, concentric. Detachable box magazine, 10 rounds. Optical sight. 1080 fps with 40-grain bullet.

This selective-fire (single-shot or autoloading) rimfire rifle was originally made by Beretta. Stocked similarly to the Mark V Deluxe, the Weatherby rimfire autoloaders were beautifully made and very expensive compared with others in their class.

SIMILAR GUNS

Mark XXII Tubular. Identical with the standard gun, this had a 15-round tube magazine beneath the barrel.

• Weatherby, bolt-action type

Roy Weatherby was the first man to promote a matched range of powerful belted-case magnum cartridges in North America. Beginning in the early 1940s, Weatherby produced several new rounds by necking and re-forming Holland & Holland magnum cartridge cases. When hostilities ended, Weatherby began his own operations in earnest, offering rifles based on FN-Mauser actions.

Schultz & Larsen actions were purchased specially for the 378 cartridge, introduced in 1953, and some left-hand guns were built on the Mathieu system. Dissatisfied with these commercial actions, however, Weatherby and his chief engineer, Fred Jennie, began work on their own rifle in 1954.

Patents were sought in 1958 and production began in San Francisco. The essence of the Mark V action was a counter-bored breech, enabling the barrel to shroud the bolt-head, and nine locking lugs were disposed at 120 degrees in three rows of three. This gave a 54-degree bolt-throw and allowed the lugs to share the external diameter of the bolt body. The extractor was set into the bolt head.

WEATHERBY-MAUSER RIFLES

Built in 1949-58 on the basis of FN-Mauser actions, these guns were chambered for the 220 Rocket and 375 H&H Magnum in addition to the 257, 270, 7mm and 300 Weatherby magnums.

THE GUNS

Deluxe rifle. These rifles chambered non-magnum cartridges—e.g., 270 Winchester or 30-06.

Deluxe Magnum rifle. These rifles had a Monte Carlo-style stock with contrasting pistol grip caps and forend tips. Quick-detachable swivels and ventilated recoil pads were standard.

MARK V SPORTING RIFLE

Made for Weatherby by Precision Founders, Inc., San Francisco (1958-9); J.P. Sauer & Sohn, Eckenförde (1959-72); and Howa Industries, Nagoya (1971 to date).

Currently in production. **Chambering:** a broad selection of Weatherby Magnums, plus other well-known cartridges. See notes. **Action:** locked by rotating nine lugs on the bolt head into engagement with the receiver walls.

DATA FOR A TYPICAL MARK V

Chambering: 378 Weatherby Magnum, belted rimless. 46.25in overall, 8.38lb empty. 26in barrel, rifling pattern not known. Internal box magazine, 2 rounds. Optical sight. 2925 fps with 300-grain bullet.

The first rifles were assembled in 1958 in Weatherby's South Gate, California, workshops from Precision Founders actions. They had a plain bolt body, a checkered bolt knob, a safety on the right side behind the bolt handle, and (prototypes only) a

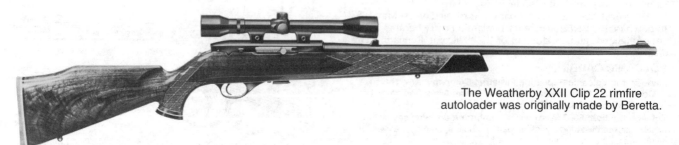

The Weatherby XXII Clip 22 rimfire autoloader was originally made by Beretta.

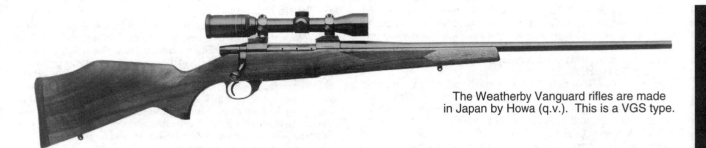

The Weatherby Vanguard rifles are made in Japan by Howa (q.v.). This is a VGS type.

two-piece bolt shroud. The awesome 460 Weatherby Magnum cartridge was specifically intended for the new gun, though most of the other options had already been offered with the FN-Mausers.

A one-piece bolt shroud was adopted in 1959, before production started in earnest; Sauer rifles also introduced the fluted bolts. The perfected Mark V was most distinctive, owing to the shape of the cocking-piece shroud. Barrels measured 24in or 26in, the latter being standard with 340, 378 or 460 cartridges and optional with the others. Several forms of barrel have been fitted over the years—there have been four 26in types—but the lengths did not change radically until 1992, when most of the 24in options were deleted.

The standard gloss-finish half-stock had a high Monte Carlo comb, skip-line checkering on the pistol grip and forend, and a separate ebony forend tip. White spacers accompanied the pistol grip cap, the forend tip, and a ventilated rubber shoulder pad. Checkering on the bolt knob was abandoned in 1960, and the old sear safety was replaced in 1962 by an improved pattern mounted on the bolt shroud.

Work began in 1963 on a short action with only six lugs (two rows of three), developed by Sauer largely by scaling-down the standard Mark V. The first full-size 340 guns also date from this period, and the 240 Weatherby Magnum cartridge appeared in 1968. In 1969, however, owing to spiraling manufacturing costs in Germany, a contract was signed with Howa in Japan; the first Nagoya-made actions were delivered in 1971. Changes were made so that the trigger could be adjusted externally, and the bolt stop—a separate component on Sauer-made rifles—became a spring-loaded plunger operated by an extension of the trigger lever.

SIMILAR GUNS

Mark V Accumark rifle, 1996 to date. Chambered for the same cartridges as the Mk V Sporter, excepting the 338 Winchester and 375 H&H magnums, this has a distinctive 26in heavy fluted barrel, black-oxidized metalwork, and a H-S Precision Pro-Series synthetic stock. The guns are typically 46.65in long and weigh 8lb.

Mark V Classicmark rifle, 1992-5. Introduced in all regular chamberings excepting 22-250 and 224 Weatherby Magnum, the Classicmark I has a straight-comb butt, a rounded forend tip, and a ventilated rubber recoil pad. The Classicmark II was a minor variant with fine wraparound checkering, a steel pistol grip cap, and an 'Old English' shoulder pad. Its metalwork had a matte finish.

Mark V Commemorative rifle, 1980. One thousand of these guns were offered in 257, 270, 7mm or 300 Weatherby Magnum to celebrate the 35th anniversary of the introduction of the Mark V.

Mark V Crown Custom rifle, 1989-95. These guns have been made in all regular Weatherby Magnum chamberings from 240 to 300, plus 30-06, and have a selected walnut stock with inlays and carving. The bolt handle is usually checkered and the bolt is damascened. Magazine floorplates are usually marked 'WEATHERBY CUSTOM'.

Mark V Euromark rifle, 1986 to date. Available in all chamberings excepting 22-250 and 224, this was a minor variant of the standard rifle with a satin-finish stock. It had conventional checkering, an ebony pistol grip cap with a maplewood diamond inlay, an ebony forend tip, and a plain black spacer ahead of a solid rubber buttplate. An improved gun with a refined stock was introduced in 1995.

Mark V Eurosport, 1995 to date. Chambered similarly to the Mk V Sporter (q.v.), this has a simpler stock with a satin oiled finish. The separate pistol grip cap and forend tip are absent.

Mark V Fibermark rifle, 1983-91. Identifiable by a textured matt-black fiberglass stock, with a black recoil pad and pistol grip cap, this had a matte-blue finish on the receiver and magazine floorplate (though the bolt was satin-chrome). An 'Alaskan' model—offered initially only in 270, 7mm, 300 or 340 Weatherby Magnum—appeared in 1992. The principal distinguishing feature is its nickel-plated metalwork.

Mark V Lazermark rifle, 1981 to date. Similar to the deluxe Mark V, this has intricate laser-cut carving on the pistol grip, forend, and cheek-piece base. Chamberings are currently restricted to 240, 257, 270, 7mm, 300, 340, 378, 416 and 460 Weatherby Magnum.

Mark V Olympic rifle, 1984. Made to celebrate the Los Angeles Olympic Games, this had a specially-selected walnut stock with an inlaid 'moving star' motif. A thousand guns were made in 257, 270, 7mm and 300 Weatherby Magnum chamberings only.

Mark V Safari Custom rifle, 1989-93. Offered only in 300, 340, 378, 416 or 460 Weatherby Magnum chamberings, this had a 24in barrel and a Euromark-style stock. A quarter-rib on the barrel carried one fixed and one folding leaf. The front swivel was carried on a barrel band. Essentially similar Safari Classic(-mark II) rifles were made for the 375 H&H Magnum cartridge in 1992-6.

The Weatherby Mark V rifle, with the original plain checkering.

The Weatherby Mark V Crown Custom rifle, showing the inlays and stock carving.

Mark V Sporter, 1993 to date. Essentially the same as the standard deluxe Mark V, this has a subdued blued finish and a high-gloss Claro walnut Monte Carlo-type half-stock. Chamberings are 257, 270, 7mm, 300 and 340 Weatherby Magnums, plus 7mm Remington Magnum, 300 Winchester Magnum, 338 Winchester Magnum and 375 H&H Magnum.

Mark V Stainless rifle, 1995 to date. Available in the same chamberings as the Mk V Sporter, this combines a stainless steel barreled action with a synthetic Monte Carlo-style stock. Checkering is molded into the pistol grip and forend.

Mark V Synthetic rifle, 1995 to date. Distinguished by a composite graphite/fiberglass half-stock with a Monte Carlo comb and cheekpiece, this is otherwise similar to the Mk V Sporter. The forend has a distinctive 'dual taper' and integrally-molded checkering.

Mark V Ultramark rifle, 1990-5. Available in all Weatherby Magnum chamberings except 224 and 460, this had a Claro walnut stock, basket-weave checkering and a jeweled bolt.

Mark V Varmintmaster rifle, 1963-91. This was announced for a variety of chamberings, including a new 224 Weatherby Magnum. Series production began in the Sauer factory in 1964.

Mark V Weathermark rifle. This was similar to the Classic-mark, but had a composite stock with raised checkering. It was offered in all regular chamberings from 240 to 300 Weatherby Magnum (24in or 26in barrels), plus 270 Winchester (22in), 7mm Remington Magnum (24in), 30-06 (22in) and 340 Weatherby Magnum (26in). The 'Weathermark Alaskan' of 1992 was a similar gun, with nickel-plating on the metalwork.

• Wesson

Benjamin Kittedge & Co. of Cincinnati, Ohio, was an enthusiastic champion of the light sporting gun patented in 1859-62 by Franklin Wesson of Springfield, Massachusetts. Though only 152 Wesson carbines were purchased by the federal government in 1863, Kittredge sold more than 2000 guns to militia in Kentucky and Illinois alone. They were not particularly efficient, but were undoubtedly handier than many caplock rivals.

WESSON CARBINE

Made by the F. Wesson Fire Arms Co., Springfield, Massachusetts, 1863-8.

Total production: 5000? **Chambering:** 44 rimfire. **Action:** the tipping barrel was locked by a catch beneath the barrel.

39.3in overall, 5.3lb empty. 24in barrel, 5-groove rifling; RH, concentric. Single-shot only. Folding-leaf rear sight. About 1100 fps with 215-grain bullet. No bayonet

The Wesson carbine had a walnut butt and a distinctive frame with two separate trigger apertures; the front lever released the barrel, which tipped forward and down to expose the chamber. Swivels lay beneath the barrel and butt. Individual guns usually bore Wesson and Kittredge markings on the barrel, which included acknowledgments of patents granted in October 1859 (no. 25,926) and November 1862 (36,925). Like many guns of its day, the Wesson lacked an extractor and stubborn cases often had to be punched out of the chamber with a ramrod.

• White

Designed by LeRoy White of Waterbury, Connecticut, who was granted U.S. patent 37,376 in January 1863, this carbine relied on an underlever to slide the hammer/trigger unit backward. The separate forend was held by a single band, swivels lay beneath the band and butt, and a small folding-leaf rear sight was brazed to the barrel ahead of the chamber. Three White carbines were tested unsuccessfully by the U.S. Army in 1865, as Guns No. 74-6.

• Whitney

Resembling the Remington rolling block externally, the original Whitney action was based on a patent granted to Theodore Laidley (q.v.) and C.A. Emery in May 1866. The Laidley-Emery rifle was claimed to be safer than the Remington, but was undoubtedly more complicated. Whitney then produced a blatant copy of the Remington rolling-block action, before exploiting a laterally-pivoting breech-block system patented by Eli Whitney III in May 1874. Known as the Phoenix, this enjoyed a short-lived popularity owing to competitive price, but was never able to challenge Ballards, Remingtons and Winchesters on the target range.

LAIDLEY-EMERY PATTERNS

The Whitney version of the Laidley-Emery system had an auxiliary cam which locked as the breech was closed; the hammer simply struck the firing pin and played no other part in the operating cycle. The action loaded at half-cock.

The rifle was hard to distinguish from a Remington at a glance, but had an extra lateral screw through the action. What appeared to be a retainer-plate on the left side of the breech for the major axis pins was two elongated lipped pin-heads locked by a central screw. Some guns of this type were sold to Mexico (q.v.) in the 1870s.

SPORTING MODEL

Made from 1872-3 by the Whitney Arms Company of Whitneyville, Connecticut, this was offered as a rifle or carbine in a variety of chamberings: 38 Long rimfire, 38-40 Winchester, 40-50 Sharps (necked), 40-70 Sharps (necked), 44-40 Winchester, 44-60 Sharps (necked), 44-77 Sharps (necked), 44-90 Sharps (necked), 44-100 Remington, 45-100 Sharps (straight), 45-70 Government, 50-70 Government and others. The round, half-octagon or fully-octagonal barrels measured 24-30in. Straight grip butts and short slender forends were standard, but schnabel tips and checkering could be supplied to order. A typical rifle chambered for the 44-77 Sharps cartridge was 42.5in overall (with a 26.5in barrel) and weighed 7.8lb. Its folding-leaf rear sight was graduated to 1000yd.

CREEDMOOR MODEL

Introduced in 1875 to compete with Remington, these rifles had specially selected butts with checkered pistol grips and checkered half-length forends. A Vernier peep sight was fitted to the upper tang behind the action; the front sight was usually a globe type, often with an additional spirit level. The No. 1 rifle, chambered for 44-90 Sharps (necked) or 44-100 Remington cartridges, was offered with half- or fully-octagonal barrels (32in or 34in); the lighter No. 2, confined to 40-50 Sharps (necked) or 40-70 Sharps (necked), had barrels of 30in or 32in. A typical 32in-barreled No. 1 was about 48.25in overall and weighed 10lb.

• Whitney-Remington Patterns

NEW SYSTEM SPORTING RIFLE

The Whitney Arms Company realized that the Laidley-Emery rolling-block was unnecessarily difficult to make, and so production ceased in the early 1880s in favor of a blatant copy of the Rider-type Remington.

The only cartridges chambered in New System Whitney guns, distinguished by a rounded receiver, appear to have been the 32-20, 38-40 and 44-40 Winchester patterns. Virtually all were made as sporting rifles, with 24-28in octagonal barrels, though a few short-barreled guns are known and a special Light Carbine appeared in small numbers. Weights ranged from 5.25lb to 7.5lb. A typical 38-40 example measured 43.75in overall, had a 28in barrel rifled with four grooves, and weighed 8.85lb. Open Rocky Mountain sights were standard.

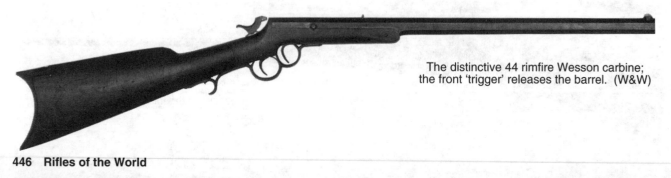

The distinctive 44 rimfire Wesson carbine; the front 'trigger' releases the barrel. (W&W)

The pivoting-lever extractor was better than most Remington designs, but omitting a Remington-type locking bar was much less desirable: the Whitney hammer could fall from full-cock even if the breech piece was open. A main-spring roller and a mechanical firing-pin retractor were added in 1886, but few of the perfected guns were made before Whitney was bought by Winchester in 1888.

WHITNEY-PHOENIX PATTERNS

The Phoenix rifle had a side-hinged breechblock, lifting up and to the right for loading, which contained the firing pin and its coil spring. The massive wrought-iron receiver was cut to accommodate the transverse breechblock and the centrally-hung hammer. A mechanical extractor was fitted, but extraction was poor and many modifications were made. The original breech-locking catch was let into the standing breech on the left side of the hammer, but was soon moved to the front right side of the receiver.

PHOENIX MILITARY MODEL

Made by the Whitney Arms Company, Whitneyville, Connecticut, about 1877-80.

Total production: not known. **Chambering options:** 43 Spanish, 45-70 Government or 50-70 Government. **Action:** the laterally pivoting breech-block was locked by the hammer.

DATA FOR A TYPICAL RIFLE

Chambering: 45-70 Government, rimmed. 50.65in overall, 9lb empty. 35in barrel, 4-groove rifling; RH, concentric. Ramp-and-leaf rear sight graduated to 1200yd. 1320 fps with 405-grain bullet. M1873 socket bayonet.

The Phoenix was available as a rifle—with a full-length forend and three screw-clamped barrel bands—or as a 7lb cavalry carbine with a single band and a ring-and-bar assembly on the right side of the receiver. It was unpopular, owing to a tendency for the breech to jam when hot, and never attracted the interest of a major army. Most rifles accepted standard socket bayonets, but Whitney advertised a brass-hilted sabre pattern as an optional accessory.

PHOENIX SPORTING RIFLE

Made by the Whitney Arms Company, Whitneyville, Connecticut, about 1877-88.

Total production: not known. **Chambering options:** 38 Long, 38-40 Winchester, 40-50 Sharps (necked or straight), 40-70 Sharps (necked or straight), 44-60 Sharps (necked), 44-77 Sharps (necked), 44-90 Sharps (necked), 44-100 Remington, 45-70 Government or 50-70 Government. **Action:** as Military Model, above.

DATA FOR A TYPICAL RIFLE

Chambering: 40-70 Sharps (straight), rimmed. 41.65in overall, 7.85lb empty. 26in barrel, 4-groove rifling; RH, concentric. Spring-leaf and elevator rear sight. 1260 fps with 330-grain bullet.

By 1880, the Phoenix sporter was being made in styles ranging from a plain hunter's gun with a round barrel and open sights to decorative guns supplied to order. Barrels measured 26-32in, and weights ranging from 7.5lb to 10lb. A carbine with a 20in barrel was also available.

SIMILAR GUNS

Phoenix Schuetzen rifle, about 1884-8. Made only for the 38 Ballard Extra Long and 40-50 Sharps (straight) cartridges, this had adjustable Vernier peep-and-globe sights. Checkering lay on the butt-wrist and forend, the butt had a cheekpiece, and a hooked Swiss-style shoulder plate was customary. Schuetzen rifles had 30in or 32in partly- or fully-octagonal barrels, and could weigh 12lb.

• Whittemore

James Whittemore, a U.S. Army officer, was responsible for 'Gun No. 36' submitted to the breechloading rifle trials of 1872. Patented in 1870-2, it had a radial-block breech with the hammer, sear and springs mounted on the block unit. It was not successful.

• Wichita

These rifles embody a bolt system with triple lugs and a 60-degree throw. Available separately, the action is neat, sturdy and effectual. All patterns have been available in right- or left-hand versions.

WICHITA CLASSIC SPORTING RIFLE

Made by Wichita Arms, Wichita, Kansas.

Total production: not known. **Chambering options:** see notes. **Action:** locked by lugs on the bolt engaging recesses in the receiver wall as the bolt handle was turned down, and by the bolt-handle base entering its seat.

DATA FOR A TYPICAL CLASSIC RIFLE

Chambering: 243 Winchester, rimless. 41in overall, 8.15lb empty. 21.2in barrel, 6-groove rifling; RH, concentric? Internal box magazine, 2 rounds. Optical sight. 3070 fps with 100-grain bullet.

Introduced in 1977, Wichita Classic Rifles had an octagonal barrel action in a select walnut half-stock with a shallow Monte Carlo comb and a slender pistol grip. The grip and forend had hand-cut checkering with spade bordering. A Niedner steel pistol grip cap and a rubber Pachmayr shoulder pad were standard. Adjustable Canjar triggers were used, and a safety catch lay behind the bolt handle.

Many guns were single-shot, but others had 'blind' magazines within the stock. The most distinctive feature was the action, with a high left side wall and three prominent gas-escape holes on the bolt.

SIMILAR GUNS

Wichita Silhouette rifle. This 1983-vintage introduction could be identified by its gray Fiberthane stock, with a high Monte Carlo comb and an upright pistol grip. The rifle weighed about 9lb owing to its heavyweight 24in barrel. The bolt was fluted.

Wichita Stainless Magnum rifle, 1980-7. These rifles could be obtained in single shot or magazine-fed form, intended for cartridges from 270 Winchester to 458 Winchester Magnum. Made with 22in or 24in barrels, they were 44.8in overall (24in barrel) and weighed 8-8.5lb.

Wichita Varmint rifle. This rifle had a heavyweight 20.2in barrel and weighed about 9lb. Like the Classic, it could be chambered for any cartridge from 17 Remington to 308 Winchester, provided the overall round-length did not exceed 2.8in.

• Wickliffe

Based on the Stevens No. 44-1/2, this dropping-block rifle was patented in 1978 by Triple-S Development Co., Inc., of Wickliffe, Ohio. The Model 76 was announced in 1976 in standard and deluxe grades, chambered for cartridges ranging from 22 Hornet to 45-70; 7mm Remington, 300 Winchester Magnum and 308 Winchester options were added in 1978-9. The standard barrel measured 26in, 22in alternatives being offered in 243 or 308 Winchester only, but production ceased in 1981.

• Wilson & Flather

William Wilson and Henry Flather of Bridesburg, Pennsylvania, were the joint recipients of U.S. patent 49,463 of August 1865. This protected a longitudinally sliding breech bolt or disc, which was unlocked by a pivoting a locking piece upward around a transverse pivot above the chamber. One gun of this type was submitted to the U.S. Army trials of 1865, but was not amongst those that were photographed and the details of its construction remain obscure.

• Winchester, autoloading type

Formed in New Haven, Connecticut, in 1866, the Winchester Repeating Arms Company succeeded the moribund New Haven Arms Company—and, therefore, to the traditions of the Volcanic Repeating Arms Company. Volcanic had made a lever-action repeater firing primer-propellant ammunition, doomed by its low power. However, this gun was refined into the Henry Rifle, chambering a more powerful rimfire cartridge; and then the Henry, suitably improved, became the Winchester Model 1866.

The Model 1873 and strengthened guns patented by John Browning (q.v.) in the 1880s brought Winchester tremendous success. Work continued after World War I, creating the Model 54 and Model 70 bolt-action rifles, until war began again in 1941.

The success of the Browning-designed 22 rimfire autoloaders made by Fabrique Nationale persuaded Winchester to develop comparable guns. Credited to Thomas C. Johnson, the M1903 was also a low powered 22 rimfire. Though it inspired centerfire derivatives, the reliance on blowback operation meant that the guns could only chamber cartridges which generated too little power to commend expensive Winchesters to huntsmen.

The French purchased a few Winchester autoloaders during the early stages of World War I to arm aviators and balloonists, who appreciated their handiness and firepower, though the magazine capacity was too limited to be truly useful in combat. No other substantial military sales have ever been authenticated,

The perfected prototype of the Winchester 'Cal. .30 Light Rifle'.

though the 351-caliber M1907 rifle, in particular, was quite popular with North American police.

Unqualified success awaited the appearance of the Winchester Light Rifle, which became the M1 Carbine. Though this was criticized for its short-range and poor hitting power compared with the M1 Garand, production of millions testified to the efficiency of the basic action.

Efforts were concentrated on sporting guns after 1945, but the company's fortunes declined appreciably in the 1960s in the face of an ill-judged change to the Model 70 and ever-increasing competition from Remington, Ruger and others. In 1983, Olin Corporation sold the Winchester gunmaking business to the U.S. Repeating Rifle Company. Under more efficient management, the Winchester reputation has been restored to much of its former glory.

Note: All Winchester center-fire barrels made after July 1905 (October 1908 for rimfire patterns) bore the company proof mark, 'WP' in an oval; this was added to receivers from July 1908 onward. 'P' in an oval, used from June 1915, indicated that the guns had been sold through the company's mail order department.

MILITARY WEAPONS

In the autumn of 1937, the Chief of Infantry suggested that the Army needed a light semi-automatic rifle with an effective range of 300yd—more potent than a pistol, but useful to men who did not need the hitting power of the new M1 Garand. The major criteria had been established by 1938: caliber to be greater than 25, weight not more than 5lb, semi-automatic (preferable) or bolt-action, a magazine containing five or seven rounds, and a fixed aperture sight.

In June 1940, the Chief of Ordnance was asked to expedite development of the light rifle as 500,000 were required immediately. Working with Winchester, the Ordnance Department staff proposed a new rimless 30 cartridge with a 110-grain bullet capable of attaining 2000 fps at the muzzle. The perfected 'Cartridge, Caliber 30 SL, M1' was standardized on 30th September. Requests for suitable rifles were circulated from 1st October 1940, and, by the beginning of May 1941, nine had been submitted for testing. Preliminary trials soon showed that only the Garand-designed Springfield Light Rifle—with a top-mounted box magazine and downward ejection—and George Hyde's distinctive pistol gripped gas-operated gun (submitted by Bendix) showed real promise.

M1 CARBINE

Made by the Winchester Repeating Arms Company, New Haven, Connecticut (828,060, 1942-5); by the Inland Manufacturing Division of the General Motors Corporation, Dayton, Ohio (2.324-2.642 million, depending on estimates, 1942-5); by the Rock-Ola Company, Chicago, Illinois (228,500, 1942-4); by the Quality Hardware & Machine Company, Chicago, Illinois (359,660, 1942-4); by the Irwin-Pedersen Arms Company, Grand Rapids, Michigan

(1,000, 1942, see notes); by the Underwood-Elliott-Fisher Company, Hartford, Connecticut (545,620, 1942-4); by the Rochester Defense Corporation, Rochester, New York (see National Postal Meter); by the Standard Products Company, Port Clinton, Ohio (247,160, 1942-4); by International Business Machines Corporation, Poughkeepsie, New York (346,500, 1943-4); by the Saginaw Steering Gear Division of the General Motors Corporation, Saginaw and Grand Rapids, Michigan (517,210, 1943-4); and by the National Postal Meter Company, Rochester, New York (413,020, 1943-4). **Total production:** 6.01-6.23 million M1, M2 and M3 Carbines for the U.S. armed forces. **Chambering:** 30 M1 Carbine, rimless. **Action:** locked by lugs on the bolt engaging the receiver; gas operated, semi-automatic.
DATA FOR POST-1943 M1 CARBINE

35.65in overall, 5.42lb without magazine. 18in barrel, 4-groove rifling; RH, concentric. Detachable box magazine, 15 or 30 rounds. Rear sight: see notes. 1900 fps with M1 Carbine ball cartridges. M4 knife bayonet.

A prototype Winchester reached Aberdeen Proving Ground on 9th August 1941, performing so well that work on an improved version began immediately. Six differing guns entered the trials that began on 15th September, but the Winchester passed its tests with flying colors and the improved Springfield Light Rifle (Garand)—which would have prevailed—was abandoned. On 30th September 1940, the Winchester design was recommended for immediate adoption; formal approval was forthcoming on 22nd October and the gun was standardized as the 'Carbine, Caliber 30, M1'. The initial requirement was set at 886,698 guns and, in November, contracts were placed with Winchester and the Inland Manufacturing Division of General Motors.

The M1 Carbine amalgamated a rotating-bolt action, adapted from an experimental Jonathan Browning rifle submitted to the U.S. Marine Corps, with a short-stroke piston credited to David Marshall Williams.

Gas bled from the bore struck a tappet back about .44in, transferring energy to the spring-loaded operating slide that unlocked the bolt. The bolt ran back to eject the spent case and cock the hammer, then returned to strip a new cartridge into the chamber. The locking lugs were engaged at the end of the return stroke.

The M1 Carbine had a pistol grip half-stock, with a screwed band retained by a spring let into the forend and a handguard running forward from the receiver ring. The magazine protruded ahead of the trigger guard web, which contained a cross-bolt safety catch. A swivel on the left side of the band was used in conjunction with a slot cut through the butt. The earliest guns had a two-position pivoting rear sight, and lacked the bayonet-lug assembly beneath the muzzle.

On 25th March 1942, Winchester licensed rights for the M1 Carbine to the U.S. government. By February, requirements had risen to 1.1 million, and five additional contractors had been recruited—Rock-Ola, the Quality Hardware & Machine Company, Irwin-Pedersen Arms Company, Underwood-Elliott-Fisher, and the Rochester Defense Corporation.

The M1 Carbine.

By the beginning of June 1942, however, only Inland had delivered guns. But this did not prevent the Army Supply Program from calculating the carbine requirements as an astonishing 4.47 million. In a third wave of expansion in August 1942, therefore, the Standard Products Company was awarded a contract to make carbines at an unprecedented rate of 45,000 per month and had delivered 111,600 by the end of the year. Inland had supplied 97,920, reaching the desired one thousand daily target by 31st December. Winchester's 1942 contribution had been 10,310, which left 3080 from Underwood and a handful from Rock-Ola and Quality Hardware.

Recruited in another wave of expansion in the Spring of 1943, International Business Machines Corporation and the Saginaw Steering Gear Division of General Motors were expected to contribute 60,000 guns per month.

The problematical Irwin-Pedersen contract and the company's Grand Rapids factory were then transferred to the General Motors Saginaw Division; all but one thousand Irwin-Pedersen marked carbines were assembled under Saginaw control. National Postal Meter, an original promoter of the Rochester Defense Corporation, began producing Carbines on its own account in February 1943; Saginaw Steering Gear's first gun appeared in May, followed by Standard Products in June and IBM in August.

After the rejection of the M1A2 (see below), the M1 receiver was adapted to accept the T21 rear sight. The magazine-retaining plunger was modified, and a new safety catch was substituted for the original sliding pattern.

By 31st December 1943, with all nine facilities participating, nearly three million guns had been delivered; Carbines were being made at a rate of more than 500,000 per month. As production was rapidly outstripping predictions, the projected Army Supply Program requirement was slashed and production at six factories stopped on 30th April 1944. Rock-Ola completed work on 31st May, leaving only Inland and Winchester making the guns.

The Bayonet-Knife M4—known during development as 'T8E1'—was approved on 10th May 1944, with a new front-band assembly incorporating a bayonet lug. This modification soon became mandatory on guns returning for repair.

By 1945, carbine production had exceeded six million. Most markings were self explanatory. However, Winchester barrels could bear 'WRA' (early), 'W' or 'PW'. Standard Products receivers displayed 'STD. PRO.' while Saginaw Steering Gear guns were marked SAGINAW S.G. (Saginaw factory) or SAGINAW S'G' (Grand Rapids factory)—though a few early Grand Rapids guns displayed IRWIN-PEDERSEN.

The oldest National Postal Meter guns were marked ROCHESTER and a few hundred displayed 'CCC' for 'Commercial Controls Corporation'. Barrels usually came from Underwood. Quality Hardware Carbines sometimes incorporated receivers made by the Union Switch & Signal Company, marked UN-QUALITY; barrels usually came from Rock-Ola. Some IBM receivers were made by Auto-Ordnance and could bear 'AO'.

Some published procurement figures show Inland production between January 1942 and July 1944 as only 1,412,691. Though one source suggests that no fewer than 754,406 carbines were made in 1945, others are much less generous and it has proved difficult to verify the final total.

SIMILAR GUNS

M1A2 Carbine. Known during development as 'M1E2' and standardized in January 1943, this was designed to overcome the limitations of the rocking-'L' rear sight. However, as the adjustable T21 rear sight required modifications to the receiver, adoption of the M1A2 was rescinded in November. The new rear sight was simply adapted to fit the standard M1.

M1E5 Carbine. This was an unsuccessful experimental pattern made largely from Arma-Steel castings.

M1E6 Carbine. Used by Frankford Arsenal for testing propellant, this had an unusually long barrel.

M1E7 Carbine. Distinguished by a Weaver M73B1 telescope sight, this was optimistically intended as a sniper's rifle. The poor ballistics of the 30 M1 cartridge restricted effective range too greatly.

Corporal Jerry Baum and Master Sergeant Eugene Savage of the 65th AAA Battalion, Ryukyus Command, Okinawa, fire the M1 Carbine 'for record' on the rifle range, 1st August 1952. US Army photograph.

M1 CARBINE
Folding-butt patterns
Made by the Inland Manufacturing Division of the General Motors Corporation, Dayton, Ohio, 1944-5.

Total production: 150,000? **Chambering:** 30 M1 Carbine, rimless. **Action:** as standard M1 Carbine, above.

DATA FOR M1A1

25.4in overall (folded), 6.2lb with empty magazine. 18in barrel, 4-groove rifling; RH, concentric. Detachable box magazine, 15 or 30 rounds. Ramp-mounted aperture sight graduated to 300yd. 1970 fps with M1 Carbine ball cartridges. M4 knife bayonet.

Experimental collapsible-stock carbines were developed in 1943 by Inland (known as M1E1) and Springfield Armory (M1E3 folding or M1E4 sliding), Springfield patterns being strengthened to withstand grenade launching. Though the M1E1 and M1E3 were standardized as the M1A1 and M1A3, only the former was made in quantity. It had a pistol grip and a skeletal butt with a reinforcing plate.

Made exclusively by Inland with the assistance of Royal Typewriters, Inc., 92,380 M1A1 Carbines had been delivered by July 1944. Work is believed to have continued into 1945, though the final total is not known.

M2 CARBINE
Made by the Winchester Repeating Arms Company, New Haven, Connecticut (17,500, 1944-5); and by the Inland Manufacturing Division of the General Motors Corporation, Dayton, Ohio (225,000, 1944-5?).

Production total: about 242,500. **Chambering:** 30 M1 Carbine, rimless. **Action:** as standard M1 Carbine, above.

35.65in overall, 5.65lb with empty magazine. 18in barrel, 4-groove rifling; RH, concentric. Detachable box magazine, 30 rounds. Ramp-mounted aperture sight graduated to 300yd. 1970 fps with M1 Carbine ball cartridges; 700-800 rds/min. M4 knife bayonet.

This was standardized on 23rd October 1944 on the basis of the experimental Inland T4 pattern. It had a new 30-round box magazine, and a selector on the left rear of the receiver to disengage the sear during automatic fire. M2 Carbines were made exclusively by Inland and Winchester, though a T17 field-conversion kit allowed M1 guns to be altered to M2 standards.

M3 CARBINE
Made by the Winchester Repeating Arms Company, New Haven, Connecticut (1110 in 1945); and by the Inland Manufacturing Division of the General Motors Corporation, Dayton, Ohio (810 in 1945).

Production total: 1920. **Chambering:** 30 M1 Carbine, rimless. Otherwise generally as M2 Carbine, excepting the omission of a rear sight.

Known during development as 'T3', this an M2 adapted for the infra-red Sniperscope M2 standardized in August 1945. The

The M3 Carbine, known during development as the 'T3', with a flash-hider and the bulky infra-red SniperScope.

infra-red lamp lay beneath the forend on the first guns, ahead of the lamp-actuating trigger, but was soon moved above it. Very few M3/Sniperscope combinations were made, owing to the end of hostilities and poor handling characteristics.

M1 CARBINES ABROAD

The tremendous quantities of M1 and M2 carbines made during World War II enabled weapons to be supplied to many foreign powers under the U.S. Military Aid Programs. Virtually all of these guns were military surplus, bearing their original U.S. military marks and numbers unless specifically defaced.

The most important recipients were South Korea and South Vietnam, acquiring 1.09 million and nearly 800,000 M1/M2 Carbines respectively in 1950-75. The guns were ideally suited to men of small stature. However, large numbers were also used in Taiwan (about 179,000); the Netherlands (170,000); Italy (159,000); France (155,000); Norway (98,000); Thailand (73,000); the Federal Republic of Germany (34,000); Uruguay (about 33,000); Greece (30,000); Burma (29,000); and Indonesia (21,000). Austria and Belgium also issued substantial quantities, believed to have run into tens of thousands.

The outstanding success of the M1 Carbine, and the ready availability of spare parts, has also persuaded manufacturers to offer guns commercially—e.g., Howa, Iver Johnson, Johnson Automatics, National Ordnance, Plainfield, and Universal.

SPORTING GUNS

MODEL 1903 SPORTING RIFLE

Made by the Winchester Repeating Arms Company, New Haven, Connecticut, 1903-32.

Total production: 126,000. **Chambering:** 22 Winchester Automatic Smokeless. **Action:** no mechanical breech lock; blowback, semi-automatic only.

DATA FOR STANDARD SPORTING RIFLE

38.2in overall, 5.75lb empty. 20in barrel, 6-groove rifling; RH, concentric. Tube magazine in butt, 10 rounds. Spring-and-slider rear sight. 1055 fps with 45-grain bullet.

Designed by Thomas C. Johnson, this concealed-hammerless gun was introduced in the summer of 1904, with a loading port on the right side of the butt. Most butts had plain straight wrists, though a few fancy rifles were made with selected walnut pistol grip butts and checkering. The action was cocked by pressing back on a rod protruding from the forend beneath the barrel.

After about 5000 guns had been made, a separate trigger lock was added to eliminate 'doubling' (firing a second shot for one press on the trigger). The firing pin was changed from bronze to steel in 1906 to reduce breakages, but few other changes were required during a 30-year production life.

SIMILAR GUNS

Model 63 rifle, 1933-58. An improved form of the M1903, chambering the popular 22LR rimfire cartridge, this was offered only in 'sporting rifle' form with plain walnut woodwork and a 20in barrel. A 23in barrel was introduced in December 1934, the shorter option being discontinued in 1936. The take-down screw locking catch was eliminated in December 1933 after a few thousand guns had been made, and post-1946 receivers were grooved to accept optical-sight mounting bases. Production totaled 174,700.

New Model 63 rifle. A 're-creation' of the original gun was announced in 1997, in Grade I (standard) and High Grade (deluxe) patterns. The standard gun has a plain walnut half-stock and forend, with subdued engraving on the grayed steel receiver; the deluxe version has select woodwork, checkering on the pistol grip and forend, and gold-inlaid bordered game scenes on the receiver. Available only in 22LR rimfire, the guns are 39in long, have 23in barrels and weigh 6.25lb.

MODEL 1905 SPORTING RIFLE

Made by the Winchester Repeating Arms Company, New Haven, Connecticut, 1905-19.

Total production: 29,110. **Chambering options:** 32 or 35 Winchester Self Loading. **Action:** as M1903, above.

DATA FOR A TYPICAL 32-CALIBER EXAMPLE

About 40in overall, 7.57lb empty. 22in barrel, 6-groove rifling; RH, concentric. Spring-leaf and elevator sight. Detachable box magazine, 5 rounds. 1400 fps with 165-grain bullet.

Delivered into stock in August 1905, made only in take-down style, this was simply a centerfire enlargement of the M1903. The general appearance of the earlier gun was retained, with a straight-wrist butt and a half-length forend. A cocking rod protruded from the forend tip, an ejection port lay on the right side of the receiver above the magazine, and a safety catch appeared on the trigger guard. Standard guns had plain woodwork, with a rubber buttplate, but select-walnut butts could be ordered. A pistol grip was standardized in 1908, and an optional 10-round magazine was introduced in October 1911.

MODEL 1907 SPORTING RIFLE

Made by the Winchester Repeating Arms Company, New Haven, Connecticut, 1906-57 (see notes).

Total production: 58,490. **Chambering:** 351 Winchester Self Loading, semi-rim. **Action:** as M1905, above.

About 39.5in overall, 7.81lb empty. 20in barrel, 6-groove rifling; RH, concentric. Spring-leaf and elevator rear sight. Detachable box magazine, 5 rounds. 1850 fps with 180-grain bullet.

Delivered into factory stock in November 1906, this had a plain pistol grip butt with a rubber buttplate, and a distinctive ribbed band at the tip of the forend. Fancy Sporting Rifles were offered with selected woodwork and special finishes, and an optional 10-round magazine appeared in October 1911. A police-style butt and forend were approved for the standard rifle in December 1937, but work ceased when war began in December 1941. A projection was added to the cocking rod in mid-summer 1948, when the magazine-release button was enlarged, and the last guns were sold from store in 1957.

SIMILAR GUNS

Police Model, 1934-7. Distinguished by a special pistol grip butt and a broad or semi-beavertail forend, this also had a checkered steel buttplate. Swivels were standard fittings, and a knife or sword bayonet could be provided.

MODEL 1910 SPORTING RIFLE

Made by the Winchester Repeating Arms Company, New Haven, Connecticut, 1910-36.

Total production: 20,790. **Chambering:** 401 Winchester Self Loading, semi-rim. **Action:** as M1905, above.

About 39.5in overall, 8.22lb empty. 20in barrel, 6-groove rifling; RH, concentric. Spring-leaf and elevator sight. Detachable box magazine, 4 rounds. 2135 fps with 200-grain bullet.

Derived from the 1907 pattern, this appeared in Spring of 1910 with a special cartridge which explored the blowback action to its limits. The M1910 was practically identical externally with the M1907, but had a larger ejection port. The standard rifle had a plain pistol grip butt with a rubber buttplate, and a half-length forend from which the cocking rod protruded. Selected stocks and butts, often finely checkered, could be supplied to order.

MODEL 74 AUTOMATIC RIFLE

Made by the Winchester Repeating Arms Company, New Haven, Connecticut, 1939-55.

Total production: 406,600. **Chambering options:** 22 Short or 22 Long Rifle rimfire. **Action:** no mechanical breech lock; blowback, semi-automatic.

46.2in overall, 6.25lb empty. 24in barrel, 6- or 4-groove rifling; RH, concentric. Tube magazine in butt, 14 (22LR) or 20 (22 Short) rounds. Spring-and-slider rear sight. 1080 fps with 40-grain bullet.

A simplified design with a conventional bolt reciprocating within a tubular receiver, this was cocked with a handle on the right side of the action and loaded through a port in the right side of the butt. Dismantling was particularly easy, as the bolt could be removed in a single piece. Distribution was hindered by the start of World War II, but the Model 74 went on to be a great success. The standard pattern had a plain walnut pistol grip half-stock with a broad or semi-beavertail forend.

THE GUNS

Model 74 rifle, 1939-42 and 1946-55. The first guns chambered the 22 Short rimfire cartridge, as the 22LR option did not appear until 1940. The last 22 Short examples were made in 1952.

Model 74 Gallery Special Rifle, 1939-42. Chambered only for the 22 Short cartridge, this was customarily found with a sheet-steel deflector fixed to the receiver to divert ejected cases forward and down. Gallery rifles could be obtained in two different chromium-plated styles.

Model 77 rifle (i), 1941. A few of these were made for evaluation with the U.S. Marine Corps immediately after the Japanese attack on Pearl Harbor. They were based on the Model 74, but had a heavy barrel, an elongated forend and a detachable eight-round box magazine. Priorities were eventually allocated elsewhere.

MODEL 77 SPORTING RIFLE

Made by the Winchester Repeating Arms Company, New Haven, Connecticut, 1955-63.

Total production: 217,200. **Chambering:** 22 Long Rifle, rimfire. **Action:** as Model 74, above.

40.35in overall, 5.55lb empty. 22in barrel, 6-groove rifling; RH, concentric. Detachable box magazine (8 rounds), or tube magazine under the barrel (15 rounds). Spring-and-slider rear sight. 1080 fps with 40-grain bullet.

This stylish autoloader offered a choice of magazines. A safety catch lay on the right side of the receiver, rails for optical-sight mounts were machined into the receiver-top, and the plain walnut half-stock had a semi-beavertail forend. The buttplate was a checkered composition type. The trigger guard and floorplate were nylon. Box-magazine guns soon proved to be less popular than their tube-magazine rivals, and were abandoned in 1962.

MODEL 55 SPORTING RIFLE

Made by the Winchester Repeating Arms Company, New Haven, Connecticut, 1957-61.

Total production: 45,100. **Chambering options:** 22 Short, 22 Long or 22 Long Rifle rimfire. **Action:** as Model 74, above.

41.6in overall, 5.25lb empty. 22in barrel, 6-groove rifling; RH, concentric. Single-shot only. Spring-and-slider rear sight. 1080 fps with 40-grain bullet.

This quirky rifle was an auto-ejector, each round being loaded manually through the top of the action before closing the chamber. Spent cases were ejected downward through the a port cut in the stock. The plain walnut pistol grip half-stock had a stamped-strip trigger guard. Though elegant and competitively priced, the lack of a magazine undoubtedly restricted sales.

MODEL 100 SPORTING RIFLE

Made by the Winchester Repeating Arms Company, New Haven, Connecticut, 1960-73.

Total production: about 263,000. **Chambering options:** 243 Winchester, 284 Winchester or 308 Winchester. **Action:** locked by lugs on the bolt rotating into the barrel extension; gas operated, semi-automatic only.

DATA FOR A TYPICAL EXAMPLE

Chambering: 308 Winchester, rimless. 42in overall, 7.48lb empty. 22in barrel, 6-groove rifling; RH, concentric. Folding-leaf rear sight. Detachable box magazine, 4 rounds. 2610 fps with 180-grain bullet.

Delivered into stock at the end of 1960, this hammerless side-ejector shared the lines of the lever-action Model 88 (q.v.). It had a one-piece stock, with basket-weave checkering on the pistol grip and round-tip forend. Synthetic buttplates and pistol grip caps were fitted; swivels lay beneath the forend and butt. The front-sight lay on a hooded ramp. A detachable four-round box magazine (three rounds in 284) lay directly under the ejection port and the safety bolt ran through the front trigger guard web.

SIMILAR GUNS

Model 100 Carbine, 1963-73. Mechanically identical with the rifle, this had a 19in barrel, a plain pistol grip stock, and a band around the forend carrying the front swivel.

MODEL 290 SPORTING RIFLE

Made by the Winchester Repeating Arms Company, New Haven, Connecticut, 1963-77.

Total production: said to have been 2.15 million (including M190). **Chambering options:** 22 Long and Long Rifle rimfire, interchangeably. **Action:** no mechanical lock; blowback, semi-automatic only.

39.5in overall, about 5lb empty. 20.5in barrel, 4-groove rifling; RH, concentric. Tube magazine beneath barrel, 15-17 rounds depending on cartridge length. Spring-leaf and elevator rear sight. 1080 fps with 40-grain bullet.

Introduced to accompany the Models 250 (lever action) and 270 (slide action), this autoloader had a round-backed aluminum alloy receiver. The hardwood butt and forend were stained to mimic walnut, though pre-1965 guns sometimes had an optional Cycolac forend. The front sight was mounted on a ramp, and a safety bolt ran laterally through the front web of the trigger guard. Impressed checkering within a decorative border was added to the pistol grip and forend in 1966. White plastic spacer plates were subsequently inserted between the woodwork and the pistol grip cap and buttplate.

SIMILAR GUNS

Model 190 rifle, 1967-78. Offered with a plain straight-comb butt, checkering being omitted to reduce manufacturing costs, this gun was numbered in the same series as the original plain-butt 290. Consequently, the two can be difficult to distinguish.

Model 190 Carbine, 1967-73. This was little more than a Model 190 with a carbine-type forend, identified by an encircling swivel-carrying band.

Model 290 Deluxe rifle, 1965-75. Made with a selected walnut butt, with a fluted Monte Carlo comb and a low-relief cheekpiece, this autoloader also had machine-cut basket-weave checkering on the pistol grip and the forend. Sling swivels lay beneath the butt and forend.

Model 490 rifle, 1975-7. An improved 290, this had a one-piece walnut half-stock with a straight-comb butt and checkering on the pistol grip and the sides of the round-tipped forend. The detachable box magazine and folding Williams-type rear sight help to distinguish this particular gun, but comparatively few were ever made.

• Winchester, block-action type

In 1883, Winchester bought manufacturing rights to the Browning (q.v.) dropping-block rifle and embarked on changes which culminated in a considerable improvement on the basic design. The best source of information about the many changes made to the Model 1885 is *The Winchester Single-Shot—a history & analysis* by John Campbell (Andrew Mowbray, 1995).

MODEL 1885 SPORTING RIFLE
High Wall and Low Wall patterns

Made by the Winchester Repeating Arms Company, New Haven, Connecticut, 1885-1919.

Total production: 139,730 (all types). **Chambering options:** see notes. **Action:** locked by closing a lever combined with the trigger guard to raise a block vertically behind the breech.

DATA FOR A TYPICAL SCHUETZEN PATTERN

Chambering: 38-55 Winchester, rimmed. 50.5in overall, 12.41lb empty. 30in barrel, 6-groove rifling; RH, concentric. Vernier sight on tang, graduated to 1200yd. 1320 fps with 255-grain bullet.

The centerfire Plain Sporting Rifle built on the 'No. 3 action' was advertised for the first time in 1885, with an octagonal barrel, a plain walnut straight-wrist butt, steel ('rifle type') or rubber ('shotgun type') shoulder plates, a schnabel-tipped forend and a simple trigger. Rear sights were open spring-leaf and elevator 'Rocky Mountain' patterns. Panels were milled out of the receiver sides from 1886, saving weight and material, and barrels were eventually made in octagon, half-octagon and round versions ranging from No. 1/2 to No. 6.

Chamberings came in amazing variety: the original November 1885 catalogue listed 22 Winchester, 32-20 Winchester, 32-40 Winchester, 38-55 Ballard, 40-50 Sharps, 40-60 Marlin, 40-60 Winchester, 40-70 Ballard, 40-90 Sharps, 40-90 Ballard, 44-40 Winchester, 44-60 Winchester, 44-77 Sharps, 45-60 Winchester, 45-75 Sharps, 45-70 Government, 45-100 Sharps and 50-90 Sharps. John Campbell lists 14 rimfire and more than 80 centerfire chamberings from 22 Short to 577 Eley.

The first 22 rimfire guns were made in May 1886, built on the 'No. 2' or low-wall action designed to facilitate loading small-caliber cartridges. Apart from a reduction in the height of metal alongside the breechblock, however, the No. 2 was identical with the standard No. 3 (or 'High Wall'). A single set trigger was made with a small adjusting screw behind the trigger lever, and there was also a unique 'close-coupled' mechanism (introduced in 1894) with two triggers set so closely that they appeared to touch.

Color case-hardening of the frames, no longer standard after 1890, was replaced by heat treatment and rust bluing. However, older actions could be returned to New Haven for refurbishment and the distinction is often blurred.

Rifles intended for smokeless cartridges had nickel-steel barrels, their breechblocks had a gas-escape port in the top surface, and several chamberings (e.g., 30-06) had a pivoting-plate safety interlock in the hammer body to intercept the receiver if gas-blast should force the hammer back prematurely. The advent of the rimless cartridges required a new extractor, developed by Frank Burton, to be set into the inner left wall of the receiver.

A change was made in 1908 to the mainspring assembly, when the leaf anchored to the underside of the barrel became a coil looped under the hammer body, around each side of the hammer-pivot pin, and up into the breechblock. A small spring-and-plunger in the receiver immediately beneath the chamber held the operating lever closed.

A take-down system, based on a patent granted to Thomas Johnson in May 1907, was introduced commercially in June 1910. The barrel and forend, held in the receiver by an interrupted-screw connection, were removed by releasing the locking catch and twisting them anti-clockwise through 90 degrees. The receivers of these guns customarily lacked milled-out side panels.

Single-shot M1885 actions have been chambered for a wide variety of non-Winchester and 'wildcat' cartridges. Typical of the non-Winchester chamberings were 25-20 Single Shot, 25-25 Stevens, 303 (British), 30-40 Krag, 32 Ideal and 50-90 Sharps—all originating prior to 1920—but many of the wildcats (e.g. 22 R-2 Lovell, 219 Wasp or 219 Improved Zipper) were developed long after the rifle had been discontinued.

SIMILAR GUNS

Note: A smooth-bore 20-gauge shotgun was built on the No. 3 Action from 1914-19. It can be distinguished by the absence of rifling.

International Match Rifle, 1909-14? A few of these guns—perhaps 30-50—were made prior to World War I. They had 30in round barrels, carbine-style single band forends, handguards above the barrel, and a Krag-type rear sight. A cork-bottomed palm-rest block was made as an integral part of the forend and a close-coupled double set trigger mechanism was fitted.

Lightweight Carbine, 1898-1905. Built on the No. 2 (low-wall) action, this was offered only in 32-30, 38-40 and 44-40 WCF. It had a 15in or 16in barrel, a straight-wrist stock, and a sling ring on the left side of the receiver.

Military Musket. A 45-70 musket with a military-style stock was touted briefly in the autumn of 1886, but attracted little attention and was soon abandoned. However, full-stock 22 RF guns were made with 28in round barrels for 'military indoor target shooting and preliminary outdoor practice' from 1886 until 1920. They included the special 'Winder Musket', named after its pro-

moter, which was introduced in 1905 in 22 Short and 22 Long Rifle. The original Winder guns had their full-length forends held by two bands, and had Hotchkiss-type rear sights; a one-band design with a finger groove in the 'bellied' forend and a Krag-type sight was substituted late in 1911; and a perfected design with a Lyman No. 53 rear sight and the receiver walls milled down to facilitate loading appeared in 1918.

Schuetzen Rifle, 1897-1919. Offered with a 30in No. 3 or No. 4 barrel, weighing 12lb or 13lb respectively, this had checkered pistol grip butt with a Swiss-pattern cheekpiece, a hooked Helm-pattern buttplate, and a double set trigger mechanism. The finger-lever had an extended spur, and a palm-rest lay beneath the forend. A mid-range Vernier peep sight lay on the tang behind the hammer. Changes were made in 1910, when the Johnson take-down system was adopted, the buttplate was changed to the Laudensack type (with a straight upper hook), and a Winchester A-5 telescope sight replaced the Vernier peep.

Standard or Military carbine. A few of these were made on the No. 3 action, with a 24in barrel, a half-length forend held by a single band, and a handguard above the barrel running from the receiver to the band. Krag-type rear sights were used. Chamberings are said to include 7x57, 30-40, 7.65x53 and 8x57, but the carbines were presumably made for military trials and other versions may exist.

Special Single Shot [Target] Rifle, 1886-1910. This was introduced with a 30in octagon barrel, a walnut pistol grip butt with a 'Swiss' cheekpiece and a short hooked buttplate. The frame was case-hardened, a single trigger was fitted, and mid-range Vernier peep and globe sights were fitted to the tang and muzzle respectively.

Special Sporting Rifle, 1887-1915. This was a deluxe version of the basic sporter, with a 'fancy walnut checkered pistol-hand butt'. The pistol grip originally had an ebony insert, but later guns had a rubber pistol grip cap. Half-octagon and round barrels, Vernier peep sights and palm rests were among the optional accessories; some guns were engraved, and others had special checkering patterns or selected woodwork.

• Winchester, bolt-action type

MODEL 1900 SPORTING RIFLE

Made by the Winchester Repeating Arms Company, New Haven, Connecticut, 1899-1902.

Total production: 105,000. **Chambering options:** 22 BB Cap, 22 CB Cap, 22 Short and 22 Long rimfire (interchangeable). **Action:** locked by the base of the bolt handle turning down in front of the receiver bridge.

DATA FOR STANDARD RIFLE

33.3in overall, 2.75lb empty. 18in barrel, 6-groove rifling; RH, concentric. Single-shot only. Fixed open rear sight. 1055 fps with 29-grain bullet.

Refined for series production by Winchester engineers, this Browning design was made in accordance with a patent granted in August 1899. It was a simple take-down design, cocked by retracting the cocking piece manually, but sold amazingly well.

The bolt could not be opened after cocking until the cocking piece fell. The plain hardwood stock lacked a buttplate, though ribs were rolled into the end of the stock. The wrist was straight. Experience suggested that the Model 1900 was too light and not sophisticated enough to compete against similar rivals, and it was rapidly superseded by the Model 1902.

SIMILAR GUNS

Note: all these guns would originally handle 22 Short and 22 Long rimfire cartridges interchangeably. Changes were made to accommodate the 22 Extra Long pattern from 1914, but, in 1927, the unpopular Extra Long was abandoned in favor of 22 Long Rifle.

Model 1902 rifle, 1902-28. Derived from the 1900 pattern, this had a heavier barrel, a short-travel trigger, a blued steel buttplate (composition material after 1907), and a rearward spur on the trigger guard forming a rudimentary pistol grip. Weight rose to about 3.15lb. The rear sight was improved by the addition of a peep, though this was reduced to the status of an optional extra in 1904.

Model 1902A rifle, 1928-31. A change was made to the sear in the late 1920s, creating this variant of the original M1902, but the designation was used only until the old-pattern guns had been sold. About 640,300 1902 and 1902A guns were made.

Thumb Trigger rifle (or 'Model 99'), 1904-23. Patented by Thomas G. Bennett, this was essentially similar to the M1902 but fired by pressure on a knurled-top trigger protruding from the stock-wrist behind the cocking piece. This was claimed to prevent a novice shooter from throwing the gun off target, but it is much more likely that the gun sold largely on novelty value. The 'Model 99' designation was added arbitrarily shortly after the end of World War I. There were 75,500 made.

Model 1904 rifle, 1904-28. This was essentially the same as the Model 1902 (q.v.), with a similarly spurred trigger guard, but was 34.25in long, had a 21in barrel and weighed about 4lb empty. The stock had a composition buttplate (hard rubber from 1925) and a noticeable schnabel tip to the forend.

Model 1904A rifle, 1928-31. This was a 'new pattern' rifle embodying a new sear. The designation was used only until Winchester had sold all the original-style guns. Total production of 1904 and 1904A guns amounted to 302,860.

MODEL 43 SPORTING RIFLE

Made by the Winchester Repeating Arms Company, New Haven, Connecticut, 1949-57.

Total production: 62,620. **Chambering options:** 218 Bee, 22 Hornet, 25-20 Winchester or 32-20 Winchester. **Action:** locked by two lugs on the bolt head rotating into the receiver when the bolt handle was turned down.

DATA FOR A TYPICAL RIFLE

Chambering: 218 Bee, rimmed. 43.5in overall, 7.05lb empty. 24in barrel, 6-groove rifling; RH, concentric? Detachable box magazine, 3 rounds. Spring-leaf and elevator rear sight. 2860 fps with 46-grain bullet.

Work on this 'Junior Model 70' began in 1944, but the first guns were not completed until 1949. They had 24in tapered barrels and plain pistol grip half-stocks with round tipped forends. The Special Rifle had checkering on the pistol grip and forend, displayed a separate pistol grip cap, and was often furnished with a Lyman No. 57A Vernier rear sight. Swivels lay beneath the butt and forend. The safety catch lay on the right side of the action, and the position of the bolt handle above the front of the trigger guard—farther forward than on other Winchesters—provided an identifying feature.

MODEL 52 SPORTING RIFLE

Made by the Winchester Repeating Arms Company, New Haven, Connecticut, 1919-79.

Total production: 125,200 (all types). **Chambering:** 22 Long Rifle. **Action:** locked by a single lug rotating into the receiver as the bolt handle was turned down, and by the bolt-handle dropping into its seat.

DATA FOR STANDARD SPORTING RIFLE

42.8in overall, 7.25lb empty. 24in barrel, 6-groove rifling; RH, concentric. Detachable box magazine, 5 or 10 rounds. Aperture rear sight on the receiver bridge. 1080 fps with 40-grain bullet.

The Model 52, patented by Thomas C. Johnson in 1919-20, owed its introduction to the familiarity gained by many Americans with bolt-action rifles during World War I. A few prototypes were made in 1919 for exhibition at the National Rifle Matches, and the first series-made rifles were delivered into store in the summer of 1920.

The original Model 52 was a simple bolt-action design. It had a 28in barrel with an integrally forged front-sight base, and weighed about 9.8lb. The box magazine was curved to handle the rimmed cartridges, though a Single Loading Adapter was introduced in March 1935.

The receiver originally had a flat top, slotted to receive the No. 82 Winchester rear sight, and the barrel was drilled to accept telescope-sight bases. The walnut half-stock had a plain pistol grip, a steel buttplate, and a finger groove (abandoned in 1932) on the forend. The cocking piece—long and unnecessarily heavy—slowed the travel of the striker, until the lightweight short-head 'Speed Lock' design appeared in August 1929.

THE GUNS

Model 52 Heavy Barrel Target Rifle (sometimes known after 1935 as 'M52A'), 1933-41. The first heavy barrels were tried as early as 1927, though they did not become an optional fitting until 1933. The guns originally had match style-stocks with a broad or semi-beavertail forend. These were replaced in 1936 by the high-comb Marksman stock (later known as the 'Marksman No. 1') for use with aperture or optical sights, and then at the end of 1937 by the Marksman No. 2 pattern with a mid-height comb. Weight averaged 11lb, depending on sights and stock density. Most guns made after the August 1935 had a adjustable five-position sling-swivel base beneath an elongated forend.

Model 52 Repeating Rifle, standard barrel (sometimes known after 1935 as 'M52A'), 1919-37. Described in the text above, this had a 28in barrel. Serial numbers with an 'A' suffix distinguished guns which had been assembled after the introduction of the Model 52B.

Model 52 Sporting Rifle (sometimes known after 1935 as 'M52A'), 1934-7. Offered with a 24in barrel and an integrally forged front-sight ramp, this was customarily fitted with a round-top receiver after 1936. The stock was a lightweight pattern with a cheekpiece on the butt, and checkering on the pistol grip and plastic-tipped forend. The pistol grip cap was hard rubber, and the buttplate was steel.

Model 52 Target Rifle, standard barrel (sometimes known after 1935 as 'M52A'), 1932-6. This had a strengthened receiver and locking lug. The stock had a plain forend, without a finger groove, and sight-bases with notches on the right sight were substituted for the original pattern in 1933; the distance between the mounts was also increased.

Model 52B Bull Gun, 1939-41 and 1945-7. Made with an extra-heavy barrel, this used the plain high-comb Marksman No. 1 stock. It weighed about 13lb.

Model 52B Heavy Barrel Target Rifle, 1937-41 and 1945-6. Distinguished by a large-diameter 28in barrel, this was a heavy version of the standard 52B Target Rifle. It weighed 11-11.5lb.

Model 52B Sporting Rifle, 1935-41 and 1945-7. The earliest guns were made with the flat-top receiver, but a new round-top pattern was introduced in 1936 and gradually replaced the earlier type (though the flat top remained optional until the end of production). The round-top receiver could accept many types of receiver sight. An improved Speed Lock appeared in May 1937; at about the same time, the awkward safety catch on the left side of the breech was replaced by a new pattern on the right side ahead of the bolt handle. Sporting Rifles generally had 24in barrels and lightweight stocks.

Model 52B Target Rifle, 1935-41 and 1945-6. Essentially the 52B action with the 28in standard-weight barrel, this introduced the adjustable sling-swivel assembly and the single shot adapter. Guns may be found with Lyman, Marble-Goss, Redfield or Winchester sights.

Model 52C Bull Barrel, 1952-61. A variation of the 52C target rifle with an ultra-heavy barrel, this could weigh more than 12lb.

Model 52C Heavy Barrel, 1947-61. Little more than a minor variant of the standard target rifle, this had a large-diameter 28in barrel and weighed about 11lb. It also had a refined form of the pre-war Marksman stock.

Model 52C Sporting Rifle, 1947. Only about a hundred of these guns were made, amalgamating the 24in barrel, the lightweight stock, and the adjustable Micro-Motion trigger.

Model 52C Target Rifle, 1947-61. The first of the improved post-war guns, this introduced changes in the receiver and an adjustable 'Micro-Motion' trigger mechanism. The standard pattern, with a 28in barrel, weighed 9.6-9.9lb.

Model 52D rifle, 1961-78. A single-shot derivative of the basic repeating-rifle action, this had a solid receiver floor, a free-floating barrel (standard or heavyweight), an adjustable bedding system, and a new stock with a straight high comb sloping up towards the rear. A new adjustable hand-stop and rail were let into the underside of the forend. Standard guns weighed 9.8lb; heavy-barrel examples weighed 11lb. Barreled actions were offered commercially from 1965 onward.

Model 52 International rifle (or 'International Target'), 1969-78. This was essentially similar to the heavy-barrel M52D, but had a distinctive thumbhole Free Rifle stock of wood laminate. The high comb and adjustable hook-pattern buttplate were accompanied by a rail under the forend for a hand-stop or palm rest. Some guns were fitted with Kenyon triggers, but others had triggers regulated to ISU instead of NRA rules. Blocks for telescope-sight mounts lay on the barrel.

Model 52 International Prone rifle, 1975-88? This was similar to the M52 International, but had a fixed-height detachable comb and a simpler fixed buttplate. A hand-stop was usually fitted to the rail under the forend, which had a sling swivel at its tip.

MODEL 54 SPORTING RIFLE

Made by the Winchester Repeating Arms Company, New Haven, Connecticut, 1925-36.

Total production: 50,150. **Chambering options:** 22 Hornet, 220 Swift, 250-3000 Savage, 257 Roberts, 270 Winchester, 7x57, 7.65x53, 30-06, 30-30 Winchester or 9x57. **Action:** locked by rotating two lugs on the bolt head into the receiver as the bolt was closed, and by a safety lug under the bolt handle entering its seat.

DATA FOR A TYPICAL STANDARD RIFLE

Chambering: 270 Winchester, rimless. 44in overall, about 7.5lb empty. 24in barrel, 6-groove rifling; RH, concentric. Internal box magazine, 5 rounds. Spring-leaf and elevator rear sight. 3140 fps with 130-grain bullet.

Developed by a team headed by Thomas Johnson on the basis of an experimental 27-caliber cartridge, this was based on the U.S. Army M1903 Springfield rifle. It had twin opposed locking lugs, a Mauser collar-pattern extractor, and a special guide-lug—patented by Frank Burton in June 1927—to smooth the bolt stroke. A three-position safety appeared on the cocking-piece shroud. The first rifles were chambered for 270 Winchester or 30-06 only and had 24in barrels. Walnut half-stocks had straight combs, with checkering on the pistol grip and forend. Shoulder plates were grooved steel, at least until 1930. The receiver ring (but not the bridge) was tapped for an optical-sight mount.

A 30-30 Winchester option was announced in 1928, but was never popular. Indeed, many rifles of this type were rechambered by Griffin & Howe and others for the harder-hitting 30-40 Krag. Three popular metric options (7mm, 7.65mm and 9mm) were added in 1930, when the grooved buttplate was replaced with a checkered pattern. Front sights were mounted on forged bases from March 1931 onward.

The 250-3000 Savage version was advertised in the early 1930s, and the adoption of the Speed Lock (1932)—with a one-piece firing pin and a modified striker spring—not only halved the firing pin travel, but also cut lock time from .0055 sec to .0033 sec. Owners of older or Plain Lock rifles could purchase replacement Speed Lock bolts; when the Model 54 was discontinued in 1936, modified Model 70-type bolts were supplied instead.

The introduction of a 22 Hornet chambering required a special cartridge pusher in the bolt head, patented by Albert Laudensack in February 1933. This feature was later perpetuated in the Model 70, together with a reduced-scale magazine inside the standard box.

A second gas vent was added in the bolt in 1934, behind the extractor collar, and a 20in barrel option was offered with the Standard Model rifle. Work ceased in the autumn of 1936 in favor of the Model 70, but not before a few Model 54 rifles had been chambered for 220 Swift or 257 Roberts cartridges. All 220-type rifles had 26in barrels.

SIMILAR GUNS

Model 54 Carbine, 1927-36. This had a 20in barrel; its half-stock lacked checkering, but had a finger groove in the forend.

Model 54 National Match Rifle, 1935-6. Made with a 24in standard barrel, production of these guns was very small. They had a target-type stock with a deep sharply-curved pistol grip and a forend which broadened ahead of the magazine. Though optical sight-mounting blocks were fitted on the chamber and barrel, Lyman vernier aperture and replaceable-element tunnel sights were also popular.

Model 54 NRA Rifle, 1931-6. Distinguished by a standard 24in barrel, this gun (made only in small numbers) also had a select-grade walnut stock. Checkering was confined to the buttplate and pistol grip.

Model 54 Sniper's Rifle, 1928-36. Identified by its 26in barrel, this also had a plain walnut stock with checkering restricted to the shoulder plate. Guns made in 1936 had plain National Match Rifle-type target stocks, and extra-heavy barrels which increased weight from 11lb to 11.75lb.

Model 54 Super Grade, 1934-6. This had a standard 24in barrel and specially selected walnut stocks with checkering on the pistol grip and forend. The forend tip was ebonite, the pistol grip cap was rubber, and a small oval cheekpiece appeared on the right side of the butt. Weight rose to about 8lb.

Model 54 Target Rifle, 1935-6. Fitted with a 24in heavy barrel, this was introduced with a standard-pattern stock—changed in 1936 to a plain National Match Rifle type. Comparatively few guns of this type were made.

MODEL 56 SPORTING RIFLE

Made by the Winchester Repeating Arms Company, New Haven, Connecticut, 1926-9

Total production: 8300. **Chambering options:** 22 Short or 22 Long Rifle. **Action:** locked by the bolt-handle base abutting on a shoulder in the receiver.

39.2in overall, 4.75lb empty. 22in barrel, 6-groove rifling; RH, concentric. Detachable box magazine, 5 or 10 rounds. Spring-and-slider rear sight. 1065 fps with a 29-grain bullet (22 Long).

Announced in the January 1927, this filled a gap between the simple Models 1902 and 1904 and the sophisticated Model 52. Unfortunately, the price was too high to guarantee success and the production life of the Model 56 was short. The 'Sporting Rifle' had a plain straight-comb walnut stock with a schnabel tipped forend, whereas the otherwise similar 'Fancy Sporting Rifle' had checkering on the pistol grip and forend.

SIMILAR GUNS

Model 57 'Accuracy Rifle', 1926-36. Offered in 22 Short (only until 1929) and 22LR rimfire, this was basically a heavier version of the Model 56 with sight bases on the barrel and receiver. The extended forend was held to the barrel with a single band, while swivels lay under the band and the butt. The Model 57 (which weighed 5.1lb without sights) was too light to be an adequate junior target rifle, and only about 18,600 were made.

MODEL 58 SPORTING RIFLE

Made by the Winchester Repeating Arms Company, New Haven, Connecticut, 1928-31

Total production: 39,000. **Chambering options:** 22 Short, 22 Long or 22 Long Rifle rimfire, interchangeably. **Action:** as Model 56, above.

33.8in overall, 3.10lb empty. 18in barrel, 6-groove rifling; RH, concentric. Single-shot only. Standing-block rear sight. 825 fps with 29-grain bullet (22 Short).

Seen as a replacement for the Models 1902 and 1904, this had a crudely formed straight-wrist hardwood stock lacking a buttplate. The action was cocked simply by pulling back on the cocking piece. Despite its low price, the unpopularity of the Model 58 was reflected in its poor sales record. It was replaced by the ill-fated Model 59 described below.

SIMILAR GUNS

Model 59 rifle, 1930. Designed as a replacement for the Model 58, this had a longer barrel and a better-shaped stock with a composition buttplate. However, it retained the same manually cocked action at a time when the rimfire guns being imported from Europe showed increasing sophistication. The Model 59 was received so badly that production lasted for less than a year; only about 9250 were made.

Model 60 rifle, 1930-4. Though little more than a Model 59 mechanically, the Model 60 had modest cosmetic improvements—e.g., chromium-plated the bolt and trigger—and changes in the firing system, which included the addition of a port in the top surface of the bolt so that the words SAFE or FIRE could show the state of cocking. A separate trigger spring was added, and a second notch added to the sear to ensure that spent 22LR cases ejected satisfactorily. Rifles made after 1933 had a 27in barrel with four-groove rifling instead of the earlier 23in 6-groove pattern, and the forend was lengthened by an inch. When the basic pattern was superseded by the Model 67, production of Model 60 and 60A rifles had amounted to 160,750.

Model 60A Target Rifle, 1933-9. About 6120 of these guns were made. They had heavy barrels, sling swivels, an extended semi-beavertail forend held by a single band, and a checkered steel buttplate. The rear sight was a Lyman No. 55W aperture pattern, mounted on the receiver bridge. Unfortunately, the Model 60A was too light to be effective and this drawback reflected in meager sales.

Model 67 rifle, 1934-42 and 1946-63. A revised form of the Model 60, sharing the same basic action, this was an attempt to launch a new model without investing too heavily in new components. It was still cocked by pulling back on the cocking piece; the bolt, safety lock and trigger were chromium plated; and the plain walnut pistol grip half-stock originally had a finger groove in the forend. Changes made during the lengthy production life included the omission of the forend finger groove from 1935 until an improved stock, with the barrel-retaining bolt recessed in the forend, was adopted in October 1937. A 22 WRF option was added in 1935. The bolt-retaining spring was omitted from January 1938, when efforts were made to smooth the bolt stroke and improve ejection by revising the bolt, sear and extractor. About 383,600 Model 67 rifles (all types) were made.

Model 67 Smooth Bore Rifle, 1936-42. Made only in small numbers, this had a 27in barrel handling 22LR and 22 Short cartridges interchangeably

Model 67 Miniature Target Boring, 1940-1. This had a 24in barrel chambered for a 22LR shot cartridge.

Model 67 Junior Rifle (also known as the "Boy's Rifle"), 1937-42. A minor variant of the standard-length rifle, this had a 20in barrel and weighed 4.2lb.

Model 67 telescope-sighted rifles, 1937-42. These guns had special sight-mounting bases on the barrels. The original pattern was offered with 2-1/2x or 5x sights with a cross-hair reticle, but this was soon replaced by a 2-3/4 x post-type reticle.

Model 677 rifle. A variant of the optically-sighted Model 67, these guns had a special barrel lacking open sights. Only about 2239 were made in 1937-9.

Model 68 rifle, 1934-42, 1946. This was a modification of the Model 67, with a hooded front-sight on a ramp and a small peep sight on a spring-leaf mounted above the chamber. Some guns also had bases for telescope-sight mounts on the barrel. Production amounted to about 100,700.

MODEL 69 SPORTING RIFLE

Made by the Winchester Repeating Arms Company, New Haven, Connecticut, 1935-63

Total production: 355,400 (all types). **Chambering options:** 22 Short, 22 Long and 22 Long Rifle interchangeably. **Action:** generally as Model 59 (q.v.).

42.6in overall, 5.25lb empty. 25in barrel, 6- or 4-groove rifling; RH, concentric. Detachable box magazine, 5 or 10 rounds. Spring-and-slider rear sight. 1080 fps with 40-grain bullet (22LR).

This arose from criticism that the earlier single-shot expedients, Models 56 and 57, could not compete with rival designs. The addition of a box magazine was a great improvement, but the greatest praise was reserved for the advent of an auto-cocking system. The round barrels were fitted with a simple front sight or a hooded blade on a ramp. The plain pistol grip half-stock had a tapered forend. An inertia-pattern firing pin was substituted for the original pattern in August 1935, and the stock was altered in October 1937 so that the barrel-retaining take-down nut was recessed entirely in the forend.

SIMILAR GUNS

Model 47 rifle, 1948-54. About 43,100 of these were made with 25in barrels, which gave a weight of about 5.25lb. The action was a single shot form of the Model 69. The bolt cocked on the opening motion, incorporated a Speed Lock, and had twin extractors to improve ejection. An automatic safety catch, alongside the bolt, was applied when the bolt was opened and had to be re-set manually before each shot. The plain walnut pistol grip stock had a composition buttplate. Most guns were fitted with a spring-and-slider rear sight, but a receiver-mounted 'peep' sight could be obtained to order. The Model 47 was unable to compete with rival designs, however, and its production life was short.

Model 69A rifle, 1937-40, 1946-63. This was a revised form of the original Model 69, cocking on the opening motion of the bolt instead of the closing stroke. The weight of the barrel was also increased.

Model 69 Target Rifle, 1940-1, 1947-63? Approved in December 1940, with a better stock than the Model 69A and swivels for a broad sling, this was chambered only for the 22LR rimfire cartridge. A Winchester peep-type rear sight was fitted.

Model 69 Match Rifle, 1940-1, 1947-63? Offered only in 22LR rimfire, this was another target-shooting derivative of the standard rifle with changes to the butt and sling swivels. The rear sight was a Lyman No. 57EW pattern.

Model 69 telescope-sighted rifles, 1937-41. These were made with additional bases on the barrels to accommodate the mounts of Winchester's 2-3/4 x and 5x optical sights.

Model 697 rifle. This was a variant of the optically-sighted Model 69, with a special barrel lacking provision for open sights. Only one thousand were made in 1938-9.

Model 72 rifle, 1938-42 and 1946-59. Made with a tube magazine beneath the 25in barrel, holding 15-20 rounds depending on cartridge length, this was introduced in the Spring of 1938 in response to demands for a greater magazine capacity than the box-equipped but otherwise similar Model 69. The plain walnut pistol grip half-stock had a semi-beavertail forend and a composition buttplate. Empty weight was about 5.7lb. The standard rear sight included a peep element (Model 72), but guns could be obtained with open or 'sporting' sights (Model 72A) and could accept 2-3/4 x or 5x optical patterns; suitable bases were provided on the barrel until 1941. Production amounted to 161,400 guns.

Model 72 Gallery Special Rifle, 1939-42. This short-lived gun was chambered only for the 22 Short rimfire cartridge, but comparatively few were ever made.

Model 75 Target Rifle, 1938-42 and 1946-58. Designed to suit purchasers who could not afford the sophistication of the Model 52, about 88,700 Model 75 rifles were made in target and sporting forms in 22LR rimfire only. The incorporation of the Speed Lock system gave surprisingly good performance and, as weight was enough to be useful, many M75 target rifles were used to train U.S. Army recruits during World War II. A typical gun had a 28in barrel, drilled and tapped to receive the Model 52 sight-mount bases. Empty weight was about 8.5lb; the detachable box magazine held five or 10 rounds, and Lyman, Redfield or Winchester aperture sights could be fitted on the receiver. The plain walnut half-stock had a higher comb than the sporting gun, with a checkered steel buttplate and a broad squared-tip forend. The stock was held to the barrel with a bolt passing laterally through an internal band, and had an adjustable swivel under the forend.

Model 75 Sporting Rifle, 1939-42, 1946-58. Introduced a few months after the target pattern, this had a 24in round barrel with the ramp for the front sight forged integrally with the muzzle. A spring leaf-and-elevator rear sight was standard, though an optional Lyman No. 57E receiver sight could be used in combination with a bead-type front sight. The stock was a plain pistol grip pattern with a hard rubber pistol grip cap and a checkered steel shoulder plate.

MODEL 70 SPORTING RIFLE
Original, or 1936 type

Made in New Haven by the Winchester Repeating Arms Company (1936-61) and by the Winchester-Western Division of Olin Industries (1962-4).

Total production: about 525,000 (all types). **Chambering options:** see notes below. **Action:** generally as Model 54, above.

DATA FOR A TYPICAL AFRICAN RIFLE

Chambering: 458 Winchester Magnum, belted rimless. 45.5in overall, 9.5lb empty. 25in barrel, 6-groove rifling; RH, concentric. Internal box magazine, 3 rounds. Folding-leaf rear sight. 2130 fps with 500-grain bullet.

The success of the Model 54 allowed Winchester's engineers to design its successor at leisure. Credited to a team led by Edwin Pugsley, with Leroy Crockett and Albert Laudensack prominent, the Model 70 of 1933 retained the basic operating system of the older gun. It had a cone breech, a partially shrouded bolt head and an improved bedding system with the front trigger guard bolt running up into the underside of the receiver instead of the recoil lug.

The bolt handle was swept down and back to clear an optical sight, and the safety catch on the cocking-piece shroud was changed to work laterally; it could be set to fire, to retract the firing-pin (yet allow the bolt to open), or to lock the bolt in the bolt way. The bolt-stop became a separate component, independent of the sear. A hinged magazine floorplate was fitted and the trigger guard became a machined steel forging.

The new gun was approved on 29th December 1934, the first rifles being delivered into store in the autumn of 1936. Known as the 'Sporting Rifle', or later also as the 'Standard Pattern', it duly appeared in the 1937 Winchester catalogue. Some of the earliest guns made for 270 Winchester and 30-06 had stripper-clip guides milled in the front edge of the receiver bridge. The top of the receiver ring and bridge had non-reflective hatching, while the receiver ring was drilled and tapped for an optical sight mount.

The standard half-stock was a refinement of the Model 54, with less drop at the heel and a broader forend. Checkering was improved. Barrels were customarily 24in or 20in, the latter being discontinued shortly after the end of World War II, though the 220 Swift and 300 H&H Magnum chamberings were always accompanied by a 26in barrel. The standard-weight 24in 375 H&H Magnum barrel was soon substituted by a heavier version and, in

February 1937, lengthened to 25in. The safety catch was altered in 1938 to operate on the right side of the bolt shroud instead of across it, and a safety-catch thumb piece was added soon afterward.

Production of the Model 70, which had stopped at the end of 1941, resumed in 1946. Few changes were made, though the upper tang was altered in 1947 to lie on top of the stock behind the receiver. The original inlet version had been prone to chipping.

A 308 Winchester chambering was introduced commercially in 1952, and the bolt knob was hollowed from 1953 onward. The 243 and 358 options date from the 1955-6, followed by 338 Winchester Magnum at the beginning of 1958 and 264 Winchester Magnum in 1959.

Unfortunately, Winchester was purchased by the giant Olin corporation in 1961 and work began to modernize the Model 70 to simplify production. All surviving versions of the original or 1936-type Model 70 were abandoned at the end of 1963, but not before a few Standard and Westerner rifles had been made for the new 300 Winchester Magnum round.

SIMILAR GUNS

Model 70 African Rifle, 1956-63. This big-game rifle was chambered specifically for the 458 Winchester Magnum cartridge; it had a 25in barrel, a three-round magazine, and a Monte Carlo-style half-stock with a sturdy rubber shoulder pad Weight was about 9.5lb.

Model 70 Alaskan Rifle, 1960-3. Chambered exclusively for 338 Winchester (three-round magazine) or 375 H&H Magnum cartridges (four rounds), this had a 25in barrel and a rubber recoil pad; guns weighed 8-8.7lb.

Model 70 Bull Gun. This specialized target rifle—which weighed 13lb—had an extra-heavy 28in barrel. Most guns were chambered for the 30-06 cartridge, but a few factory-made examples were adapted for 300 H&H Magnum. Like the National Match and Target rifles, the Bull Gun used the Marksman-pattern stock. It was finally abandoned in 1963.

Model 70 Carbine, 1936-41 and 1945-6. Distinguished by a 20in barrel, though otherwise identical with the rifle, this was chambered for only six of the standard cartridges: 22 Hornet, 250-3000 Savage, 257 Roberts, 270 Winchester, 7x57 and 30-06. It was never made in quantity, and the few post-war guns may have been assembled from parts which had remained in store.

Model 70 Featherweight Rifle (or 'Featherweight Sporter'), 1952-63. Introduced in standard and Super Grade versions, this had a tapered 22in barrel, a lightweight stock with an aluminum-alloy buttplate, and an alloy trigger guard/magazine floorplate assembly. Standard chamberings included 243, 270 and 308 Winchester, and the ubiquitous 30-06. A few guns are also believed to have been offered in 22 Hornet, 220 Swift and 257 Roberts. A 358 Winchester version encountered so many teething troubles that few suitably chambered Model 70 rifles ever made. A deluxe or 'Super Grade' Featherweight was discontinued in 1960. A 'Featherweight Magnum', dating from 1955-60, chambered the 264 Winchester Magnum cartridge.

Model 70 National Match, 1937-60. Made only in 30-06, this had a 24in barrel and weighed 9.6lb. It also had the 'Marksman' stock, with a high straight comb, a sharply curved pistol grip and a broad forend.

Model 70 Sporting Rifle (or 'Standard Rifle'), 1937-41 and 1945-6. This was the original pattern, described in the text above. It was chambered for a variety of cartridges, the most popular being 22 Hornet, 220 Swift, 257 Roberts, 270 Winchester, 30-06 and the two Holland & Holland magnum patterns, 300 and 375. Most of the guns had 24in barrels and five-round magazines, though the magnums had 26in barrels and magazines containing only four cartridges. Pre-1941 chamberings included 35 Remington, 7.65x53, 7x57, 250-3000 Savage and (perhaps) 9x57.

Model 70 Sporting Rifle (or 'Standard'), 1946-64. When work began again after the end of World War II, improvements were made in the action and stock. Though dimensions remained unchanged, chambering options were soon extended to include 243 Winchester and three Winchester Magnum cartridges: 264, 300 and 338. A few guns were also made for the 300 Savage round, and a very few for 308 Winchester.

Model 70 Super Grade Sporting Rifle, about 1936-60. This was a deluxe version, distinguished by a select-walnut stock with a Monte Carlo comb and a cheekpiece. The forend and pistol grip were extensively checkered, the forend tip was ebonite, and the pistol grip had a separate cap.

Model 70 Target Rifle, 1937-63. Originally offered in virtually every chambering associated with the Model 70 Sporting Rifle, this had a heavy 24in barrel and weighed 10.5lb without sights; the Marksman stock was standard. By the mid 1950s, only the 243 Winchester and 30-06 chamberings were available from stock.

Model 70 Varmint Rifle, 1955-63. Distinguished by a 26in barrel, a modified stock and optical-sight mounting bases, this was normally offered only in 243 Winchester though a few hundred examples were made for the 220 Swift cartridge.

Model 70 Westerner Rifle, 1960-3. Similar to the Featherweight (q.v.), this had a 26in barrel chambering the 264 Winchester Magnum cartridge. The magazine held three rounds. The Westerner was soon abandoned, but not before a few 24in-barreled gun had been offered in 300 Winchester Magnum.

MODEL 70 SPORTING RIFLE
1964 type
Made by the Winchester-Western Division of Olin Industries, New Haven, Connecticut (1964-8).

Total production: about 166,000. **Chambering options:** see text. **Action:** generally as Model 54, above.
DATA FOR A TYPICAL VARMINT RIFLE

Chambering: 243 Winchester, rimless. 44.5in overall, 9.7lb empty. 24in barrel, 6-groove rifling; RH, concentric. Internal box magazine, 5 rounds. Optical sight. 3500 fps with 80-grain bullet.

Work began in 1962 to revise the Model 70, seeking to simplify machining and cut costs. The work was entrusted to Robert Creamer and John Walsh, though much of the detailed study was sub-contracted to the Pioneer Engineering & Manufacturing Company of Warren, Michigan. Among the most important changes was the reversion to a faced-off breech instead of the earlier coned pattern. The extractor and ejector were mounted in the bolt head, and the new bolt had a separate investment-cast handle. Barrels floated freely in the forends, instead of being held by a threaded bolt.

The modified rifles, numbered from 700000 upward, were introduced commercially in 1964. However, though some of the changes were clearly improvements, the guns were poorly finished and the omission of the bolt guide lost much of the renowned smoothness of the original action.

Standard Model 70 rifles had a 22in free-floating barrel chambered for the three proprietary Winchester rounds—243, 270, 308—and the ubiquitous 30-06. The glossy Monte Carlo-pattern stock had a short steep comb, and checkering was impressed on the pistol grip and forend. Barreled actions were made available separately for the first time in 1965.

The mainspring sleeve was replaced by a 'C'-ring, to which a bearing cap was added in 1969. Standard, Magnum and Varmint stocks had been changed in 1966, when the Monte Carlo comb was raised to improve its performance with optical sights and the contours of the cheekpiece were revised to reduce the effects of recoil. A recoil bolt was added through the stock above the front web of the trigger guard. The pattern of impressed checkering was altered.

A 225 Winchester option was added in 1967, followed by 222 and 22-250 Remington chamberings, but public pressure forced the abandonment of the 1964-type action in 1971.

THE GUNS
Model 70 African Rifle, 1965-71. Made only in 458, this was offered with a 22in barrel and a three-round magazine. It was much more heavily built than the standard Sporter, and had recoil bolts beneath the chamber and ahead of the bolt handle. The stock had an ebony tip, a ventilated rubber recoil pad was fitted to the butt, and checkering was hand-cut. Special sights were fitted. One swivel lay under the butt with another on the barrel ahead of the forend tip.

Model 70 Custom Rifle (or 'Deluxe'), 1964-70. Based on the Sporter or Magnum rifles, these were made only in small quantities. Their select walnut stocks had ebony forend tips and hand-cut checkering. Quick-detachable swivels and a Williams-ramp rear sight were standard; chamberings were usually 243 Winchester, 270 Winchester, 30-06 (22in barrels, four rounds) or 300 Winchester Magnum (24in barrel, 3 rounds).

Model 70 International Army Match Rifle, 1971. These 308 guns were easily distinguished by heavy 24in barrels and massive wooden stocks with an adjustable buttplate. They weighed about

11lb without sights and had a five-round magazine. An accessory rail lay under the forend, the trigger could be adjusted externally, and a detachable five-round box magazine was used. Very few guns were made, as the 1964-type Winchester Model 70 action was soon abandoned.

Model 70 Magnum, 1964-71. Offered with a three-round magazine and a 24in barrel in 264, 300 or 338 Winchester Magnum—plus 375 H&H Magnum—this was stocked similarly to the standard Model 70 except for a rubber recoil pad. Magazines held three rounds. Weight was typically 7.8-8.4lb, depending on the density of the stock wood. The Monte Carlo comb was raised in 1966, when the cheekpiece was refined and a recoil bolt was added through the stock. The pattern of the impressed checkering was also revised. A 7mm Remington Magnum chambering was introduced in 1968.

Model 70 Mannlicher, 1969-71. Introduced in 243 Winchester, 270 Winchester, 30-06 or 308 Winchester, this had a 19in barrel and a five-cartridge magazine. The Monte Carlo stock had a full length forend, but the rifle was never popular; only a few were made.

Model 70 Standard Rifle (or 'Sporter'), 1964-71. Described in greater detail in the text (above), these usually had 22in barrels and five-round magazines; chamberings included 22-250, 223 Remington, 225 Winchester (discontinued in 1974), 243 Winchester, 270 Winchester, 308 Winchester and 30-06. The butt had a Monte Carlo comb and a cheekpiece; checkering was cut into the pistol grip and forend; and swivels were provided beneath the butt and forend.

Model 70 Target Rifle, 1964-71. These were offered with a 24in heavy barrel chambered for 30-06 or 308 cartridges. Fitted with five-round box magazines, they had mounting blocks for optical sights on the receiver ring and barrel. The plain Marksman-style stock had a high straight comb and a deep forend with an alloy hand stop. Weight was about 10.2lb.

Model 70 Varmint, 1965-71. This combined a 25in target-pattern barrel and the standard stock. Introduced in 243 Winchester only, it had mounting blocks for optical sights on the receiver ring and barrel; weight averaged 9.75lb. The stock was revised in 1966, when the Monte Carlo comb was raised. The cheekpiece was refined, a recoil bolt was added through the stock, and the checkering pattern was changed. New 222 and 22-250 Remington options appeared in 1969.

MODEL 121 SPORTING RIFLE

Made by the Winchester Repeating Arms Company, New Haven, Connecticut, 1967-73.

Total production: not known. **Chambering options:** 22 Short, Long and Long rifle rimfire, interchangeably. **Action:** locked by turning the bolt handle down into its seat in the receiver.

DATA FOR A TYPICAL EXAMPLE

39.5in overall, about 5lb empty. 20.75in barrel, 4-groove rifling; RH, concentric. Tube magazine beneath barrel, 15-21 rounds depending on cartridge length. Spring-leaf and elevator rear sight. 1080 fps with 40-grain bullet (22LR).

This modernized single-shot rifle had a plain one-piece half-stock with a low Monte Carlo comb. The front sight was attached to a short ramp above the muzzle, and the trigger guard was a plain stamped strip. The M121 was much less sophisticated than rival designs being imported from Europe—not to mention the products of some other U.S. manufacturers—and its production life was comparatively brief.

SIMILAR GUNS

Model 121 Deluxe rifle, 1967-73. A minor variant of the standard 121, this had a walnut stock, sling swivels, and a front sight mounted on a muzzle ramp.

Model 121Y rifle, 1967-73. This was a Youth's rifle, mechanically identical with the M121 but fitted with a shorter butt which reduced overall length by about 1.2in.

Model 131 rifle, 1967-73. A repeating version of the Model 121, this had a plain hardwood stock with a Monte Carlo comb. The detachable box magazine held seven rounds.

Model 135 rifle, 1967. This short-lived variant of the Model 131 chambered 22 Winchester Magnum rimfire cartridges, reducing the magazine capacity to five. It is suspected that the power of the cartridge taxed construction to its limits, as only a few guns were made.

Model 141 rifle, 1967-73. Essentially similar to the Model 131, sharing the same basic action, this had a tube magazine in the butt. Cartridge capacity varied from 13 to 19 rounds, depending on cartridge length.

Model 145 rifle, 1967. Another of the Magnum Rimfire versions of the basic rifle, this had a nine-round tube magazine in the butt. Very few were ever made.

MODEL 670 SPORTING RIFLE

Made by the Winchester-Western Division of Olin Industries, New Haven, Connecticut, 1967-73.

Total production: 20,000? **Chambering options:** 225 Winchester, 243 Winchester, 270 Winchester or 30-06. **Action:** generally as Model 54, above.

DATA FOR A TYPICAL RIFLE

Chambering: 225 Winchester, rimmed. 42.5in overall, about 7lb empty. 22in barrel, 6-groove rifling; RH, concentric. Internal box magazine, 4 rounds. Williams ramp-type rear sight. 3570 fps with 55-grain bullet.

This budget-price Model 70 had a walnut-finish beech stock, a 'blind' magazine contained entirely within the stock, and a sliding safety catch on the receiver side behind the bolt handle. The cocking piece projected from the bolt sleeve when the action was ready to fire. By 1971, chamberings had been reduced to 243 Winchester and 30-06.

SIMILAR GUNS

Model 670 Carbine, 1966-73. Mechanically identical with the standard rifle, this had a 20in barrel and measured about 40in overall.

Model 670 Magnum, 1968-73. A variant of the rifle with a 24in barrel, this was chambered for 264 or 300 Winchester Magnum cartridges.

MODEL 770 SPORTING RIFLE

Made by the Winchester-Western Division of Olin Industries, New Haven, Connecticut, 1969-71.

Total production: not known. **Chambering options:** 222 Remington, 22-250, 243 Remington, 264 Winchester Magnum, 270 Winchester, 7mm Remington Magnum, 30-06, 300 Winchester Magnum or 308 Winchester. **Action:** generally as Model 54, above.

DATA FOR A TYPICAL RIFLE

Chambering: 300 Winchester Magnum, belted rimless. 44.5in overall, 7.25lb empty. 24in barrel, 6-groove rifling; RH, concentric. Internal box magazine, 3 rounds. Williams ramp-type rear sight. 3070 fps with 180-grain bullet.

Introduced in Standard and Magnum forms, with 22in and 24in barrels respectively, this occupied a niche in the market between the Models 70 and 670. Though it retained the blind magazine, the bolt was similar to the perfected Model 70—complete with guide rib, bolt shroud and the three-position safety.

MODEL 70 SPORTING RIFLE
1968 and subsequent types

Made in New Haven, Connecticut, by the Winchester-Western Division of Olin Industries (1968-83); and by the U.S. Repeating Arms Company (1983 to date).

Total production: in excess of 1.25 million. **Chambering options:** see text. **Action:** generally as Model 54, above.

DATA FOR A TYPICAL FEATHERWEIGHT CLASSIC

Chambering: 280 Remington, rimless. 42.5in overall, 7.25lb empty. 22in barrel, 6-groove rifling; RH, concentric. Internal box magazine, 5 rounds. Williams ramp-type rear sight. 2970 fps with 150-grain bullet.

A new Model 70 appeared in 1968, beginning with gun number 866000. A 'G' prefix signified the presence of a guide slot in the bolt-head, patented by Robert Creamer in March 1969, which engaged a narrow rib in the right side of the receiver to smooth the bolt stroke. The magazine follower was revised, no longer being riveted to the spring, and finish was improved. Knurling was added to the bolt handle knob.

Introduced commercially in 1969, most of the new rifles duplicated their 1964-type equivalents despite of the changes in action. However, extensive revisions were made in the stocks. Machine-cut checkering replaced the impressed type in 1972, when the contours of the butt—especially the Monte Carlo comb—were also refined. The slab-sided forend, inspired by Weatherby patterns, had an ebonite tip and a white spacer. A short version of the basic Model 70 action was introduced in 1985 for cartridges shorter than 308 Winchester.

Note: The sale of Winchester's operations to the U.S. Repeating Arms Company in 1981 was accompanied by a change in the product range. Among the most desirable guns of this era are the few made with Winchester receiver markings and a USRA buttplate.

Most of the older guns were rapidly discontinued and the 'XTR' stock became standard, though the XTR labels disappeared when supplies of the older-style guns had been exhausted in the late 1980s. The distinctions between standard and magnum versions of specific models, arising largely from differences in barrel and cartridge capacity, are not always used—particularly if both 'cartridge groups' use actions of similar length.

The 'Classic' label applied to most post-1997 Model 70 rifles refers to the use of a claw-type extractor, a three-position safety and a straight-comb stock. Similarly, the recent advent of the BOSS (Barrel Optimizing Shooting System) adjustable barrel weight/muzzle-brake unit has also affected designations.

M70 African Rifle, 1970-84. Chambered only for the 458 Winchester Magnum round, this had a 22in barrel and weighed about 8.5lb. Two recoil bolts ran laterally through the stock, which had an ebonite forend tip.

Model 70 Collector Grade rifle, 1989-90. Denoting the highly decorative products of the Winchester Custom Shop, this represented an intermediate stage between Custom and Exhibition grades.

Model 70 Custom Rifle. Offering a superior American Black Walnut stock and more attention to detail, this was renamed 'M70 Super Grade' (q.v.) in about 1973.

Model 70 Custom Express [Classic] rifle, 1992 to date. This has been chambered for cartridges such as 375 H&H Magnum, 375 JRS, 416 Remington Magnum, 458 Winchester Magnum or 470 Capstick. It has a heavy 24in barrel (22in in 458) and a three-leaf Express rear sight.

Model 70 Custom Grade rifle. Applied in 1988-9 to old actions stocked in selected walnut, with jeweled bolts and engraving on the receiver, this term subsequently reappeared in 1990 to denote the Winchester Custom Shop equivalent of the 'off the shelf' Super Grade. The guns have selected walnut stocks and hand-honed actions. Offered in Express, Featherweight and Sharpshooter patterns, they also display a limited amount of decoration on the metalwork.

Model 70 Custom Sharpshooter II [Classic] rifle, 1992 to date. This is easily distinguished by a target-style McMillan synthetic stock with the Pillar Plus Accu Block bedding system, matte-blue finish, and a 26in stainless steel Schneider barrel (in all chamberings but 308). Options include 22-250, 30-06, 300 Winchester Magnum and 308 Winchester. The guns are 46.5in long and weigh about 11lb.

Model 70 Custom Sporting Sharpshooter II [Classic] rifle, 1993 to date. Mechanically identical with the Custom Sharpshooter, this has a gray sporting-style half-stock and a stainless steel barrel. It was introduced in 270 Winchester (discontinued in 1995), 7mm STW, and 300 Winchester Magnum.

Model 70 DBM rifle (Detachable Box Magazine), 1992-5. This was originally chambered for the 270 Winchester, 7mm Remington Magnum, 300 Winchester Magnum or 30-06 rounds; 22-250, 223 Remington and 243 Winchester were added in 1993. The major identifying characteristic was the special three-round magazine. The guns were 44.5in long, had 24in barrels and weighed 7.8-7.9lb.

Model 70 DBM-S rifle (Detachable Box Magazine, Synthetic [stock]), 1993-5. This was simply a DBM with a composite fiberglass/graphite stock.

Model 70 Exhibition Grade rifle, 1988-9. This designation was briefly applied to some of the best products of the Winchester Custom Shop, with metalwork of the finest quality and superb American Black or French walnut stocks.

Model 70 Featherweight [XTR] rifle, 1984-96. This was an amalgam of a short or medium action, a lightweight 22in barrel, and a straight-comb half-stock with checkering on the pistol grip and the schnabel-tipped forend. Weight averaged 6.6lb. Five-round magazines were standard, except magnum chamberings. Options have included 22-250, 223 Remington, 243 Winchester, 257 Roberts, 270 Winchester, 280 Remington, 7mm Remington Magnum, 7x57, 30-06, 300 Winchester Magnum, and 308 Winchester. The 257 and 7x57 versions were abandoned in 1985, but a 6.5x55 option was introduced in 1991 and 7mm-08 followed in 1992.

Model 70 Featherweight All-Terrain [Classic] rifle, 1996 to date. This was introduced only in 270 Winchester, 7mm Remington Magnum, 30-06 and 300 Winchester Magnum. It has a composite graphite/fiberglass half-stock with a schnabel tip, and a stainless steel barreled action.

Model 70 Featherweight [Classic] rifle, 1992 to date. Offered with a 22in barrel, in 22-250, 243 Winchester, 6.5x55, 270 Winches-

The Winchester Model 70 Featherweight, with riband checkering.

The Winchester Model 70 Lightweight Win-Tuff rifle.

The Winchester Model 70 Ranger Junior rifle.

The Winchester Model 70 Sporter.

ter, 280 Remington, 7mm-08, 30-06 or 308 Winchester—and also in 7mm Remington or 300 Winchester magnum chamberings—this gun combines a straight-comb Featherweight stock with a schnabel forend tip. Weight averages 7.25lb.

Model 70 Featherweight Stainless [Classic] rifle. Distinguished by a black graphite/fiberglass half-stock with a rounded forend, this was introduced in 1997 in 22-250, 243 Winchester, 270 Winchester, 7mm Remington Magnum, 300 Winchester Magnum, 30-06 and 308 Winchester. The BOSS option is available in most versions.

Model 70 Featherweight Ultra Grade rifle, 1989. Offered in 270 Winchester, only a few of these highly decorative guns were made. They had specially selected French walnut stocks, engraved actions, and came in a presentation case.

Model 70 Featherweight Winlite rifle, 1988-92. Offered only in 270 Winchester, 280 Remington or 30-06, this version had a textured McMillan fiberglass stock and weighed merely 6.25lb.

Model 70 Featherweight Win-Tuff rifle, 1992-5. Otherwise identical to the standard Featherweight design, this had a brown wood-laminate half-stock with a straight comb.

Model 70 Golden Anniversary Model, 1986-7. Produced in a 500-gun limited edition to celebrate the 50th birthday of the original Model 70, this had a 24in barrel chambering the 300 Winchester Magnum cartridge and a three-round magazine. It weighed about 7.8lb. The hand-checkered walnut stock was accompanied by scroll engraving on the metalwork and "THE RIFLEMAN'S RIFLE 1937-1987". Serial numbers ran from 50ANV1 to 50ANV500.

Model 70 Heavy Varmint [Classic] rifle, 1993 to date. Made with a 26in stainless steel barrel, giving it a weight of 10.75lb, this had a composite graphite/fiberglass stock and a blued action. The Pillar Plus Accu Block bedding system and the push-type feed were standard. Chamberings were initially restricted to 22-250 or 223 Remington, with 243 and 308 Winchester, but a 220 Swift option was added in 1994 and followed in 1997 by 222 Remington. A fluted barrel could also be obtained from 1997.

Model 70 International Army Match Rifle, 1973-81? Made only in 30-06, this was identical to the 1964-type gun except for improvements in the action. It had a heavy 24in barrel, a five-round magazine, and stripper-clip guides on the front edge of the receiver bridge. Weight averaged 11lb without sights and the stock conformed with ISU rules.

Model 70 Laredo Long-Range Hunter [Classic] rifle, 1996 to date. Offered in a gray/black synthetic stock with a broad forend and an integral Pillar Plus Accu Block bedding system, this can be obtained in 7mm Remington Magnum, 7mm STW or 300 Winchester Magnum. It measures 46.75in overall, has a 26in barrel, and weighs 9.5lb. Guns fitted with the BOSS system are also available.

Model 70 Lightweight carbine, 1984-? The walnut half-stocks fitted to these guns had straight combs and tapering forends with rounded tips. The rifles weighed 6-6.3lb—depending on type—and had 20in barrels. Sling eyes lay beneath the butt and forend. Magazines held five rounds, or six in 223 only; chamberings included 22-250 Remington, 223 Remington, 243 Winchester, 250 Savage, 270 Winchester, 30-06 or 308 Winchester.

Model 70 Lightweight rifle, 1987-95. A replacement for the otherwise similar Lightweight Carbine, this had a 22in barrel giving an overall length of 42.5in (long action); weight was about 6.5lb. Chamberings were originally 22-250, 223 Remington, 243 Winchester, 270 Winchester, 30-06 and 308 Winchester, but a 280 Remington option was added in 1988.

Model 70 Magnum rifle, 1972-81? This was similar to the M70 Standard rifle, but had a 24in barrel, a three-round magazine, an additional recoil bolt beneath the chamber, and a ventilated rubber butt pad. Chamberings included the 264 Winchester, 300 Winchester, 338 Winchester and 375 H&H magnum cartridges. Except the 375 version, a hefty 8.8lb, the guns weighed 7.7-8lb.

Model 70 Mannlicher, 1969-72. Distinguished by a 19in barrel set in a full-length stock, with a straight comb and a steel forend cap, this was offered only in 243 Winchester, 270 Winchester, 30-06 and 308 Winchester.

Model 70 Mini-Carbine. A few of these 243 Winchester guns dated from 1985-6. They were an inch shorter in the butt than the XTR Sporter.

Model 70 Ranger rifle, 1985 to date. This is a simplified version of the Model 70 Sporter with a plain hardwood stock and a push-type feed. Magazine floorplates and detachable sights were added in 1990. Chamberings have included 223 Remington, 243 Winchester, 270 Winchester and 30-06; a 7mm Remington Magnum option became available in 1997.

Model 70 Ranger Youth/Ladies rifle, 1987 to date. This is a minor variant of the Ranger with a short butt, introduced in 223 Remington, 243 Winchester and 308 Winchester. The 223 option—which had been discontinued in 1989—reappeared in 1997, accompanied by 7mm-08.

Model 70 Sharpshooter rifle, 1992-5. This was initially made to order in 300 Winchester Magnum or 308, with a Schneider barrel and a synthetic McMillan A-2 target stock. A Harris bipod brought weight up to about 11lb.

Model 70 SHB rifle ('synthetic [stock], heavy barrel'), 1992-5. Distinguished by a matted metal finish, contrasting with the machine-jeweled bolt, this was made only in 308 Winchester. Measuring 46in overall, it shared the 26in heavy barrel of the Varmint rifles and weighed about 9lb.

Model 70 SM rifle, 1992-5. Available in the same chamberings as the Model 70 Sporter, this had a distinctive black composite graphite/fiberglass half-stock and weighed about 7.8lb. The metalwork had a non-reflective finish.

Model 70 Sporter [XTR] [Classic] rifle (or 'Standard'), 1978 to date. This was originally simply an XTR version of the standard M70, with a refined walnut stock with a longer and lower Monte Carlo comb than its predecessors. A rubber buttplate was standard, together with drilled and tapped holes for optical-sight mounts on the receiver bridge and ring. The XTR suffix was dropped at the beginning of 1989. Initially offered only in 270 Winchester and 30-06 chamberings, the range was subsequently enlarged to include 22-250 and 223 Remington (from 1989), 243 Winchester (1989) and 25-06 Remington (1990). The 'custom sporter' styling, 24in barrel and five-round magazines are standard.

A magnum version was offered in 264 Winchester Magnum, 7mm Remington Magnum, 300 H&H Magnum, 300 Weatherby Magnum, 300 Winchester Magnum and 338 Winchester Magnum options. The straight-comb classic-profile stock had been adopted by 1997. The 22-250, 223, 243 and 300 H&H Magum chamberings had all been abandoned, but 270 Weatherby Magnum and 7mm STW had been introduced. The BOSS system is now being offered in 270 Winchester, 7mm Remington Magnum, 7mm STW, 300 Winchester Magnum, 30-06 and 338 Winchester Magnum.

Model 70 Sporter Stainless [Classic] rifle. This was introduced in 1997 in 270 Winchester, 7mm Remington Magnum, 7mm STW, 300 Winchester Magnum, 30-06 and 338 Winchester Magnum. It amalgamates the standard straight-comb walnut half-stock with a barreled action made of stainless steel.

Model 70 Sporter Win-Tuff rifle, 1992-4. A minor variant of the basic design, this had a brown wood-laminate half-stock with a cheekpiece and a straight comb. A rubber shoulder pad was standard. Chamberings were initially 270 Winchester, 30-06, and four magnum options—7mm Remington, 300 Weatherby, 300 Winchester and 338 Winchester.

Model 70 SSM rifle ('Synthetic Sporter, Matt [finish]'), 1992. This 24in-barreled rifle—introduced in 270 Winchester and 30-06—had a black composite fiberglass/graphite stock with checkering on the pistol grip and forend. Barrel and receiver had a non-reflective finish, and there were swivels beneath the butt and forend. A magnum version was offered for the 7mm Remington, 300 Winchester and 338 Winchester magnum cartridges.

Model 70 Stainless [Classic] rifle, 1992 to date. Featuring matte stainless steel finish on the major metal components—including the barrel, receiver and bolt—this also has a black fiberglass/graphite composite stock. By 1996, guns were being offered in 22-250, 243 Winchester, 270 Winchester, 7mm Remington Magnum, 300 Weatherby Magnum, 300 Winchester Magnum, 30-06, 308 Winchester, 338 Winchester Magnum and 375 H&H Magnum; a 270 Weatherby Magnum chambering followed in 1997, when BOSS versions of all but 22-250, 308 Winchester and 375 H&H Magnum were also introduced. Overall length is 43-45in, depending on the barrel, and weight averages 6.75lb.

Model 70 Standard rifle, 1972-80. The earliest guns of this type were similar to the 70A, but had five-round staggered-column magazines and conventional magazine floorplates; chamberings duplicated the M70A list, with the addition of short-lived 225 Winchester (1973-4 only). A 25-06 Remington option was introduced

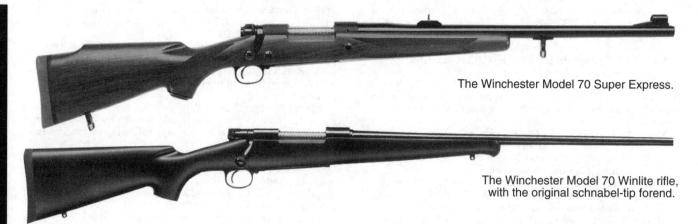

The Winchester Model 70 Super Express.

The Winchester Model 70 Winlite rifle, with the original schnabel-tip forend.

in 1972-3 (with 24in or 26in barrels). The butt had a Monte Carlo comb and a cheekpiece, an ebonite forend cap, and white spacers accompanying the buttplate and the pistol grip cap.

Model 70 Super Express [XTR] [Classic] rifle, 1983 to date. Replacements for the M70 African Rifle, chambered for 375 H&H or 458 Winchester magnum rounds and sometimes known as the 'Super Express Magnum', these impressive-looking guns had two steel recoil bolts in the stock, thermoplastic bedding, matte-black finish, open sights, and the front swivel eye on the barrel instead of the forend. They weighed 8.5lb apiece and had three-round magazines. A 416 Remington option was added in the early 1990s. The butt originally had a Monte Carlo comb, but the Classic version has a straight design.

Model 70 Super Grade rifle. A post-1973 name for the 'M70 Custom' (q.v.).

Model 70 Super Grade [Classic] rifle, 1990 to date. A deluxe version of the standard Sporter, made with a 24in barrel in 7mm Remington Magnum, 300 Winchester Magnum or 338 Winchester Magnum (though 270 and 30-06 non-Magnum options were offered from 1991), this weighs 7.8lb empty. The classic straight-comb stock has swivel eyes beneath butt and forend. Super Grade rifles have always had a non-rotating collar-type extractor and are numbered in their own series. New BOSS versions were added in 1996.

Model 70 Target rifle, 1972-80? A duplication of the original 1964 pattern, apart from the improved action, this had a high-comb 'Marksman' stock with a hand-stop and a swivel eye beneath the forend. Made only in 30-06 and 308 Winchester, with a five-round magazine, the guns had 26in barrels and weighed 10.5lb. Open sights were omitted.

Model 70 Ultimate Classic rifle, 1996 to date. This may be found with round, fluted, half-octagon or octagonal barrels. Finish may be blue or stain stainless steel; the woodwork is specially selected for its grain; and the engraving includes game scenes inlaid in gold. Chamberings were initially restricted to the 300 H&H and 300 Weatherby Magnum cartridges, but 25-06, 264 Winchester Magnum, 270 Winchester, 7mm Remington Magnum, 7mm STW, 300 Winchester Magnum and 30-06 were added in 1997.

Model 70 Ultra Match rifle, 1972-81? Similar to the M70 Target rifle, this was a 'custom grade' pattern with a 26in heavy barrel bedded in fiberglass resin, a counter-bored muzzle, and a trigger which could be adjusted externally.

Model 70 Varmint [XTR] rifle, 1969-95. Originally offered only in 222 Remington, 22-250 Remington or 243 Winchester, Varmint rifles were stocked identically with the standard M70 apart from having noticeably less drop at the heel. However, they had heavy barrels and weighed 9.5-9.8lb. The manufacturing pattern was altered to XTR standards in 1978 and a 223 Remington option was added in 1985, but the XTR label was abandoned in 1989 when another revised pattern appeared. This had a standard Sporter stock—with Monte Carlo comb and cheekpiece—plus a 26in heavyweight barrel with a counter-bored muzzle. The receiver was drilled and tapped for optical-sight mounts. Weighing about 9lb, the finalized Model 70 Varmint could be obtained in 22-250, 223 Remington or 243 Winchester. A 308 Winchester option was introduced in 1990.

Model 70 Westerner rifle, 1985-6. This made a brief appearance in the mid-1980s, chambered for the 270 Winchester, 7mm Remington Magnum, 300 Winchester Magnum, 30-06 or 308 rounds. It may simply have been the old-style Model 70A under a temporary new name.

Model 70 Win-Cam rifle, 1986-95. Available only in 270 Winchester or 30-06 Springfield, these rifles had a special warp-resistant laminated hardwood stock with a classic straight comb and green/brown camouflage finish. 24in barrels and a rubber recoil pad were standard. The receiver ring and bridge were drilled and tapped for optical-sight mounts.

Model 70 Win-Cam Lightweight rifle, 1987-95. Offered only in 270 Winchester and 30-06, with a 22in barrel, this rifle could be distinguished by its greenish laminated hardwood half-stock.

Model 70 Winlite rifle (or 'Winlight'), 1986-90. This rifle had a textured black fiberglass McMillan stock with a straight comb and conventional pistol grip. Checkering was absent. Stocks fitted to 22in-barreled Featherweight actions had a shallow schnabel tip on the forend. Chamberings were originally restricted to 270 Winchester and 30-06, but 280 Remington was added in 1987; weight was about 6.5lb and the magazine capacity was restricted to four cartridges. A magnum version had a 24in barrel, a three-round magazine and a round-tipped forend. Chambering options were initially 7mm Remington Magnum, 300 Winchester Magnum and 338 Winchester Magnum; 300 Weatherby Magnum was added in 1988.

Model 70 Win-Tuff rifle, 1986-95. Similar to the Win-Cam pattern, this had a 22in barrel and a brown laminated stock. Weight averaged 6.3lb. Guns have been chambered for 223 Remington, 243 Winchester, 270 Winchester, 30-06 or 308 Winchester.

Model 70 Win-Tuff Featherweight rifle, 1988-9 and 1992-6. This was originally chambered for the 22-250 and 243 Winchester rounds. Originally made for only one year, the basic pattern subsequently reappeared in 1992 in 22-250, 223 Remington, 243 Winchester, 270 Winchester, 30-06 or 308 Winchester. It had a 22in barrel, measured 42-42.5in overall, and weighed 6.75-7lb.

Model 70 Win-Tuff Lightweight rifle, 1987-95. Identifiable by a laminated brown hardwood stock, with checkering on the pistol grip and forend, this was chambered for cartridges including 22-250 (1988-9 only), 223 Remington (1989 onward), 243 Winchester (1988-95), 270 Winchester (1988-95), 30-06 and 308 Winchester (1989-95).

Model 70 Win-Tuff Sporter, 1992-5. This gun had a brown laminated stock. It was 44.5in overall, with a 24in barrel, and weighed 7.6-7.9lb. Chamberings included the 270 Winchester, 7mm Remington Magnum, 300 Weatherby Magnum, 300 Winchester Magnum, 30-06 Springfield and 338 Winchester Magnum rounds.

Model 70 XTR European Featherweight rifle, 1986 only. This short-lived Winchester was chambered for the 6.5x55 cartridge. It had a 22in barrel, a five-round magazine, and weighed 6.75lb. Open sights were provided.

Model 70A rifle, 1969-78. This was the original and most basic pattern. A Monte Carlo half-stock had a synthetic buttplate, with impressed checkering on the pistol grip and round-tipped forend. Standard Model 70A rifles had 22in barrels, lacked the floorplate assembly and had four-round 'blind' magazines. They were originally chambered for 222 Remington, 22-250 Remington, 243 Winchester, 270 Winchester, 30-06 or 308 Winchester cartridges. A 25-06 Remington option was introduced in 1972-3 (with 24in or 26in barrels) and discontinued in 1974. A magnum version was offered for the 264 Winchester or 300 Winchester cartridges, with 24in barrels, rubber recoil pads and three-round internal magazines.

Model 70A Police rifle, 1980-3. This short-lived 70A variant was offered with an oil-finished stock in 30-06 or 308.

Model 70A XTR rifle, 1978-? Distinguished by a high-polish blue finish, and special walnut stocks with machine-cut wraparound checkering on the forend, this had a Monte Carlo comb which was lower and appreciably longer than its predecessors. A magnum version was also made.

MODEL 310 SPORTING RIFLE

Made by the Winchester Repeating Arms Company, New Haven, Connecticut, 1972-5.

Total production: not known. **Chambering options:** 22 Short, Long and Long rifle, interchangeably. **Action:** locked by turning the bolt handle down into its seat in the receiver.

40.1in overall, about 5lb empty. 22in barrel, 4-groove rifling; RH, concentric. Tube magazine beneath barrel, 15-21 rounds depending on cartridge length. Spring-leaf and elevator rear sight. 1080 fps with 40-grain bullet (22LR).

Introduced to replace the Model 121 (q.v.), this simple single-shot rifle had a walnut half-stock with a Monte Carlo comb, checkering on the pistol grip and forend, and swivels beneath the butt and forend. Changes were made to improve the action, but the Model 310 was no more successful than its predecessor had been.

SIMILAR GUNS

Model 320 rifle, 1972-4. A repeating version of the Model 310, this had a detachable five-round box magazine.

• Winchester, lever-action type

The New Haven Arms Company, manufacturers of the Henry Rifle, was acquired by the newly formed Winchester Repeating Arms Company in 1865. The Model 1866 Winchester rifle was simply an improved Henry with a stronger extractor and, more importantly, a hinged loading gate on the right side of the frame. Patented by Nelson King in May 1866, this not only enabled the shooter to insert cartridges without taking his eyes off the target but also allowed a fixed magazine and a conventional wooden forend to be used. The new rifle was still prone to jamming if mud or dust entered through the top of the action, but it was a better weapon than the Henry. A new centerfire gun, introduced in 1873, provided the basis for a series of similar guns which ensured long-term success.

MILITARY RIFLES

The Models 1873 and 1876—together with the Browning-designed Model 1894—were offered as muskets or fully-stocked carbines, with military-style barrel bands and nose caps. They could also be fitted with bayonets. Sales were few, though 1020 M1866 rifles chambering 44 S&W centerfire cartridges were sold to Brazil in 1891.

A few 1873-type guns were sold in Central and South America, where they were favored by rural gendarmerie and irregulars. Mexico, for example, had purchased about one thousand M1866 rifles for the forces of Benito Juarez (delivered in 1867) and an unknown quantity of M1894 carbines for the 'Rurales' (rural gendarmerie) about 1903. Copies of the 1873-type rifle were also issued in Spain (q.v.). The best-known purchaser was Turkey, where

M1873 muskets were used to repulse the Russians during the battle of Plevna (1878).

Large quantities of commercial-type M1894 rifles and carbines were purchased by the British and the French at the beginning of World War I, but were invariably restricted to training purposes.

SPORTING GUNS

Note: Many of the modern re-creations, made in Japan for the Browning Arms Company, are listed under 'Browning, lever-action type'.

MODEL 1866 SPORTING RIFLE

Made by the Winchester Repeating Arms Company, New Haven and Bridgeport, Connecticut, 1866-97.

Total production: 170,100. **Action:** locked by a toggle-joint beneath the bolt.

DATA FOR A TYPICAL EXAMPLE

Chambering: 44-28-200, rimfire. 43.5in overall, 9.25lb empty. 24in barrel, 6 grooves; RH twist, concentric. Tube magazine beneath the barrel, 17 rounds. Leaf-spring and elevator rear sight. 1125 fps with 200-grain bullet.

Very few of these guns were made in 1866, as the factory moved to Bridgeport (where virtually all guns numbered below 125000 were made). The M1866 was essentially similar to the preceding Henry (q.v.), with a new loading gate on the right side of the bronze frame. A conventional wooden forend was also fitted. Guns were listed in Winchester catalogues long after the advent of the Model 1873; one thousand Model 1866 rifles were sold to Brazil as late as 1891.

THE GUNS

Model 1866 carbine. This was basically a short rifle, with a 20in round barrel held by two bands. A saddle ring normally lay on the left side of the receiver ahead of the butt, and the magazines nominally held 13 rounds. Four minor variations were made, differing in the machining of the frame and the design of the firing pin.

Model 1866 musket. Weighing about 8.3lb, this had a 27in round barrel. The magazine capacity was usually only 17 rounds—the same as the rifle—as the tube ended a few inches short of the muzzle to allow a socket bayonet to be mounted. Guns were made in the same four variants as the M1866 rifle, but had three barrel bands and sling-swivels.

Model 1866 rifle. Offered with a 24in round or octagonal barrel, this weighed 9-9.5lb. Magazines held as many as 17 rounds, though were usually loaded with fewer to reduce strain on the magazine spring. Four minor variants are recognized by collectors. Most of the changes concerned the machining of the frame, though the earliest had two screws running into the butt through the upper tang instead of the later one. The 'fourth pattern' rifle had a convertible rimfire/centerfire firing pin.

MODEL 1873 SPORTING RIFLE

Made by the Winchester Repeating Arms Company, New Haven, Connecticut, 1873-about 1924.

Total production: 720,610. **Chambering options:** 32-20 Winchester, 38-40 Winchester or 44-40 Winchester. **Action:** generally as M1866, above.

DATA FOR TYPICAL EXAMPLE

Chambering: 44-40 Winchester, rimmed. 43.75in overall, 8.87lb empty. 24in barrel, 6-groove rifling; RH, concentric. Tube magazine under barrel, 15 rounds. Spring-leaf and elevator rear sight. 1310 fps with 200-grain bullet.

The centerfire M1873 was similar to its 1866-type rimfire predecessor externally, but had an iron receiver and mounts. Unlike the flush-sided M1866, but in common with the later M1876, the 1873-pattern receiver had a prominent raised panel on the right

A Model 1866 Winchester rifle,
with an engraved brass frame. (W&W)

A 45-75 Winchester Model 1876 rifle,
with an octagon barrel. (W&W)

side. It was initially offered as a Sporting Rifle, Musket or Carbine, but decoration, barrel length and details of finish were often left to the whim of the customer. Consequently, guns could be found with half-length (six round) magazine tubes, set triggers, unusually short or extraordinarily long barrels, or shotgun-pattern butts. Unusually accurate barrels could be finished as 'One of One Thousand' (best) or 'One of One Hundred' (second-best) guns, but production amounted to only 136 and eight guns respectively.

Military-style leaf sights were favored on muskets, and folding leaves or tang-mounted Vernier peep sights could be provided on Special Sporting Rifles. The original screw-pattern lever retainer was replaced by a sliding catch in 1876 and, in 1879, alterations were made to the finger lever so that the trigger could not operate until the action was completely closed. The breech cover was altered to slide on a rib held to the receiver with two screws, a solid-face bolt was fitted, and the concave shoulder plate was supplemented by an optional straight or 'shotgun' pattern.

A 38-40 chambering introduced in 1880 was joined in 1882 by 32-20, and the original iron receiver was replaced in 1884 by a forged-steel pattern with an integral breech-cover rib.

Though the centerfire M1873 patterns were abandoned after World War I, a few guns were assembled from parts into the mid-1920s. And there are, of course, many modern reproductions of the most famous of all the Wild West rifles.

THE GUNS

Model 1873 Carbine. Distinguished by its 20in round barrel, this also had a short 12-round magazine.

Model 1873 Musket. Made with a 30in round barrel and a 17-round magazine, this had two barrel bands and a nose cap; socket bayonets were most popular, though brass-hilted sword types were also available.

Model 1873 Sporting Rifle (centerfire), 1873-1919. This was made with a 20in octagonal barrel, or a 24in round, half- or fully-octagonal pattern. Rifle magazines usually held 15 rounds.

Model 1873 Sporting Rifle (rimfire), 1885-1904. Externally similar to the standard version, this lacked the loading gate on the receiver-side.

MODEL 1876 SPORTING RIFLE

Made by the Winchester Repeating Arms Company, New Haven, Connecticut, 1876-97.

Total production: 63,870. **Chambering options:** 40-60 Winchester, 45-60 Winchester, 45-75 Winchester or 50-95 Winchester. **Action:** generally as M1873, above.

DATA FOR A TYPICAL EXAMPLE

Chambering: 50-95 Winchester, rimmed. 47.9in overall, 9.15lb empty. 26in barrel, 6-groove rifling; RH, concentric. Tube magazine under barrel, 4 rounds. Spring-leaf and elevator rear sight. 1555 fps with 300-grain bullet.

The origins of this gun lay in an experimental 45-70-405 prototype, patented by Luke Wheelock in January 1871, which was submitted unsuccessfully to the U.S. Army in 1872. Rifles chambering a powerful 45-75 cartridge were subsequently exhibited in 1876 at the Centennial Exposition in Philadelphia, and the first series-made guns were shipped from the New Haven factory in June 1877.

The M1876 was offered as a Sporting Rifle, an Express Rifle, a musket or a short-barreled carbine. Like all Winchesters of this period, however, M1876 rifles could be completed to individual requirements and came in a bewildering profusion of styles from plain to 'One of One Thousand' grades (only 54 of the latter were made).

New 40-60 and 50-95 Winchester options were added in 1879; these were followed by a trigger-lock, and a breech cover sliding on a rib held to the receiver with two screws. A change to a forged-steel receiver with an integral breech-cover rib was made in 1884, when the 40-60 chambering was announced.

THE GUNS

Note: Collectors recognize several differing manufacturing patterns.

Model 1876 Carbine. This was originally offered with a 22in barrel, customarily round, and the forend was held with a single band; carbine magazines normally held only nine rounds. Though otherwise unpopular, about 750 full-stock Model 1876 carbines were purchased by the Royal Northwest Mounted Police of Canada in 1883. They were marked 'R.N.W.P.' on the right side of the butt.

Model 1876 Express Rifle. Made with a 26in round, half- or full-octagon barrel, this was also often highly decorated.

Model 1876 Musket. Distinguished by a 32in barrel and a long forend held with two bands, this was normally accompanied by a socket bayonet. Lugs for sword patterns could be substituted on request. Magazines held 13 rounds.

Model 1876 Special Sporting Rifle. This had a pistol grip stock and was often furnished with a vernier peep sight on the tang behind the hammer.

Model 1876 Sporting Rifle. Offered as standard with a 28in round, half- or full-octagon barrel, this customarily had a 12-round magazine. A six-round half-length version was also available.

MODEL 1886 SPORTING RIFLE

Made by the Winchester Repeating Arms Company (1886-1932) and by the Winchester-Western Division of Olin Industries (1932-6), New Haven, Connecticut.

Total production: about 160,000 to 1936. **Chambering options:** 33 Winchester, 348 Winchester, 38-56 Winchester, 38-70 Winchester, 40-65 Winchester, 40-70 Winchester, 40-75 Bullard (used in 40-82 chamber), 40-82 Winchester, 45-70 Government, 45-82 Winchester or 45-85 Winchester

The Winchester Model 1886 rifle,
with a half-length magazine. (W&W)

(used in 45-90 chamber), 45-90 Winchester, 50-100 or 50-110 Express. **Action:** locked by vertically-sliding bars intercepting the bolt.

DATA FOR A TYPICAL EXAMPLE

Chambering: 50-110 Express, rimmed. 45.75in overall, 8.77lb empty. 26in barrel, 6-groove rifling; RH, concentric. Tube magazine under barrel, 4 rounds. Spring-leaf and elevator rear sight. 1605 fps with 300-grain bullet.

Though the 1876-pattern rifle was an improvement on its predecessors, its inability to handle high chamber pressures favored rivals such as Marlin. In 1883, Winchester's management were able to buy rights not only to a promising single-shot dropping-block gun developed by the Browning brothers (q.v.) but also of a lever-action breech—eventually patented by John Browning in October 1884—which was locked by sturdy vertically-sliding bars.

Production began in New Haven in 1886, after improvements to the feed mechanism had been made by William Mason. The first rifles were chambered for the 40-82, 45-70 and 45-90 cartridges, but three more options (38-56 and 40-65 Winchester, plus 50-110 Express) were offered from 1888-9, followed in 1894 by 38-70 and 40-72 Winchester. A 50-100-450 pattern became available in 1895, and 33 Winchester from 1903. Frames, buttplates and forend caps are said to have been case-hardened until 1901, but blued thereafter except to special order.

Ultra-long (28in-36in) barrels, which had been made to special order, were abandoned in 1908 and a major reduction of the growing list of chamberings was made in 1911: 38-56, 38-70, 40-65, 40-72, 40-82, 45-90 and 50-100-450 were all abandoned in this period, followed by 45-70 (and apparently, 50-110 Express) in 1920—though 45-70 was reinstated in 1928, only to be finally abandoned three years later. The 33 WCF option disappeared shortly before the M1886 was superseded by the Model 71 in 1935.

THE GUNS

Model 1886 Carbine. A full-stock carbine was described in the Winchester catalogue of 1887, but was made only in exceptionally small numbers. It was replaced in 1889 by a gun with a 22in round barrel, a straight-wrist butt, and a half-length forend.

Model 1886 Fancy Sporting Rifle. This was made with a pistol grip butt of specially-selected walnut, and had a 26in octagon barrel. A variety of decoration will be encountered.

Model 1886 Half-Magazine Rifle. A 'shotgun butt' and the usual 26in barrel options defined this pattern, in addition to a magazine tube which extended only a short distance from the forend tip.

Model 1886 Musket. About 350 of these were made, with a 30in barrel, a full-length forend retained by a single band, military sights, and provision for a socket bayonet.

Model 1886 Sporting Rifle. Made with a straight-grip butt and a concave shoulder plate, this had a 26in round, octagon or half-octagon barrel.

Model 1886 Take-Down Rifle. This appeared in 1894, but only about 350 were ever made.

Model 1886 Extra Light-Weight Rifle. Dating from 1897, this 45-70 gun had a 22in round barrel.

Model 71 rifle, 1935-57. Announced commercially on New Year's Day 1936, this was an M1886 adapted for the powerful new 348 Winchester game cartridge. Made with a 24in barrel and half-

An advertisement for the 1886-type Winchester rifle.

length four-round magazines, the rifles had checkered pistol grip butts, rubber pistol grip caps, beaver-tail forends and detachable swivels. A plain-butt gun was authorized on 6th January 1936. Some guns were sold with spring-leaf and elevator rear sights, but most had a peep pattern. A variant of the rifle with a 20in round barrel was announced in January 1937 and, on 3rd September, a long comb butt was substituted and a safety catch was added to the lower tang. Total production amounted to about 47,250, including a few deluxe examples.

MODEL 1892 SPORTING RIFLE

Made in New Haven, Connecticut, by the Winchester Repeating Arms Company (1892-1941 [all types], owned by the Western Cartridge Company from 1932 onward).

Total production: not known. **Chambering options:** 218 Bee, 25-20 Winchester, 32-20 Winchester, 357 Magnum, 38-40 Winchester, 44 Remington Magnum or 44-40 Winchester. **Action:** as M1886, above.

DATA FOR A TYPICAL EXAMPLE

Chambering: 32-20 Winchester, rimmed. 41.6in overall, 6.83lb empty. 24in barrel, 6-groove rifling; RH, concentric. Tube magazine under barrel, 5 rounds. Spring-leaf and elevator rear sight. 1290 fps with 100-grain bullet.

This reduced-scale M1886 was developed in the early 1890s partly to provide a cheaper rifle, and partly to use short-case cartridges established by the original M1873—e.g., 38-40 and 44-40. A 25-20 Winchester option was added in 1895.

THE GUNS

Model 1892 Carbine, 1893-1941. This usually had a straight-wrist butt, a band around the forend, and a round 20in barrel. Guns were also made with barrels of 12-18in, often known by the sobriquet "Trappers' Carbines". Production of carbines continued in 25-20 and 44-40 after the 1892-type rifle had been abandoned. Most guns had raised rear sights and ramp-type front sights, and

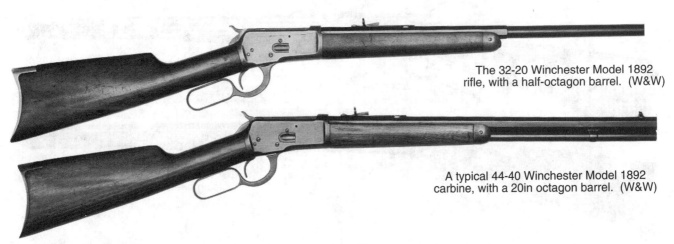

The 32-20 Winchester Model 1892 rifle, with a half-octagon barrel. (W&W)

A typical 44-40 Winchester Model 1892 carbine, with a 20in octagon barrel. (W&W)

a few will even be encountered with long Model 53-type barrels. A 218 Bee option was introduced in 1936.

Model 1892 Fancy Sporting Rifle, 1892-1930. Offered with a pistol grip butt, in any of the standard barrel styles, this could also have a half-length magazine tube.

Model 1892 Grade I and High Grade rifles, 1997. Re-creations of the original guns, made only in 45 Colt, these have a sliding safety catch on the tang behind the rebounding hammer. Grade I has a blued receiver, engraved with a pronghorn antelope and scrollwork; the High Grade, which also has selected woodwork, has the same antelope motif and bordering highlighted in gold inlay.

Model 1892 Musket, 1898-1903. The short-lived 30in-barreled Musket had a straight-wrist butt, three barrel bands, a nose cap and swivels.

Model 1892 Sporting Rifle, 1892-1932. The standard pattern had a straight-wrist butt, a concave shoulder plate, and a 24in round, octagon or half-octagon barrel. It was eventually replaced by the Models 53 and 65 (qq.v.), though production of carbines continued for a few years.

Model 1892 Take Down Rifle. This was announced in the autumn of 1893, but few were made. The magazine unscrews from the frame.

Model 53 rifle, 1924-32. An attempt to simplify the Model 1892, this offered on a 22in round barrel and a half-length six-round magazine contained in the forend. Chamberings were restricted to 25-20, 38-40 and 44-40 Winchester. The butt was usually straight-wristed, though pistol grip patterns could be obtained on request. The production total of 24,920 should be considered as an approximation, as receivers were apparently numbered in series with the Model 1892. A take-down pattern was also made in small numbers.

Model 65 rifle, 1933-47. Announced on 1st March 1933, this was an improved version of the Model 53 (i.e., the M1892) with a refined trigger and an improved front sight on a forged ramp. It was offered with a 22in round barrel in 25-20 or 32-20 Winchester, and had a pistol grip butt. A special 24in-barreled 218 Bee variant was announced in 1939, enjoying a brief period in vogue before World War II began. Production totaled only about 5700.

MODEL 1894 SPORTING RIFLE

Details of post-1936 guns will be found in a separate section, below.
Made in New Haven, Connecticut, by the Winchester Repeating Arms
   Company (1894-1936, owned by the Western Cartridge Company
   from 1932).
Total production: more than seven million (all types). **Chambering options:** 25-35 Winchester, 30-30 Winchester, 32 Winchester Special, 32-40 Winchester or 38-55 Winchester. **Action:** as M1886, above.
DATA FOR A TYPICAL EXAMPLE
   Chambering: 30-30 Winchester, rimmed. 38.15in overall, 6.9lb empty. 20in barrel, 6-groove rifling; RH, concentric. Tube magazine under barrel, 6 rounds. Spring-leaf and elevator rear sight. 2220 fps with 170-grain bullet.

This Browning design was patented in August 1894. Chambered initially for the 32-40, 38-55 or 44-40 cartridges, the Sporting Rifle (solid-frame or take-down) offered a 26in round, octagon or half-octagon barrel and straight-wrist or pistol grip butts. Most rifles had full length eight-round magazines, though a four-car-

tridge half-length pattern was common on take-down guns. Barrels, finish and accessories varied greatly.

The 25-35 and 30-30 options were announced in 1895, and the first 32 Winchester Special chamberings appeared in 1902. Though the M1894 was supplemented in 1924 by the Model 55 (q.v.), its popularity never waned and the millionth M1894 was made in 1927. The 32 Winchester Special option was withdrawn in 1930, but a raised back-sight base and a ramp-type front sight were adopted in November 1931. Assembly of rifles ceased in 1936, when all chamberings except 44-40 were withdrawn, but work on carbines continued until World War II began.

SIMILAR GUNS

Model 1894 Carbine, 1894-1941. Guns of this type usually had a 20in round barrel and a full-length (six-round) magazine, though a few four-cartridge magazines were made. Trappers' Carbines were made with barrels of 14-18in. Saddle rings were omitted from carbines made after 1925.

Model 1894 Extra Light-Weight Rifle, 1897-1918. This special design was introduced with a 22in or 26in round barrel and a shotgun-style butt. It was eventually discontinued at the end of World War I, though none had been made for some time.

Model 1894 Fancy Sporting Rifle. This had a pistol grip butt only.

Model 1894 Take-Down Rifle. Introduced in the early 1900s, but made only in small numbers, this had a magazine tube which unscrewed from the receiver.

Model 55 rifle, 1924-32. Introduced to accompany the Model 53, this 1894-type gun offered a limited range of options. Chamberings were restricted to 25-35 Winchester, 30-30 Winchester or 32 Winchester Special, and the 24in round barrel was accompanied by a half-length three-round magazine in the forend, which restricted capacity too greatly to have universal appeal. A straight-wrist butt was standard, a pistol grip pattern being offered to order. The production total of 20,580 is approximate; after about 2700 guns had been made, receivers were taken from the same series as M1894 carbines.

Model 64 rifle, 1933-57. The spartan lines of the Model 55, and the limited options available to the purchaser, restricted sales far more than Winchester had predicted. Though confined to the same basic chamberings, the Model 64 offered a longer magazine tube and a refined trigger mechanism. Standard (or 'Sporting') Rifles had a pistol grip butt and a 20in or 24in round barrel. The guns all had a hooded front-sight blade on a forged ramp. A 219 Zipper variant of the Sporting Rifle appeared in 1938, but lasted a mere three years. Total production amounted to 66,780 guns.

Model 64 rifle, modern pattern, 1972-3. About 8250 of these were made for the 30-30 cartridge, with minor changes in the action and fittings.

Model 64 Deer Rifle, 1934-9. Distinguished by a hard rubber pistol grip cap, this had a 20in or 24in round barrel, and detachable swivels.

MODEL 1895 SPORTING RIFLE

Made by the Winchester Repeating Arms Company, New Haven,
   Connecticut, 1895-1931.

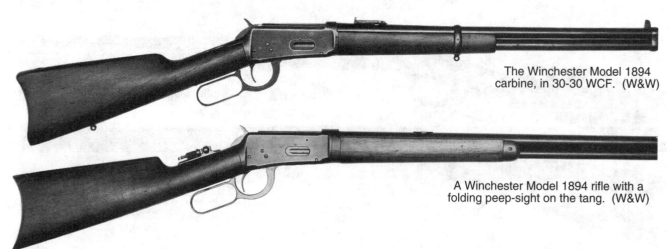

The Winchester Model 1894 carbine, in 30-30 WCF. (W&W)

A Winchester Model 1894 rifle with a folding peep-sight on the tang. (W&W)

Total production: 426,000 to 1931. **Chambering options:** 30-03, 30-06, 303 British, 30-40 Krag, 35 Winchester, 38-72 Winchester, 40-72 Winchester or 405 Winchester. **Action:** generally as M1886, above.

DATA FOR A TYPICAL EXAMPLE

Chambering: 40-72 Winchester, rimmed. 42.0in overall, 7.55lb empty. 24in barrel, 6-groove rifling; RH, concentric. Integral box magazine loaded from a stripper-clip, 5 rounds. Spring-leaf and elevator rear sight. 1405 fps with 330-grain bullet.

A considerable departure from earlier lever-action Winchesters, this box-magazine pattern was developed specifically for high-power small-caliber smokeless cartridges. The greatest military success of the 1895-pattern Winchester came in 1915, during World War I in Europe, when the beleaguered Imperial Russian government ordered 300,000 7.62mm guns. Details are included in the 'Russia (Tsarist)' chapter.

THE GUNS

Model 1895 Carbine. This was little more than a rifle with a straight-wrist butt and a 20in barrel, made only in 30-40, 30-03, 30-06 and 303. Its forend had a rounded tip.

Model 1895 Fancy Sporting Rifle. This was a deluxe version of the standard sporter with a straight-wrist or pistol grip shotgun-style butt.

Model 1895 Musket, 1896-1918. These guns were invariably stocked to the muzzle, with a short upper handguard, a finger groove in the forend, a barrel band, and a nose cap with a bayonet lug. The original pattern (30-40 Krag or 303 British) was accompanied by a proprietary knife bayonet, and the first few guns had flat-side frames. Later guns were also made in 30-03 and 30-06.

Model 1895 NRA Musket, 1905-15? Essentially similar to the U.S. Army model, this had a 30in barrel and a 1901-type Krag rear sight. Chambered for the 30 M1903 cartridge, the original version was superseded in 1908 by a 30 M1906 gun with a 24in barrel.

Model 1895 Sporting Rifle. Offered initially only in 38-72 or 40-72 Winchester, this had a round, half-round or octagon barrel. The rifle-style butt had a straight wrist. Most half-length forends had schnabel tips, and at least 5000 low-number guns had distinctive flat-side receivers. A 35 Winchester version was introduced in 1903, followed in 1904 by a 405 Winchester chambering. Barrels measuring more than 28in, previously available to order, were abandoned after 1908. The British 303 chambering was withdrawn in 1918, but the last guns were not sold from store until 1938—though it is believed that assembly had ceased in 1931.

Model 1895 Sporting Rifle, modern version. Introduced in 1997 in 270 Winchester and 30-06, with a four-round magazine, this has a two-piece underlever. A sliding hammer stop (safety catch) has been added on the tang, and the hammer is a rebounding

The Winchester Model 1895 sporting rifle, chambered for the British 303 cartridge.

The open action of a Russian-pattern M1895 Winchester rifle.

pattern. The woodwork consists of a checkered straight-comb butt and a slender schnabel-tipped forend. The rifles are 42in long, with a 24in barrel, and weigh about 8lb.

Model 1895 Take Down Rifle, 1910-14? A modified form of the standard rifle, this had a noticeable joint between the barrel/forend assembly and the remainder of the action.

Model 1895 U.S. Army Pattern, 1897-8. This was a six-shot 30-caliber derivative of the musket, with a 28in round barrel and an M1892 sword bayonet. A few rifles of this type saw service in the hands of militia and volunteers during the Spanish-American War of 1898; service-issue guns will bear 'U.S.' property mark on the frame.

MODEL 94 STANDARD CARBINE

For details of preceding pattern, see 'Model 1894' above.

Made in New Haven, Connecticut, by the Winchester Repeating Arms Company (1894-1932), by the Winchester-Western Division of Olin Industries (1932-83), and by the U.S. Repeating Arms Company (1983 to date).

Total production: more than seven million (all types). **Chambering options:** see notes. **Action:** as Model 1894, above.

DATA FOR A TYPICAL EXAMPLE

Chambering: 7x30 Waters, rimmed. 37.25in overall, 6.65lb empty. 20in barrel, 6-groove rifling; RH, concentric? Tube magazine beneath barrel, 6 rounds. Spring-leaf and elevator rear sight. 2600 fps with 139-grain bullet.

The pre-1936 history of this Browning-designed rifle will be found in the 'Model 1894' section. The 25-35 Winchester chambering was reinstated in 1940, but work virtually stopped at the end of 1941 when war began. When production began again in 1946, the standard Model 94 Carbine had a plain straight-wrist walnut butt and a half-length forend held by a single band. The front sight had a detachable hood and the receiver was drilled and tapped for optical sight mounts.

Standard Model 94 carbines made after 1984 embodied the Angle Eject feature, in 30-30 Winchester, 38-55 Winchester, 44 Remington Magnum/.44 S&W Special or 45 Colt. Magazines held six or 11 rounds, depending on whether the cartridge had been a rifle or handgun type. Sales of Model 1894/Model 94 Winchesters of all types reached seven million in 1987, but the 20in heavy barrel and Monte Carlo butt options were then abandoned. A 32 Winchester Special chambering option was introduced for the standard Model 94 in 1992.

All post-1991 guns have a safety bolt through the receiver ahead of the hammer. Changes were made in the lever system in 1992, making operation smoother and quieter; new-style guns can be distinguished by an additional link pin and set screw in the mechanism. The current standard pattern, made in 30-30 only, has been widely advertised as the 'Model 94 Walnut' to distinguish it from the Win-Tuff version.

SIMILAR GUNS

Note: Commemorative guns have not been included in this edition, as research is still underway.

Model 94 Angle Eject carbine, 1983 to date. Chambered for the 307, 356 or 375 Winchester rounds, this appeared in standard or XTR form. It was easily identified by a strange combination of a Monte Carlo comb and a straight-wrist butt. Angle Eject guns (later known as 'Side Eject') were designed to accommodate low-mounted optical sights and could be identified by the lowered right receiver wall. A lateral extension was added to the hammer spur to facilitate cocking when an optical sight was fitted, and a transfer-bar safety system was added. Swivels were usually fitted to the butt and magazine tube. The guns had 20in barrels and six-round magazines. The 356 and 375 chamberings were abandoned in 1986, though the 356 version reappeared after an absence of only two years.

Model 94 Antique carbine, 1964-84. Offered only in 30-30 Winchester, this had a color case-hardened receiver with rolled-in scrollwork. The loading gate was brass plated, and a saddle ring was fitted on the left rear side of the receiver.

Model 94 Big Bore rifle [XTR], 1983 to date. This carbine-length gun was specifically designed for the 375 Winchester cartridge, though 307 and 356 options were subsequently added. The reinforced receiver was machined from a solid billet of ordnance steel. Checkered walnut woodwork, a rubber buttplate and high-polish finish were standard. The XTR suffix was dropped in 1989, and the 1997 chamberings were restricted to the 307 and 356 cartridges.

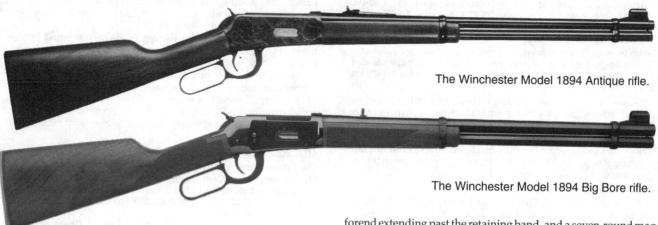

The Winchester Model 1894 Antique rifle.

The Winchester Model 1894 Big Bore rifle.

Model 94 carbine [XTR]. 'XTR'-grade woodwork—better stock finish, cut checkering—and the high-polish blue finish were extended to standard gun in 1978, causing a temporary change in designation. A 7x30 Waters chambering was introduced in 1984-5.

Model 94 Classic carbine, 1967-72. This was easily distinguished by its 20in octagon barrel.

Model 94 Classic rifle, 1967-70. Introduced with a 26in octagon barrel, this had a black-chrome receiver and forend cap; buttplates were blued, and loading gates were gold plated. Classic patterns were not popular; confined to 30-30 chambering, only about 47,000 rifles and carbines were made.

Model 94 Deluxe carbine [XTR], 1987-8. Made only in 30-30, this had a 20in barrel and a high-polish finish and a cursive 'Deluxe' rolled into the receiver. Its select woodwork had cut fleur-de-lis checkering.

Model 94 Legacy, 1996 to date. Easily distinguished by a checkered pistol grip butt and a checkered forend, this was originally offered only with a 20in carbine-type barrel chambered for the 30-30 round. A 24in barrel was introduced in 1997, together with 357 Magnum, 33 Magnum and 45 Colt chamberings.

Model 94 Long-Barrel rifle, 1988-? Guns of this type had a 24in barrel chambered for the 30-30 cartridge, an open front sight, a forend extending past the retaining band, and a seven-round magazine.

Model 94 Ranger, 1985 to date. Available only in 30-30, this had beech woodwork and a five-cartridge magazine. The front-sight hood was omitted, but the gun was identical mechanically with the standard Angle Eject Model 94.

Model 94 Saddle Ring Carbine ('SRC' or 'SRC Magnum'), 1967-72. Made only in 44 Remington Magnum, this had a 20in barrel and a prominent ring attached to an eyebolt on the left side of the receiver.

Model 94 Side Eject carbine. This name has been applied since the late 1980s to what had previously been the 'Angle Eject' design.

Model 94 Sporting rifle [XTR], 1983-8. Distinguished by a 24in barrel, this was 41.7in long, weighed about 7lb, and had a seven-round magazine. A 7x30 Waters option was introduced in 1984-5. Rifles lacked the front sight hood associated with most of the short-barrel carbines.

Model 94 Trail's End. Introduced in 1997, this offers a 20in carbine-length barrel in 357 Magnum, 44 Remington Magnum or 45 Colt. The woodwork is plain walnut, the rear sight is a spring-leaf and elevator pattern, and the front sight is an open bead. Small and large-loop versions are made.

Model 94 Trapper carbine, 1980 to date. Introduced with a 16in barrel and a shortened magazine restricted to a capacity of five 30-30 rounds instead of six, this also had the front sight moved back behind the barrel/magazine tube retaining collar. Overall length

The Winchester Model 1894 Ranger carbine, with a 4x optical sight.

The Winchester Model 1894 Trapper carbine.

The Winchester Model 1894 Win-Tuff carbine.

with the current 16in barrel is 34.25in; weight averages 6.25lb. The 44 Remington Magnum and 45 Colt options were introduced in 1985, followed by 357 Magnum in 1992.

Model 94 Win-Tuff carbine, 1987-93. Initially made only in 30-30, this gun had a laminated wood stock.

Model 94 Wrangler [II] [Angle Eject] carbine, 1981-5 and 1992 to date. Substantial quantities of these 38-55 or 32 Winchester Special guns were made with five-round magazines and a 16in barrel. Decoration was roll-engraved into the receiver, and a characteristic ultra-large lever loop was fitted. The first 8000 guns lacked the Angle Eject feature, which appeared in 1982. The M94 Wrangler (no longer distinguished by 'II' and 'Angle Eject') reappeared in 1992 in 30-30 or 44 Remington Magnum/44 S&W Special.

MODEL 88 SPORTING RIFLE

Made by the Winchester Repeating Arms Company, New Haven, Connecticut, 1955-73.

Total production: 284,000. **Chambering options:** 243 Winchester, 284 Winchester, 308 Winchester or 358 Winchester. **Action:** locked by rotating three lugs on the bolt head into recesses in the receiver.

DATA FOR A TYPICAL EXAMPLE

Chambering: 284 Winchester, rimless. 42.1in overall, 6.53lb empty. 22in barrel, 6-groove rifling; RH, concentric. Detachable box magazine, 3 rounds. Lyman No. 16A folding-leaf rear sight. 2900 fps with 150-grain bullet.

Initially chambered only for 308 and 358, this interesting rifle was developed to fire the pointed-nose cartridges that could be a source of danger in a tube magazine. The streamlined receiver contained a rotating bolt-type locking mechanism, operated by a special short-throw lever. The one-piece stock had checkering on the pistol grip and forend; a nylon grip cap and buttplate were fitted; and swivels lay beneath forend and butt. Magazine capacity was increased to five in 1956, but this seems to have strained the feed spring and a reversion to four was made in 1957.

A 243 option was announced in 1956, but the 358 chambering was abandoned in 1962 as a new 284 cartridge was being developed. Basket-weave checkering appeared in 1965.

SIMILAR GUNS

Model 88 Carbine, 1968-73. This had a 19in barrel and a plain stock with a swivel on a barrel band.

MODEL 250 SPORTING RIFLE

Made by the Winchester Repeating Arms Company, New Haven, Connecticut, 1963-73.

Total production: not known. **Chambering options:** 22 Short, 22 Long and 22 Long rifle rimfire, interchangeably. **Action:** locked by a block rising into the underside of the bolt?

DATA FOR A TYPICAL EXAMPLE

37.8in overall, about 5lb empty. 20.5in barrel, 4-groove rifling; RH, concentric. Tube magazine beneath barrel, 15-21 rounds depending on cartridge length. Spring-leaf and elevator sight. 1080 fps with 40-grain bullet.

This was the first of the '200' series of externally similar, but internally different designs. The guns all had a round-backed aluminum alloy receiver, with the ejection port on the right side, and walnut-finish hardwood butts and forends (a synthetic Cycloac forend was offered until 1965). The front sight was mounted on a ramp, a safety bolt ran laterally through the front web of the lever bow, and the magazine tube extended virtually to the muzzle. Checkering was added to the pistol grip and forend in 1966, with white plastic spacer plates between the butt, the pistol grip cap and the shoulder plate.

SIMILAR GUNS

Model 150 Carbine, 1967-73. A simplified form of the 250, this had a plain straight-wrist butt, a straight-loop lever, and a swivel-bearing band around the forend.

Model 250 Deluxe rifle, 1965-71. This had a selected walnut butt with a cheekpiece and a fluted Monte Carlo comb; basket-weave checkering was cut into the pistol grip and forend, and swivels were added.

Model 255 Magnum rifle, 1964-73. Chambered for the 22 Winchester Magnum rimfire cartridge, this was otherwise the same as the Model 250 though magazine capacity was reduced to 11 rounds. Checkering and white spacer plates were added to the stock in 1966.

Model 255 Magnum Deluxe rifle, 1965-73. This was simply a variant of the Model 255 Magnum with a Monte Carlo comb, walnut woodwork and basket-weave checkering.

MODEL 9422 SPORTING RIFLE

Made by the Winchester Repeating Arms Company, New Haven, Connecticut, 1972 to date.

Currently in production. **Chambering options:** 22 Short, 22 Long Rifle, 22 Long Rifle and 22 Winchester Magnum rimfire. **Action:** locked by a block rising into the underside of the bolt.

DATA FOR A TYPICAL MAGNUM EXAMPLE

37.15in overall, about 6lb empty. 20.5in barrel, 4-groove rifling; RH, concentric. Tube magazine beneath barrel, 11 rounds. Spring-leaf and elevator rear sight. 2000 fps with 40-grain bullet.

This was designed as a rimfire version of the M94, though internally quite different befitting the lesser power of rimfire ammunition. The most obvious external features are the squared ejection port—on the right or left side of the receiver, depending on pattern—and the position of the loading gate under the receiver. Most of the lockwork is carried on a sub-frame, rather than in the receiver forging.

SIMILAR GUNS

Model 9422 High Grade rifle, 1995 to date. Introduced with select walnut woodwork and engraved raccoon and coonhound motifs on the blued receiver, this was adapted in 1997 to celebrate the 25th anniversary of the 9422. Only 250 of the celebratory High Grade guns have been made, together with 2500 Grade I guns.

Model 9422 Standard or 'Walnut' [XTR] rifle, 1972 to date. Made in 22LR and 22 WRM, this has a 20.5in round barrel and a plain walnut straight-comb butt. The forend has a single band. From 1982 onward, the 'XTR' butt and forend were used, with checkering and a high-gloss finish, but the suffix was abandoned in 1989. The magazines hold 15-20 rounds, or only 11 in 22 Winchester Magnum rimfire.

Model 9422 Trapper, 1996 to date. This is easily distinguished by a 16.5in barrel, which reduces the capacity of the full-length magazine to 11-15 rounds.

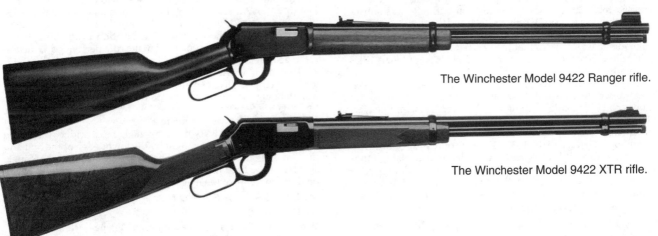

The Winchester Model 9422 Ranger rifle.

The Winchester Model 9422 XTR rifle.

Model 9422 Win-Cam rifle. Made in 22 WRM only, this had a stock and forend of brown/green camouflage laminate.

Model 9422 Win-Tuff rifle. Available in 22LR and 22 WRM rimfire, this had brown laminate woodwork.

Model 9422 XTR Classic rifle, 1985-7. Identified by its 22.5in barrel, this had a pistol grip butt and an extended forend. The buttplate was a concave steel pattern, and the lever loop was curved to follow the pistol grip.

• Winchester, slide-action type

MODEL 1890 SPORTING RIFLE

Made by the Winchester Repeating Arms Company, New Haven, Connecticut, 1890-1932.

Total production: 849,000. **Chambering options:** 22 Short, 22 Long, 22 Long Rifle or 22 Winchester Rim Fire. **Action:** locked by displacing the bolt against a shoulder in the receiver.

DATA FOR STANDARD SPORTING RIFLE

Chambering: 22 Long, rimfire. 40.2in overall, 5.75lb empty. 24in barrel, 6-groove rifling; RH, concentric. Tube magazine beneath the barrel, 11-15 rounds depending on chambering. Spring-and-slider rear sight. 1065 fps with 29-grain bullet.

Made in accordance with patents granted to John Browning in June 1888, these guns were made specifically for each individual chambering. The original chamberings were 22 Short (with a 15-round magazine), 22 Long (12) and 22 Winchester Rim Fire (12). Straight-grip butts were standard; though a pistol grip option was subsequently added, it is rarely encountered. The slide handle was circumferentially grooved. A Fancy Sporting Rifle was also made in small numbers, with a pistol grip butt selected for its figuring.

The first 15,500 rifles had a solid frame, but the advent of the take-down pattern in December 1892 caused the original pattern to be phased out. No solid-frame guns seem to have been made after 1895. Receivers were case-hardened until a blued version was substituted in 1901, and a notch was added on the top front of the receiver to allow the locking bar to engage the reciprocating bolt at the front end.

The first 22 Long Rifle examples were made in 1919, with magazines holding 11 cartridges. Production finished in the early 1930s, but sufficient rifles remained in store to permit sales to continue until World War II began.

SIMILAR GUNS

Model 1906 rifle, 1906-32. A simplified version of the M1890, this was originally chambered only for the 22 Short cartridge, with 15 rounds in the magazine; after April 1908, however, this was altered to 22 Short, 22 Long and 22 Long Rifle interchangeably—a popular decision which greatly increased sales. The butt was straight-wristed, and the cylindrical slide handle had circumferential grooves. Barrels were usually 20in long, weight averaging 5.1lb. Production amounted to about 848,000 M1906 guns of all types.

Model 1906 Expert, 1917-25. This deluxe version had a pistol grip butt and a specially-shaped plain slide handle. Expert rifles could be obtained in blue, with a nickel-plated receiver and trigger guard, or with all the metal parts nickel-plated.

Model 62 rifle, 1932-41. This was a modernized M1890, with a 23in round barrel, a shotgun-type butt, and magazine capacity increased to 14-20 rounds. A composition buttplate was substituted for the steel type in December 1934, and the slide handle was lengthened in February 1939. A change in the locking mechanism was made in May 1938 so that the bolt began to open as soon as the handle was moved back. About 409,500 M62 and M62A rifles were made.

Model 62A rifle, 1940-1, 1945-58. This modification of the 'visible-hammer' M62 was introduced at serial no. 99200, after changes had been made to strengthen the receiver. A semi-beavertail slide handle was approved in 1949, but few other alterations were made.

Model 62 Gallery Rifle, 1932-41? Made only in 22 Short, with a magazine capacity of 20 cartridges, this had a plain standing-block rear sight. From May 1936 onward, the loading port on Gallery Rifles was enlarged so that the cartridge-retaining tubes common in shooting galleries could be used more easily.

MODEL 61 SPORTING RIFLE

Made by the Winchester Repeating Arms Company, New Haven, Connecticut, 1932-63

Total production: 342,000. **Chambering options:** 22 Short, 22 Long, 22 Long Rifle, 22 WRF or 22 WMR: see text. **Action:** generally as Model 1890 (q.v.).

41.3in overall, 5.5lb empty. 24in barrel, 6-groove (later 4-groove) rifling; RH, concentric. Tube magazine beneath barrel, 14-20 rounds depending on cartridge. Spring-and-slider rear sight. 1065 fps with 29-grain bullet (22 Long).

This was a hammerless version of the Model 62, offered with a round or octagon barrel in a variety of chamberings. Some guns could handle 22 Short, Long or Long Rifle cartridges interchangeably; others, however, were chambered specifically for the 22 Short, 22LR or 22 WRF rounds. A few smooth-bore guns with shotgun-style sights were even made in 1939-41, but sales were slow. The slide handle was lengthened in December 1938 and again after World War II, but little else was done for the remainder of the production life of the Model 61.

SIMILAR GUNS

Model 61 Magnum rifle, 1960-3. Chambered for the 22 Winchester Magnum RF cartridge, this was otherwise identical with the standard Model 61.

MODEL 270 SPORTING RIFLE

Made by the Winchester Repeating Arms Company, New Haven, Connecticut, 1963-73.

Total production: not known. **Chambering options:** 22 Short, 22 Long and 22 Long rifle rimfire, interchangeably. **Action:** locked by displacing the breechblock into the receiver.

DATA FOR A TYPICAL EXAMPLE

39in overall, about 5lb empty. 20.5in barrel, 4-groove rifling; RH, concentric. Tube magazine beneath barrel, 15-21 rounds depending on cartridge length. Spring-leaf and elevator rear sight. 1080 fps with 40-grain bullet.

Introduced as part of the '200' series, this had a round-backed aluminum alloy receiver. The hardwood butts and forends had a walnut finish, though some guns were sold until 1965 with an optional synthetic Cycloac forend. The front sight was mounted on a ramp, and a safety bolt ran laterally through the front web of the trigger guard. Checkering and white plastic spacers were added to the pistol grip and forend in 1966

SIMILAR GUNS

Model 270 Deluxe rifle, 1965-73. Made with a selected walnut butt, with a fluted Monte Carlo comb and a cheekpiece, this also had basket-weave checkering on the pistol grip and the forend; unlike the similar deluxe versions of the lever-action Model 250 and the autoloading Model 290, however, the 270 Deluxe did not have sling swivels.

Model 275 Magnum rifle, 1964-70. Otherwise similar to the standard gun, this chambered the 22 Winchester Magnum rimfire cartridge and had an 11-round magazine. Checkering and white spacer plates were added to the stock and forend in 1966.

Model 275 Magnum Deluxe rifle, 1965-70. This was simply a 275 Magnum with a Monte Carlo comb and a cheekpiece on the select-walnut butt, and basket-weave checkering on the pistol grip and forend.

• Winchester-Hotchkiss

This bolt-action mechanism was designed by Benjamin Hotchkiss (q.v.), an American living in Paris, and patented in the U.S.A in August 1869. Rifles built on the basis of the French Gras pattern were exhibited at the Centennial Exposition in Philadelphia in 1876, where the obvious potential of the rifle persuaded Winchester to acquire a manufacturing license.

The tube magazine of the original guns ran up into the receiver above the trigger; five cartridges were loaded through a butt-trap, a sixth being inserted directly into the chamber if required. Each time the trigger was pressed, special cartridge stops allowed one round to move forward to the feed position.

When the Hotchkiss bolt was opened, the cartridge rim sprang upward until it could be caught by the lower edge of the bolt and pushed forward into the chamber on the closing stroke. Single shots could be fired when required by engaging the cut-off, which held the contents of the magazine in reserve.

MILITARY WEAPONS

MODEL 1878

Made by the Winchester Repeating Arms Company, New Haven, Connecticut, 1878-80.

The 1883-pattern Winchester-Hotchkiss military rifle.

Quantity: 6420 (all types) **Chambering:** 45-70, rimmed. **Action:** locked by turning the bolt guide rib down to abut the receiver ahead of the bridge.
DATA FOR U.S. ARMY TRIALS RIFLE

48.65in overall, about 9lb empty. 28.65in barrel, 3-groove rifling; RH, concentric. Tube magazine in butt, 5 rounds. Ramp-and-leaf rear sight graduated to 1200yd. About 1280 fps with standard ball rounds. M1873 socket bayonet.

A special Board of Officers reported on 23rd September 1878 that the 'Hotchkiss Magazine Gun no. 19' had won the magazine-rifle trials. About 513 1878-pattern guns were subsequently assembled in Springfield Armory in 1879 from Winchester-made actions and government pattern one-piece stocks. The barrels were held in the one-piece walnut stocks by two bands, and an 1879-type buck-horn sight lay on the barrel ahead of the split-bridge receiver. A rotary safety/magazine cut-off unit was let into the right side of the stock above the trigger guard.

SIMILAR GUNS
M1878 Carbine. Made with a 24in barrel, this usually had a short forend held by a single band.

M1878 Musket. These were offered for commercial or export sale with 32in barrels and two-band stocks. Socket or sword bayonets could be supplied to order.

M1879 Army rifle. About one thousand 1879-type Winchester-made actions were stocked and completed in Springfield Armory in 1881 for Army trials. They were similar to the Navy guns, with the new-pattern cut-off and safety catch.

M1879 carbine. Similar to the 1878 pattern, with a 24in barrel, this had an improved action.

M1879 Navy rifle. The cut-off fitted to the first Hotchkiss rifles acquired by the U.S. Navy projected above the right side of the stock, with a safety catch on the left. About 2500 were supplied directly from Winchester.

M1879 musket. Essentially similar to the M1878, this had the new-pattern cut-off and safety arrangements. When production ended in 1883, Winchester had made 16,100 second- or 1879-pattern muskets and carbines.

MODEL 1883 RIFLE
Made by the Winchester Repeating Arms Company, New Haven, Connecticut, 1883-4.
Quantity: about 750 (U.S. Army guns only). **Chambering:** 45-70, rimmed. **Action:** as M1878 rifle, above.

About 51.75in overall, 8.95lb empty. 32in barrel, 3-groove rifling; RH, concentric. Tube magazine in butt, 6 rounds. Ramp-and-leaf rear sight graduated to 1200yd. About 1300 fps with standard ball rounds. M1873 socket bayonet.

On 29th September 1882, a Board of Officers charged with testing magazine rifles reported that the Lee (q.v.) was preferred to the Chaffee-Reece and the Hotchkiss. However, as the margin of superiority was small, all three rifles were recommended for field trials. Springfield had completed its Chaffee-Reece rifles by mid-summer 1884, but late delivery of Lee (Remington) and Hotchkiss (Winchester) delayed trials until the end of the year.

The improved Hotchkiss rifle had a two-piece stock and the magazine was loaded through the top of the open action instead of the butt trap. Cartridges were simply inserted into the feed way, then pressed back and down into the magazine tube. The bolt lock and the magazine cut-off appeared on the right side of the receiver.

In December 1885, the Chief of Ordnance reported that the Lee had performed best, but also that most officers favored the Trapdoor Springfield. Winchester then attempted to sell the Hotchkiss elsewhere without ever encountering success. Military-style rifles customarily chambered the U.S. regulation 45-70-405 cartridge. A few had 32in barrels, but most measured 28in; they were reasonably popular with privately-funded state militia units, and others were sold in South and Central America.

Unfortunately, even the perfected Hotchkiss rifle was doomed by its tube magazine, which was a dangerous liability once centerfire primers and pointed-nose bullets became commonplace.

SIMILAR GUNS
Model 1883 carbine. This had a 22.5in barrel and the customary half-length forend retained by a single band. It was not made in large numbers.

SPORTING GUNS

MODEL 1883 RIFLE
Made by the Winchester Repeating Arms Company, New Haven, Connecticut, 1883-99.
Total production: 62,030 (including military weapons). **Chambering:** 45-70, rimmed. **Action:** as Model 1878, above.

45.25in overall, 8.55lb empty. 26in barrel, 3-groove rifling; RH, concentric. Tube magazine in butt, 6 rounds. Leaf rear sight graduated to 1200yd. About 1270 fps with standard ball rounds.

On 1st January 1884, Winchester announced the 'Hotchkiss Magazine Gun Model 1883' for the 40-65 or 45-70 cartridges, though there is no evidence that the smaller chambering was ever supplied. Made in standard or special Sporting Rifle grades, the guns had round, half-octagon or fully octagonal barrels; a plain straight-wrist or checkered pistol grip butt could be obtained, buttplates being concave rifle or (more rarely) the straight shotgun pattern. The half-length forend usually had a schnabel tip. Some guns had set triggers, and others were lightly engraved.

Assembly finally ceased in 1899. The perfected Hotchkiss was sturdy and reliable, but few pre-1900 purchasers liked its bolt action and butt magazine. Remaining parts were scrapped in 1913.

OTHER PATTERNS
Once sufficient Krag-Jørgensen (Army) or Lee Straight-Pull (Navy) rifles had been delivered, surviving Hotchkiss trials rifles were sold in the late 1890s. Many were altered to sporting style. Most had their barrels cut to about 24in and the forends trimmed to half-stock proportions. Work was undertaken professionally, but conversions usually retained original Army or naval marks.

• Winchester-Lee
James Lee was granted the first of a series of patents for straight-pull bolt-action rifles, improved clip-loaded magazines and a special cartridge-lifter arm in 1894. Trials undertaken in October, at the U.S. Navy's Torpedo Station in Newport, Rhode Island, convinced the U.S. Navy to adopt 236 straight-pull Lee as the M1895. A production contract was given to Winchester.

The inclined bolt was locked by a wedge-type block, which disengaged when the bolt handle was retracted. A five-round clip could be inserted in the magazine with the bolt down. Tension on the cartridge rims was released automatically as the bolt closed, allowing the clip to fall out of the bottom of the magazine after a couple of rounds had been fired.

MODEL 1895 NAVY RIFLE
Made by the Winchester Repeating Arms Company, New Haven, Connecticut, 1896-8.
Total production: about 18,000. **Chambering:** 6mm Lee (236 caliber) rimmed. **Action:** locked by camming a wedge beneath the bolt into seats in the receiver as the bolt closed.

47.6in overall, 8.13lb empty. 28in barrel, 5-groove rifling; RH, concentric. Integral clip-loaded box magazine, 5 rounds. Ramp-and-leaf rear sight graduated to 2000yd. 2560 fps with M1895 ball cartridges. M1895 knife bayonet.

The Lee rifle was adopted in May 1895, with 10,000 being ordered from Winchester. It had a conventional one-piece pistol grip walnut stock, a single barrel band and a special nose band with a bayonet lug on the right side. The fixed magazine, which protruded from the stock ahead of the trigger guard, had a dis-

The US Navy M1895 236-caliber Winchester-Lee rifle.

tinctively curved base. The extractor/ejector, the firing-pin lock and the bolt-lock actuator all gave constant trouble and production ceased in 1899. Most of the U.S. Navy service rifles were replaced by Krag-Jørgensens in the early 1900s.

WINCHESTER-LEE SPORTING RIFLE

Made by the Winchester Repeating Arms Company, New Haven, Connecticut, 1897-1904.

Total production: about 1550. **Chambering:** 6mm Lee (236 caliber) rimmed. **Action:** as M1895 rifle, above.

43.5in overall, 7.56lb empty. 24in barrel, 5-groove rifling; RH, concentric. Integral clip-loaded box magazine, 5 rounds. Spring-leaf and elevator rear sight. About 2450 fps with 112-grain bullet.

Encouraged by the the adoption of the Lee rifle for naval service, Winchester announced a sporting version in its autumn 1897 catalogue, noting that guns would be available once Navy contracts had been fulfilled. Small batches of sporting rifles were released in 1899. They had good-quality half-stocks, with a pistol grip and a shotgun-style buttplate. The forend had a finger groove and a shallow schnabel tip. However, though the tiny bullet attained a high velocity for its day, its poor knock-down capabilities did not commend themselves to hunters. As the bolt action was rarely favored by sportsmen—which must have been obvious from experience with the Hotchkiss (q.v.)—commercial sales fell far short of expectations. Universal apathy contributed to the withdrawal of the Winchester-Lee in 1904, though the last components were not scrapped until 1916.

The open action of the M1895 Winchester-Lee US Navy rifle ('Lee Straight Pull').

• Winslow

Winslow Arms Company of Camden, South Carolina, made Mauser-type sporting rifles from 1962 until the late 1980s. The actions were purchased when required from Fabrique Nationale, Zavodi Crvena Zastava and others; the guns were distinguished more by their extraordinary stocks. The Bushmaster and Plainsmaster were each offered in eight grades of finish.

At its most extreme, the Plainsmaster featured a bizarre combination of fully-curved pistol grip, exaggerated wedge-type pistol grip cap, soaring flyaway comb, basket-weave checkering and contrasting inlays.

Chamberings were supplied virtually to order, though most guns had 24in or 26in barrels; weight ranged from 7.2-7.5lb for standard cartridges to 8-9lb for the magnums.

• Wolcott

Tested by the U.S. Army in 1865 as Guns Nos. 81 and 82, Wolcott carbines were apparently made by the Starr Arms Company in accordance with U.S. patent 60,106. This was granted in November

1866 to H.H. Wolcott of Yonkers, New York, to protect an underlever action which swung the entire hammer, block and guard assembly around a pivot at the front of the action. Wolcott was the president of the Starr Arms Company at this time. The trials carbines lacked a forend and were improved from the patent pattern by 'packaging' the lockwork in a single unit. A sling ring was attached to the left side of the receiver, and a leaf-pattern rear sight lay on the barrel ahead of the breech.

• Wright & Brown

Made in accordance with U.S. patent 45,126, granted in November 1864 to Edward Wright of Buffalo, in upstate New York, three carbines of this type ('Guns No. 78-80') were tested by the U.S. Army in 1865. The breechblock lifted upward at the rear, similarly to the Allin-Springfield, and was locked by the tip of the centrally-hung hammer. The carbines had one-piece half-stocks with distinctive flats alongside the breech. The forends were each held by a single screwed band. Swivels lay on the trigger guard and the band (too close together to be truly useful), and a small folding-leaf rear sight lay on the barrel immediately ahead of the breech.

USSR

This section contains details of many rifles developed during the life of the USSR, from the revolution of 1917 until the disintegration of the Soviet bloc in the early 1990s. The demise of the Communist regime was accompanied by a rediscovery of private enterprise, and robust attempts have since been made to exploit guns – sporting and military alike – on the commercial market. A summary of these efforts will be found in the chapters devoted to 'Russia (modern)' and individual countries such as Armenia.

The mark most commonly encountered on Soviet small-arms is the hammer and sickle, often enwreathed, though a simple five-point star was used as an inspector's mark. The products of the ordnance factories in Izhevsk, Sestroretsk and Tula were identified by an arrow in a triangle, a bow and arrow, and a hammer respectively. However, the Izhevsk arrow can be difficult to read in small sizes, and the Tula mark was often corrupted into the form of 'T'. 'TOZ' -ТОЗ in Cyrillic – was customarily applied to guns made in the Tula ordnance factory (*Tulskiy Oruzheinyi Zavod*) for commercial sale. Unit markings do not appear on Soviet rifles. Serial numbers were usually four (sometimes five) digits prefixed by two Cyrillic letters: e.g., АР 1234.

Sources of reliable information are few and far between. Vladimir Fedorov's *Evolyutsiya strelkovogo oruzhiya* (1938, re-published in Germany in 1972) is a good source of pre-war details, but the best guide is *Soviet Small Arms and Ammunition* by David N. Bolotin, published by the Finnish Arms Museum Foundation in 1995.

• Degtyarev, autoloading type

Vasiliy Degtyarev is best known as a designer of machine guns, but the first of a series of similar rifles was tested extensively by the Soviet authorities in 1925. Externally similar to the modified Fedorov *Avtomaty*, the Degtyarev rifles were gas (instead of recoil) operated and locked by swinging a locking strut laterally into the right side of the receiver.

1925-TYPE RIFLE

Avtomaticheskaya vintovka sistemy Degtyareva, optniy obr. 1925g

Made in the Kovrov machine gun factory?

Total production: at least three. **Chambering:** 7.62x54, rimmed. **Action:** locked by swinging a strut attached to the bolt laterally into the receiver wall; gas operated, semi-automatic or selective fire.

About 43in overall, 10lb empty. 24.8in barrel, 4-groove rifling; RH, concentric. Integral box magazine, 5 rounds. Tangent-leaf sight graduated to 2000m (2185yd). About 2625 fps with standard ball ammunition. Knife bayonet.

This gun had a wooden stock, with a shallow Avtomat-style pistol grip and a joint in the forend ahead of the grasping groove. A short wooden barrel-top guard ran forward from the chamber to the barrel band, and a sheet-metal casing ran from the barrel band to the nose cap. The rear sight was mounted on top of the receiver; a selector lay behind the trigger; a lateral safety bolt lay in the front web of the trigger guard; and the lug on the nose cap accepted a knife bayonet. An integral magazine protruded beneath the stock, being loaded through the top of the action with a standard 1891-type stripper clip. The bolt-stop held the action open after the last spent case had been ejected.

SIMILAR GUNS

1928-type rifle. This answered a revised military specification calling for a 'peep' or aperture unit to be added to the rear sight, a 10-round magazine option to be provided, knife or sword bayonets to be replaced by integral quadrangular patterns, and the provision for automatic fire to be abandoned in an attempt to reduce weight below 8.8lb. At least one gun was made with the locking strut permanently pinned in the receiver, instead of attached to the bolt, and two with detachable magazines (10 or 15 rounds) were tested in 1930 alongside three rifles with the standard fixed five-round type.

Model 1930 rifle. This was similar to the 1928 pattern, but had an improved stock. A simplified sheet-steel forend lay between the barrel band and nose cap. The folding bayonet was retained, locking into the front of a large conical flash-hider/muzzle brake, and a detachable 10-round staggered-row magazine was fitted. This could be loaded with two five-round stripper clips, appropriate guides being milled into the breech-cover.

Though testing revealed that neither the Degtyarev rifle nor the competing Tokarev was good enough for service, production of a thousand examples of the 'Samozaryadnaya vintovka sistemy Degtyareva' was sanctioned on 28th March 1930. This 'obr. 1930g' rifle was officially adopted on 28th December 1931, but progress was so slow that the order had soon been cut to 500. The obr. 1930g was abandoned when the Simonov (q.v.) showed greater promise, and it is suspected that only a few dozen Degtyarev rifles were ever made.

• Dragunov

This was the standard Soviet bloc sniper rifle for nearly 30 years, serving in virtually all the constituent armies except Romania and independently-minded Yugoslavia. Credited to a design team led by Evgeniy Dragunov and Ivan Samoylov, the action was locked by a rotating three-lug bolt – similar to the Kalashnikov pattern – and employed a short-stroke gas piston adapted from the pre-war Tokarev.

SVD rifles have been used wherever Soviet influence was strong. Captured guns were used by the warring factions in Afghanistan, while others have appeared in Iran. Production has been undertaken in Bulgaria, the People's Republic of China, Egypt, Hungary and Poland. Most of the optical sights prove to have been made in the Soviet Union or the German Democratic Republic, but it is probable that the Chinese also make them. Markings usually determine the country of origin.

An Afghani mujehaddin with a captured Dragunov rifle.

SNIPER RIFLE
Snayperskaya Vintovka Dragunova, 'SVD'
Made by the Izhevsk ordnance factory, 1964 to date.

Total production: not known. **Chambering:** 7.62x54, rimmed. **Action:** locked by rotating three lugs on the bolt head into recesses in the receiver wall; gas operated, semi-automatic.

48.25in overall, 9.5lb without sights and magazine. 21.45in barrel, 4-groove rifling; concentric, RH. Detachable box magazine, 10 rounds. Tangent-leaf sight graduated to 1200m (1310yd). 2725 fps with standard Type L bullet. AKM or AK-74 knife bayonet.

The outcome of a protracted design study, the Dragunov was accepted for service in 1963 at the expense of prototypes submitted by – among others – Sergei Simonov and Aleksandr Konstantinov (q.v.). The first guns reached service in 1965.

Owing to the cutaway butt combined with the pistol grip, the Dragunov cannot easily be mistaken. Its slender barrel had a three-slot compensator/muzzle brake, and a two-position gas port could be adjusted with a cartridge-case rim. The trigger was a simplified version of the AK mechanism, but the combined safety lever/selector restricted it to single shots.

A selection of sights, including the 4x24 PSO-1 and the 1-PN51 image-intensifier, could be clamped onto a rail on the lower left side of the receiver. The long rubber eye cup was most distinctive, and the reticle was illuminated by power from a small battery carried in the integral mount. Optical performance was surprisingly good, and, as a bonus, the sight doubled as an infra-red emission detector.

Ribs pressed into the sides of the box magazine improved the feed of the clumsy rimmed cartridges. It has been said that development of the magazine body was particularly protracted.

The SVD is very light by modern sniper rifle standards, but is seen as an integral part of the infantry equipment – a tradition in the Soviet army dating back to the early 1930s. Western sources still proffer much conflicting data, but the Dragunov is unarguably pleasant to fire and capable of acceptable accuracy with good-quality ammunition.

MEDVED SPORTING RIFLE
Made by the Izhevsk ordnance factory, about 1963-75.

Total production: not known. **Chambering options:** see text. **Action:** as military-pattern SVD, above.

The SVD or Dragunov sniper rifle.

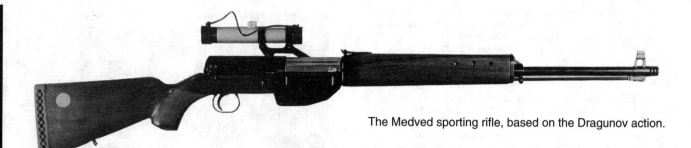

The Medved sporting rifle, based on the Dragunov action.

DATA FOR A TYPICAL 9.3MM EXAMPLE

43.7in overall, 8.25lb empty. 21.65in barrel, 4-groove rifling; concentric, RH. Integral box magazine, 5 rounds. Tangent-leaf sight graduated to 1200m (1310yd). 2330 fps with 255-grain bullet.

One of the most interesting sporting rifles made in the Soviet Union, the *Medved* ('Bear') shared the gas system and rotating-bolt lock of the SVD. The design of the receiver was refined, and a conventional straight-comb butt was fitted. Checkering appeared on the pistol grip and the forend.

Among the rifle's strangest features were the military-style open sights and a clearing rod beneath the barrel – more valuable than they might seem in sub-zero temperatures. A stubby 4x optical sight was carried in a trapezoidal mount that attached to the lower left side of the receiver above the magazine.

Most rifles were chambered for adaptations of the standard Mosin-Nagant rifle cartridge, known in Finland, where they have been loaded by Sako, as '8.2x53R' or '9.3x53R'. Efforts were made to chamber the Medved for Western European cartridges of comparable dimensions, but production had ceased by the mid 1970s.

The breech of the Medved rifle. The cover has been removed to show the bolt and the bolt carrier.

• Fedorov

For history, background and constructional details, see '**Russia, Tsarist**'.

AUTOMATIC RIFLE
Avtomata Fedorova

Made by the Kovrov machine gun factory, 1920-5.

Quantity: about 3200. Otherwise generally as Tsarist M1916, except rear sight (leaf graduated to 1500m [1640yd]?).

Production of the 1916-type Fedorov automatic rifle was optimistically scheduled to begin in Kovrov in February 1919. The first guns were actually completed in mid-September 1920; niggling manufacturing problems had hindered progress and only about a hundred had been delivered by the end of the year.

Series production began in April 1921, but field service revealed serious faults and extensive changes were made in 1923. A hold-open and a disconnector were soon added; stripper-clip guides were machined in the receiver to allow the magazine to be refilled through the open action; a simpler rear sight with only one notch appeared; and the magazine-sides were ribbed to increase rigidity.

In 1924, however, a decision was taken to develop new rifles for the standard 7.62mm rimmed cartridge and the Avtomat project was cancelled on 1st October 1925. Surviving guns were withdrawn into store in 1928. Too delicate and unreliable, they jammed easily when foul and were difficult to control when firing automatically. In 1939, however, the few Avtomaty which remained serviceable were issued for 'active service' (possibly no more than propaganda pictures) during the Winter War against Finland.

'IMPROVED AUTOMATIC RIFLE'

Work continued in the 1920s on refined versions of the Avtomat, altered to chamber the 7.62x54 rimmed rifle cartridge. In this respect at least, the rifles were little more than a reversion to the experimental patterns of 1912-14.

The 1925 type had a one-piece stock ending at the barrel band, with a characteristically shallow Avtomat-pattern pistol grip. A short wooden barrel-top guard ran from the mid-point of the grasping groove to the band, and a slotted sheet-steel casing extended forward from the band to an integral nose cap. The guns accepted knife bayonets. A fire-selector and safety lever were incorporated in the trigger mechanism, a tangent-leaf sight lay on top of the breech cover, and an integral five-round box magazine was fitted.

An Improved Avtomat was tested in January 1926 against two differing Degtyarev designs and Tokarev. However, even the best gun – one of the modified Avtomats – jammed more than 60 times in 5210 shots. The inventors were given six months to develop guns to a new specification. The new 7.62mm-caliber Fedorov rifle was completed in 1927, and, when new trials were held in June 1928, was included among the so-called 'Co-operative' ('Ko.') rifles submitted by Fedorov and Degtyarev in collusion with Urzanov, Kuznetsov and Bezrukov.

The 'Ko. No. 3' rifle (the Improved Avtomat) won the trials, though the rival Tokarev No. 2 was doing better until it suffered a major structural failure. However, nothing came of the submissions and developmental work was undertaken instead.

The 7.62mm 1928-type Fedorov retained the recoil-operated pivoting-block lock of its 6.5mm predecessors, but had a detachable box magazine and a large conical muzzle brake. The original selective-fire requirement had been abandoned, allowing weight to be saved. A bayonet with a cruciform blade could be swung forward under the muzzle until it sprang back to lock around the front-sight block. The rear sight (which had an additional 'peep' element on the notch plate) lay on the receiver above the trigger guard, there were two recoil bolts through the stock, and cooling slots were cut in the barrel casing and handguard.

Small quantities of these rifles were made for additional trials, but the post-1930 preference for gas operation brought development to an end.

• Izhevsk

Also known as 'Vostok' (a brand name applied indiscriminately to Izevsk and Tula products) or 'Ural'. The firearms history of what, until recently, was the USSR remains shrouded in mystery. Though sporting guns of all types have been made in large numbers, very little is known about their background and it is by no means clear where some of them have been made. The problem has been compounded by the existence of two separate factories in Izhevsk – the ordnance factory (Izhmash), which concentrates on military equipment, and the engineering works (Izhmekh) which makes sporting guns.

STRELA-2 TARGET RIFLE

Made by Izhevsky Mekhanichesky Zavod, about 1955-75.

Total production: not known. **Chambering:** 22, rimfire. **Action:** locked by three lugs on the bolt turning into their seats in the receiver.

55.05in overall, including butt hook, 17.5lb with sights. 29.9in barrel, 6-groove rifling; RH, concentric. Single shot only. Micro-adjustable aperture rear sight. Performance: see text.

Introduced in 1955, but rarely seen in the West until the early 1960s, this rifle had a double-trigger system incorporating a setting element; release pressure could be adjusted from about 75oz to

60oz. The chambering is said to have been for a special 5.6x18.5 cartridge, though all the guns that could be traced fired the 22 Long Rifle pattern (5.6x17). The comb of the thumbhole half-stock ran virtually straight (if slightly downward) from the pistol grip to the butt heel, and an accessory rail lay beneath the forend. Cast alloy shoulder plates usually had short straight toe hooks pierced with three lightening holes, and could be locked in the mounting-plate channel by a knurled-head wheel on the lower right side. An optional hand rest could be attached under the gun ahead of the trigger. Sights were offset to the left.

SIMILAR GUNS

SM-2. Also known as 'CM-2', this single shot 22 LR rimfire 25m or 50m target rifle has been popular as a beginner's gun. The current production variant has a hefty birch half-stock – crudely checkered on the pistol grip and the forend sides – and a competition-pattern diopter rear sight. The front sight is a replaceable-element tunnel, the trigger is adjustable from 18oz to 53oz, and the buttplate can be slid vertically in its channel plate. A typical SM-2 is about 43.2in overall (without butt spacers) and weighs 10.8lb with its sights. The 26.75in barrel has six-groove rifling.

SM-10. This gun, originally chambering a 5.6x22 cartridge instead of the subsequent 5.6x17 (22 LR rimfire) pattern, was a lighter version of the Strela-2 with a 26.75in barrel, an overall length of 47.1in, and a weight of about 10.8lb. The double trigger and thumbhole half-stock were retained. The butt-plate hook was a simple solid alloy casting.

Strela-3. This was an improved version of the Strela-2, with better sights (still offset to the left) and a refined stock. It may be found with a thumbhole butt and a Free Rifle shoulder plate with a four-hole hook bent downward at the tip, but could also be supplied (Model 3-1?) in a squared stock with checkering on the pistol grip and forend panel.

Zenit-3. This was a 7.62mm version of the SM-10, identifiable by the length of the ejection port. The rifle had a 29.9in barrel and weighed about 17.7lb; the elongated butt-plate toe hook was pierced with lightening holes, and a double-trigger unit was regarded as standard.

BK-3 TARGET RIFLE

Made by Izhevsky Mekhanichesky Zavod, Izhevsk.

Total production: not known. **Chambering:** 22 Long Rifle rimfire. **Action:** locked by three lugs on the bolt engaging recesses in the receiver as the bolt handle is turned down into its seat.

41.15in overall (without butt spacers), 10.7lb empty. 23.6in barrel, 6-groove rifling; RH, concentric. Single shot only. 6x or 10x optical sight. 1080 fps with standard cartridges.

Generally encountered under the Vostok brand, this is intended for Running Boar and moving target competitions. It embodies an improved single shot action with the locking lugs on the bolt head, and has an adjustable trigger (18-54oz). The most distinctive feature is the design of the butt, which continues straight back from the cocking piece without the wrist found on most other designs. The cheekpiece and the rubber buttplate can both be adjusted vertically.

SIMILAR GUNS

Biathlon-6 rifle. This embodies the action of the BK-3 (q.v.) with a distinctive wristless stock. The principal identifying characteristics include a rubber buttplate with an adjustable rod-type 'hook', a detachable five-shot magazine and a muzzle flap. Four magazines can be carried in the butt, which will also accept the special sling harness used in biathlon competitions. The Biathlon-6 was about 41.75in long, had a 23.6in barrel, and weighed 9.5lb with its sights

BK-5 rifle. Identical mechanically with the BK-3, this gun could often be found with an optional short barrel and a tubular extension to support the three two-piece balancing weights. The receiver was mounted on a plastic carrier, with self-adjusting inserts intended to maintain bedding pressure; the cheekpiece, buttplate and trigger were all fully adjustable. The half-stock, generally made of beech, had generous stippling on the pistol grip and forend – and, most unusually, a white line border on the guns made in the mid-1980s. The optical sight had a decidedly military appearance, but performance was very good in view of a lack of refinement. The BK-5 weighed a little under 11lb and measured 46.05in overall.

URAL-5-1 FREE RIFLE

Made by Izhevsky Mekhanichesky Zavod, Izhevsk.

Total production: substantial. **Chambering:** 22 Long Rifle rimfire. **Action:** generally as BK-3, above.

49.8in overall (butt retracted), 17.4lb empty. 27.55in barrel, 6-groove rifling; RH, concentric. Single shot only. Micro-adjustable aperture sight. 1080 fps with standard cartridges.

Intended for 50m Free Rifle and three-position shooting, this has a thumb-hole half-stock with a fully adjustable hooked butt-plate. The cheekpiece may be raised, and a full-length accessory rail beneath the forend will accept a palm-rest and a balancing-weight rod. The trigger is fully adjustable from 3.5oz (100gm) to 53oz (1500gm), and good quality competition sights are fitted. The tunnel-pattern front sight embodies a spirit level, while, most oddly, the cranked rear sight mount sets the sight-line considerably to the left of the bore axis.

SIMILAR GUNS

Ural 6-1 rifle. Intended for Standard Rifle competitions under UIT rules, this amalgamates the basic action of the Ural 5-1 (e.g., BK-3) and a conventional half-stock with extensive stippling on the pistol grip and forend. The adjustable finger-wheel butt-plate lock, channel plate and spacer system are shared with the SM-2.

BI-7-2 TARGET RIFLE

Made by Izhevsky Mekhanichesky Zavod, Izhevsk.

Production total: comparatively few. **Chambering:** 22 Long Rifle rimfire. **Action:** locked by a toggle-type bolt mechanism.

41.35in overall, 9.9lb empty. 19.7in barrel, 6-groove rifling; RH, concentric. Detachable box magazine, 5 rounds. Micro-adjustable aperture sight. 1050 fps with standard cartridges.

This rifle, introduced in the late 1970s, is locked by a toggle-type bolt comparable with that of the Anschütz-made Förtner system (see 'Anschütz' in the German section), enabling the marksman to reload with the minimum of effort. The BI-7-2 has a distinctive stock with a deepened forend ahead of the detachable box magazine, while four spare magazines are carried in spring clips on the right side of the butt. Other features include a buttplate hook, conventional diopter sights with hinged covers, and a trigger adjustable from 17.5oz (500gm) to 53oz (1500gm).

LOS-4 SPORTING RIFLE

Made by Izhevsky Mekhanichesky Zavod, Izhevsk.

Production total: not known. **Chambering options:** 7.62x51 or 9x54. **Action:** locked by three lugs on the bolt head engaging recesses in the receiver as the bolt handle is turned down.

DATA FOR A TYPICAL EXAMPLE

Chambering: 7.62x51, rimless. About 42.1in overall, 7.28lb empty. 23.6in barrel, 4-groove rifling; RH, concentric. Internal box magazine, 5 rounds. Tangent-leaf sight graduated to 500m (545yd). 2525 fps with 170-grain bullet.

Introduced about 1963, this sporting rifle may be identified by its ugly stamped-and-folded trigger guard. It introduced a quirky bolt action with the three lugs set back from the bolt face to lock in the receiver above the front of the magazine. The lugs were clearly visible toward the front of the ejection port when the mechanism was closed. LOS rifles had a crudely shaped Monte Carlo-pattern half-stock with a recoil bolt in the tapering forend. The plastic pistol grip cap and ventilated rubber shoulder pad were accompanied by white spacers. Unusually for a sporter, the gun had a chromium-plated bore and a clearing rod beneath the barrel: eminently practical in the context of a harsh northern winter.

BARS-1 SPORTING RIFLE

Made by Izhevsky Mekhanichesky Zavod, Izhevsk.

Production total: not known. **Chambering:** 5.6x40, rimless. **Action:** locked by two lugs on the bolt head engaging recesses in the receiver as the bolt handle is turned down.

About 42in overall, 5.95lb empty. 23.6in barrel, 4-groove rifling; RH, concentric. Internal box magazine, 5 rounds. Drum sight graduated to 300m (330yd). 2935 fps with 50-grain bullet?

Introduced in 1966, this gun chambered a cartridge said to have been created simply by necking the 7.62x39 case (see 'Margolin MVO', below). The Bars-1 had a birch half-stock with checkering on the pistol grip and forend. A radial safety catch lay behind the bolt on the right side of the receiver, where it could lock the bolt handle and the firing pin. The trigger guard was a simple stamped strip, and the finish was usually baked-on black paint. An optical sight could be carried in a special bracket attached to the left side of the receiver.

SV-1 TARGET RIFLE

Made by Izhevsky Mekhanichesky Zavod, Izhevsk.

Production total: not known. **Chambering:** 7.62x51, rimless. **Action:** as LOS rifle, above.

45.9in overall (without butt spacers), 10.47lb without sights. 27.55in barrel, 4-groove rifling; RH, concentric. Micro-adjustable diopter sight. 2575 fps with 170-grain bullet.

The first of the modern Soviet 300-metre target rifles was introduced in 1977-8 on the action of the LOS hunting rifle (q.v.). Though the birch stock was crudely finished, the single shot SV-1 performed very well. The buttplate could be adjusted for length and height; the anatomical pistol grip and forend were stippled; and the underside of the receiver was roughly checkered to improve bedding. The trigger was fully adjustable from 3.25lb to 4.4lb.

TsVR-1 TARGET RIFLE

Made by Izhevsky Mekhanichesky Zavod, Izhevsk.

Production total: not known. **Chambering:** 7.62x51, rimless. **Action:** as Los rifle, above.

52.55in overall (with buttplate retracted), 17.6lb with hand rest. 29.9in barrel, 4-groove rifling; RH, concentric. Micro-adjustable diopter sight. 2610 fps with 170-grain bullet.

Intended for use in 300-metre Free Rifle competitions, this 1978-vintage introduction had the standard three-lug bolt action in a massive thumb-hole half-stock. An adjustable hooked buttplate and an elevating comb were fitted, together with a refined trigger adjustable to give a pull of 3.5-53oz (100-1500gm).

Accessories included mirage bands, a hand rest, and a set of rod-mounted balance weights protruding from a block mounted in the rail under the forend. The TsVR-1 lacked the sophistication of Western rivals, but performed effectively enough on the range.

• Kalashnikov

The Kalashnikov has become one of the world's most popular weapons, serving not only regular forces with pro-Communist leanings but also countless terrorist groups from South America to the Far East. Production is said to have exceeded 70 million guns, and has been undertaken in many former Soviet bloc countries. Modified guns have even emanated from Finland, Israel and South Africa.

However, the great political changes in Europe in the 1990s have thrown the future of the whole Kalashnikov genre into question. The former Soviet manufacturing facilities were largely confined to Russia, and it will be interesting to see what weapons the armed forces of newly independent states (e.g., Latvia or the Ukraine) procure over the next decade. Even in modern Russia (q.v.), the current generation of universal rifles derived from the 5.45mm AK-74M are under threat from the Nikonov prototypes.

The Kalashnikov action taps propellant gas at the mid-point of the bore to strike a piston attached to the bolt carrier. This drives the piston/bolt carrier assembly backward and rotates the bolt out of engagement. Widely criticized for its clumsiness, low muzzle velocity and a poor-performing cartridge (from the purely technical standpoint, validly), the Kalashnikov is simple, solid, reliable, and surprisingly effective when firing automatically.

NOTE

Military and sporting guns are considered together, but the Kalashnikov – though touted commercially by the Chinese and (until recently) the Yugoslavs – cannot be considered as a genuine sporter. Except the Finnish-made Petra and the Israeli Hadar, which have much-modified stocks, few supposedly commercial Kalashnikov derivatives offer much more than improved finish. Details of the current generation of military weapons, the so-called 'Hundred Series', will be found under **'Russia, modern: Kalashnikov'**.

1946-TYPE TRIALS RIFLE

Capture of German assault rifles in 1943-4 inspired development of intermediate cartridges – begun in the USSR in the 1930s – to continue until a 7.62x39 pattern was perfected by Elizarov and Semin.

The first gun to be designed for the new ammunition was a Simonov (q.v.) carbine, batches being sent for field trials in the summer of 1944. The weapon was ordered into mass production in 1945, but none had been made by the end of World War II.

The first trial of an *Avtomat* – in Russian parlance, a hybrid of rifle and submachine gun – was undertaken with a Sudaev (q.v.) design, but this proved to be too clumsy and was eventually superseded by the Kalashnikov pattern.

Readied in a factory in Alma-Ata in 1946, with assistance from a designers' collective, the 1946-pattern Kalashnikov shared the general lines of the perfected AK but differed considerably in detail. The butt was attached to a sheet-steel shoe which had been riveted to the receiver; the rear surface of the breech cover was noticeably squared; and the charging handle, safety and selector lever all lay on the left side. The gun could thus be charged without disturbing the trigger hand, though the entire top surface of the breech was exposed as the bolt ran back.

At least five 'Avtomaty sistemy Kalashnikova, optniy obr. 1946g' (trials pattern, 1946) were made. They showed great promise, and a process of continuous refinement began in the Tula factory.

1947-TYPE TRIALS RIFLE

The '1947 No. 1' prototype differed considerably from the 1946 pattern, gaining the familiar closed-top breech cover with an ejection port on the right side. A combination safety/selector lever lay on the right side of the receiver above the trigger, possibly inspired by a similar feature on the abortive Sudaev Avtomat. The butt was inserted in the receiver; the barrel was shortened; and the forend was noticeably longer than the barrel-top guard. The design of the trigger system was also refined.

The improved Kalashnikov passed field testing with flying colors and was adopted for service in 1949. It has since been made in many guises, but they are all mechanically similar to the original trials guns of 1947.

ASSAULT RIFLE
Avtomata Kalashnikova, 'AK'

Made in the ordnance factories in Izhevsk, Tula and elsewhere, 1949-59.

Total production: at least five million. **Chambering:** 7.62x39, rimless. **Action:** locked by three lugs on the bolt head engaging recesses in the receiver wall as the bolt ran forward; gas operated, selective fire.

34.2in overall, 9.48lb with loaded magazine. 16.3in barrel, 4-groove rifling; RH, concentric. Detachable box magazine, 30 rounds. Tangent-leaf sight

The 7.62x39 AKS.

graduated to 800m (875yd). 2330 fps with M43 ball cartridges; 775±50rpm. AK knife bayonet.

The earliest guns incorporated extensive welding, stamping and pressed-metal parts, but an enforced change from stamped to machined components was made in 1951 as Soviet industry had been unable to master sheet-metal fabrication techniques gleaned from the Germans.

The rifles had wood butts and forends, pistol grips originally being laminated wood (though often replaced with coarsely checkered or ribbed plastic varieties). Buttplates were steel, with a hinged trap, and a cleaning rod was carried beneath the barrel. The rear swivel originally lay on the under-edge of the butt, but many guns will now be found with the swivel let into the left side of the wrist. Selectors were crudely marked 'AB' and 'ОД' with an electric pencil, constructional standards being adequate but not outstanding. The magazines were originally plain sided, but were subsequently ribbed to increase body-strength.

A change was made to the rear of the receiver about 1953, when, to strengthen the attachment, an extension was added to receive the tip of the butt. Laminated woodwork was standard. Selector markings were generally stamped, and shallow panels were milled in the sides of the receiver to save weight.

It has often been suggested – in the first edition of *Rifles of the World*, to name but one source – that the earliest Kalashnikov rifles lacked a bayonet lug, inferring that the Russians had developed the ungainly knife pattern only after some guns had been made. This is now known to have been untrue, and that even some of the prototype guns accepted bayonets.

SIMILAR GUNS
AKS. This was a standard Kalashnikov with a pressed-steel butt folding down and forward under the receiver. It was popular with airborne forces, tank troops, and others to whom its compact dimensions were useful.

MODIFIED ASSAULT RIFLE
Avtomata Kalshnikova Modificatsionniya, 'AKM'
Made by the Izhevsk ordnance factory, 1959–75.
Production total: at least 10 million. **Chambering:** 7.62x39, rimless. **Action:** as AK pattern, above.

34.55in overall, 8.42lb with loaded magazine. 16.35in barrel, 4-groove rifling; RH, concentric. Detachable box magazine, 30 rounds. Tangent-leaf sight graduated to 1000m (1095yd). 2330 fps with M43 ball cartridges; 650±30rpm. AKM knife bayonet.

Once Soviet industry had mastered appropriate metalworking techniques, a modified Kalashnikov Avtomat was introduced in 1959. The stamped-steel receiver – a sturdy 'U'-shape pressing – was much lighter than the original machined forging, the bolt-lock recesses were riveted in place, and the stamped receiver cover had prominent lateral ribs. The gas-piston tube of the AKM had semicircular vents immediately behind the gas-port assembly instead of the circular holes on the AK; and the bolt carrier was phosphated.

The charging handle and pistol grip were made of plastic, though the butt and forend were usually laminated wood. The oldest magazines were ribbed sheet-metal, but soon became orange-red plastic.

The most important internal change was the incorporation of a 'rate-reducer' or retarding element in the trigger system, which has often been identified as an additional mechanical safety. By

holding back the hammer after the bolt-carrier had depressed the safety sear, this reduced the rate of fire by about 15 per cent. It also added unnecessary complexity to an essentially simple design.

The impact of the bolt carrier on the bolt as the action closed was transferred from the right side (AK) to the left side (AKM), improving stability in automatic fire, and a new 1000m (1095yd) rear sight was adopted. The bayonet acquired an insulated handle to allow electrical cables to be cut in safety.

A short oblique-cut compensator was added in the early 1960s to prevent the gun climbing to the right when operating automatically, and to improve accuracy when firing from awkward positions. Forends were broadened in this era to improve grip.

A bracket could be added on the left side of the receiver to accept the NSP-2 infra-red or NSPU image-intensifier sights. Some AKM will also be found with the single shot GP-25 grenade launcher under the forend, and an additional grenade-launching sight fitted above the gas tube. A special resilient butt pad was issued to minimize the effects of recoil on the shooter's shoulder.

SIMILAR GUNS
AKMS. This was a variant of the standard gun with a folding butt, which had three rivets and a long flute on each side of the strut. The butt unit was stowed by swinging it down and forward.

AKM, silenced. Some guns will be encountered with the PBS-1 silencer and a special back-sight leaf adapted to subsonic ammunition. The two-chamber silencer relied on a rubber plug and a series of baffle plates to reduce noise.

AKMS-U. Introduced in 1975, this was a compact derivative of the AKM, measuring 28.45in overall and weighing 7.4lb with an empty magazine. The barrel was only 8.85in long, and the rear sight was reduced to a rocking-'L' pattern set for 100m (110yd) and 500m (545yd). The AKMS-U could be used as a port-firing weapon in armored personnel carriers, and has also been called 'AKR' or 'Krinkov' – apparently after the leader of the design team.

Fitted with a folding butt, the AKMS-U lacked the cleaning rod and bayonet lug of the full-length gun; instead, it had a short finned expansion chamber fitted with a conical flash-hider, and the front sight block (with a sling bar on the left side) was moved back to abut the laminated wooden barrel guard. The back-sight base was combined with the receiver-cover pivot, and a checkered plastic pistol grip was accompanied by a short wooden thumb-hole forend. Production is believed to have ceased in 1979.

MODEL 1974 ASSAULT RIFLE
Avtomata Kalashnikova obr. 74, 'AK-74'
Made by the state ordnance factories, 1975–91?
Production total: at least five million. **Chambering:** 5.45x39, rimless. **Action:** as AK rifle, above.

37.65in overall, 10.7lb with loaded 30-round magazine. 16.35in barrel, four-groove rifling; RH, concentric. Detachable box magazine, 30 or 40 rounds. Tangent-leaf sight graduated to 1000m (1095yd). 2950 fps with B-74 ball cartridges; 650±30rpm. AKM or AK-74 knife bayonet.

The 5.56mm M16 rifles captured in Vietnam in the 1960s indicated that the 7.62x39 M43 cartridge was less effective than its American rival. Experiments continued until 1973, when a 5.45mm cartridge based on the 7.62mm case was perfected. The two-piece bullet had a hollow tip within the jacket, to improve lethality by deforming against a target.

The new AK-74 had an enlarged muzzle-brake/compensator, which eventually gained two ports with the larger of the two to

The 5.54x39 AK-74. Note the design of the tactile identification groove in the butt.

the left. The ports were angled to counteract tendencies to climb to the right when firing automatically, and also facilitated cleaning.

Longitudinal grooves were cut into both sides of the butt to allow the caliber to be identified by touch. A cleaning rod, carried beneath the muzzle, could only be removed after the muzzle brake had been detached. Two lugs beneath the barrel accepted an improved wire cutter/tool bayonet, and a bracket for the 1-PN29 telescope sight could be attached to the left side of the receiver. A single shot GP-25 grenade launcher and an associated rear sight could be fitted to the forend and gas tube respectively.

The earliest guns retained butts and forends made of wood laminate or resin-impregnated wood fibers. Later guns, however, had entirely synthetic furniture.

SIMILAR GUNS

AK-74M (*Modernizovanniya*, 'modernized'). This was developed in the late 1980s as a universal-issue replacement for the AK-74 and the AKS-74. The butt retained the conventional shape, but could be swung to the left to lie alongside the receiver; rigidity in the extended position – the weakness of many stocks of this type – was enhanced by a special cam-locking catch mechanism. The AK-74M has distinctive plastic furniture, and a standardized rail on the left side of the receiver will accept the 1-PN29 optical, 1-PN51 passive infra-red or 1-PN58-2 intensifier sights.

The standard rifle is 37.15in long, weighs only 7.6lb with a loaded 30-round magazine, and has a cyclic rate of 900rpm. It was entered in the Abakan competition to determine the future assault rifle requirements of the Russian army, but has had to withstand a robust challenge from the Nikonov rifle (see **'Russia, modern'**) and the long-term future of the Kalashnikov system is still unclear.

AK-74N ('AK-74H' in Cyrillic). This was a standard AK-74 with a mount on the receiver for the 1-PN29 optical, NSP-2 infra-red, NSP-3 and 1-PN58-2 electro-optical sights.

AKS-74. This variant – popular with parachutists and vehicle crews – had a triangular skeletal butt which could be folded back along the left side of the receiver, reducing overall length to 27.55in.

AKS-74N. This was simply a folding-butt version of the AK-74N, accepting the same variety of sights.

AKS-74U. This short-barreled gun, introduced in 1979, replaced the AKMS-U (q.v.). It measured merely 26.55in overall (16.6in with butt folded), and weighed about 6lb with an empty magazine. The rocking-'L' rear sight and the pivoting breech cover/back-sight base unit of the AKMS-U were retained, but pressing a catch on the left side of the receiver behind the pistol grip allowed the AKS-74-type skeletal butt to fold back along the receiver. A small sliding retainer on the lower left side of the receiver, ahead of the magazine well, held the folded butt in place. The AKS-74U also had a short cylindrical barrel extension, apparently to act as an expansion chamber and reduce the violence of the muzzle blast.

AK-74UB. Derived from the AK-74 in the late 1970s, this was adapted to fire a noiseless SP-3 'piston seal' cartridge.

AKS-74UN. Dating from 1979, this was a variation of the AKS-74U fitted with a mount for optical or electro-optical sights. Owing to the shortness of its barrel, the AKS-74UN is best used at comparatively short ranges.

Soviet marines parade with their
AK-74 rifles: Red Square, Moscow, 1978.

AKS-74Y. This modified design had a semi-integral silencer attached to its shortened barrel, the forend and barrel casing being cut back accordingly. A silenced bolt-action grenade launcher could be fitted beneath the forend, and a special grenade-launching adapter was attached to the standard back-sight leaf.

• Konstantinov

Practically nothing is known about the experimental sniper rifle developed by Aleksandr Konstantinov to compete with the Dragunov (q.v.). Sometimes identified as the 'SVK', the gun was gas operated, locked by lugs on the bolt rotating into the receiver walls, and had a hammer-type trigger system restricted to single shots. The detachable box magazine held 10 rounds, and the tangent-leaf rear sight was graduated to 1200m (1310yd). The receiver was a sturdy pressing, most of the components were riveted together, and the barrel was held in its sleeve with a cross-pin. No gas regulator was provided, as the essence of the design lay in its simplicity.

The Konstantinov rifle had plastic furniture, two ventilated handguards retained by springs, and a detachable flash-hider. However, though batches of experimental rifles were made for trials extending over several years, they proved to be inferior to the competing Dragunov.

• Margolin

These target rifles – and a series of pistols – were the work of Mikhail Margolin, a blind but exceptionally talented sporting gunsmith working in Tula (Tulskiy Oruzheinyi Zavod).

MVO-1 TARGET RIFLE

Made by the Tula ordnance factory, about 1963-70.

Total production: not known. **Chambering:** 5.6x40, rimless. **Action:** believed to have been locked by multiple lugs on the bolt head.

48.35in overall, 9.82lb empty. 28.75in barrel, 4-groove rifling; RH, concentric. Detachable box magazine, 3 rounds. Micro-adjustable aperture rear sight. 2930 fps with 50-grain bullet?

Very little is known about the origins of this gun, which embodied a straight-pull bolt system inspired by the Canadian Ross (which was the basis for a highly successful Soviet moving-target rifle). The MVO-1 had a birch half-stock with a fixed buttplate, a cheekpiece, a high straight comb, and an unusually deep pistol grip. A flute ran the length of the upper part of the forend from the chamber to the tip. A button set into the stock ahead of the trigger guard released the box magazine.

MTs-12-1 TARGET RIFLE

Made by the Tula ordnance factory, about 1949-70.

Total production: not known. **Chambering:** 22 Long Rifle, rimfire. **Action:** locked by two pairs of two lugs on the bolt engaging recesses in the receiver walls.

49.9in overall (including butt hook), 13.78lb without accessories. 29.55in barrel, 6-groove rifling; RH, concentric. Single shot only. Micro-adjustable aperture rear sight. 1080 fps with standard ball ammunition.

Designed for three-position shooting, the MTs-12 has a distinctive straight-comb thumbhole half-stock with an amorphous schnabel tip on the forend. A forked wooden hand rest was often attached under the forend ahead of the trigger. The buttplate had a hooked toe, and could be locked in its channel plate by a knurled wheel on the right side. A setting mechanism allowed a trigger-pressure adjustment range of 1.4-53oz (40-1500gm); the set-trigger was a simple knurled rod. Unlike the Izhevsk-made Strela series, the MTs rifles had central sights.

SIMILAR GUNS

MTs-13-1. This was a larger and more powerful version of the 12-1 pattern, chambering the 7.62mm rimmed cartridge. A recoil bolt was fitted through the stock beneath the chamber, but the double-trigger mechanism was retained. The MTs-13-1 had a 29.9in barrel and weighed about 16.5lb with its competition sights and detachable hand rest. Overall length with the butt hook was about 50in.

MTs-17-1. Introduced in the late 1950s, this rifle was intended for Running Deer competitions. It was chambered for the 7.62x54R cartridge.

MTs-70-1. An improved version of the MTs-12-1, dating from 1966 and intended for use under ISU rules, this had a squared pistol grip half-stock. Checkering – possibly stippling on later guns

– appeared on the pistol grip and the forend panel. The double trigger system was retained.

MTs-80-1. This was another of the Margolin moving-target guns. It was similar to the MTs-17-1, but chambered the rimless 6.5x55 Mauser cartridge.

• Mosin-Nagant

Revolution and civil war drove the arms industry perilously close to collapse. In July 1919, Trotsky warned that new rifles were in short supply, as White forces had captured Izhevsk; Sestroretsk had been evacuated, which left only the Tula facilities intact. The crisis had passed by September 1919 and, by 1922, 1.3 million obr. 1891g rifles made in 1918-20 had supplemented 920,000 refurbished ex-Tsarist guns.

A decision was then taken to standardize the dragoon rifle once existing stocks of infantry-rifle parts had been exhausted. The first new guns were to be made in Izhevsk in 1923, and in Tula in 1924; production continued until about 1930. Details of the pre-1917 guns will be found in the **'Russia (Tsarist)'** chapter.

MODEL 1891-30 RIFLE
Vintovka obr. 1891/30g

Made by ordnance factories in Tula, Izhevsk, Sestroretsk and elsewhere.

Production total: about 17.5 million in 1930-45 alone (including 185,000 sniper rifles). **Chambering:** 7.62x54, rimmed. **Action:** locked by two lugs on a detachable bolt head rotating into recesses in the receiver behind the chamber as the bolt handle was turned down.

48.45in overall, 8.71lb empty. 28.75in barrel, 4-groove rifling; RH, concentric. Integral charger-loaded box magazine, 5 rounds. Tangent-leaf sight graduated to 2000m (2185yd). 2640 fps with Type D ball cartridges. Obr. 1891/30g socket bayonet.

Adopted on 28th April 1930, the result of trials stretching back to 1924, the perfected Soviet version of the Tsarist dragoon rifle had a simplified cylindrical receiver and a hooded front sight. The one-piece straight wrist stock retained the pre-1917 profile, but slotted oval sling anchors were fitted in the butt and forend, and the two barrel bands were retained with springs instead of screws. The rear sight was a new tangent-leaf design, and the socket bay-

The breech of a Mosin-Nagant obr. 1891/30g sniper rifle, showing the 3.5x PU sight.

onet, developed by Kabakov and Komaritskiy in 1928, had a spring catch instead of an archaic locking ring.

Finish on Soviet-made guns was notably poorer than on pre-1917 examples, but the obr. 1891/30g was solid and reliable. It was also more accurate at short ranges than its predecessors owing to greater care taken in calibrating the sights.

SIMILAR GUNS

Improved designs. The 1891/30 rifle provided the basis for many experiments undertaken in the 1930s. Some guns were given pistol grip butts, and others were converted to short-rifle proportions. Nose caps of plain Finnish type or German 'H'-form were tried with a range of sword and knife bayonets, but the goals and chronology of this work remain unclear.

Silenced rifle. A few Mosin-Nagants were used with 1.05in-diameter rubber-baffle silencers weighing about 1lb. These combinations could only fire subsonic 'partisan' ammunition, with green marks on the bullet, case or primer; otherwise, baffles were wrecked after a few rounds.

A group of volunteer women snipers, photographed on the Baltic Front in 1944.
All are armed with obr.1891/30g Mosin-Nagant rifles and PU telescope sights.

A Russian soldier in winter clothing aims his Mosin-Nagant 1891/30 rifle at an aircraft, supported by a colleague with a 14.5mm PTRS (Simonov) anti-tank rifle.

Sniper rifle (Snayperskaya vintovka). The need for an efficient sniper rifle arose from attempts to develop marksmanship made during the First Five Year Plan. After 1932, therefore, guns selected for accuracy had their bolt handles turned downward to clear the telescope sights and the side of the stock was appropriately cut away.

Russian sights were made in factory originally equipped by Carl Zeiss of Jena. The 4x PE type had a 1.2in objective lens and a field of view of 8.5 degrees; windage and elevation adjustments were internal. Optical performance was good for its day, but the sight was comparatively heavy. The earliest examples were mounted in a single-piece twin split ring mount held on the receiver ring above the chamber, but this was replaced by a twin split ring mount fitted to a dovetailed baseplate on the left of the receiver.

Use of the PU telescope, introduced in 1940 for the Tokarev sniper rifle (q.v.), was soon extended to the obr. 1891/30g. Shorter and lighter than the PE, PT and VP patterns, the 3.5x PU was carried in a twin-ring slab-side mount locking onto the left side of the receiver.

MODEL 1938 CARBINE
Karabina obr. 1938g
Made by state ordnance factories, 1939-44.

Production total: see text. **Chambering:** 7.62x54, rimmed. **Action:** as obr.1891/30g rifle, above.

40.15in overall, 7.6lb empty. 20.05in barrel, 4-groove rifling; RH, concentric. Integral charger-loaded box magazine, 5 rounds. Tangent-leaf sight graduated to 2000m (2185yd). 2575 fps with Type D ball cartridges. Obr. 1891/30g socket bayonet.

Adopted in 1939, this replaced obr. 1891/30g rifles and surviving ex-Tsarist carbines in cavalry, artillery, signals and motor-transport units. Unlike the 1907 pattern (see 'Russia, Tsarist'), the 1938-type carbine was basically a shortened infantry rifle and would accept a socket bayonet. Production exceeded two million; 687,430 were made in 1942 alone.

SIMILAR GUNS

Model 1944 carbine. Eight differing bayonets were tried on Mosin-Nagant carbines throughout May 1943. A preference for the Semin system, evident by November, allowed the obr. 1944g carbine to be standardized on 17th January 1944. It was identical with the preceding 1938 pattern, except for the special cruciform-blade bayonet pivoting on a block attached to the right side of the muzzle; weight rose to 8.9lb. Though production of this particular carbine soon ceased in the Soviet Union, work continued elsewhere – notably in China – until the late 1950s.

SPORTING GUNS

Substantial quantities of Mosin-Nagant sporting and target rifles have been made in the USSR, using actions either cannibalized from old military weapons or assembled from unused parts. Identification is still handicapped by a lack of reliable information.

BI-7.62 TARGET RIFLE
Made by Izhevsky Mekhanicheskiy Zavod, about 1963-75.

Total production: not known. **Chambering:** 7.62x54R, rimmed. **Action:** as M1891/30 rifle, above.

45.65in overall, including butt hook, 10.15lb empty. 25.6in barrel, 4-groove rifling; RH, concentric. Integral box magazine loaded from a stripper clip, 5 rounds. Micro-adjustable aperture rear sight. About 2625 fps with Type D ball cartridges.

Introduced in the early 1960s for biathlon competitions, this amalgamated a pistol grip half-stock with a standard Mosin-Nagant action – generally a reconditioned pre-1917 example, betrayed by an octagonal receiver, or from an 1891/30-type sniper rifle. Checkering appeared on the forend and pistol grip of selected guns, though standard rifles were apparently plainly finished.

The 1938-type Mosin-Nagant carbine.

The 1944-type Mosin-Nagant carbine, with permanently-attached bayonet.

The refined trigger mechanism had a lateral safety bolt through the stock. The bolt handle had a spatulate shank – dished to clear the centrally-mounted aperture rear sight – and a spherical grasping knob. A lightweight cylindrical cocking piece greatly reduced lock time. Swivels lay under the forend and butt, the latter being moved forward far enough to allow a hinged trap to be fitted. Two loaded stripper clips could be carried in the butt when required.

The hooked wooden or alloy shoulder plate slid vertically on its mount, but could be locked by a large thumb-wheel in the lower right side of the butt. The tunnel-pattern front sight, fitted on a block at the muzzle, often had a pivoting snow cover.

• Roshchepey

Yacov Roshchepey is best known for the development of an autoloading version of the 1891-type Mosin-Nagant rifle, tested in 1907-9, though the Tsarist authorities were so suspicious of its delayed-blowback operating system that nothing else was done.

In 1928, however, the inventor submitted a locked-breech gun. When the gun fired, the barrel and breech recoiled together for 6mm; a locking block beneath the tail of the bolt was then cammed down out of engagement. The bolt ran back alone, to be returned in due course by springs. A hammer-type trigger mechanism was fitted, and the box magazine held 10 rounds in a staggered row; the magazine could be loaded through the ejection port in the receiver top with the help of a stripper clip.

Testing suggested that the Roshchepey rifle was superior in some respects to rival Fedorov and Degtyarev designs, but a reliance on rimless 7.62mm cartridges (origin unknown) caused its rejection.

• Ross

Substantial quantities of unwanted Ross rifles were sent to the Soviet Union in the early 1940s, part of the Anglo-American aid schemes. These are assumed to have seen military service away from the front line, as enough of them survived to provide the basis for target rifles made in the early 1950s. Rebarreled for the 7.62x54mm rimmed cartridge, guns of this type gained the Soviet running-boar team a gold medal from the 1954 world championships. Designated 'MTs-16', they were 49.6in long, had 27.6in barrels, and weighed 9.9-11.1lb depending on their fittings or supplementary weights.

• Rukavishnikov

The automatic rifles designed by Nikolay Rukavishnikov to compete with the Tokarev and Simonov patterns were gas-operated and relied on lugs on a rotating bolt to lock the breech. Unlike their rivals, which were constructed conventionally, compact 7.62mm Rukavishnikov examples had a distinctive straight-line layout.

1938-TYPE RIFLE
Samozariadnaya vintovka sistemy Rukavishnikova, optniy obr. 1938g
Made in the Tula ordnance factory?

Total production: at least five. **Chambering:** 7.62x54, rimmed. **Action:** locked by rotating lugs on the bolt into recesses in the receiver wall; gas operated, semi-automatic.

44.7in overall, about 9.8lb empty. 23.4in barrel, 4-groove rifling; RH, concentric. Detachable box magazine, 15 (20?) rounds. Tangent-leaf sight graduated to 1500m (1640yd). 2625 fps with standard ball ammunition. Knife bayonet.

It is difficult to determine the production history of surviving guns on the basis of available information. Though they follow a single basic pattern – straight-line layout, rear sight on a riser block above the breech – individual weapons differ greatly in detail.

It is suspected, however, that the gun tested in the summer of 1938 had a machined steel receiver with a non-reciprocating charging handle on the right side beneath the rear sight. The trials are known to have criticized the Rukavishnikov as unhandy and unreliable; consequently, the modified rifle tested in the winter of 1938 may have had a pressed-steel receiver with prominent longitudinal flutes. The shaping of the parts (particularly the ventilated barrel casing) suggests a more refined design than the cumbersome machined-receiver gun. Common to both types were pistol grip butts with folding shoulder straps, short wooden handguards, and ventilated sheet-steel protectors over the gas-piston assembly.

• Serdyukov & Kraskov

SNIPER RIFLE
Vintovka Serdyukova-Kraskeski, 'VSS'
Made by Izhevsk Mekhanicheski Zavod, Izhevsk, 1990 to date?

Total production: not known. **Chambering:** 9x39mm, rimless. **Action:** locked by lugs on the bolt engaging recesses in the receiver; semi-automatic, gas operated.

35.25in overall, 6.05lb without optical sights. Barrel length not known, 4-groove rifling; RH, concentric. Detachable box magazine, 10 rounds. Optical sight. 1065 fps with standard ball ammunition.

Derived from the MA submachine gun, this interesting weapon shares its gas-system and rotating-bolt locking mechanism with the Kalashnikov assault rifles. The rifle has an integral large-diameter silencer forming the barrel casing. Propellant gas bleeds through holes in the barrel into an inner chamber containing wire-mesh baffles, and then into a second chamber before being vented to the atmosphere.

The pressed-steel breech cover and the safety lever resemble the Kalashnikov patterns in miniature, but the short synthetic forend and skeletal butt/pistol grip unit are distinctive. A tangent-leaf rear sight can be used in conjunction with a blade-type front sight in an emergency, but the VSS is intended to be used at comparatively short ranges with PSO-1 optical or 1-PN51 electro-optical sights.

SIMILAR GUNS

Assault rifle, Avtomata Serdyukova-Kraskova or 'ASS'. Essentially similar in size, weight and performance to the BSS sniper rifle, this silenced weapon chambers the same 9x39 cartridge and has the same large-diameter silencer tube enveloping the barrel. The principal differences lie in the butt, which can be swung forward along the left side of the receiver, and in the use of a twenty-round magazine.

• Simonov

These gas-operated rifles originally served the Red Army, though some captured guns were used during the Winter War by the Finns and a few were impressed into the Wehrmacht after the German invasion of Russia. The SKS, introduced after the end of World War II, has been made in several satellite and Soviet Bloc countries.

Sergei Simonov began his design work in the mid 1920s. Stung by the failure of the AVS in the mid 1930s, he improved the basic action until an effectual prototype was tested against the Tokarev in 1939. Simonov always claimed that the adoption of the SVT-38 was politically motivated, and that his gun was actually better; this conclusion was partly supported by a Soviet technical commission, which reported that the improved Simonov was easier to produce and less wasteful of raw material. But the suspicion remains that the Tokarev shot better and had a more efficient locking mechanism.

Eventually, after extensive trials, Simonov perfected the SKS carbine at the end of World War II. Though supplemented and then superseded by the Kalashnikov, the SKS remained in production in the Soviet Union until the mid 1950s. Substantial quantities remain in store, and, owing to its good balance, the SKS is still preferred for ceremonial duties.

1931-TYPE TRIALS RIFLE
Avtomaticheskaya vintovka Sistemy Simonova, optniy obr. 1931g
Made by the state ordnance factory, Izhevsk, 1931-5.

Production total: at least 410 (see notes). **Chambering:** 7.62x54, rimmed. **Action:** locked by displacing a hollow block downward into the receiver; gas operated, selective fire.

Dimensionally similar to the 1936 pattern, below. Detachable box magazine, 20 rounds. Tangent-leaf sight graduated to 1500m (1640yd). 2740 fps with Type L cartridges, cyclic rate unknown. Integral folding bayonet.

The first of these guns was submitted for trials in 1931, though the experiments were spread over several years. The Simonov is known to have been gas-operated, but has proved difficult to identify. It is believed to have had a one-piece pistol grip stock with the rear sight on top of the distinctively squared receiver immediately behind the ejection port. A short sheet-metal guard appeared above the barrel, and an additional metal section lay ahead of the chamber.

Both portions were drilled with holes to facilitate the circulation of air, and the two parts were connected by a wooden handguard with three longitudinal slots. There were no barrel bands. Two transverse recoil bolts were used and fully-automatic fire was apparently achieved by pulling the trigger back far enough to depress a blade set into the rear of the trigger guard bow.

1934-TYPE TRIALS RIFLE

Thirty more examples of the 'Avtomaticheskaya vintovka Simonova' (AVSI) were made for trials in 1933 and, on 22nd March 1934, the Soviet authorities decided to adopt the Simonov automatic rifle at the expense of the obr. 1930g Degtyarev (q.v.). More than a hundred guns were made during the year to permit extensive field testing, and about 290 additional Simonov rifles were made in 1935. It is assumed that they represented an improved form of the original obr. 1931g, but the respects in which they differed are not known.

SIMILAR GUNS

AKSI (*Avtomaticheskaya karabina Simonova*, 'Simonov automatic carbine'). This was developed in 1934 for trials against the 1935-type Tokarev. It was shorter and 400gm lighter than the Simonov rifle, but was rejected in April 1935. It is suspected that only 10-15 were ever made.

MODEL 1936 AUTOMATIC RIFLE
Avtomaticheskaya vintovka Simonova obr. 1936g, or 'AVS'

Made by the Izhevsk ordnance factory, 1937-9.
Production total: about 65,800. **Chambering:** 7.62x54, rimmed. **Action:** as 1931 pattern, above.

49.55in overall, 9.7lb with empty magazine. 24.7in barrel, 4-groove rifling; RH, concentric. Detachable box magazine, 20 rounds. Tangent-leaf sight graduated to 1500m (1640yd). 2740 fps with Type L ball cartridges; cyclic rate 600±50 rpm. AVS sword bayonet.

This improvement on the guns made in 1934-5 was ordered into full-scale production in 1936, virtually before its trials had been completed. Series production began in Izhevsk in 1937, but so many problems were encountered that only about 10,000 guns had been made by the end of the year.

The AVS had a one-piece pistol grip stock with a short sheet-metal handguard toward the muzzle. The cleaning rod was set into the right side of the stock alongside the barrel, while the distance from the pistol grip to the center of the trigger lever was too great for comfort unless the shooter had a large hand.

Experience soon revealed that the rifle had severe operating problems. It was much too light to fire automatically, the standards of manufacture were poor, and the action jammed too often owing to variations in ammunition pressure. Comparing an early undated rifle with a 1938-vintage weapon reveals that the original straight-top handguard was soon replaced by a stepped pattern with an additional locking catch; the recoil spring was strengthened; the receiver machining was simplified; the shape of the trigger guard was revised; the back-sight slider was improved; and the selector and safety catch were changed.

The AVS was controversially replaced by the simpler Tokarev (q.v.) in 1939, even though a government commission reported that the improved 1939-pattern Simonov rifle promised better reliability and was easier to make. The 1936-type AVS served through the Winter War against Finland, but the campaigns emphasized structural weakness and underscored the susceptibility to jamming. Rifles captured by the Finns may be encountered with 'SA' property marks. Others were used by the Red Army and Soviet partisans in 1941-2; a few even survived to serve the Wehrmacht.

1938-TYPE SEMI-AUTOMATIC RIFLE

The weaknesses of the AVS, which became apparent almost as soon as the first guns had been made, provoked Sergey Simonov

into developing an improved rifle. The locking system was altered to a tipping bolt – not unlike that of the rival Tokarev – and the hammer-type firing mechanism was restricted to single shots. The rifle bore an external affinity with the Tokarev SVT-38, but the receiver was noticeably squarer; the wooden stock was in two parts, with a joint immediately ahead of the rear sight base; a wooden barrel guard ran from the rear sight to the barrel band; and a ventilated sheet-metal casing ran from the band forward to the gas-port assembly. A small muzzle brake/compensator was fitted, and a short form of the AVS sword bayonet was used.

Trials undertaken in November 1938 still favored the Tokarev, which became the SVT-38 in the spring of 1939. The 1938-type Simonov had been eliminated by faults in the firing pin and extractor, but was acknowledged to be a promising design; an improved pattern was submitted in January 1939, and a commission was formed in May to consider the relative merits of the rival rifles. However, though the report broadly favored the Simonov, work on the SVT-38 had proceeded too far to persuade Stalin to rescind official adoption in favor of an untried weapon developed by an unfashionable engineer.

SIMILAR GUNS

1940-type carbine. Disappointed by the failure of the AVS and its improved successor, Simonov produced a short semi-automatic carbine in 1940. This had a fixed 10-round box magazine, a short barrel, and a 1000m rear sight. The carbine was rejected in October 1940, but had soon been replaced by an improved version.

1941-type carbine. Encouraging tests were undertaken in April 1941 with two differing 'optniy obr. 1941g' carbines, one with a 10-round magazine loaded from a special charger and the other loaded from a standard five-cartridge Mosin-Nagant charger. The guns still jammed too often during the endurance trials, but were otherwise judged to be acceptable; the five-round magazine was preferred, owing to the use of standard chargers. Fifty carbines were to be made for extended field trials, allowing the 10-round magazine to be perfected, but the German invasion of the Soviet Union prevented completion of the production order. When work recommenced in 1944, the carbine had been revised for the 7.62x39 cartridge.

The 1941 carbine was similar externally to the 1938-type rifle, apart from length, the integral magazine, a smaller rear sight, simplified receiver machining, and an elongated conical muzzle-brake/compensator.

1943-PATTERN SEMI-AUTOMATIC CARBINE

Once tests had been undertaken with captured German MP. 43 (see 'Haenel'), the first successful assault rifles, Soviet designers recommended work on guns of their own. By the end of the year, a design team led by Semin and Elizarov had adapted the 7.9mm Kurz cartridge to produce the 7.62x39 M43 round.

Concurrently with the ammunition trials, Simonov had prepared an improved version of his 1941-type carbine for the new cartridges. The 1943-pattern carbine was smaller than its predecessor, lacked the muzzle brake and had a folding knife-blade bayonet beneath the barrel. Stripper guides were moved from the receiver to the bolt carrier, and the sheet metal barrel casing was abandoned.

Several hundred carbines were sent to the Byelorussian Front in 1944, where, though susceptible to dust and prone to extraction failures, they were generally well-received. The untried weapon (sometimes known as the 'SKS-45') was promptly ordered into mass production, but the war ended before any series-built guns could be delivered. The opportunity was then taken to correct some of the most important flaws and the original introduction was temporarily rescinded.

The Simonov-designed AVS rifle of 1936.
This gun lacks its magazine.

The Simonov SKS carbine, adopted in 1945.

1945-PATTERN SIMONOV SEMI-AUTOMATIC CARBINE
Samozariadniya karabina sistemy Simonova ('SKS')
Made by the state ordnance factories in Izhevsk and elsewhere.
Production total: several million. **Chambering:** 7.62x39, rimless. **Action:** locked by tilting the tail of the bolt downward into the receiver; gas operated, semi-automatic only.

44.15in overall, 8.5lb empty. 20.45in barrel, 4-groove rifling; RH, concentric. Integral charger-loaded box magazine, 10 rounds. Tangent-leaf graduated to 800m (875yd). 2410 fps with Type PS ball cartridges. Integral folding bayonet.

Mass production of the perfected SKS – a refined form of the original wartime version – did not begin until the Spring of 1949, apparently as a safeguard against the failure of the Kalashnikov (q.v.) assault rifle. It was a conventional weapon with a pistol gripped wooden stock – laminated on some guns – and had a distinctive folding bayonet beneath the muzzle. It was easily dismantled and durable enough for arduous service.

The magazine could be loaded with single rounds or from rifle stripper clips, guides for the latter being machined on the bolt carrier face; unloading merely required the magazine housing to be unlatched and swung downward.

SIMILAR GUNS
Sniper rifle. This was an experimental adaptation of the standard carbine, dating from 1949-50. A 3.5x PU optical sight in a readily detachable two-ring mount could be clamped on a lug-plate, bolted to the left side of the receiver, and a cheekpiece was held to the butt with a strap. Surviving guns customarily retain the folding bayonet, but have the improved 1950-type trigger mechanism. The SKS was not sufficiently accurate enough to displace the special sniping version of the bolt-action obr. 1891/30g Mosin-Nagant, and so the project was abandoned.

Improved carbines. Several of these were made in 1950-3. The earliest examples retained the standard angular SKS magazine, but had improved trigger systems, better safety catches, and a pivoting trigger guard retained by a sprung latch. The later carbines also had conventional knife bayonets and detachable box magazines fitted with a depressor lever; magazines of this type could be identified by the gently rounded edge facing the trigger guard. Owing to the great success of the Kalashnikov assault rifle, however, even the most beneficial changes to the SKS had become unnecessary and work had ceased by the mid-1950s.

Sergey Simonov and his design bureau continued to develop variations of the SKS for many years, including 7.62mm sniper rifle derivatives tried in 1960 as the 'SNVS-60' and in 1963 as the 'SVS-137'. The latter is believed to have been chambered for a special rimless cartridge based on the rimmed 7.62x54 type, but details are lacking. Prototype assault rifles such as the AO-31 of 1965 and the AG-35 of 1975 were also based on Simonov principles; the AG-35, indeed, amalgamated many of the general characteristics of the SKS (including the folding bayonet) with a stamped sheet-steel receiver and an AK-type radial safety/selector lever.

SPORTING GUNS
The availability of surplus SKS actions, and large numbers of unused components, has allowed substantial numbers of sporting autoloaders to be made. Most of these have been offered – under brand names such as 'Sibir' – only since the disintegration of the Soviet Union.

• Sudaev
A gun designed by Alexey Sudaev was the first assault rifle (*Avtomat*) to be developed for the Soviet M43 7.62x39 cartridge. Tested in the Spring of 1944, it was a simple blowback with a fixed firing pin in the bolt. A radial selector lever lay on the right side of the receiver, where it closed the slot for the charging lever in its uppermost position, and a trigger-locking safety bolt ran transversely through the stock above the pistol grip. Trials soon showed that extraction was too violent and accuracy was well below expectations, so the blowback was replaced with an otherwise similar locked-breech derivative.

1944-TYPE ASSAULT RIFLE
Avtomata Sudaeva, optniy obr. 1944g
Made in the Tula ordnance factory (?), 1944-5
Total production: 50-60? **Chambering:** 7.62x39, rimless. **Action:** locked by displacing the tail of the bolt laterally into the receiver wall; recoil operated, selective fire.

Length not known, about 8.8lb empty. 22in barrel, 4-groove rifling; RH, concentric. Detachable box magazine, 30 rounds. Tangent-leaf sight graduated to 800m (875yd). 2400 fps with standard ball ammunition. Knife bayonet.

Distinguished from its unsuccessful blowback predecessor largely by the gas-piston tube above the barrel, the Sudaev assault rifle had a wooden half-stock with a separate pistol grip and a short ventilated sheet metal barrel jacket. A bipod was fitted at the muzzle, which had an integral muzzle brake/compensator and would also accept a knife bayonet.

A batch of guns (50?) was made for troop trials in 1945, but field trials proved that they were too heavy and too clumsy to appeal to the troops. Sudaev was asked to refine the design, but his death in 1946 brought work to a premature end.

• Tokarev
The earliest Tokarev rifles – 10 are said to have been made in the Tula factory in 1922 – were locked by rotating lugs on the bolt out of the receiver wall as the recoiling barrel moved the bolt carrier backward. By 1930, however, a gas-operated version had been developed and the recoil-operated prototypes were abandoned.

Despite the poor reputation the guns enjoy in the West, the Tokarev was one of the most efficient autoloading rifles to see widespread service during World War II, only the U.S. M1 Garand being made in larger numbers. However, the SVT-40 was handicapped by poor manufacture – not surprisingly, in view of the unbelievable dislocation of Soviet industry after the German invasion – and also by the clumsy Russian 7.62mm rifle cartridge. The rifle would undoubtedly have performed better with the 6.5mm Japanese cartridge chambered in the Fedorov Avtomat (q.v.). The SVT was difficult to field-strip, but had a better magazine than the U.S. M1 Garand.

Tokarev rifles were unique to the USSR; however, captured weapons were used by the Finns and Germans prior to 1945.

1925-TYPE RIFLE
Avtomaticheskaya vintovka sistemy Tokareva, optniy obr. 1925g
Made in the Kovrov machine gun factory?
Total production: at least 10. **Chambering:** 7.62x54, rimmed. **Action:** locked by rotating lugs on the bolt into recesses in the receiver wall; recoil operated, selective fire.

About 48in overall, 9.5lb empty. 24.8in barrel, 4-groove rifling; RH, concentric. Integral box magazine, 5 rounds. Pivoting-leaf sight graduated to 1500m (1640yd) or 2500m (2735yd). 2625 fps with standard ball ammunition. Knife bayonet.

The first of these guns had a one-piece wood stock with a rounded pistol grip; a slotted sheet-steel over-barrel guard ran forward from the sprung barrel band to the nose cap. The selector/safety lever lay in the guard behind the trigger, and the distinctively rounded magazine case could be released by a pivoting lever ahead of the trigger guard. The bolt was held back after the last shot had been fired, the magazine could be reloaded from a stripper clip, and a catch protruding from the right side of the stock alongside the breech could be pressed to close the bolt.

In January 1926, two of the recoil-operated Tokarevs were tried against a selection of improved Fedorov Avtomats and several

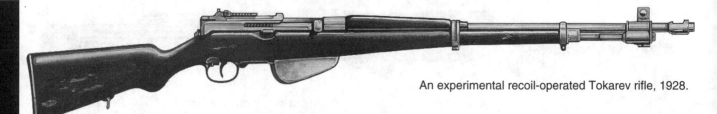

An experimental recoil-operated Tokarev rifle, 1928.

Degtyarev guns. One of the Avtomats returned the best results, and so the Tokarev patterns were rejected.

SIMILAR GUNS

1925-type carbine. Several of these were also submitted for trial, including at least one chambered for the Japanese 6.5mm semi-rimless cartridge.

1928-type rifle. This was a minor variant of the 1925 design, with a diopter or 'peep' unit added to the rear sight notch plate and an integral quadrangular bayonet pivoting on the nose cap. The rifles worked semi-automatically, as the original selective-fire requirement had been abandoned, and usually had 10-round magazines.

The major rivals of the 1928-type Tokarevs were the so-called Co-operative ('Ko.') rifles derived from the Fedorov Avtomat. The 'Ko. No. 3' rifle proved to be best; Tokarev No. 2, which had been showing promise, was eliminated when it suffered a structural failure during the endurance trial.

1930-TYPE RIFLE
Avtomaticheskaya vintovka sistemy Tokareva, optniy obr. 1930g
Made in the Tula ordnance factory?
Total production: at least two, but perhaps as many as a hundred. **Chambering:** 7.62x54, rimmed. **Action:** locked by rotating lugs on the bolt into recesses in the receiver wall; gas operated, semi-automatic fire. Data generally as 1925 pattern, above.

The first of the gas-operated Tokarev rifles shared the stock, rear sight, magazine and receiver design of the original 1925 pattern. The swivels were usually fitted beneath the butt and the rear band.

Changes were made in the design of the receiver, but the over-barrel handguard was abandoned and a new screwed nose cap was added. The most obvious difference was the gas-port assembly formed as part of the front-sight base, and the piston tube running back into the forend beneath the barrel. An open-top three-port muzzle brake/compensator was added, and a knife bayonet replaced the folding pattern to save weight. However, as the guns were semi-experimental, it is suspected that there were many minor variations in dimensions and fittings.

SIMILAR GUNS

1933-type rifle. This rifle was distinguished by several major changes. The gas system was altered so that the piston tube lay above the barrel instead of below it; the 2000m (2185yd) rear sight, changed to tangent-leaf form, was moved forward from the breech cover to a new position above the chamber; and a detachable 15-round magazine replaced the integral charger-loaded design. Most guns retained the open-top three-port muzzle brake/compensator, and are believed to have accepted an experimental knife bayonet without a muzzle ring.

1934-type carbine. This gun was developed specifically for trials against a Simonov carbine (presumably for cavalry or artillery use). It had a one-piece pistol grip stock, with a wooden handguard running to the barrel band and a perforated sheet-steel guard –

five circular holes on each side – running forward to the muzzle shroud.

The carbine was the first of the series to have the gas-piston tube separated from the front-sight block and moved back to abut the sheet-steel barrel cover. A ring-type charging handle replaced the previous ball, a smaller rear sight (1500m [1640yd]?) was fitted, and there was an additional pivoting 'peep' battle sight on the back of the breech cover. The perfected knife bayonet had a muzzle ring.

1937-type rifle (identification uncertain). Made for army trials and essentially similar to the perfected SVT-38, this was a minor variant of the 1934-type carbine with a short-stroke piston system, a 10-round magazine, and a separate mechanical hold-open. A full-length cleaning rod was set into a channel cut in the right side of the stock, and there were two screwed bands. Cooling slots were cut in the wooden barrel-top handguard, which ran from the chamber to the front band, and holes were cut in the short metal guard which ran from the front band to the gas-port assembly. Some guns had grasping grooves cut diagonally around the forend in an effort to improve grip.

1937-type carbine. This was simply a shortened version of the 1937 rifle, with only a single band and a suitably abbreviated cleaning rod in the stock channel.

MODEL 1938 TOKAREV SEMI-AUTOMATIC RIFLE
Samozaryadnaya vintovka sistemy Tokareva, obr. 1938g ('SVT' or 'SVT-38')
Made by the state ordnance factories, Tula and Izhevsk, 1939-40.
Production total: 150,000? **Chambering:** 7.62x54, rimmed. **Action:** as M1930 rifle, above. 48.05in overall, 8.7lb empty.

25in barrel, 4-groove rifling; RH, concentric. Detachable box magazine, 20 rounds. Tangent-leaf sight graduated to 1500m (1640yd). 2525 fps with Type D ball cartridges. SVT-38 sword bayonet.

Trials were held with Tokarev, Simonov and Rubashnikov rifles in the late summer of 1938. The Tokarev was an improvement of the preceding 1935-type carbine, but its barrel apparently had cooling fins. It was judged to be acceptable if the fins were discarded – they complicated manufacture – and if a hold-open and a better muzzle brake were added. A repeat of the trials in November confirmed the decision.

The SVT was adopted on 26th February 1939. It was practically identical with the 1935-pattern carbine externally, with the cleaning rod let into the right side of the stock, but was longer and had two barrel bands. The stock was made in two parts, a vertical joint being found ahead of the receiver. Four circular holes appeared in each side of the short sheet-metal handguard, and five cooling slots were cut through the woodwork over the barrel.

The rear band usually ran over the rear of the fourth slot, counting back from the muzzle. The guns had swivels on the under edge of the butt and ahead of the nose cap, and a radial safety lever could be rotated down into the back of the trigger guard behind the trigger lever. Each side of the muzzle brake had six slender slots.

The 1938-pattern Tokarev rifle (SVT-38), with a clearing-rod channel on the stock side.

The perfected 1940-type Tokarev (SVT-40), with sheet-metal forend.

A cut-down Tokarev 'partisan carbine', salvaged during the Second World War from a damaged SVT-40 rifle.

Before production could begin, however, Simonov claimed to have eliminated the faults of his AVS. A Soviet commission, after considering the comparative merits of Tokarev and Simonov rifles, concluded that the latter was not only easier to make but also less wasteful of material. Its unacceptable performance in the 1938 trials was blamed on poor manufacture.

However, mindful of the failure of the AVS, Joseph Stalin canceled work on all other automatic rifles in July 1939 to concentrate on the SVT; 4.45 million guns were required by 1942, the first rifle being exhibited on 16th July. By October 1939, mass production was underway. However, combat experience in the Winter War against Finland exposed the deficiencies of the SVT-38.

MODEL 1940 TOKAREV SEMI-AUTOMATIC RIFLE
Samozaryadnaya vintovka sistemy Tokareva, obr. 1940g ('SVT-40')
Made by the state ordnance factories in Tula (1940-5), Izhevsk (1940-1 only?) and elsewhere.
Production total: 1.8-2 million. **Chambering:** 7.62x54, rimmed.
Otherwise generally as 1938 type, above, except for the use of the SVT-40 knife bayonet.

This rifle was formally adopted on 13th April 1940 for the NCOs of the infantry and artillery, plus naval infantrymen and marines. Though many changes had been made compared with the SVT-38, the most obvious was the position of the cleaning rod, which lay under the barrel instead of being set into the stock-side. The

Guardsmen parade in Red Square in 1948, marking the 31st anniversary of the October Revolution. Note that they are carrying SVT-40 rifles.

Men of the German Wehrmacht pause for thought in eastern Russia, 1942.
Note the Tokarev rifle being shouldered by the man on the left.

SVT had an improved one-piece stock with a lengthened sheet-steel handguard/forend assembly. A recoil bolt ran through the stock beneath the cocking handle and a short grasping groove was cut into the sides of the stock below the rear sight. The magazine catch, unlike the SVT-38 pattern, could be folded back against the stock to minimize the chances of releasing the magazine accidentally.

Production steadily gathered momentum in the autumn of 1940, and the output of 1.07 million Tokarev rifles (including sniper patterns) in 1941 compared favorably with 1.29 million obr. 1891 rifles and obr. 1938g carbines. Yet success was short lived. After the German invasion of the USSR in June 1941, the Tokarev was regarded as too complicated to justify continuing production. Though a fluted chamber was introduced in 1942 to improve extraction with the poor-quality wartime ammunition, and an improved muzzle brake with two large ports on each side had soon replaced the earlier six-port pattern, production steadily declined. Work officially ceased on 3rd January 1945, but few had been made since the end of 1943.

SIMILAR GUNS

AVT-40 (*Avtomaticheskaya vintovka Tokareva*, 'Tokarev automatic rifle'). The first selective-fire rifles were made during 1942-3, when the Red Army was desperately short of machine guns, but the AVT was far too light to be successful. The guns generally had crudely shaped heavy stocks and lacked the optical sight grooves on the receiver-top.

'Partisan Carbines'. Many SVT-38 and SVT-40 rifles were cut to carbine length, probably after battle damage. They can usually be distinguished from the purpose-built SKT-40 by the rifle-type sheet-metal forend, which either retains seven cooling holes alongside the barrel or will show evidence of hasty modification – e.g.,

the hole nearest the woodwork will be cut through. This may also be true of the cooling slots in the wooden handguard.

A typical 'partisan carbine', originally a rifle made at Tula in 1941, had its barrel so greatly shortened that the sheet-steel forend was only about 1.5in long. A sling swivel was crudely screwed to the left side of the butt. Standards of workmanship were very low, suggesting that the work was undertaken somewhere other than an ordnance factory.

SKT-40 (*Samozaryadnaya karabina sistemy Tokareva*, 'Tokarev semi-automatic carbine'). A few thousand of these guns were made in the Tula ordnance factory in 1940-1. They could be distinguished from emergency wartime conversions by the design of the full-length handguard above the barrel; this had only five holes alongside the barrel (compared with seven on most rifle conversions) and only a single cooling slot was cut through the wooden handguard. All known guns have the original six-port muzzle brake, which suggests that production was stopped by the German invasion. The SKT was 41.95in long, weighed about 8.05lb empty, and had a 18.5in barrel. The standard tangent-leaf sight was retained, together with the knife bayonet.

SNT-40 or **SNVT-40** (*Snayperskaya Vintovka Tokareva*, 'Tokarev sniper rifle'). This was adopted early in October 1940 to replace the obr.1891/30 (Mosin-Nagant) pattern, but was not particularly successful: the fit of metal to metal was poor enough to compromise accuracy, and so a return to the bolt-action rifles was made.

• TOZ, autoloading type

In addition to the better known bolt-action guns described below, the Tula factory has also made a small 22 rimfire autoloading rifle under the designation 'TOZ-21'. The half-stock had a pistol grip butt and a very shallow schnabel forend tip. The magazine housing was integral with the trigger guard, the rear sight was a spring-leaf and elevator design, and a bracket for a compact optical sight could be attached to the left side of the receiver. The rifle was a simple blowback and is believed to have had an eight-round magazine. It was about 38.7in long, had a 20.5in barrel, and weighed 5.5lb.

• TOZ, bolt-action type

These rimfire target/sporting rifles are made in Tula, the range being known as 'TOZ' for *Tulskii Oruzheinyi Zavod* or 'Tula ordnance factory'. They have also been promoted in the West (misleadingly) under the brand names 'Baikal' and 'Vostok'.

TOZ-12 TARGET RIFLE

Made by Tula ordnance factory, about 1960-88.

Total production: not known, but considerable. **Chambering:** 22 Long Rifle, rimfire. **Action:** locked by the bolt-handle base entering its seat in the receiver.

44.9in overall, 8.15lb empty. 25.2in barrel, 6-groove rifling; RH, concentric. Single shot only. Micro-adjustable aperture rear sight. 1080 fps with 40-grain bullet.

This was undoubtedly intended as a basic trainer. The half-stock had a straight comb and a sling-anchor beneath the unusually elongated forend; another swivel lay beneath the butt. The sights consisted of a micro-adjustable aperture above the back of the bolt and a replaceable-element tunnel at the muzzle. The TOZ-12 was also made with a 23.6in barrel.

THE GUNS

The original TOZ sporters were single shot 22LR rimfire bolt-action guns with crudely finished birch half-stocks, belled muzzles and a military-style tangent rear sight which, taken with the general lines of the butt and the shape of the cocking-piece head, suggested that they were originally conceived as a military trainer for the Mosin-Nagant service rifle. More recent single shot 22 rimfires show detail improvements, including a capped bolt way and a safety catch immediately behind the bolt-handle recess, which may be implicit in the '-01' designation suffixes. At the time of writing, however, it is still proving impossible to catalogue the TOZ series accurately.

TOZ-8. This rifle was 43.8in long, had a 25.2in barrel and – according to W.H.B. Smith, in *The Book of Rifles* – weighed 6.9lb. A tangent-leaf sight was customary.

TOZ-8-01. Based on the TOZ-8, weighing about 8.6lb without sights, this rifle had a plain half-stock and a tangent-leaf rear sight.

TOZ-9. This was a variant of the TOZ-8 with a detachable five-round box magazine. It was slightly heavier when loaded, but only by about 3oz.

TOZ-10. A simple target-shooting variant of the basic TOZ bolt action, fitted with a vernier-type aperture rear sight, this was 46.5in long and had a 29.15in barrel; empty weight was about 11.9lb.

TOZ-16. This light single shot sporting rifle had a slender forend with a crudely formed schnabel tip. It also had a small belled weight on the muzzle.

TOZ-16-01. Sharing the action of the TOZ-8-01, this rifle has a light barrel and a slender sporting-style stock contributing to an empty weight of only 5.73lb.

TOZ-17-01. Practically identical with the current 16-01, this has a detachable five-round box magazine.

TOZ-18-01. This is identical with the 17-01 pattern, but has a rail for an optical-sight mount on the left side of the receiver. It weighs 5.7-6lb, depending on the density of the birchwood stock.

TOZ-20. According to Smith's *Book of Rifles*, this was a heavy competition rifle with an overall length of 48.4in, a 27.6in barrel and a weight of 13.4lb. Competition sights and an adjustable-length buttplate seem to have been standard fittings, though no TOZ-20 could be traced for examination.

TOZ-61. This was an oddly archaic-looking single shot Free Rifle, with a set-trigger, a hooked adjustable buttplate, a thumb-hole half-stock and a palm-rest beneath the deep square-section forend; it featured a modified TOZ-8 action, but is no longer in production.

TOZ-78. Introduced in the late 1970, this rifle embodies the action of the TOZ-18-01, but has an adjustable-pressure trigger and a superior beech or birch half-stock, modified open sights (a small block sight replacing the previous tangent-leaf pattern) and five- or 10-round magazines.

VENEZUELA

These guns are usually distinguished by the national Arms above the chamber. These comprised a shield divided into three, with a wheat sheaf and a trophy of arms and flags above a white horse. The mark was surmounted by two entwined cornucopias, and usually surrounded by a wreath.

• FN-Saive

A substantial quantity of 7x57 SAFN rifles, believed to have been about 15,000, was acquired from Fabrique Nationale in 1950-1. In 1954, however, 5,000 FAL rifles were acquired. They originally chambered a 7x49 cartridge, but were soon converted for 7.62x51.

Additional deliveries were made into the 1960s, and about 10,000 Type 50-63 Para rifles were acquired for the Guardia Nacional in 1974. These were assembled from Belgian-made components by Compaña Anonima Venezolana de Industrias Militares (CAVIM).

• Mauser

The 7mm Mo. 1910 rifle was essentially similar to the Costa Rican gun (q.v.) of the same date, but had a conventional bolt face. The army also purchased substantial quantities of 7x57 vz. 24/26 short rifles from Ceskoslovenská Zbrojovka in the early 1930s. Fabrique Nationale Mle 24/30 short rifles were acquired in the 1930s, beginning with 16,500 in 1934-5, and small quantities of FN-Mausers followed after the end of World War II.

YEMEN

• Mauser

A substantial quantity of Mle 30 short rifles was purchased from Fabrique Nationale in the late 1930s, but it is not known how (or even if) they were specially marked.

YUGOSLAVIA

'Kingdom of Croats, Serbs and Slovenes' until 1929, Yugoslavia disintegrated in the early 1990s into several autonomous republics—Bosnia-Herzegovina, Croatia, Macedonia and Slovenia. Yugoslavia exists in name alone, the territory being effectively Serbia and Montenegro. Most of the major gunmaking facilities, particularly the ZCZ factory in Kraguyevac, are still in 'Yugoslav' hands.

• Kalashnikov

These guns are still being offered commercially. Most bear the ZCZ trademark ahead of the company name and country of origin on the left side of the receiver.

MODEL 64 RIFLE

Made by the state firearms factory (Zavodi Crvena Zastava), Kraguyevac.

Chambering: 7.62x39, rimless.

Otherwise generally as Soviet AK (q.v.), except for a 1000m (1095yd) sight and a different bayonet.

The M64 of 1964 introduced a wooden pistol grip with prominent finger grooves, and an integral grenade-launching sight attached to the gas port housing (a suitable launcher replaced the muzzle brake/compensator when required). A mechanical hold-open was added internally.

Selectors were generally marked 'U', 'R' and 'J', and the 1000m rear sight was used. However, some of the rifles made for export had selectors marked in English.

SIMILAR GUNS

Model 64A. The advent of this gun in 1967 brought a shorter barrel—14.75in instead of 16.3in—and, eventually, a ribbed black plastic pistol grip.

Model 64B. Otherwise similar to the M64A, this had a folding stock with three rivets and a prominent longitudinal flute on each side.

The standard ZCZ-made
7.62x39 M70B1 Kalashnikov.

The ZCZ 7.92mm M76 sniping rifle,
derived from the Kalashnikov.

MODEL 70 RIFLE

**Made by the state firearms factory (Zavodi Crvena Zastava),
Kraguyevac.**

Chambering: 7.62x39. **Action:** as Model 64, above.

Otherwise generally as Soviet AK, except for the 1000m (1095yd) sight and a different bayonet. 5.56mm guns usually have six-groove rifling.

The Model 70, introduced about 1972, was modeled on the Soviet AKM. It generally has a stamped-sheet breech cover, a ribbed plastic pistol grip, and an improved muzzle compensator. Continual improvement led to the current models with Soviet-style spatulate compensators. The selector lever and receiver designs have also been modified.

SIMILAR GUNS

Model 70A. This was a minor variant of the Model 70 with a folding butt.

Model 70B1. This appeared about 1974. The principal change from the earlier guns lay in the addition of a ladder-type grenade launching sight above the gas tube, used in conjunction with a detachable muzzle tube. Raising the sight automatically sealed the gas port to allow the entire gas volume generated on firing to propel the grenade.

Model 70B2. A minor variant of the M70B1, this was distinguished by a folding butt.

Model 77B1. Introduced in 1977, this chambered the 7.62x51 NATO round. The receiver was suitably enlarged to accept the bulkier cartridge and a slotted muzzle brake/compensator was fitted. A grenade launcher tube and auxiliary ladder-type sights were optional extras.

Model 80. These rifles, introduced in the early 1980s, were adaptations of the Kalashnikov design for the 5.56x45 cartridge. The gas system was modified to improve performance and the longitudinally slotted compensator was used. Some guns were rifled for the U.S. M193 bullet and others for the Belgian SS109 type, the grooves (usually six) making a turn in 7.1in or 12in respectively. The M80 had a fixed wooden butt and a synthetic pistol grip. The guns could be distinguished from the 7.62x39 versions by their muzzle fittings and short straight staggered-column magazines.

Model 80A. This variant of the Model 80 had a stamped-strip butt folding down and forward beneath the receiver.

MODEL 76 SNIPER RIFLE

**Made by the state firearms factory (Zavodi Crvena Zastava),
Kraguyevac.**

Currently in production. **Chambering options:** 7.62x54R, 7.62x51 NATO or 7.9x57. **Action:** as Model 64, above.

DATA FOR A TYPICAL 7.9MM EXAMPLE

44.7in overall, 9.37lb without sights. 21.65in barrel, 4-groove rifling; RH, concentric. Detachable box magazine, 10 rounds. Tangent-leaf sight graduated to 1000m (1095yd). 2790 fps with ball cartridges. No bayonet.

Adopted as the official sniper rifle of the Yugoslav state army, exported in small numbers, this is little more than a standard Kalashnikov action enlarged to handle full-power cartridges and restricted to semi-automatic fire. The straight-comb butt, ventilated forend and hand-filling pistol grip are all wood. Barrel length and the shallow magazine distinguish the Model 76 instantly.

A mount on the receiver accepts an indigenous copy of the Soviet PSO-1 optical sight, in addition to the standard NSP-2 or NSP-3 night-vision types.

MODEL 85 AUTOMATIC RIFLE

**Made by the state firearms factory (Zavodi Crvena Zastava),
Kraguyevac.**

Currently in production. **Chambering:** 5.56x45, rimless. **Action:** as Model 64, above.

31.1in overall (22.45in with butt folded), 7.16lb without magazine. 12.4in barrel, six-groove rifling; RH, concentric. Detachable box magazine, 20 or 30 rounds Rocking-'L' sight for 100m (110yd) and 500m (545yd). 2590 fps with SS109 ball cartridges; 700±50 rpm. No bayonet.

The ZCZ 5.56mm M80.

The 24.M Mauser short rifle. (HBL)

Inspired by the Soviet AK-74 SU (q.v.), this compact weapon was introduced in 1986 principally for use in armored personnel carriers. It has a standard Yugoslavian-pattern butt, folding down and forward beneath the receiver, and a hinged breech cover doubling as the rear sight base. The cylindrical expansion chamber fitted to the muzzle has simply been copied from its Soviet counterpart. Work is currently being concentrated on 5.56mm guns in the hope of attracting export orders.

• Mauser

These usually displayed markings in Cyrillic. The guns made before 1939 also had a chamber-top crest of a crowned shield bearing a double-headed eagle, placed on a pavilion of gathered cloth. Products of Voino Tekhniki Zavod—'state technical factory'—in Kraguyevac often bore a trademark comprising 'BT3' (Cyrillic for 'VTZ') within a triangle. The chambers of post-1948 weapons had the state emblem of six torches within a circlet of wheat-ears.

THE EARLIEST GUNS

Prior to 1923, the Kingdom of Serbs, Croats and Slovenes used a selection of Serbian M1899 and M1899/07 rifles converted to 7.9x57; 7.9mm 'M24B' rifles (ex-Mexican M1912), converted at Steyr in the 1920s; and shortened ex-Turkish 'M90T' 7.9mm conversions.

POST-1923 GUNS

50,000 Mle 22 rifles were ordered from Fabrique Nationale on 14th July 1923, together with sufficient machinery to equip the Kraguyevac factory to make Mauser-type rifles. A second order for 40,000 rifles (Mle 24 short pattern?) was placed with FN on 16th February 1926; a similar quantity of vz. 24 short rifles was ordered from Ceskoslovenská Zbrojovka at the same time. Most guns were delivered in 1929-30. The last of the pre-war orders, for Mle 30 short rifles and carbines, was placed with Fabrique Nationale in 1935.

MODEL 1898K SHORT RIFLE

Many German war surplus Kar. 98k were refurbished in Yugoslavia after the end of World War II. Most of the German marks were ground away—except for 'Mod. 98' on the left rear of the receiver and a few minor Waffenamt inspectors' marks—and the post-1948 State Arms were added over the chamber. The left side of the chamber is usually marked, in Cyrillic, 'PREDUZECE 44' ('Factory no. 44').

MODEL 1948 SHORT RIFLE

Made by Voino Tekhniki Zavod, Kraguyevac, 1948-55.
Total production: not known. **Chambering:** 7.9x57, rimless. **Action:** as German Kar. 98k (q.v.).

42.7in overall, 8.86lb empty. 23.2in barrel, 4-groove rifling; RH, concentric. Internal box magazine loaded from a stripper clip, 5 rounds. Tangent-leaf sight graduated to 2000m (2185yd). About 2740 fps with ball cartridges. Czechoslovakian-type 'export' sword bayonet.

Production of this Kar. 98k variant began in 1948. The M48 shared the bucket-type buttplate and butt-slot sling attachment of its German prototype, but had a forged barrel band and an 'H'-pattern nose cap.

SIMILAR GUNS

Model 24/47. These were conversions of old Mle 24 (Belgian) and vz. 24 (Czechoslovakian) guns.

• Simonov

MODEL 59 SEMI-AUTOMATIC RIFLE

Made by Zavodi Crvena Zastava, Kraguyevac.
Total production: not known. **Chambering:** 7.62x39, rimless. **Action:** as Soviet SKS, above.
DATA FOR M59/66A1

44.1in overall, 8.85lb empty. 20.45in barrel, 4-groove rifling; RH, concentric. Integral box magazine loaded from stripper clips, 10 rounds. Tangent-leaf sight graduated to 800m (875yd). 2410 fps with Soviet Type PS ball cartridges. Integral folding bayonet.

Production of an SKS copy began in the state arsenal in 1959, the guns being modeled closely on the Soviet version—except that they generally bore English-language marks and a distinctive ZCZ trademark.

SIMILAR GUNS

Model 59/66. The basic design was modified in 1966 to include a spigot-type grenade launcher, and a grenade-launching sight which folded down behind the front-sight block when not required. The changes advanced the designation to 'Model 59/66' (subsequently '59/66A1'). Yugoslavian Simonov carbines were sold extensively on the export market, but were superseded in the 1970s by weapons based on the Kalashnikov.

The M59/66A1 Simonov carbine, with a grenade launcher.

Bibliography

Historical information and detail has been omitted from the directory text to concentrate on essentials. Readers seeking additional information should refer to the books listed below. The list is deliberately confined to books—or reprints of books—which post-date 1960 and are, therefore, reasonably accessible. The books are all published in the USA unless stated otherwise; those that emanate from Britain are listed in 'England' (or 'Scotland', if appropriate).

The list in this edition has been split by subject to make the information more accessible. The data will be continuously updated, in the hope of enlarging the bibliography some time in the future; details of new books, and those that have been missed, can be sent by way of my publisher.

1. GENERAL WORKS

Anon.: *Lists of Changes in British War Material* ('in relation to edged weapons, firearms and associated ammunition and accoutrements'). Originally published by HMSO, London, England. Edited and published in three volumes (1860-86, 1886-1900 and 1900-10) by Ian Skennerton, Margate, Queensland, Australia; 1976-9.

Anon.: *Treatise on Military Small Arms and Ammunition* ('With the Theory and Motion of a Rifle Bullet. A Textbook for the Army'). HMSO, London, England; 1888. Reprinted by Arms & Armour Press, London, England; 1971.

Ray Bearse: *Sporting Arms of the World*. Outdoor Life/Harper & Row (Times Mirror Magazines, Inc.), New York; 1976.

Edward C. Ezell: *Small Arms Today* ("Latest Reports on the World's Weapons and Ammunition"). Stackpole Books, Harrisburg, Pennsylvania, and Arms & Armour Press, London, England; second edition, 1988.

S.P. Fjestad (Ed.): *Blue Book of Gun Values*. Investment Rarities, Inc., Minneapolis, Minnesota; seventeenth edition, 1996.

James J. Grant: *Boys' Single Shot Rifles*. William Morrow & Co., New York; 1967.

—*More Single Shot Rifles*. Gun Room Press, Highland Park, New Jersey; 1984.

—*Single Shot Rifles*. The Gun Room Press, Highland Park, New Jersey; 1982.

—*Single Shot Rifles Finale*. Wolfe Publishing Company, Prescott, Arizona; 1992.

—*Still More Single Shot Rifles*. Pioneer Press, Union City, Tennessee; 1979.

W.W. Greener: *The Gun and Its Development*. Cassell & Co. Ltd, London, England; ninth edition, 1910. Reprinted by Arms & Armour Press, London, England; 1973.

—*Modern Breech Loaders*. Cassell, Petter & Galpin, London, England; 1871. Reprinted by Greenhill Books, London, England; 1985.

Julian S. Hatcher [Major General]: *Hatcher's Notebook* ('A Standard Reference Book for Shooters, Gunsmiths, Balisticians, Historians, Hunters and Collectors'). The Stackpole Company, Harrisburg, Pennsylvania, USA; third edition, 1962.

Ian V. Hogg [editor]: *Jane's Infantry Weapons*. Jane's Publishing Co. Ltd, London, England; revised annually.

—and John S. Weeks: *Military Small Arms of the 20th Century* ("A comprehensive illustrated encyclopedia of the world's small caliber firearms"). Arms & Armour Press, London, England, and DBI Books, Northbrook, Illinois; sixth edition, 1991.

Jean Huon: *Un Siècle d'Armement Mondial* ("armes à feu d'infanterie de petit calibre"). Éditions Crépin-Leblond, Paris, France; six volumes, 1976-81.

Jaroslav Lugs: *Rucni palné zbrane*. Nase Vojsko, Prague, Czechoslovakia; two volumes, 1956. Published in German as *Handfeuerwaffen* (Deutsche Militärverlag, Berlin, 1962) and in English as *Firearms Past and Present* (Ravenhill Publishing Company, London, c.1976).

George Markham: *Guns of the Elite* ('Special Forces Firearms, 1940 to the Present'). Arms & Armour Press, London, England; second edition, 1995.

J. Howard Mathews: *Firearms Identification*. Charles C. Thomas, Springfield, Illinois, USA; three volumes, 1962-73.

Daniel D. Musgrave, and Thomas B. Nelson: *The World's Assault Rifles & Automatic Carbines*. TBN Enterprises, Alexandria, Virginia, USA; c. 1966.

Rudolf Schmidt: *Die Handfeuerwaffen*. B. Schwabe, Basel, Switzerland; two volumes, 1875-8. Reprinted by Akademische Druck- und Verlagsanstalt, Graz, Austria, 1968.

Ned Schwing and Herbert Houze: *Standard Catalog of Firearms*. Krause Publications, Iola, Wisconsin; sixth edition, 1996.

Walter H.B. Smith: *The Book of Rifles*. The Stackpole Company, Harrisburg, Pennsylvania, USA; seventh edition, 1968.

—(Joseph E. Smith and Edward C. Ezell, revisers): *Small Arms of the World* ('A basic manual of small arms'). Stackpole Books, Harrisburg, Pennsylvania; eleventh edition, 1977.

Paul Wahl: *Gun Trader's Guide*. Stoeger Publishing Company, South Hackensack, New Jersey; eighteenth edition (John E. Traister, reviser), 1995.

John Walter [editor]: *Guns of the First World War* ('Rifles, handguns and ammunition, from the *Text Book of Small Arms, 1909*'). Greenhill Books, London, England; 1988.

—*The Rifle Book* ("The comprehensive one-volume guide to the world's shoulder guns"). Arms & Armour Press, London, England; 1990.

Donald D. Webster: *Military Bolt Action Rifles 1841-1918*. Museum Restoration Service, Alexandria Bay, New York, and Bloomfield, Ontario, Canada; 1993.

2. SPECIFIC TOPICS

AMMUNITION

Frank C. Barnes: *Cartridges of the World* ('The Book for Every Shooter, Collector and Handloader'). DBI Books, Inc., Northbrook, Illinois, USA; eighth edition, 1996.

Frank W. Hackley, William H. Woodin and Edward L. Scranton: *History of Modern US Military Small Arms Ammunition*. The Macmillan Company, New York, USA; volume 1 (1880-1939), 1976. The Gun Room Press, Aledo, Illinois, USA; volume 2 (1940-5), 1978.

Ian V. Hogg: *The Cartridge Guide* ('The Small Arms Ammunition Identification Manual'). Arms & Armour Press, London, England; 1982.

Charles H. Suydam: *The American Catridge*. Borden Publishing Company, Alhambra. California; 1986.

ARISAKA RIFLES

Fred L. Honeycutt, Jr: *Military Rifles of Japan*. Julin Books, Lake Park, Florida, USA; fourth edition, 1989.

ARMALITE RIFLES

R. Blake Stevens and Edward C. Ezell: *The Black Rifle. M16 Retrospective*. Collector Grade Publications, Inc., Toronto, Canada; 1987.

AUSTRIAN AND AUSTRO-HUNGARIAN RIFLES

Anton Dolleczek: *Monographie der k.u.k. österr.-ung. blanken und Handfeuer-Waffen* ('seit Errichtung des stehendes Heeres bis zur Geganwart'). L.W. Seidel & Sohn, Vienna; 1896. Reprinted by Akademische Druck- und Verlagsanstalt, Graz, Austria; 1970.

John Walter: *Firearms of the Central Powers in World War One*. The Crowood Press, Marlborough, Wiltshire, England; 1998.

BALLARD RIFLES

Willam S. Brophy, Lt.-Col.: *Marlin Firearms* ('A History of the Guns and the Company that Made Them'). Stackpole Books, Harrisburg, Pennsylvania; 1989.

BAYONETS

Anthony Carter and John Walter: *The Bayonet* ('A history of knife and sword bayonets, 1850-1970'). Arms & Armour Press, London, England; 1974.

Larry Johnson: *Japanese Bayonets* ('The Definitive Work on Japanese Bayonets 1870 to the Present'). Cedar Ridge Publications, Broken Arrow, Oklahoma; 1988.

Paul L. Kiesling: *Bayonets of the World*. Military Collectors Service, Kedichem, the Netherlands; four volumes, 1972-6.

Ian Skennerton and Robert Richardson: *British & Commonwealth Bayonets*. Published by Ian Skennerton, Margate, Queensland, Australia; 1984.

John Walter: *The German Bayonet* ('A comprehensive ilustrated history of the regulation patterns, 1871-1945'). Arms & Armour Press, London, England; 1976. A revised edition was published as *Das deutsche Bajonett, Seitengewehre 1871-1945* by Motorbuch-Verlag, Stuttgart, Germany, 1992.

BOLT-ACTION RIFLES

Frank De Haas: *Bolt Action Rifles*. DBI Books, Inc., Northfield, Illinois; 1971.

Stuart Otteson: *The Bolt Action, A Design Analysis*. Winchester Press, New York; 1976.

Donald D. Webster: *Military Bolt Action Rifles 1841-1918*. Museum Restoration Service, Alexandria Bay, New York, and Bloomfield, Ontario, Canada; 1993.

BRITISH RIFLES (GENERAL)

George Markham: *Guns of the Empire* ('Firearms of the British Soldier, 1837-1987'). Arms & Armour Press, London, England; 1990.

H.C.B. Rogers (Colonel), OBE: *Weapons of the British Soldier*. The Imperial Services Library, volume V. Seeley Service & Co. Ltd, London, England; 1960.

Bernd Rolff: *Im Dienste Ihrer Majestät* ('Gewehre und Seitengewehre der Britischen Streitkräfte und der Commonwealthländer von 1888 bis 1960'). Journal-Verlag Schwend GmbH, Schwäbisch Hall, Germany; undated (*c.* 1993).

Ian Skennerton: *British Small Arms of World War 2*. Published by the author, Margate, Queensland, Australia; 1988.

BROWNING RIFLES

John Browning and Curt Gentry: *John M. Browning, American Gunmaker*. Doubleday & Company, New York; 1964.

K.D. Kirkland: *America's Premier Gunmakers*. Bison Books, London, England; 1990.

BULLARD RIFLES

G. Scott Jamieson: *Bullard Arms*. The Boston Mills Press, Boston Mills, Ontario, Canada; 1989.

BURNSIDE RIFLES

Edward A. Hull: *The Burnside Breech Loading Carbines* (Man at Arms Monograph No. 1). Andrew Mowbray, Inc., Lincoln, Rhode Island; 1986.

COLT RIFLES

K.D. Kirkland: *America's Premier Gunmakers*. Bison Books, London, England; 1990.

James E. Serven: *Colt Firearms from 1836*. The Foundation Press, La Habra, California, USA; seventh printing, 1972.

Robert Q. Sutherland and R. Larry Wilson: *The Book of Colt Firearms*. R.Q. Sutherland, Kansas City, Missouri; 1971.

R.L. Wilson: *The Colt Heritage* ('The Official History of Colt Firearms from 1836 to the Present'). Simon & Schuster, New York, USA; undated (1979).

CZECHOSLOVAKIAN RIFLES

Miroslav Sádá (Plk. Dr.): *Ceskoslovenské Rucni Palné Zbrane a Kulomety*. Nase Vojsko, Prague, Czechoslovakia; 1971.

DREYSE NEEDLE RIFLES

Rolf Wirtgen (editor): *Das Zündnadelgewehr. Eine militärtechnische Revolution im 19. Jahrhundert.* E.S. Mittler Söhne, Herford, Germany; 1990.

FABRIQUE NATIONALE RIFLES

Anon.: *Fabrique Nationale d'Armes de Guerre S.A., Herstal, Belgique, 1889-1964.* Published by the company, Herstal-lèz-Liége, Belgium; 1964.

R. Blake Stevens: *North American FALs* ("NATO's Search for a Standard Rifle"). Collector Grade Publications, Inc., Toronto, Canada; 1979.

—*UK and Commonwealth FALs.* Collector Grade Publications, Inc., Toronto, Canada; revised (second) edition, 1987.

—and Jean E. Van Rutten: *The Metric FAL* ("The Free World's Right Arm"). Collector Grade Publications, Inc., Toronto, Canada; 1981.

FRENCH RIFLES (GENERAL)

James E. Hicks (Major): *French Military Weapons, 1717-1938.* N Flayderman & Co., New Milford, Connecticut; 1964.

Roger Marquiset and Pierre Lorain: *Armes à Feu Françaises Modèles Réglementaires.* Published privately; several volumes, 1969-72.

Jean Martin (Colonel): *Armes à Feu de l'Armée Française, 1860 à 1940* ('Historiques des évolutions précédentes; comparaison avec les armes étrangères'). Éditions Crépin-Leblond, Paris, France; 1974.

GARAND RIFLES

Bruce N. Canfield: *A Collector's Guide to the M1 Garand and the M1 Carbine.* Andrew Mowbray, Inc., Lincoln, Rhode Island; 1988.

Julian S. Hatcher (Major General): *Book of the Garand.* National Rifle Association of America; 1948. Reprinted by The Gun Room Press, Highland Park, New Jersey, USA; 1977.

E.J. Hoffschmidt: *Know Your M1 Garand Rifles.* Blacksmith Corporation, Inc., Stamford, Connecticut; 1975.

R. Blake Stevens: *US Rifle M14* ('From John Garand to the M21'). Collector Grade Publications, Inc., Toronto, Canada; second edition, 1991.

GERMAN RIFLES (GENERAL)

George Markham: *Guns of the Reich* ('Firearms of the German Forces, 1939-1945'). Arms & Armour Press, London, England; 1989.

Peter R. Senich: *The German Assault Rifle.* Paladin Press, Boulder, Colorado; 1987.

John Walter: *Firearms of the Central Powers in World War One.* The Crowood Press, Marlborough, Wiltshire, England; 1998.

—*The German Rifle* ('A comprehensive illustrated history of the standard bolt-action designs, 1871-1945'). Arms & Armour Press, London, England; 1979.

ITALIAN RIFLES (GENERAL)

Gianfranco Simone, Ruggero Belogi and Alessio Grimaldi: *Il 91* [the Mannlicher-Carcano rifle]. Editrice Ravizza, Milan, Italy; 1970.

JAPANESE RIFLES (GENERAL)

Fred L. Honeycutt, Jr: *Military Rifles of Japan.* Julin Books, Lake Park, Florida, USA; fourth edition, 1989.

George Markham: *Japanese Infantry Weapons of World War Two.* Arms & Armour Press, London, England; 1976.

KRAG RIFLES

William S. Brophy (Lieutenant Colonel): *Krag Rifles.* The Gun Room Press, Highland Park, New Jersey; 1980.

Franklin B. Mallory and Ludwig Olson: *The Krag Rifle Story.* Springfield Research Service, Silver Spring, Maryland; 1979.

LEE RIFLES

Eugene Myszkowski: *The Remington-Lee Rifle.* Excalibur Publications, Latham, New York; 1994.

E.G.B. Reynolds [Major]: *The Lee-Enfield Rifle.* Herbert Jenkins Ltd, London, England; 1960.

Ian Skennerton: *The British Service Lee* ('Lee-Metford and Lee-Enfield Rifles and Carbines, 1880-1980'). Published by the author, Margate, Queensland, Australia, in association with Arms & Armour Press, London, England; 1982.

MAYNARD RIFLES

George J. Layman: *A Guide to the Maynard Breech-Loader.* Nashoba Publications, Inc., Ayer, Massachusetts; 1993.

M1 CARBINE

Bruce N. Canfield: *A Collector's Guide to the M1 Garand and the M1 Carbine.* Andrew Mowbray, Inc., Lincoln, Rhode Island; 1988.

Larry L. Ruth: *War Baby!* ('The U.S. Caliber .30 Carbine'). Collector Grade Publications, Inc., Toronto, Ontario, Canada; 1992.

—*War Baby! Comes Home* ('The U.S. Caliber .30 Carbine Volume II'.) Collector Grade Publications, Inc., Toronto, Ontario, Canada; 1993.

MANNLICHER RIFLES

Gianfranco Simone, Ruggero Belogi and Alessio Grimaldi: *Il 91* [the Mannlicher-Carcano rifle]. Editrice Ravizza, Milan, Italy; 1970.

Konrad Edeler von Kromar: *Repetier- und Automatische Handfeuerwaffen der Systeme Ferdinand Ritter von Mannlicher.* L.W. Seidel & Sohn, Vienna, Austria; 1900. Reprinted by Journal-Verlag Schwend GmbH, Schwäbisch Hall, Germany, 1976.

Walter H.B. Smith: *Mauser, Walther & Mannlicher Firearms.* The Stackpole Company, Harrisburg, Pennsylvania, USA; 1971.

MARLIN RIFLES

William S. Brophy [Lt.-Col.]: *Marlin Firearms* ('A History of the Guns and the Company that Made Them'). Stackpole Books, Harrisburg, Pennsylvania; 1989.

MARTINI RIFLES

B.A. Temple and I.D. Skennerton: *A Treatise on the British Military Martini* ('The Martini-Henry, 1869-c.1900'). Published privately by B.A. Temple, Burbank, Australia, and in Britain by Arms & Armour Press, London, England; 1983.

—*A Treatise on the British Military Martini* ('The .40 and .303 Martinis, 1880-c.1920'). Published privately by B.A. Temple, Burbank, Australia, and in Britain by Greenhill Books, London, England; 1989.

MAUSER RIFLES

Robert W.D. Ball: *Mauser Military Rifles of the World.* Krause Publications, Iola, Wisconsin; 1996.

R.H. Korn: *Mauser-Gewehre und Mauser-Patente* ('Als Beitrag zur Entwicklung der Handfeuerwaffen in den letzten vierzig Jahren'). Ecksteins biographischem Verlag, Berlin, Germany; 1908. Reprinted by Akademische Druck- und Verlagsanstalt, Graz, Austria; 1971.

Richard D. Law: *Backbone of the Wehrmacht* ('The German K98k Rifle 1934-1945'). Collector Grade Publications, Inc., Toronto, Ontario, Canada; 1983.

—*Backbone of the Wehrmacht* ('Volume II. Sniper Variations of the German K98k Rifle'). Collector Grade Publications, Inc., Cobourg, Ontario, Canada, 1996.

Ludwig Olson: *Mauser Bolt Rifles.* F. Brownell & Son, Publishers, Inc., Montezuma, Iowa; third edition, 1976.

Walter H.B. Smith: *Mauser, Walther & Mannlicher Firearms.* The Stackpole Company, Harrisburg, Pennsylvania, USA; 1971.

John Walter: *The German Rifle* ('A comprehensive illustrated history of the standard bolt-action designs, 1871-1945'). Arms & Armour Press, London, England; 1979.

MEXICAN RIFLES (GENERAL)

James B. Hughes, Jr.: *Mexican Military Arms* ('The Cartridge Period, 1866-1967'). Deep River Armory, Houston, Texas; 1968.

MOSSBERG RIFLES

V. & C. Havlin: *Mossberg: More Gun for the Money.* Investment Rarities, Inc., Minneapolis, Minnesota; 1995.

PRUSSIAN RIFLES (GENERAL)

Rolf Wirtgen (editor): *Das Zündnadelgewehr. Eine militärtechnische Revolution im 19. Jahrhundert.* E.S. Mittler Söhne, Herford, Germany; 1990.

REMINGTON RIFLES

Robert W.D. Ball: *Remington Firearms: The Golden Age of Collecting.* Krause Publications, Iola, Wisconsin; 1995.

Alden Hatch: *Remington Arms in American History.* Remington Arms Company, Inc., Ilion, New York, USA; revised edition, 1972.

K.D. Kirkland: *America's Premier Gunmakers.* Bison Books, London, England; 1990.

SAKO RIFLES

Kalevi Huovinen: *Sako, 1921-1971* ('jakso suomalaisen asesepän kehityskaarta' ['Finnish gunmakers for fifty years']). Published by the company, Riihimäki, Finland; 1971.

SCHMIDT(-RUBIN) RIFLES

Kurt Sallaz and Michael am Rhyn: *Handfeuerwaffen Gradzug-Systeme* (part four of 'Bewaffnung und Ausrüstung der Schweizer Armee seit 1817'). Verlag Stocker-Schmid, Dietikon-Zürich, Switzerland; 1978.

SHARPS RIFLES

Frank Sellers: *Sharps Firearms.* F.W. Sellers, Denver, Colorado; 1982.

SINGLE SHOT RIFLES

Frank De Haas: *Single Shot Rifles & Actions.* DBI Books, Inc., Northfield, Illinois; revised edition, 1990.

James J. Grant: *Boys' Single Shot Rifles.* William Morrow & Co., New York; 1967.

—*More Single Shot Rifles.* Gun Room Press, Highland Park, New Jersey; 1984.

—*Single Shot Rifles.* The Gun Room Press, Highland Park, New Jersey; 1982.

—*Single Shot Rifles Finale.* Wolfe Publishing Company, Prescott, Arizona; 1992.

—*Still More Single Shot Rifles.* Pioneer Press, Union City, Tennessee; 1979.

Ned H. Roberts (Major) and Kenneth L. Waters: *The Breech-Loading Single-Shot Rifle.* Wolfe Publishing Company, Prescott, Arizona; 1995.

SNIDER RIFLES

Ian Skennerton: *A Treatise on the Snider* ("The British Soldier's Firearm, 1866- c1880"). Published by the author, Margate, Queensland, Australia; 1977.

SOVIET RIFLES

David N. Bolotin: *Soviet Small-Arms and Ammunition.* Finnish Arms Museum Foundation, Hyvinkää, Finland, and Handgun Press, Glenview, Illinois; 1995.

SPANISH RIFLES (GENERAL)

Juan L. Calvó: *Armamento Reglamentario y Auxiliar del Ejercito Español* ('Libro No.3. Modelos Portatiles de Retrocarga 1855-1922'). Published privately, Barcelona, Spain; 1977.

B. Barceló Rubi: *Armamento Portatil Español (1764-1939), una labor artillera.* Libreria Editorial San Martin, Madrid, Spain; 1976.

SPENCER RIFLES

Roy Marcot: *Spencer Firearms.* R&R Books, Livonia, New York; 1995.

SPRINGFIELD RIFLES (BOLT ACTION)

William S. Brophy (Lieutenant Colonel): *The Springfield 1903 Rifles.* Stackpole Books, Mechanicsburg, Pennsylvania; 1985.

Clark S. Campbell: *The '03 Springfields*. Ray Riling Arms Books Company, Philadelphia, Pennsylvania; 1971.

—*The '03 Era: When Smokeless Powder Revolutionized US Riflery*. Collector Grade Publications, Toronto, Ontario, Canada; 1994.

Edward C. Crossman and Roy F. Dunlap: *The Book of the Springfield*. Wolfe Publishing Company, Prescott, Arizona; 1990.

SPRINGFIELD RIFLES (SINGLE SHOT)

Joe Poyer and Craig Riesch: *The 45-70 Springfield*. North Cape Publications, Tustin, California; 1991.

M.D. Waite and B.D. Ernst: *The Trapdoor Springfield*. The Gun Room Press, Highland Park, New Jersey; 1983.

SWISS RIFLES (GENERAL)

Anon. [Schweizerischen Schützenverein, ed.]: *Hand- und Faustfeuerwaffen Schweizerische Ordonnanz 1817 bis 1967*. Verlag Huber, Frauenfeld, Switzerland; 1971.

US RIFLES (GENERAL)

John Browning and Curt Gentry: *John M. Bowning, American Gunmaker*. Doubleday & Company, New York; 1964.

David F. Butler: *United States Firearms; The First Century, 1776-1875*. Winchester Press, New York; 1971.

Claud E. Fuller: *The Breech-Loader in the Service, 1816-1917* ('A History of All Standard and Experimental U.S. Breech-Loading and Magazine Shoulder Arms'). N. Flayderman & Company, New Milford, Connecticut; 1965.

Louis Garavaglia and Charles Worman: *Firearms of the American West, 1866-1894*. University of New Mexico Press, Albuquerque, New Mexico; 1985.

Arcadi Gluckman [Colonel]: *U.S. Muskets, Rifles and Carbines*. The Stackpole Company, Harrisburg, Pennsylvania, USA; 1965.

James E. Hicks [Major]: *U.S. Military Firearms, 1776-1956*. James E. Hicks & Son, La Vineta, California; 1962.

K.D. Kirkland: *America's Premier Gunmakers*. Bison Books, London, England; 1990.

John D. McAulay: *Carbines of the Civil War*. Pioneer Press, Union City, Tennessee; 1981.

—*Civil War Breech Loading Rifles* ('A survey of the innovative Infantry arms of the American Civil War'). Andrew Mowbray, Inc., Lincoln, Rhode Island; 1987.

—*Civil War Carbines* ('Volume 2: The Early Years). Andrew Mowbray, Inc., Lincoln, Rhode Island; 1991.

George Markham: *Guns of the Wild West* ('Firearms of the American Frontier, 1849-1917'). Arms & Armour Press, London, England; 1991.

John Pitman (Briadier General): *Breech-Loading Carbines of the United States Civil War Period*. Armory Publications, Tacoma, Washington; 1987.

Joseph G. Rosa: *Guns of the American West (1776-1900)*. Arms & Armour Press, London, England; 1985.

VETTERLI RIFLES

Hugo Schneider, Michael am Rhyn, Oskar Krebs, Christian Reinhart and Robert Schiess: *Handfeuerwaffen System Vetterli* (part three of 'Bewaffnung und Ausrüstung der Schweizer Armee seit 1817'). Verlag Stocker-Schmid, Dietikon-Zürich, Switzerland; 1970.

WALTHER RIFLES

Walter H.B. Smith: *Mauser, Walther & Mannlicher Firearms*. The Stackpole Company, Harrisburg, Pennsylvania, USA; 1971.

WINCHESTER RIFLES

David F. Butler: *Winchester '73 & '76* ('The First Repeating Centerfire Rifles'). Winchester Press, New York; 1970.

John Campbell: *The Winchester Single-Shot* ('A History & Analysis'). Andrew Mowbray, Inc., Lincoln, Rhode Island; 1995.

Herbert G. Houze: *Winchester Repeating Arms Company* ('Its History & Development from 1865 to 1981'). Krause Publications, Iola, Wisconsin; 1996.

K.D. Kirkland: *America's Premier Gunmakers*. Bison Books, London, England; 1990.

George Madis: *The Winchester Book*. Taylor Publishing Company, Dallas, Texas; 1971.

Robert C. Renneberg: *The Winchester Model 94. The First 100 Years*. Krause Publications, Iola, Wisconsin; 1991.

Ned Schwing: *Winchester Slide-Action Rifles* ('Volume I: Model 1890 and Model 1906'). Krause Publications, Iola, Wisconsin: 1992.

—*Winchester Slide-Action Rifles* ('Volume II: Model 61 and Model 62'). Krause Publications, Iola, Wisconsin; 1993.

George R. Watrous: *The History of Winchester Firearms, 1866-1966*. Winchester-Western Press, New Haven, Connecticut; third edition, 1966.

Harold F. Williamson: *Winchester. The Gun that Won the West*. A.S. Barnes & Company, South Brunswick and New York, and Thomas Yoseloff Ltd, London, England; 1962.

R.L. Wilson: *Winchester, An American Legend*. Random House, New York; 1991.

Glossary

Accelerator. A mechanism, usually consisting of a lever, which increases the rearward velocity of the recoiling bolt to separate it more effectually from a recoiling barrel. Accelerators are often found in machine guns, where the goal is generally to increase the rate of fire. They may also be encountered in autoloading rifles, often simply to increase the power of the operating stroke and enhance reliability.

Aiming Tube. This was applied in Britain prior to 1914 to describe what is now better known as a 'sub-caliber adaptor' (q.v.).

Autoloading. Also known as *self-loading* or *semi-automatic*. This is a mechanism which—through force generated on firing—unlocks the breech (if appropriate), extracts and ejects the empty case, then re-cocks the firing mechanism and re-loads so that the gun will fire when the trigger is pressed again. Strictly, all semi- and fully-automatic weapons are autoloaders, though only guns in the latter group are *auto-firing*.

Automatic rifle. A gun which will continue firing until either the trigger is released or the ammunition has been expended.

Automatic safety. See 'mechanical safety'.

Azimuth adjustment. Found on a rear sight to move the point of impact vertically. Usually known as 'elevation', but sometimes incorrectly associated with *drift* or 'windage'.

Barrel band. Also known simply as 'band', this holds the barrel in the forend. It may be made in one piece or two, and retained by springs let into the forend (*sprung*) or by screws or threaded bolts (*screwed*).

Barrel extension. A frame attached to the barrel to carry the bolt or breechblock; or, alternatively, the part of the barrel behind the breech into which the bolt or breechblock may lock.

Barrel rib. A stiffener forged into the upper surface of the barrel, into which the front sight blade is formed or fixed, this is sometimes encountered in sporting guns (though much more common on shotguns). The object is to give the barrel rigidity without adding as much weight as would be required if it had been forged with a greater diameter. Half- and quarter-ribs will be encountered on sporting guns, usually to carry the sights rather than to stiffen the barrel.

Bayonet. A bladed weapon that can be attached to the muzzle of a rifle or musketoon, though not usually to a carbine. There are many differing types. A *socket bayonet* is an all-metal pattern with a short cylindrical socket, passing over the muzzle, and some method of locking the socket to the gun—a spring, a rotating collar or a sliding catch. A *knife bayonet* has a short straight blade, for the purposes of this book being defined as less than 11.8in (25cm) long; a *sword bayonet* is essentially similar to a knife pattern, but has a blade exceeding 11.8in (25cm). A *sabre bayonet* is basically a sword pattern with a curved or recurved ('yataghan') blade. A *rod bayonet* usually slides in a channel beneath the muzzle, being carried on the gun at all times.

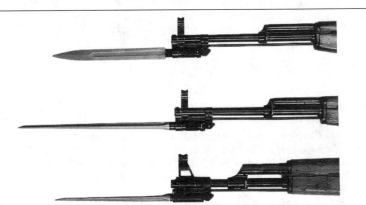

Bayonets: the Soviet SKS (top), the Chinese Type 56 Simonov rifle (center), and the Chinese Type 56-1 Kalashnikov carbine (bottom).

Belted case. See 'cartridge case'.

Block action. A mechanism relying on a block placed behind the chamber to seal the breech. It may be encountered in many differing guises. *Dropping* or *falling* blocks slide vertically downward through a mortise. The Farquharson, Sharps and Browning (Winchester) rifles are typical examples. *Rising blocks*—rarely encountered—should move vertically upward. *Swinging* blocks are common, though encountered in a variety of guises and difficult to categorize accurately. A few swing up and back. Some swing up and forward (e.g., Albini-Braendlin, Springfield-Allin). Some swing laterally backward (e.g., Restell) or forward (Milbank-Amsler). Many swing back and down (Remington rolling block, Spencer); others move down and back (Peabody, Martini). The Snider and similar breech blocks swing laterally on a longitudinal pin.

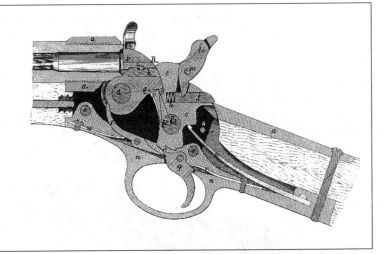

Blowback. Alternatively classed as *case projection*, this is a system of operation in which closure of the breech is undertaken simply by the inertia of the breechblock and pressure from the return spring. The breech is not locked at the moment of discharge and, therefore, the system is generally confined to low-power cartridges. Commonly encountered among pistols and submachine guns, blowback is uncommon in autoloading rifles other than rimfires and low-power centerfire sporters (e.g, the Winchesters designed by Thomas Johnson). Attempts to chamber blowback rifles for military-pattern full-power cartridges have always ended in failure, as some form of case lubrication is obligatory.

Blow-forward. The reverse of blowback operation (see above), this relies on the barrel being projected forward by chamber pressure. The empty case is ejected before a spring returns the barrel to chamber a new cartridge. Though extraction and ejection are simplified, blow-forward has too many problems to attract rifle designers: the excessive weight of the moving parts disturbs aim too easily. SIG made a few blow-forward AK-53 rifles in the early 1950s, but few other rifles of this design are known.

Bolt. This closes the breech of a gun. Used on practically all military rifles made in 1890-1940, it usually consists of a cylindrical body containing the firing pin and firing-pin spring. Several differing types of bolt have been used, but most rely on lugs rotating into the receiver (or sometimes into the barrel extension) to lock the action securely. Some guns have the lugs on the bolt body; others have them on a detachable bolt head. A few retract the lugs into the bolt during the opening stroke, and others may have a pivoting bar or locking strut.

Bolt action. A system of operation relying on a cylindrical bolt reciprocating to extract, eject, reload and cock the firing mechanism. *Straight-pull* action simply requires a handle to be pulled backward, usually transmitting a rotary motion to the bolt head by way of lugs and helical cam-tracks. Associated with the later Austro-Hungarian Mannlicher service rifles and the Swiss Schmidt(-Rubin), this system may be operated quickly when clean and properly lubricated but offers poor primary extraction. *Turning-bolt* action requires a handle to be lifted or the bolt-body rotated to disengage locking lugs before the backward movement can begin. Theoretically slower to operate than straight-pull systems, it offers better primary extraction (assuming appropriate camming surfaces are provided) and is less likely to be affected by variations in cartridge dimensions.

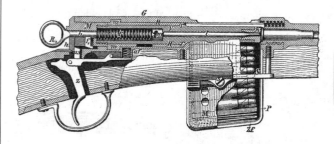 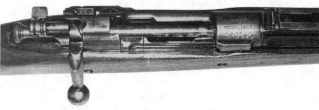

A sectional drawing of the Schmidt rifle.   The action of a Springfield-made M1903 rifle.

Bolt carrier. A component or assembly that carries or supports the bolt, commonly encountered in autoloaders. It may also control unlocking.

Bolt plug, sleeve or shroud. A housing attached to the rear of the bolt, generally surrounding the cocking piece (q.v.).

Bolt way. The portion of the receiver (q.v.) in which the bolt rides.

Bore. The axial hole through the barrel, usually rifled to spin the projectile. *Bore diameter* measurements usually exclude the depth of the rifling, though may sometimes include one groove if the number of grooves is odd instead of even.

Breech block, breechblock. Any non-cylindrical means of closing a breech. Breechblocks may take many forms—e.g., sliding vertically, pivoting laterally, or tipping upward.

Breech. The rear end of the action (q.v.), containing the breech block and giving access to the chamber. See also 'receiver'.

Breech bolt. See 'bolt', above.

Buckhorn. See 'sights'.

Butt. The part of the stock extending backward against the shooter's shoulder. It may be integral with the forend (q.v.), forming a *one-piece stock*, or a separate component. The upper edge of the butt is known as the *comb* (q.v.), which terminates at the shoulder in the *heel*. The *toe* is the lower tip of the butt, and the *grip* (q.v.), *small* or *wrist* is the narrow portion immediately behind the action facilitating the hand grip.

Butt or shoulder plate. A fixture on the end of the butt, either to protect the wood or to ease the shock of firing on the shooter's shoulder. The traditional metal pattern generally has a concave surface, known variously as *rifle type* or *crescentic*. Many sporting guns have been fitted with a straight or *shotgun* type plate, while others, especially recent ones, have had plates of rubber or injection-moulded plastic. The most powerful sporting guns have compressible buttplates, often of *ventilated* pattern. Target rifles invariably have hooked or adjustable buttplates.

Caliber, calibre. An expression of the internal diameter of a gun barrel, generally measured across the lands, but sometimes across the grooves or even—as a compromise—from the bottom of one groove to the land diametrically opposite. A caliber dimension is often an approximation and may depend on marketing strategy. The term is commonly used as a synonym for 'chambering' (q.v.), but this misleading usage should be discouraged as strongly and as quickly as possible.

Carbine. A short firearm with a barrel measuring less than 20-22in, usually—but not invariably—lacking a bayonet (cf., 'musketoon').

Substantial quantities of Sharps carbines were acquired for trials with the British cavalry in the mid 1850s.

Cartridge case. This contains the propellant and a means of igniting it. There are two major categories—*centerfire* and *rimfire*, the former containing the primer centrally in the base of the case and the latter distributing priming compound around the inside of the case rim. Some cases are straight, others may be *necked* (or 'bottle-necked') in an attempt to increase propellant capacity without affecting the case length. *Belted* cases have a raised rib or 'belt' around the body, ahead of the extraction groove, to position the cartridge accurately in the chamber. Belted cases are often very strong, and are generally confined to those rounds that develop high chamber pressures. *Rimless* cases have an extraction groove in the base, the rim being the same diameter as the case-head. They feed well from magazines, owing to the absence of projecting rims, but must be indexed on the case mouth and are often affected by headspace problems. *Rimmed* cases have a protruding rim at the base of the case, which abuts the chamber face to position the cartridge. Consequently, they index very well but are prone to rim-over-rim jams in the magazine. *Semi-rimmed* cases have an extraction groove like a rimless (q.v.) pattern, in addition to a rim offering slightly greater diameter than the case-head. Consequently, the rim can position the case correctly in the chamber but is small enough to avoid interference in the magazine.

Chamber. The enlarged and shaped area of the interior of the gun barrel at the breech, into which the cartridge fits.

Chambering. The act of cutting a chamber (q.v.) in the barrel. Alternatively, an indication of the cartridge a particular gun accepts—e.g., 'chambering 30-30 Winchester Central Fire', 'chambered for 7.62x51 NATO cartridges'. It should not be confused with caliber (q.v.), as a rifle chambering a 30-caliber cartridge may use any of several alternatives. Thus the U.S. Krag-Jørgensen M1892 (30-40 Krag rimmed), Springfield M1903 (30 M1903 or 30 M1906 rimless) and Winchester M1894 (30-30 rimmed) may all share the same nominal caliber, but they accept entirely different ammunition.

Charger. A device for loading a magazine firearm, very common in military weapons but not generally used on sporting guns. Cartridges are held in a special holder, usually made of sheet metal and often containing a spring. The action is opened, the cartridge-holder positioned at the entrance to the magazine, and the cartridges are pressed downward by the thumb. This strips them from the charger and into the magazine box. Chargers are misleadingly known as 'clips' (q.v.) in North America, or more appropriately as 'stripper clips' to avoid problems of communication between the New World and the Old.

Charger guides. A method of positioning the charger (see above) to enable the shooter to press cartridges into the magazine. Most charger-loading rifles have the guides on the front of the receiver bridge, though some early British Lee-Enfields had one guide on the bolt head and some Mausers have the left guide formed by an upward extension of the bolt-stop. Mauser is usually credited with the introduction of the charger-loaded magazine, but elements of the system may be seen in some early quick-loading devices.

Cheekpiece. Found on the side of the butt to help the shooter position his eye behind the sights, this exists in several patterns. The classical design was a plain oval, but many modern rifles have a *Monte Carlo* type with rounded contours sweeping into the pistol grip and a high comb suited to optical sights. The *Bavarian* cheekpiece has a squared lower edge, while the *Tyrolean* pattern (often wrongly called 'Swiss') has a distinctive concave surface with a curved comb.

Clip. A method of loading a magazine with several cartridges held in a special holder. The entire assembly is placed in the magazine, where a spring-loaded arm forces the cartridges upward until a fresh one is pushed into the chamber each time the bolt or breechblock reciprocates. As the last cartridge is loaded, the clip falls (or is ejected) from the weapon. Many early Mannlichers, the M1 Garand and other rifles have been clip-loaded. The system is much less flexible than a charger (stripper clip), particularly in cases—such as the Garand—where the clip is essential to the action yet cannot be replenished with single rounds when in the magazine. The term 'clip' is widely used in North America to describe a 'charger' (stripper clip). It has also gained increasing—if exasperating—popularity among European sporting-rifle manufacturers to denote a detachable box magazine.

Cocking piece. On a bolt-action rifle, an attachment to the rear of the striker, carrying a knob or spur and the sear notches.

Comb. The upper edge of the butt, extending backward from the grip (or wrist) to the heel. The classical comb is straight, but the popular *Monte Carlo* pattern curves upward at the heel—raising the line of sight—while the *Bavarian* (also known as 'Imperial' or 'Hog's Back') comb has a noticeable curve from wrist to heel. A *roll-over* comb curves over the vertical toward the non-cheek side of the stock.

Compensator. A device on the muzzle of a firearm which diverts some of the emerging gas upward, so developing a downward thrust to counteract the rise of the muzzle during rapid firing. See also 'flash hider' and 'muzzle brake'.

Cut-off. Popular on early military rifles, this restricts them to single-shot firing while holding the contents of the magazine in reserve. A typical lever-type example merely depresses the cartridges in the magazine so that the returning bolt can pass over them.

Cycle of operation. See 'operating cycle'.

Cyclic rate. Also known as *rate of fire*, this is the theoretical continuous rate of fire of an automatic weapon, assuming an unlimited supply of ammunition—i.e., ignoring the need to reload or change magazines.

Delayed blowback. This is a modified blowback (q.v.) mechanism with a restraint or brake placed on the bolt or similar breech system to delay or slow the opening movement. There is no positive breech lock. The system is also sometimes known as *hesitation* or *retarded* blowback.

Disconnecter/disconnector. A component in the trigger mechanism which disconnects the trigger from the remainder of the firing train after each shot; the shooter must release the trigger and take a fresh pressure to fire again. This prevents the gun firing continuously if pressure is accidentally or deliberately maintained on the trigger.

Double action. A mechanism in which the hammer or striker is cocked and then released by pulling through on the trigger (cf., 'Self-cocking').

Doubling. The firing of one or more shots for a single pull of the trigger, usually as a result of the disconnector (q.v.) failing.

Drift adjustment. This describes any means of moving a sight laterally to allow for the effect of crosswinds, the tendency of a projectile to 'drift' naturally laterally during its flight, or for any misalignment of the sights. The methods range from basic—sliding a slight laterally in a dovetail, for example—to the micrometric precision of the best target sights.

Ejector. A device to throw empty cases out of a gun. It is usually a fixed bar or blade which intercepts a spent case withdrawn from the breech by the extractor.

Elevation adjustment. Found on sights, this makes alterations to vary the range—usually by raising or lowering the sight block. See also 'azimuth adjustment' and 'sights'.

Extractor. This is customarily a claw attached to the bolt or breech block, which engages the rim or groove to draw the cartridge case from the chamber before presenting it to the ejector. Individual designs may differ greatly in detail.

Feed-way. That part of a weapon where a cartridge, taken from the feed system, is positioned ready to be loaded into the chamber. Rarely seen in handguns, where the distance between the magazine and the chamber is generally very short, it is much more commonly encountered on rifles and machine guns.

Fire selector. See 'selective fire'.

Firing mechanism. The trigger lever, sear(s), the hammer or striker, and all relevant pins, screws and springs.

Firing pin. See 'striker'.

Flash-hider or suppresser/suppressor. A muzzle attachment designed to minimize the effects of propellant flash, generally by using prongs or a pierced tube. It may be combined with a muzzle brake (q.v.), but efficiency is usually low.

Fluted chamber. A chamber (q.v.) with longitudinal grooves extending into the bore, but not as far as the mouth. Propellant gas flows down these grooves to 'float' the case, counteracting pressure remaining inside the case. It is associated with actions in which the breech begins opening while the residual pressure is still high. If the chamber wall was plain, internal pressure would stick the body of the cartridge case firmly against the chamber; any rearward movement of the bolt would then tear the base off the cartridge. By floating the case, there is less resistance to movement and the bolt can begin opening without risk of premature damage. Fluted chambers are most commonly encountered in delayed-blowback military rifles (e.g., CETME, Heckler & Koch G3, Swiss Stgw.57).

Follower. The mobile floor of the magazine, customarily driven by a spring, which supports the cartridges and presents them to the breech.

Forend. That part of the stock beneath the barrel, often held to the barrel by bands and/or a *nose cap*. It may extend to the muzzle or, commonly in sporting patterns, only to half length. A forend that flares outward to provide a better grip is known as a *beaver-tail*. The forend tip may be rounded; have a pronounced downward curl (*schnabel tip*); or display a curious beak derived from a pattern introduced by the Scottish gunmaker Alexander Henry in the 1870s.

Gas operation. A method of operating an autoloader by tapping part of the propellant gas from the bore to unlock the breech and propel the bolt or breechblock backward. Most early gas-operated rifles relied on intermediate rods or levers to operate the breech (*indirect* gas operation) but, inspired by the ArmaLite series, many modern designs lead gas straight back to strike the bolt or bolt carrier (*direct* gas operation). The direct method is simpler, but more prone to fouling.

Springfield Armory "Tanker" Garand.

A Colt AR-15 A2 Sporter II (M16A1 type).

Grip. (i) A part of the butt (q.v.) between the action and the comb, also known as the wrist. (ii) A separate hand grip, either behind the trigger or beneath the forend, commonly fitted either to compensate for the use of a straight-line stock or to improve control in automatic fire.

Hammerless. Truly hammerless rifles rely on nothing but a striker to fire the primer cap; 'pseudo hammerless' designs may be similar externally, but have an unseen hammer inside the frame.

Hinged frame. A gun in which the barrel forms a separate unit attached to the frame by a hinge bolt, so that by releasing a catch the barrel can be tipped down to expose the chambers. The barrel usually tips downward. Widely associated with shotguns and shotgun-type double rifles, the system is also known as 'break-open'.

Inertia firing pin. See 'striker'.

Lands. The raised portions of a gun-barrel bore between the grooves of the rifling.

Lever action. A mechanism that relies on a lever or system of levers to open the breech, extract, eject, reload and then re-lock. The lever usually works a reciprocating bolt or breechblock, though exceptions to this general rule have been made. The Winchester M1873 or Marlin M1895 typify lever-action rifles, but many differing patterns have been made. The term is now normally confined to magazine rifles (strictly, 'lever-action repeaters'); otherwise, it could be applied to many single-shot block-action guns.

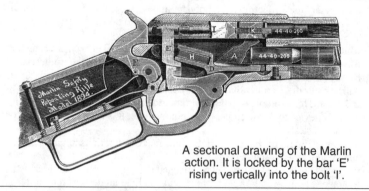

A sectional drawing of the Marlin action. It is locked by the bar 'E' rising vertically into the bolt 'I'.

Loaded-chamber indicator. A pin, blade or other device—sometimes combined with the extractor—which gives visual and tactile indication of the presence of a cartridge in the chamber.

Lock time. The period that elapses between pressing the trigger and the impact of the hammer, striker or firing-pin on the primer of a chambered cartridge. The shortest possible lock time is desirable to reduce the chance of a shift in aim during the period in which the striker is falling. Lock times as short as two milliseconds (.002 sec) will be encountered in bolt-action target rifles, which usually have a short light striker propelled very rapidly, but some military rifles record a ponderous ten milliseconds (.01 sec). This is because a heavy cocking piece—and sometimes even the safety catch—may be attached directly to the striker. The fastest lock time of standard military rifles is generally regarded as the German Gew. 98 at about five milliseconds, closely followed by the 1905-pattern Japanese Arisaka. Among the slowest are the U.S. Krag-Jørgensen and some of the early Mannlichers (about eight milliseconds), with the Gew. 88 at nine milliseconds or worse.

Lock-work, lockwork. An expression covering the whole of the mechanism necessary to fire a weapon, from the trigger through to the hammer or striker.

Long recoil. See 'recoil operation'.

Magazine. The container in which the cartridges are held to permit continuous fire. Magazines take many differing forms. Among the earliest were tubes, usually contained in the forend beneath the barrel (e.g., Henry, Vetterli, Winchester) or, more rarely, in the butt (Chaffee-Reece, Hotchkiss). These were superseded by box patterns, credited—though not without dispute—to James Lee. Some boxes were *detachable*, others have been fixed. Fixed magazines are described here as *internal* if they are carried entirely inside the stock (introduced on the Spanish Mauser of 1893) and *fixed* or *integral* if they project externally but are part of the receiver or frame (e.g., most Mannlichers, Mosin-Nagant). Some of the earlier Mausers, such as the Argentine gun of 1891 have *semi-integral* magazines, which can be removed with the aid of a tool but are not genuinely readily detachable. Magazines described as *blind* are carried internally, but are not visible from the outside of the gun owing to the lack of a floorplate. Other patterns to have reached service status include a *pan* (lateral) magazine, featured by the Krag-Jørgensen, or the *spool* or 'rotary' mechanism embodied in Mannlicher-Schönauer and similar guns. Military magazines may be loaded from chargers (stripper clips) or with clips (qq.v.).

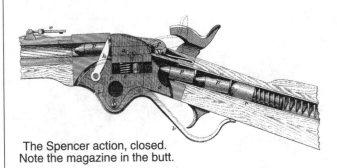

The Spencer action, closed.
Note the magazine in the butt.

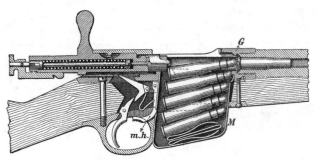

A sectional drawing of the 1879-type Lee rifle.

Magazine safety. A system ensuring that the firing mechanism will not function if the magazine is removed. The objective is to prevent a common accident where the magazine is removed and a live round remains in the chamber. Safeties of this type are unpopular on military weapons, which would otherwise be prevented from firing single shots by the absence of a magazine, but are often obligatory on guns destined for the commercial market.

Mainspring. The spring that propels the hammer or striker into the primer of a chambered cartridge.

Mechanical safety. A method of ensuring that the action does not fire before the breech is properly closed. A mechanical safety is obligatory in an autoloader, but is also present in most manually-operated rifles to ensure that the striker cannot reach the primer of a chambered round until the locking mechanism is engaged.

Musketoon. A short-barreled firearm, usually accepting a bayonet (cf., 'carbine').

Muzzle brake. An attachment similar to a compensator, intended to turn the emerging gases and drive them rearward. This counteracts the recoil sensation by thrusting the muzzle forward. The effectiveness of muzzle brakes varies, as utility has to be balanced against the unpleasant consequences of directing gas-blast sideways or backward.

Non-ejecting, non-ejector. A class of gun unable to eject spent cartridges—generally double rifles, though many early military rifles lacked ejectors and some dropping-block patterns can be set to extract only partially. The feature is useful to those who do not want to lose spent cases or to have them damaged during ejection.

Nose cap. The band or fitting nearest the muzzle. The term is usually applied to a military rifle, where the nose cap will often carry a lug for the bayonet and anchor the cleaning rod.

Operating cycle. This is simply the complete routine required for the satisfactory functioning of an automatic weapon—firing, unlocking the breech, extracting, ejecting, cocking, feeding, chambering and breech-locking. (Note: not all functions may be present, some may overlap, and the order of their occurrence may vary.)

Proof mark. Applied by an official body ('proof house') to certify that a gun is strong enough to withstand the rigours of continual use. Proof is closely regulated in most European countries, where there are mandatory procedures and severe penalties for disobedience; in the U.S., however, proof is left to the discretion of individual manufacturers.

Pump action. See 'slide action'.

Quick-loader. A method of holding cartridges so that they are readily available for insertion in the chamber. The term is associated with single-shot rifles, though a charger and even a clip are quick-loaders of a particular form. A typical loader may take the form of a spring-clip attached to the breech, or a wooden block screwed to the forend.

Receiver. A term applied to the frame of a rifle. The sides of a *solid* bridge receiver are connected above the bolt or breechblock, while a *split-bridge* receiver allows the bolt or operating handle to pass through.

Recoil. A force generated by firing, opposing the forward motion of the projectile.

Recoil bolt. A transverse bolt through the stock, acting in concert with the recoil lug (below) to spread the force that may otherwise split or damage the woodwork.

Recoil lug. A projection on the underside of the breech designed to spread the recoil force to a greater area of the stock than a bolt running up through the trigger guard, tang or magazine floorplate into the receiver.

Recoil operation. The recoil (q.v.) force can be harnessed to operate an autoloading action. *Long* recoil relies on the barrel and breech recoiling locked together for a distance at least as long as a complete unfired cartridge. At the end of this stroke, the bolt is unlocked and held while the barrel runs back to its forward position. During this movement, the cartridge case is extracted and ejected and a fresh round rises into the feedway. The bolt is then released, runs forward to chamber a round, locks, and the gun is ready to fire. Long recoil is uncommon, however. *Short* recoil is similar to long recoil, but the distance traversed by the components before unlocking occurs is less than the length of a complete unfired cartridge.

Recoil spring. See 'return spring'.

Return spring. The spring in an autoloader which returns the bolt or breechblock after firing; sometimes less accurately called the 'recoil spring'.

Ribbed barrel. See 'barrel rib'.

Rifling. This is the means by which spin is imparted to a bullet in the period before it emerges from the muzzle. Rifling generally comprises *grooves* separated by *lands*, though the details vary appreciably; some early guns (e.g., the U.S. 45 M1873 Springfield) have three grooves, while others (such as modern Marlins) may have 20 or more. *Concentric* rifling has its grooves and lands cut on the basis of concentric circles. *Polygonal* rifling is formed of several equal sides and has no obvious grooves. British Metford-type polygonal rifling was seven-sided (heptagonal), though the British Whitworth and Danish Rasmussen patterns were six-sided (hexagonal). *Ratchet* rifling is little more than a series of stepped arcs, being known as 'reverse ratchet' if it opposes the direction of twist. Patterns that fit none of these categories are classed here as *composite* rifling, though the term covers a multitude of differing styles. The direction of twist, when viewed from the breech to the muzzle, may be *left* (anti- or counter-clockwise) or *right* (clockwise). *Pitch* describes the rate at which the rifling turns about the axis of the bore: 'fast pitch' turns very rapidly, while 'slow pitch' barrels have rifling that turns so slowly that, in extreme cases, it may appear to be straight. *Progressive* rifling (also known as 'gain-twist') starts with a slow spiral and then quickens towards the muzzle; *progressive-depth* rifling is usually deeper at the breech than at the muzzle.

Rimless or rimmed case. See 'cartridge case'.

Rocky Mountain Sight. See 'sights'.

Schnabel tip. See 'forend'. Occasionally rendered colloquially as 'snobble'.

Schuetzen, Schützen. This term, which means 'marksmen' in German, is applied to a particular type of target shooting (and, by extension, target rifle) originating in central Europe and then popularized in the U.S. in the 19th Century. The rifles usually have elaborate set triggers, palm rests beneath the forends, exaggerated cheekpieces and combs, hooked buttplates, and fully adjustable sights.

A detail view of an Aydt rifle.

Sealed Pattern. Unique to the British Army and its colonial counterparts, this term denotes government acceptance. It arose from the attachment of a War Office (wax) seal—in the form of the Royal Arms—to guns and other stores approved or 'sealed' to guide manufacture. As a 'Sealed Pattern' gun was deemed to be dimensionally correct, all manufacturing patterns and gauges had to comply with it.

Sear. An intermediate component or series of components ('sear train') linking the trigger with the hammer or firing pin, holding the latter back until released by trigger pressure.

Selecter/selector. See 'selective fire'.

Selective-fire. A gun that may, when required, be set (with the 'selector') to fire single shots, multi-shot bursts or fully automatically. The selector is often combined with the manual safety catch.

Self-cocking. A firing mechanism in which the action of cocking the hammer or firing pin is performed automatically either by the breech mechanism or by pulling back the trigger (cf., 'double action'). Note that it is not released automatically, but instead requires an additional external stimulus.

Self-loading. See 'autoloading'.

Semi-automatic rifle. A gun that fires once for each pull on the trigger and reloads automatically, but requires the shooter to release the trigger lever before another shot can be fired (cf., 'automatic rifle').

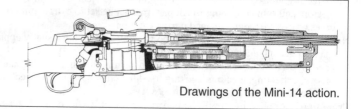

Drawings of the Mini-14 action.

Semi-rimmed case. See 'cartridge case'.

Set trigger. A mechanism, commonly used on target guns, with a lever or button to 'set' the trigger by taking up all the slack in the system; thereafter, a very slight pressure on the trigger is sufficient to fire. Set triggers come in many differing designs, some of which combine the function of the setting and trigger levers in a single component.

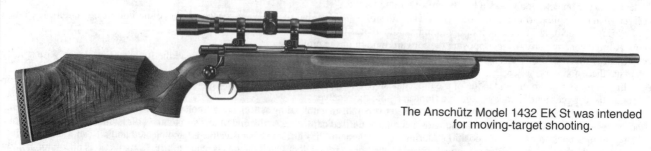

The Anschütz Model 1432 EK St was intended for moving-target shooting.

Short recoil. See 'recoil operation'.

Sights. Most rifles have sights at the muzzle (*front* sight) and at the breech (*rear* sight). Front sights are usually blades, inverted-'V' blades (known as *barleycorn* patterns) or beads. Target rifles may offer exchangeable-element tunnel or globe sights, often with integral spirit levels and wind gauges. The simplest rear sights are standing open notches. Popular in the North America, the *leaf-and-elevator* sight usually consists of a flat spring—bent into an open notch—with a sliding stepped plate controlling elevation; alternatively, a screw may raise the leaf. These were originally known as *Rocky Mountain sights* when fitted with a *buckhorn* sighting notch. Other sights popular on sporting rifles include vertically sliding plates controlled by finger-wheels, and the so-called *express* sights with a rank of several folding leaves. The *Cape* sight (a useful, but apparently artificial designation) was a variant of the express pattern with several small folding leaves and a large leaf-and-slider for longer ranges. The earliest military rifles retained the traditional *ramp-and-leaf* sight introduced on the rifle-muskets of the 1850s. A slider on the folding leaf acted in concert with ramps on the base (stepped or continuously curved) to adjust the range for distances up to about 500yd, whereafter raising the leaf allowed longer ranges to be set. A fixed 'battle sight' was usually cut into the leaf-pivot block. Variations of these sights, and simpler patterns without the stepped base, lasted until World War I. They were replaced by the *tangent-leaf* sight, which

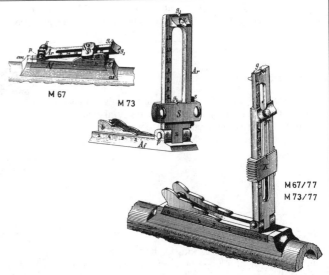

The three different Werndl rear sights help identification.

relied on the slider and side-ramps for its entire range of adjustment, and then by a selection of aperture patterns. True *tangent* sights are rarely encountered, the most common taking the form of an arm pivoted on a quadrant block to adjust the range. Target rifles often have micrometer-adjustable rear sights of the utmost sophistication on the barrel near the breech, on the breech itself, or on the upper tang behind the breech. Guns intended for long-range shooting in the supine ('back') position may have their rear sight on the comb of the butt by the heel.

Silencer. A device attached to the muzzle of a gun—or incorporated in its construction—whereby the gases emerging from the barrel are trapped, then circulated in expansion chambers to allow their temperature and pressure to drop before release to the atmosphere occurs. This prevents the usual noise of the muzzle blast by reducing the velocity of the emerging gases below the speed of sound (about 1120ft/sec at sea level). Silencers are rarely encountered on rifles, as the excessive muzzle velocity of most cartridges forces special low-power subsonic ammunition to be used.

Slide action. An operating system relying on the reciprocating motion of a forward hand grip to unlock the breech, extract, eject, cock the firing mechanism, then reload and re-lock. The first successful method was developed by Sylvester Roper and Christopher Spencer in the 1880s, but experiments had begun many years earlier.

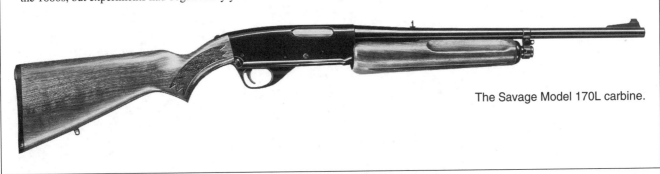

The Savage Model 170L carbine.

Standing breech. The fixed part of the frame that abuts the base of the cartridge in the firing position, carrying the firing pin or the firing-pin bush. The term is usually applied to single-shot dropping-block rifles or break-open patterns.

Stock. That part of the gun that contains or supports the barrel and action. It comprises the butt, grip and forend, but may be made in one piece or two. Originally wood, military stocks are now generally synthetic. Wood retains a tenuous pre-eminence among the sporting patterns despite an ever-increasing challenge from fiberglass, Kevlar and other synthetics offering durability and warp resistance. A one-piece sporting stock extending to the muzzle is normally called a *Mannlicher* pattern, on no particular authority; full-length stocks have been used since the dawn of gunsmithing era.

Striker. Also known as the 'firing pin', this is driven by a spring to acquire sufficient energy to fire the cartridge primer. There is confusion over the terms 'striker' and 'firing pin', but these are widely regarded as exchangeable. The term *inertia* firing pin is strictly applied only to a floating pin which is struck forward by the hammer to reach the primer of a chambered round, and then driven or cammed back to allow the breech to open; however, the term is now generally extended to include the spring-opposed or rebounding pattern. A *rebounding* (or 'flying') firing pin is shorter than the distance between the hammer and the primer of a chambered cartridge, being struck forward when required and then pushed back into the breechblock or bolt by a small coil spring.

Sub-caliber adapter/sub-calibre adaptor (or liner). This may be inserted permanently into a barrel as a 'liner', generally to alter caliber, or to serve as an 'adapter' when required—usually to permit training with low-cost rimfire ammunition. The adapter was originally known as an 'Aiming Tube' in Britain, but then became a 'Morris Tube' after a particularly notable patentee.

Tang. A rearward extension of the receiver, usually anchoring the butt to the receiver or frame.

Take-down. Originating in North America, this term denotes that a gun may be instantaneously dismantled into its major sub-assemblies for convenience. Most examples split into the barrel/forend and breech/butt.

The 1894-type Marlin 'take-down' rifle broken into its major components.

Toggle lock. A method of locking the bolt or breechblock by using a multiple-lever linkage to connect the locking block to the actuating mechanism, by way of a hinge or intermediate link. The central hinge is placed so that any thrust generated on firing tends to keep the action closed. However, the breech opens with a minimum of effort when the strut-like resistance is broken. A feature of many early dropping-block rifles, where it was used to retain the block in its uppermost position, a rudimentary toggle-lock has been used in the Henry rifle of 1860 and all pre-1876 lever-action Winchesters. It is associated with the Maxim machine gun and the Parabellum or Luger pistol, in conjunction with a locked breech, and also appeared in the delayed-blowback Pedersen rifle. However, autoloading togglelocks demand accurate machining and consistent ammunition performance to operate satisfactorily. The machine guns worked very well in an era in which high manufacturing costs and excessive weight were not regarded critically, but none of the autoloading rifles (e.g., Heinemann, Pedersen) has been particularly successful.

Ventilated rib. A barrel rib (q.v.) in which the rib is held away from the barrel by a series of supports, allowing air to circulate beneath it. The objective is to cool the barrel and, by so doing, prevent heat rising from the barrel surface disturbing the sight line. Though widely used on thin-barreled shotguns, ventilated ribs are much less common on sporting rifles.

Windage adjustment. See 'drift adjustment'.

Wrist. See 'butt'.

MAKER AND MODEL INDEX

ARGENTINA, 9
- Buenos Aires, 9
- Enfield, 9
- FMAP, 9
  MODEL 83 AUTOMATIC RIFLE
    Fusil Automatico del Republica de
    Argentina Modelo 83, 'FARA 83', 9
- FN (FMAP) ,9
  FAL-TYPE AUTOMATIC RIFLES
    Fusil Semiautomatico Livano, 'FSL' ,9
- Garand, 10
- Mauser, 10
  MODEL 1891 RIFLE
    Fusil Mauser Argentino Mo.1891, 10
  MODEL 1909 RIFLE
    Fusil Mauser Argentino Mo. 1909, 10
- Remington, 10

ARMENIAN REPUBLIC, 10
- Kalashnikov, 10
  ASSAULT RIFLE MODEL 3 AK-3, 10

AUSTRALIA, 10
- FN (Lithgow), 11
  L1A1 RIFLE, 11
- Lee-Enfield, 11
  NUMBER 1 MARK 3* H (T) (AUST.)
    RIFLE
    Sniper rifle, 11
  NUMBER 1 MARK 3 RIFLE, SHORT
    PATTERN, 11
  NUMBER 6 RIFLE, 11
- Martini, 11
- Parker-Hale, 12
- Sportco, 12
  SPORTCO MODEL 71S RIFLE, 12
  SPORTCO HORNET RIFLE, 12
  SPORTCO MODEL 44 RIFLE, 12
- Steyr (Lithgow), 12

AUSTRIA, 12
- Dschulnigg, 12
  SPORTING RIFLE, 13
- FN (Steyr), 13
  MODEL 58 ASSAULT RIFLE
    Sturmgewehr 58, StG. 58, 13
- Mannlicher, 13
  MODEL 1895/24 SHORT RIFLE, 13
  M1930 SHORT RIFLE, 13
  REPETIER-PIRSCHBÜCHSE, 13
- Mauser, 14
- Sodia, 14
  MODEL 1963 RIFLE, 14
  Steyr, autoloading type, 14
  ARMEE-UNIVERSAL-GEWEHR
    (AUG)
    Sturmgewehr 77, or StG. 77, 14
  Steyr, bolt-action type, 15
  MODEL 69 SNIPER RIFLE
    Scharfschützengewehr 69, SSG 69, 15
  RIMFIRE PATTERNS, 15
  MODEL 1969 RIFLE
    Alternatively known as 'Model 67', 15
  MODEL 72 SPORTING RIFLE, 17
  MODEL 96 SBS SPORTING RIFLE
    'Safe Bolt System', 17
- Voere, autoloading type, 17
  MODEL 2185 MATCH RIFLE
    Präzisions-Selbstlade-Sportbüchse
    M2185, 17
- Voere, bolt-action type, 17
  TITAN II
    Also known as 'Model 225' or 'Mauser
    Model 99', 17
  TITAN MENOR, 19
  TITAN III
    Also known as 'Model 226', 19
  VEC-91 SPORTING RIFLE
    Also known as 'Lightning' in the USA,
    19
- Winkler, 20

AUSTRIA-HUNGARY, 20
- Andrs, 20
- Barth & Hohenbrück, 20
- Früwirth, 20

MODEL 1872 GENDARMERIE
  CARBINE, 20
- Jurnitschek, 20
- Krnka, block-action type, 20
  BAR-LOCK GUNS, 20
  RAPID-LOADING RIFLES, 20
- Krnka, bolt-action type, 21
  1889-TYPE RIFLES, 21
- Kropatschek, 21
  MODEL 1881 GENDARMERIE
    CARBINE
    Sometimes known as 'M1874/81', 21
  1881-TYPE TRIALS RIFLES, 21
- Mannlicher, autoloading type, 21
  HANDMITRAILLEUSE, 21
  1891-TYPE AUTOMATIC RIFLE, 22
  MODEL 1893 SEMI-AUTOMATIC
    RIFLE, 22
  MODEL 1895 SEMI-AUTOMATIC
    RIFLE, 22
  MODEL 1900 SEMI-AUTOMATIC
    RIFLE, 22
- Mannlicher, bolt-action type, 22
  1880-TYPE RIFLE
    Repetir-Gewehr mit Rohrbündel-
    Magazin in Kolben, 22
  1881-TYPE RIFLE
    Repetir-Gewehr mit anhangbarem
    Magazin M1881, 22
  1884-TYPE RIFLE, 23
  1885-TYPE TRIALS RIFLE
    Repetier-Gewehr 'Österreichische
    Vorlage', 23
  MODEL 1886 RIFLE
    Infanterie-Repetier-Gewehr M1886,
    23
  1887-TYPE RIFLE
    Repetir-Gewehr mit Trommel
    Magazin M1887, 23
  1887/88-TYPE RIFLE, 23
  MODEL 1888 RIFLE
    Infanterie-Repetier-Gewehr M1888,
    24
  MODEL 1890 CAVALRY CARBINE
    Kavallerie-Repetier-Karabiner, 24
  1894-TYPE RIFLE
    Repetier-Gewehr mit Packetladung
    M1894, 24
  MODEL 1895 RIFLE
    Repetier-Gewehr M1895, 24
  1896-TYPE RIFLE
    Repetier-Gewehr mit Packetladung
    M1896, 24
  MODEL 1904 RIFLE, 24
  REPETIER-PIRSCHBÜCHSE, 25
- Mosin-Nagant, 25
- Odkolek, 25
  1889-TYPE RIFLE, 25
  1903-TYPE RIFLE, 25
- Schönauer, 25
- Schulhof, 25
- Spitalsky, 26
- Wangler, 26
- Wänzl, 26
  MODEL 1866 RIFLE
    Infanterie-Gewehr M1863/66, 26
- Werndl, 26
  MODEL 1867 RIFLE
    Infanterie- und Jägergewehr M1867,
    26
  MODEL 1867 CARBINE
    Karabiner M1867, 27
  MODEL 1873 RIFLE
    Infanterie- und Jägergewehr M1873,
    27
  MODEL 1873 CARBINE
    Karabiner M1873, 27
  MODEL 1877 RIFLE
    Infanterie- und Jägergewehr M1877,
    27
  MODEL 1877 CARBINE
    Karabiner M1877, 27

BADEN, 28
- Terry, 28

BAVARIA, 28
- Chassepot, 28
- Podewils, 28

MODEL 1858/67 RIFLE,, 28
- Spörer & Harl, 29
- Werder, 29
  MODEL 1869 RIFLE
    Rückladungsgewehr M/1869, System
    Werder, 29
  MODEL 1869 CARBINE, 29
  NEW MODEL 1869 RIFLE
    Rückladungsgewehr M/1869, neues
    Muster, 29

BELGIUM, 29
- Albini-Braendlin, 30
  MODEL 1867 RIFLE
    Fusil d'Infanterie Mle 1867, 30
- Clément, 30
  CLÉMENT AUTOMATIC CARBINE
    Carabine Automatique 'Clément', 30
- Comblain, 30
  MODEL 1870 CIVIL GUARD
    CARBINE
    Carabine de la Garde Civique Mle
    1870, 31
  MODEL 1871 SHORT RIFLE
    Mousqueton Mle 1871, 31
- Dumoulin, 31
  MR-2 SPORTING RIFLE, 31
  RIMFIRE GUNS, 31
- Engh, 31
- Fabrique Nationale, auto-loading
  type, 31
  BROWNING AUTOMATIC CARBINE
    Carabine Automatique Browning or
    'Auto-22', 31
  HIGH-POWER SEMI-AUTOMATIC
    RIFLE, 32
  LIGHT AUTOMATIC CARBINE
    Carabine Automatique Légère, 'CAL',
    32
  BROWNING AUTOMATIC
    SPORTING RIFLE
    Also known as 'BAR', 32
  FN AUTOMATIC CARBINE
    Fabrique Nationale Carabine, 'FNC',
    33
  OTHERS, 33
- Fabrique Nationale, bolt-action type,
  33
  FN-CARABINE, 33
  22 T-BOLT RIFLE, 33
- Fabrique Nationale, break-open
  type, 34
  EXPRESS DOUBLE RIFLE, 34
- Fabrique Nationale, slide-action
  type, 34
  BROWNING REPEATING CARBINE
    Carabine à Répétition Browning,
    'Trombon', 34
- Falisse & Trapmann, 34
- FN-Saive, 34
  EARLY PROTOTYPES, 34
  MODEL 1949 RIFLE
    Fusil Semi-automatique Mle 1949
    ('SAFN'), 34
  LIGHT AUTOMATIC RIFLE
    Fusil Automatique Leger, 'FAL', 35
  OTHER USERS, 35
- FN-Sauer, 35
- Francotte, 36
- Ghaye, 36
- Larsen, 36
- Laurent, 36
- Lebeau-Courally, 36
  OVER/UNDER DOUBLE RIFLES, 36
  SIDE-BY-SIDE DOUBLE RIFLES, 36
  SINGLE RIFLE, 37
- Lecocq & Hoffmann, 37
- Lenders-Lambin, 37
- Marga(-Francotte), 37
  1888-TYPE TRIALS RIFLE, 37
- Martini-Francotte, 37
- Masquelier, 37
- Mauser (state type), 37
  MODEL 1889 RIFLE
    Fusil d'Infanterie Mle 1889, 38

MODEL 1889 CAVALRY CARBINE
  Carabine de Cavallerie, Mle 1889, 38
MODEL 1889 CADET CARBINE
  Carabine des Enfants de Troupe, Mle
  1889, 39
MODEL 1889 GENDARMERIE AND
  ARTILLERY CARBINE
  Carabine pour le Gendarmerie à Pied et
  de l'Artillerie de Fortresse, Mle 1889
  ('carbine for dismounted gendarmerie
  and fortress artillery'), 39
MODEL 1889 GENDARMERIE
  CARBINE
  Carabine pour Gendarmerie à Cheval,
  Mle 1889
  ('carbine for mounted gendarmerie'),
  39
MODEL 1889 CYCLISTS' CARBINE
  Carabine pour les Cyclistes de la Garde
  Civique, Mle 1889 ('carbine for the
  cyclists of the civil guard'), 39
MODEL 1916 CARBINE
  Carabine pour Mitrailleurs, Batteries
  d'Infanterie et Agents de
  Transmission, Mle 1916 ('carbine for
  machine gunners, infantry-gun crews
  and despatch riders'), 39
MODEL 1935 SHORT RIFLE
  Fusil Mle 1935, 39
MODEL 1889/36 SHORT RIFLE
  Fusil Mle 1889/36, 39
- Mauser (FN type), 40
  MODEL 1922 RIFLE
    Fusil d'Infanterie Mle 1922, 40
  MODEL 1924 SHORT RIFLE
    Fusil Court Mle 1924, 40
  MODEL 1935/46 SHORT RIFLE
    Fusil Mle 1935/46, 40
  MODEL 30-11 SNIPER RIFLE, 41
  POST-1924 SPORTING RIFLES, 41
  200-SERIES GUNS, 41
  300-SERIES GUNS, 41
- Mauser, other types, 41
- Montigny, 42
- Nagant, 42
- Pieper (Bayard), autoloading type,
  42
  BAYARD SEMI-AUTOMATIC
    CARBINE, 42
- Pieper (Henri), bolt-action type, 42
  1888-TYPE TRIALS RIFLE, 42
- Pieper (Henri), lever-action type, 42
- Pieper (Henri), revolving-cylinder
  type, 42
- Pieper (Nicolas), autoloading type,
  42
  PIEPER SEMI-AUTOMATIC
    CARBINE, 42
- Raick, 42
  MODEL 155 SPORTING RIFLE, 43
- Terssen, 43
  MODEL 1777-1868 RIFLE
    Fusil d'Infanterie Mle 1777-1868, 43
  MODEL 1848-68 MUSKETOON, 43

BOLIVIA, 43
  MAUSER RIFLES., 43
  REMINGTON-LEE RIFLES, 43
  SIG RIFLES, 43

BRAZIL, 43
- Chuchu, 43
- Comblain, 43
  MODEL 1874 RIFLE, 43
- FN-Saive (Imbel), 44
- Garand, 44
- Mannlicher, 44
- Mauser, 44
  MODEL 1894 RIFLE, 44
  MODEL 1904 RIFLE
    Also known as the 'Mo. 1907', 44
  MODEL 1908/34 RIFLE, 45
- Pieper, 45
  MODEL 1894 RIFLE, 45
- Rossi, lever-action type, 45
  MODEL 67 PUMA RIFLE, 45
- Rossi, slide-action type, 46

MODEL 37 GALLERY RIFLE, 46
• Vergueiro, 46
BRITAIN, 46
• **Accuracy International, 46**
L96A1 SNIPER RIFLE
Also known as Model 'PM', 47
'AW' SNIPER RIFLE
Also known as the 'Arctic Warfare' pattern, 47
• **Adams, 48**
• **Anson & Deeley, 48**
• **Arisaka, 48**
• **Armalon, 48**
ARMALON BGR
'British-German Rifle', 48
ARMALON PR 'Practical Rifle', 48
ARMALON PC 'Pistol Carbine', 48
• **Aston, 49**
• **Atkin, Grant & Lang, 49**
• **Bacon, 49**
FIRST-PATTERN GUNS, 50
IMPROVED-PATTERN GUNS, 50
• **Banks, 50**
• **BMS, 50**
MILCAM RIFLE, 50
• **Braendlin, 50**
• **Brand, 50**
• **BSA, auto-loading type, 50**
MODEL 28-P RIFLE, 51
RALOCK SPORTING RIFLE, 51
ARMATIC SPORTING RIFLE, 51
• **BSA, bolt-action type, 51**
NUMBER 1 RIMFIRE RIFLE, 51
SPORTSMAN RIFLE, 51
ROYAL SPORTING RIFLE
Also known as 'Hunter', 52
SUPERSPORT FIVE SPORTING RIFLE, 52
MAJESTIC-SERIES SPORTING RIFLES, 52
MONARCH SPORTING RIFLE, 52
CF-2 SPORTING RIFLES, 52
CFT TARGET RIFLE, 53
• **BSA, slide-action type, 53**
• **BSA-Adams, 53**
TRIALS PATTERN, 53
• **BSA-Enfield, 53**
HIGH-POWER MODEL
Also known as 'Model 1923', 53
LATER GUNS, 54
• **BSA-Lee, 54**
HIGH-VELOCITY SPORTING PATTERN RIFLES, 54
MAGAZINE SPORTING PATTERN CARBINES, 54
• **BSA-Martini, 54**
SMALL-BORE RIFLES, 54
INTERNATIONAL TARGET RIFLES, 55
• **BSA-Mauser, 55**
• **BSA-Norman, block-action type, 55**
INDIA POLICE CARBINE, 55
• **BSA-Norman, bolt-action type, 55**
EXPERIMENTAL MILITARY RIFLE, 56
• **BSA-Thompson, 56**
• **Burton, block-action type, 56**
1858-TYPE CARBINE, 56
TRIALS-PATTERN RIFLE, 56
• **Burton, bolt-action type, 56**
TRIALS-PATTERN RIFLE, 56
• **Carter & Edwards, 56**
1866-PATENT GUNS, 56
1867-PATENT GUNS, 57
1869-PATENT GUNS, 57
• **Churchill, 57**
'ONE OF ONE THOUSAND' RIFLE, 57
• **Cogswell & Harrison, block-action type, 57**
• **Cogswell & Harrison, bolt-action type, 57**
CERTUS EXPERT MARKSMAN'S RIFLE, 57
CERTUS EXPRESS SPORTING RIFLE, 57

• **Cogswell & Harrison, break-open type, 58**
HIGH VELOCITY DOUBLE RIFLE, 58
• **Cogswell & Harrison (Mauser), 58**
SUPER HIGH VELOCITY SPORTING RIFLE, 58
• **Cooper, block-action type, 58**
• **Cooper, toggle-action type, 58**
• **Daw, 59**
• **Deeley & Edge, 59**
BREECH-LOADING MILITARY RIFLE 1877 pattern, 59
IMPROVED SPORTING RIFLE 1881 pattern, 59
• **De Lisle, 59**
DE LISLE CARBINE, 59
• **Dickson, 59**
• **Dougall, 59**
• **Enfield, auto-loading type, 59**
SLEM RIFLE, 59
INDIVIDUAL WEAPON Also known as the IW, SA-80 or L85, 60
• **Enfield, bolt-action type, 60**
PATTERN 1913 RIFLE, 61
PATTERN 1914 RIFLE, 61
SNIPER RIFLE, EXPERIMENTAL MODEL, 62
• **Enfield-Martini, 62**
MARK I RIFLE, 62
• **Esser-Barratt, 62**
MILITARY-PATTERN TRIALS RIFLE, 62
• **Farquhar & Hill, 62**
THE EARLY GUNS, 62
IMPROVED DESIGNS, 62
• **Farquharson, 63**
MILITARY RIFLE Gibbs-Farquharson-Metford Pattern, 63
SPORTING RIFLE
Jeffrey-Farquharson Improved or 1904 Pattern, 63
• **Field, 63**
MATCH RIFLE
Greener-Field Pattern, 63
• **Firearms Company, 63**
ALPINE MODEL RIFLE, 63
• **FN-Saive (Enfield), 63**
L1A1 RIFLE, 64
• **Fraser, 64**
IMPROVED BREECH-LOADING RIFLE, 64
• **Gamwell, 64**
• **Gibbs, 64**
• **Godsal, 64**
EXPERIMENTAL RIFLE, 65
• **Green, 65**
TRIALS RIFLE, 65
SPORTING RIFLES, 65
• **Greene, 65**
TRIALS CARBINE, 65
• **Greener, bolt-action type, 65**
• **Greener, break-open type, 66**
• **Greener-Martini, 66**
ROOK RIFLE
Also known as the 'Rook & Rabbit Rifle', 66
TRADE AND OTHER PATTERNS, 66
• **Griffiths & Woodgate, 66**
EXPERIMENTAL RIFLE
1892 patent type, 66
• **Hall, 66**
• **Hallé, 67**
MILITARY-PATTERN TRIALS RIFLE, 67
• **Heckler & Koch (Enfield), 67**
• **Henry, 67**
MILITARY PATTERN, 67
SPORTING PATTERN, 67
• **Holland & Holland, 68**
• **Januszewski (Janson), 68**
EM-2 RIFLE
Rifle, Automatic, 280in, EM-2 (CEAD), codenamed 'Yellow Acorn' or 'Mamba', 68
• **Jeffrey, 68**

• **Jeffries, 68**
• **Jenks, 68**
• **Jones, block-action type, 69**
IMPROVED MODEL RIFLE, 69
• **Jones, break-open type, 69**
• **Kerr, 69**
• **Lancaster, 69**
• **Lang, 69**
• **Lee-Burton, 69**
IMPROVED LEE RIFLE WITH BURTON MAGAZINE, 70
• **Lee-Enfield, 70**
MARK I RIFLE, 70
MARK I CARBINE, 70
NO. 1 IMPROVED PATTERN RIFLE, 70
MODIFIED (SHORTENED) PATTERN RIFLE, 71
MARK I SHORT RIFLE, 71
MARK III SHORT RIFLE, 71
.22 MARK I SHORT RIFLE, 72
.22 MARK I RIFLE
Alternatively known as '.22 Mark I Long Rifle', 72
PATTERN 1914 22 RIFLE, 72
PATTERN 1918 22 RIFLE, 73
MARK V SHORT RIFLE, 73
NUMBER 4 MARK I RIFLE, 73
NUMBER 5 MARK 1 RIFLE
'Lee-Enfield Jungle Carbine', 74
NUMBER 7 MARK 1 RIFLE, 74
L8A1 RIFLE, 75
• **Lee-Metford, 75**
THE FIRST STEPS, 75
TRIALS PATTERNS, 76
MARK I RIFLE, 76
MARK II RIFLE, 76
MARK I CARBINE, 76
AIMING-TUBE GUNS, 76
• **Leetch, 76**
BREECH-LOADING CARBINE
Military pattern, 77
• **Manceaux, 77**
TRIALS CARBINE, 77
• **Mannlicher, 77**
• **Martini-Enfield, 77**
MARK I RIFLE, 77
MARK I CAVALRY CARBINE, 78
MARK I ARTILLERY CARBINE, 78
COLONIAL PATTERNS, 78
• **Martini-Henry, 78**
BACKGROUND, 78
THE FIRST STEPS, 78
TRIALS RIFLE, 78
MARK I RIFLE, 79
MARK II RIFLE, 79
MARK I CAVALRY CARBINE, 79
GARRISON ARTILLERY CARBINE, 79
MARK I ARTILLERY CARBINE, 79
MARK III RIFLE, 79
PATTERN 1882 RIFLE, 80
MARK IV RIFLE First pattern, 80
MARK IV RIFLE Later pattern, 80
MARK II ARTILLERY CARBINE, 80
• **Martini-Metford, 80**
MARK I RIFLE, 80
MARK II RIFLE, 80
MARK I CAVALRY CARBINE, 80
MARK I ARTILLERY CARBINE, 81
COLONIAL PATTERNS, 81
• **Martini sporting guns, 81**
FIELD-MARTINI SPORTING RIFLE, 81
• **Mauser, 82**
TYPICAL RIFLES, 82
• **Midland, 82**
• **Morris, 82**
• **Needham, 82**
• **Parker (Lee-Enfield), 82**
• **Parker-Hale (Lee-Enfield), 82**
SPORTING MODEL RIFLE, 82
• **Parker-Hale (Mauser), 82**
MODEL 1000 SAFARI RIFLE, 83
MODEL 1100 RIFLE, 83
MODEL 1200 SUPER SAFARI RIFLE, 83
MODEL 1261 RIFLE, 83

MODEL 81 CLASSIC RIFLE, 83
MODEL 1200 SUPER RIFLE, 83
MODEL 1100 RIFLE, 84
MODEL 82 SNIPER RIFLE, 84
MODEL 85 SNIPER RIFLE, 84
• **Prince, 85**
TRIALS CARBINE, 85
• **Purdey, 85**
• **Reilly-Comblain, 85**
• **Remington-Lee, 85**
• **Restell, 86**
TRIALS CARBINE, 86
• **Rexer, 86**
MILITARY-PATTERN TRIALS RIFLE, 86
• **Richards, bolt type, 86**
• **Richards, lifting-block type, 86**
PATTERN NO. 1 CARBINE, 86
MILITARY RIFLES, 87
• **Richards, dropping-block type, 87**
BREECH-LOADING RIFLE
Also known as the 'Patent Central-Fire Breech-Loading Military & Sporting Rifle', 87
• **Rigby, 87**
RIGBY 243 RIFLE, 87
• **Ross, 88**
• **Sharps, 88**
PATTERN 1855 CARBINE, 88
• **Shephard, 88**
• **Snider, 88**
THE FIRST STEPS, 88
CONVERTED PATTERN 1853 RIFLE, PATTERN NO. 1, 88
CONVERTED P/1855 ENGINEER CARBINE, 89
CONVERTED P/1858 NAVAL SHORT RIFLE, 89
CONVERTED PATTERN 1856 CAVALRY CARBINE, 89
CONVERTED PATTERN 1860 SERJEANT'S RIFLES, 89
CONVERTED PATTERN 1861 ARTILLERY CARBINE, 90
ROYAL IRISH CONSTABULARY PATTERN, 90
YEOMANRY CARBINE, 90
GAOL, OR CONVICT CIVIL GUARD CARBINE, 90
INDIA AND COLONIAL PATTERNS, 90
• **Soper, 91**
IMPROVED BREECH-LOADING RIFLE, 91
• **Storm, 91**
TRIALS RIFLE, 91
• **Swinburn, 91**
MODEL 1875 RIFLE, 91
IMPROVED SPORTING RIFLE, 92
• **Terry, 92**
PATTERN NO. 1 CARBINE, 92
IMPROVED PATTERN, 92
SPORTING RIFLE, 92
• **Thorneycroft, 93**
• **Thorpe, 93**
EM-1 RIFLE
Rifle, Experimental, 280in EM-1 (CEAD), code name 'Cobra', 93
• **Turner, 93**
• **Vickers, 93**
• **War Office, 94**
WAR OFFICE MINIATURE RIFLE, 94
• **Wilson, 94**
1859-PATENT TRIALS RIFLE, 94
1867-PATENT TRIALS RIFLE, 95
• **Wood, 95**
• **Woodgate, 95**
• **Wyley, 95**

BULGARIA, 95
• **Berdan, 95**
• **Kalashnikov, 95**
• **Mannlicher, 95**

BURMA (MYANMAR), 95
• Heckler & Koch, 95

CANADA, 96
• ArmaLite (Diemaco), 96
• FN-Saive (Long Branch), 96
  C1 AUTOMATIC RIFLE, 96
• Lakefield, autoloading type, 96
  MODEL 64B SPORTING RIFLE, 96
• Lakefield, bolt-action type, 96
  MARK I SPORTING RIFLE, 97
• Lee-Enfield, 97
  NUMBER 4 MARK I* RIFLE, 97
  NUMBER 4 MARK I* (T) RIFLE, 97
  NUMBER 4 LIGHTWEIGHT RIFLE, 97
• Parker-Hale, 97
• Ross, 97
  MARK I RIFLE
    Also known as 'Military Model 1905', 98
  MARK III RIFLE
    Also known as 'Military Model 1910' or (misleadingly) as the 'Model 1912', 98
  1897-TYPE SPORTING RIFLE, 99
  1900-TYPE SPORTING RIFLE, 99
  1903-TYPE SPORTING RIFLE, 99
  MILITARY-TYPE SPORTING RIFLES, 99
  MODEL R SPORTING RIFLE, 99
  RIMFIRE SPORTING RIFLE, 100
  MODEL R-1910 SPORTING RIFLE, 100
• Savage, 100
  MODEL 1899 RIFLE, 100

CHILE, 100
• Mannlicher, 100
• Mauser, 100
  MODEL 1895 RIFLE, 100
  MODEL 1904 RIFLE, 100
  MODEL 1912 RIFLE, 101
• Remington, 101
• SIG, 101
• Winchester, 101

CHINA (EMPIRE), 101
• Haenel, 101
  1907-TYPE TRIALS RIFLE, 101
• Mauser, 101
  THE EARLY GUNS, 101
  1906-TYPE TRIALS RIFLE, 101
• Reichsgewehr, 101
• Remington-Lee, 102
  MODEL 1882 RIFLE, 102

CHINA (REPUBLIC), 102
• Arisaka, 102
• Lee-Enfield, 102
• Mannlicher, 102
  HANYANG RIFLE, 102
• Mauser, 102
  MODEL 1907 RIFLE, 102
  MODEL 21 SHORT RIFLE, 102
  CHIANG KAI-SHEK SHORT RIFLE, 102
  OTHER PATTERNS, 102

CHINA (PRC), 102
• ArmaLite (Norinco), 102
• Kalashnikov, 102
  TYPE 56 ASSAULT RIFLE, 102
• Mosin-Nagant, 103
• Simonov, 103
  TYPE 56 RIFLE, 103
• State designs, 104
  TYPE 63 RIFLE, 104

COLOMBIA, 104
• Mauser, 104

CONFEDERATE STATES OF AMERICA, 104
• Bilharz & Hall Carbines, 104
• Le Mat Revolver Carbines, 104
• Morse Carbines, 105
• Read Carbines, 105
• Robinson Carbines, 105

• Tarpley Carbines, 105

CONGO FREE STATE, 105
• MAUSER, 105

COSTA RICA, 105
• Mauser, 105
  MODEL 1895 RIFLE, 105
  MODEL 1910 RIFLE, 105
  OTHER PATTERNS, 105

CUBA, 105
• Krag-Jørgensen, 105
• Remington-Lee, 105
• Winchester, 106

CZECHOSLOVAKIA, 106
• Ceská Zbrojovka, auto-loading type, 106
  'HB' AUTOMATIC RIFLE, 106
  MODEL 'S' AUTOMATIC RIFLE, 106
  MODEL 38 AUTOMATIC RIFLE
    Samocinná puska CZ 38, 106
  MODEL 2000 ASSAULT RIFLE
    Formerly known as LADA, 107
• Ceská Zbrojovka, bolt-action type, 107
  CZ 452-2E SPORTING RIFLE, 107
  CZ 527 SPORTING RIFLE
    Also known as the 'Fox', 108
  CZ 537 SPORTING RIFLE, 108
  CZ 550 SPORTING RIFLE, 108
  CZ 700 SNIPER RIFLE
    Odstrelovacská puska CZ 700 Sniper, 109
• Galas, 109
  ZG 47 SPORTING RIFLE, 109
• Holek, auto-loading type, 109
  MODEL 29 AUTOMATIC RIFLE, 109
  MODEL 58 ASSAULT RIFLE
    Samopal vz. 58, 110
• Holek, bolt-action type, 110
• Janecek, 110
• Koucky, auto-loading type, 110
  ZK 371 AUTOMATIC RIFLE
    Samocinná puska ZK 371, 110
  ZK 381 AUTOMATIC RIFLE
    Samocinná puska ZK 381, 110
  ZK 391 AUTOMATIC RIFLE
    Samocinná puska ZK 391, 111
  ZK 420 AUTOMATIC RIFLE
    Samocinná puska ZK 420, 111
  ZK 425 AUTOMATIC RIFLE, 111
  ZK 472 AUTOMATIC RIFLE, 111
  ZKW 561 SPORTING RIFLE, 111
• Koucky, bolt-action type, 111
  ZKM 451 SPORTING RIFLE
    Also known as the 'Brno Model 1', 111
  ZKW 465 SPORTING RIFLE
    Also known as 'CZ 365', 112
  ZKK 600 SPORTING RIFLE, 112
  ZKB 680 FOX II SPORTING RIFLE, 113
• Kratochvil, 113
  MODEL 52 AUTOMATIC RIFLE
    7.62mm Samonabijecki puska vz. 52, 113
• Kyncl, 113
• Mauser (CSZ, ZB), 113
  MAUSER-JELEN TRIALS RIFLE
    Short rifle: Puska Mauser-Jelená, 113
  MODEL 1898/22 RIFLE
    Puska vz. 98/22, 114
  MODEL 1924 SHORT RIFLE
    Krátká puska vz. 24, 114
  MODEL 1933 GENDARMERIE CARBINE
    Krátká puska vz.33 pro cetnictvo a financi stráz, 114
  MODEL 1898/29 RIFLE
    Puska vz. 98/29, 114
  MODEL 21 SPORTING RIFLE
    Also known as 'Model 21H', 115
• Mosin-Nagant, 115
  MODEL 1954 SNIPER RIFLE
    Odstrelovacská Puska vz. 54, 115

DENMARK, 115
• Bang, 115
• Heckler & Koch, 116
• Krag-Jørgensen, 116
  MODEL 1889 RIFLE Gevær m/89, 116

MODEL 1889 CAVALRY CARBINE
  Ryttergevær or Rytterkarabin m/89, 116
MODEL 1889 ENGINEER CARBINE
  Ingeniørkarabin m/89, 116
MODEL 1889-23 CAVALRY CARBINE
  Rytterkarabin m/89-23, 116
MODEL 1889-24 INFANTRY CARBINE
  Fodfolksskarabin m/89-24, 116
MODEL 1889-24 ARTILLERY CARBINE
  Artillerikarabin m/89-24, 117
MODEL 1928 RIFLE, 117
• Krag-Petersson, 117
  MODEL 1877 NAVY CARBINES
    Flådens magasin-karabin m/1877, 117
• Løbnitz, 117
• Madsen, autoloading type, 117
  MADSEN-LJUNGMANN AUTOMATIC RIFLE
  LIGHT AUTOMATIC RIFLE
    Also known as 'LAR' or 'Madsen A-Carbine', 118
• Madsen, bolt-action type, 118
  MODEL 47 RIFLE
    'Madsen Light Military Rifle', 118
• Remington, 118
  MODEL 1867 RIFLE
    Bagladeriffel m/1867, 118
  MODEL 1867 CARBINE
    Karabinen for rytter, artilleri og ingeniør, m/1867, 119
  MODEL 1867/93 NAVY RIFLE
    Flådens Bagladeriffel m/1867/93, 119
  MODEL 1867/96 CAVALRY CARBINE
    Rytterkarabin m/1867/96, 119
• Schultz & Larsen, 119
  MODEL 1942 POLICE RIFLE
    Rigspolitikarabin m/42 (Rplt.42), 119
  MODEL 54 SPORTING RIFLE, 119
  MODEL 52 TARGET RIFLE, 120
• Snider, 120
  M1848-65 SHORT RIFLE
    Bagladeriffel m/1848-65, 120
  M1853-66 NAVY RIFLE
    Flådens Bagladeriffel m/53-66, 120

DOMINICAN REPUBLIC, 120
• Cristobal, 120
  CRISTOBAL CARBINE MODEL 2, 120
  MODEL 62 RIFLE, 120
• Mauser, 121

ECUADOR, 121
• Mauser, 121
  PRE-1914 PATTERNS, 121
  LATER PATTERNS, 121

EGYPT, 121
• FN-Saive, 121
• Kalashnikov, 121
• Ljungmann, 121
  HAKIM RIFLE, 121
  RASHID RIFLE, 121
• Remington, 121
  MODEL 1868 RIFLE, 121

EL SALVADOR, 122
  Mauser, 122

ESTONIA, 122
  Mauser, 122

ETHIOPIA, 122
  Mauser, 122

FINLAND, 122
• Kalashnikov, 122
  MODEL 1960 ASSAULT RIFLE
    Rynnakkokivääri m/60, 122
  MODEL 1962 ASSAULT RIFLE
    Rynnakkokivääri m/62, 122
  MODEL 1971 ASSAULT RIFLE
    Rynnakkokivääri m/71, 123
  MODEL 1976 ASSAULT RIFLE
    Rynnakkokivääri m/62/76, 123
  MODEL 95 ASSAULT RIFLE
    Rynnakkokivääri m/95 PT, 124
  PETRA SPORTING RIFLE, 124
• Mannlicher, 124
• Mauser, 124

• Mosin-Nagant, 124
  MODEL 1891 RIFLE Kivääri m/91, 124
  MODEL 1924 RIFLE Kivääri m/24, 124
  MODEL 1927 SHORT RIFLE, ARMY TYPE Kivääri m/27, 125
  MODEL 1928 SHORT RIFLE, PROTECTIVE CORPS Sk.Y kivääri m/28, 125
  MODEL 1928-30 SHORT RIFLE, PROTECTIVE CORPS Sk.Y. kivääri m/28-30, 125
  MODEL 1939 SHORT RIFLE Kivääri m/39, 125
  SNIPER RIFLES, 125
• Pelo, 126
• Sako, bolt-action type, 126
  L-46 SPORTING RIFLE, 126
  P-46 SPORTING RIFLE, 126
  L-461 SPORTING RIFLE, 126
  L-57 SPORTING RIFLE, 127
  L-579 SPORTING RIFLE, 127
  L-61 SPORTING RIFLES, 128
  P-72 SPORTING RIFLE
    Also known as 'Finnscout', 129
  TRG SPORTING RIFLE, 130
  SSR MARK 1 SILENCED RIFLE, 130
  FINNFIRE SPORTING RIFLE, 130
• Sako, lever-action type, 131
  VL-63 SPORTING RIFLE
    Finnwolf, 131
• Tampeeren Asepaja, 131
  FINNBIATHLON-22 TARGET RIFLE, 131
• Tikka, bolt-action type, 131
  MODEL 55 SPORTING RIFLE, 131
  MODEL 65 SPORTING RIFLE, 132
  TIKKA 590 POPULAR SPORTING RIFLE, 132
  TIKKA 690 POPULAR SPORTING RIFLE, 132
  TIKKA 690 MAGNUM SPORTING RIFLES, 132
  TIKKA 595 MASTER SPORTING RIFLE, 133
• Tikka, break-open type, 133
  TIKKA 512-S EXPRESS DOUBLE RIFLE, 133
• Valmet, bolt-action type, 133
  ORAVA SPORTING RIFLE, 133
  ERÄ SPORTING RIFLE, 133
  FINNISH LION ISU STANDARD TARGET RIFLE, 133
  MODEL 86 SNIPER RIFLE, 134
• Valmet, break-open type, 134
  MODEL 412-S DOUBLE RIFLE, 134

FRANCE, 134
• Albini-Braendlin, 134
• APX, 134
• Bérenger, 134
• Berdan, 134
• Berthier, autoloading type, 135
• Berthier, bolt-action type, 135
  THE FIRST STEPS, 135
  MODEL 1890 CAVALRY CARBINE
    Carabine de Cavallerie Mle 1890, 135
  MODEL 1890 CUIRASSIER CARBINE
    Carabine de Cuirassiers Mle 1890, 135
  MODEL 1890 GENDARMERIE CARBINE
    Carabine de Gendarmerie Mle 1890, 136
  MODEL 1892 ARTILLERY MUSKETOON
    Mousqueton d'Artillerie Mle 1890, 136
  MODEL 1902 COLONIAL RIFLE
    Fusil Mle 1902, 136
  MODEL 1907 COLONIAL RIFLE
    Fusil Mle 1907, 136
  MODEL 1907/15 RIFLE
    Fusil d'Infanterie Mle 1907/15, 136
  MODEL 1916 RIFLE
    Fusil d'Infanterie Mle 1916, 136
  MODEL 1892-16 ARTILLERY MUSKETOON
    Mousqueton d'Artillerie Mle 1892 M. 16, 137
  MODEL 1907-15-34 SHORT RIFLE
    Fusil d'Infanterie Mle 07/15 M. 34, 137

MODEL 1902-37 SHORT RIFLE
Fusil Mle 1902/37, 137
• **Carcano, 137**
• **Chabot, 137**
• **Chapuis Armes, 137**
OURAL EXEL SINGLE RIFLE, 138
PROGRESS UGEX DOUBLE RIFLE, 138
SUPER ORION C-5 DOUBLE RIFLE, 138
• **Pierre Chapuis, 139**
• **Chassepot, 139**
TRIALS GUNS
Fusils et carabines Chassepot des essais, 139
1865-TYPE TRIALS RIFLE
Fusil Chassepot des essais du camp de Châlons, 139
MODEL 1866 RIFLE
Fusil d'Infanterie Mle 1866, 140
MODEL 1866 COLONIAL RIFLE
Fusil pour la cavalerie d'Afrique, 140
MODEL 1866 CAVALRY CARBINE
Carabine de Cavallerie Mle 1866, 140
Model 1866 GENDARMERIE CARBINES
Carabine de Gendarmerie à Cheval Mle 1866 and Carabine de Gendarmerie à Pied Mle 1866, 141
MODEL 1866 ARTILLERY MUSKETOON
Mousqueton d'Artillerie Mle 1866, 141
• **Clair, 141**
• **CTV, 141**
• **Daudetau, 141**
MODEL 1896 NAVY RIFLE
Experimental pattern, 141
• **Descoutoures, 141**
• **ENT, 142**
• **Gallager, 142**
• **Gastinne-Renette, 142**
• **Gaucher, 142**
MODEL B-3 COLIBRI SPORTING RIFLE, 142
• **Gévelot, autoloading type, 142**
MODEL A SPORTING RIFLE, 142
MODEL E SPORTING RIFLE, 142
• **Gévelot, lever-action type, 143**
• **Gras, 143**
MODEL 1874 RIFLE
Fusil d'Infanterie Mle 1874, 143
MODEL 1874 CAVALRY CARBINE
Carabine de Cavallerie Mle 1874, 143
MODEL 1874 MOUNTED GENDARMERIE CARBINE
Carabine de Gendarmerie à Cheval Mle 1874, 143
MODEL 1874 DISMOUNTED GENDARMERIE CARBINE
Carabine de Gendarmerie à Pied Mle 1874, 144
MODEL 1874 ARTILLERY MUSKETOON
Mousqueton d'Artillerie Mle 1874, 144
MODEL 1874/80/14 RIFLE
Fusil Mle 1874 M.80 M.14, 144
GRAS-CHASSEPOT TRAINING RIFLES, 144
NOUVELLE TARGET RIFLE, 144
• **Heckler & Koch (MAS), 144**
• **Joslyn, 144**
• **Kropatschek, 144**
MODEL 1878 NAVY RIFLE
Fusil de Marine Mle 1878, 145
MODEL 1884 RIFLE
Fusil d'Infanterie Mle 1884, 145
MODEL 1885 RIFLE
Fusil d'Infanterie Mle 1885, 145
• **Lardinois, 145**
• **Lebel, 145**
THE FIRST STEPS, 146
MODEL 1886 RIFLE
Fusil d'Infanterie Mle 1886, 146
MODEL 1886/35 SHORT RIFLE
Fusil Mle 1886 R.35, 147
• **Lefaucheux, 147**

• **Manceaux & Vieillard, 147**
1862-TYPE TRIALS RIFLE, 147
• **Manufrance, autoloading type, 147**
CARABINE REINA, 147
• **Manufrance, bolt-action type, 147**
BUFFALO CARBINE, 148
RIVAL SPORTING CARBINE
Carabine à Répétition 'Rival', 148
RIVAL SPORTING RIFLE, 149
POPULAIRE CARBINE, 149
• **Manufrance, break-open type, 149**
EXPRESS, 149
EXPRESS IDEAL, 149
• **MAS, autoloading type, 149**
MAS 44 RIFLE
Fusil automatique MAS 44, 149
MAS 49/56 RIFLE
Fusil automatique MAS 49/56, 150
MAS 56 RIFLE, 150
MAS 62 RIFLE
Fusil d'Assaut MAS 56, 150
MAS ASSAULT RIFLE
Fusil d'Assaut MAS, 'FA MAS' or 'FAMAS', 151
• **MAS, bolt type, 151**
THE EARLIEST GUNS, 151
MAS 36 SHORT RIFLE
Fusil MAS 36, 151
FR F-1 TYPE A Fusil à Répétition, Modèle F-1 Type A, 152
• **Mauser, 152**
M1898 SHORT RIFLE, 152
• **Meunier, 152**
FUSIL A6, 152
• **Peabody, 152**
• **PGM, 152**
ULTIMA RATIO SNIPER RIFLE, 153
ULTIMA RATIO HECATE II RIFLE, 153
• **Plastow, 153**
• **Remington, 153**
MODEL 1915 RIFLE, 153
• **Robert, 153**
1833-TYPE TRIALS RIFLE, 153
• **Roberts, 153**
• **RSC, 154**
MODEL 1917 RIFLE
Fusil Mle 1917, 154
MODEL 1918 SHORT RIFLE
Fusil Mle 1918, 154
• **Sharps, 154**
• **SIG (Manurhin), 154**
• **SMFM, 154**
MODEL 702 SPORTING RIFLE
'Modèle 702 Olympique', 154
• **Snider, 155**
• **Springfield(-Allin), 155**
• **STA, 155**
• **Tabatière, 155**
M1867 RIFLE
Fusil d'Infanterie Mle 1867, 155
M1867 RIFLE
Fusil de Dragon Mle 1867, 155
M1867 CARBINE
Carabine de Chasseurs Mle 1867, 155
OTHER CONVERSIONS, 155
• **Treuille de Beaulieu, 155**
MODEL 1854 ROYAL BODYGUARD MUSKETOON
Mousqueton de Corps de Cent Gardes, 155
• **Unique, autoloading type, 155**
MODEL X51 SPORTING RIFLE, 156
• **Unique, bolt-action type, 156**
MODEL T66 MATCH RIFLE, 156
MODEL T2000 STANDARD RIFLE, 157
TGC SPORTING RIFLE
Fusil de Chasse, 158
• **Warner, 158**
• **Wilson, 158**
GERMANY, 158
• **Anschütz, autoloading type, 159**
MODEL 520 SPORTING RIFLE, 159
• **Anschütz, bolt-action type, 159**
1360-SERIES SPORTING RIFLES, 159
1380-SERIES SPORTING RIFLES, 160

1400-SERIES FLOBERT II SPORTING RIFLES, 160
1400-SERIES FLOBERT II TARGET RIFLES, 160
MODEL 64 MS, 161
1400-SERIES MATCH 64 TARGET RIFLES, 161
1400-SERIES MATCH 64 SPORTING RIFLES, 161
1500-SERIES MATCH 64 SPORTING RIFLES, 161
MODEL 54/MATCH 54 ACTION, 162
1400-SERIES MATCH 54 TARGET RIFLES, 162
1400-SERIES MATCH 54 SPORTING RIFLES, 163
1430-SERIES SPORTING RIFLES, 163
1520-SERIES SPORTING RIFLES, 164
1530-SERIES SPORTING RIFLES, 164
MODEL 1568 SPORTING RIFLE (i), 164
MODEL 1568 SPORTING RIFLE (ii), 165
1700-SERIES SPORTING RIFLES, 165
1800-SERIES TARGET RIFLES, 165
1900-SERIES TARGET RIFLES, 166
GERMANY, 166
2000-SERIES TARGET RIFLES, 167
MODEL 5418 TARGET RIFLE, 167
BR-50 TARGET RIFLE, 167
BAVARIAN SERIES, 167
• **Anschütz-Förtner, 167**
MODEL 1827 BT TARGET RIFLE, 167
• **Aydt, 167**
HAENEL-AYDT TARGET RIFLE, 168
AYDT-REFORM TARGET RIFLE, 168
• **Blaser, block-action type, 168**
BL-820 SPORTING RIFLE, 168
• **Blaser, bolt-action type, 168**
R-84 SPORTING RIFLE, 169
R-93 STANDARD SPORTING RIFLE, 169
• **Blaser, break-open type, 170**
K-77A STANDARD SPORTING RIFLE, 170
K-95 STANDARD SPORTING RIFLE, 170
B-750/88 SPORTING RIFLE
Bergstutzen 750/88, 170
• **Bock, 171**
• **Bornmüller, Simson & Luck, 171**
• **Brennecke, 171**
• **Brenneke-Mauser Sporting Rifles, 171**
• **Büchel, 171**
TELL SPORTING RIFLE, 171
• **Burgsmüller, 171**
• **Chassepot, 171**
• **Dornheim, 171**
• **Dreyse, 171**
SPORTING RIFLE, 172
REPEATING RIFLES, 172
• **DWM, 172**
• **Erma, autoloading type, 172**
MODEL 1 CARBINE
EM-1, also known as 'Model 69'?, 172
MODEL SG-22 CARBINE ESG-22, 172
• **Erma, bolt-action type, 173**
MODEL 1 SPORTING RIFLE
Erma-Kleinkaliberbüchse Sportmodell Nr. 1, 173
MODEL 61 RIFLE
Erma-Gewehr 61, or 'E-61', 173
MODEL 100 SNIPER RIFLE
SR-100, 173
• **Erma, lever-action type, 173**
MODEL 712 SPORTING RIFLE
Erma-Gewehr 712, 'EG-712', 173
• **Erma, slide-action type, 173**
MODEL 722 SPORTING RIFLE
Erma-Gewehr 722, 'EG-722', 173
• **Feinwerkbau, 174**
MODEL 2000 ISU STANDARD RIFLE
Alternatively known as 'UIT Standard', 174
MODEL 2600 ISU UNIVERSAL RIFLE, 174
MODEL 2602 ISU UNIVERSAL RIFLE, 174

• **FN-Saive, 175**
• **Frankonia, 175**
FAVORIT SPORTING RIFLE, 175
• **Gehmann, 175**
• **Genschow, 175**
• **Gercke, 175**
• **Gustloff, 175**
MODEL 1-5 PEOPLE'S RIFLE
Volksgerät or Volksgewehr 1-5, 'VG. 1-5', 175
• **Haenel, autoloading type, 176**
MODEL 42 (H) ASSAULT RIFLE
Maschinenkarabiner 42 (H), 'MKb. 42 (H)', 176
MODEL 43 ASSAULT RIFLE
Maschinenpistole 43, 'MP 43', 176
• **Haenel, bolt-action type, 177**
MODEL 1907 RIFLE
Aptierte Haenel-Gewehr M1907, 177
MODEL 1909 SPORTING RIFLE
Haenel-Jagdbüchse M1909, 177
• **Halbe & Gerlich, 177**
• **Heckler & Koch, 177**
BACKGROUND, 177
MODEL 3 AUTOMATIC RIFLE
Gewehr 3, 178
MODEL 32 AUTOMATIC RIFLE
Gewehr HK32, 179
MODEL 33 AUTOMATIC RIFLE
Gewehr HK33, 179
MODEL 36 AUTOMATIC RIFLE
Gewehr HK36, 180
MODEL 41 AUTOMATIC RIFLE
Gewehr 41, 180
MODEL 1 PRECISION SNIPER RIFLE
Präzisions-Scharfschützengewehr 1, 'PSG-1', 180
MODEL 3 MILITARY SNIPER RIFLE
Militär-Scharfschützengewehr 3, 'MSG-3', 181
MODEL R3 AUTOMATIC RIFLE
Gewehr R3, 181
SL-6 SPORTING RIFLE, 182
HK770 SPORTING RIFLE, 182
• **Heinemann, 182**
• **Heym, block-action type, 183**
MODEL 550 COMBI DOUBLE RIFLE, 183
• **Heym, bolt-action type, 183**
MODEL 20 SPORTING RIFLE
Usually known as 'SR 20', 183
MODEL 30 SPORTING RIFLE
Usually known as 'SR 30', 184
MAGNUM EXPRESS SPORTING RIFLE, 184
• **Heym, break-open type, 184**
MODEL 25BS DOUBLE RIFLE, 184
MODEL 37BK TRIPLE RIFLE, 184
MODEL 44B SPORTING RIFLE, 184
MODEL 55B DOUBLE RIFLE, 185
MODEL 80B DOUBLE RIFLE, 185
MODEL 88B DOUBLE RIFLE, 185
• **Heym-Ruger, 186**
HR 30 SPORTING RIFLE, 186
• **Hoster, 186**
• **Jäger, 186**
HEROLD SPORTING RIFLE
Herold-Repetierbüchse, 186
• **Kalashnikov, 186**
KALASHNIKOV MACHINE PISTOL
Maschinenpistole Kalashnikow, MPi-K, 186
• **Keppeler & Fritz, 187**
STANDARD RIFLE
Grosskaliber-Standardgewehr, 187
• **Kind, 187**
MERKUR SPORTING RIFLE, 187
• **Krico, autoloading type, 188**
MODEL 260 SPORTING RIFLE, 188
• **Krico, bolt-action type, 188**
MODEL 120 SPORTING RIFLE, 188
MODEL 300E SPORTING RIFLE, 188
MODEL 400D SPORTING RIFLE, 189
MODEL 530S TARGET RIFLE, 189
MODEL 600 SPORTING RIFLE, 190
MODEL 701 SPORTING RIFLE, 191
THE VOHBURG-IRSCHING RANGE, 192
300-SERIES SPORTING RIFLES, 192

400 SERIES SPORTING RIFLES, 192
600-SERIES SPORTING RIFLES, 192
700-SERIES SPORTING RIFLES, 192
MODEL 902 SPORTING RIFLE, 192
• **Krieghoff, autoloading type, 192**
HIGH-POWER AUTOLOADING
RIFLE, 192
• **Krieghoff, break-open type, 192**
CLASSIC STANDARD DOUBLE
RIFLE, 193
HUBERTUS STANDARD SPORTING
RIFLE, 193
TECK DOUBLE RIFLE, 193
ULM DOUBLE RIFLE, 194
ULTRA-20 DOUBLE RIFLE, 194
• **Langenhan, 194**
'F.L.' TARGET RIFLE
'F.L.'-Kleinkaliberbüchse, 194
• **Lettow, 194**
• **Lindner, 194**
• **Luger, 194**
• **Mannlicher, 194**
MODEL 1898/40 SHORT RIFLE
Gewehr 98/40, 195
• **Mauser, autoloading type, 195**
C/98 AUTOMATIC RIFLE, 195
C/02 AUTOMATIC RIFLE, 195
C/06-08 AUTOMATIC RIFLE, 195
MODEL 1915 AUTOMATIC RIFLE
Mauser Flieger-Gewehr und Flieger-
Karabiner, 195
MODEL 35 AUTOMATIC RIFLE, 196
MODEL 41 RIFLE
Gewehr 41 (M), 196
GERÄT 06 ASSAULT RIFLE, 196
OTHER RIFLES, 196
• **Mauser, bolt-action type, 196**
MODEL 1871 RIFLE
Infanterie-Gewehr M1871, 196
MODEL 1871 SHORT RIFLE
Jägerbüchse M1871, 197
MODEL 1871 CARBINE
Karabiner M1871, 197
MODEL 1882 RIFLE, 198
MODEL 1871/84 RIFLE
Infanterie-Gewehr M1871/84, 198
MODEL 1896 RIFLE
Kleinkalibriges-Gewehr M1896, 198
MODEL 1888/97 RIFLE
Infanterie-Gewehr M1888/97 ('Gew.
88/97'), 198
MODEL 1898 RIFLE
Infanterie-Gewehr M1898 or 'Gewehr
98', 199
MODEL 1898 CARBINE
Karabiner 98, 200
MODEL 1898A CARBINE
Karabiner 98A, 200
MODEL 1898 AZ CARBINE
Karabiner 98 AZ, 200
MODEL 1898K SHORT RIFLE
Karabiner 98k, 200
MODEL 24 (T) SHORT RIFLE
Gewehr 24 (t), 201
MODEL 29 (P) SHORT RIFLE
Gewehr 29 (p), 201
MODEL 29/40 SHORT RIFLE
Gewehr 29/40, 201
MODEL 33/40 SHORT RIFLE
Gewehr 33/40, 202
MODEL 1898 PEOPLE'S RIFLE
Volkskarabiner 98, 'VK. 98', 202
MODEL 1933 SHORT RIFLE
Mauser Standard-Model, 202
MODEL 93 SNIPER RIFLE
Also known as 'SR 93', 202
MODEL 1898 SPORTING RIFLE
Pirschbüchse C/98, 203
MILITIA MODEL
Wehrmannbüchse und
Einheitsgewehr, 203
MODEL 1908 SPORTING RIFLE
Mauser-Pirschbüsche C/98-08, 203
MODEL 1908 SPORTING CARBINE
Mauser-Pirschbüsche C/98-08, 203
MODEL 1908 ARMY RIFLE
Mauser-Armee-Pirschbüsche C/98-
08, 203
MODEL 1908 BIG-GAME RIFLE
Mauser-Afrika-Pirschbüsche C/98-08,
203
MODEL A SPORTING RIFLE, 204
MODEL 2000 SPORTING RIFLE, 204

MODEL 77S SPORTING RIFLE
Jagdrepetier Modell 77S, 204
MODEL 86 SNIPER RIFLE
Scharfschützengewehr 86, 'SG 86' or
'SR 86', 205
MODEL 66S SPORTING RIFLE, 205
MODEL 300 SPORTING RIFLE
M.W.-Karabiner Eb 300, 206
MODEL 340
M.W.-Sportbüchse Es 340, 206
MODEL 350
M.W.-Meisterschafts Kleinkaliber
Büchse Es 350, 206
MODEL 410
M.W.-Mehrlader-Karabiner Mm 410,
206
GERMAN SPORTS MODEL
Deutsches Sportmodell ('DSM'), 207
OTHER SPORTERS, 207
• **Mayer & Grammelspacher, 208**
MODEL 820S TARGET RIFLE, 208
• **Merkel, 208**
• **Mosin-Nagant, 209**
• **Müller & Greiss, 209**
• **Oesterreich, 209**
• **Reichsgewehr (Mannlicher), 209**
MODEL 1888 RIFLE Gewehr 88, 209
MODEL 1888 CARBINE
Karabiner 88, 210
MODEL 1888 SPORTING RIFLE, 210
• **Rheinmetall (Dreyse), autoloading
type, 210**
DREYSE SEMI-AUTOMATIC
CARBINE
Dreyse-Selbstladekarabiner, 210
• **Rheinmetall (Dreyse), bolt-action
type, 211**
DREYSE SPORTING RIFLES, 211
DREYSE TARGET RIFLES, 211
• **Rheinmetall-Stange, 211**
BACKGROUND, 211
MODEL 42 PARATROOP RIFLE
First pattern: Fallschirmjägergewehr
42 or FG. 42 I, 211
MODEL 42 PARATROOP RIFLE
Second pattern:
Fallschirmjägergewehr 42 or FG. 42 II,
211
• **Rhöner, bolt-action type, 212**
MODEL 69A SPORTING RIFLE, 212
• **Rhöner, break-open type, 212**
MODEL 75 SPORTING RIFLE, 212
• **RWS, 213**
• **Sauer, 213**
MODEL 80 SPORTING RIFLE, 213
SSG 2000 SNIPER RIFLE
Scharfschützengewehr 2000, 214
MODEL 200 SPORTING RIFLE, 214
• **Sauer-Weatherby, 215**
SAUER-WEATHERBY SPORTING
RIFLE, 215
• **Schilling, 215**
• **Schmidt & Habermann,
block-action type, 215**
STANDARD PATTERN, 215
• **Schmidt & Habermann, bolt-action
type, 215**
• **Schüler, 215**
• **Sempert & Krieghoff, 215**
• **Simonov, 216**
KARABINER-S, 216
• **Simson, 216**
PRECISION CARBINE
Simson-Präzisions-Karabiner, 216
SPORTING GUN
Simson-Sportbüchse, 216
• **Stahl, 216**
• **Thälmann, 216**
MODEL 91 SPORTING RIFLE, 216
• **Tirmax, 216**
TIRMAX AUTOMATIC CARBINE,
216
• **Voere, autoloading type, 217**
MODEL 2114S SPORTING RIFLE, 217
MODEL 0014 SPORTING RIFLE, 217
MODEL 2185 SPORTING RIFLE, 217

• **Voere, bolt-action type, 217**
GARDEN GUN, 217
MODEL 2055 SPORTING RIFLE, 217
MODEL 2155 SPORTING RIFLE
Repetierbüchse M2155, 217
MODEL 2202 SPORTING RIFLE, 218
MODEL 2107 SPORTING RIFLE, 218
TITAN 2130 E
Also known as the 'Shihar', 219
• **Vom Hofe, 219**
• **Walther, autoloading type, 219**
MODEL 1 SPORTING RIFLE
Walther-Selbstlade-Kleinkaliberbüchs
e Modell 1, 219
MODEL 41 RIFLE Gewehr 41 (W), 219
MODEL 42 (W) ASSAULT RIFLE
Maschinenkarabiner 42 (W), MKb. 42
(W), 220
MODEL 43 RIFLE Gewehr 43, 220
WA2000 SNIPING RIFLE, 220
• **Walther, block-action type, 221**
UIT-BV-UNIVERSAL TARGET
RIFLE, 221
• **Walther, bolt-action type, 221**
MODEL V SPORTING RIFLE
Walther-Kleinkaliberbüchse Modell
V, 221
POST-WAR GUNS, 222
KKJ SPORTING RIFLE, 222
MODEL A SPORTING RIFLE, 223
UIT-SPECIAL TARGET RIFLE, 223
MODEL JR SPORTING RIFLE
Jagd-Repetier-Gewehr, 224
• **Weihrauch, block-action type, 224**
HW 52 SPORTING RIFLE, 225
• **Weihrauch, bolt-action type, 225**
HW 60J SPORTING RIFLE, 225

GREECE, 226
• **Gras, 226**
• **Heckler & Koch (EBO), 226**
• **Mannlicher, 226**
MODEL 1903 RIFLE, 226
MODEL 1903/14 RIFLE, 226
• **Mauser, 226**
• **Mylona, 226**

GUATEMALA, 226
Mauser, 226

HAITI, 227
• **Remington-Lee, 227**

HESSEN, 227
• **Chassepot, 227**

HONDURAS, 227
• **Mauser, 227**
• **Remington (Enfield), 227**

HUNGARY, 227
• **Kalashnikov, 227**
MODEL 55 ASSAULT RIFLE, 227
• **Mannlicher, 227**
MODEL 1935 SHORT RIFLE
Huzagol 35.M, 227
MODEL 1943 SHORT RIFLE
Huzagol 43.M, 227
• **Mosin-Nagant, 228**

INDIA, 229
• **FN-Saive (Ishapur), 229**
• **Kalashnikov (Ishapur), 229**
INSAS ASSAULT RIFLE, 229
• **Lee-Enfield, 229**
INDIA PATTERN LEE-ENFIELDS,
229

INDONESIA, 229
• **Arisaka, 229**
• **Garand, 229**

IRAN, 229
• **Heckler & Koch, 229**

IRAQ, 230
• **Lee-Enfield, 230**

IRELAND (EIRE), 230
• **Lee-Enfield, 230**

ISRAEL, 230
• **FN-Saive (IMI), 230**

• **Galil (Kalashnikov), 230**
GALIL AUTOMATIC RIFLE, 230
• **Mauser, 231**

ITALY, 231
• **Armaguerra (Revelli), 231**
MODEL 39 AUTOMATIC RIFLE
'Fucile Armaguerra Mo. 39', 231
• **Armi-Jager, autoloading type, 231**
MODEL AP-61 SPORTING RIFLE, 231
MODEL AP-66 SPORTING RIFLE, 231
MODEL AP-74 SPORTING RIFLE, 232
• **Armi-Jager, bolt-action type, 232**
MODEL AP-62 TARGET RIFLE, 232
MODEL AP-65 UNIVERSAL
SPORTING RIFLE, 232
• **Beretta, autoloading type, 232**
MODEL 1931 RIFLE Fucile automatico
Beretta Mo. 931, 232
MODEL 1957 CARBINE
Also known as 'P-30', 233
U.S. M4 knife bayonet, 233
BM-59 RIFLE Fucile automatico
Beretta, Mo. 1959, 233
AUTOMATIC CARBINE Carabine
automatiche Beretta, 'CAB', 233
MODEL 70 ASSAULT RIFLE
Fucile d'Assalto AR-70, 234
MODEL 70-90 ASSAULT RIFLE
Fucile d'Assalto AR-70/90, 234
• **Beretta, bolt-action type, 235**
SUPER OLIMPIA TARGET RIFLE,
235
MODEL 500 SPORTING RIFLE, 235
• **Beretta, break-open type, 236**
THE BASIC PATTERNS, 236
• **Bernardelli, 236**
SEMI-AUTOMATIC CARBINE
Carabine Semi-Automatiche ('CSA'),
236
• **Breda, 237**
MODEL PG SHORT RIFLE
Moschetto Automatico Breda Mo. PG,
237
• **Carcano, 237**
MODEL 1860/67 RIFLE
Fucile di Fanteria Mo. 1860/67, 237
MODEL 1856/67 CARBINE
Carabina di Bersaglieri Mo. 1856/67,
237
MODEL 1844/67 ARTILLERY
MUSKETOON Moschetto di
Artigliera Mo. 1844/67, 237
MODEL 1860/67 GENDARMERIE
MUSKETOON Moschetto di
Carabinieri Mo. 1860/67, 237
• **Cei-Rigotti, 238**
• **Daffini, 238**
• **Doersch & von Baumgarten, 238**
• **FAVS, 238**
• **Franchi, 238**
• **Garand, 238**
• **Mannlicher-Carcano, 238**
MODEL 1891 RIFLE
Fucile di Fanteria Mo. 1891, 238
MODEL 1891 CAVALRY CARBINE
Moschetto Mo. 1891, 239
MODEL 1891 TS CARBINE
Moschetto Mo. 1891 per Truppe
Speciali, 239
MODEL 1891-24 CARBINE
Moschetto Mo. 1891-24, 240
MODEL 1891-38 SHORT RIFLE
Fucile Mo. 1891-38, 240
MODEL 1891-38 CARBINE
Moschetto Mo. 1891-38, 240
MODEL 1938 SHORT RIFLE
Fucile Mo. 1938, 240
MODEL 1938 CARBINE
Moschetto Mo. 1938, 240
MODEL 1940 RIFLE, 240
MODEL 1941 RIFLE, 240
MODEL 1938-43 SHORT RIFLE
Moschetto Mo. 1938-43, 240
• **Mauser, 240**
• **Pedersoli, 240**
KODIAK MARK IV DOUBLE RIFLE,
241
REMINGTON ROLLING BLOCK
RIFLE, 241

SHARPS DROPPING-BLOCK RIFLE, 241
SPRINGFIELD-ALLIN RIFLE, 241
• Perugini-Visini, 242
• Pieri, 242
• Pietta, 242
SMITH BREECH-LOADING CARBINE, 242
• Rizzini (FAIR Techni-Mec), 242
SAFARI DOUBLE RIFLE, 242
• SAB, bolt action type, 242
RGZ 1000 GAME RIFLE, 242
• SAB, break-open type, 243
MUSTANG SPORTING RIFLE, 243
SAFARI EXPRESS DOUBLE RIFLE, 243
• Sabatti, 243
• Scotti, 243
• Uberti, 243
1860-PATTERN HENRY RIFLE, 243
1866-PATTERN WINCHESTER SPORTING RIFLE, 244
Also known as '1866 Yellow Boy', 244
1873-PATTERN WINCHESTER SPORTING RIFLE, 244
• Vetterli, 244
MODEL 1870 RIFLE
Fucile di Fanteria Mo. 1870, 244
MODEL 1870 TS SHORT RIFLE
Moschetto per Truppe Speciali Mo. 1870, 245
MODEL 1870 CAVALRY CARBINE
Moschetto Mo. 1870, 245
MODEL 1882 NAVY RIFLE
Fucile di Marina Mo. 1882, 245
MODEL 1870-87-15 RIFLE
Fucile di Fanteria Mo. 1870/87/15, 245
• Zanardini, 246
• Zoli (Angelo), 246
• Zoli (Antonio), bolt-action type, 246
AZ 1900 SPORTING RIFLE, 246
• Zoli (Antonio), break-open type, 246
EXPRESS DOUBLE RIFLE, 246
SAVANA EXPRESS RIFLE, 247

JAPAN, 247
• Arisaka, 247
MODEL 1896 TRIALS RIFLE
Meiji 29th Year Type, 247
MODEL 1897 RIFLE
Meiji 30th Year Type, 247
MODEL 1902 RIFLE
Meiji 35th Year Type, 248
MODEL 1905 RIFLE
Meiji 38th Year Type, 248
MODEL 1905 CARBINE
Meiji 38th Year Type, 248
MODEL 1911 CAVALRY CARBINE
Meiji 44th Year Type, 248
MODEL 1939 RIFLE, 248
PARATROOP RIFLES, 249
All data for Type 2, 249
TRAINING RIFLES, 249
EMERGENCY RIFLES, 250
SPECIAL NAVY RIFLE, 250
• Chassepot, 250
• Garand, 250
TYPE 5 AUTOMATIC RIFLE, 250
• Howa, autoloading type, 250
TYPE 64 RIFLE
64-Shiki jidoju, 250
• Howa, bolt-action type, 250
MODEL 1500 SPORTING RIFLE, 250
• Mannlicher-Carcano, 251
I-TYPE RIFLE, 251
• Mauser, 251
• Murata, 252
MODEL 1880 RIFLE
Meiji 13th Year Type, 252
MODEL 1889 RIFLE
Meiji 22nd Year Type, 252
• Simple Rifles, 252

KOREA (PRK), 252
• Kalashnikov, 252
• Mosin-Nagant, 252
• Simonov, 253

KOREA (REPUBLIC), 253
• Arisaka, 253
• ArmaLite, 253
• Dae Woo, 253
K1 AUTOMATIC CARBINE, 253

LATVIA, 253
• Mauser, 253

LIBERIA, 253
• Mauser, 253

LITHUANIA, 253
• Mauser, 253

LUXEMBOURG, 253
• Mauser, 253

MANCHURIA, 254
• Mauser, 254

MEXICO, 254
• Arisaka, 254
• FN-Saive, 254
• Mauser, 254
MODEL 1893, 254
MODEL 1895 RIFLE
Fusil Mauser Mexicano Mo. 1895, 254
MODEL 1902 RIFLE
Fusil Mauser Mexicano Mo. 1902, 254
MODEL 1907 RIFLE
Fusil Mauser Mexicano Mo. 1907, 254
MODEL 1910 RIFLE
Fusil Mauser Mexicano Mo. 1910, 254
MODEL 1912 RIFLE
Fusil Mauser Mexicano Mo. 1912, 255
MODEL 1924 SHORT RIFLE
Fusil Mauser Mexicano Mo. 1924, 255
MODEL 1936 SHORT RIFLE
Fusil Mauser Mexicano Mo. 1936, 255
MODEL 1954 SHORT RIFLE
Fusil Mauser Mexicano Mo. 1954, 255
• Mondragon, autoloading type, 255
MODEL 1908 RIFLE
Fusil Automatico de 7mm 'Porfirio Diaz', Modelo de 1908, 256
• Mondragon, bolt-action type, 256
1893-TYPE RIFLE, 256
• Pieper, 256
MODEL 1893 CARBINE, 256
• Remington, 256
MODEL 1897 RIFLE, 256
• Whitney, 257
WHITNEY MILITARY MODEL, 257

MOROCCO, 257
• Beretta, 257
• Garand, 257

NETHERLANDS, 257
• Beaumont, 257
MODEL 1871 RIFLE
Infanterie-Geweer M1871, 257
• Kalashnikov (NWM), 258
• Mannlicher, 258
TRIALS RIFLES, 258
MODEL 1895 RIFLE
Infanterie-Geweer M1895, 258
MODEL 1895 CARBINE NO. 1
Karabijn M1895 A.1, 258
• Mauser, 259
MODEL 1948 GENDARMERIE CARBINE, 259

NEW ZEALAND, 259
• Lee-Enfield, 259
• Parker-Hale, 259
• Remington-Lee, 259

NICARAGUA, 259
• Mauser, 259

NIGERIA, 259
• FN-Saive, 259
• Garand, 259

NORWAY, 259
• Heckler & Koch, 259
• Jarmann, 259
MODEL 1884
Infantry rifle: Jarmann Repetergevær M /1884, 260

• Kammerladningsgevær, 260
MODEL 1842 RIFLE
Kammerladningsgevær M/1842, 260
MODEL 1846 RIFLE
Kammerladningsgevær M/1846, 260
MODEL 1848 CADET RIFLE
'Officers Academy rifle': Krigsskolens kammerladningsgevær M/1848 med sabelbajonett, 260
MODEL 1849 RIFLE
Kammerladningsgevær M/1849, 260
MODEL 1855 RIFLE
Kammerladningsgevær M/1855, 260
MODEL 1857 CAVALRY CARBINE
Kammerladnings-kavalenkarabin M/1857, 261
MODEL 1859 SHORT RIFLE
Kort kammerladningsgevær M/1859, 261
MODEL 1860 RIFLE
Kammerladningsgevær M/1860, 261
MODEL 1860 SHORT RIFLE
Kort kammerladningsgevær M/1860 med sabelbajonett, 261
MODEL 1862/66 FOOT ARTILLERY CARBINE
Kammerladningskarabin for fotartilleriet M/1862/66, 261
MODEL 1865 CAVALRY CARBINE
Kammerladnings-kavalenkarabin M/1865, 261
• Kongsberg, 261
CLASSIC SPORTING RIFLE, 261
• Krag-Jørgensen, 261
MODEL 1894 RIFLE
Krag-Jørgensengevær M/1894, 262
MODEL 1895 CAVALRY CARBINE
Krag-Jørgensenkarabin for Kavaleriet M/1895, 262
MODEL 1897 MOUNTAIN ARTILLERY AND ENGINEER CARBINE
Krag-Jørgensenkarabin for bergartilleriet og ingeniørvåpnet M/1897, 263
MODEL 1904 ENGINEER CARBINE
Krag-Jørgensenkarabin for ingeniørvåpnet M/1904, 263
MODEL 1912 SHORT RIFLE
Krag-Jørgensenkarabin M/1912, 263
MODEL 1930 MARKSMAN'S RIFLE
Skarpskyttegevær M/1930, 263
MODEL 1894, 263
MODEL 1948, 263
• Krag-Petersson, 263
MODEL 1876 NAVY RIFLE
Marinen Repetergevær M/1876, 263
• Landmark, 263
• Lund, 263
MODEL 1860/67 RIFLE
Langt Lunds gevær M/1860/67, 264
MODEL 1860/67 SHORT RIFLE
Kort Lunds gevær M/1860/67, 264
MODEL 1865/69 CAVALRY CARBINE Lunds karabin for kavaleriet M1865/69, 264
MODEL 1866/69 ARTILLERY CARBINE Lunds karabin for artilleriet M/1866/69, 264
• Mauser, 264
MODEL 59 RIFLE, 264
NM149MS TARGET RIFLE, 265
• Remington, 265
MODEL 1867 RIFLE
Remingtongevær M/1867, 265
MODEL 1888 CAVALRY CARBINE
Remingtonkarabin for kavaleriet M/1888, 265
MODEL 1891 CAVALRY CARBINE
Remingtonkarabin for kavaleriet M/1891, 265

ORANGE FREE STATE, 265
• Mauser, 265
MODEL 1896 RIFLE, 265

PAKISTAN, 265
• Heckler & Koch, 265

PARAGUAY, 266
• Mauser, 266
PRE-1900 PATTERNS, 266
MODEL 1907 RIFLE, 266
MODEL 1927 RIFLE, 266

OTHER PATTERNS, 266

PERSIA, 266
• Mauser, 266
MODEL 1310 RIFLE, 266
MODEL 1328 SHORT RIFLE, 266
OTHER GUNS, 266

PERU, 266
• Mauser, 267
MODEL 1891 RIFLE, 267
MODEL 1909 RIFLE, 267
OTHER PATTERNS, 267
• Remington-Lee, 267

PHILIPPINES, 267
• ArmaLite, 267
• Arms Corporation, autoloading type, 267
MODEL 1600 SPORTING RIFLE
Also known as 'Model 16P', 267
MODEL 2000P SPORTING RIFLE
Originally known as the 'Model 20P', 267
MODEL 50-S SPORTING RIFLE, 267
MODEL AK-22S SPORTING RIFLE, 267
• Arms Corporation, bolt-action type, 267
MODEL 1400P SPORTING RIFLE
Also known as 'Model 14P', 267
MODEL 1800 SPORTING RIFLE, 268

POLAND, 268
• Kalashnikov, 268
KALASHNIKOV MACHINE PISTOL, 268
MODEL 88 ASSAULT RIFLE
Karabinek automatyczny wz. 88, Kbk. wz. 88, 268
• Mauser, 268
MODEL 1898 RIFLE Pusek wz. 98, 268
MODEL 1929 SHORT RIFLE
Karabinek wz. 1929, 268
• Mosin-Nagant, 268
MODEL 91/98/25 RIFLE, 268

PORTUGAL, 268
• Guedes, 268
MODEL 1885 RIFLE, 269
• Heckler & Koch (FBP), 269
• Kropatschek, 269
MODEL 1886 RIFLE
Espingarda Mo. 1886, 269
MODEL 1886 SHORT RIFLE
Mosqueton Mo. 1886, 269
MODEL 1886 CARBINE, 269
• Mannlicher, 270
TRIALS RIFLES, 270
• Mauser, 270
MODEL 1937 SHORT RIFLE
Espingarda Mo. 937, 270
• Richards, 270
• Snider, 270
• Vergueiro, 270
MODEL 1904 RIFLE
Espingarda 6.5 Mo. 1904, 270

PRUSSIA, 270
• Bock, 271
• Bornmüller, 271
• Chassepot, 271
MODEL 1871 CARBINE
Aptierter Chassepot-Karabiner M1871, 271
• Doersch & von Baumgarten, 272
• Dreyse, 272
MODEL 1841 RIFLE
Leichte-Percussions-Gewehr M1841, 272
MODEL 1849 SHARPSHOOTER'S RIFLE Jägerbüchse M1849, 273
MODEL 1854 SHARPSHOOTER'S RIFLE Zündnadelbüchse M1854, 273
MODEL 1855 CAVALRY CARBINE
Karabiner M1855, 273
MODEL 1860 FUSILIER RIFLE
Zündnadel-Füsiliergewehr M1860, 274
MODEL 1862 RIFLE
Zündnadelgewehr M1862, 274

MODEL 1865 SHARPSHOOTER'S
  RIFLE Jägerbüchse M1865, 274
PIONEER RIFLE, U/M PATTERN
  Zündnadel-Pioniergewehr u/M, 275
MODEL 1869 PIONEER RIFLE
  Zündnadel-Pioniergewehr M1869, 275
OBSOLESCENT PATTERNS, 275
• Luck, 276
• Poppenburg, 276
• Spangenberg & Sauer, 276
ROMANIA, 276
• Kalashnikov, 276
• Mannlicher, 276
  MODEL 1892 RIFLE, 276
  MODEL 1893 RIFLE, 277
• Mauser, 277
• Peabody, 277
• Peabody-Martini, 277
  MODEL 1879 RIFLE, 277
RUSSIA, MODERN, 277
• Kalashnikov, 277
  MODEL 101 ASSAULT RIFLE
    Avtomat Kalashnikova, obr. 101, 277
• Nikonov, 278
  MODEL 94 ASSAULT RIFLE
    Avtomat Nikonova obr. 94, 'AN-94',
    278
RUSSIA, TSARIST, 278
• Arisaka, 278
• Baranov, 278
• Berdan, block-action type, 278
  MODEL 1868 RIFLE
    Pekhnotniya vintovka Berdana obr.
    1868g, 278
• Berdan, bolt-action type, 278
  MODEL 1870 RIFLE
    Pekhotniya vintovka Berdana obr.
    1870g, 278
  MODEL 1870 CARBINE
    Karabina Berdana obr. 1870g, 279
  MODEL 1870 DRAGOON RIFLE
    Dragunskaya vintovka Berdana obr.
    1870g, 279
  THREE LINE BERDAN-MODEL
    RIFLE Drelineinaya Pekhotniya
    vintovka Berdana, 279
• Fedorov, 279
  MODEL 1913 TRIALS RIFLE
    Avtomaticheskaya vintovka V.
    Fedorova optniy obr. 1913g, 279
  MODEL 1916 RIFLE
    Avtomaticheskaya vintovka V.
    Fedorova obr. 1916g, 280
• Gillet-Trummer, 280
• Greene, 280
  SHARPSHOOTER'S RIFLE, 280
• Karle, 280
  MODEL 1867 RIFLE, 280
• Krnka, 281
  MODEL 1869 RIFLE, 281
• Mosin-Nagant, 281
  THE FIRST STEPS, 281
  MODEL 1891 RIFLE
    Pekhotniya vintovka obr. 1891g, 281
  MODEL 1891 COSSACK RIFLE
    Kazachya vintovka obr. 1891g, 281
  MODEL 1907 CARBINE
    Karabin obr. 1907g, 282
• Nagant, 282
• Norman (Terry), 282
  MODEL 1866 RIFLE, 282
• Winchester, 282
  MODEL 1915 RIFLE
    Vintovka Vinchestya, obr. 1915g, 282
SAUDI ARABIA, 283
• Heckler & Koch (al-Khardj), 283
• Mauser, 283
SAXONY, 283
• Chassepot, 283
  MODEL 1873 CARBINE
    Aptierter Chassepot-Karabiner M
    1873, 283
• Drechsler, 283

SERBIA, 283
• Green, 283
  MODEL 1867 RIFLE Gryn-Puska, 283
• Martini, 284
• Mauser, 284
  MODEL 1878/80 RIFLE, 284
  MODEL 1885 CAVALRY CARBINE
    Also known as the 'Mauser-Koká', 284
  MODEL 1880/06 AND MODEL
    1880/07 RIFLES Also known as
    'M80/6' or 'M80/7', 284
  MODEL 1899 RIFLE, 284
  MODEL 1910 RIFLE, 285
SIAM, 285
• Arisaka, 285
• Mannlicher, 285
• Mauser, 285
  MODEL 1902 RIFLE
    Also known as 'Type 45', 285
  MODEL 1904
    Possibly known as the 'Type 47', 285
  MODEL 1923 SHORT RIFLE
    Also known as Type 66, 285
SINGAPORE, 285
• ArmaLite, 285
• Chartered Industries, 285
  SA-80 AUTOMATIC RIFLE, 285
  SR-88 ASSAULT RIFLE, 286
SOUTH AFRICA, 286
• FN-Saive (Lyttelton), 286
• Galil (Lyttelton), 286
• Lee-Enfield, 286
• Musgrave, 287
  RSA NR-1 RIFLE, 287
  NR-5 SPORTING RIFLE, 287
• Vergueiro, 287
SPAIN, 287
• Amiel, 287
• Berdan, 287
  MODEL 1867 RIFLE
    Fusil para Infanteria Mo. 1867, 287
  M1867 SHORT RIFLE
    Fusil para Cazadores Mo. 1867, 287
  MODEL 1867 CARBINE
    Carabina para Artilleria e Ingenieros
    Mo. 1867, 287
  MODEL 1867 NAVY RIFLE, 288
• CETME, 288
  CETME ASSAULT RIFLE, 7.62MM
    Fusil d'Asalto CETME, 288
  CETME ASSAULT RIFLE, 5.56MM,
    289
• García Saez, 289
• La Rosa, 289
  EXPERIMENTAL SHORT RIFLE, 289
    Carabina La Rosa, 289
• Mata, 290
• Mauser: bolt-action, 290
  MODEL 1891 TRIALS RIFLE
    Fusil Mauser Mo. 1891, 290
  MODEL 1892 RIFLE
    Fusil Mauser Español Mo. 1892, 290
  MODEL 1892 CARBINE
    Carabina Mauser Española Mo. 1892,
    290
  MODEL 1893 RIFLE
    Fusil Mauser Español Mo. 1893, 290
  MODEL 1895 CARBINE
    Carabina Mauser Española para Plazas
    Montadas Mo. 1895, 291
  MODEL 1913 SHORT RIFLE
    Mosqueton Mauser Español Mo. 1913,
    291
  MODEL 1916 SHORT RIFLE
    Mosqueton Mauser Español Mo. 1916,
    291
  MODEL 1898 CONVERSIONS, 292
  STANDARD MODEL RIFLE, 292
  MODEL 1943 RIFLE
    Fusil Mauser Español Mo. 1943, 292
  MODEL 8 RIFLE
    Fusil a Repetición Mo. 8, 'FR-8', 292
  OTHER GUNS, 292
• Núñez de Castro, 292
  EXPERIMENTAL RIFLE
    Fusil de Retrocarga Núñez de Castro,
    292

• Peabody, 292
  COLONIAL MODEL RIFLE
    Fusil Peabody do Ejercito de Ultramar,
    292
• Remington, 292
  AMERICAN-PATTERN RIFLE
    Fusil Remington Norteamericano, 292
  MODEL 1870 CARBINE
    Carabina Remington para Carabineros,
    Mo. 1870, 292
  SHORT RIFLE Mosqueton Remington,
    'fabricación Vascongada', 293
  ROYAL BODYGUARD RIFLE
    Fusil Remington para Guardias del
    Rey, 293
  MODEL 1871 RIFLE
    Fusil Remington Mo. 1871, 293
  MODEL 1871 SHORT RIFLE
    Mosqueton Remington Mo. 1871, 293
  MODEL 1871 CARBINE
    Tercerola Remington Mo. 1871, 293
  MODEL 1874 SHORT RIFLE
    Mosqueton Remington Mo. 1874, 293
  MODEL 1889 CARBINE
    Carabina Remington para Dragones,
    Mo. 1889, 293
• Snider, 294
  SHORT RIFLE, 294
• Soriano, 294
• Winchester, 294
  MODEL 1873 CARBINE
    Tercerola Winchester Mo. 1873, 294
SWEDEN, 294
• FN (FFV), 294
  MODEL 5 ASSAULT RIFLE
    Automatkarbin 5, Ak-5, 294
• Friberg-Kjellman, 295
• Galil (FFV), 295
• Hagström, 295
• Heckler & Koch (FFV), 295
• Husqvarna (FFV), 295
  1896-TYPE SPORTING RIFLES, 296
  1898-TYPE SPORTING RIFLES, 296
  HUSQVARNA-MAUSER SPORTING
    RIFLES, 296
  HVA SPORTING RIFLE
    Also known as 'Carl Gustaf', 296
  MODEL 2000 SPORTING RIFLE, 297
• Ljungmann (Husqvarna), 297
  MODEL 42 AUTOMATIC RIFLE
    Automatiskgevär 42 and 42.B, 297
• Mauser (Carl Gustaf), 297
  MODEL 1894 CARBINE
    Karabin M/1894, 297
  MODEL 1896 RIFLE
    Gevär M/1896, 298
  MODEL 1939 SHORT RIFLE
    Gevär M/1939, 298
• Remington, 298
• Sjögren, 298
  MILITARY-PATTERN TRIALS
    RIFLE, 298
• Stiga (Mauser), 298
SWITZERLAND, 299
• Abegg, 299
• End, 299
• Flisch, 299
• Flury, 299
• Frey, 299
• Gamma & Infanger, 299
• Grünig & Elmiger, 299
  SPORTING/TARGET RIFLES
    Matchkugelbüchsen: Standard and
    Luxusmodelle, 299
  UIT STANDARD TARGET RIFLE, 300
• Hämmerli, 300
  MODEL 700 SPORTING RIFLE, 300
  OTHER TYPES, 300
• Heeren, 300
  HEEREN-GLASER SPORTING
    RIFLE, 301
  WÜRTHRICH-HEEREN SPORTING
    RIFLE, 301
• Kaestli, 301
• Mannlicher, 301
  MODEL 1893 CARBINE
    Repetier-Karabiner M1893, 301

• Martini, 301
  HÄMMERLI-MARTINI TARGET
    RIFLE, 301
• Milbank-Amsler, 302
  MODEL 1851-67 SHORT RIFLE, 302
• Neuhausen, 302
  NEUHAUSEN TRIALS RIFLE, 302
• Pauly, 302
• Peabody, 302
  MODEL 1867 ENGINEER RIFLE
    Genie-Gewehr system Peabody
    M1867, 302
• Schmidt (-Rubin), 303
  THE EARLIEST TRIALS RIFLES, 303
  MODEL 1889 RIFLE
    Infanterie-Repetier-Gewehr M1889,
    303
  MODEL 1889/96 RIFLE
    Infanterie-Repetier-Gewehr
    M1889/96, 303
  MODEL 1897 CADET RIFLE
    Kadettengewehr M1897, 303
  MODEL 1900 SHORT RIFLE
    Kurzgewehr M1900, 303
  MODEL 1905 CAVALRY CARBINE
    Kavallerie-Karabiner M1905, 304
  MODEL 1911 RIFLE
    Gewehr 11, 304
  MODEL 1911 CARBINE
    Karabiner 11, 304
  MODEL 1931 SHORT RIFLE
    Karabiner 31, 304
  SNIPER RIFLE MODEL 1931/42
    Zielfernrohr-Karabiner 31/42, 304
  SNIPER RIFLE MODEL 1955
    Zielfernrohr-Karabiner 55, 305
• SIG, 305
  MODEL 46 AUTOMATIC RIFLE
    Selbstlade-Karabiner Modell 46, 'SK-
    46', 305
  MODEL 53 AUTOMATIC CARBINE
    Automatische-Karabiner Modell 53,
    'AK-53', 306
  MODEL 55 AUTOMATIC RIFLE
    Also known as 'AM-55', 306
  MODEL 510 AUTOMATIC RIFLE
    Also known as SG 510 or Stgw. 57,
    306
  MODEL 530 AUTOMATIC RIFLE
    Also known as SG 530, 307
  MODEL 540 AUTOMATIC RIFLE
    Also known as SG 540, 307
  MODEL 550 AUTOMATIC RIFLE
    Also known as SG 550, 307
• SIG-Sauer, 308
  MODEL 3000 SNIPER RIFLE
    Scharfschützengewehr 3000, 'SSG
    3000', 308
• Stamm, 308
• Tanner, 308
  STANDARD UIT-STUTZER, 308
  SUPER MATCH 50M CARBINE, 309
  FREE RIFLE Matchstutzer 300m, 309
  UIT SHORT RIFLE UIT-Stutzer, 309
• Vetterli, 310
  TRIALS RIFLE, 1867, 310
  MODEL-1869 RIFLE
    Repetier-Gewehr M1869, 310
  MODEL 1870 CADET RIFLE
    Kadetten-Gewehr M1870, 310
  MODEL 1871 CARBINE
    Repetier-Karabiner M1871, 310
  MODEL 1871 SHORT RIFLE
    Repetier-Stutzer M1871, 310
  MODEL 1878 RIFLE
    Repetier-Gewehr M1878, 311
  MODEL 1878 CARBINE
    Repetier-Karabiner M1878, 311
  MODEL 1878 BORDER-GUARD
    CARBINE
    Repetier-Karabiner für
    Grenzwächterkorps, M1878, 311
  MODEL 1881 SHORT RIFLE
    Repetier-Stutzer M1881, 311
  POLICE CARBINES, 311
TAIWAN, 312
• Armalite, 312
• Garand, 312
THAILAND, 312
• Arisaka, 312

TRANSVAAL (ZAR), 312
• Mauser, 312
   MODEL 1896 RIFLE, 312
• Richards, 312
   RICHARDS-MARTINI RIFLE, 312
TURKEY, 312
• Berthier, 312
• Heckler & Koch, 312
• Mauser, 312
   MODEL 1887 RIFLE, 312
   MODEL 1890 RIFLE, 313
   MODEL 1893 RIFLE, 313
   MODEL 1903 RIFLE, 313
   MODEL 1908 CARBINE, 313
• Peabody, 313
• Peabody-Martini, 314
   MODEL 1874 RIFLE, 314
• Reichsgewehr (Mannlicher), 314
URUGUAY, 314
• Daudetau-Mauser, 314
• Mauser, 314
   PRE-1914 PATTERNS, 314
   POST-1914 PATTERNS, 314
• Remington, 314
U.S.A., 314
• Allen (Ethan), block-action type, 314
   SPORTING RIFLE, 314
• Allen (Ethan), plug-action type, 314
• Allen (Hiram), 314
• Alpha Arms, 315
   ALPHA MODEL 1 SPORTING RIFLE, 315
   ALPHA JAGUAR SPORTING RIFLE, 315
• AMAC, 315
• American Industries (Calico), 315
   M-100 CARBINE, 315
• AMT, autoloading type, 315
   LIGHTNING SPORTING RIFE, 315
• AMT, bolt-action type, 315
   AMT SPORTING RIFLE, 315
• ArmaLite, 316
   ARMALITE AR-10 RIFLE, 316
   ARMALITE AR-15 RIFLE, 316
   XM16 AND M16 RIFLES, 317
   XM16E1 RIFLE, 317
   M16A1 RIFLE, 317
   XM16E2 AND M16A2 RIFLES, 317
   COMMERCIAL AND OTHER AR-15/M16-TYPE GUNS, 318
   OTHER AR-15/M16 SERIES USERS, 320
   ARMALITE AR-18 RIFLE, 321
• Armstrong & Taylor, 321
• A-Square, 321
   HANNIBAL MODEL SPORTING RIFLE, 321
   CAESAR MODEL SPORTING RIFLE, 321
• Auto-Ordnance, 321
• Ball, 321
   REPEATING CARBINE, 322
• Ballard, 322
   1865 TRIALS CARBINE, 322
   NO. 1 HUNTING RIFLE, 322
• Bannerman, 323
   MANNLICHER-SPRINGFIELD RIFLE, 323
   MAUSER-SPRINGFIELD RIFLE, 323
• Beal, 323
• Beals, 323
• Berdan, block-action type, 323
• Berdan, bolt-action type, 324
• Bighorn, 324
• Blake, 324
• Boswell, 324
• Broadwell, 324
• Broughton, 324
• Brown, 324
• Browning, autoloading type, 324
• Browning, block-action type, 324
   1878-PATTERN RIFLE, 325

   MODEL 78 SPORTING RIFLE
      Also known as 'B-78', 325
   MODEL 1885 SPORTING RIFLE, 325
• Browning, bolt-action type, 325
   BROWNING-MAUSER SPORTING RIFLE, 325
   BROWNING-SAKO SPORTING RIFLE, 326
   BBR LIGHTNING SPORTING RIFLE, 326
   A-BOLT HUNTER, 326
• Browning, lever-action type, 326
   MODEL 1886 SPORTING RIFLE, 326
   MODEL 92 SPORTING RIFLE
      Also known as 'B-92', 327
   MODEL 1895 SPORTING RIFLE, 327
   BLR SPORTING RIFLE, 327
• Brown Standard, 327
• Bruce, 328
• Bullard, block-action type, 328
   TARGET RIFLE, 328
• Bullard, lever-action type, 328
   LEVER-ACTION SPORTING RIFLE, 328
• Burgess, 328
   BURGESS REPEATING RIFLE
      Also known as 'Whitney-Burgess' or 'Whitney-Kennedy', 328
• Burke, 328
• Burnside, 329
   BURNSIDE CARBINE, BRISTOL TYPE 'First Pattern', 1856, 329
   BURNSIDE CARBINE, FOSTER TYPE 'Second Pattern', 1860, 329
   BURNSIDE CARBINE, HARTSHORN TYPE 'Fourth pattern', 'New Model' or 'M1863', 329
   MODEL 1865 CARBINE, 330
• Burton, 330
   1859-PATENT RIFLE, 330
• Bushmaster, 330
• Century, 330
• Chaffee-Reece, 330
   MODEL 1882 RIFLE, 331
• Champlin, 331
   SPORTING RIFLE, 331
• Charter Arms, 331
• Chipmunk, 331
• Clerke, 331
• Cochran, 331
• Coleman, 331
• Colt, autoloading type, 331
   COLTEER SPORTING RIFLE, 331
• Colt, bolt-action type, 331
   COLTEER SPORTING RIFLE, 331
   COLT-ROOT PATTERNS, 332
   COLTSMAN STANDARD SPORTING RIFLE Mauser type; originally known as 'Model 57', 332
   COLTSMAN STANDARD SPORTING RIFLE Sako type, 332
   COLT-SAUER SPORTING RIFLE, 332
• Colt, lever-action type, 332
   NEW MAGAZINE RIFLE
      Also known as 'Colt Burgess', 332
• Colt, slide-action type, 332
   LIGHTNING MAGAZINE RIFLE, 332
   LIGHTNING EXPRESS RIFLE, 333
• Conover (Empire), 333
• Conroy, 333
• Cooper, 333
   MODEL 21 VARMINT EXTREME RIFLE Classic pattern, 333
   MODEL 22 PRO-VARMINT EXTREME RIFLE, 333
• Crescent, 334
   SPORTING RIFLE, 334
• Cullen, 334
• Daisy, 334
   MODEL 2201 LEGACY SPORTING RIFLE, 334
• Dakota, 334
   DAKOTA 76 CLASSIC RIFLE, 334
• Davenport, 334
   BROWNIE SPORTING RIFLE, 334
• Dodge, 335

• DuBiel, 335
   DUBIEL SPORTING RIFLE, 335
• Durst, 335
• Elliott, 335
• Enfield, 335
   MODEL 1917, 335
• Evans, 336
   PATENT MAGAZINE RIFLE, 336
   NEW MODEL PATENT RIFLE, 336
• Fajen, 336
• Field, 336
• Firearms International, 336
• Fitzgerald, 336
• FN-Saive, 336
• Fogerty, bolt-action type, 336
   MILITARY-MODEL RIFLE, 337
• Fogerty, lever-action type, 337
   MILITARY-MODEL RIFLE, 1868 TYPE, 337
   SPORTING-MODEL RIFLE, 337
• Franklin, 337
• Freeman, 337
• Gallager, 337
   1861-PATTERN CARBINE, 338
• Garand, 338
   THE FIRST STEPS, 338
   THE EARLY DESIGNS, 338
   M1 RIFLE, 339
   M14 RIFLE, 340
   OTHER USERS, 340
• Gibbs, bolt-action type, 341
• Gibbs, break-open type, 341
   BREECH-LOADING CARBINE, 341
• Golden Eagle, 341
• Golden State, 341
• Goulding, 341
• Gray, 341
• Greene, 341
   GREENE RIFLE, 341
• Grendel, 342
   S-16 SNIPER RIFLE, 342
• Grillett, 342
• Gross, 342
   GROSS CARBINE, 342
• Gwyn & Campbell, 342
   GWYN & CAMPBELL CARBINE, 342
• Hall, 342
   MODEL 1819 RIFLE, 343
   MODEL 1833 CARBINE, 343
   MODEL 1840 CARBINE
      Patch and Huger types, 343
   MODEL 1841 RIFLE, 344
• Hammond, 344
• Hampden, 344
• Harrington & Richardson, autoloading type, 344
   MODEL 60 SPORTING RIFLE, 344
   MODEL 360 ULTRA AUTOMATIC RIFLE, 344
   MODEL 800 LYNX RIFLE, 344
   MODEL 755 SAHARA RIFLE, 344
   MODEL 700 SPORTING RIFLE, 344
• Harrington & Richardson, bolt-action type, 344
   MODEL 265 "REG'LAR" RIFLE, 344
   MODEL 300 SPORTING RIFLE, 345
   MODEL 300 ULTRA RIFLE, 345
   MODEL 5200 SPORTING RIFLE, 345
• Harrington & Richardson, break-open type, 345
   MODEL 158 TOPPER JET SPORTING RIFLE, 345
• Harrington & Richardson, block-action type, 345
   H&R CENTENNIAL RIFLE, 345
• Harrington & Richardson, slide-action type, 346
   MODEL 422 SPORTING RIFLE, 346
• Hartung (Klein), 346
• Harvey, 346
   T25 RIFLE, 346
• Hayden, 346

• Henry, 346
   HENRY'S PATENT REPEATING RIFLE, 346
• High-Standard, 347
• Hoffmann, 347
• Holden, 347
• Hopkins & Allen, 347
   NO. 722 SPORTING RIFLE, 347
   NO. 822 SPORTING RIFLE, 347
   NO. 922 SPORTING RIFLE
      Originally known as the 'Junior Model', 348
• Hotchkiss, 348
• Howard, 348
   THUNDERBOLT RIFLE, 348
• Howe, 348
• HS Precision, 348
• Hubbell, 348
   1844-PATENT GUNS, 348
   1867-PATENT GUNS, 348
• Hyper, 348
• Ithaca, 348
   MODEL 49 SADDLEGUN, 348
• Iver Johnson, 349
   PM-30 CARBINE, 349
• Jaeger, 349
   AFRICAN RIFLE, 349
• Jenks (Barton), 349
• Jenks (William), 349
   MODEL 1839 MUSKETOON, 349
   MODEL 1841 NAVY MUSKET, 350
   MODEL 1845 NAVY CARBINE, 350
• Jennings, 350
   HUNT-JENNINGS RIFLE, 350
• Johnson, autoloading type, 351
   MODEL 1941 RIFLE, 351
• Johnson, swinging-barrel type, 351
• Johnson Associates, 351
• Joslyn, 351
   MODEL 1855 NAVY RIFLE, 351
   MODEL 1861 CARBINE, 351
   MODEL 1865 RIFLE, 352
• Joslyn-Tomes, 352
• Kimber, 352
   MODEL 82 SPORTER, 352
   MODEL 82C SPORTING RIFLE, 353
   MODEL 84 SPORTER Also known as the 'Model 84 Mini-Mauser', 353
   MODEL 84C CLASSIC SPORTING RIFLE, 354
   MODEL 89 BIG-GAME RIFLE, 354
   K770 CUSTOM SPORTING RIFLE, 354
• Knight, 354
   MODEL 25 MATCH RIFLE
      Also known as 'SR-25 Match', 354
• Kodiak, 354
   MODEL 98 SPORTING RIFLE, 355
• Krag-Jørgensen, 355
   MODEL 1892 RIFLE
      'U.S. Magazine Rifle, Caliber 30, Model of 1892', 355
   MODEL 1896 RIFLE, 355
   MODEL 1896 CARBINE, 355
   MODEL 1898 RIFLE, 355
   PHILIPPINE CONSTABULARY RIFLE, 356
• Laidley, 356
• Lamson, 357
• Lee, block-action type, 357
   1866-PATTERN RIFLE, 357
   1871-PATTERN RIFLE, 357
   1871-PATTERN RIFLE, 357
   1872-PATTERN RIFLE, 357
   MODEL 1875 RIFLE, 357
   1877-PATTERN RIFLE, 357
   MAGAZINE RIFLE, 357
• Lee, bolt-action type, 357
   MAGAZINE RIFLE, MILITARY PATTERN
      Also known as the 'Model 1879', 358
• Lee, pivoting-barrel type, 358
   BREECH-LOADING CARBINE, 358
   SPORTING RIFLE, 358
• Lee-Cook, 358
   EXPERIMENTAL RIFLE, 358

- **Lindner, 358**
  CONVERTED MODEL 1841 RIFLE, 358
  MODEL 1861 CARBINE, 359
- **Ljutic, 359**
  SPACE RIFLE, 359
- **McMillan, 359**
  SIGNATURE CLASSIC SPORTER, 359
  MODEL 86 SNIPER RIFLE, 360
- **Marathon, 360**
- **Marlin, autoloading type, 360**
  MODEL 50 SPORTING RIFLE, 360
  MODEL A-1 SPORTING RIFLE, 360
  MODEL 88-C SPORTING RIFLE, 360
  MODEL 99 SPORTING RIFLE, 361
  MODEL 45 CARBINE, 362
  GLENFIELD SERIES, 362
- **Marlin, bolt-action type, 362**
  MODEL 65 SPORTING RIFLE, 362
  MODEL 100 SPORTING RIFLE, 362
  MODEL 80 SPORTING RIFLE, 362
  MODEL 322 SPORTING RIFLE, 363
  MODEL 122 SPORTING RIFLE, 363
  MODEL 980 SPORTING RIFLE, 363
  MODEL 780 SPORTING RIFLE, 363
  MODEL 15 SPORTING RIFLE, 364
  MODEL 2000 TARGET RIFLE, 364
  MODEL MR-7 SPORTING RIFLE, 364
  GLENFIELD SERIES, 364
- **Marlin, lever-action type, 364**
  MODEL 1881 SPORTING RIFLE
    Known prior to 1888 simply as the 'Marlin Repeating Rifle', 364
  MODEL 1888 SPORTING RIFLE, 365
  MODEL 1889 SPORTING RIFLE
    Also known as 'Marlin New Safety Repeater', 365
  MODEL 1891 SPORTING RIFLE
    Also known as 'Marlin Safety Rifle, Model 1891', 365
  MODEL 1892 SPORTING RIFLE
    Known from 1905 as the 'Model 92', 365
  MODEL 1893 SPORTING RIFLE
    Renamed 'Model 93' in 1905, 365
  MODEL 1894 SPORTING RIFLE
    Renamed 'Model 94' in 1906, 366
  MODEL 1895 SPORTING RIFLE
    Known as 'Model 95' after 1905, 366
  MODEL 1897 SPORTING RIFLE
    Renamed 'Model 97' in 1905, 367
  MODEL 1936 SPORTING RIFLE
    Renamed 'Model 36' in 1937, 367
  MODEL 336 SPORTING RIFLE, 367
  MODEL 39 SPORTING RIFLE, 368
  MODEL 56 LEVERMATIC SPORTING RIFLE, 369
  MODEL 444 SPORTING RIFLE, 369
  GLENFIELD MODEL 36G SPORTING CARBINE, 369
  NEW MODEL 1894 SPORTING RIFLE, 369
  NEW MODEL 1895 SPORTING RIFLE, 370
  MODEL 375 SPORTING RIFLE, 370
  OTHER PATTERNS, 370
- **Marlin, slide-action type, 370**
  MODEL 18 SPORTING RIFLE
    'Marlin Baby Featherweight Repeater No. 18', 370
  MODEL 27 SPORTING RIFLE, 371
  MODEL 32 SPORTING RIFLE, 371
- **Marston, 371**
  BREECHLOADING SPORTING RIFLE, 371
- **Mauser, 371**
- **Maynard, 371**
  CAPLOCK CARBINE, 372
  MODEL 1873 SPORTING RIFLE, 372
  MODEL 1882 SPORTING RIFLE, 373
- **Meigs, 373**
- **Merrill, 373**
  MERRILL-JENKS CARBINE, 373
  IMPROVED JENKS-PATTERN RIFLE, MODEL 1858, 373
  IMPROVED JENKS-PATTERN CARBINE, MODEL 1858, 373
- **Merrill, Latrobe & Thomas, 373**
  1856-PATENT CARBINE, 373
- **Milbank, 373**

- **Miller, 374**
- **Mix & Horton, 374**
- **Montana Armory, 374**
- **Morgenstern, 374**
- **Morse, 374**
  MORSE RIFLE, 374
- **Mosin-Nagant, 374**
- **Mossberg, autoloading type, 375**
  MODEL 50 SPORTING RIFLE, 375
  MODEL 151M SPORTING RIFLE, 375
  MODEL 350K SPORTING RIFLE, 375
  MODEL 430 SPORTING RIFLE, 375
- **Mossberg, block-action type, 375**
  MODEL L SPORTING RIFLE, 375
- **Mossberg, bolt-action type, 375**
  MODEL B SPORTING RIFLE, 375
  MODEL 10 SPORTING RIFLE, 376
  MODEL 14 SPORTING RIFLE, 376
  MODEL 25 SPORTING RIFLE, 376
  MODEL 25A SPORTING RIFLE, 376
  MODEL 26B SPORTING RIFLE, 376
  MODEL 142A SPORTING CARBINE, 377
  MODEL 146B SPORTING RIFLE, 377
  MODEL 340B SPORTING RIFLE, 377
  MODEL 640K SPORTING RIFLE
    Also known as 'Chuckster', 378
  MODEL 800 SPORTING RIFLE, 378
  MODEL 810 SPORTING RIFLE, 379
  RM-7 SPORTING RIFLE, 379
  PEDERSEN SERIES, 379
  WESTERN FIELD SERIES, 379
  SAKO PATTERNS, 379
- **Mossberg, lever-action type, 379**
  MODEL 400 SPORTING RIFLE
    Also known as 'Palomino', 379
  MODEL 472 SPORTING RIFLE, 380
  PEDERSEN SERIES, 380
  WESTERN FIELD SERIES, 380
- **Mossberg, slide-action type, 380**
  MODEL K SPORTING RIFLE, 380
- **Mullins, 380**
- **National, 380**
  NATIONAL CARBINE, 380
- **National Ordnance, 380**
- **Navy Arms, 381**
- **Needham, 381**
- **New England Firearms, 381**
  HANDI-RIFLE, 381
- **Newton, 381**
  SPORTING RIFLE, 381
  SPORTING RIFLE Second or 'Buffalo Newton' pattern, 381
  LEVERBOLT RIFLE, 382
- **Opus, 382**
- **Page-Lewis, 382**
  MODEL A TARGET RIFLE, 382
- **Palmer, 382**
  PALMER CARBINE, 382
- **Parkhurst-Lee, 382**
- **Peabody, 382**
  TRIALS-PATTERN MILITARY CARBINE, 382
  MILITARY MODEL RIFLE, 382
  SPORTING GUN, 383
- **Peabody-Martini, 383**
  IMPROVED SPORTING RIFLE, 383
- **Pedersen, 383**
  T1 RIFLE, 383
- **Percy, 383**
- **Perry, 384**
  PERRY CARBINE, 384
- **Pitcher, 384**
- **Plainfield, 384**
- **Poultney, 384**
- **Rahn, 384**
- **Ranger, 384**
  RANGER SPORTING RIFLE, 384
- **Red Willow, 385**
- **Remington, autoloading type, 385**
  MODEL 8 SPORTING RIFLE
    Subsequently known as the 'Model 8A', 385

  MODEL 16 SPORTING RIFLE
    Subsequently known as 'Model 16A', 385
  MODEL 24 SPORTING RIFLE
    Subsequently known as 'Model 24A', 385
  MODEL 550A SPORTING RIFLE, 385
  MODEL 740A WOODSMASTER RIFLE, 385
  MODEL 552A SPEEDMASTER RIFLE, 386
  NYLON 66 SPORTING RIFLE, 386
  MODEL FOUR SPORTING RIFLE, 387
  MODEL 522 VIPER SPORTING RIFLE, 387
- **Remington, block-action type, 387**
  MODEL 1864 REMINGTON-GEIGER CARBINE, 387
  LATER PATTERNS, 387
  MODEL 1870 NAVY RIFLE, 388
  MODEL 1871 RIFLE, 388
  NO. 1 SPORTING RIFLE, 388
  LIGHT MODEL SPORTING CARBINE, 389
  NO. 5 MILITARY/SPORTING RIFLE, 389
  NO. 4 SPORTING RIFLE, 389
  NO. 6 SPORTING RIFLE, 389
  NO. 7 SPORTING RIFLE, 389
- **Remington, bolt-action type, 390**
  MODEL 30 SPORTING RIFLE, 390
  MODEL 30S SPORTING RIFLE, 390
  MODEL 33 SPORTING RIFLE, 390
  MODEL 37 RANGEMASTER RIFLE, 390
  MODEL 41A TARGETMASTER RIFLE, 390
  MODEL 720 SPORTING RIFLE, 391
  MODEL 721A SPORTING RIFLE, 391
  MODEL 722A SPORTING RIFLE, 392
  MODEL 725ADL SPORTING RIFLE, 392
  MODEL 40 TARGET RIFLE, 392
  NYLON 11 SPORTING RIFLE, 393
  MODEL 700 SPORTING RIFLE, 393
  MODEL 600 SPORTING RIFLE, 395
  MODEL 788 SPORTING RIFLE, 395
  MODEL 540X TARGET RIFLE, 396
  MODEL 580 SPORTING RIFLE, 396
  MODEL SEVEN, 397
  MODEL 78 SPORTING RIFLE, 397
  MODEL 24 SNIPER RIFLE
    Part of the 'M24 Sniping System', 397
- **Remington, lever-action type, 397**
  NYLON 76 TRAIL RIDER RIFLE, 397
- **Remington, slide-action type, 398**
  MODEL 12 SPORTING RIFLE
    Subsequently known as 'Model 12A', 398
  MODEL 14 SPORTING RIFLE, 398
  MODEL 121A FIELDMASTER RIFLE, 398
  MODEL 141A SPORTING RIFLE, 398
  MODEL 760 GAMEMASTER SPORTING RIFLE, 398
  MODEL 572A FIELDMASTER RIFLE, 399
  MODEL SIX SPORTING RIFLE, 399
- **Remington-Hepburn, 399**
  NO. 3 SPORTING RIFLE, 399
- **Remington-Keene, 400**
  REMINGTON-KEENE MILITARY MUSKET
    Also known as 'Model 1880', 400
- **Remington-Lee, 400**
  MAGAZINE RIFLE
    Also known as the 'Model 1882', 400
  IMPROVED MAGAZINE RIFLE
    Also known as 'Model 1885', 400
  SMALL-BORE MAGAZINE RIFLE
    Also known as 'M1899', 401
  BLACK POWDER SPORTING RIFLE, 401
  SMALL-BORE SPORTING RIFLE, 401
- **Richardson, 401**
- **Roberts, 402**
- **Robertson & Simpson, 402**
- **Robinson, 402**
  MAGAZINE SPORTING RIFLE, 402
- **Roper, 402**
  EARLY PROGRESS, 402

  ROPER SPORTING RIFLE, 402
  CLOVERLEAF RIFLES, 402
- **Rowe, 402**
- **Ruger, autoloading type, 403**
  MODEL 10/22 CARBINE Also known as '10/22-R' and '10/22-RB', 403
  MODEL 44 CARBINE
    Also known as 'Model 44-R', 403
  MINI-14 RIFLE, 403
  XGI RIFLE, 404
- **Ruger, block-action type, 404**
  NUMBER 1 STANDARD RIFLE
    Also known as the '1-B' pattern, 404
  NUMBER 3 RIFLE, 405
- **Ruger, bolt-action type, 405**
  MODEL 77 SPORTING RIFLE
    Also known as '77-R' and '77-RS', 406
  MODEL 77/22 SPORTING RIFLE
    Also known as the Model 77/22-R, 407
- **Ruger, lever-action type, 408**
  MODEL 96/44 SPORTING RIFLE, 408
- **Russell (-Livermore), 408**
- **Savage, autoloading type, 408**
  MODEL 1912 SPORTING RIFLE, 408
  MODEL 6 SPORTING RIFLE, 408
- **Savage, block-action type, 408**
  MODEL 71 FAVORITE RIFLE, 408
  MODEL 89 SPORTING CARBINE, 409
- **Savage, bolt-action type, 409**
  MODEL 1904 SPORTING RIFLE, 409
  MODEL 3 SPORTING RIFLE, 409
  MODEL 4 SPORTING RIFLE, 409
  MODEL 19 NRA TARGET RIFLE, 410
  MODEL 20 SPORTING RIFLE, 410
  MODEL 23A SPORTING RIFLE, 410
  MODEL 40 SPORTING RIFLE, 410
  MODEL 340 SPORTING RIFLE, 411
  MODEL 110 SPORTING RIFLE, 411
  MODEL 34 SPORTING RIFLE
    Sold under the 'Savage-Stevens' or 'Stevens' brands, 413
  MODEL 111 CHIEFTAIN SPORTING RIFLE, 414
  MODEL 111 CLASSIC HUNTER SPORTING RIFLE, 414
  MODEL 112V SPORTING RIFLE, 414
  MODEL 114CU SPORTING RIFLE, 415
  MODEL 116FSS SPORTING RIFLE, 415
- **Savage, break-open type, 416**
  MODEL 219 SPORTING RIFLE, 416
- **Savage, lever-action type, 416**
  MODEL 1895 RIFLE AND CARBINE, 416
  MODEL 1895 SPORTING RIFLE, 416
  MODEL 1899 SPORTING RIFLE, 416
  MODEL 99A SPORTING RIFLE, 416
  MODEL 99 SPORTING RIFLE
    Post-war patterns, 417
- **Savage, slide-action type, 417**
  MODEL 1903 SPORTING RIFLE, 418
  MODEL 1914 SPORTING RIFLE
    Also known as the 'Model 14', 418
  MODEL 170 SPORTING RIFLE, 418
- **Schenkl, 418**
- **Schroeder, Salewski & Schmidt, 418**
  NEEDLE CARBINE, 418
- **Sears, Roebuck, 418**
- **Sharps (i), 418**
  1851-PATTERN CARBINE, 419
  1855-PATTERN CARBINE, 419
  MODEL 1859 RIFLE
    Also known as 'New Model', 419
  MODEL 1863 RIFLE AND CARBINE, 420
  THE FIRST CARTRIDGE GUNS, 420
  THE NEW CARTRIDGE GUNS, 420
  MODEL 1870 RIFLE, 420
  MILITARY MODEL, 420
  1848-PATTERN RIFLE, 420
  IMPROVED BREECH-LOADING SPORTING RIFLE, 421
  NEW MODEL SPORTING RIFLE, 421
  LONG RANGE OR CREEDMOOR RIFLE, 421
  MID-RANGE RIFLE, NO. 1 PATTERN, 421
  LONG-RANGE RIFLE NO. 1, 422

NEW OR ENGLISH MODEL, 1875 PATTERN, 422
OTHER PATTERNS, 422
MODERN RE-CREATIONS, 422
• **Sharps (ii), 422**
MODEL 1874 GUNS, 422
MODEL 1875 GUNS, 422
• **Sharps-Borchardt, 422**
NEW MODEL MILITARY RIFLE, 422
NEW MODEL SPORTING RIFLE, 422
MODERN RE-CREATIONS, 423
• **Sharps & Hankins, 423**
OLD MODEL NAVY RIFLE, 423
OLD MODEL CARBINE, 423
• **Shilen, 423**
DGA SPORTING RIFLE, 423
• **Shiloh, 424**
SHILOH SHARPS RIFLES, 424
• **Smith (Dexter), 424**
• **Smith (Gilbert), 424**
SMITH CARBINE, 425
• **Smith (Isaac), 425**
• **Smith & Wesson, 425**
MODEL A SPORTING RIFLE, 425
MODEL 1500, 425
• **Smoot, 425**
• **Sneider, 426**
• **Snell, 426**
• **Snider, 426**
• **Spencer, 426**
MODEL 1860 NAVY RIFLE, 426
MODEL 1860 CARBINE, 427
• **Spencer-Roper, 427**
SPENCER-ROPER RIFLE, 427
• **Springfield, bolt-action type, 427**
MODEL 1901 RIFLE, 427
MODEL 1903 SHORT RIFLE, 427
MODEL 1903A3 SHORT RIFLE, 429
INTERNATIONAL MATCH RIFLE, 429
MODEL 1903 NATIONAL MATCH RIFLE, 429
MODEL 1903 'MATCH SPRINGFIELD' RIFLE, 430
MODEL 1922 RIFLE, 430
MODEL 1903 NRA SPORTER, 430
MODEL 1903 'STYLE T' RIFLE, 430
SEDGLEY SPRINGFIELD SPORTER, 430
• **Springfield (-Allin), 430**
MODEL 1866 RIFLE, 431
MODEL 1868 RIFLE, 431
MODEL 1870 RIFLE, 431
MODEL 1873 RIFLE, 431
MODEL 1875 OFFICER'S RIFLE, 432
LONG RANGE RIFLE, 432
MARKSMAN'S RIFLE, 432
MODEL 1880 RIFLE, 432
MODEL 1882 SHORT RIFLE, 432
MODEL 1882 CARBINE, 432
MODEL 1884 RIFLE, 432
MODEL 1888 RIFLE, 433
• **Springfield Armory, Inc., 433**
M1A RIFLE, 433
• **Standard (Smith), 434**
STANDARD RIFLE MODEL G, 434
• **Starr, 434**
MODEL 1858 CARBINE, 434
MODEL 1865 CARBINE, 434
• **Stevens (J.), autoloading type, 434**
MODEL 57 SPORTING RIFLE, 434
• **Stevens (J.), block-action type, 435**
'SIDEPLATE' SPORTING RIFLE, 435
'LITTLE SCOUT' SPORTING RIFLE
Also known as No. 14, 435
'FAVORITE MODEL' SPORTING RIFLE, 435
'IDEAL MODEL' SPORTING RIFLE, 435
'CRACK-SHOT' SPORTING RIFLE, 436
'IMPROVED IDEAL MODEL' SPORTING RIFLE
Also known as No. 44-1/2, 436
'CRACK SHOT' SPORTING RIFLE
Also known as No. 26, 436
'NEW MODEL WALNUT HILL' TARGET RIFLE
Also known as 'No. 417', 436

• **Stevens (J.), bolt-action type, 436**
'LITTLE KRAG' SPORTING RIFLE, 437
NO. 15 SPORTING RIFLE, 437
NO. 53 SPORTING RIFLE, 437
MODEL 66 SPORTING RIFLE, 437
MODEL 82 SPORTING RIFLE, 437
MODEL 84 SPORTING RIFLE, 437
• **Stevens (J.), break-open type, 437**
'TIP-UP' SPORTING RIFLE, 437
'MAYNARD JUNIOR' SPORTING RIFLE
Also known as 'No. 15', 438
• **Stevens (J.), slide-action type, 438**
'VISIBLE LOADING' SPORTING RIFLE
Also known as 'No. 70', 438
• **Stevens (J.), swinging-barrel type, 438**
'SURE-SHOT' SPORTING RIFLE, 438
• **Stevens (W.X.), 439**
• **Stoner, 439**
MODEL 62 RIFLE, 439
MODEL 63 RIFLE, 439
• **Storm, 439**
STORM RIFLE, 439
• **Straw, 439**
• **Symmes, 439**
BREECH-LOADING CARBINE, 440
• **Thomas, 440**
• **Thompson, 440**
• **Thompson/Center, 440**
CONTENDER CARBINE, 440
TCR MODEL 83 HUNTER SPORTING RIFLE, 440
ENCORE CARBINE, 441
• **Tiesing, 441**
• **Trabue, 441**
• **Triplett & Scott, 441**
MAGAZINE CARBINE, 441
• **Ultra Light, 441**
MODEL 20 SPORTING RIFLE, 441
• **Underwood, 442**
• **Universal, 442**
UNIVERSAL M1 CARBINES, 442
• **Updegraff, 443**
• **Van Choate, 443**
• **Varner, 443**
• **Voere (KDF), 443**
K-15 AMERICAN SPORTING RIFLE, 443
• **Volcanic, 443**
VOLCANIC CARBINE, 443
• **Ward-Burton, 443**
MODEL 1871 TRIALS RIFLE, 443
• **Warner, 444**
MODEL 1864 CARBINE, 444
• **Weatherby, autoloading type, 444**
MARK XXII SPORTING RIFLE, 444
• **Weatherby, bolt-action type, 444**
WEATHERBY-MAUSER RIFLES, 444
MARK V SPORTING RIFLE, 444
• **Wesson, 446**
WESSON CARBINE, 446
• **White, 446**
• **Whitney, 446**
LAIDLEY-EMERY PATTERNS, 446
SPORTING MODEL, 446
CREEDMOOR MODEL, 446
• **Whitney-Remington Patterns, 446**
NEW SYSTEM SPORTING RIFLE, 446
WHITNEY-PHOENIX PATTERNS, 447
PHOENIX MILITARY MODEL, 447
PHOENIX SPORTING RIFLE, 447
• **Whittemore, 447**
• **Wichita, 447**
WICHITA CLASSIC SPORTING RIFLE, 447
• **Wickliffe, 447**
• **Wilson & Flather, 447**
• **Winchester, autoloading type, 447**
M1 CARBINE, 448
M1 CARBINE
Folding-butt patterns, 449

M2 CARBINE, 449
M3 CARBINE, 449
M1 CARBINES ABROAD, 450
MODEL 1903 SPORTING RIFLE, 450
MODEL 1905 SPORTING RIFLE, 450
MODEL 1907 SPORTING RIFLE, 450
MODEL 1910 SPORTING RIFLE, 450
MODEL 74 AUTOMATIC RIFLE, 451
MODEL 77 SPORTING RIFLE, 451
MODEL 55 SPORTING RIFLE, 451
MODEL 100 SPORTING RIFLE, 451
MODEL 290 SPORTING RIFLE, 451
• **Winchester, block-action type, 451**
MODEL 1885 SPORTING RIFLE
High Wall and Low Wall patterns, 451
• **Winchester, bolt-action type, 452**
MODEL 1900 SPORTING RIFLE, 452
MODEL 43 SPORTING RIFLE, 453
MODEL 52 SPORTING RIFLE, 453
MODEL 54 SPORTING RIFLE, 453
MODEL 56 SPORTING RIFLE, 454
MODEL 58 SPORTING RIFLE, 454
MODEL 69 SPORTING RIFLE, 455
MODEL 70 SPORTING RIFLE
Original, or 1936 type, 455
MODEL 70 SPORTING RIFLE
1964 type, 456
MODEL 121 SPORTING RIFLE, 457
MODEL 670 SPORTING RIFLE, 457
MODEL 770 SPORTING RIFLE, 457
MODEL 70 SPORTING RIFLE
1968 and subsequent types, 457
MODEL 310 SPORTING RIFLE, 461
• **Winchester, lever-action type, 461**
MODEL 1866 SPORTING RIFLE, 461
MODEL 1873 SPORTING RIFLE, 461
MODEL 1876 SPORTING RIFLE, 462
MODEL 1886 SPORTING RIFLE, 462
MODEL 1892 SPORTING RIFLE, 463
MODEL 1894 SPORTING RIFLE, 464
MODEL 1895 SPORTING RIFLE, 464
MODEL 94 STANDARD CARBINE, 465
MODEL 88 SPORTING RIFLE, 467
MODEL 250 SPORTING RIFLE, 467
MODEL 9422 SPORTING RIFLE, 467
• **Winchester, slide-action type, 468**
MODEL 1890 SPORTING RIFLE, 468
MODEL 61 SPORTING RIFLE, 468
MODEL 270 SPORTING RIFLE, 468
• **Winchester-Hotchkiss, 468**
MODEL 1878, 468
MODEL 1883 RIFLE, 469
MODEL 1883 RIFLE, 469
OTHER PATTERNS, 469
• **Winchester-Lee, 469**
MODEL 1895 NAVY RIFLE, 469
WINCHESTER-LEE SPORTING RIFLE, 470
• **Winslow, 470**
• **Wolcott, 470**
• **Wright & Brown, 470**
USSR, 470
• **Degtyarev, autoloading type, 470**
1925-TYPE RIFLE
Avtomaticheskaya vintovka sistemy Degtyareva, optniy obr. 1925g, 470
• **Dragunov, 471**
SNIPER RIFLE
Snayperskaya Vintovka Dragunova, 'SVD', 471
MEDVED SPORTING RIFLE, 471
• **Fedorov, 472**
AUTOMATIC RIFLE
Avtomata Fedorova, 472
'IMPROVED AUTOMATIC RIFLE', 472
• **Izhevsk, 472**
STRELA-2 TARGET RIFLE, 472
BK-3 TARGET RIFLE, 473
URAL-5-1 FREE RIFLE, 473
BI-7-2 TARGET RIFLE, 473
LOS-4 SPORTING RIFLE, 473
BARS-1 SPORTING RIFLE, 473
SV-1 TARGET RIFLE, 474
TsVR-1 TARGET RIFLE, 474
• **Kalashnikov, 474**
1946-TYPE TRIALS RIFLE, 474
1947-TYPE TRIALS RIFLE, 474
ASSAULT RIFLE
Avtomata Kalashnikova, 'AK', 474

MODIFIED ASSAULT RIFLE
Avtomata Kalashnikova Modificatsionniya, 'AKM', 475
MODEL 1974 ASSAULT RIFLE
Avtomata Kalashnikova obr. 74, 'AK-74', 475
• **Konstantinov, 476**
• **Margolin, 476**
MVO-1 TARGET RIFLE, 476
MTs-12-1 TARGET RIFLE, 476
• **Mosin-Nagant, 477**
MODEL 1891-30 RIFLE
Vintovka obr. 1891/30g, 477
MODEL 1938 CARBINE
Karabina obr. 1938g, 478
BI-7.62 TARGET RIFLE, 478
• **Roshchepey, 479**
• **Ross, 479**
• **Rukavishnikov, 479**
1938-TYPE RIFLE
Samozariadnaya vintovka sistemy Rukavishnikova, optniy obr. 1938g, 479
• **Serdyukov & Kraskov, 479**
SNIPER RIFLE
Vintovka Serdyukova-Kraskova, 'VSS', 479
• **Simonov, 479**
1931-TYPE TRIALS RIFLE
Avtomaticheskaya vintovka Sistemy Simonova, optniy obr. 1931g, 479
1934-TYPE TRIALS RIFLE, 480
MODEL 1936 AUTOMATIC RIFLE
Avtomaticheskaya vintovka Simonova obr. 1936g, or 'AVS', 480
1938-TYPE SEMI-AUTOMATIC RIFLE, 480
1943-PATTERN SEMI-AUTOMATIC CARBINE, 480
1945-PATTERN SIMONOV SEMI-AUTOMATIC CARBINE
Samozariadniya karabina sistemy Simonova ('SKS'), 481
• **Sudaev, 481**
1944-TYPE ASSAULT RIFLE
Avtomata Sudaeva, optniy obr. 1944g, 481
• **Tokarev, 481**
1925-TYPE RIFLE
Avtomaticheskaya vintovka sistemy Tokareva, optniy obr. 1925g, 481
1930-TYPE RIFLE
Avtomaticheskaya vintovka sistemy Tokareva, optniy obr. 1930g, 482
MODEL 1938 TOKAREV SEMI-AUTOMATIC RIFLE
Samozaryadnaya vintovka sistemy Tokareva, obr. 1938g ('SVT' or 'SVT-38'), 482
MODEL 1940 TOKAREV SEMI-AUTOMATIC RIFLE
Samozaryadnaya vintovka sistemy Tokareva, obr. 1940g ('SVT-40'), 483
• **TOZ, autoloading type, 484**
• **TOZ, bolt-action type, 485**
TOZ-12 TARGET RIFLE, 485
VENEZUELA, 485
• **FN-Saive, 485**
• **Mauser, 485**
YEMEN, 485
• **Mauser, 485**
YUGOSLAVIA, 485
• **Kalashnikov, 485**
MODEL 64 RIFLE, 485
MODEL 70 RIFLE, 486
MODEL 76 SNIPER RIFLE, 486
MODEL 85 AUTOMATIC RIFLE, 486
• **Mauser, 487**
THE EARLIEST GUNS, 487
POST-1923 GUNS, 487
MODEL 1898K SHORT RIFLE, 487
MODEL 1948 SHORT RIFLE, 487
• **Simonov, 487**
MODEL 59 SEMI-AUTOMATIC RIFLE, 487

FIRE UP WITH THESE RESOURCE GUIDES

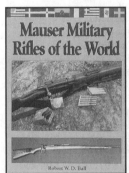
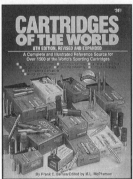

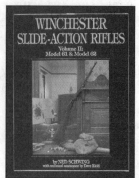
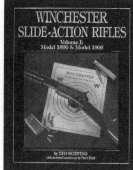

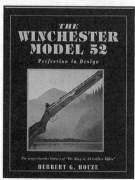
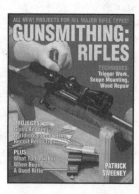
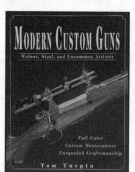